DATE DUE			

About the Editor

Priscilla Cheng Geahigan is professor of library science and director of the Consumer and Family Sciences Library at Purdue University. She is editor of *U.S. and Canadian Businesses 1955 to 1987: A Bibliography,* co-editor of *Business Serials of the U.S. Government* and *Industrial Relations Theses and Dissertations 1978-1981,* and author of numerous journal articles. She was the 1991-92 chair of Business Reference and Services Section (BRASS) of the American Library Association.

AMERICAN BUSINESS CLIMATE & ECONOMIC PROFILES

AMERICAN
BUSINESS
CLIMATE
& ECONOMIC
PROFILES

A Concise Compilation of
Facts, Rankings, Incentives,
and Resource Listings, for all
319 Metropolitan Statistical
Areas (MSAs) and the 50 States

Priscilla Cheng Geahigan, Editor

Gale Research Inc. • *DETROIT* • *WASHINGTON, D.C.* • *LONDON*

Priscilla Cheng Geahigan, *Editor*

Gale Research Inc. Staff

Lawrence W. Baker, Christine B. Hammes, *Senior Developmental Editors*
Leslie Joseph, Carol Nagel, *Developmental Editors*
Kelle Sisung, *Associate Developmental Editor*

Mary Beth Trimper, *Production Director*
Evi Seoud, *Assistant Production Manager*
Shanna Heilveil, *Production Assistant*

Cynthia Baldwin, *Art Director*
Barbara J. Yarrow, *Graphic Services Supervisor*
Mark C. Howell, *Cover Designer*

This book is printed on acid-free paper that meets the minimum requirements of American National Standard for Information Sciences—Permanence Paper for Printed Library Materials, ANSI Z39, 48-1984. ⊚™

This book is printed on recycled paper that meets Environmental Protection Agency standards. ♻

ISBN 0-8103-5545-0
Printed in the United States of America by Gale Research Inc.
Published simultaneously in the United Kingdom
by Gale Research International Limited
(An affiliated company of Gale Research Inc.)

The trademark **ITP** is used under license.

10 9 8 7 6 5 4 3 2 1

CONTENTS

CALIFORNIA (Continued)

COLORADO 119

CONNECTICUT 139

DELAWARE 161

DISTRICT OF COLUMBIA 169

FLORIDA 177

PART II: ECONOMIC RANKINGS

INTRODUCTION

During the last decade, state governments have become increasingly competitive in their efforts to attract new tourism, manufacturing, and industry to their home regions. Realizing that a healthy and growing economy requires the influx of new investment capital, states have begun to establish trade offices overseas, to actively promote their regions in the media, to establish enterprise zones in urban areas with high unemployment, and to offer incentive packages to outside investors. This has created an unprecedented opportunity for both U.S. and foreign entrepreneurs interested in establishing new businesses or relocating existing businesses. Now more than ever, it is important for business people and corporate executives to choose locations for their businesses with care and deliberation. *American Business Climate and Economic Profiles* is designed to help them to investigate the business climate of each of the fifty states and the district of Columbia, and the metropolitan statistical areas within each state. While aimed principally at entrepreneurs and corporate executives, state economic development professionals might also find this book convenient in comparing data between states and regions.

Terminology

Metropolitan Statistical Area (MSA)

Metropolitan Statistical Areas are regions containing a central city or urban area with a population of 50,000 or more people. Contiguous counties are included when they have close social and economic links with the area's population center.

Enterprise Zones

Enterprise zones are areas targeted for business growth, residential investment, and job creation. Enterprise zone programs are usually state/local partnerships that promote development in urban and depressed areas through economic incentives. Any property owner or firm located within the zone boundaries making a significant investment in the improvement of their property may be eligible for a variety of benefits. Firms that move to, or expand in, enterprise zones may be eligible for corporate tax credits, property tax abatement, exemption from certain states' sales and use taxes, state grants for the creation of new full time jobs, job training and placement assistance, as well as a variety of added local incentives.

Foreign Trade Zones

Foreign trade zones, also knows as free trade zones or free ports, are so designated by the U.S. Department of Commerce and operate under the supervision of the U.S. Customs Service. Foreign trade zones are considered to be within the continental limits of the United States but are not considered to be in the U.S. Customs territory. Merchandise can be brought into a foreign trade zone without the usual immediate formal customs entry. Domestic goods moved into a zone for export are considered exported upon entering the zone for purpose of excise tax rebates and customs drawback procedures.

The business advantage of a zone is that, for customs purposes, it is treated as though it were located outside the United States. Imported goods may be brought into a foreign trade zone without payment of customs duties, payment of government excise taxes, formal custom entry, etc.

U.S. Small Business Administration (SBA) Loans

The SBA is an independent federal agency that assists and counsels American small businesses. Any small business with net assets under $6,000,000 looking to obtain long-term financing for construction, modernization, or conversion of its plants (including the purchase of land, buildings, machinery, or equipment) can avail themselves of SBA services.

SBA 504 Loan Program—The SBA 504 Loan Programs are financial packages requiring the cooperation of the SBA, a certified development company, and private lenders. The private lender usually provides the first 50% of the total project cost. The SBA is authorized to provide up to 40% or $750,000 of a total package by issuing 100% guaranteed bonds sold in the capital market. The remaining 10% is provided by the small business itself.

SBA 7A Loan Program—The SBA may guarantee up to $750,000 or 90%, whichever is less, of conventional bank loans for most types of business. Proceeds may be used for construction or expansion, plant acquisition, leasehold improvements, machinery and equipment, and working capital.

Standard Industrial Classification (SIC)

The four-digit SIC codes are based on the *Standard Industrial Classification Manual 1987,* published by the U.S. Executive

Office of the President, Office of Management and Budget.

Data Compilation

Much data were collected from various state and regional Chamber of Commerce and Economic Development Offices, the Bureau of the Census, and the Bureau of Labor Statistics. Additional information was obtained from electronic sources through state data centers.

Format of the Book

ABCEP is divided into two parts: Economic Profiles (Part I) and Rankings (Part II). Part I groups the 319 MSAs into the 50 states and District of Columbia. Each "state" section opens with a list of the MSAs in that state, as well as a map showing county and MSA boundaries. Statistics covering such categories as Population, Civilian Labor Force, Employer Unemployment Contributions, Gross State Product, Capital Expenditures of Manufacturing Industries, State Tax Rates, Income, State Business Incentives and Assistance, and Major Companies in the State are given. In the MSA portion of Part I, such topics as Geographic Profile, Ranking Highlights, Quality of Life Indexes, Population, Unemployment, Business Climate, and Major Businesses break down statistics for individual MSAs.

In Part II, all MSAs are grouped together to show how they rank in 22 categories, such as Land Area, Population Growth, Unemployment Rate, Labor Force Size, Hospital Beds per 1,000 People, and Violent Crime per 1,000 Inhabitants.

Acknowledgments

The editor wishes to thank the American Chamber of Commerce for its permission to use data from its *ACCRA Cost of Living Index*. Thanks also need to be extended to David Rouse of the Chicago Public Library and John Schmittroth of Gale Research for their help and inspiration. Additional thanks are due to Gale Research's editorial staff, especially Christine Hammes, Leslie Joseph, Carol Nagel, and Lawrence Baker for their patience and guidance throughout the project. Finally, special thanks go to Timothy and Susan Gall at Eastword Publications Development, Inc. for their research and typesetting work at the tail end of this project.

Priscilla Cheng Geahigan

PART I: ECONOMIC PROFILES

ALABAMA

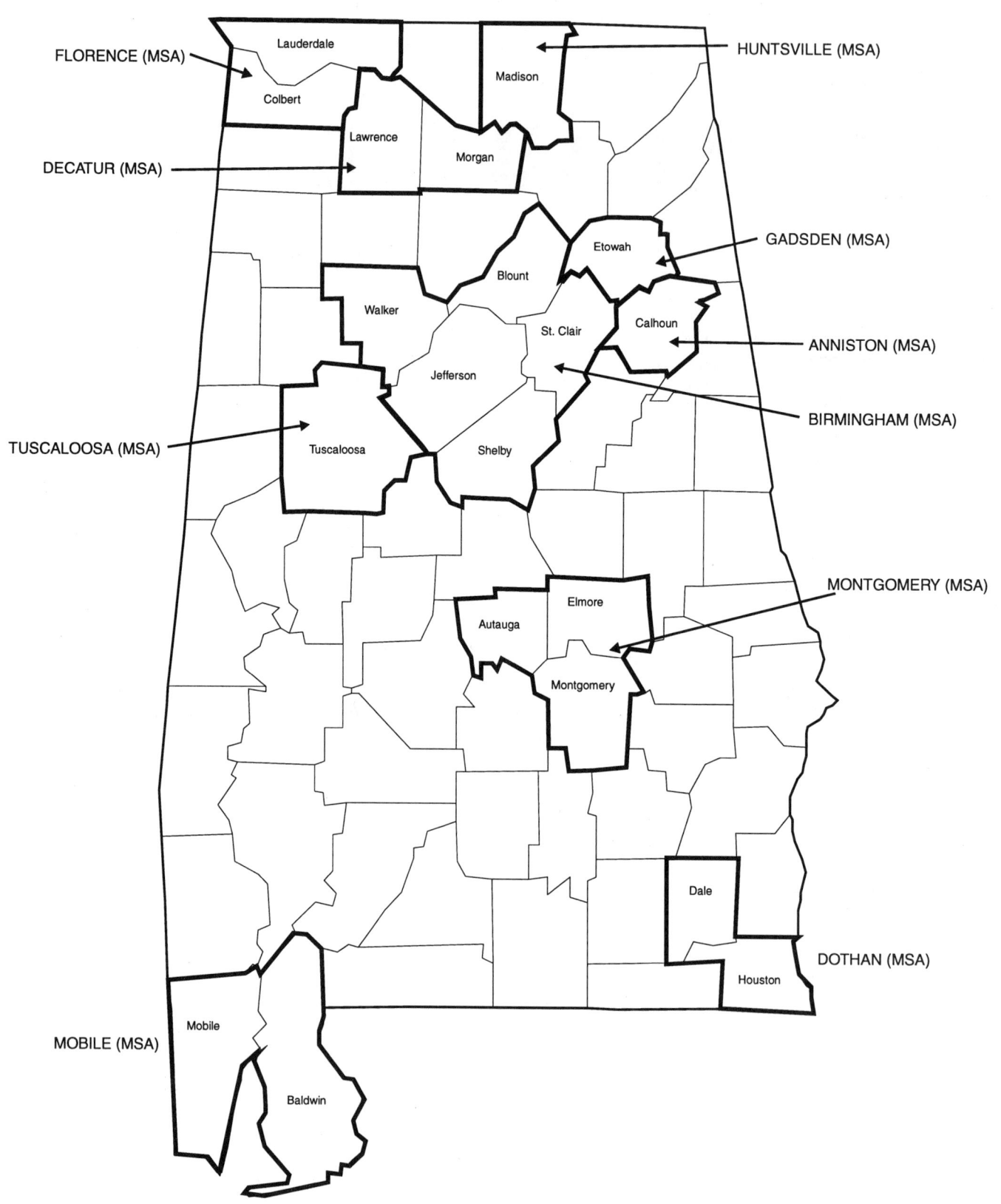

FLORENCE (MSA)

HUNTSVILLE (MSA)

Lauderdale

Colbert

Madison

DECATUR (MSA)

Lawrence

Morgan

GADSDEN (MSA)

Etowah

Blount

Walker

St. Clair

Calhoun

ANNISTON (MSA)

Jefferson

BIRMINGHAM (MSA)

TUSCALOOSA (MSA)

Tuscaloosa

Shelby

Elmore

MONTGOMERY (MSA)

Autauga

Montgomery

Dale

DOTHAN (MSA)

Houston

Mobile

MOBILE (MSA)

Baldwin

ALABAMA

Population
1990: 4,040,587
1980: 3,893,888

Age
Ages 18 to 20: 205,557
Ages 21 to 24: 237,778
Ages 25 to 44: 1,232,067
Ages 45 to 54: 419,421
Ages 55 to 59: 183,677
Ages 60 to 64: 180,310
Median age: 33.0

Race
White: 2,975,797
Black: 1,020,705
Asian/Pacific Islander: 21,797
Native American: 16,506
Hispanic origin: 24,629

Households
Total: 1,506,790
Persons per household: 2.62

Sex
Male: 1,936,162
Female: 2,104,425

Population Migration
Domestic migration: 108,000
International migration: 16,000

Projection of the Population in 1995
Total: 4,189,000
18 to 64: 2,511,000

Civilian Labor Force
1993: 1,945,000
1992: 1,913,500
1991: 1,885,300
1990: 1,855,700

Manufacturing
1995 Projection: 411,800
1992: 380,600
1991: 379,100
1990: 381,800
1989: 381,100

Services
1995 Projection: 464,300
1992: 345,400
1991: 329,100
1990: 322,600
1989: 305,000

Wholesale and Retail Trade
1995 Projection: 419,400
1992: 366,300
1991: 356,700
1990: 364,800
1989: 359,200

Unemployment Rate
1993: 8.1%
1992: 7.1%
1991: 6.7%
1990: 6.5%

Employer Unemployment Contributions

Contribution Rate
1992: 1.13%
1991: 1.00%
1990: 1.35%

Average Weekly Benefit
1992: $122.52
1991: $120.41
1990: $116.64

Gross State Product (Million $)
1989: $67,886
1988: $64,059
1987: $59,547
1979: $33,004
Growth rate, 1979 to 1989: 105.7%

Capital Expenditures of Manufacturing Industries
1990: $2,857,600,000
1989: $2,137,600,000
1988: $1,990,300,000
1987: $1,360,100,000

State Tax Rates

Individual income: Range from 2% ($1,000 or less) to 5% (above $6,000).

Corporate income: 5% of total taxable net income.

General property: Sum of state and local rates. Assessed at 30% of fair market value of utitlity property, 20% of fair market value of property not otherwise classified; 10% of residential property; 15% of passenger cars and trucks of 8,000 lbs. or less.

General sales: 4%

Gasoline: 11¢ per gallon

Income

Median income for a 4 person family: $34,930

Personal per Capita Income

1992: $16,220

1991: $15,526

1990: $14,899

Disposable per Capita Income

1992: $14,533

1991: $13,851

1990: $13,230

Private Employment Weekly Wages

Average

1989: $369

1988: $358

1987: $358

Manufacturing

1989: $345

1988: $407

1987: $393

Services

1989: $357

1988: $343

1987: $332

Wholesale

1989: $453

1988: $439

1987: $418

Retail

1989: $210

1988: $207

1987: $200

Highway Statistics

Total Highway Miles

1990: 90,672

1989: 90,535

1988: 90,418

Federal Highway Aid

1991: $216,489,000

1990: $211,870,000

1989: $257,922,000

Electricity

Average Cost per Kilowatt Hour

1990: 5.58¢

1989: 5.75¢

1988: 5.52¢

Housing (1990)

Owner occupied units: 1,061,897

Median house value: $53,700

Renter occupied units: 444,893

Median rent: $229

Total vacant units: 163,589

Homeowner vacancy rate: 1.8%

Rental vacancy rate: 9.3%

State Business Incentives and Assistance

Enterprise Zone Incentives

The Alabama Enterprise Zone Act was passed by the Alabama legislature in 1987. The act authorized state tax and non-tax incentives. The incentives for the 27 enterprise zones across the state include:

1) A business operation in the zone may qualify for up to a $2,500 tax credit per new permanent employee hired. This tax credit may be applied in all Alabama Enterprise zones, to any Alabama Income Tax liability or any Alabama Corporate Franchise Tax liability.

2) Employers may receive an exemption from Alabama Sales and Use taxes on the purchase of the materials used in the construction of a building or any addition or improvement thereon for housing any legitimate zone business and on machinery and equipment used in the zone.

3) Employers may receive certain exemptions from Alabama Income and Corporate Franchise taxes for a period of five years.

Financial and Business Assistance

Industrial Development Bonds. Can be used to finance land, building, machinery and equipment for new or expanding industry. The facility may also be exempt from ad valorem and sales and use taxes.

The State Economic Development Loan Fund. Can be used by manufacturers to purchase land, buildings, machinery and equipment.

The State Economic Development Infrastructure Grant Program. Can provide grants to local governments for public infrastructure to facilitate the location of a new or expanding business.

The SBA 504 Loan Program. Can provide small business with a better financial package than otherwise may be available.

The SBA 7a Loan Program. Can provide small businesses with long term financing for real estate acquisition, building construction, renovation, machinery, inventory, and working capital.

The Economic Development Administration Business Loan

Guarantees. Can be used to provide financial assistance to firms that create permanent jobs.

The Economic Development Administration's Public Works and Development Facilities Program. Will assist communities to encourage business expansion by providing grants for infrastructure development.

The Industrial Site Preparation Grant Program. May provide state grants to help new and expanding manufacturing industries pay for industrial site preparation.

The Wallace Plan for Linked Deposits. A public/private partnership. The state treasurer will use a small portion of the state's investment portfolio to deposit with Alabama banks, and link these deposits to individual loans made eligible to small businesses.

Alabama allows federal income tax to be deducted before computing state income tax.

Alabama provides exemptions on corporate income tax, ad valorem tax, franchise tax, and sales tax for the amount invested in pollution control equipment.

Employers located in a labor surplus area, as classified by the Department of Labor, can be given preference in bidding on federal procurement contracts.

Education and Training

Alabama Industrial Development Training Institute. This program will recruit and train employees to the company's specifications at no cost to the company.

The Job Training Partnership Act Funds, an education and training program, was created in July 1989. The funds will assist companies in hiring and training employees.

The Skills Training Education Program provides assistance throughout the state in training of workers and creation of jobs for these trained individuals.

State Offices

Real estate: Real Estate Commission, D. Phillip Lasater, Exec Director, State Capitol, 750 Washington Avenue, Montgomery, AL 36130. 205-242-5544

Chamber of commerce: Business Council of Alabama, E. Clark Richardson, President, 468 S. Perry St., PO Box 76, Montgomery, AL 36195-5401. 205-834-6000

Economic development: Alabama Development Office, Jack Hammontree, Director, State Capitol, 135 S. Union St., Montgomery, AL 36130. 800-248-0033, 205-263-0048, FAX 205-265-5078

Department of Economic and Community Affairs, Planning and Economic Development Division, Don C. Hines, Division Chief, PO Box 250347, 3465 Norman Bridge Road, Montgomery, AL 36125-0347. 205-284-8705

Department of Economic and Community Affairs, Enterprise Zone Office, Charles R. Reynolds, Coordinator, PO Box 250347, 3465 Norman Bridge Road, Montgomery, AL 36125-0347. 205-284-8784

Alabama Resource Development Committee, C. Ray Sanders, Chairman, PO Box 2641, Birmingham, AL 35291-

0630. 205-250-4546, FAX 205-250-4891

Small Business Development Consortium, Jeff Gibbs, State Director, University of Alabama in Birmingham, 1717 11th Avenue S., Ste. 419, Birmingham, AL 35294-4410. 205-934-7260

Environmental affairs: Department of Environmental Management, Leigh Pegues, Director, 1751 Cong. W. L. Dickinson Drive, Montgomery, AL 36130. 205-242-7706

Labor: Department of Labor, Robin Rea, Commissioner, 64 N. Union St., Montgomery, AL 36130. 205-242-3460

Unemployment: Department of Industrial Relations, Unemployment Compensation Division, James C. Hollon, Administrator, 649 Monroe St., Montgomery, AL 36130. 205-242-5415

Worker's compensation: Department of Industrial Relations, Workmen's Compensation Division, Marcus A. Davis, Chief, 649 Monroe St., Montgomery, AL 36130. 205-242-5420

Occupational safety and health: Department of Labor, Robin Rea, Commissioner, 64 N. Union St., Montgomery, AL 36130. 205-242-3460

Secretary of state: Secretary of State's Office, Perry Hand, Secretary of State, Statehouse Building, Montgomery, AL 36130. 205-242-7200

Taxation and revenue: Revenue Department, James M. Sizemore, Jr., Commissioner, Gordon Persons Building, Montgomery, AL 36130. 205-242-3366

Designated Zones for Economic Development

Enterprise Zones

Enacted in: 1987

No. of established zones: 27

Cities

Birmingham

Montgomery

Prichard

Counties

Barbour

Bullock

Butler

Cherokee

Clarke

Clay

Covington

Dallas

Escambia

Etowah

Jackson

Lawrence

Lowndes

Macon

Mobile

Monroe

Perry

Pickens
Pike
Randolph
Russell
Sumter
Talladega
Wilcox

Foreign Trade Zones

Foreign Trade Zone No. 98, Birmingham, Alabama, Grantee/Operator: City of Birmingham, Mayor's Office, City of Birmingham, Virginia Riley, Birmingham City Hall, Birmingham, AL 35203, 205-254-2277

Foreign Trade Zone No. 83, Huntsville, Alabama, Grantee/ Operator: Huntsville-Madison County Airport Authority, Eugene B. Conrad, Jr., A.A.E., 1000 Glenn Hearn Boulevard, Box 20008, Huntsville, AL 35824, 205-772-9395

Foreign Trade Zone No. 82, Mobile, Alabama, Grantee: City of Mobile, Operator: Mobile Airport Authority, Dan Dupont, Bldg. 11, Brookley Complex, Mobile, AL 36615, 205-438-7334

Labor Unions

Aluminum, Brick and Glass Workers, International Union (AFL-CIO)

Automobile, Aerospace & Agricultural Implement Workers of America, International Union, United (UAW AFL-CIO)

Bakery, Confectionery & Tobacco Workers International Union (AFL-CIO)

Boilermakers, Iron Shipbuilders, Blacksmiths, Forgers and Helpers, International Brotherhood of (AFL-CIO)

Chemical Workers Union, International (AFL-CIO)

Clothing and Textile Workers Union, Amalgamated (AFL-CIO)

Electrical Workers, International Brotherhood of (AFL-CIO)

Food and Commercial Workers International Union, United (AFL-CIO)

Glass, Molders, Pottery, Plastics and Allied Workers International Union (AFL-CIO)

Laborers' International Union of North America (AFL-CIO)

Ladies' Garment Workers' Union, International (AFL-CIO)

Major Companies in the State

Company name	Fortune 500 Rank	City	Telephone	SIC number
Fortune 500 Companies				
Blount Inc.	469	Montgomery	205-244-4000	1541
Intergraph Corp.	315	Huntsville	205-730-2000	3571
Russell Corp.	384	Alexander City	205-329-4000	2253
Sci. Systems Inc.	349	Huntsville	305-882-4600	3672
Vulcan Materials Co.	339	Birmingham	205-877-3000	3281
Other Major Companies in the State				
Alabama Power		Birmingham	205-250-1000	4911
Amsouth Bancorporation		Birmingham	205-320-7151	6712
Big B Inc. Bessemer		Birmingham	205-424-3421	5912
Birmingham Steel Corp.		Birmingham	205-985-9290	3312
Bruno S. Inc.		Birmingham	205-940-9400	5411
Central Bancshares of The South Inc.		Birmingham	205-933-3000	6712
Delchamps Inc.		Mobile	205-433-0431	5411
Durr Fillauer Medical Inc.		Montgomery	205-241-8800	5122
First Alabama Bancshares Inc.		Montgomery	205-832-8490	6712
Kinder Care Learning Centers Inc.		Montgomery	205-277-5090	8351
Morrison Inc.		Mobile	205-344-3000	5812
Piggly Wiggly Alabama Distributing Co. Inc.		Bessemer	205-426-2400	5141
Protective Life Corp.		Birmingham	205-879-9230	6311
Protective Life Insurance Co.		Birmingham	205-879-9230	6311
Sonat Inc.		Birmingham	205-325-3800	4923
South Central Bell Telephone Co.		Birmingham	205-321-1000	4813
Southern Natural Gas Co.		Birmingham	205-325-7410	4924
Southtrust Corp.		Birmingham	205-254-5509	6712
Torchmark Corp.		Birmingham	205-325-4200	6321

Paperworkers International Union, United (AFL-CIO)
Retail, Wholesale and Department Store Union (AFL-CIO)
Rubber, Cork, Linoleum and Plastic Workers of America, United (AFL-CIO)
Sheet Metal Workers' International Association (AFL-CIO)
Steelworkers of America, United (AFL-CIO)
Teamsters, Chauffeurs, Warehousemen and Helpers of America, International Brotherhood of (AFL-CIO)

Universities with Ph.D. Programs
Alabama Agricultural and Mechanical University, Normal
Auburn University, Auburn
Auburn University at Montgomery, Montgomery
Faulkner University, Montgomery
Samford University, Birmingham
Tuskegee University, Tuskegee
University of Alabama, Tuscaloosa
University of Alabama at Birmingham, Birmingham
University of Alabama in Huntsville, Huntsville
University of South Alabama, Mobile

Sources of Additional Information
Annual Report. Alabama Department of Economic and Community Affairs, 1990. 36p.
Directory of Alabama State Services. Alabama Department of Economic and Community Affairs, 4th ed., 1989. 101p.
Executive Summary of Alabama's Advantages. Alabama Development Office, 1989. 11p.
The State of Alabama, Open for Business, Available Buildings List. Alabama Development Office, February 1991. np.

ANNISTON, AL (MSA)

Geographic Profile
Land Area
608.5 square miles
Counties and Parishes
Calhoun

Ranking Highlights
271　*out of 319 in total* **land area**
214　*out of 319 in* **population growth,** *1970–1990*
238　*out of 310 in having the lowest* **unemployment** *rate*
284　*out of 310 in size of* **labor force**
250　*out of 318 in percentage of* **college graduates**
270　*out of 292 in per capita personal* **income**
254　*out of 319 in number of* **manufacturing establishments**
294　*out of 318 in* **physicians** *per 1000 people*
129　*out of 318 in* **hospital beds** *per 1000 people*
　46　*out of 267 in fewest* **crimes** *per 1000 people*
163　*out of 266 in fewest* **violent crimes** *per 1000 people*
　23　*out of 319 in per capita* **federal funds and grants**

Quality of Life Indexes (Rate per 1000 population)
Crime rate in 1991:	41.7
Violent crime rate in 1991:	7.3
Physicians rate in 1992:	1.09
Hospital bed rate in 1991:	4.19

Population (1990)
Total Population and Growth Rate
1990: 116,034
1980: 119,761
1970: 103,092
Growth rate 1970–1990: 13%
Race and Hispanic Origin
White: 80.0%
Black: 18.6%
Asian/Pacific Islander: 0.7%
Native American: 0.3%
Hispanic origin: 1.1%
White not Hispanic: 79.4%
Age
Ages 18 to 20: 6.5%
Ages 21 to 24: 6.4%
Ages 25 to 44: 30.4%
Ages 45 to 54: 10.2%
Ages 55 to 59: 4.7%
Ages 60 to 64: 4.5%
Ages 65 plus: 12.4%

Educational Attainment (1990)
Percent having completed high school: 67.4%
Percent having completed college: 14.2%
Elementary and high school enrollment: 20,490

Federal Funds and Grants Received
Total received in 1989: $752,600,000
Funds received per capita: $6,103

Civilian Labor Force
1993 (April): 52,452
1992 average: 52,443
1991 average: 51,271
1990 average: 50,782

Unemployment
1993 (April): 8.2%
1992 average: 8.3%
1991 average: 7.3%
1990 average: 7.0%

Average Annual Pay
1988: $17,832
1987: $17,617
1985: $16,423

Per Capita Personal Income
1991: $14,434
1990: $13,817
1989: $13,090

Business Climate (1987)
Manufacturing
Number of establishments in 1987: 143
Shipments in 1987 ($1,000): $773,500
Employees in 1987: 10,700
Change in employment, 1982 to 1987: 8.1%
Average annual pay for manufacturing work, 1989: $17,942
Average annual pay for production work, 1987: $14,759

Wholesale Trade
Number of establishments in 1987: 139
Total sales in 1987 ($1,000): $528,400
Change in sales, 1982 to 1987: 2.7%

Retail Trade
Number of establishments in 1987: 672
Total sales in 1987 ($1,000): $528,400
Retail sales per household in 1987: $13,758
Average annual pay in 1989: $10,745

Service Industry
Selected receipts in 1987 ($1,000): $142,900
Average annual pay in 1989: $15,069

Housing
Total number of units in 1990: 46,753
Occupied units in 1990: 42,983
Owner-occupied units in 1990: 70.3%
1993 ACCRA average cost: N/A
1993 ACCRA average rent for an apartment: N/A

Chamber of Commerce
Calhoun County Chamber of Commerce, Larry Sylvester, Manager, 801 Noble St., PO Box 1087, Anniston, AL 36202. 205-237-3536, FAX 205-237-4338

Major Businesses

Company	SIC	Telephone
Auto Custom Carpets, Inc.	2273	(205) 236-1118
Chalk-Line Inc.	5136	(205) 238-1540
Cooper Chevrolet Inc.	5511	(205) 236-4481
King Motor Co. Inc.	5511	(205) 831-5300
Mc Whorter & Co. Inc.	1542	(205) 238-8545
Regional Health Services	8062	(205) 235-5050
Southern Tool Inc.	3324	(205) 831-2811
Southtrust Bank Calhoun County	6021	(205) 238-1000
Stringfellow, Susie	8062	(205) 235-8900
Superior Oldsmobile Buick	5511	(205) 237-1656
Tape-Craft Corp.	2241	(205) 236-2535
Wakefield's Inc.	5651	(205) 237-9521

Colleges and Universities
Harry M. Ayers State Technical College, Anniston

BIRMINGHAM, AL (MSA)

Geographic Profile

Land Area

3981.7 square miles

Counties and Parishes

Blount

Jefferson

St. Clair

Shelby

Walker

Additional Cities/Towns within Area

Bessemer

Ranking Highlights

28　*out of 319 in total* **land area**

204　*out of 319 in* **population growth,** *1970–1990*

104　*out of 310 in having the lowest* **unemployment** *rate*

61　*out of 310 in size of* **labor force**

165　*out of 318 in percentage of* **college graduates**

104　*out of 292 in per capita personal* **income**

62　*out of 319 in number of* **manufacturing establishments**

36　*out of 318 in* **physicians** *per 1000 people*

37　*out of 318 in* **hospital beds** *per 1000 people*

168　*out of 267 in fewest* **crimes** *per 1000 people*

246　*out of 266 in fewest* **violent crimes** *per 1000 people*

209　*out of 319 in per capita* **federal funds and grants**

Quality of Life Indexes (Rate per 1000 population)

Crime rate in 1991:	66.6
Violent crime rate in 1991:	11.3
Physicians rate in 1992:	2.87
Hospital bed rate in 1991:	5.76

ACCRA Cost of Living Indexes

(First quarter 1993, average = 100)

Composite index:	99.4
Utilities index:	117.9
Housing index:	99.7

Overview

Birmingham is the central city of a five-county metropolitan area. It is one of the Southeast's major centers for healthcare, finance, education, manufacturing, research, engineering and distribution. It is the wholesale and retail trade center of the state as well. Items and goods produced in the state include pipe, wrought iron furniture, fabricated metal products, paint, apparel, electronics, chemicals, office furniture, containers, paper products, truck bodies, plastics, processed food products, aircraft components, machinery, aerial lift equipment, pet food, building products, and fire extinguishers.

Birmingham's largest employer, which is now the largest employer in the state, is the University of Alabama at Bir-

mingham, which provides some 15,600 jobs. Three major Birmingham employers, American Cast Iron Pipe Company, Alabama Gas Corporation and BE&K were included in the 1993 edition of *The 100 Best Companies to Work for in America.* Other large employers include South Central Bell, Alabama Power Company, Baptist Medical Centers, South Trust Bank, AmSouth Bank, Bruno's, Inc., Drummond Company, and USX, Inc.

Birmingham is served by three interstate highways and five major federal routes, four interstate rail carriers, ten major airlines, seven air freight companies, nearly 100 trucking operations and five barge lines, which connect Birmingham to 16,000 miles of waterways via the Warrior/Tennessee/Tombigbee system.

The just-completed expansion of the Birmingham-Jefferson Civic Center complex includes the 771-room Sheraton Civic Center Hotel. Included in the Civic Center is the Medical Forum, the world's first center dedicated to continuing medical education and medical products marketing. There are 364,000 square feet of space in the Center's exhibition hall adjacent to a 17,000-seat coliseum. Tourism has been boosted by the opening of the Civil Rights Institute, which drew 100,000 visitors in its first ten months of operations. Between 1985 and 1988 four million square feet of office space was added to the metropolitan area's inventory, which currently totals 12.7 million square feet. Rental rates range from $5.50 to $18.00 per square foot. The largest building opening in 1993 was the regional headquarters of State Farm Insurance. The $104 million Kirklin Clinic was completed in 1992.

The CSX, the Burlington Northern, the Norfolk Southern, and the Birmingham Southern Railroads haul freight to and from the metropolitan area; in all, they handle more than ten thousand containers per month. More than one hundred truck lines, many with nationwide service, and five air-cargo firms move goods and products for Birmingham companies. Birmingham's Airport Industrial Park is designated as a Foreign Trade Zone. General commodities are transported economically on barges along the nearby Warrior-Tombigbee River System and the Tennessee-Tombigbee Waterway to other inland cities and through the Port of Mobile to foreign countries.

Ten airlines offer direct service to and from Birmingham Municipal Airport and about sixty cities. More than two million passengers flew in and out of the city in 1991, an increase of 45 percent from 1985. The airport, ten minutes from downtown, is undergoing a $100 million expansion. It also added a second runway and fifteen hundred additional parking spaces. Four interstate highways bring motorists into Birmingham: Interstates 20 or 59 from the northeast or southwest; Interstate 65 from north or south; and Interstate 459, which loops to the southeast of the city. U.S. Highway 280 enters from the southeast, U.S. 31 from the north, U.S. 78 from the northwest, and U.S. 11 from the southwest and northeast. AMTRAK offers daily passenger service to Birmingham from New Orleans, Louisiana and New York City.

Population (1990)

Total Population and Growth Rate
1990: 907,810
1980: 883,993
1970: 794,083
Growth rate 1970–1990: 14%

Race and Hispanic Origin
White: 72.2%
Black: 27.1%
Asian/Pacific Islander: 0.4%
Native American: 0.2%
Hispanic origin: 0.4%
White not Hispanic: 71.9%

Age
Ages 18 to 20: 4.3%
Ages 21 to 24: 5.6%
Ages 25 to 44: 32.3%
Ages 45 to 54: 10.2%
Ages 55 to 59: 4.4%
Ages 60 to 64: 4.6%
Ages 65 plus: 13.2%

Educational Attainment (1990)
Percent having completed high school: 71.7%
Percent having completed college: 18.7%
Elementary and high school enrollment: 157,988

Federal Funds and Grants Received
Total received in 1989: $2,493,900,000
Funds received per capita: $2,701

Civilian Labor Force
1993 (April): 455,308
1992 average: 448,689
1991 average: 438,673
1990 average: 439,028

Unemployment
1993 (April): 5.6%
1992 average: 6.1%
1991 average: 5.7%
1990 average: 5.4%

Average Annual Pay
1988: $20,775
1987: $19,917
1985: $18,672

Per Capita Personal Income
1991: $18,210
1990: $17,634
1989: $16,490

Business Climate (1987)

Manufacturing
Number of establishments in 1987: 1,150
Shipments in 1987 ($1,000): $5,748,000
Employees in 1987: 51,600
Change in employment, 1982 to 1987: -3.0%
Average annual pay for manufacturing work, 1989: $23,292
Average annual pay for production work, 1987: $18,319

Wholesale Trade
Number of establishments in 1987: 2,068
Total sales in 1987 ($1,000): $10,610,400
Change in sales, 1982 to 1987: 22.8%

Retail Trade
Number of establishments in 1987: 5,364
Total sales in 1987 ($1,000): $10,610,400
Retail sales per household in 1987: $15,873
Average annual pay in 1989: $11,726

Service Industry
Selected receipts in 1987 ($1,000): $2,947,800
Average annual pay in 1989: $19,986

Office Real Estate (1992)
Average class A Central Business District rental range per sq. ft: $14.25

Vacancy Rates
All areas: 15.5%

Vacancy Rates in Central Business District
Class A space: 13.2%
Class B space: 26.1%

Vacancy Rates Outside Central Business District
Class A space: 6.9%
Class B space: 54.9%

Housing
Total number of units in 1990: 376,897
Occupied units in 1990: 345,328
Owner-occupied units in 1990: 69.0%
1993 ACCRA average cost: $116,400
1993 ACCRA average rent for an apartment: $471

Chamber of Commerce
Birmingham Area Chamber of Commerce, Don A. Newton, President, 2027 First Ave. N., PO Box 10127, Birmingham, AL 35202. 205-323-5461, FAX 205-250-7669

Economic Development Office
City of Birmingham Office of Economic Development, C. Mark Smith, Director, 710 N. 20th St., Birmingham, AL 35203. 205-254-2799, FAX 205-254-7741

Major Businesses

Company Name	SIC	Phone
Alabama Power Co.	4911	(205) 250-1000
Amsouth Bank National	6021	(205) 663-9165

Major Businesses (Continued)

Company Name	SIC	Phone
Amsouth Bancorporation	6021	(205) 320-7151
Amsouth Bank National	6021	(205) 326-5120
Baptist Medical Centers	8062	(205) 322-9300
Bellsouth Services Inc.	7374	(205) 977-1680
Big B, Inc.	5912	(205) 424-3421
Birmingham Steel Corp.	3312	(205) 985-9290
Blue Cross Blue Shield of Alabama	6324	(205) 988-2100
Bruno's Inc.	5411	(205) 940-9400
Central Bank of the South	6022	(205) 933-3000
Drummond Co. Inc.	1221	(205) 945-6500
Ebsco Industries, Inc.	5192	(205) 991-6600
Harbert Corp.	1622	(205) 987-5500
Harbert International, Inc.	1611	(205) 987-5500
Liberty National Life Insurance Co.	6311	(205) 325-2722
Mc Griff, Seibels & Williams	6411	(205) 252-9871
Motion Industries Inc.	5085	(205) 956-1122
Parisian Inc.	5651	(205) 940-4000
Protective Life Corp.	6311	(205) 879-9230
Protective Life Insurance Co.	6311	(205) 879-9230
Rust International Corp.	7389	(205) 995-7878
Sonat Inc.	4922	(205) 325-3800
South Central Bell Tele Communications	4813	(205) 321-1000
Southern Natural Gas Co.	4922	(205) 325-7410
Southtrust Bank Alabama	6022	(205) 254-5000
Southtrust Corp.	6022	(205) 254-5000
Torchmark Corp.	6321	(205) 325-4200
United States Pipe Foundry Co.	3321	(205) 254-7000
Vulcan Materials Co.	1422	(205) 877-3000

Colleges and Universities

Birmingham-Southern College, Birmingham
Herzing Institute, Birmingham
Jefferson State Community College, Birmingham
Lawson State Community College, Birmingham
Miles College, Birmingham
Rets Electronic Institute, Birmingham
Samford University, Birmingham
Southern Institute, Birmingham
Southern Junior College, Birmingham
University of Alabama at Birmingham, Birmingham
Bessemer State Technical College, Bessemer

DECATUR, AL (MSA)

Geographic Profile

Land Area

1275.7 square miles

Counties and Parishes

Lawrence
Morgan

Ranking Highlights

152 *out of 319 in total* **land area**
160 *out of 319 in* **population growth,** *1970–1990*
238 *out of 310 in having the lowest* **unemployment** *rate*
263 *out of 310 in size of* **labor force**
277 *out of 318 in percentage of* **college graduates**
230 *out of 292 in per capita personal* **income**
211 *out of 319 in number of* **manufacturing establishments**
312 *out of 318 in* **physicians** *per 1000 people*
146 *out of 318 in* **hospital beds** *per 1000 people*
34 *out of 267 in fewest* **crimes** *per 1000 people*
63 *out of 266 in fewest* **violent crimes** *per 1000 people*
158 *out of 319 in per capita* **federal funds and grants**

Quality of Life Indexes (Rate per 1000 population)

Crime rate in 1991:	39.5
Violent crime rate in 1991:	3.7
Physicians rate in 1992:	0.92
Hospital bed rate in 1991:	4.04

ACCRA Cost of Living Indexes

(First quarter 1993, average = 100)

Composite index:	89.9
Utilities index:	89.2
Housing index:	78.7

Population (1990)

Total Population and Growth Rate

1990: 131,556
1980: 120,401
1970: 104,587
Growth rate 1970–1990: 26%

Race and Hispanic Origin

White: 86.4%
Black: 11.3%
Asian/Pacific Islander: 0.3%
Native American: 1.9%
Hispanic origin: 0.5%
White not Hispanic: 86.1%

Age

Ages 18 to 20: 4.3%
Ages 21 to 24: 5.5%
Ages 25 to 44: 31.7%
Ages 45 to 54: 11.4%
Ages 55 to 59: 4.7%

Ages 60 to 64: 4.3%
Ages 65 plus: 11.7%

Educational Attainment (1990)

Percent having completed high school: 66.2%
Percent having completed college: 13.3%
Elementary and high school enrollment: 24,087

Federal Funds and Grants Received

Total received in 1989: $408,100,000
Funds received per capita: $3,077

Civilian Labor Force

1993 (April):   61,552
1992 average: 61,406
1991 average: 62,142
1990 average: 61,479

Unemployment

1993 (April):   7.1%
1992 average: 8.3%
1991 average: 7.9%
1990 average: 7.3%

Average Annual Pay

1988: $19,057
1987: $18,607
1985: $17,424

Per Capita Personal Income

1991: $15,631
1990: $15,056
1989: $13,998

Business Climate (1987)

Manufacturing

Number of establishments in 1987: 211
Shipments in 1987 ($1,000): N/A
Employees in 1987: N/A
Change in employment, 1982 to 1987: N/A
Average annual pay for manufacturing work, 1989: $26,593
Average annual pay for production work, 1987: N/A

Wholesale Trade

Number of establishments in 1987: 197
Total sales in 1987 ($1,000): $472,300
Change in sales, 1982 to 1987: 2.6%

Retail Trade

Number of establishments in 1987: 748
Total sales in 1987 ($1,000): $472,300
Retail sales per household in 1987: $17,494
Average annual pay in 1989: $10,445

Service Industry

Selected receipts in 1987 ($1,000): $209,900
Average annual pay in 1989: $15,367

Housing

Total number of units in 1990: 52,631
Occupied units in 1990: 49,209

Owner-occupied units in 1990: 73.9%
1993 ACCRA average cost: $89,500
1993 ACCRA average rent for an apartment: $385

Chamber of Commerce

Decatur Chamber of Commerce, John Seymour, President, 515 6th Ave., PO Box 2003, Decatur, AL 35602-2003. 205-353-5312, FAX 205-353-2384

Economic Development Office

Morgan County Industry Development Association, Tommy Ed Roberts, Exec. Director, PO Box 2026, Decatur, AL 35602. 205-353-1213, FAX 205-353-0407

Economic Development Organizations

North Alabama Industry Development Association, John R. Washburn, Exec. Director, 251 Johnston St., S.E., PO Box 1668, Decatur, AL 35602. 205-353-9450, FAX 205-353-5982

Major Businesses

Company Name	Sic	Phone
Alafirst Bancshares, Inc.	6712	(205) 353-2530
Central Bank of the South	6021	(205) 552-4011
Decatur Coca-Cola Bottling	5149	(205) 353-9211
Decatur Transit, Inc.	4214	(205) 353-9601
Gobble-Fite Lumber Co.	5031	(205) 353-5713
Tennessee Valley Printing	2711	(205) 353-4612
Wolverine Tube, Inc.	3351	(205) 353-1310

Colleges and Universities

John C. Calhoun State Community College, Decatur

DOTHAN, AL (MSA)

Geographic Profile

Land Area
1141.5 square miles

Counties and Parishes
Dale
Houston

Ranking Highlights

177 *out of 319 in total* **land area**
180 *out of 319 in* **population growth,** *1970–1990*
139 *out of 310 in having the lowest* **unemployment** *rate*
266 *out of 310 in size of* **labor force**
246 *out of 318 in percentage of* **college graduates**
236 *out of 292 in per capita personal* **income**
245 *out of 319 in number of* **manufacturing establishments**
180 *out of 318 in* **physicians** *per 1000 people*
55 *out of 318 in* **hospital beds** *per 1000 people*
132 *out of 267 in fewest* **crimes** *per 1000 people*
193 *out of 266 in fewest* **violent crimes** *per 1000 people*
37 *out of 319 in per capita* **federal funds and grants**

Quality of Life Indexes (Rate per 1000 population)

Crime rate in 1991:	60.3
Violent crime rate in 1991:	8.3
Physicians rate in 1992:	1.73
Hospital bed rate in 1991:	5.38

ACCRA Cost of Living Indexes

(First quarter 1993, average = 100)
Composite index: 87.4
Utilities index: 96.6
Housing index: 80.2

Population (1990)

Total Population and Growth Rate
1990: 130,964
1980: 122,453
1970: 109,569
Growth rate 1970–1990: 20%

Race and Hispanic Origin
White: 77.0%
Black: 21.2%
Asian/Pacific Islander: 0.9%
Native American: 0.4%
Hispanic origin: 1.3%
White not Hispanic: 46.3%

Age
Ages 18 to 20: 4.7%
Ages 21 to 24: 6.2%
Ages 25 to 44: 31.7%
Ages 45 to 54: 10.1%
Ages 55 to 59: 4.2%
Ages 60 to 64: 4.1%
Ages 65 plus: 11.3%

Educational Attainment (1990)

Percent having completed high school: 70.4%
Percent having completed college: 14.5%
Elementary and high school enrollment: 24,972

Federal Funds and Grants Received

Total received in 1989: $673,000,000
Funds received per capita: $5,135

Civilian Labor Force

1993 (April): 59,795
1992 average: 59,719
1991 average: 58,779
1990 average: 58,650

Unemployment

1993 (April): 7.4%
1992 average: 6.7%
1991 average: 6.2%
1990 average: 5.7%

Average Annual Pay

1988: $18,239
1987: $17,637
1985: $16,264

Per Capita Personal Income

1991: $15,564
1990: $14,828
1989: $14,038

Business Climate (1987)

Manufacturing
Number of establishments in 1987: 148
Shipments in 1987 ($1,000): $895,000
Employees in 1987: 10,200
Change in employment, 1982 to 1987: -5.6%
Average annual pay for manufacturing work, 1989: $20,321
Average annual pay for production work, 1987: $14,899

Wholesale Trade
Number of establishments in 1987: 260
Total sales in 1987 ($1,000): $759,200
Change in sales, 1982 to 1987: 32.4%

Retail Trade
Number of establishments in 1987: 995
Total sales in 1987 ($1,000): $759,200
Retail sales per household in 1987: $17,723
Average annual pay in 1989: $10,712

Service Industry
Selected receipts in 1987 ($1,000): $310,700
Average annual pay in 1989: $19,048

Housing

Total number of units in 1990: 52,628
Occupied units in 1990: 48,418

Owner-occupied units in 1990: 65.2%
1993 ACCRA average cost: $96,000
1993 ACCRA average rent for an apartment: $350

Chamber of Commerce

Dothan Area Chamber of Commerce, J. Dale Hubbard, President, 706 Honeysuckle Rd., PO Box 638, Dothan, AL 36302. 205-792-5138, FAX 205-793-9869

Major Businesses

Company	SIC	Telephone
Dunbarton Corp.	3442	(205) 794-0661
First Alabama Bank	6022	(205) 677-2400

Colleges and Universities

George C. Wallace State Community College, Dothan
Troy State University at Dothan, Dothan

FLORENCE, AL (MSA)

Geographic Profile

Land Area

1264.1 square miles

Counties and Parishes

Colbert
Lauderdale

Ranking Highlights

154 *out of 319 in total* **land area**
218 *out of 319 in* **population growth,** *1970–1990*
201 *out of 310 in having the lowest* **unemployment** *rate*
258 *out of 310 in size of* **labor force**
246 *out of 318 in percentage of* **college graduates**
268 *out of 292 in per capita personal* **income**
208 *out of 319 in number of* **manufacturing establishments**
238 *out of 318 in* **physicians** *per 1000 people*
17 *out of 318 in* **hospital beds** *per 1000 people*
17 *out of 267 in fewest* **crimes** *per 1000 people*
53 *out of 266 in fewest* **violent crimes** *per 1000 people*
164 *out of 319 in per capita* **federal funds and grants**

Quality of Life Indexes (Rate per 1000 population)

Crime rate in 1991:	34.5
Violent crime rate in 1991:	3.2
Physicians rate in 1992:	1.43
Hospital bed rate in 1991:	6.96

ACCRA Cost of Living Indexes

(First quarter 1993, average = 100)

Composite index:	92.7
Utilities index:	92.8
Housing index:	92.9

Population (1990)

Total Population and Growth Rate

1990: 131,327
1980: 135,065
1970: 117,743
Growth rate 1970-1990: 12%

Race and Hispanic Origin

White: 87.1%
Black: 12.4%
Asian/Pacific Islander: 0.2%
Native American: 0.2%
Hispanic origin: 0.4%
White not Hispanic: 86.8%

Age

Ages 18 to 20: 4.9%
Ages 21 to 24: 5.8%
Ages 25 to 44: 29.3%
Ages 45 to 54: 11.4%
Ages 55 to 59: 5.1%

Ages 60 to 64: 5%
Ages 65 plus: 14.4%

Educational Attainment (1990)
Percent having completed high school: 66.8%
Percent having completed college: 14.5%
Elementary and high school enrollment: 22,002

Federal Funds and Grants Received
Total received in 1989: $412,900,000
Funds received per capita: $3,046

Civilian Labor Force
1993 (April): 63,841
1992 average: 63,090
1991 average: 62,174
1990 average: 61,814

Unemployment
1993 (April): 7.1%
1992 average: 7.5%
1991 average: 7.8%
1990 average: 7.1%

Average Annual Pay
1988: $18,322
1987: $17,584
1985: $16,815

Per Capita Personal Income
1991: $14,600
1990: $14,084
1989: $12,798

Business Climate (1987)
Manufacturing
Number of establishments in 1987: 214
Shipments in 1987 ($1,000): $2,037,200
Employees in 1987: 12,200
Change in employment, 1982 to 1987: 3.4%
Average annual pay for manufacturing work, 1989: $22,585
Average annual pay for production work, 1987: $19,200

Wholesale Trade
Number of establishments in 1987: 213
Total sales in 1987 ($1,000): $433,100
Change in sales, 1982 to 1987: 17.9%

Retail Trade
Number of establishments in 1987: 879
Total sales in 1987 ($1,000): $433,100
Retail sales per household in 1987: $13,501
Average annual pay in 1989: $9,757

Service Industry
Selected receipts in 1987 ($1,000): $206,100
Average annual pay in 1989: $16,579

Housing
Total number of units in 1990: 55,334
Occupied units in 1990: 51,001

Owner-occupied units in 1990: 74.1%
1993 ACCRA average cost: $103,417
1993 ACCRA average rent for an apartment: $482

Chamber of Commerce
Chamber of Commerce of the Shoals, Eugene Seaton, Exec. Director, 104 S. Pine St., Florence, AL 35630. 205-764-4661, FAX 205-766-9017

Major Businesses

Company	SIC	Telephone
Alabama-Tennessee Natural Gas Co.	4923	(205) 383-3631
Alatenn Resources, Inc.	4924	(205) 383-3631
Bevis Custom Furniture Inc.	2521	(205) 766-6497
Bigbee Steel Building Inc.	3448	(205) 383-7322
Colbert County Northwest Alabama	8062	(205) 386-4196
Craig, B. H. Construction	1542	(205) 766-3350
Darby, E. H. & Co.	7513	(205) 383-3261
Darby, R. G. Co. Inc.	5031	(205) 767-4680
First National Bank Florence	6021	(205) 767-8400
First United Bancorp Inc.	6021	(205) 767-8400
L & L Services Inc.	7374	(205) 383-6940
Lewis Electric Supply Co.	5063	(205) 383-0681
Martin Industries Inc.	3433	(205) 767-0330
Muscle Shoals Mack Sales	5511	(205) 383-9546
North Alabama Gas District	4924	(205) 383-3306
Pressure Concrete Construction	1771	(205) 764-5941
Public Hospital Board Lauderdale County	8062	(205) 767-9191
R & D Trucking Co. Inc.	4213	(205) 767-4994
Robbins Tire & Rubber Co.	3011	(205) 383-5441
Rogers Inc.	5311	(205) 764-8261
Season Sportswear Inc.	2329	(205) 247-5425
Sheffeld Power Water Gas Department	4931	(205) 383-5221
Stephenson, Nelda Chevrolet	5511	(205) 764-4551
Tee Jays Manufacturing Co.	2253	(205) 767-0560
Tennessee River Inc.	2253	(205) 767-5220
Whitesell Manufacturing	3452	(205) 381-3911

Colleges and Universities
University of North Alabama, Florence

GADSDEN, AL (MSA)

Geographic Profile
Land Area
534.8 square miles

Counties and Parishes
Etowah

Ranking Highlights
285 *out of 319 in total* **land area**
236 *out of 319 in* **population growth,** *1970–1990*
254 *out of 310 in having the lowest* **unemployment** *rate*
300 *out of 310 in size of* **labor force**
314 *out of 318 in percentage of* **college graduates**
280 *out of 292 in per capita personal* **income**
285 *out of 319 in number of* **manufacturing establishments**
196 *out of 318 in* **physicians** *per 1000 people*
 54 *out of 318 in* **hospital beds** *per 1000 people*
157 *out of 267 in fewest* **crimes** *per 1000 people*
212 *out of 266 in fewest* **violent crimes** *per 1000 people*
228 *out of 319 in per capita* **federal funds and grants**

Quality of Life Indexes (Rate per 1000 population)
Crime rate in 1991:   65.0
Violent crime rate in 1991:   9.4
Physicians rate in 1992:   1.66
Hospital bed rate in 1991:   5.39

ACCRA Cost of Living Indexes
(First quarter 1993, average = 100)
Composite index: 92.0
Utilities index: 116.2
Housing index: 73.7

Overview
Gadsden and Etowah County are situated 60 miles northeast of Birmingham, 95 miles southwest of Chattanooga, Tennessee, and some 110 miles west of Atlanta, Georgia. They lie in the northeast Alabama foothills of the Appalachian Mountains. The Coosa River flows south through this area to a juncture with the Alabama River. Gadsden is served by the Gadsden Municipal Airport and the Birmingham Municipal Airport (60 miles southwest). Intersecting highways are Interstate 59, U.S. 11, U.S. 278, U.S. 431, U.S. 411, and Alabama 77. Rail services are provided by Norfolk Southern and CSX Transportation.

Population (1990)
Total Population and Growth Rate
1990: 99,840
1980: 103,057
1970: 94,144
Growth rate 1970–1990: 6%

Race and Hispanic Origin
White: 85.4%
Black: 13.8%
Asian/Pacific Islander: 0.4%
Native American: 0.3%
Hispanic origin: 0.3%
White not Hispanic: 85.2%

Age
Ages 18 to 20: 4.6%
Ages 21 to 24: 5.1%
Ages 25 to 44: 28.8%
Ages 45 to 54: 10.8%
Ages 55 to 59: 5%
Ages 60 to 64: 5.3%
Ages 65 plus: 15.9%

Educational Attainment (1990)
Percent having completed high school: 64.1%
Percent having completed college: 10.2%
Elementary and high school enrollment: 17,725

Federal Funds and Grants Received
Total received in 1989: $266,800,000
Funds received per capita: $2,594

Civilian Labor Force
1993 (April):   42,356
1992 average: 41,920
1991 average: 41,684
1990 average: 42,324

Unemployment
1993 (April): 7.4%
1992 average: 8.9%
1991 average: 10.3%
1990 average: 10.7%

Average Annual Pay
1988: $20,138
1987: $19,444
1985: $17,719

Per Capita Personal Income
1991: $13,739
1990: $13,299
1989: $12,769

Business Climate (1987)
Manufacturing
Number of establishments in 1987: 110
Shipments in 1987 ($1,000): $1,341,100
Employees in 1987: 11,100
Change in employment, 1982 to 1987: 3.7%
Average annual pay for manufacturing work in 1989: $26,318
Average annual pay for production work in 1987: $24,556

Wholesale Trade
Number of establishments in 1987: 137
Total sales in 1987 ($1,000): $333,000
Change in sales, 1982 to 1987: 56.2%

Retail Trade
Number of establishments in 1987: 616
Total sales in 1987 ($1,000): $333,000
Retail sales per household in 1987: $13,630
Average annual pay in 1989: $10,029

Service Industry
Selected receipts in 1987 ($1,000): $141,300
Average annual pay in 1989: $18,899

Housing
Total number of units in 1990: 41,787
Occupied units in 1990: 38,675
Owner-occupied units in 1990: 74.0%
1993 ACCRA average cost: $84,760
1993 ACCRA average rent for an apartment: $346

Chamber of Commerce
Gadsden-Etowah Chamber of Commerce, Tom Quinn, Executive Vice President, One Commerce Square, PO Box 185, Gadsden, AL 35902. 205-543-3472, FAX 205-543-3477

Economic Development Office
Gadsden-Etowah County Industrial Development Authority, Michael McCain, Exec Director, PO Box 271, Gadsden, AL 35902-0271. 205-543-9423, FAX 205-547-2351

Economic Development Organizations
Gadsen Board of Realtors, 406 Duncan, Gadsden, AL 35901. 205-543-7987

Alabama State Employment Service, Elmus Humphrey, Manager, 117 N. 7th St., Gadsden, AL 35901. 205-546-4667

City of Gadsden Planning Department, Ronald Carr, City Manager, PO Box 267, Gadsden, AL 35902. 205-549-4520

Etowah County Commission, Robert Hitt, Chairman, 800 Forrest Ave., Gadsden, AL 35901. 205-549-5300

Local Incentives for Business
Financing Incentives: Industrial revenue bonds (IRB), tax-free or taxable, revolving loan fund.

Local Real Estate Tax Exemptions/Abatements: 100% for up to 20 years if IRB financed. Approximately 65% for up to 10 years if conventionally financed.

Local Property Tax Exemptions on Production Machinery and Equipment: 100% for up to 20 years if financed with IRB proceeds. Approximately 65% for up to 10 years if conventionally financed.

Local Property Tax Exemption/Abatements on Pollution Control Equipment: 100% exempt.

Local Property Tax Exemptions/Abatements on Inventories: No ad valorem taxes are assessed on raw materials, work in process or finished goods. No inventory taxes.

Corporate Income Tax Credits on Job Creation and/or Capital Investment: Up to $2,500 per employee, when site is in a qualified state enterprise zone; credits can also be applied against corporate franchise tax.

Sales for Exemptions on Construction Materials, Purchases of Production Machinery and Equipment, Purchases of Raw Matrials: 100% on construction materials, furniture, equipment and machinery.

State Local Aid in Site Infrastructured Improvements: State site preparation grant of up to $150,000 is possible. Most sites are fully infrastructured.

Manpower Training: The Alabama Industrial Development Training Institute, a division of the Department of Postsecondary Education, would make a specific training assistance proposal to prospective industries. The Institute will conduct pre-hire and on-the-job training to the employer's specifications free of charge.

In-house training under the Job Training Partnership Act, with partial salary reimbursements and federal income tax credits, can be handled by the East Alabama Skills Center. For hiring and training eligible employees, employers can be reimbursed for up to 50% of salaries for a negotiated period of time.

Industrial Sites
Industrial Development Board, City of Gadsden, C.B. Collier, Secretary, 122 Oak Circle, Gadsden, AL 35901. 205-442-3492

Major Businesses

Company	SIC	Telephone
Baptist Hospital of Gadsden	8062	(205) 543-4096
Belk-Hudson Co. Inc.	5311	(205) 547-8621
Boatner Construction Co	1541	(205) 442-3820
Copeland Building Co. Inc.	1542	(205) 543-7120
Culp Industries Inc.	5093	(205) 538-7891
Dairymans Supply Co.-Alabama	5051	(205) 492-9560
Dawson Construction Co.	1542	(205) 547-2566
Gregerson's Foods, Inc.	5411	(205) 549-0644
Hollar Co. Inc.	5411	(205) 547-1644
Life Insurance Co. of Alabama	6311	(205) 543-2022
Mid-South Industries, Inc.	3634	(205) 442-3287
Osborn Transportation Inc.	4213	(205) 442-2514
Phillips, IRA Inc.	5171	(205) 547-0591
Pierson Chevrolet Inc.	5511	(205) 546-3391
Wallace Construction Co.	1542	(205) 442-2658

Colleges and Universities
Gadsden State Community College, Gadsden. Offers two-year terminal courses in civil engineering technology and mechanical engineering technology. The College is a partner in the Tom Bevill Center for Advanced Manufacturing Technology and works with the state AIDT program.

Additional Information
Etowah County, Alabama. Gadsden-Etowah Chamber of Commerce, 1989. 48p.

HUNTSVILLE, AL (MSA)

Geographic Profile

Land Area

805.0 square miles

Counties and Parishes

Madison

Ranking Highlights

235 *out of 319 in total* **land area**

142 *out of 319 in* **population growth,** *1970–1990*

47 *out of 310 in having the lowest* **unemployment** *rate*

152 *out of 310 in size of* **labor force**

25 *out of 318 in the percentage of* **college graduates**

84 *out of 292 in per capita personal* **income**

167 *out of 319 in number of* **manufacturing establishments**

166 *out of 318 in* **physicians** *per 1000 people*

153 *out of 318 in* **hospital beds** *per 1000 people*

N/A *out of 267 in fewest* **crimes** *per 1000 people*

N/A *out of 266 in fewest* **violent crimes** *per 1000 people*

3 *out of 319 in per capita* **federal funds and grants**

Quality of Life Indexes (Rate per 1000 population)

Crime rate in 1991:	N/A
Violent crime rate in 1991:	N/A
Physicians rate in 1992:	1.78
Hospital bed rate in 1991:	3.91

ACCRA Cost of Living Indexes

(First quarter 1993, average = 100)

Composite index:	97.2
Utilities index:	94.1
Housing index:	91.3

Population (1990)

Total Population and Growth Rate

1990: 238,912

1980: 196,966

1970: 186,540

Growth rate 1970–1990: 28%

Race and Hispanic Origin

White: 77.1%

Black: 20.1%

Asian/Pacific Islander: 1.8%

Native American: 0.7%

Hispanic origin: 1.2%

White not Hispanic: 76.3%

Age

Ages 18 to 20: 5.1%

Ages 21 to 24: 6.4%

Ages 25 to 44: 34.8%

Ages 45 to 54: 11.3%

Ages 55 to 59: 4.9%

Ages 60 to 64: 3.9%

Ages 65 plus: 9%

Educational Attainment (1990)

Percent having completed high school: 80.2%

Percent having completed college: 30.1%

Elementary and high school enrollment: 38,618

Federal Funds and Grants Received

Total received in 1989: $2,711,100,000

Funds received per capita: $11,453

Civilian Labor Force

1993 (April): 138,054

1992 average: 136,337

1991 average: 134,162

1990 average: 133,713

Unemployment

1993 (April): 4.8%

1992 average: 4.8%

1991 average: 5.2%

1990 average: 4.7%

Average Annual Pay

1988: $23,480

1987: $22,406

1985: $20,261

Per Capita Personal Income

1991: $18,763

1990: $18,092

1989: $16,954

Business Climate (1987)

Manufacturing

Number of establishments in 1987: 293

Shipments in 1987 ($1,000): $3,427,200

Employees in 1987: 25,600

Change in employment, 1982 to 1987: 7.6%

Average annual pay for manufacturing work in 1989: $29,899

Average annual pay for production work in 1987: $23,640

Wholesale Trade

Number of establishments in 1987: 404

Total sales in 1987 ($1,000): $1,506,200

Change in sales, 1982 to 1987: 84.0%

Retail Trade

Number of establishments in 1987: 1,460

Total sales in 1987 ($1,000): $1,506,200

Retail sales per household in 1987: $17,312

Average annual pay in 1989: $10,774

Service Industry

Selected receipts in 1987 ($1,000): $1,247,600

Average annual pay in 1989: $25,039

Housing

Total number of units in 1990: 97,855

Occupied units in 1990: 91,208
Owner-occupied units in 1990: 65.1%
1993 ACCRA average cost: $105,111
1993 ACCRA average rent for an apartment: $441

Chamber of Commerce

Huntsville-Madison County Chamber of Commerce, Larry J. Waller, President, 225 Church St., N.W., PO Box 408, Huntsville, AL 35801. 205-535-2000, FAX 205-535-2015

Economic Development Office

Dept. of Planning & Econ. Dev., Madison County Commisssion, Peggy Barnard, Director, Madison County Courthouse, 7th fl. Huntsville, AL 35801. 205-532-3505, FAX 205-532-3704

Major Businesses

Company	SIC	Telephone
Anderson, Woody Ford	5511	(205) 539-9441
Avex Electronics Inc.	3674	(205) 722-6000
Bethco Inc.	5045	(205) 830-8950
Colsa Inc.	7373	(205) 830-5412
Comptronix Corp.	3672	(205) 582-1800
Gold Star of America Inc.	3651	(205) 772-0623
Halsey, W. L. Grocery	5141	(205) 772-9691
Huntsville Hospital	8062	(205) 533-8020
Intergraph Corp.	7373	(205) 730-2000
Kilpatrick Chevrolet Inc.	5511	(205) 593-4253
Nichols Research Corp.	7371	(205) 883-1140
ONA Corp.	3621	(205) 772-9671
Phoenix Microsystems Inc.	3825	(205) 721-1200
Redstone Federal Credit	6141	(205) 837-6110
Schrimsher, J. T. Co. Inc.	1541	(205) 534-1696
SCI Manufacturing Inc.	3679	(205) 882-4800
SCI Systems Inc.	3571	(205) 882-4800
SCI Technology, Inc.	7373	(205) 882-4800
Shelby Contracting Co. Inc.	1611	(205) 533-4727
Sikes, Jeff Inc.	5511	(205) 881-1881
Spencer Companies Inc.	5171	(205) 533-1150
Universal Data Systems	3661	(205) 430-8000
USBI Booster Production	3764	(205) 721-2400

Colleges and Universities

J. F. Drake State Technical College, Huntsville
Oakwood College, Huntsville
University of Alabama in Huntsville, Huntsville

MOBILE, AL (MSA)

Geographic Profile

Land Area
2829.9 square miles

Counties and Parishes
Baldwin
Mobile

Ranking Highlights

  52 *out of 319 in total* **land area**
154 *out of 319 in* **population growth,** *1970–1990*
219 *out of 310 in having the lowest* **unemployment** *rate*
102 *out of 310 in size of* **labor force**
225 *out of 318 in percentage of* **college graduates**
253 *out of 292 in per capita personal* **income**
112 *out of 319 in number of* **manufacturing establishments**
130 *out of 318 in* **physicians** *per 1000 people*
  83 *out of 318 in* **hospital beds** *per 1000 people*
N/A *out of 267 in fewest* **crimes** *per 1000 people*
N/A *out of 266 in fewest* **violent crimes** *per 1000 people*
222 *out of 319 in per capita* **federal funds and grants**

Quality of Life Indexes (Rate per 1000 population)

Crime rate in 1991:	N/A
Violent crime rate in 1991:	N/A
Physicians rate in 1992:	1.94
Hospital bed rate in 1991:	4.9

ACCRA Cost of Living Indexes

(First quarter 1993, average = 100)
Composite index: 94.4
Utilities index: 110.7
Housing index: 77.7

Overview

Mobile is located in southwest Alabama at the head of Mobile Bay, thirty-one miles from the Gulf of Mexico. It is the second largest metropolitan area in Alabama and the state's major port.

The metropolitan area, which includes Mobile and Baldwin counties, covers an area of 2,829 square miles. The dominant urban area is the City of Mobile, which includes 141.9 square miles of the 1,238 square miles in Mobile County. In September 1992 *Money* magazine rated Mobile the fifty-sixth best metro area in which to live among the top 300 metropolitan areas in the United States.

In 1990, the *American Business Information* magazine ranked it eleventh among the 100 major metropolitan areas in the United States for business growth. From 1985 to 1990, ninety-five new companies were created and 288 existing companies were expanded, resulting in 11,211 new jobs. Items and goods produced in the area include paper, aircraft engines, aluminum, chemicals and paints, cement, apparel, pumps, batteries, ship-related items, rayon fibers, and bakery products.

Mobile, long recognized as a prime port location, is experiencing a period of strong growth. It served more than thirteen hundred ships in 1991. A new $12 million warehouse was opened in 1991 by the Alabama State Docks Department, which has more than doubled its general cargo tonnage handling from 1987 to 1991, and brings in a revenue of more than $45 million. Mobile's importance as the center of a far-reaching distribution network is further enhanced by the Brookly Complex, a designated Foreign Trade Zone serviced by two railroads and two aviation runways. Sixty-five motor freight lines are certified to transport interstate shipments to and from the Mobile area.

The Mobile Regional Airport is located approximately fourteen miles from downtown Mobile. Air travelers are serviced by six major air carriers and commuter airlines. The Downtown Airport at Brookley is a 1,700-acre transportation terminal favored by private and corporate planes for its proximity to downtown Mobile, which is only four minutes away by car. Motorists may reach Mobile via two interstate highways, I-10 and I-65, and by U.S. highways 31, 43, 45, 90, and 98. A new $100 million interstate spur completed in 1993 connects I-65 and I-10 in downtown Mobile. In addition, several state roads head into the city. AMTRAK provides passenger rail service between Mobile and New Orleans, Louisiana, Atlanta, Georgia, and New York City.

Population (1990)

Total Population and Growth Rate
1990: 476,923
1980: 443,536
1970: 376,690
Growth rate 1970–1990: 27%

Race and Hispanic Origin
White: 71.2%
Black: 27.4%
Asian/Pacific Islander: 0.8%
Native American: 0.5%
Hispanic origin: 0.9%
White not Hispanic: 70.5%

Age
Ages 18 to 20: 4.6%
Ages 21 to 24: 5.4%
Ages 25 to 44: 30.5%
Ages 45 to 54: 10.2%
Ages 55 to 59: 4.3%
Ages 60 to 64: 4.4%
Ages 65 plus: 12.5%

Educational Attainment (1990)
Percent having completed high school: 70.8%
Percent having completed college: 15.8%
Elementary and high school enrollment: 92,260

Federal Funds and Grants Received
Total received in 1989: $1,269,700,000
Funds received per capita: $2,615

Civilian Labor Force
1993 (April): 231,150
1992 average: 225,358
1991 average: 217,310
1990 average: 210,662

Unemployment
1993 (April): 7.5%
1992 average: 7.9%
1991 average: 7.0%
1990 average: 6.9%

Average Annual Pay
1988: $18,454
1987: $17,866
1985: $16,781

Per Capita Personal Income
1991: $15,134
1990: $14,268
1989: $13,335

Business Climate (1987)

Manufacturing
Number of establishments in 1987: 517
Shipments in 1987 ($1,000): $4,592,900
Employees in 1987: 25,000
Change in employment, 1982 to 1987: -11.0%
Average annual pay for manufacturing work in 1989: $26,456
Average annual pay for production work in 1987: $21,519

Wholesale Trade
Number of establishments in 1987: 917
Total sales in 1987 ($1,000): $2,890,800
Change in sales, 1982 to 1987: 21.3%

Retail Trade
Number of establishments in 1987: 2,982
Total sales in 1987 ($1,000): $2,890,800
Retail sales per household in 1987: $15,619
Average annual pay in 1989: $11,326

Service Industry
Selected receipts in 1987 ($1,000): $1,061,100
Average annual pay in 1989: $17,888

Office Real Estate (1992)
Office space inventory: square feet
Average class A Central Business District rental range per sq. ft: $10.00

Vacancy Rates
All areas: 17.4%

Vacancy Rates in Central Business District
Class A space: 25.0%
Class B space: 25.0%

Vacancy Rates Outside Central Business District

Class A space: 6.0%

Class B space: 6.0%

Housing

Total number of units in 1990: 202,153

Occupied units in 1990: 173,943

Owner-occupied units in 1990: 69.3%

1993 ACCRA average cost: $92,260

1993 ACCRA average rent for an apartment: $352

Chamber of Commerce

Mobile Area Chamber of Commerce, Jay A. Garner, Sr. Vice Pres., Economic Development, 451 Government St., PO Box 2187, Mobile, AL 36652. 205-433-6951, FAX 205-432-1143

Economic Development Office

Mobile Airport Auth.-Brookley Complex, Larry Cook, Manager, 1891 9th St., Mobile, AL 36615. 205-438-7334, FAX 205-694-7667

Industrial Sites

Mobile Commerce Park. A cooperative venture of the City of Mobile, the industrial development boards of the city and county within the MSA, the Mobile Water and Sewer Board, utility companies and the Mobile Area Chamber of Commerce.

Business Innovation Center. A cooperative venture of the City of Mobile, the County of Mobile, the University of South Alabama and the Mobile Area Chamber of Commerce.

Major Businesses

Company	SIC	Telephone
Alabama State Docks Department	4491	(205) 690-6112
Altus Bank Inc.	6035	(205) 473-0500
Bama Sea Products Inc.	5146	(205) 824-2050
Bay Chevrolet Inc.	5511	(205) 476-8080
Bender Shipbuilding & Repair	3731	(205) 431-8000
Big 10 Tire Store Inc.	5531	(205) 639-0692
Bon Secour Fisheries Inc.	5146	(205) 949-7411
Bullard, Joe Oldsmobile Inc.	5511	(205) 471-6141
Cooper/T. Smith Corp.	4491	(205) 431-6100
Delchamps Inc.	5411	(205) 433-0431
Gayfer C J Co. Inc.	5311	(205) 471-6000
Graham, John E. & Sons	4499	(205) 824-4136
Greer, Autry And Sons, Inc.	5411	(205) 457-8655
Infirmary Health Systems	8062	(205) 431-4901
International Industries	1241	(205) 344-2700
Mannor Corp.	2325	(205) 937-6767
Midtown Restaurant Corp.	5812	(205) 661-6191
Mitchell Co.	6512	(205) 476-1200
Mitchell Homes	1521	(205) 476-1200
Mobile Gas Service Corp.	4923	(205) 476-2720

Major Businesses (Continued)

Company	SIC	Telephone
Mobile Infirmary Medical Center	8062	(205) 431-2400
Mobile Paint Manufacturing Co.	2851	(205) 443-6110
Morrison Inc.	5812	(205) 344-3000
Morrisons Custom Management Services	8742	(205) 344-3000
QMS Inc.	3577	(205) 633-4300
Standard Furniture Manufacturing Co.	2511	(205) 937-6741
Trail Pontiac-GMC Truck Inc.	5511	(205) 476-4141
University South Alabama Medical	8062	(205) 471-7000

Colleges and Universities

Bishop State Community College, Mobile

Mobile College, Mobile

Southwest State Technical College, Mobile

Spring Hill College, Mobile

University of South Alabama, Mobile

Additional Information

Mobile, Alabama Community Profile, 1990. Mobile Area Chamber of Commerce, Economic Development Dept., 1990. 4p.

The Mobile Market, a publication summarizing the demographics of the Mobile Area. Mobile Area Chamber of Commerce, Economic Development Department, March 1990. 6p.

Mobile's Economic Review, 1985-1990. Mobile Area Chamber of Commerce, January 1991. 4p.

MONTGOMERY, AL (MSA)

Geographic Profile

Land Area

2007.5 square miles

Counties and Parishes

Autauga

Elmore

Montgomery

Ranking Highlights

92 *out of 319 in total* **land area**

136 *out of 319 in* **population growth,** *1970–1990*

121 *out of 310 in having the lowest* **unemployment** *rate*

147 *out of 310 in size of* **labor force**

117 *out of 318 in percentage of* **college graduates**

153 *out of 292 in per capita personal* **income**

153 *out of 319 in number of* **manufacturing establishments**

212 *out of 318 in* **physicians** *per 1000 people*

116 *out of 318 in* **hospital beds** *per 1000 people*

197 *out of 267 in fewest* **crimes** *per 1000 people*

197 *out of 266 in fewest* **violent crimes** *per 1000 people*

53 *out of 319 in per capita* **federal funds and grants**

Quality of Life Indexes (Rate per 1000 population)

Crime rate in 1991:	71.3
Violent crime rate in 1991:	8.5
Physicians rate in 1992:	1.56
Hospital bed rate in 1991:	4.4

ACCRA Cost of Living Indexes

(First quarter 1993, average = 100)

Composite index:	98.7
Utilities index:	122.3
Housing index:	81.0

Population (1990)

Total Population and Growth Rate

1990: 292,517

1980: 272,687

1970: 225,911

Growth rate 1970–1990: 29%

Race and Hispanic Origin

White: 63.0%

Black: 36.0%

Asian/Pacific Islander: 0.6%

Native American: 0.2%

Hispanic origin: 0.7%

White not Hispanic: 62.6%

Age

Ages 18 to 20: 5.2%

Ages 21 to 24: 5.8%

Ages 25 to 44: 32%

Ages 45 to 54: 10%

Ages 55 to 59: 4.3%

Ages 60 to 64: 3.9%

Ages 65 plus: 11.4%

Educational Attainment (1990)

Percent having completed high school: 73.2%

Percent having completed college: 21.1%

Elementary and high school enrollment: 56,117

Federal Funds and Grants Received

Total received in 1989: $1,377,700,000

Funds received per capita: $4,581

Civilian Labor Force

1993 (April): 144,548

1992 average: 140,573

1991 average: 135,982

1990 average: 137,718

Unemployment

1993 (April): 6.5%

1992 average: 6.4%

1991 average: 6.2%

1990 average: 6.2%

Average Annual Pay

1988: $18,525

1987: $17,956

1985: $16,809

Per Capita Personal Income

1991: $17,158

1990: $16,519

1989: $15,523

Business Climate (1987)

Manufacturing

Number of establishments in 1987: 337

Shipments in 1987 ($1,000): $1,895,200

Employees in 1987: 18,600

Change in employment, 1982 to 1987: 21.6%

Average annual pay for manufacturing work in 1989: $20,671

Average annual pay for production work in 1987: $16,482

Wholesale Trade

Number of establishments in 1987: 521

Total sales in 1987 ($1,000): $2,486,300

Change in sales, 1982 to 1987: 17.3%

Retail Trade

Number of establishments in 1987: 1,647

Total sales in 1987 ($1,000): $2,486,300

Retail sales per household in 1987: $16,188

Average annual pay in 1989: $11,531

Service Industry

Selected receipts in 1987 ($1,000): $686,700

Average annual pay in 1989: $17,925

Housing
Total number of units in 1990: 116,754
Occupied units in 1990: 105,531
Owner-occupied units in 1990: 67.1%
1993 ACCRA average cost: $91,897
1993 ACCRA average rent for an apartment: $416

Chamber of Commerce
Montgomery Area Chamber of Commerce, Randall L. George, President, 41 Commerce St., PO Box 79, Montgomery, AL 36101. 205-834-5200, FAX 205-265-4745

Major Businesses

Company	SIC	Telephone
Alfa Insurance Corp.	6331	(205) 288-3900
Amret Inc.	5651	(205) 942-1234
Baptist Medical Center	8062	(205) 288-2100
Blount Inc.	1542	(205) 244-4000
Brewbaker Motors Inc.	5511	(205) 279-0174
Caddell Construction Co., Inc.	1541	(205) 272-7723
Capitol Chevrolet Inc.	5511	(205) 272-8700
CCC Associates Co.	0181	(205) 272-2140
Cobb-Pontiac, Cadillac Inc.	5511	(205) 277-3480
Colonial Bancgroup Inc.	6022	(205) 240-5000
Durr-Fillauer Medical, Inc.	5122	(205) 241-8800
Enstar Specialty Retail	5661	(205) 270-2120
First Alabama Bancshares	6712	(205) 832-8011
First Alabama Bank	6022	(205) 832-8011
Hudson-Thompson Inc.	5141	(205) 288-6250
Ingram, Jack Motors Inc.	5511	(205) 277-5700
Jackson Hospital & Clinic	8062	(205) 293-8834
National Industries Inc.	3694	(205) 277-1551
Norment Industries Inc.	1731	(205) 281-8440
Prattville Mfg. Inc.	3714	(205) 365-2145
Sabel Industries, Inc.	5051	(205) 265-6771
Smith Industries Inc.	3432	(205) 277-8520
Southeastern Energy Corp.	5172	(205) 265-2501
Southern Granty Insurance Co.	6331	(205) 270-6000
Sylvest Poultry Inc.	2015	(205) 281-0400
Taylor, T. H. Inc.	1541	(205) 277-3600
Weil Brothers-Cotton Inc.	5159	(205) 269-1551

Colleges and Universities
Alabama State University, Montgomery
Auburn University at Montgomery, Montgomery
Draughons Junior College, Montgomery
Faulkner University, Montgomery
Huntingdon College, Montgomery
John M. Patterson State Technical College, Montgomery
Trenholm State Technical College, Montgomery
Troy State University in Montgomery, Montgomery

TUSCALOOSA, AL (MSA)

Geographic Profile
Land Area
1325.3 square miles

Counties and Parishes
Tuscaloosa

Ranking Highlights
149 *out of 319 in total* land area
133 *out of 319 in* population growth, *1970–1990*
 92 *out of 310 in having the lowest* unemployment *rate*
225 *out of 310 in size of* labor force
139 *out of 318 in percentage of* college graduates
246 *out of 292 in per capita personal* income
244 *out of 319 in number of* manufacturing establishments
139 *out of 318 in* physicians *per 1000 people*
 86 *out of 318 in* hospital beds *per 1000 people*
230 *out of 267 in fewest* crimes *per 1000 people*
218 *out of 266 in fewest* violent crimes *per 1000 people*
241 *out of 319 in per capita* federal funds and grants

Quality of Life Indexes (Rate per 1000 population)
Crime rate in 1991:   81.3
Violent crime rate in 1991:   9.7
Physicians rate in 1992:   1.89
Hospital bed rate in 1991:   4.86

ACCRA Cost of Living Indexes
(First quarter 1993, average = 100)
Composite index: 96.7
Utilities index: 115.9
Housing index: 83.2

Population (1990)
Total Population and Growth Rate
1990: 150,522
1980: 137,541
1970: 116,029
Growth rate 1970–1990: 30%

Race and Hispanic Origin
White: 72.7%
Black: 26.2%
Asian/Pacific Islander: 0.8%
Native American: 0.2%
Hispanic origin: 0.6%
White not Hispanic: 72.3%

Age
Ages 18 to 20: 8.7%
Ages 21 to 24: 8.9%
Ages 25 to 44: 30%
Ages 45 to 54: 9.2%
Ages 55 to 59: 4.1%

Ages 60 to 64: 4.2%
Ages 65 plus: 11.3%

Educational Attainment (1990)
Percent having completed high school: 69.6%
Percent having completed college: 20.0%
Elementary and high school enrollment: 24,908

Federal Funds and Grants Received
Total received in 1989: $366,900,000
Funds received per capita: $2,524

Civilian Labor Force
1993 (April):   75,574
1992 average: 73,496
1991 average: 73,749
1990 average: 73,778

Unemployment
1993 (April): 5.6%
1992 average: 5.9%
1991 average: 5.4%
1990 average: 5.0%

Average Annual Pay
1988: $19,497
1987: $18,983
1985: $17,805

Per Capita Personal Income
1991: $15,236
1990: $14,797
1989: $13,628

Business Climate (1987)
Manufacturing
Number of establishments in 1987: 152
Shipments in 1987 ($1,000): $1,392,200
Employees in 1987: 8,700
Change in employment, 1982 to 1987: 22.5%
Average annual pay for manufacturing work in 1989: $25,361
Average annual pay for production work in 1987: $22,954

Wholesale Trade
Number of establishments in 1987: 167
Total sales in 1987 ($1,000): $392,000
Change in sales, 1982 to 1987: 38.6%

Retail Trade
Number of establishments in 1987: 920
Total sales in 1987 ($1,000): $392,000
Retail sales per household in 1987: $16,052
Average annual pay in 1989: $10,403

Service Industry
Selected receipts in 1987 ($1,000): $244,800
Average annual pay in 1989: $16,250

Housing
Total number of units in 1990: 58,740
Occupied units in 1990: 55,354
Owner-occupied units in 1990: 61.5%
1993 ACCRA average cost: $93,760
1993 ACCRA average rent for an apartment: $425

Chamber of Commerce
West Alabama Chamber of Commerce, Johnnie R. Aycock, Exec. Vice President, 2200 University Blvd., PO Box 020410, Tuscaloosa, AL 35402. 205-758-7588, FAX 205-391-0565

Economic Development Office
Tuscaloosa County Industrial Development Authority, J. Dara Longgrear, Exec. Director, 2204 University Blvd., PO Box 030167, Tuscaloosa, AL 35403-0167. 205-349-1414, FAX 205-349-1416

Major Businesses

Company	SIC	Telephone
Alabama Feed Mills Inc.	2048	(205) 752-2588
Armstrong Oil Co. Inc.	5171	(205) 349-1666
Barkley Pontiac-Cadillac GMC	5511	(205) 556-6600
Black Warrior Methane Corp.	1311	(205) 556-6000
Bunn, S. T. Construction Co.	1611	(205) 752-8195
C & H Mining Co. Inc.	1231	(205) 556-6239
Campbell & Associates Inc.	1541	(205) 758-6605
Coral Industries Inc.	3231	(205) 345-1013
DCH Healthcare Authority	8062	(205) 759-7111
Deloach B. Lincoln Mercury	5511	(205) 758-9015
Friday Lumber Co. Inc.	5211	(205) 345-3515
Friday Oil Co. Inc.	5171	(205) 759-4291
G B M Services Inc.	5511	(205) 345-8040
Gulf States Paper Corp.	2611	(205) 553-6200
H M C Bridge Co.	1622	(205) 345-6061
Harco Drug Inc.	5912	(205) 345-2400
House Doctor	1521	(205) 752-7884
Howell Lumber Co. Inc.	5031	(205) 339-4838
Industrial Warehouse Services	4225	(205) 759-1290
Krupp Oil Co. Inc.	5171	(205) 553-7503
Mc Abee Construction Inc.	1711	(205) 349-2212
Peco Foods Inc.	0254	(205) 345-3955
Plott, John Co. Inc.	1623	(205) 345-5678
Pugh, Roland Construction	1623	(205) 339-4321
Southland National Insurance	6311	(205) 345-7410
Spillers Associated Furniture	5712	(205) 391-0300
Townsend Ford Inc.	5511	(205) 752-0401
Walter, Jim Resources Inc.	1222	(205) 254-7481
West Alabama General Hospital	8062	(205) 339-5100
Zeigler, R. L. Co., Inc.	2013	(205) 758-3621

Colleges and Universities
Shelton State Community College, Tuscaloosa
Stillman College, Tuscaloosa
University of Alabama, Tuscaloosa

ALASKA

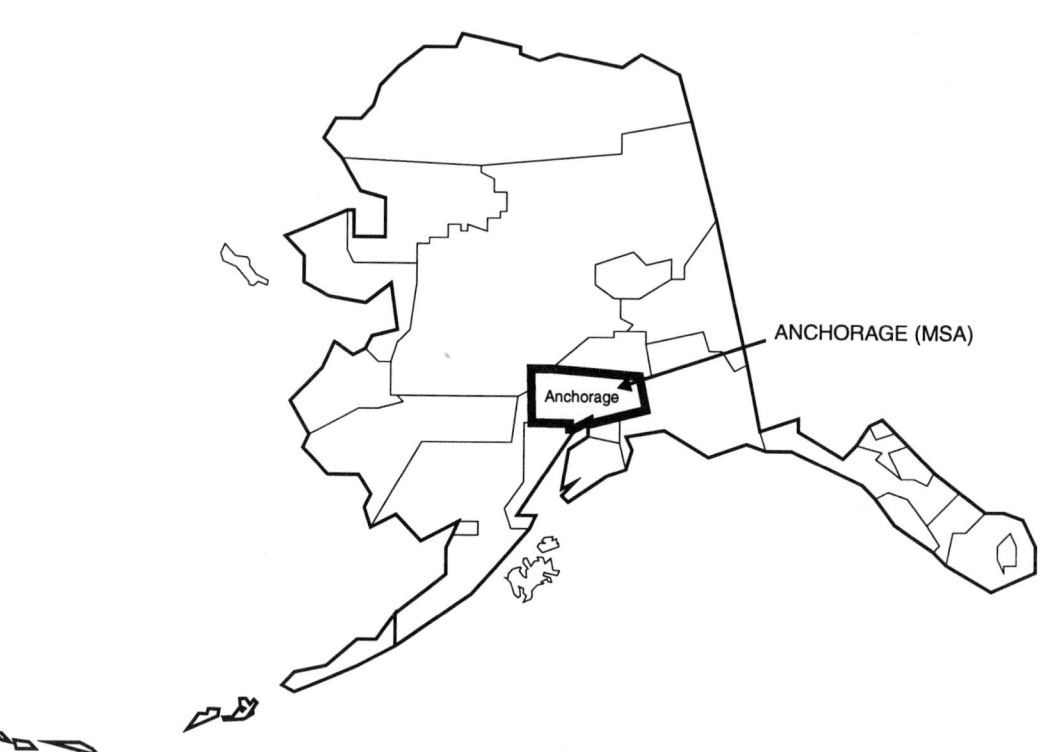

ANCHORAGE (MSA)

Anchorage

ALASKA

Population
1990: 550,043
1980: 401,851

Age
Ages 18 to 20: 22,934
Ages 21 to 24: 32,913
Ages 25 to 44: 216,062
Ages 45 to 54: 53,929
Ages 55 to 59: 16,595
Ages 60 to 64: 12,897
Median age: 29.4

Race
White: 415,492
Black: 22,451
Asian/Pacific Islander: 19,728
Native American: 85,698
Hispanic origin: 17,803

Households
Total: 188,915
Persons per household: 2.80

Sex
Male: 289,867
Female: 260,176

Population Migration
Domestic migration: -56,000
International migration: 7,000

Projection of the Population in 1995
Total: 540,000
18 to 64: 350,000

Civilian Labor Force
1993: 256,900
1992: 257,000
1991: 258,400
1990: 248,000

Manufacturing
1995 Projection: 15,800
1992: 18,000
1991: 11,800
1990: 11,300
1989: 11,600

Services
1995 Projection: 75,500
1992: 53,700
1991: 50,500
1990: 49,700
1989: 46,900

Wholesale and Retail Trade
1995 Projection: 50,900
1992: 47,900
1991: 46,800
1990: 46,400
1989: 44,900

Unemployment Rate
1993: 10.4%
1992: 11.6%
1991: 7.7%
1990: 8.4%

Employer Unemployment Contributions
Contribution Rate
1992: 2.65%
1991: 3.16%
1990: 4.11%

Average Weekly Benefit
1992: $170.32
1991: $170.00
1990: $162.76

Gross State Product (Million $)
1989: $19,582
1988: $17,681
1987: $16,994
1979: $9,201
Growth rate, 1979 to 1989: 112.8%

Capital Expenditures of Manufacturing Industries
1990: $93,600,000
1989: $102,100,000
1988: $58,300,000
1987: $68,600,000

State Tax Rates
Individual income: None

Corporate income: Range from 1% ($10,000 or less) to 9.4% (above $90,000).

General property: Maximum of 3%, rates fixed locally. Assessed at full and true value.

General sales: None

Gasoline: 8¢ per gallon

Income

Median income for a 4 person family: $48,411

Personal per Capita Income

1992: $21,603

1991: $21,144

1990: $20,867

Disposable per Capita Income

1992: $19,093

1991: $18,569

1990: $18,303

Private Employment Weekly Wages

Average

1989: $546

1988: $503

1987: $503

Manufacturing

1989: $502

1988: $494

1987: $488

Services

1989: $425

1988: $399

1987: $390

Wholesale

1989: N/A

1988: $570

1987: $573

Retail

1989: $309

1988: $294

1987: $294

Highway Statistics

Total Highway Miles

1990: 13,485

1989: 12,272

1988: 12,189

Federal Highway Aid

1991: $151,720,000

1990: $150,749,000

1989: $153,453,000

Electricity

Average Cost per Kilowatt Hour

1990: 8.61¢

1989: 9.12¢

1988: 9.26¢

Housing (1990)

Owner occupied units: 105,989

Median house value: $94,400

Renter occupied units: 82,926

Median rent: $503

Total vacant units: 43,693

Homeowner vacancy rate: 4.5%

Rental vacancy rate: 8.5%

State Business Incentives and Assistance

Financial and Business Assistance

State Capital Matching Grants Program. Administered by the Alaska Department of Commerce and Economic Development, this program is designed to assist communities in meeting the matching requirements of federal and other non-state agencies. It will help to provide an eligible applicant with matching funds if local funds are not available.

Small Business and Export Federally Guaranteed Loan Program. This program may purchase the federally guaranteed portion of loans made by private financial institutions. It could also help finance working capital, inventory, construction, and other types of projects.

Export Assistant Program. Administered by the Alaska Industrial Development and Export Authority, this program is designed to facilitate the export of Alaskan goods, services, and raw materials by guaranteeing loans made for eligible export transactions.

Alaska Regional Development Organizations Program. Administered by the Alaska Department of Commerce and Economic Development, Business Development Division, this program is designed to assist economic development at the regional and local levels through regional development organizations. Matching grants of up to $50,000 per year for financial and technical assistance are provided to each region that qualifies.

Alaska Science & Technology Foundation. Established in 1988, ASTF is a public corporation promoting and enhancing through basic research: economic development and technological innovation, telecommunications, and development of Alaskan scientific capabilities. A $100 endowment enables ASTF to annually fund up to $8.5 million in innovation grants.

Education and Training

Job Training Partnership Act. This program operates with funding from the U.S. Department of Labor. It provides job training and other employment related services.

State Offices

Real estate: Department of Commerce & Economic Development, Real Estate Commission, James L. Magowan, Exec Director, 3601 C St., Room 798, Anchorage, AK 99503. 907-563-2169

Chamber of commerce: Alaska State Chamber of Commerce, George Krusz, President, 217 2nd St. #201, Juneau, AK 99801. 907-586-2323

Economic development: Commerce & Economic Development Department, Alaska Industrial Development Authority, William Scott, Exec Director, 480 W. Tudor, Anchorage, AK 99503. 907-561-8050

Alaska State Office of International Trade, Robert Poe, Director, 3601 C St., Ste. 742, Anchorage, AK 99503. 907-561-5585

Community and Regional Affairs Department, Municipal and Regional Assistance Division, Mary Rutherford, Director, 949 E 36th Ave., Room 410, Anchorage, AK 95508. 907-561-8586

Juneau Economic Development Council, Jim Kohler, Director, 124 W. 5th St., Juneau, AK 99801. 907-463-3662

Alaska Science and Technology Foundation, John W. Sibert, Exec Director, 550 W. 7th Avenue, Ste. 360, Anchorage, AK 99501-3555. 907-272-4333

Alaska Business Development Center, Inc., Gary Selk, President, 821 N St. #103, Anchorage, AK 99501. 907-279-7427

Small Business Development Center, Jan Fredericks, State Director, Anchorage Community College, 7th Avenue, Ste. 115, Anchorage, AK 99501. 907-274-7232

Environmental affairs: Environmental Quality Division, Larry Dietrick, Director, PO Box O, Juneau, AK 99811-1800. 907-465-2640

Labor: Department of Labor, Jim Sampson, Commissioner, PO Box 21149, Juneau, AK 99802-1149. 907-465-2700

Unemployment: Department of Labor, Employment Security Division, Joseph Sitton, Director, PO Box 3-7000, Juneau, AK 99802-1218. 907-465-2712

Worker's compensation: Department of Labor, Workers' Compensation Division, Jacquelyn McClintock, Director, PO Box 25512, Juneau, AK 99802-5512. 907-465-2790

Occupational safety and health: Department of Labor, Occupational Safety and Health Section, Richard Arab, Deputy Director, PO Box 21149, Juneau, AK 99802-1149. 907-465-4855

Secretary of state: Lieutenant Governor's Office, Stephen McAlpine, Lieutenant Governor, PO Box AA, Juneau, AK 99811. 907-465-3520

Taxation and revenue: Revenue Department, Hugh Malone, Commissioner, PO Box S, State Office Building, Juneau, AK 99811. 907-465-2300

Designated Zones for Economic Development

Enterprise Zones
No program

Foreign Trade Zones
Foreign Trade Zone No. 160, Anchorage, Alaska. Grantee: Municipality of Anchorage, Larry Dinneen, PO Box 196650, Anchorage, AK 99519-6650, 907-343-4431

Foreign Trade Zone No. 159, St. Paul, Alaska. Grantee: City of St. Paul, Vernon C. McCorkle, Pouch 1, St. Paul Island, AK 99660, 907-546-2331

Foreign Trade Zone No. 108, Valdez, Alaska. Grantee: The City of Valdez, Alaska, Thomas McAlister, City Hall, PO Box 307, Valdez, AK 99686, 907-835-4313

Labor Unions
Food and Commercial Workers International Union, United (AFL-CIO)

National Education Association

Universities with Ph.D. Programs
Alaska Pacific University, Anchorage
University of Alaska Fairbanks, Fairbanks

Major Companies in the State

Company name	City	Telephone	SIC number
Fortune 500 Companies			
None			
Other Major Companies in the State			
National Bancorp of Alaska Inc.	Anchorage	907-276-1132	6712
Chugach Electric Association Inc.	Anchorage	907-563-7494	4911
General Communication Inc.	Anchorage	907-265-5600	4813
Martech USA Inc.	Anchorage	907-561-1970	4959
Sphinx Mining Inc.	Fairbanks	907-452-2639	1041
Fairview Mountain Gold Inc.	Big Lake	907-892-6297	1041

ANCHORAGE, AK (MSA)

Geographic Profile

Land Area

1697.7 square miles

Counties and Parishes

Anchorage Borough

Ranking Highlights

114 *out of 319 in total* **land area**

 35 *out of 319 in* **population growth,** *1970–1990*

184 *out of 310 in having the lowest* **unemployment** *rate*

173 *out of 310 in size of* **labor force**

 40 *out of 318 in percentage of* **college graduates**

 11 *out of 292 in per capita personal* **income**

249 *out of 319 in number of* **manufacturing establishments**

175 *out of 318 in* **physicians** *per 1000 people*

224 *out of 318 in* **hospital beds** *per 1000 people*

170 *out of 267 in fewest* **crimes** *per 1000 people*

157 *out of 266 in fewest* **violent crimes** *per 1000 people*

 33 *out of 319 in per capita* **federal funds and grants**

Quality of Life Indexes (Rate per 1000 population)

Crime rate in 1991:	66.9
Violent crime rate in 1991:	7.1
Physicians rate in 1992:	1.75
Hospital bed rate in 1991:	3.15

ACCRA Cost of Living Indexes

(First quarter 1993, average = 100)

Composite index:	132.9
Utilities index:	102.0
Housing index:	141.0

Overview

The largest city in Alaska, Anchorage is home to 40% of Alaskans. The city is the state's commercial and financial center. Population, office space, and housing tripled between 1973 and 1984 when development of the Prudhoe Bay oilfields and construction of the Trans-Alaska pipeline dramatically altered the state's economy.

Wholesale, retail, and service industries provide 40 percent of the jobs in the area. However, tourism and sport fishing are becoming increasingly important to Anchorage, bringing in more than one million visitors annually. The endorsement of Anchorage by the U.S. Olympic Committee as its choice for the site of the 1994 Winter Olympic Games is expected to increase the city's development as a winter and off-season visitor destination. Items and goods produced in the state include fisheries' products, wood and wood products, petroleum products, coal, and minerals.

Anchorage is 360 miles from Fairbanks. They are connected by the George Parks Highway and the Glenn Highway. The Anchorage-Seward Highway runs south from Anchorage to the Kenai Peninsula. It is also served by the Alaska-Canadian (Alcan) Highway.

The Alaska Railroad transports goods and passengers between Anchorage and Seattle, and the rest of the continental U.S. In addition, the Port of Anchorage is served by two U.S. container lines on a regular schedule, one barge line regularly, and several others on a charter basis.

Air transport is served by the Anchorage International Airport, in the heart of the city. It is the 38th most active airport in the nation. Anchorage is 3,377 miles from New York City, 3,463 miles from Tokyo, Japan, and 4,430 miles from Frankfurt, West Germany. It serves as a stopover point for many international flights between Europe and Asia.

Population (1990)

Total Population and Growth Rate

1990: 226,338

1980: 174,431

1970: 126,385

Growth rate 1970–1990: 79%

Race and Hispanic Origin

White: 80.7%

Black: 6.4%

Asian/Pacific Islander: 4.8%

Native American: 6.4%

Hispanic origin: 4.1%

White not Hispanic: 78.7%

Age

Ages 18 to 20: 4.4%

Ages 21 to 24: 6.2%

Ages 25 to 44: 40.7%

Ages 45 to 54: 10.3%

Ages 55 to 59: 3.1%

Ages 60 to 64: 2.3%

Ages 65 plus: 3.6%

Educational Attainment (1990)

Percent having completed high school: 90.4%

Percent having completed college: 26.9%

Elementary and high school enrollment: 39,993

Federal Funds and Grants Received

Total received in 1989: $1,151,100,000

Funds received per capita: $5,268

Civilian Labor Force

1993 (April):   121,761

1992 average: 117,700

1991 average: 116,738

1990 average: 117,215

Unemployment

1993 (April):   6.4%

1992 average: 7.3%

1991 average: 6.7%

1990 average: 5.2%

Average Annual Pay
1988: $28,715
1987: $28,486
1985: $28,236

Per Capita Personal Income
1991: $24,464
1990: $24,340
1989: $22,637

Business Climate (1987)

Manufacturing
Number of establishments in 1987: 146
Shipments in 1987 ($1,000): $714,100
Employees in 1987: 2,300
Change in employment, 1982 to 1987: -17.9%
Average annual pay for manufacturing work, 1989: $23,532
Average annual pay for production work, 1987: $23,077

Wholesale Trade
Number of establishments in 1987: 479
Total sales in 1987 ($1,000): $1,708,500
Change in sales, 1982 to 1987: -9.4%

Retail Trade
Number of establishments in 1987: 1,403
Total sales in 1987 ($1,000): $1,708,500
Retail sales per household in 1987: $22,944
Average annual pay in 1989: $16,801

Service Industry
Selected receipts in 1987 ($1,000): $1,064,100
Average annual pay in 1989: $22,699

Housing
Total number of units in 1990: 94,153
Occupied units in 1990: 82,702
Owner-occupied units in 1990: 52.8%
1993 ACCRA average cost: $155,913
1993 ACCRA average rent for an apartment: $720

Chamber of Commerce
Anchorage Chamber of Commerce, Carol Heyman, President, 441 W. 5th Ave. #300, Anchorage, AK 99501-2365. 907-272-2401

Economic Development Office
Anchorage Economic Development Corp., Scott Hawkins, President, 550 W. 7th Ave. #1130, Anchorage, AK 99501. 907-258-3700 or 800-462-7275, FAX 907-258-6646

Economic Development Organizations
Alaska Industry Development & Export Authority, Bert Wagnon, Exec. Director, 1577 C St. #304, Anchorage, AL 99501. 907-561-8050

Private Industry Council, Director, 825 L St., Anchorage, AK 99501. 907-343-6560

Municipality of Anchorage, Dept. of Economic Development and Planning, Director, 632 W. 6th Ave., Rm. 505, Anchorage, AK 99501. 907-343-4222

Local Incentives for Business
Property Tax Abatement. The Anchorage Economic Development Corp. (AEDC) can arrange abatement of local property and inventory taxes for new primary industry when appropriate and necessary.

Infrastructure Funding. The AEDC can arrange funding for improvements to publicly owned infrastructure and can also arrange the use of municipal revenue bonds.

The Alaska Industrial Development and Export Authority. A public corporation of the state that assists businesses in securing long term financing for capital investments at moderate fixed-interest rates.

Industrial Sites
Port Industrial Park. 110 acres, located next to the Port of Anchorage terminal facility. Arrangements for term storage can be made in advance of vessel or cargo arrival.

Major Businesses

Company	SIC	Telephone
Alascom Inc.	4813	(907) 264-7000
Alaska Basic Industries	6719	(907) 274-5691
Alaska Builders Cache	2431	(907) 277-6565
Alaska Cleaners	7213	(907) 265-4800
Alaska Industrial Hardware	5072	(907) 276-7201
Alaska Precious Metals	5094	(907) 562-6484
Anchorage Cold Storage Co.	5149	(907) 272-8511
Anchorage Sand & Gravel Co.	3273	(907) 274-5691
Arco Alaska, Inc.	1311	(907) 276-1215
Bristol Bay Native Corp.	6719	(907) 278-3602
Brown's Electrical Supply	5063	(907) 272-2259
Construction & Rigging	1542	(907) 563-3422
ERA Helicopters, Inc.	4512	(907) 248-4422
General Communication, Inc.	4813	(907) 265-5600
Geonex Itech, Inc.	8713	(907) 278-1571
J. B. Gottstein & Co.	5141	(907) 561-1944
Jack White Co.	6531	(907) 563-5500
Key Bank of Alaska	6029	(907) 562-6100
Key Trust Co.	6022	(907) 561-5233
Markair, Inc.	4522	(907) 243-1414
Martech USA, Inc.	1389	(907) 561-1970
National Bancorp of Alaska	6712	(907) 276-1132
National Bank of Alaska	6021	(907) 276-1132
Northrim Bank	6022	(907) 562-0062
Reeve Aleutian Airways	4512	(907) 243-1112
Security Pacific Bank	6022	(907) 276-8080
Sheet Metal, Inc.	3444	(907) 562-2663
Tesoro-Alaska Petroleum	2911	(907) 561-5521
Transalaska Data Systems	3571	(907) 522-1776

Colleges and Universities
Alaska Pacific University, Anchorage
University of Alaska Anchorage, Anchorage

Additional Information

Anchorage, Alaska: Come North to the Future. Anchorage
Economic Development Corp., 1989. n.p.

Anchorage Chamber of Commerce. *Recent Chamber Activity Headlines.* 1989. 40p.

Anchorage, North to the Future: Community Profile.
Anchorage Economic Development Corp., n.d. 45p.

ARIZONA

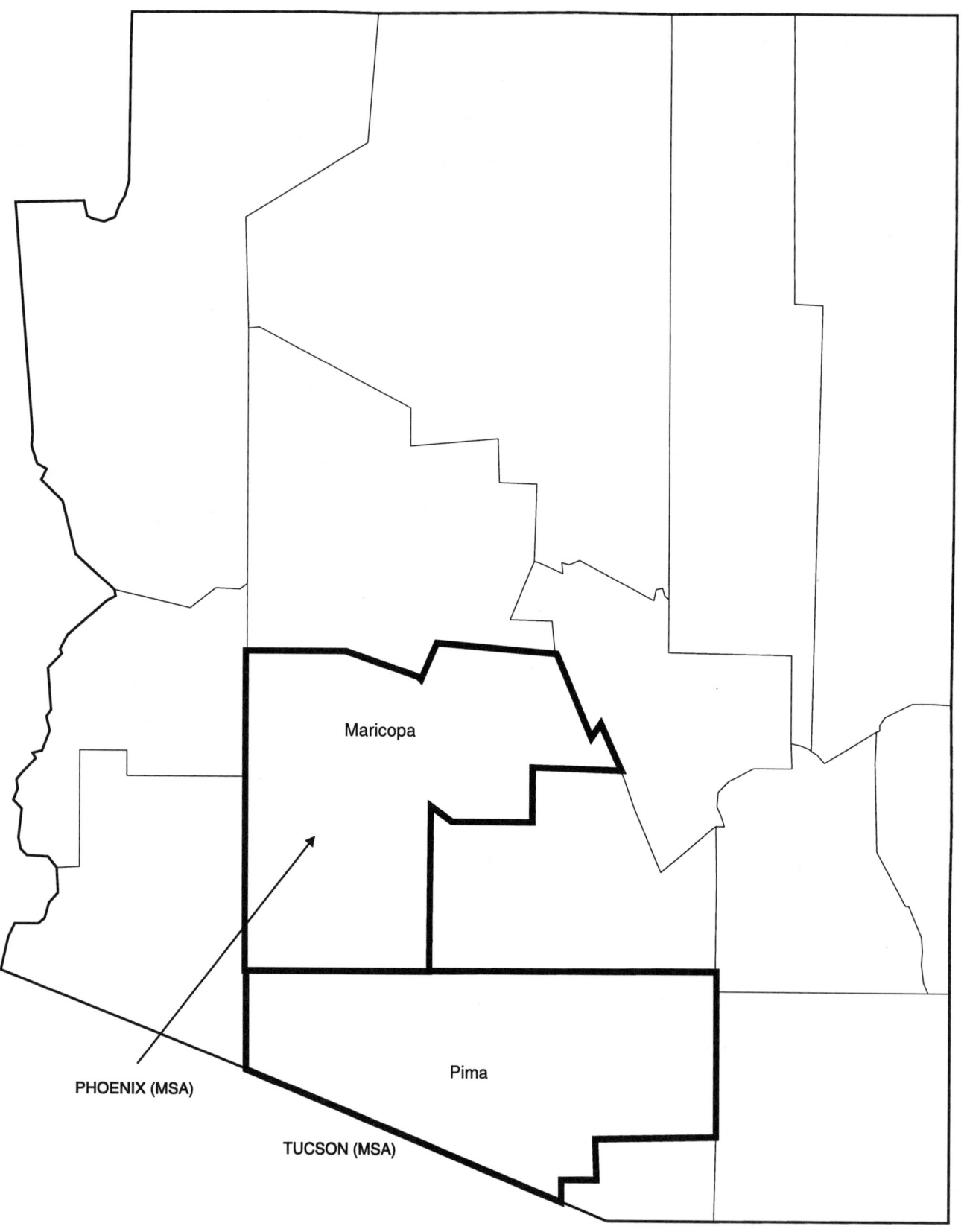

Maricopa

Pima

PHOENIX (MSA)

TUCSON (MSA)

ARIZONA

Population
1990: 3,665,228
1980: 2,718,215

Age
Ages 18 to 20: 172,063
Ages 21 to 24: 220,617
Ages 25 to 44: 1,163,607
Ages 45 to 54: 349,516
Ages 55 to 59: 146,658
Ages 60 to 64: 152,874
Median age: 32.2

Race
White: 2,963,186
Black: 110,524
Asian/Pacific Islander: 55,206
Native American: 203,527
Hispanic origin: 688,338

Households
Total: 1,368,843
Persons per household: 2.62

Sex
Male: 1,810,691
Female: 1,854,537

Population Migration
Domestic migration: 511,000
International migration: 37,000

Projection of the Population in 1995
Total: 3,957,000
18 to 64: 2,351,000

Civilian Labor Force
1993: 1,759,000
1992: 1,753,300
1991: 1,716,400
1990: 1,683,900

Manufacturing
1995 Projection: 217,600
1992: 171,600
1991: 177,700
1990: 184,800
1989: 188,500

Services
1995 Projection: 620,500

1992: 424,500
1991: 429,900
1990: 416,200
1989: 402,100

Wholesale and Retail Trade
1995 Projection: 450,400
1992: 376,600
1991: 390,400
1990: 388,900
1989: 385,800

Unemployment Rate
1993: 7.7%
1992: 8.7%
1991: 5.0%
1990: 4.6%

Employer Unemployment Contributions
Contribution Rate
1992: 1.11%
1991: 1.04%
1990: 1.19%

Average Weekly Benefit
1992: $149.58
1991: $151.73
1990: $136.05

Gross State Product (Million $)
1989: $65,306
1988: $62,375
1987: $58,480
1979: $26,868
Growth rate, 1979 to 1989: 143.1%

Capital Expenditures of Manufacturing Industries
1990: $876,300,000
1989: $924,700,000
1988: $943,400,000
1987: $836,900,000

State Tax Rates
Individual income: Range from 3.8% ($20,000 or less) to 7% (above $300,000).
Corporate income: 9.3% of taxable net income.
General property: Sum of state and local rates. Assessed at

market value of real and personal property, range from 5% to 30% depending on classification.

General sales: 5%

Gasoline: 18¢ per gallon

Income

Median income for a 4 person family: $38,347

Personal per Capita Income

1992: $17,119

1991: $16,594

1990: $16,169

Disposable per Capita Income

1992: $15,179

1991: $14,633

1990: $14,244

Private Employment Weekly Wages

Average

1989: $389

1988: $382

1987: $382

Manufacturing

1989: $366

1988: $528

1987: $502

Services

1989: $365

1988: $356

1987: $337

Wholesale

1989: $493

1988: $474

1987: $454

Retail

1989: $235

1988: $232

1987: $226

Highway Statistics

Total Highway Miles

1990: 51,612

1989: 57,398

1988: 70,282

Federal Highway Aid

1991: $166,011,000

1990: $168,414,000

1989: $129,911,000

Electricity

Average Cost per Kilowatt Hour

1990: 7.75¢

1989: 7.52¢

1988: 7.53¢

Housing (1990)

Owner occupied units: 878,561

Median house value: $80,100

Renter occupied units: 490,282

Median rent: $370

Total vacant units: 290,587

Homeowner vacancy rate: 3.6%

Rental vacancy rate: 15.3%

State Business Incentives and Assistance

Enterprise Zone Incentives

Tax Incentives For Enterprise Zones. Business must certify that at least 35% of their new qualified employees are residents of the zone. Tax credits for hiring employees who qualify for the Job Training Partnership Act include: 1) 1/4 of the taxable wages paid to each qualified employee in the first year, not to exceed $1,000; 2) 1/3 of the taxable wages paid to each previously qualified employee in the second year of continuous employment, not to exceed $1,500; 3)1/2 the taxable wages paid to each previously qualified employee in the third year of continuous employment, not to exceed $2,500.

Financial And Business Assistance

Business and Trade. The Business and Trade Division assists companies considering expanding or relocating in the state and companies interested in exporting to other countries.

Cooperative Advertising Program. A matching grant program operated by the Arizona Office of Tourism, it offers assistance in advertising and promotions.

Education And Training

Trade Readjustment Act. This job service registers, interviews, and provides job placement services to individuals who are displaced due to foreign competition.

Job Training Partnership Act. This program operates with funding from the U.S. Department of Labor. It provides job training and other employment related services.

State Offices

Real estate: Real Estate Department, Joe Sotelo, Commissioner, 202 E. Earl Drive, 4th fl., Phoenix, AZ 85012. 602-255-4697

Chamber of commerce: Arizona State Chamber of Commerce, President, 1221 E. Osborn Road #100, Phoenix, AZ 85014. 602-248-9172

Economic development: Arizona Dept. of Commerce, Business & Trade Division, Lois Yates, Assistant Director, 1700 W. Washington, 5th Fl, Phoenix, AZ 85007. 602-255-5374

Arizona Dept. of Commerce, Mobin Qaheri, Senior Economic Specialist, 3800 N. Central Avenue, Phoenix, AZ 85912. 602-280-1321

Small Business Development Center, David Smith, State Director, Gateway Community College, 108 N 40th Street, Phoenix, AZ 85034. 602-393-5225

Major Companies in the State

Company name	Fortune 500 rank	City	Telephone	SIC number
Fortune 500 Companies				
Magma Copper Co.	397	Tucson	602-575-5600	3351
Phelps Dodge Corp.	180	Phoenix	602-234-8100	3331
Worthen Banking Corp.		Little Rock	501-378-1521	6712

Environmental affairs: Environmental Quality Department, Randolph Wood, Director, 2005 N Central, Phoenix, AZ 85004. 602-257-6917

Labor: Industrial Commission, 800 W Washington St., PO Box 19070, Phoenix, AZ 85005-9070. 602-542-4411

Unemployment: Economic Security Department, Unemployment Insurance Administration, Tom Vaughn, Director, 1717 W Jefferson St., PO Box 6123, Phoenix, AZ 85005. 602-542-3667

Worker's compensation: Insurance Department, Susan Gallinger, Director, 303 North 3rd Street, Ste. 1100, Phoenix, AZ 85012. 602-255-5400

Occupational safety and health: Industrial Commission, Occupational Safety Division, Tim Arbogast, Director, 800 West Washington Street, Phoenix, AZ 85007. 602-542-5796

Secretary of state: Secretary of the State Office, Jim Shumway, Secretary of State, 1700 West Washington, West Wing, Phoenix, AZ 85007. 602-542-4285

Taxation and revenue: Revenue Department, Paul Waddell, Director, 1600 West Monroe, Room 910, Phoenix, AZ 85007. 602-542-3572

Designated Zones for Economic Development

Enterprise Zones

Enacted in: 1989

No. of established zones: 11

Greenlee County
Huachuca
Novajo County
Phoenix
Pima County
Pinal County
Santa Cruz County
South Tucson
Tempe
Tucson
Yuma County

Foreign Trade Zones

Foreign Trade Zone No. 60, Nogales, Arizona, Grantee: Border Industrial Development, Inc., Duke H. Potty, PO Box 1688, Nogales, AZ 85628, 602-281-1212

Foreign Trade Zone No. 174, Pima County, Arizona, Grantee: Arizona Technology Foreign-Trade Zone, Inc., Sarah G. Blake, President, 1745 North Campbell Avenue, Tucson, AZ 85719, 602-323-9759

Foreign Trade Zone No. 75, Phoenix, Arizona, Grantee: City of Phoenix, Paul Katsenes, Community & Economic Development Department, One North First Street, Ste. 700, Phoenix, AZ 85004-2357, 602-495-5332 (or 602-262-5040 switchboard)

Foreign Trade Zone No. 139, Sierra Vista, Arizona, Grantee: Sierra Vista Economic Development Foundation, Inc., Joseph Luce, PO Box 2380, Sierra Vista, AZ 85636, 602-459-6070.

Foreign Trade Zone No. 48, Tucson, Arizona, Grantee: Papago-Tucson FTZ Corporation, Operator: Northill-Papago, Ltd., Sherry Francis, 7800 South Nogales Highway, Tucson, AZ 85706, 602-741-1940

Labor Unions

Aluminum, Brick and Glass Workers, International Union (AFL-CIO)

Carpenters and Joiners of America, United Brotherhood of (AFL-CIO)

National Education Association

Operating Engineers, International Union of (AFL-CIO)

Universities with Ph.D. Programs

Arizona State University, Tempe
Northern Arizona University, Flagstaff
University of Arizona, Tucson

PHOENIX, AZ (MSA)

Geographic Profile
Land Area
9204.1 square miles

Counties and Parishes
Maricopa

Additional Cities/Towns within Area
Mesa
Scottsdale
Tempe

Ranking Highlights
  2 *out of 319 in total* land area
11 *out of 319 in* population growth, *1970–1990*
121 *out of 310 in having the lowest* unemployment *rate*
20 *out of 310 in size of* labor force
94 *out of 318 in the percentage of* college graduates
106 *out of 292 in per capita personal* income
24 *out of 319 in number of* manufacturing establishments
122 *out of 318 in* physicians *per 1000 people*
251 *out of 318 in* hospital beds *per 1000 people*
231 *out of 367 in fewest* crimes *per 1000 people*
177 *out of 266 in fewest* violent crimes *per 1000 people*
136 *out of 319 in per capita* federal funds and grants

Quality of Life Indexes (Rate per 1000 population)
Crime rate in 1991:   81.8
Violent crime rate in 1991:   7.7
Physicians rate in 1992:   2
Hospital bed rate in 1991:   2.88

ACCRA Cost of Living Indexes
(First quarter 1993, average = 100)
Composite index: 99.5
Utilities index: 89.2
Housing index: 92.8

Overview
Phoenix is located 379 miles east of Los Angeles, California, 285 miles south-east of Las Vegas, Nevada, 460 miles west of Albuquerque, New Mexico, and 645 miles south of Salt Lake City, Utah.

Manufacturing and tourism form the base of the city's economy. Major industrial products manufactured by companies located in the metropolitan area include aircraft parts, electronic equipment, agricultural chemicals, radios, air-conditioning equipment, leather goods, and native American crafts. Manufacturing growth in Phoenix is expected to be strong in the aerospace industries, land-intensive manufacturing uses, and distribution facilities. High technology industries employ over half of the region's total manufacturing employment. Thirty-five percent of the state's entire labor force works in Phoenix and 64 percent

works in the metropolitan area.

Tourism is an especially vital part of the economy. Nearly seven million visitors from the United States and Canada are attracted annually to the warm weather and sunshine, making Phoenix an important resort center. Direct flights from Phoenix to Nagoya, Japan, initiated in 1991, have brought increasing numbers of Japanese tourists to Phoenix.

During the past three decades, as the result of the population boom, the economy of Phoenix has expanded in the areas of technology and service industries. This shift has brought record increases in office construction and occupancy. From 1984 to 1991, the amount of occupied office space in metropolitan Phoenix grew from 2.6 million square feet to thirty million square feet. Keeping pace with moderating trends in the economy, however, construction of new facilities has slowed.

Phoenix is located at the center of market areas stretching along interstate highways from southern California to western Texas, Colorado, Utah, and Mexico. More than one hundred fifty companies provide motor freight service. Rail service is available from three major railroads. The Phoenix metropolitan area economy benefits from air cargo service through Skyharbor International Airport.

Population (1990)
Total Population and Growth Rate
1990: 2,122,101
1980: 1,509,175
1970: 971,228
Growth rate 1970–1990: 118%

Race and Hispanic Origin
White: 84.8%
Black: 3.5%
Asian/Pacific Islander: 1.7%
Native American: 1.8%
Hispanic origin: 16.3%
White not Hispanic: 77.1%

Age
Ages 18 to 20: 4.5%
Ages 21 to 24: 6.2%
Ages 25 to 44: 33.4%
Ages 45 to 54: 9.6%
Ages 55 to 59: 3.8%
Ages 60 to 64: 3.8%
Ages 65 plus: 12.5%

Educational Attainment (1990)
Percent having completed high school: 81.5%
Percent having completed college: 22.1%
Elementary and high school enrollment: 351,130

Federal Funds and Grants Received
Total received in 1989: $6,642,000,000
Funds received per capita: $3,273

Civilian Labor Force

1993 (April): 1,058,894
1992 average: 1,057,209
1991 average: 1,054,864
1990 average: 1,080,448

Unemployment

1993 (April): 4.9%
1992 average: 6.4%
1991 average: 4.9%
1990 average: 4.3%

Average Annual Pay

1988: $21,438
1987: $20,612
1985: $18,769

Per Capita Personal Income

1991: $18,156
1990: $17,834
1989: $17,148

Business Climate (1987)

Manufacturing

Number of establishments in 1987: 2,803
Shipments in 1987 ($1,000): $14,061,800
Employees in 1987: 135,800
Change in employment, 1982 to 1987: 25.7%
Average annual pay for manufacturing work in 1989: $28,959
Average annual pay for production work in 1987: $21,262

Wholesale Trade

Number of establishments in 1987: 3,984
Total sales in 1987 ($1,000): $16,991,100
Change in sales, 1982 to 1987: 55.7%

Retail Trade

Number of establishments in 1987: 11,133
Total sales in 1987 ($1,000): $16,991,100
Retail sales per household in 1987: $17,903
Average annual pay in 1989: $12,922

Service Industry

Selected receipts in 1987 ($1,000): $7,765,100
Average annual pay in 1989: $20,241

Office Real Estate (1992)

Office space inventory: 22,906,708 square feet
Average class A Central Business District rental range per sq. ft: $16.49

Vacancy Rates

All areas: 21.6%

Vacancy Rates in Central Business District

Class A space: 23.4%
Class B space: 20.2%

Vacancy Rates Outside Central Business District

Class A space: 23.4%
Class B space: 21.8%

Housing

Total number of units in 1990: 952,041
Occupied units in 1990: 807,560
Owner-occupied units in 1990: 63.3%
1993 ACCRA average cost: $100,748
1993 ACCRA average rent for an apartment: $531

Chamber of Commerce

Phoenix Chamber of Commerce, Val Manning, Economic Development Office, 34 W. Monroe, Ste. 900, Phoenix, AZ 85003. 602-254-5521, FAX 602-495-8913

Economic Development Office

Phoenix Economic Growth Corp., Ken Husband, Exec. Director, 1 N. 1st St., Ste. 103, Phoenix, AZ 85004. 602-253-9747, FAX 602-253-9795

Economic Development Organizations

Greater Phoenix Economic Council, Ioanna Morfessis, Exec. Director, 2 N. Central Ave., Ste. M 210, Phoenix, AZ 85004. 602-256-7700, FAX 602-256-7744

City of Phoenix, Economic Development Executive Office, Dave Kritor, Economic Development Officer, 40 N. Central #2850, Phoenix, AZ 85004. 602-534-1915

Greater Phoenix Partnership, Inc., David Maurer, Exec. Director, 2800 N. 44th Street #360, Phoenix, AZ 85008. 602-468-9494

Maricopa County Government, Guido Ardaya, Principal Planner-Economic Development, 111 S. 3rd Ave., Rm. 403, Phoenix, AZ 85003. 602-261-7206.

Mesa Economic Growth Association, Phil Gardner, Exec. Director, 100 N. Center St., Mesa, AZ 85201. 602-644-2398, FAX 602-644-3458

Scottsdale Chamber of Commerce, Rod Robertson, Director, Economic Development, 7333 Scottsdale Mall, Scottsdale, AZ 85251. 602-945-8481, FAX 602-947-4523

City of Tempe, Janice M. Schaefer, Economic Development Administrator, PO Box 5002/31, E. 5th St., 3rd fl., Tempe, AZ 85281. 602-350-8036, FAX 602-350-8990

South Mountain Chamber of Commerce, Mr. Charles E. Magley, President, 5245 S. 5th St., PO Box 8172, Phoenix AZ 85066-8172. 602-268-0068

Phoenix Board of Realtors, 5033 N. 19th Ave., Phoenix, AZ 85013. 602-246-1012

Maricopa Community Colleges, Bertha Landrum, Director, Economic Development, 3910 E. Washington, Phoenix, AZ 85034. 602-392-2400

Maricopa County Planning & Zoning, Don E. McDaniel, Jr., Director, 111 S. 3rd Ave., Phoenix, AZ 85007. 602-262-3951

Arizona Corporation Commission, Marcia Weeks, Commissioner, 1200 W. Washington St., Phoenix, AZ 85007. 602-542-3026

Arizona Economic Council, Scott Eubanks, President, 2901 N. Central Ave., Ste. 1500, Phoenix, AZ 85012. 602-230-0095

Arizona Dept. of Commerce, Commissioner, 3800 N. Central Ave., Ste. 1500, Phoenix, AZ 85012. 602-280-1300

Major Businesses

Company	SIC	Telephone
Abco Markets Inc.	5411	(602) 248-9276
America West Airlines, Inc.	4512	(602) 894-0800
Arizona Public Services Co.	4911	(602) 250-1000
Armour and Co.	2841	(602) 248-2800
Circle K Convenience Store	5541	(602) 253-9600
Circle K Corp.	5411	(602) 253-9600
Dial Corporation	2841	(602) 248-2800
First Interstate Bank	6021	(602) 528-6000
Greyhound Dial Corp.	5812	(602) 248-4000
McDonnell Douglas Helicopter	3721	(602) 891-3000
Northern Automotive Corp.	5531	(602) 265-9200
Phelps Dodge Corp.	1021	(602) 234-8100
Pinnacle West Capital Corp.	4911	(602) 234-1142
Samaritan Foundation	8062	(602) 495-4000
Scottsdale Insurance Co.	6331	(602) 948-0505
Security Pacific Bancorp	6036	(602) 262-2000
Valley National Bank of Arizona	6021	(602) 221-2900
Valley National Corp.	6021	(602) 261-2900

Colleges and Universities

Devry Institute of Technology, Phoenix
Gateway Community College, Phoenix
Grand Cannon University, Phoenix
ITT Technical Institute, Phoenix
Lamson Junior College, Phoenix
Phoenix College, Phoenix
Rio Salado Community College, Phoenix
South Mountain Community College, Phoenix
Southwestern College, Phoenix
University of Phoenix, Phoenix
Lamson Junior College, Mesa
Mesa Community College, Mesa
Scottsdale Community College, Scottsdale
Arizona State University, Tempe. Known for its graduate program in international management.

Additional Information

Greater Phoenix, Introduction to a Dynamic Marketplace. Greater Phoenix Economic Council, 1990. (multiple page nos.)

TUCSON, AZ (MSA

Geographic Profile

Land Area
9187.0 square miles

Counties and Parishes
Pima

Ranking Highlights

3 *out of 319 in total* land area
23 *out of 319 in* population growth, *1970–1990*
60 *out of 310 in having the lowest* unemployment *rate*
78 *out of 310 in size of* labor force
78 *out of 318 in the percentage of* college graduates
209 *out of 292 in per capita personal* income
93 *out of 319 in number of* manufacturing establishments
50 *out of 318 in* physicians *per 1000 people*
239 *out of 318 in* hospital beds *per 1000 people*
236 *out of 267 in fewest* crimes *per 1000 people*
150 *out of 266 in fewest* violent crimes *per 1000 people*
44 *out of 319 in per capita* federal funds and grants

Quality of Life Indexes (Rate per 1000 population)

Crime rate in 1991:	83.6
Violent crime rate in 1991:	6.9
Physicians rate in 1992:	2.72
Hospital bed rate in 1991:	3.02

ACCRA Cost of Living Indexes
(First quarter 1993, average = 100)
Composite index: 102.8
Utilities index: 99.9
Housing index: 97.7

Population (1990)

Total Population and Growth Rate
1990: 666,880
1980: 531,443
1970: 351,667
Growth rate 1970–1990: 90%

Race and Hispanic Origin
White: 78.7%
Black: 3.1%
Asian/Pacific Islander: 1.8%
Native American: 3.0%
Hispanic origin: 24.5%
White not Hispanic: 68.2%

Age
Ages 18 to 20: 5.3%
Ages 21 to 24: 6.5%
Ages 25 to 44: 31.8%
Ages 45 to 54: 9.3%
Ages 55 to 59: 4.1%
Ages 60 to 64: 4.3%
Ages 65 plus: 13.7%

Educational Attainment (1990)
Percent having completed high school: 80.5%
Percent having completed college: 23.3%
Elementary and high school enrollment: 108,264

Federal Funds and Grants Received
Total received in 1989: $3,071,900,000
Funds received per capita: $4,830

Civilian Labor Force
1993 (April):   322,804
1992 average: 321,450
1991 average: 311,745
1990 average: 309,760

Unemployment
1993 (April):   4.1%
1992 average: 5.2%
1991 average: 3.9%
1990 average: 4.2%

Average Annual Pay
1988: $19,106
1987: $18,566
1985: $17,351

Per Capita Personal Income
1991: $16,087
1990: $15,300
1989: $14,956

Business Climate (1987)
Manufacturing
Number of establishments in 1987: 686
Shipments in 1987 ($1,000): $3,608,800
Employees in 1987: 30,700
Change in employment, 1982 to 1987: 16.3%
Average annual pay for manufacturing work, 1989: $31,353
Average annual pay for production work, 1987: $17,397

Wholesale Trade
Number of establishments in 1987: 911
Total sales in 1987 ($1,000): $1,607,400
Change in sales, 1982 to 1987: 12.1%

Retail Trade
Number of establishments in 1987: 3,675
Total sales in 1987 ($1,000): $1,607,400
Retail sales per household in 1987: $15,407
Average annual pay in 1989: $11,404

Service Industry
Selected receipts in 1987 ($1,000): $1,915,200
Average annual pay in 1989: $17,615

Office Real Estate (1992)
Office space inventory: 6,393,719 square feet
Average class A Central Business District rental range per sq. ft: $18.50

Vacancy Rates
All areas: 20.9%

Vacancy Rates in Central Business District
Class A space: 18.0%
Class B space: 17.1%

Vacancy Rates Outside Central Business District
Class A space: 20.4%
Class B space: 26.2%

Housing
Total number of units in 1990: 298,207
Occupied units in 1990: 261,792
Owner-occupied units in 1990: 60.9%
1993 ACCRA average cost: $112,000
1993 ACCRA average rent for an apartment: $477

Chamber of Commerce
Tucson Metropolitan Chamber of Commerce, John Camper, President, 465 W. St. Mary's Rd., PO Box 991, Tucson, AZ 85702. 602-792-1212, FAX 602-882-5704

Economic Development Office
Greater Tucson Economic Council, Andrew Flores, President, 33 N. Stone Ave. #800, Tucson, AZ 85701-1404. 602-882-5079, FAX 602-622-6413

Economic Development Organizations
Tucson Economic Development Corp., William Stephenson, Exec. Director, 465 W. St. Mary's Rd. #200, Tucson, AZ 85701. 602-623-3673

Major Businesses

Company	SIC	Telephone
Avent, Inc.	2389	(602) 294-1455
Beaudry Motor Co.	5511	(602) 748-1000
Breck, Bill Dodge, Inc.	5511	(602) 745-1000
Burr-Brown Corp.	3674	(602) 746-1111
Carondelet Health	8062	(602) 622-5833
Century Power Corp.	4911	(602) 577-3747
City Meat & Provisions Co.	5147	(602) 622-0584
Click, Jim Ford Inc.	5511	(602) 747-2000
Coleman Products Co.	3714	(602) 897-4021
Cyprus Sierrita Corp.	1021	(602) 791-2950
Golden Eagle Distributors	5181	(602) 884-5999
Holderness, Ed Supplies Inc.	5031	(602) 889-1300
Holmes, Tuttle Ford Inc.	5511	(602) 292-3600
ITT Powersystems Corp.	3661	(602) 889-7600
Kalil Bottling Co.	2086	(602) 624-1788
Mackey, Don Oldsmobile-Cadillac	5511	(602) 624-0481
Maya Construction Co.	1611	(602) 624-8502
Pima Financial Service Co.	6162	(602) 747-8484
Pima Savings & Loan Association	6036	(602) 747-8484
R. A. Homes, Inc.	1521	(602) 326-4383
Royal Buick Co. Inc.	5511	(602) 795-0760
Sundt Corp.	1542	(602) 748-7555
Tmcare	8062	(602) 327-5461
Tucson Electric Power Co.	4911	(602) 622-6661

Major Businesses (Continued)

Company	SIC	Telephone
Tucson Medical Center	8062	(602) 327-5461
University Medical Center	8062	(602) 626-0111
Warehouse Supermarkets	5411	(602) 791-9933
Watson Chevrolet Inc.	5511	(602) 292-1500
Western Copper Supplies	5051	(602) 623-1262

Colleges and Universities

Chaparral Career Arizona, Tucson
ITT Technical Institute, Tucson
Pima Community College, Tucson
University of Arizona, Tucson

ARKANSAS

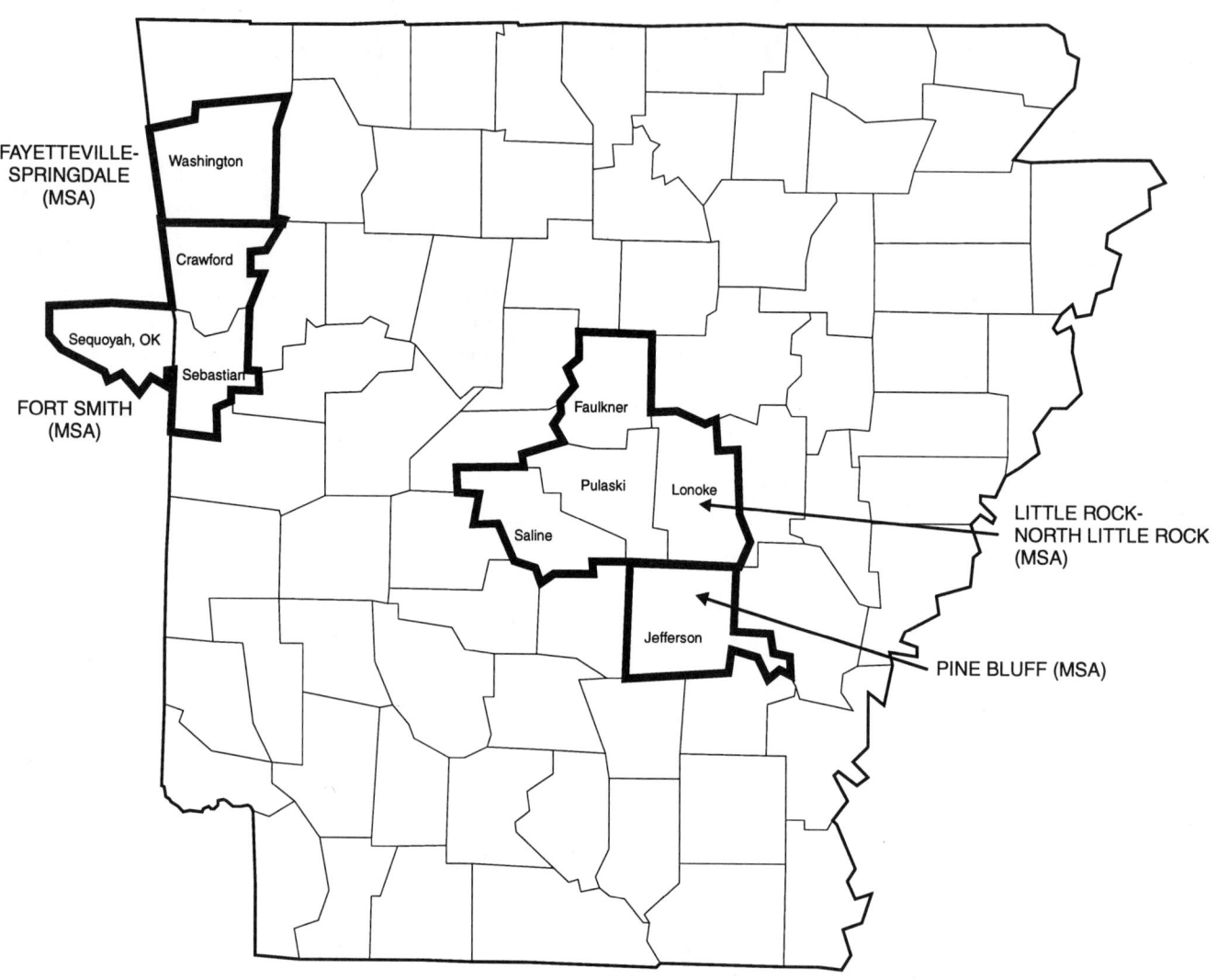

FAYETTEVILLE-
SPRINGDALE
(MSA)

Washington

Crawford

Sequoyah, OK

FORT SMITH
(MSA)

Sebastian

Faulkner

Pulaski

Lonoke

Saline

Jefferson

LITTLE ROCK-
NORTH LITTLE ROCK
(MSA)

PINE BLUFF (MSA)

ARKANSAS

Population
1990: 2,350,725
1980: 2,285,435

Age
Ages 18 to 20: 109,879
Ages 21 to 24: 127,177
Ages 25 to 44: 685,748
Ages 45 to 54: 243,337
Ages 55 to 59: 105,811
Ages 60 to 64: 107,584
Median age: 33.8

Race
White: 1,944,744
Black: 373,912
Asian/Pacific Islander: 12,530
Native American: 12,773
Hispanic origin: 19,876

Households
Total: 891,179
Persons per household: 2.57

Sex
Male: 1,133,076
Female: 1,217,649

Population Migration
Domestic migration: 33,000
International migration: 10,000

Projection of the Population in 1995
Total: 2,476,000
18 to 64: 1,439,000

Civilian Labor Force
1993: 1,100,600
1992: 1,141,200
1991: 1,126,400
1990: 1,135,300

Manufacturing
1995 Projection: 244,600
1992: 236,500
1991: 239,000
1990: 232,000
1989: 228,800

Services
1995 Projection: 284,300

1992: 210,200
1991: 205,900
1990: 195,100
1989: 176,100

Wholesale and Retail Trade
1995 Projection: 247,400
1992: 213,000
1991: 216,200
1990: 210,900
1989: 211,600

Unemployment Rate
1993: 8.3%
1992: 8.5%
1991: 7.2%
1990: 6.8%

Employer Unemployment Contributions
Contribution Rate
1992: 2.20%
1991: 2.09%
1990: 2.20%

Average Weekly Benefit
1992: $156.33
1991: $157.25
1990: $133.28

Gross State Product (Million $)
1989: $37,169
1988: $35,130
1987: $32,708
1979: $19,075
Growth rate, 1979 to 1989: 94.9%

Capital Expenditures of Manufacturing Industries
1990: $1,172,900,000
1989: $988,800,000
1988: $778,000,000
1987: $891,500,000

State Tax Rates
Individual income: Range from 1% ($2,999 or less) to 7% (above $25,000).
Corporate income: Range from 1% ($3,000 or less) to 6.5% (above $100,000).

General property: Sum of all local rates, no state levy. Assessed at 20% of true market value of real and personal property.

General sales: 4.5%

Gasoline: 18.5¢ per gallon

Income

Median income for a 4-person family: $31,853

Personal per Capita Income
1992: $15,439
1991: $14,636
1990: $14,037

Disposable per Capita Income
1992: $13,879
1991: $13,097
1990: $12,506

Private Employment Weekly Wages

Average
1989: $329
1988: $322
1987: $322

Manufacturing
1989: $312
1988: $364
1987: $354

Services
1989: $300
1988: $293
1987: $284

Wholesale
1989: $411
1988: $396
1987: $380

Retail
1989: $206
1988: $204
1987: $197

Highway Statistics

Total Highway Miles
1990: 77,085
1989: 77,122
1988: 77,094

Federal Highway Aid
1991: $139,540,000
1990: $140,452,000
1989: $137,041,000

Electricity

Average Cost per Kilowatt Hour
1990: 6.70¢
1989: 6.42¢
1988: 6.48¢

Housing (1990)

Owner occupied units: 619,938
Median house value: $46,300
Renter occupied units: 271,241
Median rent: $230
Total vacant units: 109,488
Homeowner vacancy rate: 2.4%
Rental vacancy rate: 10.4%

State Business Incentives and Assistance

Enterprise Zone Incentives

Tax Incentives For Enterprise Zones. Business must certify that at least 35% of their new qualified employees are residents of the zone. Tax credits for hiring employees who qualify for the Job Training Partnership Act include: 1) 1/4 of the taxable wages paid to each qualified employee in the first year, not to exceed $1,000; 2) 1/3 of the taxable wages paid to each previously qualified employee in the second year of continuous employment, not to exceed $1,500; 3) 1/2 the taxable wages paid to each previously qualified employee in the third year of continuous employment, not to exceed $2,500.

The Arkansas Enterprise Zone Program offers these incentives:

1. a $2,000 state income tax credit per net new employee.
2. a refund of state sales and use taxes on the purchase of materials used in construction of a new facility or expansion of an existing facility.
3. a refund of state sales and use taxes on machinery and equipment to be used in connection with the business.

Financial and Business Assistance

Arkansas offers a credit against a manufacturer's sales and use tax liability of 7% of the total project cost when the investment exceeds $5 million. The investment must be in construction or expansion of an existing operation. Construction or expansion includes modernization of old plants through major modifications or replacement of obsolete machinery. The credit cannot exceed 50% of the tax liability for the reporting period. The credit has a six-year carryover period. For more information, contact the Arkansas Industrial Development Commission.

Research & Development Tax Credit Program. Managed by the Arkansas Science & Technology Authority, the program provides incentives to Arkansas industry to participate in the Arkansas Science & Technology Authority's Applied Research Grant Program or similar research programs. The program encourages investment by industry in the transfer of science and technology from Arkansas colleges and universities.

Seed Capital Investment Program. Managed by the Arkansas Science & Technology Authority, the program fosters the formation and development of innovative, technology-based business enterprises that will stimulate the economy of Arkansas.

Applied Research Grant Program. Managed by the Arkansas Science & Technology Authority, the program encourages, establishes and supports applied research in science and engineering by providing a cash match to Arkansas colleges and universities for contributions of funds and new equipment from private industry and other private sources.

Business Incubator Program. Managed by the Arkansas Science & Technology Authority, the program increases the survival rate of new, technology-based business in Arkansas.

Education and Training

Governor's Dislocated Worker Task Force. The task force utilizes the expertise of the Employment Security Division, the Industrial Development Commission, and the Arkansas AFL-CIO. These agencies serve affected workers by helping communities organize and local leaders respond to plant closings and mass layoffs.

Job Training Partnership Act. This program operates with funding from the U.S. Department of Labor. It provides job training and other employment related services.

State Offices

Real estate: Real Estate Comm., Roy Bilheimer, Exec Sec., 612 Summit, Little Rock, AR 72201. 501-682-2732

Chamber of commerce: Arkansas State Chamber of Commerce, Ron Russell, Exec Director, PO Box 3645, 412 Cross St., Little Rock, AR 72203. 501-374-9225

Economic development: Arkansas Industrial Development Commission, David Harrington, Exec Director, One State Capitol Mall, Room 46-300, Little Rock, AR 72201. 501-682-1121, FAX 501-682-7341

Arkansas Industrial Development Commission, Enterprise Zone Program, Armando Plata, Jr., Enterprise Zone Coordinator, One State Capitol Mall, Little Rock, AR 72201. 501-682-7384

Arkansas Development Finance Authority, Bob Nash, President, 100 S. Main St., Ste. 200, Little Rock, AR 72201. 501-682-5900

Arkansas Capitol Corporation, Sam Walls, Executive Director, 800 Pyramid Place, 221 W. Second St., Little Rock, AR 72201. 801-374-9247

Arkansas Science and Technology Authority, J.P. Gentry, Vice President Research, 100 Main St., Ste. 450, Little Rock, AR 72201. 501-324-9006

Arkansas Science and Technology Authority, Business Incubator Program, Chuck Myers, Program Manager, 100 Main Street., Ste. 450, Little Rock, AR 72201. 501-324-9006

Small Business Development Center, Paul McGinnis, State Director, University of Arkansas, Little Rock Technology Center Building, 100 S. Main St., Ste. 401, Little Rock, AR 72201. 501-324-9043

Environmental affairs: Pollution Control and Ecology Department, Randall Mathis, Director, 8001 National Drive, Little Rock, AR 72201. 501-562-7444

Labor: Dept. of Labor, J.L. Terwillinger, Director, 10421 W. Markham, Little Rock, AR 72201. 501-682-4500

Unemployment: Employment Security Division, William D. Gaddy, Director, Employment Security Bldg., PO Box 2981, 2 State Capitol Mall, Little Rock, AR 72203. 501-682-2121

Worker's compensation: Workers Compensation Commission, James Daniel, Chairman, Justice Bldg., 2nd fl., 625 Marshall St., Little Rock, AR 72201. 501-682-3930

Occupational safety and health: Dept. of Labor, Occupational Safety and Health, Edwin Daven, Safety Section, 10421 W. Markham St., Little Rock, AR 72205. 501-682-4500

Secretary of state: Secretary of State Office, W.J. Bill McCuen, Secretary of State, 256 State Capitol, Little Rock, AR 72201. 501-682-1010

Taxation and revenue: Dept. of Finance and Administration, Jim Pledger, Director, 401 Dept. of Finance and Administration Bldg., 1509 W. Seventh St., Little Rock, AR 72201. 501-682-2242

Designated Zones for Economic Development

Enterprise Zones

Enacted in: 1983

No. of established zones: 456

For location information, please contact: Arkansas Industrial Development Commission, Armando Plata Jr., Enterprise Zone Coordinator, One State Capitol Mall, Little Rock, AR 72201. 501-682-7384

Foreign Trade Zones

Foreign Trade Zone No. 14, Little Rock, Arkansas. Grantee: Arkansas Dept. of Industrial Development, Operator: Little Rock Port Authority, Robert Brave, 7500 Lindsey Road, Little Rock, AR 72206, 501-490-1468

Labor Unions

Food and Commercial Workers International Union, United (AFL-CIO)

Paperworkers International Union, United (AFL-CIO)

Universities with Ph.D. Programs

University of Arkansas, Fayetteville

University of Arkansas at Little Rock, Little Rock

Sources of Additional Information

A Summary of Taxes in Arkansas. Arkansas Industrial Development Commission, April 1990. 24p. [Prepared by Univ. of Arkansas, Research and Public Service, Div. of Regional Economic Analysis. Publication 90-6]

Arkansas State and County Economic Data. Arkansas Industrial Development Commission, April 1990. 19p. [Prepared by University of Arkansas, Research and Public Service, Div. of Regional Economic Analysis. Publication 90-5]

Largest and Major Employers in Arkansas. Arkansas Industrial Development Commission, Research Section, August 15, 1990. 12p.

Postsecondary Educational Opportunities in Arkansas, Directory 1989-91. Arkansas Dept. of Education (501-682-1505) and Arkansas Dept. of Higher Education (501-371-1441), n.d. 106p.

1990 Arkansas Manufacturing Wage Survey. Arkansas Industrial Development Commission, Research Section, May 1990. np.

Companies Doing Business in Arkansas

Company	Fortune 500 rank	City	Telephone	SIC
Fortune 500 Companies				
Hudson Foods Inc.	405	Rogers	501-636-1100	2015
Murphy Oil Corp.	249	El Dorado	501-862-6411	2911
Riceland Foods Inc.	466	Stuttgart	501-673-5500	2075
Tyson Foods Inc.	118	Springdale	501-756-4000	2015
Other Major Companies in the State				
ABF Freight System Inc.		Fort Smith	501-785-8700	4213
Acxiom Corp.		Conway	501-450-1424	7374
Alltel Corp.		Little Rock	501-661-8000	4813
Arkansas Best Corp.		Fort Smith	501-785-6000	4213
Arkansas Electric Cooperative Corp.		Little Rock	501-570-2200	4911
Arkansas Freightways Corp.		Harrison	501-741-9000	4011
Arkansas Power & Light Co.		Little Rock	501-377-4000	4911
Baldor Electric Co.		Fort Smith	501-646-4711	3621
Beverly Enterprises Inc.		Fort Smith	501-452-6712	8051
Dillard Department Stores Inc.		Little Rock	501-376-5200	5311
Environmental Systems Co.		Little Rock	501-223-4100	4953
Fairfield Communities Inc.		Little Rock	501-664-6000	6552
First Commercial Corp.		Little Rock	501-371-7000	6712
First United Bancshares Inc. Arkansas		El Dorado	501-863-3181	6712
J B Hunt Transport Services Inc		Lowell	501-820-0000	4213
Southwestern Energy Co.		Fayetteville	501-521-1141	1311
Tcby Enterprises Inc.		Little Rock	501-688-8229	5451
Treadco Inc.		Fort Smith	501-785-6000	7534
Wal Mart Stores Inc.		Bentonville	501-273-4000	5311
Worthen Banking Corp.		Little Rock	501-378-1521	6712

FAYETTEVILLE–SPRINGDALE, AR (MSA)

Geographic Profile

Land Area
950.2 square miles

Counties and Parishes
Washington

Ranking Highlights

207 *out of 319 in total* **land area**
79 *out of 319 in* **population growth**, *1970–1990*
12 *out of 310 in having the lowest* **unemployment** *rate*
242 *out of 310 in size of* **labor force**
137 *out of 318 in the percentage of* **college graduates**
216 *out of 292 in per capita personal* **income**
260 *out of 319 in number of* **manufacturing establishments**
144 *out of 318 in* **physicians** *per 1000 people*
38 *out of 318 in* **hospital beds** *per 1000 people*
96 *out of 267 in fewest* **crimes** *per 1000 people*
25 *out of 266 in fewest* **violent crimes** *per 1000 people*
223 *out of 319 in per capita* **federal funds and grants**

Quality of Life Indexes (Rate per 1000 population)

Crime rate in 1991:	53.9
Violent crime rate in 1991:	2.2
Physicians rate in 1992:	1.86
Hospital bed rate in 1991:	5.74

ACCRA Cost of Living Indexes

(First quarter 1993, average = 100)

Composite index:	89.7
Utilities index:	86.4
Housing index:	76.9

Overview

Springdale is located in northwest Arkansas in the Ozarks on Arkansas Highway 412 and U.S. 71. The nearest interstate highway is I-40, 50 miles away. It is located about 325 miles from Dallas, Texas and 236 miles from Kansas City, Missouri. Rail service is provided by the Arkansas/Missouri Railroad. Springdale has its own public airport and a commercial airport is 10 miles away.

Population (1990)

Total Population and Growth Rate
1990: 113,409
1980: 100,494
1970: 77,370
Growth rate 1970–1990: 47%

Race and Hispanic Origin
White: 95.9%
Black: 1.5%
Asian/Pacific Islander: 0.9%
Native American: 1.3%
Hispanic origin: 1.3%
White not Hispanic: 95.0%

Age
Ages 18 to 20: 7%
Ages 21 to 24: 8.2%
Ages 25 to 44: 31.3%
Ages 45 to 54: 9.8%
Ages 55 to 59: 4%
Ages 60 to 64: 3.7%
Ages 65 plus: 11.3%

Educational Attainment (1990)

Percent having completed high school: 73.2%
Percent having completed college: 20.0%
Elementary and high school enrollment: 1,827

Federal Funds and Grants Received

Total received in 1989: $289,200,000
Funds received per capita: $2,614

Civilian Labor Force

1993 (April): 68,098
1992 average: 66,543
1991 average: 63,242
1990 average: 63,978

Unemployment

1993 (April): 3.2%
1992 average: 3.6%
1991 average: 3.7%
1990 average: 3.5%

Average Annual Pay

1988: $17,087
1987: $16,657
1985: $15,109

Per Capita Personal Income

1991: $15,987
1990: $15,634
1989: $14,555

Business Climate (1987)

Manufacturing
Number of establishments in 1987: 140
Shipments in 1987 ($1,000): $1,027,100
Employees in 1987: 9,800
Change in employment, 1982 to 1987: 24.1%
Average annual pay for manufacturing work in 1989: $19,881
Average annual pay for production work in 1987: $15,408

Wholesale Trade
Number of establishments in 1987: 225
Total sales in 1987 ($1,000): $904,400
Change in sales, 1982 to 1987: 58.9%

Retail Trade
Number of establishments in 1987: 732

Total sales in 1987 ($1,000): $904,400
Retail sales per household in 1987: $18,343
Average annual pay in 1989: $10,171

Service Industry
Selected receipts in 1987 ($1,000): $191,200
Average annual pay in 1989: $14,575

Housing
Total number of units in 1990: 47,349
Occupied units in 1990: 43,372
Owner-occupied units in 1990: 61.6%
1993 ACCRA average cost: $88,675
1993 ACCRA average rent for an apartment: $400

Chamber of Commerce
Fayetteville Chamber of Commerce, Steven M. Ward, President, 123 W. Mountain St., PO Box 4216, Fayetteville, AR 72701. 501-521-1710, FAX 501-521-1791

Economic Development Office
Springdale Chamber of Commerce, Lee Zachary, President, PO Box 166, 700 W. Emma, Springdale, AR 72765. 501-756-4694, FAX 501-751-4699

Local Incentives for Business
Industrial Financing
Methods: Conventional, Industrial Revenue Bonds, Industrial Foundation, and Municipal Tax Bonds

Major Businesses

Company	SIC	Telephone
Arkansas Western Gas Co.	4923	(501) 521-1141
Continental Ozark Inc.	5171	(501) 521-5565
Harp's Food Stores Inc.	5411	(501) 751-7601
Herider Farms Inc.	0251	(501) 442-4966
Hudson Foods Inc.	0252	(501) 636-1100
Hunt, J. B. Transport, Inc.	4213	(501) 659-8800
Jones Truck Lines, Inc.	4213	(501) 751-4806
JTL Intermediate Co.	4213	(501) 751-4806
Kuhn's-Big K Stores Corp.	5311	(501) 273-7741
National Home Centers	5211	(501) 756-6145
North Arkansas Wholesale	5023	(501) 273-4000
PAM Transportation Services	4213	(501) 361-9111
Schmieding Enterprises Inc.	5148	(501) 751-4517
Shaw, Willis, Express Inc.	4213	(501) 248-7261
Southwestern Energy Co.	4923	(501) 521-1141
Tyson Foods Inc.	0251	(501) 756-4000
Wal-Mart Stores Inc.	5311	(501) 273-4000
Weaver, Victor F., Inc.	2015	(501) 756-4000

Colleges and Universities
University of Arkansas, Fayetteville

LITTLE ROCK–NORTH LITTLE ROCK, AR (MSA)

Geographic Profile
Land Area
2908.6 square miles

Counties and Parishes
Faulkner
Lonoke
Pulaski
Saline

Additional Cities/Towns within Area
Jacksonville

Ranking Highlights
49 *out of 319 in total* land area
116 *out of 319 in* population growth, *1970–1990*
104 *out of 310 in having the lowest* unemployment *rate*
84 *out of 310 in size of* labor force
130 *out of 318 in the percentage of* college graduates
137 *out of 292 in per capita personal* income
103 *out of 319 in number of* manufacturing establishments
26 *out of 318 in* physicians *per 1000 people*
33 *out of 318 in* hospital beds *per 1000 people*
257 *out of 267 in fewest* crimes *per 1000 people*
261 *out of 266 in fewest* violent crimes *per 1000 people*
120 *out of 319 in per capita* federal funds and grants

Quality of Life Indexes (Rate per 1000 population)
Crime rate in 1991:	93.5
Violent crime rate in 1991:	14.1
Physicians rate in 1992:	3.14
Hospital bed rate in 1991:	5.87

ACCRA Cost of Living Indexes
(First quarter 1993, average = 100)
Composite index: 91.5
Utilities index: 115.6
Housing index: 81.6

Overview
Little Rock, the state's capital, is located in the center of Arkansas. The state's two mountain ranges lie to the northwest and include the Ozark National Forest and the Ouachita National Forest. The Grand Prairie stretches south and east from Little Rock.

The city's economy is dominated by traditional industries like lumber, poultry, oil and gas. Medical facilities, banks, and other service industries are also important to the economy, and their presence has in turn attracted to the area other companies that offer a variety of support services, especially those that are computer-related. Local, state, and federal government have been Little Rock's major employers for many years.

Because of its strategic location, Little Rock serves as a center for trade. The Little Rock Port Industrial Park offers some of the finest facilities on the Arkansas River, enabling the city to promote itself not only as a distribution center for the state's agricultural products, but also for its increasing number of manufactured goods. Cotton and soybeans are the major products at the city's nearby farms, and the country's largest supply of bauxite is mined in the city's outskirts. Items and goods produced in the area include metals, chemicals, apparel, food products, machinery, textiles, paper products, and wood furniture.

The city's main asset, however, is its port. The development of the Arkansas River into a year-round barge navigation route has meant that a city as far west as Tulsa, Oklahoma, has access to the Mississippi River. Consequently, a variety of products pass through the port, including sand and gravel, wheat, soybeans, petroleum, iron, steel, stone, and chemicals. South American bauxite is unloaded at Little Rock, bound for the central Arkansas aluminum industry, while Arkansas-produced coal is loaded for shipment to Japan. Furthermore, the Little Rock Port Industrial Park has been designated as a Foreign Trade Zone, enabling goods to be stored or processed without payment of customs duty until they are moved out of the zone and into normal domestic channels. Little Rock is also a U.S. Customs Port of Entry for both freight and passengers. Recent improvements and enhancements of the port take advantage of increased traffic on the Arkansas River.

The greater Little Rock area is served by three railroads: Union Pacific Railroad, Amtrak and Cotton Belt/Southern Pacific. The port industrial park is served by the Little Rock Port Railroad (switching) with direct in-park interchange with Union Pacific. Interstates 30, 40, 430, 440, 630, and U.S. highways 64, 65, 67, 70, and 167 intersect the metropolitan area. The McClellan-Kerr Arkansas River Navigation System is four hundred and forty-five miles long with 17 locks and dams and is a year-round water-way system into the Southwest. Through the McClellan-Kerr System, shippers have access to deep water ports for international trade. There are over seventy franchised motor carriers with terminals in the Greater Little Rock Area. The Little Rock Regional Airport is located within the city limits and is only three miles from downtown. It is served by nine major air carriers. The airport's new 7,200 feet parallel runway was opened in 1991. The airport also has facilities for private planes and corporate aircraft.

Population (1990)

Total Population and Growth Rate
1990: 513,117
1980: 474,463
1970: 381,123
Growth rate 1970–1990: 35%

Race and Hispanic Origin
White: 78.9%
Black: 19.9%
Asian/Pacific Islander: 0.7%
Native American: 0.4%
Hispanic origin: 0.8%
White not Hispanic: 78.4%

Age
Ages 18 to 20: 4.7%
Ages 21 to 24: 5.9%
Ages 25 to 44: 33.3%
Ages 45 to 54: 10.3%
Ages 55 to 59: 4.1%
Ages 60 to 64: 3.9%
Ages 65 plus: 11.4%

Educational Attainment (1990)
Percent having completed high school: 76.6%
Percent having completed college: 20.4%
Elementary and high school enrollment: 91,181

Federal Funds and Grants Received
Total received in 1989: $1,741,900,000
Funds received per capita: $3,395

Civilian Labor Force
1993 (April):   273,724
1992 average: 274,133
1991 average: 266,538
1990 average: 268,851

Unemployment
1993 (April):   5.1%
1992 average: 6.1%
1991 average: 6.2%
1990 average: 5.9%

Average Annual Pay
1988: $19,252
1987: $18,912
1985: $17,662

Per Capita Personal Income
1991: $17,610
1990: $16,898
1989: $15,796

Business Climate (1987)

Manufacturing
Number of establishments in 1987: 590
Shipments in 1987 ($1,000): $3,785,000
Employees in 1987: 31,100
Change in employment, 1982 to 1987: -8.3%
Average annual pay for manufacturing work in 1989: $21,740
Average annual pay for production work in 1987: $17,898

Wholesale Trade
Number of establishments in 1987: 1,140

Total sales in 1987 ($1,000): $6,156,100
Change in sales, 1982 to 1987: 23.2%

Retail Trade

Number of establishments in 1987: 3,256
Total sales in 1987 ($1,000): $6,156,100
Retail sales per household in 1987: $16,893
Average annual pay in 1989: $11,699

Service Industry

Selected receipts in 1987 ($1,000): $1,399,700
Average annual pay in 1989: $18,203

Office Real Estate (1992)

*Average class A Central Business District rental range per
  sq. ft: $13.50*

Vacancy Rates

All areas: 12.9%

Vacancy Rates in Central Business District

Class A space: 13.3%
Class B space: 20.2%

Vacancy Rates Outside Central Business District

Class A space: 9.1%
Class B space: 7.7%

Housing

Total number of units in 1990: 214,546
Occupied units in 1990: 195,437
Owner-occupied units in 1990: 64.8%
1993 ACCRA average cost: $92,750
1993 ACCRA average rent for an apartment: $412

Chamber of Commerce

Greater Little Rock Chamber of Commerce, Paul H. Harvel,
  President, 1 Spring St., PO Box 1, Little Rock, AR 72201.
  501-374-4871, FAX 501-374-6018

Economic Development Office

Little Rock Port Authority, Robert Brave, Exec. Director,
  7500 Lindsey Rd., Little Rock, AR 72206. 501-490-1468,
  FAX 501-490-1800

Major Businesses

Company	SIC	Telephone
AFCO Metals Inc.	5051	(501) 490-2255
Affiliated Food Stores Inc.	5141	(501) 455-3590
Arkansas Blue Cross Blue Shield	6324	(501) 378-2000
Arkansas Electric Coop Co.	4911	(501) 570-2200
Arkansas Power & Light	4911	(501) 377-4000
Baptist Medical System	8062	(501) 227-2000
Coca-Cola Bottling Co. of Arkansas	2086	(501) 569-2700
Dillard Department Stores	5311	(501) 376-5200
Environmental Systems	4953	(501) 223-4100
Fairfield Communities Inc.	1522	(501) 664-6000
First Commercial Corp.	6021	(501) 371-7000
Harvest Foods, Inc.	5411	(501) 562-3583

Major Businesses (Continued)

Company	SIC	Telephone
Sales Marketing Group, Inc.	5141	(501) 375-8121
Shur-Valu Stamps, Inc.	2026	(501) 455-3590
Southern Farmers Association	5191	(501) 945-2371
Stephens Inc.	6211	(501) 374-4361
Systematics, Inc.	7374	(501) 223-5100
TCBY Enterprises Inc.	2024	(501) 688-8229
Tenenbaum, A. Co. Inc.	5093	(501) 945-0881
Worthen Banking Corp.	6021	(501) 378-1521

Colleges and Universities

Arkansas Baptist College, Little Rock
Capital City Junior College of Business, Little Rock
National Education Center-Arkansas College of Technology
  Campus, Little Rock
Philander Smith College, Little Rock
University of Arkansas at Little Rock, Little Rock
University of Arkansas for Medical Sciences, Little Rock
Shorter College, North Little Rock

PINE BLUFF, AR (MSA)

Geographic Profile

Land Area

884.8 square miles

Counties and Parishes

Jefferson

Ranking Highlights

223 *out of 319 in total* land area

272 *out of 319 in* population growth, *1970–1990*

290 *out of 310 in having the lowest* unemployment *rate*

306 *out of 310 in size of* labor force

243 *out of 318 in the percentage of* college graduates

278 *out of 292 in per capita personal* income

305 *out of 319 in number of* manufacturing establishments

232 *out of 318 in* physicians *per 1000 people*

45 *out of 318 in* hospital beds *per 1000 people*

206 *out of 267 in fewest* crimes *per 1000 people*

241 *out of 266 in fewest* violent crimes *per 1000 people*

68 *out of 319 in per capita* federal funds and grants

Quality of Life Indexes (Rate per 1000 population)

Crime rate in 1991:	72.8
Violent crime rate in 1991:	10.9
Physicians rate in 1992:	1.47
Hospital bed rate in 1991:	5.61

ACCRA Cost of Living Indexes

(First quarter 1993, average = 100)

Composite index:	N/A
Utilities index:	N/A
Housing index:	N/A

Overview

Pine Bluff is located 38 miles southeast of the state capitol, Little Rock. The area is a transportation center for agriculture and industry. The city has one of the largest slack water harbors on the navigable Arkansas River, 55 miles upstream from its confluence with the Mississippi. Adjacent to the port area, two railroads, the Southern Pacific and Union Pacific, maintain major facilities. An executive jet airport, access to commercial air service within 45 minutes, and a network of national or state highways radiating from the city are also available: U.S. 65, U.S. 79, U.S. 270, and U.S. 425. In its 1990 economic development strategies report, KPMG Peat Marwick said, "Pine Bluff is a leading edge center of manufacturing in the mid-south, and a symbol of the viability of manufacturing in the American economy." About 20% of the labor force is employed in manufacturing, well above the national average. Annual capital investment in new or expanding area industry has exceeded $80 million in each of the last eight years

The Convention Center is the largest in the state, and nearby a new Arts and Science Center is being developed. The city is surrounded by forests and some of the richest farm lands in the world. Principal agricultural production is in timber, cotton, rice and soybeans.

Population (1990)

Total Population and Growth Rate

1990: 85,487

1980: 90,718

1970: 85,329

Growth rate 1970–1990: 0%

Race and Hispanic Origin

White: 56.0%

Black: 43.1%

Asian/Pacific Islander: 0.4%

Native American: 0.3%

Hispanic origin: 0.5%

White not Hispanic: 55.8%

Age

Ages 18 to 20: 5.7%

Ages 21 to 24: 5.7%

Ages 25 to 44: 28.7%

Ages 45 to 54: 9.8%

Ages 55 to 59: 4%

Ages 60 to 64: 4.2%

Ages 65 plus: 13.5%

Educational Attainment (1990)

Percent having completed high school: 65.9%

Percent having completed college: 14.6%

Elementary and high school enrollment: 17,045

Federal Funds and Grants Received

Total received in 1989: $370,900,000

Funds received per capita: $4,085

Civilian Labor Force

1993 (April):	36,688
1992 average:	37,146
1991 average:	36,813
1990 average:	37,559

Unemployment

1993 (April):	9.3%
1992 average:	10.9%
1991 average:	10.5%
1990 average:	8.4%

Average Annual Pay

1988: $18,570

1987: $18,143

1985: $16,913

Per Capita Personal Income

1991: $13,749

1990: $13,345

1989: $12,570

Business Climate (1987)

Manufacturing

Number of establishments in 1987: 87

Shipments in 1987 ($1,000): $902,900

Employees in 1987: 5,800

Change in employment, 1982 to 1987: 3.6%

Average annual pay for manufacturing work in 1989: $24,137

Average annual pay for production work in 1987: $22,867

Wholesale Trade

Number of establishments in 1987: 124

Total sales in 1987 ($1,000): $272,200

Change in sales, 1982 to 1987: -16.3%

Retail Trade

Number of establishments in 1987: 560

Total sales in 1987 ($1,000): $272,200

Retail sales per household in 1987: $14,433

Average annual pay in 1989: $10,032

Service Industry

Selected receipts in 1987 ($1,000): $128,400

Average annual pay in 1989: $16,298

Housing

Total number of units in 1990: 33,311

Occupied units in 1990: 30,001

Owner-occupied units in 1990: 67.1%

1993 ACCRA average cost: N/A

1993 ACCRA average rent for an apartment: N/A

Chamber of Commerce

Greater Pine Bluff Chamber of Commerce, Jim Berry, President, 612 W. 5th St., PO Box 5069, Pine Bluff, AR 71611. 501-535-0110, FAX 501-543-4593

Economic Development Office

Jefferson County Industry Foundation, Wallace Gieringer, President, PO Box 6866, 121 W. 6th Ave. #200, Pine Bluff, AR 71601. 501-535-7189, FAX 501-535-1643

Economic Development Organizations

Jefferson County Industrial Foundation, W.A. Gieringer, President, PO Box 6866, 121 W. 6th St., Ste. 200, Pine Bluff, AR 71611. 501-535-7189, FAX 501-535-1643

Pine Bluff-Jefferson County Port Authority, W.A. Gieringer, Exec. Director, PO Box 6866, Pine Bluff, AR 71611. 501-535-7189, FAX 501-535-1643

Pine Bluff Downtown Development, Montine McNulty, Exec. Director, 512 S. Pine, Ste. 301, Pine Bluff, AR 71601. 501-536-8742

Southeast Arkansas Economic Development District, Glenn Bell, Director, PO Box 6806, Pine Bluff, AR 71611. 501-536-1971

City of Pine Bluff, Carolyn Robinson, Mayor, 200 E. 8th St., Pine Bluff, AR 71601. 501-543-1855

Pine Bluff Planning Dept., Jeff Hawkins, Director, 200 E. 8th St., Pine Bluff, AR 71601. 501-543-1898

Southeast Arkansas Regional Planning Commission, Alan Skinner, Assistant Director, PO Box 8398, Pine Bluff, AR 71611. 501-534-4247

Arkansas Employment Security Div., Wanda Neal, Manager, PO Box 8308, Pine Bluff, AR 71611. 501-534-1920

Industrial Sites

Harbor Industrial District (372 acres), Pine Bluff-Jefferson County Port Authority, PO BOx 6866, Pine Bluff, AR 71611. 501-535-7189, FAX 501-535-1643

Jefferson Industrial Park (785 acres), Jefferson County Industrial Foundation, PO Box 6866, 121 W. 6th St., Ste. 200, Pine Bluff, AR 71611. 501-535-7189, FAX 501-535-1643

Major Businesses

Company	SIC	Telephone
Arkansas Mill Supply Co.	5085	(501) 534-6540
Arkansas Oak Flooring Co.	2426	(501) 534-3110
Century Tube Corp.	3312	(501) 535-6200
Farmers Supply Association	5191	(501) 534-0541
Hixson Lumber Sales Inc.	5031	(501) 535-1436
Jefferson Hospital Association	8062	(501) 541-7100
MK Distributors, Inc.	5181	(501) 534-0364
Mad Butcher Inc.	5411	(501) 535-6356
National Bank of Commerce	6021	(501) 541-8000
Nelson, Knox Oil Co. Inc.	5171	(501) 534-4941
Pearson, Ben, Inc.	3534	(501) 534-6411
Pine Bluff Warehouse Co.	4225	(501) 535-6464
Simmons First National Bank	6021	(501) 541-1000
Strong Systems, Inc.	3295	(501) 536-1251

Colleges and Universities

University of Arkansas at Pine Bluff. Offers bachelor degree programs in arts & sciences, education, agriculture, home economics and technologies, and business and management. Some graduate level courses are offered.

Additional Information

Harbor Industrial District. Jefferson County Industrial Foundation, n.d. 4p.

Jefferson Industrial Park. Jefferson County Industrial Foundation, n.d. 4p.

Pine Bluff, Arkansas, Community Data. Jefferson County Industrial Foundation, n.d. 4p.

FORT SMITH, AR–OK (MSA)

Geographic Profile

Land Area

1805.7 square miles

Counties and Parishes

Arkansas:

Crawford

Sebastian

Oklahoma:

Sequoyah

Ranking Highlights

104 *out of 319 in total* land area

107 *out of 319 in* population growth, *1970–1990*

184 *out of 310 in having the lowest* unemployment *rate*

195 *out of 310 in size of* labor force

300 *out of 318 in the percentage of* college graduates

272 *out of 292 in per capita personal* income

165 *out of 319 in number of* manufacturing establishments

193 *out of 318 in* physicians *per 1000 people*

31 *out of 318 in* hospital beds *per 1000 people*

85 *out of 267 in fewest* crimes *per 1000 people*

87 *out of 266 in fewest* violent crimes *per 1000 people*

232 *out of 319 in per capita* federal funds and grants

Quality of Life Indexes (Rate per 1000 population)

Crime rate in 1991:	50.6
Violent crime rate in 1991:	4.4
Physicians rate in 1992:	1.67
Hospital bed rate in 1991:	5.88

ACCRA Cost of Living Indexes

(First quarter 1993, average = 100)

Composite index:	89.3
Utilities index:	100.8
Housing index:	70.7

Overview

Fort Smith, Arkansas, is located on the Arkansas-Oklahoma border. The city is between two U.S. Government Forest Reserves, the Ozark National Forest to the north and Ouachita National Forest to the south. It is situated on U.S. Highways 71, 64 and 271. The city has transcontinental highway links with the east and west coasts by means of Interstate Highways 40 and 540.

Fort Smith is located in the center of the largest producing natural gas field in the nation and, as a result has low residential, commercial and industrial gas rates. Electricity rates are also among the lowest in the nation. Three municipally-owned lakes in the Boston Mountains north of Fort Smith provide the city with water.

There are over 200 manufacturing plants in the area. Over the past 25 years, 111 new plants began production creating 6,474 jobs. In the same period, there were 782 expansions, creating 20,126 jobs.

Fort Smith Municipal Airport hosts American Eagle, Atlantic Southeast, Northwest Airlink, and TWA/Air Midwest Airlines. The airport has an 8,000 foot runway, the largest in the state.

Rail service is provided by the Kansas City Southern, Fort Smith Railroad and Missouri-Arkansas railroads. Reciprocal switching gives industry a choice of service by the three rail carriers. Twenty-seven motor freight lines maintain daily schedules, giving overnight service to Fort Smith's trade territory and between Fort Smith and principal Southwest and Midwest markets. Low cost transportation by barge between Fort Smith and points on the navigable waterways is available by water common or contract carriers certified by the Interstate Commerce Commission to serve Fort Smith. The public port in Fort Smith is in operation with on-site warehousing facilities.

Population (1990)

Total Population and Growth Rate

1990: 175,911

1980: 162,813

1970: 128,284

Growth rate 1970–1990: 37%

Race and Hispanic Origin

White: 88.4%

Black: 3.9%

Asian/Pacific Islander: 2.1%

Native American: 5.1%

Hispanic origin: 1.2%

White not Hispanic: 87.8%

Age

Ages 18 to 20: 4.2%

Ages 21 to 24: 5.2%

Ages 25 to 44: 30.4%

Ages 45 to 54: 10.9%

Ages 55 to 59: 4.4%

Ages 60 to 64: 4.2%

Ages 65 plus: 13.4%

Educational Attainment (1990)

Percent having completed high school: 67.5%

Percent having completed college: 11.8%

Elementary and high school enrollment: 32,779

Federal Funds and Grants Received

Total received in 1989: $466,800,000

Funds received per capita: $2,583

Civilian Labor Force

1993 (April):	92,092
1992 average:	93,084
1991 average:	91,859
1990 average:	93,169

Unemployment

1993 (April): 6.2%
1992 average: 7.3%
1991 average: 8.1%
1990 average: 7.5%

Average Annual Pay

1988: $17,557
1987: $17,007
1985: $16,215

Per Capita Personal Income

1991: $14,324
1990: $13,997
1989: $13,187

Business Climate (1987)

Manufacturing

Number of establishments in 1987: 298
Shipments in 1987 ($1,000): $3,402,100
Employees in 1987: 25,900
Change in employment, 1982 to 1987: 34.9%
Average annual pay for manufacturing work, 1989: $20,466
Average annual pay for production work, 987: $17,648

Wholesale Trade

Number of establishments in 1987: 352
Total sales in 1987 ($1,000): $818,600
Change in sales, 1982 to 1987: 3.9%

Retail Trade

Number of establishments in 1987: 1,239
Total sales in 1987 ($1,000): $818,600
Retail sales per household in 1987: $14,798
Average annual pay in 1989: $10,257

Service Industry

Selected receipts in 1987 ($1,000): $389,100
Average annual pay in 1989: $15,666

Housing

Total number of units in 1990: 74,646
Occupied units in 1990: 66,884
Owner-occupied units in 1990: 69.4%
1993 ACCRA average cost: $79,200
1993 ACCRA average rent for an apartment: $368

Chamber of Commerce

Fort Smith Chamber of Commerce, Billy Dooly, President, 612 Garrison Ave., PO Box 1668, Fort Smith, AR 72902. 501-783-6118, FAX 501-783-6110

Economic Development Office

Fort Smith Economic Development, Billy Dooly, President, 612 Garrison Ave., PO Box 1668, Fort Smith, AR 72902. 501-783-6118, FAX 501-783-6110

Major Businesses

Company	SIC	Telephone
A B C Treadco Inc.	7534	(501) 785-6000
ABF Freight System, Inc.	4213	(501) 785-6000
Air Systems Inc.	3444	(501) 646-8386
Arkansas Best Corp.	4213	(501) 785-6000
Arkansas Oklahoma Gas Corp.	4923	(501) 783-3181
Baldor Electric Co.	3621	(501) 646-4711
Carco Capital Corp.	7513	(501) 441-3200
Carco Rentals, Inc.	7359	(501) 441-3200
CCC Express, Inc.	4213	(501) 441-3200
Co-Plas, Inc.	2851	(501) 646-7865
Donrey Inc.	2711	(501) 785-7810
Farmers Cooperative	5191	(501) 783-8959
First America Federal Saving	6035	(501) 782-8901
First National Bank Inc.	6021	(501) 782-2041
Flanders Industries Inc.	2514	(501) 785-2351
Fort Smith Chair Co.	2519	(501) 785-4411
J & B Supply Inc.	5074	(501) 782-7933
K-Mac Enterprises, Inc.	5812	(501) 646-2053
Riverside Furniture Corp.	2511	(501) 785-8100
Sisters Mercy St. Edwards Mercy Hospital	8062	(501) 484-6000
Sparks Regional Medical Center	8062	(501) 441-4000
Superior Federal Bank	6035	(501) 452-8900
Trans States Lines Inc.	4213	(501) 648-4400
USA Truck Inc.	4213	(501) 471-2500
Warmack & Co.	6512	(501) 452-1000
Weldon, Williams & Lick	2759	(501) 783-4113
Wortz Co.	2052	(918) 647-8630

CALIFORNIA

REDDING (MSA)

CHINO (MSA)

YUBA CITY (MSA)

SACRAMENTO (MSA)

SANTA ROSA-
PETALUMA (PMSA)

VALLEJO-FAIRFIELD-
NAPA (PMSA)

STOCKTON (MSA)

SAN FRANCISCO
(MSA)

OAKLAND (PMSA)

MODESTO (MSA)

SAN JOSE (MSA)

SANTA CRUZ (PMSA)

MERCED (MSA)

FRESNO (MSA)

VISALIA-TULARE-
PORTERVILLE (MSA)

RIVERSIDE-
SAN BERNARDINO
(PMSA)

SALINAS-SEASIDE-MONTEREY
(MSA)

BAKERSFIELD (MSA)

SANTA BARBARA-SANTA MARIA-
LOMPOC (MSA)

OXNARD-VENTURA (PMSA)

LOS ANGELES-LONG BEACH (PMSA)

ANAHEIM-SANTA ANA (PMSA)

SAN DIEGO (MSA)

Shasta

Butte

Sutter Yuba Placer

Yolo El Dorado

Sonoma Napa Sacramento

Solano

Marin San Joaquin

Contra Costa

San Francisco Alameda Stanislaus

San Mateo

Santa Clara Merced

Santa Cruz

Fresno Inyo

Tulare

Monterey

Kern

Santa Barbara San Bernardino

Ventura Los Angeles

Orange Riverside

San Diego

CALIFORNIA

Population
1990: 29,760,021
1980: 23,667,902

Age
Ages 18 to 20: 1,411,200
Ages 21 to 24: 2,001,057
Ages 25 to 44: 10,325,692
Ages 45 to 54: 2,902,569
Ages 55 to 59: 1,133,907
Ages 60 to 64: 1,099,319
Median age: 31.5

Race
White: 20,524,327
Black: 2,208,801
Asian/Pacific Islander: 2,845,659
Native American: 242,164
Hispanic origin: 7,687,938

Households
Total: 10,381,206
Persons per household: 2.79

Sex
Male: 14,897,627
Female: 14,862,394

Population Migration
Domestic migration: 502,000
International migration: 1,843,000

Projection of the Population in 1995
Total: 31,373,000
18 to 64: 19,698,000

Civilian Labor Force
1993: 15,122,600
1992: 14,975,200
1991: 14,685,000
1990: 14,441,600

Manufacturing
1995 Projection: 2,332,800
1992: 1,889,600
1991: 1,998,500
1990: 2,087,800
1989: 2,148,600

Services
1995 Projection: 5,416,600
1992: 3,420,400
1991: 3,584,200
1990: 3,540,900
1989: 3,337,200

Wholesale and Retail Trade
1995 Projection: 3,701,000
1992: 2,832,600
1991: 3,049,800
1990: 3,109,100
1989: 3,088,800

Unemployment Rate
1993: 9.8%
1992: 8.5%
1991: 7.0%
1990: 5.5%

Employer Unemployment Contributions

Contribution Rate
1992: 2.54%
1991: 2.01%
1990: 2.07%

Average Weekly Benefit
1992: $156.62
1991: $153.68
1990: $132.51

Gross State Product (Million $)
1989: $697,381
1988: $642,309
1987: $589,311
1979: $288,244
Growth rate, 1979 to 1989: 141.9%

Capital Expenditures of Manufacturing Industries
1990: $9,641,500,000
1989: $9,373,700,000
1988: $8,265,200,000
1987: $8,571,700,000

State Tax Rates

Individual income: Range from 1% ($4,394 or less) to 11% (above $200,000).

Corporate income: 9.3% of taxable net income.

General property: Local collections, assessed at 100% of full cash value.

General sales: 6%

Gasoline: 17¢ per gallon

Income

Median income for a 4 person family: $42,813

Personal per Capita Income

1992: $21,278

1991: $20,805

1990: $20,547

Disposable per Capita Income

1992: $18,495

1991: $17,959

1990: $17,596

Private Employment Weekly Wages

Average

1989: $470

1988: $456

1987: $456

Manufacturing

1989: $437

1988: $562

1987: $537

Services

1989: $459

1988: $448

1987: $426

Wholesale

1989: $582

1988: $565

1987: $528

Retail

1989: $277

1988: $267

1987: $256

Highway Statistics

Total Highway Miles

1990: 163,574

1989: 164,298

1988: 162,562

Federal Highway Aid

1991: $1,058,814,000

1990: $1,138,101,000

1989: $1,006,336,000

Electricity

Average Cost per Kilowatt Hour

1990: 8.82¢

1989: 8.38¢

1988: 7.94¢

Housing (1990)

Owner occupied units: 5,773,943

Median house value: $195,500

Renter occupied units: 4,607,263

Median rent: $561

Total vacant units: 801,676

Homeowner vacancy rate: 2.0%

Rental vacancy rate: 5.9%

State Business Incentives and Assistance

Enterprise Zone Incentives

California has enacted two enterprise zone programs to stimulate growth in selected areas of the state. Ten areas have been designated as enterprise zones and nine areas as employment and economic incentive areas. State and local incentives are available to businesses located within these zones. Legislation provides the following state incentives to new and expanding enterprise zone and employment incentive area companies:

1. Tax credits of up to $1.3 million for sales and use taxes paid on machinery purchase.
2. Tax credits of up to $19,000 per qualified employee hired.
3. Interest deductions for lenders on loans to firms within the zones.
4. 100% net operating loss carry forward for all firms.
5. Accelerated expensing deduction for a business purchase of certain property.
6. Five years to use tax credits.

In addition to state tax incentives, local permit and construction related fees are often reduced or eliminated in enterprise zones. Communities also offer expeditious processing of plans and permits. Enterprise zone businesses also receive marketing assistance at no cost. Up to 2,000 sales leads are provided through the Sales Development Program. The program serves a host of non-retail industries that do business on a state, regional or national basis.

Foreign Trade Zone Incentives

By operating in a trade zone, foreign or domestic merchandise may be brought into United States for shipment to a third country, either in its original or completely altered conditions without formal customs entry or payment of customs duties or excise taxes. Within this area, the goods are considered to be outside U.S. customs territory, but within international commerce territory.

Financial and Business Assistance

Tax-Exempt Industrial Development Bonds. Companies qualifying for industrial development bond financing receive approval for a project through a local industrial development authority. An eligible bond project can be the construction of a new plant, expansion of an existing plant, or replacement of part or all of an existing plant. Industrial activities eligible for financing include assembly, fabrication, manufacturing and processing. Warehousing, if in support of a manufacturing facility, may also be an eligible activity. This program was scheduled to end on September 30, 1990.

Taxable Industrial Development Bonds. Taxable IDB can be used for a variety of projects with proceeds going towards land, property, machinery, or permanent working capital. Loans, as low as $250,000 with no maximum, can be issued for 20 to 30 years. The interest created is approximately 80% of prime.

Permit Assistance. The Office of Permit Assistance, in the Governor's Office of Planning and Research, assists businesses in identifying the permits needed for development projects. The office is also the central point of contact for obtaining information on the environmental and project review process.

Rural Economic Development Infrastructure Program. The California Department of Commerce provides capital designed to assist rural municipalities in financing off-site public infrastructure improvements necessary to accommodate the retention and expansion of businesses. The program can offer below market rate financing up to $2 million per project. Eligible improvements include sewer and water facilities; streets, highways, curbs and gutters; bridges; rail spurs; and other infrastructure improvement necessary for private industrial or commercial development. For more information, contact the Office of Local Development.

Community Development Block Grant. Local governments may apply to this program for funding of economic development projects. The State of California receives approximately $20 million each year from the U.S. Dept. of Housing and Urban Development. 30% is made available to eligible counties and cities to finance business development projects that create or retain permanent private sector jobs. Cities under 50,000 and counties under 200,000 populations are eligible for grants up to $500,000 per year. Grants are used to make loans to businesses for business expansion. The business concern must provide $2 for every $1 of Grant funds. For more information, contact the Office of Local Development.

Pollution Control and Solid Waste Financing. The California Pollution Control Financing Authority, an independent state agency, provides tax exempt financing for companies to perform projects in compliance with pollution control and solid waste regulations. This includes projects that convert a valueless waste product into a useful product that can be sold at a profit. The full qualifying amount of the project can be financed tax exempt. The Authority can also offer financing to businesses that qualify under federal tax regulations for small issue private activity bonds, limiting $10 million per project.

Energy Cogeneration. Cogeneration is the simultaneous

production of electricity and useful thermal energy from the same initial fuel source. Through cogeneration, firms receive clean, stable, continuous power while reducing operation costs. The California Energy Commission can provide funds for project feasibility studies for firms investigating the possibility of cogeneration for the first time. The California Alternative Energy Source Financing Authority can provide low-interest loans available by selling tax exempt bonds. Companies with qualified projects are eligible for accelerated depreciation allowed by state and federal tax laws.

Urban Waterfront Area Restoration Financing Authority. This program is designed to encourage commercial activity in urban waterfront areas. The Authority is empowered to issue up to $650 million in revenue bonds for waterfront restoration projects.

California Small Business Loan Guarantee Program. The state offers more than $30 million for loan guarantees to qualified small business for short term credit and lines of credit. The applicant must be a small business with three years or more of operational record and unable to service a loan with a bank or lender. The maximum amount of the loan guarantee cannot exceed 90% or $350,000.

California Competitive Technology Program. This program enhances private sector competitiveness by providing matching funds for collaborative research projects, R&D consortia, and technology transfer innovation efforts. It facilitates the transfer of knowledge from research institutions to the private sector. These joint efforts are geared to the commercialization of products or processes which will contribute to the competitiveness of California firms and the creation and retention of jobs in the state.

Microelectronics Innovation and Computer Research. This program brings industry, state government, and academia together for the advancement of research and education in microelectronics technology. The state and industry jointly find innovative research projects proposed and carried out by University of California faculty members. University funds for the projects are matched by industrial contributions on a project-by-project basis.

Education And Training

Job Service Program. The California Employment Development Department (EDD) is responsible for the Job Service program. This program is designed to assist businesses in reducing personnel costs. EDD refers qualified applicants to employers and provides demographic data and current or projected labor supply information. Employers may also use EDD offices to interview pre-screened applicants.

California Employment Training Panel. Financed through state unemployment funds, ETP provides money to train the workforce a new or expanding business may need. This program focuses on experienced workers who are either unemployed or may soon be displaced.

Job Training Partnership Act. JTPA is a state-administered, federally-financed program providing job training services and incentives to businesses. Local Private Industry Councils have the responsibility for allocating JTPA funds to ensure that eligible people in their area receive the training needed for available jobs. Eligible participants include dislocated workers, economically disadvantaged individuals and youth. Services and financial incentives available to businesses include recruitment, prescreening, and training of applicants. A subsidy of 50% on-the-job training wage for up to six months may also be negotiated.

State Offices

Real estate: Real Estate Department, James A. Edmonds, Jr., Commissioner, Box 187000, Sacramento, CA 95818-7000. 916-739-3600

Chamber of commerce: California State Chamber of Commerce, Kirk West, President, 1215 K St., 12th Fl, PO Box 1736, Sacramento, CA 95812-1736. 916-444-6670

Economic development: Dept. of Commerce, Business and Government Affairs, Anne Sheehan, Director, 1121 L St. Ste. 600, Sacramento, CA 95814. 916-322-0414

Dept. of Commerce, Office of Business Development, Janet Turner, Director, 801 K Street, Ste. 1700, Sacramento, CA 95814. 916-322-5665, FAX 916-322-3524

Dept. of Commerce, Enterprise Zone Programs, Paul Hiller, Manager, 801 K Street, Ste. 1700, Sacramento, CA 95814. 916-324-8211, FAX 916-322-3524

Dept. of Commerce, Office of Business Development, San Jose Field Office, Art Taylor, Manager, 111 N. Market Street, Ste. 815, San Jose, CA 95113. 408-277-9799

Dept. of Commerce, Office of Business Development, Los Angeles Field Office, Laurel Shockley, Manager, 200 E. Del Mar, Ste. 204, Pasadena, CA 91105. 818-568-9856

Dept. of Commerce, Office of Foreign Investment, Allan Melkesian, Director, 1121 L St. Ste. 600, Sacramento, CA 95814. 916-322-3518

Office of Competitive Technology, Thomas Walters, Director, 200 E. Del Mar Ave., Ste. 204, Pasadena, CA 91105. 818-405-1060

Dept. of Commerce, Office of Local Development, Brian McMahon, Director, 801 K Street, Ste. 1700, Sacramento, CA, 95814. 916-445-6546

Dept. of Commerce, Office of Small Business, Richard Nelson, Director, 801 K Street, Ste. 1600, Sacramento, CA, 95814. 916-322-3596

Environmental affairs: Environmental Affairs Agency, Jananne Sharpless, Secretary, PO Box 2815, 1102 Q Street, Sacramento, CA 95814. 916-322-5840

Labor: Industrial Relations Department, Ron Rinaldi, Director, PO Box 603, San Francisco, CA 94101. 415-557-3356

Unemployment: Unemployment Insurance Appeals Board, Robert Harvey, Chairperson, PO Box 944275, Sacramento, CA 94244-2750. 916-445-5678

Worker's compensation: Industrial Relations Department, Ron Rinaldi, Director, PO Box 603, San Francisco, CA 94101. 415-557-3356

Occupational safety and health: Industrial Relations Department, Occupational Safety and Health Division, Robert Stranberg, Director, PO Box 603, San Francisco, CA 94101. 415-557-1946

Secretary of state: Secretary of State, March Fong Eu, Secretary of State, 1230 J Street, Sacramento, CA 95814. 916-445-6371

Taxation and revenue: Tax Administration Division, Myron Siedorf, Tax Attorney, 3301 C Street, Ste. 301, Sacramento, CA 95816. 916-445-7392

Designated Zones for Economic Development
Enterprise Zones
Enacted in: 1984

No. of established zones: 20, plus 9 Employment Incentive Areas.

Altadena/Pasadena
Bakersfield
Coachella Valley
Calexico
Colton
Delano
Eureka
Fresno
Huntington Park
Long Beach
Los Angeles, Central City
Los Angeles, Pacoima
Lynwood
Madera
Marysville
Merced/Atwater
Oroville
Pittsburg
Porterville
Rialto
Richmond
Riverside
Sacramento
San Diego
San Francisco
San Jose
Shasta Metro area
South Gate
West Sacramento
Yuba City

Foreign Trade Zones
Foreign Trade Zone No. 50, Long Beach, California, Grantee: Board of Harbor Commissioners of the Port of Long Beach, Gerry Haugan, 925 Harbor Plaza Drive,

Major Companies in the State

Company name	Fortune 500 rank	City	Telephone	SIC number
Fortune 500 Companies				
Advanced Micro Devices Inc.	270	Sunnyvale	408-732-2400	3674
Allergan Inc.	381	Irvine	714-752-4500	3851
Amdahl Corp.	182	Sunnyvale	408-746-6000	3571
Amgen Inc.	326	Thousand Oaks	805-447-1000	2834
Apple Computer Inc.	76	Cupertino	408-996-1010	3571
Applied Materials Inc.	424	Santa Clara	408-727-5555	3559
AST Research Inc.	368	Irvine	714-727-4141	3571
Atlantic Richfield Co.	22	Los Angeles	213-486-3511	1311
Avery Dennison Corp.	177	Pasadena	818-304-2000	2672
Beckman Instruments Inc.	379	Fullerton	714-871-4848	3821
Chevron Corp.	8	San Francisco	415-894-7700	2911
Clorox Co.	246	Oakland	510-271-7000	2842
Conner Peripherals Inc.	203	San Jose	408-456-4500	3572
Del Monte Foods Co.	280	San Francisco	415-442-4000	2033
Fleetwood Enterprises Inc.	260	Riverside	909-351-3500	3716
Hewlett Packard Co.	24	Palo Alto	415-857-1501	3571
Homestake Mining Co.	451	San Francisco	415-981-8150	1041
Intel Corp.	93	Santa Clara	408-765-8080	3674
Levi Strauss Associates Inc.	99	San Francisco	415-544-6000	2325
Litton Industries Inc.	95	Beverly Hills	310-859-5000	3812
Lockheed Corp.	45	Calabasas	818-876-2000	3761
LSI Logic Corp.	475	Milpitas	408-433-8000	3674
Magnetek Inc.	310	Los Angeles	310-473-6681	3621
Mattel Inc.	230	El Segundo	310-524-2000	3942
Maxtor Corp.	352	San Jose	408-432-1700	3572
National Semiconductor Corp.	243	Santa Clara	408-721-5000	3674
Northrop Corp.	100	Los Angeles	310-553-6262	3721
Occidental Petroleum Corp.	56	Los Angeles	310-208-8800	2812
Potlatch Corp.	287	San Francisco	415-576-8800	2631
Quantum Corp.	327	Milpitas	408-894-4000	3572
Raychem Corp.	295	Menlo Park	415-361-3333	3678
Rockwell International Corp.	43	Seal Beach	310-797-3311	3823
Rohr Inc.	300	Chula Vista	619-691-4111	3728
Seagate Technology Inc.	164	Scotts Valley	408-438-6550	3572
Silicon Graphics Inc.	393	Mountain View	415-960-1980	3571
Sun Diamond Growers of Calif.	476	Pleasanton	510-463-8200	0173
Sun Microsystems Inc.	139	Mountain View	415-960-1300	3571
Tandem Computers Inc.	217	Cupertino	408-285-6000	3571
Teledyne Inc.	163	Los Angeles	310-277-3311	3724
Times Mirror Co.	138	Los Angeles	213-237-3700	2711
Tri Valley Growers Inc.	411	San Francisco	415-445-1600	2033
Unocal Corp.	55	Los Angeles	213-977-7600	2911
Varian Associates Inc.	298	Palo Alto	415-493-4000	3671
Western Digital Corp.	371	Irvine	714-932-5000	3572
Other Major Companies in the State				
Bankamerica Corp.		San Francisco	415-622-2091	6712
Bergen Brunswig Corp.		Orange	714-385-4000	5122

Major Companies in the State (Continued)

Company name	Fortune 500 rank	City	Telephone	SIC number
First Interstate Bancorp		Los Angeles	213-614-3001	6712
Fluor Corp.		Irvine	714-975-2000	1541
H F Ahmanson & Co.		Irwindale	818-960-6311	6712
Mckesson Corp.		San Francisco	415-983-8300	5122
Pacific Bell		San Francisco	415-542-9000	4813
Pacific Enterprises		Los Angeles	213-895-5000	4923
Pacific Gas & Electric Co.		San Francisco	415-973-7000	4931
Pacific Telesis Group		San Francisco	415-394-3000	4813
Price Co.		San Diego	619-581-4600	5331
Safeway Inc.		Oakland	510-891-3000	5411
SCECorp		Rosemead	818-302-2222	4911
Security Pacific Corp.		Los Angeles	213-345-4540	6712
Southern California Edison Co.		Rosemead	818-302-1212	4911
Transamerica Corp.		San Francisco	415-983-4000	6311
Union Oil Co. of California		Los Angeles	213-977-7600	1311
Vons Companies Inc.		Arcadia	818-821-7000	5411
Walt Disney Co.		Burbank	818-560-1000	7996
Wells Fargo & Co.		San Francisco	415-477-1000	6712

Long Beach, CA 90802, 213-590-4162

Foreign Trade Zone No. 56, Oakland, California, Operator: Pacific American Warehousing & Trucking Co., Grantee: City of Oakland, Ronald E. Hothem, 9401 San Leandro, Oakland, CA 94603, 415-568-8500

Foreign Trade Zone No. 153, San Diego, California, Grantee: City of San Diego, Kurt A. Chilcott, Economic Development Division, Security Pacific Plaza, 1200 Third Ave., Ste. 1620, San Diego, CA 92101, 619-236-6550

Foreign Trade Zone No. 3, San Francisco, California, Grantee: San Francisco Port Commission, Operator: Foreign Trade Services, Inc., Ed Osgood, Pier 23, San Francisco, CA 94111, 415-391-0176

Foreign Trade Zone No. 18, San Jose, California, Grantee: City of San Jose, Ruani Weerakoon, 101 Park Center Plaza, Ste. 1100, San Jose, CA 95113, 408-277-5823

Foreign Trade Zone No. 143, West Sacramento, California, Grantee: Port of Sacramento, Dennis Clark, World Trade Center, West Sacramento, CA 95691, 916-371-8000

Labor Unions

Air Line Pilots Association, International (AFL-CIO)

Association of California State Attorneys

Automobile, Aerospace & Agricultural Implement Workers of America, International Union, United (UAW AFL-CIO)

California Association of Highway Patrolmen

California Association of Professional Scientists

California Correctional Peace Officers Association

California Faculty Association

California School Employees Association

California Union of Safety Employees

Carpenters and Joiners of America, United Brotherhood of (AFL-CIO)

Classified School Employees Association

Communications Workers of America (AFL-CIO)

Distillery, Wine and Allied Workers' International Union (AFL-CIO)

Electrical Workers, International Brotherhood of (AFL-CIO)

Fire Fighters, International Association of (AFL-CIO)

Food and Commercial Workers International Union, United (AFL-CIO)

Hotel Employees and Restaurant Employees International Union (AFL-CIO)

Ladies' Garment Workers' Union, International (AFL-CIO)

Lonshoremen's and Warehousemen's Union, International (AFL-CIO)

Machinists and Aerospace Workers, International Association of (AFL-CIO)

Monterey County Employees Association

National Education Association

Nurses' Association, American

Office and Professional Employees International Union (AFL-CIO)

Painters and Allied Trades of The United States and Canada, International Brotherhood of (AFL-CIO)

Professional Engineers in California Government

Public Employee Association of Riverside County

San Bernardino Public Employee Association

San Diego County Deputy Sheriffs Association

Seafarers' International Union of North America (AFL-CIO)

Service Employees' International Union (AFL-CIO)

State, County and Municipal Employees, American Federation of (AFL-CIO)

Support Service Unit (Riverside County)

Teamsters, Chauffeurs, Warehousemen and Helpers of America, International Brotherhood of (AFL-CIO)

Teachers, American Federation of (AFL-CIO)

Theatrical Stage Employees and Moving Picture Machine Operators of the United States and Canada, International Alliance of (AFL-CIO)

Trades and Maintenance

Transit Union, Amalgamated (AFL-CIO)

Transport Workers Union of America (AFL-CIO)

Union of American Physicians and Dentists

United Teachers of Los Angeles

United Transportation Union (AFL-CIO)

Utility Workers Union of America (AFL-CIO)

Universities with Ph.D. Programs

Biola University, La Mirada

California Institute of Technology, Pasadena

California State University, Los Angeles

Golden Gate University, San Francisco

Humphreys College, Stockton

Loma Linda University, Riverside

Los Angeles College of Chiropractic, Whittier

Loyola Marymount University, Los Angeles

National University, San Diego

Northrop University, Los Angeles

Pepperdine University, Culver City

Pepperdine University, Malibu

San Diego State University, San Diego

San Francisco State University, San Francisco

Santa Clara University, Santa Clara

Sierra University: A University Without Walls, Costa Mesa

Southern California College of Optometry, Fullerton

Stanford University, Stanford

United States International University, San Diego

University of California At Berkeley, Berkeley

University of California, Davis, Davis

University of California, Irvine, Irvine

University of California, Los Angeles, Los Angeles

University of California, Riverside, Riverside

University of California, San Diego, La Jolla

University of California, San Francisco, San Francisco

University of California, Santa Barbara, Santa Barbara

University of California, Santa Cruz, Santa Cruz

University of La Verne, La Verne

University of San Diego, San Diego

University of San Francisco, San Francisco

University of Southern California, Los Angeles

University of the Pacific, Stockton

University of West Los Angeles, Los Angeles

Sources of Additional Information

Environmental Permits. California Dept. of Commerce, Office of Economic Research, n.d. np.

The Facts. California Dept. of Commerce, 1988. 16p.

The Californias, Business Incentives. California Dept. of Commerce, Office of Business Development, n.d. 14p.

The Californias, Investment Guide. California Dept. of Commerce, Office of Business Development, June 1989. 20p.

The Californias, Tax Profiles. California Dept. of Commerce, Office of Business Development, n.d. 16p.

Services, California Department of Commerce. California Dept. of Commerce, January 1990. 23p.

A-Z, Everything You Ever Want to Know About Running A Small Business [in California]. California Dept. of Commerce, n.d. 8p.

The Californias Economic Review. Dept. of Commerce, Office of Economic Research (916-324-5853). Quarterly publication.

Bear Traces. Dept. of Commerce, Office of Marketing and Communications (916-324-8213). Quarterly publication.

ANAHEIM–SANTA ANA, CA (PMSA)

Geographic Profile

Land Area
789.7 square miles

Counties and Parishes
Orange

Ranking Highlights

241 *out of 319 in total* **land area**
46 *out of 319 in* **population growth,** *1970–1990*
104 *out of 310 in having the lowest* **unemployment** *rate*
12 *out of 310 in size of* **labor force**
32 *out of 318 in the percentage of* **college graduates**
N/A *out of 292 in per capita personal* **income**
7 *out of 319 in number of* **manufacturing establishments**
71 *out of 318 in* **physicians** *per 1000 people*
265 *out of 318 in* **hospital beds** *per 1000 people*
123 *out of 267 in fewest* **crimes** *per 1000 people*
122 *out of 266 in fewest* **violent crimes** *per 1000 people*
125 *out of 319 in per capita* **federal funds and grants**

Quality of Life Indexes (Rate per 1000 population)

Crime rate in 1991:	58.7
Violent crime rate in 1991:	5.7
Physicians rate in 1992:	2.46
Hospital bed rate in 1991:	2.64

ACCRA Cost of Living Indexes

(First quarter 1993, average = 100)
Composite index: N/A
Utilities index: N/A
Housing index: N/A

Population (1990)

Total Population and Growth Rate
1990: 2,410,556
1980: 1,932,921
1970: 1,421,233
Growth rate 1970–1990: 70%

Race and Hispanic Origin
White: 78.6%
Black: 1.8%
Asian/Pacific Islander: 10.3%
Native American: 0.5%
Hispanic origin: 23.4%
White not Hispanic: 64.5%

Age
Ages 18 to 20: 5%
Ages 21 to 24: 7.5%
Ages 25 to 44: 35.8%
Ages 45 to 54: 10.6%
Ages 55 to 59: 4%

Ages 60 to 64: 3.5%
Ages 65 plus: 9.2%

Educational Attainment (1990)

Percent having completed high school: 81.2%
Percent having completed college: 27.8%
Elementary and high school enrollment: 392,695

Federal Funds and Grants Received

Total received in 1989: $7,516,500,000
Funds received per capita: $3,330

Civilian Labor Force

1993 (April): 1,382,574
1992 average: 1,374,144
1991 average: 1,345,808
1990 average: 1,371,444

Unemployment

1993 (April): 6.0%
1992 average: 6.1%
1991 average: 4.8%
1990 average: 3.3%

Average Annual Pay

1988: $24,264
1987: $22,994
1985: $20,861

Per Capita Personal Income

1991: N/A
1990: N/A
1989: N/A

Business Climate (1987)

Manufacturing
Number of establishments in 1987: 5,855
Shipments in 1987 ($1,000): $25,887,400
Employees in 1987: 254,600
Change in employment, 1982 to 1987: 9.6%
Average annual pay for manufacturing work in 1989: $30,254
Average annual pay for production work in 1987: $20,965

Wholesale Trade
Number of establishments in 1987: 6,055
Total sales in 1987 ($1,000): $47,128,500
Change in sales, 1982 to 1987: 113.7%

Retail Trade
Number of establishments in 1987: 13,385
Total sales in 1987 ($1,000): $47,128,500
Retail sales per household in 1987: $21,962
Average annual pay in 1989: $14,761

Service Industry
Selected receipts in 1987 ($1,000): $13,959,700
Average annual pay in 1989: $23,713

Housing

Total number of units in 1990: 875,072

Occupied units in 1990: 827,066
Owner-occupied units in 1990: 60.1%
1993 ACCRA average cost: N/A
1993 ACCRA average rent for an apartment: N/A

Chamber of Commerce

Anaheim Chamber of Commerce, Allan B. Hughes, Exec. Director, 100 S. Anaheim Blvd. #300, Anaheim, CA 92805. 714-758-0222

Major Businesses

Company	SIC	Telephone
Avco Financial Services	6141	(714) 553-1200
Beatrice/Hunt-Wesson, Inc.	2033	(714) 680-1000
Beckman Instruments Inc.	3826	(714) 871-4848
Bergen Brunswig Corp.	5122	(714) 385-4000
Best Holding Corp.	4213	(714) 759-5585
Burlington Air Express	4731	(714) 752-4000
Calcomp Inc.	3577	(714) 821-2000
Crysen Trading & Marketing	6211	(714) 835-6505
Daniel International Corp.	1541	(714) 975-2000
Denny's Inc.	5812	(714) 251-5000
First American Financial	6361	(714) 558-3211
First American Title Insurance Co.	6361	(714) 558-3211
Fluor Corp.	1541	(714) 975-2000
Fluor Daniel, Inc.	8711	(714) 975-2000
Hyundai Motor America	5012	(714) 965-3000
Karcher, Carl Enterprises	5812	(714) 774-5796
Lyon, William Co.	1531	(714) 833-3600
Mitsubishi Consumer Electric	3651	(714) 261-3200
Pacific Mutual Life Insurance Co.	6311	(714) 640-3011
Pacificare Health Systems	6324	(714) 952-1121
Petro-Diamond Inc.	5172	(714) 553-0112
Restaurant Enterprise Group Inc.	5812	(714) 852-5700
St Joe Minerals Corp.	1031	(714) 975-2000
St Joseph Health System	8062	(714) 997-7690
Standard Pacific	1531	(714) 546-1161
Sunrich Mercantile Corp.	5199	(714) 738-2000
Taco Bell Corp.	5812	(714) 863-4500
Western Digital Corp.	3674	(714) 932-5000
Yamaha Motor Corp.	5012	(714) 761-7300

Colleges and Universities

Control Data Institute, Santa Ana
Rancho Santiago College, Santa Ana

BAKERSFIELD, CA (MSA)

Geographic Profile

Land Area
8141.6 square miles

Counties and Parishes
Kern

Ranking Highlights

4 *out of 319 in total* **land area**
57 *out of 319 in* **population growth,** *1970–1990*
305 *out of 310 in having the lowest* **unemployment** *rate*
90 *out of 310 in size of* **labor force**
276 *out of 318 in the percentage of* **college graduates**
223 *out of 292 in per capita personal* **income**
149 *out of 319 in number of* **manufacturing establishments**
273 *out of 318 in* **physicians** *per 1000 people*
291 *out of 318 in* **hospital beds** *per 1000 people*
161 *out of 267 in fewest* **crimes** *per 1000 people*
208 *out of 266 in fewest* **violent crimes** *per 1000 people*
93 *out of 319 in per capita* **federal funds and grants***out of 319 in per capita* **federal funds and grants**

Quality of Life Indexes (Rate per 1000 population)

Crime rate in 1991:	65.6
Violent crime rate in 1991:	9.2
Physicians rate in 1992:	1.25
Hospital bed rate in 1991:	2.2

ACCRA Cost of Living Indexes
(First quarter 1993, average = 100)

Composite index:	113.6
Utilities index:	115.6
Housing index:	114.4

Overview

The Bakersfield MSA is located 90 minutes from Los Angeles, two hours from the Pacific Ocean and 3.5 hours from the Bay Area. Kern County is the largest oil producing county and third in agriculture in the United States. Bakersfield is the county seat, and the principal metropolitan city, of Kern County.

Three major highways serve the area: State Highway 99 travels the length of the state bisecting Bakersfield. Interstate 5, 25 miles west of Bakersfield, connects to San Francisco in five hours and two hours south to Los Angeles. Highway 58 links Bakersfield to the east. The region is served by 13 public, four private, and two government (Edwards AFB and NWC China Lake) airports. Direct commercial flights are available to Dallas, Texas, Los Angeles, San Jose, and Sacramento. Amtrak passenger train travel the length of the Central Valley to the Pacific Northwest.

Kern County has three community colleges and one university. Each will customize its courses to meet the needs of businesses in the area.

Cultural organizations include the Bakersfield Civic Light Opera, Bakersfield Museum of Art, Bakersfield Community Concern Association, Bakersfield Community Theatre, Bakersfield Jazz Festival, Beethovan Festival, Bakersfield Symphony Orchestra, Comedy Sportz, Vaudeville Express Melodrama Theatre, and many more.

Population (1990)

Total Population and Growth Rate

1990: 543,477
1980: 403,089
1970: 330,234
Growth rate 1970-1990: 65%

Race and Hispanic Origin

White: 69.6%
Black: 5.5%
Asian/Pacific Islander: 3.0%
Native American: 1.3%
Hispanic origin: 28.0%
White not Hispanic: 62.7%

Age

Ages 18 to 20: 4.3%
Ages 21 to 24: 5.8%
Ages 25 to 44: 32.6%
Ages 45 to 54: 9%
Ages 55 to 59: 3.6%
Ages 60 to 64: 3.6%
Ages 65 plus: 9.7%

Educational Attainment (1990)

Percent having completed high school: 67.6%
Percent having completed college: 13.3%
Elementary and high school enrollment: 111,274

Federal Funds and Grants Received

Total received in 1989: $1,891,300,000
Funds received per capita: $3,637

Civilian Labor Force

1993 (April): 274,183
1992 average: 262,147
1991 average: 248,129
1990 average: 237,437

Unemployment

1993 (April): 13.6%
1992 average: 15.1%
1991 average: 11.8%
1990 average: 10.5%

Average Annual Pay

1988: $20,377
1987: $19,509
1985: $19,017

Per Capita Personal Income

1991: $15,791
1990: $15,639

1989: $14,760

Business Climate (1987)

Manufacturing

Number of establishments in 1987: 357
Shipments in 1987 ($1,000): $1,455,200
Employees in 1987: 7,700
Change in employment, 1982 to 1987: -8.3%
Average annual pay for manufacturing work in 1989: $28,975
Average annual pay for production work in 1987: $19,275

Wholesale Trade

Number of establishments in 1987: 752
Total sales in 1987 ($1,000): $3,335,500
Change in sales, 1982 to 1987: 2.9%

Retail Trade

Number of establishments in 1987: 2,745
Total sales in 1987 ($1,000): $3,335,500
Retail sales per household in 1987: $15,349
Average annual pay in 1989: $12,404

Service Industry

Selected receipts in 1987 ($1,000): $1,185,400
Average annual pay in 1989: $19,872

Housing

Total number of units in 1990: 198,636
Occupied units in 1990: 181,480
Owner-occupied units in 1990: 59.3%
1993 ACCRA average cost: $129,148
1993 ACCRA average rent for an apartment: $573

Chamber of Commerce

Greater Bakersfield Chamber of Commerce, Chris Frank, Exec. Vice President, PO Box 1947, 1033 Truxtun Ave., Bakersfield, CA 93301. 805-327-4421, FAX 805-325-7074

Economic Development Office

Kern Economic Development Corp., Michael S. Ammann, President, PO Box 1312, 2101 Oak St., Bakersfield, CA 93302. 805-861-2774, FAX 805-861-2017

Economic Development Organizations

County of Kern Economic Development, Paul Sippel, Manager, 2700 M Street, Bakersfield, CA 93301. 805-861-2041

Kern County Board of Trade, Ann Gutcher, Manager, 2101 Oak Street, PO Bin 1312, Bakersfield, CA 93302. 805-861-2367, FAX 805-861-2017

City of Bakersfield, Economic and Community Development Dept., Charles Webb, Economic Development Associate, 515 Truxtun Ave., Bakersfield, CA 93301. 805-326-3765, FAX 805-328-1548

Bakersfield Board of Realtors, Karen Wass, President, PO Box 2306, Bakersfield, CA 93309-2306. 805-325-7221

Employer Training Resource (Private Industry Council),

Peter Parra, Director, 2001 28th St., Bakersfield, CA 93301. 805-861-2495

Bakersfield College, ROP, WESTEC, Larry Fannucchi, Program Manager, 1801 Panorama Dr., Bakersfield, CA 93305. 805-393-4571

Weil Institute (Entrepreneurs Group), Debra Orr-Carpenter, 1801 Panorama Dr., Bakersfield, CA 93305. 805-395-4148

Kern County Resource Management Agency Planning Dept., Randy Abbott, Resource Director, 2700 M Street, Bakersfield, CA 93301. 805-861-3502

Board of Supervisors, Kern County, Karl Hettinger, 1415 Truxtun Ave., 7th fl., Bakersfield, CA 93301. 805-861-3213

Employment Development Dept., Maggie Sabovich, Employment Service Public Relations, 1401 S. H St., Bakersfield, CA 93304. 805-395-2500

City of Bakesfield Planning Dept., Jack Hardisty, Director, 1501 Truxtun Ave., Bakersfield, CA 93301. 805-326-3733

Local Incentives for Business

Industrial Development Bonds.

Metropolitan Bakersfield Incentive Area - State tax credits.

State and Local Financial Incentives

California Enterprise Zone Program.

State of California Employment Training Panel. Up to $2,500 per employee is available depending on the details of the project.

Possibility of purchasing city owned property below market value.

In-Kind Service Incentives

Free services from the Kern Economic Development Corporation.

The City will assign a staff person to coordinate and communicate with all the necessary city departments regarding approvals and permits.

Incentives to Offset the Relocation Costs

Some development costs may be negotiated and a payment schedule arranged over several years.

Posibility of negotiating mortgage rates and swing loans at preferred rates with a local bank for those employees that relocate to the area.

Possibility of negotiating favorable hotel/motel rates with the local providers.

Industrial Sites

Airport Business Park

Bakersfield Airport Business Center

North Meadow

Major Businesses

Company	SIC	Telephone
ARB Inc.	1623	(805) 831-7575

Major Businesses (Continued)

Company	SIC	Telephone
Bakersfeld Memorial Hospital Association	8062	(805) 327-1792
Bakersfield Dodge, Inc.	5511	(805) 323-7961
Berry Petroleum Co.	1311	(805) 769-8811
Bolthouse, William Farms Inc.	0723	(805) 366-7205
Cactus Gold Mines Co	1041	(805) 256-2686
California Bancorp Inc.	6022	(805) 395-5800
California-World Produce Sales Inc.	5148	(805) 845-3724
Calcot Ltd.	5159	(805) 327-5961
California Republic Bank	6022	(805) 395-5800
Calzona Box & Lumber Co.	5085	(805) 845-0723
Coleman Homes Inc.	1521	(805) 326-1141
Colombo Construction Co.	1542	(805) 327-5934
Community First Bank	6022	(805) 395-3200
Contel of Texas, Inc.	4813	(805) 328-2200
Contel of The Northwest	4813	(805) 328-2200
Contel of The West	4813	(805) 328-2200
Delano Regional Medical Center	8062	(805) 725-4800
Freymiller Trucking Inc.	4213	(805) 397-4151
Gary Drilling Co.	1381	(805) 589-0111
Giumarra Vineyards Corp.	0172	(805) 395-7000
Hill Top Developers Inc.	1531	(805) 324-4561
Hopper Inc.	5051	(805) 861-7000
Houchin Enterprises, Inc.	6719	(805) 764-5111
Jaco Oil Co.	5541	(805) 393-7000
Jaco-Hill Co.	6512	(805) 393-7000
Jamieson-Hill A General Partner	5541	(805) 393-7000
Kern County Water Agency	4941	(805) 393-6200
Luna Corp.	5148	(805) 327-0067
M. P. Vacuum Truck Service	4953	(805) 393-1151
Mercy Hospital, Bakersfield	8062	(805) 327-3371
Occidental International	1382	(805) 321-6000
Pacific World of Bakersfield	2491	(805) 833-0429
Pandol Brosthers Inc.	5148	(805) 725-3755
Paramount Farms	0762	(805) 393-5121
Ragsdale, R. L. Inc.	5172	(805) 327-7212
San Joaquin Community Hospital	8062	(805) 395-3000
Sangera Autohaus	5511	(805) 836-3737
Smith, Jess & Sons Inc.	5159	(805) 325-7231
Sun World International	0723	(805) 833-6460
Tenneco West Inc.	6519	(805) 328-7040
Three-Way Chevrolet Co.	5511	(805) 322-3929
Wheeler Ridge-Maricopa	4971	(805) 858-2281
Wright, Bill Toyota Inc.	5511	(805) 398-8697
Yurosek, Mike & Son Inc.	0723	(805) 845-3764
Zond Group Inc.	4911	(805) 822-6835

Colleges and Universities

Bakersfield College, Bakersfield

California State University, Bakersfield (5,686 students).

Offers degrees in Business/Management, Accounting, Engineering, Computer Science, etc.

Additional Information

Bakersfield, the Official Visitors Guide. Greater Bakersfield Convention & Visitors Bureau (1033 Truxtun Ave., Bakersfield, CA 93301), 1989. 40p.

Kern County Statistical and Economic Data Profile, 1990. Kern County Board of Trade, 1990. 47p.

Marcoa's Official 1990-91 Greater Bakersfield Area Relocation Journal. Maricoa Publishing Inc., (PO Box 1000, San Diego, CA 92138), 1990. 69p.

Metropolitan Bakersfield. City of Bakersfield, Economic and Community Development Dept., n.d. 20p.

CHICO, CA (MSA)

Geographic Profile

Land Area
1639.6 square miles

Counties and Parishes
Butte

Ranking Highlights

120 *out of 319 in total* **land area**

36 *out of 319 in* **population growth,** *1970–1990*

293 *out of 310 in having the lowest* **unemployment** *rate*

206 *out of 310 in size of* **labor force**

148 *out of 318 in the percentage of* **college graduates**

252 *out of 292 in per capita personal* **income**

204 *out of 319 in number of* **manufacturing establishments**

157 *out of 318 in* **physicians** *per 1000 people*

201 *out of 318 in* **hospital beds** *per 1000 people*

71 *out of 267 in fewest* **crimes** *per 1000 people*

93 *out of 266 in fewest* **violent crimes** *per 1000 people*

194 *out of 319 in per capita* **federal funds and grants**

Quality of Life Indexes (Rate per 1000 population)

Crime rate in 1991: 48.1

Violent crime rate in 1991: 4.6

Physicians rate in 1992: 1.81

Hospital bed rate in 1991: 3.43

ACCRA Cost of Living Indexes

(First quarter 1993, average = 100)

Composite index: N/A

Utilities index: N/A

Housing index: N/A

Population (1990)

Total Population and Growth Rate

1990: 182,120

1980: 143,851

1970: 101,969

Growth rate 1970–1990: 79%

Race and Hispanic Origin

White: 90.7%

Black: 1.3%

Asian/Pacific Islander: 2.8%

Native American: 1.8%

Hispanic origin: 7.5%

White not Hispanic: 86.9%

Age

Ages 18 to 20: 5.8%

Ages 21 to 24: 7.9%

Ages 25 to 44: 28.4%

Ages 45 to 54: 8.7%

Ages 55 to 59: 3.8%

Ages 60 to 64: 4.6%

Ages 65 plus: 17.3%

Educational Attainment (1990)
Percent having completed high school: 77.6%
Percent having completed college: 19.5%
Elementary and high school enrollment: 27,899

Federal Funds and Grants Received
Total received in 1989: $494,800,000
Funds received per capita: $2,836

Civilian Labor Force
1993 (April): 82,097
1992 average: 81,419
1991 average: 77,500
1990 average: 76,019

Unemployment
1993 (April): 11.4%
1992 average: 11.6%
1991 average: 9.4%
1990 average: 7.5%

Average Annual Pay
1988: $16,878
1987: $16,438
1985: $15,045

Per Capita Personal Income
1991: $15,172
1990: $14,900
1989: $14,104

Business Climate (1987)
Manufacturing
Number of establishments in 1987: 222
Shipments in 1987 ($1,000): $671,000
Employees in 1987: 5,700
Change in employment, 1982 to 1987: 29.5%
Average annual pay for manufacturing work in 1989: $20,723
Average annual pay for production work in 1987: $17,841

Wholesale Trade
Number of establishments in 1987: 238
Total sales in 1987 ($1,000): $569,200
Change in sales, 1982 to 1987: 48.3%

Retail Trade
Number of establishments in 1987: 1,145
Total sales in 1987 ($1,000): $569,200
Retail sales per household in 1987: $12,999
Average annual pay in 1989: $11,177

Service Industry
Selected receipts in 1987 ($1,000): $343,300
Average annual pay in 1989: $17,018

Housing
Total number of units in 1990: 76,115
Occupied units in 1990: 71,665

Owner-occupied units in 1990: 60.9%
1993 ACCRA average cost: N/A
1993 ACCRA average rent for an apartment: N/A

Chamber of Commerce
Greater Chico Chamber of Commerce, Bob Linscheid, CEO, 500 Main St., PO Box 3038, Chico, CA 95928. 916-891-5556, FAX 916-891-3613

Economic Development Office
The Business Center, Jon Gregory, General Manager, 1001 Willow St., PO Box 6250, Chico, CA 95927. 916-893-8732

Major Businesses

Company	SIC	Telephone
Associated Students/California	8221	(916) 895-6411
Besegh & Rabo Inc.	5145	(916) 342-1857
Cost Less Foods, Inc.	5411	(916) 894-2678
Enloe, N. T. Memorial Hospital	8062	(916) 891-7300
Feather River Hospital	8062	(916) 877-9361
Knudsen & Sons Inc.	2033	(916) 891-1517
Netco Foods, Inc.	5411	(916) 894-1050
O.P.T.I.O.N. Care	6794	(916) 893-5830
Orohealth Corp.	6719	(916) 533-8500
Oroville Hospital	8062	(916) 533-8500
Pacific Oroville Power Inc.	4911	(916) 532-0597
Patterson, Chuck Inc.	5511	(916) 895-1771
Shastan Co.	1521	(916) 894-2027
Stash Distributing Inc.	5181	(916) 891-6000
Sunseri Construction, Inc.	1541	(916) 891-6444
Tri Counties Bank	6029	(916) 893-8222
Trico Bancshares	6712	(916) 893-8222
Vanella Oil Inc.	5171	(916) 342-5582
Western Woods, Inc.	5031	(916) 343-5821

Colleges and Universities
California State University, Chico, Chico

FRESNO, CA (MSA)

Geographic Profile
Land Area
5963.2 square miles

Counties and Parishes
Fresno

Ranking Highlights
8 *out of 319 in total* **land area**
62 *out of 319 in* **population growth**, *1970–1990*
304 *out of 310 in having the lowest* **unemployment** *rate*
74 *out of 310 in size of* **labor force**
195 *out of 318 in the percentage of* **college graduates**
214 *out of 292 in per capita personal* **income**
94 *out of 319 in number of* **manufacturing establishments**
175 *out of 318 in* **physicians** *per 1000 people*
274 *out of 318 in* **hospital beds** *per 1000 people*
254 *out of 267 in fewest* **crimes** *per 1000 people*
234 *out of 266 in fewest* **violent crimes** *per 1000 people*
266 *out of 319 in per capita* **federal funds and grants**

Quality of Life Indexes (Rate per 1000 population)
Crime rate in 1991:	91.0
Violent crime rate in 1991:	10.2
Physicians rate in 1992:	1.75
Hospital bed rate in 1991:	2.52

ACCRA Cost of Living Indexes
(First quarter 1993, average = 100)
Composite index:	N/A
Utilities index:	N/A
Housing index:	N/A

Overview
Fresno is the county seat of the large agricultural producing Fresno County. Fresno is located 184 miles southeast of San Francisco and 222 miles northwest of Los Angeles. It is 122 miles from Stockton, the nearest seaport, and within 90 minutes of three National Parks.

Fresno has access to State Highways 99, 41 (north-south), 180 (east-west) and 168 (north to the Sierras). Interstate 5 is 40 miles west of the city. Rail freight service is provided by the Santa Fe Railway and the Southern Pacific Railroad. The Fresno Air Terminal provides regularly scheduled passenger and freight srvice to the nation's major cities. General aviation services are handled by Chandler Field in the downtown area of Fresno.

There are approximately 4,770 acres within the Fresno area which are vacant and zoned for light industry and 4,221 acres for heavy industry. Most parcels range in size from 1/2 acre to 10 acres and some larger parcels are available in sizes of 20 to 100 acres.

It is currently estimated that approximately 12% of Fresno County's employees are unionized, down from a high of 20% in 1981.

Population (1990)
Total Population and Growth Rate
1990: 667,490
1980: 514,621
1970: 413,329
Growth rate 1970–1990: 61%

Race and Hispanic Origin
White: 63.3%
Black: 5.0%
Asian/Pacific Islander: 8.6%
Native American: 1.1%
Hispanic origin: 35.5%
White not Hispanic: 50.7%

Age
Ages 18 to 20: 4.7%
Ages 21 to 24: 6.5%
Ages 25 to 44: 31.2%
Ages 45 to 54: 8.8%
Ages 55 to 59: 3.5%
Ages 60 to 64: 3.6%
Ages 65 plus: 10.4%

Educational Attainment (1990)
Percent having completed high school: 66.2%
Percent having completed college: 16.9%
Elementary and high school enrollment: 141,261

Federal Funds and Grants Received
Total received in 1989: $1,433,300,000
Funds received per capita: $2,331

Civilian Labor Force
1993 (April): 362,380
1992 average: 343,006
1991 average: 317,589
1990 average: 314,431

Unemployment
1993 (April): 13.4%
1992 average: 14.5%
1991 average: 12.6%
1990 average: 10.5%

Average Annual Pay
1988: $17,908
1987: $16,818
1985: $15,361

Per Capita Personal Income
1991: $15,994
1990: $15,926
1989: $15,023

Business Climate (1987)
Manufacturing
Number of establishments in 1987: 678

Shipments in 1987 ($1,000): $3,172,600

Employees in 1987: 21,100

Change in employment, 1982 to 1987: -0.5%

Average annual pay for manufacturing work in 1989: $21,742

Average annual pay for production work in 1987: $17,736

Wholesale Trade

Number of establishments in 1987: 1,129

Total sales in 1987 ($1,000): $4,557,500

Change in sales, 1982 to 1987: 5.3%

Retail Trade

Number of establishments in 1987: 3,403

Total sales in 1987 ($1,000): $4,557,500

Retail sales per household in 1987: $16,438

Average annual pay in 1989: $13,404

Service Industry

Selected receipts in 1987 ($1,000): $1,448,900

Average annual pay in 1989: $19,062

Office Real Estate (1992)

Office space inventory: 11,332,700 square feet

Average class A Central Business District rental range per sq. ft: $17.70

Vacancy Rates

All areas: 13.0%

Vacancy Rates in Central Business District

Class A space: 0.1%

Class B space: 36.2%

Vacancy Rates Outside Central Business District

Class A space: 4.2%

Class B space: 14.5%

Housing

Total number of units in 1990: 235,563

Occupied units in 1990: 220,933

Owner-occupied units in 1990: 54.3%

1993 ACCRA average cost: N/A

1993 ACCRA average rent for an apartment: N/A

Chamber of Commerce

Fresno Chamber of Commerce, Stebbins Dean, Exec. Vice President, PO Box 1469, 2331 Fresno St., Fresno, CA 93721. 209-233-4651, FAX 209-233-6631

Economic Development Office

Fresno County Economic Development Corp., John Quiring, President, 2344 Tulare St. Ste. 100, Fresno, CA 93721. 209-233-2564, FAX 209-233-2156

Industrial Sites

There are 21 industrial parks. Sale prices range from $0.75 to $1.35 per square foot for unfurnished industrial sites and from $1.50 to $2.25 per square foot for furnished industrial sites.

Major Businesses

Company	SIC	Telephone
Arcadian Motor Carriers	4213	(209) 896-2665
Bank of Fresno	6022	(209) 221-2265
Biedermann International	5172	(209) 294-1212
Bingham Toyota, Inc.	5511	(209) 291-5544
Community Hospitals-Central	8062	(209) 442-6000
D M C Construction Inc.	1542	(209) 275-7011
Danish Creamery Association	2026	(209) 233-5154
Enoch Packing Co. Inc.	0723	(209) 888-2151
Fowler Packing Co. Inc.	0723	(209) 834-5911
Fresno Truck Center	5531	(209) 486-4310
Gamel, Dan, Inc.	5561	(209) 268-0151
Gottschalk, E. & Co. Inc.	5311	(209) 485-1111
Gottschalks Inc.	5311	(209) 485-1111
Harris Farms, Inc.	0191	(209) 884-2435
Herwaldt, Lou Olds, Inc.	5511	(209) 431-2020
Kaweah Construction Co.	1629	(209) 252-9492
Mendelson-Zeller Co. Inc.	5148	(209) 454-8400
Pierce Lathing Co.	1742	(209) 441-1551
Producers Cotton Oil Co.	0724	(209) 442-4400
Ranchers Cotton Oil	2074	(209) 268-5353
Richland Sales Co.	0723	(209) 591-0632
Riverbend International	0723	(209) 787-2501
Saint Agnes Hospital	8062	(209) 449-3000
Sanden of America Inc.	3581	(209) 439-1770
Seabrook Foods, Inc.	5142	(209) 252-2836
Spencer Enterprises, Inc.	1522	(209) 252-4043
Sun-Maid Growers of California	2034	(209) 896-8000
Valley Medical Center of Fresno	8062	(209) 453-4000
Vie-Del Co.	2084	(209) 834-2525
Westair Holding, Inc.	4512	(209) 294-6915

Colleges and Universities

California State University, Fresno, Fresno

Fresno City College, Fresno

Fresno Pacific College, Fresno

Heald Engineering College, Fresno

LOS ANGELES–LONG BEACH, CA (PMSA)

Geographic Profile

Land Area

4060.0 square miles

Counties and Parishes

Los Angeles

Additional Cities/Towns within Area

Burbank

Pasadena

Pomona

Ranking Highlights

26 *out of 319 in total* **land area**

159 *out of 319 in* **population growth,** *1970–1990*

276 *out of 310 in having the lowest* **unemployment** *rate*

1 *out of 310 in size of* **labor force**

90 *out of 318 in the percentage of* **college graduates**

35 *out of 292 in per capita personal* **income**

1 *out of 319 in number of* **manufacturing establishments**

74 *out of 318 in* **physicians** *per 1000 people*

227 *out of 318 in* **hospital beds** *per 1000 people*

221 *out of 267 in fewest* **crimes** *per 1000 people*

264 *out of 266 in fewest* **violent crimes** *per 1000 people*

106 *out of 319 in per capita* **federal funds and grants**

Quality of Life Indexes (Rate per 1000 population)

Crime rate in 1991:	76.2
Violent crime rate in 1991:	18.0
Physicians rate in 1992:	2.43
Hospital bed rate in 1991:	3.13

ACCRA Cost of Living Indexes

(First quarter 1993, average = 100)

Composite index:	127.9
Utilities index:	83.3
Housing index:	173.4

Overview

Los Angeles possesses a diverse economy with no single dominant industry. The city is the largest manufacturing center in the West, one of the world's busiest ports, a major financial and banking center, and the largest retail market in the United States. International trade is today the strongest element in the regional economy.

Manufacturing has traditionally been led by the aerospace and defense industries, which employed almost one-third of the manufacturing workforce. Between 1988 and 1993, however, the region lost one hundred fifty thousand aerospace and weapons jobs as defense spending began to decline nationwide. Steel fabrication is the second largest industry in manufacturing, followed closely by fashion apparel. In the United States, only Detroit, Michigan pro-duces more automobiles than the Los Angeles area. The manufacture of heavy machinery for the agricultural, construction, mining, and oil industries contributes significantly to the local economy. Los Angeles is also a major producer of furniture and fixtures, as well as petroleum products and chemicals, print material, rubber goods, electronic equipment, glass, pottery, ceramics, and cement products.

Los Angeles is the nation's largest port in terms of value of goods handled and tonnage, having taken the lead over the ports of New York City in 1989. Proximity to the major Pacific manufacturing nations—Japan, Korea, and Taiwan—and easy access to transcontinental rail and truck shipping, plus the large commercial facilities available at Los Angeles International Airport make the Los Angeles Customs District the largest in the nation. The city's prominence in international trade is evidenced by the more than forty U.S. headquarters of foreign companies located in the area.

The banking and finance industry in Los Angeles is one of the largest in the United States. Over one hundred foreign and countless domestic banks operate branches in Los Angeles, along with many financial law firms and investment banks. Entertainment, in the form of film, television, and music production, is the best known industry in Los Angeles. It employs a very small percentage of the labor force, but focuses worldwide attention on the city, making Los Angeles a major tourist destination.

Other prominent industries in the Los Angeles area include health services, education, high-technology research and development, professional fields such as architecture and engineering, and a large construction business, both commercial and residential.

Items and goods produced in the area include agricultural and seafood products, aircraft and aircraft parts, furniture fixtures, ordnance missiles, electrical equipment, stone, clay, glass, apparel, fabricated metals, rubber, plastic, motion pictures, petroleum, and coal.

The Los Angeles-Long Beach Port System is the largest in the country in terms of value of goods handled and tonnage. Import and export shipping through Los Angeles International Airport is also heavy, and the city's Free Trade Zone status is conducive to foreign trade. Several major transcontinental rail systems, used by a number of rail shipping companies, terminate in Los Angeles, and all of the major interstate truck companies maintain large facilities in the metropolitan area. Los Angeles plans to spend $150 billion over the next thirty years on a 400-mile metro system to include light-, heavy-, and commuter-rail systems. Los Angeles International Airport (LAX), just west of the downtown area, is the third largest airport in the world in terms of passengers handled, and the airport is served by more than eighty-five major airlines with over seven hundred flights daily.

The major convention and meeting facility in Los Angeles is the Los Angeles Convention Center. Situated on sixty-three landscaped acres, the complex is centrally located within easy access of hotels, restaurants, nightlife, shops, recreational activities, and sightseeing attractions. A $500 million expansion scheduled for completion in late 1993 more than doubled the size of the center to 810,000 square feet, making it the largest convention facility on the West Coast. With more than eighty-six thousand hotel rooms in the city, Los Angeles continues to add hotels; at least five major hotels were to be constructed between 1992 and 1995.

Three interstate highways converge in the Los Angeles area: I-5 approaching from Canada in the north, I-15 from Las Vegas, Nevada to the east, and I-10 connecting Los Angeles with Arizona and the Southwest. State Highway 1, the Pacific Coastal Highway, skirts the city along the ocean.

Population (1990)

Total Population and Growth Rate
1990: 8,863,164
1980: 7,477,239
1970: 7,041,980
Growth rate 1970–1990: 26%

Race and Hispanic Origin
White: 56.8%
Black: 11.2%
Asian/Pacific Islander: 10.8%
Native American: 0.5%
Hispanic origin: 37.8%
White not Hispanic: 40.8%

Age
Ages 18 to 20:　5%
Ages 21 to 24: 7.3%
Ages 25 to 44: 34.9%
Ages 45 to 54: 9.5%
Ages 55 to 59: 3.7%
Ages 60 to 64: 3.6%
Ages 65 plus: 9.7%

Educational Attainment (1990)
Percent having completed high school: 70.0%
Percent having completed college: 22.3%
Elementary and high school enrollment: 16,159.4

Federal Funds and Grants Received ($1000)
Total received in 1989: 30,039,300
Funds received per capita: 3,498

Civilian Labor Force
1993 (April): 4,504,000
1992 average: 4,535,300
1991 average: 4,503,000
1990 average: 4,428,000

Unemployment
1993 (April):　9.1%

1992 average: 9.6%
1991 average: 8.0%
1990 average: 5.8%

Average Annual Pay
1988: $26,019
1987: $25,005
1985: $22,326

Per Capita Personal Income
1991: $20,967
1990: $20,744
1989: $19,856

Business Climate (1987)

Manufacturing
Number of establishments in 1987: 19,753
Shipments in 1987 ($1,000): $99,888,600
Employees in 1987: 881,000
Change in employment, 1982 to 1987: 1.7%
Average annual pay for manufacturing work in 1989: $28,999
Average annual pay for production work in 1987: $20,172

Wholesale Trade
Number of establishments in 1987: 19,688
Total sales in 1987 ($1,000): $141,729,200
Change in sales, 1982 to 1987: 42.7%

Retail Trade
Number of establishments in 1987: 43,606
Total sales in 1987 ($1,000): $141,729,200
Retail sales per household in 1987: $17,459
Average annual pay in 1989: $15,365

Service Industry
Selected receipts in 1987 ($1,000): $52,548,600
Average annual pay in 1989: $26,333

Office Real Estate (1992)
Office space inventory:
　Los Angeles-Central31,2000,167
　Los Angeles-Orange County54,496,689
　Los Angeles-San Bernardino County8,925,601
　Los Angeles-San Fernando Valley23,640,000
　Los Angeles-San Gabriel Valley8,450,000
　Los Angeles-South Bay30,229,769
　Los Angeles-West　51,750,000
Average class A Central Business District rental range per sq. ft: $25.00

Vacancy Rates
All areas: 21.0%

Vacancy Rates in Central Business District
Class A space: 27.5%
Class B space: 23.4%

Vacancy Rates Outside Central Business District
Class A space: N/A
Class B space: N/A

Housing

Total number of units in 1990: 3,163,343

Occupied units in 1990: 2,989,552

Owner-occupied units in 1990: 48.2%

1993 ACCRA average cost: $206,960

1993 ACCRA average rent for an apartment: $741

Chamber of Commerce

Los Angeles Area Chamber of Commerce, Ray Remy, President, 404 S. Bixel Street, PO Box 4696, Los Angeles, CA 90051-1696. 213-629-0602, FAX 213-629-0708

Economic Development Office

Los Angeles Business Council, Lori Pye, President, 10880 Wilshire Blvd. #1103, Los Angeles, CA 90024. 310-475-4574, FAX 310-475-1427

Economic Development Organizations

Long Beach Area Chamber of Commerce, John Higginson, President, One World Trade Center #350, Long Beach, CA 90831-0350. 213-436-1251, FAX 213-436-7099

Economic Development Bureau, Gerald R. Miller, Manager, Business Development Center, 230 Pine Ave., 3rd fl., Long Beach, CA 90802. 213-590-6095

Board of Realtors (Long Beach), 213-424-8687

Major Businesses

Company	SIC	Telephone
Ahmanson (H.F.) and Co.	6035	(818) 960-6311
American Isuzu Motors Inc.	5012	(213) 949-0611
Atlantic Richfield Co.	1311	(213) 625-2132
Avery International Corp.	2672	(818) 304-2000
Blue Cross of California	6324	(818) 703-3413
California Federal Bank	6035	(213) 932-4200
Canadian Petroleum Ltd.	2911	(213) 275-6100
Carnation Co.	2023	(213) 932-6000
Carter Hawley Hale Stores	5311	(213) 620-0150
Castle & Cooke, Inc.	0179	(213) 824-1500
Certified Grocers of California	5141	(213) 726-2601
Coast Federal Bank	6035	(213) 688-2000
Columbia Savings & Loan Association	6036	(213) 657-6134
Computer Sciences Corp.	7373	(213) 615-0311
Disney, Walt Co. (Inc.)	7996	(818) 560-1000
Executive Life Insurance Co.	6311	(213) 312-1000
Farmers Group Inc.	6331	(213) 932-3200
Farmers Insurance Exchange	6331	(213) 932-3441
First Executive Corp.	6311	(213) 312-1000
First Interstate Bancorp	6021	(213) 614-3001
First Interstate Bank	6022	(213) 614-4111
Gibraltar Financial Corp.	6035	(213) 278-2941
Glendale Federal Bank	6035	(818) 500-2000
Glenfed, Inc.	6035	(818) 500-2000
Great Western Bank	6035	(213) 852-3411
Great Western Financial Co.	6035	(213) 852-3411

Major Businesses (Continued)

Company	SIC	Telephone
Home Savings of America	6035	(818) 960-6311
Hughes Aircraft Co.	3669	(213) 568-7200
Hughes Markets Inc.	5411	(213) 227-8211
Kaufman & Broad Home Corp.	1531	(213) 312-5000
Litton Industries, Inc.	3812	(213) 859-5000
Litton Systems Inc.	3812	(213) 859-5000
Lockheed Corp.	3761	(818) 712-2000
Mattel, Inc.	3944	(213) 978-5150
Maxxam Group Inc.	1099	(213) 474-6264
MCA Inc.	7812	(818) 777-1000
Merisel International	5045	(213) 615-3080
National Medical Enterprise	8063	(213) 315-8000
Nissan Motor Corp. In USA	5012	(213) 532-3111
NME Hospitals, Inc.	8062	(213) 452-4444
Northrop Corp.	3721	(213) 553-6262
Occidental Petroleum Corp.	2011	(213) 208-8800
Occidental Petroleum Investments	1311	(213) 879-1700
P M C Inc.	5051	(818) 896-1101
Pacific Enterprises	4923	(213) 895-5000
Paramount Pictures Corp.	7812	(213) 468-5065
Ralphs Grocery Co.	5411	(213) 637-1101
Rockwell International Co.	3721	(213) 647-5000
Rykoff-Sexton, Inc.	5141	(213) 622-4131
SCE Corp.	4911	(818) 302-1212
Security Pacific Corp.	6021	(213) 345-6211
Security Pacific National Bank	6021	(213) 345-6211
Southern California Edison Co.	4911	(818) 302-1212
Southern California Gas Co.	4924	(213) 689-2345
Southern California Medical	6324	(818) 405-5715
Sun Life Insurance Co.	6311	(213) 312-5000
Teledyne, Inc.	3724	(213) 277-3311
Teledyne Industries Inc.	3724	(213) 277-3311
Thrifty Corp.	5912	(213) 251-6000
Thrifty Oil Co Inc.	5541	(213) 923-9876
Times Mirror Co.	2711	(213) 237-3700
Tosco Corp.	2911	(213) 207-7107
Transamerica Finance Group	6141	(213) 742-4321
Transamerica Occidental Life	6311	(213) 742-2111
Unihealth America	8062	(818) 566-6300
Union Oil Co. of California	2911	(213) 977-7600
Vons Companies Inc.	5411	(818) 821-7000
Wickes Companies, Inc.	5211	(213) 452-0161

Colleges and Universities

American Academy of Dramatic Arts/west, Pasadena

American College for the Applied Arts, Los Angeles

Art Center College of Design, Pasadena

Brooks College, Long Beach

California Institute of Technology, Pasadena

California State University, Long Beach, Long Beach

(32,000 students), Offers 65 baccalaureate and 50 advanced degree programs incuding Applied Arts and Sciences, Business Administration, Education, Engineering, and Public Policy and Administration.

California State Polytechnic University, Pomona, Pomona

California State University, Los Angeles, Los Angeles

Charles R. Drew University, Los Angeles

Fashion Institute of Design and Merchandising, Los Angeles Campus, Los Angeles

Long Beach City College, Long Beach

Los Angeles City College, Los Angeles

Los Angeles Southwest College, Los Angeles

Los Angeles Trade-Technical College, Los Angeles

Loyola Marymount University, Los Angeles

Mount St. Mary's College, Los Angeles

National Technical Schools, Los Angeles

Northrop University, Los Angeles

Occidental College, Los Angeles

Otis Art Institute of Parsons School of Design, New School for Social Research, Los Angeles

Pacific Oaks College, Pasadena

Pasadena City College, Pasadena

University of California, Los Angeles, Los Angeles

University of Judaism, Los Angeles

University of Southern California, Los Angeles

University of West Los Angeles, Los Angeles

Additional Information

Long Beach Economic Forecast. California State University, Long Beach, Office of Economic Research (1250 Bellflower Blvd., Long Beach, CA 90840-4607), November, 1990. 32p.

Long Beach, New Resident Guide. Long Beach Area Chamber of Commerce, March 1991. 21p.

MERCED, CA (MSA)

Geographic Profile

Land Area

1928.9 square miles

Counties and Parishes

Merced

Ranking Highlights

97 *out of 319 in total* **land area**

45 *out of 319 in* **population growth,** *1970–1990*

308 *out of 310 in having the lowest* **unemployment** *rate*

209 *out of 310 in size of* **labor force**

296 *out of 318 in the percentage of* **college graduates**

282 *out of 292 in per capita personal* **income**

274 *out of 319 in number of* **manufacturing establishments**

297 *out of 318 in* **physicians** *per 1000 people*

308 *out of 318 in* **hospital beds** *per 1000 people*

69 *out of 267 in fewest* **crimes** *per 1000 people*

98 *out of 266 in fewest* **violent crimes** *per 1000 people*

166 *out of 319 in per capita* **federal funds and grants** *out of 319 in per capita* **federal funds and grants**

Quality of Life Indexes (Rate per 1000 population)

Crime rate in 1991:	47.2
Violent crime rate in 1991:	4.8
Physicians rate in 1992:	1.08
Hospital bed rate in 1991:	1.89

ACCRA Cost of Living Indexes

(First quarter 1993, average = 100)

Composite index:	N/A
Utilities index:	N/A
Housing index:	N/A

Overview

The City of Atwater is in Merced County, which is located in the center of the San Joaquin Valley. Atwater is located approximately 265 miles northwest of Los Angeles, approximately 123 miles south and east of San Francisco, and about 108 miles south of Sacramento.

The City is serviced by State Highway 99, a major transportation link. In Merced, the County seat, five miles southwest there are 16 main truck carriers with regional and national connections, air commuter service to Los Angeles and San Francisco, and bus service provided by Greyhound, Continental Trailways, California Yosemite Tours, Via Charger Lines, and the Merced Area Regional Transit System. There is a deepwater port available in Stockton, 67 miles north of Merced.

Atwater is serviced by Pacific Gas and Electric and Pacific Bell telephone. The city water system has a pumping capacity of 11 million gallons per day. Current peak daily water usage is six million gallons per day. Current sewer (the system serves Atwater and Winton) capacity for the city is 10 million gallons per day with average daily usage of 6.5 million gallons per day. Existing capacities are adequate to accommodate planned future growth.

Merced College is the only institution of higher education in Merced County; however, Merced has been picked as one of the Central Valley locations being considered as the possible site of a new University of California campus. The Merced site is located at the eastern edge of Lake Yosemite, a short distance north of Merced. Should the Merced site be selected, the entire area would potentially be enhanced. The anticipated time frame for the site selection is 1993 or 1994.

The economy of Merced County is based primarily on agriculture. For the 1992 crop year, the grow value of Merced County's agriculture amounted to $1,070,181,000. This figure represents a 3.8% increase above the previous crop year. With the drought officially over and a decrease in the salmonella scare, the 1993 crop year is expected to be good. The commodities with the highest overall contributory value were, in order, milk, chickens, almonds, cotton, cattle, alfalfa, tomatoes, sweet potatoes, turkeys, eggs, wine grapes, and corn silage.

Castle Air Force Base, a Strategic Air Command training facility, is also of considerable significance to both the city and the county. In 1992, 4,940 active duty military and 1,131 civilian employees shared an annual payroll of $125,143,742. An additional 6,847 local military retirees have an annual payroll of $97,066,671. Of particular importance is the fact that in April 1991 it was announced that Castle AFB was included on the military base closure list. This list has since been affirmed by the President and Congress. Employment figures for Castle will continue to decline somewhat until October 1994, when the decline will accelerate. By March 1995 over 50% of the current 4,940 active duty personnel and their families will have been transferred. The 1,131 civilian employees will be given the opportunity to transfer to other civil service positions in this and other areas of the country.

Population (1990)
Total Population and Growth Rate
1990: 178,403
1980: 134,558
1970: 104,629
Growth rate 1970–1990: 71%

Race and Hispanic Origin
White: 67.4%
Black: 4.8%
Asian/Pacific Islander: 8.5%
Native American: 0.8%
Hispanic origin: 32.6%
White not Hispanic: 54.2%

Age
Ages 18 to 20: 4.6%
Ages 21 to 24: 6.2%
Ages 25 to 44: 30.6%
Ages 45 to 54: 8.3%
Ages 55 to 59: 3.7%
Ages 60 to 64: 3.4%
Ages 65 plus: 9.2%

Educational Attainment (1990)
Percent having completed high school: 63.1%
Percent having completed college: 12.0%
Elementary and high school enrollment: 41,371

Federal Funds and Grants Received
Total received in 1989: $516,500,000
Funds received per capita: $3,038

Civilian Labor Force
1993 (April):   83,829
1992 average: 80,386
1991 average: 75,412
1990 average: 72,012

Unemployment
1993 (April): 15.7%
1992 average: 16.5%
1991 average: 14.6%
1990 average: 12.2%

Average Annual Pay
1988: $16,242
1987: $15,538
1985: $14,895

Per Capita Personal Income
1991: $13,403
1990: $13,358
1989: $12,866

Business Climate (1987)
Manufacturing
Number of establishments in 1987: 120
Shipments in 1987 ($1,000): $1,322,600
Employees in 1987: 7,300
Change in employment, 1982 to 1987: -3.9%
Average annual pay for manufacturing work in 1989: $19,788
Average annual pay for production work in 1987: $17,621

Wholesale Trade
Number of establishments in 1987: 154
Total sales in 1987 ($1,000): $578,400
Change in sales, 1982 to 1987: 55.5%

Retail Trade
Number of establishments in 1987: 765
Total sales in 1987 ($1,000): $578,400
Retail sales per household in 1987: $12,284
Average annual pay in 1989: $11,750

Service Industry
Selected receipts in 1987 ($1,000): $169,400
Average annual pay in 1989: $16,019

Housing

Total number of units in 1990: 58,410
Occupied units in 1990: 55,331
Owner-occupied units in 1990: 54.4%
1993 ACCRA average cost: N/A
1993 ACCRA average rent for an apartment: N/A

Chamber of Commerce

Merced Chamber of Commerce, Dorothea J. Cook, Exec Director, 690 W. 16th St., Merced, CA 95340. 209-384-3333, FAX 209-384-8472

Economic Development Office

Merced County Chamber of Commerce, Sally Vaught, Exec. Director., 732 W. 18th St., PO Box 1112, Merced, CA 95340. 209-722-3864, FAX 209-722-2406

Economic Development Organizations

Merced County Office of Economic & Strategic Dev., Karen Prentiss, Deputy County Administrator, 1632 N St., Merced, CA 95340. 209-385-7312, FAX 209-383-4959

Major Businesses

Company	SIC	Telephone
Lesher Newspapers, Inc.	2711	(209) 722-1511

Colleges and Universities

Merced College, Merced

MODESTO, CA (MSA)

Geographic Profile

Land Area
1494.6 square miles

Counties and Parishes
Stanislaus

Additional Cities/Towns within Area
Turlock

Ranking Highlights

134 *out of 319 in total* **land area**
 22 *out of 319 in* **population growth,** *1970–1990*
307 *out of 310 in having the lowest* **unemployment** *rate*
125 *out of 310 in size of* **labor force**
280 *out of 318 in the percentage of* **college graduates**
248 *out of 292 in per capita personal* **income**
143 *out of 319 in number of* **manufacturing establishments**
217 *out of 318 in* **physicians** *per 1000 people*
189 *out of 318 in* **hospital beds** *per 1000 people*
172 *out of 267 in fewest* **crimes** *per 1000 people*
186 *out of 266 in fewest* **violent crimes** *per 1000 people*
297 *out of 319 in per capita* **federal funds and grants**

Quality of Life Indexes (Rate per 1000 population)

Crime rate in 1991:   67.3
Violent crime rate in 1991:   8.0
Physicians rate in 1992:   1.55
Hospital bed rate in 1991:   3.52

ACCRA Cost of Living Indexes

(First quarter 1993, average = 100)
Composite index: N/A
Utilities index: N/A
Housing index: N/A

Overview

Highways: Interstate 5, Highways 99 and 132
Rail Services: Southern Pacific, Santa Fe, Union Pacific
Airports: Modesto, Stockton
Location: 90 miles south of San Francisco, 300 miles north of Los Angeles, 80 miles from Sacramento.
Local government annual budget: $330,000,000. $255,000,000 contributed from state and federal governments. $75,000,000 from local sales, property, and other tax revenue.

Population (1990)

Total Population and Growth Rate
1990: 370,522
1980: 265,900
1970: 194,506
Growth rate 1970–1990: 90%

Race and Hispanic Origin
White: 80.2%

Black: 1.7%
Asian/Pacific Islander: 5.2%
Native American: 1.1%
Hispanic origin: 21.8%
White not Hispanic: 70.5%

Age
Ages 18 to 20: 4.2%
Ages 21 to 24: 5.6%
Ages 25 to 44: 32.2%
Ages 45 to 54: 9.3%
Ages 55 to 59: 3.6%
Ages 60 to 64: 3.6%
Ages 65 plus: 10.8%

Educational Attainment (1990)
Percent having completed high school: 68.4%
Percent having completed college: 13.0%
Elementary and high school enrollment: 74,366

Federal Funds and Grants Received
Total received in 1989: $732,500,000
Funds received per capita: $2,148

Civilian Labor Force
1993 (April): 182,477
1992 average: 180,044
1991 average: 168,885
1990 average: 164,375

Unemployment
1993 (April): 17.7%
1992 average: 16.0%
1991 average: 14.3%
1990 average: 11.5%

Average Annual Pay
1988: $18,655
1987: $17,934
1985: $16,728

Per Capita Personal Income
1991: $15,221
1990: $15,119
1989: $14,375

Business Climate (1987)
Manufacturing
Number of establishments in 1987: 379
Shipments in 1987 ($1,000): $4,625,400
Employees in 1987: 23,200
Change in employment, 1982 to 1987: 5.9%
Average annual pay for manufacturing work in 1989: $23,665
Average annual pay for production work in 1987: $20,397

Wholesale Trade
Number of establishments in 1987: 469
Total sales in 1987 ($1,000): $1,331,000
Change in sales, 1982 to 1987: 30.0%

Retail Trade
Number of establishments in 1987: 1,812
Total sales in 1987 ($1,000): $1,331,000
Retail sales per household in 1987: $17,050
Average annual pay in 1989: $12,437

Service Industry
Selected receipts in 1987 ($1,000): $747,800
Average annual pay in 1989: $18,834

Housing
Total number of units in 1990: 132,027
Occupied units in 1990: 125,375
Owner-occupied units in 1990: 60.7%
1993 ACCRA average cost: N/A
1993 ACCRA average rent for an apartment: N/A

Chamber of Commerce
Modesto Chamber of Commerce, Bill Seavy, CEO, PO Box 844, 1114 J St., Modesto, CA 95353. 209-577-5757, FAX 209-577-2673

Economic Development Office
Stanislaus County Economic Development Corp., William Carney, Exec. Director, 1012 Eleventh St., Ste. 300, Modesto, CA 95354. 209-521-9333, FAX 209-521-9373

Local Incentives for Business
Industrial Revenue Bonds
SBA 504 financing
Fast-Track permit processing

Major Businesses

Company	SIC	Telephone
Acme Construction Co. Inc.	1542	(209) 523-2674
Associated Feed & Supply	5191	(209) 667-2708
Beard Land & Investment Co.	4011	(209) 524-4631
Berry Distributing Co.	5141	(209) 527-1875
Brower, C. W., Inc.	5411	(209) 523-5447
California-Almond, Inc.	0723	(209) 883-0483
Central Valley Chrysler Inc.	5511	(209) 526-3300
Dimare Enterprises, Inc.	0174	(209) 862-2872
Emanuel Medical Center, Inc.	8062	(209) 667-4200
Ferry-Morse Seed California	0181	(209) 579-7333
Franco Construction, Inc.	6513	(209) 667-1810
Frontier Dodge, Inc.	5511	(209) 524-6811
Gallo, E. & J. Winery	2084	(209) 579-3111
Heath Motor Ltd., Inc.	5511	(209) 529-2933
Heritage Ford, Inc.	5511	(209) 529-5110
Hilmar Farmers Warehouse	2048	(209) 632-2424
Major-Sysco Food Service	5141	(209) 527-7700
Memorial Hospitals Association	8062	(209) 526-4500
Modesto Irrigation Distribution	4911	(209) 526-7373
MTC Distributing	5194	(209) 523-6449
Pacific Aluminum Corp.	3354	(209) 521-6400
Pallios Brothers Inc.	5411	(209) 538-3000

Major Businesses (Continued)

Company	SIC	Telephone
Patton Music Co. Inc.	5993	(209) 529-6500
Rule-Dale Enterprises, Inc.	5511	(209) 529-5300
Save Mart Supermarkets	5411	(209) 577-1600
Stanislaus Farm Supplies Co.	5191	(209) 538-7070
Sun Valley Farms	0252	(209) 545-1615
Turlock Irrigation Distribution	4911	(209) 632-3861
Veterinary Services, Inc.	5047	(209) 522-5281
Vine, E. R. & Sons, Inc.	5171	(209) 537-0723

Colleges and Universities

California State University, Stanislaus, Turlock

Modesto Junior College, Modesto

Additional Information

Doing Business in Stanislaus County. Stanislaus County Economic Development Corp., December 1990. np.

Modesto, Stanislaus County, California, Community Economic Profile. Modesto Chamber of Commerce, July 1990. 4p.

Statistical Update, Data on Stanislaus County and Its Nine Cities. Stanislaus County Economic Development Corp. Published bimonthly. 4p.

OAKLAND, CA (PMSA)

Geographic Profile

Land Area

1457.8 square miles

Counties and Parishes

Alameda

Contra Costa

Additional Cities/Towns within Area

Berkeley

Livermore

Ranking Highlights

139 *out of 319 in total* **land area**

145 *out of 319 in* **population growth,** *1970–1990*

128 *out of 310 in having the lowest* **unemployment** *rate*

19 *out of 310 in size of* **labor force**

26 *out of 318 in the percentage of* **college graduates**

12 *out of 292 in per capita personal* **income**

20 *out of 319 in number of* **manufacturing establishments**

94 *out of 318 in* **physicians** *per 1000 people*

278 *out of 318 in* **hospital beds** *per 1000 people*

214 *out of 267 in fewest* **crimes** *per 1000 people*

236 *out of 266 in fewest* **violent crimes** *per 1000 people*

97 *out of 319 in per capita* **federal funds and grants**

Quality of Life Indexes (Rate per 1000 population)

Crime rate in 1991:	74.6
Violent crime rate in 1991:	10.4
Physicians rate in 1992:	2.25
Hospital bed rate in 1991:	2.43

ACCRA Cost of Living Indexes

(First quarter 1993, average = 100)

Composite index:	N/A
Utilities index:	N/A
Housing index:	N/A

Overview

The city of Oakland is known as the heart of the East Bay section of the San Francisco Bay Area. It is a heavily populated and industrialized belt that is home to about half the residents of the San Francisco-Oakland urban area. Approximately 25 percent of Oakland's work force is employed in the wholesale and retail trade. The city has more than 750 manufacturing plants employing nearly 20 percent of the city's workers. Shipbuilding has flourished along the city's inner harbor. Other major industries include electrical equipment, chemicals, glass, automobiles and trucks, and pharmaceuticals. items and goods produced in the area include processed foods, transportation equipment, fabricated metal products, non-electrical machinery, electrical equipment, and clay and glass products

Oakland's business community has faced some major

problems in recent years. The Loma Prieta Earthquake in 1989 not only caused physical damage but caused many companies to consider relocation. Although Alameda County had economic growth of 12 percent in the 1980s, Oakland did not participate in that growth but showed a decline of one percent. Major plant closures in the late 1980s and 1990s included Gerber Products, General Electric, National Lead, American Can, and Oakland's largest manufacturing facility, Transamerican Delaval, which had employed sixteen hundred workers. The ripple effect of these closures led to the closings of numerous small businesses that had been suppliers to these firms. The city has applied for a designated Urban Enterprise Zone to help alleviate the employment situation, particularly for inner city residents.

The Port of Oakland is the largest container port on the North American Pacific Coast. Annual container traffic ranks among the top ten nationally and top twenty worldwide. The Port of Oakland occupies 19 miles on the mainland shore of San Francisco Bay, one of the finest natural harbors in the world. There are more than 550 acres of marine terminal facilities, twenty-seven deepwater berths, and twenty-nine container cranes. On-dock storage space exceeds six hundred thousand square feet. As of late 1992, the port, which has the potential to become a *super port* linking sea, air and land transportation for all of Northern California, faced a serious problem in its efforts to expand its facilities to handle today's enormous super-sized ships. Although Congress appropriated funds in 1986 for dredging to deepen the harbor, no dredging has been accomplished because each time a site is proposed, organizations have blocked the project through complicated lawsuits. The long-term fate of the port is yet to be seen.

Oakland can be reached from San Francisco by traveling east across the Bay Bridge via Interstate 80 and continuing south to Oakland on I-580 or I-980. Oakland International Airport is located only twelve minutes from downtown. A total of eleven airlines serve Oakland International Airport, with 131 daily inbound/outbound flights and approximately seventeen thousand daily passengers. The airport has major thoroughfares to Denver, Colorado, Chicago, Illinois, Dallas, Texas, Seattle, Washington, Portland, Oregon, and Los Angeles.

Population (1990)

Total Population and Growth Rate
1990: 2,082,914
1980: 1,761,710
1970: 1,627,562
Growth rate 1970–1990: 28%

Race and Hispanic Origin
White: 65.9%
Black: 14.6%
Asian/Pacific Islander: 12.9%

Native American: 0.7%
Hispanic origin: 13.1%
White not Hispanic: 59.5%

Age
Ages 18 to 20: 4.3%
Ages 21 to 24: 6.1%
Ages 25 to 44: 36.1%
Ages 45 to 54: 10.8%
Ages 55 to 59: 3.9%
Ages 60 to 64: 3.7%
Ages 65 plus: 10.7%

Educational Attainment (1990)
Percent having completed high school: 83.4%
Percent having completed college: 29.9%
Elementary and high school enrollment: 328,709

Federal Funds and Grants Received
Total received in 1989: $7,222,900,000
Funds received per capita: $3,600

Civilian Labor Force
1993 (April): 1,124,639
1992 average: 1,117,769
1991 average: 1,098,503
1990 average: 1,097,118

Unemployment
1993 (April): 6.4%
1992 average: 6.5%
1991 average: 5.4%
1990 average: 4.1%

Average Annual Pay
1988: $25,183
1987: $23,972
1985: $21,756

Per Capita Personal Income
1991: $23,545
1990: $23,135
1989: $22,008

Business Climate (1987)

Manufacturing
Number of establishments in 1987: 3,211
Shipments in 1987 ($1,000): $22,629,100
Employees in 1987: 107,000
Change in employment, 1982 to 1987: 2.2%
Average annual pay for manufacturing work, 1989: $31,822
Average annual pay for production work, 1987: $24,044

Wholesale Trade
Number of establishments in 1987: 3,884
Total sales in 1987 ($1,000): $30,306,700
Change in sales, 1982 to 1987: 78.4%

Retail Trade
Number of establishments in 1987: 10,924
Total sales in 1987 ($1,000): $30,306,700

Retail sales per household in 1987: $17,100
Average annual pay in 1989: $15,925

Service Industry
Selected receipts in 1987 ($1,000): $7,793,800
Average annual pay in 1989: $23,256

Office Real Estate (1992)

Office space inventory: 19,390,972 square feet
Average class A Central Business District rental range per sq. ft: $24.24

Vacancy Rates
All areas: 16.4%

Vacancy Rates in Central Business District
Class A space: 13.1%
Class B space: 12.4%

Vacancy Rates Outside Central Business District
Class A space: 34.0%
Class B space: 17.7%

Housing

Total number of units in 1990: 820,279
Occupied units in 1990: 779,806
Owner-occupied units in 1990: 58.8%
1993 ACCRA average cost: N/A
1993 ACCRA average rent for an apartment: N/A

Chamber of Commerce

Oakland Chamber of Commerce, Robert L. Toney, President, 475 14th St., Oakland, CA 94612. 415-874-4800, FAX 510-839-8817

Economic Development Office

City of Oakland Economic Development & Employment, Julia T. Brown, Director, 1333 Broadway #900, Oakland, CA 94612. 510-238-3015

Economic Development Organizations

Oakland International Trade Center, N.S. Tsui, President, 1714 Franklin Street, Oakland, CA 94612. 510-465-7012
Oakland Office of Economic Development, Bruce Kern, Director, 1221 Oak Street #555, Oakland, CA 94612. 510-272-6984, FAX 510-272-5007

Major Businesses

Company	SIC	Telephone
American Brass & Iron Foundry	3321	(415) 632-3467
American President Corp.	4412	(415) 272-8000
Civic Bank of Commerce	6022	(415) 836-6500
Clorox Co.	2842	(415) 271-7000
Cochran & Celli	5511	(415) 444-0055
Conklin Brothers of Oakland	1752	(415) 836-2867
Cornnuts, Inc.	2096	(415) 523-3949
Custom Alloy Scrap Sales	3341	(415) 893-6476
Cutter Lumber Products	2448	(415) 444-5959
Dreyer's Grand Ice Cream	2024	(415) 652-8187

Major Businesses (Continued)

Company	SIC	Telephone
Equitec Financial Group	6531	(415) 430-9900
Fabco Automotive Corp.	3537	(415) 658-7070
Frank W. Dunne Co.	2851	(415) 652-1200
Gallagher & Burk, Inc.	1429	(415) 261-0466
Gardiner Mfg. Co.	3462	(415) 832-7823
General Grinding Inc.	3599	(415) 261-5557
Granny Goose Foods Inc.	2096	(415) 635-5400
Hayes Manufacturing Co.	2512	(415) 534-4511
Henry Conversano & Association	7389	(415) 547-6890
Hooper's Confections, Inc.	2064	(415) 654-3373
Imacc Corp.	3412	(415) 652-6847
Industrial Steam Division	3443	(415) 261-8738
J. L. Henderson & Co.	5088	(415) 839-1900
L. N. Curtis & Sons	5087	(415) 839-5111
Morehouse Foods Inc.	2035	(415) 652-7980
Mother's Cake & Cookie Co.	2052	(415) 569-2323
Nor-Cal Metal Fabricators	3499	(415) 836-1451
Oakland Mfg. Co.	3429	(415) 832-7823
Oakland Tribune Inc.	2711	(415) 645-2000
Pacific Electric Motor Co.	3699	(415) 569-7621
Pacific Pipe Co.	5074	(415) 452-0122
Pacific Venture Finance	6799	(415) 729-7253
Paco Pumps Inc.	3561	(415) 639-3200
Parisian Bakeries, Inc.	2051	(415) 641-1000
Phoenix Iron Works	3321	(415) 465-9900
Ransome Co.	1611	(415) 430-1900
S. T. Johnson Co.	3433	(415) 652-6000
Safeway Inc.	5411	(415) 891-3000
San Francisco French Bread	2051	(415) 641-5511
Service Brass & Aluminum	3494	(415) 261-5733
Sierra Capital Companies	6798	(415) 444-3132
Sono-Ceil Co.	1742	(415) 834-4524
Tulloch Construction Inc.	1541	(415) 655-3400
United Beverage Inc.	5181	(415) 832-6081
United Plastics Corp.	3089	(415) 562-9828
Wellmade Metal Products Co.	3499	(415) 562-1878
Western Door & Sash Co.	5031	(415) 535-2000
White Brothers	5031	(415) 261-1600

Colleges and Universities

Armstrong College, Berkeley
California College of Arts and Crafts, Oakland
Heald College, Oakland
Holy Names College, Oakland
Laney College, Oakland
Merritt College, Oakland
Mills College, Oakland
Patten College, Oakland
Samuel Merritt College, Oakland
University of California at Berkeley, Berkeley
Vista College, Berkeley

OXNARD-VENTURA, CA (PMSA)

Geographic Profile

Land Area

1846.0 square miles

Counties and Parishes

Ventura

Ranking Highlights

102 *out of 319 in total* **land area**

39 *out of 319 in* **population growth**, *1970–1990*

242 *out of 310 in having the lowest* **unemployment** *rate*

68 *out of 310 in size of* **labor force**

80 *out of 318 in the percentage of* **college graduates**

N/A *out of 292 in per capita personal* **income**

76 *out of 319 in number of* **manufacturing establishments**

175 *out of 318 in* **physicians** *per 1000 people*

305 *out of 318 in* **hospital beds** *per 1000 people*

55 *out of 267 in fewest* **crimes** *per 1000 people*

115 *out of 266 in fewest* **violent crimes** *per 1000 people*

133 *out of 319 in per capita* **federal funds and grants**

Quality of Life Indexes (Rate per 1000 population)

Crime rate in 1991:	44.3
Violent crime rate in 1991:	5.3
Physicians rate in 1992:	1.75
Hospital bed rate in 1991:	2.05

ACCRA Cost of Living Indexes

(First quarter 1993, average = 100)

Composite index:	N/A
Utilities index:	N/A
Housing index:	N/A

Overview

Ventura County is located at the approximate midway point between Los Angeles and Santa Barbara and is linked to these areas by several highways. The largest and most heavily traveled highways are U.S. 101, the Ventura Freeway; the 118 Simi Valley Freeway; Pacific Coast Highway 1; Highway 23, which connects Moorpark to Thousand Oaks and U.S. 101; Highway 33, which connects Ventura and Ojai; and Highway 126, which runs through the Fillmore and Santa Paula areas. 118 and 126 connect to Interstate 5 in Los Angeles County.

Ventura County possesses a diverse economy and large labor force. Strong industries include agriculture, oil, aerospace, advanced technologies, tourism, automotive, and military testing and development.

Ventura County rates 10th in agricultural production in California at a gross value of $723,845,000 for 1990. The oil industry, like agriculture, has been a mainstay of the economy for some time. Offshore and hillside drilling pro-duce more than 19 million barrels of oil a year.

The naval Construction Battalion, one of two "Seabee" centers in the United States is the second-largest civilian employer in the County with a total payroll exceeding $420 million annually. The County government employs close to 6,788 people.

The Southern Pacific Railroad serves Ventura County's industrial areas running 30 trains daily, piggyback service, and providing available industrial sidings. Ventura County Railway, a privately owned shortlined railroad, serves the industrial areas of south Oxnard, the Port of Hueneme, and the U.S. Navy Construction Battalion Center. Commuter air service is available from the Oxnard Airport. Other airports serving Ventura County are Camarillo Airport and the Santa Paula Airport, both general aviation facilities. Ventura County is approximately 62 miles from Los Angeles International Airport and 55 miles from Burbank Airport.

Natural gas service for Ventura County is uniformly provided by the Southern California Gas Company with electricity provided by Southern California Edison. Telephone service is provided by either Pacific Bell or GTE California.

The commercial, deepwater seaport Port of Hueneme is located in the City of Port Hueneme in southern Ventura County. The Port of Hueneme consists of two separate parts: commercial international trade facilities and operations under the control and administration of the Oxnard Harbor District; military facilities and operations under the control of the U.S. Naval Construction Battalion Center, Port Hueneme.

Population (1990)

Total Population and Growth Rate

1990: 669,016

1980: 529,174

1970: 378,497

Growth rate 1970–1990: 77%

Race and Hispanic Origin

White: 79.1%

Black: 2.3%

Asian/Pacific Islander: 5.2%

Native American: 0.7%

Hispanic origin: 26.4%

White not Hispanic: 65.9%

Age

Ages 18 to 20: 4.7%

Ages 21 to 24: 6%

Ages 25 to 44: 34.5%

Ages 45 to 54: 10.7%

Ages 55 to 59: 3.9%

Ages 60 to 64: 3.4%

Ages 65 plus: 9.4%

Educational Attainment (1990)

Percent having completed high school: 79.4%

Percent having completed college: 23.0%

Elementary and high school enrollment: 122,565

Federal Funds and Grants Received
Total received in 1989: $2,129,300,000
Funds received per capita: $3,290

Civilian Labor Force
1993 (April):   389,675
1992 average: 384,528
1991 average: 375,954
1990 average: 375,932

Unemployment
1993 (April):   7.5%
1992 average: 8.4%
1991 average: 7.0%
1990 average: 5.5%

Average Annual Pay
1988: $22,275
1987: $21,399
1985: $19,311

Per Capita Personal Income
1991: N/A
1990: N/A
1989: N/A

Business Climate (1987)
Manufacturing
Number of establishments in 1987: 836
Shipments in 1987 ($1,000): $3,671,900
Employees in 1987: 34,600
Change in employment, 1982 to 1987: 28.6%
Average annual pay for manufacturing work in 1989: $28,600
Average annual pay for production work in 1987: $20,839

Wholesale Trade
Number of establishments in 1987: 867
Total sales in 1987 ($1,000): $6,306,100
Change in sales, 1982 to 1987: 113.8%

Retail Trade
Number of establishments in 1987: 3,328
Total sales in 1987 ($1,000): $6,306,100
Retail sales per household in 1987: $20,371
Average annual pay in 1989: $13,317

Service Industry
Selected receipts in 1987 ($1,000): $1,910,400
Average annual pay in 1989: $21,825

Housing
Total number of units in 1990: 228,478
Occupied units in 1990: 217,298
Owner-occupied units in 1990: 65.5%
1993 ACCRA average cost: N/A
1993 ACCRA average rent for an apartment: N/A

Chamber of Commerce
Oxnard Area Chamber of Commerce, George Scarvelis, Exec. Director, 500 Esplanade Dr. #1230, PO Box 867, Oxnard, CA 93032. 805-485-5255, FAX 805-485-4057

Economic Development Office
Ventura County Economic Development Association, Nancy M. Williams, Exec. Director, 500 Esplanade Dr. #810, Oxnard, CA 93030. 805-988-1106

Economic Development Organizations
Oxnard Economic Development Department, Steven L. Kinney, Economic Development Director, 300 W. 3rd St., Oxnard, CA 93030. 805-984-4611, FAX 805-486-9462

Local Incentives for Business
The city has financing programs to aid both small and large businesses including: Industrial Development Bonds, Revolving Loan Fund, and Commercial Rehabilitation Loan Program.

Industrial Sites
Oxnard Town Center (265 acres). A proposed mixed use development.
Northeast Industrial Park (1600 acres). Planned for: Del Norte Business Park (60 acres), Maulhardt Industrial Center (100 acres). Northfield Business Park (152 acres), McInnes Ranch (236 acres), Seagate Business Park (85 acres). Sammis Business Park (65 acres), and the Camino Real Business Park (45 acres).
McGrath Business Park (75-136 acres).
Hueneme Assessment District (98 acres). For industrial development
Plaza Del Norte Commercial and Industrial Park (204 acres). Includes an auto center with eight dealers, retail office, and industrial projects.
Financial Plaza. Consists of 600,000 square feet of office space, several restaurants, a helipad, and a hotel.

Major Businesses

Company	SIC	Telephone
Amgen Inc.	8731	(805) 499-5725
Bugle Boy Industries Inc.	2329	(805) 582-1010
Cardkey Systems, Inc.	5065	(805) 522-5555
Community Memorial Hospital	8062	(805) 648-7811
Everest & Jennings International	3842	(805) 987-6911
G & H Technology Inc.	3678	(805) 484-0543
G T E L Corp.	5999	(805) 373-5000
Grindall & Associates Inc.	6552	(805) 379-1182
Los Robles Regional Medical Co.	8062	(805) 497-2727
Lost Arrow Corp.	2329	(805) 643-8616
Merchants Home Delivery Service	4213	(805) 485-7979
Pacific Coast Ford Corp.	5511	(805) 983-6511
Pacifica Corp.	1521	(805) 495-9494
Patagonia Inc.	2329	(805) 643-8616

Major Businesses (Continued)

Company	SIC	Telephone
Pleasant Travel Service	4724	(818) 991-3390
Saticoy Lemon Association	0723	(805) 654-6500
Security Pacific Automobile Financial	6159	(805) 496-1961
St. Johns Regional Medical Center	8062	(805) 988-2500
Tandon Corp.	3571	(805) 523-0340
Told Corp.	6552	(805) 487-4300
Western States Import Co.	5091	(805) 484-8130

Colleges and Universities

Moorpark College (10,500 students). Offers undergraduate and technical training programs.

Oxnard College, Oxnard

Ventura College, Ventura

Additional Information

Oxnard, California, Office and Industrial Opportunities. Oxnard Economic Development Department, December 1989. 30p.

Oxnard, California, Retail Opportunities. Oxnard Economic Development Department, December 1989. 27p.

REDDING, CA (MSA)

Geographic Profile

Land Area

3785.7 square miles

Counties and Parishes

Shasta

Ranking Highlights

31 *out of 319 in total* land area

25 *out of 319 in* population growth, *1970–1990*

298 *out of 310 in having the lowest* unemployment *rate*

238 *out of 310 in size of* labor force

266 *out of 318 in the percentage of* college graduates

182 *out of 292 in per capita personal* income

192 *out of 319 in number of* manufacturing establishments

154 *out of 318 in* physicians *per 1000 people*

220 *out of 318 in* hospital beds *per 1000 people*

79 *out of 267 in fewest* crimes *per 1000 people*

85 *out of 266 in fewest* violent crimes *per 1000 people*

157 *out of 319 in per capita* federal funds and grants

Quality of Life Indexes (Rate per 1000 population)

Crime rate in 1991:	48.9
Violent crime rate in 1991:	4.4
Physicians rate in 1992:	1.82
Hospital bed rate in 1991:	3.18

ACCRA Cost of Living Indexes

(First quarter 1993, average = 100)

Composite index:	N/A
Utilities index:	N/A
Housing index:	N/A

Overview

The metropolitan area of Shasta County lies astride the Sacramento River about 160 miles north of the State Capitol in Sacramento and 230 miles north of San Francisco, equidistant between Seattle, Washington and Los Angeles. Major highways include the north/south Interstate 5 and the east/west State highways 299 and 44. The City of Redding is consistently ranked by the California Department of Finance as being in the top 10 fastest growing cities in California with populations under 200,000.

Redding Municipal Airport provides commercial air transportation to Sacramento, San Francisco and San Jose. General air service available at the Benton Airpark, Enterprise Skypark, and Redding Sky Ranch. Rail services to the area are provided by the Southern Pacific, Burlington Northern, and the McCloud River Railroads.

Population (1990)

Total Population and Growth Rate

1990: 147,036

1980: 115,613

1970: 77,640

Growth rate 1970–1990: 89%

Race and Hispanic Origin

White: 93.8%

Black: .7%

Asian/Pacific Islander: 1.8%

Native American: 2.7%

Hispanic origin: 3.8%

White not Hispanic: 91.1%

Age

Ages 18 to 20: 3.8%

Ages 21 to 24: 4.3%

Ages 25 to 44: 30.2%

Ages 45 to 54: 11%

Ages 55 to 59: 4.4%

Ages 60 to 64: 4.7%

Ages 65 plus: 14.1%

Educational Attainment (1990)

Percent having completed high school: 78.4%

Percent having completed college: 13.7%

Elementary and high school enrollment: 27,192

Federal Funds and Grants Received

Total received in 1989: $431,300,000

Funds received per capita: $3,086

Civilian Labor Force

1993 (April): 69,232

1992 average: 68,697

1991 average: 65,249

1990 average: 63,084

Unemployment

1993 (April): 11.4%

1992 average: 12.5%

1991 average: 10.3%

1990 average: 8.4%

Average Annual Pay

1988: $19,403

1987: $18,451

1985: $17,255

Per Capita Personal Income

1991: $16,579

1990: $16,383

1989: $15,252

Business Climate (1987)

Manufacturing

Number of establishments in 1987: 239

Shipments in 1987 ($1,000): $732,100

Employees in 1987: 5,000

Change in employment, 1982 to 1987: 16.3%

Average annual pay for manufacturing work in 1989: $29,022

Average annual pay for production work in 1987: $22,946

Wholesale Trade

Number of establishments in 1987: 262

Total sales in 1987 ($1,000): $651,100

Change in sales, 1982 to 1987: 62.9%

Retail Trade

Number of establishments in 1987: 972

Total sales in 1987 ($1,000): $651,100

Retail sales per household in 1987: $16,928

Average annual pay in 1989: $12,441

Service Industry

Selected receipts in 1987 ($1,000): $348,800

Average annual pay in 1989: $18,316

Housing

Total number of units in 1990: 60,552

Occupied units in 1990: 55,966

Owner-occupied units in 1990: 64.5%

1993 ACCRA average cost: N/A

1993 ACCRA average rent for an apartment: N/A

Chamber of Commerce

Greater Redding Chamber of Commerce, David Lee Gibson, Director, PO Box 1180, 747 Auditorium Drive, Redding, CA 96001. 916-225-4433, FAX 916-225-4398

Economic Development Office

Superior California Development Council, Inc., Burce Daniels, Exec. Officer, 737 Auditorium Dr. #D, Redding, CA 96001. 916-241-8720

Economic Development Organizations

Economic Development Corp. of Shasta County, James G. Zauher, General Manager, 737 Auditorium Drive, Ste. D, Redding, CA 96001. 916-225-5300, FAX 916-225-5303

Shasta County Board of Realtors, Marie Whitaere, 840 Remor Street, Redding, CA 96002. 916-223-0410

Private Industry Council, Don Perry, Exec Director, 1220 Sacramento St., Redding, CA 96001. 916-246-7911

Manufacturers Association, Kent Daag, Manager, 2410 Larkspur, Redding, CA 96002. 916-221-5556

Local Incentives for Business

Finalist in California Enterprise Zone Program, which, if designated, would offer tax incentives to new and expanding businesses.

Industrial Sites

Redding Municipal Airport (1,105 acres) These planned industrial sites are located adjacent to the airport, 5-15 minutes from Highway 44 and I-5.

Mountain Lakes Industrial Park (530 acres). Adjacent to I-5 with rail spur.

Peterson Industrial Park (40 acres).

Shasta Dam Public Utilities District Planned Industrial Park (240 acres).

Major Businesses

Company	SIC	Telephone
Boone's Wholesale Inc.	5141	(916) 241-4631
Crystal Creek Construction	1611	(916) 244-2155
Denham, S. J. Inc.	5511	(916) 241-1756
Fletcher Forest Products	2411	(916) 336-6263
Gifford Associates Inc.	1542	(916) 243-8287
Hawkey Transportation Inc.	4213	(916) 241-1203
Jones, Edwin B., Jr.	1542	(916) 547-4448
Ladd, Roy E. Inc.	1611	(916) 241-6102
Lassen Canyon Nursery Inc.	0171	(916) 223-1075
Mercy Hospital of Redding	8062	(916) 225-6368
Moss Lumber Co. Inc.	5211	(916) 244-0700
North Valley Bancorp	6022	(916) 221-8400
Redding 76 Auto/Truck	5541	(916) 221-4760
Redding F. B. Hart Co.	5511	(916) 246-2460
Redding Lumber Transportation	4213	(916) 241-8193
Shasta-Siskiyou Transportation	5171	(916) 241-1167
Sierra Pacific Industries	2421	(916) 275-8812
Stimpel-Wiebelhaus Inc.	1611	(916) 223-6605
Toney, Ray & Associates Inc.	1542	(916) 241-6691
Tullis & Associates Inc.	1011	(916) 241-5105
West Side Markets, Inc.	5411	(916) 223-2093
Wood, J. W. Co. Inc.	5074	(916) 222-0423

Colleges and Universities

Shasta College, Redding (13,000 students) Two year, fully accredited. Offers a variety of occupational and transfer programs.

Simpson College, Redding

Additional Information

Growing Responsibility in a Priceless Environment, a Report on the State of the City of Redding, California. Redding City Council, January 1991. np.

The Right Place for Industry and Quality Living–Shasta Dam Area. Shasta Dam Area Public Utility District, n.d. 10p.

Shasta Country. Shasta Economic Development Corporation, n.d. n.p. (Brochure with inserted fact sheets.)

RIVERSIDE–SAN BERNARDINO, CA (PMSA)

Geographic Profile

Land Area

27269.9 square miles

Counties and Parishes

Riverside

San Bernardino

Additional Cities/Towns within Area

Palm Springs

Ranking Highlights

   1 *out of 319 in total* land area

   9 *out of 319 in* population growth, *1970–1990*

291 *out of 310 in having the lowest* unemployment *rate*

 18 *out of 310 in size of* labor force

237 *out of 318 in the percentage of* college graduates

177 *out of 292 in per capita personal* income

 31 *out of 319 in number of* manufacturing establishments

229 *out of 318 in* physicians *per 1000 people*

289 *out of 318 in* hospital beds *per 1000 people*

N/A *out of 267 in fewest* crimes *per 1000 people*

N/A *out of 266 in fewest* violent crimes *per 1000 people*

199 *out of 319 in per capita* federal funds and grants*out of 319 in per capita* federal funds and grants

Quality of Life Indexes (Rate per 1000 population)

Crime rate in 1991:	N/A
Violent crime rate in 1991:	N/A
Physicians rate in 1992:	1.49
Hospital bed rate in 1991:	2.23

ACCRA Cost of Living Indexes

(First quarter 1993, average = 100)

Composite index:	116.1
Utilities index:	72.0
Housing index:	128.5

Overview

Riverside-San Bernardino is located about 50 miles from Los Angeles and about 100 miles from San Diego. The economy and labor force have changed with the rapid growth of recent years. While agriculture, particularly oranges, has been the primary industry in Riverside, the city, with important trade and service center activities, has evolved into the business and industrial center of the Inland Empire area. Retail sales for Riverside have increased by eighty percent since 1980. Retail sales grew both because of an increasing local population and expansion in the quality and variety of goods for sale. Goods produced in the area include manufactured homes, recreational vehicles, electronic components, aircraft parts, and citrus-packing.

Riverside is adjacent to one of the major rail-freight centers in the state. Rail service to the city includes a main line of the Atchison, Topeka & Santa Fe, with four local freights daily; a branch line of the Southern Pacific Railroad, with one local freight daily; and a main line for the Union Pacific Railroad, with two local freights daily. The Riverside Municipal Airport accommodates private aircraft, charter services, and air-related businesses. More than sixty-five trucking companies are based in or have facilities in Riverside and provide a broad range of interstate, regional, and local freight services.

Interstate highways in the area include I-215, which runs north-south, and I-10, which runs east-west just north of the city of Riverside. Other major freeways in the area are State Highways 60 (the Pomona Freeway) and 91 (the Riverside Freeway). These routes provide direct access to metropolitan areas of Los Angeles and Orange County.

Population (1990)

Total Population and Growth Rate
1990: 2,588,793
1980: 1,558,215
1970: 1,139,149
Growth rate 1970–1990: 127%

Race and Hispanic Origin
White: 74.6%
Black: 6.9%
Asian/Pacific Islander: 3.9%
Native American: 1.0%
Hispanic origin: 26.5%
White not Hispanic: 62.4%

Age
Ages 18 to 20: 4.4%
Ages 21 to 24: 6%
Ages 25 to 44: 33.3%
Ages 45 to 54: 8.6%
Ages 55 to 59: 3.5%
Ages 60 to 64: 3.6%
Ages 65 plus: 10.8%

Educational Attainment (1990)
Percent having completed high school: 74.8%
Percent having completed college: 14.8%
Elementary and high school enrollment: 501,935

Federal Funds and Grants Received
Total received in 1989: $6,372,400,000
Funds received per capita: $2,798

Civilian Labor Force
1993 (April): 1,146,361
1992 average: 1,137,617
1991 average: 1,088,381
1990 average: 1,066,615

Unemployment
1993 (April): 10.9%
1992 average: 11.0%
1991 average: 9.2%
1990 average: 6.5%

Average Annual Pay
1988: $20,212
1987: $19,301
1985: $17,300

Per Capita Personal Income
1991: $16,707
1990: $16,802
1989: $16,172

Business Climate (1987)

Manufacturing
Number of establishments in 1987: 2,494
Shipments in 1987 ($1,000): $9,445,300
Employees in 1987: 85,600
Change in employment, 1982 to 1987: 37.2%
Average annual pay for manufacturing work in 1989: $25,664
Average annual pay for production work in 1987: $18,738

Wholesale Trade
Number of establishments in 1987: 2,308
Total sales in 1987 ($1,000): $8,356,100
Change in sales, 1982 to 1987: 55.8%

Retail Trade
Number of establishments in 1987: 10,689
Total sales in 1987 ($1,000): $8,356,100
Retail sales per household in 1987: $16,571
Average annual pay in 1989: $13,482

Service Industry
Selected receipts in 1987 ($1,000): $4,715,600
Average annual pay in 1989: $19,287

Housing
Total number of units in 1990: 1,026,179
Occupied units in 1990: 866,804
Owner-occupied units in 1990: 65.2%
1993 ACCRA average cost: $149,450
1993 ACCRA average rent for an apartment: $619

Chamber of Commerce
Greater Riverside Chamber of Commerce, Art Pick, Exec. Vice President, 4261 Main St., Riverside, CA 92501. 714-683-7100, FAX 714-683-2670

Economic Development Office
Riverside County Economic Development Agency, David McElroy, Director, PO Box 1180, 3499 10th St., Riverside, CA 92502. 714-788-9770, FAX 714-788-1415

Economic Development Organizations
Riverside Area Board of Realtors, Frank Heyming, President, 3690 Elizabeth St., Riverside, CA 92506. 714-684-1221

Economic Development Partnership, Inc. Stephen Albright, President, 3750 University Ave., Ste. 260, Riverside, CA

92501. 714-781-9000Indland Empire Economic Council, Steve Pontell, President, 800 N. Haven Ave., Ontario, CA 91764. 714-941-7877

County of San Bernardino, Dept. of Economic and Community Development, 474 W. 5th St., San Bernardino, CA 92415-0040. 714-387-4573

Local Incentives for Business

Industrial Development Bonds

Permit Fast Tracking

Redevelopment Area Incentives

State Tax Credits, Agua Mansa Enterprise Zone (includes parts of Riverside and San Bernardino Counties)

County Development Block Grant Program

Grants

Housing Loan Fund Program

Economic Development Loans. Gap loans up to $500,000 for 10 to 15 years may be used for: land acquisition, construction costs, architect and engineering professional fees, capital equipment purchases, etc.

Major Businesses

Company	SIC	Telephone
Boral Concrete Products	3272	(714) 888-7077
Boral Industries Inc.	3272	(714) 822-4407
Bourns Inc.	3825	(714) 781-5690
California Steel Industries	3312	(714) 350-6200
Coast Grain Co.	2048	(714) 983-9766
Contel of California, Inc.	4813	(619) 245-0511
Data-Design Laboratories	3672	(714) 987-2511
Desert Hospital District	8062	(619) 323-6511
Deutsch Engineering	3678	(714) 849-7844
Eastern Municipal Water Distribution	4941	(714) 925-7676
Eisenhower Medical Center	8062	(619) 340-3911
Fleetwood Enterprises, Inc.	3716	(714) 351-3500
Forecast Mortgage Corp.	6552	(714) 987-7788
Harris Co., The	5311	(714) 889-0444
Hub Distributing, Inc.	5399	(714) 988-6431
Kasler Corp.	1611	(714) 884-4811
King Bearing, Inc.	5085	(714) 279-1170
Loma Linda University Medical Center	8062	(714) 796-7311
MIS Industries Inc.	5063	(714) 279-1170
Riverside Community Hospital	8062	(714) 788-3100
San Antonio Community Hospital	8062	(714) 985-2811
Stater Brothers Inc.	5411	(714) 783-5000

Colleges and Universities

California Baptist College, Riverside

California State University, San Bernardino, San Bernardino

ITT Technical Institute, San Bernardino

Loma Linda University, Riverside

National Education Center-Skadron College of Business Campus, San Bernardino

Riverside Community College, Riverside

San Bernardino Valley College, San Bernardino

University of California, Riverside, Riverside

Additional Information

Economic Development Agency Financing Incentives and Programs. Riverside County Economic Development Agency, n.d. 2p.

Riverside County Instant Site Selector. Riverside County Economic Development Agency, 1990. 4p.

Riverside County Tax System Overview. Riverside County Economic Development Agency, 1990. 4p.

SACRAMENTO, CA (MSA)

Geographic Profile

Land Area

5094.0 square miles

Counties and Parishes

El Dorado
Placer
Sacramento
Yolo

Additional Cities/Towns within Area

Davis
Roseville
Woodland

Ranking Highlights

13 *out of 319 in total* **land area**

40 *out of 319 in* **population growth,** *1970–1990*

219 *out of 310 in having the lowest* **unemployment** *rate*

31 *out of 310 in size of* **labor force**

73 *out of 318 in the percentage of* **college graduates**

61 *out of 292 in per capita personal* **income**

50 *out of 319 in number of* **manufacturing establishments**

102 *out of 318 in* **physicians** *per 1000 people*

238 *out of 318 in* **hospital beds** *per 1000 people*

158 *out of 267 in fewest* **crimes** *per 1000 people*

202 *out of 266 in fewest* **violent crimes** *per 1000 people*

183 *out of 319 in per capita* **federal funds and grants**

Quality of Life Indexes (Rate per 1000 population)

Crime rate in 1991:	72.1
Violent crime rate in 1991:	7.9
Physicians rate in 1992:	2.16
Hospital bed rate in 1991:	2.37

ACCRA Cost of Living Indexes

(First quarter 1993, average = 100)

Composite index:	N/A
Utilities index:	N/A
Housing index:	N/A

Overview

Sacramento began as a city rich from gold and railroad money. Productive mines still operate in the area, and the city remains an important transportation center. Sacramento's deep-water port, connected to the San Francisco Bay via a 43-mile channel, is an important West Coast hub for the handling of cargo from ocean-going ships. As the junction of the state's major railroad, the Southern Pacific Transportation Company, Sacramento maintains its position at the top of the rail transportation industry.

The economy is broadly based: mining and transportation are supplemented by agriculture and food production, military defense, manufacturing, government, and services.

Sacramento companies produce, can and package, and market food grown in the fertile Sacramento Valley; among the region's products are fruits and vegetables, rice and other grains, meat, beet sugar, and almonds. The military and the national space program have long been a vital part of the city's economic life, although of the three defense installations—Mather Air Force Base, McClellan Air Force Base, and Sacramento Army Depot—located in the area, two are scheduled to close. Mining equipment and lumber are also produced in Sacramento. Sacramento is the state capital and the state government is one of the city's largest employers. Service industries are growing rapidly, however, and are expected to overtake government employment in the 1990s. Items and goods produced in the area include dairy products, feeds, meat, brick and clay products, rocket engines and guided missiles, mining equipment, and lumber boxes

Hotels and motels in the metropolitan area provide ten thousand rooms and offer meeting facilities for large and small groups.

The Sacramento Metropolitan Airport, 12 miles northwest of downtown, receives service from 12 major domestic airlines and five commuter airlines. Also in Sacramento, the Executive Airport serves private planes. The primary north-south routes to Sacramento are I-5 (the Pan American Highway) and U.S. 90; the major east-west routes are I-80 and U.S. 50, connecting Sacramento to San Francisco to the southwest and Lake Tahoe to the northeast.

Population (1990)

Total Population and Growth Rate

1990: 1,481,102
1980: 1,099,814
1970: 847,626
Growth rate 1970–1990: 75%

Race and Hispanic Origin

White: 79.0%
Black: 6.9%
Asian/Pacific Islander: 7.7%
Native American: 1.1%
Hispanic origin: 11.6%
White not Hispanic: 73.2%

Age

Ages 18 to 20: 4.4%
Ages 21 to 24: 6.1%
Ages 25 to 44: 34.8%
Ages 45 to 54: 9.9%
Ages 55 to 59: 4%
Ages 60 to 64: 3.9%
Ages 65 plus: 10.8%

Educational Attainment (1990)

Percent having completed high school: 82.6%
Percent having completed college: 23.4%
Elementary and high school enrollment: 251,963

Federal Funds and Grants Received
Total received in 1989: $7,746,400,000
Funds received per capita: $5,592

Civilian Labor Force
1993 (April): 789,636
1992 average: 784,443
1991 average: 764,830
1990 average: 744,203

Unemployment
1993 (April): 7.6%
1992 average: 7.9%
1991 average: 6.4%
1990 average: 4.7%

Average Annual Pay
1988: $21,933
1987: $21,047
1985: $19,220

Per Capita Personal Income
1991: $19,540
1990: $19,026
1989: $17,914

Business Climate (1987)

Manufacturing
Number of establishments in 1987: 1,415
Shipments in 1987 ($1,000): $5,495,700
Employees in 1987: 41,600
Change in employment, 1982 to 1987: 32.1%
Average annual pay for manufacturing work in 1989: $27,801
Average annual pay for production work in 1987: $20,281

Wholesale Trade
Number of establishments in 1987: 2,083
Total sales in 1987 ($1,000): $8,615,500
Change in sales, 1982 to 1987: 56.0%

Retail Trade
Number of establishments in 1987: 7,894
Total sales in 1987 ($1,000): $8,615,500
Retail sales per household in 1987: $17,218
Average annual pay in 1989: $13,106

Service Industry
Selected receipts in 1987 ($1,000): $4,092,100
Average annual pay in 1989: $20,539

Office Real Estate (1992)
Office space inventory: 33,016,000 square feet
Average class A Central Business District rental range per sq. ft: $27.00

Vacancy Rates
All areas: 15.7%

Vacancy Rates in Central Business District
Class A space: 11.0%
Class B space: 7.0%

Vacancy Rates Outside Central Business District
Class A space: 10.3%
Class B space: 24.6%

Housing
Total number of units in 1990: 609,904
Occupied units in 1990: 556,448
Owner-occupied units in 1990: 59.0%
1993 ACCRA average cost: N/A
1993 ACCRA average rent for an apartment: N/A

Chamber of Commerce
Sacramento Metro Chamber of Commerce, Donald I. Barber, CEO, 917 7th St., PO Box 1017, Sacramento, CA 95812-1017. 916-443-3771, FAX 916-443-2672

Economic Development Office
Office of Business Development, Dept. of Commerce, Janet Turner, Director, 1121 L St. #600, Sacramento, CA 95814. 916-322-5665

Economic Development Organizations
Assembly Economic Development International Trade & Technologies, Sam Farr, Director, State Capitol Bldg., Room 3120, Sacramento, CA 95814. 916-445-0424

Sacramento Area Commerce & Trade Organization, Alan Giannini, Exec Director, 300 Capitol Mall #1210, Sacramento, CA 95814-4338. 916-441-2144

Office of Small Business, Richard Nelson, Director, 1121 L Street #600, Sacramento, CA 95814. 916-445-6545

Major Businesses

Company	SIC	Telephone
Adventist Health Systems	8062	(916) 781-2000
Aerojet-General Corp.	3764	(916) 351-8500
Bel Air Mart	5411	(916) 929-6342
California Almond	5145	(916) 442-0771
Diamond Lumber Inc.	5031	(916) 483-9593
Iron-Oak Supply Corp.	5074	(916) 484-5100
MTS Inc.	5735	(916) 373-2500
MWC Inc.	5122	(916) 985-5000
Mc Clatchy Newspapers, Inc.	2711	(916) 321-1000
Mc Kenzie Realty & Investments	6162	(916) 920-3648
Mercy Healthcare Sacramento	8062	(916) 920-9400
Michigan General Corp.	5031	(916) 485-8737
Pacific Coast Building	5031	(916) 444-9304
Pacific Standard Life Insurance Co.	6311	(916) 756-3030
Puregro Co.	5191	(916) 372-7011
Raley's	5411	(916) 373-3333
Sacramento Health	6719	(916) 733-8800
Teichert, Inc.	1611	(916) 484-3011
Western Farm Credit Bank	6159	(916) 485-6000
Wickland Oil Co.	5171	(916) 921-1100

Colleges and Universities

American River College, Sacramento
California State University, Sacramento
Cosumnes River College, Sacramento
ITT Technical Institute, Sacramento
Sacramento City College, Sacramento
University of California, Davis

SALINAS–SEASIDE–MONTEREY, CA (MSA)

Geographic Profile

Land Area

3321.9 square miles

Counties and Parishes

Monterey

Ranking Highlights

42 *out of 319 in total* **land area**

85 *out of 319 in* **population growth,** *1970–1990*

297 *out of 310 in having the lowest* **unemployment** *rate*

130 *out of 310 in size of* **labor force**

105 *out of 318 in the percentage of* **college graduates**

60 *out of 292 in per capita personal* **income**

186 *out of 319 in number of* **manufacturing establishments**

238 *out of 318 in* **physicians** *per 1000 people*

313 *out of 318 in* **hospital beds** *per 1000 people*

80 *out of 267 in fewest* **crimes** *per 1000 people*

132 *out of 266 in fewest* **violent crimes** *per 1000 people*

58 *out of 319 in per capita* **federal funds and grants**

Quality of Life Indexes (Rate per 1000 population)

Crime rate in 1991:	49.2
Violent crime rate in 1991:	6.3
Physicians rate in 1992:	1.43
Hospital bed rate in 1991:	1.69

ACCRA Cost of Living Indexes

(First quarter 1993, average = 100)

Composite index:	N/A
Utilities index:	N/A
Housing index:	N/A

Overview

The Salinas-Seaside-Monterey Metropolitan Area has the same boundary as Monterey County. Monterey County is situated along the California coastline, almost at its midpoint. The county is 106 miles south of San Francisco and 241 miles north of Los Angeles. In the county's eastern portion lies the Salinas Valley, a rich agricultural center and one of the nation's major vegetable producing areas. Salinas, located eight miles from Monterey Bay and at the head of the Salinas Valley, is the county's government seat and largest city. With more than 100 major industrial and manufacturing facilities, it is the retail trade center for the region.

The county's largest industries, in terms of numbers of employees, are retail trade (18.1%), services (12.1%), government (21.2%) and agriculture (16.3%). Agriculture and agricultural related businesses remain the major employment base in Monterey County. The largest employers are Bud of California, 3,000; County of Monterey, 2,160; Household Credit, 1,800; Bruce Church, 1,500; D'Arrigo

Brothers, 1,500; Salinas Valley Memorial Hospital, 1,130; and Tanimura & Antle, 1,000.

There are 1,610 and 1,736 gross acres in the Salinas city limits zoned for light to heavy industry; about 10% to 11% is vacant and available in parcels ranging in size from 1 to 40 acres. Typical sales prices during 1989-1990 ranged from $2.25 to $3.75 per square foot. Sizes of sewer lines range from 8 to 12 inches.

The major north-south freeway, U.S. Highway 101, traverses Salinas, and State Highways 68 and 183 connect with the Monterey Peninsula. The Salinas Municipal Airport has a lighted 5,026 foot runway, flight service station and control tower. The city offers airport T-hangars and leased land and buildings. Commercial airlines serve nearby Monterey Peninsula Airport. Additional service is available through the San Jose and San Francisco International Airports, approximately two hours north. Southern Pacific's main line, with daily Amtrack service, connects with San Francisco and Los Angeles.

Commercial air flights are available from Monterey Peninsula Airport, 20 miles away. The local

Population (1990)

Total Population and Growth Rate
1990: 355,660
1980: 290,444
1970: 247,450
Growth rate 1970–1990: 44%

Race and Hispanic Origin
White: 63.8%
Black: 6.4%
Asian/Pacific Islander: 7.8%
Native American: 0.8%
Hispanic origin: 33.6%
White not Hispanic: 52.3%

Age
Ages 18 to 20: 5.5%
Ages 21 to 24: 7.6%
Ages 25 to 44: 34.2%
Ages 45 to 54: 8.4%
Ages 55 to 59: 3.5%
Ages 60 to 64: 3.5%
Ages 65 plus: 9.8%

Educational Attainment (1990)
Percent having completed high school: 72.9%
Percent having completed college: 21.5%
Elementary and high school enrollment: 63,863

Federal Funds and Grants Received ($1000)
Total received in 1989: 1,553,200
Funds received per capita: 4,454

Civilian Labor Force
1993 (April): 174,999
1992 average: 170,840
1991 average: 161,052
1990 average: 159,673

Unemployment
1993 (April): 10.0%
1992 average: 12.2%
1991 average: 10.9%
1990 average: 9.0%

Average Annual Pay
1988: $18,860
1987: $18,223
1985: $16,991

Per Capita Personal Income
1991: $19,572
1990: $19,223
1989: $18,028

Business Climate (1987)

Manufacturing
Number of establishments in 1987: 252
Shipments in 1987 ($1,000): $1,195,100
Employees in 1987: 7,800
Change in employment, 1982 to 1987: -7.1%
Average annual pay for manufacturing work in 1989: $24,081
Average annual pay for production work in 1987: $20,755

Wholesale Trade
Number of establishments in 1987: 460
Total sales in 1987 ($1,000): $1,680,200
Change in sales, 1982 to 1987: 61.3%

Retail Trade
Number of establishments in 1987: 2,220
Total sales in 1987 ($1,000): $1,680,200
Retail sales per household in 1987: $16,770
Average annual pay in 1989: $13,526

Service Industry
Selected receipts in 1987 ($1,000): $933,500
Average annual pay in 1989: $18,342

Housing
Total number of units in 1990: 121,224
Occupied units in 1990: 112,965
Owner-occupied units in 1990: 50.6%
1993 ACCRA average cost: N/A
1993 ACCRA average rent for an apartment: N/A

Chamber of Commerce
Salinas Area Chamber of Commerce, Carol Kurtz, Exec. Director, PO Box 1170, 119 E. Alisal St., Salinas, CA 93902. 408-424-7611, FAX 408-424-8639

Economic Development Office
Economic Development Corp. of Monterey County, Virginia L. Cooper, Exec. Director, 340-22 El Camino Real, S., Salinas, CA 93901. 408-754-6807, FAX 408-754-5633

Major Businesses

Company	SIC	Telephone
Antle, Bud Inc.	0723	(408) 422-8871
Associated Produce Distributors	4212	(408) 633-3335
Baillie, Jack T. Co. Inc.	0161	(408) 422-9862
Bengard, Tom Ranch Inc.	0161	(408) 422-9021
Bruhn, Dick Inc.	5651	(408) 758-4684
California Capital Insurance	6331	(408) 649-1155
Church, Bruce, Inc.	0161	(408) 758-4421
Community Hospital	8062	(408) 624-5311
D'arrigo Brothers of California	0161	(408) 424-3955
Design Professionals Insurance Co.	6351	(408) 649-5522
Fairway Stores Inc.	5411	(408) 633-3306
Fresh International Corp.	0723	(408) 422-5334
Fresh Western Marketing,	5148	(408) 758-1390
Landmark Land Company, Inc.	6552	(408) 625-4060
Lantis Corp.	3537	(408) 754-6202
Mann Packing Co., Inc.	0723	(408) 422-7405
Merrill Farms	0161	(408) 424-7365
Mills Distributing Co.	5148	(408) 424-2591
Mivco Packing Co.	0161	(408) 422-4479
Monterey Savings & Loan Association	6036	(408) 375-1500
Nunes Co. Inc.	5148	(408) 424-2704
Nunes Vegetables, Inc.	0161	(408) 757-1521
Oshita International, Inc.	0161	(408) 758-7800
Salinas Valley Ford Inc.	5511	(408) 758-4444
Salinas Valley Memorial Hospital District	8062	(408) 757-4333
Sam Linder Town Country	5511	(408) 424-6455
Vegetable Grower Supply Co.	5199	(408) 424-4897

Colleges and Universities

Hartnell College, Salinas
Monterey Institute of International Studies, Monterey
Monterey Peninsula College, Monterey

Additional Information

Community Economic Profile for Salinas, Monterey County, California. Salinas Area Chamber of Commerce, November 1990. [4p.]

Salinas-Seaside-Monterey Metropolitan Statistical Area, Annual Planning Information. State of California, Employment Development Department, June 1990. 89p.

SAN DIEGO, CA (MSA)

Geographic Profile

Land Area
4204.5 square miles

Counties and Parishes
San Diego

Additional Cities/Towns within Area
Escondido

Ranking Highlights

24 *out of 319 in total* land area
31 *out of 319 in* population growth, *1970–1990*
191 *out of 310 in having the lowest* unemployment *rate*
16 *out of 310 in size of* labor force
55 *out of 318 in the percentage of* college graduates
57 *out of 292 in per capita personal* income
22 *out of 319 in number of* manufacturing establishments
91 *out of 318 in* physicians *per 1000 people*
276 *out of 318 in* hospital beds *per 1000 people*
181 *out of 267 in fewest* crimes *per 1000 people*
219 *out of 266 in fewest* violent crimes *per 1000 people*
43 *out of 319 in per capita* federal funds and grants

Quality of Life Indexes (Rate per 1000 population)

Crime rate in 1991:	68.2
Violent crime rate in 1991:	9.7
Physicians rate in 1992:	2.27
Hospital bed rate in 1991:	2.47

ACCRA Cost of Living Indexes

(First quarter 1993, average = 100)

Composite index:	130.4
Utilities index:	72.9
Housing index:	190.0

Overview

San Diego County is approximately the same size as the state of Connecticut. It is the nineteenth most populous metropolitan area in the United States. The physical, social and economic development of the region has been influenced by its unique geography, which includes 70 miles of coastline, broad valleys, lakes, forested mountains, and the desert.

San Diego sits on the edge of the Pacific Rim and Mexican markets and is a neighbor to Tijuana, Mexico, which is the home of over 600 "Twin Plant" operations including firms such as Honeywell, Mattel, Sony and Kodak. These operations utilize San Diego's local resources and San Diego acts as the distribution and final assembly locations for most of the firms. Manufacturing is San Diego's leading industry. The aerospace, transportation, and shipbuilding sectors contribute $4 billion to the more than $14.5 billion in manufactured goods produced there annually.

Companies that develop and produce such goods as computers, electric components and telecommunication systems are responsible for the employment of over 72,000 people. The rapidly growing biotechnology industry employs over 14,000 people. Over 145 biotechnology and biomedical companies currently exist in San Diego County, making San Diego the fourth largest research and development center in the world.

Since the founding of San Diego, the city's economy has been tied to its natural harbor, which today is one of California's five major ports. It is an important link in the nation's international shipping trade; more than one hundred merchant ships from over twenty-four nations make regular stops in the harbor, which is equipped with commercial docking and loading facilities. The port's modern, well-equipped marinas accommodate private yachts, pleasure craft, and charter fishing fleets. While commercial fishing is still a viable industry, it has recently been overtaken by sport fishing.

San Diego's harbor has had the most significant impact on the local economy, however, through the Eleventh Naval District Headquarters, the base for the U.S. Navy Pacific fleet, which is located on the bay. The military/defense industry is the city's second largest economic sector. San Diego County is home to one of every five U.S. Navy ships and one in five U.S. marines, plus many major companies working on U.S. Department of Defense contracts. This segment of the economy brings in nearly $10 billion annually.

The fourth largest segment of the economy is agriculture. San Diego is the nation's top producer of nursery products, flowers, and foliage plants.

San Diego's new convention center has spurred the development of hotels and retail establishments. Other significant recent development includes the $3 billion renovation of Gaslamp Quarter and the opening of a second location of the Museum of Contemporary Art in 1993.

San Diego has a well developed highway system. Interstate 5 from Los Angeles, Nevada, and I-15 from Las Vegas meet in San Diego and continue to the Mexican border. I-8 enters San Diego from the east. San Diego's commute time to and from work ranked second best when compared to 20 other similar metropolitan cities in the nation.

Fourteen major airlines serve the major commercial airport and 27 other public, private and military airports serve the area.

Population (1990)

Total Population and Growth Rate
1990: 2,498,016
1980: 1,861,846
1970: 1,357,854
Growth rate 1970–1990: 84%

Race and Hispanic Origin
White: 74.9%
Black: 6.4%
Asian/Pacific Islander: 7.9%
Native American: 0.8%
Hispanic origin: 20.4%
White not Hispanic: 65.4%

Age
Ages 18 to 20: 5.6%
Ages 21 to 24: 8%
Ages 25 to 44: 35.2%
Ages 45 to 54: 8.8%
Ages 55 to 59: 3.5%
Ages 60 to 64: 3.6%
Ages 65 plus: 10.9%

Educational Attainment (1990)
Percent having completed high school: 81.9%
Percent having completed college: 25.3%
Elementary and high school enrollment: 397,787

Federal Funds and Grants Received
Total received in 1989: $11,531,700,000
Funds received per capita: $4,865

Civilian Labor Force
1993 (April): 1,201,554
1992 average: 1,195,619
1991 average: 1,176,266
1990 average: 1,174,577

Unemployment
1993 (April): 7.6%
1992 average: 7.4%
1991 average: 6.1%
1990 average: 4.4%

Average Annual Pay
1988: $22,183
1987: $21,051
1985: $19,154

Per Capita Personal Income
1991: $19,799
1990: $19,341
1989: $18,824

Business Climate (1987)

Manufacturing
Number of establishments in 1987: 3,041
Shipments in 1987 ($1,000): $10,996,600
Employees in 1987: 120,000
Change in employment, 1982 to 1987: 7.6%
Average annual pay for manufacturing work in 1989: $29,966
Average annual pay for production work in 1987: $20,313

Wholesale Trade
Number of establishments in 1987: 3,415
Total sales in 1987 ($1,000): $9,950,200
Change in sales, 1982 to 1987: 36.4%

Retail Trade
Number of establishments in 1987: 12,733
Total sales in 1987 ($1,000): $9,950,200
Retail sales per household in 1987: $18,111
Average annual pay in 1989: $13,201

Service Industry
Selected receipts in 1987 ($1,000): $8,938,000
Average annual pay in 1989: $21,606

Office Real Estate (1992)
Office space inventory: 43,076,205 square feet
Average class A Central Business District rental range per sq. ft: $18.00

Vacancy Rates
All areas: 17.0%

Vacancy Rates in Central Business District
Class A space: 16.2%
Class B space: 21.6%

Vacancy Rates Outside Central Business District
Class A space: 18.0%
Class B space: 13.9%

Housing
Total number of units in 1990: 946,240
Occupied units in 1990: 887,403
Owner-occupied units in 1990: 53.8%
1993 ACCRA average cost: $223,600
1993 ACCRA average rent for an apartment: $900

Chamber of Commerce
Greater San Diego Chamber of Commerce, Lee Grissom, President, 110 W. C St. #1600, San Diego, CA 92101. 619-232-0124

Economic Development Office
Economic Development Corp., Daniel Pegg, President, 701 B St. #1850, San Diego, CA 92101. 619-234-8484, FAX 619-234-1935

Economic Development Organizations
San Diego Unified Port District, Don L. Nay, Port Director, 3165 Pacific Highway, PO Box 488, San Diego, CA 92112. 619-291-3900, 800-854-275

Major Businesses

Company	SIC	Telephone
Advanced Marketing Service	5192	(619) 581-2232
Big Bear Super Market	5411	(619) 263-3161
Bumble Bee Seafoods Inc.	2091	(619) 560-0404
Cipher Data Products, Inc.	3572	(619) 693-7200
Cubic Corp.	3699	(619) 277-6780
Ellco Leasing Corp.	7377	(619) 458-4400
First Capital Life Insurance	6311	(619) 452-9060
Foodmaker, Inc.	5812	(619) 571-2121
Forte Hotels International	7011	(619) 448-1884

Major Businesses (Continued)

Company	SIC	Telephone
General Dynmics Commercial	4789	(619) 496-4000
Golden Eagle Insurance Co.	6331	(619) 463-5800
Great American Savings Bank	6036	(619) 231-1885
Hahn, Ernest W. Inc.	6512	(619) 546-1001
Home Federal Corp.	6035	(619) 699-8000
Homefed Bank	6035	(619) 699-8000
Imperial Corp. of America	6411	(619) 292-3000
Intermark Inc.	5712	(619) 459-3841
JWP West Inc.	1711	(619) 283-3181
Kyocera America, Inc.	3253	(619) 576-2600
National Shipbuilding Company	3731	(619) 696-7000
Ocean Garden Products Inc.	5146	(619) 571-5002
Pacific Diversified Capital Co.	3829	(619) 571-7322
Paragon Restaurant Group	5812	(619) 292-8050
Price Co.	5199	(619) 581-4600
Rohr Industries, Inc.	3728	(619) 691-4111
San Diego Gas & Electric Co.	4911	(619) 696-2000
San Diego Hospital Association	8062	(619) 541-4375
Sanyo Manufacturing Corp.	3651	(619) 661-6029
Science Applications International	8731	(619) 546-6000
Scripps Memorial Corp.	8062	(619) 457-4123
Security Pacific Financial Systems	6141	(619) 578-6150
Solar Turbines, Inc.	3511	(619) 544-5000
Southwest Marine Inc.	3731	(619) 238-1000
Triton Group Ltd.	3724	(619) 459-3841
Trusthouse Forte Inc.	7011	(619) 355-4545
VSR Acquisition Corp.	5812	(619) 292-8050
Wimpey, George Inc.	1521	(619) 260-1109

Colleges and Universities
Kelsey Jenney Business College, San Diego
National University, San Diego
Point Loma Nazarene College, San Diego
San Diego City College, San Diego
San Diego MESA College, San Diego
San Diego Miramar College, San Diego
San Diego State University, San Diego
United States International University, San Diego
University of San Diego, San Diego

SAN FRANCISCO, CA (PMSA)

Geographic Profile

Land Area

1015.6 square miles

Counties and Parishes

Marin

San Francisco

San Mateo

Ranking Highlights

198 *out of 319 in total* **land area**

230 *out of 319 in* **population growth,** *1970–1990*

104 *out of 310 in having the lowest* **unemployment** *rate*

27 *out of 310 in size of* **labor force**

9 *out of 318 in the percentage of* **college graduates**

1 *out of 292 in per capita personal* **income**

21 *out of 319 in number of* **manufacturing establishments**

10 *out of 318 in* **physicians** *per 1000 people*

178 *out of 318 in* **hospital beds** *per 1000 people*

177 *out of 267 in fewest* **crimes** *per 1000 people*

224 *out of 266 in fewest* **violent crimes** *per 1000 people*

100 *out of 319 in per capita* **federal funds and grants**

Quality of Life Indexes (Rate per 1000 population)

Crime rate in 1991:	67.9
Violent crime rate in 1991:	9.8
Physicians rate in 1992:	4.21
Hospital bed rate in 1991:	3.6

ACCRA Cost of Living Indexes

(First quarter 1993, average = 100)

Composite index:	N/A
Utilities index:	N/A
Housing index:	N/A

Overview

San Francisco is one of the few truly international cities in the United States. Almost half of the inhabitants of the Bay Area were born outside of the United States or have at least one non-native parent. The city is a major financial and insurance center, an international port, and the gateway to Silicon Valley, America's premier high-technology center. The consistently spring-like weather and unique atmosphere attract corporations as well as visitors.

Because of its natural, landlocked harbor, San Francisco has profited from trade and shipping since its early days. Today, more than forty deep-water piers serve ships from every nation. Rivers heading inland connect the port with the major agricultural areas of the Sacramento and San Joaquin valleys, providing easy access to international markets. The major imported goods are crude oil and petroleum products, followed closely by agricultural products, mainly green coffee, which is processed at numerous plants in the area. Shipping provides eighty thousand jobs and nearly $11 billion in annual revenue.

The city is also a major financial center, home to the U.S. headquarters of two of the world's five largest banks, as well as the nation's largest bank and a number of major insurance companies, including Transamerica and Fireman's Fund. Over eighty foreign banks maintain branches in the city, as does the Federal Reserve, the United States Mint, and numerous other U.S. banks. San Francisco is also the site of the Pacific Stock Exchange.

Nearby Silicon Valley, along with Stanford University, are considered to be among the places where the worldwide technology boom began, and they remain on the leading edge today. More than one thousand San Francisco area companies produce computers, semiconductors and related components, scientific instruments, and various other electronic systems and equipment. Aerospace industries such as the National Aeronautic and Space Administration (NASA) and Lockheed also maintain major research facilities in the area.

Another emerging high-technology industry is medical science; nearly one hundred companies in the Bay Area are setting the pace in research and development of pharmaceutical products, medical electronics, bionics, and genetic engineering. Almost one third of the total worldwide biotechnology workforce is employed in San Francisco and the surrounding region. Other prominent industries include tourism, which employs over sixty thousand area residents; fashion apparel, with over one thousand companies in retail sales and manufacturing; and restaurants, with over twenty-five hundred outlets leading the nation in sales per capita.

The city of San Francisco hosts nearly one thousand conventions annually. The city has nearly thirty thousand hotel rooms available, having increased its room inventory 16 percent between 1988 and 1992. All the rooms are within easy traveling distance of the main convention sites. Most of the major hotels in the area provide ample meeting space, ballrooms, registration lobbies, and exhibit areas.

The San Francisco International Airport is the fifth busiest in the nation, handling more than thirteen hundred flights a day from thirty-four major airlines. An efficient customs clearance, modern facilities, and computerized ground transportation information make the airport easy to use. Many of the downtown hotels offer free transportation to and from the airport.

The city is at the intersection of several major highways. U.S. 101 and S.R. 1, the Pacific Coastal Highway, converge on San Francisco from the north and south. From the east, Interstate 80 and U.S. 50 serve the city. Interstate Loops 580 and 680 provide access to Interstate 5, the major north-south route from Canada to Mexico.

Population (1990)

Total Population and Growth Rate

1990: 1,603,678

1980: 1,488,895
1970: 1,481,687
Growth rate 1970–1990: 8%

Race and Hispanic Origin
White: 66.0%
Black: 87.6%
Asian/Pacific Islander: 20.6%
Native American: 0.5%
Hispanic origin: 14.5%
White not Hispanic: 57.6%

Age
Ages 18 to 20: 3.5%
Ages 21 to 24: 6.1%
Ages 25 to 44: 37.9%
Ages 45 to 54: 11.3%
Ages 55 to 59: 4.4%
Ages 60 to 64: 4.4%
Ages 65 plus: 13.3%

Educational Attainment (1990)
Percent having completed high school: 82.4%
Percent having completed college: 34.9%
Elementary and high school enrollment: 205,112

Federal Funds and Grants Received
Total received in 1989: $5,676,800,000
Funds received per capita: $3,570

Civilian Labor Force
1993 (April): 885,264
1992 average: 878,085
1991 average: 869,408
1990 average: 875,537

Unemployment
1993 (April): 5.9%
1992 average: 6.1%
1991 average: 4.8%
1990 average: 3.5%

Average Annual Pay
1988: $27,859
1987: $26,594
1985: $24,146

Per Capita Personal Income
1991: $30,555
1990: $29,828
1989: $27,802

Business Climate (1987)
Manufacturing
Number of establishments in 1987: 3,153
Shipments in 1987 ($1,000): $9,053,100
Employees in 1987: 81,900
Change in employment, 1982 to 1987: -12.2%
Average annual pay for manufacturing work in 1989: $32,469

Average annual pay for production work in 1987: $19,681
Wholesale Trade
Number of establishments in 1987: 4,621
Total sales in 1987 ($1,000): $27,282,500
Change in sales, 1982 to 1987: 11.2%
Retail Trade
Number of establishments in 1987: 12,455
Total sales in 1987 ($1,000): $27,282,500
Retail sales per household in 1987: $18,519
Average annual pay in 1989: $15,956
Service Industry
Selected receipts in 1987 ($1,000): $13,378,900
Average annual pay in 1989: $26,156

Office Real Estate (1992)
Office space inventory: 58,232,000 square feet
Average class A Central Business District rental range per sq. ft: $22.63
Vacancy Rates
All areas: 15.5%
Vacancy Rates in Central Business District
Class A space: 14.9%
Class B space: 16.5%
Vacancy Rates Outside Central Business District
Class A space: 11.0%
Class B space: 17.8%

Housing
Total number of units in 1990: 680,010
Occupied units in 1990: 642,504
Owner-occupied units in 1990: 48.3%
1993 ACCRA average cost: N/A
1993 ACCRA average rent for an apartment: N/A

Chamber of Commerce
San Francisco Chamber of Commerce, Harry Orbelian, Sr. Vice President, 465 California St., San Francisco, CA 94104. 415-392-4511

Economic Development Office
San Francisco Economic Development Corp., Kent O. Sims, President, 465 California St. #831, San Francisco, CA 94104. 415-381-1209

Economic Development Organizations
Mission Economic Development Association, Roberto Barragan, Exec Director, 2601 Mission Street, 9th fl., San Francisco, CA 94110. 415-282-3334

Major Businesses

Company	SIC	Telephone
Bank /America National Trust & Savings Association	6021	(415) 622-3657
Bankamerica Corp.	6021	(415) 622-2091
Bechtel Corp.	1629	(415) 768-1234

Major Businesses (Continued)

Company	SIC	Telephone
Bechtel Group, Inc.	1629	(415) 768-1234
California Physicians Service	6324	(415) 445-5000
Chevron Chemical Co.	2821	(415) 842-5500
Chevron Corp.	2911	(415) 894-7700
Chevron U.S.A., Inc.	1311	(415) 894-7700
Consolidated Freightways	4213	(415) 326-1700
Dalgety, Inc.	5113	(415) 572-8000
Federal Home Loan Bank San Francisco	6111	(415) 393-1000
Federal Reserve	6019	(415) 974-2000
Firemans Fund Insurance Co.	6331	(415) 899-2000
First Nationwide Financial	6035	(415) 772-1400
Fleming Foods West, Inc.	5141	(415) 847-4000
Kaiser Foundation Health	6324	(415) 271-5910
Kaiser Foundation Hospital	8062	(415) 271-5910
Lucky Stores, Inc.	5411	(415) 833-6000
McKesson Corp.	5122	(415) 983-8300
Mervyn's	5311	(415) 785-8800
Pacific Bell	4813	(415) 542-9000
Pacific Gas and Electric Co.	4911	(415) 972-7000
Pacific Telesis Group	4813	(415) 394-3000
Safeway Stores, Inc.	5411	(415) 891-3000
Southern Pacific Transportation Co.	4011	(415) 541-1000
Strauss, Levi Associates	2325	(415) 544-6000
Transamerica Corp.	6311	(415) 983-4000
Wells Fargo & Co.	6021	(415) 396-7403
Wells Fargo Bank	6021	(415) 396-0123

Colleges and Universities

Academy of Art College, San Francisco

City College of San Francisco, San Francisco

Fashion Institute of Design and Merchandising, San Francisco Campus, San Francisco

Golden Gate University, San Francisco

Heald Business College, San Francisco

Heald Institute of Technology, San Francisco

Lincoln University, San Francisco

Los Angeles Mission College, San Fernando

Louise Salinger Academy of Fashion, San Francisco

New College of California, San Francisco

San Francisco Art Institute, San Francisco

San Francisco College of Mortuary Science, San Francisco

San Francisco Conservatory of Music, San Francisco

San Francisco State University, San Francisco

University of California, San Francisco, San Francisco

University of San Francisco, San Francisco

SAN JOSE, CA (PMSA)

Geographic Profile

Land Area

1291.2 square miles

Counties and Parishes

Santa Clara

Additional Cities/Towns within Area

Palo Alto

Ranking Highlights

151 *out of 319 in total* land area

96 *out of 319 in* population growth, *1970–1990*

149 *out of 310 in having the lowest* unemployment *rate*

29 *out of 310 in size of* labor force

16 *out of 318 in the percentage of* college graduates

6 *out of 292 in per capita personal* income

19 *out of 319 in number of* manufacturing establishments

61 *out of 318 in* physicians *per 1000 people*

289 *out of 318 in* hospital beds *per 1000 people*

82 *out of 267 in fewest* crimes *per 1000 people*

113 *out of 266 in fewest* violent crimes *per 1000 people*

36 *out of 319 in per capita* federal funds and grants

Quality of Life Indexes (Rate per 1000 population)

Crime rate in 1991:	50.4
Violent crime rate in 1991:	5.2
Physicians rate in 1992:	2.52
Hospital bed rate in 1991:	2.23

ACCRA Cost of Living Indexes

(First quarter 1993, average = 100)

Composite index:	N/A
Utilities index:	N/A
Housing index:	N/A

Overview

The rapid expansion of high-technology industries triggered uninterrupted growth in the Silicon Valley—San Jose and Santa Clara County—from the 1950s through the early 1980s. The 1985 recession, however, left a stagnant economy, pointing to a need to diversify the economic base of the area. Studies have indicated, specifically, that high-technology companies must move toward decreased reliance on the defense industry. Already progress is apparent, with businesses in San Jose and Santa Clara County showing less than 20 percent of their budgets devoted to government contracts. The city was encouraged by a 1992 study that reported the nation's beleaguered semiconductor industry claimed 43.8 percent of the world market, up from a low of 36.9 percent in 1988.

Manufacturing continues to be an important sector of the metropolitan area economy, accounting for nearly a third of the labor force. San Jose maintains its traditional ties with agriculture as the processing and shipping center for fruits, vegetables, wines, and spirits produced in the region. Items and goods produced in the area include canning and dried-fruit packing machinery, missiles, rocket boosters, computers, atomic electrical equipment, fruit, vegetable, and fish cans, dairy products, chemicals, aluminum, paint, fiberglass, and matches

A major recent development in San Jose is the $140 million convention center, which has spurred the development and renovation of nearby hotels. Other developments include the new San Jose Arena and a cultural center and commercial complex to be built in historic Japantown.

Forty-eight percent of the traffic at San Jose International Airport is business related, which makes the facility an important factor in the Silicon Valley economy. Revenues from freight shipments average more than $10 million annually. Three air cargo carriers and nine air freight services maintain facilities at the airport. Two major rail freight lines and a number of motor freight carriers also operate in the metropolitan area.

Three interstate highways serve San Jose: I-680 (north-south), which becomes I-280 (east-west); I-880 (north-south); and I-101 (northeast-southwest).

Population (1990)

Total Population and Growth Rate
1990: 1,497,577
1980: 1,295,071
1970: 1,065,313
Growth rate 1970–1990: 41%

Race and Hispanic Origin
White: 68.9%
Black: 3.8%
Asian/Pacific Islander: 17.5%
Native American: 0.6%
Hispanic origin: 21.0%
White not Hispanic: 58.1%

Age
Ages 18 to 20: 4.7%
Ages 21 to 24: 6.7%
Ages 25 to 44: 37.5%
Ages 45 to 54: 10.9%
Ages 55 to 59: 4%
Ages 60 to 64: 3.5%
Ages 65 plus: 8.7%

Educational Attainment (1990)
Percent having completed high school: 9.9820%
Percent having completed college: 32.6%
Elementary and high school enrollment: 237,043

Federal Funds and Grants Received
Total received in 1989: $7,369,200,000
Funds received per capita: $5,146

Civilian Labor Force
1993 (April): 822,414
1992 average: 821,953
1991 average: 814,876
1990 average: 817,658

Unemployment
1993 (April): 6.6%
1992 average: 6.8%
1991 average: 5.5%
1990 average: 4.0%

Average Annual Pay
1988: $29,521
1987: $27,748
1985: $25,050

Per Capita Personal Income
1991: $25,955
1990: $25,201
1989: $23,913

Business Climate (1987)

Manufacturing
Number of establishments in 1987: 3,298
Shipments in 1987 ($1,000): $32,056,600
Employees in 1987: 275,700
Change in employment, 1982 to 1987: -0.3%
Average annual pay for manufacturing work in 1989: $40,822
Average annual pay for production work in 1987: $24,500

Wholesale Trade
Number of establishments in 1987: 2,886
Total sales in 1987 ($1,000): $21,700,500
Change in sales, 1982 to 1987: 76.3%

Retail Trade
Number of establishments in 1987: 7,991
Total sales in 1987 ($1,000): $21,700,500
Retail sales per household in 1987: $20,335
Average annual pay in 1989: $14,872

Service Industry
Selected receipts in 1987 ($1,000): $8,516,400
Average annual pay in 1989: $26,606

Housing
Total number of units in 1990: 540,240
Occupied units in 1990: 520,180
Owner-occupied units in 1990: 59.1%
1993 ACCRA average cost: N/A
1993 ACCRA average rent for an apartment: N/A

Chamber of Commerce
San Jose Chamber of Commerce, Steven J. Tedesco, President, 180 S. Market St., PO Box 611208, San Jose, CA 95161-1208. 408-998-7000

Economic Development Office
San Jose Development Corp., Richard Rios, President, 380

N. First St. #202, San Jose, CA 95112. 408-298-8455

Major Businesses

Company	SIC	Telephone
Advanced Micro Devices	3674	(408) 732-2400
Amdahl Corp.	3571	(408) 746-6000
Apple Computer Inc.	3571	(408) 996-1010
Businessland, Inc.	5734	(408) 437-0400
Conner Peripherals, Inc.	3572	(408) 433-3340
Emery Air Freight Corp.	4513	(408) 855-9100
Fujitsu America Inc.	3575	(408) 432-1300
Fujitsu Microelectronics	3674	(408) 922-9000
Hewlett-Packard Co.	3571	(415) 857-1501
Hitachi Data Systems Corp.	5045	(408) 970-1000
Intel Corp.	3674	(408) 987-8080
Lockheed Missiles & Space	3761	(408) 742-4321
LSI Logic Corp.	3674	(408) 433-8000
National Semiconductor Co.	3674	(408) 721-5000
NEC Electronics Inc.	3674	(415) 960-6000
Sun Microsystems, Inc.	3571	(415) 960-1300
Syntex (USA) Inc.	2834	(415) 855-5050
Syntex Laboratories Inc.	2834	(415) 855-5050
Tandem Computers Inc.	3571	(408) 725-6000
Varian Associates Inc.	3671	(415) 493-4000

Colleges and Universities

Evergreen Valley College, San Jose
Heald Institute of Technology, San Jose
National Hispanic University, San Jose
San Jose Christian College, San Jose
San Jose City College, San Jose
San Jose State University, San Jose

SANTA BARBARA–SANTA MARIA–LOMPOC, CA (MSA)

Geographic Profile

Land Area
2738.5 square miles

Counties and Parishes
Santa Barbara

Ranking Highlights

 58 *out of 319 in total* **land area**
 98 *out of 319 in* **population growth,** *1970–1990*
212 *out of 310 in having the lowest* **unemployment** *rate*
119 *out of 310 in size of* **labor force**
 44 *out of 318 in the percentage of* **college graduates**
 20 *out of 292 in per capita personal* **income**
110 *out of 319 in number of* **manufacturing establishments**
 84 *out of 318 in* **physicians** *per 1000 people*
256 *out of 318 in* **hospital beds** *per 1000 people*
 75 *out of 267 in fewest* **crimes** *per 1000 people*
102 *out of 266 in fewest* **violent crimes** *per 1000 people*
 59 *out of 319 in per capita* **federal funds and grants**

Quality of Life Indexes (Rate per 1000 population)

Crime rate in 1991:	48.5
Violent crime rate in 1991:	5.0
Physicians rate in 1992:	2.35
Hospital bed rate in 1991:	2.79

ACCRA Cost of Living Indexes

(First quarter 1993, average = 100)
Composite index:	N/A
Utilities index:	N/A
Housing index:	N/A

Overview

Santa Maria Public Airport is served by Delta Connection, American Eagle, and United Express.

Lompoc is located on California State Highways 1 and 246, 55 miles north of Santa Barbara and 155 miles north of Los Angeles. Rail service is provided by the Southern Pacific Railroad. Lompoc Airport offers charter service, and general air services. Airline service from Santa Barbara and Santa Maria connects to major California terminals and other national points.

Population (1990)

Total Population and Growth Rate
1990: 369,608
1980: 298,694
1970: 264,324
Growth rate 1970–1990: 40%

Race and Hispanic Origin
White: 77.2%

Black: 2.8%
Asian/Pacific Islander: 4.4%
Native American: 0.9%
Hispanic origin: 26.6%
White not Hispanic: 66.1%

Age
Ages 18 to 20: 6.6%
Ages 21 to 24: 8%
Ages 25 to 44: 32.7%
Ages 45 to 54: 9.3%
Ages 55 to 59: 3.9%
Ages 60 to 64: 3.9%
Ages 65 plus: 12.3%

Educational Attainment (1990)
Percent having completed high school: 80.0%
Percent having completed college: 26.6%
Elementary and high school enrollment: 56,308

Federal Funds and Grants Received ($1000)
Total received in 1989: 1,526,000
Funds received per capita: 4,447

Civilian Labor Force
1993 (April): 183,390
1992 average: 184,102
1991 average: 183,475
1990 average: 181,033

Unemployment
1993 (April): 7.3%
1992 average: 7.8%
1991 average: 6.0%
1990 average: 4.5%

Average Annual Pay
1988: $21,111
1987: $20,389
1985: $18,957

Per Capita Personal Income
1991: $22,611
1990: $21,607
1989: $20,942

Business Climate (1987)
Manufacturing
Number of establishments in 1987: 523
Shipments in 1987 ($1,000): $1,733,600
Employees in 1987: 20,200
Change in employment, 1982 to 1987: 2.5%
Average annual pay for manufacturing work in 1989: $32,734
Average annual pay for production work in 1987: $19,058

Wholesale Trade
Number of establishments in 1987: 538
Total sales in 1987 ($1,000): $1,114,300
Change in sales, 1982 to 1987: 26.8%

Retail Trade
Number of establishments in 1987: 2,512
Total sales in 1987 ($1,000): $1,114,300
Retail sales per household in 1987: $17,609
Average annual pay in 1989: $12,283

Service Industry
Selected receipts in 1987 ($1,000): $1,447,500
Average annual pay in 1989: $20,975

Housing
Total number of units in 1990: 138,149
Occupied units in 1990: 129,802
Owner-occupied units in 1990: 54.7%
1993 ACCRA average cost: N/A
1993 ACCRA average rent for an apartment: N/A

Chamber of Commerce
Santa Barbara County Chamber of Commerce, Steve Cushman, Exec. Director, 504 State Street, PO Box 299, Santa Barbara, CA 93103. 805-965-3023, FAX 805-966-5954

Economic Development Office
Santa Maria Valley Chamber of Commerce, PO Box 377, 614 S. Broadway, Santa Maria, CA 93454. 805-925-2403, FAX 805-928-7559

Economic Development Organizations
Santa Maria Valley Economic Development Association, Bob Boyster, Exec. director, 428E S. Broadway, Santa Maria, CA 93454. 805-922-7737, FAX 805-349-9875

Economic Development Association, Bob Royster, Director, 428R S. Broadway, Santa Maria, CA 93454. 805-922-7737

Private Industry Council, Frank Bartilet, Exec. Director, 228C W. Carrillo, Santa Barbara, CA 93103. 805-568-2286

Board of Realtors of Santa Maria, 222 West Carmen Ln., Santa Maria, CA 93454. 805-568-2286

Lompoc Valley Chamber of Commerce, Robert P. Hatch, Exec. Vice President, 111 S. I St., Lompoc, CA 93436. 805-736-4567

Lompoc Valley Board of Realtors, Sheila Centeno, PO Box 698139 N. G St., Lompoc, CA 93436. 805-736-1288

Community Development Dept., City of Lompoc (Zoning Information), 100 Civic Center Plaza, Lompoc, CA 93438. 805-736-2341

California State Employment Development Dept., 304 W. Carmen, Santa Maria, CA 93454. 805-734-3433

Industrial Sites
Skyway Business Park, Skyway Drive, Santa Maria, CA 93455.

There are approximately 190 acres of industrial land available in Lompoc. Parcels of 0.5 to 40 acres are offered within the city limits. Prices for undeveloped land start at $30,000 to $45,000 per acre.

The Central Ave. Specific Plan (130 acres). Located adjacent to the Lompoc Airport, includes parcels from one acre to 40 acres in size. All accessible to city services and utilities, the City of Lompoc adopted a specific plan to encourage business park and industrial firms to locate in the area. For more information, contact: Mr. Gene L. Wahlers, City Administration, Lompoc City Hall, 100 Civic Center Plaza, Lompoc, CA 93438. 805-736-1261.

Major Businesses

Company	SIC	Telephone
A-M Homes	1521	(805) 965-0550
Applied Magnetics Corp.	3572	(805) 683-5353
Carrows Restaurants Inc.	5812	(805) 963-7805
Casino USA Inc.	5141	(805) 564-6700
County Bank	6035	(805) 682-2400
Financial Corp. Santa Barbara	6036	(805) 963-9252
General Research Corp.	8732	(805) 964-7724
Jordanos' Inc.	5181	(805) 964-0611
Mentor Corp.	3842	(805) 967-3451
Mission Industries	7213	(805) 682-8588
Mission Research Corp.	8731	(805) 963-8761
Nanco Enterprises Inc.	3589	(805) 564-1410
Pacific Beverages Co. Inc.	5181	(805) 964-0611
Richards, R. P. Inc.	1711	(805) 683-1511
Santa Barbara Bancorp	6022	(805) 564-6300
Santa Barbara Bank And Trust	6022	(805) 564-6300
Santa Barbara Research	8731	(805) 968-3511
Santa Barbara Cottage Hospital	8062	(805) 682-7111
Santa Barbara Savings & Loan Association	6035	(805) 682-5000
Soverign Life Insurance of California	6311	(805) 963-7871
Williams Brothers Markets Inc.	5411	(805) 922-7373

Colleges and Universities

Allan Hancock College, Santa Maria
Antioch University Santa Barbara, Santa Barbara
Brooks Institute of Photography, Santa Barbara
Santa Barbara City College, Santa Barbara
University of California, Santa Barbara, Santa Barbara

Additional Information

Lompoc 1990, Community and Economic Profile. Lompoc Valley Chamber of Commerce, n.d. 6p.

SANTA CRUZ, CA (PMSA)

Geographic Profile

Land Area
445.8 square miles

Counties and Parishes
Santa Cruz

Ranking Highlights

305　*out of 319 in total* **land area**
　28　*out of 319 in* **population growth,** *1970–1990*
266　*out of 310 in having the lowest* **unemployment** *rate*
142　*out of 310 in size of* **labor force**
　28　*out of 318 in the percentage of* **college graduates**
　23　*out of 292 in per capita personal* **income**
145　*out of 319 in number of* **manufacturing establishments**
171　*out of 318 in* **physicians** *per 1000 people*
312　*out of 318 in* **hospital beds** *per 1000 people*
118　*out of 267 in fewest* **crimes** *per 1000 people*
116　*out of 266 in fewest* **violent crimes** *per 1000 people*
308　*out of 319 in per capita* **federal funds and grants**

Quality of Life Indexes (Rate per 1000 population)

Crime rate in 1991:	58.4
Violent crime rate in 1991:	5.3
Physicians rate in 1992:	1.76
Hospital bed rate in 1991:	1.7

ACCRA Cost of Living Indexes

(First quarter 1993, average = 100)
Composite index:　N/A
Utilities index:　N/A
Housing index:　N/A

Overview

The Santa Cruz Metropolitan Statistical Area comprises all of Santa Cruz County. Two-thirds of the county is considered to be forest land by the United States Dept. of Agriculture. Within its borders are six State Parks. Santa Cruz County is a vacation and recreation area. The City of Santa Cruz, the largest city and the county seat, features beaches and a boardwalk.

Four major highways connect Santa Cruz with adjacent counties. Highway 1 leads along the coast. Highways 9 and 17 traverse the county from the City of Santa Cruz across the Santa Cruz mountains into Santa Clara County. Highway 152 leads to neighboring Santa Clara County.

Population (1990)

Total Population and Growth Rate
1990: 229,734
1980: 188,141
1970: 123,790
Growth rate 1970–1990: 86%

Race and Hispanic Origin
White: 83.9%
Black: 1.1%
Asian/Pacific Islander: 3.7%
Native American: 0.8%
Hispanic origin: 20.4%
White not Hispanic: 74.5%

Age
Ages 18 to 20: 5.6%
Ages 21 to 24: 6.6%
Ages 25 to 44: 36.4%
Ages 45 to 54: 9.7%
Ages 55 to 59: 3.3%
Ages 60 to 64: 3.3%
Ages 65 plus: 11.3%

Educational Attainment (1990)
Percent having completed high school: 81.9%
Percent having completed college: 29.7%
Elementary and high school enrollment: 36,017

Federal Funds and Grants Received
Total received in 1989: $431,500,000
Funds received per capita: $1,903

Civilian Labor Force
1993 (April):　149,660
1992 average:　144,502
1991 average:　141,045
1990 average:　135,807

Unemployment
1993 (April):　8.1%
1992 average:　9.2%
1991 average:　8.0%
1990 average:　6.3%

Average Annual Pay
1988: $18,702
1987: $17,959
1985: $15,826

Per Capita Personal Income
1991: $22,554
1990: $21,558
1989: $18,799

Business Climate (1987)
Manufacturing
Number of establishments in 1987: 375
Shipments in 1987 ($1,000): $2,076,700
Employees in 1987: 12,200
Change in employment, 1982 to 1987: 8.0%
Average annual pay for manufacturing work in 1989: $25,481
Average annual pay for production work in 1987: $17,571

Wholesale Trade
Number of establishments in 1987: 328

Total sales in 1987 ($1,000): $893,000
Change in sales, 1982 to 1987: 70.7%

Retail Trade
Number of establishments in 1987: 1,541
Total sales in 1987 ($1,000): $893,000
Retail sales per household in 1987: $17,759
Average annual pay in 1989: $12,578

Service Industry
Selected receipts in 1987 ($1,000): $601,500
Average annual pay in 1989: $19,104

Housing
Total number of units in 1990: 91,878
Occupied units in 1990: 83,566
Owner-occupied units in 1990: 59.9%
1993 ACCRA average cost: N/A
1993 ACCRA average rent for an apartment: N/A

Chamber of Commerce
Santa Cruz Area Chamber of Commerce, John Lisher, Exec. Director, 1543 Pacific Ave., PO Box 921, Santa Cruz, CA 95061. 408-423-1111

Economic Development Office
City of Santa Cruz, Dept. of Planning and Community Development, Kathy Barbara, Principal Planner, 809 Center, Room 206, Santa Cruz, CA 95060. 408-429-3441

Major Businesses

Company	SIC	Telephone
A C S Communications Inc.	3661	(408) 438-3883
Beta Technology, Inc.	3561	(408) 426-5890
Beverly Fabrics Inc.	5949	(408) 475-2811
Bogard Construction Inc.	1542	(408) 426-8191
Borland International Inc.	7371	(408) 438-8400
Coastal Berry Corp.	4213	(408) 724-1366
Dominican Santa Cruz Hospital	8062	(408) 462-7700
E-MU Systems, Inc.	3931	(408) 438-1921
Fmali Herb Co Inc.	2099	(408) 423-7913
Ford, Charles Co. Inc.	5311	(408) 722-3341
Granite Construction Co.	1611	(408) 724-1011
Holcomb Corp.	1531	(408) 688-6807
Inn Foods, Inc.	5142	(408) 724-2026
Interphase Technologies	3663	(408) 426-2007
NHS Inc.	3949	(408) 475-9434
Naturipe Berry Growers	0723	(408) 722-2430
New West Fruit Corp.	5148	(408) 728-1773
North Bay Ford-Lincoln-Mercury	5511	(408) 423-4550
Salz Leathers, Inc.	3111	(408) 423-4470
San Lorenzo Lumber Co. Inc.	5211	(408) 426-1020
Santa Cruz Motors	5511	(408) 427-1155
Santa Cruz Operation Inc.	7371	(408) 425-7222
Santa Cruz Seaside Co.	7996	(408) 423-5590
Seagate Technology, Inc.	3572	(408) 438-6550

Major Businesses (Continued)

Company	SIC	Telephone
Shaw, Richard A. Inc.	0723	(408) 728-2281
Skyway Freight Systems Inc.	4731	(408) 722-3133
Southwest Truck Service	4213	(408) 724-8514
Threshold Enterprises Ltd.	2833	(408) 438-6851
U. S. Flowers	5193	(408) 722-2912
Watsonville Community Hospital	8062	(408) 724-4741

Colleges and Universities

University of California, Santa Cruz, Santa Cruz

Additional Information

Santa Cruz, Metropolitan Statistical Area, Annual Planning Information. State of California, Employment Development Dept., June 1990. 86p.

SANTA ROSA-PETALUMA, CA (PMSA)

Geographic Profile

Land Area

1576.2 square miles

Counties and Parishes

Sonoma

Ranking Highlights

125 *out of 319 in total* **land area**

24 *out of 319 in* **population growth**, *1970–1990*

174 *out of 310 in having the lowest* **unemployment** *rate*

103 *out of 310 in size of* **labor force**

69 *out of 318 in the percentage of* **college graduates**

25 *out of 292 in per capita personal* **income**

96 *out of 319 in number of* **manufacturing establishments**

100 *out of 318 in* **physicians** *per 1000 people*

303 *out of 318 in* **hospital beds** *per 1000 people*

68 *out of 267 in fewest* **crimes** *per 1000 people*

88 *out of 266 in fewest* **violent crimes** *per 1000 people*

257 *out of 319 in per capita* **federal funds and grants**

Quality of Life Indexes (Rate per 1000 population)

Crime rate in 1991:	46.8
Violent crime rate in 1991:	4.4
Physicians rate in 1992:	2.22
Hospital bed rate in 1991:	2.06

ACCRA Cost of Living Indexes

(First quarter 1993, average = 100)

Composite index:	N/A
Utilities index:	N/A
Housing index:	N/A

Overview

Located in a narrow valley at the top of San Pablo Bay, with the Sonoma Mountains to the east and a range of low hills to the west, Petaluma sits astride Highway 101, 38 miles from San Francisco to the south and 20 miles from the Pacific coastline to the west. Through Highway 116, Petaluma connects with Highway 37 and Interstate 80 serving Central Valley points. The Petaluma River penetrates the heart of the city.

Rail Service is provided by Northwestern Pacific, interchange with Southern Pacific at Schellville, and Santa Fe at Richmond. The local Petaluma Airport provides general air service. Regular scheduled passenger and air freight service from Sonoma County Airport located 27 miles north of Petaluma.

Population (1990)

Total Population and Growth Rate

1990: 388,222

1980: 299,681

1970: 204,885
Growth rate 1970–1990: 89%

Race and Hispanic Origin

White: 90.6%
Black: 1.4%
Asian/Pacific Islander: 2.8%
Native American: 1.1%
Hispanic origin: 10.6%
White not Hispanic: 84.3%

Age

Ages 18 to 20: 4%
Ages 21 to 24: 5%
Ages 25 to 44: 35.1%
Ages 45 to 54: 10.4%
Ages 55 to 59: 3.7%
Ages 60 to 64: 3.8%
Ages 65 plus: 13.4%

Educational Attainment (1990)

Percent having completed high school: 84.4%
Percent having completed college: 24.5%
Elementary and high school enrollment: 61,391

Federal Funds and Grants Received

Total received in 1989: $877,900,000
Funds received per capita: $2,399

Civilian Labor Force

1993 (April):   221,061
1992 average: 219,845
1991 average: 214,119
1990 average: 208,493

Unemployment

1993 (April):   6.3%
1992 average: 7.1%
1991 average: 5.7%
1990 average: 4.2%

Average Annual Pay

1988: $20,286
1987: $19,601
1985: $17,775

Per Capita Personal Income

1991: $22,156
1990: $21,549
1989: $20,940

Business Climate (1987)

Manufacturing

Number of establishments in 1987: 657
Shipments in 1987 ($1,000): $2,088,000
Employees in 1987: 19,200
Change in employment, 1982 to 1987: 35.2%
Average annual pay for manufacturing work in 1989: $26,324
Average annual pay for production work in 1987: $21,000

Wholesale Trade

Number of establishments in 1987: 596
Total sales in 1987 ($1,000): $1,690,500
Change in sales, 1982 to 1987: 58.2%

Retail Trade

Number of establishments in 1987: 2,427
Total sales in 1987 ($1,000): $1,690,500
Retail sales per household in 1987: $17,483
Average annual pay in 1989: $13,738

Service Industry

Selected receipts in 1987 ($1,000): $931,900
Average annual pay in 1989: $17,378

Office Real Estate (1992)

Office space inventory: N/A
Average class A Central Business District rental range per sq. ft: N/A

Vacancy Rates

All areas: N/A

Vacancy Rates in Central Business District

Class A space: 12.3%
Class B space: 12.1%

Vacancy Rates Outside Central Business District

Class A space: N/A
Class B space: N/A

Housing

Total number of units in 1990: 161,062
Occupied units in 1990: 149,011
Owner-occupied units in 1990: 62.9%
1993 ACCRA average cost: N/A
1993 ACCRA average rent for an apartment: N/A

Chamber of Commerce

Santa Rosa Chamber of Commerce, Keith A. Woods, President, 637 1st. St., Santa Rosa, CA 95404. 707-545-1414, FAX 707-545-6914

Economic Development Office

Petaluma Area Chamber of Commerce, Terre McRae, Exec. Director, 215 Howard St., Petaluma, CA 94952-2760. 707-762-2785, FAX 707-762-4721

Economic Development Organizations

Northbay Economic Development, Daniel Apodaca, President, 131 Stony Circle #450, Santa Rosa, CA 95401. 707-578-2331

City of Petaluma, Community Development & Planning, Warren Salmons, Director, PO Box 61, 11 English St., Petaluma, CA 94953-0061. 707-778-4301

County of Sonoma, Economic Development Board, 3033 Cleveland Ave., Ste.. 111, Santa Rosa, CA 95403. 707-527-2406

City of Petaluma, Planning and Building Divisions, PO Box 61, Room 100, 11 English Street, Petaluma, CA 94953-0061. 707-778-4301

City of Petaluma, Finance Dept., PO Box 61, Room 1, 11 English Street, Petaluma, CA 94953-0061. 707-778-4354

City of Petaluma, Employment Development Dept., 715 Northpoint, Ste.. G, Petaluma, CA 94952. 707-762-4501

County of Sonoma, Planning Office, Planning Director, 575 Administration Dr., Room 105-A, Santa Rosa, CA 95403. 707-527-3689

County of Sonoma, Small Business Center, 3033 Cleveland Ave., Ste.. 111, Santa Rosa, CA 95403. 707-527-2407

State of California, Employment Development Dept., 715 N. Point Blvd., Ste.. G, Petaluma, CA 94975. 707-762-4501

Industrial Sites

Cader Lane Industrial Park, Edna Buddem 790 DeLong Ave., Ste. 7, Novato, CA 94947. 415-892-4763

Foundry Wharf Business Park, K. Walter Haake, 615 Second St., Petaluma, CA 94952. 707-762-5999

Lakeville Business Park, George Wagner, 1001 Larkspur Landing Cir., Larkspur, CA 94939

Mar Mon Medical Park, Lou Sabella, 1301 Redwood Way, Ste. 165, Petaluma, CA 94952. 707-664-1400

Oakmead North Bay Industrial Park, Chris Castellucci, 1301 Redwood Way, Ste. 165, Petaluma, CA 94952. 707-664-1400

Petaluma Industrial Park, Irv Marcus, 1150 Industrial Ave., Ste.. E, 707-765-1900

Redwood Business Park, Bill White, 1301 Redwood Way, Ste.. 240, Petaluma, CA 94952. 707-795-4477

South Point Industrial Park, Charles Peaslee, 1364 N. McDowell Blvd., Petaluma, CA 94952. 707-763-6819

Woodside Business Park, Carlos Telleria, 1360 Industrial Dr., Ste.. D, Petaluma, CA 94952. 707-763-1966

Major Businesses

Company	SIC	Telephone
American Home Shield Corp.	6351	(707) 578-2800
American Home Shield of California	6351	(707) 578-2800
Apollo Leasing Co. Ltd.	6159	(707) 763-1700
Blevins, J. H. Co. Inc.	2421	(707) 894-4201
California Coop Creamery	2023	(707) 763-1931
Clover-Stornetta Farms, Inc.	2026	(707) 778-8448
Codding Enterprises	6512	(707) 584-7550
Exchange Bank	6036	(707) 545-6220
Gagmars, Inc.	5411	(707) 546-6877
Hunt & Behrens, Inc.	5999	(707) 762-4594
Imco Realty Services	6162	(707) 546-3310
Mc Phail's, Inc.	5722	(707) 457-9700
Milk Products, Inc.	5143	(707) 573-3300
Molsberry Markets, Inc.	5411	(707) 546-5041
New Zealand Milk Products	5143	(707) 664-1000
North Bay Construction, Inc.	1794	(707) 763-2891
North Coast Farm Credit Services	6159	(707) 838-4866

Major Businesses (Continued)

Company	SIC	Telephone
Northbay Savings Bank	6036	(707) 778-3300
Optical Coating Laborator	3479	(707) 545-6440
Oxford Energy Co.	4911	(707) 575-3939
Petaluma Hospital District	8062	(707) 778-1111
Precision Redwood Manufacturing Co.	2421	(707) 894-5263
Redwood Oil Co.	5172	(707) 546-0766
Santa Rosa Memorial Hospital	8062	(707) 546-3210
Tegal Corp.	3559	(707) 763-5600
Transworld Systems, Inc.	7322	(707) 584-4225
Vacu-Dry Co.	2034	(707) 578-5656
Wright Contracting, Inc.	1541	(707) 528-1172
Yaeger & Kirk, Inc.	5211	(707) 545-3883
Yardbirds Electric & Plumbing	5251	(707) 762-5600

Colleges and Universities

Empire College, Santa Rosa. Private business school.

Santa Rosa Junior College, Santa Rosa

Sonoma State University, Rohnert Park

World College West, Petaluma

Additional Information

Economic Profile Packet. Petaluma Area Chamber of Commerce, n.d.

Petaluma Business Park and Industrial Development Survey. Petaluma Area Chamber of Commerce, Community Development and Planning Dept., 1989. 72p.

STOCKTON, CA (MSA)

Geographic Profile

Land Area
1399.4 square miles

Counties and Parishes
San Joaquin

Additional Cities/Towns within Area
Lodi

Ranking Highlights

144 *out of 319 in total* **land area**
54 *out of 319 in* **population growth,** *1970–1990*
303 *out of 310 in having the lowest* **unemployment** *rate*
106 *out of 310 in size of* **labor force**
279 *out of 318 in the percentage of* **college graduates**
233 *out of 292 in per capita personal* **income**
109 *out of 319 in number of* **manufacturing establishments**
243 *out of 318 in* **physicians** *per 1000 people*
222 *out of 318 in* **hospital beds** *per 1000 people*
238 *out of 267 in fewest* **crimes** *per 1000 people*
202 *out of 266 in fewest* **violent crimes** *per 1000 people*
252 *out of 319 in per capita* **federal funds and grants**

Quality of Life Indexes (Rate per 1000 population)

Crime rate in 1991:	83.9
Violent crime rate in 1991:	8.9
Physicians rate in 1992:	1.42
Hospital bed rate in 1991:	2.19

ACCRA Cost of Living Indexes

(First quarter 1993, average = 100)
Composite index: N/A
Utilities index: N/A
Housing index: N/A

Population (1990)

Total Population and Growth Rate
1990: 480,628
1980: 347,342
1970: 291,073
Growth rate 1970–1990: 65%

Race and Hispanic Origin
White: 73.5%
Black: 5.6%
Asian/Pacific Islander: 12.4%
Native American: 1.1%
Hispanic origin: 23.4%
White not Hispanic: 58.8%

Age
Ages 18 to 20: 4.5%
Ages 21 to 24: 5.9%
Ages 25 to 44: 32.2%
Ages 45 to 54: 9.3%
Ages 55 to 59: 3.6%
Ages 60 to 64: 3.7%
Ages 65 plus: 11.1%

Educational Attainment (1990)

Percent having completed high school: 68.6%
Percent having completed college: 13.2%
Elementary and high school enrollment: 95,423

Federal Funds and Grants Received

Total received in 1989: $1,109,700,000
Funds received per capita: $2,435

Civilian Labor Force

1993 (April):   221,616
1992 average: 212,950
1991 average: 203,769
1990 average: 198,233

Unemployment

1993 (April): 13.6%
1992 average: 14.3%
1991 average: 12.0%
1990 average: 9.8%

Average Annual Pay

1988: $19,543
1987: $18,961
1985: $17,468

Per Capita Personal Income

1991: $15,582
1990: $15,211
1989: $14,712

Business Climate (1987)

Manufacturing
Number of establishments in 1987: 535
Shipments in 1987 ($1,000): $3,974,300
Employees in 1987: 25,800
Change in employment, 1982 to 1987: 32.3%
Average annual pay for manufacturing work in 1989: $24,846
Average annual pay for production work in 1987: $20,634

Wholesale Trade
Number of establishments in 1987: 631
Total sales in 1987 ($1,000): $2,672,700
Change in sales, 1982 to 1987: 0%

Retail Trade
Number of establishments in 1987: 2,261
Total sales in 1987 ($1,000): $2,672,700
Retail sales per household in 1987: $15,288
Average annual pay in 1989: $12,492

Service Industry
Selected receipts in 1987 ($1,000): $865,200
Average annual pay in 1989: $18,879

Housing

Total number of units in 1990: 166,274

Occupied units in 1990: 158,156

Owner-occupied units in 1990: 57.6%

1993 ACCRA average cost: N/A

1993 ACCRA average rent for an apartment: N/A

Chamber of Commerce

Greater Stockton Chamber of Commerce, Paula J. Edwards, CEO, 445 W. Weber #220, Stockton, CA 95203. 209-466-7066, FAX 209-466-5271

Economic Development Office

San Joaquin County Economic Development Association, Sylvin Lange, Industrial Development Manager, 709 N. Center St. #2A, Stockton, CA 95202. 209-465-5931

Major Businesses

Company	SIC	Telephone
Alpine Packing Co.	2011	(209) 477-2691
American Moulding & Millwork	2431	(209) 946-5800
American Savings Bank	6035	(209) 546-6050
Bank of Stockton	6022	(209) 464-8781
Beck Development Co. Inc.	1521	(209) 957-0331
Big Valley Ford, Inc.	5511	(209) 956-6711
California Ammonia Co.	5169	(209) 982-1000
Catwil Corp.	1522	(209) 957-5981
Chase Chevrolet Co.	5511	(209) 946-6600
Dameron Hospital Association	8062	(209) 944-5550
Diamond Walnut Growers, Inc.	0723	(209) 467-6000
Farmers & Merchants Bank	6022	(209) 334-1101
Golden Gate Fresh Foods	2013	(209) 368-5117
Grupe Co. Inc.	1531	(209) 473-6000
Guild Wineries & Distillery	2084	(209) 368-5151
Hogan Manufacturing Inc.	3999	(209) 838-7323
Klein Bros. Ltd.	5153	(209) 948-6802
Lodi Development, Inc.	6552	(209) 333-0300
Lodi Memorial Hospital Association	8062	(209) 334-3411
National Medical Enterprises	8062	(209) 823-3111
Port Stockton Food Distributors	5141	(209) 948-1814
R E Development Corp.	6552	(209) 951-5444
Reynolds Packing Co.	0723	(209) 369-2725
San Joaquin Health Care Facilities	8062	(209) 468-6000
Spanos, A.G. Construction	1522	(209) 478-7954
St. Josephs Hospital of Stockton	8062	(209) 943-2000
Stockton Savings Bank	6036	(209) 948-6870
Union Safe Deposit Bank	6022	(209) 946-5011
Valley Electric Co. of Stockton	5063	(209) 948-1911
Wood, Claude C. Co.	1611	(209) 334-0790

Colleges and Universities

Humphreys College, Stockton

San Joaquin Delta College, Stockton

University of the Pacific, Stockton

VALLEJO–FAIRFIELD–NAPA, CA (PMSA)

Geographic Profile

Land Area

1582.0 square miles

Counties and Parishes

Napa

Solano

Ranking Highlights

123 *out of 319 in total* **land area**

　34 *out of 319 in* **population growth**, *1970–1990*

226 *out of 310 in having the lowest* **unemployment** *rate*

105 *out of 310 in size of* **labor force**

143 *out of 318 in the percentage of* **college graduates**

　76 *out of 292 in per capita personal* **income**

125 *out of 319 in number of* **manufacturing establishments**

144 *out of 318 in* **physicians** *per 1000 people*

207 *out of 318 in* **hospital beds** *per 1000 people*

117 *out of 267 in fewest* **crimes** *per 1000 people*

173 *out of 266 in fewest* **violent crimes** *per 1000 people*

　65 *out of 319 in per capita* **federal funds and grants**

Quality of Life Indexes (Rate per 1000 population)

Crime rate in 1991:	58.2
Violent crime rate in 1991:	7.5
Physicians rate in 1992:	1.86
Hospital bed rate in 1991:	3.37

ACCRA Cost of Living Indexes

(First quarter 1993, average = 100)

Composite index:	N/A
Utilities index:	N/A
Housing index:	N/A

Overview

This area is about 45 miles from Oakland, 50 miles from San Francisco, and 60 miles from Sacramento. Interstate 80 connects Vallejo and Fairfield, and U.S. 101 is about 25 miles west of Napa.

There are approximately 30 manufacturing plants in the area. Leading group classes of products are: steel products, building materials, clothing, paper boxes, computer graphics, switches, wine, brandy and champagne.

The Napa area is only marginally unionized with some concentration in winery production and grocery stores. Wage rates are commonly below much of the Bay Area and comparable with Sonoma and Solano counties. Business relocations to Napa have increased notably beginning in 1989 with concentrations in the areas of light manufacturing, distribution and insurance.

Napa County Airport provides general aviation services. It has a FAA traffic control tower which can accommodate small- to medium-sized jets. Commuter and charter planes link this area to national and international airports at San Francisco, Oakland and Sacramento. Rail service is provided by the Southern Pacific, Santa Fe Railroads, and the Napa Valley Wine Train.

Population (1990)

Total Population and Growth Rate

1990: 451,186

1980: 334,402

1970: 251,129

Growth rate 1970–1990: 80%

Race and Hispanic Origin

White: 72.2%

Black: 10.4%

Asian/Pacific Islander: 10.4%

Native American: 0.9%

Hispanic origin: 13.6%

White not Hispanic: 65.8%

Age

Ages 18 to 20: 4.3%

Ages 21 to 24: 5.8%

Ages 25 to 44: 35.3%

Ages 45 to 54: 9.9%

Ages 55 to 59: 3.8%

Ages 60 to 64: 3.4%

Ages 65 plus: 10.2%

Educational Attainment (1990)

Percent having completed high school: 82.2%

Percent having completed college: 19.7%

Elementary and high school enrollment: 80,302

Federal Funds and Grants Received

Total received in 1989: $1,780,000,000

Funds received per capita: $4,231

Civilian Labor Force

1993 (April): 214,981

1992 average: 213,109

1991 average: 203,141

1990 average: 201,374

Unemployment

1993 (April): 8.2%

1992 average: 8.0%

1991 average: 6.7%

1990 average: 5.3%

Average Annual Pay

1988: $21,431

1987: $20,773

1985: $19,562

Per Capita Personal Income

1991: $19,086

1990: $18,648

1989: $17,787

Business Climate (1987)

Manufacturing

Number of establishments in 1987: 430

Shipments in 1987 ($1,000): $2,675,500

Employees in 1987: 11,000

Change in employment, 1982 to 1987: 4.8%

Average annual pay for manufacturing work in 1989: $26,569

Average annual pay for production work in 1987: $22,471

Wholesale Trade

Number of establishments in 1987: 399

Total sales in 1987 ($1,000): $1,539,200

Change in sales, 1982 to 1987: 43.7%

Retail Trade

Number of establishments in 1987: 2,180

Total sales in 1987 ($1,000): $1,539,200

Retail sales per household in 1987: $14,909

Average annual pay in 1989: $13,416

Service Industry

Selected receipts in 1987 ($1,000): $782,700

Average annual pay in 1989: $18,521

Housing

Total number of units in 1990: 163,732

Occupied units in 1990: 154,741

Owner-occupied units in 1990: 63.3%

1993 ACCRA average cost: N/A

1993 ACCRA average rent for an apartment: N/A

Chamber of Commerce

Vallejo Chamber of Commerce, Robert E. Whyte, Exec. Vice President, #2 Florida St., Vallejo, CA 94590. 707-644-5551, FAX 707-644-5590

Economic Development Office

Napa Chamber of Commerce, Jim Ford, Exec. Director, 1556 1st St., PO Box 636, Napa, CA 94559-0636. 707-226-7455, FAX 707-226-1171

Economic Development Organizations

City of Vallejo Economic Development Dept., Alvaro P. de Silva, Director, 555 Santa Clara St., PO Box 3068, Vallejo, CA 94590. 707-648-4444

Napa City/County Development Corp, Angela Pieper, Exec. Director, 100 Coombs St., Napa, CA 94556. 707-253-3212, FAX 707-255-0972

Napa County Board of Realtors, Mary Rasmussen, Exec. Vice President, 2045 Jefferson St., Napa, CA 94558. 707-255-1040

Napa Valley Private Industry Council, Donna De Weerd, Director, 2447 Old Sonoma Rd., Napa, CA 94558. 707-253-4339

Napa Valley College Small Business Center, Patti Peters, Exec. Director, 100 Coombs St., Napa, CA 94556. 707-253-3210

California State Employment Development Dept., Carol

Palomo, Manager, 895 Trancas St., Napa, CA 94558. 707-226-9947

Napa County Planning Dept., Jeff Redding, Planning Director, 1195 3rd St., Napa, CA 94559. 707-253-4416

Napa County Board of Supervisors, Paul Battisti, Chairman, 1195 3rd St., Napa, CA 94559. 707-253-4421

City of Napa, Mayor's Office, 955 School St., Napa, CA 94559. 707-257-9613

Local Incentives for Business

The Napa City/County Development Corp. Provides financial information on SBA Loans (502, 504, and 7A) for buildings, equipment and operating capital, funds available through State sources and venture capitalists, and the Revolving Loan Fund, guaranteed long-term loans at low-interest rates, sponsored by the Napa City and County.

Business and financial counseling. NCCDC's staff and the Service Corps of Retired Executives help new or established companies solve problems. Napa Valley College also trains entrepreneurs in the basics of business.

Site inventory computerized. NCCDC keeps a current inventory of available commercial and industrial sites for new or additional locations.

Industrial Development Bonds. Taxable and non-taxable industrial development bonds and funding for land, buildings and capital improvement.

Employee Training. NCCDC and the Private Industry Council work together to provide trained employees for businesses, some at no cost to employers.

Industrial Sites

Chardonnay Business Park

Enterprise Industrial Park

Green Island Industrial Park

Napa Airport Corporate Park

Napa Valley Business Park

Napa Valley Corporate Park

Napa Valley Gateway Business Park

Major Businesses

Company	SIC	Telephone
APM, Inc.	2499	(707) 745-8060
Barber Auto Sales	5511	(707) 648-8500
Big O Tires, Inc.	5014	(707) 446-4444
Bill's Drugs, Inc.	5331	(707) 747-0500
California Erectors Bay	1791	(707) 746-1990
Campbell's Carpets Inc.	5023	(707) 747-4000
Corey Delta Inc.	1711	(707) 745-8932
Dag Builders	1542	(707) 257-0737
Diablo Timber	5031	(707) 252-6142
Doctor's Co.	6411	(707) 226-7160
First Northern Bank	6022	(916) 678-3041
Greene Motors, Inc.	5511	(707) 553-1100
Institutional Financing Service	3961	(707) 746-7600

Major Businesses (Continued)

Company	SIC	Telephone
Kelley, Loran & Gibber	1521	(707) 429-8220
M & H Tobacco Co, Inc.	5194	(707) 643-4526
Mid Valley Dairy Co.	2026	(707) 864-0502
Mondavi, Robert Winery, Inc.	2084	(707) 963-9611
Napa Valley Bancorp	6022	(707) 257-4900
Napa Valley Bank	6022	(707) 255-8300
Northbay Hospital Group	8062	(707) 429-3600
Queen of The Valley	8062	(707) 252-4411
R & R Warehouse, Inc.	5411	(707) 644-5531
Sawyer of Napa, Inc.	2386	(707) 253-1000
Sutter Home Winery, Inc.	2084	(707) 963-3104
Sutter Solano Medical Center	8062	(707) 554-4444
Underground Construction	1623	(707) 746-8800
Vallerga's Drive-In Market	5411	(707) 253-2620
Vintage Companies, Inc.	6552	(707) 226-8403
Westminister Development	6552	(707) 252-4611
Wilson-Cornelius Ford	5511	(707) 643-2511

Colleges and Universities

California Maritime Academy, Vallejo
Napa Valley College, Napa . Two year college.
Pacific Union College, Angwin

Additional Information

Napa Resource Directory 1989. Napa City County Development Corp., 1990. 50p.

Napa Valley on the Move. Napa City County Development Corp., 1990. 20p.

VISALIA–TULARE–PORTERVILLE, CA (MSA)

Geographic Profile

Land Area
4824.3 square miles

Counties and Parishes
Tulare

Ranking Highlights

17 *out of 319 in total* **land area**
53 *out of 319 in* **population growth,** *1970–1990*
306 *out of 310 in having the lowest* **unemployment** *rate*
135 *out of 310 in size of* **labor force**
300 *out of 318 in the percentage of* **college graduates**
273 *out of 292 in per capita personal* **income**
164 *out of 319 in number of* **manufacturing establishments**
298 *out of 318 in* **physicians** *per 1000 people*
300 *out of 318 in* **hospital beds** *per 1000 people*
113 *out of 267 in fewest* **crimes** *per 1000 people*
137 *out of 266 in fewest* **violent crimes** *per 1000 people*
178 *out of 319 in per capita* **federal funds and grants**

Quality of Life Indexes (Rate per 1000 population)

Crime rate in 1991:	61.2
Violent crime rate in 1991:	7.7
Physicians rate in 1992:	1.07
Hospital bed rate in 1991:	2.1

ACCRA Cost of Living Indexes

(First quarter 1993, average = 100)
Composite index: 115.8
Utilities index: 122.7
Housing index: 116.4

Overview

Tulare County is located 183 miles north of Los Angeles and 228 miles south of San Francisco. State Highways 99 and 65 are the primary north-south routes and highways 198, 137 and 190 are the primary east-west routes.

Visalia provides commuter flight service to Sacramento, San Francisco, and Los Angeles. Southern Pacific and Santa Fe Railroads provide rail service.

Population (1990)

Total Population and Growth Rate
1990: 311,921
1980: 245,738
1970: 188,322
Growth rate 1970–1990: 66%

Race and Hispanic Origin
White: 65.7%
Black: 1.5%
Asian/Pacific Islander: 4.3%

Native American: 1.3%
Hispanic origin: 38.8%
White not Hispanic: 54.6%

Age

Ages 18 to 20: 4.6%
Ages 21 to 24: 5.6%
Ages 25 to 44: 29.7%
Ages 45 to 54: 9%
Ages 55 to 59: 3.7%
Ages 60 to 64: 3.5%
Ages 65 plus: 10.8%

Educational Attainment (1990)

Percent having completed high school: 60.2%
Percent having completed college: 11.8%
Elementary and high school enrollment: 71,177

Federal Funds and Grants Received

Total received in 1989: $678,400,000
Funds received per capita: $2,277

Civilian Labor Force

1993 (April):   168,977
1992 average: 160,094
1991 average: 142,775
1990 average: 132,352

Unemployment

1993 (April): 13.7%
1992 average: 15.3%
1991 average: 17.1%
1990 average: 11.9%

Average Annual Pay

1988: $15,199
1987: $15,164
1985: $14,078

Per Capita Personal Income

1991: $14,248
1990: $14,515
1989: $13,514

Business Climate (1987)

Manufacturing

Number of establishments in 1987: 301
Shipments in 1987 ($1,000): $1,688,600
Employees in 1987: 11,200
Change in employment, 1982 to 1987: 3.7%
Average annual pay for manufacturing work in 1989: $22,534
Average annual pay for production work in 1987: $17,917

Wholesale Trade

Number of establishments in 1987: 390
Total sales in 1987 ($1,000): $1,558,600
Change in sales, 1982 to 1987: 8.7%

Retail Trade

Number of establishments in 1987: 1,558
Total sales in 1987 ($1,000): $1,558,600
Retail sales per household in 1987: $13,592
Average annual pay in 1989: $11,822

Service Industry

Selected receipts in 1987 ($1,000): $397,100
Average annual pay in 1989: $15,939

Housing

Total number of units in 1990: 105,013
Occupied units in 1990: 97,861
Owner-occupied units in 1990: 60.1%
1993 ACCRA average cost: $139,600
1993 ACCRA average rent for an apartment: $514

Chamber of Commerce

Visalia Chamber of Commerce, Diane P. Muro, Exec. Vice President, 720 W. Mineral King, Visalia, CA 93291. 209-734-5876

Economic Development Office

Tulare County Economic Development Corp., Robert B. Jensen, Exec. Director, PO Box 5033, 2380 W. Whitendale Ave., Visalia, CA 93278. 209-627-0766, FAX 209-627-8149

Economic Development Organizations

Tulare County Private Industry Council, Joe Daniel, Director, 2374 W. Whitendale Ave., Visalia, CA 93278. 209-625-9222

Visalia Board of Realtors, Inc., Janet Carr, Exec. Officer, 301 W. Noble Ave., Visalia, CA 93277. 209-627-1776

Tulare Industrial Park, Lynn Dredge, City Manager, Tulare, CA 93274. 209-686-2452

Visalia Industrial Park, Sheryl Timmons, Economic Development Manager, City of Visalia, Visalia, CA 93291. 209-738-3393

Porterville Industrial Park, Vickie Maples, Development Associate, City of Porterville, Porterville, CA. 209-782-7466

California Employment Development Dept., Bert Flores, Office Manager, 2523 S. Mooney Blvd, Visalia, CA 93278. 209-733-3706

Tulare County Private Industry Council, JTPA, Carmen Jacobo, 2374 W. Whitendale Ave., Visalia, CA 93278. 209-625-9222

Local Incentives for Business

Job Training Assistance Programs:

Private Industry Council. Coordinates training programs for Job Training Partnership Act.

Employment Training Panel. Employer reimbursement for job training.

Targeted Job Tax Credit. Credit of up to 50% of wages.

Work Incentive Program. Tax credit for training.

Loans for Business Expansion:

1. Tulare County Loan Fund. Interest rate fixed at the prime rate or the prime rate plus 1% point for machinery and equipment, working capital, and acquisition of existing buildings. Machinery and equipment terms are up to 10 years, working capital terms up to seven years, and real estate terms up to 20 years.
2. Industrial Development Revenue Bonds. Typically less expensive than conventional financing. Maximum project size $10 million. Minimum project size $1 million. Maximum term 40 years.

Industrial Sites

Contact:
Porterville Industrial Park
Tulare Industrial Park
Visalia Industrial Park

Major Businesses

Company	SIC	Telephone
Atkins, Claude E. Enterprises	1542	(209) 733-7350
Big John's Food King, Inc.	5411	(209) 732-5627
Brott Mechanical	1711	(209) 688-7571
California Citrus Produce	2037	(209) 562-5169
Coehlo Meat Co.	5147	(209) 688-2839
Dairymans Coop Creamery	2026	(209) 685-6800
Dinuba Timber Industries	2421	(209) 591-2000
Gang Nails Truss Inc.	2439	(209) 651-2121
Griggs, Jack, Inc.	5171	(209) 592-3154
Kaweah Delta Hospital District	8062	(209) 625-2211
Kings County Truck Lines	4213	(209) 686-2857
Lawrence Tractor Co.	5083	(209) 734-7406
Linder Equipment Co.	5999	(209) 685-5000
Lindsay Hospital Medical Center	8062	(209) 562-4955
Lindsay Olive Growers	2033	(209) 562-5121
Nash De Camp Co.	0723	(209) 651-1850
Parks, R. M., Inc.	5171	(209) 784-2384
Putnam-Windh, Inc.	5511	(209) 627-4444
Razzari-Visalia, Inc.	5511	(209) 625-1000
Ruiz Food Products, Inc.	2038	(209) 688-2972
Sequoia Pacific Holdings	2752	(209) 592-2191
Sierra View Local Hospital District	8062	(209) 784-1110
Smith's Complete Market	5411	(209) 784-2244
Stone Merle Chevrolet Corp.	5511	(209) 686-8356
Synanon Church Inc.	5199	(209) 337-2885
T & C Foods, Inc.	5411	(209) 784-6428
Tri-Ex Tower Corp.	3441	(209) 651-2171
Tulare Local Hospital District	8062	(209) 688-0821
Walco International, Inc.	5122	(209) 781-3510
Young's, Jack Super Market	5411	(209) 625-9252

Colleges and Universities

College of the Sequoias, Visalia
Porterville College, Porterville
Golden State Business College
Galen College of Medical & Dental Assistants

YUBA CITY, CA (MSA)

Geographic Profile

Land Area
1233.1 square miles

Counties and Parishes
Sutter
Yuba

Ranking Highlights

160 *out of 319 in total* **land area**

 92 *out of 319 in* **population growth**, *1970–1990*

310 *out of 310 in having the lowest* **unemployment** *rate*

283 *out of 310 in size of* **labor force**

288 *out of 318 in the percentage of* **college graduates**

260 *out of 292 in per capita personal* **income**

278 *out of 319 in number of* **manufacturing establishments**

N/A *out of 318 in* **physicians** *per 1000 people*

301 *out of 318 in* **hospital beds** *per 1000 people*

 97 *out of 267 in fewest* **crimes** *per 1000 people*

164 *out of 266 in fewest* **violent crimes** *per 1000 people*

 85 *out of 319 in per capita* **federal funds and grants**

Quality of Life Indexes (Rate per 1000 population)

Crime rate in 1991:	54.1
Violent crime rate in 1991:	7.3
Physicians rate in 1992:	N/A
Hospital bed rate in 1991:	2.09

ACCRA Cost of Living Indexes

(First quarter 1993, average = 100)

Composite index:	N/A
Utilities index:	N/A
Housing index:	N/A

Population (1990)

Total Population and Growth Rate
1990: 122,643
1980: 101,979
1970: 86,671
Growth rate 1970–1990: 42%

Race and Hispanic Origin
White: 77.5%
Black: 2.8%
Asian/Pacific Islander: 9.0%
Native American: 2.1%
Hispanic origin: 14.1%
White not Hispanic: 72.6%

Age
Ages 18 to 20: 4.3%
Ages 21 to 24: 5.7%
Ages 25 to 44: 30.4%
Ages 45 to 54: 9.8%
Ages 55 to 59: 4.4%
Ages 60 to 64: 4.1%
Ages 65 plus: 11.2%

Educational Attainment (1990)

Percent having completed high school: 70.5%
Percent having completed college: 12.7%
Elementary and high school enrollment: 24,529

Federal Funds and Grants Received

Total received in 1989: $446,800,000
Funds received per capita: $3,772

Civilian Labor Force

1993 (April):	55,287
1992 average:	53,937
1991 average:	50,046
1990 average:	47,639

Unemployment

1993 (April): 17.7%
1992 average: 18.1%
1991 average: 16.2%
1990 average: 13.0%

Average Annual Pay

1988: $17,330
1987: $16,398
1985: $15,139

Per Capita Personal Income

1991: $15,016
1990: $14,237
1989: $13,654

Business Climate (1987)

Manufacturing
Number of establishments in 1987: 117
Shipments in 1987 ($1,000): $512,700
Employees in 1987: 3,100
Change in employment, 1982 to 1987: -3.1%
Average annual pay for manufacturing work in 1989: $19,576
Average annual pay for production work in 1987: $19,583

Wholesale Trade
Number of establishments in 1987: 142
Total sales in 1987 ($1,000): $269,000
Change in sales, 1982 to 1987: 10.4%

Retail Trade
Number of establishments in 1987: 609
Total sales in 1987 ($1,000): $269,000
Retail sales per household in 1987: $12,695
Average annual pay in 1989: $11,255

Service Industry
Selected receipts in 1987 ($1,000): $153,200
Average annual pay in 1989: $19,043

Housing

Total number of units in 1990: 45,408

Occupied units in 1990: 42,887
Owner-occupied units in 1990: 55.9%
1993 ACCRA average cost: N/A
1993 ACCRA average rent for an apartment: N/A

Chamber of Commerce

City of Yuba City, Economic Development, Jon Whiteman,
Director, 1201 Civic Center Blvd., Yuba City, CA 95993.
916-741-4697, FAX 916-741-4694

Major Businesses

Company	SIC	Telephone
Amarel Grain Co.	5153	(916) 674-5166
Baldwin Contracting Co.	1611	(916) 742-5141
Bond Gold Placer Corp.	1041	(916) 742-7164
Booth, Frank M. Inc.	1711	(916) 742-7134
Bradley's Department Store	5311	(916) 743-5441
Close, Frank R. & Son Inc.	5211	(916) 755-0055
D & H Transportation	4214	(916) 674-5746
Daoust Chevrolet Co., Inc.	5511	(916) 743-9233
Dillen Shoe Corp.	5661	(916) 674-7780
Eagle Moulding Co., Inc.	2431	(916) 673-6517
Feather River State Bank	6022	(916) 671-6343
Fremont Hospital	8062	(916) 671-2220
Geweke, Larry Ford Inc.	5511	(916) 743-7301
Hust Bros. Inc.	5013	(916) 743-1561
Jaeger Construction, Inc.	1611	(916) 673-3885
Jarvis, M. A. Co.	1522	(916) 674-3582
Lamon Construction Co. Inc.	1542	(916) 671-1370
Midvalley Toyota Inc.	5511	(916) 673-5661
Peavey Marts Inc.	5251	(916) 673-9607
Rideout Hospital Foundation	8062	(916) 742-7381
Speckert Building	5031	(916) 742-2325
Sunset Moulding Co.	2431	(916) 695-1801
Sunsweet Dryers	2034	(916) 674-5010
Sunsweet Growers, Inc.	2034	(916) 674-5010
Superior Beverage Co. of Marysville	5181	(916) 673-6800
Wheeler Oldsmobile Cadillac	5511	(916) 673-9160
Yuba County Water Agency	4911	(916) 741-6278
Yuba River Moulding & Millwork	2431	(916) 742-2168
Yuba Trucking Inc.	4212	(916) 743-9293

Colleges and Universities

None

COLORADO

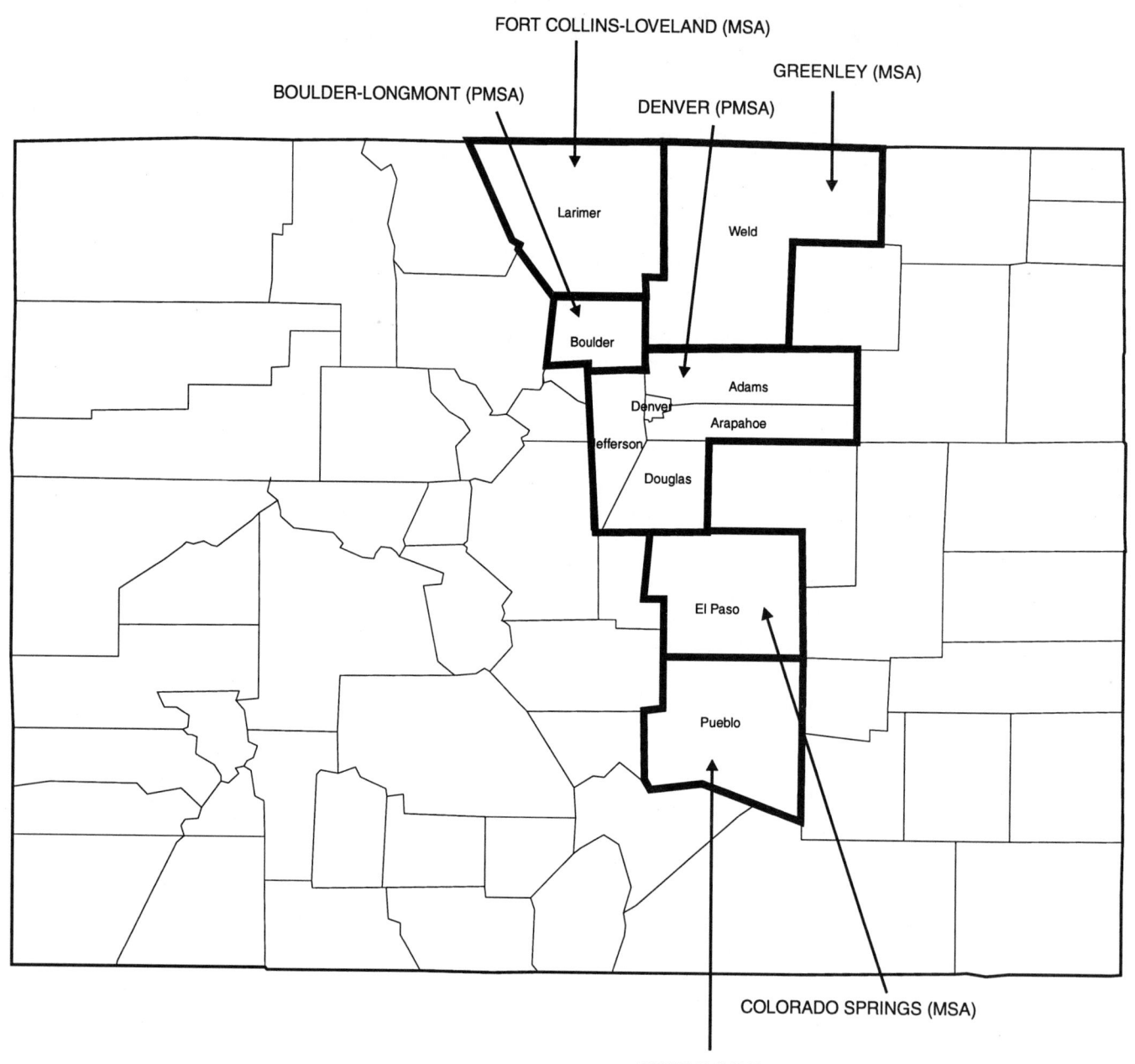

FORT COLLINS-LOVELAND (MSA)

GREENLEY (MSA)

BOULDER-LONGMONT (PMSA)

DENVER (PMSA)

Larimer

Weld

Boulder

Adams

Denver

Arapahoe

Jefferson

Douglas

El Paso

Pueblo

COLORADO SPRINGS (MSA)

PUEBLO (MSA)

COLORADO

Population
1990: 3,294,394
1980: 2,889,964

Age
Ages 18 to 20: 148,197
Ages 21 to 24: 187,328
Ages 25 to 44: 1,179,936
Ages 45 to 54: 336,671
Ages 55 to 59: 130,193
Ages 60 to 64: 121,360
Median age: 32.5

Race
White: 2,905,474
Black: 133,146
Asian/Pacific Islander: 59,862
Native American: 27,776
Hispanic origin: 424,302

Households
Total: 1,282,489
Persons per household: 2.51

Sex
Male: 1,631,295
Female: 1,663,099

Population Migration
Domestic migration: -81,000
International migration: 52,000

Projection of the Population in 1995
Total: 3,596,000
18 to 64: 2,296,000

Civilian Labor Force
1993: 1,774,600
1992: 1,796,000
1991: 1,753,300
1990: 1,684,600

Manufacturing
1995 Projection: 209,700
1992: 184,800
1991: 190,800
1990: 193,800
1989: 194,800

Services
1995 Projection: 636,100

1992: 411,800
1991: 422,300
1990: 411,300
1989: 385,300

Wholesale and Retail Trade
1995 Projection: 452,400
1992: 385,500
1991: 385,700
1990: 383,700
1989: 367,700

Unemployment Rate
1993: 6.3%
1992: 6.0%
1991: 4.7%
1990: 5.3%

Employer Unemployment Contributions
Contribution Rate
1992: 1.40%
1991: 1.30%
1990: 1.60%

Average Weekly Benefit
1992: $183.12
1991: $183.27
1990: $168.84

Gross State Product (Million $)
1989: $66,180
1988: $62,490
1987: $59,630
1979: $33,212
Growth rate, 1979 to 1989: 99.3%

Capital Expenditures of Manufacturing Industries
1990: $849,900,000
1989: $870,400,000
1988: $794,800,000
1987: $791,500,000

State Tax Rates
Individual income: 5% of federal taxable income.
Corporate income: Range from 5% ($50,000 or less) to 5.4% (above $50,000).
General property: Sum of state and local rates. Assessed at

actual value of real property and tangible pesonal property. Residential realty is assessed at 21% of actual value. All other property is assessed at 29% of actual value.

General sales: 3%

Gasoline: 22¢ per gallon

Income

Median income for a 4 person family: $40,265

Personal per Capita Income

1992: $20,124

1991: $19,395

1990: $18,795

Disposable per Capita Income

1992: $17,517

1991: $19,793

1990: $16,219

Private Employment Weekly Wages

Average

1989: $415

1988: $406

1987: $406

Manufacturing

1989: $392

1988: $548

1987: $527

Services

1989: $378

1988: $366

1987: $344

Wholesale

1989: $533

1988: $519

1987: $500

Retail

1989: $229

1988: $224

1987: $221

Highway Statistics

Total Highway Miles

1990: 77,680

1989: 77,361

1988: 77,149

Federal Highway Aid

1991: $169,432,000

1990: $180,459,000

1989: $186,442,000

Electricity

Average Cost per Kilowatt Hour

1990: 5.85¢

1989: 5.96¢

1988: 5.95¢

Housing (1990)

Owner occupied units: 798,277

Median house value: $82,700

Renter occupied units: 484,212

Median rent: $362

Total vacant units: 194,860

Homeowner vacancy rate: 3.3%

Rental vacancy rate: 11.4%

State Business Incentives and Assistance

Enterprise Zone Incentives

1) 3% Investment Tax Credit (ITC). Colorado law limits ITCs to 100% of the first $5,000 in tax liability, plus 25% of tax liability in excess of $5,000.

2) $500 refundable credit per new business facility employee, exceeding one, engaged or maintained during the taxable year. A new business facility is a revenue-producing enterprise (excluding passive real estate investment) newly constructed, acquired, or leased to the taxpayer; or expanded with an investment of at least $1 million, or, if less, double the original investment or adding at least 10 employees; and not replacing another facility used by the same or related taxpayer for a similar enterprise.

3) Exemption from state sales and use taxes on the purchase of machinery or machine tools for use in manufacturing, to the extent purchased do not exceed $10,000,000 per year. Local governments may exempt such purchases from local sales and use taxes.

Financial and Business Assistance

Industrial Development Bond. IDBs may be issued by local governments to promote industry and attract businesses to locate facilities in the state. IDB financing is available for manufacturing, industrial, and commercial projects. The maximum term of any individual bond issue is 40 years.

Private Activity Bond. This allocation program provides industry with tax-exempt private activity bonds to encourage investment in creating and sustaining jobs, redevelopment projects, and financing infrastructure facilities.

Economic Development Commission Fund. The state Commission allocates funds for business incentives projects such as infrastructure improvements and site development costs anywhere in the state. The state may also loan these funds to private businesses through local non-profit economic development organizations.

Colorado Initiatives. The program provides intensive assistance to rural communities. This is a unique combination of technical and financial assistance targeted to rural communities. It is a joint effort between the Department of Local Affairs, the University of Colorado at Denver and Mountain Bell.

Education and Training

Customized Training Program. The Colorado FIRST Customized Training Program tries to create new jobs for state residents by providing trained workers for new and expanding firms in the state. The customized pre-employment or on-the-job trainings are administered by the Colorado Community College and Occupational Education System.

Colorado Existing Industry Training Program. This program is designed to provide job-specific and short-term retraining to workers of companies undergoing major technological changes, or where training is deemed crucial for the company and for worker retention.

Job Training Partnership Act. This program operates with funding from the U.S. Department of Labor. It provides job training and other employment related services.

State Offices

Real estate: Real Estate Commission, Michael Gorham, Director, 1776 Logan St., 4th fl., Denver, CO 80203. 303-894-2166

Chamber of commerce: Colorado Association of Commerce & Industry, George S. Dibble Jr., President, 1776 Lincoln St. #1200, Denver, CO 80203-1029. 303-831-7411

Economic development: Office of the Governor, Economic Development Office, J. Fredrick Niehaus, Special Asst. to Governor, 1625 Broadway St. #1710, Denver, CO 80202. 303-892-3840

Colorado Dept. of Local Affairs (Enterprise Zones Office), Evan Metcalf, 1313 Sherman St., Room 518, Denver, CO 80203. 303-866-2205

Small Business Development Center, Rick Garcia, State Director, 1625 Broadway, Ste. 1710, Denver, CO 80202. 303-892-3809

Department of Local Affairs, Colorado Initiatives, T. Michael Smith, 1313 Sherman, Room 518, Denver, CO 80203. 303-866-2156

Environmental affairs: Health and Environment Protection Office, Denver, CO 80220. 303-331-4513

Labor: Labor & Employment Department, John J. Donlon, Exec Director, 600 Grant St., Ste. 900, Denver, CO 80236. 303-837-3801

Major Companies in Colorado

Company name	Fortune 500 rank	City	Telephone	SIC
Fortune 500 Companies				
Adolph Coors Co.	220	Golden	303-279-6565	2082
Cyprus Minerals Co.	253	Englewood	303-643-5000	1021
Manville Corp.	206	Denver	303-978-2000	2631
Newmont Mining Corp.	473	Denver	303-863-7414	1041
Storage Technology Corp.	261	Louisville	303-673-5151	3674
Total Petroleum North America Ltd	189	Denver	303-291-2000	2911
Other Major Companies in the State				
Affiliated Bankshares of Colorado Inc.		Denver	303-296-7788	6712
Apache Corp.		Denver	303-837-5000	1311
Associated Natural Gas Corp.		Denver	303-595-3331	1311
CF&I Steel Corp.		Pueblo	719-561-7103	3312
Colorado Interstate Gas Co.		Colorado Springs	719-473-2300	4923
Colorado National Bankshares Inc.		Denver	303-629-1968	6712
K N Energy Inc.		Lakewood	303-989-1740	4923
M D C Holdings Inc.		Denver	303-773-1100	1531
Miniscribe Corp.		Denver	415-576-3376	3572
Mountain States Telephone & Telegraph Co.		Denver	303-896-3099	4813
Newmont Gold Co.		Denver	303-863-7414	1041
Public Service Co. of Colorado		Denver	303-571-7511	4931
Tele Communications Inc.		Englewood	303-267-5500	4841
Total Petroleum North America Ltd.		Denver	303-291-2000	2911
U S West Communications Inc.		Denver	303-896-2355	4813
U S West Inc.		Englewood	303-793-6500	4813
United Artists Entertainment Co.		Englewood	303-843-8600	4841
United Banks of Colorado Inc.		Denver	303-861-4700	6712
Vicorp Restaurants Inc.		Denver	303-296-2121	5812
Western Capital Investment Corp.		Denver	303-623-5577	6712

Unemployment: Labor & Employment Department, Unemployment Insurance Office, Robert Hale, Director, 600 Grant St., Ste. 900, Denver, CO 80236. 303-866-6389

Worker's compensation: Labor Division, Workers Compensation Section, Ruth Anne Gartland, Director, 1313 Sherman St., Room 314, Denver, CO 80203. 303-866-2861

Occupational safety and health: Labor & Employment Department, John J. Donlon, Exec Director, 600 Grant St., Ste. 900, Denver, CO 80236. 303-837-3801

Secretary of state: State Department, Natalie Meyer, Secretary of State, 1560 Broadway, Ste. 200, Denver, CO 80202. 303-894-2211

Taxation and revenue: Revenue Department, John J. Tipton, Exec Director, 1375 Sherman St., Denver, CO 80261. 303-866-3091

Designated Zones for Economic Development

Enterprise Zones

Enacted in: 1986

No. of established zones: 16

Foreign Trade Zones

Foreign Trade Zone No. 112, Colorado Springs, Colorado, Grantee: Colorado Springs Foreign-Trade Zone, Inc., Robert K. Scott, PO Drawer B, Colorado Springs, CO 80901, 719-471-8183

Foreign Trade Zone No. 123, Denver, Colorado, Grantee: City and County of Denver, Operator: Aspen Distribution, Don Cooper, 5401 Oswego St., PO Box 39108, Denver, CO 80239, 303-371-2511

Labor Unions

Bakery, Confectionery & Tobacco Workers International Union (AFL-CIO)

Electrical Workers, International Brotherhood of (AFL-CIO)

Laborers' International Union of North America (AFL-CIO)

National Education Association

Rubber, Cork, Linoleum and Plastic Workers of America, United (AFL-CIO)

Transit Union, Amalgamated (AFL-CIO)

Universities with Ph.D. Programs

Colorado State University, Fort Collins

University of Colorado at Boulder, Boulder

University of Colorado at Colorado Springs, Colorado Springs

University of Colorado at Denver, Denver

University of Colorado Health Sciences Center, Denver

University of Denver, Denver

University of Northern Colorado, Greeley

BOULDER–LONGMONT, CO (PMSA)

Geographic Profile

Land Area

742.5 square miles

Counties and Parishes

Boulder

Ranking Highlights

246 *out of 319 in total* land area

44 *out of 319 in* population growth, *1970–1990*

20 *out of 310 in having the lowest* unemployment *rate*

143 *out of 310 in size of* labor force

2 *out of 318 in the percentage of* college graduates

24 *out of 292 in per capita personal* income

113 *out of 319 in number of* manufacturing establishments

106 *out of 318 in* physicians *per 1000 people*

311 *out of 318 in* hospital beds *per 1000 people*

137 *out of 267 in fewest* crimes *per 1000 people*

39 *out of 266 in fewest* violent crimes *per 1000 people*

119 *out of 319 in per capita* federal funds and grants

Quality of Life Indexes (Rate per 1000 population)

Crime rate in 1991:	61.2
Violent crime rate in 1991:	2.8
Physicians rate in 1992:	2.1
Hospital bed rate in 1991:	1.72

ACCRA Cost of Living Indexes

(First quarter 1993, average = 100)

Composite index:	N/A
Utilities index:	N/A
Housing index:	N/A

Overview

Boulder and Longmont together formed the PMSA as designated by the Bureau of the Census. Boulder is 15 miles south of Longmont. Denver is located about 15 miles south east of the Boulder-Longmont PMSA.

The strength of this area is the University of Colorado and Government Research; National Center for Atmospheric Research, National Oceanic and Atmospheric Administration, and the National Bureau of Standards. The Boulder campus of the University of Colorado is internationally recognized for its research accomplishments in the fields of space science technology, molecular, cellular and developmental biology; atomic, molecular and optical physics; and electrical and computer engineering. It received over $60 million in sponsored research from various federal agencies in one year and is ranked seventh among the top ten leading public universities receiving funds from NASA. The Boulder campus of the University of Colorado is the location of a Business Research Division, the Center for Economic

Analysis, a Small Business Assistance Center, the Colorado Technical Reference Center, an International Center for Energy and Economic Development, and a Laboratory of Education Research.

Highways servicing the area include U.S. 36, U.S. 287, I-25,and state highways 93, 7, 119, 72, 66, 52,and 128. Interstate 25, Colorado's major north-south highway, runs just to the east of Boulder. The Boulder-Denver Turnpike connects the two cities, and I-70 at Denver provides links east and west. Other major highways include U.S. 36 and 287. Rail service is provided by the Colorado and Southern Railroad, part of the Burlington Northern System. The Stapleton International Airport is 35 miles from Boulder. Local airports include the Boulder Municipal Airport, Longmont Vance Brand Airport, Tri-County Airport, and the Jefferson County Airport.

Population (1990)

Total Population and Growth Rate
1990: 225,339
1980: 189,625
1970: 131,889
Growth rate 1970–1990: 71%

Race and Hispanic Origin
White: 93.3%
Black: .9%
Asian/Pacific Islander: 2.4%
Native American: 0.6%
Hispanic origin: 6.7%
White not Hispanic: 89.5%

Age
Ages 18 to 20: 6.7%
Ages 21 to 24: 7.9%
Ages 25 to 44: 38.3%
Ages 45 to 54: 10.2%
Ages 55 to 59: 3.4%
Ages 60 to 64: 2.8%
Ages 65 plus: 7.6%

Educational Attainment (1990)
Percent having completed high school: 91.3%
Percent having completed college: 42.1%
Elementary and high school enrollment: 33,110

Federal Funds and Grants Received
Total received in 1989: $740,500,000
Funds received per capita: $3,398

Civilian Labor Force
1993 (April): 147,129
1992 average: 143,591
1991 average: 141,333
1990 average: 139,277

Unemployment
1993 (April): 4.1%
1992 average: 4.1%

1991 average: 3.5%
1990 average: 3.7%

Average Annual Pay
1988: $21,390
1987: $20,807
1985: $18,849

Per Capita Personal Income
1991: $22,169
1990: $21,604
1989: $20,335

Business Climate (1987)

Manufacturing
Number of establishments in 1987: 507
Shipments in 1987 ($1,000): $2,744,200
Employees in 1987: 29,500
Change in employment, 1982 to 1987: -6.1%
Average annual pay for manufacturing work in 1989: $31,421
Average annual pay for production work in 1987: $18,216

Wholesale Trade
Number of establishments in 1987: 395
Total sales in 1987 ($1,000): $1,062,600
Change in sales, 1982 to 1987: 135.1%

Retail Trade
Number of establishments in 1987: 1,585
Total sales in 1987 ($1,000): $1,062,600
Retail sales per household in 1987: $18,686
Average annual pay in 1989: $10,885

Service Industry
Selected receipts in 1987 ($1,000): $847,200
Average annual pay in 1989: $20,579

Housing
Total number of units in 1990: 94,621
Occupied units in 1990: 88,402
Owner-occupied units in 1990: 61.1%
1993 ACCRA average cost: N/A
1993 ACCRA average rent for an apartment: N/A

Chamber of Commerce
Boulder Chamber of Commerce, Denis Nock, President, 2440 Pearl St., PO Box 73, Boulder, CO 80306. 303-442-1044, FAX 303-938-8837

Economic Development Office
Longmont Area Chamber of Commerce, Brian O'Hanlon, President, 528 N. Main St., Longmont, CO 80501. 303-776-5295, FAX 303-442-5657

Economic Development Organizations
Boulder Development Commission , Pamela K. Schwab, Economic Development Coordinator, 2440 Pearl St., PO Box 73, Boulder, CO 80306. 303-442-1044, FAX 303-938-8837

Longmont Economic Development Association, John Reardon, President, PO Box 842, Longmont, CO 80502. 303-651-0128, FAX 303-442-6673

Boulder Technology Incubator, Dr. Robert J. Calcaterra, Exec Director. PO Box 8005, Ste. 215, Boulder, CO 80306. 303-449-3323

Economic Development Association of Longmont, PO Box 842, Longmont, CO 80502. 303-651-0128

Local Incentives for Business

The Colorado Quality Investment Capital Program is a finanial program funded by the Colorado State Treasurer. It provides fixed note financing for small business loans guaranteed by the Small Business Administration.

Small business support is also available through assistance programs run by the Chamber of Commerce. Call for more information on the current programs being offered.

No inventory tax.

Industrial Sites

Research Park, University of Colorado at Boulder (143 acres). Jeffrey S. Lipton, Director, Telecommunication Center, Campus Box 317, Boulder, CO 80309-0317, FAX 303-492-5105

Major Businesses

Company	SIC	Telephone
Avedon Engineering, Inc.	3089	(303) 772-2633
Bioenergy Nutrients, Inc.	2834	(303) 530-2508
Boulder Tobacco & Candy Co.	5145	(303) 443-7111
Cell Technology, Inc.	8731	(303) 443-8155
Colorado Brick Co.	3251	(303) 449-1227
Crystal Venture Corp.	9999	(303) 447-0505
Data Display Corp.	3993	(303) 494-9400
Denver Autometrics	3823	(303) 530-1600
Destron/Idi Inc.	3669	(303) 444-5306
Discovery Technologies, Inc.	3844	(303) 651-6500
Discovery Technologies	3845	(303) 651-6500
Engineering Measurements	3823	(303) 651-0550
Exabyte Corp.	3572	(303) 442-4333
Good Times Restaurants Inc.	5812	(303) 449-6162
Granville-Phillips Co.	3823	(303) 443-7660
Hauser Chemical Research	8731	(303) 443-4662
Leanin Tree Inc.		(303) 443-1442
National Securities Holdings	6211	(303) 443-6830
NBI, Inc.	7372	(303) 444-5710
Premium Enterprises, Inc.	7549	(303) 772-1253
Satellite Information Systems	7371	(303) 449-0442
Scientech, Inc.	3821	(303) 444-1361
Somatogen, Inc.	8731	(303) 440-9988
Spectrum Datatech, Inc.	5112	(303) 652-3586
Staodyn, Inc.	3841	(303) 772-3631
Synergen, Inc.	2834	(303) 938-6200
Times-Call Publishing Co.	2711	(303) 776-2244
United Bank of Boulder	6021	(303) 442-0351

Major Businesses (Continued)

Company	SIC	Telephone
Vac-Tec Systems, Inc.	3559	(303) 530-2700
Valleylab, Inc.	3841	(303) 530-2300
Western Mobile Inc.	1611	(303) 428-0800
Westview Press, Inc.	2731	(303) 444-3541
Wiland Services, Inc.	7371	(303) 530-0606
Xedar Corp.	3861	(303) 443-6441

Colleges and Universities

Naropa Institute, Boulder

University of Colorado at Boulder, Boulder (25,176 students). Offers over 4,000 courses and 180 fields of study.

Additional Information

The Spirit of Inquiry, The University of Colorado at Boulder Research Park. University of Colorado at Boulder, n.d. n.p.

Boulder, Colorado, Demographics. Boulder Development Commission, Boulder Chamber of Commerce, n.d. 4p.

Longmont Community Data Summary. Longmont Area Chamber of Commerce, January 1991. 4p.

1991 Economic Development Program. Boulder Development Commission, Boulder Chamber of Commerce, n.d. 10p.

Boulder Technology Incubator. Boulder Economic Development Commission, Boulder Chamber of Commerce, n.d. [brochure]

The Boulder Business Barometer. Boulder Economic Development Commission, Boulder Chamber of Commerce. Quarterly publication.

Boulder, Colorado, A Community Profile. Boulder Economic Development Commission, Boulder Chamber of Commerce, n.d. n.p.

Longmont, Colorado, U.S.A. Economic Development Association of Longmont, n.d. np.

COLORADO SPRINGS, CO (MSA)

Geographic Profile

Land Area

2126.7 square miles

Counties and Parishes

El Paso

Ranking Highlights

82 *out of 319 in total* **land area**

48 *out of 319 in* **population growth,** *1970–1990*

157 *out of 310 in having the lowest* **unemployment** *rate*

114 *out of 310 in size of* **labor force**

52 *out of 318 in the percentage of* **college graduates**

131 *out of 292 in per capita personal* **income**

128 *out of 319 in number of* **manufacturing establishments**

234 *out of 318 in* **physicians** *per 1000 people*

269 *out of 318 in* **hospital beds** *per 1000 people*

143 *out of 267 in fewest* **crimes** *per 1000 people*

81 *out of 266 in fewest* **violent crimes** *per 1000 people*

22 *out of 319 in per capita* **federal funds and grants**

Quality of Life Indexes (Rate per 1000 population)

Crime rate in 1991:	62.0
Violent crime rate in 1991:	4.2
Physicians rate in 1992:	1.46
Hospital bed rate in 1991:	2.58

ACCRA Cost of Living Indexes

(First quarter 1993, average = 100)

Composite index:	94.3
Utilities index:	75.2
Housing index:	92.2

Overview

Colorado Springs is located 65 miles south of Denver and 45 miles north of Pueblo. It is accessed by Interstate Highway 25, U.S. Highways 85, and 87, State Highway 24 and Routes 83, 27,2,94, and 115. Rail service is provided by Atchison; Topeka; Santa Fe; Burlington Northern; and the Denver & Rio Grande Western railroads. Air service is provided by the Corlorado Springs Airport and Stapleton International Airport, 65 miles north.

Population (1990)

Total Population and Growth Rate

1990: 397,014

1980: 309,424

1970: 235,972

Growth rate 1970–1990: 68%

Race and Hispanic Origin

White: 86.0%

Black: 7.2%

Asian/Pacific Islander: 2.5%

Native American: 0.8%

Hispanic origin: 8.7%

White not Hispanic: 81.2%

Age

Ages 18 to 20: 5.2%

Ages 21 to 24: 6.9%

Ages 25 to 44: 35.7%

Ages 45 to 54: 9.6%

Ages 55 to 59: 3.8%

Ages 60 to 64: 3.2%

Ages 65 plus: 8%

Educational Attainment (1990)

Percent having completed high school: 88.3%

Percent having completed college: 25.8%

Elementary and high school enrollment: 68,291

Federal Funds and Grants Received

Total received in 1989: $2,445,200,000

Funds received per capita: $6,208

Civilian Labor Force

1993 (April): 195,630

1992 average: 191,374

1991 average: 188,602

1990 average: 190,149

Unemployment

1993 (April): 6.8%

1992 average: 6.9%

1991 average: 6.1%

1990 average: 6.3%

Average Annual Pay

1988: $19,627

1987: $18,986

1985: $17,517

Per Capita Personal Income

1991: $17,651

1990: $16,807

1989: $16,474

Business Climate (1987)

Manufacturing

Number of establishments in 1987: 419

Shipments in 1987 ($1,000): $2,111,900

Employees in 1987: 22,200

Change in employment, 1982 to 1987: 20.0%

Average annual pay for manufacturing work in 1989: $28,891

Average annual pay for production work in 1987: $19,414

Wholesale Trade

Number of establishments in 1987: 537

Total sales in 1987 ($1,000): $986,400

Change in sales, 1982 to 1987: 64.5%

Retail Trade

Number of establishments in 1987: 2,458
Total sales in 1987 ($1,000): $986,400
Retail sales per household in 1987: $16,371
Average annual pay in 1989: $10,866

Service Industry

Selected receipts in 1987 ($1,000): $1,181,100
Average annual pay in 1989: $19,068

Office Real Estate (1992)

Average class A Central Business District rental range per sq. ft: $14.03

Vacancy Rates

All areas: 17.1%

Vacancy Rates in Central Business District

Class A space: 20.2%
Class B space: N/A

Vacancy Rates Outside Central Business District

Class A space: 16.3%
Class B space: N/A

Housing

Total number of units in 1990: 165,056
Occupied units in 1990: 146,965
Owner-occupied units in 1990: 57.4%
1993 ACCRA average cost: $111,000
1993 ACCRA average rent for an apartment: $384

Chamber of Commerce

Colorado Springs Chamber of Commerce, John D. Fowler, President, 2 N. Cascade Ave. #110, PO Drawer B, Colorado Springs, CO 80901-3002. 719-635-1551, FAX 719-635-1571

Economic Development Office

Greater Colorado Springs Economic Development Council, Robert Scott, President, 2 N. Cascade Ave., PO Drawer B, Colorado Springs, CO 80901. 719-471-8183, 719-471-9733

Local Incentives for Business

SBA 504 Loan Program. The Pikes Peak Regional Development Corporation makes loans under the guidelines of the SBA 504 Program. Small loans of up to $50,000 may be available at below market rates for some businesses.

Colorado Economic Development Commission Loan Fund. The Commission has limited funds available for low-interest loans which are made available, on a matching basis with local communities, to expanding and relocating companies. This gap financing can be for fixed assets or working capital.

Colorado Housing and Finance Authority. Bonds can be issued to finance buildings and equipment at below-market rates and low costs of issuance.

Private Incentives. Various programs are available from local businesses to assist with moving costs, discounts in home purchases, home mortgages, home purchase costs, office equipment purchases, hotel rooms, banking packages, education assistance, spouse reemployment, relocation assistance, etc. depending upon situation.

Vocational Training Funding. Customized training is provided for new employees by the State of Colorado, the local Pikes Peak Private Industry Council, and Pikes Peak Community College. The Private Industry Council provides: (1) On the job training which allows employers to develop a training program and receive reimbursement for up to half of the wages paid during the training period; (2) Targeted Tax Credit which enables employers to receive direct dollar-for-dollar tax credits for hiring individuals in targeted employee groups; (3) Customized Training to be conducted in a classroom setting, on the job, or combination of both.

Tax Incentives. Tax incentives have been built into the tax codes of state and local taxing authorities. Examples include no state sales tax on manufacturing equipment, no inventory tax, and others. Amendment to Sales and Use Tax Code provides for a declining tax rate as investment in machinery increases with an exemption of taxes above a $20 million annual investment.

Enterprise Zone. Some of the advantages are: (1) a $500 Colorado Income Tax Credit refund is available per position established before January 1, 1994; (2) investment tax credit of 3% on machinery and equipment; (3) a 3% R&D tax credit which applies to incremental increase each year; (4) if the company pays at least half the coverage of a health insurance program, there is a $200 credit for year one and year two per position established; (5) 25% credit for expenditures to rehabilitate older vacant buildings.

Other City Incentives: The city can waive utility deposits for credit worthy companies. It also has the ability to lease city owned property for 99 years. The city's Economic Development Response Team will provide expeditious handling of permits and reviews to assure timely approvals.

Major Businesses

Company	SIC	Telephone
Boddington Lumber Co. Inc.	5031	(719) 578-4400
Brookhart's Inc.	5211	(719) 471-4500
Calin Dodge Inc.	5511	(719) 475-8550
Cobb Mechanical Contractors	1711	(719) 471-8958
Colorado Interstate Gas Co.	4923	(719) 473-2300
Colorado National Bank Exchange	6021	(719) 473-1333
Daniels Motors, Inc.	5511	(719) 632-5591
First National Bank	6021	(719) 471-5000
Johnson G. E. Construction	1542	(719) 473-5321
Laser Magnetic Storage Inc.	3572	(719) 593-7900
Long, Phil Ford Inc.	5511	(719) 633-6661

Major Businesses (Continued)

Company	SIC	Telephone
Memorial Hospital	8062	(719) 475-5011
National Systems & Research	7373	(719) 590-8880
Penrose-St. Francis	8062	(719) 630-5000
Sinton Dairy Foods Co.	2026	(719) 633-3821
TGS Technology Inc.	7384	(719) 531-9114
United Bank Colorado Spring National	6021	(719) 636-1361
Wigand Corp.	2431	(719) 599-8887

Colleges and Universities

Beth-El College of Nursing, Colorado Springs
Blair Junior College, Colorado Springs
Colorado College, Colorado Springs
Colorado Technical College, Colorado Springs
Pikes Peak Community College, Colorado Springs
United States Air Force Academy, Colorado Springs
University of Colorado at Colorado Springs, Colorado Springs
University of Phoenix at Colorado Springs, Colorado Springs

DENVER, CO (PMSA)

Geographic Profile

Land Area
3760.9 square miles

Counties and Parishes
Adams
Arapahoe
Denver
Douglas
Jefferson

Ranking Highlights

32 *out of 319 in total* **land area**
77 *out of 319 in* **population growth,** *1970–1990*
82 *out of 310 in having the lowest* **unemployment** *rate*
26 *out of 310 in size of* **labor force**
31 *out of 318 in the percentage of* **college graduates**
30 *out of 292 in per capita personal* **income**
30 *out of 319 in number of* **manufacturing establishments**
53 *out of 318 in* **physicians** *per 1000 people*
231 *out of 318 in* **hospital beds** *per 1000 people*
165 *out of 267 in fewest* **crimes** *per 1000 people*
166 *out of 266 in fewest* **violent crimes** *per 1000 people*
56 *out of 319 in per capita* **federal funds and grants**

Quality of Life Indexes (Rate per 1000 population)

Crime rate in 1991: 66.2
Violent crime rate in 1991: 7.3
Physicians rate in 1992: 2.64
Hospital bed rate in 1991: 3.09

ACCRA Cost of Living Indexes
(First quarter 1993, average = 100)
Composite index: 105.4
Utilities index: 90.2
Housing index: 112.6

Overview

Denver is the capital of Colorado and the center of the Rocky Mountain region. Following record economic and population growth in the 1950s, Denver weathered reversals tied to the fluctuating petroleum market in the 1970s and 1980s. By the late 1980s the city had taken measures toward establishing a diversified economic base. More than one hundred companies in the Denver metropolitan area employ more than five hundred workers each in a range of fields such as air transportation, telecommunications, aerospace, and manufacturing. The city is also a major energy research center and a regional headquarters for government agencies. The metropolitan area was identified by *Fortune* magazine as one of the top ten most desirable locations in the United States and *INC.* magazine rates Colorado the third best state for small businesses.

The financial and commercial capital of the Rocky Mountain region, Denver's downtown banking district—dubbed the Wall Street of the Rockies—consists of major national and international institutions. The city is the transportation hub for a large portion of the western United States; consumer and industrial goods are transported by air, rail, and truck through Denver to 34.4 million people annually. In 1985 Denver became a Foreign Trade Zone, providing advantages to companies involved in international trade.

The new $3.2 billion Denver International Airport will provide nonstop service to more than 100 U.S. cities and will accommodate as many as 34 million passengers in its first year of operation. The airport has become one of the largest air cargo hubs in the nation and handles more than 500 million pounds of freight and more than 160 million pounds of mail. It is predicted that the new airport will be the third busiest in the country by the year 2000.

Denver is also home to the Broncos football team, the Nuggets basketball team, and the new Colorado Rockies baseball team. Within an hour's drive of the center of downtown, the Rocky Mountains provide year round outdoor recreational opportunities.

Denver is at the crossroads of three major interstate highways. Colorado 470, completed in 1990, is the southwest quarter of a new beltway highway system area that will encircle the metro area and provide easy access to the new airport. The first segment of the eastern half of the new beltway has been completed.

Population (1990)

Total Population and Growth Rate
1990: 1,622,980
1980: 1,428,836
1970: 1,106,384
Growth rate 1970–1990: 47%

Race and Hispanic Origin
White: 85.6%
Black: 5.9%
Asian/Pacific Islander: 2.3%
Native American: 0.8%
Hispanic origin: 13.0%
White not Hispanic: 78.4%

Age
Ages 18 to 20: 3.8%
Ages 21 to 24: 5.2%
Ages 25 to 44: 37.5%
Ages 45 to 54: 10.6%
Ages 55 to 59: 4%
Ages 60 to 64: 3.6%
Ages 65 plus: 9.4%

Educational Attainment (1990)
Percent having completed high school: 85.5%
Percent having completed college: 28.9%
Elementary and high school enrollment: 270,774

Federal Funds and Grants Received
Total received in 1989: $7,425,800,000
Funds received per capita: $4,528

Civilian Labor Force
1993 (April):   908,276
1992 average: 890,231
1991 average: 892,656
1990 average: 896,121

Unemployment
1993 (April):   5.7%
1992 average: 5.7%
1991 average: 4.6%
1990 average: 4.6%

Average Annual Pay
1988: $23,641
1987: $22,895
1985: $21,498

Per Capita Personal Income
1991: $21,441
1990: $20,802
1989: $19,646

Business Climate (1987)

Manufacturing
Number of establishments in 1987: 2,505
Shipments in 1987 ($1,000): $12,120,000
Employees in 1987: 96,400
Change in employment, 1982 to 1987: 0%
Average annual pay for manufacturing work in 1989: $30,995
Average annual pay for production work in 1987: $24,567

Wholesale Trade
Number of establishments in 1987: 4,320
Total sales in 1987 ($1,000): $24,141,400
Change in sales, 1982 to 1987: 0%

Retail Trade
Number of establishments in 1987: 9,991
Total sales in 1987 ($1,000): $24,141,400
Retail sales per household in 1987: $16,615
Average annual pay in 1989: $12,974

Service Industry
Selected receipts in 1987 ($1,000): $7,480,800
Average annual pay in 1989: $21,611

Office Real Estate (1992)
Office space inventory: 55,479,674 square feet
Average class A Central Business District rental range per sq. ft: $14.00

Vacancy Rates
All areas: 18.3%

Vacancy Rates in Central Business District
Class A space: 14.5%
Class B space: 25.1%

Vacancy Rates Outside Central Business District

Class A space: 17.3%
Class B space: 17.8%

Housing

Total number of units in 1990: 716,150
Occupied units in 1990: 649,404
Owner-occupied units in 1990: 61.6%
1993 ACCRA average cost: $125,200
1993 ACCRA average rent for an apartment: $604

Chamber of Commerce

Greater Denver Chamber of Commerce, Richard C. D. Fleming, President, 1600 Sherman St., Denver, CO 80203-1620. 303-894-8500, FAX 303-534-3200

Economic Development Office

Mayor's Office of Economic Development, John Huggins, Director, 216 16th St. #1000, Denver, CO 80202. 303-640-7100, FAX 303-640-7059

Economic Development Organizations

Adams County Economic Development, Inc., Jack Keever, President, 11990 N. Grant St., #220, Denver, CO 80233. 303-837-4717

The Downtown Denver Partnership, Inc., William E. Mosher, President, 511 16th St., #200, Denver, CO 80202. 303-534-6161, FAX 303-534-2803

Metro Denver Network, Dolores Wilson, 1445 Market St., Denver, CO 80202. 303-534-8500

Industrial Sites

Academy Park (230 acres)
Aurora Business Center (900 acres)
Aurora Centre Tech (360 acres)
Center Point (112 acres)
Centennial Airport Center (580 acres)
Centennial Valley (320 acres)
Church Range Home Place (415 acres)
Colorado Tech Center (600 acres)
Coors Technology Center (375 acres)
Denver Business Center (256 acres)
Denver Technology Center (776 acres)
Denver West Office Park (750 acres)
Dove Valley Business Park (1,000 acres)
Flatirons Industrial Park (260 acres)
Greenwood Plaza (600 acres)
Highlands Ranch (930 acres)
Interlocken Business Park (570 acres)
Inverness Business Park (980 acres)
Irondale Industrial Park (196 acres)
Ken-Caryl Business Center (300 acres)
Genesee Business Center (120 acres)
Jefferson Center (4,400 acres)
Meridian International Business Center (1,158 acres)
Montbello Industrial Park (600 acres)
Northglenn Industrial Park (100 acres)

Park Centre (460 acres)
Red Rocks Center (320 acres)
Regency West (125 acres)
South Park (267 acres)
Stapleton Industrial Park (186 acres)
Upland I, II & III (823 acres)
Washington Center (287 acres)
Westminster Crossing (300 acres)

Industrial space costs per square foot in the area range from $1.50-$2.25 for warehousing and manufacturing and $4.25-$5.50 for R&D.s

Major Businesses

Company	SIC	Telephone
Advent Health System Rocky Mountain	8062	(303) 778-5736
Affiliated Bankshares	6029	(303) 296-7788
Amdura Corp.	5072	(303) 377-8400
ANR Freight System, Inc.	4213	(303) 278-9900
Anschutz Corp.	4111	(303) 298-1000
Apache Corp.	1311	(303) 837-5000
Asset Investors Corp.	6799	(303) 793-2703
Associated Natural Gas Co.	4923	(303) 595-3331
Betawest Properties, Inc.	6531	(303) 292-7000
Border Fuel Supply Corp.	5172	(303) 770-1600
Butler Paper Co., Inc.	5111	(303) 790-8343
Capitol Life Insurance Co.	6321	(303) 861-4065
Champion Boxed Beef Co.	5147	(303) 288-1003
Cobank National Bank	6111	(303) 740-4000
Cobe Laboratories, Inc.	3841	(303) 232-6800
Colorado National Bankshares	6021	(303) 629-1968
Coors, Adolph Co.	2082	(303) 279-6565
Cyprus Coal Co.	1222	(303) 643-5100
Cyprus Metals Co.	1021	(303) 643-5000
Cyprus Minerals Co.	1021	(303) 643-5000
Cyprus Mines Corp.	1221	(303) 643-5000
Denver Rio Grande	4011	(303) 629-5533
Frontier Oil and Refining Co.	2911	(303) 860-6100
Frontier Oil Corp.	2911	(303) 860-6100
Gates Corp.	3052	(303) 744-1911
Gates Rubber Co.	3052	(303) 744-1911
Gillett Holdings Inc.	2011	(303) 292-0045
Great Western Life & Annuity Insurance	6311	(303) 889-3000
Hamilton Oil Corp.	1311	(303) 863-3000
K N Energy, Inc.	4923	(303) 989-1740
Leprino Foods Co.	2022	(303) 480-2600
Litvak Meat Co.	2011	(303) 288-0766
M. D. C. Holdings Inc.	6552	(303) 773-1100
Mail-Well Envelope Co.	2677	(303) 790-8023
Manville Corp.	3296	(303) 978-2000
Mountain States Telephone Telegraph	4813	(303) 896-2355

Major Businesses (Continued)

Company	SIC	Telephone
Natkin Group Inc.	1711	(303) 761-6603
Newmont Gold Co.	1041	(303) 863-7414
Newmont Mining Corp.	1041	(303) 863-7414
Nobel Sysco Food Services	5141	(303) 458-4000
Pace Membership Warehouse	5141	(303) 364-0700
PCL Construction Services	1542	(303) 753-6600
PCL Enterprises Inc.	1542	(303) 753-6554
Pittsburg Midway Coal Mining	1221	(303) 930-3600
Public Service Co. of Colorado	4911	(303) 571-7511
Rio Grande Holding, Inc.	4011	(303) 595-2254
Rocky Mountain Hospital & Medical Service	6324	(303) 831-2131
Samsonite Corp.	3161	(303) 373-2000
Security Life of Denver	6311	(303) 860-1290
St. Anthony Healthcare Corp.	8062	(303) 629-3511
Stolte Inc.	1542	(303) 595-0925
Storage Technology Corp.	3572	(303) 673-5151
TCI Central Inc.	4841	(303) 987-9552
Tele-Communications, Inc.	4841	(303) 721-5500
Texaco Trading And Transportation	5172	(303) 861-4475
Total Petroleum Inc.	2911	(303) 291-2000
U S West Direct Co.	2741	(303) 337-8888
U. S. West Financial Service	6159	(303) 773-2363
U. S. West Inc.	4813	(303) 793-6500
U. S. West Marketing Resources	2741	(303) 696-2900
United Bank of Denver	6021	(303) 861-8811
Vicorp Restaurants Inc.	5812	(303) 296-2121
Walter, Jim Papers, Inc.	5111	(303) 790-8343
Western Capital Investment	6035	(303) 623-5577
Western Dairymen Cooperation	5143	(303) 451-0422
Western Sugar Co.	2063	(303) 830-3939

Colleges and Universities

Bel-Rea Institute of Animal Technology, Denver
Colorado Institute of Art, Denver
Community College of Denver, Denver
Denver Automotive and Diesel College, Denver
Denver Institute of Technology, Denver
Denver Technical College, Denver
Metropolitan State College, Denver
Parks Junior College, Denver
Regis College, Denver
Rocky Mountain College of Art and Design, Denver
University of Colorado at Denver, Denver
University of Colorado Health Sciences Center, Denver
University of Denver, Denver

Additional Information

Business Barometers, Denver Metropolitan Area. Greater Denver Chamber of Commerce, monthly. 4p.
Denver. Metro Denver Network. Quarterly.

Greater Denver Community Guidebook, Living, Working and Doing Business in the Six-County Metro Area. Greater Denver Chamber of Commerce, 1991. 84p.
Metro Denver Economic Focus. Greater Denver Chamber of Commerce, Economic Development Group, May 1990. 4p.
1991 Metro Denver Economic Profile. Greater Denver Chamber of Commerce, 1991. 58p.

FORT COLLINS–LOVELAND, CO (MSA)

Geographic Profile

Land Area

2601.4 square miles

Counties and Parishes

Larimer

Ranking Highlights

 65 *out of 319 in total* **land area**

 18 *out of 319 in* **population growth,** *1970–1990*

 29 *out of 310 in having the lowest* **unemployment** *rate*

183 *out of 310 in size of* **labor force**

 17 *out of 318 in the percentage of* **college graduates**

129 *out of 292 in per capita personal* **income**

178 *out of 319 in number of* **manufacturing establishments**

212 *out of 318 in* **physicians** *per 1000 people*

291 *out of 318 in* **hospital beds** *per 1000 people*

N/A *out of 267 in fewest* **crimes** *per 1000 people*

N/A *out of 266 in fewest* **violent crimes** *per 1000 people*

296 *out of 319 in per capita* **federal funds and grants**

Quality of Life Indexes (Rate per 1000 population)

Crime rate in 1991:	N/A
Violent crime rate in 1991:	N/A
Physicians rate in 1992:	1.56
Hospital bed rate in 1991:	2.2

ACCRA Cost of Living Indexes

(First quarter 1993, average = 100)

Composite index:	103.8
Utilities index:	73.3
Housing index:	115.7

Overview

Fort Collins is located abot 65 miles north of Denver, along the banks of the Cache La Poudre River, at the foothills of the Rockies on the Eastern Plains at an elevation of 4,979 feet above sea level.

Colorado State University and the Colorado State University Research Foundation play major roles in attracting and supporting high technology business and industry. CSU has created a consortium to help Colorado companies effectively use new technologies to solve their manufacturing problems. The Manufacturing Excellence Center was created to supplement companies' in-house expertise in engineering, accounting, marketing, software engineering, and other areas.

Denver International Airport is less than one hour's drive to the south. The Fort Collins/Loveland Airport and the Downtown Fort Collins Airport provide facilities for private aircraft and corporate aviation. A commuter service has seven daily flights to and from Denver. Motor connections can be easily made with I-25 adjacent to the city, I-80 forty miles north, and I-70 sixty miles south.

Population (1990)

Total Population and Growth Rate

1990: 186,136

1980: 149,184

1970: 89,900

Growth rate 1970–1990: 107%

Race and Hispanic Origin

White: 94.5%

Black: .6%

Asian/Pacific Islander: 1.5%

Native American: 0.6%

Hispanic origin: 6.6%

White not Hispanic: 90.9%

Age

Ages 18 to 20: 6.7%

Ages 21 to 24: 7.5%

Ages 25 to 44: 34.9%

Ages 45 to 54: 9.4%

Ages 55 to 59: 3.4%

Ages 60 to 64: 3.2%

Ages 65 plus: 9.6%

Educational Attainment (1990)

Percent having completed high school: 88.6%

Percent having completed college: 32.3%

Elementary and high school enrollment: 30,942

Federal Funds and Grants Received

Total received in 1989: $391,700,000

Funds received per capita: $2,152

Civilian Labor Force

1993 (April):   105,920

1992 average: 104,082

1991 average: 103,773

1990 average: 102,633

Unemployment

1993 (April):   4.1%

1992 average: 4.5%

1991 average: 4.1%

1990 average: 4.4%

Average Annual Pay

1988: $19,637

1987: $18,952

1985: $17,526

Per Capita Personal Income

1991: $17,657

1990: $17,162

1989: $16,127

Business Climate (1987)

Manufacturing

Number of establishments in 1987: 274
Shipments in 1987 ($1,000): $1,124,300
Employees in 1987: 12,500
Change in employment, 1982 to 1987: -1.6%
Average annual pay for manufacturing work, 1989: $30,345
Average annual pay for production work, 1987: $23,667

Wholesale Trade

Number of establishments in 1987: 293
Total sales in 1987 ($1,000): $522,900
Change in sales, 1982 to 1987: 45.6%

Retail Trade

Number of establishments in 1987: 1,269
Total sales in 1987 ($1,000): $522,900
Retail sales per household in 1987: $15,697
Average annual pay in 1989: $10,234

Service Industry

Selected receipts in 1987 ($1,000): $358,000
Average annual pay in 1989: $15,489

Office Real Estate (1992)

Office space inventory: N/A
Average class A Central Business District rental range per sq. ft: $14.00

Vacancy Rates

All areas: 39%

Vacancy Rates in Central Business District

Class A space: N/A
Class B space: N/A

Vacancy Rates Outside Central Business District

Class A space: N/A
Class B space: N/A

Housing

Total number of units in 1990: 77,811
Occupied units in 1990: 70,472
Owner-occupied units in 1990: 62.9%
1993 ACCRA average cost: $137,190
1993 ACCRA average rent for an apartment: $507

Chamber of Commerce

Fort Collins Chamber of Commerce, Mike Hauser, Exec. Vice President, 225 S. Meldrum St., PO Drawer D, Fort Collins, CO 80521. 303-482-3746, FAX 303-482-5219

Economic Development Office

Fort Collins, Inc., Ed Stoner, Exec. Director, PO Box 1849, 225 S. Meldrum St., Fort Collins, CO 80521. 303-221-0861, FAX 303-221-5219

Economic Development Organizations

Loveland Chamber of Commerce, Patricia A. Farnham, Exec. Director, 114 E. 5th St., PO Box 7058, Loveland, CO 80537. 800-667-5971, 303-667-6311, FAX 303-667-5211

Loveland Economic Development Council, Richard Greenberg, Exec. Director, 200 E. 7th St. #302, Loveland, CO 80537. 303-667-0905, FAX 303-669-4680

Loveland Info EDC, Joe Richards, Exec. Director, 926 Logan Court, Loveland, CO 80538. 303-667-6311

Colorado State University, Manufacturing Excellence Center, Dr. Wade Troxell, Assoc. Director, Colorado Springs, CO. 303-491-6618

Local Incentives for Business

Development. Local incentives include waiver of development and permit fees from the city and county and participation in infrastructure. Financial assistance package could be arranged on a case by case basis.

Employee Training. Larimer County Employment and Training will handle all applications, testing, and interviews to the company's specifications. Front Range Community College offers contracted customized training. It also offers assistance with applications to Colorado FIRST, JTPA and Targeted Jobs Tax Credit.

Major Businesses

Company	SIC	Telephone
Advanced Energy Industries	3679	(303) 221-4670
American Natural Gas Corp.	1311	(303) 226-1606
Baldwin Construction, Inc.	1542	(303) 482-7722
Cloverleaf Kennel Club Inc.	7948	(303) 667-6211
Colorado Steel & Wire Co.	3312	(303) 667-9390
Comlinear Corp.	3674	(303) 226-0500
Connell Resources Inc.	1611	(303) 667-1238
First National Bank In Loveland	6021	(303) 224-2276
Forney Industries Inc.	5084	(303) 482-7271
Gracon Corp.	1623	(303) 667-2203
Hach Co.	3826	(303) 669-3050
Home Federal Savings Bank	6035	(303) 482-3216
Innovative Companies Inc.	2541	(303) 223-7779
Markley Motors Inc.	5511	(303) 226-2213
Platte River Power Authority	4911	(303) 226-4000
Poudre Valley Hospital	8062	(303) 482-4111
Poudre Valley Rural Electric	4911	(303) 226-1234
Schrader Oil Co.	5541	(303) 484-1225
Steele's Market, Inc.	5411	(303) 226-3086
Vipont Pharmaceutical, Inc.	2844	(303) 482-3126
Yancey's Food Service Co.	5141	(303) 484-3123

Colleges and Universities

Colorado State University, Fort Collins (20,000 students).
Front Range Community College (3,000 students).

Additional Information

Profile - Fort Collins, Colorado. Fort Collins, Inc., n.d. 16p.
Fort Collins Trends, A Quarterly review of Current Social and Economic Conditions. City of Fort Collins, Planning Dept., October 1990. 66p.

GREELEY, CO (MSA)

Geographic Profile

Land Area
3992.8 square miles

Counties and Parishes
Weld

Ranking Highlights

27 *out of 319 in total* **land area**

75 *out of 319 in* **population growth,** *1970–1990*

64 *out of 310 in having the lowest* **unemployment** *rate*

235 *out of 310 in size of* **labor force**

169 *out of 318 in the percentage of* **college graduates**

211 *out of 292 in per capita personal* **income**

257 *out of 319 in number of* **manufacturing establishments**

246 *out of 318 in* **physicians** *per 1000 people*

296 *out of 318 in* **hospital beds** *per 1000 people*

120 *out of 267 in fewest* **crimes** *per 1000 people*

69 *out of 266 in fewest* **violent crimes** *per 1000 people*

311 *out of 319 in per capita* **federal funds and grants**

Quality of Life Indexes (Rate per 1000 population)

Crime rate in 1991:	58.5
Violent crime rate in 1991:	3.8
Physicians rate in 1992:	1.41
Hospital bed rate in 1991:	2.13

ACCRA Cost of Living Indexes

(First quarter 1993, average = 100)

Composite index:	N/A
Utilities index:	N/A
Housing index:	N/A

Overview

The past two decades have seen Weld County change from a predominantly agriculture and agri-business dependent economy to a diverse industry base, including high-tech manufacturing and development. There are eight Fortune 500 companies located in Weld County, including: Hewlett-Packard, Eastman Kodak, State Farm Insurance Regional Headquarters, W.R. Grace, Adolph Coors Co., R.R. Donnelley & Sons, Anheuser-Busch, and ConAgra. Two and a half million acres are devoted to agriculture with more than 96% of that area devoted to farming and raising livestock.

Weld County is ranked No. 1 in the nation in value of livestock, poultry and their products; sheep and lambs inventory; sheep and lambs sold; number of cattle and calves sold; and the number of cattle fattened on grain. Weld has had between 35-45% of all cattle on feed in Colorado, varying from 300,000 to 450,000 head, depending on the market. Weld is also becoming more important as a milk producing county, with about 43% of the state's dairy herds here.

In field crops, Weld produces 21% of the grain corn in Colorado, with a market value of nearly $63 million in 1989. Some of the other big producers were potatoes at $6 million, winter wheat at $17 million, barley at $4.6 million, beans $20.5 million, hay at $42 million and other field crops at $18.5 million. Much of the crop production, as well as the livestock, provide considerable employment in the processing, shipping and marketing areas. It is estimated that about 31% of the employment in Weld County has a relationship to agriculture.

Weld County has one of the world's largest irrigating areas: 420,000 acres in Weld County are irrigated by a combination of mountain run-off, over 5,000 acres by irrigation wells, and over 40,000 acres irrigated by pivot sprinklers. There are enough water resources to serve it into the 21st century.

The county is the second highest oil and natural gas producing county in Colorado, and is rapidly approaching number one. Weld County has experienced a continued, steady population growth rate of approximately 10% per decade, which is more than the national average of 8%. Greeley and Weld County have been designated a state Enterprise Zone, allowing qualified businesses to take credit against their state income taxes for equipment investment and jobs.

Two interstate highways, I-25 and I-76 and two U.S.highways, U.S. 34 & U.S. 85 serve the county, and two additional interstate highways border Weld County, I-70 and I-80. Fourteen motor freight firms and three railroads provide freight service. Commercial air service is provided by 18 carriers operating from Denver's Stapleton Airport to 186 cities and nine countries; the airport is an hour's drive from the county's population centers. The new Denver international airport under construction will be located at the southern edge of Weld County, about 45 minutes from Greeley.

Six major ski areas are located within a two-hour drive. Weld County is home to the oldest philharmonic orchestra west of the Mississippi River,and is the site of the largest civic auditorium in northern Colorado. Rocky Mountain National Park,is 50 miles to the west.

Population (1990)

Total Population and Growth Rate
1990: 131,821
1980: 123,438
1970: 89,297
Growth rate 1970–1990: 48%

Race and Hispanic Origin
White: 88.9%
Black: .4%
Asian/Pacific Islander: 0.9%
Native American: 0.6%
Hispanic origin: 20.9%
White not Hispanic: 77.4%

Age

Ages 18 to 20: 6.4%
Ages 21 to 24: 6.8%
Ages 25 to 44: 31.7%
Ages 45 to 54: 9.6%
Ages 55 to 59: 3.8%
Ages 60 to 64: 3.5%
Ages 65 plus: 10.2%

Educational Attainment (1990)

Percent having completed high school: 74.5%
Percent having completed college: 18.4%
Elementary and high school enrollment: 24,519

Federal Funds and Grants Received

Total received in 1989: $244,600,000
Funds received per capita: $1,796

Civilian Labor Force

1993 (April): 69,780
1992 average: 69,547
1991 average: 70,316
1990 average: 68,907

Unemployment

1993 (April): 5.2%
1992 average: 5.3%
1991 average: 4.5%
1990 average: 5.0%

Average Annual Pay

1988: $19,009
1987: $18,293
1985: $17,335

Per Capita Personal Income

1991: $16,052
1990: $15,518
1989: $14,827

Business Climate (1987)

Manufacturing

Number of establishments in 1987: 142
Shipments in 1987 ($1,000): $3,037,100
Employees in 1987: 7,900
Change in employment, 1982 to 1987: 16.2%
Average annual pay for manufacturing work in 1989: $27,120
Average annual pay for production work in 1987: $20,840

Wholesale Trade

Number of establishments in 1987: 241
Total sales in 1987 ($1,000): $583,100
Change in sales, 1982 to 1987: -4.1%

Retail Trade

Number of establishments in 1987: 672
Total sales in 1987 ($1,000): $583,100
Retail sales per household in 1987: $11,225
Average annual pay in 1989: $10,190

Service Industry

Selected receipts in 1987 ($1,000): $165,600
Average annual pay in 1989: $15,364

Housing

Total number of units in 1990: 51,138
Occupied units in 1990: 47,470
Owner-occupied units in 1990: 61.2%
1993 ACCRA average cost: N/A
1993 ACCRA average rent for an apartment: N/A

Chamber of Commerce

Greeley-Weld Area Chamber of Commerce, Pamela Ross, President, 1407 8th Ave., Greeley, CO 80631-4603. 303-352-3566, FAX 303-352-3572

Economic Development Office

Greeley/Weld Economic Development Action Partnership, William J. Argo, President, 810 9th St., 2nd Fl., PO Box S., Greeley, CO 80632. 303-356-4565, FAX 303-352-2436

Economic Development Organizations

Greeley Board of Realtors, Steve Case, President, 819 11th St., Greeley, CO. 303-353-8884

Weld County Human Resources, Director, 1551 N. 17th Ave., Greeley, CO. 303-353-3800

Weld County Planning, Chuck Cuntiff, Director, PO Box 758, Greeley, CO. 303-356-4000

Weld County Commissioners, Coorden Lacey, PO Box 758, Greeley, CO. 303-356-4000

Local Incentives for Business

Enterprise Zone. Weld County has a state designated enterprise zone in 16 municipalities including Greeley offering substantial state income tax credits for businesses locating within the zone.

Revolving Loan Fund. The RLF was created to help fill the financial gaps (maximum $100,000) between the amount needed for business venture or expansion and the amount secured through various sources. This GAP financing is or manufacturing projects that create new jobs.

Waivers of Fees & Permits. Waivers for new industrial construction are available in several Weld cities.

Special Incentive Packages. The Greeley/Weld Economic Development Action Partnership will prepare a full proposal for industrial employers related to financing, incentives, rates, labor, etc.s

Major Businesses

Company	SIC	Telephone
Agland Inc.	2048	(303) 454-3391
Armadillo Club, Inc.	5812	(303) 284-5587
D S C O Inc.	7513	(303) 352-6760
Electronic Fab Technology	3823	(303) 353-3100
Formby Ford Inc.	5511	(303) 857-2787
Garnsey & Wheeler Co.	5511	(303) 352-9174

Major Businesses (Continued)

Company	SIC	Telephone
Hydraulics Unlimited Mfg.	3536	(303) 454-2291
Loveland Industries Inc.	2879	(303) 356-8920
Miller Diversified Corp.	0211	(303) 284-5556
Monfort, Inc.	2011	(303) 353-2311
Monfort Food Distributing Co.	5147	(303) 353-2311
Monfort Transportation Inc.	4213	(303) 353-2311
Newco Inc.	5063	(303) 352-5024
Nor-Colo Distributing Co.	5181	(303) 352-8161
North Colorado Medical Center	8062	(303) 352-4121
Phelps Inc.	1542	(303) 352-6565
Roche Constructors, Inc.	1542	(303) 356-3611
Roggen Farmers Elevator	5153	(303) 849-5506
Sipco, Inc.	2011	(303) 351-0083
Swift Independent Corp.	2011	(303) 353-2311
Swift Independent Holding	2011	(303) 353-2311
Union Colony Bank	6022	(303) 356-7000
United Bank of Greeley National	6022	(303) 356-1000
Val-Agri Inc.	2011	(303) 353-2311
Webster Feed Lots Inc.	0211	(303) 353-4304
Weld County Garage	5511	(303) 352-1313
Winoco, Inc.	5051	(303) 352-6722

Colleges and Universities

Aims Community College, Greeley

University of Northern Colorado, Greeley

Additional Information

Demographic Profile, Greeley/Weld County, Colorado. Greeley/Weld Economic Development Action Partnership, March 1991. np.

Greeley/Weld Urban Enterprise Zone, State Tax Incentives. Greeley/Weld Office of Economic Development, n.d. 6p.

PUEBLO, CO (MSA)

Geographic Profile

Land Area

2388.8 square miles

Counties and Parishes

Pueblo

Ranking Highlights

73 *out of 319 in total* **land area**

249 *out of 319 in* **population growth**, *1970–1990*

212 *out of 310 in having the lowest* **unemployment** *rate*

286 *out of 310 in size of* **labor force**

256 *out of 318 in the percentage of* **college graduates**

265 *out of 292 in per capita personal* **income**

299 *out of 319 in number of* **manufacturing establishments**

109 *out of 318 in* **physicians** *per 1000 people*

111 *out of 318 in* **hospital beds** *per 1000 people*

182 *out of 267 in fewest* **crimes** *per 1000 people*

258 *out of 266 in fewest* **violent crimes** *per 1000 people*

155 *out of 319 in per capita* **federal funds and grants**

Quality of Life Indexes (Rate per 1000 population)

Crime rate in 1991:	68.5
Violent crime rate in 1991:	13.4
Physicians rate in 1992:	2.07
Hospital bed rate in 1991:	4.51

ACCRA Cost of Living Indexes

(First quarter 1993, average = 100)

Composite index:	84.7
Utilities index:	79.0
Housing index:	71.9

Population (1990)

Total Population and Growth Rate

1990: 123,051

1980: 125,972

1970: 118,238

Growth rate 1970–1990: 4%

Race and Hispanic Origin

White: 84.8%

Black: 1.8%

Asian/Pacific Islander: 0.6%

Native American: 0.8%

Hispanic origin: 35.8%

White not Hispanic: 61.3%

Age

Ages 18 to 20: 4.3%

Ages 21 to 24: 4.9%

Ages 25 to 44: 29.5%

Ages 45 to 54: 9.8%

Ages 55 to 59: 4.8%

Ages 60 to 64: 5.2%

Ages 65 plus: 15.2%

Educational Attainment (1990)

Percent having completed high school: 73.9%
Percent having completed college: 14.0%
Elementary and high school enrollment: 22,129

Federal Funds and Grants Received

Total received in 1989: $396,200,000
Funds received per capita: $3,104

Civilian Labor Force

1993 (April):	52,123
1992 average:	51,864
1991 average:	52,949
1990 average:	52,916

Unemployment

1993 (April): 7.8%
1992 average: 7.8%
1991 average: 7.0%
1990 average: 6.7%

Average Annual Pay

1988: $17,323
1987: $16,714
1985: $16,353

Per Capita Personal Income

1991: $14,795
1990: $14,014
1989: $13,252

Business Climate (1987)

Manufacturing

Number of establishments in 1987: 95
Shipments in 1987 ($1,000): $467,200
Employees in 1987: 3,600
Change in employment, 1982 to 1987: -36.8%
Average annual pay for manufacturing work in 1989: $24,834
Average annual pay for production work in 1987: $23,917

Wholesale Trade

Number of establishments in 1987: 137
Total sales in 1987 ($1,000): $247,800
Change in sales, 1982 to 1987: 6.2%

Retail Trade

Number of establishments in 1987: 842
Total sales in 1987 ($1,000): $247,800
Retail sales per household in 1987: $13,652
Average annual pay in 1989: $10,268

Service Industry

Selected receipts in 1987 ($1,000): $193,400
Average annual pay in 1989: $14,829

Housing

Total number of units in 1990: 50,872
Occupied units in 1990: 47,057

Owner-occupied units in 1990: 67.9%
1993 ACCRA average cost: $82,033
1993 ACCRA average rent for an apartment: $353

Chamber of Commerce

Pueblo Chamber of Commerce, Meme Dunckel, President, 302 N. Santa Fe Ave., PO Box 697, Pueblo, CO 81002. 719-542-1704, FAX 719-542-1624

Economic Development Office

Southern Colorado Economic Development District, David Grimes, Exec. Director, 212 W. 13th St., Pueblo, CO 81003. 719-545-8680

Major Businesses

Company	SIC	Telephone
Bassett Construction Co.	1542	(719) 544-6391
Board of Water Works of Pueblo	4941	(719) 584-0250
Brice, Cliff Stations Inc.	5541	(719) 543-3934
C F & I Steel Corp.	3312	(719) 561-6000
Colorado Wyoming Railway Co.	4011	(719) 561-6358
Houston H. W. Construction Co.	1542	(719) 544-2791
Industrial Gas Products	2813	(719) 543-1122
Kirkland, James H. Construction	1611	(719) 489-3385
Parkview Health System	8062	(719) 584-4000
Pueblo Bank & Trust Co.	6022	(719) 545-1834
Pueblo Housing Authority	6531	(719) 544-6230
San Isabel Electric Association	4911	(719) 547-2160
Whitlock, H. E., Inc.	1542	(719) 544-9475
Whitlock Service Corp.	1542	(719) 544-9475
Wilcoxson Buick-Cadillac	5511	(719) 544-4423

Colleges and Universities

Pueblo Community College, Pueblo
University of Southern Colorado, Pueblo

CONNECTICUT

HARTFORD-NEW BRITAIN-
MIDDLETOWN-BRISTOL (NECMA)

RHODE
ISLAND

NEW LONDON-NORWICH (NECMA)

NEW HAVEN-WATERBURY-
MERIDEN (NECMA)

BRIDGEPORT-STAMFORD-
NORWALK-DANBURY (NECMA)

CONNECTICUT

Population
1990: 3,287,116
1980: 3,107,576

Age
Ages 18 to 20: 145,274
Ages 21 to 24: 200,159
Ages 25 to 44: 1,094,878
Ages 45 to 54: 356,042
Ages 55 to 59: 147,022
Ages 60 to 64: 148,253
Median age: 34.4

Race
White: 2,859,353
Black: 274,269
Asian/Pacific Islander: 50,698
Native American: 6,654
Hispanic origin: 213,116

Households
Total: 1,230,479
Persons per household: 2.59

Sex
Male: 1,592,873
Female: 1,694,243

Population Migration
Domestic migration: 15,000
International migration: 69,000

Projection of the Population in 1995
Total: 3,392,000
18 to 64: 2,133,000

Civilian Labor Force
1993: 1,745,900
1992: 1,818,100
1991: 1,799,700
1990: 1,758,700

Manufacturing
1995 Projection: 371,900
1992: 305,700
1991: 322,300
1990: 337,600
1989: 357,800

Services
1995 Projection: 627,300

1992: 420,100
1991: 433,100
1990: 439,400
1989: 433,100

Wholesale and Retail Trade
1995 Projection: 456,200
1992: 332,500
1991: 358,600
1990: 378,100
1989: 400,400

Unemployment Rate
1993: 7.5%
1992: 8.0%
1991: 5.8%
1990: 5.0%

Employer Unemployment Contributions
Contribution Rate
1992: 2.80%
1991: 2.20%
1990: 1.82%

Average Weekly Benefit
1992: $227.41
1991: $219.99
1990: $201.57

Gross State Product (Million $)
1989: $88,863
1988: $85,651
1987: $78,420
1979: $36,695
Growth rate, 1979 to 1989: 142.2%

Capital Expenditures of Manufacturing Industries
1990: $1,441,200,000
1989: $1,374,700,000
1988: $1,238,500,000
1987: $1,293,300,000

State Tax Rates
Individual income: 4.5% of all taxable income.
Corporate income: 11.5% of taxable net income.
General property: Rates fixed locally. Assessed at actual value of real and personal property.

General sales: 6%
Gasoline: 26¢ per gallon

Income
Median income for a 4 person family: $53,313

Personal per Capita Income
1992: $26,979
1991: $25,968
1990: $25,528

Disposable per Capita Income
1992: $22,891
1991: $22,082
1990: $21,699

Private Employment Weekly Wages
Average
1989: $526
1988: $505
1987: $505

Manufacturing
1989: $468
1988: $614
1987: $578

Services
1989: $462
1988: $435
1987: $400

Wholesale
1989: $727
1988: $702
1987: $629

Retail
1989: $294
1988: $280
1987: $260

Highway Statistics
Total Highway Miles
1990: 19,991
1989: 19,914
1988: 19,798

Federal Highway Aid
1991: $346,917,000
1990: $321,886,000
1989: $265,065,000

Electricity
Average Cost per Kilowatt Hour
1990: 9.17¢
1989: 8.77¢
1988: 8.37¢

Housing (1990)
Owner occupied units: 807,481
Median house value: $177,800

Renter occupied units: 422,998
Median rent: $510
Total vacant units: 90,371
Homeowner vacancy rate: 1.9%
Rental vacancy rate: 6.9%

State Business Incentives and Assistance
Enterprise Zones Incentives
Urban Enterprise Zone Program. Offers expanded incentives for companies involving themselves in the 11 state designated zones. Special investment incentives for manufacturers, commercial businesses, retailers, and residential property owners undertaking new capital investments. Special financing programs include low-cost working capital, venture capital, and small-business loans. Incentives include a seven-year graduated deferral of any increases in property taxes attributable to new improvements. Added incentives for manufacturers and research-and-development facilities include 80% abatement of property taxes, 50% state corporate business tax reductions, and $1,500 grants for each new job created within a two-year period.

Urban Jobs Program. Benefits firms undertaking projects in 28 targeted municipalities. It offers $500 grants for each new, permanent full-time job.

Financial and Business Assistance
Connecticut Development Authority. Helps companies undertake new capital expansions covering the cost of land, the construction, purchase, improvement or expansion of buildings, and the purchase and installation of machinery and equipment. Project types include manufacturing, research and development, and distribution, warehouse and office facilities. Pollution control and energy conservation projects also are eligible. Options include the Umbrella Bond program for loans of up to $5 million, in conjunction with bank participation in the form of limited letters of credit; the Self-Substaining Industrial Revenue Bond program for projects up to $10 million, and the Mortgage Insurance program to insure mortgage loans on buildings up to $10 million, and machinery and equipment up to $5 million.

Connecticut Innovations, Inc. Provides up to 60% of eligible development costs of specific projects, from initial concept through fabrication of the production-ready prototype. Loans of up to $200,000 are also offered to help get new products produced. A limited royalty on the sales of the sponsored product is required.

Connecticut Business Development Corporation. Arranges SBA-guaranteed debenture financing for fixed-asset projects on a second mortgage basis. The second mortgage cannot exceed $500,000, or 40% of the project cost. The net worth of the business must be less than $6 million, and its after-tax profit for each of the last two years must be less than $2 million.

Connecticut Technology Assistance Center. Administered

Major Companies in the State

Company name	Fortune 500 rank	City	Telephone	SIC number
Fortune 500 Companies				
American Brands Inc.	57	Old Greenwich	203-698-5000	2111
Bowater Inc.	273	Darien	203-656-7200	2621
Champion International Corp.	109	Stamford	203-358-7000	2621
Crane Co.	291	Stamford	203-363-7300	3491
Crystal Brands Inc.	428	Southport	203-254-6200	2321
Dexter Corp.	366	Windsor Locks	203-627-9051	2297
Duracell International Inc.	259	Bethel	203-796-4000	3691
Echlin Inc.	237	Branford	203-481-5751	3714
First Brands Corp.	360	Danbury	203-731-2300	3081
General Electric Co.	5	Fairfield	203-373-2211	3724
General Signal Corp.	257	Stamford	203-357-8800	3823
Hubbell Inc.	407	Orange	203-799-4100	3643
ITT Rayonier Inc.	364	Stamford	203-348-7000	2611
Kaman Corp.	414	Bloomfield	203-243-7100	5085
Loctite Corp.	484	Hartford	203-520-5000	2891
Olin Corp.	191	Stamford	203-356-2000	2822
Perkin Elmer Corp.	375	Norwalk	203-762-1000	3826
Pitney Bowes Inc.	144	Stamford	203-356-5000	3579
Silgan Corp.	474	Stamford	203-975-7110	3411
Stanley Works	209	New Britain	203-225-5111	3423
Tosco Corp.	212	Stamford	203-977-1000	2911
UCC Investors Holding Inc.	395	Middlebury	203-573-2000	2879
Union Carbide Corp.	88	Danbury	203-794-2000	2821
United States Surgical Corp.	311	Norwalk	203-845-1000	3841
United Technologies Corp.	16	Hartford	203-728-7000	3585
UST Inc.	356	Greenwich	203-661-1100	2131
Xerox Corp.	21	Stamford	203-968-3000	3861
Other Major Companies in the State				
Aetna Life & Casualty Co.		Hartford	203-273-0123	6311
Ames Department Stores Inc.		Rocky Hill	203-257-2000	5331
Caldor Corp.		Norwalk	203-849-2000	5331
Connecticut Light & Power Co.		Berlin	203-665-5000	4911
General Electric Capital Corp.		Stamford	203-357-4000	6153
General Electric Financial Services Inc.		Stamford	203-357-4000	6153
General Re Corp.		Stamford	203-328-5000	6331
GND Holdings Corp.		Riverside	203-637-0511	5411
GTE Corp.		Stamford	203-965-2000	4813
GU Acquisition Corp.		Westport	203-222-1368	5411
Hartford Fire Insurance Co.		Hartford	203-547-5000	6331
Kiewit Continental Inc.		Norwalk	203-855-5900	3411
Pittston Co.		Stamford	203-978-5200	4731
Primerica Holdings Inc.		Greenwich	203-862-2050	6211
Shawmut National Corp.		Hartford	203-728-2000	6712
Southern New England Telecommun Corp.		New Haven	203-771-5200	4813
Travelers Corp.		Hartford	203-277-0111	6331
Travelers Insurance Co.		Hartford	203-277-0111	6311
Union Carbide Chemicals & Plastics Co. Inc.		Danbury	203-794-2000	2821
United Parcel Service of America Inc.		Greenwich	203-862-6000	4215

by Connecticut Innovations, Inc., is the state's clearing-house for information on all public and private sector services, programs and resources available to help high-technology firms and entrepreneurs planning to establish or expand operations in Connecticut. It also offers cooperative high-tech R&D grants. These grants assist small businesses expand their research capabilities, using the resources and facilities of the state's colleges and universities. Grants of up to $200,000 are awarded to help with the cost of joint high-tech research projects. Firms dealing in aerospace, biotechnology, computer applications, energy systems, materials technology, medical technology, and telecommunications are eligible.

Sales Contact Centers. Help generate new sales by matching manufacturers with the purchasing executives of large corporations. It also helps manufacturers to locate suppliers.

Export Assistance. Assists manufacturers selling or looking to sell their products overseas. Will also try to match Connecticut firms with overseas companies interested in undertaking join-venture projects and licensing agreements.

Industrial Parks. State subsidized and provide ready-to-build sites complete with utility and infrastructure improvements. The 80-acre Science Park in New Haven, the state's high-technology industrial park, is providing firms and entrepreneurs with a working link with the scientific and technical resources of Yale University. The 390-acre ConnTech Park is the high-technology industrial park linked to the University of Connecticut at Storrs. It includes industrial research sites and an incubator building.

Mini-Industrial Parks. Provide low-cost space in existing buildings.

Incubator Parks. Feature building space for lease by start-up enterprises.

High-Tech Parks. Provide firms with access to the resources of the state's major universities.

Education and Training

The state helps employers to design and implement customized job-training programs. An inter-agency team identifies and accesses the training and educational resources necessary to upgrade an existing workforce. The team also assists companies with the recruitment and training of new employees.

Job Training Partnership Act. This program operates with funding from the U.S. Department of Labor. It provides job training and other employment related services.

State Offices

Real estate: Real Estate Commission, Laurence Hannafin, Exec Director, 165 Capitol Ave., Hartford, CT 06106. 203-566-5130

Chamber of commerce: Connecticut Business & Industry Association, Kenneth O. Decko, President, 370 Asylum Ave., Hartford, CT 06103-2022. 203-547-1661

Economic development: Connecticut Dept. of Economic Development, International Division, Matthew J. Broder, Director, 865 Brook Street, Rocky Hill, CT 06067-3405. 203-258-4258, FAX 203-529-0535

Connecticut Dept. of Economic Development, Business Recruitment, James Musante, Director, 865 Brook Street, Rocky Hill, CT 06067-3405. 203-258-4245, FAX 203-529-0535

Connecticut Dept. of Economic Development, Small Business Affairs, Leslie Twibble, Director, 865 Brook Street, Rocky Hill, CT 06067-3405. 203-258-4275

State of Connecticut, Shyama Jaipershad, Enterprise Zones Program Manager, 865 Brook Street, Rocky Hill, CT 06067-3405. 203-258-4227

Small Business Development Center, John P. O'Connor, State Director, University of Connecticut, Box U-41, 368 Fairfield Road, Room 422, Storrs, CT 06268. 203-486-4135

Environmental affairs: Dept. of Environmental Protection, Leslie Carothers, Commissioner, 165 Capitol Ave., Hartford, CT 06106. 203-566-2110

Labor: Dept. of Labor, Betty L. Tianti, Commissioner, 200 Folly Brook Blvd., Wethersfield, CT 06109-1114. 203-566-5160

Unemployment: Dept. of Labor, Employment Security Division, John C. Souchuns, Director, 200 Folly Brook Blvd., Wethersfield, CT 06109-1114. 203-566-5160

Worker's compensation: Workers' Compensation Commission, John Arcudi, Chairman, 1890 Dixwell Ave., Hamden, CT 06514. 203-789-7783

Occupational safety and health: Dept. of Labor, Occupational Safety and Health Division, Emil J. Caruso, Director, 200 Folly Brook Blvd., Wethersfield, CT 06109-1114. 203-566-4550

Secretary of state: Secretary of State Office, Julia H. Tashjian, Secretary of State, 210 Capitol Ave., Hartford, CT 06106. 203-566-4135

Taxation and revenue: Dept. of Revenue Services, James F. Meehan, Commissioner, 92 Farmington Ave., Hartford, CT 06105. 203-297-5650

Designated Zones for Economic Development

Enterprise Zones

Enacted in: 1982

No. of established zones: 11

  Bridgeport
  Hamden
  Hartford
  Meriden
  New Britain
  New Haven
  New London

Norwalk
Norwich
Waterbury
Windham

Foreign Trade Zones

Foreign Trade Zone No. 76, Bridgeport, Connecticut, Grantee/Operator: City of Bridgeport, Edward Lavernoich, City Hall, 45 Lyon Terrace, Bridgeport, CT 06604, 203-576-8229

Foreign Trade Zone No. 162, North Haven, Connecticut, Grantee: Greater New Haven Chamber of Commerce, Fabio Sampoli, 195 Church Street, New Haven, CT 06506, 203-787-6735

Foreign Trade Zone No. 71, Windsor Locks, Connecticut, Grantee: Industrial Development Commission of Windsor Locks, R. Clifford Randall, Town Office Building, 50 Church Street, PO Box L, Windsor Locks, CT 06096, 203-627-1444

Labor Unions

Carpenters and Joiners of America, United Brotherhood of (AFL-CIO)

Congress of Connecticut Community Colleges

Electrical Workers, International Brotherhood of (AFL-CIO)

Food and Commercial Workers International Union, United (AFL-CIO)

Hotel Employees and Restaurant Employees International Union (AFL-CIO)

Laborers' International Union of North America (AFL-CIO)

Machinists and Aerospace Workers, International Association of (AFL-CIO)

Plumbing and Pipe Fitting Industry of The United States and Canada, United Association of, Journeymen and Aprentices of the (AFL-CIO)

State, County and Municipal Employees, American Federation of (AFL-CIO)

Universities with Ph.D. Programs

University of Bridgeport, Bridgeport
University of Hartford, West Hartford
University of New Haven, West Haven
Yale University, New Haven

BRIDGEPORT–STAMFORD–NORWALK–DANBURY, CT (NECMA)

Geographic Profile

Land Area

625.9 square miles

Counties and Parishes

Bridgeport
Danbury
Fairfield
Litchfield
New Haven
Norwalk
Stamford

Additional Cities/Towns within Area

Bridgeport

Fairfield County:
  Bridgeport
  Easton
  Fairfield
  Monroe
  Shelton
  Stratford
  Trumbull

New Haven County:
  Ansonia
  Beacon Falls
  Derby
  Milfor
  Oxford
  Seymour

Danbury

Fairfield County:
  Bethel
  Brookfield
  New Fairfield
  Newtown
  Redding
  Ridgefield
  Sherman

Litchfield County:
  Bridgewater
  New Milford
  Norwalk
  Weston
  Westport
  Wilton

Stamford

  Darien
  Greenwich

New Canaan

Ranking Highlights

267 *out of 319 in total* **land area**

246 *out of 319 in* **population growth,** *1970–1990*

149 *out of 310 in having the lowest* **unemployment** *rate*

46 *out of 310 in size of* **labor force**

49 *out of 318 in the percentage of* **college graduates**

N/A *out of 292 in per capita personal* **income**

40 *out of 319 in number of* **manufacturing establishments**

39 *out of 318 in* **physicians** *per 1000 people*

187 *out of 318 in* **hospital beds** *per 1000 people*

143 *out of 267 in fewest* **crimes** *per 1000 people*

162 *out of 266 in fewest* **violent crimes** *per 1000 people*

54 *out of 319 in per capita* **federal funds and grants**

Quality of Life Indexes (Rate per 1000 population)

Crime rate in 1991:	62.0
Violent crime rate in 1991:	7.3
Physicians rate in 1992:	2.83
Hospital bed rate in 1991:	3.54

ACCRA Cost of Living Indexes

(First quarter 1993, average = 100)

Composite index:	N/A
Utilities index:	N/A
Housing index:	N/A

Overview

The major highways serving the area include Interstate Highway 95 and State Routes 8 and 25. Rail service is provided by Genrail. Passenger commuter service is provided by the New York area commuter rail, Metro North, and Amtrak's Northeast corridor routes. For the purpose of air travel, this area is considered part of the New York City hub. Kennedy International Airport in Queens and LaGuardia in New York are an hour's drive from Stamford and offer full international, domestic, commuter, and freight service. Newark International Airport is a little more than an hour away.

Bridgeport

A smokestack city known for its defense-related manufacturing activities and port facilities, Bridgeport, the largest city in Connecticut, has been devastated in recent years by the loss of its manufacturing base as a result of the end of the Cold War between the United States and the former Soviet Union. Afflicted by an eroding tax base, growing welfare population, and other economic woes, Bridgeport declared itself bankrupt in 1991. The city is the fourth largest financial center in New England.

Manufacturing and trade, long mainstays in the Bridgeport economy, are being increasingly supplemented by the service-producing industries, particularly personal, business and health services, as Bridgeport seeks to diversify. The city is one of the largest financial centers in the Northeast, but the banking crisis had reduced the number of banks with

headquarters there from eleven to just three by 1992. The defense industry, for many years a vital part of the city's economy, has been hard hit by layoffs in recent years with no relief expected. Wholesale and retail trade thrive thanks to the city's strategic location as a deep–sea port, a crossroads of interstate highways, and a hub of railroad lines. Items and goods produced in the area include transportation equipment, women's underwear, electrical supplies, machinery and machine tools and fabricated metals.

Bridgeport's development strategy centers around improvements to the Port of Bridgeport and its transportation linkages to attract small manufacturers; the object is to favorably position the city for increased international trade. Bridgeport Harbor is one of three deep–water ports in the state. Its Cilco Terminal is one of New England's busiest deep draft ports; facilities include COMEX, bonded warehousing, and wet and dry storage. Conrail operates a major freight yard nearby.

Danbury, CT

Danbury, formerly known as the Hat Capital of the World and official supplier of silk top hats to presidents, is perhaps best known today as the headquarters of Union Carbide and other industries that have moved out of metropolitan areas. Danbury is located near the beautiful rural area of Connecticut known as Litchfield Hills, an affluent region where per capita income is among the highest in the country. Combining beautiful surroundings with access to the amenities of large city life, Danbury was chosen by *Money* magazine in 1988 as the best place to live in the country.

Danbury's economic mix retains a manufacturing–industrial base of 25 percent, far above the state average. More than 3,000 manufacturing firms are located in the area. The four occupational categories—executive/managerial, professional/technical, secretarial/clerical, and production/other—are well represented. Major non–manufacturing sectors are construction; wholesale and retail trade; and finance, insurance, and real estate. Retail trade is an important contributor to the local economy, centered around the 1.5–million–square–foot Danbury Fair Mall.

Items and goods produced in Danbury include surgical instruments and supplies, electronic and railroad testing equipment, silverware, aluminum foil, aircraft parts, rubber tile, air conditioning equipment, steam generators, plastics, glue, textiles, and ball and roller bearings.

Stamford

Connecticut's Fairfield County, with its keystone cities of Stamford, Norwalk, and Greenwich, is one of the nation's most popular addresses for corporate headquarters. Stamford, Norwalk, and Greenwich are also known for their research and development activities and their manufacture of high-technology products for a number of industries. Much of this activity is defense oriented, and with the end of the Cold War between the United States and the former

Soviet Union, the industry faces an uncertain future.

Traditionally, Stamford has been known for its manufacturing, retail, and research activities, as have the adjacent cities of Norwalk and Greenwich. In the 1980s, however, southwestern Connecticut blossomed, its real estate growing ever more attractive as the cost of doing business in New York City skyrocketed. By 1990, Stamford boasted the third largest concentration of Fortune 500 headquarters in the country. The city's downtown had been demolished and replaced by corporate headquarters. Hard hit by the recession of the early nineties, Stamford companies face layoffs, new buildings stand empty, and new businesses are looking elsewhere for space in office parks.

Fortune 500 industrial companies with headquarters in Stamford include: Xerox Corporation; Champion International Corporation (wood and paper products); Combustion Engineering Inc.; Pitney Bowes Inc.; Olin Corporation; General Signal Corporation; American Maize Products; and Sprague Technologies. Items and goods produced in the area include chemicals, electrical and electronic equipment, drugs, cosmetics, machinery, aircraft, metals, die casting, and apparel and textile products.

Population (1990)

Total Population and Growth Rate
1990: 827,654
1980: 807,143
1970: 792,814
Growth rate 1970–1990: 4%

Race and Hispanic Origin
White: 86.2%
Black: 8.8%
Asian/Pacific Islander: 1.9%
Native American: 0.2%
Hispanic origin: 7.7%
White not Hispanic: 81.8%

Age
Ages 18 to 20: 4.4%
Ages 21 to 24: 6.6%
Ages 25 to 44: 38.5%
Ages 45 to 54: 13.7%
Ages 55 to 59: 5.7%
Ages 60 to 64: 5.5%
Ages 65 plus: 15.5%

Educational Attainment (1990)
Percent having completed high school: 81.0%
Percent having completed college: 26.1%
Elementary and high school enrollment: 144,441

Federal Funds and Grants Received
Total received in 1989: $3,723,800,000
Funds received per capita: $4,556

Civilian Labor Force
1993 (April): 536,242

1992 average: 543,455
1991 average: 547,700
1990 average: 543,028

Unemployment
1993 (April): 6.0%
1992 average: 6.8%
1991 average: 6.0%
1990 average: 4.8%

Average Annual Pay
1988: $30,535
1987: $27,832
1985: $23,970

Per Capita Personal Income
1991: N/A
1990: N/A
1989: N/A

Business Climate (1987)

Manufacturing
Number of establishments in 1987: 1,796
Shipments in 1987 ($1,000): $10,833,000
Employees in 1987: 117,000
Change in employment, 1982 to 1987: -11.7%
Average annual pay for manufacturing work in 1989: $39,140
Average annual pay for production work in 1987: $22,878

Wholesale Trade
Number of establishments in 1987: 1,926
Total sales in 1987 ($1,000): $29,767,200
Change in sales, 1982 to 1987: 62.0%

Retail Trade
Number of establishments in 1987: 5,838
Total sales in 1987 ($1,000): $29,767,200
Retail sales per household in 1987: $24,274
Average annual pay in 1989: $17,184

Service Industry
Selected receipts in 1987 ($1,000): $4,791,600
Average annual pay in 1989: $28,789

Office Real Estate (1992)
Office space inventory: 41,217,514 square feet
Average class A Central Business District rental range per sq. ft: $17.01

Vacancy Rates
All areas: 25.8%

Vacancy Rates in Central Business District
Class A space: 20.3%
Class B space: 26.4%

Vacancy Rates Outside Central Business District
Class A space: 27.4%
Class B space: 25.0%

Housing
Total number of units in 1990: 378,102

Occupied units in 1990: 355,375
Owner-occupied units in 1990: 68.8%
1993 ACCRA average cost: N/A
1993 ACCRA average rent for an apartment: N/A

Chamber of Commerce

Bridgeport Regional Business Council, Paul S. Timpanelli, President, PO Box 999, 10 Middle St., 14th Fl., Bridgeport, CT 06601-0999. 203-335-3800

Economic Development Office

Greater Danbury Chamber of Commerce, Clarice Osiecki, President, 72 West St., Danbury, CT 06810. 203-743-5565

Economic Development Organizations

City of Bridgeport, Office of Planning & Economic Development, Daniel J. McCormick, Director, 45 Lyon Terrace, Room 301, Bridgeport, CT 06604. 203-576-7221, FAX 203-332-5568

Stamford Economic Development, Christopher Bruhl, President, 1 Landmark Square #230, Stamford, CT 06901. 203-359-3220, FAX 203-967-8294

Foreign Trade Zone #76, Michael Freimuth, 45 Lyon Terrace #212, City Hall, Bridgeport CT 06604. 203-576-7755

Bridgeport Foreign Trade Zone Development Corp., William A. Hooton, 939 Barnum Ave., Bridgeport, CT 06608. 203-335-3885

Greater Bridgeport Board of Realtors, 961 Huntington Turnpike, Bridgeport, CT 06610. 203-374-2150

Connecticut World Trade Association, Daniel J. McCormick, 360 Fairfield Ave., Bridgeport, CT 06604. 203-336-5353

Greater Norwalk Chamber of Commerce, Sheldon R. Gerarden, President, 101 East Ave., PO Box 668, Norwalk, CT 06852. 203-866-2521

Southwestern Area Commerce & Industry Assn., Harry P. Harris, Vice President, 1 Landmark Square, Stamford, CT 06901. 203-359-3220

Economic Development, Joe Ercalano, Director, 1 Landmark Square, Stamford, CT 06901. 203-359-3220

Greater Bridgeport Regional Planning Agency, James T. Wang, Exec. Director, 525 Water St., 3rd Fl., Bridgeport, CT 06604. 203-366-5405

City of Bridgeport, Dept. of Planning, Michael P. Nidoh, Director, 45 Lyon Terrace, Room 211, Bridgeport, CT 06604. 203-576-7760

City of Bridgeport, Zoning Dept., William Shaw, Chief Zoning Officer, 45 Lyon Terrace, Room 206, Bridgeport, CT 06604. 203-576-7217

Private Industry Council, Director, 181 Midddle St., Bridgeport, CT 06604.

Local Incentives for Business

Negotiated Property Tax Incentives for major real estate development projects.

State mandated property tax deferrals for real property, improvement in Urban Enterprise Zone, and Housing redevelopment areas. Individuals or firms undertaking real estate development projects with construction costs of $3,000,000 or more may be eligible for a development tax incentive. Tax incentives are available for smaller property improvements within the city's Urban Enterprise Zone, East End Development Area and West End Development Areas. The city may fix the property tax assessment on improved real property, forgiving all or part of new taxes attributable to property improvements for a number of years.

Property tax, state corporate income tax, and job training grants for new or expanding manufacturers.

Customs cost management for importers in Foreign Trade Zone.

Industrial Sites

Boston Avenue Industrial Park, Mark R. Trinkley, President 203-374-2150

International Enterprise Park, William A. Hooton, Bridgeport Foreign Trade Zone Development Corp., 939 Barnum Ave., Bridgeport, CT, 06608. 203-335-3885

Major Businesses

Company	SIC	Telephone
Allied Lyons North America	2086	(203) 925-4400
American Frozen Foods Inc.	5421	(203) 378-7900
Babcock Industries Inc.	3089	(203) 255-7100
Bank Mart Inc.	6035	(203) 579-5400
Bic Corp.	3999	(203) 783-2000
Blau, Barry & Partners Inc.	7311	(203) 254-3700
Bridgeport Hospital Inc.	8062	(203) 384-3000
Carter, William Co.	2254	(203) 926-5000
Cartier Inc. (Delaware Corp.)	5944	(203) 925-6500
Citytrust	6022	(203) 384-5212
Citytrust Bancorp Inc.	6022	(203) 384-5400
Connecticut Energy Corp.	4924	(203) 382-8111
Connecticut Jai Alai Inc.	7941	(203) 877-4242
Dictaphone Corp.	3579	(203) 381-7000
Doctor's Associates Inc.	6794	(203) 877-4281
Dorr-Oliver Inc.	3569	(203) 876-5400
Fair Auto Supply Inc.	5013	(203) 377-0075
FKI Holdings Inc.	3089	(203) 255-7100
General Electric Technical Service	8711	(203) 382-2000
General Electric Co.	3724	(203) 373-2211
Golf Digest/Tennis Inc.	2721	(203) 373-7000
Hydraulic Co.	4941	(203) 367-6621
Keeler Brass Co.	3469	(203) 255-7100
Koenig Artist Supplies Inc.	5199	(203) 877-4541
Koenig Corp.	5199	(203) 877-4541
Lafayette Bank & Trust Co.	6022	(203) 336-6200
Mechanics & Farmers Savings Bank	6035	(203) 382-6363

Major Businesses (Continued)

Company	SIC	Telephone
People's Bank	6036	(203) 579-7171
Pilot Corp. of America	5112	(203) 377-8800
Remington Products Inc.	3634	(203) 367-4400
Rhone-Poulenc Basic Chemical	2819	(203) 925-3300
RVI Acquisition Corp.	2834	(203) 925-6000
Southern Connecticut Gas Co.	4924	(203) 382-8111
Southern Connecticut Health	8062	(203) 384-3000
St. Vincent Health Service	8062	(203) 576-6000
St. Vincent's Medical Center	8062	(203) 576-6000
Tetley Inc.	2095	(203) 929-9200
Tetra Pak, Inc.	2671	(203) 929-3200
Town Fair Tire Centers Inc.	5531	(203) 378-8625
Trusthouse Forte Food Service	5812	(203) 268-3663
Warnaco Inc.	2321	(203) 579-8272

Colleges and Universities

Beth Benjamin Academy of Connecticut, Stamford
Bridgeport Engineering Institute, Fairfield
Bullard Havens Regional Vocational Technical School
Connecticut Business Institute
Fairfield University, Fairfield
Housantic Community College, Bridgeport
Katharine Gibbs School, Norwalk
Norwalk Community College, Norwalk
Norwalk State Technical College, Norwalk
Sacred Heart University, Fairfield
St. Basil's College, Stamford
University of Bridgeport, Bridgeport
University of Connecticut at Stamford, Stamford

HARTFORD–NEW BRITAIN–MIDDLETOWN–BRISTOL, CT (NECMA)

Geographic Profile

Land Area

1514.9 square miles

Counties and Parishes

Hartford
Hartford (part)
Litchfield (part)
Middlesex (part)
New London (part)
Tolland (part)
Bristol
Hartford (part)
Litchfield (part)
Middletown
Middlesex
New Britain
Hartford (part)

Additional Cities/Towns within Area

Hartford
Hartford County:
　West Hartford
　Wethersfield
　Windsor
　Windsor Locks
Litchfield County:
　Barkhamsted
　New Hartford
Middlesex County:
　East Haddam
New London County:
　Colchester
Tolland County:
　Andover
　Bolton
　Columbia
　Coventry
　Ellington
　Hebron
　Somers
　Stafford
　Tolland
　Vernon
　Willington
Bristol
Hartford County:
　Burlington
Litchfield County:

Plymouth
Middletown
  Cromwell
  Durham
  East Hampton
  Haddam
  Middlefield
  Portland
New Britain
  Berlin
  Plainville
  Southington

Ranking Highlights

130 *out of 319 in total* **land area**

229 *out of 319 in* **population growth,** *1970–1990*

212 *out of 310 in having the lowest* **unemployment** *rate*

43 *out of 310 in size of* **labor force**

50 *out of 318 in the percentage of* **college graduates**

9 *out of 292 in per capita personal* **income**

36 *out of 319 in number of* **manufacturing establishments**

42 *out of 318 in* **physicians** *per 1000 people*

219 *out of 318 in* **hospital beds** *per 1000 people*

111 *out of 267 in fewest* **crimes** *per 1000 people*

140 *out of 266 in fewest* **violent crimes** *per 1000 people*

67 *out of 319 in per capita* **federal funds and grants**

Quality of Life Indexes (Rate per 1000 population)

Crime rate in 1991:	57.0
Violent crime rate in 1991:	6.5
Physicians rate in 1992:	2.8
Hospital bed rate in 1991:	3.19

ACCRA Cost of Living Indexes
(First quarter 1993, average = 100)

Composite index:	129.1
Utilities index:	139.7
Housing index:	152.7

Overview

Hartford

Hartford is located 105 miles north of New York and 80 miles sorthwest of Boston, at the junction of Interstate Highways 84 and 91. It is served by the Brainard Airport and the Bradley International Airport. H artford, Connecticut's state capital and second largest city, is known as the insurance capital of the world. Today, the insurance industry is beset with economic woes, and in spite of the fact that Connecticut is one of the country's richest states, Hartford is ranked as one of the nation's poorest municipalities.

Manufacturers in the Hartford region, including United Technologies, headquartered there, produce high–technology products for a world market. Government is a major economic sector in Hartford, with employees working in the state capitol building, legislature, libraries, and supreme court.

Items and goods produced in the area include jet engines and aerospace products; fiber optics; chemicals; and bio-medical pharmaceutical products

Hartford, New England's second busiest retail market, benefits from its location on the Connecticut River and at the apex of several major interstate highways. The Connecticut River can accommodate barge and coastal tanker traffic; the river and two major interstate highways give Greater Hartford quick and direct access to commercial ports in New Haven, Bridgeport, and New London, with a convenient sea link to the Port of New York. Greater Hartford has benefitted from the state's $6.5 billion highway improvement program, which continues in the 1990s. Freight rail service is provided by Boston and Maine Corporation and Consolidated Rail Corporation Bradley International Airport, 15 miles north of the city, handles 100,000 tons of air cargo each year. The Hartford-Brainard Airport provides freight service. Hartford Dispatch International, based in East Hartford, is considered one of the country's foremost movers of commodities.

Bradley International Airport, a medium-sized hub and regional facility, is located 12 miles north of downtown Hartford in Windsor Locks. The airport offers 117 flights daily on eighteen carriers. Brainard Field, built in 1921 and located in the southeast corner of the city, was the nation's first municipally-owned airport. Now state-owned, the airport is used for charter, instruction, and private aircraft.

Bristol

Bristol is located close to several major markets. Hartford is 16 miles away and the New Haven area is 25 miles away. New York and Boston each lie within 100 miles of Bristol, and both are directly accessible by interstate highway. Connecticut's major east-west highway, Interstate 84, is two miles south, off of Route 229 in Bristol. Route 72 through Bristol also connects Interstate 84 with Interstate 91, providing access to New Haven and New York City to the south and Hartford and Springfield, Massachusetts, to the north. Route 6, one of the country's original trans-continental highways, runs through Bristol as part of its 3,234 mile expanse stretching from Cape Cod to California. Bristol is 35 miles from Bradley International Airport, serving the Hartford and Springfield areas, and closer to several smaller airfields which can accommodate corporate jets. Helicopter service is available to Bristol's 229 Technology Park. Rail freight is in service locally.

Bristol's industry dates back to the late 1700's. For many years, the manufacture of clocks and watches was the city's principal industry, earning its recognition as the Clockmaking Capital of the World. The E. Ingraham Company and the Sessions Clock Company emerged as the city's most renowned clock manufacturers.

At present over 170 manufacturing firms form Bristol's economic base, manufacturing goods from screw machine products, glass cutters, electrical items and plastics to synchronous motors, timing devices, metal stamping, steel, wire springs, screws and machine tools.

`The City's three largest industrial employers—Delco Chassis Division of GM, the Barnes Group, Inc. and Dana/Superior Electric Compan—had their origins in Bristol, beginning as small manufacturing operations. Delco Chassis Division of General Motors has as its major product line spindle bearings for General Motors cars and continues to expand its automotive product lines. It is also a major manufacturer of ball and roller bearings for commercial and automotive uses. Dana/Superior Electric Company, one of the 100 largest manufacturing firms in Connecticut, is known for the production of electric and electrical voltage conditioning and motion control products. The Barnes Group (formerly Associated Spring Corporation), with corporate headquarters in Bristol, is one of the world's leading producers of precision mechanical springs. It employs more than 4,700 people in its manufacturing and distribution operations located mainly in North and South America.

Population (1990)

Total Population and Growth Rate
1990: 1,123,678
1980: 1,051,606
1970: 1,035,195
Growth rate 1970–1990: 9%

Race and Hispanic Origin
White: 86.0%
Black: 8.7%
Asian/Pacific Islander: 1.5%
Native American: 0.2%
Hispanic origin: 7.0%
White not Hispanic: 83.1%

Age
Ages 18 to 20: 4.1%
Ages 21 to 24: 5.9%
Ages 25 to 44: 32.8%
Ages 45 to 54: 10.4%
Ages 55 to 59: 4.3%
Ages 60 to 64: 4.3%
Ages 65 plus: 12.9%

Educational Attainment (1990)
Percent having completed high school: 78.8%
Percent having completed college: 26.0%
Elementary and high school enrollment: 164,135

Federal Funds and Grants Received
Total received in 1989: $4,569,900,000
Funds received per capita: $4,123

Civilian Labor Force
1993 (April):   577,895
1992 average: 594,564
1991 average: 605,200
1990 average: 601,202

Unemployment
1993 (April):   7.7%
1992 average: 7.8%
1991 average: 6.8%
1990 average: 4.8%

Average Annual Pay
1988: $25,787
1987: $24,151
1985: $21,042

Per Capita Personal Income
1991: $24,911
1990: $24,443
1989: $23,392

Business Climate (1987)

Manufacturing
Number of establishments in 1987: 2,229
Shipments in 1987 ($1,000): $13,012,600
Employees in 1987: 132,700
Change in employment, 1982 to 1987: -6.9%
Average annual pay for manufacturing work in 1989: $33,116
Average annual pay for production work in 1987: $23,356

Wholesale Trade
Number of establishments in 1987: 2,003
Total sales in 1987 ($1,000): $9,976,300
Change in sales, 1982 to 1987: 37.9%

Retail Trade
Number of establishments in 1987: 7,049
Total sales in 1987 ($1,000): $9,976,300
Retail sales per household in 1987: $20,719
Average annual pay in 1989: $14,773

Service Industry
Selected receipts in 1987 ($1,000): $4,395,800
Average annual pay in 1989: $22,899

Office Real Estate (1992)
Office space inventory: N/A
Average class A Central Business District rental range per sq. ft: $19.00

Vacancy Rates
All areas: 15.7%

Vacancy Rates in Central Business District
Class A space: 16.8%
Class B space: 18.2%

Vacancy Rates Outside Central Business District
Class A space: 11.9%
Class B space: 34.1%

Housing
Total number of units in 1990: 434,791
Occupied units in 1990: 411,539
Owner-occupied units in 1990: 64.5%
1993 ACCRA average cost: $176,000

1993 ACCRA average rent for an apartment: $735

Chamber of Commerce

Greater Hartford Chamber of Commerce, Hector Torres, Director of Economic Development, 250 Constitution Plaza, Hartford, CT 06103. 203-525-4451, FAX 203-293-2592

Economic Development Office

Bristol Chamber of Commerce, John J. Leone, Jr., Exec. Director, 17 Riverside Ave., PO Box 2658, Bristol, CT 06010. 203-589-4111, FAX 203-585-5890

Economic Development Organizations

Middlesex County Chamber of Commerce, Lawrence McHugh, President, 393 Main St., Middletown, CT 06457. 203-347-6924, FAX 203-346-1043

New Britain Municipal Economic Development Agency, David Prendergast, Exec. Director, 1 Central Park Plaza, New Britain, CT 06051. 203-225-5507

Bristol Development Authority, Exec. Director, 111 North St., 229 Technology Park, Bristol, CT 06010. 203-584-7971

Greater Hartford Association of Realtors, Inc., Lynda M. Wilson, President, 65 Kane St., West Hartford, CT 06119. 203-236-2561

Hartford Private Industry Council, Rich Pearson, Director, 2 Holcomb St., Hartford, CT 06112

Hartford Enterprise Zone, Beverley Marshall-Dawes, Manager, 942 Main St., Hartford, CT 06103. 203-722-6430

Connecticut Business and Industrial Association, Ken Decko, President, 370 Asylum Ave., CT 06103. 203-547-4064

Hartford Area Business Economists, Anne Wingate, President, c/o SCORE, 61 Woodland St., Hartford, CT 06105. 203-566-4064

Connecticut Association of Municipal Development Commissions, Fernando Rosa, President, 15 Lewis St., Hartford, CT 06103. 203-527-1301

Middlesex County Chamber of Commerce, Lawrence McHugh, President, 393 Main St., Middletown, CT 06457. 203-347-6924

Middlesex Industrial Development Corporation, Michelle Stronz, Exec. Director, 393 Main St., Middletown, CT 06457. 203-347-7291, FAX 203-638-3946

Meriden-Middlesex Private Industry Council, Inc., Robyn Bugbee, Exec. Director, 393 Main St., Middletown, CT 06457. 203-347-7291

Industry for Middletown, Michelle Stronz, Exec. Director, 393 Main St., Middletown, CT, 06457. 203-347-7291, FAX 203-638-3946

City of Middletown Municipal Development, Linda Ozga, DeKoven Dr., Middletown, CT 06457. 203-344-3419

New Britain Chamber of Commerce, Robert T. MacBain, Exec. Vice President, 1 Central Park Plaza, New Britain, CT 06051. 203-229-1665

Local Incentives for Business

The Greater Hartford Business Development Center, Inc. GHBDC provides financing to Hartford-based businesses or businesses contemplating a relocation to Hartford for the acquisition of, or renovations to, real estate, the purchase of machinery and equipment, working capital, leasehold improvements and labor expenses and materials for contractors with specifically assignable contracts. Interest rates are fixed and usually below prevailing commercial rates. Assistance can also be provided in long-term financing to existing businesses that are considering a major expansion.

Assessment Fixing Agreements. The City can enter into a written agreement fixing the assessment on real property or air space and all improvements for a period of not more than seven years with a property owner or prospective owner proposing a development of at least $3 million.

Commercial Rehab Tax Deferral Program. The program freezes the assessment of property while rehabilitation is underway and during the first year following completion. The assessment increase attributed to the renovations is phased in over a five to seven year period so full taxes are not immediately paid.

Industrial Sites

Hartford

Hartford Enterprise Zone (see address above).

Middletown

Aetna Insurance Co.

Cheeseborough Ponds

EIS/Standard Motor Products

Pratt & Whitney

R.R. Donnelly

Raymond Engineering

Industry for Middletown (see address above).

Major Businesses

Company	SIC	Telephone
Advest Group Inc.	6211	(203) 525-1421
Advo-System Inc.	7331	(203) 285-6100
Aetna Casualty & Surety Co.	6331	(203) 273-0123
Aetna Life And Casulty Co.	6311	(203) 273-0123
Aetna Life Insurance & Annuities	6311	(203) 273-0123
Aetna Life Insurance Co.	6311	(203) 273-0123
AKD Inc.	6719	(203) 563-8234
Allied Grocers Cooperative Inc.	5141	(203) 688-8341
American Nuclear Insurers	6331	(203) 677-7305
Ames Department Stores Inc.	5311	(203) 563-8234
Carrier Corp.	3585	(203) 674-3000
Charter Oak Fire Insurance Co.	6331	(203) 277-0111
Chase Enterprises	6552	(203) 549-1674
Cigna Healthplan Inc.	6324	(203) 726-6000

Major Businesses (Continued)

Company	SIC	Telephone
Connecticut Yankee Atomic Power	4911	(203) 267-9279
Connectcut Housing Financial Authority	6162	(203) 721-9501
Connecticut Bank & Trust Co.	6021	(203) 244-5000
Connecticut General Life Insurance	6311	(203) 726-6000
Connecticut General Corp.	6311	(203) 726-6000
Connecticut Mutual Life Insurance Co.	6311	(203) 727-6500
Connecticut National Bank	6021	(203) 728-2000
Connecticut Natural Gas Co.	4924	(203) 727-3000
Dairy Mart Convenience Store	5411	(203) 741-3611
Dexter Corp.	2891	(203) 627-9051
Eastern Retailers Service	5311	(203) 563-8234
FNS Holding Co. Inc.	5411	(203) 627-9311
Gerber Scientific Inc.	3559	(203) 644-1551
Hartford Accident/Indemnities	6321	(203) 547-5000
Hartford Fire Insurance Co.	6331	(203) 547-5000
Hartford Hospital	8062	(203) 524-3011
Hartford Life Accident Insurance	6311	(203) 843-8216
Hartford Life Insurance Co.	6311	(203) 547-5000
Hartford National Corp.	6021	(203) 728-2000
Heublein, Inc.	2085	(203) 240-5000
Industrial Risk Insurers	6331	(203) 520-7300
Kaman Aerospace Corp.	3721	(203) 242-4461
Kaman Corp.	3721	(203) 243-8311
Kaman Industrial Technologies	5085	(203) 243-8311
Kollmorgen Corp.	3825	(203) 651-3757
Kollmorgen Corp.	3621	(203) 651-3757
Konica Business Machines	5044	(203) 683-2222
Loctite Corp.	2891	(203) 520-5000
North American Ventures	4581	(203) 528-0232
Northeast Savings	6035	(203) 280-1000
Orion Group, Inc.	6331	(203) 674-6600
Otis Elevator Co.	3534	(203) 674-4000
Phoenix Insurance Co.	6331	(203) 277-0111
Phoenix Mutual Life Insurance	6311	(203) 275-5000
Security-Connecticut	6311	(203) 677-8621
Shawmut National Corp.	6021	(203) 728-2000
Society for Savings	6022	(203) 727-5000
Society for Savings Bank Corp.	6022	(203) 727-5440
Stanadyne Automotive Corp.	3714	(203) 525-0821
Standard Fire Insurance	6331	(203) 273-0123
Sweet Life Foods, Inc.	5141	(203) 623-1681
Travelers Corp.	6331	(203) 277-0111
Travelers Indemnity Co.	6351	(203) 277-0111
Travelers Insurance Co.	6311	(203) 277-0111
Travelers Life Insurance Co.	6331	(203) 277-0111
United Technologies Corp.	3724	(203) 728-7000
Yankee Gas Services Co.	4924	(203) 721-2000

Colleges and Universities

A.I. Prince Vocational Technical School, Hartford
Briarwood College, Southington
Central Connecticut State University, New Britain
Greater Hartford Community College, Hartford
Hartford College for Women, Hartford
Hartford State Technical College, Hartford
Holy Apostles College, Cromwell
Middlesex Community College, Middletown
Morse School of Business, Hartford
St. Francis Hospital School of Nursing, Hartford
St. Joseph College, West Hartford
Trinity College, Hartford
University of Connecticut at Hartford, West Hartford
University of Hartford, West Hartford
Wesleyan University, Middletown

Additional Information

FactPak, an Informational Profile on the Greater Hartford Region. The Greater Hartford Chamber of Commerce, n.d. 15p.

NEW HAVEN–WATERBURY–MERIDEN, CT (NECMA)

Geographic Profile

Land Area
605.8 square miles

Counties and Parishes
Middlesex (part)
New Haven (part)
Waterbury
Litchfield (part)
New Haven (part)

Additional Cities/Towns within Area
Middlesex County:
  Clinton
  Killingworth
New Haven County:
  Bethany
  Branford
  Cheshire
  East Haven
  Guilford
  Hamden
  Madison
  Meriden
  North Branford
  North Haven
  Orange
  Wallingford
  West Haven
  Woodbridge
  Waterbury
Litchfield County:
  Bethlehem
  Thomaston
  Watertown
  Woodbury
New Haven County:
  Middlebury
  Naugatuck
  Prospect
  Southbury
  Waterbury
  Wolcott

Ranking Highlights

273 *out of 319 in total* **land area**
231 *out of 319 in* **population growth**, *1970–1990*
234 *out of 310 in having the lowest* **unemployment** *rate*
67 *out of 310 in size of* **labor force**
61 *out of 318 in the percentage of* **college graduates**
3 *out of 292 in per capita personal* **income**

41 *out of 319 in number of* **manufacturing establishments**
16 *out of 318 in* **physicians** *per 1000 people*
264 *out of 318 in* **hospital beds** *per 1000 people*
179 *out of 267 in fewest* **crimes** *per 1000 people*
180 *out of 266 in fewest* **violent crimes** *per 1000 people*
188 *out of 319 in per capita* **federal funds and grants**

Quality of Life Indexes (Rate per 1000 population)

Crime rate in 1991:   68.0
Violent crime rate in 1991:   7.8
Physicians rate in 1992:   3.53
Hospital bed rate in 1991:   2.66

ACCRA Cost of Living Indexes
(First quarter 1993, average = 100)
Composite index: 127.4
Utilities index: 135.6
Housing index: 157.4

Overview

New Haven is situated on Long Island Sound 40 miles south of Hartford, 75 miles north of New York City, and 135 miles from Boston, Massachusetts. Connecticut is the southermost and westernmost of the New England states. New Haven is accessible via air through commuter service from the New York airports to Tweed-New Haven airport, three miles from downtown New Haven. International and domestic service is also available at Bradley International Airport at Hartford.

Amtrak and Metro-North commuter service provide rail commuter services for passengers traveling the New York-Connecticut-Boston corridor. Interstate Highways 91 and 95 intersect in New Haven. U.S. Routes 1 and 5, the Merrit/Wilbur Cross Parkway and Connecticut Route 34 all connect to New Haven.

New Haven has a deep draft port offering facilities such as COMEX and bonded warehouses, and wet and dry storage. The liquid terminal has a storage capacity of over 2.5 million barrels.

Population (1990)

Total Population and Growth Rate
1990: 804,219
1980: 761,325
1970: 744,948
Growth rate 1970–1990: 8%

Race and Hispanic Origin
White: 84.9%
Black: 10.6%
Asian/Pacific Islander: 1.3%
Native American: 0.2%
Hispanic origin: 6.6%
White not Hispanic: 81.7%

Age
Ages 18 to 20: 4.3%
Ages 21 to 24: 5.8%

Ages 25 to 44: 30.9%
Ages 45 to 54: 9.5%
Ages 55 to 59: 3.9%
Ages 60 to 64: 4.1%
Ages 65 plus: 13.6%

Educational Attainment (1990)

Percent having completed high school: 77.6%
Percent having completed college: 24.9%
Elementary and high school enrollment: 112,399

Federal Funds and Grants Received

Total received in 1989: $2,313,700,000
Funds received per capita: $2,912

Civilian Labor Force

1993 (April):   380,004
1992 average: 390,296
1991 average: 392,200
1990 average: 390,721

Unemployment

1993 (April):   7.9%
1992 average: 8.2%
1991 average: 7.3%
1990 average: 5.6%

Average Annual Pay

1988: $23,754
1987: $22,009
1985: $19,193

Per Capita Personal Income

1991: $28,021
1990: $27,602
1989: $26,281

Business Climate (1987)

Manufacturing

Number of establishments in 1987: 1,795
Shipments in 1987 ($1,000): $7,374,400
Employees in 1987: 76,200
Change in employment, 1982 to 1987: -8.4%
Average annual pay for manufacturing work in 1989: $29,010
Average annual pay for production work in 1987: $20,571

Wholesale Trade

Number of establishments in 1987: 1,577
Total sales in 1987 ($1,000): $7,734,300
Change in sales, 1982 to 1987: 28.3%

Retail Trade

Number of establishments in 1987: 5,222
Total sales in 1987 ($1,000): $7,734,300
Retail sales per household in 1987: $20,004
Average annual pay in 1989: $14,799

Service Industry

Selected receipts in 1987 ($1,000): $2,409,100
Average annual pay in 1989: $22,500

Office Real Estate (1992)

Office space inventory: 9,800,000 square feet
Average class A Central Business District rental range per sq. ft: $16.00

Vacancy Rates

All areas: 27.6%

Vacancy Rates in Central Business District

Class A space: 32.4%
Class B space: 78.6%

Vacancy Rates Outside Central Business District

Class A space: 22.6%
Class B space: 10.9%

Housing

Total number of units in 1990: 214,831
Occupied units in 1990: 199,726
Owner-occupied units in 1990: 62.4%
1993 ACCRA average cost: N/A
1993 ACCRA average rent for an apartment: N/A

Chamber of Commerce

Greater New Haven Chamber of Commerce, Fabio Sampoli, Vice President for Economic Development, 195 Church St., PO Box 1445, New Haven, CT 06506. 203-787-6735, FAX 203-787-6730

Economic Development Office

City of New Haven, Office of Business Development, Sal Braucati, Director, 95 Orange St., New Haven, CT 06511. 203-787-7059

Economic Development Organizations

Waterbury Development Agency, Howard Plomann, Exec. Director, 101 S. Main St., Waterbury, CT 06706. 203-757-9621, FAX 203-596-7977

Greater New Haven Board of Realtors, Roberta O'Hare, Exec. Vice President, 154 Derby Ave., New Haven, CT 06511. 203-787-5891

Private Industry Council, Bill Villaue, Exec. Director, 580 Erasso Blvd., New Haven, CT 06519. 203-624-1493

Science Park Development Corporation, Will Einsberg, President, 5 Science Park, New Haven, CT 06511. 203-786-5000

New Haven Downtown Council, PO Box 1456, 195 Church St., New Haven, CT 06506. 800-722-8886, 203-777-9000

New Haven Development Corp., Paul Goodwin, President, 770 Chapel St., New Haven, CT 06510. 203-787-7059

New Haven Community Investment Corp., Frederick G. Fischer, President, 770 Chapel St., New Haven, CT 06510. 203-787-6023

New Haven Enterprise Development Corporation, Office of Business Development, Irving L. Finley, Director of Minority and Disadvantaged Business Assistance Program, 770 Chapel St., New Haven, CT 06510. 203-787-6452

Technology Investment Fund, Inc., Paul Goodwin, President, 770 Chapel St., New Haven, CT 06510. 203-787-7059

Greater Waterbury Chamber of Commerce, Frank D. Fulco, President, 32 N. Main St., PO Box 1469, Waterbury, CT 06721. 203-757-0701

City of New Haven, Development Administration, Yaska Escalua, Development Administrator, 95 Orange St., New Haven, CT 06511. 203-787-8333

City of New Haven, City Plan Dept., John McEuerthy, Director, Development Administrator, 95 Orange St., New Haven, CT 06511. 203-787-6380

Jobs Center -- New Haven, Raymond Lopes, Director, 25 Science Park, New Haven, CT 06511. 203-865-4357

Local Incentives for Business

New Haven Enterprise Zone. New Haven's enterprise zone, at over 700 acres and including a Science Park, is the largest among the ten in the state. Please see Connecticut State Profile for more information.

The Municipal Industrial Park Programs provide low-cost industrial sites.

Assessment Deferral Program. It assists property owners undertaking rehabilitation which will increase the assessment of the property by 35% or more. The program saves property owners money by freezing the assessment of the property while the rehaiblitation is underway and during the first year afterward and phasing in the assessment increase caused by the rehabilitation at 20% per year over the next five years.

New Haven Community Investment Corp. Under the regulations of the SBA the NHCIC can offer the following financial services; issues SBA 503/504 Loans; issues SBA 7A Loan; issues working capital loans up to $50,000, financed jointly by city grants and private debenture sales, to existing or start-up firms. Project must generate jobs which will be available to New Haven residents.

Technology Investment Fund, Inc. TIF invests in technology-based start-up ventures which have the potential for substantial growth, financial success and significant job creation. Through the basic investment fund, TIF will provide up to $100,000 in near-equity financing by receiving either royalty rights or rights to purchase some of the company's equity at a set price.

A second program is the Business Creation Fund. TIF offers a short-term loan at below market interest rates with certain rights to TIF to invest in the company.

Industrial Sites

Science Park (80 acres). Located within a state Urban Enterprise Zone, this high-technology industrial park provides businesses with a working link with the scientific and technical resources of Yale University.

Science Park Development Corp. (see address above)

Major Businesses

Company	SIC	Telephone
ABS Pumps, Inc.	3561	(203) 238-2700
Ami Industries Inc.	1611	(203) 238-9160
Amphenol Corp.	3825	(203) 265-8500
Amstar Corp.	3546	(203) 777-2274
Automotive Controls Corp.	3694	(203) 481-5771
Blue Cross Blue Shield of Connecticut	6324	(203) 239-4911
Canberra Industries Inc.	3829	(203) 238-2351
Central Bank	6035	(203) 238-2300
Century Toyota Inc.	5511	(203) 269-7753
Cenvest Inc.	6035	(203) 238-2300
Condere Corp.	3011	(203) 287-2200
Connecticut Steel Corp.	3312	(203) 239-9947
Dataproducts New England	3577	(203) 265-7151
Dime Savings Bank of Wallingford	6035	(203) 269-8881
Echlin Inc.	3714	(203) 481-5751
Essex Industries Inc.	3429	(203) 777-2274
First Constitution Financial	6036	(203) 782-4570
First Constitution Bank	6035	(203) 782-4500
Fusco Corp.	1542	(203) 777-7451
Harte Chevrolet Inc.	5511	(203) 237-5561
Hospital of St. Raphael Inc.	8062	(203) 789-3000
Hubbell Inc.	3643	(203) 799-4100
LPL Technologies Inc.	3643	(203) 265-8500
Lane Construction Corp.	1629	(203) 235-3351
Lane Industries InCorp.	1629	(203) 235-3351
Lyon & Billard Co.	5211	(203) 235-4487
Mcdermott, David Chevrolet	5511	(203) 562-0101
Meriden Record Co.	2711	(203) 235-1661
Meriden-Wallingford Hospital	8062	(203) 238-8202
Miller Co.	3351	(203) 235-4474
New Haven Savings Bank	6036	(203) 787-1111
Pearce H. Real Estate Co.	6531	(203) 281-3400
Pirelli Armstrong Tire Co.	3011	(203) 784-2200
Roberts Chrysler Plymouth	5511	(203) 235-1667
Roberts Dodge Inc.	5511	(203) 237-8474
Saab-Scania of America Inc.	5012	(203) 795-5671
Simkins Industries, Inc.	2631	(203) 787-7171
Southern New England Telecommunication	4813	(203) 771-5200
St. Raphael Corp.	8062	(203) 789-3000
Times Fiber Communication	3357	(203) 265-8500
Ulbrich of California	5051	(203) 239-4481
United Illuminating Co. Inc.	4911	(203) 787-7200
World War II Veterans Memorial	8062	(203) 237-5531
Wyatt, Inc.	5171	(203) 483-4400
Yale-New Haven Hospital	8062	(203) 785-4242

Colleges and Universities

Albertus Magnus College, New Haven

Greater New Haven State Technical College, North Haven

Mattatuck Community College, Waterbury
Paier College of Art, Inc., Hamden
Quinnipiac College, Hamden
South Central Community College, New Haven
Southern Connecticut State University, New Haven
Telkyo Post University, Waterbury
University of Connecticut at Waterbury, Waterbury
University of New Haven, West Haven
Yale University, New Haven

Additional Information

New Haven in Brief. New Haven Downtown Council, n.d. [9p.]

New Haven's Science Park Nurtures Start-Up Businesses. New Haven Downtown Council, August 16, 1989. 3p. (news release)

New Haven Becomes Center of Connecticut's Biomedical Corridor. New Haven Downtown Council, September 1988. 3p. (news release)

Package of Information Outlining the Programs Offered by the New Haven Development Corporation, New Haven Community Investment Corporation, Technology Investment Fund, Inc., and the New Haven Enterprise Development Corporation City of New Haven, Office of Business Development, n.d. [folder]

NEW LONDON–NORWICH, CT–RI (NECMA)

Geographic Profile

Land Area
666.1 square miles

Counties and Parishes
Connecticut:
　New London (part)
　Windham (part)
Rhode Island:
　Washington (part)

Additional Cities/Towns within Area
New London County:
　Bozrah
　East Lyme
　Franlin
　Griswold
　Groton
　Ledyard
　Lisbon
　Montville
　North Stonington
　Norwich
　Old Lyme
　Preston
　Salem
　Sprague
　Stonington
　Waterford
Washington County:
　Hopkinton
　Westerly
Windham County:
　Canterbury

Ranking Highlights

260　*out of 319 in total* **land area**
224　*out of 319 in* **population growth**, *1970–1990*
166　*out of 310 in having the lowest* **unemployment** *rate*
149　*out of 310 in size of* **labor force**
114　*out of 318 in the percentage of* **college graduates**
37　*out of 292 in per capita personal* **income**
185　*out of 319 in number of* **manufacturing establishments**
154　*out of 318 in* **physicians** *per 1000 people*
272　*out of 318 in* **hospital beds** *per 1000 people*
26　*out of 267 in fewest* **crimes** *per 1000 people*
56　*out of 266 in fewest* **violent crimes** *per 1000 people*
1　*out of 319 in per capita* **federal funds and grants**

Quality of Life Indexes (Rate per 1000 population)
Crime rate in 1991:　　37.2
Violent crime rate in 1991:　　3.3

Physicians rate in 1992:   1.82
Hospital bed rate in 1991:   2.57

ACCRA Cost of Living Indexes
(First quarter 1993, average = 100)
Composite index: N/A
Utilities index: N/A
Housing index: N/A

Overview

The New London-Norwich MSA is about midway between New York City and Boston, Massachusetts, about 2 5 hours drive from either city. Interstate Highway 395 and State Route 32 link New London and Norwich together as a MSA.

Rail service to Norwich is provided by Central Vermont and Providence & Worcester Railways.

Air service in this area is provided by the local Groton/New London Airport and the Bradley International Airport in Hartford, a 60 mile distance.Population (1990)

Total Population and Growth Rate
1990: 254,957
1980: 238,409
1970: 230,654
Growth rate 1970–1990: 11%

Race and Hispanic Origin
White: 92.2%
Black: 4.5%
Asian/Pacific Islander: 1.3%
Native American: 0.5%
Hispanic origin: 3.2%
White not Hispanic: 90.6%

Age
Ages 18 to 20: 5.2%
Ages 21 to 24: 7.3%
Ages 25 to 44: 35.3%
Ages 45 to 54: 10.3%
Ages 55 to 59: 4.4%
Ages 60 to 64: 4.5%
Ages 65 plus: 13%

Educational Attainment (1990)
Percent having completed high school: 80.0%
Percent having completed college: 21.2%
Elementary and high school enrollment: 39,591

Federal Funds and Grants Received
Total received in 1989: $3,613,200,000
Funds received per capita: $14,591

Civilian Labor Force
1993 (April):   137,855
1992 average: 138,735
1991 average: 135,499
1990 average: 132,615

Unemployment
1993 (April):   6.4%
1992 average: 7.0%
1991 average: 6.7%
1990 average: 5.6%

Average Annual Pay
1988: $23,108
1987: $21,812
1985: $20,716

Per Capita Personal Income
1991: $20,863
1990: $20,269
1989: $19,667

Business Climate (1987)
Manufacturing
Number of establishments in 1987: 255
Shipments in 1987 ($1,000): $2,930,900
Employees in 1987: 34,200
Change in employment, 1982 to 1987: -2.6%
Average annual pay for manufacturing work in 1989: $30,651
Average annual pay for production work in 1987: $24,049

Wholesale Trade
Number of establishments in 1987: 261
Total sales in 1987 ($1,000): $636,500
Change in sales, 1982 to 1987: 27.3%

Retail Trade
Number of establishments in 1987: 1,822
Total sales in 1987 ($1,000): $636,500
Retail sales per household in 1987: $20,351
Average annual pay in 1989: $13,244

Service Industry
Selected receipts in 1987 ($1,000): $639,900
Average annual pay in 1989: $20,467

Housing
Total number of units in 1990: 110,752
Occupied units in 1990: 98,148
Owner-occupied units in 1990: 63.8%
1993 ACCRA average cost: N/A
1993 ACCRA average rent for an apartment: N/A

Chamber of Commerce
Southeastern Connecticut Chamber of Commerce, William D. Moore, President, 105 Huntington St., New London, CT 06320. 203-443-8332, FAX 203-444-1529

Economic Development Office
Eastern Connecticut Chamber of Commerce, A.M. Danielson, President, 35 Main St., Norwich, CT 06360. 203-887-1647, FAX 203-889-7615

Economic Development Organizations
City of Norwich, Office of Community Development, Peter Lent, Corporation and Economic Development Coordina-

tor, City Hall, 100 Broadway, Norwich, CT 06360. 203-886-2381, ext. 226

Greater Norwich Board of Realtors, Pat Udell, 1 Washington St., Norwich, CT 06360. 203-886-1533

Southeastern Connecticut Private Industry Council, John Beauregard, PO Box 215, Jewett City, CT 06351. 203-889-5241

Southeastern Connecticut Regional Planning Agency, Director, 139 Boswell Ave., Norwich, CT 06320. 203-889-2324

Local Incentives for Business

State Department of Economic Development: Norwich Urban Enterprise Zone, Norwich Urban Jobs Program, Target Investment Community - Manufacturers Assisstance Act of 1990, Connecticut Development Authority Low-Cost Financing, Connecticut Innovations Inc. (Product Development Assistance)

City of Norwich Downtown Programs:, Facade Restoration Grants, Rental Retail Subsidy Program, Commercial Construction Loan Program, Property tax assessment deferrals

Industrial Sites

Norwich Industrial Park. Norwich Office of Community Development, Corporation and Economic Development Coordinator (see address above).

Major Businesses

Company	SIC	Telephone
Arrow Paper & Supply Co. Inc.	5113	(203) 886-5141
Backus, William Hospital	8062	(203) 889-8331
Car Service Inc.	5511	(203) 447-3141
Chelsea Groton Savings Bank	6035	(203) 823-4800
Coastal Savings Bank	6035	(203) 447-5000
Electric Boat Community Federal	6111	(203) 446-8085
Lawrence and Memorial Hospital	8062	(203) 442-0711
Mallon Chevrolet Inc.	5511	(203) 889-3333
Moore Co.	2258	(401) 596-2816
Napert Construction Inc.	1522	(203) 442-6585
NESB Corp.	6036	(203) 444-3400
New London County Mutual Inc.	6331	(203) 887-3553
Norwich Savings Society	6035	(203) 889-2621
Plastic Wire Cable Credit	6111	(203) 376-4411
Sonalysts Inc.	8711	(203) 442-4355
Sully's Auto Sales & Service	5511	(203) 443-8432
Washington Trust Co.	6022	(401) 348-1200
Westerly Hospital Inc.	2221	(203) 535-1050

Colleges and Universities

Connecticut College, New London

Mitchell College, New London

Mohegan Community College, Norwich

Thames Valley State Technical College, Norwich

United States Coast Guard Academy, New London

University of Connecticut at Avery Point, Groton

Additional Information

Demographic Information. City of Norwich, Connecticut, Office of Economic Development, n.d. 4p.

DELAWARE

WILMINGTON, DE-NJ-MD (PMSA)

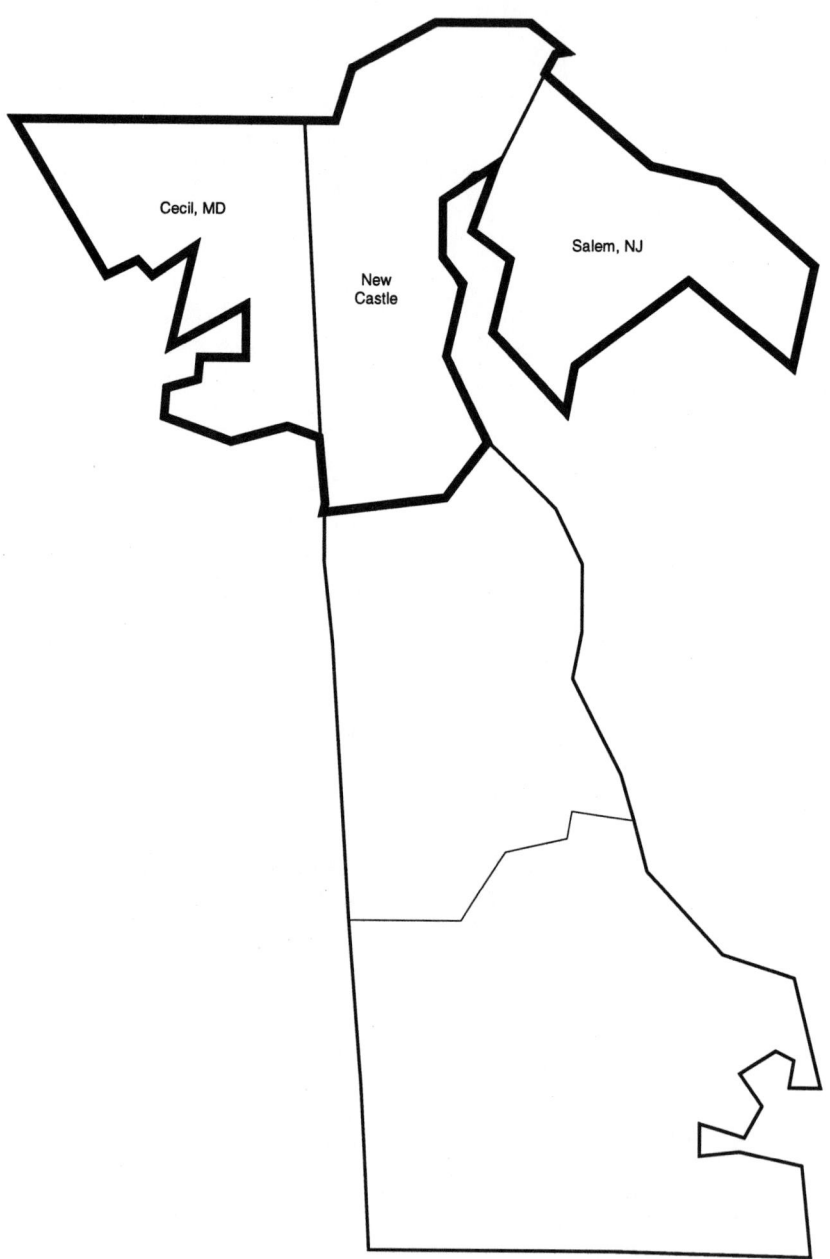

Cecil, MD

New
Castle

Salem, NJ

DELAWARE

Population

1990: 666,168
1980: 594,338

Age

Ages 18 to 20: 33,586
Ages 21 to 24: 42,647
Ages 25 to 44: 217,981
Ages 45 to 54: 68,114
Ages 55 to 59: 29,861
Ages 60 to 64: 29,903
Median age: 32.9

Race

White: 535,094
Black: 112,460
Asian/Pacific Islander: 9,057
Native American: 2,019
Hispanic origin: 15,820

Households

Total: 247,497
Persons per household: 2.61

Sex

Male: 322,968
Female: 343,200

Population Migration

Domestic migration: 40,000
International migration: 5,000

Projection of the Population in 1995

Total: 725,000
18 to 64: 456,000

Civilian Labor Force

1993: 376,800
1992: 368,900
1991: 363,800
1990: 361,400

Manufacturing

1995 Projection: 73,000
1992: 67,600
1991: 71,100
1990: 69,700
1989: 72,900

Services

1995 Projection: 115,200

1992: 85,800
1991: 84,100
1990: 84,400
1989: 83,700

Wholesale and Retail Trade

1995 Projection: 88,000
1992: 75,400
1991: 75,400
1990: 77,400
1989: 76,600

Unemployment Rate

1993: 5.0%
1992: 6.3%
1991: 6.1%
1990: 5.2%

Employer Unemployment Contributions

Contribution Rate

1992: 1.90%
1991: 2.40%
1990: 2.30%

Average Weekly Benefit

1992: $179.01
1991: $177.89
1990: $174.93

Gross State Product (Million $)

1989: $15,418
1988: $14,275
1987: $12,823
1979: $6,544
Growth rate, 1979 to 1989: 135.6%

Capital Expenditures of Manufacturing Industries

1990: $358,400,000
1989: $335,200,000
1988: $280,700,000
1987: $276,900,000

State Tax Rates

Individual income: Range from 3.2% ($5,000 or less) to 7.7% (above $40,000).
Corporate income: 8.7% of taxable income.
General property: Local collections, no state levy.

General sales: None

Gasoline: 19¢ per gallon

Income

Median income for a 4 person family: $42,790

Personal per Capita Income

1992: $21,451

1991: $20,935

1990: $20,709

Disposable per Capita Income

1992: $18,300

1991: $17,798

1990: $17,521

Private Employment Weekly Wages

Average

1989: $447

1988: $423

1987: $423

Manufacturing

1989: $400

1988: $650

1987: $627

Services

1989: $362

1988: $340

1987: $304

Wholesale

1989: $539

1988: $515

1987: $478

Retail

1989: $226

1988: $216

1987: $204

Highway Statistics

Total Highway Miles

1990: 5,444

1989: 5,417

1988: 5,387

Federal Highway Aid

1991: $50,328,000

1990: $50,037,000

1989: $50,339,000

Electricity

Average Cost per Kilowatt Hour

1990: 6.37¢

1989: 6.34¢

1988: 6.76¢

Housing (1990)

Owner occupied units: 173,813

Median house value: $100,100

Renter occupied units: 73,684

Median rent: $425

Total vacant units: 42,422

Homeowner vacancy rate: 2.3%

Rental vacancy rate: 7.8%

State Business Incentives and Assistance

Financial and Business Assistance

The Delaware Economic Development Authority, a subsidiary of the Delaware Development Office, offers comprehensive assistance to loan packaging by utilizing existing state and federal programs which include:

Industrial Revenue Bonds. Industrial Revenue Bonds are available for loans of $250,000 to $10,000,000. For additional details, contact the Delaware Development Office.

SBA 7a Loan Program. The eligibility of an applicant depends on the size and nature of the business. Suggested size of the loan is $25,000 to $500,000 and may be used for working capital and/or fixed assets. The interest rate and term of financing are negotiated with the bank. The SBA may guarantee up to 90% of the bank loan.

SBA 504 Loan Program. Eligible applicants are small businesses that will be the direct users of assets purchased with SBA 504 financing. The funds may only be used to purchase fixed assets. Suggested size of the loan is between $145,000 and $500,000. Normal project loan structuring is 50% from a bank, 40% SBA funds, and 10% applicant equity. Loans are for 10 and 20 years and rates will be approximately 0.75% point above the rates for U.S. Treasury Bonds of similar maturity. The loan recipient should employ one new employee for each $15,000 of the project costs.

Economic Development Fund. This fund provides below market fixed rate financing for manufacturing, wholesale, research and development laboratories or facilities and incubator service firms. Loans my be used for new construction, building acquisition and renovation, and machinery and equipment purchases.

Small Business Revolving Loan and Credit Enhancement Fund. The fund provides below market rate gap financing or purchases financial institution credit enhancements on behalf of small businesses. To qualify, a small business must have less than 100 employees and increase or retain permanent full-time jobs The fund may be used for loans up to 25% of the total capital required, but not to exceed $100,000.

Tax Credits. Targeted industries locating or expanding operations in Delaware are eligible for corporate income tax credits and gross receipts tax reductions if they invest a minimum of $200,000 in a new or expanded facility and employ a minimum of five new employees. Target industries are defined as manufacturers; wholesalers; laboratories or similar facilities used for scientific, agricultural or industrial research, development or testing; any combinations of these activities; and the administration or management required to support any of these functions. Tax credits are $250 for each $100,000 investment and $250 for each new qualified employee for which at least $40,000 in new investment has been made. In any single year, credits cannot exceed 50% of a firm's pre-credit tax liability. Unused credits can be carried forward throughout the 10 year life of the credits. Gross receipts taxes are reduced on a declining scale over a 10-year period ranging from a 90% reduction in the first year to a 5% reduction in the tenth year. Qualified firms located in selected geographic areas will receive additional tax credits.

Technological Outreach. A joint research effort between the University of Delaware and private industry for the purpose of technology transfer to those participating businesses.

Education and Training

Job Training Partnership Act. This program operates with funding from the U.S. Department of Labor. It provides job training and other employment related services.

State Offices

Real estate: Real Estate Commission, Dorothy F. Baker, Administrative Assistant, PO Box 1401, Margaret M.

O'Neill Bldg., 2nd fl., Federal & Court Stations, Dover, DE 19903. 302-736-4186

Chamber of commerce: Delaware State Chamber of Commerce, John M. Burris, President, One Commerce Center Suite 200, Wilmington, DE 19801. 302-655-7221

Economic development: Delaware Development Office, John J. Casey, Jr., Director, PO Box 1401, 99 Kings Highway., Dover, DE 19903. 302-736-4271, FAX 302-736-5749

Delaware Development Office, Business Research, Douglas Clendaniel, Director, PO Box 1401, 99 Kings Highway, Dover, DE 19903. 302-739-4271

Delaware Development Office (Enterprize Zones Office), Dorothy Sbriglia, Senior Business Development Rep., 99 Kings Highway, Dover, DE 19903. 302-739-4271

Technological Outreach, Harvey Stone, Special Assistant to the President, University of Delaware, Newark, DE 19711. 302-451-2862

Small Business Development Center, Linda L. Fayerweather, State Director, University of Delaware, 005 Purnell Hall, Newark, DE 19711. 302-451-2747

Environmental affairs: Dept. of Natural Resources and Environmnetal Control, Edwin H. Clark II, Secretary, 89

Major Companies in the State

Company name	Fortune 500 rank	City	Telephone	SIC number
Fortune 500 Companies				
E I Du Pont De Nemours & Co.	9	Wilmington	302-774-1000	2911
Hercules Inc.	166	Wilmington	302-594-5000	2869
Other Major Companies in the State				
Advanta Corp.		Claymont	302-791-4400	6021
Airgas Inc.		Wilmington	215-687-5253	5169
American Express Credit Corp.		Wilmington	302-594-3360	6141
Beneficial Corp.		Wilmington	302-798-0800	6141
Coltec Holdings Inc.		Wilmington	302-654-7539	3728
Columbia Gas System Inc.		Wilmington	302-429-5000	4923
Consolidated Stores Corp.		Wilmington	302-478-4896	5331
DCNY Corp.		Wilmington	302-421-7900	6211
Delmarva Power & Light Co.		Wilmington	302-429-3649	4931
Delphi Financial Group Inc.		Wilmington	302-478-5142	6311
Diamond State Telephone Co.		Wilmington	302-427-7750	4813
Discover Credit Corp.		Greenville	302-888-3190	6799
G I Holdings Inc.		Wilmington	302-429-8525	2869
International Specialty Products Inc.		Wilmington	302-429-8554	2819
Mary Kay Corp.		Wilmington	302-998-0592	5963
Mercantile Stores Co. Inc.		Wilmington	302-575-1816	5311
Norton Simon Inc.		Wilmington	302-428-3949	2033
Rollins Environmental Services Inc.		Wilmington	302-479-3455	4953
Rollins Truck Leasing Corp.		Wilmington	302-479-2700	7519
Sears Roebuck Acceptance Corp.		Greenville	302-888-3112	6153

Kings Highway, Dover, DE 19901. 302-739-4506

Labor: Dept. of Labor, Jan Ewing Robinson, Secretary of Labor, Carvel State Office Bldg., 820 N. French St., Wilmington, DE 19801. 302-577-2710

Unemployment: Division of Unemployment Insurance, W. Thomas MacPherson, Director, Dept. of Labor Bldg., University Office Plaza, Newark, DE 19714-9029. 302-368-6730

Worker's compensation: Dept. of Labor, Jan Ewing Robinson, Secretary of Labor, Carvel State Office Bldg., 820 N. French St., Wilmington, DE 19801. 302-577-2710

Occupational safety and health: Industrial Accident Board, John F. Kirk, Jr., Director, Carvel State Office Bldg., 820 N. French St., Wilmington, DE 19801. 302-739-4506

Secretary of state: Dept. of State, Michael Harkins, Secretary of State, Townsend Bldg., Dover, DE 19901. 302-736-4111

Taxation and revenue: Dept. of Finance, Scott R. Douglass, Secretary of Finance, Thomas Collins Bldg., US 13 and River Rd., Dover, DE 19901. 302-739-4201

Designated Zones for Economic Development

Enterprise Zones
Enacted in: 1984
No. of established zones: 30

Foreign Trade Zones
Foreign Trade Zone No. 99, Wilmington, Delaware, Grantee/ Operator: State of Delaware, Dorothy Sbriglia, Delaware Development Office, Dover, DE 19901, 302-736-4271

Labor Unions
Operating Engineers, International Union of (AFL-CIO)
Seaford Nylon Employees Council

Universities with Ph.D. Programs
University of Delaware, Newark

Sources of Additional Information
Delaware Wage Survey, Business Services Sector. Delaware Development Office, Business Research Section, April 1990. 32p.

Delaware Wage Survey, Manufacturing Sector. Delaware Development Office, Business Research Section, March 1990. 63p.

Education: Delaware's Renewable Resource. Delaware Development Office, n.d. [packet]

In Delaware Your Business Has All the Right Connections. Delaware Development Office, n.d. 15p.

WILMINGTON, DE–NJ–MD (PMSA)

Geographic Profile

Land Area
1112.3 square miles

Counties and Parishes
Delaware:
 New Castle
Maryland:
 Cecil
New Jersey:
 Salem

Ranking Highlights
180 *out of 319 in total* land area
195 *out of 319 in* population growth, *1970–1990*
 99 *out of 310 in having the lowest* unemployment *rate*
 80 *out of 310 in size of* labor force
 94 *out of 318 in the percentage of* college graduates
 18 *out of 292 in per capita personal* income
107 *out of 319 in number of* manufacturing establishments
 61 *out of 318 in* physicians *per 1000 people*
217 *out of 318 in* hospital beds *per 1000 people*
107 *out of 267 in fewest* crimes *per 1000 people*
137 *out of 266 in fewest* violent crimes *per 1000 people*
175 *out of 319 in per capita* federal funds and grants

Quality of Life Indexes (Rate per 1000 population)
Crime rate in 1991: 56.2
Violent crime rate in 1991: 6.4
Physicians rate in 1992: 2.52
Hospital bed rate in 1991: 3.22

ACCRA Cost of Living Indexes (First quarter 1993, average = 100)
Composite index: 113.6
Utilities index: 115.0
Housing index: 121.5

Overview
Since 1980, the Wilmington economy has been transformed from one dominated almost exclusively by the chemical industry to one supported by a diverse employment base in terms of type and size. The Financial Center Development Act of 1981 brought large financial institutions and their operations to the City's downtown business district. As a result, commercial office space grew from a total of 4.5 million square feet to over 7.4 million square feet. During that same period of time, more than 5,000 jobs were created and the investment of over $600 million in real estate projects occurred in the City.

A new initiative in the City's development plan is in the convention/tourism industry. The cornerstone of this initiative is the development of a convention/civic center to be located in the City's central business district. The plan, as developed to date, calls for the development of a 165,000 square foot facility including 65,000 square feet of contiguous flat floor space in the main exhibit hall. The facility, to be called the First State Center, will be developed with funding from both the City and the State of Delaware.

Population (1990)

Total Population and Growth Rate

1990: 578,587
1980: 523,221
1970: 499,493
Growth rate 1970–1990: 16%

Race and Hispanic Origin

White: 82.5%
Black: 14.8%
Asian/Pacific Islander: 1.3%
Native American: 0.2%
Hispanic origin: 2.4%
White not Hispanic: 81.4%

Age

Ages 18 to 20: 5.1%
Ages 21 to 24: 6.4%
Ages 25 to 44: 33.2%
Ages 45 to 54: 10.4%
Ages 55 to 59: 4.4%
Ages 60 to 64: 4.3%
Ages 65 plus: 11.6%

Educational Attainment (1990)

Percent having completed high school: 78.7%
Percent having completed college: 22.1%
Elementary and high school enrollment: 94,690

Federal Funds and Grants Received

Total received in 1989: $1,709,000,000
Funds received per capita: $2,980

Civilian Labor Force

1993 (April): 315,292
1992 average: 316,071
1991 average: 313,718
1990 average: 313,467

Unemployment

1993 (April): 4.6%
1992 average: 6.0%
1991 average: 6.5%
1990 average: 5.3%

Average Annual Pay

1988: $23,611
1987: $22,266
1985: $21,169

Per Capita Personal Income

1991: $22,668

1990: $22,477
1989: $21,140

Business Climate (1987)

Manufacturing

Number of establishments in 1987: 542
Shipments in 1987 ($1,000): $9,366,600
Employees in 1987: 56,600
Change in employment, 1982 to 1987: -8.4%
Average annual pay for manufacturing work in 1989: $40,199
Average annual pay for production work in 1987: $28,078

Wholesale Trade

Number of establishments in 1987: 805
Total sales in 1987 ($1,000): $7,188,400
Change in sales, 1982 to 1987: 5.1%

Retail Trade

Number of establishments in 1987: 3,206
Total sales in 1987 ($1,000): $7,188,400
Retail sales per household in 1987: $20,334
Average annual pay in 1989: $11,977

Service Industry

Selected receipts in 1987 ($1,000): $1,914,500
Average annual pay in 1989: $19,407

Office Real Estate (1992)

Office space inventory: 10,039,625 square feet
Average class A Central Business District rental range per sq. ft: $18.76

Vacancy Rates

All areas: 18.6%

Vacancy Rates in Central Business District

Class A space: 18.6%
Class B space: 27.0%

Vacancy Rates Outside Central Business District

Class A space: 14.2%
Class B space: 19.8%

Housing

Total number of units in 1990: 226,565
Occupied units in 1990: 212,680
Owner-occupied units in 1990: 69.5%
1993 ACCRA average cost: $143,680
1993 ACCRA average rent for an apartment: $525

Chamber of Commerce

New Castle County Chamber of Commerce, Fredric M. Rohm, President, PO Box 11247, County Commerce Office Park, Wilmington, DE 19850-1247. 302-737-4343, FAX 302-737-8450

Economic Development Office

Wilmington Economic Development Corp., Edwin Nutter, Exec. Director, 305-A Market St. Mall, Wilmington, DE 19801. 302-571-9088

Economic Development Organizations

New Castle County Economic Development Corp., President, 704 King St., First Federal Plaza #536, Wilmington, DE 19801. 302-656-5050

New Castle County Board of Realtors, Leslie Segall, President, PO Box 2086, 3615 Miller Rd., Wilmington, DE 19899. 302-762-4800

Industrial Sites

Airport Industrial Park, New Castle 302-322-9500

Boulden Interstate Park, Wilmington 302-658-2005

Boxwood Commerce Center, Wilmington 302-658-6681

Center Point Business Park, New Castle 302-322-9500

Delaware River Industrial Park, Wilmington 302-478-1190

Enterprise Busienss Park, New Castle 302-322-9500

First State Industrial Park, Wilmington 302-429-7353

Germay Industrial Park, Wilmington 302-655-9621

Harmony Business Park, New Castle 302-324-5100

Interchange Business Park, New Castle 302-322-9500

Lukens/Riveredge Park, New Castle 302-323-9700

Middletown Industrial Park, Wilmington 302-656-6686

Old Baltimore Industrial Park, Wilmington 302-429-0800

Pencader Corporate Center, New Castle 302-322-9500

Sandy Brae Indutrial Park, Wilmington 302-658-6681

Southgate Industrial Park, New Castle 302-324-5100

West Milford Industrial Park, New Castle 302-323-9700

Major Businesses

Company	SIC	Telephone
American International	6411	(302) 594-2000
American Life Insurance Co.	6311	(302) 594-2000
Bank of New York Delaware	6022	(302) 651-2000
Beneficial Corp.	6141	(302) 798-0800
Cigna Holdings Inc.	6311	(302) 479-6800
Citicorp Banking Corp.	6162	(302) 323-3142
Citicorp Holdings, Inc.	6021	(302) 323-3102
Columbia Gas System Inc.	4924	(302) 429-5000
Delaware Capital Holdings	5084	(302) 652-8759
Delmarva Power & Light Co.	4911	(302) 429-3011
Dixons US Holdings Inc.	3312	(302) 478-9330
Gore, W. L. & Associates Inc.	3357	(302) 738-4880
Greenwood Trust Co.	6022	(302) 323-7130
Hercules Incorporated	2821	(302) 594-5000
Himont Inc.	2821	(302) 996-6000
Holzmann, Philipp USA, Inc.	1542	(302) 651-9164
ICI Americas Inc.	2879	(302) 886-3000
INA Financial Corp.	6321	(302) 479-6214
Mercantile Stores Co.	5311	(302) 575-1816
NBD Delaware Bank	6022	(302) 453-5890
Nestle Holdings Inc.	2023	(302) 658-8021
Shell Energy Resources Inc.	1382	(302) 731-7474
Shell Petroleum Inc.	2911	(302) 658-5704
Tate & Lyle Inc.	5149	(302) 478-4773

Colleges and Universities

Brandywine College of Widener University, Wilmington, DE

Goldey-Beacom College, Wilmington, DE

DISTRICT OF COLUMBIA

WASHINGTON, DE-MD-VA (MSA)

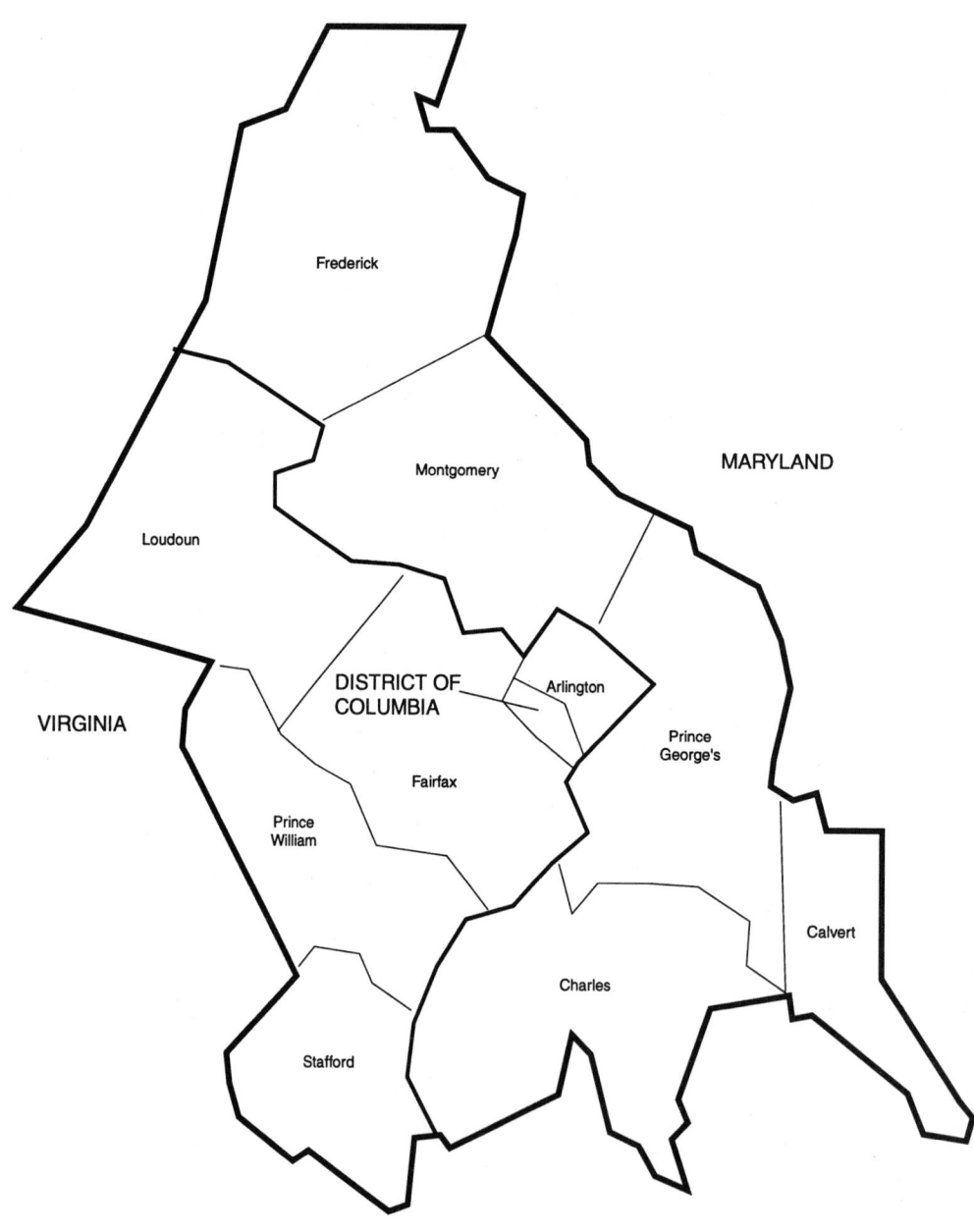

DISTRICT OF COLUMBIA

Population
1990: 606,900
1980: 638,333

Age
Ages 18 to 20: 35,291
Ages 21 to 24: 47,267
Ages 25 to 44: 216,472
Ages 45 to 54: 62,031
Ages 55 to 59: 25,441
Ages 60 to 64: 25,459
Median age: 33.5

Race
White: 179,667
Black: 399,604
Asian/Pacific Islander: 11,214
Native American: 1,466
Hispanic origin: 32,710

Households
Total: 249,634
Persons per household: 2.26

Sex
Male: 282,970
Female: 323,930

Population Migration
Domestic migration: -55,000
International migration: 24,000

Projection of the Population in 1995
Total: 617,000
18 to 64: 398,000

Civilian Labor Force
1993: 262,500
1992: 284,500
1991: 287,900
1990: 303,200

Manufacturing
1995 Projection: 18,800
1992: 14,000
1991: 15,100
1990: 15,600
1989: 16,100

Services
1995 Projection: 332,300

1992: 255,600
1991: 262,500
1990: 263,400
1989: 259,500

Wholesale and Retail Trade
1995 Projection: 73,400
1992: 54,700
1991: 59,800
1990: 62,100
1989: 66,400

Unemployment Rate
1993: 9.9%
1992: 8.4%
1991: 7.2%
1990: 5.6%

Employer Unemployment Contributions
Contribution Rate
1992: 2.80%
1991: 2.00%
1990: 2.00%

Average Weekly Benefit
1992: $228.15
1991: $231.14
1990: $213.09

Gross State Product (Million $)
1989: $39,363
1988: $36,759
1987: $33,486
1979: $17,778
Growth rate, 1979 to 1989: 121.4%

Capital Expenditures of Manufacturing Industries
1990: $41,400,000
1989: $44,100,000
1988: $40,000,000
1987: $43,600,000

State Tax Rates
Individual income: Range from 6% ($10,000 or less) to 9.5% (above $20,000).
Corporate income: 10% of total taxable income, with a 5% surtax imposed.

General property: $1.06 per $100 assessed value for residential property occupied by owners.

General sales: 6%

Gasoline: 18¢ per gallon

Income

Median income for a 4 person family: $40,574

Personal per Capita Income

1992: $26,360

1991: $24,916

1990: $23,885

Disposable per Capita Income

1992: $22,101

1991: $20,705

1990: $19,559

Private Employment Weekly Wages

Average

1989: $572

1988: $535

1987: $535

Manufacturing

1989: $497

1988: $710

1987: $658

Services

1989: $581

1988: $548

1987: $510

Wholesale

1989: $726

1988: $675

1987: $620

Retail

1989: $274

1988: $261

1987: $248

Highway Statistics

Total Highway Miles

1990: 1,102

1989: 1,102

1988: 1,102

Federal Highway Aid

1991: $92,914,000

1990: $90,853,000

1989: $108,490,000

Electricity

Average Cost per Kilowatt Hour

1990: 5.94¢

1989: 5.88¢

1988: 6.14¢

Housing (1990)

Owner occupied units: 97,108

Median house value: $123,900

Renter occupied units: 152,526

Median rent: $441

Total vacant units: 28,855

Homeowner vacancy rate: 3.1%

Rental vacancy rate: 7.9%

State Business Incentives and Assistance

Enterprise Zone Incentives

1) Real property tax abatement for new construction and rehabilitation of commercial and industrial facilities.
2) 50% credits for two years on business franchise taxes (corporate income tax) for wages paid to qualified employees and workman's compensation paid for qualified employees. The credits are capped at $7,500 per qualified employee and 30% of net income of the business. The credits may be carried over for five years.
3) Five-year carry over credit on business franchise taxes equal to the difference between the fair market rental value and the actual rent charged for child development centers located in property owner's facility.
4) Five-year 100% real property tax abatement for first time low and moderate income homeowners; with recordation and transfer taxes exemptions.

Education and Training

Job Training Partnership Act. This program operates with funding from the U.S. Department of Labor. It provides job training and other employment related services.

State Offices

Real estate: Consumer and Regulatory Affairs Department, Real Estate Commission, Rosalind W. Styles, Contract Representative, PO Box 37200, 614 H Street NW, Room 923, Washington DC 20001. 202-727-7468

Chamber of commerce: District of Columbia Chamber of Commerce, Robert Titus, President, 1411 K Street N.W., 6th fl., Washington DC 20005. 202-347-7201

Economic development: Office of Business & Economic Development, Raymond A. Skinner, Exec Director, 1111 E St. N.W. #700, Washington DC 20004. 202-727-6600

Development Zone Program, John Moore, Development Zone Administrator, 3101 Martin Luther King, Jr. Ave. S.E., Washington DC 20032. 202-404-1022

Environmental affairs: Public Works Department, Environmental Policy Division, Keneth Laden, Director, 2000 14th Street NW, 6th FL., Washington DC 20009. 202-939-8115

Labor: Employment Services Department, F. Alexis H. Roberson, Director, 500 C Street NW, Washington DC 20001. 202-639-1000

Unemployment: Employment Services Department, F. Alexis H. Roberson, Director, 500 C Street NW, Washington DC 20001. 202-639-1000

Worker's compensation: Employment Services Department, F. Alexis H. Roberson, Director, 500 C Street NW, Washington DC 20001. 202-639-1000

Occupational safety and health: Consumer and Regulatory Affairs Department, Donald Murray, Director, 614 H Street NW, Room 1120, Washington DC 20001. 202-727-7170

Secretary of state: Secretary Office, Teri Y. Doke, Secretary, 1350 Pennsylvania Ave. NW, Washington DC 20004. 202-727-6306

Taxation and revenue: Finance and Revenue Department, Harold L. Thomas, Director, Room 4136, 300 Indiana Ave. NE, Washington DC 20001. 202-727-6020

Designated Zones for Economic Development

Enterprise Zones

Enacted in: 1988
No. of established zones: 3

Foreign Trade Zones

Foreign Trade Zone No. 137, Washington Dulles Intl. Airport, Grantee: Washington Dulles Foreign-Trade Zone, Vincent Rivellese, PO Box 17349, Washington Dulles Intl. Airport, Washington, D.C. 20041, 703-661-8040

Labor Unions

Electrical Workers, International Brotherhood of (AFL-CIO)

Laborers' International Union of North America (AFL-CIO)

Nurses' Association, American

Universities with Ph.D. Programs

American University, Washington DC

Catholic University of America, Washington DC

Gallaudet University, Washington, DC

Georgetown University, Washington DC

George Washington University, Washington DC

Major Companies in the State

Company name	Fortune 500 rank	City	Telephone	SIC number
Fortune 500 Companies				
Danaher Corp.	367	Washington	202-828-0850	3423
Harman International Industries Inc.	490	Washington	202-393-1101	3651
Washington Post Co.	277	Washington	202-334-6000	2711
Other Major Companies in the State				
Abigail Adams National Bancorp Inc.		Washington	202-466-4090	6712
Allied Capital Corp.		Washington	202-331-1112	6726
Bet Holdings Inc.		Washington	202-337-5260	4841
Bresler & Reiner Inc.		Washington	202-488-8800	6552
Bureau of National Affairs Inc.		Washington	202-452-4200	2721
Century Bancshares Inc.		Washington	202-463-8710	6712
Chesapeake & Potomac Telephone Co.		Washington	202-392-1324	4813
Communications Satellite Corp.		Washington	202-863-6000	3663
Geico Corp.		Washington	301-986-3000	6331
Home Federal Savings Bank Washington DC		Washington	202-537-8800	6035
Independence Federal Savings Bank		Washington	202-628-5500	6035
James Madison Ltd.		Washington	202-429-7700	6712
MCI Communications Corp.		Washington	202-872-1600	4813
National Consumer Cooperative Bank		Washington	202-745-4610	6111
National Cooperative Bank		Washington	202-745-4610	6021
Potomac Electric Power Co.		Washington	202-872-2456	4911
Riggs National Corp.		Washington	202-835-6000	6712
Washington Bancorporation		Washington	202-429-7700	6712
Washington Gas Light Co.		Washington	703-750-4440	4923
Western Pacific Industries Inc.		Washington	202-828-0850	3824

WASHINGTON, DC–MD–VA (MSA)

Geographic Profile

Land Area

3966.7 square miles

Counties and Parishes

District of Columbia:

District of Columbia

Maryland:

Calvert

Charles

Frederick

Montgomery

Prince George's

Virginia:

Arlington

Fairfax

Loudoun

Prince William

Stafford

Additional Cities/Towns within Area

Alexandria

Arlington

Fairfax

Falls Church

Frederick

Manassas

Manassas Park

Ranking Highlights

29   *out of 319 in total* **land area**

137   *out of 319 in* **population growth,** *1970–1990*

51   *out of 310 in having the lowest* **unemployment** *rate*

5   *out of 310 in size of* **labor force**

4   *out of 318 in the percentage of* **college graduates**

8   *out of 292 in per capita personal* **income**

26   *out of 319 in number of* **manufacturing establishments**

28   *out of 318 in* **physicians** *per 1000 people*

263   *out of 318 in* **hospital beds** *per 1000 people*

126   *out of 267 in fewest* **crimes** *per 1000 people*

181   *out of 266 in fewest* **violent crimes** *per 1000 people*

4   *out of 319 in per capita* **federal funds and grants**

Quality of Life Indexes (Rate per 1000 population)

Crime rate in 1991:	59.0
Violent crime rate in 1991:	7.9
Physicians rate in 1992:	3.09
Hospital bed rate in 1991:	2.68

ACCRA Cost of Living Indexes

(First quarter 1993, average = 100)

Composite index: 133.8

Utilities index: 114.1

Housing index: 166.6

Overview

Washington, D.C. holds a worldwide reputation as a cosmopolitan city rich in museums, monuments, culture and political power. From the Hill, where the U.S. Capitol sits, to Embassy Row, home to much of the foreign diplomatic corps in Washington, the wide avenues hum with the business of America.

People often think of Washington, D.C. as a company town, where most people work for the federal government. However, as of the 1990s, only one of six workers in the area was on the government payroll. That figure is down from one in four in 1977. By contrast, there has been a great deal of growth in the private service sector, which now accounts for one of every three jobs. Still, many of these employees work for companies who rely on government contracts. As the largest consumer of technological equipment and service in the world, the federal government stimulates business through purchases, research and development funding, and grant and loan programs. As a result, Washington is a magnet for growth industries, such as biotechnology, telecommunications, information and computer firms, and many service industries. Forty-three of the major *Fortune* 50 companies have offices in the District, which is also the location of leading world, national, and regional financial institutions.

There are many publishing and printing companies in the area to produce the vast array of documents generated by the federal government. In addition, the city is the site of hundreds of national association headquarters and lobby groups who need a presence in the District to attempt to influence the legislation process on their own behalf.

The Capital offers more than twenty million square feet of office space, nearly half of it opened since 1980. A key to office development has been the growth of the Metrorail subway stations. Commercial projects have typically followed the opening of new subway stops. Many of the buildings are connected directly to the stations through underground tunnels which also serve retail stores and restaurants.

Baltimore-Washington International Airport handles the bulk of air freight in the area. For shipping, Washington has its own port and benefits from nearby facilities in Baltimore, Maryland; Norfolk, Virginia; and Alexandria, Virginia.

The Washington Convention Center, completed in 1983 and located on a 9.7-acre site—close to the Metro subway system—halfway between the White House and the Capitol, offers 378,000 square feet of exhibit space, forty meetings rooms, and seating for 20,000 people. The Washington area offers more than forty-two thousand hotel rooms.

Population (1990)

Total Population and Growth Rate
1990: 3,923,574
1980: 3,250,921
1970: 3,040,307
Growth rate 1970–1990: 29%

Race and Hispanic Origin
White: 65.7%
Black: 26.6%
Asian/Pacific Islander: 5.2%
Native American: 0.3%
Hispanic origin: 5.7%
White not Hispanic: 62.7%

Age
Ages 18 to 20: 4.3%
Ages 21 to 24: 6.7%
Ages 25 to 44: 37.9%
Ages 45 to 54: 11.5%
Ages 55 to 59: 4%
Ages 60 to 64: 3.4%
Ages 65 plus: 8.6%

Educational Attainment (1990)
Percent having completed high school: 85.2%
Percent having completed college: 38.5%
Elementary and high school enrollment: 598,403

Federal Funds and Grants Received
Total received in 1989: $36,649,900,000
Funds received per capita: $9,815

Civilian Labor Force
1993 (April): 2,256,179
1992 average: 2,262,748
1991 average: 2,228,960
1990 average: 2,212,178

Unemployment
1993 (April): 4.4%
1992 average: 5.0%
1991 average: 4.5%
1990 average: 3.4%

Average Annual Pay
1988: $26,784
1987: $25,210
1985: $22,727

Per Capita Personal Income
1991: $25,338
1990: $24,797
1989: $23,840

Business Climate (1987)

Manufacturing
Number of establishments in 1987: 2,744
Shipments in 1987 ($1,000): $10,859,300
Employees in 1987: 103,200

Change in employment, 1982 to 1987: 0%
Average annual pay for manufacturing work in 1989: $33,631
Average annual pay for production work in 1987: $21,672

Wholesale Trade
Number of establishments in 1987: 4,353
Total sales in 1987 ($1,000): $31,241,900
Change in sales, 1982 to 1987: 0%

Retail Trade
Number of establishments in 1987: 19,814
Total sales in 1987 ($1,000): $31,241,900
Retail sales per household in 1987: $20,636
Average annual pay in 1989: $15,325

Service Industry
Selected receipts in 1987 ($1,000): $26,899,400
Average annual pay in 1989: $27,980

Office Real Estate (1992)
Office space inventory: 260,767,087
Average class A Central Business District rental range per sq. ft: $30.00

Vacancy Rates
All areas: 15.9%

Vacancy Rates in Central Business District
Class A space: 14.9%
Class B space: N/A

Vacancy Rates Outside Central Business District
Class A space: 16.5%
Class B space: N/A

Housing
Total number of units in 1990: 1,556,749
Occupied units in 1990: 1,459,358
Owner-occupied units in 1990: 60.5%
1993 ACCRA average cost: $184,984
1993 ACCRA average rent for an apartment: $939

Chamber of Commerce
District of Columbia Chamber of Commerce, Robert Titus, President, 1411 K St. N.W., Washington, DC 20005. 202-347-7201

Economic Development Office
DC Office of Business & Economic Development, Charles E. Countee, Exec. Director, 717 14th St. N.W., Washington, DC 20005. 202-727-6600, FAX 202-727-3787

Economic Development Organizations
Greater Washington Board of Trade, Alan Gesser, Director, 1129 20th St. N.W., Washington DC 20036. 202-857-5966, FAX 202-223-2648

Major Businesses

Company	SIC	Telephone
British Aerospace Holding	5088	(703) 478-9420

Major Businesses (Continued)

Company	SIC	Telephone
Clark Construction Group	1542	(301) 657-7100
Federal Deposit Insurance	6399	(202) 898-6974
Federal Home Loan Mortgage Co.	6111	(703) 733-4368
Federal National Mortgage	6111	(202) 752-7000
First American Bankshares	6022	(202) 383-1400
Gannett Co. Inc.	2711	(703) 284-6000
Geico Corp.	6331	(202) 986-3000
Giant Food Inc.	5411	(301) 341-4100
Giant of Maryland Inc.	5411	(301) 341-4100
Government Employees Insurance	6331	(202) 986-3000
Group Hospitalization Medical	6324	(202) 479-8000
Hechinger Co.	5211	(301) 341-1000
Inter-American Development Bank	6082	(202) 623-1000
International Monetary	6111	(202) 623-7000
Lafarge Corp.	3241	(703) 264-3600
Marriott Corp.	5812	(202) 897-9000
Mars Inc.	2064	(703) 821-4900
Martin Marietta Corp.	3761	(301) 897-6000
MCI Communications Corp.	4813	(202) 872-1600
National Railroad Pass Co.	4011	(202) 906-3000
Peoples Drug Stores Inc.	5912	(703) 750-6100
Potomac Electric Power Co.	4911	(202) 872-2000
Sovran Bank-DC National	6021	(202) 955-8700
Student Loan Marketing Association	6111	(202) 333-8000
USAir Group, Inc.	4512	(703) 418-7000
Washington Post Co.	2711	(202) 334-6000

Colleges and Universities

American University, Washington, D.C.
Catholic University of America, Washington, D.C.
Corcoran School of Art, Washington, D.C.
Frederick Community College, Frederick, MD
Gallaudet University, Washington, D.C.
George Washington University, Washington, D.C.
Georgetown University, Washington, D.C.
Hood College, Frederick, MD
Howard University, Washington, D.C.
Mount Vernon College, Washington, D.C.
Oblate College, Washington, D.C.
Southeastern University, Washington, D.C.
Strayer College, Washington, D.C.
Trinity College, Washington, D.C.
University of the District of Columbia, Washington, D.C.

FLORIDA

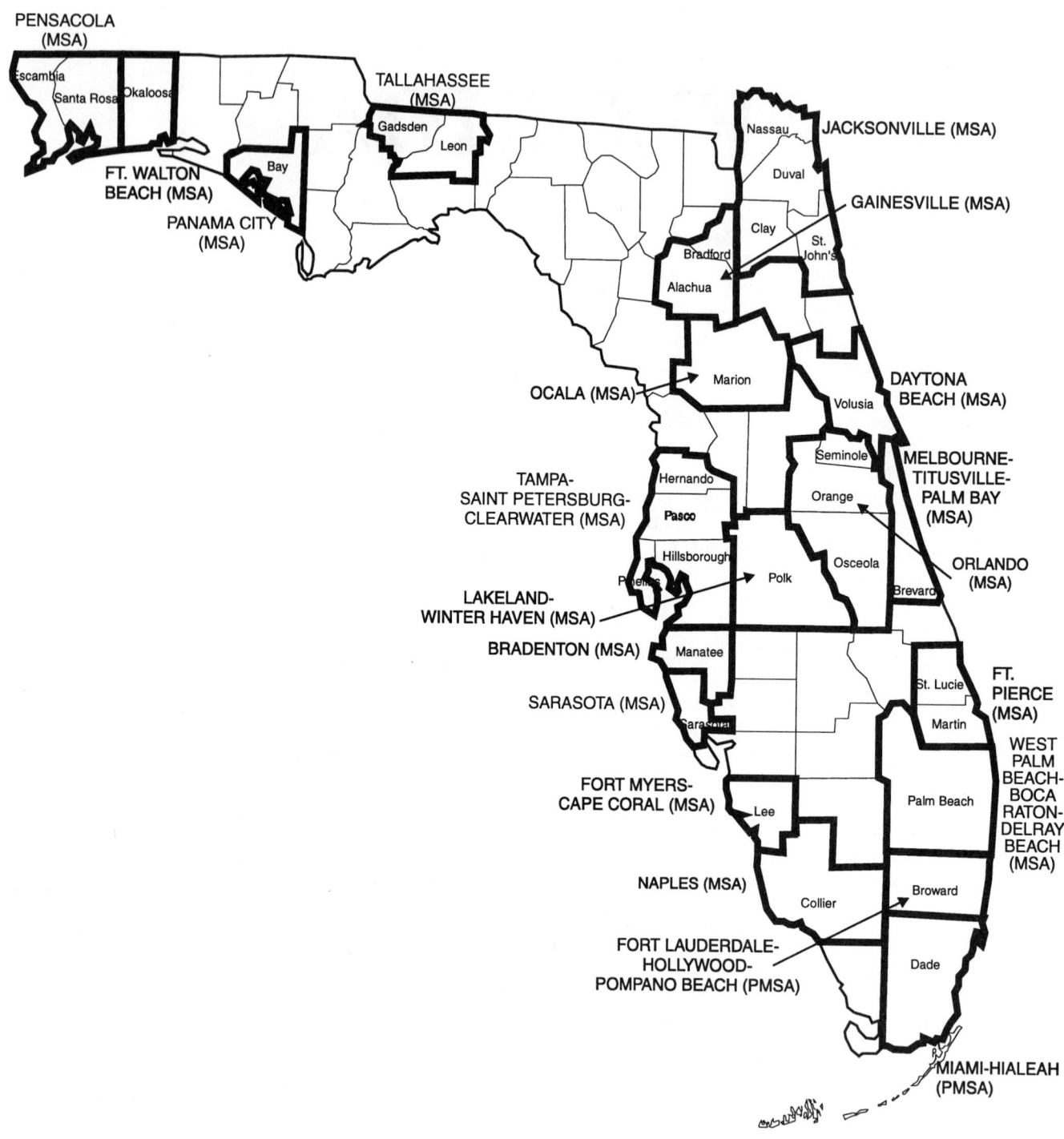

PENSACOLA
(MSA)

Escambia

Santa Rosa Okaloosa

FT. WALTON
BEACH (MSA)

PANAMA CITY
(MSA)

Bay

TALLAHASSEE
(MSA)

Gadsden Leon

JACKSONVILLE (MSA)

Nassau

Duval

Clay

Bradford St. John's

GAINESVILLE (MSA)

Alachua

OCALA (MSA)

Marion

Volusia

DAYTONA
BEACH (MSA)

Seminole

MELBOURNE-
TITUSVILLE-
PALM BAY
(MSA)

TAMPA-
SAINT PETERSBURG-
CLEARWATER (MSA)

Hernando

Pasco

Orange

ORLANDO
(MSA)

Hillsborough

Osceola

Pinellas

Polk

Brevard

LAKELAND-
WINTER HAVEN (MSA)

BRADENTON (MSA)

Manatee

St. Lucie

FT.
PIERCE
(MSA)

SARASOTA (MSA)

Sarasota

Martin

WEST
PALM
BEACH-
BOCA
RATON-
DELRAY
BEACH
(MSA)

FORT MYERS-
CAPE CORAL (MSA)

Lee

Palm Beach

NAPLES (MSA)

Collier

Broward

FORT LAUDERDALE-
HOLLYWOOD-
POMPANO BEACH (PMSA)

Dade

MIAMI-HIALEAH
(PMSA)

FLORIDA

Population
1990: 12,937,926
1980: 9,746,324

Age
Ages 18 to 20: 522,755
Ages 21 to 24: 692,902
Ages 25 to 44: 3,927,400
Ages 45 to 54: 1,291,611
Ages 55 to 59: 588,552
Ages 60 to 64: 679,038
Median age: 36.4

Race
White: 10,749,285
Black: 1,759,534
Asian/Pacific Islander: 154,302
Native American: 36,335
Hispanic origin: 1,574,143

Households
Total: 5,134,869
Persons per household: 2.46

Sex
Male: 6,261,719
Female: 6,676,207

Population Migration
Domestic migration: 1,975,000
International migration: 290,000

Projection of the Population in 1995
Total: 13,712,000
18 to 64: 8,132,000

Civilian Labor Force
1993: 6,530,500
1992: 6,438,200
1991: 6,424,000
1990: 6,183,600

Manufacturing
1995 Projection: 601,500
1992: 480,700
1991: 496,100
1990: 514,000
1989: 547,900

Services
1995 Projection: 2,277,300

1992: 1,685,000
1991: 1,667,100
1990: 1,629,600
1989: 1,544,700

Wholesale and Retail Trade
1995 Projection: 1,775,000
1992: 1,409,200
1991: 1,453,700
1990: 1,494,900
1989: 1,504,500

Unemployment Rate
1993: 7.9%
1992: 8.6%
1991: 6.3%
1990: 5.8%

Employer Unemployment Contributions
Contribution Rate
1992: 1.49%
1991: 0.93%
1990: 0.73%

Average Weekly Benefit
1992: $168.33
1991: $163.75
1990: $147.22

Gross State Product (Million $)
1989: $226,964
1988: $212,761
1987: $194,884
1979: $85,142
Growth rate, 1979 to 1989: 166.6%

Capital Expenditures of Manufacturing Industries
1990: $1,866,900,000
1989: $1,887,300,000
1988: $1,929,200,000
1987: $1,910,700,000

State Tax Rates
Individual income: None
Corporate income: 5.5% of federal taxable income.
General property: No state levy on realty or tangible property. Rates fixed locally. 1.5 mills per dollar of all intangible properties.

General sales: 6%

Gasoline: 4¢ per gallon

Income

Median income for a 4 person family: $37,399

Personal per Capita Income

1992: $19,397

1991: $18,985

1990: $18,606

Disposable per Capita Income

1992: $17,246

1991: $16,813

1990: $16,366

Private Employment Weekly Wages

Average

1989: $376

1988: $367

1987: $367

Manufacturing

1989: $351

1988: $451

1987: $429

Services

1989: $383

1988: $369

1987: $351

Wholesale

1989: $520

1988: $506

1987: $470

Retail

1989: $238

1988: $233

1987: $226

Highway Statistics

Total Highway Miles

1990: 108,085

1989: 107,955

1988: 104,589

Federal Highway Aid

1991: $502,550,000

1990: $359,134,000

1989: $509,518,000

Electricity

Average Cost per Kilowatt Hour

1990: 7.06¢

1989: 6.93¢

1988: 7.05¢

Housing (1990)

Owner occupied units: 3,452,160

Median house value: $77,100

Renter occupied units: 1,682,709

Median rent: $402

Total vacant units: 965,393

Homeowner vacancy rate: 3.4%

Rental vacancy rate: 12.4%

State Business Incentives and Assistance

Enterprise Zone Incentives

Florida's Enterprise Zone Program offers substantial tax/area incentives to businesses who invest their resources in designated declining areas or who employ zone residents and other targeted employees.

Corporate income tax credits for community contributions, hiring targeted individuals and property taxes paid on new or expanding businesses.

Sales tax credit for hiring persons who are enterprise zone residents, AFDC recipients, or JTPA economically disadvantaged. Sales tax exemptions for building materials, business property, and electricity used in an enterprise zone.

Has eight foreign trade zones located in the state and 13 world trade councils and international associations.

Financial and Business Assistance

Tax Incentives. No annual franchise tax levied on stock or equity. Exemptions from the sales and use taxes for manufacturing or processing equipment for new businesses. Partial exemptions for such machinery purchased by existing firms undergoing expansion. Sales and use taxes exemptions for the entertainment industry (motion picture, television, and recording production). Tax exemptions for commercial space activity. Launch vehicles, payloads, and fuel are exempt from the sales and use taxes. Rocket fuel is exempt from taxation as fuel. Machinery and equipment purchased to produce items for exclusive use at Spaceport Florida are exempt from the sales and use taxes. No sales and use taxes on equipment and machinery used in recycling. No sales and use taxes on cogeneration of electricity. Use tax exemption for research and development labor costs. Farm equipment taxed at 3%. No sales tax on containers and packaging, or materials in a final product. No sales and use taxes on boiler fuels. No tax on inventory or goods-in-transit. Local option ad valorem tax exemption. Pollution control equipment assessed at salvage value for property taxes. No state-level ad valorem tax. Local tax increment financing for redevelopment.

Industrial Development Bond. IDB financing authorized for research and development parks, industrial and office buildings, warehouses and distribution facilities, machinery and equipment purchases.

Florida First Capital Finance Corporation. A non-profit corporation certified to participate in Small Business Administration financing programs.

Community Development Corporation Support and Assistance Program. Provides funds to local community development corporations for use in making loans for establishing new businesses, providing financial assistance to existing businesses or purchasing equity interests in businesses.

State procurement incentives. Permits spending up to 10% more for products made from recovered materials.

Research and Development. a) Over 200 special research and service institutes through the State University System available for technical assistance and research; b) Nine university-related research parks in which firms may build facilities to access university resources and expertise; c) The Applied Research Grants Program provides match funding for university research which has commercialization potential. Partnerships between universities and industries are encouraged during all phases of research, and are required for developmental and operational phase projects; d) Six technology transfer centers to assist small and medium size manufacturing companies to adapt tech-

nological advances necessary to enhance productivity and competitiveness.

Site Selection. Computerized profiles for 67 counties. Computerized directory of available industrial buildings. Comparison of taxes and other location factors for Florida and other states.

Marketing. Export assistance, including: export finance office, trade missions, trade shows, and in-plant consultations. Provides trade leads database and statewide business assistance hot-line 1-800-342-0771 (in Florida).

Education and Training

Centers of Electronic Emphasis and Centers of Electronic Specialization are public/private partnerships with industry to supply skilled employees for high technology industries.

Florida Occupation Information System maintains a statewide and local computerized occupation data bank. Data on occupational demand, occupational supply, and occu-

Major Companies in the State

Company name	Fortune 500 rank	City	Telephone	SIC number
Fortune 500 Companies				
Anchor Glass Container Corp.	320	Tampa	813-884-0000	3221
Brooke Group Ltd	376	Miami	305-533-0800	2111
DWG Corp.	301	Miami Beach	305-866-7771	2261
Harris Corp. Fla	156	Melbourne	407-727-9100	3812
Knight Ridder Inc.	198	Miami	305-376-3800	2711
St. Joe Paper Co.	489	Jacksonville	904-396-6600	2653
W. R. Grace & Co.	83	Boca Raton	407-362-2000	2671
Other Major Companies in the State				
American Bankers Insurance Group Inc.		Miami	305-253-2244	6331
Barnett Banks Inc.		Jacksonville	904-791-7720	6712
Carnival Cruise Lines Inc.		Miami	305-599-2600	4481
Eastern Air Lines Inc.		Miami	305-873-2211	4512
Florida Power & Light Co.		Juno Beach	407-694-4646	4911
Florida Power Corp.		St Petersburg	813-866-5151	4911
Florida Progress Corp.		St Petersburg	813-824-6400	4911
FPL Group Capital Inc.		Juno Beach	407-694-4646	6331
FPL Group Inc.		Juno Beach	407-694-4646	4911
GTE Florida Inc.		Tampa	813-224-4011	4813
GTE South Inc.		Tampa	813-224-4011	4813
Home Shopping Network Inc.		St Petersburg	813-572-8585	5963
Jack Eckerd Corp.		Largo	813-397-7461	5912
Kash N Karry Food Stores Inc.		Tampa	813-621-0200	5411
Publix Super Markets Inc.		Lakeland	813-688-1188	5411
Ryder System Inc.		Miami	305-593-3726	7513
Southeast Banking Corp.		Miami	305-375-7500	6712
Tampa Electric Co.		Tampa	813-228-4111	4911
Teco Energy Inc.		Tampa	813-228-4111	4911
Winn Dixie Stores Inc.		Jacksonville	904-783-5000	5411

pation characteristics are available.

Job Training Partnership Act. This program operates with funding from the U.S. Department of Labor. It provides job training and other employment related services.

State Offices

Real estate: Real Estate Commission, Darlene Keller, Director, PO Box 1900, Orlando, FL 32802. 407-423-6053

Chamber of commerce: Florida State Chamber of Commerce, Michelle Orlando, Director of Services, PO Box 11309, 136 S. Bronough St., Tallahassee, FL 32301. 904-222-2831

Economic development: Dept. of Commerce, Division of Economic Development, Stephen Mayberry, Director, 107 W. Gaines St., Tallahassee, FL 32399-2000. 904-488-6300

Dept. of Business Regulation, Stephen R. MacNamara, Secretary, 725 South Bronough, Tallahassee, FL 32399-1000. 904-488-7114

Florida Dept. of Community Affairs (Enterprize Zones Office), Tony Collins, Community Assistance Consultant, 2740 Centerview Drive, Tallahassee, FL 32399-2000. 904-488-3581

Small Business Development Center, Jerry Cartwright, State Director, University of West Florida, Building 38, Pensacola, FL 32514. 904-474-3016

Environmental affairs: Dept. of Environmental Regulation, Carol Browner, Secretary, 2600 Blairstone Rd., Twin Towers Bldg., Tallahassee, FL 32399-2400. 904-488-4805

Labor: Dept. of Labor and Employment Security, Div. of Labor, Employment and Training, Skip Johnson, Director, Rm 300, Atkins Bldg., Tallahassee, FL 32399-0667. 904-488-7228

Unemployment: Dept. of Labor and Employment Security, Div. of Unemployment Compensation, Michael Switzer, Director, Suite 201, Caldwell Bldg., Tallahassee, FL 32399. 904-488-6093

Worker's compensation: Dept. of Labor and Employment Security, Div. of Worker's Compensation, Charlie Macon, Director, Ashley Bldg., Room 201, 1321 Executive Center Drive East, Tallahassee, FL 32399-0680. 904-488-2514

Occupational safety and health: Dept. of Labor and Employment Security, Bureau of Industrial Safety & Health, Gary Strobel, Chief, 2002 Old St. Augustine Rd., Suite 45, Bldg. E, Tallahassee, FL 32399-0663. 904-488-3044

Secretary of state: Dept. of State, Jim Smith, Secretary of State, The Capitol Plaza Level, Rm 2, Tallahassee, FL 32399-0250. 904-488-3680

Taxation and revenue: Dept. of Revenue, Tom Herndon, Director, 501 E. Calhoun St., Carlton Bldg., Tallahassee, FL 32399-0100. 904-488-6387 or 800-226-3411

Designated Zones for Economic Development

Enterprise Zones

Enacted in: 1984

No. of established zones: 30

Foreign Trade Zones

Foreign Trade Zone No. 136, Brevard County, Florida, Grantee: Canaveral Port Authority, Max Willis, PO Box 267, Port Canaveral Station, Cape Canaveral, FL 32920, 407-783-7833

Foreign Trade Zone No. 166, Homestead, Florida, Grantee: Vison Foreign-Trade Zone, Inc., Nic Walker, 15600 S.W. 288 Street, Suite 304, Homestead, FL 33033, 305-247-7082

Foreign Trade Zone No. 64, Jacksonville, Florida, Grantee: Jacksonville Port Authority, Neil Ganzel, PO Box 3005, Jacksonville, FL 32206, 904-630-3070

Foreign Trade Zone No. 169, Manatee County, Florida, Grantee: Manatee County Port Authority, Claude E. McGavic, Route 1/Tampa Bay, Palmetto, FL 34221, 813-722-6621 or 229-1051

Foreign Trade Zone No. 32, Miami, Florida, Grantee: Greater Miami Foreign Trade Zone, Inc., Sandra Gonzalez, Omni International Complex, 1601 Biscayne Blvd., Miami, FL 33132, 305-350-7700

Foreign Trade Zone No. 180, Miami (Wynwood), Florida, Grantee/Operator: Wynwood Community Economic Development Corp., William Rios, Executive Director, 225 NE 34th Street, Suite 209, Miami, FL 33137, 305-576-0440

Foreign Trade Zone No. 42, Orlando, Florida, Grantee/Operator: Greater Orlando Aviation Authority, Linda Smith, 9055 Tradeport Drive, Orlando, FL 32827, 407-859-9485

Foreign Trade Zone No. 135, Palm Beach County, Florida, Grantee: Port of Palm Beach District, Colonel Frank Donahue, PO Box 761, Palm Beach, FL 33480, 407-832-4556

Foreign Trade Zone No. 65, Panama City, Florida, Grantee/Operator: Panama City Port Authority, Tommy L. Berry, PO Box 15095, Panama City, FL 32406, 904-763-8471

Foreign Trade Zone No. 25, Port Everglades, Florida, Grantee/Operator: Port Everglades Port Authority, Doug Madora, 1850 Eller Drive, Ft. Lauderdale, FL 33316, 305-523-3404

Foreign Trade Zone No. 79, Tampa, Florida, Grantee: City of Tampa, Operator: Tampa FTZ Board, Inc., Robert E. Perkins, Jr., PO Box 3324, Tampa, FL 33601, 813-273-5202

Labor Unions

Association of Educational Secretaries and Office Personnel

Automobile, Aerospace & Agricultural Implement Workers of America, International Union, United (UAW AFL-CIO)

Boilermakers, Iron Shipbuilders, Blacksmiths, Forgers and

Helpers, International Brotherhood of (AFL-CIO)

Electrical Workers, International Brotherhood of (AFL-CIO)

Firemen and Oilers, International Brotherhood of (AFL-CIO)

Food and Commercial Workers International Union, United (AFL-CIO)

Hotel Employees and Restaurant Employees International Union (AFL-CIO)

Marine Engineers' Beneficial Association, National (AFL-CIO)

National Education Association

National Fraternal Order of Police

Nurses' Association, American

Painters and Allied Trades of The United States and Canada, International Brotherhood of (AFL-CIO)

State, County and Municipal Employees, American Federation of (AFL-CIO)

Teamsters, Chauffeurs, Warehousemen and Helpers of America, International Brotherhood of (AFL-CIO)

Teachers, American Federation of (AFL-CIO)

Transport Workers Union of America (AFL-CIO)

Universities with Ph.D. Programs

Florida Agricultural and Mechanical University, Tallahassee

Florida Atlantic University, Boca Raton

Florida Institute of Technology, Melbourne

Florida International University, Miami

Florida State University, Tallahassee

Nova University, Fort Lauderdale

St. Thomas University, Miami

University of Central Florida, Orlando

University of Florida, Gainesville

University of Miami, Coral Gables

University of South Florida, Tampa

Sources of Additional Information

Florida and the Other Forty-Nine, 1989: Florida's Business and Demographic Climate with National and State Comparisons. Florida Dept. of Commerce, Div. of Economic Development, Bureau of Economic Analysis, February 1990. 112p.

The Florida Economy, An Analysis of the Economy and Its Industrial Structure. Florida Dept. of Commerce, Div. of Economic Development, Bureau of Economic Analysis, January 1987. 121p.

1988 Florida Directory. [Florida Dept. of Commerce, Div. of Economic Development, Bureau of Economic Analysis], n.d., 12p.

High Tech in Florida: Is the Sky the Limit? Market Supplements, Aviation Week & Space Technology, November 28, 1988. pp.49-68.

Florida, Flexes Its Economic Muscle. Special Advertising Section, Business Week, September 17, 1990.

Florida, A Guide for Decision Makers. Florida Dept. of Commerce, Div. of Economic Development, n.d. np.

Florida Seaports. Florida Dept. of Commerce, Div. of Economic Development, n.d. [packet]

Florida Facts, Information on Florida Taxes and Fees. Florida Dept. of Commerce, Div. of Economic Development, January 1991, 6p.

Florida Facts, Florida's Business Advantages and Incentives. Florida Dept. of Commerce, Div. of Economic Development, September, 1990, [3p.]

BRADENTON, FL (MSA)

Geographic Profile

Land Area

741.2 square miles

Counties and Parishes

Manatee

Ranking Highlights

247 *out of 319 in total* land area

12 *out of 319 in* population growth, *1970–1990*

114 *out of 310 in having the lowest* unemployment *rate*

181 *out of 310 in size of* labor force

229 *out of 318 in the percentage of* college graduates

N/A *out of 292 in per capita personal* income

207 *out of 319 in number of* manufacturing establishments

224 *out of 318 in* physicians *per 1000 people*

146 *out of 318 in* hospital beds *per 1000 people*

225 *out of 267 in fewest* crimes *per 1000 people*

238 *out of 266 in fewest* violent crimes *per 1000 people*

128 *out of 319 in per capita* federal funds and grants

Quality of Life Indexes (Rate per 1000 population)

Crime rate in 1991:	79.1
Violent crime rate in 1991:	10.6
Physicians rate in 1992:	1.54
Hospital bed rate in 1991:	4.04

ACCRA Cost of Living Indexes

(First quarter 1993, average = 100)

Composite index:	N/A
Utilities index:	N/A
Housing index:	N/A

Population (1990)

Total Population and Growth Rate

1990: 211,707

1980: 148,445

1970: 97,115

Growth rate 1970–1990: 118%

Race and Hispanic Origin

White: 89.9%

Black: 7.7%

Asian/Pacific Islander: 0.6%

Native American: 0.2%

Hispanic origin: 4.5%

White not Hispanic: 87.2%

Age

Ages 18 to 20: 3.1%

Ages 21 to 24: 4.2%

Ages 25 to 44: 25.7%

Ages 45 to 54: 8.8%

Ages 55 to 59: 4.5%

Ages 60 to 64: 6.5%

Ages 65 plus: 28.1%

Educational Attainment (1990)

Percent having completed high school: 75.6%

Percent having completed college: 15.5%

Elementary and high school enrollment: 26,221

Federal Funds and Grants Received

Total received in 1989: $620,200,000

Funds received per capita: $3,318

Civilian Labor Force

1993 (April): 120,432

1992 average: 107,357

1991 average: 97,469

1990 average: 92.750

Unemployment

1993 (April): 4.8%

1992 average: 6.2%

1991 average: 5.8%

1990 average: 4.6%

Average Annual Pay

1988: $16,740

1987: $16,349

1985: $14,857

Per Capita Personal Income

1991: N/A

1990: N/A

1989: N/A

Business Climate (1987)

Manufacturing

Number of establishments in 1987: 215

Shipments in 1987 ($1,000): $1,502,800

Employees in 1987: 9,300

Change in employment, 1982 to 1987: 60.3%

Average annual pay for manufacturing work in 1989: $23,577

Average annual pay for production work in 1987: $17,545

Wholesale Trade

Number of establishments in 1987: 197

Total sales in 1987 ($1,000): $1,058,200

Change in sales, 1982 to 1987: 224.0%

Retail Trade

Number of establishments in 1987: 1,172

Total sales in 1987 ($1,000): $1,058,200

Retail sales per household in 1987: $16,698

Average annual pay in 1989: $11,727

Service Industry

Selected receipts in 1987 ($1,000): $462,500

Average annual pay in 1989: $16,902

Housing

Total number of units in 1990: 115,245

Occupied units in 1990: 91,060

Owner-occupied units in 1990: 70.9%
1993 ACCRA average cost: N/A
1993 ACCRA average rent for an apartment: N/A

Chamber of Commerce

Manatee County Chamber of Commerce, Robert P. Bartz, President, PO Box 321, 222 10th St. W., Bradenton, FL 34206. 813-748-3411, FAX 813-745-1877

Economic Development Office

Bradenton Downtown Development Authority, W.T. Mills, Jr., Exec. Director, 1001 3rd Ave. W. #350, Bradenton, FL 34206. 813-748-7949

Major Businesses

Company	SIC	Telephone
Barnett Bank of Manatee	6021	(813) 755-8889
Beall's Department Stores	5651	(813) 747-2355
Butler, H. Footwear Inc.	5661	(813) 748-8288
Citizens & Southern National Bank	6022	(813) 722-3271
Etsell Inc.	7389	(813) 383-3420
Graham, Bill Ford Co.	5511	(813) 747-3711
HCA Blake, L. W. Hospital	8062	(813) 792-6611
Hilliard Bros. Inc.	5511	(813) 748-6886
Miller Trailers Inc.	3715	(813) 748-3900
Pacific Tomato Growers	0161	(813) 722-3291
Prince Contracting Co., Inc.	1629	(813) 722-7707
Pursley Inc.	0181	(813) 756-8441
Rossignol L. F. Development	6552	(813) 351-5802
Schroeder Manatee Inc.	0174	(813) 755-1637
Southern Agricultural Insecticides	5191	(813) 722-3285
Staff Leasing Inc.	7363	(813) 748-4540
Stimus, Tom Chrysler Plymouth	5511	(813) 746-7153
Stimus, Tom Auto Sales Inc.	5511	(813) 748-0700
Sun Coast Beef & Provision	5147	(813) 722-3229
Taylor & Fulton Inc.	0723	(813) 729-3883
Trilectron Industries Inc.	3728	(813) 723-1841
Tropicana Products Inc.	2033	(813) 747-4461

Colleges and Universities

Manatee Community College, Bradenton

DAYTONA BEACH, FL (MSA)

Geographic Profile

Land Area

1105.9 square miles

Counties and Parishes

Volusia

Ranking Highlights

184 *out of 319 in total* land area
　10 *out of 319 in* population growth, *1970–1990*
219 *out of 310 in having the lowest* unemployment *rate*
132 *out of 310 in size of* labor force
237 *out of 318 in the percentage of* college graduates
224 *out of 292 in per capita personal* income
148 *out of 319 in number of* manufacturing establishments
254 *out of 318 in* physicians *per 1000 people*
175 *out of 318 in* hospital beds *per 1000 people*
210 *out of 267 in fewest* crimes *per 1000 people*
205 *out of 266 in fewest* violent crimes *per 1000 people*
111 *out of 319 in per capita* federal funds and grants

Quality of Life Indexes (Rate per 1000 population)

Crime rate in 1991:	73.8
Violent crime rate in 1991:	9.1
Physicians rate in 1992:	1.36
Hospital bed rate in 1991:	3.64

ACCRA Cost of Living Indexes

(First quarter 1993, average = 100)
Composite index:	N/A
Utilities index:	N/A
Housing index:	N/A

Population (1990)

Total Population and Growth Rate

1990: 370,712
1980: 258,762
1970: 169,487
Growth rate 1970–1990: 119%

Race and Hispanic Origin

White: 88.6%
Black: 9.0%
Asian/Pacific Islander: 0.7%
Native American: 0.2%
Hispanic origin: 4.0%
White not Hispanic: 86.1%

Age

Ages 18 to 20: 4.3%
Ages 21 to 24: 5.2%
Ages 25 to 44: 27.8%
Ages 45 to 54: 9.4%
Ages 55 to 59: 4.8%

Ages 60 to 64: 6.1%
Ages 65 plus: 22.8%

Educational Attainment (1990)
Percent having completed high school: 75.4%
Percent having completed college: 14.8%
Elementary and high school enrollment: 48,207

Federal Funds and Grants Received
Total received in 1989: $1,206,900,000
Funds received per capita: $3,464

Civilian Labor Force
1993 (April): 170,713
1992 average: 164,598
1991 average: 161,699
1990 average: 159,365

Unemployment
1993 (April): 6.8%
1992 average: 7.9%
1991 average: 6.9%
1990 average: 5.6%

Average Annual Pay
1988: $16,231
1987: $15,639
1985: $14,122

Per Capita Personal Income
1991: $15,742
1990: $15,574
1989: $15,161

Business Climate (1987)
Manufacturing
Number of establishments in 1987: 359
Shipments in 1987 ($1,000): $1,029,700
Employees in 1987: 12,600
Change in employment, 1982 to 1987: 37.0%
Average annual pay for manufacturing work in 1989: $22,047
Average annual pay for production work in 1987: $15,526

Wholesale Trade
Number of establishments in 1987: 449
Total sales in 1987 ($1,000): $662,300
Change in sales, 1982 to 1987: 69.3%

Retail Trade
Number of establishments in 1987: 2,440
Total sales in 1987 ($1,000): $662,300
Retail sales per household in 1987: $16,649
Average annual pay in 1989: $10,992

Service Industry
Selected receipts in 1987 ($1,000): $925,000
Average annual pay in 1989: $15,973

Housing
Total number of units in 1990: 180,972

Occupied units in 1990: 153,416
Owner-occupied units in 1990: 71.9%
1993 ACCRA average cost: N/A
1993 ACCRA average rent for an apartment: N/A

Chamber of Commerce
Daytona Beach-Halifax Area Chamber of Commerce, George Mirabal, President, 126 E. Orange Ave., PO Box 2475, Daytona Beach, FL 32115-2775. 800-854-1234, 904-255-0981, FAX 904-255-5478

Economic Development Office
Volusia County Business Development Corp., Jim Reichardt, Exec Director, 101 Corsair Dr., Suite 103, Daytona Beach, FL 32014. 904-255-8888

Major Businesses

Company	SIC	Telephone
Aluma Shield Industries	3585	(904) 255-5391
Barnett Bank Volusia	6022	(904) 734-2311
Charles Wayne Group	1521	(904) 238-3500
City Provisioners Inc.	5142	(904) 673-2443
Consolidated-Tomoka Land Co.	6531	(904) 255-7558
Crane Cams Inc.	3714	(904) 252-1151
Deland Ford Lincoln Mercury	5511	(904) 774-7000
Delco Oil Inc.	5172	(904) 734-6654
Dunn Corp.	5211	(904) 252-8318
FAME Plastics Inc.	3089	(904) 274-2700
Fornell Enterprises Inc.	5171	(904) 252-3411
Homac Manufacturing Co. Inc.	3643	(904) 677-9110
International Speedway Co.	7948	(904) 253-6711
Jon Hall Chevrolet	5511	(904) 255-4444
Martin Paving Co.	1611	(904) 761-8383
Memorial Health Systems	8062	(904) 677-6900
Seco Dairies of Florida	7389	(904) 734-3906
Security First Federal	6035	(904) 274-1300
Sun Bank of Volusia County	6022	(904) 255-4400
West Volusia Memorial Hospital	8062	(904) 734-3320

Colleges and Universities
Bethune-Cookman College, Daytona Beach
Daytona Beach Community College, Daytona Beach
Embry-Riddle Aeronautical University, Daytona Beach
Embry-Riddle Aeronautical University, College of Continuing Education, Daytona Beach

FORT LAUDERDALE–HOLLYWOOD–POMPANO BEACH, FL (PMSA)

Geographic Profile

Land Area
1208.9 square miles

Counties and Parishes
Broward

Ranking Highlights

163 *out of 319 in total* **land area**
19 *out of 319 in* **population growth**, *1970–1990*
230 *out of 310 in having the lowest* **unemployment** *rate*
36 *out of 310 in size of* **labor force**
163 *out of 318 in the percentage of* **college graduates**
19 *out of 292 in per capita personal* **income**
42 *out of 319 in number of* **manufacturing establishments**
126 *out of 318 in* **physicians** *per 1000 people*
114 *out of 318 in* **hospital beds** *per 1000 people*
241 *out of 267 in fewest* **crimes** *per 1000 people*
203 *out of 266 in fewest* **violent crimes** *per 1000 people*
153 *out of 319 in per capita* **federal funds and grants**

Quality of Life Indexes (Rate per 1000 population)

Crime rate in 1991:	85.1
Violent crime rate in 1991:	9.1
Physicians rate in 1992:	1.97
Hospital bed rate in 1991:	4.42

ACCRA Cost of Living Indexes

(First quarter 1993, average = 100)

Composite index:	N/A
Utilities index:	N/A
Housing index:	N/A

Overview

Major businesses in Broward County include manufacturing, service, agribusiness, high-technology and biomedical firms as well as the strong economic activity related to retailing and tourism.

In its position between Miami and West Palm Beach, Broward County provides access to a current consumer market exceeding four million people. Projections call for this figure to double by the year 2020, expanding to some 8.5 million people.

Broward County is served by Interstate 95, Interstate 75, Interstate 595, Florida's Turnpike and the Sawgrass Expressway. Fort Lauderdale/Hollywood International Airport and Port Everglades are located here. Two other major international airports and seaports are within an hours drive. Major recent economic activity in the area includes: 1) Federal Express announced a 70,000-square foot expansion of its office and distribution facilities at Fort Lauderdale/Hol-

lywood International Airport. The potential exists for hundreds of new jobs to be added; 2) The Florida Department of Transportation consolidated and relocated its district headquarters and administrative offices within Broward County, occupying more than 100,000 square feet of space and employing nearly 500 people; 3) Home Depot USA, Inc. opened a 151,000-square-foot distribution center employing 45 people. 4) Magnivision, a manufacturer of reading glasses, relocated to Broward County. The firm moved into 70,000 square feet of space and employed 150 people; and 5) Baxter Healthcare Corp., Prescription Services Division will open a new business at Meridian Business Campus at Weston. The mail service pharmacy will occupy 60,000 sq. ft. of office and distribution space and eventually employ 300 people.

Downtown Fort Lauderdale has been the site of major recent development activity, with completion of the 270,000-square-foot New River Centre, the 214,500-square-foot First Union Center, and the 216,000-square-foot Sun Bank Tower. Blockbuster Entertainment Corporation consolidated its headquarters operations into a new downtown office tower, as well. New office construction also has continued in the County's western communities, including Plantation, Sunrise and Coral Springs.

Population (1990)

Total Population and Growth Rate
1990: 1,255,488
1980: 1,018,257
1970: 620,100
Growth rate 1970–1990: 102%

Race and Hispanic Origin
White: 81.7%
Black: 15.4%
Asian/Pacific Islander: 1.4%
Native American: 0.2%
Hispanic origin: 8.6%
White not Hispanic: 74.9%

Age
Ages 18 to 20: 3.3%
Ages 21 to 24: 4.9%
Ages 25 to 44: 31.9%
Ages 45 to 54: 9.9%
Ages 55 to 59: 4.1%
Ages 60 to 64: 4.7%
Ages 65 plus: 20.8%

Educational Attainment (1990)

Percent having completed high school: 76.8%
Percent having completed college: 18.8%
Elementary and high school enrollment: 168,078

Federal Funds and Grants Received

Total received in 1989: $3,690,100,000
Funds received per capita: $3,109

Civilian Labor Force
1993 (April): 716,765
1992 average: 688,270
1991 average: 673,521
1990 average: 662,879

Unemployment
1993 (April): 6.8%
1992 average: 8.1%
1991 average: 7.4%
1990 average: 5.5%

Average Annual Pay
1988: $20,983
1987: $19,913
1985: $17,675

Per Capita Personal Income
1991: $22,620
1990: $22,478
1989: $21,764

Business Climate (1987)

Manufacturing
Number of establishments in 1987: 1,790
Shipments in 1987 ($1,000): $3,746,300
Employees in 1987: 43,300
Change in employment, 1982 to 1987: 7.4%
Average annual pay for manufacturing work in 1989: $25,552
Average annual pay for production work in 1987: $17,027

Wholesale Trade
Number of establishments in 1987: 3,064
Total sales in 1987 ($1,000): $11,773,100
Change in sales, 1982 to 1987: 54.9%

Retail Trade
Number of establishments in 1987: 8,625
Total sales in 1987 ($1,000): $11,773,100
Retail sales per household in 1987: $19,718
Average annual pay in 1989: $13,101

Service Industry
Selected receipts in 1987 ($1,000): $5,457,100
Average annual pay in 1989: $21,338

Office Real Estate (1992)
Office space inventory: 15,932,882square feet
Average class A Central Business District rental range per sq. ft: $20.71

Vacancy Rates
All areas: 23.4%

Vacancy Rates in Central Business District
Class A space: 27.1%
Class B space: 11.6%

Vacancy Rates Outside Central Business District
Class A space: 22.2%
Class B space: 23.8%

Housing
Total number of units in 1990: 628,660
Occupied units in 1990: 528,442
Owner-occupied units in 1990: 68.0%
1993 ACCRA average cost: N/A
1993 ACCRA average rent for an apartment: N/A

Chamber of Commerce
Fort Lauderdale Chamber of Commerce, Richard G. Clark, President, 512 N.E. 3rd Ave., PO Box 14516, Fort Lauderdale, FL 33302-4516. 305-462-6000, FAX 305-527-8766

Economic Development Office
Broward Economic Development Council, Inc., James A. Garver, President, 200 E. Las Olas Blvd. Suite 1850, Fort Lauderdale, FL 33301. 305-524-3113, FAX 305-524-316

Major Businesses

Company	SIC	Telephone
Bankatlantic Federal Savings	6035	(305) 760-5016
Blockbuster Entertainment	7841	(305) 524-8200
Blockbuster Videos Inc.	7841	(305) 524-8400
Burnup & Sims Inc.	1623	(305) 587-4512
Capital Factors Inc.	6153	(305) 730-2900
Citizens Southern National Bank	6022	(305) 765-2000
Encore Computer Corp.	3571	(305) 587-2900
Florida Supermarkets Inc.	5411	(305) 786-3900
Holy Cross Hospital Inc.	8062	(305) 771-8000
JM Family Enterprises Inc.	5012	(305) 429-2000
Jan-Bell Marketing Inc.	3911	(305) 846-8000
King Motor Co. of Ft. Lauderdale	5511	(305) 764-2122
Loren Industries Inc.	3915	(305) 920-6622
Moran, Jim Pontiac Inc.	5511	(305) 961-8950
Morse, Ed Chevrolet Inc.	5511	(305) 733-6000
Morse Operations Inc.	5511	(305) 568-0770
National Bancard Corp.	7389	(305) 785-2100
News & Sun Sentinel Co.	2711	(305) 761-4000
North Broward Hospital District	8062	(305) 355-5107
Personnel Pool of America	6794	(305) 938-7600
Racal Data Communications	3661	(305) 475-1601
Rooney, Frank J. Inc.	1542	(305) 565-2771
Rooney Enterprises Inc.	1542	(305) 565-2771
Sensormatic Electronics Co.	3812	(305) 427-9700
South Broward Hospital	8062	(305) 987-2000
Southeast Toyota Distribution	5012	(305) 429-2000
Sun Bank/South Florida National	6021	(305) 467-5000
Tarmac Florida Inc.	3273	(305) 481-2800
VGC Corp.	5043	(305) 722-3000
Xtra Super Food Centers	5411	(305) 977-2500

Colleges and Universities
Art Institute of Fort Lauderdale, Fort Lauderdale
Broward Community College, Fort Lauderdale
Fort Lauderdale College, Fort Lauderdale

National Education Center-Bauder College Campus, Fort
Lauderdale
Nova University, Fort Lauderdale
Prospect Hall College, Hollywood

FORT MYERS–CAPE CORAL, FL (MSA)

Geographic Profile

Land Area
803.6 square miles

Counties and Parishes
Lee

Ranking Highlights

236 *out of 319 in total* **land area**
  2 *out of 319 in* **population growth,** *1970–1990*
208 *out of 310 in having the lowest* **unemployment** *rate*
137 *out of 310 in size of* **labor force**
213 *out of 318 in the percentage of* **college graduates**
 65 *out of 292 in per capita personal* **income**
162 *out of 319 in number of* **manufacturing establishments**
201 *out of 318 in* **physicians** *per 1000 people*
180 *out of 318 in* **hospital beds** *per 1000 people*
N/A *out of 267 in fewest* **crimes** *per 1000 people*
N/A *out of 266 in fewest* **violent crimes** *per 1000 people*
147 *out of 319 in per capita* **federal funds and grants**

Quality of Life Indexes (Rate per 1000 population)

Crime rate in 1991:	N/A
Violent crime rate in 1991:	N/A
Physicians rate in 1992:	1.62
Hospital bed rate in 1991:	3.59

ACCRA Cost of Living Indexes

(First quarter 1993, average = 100)

Composite index:	N/A
Utilities index:	N/A
Housing index:	N/A

Overview

Lee County, the center of southwest Florida, is located 123 miles south of Tampa on the Gulf of Mexico and is equal distance from Miami. The county seat of Lee County is Fort Myers. Metropolitan Fort Myers is the hub of a five county trade area: Charlotte to the north, Collier to the south and Glades and Hendry to the east.

Fort Myers is the western terminus of the cross state Okeechobee Waterway, linking the Gulf of Mexico and the Atlantic Ocean. Major airlines operate from the Southwest Florida Regional Airport. Area private aviation facilities include Page Field located in Lee County; Punta Gorda Airfield, located in Charlotte County; and Naples Airport & Marco Island/Immokalee Airfield, located in Collier County. Local freight rail service ties into the state-wide rail network. Motor freight to and from points across the nation has grown steadily to meet the area's demands. There are general commodity truck lines providing intrastate and interstate service. Lee County currently has interstate carriers, air freight forwarders, liquid petroleum and chemical haulers and truck brokers servicing the area. Air charter service is provided by several companies.

Interstate 75 is now complete from Tampa to Naples, and ties into "Alligator Alley", Florida's cross state expressway.

Consistent with regional growth patterns, the tri-county labor force has averaged a growth rate of 8.5 percent per year since 1985 bringing the total in 1990 to over 273,789. Unemployment has, since 1980, been well below the national average. Climate and location have attracted light industry to the area for the last 20 years. Tourism, agriculture and construction are the main industries.

The total land area of the three coastal county region is 3,487 square miles. Much of this land is inexpensive and undeveloped, and is available for industrial and commercial growth.

Population (1990)

Total Population and Growth Rate
1990: 335,113
1980: 205,266
1970: 105,216
Growth rate 1970–1990: 219%

Race and Hispanic Origin
White: 91.4%
Black: 6.6%
Asian/Pacific Islander: 0.6%
Native American: 0.2%
Hispanic origin: 4.5%
White not Hispanic: 88.3%

Age
Ages 18 to 20: 3.1%
Ages 21 to 24: 4.3%
Ages 25 to 44: 26.6%
Ages 45 to 54: 9.5%
Ages 55 to 59: 5.1%
Ages 60 to 64: 7%
Ages 65 plus: 24.8%

Educational Attainment (1990)
Percent having completed high school: 76.9%
Percent having completed college: 16.4%
Elementary and high school enrollment: 42,600

Federal Funds and Grants Received
Total received in 1989: $981,600,000
Funds received per capita: $3,175

Civilian Labor Force
1993 (April): 162,809
1992 average: 155,945
1991 average: 152,578
1990 average: 150,838

Unemployment
1993 (April): 6.1%
1992 average: 7.7%
1991 average: 6.4%
1990 average: 4.4%

Average Annual Pay
1988: $17,753
1987: $16,843
1985: $14,843

Per Capita Personal Income
1991: $19,392
1990: $19,150
1989: $18,629

Business Climate (1987)

Manufacturing
Number of establishments in 1987: 305
Shipments in 1987 ($1,000): $452,000
Employees in 1987: 5,600
Change in employment, 1982 to 1987: 40.0%
Average annual pay for manufacturing work in 1989: $20,227
Average annual pay for production work in 1987: $15,306

Wholesale Trade
Number of establishments in 1987: 538
Total sales in 1987 ($1,000): $954,100
Change in sales, 1982 to 1987: 63.6%

Retail Trade
Number of establishments in 1987: 2,369
Total sales in 1987 ($1,000): $954,100
Retail sales per household in 1987: $20,068
Average annual pay in 1989: $12,410

Service Industry
Selected receipts in 1987 ($1,000): $975,200
Average annual pay in 1989: $19,713

Housing
Total number of units in 1990: 189,051
Occupied units in 1990: 140,124
Owner-occupied units in 1990: 72.1%
1993 ACCRA average cost: N/A
1993 ACCRA average rent for an apartment: N/A

Chamber of Commerce
Greater Fort Myers Chamber of Commerce, Marietta Mudgett, Exec. Director, PO Box 9289, 2310 Edwards Dr., Fort Myers, FL 33902. 813-332-3624, FAX 813-332-6659

Economic Development Office
Chamber of Southwest Florida, Steve Tirey, President, 8191 College Parkway #306, PO Box 1290, Fort Myers, FL 33919-5121. 813-433-3321, FAX 813-433-3598

Economic Development Organizations
Lee County Industrial Development Authority, Elaine McLaughlin, Exec. Director, PO Drawer 910, Fort Myers, FL 33902. 813-335-2346, FAX 813-334-1106

Lee County Business Development Corp. of Southwest Florida, R. Lee Menzies, President, PO Box 2472, Fort Myers, FL 33902. 813-332-5880

Major Businesses

Company	SIC	Telephone
A Medical Personnel Service	7361	(813) 334-4144
Branch, Bill Chevrolet Inc.	5511	(813) 936-8561
Cape Coral Medical Center	8062	(813) 574-2323
Dixie Buick Inc.	5511	(813) 332-1103
First Federal Savings & Loan	6035	(813) 334-4106
Ft. Myers Lincoln Mercury	5511	(813) 433-2277
Galeana Chrysler Plymouth	5511	(813) 481-2600
Hospital Bd. of Directors Lee County	8062	(813) 332-1111
Lee County Electric	4911	(813) 995-2121
Lehigh Corp.	6552	(813) 369-2121
Mariner Group Inc.	5712	(813) 481-2011
Munters Corp.	3585	(813) 936-1555
Raymond Building Supply Co.	5211	(813) 995-5467
Resort Development International	1531	(813) 936-5800
Robb & Stucky Ltd.	5712	(813) 936-8541
Rutledge, H. D. & Son Inc.	1542	(813) 936-4726
South Seas Resort	7011	(813) 481-2011
Southwest Florida Regional	8062	(813) 939-1147
Tesone Development Corp.	6515	(813) 947-1515
Wright Construction Corp.	1542	(813) 481-5000

Colleges and Universities

Edison Community College, Fort Myers

FORT PIERCE, FL (MSA)

Geographic Profile

Land Area

1128.2 square miles

Counties and Parishes

Martin

St. Lucie

Ranking Highlights

179 *out of 319 in total* **land area**

3 *out of 319 in* **population growth,** *1970–1990*

301 *out of 310 in having the lowest* **unemployment** *rate*

178 *out of 310 in size of* **labor force**

219 *out of 318 in the percentage of* **college graduates**

44 *out of 292 in per capita personal* **income**

199 *out of 319 in number of* **manufacturing establishments**

234 *out of 318 in* **physicians** *per 1000 people*

255 *out of 318 in* **hospital beds** *per 1000 people*

131 *out of 267 in fewest* **crimes** *per 1000 people*

146 *out of 266 in fewest* **violent crimes** *per 1000 people*

167 *out of 319 in per capita* **federal funds and grants**

Quality of Life Indexes (Rate per 1000 population)

Crime rate in 1991:	60.2
Violent crime rate in 1991:	6.7
Physicians rate in 1992:	1.46
Hospital bed rate in 1991:	2.8

ACCRA Cost of Living Indexes

(First quarter 1993, average = 100)

Composite index:	N/A
Utilities index:	N/A
Housing index:	N/A

Population (1990)

Total Population and Growth Rate

1990: 251,071

1980: 151,196

1970: 78,871

Growth rate 1970–1990: 218%

Race and Hispanic Origin

White: 85.3%

Black: 12.2%

Asian/Pacific Islander: 0.6%

Native American: 0.2%

Hispanic origin: 4.3%

White not Hispanic: 82.9%

Age

Ages 18 to 20: 3.1%

Ages 21 to 24: 4.1%

Ages 25 to 44: 27.4%

Ages 45 to 54: 9.3%

Ages 55 to 59: 4.9%

Ages 60 to 64: 6.7%
Ages 65 plus: 23.6%

Educational Attainment (1990)

Percent having completed high school: 75.1%
Percent having completed college: 16.1%
Elementary and high school enrollment: 34,475

Federal Funds and Grants Received

Total received in 1989: $702,900,000
Funds received per capita: $3,032

Civilian Labor Force

1993 (April):   110,026
1992 average: 110,202
1991 average: 107,849
1990 average: 108,521

Unemployment

1993 (April): 10.6%
1992 average: 13.9%
1991 average: 12.2%
1990 average: 10.5%

Average Annual Pay

1988: $17,787
1987: $16,895
1985: $15,008

Per Capita Personal Income

1991: $20,447
1990: $20,215
1989: $19,284

Business Climate (1987)

Manufacturing

Number of establishments in 1987: 231
Shipments in 1987 ($1,000): $700,200
Employees in 1987: 6,400
Change in employment, 1982 to 1987: 33.3%
Average annual pay for manufacturing work in 1989: $22,926
Average annual pay for production work in 1987: $17,610

Wholesale Trade

Number of establishments in 1987: 309
Total sales in 1987 ($1,000): $659,800
Change in sales, 1982 to 1987: 70.2%

Retail Trade

Number of establishments in 1987: 1,563
Total sales in 1987 ($1,000): $659,800
Retail sales per household in 1987: $18,442
Average annual pay in 1989: $12,275

Service Industry

Selected receipts in 1987 ($1,000): $572,800
Average annual pay in 1989: $19,486

Housing

Total number of units in 1990: 128,042

Occupied units in 1990: 101,196
Owner-occupied units in 1990: 74.0%
1993 ACCRA average cost: N/A
1993 ACCRA average rent for an apartment: N/A

Chamber of Commerce

Port Pierce-Saint Lucie County Chamber of Commerce, Bruce Abernethy, Exec. Vice President, 2200 Virginia Ave., Fort Pierce, FL 34982. 407-461-2700, FAX 407-461-9084

Economic Development Office

St. Lucie County Economic Development Council, Al Rivett, Exec. Director, 900 Virginia Ave. #16, Fort Pierce, FL 34982. 407-460-6700

Economic Development Organizations

Martin County Chamber of Commerce, Ray Navitsky, Exec. Vice President, 1650 S. Kanner Highway, Stuart, FL 34994. 407-283-3366

Major Businesses

Company	SIC	Telephone
Mullins Inc.	4212	(407) 461-6147
Sunbank/Treasure Coast	6022	(407) 461-6300
Zeroll Co.	3469	(407) 461-3811

Colleges and Universities

Indian River Community College, Fort Pierce

FORT WALTON BEACH, FL (MSA)

Geographic Profile

Land Area

935.8 square miles

Counties and Parishes

Okaloosa

Ranking Highlights

210 *out of 319 in total* **land area**

 60 *out of 319 in* **population growth,** *1970–1990*

139 *out of 310 in having the lowest* **unemployment** *rate*

233 *out of 310 in size of* **labor force**

120 *out of 318 in the percentage of* **college graduates**

184 *out of 292 in per capita personal* **income**

279 *out of 319 in number of* **manufacturing establishments**

268 *out of 318 in* **physicians** *per 1000 people*

208 *out of 318 in* **hospital beds** *per 1000 people*

N/A *out of 267 in fewest* **crimes** *per 1000 people*

N/A *out of 266 in fewest* **violent crimes** *per 1000 people*

 12 *out of 319 in per capita* **federal funds and grants**

Quality of Life Indexes (Rate per 1000 population)

Crime rate in 1991:   N/A

Violent crime rate in 1991:   N/A

Physicians rate in 1992:   1.28

Hospital bed rate in 1991:   3.35

ACCRA Cost of Living Indexes

(First quarter 1993, average = 100)

Composite index: N/A

Utilities index: N/A

Housing index: N/A

Population (1990)

Total Population and Growth Rate

1990: 143,776

1980: 109,920

1970: 88,187

Growth rate 1970–1990: 63%

Race and Hispanic Origin

White: 87.1%

Black: 9.0%

Asian/Pacific Islander: 2.5%

Native American: 0.5%

Hispanic origin: 3.1%

White not Hispanic: 85.0%

Age

Ages 18 to 20: 4.3%

Ages 21 to 24: 6.7%

Ages 25 to 44: 34.4%

Ages 45 to 54: 10.4%

Ages 55 to 59:   5%

Ages 60 to 64: 4.1%

Ages 65 plus: 9.3%

Educational Attainment (1990)

Percent having completed high school: 83.8%

Percent having completed college: 21.0%

Elementary and high school enrollment: 24,187

Federal Funds and Grants Received ($1000)

Total received in 1989: 1,170,400

Funds received per capita: 7,772

Civilian Labor Force

1993 (April):   72,752

1992 average: 69,600

1991 average: 67,146

1990 average: 66,056

Unemployment

1993 (April):   5.9%

1992 average: 6.6%

1991 average: 6.7%

1990 average: 6.2%

Average Annual Pay

1988: $16,140

1987: $15,644

1985: $14,185

Per Capita Personal Income

1991: $16,574

1990: $15,832

1989: $15,038

Business Climate (1987)

Manufacturing

Number of establishments in 1987: 115

Shipments in 1987 ($1,000): $290,800

Employees in 1987: 4,700

Change in employment, 1982 to 1987: 56.7%

Average annual pay for manufacturing work in 1989: $18,956

Average annual pay for production work in 1987: $13,556

Wholesale Trade

Number of establishments in 1987: 163

Total sales in 1987 ($1,000): $328,300

Change in sales, 1982 to 1987: 150.7%

Retail Trade

Number of establishments in 1987: 1,142

Total sales in 1987 ($1,000): $328,300

Retail sales per household in 1987: $17,094

Average annual pay in 1989: $9,856

Service Industry

Selected receipts in 1987 ($1,000): $424,400

Average annual pay in 1989: $17,252

Housing

Total number of units in 1990: 62,569

Occupied units in 1990: 53,313
Owner-occupied units in 1990: 62.2%
1993 ACCRA average cost: N/A
1993 ACCRA average rent for an apartment: N/A

Chamber of Commerce

Greater Fort Walton Beach Chamber of Commerce, Roger Peters, Exec. Director, 34 Miracle Strip Pkwy. S.E., PO Drawer 640, Fort Walton Beach, FL 32549. 904-244-8191, FAX 904-244-1935

Economic Development Office

Economic Development Council of Okaloosa County, Jim Breitenfield, Exec Director, 81 Beal Pkwy. S.E. Suite 8, Fort Walton Beach, FL 32548. 904-243-5812, FAX 904-664-5547

Major Businesses

Company	SIC	Telephone
Black-Jack Inc.	5511	(904) 244-7151
Crestview Aerospace Corp.	3728	(904) 682-2746
D & H Oil and Gas Co., Inc.	5541	(904) 678-8735
First National Bank & Trust	6021	(904) 243-7111
Hood, Preston Chevrolet	5511	(904) 244-3181
Lee Chrysler/Plymouth/Dodge	5511	(904) 244-7611
Lee Pontiac-Oldsmobile Inc.	5511	(904) 243-3123
Metric Systems Corp.	3812	(904) 244-9600
Nugget Oil Inc.	5541	(904) 682-4713
Okaloosa County Gas District	4923	(904) 678-2123
Quality Imports Inc.	5511	(904) 863-2161
Sandestin Corp.	7011	(904) 267-8118
Tate Oil Co. Inc.	5171	(904) 682-5127
Taylor, Sam Buick-Cadillac	5511	(904) 244-5165
Vanguard Bank & Trust Co.	6021	(904) 678-4141
Ver-Val Enterprises Inc.	3444	(904) 244-7931
Vitro Services Corp.	8734	(904) 244-7711
Watts, Edwin Golf Shop Inc.	5941	(904) 244-2066
Williams Electric Co. Inc.	1731	(904) 862-1171

GAINESVILLE, FL (MSA)

Geographic Profile

Land Area
1167.5 square miles

Counties and Parishes
Alachua
Bradford

Ranking Highlights

172 *out of 319 in total* **land area**
43 *out of 319 in* **population growth,** *1970–1990*
48 *out of 310 in having the lowest* **unemployment** *rate*
176 *out of 310 in size of* **labor force**
21 *out of 318 in the percentage of* **college graduates**
175 *out of 292 in per capita personal* **income**
220 *out of 319 in number of* **manufacturing establishments**
6 *out of 318 in* **physicians** *per 1000 people*
49 *out of 318 in* **hospital beds** *per 1000 people*
258 *out of 267 in fewest* **crimes** *per 1000 people*
248 *out of 266 in fewest* **violent crimes** *per 1000 people*
205 *out of 319 in per capita* **federal funds and grants**

Quality of Life Indexes (Rate per 1000 population)

Crime rate in 1991:	94.6
Violent crime rate in 1991:	11.5
Physicians rate in 1992:	5.41
Hospital bed rate in 1991:	5.55

ACCRA Cost of Living Indexes

(First quarter 1993, average = 100)
Composite index: N/A
Utilities index: N/A
Housing index: N/A

Population (1990)

Total Population and Growth Rate
1990: 204,111
1980: 171,392
1970: 119,389
Growth rate 1970–1990: 71%

Race and Hispanic Origin
White: 77.6%
Black: 19.1%
Asian/Pacific Islander: 2.3%
Native American: 0.2%
Hispanic origin: 3.5%
White not Hispanic: 75.0%

Age
Ages 18 to 20: 9.8%
Ages 21 to 24: 10.8%
Ages 25 to 44: 32.7%
Ages 45 to 54: 8.5%
Ages 55 to 59: 3.3%

Ages 60 to 64: 3.3%
Ages 65 plus: 9.6%

Educational Attainment (1990)
Percent having completed high school: 80.5%
Percent having completed college: 31.2%
Elementary and high school enrollment: 29,051

Federal Funds and Grants Received
Total received in 1989: $568,300,000
Funds received per capita: $2,737

Civilian Labor Force
1993 (April): 117,145
1992 average: 113,093
1991 average: 111,725
1990 average: 109,192

Unemployment
1993 (April): 4.3%
1992 average: 4.9%
1991 average: 4.3%
1990 average: 3.5%

Average Annual Pay
1988: $17,355
1987: $16,552
1985: $15,467

Per Capita Personal Income
1991: $16,743
1990: $16,139
1989: $15,151

Business Climate (1987)
Manufacturing
Number of establishments in 1987: 198
Shipments in 1987 ($1,000): $725,900
Employees in 1987: 5,900
Change in employment, 1982 to 1987: 28.3%
Average annual pay for manufacturing work in 1989: $21,602
Average annual pay for production work in 1987: $16,907

Wholesale Trade
Number of establishments in 1987: 239
Total sales in 1987 ($1,000): $461,500
Change in sales, 1982 to 1987: 9.6%

Retail Trade
Number of establishments in 1987: 1,338
Total sales in 1987 ($1,000): $461,500
Retail sales per household in 1987: $17,470
Average annual pay in 1989: $9,951

Service Industry
Selected receipts in 1987 ($1,000): $515,700
Average annual pay in 1989: $18,671

Office Real Estate (1992)
Office space inventory: 1,470,000 square feet

Average class A Central Business District rental range per sq. ft: $15.00

Vacancy Rates
All areas: 9.2%

Vacancy Rates in Central Business District
Class A space: 2.9%
Class B space: 16.7%

Vacancy Rates Outside Central Business District
Class A space: 3.3%
Class B space: 10.0%

Housing
Total number of units in 1990: 87,121
Occupied units in 1990: 78,451
Owner-occupied units in 1990: 56.2%
1993 ACCRA average cost: N/A
1993 ACCRA average rent for an apartment: N/A

Chamber of Commerce
Gainesville Area Chamber of Commerce, Robert C. Douglass Jr., Exec. Vice President, PO Box 1187, 300 E. University Ave., Gainesville, FL 32602. 904-336-7100, FAX 904-336-7141

Economic Development Office
Bradford County Economic Development Corp., Charles D. McKeown, Exec Director, PO Box 576, Starke, FL 32091. 904-964-7375

Industrial Sites
Florida Progress Center (457 acres) Affiliated with University of Florida. For more information, please contact: Ms. Sandra Burgess, Manager, 1 Progress Blvd., PO Box 10, Alachua, Florida 32615. 904-462-4040

Major Businesses

Company	SIC	Telephone
Bear Archery Inc.	3949	(904) 376-2327
Campus Communications, Inc.	2711	(904) 376-4446
Environmental Science	8711	(904) 332-3318
Gates Energy Products, Inc.	3715	(904) 462-3911
Mammatech Corp.	5047	(904) 375-0607
Phoenix Advanced Technology	6794	(904) 372-9585
Quadrex Corp.	8999	(904) 373-6066
Quadrex Environmental Co.	3559	(904) 373-6066
Quadrex International Corp.	8748	(904) 373-6066

Colleges and Universities
Santa Fe Community College, Gainesville
University of Florida, Gainesville

JACKSONVILLE, FL (MSA)

Geographic Profile

Land Area

2635.7 square miles

Counties and Parishes

Clay

Duval

Nassau

St. Johns

Ranking Highlights

61 *out of 319 in total* **land area**

74 *out of 319 in* **population growth,** *1970–1990*

166 *out of 310 in having the lowest* **unemployment** *rate*

57 *out of 310 in size of* **labor force**

168 *out of 318 in the percentage of* **college graduates**

117 *out of 292 in per capita personal* **income**

70 *out of 319 in number of* **manufacturing establishments**

107 *out of 318 in* **physicians** *per 1000 people*

191 *out of 318 in* **hospital beds** *per 1000 people*

256 *out of 267 in fewest* **crimes** *per 1000 people*

262 *out of 266 in fewest* **violent crimes** *per 1000 people*

80 *out of 319 in per capita* **federal funds and grants**

Quality of Life Indexes (Rate per 1000 population)

Crime rate in 1991:	92.0
Violent crime rate in 1991:	14.5
Physicians rate in 1992:	2.09
Hospital bed rate in 1991:	3.51

ACCRA Cost of Living Indexes

(First quarter 1993, average = 100)

Composite index:	94.6
Utilities index:	101.0
Housing index:	81.1

Overview

Jacksonville is the main insurance and financial center of the state of Florida. In addition, it is the major distribution and transportation center of the southeast, with many wholesale and retail warehouses. Ship building, along with ship repair, play a substantial role in the local economy. One area of especially strong growth in the 1980s and 1990s was the service industry. Some of the city's major service sector employers are American Express Travel Related Services, AT & T Universal Card Services, AT & T Transtech, the Professional Golfer's Association Tour, the ATP, Association of Tennis Professionals, Prudential Insurance Company, and Merrill Lynch. The city is a transportation hub with a thirty-six-foot deepwater port, a rail system served by three railroads, and a highway system that links the city to three major interstates.

The largest product of Jackson's more than seven hundred factories is processed foods. Other manufacturers include Vistakon (contact lenses), Florida Publishing, Anheuser-Busch Inc., Revlon Professional Products, Lamborghini, SuperStock (photo stock service), American Tourister, and Maxwell House. Efforts are being made to recruit new businesses in the fields of distribution, bio-medical production, aviation, transportation, equipment, instruments and controls, building products, and consumer goods.

Jacksonville, home of the Mayo Clinic and Nemours Children's Clinic, is a major health care center in Florida and is projected to be a major health care center for the entire U.S. by the year 2005. The three Naval Air Stations within the city limits and Mayport Naval Base and Kings Bay Submarine Base nearby, give Jacksonville the largest military presence in the United States. The total economic impact of the bases on the community is $1.7 billion annually.

The area has 396 import/export firms and twenty-five customs house brokers and freight forwarders. The city is home to Foreign Trade Zone #64 and there are designated customs facilities at the Jacksonville International Airport. Major exports include linerboard, paper products, automobiles and parts, clay, metals, phosphate, foods, citrus fruit, and consumer goods. The major imports are containers, automobiles, lumber, steel, coffee, and bulk commodities.

The hub of three major highways, I-10, I-95 and U.S. 1 converge on the city, providing a straight shipping line to the Midwest, West and Northeast. Jacksonville is served by one-hundred and thirty trucking lines and three major railroads, as well as the Greyhound and Trailways intra- and interstate bus lines. As the largest deepwater port in the South Atlantic, Jacksonville is the leading port in the United States for automobile import. Thirty international shipping lines connect Jacksonville with seventy-five foreign countries. Jacksonville International Airport (JIA) is served by seven major airlines and three regional airlines. There are more than two hundred flights in and out of the city every day. In addition to JIA, Jacksonville has two general aviation facilities, Craig Airfield and Herlong Airfield.

Population (1990)

Total Population and Growth Rate

1990: 906,727

1980: 722,252

1970: 612,585

Growth rate 1970–1990: 48%

Race and Hispanic Origin

White: 77.4%

Black: 20.0%

Asian/Pacific Islander: 1.7%

Native American: 0.3%

Hispanic origin: 2.5%

White not Hispanic: 75.8%

Age

Ages 18 to 20: 4.6%

Ages 21 to 24: 6.2%

Ages 25 to 44: 34.1%
Ages 45 to 54: 10%
Ages 55 to 59: 4%
Ages 60 to 64: 4.1%
Ages 65 plus: 10.9%

Educational Attainment (1990)

Percent having completed high school: 77.4%
Percent having completed college: 18.6%
Elementary and high school enrollment: 152,929

Federal Funds and Grants Received

Total received in 1989: $3,528,500,000
Funds received per capita: $3,929

Civilian Labor Force

1993 (April): 482,536
1992 average: 470,430
1991 average: 469,973
1990 average: 461,863

Unemployment

1993 (April): 6.1%
1992 average: 7.0%
1991 average: 6.6%
1990 average: 5.5%

Average Annual Pay

1988: $19,987
1987: $19,141
1985: $17,513

Per Capita Personal Income

1991: $17,937
1990: $17,561
1989: $16,799

Business Climate (1987)

Manufacturing

Number of establishments in 1987: 942
Shipments in 1987 ($1,000): $5,936,300
Employees in 1987: 35,400
Change in employment, 1982 to 1987: 9.3%
Average annual pay for manufacturing work in 1989: $24,937
Average annual pay for production work in 1987: $20,148

Wholesale Trade

Number of establishments in 1987: 1,756
Total sales in 1987 ($1,000): $15,425,400
Change in sales, 1982 to 1987: 0%

Retail Trade

Number of establishments in 1987: 5,825
Total sales in 1987 ($1,000): $15,425,400
Retail sales per household in 1987: $18,197
Average annual pay in 1989: $12,275

Service Industry

Selected receipts in 1987 ($1,000): $3,000,600
Average annual pay in 1989: $19,231

Office Real Estate (1992)

Office space inventory: 13,227,358 square feet
Average class A Central Business District rental range per sq. ft: $15.75

Vacancy Rates

All areas: 19.3%

Vacancy Rates in Central Business District

Class A space: 13.1%
Class B space: 34.1%

Vacancy Rates Outside Central Business District

Class A space: 16.2%
Class B space: 24.8%

Housing

Total number of units in 1990: 384,360
Occupied units in 1990: 343,526
Owner-occupied units in 1990: 64.8%
1993 ACCRA average cost: $87,957
1993 ACCRA average rent for an apartment: $467

Chamber of Commerce

Jacksonville Area Chamber of Commerce, Walter M. Lee III, President, PO Box 329, 3 Independent Dr., Jacksonville, FL 32202. 904-366-6600, FAX 904-632-0617

Economic Development Office

Jacksonville Port Authority, Joseph Strain, Marketing Director, PO Box 3005, 2831 Talleyrand Ave., Jacksonville, FL 32206-3496. 904-630-3070, FAX 904-630-3066

Economic Development Organizations

Jacksonville Downtown Development Authority, Frank R. Nero, Exec. Director, 128 E. Forsyth #600, Jacksonville, FL 32202. 904-630-1913, FAX 904-630-2919

Clay County Economic Development Council, Tracy McDaniel, Exec. Secretary, PO Box 1838, Orange Park, FL 32067. 904-264-7373

Amelia Island/Fernandina Beach Chamber of Commerce (Nassau County), Kristey L. Nielson, Exec. Director, PO Box 472, Fernanadina Beach, FL 32034. 904-261-3248

St. Johns County/St. Augustine Chamber of Commerce, Committee of 100, Paul Merchant, Exec. Director, PO Box 0, St. Augustine, FL 32085-0119. 904-829-5683

Industrial Sites

First Coast Technology Park (275 acres). Affiliated with University of North Florida. For more information, please contact: Mr. William A. Ingram, Exec. Director, University of North Florida, 4567 St. John's Bluff Road, S., Jacksonville, FL 32216. 904-646-2500

Major Businesses

Company	SIC	Telephone
American Heritage Life Insurance	6321	(904) 354-1776
American Transtech Inc.	6289	(904) 636-1000
Barnett Banks Inc.	6021	(904) 791-7720

Major Businesses (Continued)

Company	SIC	Telephone
Barnett Bank of Jacksonville	6021	(904) 791-7500
Blue Cross/Blue Shield of Florida	6324	(904) 791-6111
Cain & Bultman Inc.	5064	(904) 356-4812
First Union National Bank of Florida	6021	(904) 632-6565
First Union Corp. of Florida	6021	(904) 361-3651
Florida Rock Industries Inc.	3273	(904) 355-1781
Gate Petroleum Co.	5541	(904) 737-7220
Gulf Life Insurance Co.	6311	(904) 390-7000
Health Options Inc.	6324	(904) 731-1037
Independent Insurance Group	6311	(904) 358-5151
Independent Life Accident Insurance	6311	(904) 358-5151
Jacksonville Electric Authority	4911	(904) 632-7620
National Merchandise Co.	5122	(904) 350-9500
RPC Inc.	5082	(904) 737-7730
St. John's River Power	4911	(904) 751-7700
St. Joe Container Co.	2653	(904) 396-6600
St. Joe Forest Products Co.	2621	(904) 396-6600
St. Joe Paper Co.	2631	(904) 396-6600
St. Johns River Power Park	4911	(904) 751-7700
St. Vincent De Paul	8062	(904) 389-1400
Trailer Marine Transportation	4424	(904) 727-2200
Transmark USA Inc.	6311	(904) 733-9658
Winn-Dixie Atlanta Inc.	5411	(904) 783-5000
Winn-Dixie Charlotte, Inc.	5411	(904) 783-5000
Winn-Dixie Montgomery Inc.	5411	(904) 783-5000
Winn-Dixie Raleigh Inc.	5411	(904) 783-5000
Winn-Dixie Stores Inc.	5411	(904) 783-5000

Colleges and Universities

Edward Waters College, Jacksonville
Flagler Career Institute, Jacksonville
Florida Community College at Jacksonville
Jacksonville University, Jacksonville
Jones College, Jacksonville
University of North Florida, Jacksonville

LAKELAND–WINTER HAVEN, FL (MSA)

Geographic Profile

Land Area
1874.9 square miles

Counties and Parishes
Polk

Ranking Highlights

101 *out of 319 in total* **land area**
 37 *out of 319 in* **population growth,** *1970–1990*
292 *out of 310 in having the lowest* **unemployment** *rate*
123 *out of 310 in size of* **labor force**
284 *out of 318 in the percentage of* **college graduates**
244 *out of 292 in per capita personal* **income**
119 *out of 319 in number of* **manufacturing establishments**
262 *out of 318 in* **physicians** *per 1000 people*
220 *out of 318 in* **hospital beds** *per 1000 people*
259 *out of 267 in fewest* **crimes** *per 1000 people*
226 *out of 266 in fewest* **violent crimes** *per 1000 people*
236 *out of 319 in per capita* **federal funds and grants**

Quality of Life Indexes (Rate per 1000 population)

Crime rate in 1991:	97.2
Violent crime rate in 1991:	9.9
Physicians rate in 1992:	1.32
Hospital bed rate in 1991:	3.18

ACCRA Cost of Living Indexes

(First quarter 1993, average = 100)

Composite index:	N/A
Utilities index:	N/A
Housing index:	N/A

Population (1990)

Total Population and Growth Rate
1990: 405,382
1980: 321,652
1970: 228,515
Growth rate 1970–1990: 77%

Race and Hispanic Origin
White: 84.4%
Black: 13.4%
Asian/Pacific Islander: 0.6%
Native American: 0.3%
Hispanic origin: 4.1%
White not Hispanic: 81.8%

Age
Ages 18 to 20: 4.1%
Ages 21 to 24: 5.1%
Ages 25 to 44: 27.9%
Ages 45 to 54: 10%
Ages 55 to 59: 4.7%

Ages 60 to 64: 5.6%
Ages 65 plus: 18.6%

Educational Attainment (1990)
Percent having completed high school: 68.0%
Percent having completed college: 12.9%
Elementary and high school enrollment: 64,695

Federal Funds and Grants Received
Total received in 1989: $1,009,800,000
Funds received per capita: $2,551

Civilian Labor Force
1993 (April): 184,305
1992 average: 181,416
1991 average: 180,659
1990 average: 181,254

Unemployment
1993 (April): 9.2%
1992 average: 11.3%
1991 average: 10.1%
1990 average: 9.8%

Average Annual Pay
1988: $17,861
1987: $17,209
1985: $15,789

Per Capita Personal Income
1991: $15,241
1990: $14,803
1989: $14,520

Business Climate (1987)
Manufacturing
Number of establishments in 1987: 469
Shipments in 1987 ($1,000): $4,109,300
Employees in 1987: 20,700
Change in employment, 1982 to 1987: 6.2%
Average annual pay for manufacturing work in 1989: $22,340
Average annual pay for production work in 1987: $17,007

Wholesale Trade
Number of establishments in 1987: 634
Total sales in 1987 ($1,000): $2,462,600
Change in sales, 1982 to 1987: 37.8%

Retail Trade
Number of establishments in 1987: 2,329
Total sales in 1987 ($1,000): $2,462,600
Retail sales per household in 1987: $16,101
Average annual pay in 1989: $12,969

Service Industry
Selected receipts in 1987 ($1,000): $842,000
Average annual pay in 1989: $17,635

Housing
Total number of units in 1990: 186,225
Occupied units in 1990: 155,969
Owner-occupied units in 1990: 70.5%
1993 ACCRA average cost: N/A
1993 ACCRA average rent for an apartment: N/A

Chamber of Commerce
Lakeland Area Chamber of Commerce, Susan H. Darden, Exec. Vice President, 35 Lake Morton Dr., PO Box 3607, Lakeland, FL 33802. 813-688-8551, FAX 813-683-7454

Economic Development Office
Lakeland Economic Development Council, Steven Scruggs, Director, 35 Lake Morton Dr., PO Box 3607, Lakeland, FL 33802. 813-687-3788, FAX 813-683-7454

Economic Development Organizations
Lakeland Downtown Development Authority, James H. Edwards, Exec. Director, 207 S. Tennessee Ave., Lakeland, FL 33801. 813-687-8910, FAX 813-683-2783

Economic Development Council of Polk County, James C. Brantley, Director, Economic Development, PO Box 1909, Bartow, FL 33830. 813-533-1755

Winter Haven Commission of 100, Joyce Davis, Director, PO Box 1420, Winter Haven, FL 33882-1420. 813-294-9454

Major Businesses

Company	SIC	Telephone
Badcock, W. S. Corp.	5712	(813) 425-4921
Bartow Ford Co.	5511	(813) 533-0425
Bowen Brothers Inc.	5148	(813) 299-1183
Century Group Inc.	6552	(813) 533-3533
Citrus World Inc.	2037	(813) 676-1411
Colorado Boxed Beef Co.	5147	(813) 967-0636
Conserv Inc.	2819	(813) 425-1164
Kaplan Industries Inc.	2011	(813) 533-0685
Lakeland Regional Medical Center	8062	(813) 687-1100
Malone, E. B. Corp.	2515	(813) 676-6061
Master Merchants Inc.	7389	(813) 688-0042
Meritor Savings	6035	(813) 294-3101
Mid Florida Medical Service	8062	(813) 297-1895
Mutual Wholesale Co., Inc.	5142	(813) 688-0042
Orange-Co., Inc.	0174	(813) 439-1585
Publix Super Markets Inc.	5411	(813) 688-1188
Scotty's Inc.	5211	(813) 299-1111
Sikes Corp.	3253	(813) 687-7171
Watkins Motor Lines, Inc.	4213	(813) 687-4545
Winter Haven Hospital Inc.	8062	(813) 293-1121

Colleges and Universities
Florida Southern College, Lakeland
Southeastern College of the Assemblies of God, Lakeland
Tampa College-Lakeland, Lakeland
Polk Community College, Winter Haven

MELBOURNE–TITUSVILLE–PALM BAY, FL (MSA)

Geographic Profile

Land Area
1018.5 square miles

Counties and Parishes
Brevard

Ranking Highlights

197 *out of 319 in total* **land area**
42 *out of 319 in* **population growth,** *1970–1990*
230 *out of 310 in having the lowest* **unemployment** *rate*
107 *out of 310 in size of* **labor force**
130 *out of 318 in the percentage of* **college graduates**
112 *out of 292 in per capita personal* **income**
139 *out of 319 in number of* **manufacturing establishments**
238 *out of 318 in* **physicians** *per 1000 people*
259 *out of 318 in* **hospital beds** *per 1000 people*
190 *out of 267 in fewest* **crimes** *per 1000 people*
169 *out of 266 in fewest* **violent crimes** *per 1000 people*
7 *out of 319 in per capita* **federal funds and grants**

Quality of Life Indexes (Rate per 1000 population)

Crime rate in 1991:	70.4
Violent crime rate in 1991:	7.3
Physicians rate in 1992:	1.43
Hospital bed rate in 1991:	2.72

ACCRA Cost of Living Indexes

(First quarter 1993, average = 100)
Composite index:　N/A
Utilities index:　　N/A
Housing index:　　N/A

Population (1990)

Total Population and Growth Rate
1990: 398,978
1980: 272,959
1970: 230,006
Growth rate 1970–1990: 73%

Race and Hispanic Origin
White: 89.8%
Black: 7.9%
Asian/Pacific Islander: 1.3%
Native American: 0.3%
Hispanic origin: 3.1%
White not Hispanic: 87.5%

Age
Ages 18 to 20: 3.7%
Ages 21 to 24: 5%
Ages 25 to 44: 31.2%
Ages 45 to 54: 10.5%
Ages 55 to 59: 5.3%
Ages 60 to 64: 5.7%
Ages 65 plus: 16.6%

Educational Attainment (1990)

Percent having completed high school: 82.3%
Percent having completed college: 20.4%
Elementary and high school enrollment: 55,740

Federal Funds and Grants Received ($1000)

Total received in 1989: 3,182,700
Funds received per capita: 8,197

Civilian Labor Force

1993 (April): 204,405
1992 average: 201,777
1991 average: 199,930
1990 average: 197,012

Unemployment

1993 (April): 7.8%
1992 average: 8.1%
1991 average: 7.1%
1990 average: 5.5%

Average Annual Pay

1988: $21,441
1987: $20,621
1985: $18,898

Per Capita Personal Income

1991: $18,009
1990: $17,629
1989: $17,060

Business Climate (1987)

Manufacturing
Number of establishments in 1987: 387
Shipments in 1987 ($1,000): $2,500,100
Employees in 1987: 24,300
Change in employment, 1982 to 1987: 6.1%
Average annual pay for manufacturing work in 1989: $31,243
Average annual pay for production work in 1987: $19,676

Wholesale Trade
Number of establishments in 1987: 456
Total sales in 1987 ($1,000): $1,158,800
Change in sales, 1982 to 1987: 54.0%

Retail Trade
Number of establishments in 1987: 2,387
Total sales in 1987 ($1,000): $1,158,800
Retail sales per household in 1987: $16,086
Average annual pay in 1989: $11,265

Service Industry
Selected receipts in 1987 ($1,000): $1,751,400
Average annual pay in 1989: $24,679

Office Real Estate (1992)

Office space inventory: 803,230 square feet

Average class A Central Business District rental range per sq. ft: $14.50

Vacancy Rates
All areas: 23.8%

Vacancy Rates in Central Business District
Class A space: N/A
Class B space: N/A

Vacancy Rates Outside Central Business District
Class A space: 23.8%
Class B space: N/A

Housing
Total number of units in 1990: 185,150
Occupied units in 1990: 161,365
Owner-occupied units in 1990: 69.2%
1993 ACCRA average cost: N/A
1993 ACCRA average rent for an apartment: N/A

Chamber of Commerce
Melbourne-Palm Bay Area Chamber of Commerce, Larry Malta, President, 1005 E. Strawbridge Ave., Melbourne, FL 32901. 407-724-5400, FAX 407-725-2093

Economic Development Office
Titusville Area Chamber of Commerce, John Marshall Hobbs, President, PO Drawer 2767, 2000 S. Washington Ave., Titusville, FL 32780. 407-267-3036

Economic Development Organizations
Brevard Economic Development Corp., Lawrence Wuensch, President, 6767 N. Wickham Rd #306, Melbourne 32940. 407-242-1800, FAX 407-242-2999

Space Coast Development Commission, Bob Allen, Exec Director, 2000 S. Washington Ave. #2, Titusville, FL 32780. 407-269-3221

Major Businesses

Company	SIC	Telephone
BAMSI Inc.	7371	(407) 269-4193
Boeing Aerospace Corperation	3724	(407) 783-0220
Boniface Chrysler-Dodge Inc.	5511	(407) 452-8181
Cape Canaveral Hospital	8062	(407) 799-7111
DBA Systems Inc.	3861	(407) 725-3711
EG & G Florida Inc.	8711	(407) 631-7300
Engineering and Technical	3663	(407) 724-5678
Harris Corp.	3663	(407) 727-9100
Holiday Builders Inc.	1521	(407) 951-4407
Holmes Regional Medical Co.	8062	(407) 727-7000
Indian River Colony Club	6552	(407) 255-6000
Lane Pontiac-Buick Inc.	5511	(407) 724-5263
Mercedes Homes Inc.	1521	(407) 259-8409
Murphy Olds-Toyota-GMC	5511	(407) 727-2830
North Brevard County Hospital	8062	(407) 268-6111
Opto Mechanik Inc.	3827	(407) 254-1212
Osman, Vic Lincoln Mercury	5511	(407) 725-1100

Major Businesses (Continued)

Company	SIC	Telephone
Pan Am World Services, Inc.	4581	(407) 784-7100
Premier Cruise Lines Ltd.	4481	(407) 783-5061
Relm Communications of Florida	3663	(407) 984-1414
Ron Jon Surf Shop of Florida	5699	(407) 799-8888
Rossi Electronics Inc.	3672	(407) 676-6925
Steele, Bob Chevrolet Inc.	5511	(407) 452-6700
Sutherlin Jake Olds Cadillac	5511	(407) 453-2050
Technology Service Group	7629	(407) 768-1551
Triple T Inns Inc.	7011	(407) 725-7500
United Savings of America	6035	(407) 723-1531
United Southern Assurance	6331	(407) 984-2941
W & J Construction Corp.	1541	(407) 632-7660
Wuesthoff Memorial Hospital	8062	(407) 636-2211

Colleges and Universities
Florida Institute of Technology, Melbourne
Phillips Junior College of Business, Melbourne

MIAMI-HIALEAH, FL (PMSA)

Geographic Profile

Land Area
1944.5 square miles

Counties and Parishes
Dade

Places
Miami Beach

Ranking Highlights

  96 *out of 319 in total* **land area**

  69 *out of 319 in* **population growth,** *1970–1990*

282 *out of 310 in having the lowest* **unemployment** *rate*

  23 *out of 310 in size of* **labor force**

163 *out of 318 in the percentage of* **college graduates**

102 *out of 292 in per capita personal* **income**

  17 *out of 319 in number of* **manufacturing establishments**

  29 *out of 318 in* **physicians** *per 1000 people*

107 *out of 318 in* **hospital beds** *per 1000 people*

267 *out of 267 in fewest* **crimes** *per 1000 people*

266 *out of 266 in fewest* **violent crimes** *per 1000 people*

180 *out of 319 in per capita* **federal funds and grants**

Quality of Life Indexes (Rate per 1000 population)

Crime rate in 1991:	127.9
Violent crime rate in 1991:	21.9
Physicians rate in 1992:	3.06
Hospital bed rate in 1991:	4.56

ACCRA Cost of Living Indexes
(First quarter 1993, average = 100)

Composite index:	108.2
Utilities index:	126.4
Housing index:	108.3

Overview

For most of Miami's history, its economy has been based on tourism. While tourism continues to be a principal industry in Miami, its economy has increasingly adapted an international focus. The port of Miami, Miami International Airport, and the Miami Free Trade Zone have contributed to Miami's importance in the world market. In keeping with the new international image of the city, the tourist industry has also taken on an added dimension. Miami is the world's busiest cruise port, while the Greater Miami Airport is served by more airlines than any other U.S. city, and ranks among the highest in the world in the number of travelers passing through its gates.

Within the past decade, Miami's economic base has become more diversified: two-thirds of incomes and jobs are related to international banking and trade. Today more than ninety banks and foreign agencies are located in downtown Miami. Miami's international business community has come to include many businesses from Europe and Asia, as well as South America and the Caribbean. The major sectors of Miami's economy, including services, trade, retail banking, manufacturing, and real estate, all reflect an international orientation. The area has become a printing and publishing hub for the Americas, with a thriving industry in English and Spanish publications, and is also a leading apparel and textile center. Some major manufacturers include Coulter Corporation, Suave Shoe Corporation, Cordis Corporation, and Gator Industries, Inc. Other private-sector employers include Publix Super Markets, Southern Bell, American Airlines and Burdines Department Stores.

In contrast to its strong international development, the old local economy has experienced serious problems. The 1990s saw the demise of long-time Miami companies such as Eastern Airlines, Inc., Southwest Banking Corp., and CenTrust Savings & Loan. However, due to the benefits of the Florida tax structure, which has no personal income tax, and one of the lowest state corporate rates in the country, Miami is attracting new business and investment. Major development projects during the 1990s have included among others: the Brickell and Omni Components of the $240 million Metrorail system; the $30 million Bayfront Park Redevelopment Project; and a major $1.5 million renovation of Gusman Center for the Performing Arts. The Miami Beach Convention Center, which underwent a $93 million renovation and expansion in 1990, is the center of Miami Beach renovation.

The economic vitality of Miami comes in large measure from the three major railway systems linking the city with all parts of the country and from a network of 5,640 miles of roadway that provides delivery and receiving routes for the twenty-nine motor freight lines operating in the area. The Miami Free Trade Zone's principal function is importing for domestic U.S. consumption. Fifteen minutes from the seaport and five minutes from the airport, the free trade zone is one of the largest duty-free zones in the United States. The Port of Miami, located on Dodge Island within five minutes of Interstate 95, accommodates fifty steamship lines and has access to virtually every port in the world. In addition to being the world's largest cruise port, the Port of Miami has, within the last two decades, achieved dominance in international commerce, second only to New York City in commercial tonnage. Miami International Airport is a hub of both domestic and international trade whose one-hundred and fifty all-cargo flights weekly to U.S. and foreign cities make it the world's fifth busiest cargo airport. It is the primary commerce link between North and South America.

Population (1990)

Total Population and Growth Rate

1990: 1,937,094

1980: 1,625,509

1970: 1,267,792
Growth rate 1970–1990: 53%

Race and Hispanic Origin
White: 72.9%
Black: 20.5%
Asian/Pacific Islander: 1.4%
Native American: 0.2%
Hispanic origin: 49.2%
White not Hispanic: 30.2%

Age
Ages 18 to 20: 4.2%
Ages 21 to 24: 5.8%
Ages 25 to 44: 31.5%
Ages 45 to 54: 10.9%
Ages 55 to 59: 4.7%
Ages 60 to 64: 4.7%
Ages 65 plus: 14%

Educational Attainment (1990)
Percent having completed high school: 65.0%
Percent having completed college: 18.8%
Elementary and high school enrollment: 325,869

Federal Funds and Grants Received ($1000)
Total received in 1989: 5,376,700
Funds received per capita: 2,965

Civilian Labor Force
1993 (April): 996,679
1992 average: 979,613
1991 average: 962,089
1990 average: 956,188

Unemployment
1993 (April): 7.7%
1992 average: 10.0%
1991 average: 8.7%
1990 average: 6.7%

Average Annual Pay
1988: $21,871
1987: $20,988
1985: $18,877

Per Capita Personal Income
1991: $18,252
1990: $17,871
1989: $17,292

Business Climate (1987)
Manufacturing
Number of establishments in 1987: 3,395
Shipments in 1987 ($1,000): $6,734,400
Employees in 1987: 89,300
Change in employment, 1982 to 1987: -9.2%
Average annual pay for manufacturing work in 1989: $20,147
Average annual pay for production work in 1987: $14,150

Wholesale Trade
Number of establishments in 1987: 6,860
Total sales in 1987 ($1,000): $21,772,300
Change in sales, 1982 to 1987: 42.4%

Retail Trade
Number of establishments in 1987: 13,136
Total sales in 1987 ($1,000): $21,772,300
Retail sales per household in 1987: $18,757
Average annual pay in 1989: $14,093

Service Industry
Selected receipts in 1987 ($1,000): $7,934,600
Average annual pay in 1989: $22,368

Office Real Estate (1992)
Office space inventory: 30,260,000 square feet
Average class A Central Business District rental range per sq. ft: $25.00

Vacancy Rates
All areas: 24.5%

Vacancy Rates in Central Business District
Class A space: 29.9%
Class B space: 34.0%

Vacancy Rates Outside Central Business District
Class A space: 20.3%
Class B space: 19.7%

Housing
Total number of units in 1990: 771,288
Occupied units in 1990: 692,355
Owner-occupied units in 1990: 54.3%
1993 ACCRA average cost: $114,939
1993 ACCRA average rent for an apartment: $656

Chamber of Commerce
Greater Miami Chamber of Commerce, William O. Cullom, President, 1601 Biscayne Blvd., Omni Complex, Miami, FL 33132. 305-350-7700, FAX 305-374-6902

Economic Development Office
Hialeah Chamber of Commerce & Industry, Vicente P. Rodriguez, President, 60 E. 3rd St. #201, PO Box 1329, Hialeah, FL 33010. 305-888-8686

Economic Development Organizations
Dade County Industry Development Authority, James D. Wagner, Jr., Exec. Director, World Trade Center Bldg., Suite 2440, 80S.W. 8th St., Miami, FL 33130. 305-579-0070, FAX 305-375-0271

Downtown Development Authority of Miami, Matthew Schwartz, Exec. Director, 1 Biscayne Tower #1818, Miami, FL 33131. 305-579-6675, FAX 305-371-2423

Hialeah Office of Economic Development, Daniel DeLoach, Director, 501 Palm Ave., Hialeah, FL, 33011. 305-884-1219

Industrial Sites
South Campus of the University of Miami (107 acres).

Affiliated with University of Miami School of Medicine. For more information, please contact: Dr. Robert Rubin, Vice Provost for Research and Deputy Dean, Research and Graduate Studies, University of Miami School of Medicine, 1600 N.W. 10th Ave., R-64, Miami, FL 33101. 305-547-6626

Major Businesses

Company	SIC	Telephone
Alden John Life Insurance Co.	6311	(305) 470-3100
American Bankers Insurance Group	6331	(305) 253-2244
American Breeding Service	0751	(305) 822-8217
American Savings Loan Associationn of Florida	6035	(305) 653-5353
APL Corp.	1731	(305) 866-7771
Bacardi Imports Inc.	5182	(305) 573-8511
Barnett Bank South Florida	6029	(305) 350-7100
Carnival Cruise Lines, Inc.	4481	(305) 573-6030
Centrust Bank	6036	(305) 376-5094
Citizens & Southern International	6082	(305) 358-0327
Coastal Fuels Marketing Inc.	5172	(305) 551-5200
Continental Companies	8741	(305) 445-2493
Coulter Corp.	3821	(305) 885-0131
Coulter Electronics Inc.	3826	(305) 885-0131
DWG Corp.	2211	(305) 866-7771
Eastern Air Lines, Inc.	4512	(305) 873-2211
ESSO Standard Oil Ltd.	2911	(305) 441-6000
Florida Power & Light	4911	(305) 552-3552
Kloster Cruise Ltd.	4481	(305) 447-9660
Knight-Ridder Inc.	2711	(305) 376-3800
PPI Del Monte Tropical Fruit Co.	5148	(305) 441-8400
Resorts International Inc.	7011	(305) 891-2500
Ryder System Inc.	7513	(305) 593-3726
Ryder Truck Rental Inc.	7513	(305) 593-3726
SCI Holdings Inc.	4841	(305) 899-1000
Southeast Bank, National	6021	(305) 375-7988
Southeast Banking Corp.	6021	(305) 375-7500
Storer Communication Inc.	4841	(305) 899-1000
Transcapital Financial Co	6036	(305) 536-1400
Wackenhut Corp.	7381	(305) 666-5656

Colleges and Universities

Barry University, Miami Shores
Flagler Career Institute, Miami
Florida International University, Miami
Florida Memorial College, Miami
International Fine Arts College, Miami
Miami Christian College, Miami
Miami-Dade Community College, Miami
St. Thomas University, Miami
Talmudical College of Florida, Miami Beach

NAPLES, FL (MSA)

Geographic Profile
Land Area
2025.5 square miles
Counties and Parishes
Collier

Ranking Highlights
89 *out of 319 in total* **land area**
1 *out of 319 in* **population growth**, *1970–1990*
268 *out of 310 in having the lowest* **unemployment** *rate*
216 *out of 310 in size of* **labor force**
90 *out of 318 in the percentage of* **college graduates**
5 *out of 292 in per capita personal* **income**
265 *out of 319 in number of* **manufacturing establishments**
134 *out of 318 in* **physicians** *per 1000 people*
254 *out of 318 in* **hospital beds** *per 1000 people*
133 *out of 267 in fewest* **crimes** *per 1000 people*
195 *out of 266 in fewest* **violent crimes** *per 1000 people*
144 *out of 319 in per capita* **federal funds and grants**

Quality of Life Indexes (Rate per 1000 population)
Crime rate in 1991:	60.4
Violent crime rate in 1991:	8.5
Physicians rate in 1992:	1.91
Hospital bed rate in 1991:	2.83

ACCRA Cost of Living Indexes
(First quarter 1993, average = 100)
Composite index: N/A
Utilities index: N/A
Housing index: N/A

Population (1990)
Total Population and Growth Rate
1990: 152,099
1980: 85,971
1970: 38,040
Growth rate 1970–1990: 300%
Race and Hispanic Origin
White: 91.4%
Black: 4.6%
Asian/Pacific Islander: 0.4%
Native American: 0.3%
Hispanic origin: 13.6%
White not Hispanic: 82.0%
Age
Ages 18 to 20: 3.2%
Ages 21 to 24: 4.6%
Ages 25 to 44: 27.4%
Ages 45 to 54: 10%
Ages 55 to 59: 5.1%
Ages 60 to 64: 6.9%
Ages 65 plus: 22.7%

Educational Attainment (1990)

Percent having completed high school: 79.0%
Percent having completed college: 22.3%
Elementary and high school enrollment: 20,035

Federal Funds and Grants Received ($1000)

Total received in 1989: 443,800
Funds received per capita: 3,203

Civilian Labor Force

1993 (April):   79,558
1992 average: 77,219
1991 average: 79,175
1990 average: 76,019

Unemployment

1993 (April):   5.7%
1992 average: 9.3%
1991 average: 7.5%
1990 average: 5.5%

Average Annual Pay

1988: $16,084
1987: $15,285
1985: $13,750

Per Capita Personal Income

1991: $26,935
1990: $26,920
1989: $25,745

Business Climate (1987)

Manufacturing

Number of establishments in 1987: 136
Shipments in 1987 ($1,000): $129,700
Employees in 1987: 1,500
Change in employment, 1982 to 1987: 50.0%
Average annual pay for manufacturing work, 1989: $21,586
Average annual pay for production work, 1987: $16,111

Wholesale Trade

Number of establishments in 1987: 214
Total sales in 1987 ($1,000): $346,600
Change in sales, 1982 to 1987: 93.7%

Retail Trade

Number of establishments in 1987: 1,236
Total sales in 1987 ($1,000): $346,600
Retail sales per household in 1987: $21,022
Average annual pay in 1989: $13,010

Service Industry

Selected receipts in 1987 ($1,000): $522,400
Average annual pay in 1989: $19,093

Housing

Total number of units in 1990: 94,165
Occupied units in 1990: 61,703
Owner-occupied units in 1990: 70.2%
1993 ACCRA average cost: N/A
1993 ACCRA average rent for an apartment: N/A

Chamber of Commerce

Naples Area Chamber of Commerce, Edward J. Oates, Jr., Exec. Director, 3620 Tamiami Trail N. Naples, FL 33940. 813-262-6141, FAX 813-262-8374

Economic Development Office

Collier County Economic Development Council, Ross Obley, President, 4501 Tamiami Trail N. Suite 106, Naples, FL 33940. 813-263-8989, FAX 813-263-6021

Major Businesses

Company	SIC	Telephone
Bancflorida	6035	(813) 597-1611
Bancflorida Financial Corp.	6712	(800) 321-2262
Dev-Tech Corp.	6531	(813) 591-1770
Flea Fair USA Inc.	6512	(813) 566-9600
Health Management Association	8062	(813) 598-3131
Krehling Industries, Inc.	3273	(813) 597-3162

OCALA, FL (MSA)

Geographic Profile

Land Area

1579.0 square miles

Counties and Parishes

Marion

Ranking Highlights

124 *out of 319 in total* **land area**

4 *out of 319 in* **population growth**, *1970–1990*

259 *out of 310 in having the lowest* **unemployment** *rate*

203 *out of 310 in size of* **labor force**

304 *out of 318 in the percentage of* **college graduates**

274 *out of 292 in per capita personal* **income**

213 *out of 319 in number of* **manufacturing establishments**

277 *out of 318 in* **physicians** *per 1000 people*

285 *out of 318 in* **hospital beds** *per 1000 people*

179 *out of 267 in fewest* **crimes** *per 1000 people*

233 *out of 266 in fewest* **violent crimes** *per 1000 people*

178 *out of 319 in per capita* **federal funds and grants**

Quality of Life Indexes (Rate per 1000 population)

Crime rate in 1991:	68.0
Violent crime rate in 1991:	10.2
Physicians rate in 1992:	1.24
Hospital bed rate in 1991:	2.31

ACCRA Cost of Living Indexes

(First quarter 1993, average = 100)

Composite index:	N/A
Utilities index:	N/A
Housing index:	N/A

Population (1990)

Total Population and Growth Rate

1990: 194,833

1980: 122,488

1970: 69,030

Growth rate 1970–1990: 182%

Race and Hispanic Origin

White: 85.8%

Black: 12.8%

Asian/Pacific Islander: 0.5%

Native American: 0.3%

Hispanic origin: 3.0%

White not Hispanic: 83.6%

Age

Ages 18 to 20: 3.5%

Ages 21 to 24: 4.3%

Ages 25 to 44: 26.2%

Ages 45 to 54: 9.8%

Ages 55 to 59: 5.1%

Ages 60 to 64: 6.8%

Ages 65 plus: 22.2%

Educational Attainment (1990)

Percent having completed high school: 69.6%

Percent having completed college: 11.5%

Elementary and high school enrollment: 28,336

Federal Funds and Grants Received

Total received in 1989: $563,700,000

Funds received per capita: $2,970

Civilian Labor Force

1993 (April):	87,089
1992 average:	84,136
1991 average:	82,265
1990 average:	80,689

Unemployment

1993 (April): 8.7%

1992 average: 9.0%

1991 average: 8.6%

1990 average: 6.9%

Average Annual Pay

1988: $16,033

1987: $15,418

1985: $14,040

Per Capita Personal Income

1991: $14,158

1990: $13,835

1989: $13,456

Business Climate (1987)

Manufacturing

Number of establishments in 1987: 208

Shipments in 1987 ($1,000): $545,900

Employees in 1987: 6,500

Change in employment, 1982 to 1987: 12.1%

Average annual pay for manufacturing work in 1989: $19,236

Average annual pay for production work in 1987: $15,065

Wholesale Trade

Number of establishments in 1987: 311

Total sales in 1987 ($1,000): $1,075,900

Change in sales, 1982 to 1987: 31.1%

Retail Trade

Number of establishments in 1987: 1,216

Total sales in 1987 ($1,000): $1,075,900

Retail sales per household in 1987: $16,529

Average annual pay in 1989: $11,085

Service Industry

Selected receipts in 1987 ($1,000): $376,200

Average annual pay in 1989: $17,552

Housing

Total number of units in 1990: 94,567

Occupied units in 1990: 78,177

Owner-occupied units in 1990: 75.6%
1993 ACCRA average cost: N/A
1993 ACCRA average rent for an apartment: N/A

Chamber of Commerce

Ocala-Marion County Chamber of Commerce, Jack E. Peake, Exec. Vice President, 110 E. Silver Springs Blvd., PO Box 1210, Ocala, FL 32678. 904-629-8051, FAX 904-629-7651

Economic Development Office

Ocala/Marion County Economic Development Council, Brett B. Wattles, Exec. Vice President, PO Box 459, 110 E. Silver Springs Blvd., Ocala, FL 32678. 904-629-2757, FAX 904-629-1581

Major Businesses

Company	SIC	Telephone
Adkins, Kenneth Inc.	5511	(904) 867-1800
Barnett Bank of Marion County	6022	(904) 732-2212
Big Sun Healthcare System	8062	(904) 351-7325
Branch Properties Inc.	2048	(904) 732-4143
Carter, Dave of Florida Inc.	5063	(904) 732-3317
Certified Grocers of Florida	5141	(904) 245-5151
Colonial Paper Co., Inc.	5113	(904) 622-4171
Deluca Toyota Inc.	5511	(904) 732-0770
Edwards Construction	1541	(904) 854-6266
Falcon Corp.	5063	(904) 732-2992
Florida Seed Co. Inc.	5191	(904) 245-0166
Intrastate Wholesale of Florida	5141	(904) 351-2455
K and J Industries of Ocala	5013	(904) 732-0688
Kwik King Food Stores Inc.	5411	(904) 732-4464
Marion Community Hospital	8062	(904) 732-2700
Mark III Industries Inc.	5012	(904) 732-5878
Microdyne Corp.	3663	(904) 687-4633
Mid-State Federal Savings Bank	6035	(904) 854-0177
Nobility Homes Inc.	2451	(904) 732-5157
Pine Street Motors Inc.	5511	(904) 732-2866
Pioneer Products Inc.	2064	(904) 622-3134
Rallye Motors Inc.	5511	(904) 732-6035
Sun Bank of Ocala	6022	(904) 368-6200

Colleges and Universities

Central Florida Community College, Ocala

ORLANDO, FL (MSA)

Geographic Profile

Land Area
2537.9 square miles

Counties and Parishes
Orange
Osceola
Seminole

Ranking Highlights

68 *out of 319 in total* **land area**
7 *out of 319 in* **population growth,** *1970–1990*
166 *out of 310 in having the lowest* **unemployment** *rate*
39 *out of 310 in size of* **labor force**
103 *out of 318 in the percentage of* **college graduates**
122 *out of 292 in per capita personal* **income**
55 *out of 319 in number of* **manufacturing establishments**
162 *out of 318 in* **physicians** *per 1000 people*
209 *out of 318 in* **hospital beds** *per 1000 people*
N/A *out of 267 in fewest* **crimes** *per 1000 people*
N/A *out of 266 in fewest* **violent crimes** *per 1000 people*
77 *out of 319 in per capita* **federal funds and grants**

Quality of Life Indexes (Rate per 1000 population)

Crime rate in 1991:	N/A
Violent crime rate in 1991:	N/A
Physicians rate in 1992:	1.79
Hospital bed rate in 1991:	3.33

ACCRA Cost of Living Indexes
(First quarter 1993, average = 100)
Composite index: 98.2
Utilities index: 100.3
Housing index: 95.4

Overview

Located in the heart of the fourth largest and fastest growing state in the United States, Metro Orlando is attractive to a breadth of industries, including banking and finance, manufacturing and high technology. Major companies in the area include Siemens Stromberg-Carlson, Westinghouse Electric Corporation, Walt Disney Company, AT&T, Tupperware Worldwide and American Automobile Association. *Fortune* magazine named Orlando one of the top 10 cities for global competitiveness in the United States.

The 15,000-acre Orlando International Airport (OIA) has over 20 carriers making a total of 800 flights daily. It is the 15th busiest airport in the United States and 24th busiest in the world. Additionally, two deep water ports and one shallow water port are accessible within 50 miles.

The University of Central Florida, with more than 22,000 students, features technical curriculums in engineering and computer science. It houses two research institutes, the Institute for Simulation and Training and the Center for

Research in Electro-Optics and Lasers. Metro Orlando's work force is nearly 700,000 with the largest percentage being young (18-44 years old) and skilled. Florida's "Right-to-Work" law accounts for less than 10 percent of the manufacturing work force being unionized. Over the past five years, hundreds of new and expanding companies have moved into the region, representing more than $1 billion of investment and revenue, more than 30,000 new jobs and over 15 million square feet of office and industrial space leased or constructed.

Population (1990)
Total Population and Growth Rate
1990: 1,072,748
1980: 699,904
1970: 453,270
Growth rate 1970–1990: 137%

Race and Hispanic Origin
White: 82.9%
Black: 12.4%
Asian/Pacific Islander: 1.9%
Native American: 0.3%
Hispanic origin: 9.0%
White not Hispanic: 76.8%

Age
Ages 18 to 20: 5%
Ages 21 to 24: 6.6%
Ages 25 to 44: 35.1%
Ages 45 to 54: 10%
Ages 55 to 59: 4.1%
Ages 60 to 64: 4%
Ages 65 plus: 10.9%

Educational Attainment (1990)
Percent having completed high school: 79.9%
Percent having completed college: 21.6%
Elementary and high school enrollment: 168,901

Federal Funds and Grants Received
Total received in 1989: $3,859,600,000
Funds received per capita: $3,974

Civilian Labor Force
1993 (April): 696,657
1992 average: 665,685
1991 average: 641,480
1990 average: 642,159

Unemployment
1993 (April): 5.9%
1992 average: 7.0%
1991 average: 6.5%
1990 average: 5.3%

Average Annual Pay
1988: $19,930
1987: $18,923
1985: $17,310

Per Capita Personal Income
1991: $17,832
1990: $17,562
1989: $17,018

Business Climate (1987)
Manufacturing
Number of establishments in 1987: 1,249
Shipments in 1987 ($1,000): $5,655,300
Employees in 1987: 51,900
Change in employment, 1982 to 1987: 33.8%
Average annual pay for manufacturing work, 1989: $28,413
Average annual pay for production work, 1987: $17,331

Wholesale Trade
Number of establishments in 1987: 2,306
Total sales in 1987 ($1,000): $11,433,100
Change in sales, 1982 to 1987: 107.2%

Retail Trade
Number of establishments in 1987: 6,388
Total sales in 1987 ($1,000): $11,433,100
Retail sales per household in 1987: $22,124
Average annual pay in 1989: $12,472

Service Industry
Selected receipts in 1987 ($1,000): $6,453,700
Average annual pay in 1989: $19,526

Office Real Estate (1992)
Office space inventory: 22,935,990 square feet
Average class A Central Business District rental range per sq. ft: $18.00

Vacancy Rates
All areas: 16.6%

Vacancy Rates in Central Business District
Class A space: 14.1%
Class B space: 34.8%

Vacancy Rates Outside Central Business District
Class A space: 16.6%
Class B space: 14.7%

Housing
Total number of units in 1990: 448,490
Occupied units in 1990: 401,659
Owner-occupied units in 1990: 61.9%
1993 ACCRA average cost: $104,112
1993 ACCRA average rent for an apartment: $556

Chamber of Commerce
Greater Orlando Chamber of Commerce, Jacob V. Stuart, Exec. Vice President, 75 E. Ivanhoe Blvd., PO Box 1234, Orlando, FL 32802. 407-425-1234

Economic Development Office
Economic Development Commission of Mid-Florida, Inc., Michael B. Cooney, Vice President of Economic Develop-

ment, 200 E. Robinson St. #600, Orlando, FL 32801. 407-422-7159, FAX 407-843-9514

Economic Development Organizations

Kissimmee/St. Cloud Economic Development Council (Oscelola County), Michael Bobroff, Director, Economic Development, 320 E. Monument Ave., Kissimmee, FL 32741. 407-847-3174

Seminole County Industrial Development Commission of Mid-Florida, Inc., Roy L. Harris, Jr., President, PO Box 2144, Orlando, FL 32802. 407-422-7159

Industrial Sites

Central Florida Research Park (1,027 acres). Affiliated with University of Central Florida. For more information, please contact:

Mr. Joe Wallace, Marketing Director, 12424 Research Parkway Suite 100, Orlando, FL 32826. 407-282-3944

Major Businesses

Company	SIC	Telephone
Adventist Health System/Sunbelt	8062	(407) 897-1919
Alabama Acquisition Corp.	5411	(407) 263-3804
Bairnco Corp.	3679	(407) 875-2222
Catalina Homes Ltd.	1521	(407) 297-0514
Citrus Central Inc.	3411	(407) 889-4101
Duda, A. & Sons Inc.	0161	(407) 365-2111
Federal Home Life Insurance Co.	6211	(407) 345-2600
Florida Hospital Medical	8062	(407) 896-6611
Goodings Supermarket Inc.	5411	(407) 869-8300
Guthrie North America Inc.	4581	(407) 351-1444
Harcourt Brace Jovanovich	2731	(407) 345-2000
Harvest Life Insurance Co.	6311	(407) 345-2600
Holler, Roger Chevrolet Co.	5511	(407) 645-1234
Hubbard Construction Co.	1611	(407) 645-5500
Hughes Supply Inc.	5074	(407) 841-4755
Maynard Electronics Inc.	3674	(407) 263-3500
McInerney Ford Inc.	5511	(407) 275-3200
Munford Inc.	5411	(407) 331-4300
Orlando Regional Medical	8011	(407) 841-5111
Orlando Utilities Commission	4931	(407) 423-9100
Page Avjet Corp.	4581	(407) 351-1444
PHF Life Insurance Co.	6311	(407) 345-6480
Potter, Luke Dodge Inc.	5511	(407) 644-1919
Sanderlin, W. M. Corp.	1521	(407) 297-0514
Sentinel Commnications Co.	2711	(407) 420-5000
Silver Spring Citrus Cooperative	2033	(407) 656-1122
Stromberg-Carlson Corp.	3661	(407) 333-5000
Sun Bank National Association	6021	(407) 237-4141
Sun Banks Inc.	6021	(407) 237-4585
United Telephone Co. of Florida	4813	(407) 889-6000

Colleges and Universities

Orlando College, Orlando
Southern College, Orlando
University of Central Florida, Orlando
Valencia Community College, Orlando

PANAMA CITY, FL (MSA)

Geographic Profile
Land Area
763.7 square miles

Counties and Parishes
Bay

Ranking Highlights
243 *out of 319 in total* **land area**
47 *out of 319 in* **population growth**, *1970–1990*
226 *out of 310 in having the lowest* **unemployment** *rate*
244 *out of 310 in size of* **labor force**
124 *out of 318 in the percentage of* **college graduates**
234 *out of 292 in per capita personal* **income**
281 *out of 319 in number of* **manufacturing establishments**
262 *out of 318 in* **physicians** *per 1000 people*
164 *out of 318 in* **hospital beds** *per 1000 people*
173 *out of 267 in fewest* **crimes** *per 1000 people*
144 *out of 266 in fewest* **violent crimes** *per 1000 people*
49 *out of 319 in per capita* **federal funds and grants**

Quality of Life Indexes (Rate per 1000 population)
Crime rate in 1991:   67.4
Violent crime rate in 1991:   6.7
Physicians rate in 1992:   1.32
Hospital bed rate in 1991:   3.76

ACCRA Cost of Living Indexes
(First quarter 1993, average = 100)
Composite index: N/A
Utilities index: N/A
Housing index: N/A

Population (1990)
Total Population and Growth Rate
1990: 126,994
1980: 97,740
1970: 75,283
Growth rate 1970–1990: 69%

Race and Hispanic Origin
White: 86.3%
Black: 10.8%
Asian/Pacific Islander: 1.8%
Native American: 0.7%
Hispanic origin: 1.8%
White not Hispanic: 85.0%

Age
Ages 18 to 20: 4.3%
Ages 21 to 24: 5.6%
Ages 25 to 44: 32.3%
Ages 45 to 54: 10.8%
Ages 55 to 59: 4.8%
Ages 60 to 64: 4.8%
Ages 65 plus: 12%

Educational Attainment (1990)
Percent having completed high school: 74.7%
Percent having completed college: 15.7%
Elementary and high school enrollment: 21,615

Federal Funds and Grants Received
Total received in 1989: $584,900,000
Funds received per capita: $4,661

Civilian Labor Force
1993 (April):   70,792
1992 average: 66,299
1991 average: 63,866
1990 average: 63,047

Unemployment
1993 (April):   7.5%
1992 average: 8.9%
1991 average: 8.0%
1990 average: 8.3%

Average Annual Pay
1988: $16,102
1987: $15,379
1985: $14,284

Per Capita Personal Income
1991: $15,580
1990: $14,812
1989: $13,866

Business Climate (1987)
Manufacturing
Number of establishments in 1987: 114
Shipments in 1987 ($1,000): $447,200
Employees in 1987: 2,800
Change in employment, 1982 to 1987: -26.3%
Average annual pay for manufacturing work, 1989: $24,579
Average annual pay for production work, 1987: $21,773

Wholesale Trade
Number of establishments in 1987: 198
Total sales in 1987 ($1,000): $379,900
Change in sales, 1982 to 1987: 26.5%

Retail Trade
Number of establishments in 1987: 1,136
Total sales in 1987 ($1,000): $379,900
Retail sales per household in 1987: $18,746
Average annual pay in 1989: $9,930

Service Industry
Selected receipts in 1987 ($1,000): $328,900
Average annual pay in 1989: $15,888

Housing
Total number of units in 1990: 65,999
Occupied units in 1990: 48,938

Owner-occupied units in 1990: 65.5%
1993 ACCRA average cost: N/A
1993 ACCRA average rent for an apartment: N/A

Chamber of Commerce

Bay County Chamber of Commerce, Frank J. Bacen Jr., Exec. Vice President, PO Box 1850, 235 W. 5th St., Panama City, FL 32402. 904-785-5206, FAX 904-763-6229

Major Businesses

Company	SIC	Telephone
Alvin's Stores Inc.	5699	(904) 234-8897
Arizona Chemical Co., Inc.	2861	(904) 785-6700
Bay Bank & Trust Co.	6029	(904) 769-3333
Bay Hospital Inc.	8062	(904) 769-8341
Bay Medical Center	8062	(904) 769-1511
Florida First Federal Savings	6035	(904) 872-7000
Hull Oil Co.	5171	(904) 763-1746
Lloyd Pontiac Cadillac Inc.	5511	(904) 763-6575
Major Development Co.	1522	(904) 234-7356
Northwest Campers Inc.	5561	(904) 763-3945
Panama City Toyota Inc.	5511	(904) 769-3377
Royal American Cnstruction Co.	1522	(904) 769-8981
Sun Commercial Bank	6022	(904) 769-4811
Sunshine-Jr. Stores Inc.	5411	(904) 769-1661
Thomas, Tommy Chevrolet Inc.	5511	(904) 785-5222
Tyndall Federal Credit Union	6111	(904) 769-9999
West Florida Natural Gas Co.	4923	(904) 872-6100

Colleges and Universities

Gulf Coast Community College, Panama City

PENSACOLA, FL (MSA)

Geographic Profile

Land Area
1679.5 square miles

Counties and Parishes
Escambis
Santa Rosa

Ranking Highlights

117 *out of 319 in total* land area
91 *out of 319 in* population growth, *1970–1990*
99 *out of 310 in having the lowest* unemployment *rate*
138 *out of 310 in size of* labor force
172 *out of 318 in the percentage of* college graduates
243 *out of 292 in per capita personal* income
182 *out of 319 in number of* manufacturing establishments
166 *out of 318 in* physicians *per 1000 people*
66 *out of 318 in* hospital beds *per 1000 people*
N/A *out of 267 in fewest* crimes *per 1000 people*
N/A *out of 266 in fewest* violent crimes *per 1000 people*
51 *out of 319 in per capita* federal funds and grants

Quality of Life Indexes (Rate per 1000 population)

Crime rate in 1991:   78.8
Violent crime rate in 1991:   N/A
Physicians rate in 1992:   1.78
Hospital bed rate in 1991:   5.21

ACCRA Cost of Living Indexes

(First quarter 1993, average = 100)
Composite index: N/A
Utilities index: N/A
Housing index: N/A

Overview

Pensacola is situated in a warm temperate zone, with a climate typical of the region along the upper Gulf Coast. The winters are mild and the summer heat is tempered by the southerly prevailing winds from the Gulf of Mexico. The city averages 343 days of sunshine a year. Unusual weather phenomena such as hurricanes and tornadoes have occurred, but such phenomena are far less frequent or severe than in many other parts of the Southeast. Late summer and fall are the seasons of highest winds.

Major employers include Monsanto Company, Gulf Power Company, Champion International Corporation, Instrument Control Service, Westinghouse Electric Corporation, Armstrong World Industries, American Cyanamid Company, Stone Container Corporation and Pacer Industries.

The Port of Pensacola is northwest Florida's leading deepwater port. It is located on the Gulf of Mexico, 11 miles from the sea buoy and offers stevedoring and marine terminal services for any description of break-bulk and unitized freight, specializing in bagged agriculture products, forest products, steel products and project cargoes. Port site is comprised of approximately 50 acres. The Port is served by The Burlington Northern Railroad and the CSX Transportation System.

Pensacola Regional Airport is a commercial airport served by ComAir, Continental, Delta, ASA, American Eagle, Northwest Airlink and US Air. Pensacola Regional Airport has an instrument approach runway of 7,000 feet and a non-instrument approach runway of 6,000 feet.

The multi-purpose Pensacola Civic Center, which opened in 1985, seats 10,000 plus and features 12 meeting rooms, 23,000 square feet of exhibit space and parking for 2,000. The city owned Bayfront Auditorium has a seating capacity of 3000 for concerts or state events.

Population (1990)

Total Population and Growth Rate
1990: 344,406
1980: 289,782
1970: 243,075
Growth rate 1970–1990: 42%

Race and Hispanic Origin
White: 80.6%
Black: 16.2%
Asian/Pacific Islander: 1.7%
Native American: 1.0%
Hispanic origin: 1.8%
White not Hispanic: 79.4%

Age
Ages 18 to 20: 5.1%
Ages 21 to 24: 6.3%
Ages 25 to 44: 31.8%
Ages 45 to 54: 10.7%
Ages 55 to 59: 4.6%
Ages 60 to 64: 4.4%
Ages 65 plus: 11.3%

Educational Attainment (1990)
Percent having completed high school: 76.7%
Percent having completed college: 18.3%
Elementary and high school enrollment: 57,730

Federal Funds and Grants Received
Total received in 1989: $1,615,200,000
Funds received per capita: $4,616

Civilian Labor Force
1993 (April):   161,417
1992 average: 154,928
1991 average: 152,776
1990 average: 150,622

Unemployment
1993 (April): 5.6%
1992 average: 6.0%
1991 average: 6.1%
1990 average: 6.0%

Average Annual Pay
1988: $18,059
1987: $17,286
1985: $16,221

Per Capita Personal Income
1991: $15,328
1990: $14,788
1989: $14,077

Business Climate (1987)

Manufacturing
Number of establishments in 1987: 262
Shipments in 1987 ($1,000): $1,836,700
Employees in 1987: 10,800
Change in employment, 1982 to 1987: -9.2%
Average annual pay for manufacturing work in 1989: $27,647
Average annual pay for production work in 1987: $23,627

Wholesale Trade
Number of establishments in 1987: 495
Total sales in 1987 ($1,000): $1,193,300
Change in sales, 1982 to 1987: 26.9%

Retail Trade
Number of establishments in 1987: 2,154
Total sales in 1987 ($1,000): $1,193,300
Retail sales per household in 1987: $15,795
Average annual pay in 1989: $10,184

Service Industry
Selected receipts in 1987 ($1,000): $778,300
Average annual pay in 1989: $17,311

Housing
Total number of units in 1990: 145,061
Occupied units in 1990: 128,508
Owner-occupied units in 1990: 67.2%
1993 ACCRA average cost: N/A
1993 ACCRA average rent for an apartment: N/A

Chamber of Commerce
Pensacola Area Chamber of Commerce, Joe F. Ragland, Exec. Vice President, PO Box 550, 117 W. Garden St., Pensacola, FL 32593. 904-438-4081, FAX 904-438-6369

Economic Development Office
Pensacola-Escambia Development Commisssion, Frank Tamberrino, Exec. Director, 117 W. Garden St., Pensacola, FL 32501. 904-433-3065

Economic Development Organizations
Santa Rosa County Industrial Devlopment Authority, Richard D. Sorenson, Exec Director, 1099 Old Bagdad Highway, Milton, FL 32570. 904-994-8329, 904-623-0174

Major Businesses

Company	SIC	Telephone
American Fidelity Life Insurance	6311	(904) 456-7401
Bank South of Pensacola Inc.	6021	(904) 444-3200
Baptist Health Care Corp.	8062	(904) 434-4805
Baptist Hospital	8062	(904) 434-4011
Barnett Bank of West Florida	6022	(904) 432-0271
Bear, Lewis Co., Inc.	5141	(904) 438-9651
Greenhut Construction Co.	1542	(904) 433-5421
Gulf Power Co.	4911	(904) 444-6111
Hill-Kelly Dodge Inc.	5511	(904) 476-9078
Instrument Control Service	8711	(904) 968-2191
International Utility Supply	2491	(904) 433-0995
Mitchell Motors Inc.	5511	(904) 476-6002
Mocar Oil Co. Inc.	5171	(904) 456-6669
Pacer Industries Inc.	3429	(904) 476-0907
Pensacola Chrysler-Plymouth	5511	(904) 477-3385
Sacred Heart Hospital of Pensacola	8062	(904) 474-7000
Sansing Chevrolet Inc.	5511	(904) 476-2480
Southern Erectors Inc.	1791	(904) 944-0013
Southern Home Savings Bank	6022	(904) 433-4663
Whibbs Vince Pontiac-GMC	5511	(904) 433-7671

Colleges and Universities

Pensacola Junior College, Pensacola
University of West Florida, Pensacola

SARASOTA, FL (MSA)

Geographic Profile

Land Area
571.8 square miles

Counties and Parishes
Sarasota

Ranking Highlights

278 *out of 319 in total* **land area**
8 *out of 319 in* **population growth,** *1970–1990*
92 *out of 310 in having the lowest* **unemployment** *rate*
160 *out of 310 in size of* **labor force**
98 *out of 318 in the percentage of* **college graduates**
21 *out of 292 in per capita personal* **income**
127 *out of 319 in number of* **manufacturing establishments**
79 *out of 318 in* **physicians** *per 1000 people*
82 *out of 318 in* **hospital beds** *per 1000 people*
199 *out of 267 in fewest* **crimes** *per 1000 people*
127 *out of 266 in fewest* **violent crimes** *per 1000 people*
64 *out of 319 in per capita* **federal funds and grants**

Quality of Life Indexes (Rate per 1000 population)

Crime rate in 1991:	71.7
Violent crime rate in 1991:	6.1
Physicians rate in 1992:	2.39
Hospital bed rate in 1991:	4.91

ACCRA Cost of Living Indexes
(First quarter 1993, average = 100)

Composite index:	N/A
Utilities index:	N/A
Housing index:	N/A

Population (1990)

Total Population and Growth Rate
1990: 277,776
1980: 202,251
1970: 120,413
Growth rate 1970–1990: 131%

Race and Hispanic Origin
White: 94.6%
Black: 4.3%
Asian/Pacific Islander: 0.5%
Native American: 0.2%
Hispanic origin: 2.1%
White not Hispanic: 92.9%

Age
Ages 18 to 20: 2.7%
Ages 21 to 24: 3.5%
Ages 25 to 44: 24%
Ages 45 to 54: 9.5%
Ages 55 to 59: 5.1%

Ages 60 to 64: 7.3%
Ages 65 plus: 32.2%

Educational Attainment (1990)
Percent having completed high school: 81.3%
Percent having completed college: 21.9%
Elementary and high school enrollment: 28,649

Federal Funds and Grants Received ($1000)
Total received in 1989: 1,105,800
Funds received per capita: 4,243

Civilian Labor Force
1993 (April): 133,032
1992 average: 129,412
1991 average: 130,515
1990 average: 127,325

Unemployment
1993 (April): 5.1%
1992 average: 5.9%
1991 average: 5.1%
1990 average: 4.1%

Average Annual Pay
1988: $17,839
1987: $17,163
1985: $15,341

Per Capita Personal Income
1991: $22,580
1990: $22,232
1989: $21,623

Business Climate (1987)

Manufacturing
Number of establishments in 1987: 427
Shipments in 1987 ($1,000): $692,200
Employees in 1987: 8,900
Change in employment, 1982 to 1987: 17.1%
Average annual pay for manufacturing work in 1989: $22,363
Average annual pay for production work in 1987: $15,804

Wholesale Trade
Number of establishments in 1987: 470
Total sales in 1987 ($1,000): $788,600
Change in sales, 1982 to 1987: 77.2%

Retail Trade
Number of establishments in 1987: 2,217
Total sales in 1987 ($1,000): $788,600
Retail sales per household in 1987: $20,398
Average annual pay in 1989: $12,367

Service Industry
Selected receipts in 1987 ($1,000): $1,046,300
Average annual pay in 1989: $18,490

Housing
Total number of units in 1990: 157,055

Occupied units in 1990: 125,493
Owner-occupied units in 1990: 76.2%
1993 ACCRA average cost: N/A
1993 ACCRA average rent for an apartment: N/A

Chamber of Commerce
Sarasota Chamber of Commerce, David L. May, President, PO Box 308, 1819 Main St. #240, Sarasota, FL 33578. 813-955-8187, FAX 813-366-5621

Economic Development Office
Triangle Economic Development Authority, Inc., Sarasota County, Jodi Struble, Exec. Director, PO Box 3377, Port Charlotte, FL 33949-3377. 813-627-0031

Major Businesses

Company	SIC	Telephone
Apac-Florida Inc.	1611	(813) 355-7178
Coast Federal Savings & Loan Association	6035	(813) 366-7000
Dooley & Mack Constructor	1542	(813) 921-4636
Duncan Aircraft	5599	(813) 484-9704
First Federal Savings Loan	6035	(813) 474-3205
First National Bank	6021	(813) 488-7771
Florida Cities Water Co.	4941	(813) 924-1128
Florida Construction Commerce	6411	(813) 955-2811
Florida Westcoast Banks Inc.	6021	(813) 488-7771
Gator Asphalt Co.	2951	(813) 355-9306
Germain Hyundai Inc.	5511	(813) 921-5001
Halfacre, Bill Inc.	1542	(813) 351-6521
Kalin Enterprises Inc.	5712	(813) 924-1271
Kent, Wendel and Co.	1611	(813) 355-8575
Kimal Lumber Co., Inc.	5211	(813) 484-9721
London International U. S. Holdings	2834	(813) 365-1600
Maran Grove Corp.	0174	(813) 378-1794
Matthews Currie Ford Co.	5511	(813) 488-6787
Mills, W. G. Inc.	1542	(813) 758-6441
Murray Chris-Craft Cruise	3731	(813) 954-8814
Paver Development Corp.	6552	(813) 922-3516
Sarasota County Public Hospital	8062	(813) 955-1111
Snelling And Snelling Inc.	7363	(813) 922-9616
Southern Grocery Co.	5141	(813) 355-5151
Southpointe Motorcars Inc.	5511	(813) 923-2700
Stinnett's Pontiac Service	5511	(813) 922-3553
Sun Bank/Sarasota County National	6021	(813) 365-4000
Tropitone Furniture Co.	2514	(813) 355-2715
Venice Hospital Inc.	8062	(813) 485-7711

Colleges and Universities
New College of the University of South Florida, Sarasota
Ringling School of Art and Design, Sarasota

TALLAHASSEE, FL (MSA)

Geographic Profile

Land Area

1183.0 square miles

Counties and Parishes

Gadsden

Leon

Ranking Highlights

167 *out of 319 in total* **land area**

 58 *out of 319 in* **population growth,** *1970–1990*

 26 *out of 310 in having the lowest* **unemployment** *rate*

144 *out of 310 in size of* **labor force**

110 *out of 318 in the percentage of* **college graduates**

190 *out of 292 in per capita personal* **income**

215 *out of 319 in number of* **manufacturing establishments**

130 *out of 318 in* **physicians** *per 1000 people*

 91 *out of 318 in* **hospital beds** *per 1000 people*

265 *out of 267 in fewest* **crimes** *per 1000 people*

263 *out of 266 in fewest* **violent crimes** *per 1000 people*

 38 *out of 319 in per capita* **federal funds and grants**

Quality of Life Indexes (Rate per 1000 population)

Crime rate in 1991:   113.5

Violent crime rate in 1991:   16.7

Physicians rate in 1992:   1.94

Hospital bed rate in 1991:   4.76

ACCRA Cost of Living Indexes

(First quarter 1993, average = 100)

Composite index: 97.4

Utilities index: 103.2

Housing index: 93.0

Population (1990)

Total Population and Growth Rate

1990: 233,598

1980: 190,329

1970: 142,231

Growth rate 1970–1990: 64%

Race and Hispanic Origin

White: 67.8%

Black: 30.1%

Asian/Pacific Islander: 1.2%

Native American: 0.2%

Hispanic origin: 2.4%

White not Hispanic: 66.2%

Age

Ages 18 to 20: 8.9%

Ages 21 to 24: 9.8%

Ages 25 to 44: 33%

Ages 45 to 54: 9.1%

Ages 55 to 59: 3.3%

Ages 60 to 64: 3.2%

Ages 65 plus: 9%

Educational Attainment (1990)

Percent having completed high school: 80.3%

Percent having completed college: 21.4%

Elementary and high school enrollment: 36,923

Federal Funds and Grants Received

Total received in 1989: $1,171,400,000

Funds received per capita: $5,124

Civilian Labor Force

1993 (April):   147,430

1992 average: 142,968

1991 average: 139,858

1990 average: 138,124

Unemployment

1993 (April): 4.2%

1992 average: 4.4%

1991 average: 4.4%

1990 average: 4.1%

Average Annual Pay

1988: $17,951

1987: $17,025

1985: $15,297

Per Capita Personal Income

1991: $16,422

1990: $15,818

1989: $14,874

Business Climate (1987)

Manufacturing

Number of establishments in 1987: 205

Shipments in 1987 ($1,000): $343,000

Employees in 1987: 4,500

Change in employment, 1982 to 1987: 0%

Average annual pay for manufacturing work, 1989: $18,453

Average annual pay for production work, 1987: $14,059

Wholesale Trade

Number of establishments in 1987: 303

Total sales in 1987 ($1,000): $988,200

Change in sales, 1982 to 1987: 77.4%

Retail Trade

Number of establishments in 1987: 1,398

Total sales in 1987 ($1,000): $988,200

Retail sales per household in 1987: $17,444

Average annual pay in 1989: $9,906

Service Industry

Selected receipts in 1987 ($1,000): $670,500

Average annual pay in 1989: $19,690

Housing

Total number of units in 1990: 96,184

Occupied units in 1990: 88,233

Owner-occupied units in 1990: 59.7%

1993 ACCRA average cost: $108,177

1993 ACCRA average rent for an apartment: $437

Chamber of Commerce

Tallahassee Area Chamber of Commerce, Robert Bone, President, PO Box 1639, 100 N. Duval St., Tallahassee, FL 32302. 904-224-8116, FAX 904-561-3860

Industrial Sites

Innovation Park Tallahassee (220 acres). Affiliated with Florida State University and Florida A&M University. For more information, please contact: Mr. W.T. Gaupin, Marketing Director, 1673 W. Dirac Dr., Tallahassee, FL 32310. 904-575-6381

Major Businesses

Company	SIC	Telephone
Ajax Construction Co., Inc. Tallahassee	1542	(904) 224-9571
Astro Travel & Tours Inc.	4724	(904) 222-2023
Barnett Bank of Tallahassee	6022	(904) 224-1111
Bill's Book Store Inc.	5942	(904) 224-3178
Blankenship & Lee Inc.	1623	(904) 878-2413
Capital City Bank Group Inc.	6022	(904) 224-1171
Capital City First National Bank	6022	(904) 224-1171
Cawthon, Rainey Distribution	5171	(904) 222-1948
Chenoweth Distributing Ltd.	5181	(904) 576-1294
Cook, J. Kinson Inc.	1542	(904) 576-0119
Council Brothers Inc.	1711	(904) 576-1202
Crowder Jim	1794	(904) 576-7176
Culpepper Construction Co.	1542	(904) 224-3146
EDP Systems Inc.	7371	(904) 575-0179
Homes and Land Publishing	2721	(904) 576-2724
Investors Companies of Florida	6719	(904) 224-6900
Johnson, Gary Inc.	5531	(904) 656-2333
Killearn Properties Inc.	6552	(904) 893-2111
McKenzie Tank Lines Inc.	4213	(904) 576-1221
Monk's Office Machine	5999	(904) 878-7133
National Research & Technology	3672	(904) 576-0133
Pafford Oil Co. Inc.	5171	(904) 224-7434
Premium Assignment Corp.	6141	(904) 893-1191
Rose Printing Co. Inc.	2732	(904) 576-4151
Skagfield Corp.	2591	(904) 878-1144
Southeast Community Health	8062	(904) 681-5675
Sperry & Associates Inc.	1542	(904) 562-1101
Tallahassee Memorial Regional	8062	(904) 681-5238
Terminal Service Co. Inc.	3715	(904) 576-1221
Tri State Supply Inc.	5063	(904) 575-9674

Colleges and Universities

Florida Agricultural and Mechanical University, Tallahassee

Florida State University, Tallahassee

Tallahassee Community College, Tallahassee

TAMPA–SAINT PETERSBURG–CLEARWATER, FL (MSA)

Geographic Profile

Land Area

2554.5 square miles

Counties and Parishes

Hernando

Hillsborough

Pasco

Pinellas

Ranking Highlights

67 *out of 319 in total* land area

26 *out of 319 in* population growth, *1970–1990*

174 *out of 310 in having the lowest* unemployment *rate*

21 *out of 310 in size of* labor force

188 *out of 318 in the percentage of* college graduates

93 *out of 292 in per capita personal* income

28 *out of 319 in number of* manufacturing establishments

126 *out of 318 in* physicians *per 1000 people*

141 *out of 318 in* hospital beds *per 1000 people*

234 *out of 267 in fewest* crimes *per 1000 people*

254 *out of 266 in fewest* violent crimes *per 1000 people*

98 *out of 319 in per capita* federal funds and grants

Quality of Life Indexes (Rate per 1000 population)

Crime rate in 1991:	82.7
Violent crime rate in 1991:	12.6
Physicians rate in 1992:	1.97
Hospital bed rate in 1991:	4.09

ACCRA Cost of Living Indexes

(First quarter 1993, average = 100)

Composite index:	95.9
Utilities index:	98.6
Housing index:	94.8

Population (1990)

Total Population and Growth Rate

1990: 2,067,959

1980: 1,613,600

1970: 1,105,553

Growth rate 1970–1990: 87%

Race and Hispanic Origin

White: 88.4%

Black: 9.0%

Asian/Pacific Islander: 1.1%

Native American: 0.3%

Hispanic origin: 6.7%

White not Hispanic: 83.1%

Age

Ages 18 to 20: 3.6%
Ages 21 to 24: 5%
Ages 25 to 44: 29.6%
Ages 45 to 54: 9.8%
Ages 55 to 59: 4.5%
Ages 60 to 64: 5.5%
Ages 65 plus: 21.6%

Educational Attainment (1990)

Percent having completed high school: 75.1%
Percent having completed college: 17.3%
Elementary and high school enrollment: 274,742

Federal Funds and Grants Received ($1000)

Total received in 1989: 7,171,800
Funds received per capita: 3,595

Civilian Labor Force

1993 (April): 1,074,482
1992 average: 1,038,694
1991 average: 1,020,490
1990 average: 1,019,735

Unemployment

1993 (April): 6.6%
1992 average: 7.1%
1991 average: 6.4%
1990 average: 5.1%

Average Annual Pay

1988: $18,714
1987: $17,911
1985: $16,410

Per Capita Personal Income

1991: $18,445
1990: $17,977
1989: $17,472

Business Climate (1987)

Manufacturing

Number of establishments in 1987: 2,546
Shipments in 1987 ($1,000): $8,547,000
Employees in 1987: 84,500
Change in employment, 1982 to 1987: 8.6%
Average annual pay for manufacturing work in 1989: $22,912
Average annual pay for production work in 1987: $16,684

Wholesale Trade

Number of establishments in 1987: 3,986
Total sales in 1987 ($1,000): $17,994,200
Change in sales, 1982 to 1987: 44.3%

Retail Trade

Number of establishments in 1987: 12,759
Total sales in 1987 ($1,000): $17,994,200
Retail sales per household in 1987: $16,820
Average annual pay in 1989: $11,987

Service Industry

Selected receipts in 1987 ($1,000): $7,526,800
Average annual pay in 1989: $18,888

Office Real Estate (1992)

Office space inventory: 20,210,309 square feet
Average class A Central Business District rental range per sq. ft: $23.45

Vacancy Rates

All areas: 19.0%

Vacancy Rates in Central Business District

Class A space: 26.3%
Class B space: 44.1%

Vacancy Rates Outside Central Business District

Class A space: 12.2%
Class B space: 15.8%

Housing

Total number of units in 1990: 1,025,064
Occupied units in 1990: 869,481
Owner-occupied units in 1990: 69.3%
1993 ACCRA average cost: $101,400
1993 ACCRA average rent for an apartment: $554

Chamber of Commerce

Greater Tampa Chamber of Commerce, Harvey A. Schmitt, Exec. Vice President, PO Box 420, 801 E. Kennedy Blvd., Tampa, FL 33601. 813-228-7777, FAX 813-223-7899

Economic Development Office

Greater Clearwater Chamber of Commerce, Peter Woodham, President, PO Box 2457, 128 N. Osceola Ave., Clearwater, FL 34617. 813-461-0011, FAX 813-449-2889

Economic Development Organizations

Tampa Port Authority, Joseph Valenti, Director, PO Box 2192, 811 Wynkoop Rd., Tampa, FL 33601. 813-248-1924, FAX 813-247-2352

St. Petersburg Housing and Economic Development Department, Tony Collins, Director, PO Box 2842, St. Petersburg, FL 33731. 813-893-7788, FAX 813-892-5465

Hernando County Economic Development Dept., Al Fluman, Economic Development Director, 2489 Broad St., Brooksville, FL 34609. 904-799-7275

Pasco County Chamber of Commerce, Committee of 100, Paul Griffin, Exec. Director, 4111 Land O'Lakes Blvd. Suite 305, Land O'Lakes, FL 34639. 813-996-4075

Pinellas Economic Development Council, David Knowlton, President, 19321 U.S. 19 N. #100, Clearwater, FL 34624. 813-535-3630, FAX 813-538-8663

Industrial Sites

Hidden River Corporate Park (513 acres). Affiliated with University of South Florida. For more information, please contact: Mr. Joseph W. Taggart, Partner, Hidden River Properties, 101 E. Kennedy Blvd. Suite 4100, Barnett Plaza, Tampa, FL 33602. 813-228-8600

Tampla Palms Commerce Park (2,000 acres). Affiliated with University of South Florida. For more information, please contact: Mr. Joseph DeTuno, President, Gulfstream Commercial Properties, 15310 Amberly Dr., Suite 300, Tampa, FL 33647. 813-972-5757

Tampa Bay Area Research and Development Park (90 acres). Affiliated with University of South Florida. For more information, please contact: Mr. John Hennessey, Exec. Director, University of South Florida, 280 Administration Bldg., Tampa, FL 33620. 813-974-2890

University Center Research and Development Park (87 acres). Affiliated with University of South Florida. For more information, please contact: Mr. Daniel Woodward, Project Manager, 7650 W. Courtney Campbell Causeway Suite 1100, Tampa, FL 33607. 813-882-0601

Major Businesses

Company	SIC	Telephone
Anchor Glass Container Co.	3221	(813) 884-0000
AT & T Paradyne Corp.	3661	(813) 530-2000
Bilzerian Partners	3812	(813) 264-7100
Celotex Corp.	3086	(813) 873-1700
Eckerd, Jack Corp.	5912	(813) 397-7461
Eckerd Drugs of Texas Inc.	5912	(813) 397-7461
Electric Fuels Corp.	1221	(813) 892-2700
Eli Witt Co. (Inc.)	5194	(813) 623-6502
First Florida Bank National	6021	(813) 224-1111
First Florida Banks Inc.	6021	(813) 224-1455
Florida Federal Savings Bank	6035	(813) 893-1131
Florida Power Corp.	4911	(813) 866-5151
Florida Progress Corp.	4911	(813) 894-8141
Florida Steel Corp.	3312	(813) 251-8811
FLS Holdings Inc.	3312	(813) 251-8811
GTE Data Services Inc.	7374	(813) 978-4000
GTE South Incorporated	4813	(813) 224-4011
Hillsborough Holdings Corp.	3321	(813) 871-4811
Kash N' Karry Food Stores	5411	(813) 621-0200
Lykes Bros. Inc.	0721	(813) 223-3981
Maas Inc.	5311	(813) 223-7525
NCNB BanCorp. Inc.	6021	(813) 224-5270
NCNB Florida Bancorp	6029	(813) 224-5270
NCNB National Bank of Florida	6021	(813) 224-5270
Seminole Electric Cooperative	4911	(813) 963-0994
Spalding & Evenflo Co.	3949	(813) 887-5200
Tampa Electric Co.	4911	(813) 228-4111
Tech Data Corp.	5045	(813) 539-7429
Teco Energy Inc.	4911	(813) 228-4111
Walter, Jim Corp.	3086	(813) 873-4000

Colleges and Universities

Clearwater Christian College, Clearwater
Eckerd College, St. Petersburg
Hillsborough Community College, Tampa

International Academy of Merchandising & Design, Tampa
International Technical Institute, Tampa
ITT Technical Institute, Tampa
National Education Center-Tampa Technical Institute Campus, Tampa
St. Petersburg Junior College, St. Petersburg
Tampa College, Tampa
United Electronics Institute, Tampa
University of South Florida, Tampa
University of Tampa, Tampa

WEST PALM BEACH–BOCA RATON–DELRAY BEACH, FL (MSA)

Geographic Profile

Land Area
2034.3 square miles

Counties and Parishes
Palm Beach

Ranking Highlights

88 *out of 319 in total* **land area**

6 *out of 319 in* **population growth,** *1970–1990*

278 *out of 310 in having the lowest* **unemployment** *rate*

62 *out of 310 in size of* **labor force**

94 *out of 318 in the percentage of* **college graduates**

2 *out of 292 in per capita personal* **income**

73 *out of 319 in number of* **manufacturing establishments**

101 *out of 318 in* **physicians** *per 1000 people*

173 *out of 318 in* **hospital beds** *per 1000 people*

N/A *out of 267 in fewest* **crimes** *per 1000 people*

N/A *out of 266 in fewest* **violent crimes** *per 1000 people*

86 *out of 319 in per capita* **federal funds and grants**

Quality of Life Indexes (Rate per 1000 population)

Crime rate in 1991:   N/A
Violent crime rate in 1991: N/A
Physicians rate in 1992:   2.17
Hospital bed rate in 1991:   3.66

ACCRA Cost of Living Indexes

(First quarter 1993, average = 100)
Composite index: 111.6
Utilities index: 120.4
Housing index: 124.0

Population (1990)

Total Population and Growth Rate
1990: 863,518
1980: 576,758
1970: 348,993
Growth rate 1970–1990: 147%

Race and Hispanic Origin
White: 84.8%
Black: 12.5%
Asian/Pacific Islander: 1.0%
Native American: 0.1%
Hispanic origin: 7.7%
White not Hispanic: 79.1%

Age
Ages 18 to 20: 3.1%
Ages 21 to 24: 4.4%
Ages 25 to 44: 29.4%

Ages 45 to 54: 9.3%
Ages 55 to 59: 4.3%
Ages 60 to 64: 5.5%
Ages 65 plus: 24.3%

Educational Attainment (1990)

Percent having completed high school: 78.8%
Percent having completed college: 22.1%
Elementary and high school enrollment: 107,976

Federal Funds and Grants Received

Total received in 1989: $3,040,200,000
Funds received per capita: $3,715

Civilian Labor Force

1993 (April):   452,330
1992 average: 441,202
1991 average: 432,404
1990 average: 427,765

Unemployment

1993 (April):   8.1%
1992 average: 9.8%
1991 average: 8.4%
1990 average: 6.6%

Average Annual Pay

1988: $21,741
1987: $20,662
1985: $18,363

Per Capita Personal Income

1991: $28,097
1990: $27,550
1989: $25,994

Business Climate (1987)

Manufacturing
Number of establishments in 1987: 861
Shipments in 1987 ($1,000): $6,405,700
Employees in 1987: 38,500
Change in employment, 1982 to 1987: 24.6%
Average annual pay for manufacturing work in 1989: $34,711
Average annual pay for production work in 1987: $20,794

Wholesale Trade
Number of establishments in 1987: 1,440
Total sales in 1987 ($1,000): $4,101,600
Change in sales, 1982 to 1987: 56.0%

Retail Trade
Number of establishments in 1987: 5,938
Total sales in 1987 ($1,000): $4,101,600
Retail sales per household in 1987: $19,139
Average annual pay in 1989: $13,579

Service Industry
Selected receipts in 1987 ($1,000): $3,262,100
Average annual pay in 1989: $21,557

Office Real Estate (1992)

Office space inventory: 6,572,000 square feet
Average class A Central Business District rental range per sq. ft: $23.00

Vacancy Rates

All areas: 20.8%

Vacancy Rates in Central Business District

Class A space: 16.0%
Class B space: 17.4%

Vacancy Rates Outside Central Business District

Class A space: 14.5%
Class B space: 33.9%

Housing

Total number of units in 1990: 461,665
Occupied units in 1990: 365,558
Owner-occupied units in 1990: 71.9%
1993 ACCRA average cost: N/A
1993 ACCRA average rent for an apartment: N/A

Chamber of Commerce

Chamber of Commerce of the Palm Beaches, Dennis Grady, Exec. Director, 401 N. Flagler Dr., PO Box 2931, West Palm Beach, FL 33402. 407-833-3711, FAX 407-833-5582

Economic Development Office

Greater Boca Raton Chamber of Commerce, M.J. Arts, President, PO Box 1390, 1800 N. Dixie Highway, Boca Raton, FL 33432. 407-395-4433, FAX 407-392-3780

Economic Development Organizations

Greater Delray Beach Chamber of Commerce, William Wood, President, 64 S.E. 5th Ave., Delray Beach, FL 33483. 407-860-2651

Business Development Board of Palm Beach County, Inc., Larry L. Pelton, President, 1555 Palm Beach Lakes Blvd. Suite 155, West Palm Beach, FL 33401. 305-684-2401, FAX 407-833-8873

Boca Raton Community Redevelopment Agency, Jorge Camejo, Exec. Director, 201 W. Palmetto Park Rd., Boca Raton, FL 33432. 407-338-7070, FAX 407-338-6837

Industrial Sites

Florida Atlantic Research and Development Park (60 acres). Affiliated with Florida Atlantic University. For more information, please contact: Dr. Jeffrey Tennant, Associate Vice President, PO Box 3091, Boca Raton, FL 33431. 407-393-3066

Major Businesses

Company	SIC	Telephone
Barnett Bank of Palm Beach	6022	(407) 838-2392
Cenvill Development Corp.	6552	(407) 533-9500
Colonial Penn Group, Inc.	6331	(407) 694-6364
Colonial Penn Holdings Inc.	6311	(407) 694-6300

Major Businesses (Continued)

Company	SIC	Telephone
Colonial Penn Life Insurance	6311	(407) 694-6300
Computer Products Inc.	3679	(407) 451-1000
Dycom Industries Inc.	1623	(407) 659-6301
Express Financial Corp.	6163	(407) 368-1771
Financial Benefit Life Insurance	6311	(407) 394-9400
First Federal Savings Palm Beach	6035	(407) 655-8511
FPL Group Capital Inc.	6331	(407) 694-6364
FPL Group Inc.	4911	(407) 694-6300
Globe Security Systems, Inc.	7381	(407) 241-9670
JFK Medical Center Inc.	8062	(407) 965-7300
Levitz Furniture Corp.	5712	(407) 994-6006
LFC Holding Corp	5712	(407) 994-6006
Lumbermens Underwriting	6331	(407) 994-1900
Office Depot, Inc.	5943	(407) 994-2131
Palm Beach Gardens Medical Center	8062	(407) 622-1411
Rinker Materials Corp.	3273	(407) 833-5555
Sahlen & Associates Inc.	7381	(407) 241-9670
Servico Inc.	7011	(407) 689-9970
Siemens Information System	3661	(407) 994-8100
St. Mary's Hospital Inc.	8062	(407) 844-6300
Steego Corp.	6799	(407) 655-9700
Summa Equity Corp.	6211	(407) 395-4459
Tire Kingdom Inc.	5531	(407) 842-4290
Tradecom, Inc.	6221	(407) 392-7100
Worldmark Corp.	3471	(407) 626-3116

Colleges and Universities

College of Boca Raton, Boca Raton
College of The Palm Beaches, West Palm Beach
Florida Atlantic University, Boca Raton
New England Institute of Technology, West Palm Beach
Northwood Institute, Florida Campus, West Palm Beach
Palm Beach Atlantic College, West Palm Beach

GEORGIA

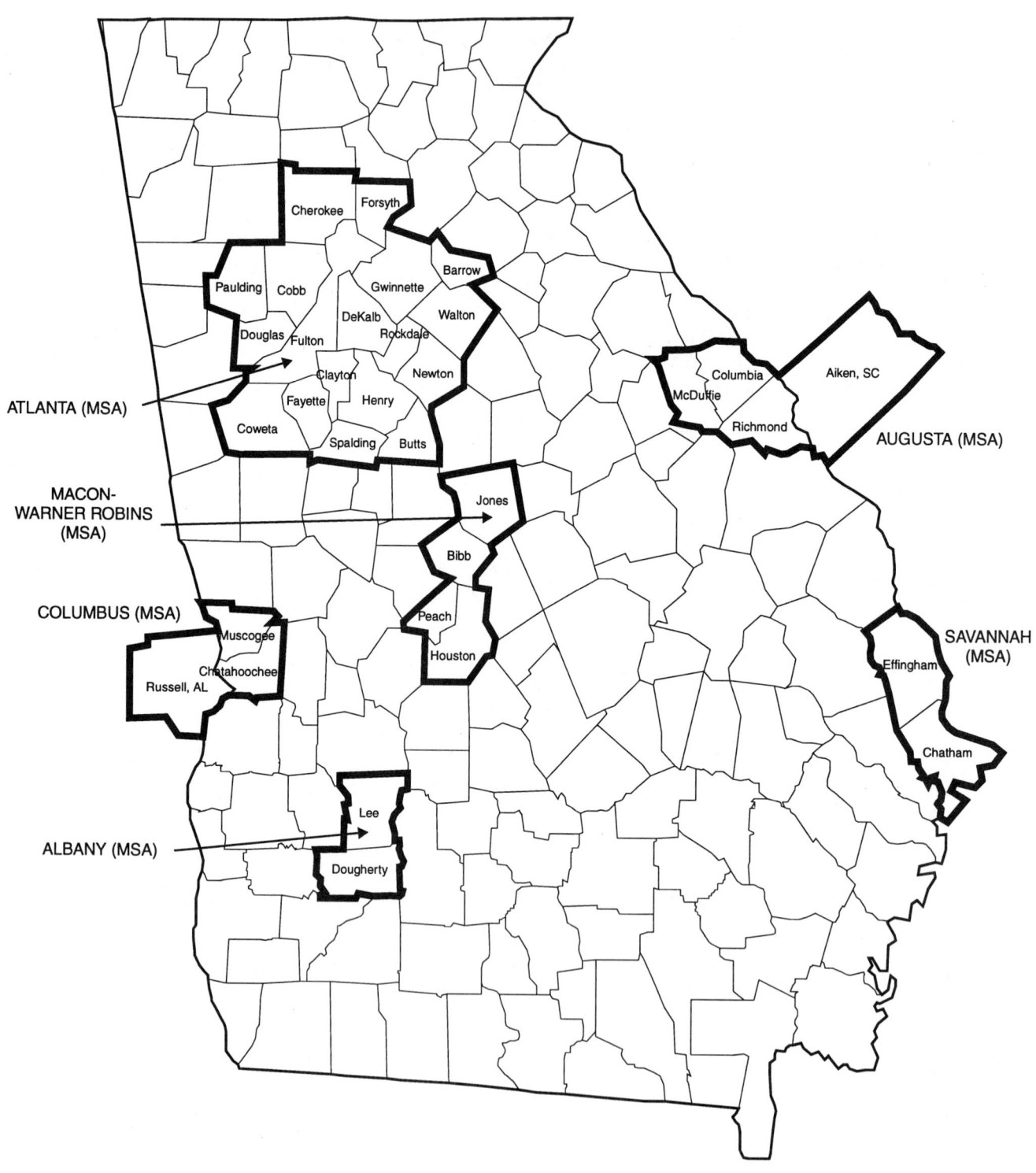

ATLANTA (MSA)

Cherokee
Forsyth
Barrow
Paulding
Cobb
Gwinnette
DeKalb
Walton
Douglas
Fulton
Rockdale
Clayton
Newton
Fayette
Henry
Coweta
Spalding
Butts

MACON-
WARNER ROBINS
(MSA)

Jones
Bibb
Peach
Houston

COLUMBUS (MSA)

Muscogee
Chatahoochee
Russell, AL

ALBANY (MSA)

Lee
Dougherty

Columbia
Aiken, SC
McDuffie
Richmond

AUGUSTA (MSA)

SAVANNAH
(MSA)

Effingham
Chatham

GEORGIA

Population
1990: 6,478,216
1980: 5,463,105

Age
Ages 18 to 20: 325,159
Ages 21 to 24: 413,425
Ages 25 to 44: 2,190,594
Ages 45 to 54: 668,951
Ages 55 to 59: 259,735
Ages 60 to 64: 238,779
Median age: 31.6

Race
White: 4,600,148
Black: 1,746,565
Asian/Pacific Islander: 75,781
Native American: 13,348
Hispanic origin: 108,922

Households
Total: 2,366,615
Persons per household: 2.66

Sex
Male: 3,144,503
Female: 3,333,713

Population Migration
Domestic migration: 618,000
International migration: 41,000

Projection of the Population in 1995
Total: 6,846,000
18 to 64: 4,253,000

Civilian Labor Force
1993: 3,261,200
1992: 3,202,400
1991: 3,194,200
1990: 3,191,300

Manufacturing
1995 Projection: 619,600
1992: 544,200
1991: 543,100
1990: 550,600
1989: 571,300

Services
1995 Projection: 936,400

1992: 672,400
1991: 644,100
1990: 650,600
1989: 629,500

Wholesale and Retail Trade
1995 Projection: 905,500
1992: 742,800
1991: 741,100
1990: 763,600
1989: 776,100

Unemployment Rate
1993: 6.8%
1992: 5.5%
1991: 5.7%
1990: 5.3%

Employer Unemployment Contributions
Contribution Rate
1992: 1.44%
1991: 1.30%
1990: 1.32%

Average Weekly Benefit
1992: $150.05
1991: $148.49
1990: $143.23

Gross State Product (Million $)
1989: $129,776
1988: $122,717
1987: $113,098
1979: $51,211
Growth rate, 1979 to 1989: 153.4%

Capital Expenditures of Manufacturing Industries
1990: $3,376,400,000
1989: $2,727,400,000
1988: $2,580,200,000
1987: $2,471,500,000

State Tax Rates
Individual income: Range from 1% ($1,000 or less) to 6% (above $10,000).
Corporate income: 6% of federal taxable income.
General property: levied at 1/4 mill, based on full market

value of real property and tangible personal property. Property is assessed at 40% of its fair market value.

General sales: 4%

Gasoline: 7.5¢ per gallon

Income

Median income for a 4 person family: $40,019

Personal per Capita Income

1992: $18,130

1991: $17,447

1990: $17,041

Disposable per Capita Income

1992: $15,943

1991: $15,272

1990: $14,816

Private Employment Weekly Wages

Average

1989: $404

1988: $394

1987: $394

Manufacturing

1989: $377

1988: $418

1987: $404

Services

1989: $387

1988: $374

1987: $351

Wholesale

1989: $578

1988: $561

1987: $528

Retail

1989: $230

1988: $227

1987: $221

Highway Statistics

Total Highway Miles

1990: 109,601

1989: 108,010

1988: 107,388

Federal Highway Aid

1991: $377,924,000

1990: $381,809,000

1989: $383,070,000

Electricity

Average Cost per Kilowatt Hour

1990: 6.49¢

1989: 6.34¢

1988: 6.25¢

Housing (1990)

Owner occupied units: 1,536,759

Median house value: $71,300

Renter occupied units: 829,856

Median rent: $344

Total vacant units: 271,803

Homeowner vacancy rate: 2.5%

Rental vacancy rate: 12.2%

State Business Incentives and Assistance

Financial and Business Assistance

Industrial Revenue Bond. With allocation approval by the Georgia Department of Community Affairs, local industrial revenue authorities may issue industrial development bonds of less than $10 million for land, buildings, and equipment financing. The terms of the bond issue may not exceed 40 years and the interest rates are negotiated with the lender.

Georgia Business Development Corporation. It offers loans to qualified companies unable to obtain conventional financing. Emphasis is placed on firms that are expanding production and on sound new ventures, preferably in manufacturing or processing. Loans range from $100,000 to $400,000, with an average of $275,000.

Small Business Investment Corporations. Georgia has six Small Business Investment Corporations. These privately owned corporations are licensed and regulated by SBA. Their services include equity financing, long-term loans, consulting, and advisory assistance to small concerns. Equity financing may be provided to small businesses through some type of equity securities. Georgia also has over 200 local development corporations that assist in securing local bank and U.S. Small Business Administration 503 loans for long-term fixed assets.

Agribusiness Loan Program. Low-interest agribusiness loans are available under the Georgia Development Authority's tax-free revenue note program. Loans are limited to $1 million, with the provision that no more than 25% or $150,000 may be used toward land purchase.

Georgia Research Consortium. Created to coordinate the resources, expertise, and facilities of Georgia's eight high technology institutions (Atlanta University Center, Emory University, Georgia State University, Georgia Technology Institute, Medical College of Georgia, Mercer University, Southern College of Technology, and University of Georgia).

The Advanced Technology Development Center (On the Georgia Tech campus). Created to stimulate growth in Georgia's high technology industry. It offers assistance programs for established as well as emerging companies. A second center in Augusta specializes in biomedical products. A third in Warner Robins encourages the growth of aerospace and defense-related industry. An ATDC administered Seed Capital Fund is available to stimulate

Major Companies in the State

Company name	Fortune 500 rank	City	Telephone	SIC number
Fortune 500 Companies				
Coca Cola Co.	34	Atlanta	404-676-2121	2087
Coca Cola Enterprises Inc.	106	Atlanta	404-676-2100	2086
Flowers Industries Inc.	387	Thomasville	912-226-9110	2051
Georgia Gulf Corp.	417	Atlanta	404-395-4500	2812
Georgia Pacific Corp.	39	Atlanta	404-521-4000	2435
Gold Kist Inc.	290	Atlanta	404-393-5000	5144
Interface Inc.	493	Lagrange	706-882-1891	2273
National Service Industries Inc.	255	Atlanta	404-853-1000	3646
Savannah Foods & Industries Inc.	324	Savannah	912-234-1261	2062
Shaw Industries Inc.	241	Dalton	706-278-3812	2273
West Point Pepperell Inc.	272	West Point	706-645-4000	2392
Other Major Companies in the State				
American Family Corp.		Columbus	404-323-3431	6321
Atlanta Gas Light Co.		Atlanta	404-584-4000	4923
Bank South Corp.		Atlanta	404-529-4529	6712
Bellsouth Corp.		Atlanta	404-249-2000	4813
Charter Medical Corp.		Macon	912-742-1161	8062
Contel Corp.		Atlanta	404-391-8000	4813
Delta Air Lines Inc.		Atlanta	404-765-2600	4512
Equifax Inc.		Atlanta	404-885-8000	6411
First Financial Management Corp.		Atlanta	404-321-0120	7374
First Wachovia Corp.		Atlanta	404-332-5000	6712
Fuqua Industries Inc.		Atlanta	404-658-9000	7384
Genuine Parts Co.		Atlanta	404-953-1700	5013
Georgia Power Co.		Atlanta	404-526-6526	4911
Gulfstream Aerospace Corp.		Savannah	912-964-3000	3721
Home Depot Inc.		Atlanta	404-433-8211	5211
Oglethorpe Power Corp.		Tucker	404-270-7600	4911
Southern Bell Telephone & Telegraph Co.		Atlanta	404-529-8611	4813
Southern Co.		Atlanta	404-393-0650	4911
Suntrust Banks Inc.		Atlanta	404-588-7711	6712
Turner Broadcasting System Inc.		Atlanta	404-827-1700	7812

small, entrepreneurial high-tech operations.

Statewide tax increment financing for redevelopment projects.

Small Business Revitalization Program to help small businesses secure long-term financing.

Georgia Development Authority low-interest agribusiness loans.

Tax credits available to new or expanding companies creating jobs in less developed counties.

Computerized trade lead program to help Georgia companies increase product exports.

Product marketing assistance through government-produced manufacturing and international trade directories.

Single point-of-contact for all State environmental regulations.

Regional Development Centers provide information about growth potentials in their areas.

Start-up space and research assistance for high technology operations.

Education and Training

Quick Start. Administered by the Georgia Department of Technical and Adult Education, this job training program is designed to help industries start up and expand their operations by developing and implementing customized training programs for companies. It is an economic development tool to attract new and expanding businesses.

Job Training Partnership Act. This program operates with funding from the U.S. Department of Labor. It provides job training and other employment related services.

State Offices

Real estate: Real Estate Commission, Charles Clar, Commissioner, 40 Pryor Street SW, Atlanta, GA 30303-3184. 404-656-3916

Chamber of commerce: Business Council of Georgia, Gene Dyson, President, 233 Peachtree St. #200, Atlanta, GA 30303-1504. 404-223-2264

Economic development: Georgia Dept. of Industry, Trade and Tourism, George Berry, Commissioner, PO Box 1776, 230 Peachtree St. N.W. #700, Atlanta, GA 30301. 404-656-3545, FAX 404-656-3567

Community Affairs Department, Ecommunity & Economic Development Division, Chantal Akridge, Director, 100 Peachtree Street, 1200 Equitable Bldg., Atlanta, GA 30303. 404-656-4143

Atlanta Economic Development Council, Walter R. Huntley, Jr., President, 230 Peachtree Street, Suite 1650, Atlanta, GA 30303. 404-658-7000

Small Business Development Center, Henry H. Logan, Acting State Director, University of Georgia, Chicopec Complex, Athens, GA 30602. 404-542-5760

Environmental affairs: Environmental Protection Division, Harold Reheis, Director, 205 Butler Street SE, Suite 1252, Atlanta, GA 30334. 404-656-4713

Labor: Labor Department, Joe Tanner, Commissioner, 148 International Blvd., Atlanta, GA 30303. 404-656-3011

Unemployment: Labor Department, Unemployment Insurance Division, Tome Lowe, Director, 148 International Blvd., Atlanta, GA 30303. 404-656-3050

Worker's compensation: Workers' Compensation Board, James W. Oxendine, Chairman, 1000 South Tower, 1 CNN Center, Atlanta, GA 30303-2788. 404-656-2034

Occupational safety and health: Transportation, Certification, Enforcement and Safety Division, Al Hatcher, Director, 1007 Virginia Ave., Hapeville, GA 30354. 404-559-6600

Secretary of state: Secretary of State, Max Cleland, Secretary of State, State Capitol, Room 214, Atlanta,GA 30334. 404-656-2881

Taxation and revenue: Revenue Department, Marcus E. Collins, Sr., Commissioner, 270 Washington Street SW, Atlanta, GA 30334. 404-656-4015

Designated Zones for Economic Development

Enterprise Zones

Enacted in: 1982

Atlanta

Fulton County

Foreign Trade Zones

Foreign Trade Zone No. 144, Brunswick, Georgia, Grantee: Brunswick Foreign-Trade Zone, Inc., B. E. Bledsoe, PO Box 130, Brunswick, GA 31521, 912-265-6900

Foreign Trade Zone No. 104, Savannah, Georgia, Grantee/Operator: Savannah Airport Commission, W. Kenneth Mattox, PO Box 2723, Savannah, GA 31402-2723, 912-964-0904 or 964-1514

Foreign Trade Zone No. 26, Shenandoah, Georgia, Grantee: Georgia Foreign Trade Zone, Inc., Christine Campbell, 400 Tradeport Blvd., Suite 400, Atlanta, GA 30354, 404-361-6000

Labor Unions

Electrical Workers, International Brotherhood of (AFL-CIO)

Food and Commercial Workers International Union, United (AFL-CIO)

Plumbing and Pipe Fitting Industry of The United States and Canada, United Association of, Journeymen and Aprentices of the (AFL-CIO)

Steelworkers of America, United (AFL-CIO)

Theatrical Stage Employees and Moving Picture Machine Operators of the United States and Canada,, International Alliance of (AFL-CIO)

Transit Union, Amalgamated (AFL-CIO)

Universities with Ph.D. Programs

Clark Atlanta University, Atlanta

Emory University, Atlanta

Georgia Institute of Technology, Atlanta

Georgia State University, Atlanta

Medical College of Georgia, Augusta

Mercer University, Macon

University of Georgia, Athens

Sources of Additional Information

1990 Georgia Manufacturing Wage Survey, Statewide Summary. Georgia Dept. of Industry, Trade and Tourism, n.d. 15p.

Georgia Opportunites in Technology. Georgia Dept. of Industry, Trade and Tourism, n.d. 16p.

Georgia Crossroads of the Southeast. Georgia Dept. of Industry, Trade and Tourism, n.d. 16p.

Georgia, the State of Business Today. Georgia Dept. of Industry, Trade and Tourism, n.d. 24p.

Georgia Economic Profile. Georgia Dept. of Industry, Trade and Tourism, n.d. 7p.

ALBANY, GA (MSA)

Geographic Profile

Land Area

685.5 square miles

Counties and Parishes

Dougherty

Lee

Places

None

Ranking Highlights

256 *out of 319 in total* **land area**

193 *out of 319 in* **population growth,** *1970–1990*

245 *out of 310 in having the lowest* **unemployment** *rate*

282 *out of 310 in size of* **labor force**

209 *out of 318 in the percentage of* **college graduates**

255 *out of 292 in per capita personal* **income**

297 *out of 319 in number of* **manufacturing establishments**

236 *out of 318 in* **physicians** *per 1000 people*

42 *out of 318 in* **hospital beds** *per 1000 people*

255 *out of 267 in fewest* **crimes** *per 1000 people*

189 *out of 266 in fewest* **violent crimes** *per 1000 people*

135 *out of 319 in per capita* **federal funds and grants**

Quality of Life Indexes (Rate per 1000 population)

Crime rate in 1991:	90.8
Violent crime rate in 1991:	8.2
Physicians rate in 1992:	1.44
Hospital bed rate in 1991:	5.66

ACCRA Cost of Living Indexes

(First quarter 1993, average = 100)

Composite index:	N/A
Utilities index:	N/A
Housing index:	N/A

Population (1990)

Total Population and Growth Rate

1990: 112,561

1980: 112,394

1970: 96,683

Growth rate 1970–1990: 16%

Race and Hispanic Origin

White: 53.3%

Black: 45.8%

Asian/Pacific Islander: 0.4%

Native American: 0.2%

Hispanic origin: 0.8%

White not Hispanic: 52.9%

Age

Ages 18 to 20: 5.7%

Ages 21 to 24: 5.9%

Ages 25 to 44: 30.9%

Ages 45 to 54: 9.5%

Ages 55 to 59: 3.9%

Ages 60 to 64: 3.8%

Ages 65 plus: 9.7%

Educational Attainment (1990)

Percent having completed high school: 67.9%

Percent having completed college: 16.5%

Elementary and high school enrollment: 24,483

Federal Funds and Grants Received

Total received in 1989: $381,100,000

Funds received per capita: $3,276

Civilian Labor Force

1993 (April): 54,093

1992 average: 54,419

1991 average: 53,246

1990 average: 54,285

Unemployment

1993 (April): 6.6%

1992 average: 8.6%

1991 average: 5.5%

1990 average: 6.5%

Average Annual Pay

1988: $19,007

1987: $17,806

1985: $17,129

Per Capita Personal Income

1991: $15,133

1990: $14,522

1989: $13,540

Business Climate (1987)

Manufacturing

Number of establishments in 1987: 97

Shipments in 1987 ($1,000): $2,123,600

Employees in 1987: 8,000

Change in employment, 1982 to 1987: -27.3%

Average annual pay for manufacturing work in 1989: $28,782

Average annual pay for production work in 1987: $24,717

Wholesale Trade

Number of establishments in 1987: 264

Total sales in 1987 ($1,000): $938,000

Change in sales, 1982 to 1987: 8.3%

Retail Trade

Number of establishments in 1987: 787

Total sales in 1987 ($1,000): $938,000

Retail sales per household in 1987: $18,353

Average annual pay in 1989: $9,968

Service Industry

Selected receipts in 1987 ($1,000): $287,200

Average annual pay in 1989: $17,517

Housing

Total number of units in 1990: 42,910
Occupied units in 1990: 392,622
Owner-occupied units in 1990: 55.7%
1993 ACCRA average cost: N/A
1993 ACCRA average rent for an apartment: N/A

Chamber of Commerce

Albany Chamber of Commerce, H.B. Dearman, Jr., Exec. Vice President, 225 W. Broad Ave., PO Box 308, Albany, GA 31702. 912-434-8700

Economic Development Office

Albany/Dougherty Economic Development Commisssion, Jones Hook, Exec. Director, PO Box 308, Albany, GA 31702. 912-434-0044, FAX 912-434-8716

Major Companies

Company	SIC	Telephone
Albany 1st Federal Savings & Loan	6035	(912) 435-2111
Alcon Associates Inc.	1629	(912) 432-7411
ATC Corp.	5084	(912) 888-1212
Bobs Candies Inc.	2064	(912) 435-2121
Chem-Nut Inc.	5191	(912) 883-7050
Engineering & Equipment Co.	5074	(912) 435-5601
First State Corp.	6719	(912) 432-8000
Flint River Textiles Inc.	2211	(912) 435-1495
Gray Communications Systems	5065	(912) 888-9390
HCA Palmyra Medical Center	8062	(912) 888-3800
Hospital Authority Albany-Dougherty	8062	(912) 883-1800
Interstate Truck Leasing	7513	(912) 883-7250
MacGregor Golf Co.	3949	(912) 888-0001
Nut Tree Pecan Co.	5159	(912) 888-2425
Pritchett Ford Co.	5511	(912) 883-3100
Taylor, Fred Co. Inc.	5012	(912) 883-5200
Trans Power Inc.	5012	(912) 883-6550
Water Gas & Light Commission	4931	(912) 883-8330
Wingate/Taylor-Maid	4213	(912) 439-8888
Woodford Plywood Inc.	5031	(912) 883-4900

Colleges and Universities

Albany State College, Albany
Darton College, Albany

ATHENS, GA (MSA)

Geographic Profile

Land Area
933.4 square miles

Counties and Parishes
Clarke
Jackson
Madison
Oconee

Places
None

Ranking Highlights

212 *out of 319 in total* land area
82 *out of 319 in* population growth, *1970–1990*
76 *out of 310 in having the lowest* unemployment *rate*
220 *out of 310 in size of* labor force
50 *out of 318 in the percentage of* college graduates
237 *out of 292 in per capita personal* income
221 *out of 319 in number of* manufacturing establishments
212 *out of 318 in* physicians *per 1000 people*
51 *out of 318 in* hospital beds *per 1000 people*
174 *out of 267 in fewest* crimes *per 1000 people*
109 *out of 266 in fewest* violent crimes *per 1000 people*
244 *out of 319 in per capita* federal funds and grants

Quality of Life Indexes (Rate per 1000 population)

Crime rate in 1991: 67.5
Violent crime rate in 1991: 5.2
Physicians rate in 1992: 1.56
Hospital bed rate in 1991: 5.43

ACCRA Cost of Living Indexes

(First quarter 1993, average = 100)
Composite index: N/A
Utilities index: N/A
Housing index: N/A

Population (1990)

Total Population and Growth Rate
1990: 156,267
1980: 130,015
1970: 107,702
Growth rate 1970–1990: 45%

Race and Hispanic Origin
White: 79.4%
Black: 18.6%
Asian/Pacific Islander: 1.5%
Native American: 0.2%
Hispanic origin: 1.3%
White not Hispanic: 78.6%

Age
Ages 18 to 20: 9.6%

Ages 21 to 24: 11%
Ages 25 to 44: 30.8%
Ages 45 to 54: 9.2%
Ages 55 to 59: 3.5%
Ages 60 to 64: 3.2%
Ages 65 plus: 9.7%

Educational Attainment (1990)

Percent having completed high school: 69.6%
Percent having completed college: 26.0%
Elementary and high school enrollment: 23,490

Federal Funds and Grants Received

Total received in 1989: $362,200,000
Funds received per capita: $2,503

Civilian Labor Force

1993 (April): 77,604
1992 average: 75,980
1991 average: 76,389
1990 average: 77,202

Unemployment

1993 (April): 3.8%
1992 average: 5.6%
1991 average: 3.9%
1990 average: 4.5%

Average Annual Pay

1988: $17,819
1987: $16,989
1985: $15,393

Per Capita Personal Income

1991: $15,428
1990: $15,028
1989: $14,202

Business Climate (1987)

Manufacturing

Number of establishments in 1987: 197
Shipments in 1987 ($1,000): $1,338,900
Employees in 1987: 15,400
Change in employment, 1982 to 1987: 9.2%
Average annual pay for manufacturing work in 1989: $18,244
Average annual pay for production work in 1987: $14,198

Wholesale Trade

Number of establishments in 1987: 218
Total sales in 1987 ($1,000): $894,700
Change in sales, 1982 to 1987: 47.7%

Retail Trade

Number of establishments in 1987: 994
Total sales in 1987 ($1,000): $894,700
Retail sales per household in 1987: $15,998
Average annual pay in 1989: $9,709

Service Industry

Selected receipts in 1987 ($1,000): $236,800

Average annual pay in 1989: $16,939

Housing

Total number of units in 1990: 62,735
Occupied units in 1990: 57,787
Owner-occupied units in 1990: 58.6%
1993 ACCRA average cost: N/A
1993 ACCRA average rent for an apartment: N/A

Chamber of Commerce

Athens Area Chamber of Commerce, Thomas B. Glaser, Exec. Director, PO Box 948, 220 College Ave. #7, Athens, GA 30601. 404-549-6800, FAX 404-549-5636

Major Companies

Company	SIC	Telephone
Allen, Heyward Motor Co., Inc.	5511	(404) 549-8580
Athens Federal Saving Bank	6035	(404) 357-7000
Craven's Pottery Inc.	5199	(404) 335-5984
Farmer, Leon and Co.	5181	(404) 353-1166
Golden Pantry Food Stores	5541	(404) 549-4945
Hospital Authority Clarke	8062	(404) 549-9977
Jackson Electric Membership Co.	4911	(404) 367-5281
Loef Co. Inc.	5093	(404) 549-6700
Seaboard Farms of Athens	2015	(404) 543-8700
Terry/Salloum Construction Co., Inc.	1541	(404) 548-1343
Trust Co. Bank Georgia	6021	(404) 354-5200
UCR Inc.	7359	(404) 353-2539

Colleges and Universities

University of Georgia, Athens

ATLANTA, GA (MSA)

Geographic Profile

Land Area
5121.5 square miles

Counties and Parishes
Barrow
Butts
Cherokee
Clayton
Cobb
Coweta
DeKalb
Douglas
Fayette
Forsyth
Fulton
Gwinnett
Henry
Newton
Paulding
Rockdale
Spalding
Walton

Places
Marietta

Ranking Highlights
12 *out of 319 in total* **land area**
49 *out of 319 in* **population growth**, *1970–1990*
128 *out of 310 in having the lowest* **unemployment** *rate*
9 *out of 310 in size of* **labor force**
42 *out of 318 in the percentage of* **college graduates**
46 *out of 292 in per capita personal* **income**
14 *out of 319 in number of* **manufacturing establishments**
107 *out of 318 in* **physicians** *per 1000 people*
195 *out of 318 in* **hospital beds** *per 1000 people*
235 *out of 267 in fewest* **crimes** *per 1000 people*
226 *out of 266 in fewest* **violent crimes** *per 1000 people*
208 *out of 319 in per capita* **federal funds and grants**

Quality of Life Indexes (Rate per 1000 population)
Crime rate in 1991:	83.2
Violent crime rate in 1991:	9.9
Physicians rate in 1992:	2.09
Hospital bed rate in 1991:	3.47

ACCRA Cost of Living Indexes
(First quarter 1993, average = 100)
Composite index:	98.6
Utilities index:	109.6
Housing index:	96.3

Overview
Georgia's capital and largest city, Atlanta is the major financial and cultural force, as well as the transportation hub, of a seven-state southeastern region that includes Georgia, Alabama, Florida, Mississippi, North Carolina, South Carolina, and Tennessee. In November 1991 *Fortune* magazine named Atlanta the "Best City of Business" in the United States.

While the Coca-Cola Company wields considerable influence in Atlanta—much of it in areas outside its immediate manufacturing concerns—no single industry or firm truly dominates the local economy. Service industries employ the largest number of workers, but trade and manufacturing are also important elements. Having such diversity, Atlanta has been slower to suffer a downturn and quicker to recover from any temporary setback than many other major American cities. More than 730 of the *Fortune* 1000 companies have offices in the city.

Atlanta's economy will be bolstered by its being chosen the host city of the 1996 Centennial Summer Olympic Games. This is expected to have a $3.5 billion economic impact on Atlanta, with more than $500 million of construction slated to be completed by 1995.

Easy access to the city, a good public transportation system, an abundance of hotel rooms (more than forty thousand in the entire metropolitan area, some thirteen thousand of which are downtown), and a mild climate have combined to make Atlanta one of the leading convention centers in the United States, by most accounts ranking just behind Chicago and New York City.

Often referred to as Atlanta's number-one economic asset, Hartsfield International Airport is one of the world's busiest transfer hubs. The huge, ultramodern facility, only 10 miles from downtown, is served by more than 20 passenger airlines that fly non-stop to more than 115 cities. Various international carriers offer non-stop service to London, Paris, Brussels, Frankfurt, Amsterdam, Mexico, and the Caribbean area. Terminals are connected by an automated underground train system. General aviation facilities in the Atlanta area number 19 (including Hartsfield).

Three major interstates—I-75, I-20, and I-85—route traffic into and out of Atlanta, making it one of the leading interstate highways centers in the nation.

Population (1990)

Total Population and Growth Rate
1990: 2,833,511
1980: 2,138,136
1970: 1,684,200
Growth rate 1970–1990: 68%

Race and Hispanic Origin
White: 71.3%
Black: 26.0%
Asian/Pacific Islander: 1.8%

Native American: 0.2%
Hispanic origin: 2.0%
White not Hispanic: 70.1%

Age
Ages 18 to 20: 4.5%
Ages 21 to 24: 6.4%
Ages 25 to 44: 37.7%
Ages 45 to 54: 10.7%
Ages 55 to 59: 3.7%
Ages 60 to 64: 3.2%
Ages 65 plus: 7.9%

Educational Attainment (1990)
Percent having completed high school: 79.5%
Percent having completed college: 26.8%
Elementary and high school enrollment: 475,880

Federal Funds and Grants Received
Total received in 1989: $7,398,300,000
Funds received per capita: $2,703

Civilian Labor Force
1993 (April): 1,580,694
1992 average: 1,534,846
1991 average: 1,505,125
1990 average: 1,524,861

Unemployment
1993 (April): 4.8%
1992 average: 6.5%
1991 average: 4.7%
1990 average: 5.1%

Average Annual Pay
1988: $23,445
1987: $22,426
1985: $20,264

Per Capita Personal Income
1991: $20,304
1990: $20,042
1989: $19,133

Business Climate (1987)
Manufacturing
Number of establishments in 1987: 3,878
Shipments in 1987 ($1,000): $28,085,700
Employees in 1987: 200,400
Change in employment, 1982 to 1987: 21.7%
Average annual pay for manufacturing work in 1989: $27,288
Average annual pay for production work in 1987: $21,042

Wholesale Trade
Number of establishments in 1987: 7,963
Total sales in 1987 ($1,000): $69,999,900
Change in sales, 1982 to 1987: 66.1%

Retail Trade
Number of establishments in 1987: 16,683
Total sales in 1987 ($1,000): $69,999,900
Retail sales per household in 1987: $20,938
Average annual pay in 1989: $13,403

Service Industry
Selected receipts in 1987 ($1,000): $12,938,200
Average annual pay in 1989: $22,555

Office Real Estate (1992)
Office space inventory: 97,144,035 square feet
Average class A Central Business District rental range per sq. ft: $22.51

Vacancy Rates
All areas: 14.9%

Vacancy Rates in Central Business District
Class A space: 16.7%
Class B space: N/A

Vacancy Rates Outside Central Business District
Class A space: 14.0%
Class B space: N/A

Housing
Total number of units in 1990: 1,174,007
Occupied units in 1990: 1,056,427
Owner-occupied units in 1990: 62.3%
1993 ACCRA average cost: $106,220
1993 ACCRA average rent for an apartment: $549

Chamber of Commerce
Atlanta Area Chamber of Commerce, Gerald L. Bartels, President, 235 International Blvd. N.W., PO Box 1740, Atlanta, GA 30301. 404-880-9000, FAX 404-586-8464

Economic Development Office
Atlanta Economic Development Corp., Walter R. Huntley Jr., President, 230 Peachtree St. #1650, Atlanta, GA 30303. 404-325-7000

Economic Development Organizations
Fulton County Development Authority, C. Clayton Powell, Chairman, 10 Park Place S. #205, Atlanta, GA 30303. 404-730-8083

Southern Industry Development Council, Robert B. Cassell, Exec. Director, 1649 Tullie Circle N.E. #105, Atlanta, GA. 30329. 404-636-0969

Major Companies

Company	SIC	Telephone
Alumax Inc.	3334	(404) 246-6600
Amoco Fabrics Fibers Co.	3069	(404) 956-9025
Apac Holdings Inc.	1611	(404) 261-2610
Ashland Engineering & Construction	8711	(404) 261-2610
Atec Inc.	8711	(404) 261-2610
Atlanta Gas Light Co.	4924	(404) 584-4000
Bellsouth Corp.	4813	(404) 249-2000
Blue Cross & Blue Shield	6324	(404) 842-8000

Major Companies (Continued)

Company	SIC	Telephone
Charter Brook Hospital Inc.	8062	(404) 457-8315
Citizens and Southern Georgia	6162	(404) 581-2121
Coca-Cola Co. Inc.	2087	(404) 676-2121
Coca-Cola Enterprises Inc.	2086	(404) 676-2100
Contel Corp.	4813	(404) 391-8000
Cox Enterprises Inc.	2711	(404) 843-5000
CSR America Inc.	3273	(404) 237-8811
Delta Air Lines Inc.	4512	(404) 765-2600
Equifax Inc.	6411	(404) 885-8000
Federal Home Loan Bank of Atlanta	6111	(404) 888-8000
Federal Reserve Bank Atlanta	6011	(404) 521-8500
First Atlanta Corp.	6712	(404) 332-5000
First Financial Mortgage Corp.	7374	(404) 321-0120
First National Bank of Atlanta	6021	(404) 332-5000
Fuqua Industries Inc.	7384	(404) 658-9000
Georgia Gulf Corp.	2812	(404) 395-4500
Georgia Power Co.	4911	(404) 526-6526
Georgia-Pacific Corp.	2436	(404) 521-4000
Gold Kist Inc.	2015	(404) 393-5000
Great Northern Nekoosa Co.	2621	(404) 521-4000
Home Depot Inc.	5211	(404) 433-8211
Hooker, L. J. Corp. Inc.	6552	(404) 329-0007
Lanier Worldwide Inc.	3579	(404) 496-9500
Macy's South Inc.	5311	(404) 221-7509
Manheim Auction	5012	(404) 843-5000
Massachusetts Indemnity	6321	(404) 381-1000
National Service Industries	3646	(404) 853-1000
Nekoosa Packaging Corp.	2653	(404) 521-4000
Oglethorpe Power Corp.	4911	(404) 270-7600
Oxford Industries Inc.	2311	(404) 659-2424
Racetrac Petroleum Inc.	5411	(404) 431-7600
Rock-Tenn Co.	2631	(404) 448-2193
Scientific-Atlanta Inc.	3663	(404) 441-4000
Sewell Plastics Inc.	3089	(404) 691-4256
Southern Bell Telephone Telegraph Co.	4813	(404) 529-2526
Southern Railway Co.	4011	(404) 529-1000
Telecom USA Inc.	4813	(404) 250-5500
Trust Co. of Georgia	6712	(404) 588-7711
Turner Broadcasting System	4833	(404) 827-1700
Williams, A. L. Corp.	6311	(404) 381-1674

Colleges and Universities

American College for the Applied Arts, Atlanta
Art Institute of Atlanta, Atlanta
Atlanta College of Art, Atlanta
Atlanta Metropolitan College, Atlanta
Balin Institute of Technology, Atlanta
Bauder Fashion College, Atlanta
Clark Atlanta University, Atlanta

Emory University, Atlanta
Georgia Institute of Technology, Atlanta
Georgia State University, Atlanta
Gupton-Jones College of Funeral Service, Atlanta
Kennesaw State College, Marietta
Massey Business College, Atlanta
Mercer University Atlanta, Atlanta
Morehouse College, Atlanta
Morris Brown College, Atlanta
Oglethorpe University, Atlanta
Southern College of Technology, Marietta
Spelman College, Atlanta

AUGUSTA, GA-SC (MSA)

Geographic Profile

Land Area
1947.0 square miles

Counties and Parishes
Georgia:
Columbia
McDuffie
Richmond
South Carolina:
Aiken

Places
None

Ranking Highlights

  95 *out of 319 in total* **land area**
110 *out of 319 in* **population growth,** *1970–1990*
121 *out of 310 in having the lowest* **unemployment** *rate*
110 *out of 310 in size of* **labor force**
175 *out of 318 in the percentage of* **college graduates**
172 *out of 292 in per capita personal* **income**
151 *out of 319 in number of* **manufacturing establishments**
  20 *out of 318 in* **physicians** *per 1000 people*
  73 *out of 318 in* **hospital beds** *per 1000 people*
189 *out of 267 in fewest* **crimes** *per 1000 people*
173 *out of 266 in fewest* **violent crimes** *per 1000 people*
   8 *out of 319 in per capita* **federal funds and grants**

Quality of Life Indexes (Rate per 1000 population)

Crime rate in 1991:	70.2
Violent crime rate in 1991:	7.5
Physicians rate in 1992:	3.29
Hospital bed rate in 1991:	5.09

ACCRA Cost of Living Indexes
(First quarter 1993, average = 100)
Composite index: 97.2
Utilities index: 103.2
Housing index: 96.1

Overview
Stretched between Georgia and South Carolina.

Population (1990)

Total Population and Growth Rate
1990: 396,809
1980: 345,923
1970: 291,063
Growth rate 1970–1990: 36%

Race and Hispanic Origin
White: 66.7%
Black: 31.1%
Asian/Pacific Islander: 1.4%
Native American: 0.2%
Hispanic origin: 1.4%
White not Hispanic: 66.0%

Age
Ages 18 to 20: 5.1%
Ages 21 to 24: 6%
Ages 25 to 44: 33.1%
Ages 45 to 54: 9.9%
Ages 55 to 59: 4.2%
Ages 60 to 64: 3.9%
Ages 65 plus: 9.9%

Educational Attainment (1990)
Percent having completed high school: 71.8%
Percent having completed college: 18.0%
Elementary and high school enrollment: 74,817

Federal Funds and Grants Received
Total received in 1989: $3,240,100,000
Funds received per capita: $8,173

Civilian Labor Force
1993 (April): 201,736
1992 average: 200,513
1991 average: 199,891
1990 average: 199,433

Unemployment
1993 (April): 5.9%
1992 average: 6.4%
1991 average: 4.7%
1990 average: 4.4%

Average Annual Pay
1988: $19,846
1987: $19,008
1985: $17,573

Per Capita Personal Income
1991: $16,792
1990: $16,483
1989: $15,201

Business Climate (1987)

Manufacturing
Number of establishments in 1987: 347
Shipments in 1987 ($1,000): $5,047,900
Employees in 1987: 38,900
Change in employment, 1982 to 1987: 5.4%
Average annual pay for manufacturing work in 1989: $31,267
Average annual pay for production work in 1987: $21,273

Wholesale Trade
Number of establishments in 1987: 476
Total sales in 1987 ($1,000): $1,361,600
Change in sales, 1982 to 1987: 32.7%

Retail Trade
Number of establishments in 1987: 2,313
Total sales in 1987 ($1,000): $1,361,600

Retail sales per household in 1987: $16,803
Average annual pay in 1989: $10,394

Service Industry
Selected receipts in 1987 ($1,000): $883,600
Average annual pay in 1989: $17,962

Housing
Total number of units in 1990: 158,342
Occupied units in 1990: 142,669
Owner-occupied units in 1990: 66.3%
1993 ACCRA average cost: $115,750
1993 ACCRA average rent for an apartment: $409

Chamber of Commerce
Metro Augusta Chamber of Commerce, Albert M. Hodge, Jr., President, 600 Broad St. Plaza, PO Box 657, Augusta, GA 30913. 404-821-1300, FAX 404-821-1330

Major Companies

Company	SIC	Telephone
A. B. Beverage Co. Inc.	5181	(404) 724-5449
American Yard Products Inc.	3524	(404) 724-0822
Augusta Newsprint Co.	2621	(404) 798-3440
Augusta Sportwear Inc.	2329	(404) 860-4633
Bankers First Corp.	6036	(404) 823-3200
Beard, Bob Ford Inc.	5511	(404) 736-3351
Boardman Petroleum Inc.	5172	(404) 736-6466
Boral Bricks Inc.	3251	(404) 722-6831
Carole Fabrics Inc.	2221	(404) 863-4742
Clearwater Finishing Inc.	2396	(803) 593-2521
DSM Chemical Augusta Inc.	2819	(404) 823-4240
Duke Buick Inc.	5511	(404) 722-0482
Fairway Ford of Augusta	5511	(404) 722-5371
First of Georgia Insurance	6331	(404) 738-0111
Forest Sales Corp.	5031	(404) 738-7786
G IW Industries Inc.	3561	(404) 863-1011
Graniteville Co.	2211	(803) 663-7231
Jones, Gerald Volkswagen	5511	(404) 738-2561
Kalmia Motors Inc.	5511	(803) 648-1301
Maxxon, R. & H. Inc.	5541	(803) 648-0458
McKnight Construction Co.	1542	(404) 863-7784
Merry Land & Investment Co.	6726	(404) 722-6756
Morris Communications Corp.	2711	(404) 724-0851
Richards, Bob Chevrolet Co.	5511	(404) 733-9411
Ruben, Milton Chevrolet Inc.	5511	(404) 868-0588
Shapiro Packing Co. Inc.	2011	(404) 722-2694
St. Joseph Hospital of Augusta	8062	(404) 737-7400
Taylor Toyota Inc.	5511	(803) 279-8400
Thermal Ceramics Inc.	3255	(404) 796-4200
Trans-Fleet Enterprises Inc/	7363	(404) 863-8143
Tranter Inc.	3443	(404) 738-7900
University Health Inc.	8062	(404) 722-9011
White, J.B. & Co.	5311	(404) 790-7070
Wyndham Baking Co., Inc.	2052	(404) 798-8600

Colleges and Universities
Augusta College, Augusta, GA
Medical College of Georgia, Augusta, GA
Paine College, Augusta, GA
Phillips College, Augusta, GA

COLUMBUS, GA–AL (MSA)

Geographic Profile

Land Area

1106.3 square miles

Counties and Parishes

Alabama:

Russell

Georgia:

Chattahoochee

Muscogee

Ranking Highlights

183 *out of 319 in total* **land area**

263 *out of 319 in* **population growth,** *1970–1990*

184 *out of 310 in having the lowest* **unemployment** *rate*

187 *out of 310 in size of* **labor force**

233 *out of 318 in the percentage of* **college graduates**

238 *out of 292 in per capita personal* **income**

217 *out of 319 in number of* **manufacturing establishments**

225 *out of 318 in* **physicians** *per 1000 people*

36 *out of 318 in* **hospital beds** *per 1000 people*

125 *out of 267 in fewest* **crimes** *per 1000 people*

126 *out of 266 in fewest* **violent crimes** *per 1000 people*

31 *out of 319 in per capita* **federal funds and grants**

Quality of Life Indexes (Rate per 1000 population)

Crime rate in 1991:	58.9
Violent crime rate in 1991:	6.4
Physicians rate in 1992:	1.53
Hospital bed rate in 1991:	5.77

ACCRA Cost of Living Indexes

(First quarter 1993, average = 100)

Composite index:	95.3
Utilities index:	98.5
Housing index:	91.0

Population (1990)

Total Population and Growth Rate

1990: 243,072

1980: 239,196

1970: 238,584

Growth rate 1970–1990: 2%

Race and Hispanic Origin

White: 59.4%

Black: 37.6%

Asian/Pacific Islander: 1.3%

Native American: 0.3%

Hispanic origin: 3.0%

White not Hispanic: 58.1%

Age

Ages 18 to 20: 6.1%

Ages 21 to 24: 7.4%

Ages 25 to 44: 31.7%

Ages 45 to 54: 9%

Ages 55 to 59: 4.2%

Ages 60 to 64: 4.1%

Ages 65 plus: 10.5%

Educational Attainment (1990)

Percent having completed high school: 69.4%

Percent having completed college: 15.1%

Elementary and high school enrollment: 42,072

Federal Funds and Grants Received

Total received in 1989: $1,306,800,000

Funds received per capita: $5,293

Civilian Labor Force

1993 (April): 101,293

1992 average: 100,095

1991 average: 97,610

1990 average: 99,961

Unemployment

1993 (April): 5.8%

1992 average: 7.3%

1991 average: 5.4%

1990 average: 6.1%

Average Annual Pay

1988: $17,368

1987: $17,004

1985: $15,291

Per Capita Personal Income

1991: $15,401

1990: $15,028

1989: $14,111

Business Climate (1987)

Manufacturing

Number of establishments in 1987: 204

Shipments in 1987 ($1,000): $2,364,500

Employees in 1987: 19,800

Change in employment, 1982 to 1987: -2.5%

Average annual pay for manufacturing work in 1989: $21,817

Average annual pay for production work in 1987: $18,378

Wholesale Trade

Number of establishments in 1987: 301

Total sales in 1987 ($1,000): $932,700

Change in sales, 1982 to 1987: 0%

Retail Trade

Number of establishments in 1987: 1,485

Total sales in 1987 ($1,000): $932,700

Retail sales per household in 1987: $16,671

Average annual pay in 1989: $10,641

Service Industry

Selected receipts in 1987 ($1,000): $515,500

Average annual pay in 1989: $15,927

Housing
Total number of units in 1990: 93,643
Occupied units in 1990: 86,241
Owner-occupied units in 1990: 55.0%
1993 ACCRA average cost: $104,500
1993 ACCRA average rent for an apartment: $444

Chamber of Commerce
Columbus Chamber of Commerce, F. Michael Gaymon, President, 1 Arsenal Place, 901 Front Ave., PO Box 1200, Columbus, GA 31902-1200. 404-327-1566, FAX 404-327-7512

Major Companies

Company	SIC	Telephone
American Family Corp.	6321	(404) 323-3431
American Family Life Assurance Co.	6321	(404) 323-3431
Bradley, W. C. Co.	3631	(404) 571-6042
Burnham Service Co.	4213	(404) 563-1120
Burnham Service Corp.	4213	(404) 563-1120
Carmike Cinemas Inc.	7832	(404) 576-3400
Columbus Foundries Inc.	3321	(404) 323-5221
Columbus Mills Inc.	2273	(404) 324-0111
Columbus Regional Health Center Systems	7389	(404) 571-1250
Communicorp Inc.	2752	(404) 324-1182
Flournoy Construction Co.	1522	(404) 324-4000
Flournoy Development Co.	6552	(404) 324-4000
Hardaway Co. Inc.	1611	(404) 322-3274
Heard, Bill Enterprises	5511	(404) 561-6213
Heard, Bill Chevrolet Inc.	5511	(404) 322-8881
Jay Pontiac - GMC Truck	5511	(404) 324-1234
Jordan Co. Inc.	6552	(404) 649-3000
Lummus Industries Inc.	3559	(404) 322-4511
Medical Center Inc.	8062	(404) 571-1000
Phoenix Medical Park Hospital	8062	(205) 291-8000
Plicon Corp.	2671	(404) 327-0234
Preacher Goolsby Inc.	5411	(404) 563-4357
R-P Packaging Inc.	2671	(404) 327-0234
Riverside Buick-Cadillac	5511	(404) 322-7301
Southeast Canners Inc.	2086	(404) 324-0040
St. Francis Hospital Inc.	8062	(404) 322-8281
Synovus Financial Corp.	6022	(404) 649-2311
Tom's Foods Inc.	2064	(404) 323-2721
Total System Services, Inc.	7374	(404) 649-2204

Colleges and Universities
Columbus College, Columbus, GA
Meadows Junior College, Columbus, GA
Phillips College, Columbus, GA

MACON–WARNER ROBINS, GA (MSA)

Geographic Profile
Land Area
1171.7 square miles

Counties and Parishes
Bibb
Houston
Jones
Peach

Ranking Highlights
171 *out of 319 in total* land area
175 *out of 319 in* population growth, *1970–1990*
117 *out of 310 in having the lowest* unemployment *rate*
157 *out of 310 in size of* labor force
216 *out of 318 in the percentage of* college graduates
181 *out of 292 in per capita personal* income
181 *out of 319 in number of* manufacturing establishments
134 *out of 318 in* physicians *per 1000 people*
96 *out of 318 in* hospital beds *per 1000 people*
145 *out of 267 in fewest* crimes *per 1000 people*
123 *out of 266 in fewest* violent crimes *per 1000 people*
40 *out of 319 in per capita* federal funds and grants

Quality of Life Indexes (Rate per 1000 population)
Crime rate in 1991:   62.2
Violent crime rate in 1991: 5.7
Physicians rate in 1992:   1.91
Hospital bed rate in 1991:   4.68

ACCRA Cost of Living Indexes
(First quarter 1993, average = 100)
Composite index: 99.1
Utilities index: 104.2
Housing index: 95.2

Population (1990)
Total Population and Growth Rate
1990: 281,103
1980: 263,591
1970: 234,550
Growth rate 1970–1990: 20%

Race and Hispanic Origin
White: 64.2%
Black: 34.6%
Asian/Pacific Islander: 0.7%
Native American: 0.2%
Hispanic origin: 1.0%
White not Hispanic: 63.6%

Age
Ages 18 to 20: 4.9%
Ages 21 to 24: 5.9%

Ages 25 to 44: 32.3%
Ages 45 to 54: 10.3%
Ages 55 to 59: 4.4%
Ages 60 to 64: 4%
Ages 65 plus: 10.8%

Educational Attainment (1990)
Percent having completed high school: 71.9%
Percent having completed college: 16.2%
Elementary and high school enrollment: 52,192

Federal Funds and Grants Received
Total received in 1989: $1,433,000,000
Funds received per capita: $4,997

Civilian Labor Force
1993 (April): 131,927
1992 average: 131,850
1991 average: 131,664
1990 average: 134,394

Unemployment
1993 (April): 5.1%
1992 average: 6.3%
1991 average: 4.2%
1990 average: 4.8%

Average Annual Pay
1988: $19,709
1987: $18,983
1985: $17,671

Per Capita Personal Income
1991: $16,611
1990: $16,157
1989: $15,394

Business Climate (1987)
Manufacturing
Number of establishments in 1987: 262
Shipments in 1987 ($1,000): $3,884,600
Employees in 1987: 18,700
Change in employment, 1982 to 1987: 5.6%
Average annual pay for manufacturing work in 1989: $28,047
Average annual pay for production work in 1987: $23,591

Wholesale Trade
Number of establishments in 1987: 431
Total sales in 1987 ($1,000): $1,423,400
Change in sales, 1982 to 1987: 0%

Retail Trade
Number of establishments in 1987: 1,855
Total sales in 1987 ($1,000): $1,423,400
Retail sales per household in 1987: $18,318
Average annual pay in 1989: $10,726

Service Industry
Selected receipts in 1987 ($1,000): $701,900
Average annual pay in 1989: $18,367

Housing
Total number of units in 1990: 111,506
Occupied units in 1990: 103,182
Owner-occupied units in 1990: 62.6%
1993 ACCRA average cost: $107,917
1993 ACCRA average rent for an apartment: $492

Chamber of Commerce
Greater Macon Chamber of Commerce, Paul Nagle, President, 305 Coliseum Dr., PO Box 169, Macon, GA 31298. 912-741-8000, FAX 912-741-8021

Economic Development Office
Warner Robins Area Chamber of Commerce, Alfred C. Walden, Exec. Vice President, 1420 Watson Blvd., Warner Robins, GA 31093. 912-922-8585, FAX 912-328-7745

Economic Development Organizations
Middle Georgia Regional Development Center, James Tonn, Exec. Director, 600 Grand Bldg., 661 Mulberry St., Macon, GA 31201. 912-751-6160, FAX 912-751-6517

Houston County Development Authority, Eric Newson, Exec. Director, 200 Carl Vinson Parkway, Warner Robins, GA 31056. 912-922-4471

Major Companies

Company	SIC	Telephone
Bank South Macon Inc.	6022	(912) 749-9300
Bearings & Drives Inc.	5085	(912) 743-6711
Belk-Matthews Co. of Macon	5311	(912) 477-2355
Bibb Co. Inc.	2211	(912) 752-6700
Boeing Georgia Inc.	3728	(912) 781-3000
GEC Automation Projects	3625	(912) 784-5200
Georgia Farm Bureau	6331	(912) 474-8411
Houston County Hospital Authority	8062	(912) 922-4281
LJL Truck Center Inc.	5012	(912) 784-3100
Macon-Bibb County Hospital Authority	8062	(912) 744-1000
Mellco Inc.	2491	(912) 987-5040
Restaurant Management Service	5812	(912) 474-5633
Security Trust Life Insuramce Co.	6311	(912) 741-2500
Shallowford Community Hospital	8062	(912) 742-1161
Smith & Sons Foods Inc.	5812	(912) 745-4759
Texprint Georgia Inc.	2262	(912) 743-0321
Tolleson Lumber Co., Inc.	2491	(912) 987-2105
Wiggins Ed Ford Lincoln-Mercury	5511	(912) 922-9131

Colleges and Universities
Crandall Junior College, Macon
Macon College, Macon
Mercer University, Macon

SAVANNAH, GA (MSA)

Geographic Profile

Land Area

919.9 square miles

Counties and Parishes

Chatham

Effingham

Ranking Highlights

215 *out of 319 in total* land area

174 *out of 319 in* population growth, *1970–1990*

139 *out of 310 in having the lowest* unemployment *rate*

169 *out of 310 in size of* labor force

183 *out of 318 in the percentage of* college graduates

152 *out of 292 in per capita personal* income

191 *out of 319 in number of* manufacturing establishments

114 *out of 318 in* physicians *per 1000 people*

81 *out of 318 in* hospital beds *per 1000 people*

276 *out of 267 in fewest* crimes *per 1000 people*

193 *out of 266 in fewest* violent crimes *per 1000 people*

71 *out of 319 in per capita* federal funds and grants

Quality of Life Indexes (Rate per 1000 population)

Crime rate in 1991:	79.5
Violent crime rate in 1991:	8.4
Physicians rate in 1992:	2.05
Hospital bed rate in 1991:	4.98

ACCRA Cost of Living Indexes

(First quarter 1993, average = 100)

Composite index:	N/A
Utilities index:	N/A
Housing index:	N/A

Overview

According to the Savannah Area Chamber of Commerce, Savannah has a four-tiered economy consisting of manufacturing and industry, retail sales, the Port of Savannah, and tourism. Manufacturing is the largest part of the economy, with 164 factories with an annual payroll exceeding $500 million. The largest plants include Union Camp, the largest producer of paper for paper bags in the United States; Gulfstream Aerospace, an executive jet aircraft manufacturer; Great Dane Trailers, which makes large truck trailers; and Savannah Foods, a sugar refinery. Savannah, with more than forty shopping centers and malls, is the retail center for a six-county area. In 1991, it had $1.78 billion in retail sales, up from $1.75 billion in 1990. The shipping and distribution industry remains another vital element of the economic mix. The Port of Savannah saw the number of ships increase from 1,678 in 1990 to 1,883 in 1991, and customs collected were $202.8 million. Tourism is an active and rapidly growing segment of the economy. The city's attractiveness as a visitor destination is enhanced by its charming historic district, accommodations and accessibility. In 1991 more than five million visitors spent $580 million, accounting for sixteen thousand jobs locally.

The military plays an important role in the economic health of the city as well. The U.S. Army 24th Infantry Division is headquartered in nearby Liberty County, forty miles away. The base has 14,800 soldiers and thirty-two hundred civilians at Fort Stewart. The command extends to Hunter Army Airfield in Savannah with four thousand soldiers and eight hundred civilians. Fort Stewart/Hunter, the largest Army base east of the Mississippi River, is coastal Georgia's largest employer, and spending exceeds $700 million per year. In addition, Savannah benefits from the District Corps of Engineers, the Army National Guard, Military Reserves, Coast Guard, and other guard and reserve units which contribute another $70 million in spending, although overall reduction is expected throughout the 1990s.

Savannah International Airport has almost seventy flights daily on American, Delta, US Air, United, United Express, ComAir, Florida Gulf, and Key Airlines (which chose Savannah as its hub in 1991). Key Airlines operates six nonstop international charter flights almost daily to eleven international destinations including Cancun and Aruba. International travelers are served by Customs, Immigration, Agriculture, and Public Health officers at the airport. The airport has ten air cargo services and Foreign Trade Zone #104 is located at the airport.

The Georgia Ports Authority added eight new shipping lines in 1991 and is scheduled to begin an $88 million expansion program in 1993. In 1990 the ports processed 16.6 million net tons. There are 119 motor carriers in Savannah, thirty freight forwarders and twenty-three customs brokers.

Interstate Highway 95 runs north and south just west of the city, and I-16 comes from the west and stops at the city's center.

Population (1990)

Total Population and Growth Rate

1990: 242,622

1980: 220,553

1970: 201,448

Growth rate 1970–1990: 20%

Race and Hispanic Origin

White: 62.9%

Black: 35.5%

Asian/Pacific Islander: 1.0%

Native American: 0.2%

Hispanic origin: 1.2%

White not Hispanic: 62.2%

Age

Ages 18 to 20: 4.8%

Ages 21 to 24: 6.2%

Ages 25 to 44: 31.8%

Ages 45 to 54: 9.7%
Ages 55 to 59: 4.1%
Ages 60 to 64: 4.3%
Ages 65 plus: 12.2%

Educational Attainment (1990)
Percent having completed high school: 72.9%
Percent having completed college: 17.5%
Elementary and high school enrollment: 43,506

Federal Funds and Grants Received
Total received in 1989: $992,800,000
Funds received per capita: 4,063

Civilian Labor Force
1993 (April): 122,368
1992 average: 119,037
1991 average: 116,073
1990 average: 117,405

Unemployment
1993 (April): 5.0%
1992 average: 6.6%
1991 average: 4.4%
1990 average: 4.9%

Average Annual Pay
1988: $19,452
1987: $18,999
1985: $17,377

Per Capita Personal Income
1991: $17,161
1990: $16,873
1989: $15,995

Business Climate (1987)
Manufacturing
Number of establishments in 1987: 244
Shipments in 1987 ($1,000): $3,194,500
Employees in 1987: 15,900
Change in employment, 1982 to 1987: 4.6%
Average annual pay for manufacturing work in 1989: $29,230
Average annual pay for production work in 1987: $25,298

Wholesale Trade
Number of establishments in 1987: 464
Total sales in 1987 ($1,000): $1,752,500
Change in sales, 1982 to 1987: 3.0%

Retail Trade
Number of establishments in 1987: 1,657
Total sales in 1987 ($1,000): $1,752,500
Retail sales per household in 1987: $18,666
Average annual pay in 1989: $10,720

Service Industry
Selected receipts in 1987 ($1,000): $625,800
Average annual pay in 1989: $19,157

Housing
Total number of units in 1990: 100,670
Occupied units in 1990: 89,870
Owner-occupied units in 1990: 60.8%
1993 ACCRA average cost: N/A
1993 ACCRA average rent for an apartment: N/A

Chamber of Commerce
Savannah Area Chamber of Commerce, Alan Beals, President, 222 W. Oglethorpe Ave., Savannah, GA 31401. 912-944-0444, FAX 912-944-0468

Major Companies

Company	SIC	Telephone
Aminco Inc.	2844	(912) 651-3400
Anderson, M. C.	1611	(912) 964-5712
Atlantic Wood Industries	2491	(912) 964-1234
Branigar Organization Inc.	6552	(912) 354-4885
Brasseler U. S. A. Inc.	5999	(912) 925-8525
Builderama Inc.	5211	(912) 927-3115
Candler General Hospital	8062	(912) 356-6152
Candler Health Services Inc.	8062	(912) 356-6152
Carson Products Co.	2844	(912) 651-3400
Center Brothers Inc.	1742	(912) 232-6491
Citizens and Southern National	6021	(912) 944-3000
Coastal Motors Sales Inc.	5511	(912) 927-1234
Colonial Oil Industries Inc.	5171	(912) 236-1331
Concorde Finance & Investments	5052	(912) 756-3990
Enmark Stations Inc.	5541	(912) 236-1331
Great Dane Trailers Inc.	3715	(912) 232-4471
Gulfstream Aerospace Corp.	3721	(912) 964-3000
Intermarine USA	3731	(912) 234-6579
Interredec Inc.	5052	(912) 756-3990
Kemira Inc.	2816	(912) 236-6171
Savannah Electric & Power Co.	4911	(912) 232-7171
Savannah Foods & Industries	2062	(912) 234-1261
Sheftall Ben Distributing	5122	(912) 236-9595
Solomons Co., Inc.	5122	(912) 234-7204
St. Joseph's Hospital	8062	(912) 925-4100
TIC-The Indus Co. Southeast	1629	(912) 234-2266
Time Saver Inc.	5411	(912) 651-8000

Colleges and Universities
Armstrong State College, Savannah
Savannah College of Art and Design, Savannah
Savannah State College, Savannah
South College, Savannah

HAWAII

o

Honolulu

HONOLULU (MSA)

HAWAII

Population
1990: 1,108,229
1980: 964,691

Age
Ages 18 to 20: 48,549
Ages 21 to 24: 72,636
Ages 25 to 44: 379,035
Ages 45 to 54: 108,775
Ages 55 to 59: 45,375
Ages 60 to 64: 48,728
Median age: 32.6

Race
White: 369,616
Black: 27,195
Asian/Pacific Islander: 685,236
Native American: 5,099
Hispanic origin: 81,390

Households
Total: 356,267
Persons per household: 3.01

Sex
Male: 563,891
Female: 544,338

Population Migration
Domestic migration: 93,000
International migration: 77,000

Projection of the Population in 1995
Total: 1,226,000
18 to 64: 768,000

Civilian Labor Force
1993: 575,400
1992: 567,600
1991: 556,800
1990: 528,000

Manufacturing
1995 Projection: 26,000
1992: 19,500
1991: 20,100
1990: 20,600
1989: 20,800

Services
1995 Projection: 214,500

1992: 162,400
1991: 161,400
1990: 157,800
1989: 148,100

Wholesale and Retail Trade
1995 Projection: 157,500
1992: 135,300
1991: 138,700
1990: 138,600
1989: 136,300

Unemployment Rate
1993: 4.8%
1992: 3.6%
1991: 2.6%
1990: 3.0%

Employer Unemployment Contributions
Contribution Rate
1992: 0.70%
1991: 1.34%
1990: 1.29%

Average Weekly Benefit
1992: $250.01
1991: $244.03
1990: $198.01

Gross State Product (Million $)
1989: $25,755
1988: $23,183
1987: $20,738
1979: $11,257
Growth rate, 1979 to 1989: 128.8%

Capital Expenditures of Manufacturing Industries
1990: $126,900,000
1989: $98,400,000
1988: $76,100,000
1987: $102,000,000

State Tax Rates
Individual income: Range from 2% ($3,000 or less) to 10% (above $41,000).
Corporate income: Range from 4.4% ($25,000 or less) to 6.4% (above $100,000).

General property: Local collections, rates fixed locally. Realty assessed at 100% of fair market value.

General sales: 4%

Gasoline: Range from 24.8¢ (Hawaii County) to 32.5¢ (Honolulu County) per gallon

Income

Median income for a 4 person family: $44,988

Personal per Capita Income
1992: $21,218
1991: $21,062
1990: $20,461

Disposable per Capita Income
1992: $17,972
1991: $17,751
1990: $17,279

Private Employment Weekly Wages

Average
1989: $397
1988: $374
1987: $374

Manufacturing
1989: $347
1988: $415
1987: $387

Services
1989: $383
1988: $367
1987: $339

Wholesale
1989: $474
1988: $452
1987: $417

Retail
1989: $259
1988: $243
1987: $224

Highway Statistics

Total Highway Miles
1990: 4,099
1989: 4,082
1988: 4,081

Federal Highway Aid
1991: $100,115,000
1990: $137,421,000
1989: $144,843,000

Electricity

Average Cost per Kilowatt Hour
1990: 9.02¢
1989: 8.06¢
1988: 7.49¢

Housing (1990)
Owner occupied units: 191,911
Median house value: $245,300
Renter occupied units: 164,356
Median rent: $599
Total vacant units: 33,543
Homeowner vacancy rate: 0.8%
Rental vacancy rate: 5.4%

State Business Incentives and Assistance

Financial and Business Assistance

Hawaii Trade Program. Operates through the Department of Business, Economic Development & Tourism (DBED) representative in Hawaii's Washington, D.C. office. Links Hawaii businesses with the procurement activities of international agencies, governments, and private businesses.

Leadtracker Program. A computerized database system for tracking and servicing various leads. The inquiries were generated from advertising in regional editions of the Wall Street Journal, Asian Wall Street Journal, and Fortune magazine.

Hawaii: the Pacific Link Program. A state-sponsored program promotes the advantages of Hawaii as a site for a corporate Pacific regional headquarters.

Business Action Center. Part of DBED, the center provides information and referral on business licenses and permits, and receives applications for direct processing. It gives statewide assistance in starting, expanding, or relocating a business.

Small Business Information Service. It provides information and referral for new and existing businesses.

Molokai Loan Program. Established in 1988, this program helps stimulate business development and growth on the island and to serve as a pilot project for similar programs in other rural areas.

Hawaii Capital Loan Program. This program provides low-interest financing for small businesses unable to obtain financing from conventional sources. It makes loans to many local high technology companies to start or expand a business. The loans may be used to finance plant conversion, construction, or acquisition of land for expansion, as well as for acquisition of equipment, machinery, supplies, and materials, or for working capital.

Hawaii Small Business Innovation Research (SBIR) Grant Program. Provides matching grants for small businesses.

Kaimuki Technology Enterprise Center (KAITEC). An incubator for small start-up high-tech companies.

Education and Training

Aloha Stat Specialized Employment and Training (ASSET). ASSET is specifically targeted for new and expanding businesses in high technology and growth industries. It helps qualified businesses to recruit, hire, and train employees. The program provides training specialists to assist in developing customized training plan designed

Major Companies in the State

Company name	Fortune 500 rank	City	Telephone	SIC number
Fortune 500 Companies				
None				
Other Major Companies in the State				
Alexander & Baldwin Inc.		Honolulu	808-525-6611	4424
Bancorp Hawaii Inc.		Honolulu	808-537-8111	6712
Barnwell Industries Inc.		Honolulu	808-836-0136	1311
Capital Investment of Hawaii Inc.		Honolulu	808-537-3981	5149
CB Bancshares Inc. Hawaii		Honolulu	808-546-2411	6712
CPB Inc.		Honolulu	808-544-0500	6712
Cyanotech Corp.		Kailua-kona	808-326-1353	2836
First Hawaiian Inc.		Honolulu	808-525-7000	6712
GTE Hawaiian Telephone Co. Inc.		Honolulu	808-546-4511	4813
HAL Inc.		Honolulu	808-525-5480	4512
Hawaii National Bancshares Inc.		Honolulu	808-528-7711	6712
Hawaiian Electric Co. Inc.		Honolulu	808-543-7771	4911
Hawaiian Electric Industries Inc.		Honolulu	808-543-5662	4911
Honfed Bank A Federal Savings Bank		Honolulu	808-546-2200	6035
Hosoi Garden Mortuary Inc.		Honolulu	808-538-3877	7261
International Holding Capital Corp.		Honolulu	808-547-5110	6712
Maui Land & Pineapple Co. Inc.		Kahului Maui	808-877-3351	0179
Pacific International Services Corp.		Honolulu	808-926-4242	7514
Pioneer Federal Bancorp Inc.		Honolulu	808-522-6690	6712

especially for each company.

Job Training Partnership Act. This program operates with funding from the U.S. Department of Labor. It provides job training and other employment related services.

State Offices

Real estate: Department of Commerce & Consumer Affairs, Real Estate Commission, Calvin Kimura, Exec Secretary, PO Box 3469, 1010 Richard Street, Honolulu, HI 96801. 808-548-7464

Chamber of commerce: Hawaii Chamber of Commerce, Robert B. Robinson, President, 725 Bishop St., Honolulu, HI 96813. 808-522-8800

Economic development: Dept. of Business, Economic Development and Tourism, Roger A. Ulveling, Director, PO Box 2359, Honolulu, HI 96804. 808-548-3033, FAX 808-523-8637

Dept. of Business, Economic Development and Tourism, Foreign Trade Zone Division, Homer Maxey, Manager, 521 Ala Moana Blvd., Pier 2, Honolulu, HI 96804. 808-548-5435

Dept. of Business, Economic Development and Tourism, Industry Promotion Division, Director, Grosvenor Center, Mauka Tower, 737 Bishop Street, Suite 1900, Honolulu, HI 96804. 808-548-6007

Dept. of Business, Economic Development and Tourism, Business Services Division, Tom Smythe, Director, Grosvenor Center, Mauka Tower, 737 Bishop Street, Suite 1900, Honolulu, HI 96804. 808-548-3081

Aloha Tower Development Corporation, Director, 33 South King Street, Suite 403, Honolulu, HI 96804. 808-548-6585

High Technology Development Corporation, William Bass, Exec Director, Mililani Technology Park, Suite 35, Honolulu, HI 96804. 808-625-5293

Kaimuki Technology Enterprise Center (KAITEC), Director, 1103 9th Ave., Honolulu, HI 96804. 808-733-2000

Dept. of Business, Economic Development and Tourism, Enterprise Zones Program, Tom Smythe, Director, Grosvenor Center, Mauka Tower, 737 Bishop Street, Suite 1900, Honolulu, HI 96804. 808-548-3081

Environmental affairs: Environmental Quality Control Office, Marvin Miura, Exec Director, 550 Halekauwila Street, Room 301, Honolulu, HI 96813. 808-548-6915

Labor: Labor and Industrial Relations Department, Mario R. Ramil, Director, 830 Punchbowl Street, Honolulu, HI 96813. 808-548-3150

Unemployment: Unemployment Insurance Division, Douglas Odo, Administrator, 830 Punchbowl Street, Honolulu, HI 96813. 808-548-7515

Worker's compensation: Labor and Industrial Relations

Department, Mario R. Ramil, Director, 830 Punchbowl Street, Honolulu, HI 96813. 808-548-3150

Occupational safety and health: Occupational Safety and Health Division, Harold Banks, Administrator, 677 Ala Moana Blvd., Suite 910, Honolulu, HI 96813. 808-548-4155

Secretary of state: Lieutenant Govenor Office, Benjamin Cayetano, Lieutenant Govenor, PO Box 3226, Honolulu, HI 96801. 808-548-2544

Taxation and revenue: Taxation Department, Richard F. Kahle, Jr., Director, PO Box 259, Honolulu, HI 96809. 808-548-7650

Designated Zones for Economic Development

Enterprise Zones

Enacted in: 1986

No. of established zones: 0

Program became operational in 1991.

Foreign Trade Zones

Foreign Trade Zone No. 9, Honolulu, Hawaii, Grantee/Operator: State of Hawaii, Homer Maxey, Pier 2, 521 Ala Moana, Honolulu, HI 96813, 808-586-2507. This is a General-Purpose Zone which includes one headquarter and five subzones:, Headquarter at Pier 2, Honolulu (17 acres of warehouse and open yard areas), Campbell Industrial Park (1,051 acres including Barbers Point Deep Draft Harbor), and Mililani Technology Park (109 acres at Mililani, Oahu).

Subzone 9A (Ewa, Oahu). Oil refinery and synthetic natural gas plant operated by subsidiaries of Pacific Resources, Inc.

Subzone 9B (Pier 23, Honolulu). Bakery-mix blending operations producing special mixes for export markets. Operated by HFM, a division of Kerr Pacific Corp.

Subzone 9C (Iwilei). A pineapple cannery and con-making plant, operated by Dole Packaged Foods.

Subzone 9D (Kahului, Maui). A pineapple cannery and can-making plant, operated by Maui Pineapple Co., Ltd.

Subzone 9E (Ewa, Oahu). An oil refinery operated by Chevron USA, Inc.

Labor Unions

Electrical Workers, International Brotherhood of (AFL-CIO)

International Longshoremen's and Warehousemen's Union

State, County and Municipal Employees, American Federation of (AFL-CIO)

Universities with Ph.D. Programs

University of Hawaii, Honolulu

Sources of Additional Information

Strategic Plan, Business & Industry Development, Marketing, Promotion. State of Hawaii, Dept. of Business and Economic Development, January 1988. 15p.

Annual Report, 1989. State of Hawaii, Dept. of Business and Economic Development, 1990. 52p.

Statistical & Economic Report. State of Hawaill, Dept. of Business, Economic Development and Tourism, Research and Economic Analysis Division, [Quarterly publication].

All About Business in Hawaii. Crossroads Press, Inc. (PO Box 833, Honolulu, HI 96808), 1990. 80p.

HONOLULU, HI (MSA)

Geographic Profile

Land Area

600.2 square miles

Counties and Parishes

Honolulu

Ranking Highlights

274 *out of 319 in total* **land area**

121 *out of 319 in* **population growth**, *1970–1990*

10 *out of 310 in having the lowest* **unemployment** *rate*

65 *out of 310 in size of* **labor force**

67 *out of 318 in the percentage of* **college graduates**

26 *out of 292 in per capita personal* **income**

82 *out of 319 in number of* **manufacturing establishments**

69 *out of 318 in* **physicians** *per 1000 people*

268 *out of 318 in* **hospital beds** *per 1000 people*

128 *out of 267 in fewest* **crimes** *per 1000 people*

31 *out of 266 in fewest* **violent crimes** *per 1000 people*

26 *out of 319 in per capita* **federal funds and grants**

Quality of Life Indexes (Rate per 1000 population)

Crime rate in 1991:	59.6
Violent crime rate in 1991:	2.4
Physicians rate in 1992:	2.47
Hospital bed rate in 1991:	2.6

ACCRA Cost of Living Indexes

(First quarter 1993, average = 100)

Composite index:	N/A
Utilities index:	N/A
Housing index:	N/A

Overview

Honolulu began its economic life in the mid-nineteenth century as a port for whalers; it was also a trade center for nations bordering the Pacific, dealing in such goods as sandalwood, whale oil, and fur. While markets for sandalwood and whale oil decreased, sugar and pineapple markets increased dramatically. In fact, the powerful sugar industry, owned mainly by Americans, engineered the downfall of Hawaii's last monarch and the islands' annexation by the United States. Today, one-fifth of the land in Honolulu County is zoned for agriculture, but fields are now giving way to new homes, and it is agreed that the sugar industry will not survive without continued federal price subsidies. Diversified agriculture is thriving, however. Honolulu is becoming the center of an aquaculture—fish growing—industry and continues to be the source of exotic flowers and plants sent to the mainland.

In addition to serving as the business and trading hub of the Hawaiian Islands, Honolulu is the transportation crossroads of the Pacific, connecting East with West. The city's well-equipped port handles cargo for several international steamship companies, and a Foreign Trade Zone is based there. Other important elements of Honolulu's economic base include tourism, military defense, research and development, and manufacturing. With millions of visitors coming each year to enjoy Honolulu's climate and beaches, tourism contributes $11 billion annually to the local economy. Pearl Harbor Naval Shipyard, Hickam Air Force Base, and the Fort Shafter U.S. Army base, which provide revenues that are unaffected by the normal business cycle, have exerted a stabilizing economic influence, although military spending is declining nationwide. As the home of the University of Hawaii at Manoa, Honolulu is a center for research and development, especially in the areas of oceanography, astrophysics, geophysics, and biomedicine. Twenty-one industrial parks in Honolulu County are sites for the production of such goods as clothing, awnings, tents, and cement.

Isolated from the mainland, Honolulu is reached primarily by plane. Honolulu International Airport, a major center for Pacific air travel, is served by thirty-one domestic and foreign airlines as well as inter-island carriers. Honolulu may also be reached by ship; cruise lines sail regularly between Honolulu and San Francisco. State legislation in 1990 authorized construction of a fixed rail system.

Population (1990)

Total Population and Growth Rate

1990: 836,231

1980: 762,565

1970: 630,528

Growth rate 1970–1990: 33%

Race and Hispanic Origin

White: 31.6%

Black: 3.1%

Asian/Pacific Islander: 63.0%

Native American: 0.4%

Hispanic origin: 6.8%

White not Hispanic: 29.9%

Age

Ages 18 to 20: 4.7%

Ages 21 to 24: 7.2%

Ages 25 to 44: 34.3%

Ages 45 to 54: 9.8%

Ages 55 to 59: 4.1%

Ages 60 to 64: 4.4%

Ages 65 plus: 11%

Educational Attainment (1990)

Percent having completed high school: 81.2%

Percent having completed college: 24.6%

Elementary and high school enrollment: 135,478

Federal Funds and Grants Received

Total received in 1989: $4,784,600,000

Funds received per capita: $5,706

Civilian Labor Force

1993 (April):   411,237
1992 average: 408,196
1991 average: 403,498
1990 average: 392,320

Unemployment

1993 (April): 3.5%
1992 average: 3.5%
1991 average: 2.3%
1990 average: 2.6%

Average Annual Pay

1988: $21,196
1987: $19,718
1985: $17,902

Per Capita Personal Income

1991: $22,102
1990: $21,440
1989: $19,638

Business Climate (1987)

Manufacturing

Number of establishments in 1987: 800
Shipments in 1987 ($1,000): $2,783,800
Employees in 1987: 16,500
Change in employment, 1982 to 1987: -7.8%
Average annual pay for manufacturing work in 1989: $23,620
Average annual pay for production work in 1987: $16,349

Wholesale Trade

Number of establishments in 1987: 1,577
Total sales in 1987 ($1,000): $4,501,800
Change in sales, 1982 to 1987: 32.7%

Retail Trade

Number of establishments in 1987: 4,918
Total sales in 1987 ($1,000): $4,501,800
Retail sales per household in 1987: $23,187
Average annual pay in 1989: $13,654

Service Industry

Selected receipts in 1987 ($1,000): $3,234,300
Average annual pay in 1989: $20,785

Office Real Estate (1992)

Office space inventory: 13,364,900 square feet
Average class A Central Business District rental range per sq. ft: $32.25

Vacancy Rates

All areas: 9.1%

Vacancy Rates in Central Business District

Class A space: 9.7%
Class B space: 7.9%

Vacancy Rates Outside Central Business District

Class A space: 9.4%
Class B space: N/A

Housing

Total number of units in 1990: 281,683
Occupied units in 1990: 265,304
Owner-occupied units in 1990: 52.0%
1993 ACCRA average cost: N/A
1993 ACCRA average rent for an apartment: N/A

Chamber of Commerce

Honolulu Japanese Chamber of Commerce, Ronald Ushijima, Exec. Vice President, 2454 S. Beretania St., Honolulu, HI 96826. 808-949-5531

Economic Development Office

Economic Development Corp. of Honolulu, Frederick Sexton, President, 1001 Bishop St. #735 Pacific Tower, Honolulu, HI 96813. 808-545-4533, FAX 808-536-3266

Economic Development Organizations

City and County of Honolulu, Cora Avinante-Tanaka, Exec. Assistant, City Hall, 530 S. King St., Honolulu, HI 96813. 808-523-4130, FAX 808-527-5552

Major Companies

Company	SIC	Telephone
Alexander & Baldwin Inc.	4424	(808) 525-6611
Aloha Airgroup Inc.	4512	(808) 836-4101
Aloha Airlines, Inc.	4512	(808) 836-4101
Amfac Agribusiness, Inc.	0179	(808) 945-8111
AQ Corp.	4512	(808) 836-4101
Azabu USA Corp.	7011	(808) 955-4811
Bancorp Hawaii Inc.	6022	(808) 537-8111
Bank of Hawaii	6022	(808) 537-8111
Brewer, C. and Co. Ltd.	0173	(808) 536-4461
Buyco Inc.	0133	(808) 536-4461
Davies, Theo H & Co Ltd.	5084	(808) 531-8531
Dillingham Construction Ltd.	1542	(808) 735-3211
Familiar, Ltd.	5641	(808) 537-9131
First Hawaiian Bank	6022	(808) 525-7000
Fletcher Construction Co. Hawaii Ltd.	1522	(808) 521-7861
Foodland Super Market Ltd.	5411	(808) 732-0791
HAL, Inc.	4512	(808) 525-5511
Hawaii Energy Resources Inc.	2911	(808) 547-3111
Hawaii Medical Service Association	6324	(808) 944-2110
Hawaiian Airlines, Inc.	4512	(808) 835-3001
Hawaiian Electric Co.	4911	(808) 543-7771
Hawaiian Electric Industries	4911	(808) 543-5662
Hawaiian Independent Refineries	2911	(808) 547-3222
Hilton Hawaiian	7011	(808) 949-4321
Honfed Bank, A Federal Savings	6035	(808) 545-6440
Kyo-Ya Co. Ltd.	7011	(808) 924-5170
Liberty House Inc.	5311	(808) 941-2345
M & E Pacific, Inc.	8711	(808) 521-3051
MNS Ltd	5912	(808) 538-6743

Major Companies (Continued)

Company	SIC	Telephone
Nissan Motor Corp. in Hawaii	5012	(808) 531-0231
Oceanic Properties Inc.	6552	(808) 548-6611
Outrigger Hotels Hawaii	7011	(808) 921-6510
Pacific Construction Co., Ltd.	1522	(808) 521-7861
Pacific Resources Inc.	2911	(808) 547-3111
Queen's Medical Center	8062	(808) 547-4329
Servco Pacific Inc.	5511	(808) 521-6511
SMK Inc.	5912	(808) 538-6743
Times Super Market Ltd.	5411	(808) 847-0811
Watkins Pacific Corp.	5031	(808) 848-2451

Colleges and Universities

Cannon's International Business College of Honolulu, Honolulu

Chaminade University of Honolulu, Honolulu

Hawaii Pacific University, Honolulu

University of Hawaii-Honolulu Community College, Honolulu

University of Hawaii-Kapiolani Community College, Honolulu

University of Hawaii at Manoa, Honolulu

IDAHO

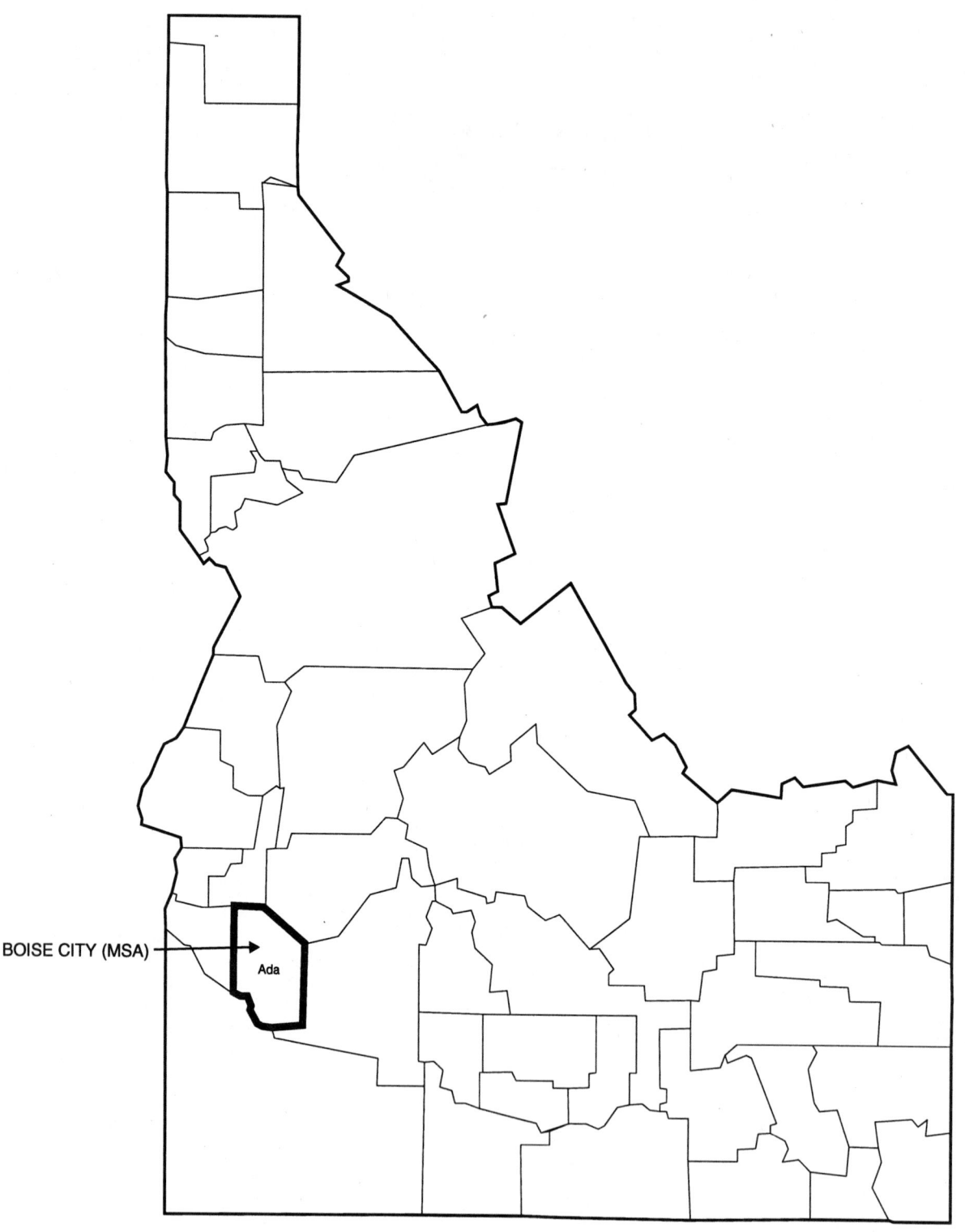

BOISE CITY (MSA)

Ada

IDAHO

Population
1990: 1,006,749
1980: 943,935

Age
Ages 18 to 20: 47,064
Ages 21 to 24: 51,183
Ages 25 to 44: 301,968
Ages 45 to 54: 98,907
Ages 55 to 59: 39,407
Ages 60 to 64: 38,550
Median age: 31.5

Race
White: 950,451
Black: 3,370
Asian/Pacific Islander: 9,365
Native American: 13,780
Hispanic origin: 52,927

Households
Total: 360,723
Persons per household: 2.73

Sex
Male: 500,956
Female: 505,793

Population Migration
Domestic migration: -65,000
International migration: 9,000

Projection of the Population in 1995
Total: 1,047,000
18 to 64: 608,000

Civilian Labor Force
1993: 513,600
1992: 506,300
1991: 499,000
1990: 493,300

Manufacturing
1995 Projection: 66,400
1992: 65,600
1991: 64,100
1990: 63,500
1989: 62,800

Services
1995 Projection: 131,700

1992: 90,500
1991: 87,100
1990: 83,000
1989: 77,100

Wholesale and Retail Trade
1995 Projection: 111,900
1992: 105,800
1991: 104,100
1990: 100,700
1989: 99,500

Unemployment Rate
1993: 8.2%
1992: 7.9%
1991: 6.4%
1990: 6.6%

Employer Unemployment Contributions
Contribution Rate
1992: 1.76%
1991: 1.32%
1990: 1.74%

Average Weekly Benefit
1992: $165.39
1991: $159.35
1990: $145.40

Gross State Product (Million $)
1989: $16,339
1988: $14,830
1987: $13,599
1979: $8,954
Growth rate, 1979 to 1989: 82.5%

Capital Expenditures of Manufacturing Industries
1990: $476,800,000
1989: $341,900,000
1988: $352,000,000
1987: $234,800,000

State Tax Rates
Individual income: Range from 2% ($1,000 or less) to 8.2% (above $20,000).
Corporate income: 8% of total taxable income.
General property: No state levy. Rates fixed locally.

General sales: 5%

Gasoline: 22¢ per gallon

Income

Median income for a 4 person family: $33,633

Personal per Capita Income

1992: $16,067

1991: $15,366

1990: $15,137

Disposable per Capita Income

1992: $14,572

1991: $13,917

1990: $13,674

Private Employment Weekly Wages

Average

1989: $346

1988: $337

1987: $337

Manufacturing

1989: $325

1988: $438

1987: $420

Services

1989: $338

1988: $331

1987: $325

Wholesale

1989: $379

1988: $363

1987: $346

Retail

1989: $208

1988: $205

1987: $196

Highway Statistics

Total Highway Miles

1990: 62,435

1989: 61,317

1988: 60,663

Federal Highway Aid

1991: $72,701,000

1990: $71,939,000

1989: $80,232,000

Electricity

Average Cost per Kilowatt Hour

1990: 3.78¢

1989: 3.79¢

1988: 3.70¢

Housing (1990)

Owner occupied units: 252,734

Median house value: $58,200

Renter occupied units: 107,989

Median rent: $261

Total vacant units: 52,604

Homeowner vacancy rate: 2.0%

Rental vacancy rate: 7.3%

State Business Incentives and Assistance

Financial and Business Assistance

Job Creation Credit. $500 corporate income tax credit for each new employee hired in the first year.

Investment Tax Credit. A 3% credit for new investments made in the state, not to exceed 50% of the tax liability for the year.

Industrial Revenue Bonds. Enables Idaho businesses to borrow up to $10 million at tax-exempt interest rates.

Export Marketing Service. The Department of Commerce provides support through International Trade workshops and seminars, and trade missions and exhibitions to bring Idaho firms in contact with business prospects in other countries.

Technology Transfer Program. The program assists existing Idaho businesses by promoting new technology and procurement for Idaho business for U.S. government facilities. The division also helps to attract hi-tech business to Idaho.

Education and Training

Dislocated Worker Project. With JPTA Title III funding, the project provides dislocated workers comprehensive employment and training services. The project places participants into unsubsidized employment.

New Industry Training Program. Administered by the Division of Vocational Education, this program provides customized pre-employment and on-the-job training for new and expanding businesses in the state.

Job Training Partnership Act. This program operates with funding from the U.S. Department of Labor. It provides job training and other employment related services.

State Offices

Real estate: Real Estate Commission, Michael P. Gray, Exec Director, 633 North 4th Street, Boise, ID 83702. 208-334-3285

Chamber of commerce: (No State Chamber of Commerce)

Economic development: Department of Commerce, Division of Economic Development, Jay Engstrom, Administrator, 700 W. State Street, Boise, ID 83720-2700. 208-334-2470, FAX 208-334-2631

Department of Commerce, Division of International Trade, David Christensen, Administrator, 700 W. State Street, Boise, ID 83720-2700. 208-334-2470, FAX 208-334-2631

Small Business Development Center, Ronald R. Hall, State Director, Boise State University, 1910 University Drive, Boise, ID 83725. 208-385-1640

Environmental affairs: Department of Health and Welfare, Division of Environmental Quality, Joe Nagel, Director,

Major Companies in the State

Company name	Fortune 500 rank	City	Telephone	SIC number
Fortune 500 Companies				
Boise Cascade Corp	134	Boise	208-384-6161	2621
Other Major Companies in the State				
Albertson, Inc.		Boise	208-385-6200	5411
Allied Silver Lead Co.		Mullan	208-752-1154	6794
Aqua Vie Beverage Corp.		Ketchum	208-726-2555	5149
BMC West Corp.		Boise	208-338-1750	5039
Coeur Alene Mines Corp.		Coeur d'alene	208-667-3511	1044
Consolidated Silver Corp.		Coeur d'alene	208-769-4100	6519
Hecla Mining Co.		Coeur d'alene	208-769-4100	1041
Helena Silver Mines Inc.		Coeur d'alene	208-667-9565	6514
Highland Gold Properties Inc.		Sandpoint	208-263-6533	1041
Idaho Co.		Boise	208-344-6308	6159
Idaho Power Co.		Boise	208-383-2200	4911
Idora Silver Mines Inc.		Coeur d'Alene	208-667-9565	6552
Independent Direct Inc.		Lewiston	208-746-3346	----
Micron Technology Inc.		Boise	208-368-4000	3674
Morrison Knudsen Corp.		Boise	208-386-5000	1629
Summit Securities Inc. Idaho		Coeur d Alene	208-667-5717	6153
Sunshine Precious Metals Inc.		Boise	208-345-0660	1044
TJ International Inc.		Boise	208-345-8500	3449
Transtector Systems Inc.		Hayden Lake	208-772-8515	3613
West One Bancorp		Boise	208-383-7000	6712

1410 North Hilton, Boise, ID 83706. 208-334-5879

Labor: Department of Labor and Industrial Services, Gary Gould, Director, 277 Main Street, Boise, ID 83720. 208-334-3950

Unemployment: Department of Employment, Unemployment Insurance Division, Richard Eardley, Director, 317 Main Street, Boise, ID 83720. 208-334-6466

Worker's compensation: Industrial Commission, Will S. Defenbach, Chairman, 317 Main Street, Boise, ID 83720. 208-334-6000

Occupational safety and health: Labor and Industrial Services Department, Safety and Labor Relations Administration, Robert D. Hayes, Administrator, State House Mall, Boise, ID 83720. 208-334-2327

Secretary of state: Secretary of the State, Pete T. Cenarrusa, Secretary of State, Statehouse, Room 203, Boise, ID 83720. 208-334-2300

Taxation and revenue: Department of Revenue and Taxation, Larry G. Looney, Chairman, 3131 West State Street, Boise, ID 83703. 208-334-3660

Designated Zones for Economic Development

Enterprise Zones

No program.

Foreign Trade Zones

None

Labor Unions

Carpenters and Joiners of America, United Brotherhood of (AFL-CIO)

Chemical and Atomic Workers

Communications Workers of America (AFL-CIO)

Electrical Workers, International Brotherhood of (AFL-CIO)

Grain Millers, American Federation of (AFL-CIO)

Laborers' International Union of North America (AFL-CIO)

Operating Engineers, International Union of (AFL-CIO)

Steelworkers of America, United (AFL-CIO)

Universities with Ph.D. Programs

Idaho State University, Pocatello

University of Idaho, Moscow

BOISE CITY, ID (MSA)

Geographic Profile

Land Area
1055.0 square miles

Counties and Parishes
Ada

Ranking Highlights

191 *out of 319 in total* land area

32 *out of 319 in* population growth, *1970–1990*

20 *out of 310 in having the lowest* unemployment *rate*

162 *out of 310 in size of* labor force

61 *out of 318 in the percentage of* college graduates

133 *out of 292 in per capita personal* income

172 *out of 319 in number of* manufacturing establishments

132 *out of 318 in* physicians *per 1000 people*

260 *out of 318 in* hospital beds *per 1000 people*

63 *out of 267 in fewest* crimes *per 1000 people*

46 *out of 266 in fewest* violent crimes *per 1000 people*

124 *out of 319 in per capita* federal funds and grants

Quality of Life Indexes (Rate per 1000 population)

Crime rate in 1991:	45.7
Violent crime rate in 1991:	3.0
Physicians rate in 1992:	1.87
Hospital bed rate in 1991:	2.71

ACCRA Cost of Living Indexes

(First quarter 1993, average = 100)

Composite index:	106.2
Utilities index:	71.5
Housing index:	121.4

Overview

Boise, the capital of Idaho and the largest city in the state, is the commercial, financial, and cultural center of the northern Rockies region. Boise began its history as a supply and service center for the mining camps in the nearby mountains. It continues today as an important commercial hub for smaller towns and agricultural establishments in the northern Rockies. In addition to mining, farming and timber have played important roles in the development of the Boise economy.

The present economy has shifted away from its traditional sources towards a more diversified base. State government is one of the city's main employers, since Boise is the capital of Idaho. Boise is the world headquarters for nine major corporations, including Albertson's, a supermarket chain; Morrison-Knudsen, an engineering and construction firm; Micron Technology, which manufactures semiconductors; and Ore-Ida Foods, a packaged and frozen food company. Tourism is a major source of revenue, providing $140 million dollars for the local economy in 1992. High technology industries are becoming an increasingly important sector,

and the Army National Guard's Gowen Field also has an economic impact.

The Boise Convention Centre opened in 1990. It features a glass-fronted eighty-five-hundred-square-foot lobby, a five thousand square foot auditorium that will seat up to 400 persons, and a twenty-five-thousand square foot central meeting space, offering fifty thousand square feet overall. Other facilities include the Boise State University Pavilion, which seats up to 12,000 persons and has 17,472 square feet of open floor space. The Western Idaho Exhibition Hall is a complex of three buildings with a total of eighty-three thousand square feet of exhibit area. There are more than three thousand hotel rooms in metropolitan Boise; most of the major hotels, including the five-hotel cluster downtown, provide meeting, banquet, and ballroom facilities.

Boise Air Terminal, located a few miles south of downtown, is served by six airlines with forty-eight flights daily. Amtrak rail service is provided at the Morrison-Knudsen Depot with two trains daily. Two major highways lead into Boise. I-84 runs east and west, connecting the metropolitan area with the West Coast and the midwestern states. U.S. 20/26 runs diagonally west to southeast through the center of the city.

Population (1990)

Total Population and Growth Rate

1990: 205,775

1980: 173,125

1970: 112,230

Growth rate 1970–1990: 83%

Race and Hispanic Origin

White: 96.7%

Black: .5%

Asian/Pacific Islander: 1.4%

Native American: 0.7%

Hispanic origin: 2.7%

White not Hispanic: 94.8%

Age

Ages 18 to 20: 4.3%

Ages 21 to 24: 5.6%

Ages 25 to 44: 34.6%

Ages 45 to 54: 10%

Ages 55 to 59: 3.6%

Ages 60 to 64: 3.3%

Ages 65 plus: 10.4%

Educational Attainment (1990)

Percent having completed high school: 87.2%

Percent having completed college: 24.9%

Elementary and high school enrollment: 38,477

Federal Funds and Grants Received

Total received in 1989: $674,600,000

Funds received per capita: $3,361

Civilian Labor Force
1993 (April):   127,084
1992 average: 125,929
1991 average: 119,871
1990 average: 117,050

Unemployment
1993 (April):   4.1%
1992 average: 4.1%
1991 average: 4.1%
1990 average: 3.8%

Average Annual Pay
1988: $20,238
1987: $19,371
1985: $18,638

Per Capita Personal Income
1991: $17,625
1990: $17,116
1989: $16,070

Business Climate (1987)

Manufacturing
Number of establishments in 1987: 284
Shipments in 1987 ($1,000): $1,473,700
Employees in 1987: 11,100
Change in employment, 1982 to 1987: 20.7%
Average annual pay for manufacturing work in 1989: $29,142
Average annual pay for production work in 1987: $19,262

Wholesale Trade
Number of establishments in 1987: 536
Total sales in 1987 ($1,000): $1,746,100
Change in sales, 1982 to 1987: 19.7%

Retail Trade
Number of establishments in 1987: 1,233
Total sales in 1987 ($1,000): $1,746,100
Retail sales per household in 1987: $15,527
Average annual pay in 1989: $12,456

Service Industry
Selected receipts in 1987 ($1,000): $566,300
Average annual pay in 1989: $17,020

Housing
Total number of units in 1990: 80,849
Occupied units in 1990: 77,471
Owner-occupied units in 1990: 69.1%
1993 ACCRA average cost: $132,675
1993 ACCRA average rent for an apartment: $676

Chamber of Commerce
Boise Area Chamber of Commerce, Jay M. Clemens, President, 300 N. 6th St., PO Box 2368, Boise, ID 83701. 208-344-5515, FAX 208-344-5849

Economic Development Office
Ida-Ore Planning and Development Association, Phil Cho-

ate, Exec. Director, 11624 W. Executive Dr., Boise, ID 83704. 208-322-7033

Industrial Sites
Central Valley Corproate Park. Contact: Robert W. Nahas, 102 S. 17th St. Suite 300, Boise, ID 83702. 208-336-6661

Boise Research Center. Contact: Ted Johnson, 9512 Fairview Ave., Boise, ID 83704. 208-375-8557

Treasure Valley Business Park. Contact: Thomas T. Wright, PO Box 2727, Boise, ID 83701. 208-343-4000

Westpark Corporate Center. Contact: James L. Boyd, PO Box 7378, Boise, ID 83707. 208-343-2300

Major Companies

Company	SIC	Telephone
Albertson's, Inc.	5411	(208) 385-6200
Blue Cross of Idaho Health	6324	(208) 345-4550
BMC Holdings Inc.	5211	(208) 338-1750
Boise Cascade Corp.	2621	(208) 384-6161
Canfor U.S.A. Corp.	2421	(208) 888-2456
Club Wholesale Concepts	5112	(208) 384-1947
Dennis Dillon Auto	5511	(208) 336-6000
First Interstate Bank of Idaho	6021	(208) 327-2000
First Security Bank of Idaho	6021	(208) 338-4000
Foodways National Inc.	2038	(208) 383-6700
Hoff Companies Inc.	2431	(208) 323-8606
Idaho Power Co.	4911	(208) 383-2200
Idaho Timber Corp.	2421	(208) 377-3000
Intermountain Gas Co.	4924	(208) 377-6000
Key Bank of Idaho	6022	(208) 334-7000
Micron Technology Inc.	3674	(208) 383-4000
Morrison Knudsen Corp.	1622	(208) 386-8000
National Projects, Inc.	1629	(208) 386-6789
Ore-Ida Foods Inc.	2037	(208) 383-6100
Preco Inc.	3714	(208) 323-1000
Rogers Brothers Seed Co.	5191	(208) 322-7272
St. Alphonsus	8062	(208) 378-2121
Sequoia Forest Industries	2421	(208) 342-8901
J. R. Simplot Co.	2037	(208) 336-2110
St. Lukes Regional Medical Center	8062	(208) 386-2222
TJ International, Inc.	2439	(208) 345-8500
Waremart, Inc.	5411	(208) 345-4298
West One Bancorp	6021	(208) 383-7000

Colleges and Universities
Boise Bible College, Boise
Boise State University, Boise
ITT Technical Institute, Boise

ILLINOIS

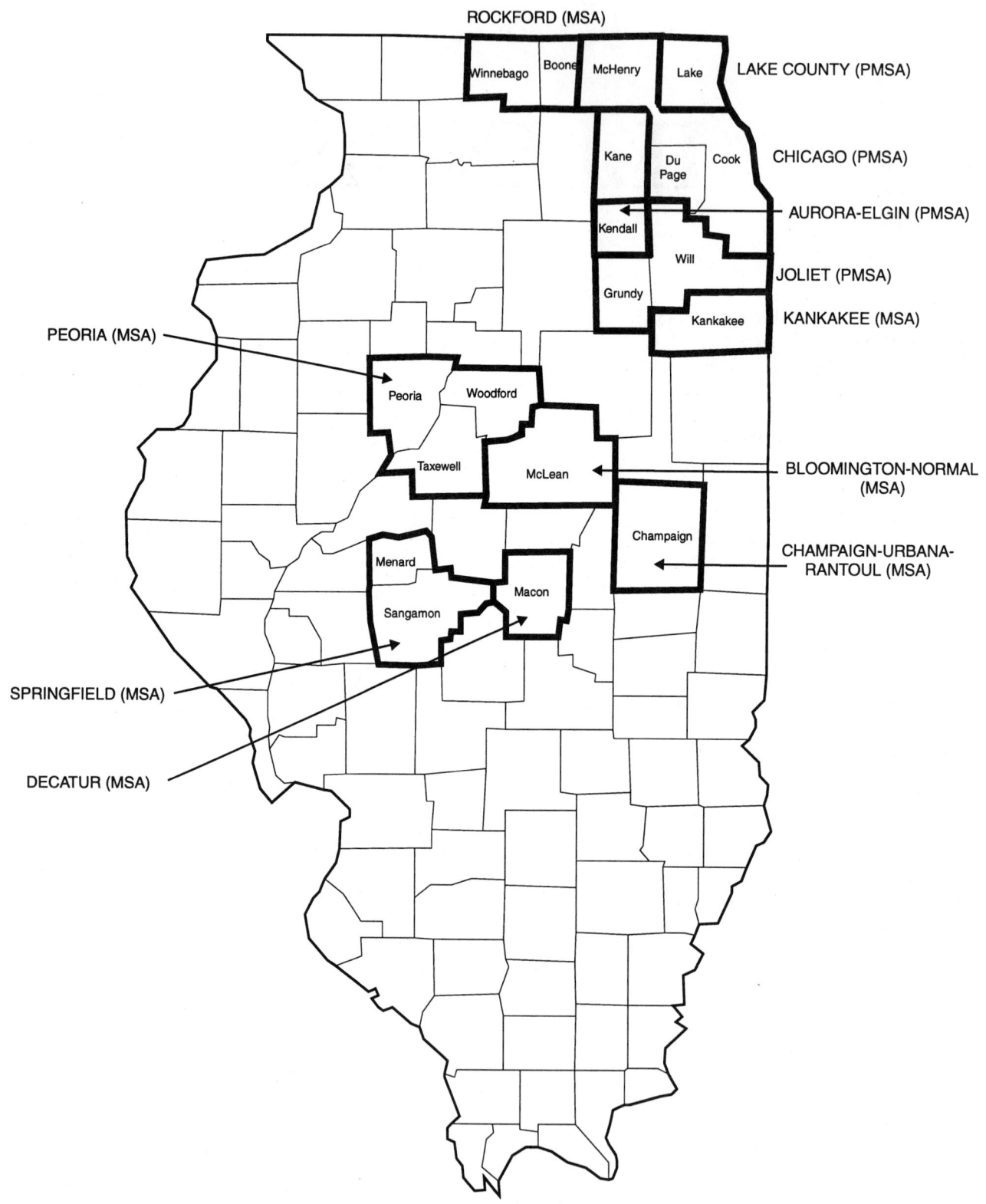

ROCKFORD (MSA)

Winnebago

Boone

McHenry

Lake

LAKE COUNTY (PMSA)

Kane

Du Page

Cook

CHICAGO (PMSA)

AURORA-ELGIN (PMSA)

Kendall

Will

JOLIET (PMSA)

Grundy

Kankakee

KANKAKEE (MSA)

PEORIA (MSA)

Peoria

Woodford

Taxewell

McLean

BLOOMINGTON-NORMAL (MSA)

Champaign

CHAMPAIGN-URBANA-RANTOUL (MSA)

Menard

Macon

Sangamon

SPRINGFIELD (MSA)

DECATUR (MSA)

ILLINOIS

Population
1990: 11,430,602
1980: 11,426,518

Age
Ages 18 to 20: 531,971
Ages 21 to 24: 680,979
Ages 25 to 44: 3,693,329
Ages 45 to 54: 1,166,727
Ages 55 to 59: 485,581
Ages 60 to 64: 489,104
Median age: 32.8

Race
White: 8,952,978
Black: 1,694,273
Asian/Pacific Islander: 285,311
Native American: 21,836
Hispanic origin: 904,446

Households
Total: 4,202,240
Persons per household: 2.65

Sex
Male: 5,552,233
Female: 5,878,369

Population Migration
Domestic migration: -730,000
International migration: 291,000

Projection of the Population in 1995
Total: 12,086,000
18 to 64: 7,482,000

Civilian Labor Force
1993: 6,028,100
1992: 6,124,200
1991: 6,049,000
1990: 6,006,300

Manufacturing
1995 Projection: 1,008,300
1992: 921,500
1991: 959,100
1990: 976,200
1989: 981,600

Services
1995 Projection: 1,951,500

1992: 1,389,200
1991: 1,355,700
1990: 1,350,400
1989: 1,284,100

Wholesale and Retail Trade
1995 Projection: 1,491,100
1992: 1,229,900
1991: 1,289,300
1990: 1,286,900
1989: 1,298,600

Unemployment Rate
1993: 7.4%
1992: 9.1%
1991: 6.5%
1990: 6.9%

Employer Unemployment Contributions
Contribution Rate
1992: 2.38%
1991: 2.35%
1990: 2.61%

Average Weekly Benefit
1992: $200.44
1991: $185.59
1990: $170.61

Gross State Product (Million $)
1989: $256,478
1988: $241,135
1987: $222,079
1979: $137,616
Growth rate, 1979 to 1989: 86.4%

Capital Expenditures of Manufacturing Industries
1990: $5,004,800,000
1989: $5,454,700,000
1988: $4,165,900,000
1987: $4,425,800,000

State Tax Rates
Individual income: 3% of federal adjusted gross income.
Corporate income: 4.8% of federal taxable income.
General property: Levied to meet local budget needs. Assessed at 33.33% of fair cash value.

General sales: 6.25%
Gasoline: 19¢ per gallon

Income

Median income for a 4 person family: $42,609

Personal per Capita Income
1992: $21,608
1991: $20,737
1990: $20,327

Disposable per Capita Income
1992: $18,914
1991: $18,052
1990: $17,584

Private Employment Weekly Wages

Average
1989: $465
1988: $454
1987: $454

Manufacturing
1989: $427
1988: $556
1987: $523

Services
1989: $419
1988: $402
1987: $379

Wholesale
1989: $598
1988: $588
1987: $536

Retail
1989: $243
1988: $235
1987: $227

Highway Statistics

Total Highway Miles
1990: 135,944
1989: 135,878
1988: 135,506

Federal Highway Aid
1991: $326,794,000
1990: $351,104,000
1989: $368,465,000

Electricity

Average Cost per Kilowatt Hour
1990: 7.00¢
1989: 7.48¢
1988: 7.32¢

Housing (1990)

Owner occupied units: 2,699,182
Median house value: $80,900

Renter occupied units: 1,503,058
Median rent: $369
Total vacant units: 304,035
Homeowner vacancy rate: 1.5%
Rental vacancy rate: 8.0%

State Business Incentives and Assistance

Financial and Business Assistance

Local Programs

Industrial Revenue Bonds. State agencies or local governments issue bonds for firms with strong credit ratings constructing or expanding industrial facilities.

Tax Increment Financing. Government provided improvements to promote development of a specific area. The resulted annual growth in property tax pays for bonds issued to fund improvements.

State Programs

Small Business Development Program. Provides direct loan from the state to businesses with fewer than 500 employees. Will fund up to 25% of project cost or $750,000, whichever is less.

Large Business Development Program. For businesses with at least 500 employees, markets outside Illinois and multi-state location options. Direct loan made from the state up to 25% of project cost or $2 million. Interest write-down grants up to 25% of project cost or $500,000 are available.

Technology Venture Investment Program. For new and advanced technology based early stage Illinois business. Provides high risk capital in the form of equity, convertible debt or royalty financing up to one half of project cost up to $500,000.

Public Infrastructure Loan & Grant Program. The state provides grants or reduced rate loans to local governments needing to finance infrastructure improvements required for economic development.

Community Development Assistance Program. Local government obtains state loans on behalf of companies. Program is for companies in cities of less than 50,000 population and not in any one of the six Community Development Block Grant counties.

Small Business Financing Fund. For Illinois companies with at least a moderately strong credit rating creating new job opportunities for low to moderate income workers. The state will finance up to 20%, but no more than $100,000 of total project costs.

Development Finance Authority Direct Loan Fund. For small or medium sized Illinois industrial firms undertaking capital projects. The State may loan up to 30% of fixed asset costs.

Illinois Development Finance Authority Pooled Bond Program for Small Business. Designed to assist small companies with industrial projects ranging in size from $200,000 to $2.5 million. IDFA issues a bond and lends money to two or more small businesses.

Illinois Farm Development Authority Agri-Industries Guarantee Program. IFDA will issue 85% guarantee for loans by local lenders to agribusinesses or farmers whose project promotes diversification of the farm economy.

Small Business Micro Loan Program. For Illinois businesses with fewer than 500 employees, the State may provide direct loan of no more than $3,000 per job created or retained, up to $100,000 limit.

Small Business Energy Conservation. For small businesses wishing to retrofit building or machinery to conserve energy, the State may provide interest subsidies to reduce total cost of project.

Illinois Fixed Rate Fund. For businesses with fewer than 500 employees. Additional state or local funds may be provided in conjunction with the SBA 7(a) Program.

Illinois Export Development Authority. The Authority may provide loans for up to 90% of export sale with a $500,000 cap for each exporting company.

Prairie State 2000. For businesses which need to retrain employees, the program may provide loans covering 100% of direct training costs or grants for 50% of those costs.

Modernization Assessment Grant Program. Grant of up to $100,000 or up to 50% of the costs of consultants, engineers, etc. may be provided to firms needing productivity or profitability improvement.

Modernization Retooling Loan Program. Loans for machinery and equipment up to $500,000, not to exceed 25% of the project, may be provided to firms needing productivity or profitability improvement.

Illinois Technology Commercialization Program. This program fosters research and development in advanced technologies, leading to new products which could be manufactured or marketed by Illinois businesses. The emphasis of the program is the linkage of the technological resources and expertise in the academic sectors with the research, engineering and commercialization needs of small business. Under this program, developing businesses may obtain work space and a business address.

Inventors Council. It accelerates technology transfer from inventors to manufacturers by providing liaison activities which help inventors license inventions to manufacturers.

Federal Programs

SBA Guaranteed Loan Program. For small business with moderately strong credit ratings unable to acquire conventional financing, SBA may provide guaranteed loans of up to $500,000.

FmHA Business and Industrial Loan Program. For businesses with projects in rural areas or cities of less than 50,000 population, this program may provide guaranteed loans for up to 90% of project costs and between $500,000 and $10 million.

Small Business Innovation Research. For companies with less than 500 employees wishing to conduct research, SBIR may provide federal grants for approved feasibility, experimental or applied research.

Export Import Bank of the United States. The program provides export loans, insurance and working capital guarantees to help financing for exporters.

Education and Training

Industrial Training Program. State grants to subsidize on-the-job training up to $1,000 per job created or retained by manufacturing firms locating or expanding in Illinois. ITP pays a portion of the salaries of new workers while they are being trained. ITP can be used to improve the skills of currently employed workers and to support on-the-job training in a wide range of skill levels.

High Impact Training Service. Funded from state and federal vocational dollars, HITS is to bridge the gap between long-term, in-school vocational training programs and the immediate short-term job training needs of business and industry. This program is available to any business that is expanding in Illinois or locating in Illinois. The State provides grants through a local educational institution to subsidize employee training. Limit to $1,200 per job created.

Job Training Partnership Act Financing Programs. JTPA provides job training for unskilled adults and youths who are economically disadvantaged and for others who face serious barriers to employment. Businesses with eligible workers requiring training, this program provides grants for up to 50% of wages during on-the-job training and up to 100% of other training costs.

State Offices

Real estate: Real Estate Division, Robert Adams, Director, 715 William Stratton Bldg., Springfield, IL 62706. 217-782-5410

Chamber of commerce: Illinois State Chamber of Commerce, Lester W. Brann Jr., President, 20 N. Wacker Dr., Suite 1960, Chicago, IL 60606-3083. 312-372-7373

Economic development: Department of Commerce & Community Affairs, Jay R. Hedges, Director, 620 East Adams Street, Springfield, IL 62706. 217-782-7500, FAX 217-785-6454

Department of Commerce & Community Affairs, Enterprise Zone Program, Tom Henderson, Manager, 620 E. Adams Street, 5th Floor, Springfield, IL 62701. 217-785-6128

Department of Commerce & Community Affairs, Small Business Assistance Bureau, Jeff Mitchell, Director, Illinois SBDC Program, 620 East Adams Street, Springfield, IL 62701. 217-524-5856

Illinois Development Finance Authority, Ronald Bean, Exec Director, 2 North LaSalle Street, Suite 980, Chicago, IL 60602. 312-793-5586

Prairie State 2000 Authority, Operations Manager, State of Illinois Center, 100 West Randolph, Suite 4-800, Chicago, IL 60601. 312-917-2700

Major Companies in the State

Company name	Fortune 500 rank	City	Telephone	SIC number
Fortune 500 Companies				
Abbott Laboratories	66	Abbott Park	708-937-6100	2834
Alberto Culver Co.	335	Melrose Park	708-450-3000	2844
AM International Inc.	483	Chicago	312-558-1966	3555
Amoco Corp.	14	Chicago	312-856-6111	2911
Amsted Industries Inc.	399	Chicago	312-645-1700	3325
Archer Daniels Midland Co.	50	Decatur	217-424-5200	2075
Baxter International Inc.	61	Deerfield	708-948-2000	2834
Brunswick Corp.	207	Lake Forest	708-735-4700	3519
CF Industries Inc.	381	Long Grove	708-438-9500	2873
Caterpillar Inc.	44	Peoria	309-675-1000	3531
Commerce Clearing House Inc.	457	Riverwoods	708-940-4600	2741
Dean Foods Co.	200	Franklin Park	708-678-1680	2026
Deere & Co.	79	Moline	309-765-8000	3523
FMC Corp.	125	Chicago	312-861-6000	3795
Fruit of the Loom Inc.	233	Chicago	312-876-1724	2322
Gaylord Container Corp.	433	Deerfield	708-405-5500	2653
General Instrument Corp.	340	Chicago	312-541-5000	3663
Great American Management & Investment	293	Chicago	312-648-5656	2297
Hartmarx Corp.	346	Chicago	312-372-6300	2311
Helene Curtis Industries Inc.	354	Chicago	312-661-0222	2844
Illinois Tool Works Inc.	168	Glenview	708-724-7500	3565
IMC Fertilizer Group Inc.	344	Northbrook	708-272-9200	2874
Imcera Group Inc.	244	Northbrook	708-564-8600	2048
Inland Steel Industries Inc.	142	Chicago	312-346-0300	3312
Interlake Corp.	437	Lisle	708-852-8800	2542
Molex Inc.	416	Lisle	708-969-4550	3643
Morton International Inc.	225	Chicago	312-807-2000	2891
Motorola Inc.	32	Schaumburg	708-576-5000	3674
Nalco Chemical Co.	283	Naperville	708-305-1000	2899
Navistar International Corp.	126	Chicago	312-836-2000	3711
Newell Co.	262	Freeport	815-235-4171	3365
Outboard Marine Corp.	341	Waukegan	708-689-6200	3519
Pittway Corp.	355	Chicago	312-831-1070	3669
Prairie Farms Dairy Inc.	458	Carlinville	217-854-2547	2026
Premark International Inc.	162	Deerfield	708-405-6000	3089
Quaker Oats Co.	98	Chicago	312-222-7111	2043
R R Donnelley & Sons Co.	117	Chicago	312-326-8000	2754
Safety Kleen Corp.	410	Elgin	708-697-8460	4953
Sara Lee Corp.	33	Chicago	312-726-2600	2251
Stone Container Corp.	101	Chicago	312-346-6600	2631
Sundstrand Corp.	247	Rockford	815-226-6000	3724
Tribune Co.	213	Chicago	312-222-9100	2711
USG Corp.	238	Chicago	312-606-4000	3275
Vigoro Corp.	494	Chicago	312-819-2020	2873
Whitman Corp.	190	Rolling Meadows	708-818-5000	2086
William Wrigley Jr. Co.	292	Chicago	312-644-2121	2067
Zenith Electronics Corp.	304	Glenview	708-391-7000	3651

Major Companies in the State (Continued)

Company name	Fortune 500 rank	City	Telephone	SIC number
Other Major Companies in the State				
American Information Technologies Corp.		Chicago	312-750-5000	4813
AON Corp.		Chicago	312-701-3000	6311
CNA Financial Corp.		Chicago	312-822-5000	6331
Commonwealth Edison Co.		Chicago	312-294-4321	4911
Continental Bank Corp.		Chicago	312-828-2345	6712
First Chicago Corp.		Chicago	312-732-4000	6712
Household Finance Corp.		Prospect Heights	708-564-5000	6141
Household International Inc.		Prospect Heights	708-564-5000	6141
Illinois Bell Telephone Co.		Chicago	312-727-9411	4813
Kemper Corp.		Long Grove	708-540-2000	6311
Kraft General Foods Inc.		Glenview	708-998-2000	2095
Mcdonald's Corp.		Oak Brook	708-575-3000	5812
Montgomery Ward Holding Corp.		Chicago	312-467-2000	5311
Navistar International Transportat Corp.		Chicago	312-836-2000	3711
Sears Roebuck & Co.		Chicago	312-875-2500	5311
UAL Corp.		Elk Grove	312-952-4000	4512
United Air Lines Inc.		Chicago	312-952-4000	4512
Walgreen Co.		Deerfield	708-940-2500	5912
Waste Management Inc.		Oak Brook	708-572-8800	4953

Environmental affairs: Environmental Protection Agency, Bernard P. Killian, Director, 2200 Churchill Road, Springfield, IL 62708. 217-782-3397

Labor: Department of Labor, Gwen R. Martin, Director, 310 S. Michigan, 10th fl., Chicago, IL 60604. 312-793-2800

Unemployment: Department of Employment Security, Sally A. Jackson, Director, 401 S. State Street, 6th fl., Chicago, IL 60605. 312-793-5700

Worker's compensation: Industrial Commission, Ray J. Rybacki, Chairman, 100 West Randolph Street, Suite 8-272, Chicago, IL 60601. 312-814-6555

Occupational safety and health: Occupational Safety and Health Administration, Regional Administrator, 230 S. Dearborn, Chicago, IL 60604. 312-353-2220

Secretary of state: Secretary of State, George Ryan, Secretary of State, Rm 213, Capitol Bldg., Springfield, IL 62756. 217-782-2201

Taxation and revenue: Dept. of Revenue, Roger D. Sweet, Director, 101 West Jefferson, Springfield, IL 62756. 217-785-2602

Designated Zones for Economic Development

Enterprise Zones
Enacted in: 1986
No. of established zones: 82
Bartonville/Peoria County
Beardstown
Belleville
Belvidere/Bone County
Bloomington/Normal/McLean County
Bureau/Putnam County
Cal-Sag (Robbins, Blue Island, Worth, Alsip and Crestwood)
Calumet City Area
Canton/Fulton County
Carmi/White County
Centralia Area
Champaign/Champaign County
Chicago (6 zones)
Chicago Heights
Cicero
Danville/Tilton
Decatur
DesPlaines River Valley (Joliet, Will County, Lockport, Rockdale and Romeoville)
Dixon/Lee County
East Peoria
East St. Louis/Washington Park
Effingham/Effingham County
Elgin
Flora/Clay County
Galesburg
Greenville
Harvey

Illinois Valley (LaSalle, Peru, Oglesby, North Utica and LaSalle County)

Kankakee County

Kankakee River Valley (Kankakee, Bradley, Boubonnais, Aroma Park and Kankakee County)

Kewanee

Lincoln/Logan County

Macomb/McDonough County

Massac County (Metropolis, Joppa, and Massac County)

Maywood

Mendota

McCook/Hodgkins

Monmouth

Morton

Mound City/Pulsaki County

Mt. Carmel

Mt. Vernon/Jefferson County

Nashville/Washington County

Olney/Richland County

Ottawa/LaSalle County

Pekin/Tazewell County

Peoria

Quad Cities (Moline, East Moline, and Silvis)

Quincy/Adams County

Rantoul

Riverbend (Alton, East Alton, Hartford, Roxana, South Roxana, Wood River, and Madison County)

Rockford

Rock Island

Southwestern Madison County (Madison, Granite City, Venice and Madison County)

Springfield

Streator/LaSalle County/Livingston County

Summit/Bedford Park

Urbana

Washington

West Frankfort

Whiteside County (Morrison, Rock Falls, Sterling, Whiteside County)

Foreign Trade Zones

Foreign Trade Zone No. 22, Chicago, Illinois, Grantee: Illinois International Port District, Anthony G. Ianello, 3600 East 95th Street, Chicago, IL 60617-5193, 312-646-4400

Foreign Trade Zone No. 31, Granite City, Illinois, Grantee/Operator: Tri-City Regional Port District, Robert Wydra, 2801 Rock Road, Granite City, IL 62040, 618-877-8444

Foreign Trade Zone No. 146, Lawrence County, Illinois, Grantee: Bi-State Authority, Lawrenceville-Vicennes Airport, Michael Smith, Route 4, Box 195, Lawrenceville, IL 62439, 618-943-5219

Foreign Trade Zone No. 114, Peoria, Illinois, Grantee: Economic Development Council, Inc., Bill Rigley, 124 S.W. Adams, Suite 300, Peoria, IL 61602-1388, 309-676-0755

Foreign Trade Zone No. 176, Rockford, Illinois, Grantee:

Greater Rockford Airport Authority, Frederick C. Ford, Executive Director, Two Airport Circle, Rockford, IL 61109, 815-965-8639

Foreign Trade Zone No. 133, Quad-City, Iowa/Illinois, Grantee: Quad-City Foreign-Trade Zone, Inc., Thomas E. Ward, 1639 Second Avenue, Suite 406, Rock Island, IL 61201, 309-788-7436 or 319-326-1005

Labor Unions

Automobile, Aerospace & Agricultural Implement Workers of America, International Union, United, (UAW AFL-CIO)

Bakery, Confectionery & Tobacco Workers International Union (AFL-CIO)

Carpenters and Joiners of America, United Brotherhood of (AFL-CIO)

Chicago Truck Drivers

Electrical Workers, International Brotherhood of (AFL-CIO)

Elgin Teachers Association

Fire Fighters, International Association of (AFL-CIO)

Food and Commercial Workers International Union, United (AFL-CIO)

Graphic Communications International Union (AFL-CIO)

Illinois State Employees Association

Iron Workers, International Association of Bridge, Structural and Ornamental (AFL-CIO)

Laborers' International Union of North America (AFL-CIO)

Machinists and Aerospace Workers, International Association of (AFL-CIO)

National Fraternal Order of Police

Nurses' Association, American

Painters and Allied Trades of The United States and Canada, International Brotherhood of (AFL-CIO)

Roofers, Waterproofers and Allied Workers, United Union of (AFL-CIO)

Service Employees' International Union (AFL-CIO)

State, County and Municipal Employees, American Federation of (AFL-CIO)

Teachers, American Federation of (AFL-CIO)

Teamsters, Chauffeurs, Warehousemen and Helpers of America, International Brotherhood of (AFL-CIO)

Theatrical Stage Employees and Moving Picture Machine Operators of the United States and Canada, International Alliance of (AFL-CIO)

United Transport Employees

Universities with Ph.D. Programs

Depaul University, Chicago

Illinois College of Optometry, Chicago

Illinois Institute of Technology, Chicago

Illinois State University, Normal

Loyola University Chicago, Chicago

National-Louis University, Evanston

Northern Illinois University, De Kalb

Northwestern University, Evanston
Rush University, Chicago
Southern Illinois University at Carbondale, Carbondale
Southern Illinois University at Edwardsville, Edwardsville
University of Chicago, Chicago
University of Health Sciences/chicago Medical School, North Chicago
University of Illinois at Chicago, Chicago
University of Illinois at Urbana-Champaign, Urbana

Sources of Additional Information

Illinois Facts. Illinois Department of Commerce and Community Affairs, 1991. 35p.

Rural Development Resource Guide. Illinois Department of Commerce and Community Affairs, May 1990. 55p.

Business Financing Programs. Illinois Department of Commerce and Community Affairs, 1988. 60p.

The Economic Development Resource Catalog. Illinois Department of Commerce and Community Affairs, Office of Urban Assistance, 1987. 128p.

AURORA–ELGIN, IL (PMSA)

Geographic Profile

Land Area
841.4 square miles

Counties and Parishes
Kane
Kendall

Ranking Highlights

228 *out of 319 in total* **land area**
139 *out of 319 in* **population growth**, *1970–1990*
212 *out of 310 in having the lowest* **unemployment** *rate*
109 *out of 310 in size of* **labor force**
120 *out of 318 in the percentage of* **college graduates**
N/A *out of 292 in per capita personal* **income**
81 *out of 319 in number of* **manufacturing establishments**
254 *out of 318 in* **physicians** *per 1000 people*
187 *out of 318 in* **hospital beds** *per 1000 people*
N/A *out of 267 in fewest* **crimes** *per 1000 people*
N/A *out of 266 in fewest* **violent crimes** *per 1000 people*
251 *out of 319 in per capita* **federal funds and grants**

Quality of Life Indexes (Rate per 1000 population)

Crime rate in 1991:	N/A
Violent crime rate in 1991:	N/A
Physicians rate in 1992:	1.36
Hospital bed rate in 1991:	3.54

ACCRA Cost of Living Indexes
(First quarter 1993, average = 100)

Composite index:	N/A
Utilities index:	N/A
Housing index:	N/A

Population (1990)

Total Population and Growth Rate
1990: 356,884
1980: 315,607
1970: 277,379
Growth rate 1970–1990: 29%

Race and Hispanic Origin
White: 76.8%
Black: 9.2%
Asian/Pacific Islander: 2.4%
Native American: 0.4%
Hispanic origin: 20.5%
White not Hispanic: 67.9%

Age
Ages 18 to 20: 4.4%
Ages 21 to 24: 5.4%
Ages 25 to 44: 33.9%
Ages 45 to 54: 10.2%
Ages 55 to 59: 3.7%

Ages 60 to 64: 3.3%
Ages 65 plus: 9.2%

Educational Attainment (1990)
Percent having completed high school: 78.4%
Percent having completed college: 21.0%
Elementary and high school enrollment: 68,934

Federal Funds and Grants Received
Total received in 1989: $869,600,000
Funds received per capita: $2,447

Civilian Labor Force
1993 (April): 199,767
1992 average: 200,564
1991 average: 194,057
1990 average: 191,268

Unemployment
1993 (April): 7.8%
1992 average: 7.8%
1991 average: 7.4%
1990 average: 5.8%

Average Annual Pay
1988: $21,309
1987: $19,924
1985: $18,701

Per Capita Personal Income
1991: N/A
1990: N/A
1989: N/A

Business Climate (1987)
Manufacturing
Number of establishments in 1987: 800
Shipments in 1987 ($1,000): $5,147,700
Employees in 1987: 38,800
Change in employment, 1982 to 1987: -5.6%
Average annual pay for manufacturing work in 1989: $28,034
Average annual pay for production work in 1987: $21,597

Wholesale Trade
Number of establishments in 1987: 624
Total sales in 1987 ($1,000): $3,511,400
Change in sales, 1982 to 1987: 143.5%

Retail Trade
Number of establishments in 1987: 1,903
Total sales in 1987 ($1,000): $3,511,400
Retail sales per household in 1987: $17,477
Average annual pay in 1989: $11,869

Service Industry
Selected receipts in 1987 ($1,000): $671,700
Average annual pay in 1989: $18,138

Housing
Total number of units in 1990: 125,243
Occupied units in 1990: 120,477
Owner-occupied units in 1990: 70.3%
1993 ACCRA average cost: N/A
1993 ACCRA average rent for an apartment: N/A

Chamber of Commerce
Greater Aurora Chamber of Commerce, Steven L. Hatcher, President, PO Box 277, Aurora, IL 60507. 708-897-9214, FAX 708-897-0469

Economic Development Office
Elgin Area Chamber of Commerce, M. Edward Kelly, Exec. Vice President, PO Box 648, 24 E. Chicago St., Elgin, IL 60121. 708-741-5660, FAX 708-741-5677

Economic Development Organizations
Aurora Economic Development Commisssion, Paul J. Borek, Exec. Director, 40 W. Downer Pl., Aurora, IL 60506. 708-897-5500, FAX 708-897-0469

Major Companies

Company	SIC	Telephone
Aero Welding & Mfg. Co.	3444	(708) 892-7677
American Gage & Machine	3694	(708) 379-1121
Arbetman Brothers & Blair, Inc.	2339	(708) 898-2500
Artistic Carton Co.	2652	(708) 741-0247
Aurora Cord & Cable Co.	2298	(708) 851-1616
Aurora Equipment Co.	2542	(708) 859-1000
Aurora Laundry Co., Inc.	7218	(708) 897-4259
Aurora National Bank	6021	(708) 844-7000
Bentson Industries Inc.	2522	(708) 896-1001
CR Industries	3714	(708) 742-7840
David C. Cook Publishing	2721	(708) 741-2400
Elgiloy Co.	3356	(708) 695-1900
Elgin Corrugated Box Co.	2653	(708) 741-2200
Elgin Diamond Products Co.	3291	(708) 742-3305
Elgin Industries	3714	(708) 742-1720
Elgin Paper Co.	5112	(708) 741-0137
Elgin Salvage & Supply Co.	7389	(708) 742-9500
Elgin Sweeper Co.	3711	(708) 741-5370
First National Bank of Elgin	6021	(708) 697-1100
FM Graphic Impressions	2759	(708) 897-8788
Geneva Construction Co.	1611	(708) 892-4357
Grayline Housewares	3496	(708) 695-3900
Henry Pratt Co.	3491	(708) 844-4000
Illinois Supply Co.	5074	(708) 892-7904
Joseph Spiess Co.	5311	(708) 741-4300
Katy Industries, Inc.	3825	(708) 379-1121
Kinney Electrical Mfg. Co.	3612	(708) 742-9600
Leewards Creative Crafts	5949	(708) 888-5702
Lyon Metal Products, Inc.	2599	(708) 892-8941
Materials Corporation	5031	(708) 697-3333
Merchants National Bank	6021	(708) 896-8531
Metal & Industrial Grinding	3291	(708) 742-3305
National Brush Co.	3991	(708) 897-9133

Major Companies (Continued)

Company	SIC	Telephone
National Engineering Co.	3559	(708) 978-0044
National Metalwares, Inc.	3312	(708) 892-9000
Nichols-Homeshield, Inc.	3354	(708) 355-5400
Northern Illinois Gas Co.	4924	(708) 983-8888
Old Second Bancorp, Inc.	6712	(708) 892-0202
Old Second National Bank	6021	(708) 892-0202
Olympic Controls Corp.	3625	(708) 742-3566
Porvene & Mckees Inc.	2431	(708) 897-9600
Precision Diamond Tool Co.	3291	(708) 888-7100
Professional Packaging Co.	5122	(708) 896-0574
R. & M. Kaufmann, Inc.	2335	(708) 898-6700
Refractory Products Co.	3255	(708) 697-2350
Richards-Wilcox	3442	(708) 897-6951
Royal Insurance Co.	6331	(312) 454-0300
Safety-Kleen Corp.	7699	(708) 697-8460
Salter Broadcasting Co.	4832	(708) 898-6668
Seigle's Home & Building	5031	(708) 742-2000
Simpson Electric Co.	3825	(708) 697-2260
Steiner Co. Inc.	3999	(708) 897-8458
Suburban Plastics Co.	3089	(708) 741-4900
Teledyne Pines	3542	(708) 896-7701
Walker Process Equipment	3589	(708) 892-7921
Weldstar Co.	5169	(708) 859-3100

Colleges and Universities

Aurora University, Aurora
Elgin Community College, Elgin
Judson College, Elgin

BLOOMINGTON–NORMAL, IL (MSA)

Geographic Profile

Land Area
1183.6 square miles

Counties and Parishes
McLean

Ranking Highlights
166 *out of 319 in total* land area
165 *out of 319 in* population growth, *1970–1990*
 34 *out of 310 in having the lowest* unemployment *rate*
207 *out of 310 in size of* labor force
 30 *out of 318 in the percentage of* college graduates
 64 *out of 292 in per capita personal* income
296 *out of 319 in number of* manufacturing establishments
262 *out of 318 in* physicians *per 1000 people*
109 *out of 318 in* hospital beds *per 1000 people*
N/A *out of 267 in fewest* crimes *per 1000 people*
N/A *out of 266 in fewest* violent crimes *per 1000 people*
272 *out of 319 in per capita* federal funds and grants

Quality of Life Indexes (Rate per 1000 population)
Crime rate in 1991:   N/A
Violent crime rate in 1991:   N/A
Physicians rate in 1992:   1.32
Hospital bed rate in 1991:   4.55

ACCRA Cost of Living Indexes
(First quarter 1993, average = 100)
Composite index: 104.4
Utilities index: 120.0
Housing index: 100.9

Population (1990)

Total Population and Growth Rate
1990: 129,180
1980: 119,149
1970: 104,389
Growth rate 1970–1990: 24%

Race and Hispanic Origin
White: 93.7%
Black: 4.3%
Asian/Pacific Islander: 1.3%
Native American: 0.2%
Hispanic origin: 1.3%
White not Hispanic: 93.0%

Age
Ages 18 to 20: 10.5%
Ages 21 to 24: 10.2%
Ages 25 to 44: 30.2%
Ages 45 to 54: 8.6%
Ages 55 to 59: 3.5%

Ages 60 to 64: 3.5%
Ages 65 plus: 10.4%

Educational Attainment (1990)
Percent having completed high school: 84.7%
Percent having completed college: 29.0%
Elementary and high school enrollment: 19,342

Federal Funds and Grants Received
Total received in 1989: $284,400,000
Funds received per capita: $2,282

Civilian Labor Force
1993 (April):   80,585
1992 average: 81,203
1991 average: 75,629
1990 average: 75,027

Unemployment
1993 (April):   4.9%
1992 average: 4.6%
1991 average: 4.6%
1990 average: 4.0%

Average Annual Pay
1988: $20,592
1987: $19,847
1985: $18,353

Per Capita Personal Income
1991: $19,401
1990: $18,894
1989: $17,876

Business Climate (1987)
Manufacturing
Number of establishments in 1987: 99
Shipments in 1987 ($1,000): $786,300
Employees in 1987: 6,400
Change in employment, 1982 to 1987: 0%
Average annual pay for manufacturing work in 1989: $28,143
Average annual pay for production work in 1987: $21,229

Wholesale Trade
Number of establishments in 1987: 241
Total sales in 1987 ($1,000): $1,111,300
Change in sales, 1982 to 1987: -16.8%

Retail Trade
Number of establishments in 1987: 811
Total sales in 1987 ($1,000): $1,111,300
Retail sales per household in 1987: $18,264
Average annual pay in 1989: $9,754

Service Industry
Selected receipts in 1987 ($1,000): $239,700
Average annual pay in 1989: $17,910

Housing
Total number of units in 1990: 49,164

Occupied units in 1990: 46,796
Owner-occupied units in 1990: 63.5%
1993 ACCRA average cost: $105,400
1993 ACCRA average rent for an apartment: $602

Chamber of Commerce
McLean County Chamber of Commerce, Dave Hawkinson, Exec. Director, 210 S. East St. PO Box 1586, Bloomington, IL 61702-1586. 309-829-6344, FAX 309-827-3940

Economic Development Office
Economic Development of the Bloomington-Normal Area, Dave Hawkinson, Exec. Director, 210 S. East St. PO Box 1586, Bloomington, IL 61702-1586. 309-829-6344, FAX 309-827-3940

Major Companies

Company	SIC	Telephone
Amberjack Ltd.	6719	(309) 766-6606
Bell Foods Inc.	5411	(309) 663-8323
Bromenn Healthcare	8062	(309) 827-4321
CC Services Inc.	8742	(309) 557-2111
Central Illinois Trucks Inc.	5012	(309) 452-8392
Champion Federal Savings Loan Association	6035	(309) 829-0456
Country Casualty Insurance	6331	(309) 557-2111
Country Investors Life Assurance	6311	(309) 557-2212
Country Life Insurance Co.	6311	(309) 557-2111
Country Mutual Insurance	6331	(309) 557-2111
Dennison Corp.	5511	(309) 663-1331
Felmley-Dickerson Co.	1542	(309) 828-4317
Growmark, Inc.	5191	(309) 557-6000
Mc Lean County Service Co.	5153	(309) 663-2392
Nestle-Beich, Inc.	2064	(309) 828-1311
Nussbaum Trucking, Inc.	4213	(309) 452-4426
State Farm Life Insurance Co.	6311	(309) 766-2311
State Farm Fire Casualty Co.	6331	(309) 766-2311
State Farm Life Accident Assurance	6311	(309) 766-2311

Colleges and Universities
Illinois State University, Normal
Illinois Wesleyan University, Bloomington
Mennonite College of Nursing, Bloomington

CHAMPAIGN–URBANA–RANTOUL, IL (MSA)

Geographic Profile

Land Area
997.2 square miles

Counties and Parishes
Champaign

Ranking Highlights

204 *out of 319 in total* **land area**
237 *out of 319 in* **population growth,** *1970–1990*
40 *out of 310 in having the lowest* **unemployment** *rate*
191 *out of 310 in size of* **labor force**
12 *out of 318 in the percentage of* **college graduates**
141 *out of 292 in per capita personal* **income**
258 *out of 319 in number of* **manufacturing establishments**
96 *out of 318 in* **physicians** *per 1000 people*
98 *out of 318 in* **hospital beds** *per 1000 people*
N/A *out of 267 in fewest* **crimes** *per 1000 people*
N/A *out of 266 in fewest* **violent crimes** *per 1000 people*
109 *out of 319 in per capita* **federal funds and grants**

Quality of Life Indexes (Rate per 1000 population)

Crime rate in 1991:   N/A
Violent crime rate in 1991:   N/A
Physicians rate in 1992:   2.24
Hospital bed rate in 1991:   4.65

ACCRA Cost of Living Indexes

(First quarter 1993, average = 100)
Composite index: 101.6
Utilities index: 112.7
Housing index: 98.9

Population (1990)

Total Population and Growth Rate
1990: 173,025
1980: 168,392
1970: 163,281
Growth rate 1970–1990: 6%

Race and Hispanic Origin
White: 84.7%
Black: 9.6%
Asian/Pacific Islander: 4.6%
Native American: 0.2%
Hispanic origin: 2.0%
White not Hispanic: 83.7%

Age
Ages 18 to 20: 11.3%
Ages 21 to 24: 11.4%
Ages 25 to 44: 32.4%
Ages 45 to 54: 7.9%
Ages 55 to 59: 3.3%
Ages 60 to 64: 3.1%
Ages 65 plus: 8.7%

Educational Attainment (1990)

Percent having completed high school: 87.5%
Percent having completed college: 34.1%
Elementary and high school enrollment: 23,043

Federal Funds and Grants Received

Total received in 1989: $597,300,000
Funds received per capita: $3,471

Civilian Labor Force

1993 (April):   96,216
1992 average: 95,560
1991 average: 93,144
1990 average: 92,241

Unemployment

1993 (April):   5.5%
1992 average: 4.7%
1991 average: 4.5%
1990 average: 3.9%

Average Annual Pay

1988: $18,745
1987: $17,918
1985: $15,068

Per Capita Personal Income

1991: $17,460
1990: $16,990
1989: $15,947

Business Climate (1987)

Manufacturing
Number of establishments in 1987: 141
Shipments in 1987 ($1,000): $1,685,700
Employees in 1987: 9,400
Change in employment, 1982 to 1987: 28.8%
Average annual pay for manufacturing work in 1989: $21,298
Average annual pay for production work in 1987: $18,359

Wholesale Trade
Number of establishments in 1987: 229
Total sales in 1987 ($1,000): $1,490,000
Change in sales, 1982 to 1987: 26.3%

Retail Trade
Number of establishments in 1987: 1,032
Total sales in 1987 ($1,000): $1,490,000
Retail sales per household in 1987: $17,998
Average annual pay in 1989: $9,558

Service Industry
Selected receipts in 1987 ($1,000): $416,700
Average annual pay in 1989: $17,999

Housing

Total number of units in 1990: 68,416

Occupied units in 1990: 63,900
Owner-occupied units in 1990: 54.5%
1993 ACCRA average cost: $111,077
1993 ACCRA average rent for an apartment: $477

Chamber of Commerce

Champaign County Chamber of Commerce, Michael W. Moore, President, PO Box 37, 100 Trade Center Dr., Suite 402, Champaign, IL 61820. 217-359-1791, FAX 217-359-1809

Economic Development Office

Rantoul Area Chamber of Commerce, Robert G. Kidd, Exec. Vice President, 117 N. Garrard St., Rantoul, IL 61866. 217-893-3323

Economic Development Organizations

Urbana-Champaign Economic Development Corp., Brian D. Crandall, Vice President, PO Box 1813, Champaign, IL 61820. 217-359-6257, FAX 217-359-1809

Industrial Sites

Interstate Research Park. Contact: Newton H. Dodds, PO Box 594, University of Illinois, Champaign, IL 61820. 217-356-1455

Major Businesses

Company	SIC	Telephone
Alltel Illinois, Inc.	4813	(217) 893-4608
Bacon and Van Buskirk Glass	1793	(217) 356-6471
Bank of Illinois in Champaign	6022	(217) 351-6500
Busey Bank	6022	(217) 384-4500
Carle Foundation	8062	(217) 337-3311
Champaign National Bank	6021	(217) 351-2800
Clifford-Jacobs Forging Co.	3462	(217) 352-5172
First American Bank-Champaign	6021	(217) 351-0500
First Busey Corp.	6712	(217) 384-4556
Fisher Farmers Coal Co.	5153	(217) 897-1111
Grand Prairie Coop Inc.	5153	(217) 598-2312
Gordon Hannagan Auction	7389	(217) 568-7117
Hill Ford Sales Inc.	5511	(217) 356-8366
Illini FS Inc.	5191	(217) 384-8300
J & R Construction Manager	1531	(217) 359-6150
Kirby Foods Inc.	5411	(217) 352-2600
Ludlow Co-Operative Elevator	5153	(217) 396-4111
Northern Illinois Water Co.	4941	(217) 352-7001
Parkhill Motor Sales Inc.	5511	(217) 352-4161
Plastic Container Corp.	3089	(217) 356-0358
Rantoul Products, Inc.	3089	(217) 892-9200
Rogers Supply Co., Inc.	5075	(217) 356-0166
Tri Star Marketing, Inc.	5541	(217) 367-8386
Twin City Pontiac Co.	5511	(217) 356-1801
Worden Martin Inc.	5511	(217) 352-7901

Colleges and Universities

Parkland College, Champaign
University of Illinois at Urbana-Champaign, Urbana

CHICAGO, IL (PMSA)

Geographic Profile

Land Area
1884.3 square miles

Counties and Parishes
Cook
DuPage
McHenry

Additional Cities/Towns within Area
Chicago Heights
Evanston

Ranking Highlights

100 *out of 319 in total* **land area**

275 *out of 319 in* **population growth,** *1970–1990*

191 *out of 310 in having the lowest* **unemployment** *rate*

3 *out of 310 in size of* **labor force**

70 *out of 318 in the percentage of* **college graduates**

17 *out of 292 in per capita personal* **income**

3 *out of 319 in number of* **manufacturing establishments**

43 *out of 318 in* **physicians** *per 1000 people*

153 *out of 318 in* **hospital beds** *per 1000 people*

N/A *out of 267 in fewest* **crimes** *per 1000 people*

N/A *out of 266 in fewest* **violent crimes** *per 1000 people*

217 *out of 319 in per capita* **federal funds and grants**

Quality of Life Indexes (Rate per 1000 population)

Crime rate in 1991:	N/A
Violent crime rate in 1991:	N/A
Physicians rate in 1992:	2.78
Hospital bed rate in 1991:	3.91

ACCRA Cost of Living Indexes

(First quarter 1993, average = 100)

Composite index:	120.6
Utilities index:	120.5
Housing index:	154.3

Overview

Chicago, the seat of Illinois's Cook County and the third largest city in the country, is the focus of a metropolitan statistical area that covers Cook, Du Page, and McHenry counties. It is a national transportation, industrial, and financial leader as well as a city of great architectural significance, ethnic diversity, and cultural wealth. The only inland urban area to rank with major East and West Coast metropolises, Chicago has achieved international status through the quality of its cultural institutions and its position as a world financial center.

Chicago's diversified economy is based on manufacturing, printing and publishing, finance and insurance, and food processing (the city is still considered the nation's candy capital) as primary sectors. A substantial industrial base and a major inland port contribute to the city's position as a national transportation and distribution center. The source of nationally distributed magazines, catalogs, educational materials, encyclopedias, and specialized publications, Chicago ranks second only to New York City in the publishing industry. The city is home to the Federal Reserve Bank, the Chicago Board of Trade, and the Chicago Mercantile Exchange and is in addition the headquarters for forty–three Fortune 500 firms.

Items and goods produced include telephone equipment, musical instruments, surgical appliances, machinery, earth-moving and agricultural equipment, steel, metal products, diesel engines, printing presses, office machines, radios and television sets, auto accessories, chemicals, soap, paint, food products and confections.

Since 1979 more than $10 billion has been spent on downtown renovation and construction in Chicago, resulting in a thriving center city. The centerpiece of Mayor Daley's economic program is a proposed $10.8 billion airport to be built on the city's southeast side that would permit the existing Midway Airport to become a cargo and freight terminal. It is predicted that this project, which may not be completed until 2005, would bring two hundred thousand jobs and $14 billion annually into the local economy.

Since its founding, Chicago has been an important transportation and distribution point; at one time it was a crucial link between the Great Lakes and Mississippi River waterways and today the city ranks among the world's busiest shipping hubs. The city became a world port in 1959 with the opening of the St. Lawrence Seaway, which provides a direct link from the Great Lakes to the Atlantic Ocean. By 1990 Illinois International Port was handling more than one hundred and fifty overseas ship arrivals annually. The state of Illinois maintains the third-highest combined mileage of railroads and paved highways in the country. Approximately seven hundred and fifty motor freight carriers serve the metropolitan area, and trucking companies ship more than 50 million tons of freight each year; railroads average more than 40 million tons. Chicago's airports handle more than one million metric tons of cargo annually.

Chicago, one of the most popular convention cities in the United States, is home to McCormick Place, the largest exhibition center in North America. Set on the edge of Lake Michigan, McCormick Place contains 1.6 million square feet of space, having been augmented in 1986 by North Hall, a two-level expansion that added more than five hundred thousand square feet. The entire complex consists of four sections, each with exhibition halls and meeting rooms. A planned expansion, scheduled for completion in 1996, will add 1.3 million square feet. McCormick Place East houses the Aries Crown Theatre. Chicago is known for its mix of gracious dowager hotels and modern glass towers with spectacular views of Lake Michigan. As a hotel city, it is constantly expanding, with more than a half–dozen major hotels being constructed in the last few years. The Sheraton Chicago Hotel and Towers, the first new convention hotel to have been built in Chicago in fourteen years, opened in March 1992.

Expocenter/Chicago, located at O'Hare Airport, features 120,000 square feet of exhibit space. The single-level facility can accommodate up to 617 booths; a hotel is on the premises, and parking for five thousand cars is available nearby. Special meeting facilities are available at museums, theaters, stadiums, corporations, and colleges and universities in the Chicago area.

A somewhat complex network of interstate highways facilitates access into the metropolitan area as well as the Loop district. Approaching from the northwest is I-94, which merges with the John F. Kennedy Expressway leading downtown. I-294 (the Tri-State Tollway), an outerbelt on the west side, joins I-80 to the south. Other westerly approaches are: State Road 5, the East-West Tollway, which becomes I-290; I-90, the North-West Tollway, which intersects I-290; and I-55, the Adlai Stevenson Expressway. Approaches from the south include I-94, the Calumet Expressway; I-57; and I-90, the Chicago Skyway; all of these merge with the Dan Ryan Expressway leading into the city. Running south of Chicago is I-80, which connects with I-55, I-57, I-90, and I-94; near the Indiana border I-80 joins I-90 to become the Northern Indiana Toll Road.

Population (1990)

Total Population and Growth Rate
1990: 6,069,974
1980: 6,060,383
1970: 6,093,287
Growth rate 1970–1990: 0%

Race and Hispanic Origin
White: 67.5%
Black: 22.0%
Asian/Pacific Islander: 3.8%
Native American: 0.2%
Hispanic origin: 12.1%
White not Hispanic: 62.3%

Age
Ages 18 to 20: 4.3%
Ages 21 to 24: 6.2%
Ages 25 to 44: 33.6%
Ages 45 to 54: 10.2%
Ages 55 to 59: 4.2%
Ages 60 to 64: 4.2%
Ages 65 plus: 11.8%

Educational Attainment (1990)
Percent having completed high school: 75.7%
Percent having completed college: 24.4%
Elementary and high school enrollment: 1,015,718

Federal Funds and Grants Received
Total received in 1989: $16,311,200,000
Funds received per capita: $2,624

Civilian Labor Force
1993 (April): 3,276,318
1992 average:3,257,492
1991 average: 3,250,275
1990 average: 3,285,526

Unemployment
1993 (April): 7.9%
1992 average: 7.4%
1991 average: 6.9%
1990 average: 5.9%

Average Annual Pay
1988: $25,691
1987: $24,059
1985: $22,166

Per Capita Personal Income
1991: $22,849
1990: $22,395
1989: $21,146

Business Climate (1987)

Manufacturing
Number of establishments in 1987: 11,742
Shipments in 1987 ($1,000): $68,935,500
Employees in 1987: 579,900
Change in employment, 1982 to 1987: -9.1%
Average annual pay for manufacturing work in 1989: $29,994
Average annual pay for production work in 1987: $21,430

Wholesale Trade
Number of establishments in 1987: 14,376
Total sales in 1987 ($1,000): $125,820,400
Change in sales, 1982 to 1987: 33.2%

Retail Trade
Number of establishments in 1987: 31,656
Total sales in 1987 ($1,000): $125,820,400
Retail sales per household in 1987: $17,049
Average annual pay in 1989: $14,159

Service Industry
Selected receipts in 1987 ($1,000): $27,337,600
Average annual pay in 1989: $24,182

Office Real Estate (1992)
Office space inventory: 152,735,637 square feet
Average class A Central Business District rental range per sq. ft: $33.45

Vacancy Rates
All areas: 22.5%

Vacancy Rates in Central Business District
Class A space: 24.6%
Class B space: 22.8%

Vacancy Rates Outside Central Business District
Class A space: 18.4%
Class B space: 22.0%

Housing
Total number of units in 1990: 2,380,355
Occupied units in 1990: 2,221,722
Owner-occupied units in 1990: 58.6%
1993 ACCRA average cost: N/A
1993 ACCRA average rent for an apartment: N/A

Chamber of Commerce
Chicagoland Chamber of Commerce, Samuel R. Mitchell, President, 200 N. LaSalle St. #600, Chicago, IL 60601. 312-580-6900, FAX 312-580-0046

Economic Development Office
Economic Development Council, Lewis F. Matuszewich, Chair, 150 N. Michigan Ave. Suite 2810, Chicago, IL 60601. 312-726-8787, FAX 312-372-7331

Economic Development Organizations
Economic Development Commission of the City of Chicago, Diana Paluch, Dept. of Planning and Development, 24 E. Congress 7th Fl., Chicago, IL 60505. 312-747-7485

Mt. Greenwood Economic Development Commission, Darlene Larsen, Exec. Director, 3052 W. 111 St., Chicago, IL 60655. 312-238-6103

Illinois Dept. of Commerce and Community Affairs, Chicago Office, 100 W. Randolph Suite 3-400, Chicago, IL 60601. 312-814-6649

Industrial Sites
Chicago Technology Park. Contact: Nina Klarich, Director, 312 Administration Office Bldg., 1737 W. Polk St., University of Illinois at Chicago, Chicago, IL 60612. 312-996-7018

Illinois Institute of Technology Research Institute. Contact: Morton J. Klein, 10 W. 35th St., Chicago, IL 60616. 312-567-4000

Evanston/University Research Park. Contact: Ronald Kysiak, Evanston Inventure, Evanston, IL 60201. 708-864-9334

Major Companies

Company	SIC	Telephone
Abbott Laboratories	2834	(708) 937-6100
Ace Hardware Corp.	5072	(708) 990-6600
Allstate Insurance Co.	6331	(708) 402-5000
Allstate Life Insurance Co.	6311	(708) 402-5199
American Drug Stores, Inc.	5912	(312) 572-5000
American Info Tchnologies	4813	(312) 750-5000
American National Can Co.	3411	(312) 399-3000
Amoco Chemical Co.	2821	(312) 856-3200
Amoco Corp.	2911	(312) 856-6111
Arthur Andersen & Co.	8721	(312) 580-0069

Major Companies (Continued)

Company	SIC	Telephone
Anixter Bros., Inc.	5065	(708) 677-2600
Aon Corp.	6321	(312) 701-3000
Atchison, Topeka	4011	(312) 347-3000
Bally Manufacturing Corp.	7011	(312) 399-1300
Bankers Life & Casualty Co.	6311	(312) 777-7000
Baxter Healthcare Corp.	2834	(312) 948-2000
Baxter International Inc.	2834	(708) 948-2000
Beatrice Co.	2033	(312) 558-4000
Borg-Warner Corp.	7381	(312) 322-8500
Robert Bosch Corp.	5013	(708) 865-5200
Leo Burnett Worldwide Inc.	7311	(312) 220-5959
Carson Pirie Scott & Co.	5311	(312) 641-8000
CBI Industries Inc.	1791	(708) 572-7000
Centel Corp.	4813	(312) 399-2500
CNA Financial Corp.	6331	(312) 822-5000
Coldwell Banker & Co.	6531	(312) 875-5200
Combined Insurance Co. of America	6321	(312) 701-3000
Comdisco, Inc.	7377	(708) 698-3000
Commonwealth Edison Co.	4911	(312) 294-4321
Continental Assurance Co.	6321	(312) 822-5000
Continental Bank Corp.	6021	(312) 828-2345
Continental Bank National	6021	(312) 828-2345
Continental Casualty Co.	6331	(312) 822-5000
Cotter & Co.	5072	(312) 975-2700
Dart Industries Inc.	3089	(708) 405-6000
Dean Foods Co.	2026	(312) 625-6200
Discover Card Services, Inc.	6153	(708) 405-0900
Dodi Inc.	5411	(708) 562-1000
Dominick's Finer Foods, Inc.	5411	(708) 562-1000
Donnelley, R. R. & Sons Co.	2754	(312) 326-8000
Farley Inc.	2322	(312) 876-1724
Federal Reserve Bank of Chicago	6011	(312) 322-5322
First Chicago Corp.	6021	(312) 732-4000
First National Bank of Chicago	6021	(312) 732-4000
FMC Corp.	3711	(312) 861-6000
Frank Consolidated Enterprises	4724	(708) 699-7000
Fruit of Loom, Inc.	2254	(312) 876-7000
Gl Sub Co.	3743	(312) 372-9500
W. W. Grainger Inc.	5063	(708) 982-9000
Great American Management & Investment	3585	(312) 648-5656
H G Group Inc.	4512	(312) 750-1234
H Group Holding, Inc.	4512	(312) 750-1234
Harris Bankcorp, Inc.	6022	(312) 461-2121
Hartmarx Corp.	5611	(312) 372-6300
Health Care Service Corp.	6324	(312) 938-7500
Household Finance Corp.	6141	(708) 564-5000
Household International	6141	(708) 564-5000
Illinois Bell Telephone Co.	4813	(312) 727-9411
Illinois Tool Works Inc.	3089	(708) 724-7500

Major Companies (Continued)

Company	SIC	Telephone
IMC Fertilizer Group, Inc.	2874	(708) 272-9200
Inland Steel Industries Inc.	3312	(312) 346-0300
Inland Steel Services Holding	5051	(312) 346-0300
ITE Corp.	5065	(312) 902-1515
Keebler Co.	2052	(312) 833-2900
Kemper Financial Companies	6311	(708) 540-2000
Komatsu Dresser Co.	3531	(708) 367-2000
Kraft General Foods, Inc.	2033	(708) 998-2000
Lumbermens Mutual Casualty Co.	6331	(708) 540-2000
Marmon Corp.	5051	(312) 372-9500
Marmon Holdings, Inc.	5051	(312) 372-9500
Marmon Industrial Corp.	3743	(312) 372-9500
Martin-Brower Co.	5113	(708) 391-4100
McDonald's Corp.	5812	(708) 575-3000
Midcon Corp.	4922	(708) 691-2500
Mitsui Grain Corp.	5153	(312) 993-5700
Montgomery Ward & Co., Inc.	5651	(312) 467-2000
Montgomery Ward Holding Co.	5311	(312) 467-2000
Moore Business Forms	2621	(708) 480-3208
Motorola, Inc.	3663	(708) 397-5000
Motorola Communications	5065	(708) 397-1000
Nalco Chemical Co.	2899	(708) 305-1000
National Holdings Co.	5411	(312) 693-5100
National Tea Co.	5411	(312) 693-5100
Natural Gas Pipeline of America	4922	(708) 691-3000
Navistar International Co.	3711	(312) 836-2000
Nicor Inc.	4924	(708) 305-9500
Northern Illinois Gas Co.	4924	(708) 983-8888
Norton Simon, Inc.	2033	(312) 782-3820
Old Republic International	6311	(312) 346-8100
Outboard Marine Corp.	3519	(708) 689-6200
Pacific Dunlop Holdings Inc.	3069	(312) 332-2878
Packaging Corp. America	2631	(708) 492-5713
Peoples Energy Corp.	4925	(312) 431-4000
Peoples Gas Light Coke Co.	4924	(312) 431-4000
Pepsi-Cola General Bottlers Div.	2086	(708) 253-1000
Premark International, Inc.	3089	(708) 405-6000
Quaker Oats Co.	2043	(312) 222-7111
Joseph T. Ryerson & Son	5051	(312) 762-2121
Santa Fe Pacific Corp.	4011	(312) 786-6000
Sara Lee Corp.	2013	(312) 726-2600
Sears Roebuck and Co.	5311	(312) 875-2500
Servicemaster Ltd. Partner	8741	(312) 964-1300
Spiegel Inc.	5961	(708) 986-8800
Square D Co.	3613	(708) 397-2600
Stone Container Corp.	2631	(312) 346-6600
Stone Southwest Corp.	2631	(312) 346-6600
Swift-Eckrich, Inc.	2013	(708) 512-1000
Terminal Freight Handling Co.	4731	(312) 875-2500
Thomson Newspapers Inc.	2711	(708) 299-5544

Major Companies (Continued)

Company	SIC	Telephone
Topco Associates Inc.	5141	(708) 676-3030
Tribune Co.	2711	(312) 222-9100
U. B. (Holdings) U. S. Ltd.	2052	(312) 833-2900
U. B. Foods U. S., Inc.	2052	(708) 833-2900
UAL Corp.	4512	(708) 952-4000
United Air Lines, Inc.	4512	(708) 952-4000
United States Gypsum Co.	3275	(312) 606-4000
USG Corp.	3275	(312) 321-4000
Walgreen Co.	5912	(708) 940-2500
Waste Management Inc.	4953	(708) 572-8800
Whitman Corp.	2032	(312) 565-3000
Zenith Electronics Corp.	3651	(708) 391-7000

Colleges and Universities

American Academy of Art, Chicago
American Conservatory of Music, Chicago
American Islamic College, Chicago
Chicago College of Commerce, Chicago
Chicago State University, Chicago
City Colleges of Chicago, Chicago City-Wide College, Chicago
City Colleges of Chicago, Harold Washington College, Chicago
City Colleges of Chicago, Harry S Truman College, Chicago
City Colleges of Chicago, Kennedy-King College, Chicago
City Colleges of Chicago, Malcolm X College, Chicago
City Colleges of Chicago, Olive-Harvey College, Chicago
City Colleges of Chicago, Richard J. Daley College, Chicago
City Colleges of Chicago, Wilbur Wright College, Chicago
Columbia College, Chicago
DePaul University, Chicago
Devry Institute of Technology, Chicago
Dr. William M. Scholl College of Podiatric Medicine, Chicago
East-West University, Chicago
Harrington Institute of Interior Design, Chicago
Illinois College of Optometry, Chicago
Illinois Institute of Technology, Chicago
Illinois Technical College, Chicago
International Academy of Merchandising & Design, Ltd., Chicago
Lexington Institute of Hospitality Careers, Chicago
Loyola University Chicago, Chicago
MacCormac Junior College, Chicago
Montay College, Chicago
Mundelein College, Chicago
Naes College, Chicago
Northeastern Illinois University, Chicago
North Park College, Chicago

Northwestern Business College, Chicago
Prairie State College, Chicago Heights
Ray College of Design, Chicago
Robert Morris College, Chicago Campus, Chicago
Roosevelt University, Chicago
Rush University, Chicago
St. Augustine College, Chicago
St. Xavier College, Chicago
School of the Art Institute of Chicago, Chicago
Spertus College of Judaica, Chicago
Telshe Yeshiva-Chicago, Chicago
University of Chicago, Chicago
University of Illinois at Chicago, Chicago
Vandercook College of Music, Chicago
Kendall College, Evanston
National-Louis University, Evanston
Northwestern University, Evanston

DECATUR, IL (MSA)

Geographic Profile
Land Area
580.6 square miles
Counties and Parishes
Macon

Ranking Highlights
277 *out of 319 in total* **land area**
304 *out of 319 in* **population growth**, *1970–1990*
266 *out of 310 in having the lowest* **unemployment** *rate*
254 *out of 310 in size of* **labor force**
237 *out of 318 in the percentage of* **college graduates**
101 *out of 292 in per capita personal* **income**
270 *out of 319 in number of* **manufacturing establishments**
248 *out of 318 in* **physicians** *per 1000 people*
25 *out of 318 in* **hospital beds** *per 1000 people*
N/A *out of 267 in fewest* **crimes** *per 1000 people*
N/A *out of 266 in fewest* **violent crimes** *per 1000 people*
269 *out of 319 in per capita* **federal funds and grants**

Quality of Life Indexes (Rate per 1000 population)
Crime rate in 1991:   N/A
Violent crime rate in 1991: N/A
Physicians rate in 1992:   1.4
Hospital bed rate in 1991:   6.19

ACCRA Cost of Living Indexes
(First quarter 1993, average = 100)
Composite index: 94.9
Utilities index: 110.5
Housing index: 81.0

Overview
Decatur is located in the center of Illinois. More than a third of the nation's population is located within 500 miles of Decatur, which lies 130 miles north of St. Louis, Missouri 180 miles south of Chicago and 165 miles west of Indianapolis, Indiana. Decatur's location allows same-day truck access to more than 60 major markets, including Chicago, St. Louis, Detroit, Michigan, Minneapolis, Minnesota, Kansas City, Missouri, and Cincinnati, Ohio.

Archer Daniels Midland (#60 on the Fortune 500), A.E. Staley, Illinois Power Company, and Federal Kemper Insurance Company have their corporate headquarters in Decatur. Caterpillar, Bridgestone/Firestone, PPG, Mueller, Wagner Castings, and Wallace Labs have manufacturing facilities here. Caterpillar, which has 3,000 workers, is the largest employer in Decatur.

Air service to Decatur is provided several times a day by Trans World Express and American Eagle. Connections are made through St. Louis and Chicago O'Hare. Decatur is United Parcel Service's downstate hub, with daily 727 air express package and freight service. A 15-minute drive will take you from one side of town to the other.

Population (1990)

Total Population and Growth Rate
1990: 117,206
1980: 131,375
1970: 125,010
Growth rate 1970–1990: -6%

Race and Hispanic Origin
White: 87.2%
Black: 12.1%
Asian/Pacific Islander: 0.4%
Native American: 0.1%
Hispanic origin: 0.5%
White not Hispanic: 86.9%

Age
Ages 18 to 20: 4.4%
Ages 21 to 24: 4.9%
Ages 25 to 44: 29.8%
Ages 45 to 54: 10.8%
Ages 55 to 59: 4.8%
Ages 60 to 64: 4.9%
Ages 65 plus: 14.6%

Educational Attainment (1990)
Percent having completed high school: 76.2%
Percent having completed college: 14.8%
Elementary and high school enrollment: 21,013

Federal Funds and Grants Received
Total received in 1989: $284,400,000
Funds received per capita: $2,300

Civilian Labor Force
1993 (April):   63,765
1992 average: 63,603
1991 average: 61,022
1990 average: 60,114

Unemployment
1993 (April):   9.7%
1992 average: 9.2%
1991 average: 8.9%
1990 average: 7.1%

Average Annual Pay
1988: $23,606
1987: $22,185
1985: $20,969

Per Capita Personal Income
1991: $18,258
1990: $17,898
1989: $16,893

Business Climate (1987)

Manufacturing
Number of establishments in 1987: 129

Shipments in 1987 ($1,000): $3,345,000
Employees in 1987: 13,100
Change in employment, 1982 to 1987: -17.1%
Average annual pay for manufacturing work in 1989: $35,288
Average annual pay for production work in 1987: $31,061

Wholesale Trade
Number of establishments in 1987: 189
Total sales in 1987 ($1,000): $3,662,400
Change in sales, 1982 to 1987: 35.5%

Retail Trade
Number of establishments in 1987: 748
Total sales in 1987 ($1,000): $3,662,400
Retail sales per household in 1987: $15,760
Average annual pay in 1989: $11,474

Service Industry
Selected receipts in 1987 ($1,000): $235,000
Average annual pay in 1989: $17,019

Housing
Total number of units in 1990: 50,049
Occupied units in 1990: 45,996
Owner-occupied units in 1990: 70.2%
1993 ACCRA average cost: $86,500
1993 ACCRA average rent for an apartment: $453

Chamber of Commerce
Metro Decatur Chamber of Commerce, Richard J. Lutovsky, President, 100 Merchant St. #100, PO Box 1031, Decatur, IL 62525. 217-422-2200, FAX 217-422-9307

Economic Development Office
Decatur-Macon County Economic Development Foundation, James Holderread, Exec Director, 100 Merchant St., PO Box 1031, Decatur, IL 62525. 217-422-2200, FAX 217-422-9307

Major Companies

Company	SIC	Telephone
ADM Feeds Corp.	2048	(217) 424-2674
ADM Trucking, Inc.	4213	(217) 424-5820
Archer Daniels Midland Co.	2075	(217) 424-5200
Black & Co.	5085	(217) 428-4424
T. A. Brinkoetter & Sons	1711	(217) 423-3493
A. W. Cash Valve Manufacturing Corp.	3491	(217) 422-8574
Christy-Foltz Inc.	1541	(217) 428-8601
Citizens National Bank of Decatur	6021	(217) 424-2000
Climate Control Inc.	3714	(217) 422-0055
Corn Belt Inc.	5171	(217) 877-4301
Decatur Memorial Hospital	8062	(217) 877-8121
DMH Health System Inc.	8062	(217) 877-8121
R. V. Evans Co. Distributors	5084	(217) 423-3631

Major Companies (Continued)

Company	SIC	Telephone
Federal Kemper Insurance Co.	6331	(217) 877-9510
First Decatur Bancshares	6021	(217) 424-1111
First Mutual Savings Bank	6036	(217) 429-2306
First National Bank of Decatur	6021	(217) 424-1111
Huston-Patterson Corp.	2752	(217) 429-5161
Illinois Power Co.	4911	(217) 424-6600
K's Merchandise Mart, Inc.	5399	(217) 875-1440
Magna Millikin Bank of Decatur	6021	(217) 429-4253
Mueller Co.	3823	(217) 423-4471
Rathje Enterprises	1731	(217) 423-2593
St. Mary's Hospital	8062	(217) 429-2966
Tabor Grain Co.	5153	(217) 424-5200

Colleges and Universities

Millikin University, Decatur
Richland Community College, Decatur

JOLIET, IL (PMSA)

Geographic Profile

Land Area
1257.4 square miles

Counties and Parishes
Grundy
Will

Ranking Highlights

156 *out of 319 in total land area*
 89 *out of 319 in population growth, 1970–1990*
226 *out of 310 in having the lowest unemployment rate*
 98 *out of 310 in size of labor force*
181 *out of 318 in the percentage of college graduates*
N/A *out of 292 in per capita personal income*
132 *out of 319 in number of manufacturing establishments*
316 *out of 318 in physicians per 1000 people*
299 *out of 318 in hospital beds per 1000 people*
N/A *out of 267 in fewest crimes per 1000 people*
N/A *out of 266 in fewest violent crimes per 1000 people*
314 *out of 319 in per capita federal funds and grants*

Quality of Life Indexes (Rate per 1000 population)

Crime rate in 1991:	N/A
Violent crime rate in 1991:	N/A
Physicians rate in 1992:	0.82
Hospital bed rate in 1991:	2.12

ACCRA Cost of Living Indexes

(First quarter 1993, average = 100)
Composite index: 112.9
Utilities index: 124.3
Housing index: 130.5

Population (1990)

Total Population and Growth Rate
1990: 389,650
1980: 355,042
1970: 274,360
Growth rate 1970–1990: 42%

Race and Hispanic Origin
White: 86.0%
Black: 9.9%
Asian/Pacific Islander: 1.3%
Native American: 0.2%
Hispanic origin: 5.3%
White not Hispanic: 83.5%

Age
Ages 18 to 20: 4.6%
Ages 21 to 24: 5.4%
Ages 25 to 44: 34%
Ages 45 to 54: 10.5%
Ages 55 to 59: 3.6%

Ages 60 to 64: 3.3%
Ages 65 plus: 9%

Educational Attainment (1990)
Percent having completed high school: 80.3%
Percent having completed college: 17.6%
Elementary and high school enrollment: 75,877

Federal Funds and Grants Received
Total received in 1989: $655,000,000
Funds received per capita: $1,727

Civilian Labor Force
1993 (April): 232,544
1992 average: 233,581
1991 average: 217,372
1990 average: 213,128

Unemployment
1993 (April): 7.8%
1992 average: 8.0%
1991 average: 7.6%
1990 average: 6.5%

Average Annual Pay
1988: $21,854
1987: $20,952
1985: $19,747

Per Capita Personal Income
1991: N/A
1990: N/A
1989: N/A

Business Climate (1987)
Manufacturing
Number of establishments in 1987: 405
Shipments in 1987 ($1,000): $6,014,100
Employees in 1987: 20,500
Change in employment, 1982 to 1987: -16.3%
Average annual pay for manufacturing work in 1989: $30,686
Average annual pay for production work in 1987: $26,493

Wholesale Trade
Number of establishments in 1987: 426
Total sales in 1987 ($1,000): $1,788,500
Change in sales, 1982 to 1987: 27.9%

Retail Trade
Number of establishments in 1987: 1,661
Total sales in 1987 ($1,000): $1,788,500
Retail sales per household in 1987: $14,004
Average annual pay in 1989: $10,643

Service Industry
Selected receipts in 1987 ($1,000): $517,600
Average annual pay in 1989: $18,403

Housing
Total number of units in 1990: 135,522

Occupied units in 1990: 128,912
Owner-occupied units in 1990: 76.7%
1993 ACCRA average cost: $156,840
1993 ACCRA average rent for an apartment: $545

Chamber of Commerce
Joliet Regional Chamber of Commerce & Industry, Lawrence J. Sak, President, 16 W. Van Buren, PO Box 752, Joliet, IL 60434. 815-727-5371

Economic Development Office
Will County Chamber of Commerce, Ruth Calvert Fitzgerald, President, 116 N. Chicago St., Suite 101, Joliet, IL 60431. 815-723-1800, FAX 815-723-6972

Economic Development Organizations
Joliet/Will County Center for Economic Development, Ruth Calvert Fitzgerald, President, 116 N. Chicago St., Suite 101, Joliet, IL 60431. 815-723-1800, FAX 815-723-6972

Major Businesses

Company	SIC	Telephone
Barrett Hardware Co.	5085	(815) 726-4341
Bill Jacobs Chevrolet	5511	(815) 725-7110
Champion Machinery Co.	3556	(815) 726-4336
First Midwest Bank/Illinois	6021	(815) 727-5222
J. Merle Jones & Sons, Inc.	5511	(815) 741-7500
Joliet Equipment Corp.	5063	(815) 727-6606
Kemmerer Bottling Group	2086	(815) 741-7777
Phillips Getschow Co.	1711	(815) 644-6116
Werden Buck Co.	5032	(815) 726-4366

Colleges and Universities
College of St. Francis, Joliet
Joliet Junior College, Joliet

KANKAKEE, IL (MSA)

Geographic Profile

Land Area
677.5 square miles

Counties and Parishes
Kankakee

Ranking Highlights

258 *out of 319 in total* **land area**
278 *out of 319 in* **population growth,** *1970–1990*
248 *out of 310 in having the lowest* **unemployment** *rate*
285 *out of 310 in size of* **labor force**
298 *out of 318 in the percentage of* **college graduates**
155 *out of 292 in per capita personal* **income**
283 *out of 319 in number of* **manufacturing establishments**
254 *out of 318 in* **physicians** *per 1000 people*
 35 *out of 318 in* **hospital beds** *per 1000 people*
N/A *out of 267 in fewest* **crimes** *per 1000 people*
N/A *out of 266 in fewest* **violent crimes** *per 1000 people*
207 *out of 319 in per capita* **federal funds and grants**

Quality of Life Indexes (Rate per 1000 population)

Crime rate in 1991:	N/A
Violent crime rate in 1991:	N/A
Physicians rate in 1992:	1.36
Hospital bed rate in 1991:	5.8

ACCRA Cost of Living Indexes

(First quarter 1993, average = 100)

Composite index:	N/A
Utilities index:	N/A
Housing index:	N/A

Population (1990)

Total Population and Growth Rate
1990: 96,255
1980: 102,926
1970: 97,250
Growth rate 1970–1990: -1%

Race and Hispanic Origin
White: 83.3%
Black: 15.0%
Asian/Pacific Islander: 0.7%
Native American: 0.2%
Hispanic origin: 2.0%
White not Hispanic: 82.3%

Age
Ages 18 to 20: 4.6%
Ages 21 to 24: 5.3%
Ages 25 to 44: 29.6%
Ages 45 to 54: 10.1%
Ages 55 to 59: 4.1%
Ages 60 to 64: 4.5%
Ages 65 plus: 13.7%

Educational Attainment (1990)

Percent having completed high school: 73.1%
Percent having completed college: 11.9%
Elementary and high school enrollment: 18,252

Federal Funds and Grants Received

Total received in 1989: $267,000,000
Funds received per capita: $2,728

Civilian Labor Force

1993 (April):	50,656
1992 average:	51,973
1991 average:	50,407
1990 average:	48,717

Unemployment

1993 (April): 8.7%
1992 average: 8.7%
1991 average: 8.2%
1990 average: 7.0%

Average Annual Pay

1988: $18,665
1987: $17,070
1985: $16,133

Per Capita Personal Income

1991: $17,080
1990: $16,630
1989: $15,283

Business Climate (1987)

Manufacturing
Number of establishments in 1987: 111
Shipments in 1987 ($1,000): $1,301,600
Employees in 1987: 7,000
Change in employment, 1982 to 1987: -13.6%
Average annual pay for manufacturing work in 1989: $28,897
Average annual pay for production work in 1987: $22,979

Wholesale Trade
Number of establishments in 1987: 140
Total sales in 1987 ($1,000): $530,600
Change in sales, 1982 to 1987: -6.2%

Retail Trade
Number of establishments in 1987: 487
Total sales in 1987 ($1,000): $530,600
Retail sales per household in 1987: $14,652
Average annual pay in 1989: $10,623

Service Industry
Selected receipts in 1987 ($1,000): $146,600
Average annual pay in 1989: $16,655

Housing

Total number of units in 1990: 37,001

Occupied units in 1990: 34,623
Owner-occupied units in 1990: 66.8%
1993 ACCRA average cost: N/A
1993 ACCRA average rent for an apartment: N/A

Chamber of Commerce

Kankakee Area Chamber of Commerce, Richard Clark, President, 4 Dearborn Square, PO Box 905, Kankakee, IL 60901. 815-933-7721

Economic Development Office

Kankakee County Economic Development Council, Patricia Blanchette, President, 4 Dearborn Square #B, Kankakee, IL 60901. 815-935-1177, FAX 815-935-1181

Major Companies

Company	SIC	Telephone
Azzarelli Builders, Inc.	1542	(815) 937-8701
Azzarelli Construction Co.	1611	(815) 937-8700
Baron-Huot Oil Co., Inc.	5171	(815) 933-3365
Consumers Illinois Water	4941	(815) 935-8803
Kankakee Distributing Co.	5182	(815) 933-4457
Kankakee Federal Savings & Loan	6035	(815) 937-2800
La Beau Bros. Inc.	5012	(815) 933-5519
Loitz Bros. Construction	1623	(815) 465-2155
Peddinghaus Corp.	3541	(815) 937-3800
Rexco, Inc.	4213	(815) 933-4466
Riverside Health System	8062	(815) 933-1671
Smith Oil Co. of Kankakee	5541	(815) 932-6411
St. Marys Hospital	8062	(815) 937-2490
Tami Leasing Inc.	7513	(815) 939-2235
A. N. Webber, Inc.	4213	(815) 939-2235

Colleges and Universities

Kankakee Community College, Kankakee
Olivet Nazarene University, Kankakee

LAKE COUNTY, IL (PMSA)

Geographic Profile

Land Area
447.8 square miles

Counties and Parishes
Lake

Additional Cities/Towns within Area
North Chicago
Waukegan

Ranking Highlights

304 *out of 319 in total* **land area**
113 *out of 319 in* **population growth**, *1970–1990*
47 *out of 310 in having the lowest* **unemployment** *rate*
77 *out of 310 in size of* **labor force**
20 *out of 318 in the percentage of* **college graduates**
N/A *out of 292 in per capita personal* **income**
86 *out of 319 in number of* **manufacturing establishments**
109 *out of 318 in* **physicians** *per 1000 people*
250 *out of 318 in* **hospital beds** *per 1000 people*
N/A *out of 267 in fewest* **crimes** *per 1000 people*
N/A *out of 266 in fewest* **violent crimes** *per 1000 people*
192 *out of 319 in per capita* **federal funds and grants**

Quality of Life Indexes (Rate per 1000 population)

Crime rate in 1991:	N/A
Violent crime rate in 1991:	N/A
Physicians rate in 1992:	2.07
Hospital bed rate in 1991:	2.9

ACCRA Cost of Living Indexes

(First quarter 1993, average = 100)
Composite index: N/A
Utilities index: N/A
Housing index: N/A

Population (1990)

Total Population and Growth Rate
1990: 516,418
1980: 440,388
1970: 382,638
Growth rate 1970–1990: 35%

Race and Hispanic Origin
White: 87.3%
Black: 6.7%
Asian/Pacific Islander: 2.4%
Native American: 0.2%
Hispanic origin: 7.5%
White not Hispanic: 83.4%

Age
Ages 18 to 20: 5.4%
Ages 21 to 24: 5.5%
Ages 25 to 44: 34.9%

Ages 45 to 54: 10.8%
Ages 55 to 59: 3.9%
Ages 60 to 64: 3.6%
Ages 65 plus: 8.4%

Educational Attainment (1990)
Percent having completed high school: 84.7%
Percent having completed college: 32.0%
Elementary and high school enrollment: 88,975

Federal Funds and Grants Received
Total received in 1989: $1,413,900,000
Funds received per capita: $2,854

Civilian Labor Force
1993 (April): 332,942
1992 average: 332,050
1991 average: 319,950
1990 average: 312,407

Unemployment
1993 (April): 4.8%
1992 average: 4.8%
1991 average: 4.6%
1990 average: 3.9%

Average Annual Pay
1988: $23,459
1987: $21,827
1985: $19,833

Per Capita Personal Income
1991: N/A
1990: N/A
1989: N/A

Business Climate (1987)
Manufacturing
Number of establishments in 1987: 760
Shipments in 1987 ($1,000): $4,816,300
Employees in 1987: 50,900
Change in employment, 1982 to 1987: 11.6%
Average annual pay for manufacturing work in 1989: $32,536
Average annual pay for production work in 1987: $20,380

Wholesale Trade
Number of establishments in 1987: 872
Total sales in 1987 ($1,000): $5,398,300
Change in sales, 1982 to 1987: 108.0%

Retail Trade
Number of establishments in 1987: 2,786
Total sales in 1987 ($1,000): $5,398,300
Retail sales per household in 1987: $22,437
Average annual pay in 1989: $13,717

Service Industry
Selected receipts in 1987 ($1,000): $1,636,900
Average annual pay in 1989: $21,683

Housing
Total number of units in 1990: 183,283
Occupied units in 1990: 173,966
Owner-occupied units in 1990: 74.2%
1993 ACCRA average cost: N/A
1993 ACCRA average rent for an apartment: N/A

Chamber of Commerce
Waukegan/Lake County Chamber of Commerce, Charles C. Isely III, President, 414 N. Sheridan Rd., Waukegan, IL 60085-4096. 708-249-3800, FAX 708-249-3802

Economic Development Office
Lake County Economic Development Commission, Cranston Byrd, Deputy Director, 18 North County Street, Room A03, Waukegan, IL 60085. 708-360-6350

Economic Development Organizations
Waukegan Port District, Mary S. Walker, Harbor Manager, PO Box 620, 55 S. Harbor Pl., Waukegan, IL 60079. 708-244-3133, FAX 708-244-1348

Colleges and Universities
Shimer College, Waukegan
University of Health Sciences/Chicago Medical School, North Chicago

PEORIA, IL (MSA)

Geographic Profile
Land Area
1796.5 square miles

Counties and Parishes
Peoria
Tazewell
Woodford

Additional Cities/Towns within Area
Pekin

Ranking Highlights
105 *out of 319 in total* **land area**
276 *out of 319 in* **population growth,** *1970–1990*
191 *out of 310 in having the lowest* **unemployment** *rate*
128 *out of 310 in size of* **labor force**
195 *out of 318 in the percentage of* **college graduates**
 96 *out of 292 in per capita personal* **income**
159 *out of 319 in number of* **manufacturing establishments**
109 *out of 318 in* **physicians** *per 1000 people*
113 *out of 318 in* **hospital beds** *per 1000 people*
N/A *out of 267 in fewest* **crimes** *per 1000 people*
N/A *out of 266 in fewest* **violent crimes** *per 1000 people*
242 *out of 319 in per capita* **federal funds and grants**

Quality of Life Indexes (Rate per 1000 population)
Crime rate in 1991:	N/A
Violent crime rate in 1991:	N/A
Physicians rate in 1992:	2.07
Hospital bed rate in 1991:	4.47

ACCRA Cost of Living Indexes
(First quarter 1993, average = 100)
Composite index: 106.3
Utilities index: 95.2
Housing index: 114.0

Overview
Peoria is the seat of Peoria County and the center of an urban complex consisting of Peoria Heights, West Peoria, Bartonville, Bellevue, East Peoria, Creve Coeur, and Pekin. The city is considered the oldest continuously inhabited American community west of the Allegheny Mountains. Another of Peoria's distinctions is its typicality: in terms of such demographic characteristics as median age and purchasing patterns, the city's general makeup is almost identical to that of the United States as a whole, thus making it an ideal test market for consumer researchers. Peoria was described in the November 1991 *Kiplinger's Personal Finance Magazine* as a "super city" where people are moving and opportunity is knocking.

Located at the center of a fertile agricultural region, with corn and soybeans as principal crops, Peoria is an important livestock and grain exporting market. Farm production in a three-county area totals more than $290 million yearly; livestock sales, particularly of hogs, consistently rank among the six to eight highest in the nation. Peoria is surrounded by rich bituminous coal fields that hold reserves estimated to last for 150 years and slated for worldwide distribution.

Manufacturing is a major industry: more than two hundred diversified firms make nearly 1,000 different products. Peoria is the headquarters of two of the largest U.S. earth-moving equipment makers, which record an average of $2 billion in shipments annually. Local companies produce more than fourteen percent of the country's internal-combustion engines and about eight percent of all construction machinery in North America. The city is also the base for several distilleries and breweries.

With access to three interstate and four federal highways, metropolitan Peoria is linked to markets nationwide by 168 motor freight carriers, 131 of which maintain local terminals, and thirteen railroads. Air cargo transfer facilities are available at Greater Peoria Regional Airport and two private airfields. Four barge lines transport more than thirty–six million tons during a year-round navigation season through the Peoria Lock and Dam, a major link from the Gulf of Mexico to the St. Lawrence Seaway. Peoria is a Foreign Trade Zone.

Population (1990)
Total Population and Growth Rate
1990: 339,172
1980: 365,864
1970: 341,979
Growth rate 1970–1990: -1%

Race and Hispanic Origin
White: 91.2%
Black: 7.4%
Asian/Pacific Islander: 0.8%
Native American: 0.2%
Hispanic origin: 1.1%
White not Hispanic: 90.5%

Age
Ages 18 to 20: 4.6%
Ages 21 to 24: 5.2%
Ages 25 to 44: 30.1%
Ages 45 to 54: 10.6%
Ages 55 to 59: 4.6%
Ages 60 to 64: 4.6%
Ages 65 plus: 13.8%

Educational Attainment (1990)
Percent having completed high school: 78.4%
Percent having completed college: 16.9%
Elementary and high school enrollment: 60,852

Federal Funds and Grants Received
Total received in 1989: $857,700,000

Funds received per capita: $2,520

Civilian Labor Force
1993 (April): 171,999
1992 average: 173,239
1991 average: 166,818
1990 average: 167,256

Unemployment
1993 (April): 7.4%
1992 average: 7.4%
1991 average: 7.0%
1990 average: 5.9%

Average Annual Pay
1988: $22,713
1987: $21,205
1985: $19,994

Per Capita Personal Income
1991: $18,383
1990: $18,139
1989: $16,999

Business Climate (1987)
Manufacturing
Number of establishments in 1987: 319
Shipments in 1987 ($1,000): $4,165,400
Employees in 1987: 29,700
Change in employment, 1982 to 1987: -34.9%
Average annual pay for manufacturing work in 1989: $38,388
Average annual pay for production work in 1987: $29,880

Wholesale Trade
Number of establishments in 1987: 645
Total sales in 1987 ($1,000): $4,710,300
Change in sales, 1982 to 1987: 1.0%

Retail Trade
Number of establishments in 1987: 2,096
Total sales in 1987 ($1,000): $4,710,300
Retail sales per household in 1987: $15,701
Average annual pay in 1989: $10,793

Service Industry
Selected receipts in 1987 ($1,000): $701,500
Average annual pay in 1989: $17,346

Housing
Total number of units in 1990: 136,458
Occupied units in 1990: 129,363
Owner-occupied units in 1990: 68.0%
1993 ACCRA average cost: $137,770
1993 ACCRA average rent for an apartment: $484

Chamber of Commerce
Peoria Area Chamber of Commerce, Rebekah Bourland, Senior Vice President, 124 S.W. Adams St. #300, Peoria, IL 61604-1388. 309-676-0755, FAX 309-676-7534

Economic Development Office
Economic Development Council, Inc., Robert Marcusse, Director, 124 S.W. Adams #300, Peoria, IL 61602. 309-676-7500

Major Companies

Company	SIC	Telephone
Becker Bros., Inc.	1542	(309) 674-1200
Burklund Distributors Inc.	5194	(309) 694-1900
Caterpillar Inc.	3531	(309) 675-1000
Caterpillar Financial Services	6159	(309) 675-6666
Central Illinois Light Co.	4931	(309) 672-5271
Cilcorp Inc.	4911	(309) 672-5167
Farmers Auto Insurance Association	6311	(309) 346-1161
First American Bank - Illinois	6021	(309) 655-5000
Fleming Packaging Corp.	2752	(309) 676-2121
C. Iber & Sons Inc.	1542	(309) 699-7291
Illinois Mutual Life & Casualty	6321	(309) 674-8255
Interstate Products Association	5154	(309) 691-5360
Klaus Radio, Inc.	5064	(309) 691-4840
Methodist Medical Center	8062	(309) 672-5522
Midwest Financial Group Inc.	6021	(309) 655-5500
OSF Healthcare System	8062	(309) 655-2869
Pekin Life Insurance Co.	6311	(309) 346-1161
Proctor Health Care Inc.	8062	(309) 691-1000
River City Construction Co.	1542	(309) 694-3120
RLI Corp.	6331	(309) 692-1000
S & K Chevrolet Co.	5511	(309) 692-4010
Scrivner of Illinois Inc.	5141	(309) 694-4211
United Financial Services	6141	(309) 688-9531
USA Financial Services Inc.	6141	(309) 688-9531

Colleges and Universities
Bradley University, Peoria
Midstate College, Peoria
St. Francis Medical Center College of Nursing, Peoria

ROCKFORD, IL (MSA)

Geographic Profile
Land Area
795.2 square miles

Counties and Parishes
Boone
Winnebago

Ranking Highlights
240 *out of 319 in total* **land area**
247 *out of 319 in* **population growth,** *1970–1990*
254 *out of 310 in having the lowest* **unemployment** *rate*
134 *out of 310 in size of* **labor force**
216 *out of 318 in the percentage of* **college graduates**
118 *out of 292 in per capita personal* **income**
84 *out of 319 in number of* **manufacturing establishments**
154 *out of 318 in* **physicians** *per 1000 people*
173 *out of 318 in* **hospital beds** *per 1000 people*
N/A *out of 267 in fewest* **crimes** *per 1000 people*
N/A *out of 266 in fewest* **violent crimes** *per 1000 people*
277 *out of 319 in per capita* **federal funds and grants**

Quality of Life Indexes (Rate per 1000 population)
Crime rate in 1991:	N/A
Violent crime rate in 1991:	N/A
Physicians rate in 1992:	1.82
Hospital bed rate in 1991:	3.66

ACCRA Cost of Living Indexes
(First quarter 1993, average = 100)
Composite index:	108.1
Utilities index:	137.8
Housing index:	107.1

Population (1990)
Total Population and Growth Rate
1990: 283,719
1980: 279,514
1970: 272,063
Growth rate 1970–1990: 4%

Race and Hispanic Origin
White: 88.7%
Black: 8.2%
Asian/Pacific Islander: 1.1%
Native American: 0.2%
Hispanic origin: 3.5%
White not Hispanic: 87.0%

Age
Ages 18 to 20: 4.2%
Ages 21 to 24: 5.4%
Ages 25 to 44: 32.2%
Ages 45 to 54: 10.7%
Ages 55 to 59: 4.3%
Ages 60 to 64: 4.4%
Ages 65 plus: 12.6%

Educational Attainment (1990)
Percent having completed high school: 76.2%
Percent having completed college: 16.2%
Elementary and high school enrollment: 48,810

Federal Funds and Grants Received
Total received in 1989: $638,600,000
Funds received per capita: $2,263

Civilian Labor Force
1993 (April): 161,232
1992 average: 160,953
1991 average: 158,942
1990 average: 156,936

Unemployment
1993 (April): 9.5%
1992 average: 8.9%
1991 average: 8.3%
1990 average: 6.4%

Average Annual Pay
1988: $22,276
1987: $20,818
1985: $19,771

Per Capita Personal Income
1991: $17,936
1990: $17,783
1989: $17,083

Business Climate (1987)
Manufacturing
Number of establishments in 1987: 772
Shipments in 1987 ($1,000): $5,274,100
Employees in 1987: 43,800
Change in employment, 1982 to 1987: -5.4%
Average annual pay for manufacturing work in 1989: $30,023
Average annual pay for production work in 1987: $24,083

Wholesale Trade
Number of establishments in 1987: 606
Total sales in 1987 ($1,000): $1,435,400
Change in sales, 1982 to 1987: 11.7%

Retail Trade
Number of establishments in 1987: 1,663
Total sales in 1987 ($1,000): $1,435,400
Retail sales per household in 1987: $16,318
Average annual pay in 1989: $11,205

Service Industry
Selected receipts in 1987 ($1,000): $675,000
Average annual pay in 1989: $17,191

Housing
Total number of units in 1990: 113,143

Occupied units in 1990: 107,677
Owner-occupied units in 1990: 68.5%
1993 ACCRA average cost: $120,650
1993 ACCRA average rent for an apartment: $525

Chamber of Commerce

Rockford Area Chamber of Commerce, Ryan Petty, President, 515 N. Court St., PO Box 1747, Rockford, IL 61110-0247. 815-987-8100, FAX 815-987-8122

Economic Development Office

Rockford Dept. of Community Development, Diane Voneida, Exec. Director, 425 E. State St., Rockford, IL 61104. 815-987-5600

Major Companies

Company	SIC	Telephone
Amcore Financial Inc.	6021	(815) 968-2241
Amerock Corp.	3429	(815) 963-9631
Anderson Industries Inc.	3714	(815) 987-9070
Atwood Industries Inc.	3714	(815) 877-5771
Barber-Colman Co.	3822	(815) 397-7400
Barber-Colman Holdings Co.	3822	(815) 397-7400
Behr, Joseph & Sons Inc.	5093	(815) 987-2600
Clarcor Inc.	3714	(815) 962-8867
Eclipse, Inc.	3433	(815) 877-3031
Elco Industries, Inc.	3452	(815) 397-5151
First Community Bancorp	6712	(815) 962-3771
Hilander Foods Inc.	5411	(815) 398-5500
Independent Freightway Inc.	4213	(815) 395-1112
Ingersoll International Inc.	3541	(815) 987-6000
Liebovich Bros., Inc.	5051	(815) 987-3200
Pacemaker Food Stores Inc.	5411	(815) 397-6080
Pioneer Financial Service	6311	(815) 987-5000
Pioneer Life Insurance of Illinois	6311	(815) 987-5000
Regal-Beloit Corp. Delaware	8062	(815) 968-6861
Rockford Products Corp.	3452	(815) 397-6000
Sundstrand Corp.	3812	(815) 226-2500
Swedish American Corp.	8062	(815) 966-2083
Swedish American Hospital Association	8062	(815) 968-4400

Colleges and Universities

Rockford College, Rockford
Rock Valley College, Rockford

SPRINGFIELD, IL (MSA)

Geographic Profile

Land Area
1182.6 square miles

Counties and Parishes
Menard
Sangamon

Ranking Highlights

168 *out of 319 in total* **land area**
223 *out of 319 in* **population growth,** *1970–1990*
 64 *out of 310 in having the lowest* **unemployment** *rate*
165 *out of 310 in size of* **labor force**
 98 *out of 318 in the percentage of* **college graduates**
 55 *out of 292 in per capita personal* **income**
266 *out of 319 in number of* **manufacturing establishments**
 23 *out of 318 in* **physicians** *per 1000 people*
  5 *out of 318 in* **hospital beds** *per 1000 people*
N/A *out of 267 in fewest* **crimes** *per 1000 people*
N/A *out of 266 in fewest* **violent crimes** *per 1000 people*
 25 *out of 319 in per capita* **federal funds and grants**

Quality of Life Indexes (Rate per 1000 population)

Crime rate in 1991:   N/A
Violent crime rate in 1991: N/A
Physicians rate in 1992:   3.18
Hospital bed rate in 1991:   8.74

ACCRA Cost of Living Indexes

(First quarter 1993, average = 100)
Composite index: 92.6
Utilities index: 89.2
Housing index: 86.1

Overview

Sangamon County serves as a retail center for central Illinois. Drawing from an 11-county trade area (Cass, Christian, Greene, Logan, Macon, Macoupin, Menard, Montgomery, Morgan, Sangamon, and Scott counties), retail sales have increased each year since 1982. Within this 11-year period, retail sales in Sangamon County have increased 56 percent.

The Springfield Trade Area is supported by more than 520,000 people in 203,300 households with a combined effective buying income of $7.51 billion.

The purchase of automotive products, general merchandise, and food accounted for $956 million or more than one-half, 55 percent, of the county's total retail sales in 1992.

Springfield is the regional health and medical-care center for central Illinois. There are three hospitals, 40 clinics and ancillary medical facilities and 20 licensed nursing homes.

Sangamon County's 1,277 farms are principally grain producers, with 918 (71.4%) producing cash grains and 315 (28%) involving livestock and other enterprises. Among these farms, 354 are 50 acres-or-less in size, 559 manage 50-499 acres, and the remaining 364 are large with 500 acres-or-more under production. Total land in farms in Sangamon County amounts to 493,253 acres or 89% of the county's land area. Local 1991 crop yields of corn (149 bu./ acre), soybeans (48.5 bu./acre), and wheat (47 bu./acre) were each above Illinois averages for these crops, (107 bu./ acre, 37.5 bu./acre, and 32 bu./acre, respectively). Livestock and cash grain production and revenues continue to be cyclical and heavily dependent upon local weather patterns.

Springfield is located in central Illinois at the intersection of Interstate Highways 55 and 72, approximately 190 miles (304 kilometers) southwest of Chicago, 100 miles (161 kilometers) northeast of St. Louis, Missouri, and 60 miles (100 kilometers) southwest of Bloomington-Normal. This location provides same-day or overnight transportation access to and from more than one-third of the nation's manufacturing firms. The following highways and interstates serve the greater Springfield area: Interstates 55 and 72, U.S. Route 36, and Illinois Routes 4, 29, 54, 97, 124, and 125. Rail service is provided for by Southern Pacific Railroad, Illinois Central Railroad, Norfolk and Southern Railroad, Chicago and North Western Transportation Company, and Chicago and Illinois Midland Railway.

Air service is provided at Capital Airport by American Airlines, American Eagle, Trans World Express, and United Express. The labor force includes concentrations of technical and administrative support personnel, service workers, and managerial and professional personnel. There are also fairly strong representations of operators, fabricators, and craft and precision production workers.

Population (1990)

Total Population and Growth Rate
1990: 189,550
1980: 187,770
1970: 171,020
Growth rate 1970–1990: 11%

Race and Hispanic Origin
White: 91.3%
Black: 7.6%
Asian/Pacific Islander: 0.7%
Native American: 0.2%
Hispanic origin: 0.7%
White not Hispanic: 90.8%

Age
Ages 18 to 20: 3.6%
Ages 21 to 24: 5%
Ages 25 to 44: 33%
Ages 45 to 54: 10.4%
Ages 55 to 59: 4.3%
Ages 60 to 64: 4.4%
Ages 65 plus: 13.8%

Educational Attainment (1990)
Percent having completed high school: 81.5%
Percent having completed college: 21.9%
Elementary and high school enrollment: 31,921

Federal Funds and Grants Received
Total received in 1989: $1,106,000,000
Funds received per capita: $5,769

Civilian Labor Force
1993 (April): 119,479
1992 average: 121,010
1991 average: 118,647
1990 average: 116,899

Unemployment
1993 (April): 5.2%
1992 average: 5.3%
1991 average: 4.9%
1990 average: 4.4%

Average Annual Pay
1988: $21,795
1987: $20,626
1985: $16,232

Per Capita Personal Income
1991: $19,822
1990: $19,360
1989: $18,231

Business Climate (1987)

Manufacturing
Number of establishments in 1987: 133
Shipments in 1987 ($1,000): $496,300
Employees in 1987: 4,400
Change in employment, 1982 to 1987: -27.9%
Average annual pay for manufacturing work in 1989: $23,509
Average annual pay for production work in 1987: $17,464

Wholesale Trade
Number of establishments in 1987: 361
Total sales in 1987 ($1,000): $1,541,300
Change in sales, 1982 to 1987: -1.7%

Retail Trade
Number of establishments in 1987: 1,222
Total sales in 1987 ($1,000): $1,541,300
Retail sales per household in 1987: $16,068
Average annual pay in 1989: $10,261

Service Industry
Selected receipts in 1987 ($1,000): $547,300
Average annual pay in 1989: $18,886

Housing
Total number of units in 1990: 81,523
Occupied units in 1990: 76,345
Owner-occupied units in 1990: 67.1%
1993 ACCRA average cost: $97,850

1993 ACCRA average rent for an apartment: $414

Chamber of Commerce

Greater Springfield Chamber of Commerce, Michael Boer, President, 3 S. Old State Capitol Plaza, Springfield, IL 62701. 217-525-1173, FAX 217-525-8768

Economic Development Office

Dept. of Community Development, Don McCarthy, Exec. Director, 231 S. 6th St., Springfield, IL 62701. 217-789-2377, FAX 217-789-2117

Major Companies

Company	SIC	Telephone
Central Illinois Public Service Co.	4911	(217) 523-3600
Chronister Oil Co.	5172	(217) 786-3200
Commonwealth Industries Co.	6311	(217) 786-4321
First National Bank of Springfield	6021	(217) 753-7530
First of America	6021	(217) 753-7100
Firstbank of Illinois Co.	6712	(217) 753-7543
Franklin Life Insurance Co.	6311	(217) 528-2011
Harper Oil Co.	5541	(217) 528-4088
Horace Mann Educators Corp.	6311	(217) 789-2500
Horace Mann Growth Fund Inc.	6722	(217) 789-2500
Horace Mann Insurance Co.	6331	(217) 789-2500
Horace Mann Life Insurance Co.	6311	(217) 789-2500
Hospital Sisters Health System	8741	(217) 522-6969
Illinois Municipal Electric	4911	(217) 789-4632
Illinois National Bank	4225	(217) 525-2112
Investors Trust Inc.	6311	(217) 786-4300
Isringhausen, Lee Robert	5511	(217) 528-2042
Landmark Ford Inc.	5511	(217) 753-5500
Marine Bank of Springfield	6022	(217) 525-9600
Marine Corp.	6022	(217) 525-9600
Memorial Medical Center	8062	(217) 788-3000
Memorial Medical Center System	8062	(217) 788-3000
Mid-Continental Companies	5511	(217) 753-5500
Robert's Foods, Inc.	5142	(217) 793-2633
Roland Machinery Co.	5082	(217) 789-7711
Springfield Electric Supply Co.	5063	(217) 788-2100
St. John's Hospital	8062	(217) 544-6464
Standard Mutual Insurance	6331	(217) 546-2894
Teachers Insurance Co.	6331	(217) 789-2500
Timberlake Sales, Inc.	6221	(217) 787-4200

Colleges and Universities

Lincoln Land Community College, Springfield
Robert Morris College, Springfield Campus, Springfield
Sangamon State University, Springfield
Springfield College In Illinois, Springfield

INDIANA

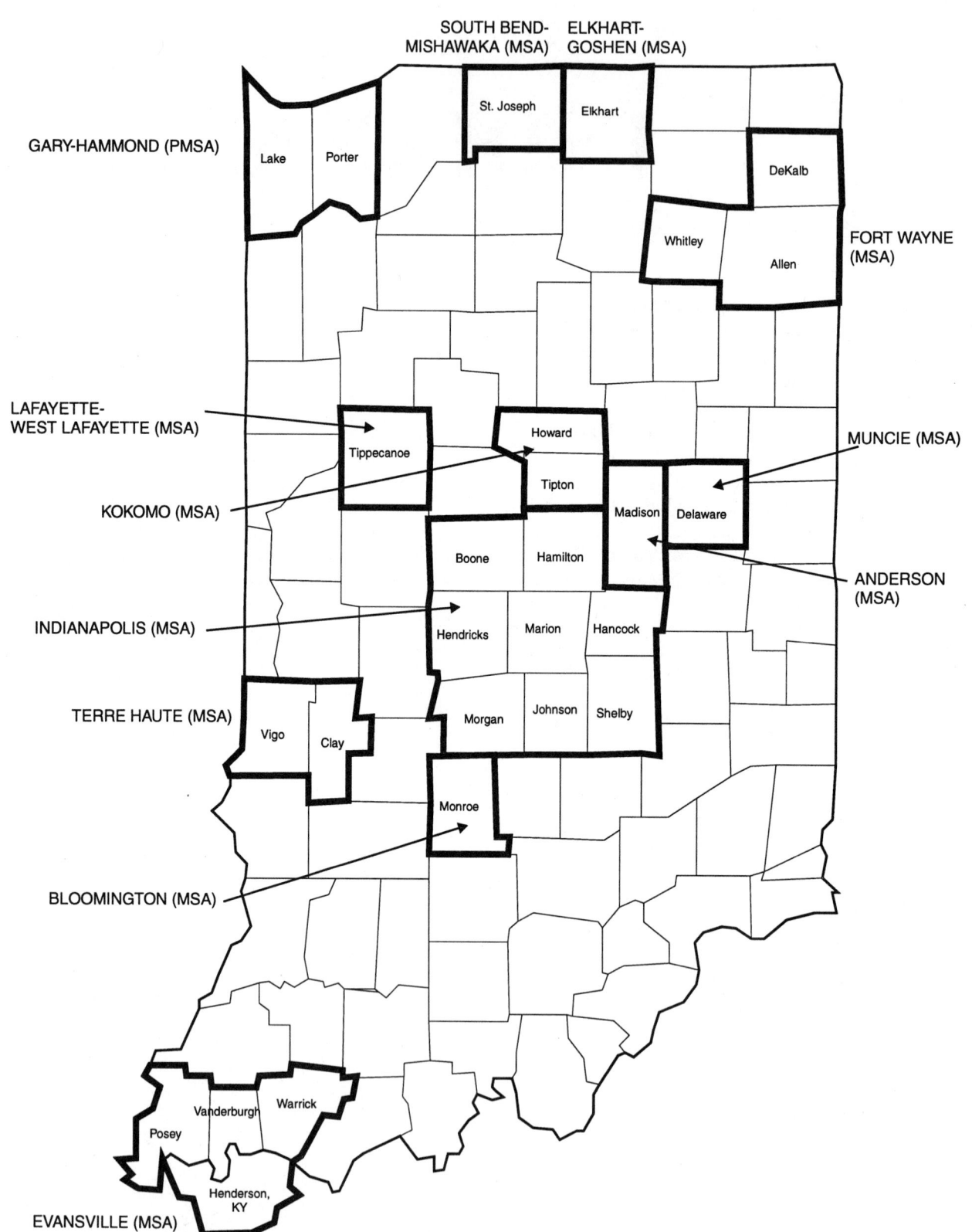

SOUTH BEND-
MISHAWAKA (MSA)

ELKHART-
GOSHEN (MSA)

GARY-HAMMOND (PMSA)

St. Joseph

Elkhart

Lake

Porter

DeKalb

Whitley

Allen

FORT WAYNE
(MSA)

LAFAYETTE-
WEST LAFAYETTE (MSA)

Tippecanoe

Howard

MUNCIE (MSA)

KOKOMO (MSA)

Tipton

Madison

Delaware

Boone

Hamilton

ANDERSON
(MSA)

INDIANAPOLIS (MSA)

Hendricks

Marion

Hancock

TERRE HAUTE (MSA)

Vigo

Clay

Morgan

Johnson

Shelby

Monroe

BLOOMINGTON (MSA)

Vanderburgh

Warrick

Posey

Henderson,
KY

EVANSVILLE (MSA)

INDIANA

Population

1990: 5,544,159
1980: 5,490,224

Age

Ages 18 to 20: 279,864
Ages 21 to 24: 325,018
Ages 25 to 44: 1,734,270
Ages 45 to 54: 570,791
Ages 55 to 59: 239,692
Ages 60 to 64: 242,364
Median age: 32.8

Race

White: 5,020,700
Black: 432,092
Asian/Pacific Islander: 37,617
Native American: 12,720
Hispanic origin: 98,788

Households

Total: 2,065,355
Persons per household: 2.61

Sex

Male: 2,688,281
Female: 2,855,878

Population Migration

Domestic migration: -83,000
International migration: 23,000

Projection of the Population in 1995

Total: 5,750,000
18 to 64: 3,539,000

Civilian Labor Force

1993: 2,764,600
1992: 2,795,800
1991: 2,810,400
1990: 2,824,300

Manufacturing

1995 Projection: 666,500
1992: 626,500
1991: 628,100
1990: 624,500
1989: 638,200

Services

1995 Projection: 763,900

1992: 552,400
1991: 553,100
1990: 537,200
1989: 515,400

Wholesale and Retail Trade

1995 Projection: 690,100
1992: 597,100
1991: 608,800
1990: 613,600
1989: 609,800

Unemployment Rate

1993: 7.1%
1992: 6.5%
1991: 5.9%
1990: 5.8%

Employer Unemployment Contributions

Contribution Rate

1992: 1.21%
1991: 1.30%
1990: 1.40%

Average Weekly Benefit

1992: $141.55
1991: $137.56
1990: $107.04

Gross State Product (Million $)

1989: $105,314
1988: $98,243
1987: $91,231
1979: $58,404
Growth rate, 1979 to 1989: 80.3%

Capital Expenditures of Manufacturing Industries

1990: $3,753,500,000
1989: $4,004,200,000
1988: $3,414,200,000
1987: $3,363,900,000

State Tax Rates

Individual income: 3.4% of adjusted gross income.
Corporate income: 3.4% of taxable income or the gross income tax, whichever is the greater. Supplemental net income tax is imposed on corporations, banks, trust com-

panies, savings associations and domestic insurers at 4.5%.

General property: Sum of state and local rates. Assessed at 33.33% of true cash value.

General sales: 5%

Gasoline: 15¢ per gallon

Income
Median income for a 4 person family: $38,201

Personal per Capita Income
1992: $18,043
1991: $17,193
1990: $16,814

Disposable per Capita Income
1992: $15,882
1991: $15,044
1990: $14,638

Private Employment Weekly Wages
Average
1989: $401
1988: $393
1987: $393

Manufacturing
1989: $379
1988: $532
1987: $513

Services
1989: $328
1988: $318
1987: $304

Wholesale
1989: $485
1988: $475
1987: $454

Retail
1989: $202
1988: $200
1987: $194

Highway Statistics
Total Highway Miles
1990: 91,908
1989: 91,744
1988: 91,588

Federal Highway Aid
1991: $268,212,000
1990: $264,092,000
1989: $298,913,000

Electricity
Average Cost per Kilowatt Hour
1990: 5.58¢
1989: 5.69¢
1988: 5.83¢

Housing (1990)
Owner occupied units: 1,450,898
Median house value: $53,900
Renter occupied units: 614,457
Median rent: $291
Total vacant units: 180,691
Homeowner vacancy rate: 1.5%
Rental vacancy rate: 8.3%

State Business Incentives and Assistance
Enterprise Zone Incentives
This program is designed to help revitalize specific distressed geographical areas and to create jobs for zone residents. Business sites are available to meet various facility requirements. Tax and financial incentives offer business the benefit of locating in these zones. Employees receive income tax credit for 10% of resident employee wages up to $1,500 per employee. Businesses also receive property tax credits on inventory.

Financial and Business Assistance
Property Tax Abatement. A major property tax deduction on assessed value that is increased through rehabilitation or new construction is available in designated economic revitalization areas. Manufacturing equipment installed in an approved economic revitalization area qualifies for a deduction from assessed value over a five-year period.

Industrial Revenue Bonds. Industrial revenue bonds make municipal bond financing possible to some corporations through local economic development organizations.

Tax Incremental Financing. Tax incremental financing gives local municipalities an innovative mechanism for infrastructure improvements and new construction in areas needing growth or rehabilitation. Bonds are issued by a local municipality to finance these improvement.

Industrial Development Infrastructure Program. This program provides grants and loans to smaller communities to develop necessary infrastructure to support new business investment.

Indiana Statewide Certified Development Corporation. This is a for-profit corporation, approved by the U.S. Small Business Administration. It is designed to provide needed long-term fixed asset financing. It can provide up to $500,000 in low-interest subordinated mortgages for small Indiana businesses.

Institute for New Business Ventures. The Institute fosters the development of new business ventures that may contribute to Indiana employment and income growth. It facilitates successful operation of new businesses by linking prospective entrepreneurs with managerial, technical and financial resources.

Corporation for Innovation Development. The Corporation is designed to encourage the entrepreneurial spirit through increased access to venture capital. Activities include providing venture capital as well as equity and financing to established industries.

Regulatory Ombudsman. This office works with business to obtain and prepare the permits required to conduct business in Indiana. The staff of the Ombudsman's office can serve as permit consultants for utility and infrastructure requirements. This office can also provide information concerning business assistance programs available through government agencies and private sources.

International Trade Specialists. International trade specialists in the Indiana Department of Commerce offer extensive support for growing businesses through expertise and resources in the international marketplace.

Government Marketing Assistant Group. Part of the Indiana Department of Commerce, this Group provides professional marketing and technical assistance at no cost to businesses to increase sales of goods and services to the Department of Defense and other federal agencies and prime government contractors.

Energy Assistance Office. This Office provides assistance in energy conservation at no charge to business.

Corporation for Science and Technology. This Corporation works with businesses that are developing innovative technologies or products for production purposes. The corporation serves as a catalyst for public, private and education sectors, drawing together respective resources to foster the development of technology-based research and industry in Indiana.

Strategic Development Fund. This program is based on a philosophy that companies in similar markets share similar problems and concerns that can be addressed most successfully by pulling their resources together. The program attempts to team up two or more Indiana businesses by offering grant or loan money in the form of matching dollars. This program is designed to foster creativity and cooperation between industrial sectors or regions of the state. Some project ideas include: marketing programs, technology deployment, cooperative research, export development programs, cooperative administrative projects, apprentice programs, and cooperative advertising.

Trade Show Assistance Program. This program provides financial assistance to Indiana companies planning to attend trade shows overseas. It is designed to help small and medium-sized companies realize their export potential through participation in international trade fairs and exhibitions. Companies can be reimbursed for up to $5,000 of the cost directly attributable to the trade show.

Education and Training

Intelenet. Intelenet utilizes fiber optic networks to link Indiana educational institutions and increase statewide access to available technological resources. Indiana businesses have accessed Intelenet through local education facilities for training and continuing education purposes.

Training For Profit. This program provides assistance in

meeting the up front costs associated with the training of newly hired employees. This program is available to existing companies that are expanding and companies in the process of locating in Indiana.

Basic Industry Retraining. This program is designed to provide essential retraining assistance for Indiana's existing manufacturing sector in the utilization of new technology and/or the creation of a new product mix.

Job Training Partnership Act. This program operates with funding from the U.S. Department of Labor. It provides job training and other employment related services.

State Offices

Real estate: Professional Licensing Agency, Gerald Quigley, Exec Director, 1021 State Office Bldg., Indianapolis, IN 46204. 317-232-3997

Indiana Association of Realtors, Inc., Richard C. Nye, Exec Vice President, PO Box 50736, 7301 N. Shadeland, Indianapolis, IN 46250. 317-842-0890

Chamber of commerce: Indiana State Chamber of Commerce, John W. Walls, President, One N. Capitol Ave., 2nd Fl, Indianapolis, IN 46204-2248. 317-264-3110

Economic development: Department of Commerce, Robert Kovach, Exec Director, One North Capitol St. Suite 700, Indianapolis, IN 46204-2248. 317-232-8800, FAX 317-232-4146

Department of Commerce, Business Development Division, Frank Sabatine, Director, One North Capitol Ave., Suite 700, Indianapolis, IN 46204-2248. 317-232-0159, FAX 317-232-4146

Small Business Development Center, Steve Thrash, Exec Director, One North Capitol Ave., Suite 420, Indianapolis, IN 46204. 317-264-6871

Department of Commerce, Enterprize Zone Programs, Art Banks, Director, One North Capitol Ave., Suite 700, Indianapolis, IN 46204. 317-232-8905

Department of Commerce, Development Finance Office, Betty Cockrum, Director, One North Capitol Ave., Suite 700, Indianapolis, IN 46204. 317 232-8782

Indiana Development Finance Authority, Peggy Boehm, Exec Director, One North Capitol Ave., Suite 320, Indianapolis, IN 46204. 317-232-4408

Department of Commerce, International Trade Division, Mercedes Plant, Director, One North Capitol Ave., Indianapolis, IN 46204. 317-232-3527

Department of Commerce, Ombudsman Office, John Humes, Ombudsman, One North Capitol Ave., Indianapolis, IN 46204. 317-232-7304

Indiana Institute for New Business Ventures, Director, One North Capitol Ave., Suite 1275, Indianapolis, IN 46204. 317-634-8418

Environmental affairs: Dept. of Environmental Management, Kathy Prosser, Commissioner, 105 S. Meridian, Indianapolis, IN 46206. 317-232-8162

Major Companies in the State

Company name	Fortune 500 rank	City	Telephone	SIC number
Fortune 500 Companies				
Anacomp Inc.	472	Indianapolis	317-844-9666	3861
Arvin Industries Inc.	228	Columbus	812-379-3000	3714
Ball Corp.	187	Muncie	317-747-6100	3411
Central Soya Co. Inc.	226	Fort Wayne	219-425-5100	2075
Clark Equipment Co.	342	South Bend	219-239-0100	3714
Cummins Engine Co. Inc.	132	Columbus	812-377-5000	3519
Eli Lilly & Co.	84	Indianapolis	317-276-2000	2834
Essex Group Inc.	380	Fort Wayne	219-461-4000	3357
Great Lakes Chemical Corp.	269	West Lafayette	317-497-6100	2819
Hillenbrand Industries Inc.	279	Batesville	812-934-7000	3161
Kimball International Inc.	477	Jasper	812-482-1600	2521
National Steel Corp.	193	Mishawaka	219-273-7000	3316
Other Major Companies in the State				
American General Finance Corp.		Evansville	812-424-8031	6141
American General Finance Inc.		Evansville	812-424-8031	6141
Bindley Western Industries Inc.		Indianapolis	317-298-9900	5122
Conseco Inc.		Carmel	317-573-6100	6311
GTE North Inc.		Westfield	317-896-6464	4813
INB Financial Corp.		Indianapolis	317-266-6000	6712
Indiana Bell Telephone Co. Inc.		Indianapolis	317-265-2266	4813
Indiana Energy Inc.		Indianapolis	317-926-3351	4923
Indiana Michigan Power Co.		Fort Wayne	219-425-2111	4911
Indianapolis Power & Light Co.		Indianapolis	317-261-8261	4911
IPALCO Enterprises Inc.		Indianapolis	317-261-8261	4911
Lincoln National Corp.		Fort Wayne	219-455-2000	6331
Marsh Supermarkets Inc.		Indianapolis	317-594-2100	5411
Mayflower Group Inc.		Carmel	317-875-1463	4213
Merchants National Corp.		Indianapolis	317-267-6100	6712
Nipsco Industries Inc.		Hammond	219-853-5200	4931
Northern Indiana Public Service Co.		Hammond	219-853-5200	4931
PSI Energy Inc.		Plainfield	317-839-9611	4911
PSI Resources Inc.		Plainfield	317-839-9611	4911
Wholesale Club Inc.		Indianapolis	317-842-0351	5399

Labor: Dept. of Labor, Kenneth Zeller, Commissioner, State Office Bldg., Room 1013, 100 N. Senate Ave., Indianapolis, IN 46204. 317-232-2378

Unemployment: Employment Security Div., Unemployment Insurance, Director, 100 N. Senate Ave., Room 238, Indianapolis, IN 46204. 317-232-8087

Worker's compensation: Worker's Compensation Board of Indiana, Rogelio Dominquez, Chairman, State Office Bldg., Room 601, 100 N. Senate Bldg., Indianapolis, IN Indianapolis, IN 46204. 317-232-3808

Occupational safety and health: State Board of Health, Div.

of Industrial Hygiene & Radiological Health, Director, Health Bldg., 1330 W. Michigan St., Indianapolis, IN 46206. 317-232-9421

Secretary of state: Secretary of State Office, Joseph H. Hogsett, Secretary of State, State House, 200 W. Washington St., Indianapolis, IN 46204. 317-232-6536

Taxation and revenue: Indiana Dept. of Revenue, John Gildea, Commissioner, One North Capitol Ave., Suite 202, 100 N. Senate Bldg., Indianapolis, IN 46204. 317-232-2101

Tax Commissioners Board, Jack L. New, Chairman, One

North Capitol Ave., Indianapolis, IN 46204. 317-232-3782

Designated Zones for Economic Development

Enterprise Zones

Enacted in: 1983

No. of established zones: 14

Mr. Bob Murray, Anderson Urban Enterprise Association, City of Anderson, P.O. Box 2100, Anderson, IN 46018, 317-646-9648

Ms. Terri Simanton, Director, Bloomington Urban Enterprise Association, P.O. Box 1996, Bloomington, IN 47402, 812-333-4276

Mr. Mark Brinson, Assistant Director, Community Development, 229 South Second Street, Elkhart, IN 46516, 219-294-5471

Mr. Alan Eric Jones, Executive Director, Urban Enterprise Association, 2425 Business Old 41, Suite 200, Evansville, IN 47711, 812-426-2490

Mr. Roy Hossler, Ft. Wayne Urban Enterprise Association, 1830 Wayne Trace, Fort Wayne, IN 46803, 219-422-2304

Mr. Jihad Muhammad, Gary Urban Enterprise Association, 504 Broadway, Suite 512, Gary, IN 46402, 219-885-2937

Mr. Patrick Reardon, Executive Director, Urban Enterprise Association, 649 Conkey Street, Hammond, IN 46534, 219-853-6512

Mr. Robert J. Hedding, Jr., Indianapolis Urban Enterprise Association, 3913 North Keystone Avenue, Indianapolis, IN 46205, 317-541-2740

Mr. Jeff Rudolph, Dept. of Urban Development & Design, City Hall, Second Floor, Kokomo, IN 46901, 317-456-7400

Ms. Mary K. Kaczka, Director, Michigan City Urban Enterprise Association, P.O. Box 9003, 200 East Michigan Blvd., Michigan City, IN 46360, 219-874-6221

Mr. Casey Foley, Executive Director, Urban Enterprise Association, City of Richmond, 50 North Fifth Street, Richmond, IN 47374, 317-983-7204

Mrs. Pamela Meyer, Community Development, 1200 County-City Building, South Bend, IN 46601, 219-284-9335

Mr. David Daghir, Madison Urban Enterprise Association, Community Development, 416 West Street, Madison, IN 47250, 812-265-8322

Mrs. Kim Gordon, Director, East Chicago, Urban Enterprise Association, 2001 E. Columbus Dr., P.O. Box 378, East Chicago, IN 46312, 219-399-7039

Mr. James Carey, Executive Director, Muncie Urban Enterprise Association, Inc., 401 S. High Street, Muncie, IN 47305, 317-741-5487

Foreign Trade Zones

Foreign Trade Zone No. 152, Burns Harbor, Indiana, Grantee: The Indiana Port Commission, James H. Hartung, 6600 U.S. Highway 12, Portage, IN 46368, 219-787-8636

Foreign Trade Zone No. 170, Clark County, Indiana, Grantee: Indiana Port Commission, Ports of Indiana, Joy D. McCarthy, 150 West Market St., Suite 603, Indianapolis, IN 46204-2819, 317-232-9200

Foreign Trade Zone No. 177, Evansville, Indiana, Grantee: Indiana Port Commission, Ports of Indiana, Joy D. McCarthy, 150 West Market Street, Suite 603, Indianapolis, IN 46204-2819, 317-232-9200

Foreign Trade Zone No. 72, Indianapolis, Indiana, Grantee: Indianapolis Airport Authority, Operator: Indianapolis Economic Development Corporation, Bill Herber, FTZ No. 72, PO Box 51681, Indianapolis, IN 46251, 317-247-1181

Foreign Trade Zone No. 125, South Bend, Indiana, Grantee: St. Joseph County Airport Authority, Operator: Material Trans Action, Kenneth Kanczuzewski, 2741 N. Foundation Dr., South Bend, IN 46634-1877, 219-233-2666

Labor Unions

Automobile, Aerospace & Agricultural Implement Workers of America, International Union, United (UAW AFL-CIO)

Carpenters and Joiners of America, United Brotherhood of (AFL-CIO)

Communications Workers of America (AFL-CIO)

Electrical Workers, International Brotherhood of (AFL-CIO)

Food and Commercial Workers International Union, United (AFL-CIO)

Iron Workers, International Association of Bridge, Structural and Ornamental (AFL-CIO)

Laborers' International Union of North America (AFL-CIO)

National Education Association

State, County and Municipal Employees, American Federation of (AFL-CIO)

Steelworkers of America, United (AFL-CIO)

Teachers, American Federation of (AFL-CIO)

Teamsters, Chauffeurs, Warehousemen and Helpers of America, International Brotherhood of (AFL-CIO)

Theatrical Stage Employees and Moving Picture Machine Operators of the United States and Canada, International Alliance of (AFL-CIO)

Woodworkers of America, International (AFL-CIO)

Universities with Ph.D. Programs

Ball State University, Muncie

Indiana State University, Terre Haute

Indiana University, Bloomington

Indiana University-Purdue University at Indianapolis, Indianapolis

Notre Dame University, Notre Dame

Purdue University, West Lafayette

ANDERSON, IN (MSA)

Geographic Profile

Land Area
452.2 square miles

Counties and Parishes
Madison

Ranking Highlights
303 *out of 319 in total* **land area**

299 *out of 319 in* **population growth,** *1970–1990*

238 *out of 310 in having the lowest* **unemployment** *rate*

270 *out of 310 in size of* **labor force**

302 *out of 318 in the percentage of* **college graduates**

N/A *out of 292 in per capita personal* **income**

267 *out of 319 in number of* **manufacturing establishments**

305 *out of 318 in* **physicians** *per 1000 people*

77 *out of 318 in* **hospital beds** *per 1000 people*

50 *out of 267 in fewest* **crimes** *per 1000 people*

68 *out of 266 in fewest* **violent crimes** *per 1000 people*

250 *out of 319 in per capita* **federal funds and grants**

Quality of Life Indexes (Rate per 1000 population)
Crime rate in 1991:	42.5
Violent crime rate in 1991:	3.8
Physicians rate in 1992:	1.04
Hospital bed rate in 1991:	5.01

ACCRA Cost of Living Indexes
(First quarter 1993, average = 100)
Composite index:	96.4
Utilities index:	95.2
Housing index:	96.9

Population (1990)

Total Population and Growth Rate
1990: 130,669

1980: 139,336

1970: 138,522

Growth rate 1970–1990: -6%

Race and Hispanic Origin
White: 91.6%

Black: 7.6%

Asian/Pacific Islander: 0.3%

Native American: 0.2%

Hispanic origin: 0.7%

White not Hispanic: 91.2%

Age
Ages 18 to 20: 4.8%

Ages 21 to 24: 5.5%

Ages 25 to 44: 30.1%

Ages 45 to 54: 11.2%

Ages 55 to 59: 4.8%

Ages 60 to 64: 4.8%

Ages 65 plus: 14%

Educational Attainment (1990)
Percent having completed high school: 73.5%

Percent having completed college: 11.7%

Elementary and high school enrollment: 22,436

Federal Funds and Grants Received
Total received in 1989: $323,600,000

Funds received per capita: $2,455

Civilian Labor Force
1993 (April):	56,497
1992 average:	58,120
1991 average:	56,599
1990 average:	58,336

Unemployment
1993 (April):	7.6%
1992 average:	8.3%
1991 average:	7.5%
1990 average:	6.5%

Average Annual Pay
1988: $23,782

1987: $21,706

1985: $21,923

Per Capita Personal Income
1991: N/A

1990: N/A

1989: N/A

Business Climate (1987)

Manufacturing
Number of establishments in 1987: 132

Shipments in 1987 ($1,000): $2,119,100

Employees in 1987: 16,800

Change in employment, 1982 to 1987: 1.2%

Average annual pay for manufacturing work in 1989: $42,165

Average annual pay for production work in 1987: $34,664

Wholesale Trade
Number of establishments in 1987: 127

Total sales in 1987 ($1,000): $274,500

Change in sales, 1982 to 1987: -8.0%

Retail Trade
Number of establishments in 1987: 773

Total sales in 1987 ($1,000): $274,500

Retail sales per household in 1987: $15,418

Average annual pay in 1989: $9,764

Service Industry
Selected receipts in 1987 ($1,000): $178,900

Average annual pay in 1989: $16,680

Housing
Total number of units in 1990: 53,353

Occupied units in 1990: 49,804
Owner-occupied units in 1990: 73.1%
1993 ACCRA average cost: $111,600
1993 ACCRA average rent for an apartment: $435

Chamber of Commerce

Anderson Area Chamber of Commerce, Duane Marsh, President, 205 W. 11th St., PO Box 469, Anderson, IN 46016. 317-642-0264

Economic Development Office

Anderson Corp. for Economic Development, John L. Hagen, Exec. Director, 205 W. 11th St., PO Box 469, Anderson, IN 46016. 317-642-1860, FAX 317-642-0266

Major Businesses

Company	SIC	Telephone
Anderson Banking Co.	6022	(317) 646-5400
Anderson Ford Lincoln Mercury	5511	(317) 649-1111
Citizens Banking Co.	6022	(317) 649-8100
Community Hospital-Anderson	8062	(317) 646-5120
Cox Super Market Inc.	5411	(317) 724-4777
Duke's GMC Inc.	5511	(317) 643-6641
E & B Paving Inc.	1611	(317) 643-5358
Emporia Grain Co.	5153	(317) 779-4404
First Citizen Bancorp	6022	(317) 649-8100
First National Bank of Madison	6021	(317) 642-4901
Madison County Farm Bureau Coop.	5153	(317) 643-6639
Paint & Assembly Corp.	3479	(317) 552-0851
Pay Less Super Markets Inc.	5411	(317) 649-3526
Prime Battery Manufacturing Co., Inc.	3691	(317) 649-4818
Ram Graphics Inc.	5131	(317) 724-7783
Red Giant Foods Inc.	2033	(317) 552-3386
Red Gold Inc.	2033	(317) 754-7527
Regenold Russ Pontiac Inc.	5511	(317) 644-2571
St. Johns Health Care Corp.	8062	(317) 646-8273
Warner Press Inc.	5049	(317) 644-7721

Colleges and Universities

Anderson University, Anderson

BLOOMINGTON, IN (MSA)

Geographic Profile

Land Area
394.4 square miles

Counties and Parishes
Monroe

Ranking Highlights

313 *out of 319 in total* **land area**
146 *out of 319 in* **population growth,** *1970–1990*
40 *out of 310 in having the lowest* **unemployment** *rate*
259 *out of 310 in size of* **labor force**
15 *out of 318 in the percentage of* **college graduates**
263 *out of 292 in per capita personal* **income**
286 *out of 319 in number of* **manufacturing establishments**
212 *out of 318 in* **physicians** *per 1000 people*
266 *out of 318 in* **hospital beds** *per 1000 people*
N/A *out of 267 in fewest* **crimes** *per 1000 people*
N/A *out of 266 in fewest* **violent crimes** *per 1000 people*
274 *out of 319 in per capita* **federal funds and grants**

Quality of Life Indexes (Rate per 1000 population)

Crime rate in 1991:	N/A
Violent crime rate in 1991:	N/A
Physicians rate in 1992:	1.56
Hospital bed rate in 1991:	2.62

ACCRA Cost of Living Indexes

(First quarter 1993, average = 100)
Composite index: 100.3
Utilities index: 99.1
Housing index: 96.6

Population (1990)

Total Population and Growth Rate
1990: 108,978
1980: 98,787
1970: 85,221
Growth rate 1970–1990: 28%

Race and Hispanic Origin
White: 94.3%
Black: 2.6%
Asian/Pacific Islander: 2.5%
Native American: 0.2%
Hispanic origin: 1.3%
White not Hispanic: 93.4%

Age
Ages 18 to 20: 15.2%
Ages 21 to 24: 13.8%
Ages 25 to 44: 29.6%
Ages 45 to 54: 8%
Ages 55 to 59: 3.3%

Ages 60 to 64: 3.2%
Ages 65 plus: 8.5%

Educational Attainment (1990)
Percent having completed high school: 82.1%
Percent having completed college: 32.9%
Elementary and high school enrollment: 13,155

Federal Funds and Grants Received
Total received in 1989: $235,100,000
Funds received per capita: $2,281

Civilian Labor Force
1993 (April):   61,939
1992 average: 62,131
1991 average: 59,597
1990 average: 60,437

Unemployment
1993 (April):   5.1%
1992 average: 4.7%
1991 average: 3.7%
1990 average: 3.3%

Average Annual Pay
1988: $17,615
1987: $17,078
1985: $15,695

Per Capita Personal Income
1991: $14,957
1990: $14,391
1989: $13,535

Business Climate (1987)

Manufacturing
Number of establishments in 1987: 108
Shipments in 1987 ($1,000): $1,616,200
Employees in 1987: 8,200
Change in employment, 1982 to 1987: 3.8%
Average annual pay for manufacturing work in 1989: $24,302
Average annual pay for production work in 1987: $20,391

Wholesale Trade
Number of establishments in 1987: 117
Total sales in 1987 ($1,000): $458,000
Change in sales, 1982 to 1987: 74.5%

Retail Trade
Number of establishments in 1987: 680
Total sales in 1987 ($1,000): $458,000
Retail sales per household in 1987: $16,859
Average annual pay in 1989: $8,970

Service Industry
Selected receipts in 1987 ($1,000): $168,300
Average annual pay in 1989: $14,965

Housing
Total number of units in 1990: 41,948

Occupied units in 1990: 39,351
Owner-occupied units in 1990: 54.8%
1993 ACCRA average cost: $105,613
1993 ACCRA average rent for an apartment: $518

Chamber of Commerce
Greater Bloomington Chamber of Commerce, Michael Brooks, Exec. Director, 116 W. 6th St. #100, PO Box 1302, Bloomington, IN 47402. 812-336-6381

Economic Development Office
Bloomington Economic Development Corp., Robert Anderson, Exec. Director, 116 W. 6th St. #100, Bloomington, IN 47401. 812-336-6381

Economic Development Organizations
Bloomington Small Business Development Center, David Miller, Director, 116 W. 6th St., Bloomington, IN 47404. 812-239-8937

Major Businesses

Company	SIC	Telephone
B & B Investments Inc.	7513	(812) 824-6741
Bank One Bloomington, NA	6021	(812) 332-6351
Bender Lumber Co., Inc.	5211	(812) 339-9730
Big Red Liquors Inc.	5921	(812) 332-0653
Black Lumber Co., Inc.	5031	(812) 332-7208
Bloomington Hospital Inc.	8062	(812) 336-6821
Curry Buick Cadillac Pontiac	5511	(812) 339-2227
Hall Signs Inc.	3993	(812) 332-9355
Harrell Mechanical Inc.	1711	(812) 339-2579
Hoosier Energy Rural Electric	4911	(812) 876-2021
Indiana University Foundation	7389	(812) 855-8311
Monroe Bancorp	6712	(812) 336-0201
Royal Chevrolet Inc.	5511	(812) 339-1161
Smithville Telephone Co., Inc.	4813	(812) 876-2211
TIS Inc.	5942	(812) 332-3307
Tarzian, Sarkes Inc.	4833	(812) 332-7251
Weddle Bros Construction	1622	(812) 339-9500

Colleges and Universities
Indiana University Bloomington, Bloomington

ELKHART–GOSHEN, IN (MSA)

Geographic Profile

Land Area
463.8 square miles

Counties and Parishes
Elkhart

Ranking Highlights

297 *out of 319 in total* **land area**
166 *out of 319 in* **population growth**, *1970–1990*
104 *out of 310 in having the lowest* **unemployment** *rate*
199 *out of 310 in size of* **labor force**
250 *out of 318 in the percentage of* **college graduates**
165 *out of 292 in per capita personal* **income**
 74 *out of 319 in number of* **manufacturing establishments**
307 *out of 318 in* **physicians** *per 1000 people*
236 *out of 318 in* **hospital beds** *per 1000 people*
 70 *out of 267 in fewest* **crimes** *per 1000 people*
 97 *out of 266 in fewest* **violent crimes** *per 1000 people*
315 *out of 319 in per capita* **federal funds and grants**

Quality of Life Indexes (Rate per 1000 population)

Crime rate in 1991:	48.0
Violent crime rate in 1991:	4.7
Physicians rate in 1992:	1.01
Hospital bed rate in 1991:	3.06

ACCRA Cost of Living Indexes
(First quarter 1993, average = 100)

Composite index:	N/A
Utilities index:	N/A
Housing index:	N/A

Overview

Elkhart tops the list of U.S. manufacturing cities, with 50 percent of its workers in manufacturing jobs. Over 100 manufacturing firms each employ 500 or more people. This fact contributes to the area's highly stable economy.

Elkhart County is a leader in the production of recreational vehicles and manufactured housing. Hundreds of manufacturers produce motor homes, travel trailers, campers, park models, mobile homes, or the products used in RVs and manufactured housing. The Elkhart area is also the "Band Instrument Capital of the World," a title earned in the last century when C.G. Conn Company became the nation's largest manufacturer of band instruments.

Despite dominance in specific fields, Elkhart County industry is highly diversified. Miles Inc. is one of the largest employers with 2,600 workers engaged in the production of prescription pharmaceuticals, diagnostics, chemicals and numerous consumer health care products.

Elkhart County offer a wide range of affordable housing.

The Elkhart-Goshen metro area of Indiana was cited as the nation's most affordable housing market among 176 metropolitan regions, according to a 1992 survey of the National Association of Home Builders.

Elkhart County has one of the world's largest freight classification systems, a Conrail switching yard where trains are assembled. Amtrak provides passenger service from a station at the center of Elkhart. Merchants and manufacturers also have access to dozens of motor freight carriers. Interstate Highways 80-90 skirt the northern edge of Elkhart and a recently completed Highway 20 Bypass provides four-lane swiftness from the city's southern edge to the northern parts of Indiana. Elkhart Municipal Airport has 6,500- and 4,000-foot runways and offers charger service. Two other private airports are located in the area. Mishawaka Pilot's Airport and Goshen Municipal Airport. Convenient Michiana Regional Airport, at South Bend, is served by nine commercial air carriers that provide direct flights to most major U.S. cities. One bus line offers regularly scheduled trips between Elkhart and Michiana Regional Airport and Chicago's O'Hare International.

Population (1990)

Total Population and Growth Rate
1990: 156,198
1980: 137,330
1970: 126,529
Growth rate 1970–1990: 23%

Race and Hispanic Origin
White: 93.8%
Black: 4.5%
Asian/Pacific Islander: 0.6%
Native American: 0.3%
Hispanic origin: 1.9%
White not Hispanic: 92.6%

Age
Ages 18 to 20: 4.3%
Ages 21 to 24: 5.9%
Ages 25 to 44: 31.8%
Ages 45 to 54: 10.3%
Ages 55 to 59: 4.1%
Ages 60 to 64: 3.9%
Ages 65 plus: 11.2%

Educational Attainment (1990)
Percent having completed high school: 72.8%
Percent having completed college: 14.2%
Elementary and high school enrollment: 28,185

Federal Funds and Grants Received
Total received in 1989: $249,200,000
Funds received per capita: $1,649

Civilian Labor Force
1993 (April): 93,524
1992 average: 90,418

1991 average: 88,234
1990 average: 92,861

Unemployment
1993 (April): 4.6%
1992 average: 6.1%
1991 average: 6.4%
1990 average: 5.7%

Average Annual Pay
1988: $19,809
1987: $19,318
1985: $17,932

Per Capita Personal Income
1991: $16,857
1990: $16,585
1989: $16,321

Business Climate (1987)

Manufacturing
Number of establishments in 1987: 855
Shipments in 1987 ($1,000): $5,760,200
Employees in 1987: 50,000
Change in employment, 1982 to 1987: 44.5%
Average annual pay for manufacturing work in 1989: $23,220
Average annual pay for production work in 1987: $17,920

Wholesale Trade
Number of establishments in 1987: 397
Total sales in 1987 ($1,000): $1,640,400
Change in sales, 1982 to 1987: 55.9%

Retail Trade
Number of establishments in 1987: 960
Total sales in 1987 ($1,000): $1,640,400
Retail sales per household in 1987: $19,764
Average annual pay in 1989: $10,606

Service Industry
Selected receipts in 1987 ($1,000): $387,000
Average annual pay in 1989: $14,227

Housing
Total number of units in 1990: 60,182
Occupied units in 1990: 56,713
Owner-occupied units in 1990: 71.8%
1993 ACCRA average cost: N/A
1993 ACCRA average rent for an apartment: N/A

Chamber of Commerce
Greater Elkhart Chamber of Commerce, Robert L. Kelso, President, 418 S. Main St., PO Box 428, Elkhart, IN 46515-0428. 219-293-1531

Economic Development Office
North Central Indiana Business Assistant Center, David Germain, President, 418 S. Main St., PO Box 428, Elkhart, IN 46515. 219-293-1531, FAX 219-294-1859

Major Businesses

Company	SIC	Telephone
Ameritrust Indiana Corp.	6021	(219) 295-2000
Bristol Corp.	3088	(219) 848-7681
Coachmen Industries, Inc.	3716	(219) 262-0123
Dometic Corp.	3632	(219) 294-2511
ESI Meats Inc.	2013	(219) 848-7661
Excel Industries Inc.	3231	(219) 264-2131
Fairmont Homes, Inc.	2451	(219) 773-7941
Holiday Rambler Corp.	3716	(219) 862-7211
Lasalle-Deitch Co., Inc.	5023	(219) 294-2661
Mallard Coach Co.	3716	(219) 773-2471
Marlette Homes Inc.	2451	(219) 825-5881
Miles Inc.	2834	(219) 264-8111
Nibco Inc.	3494	(219) 295-3000
Patrick Industries, Inc.	5031	(219) 294-7511
Schult Homes Corp.	2451	(219) 825-5881
Shelter Components Corp.	5031	(219) 262-4541
Shelter Components of Indiana	2273	(219) 262-4541
Skyline Corp.	2452	(219) 294-6521
Troyer Foods Inc.	5147	(219) 533-0302
Van American Inc.	3792	(219) 534-1418

Colleges and Universities
Goshen College, Goshen

EVANSVILLE, IN–KY (MSA)

Geographic Profile

Land Area

1467.4 square miles

Counties and Parishes

Indiana:

    Posey

    Vanderburgh

    Warrick

Kentucky:

    Henderson

Additional Cities/Towns within Area

Henderson, KY

Ranking Highlights

136 *out of 319 in total* **land area**

226 *out of 319 in* **population growth,** *1970–1990*

128 *out of 310 in having the lowest* **unemployment** *rate*

141 *out of 310 in size of* **labor force**

237 *out of 318 in the percentage of* **college graduates**

119 *out of 292 in per capita personal* **income**

131 *out of 319 in number of* **manufacturing establishments**

144 *out of 318 in* **physicians** *per 1000 people*

 58 *out of 318 in* **hospital beds** *per 1000 people*

 82 *out of 267 in fewest* **crimes** *per 1000 people*

124 *out of 266 in fewest* **violent crimes** *per 1000 people*

247 *out of 319 in per capita* **federal funds and grants**

Quality of Life Indexes (Rate per 1000 population)

Crime rate in 1991:	50.4
Violent crime rate in 1991:	5.8
Physicians rate in 1992:	1.86
Hospital bed rate in 1991:	5.33

ACCRA Cost of Living Indexes

(First quarter 1993, average = 100)

Composite index:	90.2
Utilities index:	89.3
Housing index:	87.5

Overview

The seat of Vanderburgh County, Evansville is the center of a metropolitan area that includes Warrick and Posey Counties in Indiana and Henderson County in Kentucky. Well-positioned in the days of the steamboat, the city occupies a unique prospect on a U-bend of the Ohio River.

Evansville is the industrial, agricultural, retail, and transportation center for a thirty–six-county region in Indiana, Illinois, and Kentucky. The city is situated in the heart of rich coal fields that produce more than 140 tons of coal annually and contain resources of 290 billion tons. Evansville is also located in the Illinois Oil Basin, where 53 million barrels of oil are produced each year; one hundred and fifty oil companies and oil-related firms are based in the city. Other industries in the area produce appliances, pharmaceuticals, aluminum, equipment and machinery, food products, furniture, pottery, textiles, plastics, metals, and chemicals.

A fertile farming region, part of the Midwest agricultural belt, surrounds Evansville. More than thirty–one thousand farms acres yield corn, soybeans, wheat, oats, barley, melons, apples, peaches, pears, small fruits, potatoes, and various other vegetables. Meat, fruit, and vegetable packing plants operate in the city.

Evansville retail and wholesale trade areas rank second in size in the state of Indiana. The city's financial community also serves the region with nine major banks in addition to brokerage firms, credit unions, consumer finance companies, and the loan production offices of four national and international banks.

A location near the geographic center of the nation and access to inland water transportation contribute to Evansville's position as the second largest warehousing hub in Indiana. Services include modern public warehouses, rail-barge-truck-storage facilities, and storage-in-transit privileges with the three major rail carriers. The newly remodeled terminal at Evansville Regional Airport is served by six airlines and regional carriers that schedule more than forty daily connecting or direct flights from cities in the Midwest, the South, and Pittsburgh, Pennsylvania. General aviation facilities are maintained at Evansville Regional Airport and at two smaller area airports.

A system of interstate, federal, state, and local highways provides easy access into the city within the Evansville vicinity and from points throughout the nation. Principal routes include I-164; U.S. 41; and Indiana state roads 57, 62, 65, and 66.

Population (1990)

Total Population and Growth Rate

1990: 278,990

1980: 276,252

1970: 254,515

Growth rate 1970–1990: 10%

Race and Hispanic Origin

White: 93.5%

Black: 5.8%

Asian/Pacific Islander: 0.4%

Native American: 0.2%

Hispanic origin: 0.5%

White not Hispanic: 93.1%

Age

Ages 18 to 20: 4.3%

Ages 21 to 24: 5.2%

Ages 25 to 44: 31.7%

Ages 45 to 54: 10.3%

Ages 55 to 59: 4.4%

Ages 60 to 64: 4.6%

Ages 65 plus: 14%

Educational Attainment (1990)

Percent having completed high school: 75.1%

Percent having completed college: 14.8%

Elementary and high school enrollment: 47,279

Federal Funds and Grants Received

Total received in 1989: $694,600,000

Funds received per capita: $2,470

Civilian Labor Force

1993 (April): 150,322

1992 average: 144,940

1991 average: 142,007

1990 average: 143,821

Unemployment

1993 (April): 6.4%

1992 average: 6.5%

1991 average: 5.8%

1990 average: 5.4%

Average Annual Pay

1988: $20,275

1987: $19,754

1985: $18,795

Per Capita Personal Income

1991: $17,863

1990: $17,438

1989: $16,473

Business Climate (1987)

Manufacturing

Number of establishments in 1987: 407

Shipments in 1987 ($1,000): $6,949,800

Employees in 1987: 32,000

Change in employment, 1982 to 1987: 0%

Average annual pay for manufacturing work in 1989: $28,967

Average annual pay for production work in 1987: $24,238

Wholesale Trade

Number of establishments in 1987: 614

Total sales in 1987 ($1,000): $2,671,000

Change in sales, 1982 to 1987: 19.0%

Retail Trade

Number of establishments in 1987: 1,812

Total sales in 1987 ($1,000): $2,671,000

Retail sales per household in 1987: $16,636

Average annual pay in 1989: $10,084

Service Industry

Selected receipts in 1987 ($1,000): $701,900

Average annual pay in 1989: $17,138

Housing

Total number of units in 1990: 117,896

Occupied units in 1990: 108,663

Owner-occupied units in 1990: 68.9%

1993 ACCRA average cost: $100,440

1993 ACCRA average rent for an apartment: $412

Chamber of Commerce

Metro Evansvile Chamber of Commerce, David A. Jenkins, President, 100 N.W. 2nd St. #202, Evansville, IN 47708. 812-425-8147

Economic Development Office

Evansville Regional Economic Development Corporation, Ken Robinson, Exec. Director, 100 N.W. 2nd Street, Suite 208, PO Box 20127, Evansville, IN 47708-0127. 812-423-2020, FAX 812-423-2080

Economic Development Organizations

Southwestern Indiana Small Business Development Center, Jeff Lake, Director, 100 N.W. 2nd St., Suite 200, Evansville, IN 47708. 812-425-7232

Major Businesses

Company	SIC	Telephone
American General Finance	6141	(812) 424-8031
Atlas Van Lines Inc.	4213	(812) 424-2222
Big Rivers Electric Corp.	4911	(502) 827-2561
C N B Bancshares, Inc.	6021	(812) 464-3400
Costain Coal Holdings Inc.	1222	(812) 473-8600
Costain Coal Inc.	1221	(812) 473-8600
Dar Group Investments, Inc.	5661	(812) 476-3636
Deaconess Development Corp.	8062	(812) 426-3900
Deaconess Hospital Inc.	8062	(812) 426-3000
Emge Packing Co. Inc.	2011	(812) 753-3214
Gibbs Die Casting Aluminum Co.	3363	(502) 827-1801
George Koch Sons Inc.	3363	(812) 426-9600
Mead Johnson & Co.	2099	(812) 429-5000
Merit Life Insurance Co.	6311	(812) 424-8031
Old National Bancorp	6021	(812) 464-1434
Potter & Brumfield Inc.	3625	(812) 386-1000
Southern Indiana Gas Electric Co.	4911	(812) 424-6411
St. Marys Medical Center of Evansville	8062	(812) 479-4000
Traylor Bros. Inc.	1622	(812) 477-1542

Colleges and Universities

Indiana Vocational Technical College-Southwest, Evansville

ITT Technical Institute, Evansville

Lockyear College, Evansville Campus, Evansville

University of Evansville, Evansville

University of Southern Indiana, Evansville

FORT WAYNE, IN (MSA)

Geographic Profile

Land Area

1355.7 square miles

Counties and Parishes

Allen

De Kalb

Whitley

Ranking Highlights

148 *out of 319 in total* **land area**

228 *out of 319 in* **population growth,** *1970–1990*

104 *out of 310 in having the lowest* **unemployment** *rate*

111 *out of 310 in size of* **labor force**

188 *out of 318 in the percentage of* **college graduates**

116 *out of 292 in per capita personal* **income**

95 *out of 319 in number of* **manufacturing establishments**

198 *out of 318 in* **physicians** *per 1000 people*

163 *out of 318 in* **hospital beds** *per 1000 people*

134 *out of 267 in fewest* **crimes** *per 1000 people*

62 *out of 266 in fewest* **violent crimes** *per 1000 people*

138 *out of 319 in per capita* **federal funds and grants**

Quality of Life Indexes (Rate per 1000 population)

Crime rate in 1991:	60.5
Violent crime rate in 1991:	3.7
Physicians rate in 1992:	1.65
Hospital bed rate in 1991:	3.79

ACCRA Cost of Living Indexes

(First quarter 1993, average = 100)

Composite index:	90.2
Utilities index:	108.8
Housing index:	87.1

Overview

Fort Wayne is located in the northeastern section of Indiana. Sixty-nine million people are within a radius of 300 miles. Fort Wayne has a mean annual temperature of 50 degrees Fahrenheit. Total rainfall averages 35 inches annually. The normal winter low is 30 degrees Fahrenheit while the average summer high is 82 degrees Fahrenheit.

Fort Wayne is served by two airports. Fort Wayne International Airport and Smith Field. Fort Wayne International Airport is located seven miles southwest of Fort Wayne's central business district and offers 88 scheduled passenger departures daily. It has a 12,000 foot runway. Smith Field is a secondary airport which is used exclusively for private and corporate aviation. Both Conrain and Norfolk & Southern Railway have a main line through Fort Wayne. Fort Wayne is one of the principle Midwest hubs of Norfolk & Southern Railway and is headquarters for the efficient "roadrailers" joint venture between Conrail and Norfolk & Southern called Triple Crown. Roadrailers are specially equipped truck trailers with both regular highway tires and rail wheels enabling them to be used for both modes of transportation without costly handling expenditures.

Convention facilities include the Grand Wayne Center, the Allen County War Memorial Coliseum, and the Memorial Coliseum. The Komets professional hockey team, the Fury professional basketball team, and the Wizards professional baseball team play in Fort Wayne.

Population (1990)

Total Population and Growth Rate

1990: 363,811

1980: 354,156

1970: 334,687

Growth rate 1970–1990: 9%

Race and Hispanic Origin

White: 89.8%

Black: 8.4%

Asian/Pacific Islander: 0.8%

Native American: 0.3%

Hispanic origin: 1.7%

White not Hispanic: 88.9%

Age

Ages 18 to 20: 4.3%

Ages 21 to 24: 5.5%

Ages 25 to 44: 32.8%

Ages 45 to 54: 9.8%

Ages 55 to 59: 4%

Ages 60 to 64: 4.1%

Ages 65 plus: 11.5%

Educational Attainment (1990)

Percent having completed high school: 80.6%

Percent having completed college: 17.3%

Elementary and high school enrollment: 66,355

Federal Funds and Grants Received

Total received in 1989: $1,195,000,000

Funds received per capita: $3,253

Civilian Labor Force

1993 (April): 202,625

1992 average: 199,942

1991 average: 195,999

1990 average: 200,114

Unemployment

1993 (April): 5.9%

1992 average: 6.1%

1991 average: 6.1%

1990 average: 5.3%

Average Annual Pay

1988: $21,268

1987: $20,375

1985: $18,652

Per Capita Personal Income

1991: $17,962
1990: $17,788
1989: $17,191

Business Climate (1987)

Manufacturing

Number of establishments in 1987: 674
Shipments in 1987 ($1,000): $5,055,300
Employees in 1987: 45,700
Change in employment, 1982 to 1987: 7.5%
Average annual pay for manufacturing work in 1989: $29,808
Average annual pay for production work in 1987: $21,709

Wholesale Trade

Number of establishments in 1987: 861
Total sales in 1987 ($1,000): $5,420,200
Change in sales, 1982 to 1987: 87.9%

Retail Trade

Number of establishments in 1987: 2,186
Total sales in 1987 ($1,000): $5,420,200
Retail sales per household in 1987: $18,843
Average annual pay in 1989: $10,958

Service Industry

Selected receipts in 1987 ($1,000): $1,001,300
Average annual pay in 1989: $17,302

Office Real Estate (1992)

Office space inventory: 2,581,998 square feet
Average class A Central Business District rental range per sq. ft: $15.00

Vacancy Rates

All areas: 23.9%

Vacancy Rates in Central Business District

Class A space: 4.7%
Class B space: 41.8%

Vacancy Rates Outside Central Business District

Class A space: 30.6%
Class B space: 39.1%

Housing

Total number of units in 1990: 147,376
Occupied units in 1990: 136,068
Owner-occupied units in 1990: 72.1%
1993 ACCRA average cost: $97,000
1993 ACCRA average rent for an apartment: $455

Chamber of Commerce

Fort Wayne Chamber of Commerce and Economic Development, David G. Brown, President, 826 Ewing St., Fort Wayne, IN 46802. 219-424-1435, FAX 219-426-7232

Economic Development Office

Indiana North East Development, Lincoln Schrock, Director, 203 W. Wayne St., PO Box 11099, Fort Wayne, IN 46855. 219-426-7649, FAX 219-426-4740

Economic Development Organizations

Department of Economic Development, Director, 1 Main St., Room 840, Fort Wayne, IN 46802. 219-427-1127

Fort Wayne Small Business Development Center, Cheri Maslyk, Director, 1830 Wayne Trace, Fort Wayne, IN 46803. 219-426-0040

Fort Wayne Enterprise Center, Business Incubation, John Brell, Director, 1830 Wayne Trace, Fort Wayne, IN 46803. 219-426-5700

Job Works (Fort Wayne Area Training & Development Corp.), Indiana Northeast Development, Lincoln Schrock, Director, 203 W. Wayne St., PO Box 11099, Fort Wayne, IN 46855. 219-426-7649

Major Businesses

Company	SIC	Telephone
Advance Mixer Inc.	3711	(219) 484-6691
Allen County Motors Inc.	5511	(219) 432-9545
Allen Dairy Products Inc.	2026	(219) 483-6436
Ayres, Don Pontiac Inc.	5511	(219) 484-0551
Azar's Inc.	5812	(219) 424-1972
Central Soya Co., Inc.	5153	(219) 425-5100
Central States Enterprise	5153	(219) 422-1577
CSY Agri-Processing, Inc.	5153	(219) 425-5100
Essex Group Inc.	3357	(219) 461-4000
Fort Wayne National Bank	6021	(219) 426-0555
Fort Wayne National Corp.	6712	(219) 426-0555
Franklin Electric Co., Inc.	3621	(219) 824-2900
Hagerman Construction Corp.	1542	(219) 424-1470
Hardware Wholesalers, Inc.	5072	(219) 749-8531
Indiana Michigan Power Co.	4911	(219) 425-2111
Irmscher & Sons Inc.	1541	(219) 422-5572
K & K Insurance Group Inc.	6411	(219) 427-3000
Lincoln Financial Corp.	6021	(219) 461-6000
Lincoln Foodservice Products	3589	(219) 432-9511
Lincoln National Admnistrative	8741	(219) 427-2000
Lincoln National Health Casualty Inc.	6411	(219) 427-4202
Lincoln National Bank & Trust	6021	(219) 461-6000
Lincoln National Corp.	6331	(219) 427-2000
Lincoln National Life Insurance	6311	(219) 427-2000
Lutheran Hospital of Indiana	8062	(219) 458-2001
Magnavox	3812	(219) 429-6000
F. McConnell & Sons Inc.	5194	(219) 493-6607
Medical Protective Co. Inc.	6399	(219) 485-9622
Midwestern United Life Insurance	6311	(219) 432-1551
North American Van Lines	4213	(219) 429-2511
Omnisource Corp.	5093	(219) 422-5541
Parkview Memorial Hospital	8062	(219) 484-6636
Patton Electric Co. Inc.	3634	(219) 493-3564
Perfection Biscuit Co.	2051	(219) 424-8245
Petroleum Traders Corp.	5172	(219) 432-6622

Major Businesses (Continued)

Company	SIC	Telephone
Phelps Dodge Industries Inc.	3357	(219) 458-4444
Rogers Markets Inc.	5411	(219) 423-4376
Schwartz Ford Co. Inc.	5511	(219) 724-3101
Scott's Food Stores Inc.	5411	(219) 483-9537
Seyfert Foods Inc.	2096	(219) 483-9521
Shambaugh & Son Inc.	1711	(219) 487-7777
Summcorp	6022	(219) 427-8333
Summit Bank	6022	(219) 427-8333
Tokheim Corp.	3586	(219) 423-2552
Waterfield Financial Corp.	6162	(219) 425-8411

Colleges and Universities

Indiana Institute of Technology, Fort Wayne

Indiana University-Purdue University at Fort Wayne, Fort Wayne

Indiana Vocational Technical College-Northeast, Fort Wayne

International Business College, Fort Wayne

Interstate Technical Institute, Fort Wayne

ITT Technical Institute, Fort Wayne

St. Francis College, Fort Wayne

Summit Christian College, Fort Wayne

GARY–HAMMOND, IN (PMSA)

Geographic Profile

Land Area
915.2 square miles

Counties and Parishes
Lake

Porter

Additional Cities/Towns within Area
East Chicago

Ranking Highlights

217 *out of 319 in total* land area

293 *out of 319 in* population growth, *1970–1990*

234 *out of 310 in having the lowest* unemployment *rate*

88 *out of 310 in size of* labor force

256 *out of 318 in the percentage of* college graduates

170 *out of 292 in per capita personal* income

117 *out of 319 in number of* manufacturing establishments

238 *out of 318 in* physicians *per 1000 people*

99 *out of 318 in* hospital beds *per 1000 people*

129 *out of 267 in fewest* crimes *per 1000 people*

211 *out of 266 in fewest* violent crimes *per 1000 people*

293 *out of 319 in per capita* federal funds and grants

Quality of Life Indexes (Rate per 1000 population)

Crime rate in 1991:	60.0
Violent crime rate in 1991:	9.3
Physicians rate in 1992:	1.43
Hospital bed rate in 1991:	4.62

ACCRA Cost of Living Indexes
(First quarter 1993, average = 100)

Composite index:	N/A
Utilities index:	N/A
Housing index:	N/A

Overview

The fourth largest city in Indiana, Gary is the largest U.S. city founded in the twentieth century. A leading steel producing center, it is often called the Steel City. Historically, manufacturing has been the heart of Gary and northwest Indiana. However, the steel production that revived in the late 1980s no longer totally dominates the scene. Gary's economy has been hard hit by decline of the number of people employed in the American steel industry. The Gary Chamber of Commerce points out that although jobs have decreased due primarily to automation, the amount of steel produced in Gary has actually increased as of the early 1990s. The Gary Works of the U S X Corporation can produce seven million short tons of steel annually. Three other large steel plants are in the region.

The economy is also exemplified by the following businesses, which are some of the city's major employers: Gary Steel Products Corporation, which produces machinery and air distribution products; Georgia Pacific Corporation, which makes paper products; the women's sports apparel maker Jantus Manufacturing Company; the Lehigh Portland Cement Company; and the Western Engine Company. In recent years, tourism has become one of the Gary's fastest growing industries. Gary, and Lake County, are becoming increasingly popular for people from Chicago and other urban areas who want to escape the big cities for short vacations and recreational opportunities. Genesis Convention Center can accommodate nearly 9,000 people for conventions with eleven meeting rooms that seat 40 to 400 persons.

Located about 28 miles southeast of Chicago, Gary is accessible from Interstate 65, which runs north and south, and I–94/80, which runs east and west. The Indiana Toll Road I–90 connects the Chicago Skyway to the west and the Ohio Turnpike to the east. Greyhound Trailways, Indiana, and Tri–State operate bus service into Gary. Gary Regional Airport, four miles east of the city on U.S. 12, houses Direct Air, which provides passenger service to Pittsburgh, Pennsylvania, Cleveland, Ohio, Detroit, Michigan, and Fort Wayne. Chicago's Midway airport is a thirty–minute drive while Chicago's O'Hare Airport is a one–hour drive from Gary.

Population (1990)

Total Population and Growth Rate
1990: 604,526
1980: 642,733
1970: 633,367
Growth rate 1970–1990: -5%

Race and Hispanic Origin
White: 76.2%
Black: 19.4%
Asian/Pacific Islander: 0.6%
Native American: 0.2%
Hispanic origin: 8.0%
White not Hispanic: 72.0%

Age
Ages 18 to 20: 4.5%
Ages 21 to 24: 5.2%
Ages 25 to 44: 30.9%
Ages 45 to 54: 10.5%
Ages 55 to 59: 4.5%
Ages 60 to 64: 4.5%
Ages 65 plus: 11.8%

Educational Attainment (1990)
Percent having completed high school: 75.4%
Percent having completed college: 14.0%
Elementary and high school enrollment: 118,993

Federal Funds and Grants Received
Total received in 1989: $1,335,100,000

Funds received per capita: $2,181

Civilian Labor Force
1993 (April): 263,462
1992 average: 262,395
1991 average: 261,092
1990 average: 261,244

Unemployment
1993 (April): 8.4%
1992 average: 8.2%
1991 average: 6.5%
1990 average: 5.7%

Average Annual Pay
1988: $21,961
1987: $20,934
1985: $20,401

Per Capita Personal Income
1991: $16,811
1990: $16,564
1989: $15,630

Business Climate (1987)

Manufacturing
Number of establishments in 1987: 483
Shipments in 1987 ($1,000): $13,189,500
Employees in 1987: 52,700
Change in employment, 1982 to 1987: -30.3%
Average annual pay for manufacturing work in 1989: $36,550
Average annual pay for production work in 1987: $30,760

Wholesale Trade
Number of establishments in 1987: 628
Total sales in 1987 ($1,000): $2,802,100
Change in sales, 1982 to 1987: 23.4%

Retail Trade
Number of establishments in 1987: 3,177
Total sales in 1987 ($1,000): $2,802,100
Retail sales per household in 1987: $15,269
Average annual pay in 1989: $10,077

Service Industry
Selected receipts in 1987 ($1,000): $1,182,900
Average annual pay in 1989: $17,955

Office Real Estate (1992)
Office space inventory: 2,850,000 square feet
Average class A Central Business District rental range per sq. ft: N/A

Vacancy Rates
All areas: 7.5%

Vacancy Rates in Central Business District
Class A space: N/A
Class B space: 10.0%

Vacancy Rates Outside Central Business District
Class A space: 10.0%

Class B space: 5.9%

Housing

Total number of units in 1990: 230,254
Occupied units in 1990: 215,907
Owner-occupied units in 1990: 69.3%
1993 ACCRA average cost: N/A
1993 ACCRA average rent for an apartment: N/A

Chamber of Commerce

Greater Gary Chamber of Commerce, Maxine J. Young, President, 504 Broadway Suite 324, Gary, IN 46402. 219-885-7407

Economic Development Office

North Lake Small Business Development Center, Jeanenne Holcomb, Director, 504 Broadway Suite 710, Gary, IN 46402. 219-882-2000

Economic Development Organizations

Lakeshore Private Industry Council, W.W. (Wes) Arington, 504 Broadway Suite 923, Gary, IN 46402. 219-882-0033

Globetrotters Engineering Corp., Gary Minority Business Development Center, Jeffrey Q. Williams, Director, PO Box 9007, 567 Broadway Suite 4, Gary, IN 46402. 219-883-5802

Major Businesses

Company	SIC	Telephone
Applewood Farms Inc.	5144	(219) 942-0961
Bank One Merrillville	6021	(219) 738-6000
G. W. Berkheimer Co., Inc.	5075	(219) 887-0141
Calumet Construction Corp.	1541	(219) 844-9420
Canonie Enviromental Services	1629	(219) 926-8651
Carpetland U.S.A. Inc.	5713	(219) 836-5555
Chester Inc.	2873	(219) 462-1131
Citizens Federal Savings Loan Association	6035	(219) 933-0432
Concord Life Insurance Co.	6351	(219) 836-5233
Dixie Dairy Co.	2026	(219) 885-6101
Emcor Inc.	1629	(219) 932-5036
First Bancshares Inc.	6022	(219) 769-6905
First Federal Savings Bank	6035	(219) 736-2644
First National Bank E. Chicago	6021	(219) 397-1000
J. M. Foster, Inc.	1541	(219) 949-4020
Gainer Bank National Association	6021	(219) 738-4000
Gainer Corp.	6021	(219) 738-4000
Gough Construction Co. Inc.	1531	(219) 769-1873
Jack Gray Transport, Inc.	4213	(219) 938-7020
Hammond Lead Products Inc.	2819	(219) 931-9360
Hunter Corp.	1629	(219) 762-0200
Indiana Federal Savings & Loan	6035	(219) 462-4131
Indiana Harbor Belt Co.	4013	(219) 989-4703
KAT Inc.	4213	(219) 926-3413
La-Z Recliner Shop Inc.	5712	(219) 937-3360

Major Businesses (Continued)

Company	SIC	Telephone
Lake Shore Health System	8062	(219) 882-9411
McCartin Mc Auliffe	1711	(219) 398-0233
McGill Manufacturing Co.	3562	(219) 465-2200
Mercantile National Bank	6021	(219) 932-8220
Methodist Hospitals	8062	(219) 886-4000
Midstates Distributor Inc.	5147	(219) 981-2401
Morrison Construction Co.	1711	(219) 932-5036
Morrison Inc.	1711	(219) 932-5036
Multi Media Distributing	5961	(219) 942-1155
Munster Medical Foundation	8062	(219) 836-1600
Nipsco Industries Inc.	4931	(219) 853-5200
Northern Indiana Public Service Co.	4911	(219) 853-5200
Peoples Bank	6035	(219) 836-9690
Porter Memorial Hospital	8062	(219) 465-4600
Smith Motors Inc.	5511	(219) 845-4000
St. Anthony Medical Center	8062	(219) 663-8120
St. Catherine Hospital of Indiana	8062	(219) 392-7104
Steel Transport Inc.	4213	(219) 938-2894
Superior Construction Co.	1622	(219) 886-3728
U. S. Reduction Co.	3341	(219) 836-0555
United Consumer's Club Inc.	6794	(219) 736-1100
Urschel Laboratories Inc.	3556	(219) 464-4811
Walsh & Kelly Inc.	1611	(219) 924-5900
Webb Ford Inc.	5511	(219) 924-3400
White Graphic Systems Inc.	2759	(219) 769-8067

Colleges and Universities

Indiana University Northwest, Gary
Indiana Vocational Technical College-Northwest, Gary
Purdue University Calumet, Hammond

INDIANAPOLIS, IN (MSA)

Geographic Profile

Land Area
3071.2 square miles

Counties and Parishes
Boone
Hamilton
Hancock
Hendricks
Johnson
Marion
Morgan
Shelby

Ranking Highlights
  44 *out of 319 in total* **land area**
215 *out of 319 in* **population growth,** *1970–1990*
  56 *out of 310 in having the lowest* **unemployment** *rate*
  37 *out of 310 in size of* **labor force**
117 *out of 318 in the percentage of* **college graduates**
  54 *out of 292 in per capita personal* **income**
  39 *out of 319 in number of* **manufacturing establishments**
  49 *out of 318 in* **physicians** *per 1000 people*
120 *out of 318 in* **hospital beds** *per 1000 people*
135 *out of 267 in fewest* **crimes** *per 1000 people*
167 *out of 266 in fewest* **violent crimes** *per 1000 people*
129 *out of 319 in per capita* **federal funds and grants**

Quality of Life Indexes (Rate per 1000 population)
Crime rate in 1991:	60.6
Violent crime rate in 1991:	7.3
Physicians rate in 1992:	2.73
Hospital bed rate in 1991:	4.36

ACCRA Cost of Living Indexes
(First quarter 1993, average = 100)
Composite index:	97.1
Utilities index:	95.2
Housing index:	95.1

Overview

Indianapolis is centrally located with four interstate highways converging within its boundaries. Companies headquartered here include Eli Lilly and Company and The Associated Group. Other manufacturers include Nabisco Foods, Jenn-Air, Ford Motor Company, and Boehringer Mannheim (medical products). The central and most populated county in the metro area is Marion County, with the city of Indianapolis occupying 368 of the county's 402 square miles. The Indiana University School of Medicine is among the colleges, universities, and technical schools in the city.

Indianapolis is a primary industrial, commercial, and transportation center for the Midwest. Situated in proximity to the vast agricultural region known as the corn belt and to the industrialized cities of the upper Midwest and the East, Indianapolis is supported by a diversified economic base. Prior to the 1980s, the city's principal industry was manufacturing, which has been displaced by retailing and services. Having made a conscious decision to achieve prosperity through sports, Indianapolis quadrupled its tourism trade and doubled its hotel space during the period 1984–1991, largely by hosting amateur sporting events. Each major sporting event pumps tens of millions of dollars into the economy, contributing $1.1 billion to the tourism trade in 1990, and leading to expanded business opportunities, more jobs, and increasing tax payments to the city.

The insurance industry has long been established in Indianapolis; several insurance companies have located their headquarters and regional offices in the city. With the largest stockyards east of Chicago, Indianapolis is also an important meatpacking center.

Indianapolis is a major transportation and distribution hub for the Midwest. As the most centrally located of the largest one hundred cities in the United States, Indianapolis is within 650 miles of 55 percent of all Americans, or more than 50 million households. The city is served by four interstate highways, five railroads, an international airport, and a foreign trade zone. The Indianapolis market benefits from low state–wide transportation costs: Indiana ranks among the five least costly states in most categories of manufacturing production and maintains the lowest costs in the transportation of all but two commodities. Continued expansion of the wholesale sector and the entry of more than forty–eight hundred businesses into the local economy since 1980 contribute to Indianapolis's position as a primary distribution center.

Indianapolis is gaining in prominence as a convention destination. The number of convention delegates grew from 147,150 in 1984 to 655,926 in 1991. The principal meeting facility is the Indiana Convention Center/Hoosier Dome (ICC/HD). The convention center provides more than 300,000 square feet of column-free exhibit space. A $35 million expansion scheduled for completion in 1993 would add thirty–six thousand square feet and improve the existing space; skywalks would connect the center with more than one thousand hotel rooms. The Hoosier Dome, opened in 1984, features ninety thousand square feet of space. The complex, consisting of five exhibit halls and the multi-use Dome floor, is the site of trade shows, banquets, sporting events, and concerts.

Indianapolis is linked with points throughout the nation by a network of interstate highways. Intersecting the city from east to west is I-70; I-65 passes through the downtown area from the northwest to the southeast. I-69 approaches from the northwest. All of these routes connect with I-465, which encircles the metropolitan area. Amtrak carries rail passengers into Union Station.

The Indianapolis International Airport provides non-stop flights to most major U.S. markets and has become an air-craft maintenance and air cargo center. United Airlines began building a $1 billion maintenance center in Indianapolis in 1992, and Federal Express announced a major expansion of its package sorting hub in 1993. The Indiana Convention Center and Hoosier Dome attract conventions and the city hosts numerous amateur sporting events. Indianapolis is the home of the Indianapolis 500 professional auto race.

Population (1990)

Total Population and Growth Rate
1990: 1,249,822
1980: 1,166,575
1970: 1,111,352
Growth rate 1970–1990: 12%

Race and Hispanic Origin
White: 84.9%
Black: 13.8%
Asian/Pacific Islander: 0.8%
Native American: 0.2%
Hispanic origin: 0.9%
White not Hispanic: 84.4%

Age
Ages 18 to 20: 4.1%
Ages 21 to 24: 5.8%
Ages 25 to 44: 34.2%
Ages 45 to 54: 10.2%
Ages 55 to 59: 4.2%
Ages 60 to 64: 4.1%
Ages 65 plus: 11.1%

Educational Attainment (1990)
Percent having completed high school: 78.6%
Percent having completed college: 21.1%
Elementary and high school enrollment: 212,357

Federal Funds and Grants Received
Total received in 1989: $4,097,800,000
Funds received per capita: $3,314

Civilian Labor Force
1993 (April):   703,354
1992 average: 687,552
1991 average: 683,021
1990 average: 687,219

Unemployment
1993 (April): 5.0%
1992 average: 5.1%
1991 average: 4.7%
1990 average: 4.1%

Average Annual Pay
1988: $21,877
1987: $21,081

1985: $19,494

Per Capita Personal Income
1991: $19,844
1990: $19,253
1989: $18,072

Business Climate (1987)

Manufacturing
Number of establishments in 1987: 1,813
Shipments in 1987 ($1,000): $13,274,700
Employees in 1987: 105,600
Change in employment, 1982 to 1987: -6.2%
Average annual pay for manufacturing work in 1989: $31,174
Average annual pay for production work in 1987: $24,877

Wholesale Trade
Number of establishments in 1987: 2,795
Total sales in 1987 ($1,000): $16,532,400
Change in sales, 1982 to 1987: 37.6%

Retail Trade
Number of establishments in 1987: 7,317
Total sales in 1987 ($1,000): $16,532,400
Retail sales per household in 1987: $19,764
Average annual pay in 1989: $11,809

Service Industry
Selected receipts in 1987 ($1,000): $3,989,100
Average annual pay in 1989: $19,505

Office Real Estate (1992)
Office space inventory: 20,171,300 square feet
Average class A Central Business District rental range per sq. ft: $18.00

Vacancy Rates
All areas: 22.0%

Vacancy Rates in Central Business District
Class A space: 16.7%
Class B space: 37.8%

Vacancy Rates Outside Central Business District
Class A space: 21.9%
Class B space: N/A

Housing
Total number of units in 1990: 517,893
Occupied units in 1990: 480,010
Owner-occupied units in 1990: 63.8%
1993 ACCRA average cost: $104,800
1993 ACCRA average rent for an apartment: $518

Chamber of Commerce
Indianapolis Chamber of Commerce, Thomas A. King, President, 320 N. Meridian St. #928, Indianapolis, IN 46204. 317-464-2200

Economic Development Office
Indianapolis Economic Development Corp., Timothy Monger, President, 320 N. Meridian St. #906, Indianapolis, IN

46204. 317-236-6262, FAX 317-236-6275

Economic Development Organizations

Indiana National Business Development Corp., Larry Ingraham, 1 Indiana Square, Suite 460, Indianapolis, IN 46266. 317-266-5482

Greater Indianapolis Foreign Trade Zone, William Herbert, Director, PO Box 51681, Indianapolis International Airport, Indianapolis, IN 46251. 317-247-1181

Central Indiana Small Business Development Center, Mary Alice McCord, Director, 1317 W. Michigan, Indianapolis, IN 46202. 317-274-8200

Indiana Labor & Management Council, Inc., Robert Firenze, Director, 2780 Waterfront Parkway, East Dr., Indianapolis, IN 46224. 317-293-4101

Major Businesses

Company	SIC	Telephone
Allied Companies, Inc.	5141	(317) 634-3663
Alpine Electronics Manufacturing	3651	(317) 881-7700
American Economy Insurance	6331	(317) 262-6262
American States Insurance Co.	6331	(317) 262-6262
American Trans Air Inc.	4581	(317) 247-4000
Amtran Inc.	4512	(317) 247-4000
Anacomp Inc.	7389	(317) 844-9666
Associated Insurance Co.	6324	(317) 263-8000
Baldwin & Lyons Inc.	6331	(317) 636-9800
Balkamp Inc.	5013	(317) 244-7241
Bank One, Indianapolis	6021	(317) 321-3000
Bankers National Life Insurance	6311	(317) 573-6300
Basic American Medical Inc.	8062	(317) 783-5461
Bindley Western Industries	5122	(317) 298-9900
Boehringer Mannheim Corp.	3826	(317) 845-2000
Central Newspapers Inc.	2711	(317) 633-9252
Citizens Gas & Coke Utilities	4925	(317) 924-3341
Community Hospital of Indiana	8062	(317) 353-1411
Consolidated Insurance Co.	6411	(317) 266-1234
D-A Lubricant Co.	5065	(317) 923-5321
De Mars Corp.	1542	(317) 924-9192
Dowbrands Inc.	5162	(317) 873-7000
Federal Home Loan Bank Indiana	6111	(317) 465-0200
First Indiana Corp.	6035	(317) 269-1200
General Telephone Co. of California	4813	(317) 372-6000
Geupel De Mars, Inc.	1542	(317) 924-9192
Golden Rule Financial Corp.	6321	(317) 297-4123
Golden Rule Insurance Co.	6321	(317) 297-4123
Gregg Appliances Inc.	5731	(317) 848-8710
GTE Florida Inc.	4813	(317) 224-4011
GTE Hawaiian Telephone Co.	4813	(317) 896-8325
GTE North Inc.	4813	(317) 896-6464
GTE Northwest Inc.	4813	(317) 261-5321
GTE Telecom Marketing Corp.	1731	(317) 848-8935
Harman-Motive Inc.	3651	(317) 342-5551

Major Businesses (Continued)

Company	SIC	Telephone
Health Hospital Corp.	8062	(317) 633-9600
Herff Jones, Inc.	3911	(317) 297-3740
Huber, Hunt & Nichols Inc.	1542	(317) 241-6301
Hunt Corp.	1541	(317) 241-0761
INB Financial Corp.	6021	(317) 266-6000
INB National Bank	6021	(317) 266-6000
Indiana Bell Telephone Co.	4813	(317) 265-7437
Indiana Energy Inc.	4924	(317) 926-3351
Indiana Farm Bureau Cooperate	5153	(317) 685-3000
Indiana Gas Co. Inc.	4924	(317) 926-3351
Indiana Insurance Co.	6331	(317) 266-1234
Indiana Municipal Power Age	4911	(317) 573-9955
Indiana National Bank	6021	(317) 266-5113
Indianapolis Life Insuance Co.	6311	(317) 927-6500
Indianpolis Power Light Co.	4911	(317) 261-8261
Inland Container Corp.	2653	(317) 879-4222
Inland-Rome Inc.	2631	(317) 879-4222
Intrenet, Inc.	4213	(317) 872-4011
Ipalco Enterprises Inc.	4911	(317) 261-8261
Jefferson National Life Insurance Co.	6311	(317) 635-7676
Lacy Diversified Industries	5099	(317) 237-2251
Eli Lilly and Co.	2833	(317) 276-2000
Eli Lilly International Co.	8742	(317) 276-2000
Lilly Industrial Coatings	2851	(317) 634-8512
Lincoln Income Life Insurance Co.	6311	(317) 573-6100
Mayflower Group, Inc.	4213	(317) 875-1000
Mayflower Transit, Inc.	4213	(317) 875-1000
Merchants National Corp.	6021	(317) 267-7000
Meridian Insurance Group	6331	(317) 927-8100
Methodist Hospital of Indiana	8062	(317) 924-6411
Paul Harris Stores, Inc.	5621	(317) 293-3900
PSI Energy Inc.	4911	(317) 839-9611
PSI Resources Inc.	4911	(317) 839-9611
Reilly Industries, Inc.	2865	(317) 638-7531
St. Vincent Hospital Health Care	8062	(317) 871-2345
Thomson Consumer Electronic	3651	(317) 267-5000
United Farm Bureau Family	6321	(317) 263-7200
United Farm Bureau Mutual Insurance Co.	6331	(317) 263-7200
Wabash Valley Power Assn.	4911	(317) 247-1596
Western Casualty & Surety	6331	(317) 262-6262
Western National Life Insurance Co.	6311	(317) 573-6100
Wholesale Club, Inc.	5149	(317) 842-0351
F. A. Wilhelm Construction	1541	(317) 359-5411

Colleges and Universities

Butler University, Indianapolis

George Rogers Clark College, Indianapolis

Indiana Business College, Indianapolis

Indiana University-Purdue University at Indianapolis, Indianapolis

Indiana Vocational Technical College-Central Indiana, Indianapolis

ITT Technical Institute, Indianapolis

Lincoln Technical Institute, Indianapolis

Lockyear College, Indianapolis Campus, Indianapolis

Marian College, Indianapolis

Martin Center College, Indianapolis

University of Indianapolis, Indianapolis

KOKOMO, IN (MSA)

Geographic Profile

Land Area

553.5 square miles

Counties and Parishes

Howard

Tipton

Ranking Highlights

283 *out of 319 in total* **land area**

283 *out of 319 in* **population growth,** *1970–1990*

191 *out of 310 in having the lowest* **unemployment** *rate*

290 *out of 310 in size of* **labor force**

269 *out of 318 in the percentage of* **college graduates**

125 *out of 292 in per capita personal* **income**

306 *out of 319 in number of* **manufacturing establishments**

294 *out of 318 in* **physicians** *per 1000 people*

95 *out of 318 in* **hospital beds** *per 1000 people*

40 *out of 267 in fewest* **crimes** *per 1000 people*

61 *out of 266 in fewest* **violent crimes** *per 1000 people*

281 *out of 319 in per capita* **federal funds and grants**

Quality of Life Indexes (Rate per 1000 population)

Crime rate in 1991:	40.2
Violent crime rate in 1991:	3.7
Physicians rate in 1992:	1.09
Hospital bed rate in 1991:	4.72

ACCRA Cost of Living Indexes

(First quarter 1993, average = 100)

Composite index:	N/A
Utilities index:	N/A
Housing index:	N/A

Population (1990)

Total Population and Growth Rate

1990: 96,946

1980: 103,715

1970: 99,848

Growth rate 1970–1990: -3%

Race and Hispanic Origin

White: 94.3%

Black: 4.5%

Asian/Pacific Islander: 0.5%

Native American: 0.3%

Hispanic origin: 1.2%

White not Hispanic: 93.5%

Age

Ages 18 to 20: 4.1%

Ages 21 to 24: 4.9%

Ages 25 to 44: 30.6%

Ages 45 to 54: 12.1%

Ages 55 to 59: 4.9%

Ages 60 to 64: 4.5%
Ages 65 plus: 12.2%

Educational Attainment (1990)
Percent having completed high school: 78.2%
Percent having completed college: 13.6%
Elementary and high school enrollment: 17,852

Federal Funds and Grants Received
Total received in 1989: $220,700,000
Funds received per capita: $2,231

Civilian Labor Force
1993 (April):   47,941
1992 average: 47,593
1991 average: 46,289
1990 average: 47,066

Unemployment
1993 (April):   6.2%
1992 average: 7.4%
1991 average: 8.2%
1990 average: 6.5%

Average Annual Pay
1988: $26,452
1987: $24,652
1985: $24,407

Per Capita Personal Income
1991: $17,754
1990: $17,460
1989: $16,864

Business Climate (1987)
Manufacturing
Number of establishments in 1987: 85
Shipments in 1987 ($1,000): $2,546,600
Employees in 1987: 18,500
Change in employment, 1982 to 1987: 5.1%
Average annual pay for manufacturing work in 1989: $42,609
Average annual pay for production work in 1987: $34,861

Wholesale Trade
Number of establishments in 1987: 140
Total sales in 1987 ($1,000): $362,200
Change in sales, 1982 to 1987: -29.2%

Retail Trade
Number of establishments in 1987: 675
Total sales in 1987 ($1,000): $362,200
Retail sales per household in 1987: $18,257
Average annual pay in 1989: $10,172

Service Industry
Selected receipts in 1987 ($1,000): $142,200
Average annual pay in 1989: $17,300

Housing
Total number of units in 1990: 40,247

Occupied units in 1990: 37,549
Owner-occupied units in 1990: 72.8%
1993 ACCRA average cost: N/A
1993 ACCRA average rent for an apartment: N/A

Chamber of Commerce
Kokomo/Howard County Chamber of Commerce, Margaret Johnson, President, 106 N. Washington, PO Box 731, Kokomo, IN 46903-0731. 317-457-5301

Economic Development Office
Kokomo Development Corp., President, PO Box 731, Kokomo, IN 46903-0731. 317-457-2000, FAX 317-452-4564

Economic Development Organizations
Kokoma/Howard County Small Business Development Center, Todd Moser, Director, PO Box 731, 106 N. Washington, Kokomo, IN 46903. 317-457-5301

Major Businesses

Company	SIC	Telephone
Ameritrust Bank, Howard County	6022	(317) 457-8111
Delco Electronics Corp.	3651	(317) 451-2384
First National Bank	6021	(317) 459-3911
Fleet Supply Inc.	5251	(317) 452-4038
Foust Motors Inc.	5511	(317) 675-7491
Haynes International	3313	(317) 456-6000
Howard County Community Hospital	8062	(317) 453-0702
Kokomo Chrysler-Plymouth	5511	(317) 459-8071
Kokomo Gas & Fuel Co. Inc.	4932	(317) 459-4101
H. E. McGonigal, Inc.	5511	(317) 459-0381
St. Joseph Hospital & Health	8062	(317) 452-5611
Tipton County Farm Bureau Cooperative	5153	(317) 675-8736
United Presidential Corp.	6311	(317) 453-0602
United Presidential Life Insurance	6311	(317) 453-0602

Colleges and Universities
Indiana University at Kokomo, Kokomo
Indiana Vocational Technical College-Kokomo, Kokomo

LAFAYETTE–WEST LAFAYETTE, IN (MSA)

Geographic Profile

Land Area

499.8 square miles

Counties and Parishes

Tippecanoe

Ranking Highlights

291 *out of 319 in total* **land area**

182 *out of 319 in* **population growth,** *1970–1990*

14 *out of 310 in having the lowest* **unemployment** *rate*

237 *out of 310 in size of* **labor force**

22 *out of 318 in the percentage of* **college graduates**

205 *out of 292 in per capita personal* **income**

289 *out of 319 in number of* **manufacturing establishments**

162 *out of 318 in* **physicians** *per 1000 people*

86 *out of 318 in* **hospital beds** *per 1000 people*

66 *out of 267 in fewest* **crimes** *per 1000 people*

36 *out of 266 in fewest* **violent crimes** *per 1000 people*

243 *out of 319 in per capita* **federal funds and grants**

Quality of Life Indexes (Rate per 1000 population)

Crime rate in 1991:	46.4
Violent crime rate in 1991:	2.8
Physicians rate in 1992:	1.79
Hospital bed rate in 1991:	4.86

ACCRA Cost of Living Indexes

(First quarter 1993, average = 100)

Composite index:	N/A
Utilities index:	N/A
Housing index:	N/A

Overview

The Lafayette MSA includes the City of Lafayette, the City of West Lafayette, and the other smaller communities within Tippecanoe County. It is located on Interstate 65, about 65 miles from Indianapolis and 120 miles from Chicago. It has easy access to other interstate highways and metropolitan areas. Air transportation is provided by the local Purdue University Airport and other regional airports in Indianapolis and Chicago. Rail Service includes Amtrak, Cornrail, CSX Chicago Transportation, the Norfolk Southern Corporation, and the Hoosier Lift connection to the Santa Fe Railway.

The two largest employers in the area are Purdue University and Subaru-Isuzu Automotive, Inc. Revenue generated by the local government totalled $52.7 million annually. The federal government contributed an additional $172 millions in funds and $53 millions in grants.

Population (1990)

Total Population and Growth Rate

1990: 130,598

1980: 121,702

1970: 109,378

Growth rate 1970–1990: 19%

Race and Hispanic Origin

White: 93.4%

Black: 2.0%

Asian/Pacific Islander: 3.7%

Native American: 0.2%

Hispanic origin: 1.6%

White not Hispanic: 92.4%

Age

Ages 18 to 20: 13.4%

Ages 21 to 24: 12.6%

Ages 25 to 44: 29%

Ages 45 to 54: 8.1%

Ages 55 to 59: 3.2%

Ages 60 to 64: 3.2%

Ages 65 plus: 9.4%

Educational Attainment (1990)

Percent having completed high school: 85.2%

Percent having completed college: 30.7%

Elementary and high school enrollment: 17,395

Federal Funds and Grants Received

Total received in 1989: $314,400,000

Funds received per capita: $2,508

Civilian Labor Force

1993 (April): 69,462

1992 average: 68,824

1991 average: 67,907

1990 average: 68,554

Unemployment

1993 (April): 4.4%

1992 average: 3.8%

1991 average: 3.2%

1990 average: 2.9%

Average Annual Pay

1988: $19,790

1987: $19,061

1985: $17,604

Per Capita Personal Income

1991: $16,184

1990: $15,763

1989: $14,857

Business Climate (1987)

Manufacturing

Number of establishments in 1987: 106

Shipments in 1987 ($1,000): $1,965,000

Employees in 1987: 11,700

Change in employment, 1982 to 1987: 13.6%

Average annual pay for manufacturing work in 1989: $29,833

Average annual pay for production work in 1987: $24,790

Wholesale Trade

Number of establishments in 1987: 143

Total sales in 1987 ($1,000): $261,900

Change in sales, 1982 to 1987: -18.0%

Retail Trade

Number of establishments in 1987: 743

Total sales in 1987 ($1,000): $261,900

Retail sales per household in 1987: $19,707

Average annual pay in 1989: $9,445

Service Industry

Selected receipts in 1987 ($1,000): $277,900

Average annual pay in 1989: $15,411

Housing

Total number of units in 1990: 48,134

Occupied units in 1990: 45,618

Owner-occupied units in 1990: 57.1%

1993 ACCRA average cost: N/A

1993 ACCRA average rent for an apartment: N/A

Chamber of Commerce

Greater Lafayette Chamber of Commerce, Dana Smith, President, 122 N. Third St., PO Box 348, Lafayette, IN 47905. 317-742-4041, FAX 317-742-6276

Economic Development Office

Greater Lafayette Progress, Inc., Michael Brooks, President, 122 N. 3rd St., PO Box 311, Lafayette, IN 47905. 317-742-0095, FAX 317-742-6276

Economic Development Organizations

Greater Lafayette Area Small Business Development Center, Susan Davis, Director, 224 Main St.., Lafayette, IN 47901. 317-742-0095

Lafayette Board of Realtors, Donald F. Blackburn, President, 2075 Main St., Lafayette, IN 47904. 317-742-8162

Tecumseh Area Partnership, Inc. (Private Industry Council), Director of Administration, PO Box 4729, 639 S. Earl Ave., Lafayette, IN 47903. 317-447-2610

Purdue Research Foundation, Purdue Industrial Research Park, Director, 1220 Potter Dr., Purdue University, West Lafayette, IN 47907. 317-494-1727

Indiana Department of Employment and Training Services, Director, 2301 Concord Rd., Lafayette, IN 47905. 317-474-5411

Lafayette Economic Development Commission, Commissioner, 20 N. 6th St., Lafayette, IN 47901. 317-742-8404

Tippecanoe County Area Plann Commission, Director, 20 North 3rd Street, Lafayette, IN 47902. 317-423-9242

Tippecanoe County Commission, Commisioner, 20 N. 3rd St., Lafayette, IN 47902. 317-423-9215

Tippecanoe County Economic Development Commission, Director, County Government Office Building, 20 N. 3rd. St., Lafayette, IN 47901. 317-423-9207

West Lafayette Economic Development Commission, Director, 609 W. Navajo, West Lafayette, IN 47906. 317-463-3571

Local Incentives for Business

West Lafayette, Lafayette, and Tippecanoe County Economic Development Commissions can issue tax-exempt Economic Development Bonds. Under the EDB bonds, up to 100% financing is available for land, building, on-site improvements and capital equipment. For more information, contact the three Economic Development Commission offices listed above.

Funding can be provided as incentives to hire and train qualified individuals. For more information, contact the Tecumseh Area Partnership Private Industry Council listed above.

Industrial Sites

Purdue Industrial Research Park. (77 acres). Contact: Dr. Leroy Silver , Purdue University, West Lafayette, IN 47907, 317-494-8642

Major Businesses

Company	SIC	Telephone
Andover Inc.	3694	(317) 447-1157
E/M Corp.	2899	(317) 497-6100
Egyptian Lacquer Mfg. Co.	2851	(317) 447-2136
Fairfield Mfg. Co.	3566	(317) 474-3474
Fauber Construction Co. Inc.	1771	(317) 742-1081
First Bancorp Indiana, Inc.	6035	(317) 423-2525
Great Lakes Chemical Corp.	2819	(317) 497-6100
Henry Poor Lumber Co.	5211	(317) 743-2196
INB National Bank, Northwest	6021	(317) 423-8022
Korschot's Heating & Air	5075	(317) 447-1137
Lafayette Life Insurance	6311	(317) 477-7411
Landis & Gyr Metering, Inc.	3825	(317) 742-1001
MDBS, Inc.	7372	(317) 447-1122
Microelectronics Div.	3679	(317) 463-2565
Personal Finance Co.	6141	(317) 742-1013
Qo Chemicals, Inc.	2899	(317) 497-6100
Ross Gear Div.	3594	(317) 423-5377
Rostone Corp.	2821	(317) 474-2421
Schnaible Service & Supply	5087	(317) 742-0280
Schwab Corp.	2522	(317) 447-9470
Wabash National Corp.	3537	(317) 448-1591
Warren Industries, Inc.	3944	(317) 447-2151

Colleges and Universities

Indiana Vocational Technical College-Lafayette, Lafayette, IN (1,800 students). Offers one-to-two year training programs in business, health, and trade technical areas.

Purdue University, West Lafayette, IN

Additional Information

The Fact Book, Greater Lafayette, Indiana. Greater Lafayette Progress, Inc. 224 Main Street, P.O. Box 311, Lafayette, IN 47902.

MUNCIE, IN (MSA)

Geographic Profile

Land Area

393.3 square miles

Counties and Parishes

Delaware

Ranking Highlights

314 *out of 319 in total* **land area**

309 *out of 319 in* **population growth,** *1970–1990*

139 *out of 310 in having the lowest* **unemployment** *rate*

262 *out of 310 in size of* **labor force**

209 *out of 318 in the percentage of* **college graduates**

210 *out of 292 in per capita personal* **income**

227 *out of 319 in number of* **manufacturing establishments**

128 *out of 318 in* **physicians** *per 1000 people*

138 *out of 318 in* **hospital beds** *per 1000 people*

N/A *out of 267 in fewest* **crimes** *per 1000 people*

N/A *out of 266 in fewest* **violent crimes** *per 1000 people*

283 *out of 319 in per capita* **federal funds and grants**

Quality of Life Indexes (Rate per 1000 population)

Crime rate in 1991:	N/A
Violent crime rate in 1991:	N/A
Physicians rate in 1992:	1.96
Hospital bed rate in 1991:	4.13

ACCRA Cost of Living Indexes

(First quarter 1993, average = 100)

Composite index:	99.5
Utilities index:	100.0
Housing index:	102.8

Population (1990)

Total Population and Growth Rate

1990: 119,659

1980: 128,587

1970: 129,219

Growth rate 1970–1990: -7%

Race and Hispanic Origin

White: 93.0%

Black: 6.0%

Asian/Pacific Islander: 0.5%

Native American: 0.2%

Hispanic origin: 0.7%

White not Hispanic: 92.5%

Age

Ages 18 to 20: 10.1%

Ages 21 to 24: 8.9%

Ages 25 to 44: 26.9%

Ages 45 to 54: 10.6%

Ages 55 to 59: 4.4%

Ages 60 to 64: 4.4%
Ages 65 plus: 12.7%

Educational Attainment (1990)
Percent having completed high school: 74.5%
Percent having completed college: 16.5%
Elementary and high school enrollment: 17,826

Federal Funds and Grants Received
Total received in 1989: $265,500,000
Funds received per capita: $2,211

Civilian Labor Force
1993 (April):   58,814
1992 average: 61,501
1991 average: 59,828
1990 average: 60,209

Unemployment
1993 (April):   6.6%
1992 average: 6.6%
1991 average: 6.1%
1990 average: 5.3%

Average Annual Pay
1988: $19,575
1987: $19,038
1985: $17,933

Per Capita Personal Income
1991: $16,080
1990: $15,455
1989: $14,500

Business Climate (1987)
Manufacturing
Number of establishments in 1987: 188
Shipments in 1987 ($1,000): $1,177,300
Employees in 1987: 11,200
Change in employment, 1982 to 1987: 7.7%
Average annual pay for manufacturing work in 1989: $32,252
Average annual pay for production work in 1987: $27,405

Wholesale Trade
Number of establishments in 1987: 163
Total sales in 1987 ($1,000): $445,400
Change in sales, 1982 to 1987: 11.9%

Retail Trade
Number of establishments in 1987: 758
Total sales in 1987 ($1,000): $445,400
Retail sales per household in 1987: $16,041
Average annual pay in 1989: $10,549

Service Industry
Selected receipts in 1987 ($1,000): $206,300
Average annual pay in 1989: $15,832

Housing
Total number of units in 1990: 48,793

Occupied units in 1990: 45,177
Owner-occupied units in 1990: 66.8%
1993 ACCRA average cost: $112,378
1993 ACCRA average rent for an apartment: $540

Chamber of Commerce
Muncie-Delaware County Chamber of Commerce, Russ Sloan, President, 401 S. High St., Muncie, IN 47305. 317-288-6681

Economic Development Office
East Central Small Business Development Center, Nancy Stoll, Director, PO Box 842, 401 S. High St., Muncie, IN 47308. 317-284-8144

Major Businesses

Company	SIC	Telephone
American National Bank Trust Co. Mutual	6021	(317) 747-7575
Attlin Construction Inc.	1541	(317) 289-0671
BMH Health Services Inc.	8062	(317) 286-3456
Ball Corp.	3411	(317) 747-6100
Ball Memorial Hospital Inc.	8062	(317) 747-3111
Ball-Incon Glass Packaging	3221	(317) 741-7000
City Machine Tool & Die Co.	3541	(317) 288-4431
Delaware County Farm Bureau Cooperative	5153	(317) 288-5001
Duffy Tool & Stamping Inc.	3465	(317) 288-1941
Eavey's Markets Inc.	5411	(317) 289-7057
Farmers Elevator Co. of Oakville	5153	(317) 288-1951
First Merchants Corp.	6035	(317) 747-1500
G & G Oil Co. of Indiana Inc.	5541	(317) 288-7795
Bill Gaddis Chrysler Plymouth	5511	(317) 289-2361
N. G. Gilbert Corp.	1629	(317) 284-4461
Indiana-American Water Co.	4941	(317) 288-5073
Jordan Paper Products Inc.	5113	(317) 289-7121
Lift-A-Loft Corp.	3537	(317) 288-3691
Marsh Supermarkets, Inc.	5411	(317) 759-8101
Merchants National Bank	6035	(317) 747-1500
Mid-West Metal Products	3496	(317) 289-3355
Minnetrista Corp.	5088	(317) 741-5500
Muncie Power Products, Inc.	3714	(317) 284-7721
Mutual Federal Savings Bank	6035	(317) 747-2800
Ontario Corp.	3398	(317) 747-9001
A. L. Ross & Sons Inc.	5411	(317) 284-1441
Stoops Express, Inc.	4213	(317) 378-0261
Summit Bank of Muncie	6022	(317) 747-4500
Townsend Tree Service Co.	0783	(317) 282-1234
Wise Food Co. Inc.	5411	(317) 288-9775
Yorktown Tool & Die Corp.	3544	(317) 759-7767

Colleges and Universities
Ball State University, Muncie
Indiana Vocational Technical College-Eastcentral, Muncie

SOUTH BEND – MISHAWAKA, IN (MSA)

Geographic Profile

Land Area
457.3 square miles

Counties and Parishes
St. Joseph

Ranking Highlights

300 *out of 319 in total* **land area**
268 *out of 319 in* **population growth**, *1970–1990*
128 *out of 310 in having the lowest* **unemployment** *rate*
161 *out of 310 in size of* **labor force**
153 *out of 318 in the percentage of* **college graduates**
133 *out of 292 in per capita personal* **income**
116 *out of 319 in number of* **manufacturing establishments**
171 *out of 318 in* **physicians** *per 1000 people*
166 *out of 318 in* **hospital beds** *per 1000 people*
N/A *out of 267 in fewest* **crimes** *per 1000 people*
N/A *out of 266 in fewest* **violent crimes** *per 1000 people*
104 *out of 319 in per capita* **federal funds and grants**

Quality of Life Indexes (Rate per 1000 population)

Crime rate in 1991:	N/A
Violent crime rate in 1991:	N/A
Physicians rate in 1992:	1.76
Hospital bed rate in 1991:	3.75

ACCRA Cost of Living Indexes
(First quarter 1993, average = 100)

Composite index:	94.1
Utilities index:	105.6
Housing index:	90.5

Overview

South Bend is the seat of St. Joseph County and the focus of a region known as Michiana that extends over six counties in Indiana and two counties in Michigan. Mishawaka lies to the east of South Bend; the two cities comprise a metropolitan statistical area and are in the heart of the nation's industrial belt. South Bend is home to the University of Notre Dame, which is nationally recognized for its academic excellence and its winning football teams.

South Bend's diversified economic base consists principally of wholesale and retail trade, manufacturing, services, and government. About fifty–seven hundred non–agricultural businesses are located in St. Joseph County; about 86 percent of those businesses employ fewer than 25 persons. Manufacturing industries include non-electrical machinery, transportation equipment, and rubber and various plastic products. Several construction firms that conduct business nationwide are located in the area.

South Bend is a retail center for the Michiana region, with a total market penetration of sixteen counties; sales average more than $5 billion per year. From 1979 to 1985, retail sales increased by 48.4 percent per household in St. Joseph County alone. South Bend is also emerging as a center for professional, financial, and business support services as well as marketing, telecommunications, and computer and data processing. Another primary industry in St. Joseph and Elkhart counties is tourism, which generates a significant number of jobs and revenues reaching $250 million in 1987.

Designated a Foreign Trade Zone, South Bend is a center for manufacturer suppliers and vendors throughout the United States and abroad. Six air-freight carriers ship goods through Michiana Regional Airport. A network of interstate highways, including I-80 and I-90, the nation's major east-west axis routes, provides access to more than seventy motor freight carriers. Four major rail freight lines include Conrail, which links metropolitan South Bend with Chicago, Detroit, Michigan, New York, and Boston, Massachusetts; two privately-owned railroads offer regional service. About sixty–thousand tons of freight annually are transported by four bus lines. Eight commercial airlines schedule more than one hundred direct and connecting daily flights into South Bend at the Michiana Regional Airport from all major United States cities and points abroad. The closest major airport is O'Hare in Chicago, about 120 miles away.

Population (1990)

Total Population and Growth Rate
1990: 247,052
1980: 241,617
1970: 244,827
Growth rate 1970–1990: 1%

Race and Hispanic Origin
White: 87.8%
Black: 9.8%
Asian/Pacific Islander: 1.0%
Native American: 0.3%
Hispanic origin: 2.1%
White not Hispanic: 86.8%

Age
Ages 18 to 20: 5.9%
Ages 21 to 24: 6.4%
Ages 25 to 44: 30.4%
Ages 45 to 54: 9.1%
Ages 55 to 59: 4.2%
Ages 60 to 64: 4.6%
Ages 65 plus: 14.1%

Educational Attainment (1990)

Percent having completed high school: 76.1%
Percent having completed college: 19.2%
Elementary and high school enrollment: 40,737

Federal Funds and Grants Received

Total received in 1989: $867,500,000

Funds received per capita: $3,552

Civilian Labor Force
1993 (April): 130,655
1992 average: 128,033
1991 average: 126,156
1990 average: 129,144

Unemployment
1993 (April): 5.8%
1992 average: 6.5%
1991 average: 5.7%
1990 average: 5.5%

Average Annual Pay
1988: $19,841
1987: $19,076
1985: $17,742

Per Capita Personal Income
1991: $17,625
1990: $17,193
1989: $16,487

Business Climate (1987)

Manufacturing
Number of establishments in 1987: 489
Shipments in 1987 ($1,000): $2,887,600
Employees in 1987: 23,200
Change in employment, 1982 to 1987: -2.1%
Average annual pay for manufacturing work in 1989: $27,902
Average annual pay for production work in 1987: $21,162

Wholesale Trade
Number of establishments in 1987: 501
Total sales in 1987 ($1,000): $1,597,500
Change in sales, 1982 to 1987: 11.8%

Retail Trade
Number of establishments in 1987: 1,571
Total sales in 1987 ($1,000): $1,597,500
Retail sales per household in 1987: $18,806
Average annual pay in 1989: $10,159

Service Industry
Selected receipts in 1987 ($1,000): $705,500
Average annual pay in 1989: $18,549

Office Real Estate (1992)
Office space inventory: 3,596,000 square feet
Average class A Central Business District rental range per sq. ft: $13.50

Vacancy Rates
All areas: 12.3%

Vacancy Rates in Central Business District
Class A space: 8.5%
Class B space: 22.2%

Vacancy Rates Outside Central Business District
Class A space: 4.7%

Class B space: 24.2%

Housing
Total number of units in 1990: 97,956
Occupied units in 1990: 92,365
Owner-occupied units in 1990: 72.0%
1993 ACCRA average cost: $96,228
1993 ACCRA average rent for an apartment: $532

Chamber of Commerce
South Bend-Mishawaka Area Chamber of Commerce, Stephen M. Queior, Pesident, 401 E. Colfax #310, PO Box 1677, South Bend, IN 46634. 219-234-0051

Economic Development Office
South Bend Small Business Development Center, Carolyn Anderson, Director, 300 N. Michigan, South Bend, IN 46601. 219-282-4350

Major Businesses

Company	SIC	Telephone
1st Source Bank & Subsidiaries	6022	(219) 236-2000
1st Source Corp.	6022	(219) 236-2000
Aker Plastics Co. Inc.	3088	(219) 936-3838
AM General Corp.	3711	(219) 237-6222
Automatic Technologies, Inc.	3089	(219) 289-2404
Bristol Holding Corp.	3088	(219) 232-0497
Clark Equipment Co.	3537	(219) 239-0100
Holy Cross Health System	8062	(219) 233-8558
Indiana Transportation Financial Authority	4785	(219) 674-8836
Interstate Glass Co. Inc.	5039	(219) 291-5150
Jordan Motors Inc.	5511	(219) 259-1981
Koontz-Wagner Electric Co.	1731	(219) 232-2051
Memorial Hospital of South Bend	8062	(219) 234-9041
New Energy Co. Indiana	2869	(219) 233-3116
Nyloncraft Inc.	3089	(219) 256-1521
Reinke Construction Corp.	1542	(219) 287-1561
Ristance Corp.	3357	(219) 259-6253
Schurz Communications Inc.	2711	(219) 287-1001
Sisters of St. Francis Health	8062	(219) 256-3935
Society BanCorp. of Indiana	6022	(219) 237-5373
Society Bank, Indiana	6022	(219) 237-5200
South Bend Drug Co. Inc.	5122	(219) 232-3303
South Bend Tribune Corp.	2711	(219) 233-6161
St. Joseph's Medical Center	8062	(219) 237-7111
E. H. Tepe Co., Inc.	5399	(219) 289-7711
Uniroyal Plastics Acquisition	2295	(219) 255-2181
Uniroyal Plastics Co.	3086	(219) 255-2181
Valley American Bank	6022	(219) 256-6000
Wells Aluminum Corp.	3354	(219) 234-8100
Whiteford Transport System	4213	(219) 234-1900

Colleges and Universities
Bethel College, Mishawaka

Indiana University at South Bend, South Bend
Indiana Vocational Technical College-Northcentral, South
  Bend
Michiana College, South Bend

TERRE HAUTE, IN (MSA)

Geographic Profile

Land Area
761.0 square miles

Counties and Parishes
Clay
Vigo

Ranking Highlights
244 *out of 319 in total* land area
298 *out of 319 in* population growth, *1970–1990*
128 *out of 310 in having the lowest* unemployment *rate*
257 *out of 310 in size of* labor force
213 *out of 318 in the percentage of* college graduates
257 *out of 292 in per capita personal* income
239 *out of 319 in number of* manufacturing establishments
226 *out of 318 in* physicians *per 1000 people*
 79 *out of 318 in* hospital beds *per 1000 people*
N/A *out of 267 in fewest* crimes *per 1000 people*
N/A *out of 266 in fewest* violent crimes *per 1000 people*
160 *out of 319 in per capita* federal funds and grants

Quality of Life Indexes (Rate per 1000 population)
Crime rate in 1991:   N/A
Violent crime rate in 1991: N/A
Physicians rate in 1992:   1.5
Hospital bed rate in 1991:   5

ACCRA Cost of Living Indexes
(First quarter 1993, average = 100)
Composite index: N/A
Utilities index: N/A
Housing index: N/A

Population (1990)

Total Population and Growth Rate
1990: 130,812
1980: 137,247
1970: 138,461
Growth rate 1970–1990: -6%

Race and Hispanic Origin
White: 94.0%
Black: 4.6%
Asian/Pacific Islander: 0.9%
Native American: 0.3%
Hispanic origin: 0.8%
White not Hispanic: 93.5%

Age
Ages 18 to 20: 6.8%
Ages 21 to 24: 6.8%
Ages 25 to 44: 29.2%
Ages 45 to 54: 9.5%
Ages 55 to 59: 4.1%

Ages 60 to 64: 4.6%

Ages 65 plus: 15.4%

Educational Attainment (1990)

Percent having completed high school: 76.0%

Percent having completed college: 16.4%

Elementary and high school enrollment: 20,939

Federal Funds and Grants Received

Total received in 1989: $406,800,000

Funds received per capita: $3,067

Civilian Labor Force

1993 (April):	63,074
1992 average:	63,269
1991 average:	60,699
1990 average:	60,324

Unemployment

1993 (April):	7.0%
1992 average:	6.5%
1991 average:	5.3%
1990 average:	4.6%

Average Annual Pay

1988: $18,192

1987: $18,100

1985: $16,840

Per Capita Personal Income

1991: $15,113

1990: $14,547

1989: $13,948

Business Climate (1987)

Manufacturing

Number of establishments in 1987: 161

Shipments in 1987 ($1,000): $2,034,600

Employees in 1987: 10,900

Change in employment, 1982 to 1987: -8.4%

Average annual pay for manufacturing work in 1989: $26,876

Average annual pay for production work in 1987: $25,157

Wholesale Trade

Number of establishments in 1987: 204

Total sales in 1987 ($1,000): $522,700

Change in sales, 1982 to 1987: -11.6%

Retail Trade

Number of establishments in 1987: 817

Total sales in 1987 ($1,000): $522,700

Retail sales per household in 1987: $25,592

Average annual pay in 1989: $10,812

Service Industry

Selected receipts in 1987 ($1,000): $246,100

Average annual pay in 1989: $15,022

Housing

Total number of units in 1990: 54,809

Occupied units in 1990: 49,186

Owner-occupied units in 1990: 71.2%

1993 ACCRA average cost: N/A

1993 ACCRA average rent for an apartment: N/A

Chamber of Commerce

Terre Haute Area Chamber of Commerce, Arnold D. Arrowood, President, 643 Wabash Ave., PO Box 689, Terre Haute, IN 47808. 812-232-2391

Economic Development Office

Alliance for Growth and Progress, Pat O'Leary, Director, PO Box 1830, Terre Haute, IN 47808. 812-234-2524

Economic Development Organizations

Terre Haute Area Small Business Development Center, William Minnis, Director, Indiana State University, Terre Haute, IN 47809. 812-237-7676

Entrepreneur's Alliance of Indiana, Inc., John Ridder, Director, PO Box 40609, Indianapolis, IN 46240-0609. 317-848-8920

Major Businesses

Company	SIC	Telephone
Ace Washer Supplies Inc.	5722	(812) 232-7185
B & B Food Distributors Inc.	5149	(812) 238-1438
Brentlinger Distributing	5181	(812) 232-9644
CDI Inc.	1542	(812) 232-3327
Stanley J. Clark Inc.	5171	(317) 492-3932
Doan & Decker Ford Inc.	5511	(812) 234-4831
First Financial Corp.	6022	(812) 238-6000
General Housewares Corp.	3469	(812) 232-1000
Gibco Motor Express Inc.	4212	(812) 424-9000
Growers Cooperative Inc.	5153	(812) 235-8123
Hydro-Power Inc.	5084	(812) 232-0156
Indiana Gas & Chemical Co.	4924	(812) 234-1561
Merchants National Bank Terre Haute	6021	(812) 234-5571
RJ Oil Co. Inc.	5172	(812) 877-1556
Specialty Blanks Inc.	3354	(812) 234-3002
Spence/Banks, Inc.	5171	(812) 232-3475
Stuart Moore Oil Corp.	5171	(812) 835-2931
Sunset Harbor Inc.	6512	(812) 235-6079
Sycamore Chevrolet Inc.	5511	(812) 234-6661
Templeton Coal Co. Inc.	5074	(812) 232-7037
Terre Haute Autoplex Inc.	5511	(812) 235-8111
Terre Haute First National Bank	6021	(812) 238-6000
Tri-Industries Inc.	3724	(812) 234-1591
Union Hospital, Inc.	8062	(812) 238-7000
Valley Federal Savings Bank	6036	(812) 232-0311
Vermillion County Hospital	8062	(317) 832-2451
Wabash Valley Asphalt Co.	1611	(812) 232-6094
Western Tar Products Corp.	2865	(812) 232-2384
Weston Paper and Mfg. Co.	2653	(812) 232-0521

Colleges and Universities

Indiana State University, Terre Haute

Indiana Vocational Technical College-Wabash Valley, Terre Haute

Rose-Hulman Institute of Technology, Terre Haute

IOWA

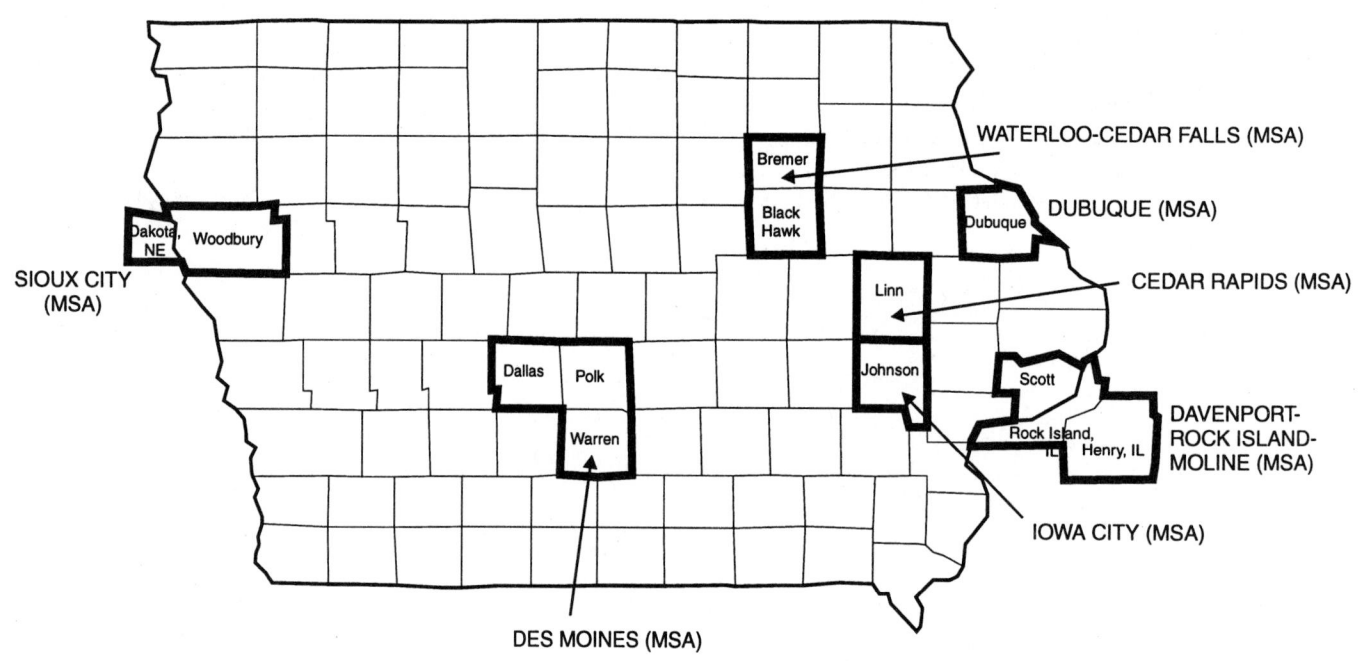

WATERLOO-CEDAR FALLS (MSA)

Bremer

Black
Hawk

DUBUQUE (MSA)

Dubuque

CEDAR RAPIDS (MSA)

Linn

Dakota,
NE

Woodbury

SIOUX CITY
(MSA)

Dallas

Polk

Johnson

Scott

Warren

Rock Island,
IL

Henry, IL

DAVENPORT-
ROCK ISLAND-
MOLINE (MSA)

IOWA CITY (MSA)

DES MOINES (MSA)

IOWA

Population
1990: 2,776,755
1980: 2,913,808

Age
Ages 18 to 20: 131,299
Ages 21 to 24: 152,414
Ages 25 to 44: 823,940
Ages 45 to 54: 274,428
Ages 55 to 59: 122,335
Ages 60 to 64: 127,353
Median age: 34.0

Race
White: 2,683,090
Black: 48,090
Asian/Pacific Islander: 25,476
Native American: 7,349
Hispanic origin: 32,647

Households
Total: 1,064,325
Persons per household: 2.52

Sex
Male: 1,344,802
Female: 1,431,953

Population Migration
Domestic migration: -251,000
International migration: 17,000

Projection of the Population in 1995
Total: 2,933,000
18 to 64: 1,762,000

Civilian Labor Force
1993: 1,556,200
1992: 1,548,700
1991: 1,504,600
1990: 1,486,700

Manufacturing
1995 Projection: 239,300
1992: 229,900
1991: 229,800
1990: 234,800
1989: 235,700

Services
1995 Projection: 441,800

1992: 306,100
1991: 300,400
1990: 293,600
1989: 281,400

Wholesale and Retail Trade
1995 Projection: 371,600
1992: 317,500
1991: 313,200
1990: 313,000
1989: 315,300

Unemployment Rate
1993: 5.1%
1992: 5.1%
1991: 4.6%
1990: 4.8%

Employer Unemployment Contributions
Contribution Rate
1992: 1.56%
1991: 1.57%
1990: 1.61%

Average Weekly Benefit
1992: $180.05
1991: $176.96
1990: $160.91

Gross State Product (Million $)
1989: $52,574
1988: $47,558
1987: $44,659
1979: $33,423
Growth rate, 1979 to 1989: 57.3%

Capital Expenditures of Manufacturing Industries
1990: $1,384,400,000
1989: $1,109,000,000
1988: $993,200,000
1987: $834,200,000

State Tax Rates
Individual income: Range from 0.4% ($1,038 or less) to 9.98% (above $45,720).
Corporate income: Range from 6% ($25,000 or less) to 12% (above $250,000).

General property: Local collections. Assessed at 100% of actual value.

General sales: 4%

Gasoline: 20¢ per gallon

Income

Median income for a 4 person family: $36,736

Personal per Capita Income

1992: $18,287

1991: $17,251

1990: $16,848

Disposable per Capita Income

1992: $16,089

1991: $15,089

1990: $14,693

Private Employment Weekly Wages

Average

1989: $346

1988: $338

1987: $338

Manufacturing

1989: $327

1988: $477

1987: $469

Services

1989: $287

1988: $277

1987: $266

Wholesale

1989: $413

1988: $400

1987: $386

Retail

1989: $186

1988: $180

1987: $174

Highway Statistics

Total Highway Miles

1990: 112,541

1989: 112,551

1988: 112,488

Federal Highway Aid

1991: $144,583,000

1990: $153,949,000

1989: $162,251,000

Electricity

Average Cost per Kilowatt Hour

1990: 5.91¢

1989: 5.91¢

1988: 6.10¢

Housing (1990)

Owner occupied units: 745,377

Median house value: $45,900

Renter occupied units: 318,948

Median rent: $261

Total vacant units: 79,344

Homeowner vacancy rate: 1.5%

Rental vacancy rate: 6.4%

State Business Incentives and Assistance

Financial and Business Assistance

Tax Incentives. Personal property and inventory tax for businesses became exempt from assessment in Iowa. 50% federal tax deductibility on state corporate tax calculation. Local option five-year partial exemption for improvements made to real property, including industrial and research service facilities. Ten-year tax exemption in urban revitalization areas.

Highway and Access Road Funding. RISE (Revitalize Iowa's Sound Economy) provides financing for highway improvements which foster economic development.

Machinery and Equipment Taxes. No state sales and use taxes on industrial machinery, equipment and computers and 70% cut in local property taxes on computers and industrial machinery and equipment.

Business Grants and Loans. The Community Economic Betterment Account program provides grants and loans to political subdivisions to promote economic development. Buy-downs of interest or principal on business loans are provided through this fund.

Other programs provide interest rate subsidies for business projects that will either create new jobs or retain jobs that would otherwise be lost. Specific programs are also available for targeted small business.

Foreign Trade Assistance Program. This program is designed to help Iowa companies enter the international marketplace by reimbursing up to 75% of their direct costs for participation in overseas trade shows and trade missions.

Iowa Procurement Outreach Center. Provides assistance to help ensure that Iowa companies are successful in winning more government contracts. Funding is provided by the State of Iowa and the U.S. Department of Defense.

Research and Development. Up to 6.5% in tax credits may be given to corporate and individual taxpayers for qualifying research activities within the state.

Wallace Technology Transfer Foundation. The Financial Assistance for Research, Development and Technology Commercialization Program offers assistance to Iowa industries for development and commercialization of advanced technologies for new products and processes.

Education and Training

Tax Credit for New Jobs. New and existing business entering into jobs-training agreements and increasing their work force by 10% may get a tax credit on their personal or corporate income taxes for every new job created (equal to $690 per employee in 1989).

Job Training Partnership Act. This program operates with funding from the U.S. Department of Labor. It provides job training and other employment related services.

State Offices

Real estate: Real Estate Commission, Kenneth L. Smith, Exec Director, 1918 SE Hulsizer Ave., Ankney, IA 50021. 515-281-7361

Chamber of commerce: Iowa Dept. of Economic Development, Rick Swalwell, Commun. Manager, 200 E. Grand St., Des Moines, IA 50309. 515-281-3251

Economic development: Iowa Dept. of Economic Development, Allan T. Thomas, Director, 200 East Grand Ave., Des Moines, IA 50309. 800-245-IOWA or 515-281-3619, FAX 515-242-4859

Iowa Dept. of Economic Development, Bureau of Business, Grants & Loans, Mike Miller, Bureau Chief, 200 East Grand Ave., Des Moines, IA 50309. 515-242-4827

Small Business Development Center, Ronald Manning, State Director, Iowa State University, College of Business Administration, 137 Lynn Ave., Ames, IA 50010. 515-292-6351

Professional Developers of Iowa, Ron Padavich, Director, 100 Court Ave., Rm. 312, Des Moines, IA 50309. 515-243-2000

Iowa Finance Authority, Executive Director, 200 E. Grand Ave., Des Moines, IA 50309. 515-281-4058

Iowa Business Development Credit Corp., Executive Director, 901 Insurance Exchange Bldg., Des Moines, IA 50309. 515-282-2164

Iowa Business Growth Co., Director, 901 Insurance Exchange Bldg., Des Moines, IA 50309. 515-282-2164

Department of Economic Development, Iowa High Technology Council, Director, 200 E. Grand Ave., Des Moines, IA 50309. 515-281-3036

Iowa Procurement Outreach Center, Allen Williams, c/o Kirkwood Community College, 6301 Kirkwood Blvd. SW, Cedar Rapids, Iowa 52406. 319-398-5665

Major Companies in the State

Company name	Fortune 500 rank	City	Telephone	SIC number
Fortune 500 Companies				
Bandag Inc.	491	Muscatine	319-262-1400	3011
Hon Industries Inc.	436	Muscatine	319-264-7400	2522
Maytag Corp.	157	Newton	515-792-8000	3633
Meredith Corp.	432	Des Moines	515-284-3000	2721
Other Major Companies in the State				
Allied Group Inc.		Des Moines	515-280-4211	6331
Banks of Iowa Inc.		Des Moines	515-245-6320	6712
Casey's General Stores Inc.		Ankeny	515-965-6100	5511
Commtron Corp.		Des Moines	515-226-3000	7822
Equitable of Iowa Companies		Des Moines	515-282-1335	6311
IE Industries Inc.		Cedar Rapids	319-398-4411	4931
IES Industries Inc.		Cedar Rapids	319-398-4411	4931
Interstate Power Co.		Dubuque	319-582-5421	4931
Iowa Electric Light & Power Co.		Cedar Rapids	319-398-4411	4931
Iowa Illinois Gas & Electric Co.		Davenport	319-326-7111	4931
Iowa Power Inc.		Des Moines	515-281-2900	4911
Iowa Public Service Co.		Sioux City	712-277-7500	4932
Iowa Resources Inc.		Des Moines	515-281-2900	4911
Lee Enterprises Inc.		Davenport	319-383-2100	2711
Midwest Energy Co.		Sioux City	712-277-7400	4923
Midwest Resources Inc.		Des Moines	515-242-4300	4931
Norwest Financial Inc.		Des Moines	515-243-2131	6141
Pioneer Hi Bred International Inc.		Des Moines	515-245-3500	5191
Statesman Group Inc.		Des Moines	515-284-7500	6311
Winnebago Industries Inc.		Forest City	515-582-3535	3716

Wallace Technology Transfer Foundation, Daniel Dittemore, 317 Sixth Ave., Suite 840, Des Moines, IA 50309. 515-243-1487

Environmental affairs: Department of Natural Resources, Environmental Protection Division, Allan Stokes, Director, Wallace State Office Bldg., E. Grand Ave., Des Moines, IA 50309. 515-281-6284

Labor: Department of Employment Services, Anne Wagner, Administrator, 1000 E. Grand Ave., Des Moines, IA 50309. 515-281-8182

Unemployment: Department of Employment Services, Mike Blank, Administrator, 1000 E. Grand Ave., Des Moines, IA 50309. 515-242-5861

Worker's compensation: Dept. of Employment Services, Sharon McDonald, Administrator, 1000 E. Grand Ave., Des Moines, IA 50309. 515-281-8338

Occupational safety and health: Department of Employment Services, Occupational Safety and Health Bureau, Mary Bryant, Administrator, 1000 E. Grand Ave., Des Moines, IA 50309. 515-281-8066

Secretary of state: Secretary of State Office, Elaine Baxter, Secretary of State, 1st fl., State Capitol Bldg., Des Moines, IA 50309. 515-281-5864

Taxation and revenue: Department of Revenue & Finance, Gerald Bair, Director, Hoover State Office Bldg., Des Moines, IA 50309. 515-281-3204

Designated Zones for Economic Development

Enterprise Zones

No program.

Foreign Trade Zones

Foreign Trade Zone No. 175, Cedar Rapids, Iowa, Grantee: Cedar Rapids Airport Commission, Larry Mullendore, Director, 2501 Wright Brothers Boulevard West, Cedar Rapids, IA 52404, 319-362-3131

Foreign Trade Zone No. 107, Des Moines, Iowa, Grantee: The Iowa Foreign Trade Zone Corporation, Centennial Warehousing Corp., Fred T. Caruthers, Jr., President, 10400 Hickman Road, Des Moines, IA 50322, 515-278-9517

Foreign Trade Zone No. 133, Quad-City, Iowa/Illinois, Grantee: Quad-City Foreign-Trade Zone, Inc., Thomas E. Ward, 1639 Second Avenue, Suite 406, Rock Island, IL 61201, 309-788-7436 or 319-326-1005

Labor Unions

Automobile, Aerospace & Agricultural Implement Workers of America, International Union, United (UAW AFL-CIO)

Carpenters and Joiners of America, United Brotherhood of (AFL-CIO)

Electrical Workers, International Brotherhood of (AFL-CIO)

Food and Commercial Workers International Union, United (AFL-CIO)

National Education Association

Operating Engineers, International Union of (AFL-CIO)

Plumbing and Pipe Fitting Industry of The United States and Canada, United Association of, Journeymen and Apprentices of the (AFL-CIO)

State, County and Municipal Employees, American Federation of (AFL-CIO)

Teamsters, Chauffeurs, Warehousemen and Helpers of America, International Brotherhood of,(AFL-CIO)

Des Moines Local American Postal Workers Union

Universities with Ph.D. Programs

Drake University, Des Moines

Iowa State University of Science and Technology, Ames

Palmer College of Chiropractic, Davenport

University of Iowa, Iowa City

University of Northern Iowa, Cedar Falls

University of Osteopathic Medicine and Health Sciences, Des Moines

Sources of Additional Information

Directory of Financial Assistance Programs. Iowa Dept. of Economic Development, September 1990. 49p.

Iowa, Manufacturing. Iowa Dept. of Economic Development, n.d. 10p.

Iowa, The Time Is Right. Iowa Dept. of Economic Development, n.d. 12p.

Iowa, Your Guide to Doing Business. Iowa Dept. of Economic Development, n.d. 56p.

CEDAR RAPIDS, IA (MSA)

Geographic Profile
Land Area
717.5 square miles

Counties and Parishes
Linn

Ranking Highlights
252 *out of 319 in total* **land area**
255 *out of 319 in* **population growth,** *1970–1990*
 34 *out of 310 in having the lowest* **unemployment** *rate*
188 *out of 310 in size of* **labor force**
105 *out of 318 in the percentage of* **college graduates**
 77 *out of 292 in per capita personal* **income**
197 *out of 319 in number of* **manufacturing establishments**
209 *out of 318 in* **physicians** *per 1000 people*
 52 *out of 318 in* **hospital beds** *per 1000 people*
N/A *out of 267 in fewest* **crimes** *per 1000 people*
N/A *out of 266 in fewest* **violent crimes** *per 1000 people*
 92 *out of 319 in per capita* **federal funds and grants**

Quality of Life Indexes (Rate per 1000 population)
Crime rate in 1991:	N/A
Violent crime rate in 1991:	N/A
Physicians rate in 1992:	1.58
Hospital bed rate in 1991:	5.42

ACCRA Cost of Living Indexes
(First quarter 1993, average = 100)
Composite index: 100.5
Utilities index: 98.0
Housing index: 102.3

Overview
Cedar Rapids preserves a small-town atmosphere in a metropolitan setting. The industrial and cultural center of eastern Iowa, the city has undergone growth and development as it gains prominence in high-technology industries and in export trade. Expansion has been carefully monitored by civic leaders, however, so that international business may be conducted at an unhurried pace and residents may maintain their midwestern traditions. Cedar Rapids is the seat of Linn County and adjoins the city of Marion.

The economy of Cedar Rapids has been traditionally based on the manufacture and processing of agricultural and food products, steel fabricating, tool and die making, and radios and electronics. Manufacturing, which continues to be an important economic sector, has been augmented by high-technology industries and transportation. The Cedar Rapids-Iowa City Corridor of Technology is one of the leading centers in the country for the defense electronics industry; the fastest-growing segment of the metropolitan area economy is telecommunications and telemarketing. Advanced research and development laboratories, an edu-

cated and productive labor force, and a mid-continent location are increasingly attracting new business and industry to Cedar Rapids.

Cedar Rapids is one of the largest exporting cities per capita in the United States, with local industries conducting commerce with points in all parts of the world. The International Trade Bureau, based in the area for more than forty years, draws its membership from banking, translation, consulting and documentation services, and marketing. Cedar Rapids is establishing trade connections with the countries of the former Soviet Union, and the telemarketing expertise of local firms will be employed to identify and penetrate other foreign markets.

A central location, efficient access, and low supply and distribution costs have contributed to the development of Cedar Rapids as a primary transportation hub in the Midwest and as the number one exporting city in the country. More than one–hundred area companies are involved in world markets, and Cedar Rapids is a designated Foreign Trade Zone. Cedar Rapids Municipal Airport's ten air cargo carriers transport more than twenty thousand tons annually. The airport was chosen by United Parcel Service (UPS) as a "central input point" for overnight service in the continental United States. Iowa is the only state bordered by two navigable rivers, and many area exports leave via water.

Three railroads, providing piggyback ramp service, move freight through Cedar Rapids to markets throughout the nation. Approximately thirty–four motor carriers, operating more than twenty local terminals, transport cargo border to border via a network of interstate highways surrounding the city. Cedar Rapids is also an important link in the emerging "information transport" industry; area companies are part of a nationwide fiber optic tele-transportation system that furnishes digital telecommunication service.

The Cedar Rapids Airport, seven miles south of the center of the city, offers direct service to ten cities on an average of seventy–four commercial flights daily. Business travelers have access to the airport's Information Center. It is estimated that the airport will board 803,000 passengers annually by the year 2006.

Cedar Rapids is linked with points throughout the nation by two interstate highways, I-380 (north-south) and I-80 (east-west). Federal highways are 30/218, which runs east to west through the south sector of Cedar Rapids, and 151, which intersects the city diagonally northeast to southwest. State routes include 150, running parallel with I-380, and east-west 94.

Population (1990)
Total Population and Growth Rate
1990: 168,767
1980: 169,775
1970: 163,213
Growth rate 1970–1990: 3%

Race and Hispanic Origin
White: 96.7%
Black: 2.0%
Asian/Pacific Islander: 0.8%
Native American: 0.2%
Hispanic origin: 0.9%
White not Hispanic: 96.0%

Age
Ages 18 to 20: 5%
Ages 21 to 24: 5.9%
Ages 25 to 44: 32.7%
Ages 45 to 54: 10.6%
Ages 55 to 59: 4.4%
Ages 60 to 64: 4.1%
Ages 65 plus: 12.1%

Educational Attainment (1990)
Percent having completed high school: 84.9%
Percent having completed college: 21.5%
Elementary and high school enrollment: 27,888

Federal Funds and Grants Received
Total received in 1989: $624,900,000
Funds received per capita: $3,644

Civilian Labor Force
1993 (April): 99,759
1992 average: 99,098
1991 average: 97,187
1990 average: 96,526

Unemployment
1993 (April): 4.3%
1992 average: 4.6%
1991 average: 5.0%
1990 average: 5.2%

Average Annual Pay
1988: $21,003
1987: $20,173
1985: $18,620

Per Capita Personal Income
1991: $19,079
1990: $18,559
1989: $17,764

Business Climate (1987)
Manufacturing
Number of establishments in 1987: 234
Shipments in 1987 ($1,000): $3,862,500
Employees in 1987: 23,400
Change in employment, 1982 to 1987: -7.9%
Average annual pay for manufacturing work in 1989: $30,730
Average annual pay for production work in 1987: $25,377
Wholesale Trade
Number of establishments in 1987: 432

Total sales in 1987 ($1,000): $1,731,600
Change in sales, 1982 to 1987: 42.1%
Retail Trade
Number of establishments in 1987: 1,100
Total sales in 1987 ($1,000): $1,731,600
Retail sales per household in 1987: $17,192
Average annual pay in 1989: $10,725
Service Industry
Selected receipts in 1987 ($1,000): $545,300
Average annual pay in 1989: $16,640

Housing
Total number of units in 1990: 68,357
Occupied units in 1990: 65,501
Owner-occupied units in 1990: 70.4%
1993 ACCRA average cost: $120,620
1993 ACCRA average rent for an apartment: $443

Chamber of Commerce
Cedar Rapids Area Chamber of Commerce, Alan R. Kenyon, President, 424 1st Ave. N.E., PO Box 74860, Cedar Rapids, IA 52407-4860. 319-398-5317, FAX 319-398-5228

Major Businesses

Company	SIC	Telephone
Aegon USA, Inc.	6311	(319) 398-8511
Allen Motor Co.	5511	(319) 366-1861
Ausa Holding Co.	6311	(319) 398-8631
Ausa Life Insurance Co., Inc.	6311	(319) 398-8511
Bankers United Life Association	6311	(319) 398-8511
Central Iowa Power	4911	(319) 366-8011
CRST International, Inc.	4213	(319) 396-4400
Galt Sand Co.,	5136	(319) 368-0300
General Services Life Insurance	6311	(319) 398-8511
Grafton Group, Inc.	5621	(319) 364-0178
I. E. Industries Inc.	4911	(319) 398-4411
Iowa Electric Light & Power Co.	4911	(319) 398-4411
F. J. Krob & Co.	5153	(319) 848-4161
Larken Inc.	7011	(319) 366-8201
Leaseamerica Corp.	6159	(319) 366-5331
Life Investors Insurance of America	6311	(319) 398-8511
Lincoln Sales & Service Inc.	7363	(319) 396-4400
Malone Freight Lines Inc.	4213	(319) 396-4400
Merchants National Bank	6021	(319) 368-4444
Mercy Medical Center Cedar Rapids	8062	(319) 398-6011
Met-Coil Systems Corp.	3542	(319) 363-6566
N. N. Investors Life Insurance	6311	(319) 398-8511
Pacific Fidelity Life Insurance	6311	(319) 398-8511
St. Luke's Methodist Hospital	8062	(319) 369-7211
Teleconnect Co.	4813	(319) 366-6600
United Fire & Casualty Co.	6331	(319) 399-5700

Major Businesses (Continued)

Company	SIC	Telephone
Vigortone Agriculture Products Inc.	2048	(319) 393-3310
West Side Unlimited Corp.	4213	(319) 390-4466
Bob Zimmerman Ford Inc.	5511	(319) 364-0181

Colleges and Universities

Coe College, Cedar Rapids
Kirkwood Community College, Cedar Rapids
Mount Mercy College, Cedar Rapids

DAVENPORT–ROCK ISLAND–MOLINE, IA–IL (MSA)

Geographic Profile

Land Area
1708.0 square miles

Counties and Parishes
Illinois:
　Henry
　Rock Island
Iowa:
　Scott

Ranking Highlights

111 *out of 319 in total* land area
286 *out of 319 in* population growth, *1970–1990*
181 *out of 310 in having the lowest* unemployment *rate*
116 *out of 310 in size of* labor force
186 *out of 318 in the percentage of* college graduates
108 *out of 292 in per capita personal* income
123 *out of 319 in number of* manufacturing establishments
271 *out of 318 in* physicians *per 1000 people*
112 *out of 318 in* hospital beds *per 1000 people*
N/A *out of 267 in fewest* crimes *per 1000 people*
N/A *out of 266 in fewest* violent crimes *per 1000 people*
121 *out of 319 in per capita* federal funds and grants

Quality of Life Indexes (Rate per 1000 population)

Crime rate in 1991:	N/A
Violent crime rate in 1991:	N/A
Physicians rate in 1992:	1.27
Hospital bed rate in 1991:	4.49

ACCRA Cost of Living Indexes
(First quarter 1993, average = 100)

Composite index:	96.4
Utilities index:	92.9
Housing index:	98.3

Overview

The Iowa-Illinois Quad Cities comprises the Davenport-Moline-Rock Island MSA located on the Mississippi River and Interstate 80, 160 miles west of Chicago. This bi-state MSA covers Scott County in Iowa and Rock Island and Henry counties in Illinois.

The community is headquarters to John Deere, Montgomery Elevator, Servus Rubber, Nichols-Homeshield Sears Manufacturing and the Rock Island Arsenal. Major manufacturers with production facilities include Alcoa, Case/IH, Ralston Purina, and Oscar Mayer. The Quad Cities also has a strong services sector and is headquarters for insurance and related companies including Modern Woodmen, Bituminous, Royal Neighbors of America and John Deere insurance companies.

Besides its strategic location and productive work force, the region's major strengths include a below-average cost of living and sophisticated infrastructure to support the area's manufacturing and transportation needs. The community is very competitive in the incentives available to new and existing growing companies. The area's 300-mile market is the largest outside of Chicago and includes over 34 million people and the major cities of Chicago, Minneapolis, Minnesota, St. Louis, Missouri, Kansas City, Missouri, and Omaha, Nebraska.

Tourism has become a major industry with the advent of riverboat gaming and both Davenport and Rock Island have casino boats on the Mississippi. The area has a wide array of convention and visitor facilities including the River Center and adjacent Adler Theater in Davenport. The newly completed 12,000 seat Mark of the Quad Cities seats over 12,000 for musical, athletic and convention events. The area is hotels/motels offer nearly 5,000 guest rooms with a new 300-room hotel nearing the start of construction.

The Quad Cities has its own U.S. Customs Port of Entry, Foreign Trade Zone and intermodal transfer station. Barge transportation gives the area access to the Gulf of Mexico and its rail service provides a connection to the Port of Montreal on the east coast. The Quad City airport in Moline has nearly 100 inbound and outbound flights daily.

Population (1990)

Total Population and Growth Rate
1990: 350,861
1980: 384,749
1970: 362,638
Growth rate 1970–1990: -3%

Race and Hispanic Origin
White: 92.0%
Black: 5.4%
Asian/Pacific Islander: 0.7%
Native American: 0.3%
Hispanic origin: 3.7%
White not Hispanic: 89.9%

Age
Ages 18 to 20: 4.3%
Ages 21 to 24: 5.2%
Ages 25 to 44: 30.7%
Ages 45 to 54: 10.5%
Ages 55 to 59: 4.4%
Ages 60 to 64: 4.5%
Ages 65 plus: 13.7%

Educational Attainment (1990)
Percent having completed high school: 79.1%
Percent having completed college: 17.4%
Elementary and high school enrollment: 63,003

Federal Funds and Grants Received
Total received in 1989: $1,233,800,000

Funds received per capita: $3,388

Civilian Labor Force
1993 (April): 187,683
1992 average: 188,413
1991 average: 183,274
1990 average: 180,956

Unemployment
1993 (April): 6.7%
1992 average: 7.2%
1991 average: 6.8%
1990 average: 5.9%

Average Annual Pay
1988: $20,805
1987: $20,459
1985: $19,635

Per Capita Personal Income
1991: $18,092
1990: $17,776
1989: $16,507

Business Climate (1987)

Manufacturing
Number of establishments in 1987: 452
Shipments in 1987 ($1,000): $5,905,900
Employees in 1987: 32,700
Change in employment, 1982 to 1987: -19.5%
Average annual pay for manufacturing work in 1989: $32,708
Average annual pay for production work in 1987: $26,038

Wholesale Trade
Number of establishments in 1987: 810
Total sales in 1987 ($1,000): $4,420,200
Change in sales, 1982 to 1987: 11.1%

Retail Trade
Number of establishments in 1987: 2,380
Total sales in 1987 ($1,000): $4,420,200
Retail sales per household in 1987: $15,651
Average annual pay in 1989: $10,759

Service Industry
Selected receipts in 1987 ($1,000): $690,100
Average annual pay in 1989: $16,025

Office Real Estate (1992)
Office space inventory: N/A
Average class A Central Business District rental range per sq. ft: N/A

Vacancy Rates
All areas: N/A

Vacancy Rates in Central Business District
Class A space: 15.7%
Class B space: 12.7%

Vacancy Rates Outside Central Business District
Class A space: N/A

Class B space: 14.8%

Housing

Total number of units in 1990: 145,587

Occupied units in 1990: 136,269

Owner-occupied units in 1990: 67.8%

1993 ACCRA average cost: N/A

1993 ACCRA average rent for an apartment: N/A

Chamber of Commerce

Davenport Chamber of Commerce, Larry S. Reed, Exec. Vice President, 112 E. 3rd St., Davenport, IA 52801. 319-322-1706, FAX 319-322-2251

Economic Development Office

Illinois Quad City Chamber of Commerce, John Verona, Exec. Manager, 1819 3rd Ave., Rock Island, IL 61201. 309-788-6311, FAX 309-788-6323

Economic Development Organizations

Illinois Quad City Chamber of Commerce, John Verona, Exec. Manager, 622 19th St., Moline, IL 61265. 309-788-6311, FAX 309-788-6323

Quad City Development Group, John C. Gardner, President, 1830 2nd Ave. Suite 200, Rock Island, IL 61201-8038. 309-788-7436, FAX 309-788-4964

Major Businesses

Company	SIC	Telephone
Bawden Printing Inc.	2752	(319) 285-4800
Bituminous Casualty Corp.	6331	(309) 786-5401
Davenport Bank & Trust Co.	6022	(319) 383-3211
John Deere Insurance Co.	6331	(309) 765-5550
Deere & Co.	3523	(309) 765-8000
Elliott Flying Service Inc.	5599	(309) 799-3183
Franciscan Health Systems	8062	(309) 793-2121
General Car & Truck Leasing	7513	(319) 386-8000
Heartland Holdings Inc.	5531	(319) 332-9922
Iowa 80 Truckstop Inc.	5541	(319) 284-6668
Iowa-Illinois Gas Electric Co.	4911	(319) 326-7111
Jaydon, Inc.	5122	(309) 787-4492
John Deere Co.	5083	(309) 765-8000
Lee Enterprises, Inc.	2711	(319) 383-2100
Modern Woodmen of America	6311	(309) 786-6481
Moline Consumers Co.	1422	(309) 757-8250
Montgomery Elevator Co.	3534	(309) 764-6771
Murphy Bros., Inc.	1623	(309) 752-1227
Rock Island Distributing	5194	(309) 787-4445
Royal Neighbors of America	6311	(309) 788-4561
Sieg Co.	5013	(319) 323-3641
St. Lukes Hospital	8062	(319) 326-6512
Swiss Valley Farms Co.	2022	(319) 391-3341
Thoms-Proestler Co.	5149	(319) 326-4041
United Medical Center Inc.	8062	(309) 757-3222
Von Maur Inc.	5311	(319) 388-2200

Colleges and Universities

Black Hawk College-Quad-Cities Campus, Moline, IL

Commonwealth Business College, Moline, IL

Hamilton Technical College, Davenport, IA

Marycrest College, Davenport, IA

Palmer College of Chiropractic, Davenport, IA

St. Ambrose University, Davenport, IA

DES MOINES, IA (MSA)

Geographic Profile

Land Area

1727.7 square miles

Counties and Parishes

Dallas

Polk

Warren

Ranking Highlights

109 *out of 319 in total* **land area**

196 *out of 319 in* **population growth,** *1970–1990*

15 *out of 310 in having the lowest* **unemployment** *rate*

93 *out of 310 in size of* **labor force**

85 *out of 318 in the percentage of* **college graduates**

41 *out of 292 in per capita personal* **income**

118 *out of 319 in number of* **manufacturing establishments**

201 *out of 318 in* **physicians** *per 1000 people*

57 *out of 318 in* **hospital beds** *per 1000 people*

N/A *out of 267 in fewest* **crimes** *per 1000 people*

N/A *out of 266 in fewest* **violent crimes** *per 1000 people*

73 *out of 319 in per capita* **federal funds and grants**

Quality of Life Indexes (Rate per 1000 population)

Crime rate in 1991:	N/A
Violent crime rate in 1991:	N/A
Physicians rate in 1992:	1.62
Hospital bed rate in 1991:	5.34

ACCRA Cost of Living Indexes

(First quarter 1993, average = 100)

Composite index: 104.1

Utilities index: 103.8

Housing index: 111.5

Overview

Des Moines' economic base consists of insurance, health services, printing and publishing, business services and government. Des Moines is located at the crossroads of Interstates 80 and 35. The Des Moines International Airport ranks 87th worldwide for air cargo tonnage and is a UPS regional hub. Iowa has among the lowest long-distance rates in the United States for companies with 800 numbers. It is located at the crossroads of all the major transcontinental fiber optics networks. Iowa's labor force is highly educated and maintains the highest literacy rates in the country. It is 36% more productive than the national average.

There are several tax advantages to locating a business within Des Moines. There are no sales or use taxes on industrial machinery, equipment and computers. In addition, there is no personal property tax on inventories of salable goods, raw materials, and goods in transit. Iowa businesses are entitled to deduct 50% of their federal income tax on state income tax forms. Businesses do not pay corporate income taxes on profits from out-of-state sales.

The City of Des Moines enacted legislation that allows taxes on new commercial/industrial construction within designated areas of the city to be abated. The most cost-effective option for new industrial/commercial construction is the 10 year declining percentage abatement. The program is designed to encourage development in urban revitalization areas. It will be offered through December 31, 1995. The City also allows taxes to be abated for five years on all new residential construction throughout the city. Taxes may be abated for 10 years in targeted areas. This program will be offered through December 31, 1995.

Des Moines maintains an affordable cost of living. It ranks 3rd out of 150 major U. S. housing markets in terms of affordability and percent of income required to meet mortgage payments on a new single-family, upscale, three-bedroom house (1990 Prudential Real Estate Study).

Population (1990)

Total Population and Growth Rate

1990: 392,928

1980: 367,561

1970: 339,647

Growth rate 1970–1990: 16%

Race and Hispanic Origin

White: 93.8%

Black: 3.8%

Asian/Pacific Islander: 1.6%

Native American: 0.3%

Hispanic origin: 1.7%

White not Hispanic: 92.7%

Age

Ages 18 to 20: 4.6%

Ages 21 to 24: 6.1%

Ages 25 to 44: 33.8%

Ages 45 to 54: 10.2%

Ages 55 to 59: 4.1%

Ages 60 to 64: 4%

Ages 65 plus: 11.7%

Educational Attainment (1990)

Percent having completed high school: 85.4%

Percent having completed college: 22.6%

Elementary and high school enrollment: 64,133

Federal Funds and Grants Received

Total received in 1989: $1,591,000,000

Funds received per capita: $4,061

Civilian Labor Force

1993 (April): 254,478

1992 average: 248,449

1991 average: 240,885

1990 average: 235,560

Unemployment

1993 (April): 3.8%

1992 average: 3.9%
1991 average: 3.8%
1990 average: 3.2%

Average Annual Pay
1988: $20,302
1987: $19,389
1985: $17,998

Per Capita Personal Income
1991: $20,570
1990: $19,962
1989: $18,674

Business Climate (1987)
Manufacturing
Number of establishments in 1987: 474
Shipments in 1987 ($1,000): $4,013,100
Employees in 1987: 24,400
Change in employment, 1982 to 1987: 4.7%
Average annual pay for manufacturing work in 1989: $26,735
Average annual pay for production work in 1987: $22,221

Wholesale Trade
Number of establishments in 1987: 1,059
Total sales in 1987 ($1,000): $5,410,600
Change in sales, 1982 to 1987: -15.4%

Retail Trade
Number of establishments in 1987: 2,596
Total sales in 1987 ($1,000): $5,410,600
Retail sales per household in 1987: $17,591
Average annual pay in 1989: $11,261

Service Industry
Selected receipts in 1987 ($1,000): $1,310,100
Average annual pay in 1989: $17,981

Office Real Estate (1992)
Office space inventory: 6,131,654 square feet
Average class A Central Business District rental range per sq. ft: $19.00

Vacancy Rates
All areas: 14.6%

Vacancy Rates in Central Business District
Class A space: 16.7%
Class B space: 9.6%

Vacancy Rates Outside Central Business District
Class A space: 12.1%
Class B space: 21.3%

Housing
Total number of units in 1990: 160,948
Occupied units in 1990: 153,100
Owner-occupied units in 1990: 66.9%
1993 ACCRA average cost: $131,400
1993 ACCRA average rent for an apartment: $506

Chamber of Commerce
Greater Des Moines Chamber of Commerce Federation, Michael Reagen, President, 601 Loutus St. #100, Des Moines, IA 50309. 515-286-4950, FAX 515-286-4974

Economic Development Office
City of Des Moines, Office of Economic Development, Scott Stricker, Administrator, Armory Bldg., 602 E. 1st St. Des Moines, IA 50308. 515-283-4004

Economic Development Organizations
Iowa Business Development Credit Corp., Don Albertson, Exec. Vice President, 505 5th Ave. #901, Des Moines, IA 50309. 515-282-2164, FAX 515-282-8031

Iowa Business Council, Myrtilla Levin, Exec. Director, 100 E. Grand St. Des Moines, IA 50309. 515-246-1700

Industrial Sites
Airport Business Park (400-1000 acres). Adjacent to the Des Moines International Airport; three miles to Interstate 235.

Guthrie Avenue Business Park (135 acres). 1/2 mile from Interstate 235, providing a direct link to Interstate Highways 80 and 35. Railroad adjacent to site.

Vandalia Acres Industrial Park (600 acres). Within one mile of the proposed relocated U.S. 65 providing a direct link to Interstate Highways 80 and 35. Accessible by rail.

Major Companies

Company	SIC	Telephone
Agri Grain Marketing	5153	(515) 224-2600
Allied Group, Inc.	6331	(515) 280-4211
American Life Casualty Insurance Co.	6311	(515) 284-7500
Casey's General Stores, Inc.	5541	(515) 965-6100
Central Life Assurance Co.	6311	(515) 283-2371
Commtron Corp.	7822	(515) 226-3000
Easter Enterprises, Inc.	5411	(515) 265-1116
Employers Mutual Casualty Co.	6331	(515) 280-2511
Equitable Life Insurance Co. of Iowa	6311	(515) 245-6911
Equitable of Iowa Companies	6311	(515) 282-1335
Federal Home Loan Bank of Des Moines	6111	(515) 243-4211
Heritage Communications Inc.	4841	(515) 246-1440
IASD Health Services Corp.	6324	(515) 245-4500
Integrated Resources	6311	(515) 223-3000
Iowa Power Inc.	4911	(515) 281-2900
Iowa Resources Inc.	4911	(515) 242-4300
Massey-Ferguson Inc.	5083	(515) 247-2011
Meredith Corp.	2721	(515) 284-3000
Meredith/Burda Corp.	2754	(515) 284-3900
Meredith/Burda Ltd.	2752	(515) 284-3000
Midland Savings Bank	6036	(515) 283-2151
Norwest Financial Inc.	6141	(515) 243-2131

Major Companies (Continued)

Company	SIC	Telephone
Norwest Financial Leasing	6159	(515) 282-3993
Norwest Financial Service	6141	(515) 243-2131
Perishable Distributors of Iowa	5147	(515) 965-6300
Pioneer Hi-Bred International	5191	(515) 245-3500
Principal Mutual Life Insurance	6311	(515) 247-5111
Ruan Financial Corp.	7353	(515) 245-2500
Statesman Group Inc.	6311	(515) 284-7500
Younkers Inc.	5311	(515) 244-1112

Colleges and Universities

American Institute of Business, Des Moines

Drake University, Des Moines

Grand View College, Des Moines

University of Osteopathic Medicine and Health Sciences, Des Moines

DUBUQUE, IA (MSA)

Geographic Profile

Land Area
608.2 square miles

Counties and Parishes
Dubuque

Ranking Highlights

272 *out of 319 in total* land area

294 *out of 319 in* population growth, *1970–1990*

76 *out of 310 in having the lowest* unemployment *rate*

292 *out of 310 in size of* labor force

200 *out of 318 in the percentage of* college graduates

189 *out of 292 in per capita personal* income

255 *out of 319 in number of* manufacturing establishments

186 *out of 318 in* physicians *per 1000 people*

24 *out of 318 in* hospital beds *per 1000 people*

N/A *out of 267 in fewest* crimes *per 1000 people*

N/A *out of 266 in fewest* violent crimes *per 1000 people*

203 *out of 319 in per capita* federal funds and grants

Quality of Life Indexes (Rate per 1000 population)

Crime rate in 1991:	36.4
Violent crime rate in 1991:	N/A
Physicians rate in 1992:	1.7
Hospital bed rate in 1991:	6.26

ACCRA Cost of Living Indexes

(First quarter 1993, average = 100)

Composite index: 102.7

Utilities index: 84.4

Housing index: 121.7

Population (1990)

Total Population and Growth Rate
1990: 86,403

1980: 93,745

1970: 90,609

Growth rate 1970–1990: -5%

Race and Hispanic Origin
White: 98.8%

Black: .4%

Asian/Pacific Islander: 0.5%

Native American: 0.1%

Hispanic origin: 0.5%

White not Hispanic: 98.5%

Age
Ages 18 to 20: 5.1%

Ages 21 to 24: 5.6%

Ages 25 to 44: 29.4%

Ages 45 to 54: 10%

Ages 55 to 59: 4.3%

Ages 60 to 64: 4.4%

Ages 65 plus: 14.1%

Educational Attainment (1990)
Percent having completed high school: 77.7%
Percent having completed college: 16.8%
Elementary and high school enrollment: 16,045

Federal Funds and Grants Received
Total received in 1989: $251,100,000
Funds received per capita: $2,762

Civilian Labor Force
1993 (April): 47,610
1992 average: 46,630
1991 average: 45,688
1990 average: 44,346

Unemployment
1993 (April): 4.4%
1992 average: 5.6%
1991 average: 6.1%
1990 average: 5.6%

Average Annual Pay
1988: $19,220
1987: $18,768
1985: $17,713

Per Capita Personal Income
1991: $16,469
1990: $15,992
1989: $14,924

Business Climate (1987)
Manufacturing
Number of establishments in 1987: 143
Shipments in 1987 ($1,000): $1,893,400
Employees in 1987: 12,200
Change in employment, 1982 to 1987: 2.5%
Average annual pay for manufacturing work in 1989: $27,373
Average annual pay for production work in 1987: $24,084

Wholesale Trade
Number of establishments in 1987: 191
Total sales in 1987 ($1,000): $506,200
Change in sales, 1982 to 1987: 3.1%

Retail Trade
Number of establishments in 1987: 650
Total sales in 1987 ($1,000): $506,200
Retail sales per household in 1987: $17,770
Average annual pay in 1989: $9,481

Service Industry
Selected receipts in 1987 ($1,000): $217,000
Average annual pay in 1989: $16,148

Housing
Total number of units in 1990: 32,053
Occupied units in 1990: 30,799
Owner-occupied units in 1990: 71.2%
1993 ACCRA average cost: $138,000
1993 ACCRA average rent for an apartment: $575

Chamber of Commerce
Dubuque Area Chamber of Commerce, J. Steven Horman, President, PO Box 705, 770 Town Clock Plaza, Dubuque, IA 52004-0705. 319-557-9200, FAX 319-557-1591

Economic Development Office
Greater Dubuque Development Corp., Hugh La Mont, Exec Director, 770 Town Clock Plaza, Dubuque, IA 52001. 319-557-9049, FAX 319-557-1591

Major Companies

Company	SIC	Telephone
Amtrust, Inc.	6022	(319) 582-1841
Bird Chevrolet Co.	5511	(319) 583-9121
William C. Brown Publishing Co.	2731	(319) 588-1451
Conlon Construction Co.	1542	(319) 583-1724
Dubuque Bank & Trust Co.	6022	(319) 589-2000
Eagle Window & Door Inc.	5031	(319) 556-2270
FDL Foods Inc.	2011	(319) 588-5400
Finley Hospital	8062	(319) 582-1881
First National Bank of Dubuque	6021	(319) 582-3655
Flexsteel Industries, Inc.	2512	(319) 556-7730
Frommelt Industries, Inc.	3537	(319) 556-2020
H & W Motor Express Co.	4213	(319) 583-7391
Interstate Power Co.	4931	(319) 582-5421
Iowa Oil Co.	5541	(319) 583-3563
Kendall/Hunt Publishing	5192	(319) 588-1451
Klauer Manufacturing Co.	3444	(319) 582-7201
A. Y. McDonald Industries	3432	(319) 583-7311
A. Y. McDonald Supply Co.	5074	(319) 583-7311
Molo Oil Co.	5171	(319) 557-7540
Rainbo Oil Co.	5171	(319) 582-7291
Riverside Tractor-Trailer	5012	(319) 557-8170
Spahn & Rose Lumber Co.	5211	(319) 582-3606
Theisen Supply Inc.	5199	(319) 556-4738
Theisen's, Inc.	5331	(319) 556-4738
Woodward Communications	2711	(319) 588-5611

Colleges and Universities
Clarke College, Dubuque
Loras College, Dubuque
University of Dubuque, Dubuque

IOWA CITY, IA (MSA)

Geographic Profile

Land Area

614.5 square miles

Counties and Parishes

Johnson

Ranking Highlights

269 *out of 319 in total* **land area**

120 *out of 319 in* **population growth,** *1970–1990*

  1 *out of 310 in having the lowest* **unemployment** *rate*

251 *out of 310 in size of* **labor force**

  1 *out of 318 in the percentage of* **college graduates**

 89 *out of 292 in per capita personal* **income**

309 *out of 319 in number of* **manufacturing establishments**

  2 *out of 318 in* **physicians** *per 1000 people*

  2 *out of 318 in* **hospital beds** *per 1000 people*

N/A *out of 267 in fewest* **crimes** *per 1000 people*

N/A *out of 266 in fewest* **violent crimes** *per 1000 people*

139 *out of 319 in per capita* **federal funds and grants**

Quality of Life Indexes (Rate per 1000 population)

Crime rate in 1991:   N/A

Violent crime rate in 1991:   N/A

Physicians rate in 1992:   10.6

Hospital bed rate in 1991:   11.53

ACCRA Cost of Living Indexes

(First quarter 1993, average = 100)

Composite index: N/A

Utilities index: N/A

Housing index: N/A

Overview

Iowa City Area experienced a 17.6% growth in population from 1980 to 1990 and is the fastest growing community in the five state upper midwest. The University of Iowa is located here.

Air service is supplied by the Cedar Rapids-Iowa City Airport. The airport is a designated Foreign Trade Zone and has recently completed an air cargo facility and an $18 million passenger terminal.

Corporations located here include Procter & Gamble, National Computer Systems, American College Testing (ACT), General Mills, Oral B Laboratories, Release International and Moore Business Forms.

Major new development projects include new 18,000 and 20,000 square foot office buildings, construction to begin on a speculative 12,000 square foot warehouse, and plans are ready for several commercial expansions. Two major hotels are undergoing renovation and a $2.7 million renovation of an existing property to a Country Inn was just completed.

Population (1990)

Total Population and Growth Rate

1990: 96,119

1980: 81,717

1970: 72,127

Growth rate 1970–1990: 33%

Race and Hispanic Origin

White: 93.3%

Black: 2.1%

Asian/Pacific Islander: 4.0%

Native American: 0.2%

Hispanic origin: 1.5%

White not Hispanic: 92.3%

Age

Ages 18 to 20:   11%

Ages 21 to 24: 13.8%

Ages 25 to 44: 34.8%

Ages 45 to 54: 7.5%

Ages 55 to 59: 2.8%

Ages 60 to 64: 2.6%

Ages 65 plus: 7.4%

Educational Attainment (1990)

Percent having completed high school: 90.6%

Percent having completed college: 44.0%

Elementary and high school enrollment: 11,524

Federal Funds and Grants Received

Total received in 1989: $281,800,000

Funds received per capita: $3,250

Civilian Labor Force

1993 (April):   66,278

1992 average: 63,850

1991 average: 63,138

1990 average: 61,798

Unemployment

1993 (April):   1.9%

1992 average: 2.0%

1991 average: 1.8%

1990 average: 1.7%

Average Annual Pay

1988: $19,238

1987: $18,304

1985: $16,678

Per Capita Personal Income

1991: $18,524

1990: $17,790

1989: $16,862

Business Climate (1987)

Manufacturing

Number of establishments in 1987: 76

Shipments in 1987 ($1,000): $985,100

Employees in 1987: 3,700

Change in employment, 1982 to 1987: 12.1%
Average annual pay for manufacturing work in 1989: $25,171
Average annual pay for production work in 1987: $21,720

Wholesale Trade
Number of establishments in 1987: 91
Total sales in 1987 ($1,000): $300,200
Change in sales, 1982 to 1987: 24.8%

Retail Trade
Number of establishments in 1987: 597
Total sales in 1987 ($1,000): $300,200
Retail sales per household in 1987: $15,830
Average annual pay in 1989: $8,839

Service Industry
Selected receipts in 1987 ($1,000): $211,600
Average annual pay in 1989: $14,941

Housing
Total number of units in 1990: 37,210
Occupied units in 1990: 36,067
Owner-occupied units in 1990: 52.7%
1993 ACCRA average cost: N/A
1993 ACCRA average rent for an apartment: N/A

Chamber of Commerce
Iowa City Chamber of Commerce, Robert Quick, Exec. Vice President, 325 E. Washington St. #100, PO Box 2358, Iowa City, IA 52244. 319-337-9637, FAX 319-338-9958

Economic Development Office
Iowa City Area Development Group, Martin J. Kelly, President, PO Box 2567, 325 E. Washington St., Iowa City, IA 52244. 319-354-3939, FAX 319-338-9958

Major Companies

Company	SIC	Telephone
Economy Advertising Co.	2759	(319) 337-9623
Iowa Book & Supply Co.	5942	(319) 337-4188

Colleges and Universities
University of Iowa, Iowa City

SIOUX CITY, IA–NE (MSA)

Geographic Profile
Land Area
1136.6 square miles
Counties and Parishes
Iowa:
  Woodbury
Nebraska:
  Dakota

Ranking Highlights
178 *out of 319 in total* land area
277 *out of 319 in* population growth, *1970–1990*
 20 *out of 310 in having the lowest* unemployment *rate*
252 *out of 310 in size of* labor force
220 *out of 318 in the percentage of* college graduates
165 *out of 292 in per capita personal* income
276 *out of 319 in number of* manufacturing establishments
204 *out of 318 in* physicians *per 1000 people*
 14 *out of 318 in* hospital beds *per 1000 people*
N/A *out of 267 in fewest* crimes *per 1000 people*
N/A *out of 266 in fewest* violent crimes *per 1000 people*
185 *out of 319 in per capita* federal funds and grants

Quality of Life Indexes (Rate per 1000 population)
Crime rate in 1991:   N/A
Violent crime rate in 1991:   N/A
Physicians rate in 1992:   1.61
Hospital bed rate in 1991:   7.16

ACCRA Cost of Living Indexes
(First quarter 1993, average = 100)
Composite index: 100.7
Utilities index: 89.2
Housing index: 114.8

Population (1990)
Total Population and Growth Rate
1990: 115,018
1980: 117,457
1970: 116,189
Growth rate 1970–1990: -1%
Race and Hispanic Origin
White: 93.5%
Black: 1.7%
Asian/Pacific Islander: 1.4%
Native American: 1.7%
Hispanic origin: 3.2%
White not Hispanic: 92.1%
Age
Ages 18 to 20: 4.4%
Ages 21 to 24: 5.2%
Ages 25 to 44: 30.1%

Ages 45 to 54: 9%
Ages 55 to 59: 4.2%
Ages 60 to 64: 4.5%
Ages 65 plus: 14.3%

Educational Attainment (1990)

Percent having completed high school: 77.9%
Percent having completed college: 16.0%
Elementary and high school enrollment: 21,713

Federal Funds and Grants Received

Total received in 1989: $340,800,000
Funds received per capita: $2,946

Civilian Labor Force

1993 (April): 64,874
1992 average: 63,715
1991 average: 62,985
1990 average: 60,860

Unemployment

1993 (April): 3.2%
1992 average: 4.1%
1991 average: 4.4%
1990 average: 3.8%

Average Annual Pay

1988: $16,933
1987: $15,935
1985: $15,599

Per Capita Personal Income

1991: $16,857
1990: $16,334
1989: $15,392

Business Climate (1987)

Manufacturing

Number of establishments in 1987: 119
Shipments in 1987 ($1,000): $2,259,700
Employees in 1987: 9,900
Change in employment, 1982 to 1987: -5.7%
Average annual pay for manufacturing work in 1989: $18,429
Average annual pay for production work in 1987: $17,164

Wholesale Trade

Number of establishments in 1987: 321
Total sales in 1987 ($1,000): $6,041,800
Change in sales, 1982 to 1987: 0%

Retail Trade

Number of establishments in 1987: 803
Total sales in 1987 ($1,000): $6,041,800
Retail sales per household in 1987: $15,849
Average annual pay in 1989: $9,306

Service Industry

Selected receipts in 1987 ($1,000): $308,500
Average annual pay in 1989: $16,496

Housing

Total number of units in 1990: 45,557
Occupied units in 1990: 42,934
Owner-occupied units in 1990: 68.5%
1993 ACCRA average cost: $134,950
1993 ACCRA average rent for an apartment: $507

Chamber of Commerce

Sioux City Chamber of Commerce, Les L. Horrell, Jr., President, 101 Pierce St., Sioux City, IA 51101. 712-255-7903, FAX 712-258-7578

Economic Development Office

Sioux Land Economic Development Corp., Ken Beekley, Director, PO Box 447, Sioux City, IA 51102. 712-279-6286, FAX 712-279-6920

Major Companies

Company	SIC	Telephone
Aalfs Manufacturing, Inc.	2325	(712) 252-1877
Bomgaars Supply Inc.	5311	(712) 277-2000
Farmers Coop Elevator Co.	5153	(712) 874-3211
First Federal Savings Loan Association	6035	(712) 277-2033
Great West Casualty Co.	6331	(402) 494-2411
Hirschbach Motor Lines, Inc.	4213	(402) 494-5000
IBP, Inc.	2011	(402) 494-2061
Iowa Public Service Co.	4924	(712) 277-7500
Klinger, W. A. Inc.	1542	(712) 277-3900
L & R Communications Ltd.	1623	(712) 252-4101
Long Lines, Ltd.	4813	(712) 943-1000
Metz Baking Co.	2051	(712) 255-7611
Metz Holdings Inc.	2051	(712) 255-7611
Midwest Capital Group Inc.	8742	(712) 277-7400
Midwest Energy Co.	4924	(712) 277-7400
PBX, Inc.	4213	(402) 241-2577
Prince Manufacturing Corp.	3594	(712) 277-4061
Riverside/Terra Corp.	5191	(712) 277-1340
Rosenthal Foods Corp.	5148	(712) 255-7943
Saunders Oil Co.	5172	(712) 277-1612
Security National Corp.	6021	(712) 277-6500
Sioux City Truck Sales Inc.	5012	(712) 252-4566
Sioux Honey Association	5149	(712) 258-0638
St. Luke Health System Inc.	8062	(712) 279-3500
State Steel Supply Co.	5051	(712) 277-4000
Terra International, Inc.	2873	(712) 277-1340
The Security National Bank	6021	(712) 277-6500

Colleges and Universities

Briar Cliff College, Sioux City, IA
Morningside College, Sioux City, IA

WATERLOO–CEDAR FALLS, IA (MSA)

Geographic Profile

Land Area

1005.3 square miles

Counties and Parishes

Black Hawk

Bremer

Ranking Highlights

202 *out of 319 in total* **land area**

301 *out of 319 in* **population growth,** *1970–1990*

82 *out of 310 in having the lowest* **unemployment** *rate*

219 *out of 310 in size of* **labor force**

192 *out of 318 in the percentage of* **college graduates**

193 *out of 292 in per capita personal* **income**

228 *out of 319 in number of* **manufacturing establishments**

229 *out of 318 in* **physicians** *per 1000 people*

79 *out of 318 in* **hospital beds** *per 1000 people*

N/A *out of 267 in fewest* **crimes** *per 1000 people*

N/A *out of 266 in fewest* **violent crimes** *per 1000 people*

187 *out of 319 in per capita* **federal funds and grants**

Quality of Life Indexes (Rate per 1000 population)

Crime rate in 1991:	51.2
Violent crime rate in 1991:	N/A
Physicians rate in 1992:	1.49
Hospital bed rate in 1991:	5

ACCRA Cost of Living Indexes

(First quarter 1993, average = 100)

Composite index:	94.8
Utilities index:	87.5
Housing index:	91.6

Population (1990)

Total Population and Growth Rate

1990: 146,611

1980: 162,781

1970: 155,653

Growth rate 1970–1990: -6%

Race and Hispanic Origin

White: 92.9%

Black: 5.9%

Asian/Pacific Islander: 0.8%

Native American: 0.2%

Hispanic origin: 0.7%

White not Hispanic: 92.5%

Age

Ages 18 to 20: 6.4%

Ages 21 to 24: 7.1%

Ages 25 to 44: 28.3%

Ages 45 to 54: 10%

Ages 55 to 59: 4.2%

Ages 60 to 64: 4.4%

Ages 65 plus: 14.1%

Educational Attainment (1990)

Percent having completed high school: 80.1%

Percent having completed college: 17.0%

Elementary and high school enrollment: 225,054

Federal Funds and Grants Received

Total received in 1989: $430,300,000

Funds received per capita: $2,913

Civilian Labor Force

1993 (April):	78,531
1992 average:	76,499
1991 average:	74,441
1990 average:	72,459

Unemployment

1993 (April): 5.6%

1992 average: 5.7%

1991 average: 5.5%

1990 average: 4.8%

Average Annual Pay

1988: $19,871

1987: $19,005

1985: $18,055

Per Capita Personal Income

1991: $16,390

1990: $15,941

1989: $14,900

Business Climate (1987)

Manufacturing

Number of establishments in 1987: 188

Shipments in 1987 ($1,000): $1,559,600

Employees in 1987: 11,900

Change in employment, 1982 to 1987: -38.3%

Average annual pay for manufacturing work in 1989: $33,880

Average annual pay for production work in 1987: $28,122

Wholesale Trade

Number of establishments in 1987: 278

Total sales in 1987 ($1,000): $680,900

Change in sales, 1982 to 1987: -28.8%

Retail Trade

Number of establishments in 1987: 1,012

Total sales in 1987 ($1,000): $680,900

Retail sales per household in 1987: $15,276

Average annual pay in 1989: $9,526

Service Industry

Selected receipts in 1987 ($1,000): $263,400

Average annual pay in 1989: $15,542

Housing

Total number of units in 1990: 58,535
Occupied units in 1990: 55,326
Owner-occupied units in 1990: 68.5%
1993 ACCRA average cost: $108,254
1993 ACCRA average rent for an apartment: $397

Chamber of Commerce

Waterloo Chamber of Commerce, Jim Lawrence, President, 215 E. 4th St., PO Box 1587, Waterloo, IA 50704. 319-233-8431, FAX 319-233-4580

Economic Development Office

Cedar Falls Chamber of Commerce, Lee Miller, President, PO Box 367, 10 Main St. Cedar Falls, IA 50613. 319-266-3593, FAX 319-277-4325

Economic Development Organizations

Waterloo Industry Development Association, Steve Brustkern, Exec. Director, 8 W. 4th St., Waterloo, IA 50701. 800-369-0513, 319-232-1156

Cedar Falls Department of Development, Bob Seymour, Community Service Manager, 217 Washington Street, Cedar Falls, IA 50613. 319-273-8506

Black Hawk County Economic Development Committee, Donald Wade, Exec. Director, 8 W. 4th St., Waterloo, IA 50701. 800-369-0513, 319-232-1156

Cedar Valley Partnership, Donald Wade, President, 8 West Fourth Street, Waterloo, IA 50701. 800-369-0513, 319-232-1156

Major Companies

Company	SIC	Telephone
Ag Services of America Inc.	5999	(319) 277-0261
Allen Health Systems, Inc.	8062	(319) 235-3941
Allen Memorial Hospital Co.	8062	(319) 235-3941
American Black Hawk	4833	(319) 291-1200
Bearing Service Co.	5085	(319) 234-6845
Cardinal Construction Co.	1542	(319) 232-5400
Cedar Valley Corp.	1611	(319) 235-9537
Community Motor Co., Inc.	5511	(319) 277-5010
Control-O-Fax Corp.	2761	(319) 234-4651
Cooperative of Hudson Inc.	5153	(319) 988-3257
Covenant Medical Center Inc.	8062	(319) 236-4111
Crossroads Ford Ltd.	5511	(319) 234-4200
Dan Deery Motor Co.	5511	(319) 277-4500
John Deery Motor Co.	5511	(319) 277-6200
Friedley Lincoln Mercury	5511	(319) 277-1140
H & H Machine Tool Co.	3312	(319) 268-0181
Iowa National Bankshares	6021	(319) 291-5200
J. S. Latta Co.	5049	(319) 266-3501
Wendell Lockard Construction	1542	(319) 235-9391
Metro Bancorporation	6712	(319) 295-3285
Midamerica Savings Bank	6035	(319) 234-5523
Municipal Electric Utilities	4911	(319) 266-1761

Major Companies (Continued)

Company	SIC	Telephone
Omega Cabinets, Ltd.	2434	(319) 236-2256
United Jackson Companies	1611	(319) 232-6909
Warren Transport Inc.	4213	(319) 233-6113
Waterloo Savings Bank	6022	(319) 235-3285
Waterloo Service Co.	5171	(319) 233-4232
WFSI-Iowa, Inc.	8062	(319) 236-4111
Windor Inc.	5031	(319) 234-1763

Colleges and Universities

Hawkeye Institute of Technology, Waterloo
University of Northern Iowa, Cedar Falls

KANSAS

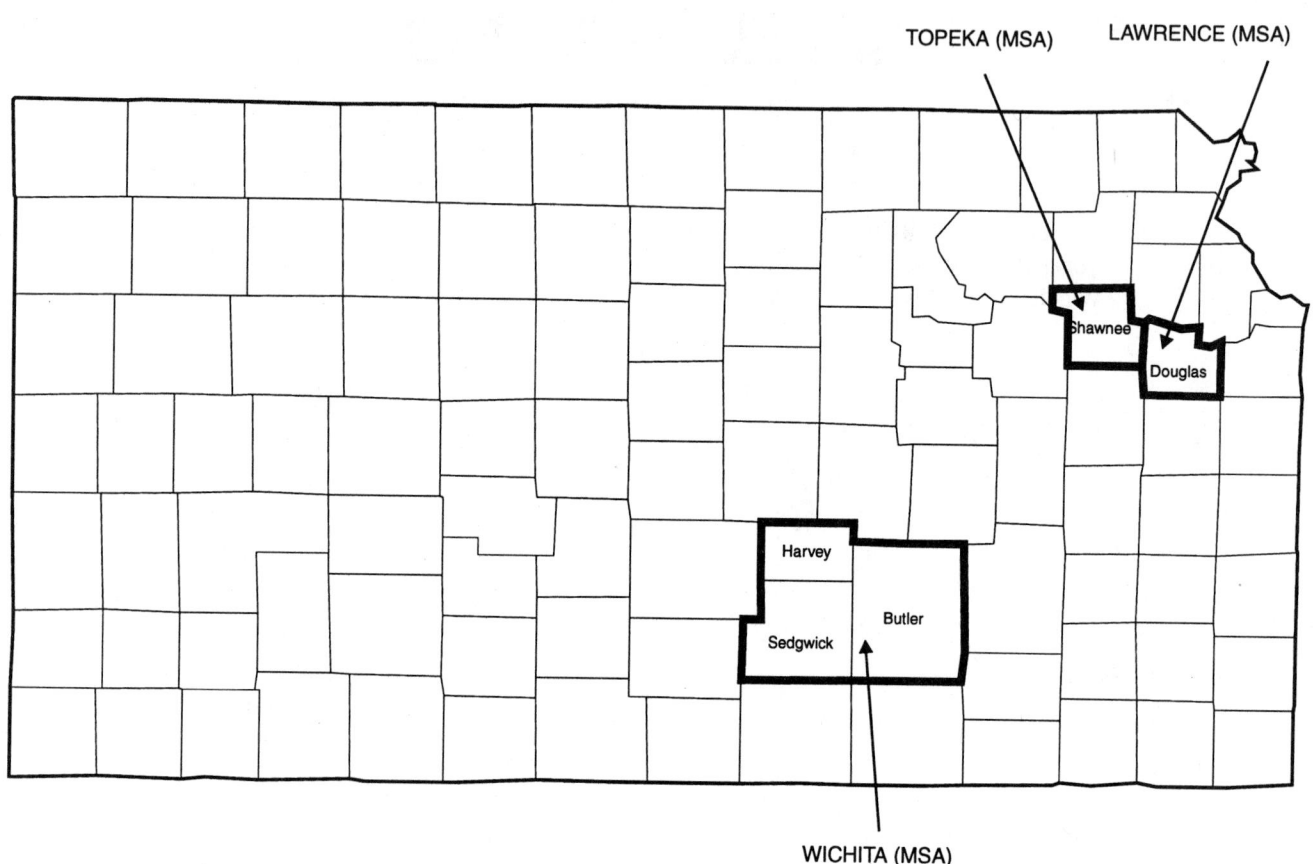

TOPEKA (MSA)

LAWRENCE (MSA)

Shawnee

Douglas

Harvey

Butler

Sedgwick

WICHITA (MSA)

KANSAS

Population
1990: 2,477,574
1980: 2,363,679

Age
Ages 18 to 20: 113,717
Ages 21 to 24: 140,776
Ages 25 to 44: 774,499
Ages 45 to 54: 235,388
Ages 55 to 59: 103,821
Ages 60 to 64: 105,188
Median age: 32.9

Race
White: 2,231,986
Black: 143,076
Asian/Pacific Islander: 31,750
Native American: 21,965
Hispanic origin: 93,670

Households
Total: 944,726
Persons per household: 2.53

Sex
Male: 1,214,645
Female: 1,262,929

Population Migration
Domestic migration: -65,000
International migration: 29,000

Projection of the Population in 1995
Total: 2,580,000
18 to 64: 1,554,000

Civilian Labor Force
1993: 1,316,800
1992: 1,323,400
1991: 1,297,400
1990: 1,267,400

Manufacturing
1995 Projection: 194,000
1992: 181,800
1991: 185,200
1990: 186,200
1989: 185,200

Services
1995 Projection: 367,800

1992: 259,100
1991: 252,100
1990: 244,500
1989: 234,100

Wholesale and Retail Trade
1995 Projection: 313,700
1992: 272,000
1991: 273,000
1990: 271,500
1989: 275,100

Unemployment Rate
1993: 4.9%
1992: 4.5%
1991: 4.8%
1990: 4.7%

Employer Unemployment Contributions
Contribution Rate
1992: 2.39%
1991: 2.41%
1990: 2.47%

Average Weekly Benefit
1992: $188.21
1991: $187.23
1990: $170.56

Gross State Product (Million $)
1989: $48,829
1988: $46,615
1987: $43,956
1979: $26,694
Growth rate, 1979 to 1989: 82.9%

Capital Expenditures of Manufacturing Industries
1990: $814,000,000
1989: $783,800,000
1988: $764,000,000
1987: $1,011,200,000

State Tax Rates
Individual income: Range from 3.65% ($35,000 or less) to 5.15% (above $35,000).
Corporate income: 4.5% of federal taxable income, with 2.25% surtax imposed.

General property: Real and tangible personal property - 30% of fair market value.

General sales: 4.25%

Gasoline: 18¢ per gallon

Income

Median income for a 4 person family: $37,938

Personal per Capita Income

1992: $19,376

1991: $18,306

1990: $17,768

Disposable per Capita Income

1992: $16,982

1991: $15,913

1990: $15,393

Private Employment Weekly Wages

Average

1989: $373

1988: $366

1987: $366

Manufacturing

1989: $354

1988: $479

1987: $468

Services

1989: $329

1988: $321

1987: $306

Wholesale

1989: $476

1988: $463

1987: $442

Retail

1989: $205

1988: $204

1987: $196

Highway Statistics

Total Highway Miles

1990: 133,578

1989: 133,156

1988: 132,965

Federal Highway Aid

1991: $134,894,000

1990: $138,826,000

1989: $140,167,000

Electricity

Average Cost per Kilowatt Hour

1990: 6.58¢

1989: 6.43¢

1988: 6.60¢

Housing (1990)

Owner occupied units: 641,762

Median house value: $52,200

Renter occupied units: 302,964

Median rent: $285

Total vacant units: 99,386

Homeowner vacancy rate: 2.3%

Rental vacancy rate: 11.1%

State Business Incentives and Assistance

Enterprise Zone Incentives

The Kansas Enterprise Zone Program provides incentives to businesses to locate or expand in distressed areas.

1) Sales tax exemption on purchases of certain tangible personal property or services.

2) Eligible for tax increment financing.

3) 10-year Employer tax credit of a) $350 for each employee living in Kansas, b) $500 for each disadvantaged employee.

4) Review and modification of regulations having a negative impact on economic viability of the zone.

5) Targeting of state programs, funds, and services.

Financial and Business Assistance

Industrial Development Bonds. Under the management of the Industrial Development Division, this program fosters development of new businesses and stability and expansion of existing businesses. It encourages industrial development and recruitment. IDBs provide funds for 100% financing of the the cost of the land, buildings, and equipment, as well as other developmental and financing costs. Eligible projects include manufacturing, industrial, commercial, health care, agricultural, and pollution control facilities.

Kansas Development Finance Authority. The Authority is authorized to issue bonds for the purpose of financing industrial enterprises, agricultural business enterprises, educational facilities, health care facilities, and housing developments. These bonds are exempt from all state, county, and municipal taxes.

Kansas Partnership Fund. The Community Development Division of the Department of Commerce was established to encourage development of Kansas communities and to provide technical assistance to communities for economic development. Administered by the Community Development Division, this Fund is a revolving loan fund to provide assistance to local communities in financing public infrastructure improvement projects to aid the expansion, relocation, and attraction of businesses.

Education and Training

Kansas Industrial Training Program. Administered by the Department of Commerce, this program provides pre-employment and on-the-job training to new and expanding industrial firms within the state. It is designed to meet the specialized training needs of new and expanding manufac-

Major Companies in the State

Company name	Fortune 500 rank	City	Telephone	SIC number
Fortune 500 Companies				
Doskocil Co., Inc.	409	South Hutchinson	316-663-1005	2013
National Coop Refinery Assn.	467	Mcpherson	316-241-2340	2911
Other Major Companies in the State				
Air Midwest Inc.		Wichita	316-942-8137	4512
Amvestors Financial Corp.		Topeka	913-232-6945	6311
Coleman Co. Inc.		Wichita	316-261-3211	3089
Collins Industries Inc.		Hutchinson	316-663-5551	3711
Comcoa Inc.		Wichita	316-683-4411	7359
First Bancorp of Kansas		Wichita	316-383-1111	6712
Fourth Financial Corp.		Wichita	316-261-4444	6712
Franklin Savings Assn.		Ottawa	913-242-6300	6036
Home Office Reference Laboratory Inc.		Lenexa	913-888-1770	8071
IFR Systems Inc.		Wichita	316-522-4981	3825
Kansas Gas & Electric Co.		Wichita	316-261-6611	4911
Kansas Power & Light Co.		Topeka	913-296-6300	4932
Midamerican Corp.		Prairie Village	913-865-0410	6712
Midwest Grain Products Inc.		Atchison	913-367-1480	2085
National Pizza Co.		Pittsburg	316-231-3390	5812
Physician Corp. of America		Wichita	316-267-8008	6324
Puritan Bennett Corp.		Overland Park	913-661-0444	3845
Union Bancshares Inc. Kansas		Wichita	316-261-4700	6712
Western Financial Corp. Kansas		Overland Park	913-339-9700	6712
Yellow Freight System Inc. of Delaware		Overland Park	913-345-1020	4213

turing, warehousing, distribution, and regional service businesses. This program also assists firms in hiring ten or more new employees.

Job Training Partnership Act. This program operates with funding from the U.S. Department of Labor. It provides job training and other employment related services.

State Offices

Real estate: Real Estate Commission, Eugene Yockers, Director, 900 Jackson Street, Room 501, Topeka, KS 66612. 913-296-3411

Chamber of commerce: Kansas Chamber of Commerce & Industry, Ed Bruske, President/CEO, 500 Bank IV Tower, Topeka, KS 66603. 913-357-6321

Economic development: Department of Commerce, Industrial Development Division, Lou Atherton, Director, 400 SW. 8th St. Suite 500, Topeka, KS 66603-3957. 913-296-3483

Department of Commerce, Enterprise Zone Program, David Ross, Coordinator, 400 SW 8th Street, Suite 500, Topeka, KS 66603-3957. 913-296-3485

Kansas Development Finance Authority, Allen Bell, President, Capitol Towers, Suite 100, 400 SW 8th Street, Topeka, KS 66603. 913-296-6747, FAX 913-296-6810

Kansas Technology Enterprise Corporation, William Brundage, President, 112 West 6th Street, Suite 400, Topeka, KS 66603. 913-296-5272

Kansas Inc., Charles Warren, President, 400 SW 8th Street, Topeka, KS 66603. 913-296-1460

Small Business Development Center, Tom Hull, State Director, Wichita State University, Campus Box 148, 17th & Yale Streets, Wichita, KS 62708. 316-689-3193

Environmental affairs: Health and Environment Department, Stanley C. Grant, Secretary, Landon State Office Bldg., 901 SW Jackson Street, Topeka, KS 66612. 913-296-1522

Labor: Human Resources Department, Ray D. Siehndel, Secretary, 401 Topeka Ave., Topeka, KS 66603. 913-296-7474

Unemployment: Human Resources Department, Ray D. Siehndel, Secretary, 401 Topeka Ave., Topeka, KS 66603. 913-296-7474

Worker's compensation: Human Resources Department, Workers Compensation Division, Robert Anderson, Director, 401 Topeka Ave., Topeka, KS 66603. 913-296-3441

Occupational safety and health: Human Resources Department, Industrial Safety & Health Division, David Wilsie, Director, 401 Topeka Ave., Topeka, KS 66603. 913-296-4386

Secretary of state: Secretary of State, Bill P. Graves, Secretary of State, Statehouse, 2nd fl., Topeka, KS 66612. 913-296-2236

Taxation and revenue: Revenue Department, Ed C. Rolfs, Secretary, 915 Harrison Street, Topeka, KS 66612-1588. 913-296-3041

Designated Zones for Economic Development

Enterprise Zones
Enacted in: 1982
No. of established zones: 255

Foreign Trade Zones
Foreign Trade Zone No. 17, Kansas City, Kansas, Grantee/Operator: Greater Kansas City FTZ, Inc., Chris Vedros, 10 Petticoat Lane, Suite 250, Kansas City, MO 64106, 816-421-7666

Foreign Trade Zone No. 161, Sedgwick County, Kansas, Grantee: Board of Commissioners of Sedgwick County, Louanna Honeycutt, 525 N. Main, Suite 343, Wichita, KS 67203, 316-268-7575

Labor Unions
Automobile, Aerospace & Agricultural Implement Workers of America, International Union, United (UAW AFL-CIO)
National Education Association
Service Employees' International Union (AFL-CIO)

Universities with Ph.D. Programs
Kansas State University, Manhattan
University of Kansas, Lawrence
University of Kansas Medical Center, Kansas City

LAWRENCE, KS (MSA)

Geographic Profile

Land Area
457.0 square miles

Counties and Parishes
Douglas

Ranking Highlights
301 *out of 319 in total* **land area**
 93 *out of 319 in* **population growth,** *1970–1990*
  6 *out of 310 in having the lowest* **unemployment** *rate*
291 *out of 310 in size of* **labor force**
  5 *out of 318 in the percentage of* **college graduates**
269 *out of 292 in per capita personal* **income**
308 *out of 319 in number of* **manufacturing establishments**
262 *out of 318 in* **physicians** *per 1000 people*
280 *out of 318 in* **hospital beds** *per 1000 people*
206 *out of 267 in fewest* **crimes** *per 1000 people*
 88 *out of 266 in fewest* **violent crimes** *per 1000 people*
227 *out of 319 in per capita* **federal funds and grants**

Quality of Life Indexes (Rate per 1000 population)
Crime rate in 1991:	72.8
Violent crime rate in 1991:	4.4
Physicians rate in 1992:	1.32
Hospital bed rate in 1991:	2.41

ACCRA Cost of Living Indexes
(First quarter 1993, average = 100)
Composite index:	93.3
Utilities index:	70.7
Housing index:	95.8

Population (1990)

Total Population and Growth Rate
1990: 81,798
1980: 67,640
1970: 57,932
Growth rate 1970–1990: 41%

Race and Hispanic Origin
White: 89.1%
Black: 4.1%
Asian/Pacific Islander: 3.2%
Native American: 2.6%
Hispanic origin: 2.6%
White not Hispanic: 87.7%

Age
Ages 18 to 20: 13.6%
Ages 21 to 24: 14.4%
Ages 25 to 44: 30.6%
Ages 45 to 54: 7.3%

Ages 55 to 59: 2.8%
Ages 60 to 64: 2.7%
Ages 65 plus: 8.1%

Educational Attainment (1990)
Percent having completed high school: 88.8%
Percent having completed college: 38.4%
Elementary and high school enrollment: 10,570

Federal Funds and Grants Received
Total received in 1989: $198,500,000
Funds received per capita: $2,596

Civilian Labor Force
1993 (April):   48,747
1992 average: 47,130
1991 average: 44,956
1990 average: 44,408

Unemployment
1993 (April):   4.3%
1992 average: 3.2%
1991 average: 3.5%
1990 average: 3.6%

Average Annual Pay
1988: $17,034
1987: $16,377
1985: $15,654

Per Capita Personal Income
1991: $14,590
1990: $14,078
1989: $13,494

Business Climate (1987)

Manufacturing
Number of establishments in 1987: 82
Shipments in 1987 ($1,000): $864,400
Employees in 1987: 4,500
Change in employment, 1982 to 1987: 7.1%
Average annual pay for manufacturing work in 1989: $23,557
Average annual pay for production work in 1987: $19,516

Wholesale Trade
Number of establishments in 1987: 96
Total sales in 1987 ($1,000): $127,300
Change in sales, 1982 to 1987: -13.2%

Retail Trade
Number of establishments in 1987: 488
Total sales in 1987 ($1,000): $127,300
Retail sales per household in 1987: $14,687
Average annual pay in 1989: $9,910

Service Industry
Selected receipts in 1987 ($1,000): $121,800
Average annual pay in 1989: $13,661

Housing
Total number of units in 1990: 31,782
Occupied units in 1990: 30,138
Owner-occupied units in 1990: 52.5%
1993 ACCRA average cost: $108,527
1993 ACCRA average rent for an apartment: $488

Chamber of Commerce
Lawrence Chamber of Commerce, Gary L. Toebben, President, 209 W. 8th St., PO Box 581, Lawrence, KS 66044. 913-843-4411

Major Businesses

Company	SIC	Telephone
Allen Press, Inc.	2752	(913) 843-1234
Jim Clark Motors, Inc.	5511	(913) 843-3055
E and E Specialties, Inc.	2653	(913) 843-9240
Farmers Cooperative Assn.	4221	(913) 842-8222
Hall-Kimbrell Environmental	8712	(913) 749-2381
Huxtable & Associates Inc.	1711	(913) 843-2910
Lawrence Memorial Hospital	8062	(913) 749-6100
Lawrence Paper Co.	2653	(913) 843-8111
Linquist Craig Hotels Restaurants	7011	(913) 841-3100
Maupintour Inc.	4725	(913) 843-1211
Laird Noller Motors Inc.	5511	(913) 843-3500
Packer Plastics Inc.	3089	(913) 842-3000
Tanana Oil Corp.	5541	(913) 749-5741
University Kansas Memorial Corp.	5942	(913) 864-4651
World Co. Inc.	2711	(913) 843-1000

Colleges and Universities
Haskell Indian Junior College, Lawrence
University of Kansas, Lawrence

TOPEKA, KS (MSA)

Geographic Profile

Land Area

549.9 square miles

Counties and Parishes

Shawnee

Ranking Highlights

284 *out of 319 in total* **land area**

252 *out of 319 in* **population growth**, *1970–1990*

 23 *out of 310 in having the lowest* **unemployment** *rate*

193 *out of 310 in size of* **labor force**

 90 *out of 318 in the percentage of* **college graduates**

 62 *out of 292 in per capita personal* **income**

269 *out of 319 in number of* **manufacturing establishments**

 56 *out of 318 in* **physicians** *per 1000 people*

140 *out of 318 in* **hospital beds** *per 1000 people*

243 *out of 267 in fewest* **crimes** *per 1000 people*

210 *out of 266 in fewest* **violent crimes** *per 1000 people*

57*out of 319 in per capita* **federal funds and grants**

Quality of Life Indexes (Rate per 1000 population)

Crime rate in 1991:	85.5
Violent crime rate in 1991:	9.3
Physicians rate in 1992:	2.58
Hospital bed rate in 1991:	4.11

ACCRA Cost of Living Indexes

(First quarter 1993, average = 100)

Composite index:	N/A
Utilities index:	N/A
Housing index:	N/A

Overview

Topeka is the seat of Shawnee County, the capital of Kansas, and center of a metropolitan statistical area that includes the rest of Shawnee County. Government and services comprise more than 50 percent of the metropolitan Topeka economy: total state, county, and city government employment accounts for over one-fourth of the work force, and more than 20 percent of area workers are on the service industry payroll. Wholesale and retail trade employs more than 20 percent of the work force. Among the Fortune 500 companies that have established manufacturing or distribution facilities in Topeka are American Bakeries; Armco, Inc.; Atchison, Topeka & Santa Fe Railway; Essex Group; Frito-Lay, Inc.; Georgia Pacific; Goodyear Tire & Rubber; and Hill's Pet Products. Topeka Quaker "Quaker Oats" Company, among the most technologically advanced pet food processors in the world, is considered an industry-wide model for management–employee cooperation. Self-regulating work teams and hiring and training procedures account for the success of the Topeka System. Other principal industries located in Topeka include flour mills, printing and publishing companies, iron foundries, creameries, and meat, poultry, and egg packing plants.

Topeka is a shipping and distribution hub that links the corn- and wheat-growing region of northeastern Kansas and the cattle-producing states of the Southwest with markets throughout the country via an efficient transportation network. The three rail freight carriers, offering piggyback service within a 60–mile radius, are the Santa Fe Railway Company, Union Pacific, and St. Louis-Southwestern. Twenty trucking companies provide overnight and second-morning delivery to major cities in the Midwest and the West. Nine air carriers operate parcel and freight facilities at Forbes Field.

The Kansas Expocentre, a multi-purpose complex that accommodates meetings, conventions, trade shows, and entertainment events, houses an arena, a concert hall, and a convention center. The arena, seating up to 10,000 people, contains 210,000 square feet of unobstructed space.

Four major commercial airlines schedule flights into Forbes Field, where the Air Terminal is slated for expansion, seven miles south of downtown Topeka. Daily commuter service is available from Kansas City. The destination for general and business aviation traffic is Phillip Billiard Field, three miles northeast of the city. Passenger rail service to Topeka is provided by Amtrak. An efficient highway network facilitates access into Topeka. Three interstate and three U.S. highways converge in Topeka: I–70, I–470, and I–335; and U.S. 24, U.S. 40, and U.S. 75.

Population (1990)

Total Population and Growth Rate

1990: 160,976

1980: 154,916

1970: 155,322

Growth rate 1970–1990: 4%

Race and Hispanic Origin

White: 87.7%

Black: 8.3%

Asian/Pacific Islander: 0.7%

Native American: 1.1%

Hispanic origin: 4.8%

White not Hispanic: 85.3%

Age

Ages 18 to 20: 3.8%

Ages 21 to 24: 5.4%

Ages 25 to 44: 32.5%

Ages 45 to 54: 10.2%

Ages 55 to 59: 4.5%

Ages 60 to 64: 4.6%

Ages 65 plus: 13.1%

Educational Attainment (1990)

Percent having completed high school: 84.4%

Percent having completed college: 22.3%

Elementary and high school enrollment: 27,250

Federal Funds and Grants Received

Total received in 1989: $740,000,000
Funds received per capita: $4,490

Civilian Labor Force

1993 (April): 95,322
1992 average: 94,320
1991 average: 92,733
1990 average: 93,360

Unemployment

1993 (April): 4.7%
1992 average: 4.2%
1991 average: 4.7%
1990 average: 4.8%

Average Annual Pay

1988: $19,472
1987: $19,084
1985: $17,929

Per Capita Personal Income

1991: $19,476
1990: $18,887
1989: $18,159

Business Climate (1987)

Manufacturing

Number of establishments in 1987: 130
Shipments in 1987 ($1,000): $1,632,600
Employees in 1987: 9,000
Change in employment, 1982 to 1987: 0%
Average annual pay for manufacturing work in 1989: $27,474
Average annual pay for production work in 1987: $24,318

Wholesale Trade

Number of establishments in 1987: 270
Total sales in 1987 ($1,000): $806,800
Change in sales, 1982 to 1987: -14.9%

Retail Trade

Number of establishments in 1987: 1,088
Total sales in 1987 ($1,000): $806,800
Retail sales per household in 1987: $16,639
Average annual pay in 1989: $11,551

Service Industry

Selected receipts in 1987 ($1,000): $425,100
Average annual pay in 1989: $17,936

Housing

Total number of units in 1990: 68,991
Occupied units in 1990: 63,768
Owner-occupied units in 1990: 66.6%
1993 ACCRA average cost: N/A
1993 ACCRA average rent for an apartment: N/A

Chamber of Commerce

Greater Topeka Chamber of Commerce, Merle Blair, President, 120 E. 6th St., Topeka, KS 66603. 913-234-2644

Economic Development Office

Topeka Community Economic Development, Al Bailey, Director, 515 S. Kansas Ave. Suite 405, Topeka, KS 66603-3415. 913-295-3711, FAX 913-295-3806

Economic Development Organizations

State of Kansas, Department of Economic Development, Roger Christianson, 503 Kansas Ave. 6th Fl. Topeka, KS 66603. 913-296-3483

Major Businesses

Company	SIC	Telephone
Adams Brothers Co. Inc.	2761	(913) 233-4101
Adams Business Forms	2761	(913) 233-4101
American Companies Inc.	2789	(913) 233-4252
American Investors Life Insurance	6311	(913) 232-6945
American Yearbook Co.	2731	(913) 266-3300
Amvestors Financial Corp.	6311	(913) 232-6945
B R B Contractors Inc.	1629	(913) 232-1245
Bank IV, Topeka	6021	(913) 295-3400
Blakely Crop-Hail Inc.	6331	(913) 232-0937
Blue Cross Blue Shield of Kansas	6324	(913) 291-7000
C G F Industries Inc.	3993	(913) 233-0541
Capitol Federal Savings & Loan	6035	(913) 235-1341
Commerce Bank & Trust	6022	(913) 267-0123
Famous Brands Distributor	5182	(913) 233-1378
Highway Oil, Inc.	5541	(913) 357-6161
Kansas Power and Light Co.	4923	(913) 296-6300
Landmark Hotel Corp.	8741	(913) 272-7500
Lee & Bueltel Construction	1542	(913) 272-9871
M-C Industries, Inc.	3841	(913) 273-3990
Martin Tractor Co. Inc.	5082	(913) 266-5770
Noller, Laird Ford Inc.	5511	(913) 235-9211
Security Benefit Life Insurance	6311	(913) 295-3000
St. Francis Hospital & Medical Center	8062	(913) 295-8000
Stauffer Communications Inc.	2711	(913) 295-1111
Stormont-Vail Regional	8062	(913) 354-6000
Veterinary Companies of America	5047	(913) 354-8523
Victory Life Insurance Co.	6311	(913) 357-6151
Volume Shoe Corp.	5661	(913) 233-5171
Whelan's, Inc.	5211	(913) 357-0321
Workingman's Friend Oil Inc.	5541	(913) 357-6161

Colleges and Universities

Washburn University of Topeka, Topeka

WICHITA, KS (MSA)

Geographic Profile

Land Area
2967.8 square miles

Counties and Parishes
Butler
Harvey
Sedgwick

Ranking Highlights

45   *out of 319 in total* **land area**
192   *out of 319 in* **population growth,** *1970–1990*
26   *out of 310 in having the lowest* **unemployment** *rate*
87   *out of 310 in size of* **labor force**
105   *out of 318 in the percentage of* **college graduates**
70   *out of 292 in per capita personal* **income**
91   *out of 319 in number of* **manufacturing establishments**
141   *out of 318 in* **physicians** *per 1000 people*
94   *out of 318 in* **hospital beds** *per 1000 people*
216   *out of 267 in fewest* **crimes** *per 1000 people*
141   *out of 266 in fewest* **violent crimes** *per 1000 people*
76   *out of 319 in per capita* **federal funds and grants**

Quality of Life Indexes (Rate per 1000 population)

Crime rate in 1991:	74.9
Violent crime rate in 1991:	6.6
Physicians rate in 1992:	1.88
Hospital bed rate in 1991:	4.73

ACCRA Cost of Living Indexes

(First quarter 1993, average = 100)

Composite index:	N/A
Utilities index:	N/A
Housing index:	N/A

Overview

Wichita, the largest city in Kansas and the seat of Sedgwick County, is the focus of a metropolitan statistical area that includes Butler and Sedgwick counties. During the early 1980s, the Wichita economy underwent setbacks caused by declines in agriculture, oil exploration, and durable goods manufacturing. Since 1987, however, growth in manufacturing has maintained a rate of 2.5 to 3.0 percent annually, particularly in the aviation sector; the services industry has also undergone expansion. Retail sales have risen steadily; in fact, in 1987 Wichita was ranked the thirtieth most affluent market in the United States. Primary areas of production are wheat growing, meat packing, flour milling, grain storage, oil refining, high technology, and telecommunications.

The aircraft industry has long been established in Wichita, and today the city is headquarters of some of the nation's leading aerospace firms. Boeing Military Airplanes is the second-largest division of the Boeing Company and Kansas's largest employer; it is also the world's largest private aerospace complex at a single site. Boeing announced in early 1993 the projected loss of up to thirty–thousand jobs industry–wide; about five thousand workers at Wichita plants were among this number. The Cessna Aircraft Company is the world's leading maker of light aircraft and corporate jets. The Beech Aircraft Corporation manufactures business and general aviation craft. Learjet Corporation headquarters and manufacturing facilities are also located in Wichita. Nearby McConnell Air Force Base, one of only four bases in the country that house the B–1 bomber, is the headquarters of the Kansas Air National Guard—the third largest in the nation.

Air cargo service is provided by thirteen freight companies based at Wichita's Mid-Continent Airport. Nine trucking companies ship goods nationwide; nine others offer intrastate delivery; and an additional seventy independent carriers are available on a contract basis. Three major railroads—Union Pacific, Burlington Northern, and Atchison, Topeka, & Santa Fe—link the city with most major continental markets.

A network of interstate, federal, and state highways links Wichita with the East and West Coasts as well as the Canadian and Mexican borders. Interstates I-35 and I-135 pass directly through metropolitan Wichita, connecting the city with I-40, I-44, and I-70. Major U.S. highways are 54 and 81; state routes include K-42, K-2, K-15, K-254, K-96, and the Kansas Turnpike.

Population (1990)

Total Population and Growth Rate
1990: 485,270
1980: 442,401
1970: 416,588
Growth rate 1970–1990: 16%

Race and Hispanic Origin
White: 87.3%
Black: 7.6%
Asian/Pacific Islander: 1.9%
Native American: 1.1%
Hispanic origin: 4.1%
White not Hispanic: 85.6%

Age
Ages 18 to 20:   4%
Ages 21 to 24:   5.5%
Ages 25 to 44: 33.1%
Ages 45 to 54:   9.3%
Ages 55 to 59:   4.2%
Ages 60 to 64:   4.1%
Ages 65 plus: 11.9%

Educational Attainment (1990)

Percent having completed high school: 82.2%
Percent having completed college: 21.5%
Elementary and high school enrollment: 86,115

Federal Funds and Grants Received
Total received in 1989: $1,922,900,000
Funds received per capita: $3,980

Civilian Labor Force
1993 (April):   263,865
1992 average: 265,028
1991 average: 257,963
1990 average: 258,271

Unemployment
1993 (April):   5.8%
1992 average: 4.4%
1991 average: 4.4%
1990 average: 4.4%

Average Annual Pay
1988: $21,547
1987: $20,897
1985: $19,565

Per Capita Personal Income
1991: $19,206
1990: $18,482
1989: $17,481

Business Climate (1987)
Manufacturing
Number of establishments in 1987: 697
Shipments in 1987 ($1,000): $8,615,400
Employees in 1987: 69,000
Change in employment, 1982 to 1987: 21.5%
Average annual pay for manufacturing work in 1989: $30,180
Average annual pay for production work in 1987: $26,421

Wholesale Trade
Number of establishments in 1987: 1,002
Total sales in 1987 ($1,000): $4,441,600
Change in sales, 1982 to 1987: -3.8%

Retail Trade
Number of establishments in 1987: 3,093
Total sales in 1987 ($1,000): $4,441,600
Retail sales per household in 1987: $17,201
Average annual pay in 1989: $11,343

Service Industry
Selected receipts in 1987 ($1,000): $1,471,800
Average annual pay in 1989: $18,754

Office Real Estate (1992)
Office space inventory: 5,626,386 square feet
Average class A Central Business District rental range per sq. ft: $13.50

Vacancy Rates
All areas: 17.4%

Vacancy Rates in Central Business District
Class A space: 13.9%
Class B space: 21.2%

Vacancy Rates Outside Central Business District
Class A space: 11.3%
Class B space: 21.0%

Housing
Total number of units in 1990: 202,521
Occupied units in 1990: 186,640
Owner-occupied units in 1990: 65.2%
1993 ACCRA average cost: N/A
1993 ACCRA average rent for an apartment: N/A

Chamber of Commerce
Wichita Area Chamber of Commerce, F. Tim Witsman, President, 350 W. Douglas Ave., Wichita, KS 67202. 316-265-7771

Economic Development Office
South Central Kansas Economic Development District, Inc., Jack E. Alumbaugh, Exec. Director, 151 N. Volutsia, Wichita, KS 67214. 800-658-1742, 316-683-4422, FAX 316-683-7326

Economic Development Organizations
Wichita-Sedgwick County Partnership for Growth. Contact: F. Tim Witsman, CEO, 350 W. Douglas Ave., Wichita, KS 67202. 316-265-2095, FAX 316-265-7502

Major Businesses

Company	SIC	Telephone
Bank IV Wichita	6021	(316) 261-4444
Beech Aircraft Corp.	3721	(316) 681-7111
Beech Holdings, Inc.	5599	(316) 681-7207
Buckeye P. H. Inc.	5812	(316) 681-9000
Cessna Aircraft Co.	3721	(316) 685-9111
Coastal Derby Co.	2911	(316) 267-0361
CSJ Health System of Wichita	8062	(316) 689-4000
Eby, Martin K. Construction	1623	(316) 268-3500
Eby Corporation	1629	(316) 268-3500
Farm Credit Bank of Wichita	6111	(316) 266-5100
First Bancorp of Kansas	6021	(316) 268-1111
Fourth Financial Corp.	6021	(316) 261-2000
Garvey Industries Inc.	1311	(316) 291-8390
Garvey International Inc.	5153	(316) 291-8390
HCA Health Services of Kansas	8062	(316) 688-2468
A. C. Houston Lumber Co.	5211	(316) 262-8491
Kansas Gas and Electric Co.	4911	(316) 261-6611
Koch Industries Inc.	2911	(316) 832-5500
Koch Refining Co. Inc.	5172	(316) 832-5500
Koch Service, Inc.	4213	(316) 832-5212
Learjet Inc.	3721	(316) 946-2000
Love Box Co. Inc.	2653	(316) 838-0851
Midwest Unlimited, Inc.	2086	(316) 682-1553
Petroleum Trading & Transportation	5172	(316) 942-3800
Pizza Hut, Inc.	5812	(316) 681-9000
Pizza Hut of America Inc.	5812	(316) 681-9000

Major Businesses (Continued)

Company	SIC	Telephone
Rent-A-Center, Inc.	7359	(316) 636-7368
Sisters Sorrowful	8062	(316) 268-5000
St. Francis Regional Medical Center	8062	(316) 268-5000
St. Joseph Medical Center	8062	(316) 685-1111

Colleges and Universities

Friends University, Wichita

Kansas Newman College, Wichita

KENTUCKY

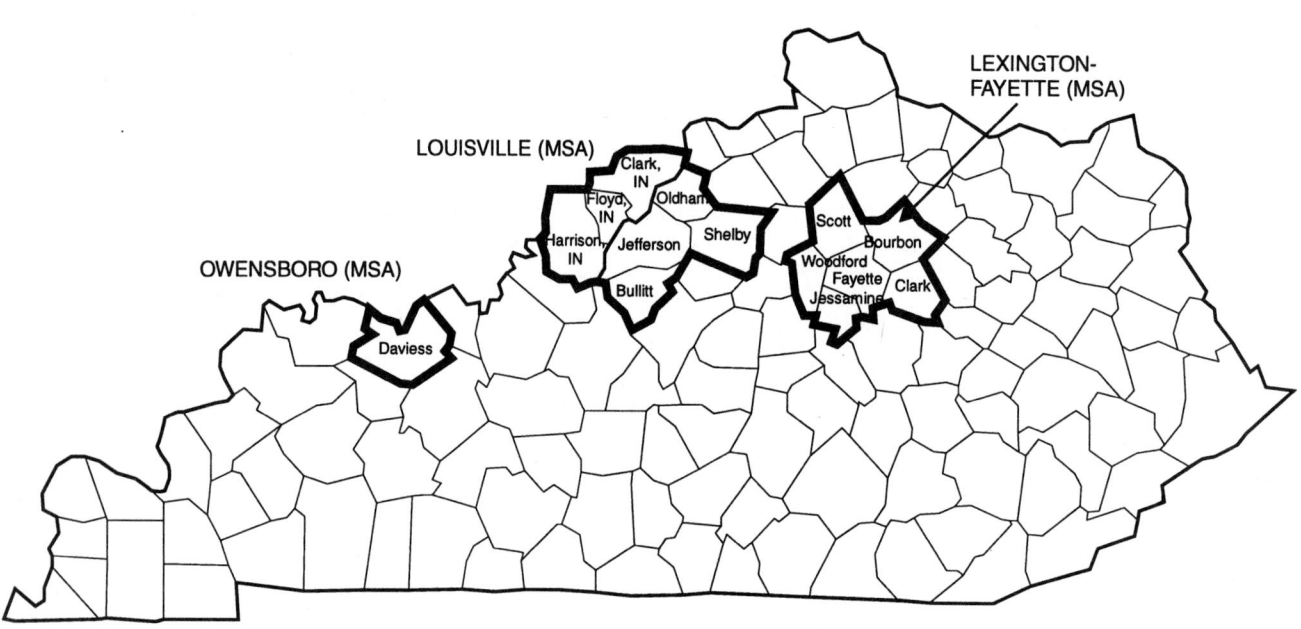

OWENSBORO (MSA)

Daviess

LOUISVILLE (MSA)

Clark, IN

Floyd, IN

Oldham

Harrison, IN

Jefferson

Shelby

Bullitt

LEXINGTON-FAYETTE (MSA)

Scott

Bourbon

Woodford

Fayette

Clark

Jessamine

KENTUCKY

Population
1990: 3,685,296
1980: 3,660,777

Age
Ages 18 to 20: 182,178
Ages 21 to 24: 217,811
Ages 25 to 44: 1,159,182
Ages 45 to 54: 382,366
Ages 55 to 59: 162,821
Ages 60 to 64: 159,999
Median age: 33.0

Race
White: 3,391,832
Black: 262,907
Asian/Pacific Islander: 17,812
Native American: 5,769
Hispanic origin: 21,984

Households
Total: 1,379,782
Persons per household: 2.60

Sex
Male: 1,785,235
Female: 1,900,061

Population Migration
Domestic migration: -117,000
International migration: 17,000

Projection of the Population in 1995
Total: 3,811,000
18 to 64: 2,325,000

Civilian Labor Force
1993: 1,741,400
1992: 1,763,300
1991: 1,728,200
1990: 1,733,500

Manufacturing
1995 Projection: 290,700
1992: 287,300
1991: 285,600
1990: 286,800
1989: 285,700

Services
1995 Projection: 464,700

1992: 350,600
1991: 340,200
1990: 332,800
1989: 319,600

Wholesale and Retail Trade
1995 Projection: 405,500
1992: 355,400
1991: 361,200
1990: 361,200
1989: 359,400

Unemployment Rate
1993: 7.1%
1992: 8.5%
1991: 6.6%
1990: 6.5%

Employer Unemployment Contributions
Contribution Rate
1992: 2.00%
1991: 2.00%
1990: 2.00%

Average Weekly Benefit
1992: $151.33
1991: $152.27
1990: $138.82

Gross State Product (Million $)
1989: $65,858
1988: $61,631
1987: $57,426
1979: $35,399
Growth rate, 1979 to 1989: 86.0%

Capital Expenditures of Manufacturing Industries
1990: $1,796,500,000
1989: $1,861,500,000
1988: $1,157,100,000
1987: $1,746,000,000

State Tax Rates
Individual income: Range from 2% ($3,000 or less) to 6% (above $8,000).
Corporate income: Range from 4% ($25,000 or less) to 8.25% (above $250,000).

General property: Sum of state and local rates. State rate on real property is at 18.9¢ per $100.

General sales: 6%

Gasoline: 15¢ per gallon

Income

Median income for a 4 person family: $34,390

Personal per Capita Income

1992: $16,534

1991: $15,626

1990: $14,984

Disposable per Capita Income

1992: $14,664

1991: $13,757

1990: $13,132

Private Employment Weekly Wages

Average

1989: $361

1988: $352

1987: $352

Manufacturing

1989: $343

1988: $465

1987: $454

Services

1989: $310

1988: $299

1987: $287

Wholesale

1989: $439

1988: $427

1987: $405

Retail

1989: $195

1988: $191

1987: $188

Highway Statistics

Total Highway Miles

1990: 69,668

1989: 69,711

1988: 69,848

Federal Highway Aid

1991: $165,022,000

1990: $159,819,000

1989: $165,356,000

Electricity

Average Cost per Kilowatt Hour

1990: 4.82¢

1989: 5.11¢

1988: 4.99¢

Housing (1990)

Owner occupied units: 960,469

Median house value: $50,500

Renter occupied units: 419,313

Median rent: $250

Total vacant units: 127,063

Homeowner vacancy rate: 1.6%

Rental vacancy rate: 8.2%

State Business Incentives and Assistance

Enterprise Zone Incentives

Businesses in enterprise zones may receive tax and other advantages for up to 20 years:

1. Exemption from state sales taxes on purchases of building materials, and new and used equipment.
2. Exemption from state usage tax on motor vehicles purchased for use in the zone.
3. Exemption from state income taxes on capital gains from the sales of land, buildings, and tangible personal property used in the conduct of business in the zone.
4. Lower interest rates on loans through state tax exemptions to lenders.
5. Possible reduction of city or county property tax rates to only 1/10 cent per $100 valuation (local government option).
6. Possible delay of up to five years for increased property tax assessments on renovated facilities (local government option).

Tax Exemptions, Reductions, and Credits:

Cities can exempt new manufacturing facilities from city occupational license (income) taxes for up to five years.

State income tax credits for debt service payments on manufacturing facilities financed by state bonds in qualifying rural development counties.

Credits against state income tax and corporation license tax for up to 40% of investments made in the state venture capital fund through 1991. Financial institutions making investments in the fund may take credits against state property taxes on shares of capital.

International Facilities:

Foreign trade zones, under U.S. Customs supervision. Goods may be exhibited, stored, assembled, or used in manufacture within the zones, with customs duties paid only if and when the goods or their end products enter U.S. customs territory. Re-exports emerge duty free.

Domestic goods moved into the zone for export are considered for purposes of excise tax rebates and customs drawback procedures.

Financial and Business Assistance

Industrial Revenue Bonds. Cities or counties may issue bonds to finance land, building, machinery and equipment, and pollution control equipment. Projects eligible for industrial revenue bond financing include manufacturing, mining facilities, transportation and parking facilities, convention centers, hotels, health facilities, and recreational facilities. Lease payments made by the companies using the buildings to retire the bonds can be offset by state income tax credits, supplemented by a payroll tax on plant workers when necessary.

SBA Loans. Low-interest SBA guaranteed loans to small businesses, for up to 40% of fixed asset costs, by the Commonwealth Small Business Development Corporation.

State Venture Capital Fund. Loans, loan guarantees, or equity investments of up to $500,000 in small businesses to develop new products and technologies. Investors in the fund receive tax credits of up to 40% of their investments.

Kentucky Development & Finance Authority. It encourages economic development, business expansion and job creation by providing low interest financial support to manufacturing, warehousing, distribution, non-retail services, agribusiness and tourism projects.

Mountain Association for Community Economic Development. It provides direct technical assistance to community organizations and individual enterprises during the planning phase of the start-up or expansion of small business.

Kentucky Infrastructure Authority. KIA was created in 1988 to provide the mechanism for funding construction of local public works projects including basic water, sewer, and solid waste facilities and other infrastructure. Includes Environmental Financing with federally assisted waste water revolving loans and a solid waste loan and grant fund; Infrastructure Revolving Loan Fund for job creation, drinking water loans and grants; and a Bond Bank for a governmental agencies program and Farmers Home Administration loan supplement program. Funds are available for all reasonable costs associated with public works projects including but not limited to acquisition, construction, professional services and interest during construction.

International Marketing. Operated by the Office of International Marketing, this program creates jobs and increases tax revenues through the development of foreign industrial investment within the state, through the promotion of the state's manufactured products for export.

Technology Transfer. Operated by the Office of Business & Technology, this program serves as a link between business and the technological resources and research capabilities of the state universities.

Community Development Block Grant Loans. Operated by the Division of Community Programs, this program provides low-interest loans obtained through the federally-funded CDBG system. Cities and counties lend grant funds to businesses for the creation or retention of jobs. The preferred use of loans funds is for fixed asset financing.

Education and Training

Kentucky's Bluegrass State Skills Corporation. An independent public corporation, it provides custom training of industrial workers to skill levels specified by industrial employers. It works with business, industry, and educational institutions to establish programs of skill training. It also assists businesses in labor force recruitment, screening, and assessment programs.

Job Training Partnership Act. This program operates with funding from the U.S. Department of Labor. It provides job training and other employment related services.

State Offices

Real estate: Real Estate Commission, James P. Daniels, Secretary, 10200 Linn Station Rd., Louisville, KY 40223. 502-425-4273

Chamber of commerce: Kentucky State Chamber of Commerce, Jeff Eger, Chief Operating Officer, PO Box 817, 425 Versailles Rd., Frankfort, KY 40601. 502-695-4700

Economic development: Kentucky Cabinet for Economic Development, Gene C. Royalty, Cabinet Secretary, Capital Plaza Tower, 24th Fl, Frankfort, KY 40601. 502-564-7670, FAX 502-564-3256

Kentucky Department of Local Government, Division of Community Programs, Libby McManis, Director, Capitol Plaza Tower, 2nd fl., Frankfort, KY 40601. 502-564-2382

Office of International Marketing, Michael Hayes, Director, Capitol Plaza Tower, Frankfort, KY 40601. 502-564-2170

Kentucky Development Finance Authority, D. Jeffrey Noel, Exec Director, Capital Plaza Tower, 24th fl., Frankfort, KY 40601. 502-564-4554

Kentucky Cabinet for Economic Development, Office of Enterprise Zone, Sara Bell, Enterprise Zone Coordinator, Capitol Plaza Tower, 23rd Floor, Frankfort, KY 40601. 502-564-7140

Kentucky Infrastructure Authority, Finance & Administration Cabinet, L. Rogers Wells Jr., Chairman, Capitol Annex, Room 075, Frankfort, KY 40601. 502-564-2611

Office of Business & Technology, Debbie Kimbrough, Exec Director, Capitol Plaza Tower, Frankfort, KY 40601. 502-564-7670

Small Business Development Center, Janet Holloway, State Director, 465 East High Street, Suite 201, Lexington, KY 40507-1941. 606-257-7668

Business Information Clearinghouse, Patti Kirk, Manager, Capitol Plaza Tower, Frankfort, KY 40601. 502-564-4252 (800-626-2250 in-state)

Kentucky Dept. of Existing Business & Industry, Bernard L. Williams, Commissioner, Capital Plaza Tower, Frankfort, KY 40601. 502-564-7140

Commonwealth Small Business Development Corp., Theresa Middleton, President, Capitol Plaza Tower, Frankfort, KY 40601. 502-564-4320

Mountain Association for Community Economic Development, Inc., Director, 210 Center Street, Berea, KY 40403. 606-986-2373

South Kentucky Industrial Development Association, James

Major Companies in the State

Company name	Fortune 500 rank	City	Telephone	SIC number
Fortune 500 Companies				
Ashland Oil Inc.	48	Ashland	606-329-3333	2911
Brown Forman Corp.	305	Louisville	502-585-1100	2085
Other Major Companies in the State				
Addington Resources Inc.		Ashland	606-928-3433	1221
Capital Holding Corp.		Louisville	502-560-2000	6311
Columbia Sussex Corp.		Fort Mitchell	606-331-0091	7011
Cumberland Federal Bancorporation Inc.		Louisville	502-562-5320	6712
First Security Corp. of Kentucky		Lexington	606-231-2642	6712
Glenmore Distilleries Co.		Louisville	502-589-0130	2085
Humana Inc.		Louisville	502-580-1000	8062
ICH Corp.		Louisville	502-894-2100	6321
Kentucky Central Life Insurance Co.		Lexington	606-253-5111	6311
Kentucky Power Co.		Ashland	606-327-1111	4911
Kentucky Utilities Co.		Lexington	606-255-2100	4911
KFC National Purchasing Cooperative Inc.		Louisville	502-896-5900	5144
LG & E Energy Corp.		Louisville	502-627-2000	4931
Liberty National Bancorp Inc.		Louisville	502-566-2000	6712
Louisville Gas & Electric Co.		Louisville	502-627-2000	4931
Midwest Communications Corp.		Highland Heights	606-781-2200	5065
NS Group Inc.		Newport	606-292-6809	3317
Steel Technologies Inc.		Louisville	502-245-2110	3312
Texas Gas Transmission Corp.		Owensboro	502-926-8686	4922
Thomas Industries Inc.		Louisville	502-893-4600	3645

Catlett, Exec. Director, PO Box 726, Hopkinsville, KY 42240.

South Kentucky Economic Development Corp., Forrest Wright, Exec. Director, 216 Poplar Ave., Somerset, KY 42501. 606-679-1951

Tri-County Economic Development Corp., James F. West, Jr., Exec. Director, PO Box 17246, Covington, KY 41017. 606-344-0040

East Kentucky Corp., Ben Ross, Exec. Director, PO Drawer 7190, Hazard, KY 41702. 606-439-0291

U.S. Economic Development Administration, Bobby D. Hunter, Economic Development Representative, 333 Waller Ave., Lexington, KY 40504. 606-233-2596

U.S. Small Business Administration, William Federhofer, District Director, Federal Building, Room 188, 600 Dr. Martin Luther King, Jr. Place, Louisville, KY 40202. 502-582-5973

Environmental affairs: Kentucky Department for Environmental Protection, Valerie Hudson, Deputy Commissioner, 18 Reilly Rd., Frankfort, KY 40601. 502-564-2150

Labor: Labor Cabinet, Division of Employment Standards & Mediation, Charles E. McCoy, Director, 1049 U.S. 127 South, Frankfort, KY 40601. 502-564-2784

Unemployment: Department for Employment Services, Division of Unemployment Insurance, A. Joe Anderson, Director, 275 East Main St., Frankfort, KY 40601. 502-564-2900

Worker's compensation: Department of Workers' Claims, Glenn Schilling, Commissioner, 1270 Louisville Rd., Frankfort, KY 40601. 502-564-5550

Occupational safety and health: Labor Cabinet, Department of Workplace Standards, Amanda Storment, Director of Compliance, Occupational Safety & Health, 1049 U.S. 127 South St., Frankfort, KY 40601. 502-564-7360

Secretary of state: Secretary of State Office, Corporation Division, John Crimmins, Director, State Capitol, Frankfort, KY 40601. 502-564-2848

Taxation and revenue: Revenue Cabinet, Department of Tax Compliance, Calvert Bratton, Commissioner, Capitol Annex, Frankfort, KY 40601. 502-564-3111

Designated Zones for Economic Development
Enterprise Zones

Enacted in: 1982

No. of established zones: 10; Ashland County, Campbell County, Covington, Hickman, Hopkinsville, Knox County,

Louisville, Lexington, Owensboro, Paducah

Foreign Trade Zones

Foreign Trade Zone No. 29, Louisville, Kentucky, Grantee/ Operator: Louisville & Jefferson County Riverport Authority, Bruce Traughber, 6900 Riverport Drive, PO Box 58010, Louisville, KY 40258, 502-935-6024, Northern Kentucky Foreign Trade Zone, Inc., PO Box 1177, 1029 Saratoga St., Newport, KY 41071, 606-261-8482

Foreign Trade Zone No. 47, Campbell County, Kentucky, Grantee/Operator: Greater Cincinnati FTZ, Inc., Neil Hensley, 300 Carew Tower, 441 Vine St., Cincinnati, OH 45202-2812, 513-579-3122

Labor Unions

Automobile, Aerospace & Agricultural Implement Workers of America, International Union, United (UAW AFL-CIO)

Communications Workers of America (AFL-CIO)

Electrical Workers, International Brotherhood of (AFL-CIO)

Food and Commercial Workers International Union, United (AFL-CIO)

Operating Engineers, International Union of (AFL-CIO)

Rubber, Cork, Linoleum and Plastic Workers of America, United (AFL-CIO)

Steelworkers of America, United (AFL-CIO)

Teamsters, Chauffeurs, Warehousemen and Helpers of America, International Brotherhood of,(AFL-CIO)

United Mine Workers

Universities with Ph.D. Programs

Northern Kentucky University, Highland Heights
Spalding University, Louisville
University of Kentucky, Lexington
University of Louisville, Louisville

LEXINGTON–FAYETTE, KY (MSA)

Geographic Profile

Land Area

1479.4 square miles

Counties and Parishes

Bourbon
Clark
Fayette
Jessamine
Scott
Woodford

Ranking Highlights

135 *out of 319 in total* **land area**

126 *out of 319 in* **population growth,** *1970–1990*

24 *out of 310 in having the lowest* **unemployment** *rate*

113 *out of 310 in size of* **labor force**

55 *out of 318 in the percentage of* **college graduates**

107 *out of 292 in per capita personal* **income**

138 *out of 319 in number of* **manufacturing establishments**

12 *out of 318 in* **physicians** *per 1000 people*

26 *out of 318 in* **hospital beds** *per 1000 people*

139 *out of 267 in fewest* **crimes** *per 1000 people*

155 *out of 266 in fewest* **violent crimes** *per 1000 people*

246 *out of 319 in per capita* **federal funds and grants**

Quality of Life Indexes (Rate per 1000 population)

Crime rate in 1991:	61.5
Violent crime rate in 1991:	7.1
Physicians rate in 1992:	3.87
Hospital bed rate in 1991:	6.12

ACCRA Cost of Living Indexes

(First quarter 1993, average = 100)

Composite index:	99.3
Utilities index:	85.0
Housing index:	100.5

Overview

Located in the Bluegrass area of Kentucky. Lexington, the second largest city in Kentucky, is 84 miles south of Cincinnati, Ohio, and 80 miles east of Louisville. Within this triangle is over one-third of Kentucky's population and over one-half of its manufacturing jobs. Lexington is internationally known as the home of majestic horses including the thoroughbred, the standardbred, the saddle horse, the Arabian, the quarterhorse and many other breeds.

The University of Kentucky and Transylvania University are located in Kentucky. Also within a 45 mile radius are Lexington Community College, Eastern Kentucky University, Georgetown College, Centre College, Berea College, Ashbury College, Kentucky State University, Midway College, Lexington Theological Seminary, Ashbury Theological Seminary and Lexington Baptist College. The University of Kentucky, Toyota, and Lexmark/IBM are the major public and private sector employers. Employment opportunities in equine-related businesses, medicine, tobacco, retail and services are also available.

A growing center for conventions, Lexington offers over 6,000 rooms in 50 hotels and motels. The Lexington Center offers 23,000-seat Rupp Arena, an 84,000 square foot exposition hall which is currently being expanded. Triangle Park, 50 shops, and the restored Opera House are at the very crossroads of downtown Lexington.

Seven major hospitals offer a full range of medical services at St. Joseph, UK's Chandler Medical Center, Good Samaritan, Central Baptist, Humana-Lexington, and two Veterans Administration Medical Centers. Additionally, special services are available through the Shriners Hospital for Crippled Children, Charter Ridge (psychiatric and addictive disease), Cardinal Hill Convalescent Hospital, Eastern State Hospital, as well as five other general hospitals in the MSA. Lexington has also developed a full range of outpatient surgery, emergency care, nursing, and senior center facilities. In 1991, there were 1,412 physicians and 269 dentists in Fayette County.

The University of Kentucky's Chandler Medical Center has achieved a number of "firsts" including: the only bone marrow transplant program in the Commonwealth, the first non-prototype Magnetic Resonance Imaging (MRI) diagnostic system in the world, as well as pioneering PASAR, a type of pacemaker developed as a new form of treatment for severe cardiac arrhythmias.

Interstate Highway 75 provides ready acess to the area from the north and south; Interstate 64, east and west; the Mountain Parkway, from far eastern Kentucky; and the Bluegrass Parkway, from the west and from Interstate 65. The Blue Grass Airport, ten minutes from downtown Lexington, is served by Air Kentucky, American Eagle, COMAIR, Delta, Eastern Metro Express, Jetstream, Piedmont, TWA, United Express, USAir and two local charter service firms. Additional air service is provided at Louisville and Cincinnati. Rail service is provided by Southern and CSX.

Population (1990)

Total Population and Growth Rate
1990: 348,428
1980: 317,548
1970: 266,701
Growth rate 1970–1990: 31%

Race and Hispanic Origin
White: 87.7%
Black: 10.7%
Asian/Pacific Islander: 1.2%
Native American: 0.2%
Hispanic origin: 0.9%
White not Hispanic: 87.1%

Age
Ages 18 to 20: 5.9%
Ages 21 to 24: 7.3%
Ages 25 to 44: 34.9%
Ages 45 to 54: 10%
Ages 55 to 59: 3.9%
Ages 60 to 64: 3.7%
Ages 65 plus: 10.3%

Educational Attainment (1990)
Percent having completed high school: 75.9%
Percent having completed college: 25.3%
Elementary and high school enrollment: 55,249

Federal Funds and Grants Received
Total received in 1989: $866,700,000
Funds received per capita: $2,491

Civilian Labor Force
1993 (April): 200,603
1992 average: 195,506
1991 average: 193,905
1990 average: 199,518

Unemployment
1993 (April): 4.7%
1992 average: 4.3%
1991 average: 4.3%
1990 average: 3.6%

Average Annual Pay
1988: $19,063
1987: $18,573
1985: $17,269

Per Capita Personal Income
1991: $18,142
1990: $17,506
1989: $16,415

Business Climate (1987)
Manufacturing
Number of establishments in 1987: 388
Shipments in 1987 ($1,000): $4,112,400
Employees in 1987: 27,100
Change in employment, 1982 to 1987: 2.3%
Average annual pay for manufacturing work in 1989: $28,544
Average annual pay for production work in 1987: $21,398

Wholesale Trade
Number of establishments in 1987: 650
Total sales in 1987 ($1,000): $3,637,100
Change in sales, 1982 to 1987: 0%

Retail Trade
Number of establishments in 1987: 2,300
Total sales in 1987 ($1,000): $3,637,100

Retail sales per household in 1987: $19,024

Average annual pay in 1989: $10,714

Service Industry

Selected receipts in 1987 ($1,000): $983,600

Average annual pay in 1989: $16,537

Housing

Total number of units in 1990: 145,229

Occupied units in 1990: 134,077

Owner-occupied units in 1990: 57.8%

1993 ACCRA average cost: $110,427

1993 ACCRA average rent for an apartment: $550

Chamber of Commerce

Greater Lexington Chamber of Commerce, Edward T. Houlihan, President, PO Box 781, 330 E. Main St., Lexington, KY 40507. 606-254-4447

Economic Development Office

Lexington-Fayette Urban County Government, Office of Econ. Development, J.R. Wihite, Director, 200 E. Main St., Lexington, KY 40507. 606-258-3131, FAX 606-258-3194

Economic Development Organizations

Bluegrass Area Development District, Jas. Sekhon, Exec. Director, 3220 Nicholasville Rd. Suite 11, South Park, Lexington, KY 40503-3382. 606-272-6656, FAX 606-273-5619

Winchester-Clark County Chamber of Commerce, Darrell Gilliam, Exec. Director, 2 S. Maple St. Suite. A, Winchester, KY 40391. 606-744-5627

Winchester-Clark County Industrial Authority, James J. Coleman, Vice Chairman, PO Box 707, Winchester, KY 40391. 606-744-4812

Georgetown-Scott County Chamber of Commerce, John A. Conner, Exec. Director, PO Box 224, Georgetown, KY 40324. 502-863-5424

Richmond-Madison County Industrial Corp., James H. Howard, Exec. Director, PO Box 247, Richmond, KY 40476. 606-624-1558

Jessamine County Industrial Foundation, Shelby Combs, Chairman, 504 N. 3rd St., Nicholasville KY 40356. 606-885-5581

Woodford County Chamber of Commerce, PO Box 442, 183 S. Main St., Versailles, KY 40383. 606-873-5122

Kentucky Dept. for Employment Services, David Owens, Office Manager, 300 S. Upper St., Lexington, KY 40508. 606-253-2330

Career Resource & Training Center, Arnold Gaither, Exec. Director, 258 Clark St., Lexington, KY 40508. 606-258-3140

Lexington-Fayette Urban County, Div. of Planning, Dale Thoma, Director, 200 E. Main St., Lexington, KY 40507. 606-258-3160

Local Incentives for Business

As an enterprise zone, business within the targeted areas of Lexington will enjoy the available state tax incentives. In addition, the city's Career Resource & Training Center provides pre-employment screening and testing services, and financial assistance for on-the-job and classroom training for new and existing workforces.

Dedication of increased property tax revenues created by business improvements for use in loans for business and site improvements.

Targeting of public financial aid through low-interest development loan programs such as industrial revenue bonds or small business loans as well as public improvements to foster area improvements.

Industrial Sites

Lexington-Fayette Urban County Government, Office of Economic Development, J.R. Wilhite, Director, 200 E. Main St., Lexington, KY 40507. 606-258-3131

Major Businesses

Company	SIC	Telephone
Appalachian Regional Health	8062	(606) 281-2440
Bradford National Life Insurance	6311	(606) 272-1111
East Kentucky Power Coop	4911	(606) 744-4812
First Security Corp. of Kentucky	6021	(606) 231-1000
James N. Gray Construction	1541	(606) 281-5000
Island Creek Corp.	1222	(606) 288-3000
Jerrico Inc.	5812	(606) 263-6000
Kentucky Central Life Insurance	6311	(606) 253-5111
Kentucky Food Stores, Inc.	5141	(606) 266-1117
Kentucky Utilities Co.	4911	(606) 255-2100
Link-Belt Construction	3531	(606) 263-5200
Long John Silver's Inc.	5812	(606) 263-6000
The Mason Co.	3483	(606) 252-4421
Mason Hanger-Silas Mason	3483	(606) 223-2277
Mid-Central Investment Co.	6141	(606) 253-5111
Toyota Motor Manufacturing	3711	(502) 868-2000
University of Kentucky Hospital	8062	(606) 233-5000

Colleges and Universities

Central Kentucky State Vocational-Technical School, Lexington

Eastern Kentucky University, Richmond

Fugazzi College, Lexington

Georgetown College, Georgetown

Lexington Community College, Lexington

Kentucky College of Business, Lexington

Transylvania University, Lexington

University of Kentucky, Lexington

Additional Information

The Lexington Economic Digest. Greater Lexington Chamber of Commerce, n.d. [8p.]

LOUISVILLE, KY–IN (MSA)

Geographic Profile

Land Area
2266.1 square miles

Counties and Parishes
Indiana:
   Clark
   Floyd
   Harrison
Kentucky:
   Bullitt
   Jefferson
   Oldham
   Shelby

Additional Cities/Towns within Area
New Albany

Ranking Highlights

  78 *out of 319 in total* **land area**

241 *out of 319 in* **population growth,** *1970–1990*

282 *out of 310 in having the lowest* **unemployment** *rate*

  50 *out of 310 in size of* **labor force**

188 *out of 318 in the percentage of* **college graduates**

  81 *out of 292 in per capita personal* **income**

  57 *out of 319 in number of* **manufacturing establishments**

  61 *out of 318 in* **physicians** *per 1000 people*

119 *out of 318 in* **hospital beds** *per 1000 people*

  60 *out of 267 in fewest* **crimes** *per 1000 people*

  99 *out of 266 in fewest* **violent crimes** *per 1000 people*

229 *out of 319 in per capita* **federal funds and grants**

Quality of Life Indexes (Rate per 1000 population)

Crime rate in 1991:	44.9
Violent crime rate in 1991:	4.9
Physicians rate in 1992:	2.52
Hospital bed rate in 1991:	4.38

ACCRA Cost of Living Indexes
(First quarter 1993, average = 100)

Composite index:	90.5
Utilities index:	79.8
Housing index:	87.0

Overview

Louisville is located halfway between Atlanta, Georgia, and Chicago and is within 500 miles of approximately 50 percent of the U.S. population. Louisville is ranked among the top 10 U.S. cities by *Places Rated Almanac*. The Greater Louisville metropolitan area lies along the Ohio River and comprises three Kentucky and four southern Indiana countries.

Through a state program, Louisville offers tax abatements to reimburse companies for up to 50% of their relocation and start-up costs. Since 1985, the Greater Louisville economy has added over 80,000 net new jobs. Major private-sector employers include United Parcel Service (10,000 employees), General Electric (9,000), Galen Health Care (6,000) and Ford (6,000). Major development projects under way or recently completed include a $650 million expansion of Ford's Louisville truck plant, a $370 million expansion of Standiford Field airport, a $100 million, 35-story Capital Holding office tower, and a $20 million national distribution center for Stride Rite.

Louisville is one of the top 20 convention cities in the nation and has the fifth-largest exhibit facility in the U.S. - the 1 million-square-foot Kentucky Fair & Exposition Center. In the fiscal year ended June 30, 1993, Louisville hosted 459 conventions–an increase of 8.8 percent from the previous year. Louisville's Standiford Field is also the location of United Parcel Service's national air-freight hub and is the 9th busiest cargo airport in the world.

Louisville has a symphony orchestra, professional opera and ballet companies, and a major performing-arts center. Churchill Downs in Louisville is home of the Kentucky Derby horse race. Louisville also hosted the Breeders' Cup, the $10 million world championship of thoroughbred horse racing, in 1988 and 1991 and will host the event again in 1994.

Population (1990)

Total Population and Growth Rate
1990: 952,662
1980: 956,426
1970: 906,752
Growth rate 1970–1990: 5%

Race and Hispanic Origin
White: 86.0%
Black: 13.1%
Asian/Pacific Islander: 0.6%
Native American: 0.2%
Hispanic origin: 0.6%
White not Hispanic: 85.6%

Age
Ages 18 to 20: 4.3%
Ages 21 to 24: 5.3%
Ages 25 to 44: 33%
Ages 45 to 54: 10.5%
Ages 55 to 59: 4.5%
Ages 60 to 64: 4.6%
Ages 65 plus: 12.6%

Educational Attainment (1990)
Percent having completed high school: 73.5%
Percent having completed college: 17.3%
Elementary and high school enrollment: 165,253

Federal Funds and Grants Received
Total received in 1989: $2,507,600,000

Funds received per capita: $2,593

Civilian Labor Force
1993 (April): 525,028
1992 average: 514,049
1991 average: 512,982
1990 average: 522,862

Unemployment
1993 (April): 5.7%
1992 average: 5.7%
1991 average: 6.1%
1990 average: 5.1%

Average Annual Pay
1988: $20,048
1987: $19,448
1985: $18,237

Per Capita Personal Income
1991: $18,912
1990: $18,283
1989: $17,116

Business Climate (1987)
Manufacturing
Number of establishments in 1987: 1,223
Shipments in 1987 ($1,000): $18,210,700
Employees in 1987: 86,100
Change in employment, 1982 to 1987: -6.3%
Average annual pay for manufacturing work in 1989: $28,757
Average annual pay for production work in 1987: $24,404

Wholesale Trade
Number of establishments in 1987: 1,896
Total sales in 1987 ($1,000): $11,140,100
Change in sales, 1982 to 1987: 47.4%

Retail Trade
Number of establishments in 1987: 5,618
Total sales in 1987 ($1,000): $11,140,100
Retail sales per household in 1987: $16,514
Average annual pay in 1989: $10,923

Service Industry
Selected receipts in 1987 ($1,000): $2,701,800
Average annual pay in 1989: $17,104

Office Real Estate (1992)
Office space inventory: 12,265,000 square feet
Average class A Central Business District rental range per sq. ft: $15.00

Vacancy Rates
All areas: 17.3%

Vacancy Rates in Central Business District
Class A space: 10.7%
Class B space: 42.4%

Vacancy Rates Outside Central Business District
Class A space: 3.2%

Class B space: 10.4%

Housing
Total number of units in 1990: 392,033
Occupied units in 1990: 367,819
Owner-occupied units in 1990: 67.5%
1993 ACCRA average cost: $96,920
1993 ACCRA average rent for an apartment: $450

Chamber of Commerce
Louisville Chamber of Commerce, Charles H. Buddeke III, President, 1 Riverfront Plaza, 5th & Jefferson Sts., Louisville, KY 40202. 502-566-5000

Economic Development Office
Greater Louisville Economic Development Partnership, Crit Luallen, President, 1 Riverfront Plaza, Louisville, KY 40202. 502-625-0200, FAX 502-625-0211

Economic Development Organizations
Louisville and Jefferson County Office for Economic Development, Paul Thistleton, Exec. Director, 401 S. 4th Ave. Suite 200, Louisville, KY 40202. 502-625-3051, FAX 502-625-3026

Louisville & Jefferson County Riverport Authority, C. Bruce Traughber, President, 6900 Riverport Dr. PO Box 58010, Louisville, KY 40258. 502-935-6024, FAX 502-935-6050

Campaign for Greater Louisville, Donald E. Doyle, President, 1 Riverfront Plaza, Louisville, KY 40202. 502-566-5066

Major Businesses

Company	SIC	Telephone
B-F Spirits Ltd.	2085	(502) 585-1100
Batus Inc.	2111	(502) 581-8000
Blue Cross & Blue Shield	6324	(502) 423-2011
Brown & Williamson Tobacco	2111	(502) 568-7000
Brown-Forman Corp.	2085	(502) 585-1100
Capital Holding Corp.	6311	(502) 560-2000
Chi-Chi's USA, Inc.	5812	(502) 426-3900
Citizens Fidelity Corp.	6022	(502) 581-2100
Comalco U.S. Holding, Inc.	3353	(502) 589-8100
Commonwealth Aluminum Corp.	3353	(502) 589-8100
Commonwealth Life Insurance Corp.	6311	(502) 587-7371
Dairymen Inc.	5143	(502) 426-6455
Entrade Corp.	4924	(502) 625-2400
Farm Credit Bank of Louisville	6159	(502) 566-7000
First Kentucky National Corp.	6021	(502) 581-4200
First National Bank of Louisville	6021	(502) 581-4200
Flav-O-Rich Inc.	2026	(502) 426-6455
Glenmore Distilleries Co.	2085	(502) 589-0130
I.C.H. Corp.	6311	(502) 897-1861
Kentucky Fried Chicken Co.	5812	(502) 456-8300
KFC Corp.	5812	(502) 456-8300

Major Businesses (Continued)

Company	SIC	Telephone
KFC National Management Co.	5812	(502) 456-8300
KFC National Purchasing Cooperative Inc.	5141	(502) 896-5900
Liberty National Bancorp	6021	(502) 566-2000
Louisville Gas & Electric Co.	4911	(502) 566-4011
Sisters of Charity of Nazarene	8062	(502) 429-5055
Thomas Industries Inc.	3646	(502) 893-4600

Colleges and Universities

Bellarmine College, Louisville

Louisville College, Louisville

Louisville Technical Institute, Louisville

National Education Center-Kentucky College of Technology Campus, Louisville

Rets Electronic Institute, Louisville

Spalding University, Louisville

Sullivan College, Louisville

University of Kentucky, Jefferson Community College, Louisville

University of Louisville, Louisville

OWENSBORO, KY (MSA)

Geographic Profile

Land Area
462.4 square miles

Counties and Parishes
Daviess

Ranking Highlights

298 *out of 319 in total* land area

225 *out of 319 in* population growth, *1970–1990*

174 *out of 310 in having the lowest* unemployment *rate*

297 *out of 310 in size of* labor force

253 *out of 318 in the percentage of* college graduates

194 *out of 292 in per capita personal* income

298 *out of 319 in number of* manufacturing establishments

217 *out of 318 in* physicians *per 1000 people*

41 *out of 318 in* hospital beds *per 1000 people*

27 *out of 267 in fewest* crimes *per 1000 people*

29 *out of 266 in fewest* violent crimes *per 1000 people*

287 *out of 319 in per capita* federal funds and grants

Quality of Life Indexes (Rate per 1000 population)

Crime rate in 1991:	37.3
Violent crime rate in 1991:	2.3
Physicians rate in 1992:	1.55
Hospital bed rate in 1991:	5.68

ACCRA Cost of Living Indexes
(First quarter 1993, average = 100)

Composite index:	91.9
Utilities index:	87.5
Housing index:	87.8

Population (1990)

Total Population and Growth Rate
1990: 87,189

1980: 85,949

1970: 79,486

Growth rate 1970–1990: 10%

Race and Hispanic Origin
White: 95.4%

Black: 4.2%

Asian/Pacific Islander: 0.3%

Native American: 0.1%

Hispanic origin: 0.4%

White not Hispanic: 95.1%

Age
Ages 18 to 20: 4.5%

Ages 21 to 24: 5.3%

Ages 25 to 44: 30.6%

Ages 45 to 54: 10.4%

Ages 55 to 59: 4.7%

Ages 60 to 64: 4.5%
Ages 65 plus: 12.8%

Educational Attainment (1990)
Percent having completed high school: 72.3%
Percent having completed college: 14.1%
Elementary and high school enrollment: 15,903

Federal Funds and Grants Received
Total received in 1989: $193,200,000
Funds received per capita: $2,202

Civilian Labor Force
1993 (April):   45,556
1992 average: 44,716
1991 average: 44,571
1990 average: 45,122

Unemployment
1993 (April):   7.7%
1992 average: 7.1%
1991 average: 6.9%
1990 average: 5.5%

Average Annual Pay
1988: $17,662
1987: $17,036
1985: $16,357

Per Capita Personal Income
1991: $16,387
1990: $15,765
1989: $14,892

Business Climate (1987)
Manufacturing
Number of establishments in 1987: 97
Shipments in 1987 ($1,000): $2,046,000
Employees in 1987: 7,500
Change in employment, 1982 to 1987: 13.6%
Average annual pay for manufacturing work in 1989: $23,285
Average annual pay for production work in 1987: $24,558

Wholesale Trade
Number of establishments in 1987: 184
Total sales in 1987 ($1,000): $531,300
Change in sales, 1982 to 1987: 5.8%

Retail Trade
Number of establishments in 1987: 697
Total sales in 1987 ($1,000): $531,300
Retail sales per household in 1987: $16,673
Average annual pay in 1989: $9,755

Service Industry
Selected receipts in 1987 ($1,000): $176,100
Average annual pay in 1989: $15,857

Housing
Total number of units in 1990: 35,041

Occupied units in 1990: 33,036
Owner-occupied units in 1990: 68.8%
1993 ACCRA average cost: $105,017
1993 ACCRA average rent for an apartment: $377

Chamber of Commerce
Owensboro-Daviess County Chamber of Commerce, Doug Frazior, President, 335 Frederica St., PO Box 825, Owensboro, KY 42302. 502-926-1860

Economic Development Office
Owensboro-Daviess County Industries, Inc. Fred R. King, Exec. Vice President, 313 Frederica St., Owensboro, KY 42301. 502-926-4339, FAX 502-926-3364

Economic Development Organizations
Green River Area Development District, Jiten Shah, Exec. Director, 3860 U.S. Highway 60 W., Owensboro, KY 42301. 502-926-4433, FAX 502-684-0714

Major Businesses

Company	SIC	Telephone
Addwest Mining Inc.	1221	(502) 684-2490
Area Bancshares Corp.	6021	(502) 926-3232
Central Bank & Trust Co.	6022	(502) 926-9666
Citizens State Bank	6022	(502) 926-2020
Emmick Oil Inc.	5171	(502) 683-2461
Green River Electric Corp.	4911	(502) 926-4141
Lincoln Service Corp.	6162	(502) 685-7100
Mercy Hospital of Owensboro	8062	(502) 686-6100
Miles Farm Supply, Inc.	5191	(502) 926-2420
Modern Welding Co.	3443	(502) 685-4400
Don Moore Chevrolet-Cadillac	5511	(502) 685-5551
Owensboro Municipal Utilities	4911	(502) 926-3200
Owensboro National Bank	6021	(502) 926-3232
Owensboro-Daviess County Hospital	8062	(502) 926-3030
Peters Construction Co.	1541	(502) 926-4520
Quality Oil Co Inc.	5171	(502) 684-0215
Roberts Motor Sales Inc.	5511	(502) 683-6282
Texas Gas Transmission Co.	4922	(502) 926-8686
Titan Contracting & Leasing	1791	(502) 683-6564
Wax Works Inc.	5099	(502) 926-0008
Western Kentucky Gas Resources	5172	(502) 685-8040
Wetzel's Super Markets	5411	(502) 684-9952
Whitehall Furniture Inc.	2521	(502) 683-3585
Winn Construction Co.	1221	(502) 683-9210
Wyndall Enterprises Inc.	5411	(502) 684-9493

Colleges and Universities
Brescia College, Owensboro, KY
Kentucky Wesleyan College, Owensboro
Owensboro Junior College of Business, Owensboro
University of Kentucky, Owensboro Community College, Owensboro

LOUISIANA

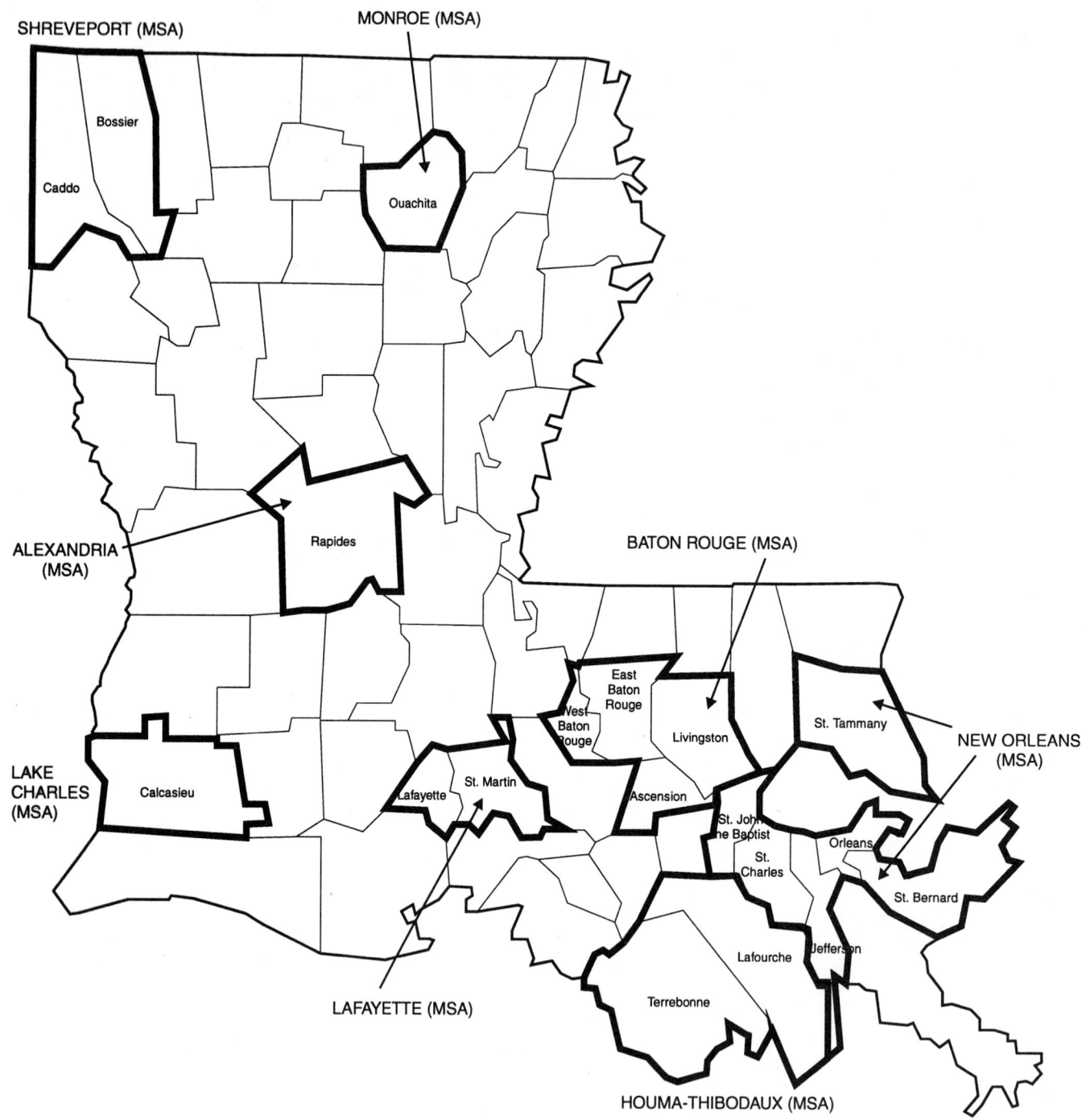

SHREVEPORT (MSA)

MONROE (MSA)

Bossier

Caddo

Ouachita

ALEXANDRIA
(MSA)

Rapides

BATON ROUGE (MSA)

East
Baton
Rouge

West
Baton
Rouge

Livingston

St. Tammany

NEW ORLEANS
(MSA)

LAKE
CHARLES
(MSA)

Calcasieu

Lafayette

St. Martin

Ascension

St. John
the Baptist

Orleans

St.
Charles

St. Bernard

Jefferson

LAFAYETTE (MSA)

Lafourche

Terrebonne

HOUMA-THIBODAUX (MSA)

LOUISIANA

Population
1990: 4,219,973
1980: 4,205,900

Age
Ages 18 to 20: 210,010
Ages 21 to 24: 254,501
Ages 25 to 44: 1,309,858
Ages 45 to 54: 406,440
Ages 55 to 59: 171,927
Ages 60 to 64: 170,977
Median age: 31.0

Race
White: 2,839,138
Black: 1,299,281
Asian/Pacific Islander: 41,099
Native American: 18,541
Hispanic origin: 93,044

Households
Total: 1,499,269
Persons per household: 2.74

Sex
Male: 2,031,386
Female: 2,188,587

Population Migration
Domestic migration: -469,000
International migration: 47,000

Projection of the Population in 1995
Total: 4,390,000
18 to 64: 2,603,000

Civilian Labor Force
1993: 1,841,900
1992: 1,940,400
1991: 1,911,500
1990: 1,802,300

Manufacturing
1995 Projection: 177,900
1992: 185,300
1991: 185,400
1990: 186,200
1989: 175,400

Services
1995 Projection: 531,100

1992: 394,700
1991: 386,600
1990: 380,600
1989: 347,400

Wholesale and Retail Trade
1995 Projection: 422,600
1992: 377,500
1991: 382,500
1990: 382,100
1989: 371,200

Unemployment Rate
1993: 8.6%
1992: 7.9%
1991: 6.8%
1990: 6.4%

Employer Unemployment Contributions
Contribution Rate
1992: 1.88%
1991: 2.03%
1990: 2.22%

Average Weekly Benefit
1992: $120.02
1991: $122.16
1990: $102.81

Gross State Product (Million $)
1989: $79,138
1988: $76,540
1987: $72,125
1979: $52,713
Growth rate, 1979 to 1989: 50.1%

Capital Expenditures of Manufacturing Industries
1990: $2,683,300,000
1989: $2,168,800,000
1988: $1,781,300,000
1987: $1,419,800,000

State Tax Rates
Individual income: Range from 2% ($10,000 or less) to 6% (above $50,000).
Corporate income: Range from 4% ($25,000 or less) to 8% (above $200,000).

General property: N/A
General sales: 4%
Gasoline: 20¢ per gallon

Income

Median income for a 4 person family: $34,406

Personal per Capita Income

1992: $15,712
1991: $15,054
1990: $14,300

Disposable per Capita Income

1992: $14,163
1991: $13,497
1990: $12,750

Private Employment Weekly Wages

Average

1989: $385
1988: $378
1987: $378

Manufacturing

1989: $365
1988: $516
1987: $500

Services

1989: $349
1988: $344
1987: $334

Wholesale

1989: $462
1988: $455
1987: $431

Retail

1989: $206
1988: $204
1987: $199

Highway Statistics

Total Highway Miles

1990: 58,620
1989: 58,521
1988: 58,422

Federal Highway Aid

1991: $212,772,000
1990: $209,631,000
1989: $269,151,000

Electricity

Average Cost per Kilowatt Hour
1990: 5.97¢
1989: 5.93¢
1988: 6.07¢

Housing (1990)

Owner occupied units: 987,919

Median house value: $58,500
Renter occupied units: 511,350
Median rent: $260
Total vacant units: 216,972
Homeowner vacancy rate: 2.7%
Rental vacancy rate: 12.5%

State Business Incentives and Assistance

Enterprise Zone Incentives

An exemption from ad valorem property taxes on manufacturing facilities and equipment for a period up to ten years.

Enterprise Zone jobs tax credits of $2,500 per job.

Enterprise Zone refunds of sales and use taxes on building materials and operating equipment.

Low-cost industrial development and pollution abatement bonds.

Freeport laws which permit manufacturers to bring raw materials into the state without having to pay a tax until after the materials have been placed in the manufacturing process.

Financial and Business Assistance

Financial Incentives Division. As part of the Department of Economic Development, the Financial Incentives Division administers economic development incentives for the state. It also provides support services to the Office of Commerce and Industry which is responsible for approving applications for certain state development incentives. The tax abatement and financial assistance programs include: Industrial Tax Exemption (ad valorem property tax), Enterprise Zone Program, Restoration Tax Abatement Program, Capital Companies Tax Credit Program, Corporate Headquarters Tax Equalization Program, Warehousing and Distribution Tax Equalization Program, Industry Assistance Program, Corporate Jobs Tax Program,and Film and Video Sales/Use Tax Refund. Additionally, the Division conducts on-site inspections of facilities that receive benefits under incentive programs to ensure that the rules and regulations of the programs are followed. Tax equalization laws which guarantee the total taxes on Louisiana industrial facilities and corporate headquarters will not exceed those of a competing location.

Louisiana Economic Development Corporation. It was organized in 1988 to stimulate the creation of venture capital in Louisiana and to encourage the development of minority-owned and women-owned business, as well as small business in general. Its programs include: Small Business Innovation Research Matching Grant Program, Venture Capital Incentive Program, Minority and Women's Business Development Program and Small Business Equity Program.

Market Analysis and Planning. The Market Analysis and Planning Division provides information and research services. It maintains a computerized listing of available industrial properties in the state, along with data on wages,

Major Companies in the State

Company name	Fortune 500 rank	City	Telephone	SIC number
Fortune 500 Companies				
Avondale Industries Inc.	497	Avondale	504-436-2121	3731
Freeport McMoran Inc.	252	New Orleans	504-582-4000	1479
Louisiana Land & Exploration Co.	413	New Orleans	504-566-6500	2911
McDermott Inc.	194	New Orleans	504-587-4411	3511
Other Major Companies in the State				
Al Copeland Enterprises Inc.		Jefferson	504-733-4300	5812
ARKLA Inc.		Shreveport	318-429-2700	4923
Central Louisiana Electric Co. Inc.		Pineville	318-484-7400	4911
Century Telephone Enterprises Inc.		Monroe	318-388-9500	4813
Entergy Corp.		New Orleans	504-529-5262	4911
First Commerce Corp. Louisiana		New Orleans	504-561-1371	6712
Hibernia Corp.		New Orleans	504-587-3297	6712
International Shipholding Corp.		New Orleans	504-529-5461	4412
Louisiana Power & Light Co.		New Orleans	504-595-3100	4911
McDermott International Inc.		New Orleans	504-587-5400	3621
MMR Holding Corp.		Baton Rouge	504-753-2701	1731
New Orleans Public Service Inc.		New Orleans	504-595-3100	4931
Ocean Drilling & Exploration Co.		New Orleans	504-561-2811	1311
Petroleum Helicopters Inc.		New Orleans	504-733-6790	4522
Piccadilly Cafeterias Inc.		Baton Rouge	504-293-9440	5812
Premier Bancorp Inc.		Baton Rouge	504-332-7277	6712
Southwestern Electric Power Co.		Shreveport	318-222-2141	4911
Tidewater Inc.		New Orleans	504-568-1010	4499
United Financial Corp.		Baton Rouge	504-924-6007	6311
Whitney Holding Corp.		New Orleans	504-586-7272	6712

utilities, transportation and other advantages Louisiana offers to new or expanding businesses. Profiles on more than 100 Louisiana communities and all 64 parishes are also maintained.

International Trade. The International Trade Division is responsible for providing guidance to Louisiana firms interested in exporting goods and services. It also conducts educational seminars and meetings on export opportunities and procedures, arranges meetings and appointments with foreign buyers and alerts companies to events such as international trade shows and conferences. A major function of the division is to represent Louisiana companies at overseas trade shows and to collect trade leads for dissemination to participating firms. The division also helps sponsor overseas missions and assists Louisiana companies in finding overseas distributors and agents for their products and services.

Education and Training

Start-Up Training. Administered by the Office of Commerce and Industry, this program is designed to provide customized, short-term pre-employment and on-the-job training for employees of new and expanding manufacturing companies. Selection of a company to receive job training assistance is based upon the creation of new, or the saving of existing, manufacturing jobs. The program staff provides assistance in recruiting and selecting trainees. At least 10 trainees are necessary for a training program to be established.

Job Training Partnership Act. This program operates with funding from the U.S. Department of Labor. It provides job training and other employment related services.

State Offices

Real estate: Real Estate Commission, Ron Brooks, Chairman, PO Box 14785, Baton Rouge, LA 70898. 504-925-4771

Chamber of commerce: Louisiana Association of Business & Industry, Maridel Avery, Marketing Director, PO Box 80258, 3113 Valley Creek Dr., Baton Rouge, LA 70898. 504-928-5388

Economic development: Louisiana Department of Economic Development, Kristen Nyrop, Secretary, PO Box 94185, 101 France St., Baton Rouge, LA 70804-9185.

504-342-5359, FAX 504-342-5389

Department of Economic Development, Office of Commerce & Industry, Paul Adams, Finance Director, PO Box 94185, 101 France St., Baton Rouge, LA 70804-9185. 504-342-5399, FAX 504-342-5389

Department of Economic Development, Office of Commerce & Industry, International Trade Division, Bill Jackson, Director, PO Box 94185, 101 France St., Baton Rouge, LA 70804-9185. 504-342-4320, FAX 504-342-5389

Department of Economic Development, Office of Commerce & Industry, Market Analysis & Planning Division, Dianne Barksdale, Director, PO Box 94185, 101 France St., Baton Rouge, LA 70804-9185. 504-342-3072, FAX 504-342-5389

Department of Commerce, Enterprise Zone Program, Laverne Jasek, Coordinator, P.O. Box 94185, Baton Rouge, LA 70804-9185. 504-342-5402

Small Business Development Center, John Baker, State Director, Northeast Louisiana University, Administrative Bldg., Room 2-57, University Drive, Monroe, LA 71209. 318-342-2464

Department of Economic Development, Economic Development Corporation, Mike Williams, Interim Exec Director, PO Box 94185, Baton Rouge, LA 70804-9185. 504-342-5675

Environmental affairs: Department of Environmental Quality, Paul H. Templet, Secretary, PO Box 4066, Baton Rouge, LA 70804-4066. 504-342-9103

Labor: Department of Labor, Phyllis Mouton, Secretary, PO Box 94094, Baton Rouge, LA 70804-9094. 504-342-3011

Unemployment: Department of Labor, Office of Employment Security, Wayne Cox, Administrator, PO Box 94094, Baton Rouge, LA 70804-9094. 504-342-3017

Worker's compensation: Department of Labor, Office of Workers' Compensation, Stephen Cavanaugh, Assistant Secretary, PO Box 94094, Baton Rouge, LA 70804-9094. 504-342-7836

Occupational safety and health: Department of Labor, Phyllis Mouton, Secretary, PO Box 94094, Baton Rouge, LA 70804-9094. 504-342-3011

Secretary of state: Secretary of State's Office, W. Fox McKeithen, Secretary of State, PO Box 94125, Baton Rouge, LA 70804-9125. 504-922-1000

Taxation and revenue: Dept. of Revenue & Taxation, Arnold A. Broussard, Secretary, PO Box 201, Baton Rouge, LA 70821. 504-925-7680

Designated Zones for Economic Development

Enterprise Zones
Enacted in: 1981
No. of established zones: 750

Foreign Trade Zones
Foreign Trade Zone No. 124, Gramercy, Louisiana,

Grantee: South Louisiana Port Commission, Richard J. Clements, PO Drawer K, La Place, LA 70068-1109, 504-652-9278

Foreign Trade Zone No. 87, Lake Charles, Louisiana, Grantee/Operator: Lake Charles Harbor & Terminal District, Pat Ford, PO Box AAA, Lake Charles, LA 70602, 318-439-3661

Foreign Trade Zone No. 2, New Orleans, Louisiana, Grantee/Operator: Board of Commissioners of the Port of New Orleans, Robert Dee, PO Box 60046, New Orleans, LA 70160, 504-897-0189

Foreign Trade Zone No. 145, Shreveport, Louisiana, Grantee: Caddo-Bossier Parishes Port Commission, John W. Holt, Jr., PO Box 1983, Shreveport, LA 71166, 318-636-7266

Foreign Trade Zone No. 154, Baton Rouge, Louisiana, Grantee: Greater Baton Rouge Port Commission, Karen St. Cyr, PO Box 380, Port Allen, LA 70767-0380, 504-387-4207

Labor Unions
Food and Commercial Workers International Union, United (AFL-CIO)

Jefferson Federation of Teachers

Machinists and Aerospace Workers, International Association of (AFL-CIO)

Plumbing and Pipe Fitting Industry of The United States and Canada, United Association of, Journeymen and Apprentices of the (AFL-CIO)

Universities with Ph.D. Programs
Grambling State University

Louisiana State University and Agricultural and Mechanical College, Baton Rouge

Louisiana State University Medical Center, New Orleans

Louisiana State University Medical Center, Shreveport

Louisiana Tech University, Ruston

Loyola University, New Orleans, New Orleans

Northeast Louisiana University, Monroe

Southern University and Agricultural and Mechanical College, Baton Rouge

Tulane University, New Orleans

University of New Orleans, New Orleans

University of Southwestern Louisiana, Lafayette

ALEXANDRIA, LA (MSA)

Geographic Profile

Land Area

1322.7 square miles

Counties and Parishes

Rapides

Ranking Highlights

150　*out of 319 in total* **land area**

219　*out of 319 in* **population growth,** *1970–1990*

184　*out of 310 in having the lowest* **unemployment** *rate*

269　*out of 310 in size of* **labor force**

243　*out of 318 in the percentage of* **college graduates**

247　*out of 292 in per capita personal* **income**

288　*out of 319 in number of* **manufacturing establishments**

162　*out of 318 in* **physicians** *per 1000 people*

34　*out of 318 in* **hospital beds** *per 1000 people*

109　*out of 267 in fewest* **crimes** *per 1000 people*

105　*out of 266 in fewest* **violent crimes** *per 1000 people*

96　*out of 319 in per capita* **federal funds and grants**

Quality of Life Indexes (Rate per 1000 population)

Crime rate in 1991:	56.8
Violent crime rate in 1991:	5.0
Physicians rate in 1992:	1.79
Hospital bed rate in 1991:	5.84

ACCRA Cost of Living Indexes

(First quarter 1993, average = 100)

Composite index:	92.2
Utilities index:	90.4
Housing index:	83.5

Population (1990)

Total Population and Growth Rate

1990: 131,556

1980: 135,282

1970: 118,078

Growth rate 1970–1990: 11%

Race and Hispanic Origin

White: 70.7%

Black: 28.0%

Asian/Pacific Islander: 0.7%

Native American: 0.4%

Hispanic origin: 1.2%

White not Hispanic: 69.9%

Age

Ages 18 to 20: 4.5%

Ages 21 to 24: 5.8%

Ages 25 to 44: 30.3%

Ages 45 to 54: 9.9%

Ages 55 to 59: 4.4%

Ages 60 to 64: 4%

Ages 65 plus: 12%

Educational Attainment (1990)

Percent having completed high school: 69.0%

Percent having completed college: 14.6%

Elementary and high school enrollment: 25,626

Federal Funds and Grants Received

Total received in 1989: $497,100,000

Funds received per capita: $3,606

Civilian Labor Force

1993 (April):　57,882

1992 average:　58,587

1991 average:　59,264

1990 average:　57,947

Unemployment

1993 (April):　6.3%

1992 average:　7.3%

1991 average:　7.1%

1990 average:　6.3%

Average Annual Pay

1988: $16,626

1987: $16,120

1985: $15,339

Per Capita Personal Income

1991: $15,230

1990: $14,296

1989: $13,283

Business Climate (1987)

Manufacturing

Number of establishments in 1987: 106

Shipments in 1987 ($1,000): $731,600

Employees in 1987: 4,100

Change in employment, 1982 to 1987: 10.8%

Average annual pay for manufacturing work in 1989: $24,832

Average annual pay for production work in 1987: $18,500

Wholesale Trade

Number of establishments in 1987: 228

Total sales in 1987 ($1,000): $425,800

Change in sales, 1982 to 1987: -17.7%

Retail Trade

Number of establishments in 1987: 832

Total sales in 1987 ($1,000): $425,800

Retail sales per household in 1987: $15,291

Average annual pay in 1989: $10,317

Service Industry

Selected receipts in 1987 ($1,000): $289,400

Average annual pay in 1989: $16,297

Housing

Total number of units in 1990: 51,239

Occupied units in 1990: 45,941
Owner-occupied units in 1990: 66.5%
1993 ACCRA average cost: $93,700
1993 ACCRA average rent for an apartment: $430

Chamber of Commerce

Central Louisiana Chamber of Commerce, John Stroud, Exec. Vice President, 802 3rd St., PO Box 992, Alexandria, LA 71309. 318-442-6671

Economic Development Office

Kisatchie Delta Regional Planning & Development District, Robert Wagner, Exec. Director, 5212 Rue Verdun, PO Box 12248, Alexandria, LA 71315. 318-487-5454, FAX 318-487-5451

Major Businesses

Company	SIC	Telephone
Afco Industries Inc.	3089	(318) 448-1651
Avoyelles Wholesale Grocery Co.	5141	(318) 442-8865
Baker Manufacturing Co.	2542	(318) 445-3601
Central Louisiana Electric	4911	(318) 484-7400
Central State Life Insurance	6311	(318) 443-3666
Crest Industries, Inc.	1629	(318) 448-8287
Estorge Drug Co. of Rapide	5122	(318) 442-3356
Roy O. Martin Lumber Co.	2491	(318) 448-0405
Rapides Bank & Trust Co.	6022	(318) 487-2431
Rapides Regional Medical Center	8062	(318) 473-3150
St. Frances Cabrini Hospital	8062	(318) 487-1122
Walker Oldsmobile Co., Inc.	5511	(318) 445-6421

Colleges and Universities

Louisiana College, Alexandria-Pineville
Louisiana State University at Alexandria, Alexandria

BATON ROUGE, LA (MSA)

Geographic Profile

Land Area

1586.5 square miles

Counties and Parishes

Ascension
East Baton Rouge
Livingston
West Baton Rouge

Ranking Highlights

122 *out of 319 in total* land area
 95 *out of 319 in* population growth, *1970–1990*
121 *out of 310 in having the lowest* unemployment *rate*
 83 *out of 310 in size of* labor force
 88 *out of 318 in the percentage of* college graduates
 16 *out of 292 in per capita personal* income
122 *out of 319 in number of* manufacturing establishments
206 *out of 318 in* physicians *per 1000 people*
168 *out of 318 in* hospital beds *per 1000 people*
248 *out of 267 in fewest* crimes *per 1000 people*
255 *out of 266 in fewest* violent crimes *per 1000 people*
210 *out of 319 in per capita* federal funds and grants

Quality of Life Indexes (Rate per 1000 population)

Crime rate in 1991:	87.8
Violent crime rate in 1991:	12.9
Physicians rate in 1992:	1.6
Hospital bed rate in 1991:	3.74

ACCRA Cost of Living Indexes

(First quarter 1993, average = 100)
Composite index: 101.0
Utilities index: 129.8
Housing index: 93.9

Overview

Baton Rouge is the state capital of Louisiana and the county seat of Baton Rouge Parish. Situated on the Mississippi River, in the heart of the state, the city is an important center in the "Sun Belt" market. With one of the nation's largest deep-water ports, which is equipped to handle both ocean-going vessels and river barges, Baton Rouge is the fastest growing city in the state of Louisiana. The continuing development of the retail trade in the sunbelt helps explain Baton Rouge's growing economy. Like other cities in oil-producing states, Baton Rouge experienced some economic instability as a result of the drop in world oil prices in the mid-1980s. For this reason, Baton Rouge shifted away from reliance on industry to emphasize the business sector. In the Greater Baton Rouge area a natural resources basin exists, giving industries inexpensive access to the natural resources of gas, oil, water, timberland, sulphur, salt, and other raw materials.

Items and goods produced in the area include petrochemicals, rubber, plastic, wood, paper products, food, concrete, and scientific instruments.

Three major railroads furnish daily service, connecting Baton Rouge with key points throughout the country. A system of interstate highways permits access to and from Baton Rouge for more than fifty common motor carriers that ship a broad range of materials through the area. More than fifty barge and steamship companies offer services to the interior of the United States.

The principal convention facility in Baton Rouge is the Riverside Centroplex, which is located downtown on the bank of the Mississippi. The complex includes a twelve thousand-seat arena, seventy-two thousand square feet of exhibit space, eight meeting rooms (seating 25 to 12,000), a twenty-one hundred-seat theatre, and dining and banquet facilities. Many of the Baton Rouge metropolitan area's fifty-eight hotels and motels (with more than six thousand rooms combined) offer convention and meeting facilities.

Located off Interstate 110 approximately five miles north of downtown Baton Rouge, the Baton Rouge Metropolitan Airport is served by five major airlines and one regional carrier. The recently renovated facility provides direct service to twenty-four cities, with connecting service also available through major southern cities.

The major routes into Baton Rouge by car are Interstates 10, 12, and 55. Interstate 10, which runs across the continent from Jacksonville, Fla., to Los Angeles, California, gives the motorist a fine view of Baton Rouge. Interstate 55 connects the city with points as far north as Chicago, Illinois.

Population (1990)

Total Population and Growth Rate
1990: 528,264
1980: 494,151
1970: 375,628
Growth rate 1970–1990: 41%

Race and Hispanic Origin
White: 68.8%
Black: 29.6%
Asian/Pacific Islander: 1.1%
Native American: 0.2%
Hispanic origin: 1.4%
White not Hispanic: 67.8%

Age
Ages 18 to 20:   6%
Ages 21 to 24: 6.9%
Ages 25 to 44: 32.8%
Ages 45 to 54: 9.6%
Ages 55 to 59: 3.6%
Ages 60 to 64: 3.5%
Ages 65 plus: 8.9%

Educational Attainment (1990)
Percent having completed high school: 76.8%
Percent having completed college: 22.4%
Elementary and high school enrollment: 102,584

Federal Funds and Grants Received
Total received in 1989: $1,448,900,000
Funds received per capita: $2,700

Civilian Labor Force
1993 (April):   281,009
1992 average: 282,670
1991 average: 281,030
1990 average: 269,861

Unemployment
1993 (April):   6.3%
1992 average: 6.4%
1991 average: 6.2%
1990 average: 5.4%

Average Annual Pay
1988: $19,901
1987: $19,154
1985: $18,587

Per Capita Personal Income
1991: $23,319
1990: $23,002
1989: $22,733

Business Climate (1987)

Manufacturing
Number of establishments in 1987: 456
Shipments in 1987 ($1,000): $10,711,500
Employees in 1987: 19,200
Change in employment, 1982 to 1987: -24.7%
Average annual pay for manufacturing work in 1989: $36,057
Average annual pay for production work in 1987: $28,561

Wholesale Trade
Number of establishments in 1987: 994
Total sales in 1987 ($1,000): $3,248,200
Change in sales, 1982 to 1987: -41.1%

Retail Trade
Number of establishments in 1987: 2,939
Total sales in 1987 ($1,000): $3,248,200
Retail sales per household in 1987: $16,064
Average annual pay in 1989: $10,776

Service Industry
Selected receipts in 1987 ($1,000): $1,417,200
Average annual pay in 1989: $18,901

Housing
Total number of units in 1990: 212,078
Occupied units in 1990: 188,377
Owner-occupied units in 1990: 65.3%
1993 ACCRA average cost: $105,000

1993 ACCRA average rent for an apartment: $476

Chamber of Commerce

Greater Baton Rouge Chamber of Commerce, William Little, President, 564 Laurel St., PO Box 3217, Baton Rouge, LA 70821. 504-381-7125

Economic Development Office

Capital Regional Planning Commission, Don Neisler, Exec. Director, 333 N. 19th St. PO Box 3355, Raton Rouge, LA 70821. 504-383-5303

Economic Development Organizations

Council for a Better Louisiana, Harold Suire, President, PO Box 4308, Baton Rouge, LA 70821. 504-344-2225, FAX 504-338-9470

Major Businesses

Company	SIC	Telephone
Anco Insulations, Inc.	1742	(504) 924-7261
Armtek Corp.	2822	(504) 355-5655
Associated Grocers Inc.	5141	(504) 769-2020
Audubon Insurance Co.	6331	(504) 293-5900
Barnard and Burk Group, Inc.	8711	(504) 293-4000
Baton Rouge General Medical Center	8062	(504) 387-7000
City National Bank of Baton Rouge	6021	(504) 387-2151
Copolymer Rubber & Chemical	2822	(504) 355-5655
Dixie Electric Membership	4911	(504) 261-1221
Fifth Generation Systems	7371	(504) 291-7221
General Health, Inc.	8062	(504) 924-4324
Guaranty Broadcasting Corp.	4832	(504) 383-9999
Louisiana Health Services Indemnity	6324	(504) 295-3307
Maison Blanche, Inc.	5311	(504) 389-7000
MMR Constructors Inc.	1731	(504) 291-7000
MMR Corp	1731	(504) 293-2701
MMR Holding Corp.	1731	(504) 292-3500
The Newtron Group, Inc.	1731	(504) 927-8921
Our Lady Lake Regional Medical Center	8062	(504) 765-6565
Piccadilly Cafeterias, Inc.	5812	(504) 293-9440
Premier Bancorp, Inc.	6712	(504) 334-7000
Premier Bank National	6021	(504) 334-7000
Rubicon Inc.	2865	(504) 673-6141
Schuylkill Metals Corp	3341	(504) 775-3040
Stupp Corp.	3317	(504) 775-8800
Triad Chemical	2873	(504) 473-9231
Turner Investments, Ltd.	1541	(504) 356-1301
Union National Life Insurance	6311	(504) 927-3430
United Companies Financial	6311	(504) 924-6007
United Companies Life Insurance Co.	6411	(504) 924-6007

Colleges and Universities

Louisiana State University and Agricultural and Mechanical College, Baton Rouge

Southern University and Agricultural and Mechanical College, Baton Rouge

HOUMA–THIBODAUX, LA (MSA)

Geographic Profile

Land Area

2339.9 square miles

Counties and Parishes

Lafourche

Terrebonne

Ranking Highlights

    75 *out of 319 in total* **land area**
   158 *out of 319 in* **population growth,** *1970–1990*
   269 *out of 310 in having the lowest* **unemployment** *rate*
   231 *out of 310 in size of* **labor force**
   317 *out of 318 in the percentage of* **college graduates**
   283 *out of 292 in per capita personal* **income**
   230 *out of 319 in number of* **manufacturing establishments**
   311 *out of 318 in* **physicians** *per 1000 people*
   191 *out of 318 in* **hospital beds** *per 1000 people*
   N/A *out of 267 in fewest* **crimes** *per 1000 people*
   N/A *out of 266 in fewest* **violent crimes** *per 1000 people*
   309 *out of 319 in per capita* **federal funds and grants**

Quality of Life Indexes (Rate per 1000 population)

Crime rate in 1991:	N/A
Violent crime rate in 1991:	N/A
Physicians rate in 1992:	0.96
Hospital bed rate in 1991:	3.51

ACCRA Cost of Living Indexes

(First quarter 1993, average = 100)

Composite index:	N/A
Utilities index:	N/A
Housing index:	N/A

Population (1990)

Total Population and Growth Rate

1990: 182,842

1980: 176,876

1970: 144,990

Growth rate 1970–1990: 26%

Race and Hispanic Origin

White: 80.6%

Black: 14.6%

Asian/Pacific Islander: 0.7%

Native American: 3.7%

Hispanic origin: 1.4%

White not Hispanic: 79.6%

Age

Ages 18 to 20: 4.8%

Ages 21 to 24: 6.4%

Ages 25 to 44: 31.3%

Ages 45 to 54: 9.8%

Ages 55 to 59: 4%

Ages 60 to 64: 3.6%

Ages 65 plus: 8.8%

Educational Attainment (1990)

Percent having completed high school: 58.0%

Percent having completed college: 9.7%

Elementary and high school enrollment: 39,850

Federal Funds and Grants Received

Total received in 1989: $344,900,000

Funds received per capita: $1,883

Civilian Labor Force

1993 (April):   69,071

1992 average: 70,602

1991 average: 71,688

1990 average: 69,419

Unemployment

1993 (April): 7.8%

1992 average: 9.4%

1991 average: 6.6%

1990 average: 5.5%

Average Annual Pay

1988: $18,530

1987: $17,957

1985: $18,196

Per Capita Personal Income

1991: $13,152

1990: $12,577

1989: $11,614

Business Climate (1987)

Manufacturing

Number of establishments in 1987: 178

Shipments in 1987 ($1,000): $441,500

Employees in 1987: 3,700

Change in employment, 1982 to 1987: -50.0%

Average annual pay for manufacturing work in 1989: $22,115

Average annual pay for production work in 1987: $17,423

Wholesale Trade

Number of establishments in 1987: 340

Total sales in 1987 ($1,000): $578,900

Change in sales, 1982 to 1987: -32.0%

Retail Trade

Number of establishments in 1987: 1,104

Total sales in 1987 ($1,000): $578,900

Retail sales per household in 1987: $14,560

Average annual pay in 1989: $10,907

Service Industry

Selected receipts in 1987 ($1,000): $316,800

Average annual pay in 1989: $19,631

Housing

Total number of units in 1990: 66,748
Occupied units in 1990: 60,672
Owner-occupied units in 1990: 74.4%
1993 ACCRA average cost: N/A
1993 ACCRA average rent for an apartment: N/A

Chamber of Commerce

Houma-Terrebonne Chamber of Commerce, A.C. Fondren, Exec. Vice President, 1700 St. Charles St., PO Box 328, Houma, LA 70361. 504-876-5600

Economic Development Office

Terrebonne Economic Development District Commission, sharon T. Ropollo, President, 600 E. Main St. #301, First National Bank, Houma, LA 70360. 504-879-2421, FAX 504-857-3134

Major Businesses

Company	SIC	Telephone
A.M. & J.C. Dupont, Inc.	5331	(504) 851-1005
American Bancshares of Houma	6712	(504) 873-7357
First National Bankshares	6712	(504) 868-1660
Gemoco	3423	(504) 872-3266
Gibbons & Lefort Inc.	5172	(504) 447-3345
Premier Bank of Houma	6022	(504) 876-7800

Colleges and Universities

Nicholls State University, Thibodaux

LAFAYETTE, LA (MSA)

Geographic Profile

Land Area
1009.8 square miles

Counties and Parishes
Lafayette
St. Martin

Ranking Highlights

201 *out of 319 in total* **land area**
 84 *out of 319 in* **population growth,** *1970–1990*
174 *out of 310 in having the lowest* **unemployment** *rate*
180 *out of 310 in size of* **labor force**
153 *out of 318 in the percentage of* **college graduates**
275 *out of 292 in per capita personal* **income**
212 *out of 319 in number of* **manufacturing establishments**
183 *out of 318 in* **physicians** *per 1000 people*
 76 *out of 318 in* **hospital beds** *per 1000 people*
 94 *out of 267 in fewest* **crimes** *per 1000 people*
128 *out of 266 in fewest* **violent crimes** *per 1000 people*
312 *out of 319 in per capita* **federal funds and grants**

Quality of Life Indexes (Rate per 1000 population)

Crime rate in 1991:	53.4
Violent crime rate in 1991:	6.1
Physicians rate in 1992:	1.72
Hospital bed rate in 1991:	5.02

ACCRA Cost of Living Indexes

(First quarter 1993, average = 100)
Composite index: N/A
Utilities index: N/A
Housing index: N/A

Population (1990)

Total Population and Growth Rate
1990: 208,740
1980: 190,231
1970: 144,096
Growth rate 1970–1990: 45%

Race and Hispanic Origin
White: 73.8%
Black: 24.6%
Asian/Pacific Islander: 0.9%
Native American: 0.2%
Hispanic origin: 1.5%
White not Hispanic: 72.8%

Age
Ages 18 to 20: 5.2%
Ages 21 to 24: 6.6%
Ages 25 to 44: 33.4%
Ages 45 to 54: 9.1%
Ages 55 to 59: 3.9%

Ages 60 to 64: 3.5%
Ages 65 plus: 8.5%

Educational Attainment (1990)
Percent having completed high school: 69.3%
Percent having completed college: 19.2%
Elementary and high school enrollment: 41,796

Federal Funds and Grants Received
Total received in 1989: $373,900,000
Funds received per capita: $1,783

Civilian Labor Force
1993 (April): 106,003
1992 average: 108,523
1991 average: 111,075
1990 average: 104,643

Unemployment
1993 (April): 5.8%
1992 average: 7.1%
1991 average: 5.4%
1990 average: 4.7%

Average Annual Pay
1988: $20,223
1987: $19,397
1985: $19,655

Per Capita Personal Income
1991: $14,215
1990: $13,566
1989: $12,306

Business Climate (1987)
Manufacturing
Number of establishments in 1987: 208
Shipments in 1987 ($1,000): $635,800
Employees in 1987: 5,900
Change in employment, 1982 to 1987: -24.4%
Average annual pay for manufacturing work in 1989: $18,725
Average annual pay for production work in 1987: $16,907

Wholesale Trade
Number of establishments in 1987: 555
Total sales in 1987 ($1,000): $1,357,300
Change in sales, 1982 to 1987: -40.5%

Retail Trade
Number of establishments in 1987: 1,345
Total sales in 1987 ($1,000): $1,357,300
Retail sales per household in 1987: $16,442
Average annual pay in 1989: $10,501

Service Industry
Selected receipts in 1987 ($1,000): $710,400
Average annual pay in 1989: $20,740

Housing
Total number of units in 1990: 85,023

Occupied units in 1990: 75,045
Owner-occupied units in 1990: 64.9%
1993 ACCRA average cost: N/A
1993 ACCRA average rent for an apartment: N/A

Chamber of Commerce
Greater Lafayette Chamber of Commerce, Robert M. Guidry, Exec. Vice President, 804 E. St. Mary Blvd., PO Box 51307, Lafayette, LA 70503. 318-233-2705

Economic Development Office
Lafayette Economic Development Authority, Curtis Hoglan, President, 315 Audobon Blvd., PO Drawer 51439, Lafayette, LA 70505-1439. 318-234-2986, FAX 318-234-3009

Major Businesses

Company	SIC	Telephone
Abdalla's Lafayette, Inc.	5651	(318) 261-2418
Ace Transportation Inc.	4213	(318) 837-4567
Advanced Environmental Technical	1389	(318) 232-2000
Aluminum & Stainless Inc.	5051	(318) 837-4381
Argosy Offshore Ltd.	4449	(318) 235-1296
Estorge Drug Co. Inc.	5122	(318) 234-5174
Hamilton Medical Center	8062	(318) 981-2949
Hub City Ford Inc.	5511	(318) 233-4500
Lafayette Bldg. Association	6035	(318) 232-4631
Lafayette General Hospital	8062	(318) 261-7375
Louisiana Energy Power Authority	4911	(318) 269-4046
Macro Oil Co. Inc.	5172	(318) 234-4583
Mallard Bay Drilling Inc.	1381	(318) 233-4922
Norman Offshore Pipelines	1623	(318) 237-1444
Offshore Logistics, Inc.	4522	(318) 233-1221
Oilfield Service Corp. America	5169	(318) 837-6047
Our Lady of Lourdes Regio	8062	(318) 234-7381
Service Chevrolet Inc.	5511	(318) 234-9411
Southwest Louisiana Electric Membership	4911	(318) 237-5112
Woodson Construction Co.	1623	(318) 233-8224

Colleges and Universities
University of Southwestern Louisiana, Lafayette

LAKE CHARLES, LA (MSA)

Geographic Profile

Land Area

1071.2 square miles

Counties and Parishes

Calcasieu

Ranking Highlights

185 *out of 319 in total* **land area**

198 *out of 319 in* **population growth,** *1970–1990*

265 *out of 310 in having the lowest* **unemployment** *rate*

204 *out of 310 in size of* **labor force**

242 *out of 318 in the percentage of* **college graduates**

241 *out of 292 in per capita personal* **income**

273 *out of 319 in number of* **manufacturing establishments**

243 *out of 318 in* **physicians** *per 1000 people*

 75 *out of 318 in* **hospital beds** *per 1000 people*

N/A *out of 267 in fewest* **crimes** *per 1000 people*

N/A *out of 266 in fewest* **violent crimes** *per 1000 people*

181 *out of 319 in per capita* **federal funds and grants**

Quality of Life Indexes (Rate per 1000 population)

Crime rate in 1991:	N/A
Violent crime rate in 1991:	N/A
Physicians rate in 1992:	1.42
Hospital bed rate in 1991:	5.03

ACCRA Cost of Living Indexes

(First quarter 1993, average = 100)

Composite index:	95.6
Utilities index:	103.3
Housing index:	81.4

Overview

Located in the southwest part of the state, Lake Charles is adjacent to Interstate 10. Its industrial base has a concentration of petrochemical companies. The Port of Lake Charles, the twelfth largest seaport in the United States, is located here with aircargo and aircraft-related industries located at Chennault Industrial Airpark. The area is served by three railroads and thirteen freight carriers. Scheduled air service is through Lake Charles Regional Airport.

Population (1990)

Total Population and Growth Rate

1990: 168,134

1980: 167,223

1970: 145,415

Growth rate 1970–1990: 16%

Race and Hispanic Origin

White: 76.2%

Black: 22.9%

Asian/Pacific Islander: 0.4%

Native American: 0.2%

Hispanic origin: 1.1%

White not Hispanic: 75.5%

Age

Ages 18 to 20: 4.6%

Ages 21 to 24: 5.5%

Ages 25 to 44: 30.9%

Ages 45 to 54: 10%

Ages 55 to 59: 4.5%

Ages 60 to 64: 4.4%

Ages 65 plus: 10.8%

Educational Attainment (1990)

Percent having completed high school: 70.3%

Percent having completed college: 14.7%

Elementary and high school enrollment: 34,221

Federal Funds and Grants Received

Total received in 1989: $510,900,000

Funds received per capita: $2,964

Civilian Labor Force

1993 (April):   81,934

1992 average: 83,767

1991 average: 83,552

1990 average: 78,838

Unemployment

1993 (April):   7.9%

1992 average: 9.1%

1991 average: 7.8%

1990 average: 6.4%

Average Annual Pay

1988: $20,734

1987: $20,180

1985: $19,149

Per Capita Personal Income

1991: $15,363

1990: $14,613

1989: $13,391

Business Climate (1987)

Manufacturing

Number of establishments in 1987: 121

Shipments in 1987 ($1,000): $5,679,300

Employees in 1987: 9,500

Change in employment, 1982 to 1987: -12.0%

Average annual pay for manufacturing work in 1989: $34,769

Average annual pay for production work in 1987: $30,742

Wholesale Trade

Number of establishments in 1987: 295

Total sales in 1987 ($1,000): $1,585,600

Change in sales, 1982 to 1987: 130.1%

Retail Trade

Number of establishments in 1987: 966

Total sales in 1987 ($1,000): $1,585,600

Retail sales per household in 1987: $14,651

Average annual pay in 1989: $10,082

Service Industry

Selected receipts in 1987 ($1,000): $366,500

Average annual pay in 1989: $17,965

Housing

Total number of units in 1990: 66,426

Occupied units in 1990: 60,328

Owner-occupied units in 1990: 70.4%

1993 ACCRA average cost: $90,250

1993 ACCRA average rent for an apartment: $425

Chamber of Commerce

Southwest Louisiana Chamber of Commerce, Joseph W. Cironi, President, 900 N. Lakeshore Dr., PO Box 3109, Lake Charles, LA 70602. 318-433-3632

Economic Development Office

The Southwest Louisana Foundation, C. Thomas Robinson, Vice President of Econ. Dev., 900 N. Lakeshore Dr. PO Box 3109, Lake Charles, LA 70602. 318-433-3632, FAX 318-436-3727

Major Businesses

Company	SIC	Telephone
Calcasieu-Marine National	6021	(318) 439-4541
Central Crude, Inc.	4213	(318) 436-1000
Davidson Louisiana, Inc.	5031	(318) 439-8393
Farmer's Rice Milling Co.	2044	(318) 433-6355
First Federal Savings & Loan	6035	(318) 433-3611
First National Bank of Lake Charles	6021	(318) 477-7630
Lake Charles Nissan Inc.	5511	(318) 477-8038
Lake Chrales Habor Terminal District	6512	(318) 439-3661
Lakeside Bancshares Inc.	6021	(318) 433-2265
Lakeside National Bank of Lake Charles	6021	(318) 433-2265
Louisiana Savings Association	6035	(318) 436-7283
Magnolia Life Insurance Co.	6311	(318) 433-1405
F. Miller & Sons Inc.	1542	(318) 439-4552
Miller Livestock Markets	5154	(318) 786-2995
Premier National Bank of Lake Charles	6021	(318) 436-0531
Pumpelly Oil Inc.	5172	(318) 436-3361
Southwest Louisiana Hospital Association	8062	(318) 494-3000
St. Patrick Hospital Inc.	8062	(318) 491-7730
Stine Inc.	5211	(318) 527-0121
West Cameron Hospital	8062	(318) 527-7035

Colleges and Universities

McNeese State University, Lake Charles

MONROE, LA (MSA)

Geographic Profile

Land Area

611.0 square miles

Counties and Parishes

Ouachita

Ranking Highlights

270 *out of 319 in* total land area

167 *out of 319 in* population growth, *1970–1990*

157 *out of 310 in having the lowest* unemployment *rate*

232 *out of 310 in size of* labor force

161 *out of 318 in the percentage of* college graduates

271 *out of 292 in per capita personal* income

238 *out of 319 in number of* manufacturing establishments

180 *out of 318 in* physicians *per 1000 people*

10 *out of 318 in* hospital beds *per 1000 people*

204 *out of 267 in fewest* crimes *per 1000 people*

201 *out of 266 in fewest* violent crimes *per 1000 people*

286 *out of 319 in per capita* federal funds and grants

Quality of Life Indexes (Rate per 1000 population)

Crime rate in 1991: 72.5

Violent crime rate in 1991: 8.9

Physicians rate in 1992: 1.73

Hospital bed rate in 1991: 7.34

ACCRA Cost of Living Indexes

(First quarter 1993, average = 100)

Composite index: 97.8

Utilities index: 130.7

Housing index: 80.2

Population (1990)

Total Population and Growth Rate

1990: 142,191

1980: 139,241

1970: 115,387

Growth rate 1970–1990: 23%

Race and Hispanic Origin

White: 68.1%

Black: 31.0%

Asian/Pacific Islander: 0.5%

Native American: 0.2%

Hispanic origin: 0.8%

White not Hispanic: 67.5%

Age

Ages 18 to 20: 5.8%

Ages 21 to 24: 6.8%

Ages 25 to 44: 29.3%

Ages 45 to 54: 9.4%

Ages 55 to 59: 4.1%

Ages 60 to 64:   4%
Ages 65 plus: 11.3%

Educational Attainment (1990)
Percent having completed high school: 71.6%
Percent having completed college: 18.9%
Elementary and high school enrollment: 28,271

Federal Funds and Grants Received
Total received in 1989: $317,500,000
Funds received per capita: $2,205

Civilian Labor Force
1993 (April):   68,833
1992 average: 70,471
1991 average: 71,299
1990 average: 68,572

Unemployment
1993 (April):   7.1%
1992 average: 6.9%
1991 average: 6.4%
1990 average: 5.8%

Average Annual Pay
1988: $18,403
1987: $17,625
1985: $16,777

Per Capita Personal Income
1991: $14,396
1990: $13,662
1989: $12,820

Business Climate (1987)
Manufacturing
Number of establishments in 1987: 161
Shipments in 1987 ($1,000): $1,234,000
Employees in 1987: 7,100
Change in employment, 1982 to 1987: -4.1%
Average annual pay for manufacturing work in 1989: $28,925
Average annual pay for production work in 1987: $25,313

Wholesale Trade
Number of establishments in 1987: 333
Total sales in 1987 ($1,000): $1,101,100
Change in sales, 1982 to 1987: 19.6%

Retail Trade
Number of establishments in 1987: 1,012
Total sales in 1987 ($1,000): $1,101,100
Retail sales per household in 1987: $17,603
Average annual pay in 1989: $10,739

Service Industry
Selected receipts in 1987 ($1,000): $380,900
Average annual pay in 1989: $18,983

Housing
Total number of units in 1990: 56,300

Occupied units in 1990: 50,518
Owner-occupied units in 1990: 64.8%
1993 ACCRA average cost: $87,040
1993 ACCRA average rent for an apartment: $442

Chamber of Commerce
Monroe Chamber of Commerce, Robert D. Daily, President, 300 Washington St. #104, Monroe, LA 71201. 318-323-3461

Economic Development Office
North Delta Regional Planning and Development District, David Creed, Exec. Director, 2115 Justice St., Monroe, LA 71201. 318-387-2572, FAX 318-387-9054

Economic Development Organizations
Quachita Enterprise Corp., Don Giffen, President, 141 DeSiard St. #511, Monroe, LA 71201. 318-837-0787, FAX 318-387-8529

Major Businesses

Company	SIC	Telephone
Allied Building Stores Inc.	5031	(318) 343-7200
Breck Construction Co. Inc.	1542	(318) 387-3300
Central Bank	6022	(318) 362-8500
Central Oil & Supply Corp.	5171	(318) 388-2602
Century Telephone Enterprise	4813	(318) 388-9500
Lee Edwards, Inc.	5511	(318) 325-4681
Evangeline Telephone Co. Inc.	4813	(318) 388-9636
Evans Oil Co. Inc.	5171	(318) 345-1502
First American Bank & Trust	6022	(318) 362-8200
First National Bank of West Monroe	6021	(318) 387-8330
Glenwood Regional Medical Center	8062	(318) 329-4200
HCA Health Service of Louisiana	8062	(318) 388-1946
Interface, Inc.	1711	(318) 388-2341
James Machine Works Inc.	3443	(318) 322-6104
Long Distance Savers Inc.	4813	(318) 323-8600
Manville Forest Products	2621	(318) 362-2000
Merchants Dutch Express Inc.	4213	(318) 322-2888
Monroe Iron & Metal Co., Inc.	5093	(318) 325-4636
Northeast Louisiana Wholesale Oil & Gas	5172	(318) 322-3195
Scott-Hixson Ford Inc.	5511	(318) 388-3300
St. Francis Medical Center	8062	(318) 362-4112
Troy and Nichols Inc.	6162	(318) 388-3900

Colleges and Universities
Northeast Louisiana University, Monroe

NEW ORLEANS, LA (MSA)

Geographic Profile

Land Area

2308.8 square miles

Counties and Parishes

Jefferson

Orleans

St. Bernard

St. Charles

St. John the Baptist

St. Tammany

Additional Cities/Towns within Area

Slidell

Ranking Highlights

76 *out of 319 in total* **land area**

213 *out of 319 in* **population growth,** *1970–1990*

166 *out of 310 in having the lowest* **unemployment** *rate*

45 *out of 310 in size of* **labor force**

143 *out of 318 in the percentage of* **college graduates**

162 *out of 292 in per capita personal* **income**

71 *out of 319 in number of* **manufacturing establishments**

24 *out of 318 in* **physicians** *per 1000 people*

65 *out of 318 in* **hospital beds** *per 1000 people*

249 *out of 267 in fewest* **crimes** *per 1000 people*

260 *out of 266 in fewest* **violent crimes** *per 1000 people*

89 *out of 319 in per capita* **federal funds and grants**

Quality of Life Indexes (Rate per 1000 population)

Crime rate in 1991:	88.4
Violent crime rate in 1991:	14.1
Physicians rate in 1992:	3.17
Hospital bed rate in 1991:	5.23

ACCRA Cost of Living Indexes

(First quarter 1993, average = 100)

Composite index:	95.6
Utilities index:	125.9
Housing index:	82.9

Overview

The New Orleans economy is dominated by four major sectors: petroleum, the port, tourism, and construction. More than one thousand products are manufactured in the city, ranging from processed foods and space hardware to a wide range of petrochemicals. Oil and natural gas are main area resources, vying with port activity as the top industry. Boasting attractions such as its magnetic French Quarter and the Mardi Gras, America's leading festival, New Orleans has a history of solid tourist trade. In a city with more than seven million visitors annually, the hospitality business supplies jobs in the service sector such as accommodations and restaurants. In the 1980s, more than $300 million was invested in projects such as new convention facilities, the Riverwalk, and shopping malls. The projects have promoted additional tourism, which some predict will outrank the city's other industries in the future.

New Orleans's largest private employer is the Avondale Ship Yards, where workers build and repair vessels for the Navy and merchant fleets. Martin Marietta, manufacturers of fuel tanks and other parts for NASA space projects, uses a large work force at its New Orleans operations. In recent years the economy has diversified into such varied fields as health services, aerospace and research and technology.

The Port of New Orleans, the largest inland port in the United States, is a hub of national and international transportation. Seventy percent of the nation's waterways drain through the Port of New Orleans, which operates a Foreign Trade Zone, where foreign and domestic goods can be stored and processed without being subject to U.S. customs and regulations. Commercial vessels and ship tonnage entering and leaving the area make the Port of New Orleans one of the world's busiest harbors, with imports and exports serving the iron and steel, manufacturing, agricultural, and petrochemical industries. Port-related activities involve shipbuilding and repair, grain elevators, coal terminals, warehouses, and distribution facilities, as well as steamship agencies, importers and exporters, international banks, transportation services, and foreign consular or trade offices. The Port is also a departure point for a variety of pleasure cruises to Caribbean destinations and for upriver riverboat and paddlewheel cruises.

More than ten thousand hotel guest rooms are available downtown, and close to fifteen thousand more are found in the metropolitan area. The New Orleans Convention Center, located on the Mississippi River in the heart of the business district and within easy walking distance of the French Quarter, offers the largest single exhibit space. The Convention Center offers more than seven hundred thousand square feet of facilities with more than 100 meeting rooms.

The New Orleans International Airport, which is located west of the city in Kenner, provides full service on more than fifteen major carriers to every part of the United States with flights to and from South and Central America. As of 1992, 4,145 domestic flights and one hundred international flights originated from the airport monthly. A $40 million expansion begins its third phase in 1993. Private planes and corporate and charter flights often prefer to use Lakefront Airport, on the Lake Pontchartrain coast near the central business district. Interstate Highways I-59, I-55, and U.S. 61 approach New Orleans from the north, while I-10 and U.S. 90 carry east-west drivers into the city. Auto ferries cross the Mississippi at various locations. Overnight AMTRAK trains from and to Chicago, Washington, D.C., and western locales arrive at and depart from the Union Passenger Railroad Terminal.

Population (1990)

Total Population and Growth Rate

1990: 1,238,816

1980: 1,256,668

1970: 1,099,833

Growth rate 1970–1990: 13%

Race and Hispanic Origin

White: 62.2%

Black: 34.7%

Asian/Pacific Islander: 1.7%

Native American: 0.3%

Hispanic origin: 4.3%

White not Hispanic: 59.3%

Age

Ages 18 to 20: 4.5%

Ages 21 to 24: 5.8%

Ages 25 to 44: 32.7%

Ages 45 to 54: 9.8%

Ages 55 to 59: 4%

Ages 60 to 64: 4.2%

Ages 65 plus: 11%

Educational Attainment (1990)

Percent having completed high school: 72.3%

Percent having completed college: 19.7%

Elementary and high school enrollment: 237,365

Federal Funds and Grants Received

Total received in 1989: $4,824,400,000

Funds received per capita: $3,691

Civilian Labor Force

1993 (April): 569,854

1992 average: 578,455

1991 average: 586,342

1990 average: 575,957

Unemployment

1993 (April): 6.9%

1992 average: 7.0%

1991 average: 6.1%

1990 average: 5.7%

Average Annual Pay

1988: $20,389

1987: $19,788

1985: $19,030

Per Capita Personal Income

1991: $16,959

1990: $16,314

1989: $15,181

Business Climate (1987)

Manufacturing

Number of establishments in 1987: 937

Shipments in 1987 ($1,000): $13,466,000

Employees in 1987: 43,100

Change in employment, 1982 to 1987: -21.8%

Average annual pay for manufacturing work in 1989: $27,609

Average annual pay for production work in 1987: $24,766

Wholesale Trade

Number of establishments in 1987: 2,461

Total sales in 1987 ($1,000): $15,342,500

Change in sales, 1982 to 1987: -5.7%

Retail Trade

Number of establishments in 1987: 7,220

Total sales in 1987 ($1,000): $15,342,500

Retail sales per household in 1987: $14,923

Average annual pay in 1989: $11,148

Service Industry

Selected receipts in 1987 ($1,000): $4,573,700

Average annual pay in 1989: $18,933

Office Real Estate (1992)

Office space inventory: 20,373,205 square feet

Average class A Central Business District rental range per sq. ft: $16.00

Vacancy Rates

All areas: 23.6%

Vacancy Rates in Central Business District

Class A space: 21.6%

Class B space: 36.5%

Vacancy Rates Outside Central Business District

Class A space: 11.7%

Class B space: 10.7%

Housing

Total number of units in 1990: 524,056

Occupied units in 1990: 455,178

Owner-occupied units in 1990: 58.0%

1993 ACCRA average cost: $88,000

1993 ACCRA average rent for an apartment: $508

Chamber of Commerce

New Orleans & River Regional Chamber of Commerce, David H. Jones, President, 301 Camp St., PO Box 30240, New Orleans, LA 70190. 504-527-6900

Economic Development Office

Regional Planning Commission, John LeBourgeois, Exec. Director, 333 Saint Charles Ave. Suite 1100, New Orleans, LA 70130. 504-568-6611, FAX 504-568-6643

Major Businesses

Company	SIC	Telephone
Avondale Industries Inc.	3731	(504) 436-2121
Babcock & Wilcox Co.	3511	(504) 587-5400
CNG Producing Co.	1382	(504) 593-7000
Conco Holding Co.	5141	(504) 834-4082
Consolidated Companies	5141	(504) 834-4082

Major Businesses (Continued)

Company	SIC	Telephone
Entergy Corp.	4911	(504) 529-5262
First Commerce Corp.	6021	(504) 561-1371
Freeport Indonesia Inc.	1021	(504) 582-4000
Freeport McMoran Rescue	2874	(504) 582-4000
Freeport Minerals Co.	1479	(504) 582-4000
Freeport-McMoran Copper Co.	1021	(504) 582-4000
Freeport-McMoran Inc.	1479	(504) 582-4000
Freeprt-McMoran Energy Partners	1382	(504) 582-4000
Hibernia Corp.	6021	(504) 586-5552
Hibernia National Bank in New Orleans	6021	(504) 586-5552
International Shipholding	4412	(504) 529-5461
K & B, Inc.	5912	(504) 586-1234
Latter & Blum Inc.	6531	(504) 525-1311
Louisana Land Exploration	1311	(504) 566-6500
Louisiana Power & Light Co.	4911	(504) 595-3100
Lykes Bros Steamship Co.	4412	(504) 523-6611
McDermott Inc.	3511	(504) 587-4411
McDermott International	3511	(504) 587-5400
New Orleans Public Service	4931	(504) 595-3100
Oak Tree Savings Bank	6036	(504) 588-9313
Ocean Drilling Exploration Co.	1311	(504) 561-2811
Pan American Life Insurance	6311	(504) 566-1300
Wm. B. Reily & Co.	2095	(504) 524-6131
Schwegmann Giant Super Market	5411	(504) 947-9921

Colleges and Universities

Delgado Community College, New Orleans
Dillard University, New Orleans
Grantham College of Engineering, Slidell
Louisiana State University Medical Center, New Orleans
Loyola University, New Orleans, New Orleans
Our Lady of Holy Cross College, New Orleans
Phillips Junior College, New Orleans
Southern University At New Orleans, New Orleans
Tulane University, New Orleans
University of New Orleans, New Orleans

SHREVEPORT, LA (MSA)

Geographic Profile

Land Area
1720.6 square miles

Counties and Parishes
Bossier
Caddo

Additional Cities/Towns within Area
Bossier City

Ranking Highlights

110 *out of 319 in total* **land area**
212 *out of 319 in* **population growth,** *1970–1990*
181 *out of 310 in having the lowest* **unemployment** *rate*
136 *out of 310 in size of* **labor force**
184 *out of 318 in the percentage of* **college graduates**
221 *out of 292 in per capita personal* **income**
152 *out of 319 in number of* **manufacturing establishments**
36 *out of 318 in* **physicians** *per 1000 people*
28 *out of 318 in* **hospital beds** *per 1000 people*
228 *out of 267 in fewest* **crimes** *per 1000 people*
209 *out of 266 in fewest* **violent crimes** *per 1000 people*
91 *out of 319 in per capita* **federal funds and grants**

Quality of Life Indexes (Rate per 1000 population)

Crime rate in 1991:   79.7
Violent crime rate in 1991:   9.3
Physicians rate in 1992:   2.87
Hospital bed rate in 1991:   6.08

ACCRA Cost of Living Indexes

(First quarter 1993, average = 100)
Composite index: N/A
Utilities index: N/A
Housing index: N/A

Population (1990)

Total Population and Growth Rate
1990: 334,341
1980: 333,158
1970: 296,061
Growth rate 1970–1990: 13%

Race and Hispanic Origin
White: 63.9%
Black: 35.0%
Asian/Pacific Islander: 0.6%
Native American: 0.3%
Hispanic origin: 1.3%
White not Hispanic: 63.0%

Age
Ages 18 to 20: 4.4%
Ages 21 to 24: 5.4%
Ages 25 to 44: 30.7%

Ages 45 to 54: 9.9%
Ages 55 to 59: 4.4%
Ages 60 to 64: 4.3%
Ages 65 plus: 12.2%

Educational Attainment (1990)

Percent having completed high school: 74.8%
Percent having completed college: 17.5%
Elementary and high school enrollment: 66,082

Federal Funds and Grants Received

Total received in 1989: $1,308,900,000
Funds received per capita: $3,645

Civilian Labor Force

1993 (April): 156,817
1992 average: 157,887
1991 average: 156,381
1990 average: 154,026

Unemployment

1993 (April): 6.3%
1992 average: 7.2%
1991 average: 7.2%
1990 average: 6.7%

Average Annual Pay

1988: $19,292
1987: $18,694
1985: $17,864

Per Capita Personal Income

1991: $15,897
1990: $15,050
1989: $14,226

Business Climate (1987)

Manufacturing

Number of establishments in 1987: 344
Shipments in 1987 ($1,000): $4,556,600
Employees in 1987: 19,300
Change in employment, 1982 to 1987: -20.2%
Average annual pay for manufacturing work in 1989: $27,005
Average annual pay for production work in 1987: $24,317

Wholesale Trade

Number of establishments in 1987: 759
Total sales in 1987 ($1,000): $2,362,400
Change in sales, 1982 to 1987: -31.0%

Retail Trade

Number of establishments in 1987: 2,105
Total sales in 1987 ($1,000): $2,362,400
Retail sales per household in 1987: $14,830
Average annual pay in 1989: $11,085

Service Industry

Selected receipts in 1987 ($1,000): $888,500
Average annual pay in 1989: $17,801

Office Real Estate (1992)

Office space inventory: 3,753,205 square feet
Average class A Central Business District rental range per sq. ft: $11.00

Vacancy Rates

All areas: 24.2%

Vacancy Rates in Central Business District

Class A space: 21.8%
Class B space: 17.5%

Vacancy Rates Outside Central Business District

Class A space: 21.4%
Class B space: 35.9%

Housing

Total number of units in 1990: 142,609
Occupied units in 1990: 123,966
Owner-occupied units in 1990: 65.0%
1993 ACCRA average cost: N/A
1993 ACCRA average rent for an apartment: N/A

Chamber of Commerce

Shreveport Chamber of Commerce, Stuart A. Bach, Exec. Vice President, 400 Edwards St., PO Box 20074, Shreveport, LA 71120. 318-677-2500

Economic Development Office

Greater Shreveport Economic Development Foundation, Michael Philpot, Manager, 400 Edwards St., PO Box 20074, Shreveport, LA 71120. 318-677-2500, FAX 318-677-2541

Economic Development Organizations

Greater Bossier Economic Development Foundation, Don Pierson, Exec. Director, 710. Benton Rd., Bossier City, LA 71111. 318-746-0252

The Coordinator and Development Corporation, M.D. LeComte, President, 5210 Hollywood Ave., PO Box 37005, Shreveport, LA 71133. 318-632-2022, FAX 318-632-2099

Major Businesses

Company	SIC	Telephone
Aeropres Corp.	5172	(318) 221-6282
Allright Shreveport Inc.	7521	(318) 425-7502
Arkla Exploration Co.	1311	(318) 429-2841
Arkla Inc.	4922	(318) 429-2700
Atlas Processing Co.	2911	(318) 636-2711
Beall Ladymon Corp.	5651	(318) 869-3121
Commercial National Bank	6021	(318) 429-1000
Courtesy Chevrolet Inc.	5511	(318) 425-3471
Crystal Oil Co.	1311	(318) 222-7791
Bill Hanna Ford Inc.	5511	(318) 222-1131
Harrison Co. Inc.	5194	(318) 221-4191
Kenyan Enterprises Inc.	5411	(318) 539-9116
Melton Truck Lines Inc.	4213	(318) 222-7661

Major Businesses (Continued)

Company	SIC	Telephone
Netherton Co. Inc.	1629	(318) 635-9721
Pel State Oil Co. Inc.	5541	(318) 868-4458
Peters Ward Investment Corp.	5541	(318) 868-4458
Pioneer Bancshares Corp.	6022	(318) 429-6000
Rountree Olds-Cadillac	5511	(318) 798-7150
Sisters of Charity	8062	(318) 227-4500
Southwestern Electric Power Co.	4911	(318) 222-2141
Specialty Oil Co. Inc.	5172	(318) 687-8000
V.I.P., Inc.	3732	(318) 375-3241
Westland Oil Co. Inc.	2992	(318) 688-1300
J. Williams Shreveport Lincoln Mercury	5511	(318) 861-3561
Willis-Knighton Medical Center	8062	(318) 632-4600
Wray Ford Inc.	5511	(318) 686-7300

Colleges and Universities

Centenary College of Louisiana, Shreveport

Louisiana State University in Shreveport, Shreveport

Southern University, Shreveport-Bossier City Campus, Shreveport

Bossier Parish Community College, Bossier City

MAINE

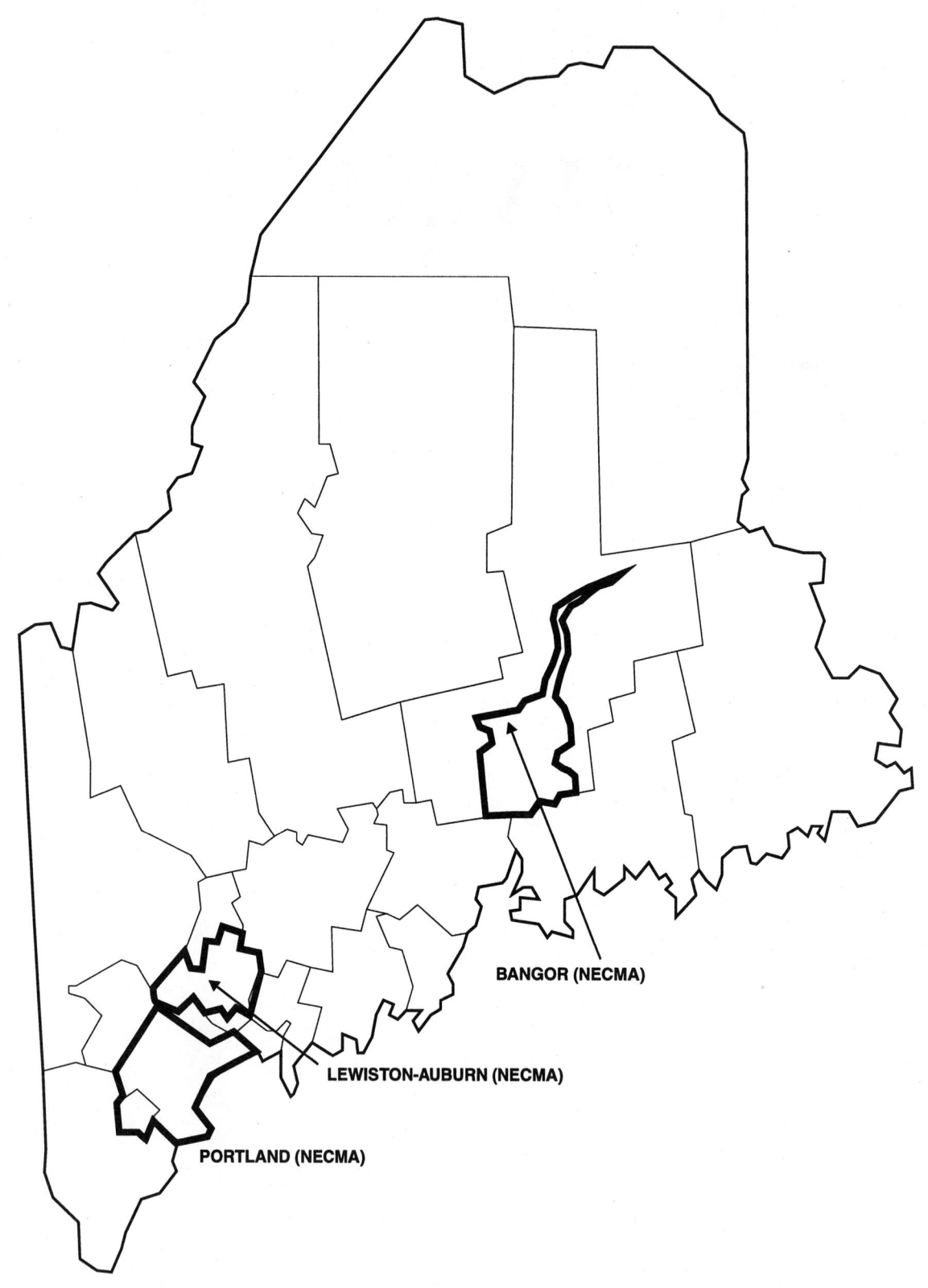

BANGOR (NECMA)

LEWISTON-AUBURN (NECMA)

PORTLAND (NECMA)

MAINE

Population
1990: 1,227,928
1980: 1,124,660

Age
Ages 18 to 20: 56,232
Ages 21 to 24: 67,540
Ages 25 to 44: 398,580
Ages 45 to 54: 124,751
Ages 55 to 59: 54,216
Ages 60 to 64: 54,234
Median age: 33.9

Race
White: 1,208,360
Black: 5,138
Asian/Pacific Islander: 6,683
Native American: 5,998
Hispanic origin: 6,829

Households
Total: 465,312
Persons per household: 2.56

Sex
Male: 597,850
Female: 630,078

Population Migration
Domestic migration: 71,000
International migration: 1,000

Projection of the Population in 1995
Total: 1,271,000
18 to 64: 780,000

Civilian Labor Force
1993: 649,800
1992: 647,600
1991: 648,500
1990: 619,700

Manufacturing
1995 Projection: 114,500
1992: 92,300
1991: 95,300
1990: 99,400
1989: 106,200

Services
1995 Projection: 193,100

1992: 129,400
1991: 124,700
1990: 126,600
1989: 123,400

Wholesale and Retail Trade
1995 Projection: 167,900
1992: 128,000
1991: 127,000
1990: 133,400
1989: 142,700

Unemployment Rate
1993: 9.2%
1992: 8.8%
1991: 8.0%
1990: 5.2%

Employer Unemployment Contributions
Contribution Rate
1992: 3.15%
1991: 2.40%
1990: 2.31%

Average Weekly Benefit
1992: $165.54
1991: $164.72
1990: $159.55

Gross State Product (Million $)
1989: $23,474
1988: $22,129
1987: $19,898
1979: $9,554
Growth rate, 1979 to 1989: 145.7%

Capital Expenditures of Manufacturing Industries
1990: $705,300,000
1989: $954,900,000
1988: $623,300,000
1987: $539,400,000

State Tax Rates
Individual income: Range from 2.1% ($4,150 or less) to 9.89% (above $37,500).

Corporate income: Range from 3.5% ($25,000 or less) to 8.93% (above $250,000), with 10% surtax imposed.

General property: Rates fixed locally, based on just value of real and personal property. Assessed to actual value at 33.33% to 75%.

General sales: 6%

Gasoline: 17¢ per gallon

Income

Median income for a 4 person family: $38,336

Personal per Capita Income

1992: $18,226

1991: $17,442

1990: $17,125

Disposable per Capita Income

1992: $16,298

1991: $15,550

1990: $15,119

Private Employment Weekly Wages

Average

1989: $361

1988: $346

1987: $346

Manufacturing

1989: $329

1988: $428

1987: $409

Services

1989: $332

1988: $314

1987: $292

Wholesale

1989: $475

1988: $454

1987: $424

Retail

1989: $221

1988: $215

1987: $205

Highway Statistics

Total Highway Miles

1990: 22,389

1989: 22,240

1988: 21,966

Federal Highway Aid

1991: $60,491,000

1990: $60,132,000

1989: $60,876,000

Electricity

Average Cost per Kilowatt Hour

1990: 7.64¢

1989: 7.01¢

1988: 6.70¢

Housing (1990)

Owner occupied units: 327,888

Median house value: $87,400

Renter occupied units: 137,424

Median rent: $358

Total vacant units: 121,733

Homeowner vacancy rate: 1.8%

Rental vacancy rate: 8.4%

State Business Incentives and Assistance

Financial and Business Assistance

The Finance Authority of Maine (FAME) operates all state business financing programs. It offers a wide array of financial assistance programs for state business which include:

Commercial Loan Insurance Program. Designed to promote economic development by providing business borrowers access to capital that would otherwise be denied by a lender due to an unacceptable level of credit risk. FAME will insure up to 90% (not to exceed $7,000,000 for most projects) of a commercial loan. This program works in cooperation with local lending institutions and bond underwriters.

Small Business Loan Insurance Program. designed to specifically help small businesses that cannot obtain conventional financing. FAME can insure up to 85% of a loan to maximum loan insurance exposure of $500,000. These businesses must employ 20 or fewer employees or have gross annual sales of less than $2.5 million.

SMART-E Bond. A tax-exempt, fixed-asset financing program for manufacturing facilities. Assets that can be financed with loan proceeds include land and depreciable assets. FAME will finance up to 90% of a loan by grouping it with other similar loans and selling tax-exempt bonds to finance the loans. With maximum size loan of $7,000,000 this program benefits borrowers by providing a low, fixed-interest rate on 90% of a loan for up to 15 years.

SMART Bond. Similar to the SMART-E Bond Program. It is available to those businesses who are not eligible for tax-exempt financing.

Municipal Securities Approval Program. Maine municipalities are empowered, with the approval of FAME, to issue tax-exempt Industrial Revenue Bonds to finance any project authorized under the United State's Internal Revenue Code, Section 103, except retail stores and office space. Proceeds from the sale of municipal Industrial Revenue Bonds may be used for land, buildings, machinery and equipment, financing and interest charges, engineering, legal services, surveys, cost estimates and studies.

Maine Job Start Program. A revolving loan program designed to provide the eligible small business person with the necessary capital to start, strengthen or expand a business operation. The maximum available loan is $10,000 with an interest rate 2% below the prime rate.

Pine Tree Partnership Fund Grant Program. Designed to help foster innovation and development of new technology products. Small businesses can apply for matching grants of up to $5,000. These grants are intended to help perform research as well as to develop and introduce advanced technology and services into the marketplace.

Occupational Safety Loan Fund. Provides targeted direct loans to Maine businesses seeking to make workplace safety improvements. A business may borrow up to $50,000 for a period of up to 10 years, at 3% fixed interest rate.

Jobs and Investment Tax Credit. Businesses, other than public utilities, who make an investment in Maine qualify for an investment tax credit. By investing at least $5 million in a taxable year which qualifies under the IRS Investment Credit provisions and increase wages in the same taxable year by $1.4 million, the taxpayer qualifies for a state income tax credit equal to the federal investment credit, limited to $300,000 or the amount of tax otherwise due.

Revolving Loan Funds. Established to assist in the financing of development projects within each Economic Development District. Emphasis is on those projects which create jobs within the districts. Districts and entities have access to the business loan programs are: Northern Maine Regional Planning Commission, Caribou; Eastern Maine Development Corporation, Bangor; Androscoggin Valley Council of Governments, Auburn; Lewiston/Auburn Economic Growth Council; Coastal Enterprises Inc., Wiscasset; Northern Kennebec Regional Planning Commission, Winslow

Development Fund. As part of the Community Development Block Grant Small Cities Program, the state has set aside $750,000 for grants to communities to help finance development projects.

Tax Increment Financing. Local governing bodies may designate areas within their municipalities as development districts in order to facilitate redevelopment activities. Public financing, usually in the form of bonds, is used to provide necessary public improvements, and developers obtain financing to carry out the major redevelopment. The public debt is retired with the increase in property taxes generated by the area's reevaluation.

SBA Programs. SBA 504 program is designed to stimulate growth and expansion of small business through a public-private partnership. The emphasis is on projects which create a meaningful number of jobs in ratio to the investment. SBA 7A program makes direct, immediate participation and guaranteed 90% of loans up to $155,000 and 85% of loans up to $750,000.

Economic Development Administration. Technical Assistance grants may be made to non-profit corporations, districts or local government entities to pay for part of the cost of feasibility studies, pilot or demonstration projects, university centers, and comprehensive studies to benefit an entire area or segment of the economy. EDA's Business Loan Guarantee Program provides financial assistance to firms in distressed areas. EDA may guarantee up to 80% of the loans. Investors must provide 15 to 25% of project funding, and lenders must be at risk for the balance of the loan.

Maine Capital Corporation. A licensed Small Business Investment Company under the Federal Small Business Act, the MCC is a private for-profit corporation designed to seek long-term investment opportunities in growing and healthy Maine businesses. The MCC investment will supplement additional lending by banks and other sources. Investments of $50,00 or more will be considered.

Education and Training

Job Opportunity Zone Program. Allows designated Maine communities or regions to offer targeted incentives to businesses locating within the zone. Among the incentives offered are labor training funds and priority utilization of other business development programs such as the Community Industrial Building Program.

Job Training Partnership Act. This program operates with funding from the U.S. Department of Labor. It provides job training and other employment related services.

State Offices

Real estate: Real Estate Commission, Commissioner, State House Station 35, Augusta, ME 04333. 207-582-8727

Chamber of commerce: Maine State Chamber of Commerce & Industry, John S. Dexter Jr., President, 126 Sewall St., Augustas, ME 04330. 207-623-4568, FAX 207-622-7723

Economic development: Economic & Community Development Office, Lynn Wachtel, Commissioner, State House Station 59, Augusta, ME 04333. 800-541-5872

Finance Authority of Maine, Timothy P. Agnew, Chief Exec Officer, PO Box 949, Augusta, ME 04332-0949. 207-623-3263

Office of Community Development (Enterprise Zones Office), Leonard Dow, 193 State Street, State House Station 59, Augusta, ME 04333. 207-289-6800

Small Business Development Center, Diane Branscomb, Director, University of Southern Maine, 246 Deering Ave., Portland, ME 04102. 202-780-4420

Environmental affairs: Department of Environmental Protection, Dean C. Marriott, Commissioner, State House Station 17, Augusta, ME 04333. 207-289-7688

Labor: Department of Labor, John Fitzsimmons, Commissioner, State House 54, Augusta, ME 04332-0309. 207-289-3788

Unemployment: Department of Labor, Unemployment Insurance Commission, Gerald Conley, Commissioner, State House 54, Augusta, ME 04332-0309. 207-289-4200

Worker's compensation: Workers' Compensation Commission, Ralph L. Tucker, Chairman, State House Station 27, Augusta, ME 04333. 207-289-7086

Major Companies in the State

Company name	Fortune 500 rank	City	Telephone	SIC number
Fortune 500 Companies				
None				
Other Major Companies in the State				
Bangor Hydro Electric Co.		Bangor	207-945-5621	4911
Bar Harbor Bankshares		Bar Harbor	207-288-3314	6712
Bethel Bancorp		Bethel	207-824-2117	6712
Central Maine Power Co.		Augusta	207-623-3521	4911
Consumers Water Co.		Portland	207-773-6438	4941
First National Lincoln Corp.		Damariscotta	207-563-3195	6712
Hannaford Brothers Co.		Scarborough	207-883-2911	5411
Idexx Corp.		Portland	207-774-4334	2835
Maine Public Service Co.		Presque Isle	207-768-5811	4911
Maine Yankee Atomic Power Co.		Augusta	207-622-4868	4911
Mid Coast Bancorp Inc.		Waldoboro	207-832-7521	6712
Mid Maine Savings Bank F S B		Auburn	207-784-3581	6035
North East Insurance Co.		Scarborough	207-883-2232	6331
Penobscot Shoe Co.		Old Town	207-827-4431	3144
Peoples Heritage Financial Group Inc.		Portland	207-761-8500	6712
Suffield Financial Corp.		Westbrook	202-774-5000	6712
Sugarloaf Mountain Corp.		Kingfield	207-237-2000	7011
Union Bankshares Co.		Ellsworth	207-667-2504	6712
Unum Corp.		Portland	207-770-2211	6321
Ventrex Laboratories Inc.		Portland	207-773-7231	2835

Occupational safety and health: Department of Labor, Safety Division, Lester Wood, Administrator, State House 54, Augusta, ME 04333. 207-289-6460

Secretary of state: Office of Secretary of State, William G. Diamond, Secretary of State, State House Station 148, Augusta, ME 04333. 207-626-8400

Taxation and revenue: Bureau of Taxation, John D. LaFaver. State Tax Assessor, State House 24, Augusta, ME 04333. 207-289-2076

Designated Zones for Economic Development

Enterprise Zones

Enacted in: 1987

No. of established zones: 4

  Central Aroostock

  Katahdin Region

  Quoddy Region

  Waldo County

Foreign Trade Zones

Foreign Trade Zone No. 58, Bangor, Grantee/Operator: City of Bangor, Ken Gibb, Economic Department, City Hall, 73 Harlow Street, Bangor, ME 04401, 207-947-4842

Foreign Trade Zone No. 179, Madawaska, Maine, Grantee: Madawaska Foreign Trade Zone Corporation, Thomas F. Kent, Chairman, PO Box 250, Madawaska, ME 04756, 207-728-4273

Labor Unions

Carpenters and Joiners of America, United Brotherhood of (AFL-CIO)

Clothing and Textile Workers Union, Amalgamated (AFL-CIO)

Electrical Workers, International Brotherhood of (AFL-CIO)

Food and Commercial Workers International Union, United (AFL-CIO)

Machinists and Aerospace Workers, International Association of (AFL-CIO)

Plumbing and Pipe Fitting Industry of The United States and Canada, United Association of, Journeymen and Apprentices of the (AFL-CIO)

State, County and Municipal Employees, American Federation of (AFL-CIO)

Teachers, American Federation of (AFL-CIO)

Universities with Ph.D. Programs

University of Maine, Orono

University of New England, Biddeford

University of Southern Maine, Portland

BANGOR, ME (NECMA)

Geographic Profile

Land Area

3396.0 square miles

Counties and Parishes

Penobscot

Waldo

Additional Cities/Towns within Area

Brewer

Eddington

Glenburn

Hampden

Hermon

Holden

Kenduskeag

Old Town

Orono

Orrington

Penobscot Indian Island

Veazie

Winterport

Ranking Highlights

39 *out of 319 in total* **land area**

188 *out of 319 in* **population growth,** *1970–1990*

N/A *out of 310 in having the lowest* **unemployment** *rate*

N/A *out of 310 in size of* **labor force**

57 *out of 318 in the percentage of* **college graduates**

212 *out of 292 in per capita personal* **income**

196 *out of 319 in number of* **manufacturing establishments**

105 *out of 318 in* **physicians** *per 1000 people*

153 *out of 318 in* **hospital beds** *per 1000 people*

43 *out of 267 in fewest* **crimes** *per 1000 people*

5 *out of 266 in fewest* **violent crimes** *per 1000 people*

191 *out of 319 in per capita* **federal funds and grants**

Quality of Life Indexes (Rate per 1000 population)

Crime rate in 1991:	43.2
Violent crime rate in 1991:	1.2
Physicians rate in 1992:	1.81
Hospital bed rate in 1991:	3.45

ACCRA Cost of Living Indexes

(First quarter 1993, average = 100)

Composite index:	N/A
Utilities index:	N/A
Housing index:	N/A

Overview

Located in the Acadia region of Maine, one of the most popular and scenic destinations in the country for summer visitors, Bangor is the third largest city in the state. Known as the Queen City of Maine, Bangor is the commercial, finan-cial, and cultural center of the eastern and northern regions of the state.

Wholesale and retail trade and services are the pillars of Bangor's economy. About a fifth of the labor force is involved with government installations there, ranging from county government to the United States Navy, Air Force, Customs Service, and Federal Aviation Administration. Bangor is a focal point for the more than four million people who annually visit Acadia National Park.

Bangor is located along major highway routes to northeast metropolitan areas and Canada. Bangor & Aroostock rail lines offer freight service throughout the state with connections to Canada, Maine Central and Boston & Maine railroads. Thirty–three motor freight carriers serve Bangor, operating out of a dozen trucking terminals. The deepwater port of Searsport, twenty miles from Bangor, is well suited to the import or export of bulk and break-bulk shipments.

Bangor International Airport is a major east coast technical refueling and customs processing stop for airlines and charter jets flying the North Atlantic Great Circle Route; the airport offers a modern domestic and international terminal complex. As the northeastern terminus of Delta Airlines, the airport has direct access to major cities across the country; it is also served by Continental Express, Northwest Airlines, United Airlines and major international air charters and is a frequent alternate field for the Concord. Bangor is easily reached via Interstate 95, Maine Route 2 from the north and west, Route 9 from the northeast, and Route 1A from the east. Rail and bus service is available.

Population (1990)

Total Population and Growth Rate

1990: 146,601

1980: 137,015

1970: 125,393

Growth rate 1970–1990: 17%

Race and Hispanic Origin

White: 97.3%

Black: .5%

Asian/Pacific Islander: 0.9%

Native American: 1.1%

Hispanic origin: 0.6%

White not Hispanic: 96.9%

Age

Ages 18 to 20: 5.1%

Ages 21 to 24: 4.9%

Ages 25 to 44: 19.1%

Ages 45 to 54: 5.7%

Ages 55 to 59: 2.6%

Ages 60 to 64: 2.5%

Ages 65 plus: 7%

Educational Attainment (1990)

Percent having completed high school: 82.7%

Percent having completed college: 23.7%

Elementary and high school enrollment: 24,000

Federal Funds and Grants Received

Total received in 1989: $404,300,000
Funds received per capita: $2,860

Civilian Labor Force

1993 (April):	N/A
1992 average:	N/A
1991 average:	70,980
1990 average:	69,480

Unemployment

1993 (April):	N/A
1992 average:	N/A
1991 average:	8.0%
1990 average:	5.4%

Average Annual Pay

1988: $18,422
1987: $17,640
1985: $15,902

Per Capita Personal Income

1991: $16,043
1990: $15,649
1989: $14,937

Business Climate (1987)

Manufacturing

Number of establishments in 1987: 234
Shipments in 1987 ($1,000): $1,447,300
Employees in 1987: 13,400
Change in employment, 1982 to 1987: -10.7%
Average annual pay for manufacturing work in 1989: $25,143
Average annual pay for production work in 1987: $20,578

Wholesale Trade

Number of establishments in 1987: 243
Total sales in 1987 ($1,000): $884,400
Change in sales, 1982 to 1987: 15.7%

Retail Trade

Number of establishments in 1987: 1,054
Total sales in 1987 ($1,000): $884,400
Retail sales per household in 1987: $22,828
Average annual pay in 1989: $11,222

Service Industry

Selected receipts in 1987 ($1,000): $260,600
Average annual pay in 1989: $18,018

Housing

Total number of units in 1990: 35,448
Occupied units in 1990: 32,867
Owner-occupied units in 1990: 62.4%
1993 ACCRA average cost: N/A
1993 ACCRA average rent for an apartment: N/A

Chamber of Commerce

Greater Bangor Chamber of Commerce, Elizabeth Bell, President, 519 Main St., PO Box 1443, Bangor, ME 04401. 207-947-0307

Economic Development Office

Eastern Maine Development Corp., Michael W. Aube, President, 1 Cumberland Place, PO Box 2579, Bangor, ME 04401. 207-942-6389, FAX 207-942-3548

Industrial Sites

Bangor International Cargo Distribution Park, Bangor (75 acres)
Bangor International Industrial Park, Bangor (83 acres)
Heritage Industrial Park Park, Bangor (95 acres)
Target Industrial Circle, Bangor (3 acres)
Bangor Industrial Park & Annex, Bangor (6 acres)
Dowd Indutrial Park, Bangor (18 acres)
Bomarc Industrial Park, Bangor (33 acres)
BanAir Industrial Park, Bangor (16 acres)
Sylvan Road Industrial Park, Bangor (15 acres)
East-West Industrial Park, Brewer (12 acres)
Ammo Industrial Park, Hampden (170 acres)
Freedom Park, Hermon (65 acres)
Northern Maine Junction, Hermon (165 acres)
Old Town Industrial Park, Old Town (60 acres)

Major Businesses

Company	SIC	Telephone
Bangor & Aroostook Rr Co.	4011	(207) 848-5711
Bangor Hydro-Electric Co.	4911	(207) 945-5621
Bangor Savings Bank	6036	(207) 942-5211
Beacon Cadillac Oldsmobile	5511	(207) 945-9458
H. O. Bouchard, Inc.	4212	(207) 862-4070
Cole Enterprises	4213	(207) 942-7311
Darling's	5511	(207) 941-1240
Downeast Toyota BMW	5511	(207) 989-6400
Eastern Fine Paper Inc.	2621	(207) 989-7070
Eastern Maine Medical Center	8062	(207) 947-3711
W. S. Emerson Company, Inc.	5136	(207) 989-3410
M. D. Hardy, Inc.	1541	(207) 942-4686
Linnehan Ford-Heavy Duty	5511	(207) 942-9244
Merrill Bankshares Company	6022	(207) 945-5651
Nickerson & O'Day Inc.	1542	(207) 989-7400
Northeast Chrysler-Plymouth	5511	(207) 942-4900
Northern Products, Inc.	2452	(207) 945-6413
Parts Wholesalers Inc.	5013	(207) 941-1200
Penobscot Energy Recovery	4911	(207) 825-4566
Penobscot Shoe Company	3144	(207) 827-4431
St. Joseph Healthcare Foundation	8062	(207) 947-8311
Sure Winner Foods	5143	(207) 989-6447
Village Car Company	5511	(207) 945-9401
Village Subaru	5511	(207) 942-7364
Z. F. Steering Gear US, Inc.	3714	(207) 989-1310

Colleges and Universities

Beal College, Bangor, ME
Eastern Maine Technical College, Bangor, ME
Husson College, Bangor, ME
University of Maine, Orono, ME

LEWISTON–AUBURN, ME (NECMA)

Geographic Profile

Land Area

470.3 square miles

Counties and Parishes

Androscoggin (part)

Additional Cities/Towns within Area

Greene
Lisbon
Mechanic Falls
Poland
Sabattus

Ranking Highlights

295 *out of 319 in total* **land area**

200 *out of 319 in* **population growth,** *1970–1990*

N/A *out of 310 in having the lowest* **unemployment** *rate*

N/A *out of 310 in size of* **labor force**

153 *out of 318 in the percentage of* **college graduates**

179 *out of 292 in per capita personal* **income**

219 *out of 319 in number of* **manufacturing establishments**

110 *out of 318 in* **physicians** *per 1000 people*

106 *out of 318 in* **hospital beds** *per 1000 people*

28 *out of 267 in fewest* **crimes** *per 1000 people*

13 *out of 266 in fewest* **violent crimes** *per 1000 people*

260 *out of 319 in per capita* **federal funds and grants**

Quality of Life Indexes (Rate per 1000 population)

Crime rate in 1991:	38.0
Violent crime rate in 1991:	1.5
Physicians rate in 1992:	1.76
Hospital bed rate in 1991:	4.3

ACCRA Cost of Living Indexes

(First quarter 1993, average = 100)

Composite index:	N/A
Utilities index:	N/A
Housing index:	N/A

Overview

The Twin Cities of Lewiston and Auburn (commonly referred to as L-A), Maine, are located on the banks of the Androscoggin River in the south central section of the State of Maine. L-A is the second largest metropolitan area in the state. Lewiston was incorporated as a town in 1795 and established as a city in 1863. The city's development in the 19th and 20th centuries was closely tied to its position as a manufacturing center, particularly of textiles. In recent years, Lewiston's economy has diversified, thereby reducing its dependence on manufacturing.

The economic development agency for the Twin Cities is the Lewiston-Auburn Economic Growth Council. The

Growth Council is charged with attracting and assisting new and expanding companies in the community, and has made more than 100 business loans since 1979. It is the administrative body for the Auburn Business Development Corp. and the Lewiston Development Corporation.

Population (1990)

Total Population and Growth Rate
1990: 105,259
1980: 99,509
1970: 91,279
Growth rate 1970–1990: 15%

Race and Hispanic Origin
White: 98.5%
Black: .5%
Asian/Pacific Islander: 0.6%
Native American: 0.2%
Hispanic origin: 0.6%
White not Hispanic: 98.0%

Age
Ages 18 to 20: 4.3%
Ages 21 to 24: 5.2%
Ages 25 to 44: 26%
Ages 45 to 54: 8%
Ages 55 to 59: 3.7%
Ages 60 to 64: 3.6%
Ages 65 plus: 11.9%

Educational Attainment (1990)
Percent having completed high school: 70.6%
Percent having completed college: 12.6%
Elementary and high school enrollment: 19,000

Federal Funds and Grants Received
Total received in 1989: $247,200,000
Funds received per capita: $2,392

Civilian Labor Force
1993 (April):   N/A
1992 average: N/A
1991 average: 52,180
1990 average: 50,480

Unemployment
1993 (April):   N/A
1992 average: N/A
1991 average: 9.7%
1990 average: 7.0%

Average Annual Pay
1988: $16,812
1987: $15,877
1985: $14,141

Per Capita Personal Income
1991: $16,682
1990: $16,161
1989: $15,582

Business Climate (1987)

Manufacturing
Number of establishments in 1987: 200
Shipments in 1987 ($1,000): $821,100
Employees in 1987: 11,300
Change in employment, 1982 to 1987: -10.3%
Average annual pay for manufacturing work in 1989: $19,667
Average annual pay for production work in 1987: $14,989

Wholesale Trade
Number of establishments in 1987: 184
Total sales in 1987 ($1,000): $444,300
Change in sales, 1982 to 1987: 59.4%

Retail Trade
Number of establishments in 1987: 700
Total sales in 1987 ($1,000): $444,300
Retail sales per household in 1987: $18,638
Average annual pay in 1989: $11,050

Service Industry
Selected receipts in 1987 ($1,000): $199,900
Average annual pay in 1989: $18,051

Housing
Total number of units in 1990: 36,993
Occupied units in 1990: 33,952
Owner-occupied units in 1990: 58.5%
1993 ACCRA average cost: N/A
1993 ACCRA average rent for an apartment: N/A

Chamber of Commerce
Lewiston-Auburn Area Chamber of Commerce, James R. Saunders, President, 10 Louise Ave., Lewiston, ME, 04240. 207-783-2249

Economic Development Office
Lewiston-Auburn Economic Growth Council, Stephen Heavener, Exec Director, PO Box 1188, 95 Park St. #306, Lewiston, ME 04243. 207-784-0161, FAX 207-786-4412

Economic Development Organizations
Auburn Industrial Development Commission, Roland Miller, Director, 45 Spring Street, Auburn, ME 04210. 207-786-2421

Industrial Sites
Auburn-Lewiston Airpark, Auburn (20 acres)
Minot Avenue Industrial Park, Auburn (35 acres)
Lewiston Industrial Park, Lewiston (13 acres)
Turnpike Industrial Park, Lewiston (69 acres)
Foss Road Business Park, Lewiston (40 acres)
Route 196 Industrial Park, Lisbon (17 acres)

Major Businesses

Company	SIC	Telephone
Androscoggin Savings Bank	6036	(207) 784-9164

Major Businesses (Continued)

Company	SIC	Telephone
Auburn Motor Sales	5511	(207) 784-2321
Bachmann Companies Inc.	3441	(207) 784-2338
Central Distributors Inc.	5181	(207) 784-4026
Central Maine Healthcare	8062	(207) 795-0111
Central Maine Medical Center	8062	(207) 795-2700
Falcon Shoe Mfg Co.	3143	(207) 784-9186
Federal Distributors Inc.	5181	(207) 783-2046
Geiger Bros.	5199	(207) 783-2001
Hall & Knight Co.	5074	(207) 784-5721
Lewiston Daily Sun	2711	(207) 784-5411
W. S. Libbey Company	2591	(207) 784-6961
Louis Chevrolet Inc.	5511	(207) 784-3503
Mid Maine Savings Bank	6035	(207) 784-3581
St. Mary's General Hospital	8062	(207) 786-2901
V. I. P. Inc.	5531	(207) 784-5423

Colleges and Universities

Bates College, Lewiston, ME

Central Maine Medical Center School of Nursing, Lewiston, ME

PORTLAND, ME (NECMA)

Geographic Profile

Land Area

835.6 square miles

Counties and Parishes

Cumberland (part)

York (part)

Additional Cities/Towns within Area

Cumberland County:

Cape Elizabeth

Cumberland

Falmouth

Freeport

Gorham

Gray

North Yarmouth

Raymond

Scarborough

South Portland

Standish

Westbrook

Windham

Yarmouth

York County:

Buxton

Hollis

Old Orchard Beach

Ranking Highlights

230 *out of 319 in total* **land area**

157 *out of 319 in* **population growth,** *1970–1990*

N/A *out of 310 in having the lowest* **unemployment** *rate*

N/A *out of 310 in size of* **labor force**

32 *out of 318 in the percentage of* **college graduates**

34 *out of 292 in per capita personal* **income**

142 *out of 319 in number of* **manufacturing establishments**

28 *out of 318 in* **physicians** *per 1000 people*

116 *out of 318 in* **hospital beds** *per 1000 people*

93 *out of 267 in fewest* **crimes** *per 1000 people*

33 *out of 266 in fewest* **violent crimes** *per 1000 people*

137 *out of 319 in per capita* **federal funds and grants**

Quality of Life Indexes (Rate per 1000 population)

Crime rate in 1991:	57.0
Violent crime rate in 1991:	2.8
Physicians rate in 1992:	3.05
Hospital bed rate in 1991:	4.15

ACCRA Cost of Living Indexes
(First quarter 1993, average = 100)

Composite index:	N/A
Utilities index:	N/A
Housing index:	N/A

Overview

Portland, the largest city in Maine, is a leading wholesale distributing point for northern New England and is an important retail center, catering mostly to pedestrian shoppers. These industries, as well as tourism, received a boost when L. L. Bean, the outdoors outfitters, opened a store in nearby Freeport in 1982. Since then more than one hundred factory outlets have opened in the area. Services, especially health services, play an important part in the economy; the Maine Medical Center is one of the city's largest employers. Portland is one of the chief trading ports on the Atlantic coast and plays a major role in Maine's paper and pulp trade. The state's annual lobster catch is the largest in the country. The finance industry has a long tradition in Portland, and Northern New England's largest real estate lender is headquartered there.

The deepwater Port of Portland is one of the largest oil terminal facilities on the East Coast based on volume of tonnage handled and is the closest U.S. port to Europe. Millions of pounds of pulpwood, fish, and other food products are shipped annually through the port. Recent years have seen the investment of millions of dollars in Portland's waterfront. Regular weekly cargo container service resumed in 1991 for the first time in eleven years.

Portland is served by the Portland International Jetport, one of the largest such facilities in the Northeast, by the Maine Turnpike and I-295, and by Maine Central Railroad and Conrail freight. More than thirty interstate truck carriers have local terminals and main or branch offices there. Interstate highways 95 (Maine Turnpike) and 295 provide direct and convenient access to Portland's employment and population centers. Canadian roads join the Maine Turnpike from the north. Greyhound provides daily bus service from Boston; Canadian bus service is also available.

Population (1990)

Total Population and Growth Rate
1990: 243,135
1980: 215,789
1970: 192,528
Growth rate 1970–1990: 26%

Race and Hispanic Origin
White: 98.2%
Black: .6%
Asian/Pacific Islander: 0.9%
Native American: 0.3%
Hispanic origin: 0.6%
White not Hispanic: 97.7%

Age
Ages 18 to 20: 3.9%
Ages 21 to 24: 5.4%
Ages 25 to 44: 31.1%
Ages 45 to 54: 8.8%
Ages 55 to 59: 3.6%
Ages 60 to 64: 3.7%
Ages 65 plus: 11.4%

Educational Attainment (1990)
Percent having completed high school: 85.1%
Percent having completed college: 27.7%
Elementary and high school enrollment: 36,500

Federal Funds and Grants Received
Total received in 1989: $768,600,000
Funds received per capita: $3,264

Civilian Labor Force
1993 (April):   N/A
1992 average: N/A
1991 average: 144,090
1990 average: 144,400

Unemployment
1993 (April):   N/A
1992 average: N/A
1991 average: 5.7%
1990 average: 3.6%

Average Annual Pay
1988: $19,837
1987: $18,673
1985: $16,514

Per Capita Personal Income
1991: $21,351
1990: $21,142
1989: $20,230

Business Climate (1987)

Manufacturing
Number of establishments in 1987: 381
Shipments in 1987 ($1,000): $1,813,700
Employees in 1987: 16,200
Change in employment, 1982 to 1987: -6.9%
Average annual pay for manufacturing work in 1989: $25,628
Average annual pay for production work in 1987: $18,505

Wholesale Trade
Number of establishments in 1987: 572
Total sales in 1987 ($1,000): $3,010,000
Change in sales, 1982 to 1987: 77.0%

Retail Trade
Number of establishments in 1987: 1,953
Total sales in 1987 ($1,000): $3,010,000
Retail sales per household in 1987: $29,467
Average annual pay in 1989: $12,659

Service Industry
Selected receipts in 1987 ($1,000): $905,500
Average annual pay in 1989: $19,906

Office Real Estate (1992)
Office space inventory: 5,884,618 square feet

Average class A Central Business District rental range per sq. ft: $15.00

Vacancy Rates

All areas: 10.3%

Vacancy Rates in Central Business District

Class A space: 8.0%

Class B space: 18.3%

Vacancy Rates Outside Central Business District

Class A space: 1.2%

Class B space: 10.0%

Housing

Total number of units in 1990: 96,297

Occupied units in 1990: 84,580

Owner-occupied units in 1990: 63.5%

1993 ACCRA average cost: N/A

1993 ACCRA average rent for an apartment: N/A

Chamber of Commerce

Greater Portland Regional Chamber of Commerce, William M. Nugent, President, 142 Free St., Portland, ME 04101. 207-772-2811

Economic Development Office

Economic Development Department, Virginia Hildreth, Director, 389 Congress Park, Portland, ME 04111. 207-874-8300

Industrial Sites

Pine Tree Industrial Park (8 acres)

Stroudwater Industrial Park (75 acres)

Gorham Industrial Park, Gorham (12 acres)

Scarborough Industrial Park, Scarborough (25 acres)

Spring Point, South Portland (66 acres)

Five Star Industrial Park, Westbrook (20 acres)

Windham Business Park, Windham (8 acres)

Major Businesses

Company	SIC	Telephone
ABB Environmental Service	8748	(207) 775-5401
G. H. Bass & Co.	5661	(207) 781-3180
L. L. Bean, Inc.	5961	(207) 865-4761
Casco Northern National Bank	6021	(207) 774-8221
Cole Haan	5139	(207) 846-3721
Consumers Water Company	4941	(207) 773-6438
Diversified Foods, Inc.	5045	(207) 879-2200
Emery-Waterhouse Company	5072	(207) 775-2371
Hannaford Bros. Co.	5411	(207) 883-2911
Jordan's Meats	2013	(207) 772-5411
Maine Medical Center	8062	(207) 871-0111
Maine Savings Bank	6036	(207) 871-1111
Nelson & Small, Inc.	5023	(207) 775-5666
Peoples Heritage Savings	6022	(207) 761-8500
S. Prawer & Company	5141	(207) 775-0223
Progressive Distributors	5122	(207) 883-2911

Major Businesses (Continued)

Company	SIC	Telephone
Unum Life Insurance Company of America	6321	(207) 770-2211

Colleges and Universities

Andover College, Portland, ME

Casco Bay College, Portland, ME

Portland School of Art, Portland, ME

University of Southern Maine, Portland, ME

Southern Maine Technical College, South Portland, ME

Saint Joseph's College, Standish, ME

MARYLAND

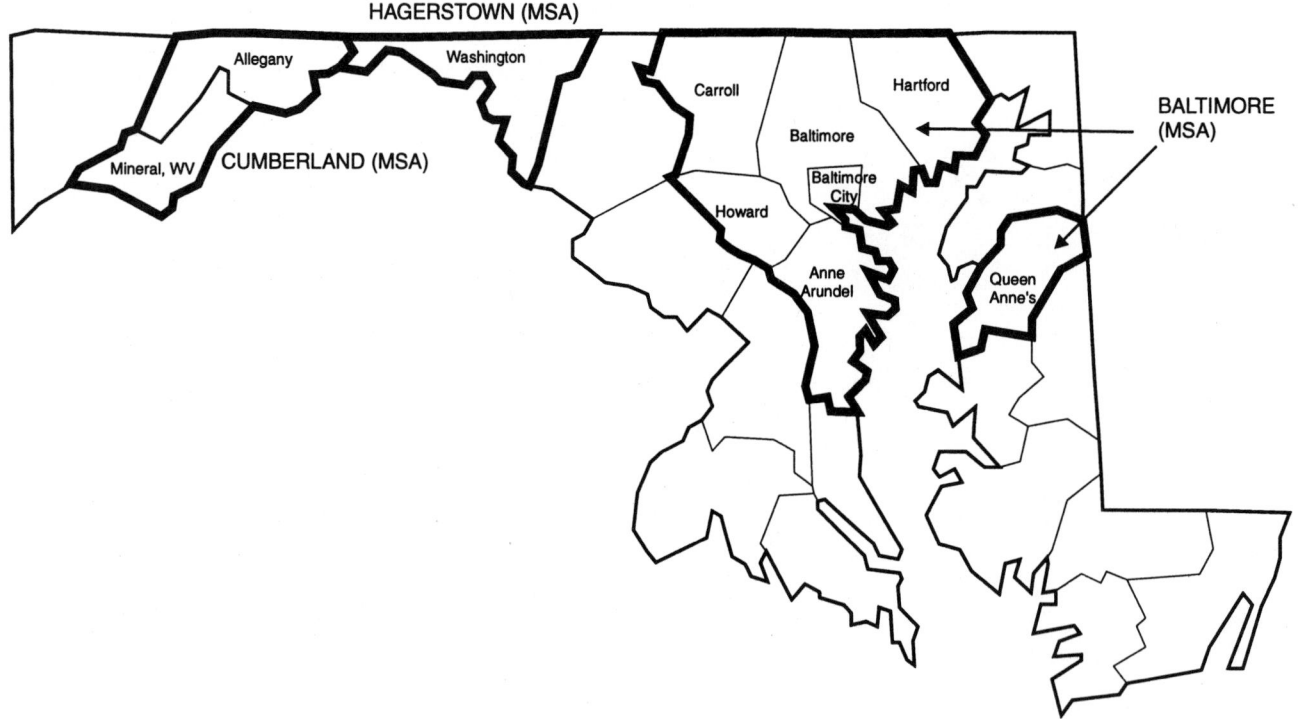

MARYLAND

Population
1990: 4,781,468
1980: 4,216,975

Age
Ages 18 to 20: 208,411
Ages 21 to 24: 296,962
Ages 25 to 44: 1,677,104
Ages 45 to 54: 521,801
Ages 55 to 59: 202,170
Ages 60 to 64: 195,297
Median age: 33.0

Race
White: 3,393,964
Black: 1,189,899
Asian/Pacific Islander: 139,719
Native American: 12,972
Hispanic origin: 125,102

Households
Total: 1,748,991
Persons per household: 2.67

Sex
Male: 2,318,671
Female: 2,462,797

Population Migration
Domestic migration: 309,000
International migration: 83,000

Projection of the Population in 1995
Total: 4,958,000
18 to 64: 3,175,000

Civilian Labor Force
1993: 2,567,400
1992: 2,570,000
1991: 2,521,900
1990: 2,510,900

Manufacturing
1995 Projection: 215,800
1992: 183,000
1991: 196,300
1990: 202,700
1989: 208,800

Services
1995 Projection: 902,600

1992: 630,200
1991: 619,900
1990: 625,700
1989: 594,900

Wholesale and Retail Trade
1995 Projection: 643,600
1992: 504,300
1991: 526,700
1990: 545,200
1989: 558,400

Unemployment Rate
1993: 6.4%
1992: 7.3%
1991: 5.6%
1990: 4.3%

Employer Unemployment Contributions
Contribution Rate
1992: 3.22%
1991: 1.47%
1990: 1.17%

Average Weekly Benefit
1992: $181.36
1991: $179.36
1990: $170.65

Gross State Product (Million $)
1989: $99,074
1988: $92,707
1987: $84,623
1979: $41,300
Growth rate, 1979 to 1989: 139.9%

Capital Expenditures of Manufacturing Industries
1990: $1,173,300,000
1989: $1,230,200,000
1988: $968,900,000
1987: $875,200,000

State Tax Rates
Individual income: Range from 2% ($1,000 or less) to 5% (above $3,000).
Corporate income: 7% of taxable net income.
General property: Sum of state and local rates. Assessed at

full cash value.
General sales: 5%
Gasoline: 18.5¢ per gallon

Income

Median income for a 4 person family: $50,145

Personal per Capita Income
1992: $22,974
1991: $22,304
1990: $21,915

Disposable per Capita Income
1992: $19,746
1991: $19,014
1990: $18,534

Private Employment Weekly Wages

Average
1989: $432
1988: $416
1987: $416

Manufacturing
1989: $393
1988: $529
1987: $509

Services
1989: $430
1988: $417
1987: $388

Wholesale
1989: $576
1988: $556
1987: $514

Retail
1989: $264
1988: $254
1987: $243

Highway Statistics

Total Highway Miles
1990: 28,752
1989: 28,495
1988: 28,233

Federal Highway Aid
1991: $244,486,000
1990: $283,730,000
1989: $269,324,000

Electricity

Average Cost per Kilowatt Hour
1990: 6.30¢
1989: 5.99¢
1988: 5.85¢

Housing (1990)

Owner occupied units: 1,137,296

Median house value: $116,500
Renter occupied units: 611,695
Median rent: $473
Total vacant units: 142,926
Homeowner vacancy rate: 1.6%
Rental vacancy rate: 6.8%

State Business Incentives and Assistance

Enterprise Zone Incentives
1) Local property taxes exempt for 10 years.
2) Wages paid to new employees, including the rehiring of laid-off workers, of $1,500 during the first year and $1,000 during the second year for disadvantaged workers, or $500 for a non-disadvantaged worker.
3) Venture Capital Guarantee Fund with $2 million in loan guarantees.
4) Larger loans for qualified businesses from Maryland's existing loan programs.

Financial and Business Assistance
Maryland Industrial Development Financing Authority. Established by the Maryland General Assembly, the Authority issues and may insure both tax-exempt and taxable industrial development bonds. IBDs encourage the expansion of businesses located in the state, to retain existing firms, and to encourage new companies to locate in the state. The bonds may be used to finance the acquisition of land, machinery and equipment, and construction. Tax-exempt IBDs enable companies to obtain financing at below-market interest rates for longer terms, and for a greater percentage of project costs than are available through conventional loans. Taxable IBDs are available to those businesses no longer eligible for tax-exempt financing.

Maryland Industrial and Commercial Redevelopment Fund. Established by the Maryland General Assembly, the Fund provides supplemental gap financing assistance to local governments to facilitate industrial and commercial redevelopment. Funds are made available from state general obligation bonds sales and are used to encourage private investment for projects that retain or create new jobs and increase tax revenue.

Maryland Industrial Land Act Program. Administered by the Department of Economic and Employment Development, this program is designed to support local economic development for the attraction of new industry and expansion of existing industry, by providing adequate land to communities where the need for industrial sites is not being met by the private real estate sector. It authorizes loans for options and acquisition of industrial land, development of industrial parks including all infrastructure improvements, and providing industry incubator facilities.

Education and Training
Maryland Industrial Training Program. Administered by the Department of Economic and Employment Develop-

Major Companies in the State

Company name	Fortune 500 rank	City	Telephone	SIC number
Fortune 500 Companies				
Black & Decker Corp.	112	Towson	410-716-3900	3546
Crown Central Petroleum Corp.	263	Baltimore	410-539-7400	2911
Martin Marietta Corp.	92	Bethesda	301-897-6000	3761
McCormick & Co. Inc.	275	Sparks	410-771-7301	2099
Other Major Companies in the State				
Baltimore Gas & Electric Co.		Baltimore	401-783-5920	4931
Caterair International Corp.		Potomac	301-309-2800	5812
Chesapeake & Potomac Telephone Co. of Md.		Baltimore	301-539-9900	4813
Commercial Credit Co.		Baltimore	410-332-3000	6141
CSX Transportation Inc.		Baltimore	301-237-2000	4011
Dart Group Corp.		Landover	301-731-1200	5531
First Maryland Bancorp		Baltimore	301-244-4000	6712
Giant Food Inc.		Landover	301-341-4100	5411
Hechinger Co.		Landover	301-341-1000	5251
Manor Care Inc.		Silver Spring	301-681-9400	8051
Marriott Corp.		Bethesda	301-380-9000	7011
Mercantile Bankshares Corp.		Baltimore	410-237-5900	6712
Merry Go Round Enterprises Inc.		Joppa	301-538-1000	5611
MNC Financial Inc.		Baltimore	301-605-5000	6712
PHH Corp.		Hunt Valley	410-771-3600	7515
Potomac Edison Co.		Hagerstown	301-790-3400	4911
Preston Corp.		Preston	301-673-7151	4213
Rouse Co.		Columbia	301-992-6000	6512
Ryland Group Inc.		Columbia	410-730-7222	1521
USF&G Corp.		Baltimore	301-547-3000	6331

ment, this program provides customized on-the-job or classroom training and employee recruitment assistance to firms starting or expanding in the state, as well as to businesses relocating from other states. The program will also assist in screening applicants for specific employment backgrounds and skills.

Partnership for Workforce Quality Program. Administered by the Department of Economic and Employment Development, this productivity enhancement program is designed to improve the productivity of the work force by upgrading workers' skills for new technologies or production processes. The Program will provide incentive grants of up to 50% of the cost of the training which can be conducted by in-house employees or by the state university or community colleges.

Job Training Partnership Act. This program operates with funding from the U.S. Department of Labor. It provides job training and other employment related services.

State Offices

Real estate: General Services Department, Real Estate Office, Deborah Ann Photiadis, Director, 301 West Preston Street, Room 1401, Baltimore, MD 21201. 301-225-4322

Chamber of commerce: Maryland State Chamber of Commerce, Peter J. Lombardi, President, 275 West St. #400, Annapolis, MD 21401-3480. 301-269-0642

Economic development: Department of Economic & Employment Development, J. Randall Evans, Secretary, 217 East Redwood Street, Baltimore, MD 21202. 301-333-6901

Department of Economic & Employment Development, Enterprise Zone Program, Jerry Wade, Administrator, 217 East Redwood Street, 11th Floor, Baltimore, MD 21202. 301-333-6950

Maryland Economic Development Corporation, Hans Mayer, Director, 36 S. Charles St. #1911, Baltimore, MD 21201. 301-625-0051

Maryland Industrial and Commercial Redevelopment Fund, Rudolph Schafert, Director, 217 East Redwood Street, Suite 2236, Baltimore, MD 21202. 301-333-4304

Maryland Industrial Development Financing Authority, Benjamimn L. Hackerman, Exec Dir., 217 East Redwood Street, 22nd fl., Baltimore, MD 21202. 301-333-4262

Small Business Development Centers, Elliott Rittenhouse, Director, 217 Redwood Street, 10th fl., Baltimore, MD 21202. 301-333-6996

Environmental affairs: Environment Department, Martin W. Walsh, Jr., Secretary, 2500 Broening Highway, Baltimore, MD 21224. 301-631-3084

Labor: Labor and Industry Division, Henry Koellein, Jr., Commissioner, 501 St. Paul Place, Baltimore, MD 21202. 301-333-4179

Unemployment: Unemployment Insurance Office, Thomas S. Wendel, Exec Director, 1100 North Eutaw Street, Room 501, Baltimore, MD 21201. 301-333-5306

Worker's compensation: Workers Compensation Commission, R. Rex Brookshire II, Secretary, 6 North Liberty Street, Baltimore, MD 21401. 301-333-4700

Occupational safety and health: Labor and Industry Division, Occupational Safety and Health Section, Milton H.F. Saul, Director, 501 St. Paul Place, Baltimore, MD 21202. 301-333-4195

Secretary of state: Secretary of State, Winfield M. Kelly, Jr., Secretary of State, 16 Francis Street, Jeffrey Bldg., Annapolis, MD 21401. 301-974-3421

Taxation and revenue: Comptroller of the Treasury, Louis Goldstein, Comptroller, Treasury Bldg., PO Box 466, Annapolis, MD 21404. 301-974-3801

Designated Zones for Economic Development

Enterprise Zones

Enacted in: 1982

No. of established zones: 17

Foreign Trade Zones

Foreign Trade Zone No. 74, Baltimore, Maryland, Grantee: City of Baltimore, Paul Gilbert, c/o Baltimore Economic Development Corporation, 36 South Charles St., Baltimore, MD 21201, 301-837-9305

Foreign Trade Zone No. 73, Baltimore/Washington Intl Airport, Maryland, Grantee: Maryland Dept. of Transportation, Operator: All Cargo Expediting Services, Inc., Robert J. Schott, PO Box 28673, BWI Airport, MD 21240, 301-859-4449

Foreign Trade Zone No. 63, Prince George's County, Maryland, Grantee: Prince George's County Government, Ed Windsor, 1300 Mercantile Land, Suite 108, Landover, MD 20785, 301-499-8170

Labor Unions

Electrical Workers, International Brotherhood of (AFL-CIO)

Fire Fighters, International Association of (AFL-CIO)

Maryland Classified Employees Association

National Education Association

National Fraternal Order of Police

Secretary and Aides Association

State, County and Municipal Employees, American Federation of (AFL-CIO)

Teachers, American Federation of (AFL-CIO)

Teachers Association of Anne Arundel County

Universities with Ph.D. Programs

Baltimore Hebrew University, Baltimore

Johns Hopkins University, Baltimore

Loyola College, Baltimore

Morgan State University, Baltimore

University of Baltimore, Baltimore

University of Maryland At Baltimore, Baltimore

University of Maryland Baltimore County, Baltimore

University of Maryland College Park, College Park

University of Maryland Eastern Shore, Princess Anne

BALTIMORE, MD (MSA)

Geographic Profile

Land Area

2609.3 square miles

Counties and Parishes

Anne Arundel

Baltimore

Carroll

Harford

Howard

Queen Anne's

Additional Cities/Towns within Area

Annapolis

Ranking Highlights

64 *out of 319 in total* **land area**

207 *out of 319 in* **population growth,** *1970–1990*

46 *out of 310 in having the lowest* **unemployment** *rate*

15 *out of 310 in size of* **labor force**

60 *out of 318 in the percentage of* **college graduates**

28 *out of 292 in per capita personal* **income**

32 *out of 319 in number of* **manufacturing establishments**

21 *out of 318 in* **physicians** *per 1000 people*

155 *out of 318 in* **hospital beds** *per 1000 people*

160 *out of 267 in fewest* **crimes** *per 1000 people*

222 *out of 266 in fewest* **violent crimes** *per 1000 people*

62 *out of 319 in per capita* **federal funds and grants**

Quality of Life Indexes (Rate per 1000 population)

Crime rate in 1991:	72.7
Violent crime rate in 1991:	12.6
Physicians rate in 1992:	3.2
Hospital bed rate in 1991:	3.41

ACCRA Cost of Living Indexes

(First quarter 1993, average = 100)

Composite index:	N/A
Utilities index:	N/A
Housing index:	N/A

Overview

Baltimore's fortuitous location on the northern Chesapeake Bay has been at the heart of its social and economic development. Farther inland than other eastern seaports, the city is convenient to landlocked areas. In 1990 *Inc.* magazine ranked Greater Baltimore in the nation's top 12 percent for business starts.

Two major employers, Westinghouse Electric Corporation, along with Martin-Marietta, concentrate on research and development of electronics and radar-controlled systems. Baltimore is also a national headquarters for advanced medical treatment and research with two pioneering teaching hospitals, Johns Hopkins Hospital and University Hospital at the University of Maryland. The Christopher Columbus Center of Marine Research and Exploration, a $163 million facility, is slated to open during the latter 1990s. Analysts estimate that the center will stimulate the creation of hundreds of new companies over a decade, and will maintain American leadership in the field of marine biotechnology.

Oriole Park at Camden Yards, which opened in 1992, represents an investment of $224 million. It is the major component in a twenty-year strategy for downtown development. Major projects underway or on the drawing board represent an investment of more than $3.5 billion and nearly twenty-thousand jobs. The Christopher Columbus Center of Marine Research and Exploration, which will cost $161 million and indicates the City's leadership in the life sciences, is being developed in the Inner Harbor. The center will contain marine biotechnology laboratories, nautical archaeology facilities, and teaching and exhibition units. City Crescent, a $37 million federal office complex, is the first major minority-owned development downtown. It will house several federal agencies. The Hopkins Bayview Research Campus is a 130-acre biomedical research park in east Baltimore that will cost $500 million and employ 5,000 people. The $600 million International Life Sciences Trade and Conference Center (Medical Mart) will employ 2,000 people.

About 350,000 people attended conventions in Baltimore in 1990, triple the number since 1980. Baltimore's largest meeting facility is the Baltimore Convention Center located at the Inner Harbor which features 115,000 square feet of unobstructed exhibit space divisible into four halls.

Baltimore-Washington International Airport is a major cargo carrier for the mid-Atlantic region. In 1990, the airport handled nearly one-hundred and thirty thousand tons of freight, an increase of 6 percent over 1989. Major railroad systems service industry throughout the Baltimore area. Several major interstate highways run through Baltimore; I-95 links Baltimore with major cities from New England to Florida, and I-70 connects it with the Midwest. More than one-hundred trucking lines also accommodate the Baltimore area.

The most significant mover of goods in the area is the port of Baltimore, the ninth largest in the nation. One hundred fifty miles closer to key midwestern markets than any other Atlantic Coast port, the port of Baltimore has lower transportation costs between its marine terminals and inland points of cargo origin or destination. Baltimore also benefits by having two access routes to its port: from the north through the Chesapeake & Delaware Canal, and from the south up the Chesapeake Bay. The new 165-acre high-technology Seagirt Marine Terminal will allow 2.5 million tons of cargo to move across its piers and will increase container capacity by half.

Population (1990)

Total Population and Growth Rate
1990: 2,382,172
1980: 2,199,497
1970: 2,089,438
Growth rate 1970–1990: 14%

Race and Hispanic Origin
White: 71.8%
Black: 25.9%
Asian/Pacific Islander: 1.8%
Native American: 0.3%
Hispanic origin: 1.3%
White not Hispanic: 71.0%

Age
Ages 18 to 20: 4.3%
Ages 21 to 24: 6.1%
Ages 25 to 44: 34.6%
Ages 45 to 54: 10.7%
Ages 55 to 59: 4.3%
Ages 60 to 64: 4.3%
Ages 65 plus: 11.7%

Educational Attainment (1990)
Percent having completed high school: 74.7%
Percent having completed college: 23.1%
Elementary and high school enrollment: 371,615

Federal Funds and Grants Received
Total received in 1989: $10,162,000,000
Funds received per capita: $4,338

Civilian Labor Force
1993 (April): 1,195,988
1992 average: 1,238,053
1991 average: 1,212,223
1990 average: 1,210,614

Unemployment
1993 (April): 7.0%
1992 average: 7.4%
1991 average: 6.6%
1990 average: 5.1%

Average Annual Pay
1988: $22,261
1987: $20,978
1985: $19,058

Per Capita Personal Income
1991: $21,874
1990: $21,551
1989: $220,499

Business Climate (1987)

Manufacturing
Number of establishments in 1987: 2,311
Shipments in 1987 ($1,000): $19,215,200
Employees in 1987: 145,200

Change in employment, 1982 to 1987: -6.0%
Average annual pay for manufacturing work in 1989: $30,709
Average annual pay for production work in 1987: $23,030

Wholesale Trade
Number of establishments in 1987: 3,657
Total sales in 1987 ($1,000): $23,407,100
Change in sales, 1982 to 1987: 42.4%

Retail Trade
Number of establishments in 1987: 13,542
Total sales in 1987 ($1,000): $23,407,100
Retail sales per household in 1987: $17,906
Average annual pay in 1989: $12,696

Service Industry
Selected receipts in 1987 ($1,000): $7,655,000
Average annual pay in 1989: $21,024

Office Real Estate (1992)
Office space inventory: 36,282,584 square feet
Average class A Central Business District rental range per sq. ft: $23.50

Vacancy Rates
All areas: 19.6%

Vacancy Rates in Central Business District
Class A space: 17.1%
Class B space: 22.1%

Vacancy Rates Outside Central Business District
Class A space: 23.3%
Class B space: 16.9%

Housing
Total number of units in 1990: 938,979
Occupied units in 1990: 880,145
Owner-occupied units in 1990: 63.7%

Chamber of Commerce
Greater Baltimore Committee, Robert Keller, Exec. Director, 111 S. Calvert St. #1500, Baltimore, MD, 21202. 301-727-2820.

Economic Development Office
Greater Annapolis Chamber of Commerce, Penny Chandler, Exec Director, One Annapolis Street, Annapolis, MD 21401. 410-268-7676, FAX 410-268-2317.

Economic Development Organizations
Baltimore Economic Development Corp., David M. Gillece, President, 36 S. Charles St. #1600, Baltimore, MD, 21201. 301-837-9305.

Greater Baltimore Community Development, Robert Keller, Exec. Director, 1111 South Calvert Street, Suite 1500. Baltimore, MD 21202. 301-727-2820.

Anne Arundel County Office of Economic Development, Jeffrey L. Stone, Exec. Director, 44 Calvert Street, Annapolis, MD 21401. 301-837-9305.

Major Businesses

Company	SIC	Telephone
American Trading and Prod.	1311	(301) 347-7000
Arcata Graphics Company	2732	(301) 783-5200
Baltimore Bancorp	6022	(301) 244-3360
Baltimore Gas and Electric Company	4911	(301) 234-5000
Bendix Field Engineering	4899	(301) 964-7000
Black & Decker Corporation	3546	(301) 583-3900
Blue Cross-Blue Shield	6324	(301) 581-3000
Bon Secours Health System	6324	(301) 442-5511
Alex Brown & Sons Incorporated	6211	(301) 727-1700
Chesapeake & Potomac Telephone Co.	4813	(301) 393-6219
Commercial Credit Company	6141	(301) 332-3000
Crown Central Holding Corp.	5411	(301) 539-7400
Crown Central Petroleum	2911	(301) 539-7400
CSX Transportation Inc.	4011	(301) 237-2000
Emhart Industries Inc.	3429	(301) 583-3900
F Z Corporation	5411	(301) 539-7400
Fidelity & Deposit Company	6351	(301) 539-0800
Fidelity & Guaranty Insurance	6331	(301) 547-3000
First Maryland Bancorp	6021	(301) 244-4000
First National Bank of Maryland	6021	(301) 244-4000
Foodarama Inc.	4225	(301) 655-8000
Golden Capital Distributors	5194	(301) 773-8600
B. Green & Company Inc.	5141	(301) 247-8300
Johns Hopkins Hospital Inc.	8062	(301) 955-4926
Maryland Casualty Company	6331	(301) 366-1000
Maryland National Bank	6021	(301) 244-5000
McCormick & Company Inc.	2099	(301) 771-6000
Mercantile Bankshares Corp.	6022	(301) 237-5900
Merry-Go-Round Enterprises	5611	(301) 538-1000
MNC Financial Inc.	6021	(301) 244-5000
Monumental General Insurance	6311	(301) 685-2900
Noxell Corporation	2844	(301) 785-7300
PHH Corporation	8741	(301) 771-1900
The Rouse Company	6512	(301) 992-6000
Ryland Acceptance Corp.	6162	(301) 730-7222
Ryland Group Inc.	1531	(301) 730-7222
Ryland Mortgage Company	6162	(301) 964-8260
SCM Chemicals Inc.	2816	(301) 783-1120
Signet Bank/Maryland	6022	(301) 332-5000
Sunbelt Beverage Corp.	5181	(301) 832-7740
UNC Incorporated	3724	(301) 266-7333
United States Fidelity Grant	6331	(301) 547-3000
USF & G Corporation	6331	(301) 547-3000
Weisman, Frederick Company	8742	(301) 760-1500
Whiting-Turner Contracting Co., Inc.	8741	(301) 821-1100
Wise Metals Co Inc.	6221	(301) 636-6500

Colleges and Universities

Baltimore Hebrew University, Baltimore, MD
Baltimore's International Culinary College, Baltimore, MD
College of Notre Dame of Maryland, Baltimore, MD
Community College of Baltimore, Baltimore, MD
Coppin State College, Baltimore, MD
Dundalk Community College, Baltimore, MD
Essex Community College, Baltimore, MD
Goucher College, Baltimore, MD
Johns Hopkins University, Baltimore, MD
Loyola College, Baltimore, MD
Maryland Institute, College of Art, Baltimore, MD
Morgan State University, Baltimore, MD
Ner Israel Rabbinical College, Baltimore, MD
Conservatory of Music, Peabody Institute of Johns Hopkins University, Baltimore, MD
Sojourner-Douglass College, Baltimore, MD
University of Baltimore, Baltimore, MD
University of Maryland At Baltimore, Baltimore, MD
University of Maryland Baltimore County, Baltimore, MD
St. John's College, Annapolis, MD
United States Naval Academy, Annapolis, MD

CUMBERLAND, MD–WV (MSA)

Geographic Profile

Land Area

753.1 square miles

Counties and Parishes

Maryland:

Allegany

West Virginia:

Mineral

Ranking Highlights

245 *out of 319 in total* land area

297 *out of 319 in* population growth, *1970–1990*

75 *out of 310 in having the lowest* unemployment *rate*

296 *out of 310 in size of* labor force

161 *out of 318 in the percentage of* college graduates

266 *out of 292 in per capita personal* income

301 *out of 319 in number of* manufacturing establishments

115 *out of 318 in* physicians *per 1000 people*

55 *out of 318 in* hospital beds *per 1000 people*

5 *out of 267 in fewest* crimes *per 1000 people*

49 *out of 266 in fewest* violent crimes *per 1000 people*

101 *out of 319 in per capita* federal funds and grants

Quality of Life Indexes (Rate per 1000 population)

Crime rate in 1991:	28.7
Violent crime rate in 1991:	3.4
Physicians rate in 1992:	1.7
Hospital bed rate in 1991:	5.3

ACCRA Cost of Living Indexes

(First quarter 1993, average = 100)

Composite index:	99.6
Utilities index:	114.1
Housing index:	101.2

Population (1990)

Total Population and Growth Rate

1990: 101,643

1980: 107,782

1970: 107,153

Growth rate 1970–1990: -5%

Race and Hispanic Origin

White: 97.2%

Black: 2.2%

Asian/Pacific Islander: 0.4%

Native American: 0.1%

Hispanic origin: 0.4%

White not Hispanic: 96.9%

Age

Ages 18 to 20: 6%

Ages 21 to 24: 5.6%

Ages 25 to 44: 26.7%

Ages 45 to 54: 10.9%

Ages 55 to 59: 5%

Ages 60 to 64: 5.6%

Ages 65 plus: 17.5%

Educational Attainment (1990)

Percent having completed high school: 71.4%

Percent having completed college: 11.5%

Elementary and high school enrollment: 15,862

Federal Funds and Grants Received

Total received in 1989: $365,300,000

Funds received per capita: $3,568

Civilian Labor Force

1993 (April): 43,881

1992 average: 45,328

1991 average: 45,288

1990 average: 44,468

Unemployment

1993 (April): 8.8%

1992 average: 10.7%

1991 average: 9.3%

1990 average: 8.0%

Average Annual Pay

1988: $18,153

1987: $17,503

1985: $16,600

Per Capita Personal Income

1991: $14,768

1990: $14,187

1989: $13,400

Business Climate (1987)

Manufacturing

Number of establishments in 1987: 91

Shipments in 1987 ($1,000): $678,200

Employees in 1987: 6,000

Change in employment, 1982 to 1987: -24.1%

Average annual pay for manufacturing work in 1989: $28,953

Average annual pay for production work in 1987: $24,289

Wholesale Trade

Number of establishments in 1987: 119

Total sales in 1987 ($1,000): $527,800

Change in sales, 1982 to 1987: 135.5%

Retail Trade

Number of establishments in 1987: 764

Total sales in 1987 ($1,000): $527,800

Retail sales per household in 1987: $14,402

Average annual pay in 1989: $9,216

Service Industry

Selected receipts in 1987 ($1,000): $195,600

Average annual pay in 1989: $16,217

Housing

Total number of units in 1990: 43,443
Occupied units in 1990: 39,615
Owner-occupied units in 1990: 71.8%
1993 ACCRA average cost: $123,250
1993 ACCRA average rent for an apartment: $426

Chamber of Commerce

Allegany County Chamber of Commerce, Charles L. Amos, Exec. Director, Bell Tower Bldg., City Hall Plaza, Cumberland, MD, 21502. 301-722-2820

Economic Development Office

Allegany County Dept. of Economic Development, David W. Edgerley, Director, 1 Commerce Dr., Cumberland, MD, 21502. 301-777-5967

Major Businesses

Company	SIC	Telephone
Carl Belt, Inc.	1541	(301) 729-8900
Black Diamond Energies Inc.	5052	(301) 724-3360
Goldsmit-Black Inc. of Maryland	5399	(301) 722-7111
Kelly-Springfield Tire Co.	3011	(301) 777-6000
Lee Tire & Rubber Co., Inc.	5014	(301) 777-6000
Memorial Hospital Medical Center	8062	(301) 777-4000
Sisters of Sacred Heart Charity Hospital	8062	(301) 759-4200
S. Schwab Company Inc.	2341	(301) 729-4488
Shaffer Ford Inc.	5511	(301) 777-3900
Spoerl's Pontiac-Cadillac	5511	(301) 722-8300
Super Shoe Stores Inc.	5661	(301) 759-4300
Wm Bancorp	6022	(301) 334-9483

Colleges and Universities

Allegany Community College, Cumberland, MD

HAGERSTOWN, MD (MSA)

Geographic Profile

Land Area
458.2 square miles

Counties and Parishes
Washington

Ranking Highlights

299 *out of 319 in total* **land area**
187 *out of 319 in* **population growth,** *1970–1990*
 60 *out of 310 in having the lowest* **unemployment** *rate*
249 *out of 310 in size of* **labor force**
162 *out of 318 in the percentage of* **college graduates**
169 *out of 292 in per capita personal* **income**
252 *out of 319 in number of* **manufacturing establishments**
147 *out of 318 in* **physicians** *per 1000 people*
208 *out of 318 in* **hospital beds** *per 1000 people*
  6 *out of 267 in fewest* **crimes** *per 1000 people*
 37 *out of 266 in fewest* **violent crimes** *per 1000 people*
148 *out of 319 in per capita* **federal funds and grants**

Quality of Life Indexes (Rate per 1000 population)

Crime rate in 1991:	29.2
Violent crime rate in 1991:	2.9
Physicians rate in 1992:	1.33
Hospital bed rate in 1991:	2.57

ACCRA Cost of Living Indexes
(First quarter 1993, average = 100)

Composite index: 103.1
Utilities index: 101.4
Housing index: 114.9

Population (1990)

Total Population and Growth Rate
1990: 121,393
1980: 113,086
1970: 103,829
Growth rate 1970–1990: 17%

Race and Hispanic Origin
White: 92.9%
Black: 6.0%
Asian/Pacific Islander: 0.7%
Native American: 0.2%
Hispanic origin: 0.7%
White not Hispanic: 92.5%

Age
Ages 18 to 20: 4.3%
Ages 21 to 24: 6.3%
Ages 25 to 44: 32.8%
Ages 45 to 54: 10.6%
Ages 55 to 59: 4.7%

Ages 60 to 64: 4.8%
Ages 65 plus: 13.8%

Educational Attainment (1990)
Percent having completed high school: 69.3%
Percent having completed college: 11.4%
Elementary and high school enrollment: 18,791

Federal Funds and Grants Received
Total received in 1989: $370,900,000
Funds received per capita: $3,149

Civilian Labor Force
1993 (April):　　62,349
1992 average:　　64,207
1991 average:　　63,493
1990 average:　　61,080

Unemployment
1993 (April):　8.0%
1992 average:　8.9%
1991 average:　8.2%
1990 average:　6.7%

Average Annual Pay
1988: $19,135
1987: $18,689
1985: $17,784

Per Capita Personal Income
1991: $16,845
1990: $16,304
1989: $15,712

Business Climate (1987)
Manufacturing
Number of establishments in 1987: 146
Shipments in 1987 ($1,000): $1,112,900
Employees in 1987: 11,500
Change in employment, 1982 to 1987: -6.5%
Average annual pay for manufacturing work in 1989: $26,082
Average annual pay for production work in 1987: $21,081

Wholesale Trade
Number of establishments in 1987: 212
Total sales in 1987 ($1,000): $724,400
Change in sales, 1982 to 1987: 65.5%

Retail Trade
Number of establishments in 1987: 774
Total sales in 1987 ($1,000): $724,400
Retail sales per household in 1987: $18,634
Average annual pay in 1989: $11,804

Service Industry
Selected receipts in 1987 ($1,000): $188,700
Average annual pay in 1989: $17,865

Housing
Total number of units in 1990: 47,448

Occupied units in 1990: 44,762
Owner-occupied units in 1990: 63.8%
1993 ACCRA average cost: $138,887
1993 ACCRA average rent for an apartment: $477

Chamber of Commerce
Hagerstown-Washington County Chamber of Commerce, Charles R. Stroh, Exec. Vice President, 14 Public Square, Hagerstown, MD, 21740. 301-739-2015

Economic Development Office
Hagerstown-Washington County Economic Development Commission, Leroy Burtner, Exec Director, Court House Annex, Hagerstown, MD, 21740. 301-791-3080

Major Businesses

Company	SIC	Telephone
A. C. & T. Co Inc.	5172	(301) 582-2700
American Moulding Inc.	2499	(301) 790-1211
Antietam Paper Company Inc.	5111	(301) 739-0600
Baer Packing Corp.	5148	(301) 739-5111
D. M. Bowman, Incorporated	4213	(301) 223-6900
Brethren Mutual Insurance Co.	6331	(301) 739-0950
Callas Contractors Inc.	1541	(301) 739-8400
Cannon Shoe Company	3143	(301) 739-1664
Cavetown Planing Mill Co.	2431	(301) 733-7940
Central Chemical Corporation	2875	(301) 733-4702
Citicorp Credit Services	7389	(301) 790-4200
Craig Paving Inc.	1611	(301) 739-9814
Ewing Oil Co Inc.	5172	(301) 790-2070
C. William Hetzer, Inc.	1541	(301) 733-7300
Home Federal Corporation	6022	(301) 733-6300
Home Federal Savings Bank	6035	(301) 733-6300
Jamison Door Co.	3442	(301) 733-3100
MacDraw Inc.	5084	(301) 223-8584
R. D. McKee, Inc.	5074	(301) 739-2525
Mid-Atlantic Bankcorp	6022	(301) 739-0850
Pangborn Corp.	3569	(301) 739-3500
Paramount Feed & Supply Inc.	5191	(301) 733-8150
Potomac Edison Company	4911	(301) 790-3400
Review & Herald Publishing Association	2721	(301) 791-7000
Sharrett Inc.	5511	(301) 739-7700
Statton Furniture Manufacturing Co.	2511	(301) 739-0360
G. A. Stewart Enterprises	5141	(301) 739-5111
Washington County Hospital Association	8062	(301) 797-2000
Western Maryland Supply	5074	(301) 739-7474
Robert F. Zeigler, Inc.	1711	(301) 733-6695

Colleges and Universities
Hagerstown Business College, Hagerstown, MD
Hagerstown Junior College, Hagerstown, MD

MASSACHUSETTS

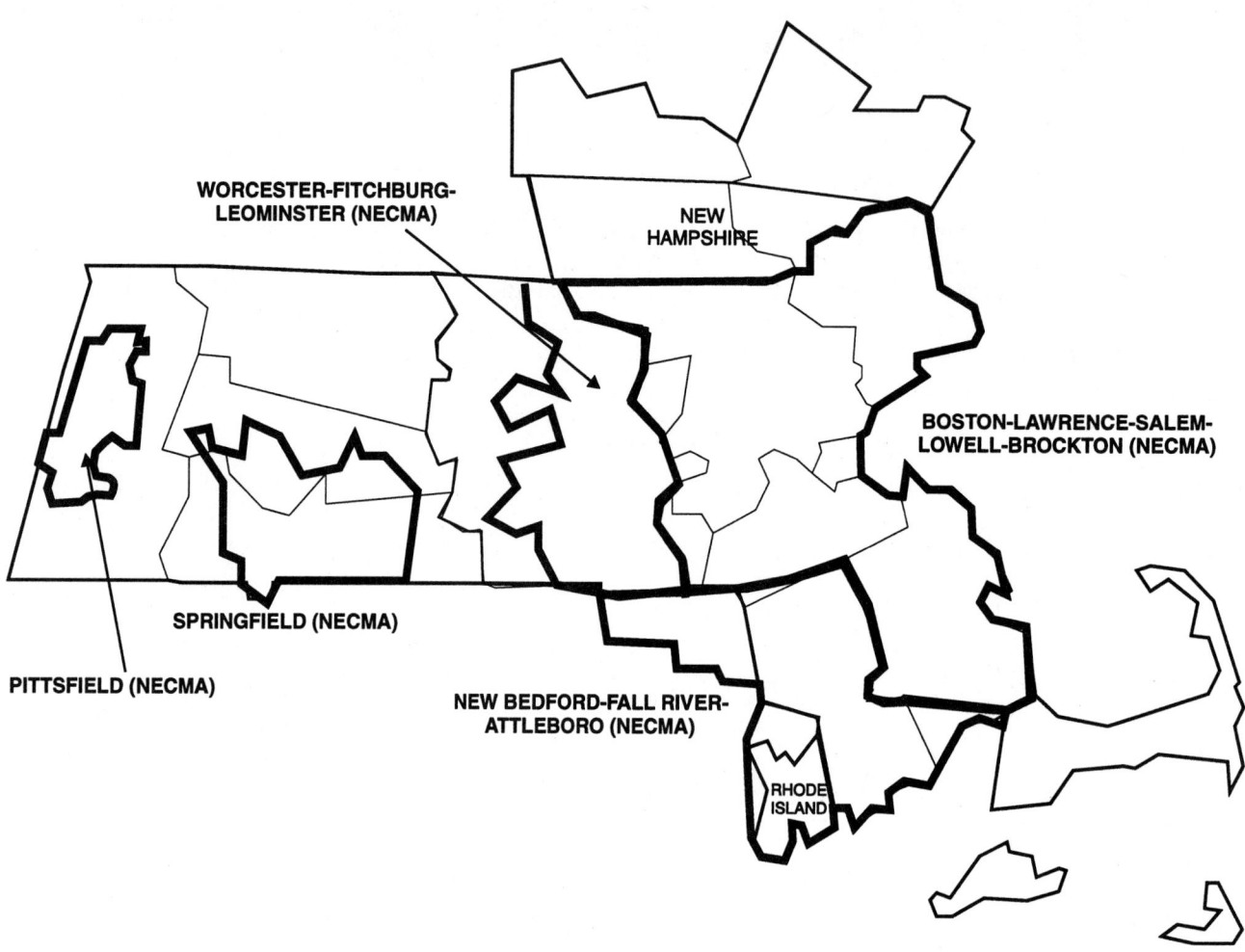

WORCESTER-FITCHBURG-
LEOMINSTER (NECMA)

NEW
HAMPSHIRE

BOSTON-LAWRENCE-SALEM-
LOWELL-BROCKTON (NECMA)

SPRINGFIELD (NECMA)

PITTSFIELD (NECMA)

NEW BEDFORD-FALL RIVER-
ATTLEBORO (NECMA)

RHODE
ISLAND

MASSACHUSETTS

Population
1990: 6,016,425
1980: 5,737,037

Age
Ages 18 to 20: 302,128
Ages 21 to 24: 406,971
Ages 25 to 44: 2,019,817
Ages 45 to 54: 600,095
Ages 55 to 59: 253,458
Ages 60 to 64: 261,597
Median age: 33.6

Race
White: 5,405,374
Black: 300,130
Asian/Pacific Islander: 143,392
Native American: 12,241
Hispanic origin: 287,549

Households
Total: 2,247,110
Persons per household: 2.58

Sex
Male: 2,888,745
Female: 3,127,680

Population Migration
Domestic migration: -203,000
International migration: 119,000

Projection of the Population in 1995
Total: 6,166,000
18 to 64: 3,935,000

Civilian Labor Force
1993: 3,150,500
1992: 3,130,600
1991: 3,117,000
1990: 3,121,900

Manufacturing
1995 Projection: 582,800
1992: 462,100
1991: 476,300
1990: 506,700
1989: 552,500

Services
1995 Projection: 1,367,300
1992: 907,300
1991: 899,900
1990: 917,300
1989: 938,500

Wholesale and Retail Trade
1995 Projection: 875,200
1992: 641,300
1991: 659,000
1990: 707,500
1989: 769,800

Unemployment Rate
1993: 8.5%
1992: 8.4%
1991: 8.4%
1990: 5.0%

Employer Unemployment Contributions
Contribution Rate
1992: 4.20%
1991: 3.70%
1990: 2.80%

Average Weekly Benefit
1992: $230.53
1991: $229.06
1990: $217.96

Gross State Product (Million $)
1989: $144,791
1988: $140,793
1987: $128,115
1979: $59,647
Growth rate, 1979 to 1989: 142.7%

Capital Expenditures of Manufacturing Industries
1990: $1,847,000,000
1989: $2,022,000,000
1988: $2,008,100,000
1987: $2,169,000,000

State Tax Rates
Individual income: No tax below $8,000 for single and $12,000 for husband and wife. Above these amounts, 5% for earned income and 10% for interest, dividends, etc.
Corporate income: 9.5% of taxable net income.

General property: No state levy. Rates fixed locally, assessed at fair cash value of real and personal property.

General sales: 5%

Gasoline: 19.1% of average price per gallon.

Income

Median income for a 4 person family: $51,799

Personal per Capita Income
1992: $24,059
1991: $23,046
1990: $22,558

Disposable per Capita Income
1992: $20,822
1991: $19,808
1990: $19,282

Private Employment Weekly Wages

Average
1989: $481
1988: $462
1987: $462

Manufacturing
1989: $430
1988: $565
1987: $525

Services
1989: $461
1988: $434
1987: $402

Wholesale
1989: $634
1988: $616
1987: $565

Retail
1989: $265
1988: $260
1987: $243

Highway Statistics

Total Highway Miles
1990: 34,076
1989: 33,807
1988: 33,809

Federal Highway Aid
1991: $949,223,000
1990: $893,150,000
1989: $349,003,000

Electricity

Average Cost per Kilowatt Hour
1990: 8.83¢
1989: 8.32¢
1988: 7.87¢

Housing (1990)
Owner occupied units: 1,331,493
Median house value: $162,800
Renter occupied units: 915,617
Median rent: $506
Total vacant units: 225,601
Homeowner vacancy rate: 1.7%
Rental vacancy rate: 6.9%

State Business Incentives and Assistance

Financial and Business Assistance

Corporation Loss Carryovers. All new corporations in Massachusetts may deduct from their taxable income losses incurred in the first five years of operation. The loss may be carried forward, terminating in the fifth year. Corporations more than five years old may carry over, but not carry back, net operating losses. Qualifying losses may be carried forward for up to five years.

Sales Tax Exemption for Machinery. Certain machinery and replacement parts used by manufacturing corporations, corporations primarily engaged in research and development, and other specialized industries such as agricultural and fishing are exempt from Massachusetts sales and use taxes.

Local Property Tax Exemption on Tangible Property. For manufacturing, R&D, agricultural, and fishing corporations, machinery, equipment, furniture and fixtures, tools, supplies, inventory, and goods in process are exempt from local property taxes. Only real estate is taxed. For non-manufacturing corporations, inventory, equipment, furniture and fixtures, tools, supplies, and goods in process are exempt from local property tax. Only machinery and real estate is taxed. Massachusetts has a special constitutional amendment, known as Proposition 2 1/2, which limits taxation to 2.5% of assessed value and restricts increases in tax rates, thus stabilizing the property tax burden.

Dividend Deduction. Corporations may deduct from net income dividends which are received from other corporations. Exceptions are from non-wholly-owned DISCs and dividends where the taxpayer owns less than 15% of the voting stock of the corporations paying the dividend.

Massachusetts Deduction-Targeted Jobs Tax Credit Program (TJTC). The federal credit is equal to 40% of the first $6,000 of the employee's first year wage (up to $2,400). Massachusetts allows a deduction to corporations for the federal Targeted Job Credit for allocable wages paid in Massachusetts. The Massachusetts Division of Employment Security determines eligibility of each employee.

Education and Training

Employee Training Programs. Employment services include customized on-the-job training, placement services, employee counseling and skills upgrading. The Employment and Training Service is operated through 15

Major Companies in the State

Company name	Fortune 500 rank	City	Telephone	SIC number
Fortune 500 Companies				
Amoskeag Co.	307	Boston	617-262-4000	2392
Cabot Corp.	265	Boston	617-345-0100	2895
Data General Corp.	328	Westboro	508-366-8911	3571
Digital Equipment Corp.	27	Maynard	508-493-5111	3571
EG&G Inc.	170	Wellesley	617-237-5100	3829
Gillette Co.	104	Boston	617-421-7000	3421
Kendall International Inc.	421	Mansfield	508-261-8000	3842
Millipore Corp.	415	Bedford	617-275-9200	3826
Ocean Spray Cranberries Inc.	336	Lakeville Middleboro	508-946-1000	2033
Polaroid Corp.	211	Cambridge	617-577-2000	3861
Raytheon Co.	54	Lexington	617-862-6600	3812
Seaboard Corp. Massachusetts	343	Newton	913-676-8800	2015
Stanhome Inc.	425	Westfield	413-562-3631	5199
Thermo Electron Corp.	362	Waltham	617-622-1000	3826
Wang Laboratories Inc.	226	Lowell	508-459-5000	7373
Other Major Companies in the State				
Bank of Boston Corp.		Boston	617-434-2200	6712
Bank of New England Corp.		Boston	617-573-0400	6712
Baybanks Inc.		Boston	617-482-1040	6712
Boston Edison Co.		Boston	617-424-2000	4911
General Cinema Corp.		Chestnut Hill	617-232-8200	7832
Hills Department Stores Inc.		Canton	617-821-1000	5311
Hills Stores Co.		Canton	617-821-1000	5311
Massachusetts Electric Co.		Westborough	508-366-9011	4911
Neiman Marcus Group Inc.		Chestnut Hill	617-232-0760	5311
New England Electric System		Westborough	508-366-9011	4911
New England Mutual Life Insurance Co.		Boston	617-578-2000	6311
New England Power Co.		Westborough	508-366-9011	4911
New England Telephone & Telegraph Co.		Boston	617-743-9800	4813
Northeast Utilities		West Springfield	413-785-5871	4911
Reebok International Ltd.		Stoughton	617-341-5000	3149
State Street Boston Corp.		Boston	617-786-3000	6712
Stop & Shop Inc.		Boston	617-380-8000	5411
TJX Companies Inc.		Framingham	508-390-1000	5651
Viacom Inc.		Dedham	617-461-1600	7812
Waban Inc.		Natick	508-651-6500	5251

locally-based service delivery systems. The employer works with the local service delivery system staff so that on-the-job training and customized training programs are tailored to their specific needs. Skills covered include electronic components assembly, data entry, computer operations, office skills, medical field skills and skills in the machine parts and precision instrument industries.

On-the-Job Training. Employers are eligible for 50% reimbursement of an employee's wage during training through on-the-job training programs. In addition, costs of on-the-

job training programs are subsidized by the federal government through various job training acts.

Bay State Skills Corporation. BSSC provides training programs for high demand industries and industries requiring retraining or upgrading of worker skills. BSSC arranges for the training to be delivered through licensed educational institutions. The State provides 50% of the cost of training and the company is expected to contribute the other 50%. Contributions from the company may be in cash or in kind. The training takes place at existing schools, colleges, and universities, and training centers in the state. If the company prefers, its own facilities and employees may be used as part of its in-kind contribution.

Job Training Partnership Act. This program operates with funding from the U.S. Department of Labor. It provides job training and other employment related services.

State Offices

Real estate: Division of Registration, Judith H. Meltzer, Director, 100 Cambridge St., 15th fl., Boston, MA 02202. 617-727-3074

Chamber of commerce: Associated Industries of Massachusetts, John Gould, President, 441 Stuart St., Boston, MA 02116. 617-262-1180

Economic development: Executive Office of Economic Affairs, Business Development Office, Joseph J. Donovan, Exec Director, 100 Cambridge St., 13th Fl, Boston, MA 02114. 617-727-3206, FAX 617-727-8797

Executive Office of Economic Affairs, Peter Lappin, Director, 1 Armory Square, Garvey Hall, Springfield, MA 01105. 413-784-1580

Massachusetts Industrial Finance Agency, Joseph D. Blair, Exec Director, 75 Federal Street., Boston, MA 02110. 617-451-2477

Massachusetts Technology Development Corp., John Hodgman, Exec Director, 131 State St., Suite 215, Boston, MA 02109. 617-723-4920

Small Business Development Center, John Ciccarelli, State Director, University of Massachusetts, School of Management, Amherst, MA 01003. 413-545-6301

Environmental affairs: Executive Office of Environmental Affairs, John P. DeVillars, Secretary, 100 Cambridge St., 20th fl., Boston, MA 02202. 617-727-9800

Labor: Executive Office of Labor, Paul J. Eustace, Secretary, 1 Ashburton Place, Room 2112, Boston, MA 02108. 617-727-6573

Unemployment: Division of Employment Security, William Luzier, Director, 1 Ashburton Place, Room 2010, Boston, MA 02108. 617-727-2200

Worker's compensation: Workers Compensation Rating and Inspection Board, Ralph Baldridge, Manager, 101 Arch St., 5th fl., Boston, MA 02110. 617-439-9030

Occupational safety and health: Labor and Industries Department, Safety & Health Planning Division, Joseph Belloli, Director, 100 Cambridge Street, Room 1100, Boston, MA 02202. 617-727-8519

Secretary of state: Secretary of the Commonwealth, Michael Joseph Connolly, Secretary of the Commonwealth, Room 337, State House, Boston, MA 02133. 617-727-9180

Taxation and revenue: Dept. of Revenue, Stephen W. Kidder, Commissioner, 100 Cambridge Street, Room 806, Boston, MA 02204. 617-727-4201

Designated Zones for Economic Development

Enterprise Zones

A program to create Economic Opportunity Areas is being considered by the state legislature.

Foreign Trade Zones

Foreign Trade Zone No. 27, Boston, Massachusetts, Grantee: Massachusetts Port Authority, Andrew Bendheim, World Trade Center, Boston, MA 02210, 617-439-5560

Foreign Trade Zone No. 28, New Bedford, Massachusetts, Grantee/Operator: City of New Bedford, Mayor's Office of Economic Development, Maureen Wells, 133 William Street, Rm. 215, New Bedford, MA 02740, 508-999-2931 Ext. 309

Labor Unions

Carpenters and Joiners of America, United Brotherhood of (AFL-CIO)

Electrical Workers, International Brotherhood of (AFL-CIO)

Food and Commercial Workers International Union, United (AFL-CIO)

Hotel Employees and Restaurant Employees International Union (AFL-CIO)

Iron Workers, International Association of Bridge, Structural and Ornamental (AFL-CIO)

Laborers' International Union of North America (AFL-CIO)

Ladies' Garment Workers' Union, International (AFL-CIO)

National Education Association

Nurses' Association, American

Plumbing and Pipe Fitting Industry of The United States and Canada, United Association of, Journeymen and Apprentices of the (AFL-CIO)

Sheet Metal Workers' International Association (AFL-CIO)

State, County and Municipal Employees, American Federation of (AFL-CIO)

Steelworkers of America, United (AFL-CIO)

Transit Union, Amalgamated (AFL-CIO)

Universities with Ph.D. Programs

American International College, Springfield

Boston University, Boston

Brandeis University, Waltham

Clark University, Worcester

Harvard University, Cambridge

Lesley College, Cambridge

Massachusetts College of Pharmacy and Allied Health Sciences, Boston

Massachusetts Institute of Technology, Cambridge

New England College of Optometry, Boston

Northeastern University, Boston

Simmons College, Boston

Smith College, Northampton

Springfield College, Springfield

Suffolk University, Boston

Tufts University, Medford
University of Lowell, Lowell
University of Massachusetts at Boston, Boston

BOSTON–LAWRENCE–SALEM–LOWELL–BROCKTON, MA (NECMA)

Geographic Profile

Land Area
2440.3 square miles

Counties and Parishes
Boston
Bristo
Essex
Middlesex
Norfolk
Plymouth
Suffolk
Worcester
Brockton
Bristol (part)
Norfolk (part)
Plymouth (part)
Lawrence-Haverhill
Massachusetts:
  Essex (part)
New Hampshire:
  Rockingham (part)
Salem
Essex (part)
Lowell
Massachusetts:
  Middlesex (part)
New Hampshire:
  Hillsborough (part)

Additional Cities/Towns within Area
Boston
Cambridge
Framingham
Lynn
Waltham
Brockton
Bristol County:
  Easton
Norfolk County:
  Avon
Plymouth County:
  Abington
  Bridgewater
  East Bridgewater
  Halifax
  West Bridgewater
  Whitman
Lawrence-Haverhill

Essex County:
  Amesbury
  Andover
  Boxford
  Georgetown
  Groveland
  Merrimac
  Methuen
  Newbury
  Newburyport
  North Andover
  Salisbury
  West Newbury
Rockingham County:
  Atkinson
  Brentwood
  Danville
  Derry
  East Kingston
  Hampstead
  Kingston
  Newton
  Plaistow
  Salem
  Sandown
  Seabrook
  Windham
Salem
Beverly
Danvers
Essex
Hamilton
Ipswich
Manchester
Marblehead
Middleton
Peabody
Rockport
Rowley
Swampscott
Topsfield
Lowell
Middlesex County:
  Billerica
  Chelmsford
  Dracut
  Dunstable
  Pepperell
  Tewksbury
  Tyngsborough
  Westford
Hillsborough County:
  Pelham

Ranking Highlights

 71 *out of 319 in total* **land area**
262 *out of 319 in* **population growth,** *1970–1990*
 52 *out of 310 in having the lowest* **unemployment** *rate*
  7 *out of 310 in size of* **labor force**
 22 *out of 318 in the percentage of* **college graduates**
 14 *out of 292 in per capita personal* **income**
  6 *out of 319 in number of* **manufacturing establishments**
 14 *out of 318 in* **physicians** *per 1000 people*
123 *out of 318 in* **hospital beds** *per 1000 people*
 83 *out of 267 in fewest* **crimes** *per 1000 people*
167 *out of 266 in fewest* **violent crimes** *per 1000 people*
 46 *out of 319 in per capita* **federal funds and grants**

Quality of Life Indexes (Rate per 1000 population)

Crime rate in 1991:	54.8
Violent crime rate in 1991:	8.3
Physicians rate in 1992:	3.6
Hospital bed rate in 1991:	4

ACCRA Cost of Living Indexes
(First quarter 1993, average = 100)

Composite index:	139.5
Utilities index:	146.3
Housing index:	181.5

Overview

During the 1980s Boston gained fame as a high technology and defense research center and a good place in which to conduct business, attributable in part to the vast network of research facilities connected with schools in the region. Boston ranked eighteenth on *Money* magazine's 1992 list of the 300 best places to live in America.

While manufacturing in Boston has lost some ground, it remains an important sector of the economy. Major industries include finance, high-technology research and development, tourism, medicine, education, commercial fishing, food processing, printing and publishing, and government. Early in its history, Boston made its name as a center for the processing of wool and the manufacture of clothing, textiles, shoes, and leather goods. While the shoe and textile industries have suffered in recent decades, they remain significant contributors to Boston's economy.

Biomedical, high–tech, and research and development activities are predicted to be the leading economic growth areas of the 1990s in the Boston region. In 1990 Boston's thirty-one hospitals and research institutes led the country with $500 million in Federal research grants.

Boston's financial district includes major banks such as the Bank of New England and First National Bank of Boston. Insurance firms such as the John Hancock Insurance Company are a significant presence there.

Boston is one of the country's top ten tourist attractions, focusing on the city's sixty–two historic sites, its nearly 2,000 restaurants, and its hundreds of hotels. Tourism is a year–long industry in Boston, which hosts 14,000,000 visitors, business executives, and conventioneers each year.

The medical schools of both Tufts University and Harvard University are located in Boston, as is Massachusetts General Hospital, the major teaching hospital for both schools. Education is a thriving segment of Boston's economy; within the city limits are ten colleges and universities, six technical schools, four art and music schools, and six junior colleges. In towns and suburbs surrounding Boston, educational institutions include many prestigious secondary and boarding schools.

As the capital of the Commonwealth of Massachusetts, Boston is the workplace of many state, as well as municipal, employees.

Shipping is a major industry in Boston: some twenty-two million tons of goods pass through the harbor each year, making it the nation's seventeenth busiest port. Today, Boston's exports include grains and metals. Its imports are petroleum products and sugar. Boston's popularity as a port is easily understood: it accommodates even the largest ocean going freighters. One of the best natural harbors in the United States, the Fort Point Channel is forty feet deep and seven miles long. Nearly forty miles of docks and wharves line the shores of Boston's inner harbor, mainly between South Boston and Charlestown. Logan International Airport, located in East Boston, is just two miles from downtown Boston. Forty-two domestic and international airlines fly into Logan for a total of more than 400 flights each day to 230 U.S. and foreign cities. One of the busiest hubs in the country, Logan can be reached by car, by public transportation on the Blue Line, and by water aboard the Airport Water Shuttle.

Boston's access routes by automobile include Interstate-90, the Massachusetts Turnpike, which is the major east-west artery. Massachusetts Service Route 9, another east-west road, accommodates suburban traffic. I-93 runs north-south through Boston where it is called the Northeast Expressway. Encircling the city is Massachusetts Service Route 128. More than seven-hundred high-technology firms have established facilities along Massachusetts SR 128 and I-495, making them heavily traveled freeways.

Lowell

The corporate headquarters of Wang Laboratories, manufacturer of information processing equipment, are located in Lowell; in its heyday, Wang employed 31,500 workers, nearly 10,000 of them in Lowell. As was the case throughout the state, by the early 1990s the computer industry in Lowell was suffering. In August 1992 Wang filed for bankruptcy court protection. The company stated that as part of its restructuring, it would cut its work force, then estimated at 13,000 employees industry–wide, by 5,000 people (38 percent). Lowell is a regional center for Fleet Bank, formerly Bank of New England, which failed in 1991. Tour-

ism is an economic mainstay, with the city welcoming about 700,000 visitors annually.

Items and goods produced in the area include textiles, yarns and threads, textile machinery, knitwear, wire and cable, plastics, computer hardware and software, electronic publishing, and printing.

The Boston & Maine Railroad, with tracks throughout the U.S. Northeast and the Canadian Maritime provinces, can also ship freight elsewhere in the United States by using a series of connector routes. The Boston & Maine runs through Lowell, which is also served by several trucking fleets.

Population (1990)

Total Population and Growth Rate
1990: 3,783,817
1980: 3,662,888
1970: 3,709,642
Growth rate 1970–1990: 2%

Race and Hispanic Origin
White: 88.5%
Black: 5.9%
Asian/Pacific Islander: 3.0%
Native American: 0.2%
Hispanic origin: 4.8%
White not Hispanic: 86.4%

Age
Ages 18 to 20: 5.2%
Ages 21 to 24: 7.4%
Ages 25 to 44: 36.7%
Ages 45 to 54: 10.8%
Ages 55 to 59: 4.5%
Ages 60 to 64: 4.4%
Ages 65 plus: 13.3%

Educational Attainment (1990)
Percent having completed high school: 82.8%
Percent having completed college: 30.6%
Elementary and high school enrollment: 595,000

Federal Funds and Grants Received
Total received in 1989: $17,873,100,000
Funds received per capita: $4,784

Civilian Labor Force
1993 (April): 2,127,484
1992 average: 2,126,580
1991 average: 2,030,900
1990 average: 2,057,200

Unemployment
1993 (April): 6.2%
1992 average: 8.0%
1991 average: 8.2%
1990 average: 5.5%

Average Annual Pay
1988: $25,731
1987: $23,888
1985: $20,817

Per Capita Personal Income
1991: $23,480
1990: $22,971
1989: $22,215

Business Climate (1987)

Manufacturing
Number of establishments in 1987: 6,796
Shipments in 1987 ($1,000): $41,855,000
Employees in 1987: 377,700
Change in employment, 1982 to 1987: -6.5%
Average annual pay for manufacturing work in 1989: $33,161
Average annual pay for production work in 1987: $21,327

Wholesale Trade
Number of establishments in 1987: 7,937
Total sales in 1987 ($1,000): $62,075,600
Change in sales, 1982 to 1987: 55.5%

Retail Trade
Number of establishments in 1987: 23,115
Total sales in 1987 ($1,000): $62,075,600
Retail sales per household in 1987: $20,700
Average annual pay in 1989: $14,586

Service Industry
Selected receipts in 1987 ($1,000): $21,971,700
Average annual pay in 1989: $25,670

Office Real Estate (1992)
Office space inventory: 84,810,000 sq. feet
Average class A Central Business District rental range per sq. ft: $22.50

Vacancy Rates
All areas: 17.2%

Vacancy Rates in Central Business District
Class A space: 13.5%
Class B space: 21.8%

Vacancy Rates Outside Central Business District
Class A space: 19.8%
Class B space: N/A

Housing
Total number of units in 1990: 1,581,202
Occupied units in 1990: 1,481,835
Owner-occupied units in 1990: 58.3%
1993 ACCRA average cost: $220,738
1993 ACCRA average rent for an apartment: $729

Chamber of Commerce
Greater Boston Chamber of Commerce, James L. Sullivan, President, 600 Atlantic Ave., Boston, MA 02210-2200. 617-227-4500

Economic Development Office
Cambridge Chamber of Commerce, Robert D. Lewis, Exec Vice President, 859 Massachusetts Ave., Cambridge, MA 02139. 617-884-4877

Economic Development Organizations
Metro West Chamber of Commerce, Michelle flaherty, President, 600 Worcester Road, Suite 4A, Framingham, MA 01701. 508-879-5600

Metro South Chamber of Commerce, A. Theodore Welte, President, 60 School St., Brockton, MA 02401. 508-586-0500

Lynn Area Chamber of Commerce, William Simons, President, 170 Union Street, Lynn, MA 01901. 617-592-2900

Waltham W. Suburban Chamber of Commerce, Theodore L. Manning, Exec Director, 500 Main Street, Waltham, MA 02154. 617-894-4700

Greater Haverhill Chamber of Commerce, Dr. Donald L. Ruhl, President, 87 Winter St., Haverhill, MA 01830. 508-373-5663

Essex North Chamber of Commerce, Steve Nichols, Chairman, 29 State Street, Newburyport, MA 01950. 508-462-6680

Salem Chamber of Commerce, Joan Gormalley, Exec Director, 32 Derby Square, Town Hall, Salem, MA 01970. 508-744-0004

Newton-Needham Chamber of Commerce, Angeljean Chiaramida, Exec Director, 437 Cherry Street, West Newton, MA 02165. 617-244-5300

WenhamSalem Chamber of Commerce, Joan P. Gormalley, Exec. Director, 32 Derby Square, Salem, MA 01970. 508-744-0004

North Shore Chamber of Commerce, Don Short, Exec Director, 7 Cherry Hill Drive, Suite 100, Danvers, MA 01923. 508-774-8565

Ipswich-Essex County Chamber of Commerce, Barbara Parsons, Exec Director, 319 Barnstable Road, Hyannis, MA 02601. 508-356-3231

Marblehead Chamber of Commerce, Dorothy Richardson, Exec Director, 62 Pleasant Street, Marblehead, MA 01945. 617-631-2868

Peabody chamber of Commerce, Jean Lebro, Exec Director, 20 Peabody Square, Peabody, MA 01960. 508-531-0384

Northern Middlesex Chamber of Commerce & Industry, Kevin E. Coughlin, President, 45 Palmer St., Lowell, MA 01852. 508-937-9300

Major Businesses

Company	SIC	Telephone
Affiliated Publications Inc.	2711	(617) 929-3035
Agar Supply Co Inc.	5147	(617) 442-8989
Algonquin Energy, Inc.	4923	(617) 254-4050
Algonquin Gas Transmission Company	4923	(617) 254-4050

Major Businesses (Continued)

Company	SIC	Telephone
Lou Allen & Sons Co., Inc.	5141	(617) 332-8200
Amoskeag Company	2211	(617) 262-4000
Analog Devices Inc.	3674	(617) 329-4700
Arkwright Mutual Insurance Company	6331	(617) 890-9300
Bain & Company	8742	(617) 572-2000
J. Baker, Inc.	5661	(617) 364-3000
Bancboston Financial Company	6153	(617) 434-4002
Bank New England Corporation	6021	(617) 742-4000
Bank of Boston Corporation	6021	(617) 434-2200
Bank of New England, NA	6021	(617) 742-4000
Bay State Gas Company	4923	(617) 828-8650
Bay State Milling Co.	2041	(617) 328-4400
Baybank Middlesex	6022	(617) 273-1700
Baybanks Inc.	6022	(617) 482-1040
Beth Israel Hospital Association	8062	(617) 735-2000
Blue Cross Blue Shield	6324	(617) 956-2000
Bolt Beranek and Newman Inc.	3571	(617) 873-2000
Bose Corporation	3651	(508) 879-7330
Boston Company Inc.	6022	(617) 956-9700
Boston Edison Company	4911	(617) 424-2000
Boston Five Bancorp	6712	(617) 742-6000
Boston Five Cents Savings Bank	6035	(617) 742-6000
Boston Gas Company	4924	(617) 742-8400
Boston Safe Deposit Trust Company	6022	(617) 722-7000
Bradlees New England Inc.	5311	(617) 380-8000
Braun Inc.	5064	(617) 592-3300
Brigham and Womens Hospital	8062	(617) 732-5500
Browning-Ferris Industries of Massachusetts	4953	(617) 265-0500
C M L Group Inc.	5611	(508) 264-4155
Cabot Corporation	1311	(617) 890-0200
Cambridge-Lee Industries	5051	(617) 783-3100
Cameron and Colby Co, Inc.	6411	(617) 357-8400
Camp Dresser & McKee Inc.	8711	(617) 621-8181
Canal Electric Company	4911	(617) 225-4000
Cargill Petroleum Inc.	5172	(617) 286-3400
Caritas Christi Inc.	8062	(617) 893-8544
Catamunt Petroleum Ltd	5172	(617) 561-7200
CDK Holding Corporation	3842	(617) 574-7000
Chelsea Industries Inc.	2673	(617) 787-9010
Ciba Corning Diagnostics	3841	(508) 359-7711
Commercial Union Corporation	6311	(617) 725-6000
Commonwealth Auto Reinsurance	6331	(617) 338-4000
Commonwealth Energy Systems	4911	(617) 225-4000
Commonwealth Gas Company	4924	(617) 225-4000
Connell Limited Partnership	3312	(617) 737-2700
Continental Cablevision Inc.	4841	(617) 742-9500
Crimson Travel Service Inc.	4724	(617) 868-2600

Major Businesses (Continued)

Company	SIC	Telephone
Cumberland Crude Processing	1311	(617) 828-4900
Cumberland Farms Inc.	5411	(617) 828-4900
James W. Daly Inc.	5122	(508) 532-6900
Dennison Manufacturing Company	2678	(508) 879-0511
Dynatech Corporation	3661	(617) 272-6100
Eastern Enterprises	4924	(617) 647-2300
Eastern Utilities Association	4911	(617) 357-9590
EG&G Inc.	8731	(617) 237-5100
Employers Fire Insurance Company	6331	(617) 725-6000
F M R Corp.	6282	(617) 570-7000
Faxon Company, Inc.	5192	(617) 329-3350
Federal Reserve Bank of Boston	6011	(617) 973-3000
James Ferrera & Sons Inc.	5141	(617) 828-6150
Fidelity Brokerage Services	6211	(617) 570-7000
Fidelity Cash Reserve Fund	6722	(617) 570-7000
Fidelity Daily Income Trust	6722	(617) 523-1919
Fidelity Distributors Corp.	6211	(617) 726-0200
Fidelity Eqity-Income Fund	6722	(617) 726-0200
Fidelity Magellan Fund	6722	(617) 570-7000
Filene's Basement Inc.	5651	(617) 239-9000
First National Bank of Boston	6021	(617) 434-2200
Fishery Products Inc.	2092	(508) 777-2660
Flatley Company	1522	(617) 848-2000
Foxboro Company, The	3823	(508) 543-8750
GCC Theaters Inc.	8741	(617) 232-8200
General Cinema Corporation	5621	(617) 232-8200
General Hospital Corporation	8062	(617) 726-2000
Gillette Company, The	3421	(617) 421-7000
Global Petroleum Corp.	5172	(617) 891-4000
Globe Newspaper Company	2711	(617) 929-2000
Grossman's Inc.	5211	(617) 848-0100
GTE Government Systems Co.	3663	(617) 890-9200
Healthco International Inc.	5047	(617) 423-6045
Heritage Travel Inc.	4724	(617) 491-0050
Hills Department Stores	5311	(617) 821-1000
Hit Or Miss Inc.	5621	(617) 344-0800
HMK Enterprises Inc.	5021	(617) 891-6660
H. P. Hood, Inc.	2026	(617) 242-0600
Houghton Mifflin Company	2731	(617) 725-5000
International Catering Co.	7389	(617) 890-6200
International Data Group	2721	(508) 875-5000
JBI Inc.	5661	(617) 364-3000
John Hancock Distributors	6211	(617) 375-1500
John Hancock Mutuall	6311	(617) 572-6000
John Hancock Subsidiaries	6311	(617) 421-4672
John Hancock Proprety Casualty	6331	(617) 236-5200
Jordan Marsh Stores Corp.	5311	(617) 357-3000

Major Businesses (Continued)

Company	SIC	Telephone
JWP Information Systems, Inc.	5045	(617) 821-4100
Kendall Company, The	3842	(617) 574-7000
Keystone Provident Life Insurance	6311	(617) 338-3500
Kimberly Quality Care Inc.	8082	(617) 951-2700
Lechmere Inc.	5731	(617) 935-8320
Lexington Insurance Co. Inc.	6331	(617) 330-1100
Liberty Insurance Corporation	6331	(617) 357-9500
Liberty Mutual Fire Insurance	6331	(617) 357-9500
Liberty Mutual Insurance Co.	6331	(617) 357-9500
Arthur D. Little, Inc.	8748	(617) 864-5770
Lotus Development Corp.	7372	(617) 577-8500
M/A-Com Inc.	3674	(617) 272-9600
Massach Financial Services	6282	(617) 954-5000
Merkert Enterprises Inc.	5141	(617) 828-4800
Metcalf & Eddy Inc.	8711	(617) 246-5200
Millipore Corporation	3826	(617) 275-9200
Mitre Corporation	8731	(617) 271-2000
Moacq Holdings Corporation	5661	(617) 828-9300
Montaup Electric Co Inc.	4911	(617) 357-9590
Montello Oil Corp.	5172	(617) 894-8800
Morse Shoe Inc.	5661	(617) 828-9300
Multibank Financial Corp.	7374	(617) 461-1820
NEDH Corp	8062	(617) 732-7000
National Amusements Inc.	7832	(617) 461-1600
NEC Technologies Inc.	5045	(508) 264-8000
Neiman-Marcus Group Inc.	5621	(617) 232-0760
New England	6371	(617) 578-2000
New England Investment Companies	6211	(617) 578-4650
New England Medical Center Hospital	8062	(617) 956-5000
New England Securities Corporation	6211	(617) 267-6600
New England Telephone and Telegraph Co.	4813	(617) 743-9800
Nynex Information Resources Co.	2741	(508) 762-1000
Perini Corporation	1542	(508) 875-6171
Polaroid Corporation	3861	(617) 577-2000
Prime Computer, Inc.	3571	(508) 655-8000
Putnam High Income Government	6722	(617) 292-1000
Raytheon Company	3812	(617) 862-6600
Raytheon Service Company	8741	(617) 272-9300
Reebok International Ltd.	3149	(617) 341-5000
Reed Publishing (USA), Inc.	2721	(617) 964-3030
Reed Publishing Holdings	2721	(617) 964-3030
RFS Carriers Holding Corp.	4213	(508) 429-5920
Rich's Department Stores	5311	(508) 741-1400
Seaboard Corporation	2015	(617) 332-8492
Seaboard Flour Corp.	2015	(617) 332-8492

Major Businesses (Continued)

Company	SIC	Telephone
Seiler Corporation	8741	(617) 890-6200
Shawmut Bank NA	6021	(617) 292-2000
Shawmut Corporation	6712	(617) 292-2000
Sheraton Corporation	7011	(617) 367-3600
Shipley Company Inc.	2869	(617) 969-5500
Somerville Lumber & Supply	5031	(617) 466-8020
St. Johnsbury Trucking Co.	4213	(508) 429-5920
State Street Bank & Trust Company	6022	(617) 786-3000
State Street Boston Corp.	6022	(617) 786-3000
Stone & Webster Engineering Corp.	8711	(617) 589-5111
Stop & Shop Companies, Inc.	5411	(617) 380-8000
Stop & Shop Holdings, Inc.	5311	(617) 380-8000
Stride Rite Corporation	3149	(617) 491-8800
Subaru of New England Inc.	5012	(617) 769-5100
Sun Carriers, Inc.	4213	(508) 429-5920
Sun Life Association of Canada	6311	(617) 237-6030
T A D Technical Services	8711	(617) 868-1650
Talbot's Inc.	5621	(617) 749-7600
Technical Aid Corporation	7363	(617) 969-3100
Teradyne Inc.	3825	(617) 482-2700
Thermo Electron Corporation	1629	(617) 622-1000
TJX Companies Inc.	5621	(508) 390-1000
Town & Country Corporation	3911	(617) 884-8500
UST Corp	6022	(617) 726-7000
Unifirst Corporation	7218	(508) 658-8888
Viacom Inc.	7812	(617) 461-1600
Waban Inc.	5211	(508) 651-6500
S. D. Warren Company	2621	(617) 423-7300
Welch Foods Inc.	2033	(508) 371-1000
Xtra Corporation	7513	(617) 367-5000

Colleges and Universities

Art Institute of Boston, Boston
Bay State College, Boston
Berklee College of Music, Boston
Boston Architectural Center, Boston
Boston Conservatory, Boston
Boston University, Boston
Bunker Hill Community College, Boston
Emerson College, Boston
Emmanuel College, Boston
Fisher College, Boston
Franklin Institute of Boston, Boston
Katharine Gibbs School, Boston
Laboure College, Boston
Massachusetts College of Art, Boston
Massachusetts College of Pharmacy And Allied Health Sciences, Boston
New England Banking Institute, Boston

New England College of Optometry, Boston
New England Conservatory of Music, Boston
Northeastern University, Boston
School of The Museum of Fine Arts, Boston
Simmons College, Boston
Suffolk University, Boston
University of Massachusetts At Boston, Boston
Harvard University, Cambridge
Lesley College, Cambridge
Massachusetts Institute of Technology, Cambridge
Framingham State College, Framingham
Bentley College, Waltham
Brandeis University, Waltham
Massasoit Community College, Brockton
Bridgewater State College, Bridgewater
Northern Essex Community College, Haverhill
Merrimack College, North Andover
Salem State College, Salem
Endicott College, Beverly
North Shore Community College, Beverly
Marian Court Junior College, Swampscott
Gordon College, Wenham
University of Lowell, Lowell

NEW BEDFORD–FALL RIVER–ATTLEBORO, MA (NECMA)

Geographic Profile

Land Area
556.0 square miles

Counties and Parishes
New Bedford
Bristol (part)
Plymouth (part)
Fall River
Massachusetts:
Bristol (part)
Rhode Island:
Newport (part)

Additional Cities/Towns within Area
New Bedford
Bristol County:
Acushnet
Dartmouth
Fairhaven
Freetown
Plymouth County:
Marion
Mattapoisett
Rochester
Fall River
Bristol County:
Somerset
Swansea
Westport
Newport County:
Little Compton
Tiverton
Attleboro
Bristol County:
North Attleborough

Ranking Highlights

282 *out of 319 in total* **land area**
208 *out of 319 in* **population growth,** *1970–1990*
N/A *out of 310 in having the lowest* **unemployment** *rate*
N/A *out of 310 in size of* **labor force**
133 *out of 318 in the percentage of* **college graduates**
N/A *out of 292 in per capita personal* **income**
　64 *out of 319 in number of* **manufacturing establishments**
161 *out of 318 in* **physicians** *per 1000 people*
243 *out of 318 in* **hospital beds** *per 1000 people*
　95 *out of 267 in fewest* **crimes** *per 1000 people*
189 *out of 266 in fewest* **violent crimes** *per 1000 people*

19 *out of 319 in per capita* **federal funds and grants**

Quality of Life Indexes (Rate per 1000 population)

Crime rate in 1991: 57.7
Violent crime rate in 1991: 9.5
Physicians rate in 1992: 1.1
Hospital bed rate in 1991: 0.83

ACCRA Cost of Living Indexes
(First quarter 1993, average = 100)

Composite index: N/A
Utilities index: N/A
Housing index: N/A

Population (1990)

Total Population and Growth Rate

1990: 506,325
1980: 474,641
1970: 444,301
Growth rate 1970–1990: 14%

Race and Hispanic Origin

White: 94.6%
Black: 1.7%
Asian/Pacific Islander: 0.7%
Native American: 0.2%
Hispanic origin: 2.8%
White not Hispanic: 93.0%

Age

Ages 18 to 20: 3.4%
Ages 21 to 24: 4.4%
Ages 25 to 44: 22%
Ages 45 to 54: 7.3%
Ages 55 to 59: 3.2%
Ages 60 to 64: 3.6%
Ages 65 plus: 11.8%

Educational Attainment (1990)

Percent having completed high school: 52.3%
Percent having completed college: 14.4%
Elementary and high school enrollment: 90,000

Federal Funds and Grants Received

Total received in 1989: $3,259,600,000
Funds received per capita: $6,749

Civilian Labor Force

1993 (April): N/A
1992 average: N/A
1991 average: 248,600
1990 average: 252,100

Unemployment

1993 (April): N/A
1992 average: N/A
1991 average: 12.3%
1990 average: 8.7%

Average Annual Pay

1988: $19,041

1987: $17,738
1985: $15,601

Per Capita Personal Income

1991: N/A
1990: N/A
1989: N/A

Business Climate (1987)

Manufacturing

Number of establishments in 1987: 1,072
Shipments in 1987 ($1,000): $5,497,100
Employees in 1987: 66,800
Change in employment, 1982 to 1987: -6.6%
Average annual pay for manufacturing work in 1989: $22,954
Average annual pay for production work in 1987: $15,914

Wholesale Trade

Number of establishments in 1987: 683
Total sales in 1987 ($1,000): $3,959,400
Change in sales, 1982 to 1987: 56.7%

Retail Trade

Number of establishments in 1987: 3,234
Total sales in 1987 ($1,000): $3,959,400
Retail sales per household in 1987: $19,708
Average annual pay in 1989: $11,860

Service Industry

Selected receipts in 1987 ($1,000): $825,600
Average annual pay in 1989: $17,550

Housing

Total number of units in 1990: 137,475
Occupied units in 1990: 126,122
Owner-occupied units in 1990: 55.4%
1993 ACCRA average cost: N/A
1993 ACCRA average rent for an apartment: N/A

Chamber of Commerce

New Bedford Area Chamber of Commerce, James H. Mathes, President, 838 Purchase St., PO Box G-827, New Bedford, MA 02740. 508-999-5231

Economic Development Office

Fall River Area Chamber of Commerce, Mark C.W. Montigny, President, 200 Pocasset St., PO Box 1871, Fall River, MA 02722. 508-676-8226

Economic Development Organizations

Economic Development Corp of Greater New Bedford, Inc., Joseph C. DeRitis, Exec Vice President, 104 William Street, 4th Fl., New Bedford, MA 02740. 508-997-9334. Mayor's Economic Development Office, James D. Oliveira, Director, 133 William St., Room 220, New Bedford, MA 02740. 508-999-2930

Major Businesses

Company	SIC	Telephone
Acushnet Co.	3949	(508) 997-2811
Alden Autoparts Warehouse	5013	(508) 673-4233
Alden Corrugated Container Corp.	2653	(508) 993-9971
Ashley Ford Sales Inc.	5511	(508) 996-5611
Ashworth Bros Inc.	3535	(508) 674-4693
Bank of Boston-Bristol NA	6021	(508) 997-6000
Barnstable County Supply	5031	(508) 947-5000
C. P. Bourg, Inc.	3579	(508) 998-2171
Cliftex Corporation	2311	(508) 999-1311
Compass Bank for Savings	6036	(508) 994-5000
Durfee Attleboro Bank	6022	(508) 679-8311
Duro Industries Inc.	2261	(508) 675-0101
Eastern Sportswear Manufacturing Co.	2369	(508) 999-5252
Epec Inc.	3672	(508) 995-5171
Fairhaven Savings Bank	6022	(508) 999-2961
Fall River Gas Company	4924	(508) 675-7811
Imtra Corporation	5088	(508) 990-2700
Karten's Jewelers Inc.	5944	(508) 999-6214
Luzo Foodservice Corporation	5141	(508) 993-9976
Monogram Industries Inc.	3315	(508) 998-1131
Morse Tool Inc. (Del)	3545	(508) 994-9611
Mutterperl Group, Ltd.	5137	(508) 993-9981
New Bedford Institution for Savings	6036	(508) 996-5000
Northeast Real Estate Development	6552	(508) 995-2205
PCI Group Inc.	3965	(508) 995-2641
Park Motors Inc.	5511	(508) 999-6479
Saint Lukes Hospital of New Bedford	8062	(508) 997-1515
Sea View Fillet Co. Inc.	2092	(508) 994-1233
Sharon-Jay Togs Inc.	5137	(508) 999-5252
Sippican Inc.	3812	(508) 748-1160
Trina Inc.	3172	(508) 678-7601
Triple Crown Seafood Co., Inc.	5146	(508) 994-7735
Universal Industries Inc.	2353	(508) 758-6101
Whaling Industries Inc.	2385	(508) 678-9061

Colleges and Universities

Southeastern Massachusetts University, North Dartmouth
Bristol Community College, Fall River

PITTSFIELD, MA (NECMA)

Geographic Profile

Land Area
931.4 square miles

Counties and Parishes
Berkshire (part)

Additional Cities/Towns within Area
Cheshire
Dalton
Hinsdale
Lanesborough
Lee
Lenox
Richmond
Stockbridge

Ranking Highlights

213 *out of 319 in total* **land area**
307 *out of 319 in* **population growth,** *1970–1990*
N/A *out of 310 in having the lowest* **unemployment** *rate*
N/A *out of 310 in size of* **labor force**
74 *out of 318 in the percentage of* **college graduates**
42 *out of 292 in per capita personal* **income**
206 *out of 319 in number of* **manufacturing establishments**
60 *out of 318 in* **physicians** *per 1000 people*
185 *out of 318 in* **hospital beds** *per 1000 people*
18 *out of 267 in fewest* **crimes** *per 1000 people*
82 *out of 266 in fewest* **violent crimes** *per 1000 people*
21 *out of 319 in per capita* **federal funds and grants**

Quality of Life Indexes (Rate per 1000 population)

Crime rate in 1991:   34.8
Violent crime rate in 1991:   4.6
Physicians rate in 1992:   2.41
Hospital bed rate in 1991:   2.99

ACCRA Cost of Living Indexes

(First quarter 1993, average = 100)
Composite index: N/A
Utilities index: N/A
Housing index: N/A

Population (1990)

Total Population and Growth Rate
1990: 139,352
1980: 145,110
1970: 149,402
Growth rate 1970–1990: -7%

Race and Hispanic Origin
White: 96.7%
Black: 2.1%
Asian/Pacific Islander: 0.7%
Native American: 0.2%

Hispanic origin: 1.0%

White not Hispanic: 96.0%

Age

Ages 18 to 20: 2.2%

Ages 21 to 24: 2.9%

Ages 25 to 44: 17.6%

Ages 45 to 54: 5.9%

Ages 55 to 59: 2.8%

Ages 60 to 64: 2.9%

Ages 65 plus: 9.5%

Educational Attainment (1990)

Percent having completed high school: 80.4%

Percent having completed college: 21.5%

Elementary and high school enrollment: 12,310

Federal Funds and Grants Received

Total received in 1989: $904,900,000

Funds received per capita: $6,525

Civilian Labor Force

1993 (April):   N/A

1992 average: N/A

1991 average: 73,600

1990 average: 74,000

Unemployment

1993 (April):   N/A

1992 average: N/A

1991 average: 10.1%

1990 average: 6.2%

Average Annual Pay

1988: $20,817

1987: $19,836

1985: $17,837

Per Capita Personal Income

1991: $20,513

1990: $20,075

1989: $19,240

Business Climate (1987)

Manufacturing

Number of establishments in 1987: 217

Shipments in 1987 ($1,000): $1,442,600

Employees in 1987: 16,400

Change in employment, 1982 to 1987: -14.6%

Average annual pay for manufacturing work in 1989: $31,348

Average annual pay for production work in 1987: $22,288

Wholesale Trade

Number of establishments in 1987: 152

Total sales in 1987 ($1,000): $277,900

Change in sales, 1982 to 1987: 14.4%

Retail Trade

Number of establishments in 1987: 1,165

Total sales in 1987 ($1,000): $277,900

Retail sales per household in 1987: $19,202

Average annual pay in 1989: $12,207

Service Industry

Selected receipts in 1987 ($1,000): $347,500

Average annual pay in 1989: $18,916

Housing

Total number of units in 1990: 35,053

Occupied units in 1990: 31,344

Owner-occupied units in 1990: 66.5%

1993 ACCRA average cost: N/A

1993 ACCRA average rent for an apartment: N/A

Chamber of Commerce

Central Berkshire Chamber of Commerce, G.C. Dodd, President, 66 West St., Pittsfield, MA 01201. 413-499-4000

Economic Development Office

Greater Lee Chamber of Commerce, Mary Bradbury, Chairman, Town Hall, Main Street, Lee, MA 01238. 413-243-0852

Economic Development Organizations

Lenox Chamber of Commerce, Beverly Reimann Marcus, Exec Director, PO Box 646, Lenox Academy, Lenox, MA 02140. 413-637-3646

Major Businesses

Company	SIC	Telephone
Bedard Brothers Auto Sales Inc.	5511	(413) 743-0014
Berkshire County Savings	6035	(413) 443-5601
Berkshire Gas Company	4924	(413) 442-1511
Berkshire Health Systems	8062	(413) 447-2000
Berkshire Life Insur Company	6311	(413) 499-4321
Berkshire Medical Center	8062	(413) 447-2000
Berkshire Mutual Insurance	6331	(413) 443-4461
Butler Wholesale Products	5141	(413) 743-3885
City Savings Bank Pittsfield	6036	(413) 443-4421
Crane & Co Inc.	2621	(413) 684-2600
Eagle Publishing Co., Inc.	2711	(413) 447-7311
Joseph Francese, Inc.	1541	(413) 442-9124
Hillcrest Hospital	8062	(413) 443-4761
Kay-Bee Toy & Hobby Shops	5945	(413) 499-0086
Lee Savings Bank	6035	(413) 243-0117
Lipton Inc.	5172	(413) 443-9191
J. H. Maxymillian, Inc.	1611	(413) 499-3050
McAndrews-King Ptc Bk Gm	5511	(413) 743-0584
Petricca Construction Inc.	1611	(413) 442-6926
Petricca Industries Inc.	1623	(413) 442-6926
Reynolds, Barnes & Hebb Inc.	6411	(413) 447-7376
Unistress Corp.	3272	(413) 442-6926

Colleges and Universities

Berkshire Community College, Pittsfield

SPRINGFIELD, MA (NECMA)

Geographic Profile

Land Area
1147.6 square miles

Counties and Parishes
Hampden (part)

Hampshire (part)

Additional Cities/Towns within Area
Hampden County:

  Agawam

  Chicopee

  East Longmeadow

  Hampden

  Holyoke

  Longmeadow

  Ludlow

  Monson

  Montgomery

  Palmer

  Russell

  Southwick

  Westfield

  West Springfield

  Wilbraham

Hampshire County:

  Belchertown

  Easthampton

  Granby

  Huntington

  Northampton

  Southampton

  South Hadley

Ranking Highlights
176 *out of 319 in total* **land area**

254 *out of 319 in* **population growth**, *1970–1990*

N/A *out of 310 in having the lowest* **unemployment** *rate*

N/A *out of 310 in size of* **labor force**

97 *out of 318 in the percentage of* **college graduates**

71 *out of 292 in per capita personal* **income**

66 *out of 319 in number of* **manufacturing establishments**

87 *out of 318 in* **physicians** *per 1000 people*

179 *out of 318 in* **hospital beds** *per 1000 people*

127 *out of 267 in fewest* **crimes** *per 1000 people*

174 *out of 266 in fewest* **violent crimes** *per 1000 people*

186 *out of 319 in per capita* **federal funds and grants**

Quality of Life Indexes (Rate per 1000 population)
Crime rate in 1991:	64.6
Violent crime rate in 1991:	8.8
Physicians rate in 1992:	2.02
Hospital bed rate in 1991:	3.07

ACCRA Cost of Living Indexes
(First quarter 1993, average = 100)

Composite index:	N/A
Utilities index:	N/A
Housing index:	N/A

Overview
Today, Springfield, one of the oldest settlements in America and the third largest city in Massachusetts, is best known for its growing service industry, which is anchored by two major insurance firms. It is the home of the Springfield Armory and a number of private firearms manufacturers.

Historically, the Springfield Armory drew skilled metal workers to the city. This manufacturing expertise has broadened to include a number of diverse concerns, and manufacturing remains a mainstay of the Springfield economy, although its twenty-nine percent share of employment in 1981 had declined by one-fourth by 1989. Most companies in the region employ fewer than fifty people. As the transportation hub of western Massachusetts, Springfield has become a major retail and wholesale trade center. Its service industry grew by fifty percent in the 1980s, anchored by two major insurance companies.

Items and goods produced in the area include women's underwear, plastic tile, surgical dressings, matches, firearms, envelopes and stationery, computer components, chemicals, machinery, electrical equipment, rubber goods, printed matter, automobile accessories, forged metals, games and toys, educational equipment

Chicopee, serves as the region's principal air cargo handling facility. Boston & Maine Railroad and a vast fleet of commercial trucks also haul freight into Springfield. Westover Metropolitan Airport and several private airports serve Springfield. Springfield is eighteen miles north of Bradley International Airport in Windsor Locks, Connecticut. Bradley offers a full range of domestic, international, and cargo flights. Shuttle buses and limousines run between the airport and Springfield.

Two major New England road arteries intersect in Springfield: the east-west running Massachusetts Turnpike (Interstate-90) and the north-south traveling Interstate-91 with its branch, Interstate-291, running through downtown.

Population (1990)

Total Population and Growth Rate
1990: 602,878

1980: 581,831

1970: 583,031

Growth rate 1970–1990: 3%

Race and Hispanic Origin
White: 86.4%

Black: 6.6%

Asian/Pacific Islander: 1.0%

Native American: 0.2%

Hispanic origin: 9.0%
White not Hispanic: 83.6%

Age

Ages 18 to 20: 4.7%
Ages 21 to 24: 5.5%
Ages 25 to 44: 27.6%
Ages 45 to 54: 8.3%
Ages 55 to 59: 3.6%
Ages 60 to 64: 4%
Ages 65 plus: 12.9%

Educational Attainment (1990)

Percent having completed high school: 74.7%
Percent having completed college: 19.0%
Elementary and high school enrollment: 97,000

Federal Funds and Grants Received

Total received in 1989: $1,731,200,000
Funds received per capita: $2,923

Civilian Labor Force

1993 (April): N/A
1992 average: N/A
1991 average: 293,200
1990 average: 295,400

Unemployment

1993 (April): N/A
1992 average: N/A
1991 average: 9.1%
1990 average: 5.7%

Average Annual Pay

1988: $20,597
1987: $19,313
1985: $17,120

Per Capita Personal Income

1991: $19,197
1990: $18,587
1989: $18,061

Business Climate (1987)

Manufacturing

Number of establishments in 1987: 1,066
Shipments in 1987 ($1,000): $6,375,600
Employees in 1987: 51,400
Change in employment, 1982 to 1987: -12.0%
Average annual pay for manufacturing work in 1989: $27,102
Average annual pay for production work in 1987: $19,799

Wholesale Trade

Number of establishments in 1987: 901
Total sales in 1987 ($1,000): $2,969,200
Change in sales, 1982 to 1987: 26.8%

Retail Trade

Number of establishments in 1987: 3,946
Total sales in 1987 ($1,000): $2,969,200

Retail sales per household in 1987: $18,244
Average annual pay in 1989: $11,815

Service Industry

Selected receipts in 1987 ($1,000): $1,304,100
Average annual pay in 1989: $19,686

Office Real Estate (1992)

Office space inventory: N/A square feet
Average class A Central Business District rental range per sq. ft: $16.00

Vacancy Rates

All areas: 25.0%

Vacancy Rates in Central Business District

Class A space: 18.5%
Class B space: 27.5%

Vacancy Rates Outside Central Business District

Class A space: 28.5%
Class B space: 33.3%

Housing

Total number of units in 1990: 207,630
Occupied units in 1990: 197,236
Owner-occupied units in 1990: 60.3%
1993 ACCRA average cost: N/A
1993 ACCRA average rent for an apartment: N/A

Chamber of Commerce

Greater Springfield Chamber of Commerce, Bill Ward, Exec Director, 1350 Main St., Springfield, MA 01115. 413-787-1555

Economic Development Office

Economic Development Partners, Marc Hanks, Managing Partner, 1350 Main St., 3rd Fl, Springfield, MA 01103. 413-787-1542

Economic Development Organizations

Greater Chicopee Chamber of Commerce, Guy Ormsby, chairman, 93 Church St., Chicopee, MA 01020. 413-594-2102

East Longmeadow Chamber of Commerce, Mike Williamson, General Manager, PO Box 221, East Longmeadow, MA 01028. 413-787-1544

Easthampton Chamber of Commerce, Marlene Krawczyk, PO Box 247, 33 Union Street, Easthampton, MA 01027. 413-527-9414

Ludlow Chamber of Commerce, William Simons, President, PO Box 136, Ludlow, MA 01056. 413-787-1551

Greater Northampton Chamber of Commerce, Paul Walker, Exec Director, 62 State Street, Northampton, MA 01060. 413-584-1900

Quabog Valley Chamber of Commerce, Maureen Solomon, Director, 418 Main Street, Palmer, MA 01069. 413-283-6149

Major Businesses

Company	SIC	Telephone
Affiliated Banc Corporation	6712	(413) 534-8000
Ampad Corporation	2678	(413) 536-3511
Bank of New England-West	6021	(413) 787-8700
Baystate Health Systems Inc.	6719	(413) 784-3345
Baystate Medical Center Inc.	8062	(413) 784-0000
Big Y Foods Inc.	5411	(413) 784-0600
Brennan College Service	5942	(413) 781-2296
Fontaine Bros Inc.	1542	(413) 781-2020
Friendly Ice Cream Corporation	5812	(413) 543-2400
JPS Elastomerics Corp.	3069	(413) 586-8750
Massachusetts Municipal Whl El	4911	(413) 589-0141
Massachusetts Mutual Life Insurance	6311	(413) 788-8411
Mercy Hospital	8062	(413) 781-9100
Mestek, Inc.	3585	(413) 568-9571
Monarch Capital Corporation	6311	(413) 781-3000
Monarch Life Insurance Co.	6311	(413) 784-2000
O'Connell Companies Inc.	1541	(413) 534-0246
Daniel O'Connell's Sons	1541	(413) 534-5667
Roberts F L & Company Inc.	5541	(413) 781-7444
Shawmut First Bank & Trust	6022	(413) 737-4321
Smith & Wesson Corp.	3484	(413) 781-8300
Springfield Institution for Savings	6035	(413) 781-8000
Stanhome Inc.	3991	(413) 562-3631
Albert Steiger, Inc.	5311	(413) 781-4211
Western Mass Electric Company	4911	(413) 785-5871

Colleges and Universities

American International College, Springfield
Springfield College, Springfield
Springfield Technical Community College, Springfield
Elms College, Chicopee
Holyoke Community College, Holyoke
Bay Path College, Longmeadow
Smith College, Northampton
Mount Holyoke College, South Hadley

WORCESTER–FITCHBURG–LEOMINSTER, MA (NECMA)

Geographic Profile

Land Area
1513.2 square miles

Counties and Parishes
Worcester
Worcester (part)
Fitchburg
Middlesex (part)
Worcester (part)

Additional Cities/Towns within Area
Worcester
Auburn
Barre
Boylston
Brookfield
Charlton
Clinton
Douglas
Dudley
East Brookfield
Grafton
Holden
Leicester
Millbury
Northborough
Northbridge
North Brookfield
Oxford
Paxton
Princeton
Rutland
Shrewsbury
Spencer
Sterling
Sutton
Uxbridge
Webster
West Boylston
Westborough
Fitchburg
Middlesex County:
　Ashby
Worcester County:
　Ashburnham
　Lunenburg
　Westminster

Ranking Highlights

131 *out of 319 in* total land area

220 *out of 319 in* population growth, *1970–1990*

N/A *out of 310 in having the lowest* unemployment *rate*

N/A *out of 310 in size of* labor force

66 *out of 318 in the percentage of* college graduates

N/A *out of 292 in per capita personal* income

48 *out of 319 in number of* manufacturing establishments

50 *out of 318 in* physicians *per 1000 people*

211 *out of 318 in* hospital beds *per 1000 people*

N/A *out of 267 in fewest* crimes *per 1000 people*

N/A *out of 266 in fewest* violent crimes *per 1000 people*

225 *out of 319 in per capita* federal funds and grants

Quality of Life Indexes (Rate per 1000 population)

Crime rate in 1991:	N/A
Violent crime rate in 1991:	N/A
Physicians rate in 1992:	2.54
Hospital bed rate in 1991:	2.45

ACCRA Cost of Living Indexes

(First quarter 1993, average = 100)

Composite index:	N/A
Utilities index:	N/A
Housing index:	N/A

Overview

Worcester, the second largest city in the Commonwealth of Massachusetts and is located at its geographic center, it is a major manufacturing, distribution, service, retail, and trading center for all of New England. Worcester's economy is diverse, with more than 5,000 firms of all types in the metropolitan area. More than 800 manufacturing firms produce products ranging from textiles to machinery. By the 1990s, however, Worcester was losing manufacturing jobs at a rate faster than the state. Worcester is home to two Fortune 500 companies: Norton, which manufactures abrasives, and Idle Wild Foods, which processes, packs, and distributes frozen foods.

Worcester's colleges and universities comprise the second-largest employer in the city. Among the city's other major areas of employment are medicine, insurance, banking, and research. Ground was broken in 1986 for the Biotechnology Research Park, one of four state–supported centers designed to spur development in high-technology industries; it includes private organizations specializing in biomedical and scientific research, testing, and instrumentation. By 1991 the park had grown to three research centers with seventeen companies and more than 1,000 employees representing an annual payroll of $44 million.

The Worcester area rail system is one of New England's largest mainline freight interchanges. The city's needs are met by two lines: Boston & Maine and Providence & Worcester Transportation. One hundred eleven common carrier truck lines use Worcester's fifty freight terminals to store goods. Air freight service is available at Worcester Municipal Airport. Worcester Airport is served by Continental and USAir, with daily flights connecting to and from nearly every area of the country. Logan International Airport near Boston is one hour to the east of Worcester.

Interstate–190 links Route 2, the Mohawk Trail, with the city of Worcester. Interstate 290 connects I–495 with the city and eventually links with the Massachusetts Turnpike, where I–290 becomes I–395, the main route south through Connecticut.

Population (1990)

Total Population and Growth Rate

1990: 709,705

1980: 646,352

1970: 637,037

Growth rate 1970–1990: 11%

Race and Hispanic Origin

White: 93.3%

Black: 2.2%

Asian/Pacific Islander: 1.8%

Native American: 0.2%

Hispanic origin: 5.1%

White not Hispanic: 91.0%

Age

Ages 18 to 20: 4%

Ages 21 to 24: 4.8%

Ages 25 to 44: 24.9%

Ages 45 to 54: 7.2%

Ages 55 to 59: 3%

Ages 60 to 64: 3.2%

Ages 65 plus: 10.7%

Educational Attainment (1990)

Percent having completed high school: 77.5%

Percent having completed college: 22.4%

Elementary and high school enrollment: 116,000

Federal Funds and Grants Received

Total received in 1989: $1,754,000,000

Funds received per capita: $2,597

Civilian Labor Force

1993 (April):	N/A
1992 average:	N/A
1991 average:	335,800
1990 average:	340,600

Unemployment

1993 (April):	N/A
1992 average:	N/A
1991 average:	10.2%
1990 average:	6.9%

Average Annual Pay

1988: $21,555

1987: $20,144

1985: $17,586

Per Capita Personal Income
1991: N/A
1990: N/A
1989: N/A

Business Climate (1987)

Manufacturing
Number of establishments in 1987: 1,469
Shipments in 1987 ($1,000): $6,736,000
Employees in 1987: 69,400
Change in employment, 1982 to 1987: -14.6%
Average annual pay for manufacturing work in 1989: $29,618
Average annual pay for production work in 1987: $19,238

Wholesale Trade
Number of establishments in 1987: 1,075
Total sales in 1987 ($1,000): $4,815,200
Change in sales, 1982 to 1987: 17.8%

Retail Trade
Number of establishments in 1987: 4,266
Total sales in 1987 ($1,000): $4,815,200
Retail sales per household in 1987: $19,285
Average annual pay in 1989: $12,356

Service Industry
Selected receipts in 1987 ($1,000): $1,838,700
Average annual pay in 1989: $19,419

Housing
Total number of units in 1990: 214,436
Occupied units in 1990: 199,700
Owner-occupied units in 1990: 60.1%
1993 ACCRA average cost: N/A
1993 ACCRA average rent for an apartment: N/A

Chamber of Commerce
Worcester Area Chamber of Commerce, William J. Short, President, 33 Waldo St., Worcester, MA 01608. 508-753-2924

Economic Development Office
North Central Massachusetts Chamber of Commerce, David L. McKeehan, President, 110 Erdman Way, Leominster, MA 01453. 508-840-4300

Economic Development Organizations
Webster-Dudley-Oxfprd Chamber of Commerce, Bernard Conti, President, PO Box 100, 154 Thompson Road, Webster, MA 01570. 508-943-0558

Industrial Development Commisssion, Michael Lanava, Exec Director, 718 Main St., Fitchburg, MA 01420. 617-345-9602, FAX 617-345-9604

Major Businesses

Company	SIC	Telephone
Astra Pharmaceutical Products	2834	(508) 366-1100

Major Businesses (Continued)

Company	SIC	Telephone
Banyan Systems Inc.	3571	(508) 898-1000
Commerce Group, Inc.	6331	(508) 943-9000
Commerce Insurance Co.	6331	(508) 943-9000
Data General Corporation	3571	(508) 366-8911
Diversified Ventures Inc.	6153	(508) 393-5300
Flexcon Company Inc.	3083	(508) 885-3973
Future Electronics Corp.	5065	(508) 366-2400
Granger Management Corporation	1542	(508) 842-8961
Hanover Insurance Company	6331	(508) 853-7200
Idle Wild Foods Inc.	2011	(508) 757-7761
Leading Edge Products Inc.	5045	(508) 836-4800
Massachusetts Electric Company	4911	(508) 366-9011
New England Electric System	4911	(508) 366-9011
New England Power Company	4911	(508) 366-9011
New England Power Service Company	1623	(508) 366-9011
Norton Company	3291	(508) 795-5000
Paul Revere	6321	(508) 799-4441
Paul Revere Life Insurance Comapny	6321	(508) 799-4441
Paul Revere Variable Annuity	6311	(508) 799-4441
Saint Vincent Healthcare	8062	(508) 798-1234
Shawmut Worcester County Bank	6021	(508) 793-4000
Sma Life Assurance Co.	6211	(508) 852-1000
Spag's Supply Inc.	5311	(508) 752-8612
State Mutual Life Assurance of America	6311	(508) 852-1000
Wonder Market Companies Inc.	5411	(508) 754-3255
Worcester County Institution	6022	(508) 831-4000
Worcester Insurance Company	6331	(508) 754-6666
Wright Line Inc.	2522	(508) 852-4300
Wyman-Gordon Company	3463	(508) 756-5111

Colleges and Universities
Assumption College, Worcester
Becker Junior College-Worcester Campus, Worcester
Clark University, Worcester
College of the Holy Cross, Worcester
Quinsigamond Community College, Worcester
Nichols College, Dudley
Becker Junior College-Leicester Campus, Leicester
Anna Maria College, Paxton
Fitchburg State College, Fitchburg

MICHIGAN

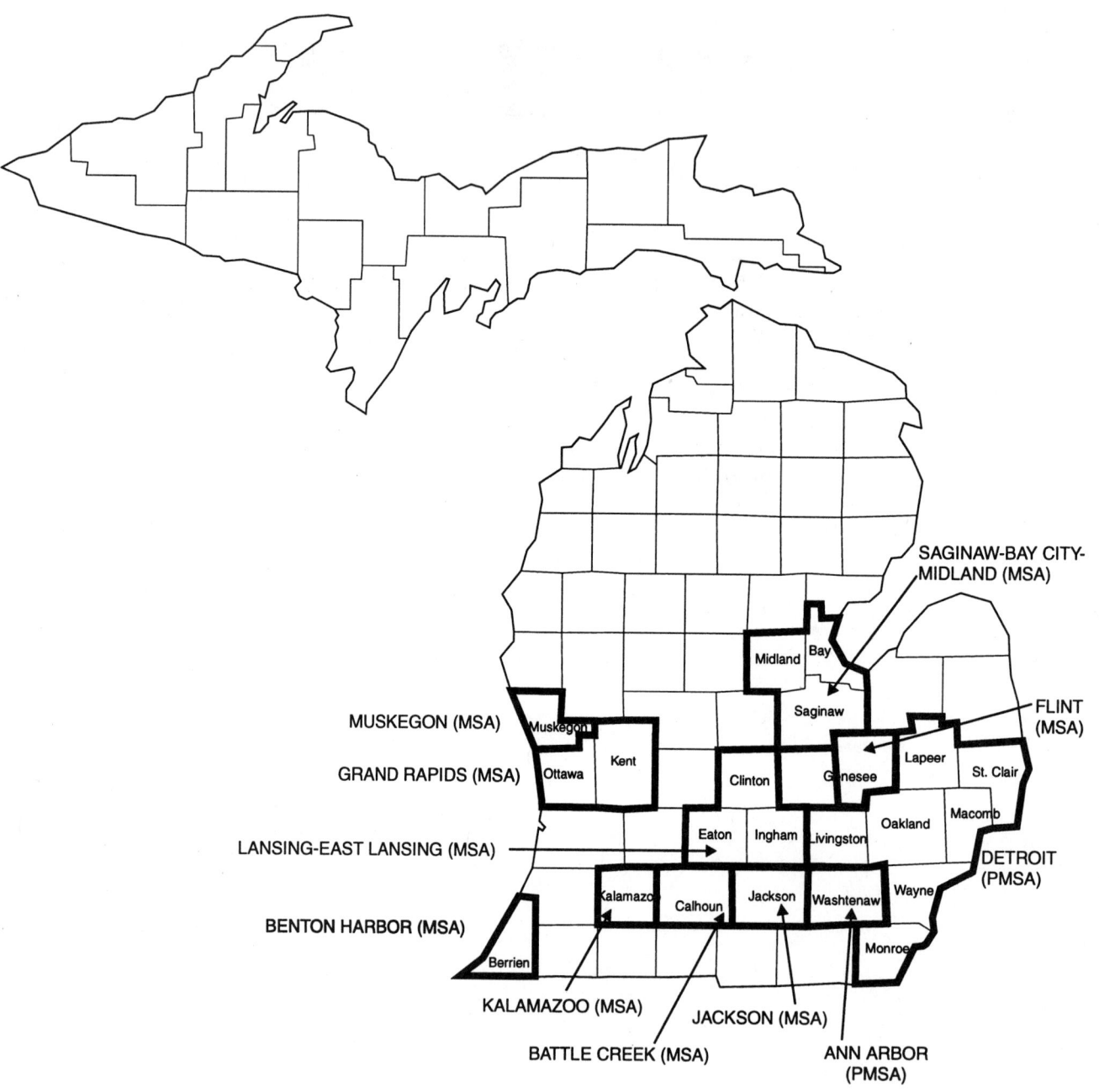

SAGINAW-BAY CITY-
MIDLAND (MSA)

Midland Bay

Saginaw

FLINT
(MSA)

MUSKEGON (MSA)   Muskegon

GRAND RAPIDS (MSA)   Ottawa   Kent   Clinton   Genesee   Lapeer   St. Clair

LANSING-EAST LANSING (MSA)   Eaton   Ingham   Livingston   Oakland   Macomb

DETROIT
(PMSA)

BENTON HARBOR (MSA)   Kalamazoo   Calhoun   Jackson   Washtenaw   Wayne

Berrien   Monroe

KALAMAZOO (MSA)   JACKSON (MSA)

BATTLE CREEK (MSA)   ANN ARBOR
(PMSA)

MICHIGAN

Population
1990: 9,295,797
1980: 9,262,078

Age
Ages 18 to 20: 449,966
Ages 21 to 24: 554,561
Ages 25 to 44: 2,980,702
Ages 45 to 54: 948,119
Ages 55 to 59: 392,787
Ages 60 to 64: 401,936
Median age: 32.6

Race
White: 7,756,086
Black: 1,291,706
Asian/Pacific Islander: 104,983
Native American: 55,638
Hispanic origin: 201,596

Households
Total: 3,419,331
Persons per household: 2.66

Sex
Male: 4,512,781
Female: 4,782,516

Population Migration
Domestic migration: -183,000
International migration: 69,000

Projection of the Population in 1995
Total: 9,552,000
18 to 64: 5,891,000

Civilian Labor Force
1993: 4,561,700
1992: 4,607,300
1991: 4,557,000
1990: 4,590,800

Manufacturing
1995 Projection: 948,600
1992: 896,500
1991: 901,300
1990: 927,200
1989: 960,200

Services
1995 Projection: 1,349,300

1992: 971,500
1991: 953,600
1990: 942,300
1989: 905,100

Wholesale and Retail Trade
1995 Projection: 1,081,200
1992: 928,500
1991: 941,300
1990: 970,100
1989: 951,400

Unemployment Rate
1993: 7.8%
1992: 9.8%
1991: 7.7%
1990: 9.4%

Employer Unemployment Contributions
Contribution Rate
1992: 4.10%
1991: 3.90%
1990: 3.80%

Average Weekly Benefit
1992: $212.43
1991: $201.50
1990: $203.86

Gross State Product (Million $)
1989: $181,827
1988: $172,653
1987: $160,930
1979: $104,587
Growth rate, 1979 to 1989: 73.9%

Capital Expenditures of Manufacturing Industries
1990: $5,604,700,000
1989: $5,938,700,000
1988: $4,073,900,000
1987: $4,793,500,000

State Tax Rates
Individual income: 4.6% on adjusted gross income.
Corporate income: 2.4% on federal taxable income.
General property: No state levy. Property assessed at 50% of true cash value. Limited to 1.5% of assessed valuation.

General sales: 4%
Gasoline: 15¢ per gallon

Income

Median income for a 4 person family: $42,825

Personal per Capita Income
1992: $19,508
1991: $18,642
1990: $18,297

Disposable per Capita Income
1992: $17,154
1991: $16,292
1990: $15,903

Private Employment Weekly Wages

Average
1989: $476
1988: $469
1987: $469

Manufacturing
1989: $447
1988: $677
1987: $635

Services
1989: $399
1988: $387
1987: $370

Wholesale
1989: $605
1988: $585
1987: $542

Retail
1989: $224
1988: $221
1987: $215

Highway Statistics

Total Highway Miles
1990: 117,449
1989: 117,996
1988: 117,895

Federal Highway Aid
1991: $325,540,000
1990: $298,710,000
1989: $332,717,000

Electricity

Average Cost per Kilowatt Hour
1990: 7.02¢
1989: 6.75¢
1988: 6.51¢

Housing (1990)

Owner occupied units: 2,427,643
Median house value: $60,600

Renter occupied units: 991,688
Median rent: $343
Total vacant units: 428,595
Homeowner vacancy rate: 1.3%
Rental vacancy rate: 7.2%

State Business Incentives and Assistance

Enterprise Zone Incentives

1) New Firms: a) exemption from the Single Business Tax, b) exemption from the Sales and Use taxes on purchases of tangible personal property; and c) 65% reduction on local property tax.

2) Expanding Firms (must invest amount equal to State Equivalent Value): a) exemption from the Single Business Tax; b) exemption from the Sales and Use taxes on purchases of tangible personal property; and c) a 65% reduction on local property tax on portion of property representing investment

3) All Other Firms, may receive a property tax credit for an amount down to the State wide average millage rate for amounts spent: a) to restore, alter, renovate, or improve real property located in the enterprise zone; b) 25% of wages paid to zone residents who have been unemployed for the previous six months; and c) cash and in-kind contributions made to local taxing units.

Financial and Business Assistance

Industrial Development Bonds. The state IDB program is administered by the Michigan Strategic Fund, a state agency guided by a nine-member board of directors. Its Industrial Development Revenue Bonds program offers low interest rate financing to businesses. It takes advantage of the federal tax exemption to reduce the cost of financing. Local government agencies may also issue IDBs for economic development purposes. The maximum bond term is 50 years. The funds may be used for machinery, equipment, buildings, site construction, warehousing, research and development facilities, etc.

Capital Access Program. This program is designed to give banks a flexible and non-bureaucratic tool to make business loans that are somewhat riskier than a conventional bank loan.

Business and Industrial Development Corporations. Administered by the Michigan Strategic Fund, the Business and Industrial Development Corporations are private financial institutions. The BIDCO helps catalyze the formation of a new industry of private financial institutions which could fill the gap between low risk/low return financing and high risk/high return financing that venture capitalists provide.

Venture Capital Fund. Administered by the Venture Capital Division of the Michigan Department of Treasury, state funds are made available for investment in qualified small business or venture capital firms under the provisions of Public Act 55. The program is targeting high growth and

Major Companies in the State

Company name	Fortune 500 rank	City	Telephone	SIC number
Fortune 500 Companies				
Chrysler Corp.	11	Highland Park	313-956-5741	3711
Dow Chemical Co.	20	Midland	517-636-1000	2821
Dow Corning Corp.	221	Midland	517-496-4000	2869
Federal Mogul Corp.	303	Southfield	313-354-7700	3714
Ford Motor Co.	3	Dearborn	313-322-3000	3711
General Motors Corp.	1	Detroit	313-556-5000	3711
Gerber Products Co.	297	Fremont	616-928-2000	2032
Herman Miller Inc.	404	Zeeland	616-654-3300	2522
Holnam Inc.	370	Dundee	313-529-4314	3241
International Controls Corp.	430	Kalamazoo	616-343-6121	3715
Kellogg Co.	87	Battle Creek	616-961-2000	2043
La Z Boy Chair Co.	481	Monroe	313-241-4414	2512
Lear Holdings Corp.	281	Southfield	313-746-1500	2531
Masco Corp.	140	Taylor	313-274-7400	3432
Masco Industries Inc.	250	Taylor	313-274-7405	3714
SPX Corp.	406	Muskegon	616-724-5000	3825
Tecumseh Products Co.	299	Tecumseh	517-423-8411	3585
Thorn Apple Valley Inc.	426	Southfield	313-552-0700	2011
Upjohn Co.	135	Kalamazoo	616-323-4000	2834
Valassis Communications Inc.	453	Livonia	313-591-3000	2752
Whirlpool Corp.	73	Benton Harbor	616-923-5000	3633
Other Major Companies in the State				
Chrysler Financial Corp.		Southfield	313-948-3060	6159
CMS Energy Corp.		Dearborn	313-436-9261	4931
Comerica Inc.		Detroit	313-222-3300	6712
Consumers Power Co.		Jackson	517-788-1030	4931
Detroit Edison Co.		Detroit	313-237-8000	4911
First of America Bank Corp.		Kalamazoo	616-376-9000	6712
Ford Holdings Inc.		Dearborn	313-322-3000	6159
Ford Motor Credit Co.		Dearborn	313-322-3000	6159
General Motors Acceptance Corp.		Detroit	313-556-1508	6141
K Mart Corp.		Troy	313-643-1000	5331
Kelly Services Inc.		Troy	313-362-4444	7363
LSS Holdings Corp.		Southfield	313-746-1500	2531
Manufacturers National Corp.		Detroit	313-222-4000	6712
MCN Corp.		Detroit	313-256-5500	4923
Michigan Bell Telephone Co.		Detroit	313-223-9900	4813
Michigan Consolidated Gas Co.		Detroit	313-965-2430	4923
Michigan National Corp.		Farmington Hills	313-473-3000	6712
NBD Bancorp Inc.		Detroit	313-225-1000	6712
PHM Corp.		Bloomfield Hills	313-647-2750	1521
Spartan Stores Inc.		Grand Rapids	616-878-2000	5141

emerging high-technology firms with unique product or service.

Location of New Business/Industry. Administered by the Location Services Division of the Department of Commerce. With state funding, the Division provides complete site and building search services to manufacturers throughout the state.

Technology Transfer Network. Administered by the Michigan Department of Commerce, the Network allows brokers to access the network to connect small to medium sized manufacturers with expert resources in research and development facilities at university centers.

Education and Training

Michigan Business and Industrial Training Program. Administered by the Governor's Office for Job Training, this program assesses companies' needs and administers training programs ranging from wage assistance to company training program development. Its services include referral and selection of trainees, orientation to work, pre-employment skills training, and on-the-job training. It also conducts upgrade training and retraining programs.

Michigan Training Incentive Fund. Administered by the Governor's Office for Job Training, this is an interest-subsidized training loan program. It provides interest subsidies for loans of up to $100,000 for training in its first year. The program allows businesses access to training expertise to upgrade worker skills.

Job Training Partnership Act. This program operates with funding from the U.S. Department of Labor. It provides job training and other employment related services.

State Offices

Real estate: Real Estate Services Division, Raymond Padgett, Director, PO Box 30026, Lansing, MI 48909. 517-373-9292

Chamber of commerce: Michigan State Chamber of Commerce, James Barrett, President, 600 S. Walnut St., Lansing, MI 48933. 517-371-2100

Economic development: Department of Commerce, Larry L. Meyer, Director, Law Bldg., 4th fl., PO Box 30004, Lansing, MI 48909. 517-373-7230

Department of Commerce, Enterprise Zone Program, John Iverson, Administrator, 525 W. Ottawa, Lansing, MI 48909. 517-335-2108

Department of Commerce, Economic Development, Alex Little, 685 W. Main St., PO Box 1208, Benton Harbor, MI 48022. 616-925-0558

Department of Treasury, Venture Capital Division, Director, PO Box 15128, Lansing, MI 48909. 517-373-4330

Manufacturing Development Group, Greg Main, Director, PO Box 30225, Lansing, MI 48909. 517-373-0601

Department of Commerce, Michigan Strategic Fund, Joanne Neuroth, Operations Director, PO Box 30234, Lansing, MI 48909. 517-373-7550

Capital Access Program, Program Manager, PO Box 30234, Lansing, MI 48909. 517-373-7551

Department of Commerce, Location Services Division, John Czarnecki, Director, PO Box 30225, Lansing, MI 48909. 517-373-9135

Department of Commerce, Technology Transfer Network, Sharon Woollard, PO Box 30225, Lansing, MI 48909. 517-335-4720

Small Business Development Center, Norman Schlafmann, State Director, Wayne State University, 2727 Second Ave., Detroit, MI 48201. 313-577-4848

Environmental affairs: Natural Resources Department, Environmental Protection, Delbert Rector, Deputy Director, PO Box 30028, Lansing, MI 48909. 517-373-7917

Labor: Labor Department, Elizabeth P. Howe, Director, 611 West Ottawa Street, PO Box 30015, Lansing, MI 48909. 517-373-9600

Unemployment: Employment Security Commission, Richard Simmons, Director, 7310 Woodward Ave., Detroit, MI 48202. 313-876-5500

Worker's compensation: Labor Department, Worker's Disbility Compensation Office, Edward Welch, Director, 611 West Ottawa Street, PO Box 30015, Lansing, MI 48909. 517-322-7296

Occupational safety and health: Labor Department, Safety and Regulation Bureau, Douglas Earle, Director, 611 West Ottawa Street, PO Box 30015, Lansing, MI 48909. 517-322-1814

Secretary of state: State Department, Richard H. Austin, Secretary of State, Treasury Bldg., 1st fl., Lansing, MI 48918. 517-373-2510

Taxation and revenue: Treasury Department, Robert A. Bowman, State Treasury, PO Box 15128, Lansing, MI 48901. 517-373-3223

Designated Zones for Economic Development

Enterprise Zones

Enacted in: 1986

No. of established zones: 1

Benton Harbor

Foreign Trade Zones

Foreign Trade Zone No. 43, Battle Creek, Michigan, Grantee: City of Battle Creek, Operator: BC/CAL/KAL Inland Port Authority of, Michael Larson, S. Central Michigan Development Corp, PO Box 1438, Battle Creek, MI 49016, 616-968-8197

Foreign Trade Zone No. 70, Detroit, Michigan, Grantee: Greater Detroit Foreign-Trade Zone, Inc., James Kellow, 174 South Clark Street, Detroit, MI 48209, 313-841-6700

Foreign Trade Zone No. 140, Flint, Michigan, Grantee: City of Flint, Bishop International Airport, Robert Hidley, G-3425 West Bristol Road, Flint, MI 48507, 313-766-8620

Foreign Trade Zone No. 16, Sault Ste. Marie, Michigan, Grantee/Operator: Economic Dev. Corp. of Sault Ste.

Marie, James F. Hendricks, 1301 W. Easterday, Sault Ste. Marie, MI 49783, 906-635-9131

Labor Unions

Automobile, Aerospace & Agricultural Implement Workers of America, International Union, United (UAW AFL-CIO)

Carpenters and Joiners of America, United Brotherhood of (AFL-CIO)

Detroit Association of Educational Employees

Electrical Workers, International Brotherhood of (AFL-CIO)

Food and Commercial Workers International Union, United (AFL-CIO)

Laborers' International Union of North America (AFL-CIO)

Machinists and Aerospace Workers, International Association of (AFL-CIO)

Michigan State Employees Association

National Education Association

Nurses' Association, American

Operating Engineers, International Union of (AFL-CIO)

Plumbing and Pipe Fitting Industry of The United States and Canada, United Association of, Journeymen and Apprentices of the (AFL-CIO)

Service Employees' International Union (AFL-CIO)

Sheet Metal Workers' International Association (AFL-CIO)

State, County and Municipal Employees, American Federation of (AFL-CIO)

Steelworkers of America, United (AFL-CIO)

Teachers, American Federation of (AFL-CIO)

Teamsters, Chauffeurs, Warehousemen and Helpers of America, International Brotherhood of (AFL-CIO)

United Products Workers

Universities with Ph.D. Programs

Central Michigan University, Mount Pleasant
Michigan State University, East Lansing
Michigan Technological University, Houghton
Oakland University, Rochester
University of Detroit, Detroit
University of Michigan, Ann Arbor

ANN ARBOR, MI (PMSA)

Geographic Profile

Land Area
710.1 square miles

Counties and Parishes
Washtenaw

Ranking Highlights

253 *out of 319 in total* **land area**
172 *out of 319 in* **population growth**, *1970–1990*
56 *out of 310 in having the lowest* **unemployment** *rate*
133 *out of 310 in size of* **labor force**
3 *out of 318 in the percentage of* **college graduates**
32 *out of 292 in per capita personal* **income**
126 *out of 319 in number of* **manufacturing establishments**
4 *out of 318 in* **physicians** *per 1000 people*
27 *out of 318 in* **hospital beds** *per 1000 people*
177 *out of 267 in fewest* **crimes** *per 1000 people*
153 *out of 266 in fewest* **violent crimes** *per 1000 people*
195 *out of 319 in per capita* **federal funds and grants**

Quality of Life Indexes (Rate per 1000 population)

Crime rate in 1991:	67.9
Violent crime rate in 1991:	6.9
Physicians rate in 1992:	6.96
Hospital bed rate in 1991:	6.11

ACCRA Cost of Living Indexes
(First quarter 1993, average = 100)

Composite index:	119.9
Utilities index:	107.9
Housing index:	137.8

Overview

Washtenaw County is located 45 minutes west of Detroit and is within overnight truck delivery of 54% of all U.S. manufacturing activity and 68% of all Canadian manufacturing activity, 45% of all U.S. personal income and 57% of all Canadian personal income, 43% of the total U.S. GNP and 65% of the total Canadian GNP. The County, with a land area of 710 square miles, is the focal point of a region known as "Automation Alley". Nearly two-thirds of all robotics, machine vision and intelligent manufacturing technologies have originated here and over 200 high technology firms and research facilities are located here.

Washtenaw County is within 30 minutes of Detroit metro airport, where 15 carriers fly more than 1000 flights to domestic and international destinations. Ann Arbor airport, the seventh busiest airport in Michigan, provides charter and private air services. Willow Run Airport in Ypsilanti is primarily a cargo handling airport with shipments of more than 300,000 tons per year. The County is criss-crossed by three major highways; I-94, running between Detroit and Chicago, Illinois.; US-23, running from Saginaw, MI to

Toledo, Ohio and connecting to I-75 which extends from Canada to Florida; M-14, running from Detroit to Ann Arbor. The County is served by 61 trucking lines, 3 major bus lines and 4 major rail lines. Washtenaw County is just 45 minutes from the busiest port serving the Great Lakes region, the Port of Detroit.

Washtenaw County is the home of the University of Michigan and Eastern Michigan University. The University of Michigan Medical Center ranks as one of the world leaders in biomedical education and research with over 8000 employees, including 740 physicians and 886 licensed beds. Music festivals, film festivals, art fairs, museums and galleries attract local, national and international artists to Washtenaw County. Washtenaw County is home to 17 performance centers, 26 theater groups, 25 dance groups and 24 music groups.

Population (1990)

Total Population and Growth Rate
1990: 282,937
1980: 264,740
1970: 234,103
Growth rate 1970–1990: 21%

Race and Hispanic Origin
White: 83.5%
Black: 11.2%
Asian/Pacific Islander: 4.1%
Native American: 0.4%
Hispanic origin: 2.0%
White not Hispanic: 82.3%

Age
Ages 18 to 20:   9%
Ages 21 to 24: 10.6%
Ages 25 to 44: 35.9%
Ages 45 to 54: 9.3%
Ages 55 to 59: 3.2%
Ages 60 to 64: 2.9%
Ages 65 plus: 7.5%

Educational Attainment (1990)
Percent having completed high school: 87.2%
Percent having completed college: 41.9%
Elementary and high school enrollment: 38,568

Federal Funds and Grants Received
Total received in 1989: $758,400,000
Funds received per capita: $2,832

Civilian Labor Force
1993 (April):   161,990
1992 average: 163,547
1991 average: 161,593
1990 average: 160,244

Unemployment
1993 (April):   3.6%
1992 average: 5.1%

1991 average: 6.0%
1990 average: 4.6%

Average Annual Pay
1988: $24,964
1987: $23,790
1985: $22,815

Per Capita Personal Income
1991: $21,369
1990: $21,267
1989: $20,484

Business Climate (1987)

Manufacturing
Number of establishments in 1987: 428
Shipments in 1987 ($1,000): $7,348,100
Employees in 1987: 39,500
Change in employment, 1982 to 1987: 31.7%
Average annual pay for manufacturing work in 1989: $37,979
Average annual pay for production work in 1987: $31,639

Wholesale Trade
Number of establishments in 1987: 376
Total sales in 1987 ($1,000): $986,000
Change in sales, 1982 to 1987: 40.8%

Retail Trade
Number of establishments in 1987: 1,565
Total sales in 1987 ($1,000): $986,000
Retail sales per household in 1987: $19,867
Average annual pay in 1989: $12,557

Service Industry
Selected receipts in 1987 ($1,000): $941,300
Average annual pay in 1989: $22,678

Housing
Total number of units in 1990: 111,256
Occupied units in 1990: 104,528
Owner-occupied units in 1990: 55.3%
1993 ACCRA average cost: $150,538
1993 ACCRA average rent for an apartment: $749

Chamber of Commerce
Ann Arbor Area Chamber of Commerce, Rodney F. Benson, President, 211 E. Huron #1, Ann Arbor, MI 48104. 313-665-4433

Economic Development Office
Washtenaw Development Council, Gretchen A. Waters, Exec. Director, 3135 S. State St., #300, Ann Arbor, MI 48108. 313-761-9317, FAX 313-761-9586

Major Businesses

Company	SIC	Telephone
Avfuel Corp.	5172	(313) 663-6466
Chelsea Milling Co.	2041	(313) 475-1361

Major Businesses (Continued)

Company	SIC	Telephone
Columbus Auto Parts Co.	3714	(313) 761-6666
Comshare, Inc.	7372	(313) 994-4800
Con-Way Central Express Inc.	4213	(313) 994-6600
Domino's Pizza Distrib.	5149	(313) 663-6300
Domino's Pizza Inc.	5812	(313) 668-4000
Domtar Gypsum Inc.	3275	(313) 930-4700
Great Lakes Bancorp	6035	(313) 769-8300
J P I Transportation Prod.	3714	(313) 663-6400
J P Industries Inc.	3714	(313) 663-6749
Manchester Plastics Inc.	3089	(313) 428-8383
NSK Corp.	3562	(313) 761-9500
Stanford Brothers Inc.	5511	(313) 996-2300
Technotrim Inc.	2399	(313) 668-0202
Tism Inc.	7941	(313) 930-3030
Unistrut Corp.	3448	(313) 930-0030
Unistrut International Co.	3448	(313) 930-0030
University Microfilms Inc.	7389	(313) 761-4700
Zantop International Airlines	4522	(313) 485-8900

Colleges and Universities

Concordia College, Ann Arbor
Eastern Michigan University, Ypsilanti
University of Michigan, Ann Arbor

BATTLE CREEK, MI (MSA)

Geographic Profile

Land Area
708.9 square miles

Counties and Parishes
Calhoun

Additional Cities/Towns within Area
None

Ranking Highlights

254 *out of 319 in total* land area
291 *out of 319 in* population growth, *1970–1990*
206 *out of 310 in having the lowest* unemployment *rate*
248 *out of 310 in size of* labor force
138 *out of 318 in the percentage of* college graduates
159 *out of 292 in per capita personal* income
210 *out of 319 in number of* manufacturing establishments
283 *out of 318 in* physicians *per 1000 people*
133 *out of 318 in* hospital beds *per 1000 people*
199 *out of 267 in fewest* crimes *per 1000 people*
207 *out of 266 in fewest* violent crimes *per 1000 people*
117 *out of 319 in per capita* federal funds and grants

Quality of Life Indexes (Rate per 1000 population)

Crime rate in 1991:	71.7
Violent crime rate in 1991:	9.2
Physicians rate in 1992:	1.18
Hospital bed rate in 1991:	4.16

ACCRA Cost of Living Indexes

(First quarter 1993, average = 100)

Composite index:	N/A
Utilities index:	N/A
Housing index:	N/A

Overview

Situated on I-94, the industrial corridor of the Midwest, Battle Creek is located midway between Chicago, Illinois and Detroit, within overnight shipping distance of 60% of the U.S. and Canadian populations. Battle Creek's close proximity to I-94 and I-69 makes Battle Creek convenient to more than forty major trucklines that serve the area. W.K. Kellogg Airport has a 10,000 foot runway. Overnight air express service is offered by five companies operating at the airport. Battle Creek is served by two rail lines, Conrail and Grand Trunk Western. The Battle Creek Inter-modal Gateway currently offers connections with Grand Trunk, Burlington Northern, Santa Fe, Canadian National, and CSX railroads. Amtrak also offers passenger service with daily runs to Chicago and Detroit.

Battle Creek has the largest industrial park in the State of Michigan. The 3,000 acre Fort Custer Industrial Park is home to over 70 companies employing over 6,000 workers.

Twenty of the 71 companies are foreign-based firms (15 Japanese, 4 German, and 1 Danish). Foreign Trade Zone #43 encompasses all of Fort Custer Industrial Park. For fiscal year 1993, the Zone has a projected combined value of merchandise in and out of the Zone of over $132 million.

Nippondenso Manufacturing USA Incorporated has invested over $180 million in a one million square foot facility in Fort Custer Industrial Park. Archway Cookies Corporate Headquarters are also located in the Park. Kellogg's World Headquarters is located in downtown Battle Creek along with the W.K. Kellogg Foundation, the largest charitable foundation in the world.

Population (1990)

Total Population and Growth Rate
1990: 135,982
1980: 141,579
1970: 141,963
Growth rate 1970–1990: -4%

Race and Hispanic Origin
White: 87.3%
Black: 10.6%
Asian/Pacific Islander: 0.8%
Native American: 0.5%
Hispanic origin: 1.9%
White not Hispanic: 86.3%

Age
Ages 18 to 20: 4.7%
Ages 21 to 24: 5.1%
Ages 25 to 44: 30.4%
Ages 45 to 54: 10.4%
Ages 55 to 59: 4.7%
Ages 60 to 64: 4.7%
Ages 65 plus: 13.4%

Educational Attainment (1990)
Percent having completed high school: 76.8%
Percent having completed college: 13.8%
Elementary and high school enrollment: 24,724

Federal Funds and Grants Received
Total received in 1989: $473,500,000
Funds received per capita: $3,401

Civilian Labor Force
1993 (April):　　65,146
1992 average:　　64,621
1991 average:　　63,329
1990 average:　　64,378

Unemployment
1993 (April):　　6.0%
1992 average:　　7.6%
1991 average:　　8.5%
1990 average:　　7.7%

Average Annual Pay
1988: $23,214
1987: $21,942
1985: $20,843

Per Capita Personal Income
1991: $17,032
1990: $16,254
1989: $15,120

Business Climate (1987)

Manufacturing
Number of establishments in 1987: 211
Shipments in 1987 ($1,000): $2,544,300
Employees in 1987: 15,300
Change in employment, 1982 to 1987: -5.6%
Average annual pay for manufacturing work, 1989: $33,194
Average annual pay for production work, 1987: $28,574

Wholesale Trade
Number of establishments in 1987: 165
Total sales in 1987 ($1,000): $539,000
Change in sales, 1982 to 1987: 38.3%

Retail Trade
Number of establishments in 1987: 878
Total sales in 1987 ($1,000): $539,000
Retail sales per household in 1987: $16,532
Average annual pay in 1989: $10,573

Service Industry
Selected receipts in 1987 ($1,000): $221,100
Average annual pay in 1989: $17,518

Housing
Total number of units in 1990: 55,619
Occupied units in 1990: 51,812
Owner-occupied units in 1990: 71.0%
1993 ACCRA average cost: N/A
1993 ACCRA average rent for an apartment: N/A

Chamber of Commerce
Battle Creek Area Chamber of Commerce, Michael J. Jackson, President, 172 W. Van Buren, Battle Creek, MI 49017. 616-962-4076

Economic Development Office
Battle Creek Unlimited, Inc., James F. Hattinger, President, 4950 W. Dickman Rd., Battle Creek, MI 49015. 616-962-7526, FAX 616-962-8096

Economic Development Organizations
Calhoun-Barry Growth Alliance,Bob Quadrozzi, Exec. Dir., 405 Hill-Brady Rd., Battle Creek, MI 49015. 616-965-4148

Major Businesses

Company	SIC	Telephone
American Fibrit, Inc.	3714	(616) 968-3000
Archway Cookies, Inc.	2052	(616) 962-4031
Battle Creek Gas Co.	4924	(616) 968-8111
Battle Creek Health Systems	8741	(616) 963-5521
Cello-Foil Products, Inc.	2673	(616) 964-7137
E. Tyden A. B. Inc.	5087	(616) 948-8080
Federated Publications Inc.	2711	(616) 964-7161
G & R Felpausch Co.	5411	(616) 945-3485
Hastings Manufacturing Co.	3714	(616) 945-2491
Hi-Lex Corp.	3496	(616) 968-0781
I I Stanley Co., Inc.	3647	(616) 964-7777
Kellogg Co.	2043	(616) 961-2000
Kellogg Sales Co	5149	(616) 961-2000
Kendall Electric, Inc.	5063	(616) 963-5585
Bill Knapp's, Michigan	5812	(616) 968-1121
Nippondenso Manufacturing	3714	(616) 965-3322
Supply Network Inc.	5087	(616) 948-8080
Transamerica Insurance Corp.s of America	6331	(616) 962-5300
Union Pump Co.	3561	(616) 966-4600
Viking Corp.	3569	(616) 945-9501

Colleges and Universities

Kellogg Community College, Battle Creek

BENTON HARBOR, MI (MSA)

Geographic Profile

Land Area
571.0 square miles

Counties and Parishes
Berrien

Ranking Highlights

279 *out of 319 in total* **land area**

280 *out of 319 in* **population growth,** *1970–1990*

259 *out of 310 in having the lowest* **unemployment** *rate*

211 *out of 310 in size of* **labor force**

203 *out of 318 in the percentage of* **college graduates**

183 *out of 292 in per capita personal* **income**

136 *out of 319 in number of* **manufacturing establishments**

281 *out of 318 in* **physicians** *per 1000 people*

124 *out of 318 in* **hospital beds** *per 1000 people*

217 *out of 267 in fewest* **crimes** *per 1000 people*

245 *out of 266 in fewest* **violent crimes** *per 1000 people*

123 *out of 319 in per capita* **federal funds and grants**

Quality of Life Indexes (Rate per 1000 population)

Crime rate in 1991:	75.2
Violent crime rate in 1991:	11.2
Physicians rate in 1992:	1.21
Hospital bed rate in 1991:	4.26

ACCRA Cost of Living Indexes
(First quarter 1993, average = 100)

Composite index:	104.5
Utilities index:	87.5
Housing index:	115.0

Population (1990)

Total Population and Growth Rate
1990: 161,378
1980: 171,276
1970: 163,940
Growth rate 1970–1990: -2%

Race and Hispanic Origin
White: 82.6%
Black: 15.4%
Asian/Pacific Islander: 0.9%
Native American: 0.4%
Hispanic origin: 1.7%
White not Hispanic: 81.7%

Age
Ages 18 to 20: 4.5%
Ages 21 to 24: 5.2%
Ages 25 to 44: 29.9%
Ages 45 to 54: 10.4%
Ages 55 to 59: 4.5%

Ages 60 to 64: 4.8%
Ages 65 plus: 13.7%

Educational Attainment (1990)
Percent having completed high school: 74.7%
Percent having completed college: 16.7%
Elementary and high school enrollment: 29,816

Federal Funds and Grants Received
Total received in 1989: $559,800,000
Funds received per capita: $3,361

Civilian Labor Force
1993 (April):   79,272
1992 average: 78,738
1991 average: 78,303
1990 average: 78,460

Unemployment
1993 (April):   7.0%
1992 average: 9.0%
1991 average: 9.1%
1990 average: 7.3%

Average Annual Pay
1988: $19,932
1987: $19,599
1985: $17,960

Per Capita Personal Income
1991: $16,576
1990: $16,060
1989: $15,527

Business Climate (1987)

Manufacturing
Number of establishments in 1987: 390
Shipments in 1987 ($1,000): $2,545,700
Employees in 1987: 22,300
Change in employment, 1982 to 1987: 12.1%
Average annual pay for manufacturing work in 1989: $26,312
Average annual pay for production work in 1987: $20,324

Wholesale Trade
Number of establishments in 1987: 231
Total sales in 1987 ($1,000): $1,451,500
Change in sales, 1982 to 1987: 74.6%

Retail Trade
Number of establishments in 1987: 1,012
Total sales in 1987 ($1,000): $1,451,500
Retail sales per household in 1987: $15,447
Average annual pay in 1989: $10,124

Service Industry
Selected receipts in 1987 ($1,000): $258,800
Average annual pay in 1989: $15,606

Housing
Total number of units in 1990: 69,532

Occupied units in 1990: 61,025
Owner-occupied units in 1990: 69.6%
1993 ACCRA average cost: $137,150
1993 ACCRA average rent for an apartment: $484

Chamber of Commerce
Twin Cities Area Chamber of Commerce, Edward J. Conrad, Exec. Vice President, 185 E. Main St., PO Box 1208, Benton Harbor, MI 49022. 616-925-0044

Economic Development Office
Benton Harbor Economic Development, Aaron Anthony, Director, 200 E. Wall St., Benton Harbor, MI 49022. 616-927-8404

Economic Development Organizations
Southwestern Michigan Commission, Wendy Walker, Associate Program Manager, 185 E. Main St., Suite 701, Benton Harbor, MI 49022. 616-925-1137, FAX 616-925-0288
Cornerstone Alliance, Duane O'Neill, President, 185 E. Main St., PO Box 428, Benton Harbor, MI 49023-0428. 616-925-6100, FAX 616-925-4471

Major Businesses

Company	SIC	Telephone
All-Phase Electric Supply	5063	(616) 926-6194
Chase Manhattan Leasing Co., Michigan	6159	(616) 697-4000
Electro-Voice Inc., Delaware	3651	(616) 695-6831
French Paper Co.	2621	(616) 683-1100
Gast Manufacturing Corp.	3563	(616) 926-6171
Imperial Printing Co.	2752	(616) 983-7105
Kapaco Group, Inc.	2621	(616) 463-3141
Leco Corp.	3821	(616) 983-5533
Mercy-Memorial Medical Center	8062	(616) 983-8300
Modern Plastics Corp.	3089	(616) 926-8201
National-Standard Co.	3315	(616) 683-8100
Old Kent Bank Southwest	6022	(616) 683-4000
Pawating Hospital Association	8062	(616) 683-5510
Shepherd Products U. S. I.	3429	(616) 983-7351
Shoreline Financial Corp.	6022	(616) 927-2251
Whirlpool Corp.	3633	(616) 926-5000
Whirlpool Financial Corp.	6159	(616) 926-5500
Wollin Products, Inc.	3089	(616) 429-3201
Worldmark Inc.	2033	(616) 461-6984

Colleges and Universities
Lake Michigan College, Benton Harbor

DETROIT, MI (PMSA)

Geographic Profile

Land Area
4465.6 square miles

Counties and Parishes
Lapeer
Livingston
Macomb
Monroe
Oakland
St. Clair
Wayne

Additional Cities/Towns within Area
Dearborn
Pontiac
Port Huron

Ranking Highlights
20 *out of 319 in total* **land area**
290 *out of 319 in* **population growth,** *1970–1990*
254 *out of 310 in having the lowest* **unemployment** *rate*
6 *out of 310 in size of* **labor force**
178 *out of 318 in the percentage of* **college graduates**
40 *out of 292 in per capita personal* **income**
4 *out of 319 in number of* **manufacturing establishments**
122 *out of 318 in* **physicians** *per 1000 people*
205 *out of 318 in* **hospital beds** *per 1000 people*
193 *out of 267 in fewest* **crimes** *per 1000 people*
231 *out of 266 in fewest* **violent crimes** *per 1000 people*
212 *out of 319 in per capita* **federal funds and grants**

Quality of Life Indexes (Rate per 1000 population)
Crime rate in 1991:	70.6
Violent crime rate in 1991:	10.0
Physicians rate in 1992:	2
Hospital bed rate in 1991:	3.38

ACCRA Cost of Living Indexes
(First quarter 1993, average = 100)
Composite index:	114.9
Utilities index:	107.8
Housing index:	131.8

Overview
Located in southeastern Michigan, Detroit is the largest city in Michigan and the sixth largest in the United States. Founded in 1701, it was named Ville de' Etroit or "City of the Strait" because of its position on the Detroit River. It is the seat for Wayne County government and occupies 140 square miles of the County's 623 square miles. Internationally known for automobile manufacturing and trade, Detroit ranks high in the production of machine tool accessories, metal fabricating, and plating. Situated on the Detroit River,

Detroit serves as a gateway to Canada. The City of Windsor, Ontario, is minutes away via a railroad tunnel, a vehicular tunnel, or the Ambassador Bridge. The City owns and operates its own general aviation airport, and has freeway access to Detroit Metropolitan and Willow Run Airports, both Wayne County facilities. Recent downtown Detroit developments include an expanded convention/exhibition facility, Cobo Hall, and several new office buildings and residential tower. A network of skywalks and the People Mover, Detroit's central automated transportation system, connect many of the downtown office and high-rise buildings. An entertainment center, known as the Theatre District, is currently being developed north of the office district.

The largest private employers include Detroit Medical Center, 10,260 employees; Chrysler Corp., 9,800 employees; and General Motors Corp., over 9,000 employers.

Major highways include I-96, I-75, U.S.10, U.S.12, U.S.24, M-5, M-39, M-85, M-102, and M-153. Rail lines include Amtrak, CSX, Conrail, Grank Trunk, and Norfolk Southern. There are 96 motor freight companies in Wayne County. The Detroit Metropolitan Airport serves Air Ontario, American, American Trans Air, British Airways, Comair, Continental, Delta, Drummond Island Air, Great Lakes Air, Mesaba Aviation, Midway, Midwest Express, Northwest Airlink, Northwest, Pan Am, Piedmont, Skyway, Southwest, TWA, United and USAir. The Detroit City airport serves Central States, Comair, Continental, Direct Air, Northcoast Executive, and Southwest. The Willow Run airport serves freight and general aviation needs. Ports in Wayne County include Detroit Marine Terminal (Scotten Street Facilities and Rouge River Facilities); Harridon Terminal, Inc., Hickman, Williams & Co.; Michigan Marine Terminal; and Nicholson Terminal & Dock (Ecorse Facility and Summit Street Facility).

Population (1990)

Total Population and Growth Rate
1990: 4,382,299
1980: 4,488,024
1970: 4,554,266
Growth rate 1970–1990: -4%

Race and Hispanic Origin
White: 76.0%
Black: 21.5%
Asian/Pacific Islander: 1.3%
Native American: 0.4%
Hispanic origin: 1.9%
White not Hispanic: 74.9%

Age
Ages 18 to 20: 4.3%
Ages 21 to 24: 5.7%
Ages 25 to 44: 32.9%
Ages 45 to 54: 10.4%
Ages 55 to 59: 4.3%

Ages 60 to 64: 4.5%
Ages 65 plus: 11.8%

Educational Attainment (1990)
Percent having completed high school: 75.7%
Percent having completed college: 17.7%
Elementary and high school enrollment: 772,532

Federal Funds and Grants Received
Total received in 1989: $11,633,500,000
Funds received per capita: $2,673

Civilian Labor Force
1993 (April):   2,160,388
1992 average: 2,141,856
1991 average: 2,114,494
1990 average: 2,147,562

Unemployment
1993 (April):   6.7%
1992 average: 8.9%
1991 average: 9.3%
1990 average: 7.5%

Average Annual Pay
1988: $26,602
1987: $25,301
1985: $23,688

Per Capita Personal Income
1991: $20,585
1990: $20,394
1989: $19,686

Business Climate (1987)
Manufacturing
Number of establishments in 1987: 8,072
Shipments in 1987 ($1,000): $74,979,100
Employees in 1987: 478,800
Change in employment, 1982 to 1987: 11.2%
Average annual pay for manufacturing work in 1989: $40,221
Average annual pay for production work in 1987: $28,803

Wholesale Trade
Number of establishments in 1987: 7,746
Total sales in 1987 ($1,000): $59,517,700
Change in sales, 1982 to 1987: 51.5%

Retail Trade
Number of establishments in 1987: 23,246
Total sales in 1987 ($1,000): $59,517,700
Retail sales per household in 1987: $17,491
Average annual pay in 1989: $12,703

Service Industry
Selected receipts in 1987 ($1,000): $14,898,100
Average annual pay in 1989: $22,861

Office Real Estate (1992)
Office space inventory: 55,651,000 square feet

Average class A Central Business District rental range per sq. ft: $16.25

Vacancy Rates
All areas: 16.0%

Vacancy Rates in Central Business District
Class A space: N/A
Class B space: N/A

Vacancy Rates Outside Central Business District
Class A space: 15.0%
Class B space: 19.2%

Housing
Total number of units in 1990: 1,714,351
Occupied units in 1990: 1,618,950
Owner-occupied units in 1990: 69.8%
1993 ACCRA average cost: N/A
1993 ACCRA average rent for an apartment: N/A

Chamber of Commerce
Greater Detroit Chamber of Commerce, Jack Steiner, Director of Research, 600 W. Lafayette Blvd., Detroit, MI 48226. 313-964-4000

Economic Development Office
Detroit Economic Growth Corp., Jack Pryor, Vice President, 150 W. Jefferson. Suite 1500, Detroit, MI 48226. 313-963-2940, FAX 313-963-8839

Economic Development Organizations
Greater Detroit/South East Michigan Business Attraction and Expansion, Michael P. Smith, Exec. Vice President, 600 W. Lafayette Blvd., Detroit, MI 48226. 313-964-4000, FAX 313-964-0531

Department of Jobs EDC, DeWitt J. Henry, Director, 323 Wayne County Bldg., 600 Randolph St., Detroit, MI 48226. 313-224-0410, FAX 313-224-0822

Wayne County Department of Jobs and Economic Development, Dewitt J. Henry, Director, 323 Wayne County Bldg., 600 Randolph St., Detroit, MI 48226. 313-224-0749, FAX 313-224-0822

Business Development Team of Wayne County, Marjorie Whittemore, Exec. Director, 323 Wayne County Bldg., 600 Randolph St., Detroit, MI 48226. 313-224-0749

Major Businesses

Company	SIC	Telephone
Abitibi-Price Corp.	5111	(313) 649-3300
Acustar Inc.	3714	(313) 528-6500
American Natural Resources Co.	4922	(313) 965-1200
American Road Insurance Co.	6331	(313) 322-9045
Ameritech Publishing Inc.	2741	(313) 524-7300
ANR Pipeline Co.	4922	(313) 496-0200
Barton-Malow Enterprises	8741	(313) 351-4500
Blue Cross/Blue Shield of Michigan	6324	(313) 225-9000

Major Businesses (Continued)

Company	SIC	Telephone
Borg-Warner Automotive Inc.	3714	(313) 649-2111
Borman's Inc.	5411	(313) 270-1000
The Budd Co.	3465	(313) 643-3500
Chrysler Corp.	3711	(313) 956-5741
Chrysler Financial Corp.	6153	(313) 948-3890
Citizens Insurance Co. of America	6331	(517) 546-2160
CMS Energy Corp.	4931	(313) 436-9200
Comerica Bank-Detroit	6022	(313) 222-3300
Comerica Inc.	6021	(313) 222-3300
Decoma International of America	5013	(313) 353-5540
Detroit Edison Co.	4911	(313) 237-8000
Detroit Medical Center	8062	(313) 745-5089
F & M Distributors Inc.	5912	(313) 758-1400
Federal-Mogul Corp.	3714	(313) 354-7700
First Federal of Michigan	6035	(313) 965-1400
Foodland Distributors	5141	(313) 523-2100
Ford Motor Co.	3711	(313) 322-3000
Ford Motor Credit Co.	6153	(313) 322-3000
G M Hughes Electronics Co.	3812	(313) 556-5000
General Dynamics Land Systems	3795	(313) 825-4000
General Motors Acceptance	6153	(313) 556-5000
General Motors Corp.	3711	(313) 556-5000
General Motors Overseas Co.	8748	(313) 974-1970
Handleman Co.	5099	(313) 362-4400
Henry Ford Health System	8062	(313) 876-2600
Highland Superstores Inc.	5731	(313) 451-3200
K Mart Corp.	5311	(313) 643-1000
K-H Corp.	3714	(313) 941-2000
Kelsey-Hayes Co.	3714	(313) 941-2000
Lear Siegler Seating Corp.	2531	(313) 746-1500
Manufacturers National Co.	6021	(313) 222-4000
Manufacturers National Bank of Detroit	6021	(313) 222-4000
Masco Corp.	3432	(313) 274-7400
Masco Industries Inc.	3714	(313) 274-7405
Michigan Bell Telephone Co.	4813	(313) 223-9900
Michigan Consolidated Gas Co.	4924	(313) 965-2430
Michigan National Bank	6021	(313) 473-3000
Motors Insurance Corp.	6331	(313) 556-5000
NBD Bancorp, Inc.	6021	(313) 225-1000
Nippondenso America Inc.	5013	(313) 350-7500
Nippondenso Sales Inc.	5013	(313) 350-7500
Perry Drug Stores Inc.	5912	(313) 334-1300
PHM Corp.	1521	(313) 644-7300
Pulte Home Corp.	1521	(313) 644-7300
Regis Inventory Specialist	7389	(313) 651-2511
Rouge Steel Co.	3312	(313) 322-3000
SGC Holding Co. Inc.	3714	(313) 832-2400
Sheller-Globe Corp.	3714	(313) 962-7311
Standard Federal Bank	6035	(313) 643-9600

Major Businesses (Continued)

Company	SIC	Telephone
The Stroh Brewery Co.	2082	(313) 446-2000
Stroh Companies Inc.	2082	(313) 446-2000
Taubman Holdings Inc.	5311	(313) 258-6800
Taubman Investment Co.	5311	(313) 258-6800
Thorn Apple Valley Inc.	2013	(313) 552-0700
Thyssen Acquisition Corp.	3465	(313) 643-3500
Thyssen Holding Corp.	3465	(313) 643-3500
Thyssen Intermediate Corp.	3465	(313) 643-3500
United Technologies Auto Holdings	3714	(313) 593-9600
United Technologies Automotive	3714	(313) 593-9600
Valassis Inserts Inc.	2752	(313) 591-3000
Volkswagen of America Inc.	5012	(313) 362-6000
Wickes Manufacturing Co.	3592	(313) 355-8000

Colleges and Universities

Center for Creative Studies-College of Art and Design, Detroit

Detroit College of Business, Dearborn

Henry Ford Community College, Dearborn

Lawrence Technological University, Southfield

Lewis College of Business, Detroit

Marygrove College, Detroit

Mercy College of Detroit, Detroit

St. Clair County Community College, Port Huron

University of Detroit, Detroit

University of Michigan-Dearborn, Dearborn

Wayne State University, Detroit

Oakland University, Rochester

FLINT, MI (MSA)

Geographic Profile

Land Area

639.7 square miles

Counties and Parishes

Genesee

Ranking Highlights

264 *out of 319 in total* **land area**

287 *out of 319 in* **population growth,** *1970–1990*

296 *out of 310 in having the lowest* **unemployment** *rate*

121 *out of 310 in size of* **labor force**

285 *out of 318 in the percentage of* **college graduates**

142 *out of 292 in per capita personal* **income**

158 *out of 319 in number of* **manufacturing establishments**

204 *out of 318 in* **physicians** *per 1000 people*

125 *out of 318 in* **hospital beds** *per 1000 people*

222 *out of 267 in fewest* **crimes** *per 1000 people*

242 *out of 266 in fewest* **violent crimes** *per 1000 people*

273 *out of 319 in per capita* **federal funds and grants**

Quality of Life Indexes (Rate per 1000 population)

Crime rate in 1991:	77.3
Violent crime rate in 1991:	10.9
Physicians rate in 1992:	1.61
Hospital bed rate in 1991:	4.25

ACCRA Cost of Living Indexes

(First quarter 1993, average = 100)

Composite index:	N/A
Utilities index:	N/A
Housing index:	N/A

Population (1990)

Total Population and Growth Rate

1990: 430,459

1980: 450,449

1970: 445,589

Growth rate 1970–1990: -3%

Race and Hispanic Origin

White: 78.2%

Black: 19.6%

Asian/Pacific Islander: 0.7%

Native American: 0.7%

Hispanic origin: 2.1%

White not Hispanic: 77.1%

Age

Ages 18 to 20: 4.6%

Ages 21 to 24: 5.7%

Ages 25 to 44: 31.9%

Ages 45 to 54: 10.8%

Ages 55 to 59: 4.6%

Ages 60 to 64: 4.2%

Ages 65 plus: 10.2%

Educational Attainment (1990)

Percent having completed high school: 76.8%

Percent having completed college: 12.8%

Elementary and high school enrollment: 84,486

Federal Funds and Grants Received

Total received in 1989: $982,800,000

Funds received per capita: $2,282

Civilian Labor Force

1993 (April): 182,489

1992 average: 183,637

1991 average: 185,170

1990 average: 183,706

Unemployment

1993 (April): 9.0%

1992 average: 12.1%

1991 average: 12.6%

1990 average: 9.8%

Average Annual Pay

1988: $26,900

1987: $25,514

1985: $26,575

Per Capita Personal Income

1991: $17,459

1990: $16,743

1989: $16,168

Business Climate (1987)

Manufacturing

Number of establishments in 1987: 323

Shipments in 1987 ($1,000): N/A

Employees in 1987: N/A

Change in employment, 1982 to 1987: N/A

Average annual pay for manufacturing work in 1989: $44,362

Average annual pay for production work in 1987: N/A

Wholesale Trade

Number of establishments in 1987: 476

Total sales in 1987 ($1,000): $1,982,700

Change in sales, 1982 to 1987: 26.1%

Retail Trade

Number of establishments in 1987: 2,559

Total sales in 1987 ($1,000): $1,982,700

Retail sales per household in 1987: $18,276

Average annual pay in 1989: $10,948

Service Industry

Selected receipts in 1987 ($1,000): $886,500

Average annual pay in 1989: $20,061

Housing

Total number of units in 1990: 170,808

Occupied units in 1990: 161,296
Owner-occupied units in 1990: 70.4%
1993 ACCRA average cost: N/A
1993 ACCRA average rent for an apartment: N/A

Chamber of Commerce

Flint Area Chamber of Commerce, Lawrence P. Ford, President. 316 W. Water St., Flint, MI 48503. 313-232-7101

Economic Development Office

Genesse County Metro Planning Commisssion, Chapin Cook, Director, 1101 Beach St., Flint, MI 48502. 313-257-3010, FAX 313-257-3185

Major Businesses

Company	SIC	Telephone
Action Auto Stores Inc.	5541	(313) 235-5600
J. Austin Oil Co.	5171	(313) 232-9141
Citizens Banking Corp.	6311	(313) 766-7500
Citizens Commercial & Savings Bank	6022	(313) 766-7500
Crown Leisure Products Inc.	2514	(517) 723-7881
Emro Propane Co.	5984	(313) 238-8200
Flint Osteopathic Hospital	8062	(313) 762-4000
Hank Graff Chevrolet Inc.	5511	(313) 653-4111
Hurley Medical Center	8062	(313) 257-9000
Kessel Food Markets Inc.	5411	(313) 733-2583
M & B Distributing Co. Inc.	5141	(313) 767-5460
McLaren General Hospital	8062	(313) 762-2000
Midland Brake Inc.	3714	(517) 723-7811
Mitchell Corp.	2396	(517) 725-2171
NBD Genesee Bank	6022	(313) 766-8000
Nu Vision Inc.	5995	(313) 767-0900
Republic Bancorp Inc.	6022	(517) 725-7337
C. J. Rogers, Inc.	1611	(313) 767-6060
St. Joseph Hospital Corp.	8062	(313) 762-8000
U. S. Brick Inc.	3251	(517) 743-3444

Colleges and Universities

Baker College of Flint, Flint
Charles Stewart Mott Community College, Flint
Detroit College of Business-Flint, Flint
GMI Engineering & Management Institute, Flint
University of Michigan-Flint, Flint

GRAND RAPIDS, MI (MSA)

Geographic Profile

Land Area
1422.0 square miles

Counties and Parishes
Kent
Ottawa

Additional Cities/Towns within Area
Holland

Ranking Highlights

143 *out of 319 in total* land area
147 *out of 319 in* population growth, *1970–1990*
166 *out of 310 in having the lowest* unemployment *rate*
66 *out of 310 in size of* labor force
134 *out of 318 in the percentage of* college graduates
113 *out of 292 in per capita personal* income
44 *out of 319 in number of* manufacturing establishments
168 *out of 318 in* physicians *per 1000 people*
269 *out of 318 in* hospital beds *per 1000 people*
100 *out of 267 in fewest* crimes *per 1000 people*
138 *out of 266 in fewest* violent crimes *per 1000 people*
290 *out of 319 in per capita* federal funds and grants

Quality of Life Indexes (Rate per 1000 population)

Crime rate in 1991: 54.4
Violent crime rate in 1991: 6.5
Physicians rate in 1992: 1.77
Hospital bed rate in 1991: 2.58

ACCRA Cost of Living Indexes

(First quarter 1993, average = 100)
Composite index: 100.9
Utilities index: 80.7
Housing index: 108.3

Overview

The seat of Kent County, Michigan, Grand Rapids is the center of a metropolitan statistical area that includes both Kent and Ottawa counties. *Kiplinger's Personal Finance Magazine* singled out Grand Rapids as a 1991 "Super City."

The furniture industry has been a mainstay of the Grand Rapids economy since the late 1800s. Today the metropolitan area is home to five of the world's leading office furniture companies: Herman Miller, Haworth, American Seating, Westinghouse, and Steelcase, Inc. Several firms also continue to produce residential furniture. The Grand Rapids manufacturing base, consisting of more than thirteen hundred companies that employ nearly one-third of the work force, has expanded to include nineteen of the twenty primary U.S. industries. General Motors, an automotive manufacturer, and Amway, manufacturer of home care products, are among the city's largest employers.

The core of the Grand Rapids manufacturing sector is made up of family-owned or small businesses. The ten largest companies in the area employ among them more than forty thousand workers, yet 90 percent of local businesses employ fewer than 50 persons.

Advertising, graphic arts, and printing comprise a substantial portion of the economic base; Grand Rapids is the sixth-largest printing community in the country. International business also plays an important role, with twenty–two foreign-owned firms located in the city and more than two hundred local firms involved in international trade. Agriculture continues to be an economic mainstay in Kent County, which is the largest apple-producing region in the state and a source for Christmas trees, dairy products, fruits and vegetables, and nursery products.

Grand Rapids was one of the first cities in the country to build a convention center and in 1987 reported a record $100 million in convention receipts. Four thousand six hundred rooms are available for lodgings in more than fifty hotels and motels, many of which also provide meeting and convention accommodations.

Ground transportation is available through more than forty motor carriers, several of which operate terminals in Grand Rapids, and three rail freight systems providing a range of services such as piggyback shipments, bulk handling, and refrigeration. Twelve air cargo companies and a deep-water port on Lake Michigan, 35 miles away in Muskegon, link Grand Rapids with world markets.

Michigan's second largest airport, Kent County International Airport, is located twenty minutes from downtown Grand Rapids. Five major airlines and six commuter services schedule 126 daily direct and connecting flights from cities in the United States, Canada, Mexico, Europe, and the Far East.

A network of interstate, federal, and state highways provides access into Grand Rapids from surrounding communities as well as points throughout the United States and Canada. Interstate highways serving the metropolitan area are I-96, I-196, and I-296. U.S. highways extending through the city are 16 and 131; state routes include 11, 44, 50, 21, and 37.

Population (1990)

Total Population and Growth Rate
1990: 688,399
1980: 601,680
1970: 539,225
Growth rate 1970–1990: 28%

Race and Hispanic Origin
White: 90.6%
Black: 6.0%
Asian/Pacific Islander: 1.1%
Native American: 0.5%

Hispanic origin: 3.3%
White not Hispanic: 89.2%

Age
Ages 18 to 20: 4.9%
Ages 21 to 24: 6.3%
Ages 25 to 44: 33.3%
Ages 45 to 54: 9.2%
Ages 55 to 59: 3.7%
Ages 60 to 64: 3.6%
Ages 65 plus: 10.5%

Educational Attainment (1990)
Percent having completed high school: 80.2%
Percent having completed college: 20.2%
Elementary and high school enrollment: 126,807

Federal Funds and Grants Received
Total received in 1989: $1,459,500,000
Funds received per capita: 2,194

Civilian Labor Force
1993 (April): 397,126
1992 average: 390,399
1991 average: 383,151
1990 average: 381,401

Unemployment
1993 (April): 5.0%
1992 average: 7.0%
1991 average: 7.2%
1990 average: 6.0%

Average Annual Pay
1988: $21,812
1987: $20,584
1985: $19,127

Per Capita Personal Income
1991: $18,008
1990: $17,624
1989: $16,905

Business Climate (1987)

Manufacturing
Number of establishments in 1987: 1,593
Shipments in 1987 ($1,000): $11,135,500
Employees in 1987: 101,500
Change in employment, 1982 to 1987: 23.0%
Average annual pay for manufacturing work in 1989: $28,902
Average annual pay for production work in 1987: $23,277

Wholesale Trade
Number of establishments in 1987: 1,541
Total sales in 1987 ($1,000): $8,740,200
Change in sales, 1982 to 1987: 55.0%

Retail Trade
Number of establishments in 1987: 3,718
Total sales in 1987 ($1,000): $8,740,200

Retail sales per household in 1987: $19,437
Average annual pay in 1989: $11,766

Service Industry

Selected receipts in 1987 ($1,000): $1,757,700
Average annual pay in 1989: $18,662

Office Real Estate (1992)

Office space inventory: 8,330,000 square feet
*Average class A Central Business District rental range per
  sq. ft:* $19.00

Vacancy Rates

All areas: 13.2%

Vacancy Rates in Central Business District

Class A space: 16.9%
Class B space: 17.4%

Vacancy Rates Outside Central Business District

Class A space: 8.8%
Class B space: 18.9%

Housing

Total number of units in 1990: 259,322
Occupied units in 1990: 244,404
Owner-occupied units in 1990: 72.5%
1993 ACCRA average cost: N/A
1993 ACCRA average rent for an apartment: N/A

Chamber of Commerce

Grand Rapids Area Chamber of Commerce, Milton W. Rohwer, President, 17 Fountain St. N.W., Grand Rapids, MI 49503. 616-771-0300

Economic Development Office

Certified Economic Development Foundation of Grand Rapids, Charles Krupp, Coordinator, 300 Monroe Ave., City Hall, 4th Fl. Grand Rapids, MI 49503. 616-456-3167

Economic Development Organizations

West Michigan Regional Planning Commission, Jonathan Edelman, Program Manager, Two Fountain Pl., Suite 240, Grand Rapids, MI 49503. 616-458-7287

The Right Place Program, Birgit Klohs, Exec. Director, 17 Fountain St. N.W., Grand Rapids, MI 49503. 616-771-0300, FAX 616-771-0318

Major Businesses

Company	SIC	Telephone
S. Abraham & Sons, Inc.	5194	(616) 247-1711
Amway Corp.	2842	(616) 676-6000
Bil Mar Foods, Inc.	2015	(616) 875-8131
Bissell, Inc.	3635	(616) 453-4451
Brooks Beverage Management	2086	(616) 396-1281
Country Fresh, Inc.	2026	(616) 243-0173
D & W Food Centers, Inc.	5411	(616) 940-3580
Donnelly Corp.	3231	(616) 394-2200
First Michigan Bank Corp.	6035	(616) 396-9000

Major Businesses (Continued)

Company	SIC	Telephone
Foremost Insurance Co.	6331	(616) 942-3000
Gantos Stores, Inc.	5621	(616) 949-7000
Gordon Food Service, Inc.	5141	(616) 530-7000
Grad, Inc.	5141	(616) 247-1711
Guardsman Products Inc.	2851	(616) 957-2600
Haworth Industries, Inc.	2522	(616) 393-3000
JSJ Corp.	3366	(616) 842-6350
Meijer Inc.	5311	(616) 453-6711
Herman Miller Inc.	2521	(616) 772-3300
Old Kent Financial Corp.	6712	(616) 771-5000
Spartan Stores Inc.	5141	(616) 878-2000
Steelcase Inc.	2522	(616) 247-2710
TNT Holland Motor Express	4213	(616) 392-3101
Transnational Motors Inc.	5012	(616) 949-7570
Universal Companies Inc.	5031	(616) 364-6161
Universal Forest Products	5031	(616) 364-6161
Wolverine World Wide Inc.	3143	(616) 866-5500

Colleges and Universities

Aquinas College, Grand Rapids
Calvin College, Grand Rapids
Davenport College of Business, Grand Rapids
Grand Rapids Junior College, Grand Rapids
Hope College, Holland
Kendall College of Art and Design, Grand Rapids

JACKSON, MI (MSA)

Geographic Profile

Land Area

706.7 square miles

Counties and Parishes

Jackson

Ranking Highlights

255 *out of 319 in total* **land area**
244 *out of 319 in* **population growth,** *1970–1990*
280 *out of 310 in having the lowest* **unemployment** *rate*
245 *out of 310 in size of* **labor force**
282 *out of 318 in the percentage of* **college graduates**
213 *out of 292 in per capita personal* **income**
157 *out of 319 in number of* **manufacturing establishments**
313 *out of 318 in* **physicians** *per 1000 people*
160 *out of 318 in* **hospital beds** *per 1000 people*
123 *out of 267 in fewest* **crimes** *per 1000 people*
256 *out of 266 in fewest* **violent crimes** *per 1000 people*
270 *out of 319 in per capita* **federal funds and grants**

Quality of Life Indexes (Rate per 1000 population)

Crime rate in 1991:	58.7
Violent crime rate in 1991:	13.0
Physicians rate in 1992:	0.91
Hospital bed rate in 1991:	3.83

ACCRA Cost of Living Indexes

(First quarter 1993, average = 100)

Composite index:	N/A
Utilities index:	N/A
Housing index:	N/A

Population (1990)

Total Population and Growth Rate

1990: 149,756
1980: 151,495
1970: 143,274
Growth rate 1970–1990: 5%

Race and Hispanic Origin

White: 90.5%
Black: 8.0%
Asian/Pacific Islander: 0.4%
Native American: 0.4%
Hispanic origin: 1.5%
White not Hispanic: 89.7%

Age

Ages 18 to 20: 4.1%
Ages 21 to 24: 5.4%
Ages 25 to 44: 33.3%
Ages 45 to 54: 10.3%
Ages 55 to 59: 4.3%
Ages 60 to 64: 4.5%
Ages 65 plus: 12.4%

Educational Attainment (1990)

Percent having completed high school: 77.7%
Percent having completed college: 12.9%
Elementary and high school enrollment: 26,132

Federal Funds and Grants Received

Total received in 1989: $342,900,000
Funds received per capita: $2,295

Civilian Labor Force

1993 (April):	65,873
1992 average:	65,791
1991 average:	64,637
1990 average:	65,930

Unemployment

1993 (April):	7.7%
1992 average:	9.9%
1991 average:	9.9%
1990 average:	7.8%

Average Annual Pay

1988: $22,233
1987: $21,188
1985: $19,538

Per Capita Personal Income

1991: $16,039
1990: $15,575
1989: $15,175

Business Climate (1987)

Manufacturing

Number of establishments in 1987: 324
Shipments in 1987 ($1,000): $1,406,800
Employees in 1987: 13,300
Change in employment, 1982 to 1987: 9.0%
Average annual pay for manufacturing work in 1989: $27,276
Average annual pay for production work in 1987: $20,467

Wholesale Trade

Number of establishments in 1987: 180
Total sales in 1987 ($1,000): $707,800
Change in sales, 1982 to 1987: 21.0%

Retail Trade

Number of establishments in 1987: 801
Total sales in 1987 ($1,000): $707,800
Retail sales per household in 1987: $15,939
Average annual pay in 1989: $11,481

Service Industry

Selected receipts in 1987 ($1,000): $262,600
Average annual pay in 1989: $17,807

Housing

Total number of units in 1990: 57,979

Occupied units in 1990: 53,660
Owner-occupied units in 1990: 73.7%
1993 ACCRA average cost: N/A
1993 ACCRA average rent for an apartment: N/A

Chamber of Commerce

Greater Jackson Chamber of Commerce, Ila J. Smith, President, 109 W. Washington Ave., PO Box 80, Jackson, MI 49201. 517-782-8221

Economic Development Office

Jackson Alliance for Business Development, Christopher M. Manegold, Exec. Director, 133 W. Michigan Ave., Jackson, MI 49201. 517-788-4455, FAX 517-788-4337

Major Businesses

Company	SIC	Telephone
Alro Steel Corp.	5051	(517) 787-5500
Camp International Inc.	3842	(517) 787-1600
Camshaft Machine Co.	3714	(517) 787-2040
CB Financial Corp.	6712	(517) 788-2711
City Bank Trust National Association	6021	(517) 788-2711
Consumers Power Co.	4911	(517) 788-0550
Dawn Food Products Inc.	2045	(517) 789-4400
Dawn/Besco Inc.	2045	(517) 787-0050
Diecast Corp.	3363	(517) 788-6100
W. A. Foote Memorial Hospital	8062	(517) 788-4883
Harris-McBurney Co.	1731	(517) 787-1800
Hayes-Albion Corp.	3322	(517) 782-9421
Heat Controller Inc.	3585	(517) 787-2100
Jackson Iron & Metal Co.	5093	(517) 787-1731
Jackson Trotting Association	7948	(517) 788-4500
Daniel L. Jacob Co. Inc.	5181	(517) 782-7191
Jacobson Stores Inc.	5311	(517) 764-6400
Kelly Distributing Co.	5172	(517) 789-8196
John Lefere Ford Inc.	5511	(517) 787-9500
Melling Tool Co.	3714	(517) 787-8172
Michigan Gas Storage Co.	4922	(517) 788-0550
Nomeco Oil & Gas Co.	1311	(517) 787-9011
Polly's Food Service Inc.	5411	(517) 787-6081
Sparton Corp.	3714	(517) 787-8600
C. Thorrez Industries Inc.	3451	(517) 750-3160
J. F. Walker Co. Inc.	5194	(517) 787-9880
Worthington Steel Co.	5051	(517) 783-2673

Colleges and Universities

Jackson Community College, Jackson

KALAMAZOO, MI (MSA)

Geographic Profile

Land Area
561.9 square miles

Counties and Parishes
Kalamazoo

Ranking Highlights

280 *out of 319 in total* **land area**
222 *out of 319 in* **population growth,** *1970–1990*
76 *out of 310 in having the lowest* **unemployment** *rate*
164 *out of 310 in size of* **labor force**
38 *out of 318 in the percentage of* **college graduates**
145 *out of 292 in per capita personal* **income**
135 *out of 319 in number of* **manufacturing establishments**
59 *out of 318 in* **physicians** *per 1000 people*
186 *out of 318 in* **hospital beds** *per 1000 people*
182 *out of 267 in fewest* **crimes** *per 1000 people*
204 *out of 266 in fewest* **violent crimes** *per 1000 people*
280 *out of 319 in per capita* **federal funds and grants**

Quality of Life Indexes (Rate per 1000 population)

Crime rate in 1991:	68.5
Violent crime rate in 1991:	9.1
Physicians rate in 1992:	2.54
Hospital bed rate in 1991:	3.55

ACCRA Cost of Living Indexes
(First quarter 1993, average = 100)
Composite index: N/A
Utilities index: N/A
Housing index: N/A

Population (1990)

Total Population and Growth Rate
1990: 223,411
1980: 212,378
1970: 201,550
Growth rate 1970–1990: 11%

Race and Hispanic Origin
White: 88.4%
Black: 8.9%
Asian/Pacific Islander: 1.4%
Native American: 0.5%
Hispanic origin: 1.8%
White not Hispanic: 87.5%

Age
Ages 18 to 20: 7.3%
Ages 21 to 24: 8.2%
Ages 25 to 44: 32.1%
Ages 45 to 54: 9.8%
Ages 55 to 59: 3.9%

Ages 60 to 64: 3.7%
Ages 65 plus: 10.6%

Educational Attainment (1990)
Percent having completed high school: 83.4%
Percent having completed college: 27.1%
Elementary and high school enrollment: 35,185

Federal Funds and Grants Received
Total received in 1989: $487,700,000
Funds received per capita: $2,238

Civilian Labor Force
1993 (April): 121,326
1992 average: 121,300
1991 average: 118,001
1990 average: 119,566

Unemployment
1993 (April): 4.1%
1992 average: 5.6%
1991 average: 5.9%
1990 average: 5.1%

Average Annual Pay
1988: $23,340
1987: $22,577
1985: $21,185

Per Capita Personal Income
1991: $17,397
1990: $16,692
1989: $16,170

Business Climate (1987)
Manufacturing
Number of establishments in 1987: 393
Shipments in 1987 ($1,000): $3,970,600
Employees in 1987: 27,900
Change in employment, 1982 to 1987: -2.4%
Average annual pay for manufacturing work in 1989: $34,390
Average annual pay for production work in 1987: $28,503

Wholesale Trade
Number of establishments in 1987: 394
Total sales in 1987 ($1,000): $1,270,200
Change in sales, 1982 to 1987: 5.0%

Retail Trade
Number of establishments in 1987: 1,343
Total sales in 1987 ($1,000): $1,270,200
Retail sales per household in 1987: $18,468
Average annual pay in 1989: $9,976

Service Industry
Selected receipts in 1987 ($1,000): $730,300
Average annual pay in 1989: $21,086

Housing
Total number of units in 1990: 88,955

Occupied units in 1990: 83,702
Owner-occupied units in 1990: 64.4%
1993 ACCRA average cost: N/A
1993 ACCRA average rent for an apartment: N/A

Chamber of Commerce
Kalamazoo County Chamber of Commerce, Mark A. V'Soske, President, 128 N. Kalamazoo Mall, PO Box 1169, Kalamazoo, MI 49005. 616-381-4000

Economic Development Office
Economic Development Department, City of Kalamazoo, Marc Ott, Manager, 241 W. South St., Kalamazoo, MI 49007-4796. 616-337-8044, FAX 616-337-8182

Economic Development Organizations
CEO Council, Inc., John F. Hanieski, President, 100 W. Michigan Ave. Suite 294, Kalamazoo, MI 49007. 616-342-0000, FAX 616-343-1151

Major Businesses

Company	SIC	Telephone
Asgrow Seed Co.	0181	(616) 323-4000
Borgess Health Alliance,	8062	(616) 383-7000
Borgess Medical Center Inc.	8062	(616) 383-7000
Bronson Healthcare Group	8099	(616) 341-6000
Bronson Methodist Hospital	8062	(616) 341-7654
L.P. Checker Motors Co.	3465	(616) 343-6121
Durametallic Corp.	3053	(616) 381-2650
Fabri-Kal Corp.	3089	(616) 385-5050
First America Bank Corp.	6022	(616) 383-9000
First of America Bank-Michigan	6021	(616) 383-9000
Gilmore Enterprises Corp.	4832	(616) 381-3490
International Controls Co.	3715	(616) 343-6121
Miller-Davis Co.	1542	(616) 345-3561
Old Kent Bank of Kalamazoo	6022	(616) 383-6700
South Haven Rubber Co.	3069	(616) 637-2116
Stryker Corp.	3841	(616) 385-2600
A. M. Todd Co.	2899	(616) 343-2603
The Upjohn Co.	2834	(616) 323-4000
Upjohn Inter-American Corp.	5122	(616) 323-4000

Colleges and Universities
Davenport College of Business, Kalamazoo Campus, Kalamazoo
Kalamazoo College, Kalamazoo
Kalamazoo Valley Community College, Kalamazoo
Nazareth College in Kalamazoo, Kalamazoo

LANSING–EAST LANSING, MI (MSA)

Geographic Profile

Land Area

1707.3 square miles

Counties and Parishes

Clinton

Eaton

Ingham

Ranking Highlights

112　*out of 319 in total* **land area**

203　*out of 319 in* **population growth**, *1970–1990*

　92　*out of 310 in having the lowest* **unemployment** *rate*

　96　*out of 310 in size of* **labor force**

　65　*out of 318 in the percentage of* **college graduates**

124　*out of 292 in per capita personal* **income**

133　*out of 319 in number of* **manufacturing establishments**

217　*out of 318 in* **physicians** *per 1000 people*

180　*out of 318 in* **hospital beds** *per 1000 people*

127　*out of 267 in fewest* **crimes** *per 1000 people*

142　*out of 266 in fewest* **violent crimes** *per 1000 people*

　95　*out of 319 in per capita* **federal funds and grants**

Quality of Life Indexes (Rate per 1000 population)

Crime rate in 1991:	59.1
Violent crime rate in 1991:	6.6
Physicians rate in 1992:	1.55
Hospital bed rate in 1991:	3.59

ACCRA Cost of Living Indexes

(First quarter 1993, average = 100)

Composite index:	104.3
Utilities index:	89.9
Housing index:	116.8

Overview

Lansing, the capital of Michigan, is the focus of a metropolitan statistical area that includes the city of East Lansing and Clinton, Eaton, and Ingham counties. Lansing is the state capital. Michigan State University is located in East Lansing and contributes to the city's strength.

Services, wholesale and retail trade, and manufacturing (primarily of transportation products) comprise the economic base of the Lansing metropolitan area. There are 430 manufacturers in the region; forty auto–related manufacturers account for 70 percent of manufacturing jobs. Nearly six hundred wholesalers employing 8,400 people are located in the Lansing region, reflecting an 18 percent increase in the number of firms and a nine percent increase in employment since 1980. Because of the region's large share of professional workers, the retailing market showed robust growth throughout the 1980s. The number of service firms in the region increased by 50 percent during the 1980s and employment rose 44 percent. Health care accounts for the largest share of the services sector, followed by business services and trade associations. Twelve insurance companies have corporate or regional offices in Lansing; four are headquartered there. Other important sectors are government, education, and transportation and public utilities.

Seven commercial airlines schedule regular daily flights into Capital City Airport, located fifteen minutes from downtown Lansing. Daily rail service to Lansing is provided by Amtrak. An efficient highway system facilitates access to Lansing and its environs. Part of a beltway circling the southern half of the city, I-96 is intersected by several major and secondary routes; east-west I-69 completes the beltway around the northern sector. I-496 bisects the downtown area westward from north-south U.S. 127 in East Lansing. Other principal highways are U.S. 27 and M-99, both running north-south, and east-west M-43.

Population (1990)

Total Population and Growth Rate

1990: 432,674

1980: 419,750

1970: 378,423

Growth rate 1970–1990: 14%

Race and Hispanic Origin

White: 88.1%

Black: 7.2%

Asian/Pacific Islander: 1.9%

Native American: 0.6%

Hispanic origin: 3.9%

White not Hispanic: 86.4%

Age

Ages 18 to 20: 7.6%

Ages 21 to 24: 8.5%

Ages 25 to 44: 32.7%

Ages 45 to 54: 9.6%

Ages 55 to 59: 3.6%

Ages 60 to 64: 3.3%

Ages 65 plus: 9%

Educational Attainment (1990)

Percent having completed high school: 84.2%

Percent having completed college: 24.7%

Elementary and high school enrollment: 74,408

Federal Funds and Grants Received

Total received in 1989: $1,550,600,000

Funds received per capita: $3,620

Civilian Labor Force

1993 (April):　242,525

1992 average:　240,471

1991 average:　238,787

1990 average:　240,985

Unemployment

1993 (April): 4.4%
1992 average: 5.9%
1991 average: 7.1%
1990 average: 6.1%

Average Annual Pay

1988: $23,055
1987: $22,141
1985: $22,046

Per Capita Personal Income

1991: $17,777
1990: $17,221
1989: $16,531

Business Climate (1987)

Manufacturing

Number of establishments in 1987: 399
Shipments in 1987 ($1,000): $7,378,500
Employees in 1987: 35,600
Change in employment, 1982 to 1987: 0%
Average annual pay for manufacturing work in 1989: $37,399
Average annual pay for production work in 1987: $31,522

Wholesale Trade

Number of establishments in 1987: 574
Total sales in 1987 ($1,000): $2,572,800
Change in sales, 1982 to 1987: 26.3%

Retail Trade

Number of establishments in 1987: 2,384
Total sales in 1987 ($1,000): $2,572,800
Retail sales per household in 1987: $18,234
Average annual pay in 1989: $10,766

Service Industry

Selected receipts in 1987 ($1,000): $893,500
Average annual pay in 1989: $18,652

Office Real Estate (1992)

Office space inventory: 5,730,000 square feet
Average class A Central Business District rental range per sq. ft: $16.50

Vacancy Rates

All areas: 17.7%

Vacancy Rates in Central Business District

Class A space: 3.6%
Class B space: 26.6%

Vacancy Rates Outside Central Business District

Class A space: 14.0%
Class B space: 26.2%

Housing

Total number of units in 1990: 165,018
Occupied units in 1990: 156,887
Owner-occupied units in 1990: 64.7%
1993 ACCRA average cost: $136,030

1993 ACCRA average rent for an apartment: $514

Chamber of Commerce

Lansing Regional Chamber of Commerce, Melvin Kent, Exec. Vice President, 510 Washtenaw, PO Box 14030, Lansing, MI 48901. 517-487-6340

Economic Development Office

Manufacturing Development Board, Gregory Main, Director, 525 W. Ottawa St., Lansing, MI 48909. 517-373-6390

Economic Development Organizations

Michigan Department of Commerce, Penelope Stump, Director, Research and Customer Assistance, PO Box 30225, Lansing, MI 48909. 517-373-9808, FAX 517-373-3872

Michigan International Office, John Field Reichardt, Director, Michigan Department of Commerce, PO Box 30225, Lansing, MI 48909. 517-373-6390, FAX 517-335-2251

Major Businesses

Company	SIC	Telephone
Accident Fund of Michigan	6331	(517) 342-4200
American Bumper & Mfg. Co.	3714	(616) 527-1220
Auto Owners Insurance Co.	6311	(517) 323-1200
Carter's Food Centers, Inc.	5411	(517) 543-7833
The Christman Co.	8741	(517) 482-1488
Clark Construction Co.	1541	(517) 372-0940
Coca-Cola Bottling Co.	2086	(517) 322-2653
Delta Dental Plan of Michigan	6324	(517) 349-6000
Farm Bureau Mutual Insurance of Michigan	6331	(517) 323-7000
Granger Associates Inc.	1541	(517) 393-1670
Granger Construction Co.	1542	(517) 393-1670
Ingham Medical Center	8062	(517) 334-2237
Lansing Grain Co.	5153	(517) 349-7630
Lansing Wholesale Grain Co.	5141	(517) 699-3555
MWC Holdings Inc.	3714	(517) 337-5700
Maxco Inc.	5051	(517) 484-1414
Michigan Education Special Services	6411	(517) 332-2581
Michigan Live Stock Exchange	5159	(517) 337-2856
Motor Wheel Corp.	3714	(517) 337-5700
Edward W. Sparrow Hospital Association	8062	(517) 483-2700

Colleges and Universities

Davenport College of Business, Lansing Campus, Lansing
Lansing Community College, Lansing
Michigan State University, East Lansing

MUSKEGON, MI (MSA)

Geographic Profile

Land Area

509.2 square miles

Counties and Parishes

Muskegon

Ranking Highlights

290 *out of 319 in total* **land area**

267 *out of 319 in* **population growth,** *1970–1990*

295 *out of 310 in having the lowest* **unemployment** *rate*

239 *out of 310 in size of* **labor force**

309 *out of 318 in the percentage of* **college graduates**

N/A *out of 292 in per capita personal* **income**

177 *out of 319 in number of* **manufacturing establishments**

301 *out of 318 in* **physicians** *per 1000 people*

133 *out of 318 in* **hospital beds** *per 1000 people*

219 *out of 267 in fewest* **crimes** *per 1000 people*

179 *out of 266 in fewest* **violent crimes** *per 1000 people*

206 *out of 319 in per capita* **federal funds and grants**

Quality of Life Indexes (Rate per 1000 population)

Crime rate in 1991:	76.0
Violent crime rate in 1991:	7.8
Physicians rate in 1992:	1.05
Hospital bed rate in 1991:	4.15

ACCRA Cost of Living Indexes

(First quarter 1993, average = 100)

Composite index:	N/A
Utilities index:	N/A
Housing index:	N/A

Population (1990)

Total Population and Growth Rate

1990: 158,983

1980: 157,589

1970: 157,426

Growth rate 1970–1990: 1%

Race and Hispanic Origin

White: 84.2%

Black: 13.6%

Asian/Pacific Islander: 0.3%

Native American: 0.8%

Hispanic origin: 2.3%

White not Hispanic: 83.1%

Age

Ages 18 to 20: 4.2%

Ages 21 to 24: 5.2%

Ages 25 to 44: 31.1%

Ages 45 to 54: 9.7%

Ages 55 to 59: 4.2%

Ages 60 to 64: 4.4%

Ages 65 plus: 13.1%

Educational Attainment (1990)

Percent having completed high school: 74.2%

Percent having completed college: 11.1%

Elementary and high school enrollment: 30,378

Federal Funds and Grants Received

Total received in 1989: $441,200,000

Funds received per capita: $2,735

Civilian Labor Force

1993 (April):	66,748
1992 average:	67,322
1991 average:	67,692
1990 average:	67,997

Unemployment

1993 (April): 9.4%

1992 average: 11.9%

1991 average: 12.0%

1990 average: 9.3%

Average Annual Pay

1988: $20,774

1987: $20,123

1985: $19,102

Per Capita Personal Income

1991: N/A

1990: N/A

1989: N/A

Business Climate (1987)

Manufacturing

Number of establishments in 1987: 275

Shipments in 1987 ($1,000): $1,999,100

Employees in 1987: 17,700

Change in employment, 1982 to 1987: 6.0%

Average annual pay for manufacturing work in 1989: $29,566

Average annual pay for production work in 1987: $24,283

Wholesale Trade

Number of establishments in 1987: 179

Total sales in 1987 ($1,000): $776,300

Change in sales, 1982 to 1987: 11.2%

Retail Trade

Number of establishments in 1987: 912

Total sales in 1987 ($1,000): $776,300

Retail sales per household in 1987: $14,542

Average annual pay in 1989: $10,480

Service Industry

Selected receipts in 1987 ($1,000): $236,100

Average annual pay in 1989: $16,500

Housing

Total number of units in 1990: 61,962

Occupied units in 1990: 57,798
Owner-occupied units in 1990: 74.4%
1993 ACCRA average cost: N/A
1993 ACCRA average rent for an apartment: N/A

Chamber of Commerce

Muskegon Area Chamber of Commerce, Mike Michalski, President, 349 W. Webster Ave., Muskegon, MI 49440. 616-722-3751

Economic Development Office

Muskegon Economic Growth Alliance, Michael C. Michalski, President, 349 W. Webster, PO Box 1087, Muskegon, MI 49443. 616-722-3751, FAX 616-728-7251

Major Businesses

Company	SIC	Telephone
Bennett Pump Co.	3586	(616) 733-1302
Brunswick Bowling & Billiards	3949	(616) 725-3300
First America Bank-Muskegon	6021	(616) 722-7683
Fisher Steel And Supply Co.	5093	(616) 722-6081
Goetze Corp. of America	3592	(616) 726-5226
Hackley Hospital	8062	(616) 726-3511
Kaydon Corp.	3562	(616) 755-3741
Kurdziel Iron Industries	3321	(616) 739-4349
Lappo Lumber Co.	5211	(616) 865-3121
Lift Tech International Inc.	3536	(616) 733-0821
Muskegon General Hospital	8062	(616) 773-3311
Plumb, Inc.	5411	(616) 759-0918
Quality Stores, Inc.	5311	(616) 744-2491
The Shaw-Walker Co.	2522	(616) 755-2270
SPX Corp.	5013	(616) 724-5000
Superior Oil Co. of Muskegon	5172	(616) 773-3225
Viking Foods, Inc.	5141	(616) 722-3151
Webb Chemical Service Corp.	5169	(616) 733-2181
Westgate Oil Co.	5541	(616) 722-0200

Colleges and Universities

Baker College of Muskegon, Muskegon
Muskegon Community College, Muskegon

SAGINAW-BAY CITY-MIDLAND, MI (MSA)

Geographic Profile

Land Area

1774.5 square miles

Counties and Parishes

Bay
Midland
Saginaw

Ranking Highlights

106 *out of 319 in total* land area
274 *out of 319 in* population growth, *1970–1990*
234 *out of 310 in having the lowest* unemployment *rate*
115 *out of 310 in size of* labor force
233 *out of 318 in the percentage of* college graduates
132 *out of 292 in per capita personal* income
129 *out of 319 in number of* manufacturing establishments
231 *out of 318 in* physicians *per 1000 people*
89 *out of 318 in* hospital beds *per 1000 people*
120 *out of 267 in fewest* crimes *per 1000 people*
206 *out of 266 in fewest* violent crimes *per 1000 people*
275 *out of 319 in per capita* federal funds and grants

Quality of Life Indexes (Rate per 1000 population)

Crime rate in 1991:	58.5
Violent crime rate in 1991:	9.1
Physicians rate in 1992:	1.48
Hospital bed rate in 1991:	4.8

ACCRA Cost of Living Indexes

(First quarter 1993, average = 100)

Composite index:	N/A
Utilities index:	N/A
Housing index:	N/A

Overview

Saginaw County's industrial base consists of heavy manufacturing, precision-parts manufacturing, tool and die, chemical, and a wide range of others. Some leading Saginaw companies are General Motors, 14,366 employees; GM Saginaw Division, 8,426 employees; GM Powertrain Group, 4,436 employees; GM Delco Chassis Saginaw Manufacturing, 1,504 employees; St. Mary's Medical Center, 1,500 employees; Saginaw General Hospital, 1,380 employees; and Ameritech, 1,346 employees.

Two-thirds of Michigan's total population are located within two hours traveling time. The total market population within 300 miles of the county exceeds 35 million.

Saginaw County is a regional medical center serving central Michigan. Five hospitals provide in-and out-patient healthcare services.

Electric and natural gas services are provided by Consumers Power Company, the principal subsidiary of CMS Energy Corporation. Electric and natural gas services are available to all new industries, regardless of size or service demands.

Telephone service in Saginaw County is provided by a choice of five telephone companies. Ameritech is the largest telephone service provider in the county, serving the City of Saginaw and several surrounding communities. Excellent interconnections exist between the four telephone companies.

The primary source of water in Saginaw County is the Saginaw-Midland Water Supply System, which is treated by the City of Saginaw. This system serves most of the urbanized areas in the country. The design capacity of the system is 50 million gallons more than the average present level of usage. The sewage treatment plants serving the City of Saginaw and most major industries in the county have been designed with a capacity of 80 million gallons per day, 50 million gallons more than average present usage.

Saginaw County is served by two certified landfills with a six-year design capacity. A solid-waste disposal plan has been prepared by the county to assure adequate long term landfill capacity beyond the existing six-year plan.

There are 2,087 miles of roads in Saginaw County, 300 of which are located in the City of Saginaw. Ten state trunk lines serve Saginaw County; M-13, M-46, M-47, M-83, M-15, M-52, M-57, M-58, M-81, and M-84. Interstate freeways I-75 and I-675 provide access to the industries highways and markets to the south, as well as to the lakes and forests of northern Michigan. Eleven interchanges on I-75 and I-675 are located in Saginaw County. Central Michigan Railway, Tuscola and Saginaw Bay Railway, CSX Transportation (Chessie), Mid-Michigan Railroad, and the Huron & Eastern Railway serve Saginaw County.

Saginaw County is served by five airports, including the state's third most active airport, Tri-City International Airport. Approximately 30 commercial flights per day offer complete passenger, air freight, and air express service including daily direct flights to Detroit, Chicago, Illinois, and Cleveland, Ohio.

The Saginaw River is one of Michigan's most important commercial harbors. Approximately 34 marine terminals are located along the river in the area from the City of Saginaw to the mouth of the river. These terminals handle approximately four million tons of cargo annually. Major commodities include limestone, sand, coal, salt, fertilizers, cement, petroleum, and chemicals.

Population (1990)

Total Population and Growth Rate
1990: 399,320
1980: 421,518
1970: 400,851
Growth rate 1970–1990: 0%

Race and Hispanic Origin
White: 86.8%
Black: 9.7%
Asian/Pacific Islander: 0.6%
Native American: 0.5%
Hispanic origin: 4.4%
White not Hispanic: 84.9%

Age
Ages 18 to 20: 4.5%
Ages 21 to 24: 5.4%
Ages 25 to 44: 31%
Ages 45 to 54: 10.9%
Ages 55 to 59: 4.3%
Ages 60 to 64: 4.3%
Ages 65 plus: 12.1%

Educational Attainment (1990)
Percent having completed high school: 76.2%
Percent having completed college: 15.1%
Elementary and high school enrollment: 76,422

Federal Funds and Grants Received
Total received in 1989: $924,900,000
Funds received per capita: $2,277

Civilian Labor Force
1993 (April):   189,114
1992 average: 190,148
1991 average: 186,926
1990 average: 186,207

Unemployment
1993 (April):   6.5%
1992 average: 8.2%
1991 average: 8.5%
1990 average: 7.6%

Average Annual Pay
1988: $24,458
1987: $23,597
1985: $22,601

Per Capita Personal Income
1991: $17,631
1990: $17,114
1989: $16,443

Business Climate (1987)

Manufacturing
Number of establishments in 1987: 412
Shipments in 1987 ($1,000): $6,080,700
Employees in 1987: 38,900
Change in employment, 1982 to 1987: 0%
Average annual pay for manufacturing work in 1989: $39,366
Average annual pay for production work in 1987: $33,384

Wholesale Trade
Number of establishments in 1987: 554

Total sales in 1987 ($1,000): $2,202,800
Change in sales, 1982 to 1987: 14.5%

Retail Trade
Number of establishments in 1987: 2,455
Total sales in 1987 ($1,000): $2,202,800
Retail sales per household in 1987: $17,427
Average annual pay in 1989: $10,436

Service Industry
Selected receipts in 1987 ($1,000): $727,000
Average annual pay in 1989: $19,276

Housing
Total number of units in 1990: 155,508
Occupied units in 1990: 148,235
Owner-occupied units in 1990: 73.6%
1993 ACCRA average cost: N/A
1993 ACCRA average rent for an apartment: N/A

Chamber of Commerce
Saginaw County Chamber of Commerce, James Bockel-man, President, 901 S. Washington Ave., Saginaw, MI, 48601. 517-752-7161

Economic Development Office
Saginaw Futrue, Inc., JoAnn Crary, Exec. Director, 301 E. Genesee, 3rd Fl., Saginaw, MI 48607. 517-754-8222, FAX 517-754-1715

Major Businesses

Company	SIC	Telephone
Agri Sales Inc.	5153	(517) 753-5432
B & K Corp.	3829	(517) 777-2111
Draper Chevrolet Co.	5511	(517) 790-0800
Duro-Last Roofing Inc.	2295	(517) 753-6486
First of America Bank-Frankenmuth	6022	(517) 652-9944
Fischer-Flack Inc.	5063	(517) 752-4181
Frankenmuth Mutual Insurance	6331	(517) 652-6121
Grant's Sysco Food Service	5149	(517) 752-3161
Michigan Sugar Co.	2063	(517) 799-7300
Peet Packing Co.	2013	(517) 845-3021
Saginaw General Hospital	8062	(517) 771-4000
Second National Bank of Saginaw	6021	(517) 776-7200
Spence Brothers	1542	(517) 752-0400
Standard Electric Co.	5063	(517) 754-2461
Star of the West Milling	2041	(517) 652-9971
Thompson Boat Co.	3732	(517) 865-8281
Jim White Lumber Sales Inc.	5031	(517) 790-6500
Wolohan Lumber Co.	5211	(517) 793-4532

Colleges and Universities
Great Lakes Junior College of Business, Saginaw
Northwood Institute, Midland

MINNESOTA

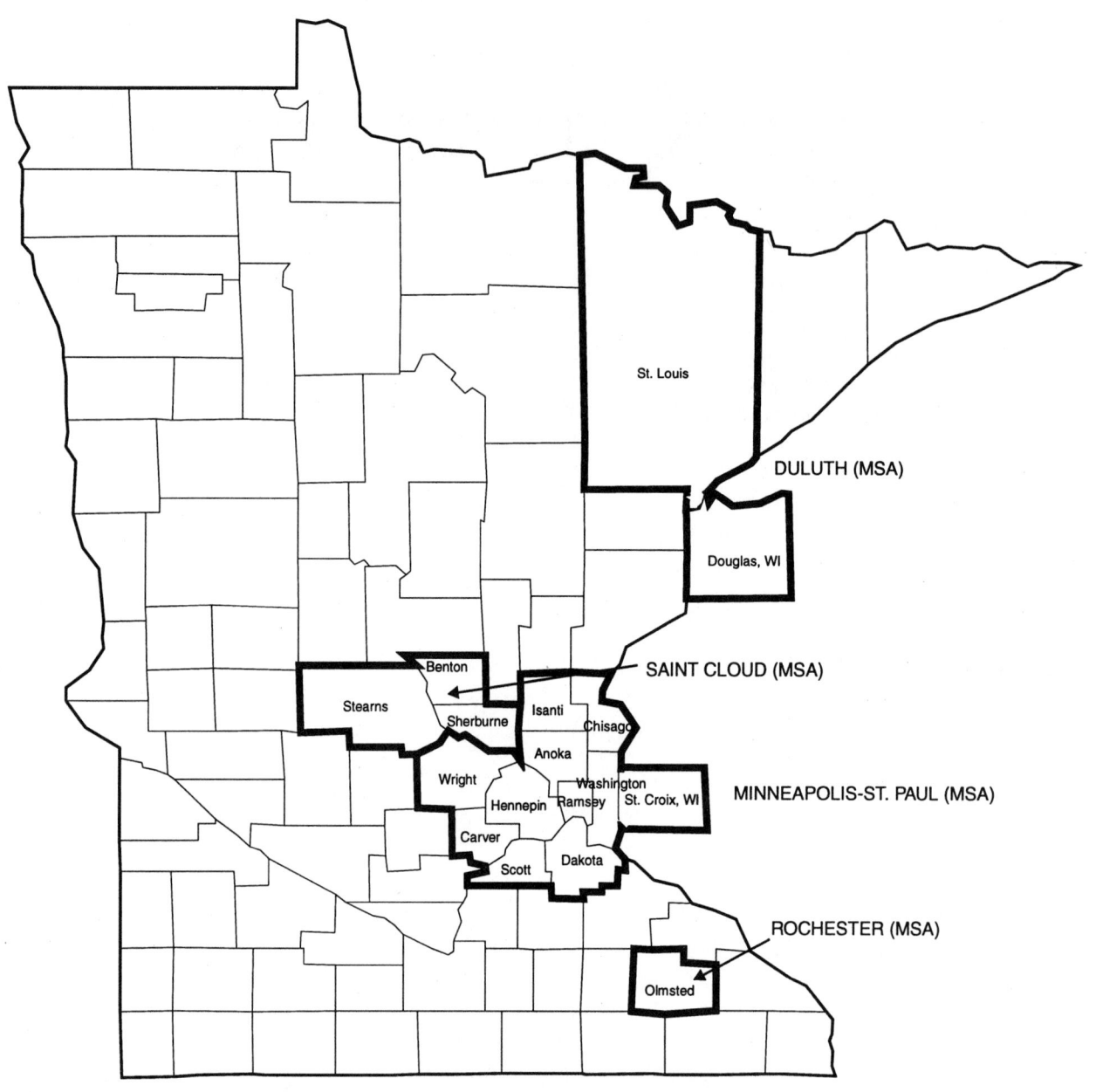

St. Louis

DULUTH (MSA)

Douglas, WI

SAINT CLOUD (MSA)

Benton

Stearns

Isanti

Sherburne

Chisago

Anoka

MINNEAPOLIS-ST. PAUL (MSA)

Wright

Washington

Hennepin

Ramsey

St. Croix, WI

Carver

Scott

Dakota

ROCHESTER (MSA)

Olmsted

MINNESOTA

Population
1990: 4,375,099
1980: 4,075,970

Age
Ages 18 to 20: 192,809
Ages 21 to 24: 250,000
Ages 25 to 44: 1,445,827
Ages 45 to 54: 428,460
Ages 55 to 59: 173,066
Ages 60 to 64: 171,220
Median age: 32.5

Race and Hispanic Origin
White: 4,130,395
Black: 94,944
Asian/Pacific Islander: 77,886
Native American: 49,909
Hispanic origin: 53,884

Households
Total: 1,647,853
Persons per household: 2.58

Sex
Male: 2,145,183
Female: 2,229,916

Population Migration
Domestic migration: -59,000
International migration: 44,000

Projection of the Population in 1995
Total: 4,538,000
18 to 64: 2,803,000

Civilian Labor Force
1993: 2,481,800
1992: 2,402,200
1991: 2,444,700
1990: 2,355,300

Manufacturing
1995 Projection: 429,500
1992: 395,800
1991: 388,400
1990: 392,800
1989: 396,000

Services
1995 Projection: 775,200

1992: 592,700
1991: 575,500
1990: 560,100
1989: 550,900

Wholesale and Retail Trade
1995 Projection: 615,200
1992: 526,900
1991: 525,000
1990: 523,300
1989: 530,400

Unemployment Rate
1993: 5.9%
1992: 6.0%
1991: 4.9%
1990: 4.9%

Employer Unemployment Contributions
Contribution Rate
1992: 1.50%
1991: 1.49%
1990: 1.96%

Average Weekly Benefit
1992: $215.30
1991: $210.98
1990: $190.36

Gross State Product (Million $)
1989: $93,559
1988: $87,238
1987: $80,881
1979: $45,555
Growth rate, 1979 to 1989: 105.4%

Capital Expenditures of Manufacturing Industries
1990: $1,827,400,000
1989: $2,013,900,000
1988: $1,709,100,000
1987: $1,765,500,000

State Tax Rates
Individual income: Range from 6% ($19,910 or less) to 8.5% (above $79,120).
Corporate income: 9.8% of total taxable income.
General property: Local collections. Rates ranged from 5%

to 50% according to classifications.
General sales: 6.5%
Gasoline: 20¢ per gallon

Income

Median income for a 4 person family: $42,365

Personal per Capita Income
1992: $20,049
1991: $19,130
1990: $18,690

Disposable per Capita Income
1992: $17,255
1991: $16,398
1990: $15,908

Private Employment Weekly Wages

Average
1989: $419
1988: $407
1987: $407

Manufacturing
1989: $386
1988: $550
1987: $522

Services
1989: $356
1988: $340
1987: $322

Wholesale
1989: $563
1988: $543
1987: $509

Retail
1989: $218
1988: $212
1987: $201

Highway Statistics

Total Highway Miles
1990: 129,397
1989: 129,553
1988: 129,644

Federal Highway Aid
1991: $160,747,000
1990: $164,103,000
1989: $185,463,000

Electricity

Average Cost per Kilowatt Hour
1990: 5.32¢
1989: 5.33¢
1988: 5.44¢

Housing (1990)

Owner occupied units: 1,183,673

Median house value: $74,000
Renter occupied units: 464,180
Median rent: $384
Total vacant units: 200,592
Homeowner vacancy rate: 1.5%
Rental vacancy rate: 7.9%

State Business Incentives and Assistance

Enterprise Zone Incentives

Competitive Zones:
1) $20,200,000 is available for tax reduction over the life of the zones, which is allocated for use by each zone.
2) Income tax credit for sales taxes paid on construction materials or equipment purchased for use in the zone.
3) Up to $3,000 income tax credit annually per new employee.
4) Income tax credit for a percentage of the cost of debt financing to construct new facilities in the zone.

Border Zones:
1) $18,8000,000 is available for tax reductions over the life of the zones.
2) Up to $1,500 income tax credit per existing worker employed in the zone.
3) State paid property tax credit for a portion of property taxes paid by existing commercial or industrial facilities located in the zone.

Financial and Business Assistance

Minnesota Fund. Administered by the Minnesota Agricultural and Economic Development Board, this program issues industrial development bonds which are backed by a state reserve for agricultural and economic development. This funds are eligible to new or expanding Minnesota businesses for creating jobs and stimulating private sector investment. Loans are made to small businesses for the portion of their fixed assets needed for expansion such as land, building, machinery and equipment, construction and renovations, and development costs.

Challenge Grant Program. Administered by the Minnesota Department of Trade and Economic Development, this program encourages private investment to provide jobs, principally for low-income persons, and promote economic development in the rural areas of the state. A Regional Revolving Loan Fund has been established.

Small Business Development Loan Program. Administered by the Minnesota Agricultural and Economic Development Board, this program was established to create jobs and provide loans for business expansions. The Board pools small business loans and issues industrial development bonds backed by a state-funded reserve. Funds may be used for acquisition of land, buildings, machinery and equipment, construction, and development costs.

Export Finance Authority. The authority guarantees loans to small and medium-sized exporters who have an export order but cannot raise the capital to fill that order. Other

Major Companies in the State

Company name	Fortune 500 rank	City	Telephone	SIC number
Fortune 500 Companies				
Alliant Techsystems Inc.	302	Edina	612-939-2000	3483
Bemis Co. Inc.	316	Minneapolis	612-376-3000	2671
Cray Research Inc.	408	Eagan	612-683-7100	3571
Deluxe Corp.	268	St. Paul	612-483-7111	2782
Ecolab Inc.	358	St. Paul	612-293-2233	7342
Farmers Union (Cenex)	238	St. Paul	612-451-5151	2911
General Mills Inc.	68	Minneapolis	612-540-2311	2043
George A. Hormel & Co.	169	Austin	507-437-5737	2013
H B Fuller Co.	372	St. Paul	612-645-3401	2891
Honeywell Inc.	86	Minneapolis	612-951-1000	3822
International Multifoods Corp.	202	Minneapolis	612-340-3300	2038
Jostens Inc.	391	Minneapolis	612-830-3300	3911
Land O'Lakes Inc.	181	Arden Hills	612-481-2222	2021
Medtronic Inc.	313	Minneapolis	612-574-4000	3845
Minnesota Mining & Manufacturing	28	St. Paul	612-733-1110	2672
Pentair Inc.	308	St. Paul	612-636-7920	3469
Toro Co.	470	Bloomington	612-888-8801	3524
Valspar Corp.	449	Minneapolis	612-332-7371	2851
Other Major Companies in the State				
Apogee Enterprises Inc.		Minneapolis	612-835-1874	1793
Best Buy Co. Inc.		Bloomington	612-896-2300	5731
Dayton Hudson Corp.		Minneapolis	612-370-6948	5331
Diversified Energies Inc.		Minneapolis	612-342-5101	4924
Fingerhut Companies Inc.		Minnetonka	612-932-3100	5961
First Bank System Inc.		Minneapolis	612-370-5100	6712
IDS Life Insurance Co.		Minneapolis	612-372-3558	6311
Minnegasco Inc.		Minneapolis	612-372-4664	4924
Musicland Group Inc.		Minneapolis	612-932-7700	5735
Musicland Stores Corp.		Minneapolis	612-932-7700	5735
Nash Finch Co.		St. Louis Park	612-929-0371	5141
North Star Universal Inc.		Minneapolis	612-546-7500	2015
Northern States Power Co. Minnesota		Minneapolis	612-330-5907	4931
Northwestern National Life Insurance Co.		Minneapolis	612-372-5432	6311
Norwest Corp.		Minneapolis	612-667-1234	6712
NWNL Companies Inc.		Minneapolis	612-372-5432	6311
St. Paul Inc.		St. Paul	612-221-7911	6331
Super Valu Stores Inc.		Eden Prairie	612-828-4000	5141
United Healthcare Corp.		Minnetonka	612-936-1300	6324

services provided include counseling exporters, bankers, and buyers on international transactions.

Economic Development Grants. Administered by the Department of Trade and Economic Development, the grants assist local units of government in meeting critical economic development needs by creating or retaining jobs and stimulating new private investment. Funds are used as gap financing loans for businesses which retain or create jobs, and stimulate additional private investment in business development.

Community Development Corporations. Administered by the Community Development Division of the Department of Trade and Economic Development, this program establishes public nonprofit corporations to provide financing and technical assistance to new and expanding businesses and communities in distressed areas of the state. The major purpose of this program is to retain and create jobs for low-income persons.

Technology Research Grants. Administered by the Greater Minnesota Corporation, a public-private partnership created by the legislature to stimulate long-term economic growth and job creation in Minnesota, these grants are awarded to projects which advance industrial technologies. The targeted projects should also have direct and marketable commercial applications and great potential for creating new jobs in the state. Projects to be considered for funding require matching funds from grantees.

Business Tax Incentives. The state has established a number of programs to provide business incentives through various tax devices. The programs include: No Minimum Tax, Two Income Formula Choices, Tax Credits for Small Businesses, Research and Development Credits, Foreign Income Deductions and Sales Tax Exemption.

Education and Training

Job Training Partnership Act. This program operates with funding from the U.S. Department of Labor. It provides job training and other employment related services.

State Offices

Real estate: Real Estate Management Division, Beerly Kroiss, 50 Sherburne Ave., St. Paul, MN 55155. 612-296-1896

Chamber of commerce: Minnesota State Chamber of Commerce, Gerald Olson, President, 480 Cedar St. #500, St. Paul, MN 55101. 612-292-4650

Economic development: Department of Trade and Economic Development, E. Peter Jillette, Commissioner, 900 American Center Bldg.,150 E. Kellogg Blvd., St. Paul, MN 55101. 612-296-6424

Department of Trade and Economic Development, Challenge Grant Program, Bob Benner, Deputy Commissioner, 900 American Center Bldg., 150 E. Kellogg Blvd., St. Paul, MN 55101. 612-297-2515

Department of Trade and Economic Development, Agricul-

tural and Economic Development Board, Director, 900 American Center Bldg., 150 E. Kellogg Blvd., St. Paul, MN 55101. 612-297-1300

Department of Trade and Economic Development, Export Finance Authority, M. Noor Doja, Director, 900 American Center Bldg., 150 E. Kellogg Blvd., St. Paul, MN 55101. 612-297-4659

Department of Trade and Economic Development, Community Development Division, Tom Helgesen, Director, 900 American Center Bldg., 150 E. Kellogg Blvd., St. Paul, MN 55101. 612-297-1363

Greater Minnesota Corporation, Patty Billings, Program Officer, 1250 International Centre II, 920 Second Avenue South, Minneapolis, MN 55402. 612-338-6666

Small Business Development Center, Randall Olson, Director, 900 American Center Building, 150 East Kellogg Blvd., St. Paul, MN 55101-1421. 612-297-5770

Environmental affairs: Pollution Control Agency, Gerald Willet, Commissioner, 520 Lafayette Road North, St. Paul, MN 55155. 612-296-7301

Labor: Labor and Industry Department, Ken Peterson, Commissioner, 443 Lafayette Road, St. Paul, MN 55155. 612-296-2342

Unemployment: Jobs and Training Department, Unemployment Insurance Unit, Terrance Clark, 390 North Robert Street, St. Paul, MN 55101. 612-296-3642

Worker's compensation: Labor and Industry Department, Ken Peterson, Commissioner, 443 Lafayette Road, St. Paul, MN 55155. 612-296-2342

Occupational safety and health: Labor and Industry Department, Occupational Safety & Health Division, Peter Clark, Administrator, 443 Lafayette Road, St. Paul, MN 55155. 612-296-4532

Secretary of state: Secretary of State, Joan Growe, Secretary of State, 180 State Office Bldg., St. Paul, MN 55155. 612-296-3266

Taxation and revenue: Revenue Department, John P. James, Commissioner, 10 River Park Plaza, St. Paul, MN 55146. 612-297-4160

Designated Zones for Economic Development

Enterprise Zones

Enacted in: 1983

No. of established zones: 16

Foreign Trade Zones

Foreign Trade Zone No. 51, Duluth, Minnesota, Grantee/Operator: Seaway Port Authority of Duluth, Henry K. Hanka, 1200 Port Terminal Drive, PO Box 18677, Duluth, MN 55816-0877, 218-727-8525.

Foreign Trade Zone No. 119, Minneapolis-St. Paul, Minnesota, Grantee: Greater Metropolitan Area FTZ Commissioner, Steven J. Anderson, 2200 Minnesota World Trade Center, 30 E. Seventh St., St. Paul, MN 55101, 612-297-4811.

Labor Unions

Electrical Workers, International Brotherhood of (AFL-CIO)

Food and Commercial Workers International Union, United (AFL-CIO)

Middle Management Association

Minnesota Association of Professional Employees

National Education Association

Service Employees' International Union (AFL-CIO)

State, County and Municipal Employees, American Federation of (AFL-CIO)

Teachers, American Federation of (AFL-CIO)

Teamsters, Chauffeurs, Warehousemen and Helpers of America, International Brotherhood of (AFL-CIO)

Woodworkers of America, International (AFL-CIO)

Universities with Ph.D. Programs

Hamline University, St. Paul

Medical Institute of Minnesota, Minneapolis

University of Minnesota, Twin Cities Campus, Minneapolis

University of St. Thomas, St. Paul

DULUTH, MN–WI (MSA)

Geographic Profile

Land Area
7534.9 square miles

Counties and Parishes
Minnesota:
St. Louis
Wisconsin:
Douglas

Additional Cities/Towns within Area
Superior, WI

Ranking Highlights

6 *out of 319 in total* **land area**

313 *out of 319 in* **population growth,** *1970–1990*

166 *out of 310 in having the lowest* **unemployment** *rate*

175 *out of 310 in size of* **labor force**

200 *out of 318 in the percentage of* **college graduates**

217 *out of 292 in per capita personal* **income**

171 *out of 319 in number of* **manufacturing establishments**

159 *out of 318 in* **physicians** *per 1000 people*

30 *out of 318 in* **hospital beds** *per 1000 people*

49 *out of 267 in fewest* **crimes** *per 1000 people*

16 *out of 266 in fewest* **violent crimes** *per 1000 people*

142 *out of 319 in per capita* **federal funds and grants**

Quality of Life Indexes (Rate per 1000 population)

Crime rate in 1991:	42.3
Violent crime rate in 1991:	1.8
Physicians rate in 1992:	1.8
Hospital bed rate in 1991:	5.96

ACCRA Cost of Living Indexes
(First quarter 1993, average = 100)

Composite index:	N/A
Utilities index:	N/A
Housing index:	N/A

Overview

The seat of St. Louis County in Minnesota, Duluth is the focus of a metropolitan statistical area comprised of both St. Louis County and Wisconsin's Douglas County. Principal industrial firms in Duluth include heavy and light manufacturing plants, food processing plants, woolen mills, lumber mills, cold storage plants, fisheries, grain elevators, and oil refineries. The city is a also a regional center for banking, retailing, and medical care for northern Minnesota, northern Wisconsin, northern Michigan, and northwestern Ontario, Canada. Arts and entertainment offerings as well as year-round recreation in a natural environment have contributed to expansion of the tourist industry in Duluth. Items and goods produced in the area include air reduction equipment, farm machinery, tractors, mining and heavy construction equipment, frozen food, canned goods and preserves, wood and wire products, Mackinaw cloth and heavy woolens.

A vital part of the Duluth economy is the Port of Duluth-Superior, which is designated a Foreign Trade Zone and ranks among the top twelve ports in the country in total volume of international and domestic cargo shipped in a ten-month season. An average of 40 million tons of cargo is handled at Duluth-Superior each year; the impact on the local economy in 1990 was $248 million. Containing over 19 square miles of water at an average depth of 27 feet, the harbor is lined by 113 docks and nearly 50 miles of commercial waterfront development. Approximately ninety-five ocean vessels and more than twelve hundred Great Lakes ships passed through the port in 1990. Duluth-Superior operates one of the largest grain-handling facilities in the world. Grain is the primary export product; domestic shipments consist mainly of iron ore and taconite, in addition to metal products, twine, machinery, coal, cement, salt, newsprint, lumber, and general cargo.

Connecting the port and the city of Duluth with inland markets are five railroads—Burlington Northern, Duluth Missabe & Iron Range, Chicago & Northwestern, Duluth Winnipeg & Pacific, and Soo Line—and nineteen motor freight carriers. Air cargo carriers serving Duluth International Airport with daily flights are Federal Express, United Parcel Service, Northwest Airlines Other Service, and U.S. Customs, Immigration, and Agriculture Services.

Duluth is the terminus point for Interstate 35, which extends from the United States-Mexico border into northern Minnesota; federal highways providing easy access into the city include U.S. 53, 61, and 2. State routes running through Duluth are 23, 39, and 194.

Population (1990)

Total Population and Growth Rate
1990: 239,971
1980: 266,650
1970: 265,350
Growth rate 1970–1990: -10%

Race and Hispanic Origin
White: 96.9%
Black: .5%
Asian/Pacific Islander: 0.6%
Native American: 1.9%
Hispanic origin: 0.5%
White not Hispanic: 96.6%

Age
Ages 18 to 20:   5%
Ages 21 to 24: 5.1%
Ages 25 to 44: 29.6%
Ages 45 to 54: 9.8%
Ages 55 to 59: 4.3%
Ages 60 to 64: 4.8%
Ages 65 plus: 16.8%

Educational Attainment (1990)
Percent having completed high school: 79.7%
Percent having completed college: 16.8%
Elementary and high school enrollment: 41,162

Federal Funds and Grants Received
Total received in 1989: $779,000,000
Funds received per capita: $3,228

Civilian Labor Force
1993 (April):   116,100
1992 average: 116,436
1991 average: 115,348
1990 average: 112,412

Unemployment
1993 (April):   8.8%
1992 average: 7.0%
1991 average: 6.4%
1990 average: 5.8%

Average Annual Pay
1988: $18,247
1987: $17,431
1985: $16,404

Per Capita Personal Income
1991: $15,979
1990: $15,200
1989: $14,321

Business Climate (1987)

Manufacturing
Number of establishments in 1987: 285
Shipments in 1987 ($1,000): $839,500
Employees in 1987: 7,900
Change in employment, 1982 to 1987: 11.3%
Average annual pay for manufacturing work in 1989: $22,140
Average annual pay for production work in 1987: $19,286

Wholesale Trade
Number of establishments in 1987: 375
Total sales in 1987 ($1,000): $1,533,300
Change in sales, 1982 to 1987: -9.3%

Retail Trade
Number of establishments in 1987: 1,840
Total sales in 1987 ($1,000): $1,533,300
Retail sales per household in 1987: $14,833
Average annual pay in 1989: $9,800

Service Industry
Selected receipts in 1987 ($1,000): $396,700
Average annual pay in 1989: $16,011

Housing
Total number of units in 1990: 116,013

Occupied units in 1990: 95,275
Owner-occupied units in 1990: 73.4%
1993 ACCRA average cost: N/A
1993 ACCRA average rent for an apartment: N/A

Chamber of Commerce

Duluth Area Chamber of Commerce, David P. Cordeau, President, 325 Harbor Dr., Duluth, MN 55802. 218-722-5501

Economic Development Office

Northeastern Minnesota Development Association, Thomas Bergh, Exec. Director, 800 Alworth Bldg., Duluth, MN 55802. 218-722-1484

Economic Development Organizations

Arrowhead Regional Development Commission, Henry Hanka, Exec. Director, 330 Canal Park Dr., Duluth, MN 55802. 218-722-5545, FAX 218-722-2335

Office of Planning and Development, Dave Sebok, Director, 400 City Hall, Duluth, MN 55802. 218-723-3556

Major Businesses

Company	SIC	Telephone
Amsoil Inc.	2992	(715) 392-7101
Duluth Winnipeg & Pacific Railroad	4011	(715) 726-9200
First Bank National Association-Duluth	6021	(218) 722-3301
Franklin Foods	2026	(218) 727-6651
Jerry Hammann Transportation	4213	(715) 394-2787
Hibbing Electronic Corp.	3672	(218) 263-8971
Inter-City Oil Co Inc.	5541	(218) 728-3641
Lakehead Constructors Inc.	1542	(715) 392-5181
Lakehead Pipe Line Co.	4612	(715) 394-1400
Maurice's Inc.	5621	(218) 727-8431
Mesabi Regional Medical Center	8062	(218) 262-4881
Miller-Dwan Medical Center	8062	(218) 727-8762
Miner's Inc.	5411	(218) 729-5882
Minnesota Power & Light Co.	4911	(218) 722-2641
Northern Drug Co.	5122	(218) 722-4791
Owens Forest Products Co.	5031	(218) 723-1151
Rathert Chevrolet, Inc.	5511	(218) 727-7481
St Luke's Hospital of Duluth	8062	(218) 726-5555
Superior Water Light Power Co.	4931	(715) 394-5511
Topeka Group, Inc.	4813	(218) 722-2641

Colleges and Universities

College of St. Scholastica, Duluth
University of Minnesota, Duluth, Duluth

MINNEAPOLIS–ST PAUL, MN–WI (MSA)

Geographic Profile

Land Area

5051.4 square miles

Counties and Parishes

Minnesota:
Anoka
Carver
Chisago
Dakota
Hennepin
Isanti
Ramsey
Scott
Washington
Wright
Wisconsin:
St. Croix

Additional Cities/Towns within Area

Bloomington

Ranking Highlights

14 *out of 319 in total* **land area**
163 *out of 319 in* **population growth,** *1970–1990*
29 *out of 310 in having the lowest* **unemployment** *rate*
11 *out of 310 in size of* **labor force**
38 *out of 318 in the percentage of* **college graduates**
29 *out of 292 in per capita personal* **income**
9 *out of 319 in number of* **manufacturing establishments**
83 *out of 318 in* **physicians** *per 1000 people*
237 *out of 318 in* **hospital beds** *per 1000 people*
106 *out of 267 in fewest* **crimes** *per 1000 people*
95 *out of 266 in fewest* **violent crimes** *per 1000 people*
159 *out of 319 in per capita* **federal funds and grants**

Quality of Life Indexes (Rate per 1000 population)

Crime rate in 1991:	55.7
Violent crime rate in 1991:	4.7
Physicians rate in 1992:	2.36
Hospital bed rate in 1991:	3.04

ACCRA Cost of Living Indexes

(First quarter 1993, average = 100)
Composite index: 104.7
Utilities index: 91.7
Housing index: 110.3

Overview

The largest city in Minnesota, Minneapolis is the seat of Hennepin County and the sister city of Saint Paul, with which it forms the Twin Cities metropolitan statistical area that includes ten counties in Minnesota and St. Croix

County in Wisconsin. The combined cities of Minneapolis and Saint Paul were chosen in 1991 by *Inc.* magazine as one of the best places in the country for growing a business and in 1992 by *Money* magazine as the fourth–best place to live in America.

Manufacturing is the primary industry in the area. Principal manufacturing areas are electronics, milling, machinery, medical products, food processing, and graphic arts. Fifteen Fortune 500 industrial companies maintain headquarters in the Twin Cities, which is among the largest commercial centers between Chicago and the West Coast. Also integral to the local economy are high-technology industries. With the University of Minnesota and other colleges and technical schools providing applied research and well-trained scientists and engineers, one of the largest concentrations of high-technology firms in the nation—more than thirteen hundred—developed in metropolitan Minneapolis–Saint Paul. An accompanying expansion of the services sector, especially health services, has attracted seventeen Fortune 500 service companies to the two cities.

Among the banks and other financial institutions that make the Twin Cities the financial center of the Upper Midwest, seven of the largest are based in Minneapolis. In addition, the headquarters of the Ninth Federal Reserve District Bank is located in the city. Local banks, savings and loan companies, venture capital concerns, and insurance companies play a major role in the economic development of the region.

The Minneapolis-Saint Paul International Airport is served by four air cargo carriers and forty air-freight forwarders. The airport handles more than 170,000 tons of freight yearly. The Twin Cities area is also linked with major United States and Canadian markets via a network of seven railroads, including the Soo Line, which is based in Minneapolis.

Considered one of the largest trucking centers in the nation, Minneapolis–Saint Paul is served by 150 motor freight companies that provide overnight and four- to five-day delivery in the Midwest and major markets in the continental United States. Vital to the Twin Cities' role as a primary transportation hub is the port of Minneapolis, which together with the port of Saint Paul processes annually more than eleven million tons of cargo to and from domestic and foreign markets.

Two major interstate highways serve Minneapolis: I-94 (east-west) and I-35 (north-south). Two belt-line freeways, I-494 and I-694, facilitate travel around the Twin-City suburbs. Seven federal and thirteen state highways link the city with points throughout the United States and Canada.

Population (1990)

Total Population and Growth Rate
1990: 2,464,124
1980: 2,137,133

1970: 1,981,951
Growth rate 1970–1990: 24%

Race and Hispanic Origin
White: 92.1%
Black: 3.6%
Asian/Pacific Islander: 2.6%
Native American: 1.0%
Hispanic origin: 1.5%
White not Hispanic: 91.3%

Age
Ages 18 to 20: 4%
Ages 21 to 24: 6.1%
Ages 25 to 44: 36.6%
Ages 45 to 54: 10%
Ages 55 to 59: 3.7%
Ages 60 to 64: 3.4%
Ages 65 plus: 9.9%

Educational Attainment (1990)
Percent having completed high school: 87.2%
Percent having completed college: 27.1%
Elementary and high school enrollment: 404,190

Federal Funds and Grants Received
Total received in 1989: $7,325,300,000
Funds received per capita: $3,068

Civilian Labor Force
1993 (April): 1,444,880
1992 average: 1,422,797
1991 average: 1,420,137
1990 average: 1,411,250

Unemployment
1993 (April): 5.3%
1992 average: 4.5%
1991 average: 4.6%
1990 average: 4.3%

Average Annual Pay
1988: $23,618
1987: $22,385
1985: $20,576

Per Capita Personal Income
1991: $21,655
1990: $21,138
1989: $20,313

Business Climate (1987)
Manufacturing
Number of establishments in 1987: 4,494
Shipments in 1987 ($1,000): $30,357,900
Employees in 1987: 250,100
Change in employment, 1982 to 1987: 3.0%
Average annual pay for manufacturing work in 1989: $32,433
Average annual pay for production work in 1987: $23,358

Wholesale Trade

Number of establishments in 1987: 5,645

Total sales in 1987 ($1,000): $44,676,400

Change in sales, 1982 to 1987: 19.5%

Retail Trade

Number of establishments in 1987: 13,311

Total sales in 1987 ($1,000): $44,676,400

Retail sales per household in 1987: $18,927

Average annual pay in 1989: $12,344

Service Industry

Selected receipts in 1987 ($1,000): $9,269,500

Average annual pay in 1989: $19,964

Office Real Estate (1992)

Office space inventory: 45,958,000 square feet

Average class A Central Business District rental range per sq. ft: $21.50

Vacancy Rates

All areas: 20.3%

Vacancy Rates in Central Business District

Class A space: 22.6%

Class B space: 25.8%

Vacancy Rates Outside Central Business District

Class A space: 16.9%

Class B space: 18.9%

Housing

Total number of units in 1990: 988,735

Occupied units in 1990: 935,516

Owner-occupied units in 1990: 68.7%

1993 ACCRA average cost: $128,112

1993 ACCRA average rent for an apartment: $503

Chamber of Commerce

Greater Minneapolis Chamber of Commerce, Connie Levi, President, 81 S. 9th St. #200, Minneapolis, MN 55402. 612-370-9132

Economic Development Office

Minneapolis Community Development Agency, J. Jensen, Exec. Director, 331 2nd Ave. S., Suite 600, Minneapolis, MN 55401. 612-673-5095

Economic Development Organizations

City of St. Paul, Department of Planning and Economic Development, Ken Johnson, Director, 25 W. 4th St., City Hall Annex, St. Paul, MN 55102. 612-228-3203

Twin Cities Reader, Mari Adamson-Bray, Dir., 5500 Wayvata Blvd. #800, Minneapolis, MN 55416. 612-591-2500

St. Paul Port Authority, James Bellus, Pres., 345 St. Peter Suite 1900, St. Paul, MN 55102. 800-328-8417

Major Businesses

Company	SIC	Telephone
Andersen Corp.	2431	(612) 439-5150
Bemis Co., Inc.	2671	(612) 340-6000
Carlson Companies, Inc.	7011	(612) 540-5000
Carlson Travel Group, Inc.	4724	(612) 449-1900
Control Data Corp.	3571	(612) 853-8100
Dayton Hudson Corp.	5311	(612) 370-6948
Deluxe Corp.	2782	(612) 483-7111
Ecolab Inc.	2841	(612) 293-2233
Fingerhut Companies Inc.	5961	(612) 932-3100
Fingerhut Corp.	5961	(612) 932-3100
First Bank National Association	6021	(612) 370-4141
First Bank System, Inc.	6021	(612) 370-5100
First Travel Corp.	4724	(612) 449-1900
General Mills Inc.	2043	(612) 540-2311
Harvest States Cooperative	5153	(612) 646-9433
Honeywell Inc.	3822	(612) 870-5200
IDS Financial Corp.	6722	(612) 372-3131
IDS Life Insurance Co Inc.	6311	(612) 372-3131
International Multifoods	5145	(612) 340-3300
Land O'Lakes, Inc.	2021	(612) 481-2222
Lutheran Brotherhood Inc.	6311	(612) 340-7000
Marshall Field & Co.	5311	(612) 370-6948
Minnesota Mining & Manufacturing Co. (3M)	2672	(612) 733-1110
Minnesota Mutual Life Insurance Co.	6311	(612) 298-3500
Nash-Finch Co.	5141	(612) 929-0371
Northern States Power Co.	4911	(612) 330-5500
Northwest Airlines, Inc.	4512	(612) 726-2111
Northwestern National Life Insurance	6311	(612) 372-5432
Norwest Corp.	6021	(612) 667-1234
NWA Inc.	4512	(612) 726-2111
NWNL Companies, Inc.	6311	(612) 372-5432
Pentair, Inc.	2621	(612) 636-7920
The Pillsbury Co.	2041	(612) 330-4966
Radisson Hotel Corp.	6794	(612) 540-5526
Share Development Corp.	6324	(612) 936-1300
St. Paul Companies, Inc.	6331	(612) 221-7911
St. Paul Fire Mar Insurance Co.	6331	(612) 221-7911
Super Valu Stores, Inc.	5141	(612) 828-4000
Tonka Corp.	3944	(612) 936-3300

Colleges and Universities

Augsburg College, Minneapolis

Bethel College, St. Paul

College of Associated Arts, St. Paul

College of St. Catherine, St. Paul

Concordia College, St. Paul

Hamline University, St. Paul

Lowthian College, Minneapolis

Macalester College, St. Paul

Medical Institute of Minnesota, Minneapolis

Metropolitan State University, St. Paul

Minneapolis College of Art and Design, Minneapolis

Minneapolis Community College, Minneapolis

National College-St. Paul Campus, St. Paul

National Education Center-Brown Institute Campus, Minneapolis

Normandale Community College, Bloomington

North Hennepin Community College, Minneapolis

Northwestern College, St. Paul

St. Mary's Campus of The College of St. Catherine, Minneapolis

St. Paul Technical College, St. Paul

University of Minnesota, Twin Cities Campus, Minneapolis

University of St. Thomas, St. Paul

ROCHESTER, MN (MSA)

Geographic Profile

Land Area

653.0 square miles

Counties and Parishes

Olmsted

Ranking Highlights

263 *out of 319 in total* **land area**

155 *out of 319 in* **population growth,** *1970–1990*

8 *out of 310 in having the lowest* **unemployment** *rate*

243 *out of 310 in size of* **labor force**

29 *out of 318 in the percentage of* **college graduates**

33 *out of 292 in per capita personal* **income**

311 *out of 319 in number of* **manufacturing establishments**

1 *out of 318 in* **physicians** *per 1000 people*

1 *out of 318 in* **hospital beds** *per 1000 people*

37 *out of 267 in fewest* **crimes** *per 1000 people*

13 *out of 266 in fewest* **violent crimes** *per 1000 people*

267 *out of 319 in per capita* **federal funds and grants**

Quality of Life Indexes (Rate per 1000 population)

Crime rate in 1991:   40.0

Violent crime rate in 1991:   1.4

Physicians rate in 1992:   17.17

Hospital bed rate in 1991:   13.5

ACCRA Cost of Living Indexes

(First quarter 1993, average = 100)

Composite index: 104.1

Utilities index: 107.7

Housing index: 104.3

Population (1990)

Total Population and Growth Rate

1990: 106,470

1980: 92,006

1970: 84,104

Growth rate 1970–1990: 27%

Race and Hispanic Origin

White: 95.7%

Black: .7%

Asian/Pacific Islander: 3.0%

Native American: 0.3%

Hispanic origin: 0.9%

White not Hispanic: 95.1%

Age

Ages 18 to 20: 3.9%

Ages 21 to 24: 5.3%

Ages 25 to 44: 35.5%

Ages 45 to 54: 10.5%

Ages 55 to 59: 3.8%

Ages 60 to 64: 3.3%
Ages 65 plus: 10%

Educational Attainment (1990)
Percent having completed high school: 88.0%
Percent having completed college: 29.5%
Elementary and high school enrollment: 18,132

Federal Funds and Grants Received
Total received in 1989: $235,100,000
Funds received per capita: $2,329

Civilian Labor Force
1993 (April): 65,903
1992 average: 66,332
1991 average: 66,618
1990 average: 64,700

Unemployment
1993 (April): 3.7%
1992 average: 3.3%
1991 average: 3.3%
1990 average: 3.2%

Average Annual Pay
1988: $22,947
1987: $22,187
1985: $20,502

Per Capita Personal Income
1991: $21,354
1990: $20,680
1989: $19,392

Business Climate (1987)
Manufacturing
Number of establishments in 1987: 66
Shipments in 1987 ($1,000): $1,762,100
Employees in 1987: 10,300
Change in employment, 1982 to 1987: 4.0%
Average annual pay for manufacturing work in 1989: $35,839
Average annual pay for production work in 1987: $22,147

Wholesale Trade
Number of establishments in 1987: 140
Total sales in 1987 ($1,000): $357,900
Change in sales, 1982 to 1987: 24.7%

Retail Trade
Number of establishments in 1987: 648
Total sales in 1987 ($1,000): $357,900
Retail sales per household in 1987: $22,373
Average annual pay in 1989: $10,233

Service Industry
Selected receipts in 1987 ($1,000): $184,000
Average annual pay in 1989: $24,107

Housing
Total number of units in 1990: 41,603

Occupied units in 1990: 40,058
Owner-occupied units in 1990: 72.4%
1993 ACCRA average cost: $109,960
1993 ACCRA average rent for an apartment: $628

Chamber of Commerce
Rochester Area Chamber of Commerce, Richard Granchalek, Exec. Vice President, 220 S. Broadway #100, Rochester , MN 55904. 507-288-1122

Economic Development Office
Rochester Area Economic Development, Gary Smith, Exec. Vice President, 220 S. Broadway #100, Rochester, MN 55904. 507-288-0208, FAX 507-282-8960

Major Businesses

Company	SIC	Telephone
Adamson Motors Inc.	5511	(507) 289-4004
All-American Coop	5153	(507) 533-4222
B & F Distributing Inc.	5171	(507) 288-9590
Byron Elevator Co.	5153	(507) 775-2323
First Bank Rochester	6021	(507) 285-7800
Greenway Cooperative Service	5541	(507) 289-4086
IBM Mid America	6111	(507) 288-3425
Kahler Corp.	7011	(507) 282-2581
Marquette Bank Rochester	6022	(507) 285-2600
Norwest Bank Rochester	6021	(507) 285-2800
Peoples Cooperative Power	4911	(507) 288-4004
Rochester Meats Inc.	5147	(507) 289-0701
Rochester Methodist Hospital	8062	(507) 286-7890
St. Mary's Hospital	8062	(507) 255-5123
Schmidt Printing Inc.	2752	(507) 288-6400
Schneider Specialized Car	4213	(507) 288-3331
Southern Minnesota Municipal Prod.	4911	(507) 285-0478
U. S. Auto & Rochester Maritime	5551	(507) 288-7620
Waters Instruments, Inc.	3699	(507) 288-7777
Weis Builders, Inc.	1542	(507) 288-2041

Colleges and Universities
Oakland University, Rochester

SAINT CLOUD, MN (MSA)

Geographic Profile

Land Area
2189.4 square miles

Counties and Parishes
Benton
Sherburne
Stearns

Ranking Highlights
79 *out of 319 in total* land area
90 *out of 319 in* population growth, *1970–1990*
76 *out of 310 in having the lowest* unemployment *rate*
182 *out of 310 in size of* labor force
195 *out of 318 in the percentage of* college graduates
264 *out of 292 in per capita personal* income
187 *out of 319 in number of* manufacturing establishments
277 *out of 318 in* physicians *per 1000 people*
199 *out of 318 in* hospital beds *per 1000 people*
13 *out of 267 in fewest* crimes *per 1000 people*
9 *out of 266 in fewest* violent crimes *per 1000 people*
300 *out of 319 in per capita* federal funds and grants

Quality of Life Indexes (Rate per 1000 population)
Crime rate in 1991:	33.5
Violent crime rate in 1991:	1.3
Physicians rate in 1992:	1.24
Hospital bed rate in 1991:	3.46

ACCRA Cost of Living Indexes
(First quarter 1993, average = 100)
Composite index:	94.0
Utilities index:	90.1
Housing index:	81.7

Overview
St. Cloud is approximately one hour northwest of Minneapolis/St. Paul and minutes from secluded woods, lakes and rivers. The economic base contains agriculture, light manufacturing, retail and a broad service sector. The optical industry in St. Cloud produces 47% of all prescription eyewear worn in the United States. The largest granite producer in the world and the number one manufacturer of lightweight coated publication paper in North America are also located here. Annual wages are three percent below the national average. Labor force productivity is nearly 10 percent above the national average. Three four-year higher education institutions have a combined enrollment of over 20,000 students and 1,000 faculty.

First class utility services are available throughout the St. Cloud area at extremely competitive rates. Northern States Power Company is the principal gas and electricity supplier. Commercial and industrial electric rates are among the lowest 25% in the nation.

Eleven major regional and national interstate trucking concerns operate out of the St. Cloud area and many have located terminals and warehouse facilities in St Cloud. St. Cloud Municipal Airport is an instrument rated facility. Rail transportation is provided by Burlington Northern.

Population (1990)

Total Population and Growth Rate
1990: 190,921
1980: 163,256
1970: 134,585
Growth rate 1970–1990: 42%

Race and Hispanic Origin
White: 98.5%
Black: .4%
Asian/Pacific Islander: 0.6%
Native American: 0.3%
Hispanic origin: 0.5%
White not Hispanic: 98.2%

Age
Ages 18 to 20: 6.9%
Ages 21 to 24: 8.4%
Ages 25 to 44: 30.8%
Ages 45 to 54: 8.4%
Ages 55 to 59: 3.4%
Ages 60 to 64: 3.3%
Ages 65 plus: 9.9%

Educational Attainment (1990)
Percent having completed high school: 79.5%
Percent having completed college: 16.9%
Elementary and high school enrollment: 36,526

Federal Funds and Grants Received
Total received in 1989: $381,000,000
Funds received per capita: $2,103

Civilian Labor Force
1993 (April): 110,657
1992 average: 107,085
1991 average: 106,944
1990 average: 102,952

Unemployment
1993 (April): 5.8%
1992 average: 5.6%
1991 average: 5.9%
1990 average: 5.7%

Average Annual Pay
1988: $17,698
1987: $17,055
1985: $15,803

Per Capita Personal Income
1991: $14,912
1990: $14,609
1989: $14,063

Business Climate (1987)

Manufacturing

Number of establishments in 1987: 250

Shipments in 1987 ($1,000): $1,290,900

Employees in 1987: 11,100

Change in employment, 1982 to 1987: 14.4%

Average annual pay for manufacturing work in 1989: $21,306

Average annual pay for production work in 1987: $18,301

Wholesale Trade

Number of establishments in 1987: 287

Total sales in 1987 ($1,000): $897,300

Change in sales, 1982 to 1987: 29.6%

Retail Trade

Number of establishments in 1987: 1,136

Total sales in 1987 ($1,000): $897,300

Retail sales per household in 1987: $32,711

Average annual pay in 1989: $11,002

Service Industry

Selected receipts in 1987 ($1,000): $263,400

Average annual pay in 1989: $15,431

Housing

Total number of units in 1990: 70,291

Occupied units in 1990: 64,354

Owner-occupied units in 1990: 72.6%

1993 ACCRA average cost: $89,269

1993 ACCRA average rent for an apartment: $448

Chamber of Commerce

Saint Cloud Area Chamber of Commerce, Thomas E. Moore, President, 26 N. 6th Ave. #100, PO Box 487, St. Cloud, MN 56302. 612-251-2940

Economic Development Office

St. Cloud Area Economic Development Partnership, Anthony Goddard, President, 26 6th Ave. N., PO Box 1091, St. Cloud, MN 56302. 612-252-2177

Major Businesses

Company	SIC	Telephone
Anderson Trucking Service	4213	(612) 255-7400
Bankers Systems, Inc.	2752	(612) 251-3060
Bauerly Brothers	1611	(612) 251-9472
Big Bear Farm Stores, Inc.	5399	(612) 251-9000
D. H. Blattner & Sons Inc.	1611	(612) 356-7351
Coborn's Inc.	5411	(612) 252-4980
Elk River Ford, Inc.	5511	(612) 441-2300
Gilleland Chevrolet Inc.	5511	(612) 251-4943
Gold'n Plump Poultry, Inc.	2015	(612) 251-3570
G. R. Herberger's, Inc.	5311	(612) 251-5351
Jack Frost, Inc.	0251	(612) 251-3570
JFC Inc.	0251	(612) 251-3570
Pan-O-Gold Baking Co.	2051	(612) 251-9361

Major Businesses (Continued)

Company	SIC	Telephone
Security Financial Group	6035	(612) 251-4500
St. Cloud Meat & Provision	5147	(612) 252-0037
United Power Association	4911	(612) 441-3121
Woodcraft Industries, Inc.	2426	(612) 252-1503
Zappco, Inc.	6712	(612) 259-8400

Colleges and Universities

St. Cloud Business College, St. Cloud

St. Cloud State University, St. Cloud

MISSISSIPPI

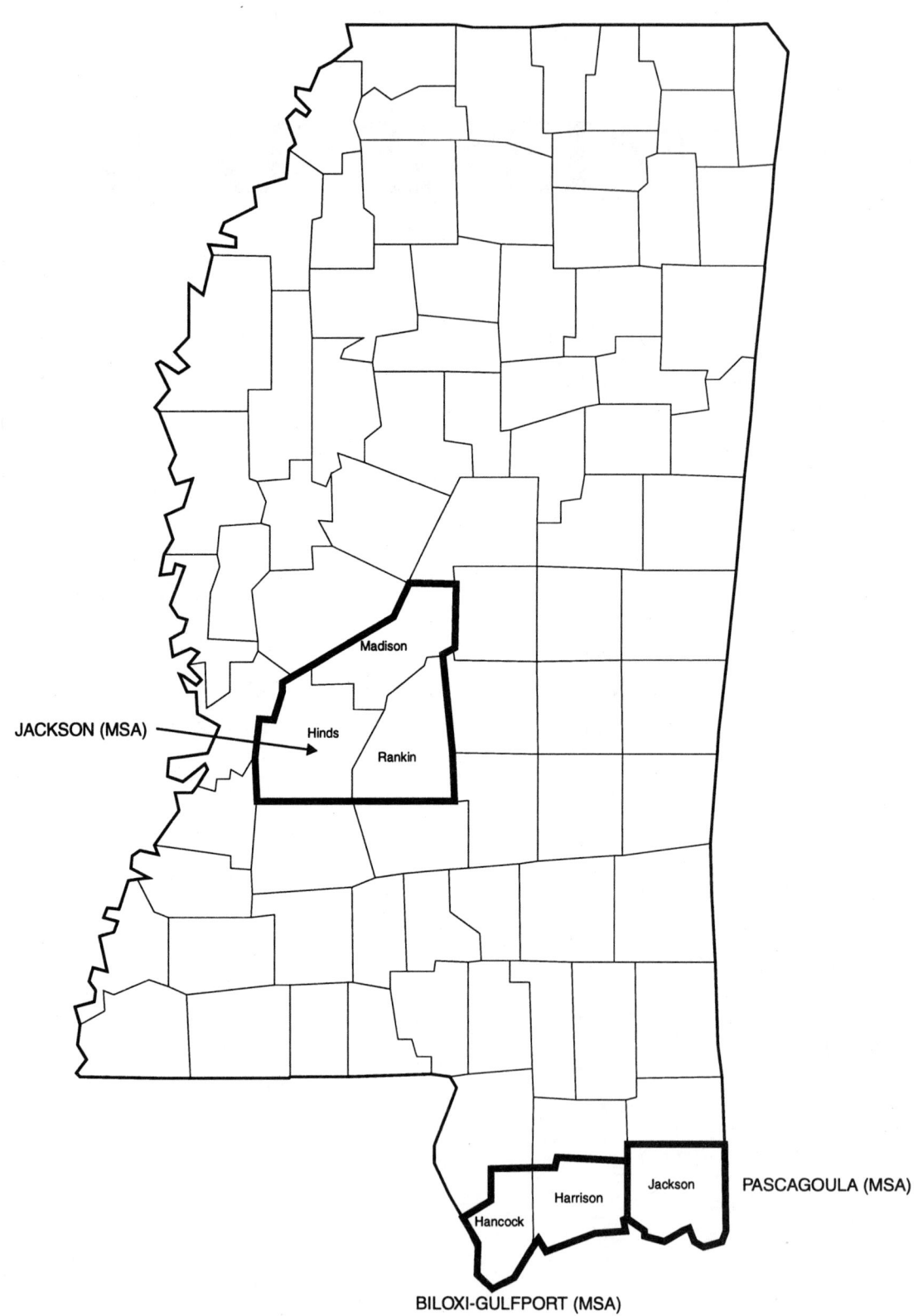

JACKSON (MSA)

Madison

Hinds

Rankin

PASCAGOULA (MSA)

Jackson

Harrison

Hancock

BILOXI-GULFPORT (MSA)

MISSISSIPPI

Population
1990: 2,573,216
1980: 2,520,638

Age
Ages 18 to 20: 141,847
Ages 21 to 24: 151,499
Ages 25 to 44: 749,584
Ages 45 to 54: 247,745
Ages 55 to 59: 107,784
Ages 60 to 64: 106,712
Median age: 31.2

Race and Hispanic Origin
White: 1,633,461
Black: 915,057
Asian/Pacific Islander: 13,016
Native American: 8,525
Hispanic origin: 15,931

Households
Total: 911,374
Persons per household: 2.75

Sex
Male: 1,230,617
Female: 1,342,599

Population Migration
Domestic migration: -53,000
International migration: 11,000

Projection of the Population in 1995
Total: 2,687,000
18 to 64: 1,551,000

Civilian Labor Force
1993: 1,159,100
1992: 1,161,400
1991: 1,195,900
1990: 1,180,200

Manufacturing
1995 Projection: 261,100
1992: 251,300
1991: 247,900
1990: 245,000
1989: 242,400

Services
1995 Projection: 242,500

1992: 176,900
1991: 167,800
1990: 162,200
1989: 154,700

Wholesale and Retail Trade
1995 Projection: 245,400
1992: 200,300
1991: 206,900
1990: 204,700
1989: 205,000

Unemployment Rate
1993: 6.6%
1992: 8.7%
1991: 8.8%
1990: 8.0%

Employer Unemployment Contributions

Contribution Rate
1992: 1.70%
1991: 0.95%
1990: 1.20%

Average Weekly Benefit
1992: $126.50
1991: $125.50
1990: $111.30

Gross State Product (Million $)
1989: $38,135
1988: $36,255
1987: $33,281
1979: $20,401
Growth rate, 1979 to 1989: 86.9%

Capital Expenditures of Manufacturing Industries
1990: $1,154,700,000
1989: $1,409,900,000
1988: $1,219,900,000
1987: $647,700,000

State Taxe Rates
Individual income: Range from 3% ($5,000 or less) to 5% (above $10,000).
Corporate income: Range from 3% ($5,000 or less) to 5% (above $10,000).

General property: Sum of local rates. Assessed at a fraction of fair market value.

General sales: 6%

Gasoline: 18¢ per gallon

Income

Median income for a 4 person family: $32,300

Personal per Capita Income

1992: $14,088

1991: $13,318

1990: $12,700

Disposable per Capita Income

1992: $13,006

1991: $12,250

1990: $11,620

Private Employment Weekly Wages

Average

1989: $322

1988: $314

1987: $314

Manufacturing

1989: $305

1988: $353

1987: $343

Services

1989: $303

1988: $295

1987: $281

Wholesale

1989: $410

1988: $396

1987: $382

Retail

1989: $195

1988: $193

1987: $191

Highway Statistics

Total Highway Miles

1990: 72,520

1989: 72,312

1988: 72,169

Federal Highway Aid

1991: $141,830,000

1990: $144,504,000

1989: $146,891,000

Electricity

Average Cost per Kilowatt Hour

1990: 6.10¢

1989: 6.18¢

1988: 6.21¢

Housing (1990)

Owner occupied units: 651,587

Median house value: $45,600

Renter occupied units: 259,787

Median rent: $215

Total vacant units: 99,049

Homeowner vacancy rate: 1.9%

Rental vacancy rate: 9.5%

State Business Incentives and Assistance

Financial and Business Assistance

Industrial Development Bonds. Issuance authorized by the Mississippi Business Finance Corporation, these bonds are limited to manufacturing and processing projects. The state issued industrial development bonds can be used to finance fixed-asset expenses and certain associated costs. The counties and municipalities issued bonds are designed to promote balanced economic development in the state by providing tax-exempt financing to new and expanding businesses for projects under $10 million. Counties and municipalities are also authorized to issue taxable industrial development bonds. Bonds proceeds may be used to acquire land, construct new buildings or expand existing facilities, and purchase new machinery and equipment. The taxable IDBs include businesses engaged in manufacturing, processing, wholesaling, distribution, and research and development.

Mississippi Business Investment Program. Administered by the Mississippi Department of Economic Development, this program is designed to make loans to local sponsors in order to install specific improvements necessary to complement investment by private companies.

Small Business Guaranty Loan Program. The Mississippi Department of Economic Development can guarantee up to 75% of long-term loans made to businesses by private lenders to assist in the development or expansion of small businesses. The maximum loan size is $500,000.

Mississippi Seed Capital Corporation. This program is set up to provide seed capital to new and expanding businesses, and provide financing to high-growth-oriented businesses. Businesses eligible for financing are corporations, partnerships, joint ventures, etc. expected to experience significant sales growth over the next five year period.

Mississippi Major Economic Impact Authority. A division of the Mississippi Department of Economic Development, the Authority issues general obligation bonds up to $20 million to improve the transportation, educational, recreational, and medical facilities of an area.

Mississippi Small Enterprise Development Finance Act. This act allows the Mississippi Business Finance Corporation to provide financing in small communities for manufacturing and processing facilities, as well as the other businesses including agricultural, aquacultural, horticul-

Major Companies in the State

Company name	Fortune 500 rank	City	Telephone	SIC number
Fortune 500 Companies				
None				
Other Major Companies in the State				
Bancorp of Mississippi Inc.		Tupelo	601-680-2000	6712
Capitol Street Corp.		Jackson	601-961-6937	6311
Deposit Guaranty Corp.		Jackson	601-354-8564	6712
Eastover Bank For Savings		Jackson	601-960-8000	6036
First Mississippi Corp.		Jackson	601-948-7550	2873
Grenada Sunburst System Corp.		Grenada	601-226-1100	6712
Hancock Fabrics Inc.		Tupelo	601-842-2834	5949
Hancock Holding Co.		Gulfport	601-868-4605	6712
KLLM Transport Services Inc.		Jackson	601-939-2545	4213
LDDS Communications Inc.		Jackson	601-364-7000	4813
Magna Bancorp Inc.		Hattiesburg	601-545-4722	6712
Midsouth Corp.		Jackson	601-353-7508	4011
Mississippi Chemical Corp.		Yazoo City	601-746-4131	2873
Mississippi Power & Light Co.		Jackson	601-969-2311	4911
Mississippi Power Co.		Gulfport	601-864-1211	4911
Mobile Telecommunication Technical Corp.		Jackson	601-944-1300	4812
Peoples Holding Co.		Tupelo	601-680-1001	6712
Sanderson Farms Inc.		Laurel	601-649-4030	2015
System Energy Resources Inc.		Jackson	601-984-9000	4911
Trustmark Corp.		Jackson	601-354-5111	6712

tural, industrial, manufacturing, processing, or research and development enterprises.

Education and Training

Industrial Training. Administered by the Industrial Services Section of the Department of Vocational and Technical Education, this program provides customized pre-employment and on-the-job training for new and expanding Mississippi companies. Training is also available to upgrade worker skills in existing firms.

Job Training Partnership Act. This program operates with funding from the U.S. Department of Labor. It provides job training and other employment related services.

State Offices

Real estate: Real Estate Commission, John W. Neeley, Administrator, 1920 Dunbarton, Jackson, MS 39216-5087. 601-987-3969

Chamber of commerce: Mississippi Economic Council, Bob W. Pittman, President, PO Box 23276, Jackson, MS 39225-3276. 601-969-0022

Economic development: Department of Economic and Community Development, J. Mac Holladay, Exec Director, PO Box 849, Jackson, MS 39205. 601-359-3449

Department of Economic Development, Enterprise Zones Office, Bill Barry, P.O. Box 849, Jackson, MS 39205. 601-359-3552

Small Business Development Center, Raleigh H. Byars, State Director, University of Mississippi, Old Chemistry Building, Suite 216, University, MS 38677. 601-232-5001

Environmental affairs: Pollution Control Bureau, Charles Chisolm, Director, PO Box 10385, Jackson, MS 39289-0385.

Labor: Labor Department, Commissioner, A.H. McCoy Federal Bldg., 100 West Capitol Street, Suite 1445, Jackson, MS 39269. 601-965-4606

Unemployment: Employment Security Commission, Linda Aldy, Exec Director, PO Box 1699, Jackson, MS 39215. 601-354-8711

Worker's compensation: Worker's Compensation Commission, J. Marshall Lusk, Jr., Chairman, PO Box 5300, Jackson, MS 39296-5300. 601-987-4200

Occupational safety and health: Labor Department, Occupational Safety and Health Administration, Director, A.H. McCoy Federal Bldg., 100 West Capitol Street, Suite 1445, Jackson, MS 39269. 601-965-4606

Secretary of state: Secretary of State, Dick Molpus, Secretary of State, PO Box 136, Jackson, MS 39205. 601-359-1350

Taxation and revenue: Tax Commission, Charles A. Marx,

Chairman and Revenue Commissioner, PO Box 22828, Jackson, MS 39225. 601-359-1098

Designated Zones for Economic Development

Enterprise Zones
No program.

Foreign Trade Zones
Foreign Trade Zone No. 92, Harrison County, Mississippi, Grantee: Greater Gulfport/Biloxi Foreign-Trade Zone, Inc., Noel Guthrie, 3825 Ridgewood Rd., Jackson, MS 39211-6453, 601-359-2902

Foreign Trade Zone No. 158, Vicksburg/Jackson, Mississippi, Grantee: Vicksburg/Jackson Foreign-Trade Zone, Inc., Jim Heidel, PO Box 709, Vicksburg, MS 39181, 601-636-4422

Universities with Ph.D. Programs
Delta State University, Cleveland
Jackson State University, Jackson
Mississippi State University, Mississippi State
University of Mississippi, Oxford
University of Southern Mississippi, Hattiesburg

BILOXI–GULFPORT, MS (MSA)

Geographic Profile

Land Area
1057.9 square miles

Counties and Parishes
Hancock
Harrison

Ranking Highlights
190 *out of 319 in total* **land area**
134 *out of 319 in* **population growth,** *1970–1990*
157 *out of 310 in having the lowest* **unemployment** *rate*
201 *out of 310 in size of* **labor force**
220 *out of 318 in the percentage of* **college graduates**
276 *out of 292 in per capita personal* **income**
237 *out of 319 in number of* **manufacturing establishments**
171 *out of 318 in* **physicians** *per 1000 people*
131 *out of 318 in* **hospital beds** *per 1000 people*
N/A *out of 267 in fewest* **crimes** *per 1000 people*
N/A *out of 266 in fewest* **violent crimes** *per 1000 people*
 32 *out of 319 in per capita* **federal funds and grants**

Quality of Life Indexes (Rate per 1000 population)
Crime rate in 1991:   N/A
Violent crime rate in 1991: N/A
Physicians rate in 1992:   1.76
Hospital bed rate in 1991:   4.18

ACCRA Cost of Living Indexes
(First quarter 1993, average = 100)
Composite index: N/A
Utilities index: N/A
Housing index: N/A

Population (1990)

Total Population and Growth Rate
1990: 197,125
1980: 182,161
1970: 151,969
Growth rate 1970–1990: 30%

Race and Hispanic Origin
White: 79.3%
Black: 17.8%
Asian/Pacific Islander: 2.3%
Native American: 0.3%
Hispanic origin: 1.8%
White not Hispanic: 78.0%

Age
Ages 18 to 20: 5.4%
Ages 21 to 24: 6.2%
Ages 25 to 44: 31.2%
Ages 45 to 54: 9.6%

Ages 55 to 59: 4.4%
Ages 60 to 64: 4.3%
Ages 65 plus: 11.4%

Educational Attainment (1990)

Percent having completed high school: 73.6%
Percent having completed college: 16.0%
Elementary and high school enrollment: 36,365

Federal Funds and Grants Received

Total received in 1989: $1,081,600,000
Funds received per capita: $5,277

Civilian Labor Force

1993 (April):   94,658
1992 average: 89,197
1991 average: 86,980
1990 average: 88,729

Unemployment

1993 (April):   5.1%
1992 average: 6.9%
1991 average: 6.6%
1990 average: 6.2%

Average Annual Pay

1988: $16,953
1987: $16,353
1985: $15,248

Per Capita Personal Income

1991: $13,930
1990: $13,313
1989: $12,507

Business Climate (1987)

Manufacturing

Number of establishments in 1987: 164
Shipments in 1987 ($1,000): $990,700
Employees in 1987: 8,000
Change in employment, 1982 to 1987: 6.7%
Average annual pay for manufacturing work in 1989: $20,989
Average annual pay for production work in 1987: $16,983

Wholesale Trade

Number of establishments in 1987: 260
Total sales in 1987 ($1,000): $430,400
Change in sales, 1982 to 1987: 8.8%

Retail Trade

Number of establishments in 1987: 1,292
Total sales in 1987 ($1,000): $430,400
Retail sales per household in 1987: $13,761
Average annual pay in 1989: $9,819

Service Industry

Selected receipts in 1987 ($1,000): $389,700
Average annual pay in 1989: $16,148

Housing

Total number of units in 1990: 84,374
Occupied units in 1990: 71,374
Owner-occupied units in 1990: 64.3%
1993 ACCRA average cost: N/A
1993 ACCRA average rent for an apartment: N/A

Chamber of Commerce

Mississippi Gulf Coast Chamber of Commerce, Martin R. Lee, Exec. Vice President, 1048 Beach Blvd., PO Box 1928, Biloxi, MS 39533. 601-374-2717

Economic Development Office

Harrison County Development Commisssion, Michael Olivier, Exec. Director, 1 Hancock Pl. Suite 1205, PO Box 569, Gulfport, MS 39502. 601-863-3807, FAX 601-863-4555

Economic Development Organizations

Southern Mississippi Planning and Development District, Leslie Newcomb, Exec. Director, 1020 32nd Ave., Gulfport, MS 39501. 601-868-2311

Major Businesses

Company	SIC	Telephone
Allen Beverages Inc.	5149	(601) 831-4343
Anderson, Roy Corp	1541	(601) 896-4000
Butch Oustalet Inc.	5511	(601) 863-5525
Coast Electric Power Association	4911	(601) 467-6535
Corso, Frank P. Inc.	5194	(601) 436-4697
Dees' Chevrolet Co.,	5511	(601) 432-2691
Equitrust Mortgage Corp.	6162	(601) 868-6432
Glass Motors Inc.	5511	(601) 896-6840
Goldin Industries Inc.	5093	(601) 896-6216
Great Southern Mercantile	5411	(601) 896-5885
Gulf National Life Insurance	6311	(601) 374-2611
Hancock Bank	6022	(601) 868-4702
Hancock Holding Co.	6022	(601) 868-4702
Mason Chamberlain Inc.	3483	(601) 467-8600
Memorial Hospital at Gulf	8062	(601) 863-1441
Merchants Bank & Trust Co.	6022	(601) 864-7332
Mississippi Power Co.	4911	(601) 864-1211
Myrick, H Gordon Inc.	1542	(601) 864-9911
Newman Lumber Co.	5031	(601) 832-1899
Peck, Pat Nissan Inc.	5511	(601) 864-6411
Peoples Bank of Biloxi	6021	(601) 435-5511
RPM Pizza Inc.	5812	(601) 832-4000
Star Chevrolet Co. Inc.	5511	(601) 928-4405
Struthers Industries Inc.	3443	(601) 864-5410

Colleges and Universities

Mississippi Gulf Coast Community College, Jefferson Davis Campus, Gulfport
Phillips Junior College of the Mississippi Gulf Coast, Gulfport

JACKSON, MS (MSA)

Geographic Profile

Land Area

2363.0 square miles

Counties and Parishes

Hinds

Madison

Rankin

Ranking Highlights

74 *out of 319 in total* **land area**

109 *out of 319 in* **population growth**, *1970–1990*

82 *out of 310 in having the lowest* **unemployment** *rate*

108 *out of 310 in size of* **labor force**

58 *out of 318 in the percentage of* **college graduates**

215 *out of 292 in per capita personal* **income**

134 *out of 319 in number of* **manufacturing establishments**

31 *out of 318 in* **physicians** *per 1000 people*

29 *out of 318 in* **hospital beds** *per 1000 people*

239 *out of 267 in fewest* **crimes** *per 1000 people*

159 *out of 266 in fewest* **violent crimes** *per 1000 people*

130 *out of 319 in per capita* **federal funds and grants**

Quality of Life Indexes (Rate per 1000 population)

Crime rate in 1991:	84.2
Violent crime rate in 1991:	7.2
Physicians rate in 1992:	3
Hospital bed rate in 1991:	6.01

ACCRA Cost of Living Indexes

(First quarter 1993, average = 100)

Composite index:	N/A
Utilities index:	N/A
Housing index:	N/A

Overview

Jackson, Mississippi's capital and largest city, is a financial center and a rapidly growing major distribution center, with interstate highways and railroads affording access to all parts of the Sun Belt. It is the site of many oil and gas corporations. Due to the diversity of business and industry, the Jackson metropolitan area has not experienced the economic downturn that many cities have in late 1980s and 1990s.

The Jackson area is home to insurance industry headquarters and relies on a varied economy that includes agriculture, government, the service sector, oil and gas drilling, and manufacturing. Trade, distribution, and high-technology firms are also important economic elements.

Equidistant from Memphis, Tennessee, to the North, New Orleans, Louisiana, to the south, as well as Atlanta, Georgia, to the east and Dallas, Texas, to the west, Jackson is advantageously positioned to serve the South's distribution needs. A transportation network of major carriers, regional airlines, major trucking lines, and rail lines operated by the Illinois Central Gulf Railroad assures Jackson's position as a vital provider of the nation's freight service. Both Jackson International Airport and Hawkins Field handle considerable freight activity. Jackson International Airport was granted port-of-entry status in 1989, permitting imported goods to enter Jackson into a free warehouse zone. Motor traffic is handled by the interstate highways, I-55 running north and south, and I-20 going east and west. Additional approaches to the city are U.S. Highways 49, 18, 80, 25, and I-220.

Population (1990)

Total Population and Growth Rate

1990: 395,396

1980: 362,038

1970: 288,643

Growth rate 1970–1990: 37%

Race and Hispanic Origin

White: 56.9%

Black: 42.5%

Asian/Pacific Islander: 0.4%

Native American: 0.1%

Hispanic origin: 0.5%

White not Hispanic: 56.6%

Age

Ages 18 to 20: 5.3%

Ages 21 to 24: 6%

Ages 25 to 44: 32.7%

Ages 45 to 54: 9.5%

Ages 55 to 59: 4%

Ages 60 to 64: 3.9%

Ages 65 plus: 10.5%

Educational Attainment (1990)

Percent having completed high school: 74.4%

Percent having completed college: 25.1%

Elementary and high school enrollment: 77,049

Federal Funds and Grants Received

Total received in 1989: $1,312,700,000

Funds received per capita: $3,313

Civilian Labor Force

1993 (April): 203,922

1992 average: 201,336

1991 average: 201,332

1990 average: 201,084

Unemployment

1993 (April): 5.3%

1992 average: 5.7%

1991 average: 6.1%

1990 average: 5.3%

Average Annual Pay

1988: $18,583

1987: $17,837
1985: $16,882

Per Capita Personal Income
1991: $15,991
1990: $15,424
1989: $14,670

Business Climate (1987)

Manufacturing
Number of establishments in 1987: 394
Shipments in 1987 ($1,000): $2,502,900
Employees in 1987: 19,500
Change in employment, 1982 to 1987: 2.1%
Average annual pay for manufacturing work in 1989: $21,389
Average annual pay for production work in 1987: $17,438

Wholesale Trade
Number of establishments in 1987: 859
Total sales in 1987 ($1,000): $3,557,700
Change in sales, 1982 to 1987: 11.2%

Retail Trade
Number of establishments in 1987: 2,409
Total sales in 1987 ($1,000): $3,557,700
Retail sales per household in 1987: $17,087
Average annual pay in 1989: $11,509

Service Industry
Selected receipts in 1987 ($1,000): $1,053,300
Average annual pay in 1989: $17,218

Office Real Estate (1992)
Office space inventory: N/A
Average class A Central Business District rental range per sq. ft: N/A

Vacancy Rates
All areas: N/A

Vacancy Rates in Central Business District
Class A space: 6.7%
Class B space: N/A

Vacancy Rates Outside Central Business District
Class A space: 6.7%
Class B space: N/A

Housing
Total number of units in 1990: 152,493
Occupied units in 1990: 140,157
Owner-occupied units in 1990: 65.7%
1993 ACCRA average cost: N/A
1993 ACCRA average rent for an apartment: N/A

Chamber of Commerce
Jackson Chamber of Commerce, Paul Latture, Jr., President, 201 S. President St., PO Box 22548, Jackson, MS 39225. 601-948-7575

Economic Development Office
Electric Power Association of Mississippi, Jack B. Rhodes, Director of Industrial Development, 2805 Greenway Dr., PO Box 7897, Jackson, MS 39284-7897. 601-922-2341

Major Businesses

Company	SIC	Telephone
Blue Cross Blue Shield	6324	(601) 932-3704
Deposit Guaranty Corp.	6021	(601) 354-8211
Deposit Guaranty National Bank	6021	(601) 354-8211
Entergy Operatons Inc.	4911	(601) 984-9000
Ergon Inc.	2911	(601) 948-3472
First Mississippi Corp.	2865	(601) 948-7550
Irby, Stuart Co.	5063	(601) 969-1811
Jitney-Jungle Stores	5411	(601) 948-0361
Lion Oil Co., Inc.	2911	(601) 948-3472
Mc Carty Processors Inc.	2015	(601) 372-7441
Mc Carty-Holman Co.	5141	(601) 948-0361
Mcrae's, Inc.	5311	(601) 968-4400
Mississippi Valley Gas Co.	4924	(601) 961-6900
Southern Farm Bureau Life Insurance	6311	(601) 981-7422
Southern Farm Bureau	6531	(601) 982-7777
Southern Jitney-Jungle Co.	5411	(601) 948-0361
Telephone Electronics Corp.	4813	(601) 764-3143
Trustmark Corp.	6021	(601) 354-5863
Trustmark National Bank	6021	(601) 354-5863
Yazoo Investment Corp.	4923	(601) 366-6421

Colleges and Universities
Belhaven College, Jackson
Jackson State University, Jackson
Millsaps College, Jackson
Phillips Junior College of Jackson, Jackson
University of Mississippi Medical Center, Jackson

PASCAGOULA, MS (MSA)

Geographic Profile

Land Area

726.6 square miles

Counties and Parishes

Jackson

Ranking Highlights

249 *out of 319 in total* **land area**

125 *out of 319 in* **population growth,** *1970–1990*

174 *out of 310 in having the lowest* **unemployment** *rate*

267 *out of 310 in size of* **labor force**

248 *out of 318 in the percentage of* **college graduates**

N/A *out of 292 in per capita personal* **income**

302 *out of 319 in number of* **manufacturing establishments**

210 *out of 318 in* **physicians** *per 1000 people*

242 *out of 318 in* **hospital beds** *per 1000 people*

N/A *out of 267 in fewest* **crimes** *per 1000 people*

N/A *out of 266 in fewest* **violent crimes** *per 1000 people*

13 *out of 319 in per capita* **federal funds and grants**

Quality of Life Indexes (Rate per 1000 population)

Crime rate in 1991:   N/A

Violent crime rate in 1991:   N/A

Physicians rate in 1992:   1.57

Hospital bed rate in 1991:   3

ACCRA Cost of Living Indexes

(First quarter 1993, average = 100)

Composite index: N/A

Utilities index: N/A

Housing index: N/A

Population (1990)

Total Population and Growth Rate

1990: 115,243

1980: 118,015

1970: 87,975

Growth rate 1970–1990: 31%

Race and Hispanic Origin

White: 78.2%

Black: 20.5%

Asian/Pacific Islander: 1.0%

Native American: 0.2%

Hispanic origin: 0.9%

White not Hispanic: 77.5%

Age

Ages 18 to 20: 4.7%

Ages 21 to 24: 5.1%

Ages 25 to 44: 31.1%

Ages 45 to 54: 11.4%

Ages 55 to 59: 4.6%

Ages 60 to 64: 4%

Ages 65 plus: 9.4%

Educational Attainment (1990)

Percent having completed high school: 74.4%

Percent having completed college: 14.4%

Elementary and high school enrollment: 24,195

Federal Funds and Grants Received

Total received in 1989: $981,200,000

Funds received per capita: $7,659

Civilian Labor Force

1993 (April):   58,049

1992 average: 59,399

1991 average: 58,223

1990 average: 54,977

Unemployment

1993 (April):   6.2%

1992 average: 7.1%

1991 average: 7.1%

1990 average: 7.7%

Average Annual Pay

1988: $21,284

1987: $20,420

1985: $19,315

Per Capita Personal Income

1991: N/A

1990: N/A

1989: N/A

Business Climate (1987)

Manufacturing

Number of establishments in 1987: 89

Shipments in 1987 ($1,000): $3,801,200

Employees in 1987: 16,800

Change in employment, 1982 to 1987: -9.7%

Average annual pay for manufacturing work in 1989: $28,516

Average annual pay for production work in 1987: $25,722

Wholesale Trade

Number of establishments in 1987: 107

Total sales in 1987 ($1,000): $498,400

Change in sales, 1982 to 1987: 29.4%

Retail Trade

Number of establishments in 1987: 671

Total sales in 1987 ($1,000): $498,400

Retail sales per household in 1987: $10,940

Average annual pay in 1989: $9,711

Service Industry

Selected receipts in 1987 ($1,000): $157,000

Average annual pay in 1989: $20,124

Housing

Total number of units in 1990: 45,542

Occupied units in 1990: 40,454
Owner-occupied units in 1990: 73.5%
1993 ACCRA average cost: N/A
1993 ACCRA average rent for an apartment: N/A

Chamber of Commerce

Jackson County Area Chamber of Commerce, Claire C. Louder, Exec. Director, 825 U.S. Hwy 90, PO Drawer P, Pascagoula, MS 39567. 601-762-3391

Economic Development Office

Jackson County Economic Development District, Linda Rosa, Director, PO Box 28, Pascagoula, MS 39567. 601-769-6263

Economic Development Organizations

Jackson County Port Authority, Department of Economic Development, Harry K. McLemore, Director, PO Box 70, Pascagoula, MS 39568-0070. 601-769-4041, FAX 601-762-7476

Major Businesses

Company	SIC	Telephone
Direct Mail Specialist, Inc.	7331	(601) 875-7900
Fletcher Construction Co.	1542	(601) 762-5792
Gulf Coast Motors Inc.	5511	(601) 762-2711
Ham Industries Inc.	3533	(601) 762-8230
Ingalls Shipbuilding Inc.	3731	(601) 935-1122
Jerry Lee's Grocery Inc.	5411	(601) 497-2730
Merchants & Marine Bank	6022	(601) 762-3311
National American Corp.	6552	(601) 497-4100
Pavco Industries, Inc.	2435	(601) 762-3172
Recreation Land Corp.	6552	(601) 497-4100
Sims Enterprises Inc.	1611	(601) 475-1147
Singing River Hospital System	8062	(601) 938-5005

MISSOURI

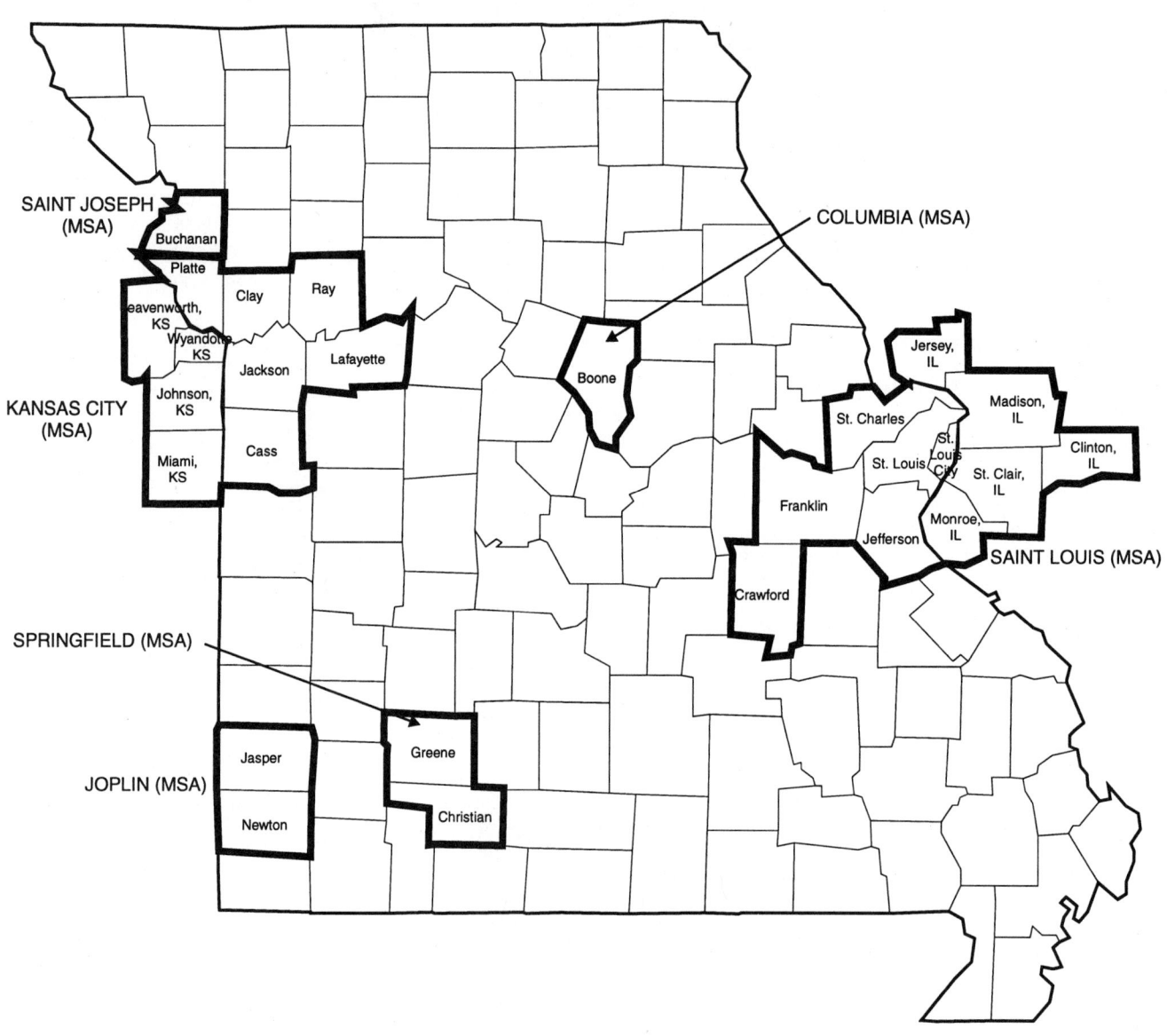

SAINT JOSEPH (MSA)

Buchanan
Platte
Clay
Ray
Leavenworth, KS
Wyandotte, KS
Jackson
Lafayette
KANSAS CITY (MSA)
Johnson, KS
Miami, KS
Cass

Boone

COLUMBIA (MSA)

Jersey, IL
St. Charles
Madison, IL
St. Louis City
Clinton, IL
St. Louis
St. Clair, IL
Franklin
Monroe, IL
Jefferson
SAINT LOUIS (MSA)
Crawford

SPRINGFIELD (MSA)

Jasper
Greene
JOPLIN (MSA)
Newton
Christian

MISSOURI

Population
1990: 5,117,073
1980: 4,916,686

Age
Ages 18 to 20: 234,368
Ages 21 to 24: 282,823
Ages 25 to 44: 1,586,813
Ages 45 to 54: 523,177
Ages 55 to 59: 228,556
Ages 60 to 64: 228,829
Median age: 33.5

Race and Hispanic Origin
White: 4,486,228
Black: 548,208
Asian/Pacific Islander: 41,277
Native American: 19,835
Hispanic origin: 61,702

Households
Total: 1,961,206
Persons per household: 2.54

Sex
Male: 2,464,315
Female: 2,652,758

Population Migration
Domestic migration: 48,000
International migration: 27,000

Projection of the Population in 1995
Total: 5,325,000
18 to 64: 3,231,000

Civilian Labor Force
1993: 2,648,500
1992: 2,728,600
1991: 2,683,400
1990: 2,574,100

Manufacturing
1995 Projection: 442,800
1992: 410,300
1991: 418,300
1990: 433,200
1989: 440,100

Services
1995 Projection: 879,900

1992: 600,600
1991: 587,400
1990: 577,800
1989: 551,000

Wholesale and Retail Trade
1995 Projection: 674,000
1992: 554,800
1991: 560,000
1990: 570,100
1989: 584,500

Unemployment Rate
1993: 6.8%
1992: 7.0%
1991: 6.5%
1990: 6.8%

Employer Unemployment Contributions
Contribution Rate
1992: 1.94%
1991: 1.54%
1990: 1.25%

Average Weekly Benefit
1992: $149.98
1991: $149.45
1990: $135.57

Gross State Product (Million $)
1989: $100,081
1988: $94,932
1987: $89,168
1979: $51,416
Growth rate, 1979 to 1989: 94.6%

Capital Expenditures of Manufacturing Industries
1990: $1,687,100,000
1989: $1,601,300,000
1988: $1,545,400,000
1987: $1,620,100,000

State Tax Rates
Individual income: Range from 1.5% ($1,000 or less) to 6% (above $9,000).
Corporate income: 5% of federal taxable income.
General property: 33.33% of true value in money for per-

sonal property. 19% of true value for residential property.

General sales: 4.225%

Gasoline: 11¢ per gallon

Income

Median income for a 4 person family: $38,478

Personal per Capita Income

1992: $18,835

1991: $17,980

1990: $17,347

Disposable per Capita Income

1992: $16,742

1991: $15,895

1990: $15,187

Private Employment Weekly Wages

Average

1989: $399

1988: $388

1987: $388

Manufacturing

1989: $375

1988: $498

1987: $482

Services

1989: $352

1988: $336

1987: $322

Wholesale

1989: $513

1988: $499

1987: $474

Retail

1989: $215

1988: $211

1987: $206

Highway Statistics

Total Highway Miles

1990: 120,527

1989: 120,077

1988: 119,888

Federal Highway Aid

1991: $257,577,000

1990: $270,953,000

1989: $287,375,000

Electricity

Average Cost per Kilowatt Hour

1990: 6.52¢

1989: 6.54¢

1988: 6.57¢

Housing (1990)

Owner occupied units: 1,348,746

Median house value: $59,800

Renter occupied units: 612,460

Median rent: $282

Total vacant units: 237,923

Homeowner vacancy rate: 2.2%

Rental vacancy rate: 10.7%

State Business Incentives and Assistance

Enterprise Zone Incentives

1) If 30% of the new employees are zone residents or are considered difficult to employ, tax credits are available for 10% of the first $10,000 in investments, 5% of the next $90,000 and 2% of the remaining qualifying investment.

2) Tax credits for new hire: a) $400 for each new job, regardless of the time of year started; b) $100 for each three months the new hire lives in the zone; c) $100 for each three months that a difficult to employ person works on the job.

3) Up to $400 in training credits for training other than JTPA or state training program.

4) State income tax exemption of 50% for 10 years to be earned by a zone business if 30% of the firm's employees are zone residents or have exhausted their unemployment compensation benefits.

5) Unused tax credits will be refunded at a rate of 40% or up to $50,000 for the first year, and 25% or up to $25,000 for the second year.

5) A minimum 50% exemption from local ad valorem property taxes for at least the first 10 years for improvements to real property. This may run for 25 years depending upon the decision of the local government.

6) Infrastructure improvements are required as part of the enterprise zone program.

Financial and Business Assistance

Industrial Development Bonds. Administered by the Missouri Department of Economic Development, this program allows local government to issue bonds for industrial development. Funds may be used to purchase, construct, expand, or improve industrial plants or sites.

Industrial Development Authorities. Administered by the Missouri Department of Economic Development, communities may form corporations called industrial development authorities that may issue industrial development bonds. When financed by IDBs issued by one of the Industrial Development Authorities, all land, buildings, and equipment are subject to real and tangible personal property taxes.

Small Business Incubator Loan Program. Administered by the Small Business Office of the Department of Economic Development, this program is designed to assist in the formation of facilities for the housing and nurturing of start-up businesses. The incubators provide shared business development services and facilities for businesses. This

Major Companies in the State

Company name	Fortune 500 rank	City	Telephone	SIC number
Fortune 500 Companies				
Anheuser Busch Companies Inc.	041	St. Louis	314-577-2000	2082
Clark Oil & Refining Corp. Missouri	204	St. Louis	314-854-9696	2911
Emerson Electric Co.	070	St. Louis	314-553-2000	3621
Farmland Industries Inc.	145	Kansas City	816-459-6000	5191
Interco Inc.	276	St. Louis	314-863-1100	2511
Interstate Bakeries Corp.	322	Kansas City	816-561-6600	2051
Jefferson Smurfit Corp.	159	St. Louis	314-746-1100	2631
Kellwood Co.	377	St. Louis	314-576-3100	2335
Leggett & Platt Inc.	319	Carthage	417-358-8131	2515
Mcdonnell Douglas Corp.	023	St. Louis	314-232-0232	3721
Mid-America Dairymen Inc.	230	Springfield	417-865-7100	2026
Monsanto Co.	060	St. Louis	314-694-1000	2824
Pet Inc.	229	St. Louis	314-622-7700	2032
Ralston Purina Co.	069	St. Louis	314-982-1000	2051
Sigma Aldrich Corp.	462	St. Louis	314-771-5765	2835
Other Major Companies in the State				
Boatmen's Bancshares Inc.		St. Louis	314-466-6000	6712
Brown Group Inc.		St. Louis	314-854-4000	3144
Clark Oil & Refining Corp. Missouri		St. Louis	314-854-9696	2911
Edison Brothers Stores Inc.		St. Louis	314-331-6000	5611
Graybar Electric Co. Inc.		St. Louis	314-727-3900	5063
H & R Block Inc.		Kansas City	816-753-6900	7291
Interstate Bakeries Corp.		Kansas City	816-561-6600	2051
Interstate Brands Corp.		Kansas City	816-561-6600	2051
ITT Financial Corp.		St. Louis	314-821-6060	6141
Marion Merrell Dow Inc.		Kansas City	816-966-4000	2834
May Department Stores Co.		St. Louis	314-342-6300	5311
Payless Cashways Inc.		Kansas City	816-234-6000	5211
Pet Inc.		St. Louis	314-622-7700	2032
Southwestern Bell Corp.		St. Louis	314-235-9800	4813
Southwestern Bell Telephone Co.		St. Louis	314-235-9800	4813
Union Electric Co.		St. Louis	314-621-3222	4931
United Telecommunications Inc.		Kansas City	913-624-3000	4813
Utilicorp United Inc.		Kansas City	816-421-6600	4932
Venture Stores Inc.		O Fallon	314-281-5500	5331
Wetterau Inc.		Hazelwood	314-524-5000	5141

program is eligible to small manufacturing, product development, and professional services firms with less than 30 full-time employees.

Action Fund Loans. Administered by the Missouri Department of Economic Development, this program provides loans to cities with populations under 50,000 and counties under 200,000. The local government will then offer low-interest loans to industries that create or retain jobs for low-income workers. These loans can by used for land, buildings, infrastructure improvements, construction, machinery or equipment, and working capital.

Missouri Linked Deposit Program (MO BUCKS). Administered by the Office of the State Treasurer, this program provides state deposits to Missouri banks, savings and loans, and credit unions who will provide loans to small businesses at rates 3% below market loan rates. Loans are available to existing Missouri small businesses with less than 10 employees and have equity less than 60% of the total assets.

Missouri Small and Existing Business Development. Administered by the Missouri Department of Economic Development, this program provides direct assistance to Missouri businesses which are seeking to start-up or expand. The program also increases the awareness of in-state assistance available through federal and state programs.

Education and Training

Missouri Customized Training Program. Administered cooperatively by the Missouri Department of Economic Development's Division of Job Development and Training and the Department of Elementary and Secondary Education's Industrial Education Section, this program is designed to assist new and expanding businesses in recruiting and training workers. It also helps existing employers in retraining and upgrading workers' skills. A company may be eligible to receive assistance to cover all training costs.

Job Training Partnership Act. This program operates with funding from the U.S. Department of Labor. It provides job training and other employment related services.

State Offices

Real estate: Real Estate Commission, Janet Thomas, Exec Director, PO Box 1339, Jefferson City, MO 65102. 314-751-2334

Chamber of commerce: Missouri State Chamber of Commerce, J.H. Frappier, Director, PO Box 149, 428 E. Capitol Ave., Jefferson City, MO 65102. 314-634-3511

Economic development: Department of Economic Development, Carl M. Koupal, Jr.,Director, PO Box 118, 301 West High St., Jefferson City, MO 65102. 314-751-4770, FAX 314-635-7385

Department of Economic Development, International Business Development Section, Director, PO Box 118, 301

West High St., Jefferson City, MO 65102. 314-751-4855, FAX 314-751-5183

Department of Economic Development, National Business Development Section, Director, PO Box 118, 301 West High St., Jefferson City, MO 65102. 314-751-4539, FAX 314-751-5183

Department of Economic Development, Small Business Office, Director, PO Box 118, 301 West High St., Jefferson City, MO 65102. 800-523-1434 or 314-751-4982

Department of Economic Development, High Technology Programs, Director, PO Box 118, 301 West High St., Jefferson City, MO 65102. 314-751-3906

Department of Economic Development, Enterprise Zone Program, Bill Green, Coordinator, P.O. Box 118, Jefferson City, MO 65102. 314-751-6994

Missouri Industrial Development Council, Pat Amick, Chairman, 204 East High St., Jefferson City, MO 65102. 314-636-7383

Office of the State Treasurer, Wendell Bailey, State Treasurer, PO Box 210, Jefferson City, MO 65102. 314-751-4123

Small Business Development Center, Max Summers, State Director, 300 University Place, Columbia, MO 65211. 314-882-4321

Environmental affairs: Natural Resources Department, Environmental Quality Division, William C. Ford, Director, PO Box 176, Jefferson City, MO 65102. 314-751-4810

Labor: Labor and Industrial Realations Department, Jerry Hunter, Director, 421 East Dunklin Street, Jefferson City, MO 65101. 314-751-4091

Unemployment: Labor and Industrial Relations Department, Employment Security Division, Tom Deuschle, Director, 421 East Dunklin Street, Jefferson City, MO 65101. 314-751-3976

Worker's compensation: Workers' Compensation Division, Richard R. Rousselot, Director, 3315 West Truman Blvd., Jefferson City, MO 65109. 314-751-4231

Occupational safety and health: Labor and Industrial Realations Department, Jerry Hunter, Director, 421 East Dunklin Street, Jefferson City, MO 65101. 314-751-4091

Secretary of state: Secretary of State, Roy D. Blunt, Secretary of State, PO Box 778, Jefferson City, MO 65102. 314-751-2379

Taxation and revenue: Revenue Department, Duane Benton, Director, PO Box 311, Jefferson City, MO 65105. 314-751-4450

Designated Zones for Economic Development

Enterprise Zones
Enacted in: 1982
No. of established zones: 37

Foreign Trade Zones
Foreign Trade Zone No. 15, Kansas City, Missouri, Grantee/Operator: Greater Kansas City FTZ, Inc., Chris

Vedros, 10 Petticoat Lane, Suite 250, Kansas City, MO 64106, 816-421-7666

Foreign Trade Zone No. 102, St. Louis, Missouri, Grantee/ Operator: St. Louis County Port Authority, Mark Tranel, 121 South Meramec, #412, St. Louis, MO 63105, 314-889-7663

Labor Unions

Chemical and Atomic Workers

Electrical Workers, International Brotherhood of (AFL-CIO)

Food and Commercial Workers International Union, United (AFL-CIO)

Laborers' International Union of North America (AFL-CIO)

Operating Engineers, International Union of (AFL-CIO)

Painters and Allied Trades of The United States and Canada, International Brotherhood of (AFL-CIO)

Transit Union, Amalgamated (AFL-CIO)

Universities with Ph.D. Programs

St. Louis College of Pharmacy, St. Louis

St. Louis University, St. Louis

University of Missouri-Columbia, Columbia

University of Missouri-Kansas City, Kansas City

University of Missouri-Rolla, Rolla

University of Missouri-St. Louis, St. Louis

Sources of Additional Information

Missouri Corporate Planner, the Missouri Advantage. Missouri Dept. of Economic Development, 1988. [Page no. by section]

COLUMBIA, MO (MSA)

Geographic Profile

Land Area

685.4 square miles

Counties and Parishes

Boone

Ranking Highlights

257 *out of 319 in total* **land area**

  99 *out of 319 in* **population growth,** *1970–1990*

    5 *out of 310 in having the lowest* **unemployment** *rate*

224 *out of 310 in size of* **labor force**

    6 *out of 318 in the percentage of* **college graduates**

123 *out of 292 in per capita personal* **income**

304 *out of 319 in number of* **manufacturing establishments**

    5 *out of 318 in* **physicians** *per 1000 people*

    4 *out of 318 in* **hospital beds** *per 1000 people*

N/A *out of 267 in fewest* **crimes** *per 1000 people*

N/A *out of 266 in fewest* **violent crimes** *per 1000 people*

213 *out of 319 in per capita* **federal funds and grants**

Quality of Life Indexes (Rate per 1000 population)

Crime rate in 1991:	N/A
Violent crime rate in 1991:	N/A
Physicians rate in 1992:	6.39
Hospital bed rate in 1991:	9.1

ACCRA Cost of Living Indexes
(First quarter 1993, average = 100)

Composite index:	91.1
Utilities index:	71.7
Housing index:	85.1

Overview

Columbia is one of only two cities nationwide to be included in *Money* Magazine's top twenty places to live during each of the past four years. Columbia is located half way between St. Louis and Kansas City I-70 at U.S. 63. The community's largest employer is the main campus of the University of Missouri (approx. 24,000 students) and the largest industry is health care and associated businesses. Columbia's seven hospitals provide health care for the majority of outstate Missouri. Toastmaster, Shelter Insurance, and the Missouri Farmers' Association have corporate headquarters in Columbia; State Farm and other insurers have state headquarters here. *Fortune* 500 companies with substantial presence in Columbia include Anheuser Bush Promotional Products, 3M, Square D, Oscar Mayer, Dana, Toastmaster and Davidson-Textron.

Columbia's regional airport provides convenient flights to St. Louis and Dallas-Ft. Worth airports.

Population (1990)

Total Population and Growth Rate
1990: 112,379
1980: 100,376
1970: 80,935
Growth rate 1970–1990: 39%

Race and Hispanic Origin
White: 89.0%
Black: 7.5%
Asian/Pacific Islander: 2.8%
Native American: 0.4%
Hispanic origin: 1.1%
White not Hispanic: 88.3%

Age
Ages 18 to 20: 10.9%
Ages 21 to 24: 11.1%
Ages 25 to 44: 33.1%
Ages 45 to 54: 8.1%
Ages 55 to 59: 2.8%
Ages 60 to 64: 2.7%
Ages 65 plus: 8.4%

Educational Attainment (1990)
Percent having completed high school: 84.8%
Percent having completed college: 36.5%
Elementary and high school enrollment: 15,612

Federal Funds and Grants Received
Total received in 1989: $282,000,000
Funds received per capita: $2,666

Civilian Labor Force
1993 (April):   73,149
1992 average: 73,883
1991 average: 71,666
1990 average: 69,092

Unemployment
1993 (April):   3.6%
1992 average: 2.9%
1991 average: 3.2%
1990 average: 2.8%

Average Annual Pay
1988: $17,964
1987: $17,291
1985: $16,035

Per Capita Personal Income
1991: $17,782
1990: $17,055
1989: $16,114

Business Climate (1987)

Manufacturing
Number of establishments in 1987: 87
Shipments in 1987 ($1,000): $439,700
Employees in 1987: 4,000

Change in employment, 1982 to 1987: 21.2%
Average annual pay for manufacturing work in 1989: $21,251
Average annual pay for production work in 1987: $18,583

Wholesale Trade
Number of establishments in 1987: 143
Total sales in 1987 ($1,000): $392,800
Change in sales, 1982 to 1987: 54.3%

Retail Trade
Number of establishments in 1987: 737
Total sales in 1987 ($1,000): $392,800
Retail sales per household in 1987: $18,319
Average annual pay in 1989: $9,585

Service Industry
Selected receipts in 1987 ($1,000): $293,500
Average annual pay in 1989: $16,580

Housing
Total number of units in 1990: 44,695
Occupied units in 1990: 41,937
Owner-occupied units in 1990: 55.0%
1993 ACCRA average cost: $97,000
1993 ACCRA average rent for an apartment: $406

Chamber of Commerce
Columbia Chamber of Commerce, Donald M. Laird, Exec. Vice President, 300 S. Providence Rd., PO Box 1016, Columbia, MO 65203. 314-874-1132

Economic Development Office
Regional Economic Development Inc., H. William Watkins, Exec. Vice President, PO Box N, Columbia, MO 65205. 314-442-8303, FAX 314-443-3986

Industrial Sites
Contact: Missouri Research Park, Rick Finholt, Exec. Director, 215 University Hall, Columbia, MO 65211. 314-882-3397

Major Businesses

Company	SIC	Telephone
Boatmen's Bank of Columbia	6022	(314) 876-6000
Boone County National Bank	6021	(314) 874-8100
Boone Electric Cooperative	4911	(314) 449-4181
A. B. Chance Co.	3612	(314) 682-5521
Commerce Bank	6021	(314) 449-3181
Datastorm Technologies	7371	(314) 474-8461
First National Bank & Trust Co.	6021	(314) 449-3911
Legend Automotive Group	5511	(314) 875-5000
Lifemark Hospital of Missouri	8062	(314) 875-9000
Little Dixie Construction	1542	(314) 449-7200
MBS Textbook Exchange Inc.	5192	(314) 874-7100
MFA Inc.	5153	(314) 874-5111
MFA Oil Co.	5171	(314) 442-0171
Mid-State Distributing Co.	5182	(314) 443-3169

Major Businesses (Continued)

Company	SIC	Telephone
Midstate Oil Co.	5541	(314) 442-0171
Midway Arms Inc.	5961	(314) 445-6363
Network Manufacturing Inc.	3713	(314) 442-0020
Semco Manufacturing Inc.	3444	(314) 443-1481
Shelter General Casualty	6331	(314) 445-8441
Shelter Insurance Co.	6331	(314) 445-8441
Shelter Life Insurance Co.	6311	(314) 445-8441
Silvey Corp.	6411	(314) 445-8411
Stephens, Temple Co.	6512	(314) 874-2939
Toastmaster Inc.	3634	(314) 445-8666
Tri-Con Industries Ltd.	2531	(314) 449-1500
Tribune Publishing Co.	2711	(314) 449-3811
University of Missouri-Columbia Hospital	8062	(314) 882-4141

Colleges and Universities

Columbia College, Columbia
Stephens College, Columbia
University of Missouri-Columbia, Columbia

JOPLIN, MO (MSA)

Geographic Profile

Land Area

1266.3 square miles

Counties and Parishes

Jasper
Newton

Ranking Highlights

153 *out of 319 in total* **land area**
179 *out of 319 in* **population growth,** *1970–1990*
 60 *out of 310 in having the lowest* **unemployment** *rate*
215 *out of 310 in size of* **labor force**
280 *out of 318 in the percentage of* **college graduates**
258 *out of 292 in per capita personal* **income**
180 *out of 319 in number of* **manufacturing establishments**
306 *out of 318 in* **physicians** *per 1000 people*
 50 *out of 318 in* **hospital beds** *per 1000 people*
 85 *out of 267 in fewest* **crimes** *per 1000 people*
 23 *out of 266 in fewest* **violent crimes** *per 1000 people*
240 *out of 319 in per capita* **federal funds and grants**

Quality of Life Indexes (Rate per 1000 population)

Crime rate in 1991:	50.6
Violent crime rate in 1991:	2.1
Physicians rate in 1992:	1.02
Hospital bed rate in 1991:	5.47

ACCRA Cost of Living Indexes

(First quarter 1993, average = 100)

Composite index:	87.1
Utilities index:	77.3
Housing index:	83.1

Overview

Joplin is located at the crossroads of major east–west and north–south highways—Interstate 44 and U.S. 71. Joplin serves as a metropolitan center for the four state area which includes Kansas, Oklahoma, Arkansas and Missouri. Joplin ranked 50th as the most livable city in America in the 1993 annual survey by *Money* Magazine. It was also selected as one of fifty towns included in the book *Best Towns in America: A Where to Go Guide for a Better Life.*

Joplin is a regional medical center for the four states with three modern, fully accredited hospitals. Joplin is the home of four major motor carriers, employing over 6,000 people. The Joplin Metropolitan Statistical Area's (MSA) major employers include transportation, food service, health care, and manufacturing of precision bearings and electronics. The Joplin Municipal Airport is served by Northwest, TWA, and Lone Star airlines. Seventeen flights per day carry passengers to St. Louis, Memphis, Tennessee, and Dallas/Fort Worth, Texas.

Population (1990)

Total Population and Growth Rate
1990: 134,910
1980: 127,513
1970: 112,833
Growth rate 1970–1990: 20%

Race and Hispanic Origin
White: 96.4%
Black: 1.0%
Asian/Pacific Islander: 0.6%
Native American: 1.8%
Hispanic origin: 0.9%
White not Hispanic: 95.8%

Age
Ages 18 to 20: 4.7%
Ages 21 to 24: 5.2%
Ages 25 to 44: 29.5%
Ages 45 to 54: 10.3%
Ages 55 to 59: 4.5%
Ages 60 to 64: 4.6%
Ages 65 plus: 15.2%

Educational Attainment (1990)
Percent having completed high school: 71.8%
Percent having completed college: 13.0%
Elementary and high school enrollment: 22,760

Federal Funds and Grants Received
Total received in 1989: $343,200,000
Funds received per capita: $2,524

Civilian Labor Force
1993 (April): 76,699
1992 average: 77,937
1991 average: 74,875
1990 average: 73,164

Unemployment
1993 (April): 5.4%
1992 average: 5.2%
1991 average: 5.8%
1990 average: 5.4%

Average Annual Pay
1988: $16,418
1987: $16,187
1985: $15,269

Per Capita Personal Income
1991: $15,092
1990: $14,339
1989: $13,657

Business Climate (1987)

Manufacturing
Number of establishments in 1987: 265
Shipments in 1987 ($1,000): $1,857,700
Employees in 1987: 16,000
Change in employment, 1982 to 1987: 16.8%
Average annual pay for manufacturing work in 1989: $19,917
Average annual pay for production work in 1987: $16,762

Wholesale Trade
Number of establishments in 1987: 294
Total sales in 1987 ($1,000): $747,100
Change in sales, 1982 to 1987: 23.3%

Retail Trade
Number of establishments in 1987: 946
Total sales in 1987 ($1,000): $747,100
Retail sales per household in 1987: $16,643
Average annual pay in 1989: $9,735

Service Industry
Selected receipts in 1987 ($1,000): $237,200
Average annual pay in 1989: $16,122

Housing
Total number of units in 1990: 57,938
Occupied units in 1990: 53,020
Owner-occupied units in 1990: 71.7%
1993 ACCRA average cost: $95,669
1993 ACCRA average rent for an apartment: $382

Chamber of Commerce
Joplin Area Chamber of Commerce, Suzanne Gilpin, General Manager, 320 E. 4th St., PO Box 1178, Joplin, MO 64802-1178. 417-624-4150

Economic Development Office
Joplin Area Economic Development Organization, Gary Tonjes, President, 303 E. 3rd St., PO Box 1355, Joplin, MO 64801. 417-624-4150

Colleges and Universities
Missouri Southern State College, Joplin
Ozark Christian College, Joplin

KANSAS CITY, MO–KS (MSA)

Geographic Profile

Land Area
4987.9 square miles

Counties and Parishes
Kansas:
  Johnson
  Leavenworth
  Miami
  Wyandotte
  Cass
Missouri:
  Clay
  Jackson
  Lafayette
  Platte
  Ray

Additional Cities/Towns within Area
Kansas City, KS
Keavenworth, KS
Olathe, KS

Ranking Highlights
16 *out of 319 in total* **land area**
206 *out of 319 in* **population growth,** *1970–1990*
58 *out of 310 in having the lowest* **unemployment** *rate*
28 *out of 310 in size of* **labor force**
73 *out of 318 in the percentage of* **college graduates**
52 *out of 292 in per capita personal* **income**
34 *out of 319 in number of* **manufacturing establishments**
96 *out of 318 in* **physicians** *per 1000 people*
121 *out of 318 in* **hospital beds** *per 1000 people*
215 *out of 267 in fewest* **crimes** *per 1000 people*
250 *out of 266 in fewest* **violent crimes** *per 1000 people*
116 *out of 319 in per capita* **federal funds and grants**

Quality of Life Indexes (Rate per 1000 population)
Crime rate in 1991:	74.8
Violent crime rate in 1991:	11.8
Physicians rate in 1992:	2.24
Hospital bed rate in 1991:	4.33

ACCRA Cost of Living Indexes
(First quarter 1993, average = 100)
Composite index:	97.5
Utilities index:	94.5
Housing index:	97.1

Overview
The Kansas City metropolitan area, the nation's biggest clean-air city, straddles the Missouri-Kansas state line. *Baring Advisor's 1993 Consensus Forecast* ranked Kansas City among the nation's top 10 cities for business relocations.

Ernst & Young's 1992 Corporate Relocation survey of national real estate executives also ranked Kansas City among the top ten most favored sites for relocations and expansions. And in 1991, *Fortune* ranked Kansas City the fourth best city in the country in which to do business.

Kansas City is located within 250 miles of the geographic and population centers of the United States. Kansas City is a principal transportation hub and is served by the nation's second leading rail center and the nation's 10th largest trucking center. Kansas City ranks first in the nation for inland foreign trade zone space. Kansas City is also the hub of a fiber optic network and growing telecommunications industry with almost 200 telecommunications companies, including the international headquarters for Sprint.

Commerce Department figures show Kansas City workers are 40% more productive than the national average, they bring $20 more per hour in value added productivity than the national average and are almost 20% above the national average in population over age 25 graduated from high school. Nearly two-thirds of the area's work force is employed in white collar jobs, and six of the area's top 25 employers are manufacturers.

According to the Metropolitan Index by the New York-based Metropolitan Consulting Group, comparative costs of operating a business in the Kansas City area rank the lowest of the nation's 30 largest metro areas. For the past five years, Kansas City has had the lowest cost of living among metro areas of 1.5 million or more. Ernst & Young's 1993 Study of Housing Costs identified Kansas City as the most affordable metro housing market in the country.

The Kansas City area is investing $5.5 billion in residential, commercial and industrial construction which includes a $130 million convention center expansion, a $76 million zoo renovation, and $48 million new runway for the city's international airport.

Population (1990)

Total Population and Growth Rate
1990: 1,566,280
1980: 1,433,464
1970: 1,373,146
Growth rate 1970–1990: 14%

Race and Hispanic Origin
White: 84.3%
Black: 12.8%
Asian/Pacific Islander: 1.1%
Native American: 0.5%
Hispanic origin: 2.9%
White not Hispanic: 82.8%

Age
Ages 18 to 20: 3.9%
Ages 21 to 24: 5.3%
Ages 25 to 44: 34.1%
Ages 45 to 54: 10.4%

Ages 55 to 59: 4.2%
Ages 60 to 64: 4.1%
Ages 65 plus: 11.6%

Educational Attainment (1990)

Percent having completed high school: 82.3%
Percent having completed college: 23.4%
Elementary and high school enrollment: 264,954

Federal Funds and Grants Received

Total received in 1989: $5,392,500,000
Funds received per capita: $3,423

Civilian Labor Force

1993 (April):   867,540
1992 average: 871,186
1991 average: 860,630
1990 average: 850,947

Unemployment

1993 (April):   5.4%
1992 average: 4.9%
1991 average: 5.6%
1990 average: 5.0%

Average Annual Pay

1988: $21,598
1987: $20,848
1985: $19,483

Per Capita Personal Income

1991: $19,963
1990: $19,336
1989: $18,534

Business Climate (1987)

Manufacturing

Number of establishments in 1987: 2,254
Shipments in 1987 ($1,000): $19,398,900
Employees in 1987: 115,400
Change in employment, 1982 to 1987: -2.8%
Average annual pay for manufacturing work in 1989: $29,295
Average annual pay for production work in 1987: $23,203

Wholesale Trade

Number of establishments in 1987: 3,710
Total sales in 1987 ($1,000): $30,074,400
Change in sales, 1982 to 1987: 22.3%

Retail Trade

Number of establishments in 1987: 9,266
Total sales in 1987 ($1,000): $30,074,400
Retail sales per household in 1987: $17,587
Average annual pay in 1989: $11,940

Service Industry

Selected receipts in 1987 ($1,000): $5,322,500
Average annual pay in 1989: $19,561

Office Real Estate (1992)

Office space inventory: 36,522,000 square feet
Average class A Central Business District rental range per sq. ft: $18.75

Vacancy Rates

All areas: 13.6%

Vacancy Rates in Central Business District

Class A space: 18.1%
Class B space: 12.0%

Vacancy Rates Outside Central Business District

Class A space: 11.9%
Class B space: 14.2%

Housing

Total number of units in 1990: 657,351
Occupied units in 1990: 602,347
Owner-occupied units in 1990: 65.4%
1993 ACCRA average cost: $104,500
1993 ACCRA average rent for an apartment: $570

Chamber of Commerce

Greater Kansas City Chamber of Commerce, Peter Levi, President, 920 Main St. #600, Kansas City, MO 64105. 816-221-2424

Economic Development Office

Kansas City Area Development Council, Robert J. Marcusse, President, 920 Main St. Suite 600, Kansas City, MO 64105. 800-522-4880, 816-221-2121

Economic Development Organizations

Platte County Economic Development Council, Inc., Burdette Fullerton, Exec. Director, 10920 Ambassador Dr. Suite 536, Kansas City, MO 64153. 816-891-8770, FAX 816-891-9108

Industrial Sites

Contact: University Park, Duana Linville, Director, 5100 Rockhill Rd., Kansas City, MO 65211. 816-276-1046

Major Businesses

Company	SIC	Telephone
Associated Wholesale Grocers	5141	(913) 321-1313
H & R Block, Inc.	7291	(816) 753-6900
Employers Reinsurance Corp.	6331	(913) 676-5200
Farmland Industries, Inc.	2911	(816) 459-6000
Federal Reserve Bank of Kansas	6011	(816) 881-2000
Ferrellgas, Inc.	6792	(816) 792-1600
Garnac Grain Co. Inc.	5153	(913) 661-6100
Government Employees Hospital	6324	(816) 753-1260
Hallmark Cards Inc.	2771	(816) 274-5111
IBC Holdings Corp.	2051	(816) 561-6600
Interstate Brands Corp.	2051	(816) 561-6600
Lee Apparel Co., Inc.	2325	(913) 384-4000
Marion Merrell Dow Inc.	2834	(816) 966-4000
Payless Cashways, Inc.	5211	(816) 234-6000

Major Businesses (Continued)

Company	SIC	Telephone
U. S. Central Credit Union	6062	(913) 661-3800
U. S. Sprint Communications	4813	(816) 276-6000
United Telecommunications	4813	(913) 676-3000
Western Auto Supply Co.	5531	(816) 346-4000
Yellow Freight System, Inc.	4213	(913) 345-3000

Colleges and Universities

Avila College, Kansas City, MO
Career Point Business School, Kansas City, MO
Devry Institute of Technology, Kansas City, MO
Donnelly College, Kansas City, KS
Kansas City Art Institute, Kansas City, MO
Kansas City Business College, Kansas City, MO
Kansas City Kansas Community College, Kansas City, KS
Maple Woods Community College, Kansas City, MO
Midamerica Nazarene College, Olathe, KS
National College, Kansas City, MO
Penn Valley Community College, Kansas City, MO
Research College of Nursing, Kansas City, MO
Rockhurst College, Kansas City, MO
University of Kansas Medical Center, Kansas City, KS
University of Missouri-Kansas City, Kansas City, MO

SAINT JOSEPH, MO (MSA)

Geographic Profile

Land Area
409.8 square miles

Counties and Parishes
Buchanan

Ranking Highlights

309 *out of 319 in total* **land area**
292 *out of 319 in* **population growth**, *1970–1990*
104 *out of 310 in having the lowest* **unemployment** *rate*
298 *out of 310 in size of* **labor force**
272 *out of 318 in the percentage of* **college graduates**
187 *out of 292 in per capita personal* **income**
293 *out of 319 in number of* **manufacturing establishments**
217 *out of 318 in* **physicians** *per 1000 people*
21 *out of 318 in* **hospital beds** *per 1000 people*
113 *out of 267 in fewest* **crimes** *per 1000 people*
96 *out of 266 in fewest* **violent crimes** *per 1000 people*
215 *out of 319 in per capita* **federal funds and grants**

Quality of Life Indexes (Rate per 1000 population)

Crime rate in 1991:	57.5
Violent crime rate in 1991:	4.7
Physicians rate in 1992:	1.55
Hospital bed rate in 1991:	6.39

ACCRA Cost of Living Indexes
(First quarter 1993, average = 100)

Composite index:	90.7
Utilities index:	87.8
Housing index:	96.1

Population (1990)

Total Population and Growth Rate
1990: 83,083
1980: 87,888
1970: 86,915
Growth rate 1970–1990: -4%

Race and Hispanic Origin
White: 95.5%
Black: 3.2%
Asian/Pacific Islander: 0.3%
Native American: 0.3%
Hispanic origin: 2.1%
White not Hispanic: 94.2%

Age
Ages 18 to 20: 4.5%
Ages 21 to 24: 5.3%
Ages 25 to 44: 29.3%
Ages 45 to 54: 9.5%
Ages 55 to 59: 4.5%

Ages 60 to 64: 4.7%
Ages 65 plus: 16.4%

Educational Attainment (1990)
Percent having completed high school: 72.1%
Percent having completed college: 13.5%
Elementary and high school enrollment: 14,278

Federal Funds and Grants Received
Total received in 1989: $226,400,000
Funds received per capita: $2,651

Civilian Labor Force
1993 (April): 42,801
1992 average: 43,573
1991 average: 43,913
1990 average: 42,768

Unemployment
1993 (April): 7.0%
1992 average: 6.1%
1991 average: 7.4%
1990 average: 6.2%

Average Annual Pay
1988: $18,527
1987: $17,726
1985: $16,436

Per Capita Personal Income
1991: $16,471
1990: $15,770
1989: $15,029

Business Climate (1987)
Manufacturing
Number of establishments in 1987: 102
Shipments in 1987 ($1,000): $1,632,100
Employees in 1987: 8,100
Change in employment, 1982 to 1987: -5.8%
Average annual pay for manufacturing work in 1989: $23,756
Average annual pay for production work in 1987: $20,583

Wholesale Trade
Number of establishments in 1987: 163
Total sales in 1987 ($1,000): $576,300
Change in sales, 1982 to 1987: -32.1%

Retail Trade
Number of establishments in 1987: 545
Total sales in 1987 ($1,000): $576,300
Retail sales per household in 1987: $16,426
Average annual pay in 1989: $10,120

Service Industry
Selected receipts in 1987 ($1,000): $146,000
Average annual pay in 1989: $15,628

Housing
Total number of units in 1990: 35,652

Occupied units in 1990: 32,486
Owner-occupied units in 1990: 68.0%
1993 ACCRA average cost: $119,100
1993 ACCRA average rent for an apartment: $343

Chamber of Commerce
St. Joseph Area Chamber of Commerce, Alan Kenyon, President, 106 S. 7th St., PO Box 1394, St. Joseph, MO 64502. 816-232-4461

Major Businesses

Company	SIC	Telephone
Ameribanc, Inc.	6022	(816) 233-2000
American National Bank of St. Joseph	6021	(816) 233-2000
Crouser International, Inc.	5012	(816) 233-9131
Heartland Health System Inc.	8062	(816) 271-7196
Heartland Hospital East	8062	(816) 271-6000
Heartland Hospital West	8062	(816) 271-7111
Herzog Contracting Corp.	1629	(816) 233-9001
Hillyard, Inc.	5169	(816) 233-1321
Hillyard Enterprises, Inc.	2842	(816) 233-1321
Interstate Ford Sales, Inc.	5511	(816) 279-7485
Marcum Oil Co.	5541	(816) 324-3224
Missouri-Nebraska Express	4213	(816) 233-3150
MNX Inc.	4213	(816) 233-3158
News-Press & Gazette Co.	4833	(816) 271-8500
Research Seeds Inc.	5191	(816) 238-7333
C. D. Smith Drug Co.	5122	(816) 232-5471
St. Joseph Light & Power Co.	4931	(816) 233-8888
St. Joseph Tobacco Co. Inc.	5194	(816) 233-8213
Tractor Leasing Inc.	4213	(816) 233-3150
Wire Rope Corp. America	3496	(816) 233-0287

Colleges and Universities
Missouri Western State College, St. Joseph
Platt Junior College, St. Joseph

SAINT LOUIS, MO–IL (MSA)

Geographic Profile

Land Area
5330.8 square miles

Counties and Parishes
Illinois:
Clinton
Jersey
Madison
Monroe
St. Clair
Missouri:
Crawford (part)
Franklin
Jefferson
St. Charles
St. Louis

Additional Cities/Towns within Area
Alton, IL
Belleville, IL
East St. Louis, IL
Granite City, IL
St. Charles, MO

Ranking Highlights
10 *out of 319 in total* **land area**
271 *out of 319 in* **population growth,** *1970–1990*
99 *out of 310 in having the lowest* **unemployment** *rate*
14 *out of 310 in size of* **labor force**
123 *out of 318 in the percentage of* **college graduates**
43 *out of 292 in per capita personal* **income**
18 *out of 319 in number of* **manufacturing establishments**
69 *out of 318 in* **physicians** *per 1000 people*
148 *out of 318 in* **hospital beds** *per 1000 people*
148 *out of 267 in fewest* **crimes** *per 1000 people*
212 *out of 266 in fewest* **violent crimes** *per 1000 people*
34 *out of 319 in per capita* **federal funds and grants**

Quality of Life Indexes (Rate per 1000 population)
Crime rate in 1991:	63.0
Violent crime rate in 1991:	9.4
Physicians rate in 1992:	2.47
Hospital bed rate in 1991:	4

ACCRA Cost of Living Indexes
(First quarter 1993, average = 100)
Composite index:	95.9
Utilities index:	105.8
Housing index:	95.2

Overview
St. Louis, the second largest city in Missouri, is the focus of the metropolitan statistical area comprised of Franklin, Jef-ferson, St. Charles, and St. Louis counties in Missouri and Clinton, Jersey, Madison, Monroe, and St. Clair counties in Illinois.

St. Louis is the headquarters of ten Fortune 500 companies as well as a primary banking and financial center for the region. Second only to Detroit, Michigan, in automobile production, St. Louis supports a strong manufacturing sector; the three major American automakers—General Motors, Chrysler, and Ford—operate assembly plants in the area. St. Louis is also the base for the Eighth Federal Reserve District Bank and several national insurance and brokerage firms.

As the nation sank into a recession in the late 1980s and early 1990s and the Pentagon began major spending cutbacks, the St. Louis area economy was jolted by massive layoffs. McDonnell Douglas, manufacturer of fighter jets, missiles, and commercial airliners, laid off nearly a quarter of its work force in 1990; it then cut its payroll from 113,000 workers industry-wide to 99,000 during the twelve-month period ending June 1992. The company then announced that it would streamline its six defense lines into two units. Hundreds of subcontractors in the area felt the effects. General Dynamics Corporation, the nation's second largest military contractor, announced in late 1991 that it would move its corporate headquarters to Falls Church, Virginia. The biggest gains in employment in recent years have been in health care, reflecting the city's growing role as a center of medical research. Manufacturing jobs have been declining steadily since 1973, while the number of service jobs increased 47 percent from 1973 to 1990.

St. Louis is a primary national center for air, land, and water transportation networks. Among the commodities shipped through the city are coal, grain, cement, petroleum products, and chemicals. The nation's third-largest rail freight hub, St. Louis is served by ten trunkline railroads and three switching lines; seventeen piggyback terminals have trailer on flat car facilities and three provide container on flat car services. Four interstate highways converge in St. Louis, affording more than one hundred trucking companies overnight to third-morning access to markets throughout the country. Ninety of these firms maintain terminals within the Commercial Truck Zone, which covers all or portions of a seven-county area. St. Louis is the nation's second-largest inland port, as well as the country's northernmost port with ice-free access year round; the port connects St. Louis via the Mississippi, Illinois, and Missouri river system with New Orleans, Louisiana, and international waterways. Air freight service is available at Lambert–St. Louis International Airport. Two Foreign Trade Zones are located in the metropolitan region.

Population (1990)

Total Population and Growth Rate
1990: 2,444,099

1980: 2,376,968
1970: 2,429,376
Growth rate 1970–1990: 1%

Race and Hispanic Origin

White: 81.2%
Black: 17.3%
Asian/Pacific Islander: 1.0%
Native American: 0.2%
Hispanic origin: 1.1%
White not Hispanic: 80.5%

Age

Ages 18 to 20: 4.1%
Ages 21 to 24: 5.4%
Ages 25 to 44: 32.5%
Ages 45 to 54: 10.2%
Ages 55 to 59: 4.4%
Ages 60 to 64: 4.4%
Ages 65 plus: 12.8%

Educational Attainment (1990)

Percent having completed high school: 76.0%
Percent having completed college: 20.7%
Elementary and high school enrollment: 418,626

Federal Funds and Grants Received

Total received in 1989: $12,915,400,00
Funds received per capita: $5,236

Civilian Labor Force

1993 (April): 1,248,434
1992 average: 1,272,909
1991 average: 1,280,619
1990 average: 1,264,147

Unemployment

1993 (April): 6.5%
1992 average: 6.0%
1991 average: 6.8%
1990 average: 5.9%

Average Annual Pay

1988: $22,735
1987: $21,793
1985: $20,368

Per Capita Personal Income

1991: $20,507
1990: $19,965
1989: $19,023

Business Climate (1987)

Manufacturing

Number of establishments in 1987: 3,351
Shipments in 1987 ($1,000): $36,176,200
Employees in 1987: 221,700
Change in employment, 1982 to 1987: 1.5%
Average annual pay for manufacturing work in 1989: $32,478

Average annual pay for production work in 1987: $24,801

Wholesale Trade

Number of establishments in 1987: 5,057
Total sales in 1987 ($1,000): $31,705,000
Change in sales, 1982 to 1987: 16.9%

Retail Trade

Number of establishments in 1987: 14,361
Total sales in 1987 ($1,000): $31,705,000
Retail sales per household in 1987: $17,055
Average annual pay in 1989: $11,961

Service Industry

Selected receipts in 1987 ($1,000): $8,035,600
Average annual pay in 1989: $19,819

Office Real Estate (1992)

Office space inventory: 34,203,346 square feet
Average class A Central Business District rental range per sq. ft: $16.50

Vacancy Rates

All areas: 28.6%

Vacancy Rates in Central Business District

Class A space: 14.6%
Class B space: 73.4%

Vacancy Rates Outside Central Business District

Class A space: 15.7%
Class B space: 27.6%

Housing

Total number of units in 1990: 1,006,011
Occupied units in 1990: 924,733
Owner-occupied units in 1990: 68.5%
1993 ACCRA average cost: $103,525
1993 ACCRA average rent for an apartment: $554

Chamber of Commerce

Saint Louis Regional Commerce and Growth Association, Ronald R. Mierzejewski, Director of Economic Development, 100 S. 4th St., Suite 500, St. Louis, MO 63102. 314-231-5555, FAX 314-444-1122

Economic Development Office

Saint Louis County Economic Council , David Alexander, Marketing Director, 121 S. Meramec Suite 412, St. Louis, MO 63105. 314-889-7663, FAX 314-889-7666

Economic Development Organizations

East St. Louis Chamber of Commerce, Norman Ross, Manager, 411 E. Broadway Room. 1008, East St. Louis, IL 62201. 618-271-2855

Belleville Economic Progress, Inc., Scott M. Schanuel, Exec. Director, 334 W. Main St., PO Box 225, Belleville, IL 62222. 618-233-2015

Industrial Sites

Contact: Missouri Research Park, Scott C. Jenkins, Dir., PO

Box 28580, St. Louis, MO 63146. 314-991-4477

Major Businesses

Company	SIC	Telephone
Anheuser-Busch Inc.	2082	(314) 577-2000
Apex Holding Co.	6719	(314) 889-9600
Boatmen's Bancshares, Inc.	6022	(314) 425-7500
Brown Group, Inc.	5661	(314) 854-4000
Center Oil Co.	5172	(314) 993-3005
Clark Oil & Refining Corp.	2911	(314) 854-9696
Container Corp. America	2631	(314) 746-1100
Continental Baking Co.	2051	(314) 982-1000
Emerson Electric Co.	3621	(314) 553-2000
G. P. & W., Inc.	5172	(314) 993-3005
General American Life Insurance	6311	(314) 231-1700
General Dynamics Corp.	3721	(314) 889-8200
Graybar Electric Co., Inc.	5063	(314) 727-3900
Interco Inc.	2511	(314) 863-1100
ITT Financial Corp.	6141	(314) 821-6060
Jefferson Smurfit Corp.	2631	(314) 746-1100
Maritz Inc.	8748	(314) 827-4000
May Department Stores Co.	5311	(314) 342-6300
Mcdonnell Douglas Corp.	3721	(314) 232-0232
Missouri Pacific Railroad Co.	4011	(314) 992-2000
Monsanto Co.	2824	(314) 694-1000
O C Oil & Refining Corp.	6719	(314) 889-9600
Peabody Holding Co. Inc.	1221	(314) 342-3400
Pet Inc.	2032	(314) 621-5400
Ralston Purina Co.	2051	(314) 982-1000
Southwestern Bell Corp.	4813	(314) 235-9800
Union Electric Co.	4911	(314) 621-3222
Wetterau Inc.	5141	(314) 524-5000

Colleges and Universities

Basic Institute of Technology, St. Louis, MO
Belleville Area College, Belleville, IL
Deaconess College of Nursing, St. Louis, MO
Fontbonne College, St. Louis, MO
Harris-Stowe State College, St. Louis, MO
ITT Technical Institute, St. Louis, MO
Lindenwood College, St. Charles, MO
Maryville College-Saint Louis, St. Louis, MO
Missouri Baptist College, St. Louis, MO
St. Charles County Community College, St. Charles, MO
St. Louis College of Pharmacy, St. Louis, MO
St. Louis Community College at Florissant Valley, St. Louis, MO
St. Louis Community College at Forest Park, St. Louis, MO
St. Louis Rabbinical College, St. Louis, MO
St. Louis University, St. Louis, MO
State Community College of East St. Louis, East St. Louis, IL
University of Missouri-St. Louis, St. Louis, MO

SPRINGFIELD, MO (MSA)

Geographic Profile

Land Area

1238.2 square miles

Counties and Parishes

Christian
Greene

Ranking Highlights

158 *out of 319 in total* land area
 86 *out of 319 in* population growth, *1970–1990*
 34 *out of 310 in having the lowest* unemployment *rate*
150 *out of 310 in size of* labor force
146 *out of 318 in the percentage of* college graduates
180 *out of 292 in per capita personal* income
144 *out of 319 in number of* manufacturing establishments
104 *out of 318 in* physicians *per 1000 people*
  8 *out of 318 in* hospital beds *per 1000 people*
113 *out of 267 in fewest* crimes *per 1000 people*
 46 *out of 266 in fewest* violent crimes *per 1000 people*
248 *out of 319 in per capita* federal funds and grants

Quality of Life Indexes (Rate per 1000 population)

Crime rate in 1991:	57.5
Violent crime rate in 1991:	3.0
Physicians rate in 1992:	2.12
Hospital bed rate in 1991:	7.42

ACCRA Cost of Living Indexes

(First quarter 1993, average = 100)

Composite index:	95.4
Utilities index:	86.6
Housing index:	82.6

Overview

Springfield, seat of Greene County, is located in the southwest corner of Missouri in the tablelands of the Ozark Mountain Plateau. Springfield is located 220 miles southwest of St. Louis, 229 miles north of Little Rock, Arkansas, 176 miles northeast of Tulsa, Oklahoma, and 175 miles southeast of Kansas City, Missouri. The altitude is 1,300 feet above sea level.

The economy is diversified with about 25% of the jobs in services; 15% in manufacturing; 16% in retail trade; 8% in wholesale trade; 5% in transportation and public utilities; 4% in finance, insurance and real estate; and 3% in construction. Larger manufacturers in the area include Advanced Circuitry Division-Litton, Sweetheart Cup, FASCO, General Electric, Gospel Publishing House, Kraft, and Paul Mueller.

The U.S. Customs Service operates a Port-of-Entry in Springfield. Springfield is the third largest retail trade market in the state and is one of the top 170 U.S. markets.

Springfield is a regional agribusiness center. Southwest

Regional Stockyards serves as a marketing point for feeder and slaughter cattle. The stockyard is the sixth largest feeder cattle operation in the United States; sales are more than $100 million annually. The majority of area farms are small, averaging 176 acres.

Meetings, trade shows, and events account for approximately $30 million direct dollars each year. Springfield has more than 4,300 lodging rooms and more than 298,000 square feet of combined exhibit space.

Air transportation is provided from the Springfield Regional Airport by U.S. Air Express, United Airlines, American Eagle, Northwest Airlink, TW Express, and TWA. Air taxi, air ambulance, and air freight services are also available. Truck transportation is provided by 42 trucklines with 22 terminals.

Springfield is supplied with utilities through the facilities of the municipally-owned City Utilities of Springfield. City Utilities supplies services of electricity, natural gas, water and mass transit (bus system). Rates are competitive with or less than those of other parts of the nation.

Population (1990)

Total Population and Growth Rate
1990: 240,593
1980: 207,704
1970: 168,053
Growth rate 1970–1990: 43%

Race and Hispanic Origin
White: 96.9%
Black: 1.6%
Asian/Pacific Islander: 0.7%
Native American: 0.6%
Hispanic origin: 0.8%
White not Hispanic: 96.3%

Age
Ages 18 to 20: 6.8%
Ages 21 to 24: 7.2%
Ages 25 to 44: 31.1%
Ages 45 to 54: 8.7%
Ages 55 to 59: 4.1%
Ages 60 to 64: 4.1%
Ages 65 plus: 13%

Educational Attainment (1990)
Percent having completed high school: 78.5%
Percent having completed college: 19.6%
Elementary and high school enrollment: 37,575

Federal Funds and Grants Received
Total received in 1989: $578,400,000
Funds received per capita: $2,469

Civilian Labor Force
1993 (April): 137,724
1992 average: 137,812

1991 average: 133,729
1990 average: 129,249

Unemployment
1993 (April): 5.4%
1992 average: 4.6%
1991 average: 5.0%
1990 average: 4.4%

Average Annual Pay
1988: $17,278
1987: $16,954
1985: $16,053

Per Capita Personal Income
1991: $16,628
1990: $15,948
1989: $15,137

Business Climate (1987)

Manufacturing
Number of establishments in 1987: 378
Shipments in 1987 ($1,000): $2,951,900
Employees in 1987: 21,200
Change in employment, 1982 to 1987: 14.6%
Average annual pay for manufacturing work in 1989: $20,966
Average annual pay for production work in 1987: $17,453

Wholesale Trade
Number of establishments in 1987: 604
Total sales in 1987 ($1,000): $3,273,300
Change in sales, 1982 to 1987: 37.1%

Retail Trade
Number of establishments in 1987: 1,648
Total sales in 1987 ($1,000): $3,273,300
Retail sales per household in 1987: $19,568
Average annual pay in 1989: $10,902

Service Industry
Selected receipts in 1987 ($1,000): $638,000
Average annual pay in 1989: $16,850

Housing
Total number of units in 1990: 100,722
Occupied units in 1990: 93,400
Owner-occupied units in 1990: 65.4%
1993 ACCRA average cost: $93,267
1993 ACCRA average rent for an apartment: $424

Chamber of Commerce
Springfield Area Chamber of Commerce, James B. Anderson, Exec. Vice President, 320 N. Jefferson, PO Box 1687, Springfield, MO 65801. 417-862-5567

Economic Development Office
Springfield Area Economic Development, Matt Jarrett, Director, PO Box 1687, Springfield, MO 65801-1687. 417-862-5567

Economic Development Organizations

Department of Planning and Development, Fred May, Director, 830 Boonville Ave., Springfield, MO 65802. 417-864-1103

Major Businesses

Company	SIC	Telephone
American National Property & Casualty	6411	(417) 887-0220
Associated Electric Cooperative	4911	(417) 881-1204
Bass Pro Shops Inc.	5961	(417) 887-1915
Boatmens National Bank of Springfield	6021	(417) 836-6000
C. B. Management Co. Inc.	5074	(417) 865-8392
Commerce Bank Springfield	6021	(417) 869-5411
Consumers Markets, Inc.	5411	(417) 866-4305
Lester E. Cox Medical Center	8062	(417) 836-3000
Friendly Ford Inc.	5511	(417) 883-4330
Great Southern Savings and Loan Association	6036	(417) 887-4400
John Q. Hammons Co.	7011	(417) 864-4300
Hiland Dairy Co.	5143	(417) 862-9311
J. C. Jones & Co., Inc.	6531	(417) 885-8000
McQueary Bros. Drug Co.	5122	(417) 869-2577
Mid-America Dairymen, Inc.	2026	(417) 865-7100
Paul Mueller Co.	3443	(417) 831-3000
New Prime, Inc.	4213	(417) 866-0001
O'Reilly Automotive Inc.	5013	(417) 862-3333
Ozark Automotive Distributors	5013	(417) 862-6708
Ozark Grocer Co.	5141	(417) 866-0884
Peterbilt of Springfield	5012	(417) 865-5355
Reliable Chevrolet Inc.	5511	(417) 887-5800
Roswil Inc.	5411	(417) 883-2555
Smitty's Supermarket Inc.	5411	(417) 831-2622
Southwest By-Products, Inc.	5199	(417) 833-1214
Springfeld Lincoln-Mercury	5511	(417) 831-2641
Springfield Remanufacturing	3519	(417) 862-3501
St. Johns Regional Health Center	8062	(417) 885-2000
Thompson Sales Co.	5511	(417) 866-6611
Trailiner Corp.	4213	(417) 866-7258

Colleges and Universities

Berean College of the Assemblies of God, Springfield
Drury College, Springfield
Evangel College, Springfield
Phillips Junior College of Springfield, Springfield
Southwest Missouri State University, Springfield

MONTANA

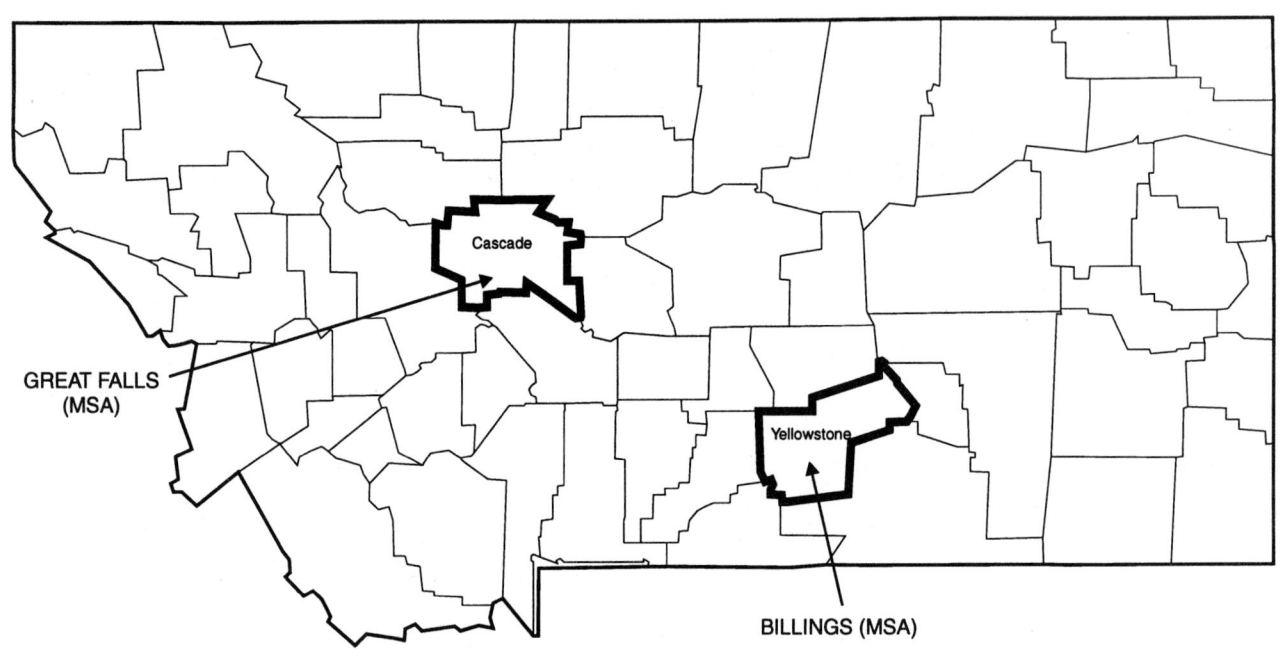

GREAT FALLS
(MSA)

Cascade

Yellowstone

BILLINGS (MSA)

MONTANA

Population
1990: 799,065
1980: 786,690

Age
Ages 18 to 20: 32,703
Ages 21 to 24: 37,308
Ages 25 to 44: 249,826
Ages 45 to 54: 82,306
Ages 55 to 59: 34,005
Ages 60 to 64: 34,316
Median age: 33.8

Race and Hispanic Origin
White: 741,111
Black: 2,381
Asian/Pacific Islander: 4,259
Native American: 47,679
Hispanic origin: 12,174

Households
Total: 306,163
Persons per household: 2.53

Sex
Male: 395,769
Female: 403,296

Population Migration
Domestic migration: -66,000
International migration: 4,000

Projection of the Population in 1995
Total: 815,000
18 to 64: 485,000

Civilian Labor Force
1993: 402,900
1992: 411,500
1991: 402,200
1990: 401,200

Manufacturing
1995 Projection: 25,000
1992: 22,600
1991: 22,800
1990: 22,700
1989: 22,500

Services
1995 Projection: 118,800

1992: 81,700
1991: 77,300
1990: 76,300
1989: 73,300

Wholesale and Retail Trade
1995 Projection: 93,500
1992: 85,300
1991: 80,100
1990: 79,600
1989: 80,000

Unemployment Rate
1993: 8.2%
1992: 9.2%
1991: 6.6%
1990: 5.9%

Employer Unemployment Contributions
Contribution Rate
1992: 1.20%
1991: 1.00%
1990: 1.30%

Average Weekly Benefit
1992: $151.06
1991: $143.65
1990: $137.38

Gross State Product (Million $)
1989: $13,104
1988: $12,178
1987: $11,771
1979: $8,554
Growth rate, 1979 to 1989: 53.2%

Capital Expenditures of Manufacturing Industries
1990: $111,000,000
1989: $119,600,000
1988: $67,900,000
1987: $97,000,000

State Taxe Rates
Individual income: Range from 2% ($1,600 or less) to 11% (above $55,000).
Corporate income: 6.8% of taxable net income, with a 5% surtax imposed.

General property: Sum of state and local rates. Assessed at market value of real and personal property.

General sales: None

Gasoline: 20.5¢ per gallon

Income

Median income for a 4 person family: $33,882

Personal per Capita Income

1992: $16,062

1991: $15,680

1990: $14,663

Disposable per Capita Income

1992: $14,064

1991: $13,736

1990: $12,747

Private Employment Weekly Wages

Average

1989: $317

1988: $310

1987: $310

Manufacturing

1989: $300

1988: $425

1987: $414

Services

1989: $281

1988: $276

1987: $267

Wholesale

1989: $405

1988: $392

1987: $381

Retail

1989: $197

1988: $190

1987: $182

Highway Statistics

Total Highway Miles

1990: 71,387

1989: 71,360

1988: 71,471

Federal Highway Aid

1991: $105,520,000

1990: $105,487,000

1989: $107,545,000

Electricity

Average Cost per Kilowatt Hour

1990: 3.96¢

1989: 4.09¢

1988: 4.20¢

Housing (1990)

Owner occupied units: 205,899

Median house value: $56,600

Renter occupied units: 100,264

Median rent: $251

Total vacant units: 54,992

Homeowner vacancy rate: 2.9%

Rental vacancy rate: 9.6%

State Business Incentives and Assistance

Financial and Business Assistance

SBDC Business Information System. An electronic bulletin board. Posts economic, demographic and business data, including state government bid solicitations, export trade opportunity leads from the U.S. Department of Commerce, and population, income and employment statistics for Montana cities and counties. Data Line: 406-444-4457; Voice Line: 406-444-2463.

Community Development Block Grant. This federally-funded grant program awards approximately $1.3 million annually to Montana cities, towns and counties, for relending by the local government to private business projects. applications are made to the Business Development Division by the local government sponsoring the project. Projects are selected for funding based on a number of criteria, including project feasibility, economic impact, and job creation for low to moderate income persons. For more information, contact Gary Morehouse, 406-444-3923.

Finance Technical Assistance. Individual consulting and group training are available to businesses in the areas of financial analysis, financial planning, loan packaging, state and private capital sources, and business tax incentives. For more information, contact Delrene Rasmussen, 406-444-3923.

International Trade. This program works to increase export sales and inward foreign investment for Montana. Trade shows and foreign buyers are matched to exporters, and special training programs are conducted to prepare more firms for export activity.

Location and Business Recruitment. This program initiates and develops relations with target industries and individual firms, and prepares and presents location data in response to inquiries received by the department. For more information, contact Rick Jones, 406-444-3923.

Montana Ambassadors. This is a membership organization, made up of approximately 200 business and university leaders from throughout the state. Members assist the Division in business recruitment projects, work with Montana manufacturers to help them market their products outside the state, and host foreign visitors and trade delegations. For more information, contact Becky Baumann, 406-444-4109.

Montana Board of Investments. The Board may purchase

debt or equity investments at market rates. The Board purchases qualified Montana Mortgages, buys the guaranteed portion of SBA loans and FmHA loans from Montana financial institutions.

Development Finance Programs. Administered by the Board of Investments, these programs are designed to help small businesses obtain capital financing. Each program operates with different eligibility criteria under state or federal law. The primary focus of all programs is to increase availability of long-term, fixed rate financing to small Montana businesses.

Coal Tax Loan Programs. The coal tax loans are administered by the Board of Investments. The program will invest in loans to businesses that will strengthen the Montana economy, that have the potential to maintain and create jobs, or that increase per capita income or future tax revenues to the people of Montana, either directly or indirectly. Loans of $500,000 to $3 million are being targeted.

Economic Development Linked Deposit Program. Through this program, the Board of Investment will place a long-term deposit with an approved financial institution on the condition that the financial institution use the proceeds of the deposit to finance a corresponding fixed-rate loan to a specific borrower that is eligible for BOI investments. These funds may be used by financial institutions to make loans for working capital, interim construction, inventory, site development, acquisition of machinery, equipment and buildings.

Business Loan Participation Program. This program is designed to allow approved Montana financial institutions to sell up to 80% of an eligible business loan to the Board of Investments. Funds will be targeted to long-term fixed-rate loans that have the potential to benefit economic development within the state.

SBA 504 Loan Participation Program. The Board of Investments may fund a portion of a project financed under the SBA 504 Program by purchasing from an originating lender up to 80% of the lender's first mortgage loan amount. All terms and rates are the same as under the Business Loan Participation Program.

Industrial Development Bond Programs. A borrower who can assume responsibility for funding its projects can have the Board of Investments issue Industrial Development Bonds under the Stand-Alone program. A borrower can accomplish funding by: direct access to the bond market through the market's recognition of financial strength of the borrower, a bank letter of credit which the bond market recognizes and accepts, or a tax-exempt loan through a bank. The Board serves as the legal issuer of the bonds and assumes no responsibility for funding the loan.

Montana Capital Companies. The Board of Investments also administers the Montana Capital Company Act, which is designated to make private venture or equity capital available within the state. Through the program, the state offers a 50% tax credit incentives (up to $150,000) to investors in qualified Montana Capital Companies, which in turn must invest these funds in small, basic Montana firms.

Advanced Technology, Inc. It is a wholly owned corporate subsidiary of the Montana State University Foundation. It was incorporated for the specific purpose of owning, managing and developing the Advanced Technology Park in Bozeman, Montana. The park is a 90-acre development, adjacent to the Montana State University campus, which makes land and other amenities available for companies engaged in high technology research, development and light manufacturing.

University Technical Assistance Program. At Montana State University, it was created to provide technical engineering and managerial assistance to those manufacturing companies in Montana that are not in a position to hire professional consultants. This program helps Montana through the transfer of technology to eligible companies.

The 49th Parallel Institute. Established by Montana State University, the Institute provides liaison between the Governor, the Montana-Western Canadian Provinces Boundary Advisory Committee, and officials of the Canadian federal and provincial governments. The purpose of the Institute is to improve U.S.-Canadian relations in the West.

Montana Science and Technology Alliance. The Alliance's purpose is to provide a source of financing for technology-based, entrepreneurial development to revitalize Montana industries and encourage new ones. It operates two financing programs: the Seed Capital Financing Program and the Research and Development Financing Program.

Property Tax Incentives. Include: 1) property assessment reductions for new or expanding industries and for certain remodeling projects; 2) property tax rate for pollution control equipment and for qualified new industries and research and development firms; and 3) property tax exemptions for business inventories and freeport merchandise.

General Individual Income and Corporation License Tax Incentives. Include: 1) a wage credit for new or expanding manufacturing corporations producing a product new to Montana; 2) a five-year exemption from taxation for research and development firms organized to engage in business in Montana for the first time; 3) exemptions for domestic international sales corporations and for investments in small business investment companies; and 4) a credit for investing in Montana capital company.

Natural resource related tax incentives include: 1) a phase-down of coal severance tax rates; 2) a reduced severance tax rate on new coal production for buyers of coal who have not previously purchased from Montana producers; 3) a 12-month net proceeds tax exemption and a 24-month severance tax exemption for new oil and gas production; 4) reduced severance tax rates for oil and natural gas strip-

Major Companies in the State

Company name	Fortune 500 rank	City	Telephone	SIC number
Fortune 500 Companies				
None				
Other Major Companies in the State				
Big Sky Transportation Co.		Billings	406-245-9449	4512
Buttrey Food & Drug Stores Co.		Great Falls	406-761-3401	5411
Diversified Realty Inc.		Great Falls	406-727-2600	6512
First Federal Savings Bank of Montana		Kalispell	406-752-7101	6035
Glacier Bancorp Inc.		Kalispell	406-756-4200	6712
GNI Inc. Montana		Great Falls	406-727-2600	6361
Great Falls Gas Co.		Great Falls	406-791-7500	4923
Montana Corp.		Great Falls	406-727-2600	6361
Montana Naturals International Inc.		Arlee	406-726-3214	2099
Montana Power Co.		Butte	406-723-5421	4931
MSR Exploration Ltd.		Cut Bank	406-873-2235	1311
Ribi Immunochem Research Inc.		Hamilton	406-363-6214	2834
Security Federal Savings Bank Montana		Billings	406-259-4571	6035
TSI Inc. Montana		Great Falls	406-727-2600	6541
UAC Inc.		Great Falls	406-727-2600	7389
United Savings Bank		Great Falls	406-761-2200	6035
United States Antimony Corp.		Thompson Falls	406-827-3523	1099
Video Lottery Technologies Inc.		Bozeman	406-586-4423	3575
Winter Sports Inc.		Whitefish	406-862-3511	7011

per well production; and 5) a severance tax rate reduction for oil production from a tertiary project.

Other Tax Incentives. Include: 1) an individual income or corporation license tax credit for investing in wind powered electrical generating equipment; 2) an individual income or corporation license tax credit for sellers of land to beginning farmers at less than 9% interest; and 3) an individual income or corporation license tax deduction for expenditures on organic fertilizer produced and used in Montana.

Education and Training

Business Start-up Training Program. Administered by the Department of Labor and Industry, it provides job training for employees of new or expanding Montana businesses. The program assists employers in recruiting and worker pre-employment skills training.

Job Training Partnership Act. This program operates with funding from the U.S. Department of Labor. It provides job training and other employment related services.

State Offices

Real estate: Commerce Department, Business Regulation Division, W. James Kembell, 1424 9th Ave., Helena, MT 59620. 406-444-3737

Chamber of commerce: Montana State Chamber of Commerce, F.H. Boles, President, PO Box 1730, 2030 11th Ave., Helena, MT 59624. 406-442-2405, FAX 406-442-2406

Economic development: Department of Commerce, Business Development Division, Evan McKinney, Deputy Administrator, 1424 9th Ave., Helena, MT 59620-0535. 406-444-4374, FAX 406-444-2808

Department of Commerce, Business Development Division, Business Recruitment Office, Rick Jones, Business Recruitment Officer, 1424 9th Ave., Helena, MT 59620-0535. 406-444-4323, FAX 406-444-2808

Department of Commerce, Business Development Division, International Trade Office, Matthew Cohn, Trade Office Director, 1424 9th Ave., Helena, MT 59620-0535. 406-444-3923, FAX 406-444-2808

Department of Commerce, Board of Investments, James R. Penner, Investment Officer, Capitol Station, Helena, MT 59620-0125. 406-442-1970, FAX 406-449-6579

Department of Commerce, Community Development Bureau, Dave Cole, Bureau Chief, Rm c-211, Cogswell Bldg., Helena, MT 59620. 406-444-3757

Department of Commerce, Local Government Assistant Division, Local Government Services Bureau, Donald L. Dooley, Bureau Chief, 1424 9th Ave., Helena, MT 59620-0535. 406-444-3010

Small Business Development Center, Evan McKinney, State

Director, Department of Commerce, 1424 9th Fl., Helena, MT 59620. 406-444-3923

Montana Science and Technology Alliance, Carl Russell, Exec Director, 46 North Last Chance Gulch, Suite 2B, Helena, MT 59620. 406-449-2778

Advanced Technology, Inc., Roger N. Flair, President, 1711 West College, Bozeman, MT 59715. 406-587-4480

University Technical Assistance Program, William R. Taylor, Director, 402 Roberts Hall, Montana State University, Bozeman, MT 59717. 406-994-3812

49th Parallel Institute, Mary Ellen Wolfe, Research Associate, 1-156 Wilson Hall, Montana State University, Bozeman, MT 59717. 406-994-6689

Environmental affairs: Dept. of Natural Resources and Conservation, Karen Barclay, Director, 1520 East Sixth Ave., Helena, MT 59620. 406-444-6699

Labor: Dept. of Labor and Industry, Mike Micone, Commissioner, Lockey and Roberts Streets, Helena, MT 59620. 406-444-3555

Unemployment: Dept. of Labor and Industry, Unemployment Insurance Div., Bob Jensen, Administrator, Lockey and Roberts Streets, Helena, MT 59620. 406-444-2723

Worker's compensation: Dept. of Labor and Industry, Employment Relations Div., Chuck Hunter, Administrator, Lockey and Roberts Streets, Helena, MT 59620. 406-444-1389,

Occupational safety and health: Dept. of Labor and Industry, Research, Safety & Training Div., Bob Anderson, Administrator, Lockey and Roberts Streets, Helena, MT 59620. 406-444-4524

Secretary of state: Secretary of State Office, Mike Cooney, Secretary of State, Rm. 225, State Capitol, Helena, MT 59620. 406-444-2034

Taxation and revenue: Dept. of Revenue, Denis L. Adams, Director, Rm. 455, Sam W. Mitchell Bldg., Helena, MT 59620. 406-444-2460

Designated Zones for Economic Development
Enterprise Zones
No program.

Foreign Trade Zones
Great Falls Foreign Trade Zone. Located at the Great Falls International Airport near the Montana-Canadian border, the Great Falls Foreign Trade Zone offers special import/export, manufacturing and warehousing benefits to businesses requiring these services. Contact: Great Falls Foreign Trade Zone #88, PO Box 3324, Great Falls, MT 59403. 406-761-5037

Universities with Ph.D. Programs
Montana State University, Bozeman
University of Montana, Missoula

Sources of Additional Information
A Guide to Montana's Economic Devlopment and Business Development Programs. Montana Dept. of Commerce, Business Development Division, January 1991. 35p.

The Sky's the Limit, Montana. Montana Dept. of Commerce, Business Development Division, n.d. [Packet]

BILLINGS, MT (MSA)

Geographic Profile

Land Area
2635.2 square miles

Counties and Parishes
Yellowstone

Ranking Highlights

  62 *out of 319 in total* **land area**
131 *out of 319 in* **population growth,** *1970–1990*
  69 *out of 310 in having the lowest* **unemployment** *rate*
241 *out of 310 in size of* **labor force**
105 *out of 318 in the percentage of* **college graduates**
138 *out of 292 in per capita personal* **income**
248 *out of 319 in number of* **manufacturing establishments**
  74 *out of 318 in* **physicians** *per 1000 people*
  84 *out of 318 in* **hospital beds** *per 1000 people*
  15 *out of 267 in fewest* **crimes** *per 1000 people*
   2 *out of 266 in fewest* **violent crimes** *per 1000 people*
224 *out of 319 in per capita* **federal funds and grants**

Quality of Life Indexes (Rate per 1000 population)

Crime rate in 1991:	34.0
Violent crime rate in 1991:	0.8
Physicians rate in 1992:	2.43
Hospital bed rate in 1991:	4.88

ACCRA Cost of Living Indexes

(First quarter 1993, average = 100)

Composite index:	104.7
Utilities index:	77.8
Housing index:	116.8

Overview

Billings is the largest city in Montana and the commercial, cultural, and industrial center of a large region of the northern Rocky Mountains. Many scenic attractions such as Yellowstone National Park are nearby, and the wide variety of available recreation activities make the Billings area a popular vacation spot.

Agriculture has been one of the leading economic forces in Billings since its founding, and it continues to play a major role today. The Yellowstone Valley and the northern Great Plains are some of the nation's most fertile areas, due to extensive irrigation. The city is the transportation, processing, and packaging center for this large, productive area. The main agricultural products include sugar beets, grain, and livestock such as cattle and sheep.

The energy industry is also an important part of the economic picture in Billings. The mountains around the city and throughout eastern Montana are a rich source of coal, oil, and natural gas. A number of refineries and purification plants are located in the Billings area to process the raw materials into usable energy resources.

Billings Logan International Airport is only two miles from the downtown district and serves most of eastern Montana and northern Wyoming with approximately forty flights daily from five major airlines. Billings is at the junction of two interstate highways: I-90, connecting the city with the Pacific Northwest and the southern Rocky Mountain states; and I-94, providing a link with the midwestern states. U.S. 87, 310, and 212 also meet in Billings.

Population (1990)

Total Population and Growth Rate
1990: 113,419
1980: 108,035
1970: 87,367
Growth rate 1970–1990: 30%

Race and Hispanic Origin
White: 95.2%
Black: .5%
Asian/Pacific Islander: 0.5%
Native American: 2.9%
Hispanic origin: 2.8%
White not Hispanic: 93.5%

Age
Ages 18 to 20: 4.1%
Ages 21 to 24: 4.8%
Ages 25 to 44: 32.7%
Ages 45 to 54: 10.3%
Ages 55 to 59: 4.3%
Ages 60 to 64: 4.3%
Ages 65 plus: 12.3%

Educational Attainment (1990)

Percent having completed high school: 83.7%
Percent having completed college: 21.5%
Elementary and high school enrollment: 20,665

Federal Funds and Grants Received

Total received in 1989: $303,700,000
Funds received per capita: $2,608

Civilian Labor Force

1993 (April):   68,071
1992 average: 66,711
1991 average: 64,565
1990 average: 64,368

Unemployment

1993 (April):   4.2%
1992 average: 5.4%
1991 average: 5.3%
1990 average: 4.8%

Average Annual Pay

1988: $18,020
1987: $17,750
1985: $17,295

Per Capita Personal Income

1991: $17,608
1990: $16,574
1989: $15,768

Business Climate (1987)

Manufacturing

Number of establishments in 1987: 147
Shipments in 1987 ($1,000): $1,109,600
Employees in 1987: 3,000
Change in employment, 1982 to 1987: -25.0%
Average annual pay for manufacturing work in 1989: $24,183
Average annual pay for production work in 1987: $22,611

Wholesale Trade

Number of establishments in 1987: 391
Total sales in 1987 ($1,000): $1,393,700
Change in sales, 1982 to 1987: -20.5%

Retail Trade

Number of establishments in 1987: 932
Total sales in 1987 ($1,000): $1,393,700
Retail sales per household in 1987: $18,731
Average annual pay in 1989: $10,858

Service Industry

Selected receipts in 1987 ($1,000): $351,000
Average annual pay in 1989: $17,137

Housing

Total number of units in 1990: 48,781
Occupied units in 1990: 44,689
Owner-occupied units in 1990: 65.7%
1993 ACCRA average cost: $146,000
1993 ACCRA average rent for an apartment: $369

Chamber of Commerce

Billings Area Chamber of Commerce-Business Development Council, Elbert Ott, President, PO Box 31177, Billings, MT 59107. 406-245-4111, FAX 406-245-7333

Economic Development Office

Billings Business Development Council, Jeanne Moller, Director, PO Box 31177, Billings, MT 59107. 406-245-4111, FAX 406-245-7333

Economic Development Organizations

Forward Billings Economic Development Council, E. Butch Ott, Exec Director, PO Box 31177, Billings, MT 59107. 406-248-7979

Treasure State Capital, Conrad Stroebe, Exec. Director, PO Box 194, Billings, MT 59103. 406-248-5678

Major Businesses

Company	SIC	Telephone
Arnlund Automotive, Inc.	5511	(406) 652-1430
Automotive & Industrial Distributors	5172	(406) 245-6443

Major Businesses (Continued)

Company	SIC	Telephone
Beall Trailers of Montana	3443	(406) 252-7163
Billings Grain Terminal	5153	(406) 245-7575
Billings Toyota Inc.	5511	(406) 245-7141
Billings Truck Center	5012	(406) 252-5121
Citizens Development Inc.	6712	(406) 252-5631
Coca-Cola Bottling Co.	2086	(406) 245-6211
Corporate Air	4522	(406) 248-1541
Deaconess Care Corp.	8062	(406) 657-4685
Deaconess Medical Center of Billings	8062	(406) 657-4000
Dyce Chemical, Inc.	5169	(406) 248-3131
Empire Sand & Gravel Co.	1611	(406) 252-8465
First Bank Montana	6021	(406) 657-8000
First Interstate Bancsystem	6021	(406) 255-5300
Fisher Construction Inc.	1542	(406) 259-2854
Frontier Chevrolet Co.	5511	(406) 259-5575
Kampgrounds of America, Inc.	7033	(406) 248-7444
Midland Dodge Inc.	5511	(406) 652-2200
Midland Implement Co.	5083	(406) 248-7771
Mountain States Petroleum	5541	(406) 252-3999
Northwest Pipe Fittings Inc.	5074	(406) 252-0142
Northwest Truck & Trailer	5012	(406) 252-5667
Norwest Bank Billings	6021	(406) 657-3400
Saint Vincent Hospital Health Ctr.	8062	(406) 657-7000
Scheels Hardware & Sport	5699	(406) 656-8962
Sector Corp.	3443	(406) 252-7163
Stockton Oil Co.	5171	(406) 245-6376
Tri-State Equipment, Inc.	5082	(406) 245-3188
United Tote, Inc.	3575	(406) 373-5507
Valley Motor Supply Co.	5013	(406) 259-4577
Waggoners Trucking	4213	(406) 248-1919
Westmoreland Resources Inc.	1222	(406) 248-7803

Colleges and Universities

Eastern Montana College, Billings
Rocky Mountain College, Billings

GREAT FALLS, MT (MSA)

Geographic Profile

Land Area

2698.0 square miles

Counties and Parishes

Cascade

Ranking Highlights

59 *out of 319 in total* land area

296 *out of 319 in* population growth, *1970–1990*

104 *out of 310 in having the lowest* unemployment *rate*

304 *out of 310 in size of* labor force

169 *out of 318 in the percentage of* college graduates

154 *out of 292 in per capita personal* income

312 *out of 319 in number of* manufacturing establishments

109 *out of 318 in* physicians *per 1000 people*

7 *out of 318 in* hospital beds *per 1000 people*

212 *out of 267 in fewest* crimes *per 1000 people*

24 *out of 266 in fewest* violent crimes *per 1000 people*

18 *out of 319 in per capita* federal funds and grants

Quality of Life Indexes (Rate per 1000 population)

Crime rate in 1991:	74.5
Violent crime rate in 1991:	2.2
Physicians rate in 1992:	2.07
Hospital bed rate in 1991:	7.57

ACCRA Cost of Living Indexes

(First quarter 1993, average = 100)

Composite index:	95.6
Utilities index:	87.8
Housing index:	83.4

Population (1990)

Total Population and Growth Rate

1990: 77,691

1980: 80,696

1970: 81,804

Growth rate 1970–1990: -5%

Race and Hispanic Origin

White: 93.1%

Black: 1.4%

Asian/Pacific Islander: 1.0%

Native American: 4.0%

Hispanic origin: 1.8%

White not Hispanic: 92.1%

Age

Ages 18 to 20: 3.8%

Ages 21 to 24: 5.3%

Ages 25 to 44: 31.6%

Ages 45 to 54: 10.3%

Ages 55 to 59: 4.4%

Ages 60 to 64: 4.2%

Ages 65 plus: 12.7%

Educational Attainment (1990)

Percent having completed high school: 82.9%

Percent having completed college: 18.4%

Elementary and high school enrollment: 13,880

Federal Funds and Grants Received

Total received in 1989: $528,400,000

Funds received per capita: $6,758

Civilian Labor Force

1993 (April):	39,572
1992 average:	40,085
1991 average:	39,127
1990 average:	39,194

Unemployment

1993 (April): 5.6%

1992 average: 6.1%

1991 average: 5.8%

1990 average: 5.0%

Average Annual Pay

1988: $17,083

1987: $16,571

1985: $16,261

Per Capita Personal Income

1991: $17,104

1990: $16,170

1989: $15,567

Business Climate (1987)

Manufacturing

Number of establishments in 1987: 60

Shipments in 1987 ($1,000): $137,600

Employees in 1987: 1,000

Change in employment, 1982 to 1987: -16.7%

Average annual pay for manufacturing work in 1989: $20,615

Average annual pay for production work in 1987: $17,667

Wholesale Trade

Number of establishments in 1987: 203

Total sales in 1987 ($1,000): $690,100

Change in sales, 1982 to 1987: -8.7%

Retail Trade

Number of establishments in 1987: 599

Total sales in 1987 ($1,000): $690,100

Retail sales per household in 1987: $16,396

Average annual pay in 1989: $11,415

Service Industry

Selected receipts in 1987 ($1,000): $167,800

Average annual pay in 1989: $16,197

Housing

Total number of units in 1990: 33,063

Occupied units in 1990: 30,133
Owner-occupied units in 1990: 63.7%
1993 ACCRA average cost: $98,900
1993 ACCRA average rent for an apartment: $351

Chamber of Commerce

Great Falls Area Chamber of Commerce, C. Dennis Anderson, President, PO Box 2127, 926 Central Ave., Great Falls, MT 59403. 406-761-4434

Economic Development Office

Great Falls Capital Corp., Don Fairchild, Exec. Director, 9 3rd St. N. Suite 305, Great Falls, MT 59401. 406-761-7978

Major Businesses

Company	SIC	Telephone
Americana Expressways, Inc.	4213	(406) 761-5454
Anderson Steel Supply Inc.	3441	(406) 761-4354
Dadco Inc.	6211	(406) 727-4200
D. A. Davidson & Co.	6211	(406) 727-4200
Farmers Union Oil Co. of Great Falls	5261	(406) 453-2436
First National Bank of Great Falls	6021	(406) 761-7200
Great Falls Gas Co.	4924	(406) 761-7100
Montana Deaconess Medical Center	8062	(406) 761-1200
Morgen & Oswood Construction Co.	1542	(406) 761-1420
Pacific Hide & Fur Depot	5051	(406) 727-6222
Pennington's Inc.	5194	(406) 453-7628
Pierce Dodge City, Inc.	5511	(406) 761-3305
Poulsen's, Inc.	5211	(406) 761-0601
Rice Motors	5511	(406) 727-9200
Sisters of Charity	8062	(406) 727-3333
Sletten Construction Co.	1541	(406) 761-7920
Transport Leasing Co.	7513	(406) 727-7500
Transystems, Inc.	4213	(406) 727-7500
Carl Weissman & Sons Inc.	5072	(406) 761-4848

Colleges and Universities

College of Great Falls, Great Falls

NEBRASKA

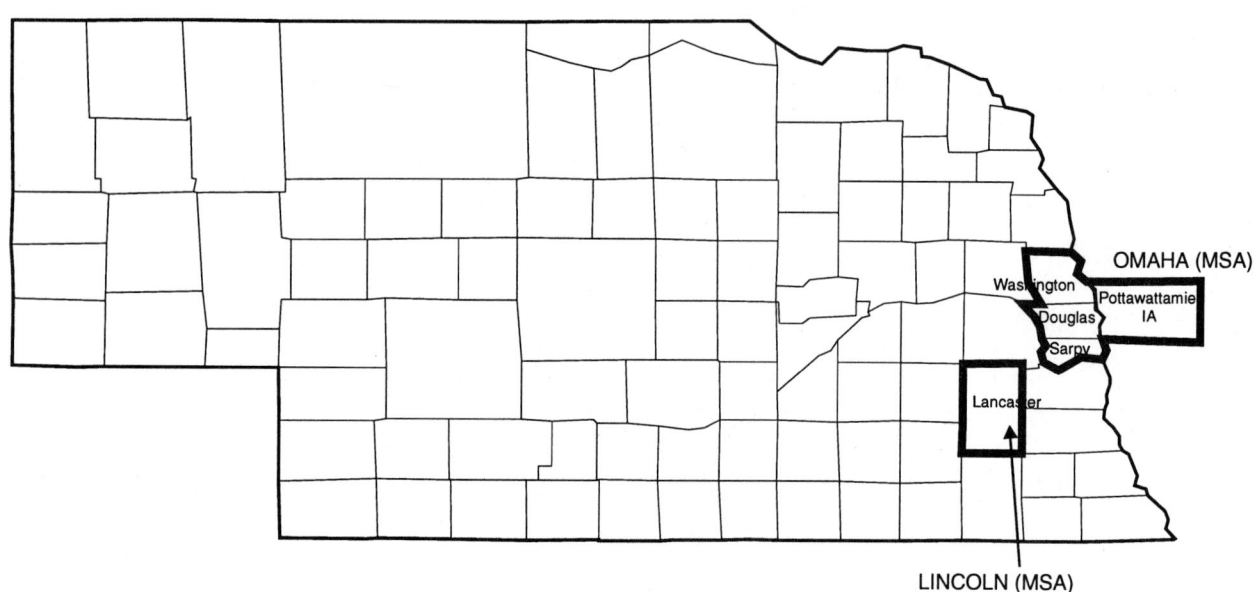

OMAHA (MSA)

Washington

Pottawattamie
IA

Douglas

Sarpy

Lancaster

LINCOLN (MSA)

NEBRASKA

Population
1990: 1,578,385
1980: 1,569,825

Age
Ages 18 to 20: 70,495
Ages 21 to 24: 85,392
Ages 25 to 44: 486,020
Ages 45 to 54: 149,389
Ages 55 to 59: 67,281
Ages 60 to 64: 67,728
Median age: 33.0

Race and Hispanic Origin
White: 1,480,558
Black: 57,404
Asian/Pacific Islander: 12,422
Native American: 12,410
Hispanic origin: 36,969

Households
Total: 602,363
Persons per household: 2.54

Sex
Male: 769,439
Female: 808,946

Population Migration
Domestic migration: -107,000
International migration: 9,000

Projection of the Population in 1995
Total: 1,657,000
18 to 64: 993,000

Civilian Labor Force
1993: 835,200
1992: 847,800
1991: 857,800
1990: 824,000

Manufacturing
1995 Projection: 104,300
1992: 100,400
1991: 103,900
1990: 101,100
1989: 96,100

Services
1995 Projection: 256,400

1992: 185,300
1991: 196,800
1990: 185,300
1989: 169,000

Wholesale and Retail Trade
1995 Projection: 219,700
1992: 188,500
1991: 197,100
1990: 192,100
1989: 188,200

Unemployment Rate
1993: 3.2%
1992: 3.5%
1991: 2.3%
1990: 2.9%

Employer Unemployment Contributions
Contribution Rate
1992: 1.24%
1991: 0.90%
1990: 1.05%

Average Weekly Benefit
1992: $139.31
1991: $137.76
1990: $120.22

Gross State Product (Million $)
1989: $31,115
1988: $28,518
1987: $26,611
1979: $17,366
Growth rate, 1979 to 1989: 79.2%

Capital Expenditures of Manufacturing Industries
1990: $413,900,000
1989: $388,000,000
1988: $366,000,000
1987: $317,900,000

State Tax Rates
Individual income: Range from 2.37% ($3,000 or less) to 6.92% (above $45,000).
Corporate income: Range from 5.6% ($50,000 or less) to 7.81% (above $50,000).

General property: Sum of local rates, valued at its actual value.

General sales: 5%

Gasoline: 23.4¢ per gallon

Income

Median income for a 4 person family: $37,902

Personal per Capita Income

1992: $19,084

1991: $17,780

1990: $17,276

Disposable per Capita Income

1992: $16,992

1991: $15,707

1990: $15,241

Private Employment Weekly Wages

Average

1989: $332

1988: $325

1987: $325

Manufacturing

1989: $310

1988: $417

1987: $400

Services

1989: $302

1988: $288

1987: $273

Wholesale

1989: $415

1988: $410

1987: $391

Retail

1989: $186

1988: $181

1987: $175

Highway Statistics

Total Highway Miles

1990: 92,403

1989: 92,459

1988: 92,495

Federal Highway Aid

1991: $95,533,000

1990: $94,487,000

1989: $97,148,000

Electricity

Average Cost per Kilowatt Hour

1990: 5.55¢

1989: 5.53¢

1988: 5.30¢

Housing (1990)

Owner occupied units: 400,394

Median house value: $50,400

Renter occupied units: 201,969

Median rent: $282

Total vacant units: 58,258

Homeowner vacancy rate: 1.7%

Rental vacancy rate: 7.7%

State Business Incentives and Assistance

Financial and Business Assistance

Nebraska Investment Finance Authority. Administered by a nine-member board appointed by the governor, the Authority was established to encourage economic and industrial development through the investment of private capital within the state. Industrial development bonds may be issued to finance eligible businesses including manufacturing or industrial enterprises involving assembling, fabricating, mixing, processing, warehousing, distributing, or transporting products; pollution control facilities; and industrial sites facilities.

Nebraska Research and Development Authority. Created by the state legislature, the Authority is designed to foster innovation in existing value-added industry, to develop new value-added industry, and to create and maintain employment in the state. The Authority is authorized to finance applied research at educational institutions, public institutions, and private enterprises. It also provides seed capital financing for existing and emerging industries. The Authority is authorized to issue bonds and can invest in projects by taking an equity position or royalty in the business created.

Nebraska Economic Development Corporation. A publicly owned and financed organization, the Corporation is funded by its membership of banks, insurance companies, and savings and loan associations and by the sale of stock to the public. This program is designed to create new jobs for the state. It provides long-term capital loans to businesses unable to secure conventional financing. The loan terms ranged from five to 15 years with interest rates about 3% above prime rate. The funds may be used for plant construction, equipment and materials, working capital, new product development, and refinancing existing debt.

Industry Recruitment Assistance. Administered by the Business Recruitment Division of the Department of Economic Development, this program provides technical assistance to communities that have undertaken a project and resource commitment to pursue industry recruitment from outside the state. Assistance includes advice on all phases of recruitment.

Nebraska Technical Assistance Center. Administered jointly by the Nebraska Department of Economic Development and the University of Nebraska-Lincoln, this program pro-

Major Companies in the State

Company name	Fortune 500 rank	City	Telephone	SIC number
Fortune 500 Companies				
AG Processing Inc.	325	Omaha	402-496-7809	2075
Berkshire Hathaway Inc.	158	Omaha	402-346-1400	6331
Conagra Inc.	17	Omaha	402-595-4000	2038
IBP Inc.	42	Dakota City	402-494-2061	2011
Other Major Companies in the State				
American Business Information Inc.		Omaha	402-593-4500	7331
California Energy Company Inc.		Omaha	402-330-8900	4911
Commercial Federal Corp.		Omaha	402-554-9200	6712
Conservative Savings Corp.		Omaha	402-334-8475	6712
Data Transmission Network Corp.		Omaha	402-390-2328	7375
First Commerce Bancshares Inc.		Lincoln	402-472-4110	6712
First National of Nebraska Inc.		Omaha	402-341-0500	6712
Firstier Financial Inc.		Omaha	402-348-6000	6712
Gibraltar Packaging Group Inc.		Hastings	402-463-1366	2657
IBP Inc.		Dakota City	402-494-2061	2011
ISCO Inc.		Lincoln	402-464-0231	3821
Lincoln Telecommunications Co.		Lincoln	402-476-5289	4813
Lindsay Manufacturing Co.		Lindsay	402-428-2131	3523
Mall Corp.		Lincoln	402-474-6093	5812
Missouri Pacific Railroad Co.		Omaha	402-271-5000	4011
Northwestern Bell Telephone Co.		Omaha	303-896-3099	4813
Pamida Holdings Corp.		Omaha	402-339-2400	5311
Terrano Corp.		Lincoln	402-483-7831	7373
Valcom Inc.		Omaha	402-392-3900	5734
Werner Enterprises Inc.		Omaha	402-895-6640	4213

vides businesses with technical assistance on engineering and manufacturing processes.

Agriculture Promotion and Development. Administered by the Department of Agriculture, this program assists companies by helping market existing agricultural products by providing information and direction for new agricultural products and by assisting in channeling resources from federal and national marketing associations.

Employment and Investment Growth Act. Administered by the Department of Revenue, this program provides state tax credits which could substantially reduce a company's tax liability. With major investments in employees and property, a company could reduce corporate income tax, sales and use taxes. Credits may be used to reduce corporate income tax or obtain a refund of sales taxes paid on purchases for use at the project. Businesses are eligible for credits for a seven-year period and accumulated credits may be used over a 15-year period.

Employment Expansion and Investment Incentive Act. Administered by the Department of Revenue, this program provides state tax credits for qualifying new and expand-

ing businesses which increase investments by at least $750,000 and increase net employment by an average of two full-time positions during a taxable year. Credits may be used to reduce a portion of the taxpayer's income tax liability or to obtain a refund of sales and use taxes paid.

Education and Training

Nebraska Job Training Program. Administered by the Department of Economic Development, this program is cosponsored by the Department of Labor. The program is jointly funded by the state, the Job Training Partnership Act program, and Community Development Block Grants. It offers pre-employment worker training for new and expanding businesses. Instructors may be the company's own employees or outside instructors selected by the state.

Job Training Partnership Act. This program operates with funding from the U.S. Department of Labor. It provides job training and other employment related services.

State Offices

Real estate: Real Estate Commission, Paul Quinlan, Director, PO Box 94667, Lincoln, NE 68509. 402-471-2004
Chamber of commerce: Nebraska Chamber of Commerce &

Industry, Jack Swartz, President, PO Box 95128, 1320 Lincoln Mall, Lincoln, NE 68509. 402-474-4422

Economic development: Nebraska Dept. of Economic Development, Steve Buttress, Director, PO Box 94666, 301 Centennial Mall South, Lincoln, NE 68509. 800-426-6505, 402-471-3111, FAX 402-471-3778

Nebraska Dept. of Economic Development, Business Recruitment Division, Mary Simmons, Division Director, PO Box 94666, 301 Centennial Mall South, Lincoln, NE 68509. 800-426-6505, 402-471-3773

Nebraska Economic Development Corporation, George Frye, Exec Vice President, 2631 O St., Lincoln, NE 68510-1340. 402-483-0382

Nebraska Investment Finance Authority, Dennis Vellek, Exec Director, 1033 O Street, Suite 304, Lincoln, NE 68508. 402-477-4406

Nebraska Research and Development Authority, Director, NBC Center, Suite 646, Lincoln, NE 68508. 800-332-0732, 402-475-5109

Nebraska Technical Assistance Center, Thomas W. Spilker, Director, West 191 Nebraska Hall, University of Nebraska-Lincoln, Lincoln, NE 68588-0535. 402-472-5600

Small Business Development Center, Robert Bernier, State Director, University of Nebraska at Omaha, Peter Kiewit Center, Omaha, NE 68182. 402-554-2521

Environmental affairs: Department of Environmental Control, Dennis Grams, Director, PO Box 98922, Lincoln, NE 68509-8922. 402-471-2186

Labor: Department of Labor, Dan Dolan, Commissioner, PO Box 94600, Lincoln, NE 68509-4600. 402-471-3405

Unemployment: Department of Labor, Unemployment Insurance Division, Allan Amsberry, Director, PO Box 94600, Lincoln, NE 68509-4600. 402-471-9979

Worker's compensation: Department of Labor, Dan Dolan, Commissioner, PO Box 94600, Lincoln, NE 68509-4600. 402-471-3405

Occupational safety and health: Department of Labor, Division of Safety (Labor & Safety Standards), Gary L. Hirsh, Director, PO Box 95024, Lincoln, NE 68509-5024. 402-471-2239

Secretary of state: Secretary of State, Allen Beermann, Secretary of State, PO Box 94608, Lincoln, NE 68509-4608. 402-471-1554

Taxation and revenue: Department of Revenue, M. Berri Balka, State Tax Commissioner, PO Box 94818, Lincoln, NE 68509-4818. 402-471-2971

Designated Zones for Economic Development

Enterprise Zones
No program.

Foreign Trade Zones
Foreign Trade Zone No. 59, Lincoln, Nebraska, Grantee/Operator: Lincoln Chamber of Commerce, Duane Vicary, 1221 N Street, Suite 320, Lincoln, NE 68508, 402-476-7511

Foreign Trade Zone No. 19, Omaha, Nebraska, Grantee/Operator: Dock Board of the City of Omaha, Jim Rhodes, Omaha-Douglas Civic Center, 1819 Farnam St., Suite 300, Omaha, NE 68183, 402-444-5272

Labor Unions
Food and Commercial Workers International Union, United (AFL-CIO)

National Education Association

State, County and Municipal Employees, American Federation of (AFL-CIO)

Universities with Ph.D. Programs
Creighton University, Omaha

University of Nebraska-Lincoln, Lincoln

University of Nebraska Medical Center, Omaha

Sources of Additional Information
Personal and Corporate Income Tax Incentives. Nebraska Department of Revenue, 1989. np.

LINCOLN, NE (MSA)

Geographic Profile

Land Area

838.9 square miles

Counties and Parishes

Lancaster

Ranking Highlights

229 *out of 319 in total* **land area**

150 *out of 319 in* **population growth,** *1970–1990*

3 *out of 310 in having the lowest* **unemployment** *rate*

154 *out of 310 in size of* **labor force**

34 *out of 318 in the percentage of* **college graduates**

95 *out of 292 in per capita personal* **income**

193 *out of 319 in number of* **manufacturing establishments**

138 *out of 318 in* **physicians** *per 1000 people*

175 *out of 318 in* **hospital beds** *per 1000 people*

220 *out of 267 in fewest* **crimes** *per 1000 people*

110 *out of 266 in fewest* **violent crimes** *per 1000 people*

134 *out of 319 in per capita* **federal funds and grants**

Quality of Life Indexes (Rate per 1000 population)

Crime rate in 1991:	76.1
Violent crime rate in 1991:	5.2
Physicians rate in 1992:	1.9
Hospital bed rate in 1991:	3.64

ACCRA Cost of Living Indexes

(First quarter 1993, average = 100)

Composite index:	89.5
Utilities index:	83.8
Housing index:	82.1

Overview

Lincoln is the capital of Nebraska and the seat of Lancaster County. Located in a grain and livestock producing region, Lincoln has since its founding been a communications, distribution, and wholesaling hub. Important industries are the manufacture and repair of locomotives, flour and feed milling, grain storage, meat packing, dairy production, and diversified manufacturing. Lincoln is also the corporate headquarters of several insurance companies.

During the 1980s Lincoln experienced sustained growth that is expected to continue at a rate of 1 percent per year throughout the 1990s. Growth has brought economic expansion, with the employment base increasing 2.5 percent annually. Retail trade, for example, has flourished since 1984, growing about five percent each year, a rate substantially above other metropolitan areas in the state. Manufacturing has also shown growth above the state average.

A number of Lincoln's local companies conduct business throughout the United States and in foreign countries. Among them are Ameritas Financial Services, Selection Research Inc./Gallup Poll, Lester Electrical, and Cook Fam-

ily Foods. Peed Corporation, publishers of national trade magazines, moved its facilities to Lincoln in 1985. Harris Laboratories, a pharmaceutical testing and research firm that serves all fifty states and twenty-seven nations abroad, underwent a major expansion in 1988, adding between four hundred and five hundred jobs to its payroll. Norden Laboratories supplies veterinary products in the United States and sixty foreign countries.

Lincoln is connected with national and world markets via two major railroads—Burlington Northern and Union Pacific—that provide piggyback transportation; twenty–two interstate and fifteen intrastate motor freight companies; and fourteen air express and freight carriers. The city is also conveniently situated within 50 miles of water transportation at Mississippi River terminals.

Lincoln Municipal Airport is served by six commercial air carriers with regularly scheduled daily direct and connecting flights from major United States cities as well as points throughout the world. Commuter service is also provided from cities in central and western Nebraska. Amtrak provides railway transportation into Lincoln.

An efficient highway system permits easy access into Lincoln. I-80 approaches from the northeast and exits due west; U.S. 6 also bisects the city from northeast to west. U.S. 34 runs northwest to south, in the center of downtown joining U.S. 77, which extends from the south, and joining Nebraska 2, which approaches from the southeast.

Population (1990)

Total Population and Growth Rate

1990: 213,641

1980: 192,884

1970: 167,972

Growth rate 1970–1990: 27%

Race and Hispanic Origin

White: 94.9%

Black: 2.2%

Asian/Pacific Islander: 1.6%

Native American: 0.6%

Hispanic origin: 1.8%

White not Hispanic: 93.9%

Age

Ages 18 to 20: 7.1%

Ages 21 to 24: 8.5%

Ages 25 to 44: 33.6%

Ages 45 to 54: 8.8%

Ages 55 to 59: 3.7%

Ages 60 to 64: 3.6%

Ages 65 plus: 10.9%

Educational Attainment (1990)

Percent having completed high school: 88.1%

Percent having completed college: 27.6%

Elementary and high school enrollment: 32,532

Federal Funds and Grants Received
Total received in 1989: $693,600,000
Funds received per capita: $3,278

Civilian Labor Force
1993 (April): 135,482
1992 average: 133,518
1991 average: 133,344
1990 average: 130,279

Unemployment
1993 (April): 2.7%
1992 average: 2.4%
1991 average: 2.2%
1990 average: 1.7%

Average Annual Pay
1988: $17,795
1987: $17,226
1985: $15,930

Per Capita Personal Income
1991: $18,429
1990: $17,692
1989: $16,567

Business Climate (1987)
Manufacturing
Number of establishments in 1987: 237
Shipments in 1987 ($1,000): $1,805,200
Employees in 1987: 13,900
Change in employment, 1982 to 1987: 12.1%
Average annual pay for manufacturing work in 1989: $24,694
Average annual pay for production work in 1987: $20,194

Wholesale Trade
Number of establishments in 1987: 353
Total sales in 1987 ($1,000): $1,808,400
Change in sales, 1982 to 1987: 32.4%

Retail Trade
Number of establishments in 1987: 1,318
Total sales in 1987 ($1,000): $1,808,400
Retail sales per household in 1987: $15,493
Average annual pay in 1989: $9,742

Service Industry
Selected receipts in 1987 ($1,000): $619,200
Average annual pay in 1989: $16,502

Housing
Total number of units in 1990: 86,734
Occupied units in 1990: 82,759
Owner-occupied units in 1990: 60.5%
1993 ACCRA average cost: $92,925
1993 ACCRA average rent for an apartment: $432

Chamber of Commerce
Lincoln Chamber of Commerce, Duane Vicary, President, 1221 N St. #320, Lincoln, NE 68508. 402-476-7511

Major Businesses

Company	SIC	Telephone
American Charter Federal	6035	(402) 435-3571
Ameritas Life Insurance	6311	(402) 467-1122
B & R Stores, Inc.	5411	(402) 464-6297
Bryan Memorial Hospital	8062	(402) 489-0200
Central Telephone Co. of Florida	4813	(402) 399-2500
Crete Carrier Corp.	4213	(402) 475-9521
Duncan Aviation Inc.	4581	(402) 475-2611
First Commerce Bancshares	6712	(402) 472-4110
First Federal Savings & Loan of Lincoln	6035	(402) 475-0521
Information Technology	7372	(402) 423-2682
Kawasaki Motor Mfg. Corp.	3949	(402) 476-6600
Lincoln Telephone & Telegraph Co.	4813	(402) 474-2211
Lincoln Telecommunications Co.	4813	(402) 474-2211
Metromail Corp.	7331	(402) 475-4591
Nebraska Book Co.	5192	(402) 467-4481
Pegler-Sysco Food Services Co.	5149	(402) 423-1031
Security Mutual Life Insurance Co.	6311	(402) 477-4141
Woodmen Accident & Life	6321	(402) 476-6500

Colleges and Universities
Lincoln School of Commerce, Lincoln
Nebraska Wesleyan University, Lincoln
Southeast Community College, Lincoln Campus, Lincoln
Union College, Lincoln
University of Nebraska-Lincoln, Lincoln

OMAHA, NE–IA (MSA)

Geographic Profile

Land Area

1916.5 square miles

Counties and Parishes

Iowa:

Pottawattamie

Nebraska:

Douglas

Sarpy

Washington

Additional Cities/Towns within Area

Council Bluffs, IA

Ranking Highlights

99 *out of 319 in total* **land area**

221 *out of 319 in* **population growth**, *1970–1990*

9 *out of 310 in having the lowest* **unemployment** *rate*

71 *out of 310 in size of* **labor force**

83 *out of 318 in the percentage of* **college graduates**

79 *out of 292 in per capita personal* **income**

89 *out of 319 in number of* **manufacturing establishments**

40 *out of 318 in* **physicians** *per 1000 people*

31 *out of 318 in* **hospital beds** *per 1000 people*

67 *out of 267 in fewest* **crimes** *per 1000 people*

119 *out of 266 in fewest* **violent crimes** *per 1000 people*

108 *out of 319 in per capita* **federal funds and grants**

Quality of Life Indexes (Rate per 1000 population)

Crime rate in 1991:	46.5
Violent crime rate in 1991:	5.5
Physicians rate in 1992:	2.82
Hospital bed rate in 1991:	5.88

ACCRA Cost of Living Indexes

(First quarter 1993, average = 100)

Composite index:	91.0
Utilities index:	94.1
Housing index:	83.9

Overview

Omaha, the seat of Douglas County, is the focus of a metropolitan statistical area that includes Douglas, Sarpy, and Washington counties in Nebraska and Pottawattamie County in Iowa. The city's development as a railroad center was augmented by the Union Stockyards and the meat-packing industry. Omaha is an insurance and telecommunications center, home to the U.S. Air Force Strategic Command, and notable for its inexpensive housing, good schools, and relatively few social and environmental problems.

There are more than fifteen thousand businesses located in the four–county metropolitan area, reflecting a growth rate of 22 percent for the period 1986–1991. The region is home to five Fortune 500 industrial companies: ConAgra, Peter Kiewit Sons, Berkshire Hathaway, AG Processing, and Valmont Industries. More than thirty other Fortune 500 companies have manufacturing plants in the metropolitan area.

The headquarters of nearly thirty insurance companies call Omaha home. Over half of the two dozen telemarketing/direct response/reservation centers operating in Omaha also have their corporate headquarters located in the metropolitan area. Numerous other large firms have their headquarters in Omaha, including Mutual of Omaha Companies, Union Pacific Railroad, Lozier Corporation, First Data Resources, I T I Marketing Services, Omaha Steaks International, Pamida, and Godfather's Pizza, Inc.

The Omaha economy is well diversified, with no industry sector accounting for more than 30 percent of total employment. Omaha has a higher concentration of its employment in finance, insurance and real estate; transportation, communications, and utilities; and services and trade jobs than does the country on average. This is offset by a relatively smaller share of total employment in the manufacturing, construction, and government sectors. Since 1980 the industry sectors that have shown the fastest growth within the Omaha metropolitan area are services, trade, and finance, insurance, and real estate.

The Port of Omaha, linking the city to the Gulf of Mexico and the Atlantic Ocean via the Missouri River and through the St. Lawrence Seaway, is an important factor in the local economy. The channel was recently expanded to a width of three hundred feet and a depth of nine feet, thus accommodating larger commercial barges. Served by a number of barge lines, the port processes more than six million tons of goods annually. The Union Pacific and four other major railroads provide freight service that is coordinated with many of the ninety trucking companies serving the metropolitan area. Four air-cargo carriers maintain facilities at Eppley Airfield.

The newly expanded terminal at Eppley Airfield, four miles northeast of downtown Omaha, is served by eight airlines with direct flights to most major United States cities and connecting flights to points throughout the world. Eppley East, on the east side of the main airfield, and Millard Airport, a reliever facility for Eppley Airfield, receive general aviation traffic.

Principal highway routes providing access to the Omaha metropolitan area are I-80 and I-29; U.S. 6, 30, 75, and 275; and Nebraska 36, 38, 50, 64, 85, 92, 131, 133, and 370.

Population (1990)

Total Population and Growth Rate

1990: 618,262

1980: 585,122

1970: 555,956

Growth rate 1970–1990: 11%

Race and Hispanic Origin
White: 89.1%
Black: 8.3%
Asian/Pacific Islander: 1.0%
Native American: 0.5%
Hispanic origin: 2.6%
White not Hispanic: 87.6%

Age
Ages 18 to 20: 4.3%
Ages 21 to 24: 5.9%
Ages 25 to 44: 33.8%
Ages 45 to 54: 9.7%
Ages 55 to 59: 4.1%
Ages 60 to 64: 3.8%
Ages 65 plus: 10.6%

Educational Attainment (1990)
Percent having completed high school: 84.4%
Percent having completed college: 22.8%
Elementary and high school enrollment: 112,173

Federal Funds and Grants Received
Total received in 1989: $2,166,200,000
Funds received per capita: $3,485

Civilian Labor Force
1993 (April):   350,187
1992 average: 345,785
1991 average: 343,731
1990 average: 340,670

Unemployment
1993 (April):   3.3%
1992 average: 3.4%
1991 average: 3.1%
1990 average: 2.6%

Average Annual Pay
1988: $19,174
1987: $18,461
1985: $17,429

Per Capita Personal Income
1991: $19,037
1990: $18,485
1989: $17,216

Business Climate (1987)
Manufacturing
Number of establishments in 1987: 702
Shipments in 1987 ($1,000): $5,553,900
Employees in 1987: 33,700
Change in employment, 1982 to 1987: -2.3%
Average annual pay for manufacturing work in 1989: $25,059
Average annual pay for production work in 1987: $20,936

Wholesale Trade
Number of establishments in 1987: 1,381
Total sales in 1987 ($1,000): $8,550,600
Change in sales, 1982 to 1987: 19.4%

Retail Trade
Number of establishments in 1987: 3,733
Total sales in 1987 ($1,000): $8,550,600
Retail sales per household in 1987: $16,623
Average annual pay in 1989: $10,614

Service Industry
Selected receipts in 1987 ($1,000): $2,153,600
Average annual pay in 1989: $17,152

Office Real Estate (1992)
Office space inventory: 13,273,000 square feet
Average class A Central Business District rental range per sq. ft: $16.75

Vacancy Rates
All areas: 18.4%

Vacancy Rates in Central Business District
Class A space: 20.9%
Class B space: 26.2%

Vacancy Rates Outside Central Business District
Class A space: 3.8%
Class B space: 32.3%

Housing
Total number of units in 1990: 247,538
Occupied units in 1990: 232,352
Owner-occupied units in 1990: 64.2%
1993 ACCRA average cost: $93,941
1993 ACCRA average rent for an apartment: $446

Chamber of Commerce
Greater Omaha Chamber of Commerce, C.R. Bell, President, 1301 Harney St., Omaha, NE 68102. 402-346-5000

Economic Development Office
Omaha Economic Development Council, Rod Moseman, Vice President, 1301 Harney St., Omaha, NE 68102. 800-852-2622, 402-346-5905, FAX 402-346-7050

Economic Development Organizations
City of Council Bluffs, Community Development Department, Donald Gross, Director, 209 Pearl St., Council Buffs, IA 51503. 712-328-4630

Major Businesses

Company	SIC	Telephone
AG Processing Inc.	2075	(402) 496-7809
Beefamerica, Inc.	2011	(402) 896-2400
Beefamerica Operating Co.	2011	(402) 896-2400
Berkshire Hathaway, Inc.	6331	(402) 346-1400
Catholic Health Corp.	8741	(402) 393-7661
Commercial Federal Corp.	6035	(402) 554-9200
Conagra Inc.	2011	(402) 978-4000
Farm Credit Bank Inc.	6159	(402) 444-3333

Major Businesses (Continued)

Company	SIC	Telephone
First National of Nebraska	6021	(402) 341-0500
Kiewit, Peter Sons'	3411	(402) 342-2052
Kiewit Construction Group	1542	(402) 342-2052
Kiewit Holdings Group Inc.	3411	(402) 342-2052
Kiewit Pacific Co.	1611	(402) 342-2052
Kiewit U.S. Co.	3411	(402) 342-2052
Mutual of Omaha Insurance Co.	6311	(402) 342-7600
Northwstern Bell Telephone Co.	4813	(402) 422-2000
Omaha Public Power Distributors	4911	(402) 636-2000
P S I, Inc.	4924	(402) 498-4490
Pacific Rail System, Inc.	4011	(402) 271-5000
Pamida Holdings Corp.	5331	(402) 339-2400
Pamida Inc.	5331	(402) 339-2400
Physicians Mutual Insurance Co.	6321	(402) 633-1000
Union Pacific Railroad Co.	4011	(402) 271-5000
United A G Cooperative, Inc.	5141	(402) 734-1250
United of Omaha Life Insurance	6311	(402) 342-7600
Valcom Inc.	5045	(402) 392-3900
Valmont Industries, Inc.	3441	(402) 359-2201
Werner Enterprises, Inc..	4213	(402) 895-6640
Woodmen World Life	6311	(402) 342-1890

Colleges and Universities

Bishop Clarkson College, Omaha, NE
College of St. Mary, Omaha, NE
Creighton University, Omaha, NE
Gateway Electronics Institute, Omaha, NE
Iowa Western Community College, Council Bluffs, IA
Metropolitan Community College, Omaha, NE
Nebraska College of Business, Omaha, NE
Nebraska Methodist College of Nursing and Allied Health, Omaha, NE
Omaha College of Health Careers, Omaha, NE
University of Nebraska at Omaha, Omaha, NE
University of Nebraska Medical Center, Omaha, NE

NEVADA

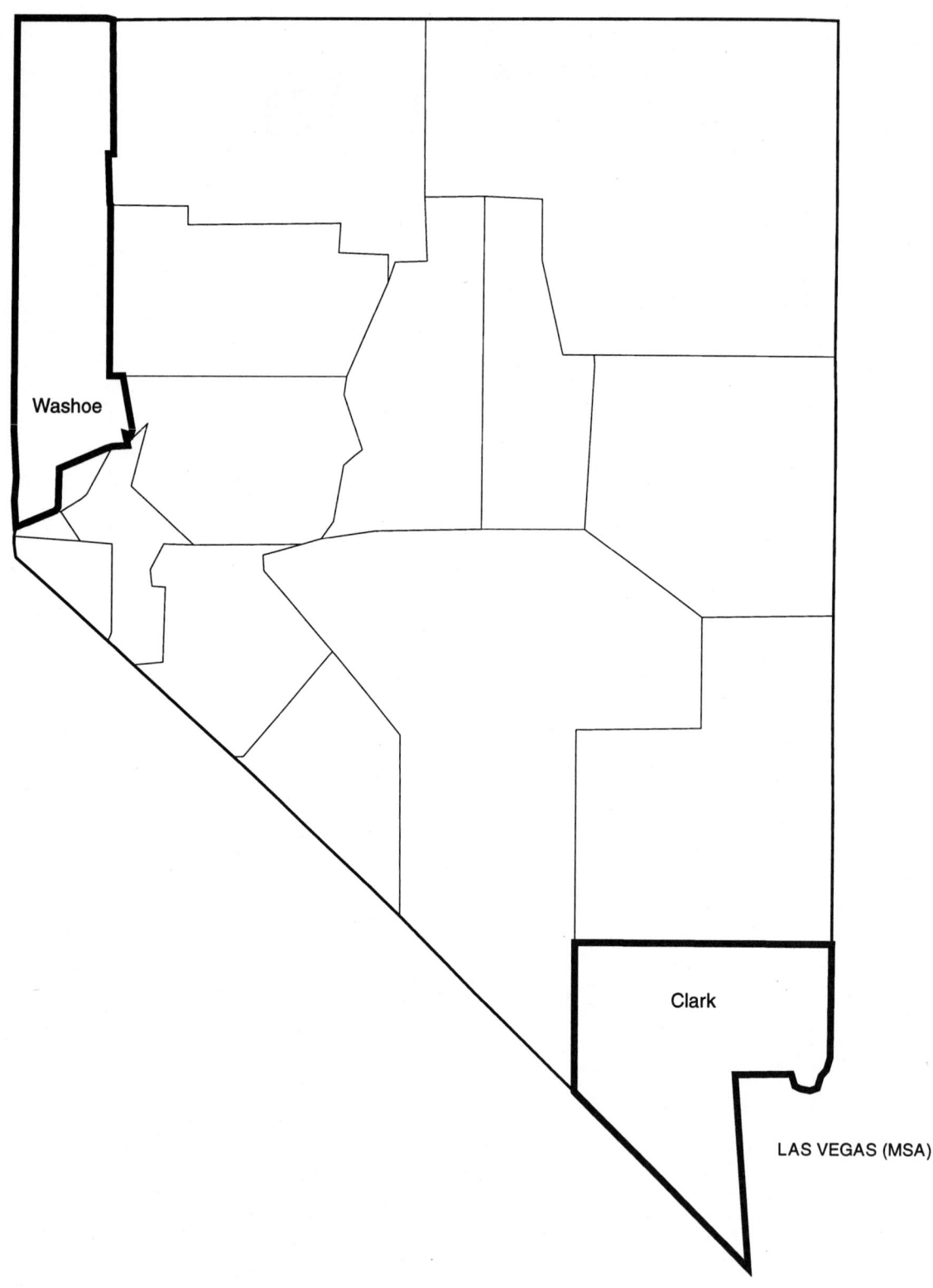

RENO (MSA)

Washoe

Clark

LAS VEGAS (MSA)

NEVADA

Population
1990: 1,201,833
1980: 800,493

Age
Ages 18 to 20: 47,863
Ages 21 to 24: 71,082
Ages 25 to 44: 414,292
Ages 45 to 54: 136,000
Ages 55 to 59: 54,681
Ages 60 to 64: 53,336
Median age: 33.3

Race and Hispanic Origin
White: 1,012,695
Black: 78,771
Asian/Pacific Islander: 38,127
Native American: 19,637
Hispanic origin: 124,419

Households
Total: 466,297
Persons per household: 2.53

Sex
Male: 611,880
Female: 589,953

Population Migration
Domestic migration: 191,000
International migration: 23,000

Projection of the Population in 1995
Total: 1,258,000
18 to 64: 798,000

Civilian Labor Force
1993: 678,100
1992: 661,900
1991: 643,100
1990: 608,200

Manufacturing
1995 Projection: 30,900
1992: 26,100
1991: 26,400
1990: 27,000
1989: 25,700

Services
1995 Projection: 346,000

1992: 284,300
1991: 276,800
1990: 274,000
1989: 258,700

Wholesale and Retail Trade
1995 Projection: 145,800
1992: 130,400
1991: 131,900
1990: 133,000
1989: 126,600

Unemployment Rate
1993: 7.5%
1992: 7.1%
1991: 5.3%
1990: 4.9%

Employer Unemployment Contributions
Contribution Rate
1992: 1.00%
1991: 1.03%
1990: 1.38%

Average Weekly Benefit
1992: $173.28
1991: $171.37
1990: $162.87

Gross State Product (Million $)
1989: $27,960
1988: $24,657
1987: $21,478
1979: $10,405
Growth rate, 1979 to 1989: 168.7%

Capital Expenditures of Manufacturing Industries
1990: $134,400,000
1989: $102,000,000
1988: $80,400,000
1987: $114,000,000

State Taxe Rates
Individual income: None
Corporate income: None
General property: Sum of state and local rates. Assessed at 35% of full cash value of real and tangible personal prop-

erty, not to exceed 5¢ per $1 of assessed valuation.
General sales: 6.5%
Gasoline: 18¢ per gallon

Income
Median income for a 4 person family: $39,737

Personal per Capita Income
1992: $20,266
1991: $19,812
1990: $19,680

Disposable per Capita Income
1992: $17,711
1991: $17,225
1990: $17,036

Private Employment Weekly Wages
Average
1989: $398
1988: $384
1987: $384

Manufacturing
1989: $363
1988: $445
1987: $432

Services
1989: $380
1988: $371
1987: $351

Wholesale
1989: $523
1988: $499
1987: $463

Retail
1989: $264
1988: $256
1987: $248

Highway Statistics
Total Highway Miles
1990: 45,524
1989: 44,856
1988: 44,833

Federal Highway Aid
1991: $71,851,000
1990: $71,289,000
1989: $72,104,000

Electricity
Average Cost per Kilowatt Hour
1990: 5.39¢
1989: 5.28¢
1988: 5.44¢

Housing (1990)
Owner occupied units: 255,388

Median house value: $95,700
Renter occupied units: 210,909
Median rent: $445
Total vacant units: 52,561
Homeowner vacancy rate: 2.3%
Rental vacancy rate: 9.1%

State Business Incentives and Assistance
Financial and Business Assistance
Sales and Use Tax Deferral. Nevada allows an interest-free sales or use tax deferral on capital goods or equipment purchases which total $100,000 or more within a one-year time frame. The determination is based on the creation of new jobs or preventing the loss of existing jobs. The program does not apply to buildings or their structural components, equipment used principally for tourism or gaming, equipment utilized by a public utility, or medical treatment equipment.

Industrial Development Revenue Bonds. To encourage manufacturing projects within the state, the Nevada Department of Commerce authorized to issue tax-exempt IDRBs. An IDRB can provide up to 100% financing for land, building, improvements and capital equipment for manufacturing firms that incur from $1 million to $10 million in development costs. The Department of Commerce can also issue taxable bonds to finance other eligible facilities, including new and existing industrial or commercial projects.

Business and Industrial Loan Guarantees. The U.S. Farmers Home Administration offers Business and Industrial Loan Guarantees specifically designed for rural ideas. The Administration contracts to reimburse the lender for losses up to a maximum of 90% of principal and interest for guaranteed loans of $2 million or less, 80% for loans over $2 million but not over $5 million, and 70% for loans over $5 million.

Nevada Revolving Loan Fund. This is an incentive financing program for small business expansion to create jobs for low-to-moderate income persons. NRLF is available to rural businesses having difficulties in obtaining necessary finance through conventional lenders.

Nevada State Development Corporation. NSDC is a private financial corporation certified by the SBA to package and service lending programs statewide. The NSDC supplies the SBA 504 Loan program. The 504 Loans are long term, below market, fixed rate, second mortgage loans that, along with a private first mortgage lender, enable a business to finance 90% of land, buildings, machinery and equipment. The maximum 504 Loan amount is $750,000.

Education and Training
Quick Start Job Training. Provides state funding for new and expanding businesses to recruit and train new employees in occupation-specific skills. The program offers intensive, short-term training in high-growth occupations

Major Companies in the State

Company name	Fortune 500 rank	City	Telephone	SIC number
Fortune 500 Companies				
None				
Other Major Companies in the State				
Amerco		Reno	702-786-0488	7513
Bally Gaming International Inc.		Las Vegas	702-896-7700	3999
Circus Circus Enterprises Inc.		Las Vegas	702-734-0410	7011
Freeport Mcmoran Copper & Gold Inc.		Reno	702-688-3000	1021
Freeport Mcmoran Copper Company Inc.		Reno	702-329-6131	1021
GNLV Finance Corp.		Las Vegas	702-385-7111	6799
GNS Finance Corp.		Las Vegas	702-791-7111	6799
Golden Nugget Finance Corp.		Las Vegas	702-791-7111	7011
Golden Nugget Inc.		Las Vegas	702-791-7111	7011
International Game Technology		Reno	702-688-0100	3999
John Deere Capital Corp.		Reno	702-786-5527	6159
Nevada Power Co.		Las Vegas	702-367-5000	4911
Sahara Resorts		Las Vegas	702-737-2111	7011
Showboat Inc.		Las Vegas	702-385-9123	7011
Sierra Health Services Inc.		Las Vegas	702-646-8112	8093
Sierra Pacific Power Co.		Reno	702-689-4286	4931
Sierra Pacific Resources		Reno	702-689-3600	4931
Southwest Gas Corp.		Las Vegas	702-876-7173	4923
Valley Capital Corp.		Las Vegas	702-654-1000	6712
FMC Gold Co.		Reno	702-827-3777	1041

ranging from entry level to skilled technical positions. Participating businesses are expected to offer an acceptable fringe benefit package and a $6.00 hourly wage. Businesses must also provide at least 25% of total training costs in equipment, material, cash, staff time or in-kind services.

Job Training Services. Provides customized training programs to new or expanding companies in recruitment, curriculum development, and classroom, as well as on-the-job, training.

Job Training Partnership Act. This program operates with funding from the U.S. Department of Labor. It provides job training and other employment related services.

State Offices

Real estate: Dept. of Commerce, Real Estate Commission, R. Lynn Luman, Administrator, Capitol Complex, Carson City, NV 89710. 702-687-4280

Chamber of commerce: Nevada State Chamber of Commerce, Fred Davis, Legal Affairs Director, PO Box 3499, Reno, NV 89505. 702-786-3030

Economic development: Commission on Economic Development, Jim Spoo, Exec Director, Capitol Complex, Carson City, NV 89710. 800-336-1600 or 702-687-4325, FAX 702-687-4450

Dept. of Commerce, Capitol Complex, Carson City, NV 89710. 702-687-4250

Nevada Commission of Economic Development (Enterprise Zones Office), Sarah Merserau, Capitol Complex, Carson City, NV 89710. 702-885-4325

Small Business Development Center, Samuel Males, State Director, Univeristy of Nevada-Reno, Business Building, Room 411, Reno, NV 89557-0100. 702-784-1717

Environmental affairs: Department of Conservation and Natural Resources, Roland Westergard, Director, Capitol Complex, Carson City, NV 89710. 702-687-4360

Labor: Labor Commission, F.T. MacDonald, Commissioner, Capitol Complex, Carson City, NV 89710. 702-687-4850

Unemployment: Employment Security Department, Unemployment Insurance Division, James Wittenburg, Administrator, Capitol Complex, Carson City, NV 89710. 702-687-4510

Worker's compensation: State Industrial Insurance System, Capitol Complex, Carson City, NV 89710. 702-687-5220

Occupational safety and health: Occupational Safety and Health Division, Capitol Complex, Carson City, NV 89710. 702-687-5240

Secretary of state: Office of Secretary of State, Cheryl Lau,

Secretary of State, Capitol Complex, Carson City, NV 89710. 702-687-5203

Taxation and revenue: Department of Taxation, John Perry Comeax, Exec Director, Capitol Complex, Carson City, NV 89710. 702-687-4892

Designated Zones for Economic Development

Enterprise Zones
Enacted in: 1983
No. of established zones: 2
Las Vegas
North Las Vegas

Foreign Trade Zones
Foreign Trade Zone No. 89, Clark County, Nevada, Grantee/Operator: Nevada Development Authority, Jerry Sandstrom, 3900 Paradise Road, Suite 155, Las Vegas, NV 89109, 702-739-8222

Foreign Trade Zone No. 126, Sparks, Nevada, Grantee: Nevada Development Authority, Operator: Nevada Foreign-Trade Services, Jeff Griffin, 728 Spice Islands Drive, Sparks, NV 89431, 702-331-8010

Labor Unions
Carpenters and Joiners of America, United Brotherhood of (AFL-CIO)
Clark County Public Employees Association
Las Vegas Employees Association
National Education Association

Universities with Ph.D. Programs
University of Nevada, Las Vegas, Las Vegas
University of Nevada, Reno, Reno

Sources of Additional Information
Business Assistance Programs. Nevada Commission on Economic Development, n.d. 13 p.

LAS VEGAS, NV (MSA)

Geographic Profile
Land Area
7910.7 square miles

Counties and Parishes
Clark

Ranking Highlights
  5 *out of 319 in total* **land area**
  5 *out of 319 in* **population growth,** *1970–1990*
149 *out of 310 in having the lowest* **unemployment** *rate*
 64 *out of 310 in size of* **labor force**
261 *out of 318 in the percentage of* **college graduates**
 90 *out of 292 in per capita personal* **income**
130 *out of 319 in number of* **manufacturing establishments**
246 *out of 318 in* **physicians** *per 1000 people*
260 *out of 318 in* **hospital beds** *per 1000 people*
189 *out of 267 in fewest* **crimes** *per 1000 people*
182 *out of 266 in fewest* **violent crimes** *per 1000 people*
 74 *out of 319 in per capita* **federal funds and grants**

Quality of Life Indexes (Rate per 1000 population)
Crime rate in 1991:	70.2
Violent crime rate in 1991:	7.9
Physicians rate in 1992:	1.41
Hospital bed rate in 1991:	2.71

ACCRA Cost of Living Indexes
(First quarter 1993, average = 100)
Composite index:	N/A
Utilities index:	N/A
Housing index:	N/A

Overview
Tourism is the major economic factor in Las Vegas, bringing to the city revenues of over $9.9 billion annually. Expansion of gaming and entertainment enterprises has produced a booming construction industry; new hotels and resorts are steadily being built to accommodate the increasing number of visitors, estimated at 21 million people per year.

While the entertainment and service industries are, collectively, the largest employers in Las Vegas, the major single employer is Nellis U.S. Air Force Base, with more than twelve thousand military and civilian personnel on its payroll. The annual economic impact of Nellis on the local economy is $684 million. Manufacturing is becoming an important industry in a city usually identified with recreation. Within five years—between 1987 and 1992—174 companies moved to Las Vegas, creating 5,659 new jobs, of which 51 percent were in the manufacturing sector.

Las Vegas is among the nation's foremost meeting destinations, with convention trade being one of the city's major industries. Las Vegas hosts more than 1.7 million convention and meeting participants annually; business is expected to increase steadily during the 1990s. Along with entertainment and recreation, well-appointed meeting facilities and luxury hotels and resorts are the attractions that consistently draw large and small groups to the city. Las Vegas boasted eighty-seven thousand hotel rooms at the end of 1992, with an additional thirty-six thousand rooms proposed or under construction.

Ten air freight carriers provide non-stop or one-stop service from McCarran International Airport to most of the largest metropolitan areas in the United States. Twenty-seven parcel services also provide facilities in Las Vegas. Union Pacific Railroad, with switching and marshalling yards downtown, links the city with markets in most states. Fifty motor freight carriers maintain terminals in the Las Vegas area. A competitive atmosphere in the local trucking industry encourages excellent rates and fast service. The newly remodeled McCarran International Airport, located five miles south of the business district, is among the busiest airports in the United States. It is served by twenty-nine airlines. The city is served by three major highways. I-15 connects Las Vegas with Los Angeles, California and Salt Lake City, Utah. U.S. 95 leads into the city from the northwest and U.S. 93/95 enters from the southeast.

Population (1990)

Total Population and Growth Rate
1990: 741,459
1980: 463,087
1970: 273,288
Growth rate 1970–1990: 171%

Race and Hispanic Origin
White: 81.3%
Black: 9.5%
Asian/Pacific Islander: 3.5%
Native American: 0.9%
Hispanic origin: 11.2%
White not Hispanic: 75.4%

Age
Ages 18 to 20:   4%
Ages 21 to 24: 6.2%
Ages 25 to 44: 34.3%
Ages 45 to 54: 11.3%
Ages 55 to 59: 4.6%
Ages 60 to 64: 4.5%
Ages 65 plus: 10.5%

Educational Attainment (1990)
Percent having completed high school: 77.3%
Percent having completed college: 13.8%
Elementary and high school enrollment: 114,577

Federal Funds and Grants Received
Total received in 1989: $2,544,600,000
Funds received per capita: $4,031

Civilian Labor Force
1993 (April):   438,588
1992 average: 422,716
1991 average: 406,748
1990 average: 385,592

Unemployment
1993 (April):   6.9%
1992 average: 6.8%
1991 average: 5.8%
1990 average: 4.9%

Average Annual Pay
1988: $20,354
1987: $19,359
1985: $18,065

Per Capita Personal Income
1991: $18,474
1990: $18,483
1989: $17,363

Business Climate (1987)

Manufacturing
Number of establishments in 1987: 408
Shipments in 1987 ($1,000): $839,800
Employees in 1987: 8,100
Change in employment, 1982 to 1987: 19.1%
Average annual pay for manufacturing work in 1989: $24,624
Average annual pay for production work in 1987: $20,000

Wholesale Trade
Number of establishments in 1987: 805
Total sales in 1987 ($1,000): $3,079,700
Change in sales, 1982 to 1987: 46.5%

Retail Trade
Number of establishments in 1987: 3,524
Total sales in 1987 ($1,000): $3,079,700
Retail sales per household in 1987: $17,601
Average annual pay in 1989: $13,713

Service Industry
Selected receipts in 1987 ($1,000): $6,999,600
Average annual pay in 1989: $20,259

Office Real Estate (1992)
Office space inventory: 7,189,790 square feet
Average class A Central Business District rental range per sq. ft: $23.00

Vacancy Rates
All areas: 12.7%

Vacancy Rates in Central Business District
Class A space: 10.1%
Class B space: N/A

Vacancy Rates Outside Central Business District
Class A space: 13.2%
Class B space: N/A

Housing

Total number of units in 1990: 317,188
Occupied units in 1990: 287,025
Owner-occupied units in 1990: 51.9%
1993 ACCRA average cost: N/A
1993 ACCRA average rent for an apartment: N/A

Chamber of Commerce

Las Vegas Chamber of Commerce, Mark Smith, President, 2301 E. Sahara Ave., Las Vegas, NV 89104. 702-457-4664

Economic Development Office

Department of Economic & Urban Development, Michael Majewski, Chief of Economic Division, 400 E. Stewart St., Las Vegas, NV 89101. 702-386-6551

Economic Development Organizations

Southern Nevada Certified Development Corp., Thomas Gutherie, President, 2770 S. Maryland Parkway Suite 212, Las Vegas, NV 89109. 702-732-3998

Major Businesses

Company	SIC	Telephone
Atlandia Design Inc.	8741	(702) 736-4556
Bally's Grand, Inc.	7011	(702) 739-4111
California Hotel & Casino	7011	(702) 456-7777
Circus Circus Enterprises	7011	(702) 734-0410
Desert Palace Inc.	7011	(702) 731-7110
Golden Nugget, Inc.	7011	(702) 385-7111
Horn & Hardart Co.	5961	(702) 369-9500
Hotel Ramada of Nevada	7993	(702) 739-2222
Humana Hospital Sunrise	8062	(702) 731-8000
Las Vegas Hilton Corp.	7011	(702) 732-5111
Nevada Power Co.	4911	(702) 367-5000
Philadelphia Freedom Corp.	6162	(702) 454-1776
Primerit Bank Federal Savings	6035	(702) 362-5555
Reynolds Electric & Engineering	7349	(702) 295-3379
Sam-Will Inc.	7993	(702) 732-6430
Southwest Gas Corp.	4923	(702) 876-7011
TNT Transport Group Inc.	4213	(702) 792-7000
Valley Bank of Nevada	6022	(702) 386-1000
Wright Companies	5172	(702) 435-4353

Colleges and Universities

University of Nevada, Las Vegas, Las Vegas

RENO, NV (MSA)

Geographic Profile

Land Area
6342.5 square miles

Counties and Parishes
Washoe

Ranking Highlights

  7 *out of 319 in total* **land area**
 15 *out of 319 in* **population growth,** *1970–1990*
117 *out of 310 in having the lowest* **unemployment** *rate*
145 *out of 310 in size of* **labor force**
123 *out of 318 in the percentage of* **college graduates**
 22 *out of 292 in per capita personal* **income**
150 *out of 319 in number of* **manufacturing establishments**
 85 *out of 318 in* **physicians** *per 1000 people*
157 *out of 318 in* **hospital beds** *per 1000 people*
185 *out of 267 in fewest* **crimes** *per 1000 people*
148 *out of 266 in fewest* **violent crimes** *per 1000 people*
262 *out of 319 in per capita* **federal funds and grants**

Quality of Life Indexes (Rate per 1000 population)

Crime rate in 1991:	69.2
Violent crime rate in 1991:	6.7
Physicians rate in 1992:	2.32
Hospital bed rate in 1991:	3.89

ACCRA Cost of Living Indexes

(First quarter 1993, average = 100)
Composite index: 108.5
Utilities index: 75.7
Housing index: 124.6

Overview

Tourism is the major industry in the Reno area. The large number of casinos and gambling institutions attract more than seven million visitors annually and add millions of dollars to the local economy each year. The casinos also support the hotel and restaurant industries. The nearby mountains draw many tourists to the highest concentration of ski resorts in America.

Light manufacturing, warehousing, distribution, and transportation have developed into important sectors of the Reno economy. Nevada's Freeport Law and the designation of 23 acres in Reno as a Foreign Trade Zone make the city an ideal location for the import and export of goods. Metropolitan Reno is also a major retail trade market and a regional center for precious metals, mining, and exploration.

Several air freight carriers operate out of Reno-Cannon International Airport, and the city's Port of Entry status and Foreign Trade Zone are helpful in the import and export of goods. Rail freight service is available from the Southern Pacific and Union Pacific-Missouri Pacific railroads. More than sixty interstate trucking companies, attracted to

Nevada by the deregulation of the trucking industry, offer coast-to-coast overland shipping.

The renovated Reno-Cannon International Airport is located three miles south of downtown Reno. The airport handles about one hundred sixty flights per day from eight major airlines and is an international Port of Entry. Passenger rail service is available from Amtrak via the California Zephyr, described as the most scenic train ride in the United States, with daily service from San Francisco, California, and Chicago. Illinois. Interstate highway 80 runs through Reno's downtown region, west to San Francisco and east to Salt Lake City. U.S. highway 395 passes just to the east of the city, connecting Reno with Portland, Washington, and Seattle, Washington, to the north and Los Angeles, California, to the south.

Population (1990)

Total Population and Growth Rate
1990: 254,667
1980: 193,623
1970: 121,068
Growth rate 1970–1990: 110%

Race and Hispanic Origin
White: 88.4%
Black: 2.2%
Asian/Pacific Islander: 3.9%
Native American: 1.9%
Hispanic origin: 9.0%
White not Hispanic: 83.4%

Age
Ages 18 to 20: 4.3%
Ages 21 to 24: 6.2%
Ages 25 to 44: 36.3%
Ages 45 to 54: 11.2%
Ages 55 to 59: 4.4%
Ages 60 to 64: 4.2%
Ages 65 plus: 10.3%

Educational Attainment (1990)
Percent having completed high school: 82.5%
Percent having completed college: 20.7%
Elementary and high school enrollment: 36,574

Federal Funds and Grants Received
Total received in 1989: $567,200,000
Funds received per capita: $2,366

Civilian Labor Force
1993 (April): 144,064
1992 average: 142,349
1991 average: 137,702
1990 average: 136,129

Unemployment
1993 (April): 6.3%
1992 average: 6.3%
1991 average: 5.0%
1990 average: 4.8%

Average Annual Pay
1988: $20,429
1987: $19,563
1985: $18,076

Per Capita Personal Income
1991: $22,561
1990: $22,122
1989: $21,461

Business Climate (1987)

Manufacturing
Number of establishments in 1987: 357
Shipments in 1987 ($1,000): $1,075,400
Employees in 1987: 9,100
Change in employment, 1982 to 1987: 8.3%
Average annual pay for manufacturing work in 1989: $25,286
Average annual pay for production work in 1987: $19,117

Wholesale Trade
Number of establishments in 1987: 555
Total sales in 1987 ($1,000): $2,066,600
Change in sales, 1982 to 1987: 38.7%

Retail Trade
Number of establishments in 1987: 1,660
Total sales in 1987 ($1,000): $2,066,600
Retail sales per household in 1987: $19,523
Average annual pay in 1989: $14,307

Service Industry
Selected receipts in 1987 ($1,000): $2,178,400
Average annual pay in 1989: $18,562

Office Real Estate (1992)
Office space inventory: 2,800,000 square feet
Average class A Central Business District rental range per sq. ft: $16.20

Vacancy Rates
All areas: 16.6%

Vacancy Rates in Central Business District
Class A space: 32.7%
Class B space: 8.3%

Vacancy Rates Outside Central Business District
Class A space: 11.3%
Class B space: 12.0%

Housing
Total number of units in 1990: 112,193
Occupied units in 1990: 102,294
Owner-occupied units in 1990: 54.1%
1993 ACCRA average cost: $142,300
1993 ACCRA average rent for an apartment: $606

Chamber of Commerce
Greater Reno-Sparks Chamber of Commerce, Ron Watson,

Exec. Vice President, 133 N. Sierra St., 3rd Fl., PO Box 3499, Reno, NV 89505. 702-786-3030

Economic Development Office

Western Nevada Economic Development Authority, Kenneth Lynn, Exec. Director, 5190 Neil Rd. #111, Reno, NV 89502. 702-322-4004

Economic Development Organizations

Sierra Pacific Resources, Darrell A. Plummer, Manager, PO Box 30150, Reno, NV 89520-3150. 702-689-3636

Major Businesses

Company	SIC	Telephone
Amerco	7513	(702) 786-0488
American Federal Savings	6035	(702) 785-8500
Clark & Sullivan Construction	1542	(702) 355-8500
Donnelly Dick Automotive	5511	(702) 786-1881
First Interstate Bank of Nevada	6022	(702) 784-3397
Harrah's Club	7999	(702) 786-3232
International Game Technologies	3999	(702) 323-5060
John Deere Capital Corp.	6153	(702) 786-5527
Jones/West Ford Inc.	5511	(702) 329-8800
Nevada Bell	4813	(702) 789-6000
Ormat Energy Systems, Inc.	1629	(702) 356-9111
Porsche Cars North America	5012	(702) 348-3000
Scolari's Warehouse Market	5411	(702) 331-7700
Sierra Pacific Power Co.	4911	(702) 689-4011
Sierra Pacific Resources	4911	(702) 689-3600
Sparks Nugget, Inc.	7011	(702) 356-3300
St. Marys Regional Medical Center	8062	(702) 323-2041
U. S. Leisure, Inc.	2511	(702) 831-4412
Washoe Health System, Inc.	6719	(702) 785-4100
Washoe Medical Center Inc.	8062	(702) 328-4100

Colleges and Universities

Reno Business College, Reno
Truckee Meadows Community College, Reno
University of Nevada, Reno, Reno

NEW HAMPSHIRE

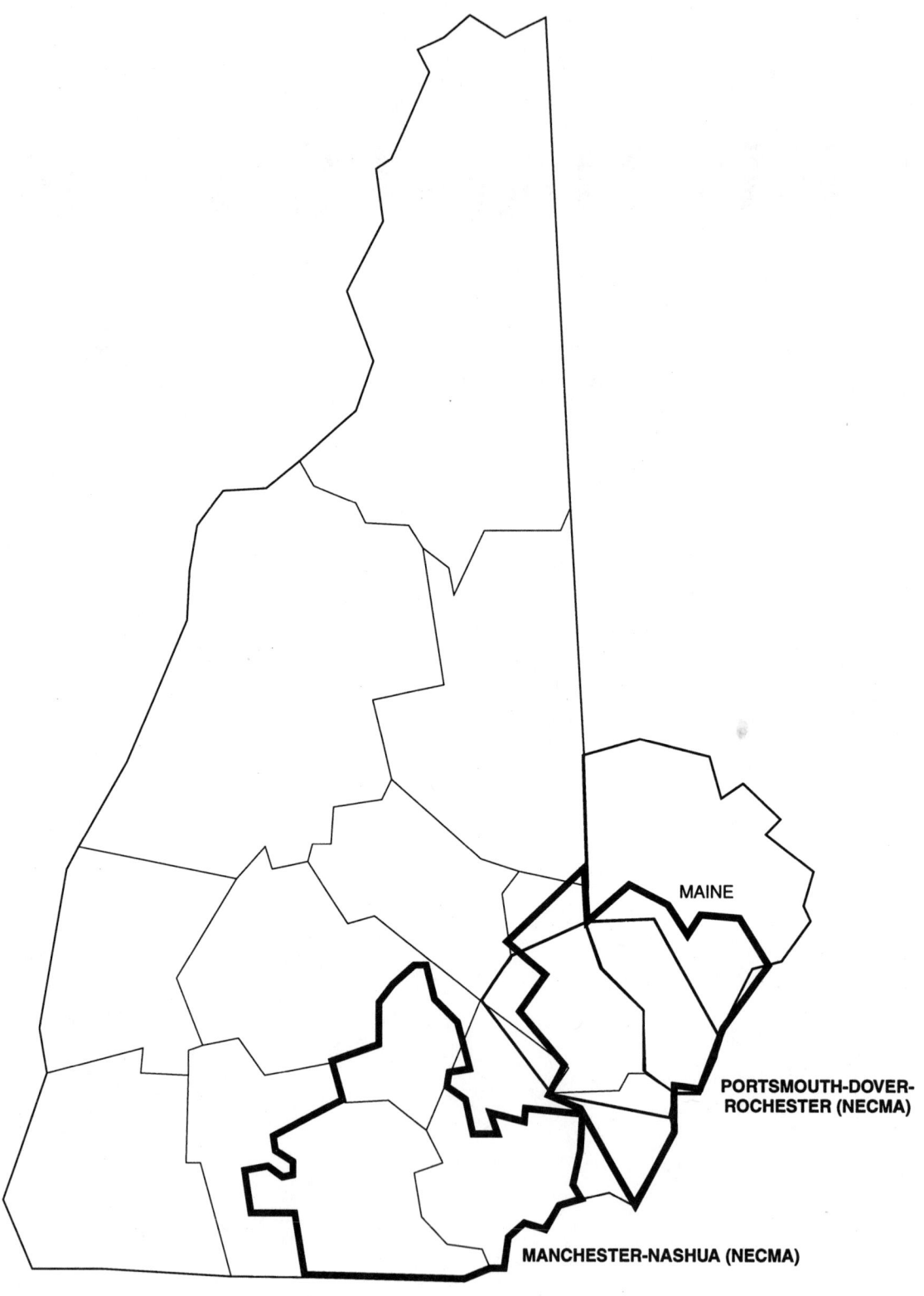

MAINE

PORTSMOUTH-DOVER-
ROCHESTER (NECMA)

MANCHESTER-NASHUA (NECMA)

NEW HAMPSHIRE

Population
1990: 1,109,252
1980: 920,610

Age
Ages 18 to 20: 52,399
Ages 21 to 24: 65,203
Ages 25 to 44: 387,455
Ages 45 to 54: 112,215
Ages 55 to 59: 44,703
Ages 60 to 64: 43,493
Median age: 32.8

Race and Hispanic Origin
White: 1,087,433
Black: 7,198
Asian/Pacific Islander: 9,343
Native American: 2,134
Hispanic origin: 11,333

Households
Total: 411,186
Persons per household: 2.62

Sex
Male: 543,544
Female: 565,708

Population Migration
Domestic migration: 162,000
International migration: 2,000

Projection of the Population in 1995
Total: 1,184,000
18 to 64: 749,000

Civilian Labor Force
1993: 642,800
1992: 628,500
1991: 643,300
1990: 622,300

Manufacturing
1995 Projection: 125,900
1992: 97,300
1991: 99,900
1990: 102,700
1989: 111,800

Services
1995 Projection: 199,500

1992: 128,900
1991: 129,400
1990: 128,600
1989: 123,000

Wholesale and Retail Trade
1995 Projection: 178,700
1992: 123,500
1991: 120,100
1990: 128,400
1989: 136,200

Unemployment Rate
1993: 8.3%
1992: 7.8%
1991: 7.1%
1990: 4.6%

Employer Unemployment Contributions

Contribution Rate
1992: 2.02%
1991: 0.80%
1990: 0.74%

Average Weekly Benefit
1992: $140.94
1991: $139.64
1990: $128.67

Gross State Product (Million $)
1989: $24,504
1988: $23,812
1987: $21,831
1979: $8,440
Growth rate, 1979 to 1989: 190.3%

Capital Expenditures of Manufacturing Industries
1990: $303,200,000
1989: $398,300,000
1988: $358,200,000
1987: $339,800,000

State Tax Rates
Individual income: None.
Corporate income: 8% of federal net income.
General property: Rates fixed locally. Assessed at full and true cash value of taxable real property and tangible per-

sonal property.

General sales: None

Gasoline: 18¢ per gallon

Income

Median income for a 4 person family: $47,983

Personal per Capita Income

1992: $22,934

1991: $21,812

1990: $21,051

Disposable per Capita Income

1992: $20,889

1991: $19,789

1990: $18,952

Private Employment Weekly Wages

Average

1989: $413

1988: $400

1987: $400

Manufacturing

1989: $373

1988: $501

1987: $471

Services

1989: $381

1988: $362

1987: $330

Wholesale

1989: $580

1988: $571

1987: $531

Retail

1989: $243

1988: $239

1987: $226

Highway Statistics

Total Highway Miles

1990: 14,836

1989: 14,803

1988: 14,711

Federal Highway Aid

1991: $54,137,000

1990: $53,481,000

1989: $54,253,000

Electricity

Average Cost per Kilowatt Hour

1990: 9.06¢

1989: 8.54¢

1988: 8.26¢

Housing (1990)

Owner occupied units: 280,372

Median house value: $129,400

Renter occupied units: 130,814

Median rent: $479

Total vacant units: 92,718

Homeowner vacancy rate: 2.7%

Rental vacancy rate: 11.8%

State Business Incentives and Assistance

Financial and Business Assistance

Industrial Development Authority. A state agency, the Authority is authorized to issue industrial development bonds. The IDBs provide financing to businesses to establish or redevelop industrial facilities. The bond funds may be used to purchase land and construct and equip a facility.

Local Industrial Development Authorities. Local governments may also establish industrial development authorities to issue industrial development bonds for property acquisition and development for manufacturing and warehousing facilities. This program is designed to help alleviate and prevent unemployment and ensure economic growth of the communities.

Tax Incentives. New Hampshire does not levy general sales tax, state personal income tax, capital gains tax, nor property tax on business inventory.

Education and Training

Job Training Services. Provides customized training programs to new or expanding companies in recruitment, curriculum development, and classroom, as well as on-the-job, training.

State Offices

Real estate: Real Estate Commission, Valerie B. Lanigan, Exec Director, 107 Pleasant Street, 3rd Fl., Concord, NH 03301. 603-271-2701

Chamber of commerce: Business & Industrial Association of New Hampshire, John D. Crosier, President, Main Street, Concord, NH 03301. 603-224-5388

Economic development: Dept. of Resources and Economic Development, Office of Business & Industrial Development, William E. Pillsbury, Jr., Director, PO Box 856, 172 Pembroke Rd., Concord, NH 03302-0856. 603-271-2591, FAX 603-271-2629

New Hampshire Industrial Development Authority, Marilyn Jewell, Exec Director, 4 Park Street, Rm 302, Concord, NH 03301. 603-271-2391

Southern New Hampshire Association of Commerce and Industry, Michael Valuk, Exec. Director, 1 Tara Blvd., Suite 211, Nashua, NH 03062. 603-891-2471

New Hampshire Small Business Development Center, Helen Goodman, Director, University of New Hampshire, 108 McConnell Hall, Durham, NH 03824. 603-862-2200

The Granite Foundation, Warren Henderson, Exec Director, 889 Elm Street, Manchester, NH 03101. 603-668-2000

Small Business Development Center, Helen Goodman, State Director, University of New Hampshire, 400 Com-

Major Companies in the State

Company name	Fortune 500 rank	City	Telephone	SIC number
Fortune 500 Companies				
Abex Inc.	429	Hampton	603-926-5911	3728
Tyco Laboratories Inc.	154	Exeter	603-778-9700	3569
Other Major Companies in the State				
Amoskeag Bank Shares Inc.		Bedford	603-627-3060	6712
Bank of New Hampshire Corp.		Manchester	603-624-6600	6712
Bankeast Corp.		Manchester	603-624-6193	6712
Cabletron Systems Inc.		Rochester	603-332-9400	3679
Dartmouth Bancorp Inc.		Manchester	603-622-2440	6712
Ekco Group Inc.		Nashua	603-888-1212	3469
Energynorth Inc.		Manchester	603-625-4000	4923
Fisher Scientific International Inc.		Hampton	603-926-5911	3821
Hadco Corp.		Salem	603-898-8000	3672
Hanover Insurance Co.		Manchester	508-853-7200	6331
Healthsource Inc.		Concord	603-225-5077	6324
Henley Properties Inc.		Hampton	603-926-5911	6552
New Hampshire Savings Bank Corp.		Concord	603-226-1212	6712
Numerica Financial Corp.		Bedford	603-472-4460	6712
Pneumo Abex Corp.		Hampton	603-926-5911	3724
Public Service Co. of New Hampshire		Manchester	603-669-4000	4911
Standex International Corp.		Salem	603-893-9701	3585
Timberland Co.		Hampton	603-926-1600	3143
Unitil Corp.		Exeter	603-772-0775	4911

mercial Street, Manchester, NH 03101. 603-625-4522

Environmental affairs: Dept. of Environmental Services, Robert W. Varney, Commissioner, 6 Hazen Drive, Concord, NH 03301. 603-271-3503

Labor: Dept. of Labor, Richard M. Flynn, Commissioner, 19 Pillsbury Street, Concord, NH 03301. 603-271-3171

Unemployment: Dept. of Employment Security, John J. Ratoff, Commissioner, 32 South Main Street, Concord, NH 03301. 603-224-3311

Worker's compensation: Dept. of Labor, Workers' Compensation Division, Richard M. Flynn, Commissioner, 19 Pillsbury Street, Concord, NH 03301. 603-271-3176

Occupational safety and health: Dept. of Labor, Occupational Safety & Health Consultation, Richard M. Flynn, Commissioner, 19 Pillsbury Street, Concord, NH 03301. 603-271-2024

Secretary of state: Corporate Division, Secretary of State, Thomas Connolly, Assistant Secretary of State, 3rd floor, State House Annex, Concord, NH 03301. 603-271-3244

Taxation and revenue: Dept. of Revenue Administration, Stanley R. Arnold, Commissioner, 61 South Spring St., Concord, NH 03301. 603-271-2191

Designated Zones for Economic Development

Enterprise Zones

No program.

Foreign Trade Zones

Foreign Trade Zone No. 81, Portsmouth, New Hampshire, Grantee/Operator: New Hampshire State Port Authority, Arlene Cohn, 555 Market Street, PO Box 506, Portsmouth, NH 03801, 603-436-8500

Labor Unions

Plumbing and Pipe Fitting Industry of The United States and Canada, United Association of, Journeymen and Apprentices of the (AFL-CIO)

State, County and Municipal Employees, American Federation of (AFL-CIO)

Universities with Ph.D. Programs

Dartmouth College, Hanover

University of New Hampshire, Durham

MANCHESTER–NASHUA, NH (NECMA)

Geographic Profile

Land Area
876.5 square miles

Counties and Parishes
Hillsborough (part)
Merrimack (part)
Rockingham (part)
Nashua
Hillsborough (part)
Rockingham (part)

Additional Cities/Towns within Area
Hillsborough County:
 Bedford
 Goffstown
Merrimack County:
 Allentown
 Hooksett
Rockingham County:
 Auburn
 Candia
Nashua
Hillsborough County:
 Amherst
 Brookline
 Hollis
 Hudson
 Litchfield
 Merrimack
 Milford
 Mount Vernon
 Wilton
Rockingham County:
 Londonderry

Ranking Highlights
225 *out of 319 in total* **land area**
 72 *out of 319 in* **population growth,** *1970–1990*
212 *out of 310 in having the lowest* **unemployment** *rate*
117 *out of 310 in size of* **labor force**
 45 *out of 318 in the percentage of* **college graduates**
N/A *out of 292 in per capita personal* **income**
 90 *out of 319 in number of* **manufacturing establishments**
190 *out of 318 in* **physicians** *per 1000 people*
247 *out of 318 in* **hospital beds** *per 1000 people*
116 *out of 267 in fewest* **crimes** *per 1000 people*
 19 *out of 266 in fewest* **violent crimes** *per 1000 people*
132 *out of 319 in per capita* **federal funds and grants**

Quality of Life Indexes (Rate per 1000 population)
Crime rate in 1991:   58.1
Violent crime rate in 1991:   1.9
Physicians rate in 1992:   1.68
Hospital bed rate in 1991:   2.95

ACCRA Cost of Living Indexes
(First quarter 1993, average = 100)
Composite index: 118.2
Utilities index: 153.2
Housing index: 117.6

Overview

Manchester
Once a single-industry town dependent on the textile industry, Manchester has diversified its economy to include manufacturing (more than 200 manufacturing firms are located there), wholesale and retail trade, information processing, and the service industry. More than eighty-five percent of the workforce is involved in sales, finance, and service companies. Manchester is considered the major insurance and financial center north of Boston, housing the area's largest savings and commercial institutions. The city is also the northeastern states' principal distribution center.

Manchester, located on the main line of the Boston & Maine Railroad, maintains excellent freight service south to Boston, Massachusetts, and north to Montreal, Quebec, Canada, and connecting lines. A large fleet of commercial trucks is also available for shipping goods to all parts of the country. Air freight service is offered at Manchester Airport, the state's major airport. Air freight lines and U.S. Customs service are also available; the industrial area surrounding the airport has been designated a Foreign Trade Zone. Daily delivery service includes Federal Express, United Parcel Service, and Airborne Express. The Merrimack River not being navigable, Manchester is not a port city; however, the Port of New Hampshire in Portsmouth is located forty-five minutes east of Manchester.

Manchester's largest convention facility is suitable for mid-sized meetings. There are twenty-two hotels and motels in the area with more than 1,200 rooms.

Increased use of Manchester Airport in recent years has brought an increase in services by major airlines and demands for expanding the facility. Non–stop flights are available to several major cities in the U.S. that offer worldwide connections.

Manchester, encircled by major highways, is the focal point of New Hampshire's interstate road system. Major north-south routes include the Frederick E. Everett Turnpike and Interstate-93, which carry traffic from Boston, through Manchester, and on to Concord. East-west arteries include U.S. Route 101, which runs east to Portsmouth on the coast, west to Keene, and southwest to Nashua. A bypass loop of I-93, named I-293, encircles the city to the west and south and handles some of the commuter traffic to the suburbs.

Nashua
Nashua, ranked the nation's best place to live by *Money*

magazine in its August 1987 issue, is New Hampshire's second largest city. Nashua, which became prominent as a cotton mill town during the Industrial Revolution, has since diversified its economic base to include service, retail, and financial firms. High-technology products and research are relative newcomers to Nashua, whose location in the Gateways Region between New Hampshire and Massachusetts makes it a prime business and transportation site.

Grant Thornton, a national accounting firm, has ranked Nashua the number one manufacturing environment in the country. The ranking was based on acceptable corporate tax and wage rates, education level of the work force, the interstate highway system, and the absence of New Hampshire sales and income taxes. More than 350 technology–related companies operate manufacturing, engineering, and research facilities in the region, and over 150 of these, employing more than 13,000 workers, are located within the city. While maintaining a strong manufacturing base, Nashua is the major retail, service, and financial center for southern Hillsborough County and adjacent Massachusetts communities. Two Nashua firms appear on the Fortune 500 list of the top U.S. manufacturing firms: Sanders Associates, a division of Lockheed International, and the Nashua Corporation.

While at one point Nashua hosted four different railroad depots, train travel declined with the advent of the automobile. Today, only the Boston & Maine rail line runs through Nashua. Five motor freight carriers service the city, which is home to a number of warehouses.

More than two thousand guest rooms and suites are available in the Gateways Region, whose principal convention site is Nashua. The largest facility in Nashua is the Sheraton Tara Hotel, with 343 guest rooms, fifteen meeting rooms, and a ballroom accommodating 1,000 people.

Boston's Logan International Airport, an hour's drive to the southeast, provides full commercial and freight air service. Regularly scheduled buses travel between Nashua and Logan daily. Just outside Nashua's northwestern city limit is Boire Field, used for corporate air travel. Boire Field is the site of the Federal Aviation Control Center that provides air traffic control for all of New England and upstate New York. Manchester Airport, about twenty–five minutes from Nashua, has daily connections to major cities.

The Nashua area is the starting point for two of the state's major four-lane highways, U.S. Route 3 and Interstate-93. Route 3, the F.E. Everett Turnpike, runs north-south through the western portion of the city. I-93 passes by the city to the east and is connected to Nashua by the east-west traveling New Hampshire Route 111.

Population (1990)

Total Population and Growth Rate
1990: 336,073
1980: 276,608
1970: 223,941
Growth rate 1970–1990: 50%

Race and Hispanic Origin
White: 97.2%
Black: .9%
Asian/Pacific Islander: 1.2%
Native American: 0.2%
Hispanic origin: 1.7%
White not Hispanic: 96.0%

Age
Ages 18 to 20: 4.2%
Ages 21 to 24: 5.8%
Ages 25 to 44: 35.8%
Ages 45 to 54: 10%
Ages 55 to 59: 3.7%
Ages 60 to 64: 3.5%
Ages 65 plus: 9.7%

Educational Attainment (1990)
Percent having completed high school: 82.3%
Percent having completed college: 26.5%
Elementary and high school enrollment: 58,212

Federal Funds and Grants Received
Total received in 1989: $1,093,000,000
Funds received per capita: $3,290

Civilian Labor Force
1993 (April): 186,400
1992 average: 185,902
1991 average: 187,580
1990 average: 190,650

Unemployment
1993 (April): 6.7%
1992 average: 7.8%
1991 average: 7.5%
1990 average: 6.1%

Average Annual Pay
1988: $22,925
1987: $21,502
1985: $18,697

Per Capita Personal Income
1991: N/A
1990: N/A
1989: N/A

Business Climate (1987)

Manufacturing
Number of establishments in 1987: 697
Shipments in 1987 ($1,000): $4,690,200
Employees in 1987: 43,900
Change in employment, 1982 to 1987: -1.1%
Average annual pay for manufacturing work in 1989: $31,116
Average annual pay for production work in 1987: $23,441

Wholesale Trade
Number of establishments in 1987: 742
Total sales in 1987 ($1,000): $3,301,000
Change in sales, 1982 to 1987: 105.3%

Retail Trade
Number of establishments in 1987: 2,265
Total sales in 1987 ($1,000): $3,301,000
Retail sales per household in 1987: $26,079
Average annual pay in 1989: $12,864

Service Industry
Selected receipts in 1987 ($1,000): $1,154,400
Average annual pay in 1989: $21,288

Office Real Estate (1992)
Office space inventory: N/A
Average class A Central Business District rental range per sq. ft: N/A

Vacancy Rates
All areas: N/A

Vacancy Rates in Central Business District
Class A space: 12.8%
Class B space: 17.4%

Vacancy Rates Outside Central Business District
Class A space: 17.4%
Class B space: 18.6%

Housing
Total number of units in 1990: 130,945
Occupied units in 1990: 121,740
Owner-occupied units in 1990: 63.7%
1993 ACCRA average cost: $125,750
1993 ACCRA average rent for an apartment: $667

Chamber of Commerce
Greater Manchester Chamber of Commerce, Thomas H. Schwieger, President, 889 Elm St., Manchester, NH 03101. 603-666-6600

Economic Development Office
Greater Nashua Chamber of Commerce, Michael J. Valuk, Exec. Director, 1 Tara Blvd. #211, Nashua, NH 03062. 603-891-2471

Economic Development Organizations
Greater Manchester Development Corp., Richard L. Hodgkinson, President, 889 Elm St., Manchester NH 03101. 603-624-6505, FAX 603-624-6308

Major Businesses

Company	SIC	Telephone
1400 Motors of Nashua Inc.	5511	(603) 888-0200
Amoskeag Bank	6035	(603) 647-3200
Amoskeag Bank Shares Inc.	6021	(603) 647-3200
Associated Grocers	5141	(603) 669-3250
Bank New Hampshire Corp.	6021	(603) 624-6600

Major Businesses (Continued)

Company	SIC	Telephone
Bankeast Corp.	6022	(603) 624-6000
Catholic Medical Center	8062	(603) 668-3545
Chemical Fabrics Corp.	2295	(603) 424-9000
Coca-Cola Bottling	5149	(603) 627-0627
Dartmouth Bancorp, Inc.	6035	(603) 485-6500
Datamedia Corp.	3571	(603) 886-1570
Dobles Chevrolet Inc.	5511	(603) 669-2450
Energynorth, Inc.	4924	(603) 625-4000
Ferrofluidics Corp.	3053	(603) 883-9800
First NH Banks Inc.	6021	(603) 668-5020
Fleet Bank-NH Inc.	6022	(603) 594-5000
Guilford Transportation	4011	(603) 429-1685
Harvey Construction	1541	(603) 668-3100
Heat Inc.	5075	(603) 889-0104
Hitchiner Manufacturing	3324	(603) 673-1100
Indian Head Banks Inc.	6712	(603) 594-5000
Lee Certified Coins Ltd.	5961	(603) 429-0869
Lockheed Sanders, Inc.	3812	(603) 885-4321
MacMulkin Chevrolet Inc.	5511	(603) 888-1121
Merchants Rent-A-Car, Inc.	5511	(603) 669-6666
Nashua Corp.	2672	(603) 880-2323
Nashua Hospital Association	8062	(603) 883-5521
Nashua Trust Co.	6022	(603) 882-2755
Nault's Truck World Inc.	5511	(603) 625-2540
New Hampshire Housing Finance	6162	(603) 472-8623
New Hampshire Insurance Co.	6331	(603) 645-7000
Numerica Financial Corp.	6035	(603) 624-2424
Numerica Savings Bank	6035	(603) 624-2424
Public Service of New Hampshire	4911	(603) 669-4000
Seaboard International Forest Products	5031	(603) 673-6800
St. Joseph Hospital	8062	(603) 882-3000
Stabile, H. J. & Son Inc.	1542	(603) 889-0318
Tulley Buick-Pontiac Co.	5511	(603) 888-0551
United Savings Bank	6035	(603) 625-2600
Worthen Industries Inc.	2891	(603) 888-5443

Colleges and Universities
Daniel Webster College, Nashua
Hesser College, Manchester
New Hampshire College, Manchester
New Hampshire Technical College, Manchester
New Hampshire Technical College, Nashua
Notre Dame College, Manchester
Rivier College, Nashua
St. Anselm College, Manchester
University of New Hampshire at Manchester, Manchester

PORTSMOUTH–DOVER–ROCHESTER, NH-ME (NECMA)

Geographic Profile

Land Area
1064.1 square miles

Counties and Parishes
New Hampshire:
　Rockingham (part)
　Strafford (part)
Maine:
　York

Additional Cities/Towns within Area
Rockingham County:
　Exeter
　Greenland
　Hampton
　New Castle
　Newfields
　Newington
　Newmarket
　North Hampton
　Rye
　Stratham
Strafford County:
　Barrington
　Durham
　Farmington
　Lee
　Madbury
　Milton
　Rollinsford
　Somersworth
York County:
　Berwick
　Eliot
　Kittery
　North Berwick
　Wells
　York

Ranking Highlights
187 *out of 319 in total* **land area**
　52 *out of 319 in* **population growth,** *1970–1990*
N/A *out of 310 in having the lowest* **unemployment** *rate*
N/A *out of 310 in size of* **labor force**
　54 *out of 318 in the percentage of* **college graduates**
N/A *out of 292 in per capita personal* **income**
104 *out of 319 in number of* **manufacturing establishments**
257 *out of 318 in* **physicians** *per 1000 people*

309 *out of 318 in* **hospital beds** *per 1000 people*
N/A *out of 267 in fewest* **crimes** *per 1000 people*
N/A *out of 266 in fewest* **violent crimes** *per 1000 people*
140 *out of 319 in per capita* **federal funds and grants**

Quality of Life Indexes (Rate per 1000 population)
Crime rate in 1991:	N/A
Violent crime rate in 1991:	N/A
Physicians rate in 1992:	1.35
Hospital bed rate in 1991:	1.84

ACCRA Cost of Living Indexes
(First quarter 1993, average = 100)
Composite index:	N/A
Utilities index:	N/A
Housing index:	N/A

Overview

Portsmouth is a part of the northeast market area that serves 36 percent of the nation's population in addition to eastern Canada. Major economic sectors in Portsmouth include tourism, the retail and service industries, and fishing and agriculture. The area's major employer is the Portsmouth Naval Shipyard across the Piscataqua River from Portsmouth. This facility, which repairs nuclear submarines, also supports attendant vendors and manufacturers, and recently completed construction of a $34 million enclosed dry dock. Pease Air Force Base in Portsmouth was one of the first military installations in the country to close as a result of the 1989 Base Closure and Realignment Act, and in March 1991, all 10,000 military personnel and their dependents left, taking with them an annual payroll of $110 million. Their departure took a heavy toll on the region's economy, already suffering as a result of the recession that began in the late 1980s.

The only seaport in the state and the only deepwater harbor between Portland, Maine, and Boston, Massachusetts, Portsmouth remains a major New England port of entry. The port, a designated Foreign Trade Zone, includes a state–operated marine terminal. Container service to Halifax and European destinations is available weekly. Public and private terminals along the Piscataqua River account for in excess of 3.5 million tons of cargo per year. In addition to the port facilities, Portsmouth shipping includes the Boston & Maine Railroad, twenty–one regular truck route carriers, United Parcel Service, and Federal Express. Air freight service is available at three commercial airports within an hour's drive; proposals for the reuse of Pease Air Force Base in Portsmouth include air travel components.

Air travelers can use facilities at Logan International Airport, one hour to Portsmouth's south in Boston, Massachusetts; at Portland International Airport, one hour to the north in Portland, Maine; or Manchester Airport in Manchester, New Hampshire, which connects the southern part of the state to Washington, New York City, Chicago, Illinois, Philadelphia, Pennsylvania, and Pittsburgh, Pennsylvania. Frequent daily limousine service is available between Logan and Portsmouth.

Interstate 95 is a direct link connecting Portsmouth with Portland, Maine, and Boston; it extends as far north as the Canadian provinces and south to Key West, Florida. The Spaulding Turnpike (Rte. 16) connects the city to Dover, Rochester, and further north to the White Mountains. U.S. Route 101 stretches west through Manchester and eventually to Keene, New Hampshire. U.S. Route 4 leads into the city from Concord to the east.

Population (1990)

Total Population and Growth Rate
1990: 350,078
1980: 275,753
1970: 209,382
Growth rate 1970–1990: 67%

Race and Hispanic Origin
White: 97.6%
Black: 1.0%
Asian/Pacific Islander: 1.0%
Native American: 0.2%
Hispanic origin: 0.9%
White not Hispanic: 97.0%

Age
Ages 18 to 20: 3.6%
Ages 21 to 24: 4.5%
Ages 25 to 44: 22%
Ages 45 to 54: 6.2%
Ages 55 to 59: 2.6%
Ages 60 to 64: 2.5%
Ages 65 plus: 7.5%

Educational Attainment (1990)
Percent having completed high school: 84.3%
Percent having completed college: 25.4%
Elementary and high school enrollment: 46,000

Federal Funds and Grants Received
Total received in 1989: $1,084,900,000
Funds received per capita: $3,244

Civilian Labor Force
1993 (April):   N/A
1992 average: N/A
1991 average: 196,530
1990 average: 194,740

Unemployment
1993 (April):   N/A
1992 average: N/A
1991 average: 7.5%
1990 average: 6.0%

Average Annual Pay
1988: $20,129
1987: $18,620

1985: $17,509

Per Capita Personal Income
1991: N/A
1990: N/A
1989: N/A

Business Climate (1987)

Manufacturing
Number of establishments in 1987: 576
Shipments in 1987 ($1,000): $4,279,400
Employees in 1987: 24,700
Change in employment, 1982 to 1987: -3.9%
Average annual pay for manufacturing work in 1989: $27,852
Average annual pay for production work in 1987: $18,481

Wholesale Trade
Number of establishments in 1987: 589
Total sales in 1987 ($1,000): $1,895,000
Change in sales, 1982 to 1987: 32.5%

Retail Trade
Number of establishments in 1987: 2,497
Total sales in 1987 ($1,000): $1,895,000
Retail sales per household in 1987: $25,964
Average annual pay in 1989: $12,251

Service Industry
Selected receipts in 1987 ($1,000): $853,300
Average annual pay in 1989: $19,073

Housing
Total number of units in 1990: 100,891
Occupied units in 1990: 84,311
Owner-occupied units in 1990: 64.9%
1993 ACCRA average cost: N/A
1993 ACCRA average rent for an apartment: N/A

Chamber of Commerce
Greater Portsmouth Chamber of Commerce, Kerry Hadley, President, 500 Market St. #16, PO Box 239, Portsmouth, NH 03801. 603-436-1118

Economic Development Office
Granite State Development Corp., Alan Abraham, 1 Cate St., 5th Fl., Portsmouth, NH 03801. 603-436-0009

Economic Development Organizations
Dover Economic Development Department, Stephen Griffin, Director, 288 Central Ave., Dover, NH 03820. 603-743-6000, FAX 603-743-6097

City of Rochester, Economic Development Department, George Bald, Acting City Manager, 31 Wakefield St., Rochester, NH 03867. 603-335-1338

Major Businesses

Company	SIC	Telephone
Abington Constructors Inc.	1541	(603) 436-5800

Major Businesses (Continued)

Company	SIC	Telephone
Bournival Inc.	5511	(603) 431-8900
Byrnes Chevrolet Inc.	5511	(603) 742-1676
Clarostat Mfg. Co. Inc.	3676	(603) 742-1120
Davidson Textron Inc.	3714	(603) 742-0720
First Coastal Banks Inc.	6021	(603) 436-7700
First National Bank of Portsmouth	6021	(603) 436-7700
Frisbie Memorial Hospital	8062	(603) 332-5211
Great Bay Bankshares, Inc.	6035	(603) 749-4149
Harris Graphics Corp.	3555	(603) 749-6600
Hilltop Chevrolet Inc.	5511	(603) 692-2121
National Sea Products Inc.	2092	(603) 431-6865
Neslab Instruments, Inc.	3821	(603) 436-9444
New Hampshire Oak Inc.	3357	(603) 926-5911
NHO Inc.	3357	(603) 926-5911
Northern Utilities, Inc.	4923	(603) 436-0310
Novel Iron Works Inc.	3441	(603) 436-7950
Omni Hotels Corp.	7011	(603) 926-8911
Omni Hotels Management Co.	7011	(603) 926-8911
PA Holdings Corp.	3812	(603) 926-5911
Portsmouth Paper Co.	5113	(603) 436-1910
Robbins Auto Parts Inc.	5013	(603) 742-2880
Seaward Corp.	1623	(207) 439-5900
Southeast Bank for Saving	6035	(603) 742-8100
Sprague Energy Corp.	5172	(603) 431-1000
Timberland Co. Inc.	3143	(603) 926-1600
Vitronics Corp.	3567	(603) 659-6550
Weathervane Seafoods Inc.	5812	(207) 439-0330
Wentworth-Douglass Hospital	8062	(603) 742-5252
Wheelabrator Technologies	1629	(603) 929-3000
York Hospital	8062	(207) 363-4321

Colleges and Universities

Mcintosh College, Dover, NH
New Hampshire Technical College, Stratham, NH
School For Lifelong Learning of The University System of
  New Hampshire, Durham, NH
University of New Hampshire, Durham, NH

NEW JERSEY

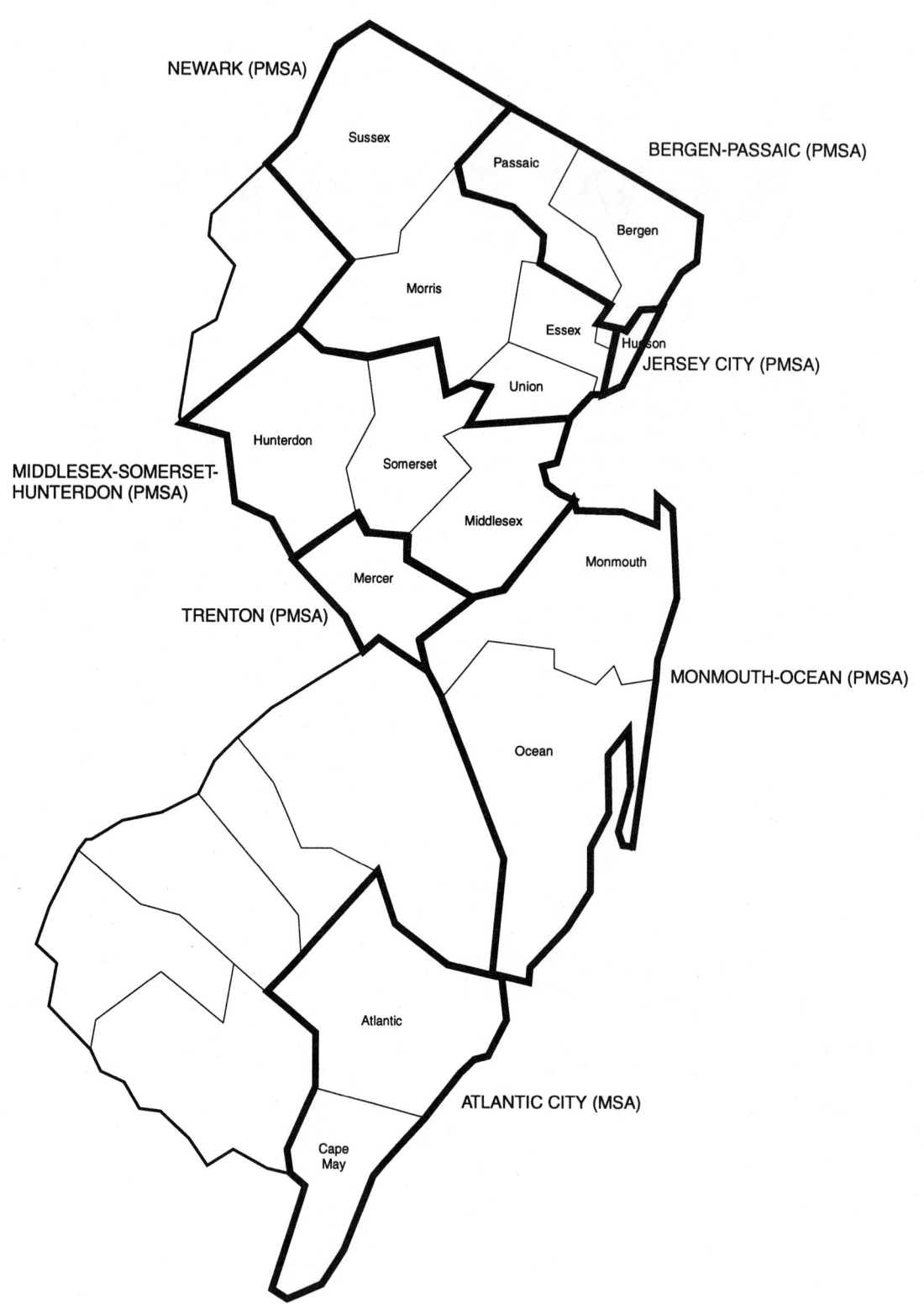

NEWARK (PMSA)

Sussex

BERGEN-PASSAIC (PMSA)

Passaic

Bergen

Morris

Essex

Hudson

JERSEY CITY (PMSA)

Union

MIDDLESEX-SOMERSET-
HUNTERDON (PMSA)

Hunterdon

Somerset

Middlesex

Monmouth

Mercer

TRENTON (PMSA)

MONMOUTH-OCEAN (PMSA)

Ocean

Atlantic

ATLANTIC CITY (MSA)

Cape
May

NEW JERSEY

Population
1990: 7,730,188
1980: 7,364,823

Age
Ages 18 to 20: 326,079
Ages 21 to 24: 453,105
Ages 25 to 44: 2,557,310
Ages 45 to 54: 843,009
Ages 55 to 59: 355,677
Ages 60 to 64: 363,521
Median age: 34.5

Race and Hispanic Origin
White: 6,130,465
Black: 1,036,825
Asian/Pacific Islander: 272,521
Native American: 14,970
Hispanic origin: 739,861

Households
Total: 2,794,711
Persons per household: 2.70

Sex
Male: 3,735,685
Female: 3,994,503

Population Migration
Domestic migration: -8,000
International migration: 205,000

Projection of the Population in 1995
Total: 8,177,000
18 to 64: 5,157,000

Civilian Labor Force
1993: 3,897,100
1992: 4,023,600
1991: 4,028,000
1990: 3,980,100

Manufacturing
1995 Projection: 662,500
1992: 527,300
1991: 542,100
1990: 584,000
1989: 650,400

Services
1995 Projection: 1,407,600

1992: 972,000
1991: 995,000
1990: 987,200
1989: 956,700

Wholesale and Retail Trade
1995 Projection: 1,078,900
1992: 808,600
1991: 870,400
1990: 898,400
1989: 925,000

Unemployment Rate
1993: 8.0%
1992: 7.6%
1991: 6.3%
1990: 5.2%

Employer Unemployment Contributions
Contribution Rate
1992: 2.00%
1991: 1.86%
1990: 1.83%

Average Weekly Benefit
1992: $234.98
1991: $227.84
1990: $209.27

Gross State Product (Million $)
1989: $203,375
1988: $193,034
1987: $174,714
1979: $81,051
Growth rate, 1979 to 1989: 150.9%

Capital Expenditures of Manufacturing Industries
1990: $2,702,200,000
1989: $2,636,000,000
1988: $2,356,000,000
1987: $2,312,500,000

State Tax Rates
Individual income: Range from 2% ($20,000 or less) to 7% (above $50,000).
Corporate income: 9% of total taxable income, with 0.375% surtax imposed.

General property: Sum of local levies. Real property valued at 20% to 100% of true value.

General sales: 7%

Gasoline: 10.5¢ per gallon

Income

Median income for a 4 person family: $53,229

Personal per Capita Income

1992: $26,457

1991: $25,369

1990: $24,977

Disposable per Capita Income

1992: $23,074

1991: $22,023

1990: $21,654

Private Employment Weekly Wages

Average

1989: $511

1988: $493

1987: $493

Manufacturing

1989: $455

1988: $592

1987: $548

Services

1989: $476

1988: $455

1987: $416

Wholesale

1989: $647

1988: $628

1987: $577

Retail

1989: $290

1988: $277

1987: $259

Highway Statistics

Total Highway Miles

1990: 34,252

1989: 34,246

1988: 34,197

Federal Highway Aid

1991: $364,533,000

1990: $352,440,000

1989: $300,557,000

Electricity

Average Cost per Kilowatt Hour

1990: 9.11¢

1989: 8.82¢

1988: 8.51¢

Housing (1990)

Owner occupied units: 1,813,381

Median house value: $162,300

Renter occupied units: 981,330

Median rent: $521

Total vacant units: 280,599

Homeowner vacancy rate: 2.5%

Rental vacancy rate: 7.4%

State Business Incentives and Assistance

Enterprise Zone Incentives

1) A one time tax credit of $1,500 for hiring residents of a city where a zone is located who have been unemployed or dependent upon public assistance for at least 90 days.

2) Credit of $500 for hiring certain other full-time employees.

3) Subsidized unemployment insurance costs, for certain new employees.

4) An eligible firm may receive an incentive tax credit of 8% of investment in the zone.

5) Sales tax exemptions for materials and for tangible personal property.

6) State regulatory relief by zone request.

7) Priority for financial assistance from New Jersey Local Development Financing Fund and Job Training Program.

Financial and Business Assistance

Advanced Technology Centers. Administered by the Commission on Science and Technology, this program is designed to assist companies getting access to state-of-the-art research in the fields of biotechnology, advanced materials, telematics, and environmental protection. By becoming affiliates of the Centers, companies can gain access to research results and possibly participate in joint research projects with individual centers.

Business Incubators Program. Administered by the Commission on Science and Technology, this program provides new technology companies with shared cost space and support services, as well as access to university facilities and research.

New Jersey Economic Development Authority. Established by the New Jersey legislature, the Authority is authorized to issue tax-exempt and taxable industrial development bonds. The IDBs help new and expanding manufacturing companies to obtain long-term loans. Tax-exempt financing may be provided for manufacturing businesses for acquisition of property and land and other facility projects. Many other businesses are elegible for taxable bond financing. Besides issuing bonds, the Authority may also guarantee partial repayment of a tax-exempt bond issue or a conventional bank loan if the guarantee will help a qualified firm to maintain or expand employment in the state.

New Jersey Local Development Financing Fund. Administered by the Urban Programs Office of the Department of Commerce and Economic Development and authorized by the Local Development Financing Fund Act, this program provides loans and grants to private developers for industrial and commercial projects in communities receiving state Urban Aid. At least 50% of the total project cost must be provided by private sources.

Small Business Assistance. Administered by the Office of Small Business Assistance of the Department of Commerce and Economic Development, this program provides business expansion and start-up counseling, financial advice and marketing and procurement assistance. Seminars are offered throughout the state as a part of the department's comprehensive outreach program.

Retention and Expansion of Existing Business. Administered by the Department of Commerce and Economic Development, this program provides a municipal level program that will seek the protection of jobs and will further the creation of new jobs. The program establishes a local volunteer task force that uses a specifically designed survey instrument to interview owners.

International Trade. Administered by the Division of International Trade of the Department of Commerce and Economic Development, this program helps New Jersey companies export their products and encourages foreign investment. It operates an overseas trade show program which assists New Jersey companies to exhibit their products overseas.

Education and Training

Office of Customized Training. Administered by the Department of Labor, this Office provides customized worker job skill training for employers. The assistance may be given in the form of on-the-job training, classroom training, retraining and upgrading skill training. For new and expanding businesses, the Office can also assist in the recruitment and screening of potential trainees.

Job Training Services. Provides customized training programs to new or expanding companies in recruitment, curriculum development, and classroom, as well as on-the-job, training.

State Offices

Real estate: Insurance Department, Real Estate Division, Daryl G. Bell, Assistant Commissioner, 20 West State Street, CN 325, Trenton, NJ 08625. 609-292-8280

Chamber of commerce: New Jersey State Chamber of Commerce, Frederick A. Westphal, President, 5 Commerce St., Newark, NJ 07102. 201-623-7070

Economic development: Department of Commerce and Economic Development, Kenneth C. LeFevre, Deputy Commissioner, 1 W. State St., CN 823, Trenton, NJ 08625. 609-292-1800

Department of Commerce and Economic Development, Office of Small Business Assistance, Director, 20 W. State St., CN-823, Trenton, NJ 08625. 609-984-4442

Department of Commerce and Economic Development,

Enterprise Zone, F. Charles Garofalo, Administrator, CN-829, Trenton, NJ 08625. 609-292-1912

Department of Commerce and Economic Development, Urban Programs, Director, One West State Street, CN-829, Trenton, NJ 08625. 609-292-2765

Department of Commerce and Economic Development, Division of International Trade, A. Philip Ferzan, Director, 153 Halsey Street, 5th Fl., Newark, NJ 07102. 201-648-3518

New Jersey Economic Development Authority, James J. Hughes, Exec Director, Capital Place One, CN-990, Trenton, NJ 08625. 609-292-1800

New Jersey Commission on Science and Technology, Director, 122 West State Street, CN-832, Trenton, NJ 08625. 609-984-1671

Small Business Development Center, Brenda Hopper, State Director, Rutger University, Ackerson Hall, 3rd Fl., Newark, NJ 07102. 201-648-5950

Environmental affairs: Environmental Protection Department, Christopher J. Duggett, Commissioner, 401 East State Street, CN 402, Trenton, NJ 08625. 609-292-2885

Labor: Labor Department, Charles Serraino, Commissioner, John Fitch Plaza, CN 110, Trenton, NJ 08625. 609-292-2323

Unemployment: Labor Department, Unemployment and Disability Insurance Division, Michael Malloy, Director, John Fitch Plaza, CN 110, Trenton, NJ 08625. 609-292-2460

Worker's compensation: Labor Department, Workers Compensation Division, Harry Parkin, Director, John Fitch Plaza, CN 110, Trenton, NJ 08625. 609-633-9843

Occupational safety and health: Labor Department, Occupational Health and Safety Consultation Office, Anthony Rossi, Director, John Fitch Plaza, CN 110, Trenton, NJ 08625. 609-984-3507

Secretary of state: State Department, Jane Burgio, Secretary of State, State Capitol Bldg., CN 300, Trenton, NJ 08625. 609-984-1900

Taxation and revenue: Treasury Department, Taxation Division, George Kelly, Jr., 50 West State Street, Trenton, NJ 08625. 609-292-5185

Designated Zones for Economic Development

Enterprise Zones

Enacted in: 1983

No. of established zones: 10

  Bridgeton
  Camden
  Elizabeth
  Jersey City
  Kearny
  Millville/Vineland
  Newark
  Orange

Major Companies in the State

Company name	Fortune 500 rank	City	Telephone	SIC number
Fortune 500 Companies				
Allied Signal Inc.	36	Morristown	201-455-2000	3724
American Cyanamid Co.	103	Wayne	201-831-2000	2834
Armco Inc.	215	Parsippany	201-316-5200	3312
BASF Corp.	107	Parsippany	201-397-2700	2821
Becton Dickinson & Co.	196	Franklin Lakes	201-847-6800	3841
Block Drug Co. Inc.	500	Jersey City	201-434-3000	2844
C. R. Bard Inc.	359	Murray Hill	908-277-8000	3841
Campbell Soup Co.	85	Camden	609-342-4800	2032
CPC International Inc.	81	Englewood Cliffs	201-894-4000	2099
Engelhard Corp.	188	Iselin	908-205-5000	3399
Federal Paper Board Co. Inc.	278	Montvale	201-391-1776	2631
GAF Corp.	349	Wayne	201-628-3000	2869
Hanson Industries North America	65	Iselin	908-603-6600	3999
Hoechst Celanese Corp.	77	Bridgewater	908-231-2000	2824
J. M. Huber Corp.	333	Edison	908-549-8600	2895
IMO Industries Inc.	374	Lawrenceville	609-896-7600	3829
Ingersoll Rand Co.	130	Woodcliff Lake	201-573-0123	3562
Johnson & Johnson	29	New Brunswick	908-524-0400	2844
Merck & Co. Inc.	47	Whitehouse Station	908-423-1000	2834
Schering Plough Corp.	123	Madison	201-822-7000	2834
Thomas & Betts Corp.	345	Bridgewater	908-685-1600	3678
Tyco Toys Inc.	423	Mt Laurel	609-234-7400	3944
Union Camp Corp.	155	Wayne	201-628-2000	2674
Warner Lambert Co.	97	Morris Plains	201-540-2000	2834
Wellman Inc.	398	Shrewsbury	908-542-7300	2824
Other Major Companies in the State				
Chubb Corp.		Warren	908-580-2000	6331
CPC International Inc.		Englewood Cliffs	201-894-4000	2099
DeTomaso Industries Inc.		Red Bank	908-842-7200	3711
First Fidelity Bancorporation		Lawrenceville	609-895-6800	6712
General Public Utilities Corp.		Parsippany	201-263-6500	4911
Great Atlantic & Pacific Tea Co. Inc.		Montvale	201-573-9700	5411
New Jersey Bell Telephone Co.		Newark	201-649-9900	4813
Public Service Electric & Gas Co.		Newark	201-430-7000	4931
Public Service Enterprise Group Inc.		Newark	201-430-7000	4931
Supermarkets General Holdings Corp.		Woodbridge	908-499-3000	5411
Toys R Us Inc.		Paramus	201-262-7800	5945

Plainfield

Trenton

Foreign Trade Zones

Foreign Trade Zone No. 44, Morris County, New Jersey, Grantee: N.J. Dept. of Commerce & Economic Development, Office of International Trade, Diane Burke, 4 Gateway Center, 10th Floor, 100 Mulberry Street, Newark, NJ 07102, 201-648-3518

Foreign Trade Zone No. 142, Salem, New Jersey, Grantee: City of Salem Port Authority, Charles Sullivan/Blanche Hogate, 465 East Broadway, Salem, NJ 08079, 609-935-6380

Foreign Trade Zone No. 49, Newark/Elizabeth, New Jersey, Grantee/Operator: Port Authority of NY and NJ, Jose Casal, One World Trade Center, Suite 34E, New York, NY 10048, 212-435-6725

Labor Unions

Chemical Workers Union, International (AFL-CIO)

Clothing and Textile Workers Union, Amalgamated (AFL-CIO)

Communications Workers of America (AFL-CIO)

Electrical Workers, International Brotherhood of (AFL-CIO)

Food and Commercial Workers International Union, United (AFL-CIO)

Glass, Molders, Pottery, Plastics and Allied Workers International Union (AFL-CIO)

Laborers' International Union of North America (AFL-CIO)

Ladies' Garment Workers' Union, International (AFL-CIO)

National Education Association

Office and Professional Employees International Union (AFL-CIO)

Plumbing and Pipe Fitting Industry of The United States and Canada, United Association of, Journeymen and Apprentices of the (AFL-CIO)

State, County and Municipal Employees, American Federation of (AFL-CIO)

Teachers, American Federation of (AFL-CIO)

Toms River Education Association

Universities with Ph.D. Programs

Drew University, Madison

Fairleigh Dickinson University, Teaneck-Hackensack Campus, Teaneck

New Jersey Institute of Technology, Newark

Princeton University, Princeton

Rutgers University, Newark

Seton Hall University, South Orange

Stevens Institute of Technology, Hoboken

ATLANTIC CITY, NJ (MSA)

Geographic Profile

Land Area

816.4 square miles

Counties and Parishes

Atlantic

Cape May

Ranking Highlights

231 *out of 319 in total* **land area**

111 *out of 319 in* **population growth,** *1970–1990*

285 *out of 310 in having the lowest* **unemployment** *rate*

118 *out of 310 in size of* **labor force**

203 *out of 318 in the percentage of* **college graduates**

10 *out of 292 in per capita personal* **income**

188 *out of 319 in number of* **manufacturing establishments**

236 *out of 318 in* **physicians** *per 1000 people*

161 *out of 318 in* **hospital beds** *per 1000 people*

263 *out of 267 in fewest* **crimes** *per 1000 people*

199 *out of 266 in fewest* **violent crimes** *per 1000 people*

174 *out of 319 in per capita* **federal funds and grants**

Quality of Life Indexes (Rate per 1000 population)

Crime rate in 1991:	102.4
Violent crime rate in 1991:	8.8
Physicians rate in 1992:	1.44
Hospital bed rate in 1991:	3.82

ACCRA Cost of Living Indexes

(First quarter 1993, average = 100)

Composite index:	N/A
Utilities index:	N/A
Housing index:	N/A

Overview

The convention and tourism industry rebuilt Atlantic City's economy in the 1980s. Now one of the nation's top tourist attractions, the city boasts twelve gambling casino/hotels, which attract 32,000,000 visitors each year. Coupled with its famous beaches and boardwalk, Atlantic City's hotel accommodations annually draw almost five thousand conventions, trade shows, and meetings. Since 1975, the casinos have funneled $5 billion back into the city's economy, in addition to creating some fifty thousand jobs.

Other industries in Atlantic City include light manufacturing, services, retail trade, real estate development, distilling, and deep sea fishing. Many of the goods produced are by-products of the convention-tourism trade. Similarly, much of the development centers around the casinos.

Twenty-three common carrier truck lines service the city. Freight shipped via air arrives at Philadelphia International Airport, Atlantic City International Airport in Pomona, and at Bader Field (Atlantic City Municipal Airport) near downtown.

The major highway into Atlantic City is the Atlantic City Expressway. U.S. 30 reaches the city via Absecon Boulevard while U.S. 40/322 parallels Albany Avenue; both are surface routes and tend to be congested. The Garden State Parkway runs north-south outside the city and is a major access route.

Population (1990)

Total Population and Growth Rate
1990: 319,416
1980: 276,385
1970: 234,597
Growth rate 1970–1990: 36%

Race and Hispanic Origin
White: 81.5%
Black: 13.9%
Asian/Pacific Islander: 1.7%
Native American: 0.2%
Hispanic origin: 5.6%
White not Hispanic: 79.0%

Age
Ages 18 to 20: 4.2%
Ages 21 to 24: 5.7%
Ages 25 to 44: 31.9%
Ages 45 to 54: 9.7%
Ages 55 to 59: 4.5%
Ages 60 to 64: 5.1%
Ages 65 plus: 16.2%

Educational Attainment (1990)
Percent having completed high school: 73.2%
Percent having completed college: 16.7%
Elementary and high school enrollment: 46,731

Federal Funds and Grants Received
Total received in 1989: $922,200,000
Funds received per capita: $2,983

Civilian Labor Force
1993 (April): 187,720
1992 average: 185,470
1991 average: 185,466
1990 average: 186,970

Unemployment
1993 (April): 9.0%
1992 average: 10.4%
1991 average: 8.6%
1990 average: 6.2%

Average Annual Pay
1988: $21,262
1987: $19,995
1985: $17,827

Per Capita Personal Income
1991: $24,856
1990: $24,575
1989: $23,507

Business Climate (1987)

Manufacturing
Number of establishments in 1987: 249
Shipments in 1987 ($1,000): $946,700
Employees in 1987: 8,400
Change in employment, 1982 to 1987: -1.2%
Average annual pay for manufacturing work in 1989: $25,327
Average annual pay for production work in 1987: $18,355

Wholesale Trade
Number of establishments in 1987: 405
Total sales in 1987 ($1,000): $1,179,400
Change in sales, 1982 to 1987: 47.4%

Retail Trade
Number of establishments in 1987: 3,077
Total sales in 1987 ($1,000): $1,179,400
Retail sales per household in 1987: $22,182
Average annual pay in 1989: $13,417

Service Industry
Selected receipts in 1987 ($1,000): $3,820,300
Average annual pay in 1989: $22,125

Housing
Total number of units in 1990: 192,414
Occupied units in 1990: 122,979
Owner-occupied units in 1990: 66.8%
1993 ACCRA average cost: N/A
1993 ACCRA average rent for an apartment: N/A

Chamber of Commerce
Greater Atlantic City Chamber of Commerce, Michael DeRogatis, President, 1301 Atlantic Ave., Atlantic City, NJ 08401. 609-345-5600

Economic Development Office
Atlantic City, Division of Economic Development, Yvonne Doggett, Director, 1333 Atlantic Ave. 7th Fl. Atlantic City, NJ 08401. 609-343-2345

Major Businesses

Company	SIC	Telephone
Adamar of New Jersey Inc.	7011	(609) 340-4000
Atlantic City Electric Co.	4911	(609) 645-4100
Atlantic City Medical Center	8062	(609) 344-4081
Atlantic City Showboat Inc.	7011	(609) 343-4000
Bally's Park Place Inc.	7011	(609) 340-2000
Boardwalk Regency Corp.	7011	(609) 348-4411
Claridge at Park Place Inc.	7993	(609) 340-3400
Claridge Hotel and Casino	7011	(609) 340-3400
Collective Federal Saving	6035	(609) 965-1234
GNAC Corp.	7011	(609) 347-7111
Great Bay Hotel & Casino	7999	(609) 441-4000

Major Businesses (Continued)

Company	SIC	Telephone
Marina Associates	7011	(609) 441-5000
Ocean Showboat Inc.	7011	(609) 343-4000
Resorts International Hotel	7011	(609) 344-6000
South Jersey Gas Co.	4923	(609) 561-9000
South Jersey Industries Inc.	4924	(609) 561-9000
Spencer Gifts, Inc.	5947	(609) 645-3300
Trump Plaza Associates	7011	(609) 441-6000

BERGEN–PASSAIC, NJ (PMSA)

Geographic Profile

Land Area
419.3 square miles

Counties and Parishes
Bergen
Passaic

Additional Cities/Towns within Area
Paterson

Ranking Highlights

308 *out of 319 in total* **land area**

303 *out of 319 in* **population growth,** *1970–1990*

234 *out of 310 in having the lowest* **unemployment** *rate*

38 *out of 310 in size of* **labor force**

36 *out of 318 in the percentage of* **college graduates**

N/A *out of 292 in per capita personal* **income**

15 *out of 319 in number of* **manufacturing establishments**

26 *out of 318 in* **physicians** *per 1000 people*

211 *out of 318 in* **hospital beds** *per 1000 people*

51 *out of 267 in fewest* **crimes** *per 1000 people*

73 *out of 266 in fewest* **violent crimes** *per 1000 people*

200 *out of 319 in per capita* **federal funds and grants**

Quality of Life Indexes (Rate per 1000 population)

Crime rate in 1991:	42.8
Violent crime rate in 1991:	3.9
Physicians rate in 1992:	3.14
Hospital bed rate in 1991:	3.28

ACCRA Cost of Living Indexes
(First quarter 1993, average = 100)

Composite index:	N/A
Utilities index:	N/A
Housing index:	N/A

Population (1990)

Total Population and Growth Rate
1990: 1,278,440
1980: 1,292,970
1970: 1,357,930
Growth rate 1970–1990: -6%

Race and Hispanic Origin
White: 81.6%
Black: 8.3%
Asian/Pacific Islander: 5.2%
Native American: 0.2%
Hispanic origin: 11.6%
White not Hispanic: 75.6%

Age
Ages 18 to 20: 3.9%

Ages 21 to 24: 5.8%
Ages 25 to 44: 32.2%
Ages 45 to 54: 11.5%
Ages 55 to 59: 5.1%
Ages 60 to 64: 5.2%
Ages 65 plus: 14.5%

Educational Attainment (1990)
Percent having completed high school: 77.3%
Percent having completed college: 27.3%
Elementary and high school enrollment: 183,220

Federal Funds and Grants Received
Total received in 1989: $3,584,800,000
Funds received per capita: $2,774

Civilian Labor Force
1993 (April): 668,410
1992 average: 677,172
1991 average: 690,849
1990 average: 707,740

Unemployment
1993 (April): 7.7%
1992 average: 8.2%
1991 average: 6.2%
1990 average: 4.5%

Average Annual Pay
1988: $26,932
1987: $24,498
1985: $21,361

Per Capita Personal Income
1991: N/A
1990: N/A
1989: N/A

Business Climate (1987)
Manufacturing
Number of establishments in 1987: 3,721
Shipments in 1987 ($1,000): $14,998,900
Employees in 1987: 162,700
Change in employment, 1982 to 1987: -2.9%
Average annual pay for manufacturing work in 1989: $31,470
Average annual pay for production work in 1987: $19,719

Wholesale Trade
Number of establishments in 1987: 4,828
Total sales in 1987 ($1,000): $57,696,700
Change in sales, 1982 to 1987: 104.7%

Retail Trade
Number of establishments in 1987: 8,707
Total sales in 1987 ($1,000): $57,696,700
Retail sales per household in 1987: $22,566
Average annual pay in 1989: $17,048

Service Industry
Selected receipts in 1987 ($1,000): $6,330,100

Average annual pay in 1989: $25,698

Housing
Total number of units in 1990: 487,329
Occupied units in 1990: 464,149
Owner-occupied units in 1990: 63.9%
1993 ACCRA average cost: N/A
1993 ACCRA average rent for an apartment: N/A

Chamber of Commerce
Clifton-Passaic Regional Chamber of Commerce, George J. Homcy, Exec. Vice President, 1033 Rte. 46, PO Box 110, Clifton, NJ 07011. 201-470-9300

Economic Development Office
Paterson, Division of Economic Development, Betty Shabazz, Director, 125 Ellison St. 2nd Fl., Paterson, NJ 07505. 201-279-5980, FAX 201-278-2981

Economic Development Organizations
Passaic County Department of Economic Development, Ronni D. Rose, Exec. Director, 317 Pennsylvania Ave., Patterson, NJ 07503. 201-881-4429, FAX 201-742-3936

Colleges and Universities
Passaic County Community College, Paterson

JERSEY CITY, NJ (PMSA)

Geographic Profile

Land Area

46.7 square miles

Counties and Parishes

Hudson

Additional Cities/Towns within Area

Hoboken

Ranking Highlights

319 *out of 319 in total* **land area**

312 *out of 319 in* **population growth,** *1970–1990*

294 *out of 310 in having the lowest* **unemployment** *rate*

86 *out of 310 in size of* **labor force**

143 *out of 318 in the percentage of* **college graduates**

N/A *out of 292 in per capita personal* **income**

52 *out of 319 in number of* **manufacturing establishments**

152 *out of 318 in* **physicians** *per 1000 people*

115 *out of 318 in* **hospital beds** *per 1000 people*

208 *out of 267 in fewest* **crimes** *per 1000 people*

251 *out of 266 in fewest* **violent crimes** *per 1000 people*

183 *out of 319 in per capita* **federal funds and grants**

Quality of Life Indexes (Rate per 1000 population)

Crime rate in 1991:	73.1
Violent crime rate in 1991:	11.9
Physicians rate in 1992:	1.83
Hospital bed rate in 1991:	4.42

ACCRA Cost of Living Indexes

(First quarter 1993, average = 100)

Composite index:	N/A
Utilities index:	N/A
Housing index:	N/A

Overview

Jersey City's economy is in a state of flux as the city lessens dependence on traditional sectors such as transportation and distribution and focuses on real estate and development. High rent and utility costs in adjacent Manhattan have prompted many New York firms to relocate partial or entire operations across the Hudson River to Jersey City. With one of the highest population densities in the country and a finite amount of geographical expansion space, Jersey City relies more and more on development to ease its crowding and to add to its tax base. Other important economic sectors in Jersey City are manufacturing and services, including finance and insurance.

Jersey City, with 11 miles of waterfront on the Hudson River, is part of the bustling Port Authority of New York and New Jersey. Port Jersey's geographic location provides excellent access to the Atlantic Ocean from the Port of New York's Upper Harbor. Docks on the Hudson River and Upper New York Bay accommodate ocean liners, freighters, and coastal and river vessels. Port Jersey is divided into a 100-acre industrial park and a modern 310–acre port with bulk capabilities, roll-on, roll-off, and breakbulk facilities. Port Jersey, whose operations are computerized, provides a large terminal for containerized shipping.

The Greenville yards of Conrail are adjacent to the port, whose own railroad complex services the port's seventeen berths and industrial complex. Truck terminals and warehousing accommodate the more than one hundred motor carriers servicing the city.

Jersey City is part of the meeting destination area known as Metro New Jersey Meadowlands, one of the state's busiest destinations; its popularity is due in part to its proximity to the attractions of Manhattan (Newark is also part of the Meadowlands destination area).

Newark International Airport, a fifteen-minute drive from Jersey City, offers comprehensive domestic and international travel service. Buses, limousines, trains, and helicopters also carry commuters between the airport and the city. The New York City airports, La Guardia and Kennedy International, are also practical access points for Jersey City. Inter- and intra-state bus lines, rapid transit, ferries, tunnels, and trains form important parts of the Jersey City transportation network. PATH, the local mass transit service, connects Jersey City with Manhattan, Newark, Harrison, and Hoboken. Major east-west arteries approaching Jersey City include Interstate-280; U.S. Routes 1 and 1A, with the Pulaski Skyway alternate; and the New Jersey Turnpike, I-78, with four exits in the city. NJ Highway 440 runs north-south through the city while I-95 bypasses it to the west.

Population (1990)

Total Population and Growth Rate

1990: 553,099

1980: 556,972

1970: 607,839

Growth rate 1970–1990: -9%

Race and Hispanic Origin

White: 68.8%

Black: 14.4%

Asian/Pacific Islander: 6.6%

Native American: 0.3%

Hispanic origin: 33.2%

White not Hispanic: 47.4%

Age

Ages 18 to 20: 4.2%

Ages 21 to 24: 6.9%

Ages 25 to 44: 34.8%

Ages 45 to 54: 10.1%

Ages 55 to 59: 4.5%

Ages 60 to 64: 4.6%

Ages 65 plus: 12.7%

Educational Attainment (1990)
Percent having completed high school: 64.1%
Percent having completed college: 19.7%
Elementary and high school enrollment: 85,531

Federal Funds and Grants Received
Total received in 1989: $1,600,800,000
Funds received per capita: $2,952

Civilian Labor Force
1993 (April): 260,927
1992 average: 267,463
1991 average: 272,777
1990 average: 276,623

Unemployment
1993 (April): 11.1%
1992 average: 11.8%
1991 average: 9.0%
1990 average: 7.4%

Average Annual Pay
1988: $24,146
1987: $22,661
1985: $20,438

Per Capita Personal Income
1991: N/A
1990: N/A
1989: N/A

Business Climate (1987)
Manufacturing
Number of establishments in 1987: 1,385
Shipments in 1987 ($1,000): $5,372,900
Employees in 1987: 46,000
Change in employment, 1982 to 1987: -23.1%
Average annual pay for manufacturing work in 1989: $25,886
Average annual pay for production work in 1987: $16,720

Wholesale Trade
Number of establishments in 1987: 1,164
Total sales in 1987 ($1,000): $10,911,000
Change in sales, 1982 to 1987: 51.2%

Retail Trade
Number of establishments in 1987: 3,365
Total sales in 1987 ($1,000): $10,911,000
Retail sales per household in 1987: $12,546
Average annual pay in 1989: $15,905

Service Industry
Selected receipts in 1987 ($1,000): $1,224,500
Average annual pay in 1989: $22,196

Housing
Total number of units in 1990: 229,682
Occupied units in 1990: 208,739
Owner-occupied units in 1990: 32.5%

1993 ACCRA average cost: N/A
1993 ACCRA average rent for an apartment: N/A

Chamber of Commerce
Hudson County Chamber of Commerce, Dominick D'Agosta, President, 574 Summit Ave. #404, Jersey City, NJ 07306. 201-653-7400

Economic Development Office
Jersey City Economic Development Corp., Thomas D. Ahern, Assistant Exec Director, 601 Pavonia Ave., Jersey City, NJ 07306. 201-420-7755

Economic Development Organizations
Hoboken Department of Planning and Community and Economic Development, Peggy E. Thomas, Director, 124 Grand St., Hoboken, NJ 07030. 201-420-2201

Major Businesses

Company	SIC	Telephone
Adidas USA Inc.	2329	(201) 580-0700
Block Drug Co., Inc.	2844	(201) 434-3000
Chubb & Son Inc.	8741	(201) 580-2000
Chubb Corp.	6331	(201) 580-2000
Drug Guild Distributors	5122	(201) 348-3700
Emerson Radio Corp.	3651	(201) 854-6600
Federal Insurance Co.	6331	(201) 580-2000
Genlyte Group Inc.	3646	(201) 864-3000
Goody Products, Inc.	3999	(201) 997-3000
Goya Foods Inc.	5141	(201) 348-4900
Hartz Mountain Corp.	2047	(201) 485-5300
Hartz Mountain Industries	6512	(201) 348-1200
Hudson County News Co. Inc.	5192	(201) 867-3600
Jamesway Corp.	5311	(201) 330-6000
K-Mart Apparel Corp.	5651	(201) 861-9100
Kuehne & Nagel Holding Inc.	4731	(201) 413-5500
Kuehne & Nagel Inc.	4731	(201) 413-5500
Loews Theatre Management	6512	(201) 319-5810
Matsushita Electric Corp.	5064	(201) 348-7000
Metromedia Co.	4813	(201) 348-3244
Miller-Wohl Co. Inc.	5621	(201) 863-9250
National Westminster Bank	6021	(201) 547-7000
National Westminster Bancorp	6021	(201) 547-7000
Ormond Shops Inc.	5621	(201) 861-5800
Panalpina Inc.	4731	(201) 451-4000
Petrie Stores Corp.	5621	(201) 866-3600
Porky Products Inc.	5147	(201) 333-2333
Soundesign Corp.	3651	(201) 434-1050
Syms Corp.	5611	(201) 902-9600

Colleges and Universities
Hudson County Community College, Jersey City
Jersey City State College, Jersey City
St. Peter's College, Jersey City
Stevens Institute of Technology, Hoboken

MIDDLESEX–SOMERSET–HUNTERDON, NJ (PMSA)

Geographic Profile

Land Area

1045.5 square miles

Counties and Parishes

Hunterdon

Middlesex

Somerset

Additional Cities/Towns within Area

New Brunswick

Perth Amboy

Ranking Highlights

192 *out of 319 in total* **land area**

177 *out of 319 in* **population growth,** *1970–1990*

149 *out of 310 in having the lowest* **unemployment** *rate*

44 *out of 310 in size of* **labor force**

24 *out of 318 in the percentage of* **college graduates**

N/A *out of 292 in per capita personal* **income**

43 *out of 319 in number of* **manufacturing establishments**

58 *out of 318 in* **physicians** *per 1000 people*

281 *out of 318 in* **hospital beds** *per 1000 people*

37 *out of 267 in fewest* **crimes** *per 1000 people*

34 *out of 266 in fewest* **violent crimes** *per 1000 people*

255 *out of 319 in per capita* **federal funds and grants**

Quality of Life Indexes (Rate per 1000 population)

Crime rate in 1991:	40.0
Violent crime rate in 1991:	2.6
Physicians rate in 1992:	2.55
Hospital bed rate in 1991:	2.39

ACCRA Cost of Living Indexes

(First quarter 1993, average = 100)

Composite index:	N/A
Utilities index:	N/A
Housing index:	N/A

Population (1990)

Total Population and Growth Rate

1990: 1,019,835

1980: 886,383

1970: 851,903

Growth rate 1970–1990: 20%

Race and Hispanic Origin

White: 84.8%

Black: 6.9%

Asian/Pacific Islander: 5.6%

Native American: 0.1%

Hispanic origin: 7.0%

White not Hispanic: 80.8%

Age

Ages 18 to 20: 4.5%

Ages 21 to 24: 6.3%

Ages 25 to 44: 35.7%

Ages 45 to 54: 11.2%

Ages 55 to 59: 4.6%

Ages 60 to 64: 4.6%

Ages 65 plus: 11.3%

Educational Attainment (1990)

Percent having completed high school: 81.8%

Percent having completed college: 30.2%

Elementary and high school enrollment: 144,713

Federal Funds and Grants Received

Total received in 1989: $2,363,700,000

Funds received per capita: $2,416

Civilian Labor Force

1993 (April): 587,624

1992 average: 591,085

1991 average: 590,240

1990 average: 589,858

Unemployment

1993 (April): 6.1%

1992 average: 6.8%

1991 average: 5.2%

1990 average: 3.7%

Average Annual Pay

1988: $27,319

1987: $25,366

1985: $22,236

Per Capita Personal Income

1991: N/A

1990: N/A

1989: N/A

Business Climate (1987)

Manufacturing

Number of establishments in 1987: 1,753

Shipments in 1987 ($1,000): $16,714,200

Employees in 1987: 110,200

Change in employment, 1982 to 1987: -5.1%

Average annual pay for manufacturing work in 1989: $34,297

Average annual pay for production work in 1987: $22,997

Wholesale Trade

Number of establishments in 1987: 2,233

Total sales in 1987 ($1,000): $20,685,300

Change in sales, 1982 to 1987: 52.3%

Retail Trade

Number of establishments in 1987: 5,785

Total sales in 1987 ($1,000): $20,685,300

Retail sales per household in 1987: $21,492

Average annual pay in 1989: $15,273

Service Industry

Selected receipts in 1987 ($1,000): $4,143,400

Average annual pay in 1989: $26,068

Housing

Total number of units in 1990: 382,814

Occupied units in 1990: 365,085

Owner-occupied units in 1990: 70.7%

1993 ACCRA average cost: N/A

1993 ACCRA average rent for an apartment: N/A

Chamber of Commerce

Middlesex Borough Chamber of Commerce, Richard G. Roy, President, PO Box 171, Middlesex, NJ 08846. 201-563-1530

Economic Development Office

New Brunswick Development Corp., Christina Foglio, Director, 390 George St., New Brunswick, NJ 08901. 908-249-2220

Economic Development Organizations

New Brunswick Housing and Development Authority, James Zullo, Exec. Director, 71 Nielson St., New Brunswick, NJ 08903. 908-745-5147, FAX 908-214-8805

Perth Amboy Department of Economic Development, Melvin Ramos, Director, 260 High St., Perth Amboy, NJ 08861. 908-826-0244, FAX 908-826-1160

Major Businesses

Company	SIC	Telephone
A D M Corp.	2672	(201) 469-0900
Acme Tube/J.L., Inc.	3317	(201) 560-8111
American Solenoid Co., Inc.	3613	(908) 560-1240
Betham Corp.	3842	(201) 356-2870
Bomar Crystal Co.	3679	(908) 356-7787
Calabrian Corp.	2869	(908) 469-0076
Coilhose Pneumatics, Inc.	3052	(908) 752-5000
Cooperheat, Inc.	3567	(908) 560-0442
D A Q Electronics, Inc.	3679	(908) 560-0050
Flexible Components, Inc.	3599	(908) 356-7330
Ingrassia Construction Co.	1542	(201) 560-1400
Jafco Industries, Inc.	2531	(908) 356-1502
Koba Corp.	3089	(201) 469-0110
Less Handling Systems, Inc.	3535	(908) 846-1550
Liberty Polymers, Inc.	3089	(908) 469-8444
Man Roland USA, Inc.	3555	(908) 469-6600
Marisol, Inc.	7389	(908) 469-5100
Mason Candlelight Co.	3641	(908) 469-4212
Materials Technology, Inc.	3497	(908) 246-1000
Philips Lighting Co.	3641	(908) 563-3000
Ronson Corp.	3728	(908) 469-8300
Royal Doulton U.S.A., Inc.	3262	(908) 356-7880
Schnitzer Alloy Products	5039	(908) 246-5200
Scientific Process & Research	3542	(908) 846-3477

Major Businesses (Continued)

Company	SIC	Telephone
Sigma Engineering & Construction	3599	(908) 356-3046
Silver Line Building Products	3442	(201) 752-8600
Testfabrics, Inc.	2211	(908) 469-6446
Vectronics Microwave Corp.	3679	(908) 356-2377
W. A. Cleary Corp.	2879	(908) 247-8000
Waldes Truarc Inc.	3499	(201) 469-7999

Colleges and Universities

Rutgers, The State University of New Jersey, College of Pharmacy, New Brunswick

Rutgers, The State University of New Jersey, Cook College, New Brunswick

Rutgers, The State University of New Jersey, Douglass College, New Brunswick

Rutgers, The State University of New Jersey, Livingston College, New Brunswick

Rutgers, The State University of New Jersey, Mason Gross School of the Arts, New Brunswick

Rutgers, The State University of New Jersey, Rutgers College, New Brunswick

Rutgers, The State University of New Jersey, University College-New Brunswick, New Brunswick

MONMOUTH–OCEAN, NJ (PMSA)

Geographic Profile

Land Area

1108.2 square miles

Counties and Parishes

Monmouth

Ocean

Ranking Highlights

181 *out of 319 in total* **land area**

76 *out of 319 in* **population growth,** *1970–1990*

226 *out of 310 in having the lowest* **unemployment** *rate*

53 *out of 310 in size of* **labor force**

87 *out of 318 in the percentage of* **college graduates**

N/A *out of 292 in per capita personal* **income**

68 *out of 319 in number of* **manufacturing establishments**

142 *out of 318 in* **physicians** *per 1000 people*

201 *out of 318 in* **hospital beds** *per 1000 people*

37 *out of 267 in fewest* **crimes** *per 1000 people*

40 *out of 266 in fewest* **violent crimes** *per 1000 people*

113 *out of 319 in per capita* **federal funds and grants**

Quality of Life Indexes (Rate per 1000 population)

Crime rate in 1991:	40.0
Violent crime rate in 1991:	2.8
Physicians rate in 1992:	1.87
Hospital bed rate in 1991:	3.43

ACCRA Cost of Living Indexes

(First quarter 1993, average = 100)

Composite index:	N/A
Utilities index:	N/A
Housing index:	N/A

Overview

No central city in this area.

Population (1990)

Total Population and Growth Rate

1990: 986,327

1980: 849,211

1970: 670,319

Growth rate 1970–1990: 47%

Race and Hispanic Origin

White: 90.8%

Black: 6.0%

Asian/Pacific Islander: 1.9%

Native American: 0.1%

Hispanic origin: 3.7%

White not Hispanic: 88.5%

Age

Ages 18 to 20: 3.7%

Ages 21 to 24: 4.9%

Ages 25 to 44: 31%

Ages 45 to 54: 10.4%

Ages 55 to 59: 4.3%

Ages 60 to 64: 4.8%

Ages 65 plus: 17.3%

Educational Attainment (1990)

Percent having completed high school: 79.3%

Percent having completed college: 22.5%

Elementary and high school enrollment: 154,044

Federal Funds and Grants Received

Total received in 1989: $3,345,900,000

Funds received per capita: $3,451

Civilian Labor Force

1993 (April): 483,948

1992 average: 486,791

1991 average: 492,297

1990 average: 491,131

Unemployment

1993 (April): 6.6%

1992 average: 8.0%

1991 average: 6.4%

1990 average: 4.8%

Average Annual Pay

1988: $22,429

1987: $21,022

1985: $18,165

Per Capita Personal Income

1991: N/A

1990: N/A

1989: N/A

Business Climate (1987)

Manufacturing

Number of establishments in 1987: 996

Shipments in 1987 ($1,000): $3,282,900

Employees in 1987: 34,800

Change in employment, 1982 to 1987: -0.3%

Average annual pay for manufacturing work in 1989: $26,958

Average annual pay for production work in 1987: $18,564

Wholesale Trade

Number of establishments in 1987: 1,412

Total sales in 1987 ($1,000): $4,056,400

Change in sales, 1982 to 1987: 137.5%

Retail Trade

Number of establishments in 1987: 6,169

Total sales in 1987 ($1,000): $4,056,400

Retail sales per household in 1987: $20,030

Average annual pay in 1989: $13,413

Service Industry

Selected receipts in 1987 ($1,000): $2,729,700

Average annual pay in 1989: $23,705

Housing

Total number of units in 1990: 438,271
Occupied units in 1990: 365,717
Owner-occupied units in 1990: 77.4%
1993 ACCRA average cost: N/A
1993 ACCRA average rent for an apartment: N/A

Chamber of Commerce

Ocean City Chamber of Commerce, Joann DelVescio, Exec. Director, PO Box 157, Ocean City, NJ 08226. 609-399-2629, FAX 609-398-3932

Economic Development Office

Department of Tourism and Economic Development, Steven Hampton, Division Director, Cape May County Airport, Terminal Bldg., Rio Grande, NJ 08242. 609-886-1755, FAX 609-886-8869

Major Businesses

Company	SIC	Telephone
Amusement Technology, Inc.	3599	(908) 918-0300
Atmos Tech Industries	3569	(908) 493-8400
I. V. Miller & Sons, Inc.	3089	(908) 493-4040
Molnar Tools, Inc.	3469	(908) 918-0580

NEWARK, NJ (PMSA)

Geographic Profile

Land Area

1219.9 square miles

Counties and Parishes

Essex
Morris
Sussex
Union

Additional Cities/Towns within Area

Elizabeth

Ranking Highlights

162 *out of 319 in total* **land area**
300 *out of 319 in* **population growth,** *1970–1990*
248 *out of 310 in having the lowest* **unemployment** *rate*
25 *out of 310 in size of* **labor force**
36 *out of 318 in the percentage of* **college graduates**
160 *out of 292 in per capita personal* **income**
13 *out of 319 in number of* **manufacturing establishments**
44 *out of 318 in* **physicians** *per 1000 people*
74 *out of 318 in* **hospital beds** *per 1000 people*
165 *out of 267 in fewest* **crimes** *per 1000 people*
235 *out of 266 in fewest* **violent crimes** *per 1000 people*
173 *out of 319 in per capita* **federal funds and grants**

Quality of Life Indexes (Rate per 1000 population)

Crime rate in 1991: 66.2
Violent crime rate in 1991: 10.3
Physicians rate in 1992: 2.77
Hospital bed rate in 1991: 5.07

ACCRA Cost of Living Indexes

(First quarter 1993, average = 100)
Composite index: N/A
Utilities index: N/A
Housing index: N/A

Overview

Newark is the largest city in a state that is the most densely populated in the country. A major east coast port of entry, Newark is a transportation, manufacturing, and education center. Its growing service economy is dominated by medical research, insurance, and high technology research and development activities. Devastated by five days of race riots in 1967, Newark has still not completely rebuilt the stores and neighborhoods destroyed in that conflagration. In the 1990s the city presents two images: one of shining steel and glass towers, the result of $6 billion in new office construction over five years; the other of century–old railroad shacks and dilapidated houses in neighborhoods with few amenities. Nevertheless, the city received an All–American Cities Award in 1991, has been cited as a "best city" for its environmental record and revitalization efforts, and its improvements have earned it the title "most livable city" according to the U.S. Conference of Mayors.

Newark lies at the heart of the great industrial stretch that begins with New York City and ends with Plainfield, New Jersey. Manufacturing is the city's most important economic activity, and most of New Jersey's factories are in this and the Trenton areas. Among the Fortune 500 companies that call Newark home are Allied (chemicals), Nabisco Brands (food products), Merck (pharmaceuticals), Warner-Lambert (pharmaceuticals), Englehard (precious metals), Schering-Plough (pharmaceuticals), and BASF Wyandotte (chemicals). Newark is also at the hub of seven major highways that combine with its railway routes and busy airport to make Newark a major mid-Atlantic distribution and wholesale and retail trade center. The area is one of the country's leading centers for the wholesale trade of chemicals and machinery. Services add greatly to Newark's commercial life; the city is the nation's third largest writer of life insurance policies and headquarters of Prudential Insurance Company of America, the world's largest insurance company. Publishing is also an economic mainstay.

Newark, with thirteen miles of waterfront along Newark Bay and the Passaic River, is part of the nation's largest containership port—the combined Newark/Elizabeth/New York City port. Port Newark/Elizabeth handles about 50 million tons of cargo and some 2,750 ships yearly. Newark handles more automobile and meat shipments than any other U.S. port. With a main channel seven thousand feet long, the 930-acre Port of Newark can berth thirty-four ships. Newark International Airport offers more than 500,000 square feet of cargo warehousing facilities either occupied or under development. Rail freight service is provided by AMTRAK and Conrail. Thirty motor freight carriers service the city.

Newark International Airport, one of the world's busiest airports, annually serves 20 million passengers carried on more than 300,000 flights. Overseas travel through the airport increased by 133 percent from 1988 to 1992, making Newark the fastest growing airport in the region.

AMTRAK, Conrail, and PATH rail lines travel into Newark's recently renovated historic Penn Station. The PATH train connects downtown Newark with New York City.

The major north-south route with access to Newark is Interstate-95, the New Jersey Turnpike. Routes from the north include I-81, I-287, the Garden State Parkway, and the New York Thruway. From the west, Newark is approached by I-78 and I-80. Other major arteries include U.S. Highways 1, 9, and 22 and state highways 21, 24, 25, 27, 78, 82, and 280.

Population (1990)

Total Population and Growth Rate

1990: 1,824,321
1980: 1,879,147

1970: 1,936,624
Growth rate 1970–1990: -6%

Race and Hispanic Origin

White: 70.2%
Black: 23.2%
Asian/Pacific Islander: 2.9%
Native American: 0.2%
Hispanic origin: 10.3%
White not Hispanic: 64.2%

Age

Ages 18 to 20: 4.2%
Ages 21 to 24: 5.9%
Ages 25 to 44: 33.1%
Ages 45 to 54: 11.4%
Ages 55 to 59: 4.7%
Ages 60 to 64: 4.6%
Ages 65 plus: 12.5%

Educational Attainment (1990)

Percent having completed high school: 76.5%
Percent having completed college: 27.3%
Elementary and high school enrollment: 288,890

Federal Funds and Grants Received

Total received in 1989: $5,653,600,000
Funds received per capita: $2,997

Civilian Labor Force

1993 (April):   917,934
1992 average: 923,578
1991 average: 938,282
1990 average: 951,132

Unemployment

1993 (April):   8.1%
1992 average: 8.7%
1991 average: 6.9%
1990 average: 5.4%

Average Annual Pay

1988: $27,648
1987: $25,536
1985: $22,739

Per Capita Personal Income

1991: $17,030
1990: $16,448
1989: $15,899

Business Climate (1987)

Manufacturing

Number of establishments in 1987: 3,887
Shipments in 1987 ($1,000): $23,336,300
Employees in 1987: 185,300
Change in employment, 1982 to 1987: -20.3%
Average annual pay for manufacturing work, 1989: $34,416
Average annual pay for production work, 1987: $22,082

Wholesale Trade
Number of establishments in 1987: 4,505
Total sales in 1987 ($1,000): $31,039,300
Change in sales, 1982 to 1987: 24.8%

Retail Trade
Number of establishments in 1987: 11,369
Total sales in 1987 ($1,000): $31,039,300
Retail sales per household in 1987: $17,266
Average annual pay in 1989: $15,931

Service Industry
Selected receipts in 1987 ($1,000): $8,573,800
Average annual pay in 1989: $26,170

Housing
Total number of units in 1990: 693,062
Occupied units in 1990: 652,035
Owner-occupied units in 1990: 59.1%
1993 ACCRA average cost: N/A
1993 ACCRA average rent for an apartment: N/A

Chamber of Commerce
Metro Newark Chamber of Commerce, Richard G. Schoon, President, 40 Clinton St., Newark, NJ 07102. 201-242-6237

Economic Development Office
Newark Economic Development Corp., Alfred Faiella, Exec Director, 744 Broad Street, Newark, NJ 07102. 201-643-2790

Economic Development Organizations
City of Elizabeth, Department of Community Development, Neil DeHaan, Director, City Hall Room 214, Elizabeth, NJ 07201. 908-820-4019

Elizabeth Development Co., Edward V. Kolling, Exec. Director, 1045 E. Jersey St., PO Box 512, Elizabeth, NJ 07207-0512. 908-289-0262

Union County Economic Development Corp., Maureen Tinen, President, 399 Westfield Ave., Elizabeth, NJ 07208. 908-527-1166, FAX 908-527-1207

Major Businesses

Company	SIC	Telephone
Ahold USA Inc.	5411	(201) 299-6590
Allied-Signal Inc.	3724	(201) 455-2000
Armco Inc.	3312	(201) 316-5200
AT&T Communications, Inc.	4813	(201) 221-2000
AT&T Technologies, Inc.	3661	(201) 771-2000
BASF Corp.	2869	(201) 397-2700
Basfin Corp.	2869	(201) 397-2700
Bell Telephone Labs Inc.	8731	(201) 582-3000
Blue Cross & Blue Shield	6324	(201) 456-2376
Crum and Forster Inc.	6331	(201) 204-3500
General Public Utilities	4911	(201) 263-6500
Hoechst Celanese Corp.	2824	(201) 231-2000

Major Businesses (Continued)

Company	SIC	Telephone
Hoechst Corp.	2833	(201) 231-2000
Labatt, John Inc.	2037	(201) 753-9311
Merck & Co. Inc.	2834	(201) 574-4000
Mutual Benefit Life Insurance	6311	(201) 481-8000
Nabisco Brands, Inc.	2052	(201) 503-2000
Nabisco Inc.	2052	(201) 884-4000
New Jersey Bell Telephone Co.	4813	(201) 649-9900
Pruco Inc.	6719	(201) 802-6000
Prudential Insurance of America	6311	(201) 802-6000
Public Service Enterprise Group	4911	(201) 430-7000
Public Service Electric & Gas Co.	4911	(201) 430-7000
Schering Corp.	2834	(201) 298-4000
Schering-Plough Corp.	2834	(201) 822-7000
Wakefern Food Corp.	5141	(201) 527-3300
Warner-Lambert Co.	2834	(201) 540-2000

Colleges and Universities
Essex County College, Newark
New Jersey Institute of Technology, Newark
Rutgers, The State University of New Jersey, College of Nursing, Newark
Rutgers, The State University of New Jersey, Newark College of Arts and Sciences, Newark
Rutgers, The State University of New Jersey, University College-Newark, Newark

TRENTON, NJ (PMSA)

Geographic Profile

Land Area

226.0 square miles

Counties and Parishes

Mercer

Ranking Highlights

317 *out of 319 in total* **land area**

234 *out of 319 in* **population growth,** *1970–1990*

128 *out of 310 in having the lowest* **unemployment** *rate*

127 *out of 310 in size of* **labor force**

40 *out of 318 in the percentage of* **college graduates**

4 *out of 292 in per capita personal* **income**

120 *out of 319 in number of* **manufacturing establishments**

51 *out of 318 in* **physicians** *per 1000 people*

60 *out of 318 in* **hospital beds** *per 1000 people*

141 *out of 267 in fewest* **crimes** *per 1000 people*

150 *out of 266 in fewest* **violent crimes** *per 1000 people*

28 *out of 319 in per capita* **federal funds and grants**

Quality of Life Indexes (Rate per 1000 population)

Crime rate in 1991:	61.6
Violent crime rate in 1991:	6.9
Physicians rate in 1992:	2.71
Hospital bed rate in 1991:	5.29

ACCRA Cost of Living Indexes

(First quarter 1993, average = 100)

Composite index:	N/A
Utilities index:	N/A
Housing index:	N/A

Overview

Mercer County is located midway between New York City and Philadelphia, Pennsylvania in New Jersey's center. It includes the City of Trenton, Townships of East Windsor, Ewing, Hamilton, Hopewell, Lawrence, Princeton, Washington and West Windsor, and the Boroughs of Hightstown, Hopewell, Pennington and Princeton. Mercer County overlaps three major markets: Suburban Manhattan-New England; Delaware Valley Region known as Pen-Jer-Del; and the Boston-Washington corridor.

The five largest employers are Princeton University, Educational Testing Service, G. E. Astro Space, General Motors and Bristol Myers-Squibb. Each has over 2,000 employees.

The Mercer County Airport has two main runways: Runway 6/24 - 6,000' x 150' and Runway 16/34 - 4,800' x 150'. Both runways have dual tandem load limits of 320,000 lbs. In addition to the airside capacities of handling the majority of the corporate and air carrier fleet aircraft, the facility provides FAA Air Traffic Control services, 24-hour Security/Fire protection, instrument landing system, and FAA approved navigation and lighting systems.

Population (1990)

Total Population and Growth Rate

1990: 325,824

1980: 307,863

1970: 304,116

Growth rate 1970–1990: 7%

Race and Hispanic Origin

White: 75.1%

Black: 18.9%

Asian/Pacific Islander: 3.1%

Native American: 0.2%

Hispanic origin: 6.0%

White not Hispanic: 72.5%

Age

Ages 18 to 20: 5.5%

Ages 21 to 24: 6.4%

Ages 25 to 44: 33%

Ages 45 to 54: 10.7%

Ages 55 to 59: 4.4%

Ages 60 to 64: 4.6%

Ages 65 plus: 13%

Educational Attainment (1990)

Percent having completed high school: 82.3%

Percent having completed college: 26.9%

Elementary and high school enrollment: 496,094

Federal Funds and Grants Received ($1000)

Total received in 1989: $1,852,200,000

Funds received per capita: $5,596

Civilian Labor Force

1993 (April): 173,303

1992 average: 175,170

1991 average: 176,759

1990 average: 176,474

Unemployment

1993 (April): 5.8%

1992 average: 6.5%

1991 average: 5.5%

1990 average: 4.1%

Average Annual Pay

1988: $26,649

1987: $24,702

1985: $21,375

Per Capita Personal Income

1991: $27,263

1990: $26,661

1989: $24,862

Business Climate (1987)

Manufacturing

Number of establishments in 1987: 468

Shipments in 1987 ($1,000): $2,593,000

Employees in 1987: 39,800

Change in employment, 1982 to 1987: 36.8%

Average annual pay for manufacturing work in 1989: $35,209

Average annual pay for production work in 1987: $23,761

Wholesale Trade
Number of establishments in 1987: 521
Total sales in 1987 ($1,000): $2,621,200
Change in sales, 1982 to 1987: 73.1%

Retail Trade
Number of establishments in 1987: 2,015
Total sales in 1987 ($1,000): $2,621,200
Retail sales per household in 1987: $19,997
Average annual pay in 1989: $14,106

Service Industry
Selected receipts in 1987 ($1,000): $1,484,400
Average annual pay in 1989: $26,023

Housing
Total number of units in 1990: 123,666
Occupied units in 1990: 116,941
Owner-occupied units in 1990: 66.5%
1993 ACCRA average cost: N/A
1993 ACCRA average rent for an apartment: N/A

Chamber of Commerce
Mercer County Chamber of Commerce, Edward F. Meara III, President, 214 W. State St., Trenton, NJ 08607. 609-393-414

Economic Development Office
Mercer County Division of Economic Development, William R. Mate, Director, Mercer County Administration Bldg., Trenton, NJ 08650. 609-989-6555, FAX 609-695-5124

Economic Development Organizations
Division of Economic Development, Department of Housing, Director, City of Trenton, 319 E. State St., Trenton, NJ 08608. 609-989-3509

New Jersey Urban Enterprise Zone Program, S. Charles Garofalo, Administrator, N20 W. State St., CN-829, Trenton, NJ 08625-0829. 609-292-1912, FAX 609-292-9145

Major Businesses

Company	SIC	Telephone
American Re-Insurance Co.	6331	(609) 243-4200
Church & Dwight Co. Inc.	2812	(609) 683-5900
Congoleum Corp.	3081	(609) 584-3601
Custodial Trust Co	6022	(609) 599-5963
Educational Testing Service	8748	(609) 921-9000
First Fidelity BanCorp.	6022	(609) 895-6800
G E American Communications	4899	(609) 987-4000
IMO Industries Inc.	3491	(609) 896-7600
Ingersoll Newspapers, Inc.	2711	(609) 683-5300
Lenox Inc.	3262	(609) 896-2800

Major Businesses (Continued)

Company	SIC	Telephone
New Jersey Mfrs. Insurance Co.	6331	(609) 883-1300
New Jersey National Bank	6021	(609) 989-5000
New Jersey National Corp.	6021	(609) 989-5000
Pullman Holding Corp.	3715	(609) 683-1770
Squibb, E. R. & Sons Inc.	2834	(609) 921-4000
Squibb Corp.	2834	(609) 921-4000
UJB Financial Corp	6712	(609) 987-3200

Colleges and Universities
Mercer County Community College, Trenton
Thomas A. Edison State College, Trenton
Trenton State College, Trenton

VINELAND–MILLVILLE–BRIDGETON, NJ (PMSA)

Geographic Profile

Land Area
489.3 square miles

Counties and Parishes
Cumberland

Ranking Highlights

294 *out of 319 in total* **land area**

210 *out of 319 in* **population growth,** *1970–1990*

301 *out of 310 in having the lowest* **unemployment** *rate*

260 *out of 310 in size of* **labor force**

312 *out of 318 in the percentage of* **college graduates**

130 *out of 292 in per capita personal* **income**

195 *out of 319 in number of* **manufacturing establishments**

268 *out of 318 in* **physicians** *per 1000 people*

158 *out of 318 in* **hospital beds** *per 1000 people*

160 *out of 267 in fewest* **crimes** *per 1000 people*

223 *out of 266 in fewest* **violent crimes** *per 1000 people*

235 *out of 319 in per capita* **federal funds and grants**

Quality of Life Indexes (Rate per 1000 population)

Crime rate in 1991:	65.5
Violent crime rate in 1991:	9.8
Physicians rate in 1992:	1.28
Hospital bed rate in 1991:	3.87

ACCRA Cost of Living Indexes

(First quarter 1993, average = 100)

Composite index:	N/A
Utilities index:	N/A
Housing index:	N/A

Population (1990)

Total Population and Growth Rate
1990: 138,053
1980: 132,866
1970: 121,374
Growth rate 1970–1990: 14%

Race and Hispanic Origin
White: 73.5%
Black: 16.9%
Asian/Pacific Islander: 0.8%
Native American: 0.9%
Hispanic origin: 13.3%
White not Hispanic: 68.9%

Age
Ages 18 to 20: 4.4%
Ages 21 to 24: 5.7%
Ages 25 to 44: 31.1%
Ages 45 to 54: 10.3%
Ages 55 to 59: 4.4%
Ages 60 to 64: 4.5%
Ages 65 plus: 13.5%

Educational Attainment (1990)

Percent having completed high school: 63.4%
Percent having completed college: 10.8%
Elementary and high school enrollment: 24,558

Federal Funds and Grants Received

Total received in 1989: $354,300,000
Funds received per capita: $2,559

Civilian Labor Force

1993 (April):	60,779
1992 average:	61,840
1991 average:	62,481
1990 average:	61,769

Unemployment

1993 (April): 11.5%
1992 average: 12.9%
1991 average: 10.7%
1990 average: 8.0%

Average Annual Pay

1988: $20,239
1987: $19,131
1985: $17,008

Per Capita Personal Income

1991: $17,654
1990: $16,937
1989: $16,031

Business Climate (1987)

Manufacturing
Number of establishments in 1987: 235
Shipments in 1987 ($1,000): $1,537,900
Employees in 1987: 15,200
Change in employment, 1982 to 1987: -12.1%
Average annual pay for manufacturing work in 1989: $23,566
Average annual pay for production work in 1987: $18,207

Wholesale Trade
Number of establishments in 1987: 225
Total sales in 1987 ($1,000): $767,900
Change in sales, 1982 to 1987: 2.4%

Retail Trade
Number of establishments in 1987: 837
Total sales in 1987 ($1,000): $767,900
Retail sales per household in 1987: $18,600
Average annual pay in 1989: $12,699

Service Industry
Selected receipts in 1987 ($1,000): $244,200
Average annual pay in 1989: $18,218

Housing

Total number of units in 1990: 50,294

Occupied units in 1990: 47,118
Owner-occupied units in 1990: 68.5%
1993 ACCRA average cost: N/A
1993 ACCRA average rent for an apartment: N/A

Chamber of Commerce

Greater Vineland Chamber of Commerce, Marianne Korn-bluh-Lods, Exec. Director, City Hall #106, 7th & Wood Sts., PO Box 489, Vineland, NJ 08360-0489. 609-691-7400

Economic Development Office

Vineland Industry Commisssion, Keith Petrosky, Exec. Director, City Hall, Seventh & Wood Sts.., Vineland, NJ 08360. 609-794-4100, FAX 609-794-4327

Economic Development Organizations

City of Bridgeton, Office of Economic Development, Dennis R. Campbell, Assistant Director, City Hall Annex, Bridgeton, NJ 08302. 609-455-3230

Millville Industry Commission, M.S. Lascarides, Director, City Hall, S. High St., Millville, NJ 08332. 609-825-7000

Cumberland County Office of Economic Development, Jonathan C. Savage, Exec. Director, 800 E. Commerce St., Bridgeton, NJ 08302. 609-453-2177, FAX 609-453-9138

Major Businesses

Company	SIC	Telephone
Airwork Corp.	4581	(609) 825-6000
Avena Coin Co.	5094	(609) 692-6343
Chancellor Land Corp.	6552	(609) 691-2400
Comar Inc.	3231	(609) 692-6100
Cumberland Dairy Inc.	2026	(609) 451-1300
Cumberland Mutual Fire Inc.	6331	(609) 451-4050
Eatmor Market Inc.	5411	(609) 455-2876
Falasca Daniel Plumbing & Heating	1711	(609) 794-2010
Farmers Merchants National Bank	6022	(609) 451-2222
IGI Inc.	2836	(609) 691-2411
Joffe Lumber & Supply Co.	5031	(609) 825-9550
Kontes Glass Co.	3231	(609) 692-8500
Landis Supermarkets Inc.	5411	(609) 691-0116
Lilliston Ford Inc.	5511	(609) 691-2020
Major Petroleum Industries	5171	(609) 451-3700
Mazzochi & Aulffo, Inc.	5943	(609) 696-1313
Morie Co. Inc.	1442	(609) 327-4500
NFI Industries Inc.	4213	(609) 691-7000
National Freight Inc.	4213	(609) 691-7000
Newcomb Medical Center	8062	(609) 691-9000
Ogren, Arthur J. Inc.	1542	(609) 692-4226
Pedroni Fuel Co.	5983	(609) 691-4855
Riggins, L. S. Oil Co.	5983	(609) 825-7600
Stanker & Galetto Inc.	1541	(609) 692-8098
Trans-National Systems	7513	(609) 794-4603

Major Businesses (Continued)

Company	SIC	Telephone
Vineland Dressed Beef Co.	2011	(609) 691-9765
Vineland Electric	4911	(609) 794-4300
Vineland Kosher Poultry	2015	(609) 692-1871
Wheaton Industries Inc.	3221	(609) 825-1400
Whibco Inc.	1446	(609) 785-2090

Colleges and Universities

Cumberland County College, Vineland

NEW MEXICO

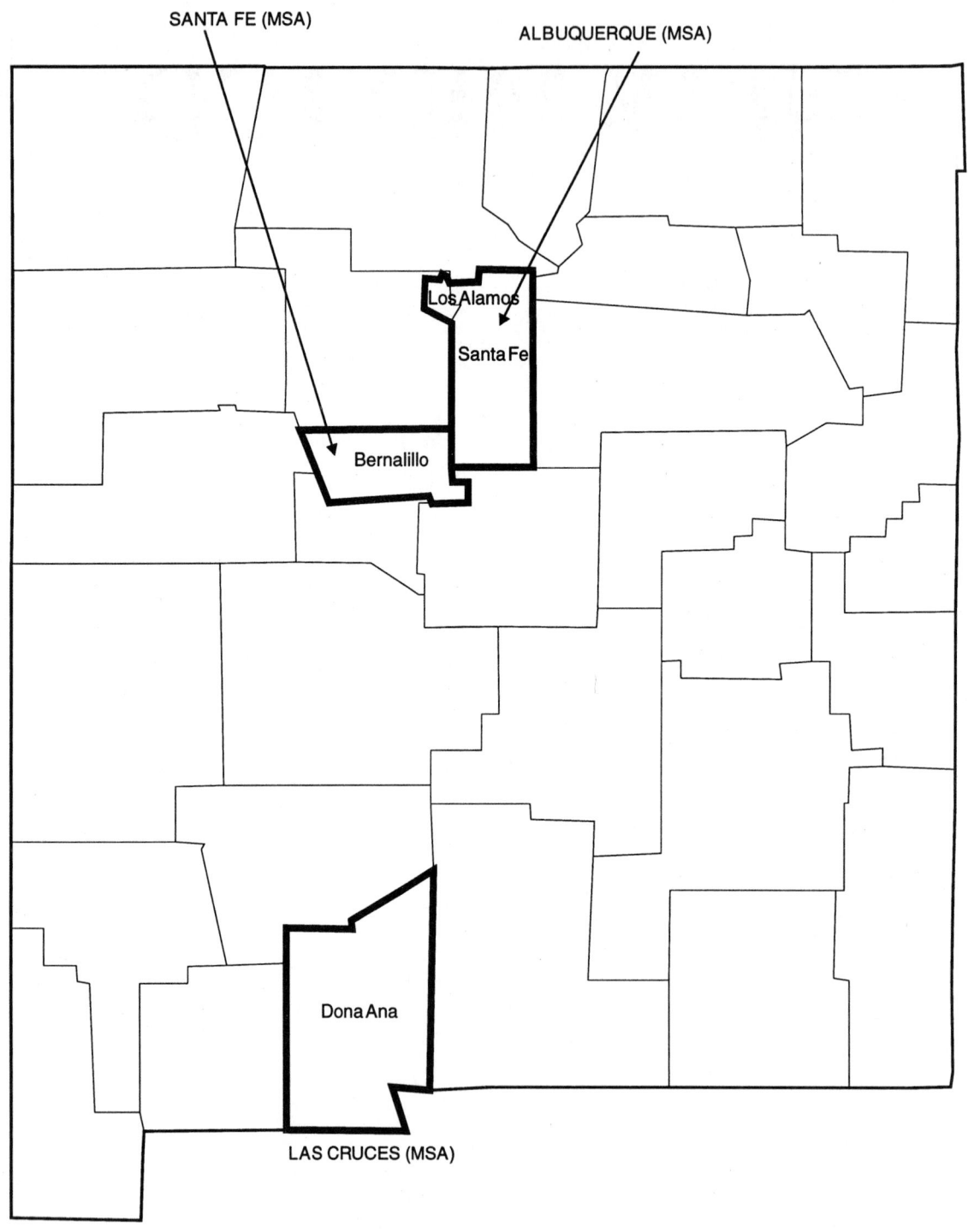

SANTA FE (MSA)

ALBUQUERQUE (MSA)

Los Alamos

Santa Fe

Bernalillo

Dona Ana

LAS CRUCES (MSA)

NEW MEXICO

Population

1990: 1,515,069
1980: 1,302,894

Age

Ages 18 to 20: 68,168
Ages 21 to 24: 83,656
Ages 25 to 44: 484,466
Ages 45 to 54: 147,448
Ages 55 to 59: 62,038
Ages 60 to 64: 59,490
Median age: 31.3

Race and Hispanic Origin

White: 1,146,028
Black: 30,210
Asian/Pacific Islander: 14,124
Native American: 134,355
Hispanic origin: 579,224

Households

Total: 542,709
Persons per household: 2.74

Sex

Male: 745,253
Female: 769,816

Population Migration

Domestic migration: 19,000
International migration: 20,000

Projection of the Population in 1995

Total: 1,621,000
18 to 64: 969,000

Civilian Labor Force

1993: 712,200
1992: 728,100
1991: 707,100
1990: 682,100

Manufacturing

1995 Projection: 46,400
1992: 40,200
1991: 40,800
1990: 42,900
1989: 42,500

Services

1995 Projection: 220,800

1992: 159,300
1991: 150,000
1990: 147,200
1989: 139,900

Wholesale and Retail Trade

1995 Projection: 164,500
1992: 141,700
1991: 141,000
1990: 139,900
1989: 137,100

Unemployment Rate

1993: 6.6%
1992: 7.5%
1991: 7.3%
1990: 5.7%

Employer Unemployment Contributions

Contribution Rate

1992: 1.52%
1991: 1.50%
1990: 1.53%

Average Weekly Benefit

1992: $141.38
1991: $141.17
1990: $129.32

Gross State Product (Million $)

1989: $25,414
1988: $24,263
1987: $23,039
1979: $14,101
Growth rate, 1979 to 1989: 80.2%

Capital Expenditures of Manufacturing Industries

1990: $300,700,000
1989: $196,800,000
1988: $176,700,000
1987: $196,400,000

State Tax Rates

Individual income: Range from 1.8% ($5,200 or less) to 8.5% (above $41,600).
Corporate income: Range from 4.8% ($500,000 or less) to 7.6% (above $1,000,000).

General property: Sum of state and local rates. Assessed at 33.33% of market value.

General sales: 5%

Gasoline: 16.2¢ per gallon

Income

Median income for a 4 person family: $31,156

Personal per Capita Income

1992: $15,353

1991: $14,709

1990: $14,124

Disposable per Capita Income

1992: $13,709

1991: $13,113

1990: $12,568

Private Employment Weekly Wages

Average

1989: $345

1988: $338

1987: $338

Manufacturing

1989: $327

1988: $412

1987: $397

Services

1989: $364

1988: $354

1987: $340

Wholesale

1989: $416

1988: $411

1987: $399

Retail

1989: $205

1988: $204

1987: $198

Highway Statistics

Total Highway Miles

1990: 54,736

1989: 54,807

1988: 53,938

Federal Highway Aid

1991: $102,373,000

1990: $102,268,000

1989: $104,516,000

Electricity

Average Cost per Kilowatt Hour

1990: 7.29¢

1989: 7.37¢

1988: 7.47¢

Housing (1990)

Owner occupied units: 365,965

Median house value: $70,100

Renter occupied units: 176,744

Median rent: $312

Total vacant units: 89,349

Homeowner vacancy rate: 2.3%

Rental vacancy rate: 11.4%

State Business Incentives and Assistance

Financial and Business Assistance

Industrial Development Bonds. Administered by the Department of Finance and Administration, Board of Finance Office, these bonds are issued by a municipality or by a county. The local agencies may exempt certain property and real estate taxes. The principal issuer of a qualified small bond issue is restricted to $10 million of capital expenditure in the county in which the project is located during a six-year period. Bonds to be issued are for manufacturing facilities only.

Community Development Revolving Loan Fund. Administered by the Economic Development Division, this program is designed to strengthen community economic development. The loans may be used for: the improvement of the community's infrastructure; acquisition of real property; construction, reconstruction, rehabilitation or installation of public facilities; site improvements and utilities; commercial or industrial buildings or structures; and other commercial or industrial property improvements.

Energy Research and Development Program. Administered by the Technology Enterprises Division of the Department of Economic Development, this program emphasizes applied research development and commercialization of new products. It provides seed capital for start-up technology-based companies.

Rio Grande Research Corridor. Authorized by the Technology Enterprises Division of the Department of Economic Development, a Science and Technology Advisory Committee was established at the Rio Grande Research Corridor. The Corridor is a center for modern science and high technology development. The Corridor links government laboratories, universities and public-private research facilities into a highly developed center and can assist companies to perform product research.

Education and Training

Industrial Development Training Program. Administered by the Department of Economic Development, this program is designed to provide financial assistance to new or expanding businesses which train residents for full-time employment. Training assistance of up to 1,040 hours per trainee is available under the program. 50% of the approved total training cost is reimbursed to the company.

Job Training Services. Provides customized training programs to new or expanding companies in recruitment, cur-

Major Companies in the State

Company name	Fortune 500 rank	City	Telephone	SIC number
Fortune 500 Companies				
None				
Other Major Companies in the State				
Diagnostek Inc.		Albuquerque	505-345-8080	5961
First National Financial Corp. New Mexico		Albuquerque	505-765-4000	6712
First Savings Bank New Mexico		Clovis	505-762-4417	6035
Home Federal Savings Bank of New Mexico		Deming	505-546-2708	6035
Hondo Oil & Gas Co.		Roswell	505-625-8700	2911
Horizon Healthcare Corp.		Albuquerque	505-881-4961	8051
Lasertechnics Inc.		Albuquerque	505-822-1123	3861
Mesa Airlines Inc.		Farmington	505-327-0271	4512
Mimbres Valley Farmers Association Inc.		Deming	505-546-2769	5399
Mutual Building & Loan Association		Las Cruces	505-524-8571	6035
Patlex Corp.		Las Cruces	505-524-4050	6794
Public Service Co. of New Mexico		Albuquerque	505-848-2700	4931
Reserve Industries Corp.		Albuquerque	505-247-2384	3339
SBS Engineering Inc.		Albuquerque	505-345-5353	3699
Security Funding Capital Corp.		Albuquerque	505-842-8155	6159
Sunwest Financial Services Inc.		Albuquerque	505-765-2403	6022
Thermo Instrument Systems Inc.		Santa Fe	617-622-1000	3826
Unico Inc. New Mexico		Farmington	505-326-2668	2911
United New Mexico Financial Corp.		Albuquerque	505-765-5086	6712
Vivigen Inc.		Santa Fe	505-438-1111	8071

riculum development, and classroom, as well as on-the-job, training.

Job Training Partnership Act. This program operates with funding from the U.S. Department of Labor. It provides job training and other employment related services.

State Offices

Real estate: Regulation and Licensing Department, Real Estate Commission, Randy Lovato, Exec Director, PO Box 25101, NE, Albuquerque, NM 87504. 505-841-6524

Chamber of commerce: Association of Commerce & Industry of New Mexico, Mark Douglas, President, 2309 Renard Place, S.E. #402, Albuquerque, NM 87106-4259. 505-842-0644

Economic development: Department of Economic Development and Tourism, Ponzi Ferraraccio, Director, 1100 St. Francis Drive, Santa Fe, NM 87503. 505-827-0305

Department of Economic Development and Tourism, Technology Enterprises Division, John Dendahl, Secretary, 1100 St. Francis Drive, Santa Fe, NM 87503. 505-827-0265

New Mexico International Trade & Development Co., Jess Hernandez Jr., President, 4007 Comanche N.E., Albuquerque, NM 87110. 505-881-2682

Environmental affairs: Health and Environment Depart-ment, Dennis C. Boyd, Secretary, 1190 St. Francis Drive, Santa Fe, NM 87503. 505-827-2613

Labor: Labor Department, Paul M. Garcia, Secretary, PO Box 1928, Albuquerque, NM 87103. 505-841-8406

Unemployment: Labor Department, Unemployment Insurance Bureau, Jimmy Sanchez, Administrator, PO Box 1928, Albuquerque, NM 87103. 505-841-8431

Worker's compensation: Worker's Compensation Division, Gerald Stuyvesant, Director, PO Box 27198, Albuquerque, NM 87102. 505-841-8787

Occupational safety and health: Regulation and Licensing Department, Ray Shollenbarger, Superintendent, PO Box 25101, NE, Albuquerque, NM 87504. 505-841-6524

Secretary of state: Secretary of State, Rebecca Vigil-Giron, Secretary of State, 400 State Capitol, Santa Fe, NM 87503. 505-827-3601

Taxation and revenue: Taxation and Revenue Department, Gail D. Reese, Secretary, PO Box 630, Santa Fe, NM 87509-0630. 505-827-0341

Designated Zones for Economic Development

Enterprise Zones

No program.

Foreign Trade Zones

Foreign Trade Zone No. 110, Albuquerque, New Mexico,

Grantee: The City of Albuquerque, Operator: Foreign-Trade Zone of New Mexico, Bob Wittington, FTZ Operators, Inc., 1414 12th Street, NW, PO Drawer 26928, Albuquerque, NM 87125, 505-842-6563

Labor Unions

State, County and Municipal Employees, American Federation of (AFL-CIO)

Universities with Ph.D. Programs

New Mexico Institute of Mining and Technology, Socorro
New Mexico State University, Las Cruces
University of New Mexico, Albuquerque

ALBUQUERQUE, NM (MSA)

Geographic Profile

Land Area
1166.2 square miles

Counties and Parishes
Bernalillo

Ranking Highlights

174 *out of 319 in total* **land area**
70 *out of 319 in* **population growth,** *1970–1990*
40 *out of 310 in having the lowest* **unemployment** *rate*
85 *out of 310 in size of* **labor force**
43 *out of 318 in the percentage of* **college graduates**
158 *out of 292 in per capita personal* **income**
102 *out of 319 in number of* **manufacturing establishments**
21 *out of 318 in* **physicians** *per 1000 people*
180 *out of 318 in* **hospital beds** *per 1000 people*
252 *out of 267 in fewest* **crimes** *per 1000 people*
252 *out of 266 in fewest* **violent crimes** *per 1000 people*
17 *out of 319 in per capita* **federal funds and grants**

Quality of Life Indexes (Rate per 1000 population)

Crime rate in 1991: 89.8
Violent crime rate in 1991: 12.0
Physicians rate in 1992: 3.22
Hospital bed rate in 1991: 3.59

ACCRA Cost of Living Indexes
(First quarter 1993, average = 100)

Composite index: 102.7
Utilities index: 95.3
Housing index: 112.4

Overview

The largest city in New Mexico, Albuquerque is also the economic center of the state. John Naisbitt, author of the best-selling *Megatrends*, calls Albuquerque one of the top ten American cities. Part of its success can be attributed to a diverse economic base—consisting of agriculture, services, manufacturing, tourism, and research and development—that prevented the general recession of the early 1990s from adversely affecting most local industries. More than 3.5 million tourists visit Albuquerque each year, to ski the Sandia Mountains and to absorb the city's rich ethnic heritage.

The Rio Grande River valley contains rich farm and pasture lands that support a sizable food industry, based mainly on fruit and produce, in the Albuquerque area. Albuquerque is also home to more than seven hundred manufacturing firms—many of them located in well-planned industrial parks—that produce such goods as trailers, food products, electronic components, neon and electric signs, hardware, and machine tools.

The Rio Grande Research Corridor sprang up in the wake of the development of nuclear research during and after

World War II. The area's major employers are part of this complex. Sandia National Laboratories, New Mexico's largest private employer, is involved in laser technology and solar energy. Kirtland U.S. Air Force Base, the sixth-largest military base in the world, is a weapons research center.

The city's economy benefits from the Santa Fe Railway and the forty motor freight carriers that link Albuquerque with major markets throughout the country. Albuquerque offers an international airport with a port of entry from Mexico. Located within the city limits, the airport is served by sixteen airlines providing one hundred eighteen flights daily. Coronado Airport, to the north of the city, furnishes landing facilities for private and corporate aircraft. Major highways servicing Albuquerque are Interstate 25, running from Canada to Mexico, and Interstate 40—formerly Route 66—intersecting the city from east to west.

The city's primary meeting place is the Albuquerque Convention Center, located in the heart of downtown. The complex, with a conference seating capacity of 6,000 people and banquet seating for 2,400 people, is in close proximity to first-class hotel accommodations and to restaurants and clubs offering a variety of entertainment.

Population (1990)

Total Population and Growth Rate
1990: 480,577
1980: 420,261
1970: 315,774
Growth rate 1970–1990: 52%

Race and Hispanic Origin
White: 76.9%
Black: 2.7%
Asian/Pacific Islander: 1.5%
Native American: 3.4%
Hispanic origin: 37.1%
White not Hispanic: 55.8%

Age
Ages 18 to 20: 4.4%
Ages 21 to 24: 6.1%
Ages 25 to 44: 34.9%
Ages 45 to 54: 10.1%
Ages 55 to 59: 4%
Ages 60 to 64: 3.8%
Ages 65 plus: 10.5%

Educational Attainment (1990)
Percent having completed high school: 82.1%
Percent having completed college: 26.7%
Elementary and high school enrollment: 82,555

Federal Funds and Grants Received
Total received in 1989: $3,368,200,000
Funds received per capita: $6,831

Civilian Labor Force
1993 (April): 275,659

1992 average: 272,004
1991 average: 267,219
1990 average: 263,247

Unemployment
1993 (April): 5.3%
1992 average: 4.7%
1991 average: 5.2%
1990 average: 5.0%

Average Annual Pay
1988: $19,719
1987: $19,162
1985: $17,980

Per Capita Personal Income
1991: $17,040
1990: $16,335
1989: $15,691

Business Climate (1987)

Manufacturing
Number of establishments in 1987: 592
Shipments in 1987 ($1,000): $1,646,100
Employees in 1987: 19,200
Change in employment, 1982 to 1987: 9.7%
Average annual pay for manufacturing work in 1989: $23,405
Average annual pay for production work in 1987: $19,664

Wholesale Trade
Number of establishments in 1987: 1,149
Total sales in 1987 ($1,000): $3,032,100
Change in sales, 1982 to 1987: 20.3%

Retail Trade
Number of establishments in 1987: 2,868
Total sales in 1987 ($1,000): $3,032,100
Retail sales per household in 1987: $17,659
Average annual pay in 1989: $11,157

Service Industry
Selected receipts in 1987 ($1,000): $2,615,300
Average annual pay in 1989: $22,240

Office Real Estate (1992)
Office space inventory: 8,487,483 square feet
Average class A Central Business District rental range per sq. ft: $14.00

Vacancy Rates
All areas: 17.4%

Vacancy Rates in Central Business District
Class A space: 14.5%
Class B space: 21.3%

Vacancy Rates Outside Central Business District
Class A space: 17.2%
Class B space: 16.8%

Housing
Total number of units in 1990: 201,235

Occupied units in 1990: 185,582
Owner-occupied units in 1990: 60.7%
1993 ACCRA average cost: $130,550
1993 ACCRA average rent for an apartment: $547

Chamber of Commerce

Greater Albuquerque Chamber of Commerce, Mrs. Terri L. Cole, President, 401 2nd St. N.W., PO Box 25100, Albuquerque, NM 87125. 505-764-3700

Economic Development Office

Albuquerque Economic Development, Inc., James A. Covell, Exec. Vice President, 851 University Blvd. S.E. Suite 203, Albuquerque, NM 87106. 505-246-6200, FAX 505-246-6219

Major Businesses

Company	SIC	Telephone
ABQ Corp.	6035	(505) 889-1000
Bradbury & Stamm Construction Co.	1542	(505) 765-1200
Diagnostek, Inc.	5961	(505) 345-8080
First Interstate Bank	6022	(505) 766-6000
First National Bank	6021	(505) 765-4000
Jaynes Corp.	1542	(505) 345-8591
New Mexico Mortgage Financial Authority	6163	(505) 843-6880
Plains Electric Transmission	4911	(505) 884-1881
Public Service Co. of New Mexico	4911	(505) 848-2700
Richardson Investments Inc.	5511	(505) 292-0000
Roadrunner Enterprises, Inc.	4213	(505) 345-8856
Roadrunner Trucking, Inc.	4213	(505) 345-8856
Sandia Corp.	8734	(505) 844-5678
Southwest Community Health	8062	(505) 823-8313
Sunwest Bank Albuquerque	6021	(505) 765-2211
Sunwest Financial Service	6021	(505) 765-2403
United Financial Corp.	6021	(505) 765-5086
ZMHC Inc.	5511	(505) 265-8711

Colleges and Universities

Albuquerque Technical Vocational Institute, Albuquerque
Parks College, Albuquerque
University of New Mexico, Albuquerque

LAS CRUCES, NM (MSA)

Geographic Profile

Land Area
3807.4 square miles

Counties and Parishes
Dona Ana

Ranking Highlights

30 *out of 319 in total* **land area**
20 *out of 319 in* **population growth,** *1970–1990*
191 *out of 310 in having the lowest* **unemployment** *rate*
265 *out of 310 in size of* **labor force**
98 *out of 318 in the percentage of* **college graduates**
287 *out of 292 in per capita personal* **income**
310 *out of 319 in number of* **manufacturing establishments**
273 *out of 318 in* **physicians** *per 1000 people*
310 *out of 318 in* **hospital beds** *per 1000 people*
158 *out of 267 in fewest* **crimes** *per 1000 people*
120 *out of 266 in fewest* **violent crimes** *per 1000 people*
42 *out of 319 in per capita* **federal funds and grants**

Quality of Life Indexes (Rate per 1000 population)

Crime rate in 1991:	65.3
Violent crime rate in 1991:	5.6
Physicians rate in 1992:	1.25
Hospital bed rate in 1991:	1.77

ACCRA Cost of Living Indexes
(First quarter 1993, average = 100)

Composite index:	100.9
Utilities index:	91.9
Housing index:	101.4

Population (1990)

Total Population and Growth Rate
1990: 135,510
1980: 96,340
1970: 69,773
Growth rate 1970–1990: 94%

Race and Hispanic Origin
White: 91.1%
Black: 1.6%
Asian/Pacific Islander: 0.9%
Native American: 0.7%
Hispanic origin: 56.4%
White not Hispanic: 40.7%

Age
Ages 18 to 20: 6.7%
Ages 21 to 24: 7.8%
Ages 25 to 44: 30.2%
Ages 45 to 54: 8.6%
Ages 55 to 59: 3.9%

Ages 60 to 64: 3.6%
Ages 65 plus: 8.8%

Educational Attainment (1990)
Percent having completed high school: 70.4%
Percent having completed college: 21.9%
Elementary and high school enrollment: 28,115

Federal Funds and Grants Received
Total received in 1989: $649,400,000
Funds received per capita: $4,919

Civilian Labor Force
1993 (April):   61,612
1992 average: 60,470
1991 average: 60,236
1990 average: 59,767

Unemployment
1993 (April):   8.8%
1992 average: 7.4%
1991 average: 7.4%
1990 average: 6.7%

Average Annual Pay
1988: $16,348
1987: $16,213
1985: $15,537

Per Capita Personal Income
1991: $11,831
1990: $11,587
1989: $10,792

Business Climate (1987)
Manufacturing
Number of establishments in 1987: 74
Shipments in 1987 ($1,000): $262,500
Employees in 1987: 2,500
Change in employment, 1982 to 1987: 25.0%
Average annual pay for manufacturing work in 1989: $19,206
Average annual pay for production work in 1987: $14,950

Wholesale Trade
Number of establishments in 1987: 129
Total sales in 1987 ($1,000): $229,800
Change in sales, 1982 to 1987: 17.6%

Retail Trade
Number of establishments in 1987: 606
Total sales in 1987 ($1,000): $229,800
Retail sales per household in 1987: $11,935
Average annual pay in 1989: $9,650

Service Industry
Selected receipts in 1987 ($1,000): $235,600
Average annual pay in 1989: $14,140

Housing
Total number of units in 1990: 49,148

Occupied units in 1990: 45,029
Owner-occupied units in 1990: 64.6%
1993 ACCRA average cost: $117,180
1993 ACCRA average rent for an apartment: $462

Chamber of Commerce
Las Cruces Chamber of Commerce, John W. Jeffers, Exec. Vice President, 760 W. Picacho, PO Drawer 519, Las Cruces, NM 88004. 505-524-1968

Economic Development Office
Las Cruces/Dona Ana County Economic Development Council, Jim Coleman, Exec Director, 400 South Main Street, Las Cruces, NM 88001. 800-462-7195, 505-524-1745

Major Businesses

Company	SIC	Telephone
Western Bank	6022	(505) 526-5544
Las Cruces TV Cable	4841	(505) 523-2531

Colleges and Universities
New Mexico State University, Las Cruces

SANTA FE, NM (MSA)

Geographic Profile

Land Area

2018.7 square miles

Counties and Parishes

Los Alamos

Santa Fe

Ranking Highlights

90 *out of 319 in total* land area

51 *out of 319 in* population growth, *1970–1990*

12 *out of 310 in having the lowest* unemployment *rate*

222 *out of 310 in size of* labor force

8 *out of 318 in the percentage of* college graduates

49 *out of 292 in per capita personal* income

268 *out of 319 in number of* manufacturing establishments

87 *out of 318 in* physicians *per 1000 people*

282 *out of 318 in* hospital beds *per 1000 people*

N/A *out of 267 in fewest* crimes *per 1000 people*

N/A *out of 266 in fewest* violent crimes *per 1000 people*

2 *out of 319 in per capita* federal funds and grants

Quality of Life Indexes (Rate per 1000 population)

Crime rate in 1991:	N/A
Violent crime rate in 1991:	N/A
Physicians rate in 1992:	2.31
Hospital bed rate in 1991:	2.38

ACCRA Cost of Living Indexes

(First quarter 1993, average = 100)

Composite index:	109.9
Utilities index:	87.0
Housing index:	138.7

Overview

Founded before Massachusetts's Plymouth Colony and the second oldest city in the United States, Santa Fe is a cultural center for the Southwest. The Santa Fe Opera Company is known throughout the world, and the city is a gathering place for writers and artists. The capital of the state of New Mexico, Santa Fe is a blend of native American, Spanish, New Mexican, and Anglo (English) cultures.

Santa Fe's economy has been based largely on tourism and state government. Because of the city's proximity to Los Alamos National Laboratory (LANL), 45 miles away, scientific research has also become a factor. Operated by the University of California and an important center for work on defense-related projects as well as superconductivity and high-energy physics, among other areas, LANL is one of the largest research laboratories in the nation. Over one third of LANL's employees live in Santa Fe, and several new research-related firms and high-technology spinoff companies have located in Santa Fe.

Santa Fe is linked with major western and midwestern markets via rail freight service provided by the Atchison, Topeka, & Santa Fe Railroad, which maintains a main line through nearby Lamy. Several rail sidings are conveniently located in the city's industrial areas. Six interstate motor freight carriers connect Santa Fe with markets on both the East and West Coasts; major parcel express lines also serve the city.

The major airport closest to Santa Fe is Albuquerque International Airport, where regular commuter service is available to Santa Fe by Mesa Airlines. Santa Fe Municipal Airport accommodates private aircraft. The principal highway routes into Santa Fe are I-25, running east and west along the southern perimeter of the city, and I-84/284, which bisects the city from north to south.

Population (1990)

Total Population and Growth Rate

1990: 117,043

1980: 93,118

1970: 69,972

Growth rate 1970–1990: 67%

Race and Hispanic Origin

White: 82.4%

Black: .6%

Asian/Pacific Islander: 0.8%

Native American: 2.5%

Hispanic origin: 43.5%

White not Hispanic: 52.9%

Age

Ages 18 to 20: 3.7%

Ages 21 to 24: 4.4%

Ages 25 to 44: 35.1%

Ages 45 to 54: 12.3%

Ages 55 to 59: 4.5%

Ages 60 to 64: 4%

Ages 65 plus: 10%

Educational Attainment (1990)

Percent having completed high school: 84.5%

Percent having completed college: 35.7%

Elementary and high school enrollment: 20,599

Federal Funds and Grants Received

Total received in 1989: $1,389,300,000

Funds received per capita: $12,353

Civilian Labor Force

1993 (April): 75,727

1992 average: 74,802

1991 average: 73,065

1990 average: 70,598

Unemployment

1993 (April): 3.9%

1992 average: 3.6%

1991 average: 3.6%

1990 average: 3.5%

Average Annual Pay
1988: $18,141
1987: $17,524
1985: $16,370

Per Capita Personal Income
1991: $20,154
1990: $19,201
1989: $17,433

Business Climate (1987)

Manufacturing
Number of establishments in 1987: 130
Shipments in 1987 ($1,000): $95,900
Employees in 1987: 1,500
Change in employment, 1982 to 1987: 7.1%
Average annual pay for manufacturing work in 1989: $19,093
Average annual pay for production work in 1987: $13,600

Wholesale Trade
Number of establishments in 1987: 135
Total sales in 1987 ($1,000): $236,500
Change in sales, 1982 to 1987: 0%

Retail Trade
Number of establishments in 1987: 890
Total sales in 1987 ($1,000): $236,500
Retail sales per household in 1987: $16,900
Average annual pay in 1989: $12,084

Service Industry
Selected receipts in 1987 ($1,000): $504,900
Average annual pay in 1989: $19,034

Housing
Total number of units in 1990: 49,029
Occupied units in 1990: 45,053
Owner-occupied units in 1990: 68.8%
1993 ACCRA average cost: $159,260
1993 ACCRA average rent for an apartment: $692

Chamber of Commerce
Santa Fe Chamber of Commerce, Catherine Zacher, Exec. Director, 333 Montezuma, PO Box 1928, Santa Fe, NM 87504. 505-983-7317

Economic Development Office
Santa Fe Economic Development, Inc., Marilyn A. Jacobs, Exec. Director, 333 Montezuma, PO Box 8184, Santa Fe, NM 87504-8184. 505-984-2842, FAX 505-989-8614

Major Businesses

Company	SIC	Telephone
Century Bank, Federal Savings	6035	(505) 982-1981
Davis & Associates, Inc.	1541	(505) 988-2894
Nambe Mills Inc.	3364	(505) 471-2912
New Mexican, Inc.	2711	(505) 983-3303

Major Businesses (Continued)

Company	SIC	Telephone
New Mexico Banquest Corp.	6712	(505) 984-7422
Thermo Instrument Systems	3829	(617) 622-1000
Viviger, Inc.	8071	(505) 438-1111

Colleges and Universities
College of Santa Fe, Santa Fe
Institute of American Indian Arts, Santa Fe
St. John's College, Santa Fe
Santa Fe Community College, Santa Fe

NEW YORK

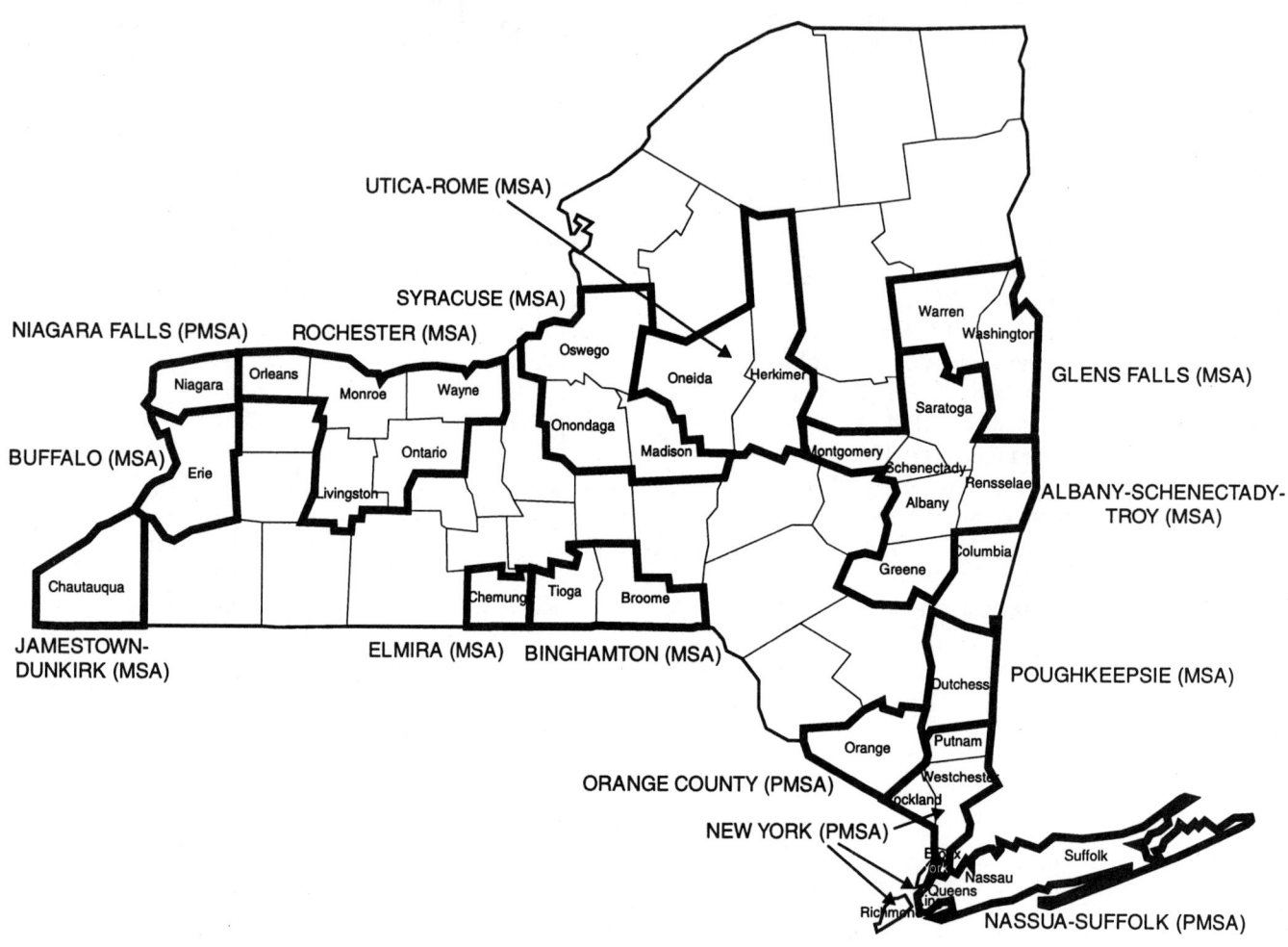

UTICA-ROME (MSA)

SYRACUSE (MSA)

NIAGARA FALLS (PMSA)   ROCHESTER (MSA)

GLENS FALLS (MSA)

BUFFALO (MSA)

ALBANY-SCHENECTADY-
TROY (MSA)

JAMESTOWN-
DUNKIRK (MSA)

ELMIRA (MSA)   BINGHAMTON (MSA)

POUGHKEEPSIE (MSA)

ORANGE COUNTY (PMSA)

NEW YORK (PMSA)

NASSUA-SUFFOLK (PMSA)

Niagara   Orleans

Monroe   Wayne

Oswego

Oneida   Herkimer

Warren

Washington

Erie

Ontario

Onondaga

Madison

Saratoga

Schenectady

Rensselae

Montgomery

Albany

Livingston

Columbia

Chautauqua

Chemung   Tioga   Broome

Greene

Dutchess

Orange

Putnam

Westcheste

ockland

Bronx
ork
Queens
in
Richmond

Nassau

Suffolk

NEW YORK

Population
1990: 17,990,455
1980: 17,558,072

Age
Ages 18 to 20: 839,066
Ages 21 to 24: 1,114,358
Ages 25 to 44: 5,862,873
Ages 45 to 54: 1,913,920
Ages 55 to 59: 811,857
Ages 60 to 64: 825,110
Median age: 33.9

Race and Hispanic Origin
White: 13,385,255
Black: 2,859,055
Asian/Pacific Islander: 693,760
Native American: 62,651
Hispanic origin: 2,214,026

Households
Total: 6,639,322
Persons per household: 2.63

Sex
Male: 8,625,673
Female: 9,364,782

Population Migration
Domestic migration: -1,556,000
International migration: 718,000

Projection of the Population in 1995
Total: 18,308,000
18 to 64: 11,435,000

Civilian Labor Force
1993: 8,562,500
1992: 8,435,100
1991: 8,536,000
1990: 8,741,100

Manufacturing
1995 Projection: 1,214,500
1992: 1,015,000
1991: 1,050,600
1990: 1,101,100
1989: 1,179,000

Services
1995 Projection: 3,382,800

1992: 2,336,400
1991: 2,373,500
1990: 2,423,200
1989: 2,391,700

Wholesale and Retail Trade
1995 Projection: 2,068,300
1992: 1,565,900
1991: 1,620,900
1990: 1,696,000
1989: 1,792,200

Unemployment Rate
1993: 9.3%
1992: 9.1%
1991: 6.4%
1990: 5.5%

Employer Unemployment Contributions

Contribution Rate
1992: 3.30%
1991: 2.26%
1990: 1.90%

Average Weekly Benefit
1992: $198.30
1991: $197.12
1990: $182.07

Gross State Product (Million $)
1989: $441,068
1988: $419,903
1987: $384,983
1979: $199,492
Growth rate, 1979 to 1989: 121.1%

Capital Expenditures of Manufacturing Industries
1990: $5,086,900,000
1989: $5,405,000,000
1988: $4,357,100,000
1987: $4,296,500,000

State Taxe Rates
Individual income: Range from 4% ($11,000 or less) to 7.875% (above $28,000).
Corporate income: 9% of taxable net income, with 15% surtax imposed.

General property: Sum of local levies. Based on full value of real property.
General sales: 4%
Gasoline: 8¢ per gallon

Income

Median income for a 4 person family: $43,693

Personal per Capita Income
1992: $23,534
1991: $22,572
1990: $22,068

Disposable per Capita Income
1992: $20,021
1991: $19,096
1990: $18,495

Private Employment Weekly Wages

Average
1989: $521
1988: $506
1987: $506

Manufacturing
1989: $472
1988: $579
1987: $542

Services
1989: $466
1988: $443
1987: $411

Wholesale
1989: $659
1988: $640
1987: $586

Retail
1989: $269
1988: $258
1987: $246

Highway Statistics

Total Highway Miles
1990: 111,242
1989: 110,964
1988: 110,613

Federal Highway Aid
1991: $674,091,000
1990: $661,697,000
1989: $658,618,000

Electricity

Average Cost per Kilowatt Hour
1990: 9.35¢
1989: 8.81¢
1988: 8.51¢

Housing (1990)

Owner occupied units: 3,464,436
Median house value: $131,600
Renter occupied units: 3,174,886
Median rent: $428
Total vacant units: 587,569
Homeowner vacancy rate: 1.9%
Rental vacancy rate: 4.9%

State Business Incentives and Assistance

Economic Development Zone Business Benefits

3% reduction in utility rates (gas, electric, steam, and water).

A tax credit for up to five years, based on wages paid to full-time employees in newly created jobs. For employees in specially targeted groups, this credit equals 25% of the total wages paid to such employees in the first year, declining to 5% in the fifth year.

An enhanced Investment Tax Credit. A one-time credit of 8-10% for any investment costs for a production business in a zone, applicable to either personal or corporate income taxes. In addition, production corporations may be entitled to a credit equaling 30% of the Investment Tax Credit in each of the three subsequent years.

Refund of sales taxes on tangible personal property used in constructing, expanding, or rehabilitating industrial or certain commercial property in an Economic Development Zone.

A credit against personal or corporate income taxes for the purchase of shares in a zone capital corporation, equal to 25% of the sum paid for any stock purchase, up to a lifetime total of $100,000 in credits.

Exemption from real property tax (100%) on improvements to zone businesses, including retail businesses, for up to five years; 75% in year 8; 50% in year nine; and 25% in year 10.

Refund of local sales taxes paid on tangible personal property used in the construction, improvement, or rehabilitation of industrial or certain commercial property.

Special, reduced electric, gas and telephone rates for the life of the zone.

The Urban Development Corporation's LIFT Program provides financial incentives to businesses and projects within zones. LIFT incentives include low interest loans, deferred interest payments, and grants for feasibility studies and employee training.

The Job Development Authority's 1-2-3 Program provides businesses a debt service deferral for the first three years for realty and machinery equipment loans.

The State Office of Business Permits and Regulatory Assistance works with local governments to expedite the issuance of both State and local business permits and licenses.

The Department of Economic Development's Skills Training Program, the Job Service Division of the State Department of Labor, the State Education Department, the Department of Social Service, and the Job Training Partnership Council combine their efforts with those of local agencies to provide job training, placement and job-readiness programs.

The Department of Education has funded the Governor's School and Business Alliance/Economic Zones linkage program for job readiness training for at-risk youths in selected high schools in zone communities.

The State Department of Economic Development provides technical assistance in government procurement contracts, export sales, and other business services.

The Department of Social Services has instituted priority status on all requests for child care development in zones, and works with the Zones Program to develop and produce criteria to best address the expressed needs of the zone communities.

Financial and Business Assistance

Direct Loan Program. Administered by the New York Job Development Authority, this program provides low interest loans for real estate, machinery and equipment to assist businesses to expand and retain jobs. Priority is given to projects that contribute to the revitalization of distressed areas. Funds are raised through the sale of tax-exempt and taxable bonds.

Industrial Access Program. Administered by the Project Development Bureau of the Department of Transportation, this program provides infrastructure financing to those economic development projects which seek to retain, attract, expand, or revitalize an industrial facility. It is designed to stimulate businesses and employment growth in the state.

Regional Economic Development Partnership Program. Administered by the Urban Development Corporation, this program is designed to help fund economic development projects at the regional level. Each of the ten economic development regions is governed by a council appointed by the Governor. The program provides low-cost loans and grants for projects such as business development, infrastructure, and tourism.

Corporation for Innovation Development Program. Administered by the Science and Technology Foundation, this program is designed to stimulate the development of innovative, technology-based new businesses with high employment growth potential. With a revolving capital fund, the Corporation provides direct and referral financial assistance and technical services to potential new business ventures.

Site and Building Selection Assistance. Administered by the Department of Commerce, this program assists firms seeking new location with comprehensive listing of available properties meeting their specifications as well as coordination of assistance with developers and realtors.

Centers for Advanced Technology. Administered by the

New York Science and Technology Foundation, the state has seven Centers covering different areas of research. This program fosters cooperative research activities between interested companies and universities with the intent of transferring technology from the laboratory to the marketplace.

Industrial Effective Program. Administered by the Department of Economic Development, this program provides management, technical, and financial assistance to industrial companies experiencing competitive problems. The program will help diagnose the company's problems and recommends productivity improvements. Financing assistance is arranged through the Urban Development Corporation.

Education and Training

Economic Development Skills Training Program. Administered by the Department of Economic Development, this program is designed to foster economic development growth through the creation or retaining of jobs. The program provides skills upgrading of existing employees and entry-level training for new employees.

Job Training Services. Provides customized training programs to new or expanding companies in recruitment, curriculum development, and classroom, as well as on-the-job, training.

Job Training Partnership Act. This program operates with funding from the U.S. Department of Labor. It provides job training and other employment related services.

State Offices

Real estate: Department of State, William E. Brown, Public Information Officer, 162 Washington Ave., Albany, NY 12231. 518-473-3678

Chamber of commerce: (No State Chamber of Commerce)

Economic development: Department of Economic Development, Vincent Tese, Commissioner, One Comerce Plaza, Albany, NY 12245. 518-474-6950

Department of Economic Development, Economic Development Zones Program, Liz J. Abzug, Director, Rm 980, One Comerce Plaza, Albany, NY 12245. 518-473-6929

Department of Transportation, Project Development Bureau, Industrial Access Program, Robert J.T. Longabough, Administrator, 5 Governor Harriman State Campus, Albany, NY 12232. 518-457-2320

New York Science and Technology Foundation, R. Graham Jones, 99 Washington Ave., 17th Fl., Albany, NY 12225. 518-474-4349

New York Science and Technology Foundation, Corporation for Innovation Development Program, Manager, Suite 1730, One Commerce Plaza, Albany, NY 12210. 518-473-9741

New York State Urban Development Corporation, President, 1515 Broadway, New York, NY 10036. 212-930-0293

Major Companies in the State

Company name	Fortune 500 rank	City	Telephone	SIC number
Fortune 500 Companies				
Agway Inc.	149	Dewitt	315-449-6431	5148
Amax Inc.	137	New York	212-856-4200	3354
Amerada Hess Corp.	91	New York	212-997-8500	2911
American Home Products Corp.	67	New York	212-878-5000	2834
American Standard Inc.	129	New York	212-703-5100	3585
Asarco Inc.	224	New York	212-510-2000	3331
Avon Products Inc.	128	New York	212-546-6015	2844
Bausch & Lomb Inc.	245	Rochester	716-338-6000	3851
Borden Inc.	74	New York	212-573-4000	2026
Bristol Myers Squibb Co.	40	New York	212-546-4000	2834
Brooke Group Ltd.	474	New York	212-486-6100	2111
Carlisle Companies Inc.	498	Syracuse	315-474-2500	2824
Carter Wallace Inc.	450	New York	212-339-5000	2834
Colgate Palmolive Co.	78	New York	212-310-2000	2844
Coltec Industries Inc.	284	New York	212-940-0400	3728
Corning Inc.	133	Corning	607-974-9000	8071
Dover Corp.	201	New York	212-922-1640	3534
Dow Jones & Co. Inc.	235	New York	212-416-2000	7375
Dresser-Rand Co.	296	Corning	607-937-6400	3511
Eastman Kodak Co.	19	Rochester	716-724-4000	3861
Fisher Price Inc.	443	East Aurora	716-687-3000	3944
Gitano Group Inc.	400	New York	212-819-0707	2339
Grumman Corp.	141	Bethpage	516-575-0574	3721
International Business Machines Co.	4	Armonk	914-765-1900	3571
International Flavors & Fragrances	329	New York	212-765-5500	2869
International Paper Co.	31	Purchase	914-397-1500	2621
K I Communications Corp.	418	New York	212-745-0100	2711
Leslie Fay Co., Inc.	419	New York	212-221-4000	2335
Loral Corp.	165	New York	212-697-1105	3812
Mark IV Industries Inc.	323	Amherst	716-689-4972	3714
Mcgraw Hill Inc.	218	New York	212-512-2000	2721
New York Times Co.	240	New York	212-556-1234	2711
North American Philips Corp.	90	New York	212-850-5000	3651
Pall Corp.	445	East Hills	516-484-5400	3841
Pepsico Inc.	15	Purchase	914-253-2000	5812
Pfizer Inc.	72	New York	212-573-2323	2834
Philip Morris Co., Inc.	7	New York	212-880-5000	2095
Ply Gem Industries Inc.	479	New York	212-832-1550	2431
Quantum Chemical Corp.	199	New York	212-949-5000	2821
Reader's Digest Association Inc.	175	Pleasantville	914-238-1000	2721
RJR Nabisco Holdings Corp.	26	New York	212-258-5600	2111
J E Seagram & Sons Inc.	120	New York	212-572-7000	2085
Sequa Corp.	232	New York	212-986-5500	3724
Tambrands Inc.	447	White Plains	914-696-6000	2676
Texaco Inc.	10	White Plains	914-253-4000	1311
UIS Inc.	435	New York	212-581-7660	4714
Ultramar Corp.	179	Tarrytown	914-333-2000	2911
Unilever United States Inc.	52	New York	212-888-1260	7389

Major Companies in the State. (Continued)

Company name	Fortune 500 rank	City	Telephone	SIC number
Varity Corp.	152	Buffalo	716-888-8000	3714
Warnaco Group Inc.	476	New York	212-661-1300	2321
Westvaco Corp.	197	New York	212-688-5000	2621
Wheeling-Pittsburgh Corp.	373	New York	212-355-5200	3312
Witco Corp.	242	New York	212-605-3800	2869

Other Major Companies in the State

Company name	Fortune 500 rank	City	Telephone	SIC number
American Express Co.		New York	212-640-2000	6211
American International Group Inc.		New York	212-770-7000	6331
American Telephone & Telegraph Co.		New York	212-605-5500	4813
Bankers Trust New York Corp.		New York	212-250-2500	6022
Chase Manhattan Corp.		New York	212-552-2222	6712
Chemical Banking Corp.		New York	212-270-6000	6712
Citicorp		New York	212-559-1000	6712
Consolidated Edison Co. of New York Inc.		New York	212-460-4600	4931
Continental Corp.		New York	212-440-3000	6331
ITT Corp.		New York	212-258-1000	6331
ITT Hartford Group Inc.		New York	212-258-1000	6331
J P Morgan & Co. Inc.		New York	212-483-2323	6712
Loew's Corp.		New York	212-545-2000	6331
Manufacturers Hanover Corp.		New York	212-270-6000	6712
Melville Corp.		Rye	914-925-4000	5651
Merrill Lynch & Co. Inc.		New York	212-449-1000	6211
Morgan Stanley Group Inc.		New York	212-703-4000	6211
New York Telephone Co.		New York	212-395-2121	4813
Nynex Corp.		New York	212-370-7400	4813
Primerica Corp.		New York	212-891-8900	6411
R H Macy & Co. Inc.		New York	212-560-4249	5311
RJR Nabisco Inc.		New York	212-258-5600	2111
Salomon Inc.		New York	212-783-7000	6211
Shearson Lehman Brothers Inc.		New York	212-298-2000	6211
Time Warner Inc.		New York	212-484-8000	7812
Woolworth Corp.		New York	212-553-2000	5331

New York Job Development Authority, Robert T. Dormer, President, 605 Third Ave., New York, NY 10158. 212-818-1700

Small Business Development Center, James L. King, State Director, SUNY Central, State University Plaza, Albany, NY 12246. 518-473-5398

Environmental affairs: Department of Environmental Conversation, Thomas C. Jorling, Commissioner, 50 Wolf Road, Albany, NY 12233. 518-457-3446

Labor: Department of Labor, Douglas Myers, Public Information Director, State Campus, Labor Department Bldg., Albany, NY 12240. 518-457-5519

Unemployment: Department of Labor, Unemployment Insurance Division, Virgil H. Hodges, Director, State Campus, Bldg 12, Albany 12240. 518-457-2878

Worker's compensation: Worker's Compensation Board,

Barbara Patton, Chairperson, 100 Broadway, Albany, NY 12241. 518-474-6670

Occupational safety and health: Department of Labor, Division of Occupational Safety & Health, Douglas Myers, Public Information Director, State Campus, Labor Department Bldg., Albany, NY 12240. 518-457-5519

Secretary of state: Department of State, Gail S. Shaffer, Secretary of State, 162 Washington Ave., Albany, NY 12231. 518-474-4750

Taxation and revenue: Department of Taxation and Finance, Karl Felsen, Public Information Director, State Campus, Tax and Finance Bldg., Albany, NY 12227. 518-457-4242

Designated Zones for Economic Development

Enterprise Zones

Enacted in: 1986

No. of established zones: 19

Auburn, Cayuga County, Ms. Lisa Barndt, Zone Coordinator, City of Auburn, 24 South Street, City Hall, Auburn, NY 13021. 315-255-4117

East Harlem, New York County, Ms. Carmen Castro, EDZ Coordinator, LDC El Barrio, 145 E. 116th Street, New York, NY 10029. 212-410-9795

East New York, Kings, Ms. Pat Catwell, East NY Local Development Corp., 116 Williams Avenue, Brooklyn, NY 11207. 718-385-6700

Elmira, Chemung County, Mr. Mike Morse, Coordinator, Elmira Downtown Development, PO Box 1416, Elmira, NY 14902. 607-734-0341

Gloversville, Fulton County, Mr. Thomas Murphy, EDZ Coordinator, Fulton County EDC, Balzano Rd., Crossroads Industrial Park, Johnstown, NY 12095. 518-773-7950

Islip, Suffolk County, Ms. Marcia Grann-O'Brien, Director of Economic Development, Town of Islip C.D.A., 267 Carleton Ave., Central Islip, NY 11722. 516-348-7676

Lackawanna, Erie County, Mr. William Egan, Planning Office, City Hall, 714 Ridge Road, Lackawanna, NY 14218. 716-827-6474

Moriah/Port Henry, Essex County, Mr. Art Norton, EDZ Coordinator, Essex Co. IDA, County Gov't Office, Elizabethtown, NY 12932. 518-873-9114

Niagara Falls, Niagara County, Mr. James Engel, Dept. of Development Services, City of Niagara Falls, 745 Main Street, City Hall, Niagara Falls, NY 14302. 716-282-3501

Ogdensburg, St. Lawrence County, Mr. Martin D. Murphy, Planner, City Hall, 330 Ford Street, Ogdensburg, NY 13669. 315-393-7150

Olean/Allegany, Cattaraugus County, Mr. George Schanzenbacher, Zone Operating Officer, Cattaraugus EDZ Corporation, 1010 Wayne St., Olean, NY 14760. 716-373-9260

Oswego, Oswego County, Mr. Eugene Saloga, Community Development Director, Community Development Office, 20 West Oneida St., 3rd Floor, Oswego, NY 13126. 315-343-3795, Mr. L. Michael Treadwell, Director, Operation Oswego County, PO Box 4067, Oswego, NY 13126. 315-343-1545

Plattsburgh, Clinton County, Ms. Rosemarie Schoonmaker, EDZ Coordinator, City of Plattsburgh, City Hall, Plattsburgh, NY 12901. 518-563-7642

Port Morris, Bronx, Mr. Jaime Gonzalez, Port Morris Local Devel. Corp., 370 149th Street, Bronx, NY 10455. 212-292-3113

South Jamaica, Queens, Mr. James Johnson, Project Director, Greater Jamaica Develop. Corp., 90-04 161st Street, Jamaica, NY 11432 718-291-0282

Syracuse, Onondaga County, Ms. Christine Abate, Coordinator, Rebuild Syracuse, Inc., 450 West Onondaga Street, Syracuse, NY 13202. 315-473-2616

Troy, Rensselaer County, Mr. Peter Swota, Zone Coordinator, City of Troy, City Hall, Troy, NY 12180. 518-270-4637

Utica, Oneida County, Ms. Jovita Bernard, EDZ Coordinator, Dept. of Urban & Economic Development, One Kennedy Plaza, Utica, NY 13502. 315-792-0181

Yonkers, Westchester County, Ms. Cynthia Wallquist, Planning Director, Dept. of Planning & Development, 87 Nepperhan Ave., Yonkers, NY 10701. 914-377-6650

Foreign Trade Zones

Foreign Trade Zone No. 121, Albany, New York, Grantee: Capital District Regional Planning Commission, Chungchin Chen, 214 Canal Square, 2nd Floor, Schenectady, NY 12305, 518-393-1715

Foreign Trade Zone No. 23, Buffalo, New York, Grantee: County of Erie, Erie County Industrial Development Agency, Constance Hoyt, Liberty Bldg., Suite 300, 424 Main St., Buffalo, NY 14202, 716-856-6525

Foreign Trade Zone No. 54, Clinton County, New York, Grantee/Operator: Clinton County Area Dev. Corp., Francis Lapham, PO Box 972, Plattsburgh, NY 12901, 518-563-3100

Foreign Trade Zone No. 1, New York City, New York, Grantee: City of New York, Operator: S & F Warehouse, Inc., Sol Braun, Brooklyn Navy Yard, Bldg. 77, Brooklyn, NY 11205, 718-834-0400

Foreign Trade Zone No. 111, JFK Int'l Airport, New York, Grantee: The City of New York, Operator: Port Authority of New York and New Jersey, Charles Seliga, JFK International Airport, Jamaica, NY 11430, 718-656-5330

Foreign Trade Zone No. 141, Monroe County, New York, Grantee: County of Monroe, New York, Lynne Clarke, Monroe County Foreign-Trade Zone, 110 County Office Bldg., 39 West Main Street, Rochester NY 14614, 716-428-5010

Foreign Trade Zone No. 34, Niagara County, New York, Grantee: County of Niagara, Operator: North American Trading and Drayage, Jodyne Morphy 2221 Niagara Falls Boulevard, Niagara Falls, NY 14304, 716-731-4900

Foreign Trade Zone No. 172, Oneida County, New York, Grantee: County of Oneida, Operator: Oneida County Industrial Development Corporation, Joseph G. Karam, Airport Terminal Building, Box 137, RR 1, Oriskany, NY 13424, 315-736-0888

Foreign Trade Zone No. 90, Onondaga, New York, Grantee: County of Onondaga, Joseph D. Russo, c/o Greater Syracuse Chamber of Commerce, 100 E. Onondaga Street, Syracuse, NY 13202, 315-470-1334

Foreign Trade Zone No. 118, Ogdensburg, New York, Grantee: Ogdensburg Bridge and Port Authority, Salvatore Pisani, Ogdensburg, NY 13669, 315-393-4080

Foreign Trade Zone No. 37, Orange County, New York, Grantee: County of Orange, Jeff Chanin, Department of Law, 275 Main Street, Goshen, NY 10924, 914-294-5151

Foreign Trade Zone No. 52, Suffolk County, New York, Grantee/Operator: County of Suffolk, Jim Mackey, 1 Trade Zone Drive, Ronkonkoma, NY 11779, 516-588-5757

Foreign Trade Zone No. 109, Watertown, New York, Grantee: The County of Jefferson, John Nichols, c/o Jefferson Industrial Development Agency, 175 Arsenal St., Watertown, NY 13601, 315-785-3226

Labor Unions

Air Line Pilots Association, International (AFL-CIO)

Automobile, Aerospace & Agricultural Implement Workers of America, International Union, United, (UAW AFL-CIO)

Bakery, Confectionery & Tobacco Workers International Union (AFL-CIO)

Carpenters and Joiners of America, United Brotherhood of (AFL-CIO)

Chemical Workers Union, International (AFL-CIO)

Communications Workers of America (AFL-CIO)

Electrical Workers, International Brotherhood of (AFL-CIO)

Electronic, Electrical, Salaried, Machine and Furniture Workers, International Union of (AFL-CIO)

Federal Employees, National Federation of

Food and Commercial Workers International Union, United (AFL-CIO)

Graphic Communications International Union (AFL-CIO)

Ilion Nylon Employees Council, Inc.

Laborers' International Union of North America (AFL-CIO)

Ladies' Garment Workers' Union, International (AFL-CIO)

National Education Association

New York State Nurses Association

The Newspaper Guild (AFL-CIO)

Novelty and Production Workers, International Union of Allied (AFL-CIO)

Nurses' Association, American

Operating Engineers, International Union of (AFL-CIO)

Plumbing and Pipe Fitting Industry of The United States and Canada, United Association of, Journeymen and Apprentices of the (AFL-CIO)

Retail, Wholesale and Department Store Union (AFL-CIO)

School Administrators, American Federation of (AFL-CIO)

Service Employees' International Union (AFL-CIO)

Sheet Metal Workers' International Association (AFL-CIO)

State, County and Municipal Employees, American Federation of (AFL-CIO)

Steelworkers of America, United (AFL-CIO)

Subway-Surface Supervisors Association

Teachers, American Federation of (AFL-CIO)

Teamsters, Chauffeurs, Warehousemen and Helpers of America, International Brotherhood of, (AFL-CIO)

Theatrical Stage Employees and Moving Picture Machine Operators of the United States and Canada, International

Alliance of (AFL-CIO)

Transit Union, Amalgamated (AFL-CIO)

Transport Workers Union of America (AFL-CIO)

United Transportation Union (AFL-CIO)

Universities with Ph.D. Programs

Adelphi University, Garden City

Albany College of Pharmacy of Union University, Albany

Alfred University, Alfred

City College of The City University of New York, New York

Clarkson University, Potsdam

Columbia University, School of Engineering and Applied Science, New York

Fordham University, New York

Hofstra University, Hempstead

John Jay College of Criminal Justice of The City University of New York, New York

Juilliard School, New York

Long Island University, Brooklyn Campus, Brooklyn

New York University, New York

Pace University, New York

Pace University, White Plains Campus, White Plains

Polytechnic University, Brooklyn Campus, Brooklyn

Rochester Institute of Technology, Rochester

St. John's University, Jamaica

State University of New York at Albany, Albany

State University of New York at Binghamton, Binghamton

State University of New York at Buffalo, Buffalo

State University of New York at Stony Brook, Stony Brook

State University of New York College of Environmental Science and Forestry, Syracuse

State University of New York Health Science Center at Brooklyn, Brooklyn

State University of New York Health Science Center at Syracuse, Syracuse

Syracuse University, Syracuse

Touro College, New York

Union College, Schenectady

University of Rochester, Rochester

Sources of Additional Information

The Fact Is, You Belong In New York State. New York State Department of Economic Development, 1990. 24p.

Institutional Directory, Postsecondary Education in New York State. The University of the State of New York [The State Education Department, Bureau of Postsecondary Research and Information Systems, Albany, NY 12230], September 1990. 74p.

ALBANY–SCHENECTADY–TROY, NY (MSA)

Geographic Profile

Land Area

3248.5 square miles

Counties and Parishes

Albany

Greene

Montgomery

Rensselaer

Saratoga

Schenectady

Ranking Highlights

43 *out of 319 in total* **land area**

232 *out of 319 in* **population growth,** *1970–1990*

99 *out of 310 in having the lowest* **unemployment** *rate*

63 *out of 310 in size of* **labor force**

73 *out of 318 in the percentage of* **college graduates**

58 *out of 292 in per capita personal* **income**

78 *out of 319 in number of* **manufacturing establishments**

87 *out of 318 in* **physicians** *per 1000 people*

151 *out of 318 in* **hospital beds** *per 1000 people*

40 *out of 267 in fewest* **crimes** *per 1000 people*

78 *out of 266 in fewest* **violent crimes** *per 1000 people*

27 *out of 319 in per capita* **federal funds and grants**

Quality of Life Indexes (Rate per 1000 population)

Crime rate in 1991:	40.2
Violent crime rate in 1991:	4.1
Physicians rate in 1992:	2.31
Hospital bed rate in 1991:	3.99

ACCRA Cost of Living Indexes

(First quarter 1993, average = 100)

Composite index:	110.9
Utilities index:	139.2
Housing index:	108.1

Overview

Trenton

Trenton, the second oldest capital in the United States, lies on the east bank of the Delaware River north of Philadelphia, Pennsylvania. Trenton is New Jersey's state capital and the county seat.

Items and goods produced in the area include refrigerated showcases, light bulbs, rubber goods, purses, automobile body hardware, pottery and porcelain products, chemicals, fabricated metal products, lumber and wood products, textiles, food products, and electronic goods.

Mercer County Airport, just minutes from Trenton in Ewing Township, offers passenger, charter, cargo, and helicopter service. The Philadelphia and New York City air-

ports, as well as Newark International Airport, are located an hour's drive away from Trenton and offer comprehensive domestic and international flight service. Rail lines serving Trenton are AMTRAK, Septa, and New Jersey Transit. One-hundred motor freight carriers service the city, taking advantage of Trenton's location along U.S. Route 1 and of the short-haul trucking to and from two of the nation's largest cities: New York and Philadelphia.

Albany

Albany is the capital and a major port and trading center for New York State. State government buildings dominate the city's skyline and governmental activities dominate the economy. State and local governments employ more than thirty percent of the Albany area work force, a phenomenon that has brought long-term stability to the economy. A network of service industries, especially restaurants and food stores, law firms, and related businesses has grown up in Albany to serve the needs of government. Area colleges and universities and an extensive health care network also play a dominant role in the city's economy. The presence of scientific research facilities has stimulated the growth of the high technology industries that are replacing traditional manufacturing industries.

Some manufacturers are based in Albany, producing such items as felt products, sporting goods, and beer, but major manufacturing is represented by national companies with divisions located throughout Albany County, including General Electric Company's plastics operation in Selkirk and its silicon plant in Waterford. The sectors of finance, insurance, and real estate enjoy a strong presence in Albany, which is the country's twentieth largest banking city and headquarters of Norstar Bancorp and KeyCorp.

As the focal point of a six-county greater metropolitan area that encompasses prime East Coast recreational areas, Albany is also affected economically by the tourists who flock to the region each year.

Inland 124 miles from New York City, the Port of Albany's thirty-two-foot channel on the Hudson River admits international ocean-going vessels and serves as an important stop on the barge canal system of the state, ultimately connecting the city with the Atlantic Ocean and the Great Lakes. The port is served by three railroads and more than one hundred motor freight carriers. Albany is within overnight trucking time of thirty-five of the country's one hundred largest retail markets.

Albany airport is an 850-acre facility that is served by fourteen carriers and offering direct jet service to some major cities. A modern superhighway network that grew up along the shores of Albany's waterways connects the city with New York City to the south via the New York State Thruway (Interstates 90 and 87), and to the Adirondack region and Lake Champlain via the Adirondack Northway (Interstate 87). Interstate 787, the Riverfront Arterial, assists inter-city travel and access to New England through connections with Interstate 90 east and U.S. Route 7. Other major highways include U.S. Routes 5, 7A, 9, 9R, and a host of county highways.

Population (1990)

Total Population and Growth Rate
1990: 874,304
1980: 835,880
1970: 811,113
Growth rate 1970–1990: 8%

Race and Hispanic Origin
White: 93.3%
Black: 4.7%
Asian/Pacific Islander: 1.2%
Native American: 0.2%
Hispanic origin: 1.3%
White not Hispanic: 9.2%

Age
Ages 18 to 20: 5.2%
Ages 21 to 24: 6.5%
Ages 25 to 44: 32.1%
Ages 45 to 54: 10%
Ages 55 to 59: 4.3%
Ages 60 to 64: 4.5%
Ages 65 plus: 14.2%

Educational Attainment (1990)
Percent having completed high school: 79.7%
Percent having completed college: 23.4%
Elementary and high school enrollment: 134,410

Federal Funds and Grants Received
Total received in 1989: $4,791,100,000
Funds received per capita: $5,631

Civilian Labor Force
1993 (April): 443,955
1992 average: 435,967
1991 average: 438,860
1990 average: 439,945

Unemployment
1993 (April): 5.0%
1992 average: 6.0%
1991 average: 5.7%
1990 average: 3.6%

Average Annual Pay
1988: $21,779
1987: $20,607
1985: $18,602

Per Capita Personal Income
1991: $19,783
1990: $19,306
1989: $18,294

Business Climate (1987)

Manufacturing
Number of establishments in 1987: 828
Shipments in 1987 ($1,000): $5,512,400
Employees in 1987: 48,000
Change in employment, 1982 to 1987: -10.4%
Average annual pay for manufacturing work in 1989: $30,590
Average annual pay for production work in 1987: $22,381

Wholesale Trade
Number of establishments in 1987: 1,408
Total sales in 1987 ($1,000): $5,702,100
Change in sales, 1982 to 1987: 20.3%

Retail Trade
Number of establishments in 1987: 5,522
Total sales in 1987 ($1,000): $5,702,100
Retail sales per household in 1987: $18,030
Average annual pay in 1989: $12,202

Service Industry
Selected receipts in 1987 ($1,000): $2,382,700
Average annual pay in 1989: $19,744

Office Real Estate (1992)
Office space inventory: 11,015,000 square feet
Average class A Central Business District rental range per sq. ft: $16.50

Vacancy Rates
All areas: 9.8%

Vacancy Rates in Central Business District
Class A space: 5.7%
Class B space: 9.9%

Vacancy Rates Outside Central Business District
Class A space: 5.1%
Class B space: 14.1%

Housing
Total number of units in 1990: 371,571
Occupied units in 1990: 335,823
Owner-occupied units in 1990: 64.1%
1993 ACCRA average cost: $116,363
1993 ACCRA average rent for an apartment: $622

Chamber of Commerce
Albany-Colonie Regional Chamber of Commerce, James M. Stewart, President, 518 Broadway, Albany, NY 12207. 518-434-1214

Economic Development Office
Center for Economic Growth Inc., Ken Wagner, Director, 1 Keycorp Pl., Suite 600, Albany, NY 12207. 518-465-8975

Economic Development Organizations
Schenectady Economic Development Corp., George Robertson, President, 1 Broadway Center Suite 750, Schenectady, NY 12305. 518-393-7252, FAX 518-393-8687

Rensselaer County Planning Office, G. Glen King, Deputy Director of Planning, 1600 7th Ave., Troy, NY 12180. 518-270-2921

Rensselaer Gateway Development Corp., Timothy Hulbert, President, 31 2nd St., Troy, NY 12180. 518-274-7020, FAX 518-272-7729

New York State Dept. of Economic Development, Capital Regional Office, Francis Quinn, Regional Director, 2 City Square, 324 Broadway, Albany, NY 12207. 518-432-2697, FAX 518-432-2697

Major Businesses

Company	SIC	Telephone
Albany International Corp.	2221	(518) 445-2200
Albany Medical Center	8062	(518) 445-5486
Albany Medical Center Hospital	8062	(518) 445-3125
Albany Savings Bank	6035	(518) 445-2000
Bellevue Builders Supply	5211	(518) 355-7190
Callanan Industries Inc.	2951	(518) 767-2222
Combined Life Insurance Co.	6321	(518) 456-9333
Davis Acoustical Corp.	1542	(518) 271-7400
Ellis Hospital	8062	(518) 382-4141
Farm Family Life Insurance	6411	(518) 436-9751
Farm Family Mutual Insurance	6331	(518) 436-9751
First Albany Companies Inc.	6211	(518) 447-8500
Garden Way Inc.	3524	(518) 235-6010
Golub Corp.	5411	(518) 355-5000
Home & City Savings Bank	6036	(518) 447-5000
I DS Life Insurance Co.	6311	(518) 458-1865
Keycorp	6021	(518) 486-8000
Memorial Hospital of Albany	8062	(518) 471-3221
NYS Thruway Authority	4785	(518) 436-2700
Norstar Bank Upstate New York	6022	(518) 447-4000
Otto Oldsmobile Cadillac	5511	(518) 869-5000
Price Chopper Operating Co.	5411	(518) 355-5000
Record Town Inc.	5735	(518) 452-1242
Rotterdam Ventures Inc.	6512	(518) 861-8516
St. Peter's Hospital	8062	(518) 454-1550
Trans World Music Corp.	5735	(518) 452-1242
Trustco Bank New York	6022	(518) 377-3311
United Community Insurance	6331	(518) 465-0457

Colleges and Universities

Albany College of Pharmacy of Union University, Albany
Bryant And Stratton Business Institute, Albany
College of Saint Rose, Albany
Hudson Valley Community College, Troy
Junior College of Albany, Albany
Maria College, Albany
Rensselaer Polytechnic Institute, Troy
Russell Sage College, Troy
Schenectady County Community College, Schenectady
State University of New York at Albany, Albany

Union College, Schenectady
University of the State of New York, Regents College Degrees, Albany

BINGHAMTON, NY (MSA)

Geographic Profile

Land Area

1225.6 square miles

Counties and Parishes

Broome

Tioga

Ranking Highlights

161 *out of 319 in total* **land area**

279 *out of 319 in* **population growth,** *1970–1990*

149 *out of 310 in having the lowest* **unemployment** *rate*

166 *out of 310 in size of* **labor force**

134 *out of 318 in the percentage of* **college graduates**

111 *out of 292 in per capita personal* **income**

161 *out of 319 in number of* **manufacturing establishments**

159 *out of 318 in* **physicians** *per 1000 people*

231 *out of 318 in* **hospital beds** *per 1000 people*

12 *out of 267 in fewest* **crimes** *per 1000 people*

17 *out of 266 in fewest* **violent crimes** *per 1000 people*

61 *out of 319 in per capita* **federal funds and grants**

Quality of Life Indexes (Rate per 1000 population)

Crime rate in 1991:	32.7
Violent crime rate in 1991:	1.9
Physicians rate in 1992:	1.8
Hospital bed rate in 1991:	3.09

ACCRA Cost of Living Indexes

(First quarter 1993, average = 100)

Composite index:	99.8
Utilities index:	118.6
Housing index:	91.7

Population (1990)

Total Population and Growth Rate

1990: 264,497

1980: 263,460

1970: 268,328

Growth rate 1970–1990: -1%

Race and Hispanic Origin

White: 96.2%

Black: 1.8%

Asian/Pacific Islander: 1.5%

Native American: 0.2%

Hispanic origin: 1.1%

White not Hispanic: 95.5%

Age

Ages 18 to 20: 5.1%

Ages 21 to 24: 6.1%

Ages 25 to 44: 31%

Ages 45 to 54: 10.4%

Ages 55 to 59: 4.6%

Ages 60 to 64: 4.7%

Ages 65 plus: 14.2%

Educational Attainment (1990)

Percent having completed high school: 79.2%

Percent having completed college: 20.2%

Elementary and high school enrollment: 41,157

Federal Funds and Grants Received

Total received in 1989: $1,131,300,000

Funds received per capita: $4,347

Civilian Labor Force

1993 (April): 121,815

1992 average: 120,461

1991 average: 121,836

1990 average: 122,840

Unemployment

1993 (April): 6.6%

1992 average: 6.8%

1991 average: 6.0%

1990 average: 4.1%

Average Annual Pay

1988: $21,315

1987: $20,635

1985: $19,047

Per Capita Personal Income

1991: $18,048

1990: $17,456

1989: $16,730

Business Climate (1987)

Manufacturing

Number of establishments in 1987: 312

Shipments in 1987 ($1,000): $3,820,500

Employees in 1987: 36,500

Change in employment, 1982 to 1987: -11.4%

Average annual pay for manufacturing work in 1989: $32,133

Average annual pay for production work in 1987: $19,735

Wholesale Trade

Number of establishments in 1987: 358

Total sales in 1987 ($1,000): $1,084,300

Change in sales, 1982 to 1987: 19.1%

Retail Trade

Number of establishments in 1987: 1,581

Total sales in 1987 ($1,000): $1,084,300

Retail sales per household in 1987: $16,647

Average annual pay in 1989: $10,389

Service Industry

Selected receipts in 1987 ($1,000): $458,600

Average annual pay in 1989: $16,254

Housing

Total number of units in 1990: 108,223

Occupied units in 1990: 100,681
Owner-occupied units in 1990: 67.9%
1993 ACCRA average cost: $102,300
1993 ACCRA average rent for an apartment: $458

Chamber of Commerce

Broome County Chamber of Commerce, Leonard J. James, Jr., President, PO Box 995, Binghamton, NY 13902. 607-772-8860

Economic Development Office

Broome County Industrial Development Agency, Mark Turner, Exec. Director, PO Box 1026, Binghamton, NY 13902. 607-772-8212

Economic Development Organizations

New York State Dept. of Economic Development, Southern Tier Regional Office, John B. McGuire, Regional Director, 164 Hawley St., Binghamton, NY 13901. 607-773-7813, FAX 607-773-7872

New York State Trade Adjust Assistance Center, John Lacey, Exec Director, 117 Hawley Street, Binghamton, NY 13901. 607-771-0875

Major Businesses

Company	SIC	Telephone
Azon Corp.	2672	(607) 797-2368
Binghamton Savings Bank	6036	(607) 779-2345
Centuri Inc.	5091	(607) 729-6316
Columbian Mutual Life Insurance	6321	(607) 724-2472
Crowley Foods Inc.	2022	(607) 722-6441
Dover Technology International	3549	(607) 773-2290
Empire Chem. Inc.	2822	(607) 729-9331
Endicott Johnson Corp.	3143	(607) 757-4000
Father & Son Shoe Stores	5661	(607) 757-4000
Great American Industries	3069	(607) 729-3475
Keuffel & Esser Co.	3952	(607) 797-2368
Our Lady of Lourdes Memorial Hospital	8062	(607) 798-5111
P L C Enterprises Inc.	3086	(607) 729-9331
Progress Capital Inc.	6153	(607) 729-9331
Public Loan Co. Inc.	6153	(607) 729-9331
Security Mutual Life Insurance	6311	(607) 723-3551
United Health Services Inc.	8062	(607) 770-6000
Universal Instruments Corp.	3559	(607) 772-7522

Colleges and Universities

Broome Community College, Binghamton
State University of New York at Binghamton, Binghamton

BUFFALO, NY (PMSA)

Geographic Profile

Land Area
1044.7 square miles

Counties and Parishes
Erie

Ranking Highlights

193 *out of 319 in total* **land area**
318 *out of 319 in* **population growth,** *1970–1990*
184 *out of 310 in having the lowest* **unemployment** *rate*
59 *out of 310 in size of* **labor force**
137 *out of 318 in the percentage of* **college graduates**
91 *out of 292 in per capita personal* **income**
54 *out of 319 in number of* **manufacturing establishments**
54 *out of 318 in* **physicians** *per 1000 people*
90 *out of 318 in* **hospital beds** *per 1000 people*
110 *out of 267 in fewest* **crimes** *per 1000 people*
196 *out of 266 in fewest* **violent crimes** *per 1000 people*
143 *out of 319 in per capita* **federal funds and grants**

Quality of Life Indexes (Rate per 1000 population)

Crime rate in 1991:	56.9
Violent crime rate in 1991:	8.5
Physicians rate in 1992:	2.6
Hospital bed rate in 1991:	4.78

ACCRA Cost of Living Indexes
(First quarter 1993, average = 100)

Composite index:	N/A
Utilities index:	N/A
Housing index:	N/A

Overview

Buffalo is the second largest city in New York State and its largest inland port. Buffalo is located at the eastern end of Lake Erie and at the head of the Niagara River; the lake has made the city one of the nation's leading inland ports, while the hydroelectric power supplied by Niagara Falls has attracted a diverse array of industries.

Following the economic decline of the 1980s, Buffalo has been able to capitalize on its strengths—location and natural resources— to build a diversified economy based on financial services (three major banks are headquartered there) and high–technology and computer equipment manufacturing while still holding on to some of its largest employers (automotive parts manufacturers and the flour industry). Buffalo has been ranked by a national magazine as one of the top five "up and coming cities" in the country. Between four and five hundred foreign–owned manufacturers have established an economic presence there, with Canada a major player and increasing interest being shown by Far Eastern countries such as Japan. Western New York is one of the state's centers of high technology and research, and retail sales is a growing segment of the region's economy.

Buffalo is located about twenty-five miles south of Niagara Falls, one of the world's premier tourist attractions drawing more than ten million visitors annually. Toronto, Ontario, is less than two hours away from Buffalo. Tourists, shoppers, and theater-goers visiting these popular spots add significantly to Buffalo's economy.

Of increasing importance to the area's economy is the University of Buffalo's two campuses in Buffalo and Amherst, which support more than fifty research centers, some of global importance. The university's technological resources are made available to private industry through its alliance with the Western New York Technology Development Center (TDC), whose goal is to create 100 new companies by 1997 while assisting existing businesses. The partnership between the university and TDC results in more than half a billion dollars in spending annually in the area.

Buffalo's port system maintains specialized grain storage, milling, and processing facilities and is said to rank first in the world in grain handling. The Port of Buffalo is an important shipping center for manufactured goods from the East Coast. Foreign trade zones operate in both Erie and Niagara counties.

Greater Buffalo International Airport can handle international and domestic air cargo. A five-year, $150 million program of improvements is in progress. Buffalo, one of the nation's largest railroad centers, is served by several major U.S. lines and one Canadian line. From a sixth to a quarter of U.S.–Canadian trade clears customs at Buffalo.

Northeast Buffalo is connected to points east by Interstate 90, which connects with Interstate 290 going south along Buffalo's eastern boundary. Northwest Buffalo is accessible via Interstate 190, which passes through the city's west side, cuts across town, and connects with Interstate 90. The city can be approached from the south via a network of highways connecting with Interstate 90. The city is connected to Canada by the Peace Bridge.

Population (1990)

Total Population and Growth Rate
1990: 968,532
1980: 1,015,472
1970: 1,113,491
Growth rate 1970–1990: -13%

Race and Hispanic Origin
White: 85.9%
Black: 11.3%
Asian/Pacific Islander: 1.1%
Native American: 0.6%
Hispanic origin: 2.3%
White not Hispanic: 84.9%

Age
Ages 18 to 20: 4.6%
Ages 21 to 24: 6.2%
Ages 25 to 44: 30.8%
Ages 45 to 54: 10%
Ages 55 to 59: 4.7%
Ages 60 to 64: 5.2%
Ages 65 plus: 15.2%

Educational Attainment (1990)
Percent having completed high school: 76.4%
Percent having completed college: 20.0%
Elementary and high school enrollment: 149,907

Federal Funds and Grants Received
Total received in 1989: $3,091,600,000
Funds received per capita: $3,225

Civilian Labor Force
1993 (April): 463,437
1992 average: 458,160
1991 average: 460,183
1990 average: 461,883

Unemployment
1993 (April): 6.5%
1992 average: 7.3%
1991 average: 6.8%
1990 average: 4.8%

Average Annual Pay
1988: $20,319
1987: $19,324
1985: $18,215

Per Capita Personal Income
1991: $18,466
1990: $17,902
1989: $16,884

Business Climate (1987)

Manufacturing
Number of establishments in 1987: 1,310
Shipments in 1987 ($1,000): $10,907,100
Employees in 1987: 80,400
Change in employment, 1982 to 1987: -8.1%
Average annual pay for manufacturing work in 1989: $29,248
Average annual pay for production work in 1987: $25,353

Wholesale Trade
Number of establishments in 1987: 1,860
Total sales in 1987 ($1,000): $10,282,700
Change in sales, 1982 to 1987: 20.6%

Retail Trade
Number of establishments in 1987: 6,006
Total sales in 1987 ($1,000): $10,282,700
Retail sales per household in 1987: $15,725
Average annual pay in 1989: $10,133

Service Industry
Selected receipts in 1987 ($1,000): $2,325,000
Average annual pay in 1989: $16,910

Office Real Estate (1992)

Office space inventory: 6,924,595 square feet

Average class A Central Business District rental range per sq. ft: $16.75

Vacancy Rates

All areas: 16.7%

Vacancy Rates in Central Business District

Class A space: 24.5%

Class B space: 13.6%

Vacancy Rates Outside Central Business District

Class A space: 5.5%

Class B space: 10.7%

Housing

Total number of units in 1990: 402,131

Occupied units in 1990: 376,994

Owner-occupied units in 1990: 63.7%

1993 ACCRA average cost: N/A

1993 ACCRA average rent for an apartment: N/A

Chamber of Commerce

Greater Buffalo Chamber of Commerce, Kevin D. Keeley, President, 107 Delaware Ave., Buffalo, NY 14202. 716-852-7100

Economic Development Office

Erie County Community Development, Ronald Coan, Director, 95 Franklin St. Room 1077, Buffalo, NY 14202. 716-846-6339

Economic Development Organizations

New York State Dept. of Economic Development, Western New York Regional Office, Leo Downing, Industrial Development Specialist, 135 Delaware Ave., Buffalo, NY 14202. 716-847-3622, FAX 716-847-3055

Western NY Economic Development Corporation, Exec. Director, 424 Main St. Suite 717, Buffalo, NY 14202. 716-856-8111, FAX 716-856-1744

Major Businesses

Company	SIC	Telephone
Blue Shield of Western NY	6324	(716) 855-7000
Calspan Corp.	8731	(716) 632-7500
Computer Task Group Inc.	7371	(716) 882-8000
Delaware North Companies	5812	(716) 858-5000
Dunlop Tire Corp.	3011	(716) 773-8200
Empire Federal Savings Bank of America	6035	(716) 845-7000
First Empire State Corp.	6712	(716) 842-5445
Goldome	6036	(716) 847-5800
Gulton Industries, Inc.	3651	(716) 689-4972
Manufactrers Traders	6022	(716) 842-4200
Marine Midland Banks Inc.	6021	(716) 841-2424
Mark IV Industries Inc.	3651	(716) 689-4972
Moog Inc.	3812	(716) 652-2000

Major Businesses (Continued)

Company	SIC	Telephone
National Fuel Gas Co.	4924	(716) 857-7000
Norstar Bank	6021	(716) 847-7200
Outokumpu American Brass	3351	(716) 879-6700
Pratt & Lambert	2851	(716) 873-6000
R F S Buffalo Holding Corp.	5411	(716) 823-3712
Rich Products Corp.	2023	(716) 878-8000
S K W Alloys Inc.	3313	(716) 285-1257
Schmitt, Peter J. Co. Inc.	5141	(716) 825-1111
Sorrento Inc.	2022	(716) 823-6262
Sportservice Corp.	5812	(716) 858-5000
Stovroff & Herman Inc.	6531	(716) 689-8101
Tops Inc.	5411	(716) 823-3712
Tops Markets, Inc.	5411	(716) 823-3712
Trico Products Corp.	3714	(716) 852-5700

Colleges and Universities

Bryant and Stratton Business Institute, Buffalo

Canisius College, Buffalo

D'youville College, Buffalo

Erie Community College, City Campus, Buffalo

Medaille College, Buffalo

State University of New York At Buffalo, Buffalo

State University of New York College at Buffalo, Buffalo

Trocaire College, Buffalo

Villa Maria College of Buffalo, Buffalo

ELMIRA, NY (MSA)

Geographic Profile

Land Area

408.2 square miles

Counties and Parishes

Chemung

Ranking Highlights

310 *out of 319 in total* **land area**

305 *out of 319 in* **population growth,** *1970–1990*

139 *out of 310 in having the lowest* **unemployment** *rate*

299 *out of 310 in size of* **labor force**

231 *out of 318 in the percentage of* **college graduates**

186 *out of 292 in per capita personal* **income**

291 *out of 319 in number of* **manufacturing establishments**

122 *out of 318 in* **physicians** *per 1000 people*

39 *out of 318 in* **hospital beds** *per 1000 people*

71 *out of 267 in fewest* **crimes** *per 1000 people*

50 *out of 266 in fewest* **violent crimes** *per 1000 people*

179 *out of 319 in per capita* **federal funds and grants**

Quality of Life Indexes (Rate per 1000 population)

Crime rate in 1991:	48.1
Violent crime rate in 1991:	3.1
Physicians rate in 1992:	2
Hospital bed rate in 1991:	5.73

ACCRA Cost of Living Indexes

(First quarter 1993, average = 100)

Composite index:	N/A
Utilities index:	N/A
Housing index:	N/A

Population (1990)

Total Population and Growth Rate

1990: 95,195

1980: 97,656

1970: 101,537

Growth rate 1970–1990: -6%

Race and Hispanic Origin

White: 92.8%

Black: 5.5%

Asian/Pacific Islander: 0.7%

Native American: 0.2%

Hispanic origin: 1.5%

White not Hispanic: 92.2%

Age

Ages 18 to 20: 4.7%

Ages 21 to 24: 5.5%

Ages 25 to 44: 30.1%

Ages 45 to 54: 10%

Ages 55 to 59: 4.5%

Ages 60 to 64: 4.8%

Ages 65 plus: 15.1%

Educational Attainment (1990)

Percent having completed high school: 77.2%

Percent having completed college: 15.4%

Elementary and high school enrollment: 16,438

Federal Funds and Grants Received

Total received in 1989: $272,000,000

Funds received per capita: $2,965

Civilian Labor Force

1993 (April):	43,066
1992 average:	42,608
1991 average:	42,918
1990 average:	44,371

Unemployment

1993 (April): 6.0%

1992 average: 6.7%

1991 average: 6.4%

1990 average: 4.4%

Average Annual Pay

1988: $18,045

1987: $17,263

1985: $16,135

Per Capita Personal Income

1991: $16,486

1990: $15,868

1989: $15,151

Business Climate (1987)

Manufacturing

Number of establishments in 1987: 102

Shipments in 1987 ($1,000): $623,100

Employees in 1987: 7,400

Change in employment, 1982 to 1987: -20.4%

Average annual pay for manufacturing work in 1989: $22,866

Average annual pay for production work in 1987: N/A

Wholesale Trade

Number of establishments in 1987: 147

Total sales in 1987 ($1,000): $549,100

Change in sales, 1982 to 1987: 12.0%

Retail Trade

Number of establishments in 1987: 620

Total sales in 1987 ($1,000): $549,100

Retail sales per household in 1987: $17,118

Average annual pay in 1989: $10,029

Service Industry

Selected receipts in 1987 ($1,000): $152,000

Average annual pay in 1989: $16,344

Housing

Total number of units in 1990: 37,290

Occupied units in 1990: 35,275
Owner-occupied units in 1990: 68.3%
1993 ACCRA average cost: N/A
1993 ACCRA average rent for an apartment: N/A

Chamber of Commerce

Chemung County Chamber of Commerce, Larry A. Bowman, President, 215 E. Church St., Elmira, NY 14901. 607-734-5137

Economic Development Office

Southern Tier Economic Growth, Inc., Robert W. Bivens, Director, PO Box 251, Elmira, NY 14902. 607-733-6513

Major Businesses

Company	SIC	Telephone
Arnot Ogden Memorial Hospital	8062	(607) 737-4100
Artistic Greetings Inc.	5961	(607) 733-5541
Booth, I. D. Inc.	5074	(607) 733-9121
Capabilities Inc.	3549	(607) 734-2006
Chemung Canal Trust Co.	6022	(607) 737-3711
Chemung Financial Corp.	6022	(607) 737-3711
Chemung Ford Inc.	5511	(607) 734-1681
Chemung Supply Corp.	5051	(607) 733-5506
Elmira Savings Bank	6035	(607) 734-3374
Hardinge Brothers Inc.	3541	(607) 734-2281
Harolds Army & Navy Store	5651	(607) 739-3826
Hilliard Corp.	3568	(607) 733-7121
Howell, F. M. & Co. Inc.	2652	(607) 734-6291
Imaging Sensing Technology	3679	(607) 796-3441
RKB Enterprises Inc.	5072	(607) 733-9115
Schweizer Aircraft Corp.	3721	(607) 739-3821
St. Joseph's Hospital	8062	(607) 733-6541

Colleges and Universities

Elmira College, Elmira

GLENS FALLS, NY (MSA)

Geographic Profile

Land Area

1705.3 square miles

Counties and Parishes

Warren
Washington

Ranking Highlights

113 *out of 319 in total* land area
194 *out of 319 in* population growth, *1970–1990*
272 *out of 310 in having the lowest* unemployment *rate*
278 *out of 310 in size of* labor force
229 *out of 318 in the percentage of* college graduates
220 *out of 292 in per capita personal* income
209 *out of 319 in number of* manufacturing establishments
212 *out of 318 in* physicians *per 1000 people*
97 *out of 318 in* hospital beds *per 1000 people*
21 *out of 267 in fewest* crimes *per 1000 people*
83 *out of 266 in fewest* violent crimes *per 1000 people*
261 *out of 319 in per capita* federal funds and grants

Quality of Life Indexes (Rate per 1000 population)

Crime rate in 1991:	35.5
Violent crime rate in 1991:	4.3
Physicians rate in 1992:	1.56
Hospital bed rate in 1991:	4.67

ACCRA Cost of Living Indexes

(First quarter 1993, average = 100)
Composite index: 107.8
Utilities index: 129.0
Housing index: 99.8

Population (1990)

Total Population and Growth Rate

1990: 118,539
1980: 109,649
1970: 102,127
Growth rate 1970–1990: 16%

Race and Hispanic Origin

White: 97.1%
Black: 2.0%
Asian/Pacific Islander: 0.3%
Native American: 0.2%
Hispanic origin: 1.5%
White not Hispanic: 96.3%

Age

Ages 18 to 20: 4.4%
Ages 21 to 24: 5.8%
Ages 25 to 44: 31.6%
Ages 45 to 54: 10.3%
Ages 55 to 59: 4.4%

Ages 60 to 64: 4.5%
Ages 65 plus: 13.8%

Educational Attainment (1990)
Percent having completed high school: 76.2%
Percent having completed college: 15.5%
Elementary and high school enrollment: 20,705

Federal Funds and Grants Received
Total received in 1989: $276,900,000
Funds received per capita: $2,384

Civilian Labor Force
1993 (April):   54,407
1992 average: 54,575
1991 average: 54,197
1990 average: 53,778

Unemployment
1993 (April):   8.1%
1992 average: 9.5%
1991 average: 8.7%
1990 average: 5.8%

Average Annual Pay
1988: $19,127
1987: $17,898
1985: $16,209

Per Capita Personal Income
1991: $15,933
1990: $15,560
1989: $14,983

Business Climate (1987)
Manufacturing
Number of establishments in 1987: 213
Shipments in 1987 ($1,000): $1,293,300
Employees in 1987: 10,900
Change in employment, 1982 to 1987: 7.9%
Average annual pay for manufacturing work in 1989: $25,307
Average annual pay for production work in 1987: $20,679

Wholesale Trade
Number of establishments in 1987: 177
Total sales in 1987 ($1,000): $442,100
Change in sales, 1982 to 1987: 62.0%

Retail Trade
Number of establishments in 1987: 1,001
Total sales in 1987 ($1,000): $442,100
Retail sales per household in 1987: $20,464
Average annual pay in 1989: $12,111

Service Industry
Selected receipts in 1987 ($1,000): $274,700
Average annual pay in 1989: $16,618

Housing
Total number of units in 1990: 55,953

Occupied units in 1990: 42,815
Owner-occupied units in 1990: 71.4%
1993 ACCRA average cost: $109,848
1993 ACCRA average rent for an apartment: $532

Chamber of Commerce
Adirondack Regional Chamber of Commerce, James A. Berg, President, 136 Warren St., Glens Falls, NY 12801. 518-798-1761

Major Businesses

Company	SIC	Telephone
4-H Transportation Co. Inc.	4213	(518) 792-6571
Ahlstrom Machinery Inc.	5084	(518) 798-9541
Ahlstrom Screen Plates Inc.	3554	(518) 761-2500
Ames Goldsmith Inc.	3399	(518) 792-5808
Arrow Financial Corp.	6712	(518) 793-4121
Carruthers, S. D. Sons Inc.	1761	(518) 638-8277
Economy Dry Goods Co. Inc.	5311	(518) 792-1141
Evergreen Bancorp Inc.	6021	(518) 792-1151
First National Bank of Glens Falls	6021	(518) 792-1151
Fort Edward Express Co. Inc.	4213	(518) 792-6571
Glens Falls Hospital	8062	(518) 792-3151
Kamtech Inc.	1796	(518) 798-6401
Kamyr Inc.	3554	(518) 793-5111
Lincoln Logs Ltd.	2452	(518) 494-4777
Mary Mc Clellan Hospital	8062	(518) 677-2611
Nemer Transportation Corp.	5511	(518) 793-2571
North American Instrument	3841	(518) 798-0067
Northern Distributing Co.	5181	(518) 792-3112
Northern Homes Inc.	2452	(518) 798-6007
Sandy Hill Corp.	3554	(518) 747-3381
Telescope Casual Furniture	2514	(518) 642-1100
Whiteman Chevrolet Inc.	5511	(518) 792-2196
Woodbury Interstate Corp.	5211	(518) 793-2505

JAMESTOWN–DUNKIRK, NY (MSA)

Geographic Profile

Land Area

1062.1 square miles

Counties and Parishes

Chautauqua

Ranking Highlights

188 *out of 319 in total* **land area**

289 *out of 319 in* **population growth**, *1970–1990*

238 *out of 310 in having the lowest* **unemployment** *rate*

253 *out of 310 in size of* **labor force**

250 *out of 318 in the percentage of* **college graduates**

231 *out of 292 in per capita personal* **income**

184 *out of 319 in number of* **manufacturing establishments**

289 *out of 318 in* **physicians** *per 1000 people*

102 *out of 318 in* **hospital beds** *per 1000 people*

29 *out of 267 in fewest* **crimes** *per 1000 people*

14 *out of 266 in fewest* **violent crimes** *per 1000 people*

182 *out of 319 in per capita* **federal funds and grants**

Quality of Life Indexes (Rate per 1000 population)

Crime rate in 1991:	38.0
Violent crime rate in 1991:	1.4
Physicians rate in 1992:	1.13
Hospital bed rate in 1991:	4.6

ACCRA Cost of Living Indexes

(First quarter 1993, average = 100)

Composite index:	102.3
Utilities index:	108.4
Housing index:	104.5

Population (1990)

Total Population and Growth Rate

1990: 141,895

1980: 146,925

1970: 147,305

Growth rate 1970–1990: -4%

Race and Hispanic Origin

White: 96.1%

Black: 1.7%

Asian/Pacific Islander: 0.4%

Native American: 0.4%

Hispanic origin: 2.9%

White not Hispanic: 94.7%

Age

Ages 18 to 20: 5.4%

Ages 21 to 24: 5.6%

Ages 25 to 44: 28.6%

Ages 45 to 54: 9.8%

Ages 55 to 59: 4.6%

Ages 60 to 64: 4.9%

Ages 65 plus: 15.7%

Educational Attainment (1990)

Percent having completed high school: 74.4%

Percent having completed college: 14.2%

Elementary and high school enrollment: 24,358

Federal Funds and Grants Received

Total received in 1989: $418,000,000

Funds received per capita: $2,957

Civilian Labor Force

1993 (April):	62,702
1992 average:	63,629
1991 average:	64,717
1990 average:	63,932

Unemployment

1993 (April):	6.5%
1992 average:	8.3%
1991 average:	7.7%
1990 average:	5.5%

Average Annual Pay

1988: N/A

1987: N/A

1985: N/A

Per Capita Personal Income

1991: $15,628

1990: $15,133

1989: $14,336

Business Climate (1987)

Manufacturing

Number of establishments in 1987: 255

Shipments in 1987 ($1,000): $1,887,700

Employees in 1987: 14,700

Change in employment, 1982 to 1987: -7.0%

Average annual pay for manufacturing work in 1989: $24,468

Average annual pay for production work in 1987: $21,143

Wholesale Trade

Number of establishments in 1987: 207

Total sales in 1987 ($1,000): $647,000

Change in sales, 1982 to 1987: 26.2%

Retail Trade

Number of establishments in 1987: 1,004

Total sales in 1987 ($1,000): $647,000

Retail sales per household in 1987: $13,159

Average annual pay in 1989: $9,628

Service Industry

Selected receipts in 1987 ($1,000): $198,900

Average annual pay in 1989: $13,545

Housing

Total number of units in 1990: 62,682

Occupied units in 1990: 53,696
Owner-occupied units in 1990: 68.6%
1993 ACCRA average cost: $117,444
1993 ACCRA average rent for an apartment: $503

Chamber of Commerce

Jamestown Area Chamber of Commerce, Charles L. Turcotte, Exec. Director, 101 W. 5th St., Jamestown, NY 14701. 716-484-1101

Economic Development Office

County of Chautauqua Industrial Development Association, David Dawson, Director, 200 Harrison St., Jamestown, NY 14701. 716-664-3262

Economic Development Organizations

New York State Economic Development Council, David Dawson, Director, 200 Harrison St., Jamestown, NY 14701. 716-664-3262

Major Businesses

Company	SIC	Telephone
Aarque Companies	3316	(716) 664-6014
Aarque Steel Corp.	3465	(716) 664-6014
Acu-Rite, Inc.	3823	(716) 661-1700
Al Tech Specialty Steel	3312	(716) 336-1000
Alltel New York, Inc.	4813	(716) 661-5400
American Locker Group Inc.	3581	(716) 664-9600
Anderson Screw Products	3451	(716) 484-1148
Blackstone Corp.	3714	(716) 665-2620
Bush Industries Inc.	2511	(716) 665-2000
C.H.C. Industries, Inc.	6719	(716) 488-1161
Chautauqua Hardware Corp.	3429	(716) 488-1161
Cliffstar Corp.	2033	(716) 366-6100
Crawford Furniture Mfg. Co.	2511	(716) 665-4227
Dahlstrom Manufacturing Co.	3442	(716) 487-0111
Dawson Metal Co., Inc.	3449	(716) 664-3815
Dunkirk Ice Cream Co., Inc.	2024	(716) 366-5400
Electronic Technology	3625	(716) 488-9699
Emco Finishing Products	2851	(716) 483-1176
Hope's Archtectural Products	3442	(716) 665-5124
Jamestown Electro Plating	3471	(716) 664-5406
Jamestown Laminating Co.	2499	(716) 665-3224
Jamestown Metal Corp.	2522	(716) 665-5410
Jamestown Metal Products	3499	(716) 665-5313
Jamestown Perforators, Inc.	3423	(716) 664-7575
Jamestown Plywood Corp.	2435	(716) 488-1984
Jamestown Royal Furniture	2512	(716) 664-5260
Jamestown Sterling	2511	(716) 665-6115
Jamestown United Parts Co.	3599	(716) 487-1195
MRC Bearings	3562	(716) 661-2600
Nog, Inc.	2066	(716) 366-3322
Phoenix Metal Fabricating	3469	(716) 483-2122
Post-Journal	2711	(716) 487-1111
Quality Markets, Inc.	5411	(716) 664-6010

Major Businesses (Continued)

Company	SIC	Telephone
Sanitary Wiping Cloth Co.	2842	(716) 664-2310
Sprinchorn & Co., Inc.	3444	(716) 484-1116
Union-National, Inc.	2434	(716) 487-1165
Van Stee Corp.	2511	(716) 664-3900
Watson Industries Inc.	2542	(716) 487-1901
Weber Knapp	3429	(716) 488-1661
Westburgh Electric, Inc.	3621	(716) 488-1172

Colleges and Universities

Jamestown Business College, Jamestown
Jamestown Community College, Jamestown

NASSAU–SUFFOLK, NY (PMSA)

Geographic Profile

Land Area

1198.0 square miles

Counties and Parishes

Nassau

Suffolk

Ranking Highlights

165 *out of 319 in total* **land area**

260 *out of 319 in* **population growth,** *1970–1990*

174 *out of 310 in having the lowest* **unemployment** *rate*

13 *out of 310 in size of* **labor force**

45 *out of 318 in the percentage of* **college graduates**

N/A *out of 292 in per capita personal* **income**

8 *out of 319 in number of* **manufacturing establishments**

17 *out of 318 in* **physicians** *per 1000 people*

194 *out of 318 in* **hospital beds** *per 1000 people*

47 *out of 267 in fewest* **crimes** *per 1000 people*

43 *out of 266 in fewest* **violent crimes** *per 1000 people*

84 *out of 319 in per capita* **federal funds and grants**

Quality of Life Indexes (Rate per 1000 population)

Crime rate in 1991:	42.0
Violent crime rate in 1991:	3.0
Physicians rate in 1992:	3.47
Hospital bed rate in 1991:	3.49

ACCRA Cost of Living Indexes

(First quarter 1993, average = 100)

Composite index:	N/A
Utilities index:	N/A
Housing index:	N/A

Overview

No central city in this area.

Population (1990)

Total Population and Growth Rate

1990: 2,609,212

1980: 2,605,813

1970: 2,555,868

Growth rate 1970–1990: 2%

Race and Hispanic Origin

White: 88.4%

Black: 7.4%

Asian/Pacific Islander: 2.4%

Native American: 0.2%

Hispanic origin: 6.3%

White not Hispanic: 84.1%

Age

Ages 18 to 20: 4.4%

Ages 21 to 24: 6%

Ages 25 to 44: 32%

Ages 45 to 54: 11.7%

Ages 55 to 59: 5.1%

Ages 60 to 64: 5.1%

Ages 65 plus: 12.4%

Educational Attainment (1990)

Percent having completed high school: 83.2%

Percent having completed college: 26.5%

Elementary and high school enrollment: 406,681

Federal Funds and Grants Received

Total received in 1989: $10,087,000,000

Funds received per capita: $3,822

Civilian Labor Force

1993 (April): 1,362,487

1992 average: 1,343,842

1991 average: 1,366,133

1990 average: 1,403,058

Unemployment

1993 (April): 6.4%

1992 average: 7.1%

1991 average: 6.0%

1990 average: 3.8%

Average Annual Pay

1988: $24,249

1987: $22,760

1985: $19,998

Per Capita Personal Income

1991: N/A

1990: N/A

1989: N/A

Business Climate (1987)

Manufacturing

Number of establishments in 1987: 4,948

Shipments in 1987 ($1,000): $17,949,200

Employees in 1987: 187,100

Change in employment, 1982 to 1987: 8.9%

Average annual pay for manufacturing work in 1989: $30,559

Average annual pay for production work in 1987: $20,353

Wholesale Trade

Number of establishments in 1987: 8,194

Total sales in 1987 ($1,000): $33,527,900

Change in sales, 1982 to 1987: 32.2%

Retail Trade

Number of establishments in 1987: 19,301

Total sales in 1987 ($1,000): $33,527,900

Retail sales per household in 1987: $24,846

Average annual pay in 1989: $15,000

Service Industry

Selected receipts in 1987 ($1,000): $11,552,700

Average annual pay in 1989: $23,068

Housing

Total number of units in 1990: 927,609

Occupied units in 1990: 856,234

Owner-occupied units in 1990: 80.3%

1993 ACCRA average cost: N/A

1993 ACCRA average rent for an apartment: N/A

Chamber of Commerce

None

Major Businesses

Company	SIC	Telephone
Allen Group Inc.	3559	(516) 293-5500
Anchor Savings Bank	6035	(516) 596-3900
Arrow Electronics Inc.	5065	(516) 391-1300
Audiovox Corp.	5065	(516) 231-7750
Avis, Inc.	7514	(516) 222-3000
Avis Rent A Car System	7514	(516) 222-3000
Avnet Inc.	5065	(516) 466-7000
Cablevision Systems Corp.	4841	(516) 364-8450
Canon USA Inc.	5044	(516) 488-6700
Computer Associates International	7372	(516) 227-3300
Dime Savings Bank of New York	6035	(516) 351-1550
Entenmann's Inc.	2051	(516) 273-6000
Esselte Business Systems	2675	(516) 741-1477
Esselte Pendaflex Corp.	2675	(516) 741-3200
European American Bancorp	6022	(516) 296-5000
Genovese Drug Stores, Inc.	5912	(516) 420-1900
Getty Petroleum Corp.	5172	(516) 338-6000
Greater New York Mortgage	6162	(516) 747-9000
Greenman Bros. Inc.	5945	(516) 293-5300
Grumman Aerospace Corp.	3721	(516) 575-0574
Grumman Allied Industries	3711	(516) 737-5400
Grumman Corp.	3721	(516) 575-0574
Grumman Data Systems Corp.	7374	(516) 682-5501
Howell, E. W. Co. Inc.	1542	(516) 621-1100
Instrument Systems Corp.	2253	(516) 938-5544
King Kullen Grocery Co. Inc.	5411	(516) 333-7100
Klockner Namasco Corp.	5051	(516) 222-0330
Long Island Lighting Co.	4911	(516) 933-4590
Long Island Savings Bank	6035	(516) 547-2000
Mel Markets Inc.	5411	(516) 794-7400
Nec America Inc.	3661	(516) 753-7000
Newmark & Lewis Inc.	5722	(516) 681-6900
Newsday Inc.	2711	(516) 454-2020
Norstar Bank	6029	(516) 547-7908
North Shore University Hospital	8062	(516) 562-0100
Olsten Corp.	7363	(516) 832-8200
Olympus Corp.	5047	(516) 364-3000
Overseas Military	5511	(516) 921-2800
Pall Corp.	3842	(516) 671-4000

Major Businesses (Continued)

Company	SIC	Telephone
Pergament Home Centers Inc.	5211	(516) 694-9300
Plexchem International Inc.	5169	(516) 271-0670
Publishers Clearing House	5961	(516) 883-5432
RIS Paper Co. Inc.	5111	(516) 742-2424
Schein, Henry Inc.	5047	(516) 621-4300
Schweber Electronics Corp.	5065	(516) 334-7474
Seaman Furniture Co.	5712	(516) 222-6011
Symbol Technologies Inc.	3577	(516) 563-2400
TDKUSA Corp.	8741	(516) 625-0100
Tambrands Inc.	2676	(516) 358-8300
Travelsavers Inc.	8743	(516) 482-3710
Waldbaum Inc.	5411	(516) 582-9300
William Penn Life Insurance	6311	(516) 328-6000

NEW YORK, NY (PMSA)

Geographic Profile

Land Area

1147.6 square miles

Counties and Parishes

Bronx

Kings

New York

Putnam

Queens

Richmond

Rockland

Westchester

Additional Cities/Towns within Area

White Plains

Ranking Highlights

175 *out of 319 in total* **land area**

302 *out of 319 in* **population growth,** *1970–1990*

283 *out of 310 in having the lowest* **unemployment** *rate*

2 *out of 310 in size of* **labor force**

67 *out of 318 in the percentage of* **college graduates**

7 *out of 292 in per capita personal* **income**

2 *out of 319 in number of* **manufacturing establishments**

14 *out of 318 in* **physicians** *per 1000 people*

102 *out of 318 in* **hospital beds** *per 1000 people*

240 *out of 267 in fewest* **crimes** *per 1000 people*

265 *out of 266 in fewest* **violent crimes** *per 1000 people*

112 *out of 319 in per capita* **federal funds and grants**

Quality of Life Indexes (Rate per 1000 population)

Crime rate in 1991:	84.8
Violent crime rate in 1991:	20.4
Physicians rate in 1992:	3.63
Hospital bed rate in 1991:	4.6

ACCRA Cost of Living Indexes

(First quarter 1993, average = 100)

Composite index:	208.7
Utilities index:	149.2
Housing index:	359.3

Overview

Hundreds of nationwide corporations make their home in New York, from finance to insurance to advertising. New York City leads the country in the number of Fortune 1000 companies headquartered there, including ninety-three of the world's largest banks, twenty-five of the country's top securities firms, and twenty-one of the country's fifty leading law firms. The city's biggest industry is publishing, with more printing plants than anywhere else in the United States publishing one-sixth of the nation's printed material. New York's clothing industry is headquartered in the Garment District near Times Square, where hundreds of factories employ more than 100,000 people. New York ranks third, after Chicago, Illinois, and Los Angeles, California, as a manufacturing center. Tourism, fueled by huge advertising campaigns, is also a key industry. More than half of tourists coming to the city list art or culture as the primary reason to visit. New York City ranks as one of the great cultural centers of the Western world, and thirty-five thousand jobs are directly attributable to the city's cultural activity with another 117,000 jobs generated indirectly. The service industries that account for seventy-eight percent of the gross state product—ranked third nationwide—are concentrated in New York City. More than nine thousand restaurants in New York City employ some 180,000 people.

High–technology railroad flat cars carry half or more of imports to the New York region from the West Coast via a land bridge that has cut the amount of tonnage handled by the ports of New York and New Jersey from a national high of fifteen percent in 1960 to six percent in 1992. The Port Authority of New York and New Jersey, which oversees New York Harbor, predicts that a shift in export manufacturing from North to South Asia may help the region restore some of its former position as an international maritime leader. The Port Authority owns and operates the twin towers of the World Trade Center, where many of the largest trading firms are based.

New York now maintains two Foreign Trade Zones—one at the Brooklyn Navy Yard and a second at Kennedy International Airport—that are legally outside U.S. Customs territory and permit importers to store or assemble goods and thus decrease certain duty charges.

New York offers large conventions and small groups an unparalleled variety of meeting place choices, from traditional convention halls to rooms in museums, racetracks, and universities. The Jacob Javits Convention Center offers nine hundred thousand square feet of exhibition space, including the largest single hall in the Western Hemisphere at 410,000 square feet, and more than one hundred other rooms.

John F. Kennedy International Airport handles more international flights—over two hundred a day—than any other airport, in addition to domestic traffic. La Guardia Airport, somewhat closer to Manhattan, offers mostly domestic connections. In late 1991 plans for a rapid rail link to these two airports and to existing mass transit lines were laid out; this job was expected to take ten years to complete. Major projects going on at La Guardia and Kennedy airports total several billion dollars. Newark International Airport in New Jersey also serves the metropolitan area.

The New Jersey Turnpike (Interstate 95) is the major artery leading into the city from the south. From the north, the New York Thruway (Interstate 87) connects with the Major Deegan Expressway, which follows the east side of the Harlem River through the Bronx. The New England

Thruway (another part of I-95) also leads into the city from the north. Interstate 80 from western New Jersey parallels I-95 as it approaches New York City.

The two main train stations, Pennsylvania and Grand Central, serve as both commuter and long-distance terminals for more than 300,000 people every day and provide AMTRAK connections. A major project being undertaken by AMTRAK and scheduled for completion by 1997 will decrease traveling time between Boston, Massachusetts, and New York to less than three hours. The Port Authority Bus Terminal—the largest in the world—is the main station for bus transportation.

Population (1990)

Total Population and Growth Rate
1990: 8,546,846
1980: 8,274,961
1970: 9,076,568
Growth rate 1970–1990: -6%

Race and Hispanic Origin
White: 56.5%
Black: 26.3%
Asian/Pacific Islander: 6.5%
Native American: 0.3%
Hispanic origin: 22.1%
White not Hispanic: 47.9%

Age
Ages 18 to 20: 4.2%
Ages 21 to 24: 6.3%
Ages 25 to 44: 33.7%
Ages 45 to 54: 10.8%
Ages 55 to 59: 4.5%
Ages 60 to 64: 4.5%
Ages 65 plus: 13%

Educational Attainment (1990)
Percent having completed high school: 70.3%
Percent having completed college: 24.6%
Elementary and high school enrollment: 1,369,144

Federal Funds and Grants Received
Total received in 1989: $29,610,700,000
Funds received per capita: $3,456

Civilian Labor Force
1993 (April): 3,928,336
1992 average: 3,954,918
1991 average: 3,962,698
1990 average: 4,013,499

Unemployment
1993 (April): 8.9%
1992 average: 10.1%
1991 average: 8.1%
1990 average: 6.2%

Average Annual Pay
1988: $30,578
1987: $28,179
1985: $24,500

Per Capita Personal Income
1991: $25,583
1990: $25,110
1989: $23,794

Business Climate (1987)

Manufacturing
Number of establishments in 1987: 16,277
Shipments in 1987 ($1,000): $54,138,000
Employees in 1987: 522,300
Change in employment, 1982 to 1987: -14.6%
Average annual pay for manufacturing work in 1989: $31,315
Average annual pay for production work in 1987: $16,826

Wholesale Trade
Number of establishments in 1987: 22,937
Total sales in 1987 ($1,000): $207,016,900
Change in sales, 1982 to 1987: 2.5%

Retail Trade
Number of establishments in 1987: 48,739
Total sales in 1987 ($1,000): $207,016,900
Retail sales per household in 1987: $12,093
Average annual pay in 1989: $16,703

Service Industry
Selected receipts in 1987 ($1,000): $49,275,400
Average annual pay in 1989: $27,934

Office Real Estate (1992)
Office space inventory: 358,543,736 square feet
Average class A Central Business District rental range per sq. ft: $38.02

Vacancy Rates
All areas: 18.2%

Vacancy Rates in Central Business District
Class A space: 16.4%
Class B space: 19.7%

Vacancy Rates Outside Central Business District
Class A space: 18.4%
Class B space: 24.9%

Housing
Total number of units in 1990: 3,449,058
Occupied units in 1990: 3,525,399
Owner-occupied units in 1990: 33.3%
1993 ACCRA average cost: $391,250
1993 ACCRA average rent for an apartment: $1,877

Chamber of Commerce
New York Chamber of Commerce and Industry, Ronald K. Shelp, President, 1 Battery Park Plaza 5th Fl., New York, NY 10004-7500. 212-493-7500, FAX 212-344-3344

Economic Development Office

East Manhattan Chamber of Commerce, Dennis Jawer, President, 1555 3rd Ave. Lower Level, New York 10128. 212-410-1070

Economic Development Organizations

New York State, Department of Economic Development, Vincent Tese, Commissioner, 1515 Broadway 52nd Fl., New York, NY 10036. 212-930-0200, FAX 212-930-0333

New York State, Department of Economic Development, New York City Regional Office, Regional Director, 50 Court St., Brooklyn, NY 11201. 718-596-4120, FAX 718-596-5169

New York State Urban Development Corp., Harold Holzer, Exec. Vice President of Public Affairs, 1515 Broadway 52nd Fl., New York NY 10036. 212-930-0307

New York State Department of Commerce, Paul Koenigsberg, 230 Park Ave., New York, NY 10169. 212-309-0431

Major Businesses

Company	SIC	Telephone
Amerada Hess Corp.	1311	(212) 997-8500
American Express Co.	6211	(212) 640-2000
American Home Products Co.	2834	(212) 878-5000
American International	6331	(212) 770-7000
American Telephone & Telegraph Co.	4813	(212) 605-5500
Bank of New York Co.	6022	(212) 495-1784
Bankers Trust New York Co.	6022	(212) 250-2500
Borden Inc.	2099	(212) 573-4000
Bristol-Myers Squibb Co.	2834	(212) 546-4000
Chase Manhattan Corp.	6021	(212) 552-2222
Chemical Banking Corp.	6021	(212) 310-6161
Citibank	6021	(212) 559-1000
Citicorp	6021	(212) 559-1000
Colgate-Palmolive Co.	2841	(212) 310-2000
Consolidated Edison Co.	4911	(212) 460-4600
Continental Corp.	6331	(212) 440-3980
Continental Grain Co.	5153	(212) 207-5100
Empire Blue Cross Blue Shield	6324	(212) 476-1000
Equitable Life Assurance Society	6311	(212) 554-1234
Exxon Corp.	1311	(212) 333-1000
Federal Reserve Bank of New York	6011	(212) 720-5000
Grace, W. R. & Co. Inc.	3081	(212) 819-5500
Gramet Holdings Corp.	5812	(201) 573-4000
Grand Metropolitan Inc.	5812	(201) 573-4000
Great Atlantic & Pacific Tea Co. Inc.	5411	(201) 573-9700
H. M. Anglo-American, Ltd	2816	(212) 888-3060
Imasco Holdings, Inc.	5912	(914) 735-1600
International Business Machines Co.	3571	(914) 765-1900
International Paper Co.	2653	(914) 397-1500

Major Businesses (Continued)

Company	SIC	Telephone
Itoh, C. & Co. (America)	5131	(212) 818-8000
ITT Corp.	6331	(212) 752-6000
Loews Corp.	6331	(212) 545-2000
Macy, R. H. & Co. Inc.	5311	(212) 560-4249
Manufacturers Hanover Corp.	6022	(212) 270-6000
Manufcturers Hanover Trust Co.	6022	(212) 286-6000
Marubeni America Corp.	5131	(212) 599-3700
Melville Corp.	5651	(914) 925-4000
Merrill Lynch & Co. Inc.	6211	(212) 449-1000
Metropolitan Life Insurance Co.	6311	(212) 578-2211
Mitsubishi International	5051	(212) 605-2000
Mitsui & Co (USA) Inc.	5051	(212) 878-4000
Mobil Oil Corp.	1311	(212) 883-4242
Morgan J. P. & Co. Inc.	6022	(212) 483-2323
Morgan Stanley Group Inc.	6211	(212) 703-4000
New York Life Insurance Co.	6311	(212) 576-7000
New York Telephone Co.	4813	(212) 395-2121
Nissho Iwai American Corp.	5051	(212) 704-6500
North American Philips Co.	3651	(212) 850-5000
Nynex Corp.	4813	(212) 370-7400
Pepsico Inc.	2087	(914) 253-2000
Pfizer Inc.	2834	(212) 573-2323
Philip Morris Companies Inc.	2111	(212) 880-5000
Primerica Corp.	6141	(212) 891-8900
RJR Nabisco, Inc.	2111	(212) 446-5600
RJR Nabisco Holdings Corp.	2111	(212) 446-5600
Salomon Brothers Holding	6211	(212) 747-7000
Salomon Inc.	6211	(212) 747-7000
Shearson Lehman Bros. Holding	6211	(212) 528-7000
Shearson Lehman Brothers	6211	(212) 298-2000
Sumitomo Corp. America	5051	(212) 207-0700
Teachers Insurance Annuities	6311	(212) 490-9000
Texaco Inc.	1311	(914) 253-4000
Texaco International Trading	5172	(914) 253-4000
Time Warner Inc.	2721	(212) 586-1212
Unilever United States, Inc.	2844	(212) 888-1260
Young & Rubicam Inc.	7311	(212) 210-3000

Colleges and Universities

American Academy Mcallister Institute of Funeral Service, New York

American Academy of Dramatic Arts, New York

Barnard College, New York

Baruch College of The City University of New York, New York

Berkeley School, White Pains, New York

Boricua College, New York

Borough of Manhattan Community College of the City University of New York, New York

City College of the City University of New York, New York

College For Human Services, New York

College of Insurance, New York

Columbia College, New York

Columbia University, School of Engineering and Applied Science, New York

Columbia University, School of General Studies, New York

Columbia University, School of Nursing, New York

Cooper Union for the Advancement of Science and Art, New York

Eugene Lang College, New School for Social Research, New York

Fashion Institute of Technology, New York

Fordham University, New York

Helene Fuld School of Nursing of Joint Diseases North General Hospital, New York

Hunter College of the City University of New York, New York

Interboro Institute, New York

John Jay College of Criminal Justice of the City University of New York, New York

Juilliard School, New York

Katharine Gibbs School, New York

Laboratory Institute of Merchandising, New York

Manhattan School of Music, New York

Mannes College of Music, New York

Marymount Manhattan College, New York

Mesivta Tifereth Jerusalem of America, New York

New School Bachelor of Arts, New School for Social Research, New York

New York School of Interior Design, New York

New York University, New York

Pace University, White Plains Campus, White Plains, New York

Parsons School of Design, New School For Social Research, New York

Phillips Beth Israel School of Nursing, New York

School of Visual Arts, New York

Stenotype Academy, New York

Taylor Business Institute, New York

Technical Career Institutes, New York

Tobe-Coburn School for Fashion Careers, New York

Touro College, New York

NIAGARA FALLS, NY (PMSA)

Geographic Profile

Land Area

523.0 square miles

Counties and Parishes

Niagara

Ranking Highlights

288 *out of 319 in total* **land area**

306 *out of 319 in* **population growth**, *1970–1990*

272 *out of 310 in having the lowest* **unemployment** *rate*

192 *out of 310 in size of* **labor force**

269 *out of 318 in the percentage of* **college graduates**

 12 *out of 292 in per capita personal* **income**

166 *out of 319 in number of* **manufacturing establishments**

298 *out of 318 in* **physicians** *per 1000 people*

144 *out of 318 in* **hospital beds** *per 1000 people*

N/A *out of 267 in fewest* **crimes** *per 1000 people*

N/A *out of 266 in fewest* **violent crimes** *per 1000 people*

196 *out of 319 in per capita* **federal funds and grants**

Quality of Life Indexes (Rate per 1000 population)

Crime rate in 1991:	N/A
Violent crime rate in 1991:	N/A
Physicians rate in 1992:	1.07
Hospital bed rate in 1991:	4.05

ACCRA Cost of Living Indexes

(First quarter 1993, average = 100)

Composite index:	N/A
Utilities index:	N/A
Housing index:	N/A

Population (1990)

Total Population and Growth Rate

1990: 220,756

1980: 227,354

1970: 235,720

Growth rate 1970–1990: -6%

Race and Hispanic Origin

White: 93.0%

Black: 5.5%

Asian/Pacific Islander: 0.4%

Native American: 0.9%

Hispanic origin: 1.0%

White not Hispanic: 92.3%

Age

Ages 18 to 20: 4.3%

Ages 21 to 24: 5.4%

Ages 25 to 44: 30.5%

Ages 45 to 54: 10%

Ages 55 to 59: 4.7%

Ages 60 to 64: 5%
Ages 65 plus: 15.2%

Educational Attainment (1990)
Percent having completed high school: 75.8%
Percent having completed college: 13.6%
Elementary and high school enrollment: 36,122

Federal Funds and Grants Received
Total received in 1989: $612,400,000
Funds received per capita: $2,823

Civilian Labor Force
1993 (April): 96,058
1992 average: 94,685
1991 average: 96,754
1990 average: 96,797

Unemployment
1993 (April): 8.2%
1992 average: 9.5%
1991 average: 8.3%
1990 average: 5.9%

Average Annual Pay
1988: $20,813
1987: $19,838
1985: $19,184

Per Capita Personal Income
1991: $23,545
1990: $23,135
1989: $22,008

Business Climate (1987)
Manufacturing
Number of establishments in 1987: 294
Shipments in 1987 ($1,000): $3,282,500
Employees in 1987: 22,700
Change in employment, 1982 to 1987: -10.3%
Average annual pay for manufacturing work in 1989: $31,409
Average annual pay for production work in 1987: $27,845

Wholesale Trade
Number of establishments in 1987: 232
Total sales in 1987 ($1,000): $513,100
Change in sales, 1982 to 1987: 26.2%

Retail Trade
Number of establishments in 1987: 1,451
Total sales in 1987 ($1,000): $513,100
Retail sales per household in 1987: $14,694
Average annual pay in 1989: $9,290

Service Industry
Selected receipts in 1987 ($1,000): $290,400
Average annual pay in 1989: $14,730

Housing
Total number of units in 1990: 90,385

Occupied units in 1990: 84,809
Owner-occupied units in 1990: 68.1%
1993 ACCRA average cost: N/A
1993 ACCRA average rent for an apartment: N/A

Chamber of Commerce
Niagara Falls Area Chamber of Commerce, Charles P. Steiner, President, 345 3rd St., Carborundum Center, Niagara Falls, NY 14303. 716-285-9141

Major Businesses

Major Businesses

Company	SIC	Telephone
Alox Corp.	2992	(716) 282-1295
Apollo Steel Corp.	3441	(716) 692-2524
Carborundum Co.	3299	(716) 278-2000
Cataract Metal Finishing	3471	(716) 282-3330
Dicamillo Baking Co., Inc.	2051	(716) 282-2341
Ferro Alloys Services, Inc.	5051	(716) 285-8401
Frontier Foundries, Inc.	3363	(716) 282-1251
Health Saver Brand Division	3842	(716) 945-2242
Helmel Engineering Products	3829	(716) 297-8644
Hiross Inc.	3443	(716) 283-6464
J. D. Calato Manufacturing	3931	(716) 285-3546
Niacet Corp.	2843	(716) 285-1474
Niagara Molded Products	3061	(716) 282-1261
Niagara Sample Book Co.	2741	(716) 284-6151
Nuttall Gear Corp.	3566	(716) 731-5180
Ohmtek, Inc.	3676	(716) 283-4025
Permanent Savings Bank	6036	(716) 285-6500
Sevenson Environmental	4953	(716) 284-0431
Shipman Printing Industries	2759	(716) 731-3281
Sicoli & Massaro, Inc.	1542	(716) 297-0484

Colleges and Universities
Niagara University, Niagara Falls

ORANGE COUNTY, NY (PMSA)

Geographic Profile

Land Area

816.4 square miles

Counties and Parishes

Orange

Ranking Highlights

232 *out of 319 in total* **land area**

100 *out of 319 in* **population growth,** *1970–1990*

174 *out of 310 in having the lowest* **unemployment** *rate*

148 *out of 310 in size of* **labor force**

N/A *out of 318 in the percentage of* **college graduates**

56 *out of 292 in per capita personal* **income**

147 *out of 319 in number of* **manufacturing establishments**

217 *out of 318 in* **physicians** *per 1000 people*

218 *out of 318 in* **hospital beds** *per 1000 people*

24 *out of 267 in fewest* **crimes** *per 1000 people*

79 *out of 266 in fewest* **violent crimes** *per 1000 people*

149 *out of 319 in per capita* **federal funds and grants**

Quality of Life Indexes (Rate per 1000 population)

Crime rate in 1991:   36.5

Violent crime rate in 1991:   4.1

Physicians rate in 1992:   1.55

Hospital bed rate in 1991:   3.2

ACCRA Cost of Living Indexes

(First quarter 1993, average = 100)

Composite index: N/A

Utilities index: N/A

Housing index: N/A

Overview

No central city in this area.

Population (1990)

Total Population and Growth Rate

1990: 307,647

1980: 259,603

1970: 221,657

Growth rate 1970–1990: 39%

Race and Hispanic Origin

White: 88.9%

Black: 7.2%

Asian/Pacific Islander: 1.2%

Native American: 0.3%

Hispanic origin: 7.0%

White not Hispanic: 84.8%

Age

Ages 18 to 20: 4.9%

Ages 21 to 24: 5.8%

Ages 25 to 44: 33.4%

Ages 45 to 54: 10.3%

Ages 55 to 59: 3.9%

Ages 60 to 64: 3.6%

Ages 65 plus: 10.4%

Educational Attainment (1990)

Percent having completed high school: N/A

Percent having completed college: N/A

Elementary and high school enrollment: 51,300

Federal Funds and Grants Received

Total received in 1989: $921,500,000

Funds received per capita: $3,139

Civilian Labor Force

1993 (April):   141,105

1992 average: 138,757

1991 average: 137,430

1990 average: 137,347

Unemployment

1993 (April):   6.8%

1992 average: 7.1%

1991 average: 6.7%

1990 average: 4.6%

Average Annual Pay

1988: $19,826

1987: $18,545

1985: $16,495

Per Capita Personal Income

1991: $19,802

1990: $19,489

1989: $18,982

Business Climate (1987)

Manufacturing

Number of establishments in 1987: 362

Shipments in 1987 ($1,000): $1,344,300

Employees in 1987: 13,600

Change in employment, 1982 to 1987: 3.8%

Average annual pay for manufacturing work in 1989: $22,162

Average annual pay for production work in 1987: $16,629

Wholesale Trade

Number of establishments in 1987: 448

Total sales in 1987 ($1,000): $2,789,600

Change in sales, 1982 to 1987: 96.1%

Retail Trade

Number of establishments in 1987: 1,854

Total sales in 1987 ($1,000): $2,789,600

Retail sales per household in 1987: $20,789

Average annual pay in 1989: $13,382

Service Industry

Selected receipts in 1987 ($1,000): $554,700

Average annual pay in 1989: $18,630

Housing

Total number of units in 1990: 110,814
Occupied units in 1990: 101,506
Owner-occupied units in 1990: 67.5%
1993 ACCRA average cost: N/A
1993 ACCRA average rent for an apartment: N/A

Chamber of Commerce

Orange County Chamber of Commerce, Christopher J. Dunleavy, Exec. Director, 24 John St., Middletown, NY 10940. 914-342-2522

POUGHKEEPSIE, NY (MSA)

Geographic Profile

Land Area

801.7 square miles

Counties and Parishes

Dutchess

Ranking Highlights

238 *out of 319 in total* **land area**
190 *out of 319 in* **population growth**, *1970–1990*
128 *out of 310 in having the lowest* **unemployment** *rate*
168 *out of 310 in size of* **labor force**
63 *out of 318 in the percentage of* **college graduates**
N/A *out of 292 in per capita personal* **income**
214 *out of 319 in number of* **manufacturing establishments**
129 *out of 318 in* **physicians** *per 1000 people*
253 *out of 318 in* **hospital beds** *per 1000 people*
22 *out of 267 in fewest* **crimes** *per 1000 people*
67 *out of 266 in fewest* **violent crimes** *per 1000 people*
284 *out of 319 in per capita* **federal funds and grants**

Quality of Life Indexes (Rate per 1000 population)

Crime rate in 1991:	35.9
Violent crime rate in 1991:	3.8
Physicians rate in 1992:	1.95
Hospital bed rate in 1991:	2.86

ACCRA Cost of Living Indexes

(First quarter 1993, average = 100)

Composite index:	N/A
Utilities index:	N/A
Housing index:	N/A

Overview

Dutchess County offers rolling hills, green valleys, clear lakes and Hudson River panoramas. Many of the nation's most important historical figures, including the Vanderbilts and Franklin Delano Roosevelts, settled here and built magnificent homes. It is located at the center of the largest consumer market in the Western Hemisphere. It is within one and one-half hours of New York City, Albany, Southern Connecticut and New Jersey.

The County is connected to national and international markets by a network of highway, rail, air, shipping and telecommunications systems. Conference centers equipped with teleconferencing and advanced computer facilities are available for business meetings.

Power and gas are available from Central Hudson Gas and Electric, which ranks lowest in pricing among investor-owned utilities in New York State for small and medium-size commercial and industrial users. Dutchess County has a well-trained work force. Nearly 70% of all high school seniors choose to pursue a higher education, and white collar employment in the County has grown twice as fast as blue collar in the last decade. Educational institutions include Vassar College, Bard and Marist College, Dutchess Community College, and the Culinary Institute of America.

Major employers in the Country include IBM, DuPont Tau Laboratories, ASD, Atlantic Design, the Texaco Research Center, Ditron, Lumb Woodworking, and Unico Special Products.

Dutchess County's natural beauty, affordable housing and cultural diversity make it the ideal place to live and raise a family. Its beauty was celebrated by the Hudson River School Painters and has been preserved in 6,000 acres of State-operated parklands that offer golf, swimming, boating, cross-country skiing, camping, fishing and many other recreational activities. Homebuyers can choose from century-old farmhouses, townhouses, village saltboxes or country estates. Renters will find apartments in new urban highrises or charming country homes. Shoppers can enjoy many of the county's leading department stores in town malls, explore boutiques and antique shops that dot the countryside, or stroll through historic downtown Poughkeepsie, the County Seat. Cultural amenities are centered around the City of Poughkeepsie. The Hudson Valley Philharmonic performs at the restored Bardavon 1869 Opera House.

Population (1990)

Total Population and Growth Rate
1990: 259,462
1980: 245,055
1970: 222,295
Growth rate 1970–1990: 17%

Race and Hispanic Origin
White: 88.3%
Black: 8.4%
Asian/Pacific Islander: 2.2%
Native American: 0.1%
Hispanic origin: 3.8%
White not Hispanic: 85.9%

Age
Ages 18 to 20: 5.1%
Ages 21 to 24: 6%
Ages 25 to 44: 34%
Ages 45 to 54: 11.1%
Ages 55 to 59: 4.5%
Ages 60 to 64: 4%
Ages 65 plus: 11.4%

Educational Attainment (1990)
Percent having completed high school: 79.8%
Percent having completed college: 24.8%
Elementary and high school enrollment: 40,481

Federal Funds and Grants Received
Total received in 1989: $578,700,000
Funds received per capita: $2,207

Civilian Labor Force
1993 (April): 118,914
1992 average: 119,184
1991 average: 125,579
1990 average: 128,963

Unemployment
1993 (April): 8.8%
1992 average: 6.5%
1991 average: 5.1%
1990 average: 3.0%

Average Annual Pay
1988: $24,478
1987: $23,514
1985: $21,501

Per Capita Personal Income
1991: N/A
1990: N/A
1989: N/A

Business Climate (1987)

Manufacturing
Number of establishments in 1987: 207
Shipments in 1987 ($1,000): $5,464,800
Employees in 1987: 30,900
Change in employment, 1982 to 1987: -5.8%
Average annual pay for manufacturing work in 1989: $39,077
Average annual pay for production work in 1987: $19,810

Wholesale Trade
Number of establishments in 1987: 294
Total sales in 1987 ($1,000): $653,500
Change in sales, 1982 to 1987: 24.5%

Retail Trade
Number of establishments in 1987: 1,688
Total sales in 1987 ($1,000): $653,500
Retail sales per household in 1987: $19,553
Average annual pay in 1989: $12,873

Service Industry
Selected receipts in 1987 ($1,000): $550,200
Average annual pay in 1989: $19,484

Housing
Total number of units in 1990: 97,632
Occupied units in 1990: 89,567
Owner-occupied units in 1990: 69.1%
1993 ACCRA average cost: N/A
1993 ACCRA average rent for an apartment: N/A

Chamber of Commerce
Poughkeepsie Area Chamber of Commerce, Ronald G. Laferriere, President, 80 Washington St., Poughkeepsie, NY 12601. 914-454-1700

Economic Development Office
Dutchess County Economic Development Corp., Gerald

McDonald, Exec. Director, 532 Albany Post Rd., Hyde Park, NY 12538. 914-229-8522, FAX 914-229-6276

Major Businesses

Company	SIC	Telephone
Adams Fairacre Farms Inc.	5431	(914) 454-4330
Audia Motor Sales Inc.	5511	(914) 677-3406
Brownell Motors Inc.	5511	(914) 831-3000
Central Hudson Gas & Electric	4911	(914) 452-2000
Dutchess Beer Distributor	5181	(914) 452-0940
Dutchess Quarry & Supply	5032	(914) 635-8151
Efco Products Inc.	2033	(914) 452-4715
Fargo Mfg. Co. Inc.	3643	(914) 471-0600
First National Bank of Rhinebec	6021	(914) 876-7041
Fishkill National Bank	6021	(914) 831-1180
Friendly of Hudson Valley	5511	(914) 454-2400
Hyde Park Motor Co Inc.	5511	(914) 229-8811
J & J Log & Lumber Corp.	2421	(914) 832-6535
Knapp, Roy C. & Sons Inc.	1541	(914) 831-0943
Mechanical Construction Co.	1711	(914) 452-6700
Mid Hudson Savings Bank	6035	(914) 896-6215
Northern Dutchess Hospital	8062	(914) 876-3001
Pawling Corp.	3069	(914) 855-1000
Pawling Savings Bank	6036	(914) 855-1333
Poughkeepsie Savings Bank	6035	(914) 431-6200
Progressive Banks, Inc.	6036	(914) 855-1333
Red Wing Properties Inc.	5032	(914) 221-2224
Redl, Herbert	1542	(914) 471-3388
Roundout Electric Inc.	1731	(914) 471-4810
Ruge's Oldsmobile Inc.	5511	(914) 876-7074
St. Francis Hospital	8062	(914) 471-2000
Spartan Motors Ltd.	5511	(914) 297-4057
Vassar Bros. Hospital	8062	(914) 431-5607

Colleges and Universities

Dutchess Community College, Poughkeepsie
Marist College, Poughkeepsie
Vassar College, Poughkeepsie

ROCHESTER, NY (MSA)

Geographic Profile

Land Area
2931.5 square miles

Counties and Parishes
Livingston
Monroe
Ontario
Orleans
Wayne

Ranking Highlights

  48 *out of 319 in total* land area
248 *out of 319 in* population growth, *1970–1990*
  69 *out of 310 in having the lowest* unemployment *rate*
  51 *out of 310 in size of* labor force
  73 *out of 318 in the percentage of* college graduates
  38 *out of 292 in per capita personal* income
  51 *out of 319 in number of* manufacturing establishments
  66 *out of 318 in* physicians *per 1000 people*
142 *out of 318 in* hospital beds *per 1000 people*
  90 *out of 267 in fewest* crimes *per 1000 people*
  59 *out of 266 in fewest* violent crimes *per 1000 people*
230 *out of 319 in per capita* federal funds and grants

Quality of Life Indexes (Rate per 1000 population)

Crime rate in 1991:	52.5
Violent crime rate in 1991:	3.4
Physicians rate in 1992:	2.5
Hospital bed rate in 1991:	4.07

ACCRA Cost of Living Indexes
(First quarter 1993, average = 100)
Composite index: 111.7
Utilities index: 114.4
Housing index: 117.3

Overview

Rochester is one of the leading manufacturing centers in the United States, dominated by Eastman Kodak, which employs about nine percent of the work force and is responsible for jobs in hundreds of the local companies that are its suppliers. In addition to other large employers such as Bausch & Lomb, Inc. and Xerox Corporation, Rochester is home to more than one thousand small companies, most of them involved in science, services, and high technology; some 125 tooling and machining companies employ more than five thousand workers. Rochester's export rate is one of the highest per capita in the country and the city is a foreign trade zone. The tourist industry adds more than $200 million annually to the local economy.

Rochester–Monroe County Airport is served by a number of airfreight and air cargo services; expansion plans include the construction of three new airfreight buildings. Rail freight service is available from Chessie Systems, and several freight forwarders operate in the city. Rochester boasts an extensive network of highways. Shipping of oversize and bulk commodities can be arranged through the New York State Barge Canal system.

The Greater Rochester International Airport, located ten minutes from downtown, is served by seven major carriers and several feeder lines. Airport facilities have been expanded to accommodate traffic that was expected to increase by seventy percent between 1985–1995. Rail service is provided by Conrail and AMTRAK. A convenient network of highways, inner- and outer-loop arterial expressways, and the New York State Thruway facilitate auto travel. From Interstate 490 at the Clinton Avenue and Plymouth Avenue exits, a color-coded sign system directs visitors to five major downtown areas of interest.

Population (1990)

Total Population and Growth Rate
1990: 1,002,410
1980: 971,230
1970: 961,516
Growth rate 1970–1990: 4%

Race and Hispanic Origin
White: 87.4%
Black: 9.4%
Asian/Pacific Islander: 1.4%
Native American: 0.3%
Hispanic origin: 3.1%
White not Hispanic: 86.1%

Age
Ages 18 to 20: 5%
Ages 21 to 24: 6.2%
Ages 25 to 44: 32.8%
Ages 45 to 54: 10.3%
Ages 55 to 59: 4.1%
Ages 60 to 64: 4.1%
Ages 65 plus: 12.4%

Educational Attainment (1990)
Percent having completed high school: 79.1%
Percent having completed college: 23.4%
Elementary and high school enrollment: 163,219

Federal Funds and Grants Received
Total received in 1989: $2,541,800,000
Funds received per capita: $2,593

Civilian Labor Force
1993 (April): 520,492
1992 average: 510,471
1991 average: 512,882
1990 average: 510,916

Unemployment
1993 (April): 4.8%
1992 average: 5.4%

1991 average: 5.0%
1990 average: 3.7%

Average Annual Pay
1988: $23,469
1987: $22,307
1985: $20,846

Per Capita Personal Income
1991: $20,784
1990: $20,161
1989: $19,279

Business Climate (1987)

Manufacturing
Number of establishments in 1987: 1,391
Shipments in 1987 ($1,000): $18,962,800
Employees in 1987: 130,200
Change in employment, 1982 to 1987: -13.4%
Average annual pay for manufacturing work in 1989: $35,816
Average annual pay for production work in 1987: $24,654

Wholesale Trade
Number of establishments in 1987: 1,652
Total sales in 1987 ($1,000): $7,598,800
Change in sales, 1982 to 1987: 38.6%

Retail Trade
Number of establishments in 1987: 5,565
Total sales in 1987 ($1,000): $7,598,800
Retail sales per household in 1987: $17,137
Average annual pay in 1989: $11,313

Service Industry
Selected receipts in 1987 ($1,000): $2,200,800
Average annual pay in 1989: $18,441

Housing
Total number of units in 1990: 399,088
Occupied units in 1990: 374,475
Owner-occupied units in 1990: 67.6%
1993 ACCRA average cost: $138,000
1993 ACCRA average rent for an apartment: $539

Chamber of Commerce
Irondequoit Council, Public Relations Dept., 55 St. Paul St., Rochester, NY 14604. 716-454-2220

Economic Development Office
County of Monroe Industrial Development Agency, Joseph C. DeRitis, Director, 1 Main St. W. #600, Rochester, NY 14614-1481. 716-325-1944

Economic Development Organizations
New York State Dept. of Economic Development, Finger Lakes Regional Office, Susan B. Lawrence, Regional Director, 121 E. Ave. Suite 220, Rochester, NY 14604. 716-325-1944, FAX 716-325-6505.

Major Businesses

Company	SIC	Telephone
Alling and Cory Co.	5111	(716) 454-1880
Bausch & Lomb Inc.	3851	(716) 338-6000
Canandaigua Wine Co.	2084	(716) 394-7900
Central Trust Co.	6022	(716) 546-4500
Champion Products Inc.	2329	(716) 385-3200
Chase Lincoln First Bank	6021	(716) 258-5000
Chase Lincoln Leaseway	6159	(716) 258-6474
Columbia Banking	6035	(716) 454-6780
Curtice Burns Foods Inc.	2096	(716) 383-1850
Eastman Kodak Co.	3861	(716) 724-4000
Genesee Corp.	2082	(716) 546-1030
Genesee Hospital Inc.	8062	(716) 263-6000
Gleason Corp.	3714	(716) 272-6000
Gleason Works, The	3541	(716) 473-1000
Griffith, W. W. Oil Co. Inc.	5171	(716) 328-3930
Interco Systems Inc.	5074	(716) 442-7380
Mc Curdy & Co. Inc.	5311	(716) 232-1000
Paychex Inc.	7374	(716) 385-6666
RCI Corp.	4813	(716) 777-8000
Roadway Motor Plazas Inc.	5541	(716) 235-3615
Rochester Community Savings Bank	6036	(716) 262-5800
Rochester Gas and Electric Corp.	4911	(716) 546-2700
Rochester General Hospital	8062	(716) 338-4000
Rochester Hospital Service	6324	(716) 454-1700
Rochester Telephone Corp.	4813	(716) 777-1000
Rumrill-Hoyt Inc.	7311	(716) 272-6100
Schlegel Corp.	3069	(716) 427-7200
Seneca Foods Corp.	2033	(716) 385-9500
University of Rochester	8221	(716) 275-2121
Wegmans Food Markets Inc.	5411	(716) 328-2550

Colleges and Universities

Bryant and Stratton Business Institute, Rochester
Monroe Community College, Rochester
Nazareth College of Rochester, Rochester
Roberts Wesleyan College, Rochester
Rochester Business Institute, Rochester
Rochester Institute of Technology, Rochester
St. John Fisher College, Rochester
Talmudical Institute of Upstate New York, Rochester
University of Rochester, Rochester

SYRACUSE, NY (MSA)

Geographic Profile

Land Area
2389.5 square miles

Counties and Parishes
Madison
Onondaga
Oswego

Ranking Highlights

72 *out of 319 in total* **land area**
251 *out of 319 in* **population growth,** *1970–1990*
157 *out of 310 in having the lowest* **unemployment** *rate*
79 *out of 310 in size of* **labor force**
102 *out of 318 in the percentage of* **college graduates**
110 *out of 292 in per capita personal* **income**
87 *out of 319 in number of* **manufacturing establishments**
81 *out of 318 in* **physicians** *per 1000 people*
205 *out of 318 in* **hospital beds** *per 1000 people*
53 *out of 267 in fewest* **crimes** *per 1000 people*
53 *out of 266 in fewest* **violent crimes** *per 1000 people*
114 *out of 319 in per capita* **federal funds and grants**

Quality of Life Indexes (Rate per 1000 population)

Crime rate in 1991:	43.3
Violent crime rate in 1991:	3.2
Physicians rate in 1992:	2.38
Hospital bed rate in 1991:	3.38

ACCRA Cost of Living Indexes
(First quarter 1993, average = 100)

Composite index: 10.34
Utilities index: 132.6
Housing index: 93.8

Overview

Syracuse is a major commercial, industrial, and transportation center for the Northeast. The economy is highly diversified; no single industry or firm dominates. Services, especially wholesale and retail trade and business and health services, are a major source of employment and revenue; several financial and insurance institutions maintain major regional centers in Syracuse. The abundance of clean water in the region has attracted corporations such as Anheuser-Busch, Miller Brewing, and Bristol-Myers Laboratories. The Nine Mile II Nuclear Power Plant resulted in the growth of the transportation and public utilities sector of the local economy during the 1980s.

Syracuse's strategic central location and well developed transportation network, including highways, water, rail, and air services, make it a transportation and distribution hub for the Northeast. More than fifty percent of U.S. manufacturing establishments are said to be located within a 750-mile radius. Two major four-lane highways intersect the area, which is served by more than one hundred sixty trucking companies. Conrail's computerized rail yard can handle twenty-two hundred cars daily; AMTRAK also provides freight service. Hancock International Airport opened a $10 million cargo facility in 1988 to serve the air freight market with six major air cargo carriers. Thirty-four miles south of Syracuse, the deep water Port of Oswego and the New York Barge Canal system provide access to the Great Lakes and overseas. The Syracuse area is a foreign trade zone.

Hancock International Airport, located eight miles from the downtown area, serves more than three million passengers annually on eight major and four commuter airlines. A $35 million expansion and renovation was scheduled for completion in 1993.

Two major four-lane highways intersect Syracuse. Interstate 81, a north-south route, passes through the center of the city. Interstate 90 (the New York State Thruway), an east-west route, crosses Interstate 81 a mile north of the city.

Population (1990)

Total Population and Growth Rate
1990: 659,864
1980: 642,971
1970: 636,596
Growth rate 1970–1990: 4%

Race and Hispanic Origin
White: 91.8%
Black: 5.9%
Asian/Pacific Islander: 1.2%
Native American: 0.6%
Hispanic origin: 1.4%
White not Hispanic: 91.0%

Age
Ages 18 to 20: 6.1%
Ages 21 to 24: 6.6%
Ages 25 to 44: 31.6%
Ages 45 to 54: 9.7%
Ages 55 to 59: 4.2%
Ages 60 to 64: 4.2%
Ages 65 plus: 12.4%

Educational Attainment (1990)
Percent having completed high school: 79.5%
Percent having completed college: 21.8%
Elementary and high school enrollment: 109,769

Federal Funds and Grants Received
Total received in 1989: $2,243,300,000
Funds received per capita: $3,450

Civilian Labor Force
1993 (April): 323,461
1992 average: 320,650
1991 average: 325,258
1990 average: 326,029

Unemployment
1993 (April): 6.3%
1992 average: 6.9%
1991 average: 6.5%
1990 average: 4.1%

Average Annual Pay
1988: $21,605
1987: $20,589
1985: $19,419

Per Capita Personal Income
1991: $18,063
1990: $17,786
1989: $16,774

Business Climate (1987)

Manufacturing
Number of establishments in 1987: 759
Shipments in 1987 ($1,000): $7,479,100
Employees in 1987: 51,900
Change in employment, 1982 to 1987: -8.3%
Average annual pay for manufacturing work in 1989: $30,861
Average annual pay for production work in 1987: $24,129

Wholesale Trade
Number of establishments in 1987: 1,422
Total sales in 1987 ($1,000): $7,926,200
Change in sales, 1982 to 1987: 33.6%

Retail Trade
Number of establishments in 1987: 4,007
Total sales in 1987 ($1,000): $7,926,200
Retail sales per household in 1987: $17,048
Average annual pay in 1989: $11,368

Service Industry
Selected receipts in 1987 ($1,000): $1,564,000
Average annual pay in 1989: $19,089

Office Real Estate (1992)
Office space inventory: 8,625,000 square feet
Average class A Central Business District rental range per sq. ft: $16.50

Vacancy Rates
All areas: 14.8%

Vacancy Rates in Central Business District
Class A space: 8.7%
Class B space: 36.7%

Vacancy Rates Outside Central Business District
Class A space: 7.3%
Class B space: 17.5%

Housing
Total number of units in 1990: 266,067
Occupied units in 1990: 243,899
Owner-occupied units in 1990: 66.2%

1993 ACCRA average cost: $104,200

1993 ACCRA average rent for an apartment: $500

Chamber of Commerce

Greater Syracuse Chamber of Commerce, Erwin G. Schultz, President, 100 E. Onondaga St., Syracuse, NY 13202. 315-470-1343

Economic Development Office

Onondaga County IDA, Sidney Devorsetz, 555 Genesee St., Syracuse, NY 13202. 315-471-2244

Economic Development Organizations

New York State Dept. of Economic Development, Central New York Regional Office, Regional Director, 333 E. Washington St., Syracuse, NY 13202. 315-428-4097, FAX 315-428-4098

Major Businesses

Company	SIC	Telephone
Agway Inc.	2033	(315) 449-7061
Agway Petroleum Corp.	5983	(315) 449-7425
American General Life Insurance Co.	6311	(315) 471-1121
Bennett Funding Group Inc.	6159	(315) 457-5000
Blue Cross and Blue Shield	6324	(315) 424-3700
Carlisle Companies Inc.	3572	(315) 474-2500
Carrols Corp.	5812	(315) 424-0513
Carrols Holdings Corp.	5812	(315) 424-0513
CIS Corp.	6159	(315) 437-1900
Community Bank Systems Inc.	6021	(315) 445-2282
Community General Hospital	8062	(315) 492-5011
Continental Information Systems	6159	(315) 437-1900
Coyne International Enterprises	7218	(315) 475-1626
Crouse Irving Memorial Hospital	8062	(315) 470-7111
Crucible Materials Corp.	3312	(315) 487-4111
Dairylea Cooperative Inc.	5143	(315) 476-9101
Eastern Milk Producers Cooperative	2026	(315) 463-0781
Fay's Drug Co. Inc.	5912	(315) 451-8000
Merchants National Bank & Trust	6021	(315) 472-5561
Niagara Mohawk Power Corp.	4911	(315) 474-1511
O'Brien & Gere Ltd.	8711	(315) 437-6100
Oneida Ltd.	3262	(315) 361-3000
Onondaga Savings Bank	6035	(315) 424-4400
P & C Food Markets Inc.	5411	(315) 457-9460
Pass & Seymour Inc.	3643	(315) 468-6211
Roth Bros. Smelting Corp.	3341	(315) 463-9500
St. Josephs Hospital Health Center	8062	(315) 448-5111
State University of New York	8062	(315) 464-8300
Syracuse China Corp.	3262	(315) 455-5671
Syracuse Supply Co.	5082	(315) 463-9511
Unity Mutual Life Insurance Co.	6311	(315) 469-7751

Colleges and Universities

Bryant and Stratton Business Institute, Syracuse
Central City Business Institute, Syracuse
Le Moyne College, Syracuse
Onondaga Community College, Syracuse
State University of New York College of Environmental Science and Forestry, Syracuse
State University of New York Health Science Center at Syracuse, Syracuse
Syracuse University, Syracuse

UTICA-ROME, NY (MSA)

Geographic Profile
Land Area
2624.6 square miles

Counties and Parishes
Herkimer
Oneida

Ranking Highlights
 63 *out of 319 in total* **land area**
308 *out of 319 in* **population growth,** *1970–1990*
201 *out of 310 in having the lowest* **unemployment** *rate*
153 *out of 310 in size of* **labor force**
223 *out of 318 in the percentage of* **college graduates**
198 *out of 292 in per capita personal* **income**
146 *out of 319 in number of* **manufacturing establishments**
232 *out of 318 in* **physicians** *per 1000 people*
211 *out of 318 in* **hospital beds** *per 1000 people*
 16 *out of 267 in fewest* **crimes** *per 1000 people*
 20 *out of 266 in fewest* **violent crimes** *per 1000 people*
 83 *out of 319 in per capita* **federal funds and grants**

Quality of Life Indexes (Rate per 1000 population)
Crime rate in 1991:   34.2
Violent crime rate in 1991:   1.9
Physicians rate in 1992:   1.47
Hospital bed rate in 1991:   3.28

ACCRA Cost of Living Indexes
(First quarter 1993, average = 100)
Composite index: 106.0
Utilities index: 129.3
Housing index: 99.2

Population (1990)
Total Population and Growth Rate
1990: 316,633
1980: 320,180
1970: 340,477
Growth rate 1970–1990: -7%

Race and Hispanic Origin
White: 94.0%
Black: 4.4%
Asian/Pacific Islander: 0.7%
Native American: 0.2%
Hispanic origin: 1.9%
White not Hispanic: 93.0%

Age
Ages 18 to 20:   5%
Ages 21 to 24:   6%
Ages 25 to 44: 29.9%
Ages 45 to 54: 9.9%
Ages 55 to 59: 4.3%
Ages 60 to 64: 4.7%
Ages 65 plus: 15.7%

Educational Attainment (1990)
Percent having completed high school: 74.6%
Percent having completed college: 15.9%
Elementary and high school enrollment: 53,185

Federal Funds and Grants Received
Total received in 1989: $1,196,600,000
Funds received per capita: $3,828

Civilian Labor Force
1993 (April):   138,036
1992 average: 136,235
1991 average: 136,892
1990 average: 137,998

Unemployment
1993 (April):   6.6%
1992 average: 7.5%
1991 average: 7.1%
1990 average: 4.6%

Average Annual Pay
1988: $18,839
1987: $18,117
1985: $16,631

Per Capita Personal Income
1991: $16,336
1990: $15,962
1989: $15,069

Business Climate (1987)
Manufacturing
Number of establishments in 1987: 367
Shipments in 1987 ($1,000): $2,449,000
Employees in 1987: 23,700
Change in employment, 1982 to 1987: -21.3%
Average annual pay for manufacturing work in 1989: $24,574
Average annual pay for production work in 1987: $19,734

Wholesale Trade
Number of establishments in 1987: 462
Total sales in 1987 ($1,000): $1,019,700
Change in sales, 1982 to 1987: -7.8%

Retail Trade
Number of establishments in 1987: 1,984
Total sales in 1987 ($1,000): $1,019,700
Retail sales per household in 1987: $14,791
Average annual pay in 1989: $10,601

Service Industry
Selected receipts in 1987 ($1,000): $491,400
Average annual pay in 1989: $15,673

Housing
Total number of units in 1990: 132,050

Occupied units in 1990: 117,498
Owner-occupied units in 1990: 66.5%
1993 ACCRA average cost: $111,500
1993 ACCRA average rent for an apartment: $487

Chamber of Commerce

Utica Area Chamber of Commerce, Alvin G. Mardon, President, 258 Genesee St., Utica, NY 13502. 315-724-3151

Economic Development Office

Rome Chamber of Commerce, Robert K. Van Slyke, President, 200 Liberty Plaza, Rome, NY 13440. 315-337-1700, FAX 315-337-1715

Economic Development Organizations

Rome Industrial Development Corp., Edward Ratazzi, Jr., Exec. Director, 200 Liberty Plaza, Rome, NY 13440. 315-337-6360, FAX 315-337-1715

NYS Dept. of Economic Dev.–Mohawk Valley Reg. Office, Donald J. Grabowski, Regional Director, 207 Genesee St., Utica, NY 13501. 315-793-2366

New York State Dept. of Economic Development, Mohawk Valley Regional Office, Regional Director, 207 Genesee St., Utica, NY 13501. 315-793-2366, FAX 315-793-2705

Major Businesses

Company	SIC	Telephone
Blask, Ed Ford Inc.	5511	(315) 736-3381
Blue Cross/Shield	6324	(315) 798-4200
Carl's Drug Co.	5912	(315) 336-1080
Casa Imports Inc.	5141	(315) 724-4189
Faxton-Children's Hospital	8062	(315) 732-3101
G&I Homes Inc.	5271	(315) 732-6136
Graphic Arts Mutual Insurance	6331	(315) 735-3321
Harden Furniture Inc.	2511	(315) 245-1000
Herkimer Petroleum Products	5541	(315) 797-7760
Herkimer Wholesale Co.	5194	(315) 732-1144
Lucas Aerospace Power Transmission	3724	(315) 793-1200
Mercer's Kwik Stop Food	5411	(315) 942-4396
Momentum Manufacturing Co.	3577	(315) 866-5300
Oneida Asbestos Removal Inc.	1799	(315) 735-6156
Par Microsystems Corp.	3578	(315) 738-0600
Par Technology Corp.	3578	(315) 738-0600
Revere Copper Products Inc.	3351	(315) 338-2324
Rome, City of	8062	(315) 336-6000
Rome Cable Corp.	3357	(315) 337-3000
Savings Bank of Utica	6035	(315) 738-5000
Scheidelman Inc.	5141	(315) 732-6186
Special Metals Corp.	3356	(315) 798-2900
St. Elizabeth Hospital	8062	(315) 798-8100
St. Lukes Memorial Hospital	8062	(315) 798-6000
Utica Fire Insurance Co. Oneida	6331	(315) 736-8211
Utica Mutual Insurance Co.	6331	(315) 735-3321
Utica National Insurance	6331	(315) 735-3321

Colleges and Universities

Mohawk Valley Community College, Utica
State University of New York Institute of Technology at Utica/Rome, Utica
Utica College of Syracuse University, Utica
Utica School of Commerce, Utica

NORTH CAROLINA

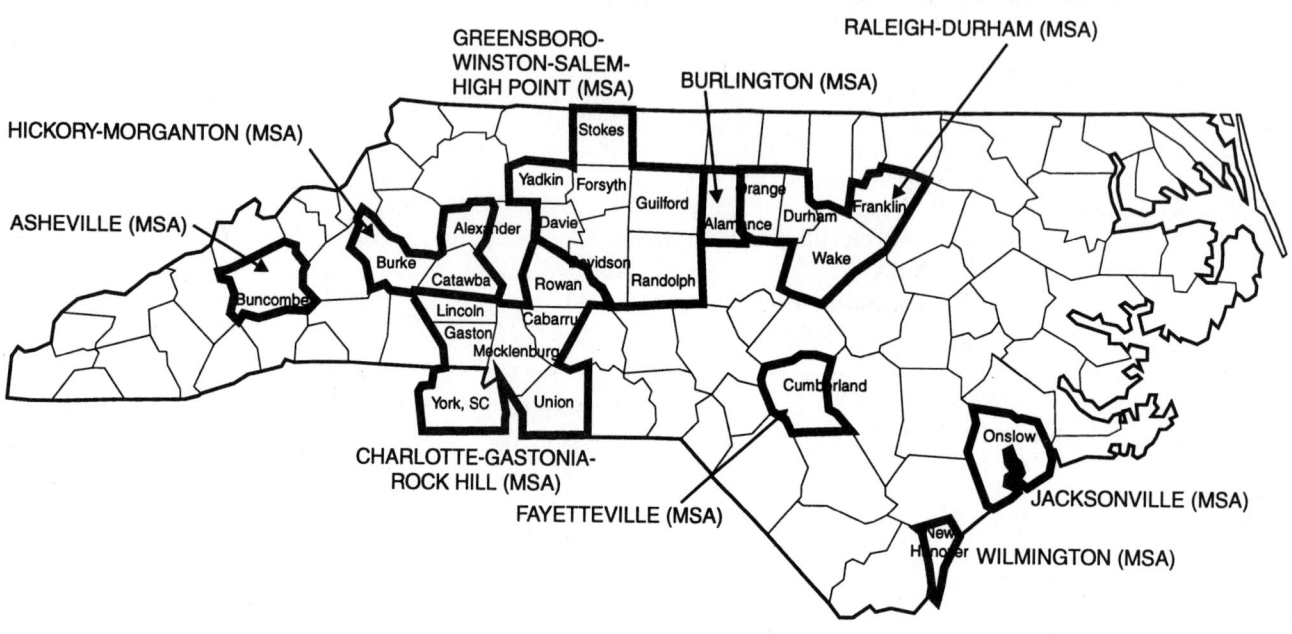

HICKORY-MORGANTON (MSA)

ASHEVILLE (MSA)

GREENSBORO-
WINSTON-SALEM-
HIGH POINT (MSA)

BURLINGTON (MSA)

RALEIGH-DURHAM (MSA)

Stokes

Yadkin   Forsyth

Guilford

Orange

Alexander   Davie

Alamance   Durham

Franklin

Burke

Davidson

Wake

Catawba   Rowan

Randolph

Lincoln

Gaston

Cabarrus

Mecklenburg

Cumberland

Onslow

JACKSONVILLE (MSA)

York, SC   Union

CHARLOTTE-GASTONIA-
ROCK HILL (MSA)

FAYETTEVILLE (MSA)

New
Hanover   WILMINGTON (MSA)

NORTH CAROLINA

Population
1990: 6,628,637
1980: 5,881,766

Age
Ages 18 to 20: 348,346
Ages 21 to 24: 432,707
Ages 25 to 44: 2,151,486
Ages 45 to 54: 698,705
Ages 55 to 59: 295,739
Ages 60 to 64: 291,164
Median age: 33.1

Race and Hispanic Origin
White: 5,008,491
Black: 1,456,323
Asian/Pacific Islander: 52,166
Native American: 80,155
Hispanic origin: 76,726

Households
Total: 2,517,026
Persons per household: 2.54

Sex
Male: 3,214,290
Female: 3,414,347

Population Migration
Domestic migration: 546,000
International migration: 30,000

Projection of the Population in 1995
Total: 6,836,000
18 to 64: 4,276,000

Civilian Labor Force
1993: 3,457,700
1992: 3,440,900
1991: 3,398,000
1990: 3,331,800

Manufacturing
1995 Projection: 918,200
1992: 832,900
1991: 837,900
1990: 849,400
1989: 867,900

Services
1995 Projection: 855,500

1992: 639,900
1991: 616,800
1990: 603,000
1989: 572,400

Wholesale and Retail Trade
1995 Projection: 843,800
1992: 713,600
1991: 720,300
1990: 735,300
1989: 742,900

Unemployment Rate
1993: 6.3%
1992: 6.7%
1991: 5.0%
1990: 4.6%

Employer Unemployment Contributions
Contribution Rate
1992: 0.99%
1991: 1.01%
1990: 1.01%

Average Weekly Benefit
1992: $162.47
1991: $162.11
1990: $152.13

Gross State Product (Million $)
1989: $130,085
1988: $121,489
1987: $112,288
1979: $54,890
Growth rate, 1979 to 1989: 137.0%

Capital Expenditures of Manufacturing Industries
1990: $3,459,000,000
1989: $3,396,800,000
1988: $3,097,800,000
1987: $2,958,700,000

State Tax Rates
Individual income: Range from 6% ($21,250 or less) to 7.75% (above $100,000).
Corporate income: 7.5% of taxable net income, with 4% surtax imposed.

General property: Rates fixed locally. Based on true cash value of real property and tangible personal property.

General sales: 4%

Gasoline: 22.6¢ per gallon

Income

Median income for a 4 person family: $38,068

Personal per Capita Income

1992: $17,667

1991: $16,848

1990: $16,383

Disposable per Capita Income

1992: $15,600

1991: $14,827

1990: $14,345

Private Employment Weekly Wages

Average

1989: $367

1988: $354

1987: $354

Manufacturing

1989: $339

1988: $397

1987: $380

Services

1989: $342

1988: $326

1987: $309

Wholesale

1989: $491

1988: $484

1987: $453

Retail

1989: $217

1988: $212

1987: $205

Highway Statistics

Total Highway Miles

1990: 94,690

1989: 94,228

1988: 93,813

Federal Highway Aid

1991: $324,255,000

1990: $235,940,000

1989: $346,034,000

Electricity

Average Cost per Kilowatt Hour

1990: 6.43¢

1989: 6.30¢

1988: 6.19¢

Housing (1990)

Owner occupied units: 1,711,817

Median house value: $65,800

Renter occupied units: 805,209

Median rent: $284

Total vacant units: 301,167

Homeowner vacancy rate: 1.8%

Rental vacancy rate: 9.2%

State Business Incentives and Assistance

Financial and Business Assistance

Industrial Development Bonds. Administered by the Department of Commerce, counties are authorized to establish authorities to issue industrial development bonds to provide tax-exempt financing for private manufacturing operations. Eligible projects are manufacturing or industrial facilities or pollution control facilities for a private company or for a public utility. The minimum amount for a bond issue is $500,000.

Incubator Facilities Program. Administered by the Technological Development Authority, the program provides one time state grants of up to $200,000 for a community to establish facilities that provide low-rent space, shared support services, and basic equipment to resident small businesses. It also provides ready access to technical, management, and entrepreneurial advice.

Innovation Research Fund. Administered by the Technological Development Authority, the funds provide up to $50,000 for the research and development activities of small businesses which include the securing of technical and management advice, purchasing of scientific equipment and materials, etc.

Industrial Building Renovation Fund. Administered by the Department of Commerce, the state provides funds in certain counties to renovate existing buildings for use as manufacturing and industrial operations. Maximum of $250,000 can be received by a company for renovation and $1,200 per job created. The funds are to be paid back at below-market interest rates.

Education and Training

Industrial Training Program. Administered by the North Carolina Department of Community Colleges, Industrial Services Division, this program provides training for new and expanding industries. The state also helps to retrain existing employees. The training is provided locally by the community colleges and technical institutes, and can be conducted on campus or within the company's facilities.

Job Training Partnership Act. This program operates with funding from the U.S. Department of Labor. It provides job training and other employment related services.

State Offices

Real estate: Real Estate Commission, Phillip T. Fisher, Exec Director, PO Box 17100, 1200 Navaho Drive, Raleigh, NC 27619. 919-733-9680

Major Companies in the State

Company name	Fortune 500 rank	City	Telephone	SIC number
Fortune 500 Companies				
Burlington Industries Equity Inc.	216	Greensboro	919-379-2000	2231
Coca Cola Bottling Co. Consolidated	460	Charlotte	704-551-4400	2086
Collins & Aikman Group Inc.	208	Charlotte	704-548-2350	5251
Cone Mills Corp.	422	Greensboro	919-379-6220	2211
Guilford Mills Inc.	485	Greensboro	919-316-4000	2258
Nucor Corp.	258	Charlotte	704-366-7000	3312
Standard Commercial Corp.	314	Wilson	919-291-5507	5194
Unifi Inc.	334	Greensboro	919-294-4410	2281
Other Major Companies In The State				
BB&T Financial Corp.		Wilson	919-399-4291	6712
Burlington Industries Capital Inc.		Greensboro	919-379-2000	2211
Carolina Freight Corp.		Cherryville	704-435-6811	4213
Carolina Power & Light Co.		Raleigh	919-546-6111	4911
Carolina Telephone & Telegraph Co.		Tarboro	919-823-9900	4813
Duke Power Co.		Charlotte	704-373-4011	4911
Family Dollar Stores Inc.		Charlotte	704-847-6961	5331
Fieldcrest Cannon Inc.		Greensboro	919-665-4300	2259
First Union Corp.		Charlotte	704-374-6565	6712
Food Lion Inc.		Salisbury	704-633-8250	5411
Ingles Markets Inc.		Asheville	704-669-2941	5411
Jefferson Pilot Corp.		Greensboro	919-691-3417	6311
Ladd Furniture Inc.		High Point	919-889-0333	2511
Lowe's Co., Inc.		North Wilkesboro	919-651-4000	5211
NCNB Corp.		Charlotte	704-386-5000	6712
Rose's Stores Inc.		Henderson	919-430-2600	5331
Ruddick Corp.		Charlotte	704-372-5404	5411
United Dominion Industries Ltd.		Charlotte	704-347-6800	1541
Wachovia Corp.		Winston-Salem	919-770-5141	6712

Chamber of commerce: North Carolina Association of Chamber of Commerce, Cynthia Cover, Exec Director, 225 Hillsborough Place #460, PO Box 1001, Raleigh, NC 27602. 919-828-0758

Economic development: Department of Commerce, Alvah Ward Jr., Director, Business/Industry Development Division, 430 North Salisbury Street, Raleigh, NC 26611. 9191-733-4151

North Carolina Technological Development Authority, Brent Lane, Exec Director, 430 North Salisbury Street, Room 4216, Raleigh, NC 27611. 919-733-7022

North Carolina Technological Development Authority, Incubator Facility Program, Melody Brown, Director, 430 North Salisbury Street, Room 4216, Raleigh, NC 27611. 919-733-7022

Small Business Development Center, Scott R. Daugherty, Exec Director, 4509 Creedmoor Road, Suite 201, Raleigh, NC 27612. 919-571-4154

Environmental affairs: Environment, Health and Natural Resources Department, William W. Cobey, Jr., Secretary, PO Box 27687, Raleigh, NC 27611. 919-733-4984

Labor: Labor Department, John C. Brooks, Commissioner, 4 West Edenton St., Raleigh, NC 27601. 919-733-7166

Unemployment: Employment Security Commission, Betsy Justus, Chairman, PO Box 25903, 700 Wade Ave., Raleigh, NC 27611. 919-733-7546

Worker's compensation: Economic and Community Development Department, State Industrial Commission, William Stephensen, Commissioner, 430 North Salisbury St., Dobbs Bldg., Raleigh, NC 27611. 919-733-4820

Occupational safety and health: Occupational Safety and Health Review Board, Ken Kiser, Chairman, 510 North Blount St., Raleigh, NC 27601. 919-733-3589

Secretary of state: Secretary of State, Rufus L. Edmisten, Secretary of State, 300 North Salisbury St., Raleigh, NC 27611. 919-733-4161

Taxation and revenue: Revenue Department, Helen A. Powers, Secretary, PO Box 25000, 2 South Salisbury St., Raleigh, NC 27640. 919-733-7211

Designated Zones for Economic Development

Enterprise Zones
No program.

Foreign Trade Zones
Zone No. 57, Mecklenburg County, North Carolina, Grantee: North Carolina Department of Commerce, Operator: Piedmont Distribution Center, Mark Mirali, 11425 Granite Street, Charlotte, NC 28273, 704-588-3277

Foreign Trade Zone No. 67, Morehead City, North Carolina, Grantee: North Carolina Dept. of Commerce, Operator: N.C. State Port Authority, Patsy Everhart, PO Box 9002, Wilmington, NC 2 8402, 919-763-1621

Foreign Trade Zone No. 93, Raleigh/Durham, North Carolina, Grantee: Triangle J Council of Governments, Pamela Davison, 100 Park Drive, PO Box 12276, Research Triangle Park, NC 27709, 919-549-0551

Foreign Trade Zone No. 66, Wilmington, North Carolina, Grantee: North Carolina Dept. of Commerce, Operator: N.C. State Port Authority, Patsy Everhart, PO Box 9002, Wilmington, NC 28402, 919-763-1621

Labor Unions
Bakery, Confectionery & Tobacco Workers International Union (AFL-CIO)

Clothing and Textile Workers Union, Amalgamated (AFL-CIO)

Electrical Workers, International Brotherhood of (AFL-CIO)

Paperworkers International Union, United (AFL-CIO)

Universities with Ph.D. Programs
Campbell University, Buies Creek
Duke University, Durham
East Carolina University, Greenville
North Carolina State University, Raleigh
University of North Carolina At Chapel Hill, Chapel Hill
University of North Carolina At Greensboro, Greensboro
Wake Forest University, Winston-Salem

ASHEVILLE, NC (MSA)

Geographic Profile

Land Area
656.3 square miles

Counties and Parishes
Buncombe

Ranking Highlights
261　*out of 319 in total* **land area**
173　*out of 319 in* **population growth,** *1970–1990*
　56　*out of 310 in having the lowest* **unemployment** *rate*
190　*out of 310 in size of* **labor force**
157　*out of 318 in the percentage of* **college graduates**
143　*out of 292 in per capita personal* **income**
170　*out of 319 in number of* **manufacturing establishments**
　47　*out of 318 in* **physicians** *per 1000 people*
133　*out of 318 in* **hospital beds** *per 1000 people*
　99　*out of 267 in fewest* **crimes** *per 1000 people*
　71　*out of 266 in fewest* **violent crimes** *per 1000 people*
193　*out of 319 in per capita* **federal funds and grants**

Quality of Life Indexes (Rate per 1000 population)
Crime rate in 1991:	54.2
Violent crime rate in 1991:	3.9
Physicians rate in 1992:	2.75
Hospital bed rate in 1991:	4.15

ACCRA Cost of Living Indexes
(First quarter 1993, average = 100)
Composite index:	N/A
Utilities index:	N/A
Housing index:	N/A

Population (1990)

Total Population and Growth Rate
1990: 174,821
1980: 160,934
1970: 145,056
Growth rate 1970–1990: 21%

Race and Hispanic Origin
White: 90.9%
Black: 8.2%
Asian/Pacific Islander: 0.4%
Native American: 0.3%
Hispanic origin: 0.7%
White not Hispanic: 90.4%

Age
Ages 18 to 20: 4.2%
Ages 21 to 24: 5.2%
Ages 25 to 44: 31.1%
Ages 45 to 54: 11.2%
Ages 55 to 59: 4.7%

Ages 60 to 64: 5.1%
Ages 65 plus: 16.1%

Educational Attainment (1990)
Percent having completed high school: 74.5%
Percent having completed college: 19.1%
Elementary and high school enrollment: 26,074

Federal Funds and Grants Received
Total received in 1989: $491,400,000
Funds received per capita: $2,839

Civilian Labor Force
1993 (April):   97,936
1992 average: 96,632
1991 average: 93,870
1990 average: 92,176

Unemployment
1993 (April):   4.4%
1992 average: 5.1%
1991 average: 4.9%
1990 average: 3.3%

Average Annual Pay
1988: $17,850
1987: $17,035
1985: $15,384

Per Capita Personal Income
1991: $17,451
1990: $16,882
1989: $15,572

Business Climate (1987)
Manufacturing
Number of establishments in 1987: 285
Shipments in 1987 ($1,000): $1,773,000
Employees in 1987: 18,700
Change in employment, 1982 to 1987: -2.1%
Average annual pay for manufacturing work in 1989: $21,046
Average annual pay for production work in 1987: $16,109

Wholesale Trade
Number of establishments in 1987: 325
Total sales in 1987 ($1,000): $872,100
Change in sales, 1982 to 1987: 44.2%

Retail Trade
Number of establishments in 1987: 1,254
Total sales in 1987 ($1,000): $872,100
Retail sales per household in 1987: $17,129
Average annual pay in 1989: $10,811

Service Industry
Selected receipts in 1987 ($1,000): $440,700
Average annual pay in 1989: $18,912

Housing
Total number of units in 1990: 77,951

Occupied units in 1990: 70,802
Owner-occupied units in 1990: 70.3%
1993 ACCRA average cost: N/A
1993 ACCRA average rent for an apartment: N/A

Chamber of Commerce
Asheville Area Chamber of Commerce, Michael W. Rollins, Exec. Vice President, 151 Haywood St., PO Box 1010, Asheville, NC 28802. 704-258-3858

Economic Development Office
Economic Development Group, Steve R. Jenkins, Senior Director, 151 Haywood St., PO Box 1010, Asheville, NC 28802. 704-258-6118

Major Businesses

Company	SIC	Telephone
Ashevlle Federal Savings & Loan	6035	(704) 254-7411
Electric Supply Co. of Asheville	5063	(704) 255-8899
Grove Park Inn Resort Inc.	7011	(704) 252-2711
Haynes, M. B. Corp.	1731	(704) 254-6141
Ingles Markets Inc.	5411	(704) 669-2941
Memorial Mission Hospital	8062	(704) 255-4000
Memorial Mission Medical Center	8062	(704) 255-4000
Milkco Inc.	2026	(704) 254-9560
Price-McNabb Advertising Agency	7311	(704) 255-2600
Revco Scientific, Inc.	3585	(704) 658-2711
Sky City Stores Inc.	5311	(704) 254-0931
Skyland Oldsmobile Inc.	5511	(704) 667-5213
Smith, Dr. T. C. Co. Inc.	5122	(704) 258-1869
St. Joseph's Hospital	8062	(704) 255-3100
Thomas Howard Co. of Asheville	5141	(704) 669-2941
Wilcox Travel Agency Inc.	4724	(704) 254-0746

Colleges and Universities
Asheville-Buncombe Technical Community College, Asheville
Blanton's Junior College, Asheville
Cecils Junior College of Business, Asheville
University of North Carolina at Asheville, Asheville

BURLINGTON, NC (MSA)

Geographic Profile

Land Area

430.7 square miles

Counties and Parishes

Alamance

Ranking Highlights

307 *out of 319 in total* land area

217 *out of 319 in* population growth, *1970–1990*

 34 *out of 310 in having the lowest* unemployment *rate*

247 *out of 310 in size of* labor force

243 *out of 318 in the percentage of* college graduates

N/A *out of 292 in per capita personal* income

163 *out of 319 in number of* manufacturing establishments

273 *out of 318 in* physicians *per 1000 people*

225 *out of 318 in* hospital beds *per 1000 people*

 91 *out of 267 in fewest* crimes *per 1000 people*

 79 *out of 266 in fewest* violent crimes *per 1000 people*

253 *out of 319 in per capita* federal funds and grants

Quality of Life Indexes (Rate per 1000 population)

Crime rate in 1991:	39.5
Violent crime rate in 1991:	4.5
Physicians rate in 1992:	1.25
Hospital bed rate in 1991:	3.14

ACCRA Cost of Living Indexes

(First quarter 1993, average = 100)

Composite index:	94.8
Utilities index:	106.0
Housing index:	99.4

Population (1990)

Total Population and Growth Rate

1990: 108,213

1980: 99,319

1970: 96,502

Growth rate 1970–1990: 12%

Race and Hispanic Origin

White: 79.8%

Black: 19.2%

Asian/Pacific Islander: 0.5%

Native American: 0.3%

Hispanic origin: 0.7%

White not Hispanic: 79.4%

Age

Ages 18 to 20: 5.4%

Ages 21 to 24: 6.1%

Ages 25 to 44: 30.6%

Ages 45 to 54: 11.1%

Ages 55 to 59: 5%

Ages 60 to 64: 5.1%

Ages 65 plus: 14.8%

Educational Attainment (1990)

Percent having completed high school: 67.9%

Percent having completed college: 14.6%

Elementary and high school enrollment: 15,833

Federal Funds and Grants Received

Total received in 1989: $257,700,000

Funds received per capita: $2,434

Civilian Labor Force

1993 (April):	64,307
1992 average:	65,262
1991 average:	66,851
1990 average:	65,439

Unemployment

1993 (April): 4.3%

1992 average: 4.6%

1991 average: 4.5%

1990 average: 3.3%

Average Annual Pay

1988: $16,188

1987: $15,489

1985: $14,199

Per Capita Personal Income

1991: N/A

1990: N/A

1989: N/A

Business Climate (1987)

Manufacturing

Number of establishments in 1987: 303

Shipments in 1987 ($1,000): $2,262,300

Employees in 1987: 24,300

Change in employment, 1982 to 1987: 14.6%

Average annual pay for manufacturing work in 1989: $18,595

Average annual pay for production work in 1987: $14,843

Wholesale Trade

Number of establishments in 1987: 185

Total sales in 1987 ($1,000): $545,100

Change in sales, 1982 to 1987: 66.7%

Retail Trade

Number of establishments in 1987: 847

Total sales in 1987 ($1,000): $545,100

Retail sales per household in 1987: $20,193

Average annual pay in 1989: $10,060

Service Industry

Selected receipts in 1987 ($1,000): $175,300

Average annual pay in 1989: $16,267

Housing

Total number of units in 1990: 45,312

Occupied units in 1990: 42,652
Owner-occupied units in 1990: 71.8%
1993 ACCRA average cost: $115,450
1993 ACCRA average rent for an apartment: $447

Chamber of Commerce

Alamance County Chamber of Commerce, William C. Wilburn, Exec. Vice President, 610 S. Lexington Ave., PO Box 450, Burlington, NC 27216. 919-228-1338

Major Businesses

Company	SIC	Telephone
Alamance County Hospital	8062	(919) 570-4130
Alamance Foods Inc.	2026	(919) 226-6392
Alamance Health Services	8062	(919) 570-5000
Alamance Memorial Hospital	8062	(919) 570-5000
B I Transportation Inc.	4213	(919) 228-2177
Bankers Insurance Co.	6331	(919) 584-3711
Byrd Food Stores Inc.	5411	(919) 227-1411
Financial First Federal Savings	6035	(919) 227-8861
Glen Raven Mills Inc.	2281	(919) 227-6211
Holt Hosiery Mills Inc.	2251	(919) 227-1431
Kingsdown Inc.	2515	(919) 563-3531
Love, W. E. & Associates	6411	(919) 226-1191
Mebane Packaging Corp.	2657	(919) 563-3516
Regent Lighting Corp.	3648	(919) 226-2411
Shirley, Dick Chevrolet Inc.	5511	(919) 229-5501
Stearns, C. A. & Co.	5511	(919) 226-6301

CHARLOTTE–GASTONIA–ROCK HILL, NC–SC, (MSA)

Geographic Profile

Land Area
3378.6 square miles

Counties and Parishes
North Carolina:
Cabarrus
Gaston
Lincoln
Meeklenburg
Rowan
Union
South Carolina:
York

Additional Cities/Towns within Area
Kannapolis

Ranking Highlights

40 *out of 319 in total* **land area**
104 *out of 319 in* **population growth,** *1970–1990*
75 *out of 310 in having the lowest* **unemployment** *rate*
41 *out of 310 in size of* **labor force**
146 *out of 318 in the percentage of* **college graduates**
85 *out of 292 in per capita personal* **income**
33 *out of 319 in number of* **manufacturing establishments**
217 *out of 318 in* **physicians** *per 1000 people*
243 *out of 318 in* **hospital beds** *per 1000 people*
227 *out of 267 in fewest* **crimes** *per 1000 people*
249 *out of 266 in fewest* **violent crimes** *per 1000 people*
305 *out of 319 in per capita* **federal funds and grants**

Quality of Life Indexes (Rate per 1000 population)

Crime rate in 1991: 80.4
Violent crime rate in 1991: 11.6
Physicians rate in 1992: 1.55
Hospital bed rate in 1991: 2.99

ACCRA Cost of Living Indexes
(First quarter 1993, average = 100)
Composite index: 99.2
Utilities index: 106.7
Housing index: 96.4

Overview

Located in one of the nation's largest urban regions, Charlotte has more than 5.4 million people living within a 100-mile radius. More than half the population of the United States can be reached from Charlotte within one hour's flight time or one day by truck. Its proximity to a wide variety of markets has led to Charlotte's maturation as a financial, distribution, and transportation center for the entire urban region. The city has developed into a major wholesale center with the highest per capita sales in the United States, ranking sixth nationally in total wholesale sales. As a result, earnings were up five percent and retail sales were up 10 percent from 1989 to 1991.

Charlotte is also becoming recognized as a national and international financial center. The city is already the major banking center of the Southeast and only New York City and San Francisco, California, have more banking resources.

Primarily a service and distribution center, Charlotte hosts other major employers in wholesale and retail trade, manufacturing, finance, and real estate. Charlotte is one of the nation's most important marketing centers for synthetic fibers, dyes, and other textile chemicals. The Charlotte Apparel Center for the Carolina-Virginia Fashion Exhibitors provides retail, exhibition, and showroom space for the textile industry.

For three years running in the 1990s, Charlotte (along with Raleigh-Durham) was identified in a Louis Harris poll as the nation's best mid-sized city for business locations. As the subsidiary headquarters for a variety of major national companies, its urban region continues to attract sophisticated industries such as micro-electronics, metal working and vehicle assembly, as well as research and development, high-technology and service-oriented international and domestic firms. Metro Charlotte has more than eleven hundred manufacturing firms and 361 of the largest industrial and service companies in the United States have facilities in the area.

Providing air service in and out of the city, Charlotte/Douglas International Airport ranked fifty-seventh worldwide in annual air-cargo volume in 1990. Both domestic and international air freight moves quickly and economically to its destination. According to an FAA-sponsored joint industry and government task force report, passenger enplanements at the airport are slated to increase by 54 percent by the year 2000, and major expansion is in the planning. Charlotte also serves as a major hub for small package express. Nine air couriers have Charlotte operations in addition to commercial passenger carriers and large freight forwarders.

Charlotte is at the center of the largest consolidated rail system in the United States. Two major rail systems, Norfolk Southern Railway and CSX Transportation link 27,000 miles of rail systems between the region and twenty-two states in the eastern half of the country. Nearly three hundred trains pass through the city each week.

Over 200 trucking companies move products and materials through the area. One-third of the nation's 100 largest trucking firms have Charlotte operations.

With more than seventeen thousand hotel rooms, Charlotte has become the major business travel center in the Carolinas and a prime meeting and convention center in the Southeast. The New Charlotte Convention Center, which will open in November 1994, is a state-of-the-art facility measuring 850,000 square feet. The exhibit space of 276,800 square feet is divisible into one to four halls. There are forty-six meeting rooms, a deluxe hotel-quality ballroom measuring thirty-five thousand square feet, and wide, light-filled concourses that converge at the heart of the center, the Grand Hall.

Driving time to the airport is usually no more than twenty minutes from home or office. For motor travel to the region, Interstates 77 and 85 intersect in Charlotte, and I-40 is a half-hour away.

Population (1990)

Total Population and Growth Rate
1990: 1,162,093
1980: 971,447
1970: 840,347
Growth rate 1970–1990: 38%

Race and Hispanic Origin
White: 78.5%
Black: 19.9%
Asian/Pacific Islander: 1.0%
Native American: 0.4%
Hispanic origin: 0.9%
White not Hispanic: 77.9%

Age
Ages 18 to 20: 4.9%
Ages 21 to 24: 6.2%
Ages 25 to 44: 34.1%
Ages 45 to 54: 10.7%
Ages 55 to 59: 4.4%
Ages 60 to 64: 4.1%
Ages 65 plus: 10.9%

Educational Attainment (1990)
Percent having completed high school: 72.5%
Percent having completed college: 19.6%
Elementary and high school enrollment: 190,748

Federal Funds and Grants Received
Total received in 1989: $2,153,700,000
Funds received per capita: $1,937

Civilian Labor Force
1993 (April):   660,664
1992 average: 657,200
1991 average: 644,336
1990 average: 643,839

Unemployment
1993 (April):   4.7%
1992 average: 5.5%
1991 average: 5.3%
1990 average: 3.5%

Average Annual Pay
1988: $20,697

1987: $19,806
1985: $17,773

Per Capita Personal Income
1991: $18,757
1990: $18,562
1989: $17,502

Business Climate (1987)

Manufacturing
Number of establishments in 1987: 2,276
Shipments in 1987 ($1,000): $17,637,700
Employees in 1987: 155,400
Change in employment, 1982 to 1987: 5.4%
Average annual pay for manufacturing work in 1989: $23,088
Average annual pay for production work in 1987: $16,969

Wholesale Trade
Number of establishments in 1987: 3,394
Total sales in 1987 ($1,000): $25,749,200
Change in sales, 1982 to 1987: 61.0%

Retail Trade
Number of establishments in 1987: 6,992
Total sales in 1987 ($1,000): $25,749,200
Retail sales per household in 1987: $18,444
Average annual pay in 1989: $12,768

Service Industry
Selected receipts in 1987 ($1,000): $3,249,100
Average annual pay in 1989: $19,176

Office Real Estate (1992)
Office space inventory: 18,770,000 square feet
Average class A Central Business District rental range per sq. ft: $21.00

Vacancy Rates
All areas: 18.0%

Vacancy Rates in Central Business District
Class A space: 20.0%
Class B space: 19.0%

Vacancy Rates Outside Central Business District
Class A space: 12.0%
Class B space: 23.0%

Housing
Total number of units in 1990: 472,913
Occupied units in 1990: 440,670
Owner-occupied units in 1990: 66.8%
1993 ACCRA average cost: $115,800
1993 ACCRA average rent for an apartment: $412

Chamber of Commerce
Charlotte Chamber of Commerce, Carroll D. Gray, President, 129 W. Trade St., PO Box 32785, Charlotte, NC 28232. 704-377-6911

Economic Development Office
Gaston County Economic Development Commisssion,

Donny Hicks, Exec. Director, 2551 Pembroke Rd., PO Box 2339, Gastonia, NC 28053. 704-867-4771, FAX 704-861-8302

Economic Development Organizations
Rock Hill Economic Development Corp., Stephen S. Turner, Director, 155 Johnston St., PO Box 11706, Rock Hill, SC 29731. 800-872-2994, 803-329-7090, FAX 803-329-7007

York County Economic Development Board, Mark Ferris, Director, PO Box 10995, Rock Hill, SC 29730. 803-324-3058, FAX 803-324-2354

Major Businesses

Company	SIC	Telephone
Associated Brokers Inc.	5141	(704) 357-1973
Barclays American Corp.	6153	(704) 339-5000
Biggers Brothers Inc.	5148	(704) 394-7121
Carolina Freight Carriers	4213	(704) 435-6811
Carolina Freight Corp.	4213	(704) 435-6811
Charlotte Mecklenburg Hospital	8062	(704) 338-2000
Coca-Cola Bottling Consolidated	2086	(704) 551-4400
Collins & Aikman Corp.	2221	(704) 547-8500
Duke Power Co.	4911	(704) 373-4011
Family Dollar Stores Inc.	5331	(704) 847-6961
Fiber Industries Inc.	2824	(704) 357-2000
First United National Bank of North Carolina	6021	(704) 374-6565
First Union Corp.	6021	(704) 374-6565
Georgetown Industries Inc.	3312	(704) 366-6901
Globe Indemnity Co.	6331	(704) 522-2000
Harris Teeter, Inc.	5411	(704) 845-3100
Jones Group Inc.	1542	(704) 553-3000
Jones J. A. Construction Co.	1542	(704) 553-3000
Lance, Inc.	2052	(704) 554-1421
Marine Midland Mortgage Co.	6162	(704) 542-1593
Mc Devitt & Street Co.	1542	(704) 357-1919
Metric Constructors Inc.	1541	(704) 554-1415
NCNB National Bank of North Carolina	6021	(704) 374-5000
Nucor Corp.	3312	(704) 366-7000
Piedmont Natural Gas Co.	4924	(704) 364-3120
Royal Group Inc.	6331	(704) 522-2000
Royal Insurance Co of America	6311	(704) 522-2000
Ruddick Corp.	5411	(704) 372-5404
Street Enterprises, Inc.	1541	(704) 357-1919
United Dominion Industries	1541	(704) 347-6800

Colleges and Universities
Central Piedmont Community College, Charlotte
Johnson C. Smith University, Charlotte
Phillips Junior College of Charlotte, Charlotte
Queens College, Charlotte
University of North Carolina at Charlotte, Charlotte

FAYETTEVILLE, NC (MSA)

Geographic Profile

Land Area

653.1 square miles

Counties and Parishes

Cumberland

Ranking Highlights

262 *out of 319 in total* **land area**

135 *out of 319 in* **population growth,** *1970–1990*

128 *out of 310 in having the lowest* **unemployment** *rate*

186 *out of 310 in size of* **labor force**

206 *out of 318 in the percentage of* **college graduates**

281 *out of 292 in per capita personal* **income**

251 *out of 319 in number of* **manufacturing establishments**

298 *out of 318 in* **physicians** *per 1000 people*

296 *out of 318 in* **hospital beds** *per 1000 people*

253 *out of 267 in fewest* **crimes** *per 1000 people*

219 *out of 266 in fewest* **violent crimes** *per 1000 people*

11 *out of 319 in per capita* **federal funds and grants**

Quality of Life Indexes (Rate per 1000 population)

Crime rate in 1991:	90.5
Violent crime rate in 1991:	9.7
Physicians rate in 1992:	1.07
Hospital bed rate in 1991:	2.13

ACCRA Cost of Living Indexes

(First quarter 1993, average = 100)

Composite index:	96.5
Utilities index:	102.3
Housing index:	85.9

Population (1990)

Total Population and Growth Rate

1990: 274,566

1980: 247,160

1970: 212,042

Growth rate 1970–1990: 29%

Race and Hispanic Origin

White: 61.9%

Black: 31.9%

Asian/Pacific Islander: 2.1%

Native American: 1.6%

Hispanic origin: 4.8%

White not Hispanic: 60.1%

Age

Ages 18 to 20: 7.3%

Ages 21 to 24: 9.8%

Ages 25 to 44: 33.9%

Ages 45 to 54: 8.4%

Ages 55 to 59: 3.6%

Ages 60 to 64: 2.9%

Ages 65 plus: 6.1%

Educational Attainment (1990)

Percent having completed high school: 80.3%

Percent having completed college: 16.6%

Elementary and high school enrollment: 48,559

Federal Funds and Grants Received

Total received in 1989: $1,998,000,000

Funds received per capita: $7,814

Civilian Labor Force

1993 (April):	105,285
1992 average:	101,619
1991 average:	97,599
1990 average:	96,162

Unemployment

1993 (April): 6.4%

1992 average: 6.5%

1991 average: 6.4%

1990 average: 4.6%

Average Annual Pay

1988: $17,549

1987: $16,417

1985: $15,135

Per Capita Personal Income

1991: $13,582

1990: $12,933

1989: $12,497

Business Climate (1987)

Manufacturing

Number of establishments in 1987: 146

Shipments in 1987 ($1,000): $2,051,400

Employees in 1987: 11,600

Change in employment, 1982 to 1987: 12.6%

Average annual pay for manufacturing work in 1989: $24,149

Average annual pay for production work in 1987: $22,364

Wholesale Trade

Number of establishments in 1987: 268

Total sales in 1987 ($1,000): $564,500

Change in sales, 1982 to 1987: -1.5%

Retail Trade

Number of establishments in 1987: 1,468

Total sales in 1987 ($1,000): $564,500

Retail sales per household in 1987: $17,650

Average annual pay in 1989: $10,736

Service Industry

Selected receipts in 1987 ($1,000): $418,000

Average annual pay in 1989: $14,258

Housing

Total number of units in 1990: 98,360

Occupied units in 1990: 91,500
Owner-occupied units in 1990: 57.7%
1993 ACCRA average cost: $97,200
1993 ACCRA average rent for an apartment: $434

Chamber of Commerce

Fayetteville Area Chamber of Commerce, John H. Swope, Exec. Vice President, 519 Ramsey St., PO Box 9, Fayetteville, NC 28301. 919-483-8133

Economic Development Office

Fayetteville Area Economic Development Corp., Danny G. Fone, Exec. Director, 519 Ramsey, PO Box 1865, Fayetteville, NC 28302. 919-483-3408, FAX 919-483-0236

Major Businesses

Company	SIC	Telephone
AAA Co. Inc.	5731	(919) 864-1322
Barnes, J. J. Inc.	1711	(919) 483-7171
Bryan Pontiac-Cadillac Co.	5511	(919) 483-1234
Cape Fear Supply Co. Inc.	5031	(919) 864-1776
Cumberland County Hospital	8062	(919) 323-6700
Dickinson Buick Co	5511	(919) 864-2411
Hercules Steel Co.	3441	(919) 488-5110
Holt Oil Co. Inc.	5171	(919) 483-5137
Lafayette Motor Sales Inc.	5511	(919) 424-0281
Li'l Thrift Food Marts Inc.	5411	(919) 433-4490
Mc Donald Lumber Co. Inc.	5211	(919) 483-0381
Mid-Atlantic Holdings Inc.	6141	(919) 485-4101
Mid-South Insurance Co.	6321	(919) 483-3185
North Crolina Natural Gas	4923	(919) 483-0315
Pate-Derby Co.	5142	(919) 483-2131
Patrick Ford Inc.	5511	(919) 867-1121
Powers-Swain Chevrolet Inc.	5511	(919) 864-9500
Public Works Commission	4931	(919) 483-1401
Quick Stop Food Mart Inc.	5541	(919) 483-9021
Shaw Food Service, Inc.	5812	(919) 323-5303
Soffe, M. J. Co.	2329	(919) 483-2500
Stewart Oldsmobile Inc.	5511	(919) 323-4400
Triangle Building Supply	5031	(919) 867-9165
Williford's Seafood	5146	(919) 483-2271

Colleges and Universities

Fayetteville State University, Fayetteville
Fayetteville Technical Community College, Fayetteville
Methodist College, Fayetteville
Phillips Junior College of Fayetteville, Fayetteville

GREENSBORO–WINSTON–SALEM–HIGH POINT, NC (MSA)

Geographic Profile

Land Area
3452.2 square miles

Counties and Parishes
Davidson
Davie
Forsyth
Guilford
Randolph
Stokes
Yadkin

Ranking Highlights

37 *out of 319 in total* **land area**
152 *out of 319 in* **population growth,** *1970–1990*
56 *out of 310 in having the lowest* **unemployment** *rate*
48 *out of 310 in size of* **labor force**
153 *out of 318 in the percentage of* **college graduates**
80 *out of 292 in per capita personal* **income**
38 *out of 319 in number of* **manufacturing establishments**
99 *out of 318 in* **physicians** *per 1000 people*
185 *out of 318 in* **hospital beds** *per 1000 people*
154 *out of 267 in fewest* **crimes** *per 1000 people*
167 *out of 266 in fewest* **violent crimes** *per 1000 people*
238 *out of 319 in per capita* **federal funds and grants**

Quality of Life Indexes (Rate per 1000 population)

Crime rate in 1991: 64.4
Violent crime rate in 1991: 7.3
Physicians rate in 1992: 2.23
Hospital bed rate in 1991: 3.56

ACCRA Cost of Living Indexes

(First quarter 1993, average = 100)
Composite index: 96.2
Utilities index: 106.0
Housing index: 94.8

Population (1990)

Total Population and Growth Rate
1990: 942,091
1980: 851,444
1970: 742,984
Growth rate 1970–1990: 27%

Race and Hispanic Origin
White: 79.4%
Black: 19.3%
Asian/Pacific Islander: 0.7%
Native American: 0.3%

Hispanic origin: 0.8%
White not Hispanic: 79.0%

Age

Ages 18 to 20: 5.1%
Ages 21 to 24: 6.2%
Ages 25 to 44: 33.1%
Ages 45 to 54: 11.2%
Ages 55 to 59: 4.7%
Ages 60 to 64: 4.6%
Ages 65 plus: 12.2%

Educational Attainment (1990)

Percent having completed high school: 72.0%
Percent having completed college: 19.2%
Elementary and high school enrollment: 145,956

Federal Funds and Grants Received

Total received in 1989: $2,351,200,000
Funds received per capita: $2,543

Civilian Labor Force

1993 (April): 536,346
1992 average: 533,458
1991 average: 520,930
1990 average: 521,212

Unemployment

1993 (April): 4.3%
1992 average: 5.1%
1991 average: 5.1%
1990 average: 3.7%

Average Annual Pay

1988: $20,204
1987: $19,150
1985: $17,528

Per Capita Personal Income

1991: $18,943
1990: $18,661
1989: $17,965

Business Climate (1987)

Manufacturing

Number of establishments in 1987: 1,977
Shipments in 1987 ($1,000): $18,949,300
Employees in 1987: 149,900
Change in employment, 1982 to 1987: 0%
Average annual pay for manufacturing work in 1989: $24,642
Average annual pay for production work in 1987: $17,648

Wholesale Trade

Number of establishments in 1987: 2,207
Total sales in 1987 ($1,000): $9,295,800
Change in sales, 1982 to 1987: 27.9%

Retail Trade

Number of establishments in 1987: 6,032
Total sales in 1987 ($1,000): $9,295,800

Retail sales per household in 1987: $17,763
Average annual pay in 1989: $12,114

Service Industry

Selected receipts in 1987 ($1,000): $2,236,300
Average annual pay in 1989: $18,282

Office Real Estate (1992)

Office space inventory: 23,625,000 square feet
Average class A Central Business District rental range per sq. ft: $17.00

Vacancy Rates

All areas: 12.5%

Vacancy Rates in Central Business District

Class A space: 12.1%
Class B space: 12.6%

Vacancy Rates Outside Central Business District

Class A space: 12.1%
Class B space: 12.6%

Housing

Total number of units in 1990: 399,004
Occupied units in 1990: 372,141
Owner-occupied units in 1990: 67.3%
1993 ACCRA average cost: $114,780
1993 ACCRA average rent for an apartment: $416

Chamber of Commerce

Greensboro Area Chamber of Commerce, T.Z. Osborne, President, 330 S. Greene St., PO Box 3246, Greensboro, NC 27402. 919-275-8675

Economic Development Office

Winston-Salem Business Inc., Robert E. Leak, Jr., President, 1920 W. 1st St., Suite 700, Winston-Salem, NC 27104. 919-723-8955, FAX 919-761-1069

Economic Development Organizations

Economic Development Commission, Daniel A. Lynch, Director, 211 S. Hamilton St., PO Box 230, High Point, NC 27261. 919-883-3419

Major Businesses

Company	SIC	Telephone
1st Home Federal Savings & Loan	6035	(919) 373-5000
Adams-Millis Corp.	2252	(919) 887-9200
Blue Bell Inc.	2325	(919) 373-3400
Burlington Industries Inc.	2211	(919) 379-2000
Carolina Medicorp Inc.	8062	(919) 760-5000
Carolina Steel Corp.	3441	(919) 275-9711
Carolina Steel Holdings	5051	(919) 275-9711
Cone, Moses H. Memorial Hospital	8062	(919) 379-3900
Culp, Inc.	2221	(919) 889-5161
Fieldcrest Cannon, Inc.	2211	(919) 665-4300
First Wachovia Corp.	6021	(919) 770-4000

Major Businesses (Continued)

Company	SIC	Telephone
Forsyth Memorial Hosptial	8062	(919) 760-5000
Galey And Lord, Inc.	2262	(919) 665-3037
Gilbarco Inc.	3586	(919) 547-5000
Guilford Mills Inc.	2258	(919) 292-7550
Halstead Industries, Inc.	3351	(919) 272-1966
Hanes Companies Inc.	5131	(919) 725-1391
Hanes Holding Co.	5131	(919) 725-1391
Integon General Insurance	6331	(919) 770-2000
Integon Life Insurance Co.	6311	(919) 770-2000
Jeffersn-Plot Life Insurance	6311	(919) 547-4000
Jefferson Pilot Corp.	6311	(919) 378-2011
Kayser-Roth Hosiery Inc.	2251	(919) 852-2030
Klaussner Corp.	2519	(919) 625-6174
Klaussner Furniture Industries	2512	(919) 625-6174
Ladd Furniture Inc.	2511	(919) 889-0333
Lowe's Food Stores Inc.	5411	(919) 659-0180
North Carolina Baptist Hospital	8062	(919) 748-2011
Old Dominion Freight Line	4213	(919) 889-5000
Piece Goods Shops Co.	5949	(919) 768-3930
Planters Lifesavers Co.	2068	(919) 741-2000
Reynolds R. J. Tobacco Co.	2111	(919) 741-5000
Reynolds R. J. Tobacco International	5194	(919) 741-5000
Salem Carpet Mills Inc.	2273	(919) 727-1200
Sara Lee Knit Products	2254	(919) 744-2400
Thomasville Furniture	2511	(919) 472-4000
Unifi Inc.	2282	(919) 294-4410
Universal Furniture Industries	2511	(919) 861-7200
Volvo G M Heavy Truck Corp.	3711	(919) 279-2000
Wachovia Bank & Trust Co.	6021	(919) 770-5000
Wachovia Corp.	6021	(919) 770-5000
Williams, A. T. Oil Co.	5541	(919) 767-6280
Work Wear Corp. Inc.	2326	(919) 299-5050

Colleges and Universities

Bennett College, Greensboro
Forsyth Technical Community College, Winston-Salem
Greensboro College, Greensboro
Guilford College, Greensboro
High Point College, High Point
John Wesley College, High Point
North Carolina Agricultural and Technical State University, Greensboro
North Carolina School of the Arts, Winston-Salem
Rutledge College of Greensboro, Greensboro
Rutledge College of Winston-Salem, Winston-Salem
Salem College, Winston-Salem
University of North Carolina at Greensboro, Greensboro
Wake Forest University, Winston-Salem

HICKORY–MORGANTON, NC (MSA)

Geographic Profile

Land Area
1167.1 square miles

Counties and Parishes
Alexander
Burke
Catawba

Ranking Highlights

173 *out of 319 in total* **land area**
130 *out of 319 in* **population growth**, *1970–1990*
69 *out of 310 in having the lowest* **unemployment** *rate*
155 *out of 310 in size of* **labor force**
294 *out of 318 in the percentage of* **college graduates**
201 *out of 292 in per capita personal* **income**
75 *out of 319 in number of* **manufacturing establishments**
258 *out of 318 in* **physicians** *per 1000 people*
195 *out of 318 in* **hospital beds** *per 1000 people*
56 *out of 267 in fewest* **crimes** *per 1000 people*
90 *out of 266 in fewest* **violent crimes** *per 1000 people*
313 *out of 319 in per capita* **federal funds and grants**

Quality of Life Indexes (Rate per 1000 population)

Crime rate in 1991: 44.4
Violent crime rate in 1991: 4.4
Physicians rate in 1992: 1.34
Hospital bed rate in 1991: 3.47

ACCRA Cost of Living Indexes
(First quarter 1993, average = 100)
Composite index: 98.4
Utilities index: 106.4
Housing index: 104.5

Population (1990)

Total Population and Growth Rate
1990: 221,700
1980: 202,711
1970: 170,703
Growth rate 1970–1990: 30%

Race and Hispanic Origin
White: 90.9%
Black: 7.9%
Asian/Pacific Islander: 0.8%
Native American: 0.2%
Hispanic origin: 0.7%
White not Hispanic: 90.5%

Age
Ages 18 to 20: 4.6%
Ages 21 to 24: 5.8%
Ages 25 to 44: 32.2%

Ages 45 to 54: 11.8%
Ages 55 to 59: 5%
Ages 60 to 64: 4.6%
Ages 65 plus: 12.2%

Educational Attainment (1990)

Percent having completed high school: 63.5%
Percent having completed college: 12.2%
Elementary and high school enrollment: 36,465

Federal Funds and Grants Received

Total received in 1989: $385,900,000
Funds received per capita: $1,737

Civilian Labor Force

1993 (April): 133,683
1992 average: 132,633
1991 average: 133,271
1990 average: 131,444

Unemployment

1993 (April): 4.1%
1992 average: 5.4%
1991 average: 6.0%
1990 average: 4.1%

Average Annual Pay

1988: $17,390
1987: $16,709
1985: $15,109

Per Capita Personal Income

1991: $16,247
1990: $15,987
1989: $15,242

Business Climate (1987)

Manufacturing

Number of establishments in 1987: 852
Shipments in 1987 ($1,000): $4,821,100
Employees in 1987: 65,800
Change in employment, 1982 to 1987: 15.2%
Average annual pay for manufacturing work in 1989: $18,625
Average annual pay for production work in 1987: $14,552

Wholesale Trade

Number of establishments in 1987: 384
Total sales in 1987 ($1,000): $1,756,000
Change in sales, 1982 to 1987: 55.2%

Retail Trade

Number of establishments in 1987: 1,535
Total sales in 1987 ($1,000): $1,756,000
Retail sales per household in 1987: $16,540
Average annual pay in 1989: $11,177

Service Industry

Selected receipts in 1987 ($1,000): $368,300
Average annual pay in 1989: $16,947

Housing

Total number of units in 1990: 91,964
Occupied units in 1990: 85,215
Owner-occupied units in 1990: 74.7%
1993 ACCRA average cost: $125,375
1993 ACCRA average rent for an apartment: $435

Chamber of Commerce

Catawba County Chamber of Commerce, Charles P. Ewart, Exec. Vice President, 470 Hwy. 70 S.W., PO Box 1828, Hickory, NC 28603. 704-328-6111

Major Businesses

Company	SIC	Telephone
Alcatel Inc.	6719	(704) 323-1120
Carolina Mills Inc.	2281	(704) 428-9911
Carolina Truck Centers Inc.	5511	(704) 328-8156
Catawba Memorial Hospital	8062	(704) 322-0450
Century Furniture Co.	2511	(704) 328-1851
Classic Leather Inc.	2512	(704) 328-2046
Clement Brothers Co.	1629	(704) 322-2850
Clement Corp.	1629	(704) 322-2850
Comm/Scope Inc.	3357	(704) 241-3142
Drillers Service Inc.	5084	(704) 322-1100
Institution Food House Inc.	5142	(704) 328-5301
Merchants Distributors	5141	(704) 323-4100
Ridgeview Inc.	2251	(704) 464-2972
Sherrill Furniture Co.	2512	(704) 322-2640
Shuford Mills Inc.	2672	(704) 328-2131
Snyder Paper Corp.	5113	(704) 328-2501
T & H Service Merchandise	5122	(704) 328-5511
Thomas & Howard Co.	5141	(704) 464-1010
VWR Textiles & Supplies	5131	(704) 322-6980
WSMP Inc.	5812	(704) 459-7626

Colleges and Universities

Catawba Valley Community College, Hickory
Lenoir-Rhyne College, Hickory

JACKSONVILLE, NC (MSA)

Geographic Profile

Land Area

766.9 square miles

Counties and Parishes

Onslow

Ranking Highlights

242 *out of 319 in total* **land area**

81 *out of 319 in* **population growth**, *1970–1990*

69 *out of 310 in having the lowest* **unemployment** *rate*

303 *out of 310 in size of* **labor force**

275 *out of 318 in the percentage of* **college graduates**

289 *out of 292 in per capita personal* **income**

319 *out of 319 in number of* **manufacturing establishments**

318 *out of 318 in* **physicians** *per 1000 people*

318 *out of 318 in* **hospital beds** *per 1000 people*

81 *out of 267 in fewest* **crimes** *per 1000 people*

76 *out of 266 in fewest* **violent crimes** *per 1000 people*

5 *out of 319 in per capita* **federal funds and grants**

Quality of Life Indexes (Rate per 1000 population)

Crime rate in 1991:   49.3

Violent crime rate in 1991:   4.0

Physicians rate in 1992:   0.77

Hospital bed rate in 1991:   0.89

ACCRA Cost of Living Indexes

(First quarter 1993, average = 100)

Composite index: N/A

Utilities index: N/A

Housing index: N/A

Population (1990)

Total Population and Growth Rate

1990: 149,838

1980: 112,784

1970: 103,126

Growth rate 1970–1990: 45%

Race and Hispanic Origin

White: 74.7%

Black: 19.9%

Asian/Pacific Islander: 2.0%

Native American: 0.6%

Hispanic origin: 5.4%

White not Hispanic: 72.7%

Age

Ages 18 to 20: 10.8%

Ages 21 to 24: 16.4%

Ages 25 to 44: 33.6%

Ages 45 to 54: 5.8%

Ages 55 to 59: 2.4%

Ages 60 to 64: 2.1%

Ages 65 plus: 4.5%

Educational Attainment (1990)

Percent having completed high school: 83.0%

Percent having completed college: 13.4%

Elementary and high school enrollment: 20,983

Federal Funds and Grants Received

Total received in 1989: $1,133,900,000

Funds received per capita: $8,967

Civilian Labor Force

1993 (April):   40,260

1992 average: 40,279

1991 average: 39,369

1990 average: 39,173

Unemployment

1993 (April): 5.9%

1992 average: 5.4%

1991 average: 5.6%

1990 average: 3.9%

Average Annual Pay

1988: $13,856

1987: $13,246

1985: $12,482

Per Capita Personal Income

1991: $10,537

1990: $9,879

1989: $10,431

Business Climate (1987)

Manufacturing

Number of establishments in 1987: 48

Shipments in 1987 ($1,000): $251,500

Employees in 1987: 3,000

Change in employment, 1982 to 1987: 25.0%

Average annual pay for manufacturing work in 1989: $14,824

Average annual pay for production work in 1987: $12,000

Wholesale Trade

Number of establishments in 1987: 85

Total sales in 1987 ($1,000): $101,500

Change in sales, 1982 to 1987: -2.9%

Retail Trade

Number of establishments in 1987: 761

Total sales in 1987 ($1,000): $101,500

Retail sales per household in 1987: $17,059

Average annual pay in 1989: $9,463

Service Industry

Selected receipts in 1987 ($1,000): $116,900

Average annual pay in 1989: $12,516

Housing

Total number of units in 1990: 47,526

Occupied units in 1990: 40,658
Owner-occupied units in 1990: 53.7%
1993 ACCRA average cost: N/A
1993 ACCRA average rent for an apartment: N/A

Chamber of Commerce

Greater Jacksonville/Onslow Chamber of Commerce, Jeffrey P. Downin, Exec. Vice President, 1 Marine Blvd. N., PO Box 765, Jacksonville, NC 28541. 919-347-3141

Economic Development Office

Onslow County EDC, President, 109 Old Bridge St., Room 108, Jacksonville, NC 28540. 919-346-9164

Major Businesses

Company	SIC	Telephone
Atlantic Coast Foods Inc.	5812	(919) 455-8111
Bailey & Associates Inc.	1542	(919) 346-4191
Belk's Dept Jacksonville	5311	(919) 353-8490
Cardinal Motors Inc.	5511	(919) 353-7700
Furniture Fair Inc.	5712	(919) 455-9595
Kennedy Oldsmobile & GMC	5511	(919) 455-1727
Lejeune Motor Co.	5511	(919) 455-1551
Marine Chevrolet Co. Inc.	5511	(919) 455-2121
National Dodge Inc.	5511	(919) 353-3777
Onslow Memorial Hospital	8062	(919) 577-2345
Padgett Motors	5511	(919) 353-1515
R & W Construction Co.	1623	(919) 455-1830
Rand Oil Co. Inc.	5171	(919) 324-3025
Rose Bros. Furniture of Jacksonville	5712	(919) 455-4424
Sanders Ford Inc.	5511	(919) 455-1911
Southerland Electric Co.	1731	(919) 347-1754

Colleges and Universities

Coastal Carolina Community College, Jacksonville

RALEIGH–DURHAM, NC (MSA)

Geographic Profile

Land Area
2015.9 square miles

Counties and Parishes
Durham
Franklin
Orange
Wake

Additional Cities/Towns within Area
Chapel Hill

Ranking Highlights

91 *out of 319 in total* land area
55 *out of 319 in* population growth, *1970–1990*
15 *out of 310 in having the lowest* unemployment *rate*
60 *out of 310 in size of* labor force
10 *out of 318 in the percentage of* college graduates
47 *out of 292 in per capita personal* income
77 *out of 319 in number of* manufacturing establishments
7 *out of 318 in* physicians *per 1000 people*
104 *out of 318 in* hospital beds *per 1000 people*
163 *out of 267 in fewest* crimes *per 1000 people*
135 *out of 266 in fewest* violent crimes *per 1000 people*
118 *out of 319 in per capita* federal funds and grants

Quality of Life Indexes (Rate per 1000 population)

Crime rate in 1991:	66.0
Violent crime rate in 1991:	6.4
Physicians rate in 1992:	4.82
Hospital bed rate in 1991:	4.58

ACCRA Cost of Living Indexes
(First quarter 1993, average = 100)
Composite index: 98.3
Utilities index: 110.0
Housing index: 97.9

Overview

For three years in the early 1990s, a Lou Harris poll rated Raleigh-Durham as one of the nation's top mid-sized cities for business locations, a designation earned because the Raleigh area was more insulated from the economic recession of the early 1990s than most other areas of the country. As the capital of North Carolina, as well as the county seat, Raleigh has city, county, state, and federal government offices and agencies. With the second largest school system in the state, as well as the many colleges and universities located in the area, education is a major employer.

Many recession-resistant high-technology and medical corporations have been attracted to Raleigh because of the outstanding educational and research facilities at area universities, such as North Carolina State University, which is home to the nation's tenth largest school of engineering, Duke University, and the University of North Carolina.

Research Triangle Park is one of the leading centers for high-technology research and development in the country. Roughly fifty corporate, academic, and government agencies in the Park employ more than thirty-two hundred workers and provide an annual payroll in excess of $1 billion.

Raleigh is an integral part of Norfolk Southern's rail service linking the east coast to Midwest markets and is in the center of CSX's 27,000 mile network serving twenty-two states and Canada. More than three hundred motor freight carriers operate in the area, which has more than forty motor freight terminals. The city is located within 500 miles of half the population of the United States. The state's 78,000-mile highway network makes the area a highway hub for the Northeast, Mid-Atlantic, and Southeast states, while providing rapid access to Midwest markets. The continuing development of the facilities at Raleigh-Durham Airport has also stimulated commercial shipping.

Raleigh-Durham International Airport, located 15 miles from downtown Raleigh, is the East Coast hub of American Airlines. Five major airlines and three commuter airlines serve the airport offering nearly three-hundred daily flights to national and international destinations, including Paris, Bermuda, St. Croix and St. Thomas, Cancun, Cozumel, and San Juan. Major airlines include American, Delta, USAir, TWA, and United. Raleigh can be reached by an extensive network of state highways and roads. Major highways approaching the city include Interstate-40, which runs east and west; U.S. Highways 1 and 401, which run north and south; U.S. Highways 64 and 70, which run east and west; and North Carolina Highways 50 (north) and 54 (west). Carolina Trailways and Greyhound Bus Lines provide service to points in the eastern United States, and AMTRAK offers rail service.

Population (1990)

Total Population and Growth Rate
1990: 735,480
1980: 560,774
1970: 446,074
Growth rate 1970–1990: 65%

Race and Hispanic Origin
White: 72.5%
Black: 24.9%
Asian/Pacific Islander: 1.9%
Native American: 0.3%
Hispanic origin: 1.2%
White not Hispanic: 71.8%

Age
Ages 18 to 20: 6.3%
Ages 21 to 24: 8%
Ages 25 to 44: 37.5%
Ages 45 to 54: 9.9%
Ages 55 to 59: 3.6%
Ages 60 to 64: 3.3%
Ages 65 plus: 8.9%

Educational Attainment (1990)
Percent having completed high school: 82.4%
Percent having completed college: 34.8%
Elementary and high school enrollment: 107,599

Federal Funds and Grants Received
Total received in 1989: $2,323,200,000
Funds received per capita: $3,399

Civilian Labor Force
1993 (April):   458,485
1992 average: 449,405
1991 average: 428,873
1990 average: 420,302

Unemployment
1993 (April):   3.8%
1992 average: 3.9%
1991 average: 3.6%
1990 average: 2.5%

Average Annual Pay
1988: $21,208
1987: $20,366
1985: $18,513

Per Capita Personal Income
1991: $20,170
1990: $19,514
1989: $18,332

Business Climate (1987)

Manufacturing
Number of establishments in 1987: 834
Shipments in 1987 ($1,000): $9,346,100
Employees in 1987: 59,400
Change in employment, 1982 to 1987: 15.8%
Average annual pay for manufacturing work in 1989: $30,578
Average annual pay for production work in 1987: $18,407

Wholesale Trade
Number of establishments in 1987: 1,313
Total sales in 1987 ($1,000): $6,546,700
Change in sales, 1982 to 1987: 66.1%

Retail Trade
Number of establishments in 1987: 4,599
Total sales in 1987 ($1,000): $6,546,700
Retail sales per household in 1987: $19,228
Average annual pay in 1989: $11,449

Service Industry
Selected receipts in 1987 ($1,000): $2,391,300
Average annual pay in 1989: $20,192

Office Real Estate (1992)

Office space inventory: 15,764,131 square feet

Average class A Central Business District rental range per sq. ft: $17.50

Vacancy Rates

All areas: 11.0%

Vacancy Rates in Central Business District

Class A space: 20.2%

Class B space: 10.8%

Vacancy Rates Outside Central Business District

Class A space: 8.8%

Class B space: 11.7%

Housing

Total number of units in 1990: 308,496

Occupied units in 1990: 287,647

Owner-occupied units in 1990: 58.9%

1993 ACCRA average cost: $113,760

1993 ACCRA average rent for an apartment: $480

Chamber of Commerce

Greater Raleigh Chamber of Commerce, R. Marc Jordan, President, 800 S. Salisbury St., PO Box 2978, Raleigh, NC, 27602. 919-833-3005

Major Businesses

Company	SIC	Telephone
Acton Corp.	6331	(919) 781-5611
Alcatel National Network System	3661	(919) 850-6000
Amerimark Building Products	3442	(919) 876-9333
B N R Inc.	8731	(919) 991-7000
Blue Cross Blue Shield	6324	(919) 489-7431
Burroughs Wellcome Co.	2834	(919) 248-3000
Carolina Power & Light Co.	4911	(919) 546-6111
CCB Financial Corp.	6022	(919) 683-7777
Durham Corp.	6311	(919) 782-6110
Durham Life Insurance Co.	6311	(919) 881-1100
Exide Electronics Group	3629	(919) 872-3020
First Citizens Bancshares	6022	(919) 755-7000
General Electric Mortage Capital	6719	(919) 846-4100
General Electric Mortage Insurance Co.	6351	(919) 846-4100
General Parts Inc.	5013	(919) 876-9813
Glaxo Inc.	2834	(919) 248-2100
Golden Corral Corp.	5812	(919) 781-9310
Investors Management Corp.	6531	(919) 781-9310
Liggett Group Inc.	2111	(919) 683-9000
Montrose Pantry Acquisition	5411	(919) 286-7000
North Carolina Farm Bureau Mutual Insurance	6331	(919) 782-1705
North Carolina Memorial Hospital	8062	(919) 966-5111
North Carolina Municipal Power	4911	(919) 832-9924

Major Businesses (Continued)

Company	SIC	Telephone
North Carolina Eastern Municipal Power	4911	(919) 832-9924
Peoples Security Life Insurance Co.	6311	(919) 687-8200
Qualex Inc.	7384	(919) 383-8535
SAS Institute Inc.	7371	(919) 677-8000
Texfi Industries Inc.	2221	(919) 783-4736

Colleges and Universities

Duke University, Durham

Durham Technical Community College, Durham

Meredith College, Raleigh

North Carolina Central University, Durham

North Carolina State University, Raleigh

Peace College, Raleigh

Phillips Junior College, Hardbarger Campus, Raleigh

Phillips Junior College of Raleigh, Raleigh

Shaw University, Raleigh

St. Augustine's College, Raleigh

St. Mary's College, Raleigh

University of North Carolina at Chapel Hill, Chapel Hill

Wake Technical Community College, Raleigh

WILMINGTON, NC (MSA)

Geographic Profile

Land Area

198.9 square miles

Counties and Parishes

New Hanover

Ranking Highlights

318 *out of 319 in total* **land area**

83 *out of 319 in* **population growth,** *1970–1990*

149 *out of 310 in having the lowest* **unemployment** *rate*

236 *out of 310 in size of* **labor force**

114 *out of 318 in the percentage of* **college graduates**

120 *out of 292 in per capita personal* **income**

243 *out of 319 in number of* **manufacturing establishments**

44 *out of 318 in* **physicians** *per 1000 people*

100 *out of 318 in* **hospital beds** *per 1000 people*

260 *out of 267 in fewest* **crimes** *per 1000 people*

190 *out of 266 in fewest* **violent crimes** *per 1000 people*

216 *out of 319 in per capita* **federal funds and grants**

Quality of Life Indexes (Rate per 1000 population)

Crime rate in 1991:	97.7
Violent crime rate in 1991:	8.3
Physicians rate in 1992:	2.77
Hospital bed rate in 1991:	4.61

ACCRA Cost of Living Indexes

(First quarter 1993, average = 100)

Composite index:	N/A
Utilities index:	N/A
Housing index:	N/A

Population (1990)

Total Population and Growth Rate

1990: 120,284

1980: 103,471

1970: 82,996

Growth rate 1970–1990: 45%

Race and Hispanic Origin

White: 78.9%

Black: 20.0%

Asian/Pacific Islander: 0.5%

Native American: 0.4%

Hispanic origin: 0.8%

White not Hispanic: 78.4%

Age

Ages 18 to 20: 6%

Ages 21 to 24: 6.5%

Ages 25 to 44: 32.5%

Ages 45 to 54: 10.7%

Ages 55 to 59: 4.4%

Ages 60 to 64: 4.6%

Ages 65 plus: 12.6%

Educational Attainment (1990)

Percent having completed high school: 78.1%

Percent having completed college: 21.2%

Elementary and high school enrollment: 19,185

Federal Funds and Grants Received

Total received in 1989: $309,400,000

Funds received per capita: $2,636

Civilian Labor Force

1993 (April):	72,314
1992 average:	68,955
1991 average:	68,136
1990 average:	65,912

Unemployment

1993 (April):	6.3%
1992 average:	6.8%
1991 average:	5.9%
1990 average:	4.2%

Average Annual Pay

1988: $17,595

1987: $16,808

1985: $15,262

Per Capita Personal Income

1991: $17,840

1990: $17,690

1989: $16,327

Business Climate (1987)

Manufacturing

Number of establishments in 1987: 154

Shipments in 1987 ($1,000): $2,004,500

Employees in 1987: 11,100

Change in employment, 1982 to 1987: -5.1%

Average annual pay for manufacturing work in 1989: $26,005

Average annual pay for production work in 1987: $23,027

Wholesale Trade

Number of establishments in 1987: 282

Total sales in 1987 ($1,000): $820,800

Change in sales, 1982 to 1987: 0.6%

Retail Trade

Number of establishments in 1987: 1,088

Total sales in 1987 ($1,000): $820,800

Retail sales per household in 1987: $20,879

Average annual pay in 1989: $10,366

Service Industry

Selected receipts in 1987 ($1,000): $399,600

Average annual pay in 1989: $16,622

Housing

Total number of units in 1990: 57,076

Occupied units in 1990: 48,139
Owner-occupied units in 1990: 62.7%
1993 ACCRA average cost: N/A
1993 ACCRA average rent for an apartment: N/A

Chamber of Commerce

Greater Wilmington Chamber of Commerce, Joseph F. Augustine, Exec. Vice President, 514 Market St., PO Box 330, Wilmington, NC 28402. 919-762-2611

Major Businesses

Company	SIC	Telephone
Becker Builders Supply Co.	5031	(919) 791-7761
Brunswick Membership	4911	(919) 754-4391
Cape Fear Memorial Hospital	8062	(919) 395-8100
Cape Industries	2869	(919) 341-5500
Carolina Savings Bank	6035	(919) 341-3200
Carolina Yacht Sales	5551	(919) 256-9901
Coopertive Savings & Loan Association	6036	(919) 343-0181
Entrepreneur Inc.	5411	(919) 395-5300
H T Restaurants Inc.	5812	(919) 799-4261
Hobbs, W. K. Inc.	5172	(919) 762-9822
Industrial Sales Co.	5085	(919) 763-5126
King, Bob Pontiac GMC Inc.	5511	(919) 799-3520
Leader Construction Co.	1542	(919) 395-6821
Linde Gases of the Southern	5084	(919) 762-6653
Lyndale Enterprises Inc.	5122	(919) 799-3320
Miller Building Corp.	1541	(919) 256-2613
Murchison, J. W., Co.	5091	(919) 763-9000
Neuwirth Motors Inc.	5511	(919) 799-1815
New Hanover Memorial Hospital	8062	(919) 343-7000
Peoples Federal Savings	6035	(919) 763-9984
Presant Industrial Supply	5074	(919) 371-2266
Qualified Personnel Inc.	7361	(919) 763-0541
Reeds Jewelers Inc.	5944	(919) 350-3100
Rippy Cadillac Oldsmobile	5511	(919) 763-2421
Schaeffer Buick Inc.	5511	(919) 392-2700
Springer-Eubank Co. Inc.	5171	(919) 343-1991
Tallberg Chevrolet Inc.	5511	(919) 791-2929
Wilson, Boney & Sons Inc.	5411	(919) 395-5161
Worsley Companies	5172	(919) 395-5300
Wright Chemical Corp.	2869	(919) 251-0234

Colleges and Universities

Cape Fear Community College, Wilmington
Martin Community College, Williamston
University of North Carolina at Wilmington

NORTH DAKOTA

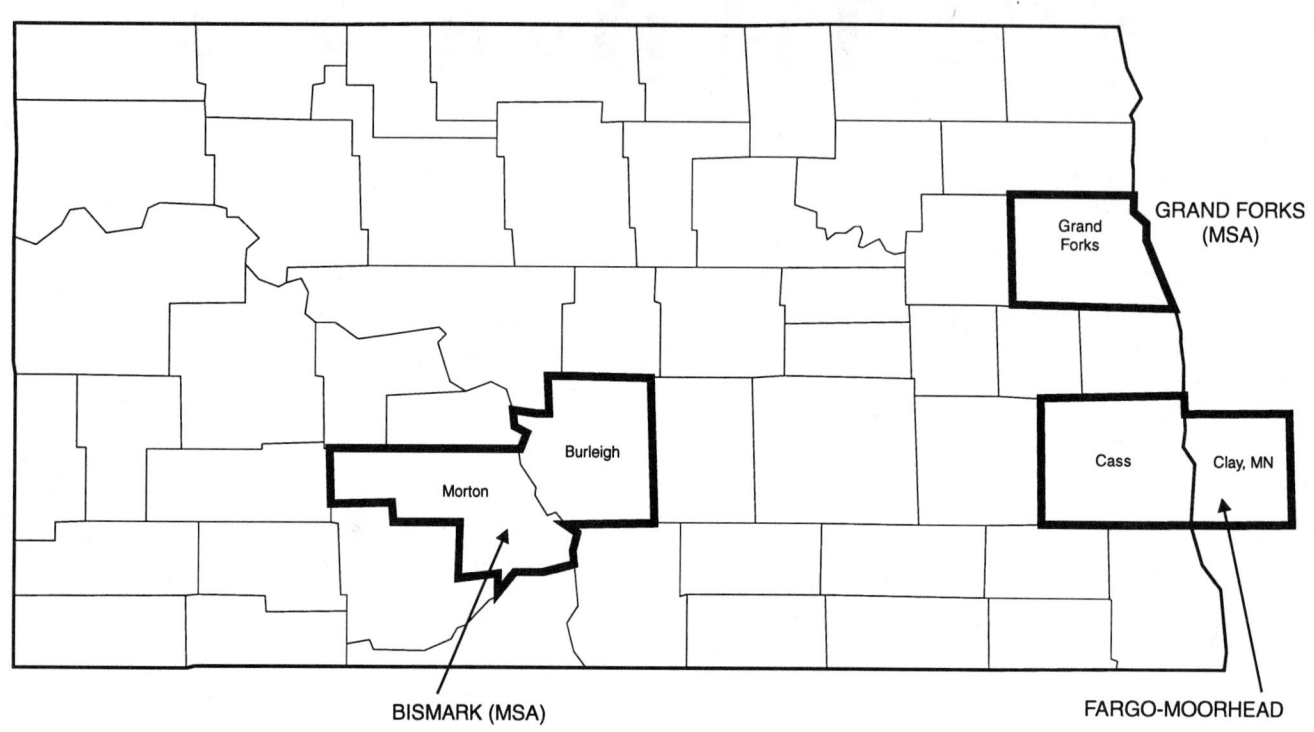

GRAND FORKS (MSA)

Grand Forks

Burleigh

Morton

Cass

Clay, MN

BISMARK (MSA)

FARGO-MOORHEAD

NORTH DAKOTA

Population
1990: 638,800
1980: 652,717

Age
Ages 18 to 20: 30,750
Ages 21 to 24: 37,103
Ages 25 to 44: 194,035
Ages 45 to 54: 57,084
Ages 55 to 59: 26,268
Ages 60 to 64: 27,120
Median age: 32.4

Race and Hispanic Origin
White: 604,142
Black: 3,524
Asian/Pacific Islander: 3,462
Native American: 25,917
Hispanic origin: 4,665

Households
Total: 240,878
Persons per household: 2.55

Sex
Male: 318,201
Female: 320,599

Population Migration
Domestic migration: -78,000
International migration: 4,000

Projection of the Population in 1995
Total: 689,000
18 to 64: 407,000

Civilian Labor Force
1993: 304,200
1992: 316,900
1991: 319,700
1990: 319,100

Manufacturing
1995 Projection: 19,600
1992: 18,300
1991: 17,900
1990: 18,000
1989: 16,900

Services
1995 Projection: 103,200

1992: 73,600
1991: 71,900
1990: 70,300
1989: 66,800

Wholesale and Retail Trade
1995 Projection: 85,600
1992: 73,200
1991: 73,300
1990: 72,700
1989: 68,800

Unemployment Rate
1993: 5.3%
1992: 5.5%
1991: 3.8%
1990: 5.1%

Employer Unemployment Contributions
Contribution Rate
1992: 1.48%
1991: 1.23%
1990: 1.64%

Average Weekly Benefit
1992: $152.22
1991: $149.71
1990: $135.09

Gross State Product (Million $)
1989: $11,231
1988: $10,042
1987: $10,193
1979: $7,715
Growth rate, 1979 to 1989: 45.6%

Capital Expenditures of Manufacturing Industries
1990: $89,600,000
1989: $87,700,000
1988: $71,800,000
1987: $47,000,000

State Tax Rates
Individual income: Range from 2.67% ($3,000 or less) to 12% (above $50,000).
Corporate income: Range from 3% ($3,000 or less) to 10.5% (above $50,000).

General property: Sum of state and local rates. 9% for residential property based on value.

General sales: 5%

Gasoline: 17¢ per gallon

Income

Median income for a 4 person family: $34,806

Personal per Capita Income
1992: $16,854
1991: $15,646
1990: $15,158

Disposable per Capita Income
1992: $15,297
1991: $14,106
1990: $13,676

Private Employment Weekly Wages

Average
1989: $317
1988: $310
1987: $310

Manufacturing
1989: $302
1988: $380
1987: $371

Services
1989: $296
1988: $290
1987: $280

Wholesale
1989: $411
1988: $394
1987: $382

Retail
1989: $179
1988: $177
1987: $173

Highway Statistics

Total Highway Miles
1990: 86,517
1989: 86,384
1988: 86,311

Federal Highway Aid
1991: $71,407,000
1990: $71,227,000
1989: $72,768,000

Electricity

Average Cost per Kilowatt Hour
1990: 5.74¢
1989: 5.79¢
1988: 6.06¢

Housing (1990)

Owner occupied units: 157,950
Median house value: $50,800
Renter occupied units: 82,928
Median rent: $266
Total vacant units: 35,462
Homeowner vacancy rate: 2.8%
Rental vacancy rate: 9.0%

State Business Incentives and Assistance

Financial and Business Assistance

Bank of North Dakota Programs. The state-owned bank serves the financial needs of the business community with several programs that are based on participation between local lenders and the Bank.

Partnership in Assisting Community Expansion Program (PACE). An interest buy-down program that provides financing to businesses through a partnership between locan lenders, local governments and the state-owned Bank of North Dakota. Funds from the PACE program are available to businesses throughout the state for projects in the manufacturing, processing, value-added processing and targeting service industries.

MATCH Program. This program is a low interest loan program that can make up to $25 million available to companies rated A or better at interest rates of .25% above the U.S. Treasury Note rate. MATCH funds can be used for acquiring land, building a plant, or for the lease or purchase of equipment and machinery. MATCH funds are available to businesses anywhere in the state in the manufacturing, processing, or value-added industries.

Business Development Loans. Administered by Bank of North Dakota, businesses may qualify for loans of up to $500,000 to finance working capital, equipment, and real property. The interest rate is set to the Bank of North Dakota base rate for the portion held by the Bank and up to 3% over the BND base rate for the portion held by the lead lender.

Small Business Development Loans. Administered by Bank of North Dakota, small businesses may qualify for loans up to $250,000 at Bank of North Dakota base for the Bank of North Dakota portion and BND base plus 3% for local lender portion of the loan. The funds can be used for working capital, equipment, and real property.

Micro Business Loan Program. Administered by Bank of North Dakota, businesses with a net worth less than $150,000 may qualify for loans of not more than $10,000. The interest rate is held to 1% below BND has rate for the portion of the loan held by BND and 4% above Bank of North Dakota base on the portion held by a local lender.

Roughrider Equity Corporation. Administered by Capital Dimensions, Inc., this program provides funding for the commercialization of technology. Funds may be made available as equity participation, loans, grants, and as a resource for feasibility studies.

Myron G. Nelson Fund. Administered by Capital Dimensions, Inc., this is a venture capital investment fund. Businesses may qualify for funds based on growth potential, management abilities, objectives, plans, and personal goal of the business's principals. Fund participation is limited to 40% of equity.

Community Development Revolving Loan Fund. Administered by the Office of Intergovernmental Assistance, businesses which will create jobs for low or moderate income people may qualify for loans up to $300,000 per project in the primary sector or $50,000 per project in the retail sector. The interest rate is based on need and averages 6%. Funds may be used for fixed assets and infrastructure.

Agricultural Product Utilization Grant. Administered by Ag Products Utilization Commission, this program provides funding and technical assistance to private industry for the establishment of agricultural processing plant for the manufacture of marketing of agricultural derived fuels, chemicals, and value-added processing.

EDA Grant. Administered by the Economic Development Administration, funds from this program are awarded to local communities for the improvement of the infrastructure in their area. Funds are limited to 80% of the cost of the project.

TRIP (Tourism and Recreation Investment Program) Loans. Administered by Bank of North Dakota, this program provides loans up to $10,000 to tourism related businesses. The interest rate is held to 1% below BND base rate for the portion of the loan held by the BND and 4% above BND base on the portion held by a local lender.

Five Year Tax Exemption. New businesses may apply for an exemption of up to five years on property tax paid to local municipalities. A business which qualifies for the property tax exemption may also receive an exemption of up to 5 years on corporate income tax due in the state of North Dakota. Businesses which do not receive, or are not eligible for, the five year corporate income tax exemption, may receive income tax credit equal to 1% of all wages and salaries paid in the for the first three years and 0.5% for the next two years.

Federal Tax Deduction. North Dakota allows a corporation to deduct the entire amount of its federal income tax liability form its income.

Research and Development Incentives. Businesses can take an income tax credit of 8% for the first $1.5 million of R & D expenditures and 4% on the excess over $1.5 million. If the tax credit exceeds the current income tax liability, unused tax credit can be carried back for three years and then forward for up to 15 years.

Investment Credits. Investors can receive an income tax deduction for investment in a North Dakota venture capital corporation and for dividends received from those investments.

Education and Training

Job Training Partnership Act. Administered by Governor's Employment and Training Forum, this federally funded program provides funds to help train the unemployed and economically disadvantaged for employment opportunities. This program can provide customized on-the-job training and subsidizes up to 100% of employment and other educational costs.

Customized Training Programs. Includes on-site classes, and in-plant training. Open ended. open exit enrollment in state-run technical schools, multiple scheduling of classroom training, coupled on-the-job training, non-credit adult education programs at the state's universities and access to multi-district vocational centers and community college programs.

Vocational Instruction Program. Provides financial and technical assistance in developing a training program to meet the needs of individual business.

Mobile Training Laboratories. The North Dakota State College of Science has mobile training laboratories that can provide short-term training in 12 program areas.

State Offices

Real estate: Real Estate Commission, Dennis Schulz, Secretary/Treasurer, 314 East Thayer, PO Box 727, Bismarck, ND 58502. 701-224-2749

Chamber of commerce: Greater North Dakota Association, Dale O. Anderson, President, PO Box 2467, 808 3rd Ave. S., Fargo, ND 58108. 701-237-9461, FAX 701-223-3081

Economic development: North Dakota Economic Development Commission, Fred A. Haeffner, Director, Liberty Memorial Bldg., 604 East Blvd., Bismarck, ND 58505-0824. 701-224-2810, FAX 701-223-3081

North Dakota Dept. of Economic Development and Finance, Charles W. Fine, Business Expansion Specialist, 1833 East Bismarck Expressway, Bismarck, ND 58504. 701-221-5300, FAX 701-221-5320

North Dakota World Trade Inc., L.R. Minton, Manager Director, Liberty Memorial Bldg., Bismarck, ND 58505. 701-224-2810

U.S. Small Business Administration, District Office, James L. Stai, District Director, 657 Second Avenue North, Room 218, Fargo, ND 58108-3086. 701-250-4421

Environmental affairs: Health and Consolidated Laboratories Dept., Dr. Robert Wentz, State Health Officer, 600 East Blvd., Bismarck, ND 58505. 701-224-2370

Labor: Labor Department, Craig Hagen, Labor Commissioner, 600 East Blvd., Bismarck, ND 58505. 701-224-2660

Unemployment: North Dakota Job Service, Mike Deisz, Exec Director, PO Box 1537, 1000 East Divide, Bismarck, ND 58501. 701-224-2825

Worker's compensation: Workers Compensation Bureau, Helen Tracy, Exec Director, 4007 North State Street, Bis-

Major Companies in the State

Company name	Fortune 500 rank	City	Telephone	SIC number
Fortune 500 Companies				
None				
Other Major Companies in the State				
Community First Bankshares Inc.		Fargo	701-235-1600	6712
Deucalion Research Inc.		Williston	701-572-6680	6799
First National Corp. North Dakota		Grand Forks	701-795-3200	6712
Fronteer Directory Company Inc.		Bismarck	701-258-4970	2741
Georesources Inc.		Williston	701-572-2020	1311
MDU Resources Group Inc.		Bismarck	701-222-7900	4931
Robertson Co., Inc.		Grand Forks	701-772-3443	5211

marck, ND 58501. 701-224-3856

Occupational safety and health: Health and Consolidated Laboratories Dept., Dr. Robert Wentz, State Health Officer, 600 East Blvd., Bismarck, ND 58505. 701-224-2370

Secretary of state: Secretary of State Office, Jim Kusler, Secretary of State, 600 East Blvd., Bismarck, ND 58505. 701-224-2905

Taxation and revenue: North Dakota State Tax Dept., Heidi Heitkamp, Tax Commissioner, 600 East Blvd., Bismarck, ND 58505. 701-224-2770

Designated Zones for Economic Development

Enterprise Zones

No program.

Foreign Trade Zones

Foreign Trade Zone No. 103, Grand Forks, North Dakota, Grantee/Operator: Grand Forks Development Foundation, Dick Olson, President, 202 North 3rd Street, Suite 300, Grand Forks, ND 58203, 701-780-9915

Universities with Ph.D. Programs

North Dakota State University, Fargo
University of North Dakota, Grand Forks

Sources of Additional Information

Discover the Spirit Doing Business in North Dakota. North Dakota Economic Development Commission, n.d. 22p.

BISMARCK, ND (MSA)

Geographic Profile

Land Area
3559.6 square miles

Counties and Parishes
Burleigh
Morto

Ranking Highlights

35 *out of 319 in total* **land area**
106 *out of 319 in* **population growth,** *1970–1990*
26 *out of 310 in having the lowest* **unemployment** *rate*
294 *out of 310 in size of* **labor force**
98 *out of 318 in the percentage of* **college graduates**
178 *out of 292 in per capita personal* **income**
307 *out of 319 in number of* **manufacturing establishments**
74 *out of 318 in* **physicians** *per 1000 people*
6 *out of 318 in* **hospital beds** *per 1000 people*
44 *out of 267 in fewest* **crimes** *per 1000 people*
1 *out of 266 in fewest* **violent crimes** *per 1000 people*
79 *out of 319 in per capita* **federal funds and grants**

Quality of Life Indexes (Rate per 1000 population)

Crime rate in 1991:	41.2
Violent crime rate in 1991:	0.7
Physicians rate in 1992:	2.43
Hospital bed rate in 1991:	7.81

ACCRA Cost of Living Indexes

(First quarter 1993, average = 100)
Composite index: N/A
Utilities index: N/A
Housing index: N/A

Population (1990)

Total Population and Growth Rate
1990: 83,831
1980: 79,988
1970: 61,024
Growth rate 1970–1990: 37%

Race and Hispanic Origin
White: 97.0%
Black: .1%
Asian/Pacific Islander: 0.3%
Native American: 2.4%
Hispanic origin: 0.5%
White not Hispanic: 96.7%

Age
Ages 18 to 20: 4.3%
Ages 21 to 24: 4.9%
Ages 25 to 44: 32.9%
Ages 45 to 54: 9.6%
Ages 55 to 59: 4.3%
Ages 60 to 64: 4.1%
Ages 65 plus: 11.5%

Educational Attainment (1990)

Percent having completed high school: 79.4%
Percent having completed college: 21.9%
Elementary and high school enrollment: 16,617

Federal Funds and Grants Received

Total received in 1989: $339,100,000
Funds received per capita: $3,954

Civilian Labor Force

1993 (April):   47,777
1992 average: 46,555
1991 average: 46,583
1990 average: 47,254

Unemployment

1993 (April):   4.8%
1992 average: 4.4%
1991 average: 4.0%
1990 average: 4.1%

Average Annual Pay

1988: $17,818
1987: $17,405
1985: $16,513

Per Capita Personal Income

1991: $16,702
1990: $15,998
1989: $14,794

Business Climate (1987)

Manufacturing
Number of establishments in 1987: 83
Shipments in 1987 ($1,000): $600,600
Employees in 1987: 1,900
Change in employment, 1982 to 1987: 0%
Average annual pay for manufacturing work in 1989: $24,489
Average annual pay for production work in 1987: $20,273

Wholesale Trade
Number of establishments in 1987: 208
Total sales in 1987 ($1,000): $533,900
Change in sales, 1982 to 1987: -3.1%

Retail Trade
Number of establishments in 1987: 640
Total sales in 1987 ($1,000): $533,900
Retail sales per household in 1987: $17,755
Average annual pay in 1989: $9,756

Service Industry
Selected receipts in 1987 ($1,000): $212,600
Average annual pay in 1989: $17,916

Housing
Total number of units in 1990: 33,270

Occupied units in 1990: 31,361
Owner-occupied units in 1990: 67.1%
1993 ACCRA average cost: N/A
1993 ACCRA average rent for an apartment: N/A

Chamber of Commerce

Bismarck Area Chamber of Commerce, President, 425 S. 7th St., PO Box 1675, Bismarck, ND 58502. 701-223-5660

Economic Development Office

Bismarck-Mandan Development Association, Russell Staiger, President, PO Box 2615, Bismarck, ND 58502. 701-222-5530

Economic Development Organizations

Cooperative Power Association, Frank J. Mattern, ND Management Rep., 911 S. 9th St., Bismarck, ND 58502. 701-235-5311

Major Businesses

Company	SIC	Telephone
BNI Coal Ltd.	1221	(701) 222-8828
Basin Cooperative Service	1221	(701) 223-0441
Basin Electric Power Cooperative	4911	(701) 223-0441
Beco Inc.	4213	(701) 843-7529
Cloverdale Foods Co.	2013	(701) 663-9511
Dan's Super Market, Inc.	5411	(701) 258-2127
Eide Ford Mercury Lincoln	5511	(701) 222-3500
Hedahls Inc.	5013	(701) 223-8393
Industrial Contractors Inc.	1711	(701) 258-9908
Joersz Food Inc.	5411	(701) 663-9885
Knife River Coal Mine Co.	1221	(701) 223-1771
MDU Resources Group Inc.	4911	(701) 222-7900
Meyer Broadcasting Co. Inc.	4833	(701) 255-5757
Midwest Motor Express Inc.	4213	(701) 223-1880
Provident Life Insurance Co.	6311	(701) 223-2120
Puklich, Stan Chevrolet	5511	(701) 223-5800
St Alexius Medical Center	8062	(701) 224-7000
Williston Basin International Pipeline	1311	(701) 222-7609

Colleges and Universities

Bismarck State College, Bismarck
Medcenter One College of Nursing, Bismarck
United Tribes Technical College, Bismarck
University of Mary, Bismarck

FARGO–MOORHEAD, ND–MN (MSA)

Geographic Profile

Land Area

2811.0 square miles

Counties and Parishes

Minnesota:
  Clay
North Dakota:
  Cass

Ranking Highlights

 53 *out of 319 in total* land area
149 *out of 319 in* population growth, *1970–1990*
 10 *out of 310 in having the lowest* unemployment *rate*
198 *out of 310 in size of* labor force
 60 *out of 318 in the percentage of* college graduates
196 *out of 292 in per capita personal* income
241 *out of 319 in number of* manufacturing establishments
 66 *out of 318 in* physicians *per 1000 people*
129 *out of 318 in* hospital beds *per 1000 people*
 45 *out of 267 in fewest* crimes *per 1000 people*
N/A *out of 266 in fewest* violent crimes *per 1000 people*
151 *out of 319 in per capita* federal funds and grants

Quality of Life Indexes (Rate per 1000 population)

Crime rate in 1991:	41.6
Violent crime rate in 1991:	N/A
Physicians rate in 1992:	2.5
Hospital bed rate in 1991:	4.19

ACCRA Cost of Living Indexes

(First quarter 1993, average = 100)
Composite index: 98.0
Utilities index: 88.7
Housing index: 99.7

Overview

Fargo is the largest city in North Dakota and the seat of Cass County. It is the focus of a metropolitan statistical area that extends over Cass County, North Dakota, and Clay County, Minnesota, where Fargo's sister city, Moorhead, is located. Founded by the Northern Pacific Railway, the city was an important transportation and marketing point for the surrounding fertile wheat-growing region. Today it is an agri-business and agricultural research center. *Money Magazine* selected Fargo as the nation's fifth most livable city in 1992. The city was declared a "Great Plains success story," with locally grown high–tech firms and a state university by *Kiplinger's Personal Finance Magazine* in 1991.

The Fargo economy is based on education, the medical industry, agricultural equipment manufacturing, retailing, and services. Because of its central location, the city is a transportation hub for the northern Midwest region. Agriculture has long been of primary importance to Fargo, as the Red River Valley area contains some of the richest farmland in the world; related industries include agribusiness and agricultural research.

The principal manufacturing employer is Case I H, makers of heavy-duty tractors. Terminals for two oil pipeline systems—Standard Oil Company of Indiana and Great Lakes Pipeline Company of Oklahoma—are located in Fargo–Moorhead. The Standard Oil pipeline is connected with the company's refinery in Whiting, Indiana, which produces more than thirty thousand barrels of oil a day.

Hector International Airport is situated ten minutes northwest of downtown Fargo. Three major airlines schedule daily flights; regular commuter service is available between Fargo and Minneapolis-St. Paul, Minnesota. Rail transportation is provided by Amtrak and bus transportation by Greyhound.

Highways serving metropolitan Fargo include I-94, extending east to west through the south sector of the city, and I-29, which runs north to south and intersects I-94. This is the only intersection of two interstate highways between western Montana and Sault Sainte Marie, Michigan. U.S. 10 and 52 are east-west routes, and U.S. 81 extends through the city from north to south. State routes serving Fargo are 20 and 294, both running east to west.

Population (1990)

Total Population and Growth Rate

1990: 153,296
1980: 137,574
1970: 120,261
Growth rate 1970–1990: 27%

Race and Hispanic Origin

White: 97.2%
Black: .3%
Asian/Pacific Islander: 0.9%
Native American: 1.0%
Hispanic origin: 1.2%
White not Hispanic: 96.6%

Age

Ages 18 to 20: 7.8%
Ages 21 to 24: 9%
Ages 25 to 44: 32.2%
Ages 45 to 54: 8.5%
Ages 55 to 59: 3.5%
Ages 60 to 64: 3.5%
Ages 65 plus: 10.5%

Educational Attainment (1990)

Percent having completed high school: 85.1%
Percent having completed college: 25.0%
Elementary and high school enrollment: 24,696

Federal Funds and Grants Received

Total received in 1989: $464,200,000
Funds received per capita: $3,129

Civilian Labor Force

1993 (April):   91,433
1992 average: 90,462
1991 average: 88,478
1990 average: 88,234

Unemployment

1993 (April):   3.5%
1992 average: 3.5%
1991 average: 3.1%
1990 average: 2.7%

Average Annual Pay

1988: $17,649
1987: $17,123
1985: $16,370

Per Capita Personal Income

1991: $16,354
1990: $15,917
1989: $14,712

Business Climate (1987)

Manufacturing

Number of establishments in 1987: 155
Shipments in 1987 ($1,000): $666,600
Employees in 1987: 4,900
Change in employment, 1982 to 1987: 4.3%
Average annual pay for manufacturing work in 1989: $20,868
Average annual pay for production work in 1987: $16,909

Wholesale Trade

Number of establishments in 1987: 474
Total sales in 1987 ($1,000): $2,142,900
Change in sales, 1982 to 1987: -6.9%

Retail Trade

Number of establishments in 1987: 978
Total sales in 1987 ($1,000): $2,142,900
Retail sales per household in 1987: $19,298
Average annual pay in 1989: $9,626

Service Industry

Selected receipts in 1987 ($1,000): $408,200
Average annual pay in 1989: $17,298

Office Real Estate (1992)

Office space inventory: 2,197,000 square feet
Average class A Central Business District rental range per sq. ft: $12.00

Vacancy Rates

All areas: 14.2%

Vacancy Rates in Central Business District

Class A space: 12.8%
Class B space: 18.7%

Vacancy Rates Outside Central Business District

Class A space: 6.5%

Class B space: 13.0%

Housing

Total number of units in 1990: 60,953

Occupied units in 1990: 57,771

Owner-occupied units in 1990: 58.9%

1993 ACCRA average cost: $114,931

1993 ACCRA average rent for an apartment: $466

Chamber of Commerce

Fargo Chamber of Commerce, John C. Campbell, President, 321 N. 4th St., PO Box 2443, Fargo, ND 58108. 701-772-7271

Economic Development Office

Fargo-Cass County Economic Development Corp., John Kramer, President, PO Box 2443, 417 Main Ave., Fargo, ND 58108-2443. 701-237-6132, FAX 701-235-6706

Industrial Sites

Fargo Industrial Park (70 acres). Contact: Dwaine Gray, President, Fargo-Cass County Development Corp., PO Box 2443, Fargo, ND 58108. 701-237-6132

Glacier Park I-29 Park (80 acres). Contact: Dwaine Gray, President, Fargo-Cass County Development Corp., PO Box 2443, Fargo, ND 58108. 701-237-6132

Glacier Park Industrial Park (640 acres). Contact: Dwaine Gray, President, Fargo-Cass County Development Corp., PO Box 2443, Fargo, ND 58108. 701-237-6132

Major Businesses

Company	SIC	Telephone
American Crystal Sugar Co.	2063	(218) 236-4400
Blue Cross	6324	(701) 282-1100
Cass-Clay Creamery, Inc.	2026	(701) 232-1566
Community First Bankshares	6022	(701) 235-1600
Dakota Health Systems	8062	(701) 280-4100
Dakota Hospital	8062	(701) 280-4100
Gateway Chevrolet, Inc.	5511	(701) 282-5522
Lutheran Health Systems	8062	(701) 293-9053
Metropolitan Federal Bank	6035	(701) 293-2600
Metropolitan Financial Co.	6035	(701) 293-2600
Northern Improvement Co.	1611	(701) 277-1225
Norwest Bank North Dakota	6021	(701) 293-4200
Pioneer Mutual Life Insurance	6311	(701) 293-3300
Service Oil Inc.	5541	(701) 277-1050
St. Luke's Hospitals	8062	(701) 234-6000
St. Lukes Association	8062	(701) 234-6000
Vanderhave USA Inc.	5191	(701) 282-7338
Vanity Shop of Grand Fork	5621	(701) 237-3330
Western States Life Insurance	6311	(701) 237-5700

Colleges and Universities

Concordia College, Moorhead, MN

Moorhead State University, Moorhead, MN

North Dakota State University, Fargo, ND

GRAND FORKS, ND (MSA)

Geographic Profile

Land Area

1437.9 square miles

Counties and Parishes

Grand Forks

Ranking Highlights

141 *out of 319 in total* **land area**

197 *out of 319 in* **population growth,** *1970–1990*

 15 *out of 310 in having the lowest* **unemployment** *rate*

308 *out of 310 in size of* **labor force**

 52 *out of 318 in the percentage of* **college graduates**

259 *out of 292 in per capita personal* **income**

317 *out of 319 in number of* **manufacturing establishments**

 85 *out of 318 in* **physicians** *per 1000 people*

 19 *out of 318 in* **hospital beds** *per 1000 people*

 62 *out of 267 in fewest* **crimes** *per 1000 people*

  8 *out of 266 in fewest* **violent crimes** *per 1000 people*

 50 *out of 319 in per capita* **federal funds and grants**

Quality of Life Indexes (Rate per 1000 population)

Crime rate in 1991:	45.4
Violent crime rate in 1991:	1.2
Physicians rate in 1992:	2.32
Hospital bed rate in 1991:	6.44

ACCRA Cost of Living Indexes

(First quarter 1993, average = 100)

Composite index:	N/A
Utilities index:	N/A
Housing index:	N/A

Overview

Grand Forks has a stable, agriculturally–based economy which has been expanding and diversifying since the early 1980s. Abundant moisture assists the growth of the hard spring wheat, corn, oats, sunflowers, durum, barley, potatoes, sugar beets, dry edible beans, and soybeans that represent its major crops, and in all its years of existence there has never been a crop failure. Cattle, sheep and hogs also contribute to the local farm economy. Plants operate for the processing of potatoes, for the conversion of locally grown mustard seed for table and commercial use, for the refining of beets into sugar, and for the pearling of barley. Much of the area's durham wheat is marketed through the North Dakota State Mill and Elevator.

While in the early 1980s almost all businesses were agriculturally based, other enterprises such as high–technology firms, a wood products company, and concrete firms now play an important role in the local economy. Some important local firms include: J. R. Simplot, which processes potatoes and other foods; American Woods, a relatively new company that produces outdoor lawn furniture; Strata Cor-

poration, which produces ready–mix concrete and handles asphalt and masonry; the American Crystal Sugar refinery; Young Manufacturing, which custom designs, engineers, and manufactures metal products; Energy Research Center, which conducts research on energy–related products; and R. D. O., which deals in processed foods.

Due to the U.S.–Canada free trade agreement, North Dakota exports have nearly doubled from $128 million in 1988 to $246 million in 1990. Canadian tourism contributed $85.3 million to the Grand Forks economy in 1990.

Grand Forks is accessible by two major highways, Interstate 29, which runs north and south, and U.S. Highway 2, which runs east and west. Grand Forks's Mark Andrews International Airport, located 4.5 miles west of the city, is served by Northwest Airlines, Mesaba Airlink, and Great Lakes Airlines, with ten arrivals and departures daily.

Population (1990)

Total Population and Growth Rate

1990: 70,683

1980: 66,100

1970: 61,102

Growth rate 1970–1990: 16%

Race and Hispanic Origin

White: 94.5%

Black: 2.0%

Asian/Pacific Islander: 1.2%

Native American: 1.8%

Hispanic origin: 1.5%

White not Hispanic: 93.6%

Age

Ages 18 to 20: 8.4%

Ages 21 to 24: 10.7%

Ages 25 to 44: 33.4%

Ages 45 to 54: 7.1%

Ages 55 to 59: 2.9%

Ages 60 to 64: 2.8%

Ages 65 plus: 8.8%

Educational Attainment (1990)

Percent having completed high school: 85.6%

Percent having completed college: 25.8%

Elementary and high school enrollment: 318,100

Federal Funds and Grants Received

Total received in 1989: $325,800,000

Funds received per capita: $4,624

Civilian Labor Force

1993 (April):	36,153
1992 average:	34,646
1991 average:	34,948
1990 average:	35,744

Unemployment

1993 (April): 4.3%

1992 average: 3.9%

1991 average: 3.3%
1990 average: 3.6%

Average Annual Pay
1988: $16,547
1987: $16,303
1985: $15,345

Per Capita Personal Income
1991: $15,020
1990: $14,621
1989: $13,542

Business Climate (1987)

Manufacturing
Number of establishments in 1987: 48
Shipments in 1987 ($1,000): $199,500
Employees in 1987: 1,500
Change in employment, 1982 to 1987: 36.4%
Average annual pay for manufacturing work in 1989: $17,764
Average annual pay for production work in 1987: $15,909

Wholesale Trade
Number of establishments in 1987: 140
Total sales in 1987 ($1,000): $332,900
Change in sales, 1982 to 1987: 11.4%

Retail Trade
Number of establishments in 1987: 494
Total sales in 1987 ($1,000): $332,900
Retail sales per household in 1987: $21,441
Average annual pay in 1989: $9,639

Service Industry
Selected receipts in 1987 ($1,000): $133,400
Average annual pay in 1989: $16,849

Housing
Total number of units in 1990: 27,085
Occupied units in 1990: 25,340
Owner-occupied units in 1990: 48.7%
1993 ACCRA average cost: N/A
1993 ACCRA average rent for an apartment: N/A

Chamber of Commerce
Grand Forks Chamber of Commerce, Bob Gustafson, President, 202 N. 3rd St., PO Box 1177, Grand Forks, ND 58201. 701-772-7271

Economic Development Office
Grand Forks Development Foundation, William J. Argo, President, 202 N. 3rd St., Suite 300, Grand Forks, ND 58203. 701-780-9915, FAX 701-780-9025

Industrial Sites
Grand Forks Industrial Park, Beverly Argo, Grand Forks Development Foundation, 202 N. 3rd St. No. 300, Grand Forks, ND 58203. 701-780-9915

Major Businesses

Company	SIC	Telephone
Acme Electric Motor Inc.	5084	(701) 746-6481
Agsco Inc.	2879	(701) 775-5325
American Federal Savings	6035	(218) 773-9711
American West Insurance Co.	6331	(701) 775-4226
Congress, Inc.	5182	(701) 772-5571
Dahlgren & Co. Inc.	2068	(218) 281-2985
Farmers Co-Op Marketing	5153	(218) 773-2407
First American Bank	6036	(218) 281-1320
First National Bank in Grand Fork	6021	(701) 795-3200
First National Corp.	6712	(701) 795-3200
G F G Foodservice, Inc.	5141	(218) 773-7414
Grand Forks Herald	2711	(701) 780-1100
Hansen Ford Sales Inc.	5511	(701) 746-6411
Manhattan National Life Insurance	6411	(701) 775-3125
Minn-Dak Growers, Ltd	0723	(701) 746-7453
Minnkota Power Cooperative	4911	(701) 795-4000
Nodak Rural Electric Cooperative	4911	(701) 746-4461
North Dakota Mill Elevator Association	2041	(701) 795-7000
Robertson Companies, Inc.	5211	(701) 772-3443
Rydell Chevrolet GMC Inc.	5511	(701) 772-7211
Square Butte Electric Co.	4911	(701) 795-4000
United Hospital	8062	(701) 780-5000
Wilcox and Malm Inc.	5511	(701) 775-4272

Colleges and Universities
University of North Dakota, Grand Forks

OHIO

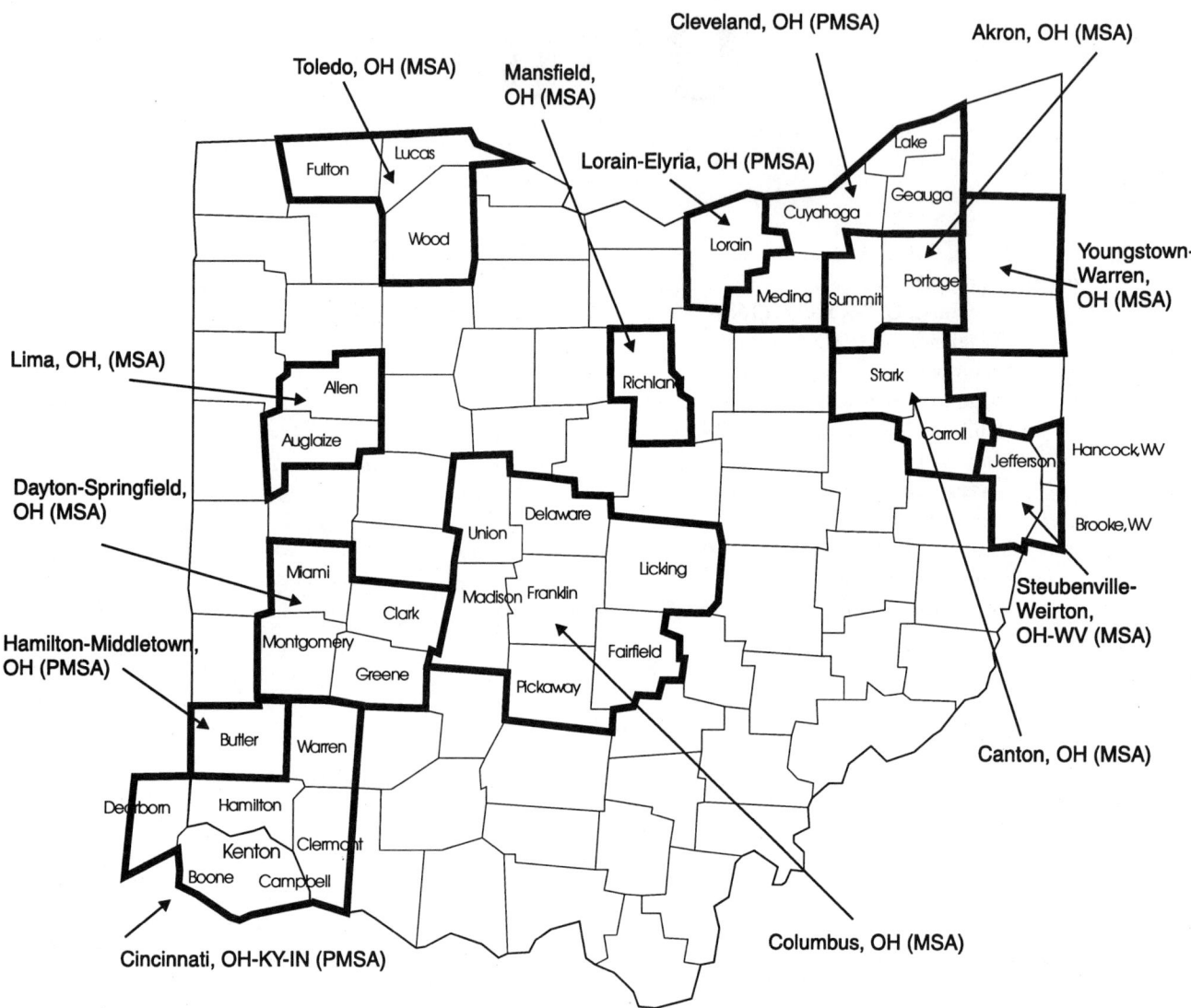

Toledo, OH (MSA)

Mansfield, OH (MSA)

Cleveland, OH (PMSA)

Akron, OH (MSA)

Lorain-Elyria, OH (PMSA)

Youngstown-Warren, OH (MSA)

Lima, OH, (MSA)

Dayton-Springfield, OH (MSA)

Hamilton-Middletown, OH (PMSA)

Steubenville-Weirton, OH-WV (MSA)

Canton, OH (MSA)

Columbus, OH (MSA)

Cincinnati, OH-KY-IN (PMSA)

Fulton

Lucas

Wood

Lake

Geauga

Cuyahoga

Lorain

Portage

Medina

Summit

Richland

Stark

Allen

Carroll

Auglaize

Jefferson

Hancock,WV

Brooke,WV

Delaware

Union

Miami

Licking

Madison

Franklin

Clark

Montgomery

Fairfield

Greene

Pickaway

Butler

Warren

Dearborn

Hamilton

Clermont

Kenton

Boone

Campbell

OHIO

Population

1990: 10,847,115
1980: 10,797,630

Age

Ages 18 to 20: 511,421
Ages 21 to 24: 624,997
Ages 25 to 44: 3,411,043
Ages 45 to 54: 1,113,443
Ages 55 to 59: 482,526
Ages 60 to 64: 496,980
Median age: 33.3

Race and Hispanic Origin

White: 9,521,756
Black: 1,154,826
Asian/Pacific Islander: 91,179
Native American: 20,358
Hispanic origin: 139,696

Households

Total: 4,087,546
Persons per household: 2.59

Sex

Male: 5,226,340
Female: 5,620,775

Population Migration

Domestic migration: -296,000
International migration: 48,000

Projection of the Population in 1995

Total: 11,117,000
18 to 64: 6,784,000

Civilian Labor Force

1993: 5,437,000
1992: 5,491,500
1991: 5,416,000
1990: 5,391,300

Manufacturing

1995 Projection: 1,122,700
1992: 1,050,600
1991: 1,079,900
1990: 1,099,900
1989: 1,121,700

Services

1995 Projection: 1,659,700

1992: 1,234,100
1991: 1,238,000
1990: 1,212,600
1989: 1,150,500

Wholesale and Retail Trade

1995 Projection: 1,335,200
1992: 1,160,000
1991: 1,200,300
1990: 1,207,600
1989: 1,218,700

Unemployment Rate

1993: 8.2%
1992: 8.0%
1991: 6.0%
1990: 7.6%

Employer Unemployment Contributions

Contribution Rate

1992: 2.80%
1991: 2.35%
1990: 2.44%

Average Weekly Benefit

1992: $183.76
1991: $179.56
1990: $157.92

Gross State Product (Million $)

1989: $211,545
1988: $201,478
1987: $186,385
1979: $117,863
Growth rate, 1979 to 1989: 79.5%

Capital Expenditures of Manufacturing Industries

1990: $6,261,500,000
1989: $5,637,300,000
1988: $4,302,200,000
1987: $4,742,200,000

State Tax Rates

Individual income: Range from 0.743% ($5,000 or less) to 6.9% (above $100,000).
Corporate income: Range from 5.1% ($50,000 or less) to 8.9% (above $50,000).

General property: Rates fixed locally, assessed at 35% of true value.

General sales: 5%

Gasoline: 21¢ per gallon

Income

Median income for a 4 person family: $41,469

Personal per Capita Income

1992: $18,624

1991: $17,767

1990: $17,422

Disposable per Capita Income

1992: $16,359

1991: $15,512

1990: $15,123

Private Employment Weekly Wages

Average

1989: $420

1988: $411

1987: $411

Manufacturing

1989: $394

1988: $570

1987: $543

Services

1989: $360

1988: $348

1987: $332

Wholesale

1989: $536

1988: $522

1987: $493

Retail

1989: $211

1988: $207

1987: $201

Highway Statistics

Total Highway Miles

1990: 113,600

1989: 113,439

1988: 113,340

Federal Highway Aid

1991: $432,659,000

1990: $457,709,000

1989: $463,065,000

Electricity

Average Cost per Kilowatt Hour

1990: 5.94¢

1989: 5.72¢

1988: 5.83¢

Housing (1990)

Owner occupied units: 2,758,149

Median house value: $63,500

Renter occupied units: 1,329,397

Median rent: $296

Total vacant units: 284,399

Homeowner vacancy rate: 1.3%

Rental vacancy rate: 7.5%

State Business Incentives and Assistance

Enterprise Zone Incentives

1) City-designated zones: Exemption of taxes on real property and tangible personal property for new businesses and the incremental value of renovated businesses up to 100% of added value for up to 10 years.

2) County-designated zones: a) exemption on real property and tangible personal property up to 100% for up to 10 years in a municipality, b) exemption for a period of up to 10 years and up to 75% of taxes of real property and tangible personal property in a township.

3) The state may provide additional benefits including: a) reductions in state corporate franchise and income taxes; b) tax credits for training programs for newly hired employees up to $1,000 per employees; c) tax credits for reimbursing newly hired employees for day care services, up to $300 per child for up to two years; and d) reductions of state payroll tax on compensations paid to qualified employees.

Financial and Business Assistance

Pooled Bond Program. Administered by the Ohio Department of Development, this program issues tax-exempt industrial development bonds to provide low cost financing for new and expanding manufacturing companies. The funds may be used for acquisition, construction, and equipping of manufacturing facilities. The IDBs can be issued as variable-rate or fixed-rate loans.

Ohio Enterprise Bond Fund. Administered by the Ohio Department of Development, this program issues taxable industrial development bonds to provide long-term financing for company projects designed to create or retain jobs in the state. Funds may be used for acquisition of land and existing facilities, new construction or renovation of facilities, and equipment. The state will issue on behalf of all borrowers investment-grade economic development revenue bonds.

Local Industrial Development Bonds. Administered by the Ohio Department of Development, local governments are authorized to issue tax-exempt IDBs to provide low cost financing for new or expanding manufacturing businesses. Projects must provide new or maintain existing jobs in the state.

Education and Training

Ohio Industrial Training Program. Administered by the Department of Development, this program is designed to

Major Companies in the State

Company name	Fortune 500 rank	City	Telephone	SIC number
Fortune 500 Companies				
A Schulman Inc.	427	Akron	216-666-3751	2821
American Greetings Corp.	264	Cleveland	216-252-7300	2771
B F Goodrich Co.	186	Akron	216-374-3985	2821
Chiquita Brands International Inc.	115	Cincinnati	513-784-8011	5148
Cincinnati Milacron Inc.	412	Cincinnati	513-841-8100	3541
Cooper Tire & Rubber Co.	317	Findlay	419-423-1321	3011
Dana Corp.	108	Toledo	419-535-4500	3714
Eagle Picher Industries Inc.	487	Cincinnati	513-721-7010	3714
Eaton Corp.	122	Cleveland	216-523-5000	3625
Ferro Corp.	330	Cleveland	216-641-8580	2899
Figgie International Inc.	318	Willoughby	216-953-2700	3569
Gencorp Inc.	223	Fairlawn	216-869-4200	3764
Goodyear Tire & Rubber Co.	38	Akron	216-796-2121	3011
Huffy Corp.	441	Miamisburg	513-866-6251	3751
Lincoln Electric Co.	394	Cleveland	216-481-8100	3548
LTV Corp.	102	Cleveland	216-622-5000	3312
Lubrizol Corp.	266	Wickliffe	216-943-4200	2992
M A Hanna Co.	286	Cleveland	216-589-4000	2821
Mead Corp.	114	Dayton	513-495-6323	5111
Nacco Industries Inc.	274	Mayfield Heights	216-449-9600	3537
Owens Corning Fiberglas Corp.	167	Toledo	419-248-8000	3296
Owens Illinois Inc.	136	Toledo	419-247-5000	3221
Parker Hannifin Corp.	192	Cleveland	216-531-3000	3594
Procter & Gamble Co.	13	Cincinnati	513-983-1100	2844
Reliance Electric Co.	267	Cleveland	216-266-5800	3621
Reynolds & Reynolds Co.	465	Dayton	513-443-2000	2761
Rubbermaid Inc.	236	Wooster	216-264-6464	3089
E W Scripps Co.	306	Wilmington	302-478-4141	2711
Sealy Corp.	463	Cleveland	216-522-1310	2515
Sherwin Williams Co.	172	Cleveland	216-566-2000	5231
Standard Products Co.	459	Cleveland	216-281-8300	3069
Standard Register Co.	440	Dayton	513-443-1000	2761
Timken Co.	254	Canton	216-438-3000	3562
Trinova Corp.	248	Maumee	419-867-2200	3492
TRW Inc.	64	Cleveland	216-291-7000	3714
Worthington Industries Inc.	363	Columbus	614-438-3210	3316
Other Major Companies in the State				
Allied Stores Corp.		Cincinnati	513-579-7000	5311
American Electric Power Co. Inc.		Columbus	614-223-1000	4911
American Financial Corp.		Cincinnati	513-579-2121	5148
Anac Holding Corp.		Twinsburg	216-425-9811	5912
Banc One Corp.		Columbus	614-248-5944	6712
Centerior Energy Corp.		Independence	216-447-3100	4911
Cleveland Electric Illuminating Co.		Cleveland	216-622-9800	4911
Federated Department Stores Inc.		Cincinnati	513-579-7000	5311
Hook Superx Inc.		Cincinnati	513-782-3000	5912
Kroger Co.		Cincinnati	513-762-4000	5411
Limited Inc.		Columbus	614-479-7000	5621

Major Companies in the State (Continued)

Company name	Fortune 500 rank	City	Telephone	SIC number
LTV Steel Company Inc.		Cleveland	216-622-5000	3312
National City Corp.		Cleveland	216-575-2000	6712
Ohio Bell Telephone Co.		Cleveland	216-822-9700	4813
Ohio Edison Co.		Akron	216-384-5100	4911
Revco Inc.		Twinsburg	216-425-9811	5912
Roadway Services Inc.		Akron	216-384-8184	4213
Society Corp.		Cleveland	216-689-3000	6712
Super Food Services Inc.		Dayton	513-439-7500	5141
United States Shoe Corp.		Cincinnati	513-527-7000	5621

help new and expanding industrial companies to create and retain jobs. It provides grants for new employees orientation programs, grants for training new or existing employees in specific skills, and grants for improving management skills.

Job Training Services. Provides customized training programs to new or expanding companies in recruitment, curriculum development, and classroom, as well as on-the-job, training.

Job Training Partnership Act. This program operates with funding from the U.S. Department of Labor. It provides job training and other employment related services.

State Offices

Real estate: Commerce Department, Real Estate Division, Peg Ritenour, Superintendent, 77 South High Street, 23rd Fl., Columbus, OH 43266-0544. 614-466-4100

Chamber of commerce: Ohio State Chamber of Commerce, Economic Development, Guy H. Ford, Director, 35 E. Gay St., 2nd Fl, Columbus, OH 43215. 614-228-4201

Economic development: Ohio Department of Development, Office of Industrial Development, Jerry Brems, Manager, PO Box 1001, 77 South High Street, 28th Fl, Columbus, OH 43266-0101. 614-466-4551, FAX 614-644-1789

Small Business Development Center, Jack Brown, State Director, Ohio Department of Development, 77 South High Street, PO Box 1001, Columbus, OH 43266-0101. 614-466-5111

Environmental affairs: Environmental Protection Agency, Richard L. Shank, Director, PO Box 1049, 1800 Watermark, Columus, OH 43266-0149. 614-644-2782

Labor: Industrial Relations Department, James W. Harris, Director, PO Box 825, 2323 West 5th Ave., Columbus, OH 43216. 614-644-2223

Unemployment: Employment Services Bureau, Unemployment Compensation Division, Doug Holmes, Administrator, 145 South Front Street, Columbus, OH 43216. 614-466-9755

Worker's compensation: Worker's Compensation Bureau, Patricia K. Barry, Administrator, 246 North High Street,

Columbus, OH 43215. 614-466-1935

Occupational safety and health: Industrial Commission, Safety and Hygiene Division, Louis Gergely, Administrator, 246 North High Street, Columbus, OH 43215. 614-466-3564

Secretary of state: Secretary of State, Bob Taft, Secretary of State, 30 East Broad Street, 14th Fl., Columbus, OH 43266-0418. 614-466-2655

Taxation and revenue: Taxation Department, Joanne Limbach, Tax Commissioner, PO Box 530, Columbus, OH 43216. 614-466-2166

Designated Zones for Economic Development

Enterprise Zones

Enacted in: 1982

No. of established zones: 223

Foreign Trade Zones

Foreign Trade Zone No. 46, Cincinnati, Ohio, Grantee/Operator: Greater Cincinnati FTZ, Inc., Neil Hensley, 300 Carew Tower, 441 Vine St., Cincinnati, OH 45202-2812, 513-579-3122

Foreign Trade Zone No. 40, Cleveland, Ohio, Grantee: Cleveland Port Authority, Roy Knapp, 101 Erieside Avenue, Cleveland, OH 44114, 216-241-8004

Foreign Trade Zone No. 101, Clinton County, Ohio, Grantee/Operator: Airborne FTZ, Inc., Mike Kuli, 145 Hunter Drive, Wilmington, OH 45177, 513-382-5591

Foreign Trade Zone No. 100, Dayton, Ohio, Grantee/Operator: Greater Dayton Foreign-Trade Zone, Inc., Harry Bumgarner, c/o Dayton Area Chamber of Commerce, Chamber Plaza, Fifth and Main, Dayton, OH 45402-2400, 513-226-8239

Foreign Trade Zone No. 151, Findlay, Ohio, Grantee: Community Development Foundation, John Kovach, Municipal Bldg., Room 310, Findlay, OH 45840, 419-424-7095

Foreign Trade Zone No. 138, Franklin County, Ohio, Grantee: Rickenbacker Port Authority, Lawrence Garrison, 2365 Fred Haise Avenue, Columbus, OH 43217-1232, 614-491-1401

Foreign Trade Zone No. 8, Toledo, Ohio, Grantee: Toledo-

Lucas County Port Authority, John Loftus, One Maritime Plaza, Toledo, OH 43604-1866, 419-243-8251

University of Dayton, Dayton
University of Toledo, Toledo

Labor Unions

Aircraft Workers Alliance Amalgamated, Inc.

Akron Education Association

Aluminum, Brick and Glass Workers, International Union (AFL-CIO)

Automobile, Aerospace & Agricultural Implement Workers of America, International Union, United, (UAW AFL-CIO)

Boilermakers, Iron Shipbuilders, Blacksmiths, Forgers and Helpers, International Brotherhood of, (AFL-CIO)

Bakery, Confectionery & Tobacco Workers International Union (AFL-CIO)

Carpenters and Joiners of America, United Brotherhood of (AFL-CIO)

Communications Workers of America (AFL-CIO)

Electrical Workers, International Brotherhood of (AFL-CIO)

Food and Commercial Workers International Union, United (AFL-CIO)

Hospital and Health Care Employees

Independent Utilities Union

Laborers' International Union of North America (AFL-CIO)

National Education Association

National Fraternal Order of Police

Paperworkers International Union, United (AFL-CIO)

Plant Protection

Plumbing and Pipe Fitting Industry of The United States and Canada, United Association of, Journeymen and Apprentices of the (AFL-CIO)

Service Employees' International Union (AFL-CIO)

State, County and Municipal Employees, American Federation of (AFL-CIO)

Steelworkers of America, United (AFL-CIO)

Teachers, American Federation of (AFL-CIO)

Teamsters, Chauffeurs, Warehousemen and Helpers of America, International Brotherhood of, (AFL-CIO)

Transit Union, Amalgamated (AFL-CIO)

Utility Workers Union of America (AFL-CIO)

Universities with Ph.D. Programs

Bowling Green State University, Bowling Green

Capital University, Columbus

Case Western Reserve University, Cleveland

Cleveland State University, Cleveland

Kent State University, Kent

Miami University, Oxford

Ohio Northern University, Ada

Ohio State University, Columbus

Ohio University, Athens

Union Institute, Cincinnati

University of Akron, Akron

University of Cincinnati, Cincinnati

AKRON, OH (PMSA)

Geographic Profile

Land Area

905.2 square miles

Counties and Parishes

Portage

Summit

Additional Cities/Towns within Area

Barberton

Kent

Ranking Highlights

219 *out of 319 in total* **land area**

285 *out of 319 in* **population growth,** *1970–1990*

157 *out of 310 in having the lowest* **unemployment** *rate*

76 *out of 310 in size of* **labor force**

151 *out of 318 in the percentage of* **college graduates**

103 *out of 292 in per capita personal* **income**

56 *out of 319 in number of* **manufacturing establishments**

119 *out of 318 in* **physicians** *per 1000 people*

161 *out of 318 in* **hospital beds** *per 1000 people*

N/A *out of 267 in fewest* **crimes** *per 1000 people*

N/A *out of 266 in fewest* **violent crimes** *per 1000 people*

237 *out of 319 in per capita* **federal funds and grants**

Quality of Life Indexes (Rate per 1000 population)

Crime rate in 1991:	N/A
Violent crime rate in 1991:	N/A
Physicians rate in 1992:	2.03
Hospital bed rate in 1991:	3.82

ACCRA Cost of Living Indexes

(First quarter 1993, average = 100)

Composite index:	94.4
Utilities index:	116.7
Housing index:	88.6

Population (1990)

Total Population and Growth Rate

1990: 657,575

1980: 660,328

1970: 679,239

Growth rate 1970–1990: -3%

Race and Hispanic Origin

White: 88.8%

Black: 9.9%

Asian/Pacific Islander: 0.9%

Native American: 0.2%

Hispanic origin: 0.6%

White not Hispanic: 88.4%

Age

Ages 18 to 20: 5.4%

Ages 21 to 24: 6.3%

Ages 25 to 44: 31.7%

Ages 45 to 54: 10.1%

Ages 55 to 59: 4.4%

Ages 60 to 64: 4.7%

Ages 65 plus: 12.9%

Educational Attainment (1990)

Percent having completed high school: 78.5%

Percent having completed college: 19.3%

Elementary and high school enrollment: 108,733

Federal Funds and Grants Received

Total received in 1989: $1,664,100,000

Funds received per capita: $2,547

Civilian Labor Force

1993 (April): 341,008

1992 average: 339,631

1991 average: 333,042

1990 average: 331,659

Unemployment

1993 (April): 5.6%

1992 average: 6.9%

1991 average: 6.0%

1990 average: 5.2%

Average Annual Pay

1988: $22,010

1987: $21,297

1985: $19,827

Per Capita Personal Income

1991: $18,234

1990: $17,992

1989: $17,025

Business Climate (1987)

Manufacturing

Number of establishments in 1987: 1,225

Shipments in 1987 ($1,000): $5,491,400

Employees in 1987: 64,600

Change in employment, 1982 to 1987: -9.3%

Average annual pay for manufacturing work in 1989: $31,514

Average annual pay for production work in 1987: $21,884

Wholesale Trade

Number of establishments in 1987: 1,134

Total sales in 1987 ($1,000): $7,160,800

Change in sales, 1982 to 1987: 41.1%

Retail Trade

Number of establishments in 1987: 3,795

Total sales in 1987 ($1,000): $7,160,800

Retail sales per household in 1987: $15,674

Average annual pay in 1989: $10,884

Service Industry

Selected receipts in 1987 ($1,000): $1,451,600

Average annual pay in 1989: $18,778

Housing
Total number of units in 1990: 263,776
Occupied units in 1990: 249,227
Owner-occupied units in 1990: 69.0%
1993 ACCRA average cost: $101,000
1993 ACCRA average rent for an apartment: $446

Chamber of Commerce
Akron Regional Development Board, Richard W. Young, President, 1 Cascade Plaza 8th Fl., Akron, OH 44308. 216-376-5550, FAX 216-379-3164

Economic Development Office
Barberton Area Chamber of Commerce, Victor Myers, Exec. Director, 503 W. Park Ave., Barberton, OH 42203. 216-745-3141. FAX 216-745-3141

Economic Development Organizations
Kent Area Chamber of Commerce, William D. Jones, Exec. Director, 152 Franklin Ave., Kent, OH 44240. 216-673-9855

Major Businesses

Company	SIC	Telephone
Albrecht, Fred W. Co.	5411	(216) 733-2861
Alltel Corp.	4813	(216) 650-7000
Brenlin Corp.	3312	(216) 762-2420
Carter-Jones Companies	5211	(216) 673-6100
Gencorp, Inc.	3764	(216) 869-4200
General Tire Inc.	3011	(216) 798-3000
Goodrich, B. F. Co.	2821	(216) 374-2000
Goodyear Energy Inc.	4922	(216) 796-2121
Goodyear Tire & Rubber Co.	3011	(216) 796-2121
Gulf States Steel	3312	(216) 762-2420
Lawson Co.	5411	(216) 923-0421
Ohio Edison Co.	4911	(216) 384-5100
Polysar Inc.	2821	(216) 836-0451
Ratners U. S. Holding Inc.	5944	(216) 668-5000
Revco D. S. Inc., Twinsburg	5912	(216) 425-9811
Roadway Express, Inc.	4213	(216) 384-1717
Roadway Services, Inc.	4213	(216) 384-8184
Schulman, A. Inc.	2821	(216) 666-3751
Sterling Inc.	5944	(216) 668-5000
Uniroyal Goodrich Tire Co.	3011	(216) 374-3000

Colleges and Universities
Kent State University, Kent
Southern Ohio College, Northeast Campus, Akron
University of Akron, Akron

CANTON, OH (MSA)

Geographic Profile
Land Area
970.9 square miles
Counties and Parishes
Carroll
Stark
Additional Cities/Towns within Area
Alliance
Massillon

Ranking Highlights
205 *out of 319 in total* **land area**
273 *out of 319 in* **population growth,** *1970–1990*
212 *out of 310 in having the lowest* **unemployment** *rate*
112 *out of 310 in size of* **labor force**
260 *out of 318 in the percentage of* **college graduates**
173 *out of 292 in per capita personal* **income**
  99 *out of 319 in number of* **manufacturing establishments**
226 *out of 318 in* **physicians** *per 1000 people*
155 *out of 318 in* **hospital beds** *per 1000 people*
  65 *out of 267 in fewest* **crimes** *per 1000 people*
102 *out of 266 in fewest* **violent crimes** *per 1000 people*
259 *out of 319 in per capita* **federal funds and grants**

Quality of Life Indexes (Rate per 1000 population)
Crime rate in 1991:   46.3
Violent crime rate in 1991:   5.0
Physicians rate in 1992:   1.5
Hospital bed rate in 1991:   3.9

ACCRA Cost of Living Indexes
(First quarter 1993, average = 100)
Composite index: 93.0
Utilities index: 102.6
Housing index: 80.4

Population (1990)
Total Population and Growth Rate
1990: 394,106
1980: 404,421
1970: 393,789
Growth rate 1970–1990: 0%
Race and Hispanic Origin
White: 92.8%
Black: 6.4%
Asian/Pacific Islander: 0.4%
Native American: 0.3%
Hispanic origin: 0.7%
White not Hispanic: 92.2%
Age
Ages 18 to 20: 4.3%
Ages 21 to 24: 5%

677

Ages 25 to 44: 30.8%
Ages 45 to 54: 10.7%
Ages 55 to 59: 4.6%
Ages 60 to 64: 5%
Ages 65 plus: 14.4%

Educational Attainment (1990)

Percent having completed high school: 75.7%
Percent having completed college: 13.9%
Elementary and high school enrollment: 68,350

Federal Funds and Grants Received

Total received in 1989: $959,900,000
Funds received per capita: $2,392

Civilian Labor Force

1993 (April): 195,294
1992 average: 198,178
1991 average: 196,459
1990 average: 195,283

Unemployment

1993 (April): 6.4%
1992 average: 7.8%
1991 average: 6.9%
1990 average: 6.2%

Average Annual Pay

1988: $19,791
1987: $18,682
1985: $18,044

Per Capita Personal Income

1991: $16,778
1990: $16,550
1989: $15,569

Business Climate (1987)

Manufacturing

Number of establishments in 1987: 643
Shipments in 1987 ($1,000): $6,122,300
Employees in 1987: 43,500
Change in employment, 1982 to 1987: -9.9%
Average annual pay for manufacturing work in 1989: $27,751
Average annual pay for production work in 1987: $23,612

Wholesale Trade

Number of establishments in 1987: 559
Total sales in 1987 ($1,000): $2,817,900
Change in sales, 1982 to 1987: 52.5%

Retail Trade

Number of establishments in 1987: 2,445
Total sales in 1987 ($1,000): $2,817,900
Retail sales per household in 1987: $15,536
Average annual pay in 1989: $9,931

Service Industry

Selected receipts in 1987 ($1,000): $767,400
Average annual pay in 1989: $16,213

Housing

Total number of units in 1990: 158,446
Occupied units in 1990: 149,240
Owner-occupied units in 1990: 70.7%
1993 ACCRA average cost: $90,000
1993 ACCRA average rent for an apartment: $397

Chamber of Commerce

Greater Canton Chamber of Commerce, Nick Navarra, President, 229 Wells Ave. N.W., Canton, OH 44703. 216-456-7253

Economic Development Office

Stark Development Board, Stephen L. Paquette, President, 800 Savannah Ave. N.E., Canton, OH 44704. 216-453-5900, FAX 216-453-1793

Economic Development Organizations

Greater Alliance Development Corp., Larry C. Pyers, President, 210 E. Main St., Alliance, OH 44601. 216-823-6260.

Massillon Development Foundation, Gene P. Boerner, Exec. Director, 137 Lincolnway E., Massillon, OH 44646. 216-833-3146

Major Businesses

Company	SIC	Telephone
Akro Corp.	3069	(216) 456-4543
Amster Kirtz Co.	5194	(216) 493-1800
Aultman Health Services Assoc.	8062	(216) 452-9911
Aultman Hospital Association	8062	(216) 452-9911
Brewster Dairy Inc.	2022	(216) 767-3492
Camelot Enterprises Inc.	5099	(216) 494-2282
Camelot Music Inc.	5735	(216) 494-2282
Campbell Oil Co. Inc.	5171	(216) 833-8555
Cardinal Operating Co.	4911	(216) 456-8173
Central Ohio Coal Co., Inc.	1221	(216) 456-8173
Central Trust Northeast Ohio	6021	(216) 455-6711
Citizens Savings Bank of Canton	6035	(216) 489-3600
Diebold, Inc.	3578	(216) 489-4000
First American Savings Bank	6035	(216) 454-3272
Fisher Foods Marketing Inc.	5411	(216) 453-5408
Flemming Foods of Ohio Inc.	5141	(216) 879-5685
John's Sporting Goods Inc.	5091	(216) 456-9100
Luntz Corp.	5093	(216) 455-0211
Nickles, Alfred Bakery Inc.	2051	(216) 879-5635
Ohio Power Co.	4911	(216) 456-8173
Redicon Corp	3411	(216) 492-7537
Republic Storage Systems	2542	(216) 438-5800
Sugardale Foods Inc.	2013	(216) 455-5253
Superior Technology Inc.	3825	(216) 452-4681
Timken Co.	3562	(216) 438-3000
Timken Mercy Medical Center	8062	(216) 489-1000

Colleges and Universities

Kent State University, Stark Campus, Canton

Malone College, Canton
Stark Technical College, Canton
Walsh College, Canton

CINCINNATI, OH–KY–IN (PMSA)

Geographic Profile

Land Area

2125.0 square miles

Counties and Parishes

Indiana
   Dearborn
Kentucky
   Boone
   Campbell
   Kenton
Ohio
   Clermont
   Hamilton
   Warren

Ranking Highlights

83   *out of 319 in total* **land area**
243   *out of 319 in* **population growth,** *1970–1990*
76   *out of 310 in having the lowest* **unemployment** *rate*
30   *out of 310 in size of* **labor force**
128   *out of 318 in the percentage of* **college graduates**
67   *out of 292 in per capita personal* **income**
35   *out of 319 in number of* **manufacturing establishments**
72   *out of 318 in* **physicians** *per 1000 people*
142   *out of 318 in* **hospital beds** *per 1000 people*
108   *out of 267 in fewest* **crimes** *per 1000 people*
139   *out of 266 in fewest* **violent crimes** *per 1000 people*
72   *out of 319 in per capita* **federal funds and grants**

Quality of Life Indexes (Rate per 1000 population)

Crime rate in 1991:	56.7
Violent crime rate in 1991:	6.5
Physicians rate in 1992:	2.45
Hospital bed rate in 1991:	4.07

ACCRA Cost of Living Indexes

(First quarter 1993, average = 100)

Composite index:	104.7
Utilities index:	100.6
Housing index:	108.1

Overview

Cincinnati, the seat of Hamilton County, is Ohio's third largest city and the center of a metropolitan statistical area comprised of Clermont, Hamilton, and Warren counties in Ohio, Kenton County in Kentucky, and Dearborn County in Indiana.

Cincinnati's diversified economic base includes manufacturing, wholesale and retail trade, insurance and finance, health services, and transportation. Known worldwide for Procter & Gamble soap products and U.S. Playing Cards, the city ranks high nationally in the value of manufacturing shipments, which totalled more than $21 billion in 1986. Fortune 500 companies that have established headquarters in Cincinnati include Procter & Gamble, Penn Central, Cincinnati Milacron Inc., Federated Department Stores Inc., Kroger Company, and U.S. Shoe Corporation. More than 340 other Fortune 500 companies maintain operations in Cincinnati. Companies that have recently relocated headquarters there include Heinz Pet Products, James River Corp., and Mercantile Stores. Retail sales average $2.6 billion annually. Banking assets total over $17 billion.

Five hundred area firms have contributed to Cincinnati's position as an international trade center, generating approximately $3 billion in sales to markets outside the United States each year. Among the export products are jet engines, machine tools, computer software, paper, and consumer goods; products imported into the city average around $2 billion yearly. Foreign investment in the local economy is increasing; ninety Cincinnati-area firms are presently owned by companies in Japan, England, Western Europe, and Canada.

Federal agencies with regional centers located in the city are the U. S. Postal Service, the U.S. Internal Revenue Service, the U.S. Environmental Protection Agency, and the National Institute for Occupational Safety and Health.

The Dr. Albert B. Sabin Cincinnati Convention Center is conveniently situated downtown and connected via the twenty-block Skywalk system with shops and stores, restaurants, entertainment and cultural activities, and hotels. The architecturally interesting entrance to the post-modern style Convention Center features the preserved facade of the historic Albee Theatre, which once stood near Fountain Square and was demolished several years ago.

The complex consists of three levels: the exhibit level contains three halls with 162,000 square feet of combined space that will accommodate up to 15,000 meeting participants; on the second level forty–one separate rooms provide banquet and meeting capacities ranging from 30 to 2,300 people; and the third level is comprised of three ballrooms that combine to offer thirty thousand square feet of space. Convention center amenities include a banquet kitchen, teleconferencing facilities, handicapped access, and adjacent parking for five thousand vehicles.

Meeting and convention accommodations can also be found at several luxury hotels clustered downtown near the Convention Center and at other hotels and motels throughout the Greater Cincinnati area. More than fifteen thousand lodging rooms are available, with more than twenty–eight hundred of them located within three blocks of the convention center.

The Cincinnati/Northern Kentucky International Airport is located in northern Kentucky, about 12 miles from the Cincinnati center city. Served by eight major commercial airlines that schedule well over six hundred commercial flights daily (including nonstop service to London, Paris, and Frankfurt), the airport is one of five Delta Airlines hubs in the United States. Highways providing access to downtown and the metropolitan region are: Interstates 71, 74, 75, 275, and 471; U.S. 22, 25, 27, 42, 50, 52, and 127; and several state and county routes.

Passenger rail service into renovated Union Terminal is available through Amtrak; bus transportation is provided by Greyhound and Southeastern Trailways.

Population (1990)

Total Population and Growth Rate
1990: 1,452,645
1980: 1,401,470
1970: 1,387,207
Growth rate 1970–1990: 5%

Race and Hispanic Origin
White: 85.8%
Black: 13.1%
Asian/Pacific Islander: 0.8%
Native American: 0.1%
Hispanic origin: 0.5%
White not Hispanic: 85.4%

Age
Ages 18 to 20: 4.4%
Ages 21 to 24: 5.8%
Ages 25 to 44: 32.5%
Ages 45 to 54: 9.8%
Ages 55 to 59: 4.3%
Ages 60 to 64: 4.3%
Ages 65 plus: 12.1%

Educational Attainment (1990)
Percent having completed high school: 74.9%
Percent having completed college: 20.5%
Elementary and high school enrollment: 253,829

Federal Funds and Grants Received
Total received in 1989: $5,883,800,000
Funds received per capita: $4,061

Civilian Labor Force
1993 (April): 796,581
1992 average: 792,858
1991 average: 785,939
1990 average: 787,587

Unemployment
1993 (April): 5.3%
1992 average: 5.6%
1991 average: 5.0%
1990 average: 42%

Average Annual Pay
1988: $21,981
1987: $21,150
1985: $19,532

Per Capita Personal Income

1991: $19,273
1990: $18,766
1989: $17,603

Business Climate (1987)

Manufacturing

Number of establishments in 1987: 2,242
Shipments in 1987 ($1,000): $22,532,600
Employees in 1987: 151,900
Change in employment, 1982 to 1987: 1.3%
Average annual pay for manufacturing work in 1989: $31,798
Average annual pay for production work in 1987: $23,999

Wholesale Trade

Number of establishments in 1987: 2,955
Total sales in 1987 ($1,000): $25,745,600
Change in sales, 1982 to 1987: 37.5%

Retail Trade

Number of establishments in 1987: 8,398
Total sales in 1987 ($1,000): $25,745,600
Retail sales per household in 1987: $17,327
Average annual pay in 1989: $11,607

Service Industry

Selected receipts in 1987 ($1,000): $4,772,400
Average annual pay in 1989: $19,024

Office Real Estate (1992)

Office space inventory: 21,887,369 square feet
Average class A Central Business District rental range per sq. ft: $22.00

Vacancy Rates

All areas: 17.1%

Vacancy Rates in Central Business District

Class A space: 11.3%
Class B space: 23.3%

Vacancy Rates Outside Central Business District

Class A space: 16.3%
Class B space: 20.5%

Housing

Total number of units in 1990: 582,376
Occupied units in 1990: 548,385
Owner-occupied units in 1990: 63.1%
1993 ACCRA average cost: $121,329
1993 ACCRA average rent for an apartment: $570

Chamber of Commerce

Greater Cincinnati Chamber of Commerce, John Williams, Jr., President, 300 Carew Tower, 441 Vine St., Cincinnati, OH 45202. 513-579-3100

Economic Development Office

Hamilton County Development Co., David K. Main, Exec. Director, 1776 Mentor Ave., Cincinnati, OH 45212. 513-632-8292

Economic Development Organizations

Cincinnati Department of Economic Development, Quentin Davis, Director, 801 Plum St., Cincinnati, OH 45202. 513-352-3950, FAX 513-352-6257

Major Businesses

Company	SIC	Telephone
Adam Wholesalers, Inc.	5031	(513) 772-9092
Allied Stores Corp.	5311	(513) 579-7000
American Financial Corp.	2011	(513) 579-2121
Bethesda, Inc.	8062	(513) 569-6111
Bloomingdale's Inc.	5311	(513) 579-7000
Central TrustCo.	6021	(513) 651-8896
Charter Co. Inc.	5172	(513) 579-2482
Chemed Corp.	2841	(513) 762-6900
Chiquita Brands International	2011	(513) 784-8000
Cincinnati Bell Inc.	4813	(513) 397-9900
Cincinnati Bell Information System	7373	(513) 784-5900
Cincinnati Gas & Electric Co.	4911	(513) 381-2000
Cincinnati Milacron Inc.	3541	(513) 841-8100
Cincinnati Milacron Marketing	5084	(513) 841-8100
Cintas Corp.	7218	(513) 489-4000
Community Mutual Insurance Co.	6324	(513) 977-8834
Drackett Co.	2842	(513) 632-1500
Dubois Chemicals Inc.	2992	(513) 762-6000
Duro Bag Mfg. Co.	2674	(606) 581-8200
Eagle-Picher Industries Inc.	3714	(513) 721-7010
Federal Home Loan Bank Cincinnati	6019	(513) 852-7500
Federated Department Store	5311	(513) 579-7000
Federated Stores Inc.	5311	(513) 579-7000
Fifth Third Bank Corp.	6022	(513) 579-5300
Gibson Greetings, Inc.	2771	(513) 841-6600
GK Technologies Inc.	3351	(513) 579-6600
Great American Holding Co.	6331	(513) 369-5000
Great American Communications Co.	4833	(513) 579-2177
Heekin Can Inc.	3411	(513) 489-3200
Hook-Superx, Inc.	5912	(513) 782-3000
Hyper Shoppes, Inc.	5411	(513) 753-7500
Hyper Shoppes (Ohio) Inc.	5411	(513) 753-7500
Joseph, David J. Co.	5093	(513) 621-8770
Kroger Co.	5411	(513) 762-4000
Litton Atomation Systems	3535	(606) 283-2202
Mazak Corp.	5084	(606) 727-5700
Merrell Dow Pharmaceuticals	2834	(513) 948-9111
Midland Enterprises Inc.	4449	(513) 721-4000
Morrell, John & Co. Inc.	2011	(513) 852-3500
National Sanitary Supply Co.	5087	(513) 762-6500
NS Group Inc.	3312	(606) 292-6809
Nutone, Inc.	3634	(513) 527-5100

Major Businesses (Continued)

Company	SIC	Telephone
Ohio National Life Insurance	6311	(513) 861-3600
PCC Technical Industries	8711	(513) 579-6600
Penn Central Corp.	3357	(513) 579-6600
Pennsylvania Co. Inc.	4899	(513) 579-6618
Procter & Gamble Co.	2841	(513) 983-1100
Procter & Gamble Distribution	5169	(513) 983-1100
Provident Bank Corp.	6022	(513) 579-2000
Richardson-Vicks Inc.	2834	(513) 983-1100
Scripps, Edward W. Trust	2711	(513) 977-3000
Scripps Howard Broadcasting Co.	4833	(513) 977-3000
SHV North America Corp.	5093	(513) 621-4014
Sisters of Charity Health	8741	(513) 922-9775
Star Banc Corp.	6021	(513) 632-4000
Star Bank National Association	6021	(513) 632-4000
Sundor Group Inc.	2033	(513) 983-1100
Thriftway Inc.	5411	(513) 984-0500
Union Central Life Insurance Co.	6311	(513) 595-2200
United States Shoe Corp.	5621	(513) 527-7000
Western Southern Life Insurance	6311	(513) 629-1800
Westinghouse Mutuals Co. of Ohio	2819	(513) 738-6200

Colleges and Universities

Antonelli Institute of Art and Photography, Cincinnati, OH
Art Academy of Cincinnati, Cincinnati, OH
Cincinnati College of Mortuary Science, Cincinnati, OH
Cincinnati Technical College, Cincinnati, OH
College of Mount St. Joseph, Cincinnati, OH
Southern Ohio College, Cincinnati Campus, Cincinnati, OH
Southwestern College of Business, Cincinnati, OH
Union Institute, Cincinnati, OH
University of Cincinnati, Cincinnati, OH
University of Cincinnati Raymond Walters College, Cincinnati, OH

CLEVELAND, OH (PMSA)

Geographic Profile

Land Area

1512.2 square miles

Counties and Parishes

Cuyahoga
Geauga
Lake
Medina

Ranking Highlights

132 *out of 319 in total* **land area**
315 *out of 319 in* **population growth,** *1970–1990*
139 *out of 310 in having the lowest* **unemployment** *rate*
24 *out of 310 in size of* **labor force**
140 *out of 318 in the percentage of* **college graduates**
51 *out of 292 in per capita personal* **income**
12 *out of 319 in number of* **manufacturing establishments**
24 *out of 318 in* **physicians** *per 1000 people*
88 *out of 318 in* **hospital beds** *per 1000 people*
75 *out of 267 in fewest* **crimes** *per 1000 people*
144 *out of 266 in fewest* **violent crimes** *per 1000 people*
146 *out of 319 in per capita* **federal funds and grants**

Quality of Life Indexes (Rate per 1000 population)

Crime rate in 1991:	48.5
Violent crime rate in 1991:	6.7
Physicians rate in 1992:	3.17
Hospital bed rate in 1991:	4.85

ACCRA Cost of Living Indexes

(First quarter 1993, average = 100)
Composite index: 109.8
Utilities index: 129.0
Housing index: 117.2

Overview

Cleveland is located midway between New York City and Chicago, Illinois, and is within a 500-mile radius of 44 percent of the U.S. population, 43 percent of U.S. business establishments, and 47 percent of U.S. industrial shipments and service receipts. It is the 13th largest consumer market in the nation. Forty-six percent of the Fortune 500 industrial corporations and 31 percent of Fortune 500 service companies are represented in Cleveland through corporate headquarters (18), major divisions, subsidiaries, and sales offices. In 1991, 68 corporations headquartered in Cleveland had annual revenues greater than $200 million. There are approximately 40,000 small businesses in Greater Cleveland, representing 97 percent of the area's total business establishments and employing 45 percent of the area's work force. The average Greater Clevelander travels 23 minutes to work.

The region has 125 public and private airports with Hopkins International Airport offering 300 scheduled passenger departures daily. The Port of Cleveland is the largest overseas general cargo port on Lake Erie and the third largest on the Great Lakes. The Port was declared a foreign trade zone in 1990 and handles 14 million tons of cargo annually.

Convention facilities include the International Exposition Center (I-X Center), the largest single building exposition facility in the world with 2.5 million square feet of indoor space, and the Cleveland Convention Center with 480,00 square feet of exhibition space. 25,000 hotel rooms are in the area with 2,300 within a 10-minute walk of the Cleveland Convention Center. Cultural and Sports organizations located in Cleveland include the Cleveland Orchestra, the Cleveland Museum of Art, the Indians baseball team, the Browns football team, and the Cavaliers basketball team.

Over the past five years more than $7 billion has been invested in new office buildings, retail centers, and recreational attractions. Major new development projects include the $362 million Gateway sports/entertainment complex, and the North Coast Harbor lakefront development. Recently completed commercial development includes the $95 million Bank One Center, the $430 million Society Bank Center, and the $400 million Tower City Center/Ritz Carlton Hotel/Skylight Office Tower.

Population (1990)

Total Population and Growth Rate
1990: 1,831,122
1980: 1,898,825
1970: 2,063,729
Growth rate 1970–1990: -11%

Race and Hispanic Origin
White: 78.4%
Black: 19.4%
Asian/Pacific Islander: 1.1%
Native American: 0.2%
Hispanic origin: 1.9%
White not Hispanic: 77.5%

Age
Ages 18 to 20:   4%
Ages 21 to 24: 5.3%
Ages 25 to 44: 31.6%
Ages 45 to 54: 10.4%
Ages 55 to 59: 4.6%
Ages 60 to 64:   5%
Ages 65 plus: 14.6%

Educational Attainment (1990)
Percent having completed high school: 75.7%
Percent having completed college: 19.9%
Elementary and high school enrollment: 299,539

Federal Funds and Grants Received
Total received in 1989: $5,879,900,000
Funds received per capita: $3,187

Civilian Labor Force
1993 (April):   936,294
1992 average: 951,180
1991 average: 943,822
1990 average: 952,639

Unemployment
1993 (April): 5.9%
1992 average: 6.6%
1991 average: 5.5%
1990 average: 4.8%

Average Annual Pay
1988: $23,051
1987: $21,985
1985: $20,713

Per Capita Personal Income
1991: $19,995
1990: $19,706
1989: $18,611

Business Climate (1987)

Manufacturing
Number of establishments in 1987: 4,155
Shipments in 1987 ($1,000): $22,056,600
Employees in 1987: 203,300
Change in employment, 1982 to 1987: -9.2%
Average annual pay for manufacturing work in 1989: $31,288
Average annual pay for production work in 1987: $24,582

Wholesale Trade
Number of establishments in 1987: 4,311
Total sales in 1987 ($1,000): $26,254,600
Change in sales, 1982 to 1987: 19.7%

Retail Trade
Number of establishments in 1987: 10,993
Total sales in 1987 ($1,000): $26,254,600
Retail sales per household in 1987: $15,991
Average annual pay in 1989: $11,485

Service Industry
Selected receipts in 1987 ($1,000): $6,310,400
Average annual pay in 1989: $21,090

Office Real Estate (1992)
Office space inventory: 35,877,555 square feet
Average class A Central Business District rental range per sq. ft: $21.00

Vacancy Rates
All areas: 23.9%

Vacancy Rates in Central Business District
Class A space: 23.7%
Class B space: 25.3%

Vacancy Rates Outside Central Business District
Class A space: 16.5%
Class B space: 41.8%

Housing

Total number of units in 1990: 758,984

Occupied units in 1990: 712,362

Owner-occupied units in 1990: 65.4%

1993 ACCRA average cost: $127,926

1993 ACCRA average rent for an apartment: $628

Chamber of Commerce

Greater Cleveland Growth Association, William H. Bryant, President, 690 Huntington Bldg., Cleveland, OH 44115. 216-621-3300

Economic Development Office

Cleveland Department of Economic Development, Joseph Marinucci, Deputy Director of Development, 601 Lakeside Ave. Room 210, City Hall, Cleveland, OH 44114. 216-664-2406, FAX 216-664-3681

Major Businesses

Company	SIC	Telephone
Alcan Aluminum Corp	3353	(216) 523-6800
American Greetings Corp.	2771	(216) 252-7300
American Seaway Foods Inc.	5141	(216) 292-7000
Ameritrust Corp.	6021	(216) 737-5000
Austin Co.	8712	(216) 382-6600
Bearings Inc.	5085	(216) 881-2838
Blue Cross & Blue Shield Mutual	6324	(216) 687-7000
BP America Inc.	2911	(216) 586-4141
BP Chemicals Inc.	2869	(216) 586-4141
BP Exploration (Alaska)	1311	(216) 586-4141
BP Oil Co. Inc.	5541	(216) 586-4141
BP Oil Supply Co.	5172	(216) 586-4141
BP Pipelines (Alaska) Inc.	4612	(216) 586-4141
CNC Holding Corp.	5945	(216) 449-4100
Centerior Energy Corp.	4911	(216) 447-3100
Cleveland Clinic Foundation	8062	(216) 444-2104
Cleveland Electric Illuminating Co.	4911	(216) 622-9800
East Ohio Gas Co.	4923	(216) 432-3232
Eaton Corp.	3714	(216) 523-5000
Federal Reserve Bank of Cleveland	6011	(216) 579-2000
Ferro Corp.	2899	(216) 641-8580
Figgie International Inc.	3569	(216) 953-2700
First National Supermarket	5411	(216) 587-7100
Fisher Foods Inc.	5411	(216) 292-7000
Glidden Co.	2851	(216) 344-8000
Gould Inc.	3825	(216) 953-5000
Growth International Industries	3089	(216) 991-9700
Hanna, M. A. Co.	3087	(216) 589-4000
Harris Wholesale Co.	5122	(216) 248-8100
Leaseway Holdings, Inc.	4213	(216) 765-5500
Leaseway Transportation Co.	4213	(216) 765-5500
Lincoln Electric Co.	3548	(216) 481-8100

Major Businesses (Continued)

Company	SIC	Telephone
LTV Steel Co. Inc.	3312	(216) 622-5000
Lubrizol Corp.	2899	(216) 943-4200
M.K. Ferguson Co.	1541	(216) 523-5600
Nacco Industries Inc.	3537	(216) 752-1000
National City Bank	6021	(216) 575-2000
National City Corp.	6021	(216) 575-2000
Ohio Bell Telephone Co.	4813	(216) 822-9700
Parker Hannifin Corp.	3594	(216) 531-3000
Picker International Inc.	3844	(216) 473-3000
Premier Industrial Corp.	5065	(216) 391-8300
Progressive Corp.	6331	(216) 464-8000
Reliance Electric Co.	3621	(216) 266-5800
Riser Foods, Inc.	5411	(216) 292-7000
Scott & Fetzer Co.	3635	(216) 892-3000
Sealy Corp.	2515	(216) 522-1310
Sherwin-Williams Co.	5231	(216) 566-2000
Society Corp.	6022	(216) 689-3000
Society National Bank	6021	(216) 689-3000
Standard Products Co.	3069	(216) 281-8300
Stouffer Foods Corp.	2038	(216) 248-3600
Stouffer Hotel Management	7011	(216) 248-3600
Sudbury Inc.	3714	(216) 464-7026
TSC Holdings Inc.	2038	(216) 248-3600
Transohio Savings Bank	6022	(216) 621-9600
TRW Inc.	3679	(216) 291-7000
White Consolidated Industries	3631	(216) 252-3700

Colleges and Universities

Case Western Reserve University, Cleveland

Cleveland Institute of Art, Cleveland

Cleveland Institute of Electronics, Cleveland

Cleveland Institute of Music, Cleveland

Cleveland State University, Cleveland

Cuyahoga Community College, Metropolitan Campus, Cleveland

Dyke College, Cleveland

ETI Technical College, Cleveland

Notre Dame College of Ohio, Cleveland

Sawyer College of Business, Cleveland

Sawyer College of Business, Cleveland Heights

COLUMBUS, OH (MSA)

Geographic Profile

Land Area

3578.9 square miles

Counties and Parishes

Delaware

Fairfield

Franklin

Licking

Madison

Pickaway

Union

Additional Cities/Towns within Area

Lancaster

Newark

Ranking Highlights

34 *out of 319 in total* **land area**

176 *out of 319 in* **population growth,** *1970–1990*

64 *out of 310 in having the lowest* **unemployment** *rate*

80 *out of 310 in size of* **labor force**

61 *out of 318 in the percentage of* **college graduates**

87 *out of 292 in per capita personal* **income**

46 *out of 319 in number of* **manufacturing establishments**

103 *out of 318 in* **physicians** *per 1000 people*

201 *out of 318 in* **hospital beds** *per 1000 people*

187 *out of 267 in fewest* **crimes** *per 1000 people*

160 *out of 266 in fewest* **violent crimes** *per 1000 people*

145 *out of 319 in per capita* **federal funds and grants**

Quality of Life Indexes (Rate per 1000 population)

Crime rate in 1991:	69.8
Violent crime rate in 1991:	7.2
Physicians rate in 1992:	2.14
Hospital bed rate in 1991:	3.43

ACCRA Cost of Living Indexes

(First quarter 1993, average = 100)

Composite index:	N/A
Utilities index:	N/A
Housing index:	N/A

Overview

Columbus is the capital of Ohio. Located in Columbus are over 50 insurance companies and 25 banks. One hundred eighty firms with revenues over $25 million are headquartered in Columbus including Adria Laboratories, Borden, CompuServe, Nationwide Insurance, Limited, Rax, Red Roof Inn and Wendy's. The service sector accounts for approximately 82 percent of the regional employment. Over one-quarter million new service-oriented jobs were created in central Ohio during the past 20 years. Approximately 15 million square feet of office space were built in the region since 1980.

Several major multi-use developments are under construction. Tuttle Crossing is a 400-acre, mixed-use development in northwest Franklin County that includes a privately funded freeway interchange. A 1.5 million square-foot regional mall is planned for the site in addition to 2 million square feet of office and 1,100 apartments. Polaris Centers of Commerce and Industry is a 1,300-acre, mixed-use development in south central Delaware County. Eight million square feet of office and light manufacturing are planned for the site. Over 370,000 square feet have been built in the past two years. A 1,000-acre site is planned to include a regional shopping mall, five million square feet of office space and warehouse uses. Local developers have assembled 4,000 acres generally referred to as the villages of New Albany. Approximately 4,000 housing units and 4.5 million square feet of associated commercial uses are planned for the site. A four-lane, limited-access highway will soon be constructed to serve this area.

Port Columbus International Airport is located 10 minutes by freeway from the central business district. Travelers can conveniently connect to virtually every major city.

Columbus is in the process of organizing an Inland Port which will allow it to become an international distribution hub in the midwest. Rickenbacker Air/Industrial Park, located in the southeast quadrant of Franklin County, combines a world-class airfield with all the economic advantages of a general purpose foreign trade zone. Approximately $200 million have been spent on infrastructure improvements to the airfield and 800 of the 1,600 acres available with in the airfield boundaries are currently serviced and ready for development. Approximately 2.5 million square feet of industrial warehousing are currently under construction in and around the airfield, including a 1.5 million square foot distribution center for Speigel.

Convention facilities include the downtown convention complex which connects 475,000 square feet of exhibition space to 900 hotel rooms. The centerpiece of the complex is the Columbus Convention Center. Other major convention venues are the vast 360 acre Ohio Exhibition Center and Veterans Memorial. There are more than 15,000 hotel rooms in the region with 2,400 of these located in downtown Columbus.

Cultural and sports organizations in Columbus include the Columbus Symphony Orchestra, Ballet Met, the Columbus Museum of Art, COSI-Ohio's Center of Science and Industry, the PGA Memorial Tournament, the Columbus Clippers, and the Ohio State Buckeyes.

Population (1990)

Total Population and Growth Rate

1990: 1,377,419

1980: 1,243,827

1970: 1,149,432
Growth rate 1970–1990: 20%

Race and Hispanic Origin
White: 86.0%
Black: 12.0%
Asian/Pacific Islander: 1.5%
Native American: 0.2%
Hispanic origin: 0.8%
White not Hispanic: 85.5%

Age
Ages 18 to 20: 5.3%
Ages 21 to 24: 7.1%
Ages 25 to 44: 34.6%
Ages 45 to 54: 9.9%
Ages 55 to 59: 4%
Ages 60 to 64: 3.9%
Ages 65 plus: 10%

Educational Attainment (1990)
Percent having completed high school: 79.7%
Percent having completed college: 23.0%
Elementary and high school enrollment: 224,737

Federal Funds and Grants Received
Total received in 1989: $4,296,200,000
Funds received per capita: $3,196

Civilian Labor Force
1993 (April): 754,816
1992 average: 761,091
1991 average: 743,756
1990 average: 739,747

Unemployment
1993 (April): 4.8%
1992 average: 5.3%
1991 average: 4.6%
1990 average: 4.4%

Average Annual Pay
1988: $21,301
1987: $20,333
1985: $19,003

Per Capita Personal Income
1991: $18,630
1990: $18,161
1989: $17,345

Business Climate (1987)
Manufacturing
Number of establishments in 1987: 1,573
Shipments in 1987 ($1,000): $15,936,600
Employees in 1987: 98,700
Change in employment, 1982 to 1987: -1.9%
Average annual pay for manufacturing work in 1989: $29,284
Average annual pay for production work in 1987: $23,341

Wholesale Trade
Number of establishments in 1987: 2,476
Total sales in 1987 ($1,000): $15,950,500
Change in sales, 1982 to 1987: 45.0%

Retail Trade
Number of establishments in 1987: 7,410
Total sales in 1987 ($1,000): $15,950,500
Retail sales per household in 1987: $17,700
Average annual pay in 1989: $12,393

Service Industry
Selected receipts in 1987 ($1,000): $4,336,700
Average annual pay in 1989: $19,506

Office Real Estate (1992)
Office space inventory: 25,010,000 square feet
Average class A Central Business District rental range per sq. ft: $20.00

Vacancy Rates
All areas: 8.8%

Vacancy Rates in Central Business District
Class A space: 5.4%
Class B space: 10.3%

Vacancy Rates Outside Central Business District
Class A space: 7.3%
Class B space: 17.3%

Housing
Total number of units in 1990: 559,446
Occupied units in 1990: 524,535
Owner-occupied units in 1990: 60.1%
1993 ACCRA average cost: N/A
1993 ACCRA average rent for an apartment: N/A

Chamber of Commerce
Columbus Chamber of Commerce, Machelle Williams, Manager, 37 N. High St., PO Box 1527, Columbus, OH 43216. 800-441-4441

Economic Development Office
Mid-Ohio Regional Planning Commisssion, William Habig, Exec. Director, 285 E. Main St., Columbus, OH 43215. 614-228-2663, FAX 614-621-2401

Major Businesses

Company	SIC	Telephone
Alexander & Alexander of Columbus	6411	(614) 228-6115
American Electric Power Co.	4911	(614) 223-1000
Banc One Corp.	6021	(614) 248-5944
Banc One Ohio Corp.	6021	(614) 248-6800
Battelle Memorial Institution	8731	(614) 424-6424
Big Bear Stores Co.	5411	(614) 464-6500
Cardinal Distribution, Inc.	5122	(614) 761-8700
Columbia Gas of Ohio, Inc.	4924	(614) 460-6000
Columbus Southern Power Co.	4911	(614) 464-7700

Major Businesses (Continued)

Company	SIC	Telephone
Consolidated Stores Corp.	5719	(614) 278-6800
Consolidated Stores International	5719	(614) 278-6800
Countrymark, Inc.	5153	(614) 548-8200
Drug Emporium, Inc.	5912	(614) 888-6876
Huntington Bancshares Inc.	6021	(614) 476-8300
Huntington National Bank	6021	(614) 476-8300
Lancaster Colony Corp.	3069	(614) 224-7141
Lane Bryant, Inc.	5621	(614) 930-9200
Limited Express, Inc.	5621	(614) 479-4000
Limited Inc.	5621	(614) 479-7000
Limited Stores Inc.	5621	(614) 479-2000
Mid-America Federal Savings & Loan	6035	(614) 278-3300
Nationwide Corp.	6311	(614) 249-7111
Nationwide Life Insurance Co.	6311	(614) 249-7111
Nationwide Mutual Fire Insurance	6331	(614) 249-7111
Nationwide Mutual Insurance Co.	6331	(614) 249-7111
Schottenstein Stores Corp	5311	(614) 221-9200
U.S. Health Corp Columbus	8062	(614) 261-5902
Warner Cable Communications	4841	(614) 792-7000
Wendy's International Inc.	5812	(614) 764-3100
Worthington Industries	3316	(614) 438-3210

Colleges and Universities

Bliss College, Columbus
Bradford School, Columbus
Capital University, Columbus
Central Ohio Technical College, Newark
Columbus College of Art and Design, Columbus
Columbus State Community College, Columbus
Devry Institute of Technology, Columbus
Franklin University, Columbus
Ohio Dominican College, Columbus
Ohio State University, Columbus
Ohio State University-Newark Campus, Newark
Ohio University-Lancaster, Lancaster
Pontifical College Josephinum, Columbus

DAYTON–SPRINGFIELD, OH (MSA)

Geographic Profile

Land Area
1683.7 square miles

Counties and Parishes
Clark
Greene
Miami
Montgomery

Ranking Highlights

116 *out of 319 in total* land area
281 *out of 319 in* population growth, *1970–1990*
128 *out of 310 in having the lowest* unemployment *rate*
 55 *out of 310 in size of* labor force
157 *out of 318 in the percentage of* college graduates
100 *out of 292 in per capita personal* income
 45 *out of 319 in number of* manufacturing establishments
152 *out of 318 in* physicians *per 1000 people*
116 *out of 318 in* hospital beds *per 1000 people*
118 *out of 267 in fewest* crimes *per 1000 people*
152 *out of 266 in fewest* violent crimes *per 1000 people*
 47 *out of 319 in per capita* federal funds and grants

Quality of Life Indexes (Rate per 1000 population)

Crime rate in 1991:	58.4
Violent crime rate in 1991:	6.9
Physicians rate in 1992:	1.83
Hospital bed rate in 1991:	4.4

ACCRA Cost of Living Indexes

(First quarter 1993, average = 100)
Composite index: 99.3
Utilities index: 99.1
Housing index: 105.4

Overview

Dayton, the seat of Ohio's Montgomery County, is the focus of a two-county metropolitan statistical area. World-famous through the pioneering efforts of the Wright brothers, today Dayton is an aviation center and home of Wright-Patterson Air Force Base, headquarters of the U. S. Air Force bomber program. Dayton, once vulnerable to severe flooding, was the site of the first comprehensive flood control project of its kind. Today the city is at the center of industrial and high-technology development, serving traditional and new markets.

Dayton's balanced economy is supported principally by manufacturing, wholesale and retail trade, and services. Nine of the nation's largest manufacturing companies have established headquarters in the city. The Dayton area is experiencing economic expansion with the establishment of multinational firms such as AGA, Burdox, Marconi Avionics, Honda, Fujitech Industries Inc., and Pioneer Electronics.

The transportation equipment industry, employing one-fifth of manufacturing workers, has been established for many years in Dayton. Two major auto makers operate divisions in the city: six General Motors plants make small trucks, diesel engines, braking systems, and other automotive components, and a Chrysler subsidiary produces air-conditioning units. Dayton has also become the site of extensive investment by Japanese auto makers.

More than fifteen hundred other firms in the Dayton area manufacture accounting systems, bicycles, castings and forgings, compressors, concrete products, washing machines, generators, hoists and jacks, industrial belts, machine tools, name plates, paints and varnishes, paper and paper-making machinery, plastics, precision gauges, tools and dies, and meat products.

Wright-Patterson Air Force Base, the research and development arm of the U.S. Air Force, is the headquarters of the Air Force Logistics Command, Air Force Material Command, and the Aeronautical Systems Division (ASD), in addition to more than one hundred other Department of Defense divisions. The new U.S. Defense Department Joint Logistics Systems Center, affiliated with Wright–Patterson, oversees the installation of new computer systems for all military services; the center is expected to generate numerous private sector jobs. The ASD at Wright–Patterson manages the U.S. Air Force bomber program; also housed at the base is the Center for Artificial Intelligence Applications (CAIA). In addition to attracting CAIA, Wright–Patterson is credited with bringing to Dayton one of the highest concentrations of aerospace/high–technology firms in the nation. More than 830 such firms employ more than twenty–three thousand scientists, engineers, technicians, and specialists actively involved in development and application in both the private and public sectors. A vital factor in the metropolitan area economy is the Miami Valley Research Park, supported by the Miami Valley Research Foundation, a private, nonprofit corporation; the 1,500-acre park is the site of corporate and government research firms.

Dayton International Airport, ranking among the nation's busiest air-freight facilities, is the midwestern hub for Emery Worldwide and a base for three other air cargo carriers. Dayton's central location places its over-the-road market of more than 5.6 million people, one of the largest in the country, within a ninety-minute drive from the city. Thirty trucking companies maintain terminals in the metropolitan area; most are located at the intersection of I-70 and I-75, twenty minutes from the airport.

Three Class I rail systems furnish rail cargo transportation, including trailer on flat car service; both CSX and Conrail operate switching yards in the city. Because of its transportation system, which affords direct access to major markets,

Dayton has become an important warehouse and distribution center.

Highways into metropolitan Dayton include two major interstate freeways, east-west I-70 and north-south I-75; I-675, a bypass, connects these highways and provides direct access to the city from Columbus and Cincinnati. U.S. 35 extends from east to west through the southern sector of Dayton. State routes leading into Dayton from points throughout the state and the immediate vicinity are 4, 202, 48, and 49—all with a general north-south orientation.

Population (1990)

Total Population and Growth Rate

1990: 951,270
1980: 942,083
1970: 974,927
Growth rate 1970–1990: -2%

Race and Hispanic Origin

White: 85.3%
Black: 13.3%
Asian/Pacific Islander: 1.0%
Native American: 0.2%
Hispanic origin: 0.8%
White not Hispanic: 84.8%

Age

Ages 18 to 20: 4.9%
Ages 21 to 24: 5.9%
Ages 25 to 44: 31.5%
Ages 45 to 54: 10.9%
Ages 55 to 59: 4.6%
Ages 60 to 64: 4.5%
Ages 65 plus: 12.4%

Educational Attainment (1990)

Percent having completed high school: 77.6%
Percent having completed college: 19.1%
Elementary and high school enrollment: 161,042

Federal Funds and Grants Received

Total received in 1989: $4,462,100,000
Funds received per capita: $4,707

Civilian Labor Force

1993 (April): 467,610
1992 average: 477,114
1991 average: 474,402
1990 average: 476,876

Unemployment

1993 (April): 5.1%
1992 average: 6.5%
1991 average: 5.8%
1990 average: 5.3%

Average Annual Pay

1988: $21,981

1987: $20,612
1985: $19,687

Per Capita Personal Income
1991: $18,302
1990: $17,808
1989: $17,011

Business Climate (1987)

Manufacturing
Number of establishments in 1987: 1,588
Shipments in 1987 ($1,000): $13,541,500
Employees in 1987: 105,900
Change in employment, 1982 to 1987: 10.2%
Average annual pay for manufacturing work in 1989: $32,031
Average annual pay for production work in 1987: $26,008

Wholesale Trade
Number of establishments in 1987: 1,472
Total sales in 1987 ($1,000): $7,756,000
Change in sales, 1982 to 1987: 45.3%

Retail Trade
Number of establishments in 1987: 5,229
Total sales in 1987 ($1,000): $7,756,000
Retail sales per household in 1987: $16,334
Average annual pay in 1989: $10,680

Service Industry
Selected receipts in 1987 ($1,000): $2,690,400
Average annual pay in 1989: $19,743

Office Real Estate (1992)
Office space inventory: 6,717,413 square feet
Average class A Central Business District rental range per sq. ft: $16.26

Vacancy Rates
All areas: 17.5%

Vacancy Rates in Central Business District
Class A space: 19.5%
Class B space: 22.8%

Vacancy Rates Outside Central Business District
Class A space: 13.1%
Class B space: 16.0%

Housing
Total number of units in 1990: 385,420
Occupied units in 1990: 364,300
Owner-occupied units in 1990: 65.7%
1993 ACCRA average cost: $119,660
1993 ACCRA average rent for an apartment: $516

Chamber of Commerce
Dayton Area Chamber of Commerce, Thomas E. Heine, President, Chamber Plaza, 5th & Main, Dayton, OH 45402-2400. 513-226-1444

Economic Development Office
City of Dayton, Department of Economic Development,

Anthony B. Char, Director, 101 W. 3rd St., PO Box 22, Dayton, OH 45401. 513-443-3623

Economic Development Organizations
City Wide Development Corp., Steve Budd, President, 40 W. 4th St. Suite 1400, Dayton, OH 45402. 513-226-0457

Dayton Development Council, William Odorizzi, Vice President, Chamber Plaza, 5th & Main Sts. Dayton, OH 45402. 513-226-8222, FAX 513-226-8294

Major Businesses

Company	SIC	Telephone
Amcast Industrial Corp.	3432	(513) 298-5251
Arnold Corp.	2761	(513) 443-2000
Bank One, Dayton	6021	(513) 449-8600
Berry, L. M. & Co.	7389	(513) 296-2121
Citfed Mortgage Corp. of America	6162	(513) 276-7100
Citizens Federal	6035	(513) 223-4234
Danis Industries Corp.	1542	(513) 228-1225
Dap Inc.	2891	(513) 667-4461
Day International Corp.	2822	(513) 224-4000
Dayco Products, Inc.	3052	(513) 226-7000
Dayton Power and Light Co.	4911	(513) 224-6000
Dayton Walther Corp.	3714	(513) 296-3113
DPL Inc.	4911	(513) 224-6000
Duriron Co. Inc.	3561	(513) 226-4000
Elder-Beerman Stores Corp.	5311	(513) 296-2700
Hobart Brothers Co.	3548	(513) 332-4000
Hobart Corp.	3589	(513) 332-3000
Huffy Corp.	3751	(513) 866-6251
Mead Corp.	2621	(513) 222-6323
Mead Data Central, Inc.	7375	(513) 865-6800
Med America Health Systems	8062	(513) 222-2200
Metromedia Steakhouses Inc.	5812	(513) 454-2400
Monarch Marking Systems Inc.	2752	(513) 865-2123
NCR Corp.	3571	(513) 445-5000
Philips Industries Inc.	3634	(513) 253-7171
Pon Holding Corp.	5812	(513) 454-2400
Reynolds and Reynolds Co.	2761	(513) 443-2000
Standard Register Co.	2761	(513) 443-1000
Super Food Services, Inc.	5141	(513) 439-7500
Wagon-Lits Travel USA Inc.	4724	(513) 435-7397

Colleges and Universities
Clark State Community College, Springfield
ITT Technical Institute, Dayton
Miami-Jacobs Junior College of Business, Dayton
Ohio Institute of Photography, Dayton
Sinclair Community College, Dayton
Southwestern College of Business, Dayton
University of Dayton, Dayton

HAMILTON–MIDDLETOWN, OH (PMSA)

Geographic Profile

Land Area

467.3 square miles

Counties and Parishes

Butler

Ranking Highlights

296 *out of 319 in total* **land area**

138 *out of 319 in* **population growth**, *1970–1990*

208 *out of 310 in having the lowest* **unemployment** *rate*

151 *out of 310 in size of* **labor force**

165 *out of 318 in the percentage of* **college graduates**

150 *out of 292 in per capita personal* **income**

168 *out of 319 in number of* **manufacturing establishments**

301 *out of 318 in* **physicians** *per 1000 people*

241 *out of 318 in* **hospital beds** *per 1000 people*

N/A *out of 267 in fewest* **crimes** *per 1000 people*

N/A *out of 266 in fewest* **violent crimes** *per 1000 people*

310 *out of 319 in per capita* **federal funds and grants**

Quality of Life Indexes (Rate per 1000 population)

Crime rate in 1991:	N/A
Violent crime rate in 1991:	N/A
Physicians rate in 1992:	1.05
Hospital bed rate in 1991:	3.01

ACCRA Cost of Living Indexes

(First quarter 1993, average = 100)

Composite index:	N/A
Utilities index:	N/A
Housing index:	N/A

Overview

The Hamilton-Middletown MSA is a 470 square mile region which follows the geographical boundaries of Butler County, Ohio. Butler County is located in the south west quadrant of Ohio, situated directly north of Cincinnati along the Interstate 75 corridor. During the last decade, the community experienced a 13% growth in population which has generated over 400 million dollars in new residential construction over the past three years.

There is a strong commitment to education in the community as it is the home of Miami University and several award winning school districts. The per capita income for Butler County residents is nearly $14,000.00 and the median household income is approximately $32,500.00.

There are approximately 7,700 businesses currently located in Butler County, including corporate headquarters for three Fortune 500 companies. Butler County is positioned within 600 miles of approximately 66% of the United States' population and buying power. Similarly, over two-thirds of the U.S. value-added manufacturing is located within overnight transport of Butler County. The Greater Cincinnati International and Dayton International airports are approximately thirty minutes from Butler County.

There are six rural enterprise zones in Butler County. Three are located in the unincorporated areas of the county and the other three are located in the cities of Hamilton, Middletown, and Monroe. Since 1990, over $510 million dollars of commercial and industrial development has taken place in the designated enterprise zones.

Population (1990)

Total Population and Growth Rate

1990: 291,479

1980: 258,787

1970: 226,207

Growth rate 1970–1990: 29%

Race and Hispanic Origin

White: 94.3%

Black: 4.5%

Asian/Pacific Islander: 0.9%

Native American: 0.1%

Hispanic origin: 0.5%

White not Hispanic: 94.0%

Age

Ages 18 to 20: 6.4%

Ages 21 to 24: 6.8%

Ages 25 to 44: 31.9%

Ages 45 to 54: 10.1%

Ages 55 to 59: 4.3%

Ages 60 to 64: 4.1%

Ages 65 plus: 10.2%

Educational Attainment (1990)

Percent having completed high school: 76.0%

Percent having completed college: 18.7%

Elementary and high school enrollment: 50,170

Federal Funds and Grants Received

Total received in 1989: $516,600,000

Funds received per capita: $1,847

Civilian Labor Force

1993 (April): 137,833

1992 average: 137,245

1991 average: 132,453

1990 average: 131,992

Unemployment

1993 (April): 7.7%

1992 average: 7.7%

1991 average: 6.6%

1990 average: 5.8%

Average Annual Pay

1988: $21,565

1987: $21,077
1985: $19,857

Per Capita Personal Income
1991: $17,200
1990: $16,768
1989: $15,939

Business Climate (1987)

Manufacturing
Number of establishments in 1987: 288
Shipments in 1987 ($1,000): $3,202,300
Employees in 1987: 22,500
Change in employment, 1982 to 1987: -11.4%
Average annual pay for manufacturing work in 1989: $33,311
Average annual pay for production work in 1987: $29,895

Wholesale Trade
Number of establishments in 1987: 328
Total sales in 1987 ($1,000): $1,182,700
Change in sales, 1982 to 1987: 11.7%

Retail Trade
Number of establishments in 1987: 1,332
Total sales in 1987 ($1,000): $1,182,700
Retail sales per household in 1987: $13,699
Average annual pay in 1989: $10,045

Service Industry
Selected receipts in 1987 ($1,000): $400,900
Average annual pay in 1989: $16,539

Housing
Total number of units in 1990: 110,353
Occupied units in 1990: 104,535
Owner-occupied units in 1990: 69.2%
1993 ACCRA average cost: N/A
1993 ACCRA average rent for an apartment: N/A

Chamber of Commerce
Greater Hamilton Chamber of Commerce, Eric Middlebrook, President, 201 Dayton St., Hamilton, OH 45013. 513-844-1500

Economic Development Office
Butler County Dept. of Economic Development, Daniel G. Evers, Administrator, 130 High St., Hamilton, OH 45011. 513-887-3402, FAX 513-887-3568

Economic Development Organizations
Hamilton Economic Development Corp., Eric Middlebrook, President, 201 Dayton St., Hamilton, OH 45013. 513-844-1500

Major Businesses

Company	SIC	Telephone
Armco Insurance Group Inc.	6331	(513) 425-4300
Baker Concrete Construction	1771	(513) 539-4000

Major Businesses (Continued)

Company	SIC	Telephone
Cincinnati Financial Corp.	6331	(513) 870-2000
Cincinnati Insurance Co.	6331	(513) 870-2000
Contech Construction Products	3443	(513) 425-5896
Crystal Tissue Co.	2621	(513) 423-0731
First Financial Bank Corp.	6022	(513) 867-4700
First National	6022	(513) 867-4700
Fort Hamilton-Hughes Healthcare	8062	(513) 867-2000
Hamilton Fixture Co.	2541	(513) 868-2144
Leshner Corp.	2211	(513) 868-3500
Mosler, Inc.	3499	(513) 867-4000
Ohio Casualty Insurance Co.	6331	(513) 867-3000
Ohio Life Insurance Co.	6311	(513) 867-3000
Pease Industries, Inc.	3442	(513) 870-3600
United Care Corp.	8062	(513) 424-2111
West American Insurance Co.	6331	(513) 867-3000

Colleges and Universities
Miami University-Hamilton Campus, Hamilton
Miami University-Middletown Campus, Middletown
Southwestern College of Business, Middletown

LIMA, OH (MSA)

Geographic Profile

Land Area
805.7 square miles

Counties and Parishes
Allen
Auglaize

Ranking Highlights
234 *out of 319 in total* land area
258 *out of 319 in* population growth, *1970–1990*
191 *out of 310 in having the lowest* unemployment *rate*
213 *out of 310 in size of* labor force
311 *out of 318 in the percentage of* college graduates
195 *out of 292 in per capita personal* income
190 *out of 319 in number of* manufacturing establishments
279 *out of 318 in* physicians *per 1000 people*
127 *out of 318 in* hospital beds *per 1000 people*
N/A *out of 267 in fewest* crimes *per 1000 people*
N/A *out of 266 in fewest* violent crimes *per 1000 people*
9 *out of 319 in per capita* federal funds and grants

Quality of Life Indexes (Rate per 1000 population)
Crime rate in 1991:   N/A
Violent crime rate in 1991: N/A
Physicians rate in 1992:   1.23
Hospital bed rate in 1991:   4.21

ACCRA Cost of Living Indexes
(First quarter 1993, average = 100)
Composite index: N/A
Utilities index: N/A
Housing index: N/A

Population (1990)

Total Population and Growth Rate
1990: 154,340
1980: 154,795
1970: 149,746
Growth rate 1970–1990: 3%

Race and Hispanic Origin
White: 91.0%
Black: 8.0%
Asian/Pacific Islander: 0.5%
Native American: 0.2%
Hispanic origin: 1.0%
White not Hispanic: 90.4%

Age
Ages 18 to 20: 4.5%
Ages 21 to 24: 5.1%
Ages 25 to 44: 30.5%
Ages 45 to 54: 9.7%
Ages 55 to 59: 4.3%
Ages 60 to 64: 4.5%
Ages 65 plus: 13.4%

Educational Attainment (1990)
Percent having completed high school: 76.2%
Percent having completed college: 10.9%
Elementary and high school enrollment: 29,477

Federal Funds and Grants Received
Total received in 1989: $1,279,800,000
Funds received per capita: $8,165

Civilian Labor Force
1993 (April):   77,844
1992 average: 78,573
1991 average: 77,818
1990 average: 78,104

Unemployment
1993 (April):   6.5%
1992 average: 7.4%
1991 average: 7.0%
1990 average: 6.7%

Average Annual Pay
1988: $20,706
1987: $20,239
1985: $18,511

Per Capita Personal Income
1991: $16,369
1990: $16,004
1989: $15,416

Business Climate (1987)

Manufacturing
Number of establishments in 1987: 247
Shipments in 1987 ($1,000): $5,792,400
Employees in 1987: 21,300
Change in employment, 1982 to 1987: 6.5%
Average annual pay for manufacturing work in 1989: $29,556
Average annual pay for production work in 1987: $26,214

Wholesale Trade
Number of establishments in 1987: 293
Total sales in 1987 ($1,000): $1,249,200
Change in sales, 1982 to 1987: 27.4%

Retail Trade
Number of establishments in 1987: 1,074
Total sales in 1987 ($1,000): $1,249,200
Retail sales per household in 1987: $17,827
Average annual pay in 1989: $9,642

Service Industry
Selected receipts in 1987 ($1,000): $253,500
Average annual pay in 1989: $15,677

Housing
Total number of units in 1990: 59,665

Occupied units in 1990: 55,384
Owner-occupied units in 1990: 73.2%
1993 ACCRA average cost: N/A
1993 ACCRA average rent for an apartment: N/A

Chamber of Commerce

Lima Area Chamber of Commerce, William L. Bassitt, President, 147 N. Main St., Lima, OH 45801. 419-222-6045

Economic Development Office

Lima/Allen County Economic Development Council, Lloyd Grim, Director, 147 N. Main St., Lima, OH 45801. 419-222-6045, FAX 419-229-0266

Major Businesses

Company	SIC	Telephone
AAP St. Mary's Corp.	3714	(419) 394-7840
AHL, Tom Chrysler-Plymouth	5511	(419) 227-0202
Airfoil Textron Inc.	3724	(419) 226-2900
All America Insurance Co.	6411	(419) 238-1010
Auglaize Farmers Cooperate	5153	(419) 738-2137
Bank One, Wapakoneta, N.A	6021	(419) 738-9261
Central Mutual Insurance Co.	6331	(419) 238-1010
Crown Equipment Corp.	3537	(419) 629-2311
Dun, R. G. Cigar Corp.	5145	(419) 227-2436
Flexible Foam Products Inc.	3069	(419) 647-4191
I & K Distributors Inc.	5141	(419) 692-6911
Joint Township District Memorial Hospital	8062	(419) 394-3335
Kennedy Manufacturing Co.	3469	(419) 238-2442
Lima Memorial Hospital	8062	(419) 228-3335
Mac Donald Enterprises Inc.	3369	(419) 647-4139
Metokote Corp.	3479	(419) 227-1100
Myers Oldsmobile-Nissan	5511	(419) 331-0396
Peterson Construction Co.	1542	(419) 657-2233
Peterson Holding Co.	1542	(419) 657-2233
St. Rita's Medical Center	8062	(419) 227-3361
Superior Metal Products Inc.	3469	(419) 228-1145
West Ohio Gas Co.	4924	(419) 226-4700

Colleges and Universities

Lima Technical College, Lima
Northwestern Business College-Technical Center, Lima
Ohio State University-Lima Campus, Lima

LORAIN–ELYRIA, OH (PMSA)

Geographic Profile

Land Area
492.6 square miles

Counties and Parishes
Lorain

Ranking Highlights

293 *out of 319 in total* land area
239 *out of 319 in* population growth, *1970–1990*
280 *out of 310 in having the lowest* unemployment *rate*
163 *out of 310 in size of* labor force
292 *out of 318 in the percentage of* college graduates
N/A *out of 292 in per capita personal* income
141 *out of 319 in number of* manufacturing establishments
294 *out of 318 in* physicians *per 1000 people*
195 *out of 318 in* hospital beds *per 1000 people*
32 *out of 267 in fewest* crimes *per 1000 people*
72 *out of 266 in fewest* violent crimes *per 1000 people*
288 *out of 319 in per capita* federal funds and grants

Quality of Life Indexes (Rate per 1000 population)

Crime rate in 1991:	38.5
Violent crime rate in 1991:	3.9
Physicians rate in 1992:	1.09
Hospital bed rate in 1991:	3.47

ACCRA Cost of Living Indexes

(First quarter 1993, average = 100)

Composite index:	N/A
Utilities index:	N/A
Housing index:	N/A

Population (1990)

Total Population and Growth Rate
1990: 271,126
1980: 274,909
1970: 256,843
Growth rate 1970–1990: 6%

Race and Hispanic Origin
White: 89.1%
Black: 7.8%
Asian/Pacific Islander: 0.5%
Native American: 0.3%
Hispanic origin: 5.6%
White not Hispanic: 85.9%

Age
Ages 18 to 20: 4.8%
Ages 21 to 24: 5.4%
Ages 25 to 44: 31.7%
Ages 45 to 54: 10.4%
Ages 55 to 59: 4.3%

Ages 60 to 64: 4.3%
Ages 65 plus: 11.6%

Educational Attainment (1990)
Percent having completed high school: 75.3%
Percent having completed college: 12.3%
Elementary and high school enrollment: 51,693

Federal Funds and Grants Received
Total received in 1989: $594,400,000
Funds received per capita: $2,198

Civilian Labor Force
1993 (April): 124,182
1992 average: 124,898
1991 average: 121,352
1990 average: 120,801

Unemployment
1993 (April): 7.1%
1992 average: 9.9%
1991 average: 9.5%
1990 average: 7.7%

Average Annual Pay
1988: $22,645
1987: $21,158
1985: $20,793

Per Capita Personal Income
1991: N/A
1990: N/A
1989: N/A

Business Climate (1987)
Manufacturing
Number of establishments in 1987: 382
Shipments in 1987 ($1,000): $9,549,200
Employees in 1987: 28,500
Change in employment, 1982 to 1987: -4.7%
Average annual pay for manufacturing work in 1989: $32,748
Average annual pay for production work in 1987: $29,685

Wholesale Trade
Number of establishments in 1987: 230
Total sales in 1987 ($1,000): $780,300
Change in sales, 1982 to 1987: 108.8%

Retail Trade
Number of establishments in 1987: 1,346
Total sales in 1987 ($1,000): $780,300
Retail sales per household in 1987: $14,556
Average annual pay in 1989: $10,194

Service Industry
Selected receipts in 1987 ($1,000): $367,500
Average annual pay in 1989: $17,312

Housing
Total number of units in 1990: 99,937

Occupied units in 1990: 96,064
Owner-occupied units in 1990: 71.9%
1993 ACCRA average cost: N/A
1993 ACCRA average rent for an apartment: N/A

Chamber of Commerce
Commerce & Industry Association of Greater Elyria, President, 360 2nd St., PO Box 179, Elyria, OH 44036. 216-322-5438

Economic Development Office
City of Lorain, Community Development Department, Stanford A. Prudoff, Director, 200 W. Erie Ave. 5th Fl., Lorain, OH 44052. 216-245-9428

Economic Development Organizations
Lorain County Department of Development, Lawrence Coyne, Director, 226 Middle Ave., Elyria, OH 44035. 216-329-5000

Major Businesses

Company	SIC	Telephone
Elyria Memorial Hospital & Medical Center	8062	(216) 329-7500
Elyria Savings & Trust National	6021	(216) 329-3000
Elyria Telephone Co.	4812	(216) 329-4000
Humility of Mary Health Center	8062	(216) 245-3569
Industrial General Corp.	3621	(216) 323-3136
Invacare Corp.	3842	(216) 329-6000
Jennings Construction Co.	1542	(216) 647-3600
LNB Bancorp, Inc.	6021	(216) 244-6000
Lakeland Community Hospital	8062	(216) 960-3000
LCB Bancorp	6022	(216) 329-8000
Lear Romec Corp.	3728	(216) 323-3211
Lorain County Bank	6022	(216) 329-8000
Lorain National Bank	6021	(216) 244-6000
Manoir-Electroalloys Corp.	3325	(216) 323-3202
Moen Inc.	3432	(216) 323-3341
Mullinax, Ed Ford Inc.	5511	(216) 984-2431
Nacscorp Inc.	5192	(216) 775-7777
Spitzer Motors of Elyria	5511	(216) 323-3311
St. Joseph Hospital & Health	8062	(216) 233-1000

Colleges and Universities
Lorain County Community College, Elyria

MANSFIELD, OH (MSA)

Geographic Profile

Land Area

497.0 square miles

Counties and Parishes

Richland

Ranking Highlights

292　*out of 319 in total* **land area**

284　*out of 319 in* **population growth,** *1970–1990*

242　*out of 310 in having the lowest* **unemployment** *rate*

255　*out of 310 in size of* **labor force**

303　*out of 318 in the percentage of* **college graduates**

242　*out of 292 in per capita personal* **income**

205　*out of 319 in number of* **manufacturing establishments**

288　*out of 318 in* **physicians** *per 1000 people*

171　*out of 318 in* **hospital beds** *per 1000 people*

149　*out of 267 in fewest* **crimes** *per 1000 people*

239　*out of 266 in fewest* **violent crimes** *per 1000 people*

291　*out of 319 in per capita* **federal funds and grants**

Quality of Life Indexes (Rate per 1000 population)

Crime rate in 1991:	63.1
Violent crime rate in 1991:	10.6
Physicians rate in 1992:	1.15
Hospital bed rate in 1991:	3.67

ACCRA Cost of Living Indexes

(First quarter 1993, average = 100)

Composite index:	97.6
Utilities index:	126.5
Housing index:	90.1

Population (1990)

Total Population and Growth Rate

1990: 126,137

1980: 131,205

1970: 129,997

Growth rate 1970–1990: -3%

Race and Hispanic Origin

White: 91.2%

Black: 7.9%

Asian/Pacific Islander: 0.5%

Native American: 0.2%

Hispanic origin: 0.7%

White not Hispanic: 90.7%

Age

Ages 18 to 20: 4.1%

Ages 21 to 24: 5.4%

Ages 25 to 44: 30.3%

Ages 45 to 54: 11.3%

Ages 55 to 59: 4.9%

Ages 60 to 64: 4.9%

Ages 65 plus: 13%

Educational Attainment (1990)

Percent having completed high school: 73.5%

Percent having completed college: 11.6%

Elementary and high school enrollment: 22,484

Federal Funds and Grants Received

Total received in 1989: $283,100,000

Funds received per capita: $2,194

Civilian Labor Force

1993 (April):	62,425
1992 average:	63,581
1991 average:	63,328
1990 average:	65,274

Unemployment

1993 (April): 7.0%

1992 average: 8.4%

1991 average: 9.4%

1990 average: 7.3%

Average Annual Pay

1988: $20,702

1987: $19,891

1985: $19,206

Per Capita Personal Income

1991: $15,348

1990: $15,236

1989: $14,740

Business Climate (1987)

Manufacturing

Number of establishments in 1987: 219

Shipments in 1987 ($1,000): $1,896,400

Employees in 1987: 18,100

Change in employment, 1982 to 1987: 2.8%

Average annual pay for manufacturing work in 1989: $30,078

Average annual pay for production work in 1987: $26,632

Wholesale Trade

Number of establishments in 1987: 211

Total sales in 1987 ($1,000): $541,300

Change in sales, 1982 to 1987: 43.1%

Retail Trade

Number of establishments in 1987: 800

Total sales in 1987 ($1,000): $541,300

Retail sales per household in 1987: $17,133

Average annual pay in 1989: $10,008

Service Industry

Selected receipts in 1987 ($1,000): $212,900

Average annual pay in 1989: $13,966

Housing

Total number of units in 1990: 50,350

Occupied units in 1990: 47,573
Owner-occupied units in 1990: 70.8%
1993 ACCRA average cost: $108,828
1993 ACCRA average rent for an apartment: $351

Chamber of Commerce

Mansfield-Richland Area Chamber of Commerce, William J. Hartnett, President, 55 N. Mulberry St., Mansfield, OH 44902. 419-522-3211

Economic Development Office

Commercial Development Department, Iwana Wagner, Manager, 30 N. Diamond St., Mansfield, OH 44902. 419-755-9793, FAX 419-755-9697

Economic Development Organizations

Richland Economic Development Corp., Richard Heupel, President, 24 W. 3rd St. Suite 204, Mansfield, OH 44902. 419-522-7332, FAX 419-522-2040

Major Businesses

Company	SIC	Telephone
Bank One Mansfield	6029	(419) 525-5500
Cousins, Inc.	3341	(419) 525-0011
Designed Metal Products Inc.	3469	(419) 524-2833
Geyer's Markets Inc.	5411	(419) 884-3443
Gorman-Rupp Co.	3561	(419) 755-1011
Heisler's Inc.	5012	(419) 522-9811
Ideal Electric Co.	3621	(419) 522-3611
Jay Plastics Inc.	3471	(419) 522-0751
Mansfield General Hospital	8062	(419) 526-8000
Neer Manufacturing Co.	3644	(419) 884-2274
Plymouth Locomotive International	3537	(419) 687-4641
Prudential Insurance Co.	6331	(419) 525-9000
Richland Trust Co.	6022	(419) 525-8700
Shafer Valve Co.	3492	(419) 529-4311
Shelby Insurance Co.	6331	(419) 347-1880
Shelby Life Insurance Co.	7389	(419) 347-1880
Therm-O-Disc Inc.	3822	(419) 525-8500
Uforma/Shelby Business Forms	2752	(419) 342-3515
United Telephone Co. of Ohio	4813	(419) 755-8011
Weidner Pontiac Inc.	5511	(419) 529-5555

Colleges and Universities

North Central Technical College, Mansfield
Ohio State University-Mansfield Campus, Mansfield

STEUBENVILLE–WEIRTON, OH–WV (MSA)

Geographic Profile

Land Area
581.5 square miles

Counties and Parishes
Ohio:
 Jefferson
West Virginia:
 Brooke
 Hancock

Ranking Highlights

276　*out of 319 in total* **land area**
319　*out of 319 in* **population growth**, *1970–1990*
265　*out of 310 in having the lowest* **unemployment** *rate*
275　*out of 310 in size of* **labor force**
318　*out of 318 in the percentage of* **college graduates**
256　*out of 292 in per capita personal* **income**
287　*out of 319 in number of* **manufacturing establishments**
308　*out of 318 in* **physicians** *per 1000 people*
 91　*out of 318 in* **hospital beds** *per 1000 people*
 3　*out of 267 in fewest* **crimes** *per 1000 people*
 85　*out of 266 in fewest* **violent crimes** *per 1000 people*
169　*out of 319 in per capita* **federal funds and grants**

Quality of Life Indexes (Rate per 1000 population)

Crime rate in 1991:	24.0
Violent crime rate in 1991:	4.4
Physicians rate in 1992:	1
Hospital bed rate in 1991:	4.76

ACCRA Cost of Living Indexes

(First quarter 1993, average = 100)
Composite index:　N/A
Utilities index:　N/A
Housing index:　N/A

Population (1990)

Total Population and Growth Rate
1990: 142,523
1980: 163,734
1970: 166,385
Growth rate 1970–1990: -14%

Race and Hispanic Origin
White: 95.5%
Black: 3.9%
Asian/Pacific Islander: 0.3%
Native American: 0.2%
Hispanic origin: 0.5%
White not Hispanic: 95.1%

Age
Ages 18 to 20: 4.6%

Ages 21 to 24: 4.6%
Ages 25 to 44: 28.6%
Ages 45 to 54: 11%
Ages 55 to 59: 5.4%
Ages 60 to 64: 6%
Ages 65 plus: 16.7%

Educational Attainment (1990)
Percent having completed high school: 72.0%
Percent having completed college: 9.5%
Elementary and high school enrollment: 24,252

Federal Funds and Grants Received
Total received in 1989: $447,700,000
Funds received per capita: $3,031

Civilian Labor Force
1993 (April):   55,914
1992 average: 55,914
1991 average: 54,648
1990 average: 56,224

Unemployment
1993 (April):   9.1%
1992 average: 9.1%
1991 average: 8.4%
1990 average: 6.5%

Average Annual Pay
1988: $21,817
1987: $20,249
1985: $19,353

Per Capita Personal Income
1991: $15,115
1990: $14,781
1989: $13,732

Business Climate (1987)
Manufacturing
Number of establishments in 1987: 107
Shipments in 1987 ($1,000): $3,176,700
Employees in 1987: 17,600
Change in employment, 1982 to 1987: -6.9%
Average annual pay for manufacturing work in 1989: $34,629
Average annual pay for production work in 1987: $27,419

Wholesale Trade
Number of establishments in 1987: 122
Total sales in 1987 ($1,000): $296,100
Change in sales, 1982 to 1987: 57.7%

Retail Trade
Number of establishments in 1987: 884
Total sales in 1987 ($1,000): $296,100
Retail sales per household in 1987: $11,727
Average annual pay in 1989: $9,124

Service Industry
Selected receipts in 1987 ($1,000): $163,300

Average annual pay in 1989: $13,770

Housing
Total number of units in 1990: 59,446
Occupied units in 1990: 55,223
Owner-occupied units in 1990: 75.4%
1993 ACCRA average cost: N/A
1993 ACCRA average rent for an apartment: N/A

Chamber of Commerce
Greater Steubenville/Jefferson Cty Chamber of Commerce, W. Curtis Klein, President, 630 Market St., PO Box 278, Steubenville, OH 43952. 614-282-6226

Economic Development Office
Jefferson Economic Development Council, Terry A. Sterling, Vice President, PO Box 278, Steubenville, OH 43952. 614-282-6226

Major Businesses

Company	SIC	Telephone
Albert Motors, Inc.	5511	(614) 283-4131
American Industries & Resources	1221	(614) 264-7704
Amitalsa Industries Inc.	5961	(614) 264-7704
Bank of Weirton	6022	(304) 797-8000
Banner Fibreboard Co.	2631	(304) 737-3711
Berkman, Louis Co.	3312	(614) 283-3722
Cattrell Companies Inc.	1711	(614) 537-2481
Choice Brands of Ohio	5181	(614) 283-3317
Colaianni Construction Inc.	1542	(614) 769-2362
Mckitrick-Harms Oldsmobile	5511	(614) 282-2571
Miners Mechanics Savings Trust	6022	(614) 283-3731
Mountaineer Bolt, Inc.	3452	(304) 737-3316
Municipal Mutual Insurance	6331	(304) 737-3371
National Church Supply Co.	2677	(304) 387-5200
National Lubricating Products	5171	(614) 598-4142
New Co-Operative Co., Inc.	5411	(614) 769-2331
Ohio Valley Hospital	8062	(614) 283-7000
Phillippi Jim Inc.	5511	(614) 537-2418
R & S Corp.	5411	(304) 564-3511
Snyder Tire & Electronics	5731	(614) 264-5543
State Park Motors Inc.	5012	(614) 765-4366
Steubenville Fruit Co. Inc.	5148	(614) 282-9786
Unibank	6022	(614) 282-0941
W. B. Coal Co. Inc.	1221	(614) 282-6503
Weir-Cove Moving & Storage	4213	(304) 748-5880
Weirton Medical Center Inc.	8062	(304) 797-6000
Weirton Steel Corp.	3312	(304) 797-2000
Weirton Wholesale Distributing	5145	(304) 748-7080
Wheeling-Nisshin Inc.	3479	(304) 527-2800
White James Cnstruction Co. Inc.	1623	(304) 748-8181

Colleges and Universities
Franciscan University of Steubenville, Steubenville
Jefferson Technical College, Steubenville

TOLEDO, OH (MSA)

Geographic Profile

Land Area

1364.6 square miles

Counties and Parishes

Fulton

Lucas

Wood

Additional Cities/Towns within Area

Bowling Green

Ranking Highlights

147 *out of 319 in total* **land area**

266 *out of 319 in* **population growth**, *1970–1990*

219 *out of 310 in having the lowest* **unemployment** *rate*

81 *out of 310 in size of* **labor force**

186 *out of 318 in the percentage of* **college graduates**

126 *out of 292 in per capita personal* **income**

69 *out of 319 in number of* **manufacturing establishments**

73 *out of 318 in* **physicians** *per 1000 people*

63 *out of 318 in* **hospital beds** *per 1000 people*

190 *out of 267 in fewest* **crimes** *per 1000 people*

147 *out of 266 in fewest* **violent crimes** *per 1000 people*

264 *out of 319 in per capita* **federal funds and grants**

Quality of Life Indexes (Rate per 1000 population)

Crime rate in 1991:	70.4
Violent crime rate in 1991:	6.7
Physicians rate in 1992:	2.44
Hospital bed rate in 1991:	5.26

ACCRA Cost of Living Indexes

(First quarter 1993, average = 100)

Composite index:	104.5
Utilities index:	121.7
Housing index:	104.8

Overview

Toledo is the seat of Ohio's Lucas County. The Toledo metropolitan statistical area encompasses the counties of Fulton, Lucas, and Wood. The city played a strategic role in the War of 1812, after which the victorious Americans enjoyed unimpeded settlement of the Northwest Territory. The site of pioneer advancements in the glass-making industry, today Toledo continues to be headquarters of international glass companies.

Manufacturing comprises approximately one-fourth of Toledo's economic base. Nearly one thousand manufacturing facilities, many of them automotive-related, are located in the metropolitan area. Toledo is home to the headquarters of such corporations as TRINOVA Corporation, Libbey-Owens-Ford Company, Owens-Corning Fiberglass Corporation, and Owens-Illinois, Inc. With thirteen major financial institutions, Toledo is also a banking and finance center for northwestern Ohio.

Medical and technologically oriented businesses are a major force in the local economy; Lucas County ranks among the fifty counties in the United States that account for 50 percent of medical industry production. Several private testing laboratories and manufacturers of medical instruments and allied products are located in the Toledo area. In addition, more than four hundred plastics, metalworking, and electronics companies adapt engineering and production capabilities to the medical device and instrument industries. Education is also an economic pillar.

The Port of Toledo, on the Maumee River, is a 150-acre domestic and international shipping facility that includes a general cargo center, mobile cargo handling gear, and covered storage space. An average of ten to fifteen million tons of coal and iron ore, grain, and general cargo are processed through the port each year; designated as a Foreign Trade Zone, the complex affords shippers deferred duty payments and tax savings on foreign goods.

Toledo is served by five railroad systems, which provide direct and interline shipping; Conrail maintains piggyback terminal facilities in the city. More than 110 truck firms link Toledo with all major metropolitan areas in the United States and points throughout Canada. Toledo Express Airport is served by seven commercial airlines providing direct and connecting flights to major cities throughout the United States. The airport also handles corporate and private aircraft. Additional general aviation services are available at Metcalf Field, operated by the Port Authority and located south of the city. Detroit Metropolitan Airport, less than an hour's drive from Toledo, is served by international as well as domestic flights.

A network of interstate, federal, and state highways facilitates access into and around the city and links Toledo to points in all sectors of the nation. Interstate 75 extends north through Michigan and south through Florida; the Ohio Turnpike (I-80 and I-90) connects Toledo with the East and West Coasts. Other highways include U.S. 24, 25, 20, and 23.

Population (1990)

Total Population and Growth Rate

1990: 614,128

1980: 616,864

1970: 606,344

Growth rate 1970–1990: 1%

Race and Hispanic Origin

White: 85.7%

Black: 11.4%

Asian/Pacific Islander: 1.0%

Native American: 0.2%

Hispanic origin: 3.3%

White not Hispanic: 84.2%

Age

Ages 18 to 20: 5.8%
Ages 21 to 24: 6.6%
Ages 25 to 44: 31.1%
Ages 45 to 54: 9.5%
Ages 55 to 59: 4.1%
Ages 60 to 64: 4.3%
Ages 65 plus: 12.4%

Educational Attainment (1990)

Percent having completed high school: 77.6%
Percent having completed college: 17.4%
Elementary and high school enrollment: 107,811

Federal Funds and Grants Received

Total received in 1989: $1,454,100,000
Funds received per capita: $2,359

Civilian Labor Force

1993 (April):   308,528
1992 average: 312,910
1991 average: 309,532
1990 average: 313,235

Unemployment

1993 (April):   6.0%
1992 average: 7.9%
1991 average: 8.4%
1990 average: 7.0%

Average Annual Pay

1988: $21,984
1987: $21,288
1985: $20,409

Per Capita Personal Income

1991: $17,713
1990: $17,416
1989: $16,861

Business Climate (1987)

Manufacturing

Number of establishments in 1987: 988
Shipments in 1987 ($1,000): $12,446,200
Employees in 1987: 63,200
Change in employment, 1982 to 1987: 4.6%
Average annual pay for manufacturing work in 1989: $33,902
Average annual pay for production work in 1987: $28,082

Wholesale Trade

Number of establishments in 1987: 1,130
Total sales in 1987 ($1,000): $5,125,900
Change in sales, 1982 to 1987: 14.4%

Retail Trade

Number of establishments in 1987: 3,847
Total sales in 1987 ($1,000): $5,125,900
Retail sales per household in 1987: $17,319
Average annual pay in 1989: $10,599

Service Industry

Selected receipts in 1987 ($1,000): $1,655,600
Average annual pay in 1989: $18,398

Office Real Estate (1992)

Office space inventory: 5,638,836 square feet
Average class A Central Business District rental range per sq. ft: $16.50

Vacancy Rates

All areas: 18.7%

Vacancy Rates in Central Business District

Class A space: 18.2%
Class B space: 25.7%

Vacancy Rates Outside Central Business District

Class A space: 13.5%
Class B space: 16.8%

Housing

Total number of units in 1990: 247,243
Occupied units in 1990: 230,681
Owner-occupied units in 1990: 66.6%
1993 ACCRA average cost: $117,625
1993 ACCRA average rent for an apartment: $525

Chamber of Commerce

Toledo Area Chamber of Commerce, J. Michael Porter, President, 218 Huron St., Toledo, OH 43604. 419-243-8191

Economic Development Office

Sea Gate Commercial Development Corp., President, 245 Summit St. #1405, Toledo, OH 43603. 419-259-8105

Major Businesses

Company	SIC	Telephone
Aeroquip Corp.	3052	(419) 867-2100
Andersons	5153	(419) 893-5050
AP Parts Manufacturing Co.	3714	(419) 259-3461
Centaur Inc.	3312	(313) 848-2915
Champion Spark Plug Co.	3694	(419) 535-2567
Dana Corp.	3714	(419) 535-4500
De Vilbiss Holding Co.	3563	(419) 470-2340
De Vilbiss Industrial Products Corp.	3563	(419) 470-2169
Diamond Financial Holding	6035	(419) 535-4776
La-Z-Boy Chair Co.	2512	(313) 242-1444
Lathrop Co.	1542	(419) 893-7000
Libbey Glass Inc.	3229	(419) 727-2263
Libbey-Owens-Ford Co.	3211	(419) 247-3736
Mid States Terminals Inc.	5153	(419) 435-7761
Monroe Auto Equipment Co.	3714	(313) 243-8000
O-I Brockway Plastics Inc.	3085	(419) 247-5000
Owens-Corning Fiberglas Co.	3296	(419) 248-8000
Owens-Illinois Inc.	3221	(419) 247-5000
Pilkington Holding Inc.	3231	(419) 247-3736

Major Businesses (Continued)

Company	SIC	Telephone
Prestolite Electric Inc.	3621	(419) 249-7600
Rudolph/Libbe Companies Inc.	1542	(419) 241-5000
Sauder Woodworking Co.	2519	(419) 446-2711
Seaway Food Town Inc.	5411	(419) 893-9401
Society Bank & Trust Inc.	6022	(419) 259-8598
Sterling Holdings Inc.	3089	(419) 867-2500
Toledo Edison Co.	4911	(419) 249-5000
Toledo Hospital	8062	(419) 471-4218
Trinova Corp.	3052	(419) 867-2200
Trustcorp Bank, Ohio	6022	(419) 259-8598
Vickers Inc.	3594	(419) 867-2600

Colleges and Universities

Bowling Green State University, Bowling Green
Davis Junior College of Business, Toledo
Owens Technical College, Toledo
Rets Institute of Technology, Toledo
Stautzenberger College, Toledo
University of Toledo, Toledo

YOUNGSTOWN–WARREN, OH (MSA)

Geographic Profile

Land Area
1031.1 square miles

Counties and Parishes
Mahoning
Trumbull

Ranking Highlights

195 *out of 319 in total* **land area**
311 *out of 319 in* **population growth**, *1970–1990*
269 *out of 310 in having the lowest* **unemployment** *rate*
101 *out of 310 in size of* **labor force**
285 *out of 318 in the percentage of* **college graduates**
225 *out of 292 in per capita personal* **income**
100 *out of 319 in number of* **manufacturing establishments**
188 *out of 318 in* **physicians** *per 1000 people*
85 *out of 318 in* **hospital beds** *per 1000 people*
N/A *out of 267 in fewest* **crimes** *per 1000 people*
N/A *out of 266 in fewest* **violent crimes** *per 1000 people*
226 *out of 319 in per capita* **federal funds and grants**

Quality of Life Indexes (Rate per 1000 population)

Crime rate in 1991:	N/A
Violent crime rate in 1991:	N/A
Physicians rate in 1992:	1.69
Hospital bed rate in 1991:	4.87

ACCRA Cost of Living Indexes

(First quarter 1993, average = 100)
Composite index: 94.0
Utilities index: 111.4
Housing index: 86.6

Population (1990)

Total Population and Growth Rate
1990: 492,619
1980: 531,350
1970: 537,124
Growth rate 1970–1990: -8%

Race and Hispanic Origin
White: 87.7%
Black: 11.1%
Asian/Pacific Islander: 0.4%
Native American: 0.2%
Hispanic origin: 1.5%
White not Hispanic: 86.9%

Age
Ages 18 to 20: 4.1%
Ages 21 to 24: 5%
Ages 25 to 44: 29.4%
Ages 45 to 54: 10.5%

Ages 55 to 59: 4.9%
Ages 60 to 64: 5.5%
Ages 65 plus: 15.8%

Educational Attainment (1990)
Percent having completed high school: 74.9%
Percent having completed college: 12.8%
Elementary and high school enrollment: 84,436

Federal Funds and Grants Received
Total received in 1989: $1,302,900,000
Funds received per capita: $2,597

Civilian Labor Force
1993 (April):   221,658
1992 average: 226,959
1991 average: 221,360
1990 average: 222,494

Unemployment
1993 (April):   8.1%
1992 average: 9.4%
1991 average: 7.3%
1990 average: 7.2%

Average Annual Pay
1988: $21,185
1987: $19,887
1985: $19,795

Per Capita Personal Income
1991: $15,739
1990: $15,375
1989: $14,640

Business Climate (1987)
Manufacturing
Number of establishments in 1987: 637
Shipments in 1987 ($1,000): $8,107,200
Employees in 1987: 49,500
Change in employment, 1982 to 1987: -4.4%
Average annual pay for manufacturing work in 1989: $35,183
Average annual pay for production work in 1987: $28,915

Wholesale Trade
Number of establishments in 1987: 695
Total sales in 1987 ($1,000): $2,859,900
Change in sales, 1982 to 1987: 24.4%

Retail Trade
Number of establishments in 1987: 3,105
Total sales in 1987 ($1,000): $2,859,900
Retail sales per household in 1987: $15,526
Average annual pay in 1989: $9,761

Service Industry
Selected receipts in 1987 ($1,000): $933,100
Average annual pay in 1989: $17,719

Housing
Total number of units in 1990: 198,448
Occupied units in 1990: 187,192
Owner-occupied units in 1990: 72.3%
1993 ACCRA average cost: $98,500
1993 ACCRA average rent for an apartment: $410

Chamber of Commerce
Youngstown Area Chamber of Commerce, John N. Moliterno, President, 200 Wick Bldg., Youngstown, OH 44503-1474. 216-744-2131

Economic Development Office
City of Youngstown Economic Development, Jeffrey Chagnot, Development Director, 26 S. Phelps St., City Hall 5th Fl., Youngstown, OH 44503. 216-742-8981, FAX 216-747-2512

Economic Development Organizations
Warren Area Chamber of Commerce-Economic Development Department, Roland L. Theriault, Vice President of Economic Development, 187 High St. N.E., PO Box 1147, Warren, OH 44482. 216-393-2565, FAX 216-393-6040

Mahoning Valley Economic Development Corp., Donald L. French, Exec. Director, 4319 Belmont Ave., Youngstown, OH 44505. 216-759-3668

Major Businesses

Company	SIC	Telephone
Commercial Intertech Corp.	3594	(216) 746-8011
Copperweld Steel Co.	3312	(216) 841-6011
CSC Industries Inc.	3312	(216) 841-6011
Debartolo Edward J. Corp.	1542	(216) 758-7292
Dollar Savings and Trust Co.	6035	(216) 744-9000
Easco Corp.	3354	(216) 545-4311
Forge Industries Inc.	5085	(216) 782-8301
Greenwood Chevrolet Inc.	5511	(216) 792-5252
Home Savings & Loan Co.	6036	(216) 742-0500
Liberty Steel Products Inc.	5051	(216) 538-2236
LTV Steel Tubular Products	3317	(216) 742-6001
Lyden Co.	5172	(216) 792-1100
Nemenz, H. P. Food Stores Inc.	5411	(216) 757-0771
Ohio Bancorp	6022	(216) 744-9000
Peerless-Winsmith Inc.	3621	(216) 395-1010
Phar-Mor Inc.	5912	(216) 746-6641
RMI Titanium Co.	3339	(216) 544-7604
St. Elizabeth Hospital	8062	(216) 746-7211
Stambaugh Thompson Co.	5211	(216) 792-9071
Standard Slag Co.	3295	(216) 743-3151
Syro Steel Co.	3444	(216) 545-4373
Tamarkin Co. Inc.	5142	(216) 792-3811
Truck World Inc.	5172	(216) 448-2210
Trumbull Industries Inc.	5074	(216) 393-6624
Trumbull Memorial Hospital	8062	(216) 841-9011
Warren Consolidated Industries	3312	(216) 841-8000

Major Businesses (Continued)

Company	SIC	Telephone
Warren General Hospital	8062	(216) 373-9000
Western Reserve Care System	8062	(216) 747-0777
YHA, Inc.	8062	(216) 747-0777

Colleges and Universities

Kent State University, Trumbull Campus, Warren
ITT Technical Institute, Youngstown
Youngstown State University, Youngstown,

OKLAHOMA

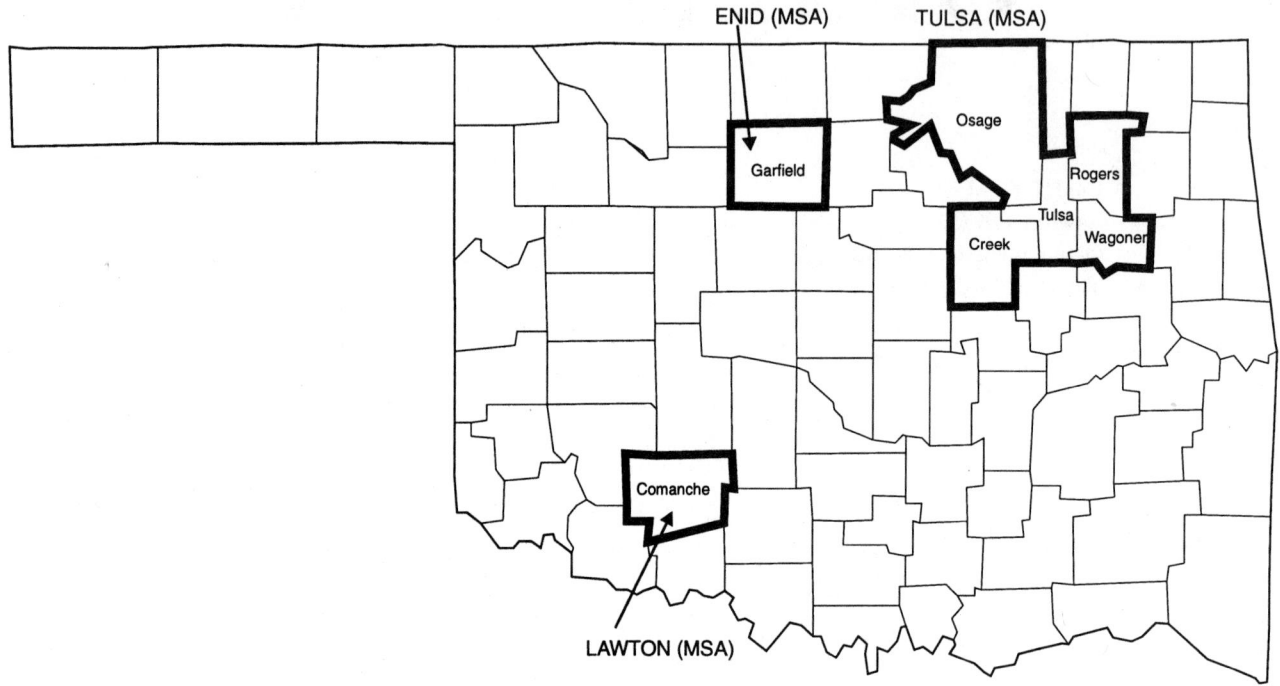

ENID (MSA)

TULSA (MSA)

Garfield

Osage

Rogers

Tulsa

Creek

Wagoner

Comanche

LAWTON (MSA)

OKLAHOMA

Population
1990: 3,145,585
1980: 3,025,290

Age
Ages 18 to 20: 148,115
Ages 21 to 24: 173,274
Ages 25 to 44: 961,560
Ages 45 to 54: 322,975
Ages 55 to 59: 141,214
Ages 60 to 64: 137,227
Median age: 33.2

Race and Hispanic Origin
White: 2,583,512
Black: 233,801
Asian/Pacific Islander: 33,563
Native American: 252,420
Hispanic origin: 86,160

Households
Total: 1,206,135
Persons per household: 2.53

Sex
Male: 1,530,819
Female: 1,614,766

Population Migration
Domestic migration: -289,000
International migration: 35,000

Projection of the Population in 1995
Total: 3,302,000
18 to 64: 1,966,000

Civilian Labor Force
1993: 1,523,700
1992: 1,518,000
1991: 1,522,400
1990: 1,500,900

Manufacturing
1995 Projection: 172,000
1992: 163,000
1991: 166,900
1990: 164,900
1989: 165,000

Services
1995 Projection: 422,700

1992: 286,900
1991: 279,300
1990: 276,700
1989: 262,500

Wholesale and Retail Trade
1995 Projection: 345,700
1992: 284,200
1991: 281,900
1990: 278,900
1989: 282,500

Unemployment Rate
1993: 6.4%
1992: 7.3%
1991: 6.3%
1990: 6.9%

Employer Unemployment Contributions
Contribution Rate
1992: 1.10%
1991: 1.34%
1990: 1.71%

Average Weekly Benefit
1992: $164.52
1991: $162.03
1990: $148.85

Gross State Product (Million $)
1989: $52,342
1988: $49,903
1987: $47,371
1979: $32,145
Growth rate, 1979 to 1989: 62.8%

Capital Expenditures of Manufacturing Industries
1990: $860,400,000
1989: $747,300,000
1988: $584,600,000
1987: $538,400,000

State Tax Rates
Individual income: Range from 0.5% ($2,000 or less) to 7% (above $21,000).
Corporate income: 6% of federal taxable income.
General property: No state levy. Local collections. Property

is taxed from 12% to 35% of fair cash value.
General sales: 4.5%
Gasoline: 16¢ per gallon

Income

Median income for a 4 person family: $34,470

Personal per Capita Income

1992: $16,198
1991: $15,570
1990: $15,154

Disposable per Capita Income

1992: $14,344
1991: $13,699
1990: $13,328

Private Employment Weekly Wages

Average

1989: $374
1988: $367
1987: $367

Manufacturing

1989: $357
1988: $469
1987: $455

Services

1989: $327
1988: $319
1987: $314

Wholesale

1989: $450
1988: $438
1987: $424

Retail

1989: $210
1988: $209
1987: $203

Highway Statistics

Total Highway Miles

1990: 111,765
1989: 111,669
1988: 111,403

Federal Highway Aid

1991: $181,358,000
1990: $191,658,000
1989: $202,053,000

Electricity

Average Cost per Kilowatt Hour
1990: 5.61¢
1989: 5.56¢
1988: 5.53¢

Housing (1990)

Owner occupied units: 821,188

Median house value: $48,100
Renter occupied units: 384,947
Median rent: $259
Total vacant units: 200,364
Homeowner vacancy rate: 3.7%
Rental vacancy rate: 14.7%

State Business Incentives and Assistance

Enterprise Zone Incentives

1) Double the regular state investment new job tax credits available elsewhere in the state.
2) Low interest loans by enterprise zone districts.

Financial and Business Assistance

Oklahoma Industrial Finance Authority. A state agency established under the Oklahoma Industrial Finance Authority Act, the Authority is designed to help with industrial development in the state by increasing and retaining jobs. It provides funding in loan packages to manufacturing or processing firms, recreational enterprises, agricultural or mineral resources processing businesses, and industrial parks.

Industrial Development Bonds. Administered by the state Department of Commerce, local governments are authorized to issue industrial development bonds to stimulate economic development. Projects targeted are manufacturing operations related and pollution control facilities. Terms are limited to 30 years.

Direct Marketing Programs for Farmers. Operated by the Market Development Division of the Department of Agriculture, this program develops direct marketing outlets for farmers by providing leadership, guidance and direction to community leaders and others in effecting farmers' markets. The program instructs farmers about direct retailing and direct wholesaling approaches.

Education and Training

Employee Training. Administered by the Department of Vocational and Technical Education, this program provides pre-employment and customized employee training for new or expanding firms.

Job Training Partnership Act. This program operates with funding from the U.S. Department of Labor. It provides job training and other employment related services.

State Offices

Real estate: Real Estate Commission, Charles C. Case, Jr., Exec Director, 4040 North Lincoln Blvd., Suite 100, Oklahoma City, OK 73105. 405-521-3387

Chamber of commerce: Oklahoma State Chamber of Commerce, Richard P. Rush, President, 4020 N. Lincoln Blvd., Oklahoma City, OK 73105. 405-424-4003

Economic development: Department of Commerce, Lon Shealy, Assistant Director, 6601 Broadway Ext., Oklahoma City, OK 73116. 405-843-9770, extension 256

Department of Commerce (Enterprise Zones Office), Barbara Clements, Manager of Business Research, P.O. Box

Major Companies in the State

Company name	Fortune 500 rank	City	Telephone	SIC number
Fortune 500 Companies				
Kerr Mcgee Corp.	147	Oklahoma City	405-270-1313	2911
Mapco Inc.	176	Tulsa	918-581-1800	2911
Phillips Petroleum Co.	37	Bartlesville	918-661-6600	2911
Other Major Companies in the State				
Bancfirst Corp.		Oklahoma City	405-270-1000	6712
Bancoklahoma Corp.		Tulsa	918-583-1232	6712
Banks of Mid America Inc.		Oklahoma City	405-231-6000	6712
C R Anthony Co.		Oklahoma City	405-278-7400	5651
CMI Corp.		Oklahoma City	405-787-6020	3531
Fleming Co., Inc.		Oklahoma City	405-840-7200	5141
Hadson Corp.		Oklahoma City	405-235-9531	5171
Helmerich & Payne Inc.		Tulsa	918-742-5531	1381
Homeland Holding Corp.		Oklahoma City	405-557-5500	5141
LSB Industries Inc.		Oklahoma City	405-235-4546	2819
Matrix Service Co.		Tulsa	918-838-8822	1389
Noble Affiliates Inc.		Ardmore	405-223-4110	1311
Oklahoma Gas & Electric Co.		Oklahoma City	405-272-3000	4911
Oneok Inc.		Tulsa	918-588-7000	4923
Parker Drilling Co.		Tulsa	918-585-8221	1381
Public Service Co. of Oklahoma		Tulsa	918-599-2000	4911
Tribune Swab Fox Companies Inc.		Tulsa	918-747-2600	2711
TSF Communications Corp.		Tulsa	918-747-2600	2711
Wheatley Corp.		Tulsa	918-446-4551	3533
Williams Companies Inc.		Tulsa	918-588-2000	4923

26980, Oklahoma City, OK 73126-0980. 405-841-5156

Oklahoma Industrial Finance Authority, Jay C. Casey, President, 205 North West 63rd Street, Suite 260, Oklahoma City, OK 73116. 405-521-2182

Development Finance Authority, Carl Clark, President, PO Box 53424, Oklahoma City, OK 73152. 405-848-9761

Corporation Commission, Bob Anthony, Chairman, Jim Thorpe Bldg., Oklahoma City, OK 73105. 405-521-2261

Small Business Development Center, Grady Pennington, State Director, Southeastern Oklahoma State University, Station A, Box 4194, Durant, OK 74701. 405-924-0277

Department of Agriculture, Market Development Division, John David, Coordinator, 2800 North Lincoln Blvd., Oklahoma City, OK 73105-4298. 405-521-3864

Environmental affairs: Pollution Control Department, Lawrence R. Edmison, Director, PO Box 53504, Oklahoma City, OK 73152. 405-271-4468

Labor: Labor Department, Dean Calhoon, Commissioner, 4001 Lincoln Blvd., Oklahoma City, OK 73105. 405-528-1500

Unemployment: Employment Security Commission, Unemployment Insurance Benefit Division, Sue Havens,

Administrator, 2401 North Lincoln Blvd., Oklahoma City, OK 73105. 405-557-7200

Worker's compensation: Workers' Compensation Court, Denver Davison Bldg., Oklahoma City, OK 73105. 405-557-7600

Occupational safety and health: Labor Department, Safety Standards Division, Jim Greenawalt, Director, 4001 Lincoln Blvd., Oklahoma City, OK 73105. 405-528-1500

Secretary of state: Secretary of State, John Kennedy, Secretary of State, 101 State Capitol Bldg., Oklahoma City, OK 73105. 405-521-3911

Taxation and revenue: Tax Commission, Business Tax Division, Randy Ross, Director, 2501 Lincoln Blvd., Oklahoma City, OK 73194. 405-521-4327

Designated Zones for Economic Development
Enterprise Zones
Enacted in: 1983
No. of established zones: 89

Foreign Trade Zones
Foreign Trade Zone No. 164, Muskogee, Oklahoma, Grantee: Muskogee City-County Port Authority, Greg

Newell, Rt. 6, Port 50, Muskogee, OK 74401, 918-687-5459

Foreign Trade Zone No. 106, Oklahoma City, Oklahoma, Grantee: The City of Oklahoma City, Office of Foreign-Trade Zone 106, Carolyn Lyon, 300 SW 7th Street, Oklahoma City, OK 73109, 405-297-2583

Foreign Trade Zone No. 53, Rogers County, Oklahoma, Grantee/Operator: City of Tulsa-Rogers County Port Authority., Robert W. Portiss, Tulsa Port of Catoosa, 5350 Cimarron Road, Catoosa, OK 74015, 918-266-2291

Labor Unions

Classroom Teachers Association

State, County and Municipal Employees, American Federation of (AFL-CIO)

Teachers, American Federation of (AFL-CIO)

Universities with Ph.D. Programs

Northeastern State University, Tahlequah

Oral Roberts University, Tulsa

University of Oklahoma, Norman

University of Oklahoma Health Sciences Center, Oklahoma City

University of Tulsa, Tulsa

ENID, OK (MSA)

Geographic Profile

Land Area

1058.5 square miles

Counties and Parishes

Garfield

Ranking Highlights

189 *out of 319 in total* **land area**

269 *out of 319 in* **population growth,** *1970–1990*

15 *out of 310 in having the lowest* **unemployment** *rate*

310 *out of 310 in size of* **labor force**

188 *out of 318 in the percentage of* **college graduates**

185 *out of 292 in per capita personal* **income**

315 *out of 319 in number of* **manufacturing establishments**

206 *out of 318 in* **physicians** *per 1000 people*

13 *out of 318 in* **hospital beds** *per 1000 people*

163 *out of 267 in fewest* **crimes** *per 1000 people*

155 *out of 266 in fewest* **violent crimes** *per 1000 people*

81 *out of 319 in per capita* **federal funds and grants**

Quality of Life Indexes (Rate per 1000 population)

Crime rate in 1991:	66.0
Violent crime rate in 1991:	7.1
Physicians rate in 1992:	1.6
Hospital bed rate in 1991:	7.16

ACCRA Cost of Living Indexes

(First quarter 1993, average = 100)

Composite index:	N/A
Utilities index:	N/A
Housing index:	N/A

Population (1990)

Total Population and Growth Rate

1990: 56,735

1980: 62,820

1970: 56,343

Growth rate 1970–1990: 1%

Race and Hispanic Origin

White: 92.4%

Black: 3.6%

Asian/Pacific Islander: 1.0%

Native American: 2.2%

Hispanic origin: 1.9%

White not Hispanic: 91.5%

Age

Ages 18 to 20: 3.6%

Ages 21 to 24: 5.1%

Ages 25 to 44: 30.2%

Ages 45 to 54: 10.1%

Ages 55 to 59: 4.6%

Ages 60 to 64: 4.7%
Ages 65 plus: 15.4%

Educational Attainment (1990)
Percent having completed high school: 76.5%
Percent having completed college: 17.3%
Elementary and high school enrollment: 10,190

Federal Funds and Grants Received
Total received in 1989: $227,100,000
Funds received per capita: $3,895

Civilian Labor Force
1993 (April):   27,539
1992 average: 27,405
1991 average: 27,349
1990 average: 27,546

Unemployment
1993 (April):   4.7%
1992 average: 3.9%
1991 average: 5.2%
1990 average: 4.3%

Average Annual Pay
1988: $17,379
1987: $16,884
1985: $16,947

Per Capita Personal Income
1991: $16,489
1990: $16,095
1989: $15,074

Business Climate (1987)
Manufacturing
Number of establishments in 1987: 56
Shipments in 1987 ($1,000): $278,500
Employees in 1987: 1,300
Change in employment, 1982 to 1987: -43.5%
Average annual pay for manufacturing work in 1989: $21,682
Average annual pay for production work in 1987: $20,750

Wholesale Trade
Number of establishments in 1987: 146
Total sales in 1987 ($1,000): $1,364,000
Change in sales, 1982 to 1987: 12.2%

Retail Trade
Number of establishments in 1987: 478
Total sales in 1987 ($1,000): $1,364,000
Retail sales per household in 1987: $13,638
Average annual pay in 1989: $9,654

Service Industry
Selected receipts in 1987 ($1,000): $133,100
Average annual pay in 1989: $16,409

Housing
Total number of units in 1990: 26,502

Occupied units in 1990: 22,460
Owner-occupied units in 1990: 69.1%
1993 ACCRA average cost: N/A
1993 ACCRA average rent for an apartment: N/A

Chamber of Commerce
Greater Enid Chamber of Commerce, Dave Osburn, President, 210 Kenwood, PO Box 907, Enid, OK 73702. 405-237-2494

Major Businesses

Company	SIC	Telephone
Central National Bank	6021	(405) 233-3535
Central Service Corp.	6712	(405) 233-3535
Cromwells, Inc.	2761	(405) 234-6561
Cummins Construction Co.	1771	(405) 233-6000
K. M. Engineering Co.	1623	(405) 234-1193
Lambert's Inc.	5621	(405) 233-2400
Luckinbill Inc.	1711	(405) 233-2026
Security National Bank	6021	(405) 234-5151
Union Equity Co-Operative	2041	(405) 233-5100
Ward Petroleum Corp.	1311	(405) 234-3229

Colleges and Universities
Phillips University, Enid

LAWTON, OK (MSA)

Geographic Profile

Land Area

1069.4 square miles

Counties and Parishes

Comanche

Ranking Highlights

186 *out of 319 in total* **land area**

257 *out of 319 in* **population growth,** *1970–1990*

64 *out of 310 in having the lowest* **unemployment** *rate*

288 *out of 310 in size of* **labor force**

169 *out of 318 in the percentage of* **college graduates**

277 *out of 292 in per capita personal* **income**

316 *out of 319 in number of* **manufacturing establishments**

286 *out of 318 in* **physicians** *per 1000 people*

229 *out of 318 in* **hospital beds** *per 1000 people*

91 *out of 267 in fewest* **crimes** *per 1000 people*

170 *out of 266 in fewest* **violent crimes** *per 1000 people*

15 *out of 319 in per capita* **federal funds and grants**

Quality of Life Indexes (Rate per 1000 population)

Crime rate in 1991:	53.2
Violent crime rate in 1991:	7.4
Physicians rate in 1992:	1.17
Hospital bed rate in 1991:	3.11

ACCRA Cost of Living Indexes

(First quarter 1993, average = 100)

Composite index:	92.5
Utilities index:	105.5
Housing index:	81.5

Population (1990)

Total Population and Growth Rate

1990: 111,486

1980: 112,456

1970: 108,144

Growth rate 1970–1990: 3%

Race and Hispanic Origin

White: 71.5%

Black: 17.9%

Asian/Pacific Islander: 2.7%

Native American: 4.6%

Hispanic origin: 6.2%

White not Hispanic: 69.2%

Age

Ages 18 to 20: 7%

Ages 21 to 24: 8.5%

Ages 25 to 44: 32.1%

Ages 45 to 54: 8.4%

Ages 55 to 59: 3.8%

Ages 60 to 64: 3.4%

Ages 65 plus: 8.6%

Educational Attainment (1990)

Percent having completed high school: 81.1%

Percent having completed college: 18.4%

Elementary and high school enrollment: 20,716

Federal Funds and Grants Received

Total received in 1989: $898,400,000

Funds received per capita: $7,531

Civilian Labor Force

1993 (April):	50,076
1992 average:	49,629
1991 average:	47,746
1990 average:	48,346

Unemployment

1993 (April):	6.3%
1992 average:	5.3%
1991 average:	6.6%
1990 average:	5.4%

Average Annual Pay

1988: $16,685

1987: $16,398

1985: $15,184

Per Capita Personal Income

1991: $13,862

1990: $13,386

1989: $12,807

Business Climate (1987)

Manufacturing

Number of establishments in 1987: 52

Shipments in 1987 ($1,000): $583,400

Employees in 1987: 3,300

Change in employment, 1982 to 1987: 22.2%

Average annual pay for manufacturing work in 1989: $26,782

Average annual pay for production work in 1987: $24,600

Wholesale Trade

Number of establishments in 1987: 100

Total sales in 1987 ($1,000): $184,000

Change in sales, 1982 to 1987: -12.1%

Retail Trade

Number of establishments in 1987: 669

Total sales in 1987 ($1,000): $184,000

Retail sales per household in 1987: $14,117

Average annual pay in 1989: $9,326

Service Industry

Selected receipts in 1987 ($1,000): $164,700

Average annual pay in 1989: $15,247

Housing

Total number of units in 1990: 43,509

Occupied units in 1990: 37,569
Owner-occupied units in 1990: 60.2%
1993 ACCRA average cost: N/A
1993 ACCRA average rent for an apartment: N/A

Chamber of Commerce

Lawton Chamber of Commerce & Industry, Owen S. Ard, President, PO Box 1376, Lawton, OK 73502. 405-355-3541

Major Businesses

Company	SIC	Telephone
American National Bank	6021	(405) 353-6500
Citizens Bank	6022	(405) 248-5970
City National Bank & Trust Co.	6021	(405) 355-3580
Comanche County Hospital Authority	8062	(405) 355-8620
Coop Services Inc.	5153	(405) 355-3703
Delluomo, Dan Inc.	5511	(405) 353-2244
Fort Sill National Bank	6021	(405) 357-9880
Glenn Oil Co. Inc.	5541	(405) 355-5701
Gordon, Milo Chrysler Plymouth	5511	(405) 355-2464
Herb's Foods Inc.	5411	(405) 357-1476
Johnson, Carey Oil Co.	5171	(405) 355-4635
Lawton Publishing Co. Inc.	2711	(405) 353-0620
Midwest Showcase Inc.	5712	(405) 353-8654
Northrop Wrldwide Aircraft	4581	(405) 353-2733
Oklahoma Drug Sales Co.	5122	(405) 355-4430
Security Bank & Trust Co.	6022	(405) 353-7700
Warner Jewelry Case Co., Inc.	3172	(405) 536-8885

Colleges and Universities

Cameron University, Lawton

OKLAHOMA CITY, OK (MSA)

Geographic Profile

Land Area
4247.4 square miles

Counties and Parishes
Canadian
Cleveland
Logan
McClain
Oklahoma
Pottawatomie

Additional Cities/Towns within Area
Norman
Shawnee

Ranking Highlights

22 *out of 319 in* **total land area**
119 *out of 319 in* **population growth,** *1970–1990*
51 *out of 310 in having the lowest* **unemployment** *rate*
52 *out of 310 in size of* **labor force**
103 *out of 318 in the percentage of* **college graduates**
171 *out of 292 in per capita personal* **income**
65 *out of 319 in number of* **manufacturing establishments**
94 *out of 318 in* **physicians** *per 1000 people*
123 *out of 318 in* **hospital beds** *per 1000 people*
229 *out of 267 in fewest* **crimes** *per 1000 people*
161 *out of 266 in fewest* **violent crimes** *per 1000 people*
88 *out of 319 in per capita* **federal funds and grants**

Quality of Life Indexes (Rate per 1000 population)

Crime rate in 1991:   80.5
Violent crime rate in 1991:   7.2
Physicians rate in 1992:   2.25
Hospital bed rate in 1991:   4.29

ACCRA Cost of Living Indexes

(First quarter 1993, average = 100)
Composite index: 90.7
Utilities index: 107.1
Housing index: 78.3

Overview

Oklahoma City was a result of the April 22, 1889 land run. It is now the state capital of Oklahoma and the state government is the area's largest employer, with over 30,000 employees. Although in its early days oil dominated its economy, Oklahoma City today hosts a wide range of businesses and employers. Agriculture, energy, aviation, goverment, manufacturing and industry all play major roles in the city's economic well-being. As one of the nation's largest processing centers for a variety of farm products, the city is home to the world's largest stocker and feeder cattle market. Many large oil and energy-related companies have headquarters or major branches in the city. Present and future growth areas include such diverse fields as aircraft, fabricated metal, computers, clothing, oil-field equipment, crude oil, back office, distribution and food processing.

Oklahoma City's Tinker Air Force Base is the largest industrial operation in Oklahoma. Tinker serves the U.S. Air Force as a repair depot and provides logistic services for the U.S. Air Force throughout the world. Tinker Air Force Base has 19,000 employees and is the city's second largest employer.

Freight such as grain, minerals, and steel products are shipped at low cost via the Arkansas River Navigation Channel. The Port of Muskogee is only 140 miles from Oklahoma City. Other freight carriers include truck lines, railroads, and the airlines.

Oklahoma City's Will Rogers World Airport, just 10 miles northwest of the city, is served by nine commercial carriers that provide more than one hundred and sixty flights daily into and out of the city. Located near the center of the United States, the city is connected to the east and west coasts and north and south borders of the nation by interstate highways I-40, I-35, I-44, I-240, and I-235. Numerous state highways and a new turnpike system provide easy access to any location in the metropolitan area.

Population (1990)

Total Population and Growth Rate

1990: 958,839
1980: 860,969
1970: 718,737
Growth rate 1970–1990: 33%

Race and Hispanic Origin

White: 81.1%
Black: 10.5%
Asian/Pacific Islander: 1.9%
Native American: 4.8%
Hispanic origin: 3.6%
White not Hispanic: 79.6%

Age

Ages 18 to 20: 5%
Ages 21 to 24: 6.1%
Ages 25 to 44: 33%
Ages 45 to 54: 10.1%
Ages 55 to 59: 4.2%
Ages 60 to 64: 4%
Ages 65 plus: 11%

Educational Attainment (1990)

Percent having completed high school: 79.2%
Percent having completed college: 21.6%
Elementary and high school enrollment: 168,499

Federal Funds and Grants Received

Total received in 1989: $3,574,600,000
Funds received per capita: $3,709

Civilian Labor Force

1993 (April):   493,011
1992 average: 492,182
1991 average: 489,195
1990 average: 501,682

Unemployment

1993 (April): 5.0%
1992 average: 5.0%
1991 average: 5.8%
1990 average: 5.4%

Average Annual Pay

1988: $19,998
1987: $19,534
1985: $19,089

Per Capita Personal Income

1991: $16,799
1990: $16,302
1989: $15,576

Business Climate (1987)

Manufacturing

Number of establishments in 1987: 1,071
Shipments in 1987 ($1,000): $9,348,300
Employees in 1987: 48,200
Change in employment, 1982 to 1987: -11.6%
Average annual pay for manufacturing work in 1989: $26,990
Average annual pay for production work in 1987: $21,915

Wholesale Trade

Number of establishments in 1987: 1,981
Total sales in 1987 ($1,000): $8,274,800
Change in sales, 1982 to 1987: -24.2%

Retail Trade

Number of establishments in 1987: 6,058
Total sales in 1987 ($1,000): $8,274,800
Retail sales per household in 1987: $15,561
Average annual pay in 1989: $11,395

Service Industry

Selected receipts in 1987 ($1,000): $2,626,600
Average annual pay in 1989: $18,356

Office Real Estate (1992)

Office space inventory: 14,960,000 square feet
Average class A Central Business District rental range per sq. ft: $16.50

Vacancy Rates

All areas: 24.7%

Vacancy Rates in Central Business District

Class A space: 30.3%
Class B space: 44.7%

Vacancy Rates Outside Central Business District

Class A space: 13.0%
Class B space: 21.6%

Housing

Total number of units in 1990: 425,043

Occupied units in 1990: 367,775

Owner-occupied units in 1990: 64.3%

1993 ACCRA average cost: $85,374

1993 ACCRA average rent for an apartment: $424

Chamber of Commerce

Oklahoma City Chamber of Commerce, Jimmy Lyles, President, 1 Santa Fe Plaza, Oklahoma City, OK 73102. 405-278-8900, FAX 405-278-8916

Economic Development Office

Oklahoma City Economic Development Foundation, Ed Bee, Director, 1 Santa Fe Plaza, Oklahoma City, OK 73102. 405-278-8900, FAX 405-278-8916

Major Businesses

Company	SIC	Telephone
All American Bottling Corp.	2086	(405) 232-1158
American Fidelity Corp.	6321	(405) 523-2000
Anthony, C. R. Co.	5311	(405) 278-7670
Anthony, C. R. Holding Corp.	5311	(405) 235-3711
Banks of Mid-America, Inc.	6021	(405) 231-6000
Baptist Medical Center	8062	(405) 949-3011
Braum, W. H. Inc.	5451	(405) 478-1656
Dealers Auto Auction of Oklahoma	5012	(405) 947-2886
Enogex Inc.	4922	(405) 525-7788
First Oklahoma Bank & Trust	6022	(405) 348-3400
Fleming Companies, Inc.	5141	(405) 840-7200
Fleming Foods of Texas, Inc.	5141	(405) 840-7200
Flickinger, S. M. Co., Inc.	5141	(405) 841-5500
Globe Life Accident Insurance Co.	6311	(405) 752-5500
Hadson Corp.	4923	(405) 235-9531
Haniel Corp.	5141	(405) 841-5500
Homeland Holding Corp.	5411	(405) 557-5500
Homeland Stores, Inc.	5411	(405) 557-5500
Jones, Fred Inc.	5511	(405) 235-2000
Kerr-McGee Corp.	2911	(405) 270-1313
Kerr-McGee Chemical Corporaiton	2819	(405) 270-1313
LSB Industries, Inc.	3585	(405) 235-4546
Musket Corp.	5541	(405) 751-9000
O G & E Co.	4911	(405) 272-3000
Oklahoma Gas and Electric Co.	4911	(405) 272-3000
Oklahoma Healthcare Corp.	8062	(405) 949-6066
Oklahoma Publishing Co.	2711	(405) 232-3311
Scrivner, Inc.	5141	(405) 841-5500
Wilson Foods Corp.	2011	(405) 525-4545

Colleges and Universities

Oklahoma Baptist University, Shawnee

Oklahoma Christian University of Science and Arts, Oklahoma City

Oklahoma City Community College, Oklahoma City

Oklahoma City University, Oklahoma City

Oklahoma State University, Oklahoma City, Oklahoma City

St. Gregory's College, Shawnee

University of Oklahoma, Norman

University of Oklahoma Health Sciences Center, Oklahoma City

TULSA, OK (MSA)

Geographic Profile

Land Area

5014.9 square miles

Counties and Parishes

Creek

Osage

Rogers

Tulsa

Wagoner

Ranking Highlights

  15 *out of 319 in total* **land area**

115 *out of 319 in* **population growth,** *1970–1990*

  89 *out of 310 in having the lowest* **unemployment** *rate*

  72 *out of 310 in size of* **labor force**

133 *out of 318 in the percentage of* **college graduates**

121 *out of 292 in per capita personal* **income**

  53 *out of 319 in number of* **manufacturing establishments**

190 *out of 318 in* **physicians** *per 1000 people*

133 *out of 318 in* **hospital beds** *per 1000 people*

151 *out of 267 in fewest* **crimes** *per 1000 people*

191 *out of 266 in fewest* **violent crimes** *per 1000 people*

279 *out of 319 in per capita* **federal funds and grants**

Quality of Life Indexes (Rate per 1000 population)

Crime rate in 1991:	63.3
Violent crime rate in 1991:	8.3
Physicians rate in 1992:	1.68
Hospital bed rate in 1991:	4.15

ACCRA Cost of Living Indexes

(First quarter 1993, average = 100)

Composite index:	89.0
Utilities index:	91.2
Housing index:	79.6

Overview

The Tulsa economy includes manufacturing, services, and research. Major industries include energy, aerospace, telecommunications, data processing, computer related products, healthcare/medical services, and financial services. Tulsa is a major market for northeast Oklahoma, northwest Arkansas, southwest Missouri and southeast Kansas. Unionization of labor force is 9.5%. Percent of time lost due to work stoppages in Oklahoma is 0.02%.

Tulsa International Airport has direct service to most major cities in the United States. Airline service is provided by seven major carriers: Delta, Continental, United, American, TWA, Northwest and Southwest. Tulsa International is 10 minutes from downtown, with three million passengers traveling through the airport each year. Tulsa's Port of Catoosa is the largest waterport located on the McClellan-Kerr Arkansas River Navigation System. The Port offers a Foreign Trade Zone, 1,500 acre industrial park, and liquid and dry cargo storage. A major railroad system is available in Tulsa with service provided by six railroads, including Burlington Northern, Union Pacific and Santa Fe.

The Oklahoma Employment Security Commission provides free screening of job applicants and the Tulsa Technology Center provides free training to employees with programs and materials tailored specifically to the needs of new or expanding industry through the Training for Industry Program. Tulsa Technology Center also provides skill enhancement and retraining to companies at 50% of the cost. Employee training is also available to employers in Tulsa, Creek and Osage counties through the local Private Industry Training Council.

Electric service is provided by Public Service Company of Oklahoma (PSO). PSO's rates are among the lowest out of 177 cities nationwide. Based on level of demand, industrial customers may expect to pay between $0.03 and $0.05 per kilowatt hour. Natural gas is supplied by Oklahoma Natural Gas Company (ONG), which is an integrated, intrastate utility. ONG's gas rates are among the lowest in the nation— 109th out of 121 cities. Average cost for 1,000 MCF is $2,817. Water supplies in Tulsa are practically unlimited. Rates average $0.91 per 1,000 gallons for industrial service. Sewage treatment is handled by three treatment plants with excess capacity to support significant growth. Industrial users may expect to pay $0.76 per 1,000 gallons of sewage.

More than 40,000 students attend universities and colleges in the Tulsa area.

Annual retail sales are $3.9 billion with 297,464 households and an average annual household income of $36,738.

Tulsa has 8,400 hotel and motel rooms to choose from. The Tulsa Convention Center provides 180,000 square feet of meeting and exhibition space.

Population (1990)

Total Population and Growth Rate

1990: 708,954

1980: 657,173

1970: 525,852

Growth rate 1970–1990: 35%

Race and Hispanic Origin

White: 83.3%

Black: 8.2%

Asian/Pacific Islander: 0.9%

Native American: 6.8%

Hispanic origin: 2.1%

White not Hispanic: 82.2%

Age

Ages 18 to 20: 4.3%

Ages 21 to 24: 5.3%

Ages 25 to 44: 32.9%

Ages 45 to 54: 10.6%

Ages 55 to 59: 4.4%

Ages 60 to 64: 4.1%
Ages 65 plus: 11.6%

Educational Attainment (1990)
Percent having completed high school: 79.4%
Percent having completed college: 20.3%
Elementary and high school enrollment: 126,116

Federal Funds and Grants Received
Total received in 1989: $1,633,400,000
Funds received per capita: $2,245

Civilian Labor Force
1993 (April): 347,596
1992 average: 344,697
1991 average: 344,353
1990 average: 345,611

Unemployment
1993 (April): 7.0%
1992 average: 5.8%
1991 average: 6.5%
1990 average: 5.4%

Average Annual Pay
1988: $21,343
1987: $20,593
1985: $19,853

Per Capita Personal Income
1991: $17,837
1990: $17,493
1989: $16,409

Business Climate (1987)
Manufacturing
Number of establishments in 1987: 1,322
Shipments in 1987 ($1,000): $5,932,800
Employees in 1987: 48,700
Change in employment, 1982 to 1987: -27.5%
Average annual pay for manufacturing work in 1989: $27,536
Average annual pay for production work in 1987: $22,861

Wholesale Trade
Number of establishments in 1987: 1,744
Total sales in 1987 ($1,000): $6,789,200
Change in sales, 1982 to 1987: -37.8%

Retail Trade
Number of establishments in 1987: 4,479
Total sales in 1987 ($1,000): $6,789,200
Retail sales per household in 1987: $14,296
Average annual pay in 1989: $11,769

Service Industry
Selected receipts in 1987 ($1,000): $2,118,000
Average annual pay in 1989: $18,855

Office Real Estate (1992)
Office space inventory: 13,948,881 square feet

Average class A Central Business District rental range per sq. ft: $11.40

Vacancy Rates
All areas: 15.4%

Vacancy Rates in Central Business District
Class A space: 12.0%
Class B space: 15.1%

Vacancy Rates Outside Central Business District
Class A space: 10.9%
Class B space: 20.6%

Housing
Total number of units in 1990: 311,890
Occupied units in 1990: 277,202
Owner-occupied units in 1990: 65.5%
1993 ACCRA average cost: $88,350
1993 ACCRA average rent for an apartment: $417

Chamber of Commerce
Metro Tulsa Chamber of Commerce, Clyde C. Cole, President, 616 S. Boston Ave., Tulsa, OK 74119. 918-585-1201, FAX 918-585-8386

Economic Development Office
Metro Tulsa Chamber of Commerce, Economic Development Division, Mickey Thompson, Vice President, 616 S. Boston Ave., Tulsa, OK 74119. 918-585-1201, FAX 918-585-8386

Economic Development Organizations
N.E. Oklahoma Economic Development Association, Bob Jackson, Chairman, 616 S. Boston Ave., Tulsa, OK 74119. 918-592-3303, FAX 918-585-8386

Major Businesses

Company	SIC	Telephone
Affiliated Food Stores Inc.	5141	(918) 446-5531
American Central Gas Co.	4923	(918) 481-6363
Bank of Oklahoma, Tulsa	6021	(918) 588-6000
Citgo Petroleum Corp.	2911	(918) 495-4000
Dover Resources Inc.	3559	(918) 481-6593
Esco Energy Inc.	1311	(918) 560-9700
Flint Industries Inc.	1542	(918) 587-8451
Group Health Service of Oklahoma	6321	(918) 560-3500
Hale-Halsell Co.	5141	(918) 835-4484
Hilti Inc.	3546	(918) 252-6000
Mapco Coal Inc.	5052	(918) 581-1800
Mapco Gas Products Inc.	5172	(918) 581-1800
Mapco Petroleum Inc.	2911	(918) 581-1800
Memorex Telex Corp.	3575	(918) 627-2333
NGL Supply Inc.	5172	(918) 481-1119
Northwest Energy Co.	4922	(918) 588-2000
Occidental Oil and Gas Co.	1311	(918) 561-3964
Oneok Inc.	4922	(918) 588-7000

Major Businesses (Continued)

Company	SIC	Telephone
Oxy Oil and Gas USA Inc.	1311	(918) 561-2211
Public Service Co. of Oklahoma	4911	(918) 599-2000
Purolator Products, Inc.	3714	(918) 492-1800
Quiktrip Corp.	5411	(918) 836-8551
Vinson Supply Co.	5084	(918) 587-6681
Williams Gas Marketing Co.	4924	(918) 588-2000
Williams Natural Gas Co.	4923	(918) 588-2000
Williams Telecommunications	4899	(918) 588-3210

Colleges and Universities

National Education Center-Spartan School of Aeronautics Campus, Tulsa

Oklahoma Junior College of Business and Technology, Tulsa

Oral Roberts University, Tulsa

Tulsa Junior College, Tulsa

University of Tulsa, Tulsa

OREGON

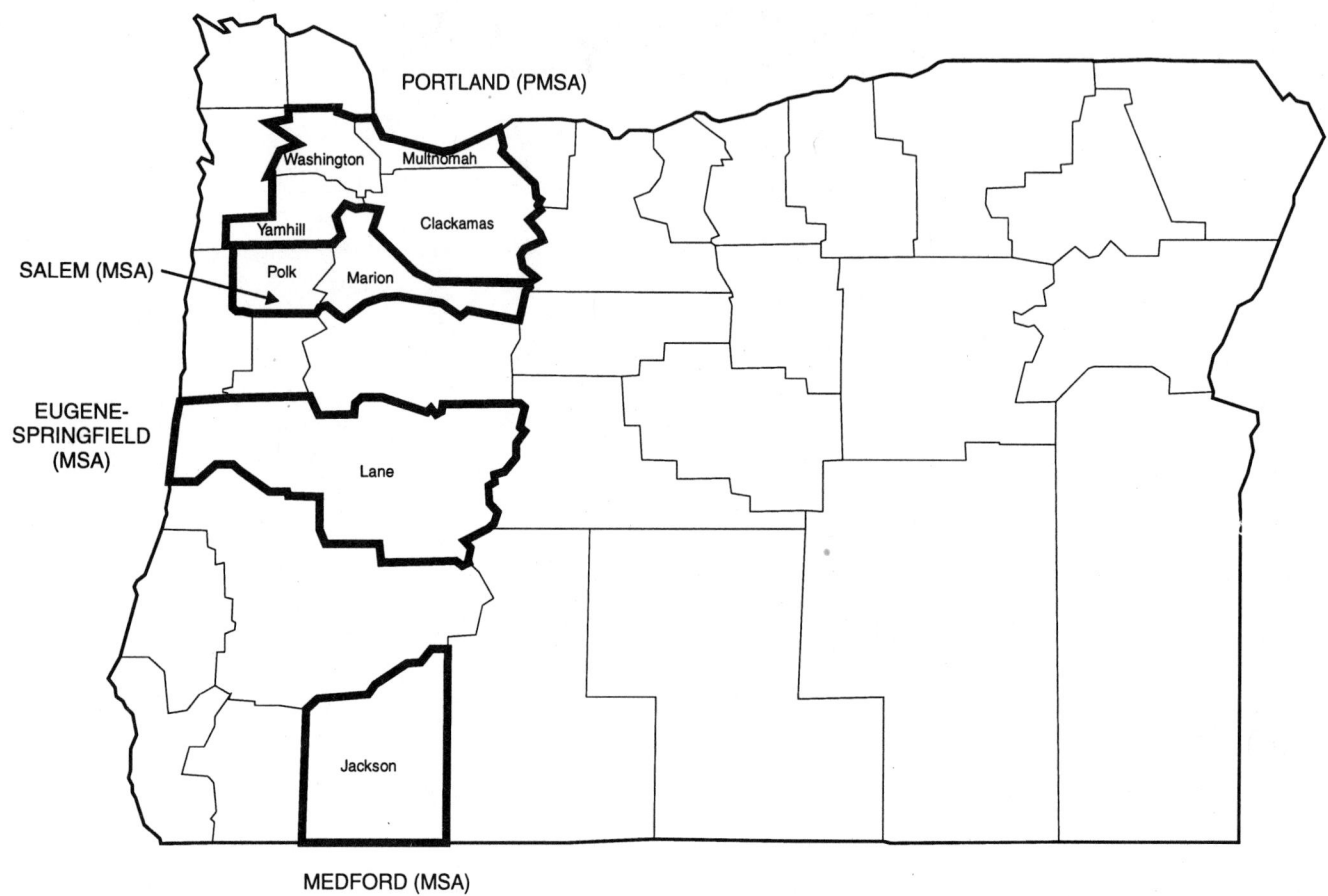

PORTLAND (PMSA)

Washington Multnomah

Clackamas

Yamhill

SALEM (MSA)

Polk Marion

EUGENE-
SPRINGFIELD
(MSA)

Lane

Jackson

MEDFORD (MSA)

OREGON

Population
1990: 2,842,321
1980: 2,633,105

Age
Ages 18 to 20: 119,327
Ages 21 to 24: 148,201
Ages 25 to 44: 926,395
Ages 45 to 54: 296,595
Ages 55 to 59: 116,011
Ages 60 to 64: 120,338
Median age: 34.5

Race and Hispanic Origin
White: 2,636,787
Black: 46,178
Asian/Pacific Islander: 69,269
Native American: 38,496
Hispanic origin: 112,707

Households
Total: 1,103,313
Persons per household: 2.52

Sex
Male: 1,397,073
Female: 1,445,248

Population Migration
Domestic migration: 74,000
International migration: 42,000

Projection of the Population in 1995
Total: 2,960,000
18 to 64: 1,809,000

Civilian Labor Force
1993: 1,519,600
1992: 1,510,900
1991: 1,480,800
1990: 1,458,600

Manufacturing
1995 Projection: 240,300
1992: 207,400
1991: 203,000
1990: 210,200
1989: 216,200

Services
1995 Projection: 446,000

1992: 309,900
1991: 309,800
1990: 300,800
1989: 281,100

Wholesale and Retail Trade
1995 Projection: 363,300
1992: 320,200
1991: 327,400
1990: 323,000
1989: 324,800

Unemployment Rate
1993: 8.3%
1992: 8.2%
1991: 5.6%
1990: 6.0%

Employer Unemployment Contributions
Contribution Rate
1992: 2.60%
1991: 2.62%
1990: 2.78%

Average Weekly Benefit
1992: $177.53
1991: $178.42
1990: $163.23

Gross State Product (Million $)
1989: $52,118
1988: $47,881
1987: $43,563
1979: $28,696
Growth rate, 1979 to 1989: 81.6%

Capital Expenditures of Manufacturing Industries
1990: $1,411,900,000
1989: $1,112,600,000
1988: $847,400,000
1987: $735,400,000

State Tax Rates
Individual income: Range from 5% ($2,000 or less) to 9% (above $5,000).
Corporate income: 6.6% of total taxable income.
General property: Sum of state and local rates. Assessed at

100% of true cash value.
General sales: None
Gasoline: 24¢ per gallon

Income

Median income for a 4 person family: $38,723

Personal per Capita Income
1992: $18,202
1991: $17,495
1990: $17,038

Disposable per Capita Income
1992: $15,614
1991: $14,976
1990: $14,557

Private Employment Weekly Wages

Average
1989: $381
1988: $369
1987: $369

Manufacturing
1989: $354
1988: $482
1987: $464

Services
1989: $340
1988: $328
1987: $314

Wholesale
1989: $501
1988: $486
1987: $458

Retail
1989: $227
1988: $220
1987: $211

Highway Statistics

Total Highway Miles
1990: 94,969
1989: 95,430
1988: 93,595

Federal Highway Aid
1991: $146,896,000
1990: $130,591,000
1989: $133,654,000

Electricity

Average Cost per Kilowatt Hour
1990: 4.17¢
1989: 4.27¢
1988: 4.25¢

Housing (1990)

Owner occupied units: 695,957
Median house value: $67,100
Renter occupied units: 407,356
Median rent: $344
Total vacant units: 90,254
Homeowner vacancy rate: 1.4%
Rental vacancy rate: 5.3%

State Business Incentives and Assistance

Enterprise Zone Incentives

Qualified businesses include new firms locating in a zone and those businesses that expand their employment within a zone by 10% in one year. An existing firm in an enterprise zone may qualify for the tax exemption without a 10% expansion in employment if the firm makes an investment of $25 million or more in qualified property. Businesses in urban zones can qualify for zone incentives by concentrating new hiring on local residents. Qualifying firms must be primarily non-retail. Exceptions are made in 24 zones where hotels, motels, and destination resorts are allowed.

Local incentives. a) educational and training opportunities; b) priority use of federal funds for economic development and job training; c) increased services (police, fire, etc.); d) reduced permit, user, business, professional and occupational fees; e) special zoning districts; and f) simplified permit application procedures.

Property tax exemption. 100% for three years to eligible business firms making an investment in qualified property.

Financial and Business Assistance

Industrial Development Bonds. Administered by the Business Finance Section of the Economic Development Department, the Oregon Economic Commission is authorized to issue tax-exempt and taxable state Industrial Development Bonds. Bond funds may be used to purchase land, buildings, or equipment and construct, expand or improve existing plants. Tax-exempt bonds are available only to manufacturing, some processing activities, and some nonprofit firms. Bonds are issued for up to 30 years.

Port Districts Industrial Development Bonds. Administered by the Ports Division of the Economic Development Department, this program authorized local port authorities to issue IDBs for financing companies locating within each district. Bond funds may be used to purchase land, buildings, equipment, construct, expand or improve existing plants. Port authorities are not limited to maritime or related industrial development.

Port Revolving Fund. Administered by the Economic Development Department, this program provides loans to port districts for improvements to port facilities. Loans may also be made to private businesses to assist financing in buildings, facilities improvements, and equipment acquisitions. These projects are usually smaller than the ones qualified for industrial development bonds.

Agricultural Marketing. Administered by the Department of Agriculture, this program assists in the development of

Major Companies in the State

Company name	Fortune 500 rank	City	Telephone	SIC number
Fortune 500 Companies				
Citgo Petroleum Corp.	53	Tulsa	918-495-4000	1311
Louisiana Pacific Corp.	210	Portland	503-221-0800	2421
Nerco Inc.	452	Portland	503-731-6600	1221
Tektronix Inc.	294	Wilsonville	503-627-7111	3825
Willamette Industries Inc.	195	Portland	503-227-5581	2621
Other Major Companies in the State				
Americold Corp.		Portland	503-624-8585	4222
Bohemia Inc.		Eugene	503-342-6262	2421
Cascade Corp.		Portland	503-227-0024	3593
Fred Meyer Inc.		Portland	503-232-8844	5311
Hyster Yale Materials Handling Inc.		Portland	503-721-6000	3537
Mentor Graphics Corp.		Wilsonville	503-685-7000	7372
Nike Inc.		Beaverton	503-671-6453	3021
Northwest Natural Gas Co.		Portland	503-226-4211	4923
Oregon Steel Mills Inc.		Portland	503-286-9651	3312
Pacificorp		Portland	503-731-2000	4911
Pacificorp Financial Services Inc.		Portland	503-222-7920	6719
Portland General Corp.		Portland	503-464-8820	4911
Portland General Electric Co.		Portland	503-464-8000	4911
Precision Castparts Corp.		Portland	503-777-3881	3369
Riedel Environmental Technologies Inc.		Portland	503-286-4656	4953
Sequent Computer Systems Inc.		Beaverton	503-626-5700	3571
Sprouse Reitz Stores Inc.		Portland	503-224-8220	5311
U S Bancorp		Portland	503-275-6111	6712
United Grocers Inc.		Milwaukie	503-653-6330	5141
WTD Industries Inc.		Portland	503-246-3440	2421

new markets or in the expansion of existing markets for agricultural commodities produced or processed in the state. This effort is directed toward development and improving overseas and domestic markets.

Infrastructure. Administered by the Economic Development Department, this program increases economic activity and creates or retains jobs by assisting local governments infrastructure by providing grants and loans. Highest priorities given where jobs will be created.

Oregon Resource and Technology Development Corporation. Governed by an eleven-member board of directors appointed by the Governor, this program is funded with proceeds of the lottery program. It is designed to improve economic development in the state by fostering innovation in existing industry and development of new industry. It will provide capital financing for the development and implementation of innovations and new technologies. The Corporation can also award, and help fund, applied research contracts to educational institutions and private enterprises.

Education and Training

Job Training Partnership Act. This program operates with funding from the U.S. Department of Labor. It provides job training and other employment related services.

State Offices

Real estate: Real Estate Agency, Morella Larsen, Commissioner, 158 12th Street NE, Salem, OR 97310. 503-378-4170

Chamber of commerce: (No State Chamber of Commerce)

Economic development: Economic Development Department, John Lively, Business Development Specialist, 44 W. Broadway, Eugene, OR 97401. 503-686-2741

Economic Development Department, Ports Division, Manager, 121 S.W. Salmon Street, Room 300, Portland, OR 97204. 503-229-5625

Economic Development Department, Enterprise Zone Program, Henry Markus, Manager, 595 Cottage Street N.E., Salem, OR 97310. 503-373-1200

Department of Agriculture, Bruce Andrews, Director, 635 Capitol Street NE, Salem, OR 97310-0110. 503-378-3774

Small Business Development Center, Edward Cutler, State Director, Lane Community College, Downtown Center, 99 West Tenth Avenue, Suite 216, Eugene, OR 97401. 503-726-2250

Oregon Research and Technology Development Corporation, John Beaulieu, President, 10300 S.W. Greenburg Road, Suite 430, Portland, OR 97223. 503-246-4844

Environmental affairs: Environmental Quality Department, Fred Hansen, Director, 811 SW 6th Ave., Portland, OR 97204. 503-229-5395

Labor: Labor and Industries Bureau, Mary Wendy Roberts, Commissioner, 1400 SW 5th Ave., Suite 409, Portland, OR 97201. 503-229-5737

Unemployment: Employment Division, Pamela Mattson, Administrator, 875 Union Street NE, Salem, OR 97311. 503-378-3211

Worker's compensation: Workers' Compensation Division, Matt Hennessee, Administrator, 200 Labor & Industries Bldg., Salem, OR 97310. 503-378-3304

Occupational safety and health: Labor and Industries Bureau, Mary Wendy Roberts, Commissioner, 1400 SW 5th Ave., Suite 409, Portland, OR 97201. 503-229-5737

Secretary of state: Secretary of State, Phil Keising, Secretary of State, 136 State Capitol, Salem, OR 97310. 503-378-4139

Taxation and revenue: Revenue Department, Richard A. Munn, Director, 457 Revenue, 955 Centre Street NE, Salem, OR 97310. 503-378-3363

Designated Zones for Economic Development

Enterprise Zones

Enacted in: 1985

No. of established zones: 30

Foreign Trade Zones

Foreign Trade Zone No. 132, Coos County, Oregon, Grantee: International Port of Coos Bay Commission, Oregon Int'l Port of Coos Ray, Paul Vogel, Port Bldg., Front & Market St., Coos Bay, OR 97420, 503-267-7678

Foreign Trade Zone No. 45, Portland, Oregon, Grantee/Operator: Port of Portland, Peggy J. Krause, PO Box 3529, Portland, OR 97208, 503-731-7537

Labor Unions

Carpenters and Joiners of America, United Brotherhood of (AFL-CIO)

Electrical Workers, International Brotherhood of (AFL-CIO)

Engineers and Architects

Laborers' International Union of North America (AFL-CIO)

Machinists and Aerospace Workers, International Association of (AFL-CIO)

National Education Association

Nurses' Association, American

Operating Engineers, International Union of (AFL-CIO)

Oregon School Employees Association

Service Employees' International Union (AFL-CIO)

Transit Union, Amalgamated (AFL-CIO)

Universities with Ph.D. Programs

Lewis and Clark College, Portland

Oregon Health Sciences University, Portland

Oregon State University, Corvallis

Pacific University, Forest Grove

Portland State University, Portland

University of Oregon, Eugene

EUGENE–SPRINGFIELD, OR (MSA)

Geographic Profile
Land Area
4554.2 square miles

Counties and Parishes
Lane

Ranking Highlights
18 *out of 319 in total* **land area**

124 *out of 319 in* **population growth,** *1970–1990*

201 *out of 310 in having the lowest* **unemployment** *rate*

139 *out of 310 in size of* **labor force**

93 *out of 318 in the percentage of* **college graduates**

206 *out of 292 in per capita personal* **income**

85 *out of 319 in number of* **manufacturing establishments**

168 *out of 318 in* **physicians** *per 1000 people*

285 *out of 318 in* **hospital beds** *per 1000 people*

103 *out of 267 in fewest* **crimes** *per 1000 people*

45 *out of 266 in fewest* **violent crimes** *per 1000 people*

245 *out of 319 in per capita* **federal funds and grants**

Quality of Life Indexes (Rate per 1000 population)
Crime rate in 1991:	55.3
Violent crime rate in 1991:	3.0
Physicians rate in 1992:	1.77
Hospital bed rate in 1991:	2.31

ACCRA Cost of Living Indexes
(First quarter 1993, average = 100)
Composite index:	N/A
Utilities index:	N/A
Housing index:	N/A

Overview
Eugene is Oregon's second largest city and the seat of Lane County. Together with Springfield it is also the second largest metropolitan area in the state. It is the commercial and cultural center for a large agricultural and timber region, as well as an important retail trade and transportation hub in the state of Oregon. Situated halfway between the ocean and the mountains, Eugene offers numerous recreational possibilities year round.

Lumber is the largest industry in the Eugene area, where a number of manufacturing concerns produce lumber and wood products. The region is the nation's largest producer of softwood lumber and plywood products. Agriculture ranks second to the wood industry in the local economy, with a wide variety of crops grown. A sizable food processing industry has grown up around the agricultural activity. Eugene serves central and southern Oregon as a retail and wholesale trade center. Services, government, and tourism are also contributors to the overall economy.

Over three thousand available hotel rooms are located in Eugene, and a number of area hotels provide extensive facilities for banquets, meetings, and conventions.

A number of air-freight services operate out of Eugene Airport; the Burlington Northern and Southern Pacific railroads provide access to transcontinental and coastal rail lines.

About thirty-five interstate truck carriers serve metropolitan Eugene via Interstate 5.

Eugene Airport is located nine miles north of Eugene and is served by five major air carriers on more than forty flights daily. The airport is a regional facility, with connections to most major cities in the West and Midwest. Amtrak provides passenger rail service.

The major north-south route from Canada to Mexico along the West Coast, I-5 runs through Eugene. U.S. 126 connects the city with the Pacific coast and eastern Oregon.

Population (1990)
Total Population and Growth Rate
1990: 282,912
1980: 275,226
1970: 215,401
Growth rate 1970–1990: 31%

Race and Hispanic Origin
White: 95.4%
Black: .7%
Asian/Pacific Islander: 2.0%
Native American: 1.1%
Hispanic origin: 2.4%
White not Hispanic: 93.8%

Age
Ages 18 to 20: 5.4%
Ages 21 to 24: 6.4%
Ages 25 to 44: 32.5%
Ages 45 to 54: 10.3%
Ages 55 to 59: 3.9%
Ages 60 to 64: 4%
Ages 65 plus: 13.1%

Educational Attainment (1990)
Percent having completed high school: 83.0%
Percent having completed college: 22.2%
Elementary and high school enrollment: 44,968

Federal Funds and Grants Received
Total received in 1989: $676,100,000
Funds received per capita: $2,503,000

Civilian Labor Force
1993 (April): 149,746
1992 average: 148,738
1991 average: 147,872
1990 average: 148,203

Unemployment
1993 (April): 7.5%

1992 average: 7.5%
1991 average: 6.5%
1990 average: 5.9%

Average Annual Pay
1988: $18,411
1987: $17,638
1985: $16,835

Per Capita Personal Income
1991: $16,145
1990: $15,760
1989: $15,083

Business Climate (1987)
Manufacturing
Number of establishments in 1987: 769
Shipments in 1987 ($1,000): $2,617,900
Employees in 1987: 20,300
Change in employment, 1982 to 1987: 20.8%
Average annual pay for manufacturing work in 1989: $24,514
Average annual pay for production work in 1987: $20,006

Wholesale Trade
Number of establishments in 1987: 532
Total sales in 1987 ($1,000): $1,803,100
Change in sales, 1982 to 1987: 37.1%

Retail Trade
Number of establishments in 1987: 1,863
Total sales in 1987 ($1,000): $1,803,100
Retail sales per household in 1987: $15,920
Average annual pay in 1989: $11,347

Service Industry
Selected receipts in 1987 ($1,000): $619,600
Average annual pay in 1989: $16,392

Housing
Total number of units in 1990: 116,676
Occupied units in 1990: 110,799
Owner-occupied units in 1990: 60.8%
1993 ACCRA average cost: N/A
1993 ACCRA average rent for an apartment: N/A

Chamber of Commerce
Eugene Area Chamber of Commerce, Larry T. Douglas, Exec. Vice President, 1401 Willamette St., PO Box 1107, Eugene, OR 97440. 503-484-1314

Economic Development Office
Eugene/Springfield Metro Partnership, John Lively, Exec. Director, PO Box 10398, 44 W. Broadway Suite 203, Eugene, OR 97440. 503-686-2741, FAX 503-686-2325

Economic Development Organizations
City of Springfield Economic Development Diision, John Tamulonis, Economic Development Manager, 225 Fifth St., Springfield, OR 503-726-3753, FAX 503-726-3689
Lane Council of Governments, Jim Zelenka, Economic Development Coordinator, 125 E. 8th Ave., Eugene, OR 97401. 503-687-4283, 503-687-4095
Planning and Development Department, Abe Farkas, Director, 72 W. Broadway, Eugene, OK 97401. 503-687-5443

Major Businesses

Company	SIC	Telephone
Betz Chevrolet-Pontiac-Oldsmobile	5511	(503) 942-4415
Bohemia Inc.	2421	(503) 342-6262
Commercial Eqp Lease Corp.	7514	(503) 484-1884
Eugene Water & Electric	4931	(503) 484-2411
Lane Plywood Inc.	2436	(503) 342-5561
Maks Wood Products Co.	5031	(503) 461-0600
Maywood-Anderson Forest Products	5031	(503) 485-1844
McDonald Candy Co.	5181	(503) 345-8421
Mckenzie–Willamette Hospital	8062	(503) 726-4400
Monaco Coach Corp.	3711	(503) 998-1068
Murphy Co.	2436	(503) 344-4747
Oregon Grocery Stores Inc.	5411	(503) 342-5779
Pacific Hospital Association	6411	(503) 686-1242
Pacific Petroleum Corp.	5172	(503) 683-4433
Pasquale Food Co. Inc.	5149	(503) 686-9600
Rosboro Lumber Co.	2436	(503) 746-8411
Springfield Utility Board	4931	(503) 746-8451
Starfire Lumber Co.	2421	(503) 942-0168
States Industries Inc.	2435	(503) 688-7871
Timber Products Co. Ltd. Partner	5031	(503) 747-3321
Troutman Investment Co.	5311	(503) 746-9611
United Pipe & Supply Co.	5083	(503) 688-6511
Wildish Land Co.	1442	(503) 485-1700
Willamette Valley Co.	5085	(503) 484-9621

Colleges and Universities
Lane Community College, Eugene
Northwest Christian College, Eugene
University of Oregon, Eugene

Additional Information
FasTrack. Eugene/Springfield Metropolitan Partnership, published quarterly. [newsletter]

MEDFORD, OR (MSA)

Geographic Profile

Land Area

2785.4 square miles

Counties and Parishes

Jackson

Ranking Highlights

  55   *out of 319 in total* **land area**

  68   *out of 319 in* **population growth,** *1970–1990*

242   *out of 310 in having the lowest* **unemployment** *rate*

217   *out of 310 in size of* **labor force**

181   *out of 318 in the percentage of* **college graduates**

218   *out of 292 in per capita personal* **income**

156   *out of 319 in number of* **manufacturing establishments**

139   *out of 318 in* **physicians** *per 1000 people*

183   *out of 318 in* **hospital beds** *per 1000 people*

  73   *out of 267 in fewest* **crimes** *per 1000 people*

  60   *out of 266 in fewest* **violent crimes** *per 1000 people*

211   *out of 319 in per capita* **federal funds and grants**

Quality of Life Indexes (Rate per 1000 population)

Crime rate in 1991:	48.3
Violent crime rate in 1991:	3.5
Physicians rate in 1992:	1.89
Hospital bed rate in 1991:	3.57

ACCRA Cost of Living Indexes

(First quarter 1993, average = 100)

Composite index:	N/A
Utilities index:	N/A
Housing index:	N/A

Population (1990)

Total Population and Growth Rate

1990: 146,389

1980: 132,456

1970: 94,533

Growth rate 1970–1990: 55%

Race and Hispanic Origin

White: 95.8%

Black: .2%

Asian/Pacific Islander: 1.0%

Native American: 1.3%

Hispanic origin: 4.1%

White not Hispanic: 93.6%

Age

Ages 18 to 20: 3.9%

Ages 21 to 24: 4.5%

Ages 25 to 44: 30%

Ages 45 to 54: 10.9%

Ages 55 to 59: 4.5%

Ages 60 to 64: 4.9%

Ages 65 plus: 16.2%

Educational Attainment (1990)

Percent having completed high school: 80.1%

Percent having completed college: 17.6%

Elementary and high school enrollment: 23,993

Federal Funds and Grants Received

Total received in 1989: $390,700,000

Funds received per capita: $2,679

Civilian Labor Force

1993 (April):	77,243
1992 average:	77,014
1991 average:	74,550
1990 average:	73,432

Unemployment

1993 (April): 8.5%

1992 average: 8.4%

1991 average: 7.6%

1990 average: 6.7%

Average Annual Pay

1988: $17,877

1987: $17,384

1985: $16,526

Per Capita Personal Income

1991: $15,953

1990: $15,570

1989: $14,772

Business Climate (1987)

Manufacturing

Number of establishments in 1987: 326

Shipments in 1987 ($1,000): $1,163,200

Employees in 1987: 8,100

Change in employment, 1982 to 1987: 42.1%

Average annual pay for manufacturing work in 1989: $23,467

Average annual pay for production work in 1987: $21,078

Wholesale Trade

Number of establishments in 1987: 263

Total sales in 1987 ($1,000): $579,400

Change in sales, 1982 to 1987: 76.3%

Retail Trade

Number of establishments in 1987: 1,022

Total sales in 1987 ($1,000): $579,400

Retail sales per household in 1987: $19,311

Average annual pay in 1989: $11,489

Service Industry

Selected receipts in 1987 ($1,000): $257,700

Average annual pay in 1989: $16,711

Housing

Total number of units in 1990: 60,376

Occupied units in 1990: 57,238
Owner-occupied units in 1990: 66.2%
1993 ACCRA average cost: N/A
1993 ACCRA average rent for an apartment: N/A

Chamber of Commerce

Medford/Jackson County Chamber of Commerce, Marilyn Yarnell, Office Manager, 304 S. Central Ave., Medford, OR 97501. 503-772-6293

Economic Development Office

Southern Oregon Regional Economic Development Inc., Corky Leister, Exec. Director, 132 W. Main St., Medford, OR 97501. 503-773-8946, FAX 503-779-0953

Major Businesses

Company	SIC	Telephone
Attaway Inc.	4213	(503) 772-8100
Bear Creek Corp.	0175	(503) 776-2362
Burrill, Eugene F. Lumber	2421	(503) 826-2221
Butler Ford Inc.	5511	(503) 482-2521
Cascade Wood Products Inc.	2431	(503) 826-2911
Combined Transport Inc.	4213	(503) 826-7486
Croman Corp.	2421	(503) 826-4455
Erickson Group Ltd.	2411	(503) 664-5544
Grange Coop Supply Association	2048	(503) 664-1261
Kogap Manufacturing Co.	2436	(503) 776-6500
Lithia Motors Inc.	5511	(503) 776-6400
Med Ply, Inc.	2436	(503) 826-3142
Medford Corp.	2436	(503) 773-7491
Medite Corp.	2493	(503) 773-2522
Rogue Valley Health Service	8062	(503) 770-4106
Rogue Valley Medical Center	8062	(503) 773-6281
Rogue Valley Physicians Service	6411	(503) 779-6464
Sherm's Thunderbird Marke	5411	(503) 779-4274
Sterling Business Forms Inc.	2761	(503) 779-3173
Sunriver Properties Oregon	6531	(503) 593-1221

PORTLAND, OR (PMSA)

Geographic Profile

Land Area

3743.0 square miles

Counties and Parishes

Clackamas
Multnomah
Washington
Yamhill

Ranking Highlights

33   *out of 319 in total* **land area**
114 *out of 319 in* **population growth,** *1970–1990*
121 *out of 310 in having the lowest* **unemployment** *rate*
35   *out of 310 in size of* **labor force**
63   *out of 318 in the percentage of* **college graduates**
69   *out of 292 in per capita personal* **income**
27   *out of 319 in number of* **manufacturing establishments**
46   *out of 318 in* **physicians** *per 1000 people*
239 *out of 318 in* **hospital beds** *per 1000 people*
175 *out of 267 in fewest* **crimes** *per 1000 people*
184 *out of 266 in fewest* **violent crimes** *per 1000 people*
198 *out of 319 in per capita* **federal funds and grants**

Quality of Life Indexes (Rate per 1000 population)

Crime rate in 1991:	67.8
Violent crime rate in 1991:	8.0
Physicians rate in 1992:	2.76
Hospital bed rate in 1991:	3.02

ACCRA Cost of Living Indexes

(First quarter 1993, average = 100)
Composite index: 109.3
Utilities index: 76.4
Housing index: 125.8

Overview

Situated on the Oregon/Washington boundary, at the confluence of the Columbia and Willamette Rivers, Portland is approximately 110 miles inland from the Pacific Ocean. Portland's employment increased by 1.9% between January 1992 and January 1993, while during the same period employment for the nation grew by just 0.6%. One of the largest sectors of the Portland economy, manufacturing, accounts for 16.1% of the area's employment. Oregon's SAT scores are first in the nation for the third consecutive year and have been in the top two rankings since 1984.

The Port of Portland continues to be one of the fastest growing air cargo centers in the United States, primarily due to its strategic location, availability of land for development, and its substantial airspace capacity. Portland International Airport (PDX) provides choice of service, competitive rates and quality cargo-handling services. Over 600 acres of airside-adjacent, choice sites are available for cargo and maintenance activities, as well as terminal expansion. PDX remains the least congested major West Coast airport. Over $350 million in airport improvements are planned over the next five years. The Port of Portland is number one in export tonnage and auto imports for the West Coast; and number one in wheat export in the United States. Portland's public transportation system (Tri-Met) was named the Best in North America in 1989. Tri-Met serves 600 square miles of the metropolitan area. MAX, a light rail line which opened in 1986, serves a 15-mile corridor from downtown Portland east to Gresham. Construction is currently underway to extend light rail service to the western portion of the metropolitan area, an 18 mile extension from downtown Portland to downtown Hillsboro.

The City of Portland has 7,500 acres of parks including Forest Park, the largest forested municipal park within a city's limits in the United States.

Population (1990)

Total Population and Growth Rate
1990: 1,239,842
1980: 1,105,750
1970: 918,889
Growth rate 1970–1990: 35%

Race and Hispanic Origin
White: 90.7%
Black: 3.1%
Asian/Pacific Islander: 3.7%
Native American: 0.9%
Hispanic origin: 3.6%
White not Hispanic: 88.8%

Age
Ages 18 to 20:   4%
Ages 21 to 24: 5.4%
Ages 25 to 44: 35.4%
Ages 45 to 54: 10.4%
Ages 55 to 59: 3.7%
Ages 60 to 64: 3.8%
Ages 65 plus: 12.2%

Educational Attainment (1990)
Percent having completed high school: 84.6%
Percent having completed college: 24.8%
Elementary and high school enrollment: 198,758

Federal Funds and Grants Received
Total received in 1989: $3,331,700,000
Funds received per capita: $2,804

Civilian Labor Force
1993 (April):   707,976
1992 average: 713,670
1991 average: 698,926
1990 average: 685,612

Unemployment
1993 (April):   6.0%

1992 average: 6.4%
1991 average: 4.7%
1990 average: 4.2%

Average Annual Pay
1988: $21,444
1987: $20,584
1985: $19,230

Per Capita Personal Income
1991: $19,235
1990: $18,744
1989: $17,844

Business Climate (1987)

Manufacturing
Number of establishments in 1987: 2,631
Shipments in 1987 ($1,000): $10,847,500
Employees in 1987: 94,100
Change in employment, 1982 to 1987: 1.2%
Average annual pay for manufacturing work in 1989: $27,920
Average annual pay for production work in 1987: $20,841

Wholesale Trade
Number of establishments in 1987: 3,403
Total sales in 1987 ($1,000): $23,849,100
Change in sales, 1982 to 1987: 10.6%

Retail Trade
Number of establishments in 1987: 7,537
Total sales in 1987 ($1,000): $23,849,100
Retail sales per household in 1987: $17,592
Average annual pay in 1989: $12,861

Service Industry
Selected receipts in 1987 ($1,000): $3,791,000
Average annual pay in 1989: $19,632

Office Real Estate (1992)
Office space inventory: 16,050,021 square feet
Average class A Central Business District rental range per sq. ft: $19.16

Vacancy Rates
All areas: 13.6%

Vacancy Rates in Central Business District
Class A space: 11.9%
Class B space: 22.2%

Vacancy Rates Outside Central Business District
Class A space: 11.7%
Class B space: 14.6%

Housing
Total number of units in 1990: 512,664
Occupied units in 1990: 487,091
Owner-occupied units in 1990: 60.7%
1993 ACCRA average cost: $142,500
1993 ACCRA average rent for an apartment: $655

Chamber of Commerce

Portland Metro Chamber of Commerce, Donald S. McClave, President, 221 N.W. 2nd Ave., Portland, OR 97209. 503-228-9411

Economic Development Office

Portland Development Commisssion, Patrick La Crosse, Exec Director, 1120 S.W. Fifth Ave. #1100, Portland, OR 97204. 503-823-3200, FAX 503-823-3368

Economic Development Organizations

Northwest Small Business Finance Corp., Robert A. Gaynor, Exec. Director, 3802 N.E. MLK Jr. Blvd. Suite 306, Portland, OR 97212. 503-284-7440, 503-284-8115

Major Businesses

Company	SIC	Telephone
Blue Cross & Blue Shield	6321	(503) 225-5221
Bonneville Power Administration	4911	(503) 230-5101
First Intrstate Bank of Oregon	6021	(503) 225-2111
FMI Associates Ltd.	5311	(503) 232-8844
Forest City Trading Group	5031	(503) 246-8500
Freightliner Corp.	3715	(503) 283-8662
Inner Pacificorp, Inc.	1221	(503) 464-6000
Kaiser Foundation Health	6324	(503) 280-2050
Louisiana-Pacific Corp.	2421	(503) 221-0800
Meyer, Fred Inc.	5311	(503) 232-8844
Nerco Coal Corp.	1221	(503) 796-6600
Nike Inc.	3149	(503) 641-6453
North Pacific Lumber Co.	5031	(503) 231-1166
Oregon State Public Employees Retirement	6733	(503) 229-5824
Pacific Telecom, Inc.	4813	(206) 696-0983
Pacificorp	4911	(503) 464-6000
Pamplin, R. B. Corp.	2211	(503) 248-1133
Pope & Talbot, Inc.	2611	(503) 228-9161
Portland Adventist Medical Center	8062	(503) 257-2500
Portland General Corp.	4911	(503) 464-8820
Portland General Electric Co.	4911	(503) 464-8000
Precision Castparts Corp.	3324	(503) 777-3881
Standard Insurance Co.	6311	(503) 248-2700
U. S. Bancorp	6021	(503) 275-6111
United Grain Corp. of Oregon	5153	(503) 228-6424
United Grocers Inc.	5141	(503) 653-6330
U. S. National Bank of Oregon	6021	(503) 275-6111
Willamette Industries, Inc.	2631	(503) 227-5581

Colleges and Universities

Bassist College, Portland
Columbia Christian College, Portland
Concordia College, Portland
ITT Technical Institute, Portland
Lewis And Clark College, Portland
Oregon Health Sciences University, Portland
Oregon Polytechnic Institute, Portland
Pacific Northwest College of Art, Portland
Portland Community College, Portland
Portland State University, Portland
Reed College, Portland
University of Portland, Portland
Warner Pacific College, Portland

SALEM, OR (MSA)

Geographic Profile

Land Area

1926.1 square miles

Counties and Parishes

Marion

Polk

Ranking Highlights

98 *out of 319 in total* **land area**

73 *out of 319 in* **population growth,** *1970–1990*

157 *out of 310 in having the lowest* **unemployment** *rate*

140 *out of 310 in size of* **labor force**

173 *out of 318 in the percentage of* **college graduates**

199 *out of 292 in per capita personal* **income**

121 *out of 319 in number of* **manufacturing establishments**

250 *out of 318 in* **physicians** *per 1000 people*

206 *out of 318 in* **hospital beds** *per 1000 people*

142 *out of 267 in fewest* **crimes** *per 1000 people*

75 *out of 266 in fewest* **violent crimes** *per 1000 people*

90 *out of 319 in per capita* **federal funds and grants**

Quality of Life Indexes (Rate per 1000 population)

Crime rate in 1991:	61.8
Violent crime rate in 1991:	4.0
Physicians rate in 1992:	1.39
Hospital bed rate in 1991:	1.95

ACCRA Cost of Living Indexes

(First quarter 1993, average = 100)

Composite index:	100.1
Utilities index:	80.2
Housing index:	96.5

Overview

Salem is the capital of Oregon and the third largest city in the state. Agriculture plays a major role in the local economy. Farming produces over $250 million worth of crops each year in the area around Salem. The city itself is an important processor of those crops, one of the largest in the nation. More than one-half billion pounds of canned and frozen foods are produced in the city annually. Lumber and other timber products are also a major industry in Salem. Government and related industries employ the largest percentage of the work force.

Manufacturing concerns are among the fastest growing industries in the area, with forty percent of the manufacturing workforce engaged in food processing. Electronics, computers, and other high-technology industries are beginning to exert a force in the local economy. Items and goods produced include berries and related products, wine, wood products, and dairy products.

Salem is situated on the main line of the Burlington Northern and Southern Pacific railroads, with more than twenty freight trains running through the city each day. Seven terminals are served by twenty-eight interstate truck lines in the city.

McNary Municipal Airport provides daily connecting flights to many major western cities via Horizon Airlines. Limousines make twelve daily round trips from Portland International Airport, 61 miles from Salem. Interstate 5, the major West Coast interstate highway, runs through Salem, and passenger rail service is available from Amtrak with two trains daily. The city is also served by a commercial busline.

Population (1990)

Total Population and Growth Rate

1990: 278,024

1980: 249,895

1970: 186,658

Growth rate 1970–1990: 49%

Race and Hispanic Origin

White: 91.8%

Black: .8%

Asian/Pacific Islander: 1.7%

Native American: 1.5%

Hispanic origin: 7.6%

White not Hispanic: 88.6%

Age

Ages 18 to 20: 4.5%

Ages 21 to 24: 5.5%

Ages 25 to 44: 31.3%

Ages 45 to 54: 10%

Ages 55 to 59: 4%

Ages 60 to 64: 4%

Ages 65 plus: 14.4%

Educational Attainment (1990)

Percent having completed high school: 78.9%

Percent having completed college: 18.2%

Elementary and high school enrollment: 47,690

Federal Funds and Grants Received

Total received in 1989: $989,800,000

Funds received per capita: $3,669

Civilian Labor Force

1993 (April): 146,155

1992 average: 146,081

1991 average: 141,496

1990 average: 140,294

Unemployment

1993 (April): 7.4%

1992 average: 6.9%

1991 average: 5.6%

1990 average: 5.4%

Average Annual Pay

1988: $17,258

1987: $16,727
1985: $15,838

Per Capita Personal Income
1991: $16,255
1990: $15,716
1989: $14,784

Business Climate (1987)
Manufacturing
Number of establishments in 1987: 463
Shipments in 1987 ($1,000): $1,500,600
Employees in 1987: 13,700
Change in employment, 1982 to 1987: 8.7%
Average annual pay for manufacturing work in 1989: $21,238
Average annual pay for production work in 1987: $16,067

Wholesale Trade
Number of establishments in 1987: 403
Total sales in 1987 ($1,000): $1,431,800
Change in sales, 1982 to 1987: 16.0%

Retail Trade
Number of establishments in 1987: 1,535
Total sales in 1987 ($1,000): $1,431,800
Retail sales per household in 1987: $14,064
Average annual pay in 1989: $10,961

Service Industry
Selected receipts in 1987 ($1,000): $485,600
Average annual pay in 1989: $15,887

Housing
Total number of units in 1990: 105,847
Occupied units in 1990: 101,661
Owner-occupied units in 1990: 63.5%
1993 ACCRA average cost: $108,656
1993 ACCRA average rent for an apartment: $490

Chamber of Commerce
Salem Area Chamber of Commerce, John Irelan, Exec. Vice President, 220 Cottage St. N.E., Salem, OR 97301. 503-581-1466

Economic Development Office
Salem Economic Development Corp., Peter Sukalac, Exec. Director, 365 Ferry St. S.E., Suite 201, Salem, OR 97301. 503-588-8326

Economic Development Organizations
Mid Willamette Valley Economic Development District, Alan Hershey, Director, 105 High St. S.E., Salem, OR 97301. 503-588-6177

Major Businesses

Company	SIC	Telephone
Agripac Inc.	2037	(503) 363-9255
Capitol Health Care Inc.	6321	(503) 364-4868

Major Businesses (Continued)

Company	SIC	Telephone
Capitol Toyota Inc.	5511	(503) 399-1011
Colson & Colson Construction Co.	1522	(503) 370-7070
Columbia Helicopters Inc.	2411	(503) 678-1222
De Lon Oldsmobile Co. Inc.	5511	(503) 581-1421
Eoff Electric Co.	5063	(503) 363-9251
Green Veneer Inc.	2421	(503) 897-2391
Morrow Crane Co., Inc.	7353	(503) 585-5721
Mountain Fir Lumber Co., Inc.	2421	(503) 399-0835
Norpac Foods Inc.	2037	(503) 769-2101
North Santiam Plywood Co.	2436	(503) 897-2391
Northwest Wood Products Inc.	5031	(503) 897-2391
Oregon Turkey Growers	2015	(503) 364-3323
Polk County Farmers Co-Op	5083	(503) 363-2332
SAIF Corp.	6321	(503) 373-8000
Salem Hospital	8062	(503) 370-5200
Santiam Midwest Lumber Co.	5031	(503) 393-1193
Truax, Merritt Inc.	5172	(503) 588-0455
Truitt Bros Inc.	2033	(503) 362-3674
Wilco Farmers	5191	(503) 845-6122

Colleges and Universities
Chemeketa Community College, Salem

PENNSYLVANIA

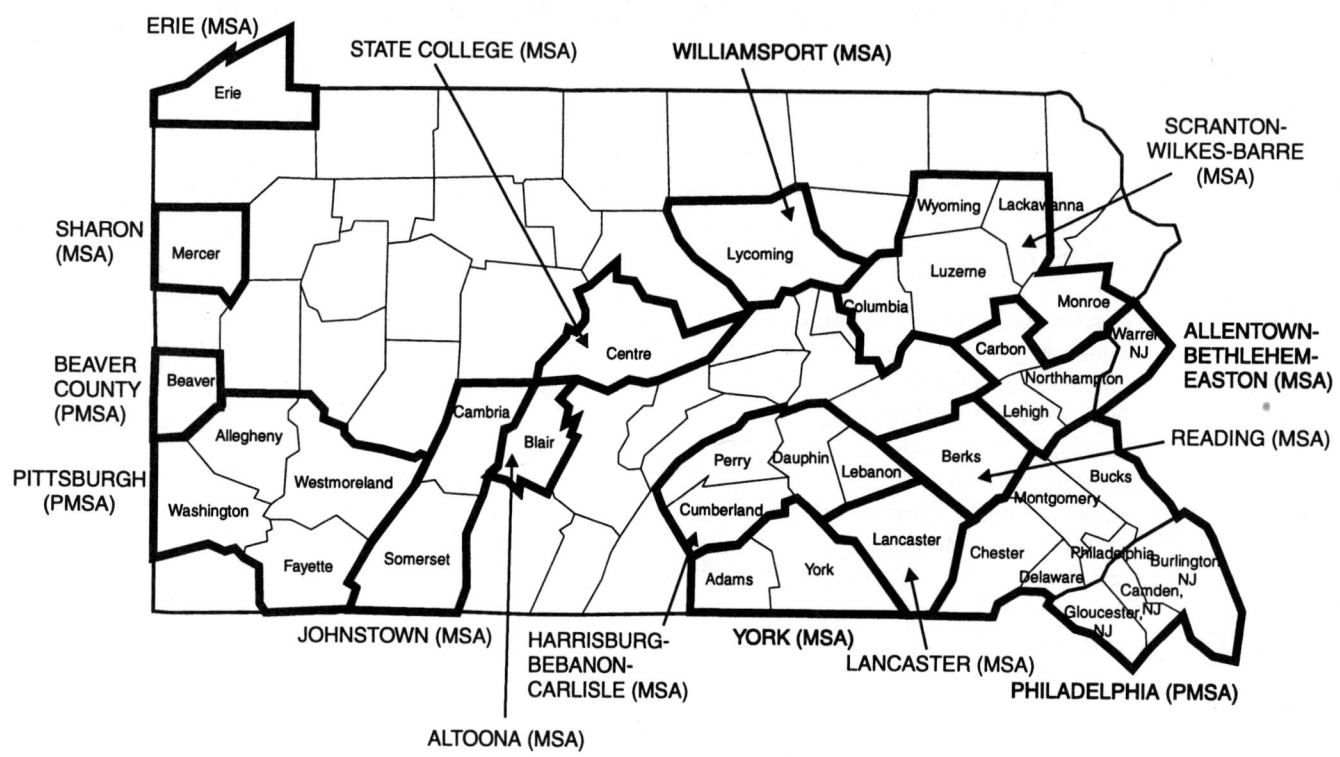

ERIE (MSA)

STATE COLLEGE (MSA)

WILLIAMSPORT (MSA)

SCRANTON-
WILKES-BARRE
(MSA)

SHARON
(MSA)

BEAVER
COUNTY
(PMSA)

PITTSBURGH
(PMSA)

ALLENTOWN-
BETHLEHEM-
EASTON (MSA)

READING (MSA)

Erie

Mercer

Beaver

Allegheny

Washington

Westmoreland

Fayette

Somerset

Cambria

Blair

Centre

Lycoming

Wyoming

Lackawanna

Luzerne

Columbia

Monroe

Carbon

Northhampton

Warren
NJ

Lehigh

Perry

Dauphin

Lebanon

Berks

Bucks

Cumberland

Montgomery

Lancaster

Chester

Philadelphia

Burlington
NJ

Adams

York

Delaware

Camden,
NJ

Gloucester,
NJ

JOHNSTOWN (MSA)

HARRISBURG-
BEBANON-
CARLISLE (MSA)

YORK (MSA)

LANCASTER (MSA)

PHILADELPHIA (PMSA)

ALTOONA (MSA)

PENNSYLVANIA

Population
1990: 11,881,643
1980: 11,863,895

Age
Ages 18 to 20: 551,216
Ages 21 to 24: 675,559
Ages 25 to 44: 3,657,323
Ages 45 to 54: 1,213,845
Ages 55 to 59: 552,378
Ages 60 to 64: 607,406
Median age: 35.0

Race and Hispanic Origin
White: 10,520,201
Black: 1,089,795
Asian/Pacific Islander: 137,438
Native American: 14,733
Hispanic origin: 232,262

Households
Total: 4,495,966
Persons per household: 2.57

Sex
Male: 5,694,265
Female: 6,187,378

Population Migration
Domestic migration: -187,000
International migration: 96,000

Projection of the Population in 1995
Total: 12,316,000
18 to 64: 7,489,000

Civilian Labor Force
1993: 5,980,300
1992: 5,977,600
1991: 5,872,000
1990: 5,860,300

Manufacturing
1995 Projection: 1,051,400
1992: 949,100
1991: 957,300
1990: 998,300
1989: 1,040,700

Services
1995 Projection: 1,963,200

1992: 1,487,500
1991: 1,489,600
1990: 1,466,300
1989: 1,392,500

Wholesale and Retail Trade
1995 Projection: 1,404,400
1992: 1,153,600
1991: 1,204,900
1990: 1,215,400
1989: 1,208,800

Unemployment Rate
1993: 8.2%
1992: 7.8%
1991: 6.3%
1990: 5.9%

Employer Unemployment Contributions
Contribution Rate
1992: 3.80%
1991: 3.40%
1990: 3.42%

Average Weekly Benefit
1992: $212.92
1991: $206.94
1990: $189.47

Gross State Product (Million $)
1989: $227,898
1988: $215,218
1987: $198,531
1979: $118,671
Growth rate, 1979 to 1989: 92.0%

Capital Expenditures of Manufacturing Industries
1990: $4,659,600,000
1989: $4,214,000,000
1988: $3,500,900,000
1987: $3,440,500,000

State Tax Rates
Individual income: 3.1% on adjusted gross income.
Corporate income: 12.25% of total taxable income.
General property: No state levy. Rates fixed locally, based on fair market value of real propety.

General sales: 6%
Gasoline: 12¢ per gallon

Income

Median income for a 4 person family: $40,404

Personal per Capita Income
1992: $20,253
1991: $19,313
1990: $18,725

Disposable per Capita Income
1992: $17,658
1991: $16,828
1990: $16,258

Private Employment Weekly Wages

Average
1989: $423
1988: $408
1987: $408

Manufacturing
1989: $387
1988: $506
1987: $481

Services
1989: $396
1988: $375
1987: $355

Wholesale
1989: $539
1988: $522
1987: $486

Retail
1989: $224
1988: $216
1987: $206

Highway Statistics

Total Highway Miles
1990: 116,508
1989: 116,277
1988: 116,084

Federal Highway Aid
1991: $497,240,000
1990: $488,317,000
1989: $486,423,000

Electricity

Average Cost per Kilowatt Hour
1990: 7.64¢
1989: 7.33¢
1988: 7.18¢

Housing (1990)

Owner occupied units: 3,176,121
Median house value: $69,700

Renter occupied units: 1,319,845
Median rent: $322
Total vacant units: 442,174
Homeowner vacancy rate: 1.5%
Rental vacancy rate: 7.2%

State Business Incentives and Assistance

Enterprise Zone Incentives

The Enterprise Zone Program places a priority on assistance to industrial manufacturing and export service firms located in designated zones. The highest priority is given to firms offering jobs with higher than minimum wages, full-time employment opportunities, provision of standard fringe benefits, and opportunities for advancement that typical retail firms do not usually provide.

State programs offer incentives to firms located in enterprise zones, including:

Pennsylvania Industrial Development Authority. Provides long-term, low-interest loans to expand existing firms engaged in manufacturing or industrial enterprises and to help out-of-state firms establish operations in Pennsylvania.

Business Infrastructure Development Program. infrastructure projects serving private companies located within the zone funded by the Commonwealth with Enterprise Zone Program funds are automatically eligible for grant assistance.

Pennsylvania Minority Business Development Authority. Low-interest loans of up to $200,000 are available to projects located within an enterprise zone.

Enterprise Zone Municipal Tax Exemption Reimbursement. Reimbursements are made to municipalities with designated enterprise zones for a portion of taxes exempted under local Economic Revitalization Tax Assistance Act. They are to be used for physical improvements on neighborhood services in the zone.

Transportation Assistance. Enterprise zones are eligible for Pennsylvania Department of Transportation assistance to improve transportation access and traffic circulation within the zone.

Neighborhood Assistance Program. NAP provides 50% Corporate Net Income Tax credits to businesses for services for low-income persons and activities that improve an impoverished area. Projects approved for the 50% tax credit and located in a designated enterprise zone may apply for an additional 20% tax credit.

Employment and Community Conservation. Priority is given to programs that provide training in advanced-technology industries and/or developing projects and that benefit residents of enterprise zones.

Enterprise Zone Tax Credit Program. Real property business investment located in an enterprise zone is eligible for a tax credit of up to 20% of the value of the investment.

Other tax credits which can be carried forward for five years, include:

1. Property tax abatements on business real property improvements at the municipal level.
2. 20% tax credit for corporations on the state Corporate Net Income Tax for the value of investments to rehabilitate or improve buildings or land located within an enterprise zone.
3. 10% credit for company projects demonstrating that jobs for low-income people will be created as a result of the investment.
4. A 50% tax credit on the state Corporate Net Income Tax for the value of cash, equipment, supply, technical assistance, or real estate contributions benefiting low-income clients or residents of impoverished areas under the Neighborhood Assistance Program.
5. A possible 20% tax credit for corporations approved for 50% tax credits by applying under Special Program Priorities identified by the Secretary of Community Affairs and approved by the Governor each year.

Other assistance in business development may include:

1. Business-plan preparation
2. Low-interest gap loans
3. Export market development assistance
4. New product market assessment
5. Technology transfer applications
6. New product technological assessment
7. Small business incubators
8. Customized job training
9. Labor-management conflict resolution assistance

Financial and Business Assistance

Pennsylvania Industrial Development Authority. Administered by the Department of Commerce, the Authority provides business loans to stimulate economic activity in areas of high unemployment. Funds may be used for land and buildings. Amount of loan and interest rate are based upon the unemployment rate of the area in which the business is located. Eligible business include manufacturing, industrial, research and development, agricultural, warehousing, computer and clerical operations firms.

Pennsylvania Technical Assistance Program. Administered by the Ben Franklin Partnership of the Department of Commerce, this program promotes technology transfer and assists firms with solving technological problems by providing research through four advanced technology centers. These centers offer joint research and development among the private sector in the technology area. It also provides small business incubator space and services.

Business Infrastructure Development Program. Administered by the Pennsylvania Industrial Development Authority of the Department of Commerce, this program was established to help local governments finance infrastructure improvements needed in their communities for recruiting businesses.

Small Business Incubator Loan Program/Ben Franklin Partnership. Administered by the Department of Commerce, this program funds the development of small business incubator facilities that provide new manufacturing or product development companies with the space and business development services needed to start up and survive in the early years of business growth.

Infrastructure Financing. Administered by the state Department of Commerce, this program is designed to upgrade and maintain facilities important to the business community in three separate areas: business infrastructure development, site development, and community facilities. For the Business Infrastructure Development Program, grants and loans are awarded to local sponsors. Private companies eligible for assistance include industrial, manufacturing, research and development, and agricultural enterprises. Eligible infrastructure improvements include energy facilities, fire and safety facilities, sewer and water systems, and transportation and disposal facilities. For the Site Development Program, ccnstruction and rehabilitation projects that are eligible include water and sewer facilities, access roads, channel realignments, and the acquisition of land. For the Community Facilities Program, projects improving water facilities, sewage collection lines, and access roads are eligible. Qualified communities include boroughs and townships with a population of less than 12,000 and municipal and county authorities serving these areas are eligible.

Education and Training

Customized Job Training Program. Administered by the Office of Program Management of the Department of Commerce, this program provides funds for training projects that result in new full-time employment opportunities, significant wage improvements, the retention of jobs that may otherwise have been lost, and other conditions that would offer substantial economic benefit to the state. It will train employees in work skills to meet specific employer's needs which may include entry-level as well as upgrade training. The program targets new start-up or expanding manufacturing, industrial, research and development, and agricultural companies which will create new jobs. Priority is given to firms located in an enterprise zone.

Training the Workforce. Administered by the state Department of Commerce, this program provides a comprehensive educational curriculum for both second and post-secondary educators and is complemented by the Customized Job Training program and the federal Job Training Partnership Act.

Job Training Partnership Act. This program operates with funding from the U.S. Department of Labor. It provides job training and other employment related services.

Major Companies in the State

Company name	Fortune 500 rank	City	Telephone	SIC number
Fortune 500 Companies				
Air Products & Chemicals Inc.	150	Allentown	215-481-4911	2813
Allegheny Ludlum Corp.	353	Pittsburgh	412-394-2800	3312
Aluminum Co. of America	49	Pittsburgh	412-553-4545	3334
Ametek Inc.	420	Paoli	215-647-2121	3823
AMP Inc.	148	Harrisburg	717-564-0100	3643
Armstrong World Industries Inc.	183	Lancaster	717-397-0611	3253
Bethlehem Steel Corp.	124	Bethlehem	215-694-2424	3312
Betz Laboratories Inc.	438	Trevose	215-355-3300	2899
Crown Cork & Seal Co. Inc.	131	Philadelphia	215-698-5100	3411
Exide Corp.	495	Reading	215-378-0500	3691
H J Heinz Co.	80	Pittsburgh	412-456-5700	2033
Harsco Corp.	256	Camp Hill	717-763-7064	3489
Hershey Foods Corp.	151	Hershey	717-534-6799	2066
Joy Technologies Inc.	482	Pittsburgh	412-562-4500	3532
Kennametal Inc.	492	Latrobe	412-539-5000	3541
Lukens Inc.	390	Coatesville	215-383-2000	3312
Miles Inc.	82	Pittsburgh	412-394-5500	2833
PPG Industries Inc.	94	Pittsburgh	412-434-3131	3211
Quaker State Corp.	401	Oil City	814-676-7676	2992
Rhone Poulenc Rorer Inc.	121	Collegeville	215-454-8000	2834
Rohm & Haas Co.	153	Philadelphia	215-592-3000	2821
Scott Paper Co.	110	Philadelphia	215-522-5000	2676
Sun Co. Inc.	59	Philadelphia	215-977-3000	2911
Unisys Corp.	62	Blue Bell	215-986-4011	3571
USX Corp.	25	Pittsburgh	412-433-1121	1311
VF Corp.	127	Wyomissing	215-378-1151	2339
Vishay Intertechnology Inc.	455	Malvern	215-644-1300	3676
Westinghouse Electric Corp.	35	Pittsburgh	412-244-2000	3812
York International Corp.	222	York	717-771-7890	3585
Other Major Companies in the State				
AHSC Holdings Corp.		Valley Forge	215-296-4480	5122
Alco Health Services Corp.		Valley Forge	215-296-4480	5122
Alco Standard Corp.		Valley Forge	215-296-8000	5111
ARA Group Inc.		Philadelphia	215-238-3000	5812
Arco Chemical Co.		Newtown Square	215-359-2000	2869
Bell Atlantic Corp.		Philadelphia	215-963-6000	4813
Bell Telephone Co. of Pennsylvania		Philadelphia	215-466-9900	4813
Cigna Corp.		Philadelphia	215-761-1000	6331
Consolidated Natural Gas Co.		Pittsburgh	412-227-1000	4923
Consolidated Rail Corp.		Philadelphia	215-977-4000	4011
Corestates Financial Corp.		Philadelphia	215-973-3806	6712
Mellon Bank Corp.		Pittsburgh	412-234-5000	6712
Paper Corporation of America		Valley Forge	215-296-4470	5111
Penn Traffic Co.		Johnstown	814-536-9900	5411
Pennsylvania Power & Light Co.		Allentown	215-774-5151	4911
Philadelphia Electric Co.		Philadelphia	215-841-4000	4931

Major Companies in the State (Continued)

Company name	Fortune 500 rank	City	Telephone	SIC number
PNC Financial Corp.		Pittsburgh	412-762-2666	6712
Reliance Insurance Co.		Philadelphia	215-864-4000	6331
Rite Aid Corp.		Shiremanstown	717-761-2633	5912
Union Pacific Corp.		Bethlehem	215-861-3200	4011

State Offices

Real estate: General Services Department, Real Estate Bureau, Director, Room 515, North Office Bldg., Harrisburg, PA 17125. 717-787-4394

Chamber of commerce: Pennsylvania Business & Industry, Clifford L. Jones, President, 222 N. 3rd St., Harrisburg, PA 17101-1596. 717-255-3252

Economic development: Pennsylvania Economic Development Partnership, Raymond R. Christman, Exec Director, 433 Forum Bldg., Harrisburg, PA 17120. 717-783-3840, FAX 717-234-4560

Pennsylvania Economic Development Partnership, Office of Enterprise Development, Emily White, Acting Director, 404 Forum Bldg., Harrisburg, PA 17120. 717-783-3950, FAX 717-234-4560

Pennsylvania Economic Development Partnership, Office of International Development, Paul Haugland, Director, 484 Forum Bldg., Harrisburg, PA 17120. 717-783-1356, FAX 717-234-4560

Pennsylvania Economic Development Partnership, Office of Small Business Advocate, Bernard A. Ryan, Jr., Small Business Advocate, 500B City Towers, Harrisburg, PA 17120. 717-783-2525, FAX 717-234-4560

Department of Commerce, Pennsylvania Industrial Development Authority, Director, 480 Forum Building, Harrisburg, PA 17120. 717-787-6245

Department of Commerce, Incubator Program, Jim Loughney, Program Manager, 352 Forum Building, Harrisburg, PA 17120. 717-787-4147

Department of Community Affairs, David S. Messner, Enterprise Zone Coordinator, 551 Forum Building, Harrisburg, PA 17120. 717-787-7402

Department of Community Affairs, Bureau of Community Planning, Regional Planning Division (Enterprise Zone Program), David S. Messner, Chief, Rm. 551, Forum Bldg., Harrisburg, PA 17120. 717-787-7402

Small Business Development Center, Gregory Higgins, State Director, The Wharton School, University of Pennsylvania, 423 Vance Hall, Philadelphia, PA 19104-6374. 215-898-1219

Pennsylvania Technical Assistance Program, Director, 248 Calder Way, Suite 306, University Park, PA 16801. 814-865-0427

Environmental affairs: Environmental Management Bureau, Richard M. Boardman, Director, PO Box 2063, 10th Fl., Fulton Bldg., Third & Locust Streets, Harrisburg, PA 17105-2063. 717-787-5027

Labor: Labor and Industry Department, 1700 Labor and Industry Bldg., Harrisburg, PA 17120. 717-787-3756

Unemployment: Labor and Industry Department, Unemployment Compensation Benefits and Allowances Bureau, Richard A. Puerzer, Director, 415 Labor and Industry Bldg., Harrisburg, PA 17120. 717-787-3547

Worker's compensation: Labor and Industry Department, Worker's Compensation Bureau, Thomas S. Cook, Director, 1171 South Cameron St., Rm. 103, Harrisburg, PA 17104-2501. 717-783-5421

Occupational safety and health: Labor and Industry Department, Patricia Halpin-Murphy, Deputy Secretary for Safety and Standards, 1700 Labor and Industry Bldg., Harrisburg, PA 17120. 717-787-3907

Secretary of state: Secretary of the Commonwealth, Christopher A. Lewis, 302 North Office Bldg., Harrisburg, PA 17120. 717-787-7630

Taxation and revenue: Revenue Department, David L. Donahoe, Secretary, 11th Fl, Strawberry Square, Harrisburg, PA 17127. 717-783-3680

Designated Zones for Economic Development

Enterprise Zones

Enacted in: 1983

No. of established zones: 42

Altoona

Beaver (Aliquippa, Ambridge, and Harmony)

Bethlehem

Braddock

City of Bradford (Lewis Run Borough, Bradford, and Foster Township)

Chester (Chester City and Chester Township)

Conshohocken and West Conshohocken Borough

Duquesne City

City of Easton and West Easton Borough

Erie

Harrisburg

Hazleton

Jeannette

Johnstown

Lancaster

Lebanon

Lock Haven (City/Bald Eagle Township, and Castanea Township)

Marcus Hook Borough/Lower Chichester Township

Marietta/Columbia Boroughs

McKeesport

Borough of Midland

Monessen

New Castle

Philadelphia (4 zones)

Pittsburgh (3 zones)

Pottsville

Reading

Sayre

Scranton

Sharon/Farrell/Wheatland/Hermitage (Shenango Valley)

Shippensburg

Tarentum

Warren

Washington (Donora, Charleroi, Allenport Boroughs and Speers Township)

West Homestead Borough

Wilkes-Barre

Wilkinsburg

Williamsport

York

Foreign Trade Zones

Foreign Trade Zone No. 35, Philadelphia, Pennsylvania, Grantee: The Philadelphia Port Corporation, Operator: Trans Freight Systems, Inc., Richard Hopkins, 8415 Envoy Avenue, Philadelphia, PA 19153, 215-365-7777

Foreign Trade Zone No. 33, Pittsburgh, Pennsylvania, Grantee: Regional Industrial Dev. Corp. of Southwestern PA, Frank Brooks Robinson, Frick Building, Suite 1220, Pittsburg, PA 15219, 412-471-3939

Foreign Trade Zone No. 24, Pittston, Pennsylvania, Grantee/Operator: Econ Dev Council of N Eastern Penn., Leonard W. Ziolkowski, 1151 Oak Street, Pittston, PA 18640-3795, 717-655-5581

Foreign Trade Zone No. 147, Reading, Pennsylvania, Grantee: FTZ Corporation of Southeastern Pennsylvania, Anthony Grimm, 645 Penn Street, Reading, PA 19601, 215-376-6766

Labor Unions

Air Line Pilots Association, International (AFL-CIO)

Automobile, Aerospace & Agricultural Implement Workers of America, International Union, United, (UAW AFL-CIO)

Boilermakers, Iron Shipbuilders, Blacksmiths, Forgers and Helpers, International Brotherhood of (AFL-CIO)

Bricklayers and Allied Craftsmen, International Union of (AFL-CIO)

Carpenters and Joiners of America, United Brotherhood of (AFL-CIO)

Electrical Workers, International Brotherhood of (AFL-CIO)

Fire Fighters, International Association of (AFL-CIO)

Food and Commercial Workers International Union, United (AFL-CIO)

Graphic Communications International Union (AFL-CIO)

Iron Workers, International Association of Bridge, Structural and Ornamental (AFL-CIO)

Laborers' International Union of North America (AFL-CIO)

Ladies' Garment Workers' Union, International (AFL-CIO)

National Education Association

National Fraternal Order of Police

Nurses' Association, American

Operating Engineers, International Union of (AFL-CIO)

Pennsylvania State Employees Association

Pennsylvania State Nurses' Association

Plumbing and Pipe Fitting Industry of The United States and Canada, United Association of Journeymen and Apprentices of the (AFL-CIO)

Rubber, Cork, Linoleum and Plastic Workers of America, United (AFL-CIO)

State, County and Municipal Employees, American Federation of (AFL-CIO)

Steelworkers of America, United (AFL-CIO)

Teamsters, Chauffeurs, Warehousemen and Helpers of America, International Brotherhood of (AFL-CIO)

Transport Workers Union of America (AFL-CIO)

Universities with Ph.D. Programs

Bryn Mawr College, Bryn Mawr

Carnegie Mellon University, Pittsburgh

Drexel University, Philadelphia

Duquesne University, Pittsburgh

Hahnemann University, Philadelphia

Indiana University of Pennsylvania, Indiana

Lehigh University, Bethlehem

Pennsylvania College of Optometry, Philadelphia

Pennsylvania State University At Harrisburg--The Capital College, Middletown

Pennsylvania State University University Park Campus, State College

Philadelphia College of Pharmacy and Science, Philadelphia

Temple University, Philadelphia

Thomas Jefferson University, Philadelphia

University of Pennsylvania, Philadelphia

University of Pittsburgh, Pittsburgh

Sources of Additional Information

The Pennsylvania Advantage. Commonwealth of Pennsylvania, Dept. of Commerce, n.d. 86p.

Pennsylvania Economic Development Partnership Business Assistance Programs. Commonwealth of Pennsylvania, Dept. of Commerce, March, 1991. 6p.

ALLENTOWN-BETHLEHEM-EASTON, PA-NJ (MSA)

Geographic Profile

Land Area

1461.0 square miles

Counties and Parishes

New Jersey:

 Warren

Pennsylvania:

 Carbon

 Lehigh

 Northampton

Ranking Highlights

137 *out of 319 in total* **land area**

199 *out of 319 in* **population growth,** *1970–1990*

219 *out of 310 in having the lowest* **unemployment** *rate*

73 *out of 310 in size of* **labor force**

178 *out of 318 in the percentage of* **college graduates**

72 *out of 292 in per capita personal* **income**

63 *out of 319 in number of* **manufacturing establishments**

150 *out of 318 in* **physicians** *per 1000 people*

138 *out of 318 in* **hospital beds** *per 1000 people*

9 *out of 267 in fewest* **crimes** *per 1000 people*

21 *out of 266 in fewest* **violent crimes** *per 1000 people*

254 *out of 319 in per capita* **federal funds and grants**

Quality of Life Indexes (Rate per 1000 population)

Crime rate in 1991:	32.0
Violent crime rate in 1991:	2.0
Physicians rate in 1992:	1.84
Hospital bed rate in 1991:	4.13

ACCRA Cost of Living Indexes

(First quarter 1993, average = 100)

Composite index:	107.3
Utilities index:	108.9
Housing index:	107.2

Population (1990)

Total Population and Growth Rate

1990: 686,688

1980: 635,481

1970: 594,382

Growth rate 1970–1990: 16%

Race and Hispanic Origin

White: 94.6%

Black: 2.0%

Asian/Pacific Islander: 1.1%

Native American: 0.1%

Hispanic origin: 4.2%

White not Hispanic: 92.8%

Age

Ages 18 to 20: 4.4%

Ages 21 to 24: 5.5%

Ages 25 to 44: 31.7%

Ages 45 to 54: 10.4%

Ages 55 to 59: 4.7%

Ages 60 to 64: 5%

Ages 65 plus: 15.2%

Educational Attainment (1990)

Percent having completed high school: 74.1%

Percent having completed college: 17.7%

Elementary and high school enrollment: 103,705

Federal Funds and Grants Received

Total received in 1989: $1,642,100,000

Funds received per capita: $2,425

Civilian Labor Force

1993 (April): 344,521

1992 average: 344,507

1991 average: 340,294

1990 average: 335,126

Unemployment

1993 (April): 6.9%

1992 average: 7.9%

1991 average: 6.9%

1990 average: 5.5%

Average Annual Pay

1988: $21,306

1987: $20,042

1985: $18,501

Per Capita Personal Income

1991: $19,176

1990: $18,759

1989: $17,979

Business Climate (1987)

Manufacturing

Number of establishments in 1987: 1,091

Shipments in 1987 ($1,000): $9,083,500

Employees in 1987: 78,100

Change in employment, 1982 to 1987: -20.0%

Average annual pay for manufacturing work in 1989: $28,130

Average annual pay for production work in 1987: $20,531

Wholesale Trade

Number of establishments in 1987: 1,026

Total sales in 1987 ($1,000): $4,012,800

Change in sales, 1982 to 1987: 23.7%

Retail Trade

Number of establishments in 1987: 4,082

Total sales in 1987 ($1,000): $4,012,800

Retail sales per household in 1987: $17,339

Average annual pay in 1989: $12,240

Service Industry

Selected receipts in 1987 ($1,000): $1,518,300
Average annual pay in 1989: $19,013

Housing

Total number of units in 1990: 277,649
Occupied units in 1990: 259,828
Owner-occupied units in 1990: 71.6%
1993 ACCRA average cost: $124,650
1993 ACCRA average rent for an apartment: $536

Chamber of Commerce

Allentown-Lehigh County Chamber of Commerce, George F. Southworth, President, 462 Walnut St., PO Box 1229, Allentown, PA 18105-1229. 215-437-9661

Economic Development Office

Allentown Economic Development Corp., Judith McGough-King, Director, 801 Hamilton Mall Suite 200, Allentown, PA 18105-1400. 215-435-8890

Economic Development Organizations

Industrial Development Corp. of Lehigh County, Donald Benner, Exec. Vice President, PO Box 1410, Allentown, PA 18105. 215-437-5581

Lehigh Valley Industrial Park, Inc., Grover H. Stainbrook, Jr., Exec. Vice President, 95 Highland Ave. Suite 310, Bethlehem, PA 18017. 215-866-4600

Easton Redevelopment Authority, David W. Luscher, Director, 650 Ferry St., Easton, PA 18042. 215-252-0500

Northampton County Development Corp., John M. Cook, Exec. Director, 157 S. 4th St., PO Box 637, Easton, PA 18044-0637. 215-253-4213

Major Businesses

Company	SIC	Telephone
A & H Sportswear Co.	2339	(215) 863-4176
Air Products and Chemical	2813	(215) 481-4911
Alice Kay (Proprietorship)	5699	(215) 791-3220
Allentown Hospital Lehigh	8062	(215) 776-8000
Allentown Osteopathic Medicine	8062	(215) 770-8300
American Enterprises, Inc.	1541	(215) 395-6871
American Manufacturing Co.	2298	(215) 797-6470
Asbury Carbons Inc.	3295	(201) 537-2155
Asbury Graphite Mills	3295	(201) 537-2155
Atlantic Processing, Inc.	5143	(215) 861-7320
B. Braun of America Inc.	3841	(215) 691-5400
Bethenergy Mines Inc.	1221	(215) 694-2424
Bethlehem Steel Corp.	3312	(215) 694-2424
Bethtran Inc.	4213	(215) 694-5908
Binney & Smith Inc.	3952	(215) 253-6271
Buckeye Partners, L. P.	4613	(215) 820-8300
Buckeye Pipe Line Co.	4613	(215) 820-8300
Burron Medical Inc.	3841	(215) 691-5400
Butz, Alvin H. Inc.	1541	(215) 395-6871

Major Businesses (Continued)

Company	SIC	Telephone
Chrysler First Business	6153	(215) 437-8042
Chrysler First Commercial	6159	(215) 437-8000
Chrysler First Inc.	6162	(215) 437-8000
Chrysler First Management	8741	(215) 437-8000
Country Miss Inc.	2339	(215) 258-9143
Daniels Cadillac-BMW Inc.	5511	(215) 820-2950
Duggan & Marcon, Inc.	1742	(215) 395-8677
Eastern Consolidated Utilities	1794	(215) 395-6784
Eastern Industries Inc.	3531	(215) 866-0932
Easton Hospital	8062	(215) 250-4000

Colleges and Universities

Cedar Crest College, Allentown
Churchman Business School, Easton
Lafayette College, Easton
Lehigh University, Bethlehem
Lincoln Technical Institute, Allentown
Moravian College, Bethlehem
Muhlenberg College, Allentown
National Education Center-Allentown Business School Campus, Allentown
Northampton County Area Community College, Bethlehem

ALTOONA, PA (MSA)

Geographic Profile

Land Area

525.9 square miles

Counties and Parishes

Blair

Ranking Highlights

287 *out of 319 in total* **land area**

288 *out of 319 in* **population growth,** *1970–1990*

248 *out of 310 in having the lowest* **unemployment** *rate*

250 *out of 310 in size of* **labor force**

313 *out of 318 in the percentage of* **college graduates**

251 *out of 292 in per capita personal* **income**

253 *out of 319 in number of* **manufacturing establishments**

198 *out of 318 in* **physicians** *per 1000 people*

77 *out of 318 in* **hospital beds** *per 1000 people*

4 *out of 267 in fewest* **crimes** *per 1000 people*

11 *out of 266 in fewest* **violent crimes** *per 1000 people*

171 *out of 319 in per capita* **federal funds and grants**

Quality of Life Indexes (Rate per 1000 population)

Crime rate in 1991:	24.6
Violent crime rate in 1991:	1.4
Physicians rate in 1992:	1.65
Hospital bed rate in 1991:	5.01

ACCRA Cost of Living Indexes

(First quarter 1993, average = 100)

Composite index:	N/A
Utilities index:	N/A
Housing index:	N/A

Population (1990)

Total Population and Growth Rate

1990: 130,542

1980: 136,621

1970: 135,356

Growth rate 1970–1990: -4%

Race and Hispanic Origin

White: 98.7%

Black: .8%

Asian/Pacific Islander: 0.3%

Native American: 0.1%

Hispanic origin: 0.3%

White not Hispanic: 98.5%

Age

Ages 18 to 20: 4.6%

Ages 21 to 24: 4.6%

Ages 25 to 44: 29%

Ages 45 to 54: 10.2%

Ages 55 to 59: 4.8%

Ages 60 to 64: 5.4%

Ages 65 plus: 17%

Educational Attainment (1990)

Percent having completed high school: 75.0%

Percent having completed college: 10.5%

Elementary and high school enrollment: 22,314

Federal Funds and Grants Received

Total received in 1989: $399,100,000

Funds received per capita: $3,011

Civilian Labor Force

1993 (April):   64,335

1992 average: 63,901

1991 average: 62,323

1990 average: 61,918

Unemployment

1993 (April):   7.3%

1992 average: 8.7%

1991 average: 9.0%

1990 average: 7.2%

Average Annual Pay

1988: $16,695

1987: $16,274

1985: $15,198

Per Capita Personal Income

1991: $15,175

1990: $14,646

1989: $13,784

Business Climate (1987)

Manufacturing

Number of establishments in 1987: 145

Shipments in 1987 ($1,000): $1,127,500

Employees in 1987: 10,300

Change in employment, 1982 to 1987: -11.2%

Average annual pay for manufacturing work in 1989: $21,370

Average annual pay for production work in 1987: $17,897

Wholesale Trade

Number of establishments in 1987: 194

Total sales in 1987 ($1,000): $1,026,900

Change in sales, 1982 to 1987: 8.2%

Retail Trade

Number of establishments in 1987: 856

Total sales in 1987 ($1,000): $1,026,900

Retail sales per household in 1987: $16,850

Average annual pay in 1989: $10,650

Service Industry

Selected receipts in 1987 ($1,000): $229,700

Average annual pay in 1989: $15,935

Housing

Total number of units in 1990: 54,349

Occupied units in 1990: 50,332
Owner-occupied units in 1990: 72.6%
1993 ACCRA average cost: N/A
1993 ACCRA average rent for an apartment: N/A

Chamber of Commerce
Altoona-Blair County Chamber of Commerce, President, 1212 12th Ave., Altoona, PA 16601. 814-943-8151

Economic Development Office
Altoona Enterprises, Inc., Robert A. Halloran, Director, 1212 12th Ave., Altoona, PA 16601. 814-944-6113

Major Businesses

Company	SIC	Telephone
Altoona Hospital	8062	(814) 946-2011
Central Pennsylvania Health	8062	(814) 946-2204
Courtesy Motor Sales Inc.	5511	(814) 944-2076
Fiore, Leonard S. Inc.	1542	(814) 946-3686
Hite Co.	5063	(814) 944-6121
Items International Inc.	5139	(814) 943-6164
Lee, W. S. & Sons, Inc.	5141	(814) 696-3535
Martin Oil Co.	5983	(814) 742-8438
Mercy Hospital	8062	(814) 949-4101
Mid State Bank & Trust Co.	6022	(814) 946-6600
Overdorff Associates	5411	(814) 695-2445
Quality Chemicals, Inc.	2869	(814) 684-4310
Roaring Spring Blank Bank Co.	2678	(814) 224-5141
Value Drug Co.	5122	(814) 944-9316
Wolf Furniture Enterprise	5712	(814) 946-1601

Colleges and Universities
Pennsylvania State University Altoona Campus, Altoona

BEAVER COUNTY, PA (PMSA)

Geographic Profile
Land Area
435.3 square miles
Counties and Parishes
Beaver

Ranking Highlights
306 *out of 319 in total* **land area**
314 *out of 319 in* **population growth**, *1970–1990*
287 *out of 310 in having the lowest* **unemployment** *rate*
256 *out of 310 in size of* **labor force**
298 *out of 318 in the percentage of* **college graduates**
N/A *out of 292 in per capita personal* **income**
231 *out of 319 in number of* **manufacturing establishments**
309 *out of 318 in* **physicians** *per 1000 people*
210 *out of 318 in* **hospital beds** *per 1000 people*
1 *out of 267 in fewest* **crimes** *per 1000 people*
48 *out of 266 in fewest* **violent crimes** *per 1000 people*
231 *out of 319 in per capita* **federal funds and grants**

Quality of Life Indexes (Rate per 1000 population)
Crime rate in 1991:   23.2
Violent crime rate in 1991:   3.0
Physicians rate in 1992:   0.99
Hospital bed rate in 1991:   3.31

ACCRA Cost of Living Indexes
(First quarter 1993, average = 100)
Composite index: N/A
Utilities index: N/A
Housing index: N/A

Overview
Close to Pittsburgh, there is no central city in this area. Beaver County is located within southwestern Pennsylvania, 20 miles southwest of Pittsburgh. Beaver County has repeatedly been recognized in national quality of life surveys, including fourth nationally by *Money* magazine and first by the *1991 Century 21* rating of suburban counties. FBI crime statistics consistently rate Beaver County as the nation's safest. Within 500 miles are more than 50 percent of the U.S. and Canadian populations and over 57 percent of the total U.S. manufacturing and service business. It is midway between Chicago, Illinois, and New York City and less than 300 miles from Toronto, Ontario, Canada, with overnight delivery to major Canadian markets.

Beaver County features proximity to a world-class international airport, the second largest in the United States in acreage. A $600 million new Terminal Facility, with over 100 gates, was completed in October 1992.

The region still produces over 10 percent of the nation's steel. The Port of Pittsburgh is the largest originating and thru-traffic river barge port.

Population (1990)

Total Population and Growth Rate
1990: 186,093
1980: 204,441
1970: 208,418
Growth rate 1970–1990: -11%

Race and Hispanic Origin
White: 93.9%
Black: 5.6%
Asian/Pacific Islander: 0.2%
Native American: 0.1%
Hispanic origin: 0.6%
White not Hispanic: 93.4%

Age
Ages 18 to 20:   4%
Ages 21 to 24: 4.5%
Ages 25 to 44: 29.3%
Ages 45 to 54: 10.5%
Ages 55 to 59: 5.3%
Ages 60 to 64: 6.1%
Ages 65 plus: 16.9%

Educational Attainment (1990)
Percent having completed high school: 74.9%
Percent having completed college: 11.9%
Elementary and high school enrollment: 29,560

Federal Funds and Grants Received
Total received in 1989: $491,600,000
Funds received per capita: $2,590

Civilian Labor Force
1993 (April):   63,437
1992 average: 63,580
1991 average: 61,123
1990 average: 60,620

Unemployment
1993 (April): 10.2%
1992 average: 10.6%
1991 average: 9.7%
1990 average: 7.7%

Average Annual Pay
1988: $19,433
1987: $19,741
1985: $19,124

Per Capita Personal Income
1991: N/A
1990: N/A
1989: N/A

Business Climate (1987)

Manufacturing
Number of establishments in 1987: 172
Shipments in 1987 ($1,000): $1,764,900
Employees in 1987: 9,800

Change in employment, 1982 to 1987: -60.3%
Average annual pay for manufacturing work in 1989: $30,563
Average annual pay for production work in 1987: $23,943

Wholesale Trade
Number of establishments in 1987: 163
Total sales in 1987 ($1,000): $377,700
Change in sales, 1982 to 1987: 13.4%

Retail Trade
Number of establishments in 1987: 988
Total sales in 1987 ($1,000): $377,700
Retail sales per household in 1987: $11,867
Average annual pay in 1989: $9,413

Service Industry
Selected receipts in 1987 ($1,000): $236,700
Average annual pay in 1989: $18,415

Housing
Total number of units in 1990: 76,336
Occupied units in 1990: 71,939
Owner-occupied units in 1990: 73.3%
1993 ACCRA average cost: N/A
1993 ACCRA average rent for an apartment: N/A

Chamber of Commerce
Beaver Valley Chamber of Commerce, Samuel J. Weber, Exec. Vice President, 1008 7th Ave., Beaver Falls, PA 15010. 412-846-6750

Economic Development Office
Beaver County Corp. for Economic Development, Clair E. Searfosse, President, 798 Turnpike St., Beaver, PA 15009. 412-728-8610

Economic Development Organizations
Beaver Falls Area Industrial Development Council, Dale S. Laughner, Director, 2601 Darlington Rd, Beaver Falls, PA 15010. 412-843-5800

Major Businesses

Company	SIC	Telephone
Baker (Michael) Corp.	8711	(412) 495-7711
Beaver Newspapers, Inc.	2711	(412) 775-3200
Beaver Trust Co.	6022	(412) 775-7800
Crain Bros. Inc.	4492	(412) 766-5880
DB & S Steel Corp.	3316	(412) 843-9400

Colleges and Universities
Geneva College, Beaver Falls

ERIE, PA (MSA)

Geographic Profile

Land Area

802.0 square miles

Counties and Parishes

Erie

Ranking Highlights

237 *out of 319 in total* **land area**

245 *out of 319 in* **population growth,** *1970–1990*

206 *out of 310 in having the lowest* **unemployment** *rate*

146 *out of 310 in size of* **labor force**

216 *out of 318 in the percentage of* **college graduates**

164 *out of 292 in per capita personal* **income**

108 *out of 319 in number of* **manufacturing establishments**

190 *out of 318 in* **physicians** *per 1000 people*

70 *out of 318 in* **hospital beds** *per 1000 people*

22 *out of 267 in fewest* **crimes** *per 1000 people*

65 *out of 266 in fewest* **violent crimes** *per 1000 people*

249 *out of 319 in per capita* **federal funds and grants**

Quality of Life Indexes (Rate per 1000 population)

Crime rate in 1991:	35.9
Violent crime rate in 1991:	3.7
Physicians rate in 1992:	1.68
Hospital bed rate in 1991:	5.14

ACCRA Cost of Living Indexes

(First quarter 1993, average = 100)

Composite index:	108.3
Utilities index:	101.7
Housing index:	117.9

Overview

Erie, the third largest city in Pennsylvania, is a major manufacturing center. Located on the southeast shore of Lake Erie, the city is the only lake port in the state. Its shoreline and protected harbor, and the availability of fresh water, offer the city unique advantages as a center of shipping and manufacturing in Pennsylvania. Erie is emerging as a top contender for job growth and livability.

Manufacturing jobs make up 30 percent of the Erie area workforce, with more than seven hundred plants manufacturing products from 135 SIC classifications. Tourism is the second largest industry, supporting more than thirty-five hundred jobs and bringing over $173 million into the economy annually. Services comprise over 20 percent of the economy, encompassing the areas of education, health care, and finance. Agriculture is still a viable industry; Erie County produces cherries and grapes.

The Port of Erie, Pennsylvania's only lake port, handles imports and exports through the St. Lawrence Seaway to the Atlantic Coast and is a major distribution center for shipping and receiving goods to and from foreign countries.

Erie is served by five commercial railway lines, nearly sixty truck and motor freight companies, and six air cargo companies, providing convenient access to large metropolitan centers throughout the United States and Ontario, Canada. Interstates 79 and 90, intersecting just south of the city, provide easy access to all points in the country.

Erie International Airport is located six miles from downtown and is served by three commercial airlines. For those approaching the city by car, access is made easy by a network of superhighways and access roads. AMTRAK carries train passengers to the city.

Population (1990)

Total Population and Growth Rate

1990: 275,572

1980: 279,780

1970: 263,654

Growth rate 1970–1990: 5%

Race and Hispanic Origin

White: 93.6%

Black: 5.2%

Asian/Pacific Islander: 0.5%

Native American: 0.2%

Hispanic origin: 1.2%

White not Hispanic: 93.0%

Age

Ages 18 to 20: 5.9%

Ages 21 to 24: 6.1%

Ages 25 to 44: 29.9%

Ages 45 to 54: 9.6%

Ages 55 to 59: 4.2%

Ages 60 to 64: 4.7%

Ages 65 plus: 13.8%

Educational Attainment (1990)

Percent having completed high school: 77.5%

Percent having completed college: 16.2%

Elementary and high school enrollment: 48,107

Federal Funds and Grants Received

Total received in 1989: $681,600,000

Funds received per capita: $2,460

Civilian Labor Force

1993 (April):	143,639
1992 average:	141,803
1991 average:	137,053
1990 average:	135,187

Unemployment

1993 (April):	6.9%
1992 average:	7.6%
1991 average:	7.1%
1990 average:	5.5%

Average Annual Pay

1988: $20,095

1987: $19,260
1985: $18,162

Per Capita Personal Income
1991: $16,886
1990: $16,239
1989: $15,284

Business Climate (1987)
Manufacturing
Number of establishments in 1987: 538
Shipments in 1987 ($1,000): $3,382,300
Employees in 1987: 34,000
Change in employment, 1982 to 1987: -10.5%
Average annual pay for manufacturing work in 1989: $27,075
Average annual pay for production work in 1987: $21,546

Wholesale Trade
Number of establishments in 1987: 402
Total sales in 1987 ($1,000): $861,100
Change in sales, 1982 to 1987: 34.6%

Retail Trade
Number of establishments in 1987: 1,753
Total sales in 1987 ($1,000): $861,100
Retail sales per household in 1987: $15,187
Average annual pay in 1989: $9,737

Service Industry
Selected receipts in 1987 ($1,000): $655,200
Average annual pay in 1989: $17,338

Housing
Total number of units in 1990: 108,585
Occupied units in 1990: 101,564
Owner-occupied units in 1990: 68.6%
1993 ACCRA average cost: $138,000
1993 ACCRA average rent for an apartment: $550

Chamber of Commerce
Erie Area Chamber of Commerce, Donald F. DiPlacido, President, 1006 State St., Erie, PA 16501. 814-454-7191

Economic Development Office
Greater Erie Industrial Development Corp., Robert H. Ploehn, Exec. Director, 2103 E. 33rd St., Erie, PA 16510. 814-899-6022

Major Businesses

Company	SIC	Telephone
American Sterilizer Co.	3842	(814) 452-3100
Autoclave Engineers, Inc.	3842	(814) 838-2071
Copes Vulcan, Inc.	3494	(814) 774-3151
Curtze, C. A. Co. Inc.	5141	(814) 452-2281
Dahlkemper, Joseph B. Co.	5399	(814) 864-4054
First National Bank of Pennsylvania	6021	(814) 871-3400
Gartner Harf Co.	5147	(814) 868-4841

Major Businesses (Continued)

Company	SIC	Telephone
Hamot Health Systems Inc.	8741	(814) 455-6711
Hamot Medical Center	8062	(814) 870-6000
Lord Corp.	3724	(814) 868-0924
Marine Bank	6022	(814) 871-9200
National Fuel Gas Supply	4924	(814) 871-8000
PHB, Inc.	3363	(814) 474-5511
Parker White Metal Co.	3363	(814) 474-5511
Ridg-U-Rak, Inc.	2542	(814) 725-8751
St. Vincent Health Center	8062	(814) 452-5000
Snap-Tite, Inc.	3429	(814) 833-6411
Spectrum Control, Inc.	3677	(814) 455-0966
Zurn Industries, Inc.	1629	(814) 452-2111

Colleges and Universities
Erie Business Center, Erie
Gannon University, Erie
Mercyhurst College, Erie
Pennsylvania State University at Erie, the Behrend College, Erie
Triangle Tech, Inc.-Erie School, Erie

HARRISBURG–LEBANON–CARLISLE, PA (MSA)

Geographic Profile

Land Area

1990.9 square miles

Counties and Parishes

Cumberland
Dauphin
Lebanon
Perry

Ranking Highlights

  94 *out of 319 in total* land area
 201 *out of 319 in* population growth, *1970–1990*
  69 *out of 310 in having the lowest* unemployment *rate*
  75 *out of 310 in size of* labor force
 177 *out of 318 in the percentage of* college graduates
  94 *out of 292 in per capita personal* income
  92 *out of 319 in number of* manufacturing establishments
  93 *out of 318 in* physicians *per 1000 people*
 148 *out of 318 in* hospital beds *per 1000 people*
 N/A *out of 267 in fewest* crimes *per 1000 people*
 N/A *out of 266 in fewest* violent crimes *per 1000 people*
  41 *out of 319 in per capita* federal funds and grants

Quality of Life Indexes (Rate per 1000 population)

Crime rate in 1991:	N/A
Violent crime rate in 1991:	N/A
Physicians rate in 1992:	2.26
Hospital bed rate in 1991:	4

ACCRA Cost of Living Indexes

(First quarter 1993, average = 100)

Composite index:	102.6
Utilities index:	124.1
Housing index:	98.8

Overview

Harrisburg is the capital of the Commonwealth of Pennsylvania. It is the metropolitan center for some four hundred communities. Its economy is diversified; eight thousand firms there represent more than five thousand types of businesses. Services (especially health) employ more than one–fifth of the labor force. National firms either headquartered in the region or with major operations there include AMP Inc. (electronic components), IBM, Hershey Foods, Harsco Corp., and Rite Aid Corp. (retailers). The largest employer, state government, provides stability to the economy and attracts attendant services. Three major military establishments are an important factor in the economy, as are two large steel mills located in the region. Excellent roads and rail transportation contribute to the city's prominence as a center for trade, warehousing, and distribution.

Located midway between Philadelphia and Pittsburgh, Harrisburg grew up from its earliest days as a transportation center. All major air, rail, and highway arteries linking the markets of the East, Midwest, and South pass through the region. There are eight public airports in the region, the largest being Harrisburg International Airport, the third busiest airport in the state and a modern facility where freight and mail are handled by eight air freight forwarders. The freight business increased from 41,512,000 pounds forwarded in 1985 to 74,786,420 pounds in 1990, and facilities continue to expand to handle that rapid growth. Numerous major interstate and U.S. highways connect the region to major metropolitan areas, and local roads are well maintained. Harrisburg has long been an important freight center. Both the Pennsylvania and Reading railroads had large yards outside the city, which are now operated by AMTRAK.

Harrisburg International Airport, eight miles south of center city, offers major airline service from some hub cities as well as short–hop commuter service. Services at Harrisburg International continue to expand to accommodate enplanements that have increased from 411,506 in 1985 to 622,506 in 1990. Seven major and commuter airlines service the airport. Capital City Airport is available for charters and business and pleasure craft. A downtown heliport is planned to serve commuting business executives. Philadelphia International Airport, 100 miles from Harrisburg, may be the most convenient destination for visitors flying in from distant locations.

Harrisburg is easily accessible by car. Interstate highways 76, 78, 81, and 83 cross in the region and connect it to major metropolitan areas. Other major highways are U.S. 11, 15, 22, 322, and 422.

Population (1990)

Total Population and Growth Rate

1990: 587,986
1980: 556,242
1970: 510,170
Growth rate 1970–1990: 15%

Race and Hispanic Origin

White: 91.3%
Black: 6.7%
Asian/Pacific Islander: 1.1%
Native American: 0.1%
Hispanic origin: 1.7%
White not Hispanic: 90.5%

Age

Ages 18 to 20: 4.7%
Ages 21 to 24: 5.8%
Ages 25 to 44: 32.2%
Ages 45 to 54: 10.6%
Ages 55 to 59: 4.7%

Ages 60 to 64: 4.8%
Ages 65 plus: 13.9%

Educational Attainment (1990)
Percent having completed high school: 76.9%
Percent having completed college: 18.0%
Elementary and high school enrollment: 90,421

Federal Funds and Grants Received
Total received in 1989: $2,918,700,000
Funds received per capita: $4,938

Civilian Labor Force
1993 (April): 343,481
1992 average: 342,912
1991 average: 339,183
1990 average: 333,191

Unemployment
1993 (April): 5.0%
1992 average: 5.4%
1991 average: 5.4%
1990 average: 4.4%

Average Annual Pay
1988: $20,598
1987: $19,599
1985: $17,947

Per Capita Personal Income
1991: $18,430
1990: $17,875
1989: $16,997

Business Climate (1987)
Manufacturing
Number of establishments in 1987: 690
Shipments in 1987 ($1,000): $6,332,300
Employees in 1987: 53,600
Change in employment, 1982 to 1987: -3.1%
Average annual pay for manufacturing work in 1989: $25,929
Average annual pay for production work in 1987: $18,982

Wholesale Trade
Number of establishments in 1987: 872
Total sales in 1987 ($1,000): $5,090,200
Change in sales, 1982 to 1987: 33.2%

Retail Trade
Number of establishments in 1987: 3,591
Total sales in 1987 ($1,000): $5,090,200
Retail sales per household in 1987: $19,172
Average annual pay in 1989: $11,119

Service Industry
Selected receipts in 1987 ($1,000): $1,640,900
Average annual pay in 1989: $18,674

Housing
Total number of units in 1990: 241,489

Occupied units in 1990: 226,353
Owner-occupied units in 1990: 68.8%
1993 ACCRA average cost: $112,340
1993 ACCRA average rent for an apartment: $537

Chamber of Commerce
Capital Region Chamber of Commerce, Matthew M. Douglas, Jr., President, 114 Walnut St., PO Box 969, Harrisburg, PA 17108. 717-232-4121

Economic Development Office
Dauphin County Office of Economic Development, Frances A. Cunningham, Director, 112 Market St. #800, PO Box 1295, Harrisburg, PA 17108. 717-257-1550, FAX 717-255-1452

Economic Development Organizations
Cumberland County Redevelopment Authority, David Nikoloff, Director, 114 N. Hanover St., Carlisle, PA 17013. 717-249-1315

Pennsylvania Department of Commerce, Raymond Christman, Secretary, Forum Bldg. Room 422, Harrisburg, PA 17120. 717-787-3003

Lebanon County Industrial Development Authority, John A. Ritter, Exec. Director, PO Box 899, Lebanon, PA 17042. 717-273-3727

Major Businesses

Company	SIC	Telephone
AMP Inc.	3643	(717) 564-0100
Capital Blue Cross Inc.	6324	(717) 541-7000
Dauphin Deposit Corp.	6022	(717) 255-2121
Gaughen, Jack Inc.	6531	(717) 761-4800
Giant Food Stores, Inc.	5411	(717) 249-4000
Gray Drug Fair Inc.	5912	(717) 761-2633
Harsco Corp.	3443	(717) 763-7064
Hershey Foods Corp.	2066	(717) 534-4001
Keystone Financial Inc.	6021	(717) 233-1555
Masland, C. H. & Sons	2273	(717) 249-1866
Medical Service Association	6324	(717) 763-3151
Pennsylvania Housing Finance	6162	(717) 780-3800
Pennsylvania Insurance	6331	(717) 234-4941
Pennsylvania TPK Commission	4785	(717) 939-9551
Phico Insurance Co.	6351	(717) 766-1122
Rite Aid Corp.	5912	(717) 761-2633
Super Rite Foods, Inc.	5141	(717) 232-6821
United Telephone Co. of Pennsylvania	4813	(717) 245-6312

Colleges and Universities
Dickinson College, Carlisle
Harrisburg Area Community College, Harrisburg
National Education Center-Thompson Institute Campus, Harrisburg

JOHNSTOWN, PA (MSA)

Geographic Profile

Land Area

1762.8 square miles

Counties and Parishes

Cambria

Somerset

Ranking Highlights

108 *out of 319 in total* **land area**

310 *out of 319 in* **population growth,** *1970–1990*

286 *out of 310 in having the lowest* **unemployment** *rate*

185 *out of 310 in size of* **labor force**

314 *out of 318 in the percentage of* **college graduates**

262 *out of 292 in per capita personal* **income**

173 *out of 319 in number of* **manufacturing establishments**

196 *out of 318 in* **physicians** *per 1000 people*

106 *out of 318 in* **hospital beds** *per 1000 people*

N/A *out of 267 in fewest* **crimes** *per 1000 people*

N/A *out of 266 in fewest* **violent crimes** *per 1000 people*

168 *out of 319 in per capita* **federal funds and grants**

Quality of Life Indexes (Rate per 1000 population)

Crime rate in 1991:	N/A
Violent crime rate in 1991:	N/A
Physicians rate in 1992:	1.66
Hospital bed rate in 1991:	4.57

ACCRA Cost of Living Indexes

(First quarter 1993, average = 100)

Composite index:	N/A
Utilities index:	N/A
Housing index:	N/A

Population (1990)

Total Population and Growth Rate

1990: 241,247

1980: 264,506

1970: 262,822

Growth rate 1970–1990: -8%

Race and Hispanic Origin

White: 98.0%

Black: 1.6%

Asian/Pacific Islander: 0.2%

Native American: 0.1%

Hispanic origin: 0.5%

White not Hispanic: 97.6%

Age

Ages 18 to 20: 4.3%

Ages 21 to 24: 4.7%

Ages 25 to 44: 28.5%

Ages 45 to 54: 9.8%

Ages 55 to 59: 4.9%

Ages 60 to 64: 5.8%

Ages 65 plus: 18.2%

Educational Attainment (1990)

Percent having completed high school: 70.5%

Percent having completed college: 10.2%

Elementary and high school enrollment: 40,819

Federal Funds and Grants Received

Total received in 1989: $759,900,000

Funds received per capita: $3,032

Civilian Labor Force

1993 (April): 104,406

1992 average: 101,987

1991 average: 99,922

1990 average: 97,838

Unemployment

1993 (April): 10.6%

1992 average: 10.5%

1991 average: 9.2%

1990 average: 7.6%

Average Annual Pay

1988: $17,503

1987: $16,880

1985: $16,092

Per Capita Personal Income

1991: $14,961

1990: $14,298

1989: $13,369

Business Climate (1987)

Manufacturing

Number of establishments in 1987: 280

Shipments in 1987 ($1,000): $1,081,800

Employees in 1987: 12,700

Change in employment, 1982 to 1987: -10.6%

Average annual pay for manufacturing work in 1989: $20,461

Average annual pay for production work in 1987: $16,290

Wholesale Trade

Number of establishments in 1987: 338

Total sales in 1987 ($1,000): $620,100

Change in sales, 1982 to 1987: -12.1%

Retail Trade

Number of establishments in 1987: 1,426

Total sales in 1987 ($1,000): $620,100

Retail sales per household in 1987: $12,186

Average annual pay in 1989: $9,808

Service Industry

Selected receipts in 1987 ($1,000): $287,800

Average annual pay in 1989: $16,541

Housing

Total number of units in 1990: 103,087

Occupied units in 1990: 91,578
Owner-occupied units in 1990: 74.6%
1993 ACCRA average cost: N/A
1993 ACCRA average rent for an apartment: N/A

Chamber of Commerce

Greater Johnstown Chamber of Commerce, Robert F. Layo, Exec. Vice President, 419 Locust St., Johnstown, PA 15901. 814-536-5107

Economic Development Office

Johnstown Area Economic Development Corp., John A. Skiavo, President, 111 Market St., Johnstown, PA 15901. 814-535-6553, FAX 814-535-8677

Major Businesses

Company	SIC	Telephone
B. T. Financial Corp.	6022	(814) 536-7801
Calandra, Frank Inc.	3532	(814) 886-4121
Conemaugh Valley Memorial Hospital	8062	(814) 533-9130
Crown American Corp.	5311	(814) 536-4441
Fetterolf Group Inc.	6331	(814) 443-4688
GB Stores	5311	(814) 536-6633
Laurel Packaging Inc.	2086	(814) 266-6005
Lee Health Services	8062	(814) 533-0751
Mincorp Inc.	1221	(814) 443-4668
P B S Coals Inc.	1221	(814) 443-4668
Penn Traffic Co.	5411	(814) 536-9900
Pennsylvania Electric Co.	4911	(814) 533-8111
Rockwood Holding Co.	6311	(814) 926-4661
Rockwood Insurance Co.	6331	(814) 926-4661
Seven D Wholesale	5031	(814) 886-8151
Usbancorp Inc.	6021	(814) 533-5300
Zamias Construction Co. Inc.	1542	(814) 535-5549

Colleges and Universities

Cambria-Rowe Business College, Johnstown, PA
University of Pittsburgh at Johnstown, Johnstown, PA

LANCASTER, PA (MSA)

Geographic Profile

Land Area
949.1 square miles

Counties and Parishes
Lancaster

Ranking Highlights

208 *out of 319 in total* **land area**
122 *out of 319 in* **population growth,** *1970–1990*
64 *out of 310 in having the lowest* **unemployment** *rate*
97 *out of 310 in size of* **labor force**
203 *out of 318 in the percentage of* **college graduates**
78 *out of 292 in per capita personal* **income**
80 *out of 319 in number of* **manufacturing establishments**
262 *out of 318 in* **physicians** *per 1000 people*
248 *out of 318 in* **hospital beds** *per 1000 people*
7 *out of 267 in fewest* **crimes** *per 1000 people*
18 *out of 266 in fewest* **violent crimes** *per 1000 people*
304 *out of 319 in per capita* **federal funds and grants**

Quality of Life Indexes (Rate per 1000 population)

Crime rate in 1991: 31.2
Violent crime rate in 1991: 1.9
Physicians rate in 1992: 1.32
Hospital bed rate in 1991: 2.94

ACCRA Cost of Living Indexes

(First quarter 1993, average = 100)
Composite index: 110.0
Utilities index: 133.8
Housing index: 116.0

Overview

Lancaster, an important industrial and agricultural center in southeastern Pennsylvania, is located in the heart of Pennsylvania Dutch country and is the county seat of Lancaster County.

Lancaster's is a widely diversified economy; industries range from manufacturing to agriculture, tourism to health care, retail trade and wholesale distribution. Many firms in the county have existed there for at least fifty and up to one hundred years, including the oldest tobacco store in the country. Tourists are attracted to the area by the picturesque and culturally distinct farming communities; most farms are family-owned.

Items and goods produced in the area include television tubes and electronic equipment, textiles, watches, farm machinery, building materials, linoleum, steel containers, ball bearings, locks, aluminum products, pharmaceuticals, toys, furniture, candy, and food products (corn is the leading crop).

Air transportation facilities are provided by the Lancaster Municipal Airport, rated among the ninety best-equipped such facilities in the country. Airline service into Lancaster Airport is provided by USAir/Allegheny Commuter and Eastern Express, with connections through Dulles International, Baltimore/Washington International, Newark International, and Kennedy International airports. Daily freight service via Conrail and at least fifty common motor carriers is available. Limousine and taxi service, as well as car rental agencies, are available. Daily passenger service to all AMTRAK service areas is also available. All of the state's major highways converge in the city with the exception of the Pennsylvania Turnpike, which interchanges at U.S. 222, PA 72, and PA 23 fifteen miles north of the city.

Population (1990)

Total Population and Growth Rate
1990: 422,822
1980: 362,346
1970: 320,079
Growth rate 1970–1990: 32%

Race and Hispanic Origin
White: 94.1%
Black: 2.4%
Asian/Pacific Islander: 1.1%
Native American: 0.1%
Hispanic origin: 3.7%
White not Hispanic: 92.9%

Age
Ages 18 to 20: 4.8%
Ages 21 to 24: 5.8%
Ages 25 to 44: 31.3%
Ages 45 to 54: 9.9%
Ages 55 to 59: 4.3%
Ages 60 to 64: 4.3%
Ages 65 plus: 13.1%

Educational Attainment (1990)
Percent having completed high school: 70.5%
Percent having completed college: 16.7%
Elementary and high school enrollment: 68,839

Federal Funds and Grants Received
Total received in 1989: $809,500,000
Funds received per capita: $1,955

Civilian Labor Force
1993 (April):   237,810
1992 average: 235,097
1991 average: 229,643
1990 average: 228,876

Unemployment
1993 (April):   4.9%
1992 average: 5.3%
1991 average: 5.3%
1990 average: 4.1%

Average Annual Pay
1988: $20,011
1987: $18,910
1985: $16,926

Per Capita Personal Income
1991: $19,071
1990: $18,884
1989: $18,015

Business Climate (1987)

Manufacturing
Number of establishments in 1987: 821
Shipments in 1987 ($1,000): $7,429,100
Employees in 1987: 60,000
Change in employment, 1982 to 1987: 4.7%
Average annual pay for manufacturing work in 1989: $25,629
Average annual pay for production work in 1987: $19,722

Wholesale Trade
Number of establishments in 1987: 700
Total sales in 1987 ($1,000): $3,466,700
Change in sales, 1982 to 1987: 62.3%

Retail Trade
Number of establishments in 1987: 2,475
Total sales in 1987 ($1,000): $3,466,700
Retail sales per household in 1987: $18,654
Average annual pay in 1989: $11,600

Service Industry
Selected receipts in 1987 ($1,000): $795,500
Average annual pay in 1989: $17,565

Housing
Total number of units in 1990: 156,462
Occupied units in 1990: 150,956
Owner-occupied units in 1990: 69.4%
1993 ACCRA average cost: $136,540
1993 ACCRA average rent for an apartment: $543

Chamber of Commerce
Lancaster Chamber of Commerce, Dan Witmer, President, 100 S. Queen St., PO Box 1558, Lancaster, PA 17603-1558. 717-397-3531

Economic Development Office
Economic Development Co. of Lancaster County, David Nicoloff, Exec Director, 100 S. Queen St., Southern Market Center, PO Box 1558, Lancaster, PA 17603-1558. 717-397-3531

Major Businesses

Company	SIC	Telephone
AC and S, Inc.	1742	(717) 397-3631
Armstrong World Industries	3996	(717) 397-0611
Burle Industries, Inc.	3699	(717) 295-6000

Major Businesses (Continued)

Company	SIC	Telephone
Burnham Corp.	3433	(717) 293-5800
Educators Mutual Life Insurance Co.	6321	(717) 397-2751
Ferranti International, Inc.	3663	(717) 285-3113
Ford New Holland, Inc.	3523	(717) 355-1121
Fulton Bank	6022	(717) 291-2411
Fulton Financial Corp.	6022	(717) 291-2411
Hamilton Bank	6022	(717) 569-8731
High Industries, Inc.	3441	(717) 293-4444
Irex Corp.	1742	(717) 397-3633
Lancaster General Hospital	8062	(717) 299-5511
Miller & Hartman, Inc.	5141	(717) 397-8261
Penn Dairies, Inc.	2026	(717) 394-5601
Pennfield Corp.	2048	(717) 299-2561
Pinnacle Mortgage Investment	6162	(717) 293-3200
Susquehanna Bancshares, Inc.	6712	(717) 626-4721
Zausner Foods Corp.	2022	(717) 354-4411

Colleges and Universities

Franklin and Marshall College, Lancaster

Palmer School, Lancaster

Thaddeus Stevens State School of Technology, Lancaster

PHILADELPHIA, PA–NJ (PMSA)

Geographic Profile

Land Area

3518.1 square miles

Counties and Parishes

New Jersey:

　Burlington

　Camden

　Gloucester

Pennsylvania:

　Bucks

　Chester

　Delaware

　Montgomery

　Philadelphia

Additional Cities/Towns within Area

Camden, NJ

Norristown, PA

Ranking Highlights

　36 *out of 319 in total* **land area**

270 *out of 319 in* **population growth,** *1970–1990*

191 *out of 310 in having the lowest* **unemployment** *rate*

　4 *out of 310 in size of* **labor force**

　83 *out of 318 in the percentage of* **college graduates**

　27 *out of 292 in per capita personal* **income**

　5 *out of 319 in number of* **manufacturing establishments**

　32 *out of 318 in* **physicians** *per 1000 people*

128 *out of 318 in* **hospital beds** *per 1000 people*

　75 *out of 267 in fewest* **crimes** *per 1000 people*

175 *out of 266 in fewest* **violent crimes** *per 1000 people*

103 *out of 319 in per capita* **federal funds and grants**

Quality of Life Indexes (Rate per 1000 population)

Crime rate in 1991:	48.5
Violent crime rate in 1991:	7.6
Physicians rate in 1992:	2.91
Hospital bed rate in 1991:	4.2

ACCRA Cost of Living Indexes

(First quarter 1993, average = 100)

Composite index:	131.1
Utilities index:	178.4
Housing index:	146.1

Overview

Manufacturing and the related distribution sector were traditionally the backbone of the Philadelphia economy. Since the end of World War II this industrial base has declined, as it has in many of the established industrial cities of the Northeast and upper Midwest, as many firms moved to new locations in the suburbs or migrated to other regions of the country. The decline in manufacturing has been offset by employment increases in the service sector, and Philadelphia considers that it has successfully made the transition to a service economy.

Computer-based businesses, banks, insurance companies, and the printing and publishing industries are doing well. The biomedical field, encompassing hospitals, medical schools, pharmaceutical firms, research institutions, manufacturers of medical instruments and supplies, and medical publishing, is flourishing in Philadelphia.

The Greater Philadelphia region has become one of the major corporate centers in the United States. Many companies are locating or expanding facilities in the area. They are attracted by the area's location at the center of the country's largest market, the access to transportation, the availability of medical, engineering, and business schools to supply technical talent, and the open land for industrial park development. Center City is still the financial, governmental, and cultural hub of the region. Concerted efforts over the last several years by government, business leaders, and concerned citizens to improve Philadelphia's reputation as a corporate host are beginning to bear fruit, and the city is being rediscovered as an attractive place to live and work.

Few cities in the country can match Philadelphia's historic attractions, and the city plays host to an estimated three million tourists a year. The new Pennsylvania Convention Center, scheduled to open in 1993, covers six city blocks in the heart of the city and offers 435,000 square feet of exhibit space, including a thirty-two thousand square foot ballroom and more than fifty meeting rooms. It encompasses historic Reading Terminal Market. Another major convention facility is the Civic Center, with 382,000 square feet of exhibit space, auditorium seating for 12,500 people, and thirty meeting rooms. Ample hotel space is available to accommodate guests and meetings; the Marriott Convention Center Hotel, scheduled to open in early 1994, added 1,200 rooms to the Center City for a total of 8,800 rooms there.

Philadelphia's port, together with the ports in southern New Jersey and Delaware, form the Ports of Philadelphia. The Ports of Philadelphia, the largest freshwater shipping complex in the world, handle the largest volume of international tonnage on the East Coast. Major imports include crude oil, fruits, iron, steel, and paper. Exports include scrap metal and petroleum products. Most of the terminals in the city are owned by a newly-formed state agency, the Philadelphia Regional Port Authority.

Two airports operate within Philadelphia's city limits: Northeast Philadelphia Airport and Philadelphia International Airport; the latter, located eight miles from the Center City, offers service to more than one hundred foreign and domestic cities and is connected with the city by a new high-speed rail line. Fourteen other airports are located within commuting distance of Philadelphia.

The city is served by the Pennsylvania and New Jersey turnpikes and by Interstate-95 and I-96. These highways and their connections allow easy access to the city from many parts of the country.

Population (1990)

Total Population and Growth Rate
1990: 4,856,881
1980: 4,716,559
1970: 4,824,110
Growth rate 1970–1990: 1%

Race and Hispanic Origin
White: 76.5%
Black: 19.1%
Asian/Pacific Islander: 2.2%
Native American: 0.2%
Hispanic origin: 3.6%
White not Hispanic: 75.3%

Age
Ages 18 to 20: 4.4%
Ages 21 to 24: 6%
Ages 25 to 44: 32.4%
Ages 45 to 54: 10.2%
Ages 55 to 59: 4.5%
Ages 60 to 64: 4.7%
Ages 65 plus: 13.5%

Educational Attainment (1990)
Percent having completed high school: 75.9%
Percent having completed college: 22.8%
Elementary and high school enrollment: 775,136

Federal Funds and Grants Received
Total received in 1989: $17,547,900,000
Funds received per capita: $3,566

Civilian Labor Force
1993 (April): 2,412,577
1992 average: 2,435,338
1991 average: 2,431,244
1990 average: 2,438,355

Unemployment
1993 (April): 7.3%
1992 average: 7.4%
1991 average: 6.4%
1990 average: 4.7%

Average Annual Pay
1988: $23,895
1987: $22,447
1985: $20,077

Per Capita Personal Income
1991: $22,014
1990: $21,381
1989: $20,232

Business Climate (1987)

Manufacturing

Number of establishments in 1987: 7,414

Shipments in 1987 ($1,000): $49,790,000

Employees in 1987: 375,200

Change in employment, 1982 to 1987: -7.7%

Average annual pay for manufacturing work in 1989: $31,171

Average annual pay for production work in 1987: $35,048

Wholesale Trade

Number of establishments in 1987: 9,641

Total sales in 1987 ($1,000): $63,054,200

Change in sales, 1982 to 1987: 38.9%

Retail Trade

Number of establishments in 1987: 27,382

Total sales in 1987 ($1,000): $63,054,200

Retail sales per household in 1987: $17,339

Average annual pay in 1989: $13,311

Service Industry

Selected receipts in 1987 ($1,000): $18,353,000

Average annual pay in 1989: $23,293

Office Real Estate (1992)

Office space inventory: 79,163,000 square feet

Average class A Central Business District rental range per sq. ft: $23.08

Vacancy Rates

All areas: 17.9%

Vacancy Rates in Central Business District

Class A space: 14.9%

Class B space: 24.7%

Vacancy Rates Outside Central Business District

Class A space: 18.2%

Class B space: 21.9%

Housing

Total number of units in 1990: 2,307,675

Occupied units in 1990: 2,154,104

Owner-occupied units in 1990: 69.4%

1993 ACCRA average cost: $169,000

1993 ACCRA average rent for an apartment: $721

Chamber of Commerce

Greater Philadelphia Chamber of Commerce, Charles Pizzi, President, 1346 Chestnut St. #800, Philadelphia, PA 19107. 215-545-1234

Economic Development Office

Philadelphia Industrial Development Corp., James McManus, Vice President, 123 S. Broad St., #2200, Philadelphia, PA 19109. 215-875-3502

Economic Development Organizations

Montgomery County Department of Commerce and Economic Development, Dwight Dundore, Director, 151 W. Marshall St., Norristown, PA 19401. 215-278-5950, FAX 215-278-5944

City of Camden, Division of Economic Development, Patrick Keating, Director, City Hall 4th Fl., Camden, NJ 08101. 609-757-7488, FAX 609-541-9668

Delaware River Port Authority, EDC, James R. Kelly, President, Bridge Plaza, Camden, NJ 08101. 609-963-6420

South Jersey Port Corp., Joseph A. Balzano, Exec. Director, 2500 Broadway, PO Box 129, Camden, NJ 08101. 609-541-8500

Major Businesses

Company	SIC	Telephone
Acme Markets Inc.	5411	(215) 889-4000
AHSC Holdings Corp.	5122	(215) 296-4480
Alco Health Services Corp.	5122	(215) 296-4480
Alco Standard Corp.	5111	(215) 296-8000
Ara Group, Inc.	5812	(215) 238-3000
Ara Leisure Service Inc.	5149	(215) 238-3000
Araserve Inc.	5812	(215) 238-3000
Arco Chemical Co.	2869	(215) 359-2000
Atlantic Petroleum Corp.	2911	(215) 768-1000
Atochem North America Inc.	2819	(215) 587-7000
Bell Atlantic Corp.	4813	(215) 963-6000
Bell Atlantic Enterprises	6159	(215) 963-6700
Bell Telephone Co. of Pennsylvania	4813	(215) 466-9900
Campbell Soup Co.	2032	(609) 342-4800
Cananwill Consumer Disc Co.	6141	(215) 496-0607
Certainteed Corp.	3296	(215) 341-7000
Cigna Corp.	6331	(215) 523-4000
Consolidated Rail Corp.	4011	(215) 977-4000
Corestates Financial Corp.	6021	(215) 973-3100
Crown Cork & Seal Co.	3411	(215) 698-5100
General Accident Corp.	6411	(215) 625-1000
INA Corp.	6331	(215) 523-4000
Independence Blue Cross	6324	(215) 241-5000
Insurance Co. of North America	6331	(215) 523-4000
Lumbermens Merchandising	5031	(215) 293-7000
Meritor Savings Bank	6022	(215) 636-6000
National Home Life Assurance Co.	6311	(215) 648-5000
Paper Corp. of America	5111	(215) 296-4470
Penn Mutual Life Insurance Co.	6311	(215) 956-8000
Philadelphia Electric Co.	4911	(215) 841-4000
Reliance Insurance Co.	6331	(215) 864-4000
Rhone-Poulenc Rorer Inc.	2834	(215) 628-6800
Rohm and Haas Co.	2851	(215) 592-3000
Scott Paper Co.	2621	(215) 522-5000
Smithkline Beecham Corp.	2834	(215) 751-4000
Subaru of America, Inc.	5012	(609) 488-8500
Sun Co. Inc.	2911	(215) 293-6000
Sun Refining and Marketing Co.	2911	(215) 977-3000

753

Major Businesses (Continued)

Company	SIC	Telephone
U.S. Healthcare Inc.	6324	(215) 628-4800
UNISYS Corp.	3571	(215) 542-4011
Wyeth Ayerst International	5122	(215) 254-4235
Wyeth-Ayerst Laboratories	2834	(215) 688-4400

Colleges and Universities

American Institute of Design, Philadelphia, PA
Art Institute of Philadelphia, Philadelphia, PA
Berean Institute, Philadelphia, PA
Chestnut Hill College, Philadelphia, PA
Community College of Philadelphia, Philadelphia, PA
Curtis Institute of Music, Philadelphia, PA
Drexel University, Philadelphia, PA
Hahnemann University, Philadelphia, PA
Holy Family College, Philadelphia, PA
Hussian School of Art, Philadelphia, PA
International Training Center, Philadelphia, PA
La Salle University, Philadelphia, PA
Lincoln Technical Institute, Philadelphia, PA
Mccarrie Schools of Health Sciences and Technology, Philadelphia, PA
Moore College of Art And Design, Philadelphia, PA
National Schools, Philadelphia, PA
Peirce Junior College, Philadelphia, PA
Pennsylvania College of Optometry, Philadelphia, PA
Philadelphia College of Pharmacy and Science, Philadelphia, PA
Philadelphia College of Textiles and Science, Philadelphia, PA
Rutgers, The State University of New Jersey, Camden College of Arts and Sciences, Camden, NJ
Rutgers, The State University of New Jersey, University College-Camden, Camden, NJ
St. Joseph's University, Philadelphia, PA
Spring Garden College, Philadelphia, PA
Talmudical Yeshiva of Philadelphia, Philadelphia, PA
Temple University, Philadelphia, PA
Thomas Jefferson University, Philadelphia, PA
Tracey-Warner School, Philadelphia, PA
University of Pennsylvania, Philadelphia, PA
University of the Arts, Philadelphia, PA

PITTSBURGH, PA (PMSA)

Geographic Profile

Land Area
3400.0 square miles

Counties and Parishes
Allegheny
Fayette
Washington
Westmoreland

Additional Cities/Towns within Area
McKeesport

Ranking Highlights

38 *out of 319 in total* **land area**
316 *out of 319 in* **population growth,** *1970–1990*
149 *out of 310 in having the lowest* **unemployment** *rate*
22 *out of 310 in size of* **labor force**
148 *out of 318 in the percentage of* **college graduates**
59 *out of 292 in per capita personal* **income**
29 *out of 319 in number of* **manufacturing establishments**
33 *out of 318 in* **physicians** *per 1000 people*
62 *out of 318 in* **hospital beds** *per 1000 people*
19 *out of 267 in fewest* **crimes** *per 1000 people*
84 *out of 266 in fewest* **violent crimes** *per 1000 people*
99 *out of 319 in per capita* **federal funds and grants**

Quality of Life Indexes (Rate per 1000 population)

Crime rate in 1991:	35.0
Violent crime rate in 1991:	4.3
Physicians rate in 1992:	2.89
Hospital bed rate in 1991:	5.27

ACCRA Cost of Living Indexes
(First quarter 1993, average = 100)

Composite index: 107.7
Utilities index: 152.8
Housing index: 97.9

Overview

With the collapse of the steel industry in the 1980s, Pittsburgh lost one out of every two manufacturing jobs. Today about eighty–five percent of the region's work force is employed in non-manufacturing industries, primarily the service sector, followed by wholesale and retail trade, government, transportation and public utilities, and finance, insurance and real estate. The service sector is the fastest growing, and almost half of the jobs are in managerial, professional, or technical positions. The city is home to the fourth largest concentration of Fortune 500 companies in the country, and more than one hundred foreign firms are headquartered there.

Research and development is the third largest industry, with more than eight hundred firms employing eighty-five thousand scientists and spending $1.5 billion annually on research. At the heart of this activity are Carnegie Mellon University and the University of Pittsburgh, which have helped transform the city into a leader in the fields of software engineering, robotics, artificial intelligence, biotechnology, and biomedicine. Filmmaking is an emerging industry; it pumped $65 million into the local economy in 1991–1992.

The City of Pittsburgh hosted 382 conventions in 1988–1990, with a total of almost one-half million attendees. The David L. Lawrence Convention Center, located two blocks from the central business district, offers three exhibit halls with a total of 131,000 square feet of unobstructed exhibit space and twenty-four meeting rooms. The Civic Arena and Exhibit Hall, also located downtown, has ninety thousand square feet of exhibit space and meeting rooms for 200 to 800 persons. The arena is covered by a retractable dome. More than 2,500 hotel rooms are available in the downtown area, many of them new or refurbished, and more than 10,000 hotel rooms are available in the county.

The Port of Pittsburgh is the country's largest inland port in terms of tonnage originating and passing through it. More than sixty-two million tons of cargo, primarily coal, are shipped annually on its three-river system. The Port offers convenient access to the nation's inland waterway system on 8,000 miles of navigable rivers flowing through twenty–four states. The port system affects almost one-half million water-dependent jobs. The Pittsburgh region boasts five class one railroads and four major interstate highways.

The three million square foot Pittsburgh International Airport opened in 1992. This state-of-the-art facility is expected to become one of the country's ten busiest airports. The old facility had been handling twenty million passengers a year on twelve major airlines offering 500 nonstop daily flights to more than 110 national and international cities.

The Pittsburgh area is at the center of an extensive highway system focused on Interstates 70, 76, and 80 (east-west) and Interstate 79 (north-south). Parkway East and Parkway West traverse the county.

Population (1990)

Total Population and Growth Rate
1990: 2,056,705
1980: 2,218,870
1970: 2,347,611
Growth rate 1970–1990: -12%

Race and Hispanic Origin
White: 90.8%
Black: 8.2%
Asian/Pacific Islander: 0.8%
Native American: 0.1%
Hispanic origin: 0.6%
White not Hispanic: 90.4%

Age
Ages 18 to 20: 4.2%
Ages 21 to 24: 5.3%
Ages 25 to 44: 30.6%
Ages 45 to 54: 10.3%
Ages 55 to 59: 4.9%
Ages 60 to 64: 5.8%
Ages 65 plus: 17.4%

Educational Attainment (1990)
Percent having completed high school: 77.4%
Percent having completed college: 19.5%
Elementary and high school enrollment: 295,399

Federal Funds and Grants Received
Total received in 1989: $7,510,300,000
Funds received per capita: $3,586

Civilian Labor Force
1993 (April): 1,032,440
1992 average: 1,032,692
1991 average: 1,004,810
1990 average: 993,181

Unemployment
1993 (April): 6.8%
1992 average: 6.8%
1991 average: 6.0%
1990 average: 4.8%

Average Annual Pay
1988: $21,945
1987: $21,019
1985: $19,558

Per Capita Personal Income
1991: $19,579
1990: $18,856
1989: $17,423

Business Climate (1987)

Manufacturing
Number of establishments in 1987: 2,518
Shipments in 1987 ($1,000): $12,433,200
Employees in 1987: 123,700
Change in employment, 1982 to 1987: -29.0%
Average annual pay for manufacturing work in 1989: $31,465
Average annual pay for production work in 1987: $23,236

Wholesale Trade
Number of establishments in 1987: 3,888
Total sales in 1987 ($1,000): $26,159,500
Change in sales, 1982 to 1987: 34.7%

Retail Trade
Number of establishments in 1987: 12,684
Total sales in 1987 ($1,000): $26,159,500
Retail sales per household in 1987: $15,007
Average annual pay in 1989: $10,969

Service Industry
Selected receipts in 1987 ($1,000): $7,658,100
Average annual pay in 1989: $21,365

Office Real Estate (1992)
Office space inventory: 28,290,377 square feet
Average class A Central Business District rental range per sq. ft: $21.50

Vacancy Rates
All areas: 12.4%

Vacancy Rates in Central Business District
Class A space: 9.1%
Class B space: 22.3%

Vacancy Rates Outside Central Business District
Class A space: 16.9%
Class B space: 11.8%

Housing
Total number of units in 1990: 879,811
Occupied units in 1990: 819,984
Owner-occupied units in 1990: 69.3%
1993 ACCRA average cost: $109,875
1993 ACCRA average rent for an apartment: $530

Chamber of Commerce
Greater Pittsburgh Chamber of Commerce, Justin T. Horan, President, 3 Gateway Center, Pittsburgh, PA 15222. 412-392-4500

Economic Development Office
Allegheny County Industrial Development Authority, Melinda Evans, Acting Manager, 445 Fort Pitt Blvd., Pittsburgh, PA 15219. 412-644-1062

Economic Development Organizations
Regional Industrial Development Corp., Frank B. Robinson, Director, 437 Grant St., Pittsburgh, PA 15219. 412-471-3939

Major Businesses

Company	SIC	Telephone
Allegheny International	3634	(412) 562-4000
Allegheny Ludlum Corp.	3312	(412) 394-2800
Aluminum Co. of America	3353	(412) 553-4545
Aristech Chemical Corp.	2821	(412) 433-2747
Bayer USA Inc.	2821	(412) 394-5500
Beazer East, Inc.	1442	(412) 227-2600
Blue Cross of Western Pennsylvania	6324	(412) 255-7000
Consolidated Natural Gas Co.	4924	(412) 227-1000
Consolidation Coal Co.	1222	(412) 831-4000
Cyclops Corp.	3312	(412) 343-4000
Cyclops Industries Inc.	3312	(412) 343-4000
Duquesne Light Co.	4911	(412) 393-6000
Fisher Scientific Co.	3826	(412) 562-8300
Fisher Scientific Group Inc.	3826	(412) 562-8300

Major Businesses (Continued)

Company	SIC	Telephone
Giant Eagle Inc.	5411	(412) 963-6200
Heinz, H. J. Co.	2033	(412) 456-5700
Mellon Bank Corp.	6021	(412) 234-5000
Mobay Corp.	2821	(412) 777-2000
National Intergroup, Inc.	5122	(412) 394-4100
National Steel Corp.	3312	(412) 394-4100
Pittsburgh National Bank	6021	(412) 762-2000
PNC Financial Corp.	6021	(412) 762-2666
PPG Industries, Inc.	3211	(412) 434-3131
Sunbeam Corp.	3634	(412) 562-4000
USX Corp.	1311	(412) 433-1121
West Penn Power Co.	4911	(412) 837-3000
Westinghouse Credit Corp.	6153	(412) 393-3000
Westinghouse Electric Corp.	3613	(412) 244-2000
Westinghouse Financial Service	6141	(412) 393-3000

Colleges and Universities
Art Institute of Pittsburgh, Pittsburgh
Carlow College, Pittsburgh
Carnegie Mellon University, Pittsburgh
Chatham College, Pittsburgh
Community College of Allegheny County Allegheny Campus, Pittsburgh
Community College of Allegheny County College Center-North, Pittsburgh
Computer Systems Institute, Pittsburgh
Dean Institute of Technology, Pittsburgh
Duff's Business Institute, Pittsburgh
Duquesne University, Pittsburgh
Electronic Institute, Pittsburgh
ICM School of Business, Pittsburgh
La Roche College, Pittsburgh
Penn Technical Institute, Pittsburgh
Pennsylvania State University Mckeesport Campus, Mckeesport
Pittsburgh Institute of Aeronautics, Pittsburgh
Pittsburgh Institute of Mortuary Science, Pittsburgh
Pittsburgh Technical Institute, Pittsburgh
Point Park College, Pittsburgh
Triangle Tech, Inc., Pittsburgh
University of Pittsburgh, Pittsburgh

READING, PA (MSA)

Geographic Profile

Land Area

859.2 square miles

Counties and Parishes

Berks

Ranking Highlights

226 *out of 319 in total* **land area**

211 *out of 319 in* **population growth,** *1970–1990*

166 *out of 310 in having the lowest* **unemployment** *rate*

122 *out of 310 in size of* **labor force**

233 *out of 318 in the percentage of* **college graduates**

 53 *out of 292 in per capita personal* **income**

101 *out of 319 in number of* **manufacturing establishments**

180 *out of 318 in* **physicians** *per 1000 people*

231 *out of 318 in* **hospital beds** *per 1000 people*

 32 *out of 267 in fewest* **crimes** *per 1000 people*

 77 *out of 266 in fewest* **violent crimes** *per 1000 people*

263 *out of 319 in per capita* **federal funds and grants**

Quality of Life Indexes (Rate per 1000 population)

Crime rate in 1991:	38.5
Violent crime rate in 1991:	4.1
Physicians rate in 1992:	1.73
Hospital bed rate in 1991:	3.09

ACCRA Cost of Living Indexes

(First quarter 1993, average = 100)

Composite index:	N/A
Utilities index:	N/A
Housing index:	N/A

Overview

The Reading Metropolitan Statistical Area (MSA) includes the City of Reading and the balance of Berks County in southeastern Pennsylvania. The Reading MSA is only 55 miles northwest of Philadelphia. The Reading MSA is within a 500-mile radius of 40% of the U.S. population and 60% of Canada's population. Reading is within 2 1/2 hours of Washington, D.C. and New York City metro areas. Overnight truck routes provide ready access to the nation's largest market area which is comprised of about 70 million people. Three deep water ports in Philadelphia, New York and Baltimore, Maryland, serve the area's manufacturing firms.

More than 500 manufacturers are located in the Reading MSA. The country, being highly industrialized, has a substantial 29% of its nonagricultural wage and salary employment in manufacturing. Products include: apparel, batteries, plastics, high alloy steel, hardware, electronic components, structural iron and steel, foundry products, specialty metals, confections, dairy products and other foods.Population (1990)

Total Population and Growth Rate

1990: 336,523

1980: 312,509

1970: 296,382

Growth rate 1970–1990: 14%

Race and Hispanic Origin

White: 93.5%

Black: 3.0%

Asian/Pacific Islander: 0.8%

Native American: 0.1%

Hispanic origin: 5.1%

White not Hispanic: 91.3%

Age

Ages 18 to 20: 4.6%

Ages 21 to 24: 5.4%

Ages 25 to 44: 30.8%

Ages 45 to 54: 10.3%

Ages 55 to 59: 4.8%

Ages 60 to 64: 5.1%

Ages 65 plus: 15.6%

Educational Attainment (1990)

Percent having completed high school: 70.0%

Percent having completed college: 15.1%

Elementary and high school enrollment: 50,724

Federal Funds and Grants Received

Total received in 1989: $777,800,000

Funds received per capita: $2,363

Civilian Labor Force

1993 (April): 181,608

1992 average: 181,445

1991 average: 176,274

1990 average: 176,869

Unemployment

1993 (April): 6.7%

1992 average: 7.0%

1991 average: 6.7%

1990 average: 5.1%

Average Annual Pay

1988: $21,157

1987: $19,979

1985: $18,106

Per Capita Personal Income

1991: $19,868

1990: $19,573

1989: $18,915

Business Climate (1987)

Manufacturing

Number of establishments in 1987: 624

Shipments in 1987 ($1,000): $5,227,500

Employees in 1987: 47,300

Change in employment, 1982 to 1987: -4.1%

Average annual pay for manufacturing work in 1989: $26,564

Average annual pay for production work in 1987: $21,812

Wholesale Trade

Number of establishments in 1987: 484

Total sales in 1987 ($1,000): $2,463,500

Change in sales, 1982 to 1987: 40.4%

Retail Trade

Number of establishments in 1987: 2,081

Total sales in 1987 ($1,000): $2,463,500

Retail sales per household in 1987: $17,101

Average annual pay in 1989: $11,896

Service Industry

Selected receipts in 1987 ($1,000): $685,300

Average annual pay in 1989: $20,169

Housing

Total number of units in 1990: 134,482

Occupied units in 1990: 127,649

Owner-occupied units in 1990: 73.9%

1993 ACCRA average cost: N/A

1993 ACCRA average rent for an apartment: N/A

Chamber of Commerce

Berks County Chamber of Commerce, Anthony F. Grimm, President, 645 Penn St., PO Box 1698, Reading, PA 19603. 215-376-6766

Economic Development Office

Greater Berks Development Fund, Edward J. Swoyer Jr., Secretary, 400 Washington St., PO Box 8621, Reading, PA 19603. 215-376-6739, FAX 215-478-9553

Major Businesses

Company	SIC	Telephone
Bank of Pennsylvania	6022	(215) 378-3600
Boscov's Department Store	5311	(215) 779-2000
Caloric Corp.	3631	(215) 682-4211
Campbell's Fresh, Inc.	0182	(215) 926-4101
Carpenter Technology Corp.	3312	(215) 371-2000
Dietrich's Milk Products	2023	(215) 929-5736
East Penn Manufacturing Co.	3691	(215) 682-6361
Exide Corp.	3691	(215) 378-0500
General Battery Corp.	3691	(215) 378-0500
Gilbert Associates, Inc.	8711	(215) 775-5900
Gilbert/Commonwealth, Inc.	8711	(215) 775-2600
Kiwi Brands, Inc.	2842	(215) 385-3041
Meridian Bancorp, Inc.	6021	(215) 320-2000
Meridian Bank	6022	(215) 320-2000
Metropolitan Edison Co.	4911	(215) 929-3601
Morgan Trailer Manufacturing Co.	3713	(215) 286-5025
National Penn Bancshares	6021	(215) 367-6001
NGK Metals Corp.	3356	(215) 921-5000

Major Businesses (Continued)

Company	SIC	Telephone
Penn Savings Bank	6035	(215) 320-8400
Penske Transportation, Inc.	7513	(215) 775-6000
Penske Truck Leasing Corp.	7513	(215) 775-6000
Ports of The World, Inc.	5311	(215) 779-2000
Reading Hospital	8062	(215) 378-6000
Reading Tube Corp.	3351	(215) 926-4141
Redner's Markets, Inc.	5411	(215) 374-4456
St. Joseph Hospital	8062	(215) 378-2000
Security of America Life Insurance	6411	(215) 372-8471
Sovereign Bancorp, Inc.	6035	(215) 320-8400
VF Corp.	2325	(215) 378-1151
Wetterau Foods Services Inc.	5141	(215) 929-5741

Colleges and Universities

Albright College, Reading

Alvernia College, Reading

Pennsylvania State University Berks Campus, Reading

Reading Area Community College, Reading

SCRANTON–WILKES-BARRE, PA (MSA)

Geographic Profile

Land Area
2839.9 square miles

Counties and Parishes
Columbia
Lackawanna
Luzerne
Monroe
Wyoming

Additional Cities/Towns within Area
Hazleton

Ranking Highlights

51 *out of 319 in total* **land area**
240 *out of 319 in* **population growth,** *1970–1990*
272 *out of 310 in having the lowest* **unemployment** *rate*
69 *out of 310 in size of* **labor force**
253 *out of 318 in the percentage of* **college graduates**
163 *out of 292 in per capita personal* **income**
61 *out of 319 in number of* **manufacturing establishments**
193 *out of 318 in* **physicians** *per 1000 people*
104 *out of 318 in* **hospital beds** *per 1000 people*
N/A *out of 267 in fewest* **crimes** *per 1000 people*
N/A *out of 266 in fewest* **violent crimes** *per 1000 people*
78 *out of 319 in per capita* **federal funds and grants**

Quality of Life Indexes (Rate per 1000 population)

Crime rate in 1991:	N/A
Violent crime rate in 1991:	N/A
Physicians rate in 1992:	1.67
Hospital bed rate in 1991:	4.58

ACCRA Cost of Living Indexes

(First quarter 1993, average = 100)
Composite index: 103.4
Utilities index: 147.3
Housing index: 107.3

Overview

Scranton, formerly known as the Anthracite Capital of the World, is the fifth–largest city in Pennsylvania. Once a one-industry town, Scranton is still dominated by manufacturing enterprises, primarily in the nondurable goods sector. The area is ranked second in the country for silk, rayon, and nylon weaving. Defense contractors also play an important role in the region's economy. The service industry, retail trade, and government make up a large part of the economic base. Tourism is said to be a growing industry.

Items and goods produced in the area include apparel and related products, plastics, compressors, automotive components, heating and air-conditioning equipment, candy, fabri-cated metal products, records and compact discs, caskets, books, furniture, chemicals, electrical equipment, glass products, tank parts, ordnance supplies, and other products for the Armed Forces.

Scranton's proximity to Northeast Corridor markets is enhanced by an excellent transportation network. Five major interstate highways are accessible within thirty miles of the city's center. Rail customers have access to four rail carriers. Fifty-eight major trucking terminals and thirty-four package delivery companies serve the area. Wilkes-Barre/Scranton International Airport, a full-service facility located nine miles south of Scranton in Avoca, maintains inland port-of-entry facilities and an adjacent foreign trade zone, enabling Scranton to accommodate a growing international market. The area has ten general service airports, three heli-ports, and ten private service airports.

Scranton is connected to the Canadian border and Maryland by Interstate 81; Interstate 84 extends to the Massachusetts Turnpike; and the northeast extension of the Pennsylvania Turnpike leads to Philadelphia. Interstate 380 provides a link to the Poconos and connects the area with Interstate 80, a principal east-west route from New York City to California.

Population (1990)

Total Population and Growth Rate
1990: 734,175
1980: 728,796
1970: 696,078
Growth rate 1970–1990: 5%

Race and Hispanic Origin
White: 98.2%
Black: 1.0%
Asian/Pacific Islander: 0.5%
Native American: 0.1%
Hispanic origin: 0.8%
White not Hispanic: 97.6%

Age
Ages 18 to 20: 5%
Ages 21 to 24: 5.4%
Ages 25 to 44: 28.7%
Ages 45 to 54: 10.1%
Ages 55 to 59: 4.7%
Ages 60 to 64: 5.6%
Ages 65 plus: 18.2%

Educational Attainment (1990)

Percent having completed high school: 73.4%
Percent having completed college: 14.1%
Elementary and high school enrollment: 108,675

Federal Funds and Grants Received

Total received in 1989: $2,915,600,000
Funds received per capita: $3,958

Civilian Labor Force
1993 (April): 376,605
1992 average: 377,499
1991 average: 367,452
1990 average: 366,478

Unemployment
1993 (April): 8.8%
1992 average: 9.5%
1991 average: 8.5%
1990 average: 6.9%

Average Annual Pay
1988: $17,618
1987: $16,866
1985: $15,368

Per Capita Personal Income
1991: $16,912
1990: $16,347
1989: $15,477

Business Climate (1987)
Manufacturing
Number of establishments in 1987: 1,166
Shipments in 1987 ($1,000): $6,812,900
Employees in 1987: 69,300
Change in employment, 1982 to 1987: 0%
Average annual pay for manufacturing work in 1989: $20,666
Average annual pay for production work in 1987: $16,921

Wholesale Trade
Number of establishments in 1987: 1,059
Total sales in 1987 ($1,000): $3,273,000
Change in sales, 1982 to 1987: 22.7%

Retail Trade
Number of establishments in 1987: 4,811
Total sales in 1987 ($1,000): $3,273,000
Retail sales per household in 1987: $15,798
Average annual pay in 1989: $10,234

Service Industry
Selected receipts in 1987 ($1,000): $1,435,600
Average annual pay in 1989: $16,344

Housing
Total number of units in 1990: 322,709
Occupied units in 1990: 280,697
Owner-occupied units in 1990: 70.0%
1993 ACCRA average cost: $119,833
1993 ACCRA average rent for an apartment: $567

Chamber of Commerce
Greater Scranton Chamber of Commerce, Austin J. Burke, President, 222 Mulberry St., PO Box 431, Scranton, PA 18501. 717-342-7711

Economic Development Office
Lackawanna County Industrial Development Authority, Kenneth S. Dolph, 200 Adams Ave. Room 413, Scranton, PA 18503. 717-963-6862

Economic Development Organizations
Greater Wilkes-Barre Industrial Fund, Inc., Frederick A. Lohman, Vice President, 67-69 Public Square, Wilkes-Barre, PA 18710-5340. 717-823-2101, FAX 717-822-5951

Greater Wilkes-Barre Partnership, Inc., Stephen M. Barroulk, President, 69 Public Square Suite 600, PO Box 5340. Wilkes-Barre, PA 18710-5340. 717-823-2101, FAX 717-822-5951

Luzerne County Office of Community Development, Gary F. Lamont, Director, 54 W. Union St., Wilkes-Barre, PA 18711. 717-824-7214

Committee for Economic Growth, Gary C. Boam, Vice President, 69 Public Square Suite 600, PO Box 5340. Wilkes-Barre, PA 18710-5340. 717-823-2101, FAX 717-822-5951

Major Businesses

Company	SIC	Telephone
Acker Drill Co. Inc.	3531	(717) 586-2061
Anemostat Products Division	3585	(717) 346-6586
C-TEC Corp.	4813	(717) 825-1100
Cleland-Simpson Co.	5311	(717) 344-7271
Crystal Soda Water Co.	2086	(717) 347-5661
Eastern Pennsylvania Supply	5074	(717) 823-1181
First Eastern Bank N.A.	6022	(717) 826-4600
First Eastern Corp.	6712	(717) 826-4623
Franklin First Financial	6712	(717) 821-7100
Giant Markets, Inc.	5411	(717) 343-2401
Gress Poultry, Inc.	2015	(717) 346-7607
Haddon Craftsmen, Inc.	2732	(717) 348-9211
Intermetro Industries Corp.	3496	(717) 825-2741
International Correspondent	8249	(717) 342-7701
J & H Concrete	3273	(717) 824-3565
Jaunty Fabric Corp.	2299	(717) 346-8421
Kay Wholesale Drug Co. Inc.	5122	(717) 823-5177
Lion Inc.	2082	(717) 823-8801
McCarthy Tire Service Co.	5013	(717) 822-3151
McKinney Products Co.	3429	(717) 346-7551
Medico Industries, Inc.	3451	(717) 825-7711
Montage Foods, Inc.	2013	(717) 347-2400
Muskin, Inc.	3949	(717) 825-4501
Penn Refrigeration Service	3585	(717) 825-5666
Pennsylvania Enterprises	4924	(717) 829-8600
Pennsylvania Gas & Water	4924	(717) 829-8600
Pennsylvania Millers Mutual	6321	(717) 822-8111
Profera's Pizza Bakery Inc.	5142	(717) 342-4181
Renold Power Transmission	3568	(717) 822-9000
Scranton Times	2711	(717) 348-9107
Simplex Industries, Inc.	2452	(717) 346-5113
Suckle Corp.	3579	(717) 346-3871

Major Businesses (Continued)

Company	SIC	Telephone
Superior Fireproof Door Co.	3442	(717) 342-3126
United Gilsonite Laboratories	2851	(717) 344-1202
W. H. Conyngham & Co.	0212	(717) 822-7188

Colleges and Universities

ICS Center For Degree Studies, Scranton
Johnson Technical Institute, Scranton
King's College, Wilkes-Barre
Lackawanna Junior College, Scranton
Marywood College, Scranton
Pennsylvania State University Hazelton Campus, Hazelton
University of Scranton, Scranton

SHARON, PA (MSA)

Geographic Profile

Land Area
671.9 square miles

Counties and Parishes
Mercer

Ranking Highlights

259 *out of 319 in total* **land area**
295 *out of 319 in* **population growth,** *1970–1990*
252 *out of 310 in having the lowest* **unemployment** *rate*
277 *out of 310 in size of* **labor force**
269 *out of 318 in the percentage of* **college graduates**
226 *out of 292 in per capita personal* **income**
234 *out of 319 in number of* **manufacturing establishments**
281 *out of 318 in* **physicians** *per 1000 people*
53 *out of 318 in* **hospital beds** *per 1000 people*
2 *out of 267 in fewest* **crimes** *per 1000 people*
33 *out of 266 in fewest* **violent crimes** *per 1000 people*
234 *out of 319 in per capita* **federal funds and grants**

Quality of Life Indexes (Rate per 1000 population)

Crime rate in 1991:   23.3
Violent crime rate in 1991:   2.6
Physicians rate in 1992:   1.21
Hospital bed rate in 1991:   5.4

ACCRA Cost of Living Indexes

(First quarter 1993, average = 100)
Composite index: 101.3
Utilities index: 102.0
Housing index: 109.6

Population (1990)

Total Population and Growth Rate
1990: 121,003
1980: 128,299
1970: 127,225
Growth rate 1970–1990: -5%

Race and Hispanic Origin
White: 94.6%
Black: 4.9%
Asian/Pacific Islander: 0.3%
Native American: 0.1%
Hispanic origin: 0.4%
White not Hispanic: 94.3%

Age
Ages 18 to 20:   5%
Ages 21 to 24: 5.3%
Ages 25 to 44:   28%
Ages 45 to 54: 10.3%
Ages 55 to 59:   5%

Ages 60 to 64: 5.7%
Ages 65 plus: 17.2%

Educational Attainment (1990)

Percent having completed high school: 75.1%
Percent having completed college: 13.6%
Elementary and high school enrollment: 19,461

Federal Funds and Grants Received

Total received in 1989: $315,600,000
Funds received per capita: $2,579

Civilian Labor Force

1993 (April):   54,164
1992 average: 54,841
1991 average: 52,693
1990 average: 52,216

Unemployment

1993 (April): 11.4%
1992 average: 8.8%
1991 average: 7.2%
1990 average: 5.3%

Average Annual Pay

1988: $18,568
1987: $17,653
1985: $17,310

Per Capita Personal Income

1991: $15,731
1990: $15,130
1989: $14,193

Business Climate (1987)

Manufacturing

Number of establishments in 1987: 169
Shipments in 1987 ($1,000): $1,521,500
Employees in 1987: 10,400
Change in employment, 1982 to 1987: -19.4%
Average annual pay for manufacturing work in 1989: $26,685
Average annual pay for production work in 1987: $23,027

Wholesale Trade

Number of establishments in 1987: 168
Total sales in 1987 ($1,000): $873,200
Change in sales, 1982 to 1987: 68.4%

Retail Trade

Number of establishments in 1987: 751
Total sales in 1987 ($1,000): $873,200
Retail sales per household in 1987: $13,358
Average annual pay in 1989: $9,419

Service Industry

Selected receipts in 1987 ($1,000): $169,300
Average annual pay in 1989: $17,570

Housing

Total number of units in 1990: 48,689

Occupied units in 1990: 45,591
Owner-occupied units in 1990: 75.0%
1993 ACCRA average cost: N/A
1993 ACCRA average rent for an apartment: N/A

Chamber of Commerce

Shenango Valley Chamber of Commerce, William Leavens, Exec. Director, 1 W. State St., Sharon, PA 16146. 412-981-5880, FAX 412-981-5480

Major Businesses

Company	SIC	Telephone
Baglier, John Buick-Cadillac	5511	(412) 981-4600
Carine and Co., Inc.	5113	(412) 346-3525
Chadderton, Ed Trucking Inc.	4213	(412) 981-5050
First Federal West PA Inc.	6035	(412) 981-1320
First National Bank of Mercer Co.	6021	(412) 588-6770
Flexospan Steel Buildings	3448	(412) 376-3698
Goldstein, MN Co. Inc.	5712	(412) 981-2900
Greenville Regional Hospital	8062	(412) 588-2100
Greenwood Pharmacy Inc.	5912	(412) 981-3800
Hodge Foundry, Inc.	3321	(412) 588-4100
Howe, George J. Co.	5145	(412) 458-9410
Jamestown Paint & Varnish	2851	(412) 932-3101
Mc Dowell National Bank	6021	(412) 981-1411
Perrine Oil Co.	5172	(412) 981-1900
Perry Brothers Coal Co.	1221	(412) 346-5555
Phillips Steel Co. Inc.	5051	(412) 981-8560
Pine Instrument Co.	3625	(412) 458-6391
Protected Home Mutual Life Insurance	6311	(412) 981-1520
Reyer, John Co.	5661	(412) 981-2200
Salem Tube, Inc.	3317	(412) 646-4301
Sharon Regional Health System	8062	(412) 983-3911
Sharon Steel Corp.	3312	(412) 981-1375
Shenango Valley Medical Center	8062	(412) 981-3500
United Community Hospital	8062	(412) 458-5442
Winner International Corp.	3429	(412) 981-1152
Yourga Trucking Inc.	4213	(412) 981-3600

Colleges and Universities

Pennsylvania State University Shenango Campus, Sharon

STATE COLLEGE, PA (MSA)

Geographic Profile

Land Area

1107.6 square miles

Counties and Parishes

Centre

Ranking Highlights

182 *out of 319 in total* land area

162 *out of 319 in* population growth, *1970–1990*

104 *out of 310 in having the lowest* unemployment *rate*

234 *out of 310 in size of* labor force

17 *out of 318 in the percentage of* college graduates

202 *out of 292 in per capita personal* income

259 *out of 319 in number of* manufacturing establishments

238 *out of 318 in* physicians *per 1000 people*

295 *out of 318 in* hospital beds *per 1000 people*

N/A *out of 267 in fewest* crimes *per 1000 people*

N/A *out of 266 in fewest* violent crimes *per 1000 people*

163 *out of 319 in per capita* federal funds and grants

Quality of Life Indexes (Rate per 1000 population)

Crime rate in 1991:	N/A
Violent crime rate in 1991:	N/A
Physicians rate in 1992:	1.43
Hospital bed rate in 1991:	2.18

ACCRA Cost of Living Indexes

(First quarter 1993, average = 100)

Composite index:	N/A
Utilities index:	N/A
Housing index:	N/A

Population (1990)

Total Population and Growth Rate

1990: 123,786

1980: 112,760

1970: 99,267

Growth rate 1970–1990: 25%

Race and Hispanic Origin

White: 94.2%

Black: 2.3%

Asian/Pacific Islander: 3.1%

Native American: 0.1%

Hispanic origin: 1.1%

White not Hispanic: 93.4%

Age

Ages 18 to 20: 12.8%

Ages 21 to 24: 15.4%

Ages 25 to 44: 29.3%

Ages 45 to 54: 8.4%

Ages 55 to 59: 3.5%

Ages 60 to 64: 3.4%

Ages 65 plus: 9%

Educational Attainment (1990)

Percent having completed high school: 83.6%

Percent having completed college: 32.3%

Elementary and high school enrollment: 14,556

Federal Funds and Grants Received

Total received in 1989: $352,700,000

Funds received per capita: $3,050

Civilian Labor Force

1993 (April):   70,198

1992 average: 69,579

1991 average: 67,738

1990 average: 66,823

Unemployment

1993 (April):   5.8%

1992 average: 6.1%

1991 average: 6.1%

1990 average: 5.3%

Average Annual Pay

1988: $19,139

1987: $18,279

1985: $16,620

Per Capita Personal Income

1991: $16,244

1990: $15,514

1989: $14,578

Business Climate (1987)

Manufacturing

Number of establishments in 1987: 141

Shipments in 1987 ($1,000): $663,500

Employees in 1987: 7,800

Change in employment, 1982 to 1987: 1.3%

Average annual pay for manufacturing work in 1989: $22,240

Average annual pay for production work in 1987: $16,821

Wholesale Trade

Number of establishments in 1987: 136

Total sales in 1987 ($1,000): $210,600

Change in sales, 1982 to 1987: 3.4%

Retail Trade

Number of establishments in 1987: 732

Total sales in 1987 ($1,000): $210,600

Retail sales per household in 1987: $17,602

Average annual pay in 1989: $9,400

Service Industry

Selected receipts in 1987 ($1,000): $324,700

Average annual pay in 1989: $18,847

Housing

Total number of units in 1990: 46,195

Occupied units in 1990: 42,683
Owner-occupied units in 1990: 59.8%
1993 ACCRA average cost: N/A
1993 ACCRA average rent for an apartment: N/A

Chamber of Commerce

State College Area Chamber of Commerce, Patricia L. Cahalen, Exec. Director, 131 Fraser St. Plaza #3, State College, PA 16801. 814-237-7644

Economic Development Office

Centre County Industrial Development Corp., Charles Mong, Exec. Director, 820 N. University Dr., State College, PA 16803. 814-234-1829, FAX 814-234-6864

Major Businesses

Company	SIC	Telephone
Bellefonte Lime Co. Inc.	3274	(814) 355-4761
C-Cor Electronics Inc.	3663	(814) 238-2461
Centre Community Hospital	8062	(814) 238-4351
Centre Oil & Gas Co.	5172	(814) 355-4749
Chemcut Corp.	3559	(814) 238-0514
Claster, M. L., & Sons, Inc.	5211	(814) 355-4851
Davidson Bros. Inc.	4213	(814) 355-5513
Dix, George A. Inc.	5511	(814) 238-6711
Don Mart Clothes Inc.	5136	(814) 342-1160
France J. H. Refractories	3255	(814) 387-6811
Hawbaker, Glenn O. Inc.	1611	(814) 237-1444
Houts, O. W. & Son Inc.	5311	(814) 238-6701
HRB Systems	3669	(814) 238-4311
HRI, Inc.	1611	(814) 238-5071
Leitzinger Imports Inc.	5511	(814) 238-2447
Management Specialist Inc.	5812	(814) 237-1622
Mellon Bank Central National Association	6021	(814) 231-2500
Merryman, R. T. Trucking	4213	(814) 342-4930
Navasky, Charles & Co. Inc.	5136	(814) 342-1160
Nittany Printing & Publishing Co.	2711	(814) 238-5000
Omega Financial Corp.	6021	(814) 237-7641
Peoples National Bank	6021	(814) 237-7641
Rider Auto	5511	(814) 234-2886
Ruetgers-Nease Chemical	2865	(814) 238-2424
S. & A. Custom Built	1521	(814) 436-8253
Stocker Chevrolet Inc.	5511	(814) 238-4905
Supelco Inc.	3826	(814) 359-3441
Uni-Marts, Inc.	5411	(814) 234-6000
Unico Corp.	1522	(814) 234-5000
United Federal Savings Bank	6035	(814) 231-1600

Colleges and Universities

Pennsylvania State University University Park Campus, State College

WILLIAMSPORT, PA (MSA)

Geographic Profile

Land Area
1234.9 square miles

Counties and Parishes
Lycoming

Ranking Highlights

159 *out of 319 in total* land area
242 *out of 319 in* population growth, *1970–1990*
230 *out of 310 in having the lowest* unemployment *rate*
261 *out of 310 in size of* labor force
292 *out of 318 in the percentage of* college graduates
203 *out of 292 in per capita personal* income
200 *out of 319 in number of* manufacturing establishments
150 *out of 318 in* physicians *per 1000 people*
43 *out of 318 in* hospital beds *per 1000 people*
N/A *out of 267 in fewest* crimes *per 1000 people*
N/A *out of 266 in fewest* violent crimes *per 1000 people*
189 *out of 319 in per capita* federal funds and grants

Quality of Life Indexes (Rate per 1000 population)

Crime rate in 1991:	N/A
Violent crime rate in 1991:	N/A
Physicians rate in 1992:	1.84
Hospital bed rate in 1991:	5.63

ACCRA Cost of Living Indexes
(First quarter 1993, average = 100)
Composite index: 110.5
Utilities index: 136.2
Housing index: 122.4

Population (1990)

Total Population and Growth Rate
1990: 118,710
1980: 118,416
1970: 113,296
Growth rate 1970–1990: 5%

Race and Hispanic Origin
White: 96.9%
Black: 2.4%
Asian/Pacific Islander: 0.4%
Native American: 0.2%
Hispanic origin: 0.5%
White not Hispanic: 96.5%

Age
Ages 18 to 20: 4.7%
Ages 21 to 24: 5.2%
Ages 25 to 44: 30.2%
Ages 45 to 54: 10.1%
Ages 55 to 59: 4.6%

Ages 60 to 64:   5%
Ages 65 plus: 15.1%

Educational Attainment (1990)
Percent having completed high school: 74.5%
Percent having completed college: 12.3%
Elementary and high school enrollment: 19,956

Federal Funds and Grants Received
Total received in 1989: $339,800,000
Funds received per capita: $2,873

Civilian Labor Force
1993 (April):   61,533
1992 average: 61,547
1991 average: 60,267
1990 average: 60,449

Unemployment
1993 (April):   8.2%
1992 average: 8.1%
1991 average: 8.0%
1990 average: 7.2%

Average Annual Pay
1988: $18,600
1987: $17,666
1985: $16,285

Per Capita Personal Income
1991: $16,234
1990: $15,816
1989: $15,084

Business Climate (1987)
Manufacturing
Number of establishments in 1987: 231
Shipments in 1987 ($1,000): $1,814,700
Employees in 1987: 17,200
Change in employment, 1982 to 1987: 16.2%
Average annual pay for manufacturing work in 1989: $22,994
Average annual pay for production work in 1987: $16,472

Wholesale Trade
Number of establishments in 1987: 182
Total sales in 1987 ($1,000): $372,200
Change in sales, 1982 to 1987: 16.2%

Retail Trade
Number of establishments in 1987: 793
Total sales in 1987 ($1,000): $372,200
Retail sales per household in 1987: $17,230
Average annual pay in 1989: $10,609

Service Industry
Selected receipts in 1987 ($1,000): $174,600
Average annual pay in 1989: $16,960

Housing
Total number of units in 1990: 49,580

Occupied units in 1990: 44,949
Owner-occupied units in 1990: 69.7%
1993 ACCRA average cost: $147,007
1993 ACCRA average rent for an apartment: $483

Chamber of Commerce
Williamsport-Lycoming Chamber of Commerce, Peter A. Loedding, President, 454 Pine St., Williamsport, PA 17701. 717-326-1971

Major Businesses

Company	SIC	Telephone
Alexander, Blaise Chevrolet	5511	(717) 368-8677
Barr Motors Inc.	5511	(717) 326-1000
Bastian Tire Sales Inc.	5014	(717) 326-9181
Brodart Co. (A Partnership)	5192	(717) 326-2461
Chromagraphic Processing	3479	(717) 323-7899
Commonwealth Bank Trust Co.	6021	(717) 327-5011
Data Papers Inc.	2761	(717) 546-2201
Divine Providence Hospital	8062	(717) 326-8101
Don Breon Ford, Inc.	5511	(717) 398-2330
Eck's Garage Inc.	5012	(717) 433-3177
Ericson Constructors, Inc.	1541	(717) 322-1105
Fry, Bill Ford Inc.	5511	(717) 368-8121
Gruenberg Oven Co., Inc.	3567	(717) 326-1755
Harrison's, Samuel & Sons	5421	(717) 322-4618
Jersey Shore State Bank	6022	(717) 398-2213
Lunaire Ltd.	3567	(717) 326-1755
Lycoming Silica Sand Co.	1442	(717) 368-2481
MHB Inc.	2013	(717) 323-3761
Mc Cormick Dray Lines Inc.	4213	(717) 546-5921
Muncy Homes Inc.	2452	(717) 546-2261
Muncy Valley Hospital	8062	(717) 546-8282
Northern Central Bank	6022	(717) 326-2611
Powell, John Chevrolet Inc.	5511	(717) 322-4611
Shirn's Pontiac-GMC Inc.	5511	(717) 326-1581
Staiman Brothers Inc.	5093	(717) 323-9494
Van Campen Motors Inc.	5511	(717) 326-0567
Webb, J. A. Inc.	4213	(717) 546-5921
Williamsport Beverage Co.	5181	(717) 494-1270
Williamsport Hospital Medical Center	8062	(717) 321-1000
Williamsport National Bank	6021	(717) 326-2431

Colleges and Universities
Lycoming College, Williamsport
Pennsylvania College of Technology, Williamsport

YORK, PA (MSA)

Geographic Profile

Land Area

1424.7 square miles

Counties and Parishes

Adams

York

Ranking Highlights

142 *out of 319 in total* **land area**

153 *out of 319 in* **population growth**, *1970–1990*

139 *out of 310 in having the lowest* **unemployment** *rate*

99 *out of 310 in size of* **labor force**

261 *out of 318 in the percentage of* **college graduates**

50 *out of 292 in per capita personal* **income**

88 *out of 319 in number of* **manufacturing establishments**

271 *out of 318 in* **physicians** *per 1000 people*

274 *out of 318 in* **hospital beds** *per 1000 people*

8 *out of 267 in fewest* **crimes** *per 1000 people*

22 *out of 266 in fewest* **violent crimes** *per 1000 people*

256 *out of 319 in per capita* **federal funds and grants**

Quality of Life Indexes (Rate per 1000 population)

Crime rate in 1991:	31.6
Violent crime rate in 1991:	2.0
Physicians rate in 1992:	1.27
Hospital bed rate in 1991:	2.52

ACCRA Cost of Living Indexes

(First quarter 1993, average = 100)

Composite index:	98.1
Utilities index:	89.3
Housing index:	101.7

Population (1990)

Total Population and Growth Rate

1990: 417,848

1980: 381,255

1970: 329,540

Growth rate 1970–1990: 27%

Race and Hispanic Origin

White: 95.7%

Black: 2.9%

Asian/Pacific Islander: 0.6%

Native American: 0.1%

Hispanic origin: 1.5%

White not Hispanic: 95.0%

Age

Ages 18 to 20: 4.4%

Ages 21 to 24: 5.4%

Ages 25 to 44: 32.7%

Ages 45 to 54: 10.8%

Ages 55 to 59: 4.6%

Ages 60 to 64: 4.5%

Ages 65 plus: 13.2%

Educational Attainment (1990)

Percent having completed high school: 72.3%

Percent having completed college: 13.8%

Elementary and high school enrollment: 66,494

Federal Funds and Grants Received

Total received in 1989: $987,400,000

Funds received per capita: $2,406

Civilian Labor Force

1993 (April):   236,669

1992 average: 232,019

1991 average: 225,828

1990 average: 223,787

Unemployment

1993 (April):   6.0%

1992 average: 6.7%

1991 average: 6.2%

1990 average: 4.9%

Average Annual Pay

1988: $19,788

1987: $18,741

1985: $17,222

Per Capita Personal Income

1991: $19,998

1990: $19,579

1989: $18,715

Business Climate (1987)

Manufacturing

Number of establishments in 1987: 759

Shipments in 1987 ($1,000): $5,962,000

Employees in 1987: 59,200

Change in employment, 1982 to 1987: -0.7%

Average annual pay for manufacturing work in 1989: $25,031

Average annual pay for production work in 1987: $19,626

Wholesale Trade

Number of establishments in 1987: 620

Total sales in 1987 ($1,000): $2,575,800

Change in sales, 1982 to 1987: 24.3%

Retail Trade

Number of establishments in 1987: 2,424

Total sales in 1987 ($1,000): $2,575,800

Retail sales per household in 1987: $17,008

Average annual pay in 1989: $11,996

Service Industry

Selected receipts in 1987 ($1,000): $662,600

Average annual pay in 1989: $17,055

Housing

Total number of units in 1990: 164,902

Occupied units in 1990: 156,733
Owner-occupied units in 1990: 74.2%
1993 ACCRA average cost: $121,750
1993 ACCRA average rent for an apartment: $465

Chamber of Commerce

York Area Chamber of Commerce, Thomas E. Donley, President, 1 Market Way E., PO Box 1229, York, PA 17405. 717-848-4000

Economic Development Office

York County Industrial Development Corp., David B. Carver, President, 1 Market Way E., York, PA 17401. 717-846-8879

Major Businesses

Company	SIC	Telephone
Baker, J. E. Co.	1422	(717) 848-1501
Baker Holding Co.	1422	(717) 848-1501
Construction Management Resource	1622	(717) 764-8521
Dentsply Holdings Inc.	3843	(717) 845-7511
Dentsply International Inc.	3843	(717) 845-7511
Farmers Bank Trust	6022	(717) 637-2291
Glatfelter, P. H. Co.	2621	(717) 225-4711
Grumbacher, S., & Son	5311	(717) 757-7660
Hanover Foods Corp.	2033	(717) 632-6000
Hanover House Industries	5961	(717) 637-6000
Helm Coal Corp.	3444	(717) 843-0021
Knouse Foods Cooperative	2033	(717) 677-8181
Nell's Inc.	5141	(717) 259-0914
Pfaltzgraff Co.	3269	(717) 848-5500
Precision Components Corp.	3443	(717) 848-1126
Scrivner of Pennsylvania	5141	(717) 755-1976
Shipley Oil Co.	5983	(717) 848-4100
Susquehanna Pfaltzgraff Co.	3269	(717) 848-5500
Voith Hydro, Inc.	3511	(717) 792-3511
Wagman, G. A. & F. C. Inc.	1622	(717) 764-8521
York Bank & Trust Co.	6022	(717) 843-8651
York Federal Savings & Loan Association	6035	(717) 846-8777
York Financial Corp.	6035	(717) 846-8777
York Holdings Corp.	3585	(717) 771-7890
York Hospital	8062	(717) 771-2345
York International Corp.	3585	(717) 771-7890
Yorktowne Paper Mills, Inc.	2631	(717) 843-8061

Colleges and Universities

Bradley Academy for the Visual Arts, York
Pennsylvania State University York Campus, York

RHODE ISLAND

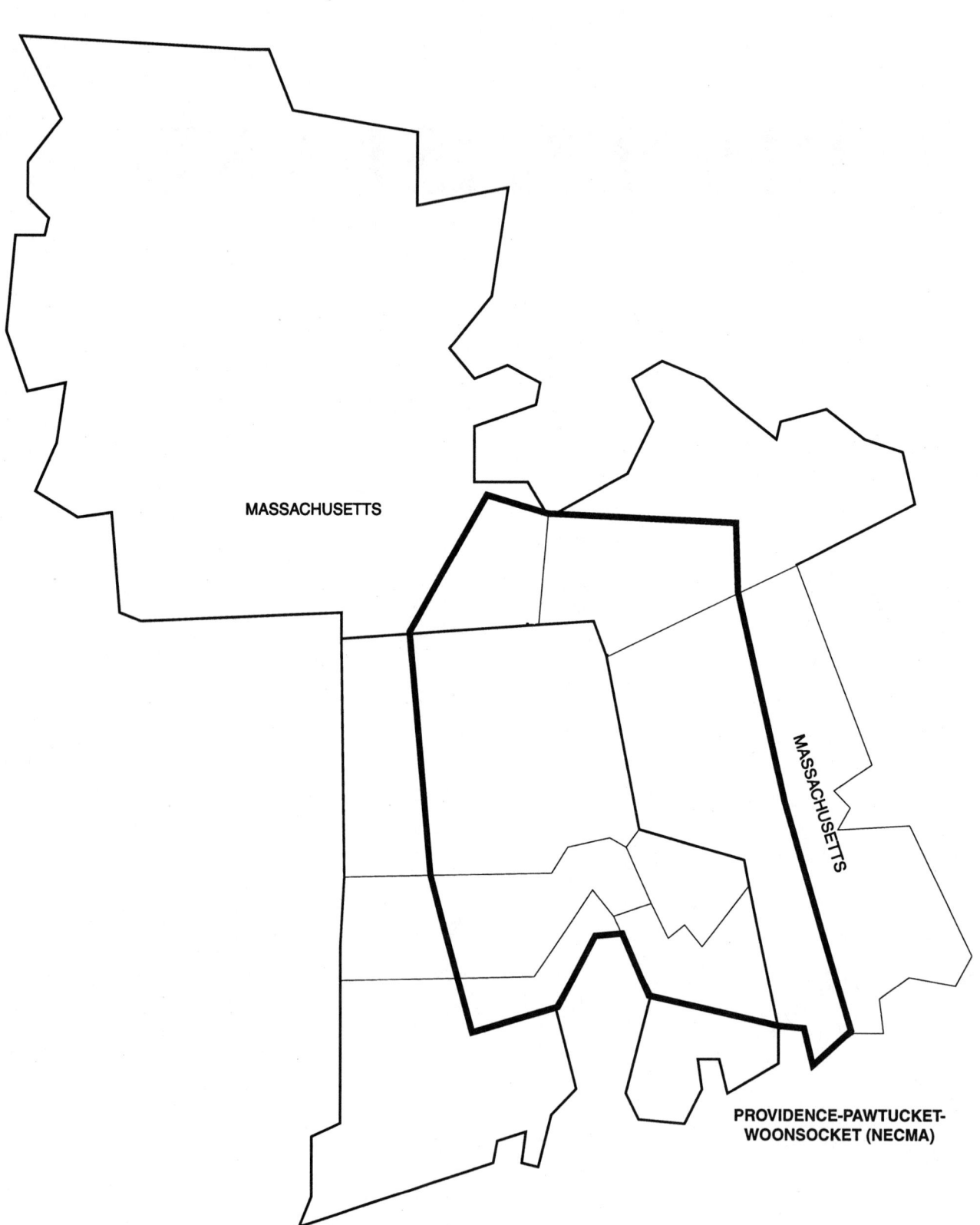

MASSACHUSETTS

MASSACHUSETTS

PROVIDENCE-PAWTUCKET-
WOONSOCKET (NECMA)

RHODE ISLAND

Population
1990: 1,003,464
1980: 947,154

Age
Ages 18 to 20: 54,930
Ages 21 to 24: 65,428
Ages 25 to 44: 321,241
Ages 45 to 54: 96,425
Ages 55 to 59: 42,077
Ages 60 to 64: 47,126
Median age: 34.0

Race and Hispanic Origin
White: 917,375
Black: 38,861
Asian/Pacific Islander: 18,325
Native American: 4,071
Hispanic origin: 45,752

Households
Total: 377,977
Persons per household: 2.55

Sex
Male: 481,496
Female: 521,968

Population Migration
Domestic migration: -5,000
International migration: 27,000

Projection of the Population in 1995
Total: 1,040,000
18 to 64: 646,000

Civilian Labor Force
1993: 522,500
1992: 516,600
1991: 514,500
1990: 513,000

Manufacturing
1995 Projection: 114,900
1992: 89,800
1991: 91,700
1990: 96,700
1989: 107,300

Services
1995 Projection: 184,000

1992: 127,200
1991: 130,600
1990: 130,400
1989: 124,800

Wholesale and Retail Trade
1995 Projection: 128,300
1992: 90,300
1991: 93,100
1990: 97,100
1989: 109,600

Unemployment Rate
1993: 8.0%
1992: 8.2%
1991: 8.1%
1990: 6.5%

Employer Unemployment Contributions

Contribution Rate
1992: 3.50%
1991: 2.50%
1990: 2.49%

Average Weekly Benefit
1992: $212.43
1991: $199.84
1990: $194.15

Gross State Product (Million $)
1989: $18,807
1988: $17,897
1987: $16,532
1979: $8,597
Growth rate, 1979 to 1989: 118.8%

Capital Expenditures of Manufacturing Industries
1990: $185,600,000
1989: $223,000,000
1988: $221,200,000
1987: $276,400,000

State Tax Rates
Individual income: 27.5% of taxpayer's modified Federal income tax.
Corporate income: 9% of taxable net income, with 11% surtax imposed.

General property: Rates fixed locally. Based on full and fair cash value of real and personal property.

General sales: 7%

Gasoline: 26¢ per gallon

Income

Median income for a 4 person family: $43,278

Personal per Capita Income

1992: $20,299

1991: $19,201

1990: $18,771

Disposable per Capita Income

1992: $17,863

1991: $16,795

1990: $16,321

Private Employment Weekly Wages

Average

1989: $391

1988: $374

1987: $374

Manufacturing

1989: $348

1988: $419

1987: $391

Services

1989: $368

1988: $349

1987: $321

Wholesale

1989: $513

1988: $502

1987: $474

Retail

1989: $238

1988: $230

1987: $215

Highway Statistics

Total Highway Miles

1990: 6,111

1989: 5,884

1988: 5,846

Federal Highway Aid

1991: $114,573,000

1990: $110,897,000

1989: $107,692,000

Electricity

Average Cost per Kilowatt Hour

1990: 9.14¢

1989: 8.26¢

1988: 7.93¢

Housing (1990)

Owner occupied units: 224,792

Median house value: $133,500

Renter occupied units: 153,185

Median rent: $416

Total vacant units: 36,595

Homeowner vacancy rate: 1.5%

Rental vacancy rate: 7.9%

State Business Incentives and Assistance

Enterprise Zone Incentives

1) Priority use of job training funds.

2) Payroll tax credit. Maximum $15,000 tax credit per employee during the first three years of zone operation. During the fourth and fifth years of operation, a credit equal to 75% of total wages and salaries of zone employees, up to $12,000 per employee, is extended. During the sixth and seventh years, a credit up to 25% of the total payroll, up to $5,000, per employee is offered.

3) Resident business owner tax deduction. $50,000 per year from net worth of income during first three years, $25,000 per year during the fourth and fifth years.

4) Enterprise Worker Tax Exemption. enterprise worker receiving more than 90% of gross income directly from a qualified business in the zone may deduct from state gross income either $5,000 or the amount earned per year for a period of two taxable years, whichever is less.

5) No property taxes levied in the first year of operation of a qualified zone business, 20% in the second year, 40% in the third year and 60% in the fourth year.

Financial and Business Assistance

Industrial Development Bonds. Administered by the Financial Services Division of the Department of Economic Development, tax-exempt IDBs may be issued for new and existing manufacturing companies. Bond proceeds may be used for industrial plants and equipments. Other manufacturing and industrial projects with new employment potential may apply for taxable IDBs.

Rhode Island Partnership for Science and Technology. Established by the state legislature, the Partnership provides state-financed matching grants for applied research and product or process development projects with high potential for retaining or creating jobs. This program will link businesses with nonprofit research institutions within the state.

Revolving Loan Fund. Administered by the Department of Economic Development, this program provides fixed-asset and working capital loans to small businesses in the state. Eligible firms are manufacturers, processors, and selected service businesses.

Education and Training

Job Development and Training. Administered by the Job Development and Training Division of the Department of Economic Development, this program provides custom-

Major Companies in the State

Company name	Fortune 500 rank	City	Telephone	SIC number
Fortune 500 Companies				
Hasbro Inc.	185	Pawtucket	401-431-8697	3944
Nortek Inc.	385	Providence	401-751-1600	3634
Sunbeam Oster Co. Inc.	365	Providence	401-831-0050	3634
Textron Inc.	63	Providence	401-421-2800	3721
Other Major Companies in the State				
A T Cross Co.		Lincoln	401-333-1200	3951
Almac's Supermarkets Inc.		East Providence	401-438-2700	5411
American Power Conversion Corp.		West Kingston	401-789-5735	3679
Astro Med Inc.		West Warwick	401-828-4000	3577
Bangor America Inc.		Woonsocket	401-765-5800	2253
Blackstone Valley Electric Co.		Lincoln	401-333-1400	4911
Brown & Sharpe Manufacturing Co.		North Kingstown	401-886-2000	3825
Eastland Financial Corp. Rhode Island		Woonsocket	401-767-3900	6712
Fleet Norstar Financial Group Inc.		Providence	401-278-5800	6712
GTECH Corp.		West Greenwich	401-392-1000	7371
GTECH Holdings Corp.		West Greenwich	401-392-1000	7371
Narragansett Electric Co.		Providence	401-781-0100	4911
Old Stone Corp.		Providence	401-278-2000	6712
Outlet Broadcasting Inc.		Providence	401-455-9200	4833
Outlet Communications Inc.		Providence	401-455-9200	4833
Providence Energy Corp.		Providence	401-272-9191	4923
Providence Gas Co.		Providence	401-272-5040	4923
Valley Resources Inc.		Cumberland	401-333-1595	4923
Victoria Creations Inc.		Warwick	401-467-7150	3961
Washington Trust Bancorp Inc.		Westerly	401-348-1200	6712

ized pre-employment and on-the-job worker training. The Division may also assist the company in applicant recruiting and screening. Any company currently located in Rhode Island or relocating to the state may qualify.

Job Training Partnership Act. This program operates with funding from the U.S. Department of Labor. It provides job training and other employment related services.

State Offices

Real estate: Business Regulations Department, Robert J. Janes, Director, 233 Richmond Street, Providence, RI 02903. 401-277-2246

Chamber of commerce: (No State Chamber of Commerce)

Economic development: Department of Economic Development, Henry Fazzano, Exec Director, 7 Jackson Walkway, Providence, RI 02903. 401-277-2601

Department of Economic Development, Financial Services Division, Virgil A. Nolan, Director, 7 Jackson Walkway, Providence, RI 02903. 401-277-2601

Department of Economic Development, Enterprise Zones Office, Jerome Lessuck, Associate Director for Small Business, 7 Jackson Walkway, Providence, RI 02903. 401-277-2601

Small Business Development Center, Douglas Jobling, State Director, Bryant College, Douglas Pike, Route 7, Smithfield, RI 02917. 401-232-6111

Rhode Island Partnership for Science and Technology, Bruce Lang, Director, 7 Jackson Walkway, Providence, RI 02903. 401-277-2601

Environmental affairs: Environmental Management Department, Robert L. Bendick, Jr., Director, 9 Hayes Street, Providence, RI 02908. 401-277-2771

Labor: Labor Department, Bernard Singleton, Director, 220 Elmwood Ave., Providence, RI 02907. 401-457-1800

Unemployment: Employment Security Department, Benifits Division, Thomas Morrissey, Administrator, 24 Mason Street, Providence, RI 02903. 401-277-3649

Worker's compensation: Workers Compensation Department, Occupational Safety Division, Jacqueline Cugini, Administrator, 610 Mantun Ave., Providence, RI 02909. 401-272-0700

Occupational safety and health: Labor Department, Bernard Singleton, Director, 220 Elmwood Ave., Providence, RI 02907. 401-457-1829

Secretary of state: Secretary of State, Kathleen S. Connell, Secretary of State, Room 217 State House, Providence, RI 02903. 401-277-2357

Taxation and revenue: Taxation Office, R. Gary Clark, Assoc Director, 289 Promenade Street, Providence, RI 02908. 401-277-3050

Designated Zones for Economic Development

Enterprise Zones

Enacted in: 1991

No. of established zones: 0, New legislation enacted in June 1991.

Foreign Trade Zones

Foreign Trade Zone No. 105, Providence and North Kingstown, Rhode Island, Grantee: Rhode Island Department of Economic Dev., Fred Santiniello, 7 Jackson Walkway, Providence, RI 02903, 401-277-3134

Labor Unions

Food and Commercial Workers International Union, United (AFL-CIO)

Plumbing and Pipe Fitting Industry of The United States and Canada, United Association of, Journeymen and Apprentices of the (AFL-CIO)

Teachers, American Federation of (AFL-CIO)

Universities with Ph.D. Programs

Brown University, Providence

Providence College, Providence

University of Rhode Island, Kingston

PROVIDENCE-PAWTUCKET-WOONSOCKET, RI (NECMA)

Geographic Profile

Land Area

940.9 square miles

Counties and Parishes

Bristol

Kent (part)

Newport (part)

Pawtucket

Providence (part)

Washington (part)

Massachusetts:

Bristol (part)

Norfolk (part)

Worcester (part)

Rhode Island:

Providence (part)

Additional Cities/Towns within Area

Bristol County:

Barrington

Bristol

Warren

Kent County:

Coventry

East Greenwich

Warwick

West Warwick

Newport County:

Jamestown

Providence County:

Cranston

East Providence

Foster

Glocester

Johnston

North Providence

Scituate

Washington County:

Exeter

Narragansett

North Kingstown

Richmond

South Kingstown

Pawtucket

Providence County:

Burrillville

Central Falls

Cumberland

Lincoln

North Smithfield
Pawtucket
Smithfield
Woonsocket
Bristol County:
   Rehoboth
   Seekonk
Norfolk County:
   Plainville
Worcester County:
   Blackstone
   Millville

Ranking Highlights

209 *out of 319 in total* **land area**
235 *out of 319 in* **population growth,** *1970–1990*
N/A *out of 310 in having the lowest* **unemployment** *rate*
N/A *out of 310 in size of* **labor force**
128 *out of 318 in the percentage of* **college graduates**
 75 *out of 292 in per capita personal* **income**
 25 *out of 319 in number of* **manufacturing establishments**
 68 *out of 318 in* **physicians** *per 1000 people*
234 *out of 318 in* **hospital beds** *per 1000 people*
 91 *out of 267 in fewest* **crimes** *per 1000 people*
107 *out of 266 in fewest* **violent crimes** *per 1000 people*
172 *out of 319 in per capita* **federal funds and grants**

Quality of Life Indexes (Rate per 1000 population)

Crime rate in 1991:   53.2
Violent crime rate in 1991:   5.1
Physicians rate in 1992:   2.49
Hospital bed rate in 1991:   3.08

ACCRA Cost of Living Indexes

(First quarter 1993, average = 100)
Composite index: N/A
Utilities index: N/A
Housing index: N/A

Overview

Providence is the state capital and the largest city in Rhode Island. A relaxed and cosmopolitan city, Providence was ranked by *Newsweek* magazine in 1989 as one of the ten growing "hot cities" in the United States, combining good jobs and affordable housing with livability and lack of pretense.

Providence is a major industrial, commercial, and financial center for New England with an economy based on manufacturing and service enterprises. The city is a major supplier of jewelry and silverware to the United States and Europe. Providence is home to four multibillion-dollar financial concerns and many smaller ones. Tourism and conventions are emerging industries. As the capital of Rhode Island, Providence supports a number of government-related jobs.

Items and goods produced in the area include jewelry, sil-

verware, and related products; electrical equipment, textiles, transportation equipment, fabricated metals, rubber and plastic goods, machinery, instruments, and primary metals.

The new Rhode Island Convention Center, scheduled for completion in December 1993, offers a total of 365,000 square feet, with one hundred thousand square feet of exhibit space, a twenty thousand square foot ballroom, and an additional seventeen thousand square feet of meeting space.

Excellent transportation facilities, including the Port of Providence, New England's second largest deepwater port and a Foreign Trade Zone, make Providence a major industrial center. The principal waterborne commodities handled at the port are petroleum products, cement, scrap metal, lumber, automobiles, and conventional and containerized general cargo. Theodore Francis Green State Airport handled twenty-one million tons of cargo in 1988 and is one of the fastest-growing medium-hub airports in the country. Direct trucking service is available to every state, Mexico, and most of Canada on a multimillion-dollar highway system. Daily rail service to Rhode Island industrial sites is provided by the Providence & Worcester Railroad, which allows access to the entire United States and Canadian rail systems. In 1991 the Providence & Worcester Railroad Company announced plans to build a rail–ship terminal in East Providence to receive overseas shipments.

Population (1990)

Total Population and Growth Rate

1990: 916,270
1980: 865,771
1970: 855,495
Growth rate 1970–1990: 7%

Race and Hispanic Origin

White: 91.6%
Black: 3.7%
Asian/Pacific Islander: 1.9%
Native American: 0.4%
Hispanic origin: 4.6%
White not Hispanic: 89.4%

Age

Ages 18 to 20: 5.7%
Ages 21 to 24: 6.6%
Ages 25 to 44: 33.1%
Ages 45 to 54: 10%
Ages 55 to 59: 4.3%
Ages 60 to 64: 4.8%
Ages 65 plus: 15.4%

Educational Attainment (1990)

Percent having completed high school: 71.8%
Percent having completed college: 20.5%
Elementary and high school enrollment: 142,000

Federal Funds and Grants Received
Total received in 1989: $2,731,900,000
Funds received per capita: $3,009

Civilian Labor Force
1993 (April):	N/A
1992 average:	N/A
1991 average:	469,800
1990 average:	471,400

Unemployment
1993 (April):	N/A
1992 average:	N/A
1991 average:	8.6%
1990 average:	6.8%

Average Annual Pay
1988: $20,089
1987: $18,696
1985: $16,709

Per Capita Personal Income
1991: $19,088
1990: $18,618
1989: $17,934

Business Climate (1987)
Manufacturing
Number of establishments in 1987: 2,791
Shipments in 1987 ($1,000): $8,611,000
Employees in 1987: 106,000
Change in employment, 1982 to 1987: -3.4%
Average annual pay for manufacturing work in 1989: $22,562
Average annual pay for production work in 1987: $16,155

Wholesale Trade
Number of establishments in 1987: 1,644
Total sales in 1987 ($1,000): $5,903,200
Change in sales, 1982 to 1987: 20.6%

Retail Trade
Number of establishments in 1987: 5,947
Total sales in 1987 ($1,000): $5,903,200
Retail sales per household in 1987: $17,176
Average annual pay in 1989: $12,460

Service Industry
Selected receipts in 1987 ($1,000): $2,289,900
Average annual pay in 1989: $19,401

Office Real Estate (1992)
Office space inventory: 5,971,565 square feet
Average class A Central Business District rental range per sq. ft: $17.41

Vacancy Rates
All areas: 20.5%

Vacancy Rates in Central Business District
Class A space: 17.0%
Class B space: N/A

Vacancy Rates Outside Central Business District
Class A space: 23.2%
Class B space: N/A

Housing
Total number of units in 1990: 398,581
Occupied units in 1990: 369,262
Owner-occupied units in 1990: 60.2%
1993 ACCRA average cost: N/A
1993 ACCRA average rent for an apartment: N/A

Chamber of Commerce
Greater Providence Chamber of Commerce, James G. Hagan, President, 30 Exchange Terrace, Providence, RI 02903. 401-231-6010

Economic Development Office
Blackstone Valley Chamber of Commerce, William J. Wood, President, 42 Park Pl., PO Box 306, Pawtucket, RI 02862. 401-722-3400

Economic Development Organizations
Department of Planning & Development, City of Pawtucket, Michael D. Cassidy, Director, 200 Main St., Pawtucket, RI 02860-4119. 401-724-5200, FAX 401-728-6637

Bristol Economic Development Commission, Gerhard G. Oswald, Director, 10 Court St., Bristol, RI 02809. 401-253-7004, FAX 401-253-1570

City of Cranston, Office of Economic Development, Kathleen Cevoli, Director, 1070 Cranston St., Cranston, RI 02910. 401-461-1000

East Providence Economic Development Commission, Jeanne Boyle, Director of Planning, 145 Taunton Ave., City Hall, East Providence, RI 02914. 401-434-3311

Lincoln Industrial Development Commission, Burton Stallwood, Chairman, 100 Old River Rd., Lincoln, RI 02865. 401-333-1100, FAX 401-333-3648

City of Pawtucket, Department of Planning and Redevelopment, Michael D. Cassidy, Director, 200 Main St., Pawtucket, RI 02860-4119. 401-724-5200, FAX 401-726-6237

City of Warwick Department of Economic Development, L. Vincent Murray, Director, Warwick City Hall, 3275 Post Rd., Warwick, RI 02886. 800-333-9035, 401-738-2000, FAX 401-738-6639

West Warwick Development Commission, James Chaput, 1170 Main St., West Warwick, RI 02893. 401-822-9215

Major Businesses

Company	SIC	Telephone
Allendale Mutual Insurance Co.	6331	(401) 275-3000
Almacs Inc.	5411	(401) 438-2700
Avco Corp.	3724	(401) 421-2800
Blue Cross & Blue Shield or Rhode Island	6324	(401) 272-8500
Brooks Drug Inc.	5912	(401) 724-9500
Brown John, Inc.	3559	(401) 884-9920

Major Businesses (Continued)

Company	SIC	Telephone
Carol Cable Co. Inc.	3357	(401) 728-7000
Citizens Financial Group	6036	(401) 456-7000
Citizens Savings Bank	6036	(401) 456-7000
Cookson America Inc.	3341	(401) 521-1000
Cranston Print Works Co.	2261	(401) 943-4800
Fleet National Bank	6021	(401) 278-6000
Fleet/Norstar Financial	6021	(401) 278-5800
Gilbane Building Co.	1541	(401) 456-5800
Hasbro Inc.	3944	(401) 727-5000
Leach & Garner Co.	3356	(508) 222-7400
Mark Steven Service Merchandising	5122	(401) 765-1500
Metropolitan Property	6331	(401) 827-2650
Narragansett Electric Co.	4911	(401) 941-1400
Nortek Inc.	3585	(401) 751-1600
Old Stone Corp.	6035	(401) 278-2000
Providence Journal Co.	2711	(401) 277-7000
RIHT Financial Corp.	6021	(401) 278-8000
Rhode Island Hospital	6021	(401) 278-8000
RWF Inc.	5143	(401) 333-4000
Sanctuary Holdings Ltd.	3559	(401) 884-9920
Stanley-Bostitch Inc.	3579	(401) 884-2500
Teknor Apex Co.	2821	(401) 725-8000
Textron Inc.	3724	(401) 421-2800

Colleges and Universities

Brown University, Providence
Community College of Rhode Island, Warwick
Johnson & Wales University, Providence
New England Institute of Technology, Warwick
Providence College, Providence
Rhode Island College, Providence
Rhode Island School of Design, Providence
Roger Williams College, Bristol

SOUTH CAROLINA

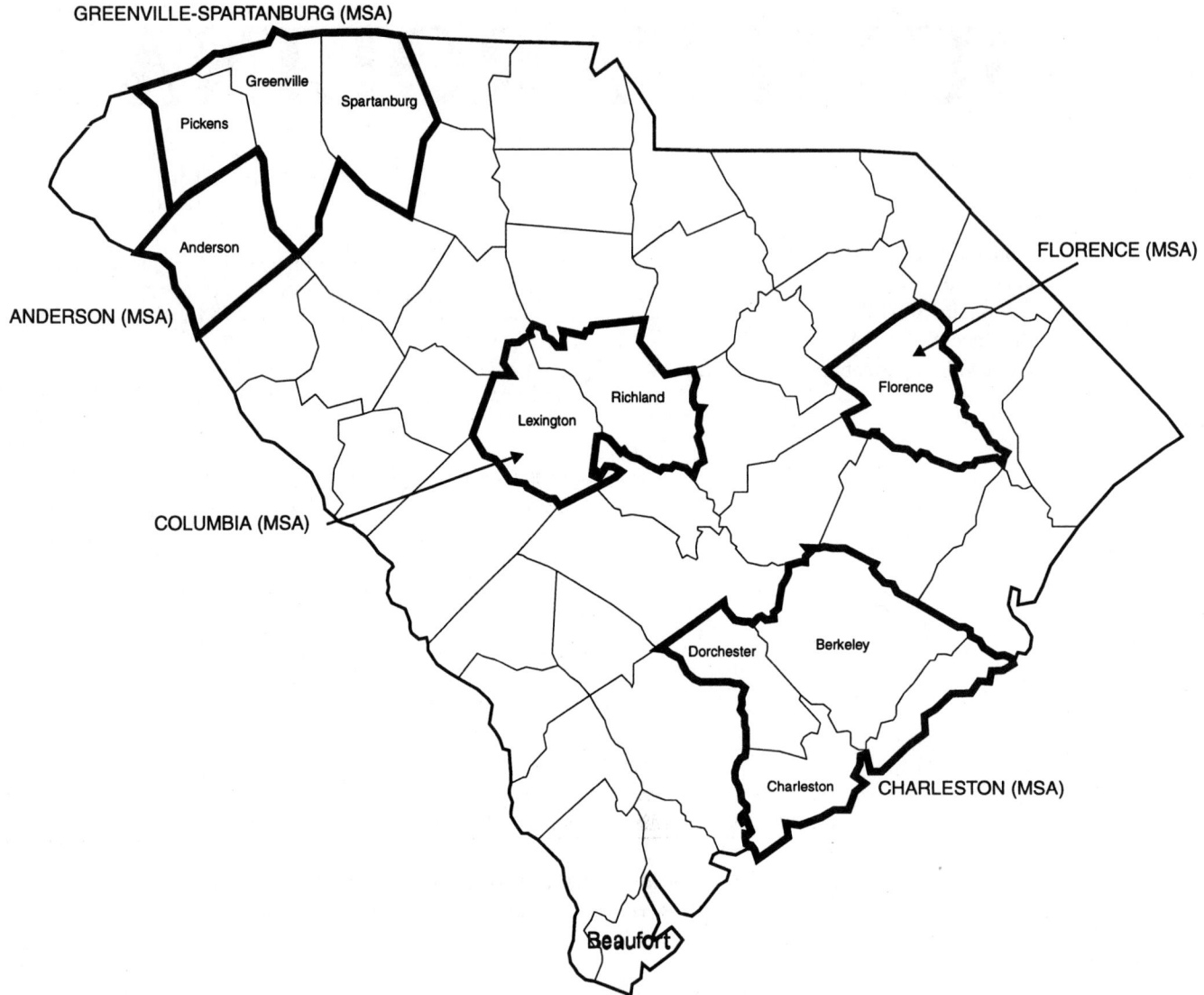

GREENVILLE-SPARTANBURG (MSA)

Greenville

Pickens

Spartanburg

FLORENCE (MSA)

ANDERSON (MSA)

Anderson

Richland

Florence

Lexington

COLUMBIA (MSA)

Dorchester

Berkeley

Charleston

CHARLESTON (MSA)

Beaufort

SOUTH CAROLINA

Population

1990: 3,485,703
1980: 3,121,820

Age

Ages 18 to 20: 185,514
Ages 21 to 24: 221,012
Ages 25 to 44: 1,114,643
Ages 45 to 54: 355,610
Ages 55 to 59: 148,762
Ages 60 to 64: 144,020
Median age: 32.0

Race and Hispanic Origin

White: 2,406,974
Black: 1,039,884
Asian/Pacific Islander: 22,382
Native American: 8,246
Hispanic origin: 30,551

Households

Total: 1,258,044
Persons per household: 2.68

Sex

Male: 1,688,510
Female: 1,798,193

Population Migration

Domestic migration: 181,000
International migration: 17,000

Projection of the Population in 1995

Total: 3,609,000
18 to 64: 2,214,000

Civilian Labor Force

1993: 1,756,900
1992: 1,763,900
1991: 1,730,900
1990: 1,680,100

Manufacturing

1995 Projection: 409,400
1992: 370,700
1991: 370,700
1990: 376,700
1989: 393,200

Services

1995 Projection: 421,100

1992: 309,200
1991: 314,200
1990: 300,900
1989: 278,800

Wholesale and Retail Trade

1995 Projection: 398,800
1992: 345,300
1991: 348,300
1990: 352,000
1989: 347,600

Unemployment Rate

1993: 6.6%
1992: 7.7%
1991: 5.7%
1990: 4.7%

Employer Unemployment Contributions

Contribution Rate

1992: 1.80%
1991: 1.82%
1990: 1.86%

Average Weekly Benefit

1992: $145.48
1991: $142.67
1990: $130.95

Gross State Product (Million $)

1989: $60,150
1988: $54,338
1987: $49,608
1979: $25,232
Growth rate, 1979 to 1989: 138.4%

Capital Expenditures of Manufacturing Industries

1990: $2,377,500,000
1989: $2,177,300,000
1988: $1,816,700,000
1987: $1,586,000,000

State Tax Rates

Individual income: Range from 2.5% ($4,200 or less) to 7% (above $10,000).
Corporate income: 5% of taxable net income.
General property: Local collections. Residential real proper-

ties taxed between 2.5% and 4% of fair market value.
General sales: 5%
Gasoline: 16¢ per gallon

Income

Median income for a 4 person family: $36,113

Personal per Capita Income
1992: $15,989
1991: $15,391
1990: $15,043

Disposable per Capita Income
1992: $14,318
1991: $13,696
1990: $13,276

Private Employment Weekly Wages

Average
1989: $352
1988: $337
1987: $337

Manufacturing
1989: $324
1988: $407
1987: $393

Services
1989: $312
1988: $297
1987: $281

Wholesale
1989: $452
1988: $437
1987: $415

Retail
1989: $206
1988: $200
1987: $192

Highway Statistics

Total Highway Miles
1990: 64,046
1989: 64,104
1988: 63,702

Federal Highway Aid
1991: $151,102,000
1990: $162,827,000
1989: $129,566,000

Electricity

Average Cost per Kilowatt Hour
1990: 5.64¢
1989: 5.64¢
1988: 5.58¢

Housing (1990)

Owner occupied units: 878,704
Median house value: $61,100
Renter occupied units: 379,340
Median rent: $276
Total vacant units: 166,111
Homeowner vacancy rate: 1.7%
Rental vacancy rate: 11.5%

State Business Incentives and Assistance

Financial and Business Assistance

Industrial Development Bonds. Established by the state legislature and governed by board of directors, the Jobs-Economic Development Authority is authorized to issue tax-exempt IDBs to promote industrial development and trade within the state. Eligible companies include manufacturers and pollution control facilities with high potential of retaining and creating jobs. Funds may be used for the acquisition of land, machinery and equipment. The Authority also issues taxable IDBs for a wide range of industrial and commercial projects not eligible for tax-exempt financing. The taxable bond proceeds may be utilized for buildings, land, equipment, working capital, and the refinancing of existing asset-based debt.

Business Loans. Established as a private corporation with banks and financial institutions as members, the Business Development Coroporation of South Carolina makes direct loans to new and expanding businesses within the state. The corporation borrows money from member institutions and charges a slightly higher rate on loans to businesses. The loans may be guaranteed by the SBA.

Education and Training

Industrial Training. Administered by the Division of Industrial and Economic Development of the State Board for Technical and Comprehensive Education, this program provides customized worker pre-employment and on-the-job training for new and expanding companies. The program also assists companies in recruiting and screening of applicants.

Job Training Partnership Act. This program operates with funding from the U.S. Department of Labor. It provides job training and other employment related services.

Multi-County Industrial Prk Incentives

In addition to the Jobs Tax Credit Program passed in 1987, the state passed a constitutional amendment in 1988 that allowed counties to enter into joint venture agreements to form multi-county industrial parks. These parks resemble enterprise zones and offer special incentives:

1) Corporate Income Tax Credits. The jobs credit is allowed for each new full-time employee job for five years beginning with years two through six after the creation of the new job: a) $1,000 per job for job increases of 10 or more in less developed counties; b) $600 per job for job increases of 18 or more in moderately developed counties; and c) $300 per job for job increases of 50 or more in developed counties.

Major Companies in the State

Company name	Fortune 500 rank	City	Telephone	SIC number
Fortune 500 Companies				
Delta Woodside Industries Inc.	439	Greenville	803-232-8301	2211
JPS Textile Group Inc.	396	Greenville	803-271-9919	2221
Sonoco Products Co.	234	Hartsville	803-383-7000	2655
Springs Industries Inc.	219	Fort Mill	803-547-1500	2392
Other Major Companies in the State				
Builders Transport Inc.		Camden	803-432-1400	4213
Clinton Mills Inc.		Columbia	803-771-4434	2211
Colonial Companies Inc.		Columbia	803-798-7000	6321
F A Computer Technologies Inc.		Greenville	803-234-0736	5045
First Federal Saving & Loan Assn. of South Carolina		Greenville	803-458-2000	6035
First Savings Bank Greenville		Greenville	803-458-2000	6035
Gates Distributing Inc.		Greenville	803-234-0736	5045
Liberty Corp.		Greenville	803-268-8283	6311
Multimedia Inc.		Greenville	803-298-4373	2711
Oneita Industries Inc.		Andrews	803-264-5225	2322
Policy Management Systems Corp.		Blythewood	803-735-4000	7372
Reeves Industries Inc. South Carolina		Spartanburg	803-576-1210	2095
Ryan's Family Steak Houses Inc.		Greer	803-879-1000	5812
Scana Corp.		Columbia	803-748-3000	4931
Seibels Bruce Group Inc.		Columbia	803-748-2000	6331
South Carolina Electric & Gas Co.		Columbia	803-748-3000	4931
South Carolina National Corp.		Columbia	803-765-3270	6712
TW Holdings Inc.		Spartanburg	803-597-8700	5812
TW Services Inc.		Spartanburg	803-597-8700	5812

2) Businesses are entitled to the greater(est) jobs tax credit allowed for the most disadvantaged county within the multi-county compact at the least job creation threshold; and, the dollar amount of the credit is increased by $500 per year for each employee during the five year tax credit window.

State Offices

Real estate: Real Estate Commission, Henry L. Jolly, Commissioner, 1201 Main Street, Suite 1500, Columbia, SC 29201. 803-737-0700

Chamber of commerce: South Carolina State Chamber of Commerce, Kenneth H. Oischlager, Exec Vice President, 1201 Main St. #1810, Columbia, SC 29201. 803-799-4601

Economic development: South Carolina State Development Board, Wayne L. Sterling, Exec Director, PO Box 927, Columbia, SC 29202. 800-868-7232, 803-737-0400, FAX 803-737-0418

South Carolina State Development Board, Economic and Industrial Development Division, Maceo Nance, Assoc. Director, PO Box 927, Columbia, SC 29202. 803-737-0400, FAX 803-737-0418

Jobs-Economic Development Authority, Elliott Franks, CEO, Suite 1750, 1201 Main Street, Columbia, SC 29201. 803-737-0079

Division of Economic Development (Enterprise Zones Office), Douglas McKay, Senior Executive, P.O. Box 11369, Columbia, SC 29211. 803-734-0420

Small Business Development Center, John M. Lenti, State Director, University of South Carolina, College of Business Administration, Columbia, SC 29208. 803-777-4907

Business Development Corporation of South Carolina, President, Suite 225, Enoree Building, 111 Executive Center Drive, Columbia, SC 29210. 803-798-4064

Environmental affairs: Health and Environmental Control Department, Michael D. Jarrett, Commissioner, 2600 Bull Street, Columbia, SC 29201. 803-734-4880

Labor: Labor Department, Virgil W. Duffie, Jr., Commissioner, PO Box 11329, Columbia, SC 29211-1329. 803-734-9594

Unemployment: Employment Security Commission, Unemployment Compensation Division, R. Michael Baker,

Administrator, PO Box 995, Columbia, SC 29202. 803-737-2787

Worker's compensation: Workers' Compensation Commission, Michael Grant LeFever, Exec Director, PO Box 1715, Columbia, SC 29202-1715. 803-737-5744

Occupational safety and health: Labor Department, Occupational Safety and Health Division, William M. Lybrand, III, Administrator, PO Box 11329, Columbia, SC 29211-1329. 803-734-9644

Secretary of state: Secretary of State, Jim Miles, Secretary of State, PO Box 11350, Columbia, SC 29211. 803-734-2155

Taxation and revenue: Tax Commission, S. Hunter Howard, Jr., Chairman, PO Box 125, Columbia, SC 29214. 803-737-9820

Designated Zones for Economic Development

Enterprise Zones

Enacted in: 1987

No. of established zones: 46

Foreign Trade Zones

Foreign Trade Zone No. 21, Dorchester County, South Carolina, Grantee: South Carolina State Ports Authority, Operator: Carolina Trade Zone, A. M. Quattlebaum, 2725 W. 5th North St., Summerville, SC 29483, 803-871-4870

Foreign Trade Zone No. 38, Spartanburg County, South Carolina, Grantee: South Carolina State Ports Authority, Operator: Carolina Trade Zone, A. M. Quattlebaum, 2725 W. 5th North St., Summerville, SC 29483, 803-871-4870

Foreign Trade Zone No. 127, West Columbia, South Carolina, Grantee/Operator: Richland-Lexington Airport District, Columbia Metropolitan Airport, Donnie Turbeville, 101 Trade Zone Drive, Suite 1A, W. Columbia, SC 29169-3911, 803-822-5013

Labor Unions

Automobile, Aerospace & Agricultural Implement Workers of America, International Union, United, (UAW AFL-CIO)

Clothing and Textile Workers Union, Amalgamated (AFL-CIO)

Electrical Workers, International Brotherhood of (AFL-CIO)

Universities with Ph.D. Programs

Bob Jones University, Greenville

Clemson University, Clemson

Medical University of South Carolina, Charleston

South Carolina State College, Orangeburg

University of South Carolina, Columbia

Sources of Additional Information

Business Incentives, South Carolina Profit from Our Ability. South Carolina State Development Board, 1991. 16p.

ANDERSON, SC (MSA)

Geographic Profile

Land Area

718.0 square miles

Counties and Parishes

Anderson

Ranking Highlights

251 *out of 319 in total* land area

105 *out of 319 in* population growth, *1970–1990*

 92 *out of 310 in having the lowest* unemployment *rate*

229 *out of 310 in size of* labor force

282 *out of 318 in the percentage of* college graduates

N/A *out of 292 in per capita personal* income

216 *out of 319 in number of* manufacturing establishments

248 *out of 318 in* physicians *per 1000 people*

225 *out of 318 in* hospital beds *per 1000 people*

 87 *out of 267 in fewest* crimes *per 1000 people*

176 *out of 266 in fewest* violent crimes *per 1000 people*

301 *out of 319 in per capita* federal funds and grants

Quality of Life Indexes (Rate per 1000 population)

Crime rate in 1991:	50.8
Violent crime rate in 1991:	7.6
Physicians rate in 1992:	1.4
Hospital bed rate in 1991:	3.14

ACCRA Cost of Living Indexes

(First quarter 1993, average = 100)

Composite index:	99.5
Utilities index:	108.8
Housing index:	100.1

Population (1990)

Total Population and Growth Rate

1990: 145,196

1980: 133,235

1970: 105,474

Growth rate 1970–1990: 38%

Race and Hispanic Origin

White: 82.9%

Black: 16.6%

Asian/Pacific Islander: 0.2%

Native American: 0.1%

Hispanic origin: 0.4%

White not Hispanic: 82.7%

Age

Ages 18 to 20: 4.6%

Ages 21 to 24: 5.3%

Ages 25 to 44: 30.5%

Ages 45 to 54: 11.6%

Ages 55 to 59: 4.9%

Ages 60 to 64: 4.7%
Ages 65 plus: 13.6%

Educational Attainment (1990)
Percent having completed high school: 64.0%
Percent having completed college: 12.9%
Elementary and high school enrollment: 25,599

Federal Funds and Grants Received
Total received in 1989: $294,200,000
Funds received per capita: $2,056

Civilian Labor Force
1993 (April):   73,731
1992 average: 72,664
1991 average: 70,247
1990 average: 71,082

Unemployment
1993 (April): 5.9%
1992 average: 5.9%
1991 average: 6.6%
1990 average: 5.3%

Average Annual Pay
1988: $17,082
1987: $16,640
1985: $15,349

Per Capita Personal Income
1991: N/A
1990: N/A
1989: N/A

Business Climate (1987)
Manufacturing
Number of establishments in 1987: 204
Shipments in 1987 ($1,000): $2,026,900
Employees in 1987: 19,900
Change in employment, 1982 to 1987: -10.0%
Average annual pay for manufacturing work in 1989: $21,064
Average annual pay for production work in 1987: $17,521

Wholesale Trade
Number of establishments in 1987: 196
Total sales in 1987 ($1,000): $551,500
Change in sales, 1982 to 1987: 8.7%

Retail Trade
Number of establishments in 1987: 940
Total sales in 1987 ($1,000): $551,500
Retail sales per household in 1987: $14,804
Average annual pay in 1989: $10,137

Service Industry
Selected receipts in 1987 ($1,000): $177,400
Average annual pay in 1989: $14,921

Housing
Total number of units in 1990: 60,745

Occupied units in 1990: 55,481
Owner-occupied units in 1990: 75.2%
1993 ACCRA average cost: N/A
1993 ACCRA average rent for an apartment: N/A

Chamber of Commerce
Anderson Area Chamber of Commerce, J. Charles McFall, President, 706 E. Greenville St., PO Box 1568, Anderson, SC 29622. 803-226-3454

Economic Development Office
Anderson County Planning and Development Board, Rusty Burns, Exec. Director, 126 N. McDuffie St., Anderson, SC 29621. 803-260-4043

Major Businesses

Company	SIC	Telephone
Am-Can Transport Service	4213	(803) 226-3477
Anderson Auto Parts Co. Inc.	5013	(803) 226-1503
Anderson Memorial Hospital	8062	(803) 261-1000
First United Bancorporation	6021	(803) 224-1112
Foundry & Steel Inc.	3599	(803) 226-0381
Glamourette Fashion Mills	2253	(803) 225-6232
Hampshire Group Ltd.	2253	(803) 225-6232
Hampshire-Designers Inc.	2253	(803) 225-6232
Hayes, Ralph Motors Inc.	5511	(803) 226-1571
Kelly, R. N. Cotton Merchants	5159	(803) 224-0951
Moorehead, Ken Oil Co.	5541	(803) 226-6076
Myers, Frank Motors Inc.	5511	(803) 226-6147
Pat Huges Chevrolet Inc.	5511	(803) 369-7303
Perpetual Federal Savings	6035	(803) 225-0241
Smith's, S. S. Lumber Co., Inc.	5211	(803) 338-6363
Travelers Petroleum Inc.	5541	(803) 225-4676

Colleges and Universities
Anderson College, Anderson

CHARLESTON, SC (MSA)

Geographic Profile

Land Area

2591.8 square miles

Counties and Parishes

Berkeley

Charleston

Dorchester

Ranking Highlights

66 *out of 319 in total* **land area**

71 *out of 319 in* **population growth,** *1970–1990*

82 *out of 310 in having the lowest* **unemployment** *rate*

94 *out of 310 in size of* **labor force**

161 *out of 318 in the percentage of* **college graduates**

250 *out of 292 in per capita personal* **income**

137 *out of 319 in number of* **manufacturing establishments**

38 *out of 318 in* **physicians** *per 1000 people*

159 *out of 318 in* **hospital beds** *per 1000 people*

221 *out of 267 in fewest* **crimes** *per 1000 people*

193 *out of 266 in fewest* **violent crimes** *per 1000 people*

45 *out of 319 in per capita* **federal funds and grants**

Quality of Life Indexes (Rate per 1000 population)

Crime rate in 1991: 74.5

Violent crime rate in 1991: 9.7

Physicians rate in 1992: 2.86

Hospital bed rate in 1991: 3.86

ACCRA Cost of Living Indexes

(First quarter 1993, average = 100)

Composite index: 100.8

Utilities index: 98.5

Housing index: 101.5

Overview

Charleston is the flagship city of three South Carolina counties collectively known as the Trident. Sharing social, economic, and political ties, Charleston, Dorchester, and Berkeley counties cover 2,600 square miles of what is called the Low-Country.

The economy in the Charleston Trident area rests upon several bases. Ever since its move to the Charleston area in 1901, the military has proved to be a stabilizing economic factor. The Charleston Naval Base in North Charleston employs both military and civilian personnel, pumping a substantial sum into the Trident economy. The base is home to both surface ships and submarines, and is one of the navy's largest submarine bases. Charleston Air Force Base employs active and reserve personnel, as well as civilian workers, and also adds substantially to the Trident's economic foundation.

Tourism is another significant factor in the area's economy. The Charleston Trident Chamber of Commerce has long been interested in promoting Charleston as a place to visit, and despite wars, fires, hurricanes, and earthquakes, Charleston has preserved and restored hundreds of historic buildings that draw some 2.5 million tourists per year. More than $800 million is brought to the area each year by tourism.

The Port of Charleston, governed by a computer system that links all port services into one integrated program, is known as one of the most efficient ports in the world. More than eighty-eight shipping lines provide regular freight services to key ports on the globe, thirteen corporations operate port facilities in Charleston, and the South Carolina Ports Authority oversees four terminals for cargo. In addition, four major shipyards operate in the Trident area. Almost one hundred motor freight lines serve the Charleston Trident, delivering truckload shipments overnight to destinations within a 450-mile radius. The Norfolk-Southern, the CSX and the South Carolina Rail Road Commission also serve the Trident area.

Charleston International Airport, which is located in North Charleston, serves 1.3 million passengers annually. Four major airlines offer more than seventy national and international flights daily. Other airports in the Trident include the Charleston Executive Airport on John's Island, St. George and Summerville airports in Dorchester County, Berkeley County Airport at Moncks Corner, and the Mt. Pleasant airport.

The major approach from the north and south is U.S. Highway 17, a favorite coastal route. Interstate 26, which terminates at Charleston, approaches from the west and links with Interstate 95 running north-south. U.S. Highway 52, paralleling Interstate 26 west of Charleston, and U.S. Highway 701 both approach Charleston from the north. Interstate 526, the Mark Clark Expressway, which forms a semicircle across the region from St. John's Island in the west to east of the Cooper River, was scheduled for completion in 1992.

Population (1990)

Total Population and Growth Rate

1990: 506,875

1980: 430,346

1970: 336,036

Growth rate 1970–1990: 51%

Race and Hispanic Origin

White: 67.8%

Black: 30.2%

Asian/Pacific Islander: 1.2%

Native American: 0.3%

Hispanic origin: 1.5%

White not Hispanic: 67.0%

Age

Ages 18 to 20: 5.4%

Ages 21 to 24: 7.6%

Ages 25 to 44: 34.7%
Ages 45 to 54: 9.2%
Ages 55 to 59: 3.5%
Ages 60 to 64: 3.4%
Ages 65 plus: 8.6%

Educational Attainment (1990)

Percent having completed high school: 75.7%
Percent having completed college: 18.9%
Elementary and high school enrollment: 92,218

Federal Funds and Grants Received

Total received in 1989: $2,456,500,000
Funds received per capita: $4,809

Civilian Labor Force

1993 (April):   247,989
1992 average: 244,014
1991 average: 242,200
1990 average: 235,912

Unemployment

1993 (April):   6.5%
1992 average: 5.7%
1991 average: 4.8%
1990 average: 3.4%

Average Annual Pay

1988: $17,927
1987: $17,167
1985: $16,004

Per Capita Personal Income

1991: $15,200
1990: $14,897
1989: $12,642

Business Climate (1987)

Manufacturing

Number of establishments in 1987: 389
Shipments in 1987 ($1,000): $3,507,800
Employees in 1987: 20,300
Change in employment, 1982 to 1987: 4.6%
Average annual pay for manufacturing work in 1989: $25,013
Average annual pay for production work in 1987: $18,964

Wholesale Trade

Number of establishments in 1987: 645
Total sales in 1987 ($1,000): $2,887,600
Change in sales, 1982 to 1987: 44.4%

Retail Trade

Number of establishments in 1987: 3,015
Total sales in 1987 ($1,000): $2,887,600
Retail sales per household in 1987: $17,319
Average annual pay in 1989: $10,380

Service Industry

Selected receipts in 1987 ($1,000): $1,034,700
Average annual pay in 1989: $15,344

Office Real Estate (1992)

Office space inventory: 2,524,000 square feet
Average class A Central Business District rental range per sq. ft: $21.00

Vacancy Rates

All areas: 16.4%

Vacancy Rates in Central Business District

Class A space: 15.3%
Class B space: 12.6%

Vacancy Rates Outside Central Business District

Class A space: 13.9%
Class B space: 19.4%

Housing

Total number of units in 1990: 199,879
Occupied units in 1990: 177,668
Owner-occupied units in 1990: 62.6%
1993 ACCRA average cost: $112,683
1993 ACCRA average rent for an apartment: $547

Chamber of Commerce

Charleston Trident Chamber of Commerce, President, 81 Mary St., PO Box 975, Charleston, SC 29402. 803-577-2510

Economic Development Office

Charleston Trident Development Board, Tom Long, Vice President, 81 Mary St., PO Box 975, Charleston, SC 29402. 803-577-2510, FAX 803-723-4853

Major Businesses

Company	SIC	Telephone
American Mutual Fire Insurance	6331	(803) 571-0510
Berkeley Electric Cooperate	4911	(803) 761-8200
Bon-Secours	8062	(803) 577-1000
Burris Chemical Inc.	5169	(803) 554-7511
Cameron & Barkley Co.	5085	(803) 554-9550
Charleston Naval Shipyard	6141	(803) 797-8300
Commissioner of Public Works	4941	(803) 724-6800
Evening Post Publishing Co.	2711	(803) 577-7111
First Federal Savings & Loan	6035	(803) 724-0800
Giant Cement Co.	3241	(803) 496-7880
Giant Group Ltd.	3241	(803) 496-7880
Goer Manufacturing Co.	2541	(803) 747-5721
Granite Services, Inc.	7363	(803) 875-5800
Honda Cars of Charleston	5511	(803) 571-6910
Intertech Group Inc.	2819	(803) 744-5174
Jones Ford Inc.	5511	(803) 744-3311
Macalloy Corp.	3313	(803) 722-8355
Palmetto Ford Inc.	5511	(803) 571-3673
Pearlstine Distributors Inc.	5181	(803) 554-1022
Piggly Wiggly Carolina Co.	5141	(803) 554-9880
Public Savings Life Insurance	6311	(803) 577-9930
Reed, Gene Chevrolet Inc.	5511	(803) 747-9681

Major Businesses (Continued) (Continued)

Company	SIC	Telephone
Roper Hospital	8062	(803) 724-2900
Siebe North Inc.	3842	(803) 554-0660
South Carolina Public Service Authority	4911	(803) 761-8000
Stokes Cycle Center Inc.	5511	(803) 572-7300
Sunbelt Coca Cola Bottling	2086	(803) 875-8010
Utilities Construction Co., Inc.	1623	(803) 722-0161
Westvaco Development Corp.	2421	(803) 871-2850

Colleges and Universities

Baptist College at Charleston, Charleston

The Citadel, The Military College of South Carolina, Charleston

College of Charleston, Charleston

Johnson & Wales University at Charleston, Charleston

Medical University of South Carolina, Charleston

Nielsen Electronics Institute, Charleston

Trident Technical College, Charleston

COLUMBIA, SC (MSA)

Geographic Profile

Land Area

1457.4 square miles

Counties and Parishes

Lexington

Richland

Ranking Highlights

140 *out of 319 in total* **land area**

97 *out of 319 in* **population growth,** *1970–1990*

40 *out of 310 in having the lowest* **unemployment** *rate*

92 *out of 310 in size of* **labor force**

55 *out of 318 in the percentage of* **college graduates**

127 *out of 292 in per capita personal* **income**

124 *out of 319 in number of* **manufacturing establishments**

61 *out of 318 in* **physicians** *per 1000 people*

216 *out of 318 in* **hospital beds** *per 1000 people*

209 *out of 267 in fewest* **crimes** *per 1000 people*

247 *out of 266 in fewest* **violent crimes** *per 1000 people*

75 *out of 319 in per capita* **federal funds and grants**

Quality of Life Indexes (Rate per 1000 population)

Crime rate in 1991:	73.2
Violent crime rate in 1991:	11.5
Physicians rate in 1992:	2.52
Hospital bed rate in 1991:	3.23

ACCRA Cost of Living Indexes

(First quarter 1993, average = 100)

Composite index:	95.8
Utilities index:	96.3
Housing index:	102.2

Overview

Columbia is located halfway between New York City and Miami, Florida, and is in the geographic center of the state of South Carolina. Columbia, the capital of South Carolina, is one of America's first planned communities. The region is also the retail and medical center of central South Carolina.

Greater Columbia's retail trading has over $5.5 billion in annual retail sales and $9.0 billion in industrial/commercial purchasing power. Within 500 miles of Columbia (approximately one day's driving time) there is an estimated 64.5 million population. Industrial/commercial shipments in this radium accounts for approximately 26% of the nation. Median household Effective Buying Income (EBI) in the Columbia MSA is $25,700.

Three interstate highway systems service the Columbia region: I-20, I-26 and I-77. Two additional interstate highways, I-85 and I-95, are within 90 miles of Columbia. Two major rail networks, the Norfolk-Southern and CSX Systems, provide freight service to the region. The Columbia Metropolitan Airport is located six miles southwest of

Columbia's central business district. The airport has an air cargo terminal, the Columbia Airport Enterprise Park and Foreign Trade Zone #127. The airport terminal is undergoing a $38 million renovation. The port of Charleston, the second busiest seaport on the East Coast, is less than a two-hour drive from Columbia via I-26.

Population (1990)

Total Population and Growth Rate
1990: 453,331
1980: 409,953
1970: 322,880
Growth rate 1970–1990: 40%

Race and Hispanic Origin
White: 67.8%
Black: 30.4%
Asian/Pacific Islander: 1.1%
Native American: 0.2%
Hispanic origin: 1.3%
White not Hispanic: 67.2%

Age
Ages 18 to 20: 6%
Ages 21 to 24: 7.1%
Ages 25 to 44: 35.2%
Ages 45 to 54: 9.9%
Ages 55 to 59: 3.9%
Ages 60 to 64: 3.6%
Ages 65 plus: 9.3%

Educational Attainment (1990)
Percent having completed high school: 78.6%
Percent having completed college: 25.3%
Elementary and high school enrollment: 78,523

Federal Funds and Grants Received
Total received in 1989: $1,835,300,000
Funds received per capita: $4,021

Civilian Labor Force
1993 (April): 254,138
1992 average: 248,551
1991 average: 246,176
1990 average: 243,711

Unemployment
1993 (April): 5.6%
1992 average: 4.7%
1991 average: 4.4%
1990 average: 3.4%

Average Annual Pay
1988: $18,842
1987: $18,114
1985: $16,553

Per Capita Personal Income
1991: $17,708
1990: $17,421
1989: $16,405

Business Climate (1987)

Manufacturing
Number of establishments in 1987: 448
Shipments in 1987 ($1,000): $3,622,000
Employees in 1987: 27,000
Change in employment, 1982 to 1987: 4.2%
Average annual pay for manufacturing work in 1989: $23,607
Average annual pay for production work in 1987: $18,388

Wholesale Trade
Number of establishments in 1987: 927
Total sales in 1987 ($1,000): $3,201,600
Change in sales, 1982 to 1987: 50.8%

Retail Trade
Number of establishments in 1987: 2,792
Total sales in 1987 ($1,000): $3,201,600
Retail sales per household in 1987: $17,435
Average annual pay in 1989: $11,125

Service Industry
Selected receipts in 1987 ($1,000): $1,209,100
Average annual pay in 1989: $17,792

Office Real Estate (1992)
Office space inventory: 8,990,000 square feet
Average class A Central Business District rental range per sq. ft: $14.50

Vacancy Rates
All areas: 18.0%

Vacancy Rates in Central Business District
Class A space: 16.0%
Class B space: 18.0%

Vacancy Rates Outside Central Business District
Class A space: 18.0%
Class B space: 22.0%

Housing
Total number of units in 1990: 177,120
Occupied units in 1990: 163,223
Owner-occupied units in 1990: 65.6%
1993 ACCRA average cost: $112,400
1993 ACCRA average rent for an apartment: $545

Chamber of Commerce
Greater Columbia Chamber of Commerce, Nevin Limburg, President, 930 Richland St., Columbia, SC 29201. 803-733-1110, FAX 803-733-1149

Economic Development Office
Greater Columbia Chamber of Commerce, Economic Development Division, Mike Eads, Sr., Director, 1308 Laurel St., PO Box 1360, Columbia, SC 29202. 803-733-1140, FAX 803-733-1149

Economic Development Organizations

Palmetto Economic Development Corp., Ralph Thomas, President, 1201 Main St., Suite 1710, Columbia, SC 29201. 803-254-9211, FAX 803-771-0233

Major Businesses

Company	SIC	Telephone
Arnold, Ben Co. Inc.	5182	(803) 251-3456
AT & T Nassau Metals Corp.	3341	(803) 796-4720
Blue Cross Blue Shield of South Carolina	6324	(803) 788-3860
Central Electric Power	4911	(803) 779-4975
Citizens & Southern South Carolina Co.	6712	(803) 343-7611
Colonial Life Accident Insurance	6321	(803) 798-7000
Farm Credit Bank of Columbia	6111	(803) 799-5000
First Citizens Bank & Trust	6022	(803) 771-8700
First Ctzens BanCorp.	6712	(803) 771-8700
Hudson Jim Oldsmobile-GMC	5511	(803) 783-0110
Kahn, M. B. Construction Co.	1542	(803) 736-2950
Laidlaw Environmental Service	4953	(803) 798-2993
Lexington Medical Center	8062	(803) 791-2000
NCNB South Carolina	6022	(803) 771-2110
Owen Steel Co. Inc.	3441	(803) 251-7680
Policy Management Systems	7372	(803) 735-4000
Richland Memorial Hospital	8062	(803) 765-6512
Scana Corp.	4911	(803) 748-3000
Seibels, Bruce Group Inc.	6411	(803) 748-2000
Shakespeare Co.	3949	(803) 754-7011
South Carolina Federal Savings	6035	(803) 254-1500
South Carolina Insurance Co.	6331	(803) 748-2000
South Carolina National Bank	6021	(803) 765-3000
South Carolina National Co.	6712	(803) 765-3000
South Carolina Pipeline Co.	4923	(803) 788-3220
South Carolina Tees Inc.	5136	(803) 256-1393
South Carolina Baptist Hospital	8062	(803) 771-5010
South Carolina Electric Gas Co.	4911	(803) 748-3000
Southeastern Freight Line	4213	(803) 794-7300
Thomas & Howard Co. Inc.	5141	(803) 788-5520

Colleges and Universities

Allen University, Columbia
Benedict College, Columbia
Columbia College, Columbia
Columbia Junior College of Business, Columbia
Midlands Technical College, Columbia
Phillips Junior College of Columbia, Columbia
University of South Carolina, Columbia

FLORENCE, SC (MSA)

Geographic Profile

Land Area

799.2 square miles

Counties and Parishes

Florence

Ranking Highlights

239 *out of 319 in total* land area
148 *out of 319 in* population growth, *1970–1990*
121 *out of 310 in having the lowest* unemployment *rate*
264 *out of 310 in size of* labor force
237 *out of 318 in the percentage of* college graduates
240 *out of 292 in per capita personal* income
256 *out of 319 in number of* manufacturing establishments
134 *out of 318 in* physicians *per 1000 people*
 21 *out of 318 in* hospital beds *per 1000 people*
202 *out of 267 in fewest* crimes *per 1000 people*
243 *out of 266 in fewest* violent crimes *per 1000 people*
292 *out of 319 in per capita* federal funds and grants

Quality of Life Indexes (Rate per 1000 population)

Crime rate in 1991:	72.1
Violent crime rate in 1991:	11.0
Physicians rate in 1992:	1.91
Hospital bed rate in 1991:	6.39

ACCRA Cost of Living Indexes

(First quarter 1993, average = 100)

Composite index: 91.5
Utilities index: 102.4
Housing index: 83.8

Population (1990)

Total Population and Growth Rate

1990: 114,344
1980: 110,163
1970: 89,636
Growth rate 1970–1990: 28%

Race and Hispanic Origin

White: 60.8%
Black: 38.7%
Asian/Pacific Islander: 0.3%
Native American: 0.1%
Hispanic origin: 0.4%
White not Hispanic: 60.6%

Age

Ages 18 to 20: 4.9%
Ages 21 to 24: 5.7%
Ages 25 to 44: 31.1%
Ages 45 to 54: 10.5%
Ages 55 to 59: 4.3%

Ages 60 to 64: 4%
Ages 65 plus: 11.1%

Educational Attainment (1990)

Percent having completed high school: 64.3%
Percent having completed college: 14.8%
Elementary and high school enrollment: 23,810

Federal Funds and Grants Received

Total received in 1989: $257,900,000
Funds received per capita: $2,186

Civilian Labor Force

1993 (April):   61,902
1992 average: 60,614
1991 average: 59,375
1990 average: 57,991

Unemployment

1993 (April): 7.8%
1992 average: 6.4%
1991 average: 5.9%
1990 average: 4.5%

Average Annual Pay

1988: $17,188
1987: $16,537
1985: $15,478

Per Capita Personal Income

1991: $15,369
1990: $14,867
1989: $13,149

Business Climate (1987)

Manufacturing

Number of establishments in 1987: 143
Shipments in 1987 ($1,000): $1,205,900
Employees in 1987: 11,500
Change in employment, 1982 to 1987: -5.7%
Average annual pay for manufacturing work in 1989: $21,155
Average annual pay for production work in 1987: $16,782

Wholesale Trade

Number of establishments in 1987: 241
Total sales in 1987 ($1,000): $656,300
Change in sales, 1982 to 1987: 25.5%

Retail Trade

Number of establishments in 1987: 877
Total sales in 1987 ($1,000): $656,300
Retail sales per household in 1987: $18,255
Average annual pay in 1989: $11,031

Service Industry

Selected receipts in 1987 ($1,000): $231,600
Average annual pay in 1989: $16,846

Housing

Total number of units in 1990: 43,209

Occupied units in 1990: 40,217
Owner-occupied units in 1990: 70.5%
1993 ACCRA average cost: $95,575
1993 ACCRA average rent for an apartment: $401

Chamber of Commerce

Greater Florence Chamber of Commerce, Douglas M. Everett, President, 610 W. Palmetto St., PO Box 948, Florence, SC 29501. 803-665-0515

Economic Development Office

Florence County Economic Development Commisssion, Curtis Hoglan, Director, 181 E. Evans St., BTC 123, Florence, SC 29501. 803-664-2866, FAX 803-664-2819

Major Businesses

Company	SIC	Telephone
Bruce Hospital System	8062	(803) 664-3000
Esab Group Inc.	3548	(803) 669-4411
Florence General Hospital	8062	(803) 667-3200
Gilbert Construction Co.	1542	(803) 669-3428
Horne Ford Inc.	5511	(803) 669-2121
King Drug Co. of Florence	5122	(803) 662-0411
McCalls Inc. of Johnsonville	5075	(803) 386-3323
McLeod Regional Medical Center	8062	(803) 667-2000
Poston Packing Co. Inc.	5147	(803) 662-1376
Powers Construction Co. Inc.	1542	(803) 669-5213
Prime Rate Inc.	6153	(803) 669-0937
Rainwater Gas & Oil Co. Inc.	5541	(803) 662-1525
Tomlinson Sales Co. Inc.	5023	(803) 669-1854
Transouth Financial Corp.	6141	(803) 662-9341
Wise Construction Co., Inc.	1542	(803) 662-7521
Yarborough, Cale Enterprise	5812	(803) 667-8843
Yarborough Cale Motors	5521	(803) 669-5556

Colleges and Universities

Florence-Darlington Technical College, Florence
Francis Marion College, Florence

GREENVILLE–SPARTANBURG, SC (MSA)

Geographic Profile

Land Area

2100.0 square miles

Counties and Parishes

Greensville

Pickens

Spartanburg

Ranking Highlights

86 *out of 319 in total* **land area**

112 *out of 319 in* **population growth**, *1970–1990*

51 *out of 310 in having the lowest* **unemployment** *rate*

70 *out of 310 in size of* **labor force**

175 *out of 318 in the percentage of* **college graduates**

176 *out of 292 in per capita personal* **income**

60 *out of 319 in number of* **manufacturing establishments**

162 *out of 318 in* **physicians** *per 1000 people*

177 *out of 318 in* **hospital beds** *per 1000 people*

149 *out of 267 in fewest* **crimes** *per 1000 people*

230 *out of 266 in fewest* **violent crimes** *per 1000 people*

306 *out of 319 in per capita* **federal funds and grants**

Quality of Life Indexes (Rate per 1000 population)

Crime rate in 1991:	63.1
Violent crime rate in 1991:	10.0
Physicians rate in 1992:	1.79
Hospital bed rate in 1991:	3.62

ACCRA Cost of Living Indexes

(First quarter 1993, average = 100)

Composite index:	99.5
Utilities index:	108.8
Housing index:	100.1

Population (1990)

Total Population and Growth Rate

1990: 640,861

1980: 570,210

1970: 473,454

Growth rate 1970–1990: 35%

Race and Hispanic Origin

White: 81.6%

Black: 17.4%

Asian/Pacific Islander: 0.7%

Native American: 0.1%

Hispanic origin: 0.8%

White not Hispanic: 81.0%

Age

Ages 18 to 20: 5.8%

Ages 21 to 24: 6.5%

Ages 25 to 44: 31.7%

Ages 45 to 54: 11%

Ages 55 to 59: 4.5%

Ages 60 to 64: 4.2%

Ages 65 plus: 12.1%

Educational Attainment (1990)

Percent having completed high school: 67.7%

Percent having completed college: 18.0%

Elementary and high school enrollment: 108,082

Federal Funds and Grants Received

Total received in 1989: $1,186,400,000

Funds received per capita: $1,909

Civilian Labor Force

1993 (April): 354,592

1992 average: 349,314

1991 average: 344,748

1990 average: 342,271

Unemployment

1993 (April): 5.1%

1992 average: 5.0%

1991 average: 5.1%

1990 average: 4.0%

Average Annual Pay

1988: $19,234

1987: $18,279

1985: $16,839

Per Capita Personal Income

1991: $16,729

1990: $16,154

1989: $14,927

Business Climate (1987)

Manufacturing

Number of establishments in 1987: 1,172

Shipments in 1987 ($1,000): $10,545,500

Employees in 1987: 99,200

Change in employment, 1982 to 1987: -3.8%

Average annual pay for manufacturing work in 1989: $22,991

Average annual pay for production work in 1987: $16,920

Wholesale Trade

Number of establishments in 1987: 1,384

Total sales in 1987 ($1,000): $5,676,400

Change in sales, 1982 to 1987: 27.8%

Retail Trade

Number of establishments in 1987: 4,078

Total sales in 1987 ($1,000): $5,676,400

Retail sales per household in 1987: $16,682

Average annual pay in 1989: $11,522

Service Industry

Selected receipts in 1987 ($1,000): $1,565,200

Average annual pay in 1989: $17,627

Office Real Estate (1992)

Office space inventory: 5,870,000 square feet

Average class A Central Business District rental range per sq. ft: $17.50

Vacancy Rates

All areas: 12.8%

Vacancy Rates in Central Business District

Class A space: 9.5%

Class B space: 13.7%

Vacancy Rates Outside Central Business District

Class A space: 15.9%

Class B space: 11.8%

Housing

Total number of units in 1990: 257,437

Occupied units in 1990: 240,803

Owner-occupied units in 1990: 68.4%

1993 ACCRA average cost: $113,000

1993 ACCRA average rent for an apartment: $502

Chamber of Commerce

Greater Greenville Chamber of Commerce, Harvey A. Schmitt, President, 24 Cleveland St., PO Box 10048, Greenville, SC 29603. 803-242-1050

Economic Development Office

Spartanburg Development Association, Darrell Jennewine, President, 1004 S. Pine Street, Spartanburg, SC 29302. 803-585-1007

Economic Development Organizations

Spartanburg Development Council, Jerri Greene, Director, BTC 11, 145 N. Church St. Suite 120, Spartanurg, SC 29301. 803-591-4245

Major Businesses

Company	SIC	Telephone
Alice Manufacturing Co.	2211	(803) 859-6323
Amreal Corp.	6531	(803) 239-1000
Bi-Lo Inc.	5411	(803) 234-1600
Canal Insurance Co.	6331	(803) 242-5365
Coats & Clark, Inc.	2284	(803) 234-0331
Coats & Clarks Sales Corp.	5131	(803) 234-0331
Community Cash Stores Inc.	5411	(803) 576-0260
Cosmos Broadcasting Corp.	4833	(803) 292-4370
Delta Mills, Inc.	2211	(803) 879-6700
Delta Woodside Industries	2211	(803) 232-8301
First Federal Savings & Loan Assoc.	6035	(803) 458-2000
First Union Corp Service	6021	(803) 255-8000
Greenville Hospital System	8062	(803) 242-7984
JPS Converter & Industrial	2211	(803) 239-4800
JPS Textile Group Inc.	2211	(803) 271-9919
Kemet Electronics Corp.	3675	(803) 963-6300
Liberty Capital Advisors	6282	(803) 268-8111

Major Businesses (Continued)

Company	SIC	Telephone
Liberty Life Insurance Co.	6311	(803) 268-8111
Lockwood Greene Engineers	8711	(803) 578-2000
Mayfair Mills Inc.	2211	(803) 576-2610
Metromont Materials Corp.	3272	(803) 585-4241
Michelin Tire Corp.	3011	(803) 458-5000
Multimedia Inc.	4833	(803) 298-4373
Phillips Fibers Corp.	2282	(803) 242-6600
Piedmont Municipal Power	4911	(803) 877-9632
PYA/Monarch Inc.	5141	(803) 233-9933
Reeves Brothers Inc.	2211	(803) 576-1210
Reeves Industries Inc.	2211	(803) 576-1210
Ryan's Family Steak House	5812	(803) 879-1000
Ryobi Motor Products Corp.	3546	(803) 878-6331
Smith, J. M. Corp.	5122	(803) 582-1216
Spartan Mills	2211	(803) 574-0211
Spartanburg Regional Medical	8062	(803) 591-6000
State at Property Casulty	6331	(803) 877-3311
Suitt Construction Co., Inc.	1541	(803) 250-5000
TW Services Inc.	5812	(803) 579-1220
Woodside Mills Inc.	2211	(803) 255-4100

Colleges and Universities

Bob Jones University, Greenville

Converse College, Spartanburg

Furman University, Greenville

Greenville Technical College, Greenville

Rutledge College of Greenville, Greenville

Rutledge College of Spartanburg, Spartanburg

Spartanburg Methodist College, Spartanburg

Spartanburg Technical College, Spartanburg

University of South Carolina at Spartanburg, Spartanburg

SOUTH DAKOTA

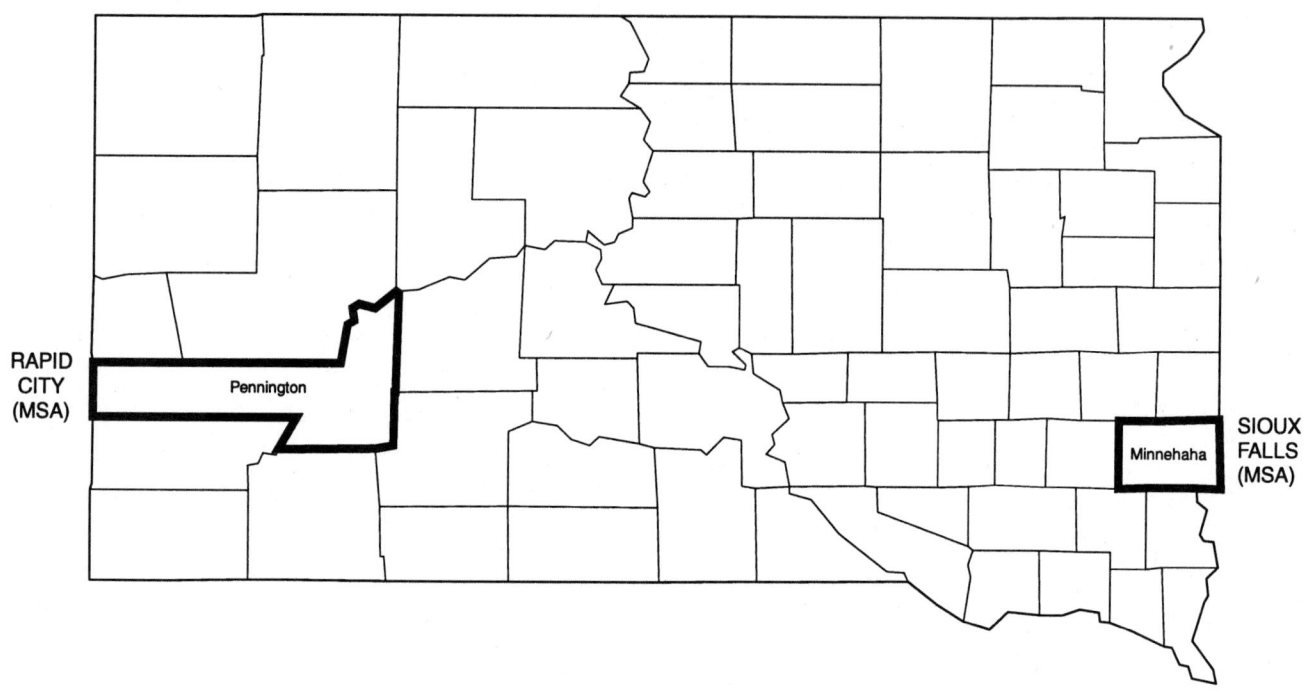

RAPID
CITY
(MSA)

Pennington

SIOUX
FALLS
(MSA)

Minnehaha

SOUTH DAKOTA

Population
1990: 696,004
1980: 690,768

Age
Ages 18 to 20: 31,014
Ages 21 to 24: 37,099
Ages 25 to 44: 204,629
Ages 45 to 54: 62,669
Ages 55 to 59: 29,218
Ages 60 to 64: 30,582
Median age: 32.5

Race and Hispanic Origin
White: 637,515
Black: 3,258
Asian/Pacific Islander: 3,123
Native American: 50,575
Hispanic origin: 5,252

Households
Total: 259,034
Persons per household: 2.59

Sex
Male: 342,498
Female: 353,506

Population Migration
Domestic migration: -38,000
International migration: 2,000

Projection of the Population in 1995
Total: 739,000
18 to 64: 433,000

Civilian Labor Force
1993: 357,100
1992: 368,200
1991: 357,800
1990: 351,300

Manufacturing
1995 Projection: 37,100
1992: 36,900
1991: 36,800
1990: 34,000
1989: 31,300

Services
1995 Projection: 103,100

1992: 78,000
1991: 74,100
1990: 71,400
1989: 67,000

Wholesale and Retail Trade
1995 Projection: 89,400
1992: 79,800
1991: 80,500
1990: 78,100
1989: 74,300

Unemployment Rate
1993: 4.3%
1992: 3.7%
1991: 3.3%
1990: 4.4%

Employer Unemployment Contributions

Contribution Rate
1992: 0.62%
1991: 0.52%
1990: 0.66%

Average Weekly Benefit
1992: $134.87
1991: $132.39
1990: $118.90

Gross State Product (Million $)
1989: $11,135
1988: $10,123
1987: $9,777
1979: $6,907
Growth rate, 1979 to 1989: 61.2%

Capital Expenditures of Manufacturing Industries
1990: $77,100,000
1989: $81,200,000
1988: $83,600,000
1987: $79,300,000

State Tax Rates
Individual income: None
Corporate income: None for manufacturing businesses.
General property: Local collections. Rates fixed locally, based on true and full value of propety.

General sales: 4%
Gasoline: 18¢ per gallon

Income

Median income for a 4 person family: $32,829

Personal per Capita Income
1992: $16,558
1991: $16,095
1990: $15,566

Disposable per Capita Income
1992: $15,082
1991: $14,644
1990: $14,081

Private Employment Weekly Wages

Average
1989: $292
1988: $286
1987: $286

Manufacturing
1989: $277
1988: $349
1987: $341

Services
1989: $272
1988: $263
1987: $253

Wholesale
1989: $364
1988: $353
1987: $339

Retail
1989: $178
1988: $174
1987: $170

Highway Statistics

Total Highway Miles
1990: 74,696
1989: 73,378
1988: 73,420

Federal Highway Aid
1991: $78,150,000
1990: $78,302,000
1989: $80,480,000

Electricity

Average Cost per Kilowatt Hour
1990: 6.06¢
1989: 6.04¢
1988: 5.52¢

Housing (1990)

Owner occupied units: 171,161
Median house value: $45,200

Renter occupied units: 87,873
Median rent: $242
Total vacant units: 33,402
Homeowner vacancy rate: 1.8%
Rental vacancy rate: 7.3%

State Business Incentives and Assistance

Financial and Business Assistance

Revolving Economic Development and Initiative Fund (REDI Fund). This program is designed to provide low interest revolving loans to businesses for the creation of primary jobs, capital investment and the diversification of South Dakota's economy. The REDI Fund may provide up to 45% of the total project cost and requires the applicant to secure the matching funds before applying for the fund, including a 10% minimum equity contribution. Business located in an enterprise zone may petition for loan participation of up to 75% of the total project costs. Interest rates have been initially set at 3%. The loans are amortized over a period of time, up to 20 years, with a balloon after five years. Costs eligible for participation include: the purchase of land and the associated site improvements; construction, acquisition, or renovation of buildings; fees, services and other costs associated with construction; the purchase and installation of machinery and equipment; trade receivables; inventory; and other working capital needs.

Economic Development Finance Authority. This program allows enterprises to pool development bonds for the purpose of machinery and equipment purchase, of construction and any site, structure, facility, service or utility for the storage, distribution or manufacturing of products. Working capital, refinancing and venture capital are not eligible project costs. Generally, the Authority will not consider loan requests for enterprises for amounts less that $300,000 and will not pool projects unless the pool volume is $1 million or more. The maximum term of the loan may not exceed the useful life of the assets purchased with the loan proceeds or 20 years, whichever is less. The loan amount, minus the amount required to be deposited into the Debt Service Reserve Account, may not exceed 80% of the appraised fair market value of the mortgaged property as improved, or 75% of the appraised fair market value of machinery and equipment.

Community Development Block Grant Community Projects Account. With funds provided by the U.S. Department of Housing and Urban Development, this program provides grants to units of general local governments in non-metropolitan areas to fund projects which benefit low and moderate income persons. Each unit of government may apply for one grant for the unit itself and one on behalf of an ineligible applicant such as an area development corporation, rural water system, sanitary district or other legally organized entity. A minimum local share match of 40% of the project cost will be required.

Community Development Block Grant Special Projects Account. This account is used to provide grants to units of local government allowing them to take advantage of an unexpected opportunity that would be lost.

SBA 504 Loan Program. This program offers subordinated mortgage financing to small businesses with less than $6 million net worth and averaged net profits of less than $2 million during the previous two years. The loans are available for fixed asset purchases of land, building, and equipment with a useful life of 10 years or more. No working capital, inventory, venture capital or refinancing is allowed. This program has a 50-40-10 structure where 50% of the project is financed by a regulated lender. 40% (up to $500,000) is provided by the South Dakota Development Corporation which sells debentures guaranteed by SBA. 10% is provided by the borrower.

Industrial Park Road Financing. This program is administered by the State Department of Transportation and provides funding for road construction in an industrial park. The DOT has a maximum expenditure authority of $500,000 per year for construction of access roads dedicated to public use.

Industrial Revenue Bonds. Industrial revenue bonds may be issued by any municipality, county or sanitary district to stimulate and develop the general economic welfare and prosperity of the state; assist in the furtherance of post secondary vocational-technical education; and promote the health and welfare of all users of health services and, in particular, the domestic well-being of the elderly and the handicapped. Promotion of the general economic welfare and prosperity of the state may be accomplished through an issuance of bonds to encourage and/or assist in the location of a new business or to assist in the expansion of an existing business.

Community Service Block Grant. This program is an anti-poverty block grant program. Municipalities must apply to the Office of the Governor to be considered under the state cap of $200 million. Funds are to be channeled towards those services and activities that will have an impact on the causes of poverty. This includes setting up a revolving loan fund to assist small businesses to assist low-income people to secure and retain employment.

Industrial Development Grant. This program allows public bodies and non-profit organizations serving rural areas to secure grants of up to $500,000. The grant funds may be used to finance and develop small and emerging private business enterprises in rural areas.

Economic Development Administration. This office is to provide assistance to economically distressed areas in order to alleviate conditions of substantial and persistent unemployment and underemployment and to establish stable and diversified economies. Grants may be awarded for such public facilities as water and sewer systems, access roads to industrial parks or areas, port facilities, railroad sidings and spurs, vocational schools, flood control projects and site improvements for industrial parks.

Farmers Home Administration Guaranteed Business and Industrial Loans. This program is designed to create and maintain employment and to improve the economic and environmental climate in rural communities. The FmHA may guarantee up to 90% of quality loans to businesses and industries to benefit rural areas.

Education and Training

Job Training Partnership Act. This program operates with funding from the U.S. Department of Labor. It provides job training and other employment related services.

State Offices

Real estate: Real Estate Commission, Jack Burchill, Secretary-Treasurer, Sahr Building, Suite 212, Pierre, SD 57501. 605-773-5032

Chamber of commerce: Industry & Commerce Association of South Dakota, Julie M. Johnson, President, PO Box 190, Pierre, SD 57501. 605-224-6161, FAX 605-224-6163

Economic development: Governor's Office of Economic Development, Darrell Butterwick, Commissioner, 711 Wells Ave., Capitol Lake Plaza, Pierre, SD 57501. 605-773-5032 or 800-872-6190

Governor's Office of Economic Development, Export, Trade and Marketing Division, Director, 711 Wells Ave., Capitol Lake Plaza, Pierre, SD 57501. 605-773-5735 or 800-872-6190

Governor's Development Board, Paul S. Ness, 1213 N. 3rd St., Aberdeen, SD, 57401. 605-229-3156

Department of Commerce, Economic Development Administration, Director, Federal Bldg., Pierre, SD 57501. 605-224-8280

Small Business Development Center, Donald Greenfield, State Director, School of Business, University of South Dakota, 414 East Clark Street, Vermillion, SD 57069. 605-677-5272

Small Business Development Center, Lynn Eichler, Director, 105 S. Euclid, Pierre, SD 57501. 605-773-5941

Procurement Technical Assistance Center, Director, Business Research Bureau, School of Business, University of South Dakota, 414 East Clark Street, Vermillion, SD 57069. 605-677-5287

U.S. Farmers Home Administration, Marvis Hogen, State Director, 200 4th Street SW, Huron, SD 57350. 605-353-1430

Sioux Falls. Forward Sioux Falls, Director, 315 S. Phillips Ave., Sioux Falls, SD 57102.

Enterprise Development Center, Francis McGowan, Director, Dakota State College, Madison, SD 57042. 605-256-5555

Environmental affairs: Dept. of Water and Natural Resources, Robert Roberts, Secretary, Joe Foss Bldg., 523 East Capitol, Pierre, SD 57501. 605-773-3151

Major Companies in the State

Company name	Fortune 500 rank	City	Telephone	SIC number
Fortune 500 Companies				
Gateway 2000	331	Sioux City	605-232-2000	5734
Other Major Companies in the State				
Black Hills Corp.		Rapid City	605-348-1700	4911
Concorde Holdings Corp.		Rapid City	605-342-7224	6799
Creek Gold Corp.		Rapid City	605-342-7265	1041
Dacotah Bank Holding Co.		Aberdeen	605-225-4850	6712
Dakota Bancorp Inc.		Watertown	605-886-6966	6712
Evro Financial Corp.		Rapid City	605-348-9187	6552
Northwestern Public Service Co.		Huron	605-352-8411	4931
Raven Industries Inc.		Sioux Falls	605-336-2750	3081

Labor: Labor Department, Peter deHueck, Secretary, Statehouse, Pierre, SD 57501. 605-773-3101

Unemployment: Labor Department, Unemployment Insurance Division, Donald Kattke, Director, PO Box 4730, 420 South Roosevelt, Aberdeen, SD 57402-4730. 605-622-2452

Worker's compensation: Labor Department, Labor & Management Division, Bill Enberg, Director, Kneip Bldg., 700 Governors Drive, Pierre, SD 57501-2277. 605-773-3681

Occupational safety and health: None

Secretary of state: Office of the Secretary of State, Joyce Hazeltine, Secretary of State, Statehouse, Pierre, SD 57501. 605-773-3537

Taxation and revenue: Dept. of Revenue, Ron Schreiner, Secretary of Revenue, Kneip Bldg., 700 Governors Drive, Pierre, SD 57501-2276. 605-773-3311

Designated Zones for Economic Development

Enterprise Zones
No program.

Foreign Trade Zones
None

Labor Unions
Food and Commercial Workers International Union, United (AFL-CIO)

National Education Association

State, County and Municipal Employees, American Federation of (AFL-CIO)

Universities with Ph.D. Programs
South Dakota School of Mines and Technology, Rapid City

South Dakota State University, Brookings

University of South Dakota, Vermillion

Sources of Additional Information
Economic Development Programs, South Dakota Programs Available to Assist Businesses and Communities Help

Themselves. Governor's Office of Economic Development, November 1990. 82p.

RAPID CITY, SD (MSA)

Geographic Profile

Land Area
2776.4 square miles

Counties and Parishes
Pennington

Ranking Highlights

- 56 *out of 319 in total* **land area**
- 108 *out of 319 in* **population growth,** *1970–1990*
- 6 *out of 310 in having the lowest* **unemployment** *rate*
- 302 *out of 310 in size of* **labor force**
- 114 *out of 318 in the percentage of* **college graduates**
- 208 *out of 292 in per capita personal* **income**
- 292 *out of 319 in number of* **manufacturing establishments**
- 132 *out of 318 in* **physicians** *per 1000 people*
- 166 *out of 318 in* **hospital beds** *per 1000 people*
- 136 *out of 267 in fewest* **crimes** *per 1000 people*
- 101 *out of 266 in fewest* **violent crimes** *per 1000 people*
- 55 *out of 319 in per capita* **federal funds and grants**

Quality of Life Indexes (Rate per 1000 population)

Crime rate in 1991:	60.9
Violent crime rate in 1991:	4.9
Physicians rate in 1992:	1.92
Hospital bed rate in 1991:	3.75

ACCRA Cost of Living Indexes
(First quarter 1993, average = 100)

Composite index:	N/A
Utilities index:	N/A
Housing index:	N/A

Overview

Agriculture, tourism, and Ellsworth Air Force Base are the major factors in Rapid City's economy. The area is also known for the manufacture of high–value, low–bulk items that can be swiftly shipped to market or assembly centers in other parts of the nation. Agriculture, and all that goes with it, is the number one industry in South Dakota, and Rapid City is the regional trade center for farm–ranch activity in the southwest part of the state and neighboring counties in Montana, Wyoming, and Nebraska. Cattle and sheep production dominate the agricultural scene, as well as processing and packing of meat and meat byproducts, but the cultivation of small grains is also important. Services offered to area farmers and ranchers include selling of new and used farm equipment, spare parts and repairs, and flour milling.

The South Dakota Cement Plant, a state–owned facility, is equipped with high capacity, environmentally sound equipment to produce high–quality cement for multi-state distribution. Other important industrial and employment institutions include several large construction companies, rock quarries, steel fabrication firms, and trucking firms. Several light industries and services located in the city include manufacturing of computer parts, printing, Indian crafts, and headquarters for insurance companies and other businesses. Regional or headquarters facilities of many state and federal offices also operate in the city.

Each year the $69.8 million payroll for workers at Ellsworth Air Force Base, the largest employer in the state, boosts the local economy. Community leaders are working together to counter the loss of military personnel as the federal government implements its military reductions.

Within half a day's drive of Rapid City are five of the country's most famous national park areas: Mount Rushmore National Memorial, Devil's Tower National Monument, Badlands National Park, Jewel Cave National Monument, and Wind Cave National Park. With its variety of restaurants, more than twenty–seven hundred hotel/motel rooms and many modern campgrounds, Rapid City benefits from a large annual tourist trade.

Rapid City is served by the Chicago Northwestern Railroad and offers piggyback service with daily switching service. Nearly forty motor freight carriers, as well as terminals, are located in Rapid City. Parcel service is provided by United Parcel. The new Rapid City Regional Airport, 10 miles east of the city, is the third most active airport in the Northern Rockies. It offers nearly fifty flights a day to and from Sioux Falls, Minneapolis, Minnesota, Salt Lake City, Utah, Chicago, Illinois, and Denver, Colorado. The airport had more than three hundred thousand boardings and departures in 1991. Three fixed–base operators provide charter service. Several wide, modern highways intersect in the city including Interstate 90, which runs east and west; State Highway 79, which runs north and south; U.S. Highway 14, which cuts through the city on an angle running northwest to southeast; and U.S. Highway 16, which approaches the city center from the south. Six highways lead from the north, west, and south into the canyons and mountains. Bus service is provided by Jack Rabbit Lines, Stagecoach West, and Gray Line of the Black Hills.

Population (1990)

Total Population and Growth Rate

1990: 81,343
1980: 70,361
1970: 59,349
Growth rate 1970–1990: 37%

Race and Hispanic Origin

White: 89.5%
Black: 1.6%
Asian/Pacific Islander: 1.1%
Native American: 7.2%
Hispanic origin: 2.2%
White not Hispanic: 88.4%

Age
Ages 18 to 20: 4.4%
Ages 21 to 24: 6.6%
Ages 25 to 44: 33.3%
Ages 45 to 54: 8.9%
Ages 55 to 59: 3.9%
Ages 60 to 64: 3.7%
Ages 65 plus: 10%

Educational Attainment (1990)
Percent having completed high school: 84.8%
Percent having completed college: 21.2%
Elementary and high school enrollment: 14,776

Federal Funds and Grants Received
Total received in 1989: $372,100,000
Funds received per capita: $4,537

Civilian Labor Force
1993 (April):   41,021
1992 average: 40,944
1991 average: 40,965
1990 average: 40,347

Unemployment
1993 (April):   3.6%
1992 average: 3.2%
1991 average: 3.6%
1990 average: 3.6%

Average Annual Pay
1988: $15,960
1987: $15,491
1985: $14,607

Per Capita Personal Income
1991: $16,106
1990: $15,640
1989: $14,562

Business Climate (1987)
Manufacturing
Number of establishments in 1987: 102
Shipments in 1987 ($1,000): $398,200
Employees in 1987: 3,500
Change in employment, 1982 to 1987: 12.9%
Average annual pay for manufacturing work in 1989: $18,565
Average annual pay for production work in 1987: $15,583

Wholesale Trade
Number of establishments in 1987: 167
Total sales in 1987 ($1,000): $388,200
Change in sales, 1982 to 1987: 37.6%

Retail Trade
Number of establishments in 1987: 678
Total sales in 1987 ($1,000): $388,200
Retail sales per household in 1987: $21,904
Average annual pay in 1989: $10,480

Service Industry
Selected receipts in 1987 ($1,000): $192,200
Average annual pay in 1989: $14,324

Housing
Total number of units in 1990: 33,741
Occupied units in 1990: 30,553
Owner-occupied units in 1990: 61.4%
1993 ACCRA average cost: N/A
1993 ACCRA average rent for an apartment: N/A

Chamber of Commerce
Rapid City Area Chamber of Commerce, John D. Schmit, President, 444 Mt. Rushmore Rd. N., PO Box 747, Rapid City, SD 57709. 605-343-1620

Economic Development Office
Old West Trail Foundation, David Bohling, Exec. Director, 1604 Mountain View Rd., Suite 108, PO Box 2554, Rapid City, SD 57709-2554. 605-343-7677, FAX 605-343-7678

Economic Development Organizations
Rapid City Area Economic Development Partnership, Robert De Mersseman, President, PO Box 747, Rapid City, SD 57709. 605-343-1880, FAX 605-343-1916

Major Businesses

Company	SIC	Telephone
Black Hills Corp.	4911	(605) 348-1700
Black Hills Milk Producer	5143	(605) 342-3780
Brink Electric Construction Co.	1731	(605) 342-6966
Coleman-Frizzell Inc.	3911	(605) 348-1799
First Federal Savings Bank of South Dakota	6035	(605) 394-6800
Heavy Constructors Inc.	1542	(605) 342-3152
Hills Materials Co.	1611	(605) 342-3875
Lien, Pete & Sons Inc.	3441	(605) 342-7224
McKie Ford, Inc.	5511	(605) 348-0008
MG Oil Inc.	5172	(605) 342-0527
Moyle Petroleum Co., Inc.	5541	(605) 343-1966
Northwestern Engineering Co.	1611	(605) 394-3300
Prairie States Life Insurance Co.	6311	(605) 348-1262
Rapid Chevrolet Co. Inc.	5511	(605) 343-1282
Rapid City Regional Hospital	8062	(605) 341-1000
Rapid Motors Inc.	5511	(605) 348-4500
Rushmore Electric Power Co.	4911	(605) 342-4759
Rushmore Health System, Inc.	6719	(605) 341-1000
Wyodak Resources Development	1222	(605) 348-1700

Colleges and Universities
National College, Rapid City
South Dakota School of Mines and Technology, Rapid City

SIOUX FALLS, SD (MSA)

Geographic Profile

Land Area

809.2 square miles

Counties and Parishes

Minnehaha

Ranking Highlights

233 *out of 319 in total* **land area**

127 *out of 319 in* **population growth,** *1970–1990*

2 *out of 310 in having the lowest* **unemployment** *rate*

212 *out of 310 in size of* **labor force**

112 *out of 318 in the percentage of* **college graduates**

88 *out of 292 in per capita personal* **income**

264 *out of 319 in number of* **manufacturing establishments**

19 *out of 318 in* **physicians** *per 1000 people*

9 *out of 318 in* **hospital beds** *per 1000 people*

61 *out of 267 in fewest* **crimes** *per 1000 people*

51 *out of 266 in fewest* **violent crimes** *per 1000 people*

154 *out of 319 in per capita* **federal funds and grants**

Quality of Life Indexes (Rate per 1000 population)

Crime rate in 1991:   45.0

Violent crime rate in 1991:   3.2

Physicians rate in 1992:   3.3

Hospital bed rate in 1991:   7.37

ACCRA Cost of Living Indexes

(First quarter 1993, average = 100)

Composite index: 93.2

Utilities index: 90.4

Housing index: 94.2

Overview

The Sioux Falls economy—comprised of a diversity of sectors, including finance, health care, retailing, agriculture, and wholesale distribution—continues a steady expansion. Evidence can be found in figures for new construction, which showed an increase of 150 percent between 1980 and 1992. The city is the national headquarters for the finance services divisions of several large companies including Citibank (South Dakota). The international credit card processing facility for Citibank employs 2,800 people. Credit card and financial services operations of Bank of New York, Dial Bank, and Sears Payment Systems are also located in Sioux Falls. The main offices of state and regional banks, as well as brokerage and insurance firms with nationwide connections, are based in the downtown financial district.

The medical industry figures significantly in the city's economic stability. Sioux Falls has emerged as a regional health care center, with the two major hospitals ranking among the top ten employers in the metropolitan area; private physician clinics employ more than one thousand workers. Retailing is another important sector; sales between 1982

and 1992 increased over 70 percent, and taxable sales now exceed $1.3 billion per year.

Set in a fertile agricultural region and the site of one of the world's largest stockyards, Sioux Falls has traditionally been a center for the agricultural industry: John Morrell & Company, a meat packer, is the city's largest employer, for instance, and agricultural cash receipts now top $3 billion annually. Among the agriculture-related activities are meat processing and packing, the production of dairy and bakery items, livestock feed milling, and the manufacture of farm implements and equipment. General manufacturing and granite quarries also contribute to the local economy.

Wholesale distributing remains a primary industry in Sioux Falls, which has long been a hub for the distribution of automobiles, trucks, food, fuel, oil, gasoline, machinery, plastics, and paper products. The city is served by the Chicago & Northwestern and Ellis & Eastern railroads. Thirty-eight motor freight carriers transport goods through Sioux Falls to markets throughout the United States.

The largest air facility in South Dakota, Sioux Falls Regional Airport at Joe Foss Field, is the destination for air traffic into Sioux Falls. Six commercial carriers schedule daily flights at remodeled Costello Terminal, providing direct or connecting service to most major cities in the country. Air freight tonnage out of Joe Foss Field was up more than 400 percent from 1987 to 1992.

East-west I-90, joining Boston, Massachusetts, and Seattle, Washington, and north-south I-29, connecting metropolitan Kansas City, Missouri, with Winnipeg, Canada, intersect northwest of Sioux Falls. I-229, a beltway around the eastern sector of the city, links I-90 and I-29. U.S. highways 18 and 81 also serve the area.

Population (1990)

Total Population and Growth Rate

1990: 123,809

1980: 109,435

1970: 95,209

Growth rate 1970–1990: 30%

Race and Hispanic Origin

White: 97.3%

Black: .6%

Asian/Pacific Islander: 0.6%

Native American: 1.4%

Hispanic origin: 0.5%

White not Hispanic: 97.0%

Age

Ages 18 to 20: 4.4%

Ages 21 to 24: 6.2%

Ages 25 to 44: 34.1%

Ages 45 to 54: 8.9%

Ages 55 to 59: 3.8%

Ages 60 to 64: 3.8%

Ages 65 plus: 11.6%

Educational Attainment (1990)
Percent having completed high school: 83.1%
Percent having completed college: 21.3%
Elementary and high school enrollment: 21,013

Federal Funds and Grants Received
Total received in 1989: $390,000,000
Funds received per capita: $3,108

Civilian Labor Force
1993 (April):   77,832
1992 average: 78,590
1991 average: 77,450
1990 average: 75,833

Unemployment
1993 (April):   2.2%
1992 average: 2.3%
1991 average: 2.5%
1990 average: 2.7%

Average Annual Pay
1988: $17,942
1987: $17,456
1985: $16,253

Per Capita Personal Income
1991: $18,597
1990: $17,968
1989: $16,398

Business Climate (1987)
Manufacturing
Number of establishments in 1987: 138
Shipments in 1987 ($1,000): $1,518,200
Employees in 1987: 8,900
Change in employment, 1982 to 1987: 7.2%
Average annual pay for manufacturing work in 1989: $20,445
Average annual pay for production work in 1987: $15,937

Wholesale Trade
Number of establishments in 1987: 375
Total sales in 1987 ($1,000): $1,439,800
Change in sales, 1982 to 1987: -3.3%

Retail Trade
Number of establishments in 1987: 875
Total sales in 1987 ($1,000): $1,439,800
Retail sales per household in 1987: $19,341
Average annual pay in 1989: $10,598

Service Industry
Selected receipts in 1987 ($1,000): $351,700
Average annual pay in 1989: $18,326

Housing
Total number of units in 1990: 49,780
Occupied units in 1990: 47,681
Owner-occupied units in 1990: 62.3%
1993 ACCRA average cost: $99,890

1993 ACCRA average rent for an apartment: $541

Chamber of Commerce
Sioux Falls Area Chamber of Commerce, Evan C. Nolte, Exec. Vice President, 315 S. Phillips Ave., PO Box 1425, Sioux Falls, SD 57101. 605-336-1620

Economic Development Office
Sioux Falls Development Foundation, Roger Hainje, President, 315 S. Phillips, PO Box 907, Sioux Falls, SD 57101. 800-658-3373, 605-339-0103, FAX 605-339-0055

Economic Development Organizations
Business Recruitment Council, Virginia Dettman, Chairman, 408 E. 21st St., Sioux Falls, SD 57102. 605-334-6000

Major Businesses

Company	SIC	Telephone
A. W. Corp.	2673	(605) 334-0334
Action Carrier Inc.	4213	(605) 335-5500
American Western Corp.	2673	(605) 334-0334
Austad Co.	5961	(605) 336-3135
Chris Cam Corp.	5113	(605) 336-1190
Citibank (South Dakota)	6021	(605) 331-2626
Dixie Bag Corp.	2673	(605) 334-0334
Everist, L. G., Inc.	1429	(605) 334-5000
First Bank of South Dakota	6021	(605) 339-8600
First National Bank in Sioux Falls	6021	(605) 335-5100
Home Federal Savings & Loan Association	6035	(605) 336-2470
Lewis Drugs, Inc.	5912	(605) 333-2800
Midland National Life Insurance	6311	(605) 335-5700
Missouri Basin	4911	(605) 338-4042
Norwest Bank of South Dakota	6021	(605) 339-7300
Pam Oil, Inc.	5172	(605) 336-1788
Presentation Health System	8741	(605) 331-4999
Presentation Sisters Inc.	8062	(605) 339-8000
Ramkota Inc.	7011	(605) 334-2371
Raven Industries, Inc.	3721	(605) 336-2750
Schulte, Terry Chevrolet	5511	(605) 336-1700
Sioux Falls Construction	1542	(605) 336-1640
Sioux Valley Hospital Assn.	8062	(605) 333-1000
South Dakota Medical Service	6324	(605) 336-1976
Sunshine Food Markets	5411	(605) 336-2505
Thompson Bros. Inc.	4213	(605) 334-4187
Western Bank	6022	(605) 335-5300
Western Surety Co.	6351	(605) 336-0850
Zip Feed Mills, Inc.	2048	(605) 336-3330

Colleges and Universities
Augustana College, Sioux Falls
Kilian Community College, Sioux Falls
National College-Sioux Falls Branch, Sioux Falls
Sioux Falls College, Sioux Falls

TENNESSEE

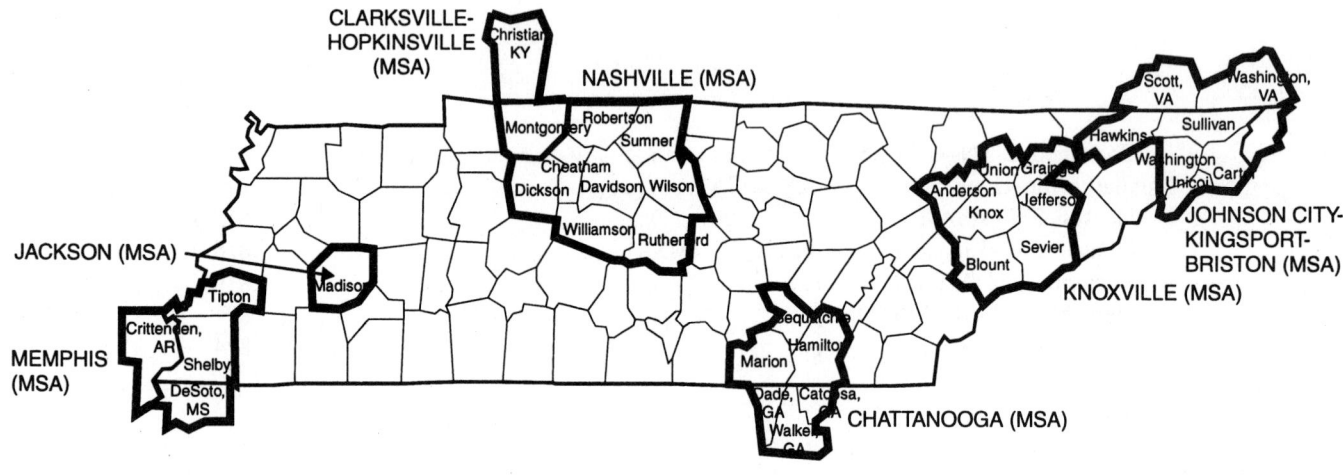

TENNESSEE

Population
1990: 4,877,185
1980: 4,591,120

Age
Ages 18 to 20: 238,948
Ages 21 to 24: 288,707
Ages 25 to 44: 1,553,309
Ages 45 to 54: 526,210
Ages 55 to 59: 220,952
Ages 60 to 64: 213,637
Median age: 33.6

Race and Hispanic Origin
White: 4,048,068
Black: 778,035
Asian/Pacific Islander: 31,839
Native American: 10,039
Hispanic origin: 32,741

Households
Total: 1,853,725
Persons per household: 2.56

Sex
Male: 2,348,928
Female: 2,528,257

Population Migration
Domestic migration: 296,000
International migration: 21,000

Projection of the Population in 1995
Total: 5,184,000
18 to 64: 3,196,000

Civilian Labor Force
1993: 2,424,500
1992: 2,428,300
1991: 2,413,700
1990: 2,359,600

Manufacturing
1995 Projection: 540,900
1992: 513,000
1991: 514,600
1990: 517,100
1989: 524,200

Services
1995 Projection: 719,000

1992: 534,600
1991: 494,000
1990: 485,700
1989: 472,200

Wholesale and Retail Trade
1995 Projection: 620,600
1992: 518,600
1991: 525,900
1990: 528,100
1989: 518,100

Unemployment Rate
1993: 7.3%
1992: 7.9%
1991: 6.6%
1990: 5.3%

Employer Unemployment Contributions
Contribution Rate
1992: 1.71%
1991: 1.60%
1990: 1.61%

Average Weekly Benefit
1992: $129.10
1991: $128.93
1990: $113.68

Gross State Product (Million $)
1989: $92,267
1988: $86,949
1987: $80,507
1979: $42,252
Growth rate, 1979 to 1989: 118.4%

Capital Expenditures of Manufacturing Industries
1990: $3,337,000,000
1989: $2,777,000,000
1988: $2,148,000,000
1987: $1,904,700,000

State Tax Rates
Individual income: None.
Corporate income: 6% of total net income.
General property: Rates fixed locally. Realty is assessed at 55% of actual value. $7,500 personal property exemption.

General sales: 5.5%
Gasoline: 20¢ per gallon

Income

Median income for a 4 person family: $34,882

Personal per Capita Income
1992: $17,341
1991: $16,478
1990: $15,869

Disposable per Capita Income
1992: $15,820
1991: $14,976
1990: $14,282

Private Employment Weekly Wages

Average
1989: $373
1988: $363
1987: $363

Manufacturing
1989: $350
1988: $417
1987: $400

Services
1989: $357
1988: $343
1987: $331

Wholesale
1989: $479
1988: $468
1987: $441

Retail
1989: $216
1988: $215
1987: $209

Highway Statistics

Total Highway Miles
1990: 84,639
1989: 84,081
1988: 83,638

Federal Highway Aid
1991: $222,018,000
1990: $249,224,000
1989: $277,036,000

Electricity

Average Cost per Kilowatt Hour
1990: 5.24¢
1989: 5.26¢
1988: 5.60¢

Housing (1990)

Owner occupied units: 1,261,118
Median house value: $58,400

Renter occupied units: 592,607
Median rent: $273
Total vacant units: 172,342
Homeowner vacancy rate: 2.1%
Rental vacancy rate: 9.6%

State Business Incentives and Assistance

Enterprise Zone Incentives

1) Job creation payments of up to $1,000 per net new employee.
2) Reimbursement of 1.33% of the purchase price of industrial machinery for use within the zone.
3) Reimbursement of 20% of the qualified business's contribution to a public school within an enterprise zone.
4) Reimbursement of sales and use taxes (local and state) for building materials bought by qualified businesses within the zone.

Financial and Business Assistance

Industrial Development Bonds. Administered by the Department of Economic and Community Development, local Industrial Development Boards are established by municipalities to issue tax-exempt IDBs. The IDBs provide low-cost financing for expansions in companies engaged in manufacturing, processing, and assembling products. Financing can also be provided for distribution facilities, ports or port facilities, and pollution control facilities. Loan proceeds may be used to acquire or construct the facilities.

Industrial Infrastructure Program. Administered by the Department of Economic and Community Development, this program makes grants and loans to local governments and businesses for infrastructure improvements and for job training. Eligible improvement projects include water systems, wastewater systems, transportation systems, site improvements, electrical and natural gas systems, and other infrastructure improvements required to support economic growth.

Education and Training

Industrial Training Service. Administered by the Industrial Training Services Division of the Department of Economic and Community Development, this program is designed to assist training of state residents for new and expanding businesses. The Department of Employment Security assists companies in recruiting, testing, and screening trainees and the Industrial Training Services Division provides basic skill training for potential employees through pre-employment training. Any new or expanding industry anticipating 25 or more new employees in a 12-month period is eligible. The Division also provides a similar on-the-job training program.

Job Training Partnership Act. This program operates with funding from the U.S. Department of Labor. It provides job training and other employment related services.

Major Companies in the State

Comapny name	Fortune 500 rank	City	Telephone	SIC number
Fortune 500 Companies				
Arcadian Corp.	496	Memphis	901-758-5200	2873
Other Major Companies in the State				
Autozone Inc.		Memphis	901-325-4600	5013
Constar International Inc.		Chattanooga	615-267-2973	3085
Dollar General Corp.		Nashville	615-386-4000	5331
Federal Express Corp.		Memphis	901-369-3600	4513
First American Corp. Tennessee		Nashville	615-748-2000	6712
First Tennessee National Corp.		Memphis	901-523-4027	6712
Gaylord Entertainment Co.		Nashville	615-871-6776	7011
Genesco Inc.		Nashville	615-367-7000	5661
HCA Hospital Corp. of America		Nashville	615-327-9551	8062
Healthtrust Inc. The Hospital Co.		Nashville	615-383-4444	8062
Hospital Corp. of America		Nashville	615-327-9551	8062
Johnston Coca Cola Bottling Group Inc.		Chattanooga	404-676-2100	2086
Promus Co., Inc.		Memphis	901-762-8600	7011
Provident Life & Accident Insurance Co.		Chattanooga	615-755-1011	6311
Provident Life Capital Corp.		Chattanooga	615-755-1011	6311
Service Merchandise Co. Inc.		Brentwood	615-660-6000	5399
Shoney's Inc.		Nashville	615-391-5201	5812
TBC Corp.		Memphis	901-363-8030	5014

State Offices

Real estate: Commerce and Insurance Department, Real Estate Commission, Bruce Lynn, 500 James Robertson Parkway, Nashville, TN 37243-0566. 615-741-2273

Chamber of commerce: (No State Chamber of Commerce)

Economic development: Tennessee Industrial Development Council, Joel Connell, President, PO Box 1704, Knoxville, TN 37901. 615-523-2999

Economic and Community Development Department, Carl Johnson, Commissioner, 320 6th Ave. North, Rachel Jackson Building, Nashville, TN 37243-0405. 615-741-1888

Economic and Community Development Department (Enterprise Zones Office), Don Waller, Director of Local Planning, 320 6th Ave. North, Rachel Jackson Building, Nashville, TN 37243-0405. 615-741-2211

Small Business Development Center, Kenneth Burns, State Director, Memphis State Univeristy, Memphis, TN 38152. 901-678-2500

Environmental affairs: Health and Environment Department, J.W. Luna, Commissioner, 313 Cordell Hull Bldg., Nashville, TN 37219. 615-741-3111

Labor: Labor Department, James R. White, Commissioner, 501 Union Bldg., Nashville, TN 37243-0655. 615-741-2582

Unemployment: Employment Security Department, Unemployment Insurance Division, Hazel Albert, Assistant Commissioner, 12th Fl., Volunteer Plaza Bldg., Nashville, TN 37245-0001. 615-741-3178

Worker's compensation: Labor Department, Worker's Compensation Division, Sue Ann Head, Administrator, 501 Union Building, Nashville, TN 37243-0655. 615-741-2395

Occupational safety and health: Labor Department, Occupational Safety Division, Robert Taylor, Administrator, 501 Union Building, Nashville, TN 37243-0655. 615-741-2793

Secretary of state: Secretary of State, Bryant Millsaps, Secretary of State, State Capitol, 1st Fl., Nashville, TN 37214. 615-741-2816

Taxation and revenue: Revenue Department, Joe B. Huddleston, Commissioner, 1200 Andrew Jackson Bldg., Nashville, TN 37242. 615-741-2461

Designated Zones for Economic Development

Enterprise Zones

Enacted in: 1984

No. of established zones: 1

North Memphis

Foreign Trade Zones

Foreign Trade Zone No. 134, Chattanooga, Tennessee, Grantee: Partners for Economic Progress, Inc., Robert

McAuley, 1001 Market Street, Chattanooga, TN 37402, 615-752-4305

Foreign Trade Zone No. 148, Knoxville, Tennessee, Grantee: Industrial Dev. Board of Blount County, Jeff Deardorff, c/o Tennessee Technology Foundation, PO Box 23184, Knoxville, TN 37933-1184, 615-694-6772

Foreign Trade Zone No. 77, Memphis, Tennessee, Grantee: The City of Memphis, Maggie Conway, Memphis & Shelby County, Division of Planning & Develop., 125 Mid-American Mall, Room 468, Memphis, TN 38103, 901-576-7107

Foreign Trade Zone No. 78, Nashville, Tennessee, Grantee: Metropolitan Nashville Port Authority, Robert Gallen, 214 Second Ave. North, Ste. 1, Nashville, TN 37201, 615-862-6029

Labor Unions

Clothing and Textile Workers Union, Amalgamated (AFL-CIO)

National Education Association

National Fraternal Order of Police

Paperworkers International Union, United (AFL-CIO)

Sheet Metal Workers' International Association (AFL-CIO)

Universities with Ph.D. Programs

East Tennessee State University, Johnson City

Memphis State University, Memphis

Middle Tennessee State University, Murfreesboro

Tennessee State University, Nashville

Tennessee Temple University, Chattanooga

University of Tennessee, Knoxville, Knoxville

University of Tennessee, Memphis, Memphis

University of The South, Sewanee

Vanderbilt University, Nashville

CHATTANOOGA, TN–GA (MSA)

Geographic Profile

Land Area
2090.6 square miles

Counties and Parishes
Georgia:
  Catoosa
  Dade
  Walker
Tennessee:
  Hamilton
  Marion
  Sequatchie

Ranking Highlights

87 *out of 319 in total* **land area**

189 *out of 319 in* **population growth,** *1970–1990*

104 *out of 310 in having the lowest* **unemployment** *rate*

104 *out of 310 in size of* **labor force**

226 *out of 318 in the percentage of* **college graduates**

156 *out of 292 in per capita personal* **income**

97 *out of 319 in number of* **manufacturing establishments**

132 *out of 318 in* **physicians** *per 1000 people*

100 *out of 318 in* **hospital beds** *per 1000 people*

154 *out of 267 in fewest* **crimes** *per 1000 people*

214 *out of 266 in fewest* **violent crimes** *per 1000 people*

127 *out of 319 in per capita* **federal funds and grants**

Quality of Life Indexes (Rate per 1000 population)

Crime rate in 1991:	64.4
Violent crime rate in 1991:	9.4
Physicians rate in 1992:	1.92
Hospital bed rate in 1991:	4.61

ACCRA Cost of Living Indexes
(First quarter 1993, average = 100)

Composite index:	91.3
Utilities index:	97.6
Housing index:	87.4

Overview

Chattanooga, the hub of a thriving economic region, is located at the crossroads of three states: Alabama, Georgia, and Tennessee. Among the city's economic advantages are abundant natural resources, a strong tourism industry, a trained labor force, and a centralized location. An extensive system of highway, air, water, and rail transportation helps make the city a major transportation and distribution center. In addition, the city has a designated Foreign Trade Zone.

One of the nation's oldest manufacturing cities, Chattanooga has 22.1 percent of its employment in that sector, which produces more than one thousand classified products.

As the city approaches the twenty-first century, it is emerging as a diversified and profitable business location with no single dominant industry.

Locally based Provident Life is a *Fortune 500* service company and Dixie Yarns is a *Fortune 500* industrial company. Other large companies with headquarters in the city include Blue Cross/Blue Shield of Tennessee, Brock Candy Company, Chattem Inc., Constart International, The Krystal Company, McKee Banking Company, North American Royalties, and Olan Mills, Inc.

The city is the headquarters for the Division of Power of the Tennessee Valley Authority (TVA), the largest utility in the United States. TVA is a federal corporation that works to develop the natural resources of the Tennessee Valley. Chattanooga is in an enviable position: both electricity and natural gas are readily available at very reasonable rates. Water supplies are also plentiful and sewage treatment has considerable excess capacity to support industrial expansion. In addition, TVA and its power distributors offer a growth credit program that provides significant savings to new commercial and industrial customers requiring a large capacity.

Chattanooga is located on the crossroads of several major U.S. highways, including Interstates 75, 24, and 59. The city is within one day's drive of nearly one-third of the major U.S. markets and population, and within 140 miles of Nashville, Atlanta, Georgia, Knoxville, Huntsville, Alabama, and Birmingham, Alabama. More than one hundred common and contract carriers with ninety-six local terminals serve the area. Chattanooga is the distribution center for the region which includes southeast Tennessee, northwest Georgia, southwest North Carolina, northeast Alabama, and parts of several neighboring states. Chattanooga remains an important port as a result of the Tennessee Valley Authority's system of locks and dams, and the Tombigbee waterway which saves days, miles, and dollars on shipments to and from ports along the Ohio and Mississippi Rivers and the Gulf of Mexico. Freight rail transportation is served by divisions of the CSX transportation system and the Norfolk Southern Railway. Air cargo service carriers operate out of Chattanooga Metropolitan Airport/Lovell Field. Jet service via Delta Air Lines and USAir is available to Chattanooga Metropolitan Airport/Lovell Field, which is just fifteen minutes from downtown. Commuter service is offered by American Eagle, Comair, CC Air, Northwest Airlink, and ASA Airlines.

Population (1990)

Total Population and Growth Rate
1990: 433,210
1980: 426,443
1970: 370,857
Growth rate 1970–1990: 17%

Race and Hispanic Origin
White: 85.5%
Black: 13.4%
Asian/Pacific Islander: 0.7%
Native American: 0.2%
Hispanic origin: 0.6%
White not Hispanic: 85.2%

Age
Ages 18 to 20: 4.6%
Ages 21 to 24: 5.5%
Ages 25 to 44: 31.4%
Ages 45 to 54: 11.2%
Ages 55 to 59: 4.9%
Ages 60 to 64: 4.7%
Ages 65 plus: 13%

Educational Attainment (1990)
Percent having completed high school: 67.7%
Percent having completed college: 15.7%
Elementary and high school enrollment: 73,095

Federal Funds and Grants Received
Total received in 1989: $1,455,100,000
Funds received per capita: $3,321,000

Civilian Labor Force
1993 (April): 212,381
1992 average: 213,898
1991 average: 212,915
1990 average: 211,963

Unemployment
1993 (April): 5.3%
1992 average: 6.1%
1991 average: 6.0%
1990 average: 4.6%

Average Annual Pay
1988: $19,730
1987: $18,766
1985: $17,001

Per Capita Personal Income
1991: $17,069
1990: $16,558
1989: $15,720

Business Climate (1987)

Manufacturing
Number of establishments in 1987: 644
Shipments in 1987 ($1,000): $5,744,300
Employees in 1987: 44,200
Change in employment, 1982 to 1987: -3.5%
Average annual pay for manufacturing work in 1989: $21,977
Average annual pay for production work in 1987: $17,212

Wholesale Trade
Number of establishments in 1987: 944

Total sales in 1987 ($1,000): $4,213,800
Change in sales, 1982 to 1987: 0%

Retail Trade
Number of establishments in 1987: 2,702
Total sales in 1987 ($1,000): $4,213,800
Retail sales per household in 1987: $16,261
Average annual pay in 1989: $10,911

Service Industry
Selected receipts in 1987 ($1,000): $1,120,600
Average annual pay in 1989: $17,586

Office Real Estate (1992)
Office space inventory: 3,727,590 square feet
Average class A Central Business District rental range per sq. ft: $13.75

Vacancy Rates
All areas: 18%

Vacancy Rates in Central Business District
Class A space: 2.0%
Class B space: 21.7%

Vacancy Rates Outside Central Business District
Class A space: 7.8%
Class B space: 17.1%

Housing
Total number of units in 1990: 181,276
Occupied units in 1990: 166,404
Owner-occupied units in 1990: 68.4%
1993 ACCRA average cost: $91,380
1993 ACCRA average rent for an apartment: $537

Chamber of Commerce
Chattanooga Area Chamber of Commerce, James G. Vaughan, Jr., Exec. Vice President, 1001 Market St., Chattanooga, TN 37402. 615-756-2121

Major Businesses

Company	SIC	Telephone
Ahlstrom Filtration Inc.	2621	(615) 821-4090
Astec Industries Inc.	3531	(615) 867-4210
Blue Cross & Blue Shield	6324	(615) 755-5600
Buster Brown Apparel Inc.	2369	(615) 629-2531
Chattanooga-Hamilton	8062	(615) 778-7000
Constar International Inc.	3089	(615) 267-2973
Dixie Saving Stores Inc.	5141	(615) 266-5151
Dixie Yarns, Inc.	2281	(615) 698-2501
EMJ Corp.	1542	(615) 855-1550
Electric Power Board of Chattanooga	4911	(615) 756-2706
Filtration Sciences Inc.	2621	(615) 821-4090
Heil Co.	3713	(615) 899-9100
Johnston Coca-Cola Bottling	2086	(615) 756-1202
Krystal Co., Inc.	5812	(615) 756-5100
McKee Baking Co.	2051	(615) 238-7111

Major Businesses (Continued)

Company	SIC	Telephone
North American Royalties	3321	(615) 265-3181
Olan Mills Inc.	7221	(615) 622-5141
Provident Life & Accident Insurance	6311	(615) 755-1011
Provident Life Capital Co.	6311	(615) 755-1011
Provident National Assurance Co.	6211	(615) 755-1901
Red Food Stores Inc.	5141	(615) 892-8029
Roper Corp.	3631	(404) 638-5100
SCT Yarns Inc.	2281	(615) 622-3131
Seaboard Farms of Chattanooga	2015	(615) 756-2471
Signal Apparel Co., Inc.	2329	(615) 756-8146
Siskin Steel And Supply Co.	5051	(615) 756-3671
Volunteer State Life Insurance	6311	(615) 756-2887

Colleges and Universities
Chattanooga State Technical Community College, Chattanooga, TN
Edmondson Junior College, Chattanooga, TN
Mckenzie College, Chattanooga, TN
Tennessee Temple University, Chattanooga, TN
University of Tennessee at Chattanooga, Chattanooga, TN

CLARKSVILLE–HOPKINSVILLE, TN–KY (MSA)

Geographic Profile

Land Area

1260.5 square miles

Counties and Parishes

Kentucky:

Christian

Tennessee:

Montgomery

Ranking Highlights

155 *out of 319 in total* land area

87 *out of 319 in* population growth, *1970–1990*

212 *out of 310 in having the lowest* unemployment *rate*

276 *out of 310 in size of* labor force

256 *out of 318 in the percentage of* college graduates

285 *out of 292 in per capita personal* income

277 *out of 319 in number of* manufacturing establishments

301 *out of 318 in* physicians *per 1000 people*

307 *out of 318 in* hospital beds *per 1000 people*

93 *out of 267 in fewest* crimes *per 1000 people*

244 *out of 266 in fewest* violent crimes *per 1000 people*

20 *out of 319 in per capita* federal funds and grants

Quality of Life Indexes (Rate per 1000 population)

Crime rate in 1991:	53.3
Violent crime rate in 1991:	11.1
Physicians rate in 1992:	1.05
Hospital bed rate in 1991:	1.92

ACCRA Cost of Living Indexes

(First quarter 1993, average = 100)

Composite index:	89.7
Utilities index:	92.9
Housing index:	80.5

Population (1990)

Total Population and Growth Rate

1990: 169,439

1980: 150,220

1970: 118,945

Growth rate 1970–1990: 42%

Race and Hispanic Origin

White: 75.9%

Black: 20.5%

Asian/Pacific Islander: 1.6%

Native American: 0.4%

Hispanic origin: 3.3%

White not Hispanic: 74.5%

Age

Ages 18 to 20: 6.6%

Ages 21 to 24: 10%

Ages 25 to 44: 33.2%

Ages 45 to 54: 8.3%

Ages 55 to 59: 3.6%

Ages 60 to 64: 3.4%

Ages 65 plus: 8.7%

Educational Attainment (1990)

Percent having completed high school: 75.6%

Percent having completed college: 14.0%

Elementary and high school enrollment: 27,866

Federal Funds and Grants Received

Total received in 1989: $1,052,700,000

Funds received per capita: $6,627

Civilian Labor Force

1993 (April):   41,977

1992 average: 54,925

1991 average: 55,180

1990 average: 55,380

Unemployment

1993 (April):   6.0%

1992 average: 7.8%

1991 average: 8.4%

1990 average: 6.5%

Average Annual Pay

1988: $15,767

1987: $15,282

1985: $14,342

Per Capita Personal Income

1991: $13,033

1990: $12,338

1989: $12,142

Business Climate (1987)

Manufacturing

Number of establishments in 1987: 117

Shipments in 1987 ($1,000): $945,100

Employees in 1987: 9,300

Change in employment, 1982 to 1987: -1.1%

Average annual pay for manufacturing work in 1989: $20,703

Average annual pay for production work in 1987: $16,529

Wholesale Trade

Number of establishments in 1987: 195

Total sales in 1987 ($1,000): $468,900

Change in sales, 1982 to 1987: 12.4%

Retail Trade

Number of establishments in 1987: 970

Total sales in 1987 ($1,000): $468,900

Retail sales per household in 1987: $16,603

Average annual pay in 1989: $9,965

Service Industry

Selected receipts in 1987 ($1,000): $155,200

Average annual pay in 1989: $12,708

Housing

Total number of units in 1990: 60,662

Occupied units in 1990: 55,981

Owner-occupied units in 1990: 58.1%

1993 ACCRA average cost: $93,390

1993 ACCRA average rent for an apartment: $378

Chamber of Commerce

Clarksville Area Chamber of Commerce, William Harpel, Exec. Director, 312 Madison St., PO Box 883, Clarksville, TN 37041-0883. 615-647-2331

Economic Development Office

Clarksville/Montgomery County Industrial Development Commisssion, Glen E. Kelley, Exec. Director, 312 Madison St., PO Box 883, Clarksville, TN 37040. 615-647-8011, FAX 615-645-1574

Economic Development Organizations

Industrial Development Board of Montgomery County, Glen E. Kelley, Exec. Director, 312 Madison St., PO Box 883,Clarksville, TN 37041. 615-647-8011, FAX 615-645-1574

Hopkinsville-Christian County Economic Development Council, Richard C. Parks, Exec. Diretor, 1209 S. Virginia St., PO Box 1382, Hopkinsville, KY 42241. 502-885-1499, FAX 502-86-2059

Pennyrile Area Development District, John Adams, Exec. Director, 300 Hammond Dr., Hopkinsville, KY 42240. 502-886-9484, FAX 502-886-3211

Major Businesses

Company	SIC	Telephone
Acme Boot Co., Inc.	3143	(615) 552-2000
Arnold, Max & Sons Inc.	5171	(502) 885-8488
Averitt Lumber Co., Inc.	2421	(615) 647-8394
Beach Oil Co., Inc.	5171	(615) 358-9303
Corlew, James Chevrolet Inc.	5511	(615) 552-2020
Cumberland Electric Membership	4911	(615) 645-2481
Electric Plant Board	4911	(502) 887-4210
First City Bank & Trust Co.	6022	(502) 887-2265
Flynn Enterprises Inc.	2325	(502) 886-0223
Hopkinsville Elevator Co.	5153	(502) 886-5191
Hopkinsville Federal Savings	6035	(502) 885-1171
Hopkinsville Milling Co.	2041	(502) 886-1231
Jackson-Parman Corp.	5171	(615) 648-4771
Jenkins & Wynne Ford Inc.	5511	(615) 647-3353
Jennie Stuart Medical Center	8062	(502) 887-0100
Kentogs Corp.	2325	(502) 886-6349
Kentucky Derby Hosiery Co.	2252	(502) 886-0131
Little River Ford/Toyota Inc.	5511	(502) 886-8131

Major Businesses (Continued)

Company	SIC	Telephone
Matthews, Gary Motors Inc.	5511	(615) 552-7100
Memorial General Hospital District	8062	(615) 552-6622
Orgain Building Supply Co.	5211	(615) 647-1567
Parks-Belk Co. Clarksville	5311	(615) 552-0960
Pennyrile Rural Electric Co.	4911	(502) 886-2555
Sisk Motor Co. Inc.	5511	(502) 885-9003
Sovran Bank/Kentucky	6022	(502) 886-5151
White Hydraulics Inc.	3511	(502) 885-1110

Colleges and Universities

Austin Peay State University, Clarksville, TN

University of Kentucky, Hopkinsville Community College, Hopkinsville, KY

JACKSON, TN (MSA)

Geographic Profile

Land Area

557.1 square miles

Counties and Parishes

Madison

Ranking Highlights

281 *out of 319 in total* **land area**

183 *out of 319 in* **population growth,** *1970–1990*

92 *out of 310 in having the lowest* **unemployment** *rate*

301 *out of 310 in size of* **labor force**

206 *out of 318 in the percentage of* **college graduates**

N/A *out of 292 in per capita personal* **income**

295 *out of 319 in number of* **manufacturing establishments**

56 *out of 318 in* **physicians** *per 1000 people*

3 *out of 318 in* **hospital beds** *per 1000 people*

246 *out of 267 in fewest* **crimes** *per 1000 people*

259 *out of 266 in fewest* **violent crimes** *per 1000 people*

204 *out of 319 in per capita* **federal funds and grants**

Quality of Life Indexes (Rate per 1000 population)

Crime rate in 1991:	87.0
Violent crime rate in 1991:	13.6
Physicians rate in 1992:	2.58
Hospital bed rate in 1991:	10.62

ACCRA Cost of Living Indexes

(First quarter 1993, average = 100)

Composite index:	98.8
Utilities index:	96.7
Housing index:	88.8

Population (1990)

Total Population and Growth Rate

1990: 77,982

1980: 74,546

1970: 65,774

Growth rate 1970–1990: 19%

Race and Hispanic Origin

White: 68.5%

Black: 31.0%

Asian/Pacific Islander: 0.3%

Native American: 0.1%

Hispanic origin: 0.5%

White not Hispanic: 68.2%

Age

Ages 18 to 20: 5.4%

Ages 21 to 24: 5.7%

Ages 25 to 44: 31%

Ages 45 to 54: 9.6%

Ages 55 to 59: 4.2%

Ages 60 to 64: 4.3%

Ages 65 plus: 13.8%

Educational Attainment (1990)

Percent having completed high school: 68.3%

Percent having completed college: 16.6%

Elementary and high school enrollment: 13,925

Federal Funds and Grants Received

Total received in 1989: $215,500,000

Funds received per capita: $2,754

Civilian Labor Force

1993 (April): 41,977

1992 average: 41,891

1991 average: 41,752

1990 average: 39,573

Unemployment

1993 (April): 6.0%

1992 average: 5.9%

1991 average: 5.6%

1990 average: 5.0%

Average Annual Pay

1988: $18,016

1987: $17,550

1985: $15,812

Per Capita Personal Income

1991: N/A

1990: N/A

1989: N/A

Business Climate (1987)

Manufacturing

Number of establishments in 1987: 100

Shipments in 1987 ($1,000): $1,341,200

Employees in 1987: 8,500

Change in employment, 1982 to 1987: 4.9%

Average annual pay for manufacturing work in 1989: $23,359

Average annual pay for production work in 1987: $19,516

Wholesale Trade

Number of establishments in 1987: 167

Total sales in 1987 ($1,000): $453,100

Change in sales, 1982 to 1987: -23.3%

Retail Trade

Number of establishments in 1987: 584

Total sales in 1987 ($1,000): $453,100

Retail sales per household in 1987: $19,836

Average annual pay in 1989: $10,466

Service Industry

Selected receipts in 1987 ($1,000): $208,900

Average annual pay in 1989: $17,933

Housing

Total number of units in 1990: 31,809

Occupied units in 1990: 29,609
Owner-occupied units in 1990: 65.4%
1993 ACCRA average cost: $94,300
1993 ACCRA average rent for an apartment: $523

Chamber of Commerce

Jackson Area Chamber of Commerce, Christopher A. Clifton, President, 197 Auditorium Dr., PO Box 1904, Jackson, TN 38301. 901-423-2200

Economic Development Office

West Tennessee Industry Association, Alf Barnette, Exec. Vice President, 26 Conrad Dr., Jackson, TN 38305. 901-668-4300, FAX 901-668-7554

Major Businesses

Company	SIC	Telephone
Beare Co.	4222	(901) 422-7100
Duck's Carpet, Inc.	5713	(901) 424-2871
First American National Bank	6021	(901) 422-9700
Jackson National Bank	6021	(901) 422-9200
Jackson Wood Products	2435	(901) 427-2791
Kelly Foods Inc.	2032	(901) 424-2255
Noma Outdoor Products, Inc.	3523	(901) 422-1690
Volunteer Bancshares, Inc.	6712	(901) 422-9200

Colleges and Universities

Jackson State Community College, Jackson
Lambuth College, Jackson
Lane College, Jackson
Union University, Jackson

JOHNSON CITY–KINGSPORT–BRISTOL, TN–VA (MSA)

Geographic Profile

Land Area

2865.6 square miles

Counties and Parishes

Tennessee:
  Carter
  Hawkins
  Sullivan
  Unicoi
  Washington
Virginia:
  Bristol
  Scott
  Washington

Additional Cities/Towns within Area

Bristol, VA

Ranking Highlights

50 *out of 319 in total* **land area**
191 *out of 319 in* **population growth,** *1970–1990*
89 *out of 310 in having the lowest* **unemployment** *rate*
100 *out of 310 in size of* **labor force**
261 *out of 318 in the percentage of* **college graduates**
254 *out of 292 in per capita personal* **income**
115 *out of 319 in number of* **manufacturing establishments**
114 *out of 318 in* **physicians** *per 1000 people*
110 *out of 318 in* **hospital beds** *per 1000 people*
20 *out of 267 in fewest* **crimes** *per 1000 people*
41 *out of 266 in fewest* **violent crimes** *per 1000 people*
94 *out of 319 in per capita* **federal funds and grants**

Quality of Life Indexes (Rate per 1000 population)

Crime rate in 1991:	35.3
Violent crime rate in 1991:	2.8
Physicians rate in 1992:	2.05
Hospital bed rate in 1991:	4.52

ACCRA Cost of Living Indexes

(First quarter 1993, average = 100)
Composite index: 97.4
Utilities index: 85.5
Housing index: 101.1

Overview

Johnson City is located in Washington County of northeast Tennessee, 22 miles from the Virginia state line and 36 miles from the North Carolina state line; 90 miles northeast of Knoxville and 160 miles southwest of Roanoke, VA. Johnson City-Kingsport-Bristol is the fourth largest metropolitan statistical area in the state of Tennessee. It is served by Intersates 81 and 181, U.S. Highways 11E, 19W, 321 and 411, and state routes 34, 36 and 75. In September, 1993, *Money* Magazine rated Johnson City as the 34th best place in the country to live.

Johnson City's business base included educational, medical, manufacturing and distribution. Johnson City is home to East Tennessee State University, The Quillen College of Medicine, and a large Veterans Administration campus. The cost of living is consistently below both the state and national average. The climate is temperate and the unemployment rage averages five percent annually.

The local Tri-City Regional Airport provides general air transportation service. Rail service is provided by the CSX and Norfolk-Southern Railways.

Population (1990)

Total Population and Growth Rate
1990: 436,047
1980: 433,638
1970: 373,591
Growth rate 1970–1990: 17%

Race and Hispanic Origin
White: 97.4%
Black: 2.0%
Asian/Pacific Islander: 0.3%
Native American: 0.2%
Hispanic origin: 0.4%
White not Hispanic: 97.1%

Age
Ages 18 to 20: 4.8%
Ages 21 to 24: 5.7%
Ages 25 to 44: 30.2%
Ages 45 to 54: 12.1%
Ages 55 to 59: 5.1%
Ages 60 to 64: 5.1%
Ages 65 plus: 14.6%

Educational Attainment (1990)
Percent having completed high school: 63.1%
Percent having completed college: 13.8%
Elementary and high school enrollment: 68,196

Federal Funds and Grants Received
Total received in 1989: $1,605,400,000
Funds received per capita: $3,630

Civilian Labor Force
1993 (April):   226,411
1992 average: 227,784
1991 average: 229,365
1990 average: 221,968

Unemployment
1993 (April):   6.2%
1992 average: 5.8%
1991 average: 5.5%
1990 average: 4.5%

Average Annual Pay
1988: $19,048
1987: $18,402
1985: $16,938

Per Capita Personal Income
1991: $15,121
1990: $14,609
1989: $13,562

Business Climate (1987)

Manufacturing
Number of establishments in 1987: 494
Shipments in 1987 ($1,000): $6,594,600
Employees in 1987: 52,800
Change in employment, 1982 to 1987: -0.2%
Average annual pay for manufacturing work in 1989: $25,440
Average annual pay for production work in 1987: $20,550

Wholesale Trade
Number of establishments in 1987: 605
Total sales in 1987 ($1,000): $3,622,200
Change in sales, 1982 to 1987: 0%

Retail Trade
Number of establishments in 1987: 2,459
Total sales in 1987 ($1,000): $3,622,200
Retail sales per household in 1987: $13,327
Average annual pay in 1989: $9,985

Service Industry
Selected receipts in 1987 ($1,000): $681,900
Average annual pay in 1989: $17,795

Housing
Total number of units in 1990: 183,995
Occupied units in 1990: 170,569
Owner-occupied units in 1990: 73.7%
1993 ACCRA average cost: $116,932
1993 ACCRA average rent for an apartment: $490

Chamber of Commerce
Johnson City-Washington County Area Chamber of Commerce, Gary M. Mabrey, III, President, PO Box 180, 603 E. Market St., Johnson City, TN 37605. 615-926-2141

Economic Development Office
Johnson City-Jonesborough-Washington County Economic Development Board, Inc., Eddie Williams, Exec. Director, PO Box 599, Johnson City, TN 37605. 800-543-4392, 615-434-2020, FAX 615-926-7360

Economic Development Organizations
First Tennessee Development District, Susan F. Roberts, Exec. Director, 207 N. Boone St. #800, Johnson City, TN 37604. 615-928-0224
Johnson City Board of Realtors, Dianna Summie, Exec.

Director, 1907 B Roan St., Johnson City, TN 37601. 615-926-2511

First Tennessee Private Industry Council, Bob East, 2514 Wesley St., Johnson City, TN 37601. 615-282-1662

Johnson City Development Authority, Dan Porter, Director, PO Box 599, Johnson City, TN 37605. 615-928-2988

Local Incentives for Business

Tennessee has no personal income tax and is a right to work state.

Johnson City offers free industrial training, local J.T.P.A. services, and grant and loan assistance.

Industrial Sites

Contact: Johnson City-Jonesborough-Washington County Economic Development Board. Address included above.

Major Businesses

Company	SIC	Telephone
Arcata Graphics/Kingsport	2732	(615) 378-1000
Bristol Metals Inc.	3498	(615) 968-2151
Bristol Regional Medical Center	8062	(615) 968-6000
Camac Corp.	2824	(703) 669-1161
Campbell Corp.	5511	(615) 968-5600
Charter Federal Savings	6035	(703) 669-5101
Eastman Chemical Products	5162	(615) 229-2000
First American National	6021	(615) 229-0100
General Shale Products Co.	3251	(615) 282-4661
Heritage Federal Bank	6035	(615) 378-8000
Hill, Don Enterprises	5511	(615) 246-6611
Holston Valley Hospital & Medical Center	8062	(615) 246-3322
Johnson City Medical Center	8062	(615) 461-6111
Kingsport Power Co.	4911	(615) 378-5000
Mid Mountain Foods Inc.	5141	(703) 628-3105
Morrison Molded Fiberglas	3089	(703) 669-1181
North American Rayon Corp.	2281	(615) 542-2141
Paty Co. Inc.	5251	(615) 538-8101
Simmons Rand Co.	3532	(703) 669-9171
United Intr-Mountain Tele Co.	4813	(615) 968-8121
White's Discount Food Mart	5411	(615) 926-0779

Colleges and Universities

Bristol University, Bristol, TN

Draughons Junior College, Johnson City, TN

East Tennessee State University, Johnson City, TN

King College, Bristol, TN

Milligan College, Johnson City, TN

Quillen College of Medicine, Johnson City, TN

Virginia Intermont College, Bristol, VA

Additional Information

Johnson City Business. Johnson City/Washington County Area Chamber of Commerce and Johnson City-Jonesborough-Washington County Economic Development Board, a Bi-monthly publication.

Johnson City/Jonesborough/Washington County and the Tri-Cities MSA, Economic & Demographic Profile. Johnson City-Jonesborough-Washington County Economic Development Board, n.d. 4p.

The Med-Tech Corridor, Leading Johnson City into the 21st Century (Johnson City Business, Special Edition). Johnson City/Washington County Area Chamber of Commerce and Johnson City-Jonesborough-Washington County Economic Development Board. January/February 1991.

KNOXVILLE, TN (MSA)

Geographic Profile

Land Area
2774.7 square miles

Counties and Parishes
Anderson
Blount
Grainger
Jefferson
Knox
Sevier
Union

Additional Cities/Towns within Area
Oak Ridge

Ranking Highlights
57 *out of 319 in total* land area
151 *out of 319 in* population growth, *1970–1990*
82 *out of 310 in having the lowest* unemployment *rate*
82 *out of 310 in size of* labor force
153 *out of 318 in the percentage of* college graduates
168 *out of 292 in per capita personal* income
83 *out of 319 in number of* manufacturing establishments
96 *out of 318 in* physicians *per 1000 people*
93 *out of 318 in* hospital beds *per 1000 people*
89 *out of 267 in fewest* crimes *per 1000 people*
131 *out of 266 in fewest* violent crimes *per 1000 people*
30 *out of 319 in per capita* federal funds and grants

Quality of Life Indexes (Rate per 1000 population)
Crime rate in 1991:	51.9
Violent crime rate in 1991:	6.3
Physicians rate in 1992:	2.24
Hospital bed rate in 1991:	4.74

ACCRA Cost of Living Indexes
(First quarter 1993, average = 100)
Composite index:	93.2
Utilities index:	97.6
Housing index:	88.2

Overview
The economy of the Greater Knoxville Area is highly diversified with no one employment sector accounting for more than 25 percent of the area's total employment. Knoxville's economy is bolstered by the presence of the Tennessee Valley Authority headquarters and the University of Tennessee at Knoxville. Added benefits accrue with the location of three major U.S. Department of Energy facilities in the area, including Oak Ridge National Laboratory in nearby Oak Ridge. These institutions provide unlimited education and training opportunities for area businesses and are active in a cooperative technology transfer program that has successfully spawned numerous spin-off companies.

As another nurturing aspect of the local business climate, the area features an unusually high number of incubator facilities, particularly in Oak Ridge—a city whose roots can be traced to the Manhattan Project of the late 1930s and early 1940s.

Knoxville is at the center of the eastern half of the United States, situated within 500 miles of 50 percent of America's marketplace. Location is one important reasons why many manufacturing businesses have relocated or expanded in the area. In Knox Country from 1980 through 1990, more than $177 million was invested in seventy-three industrial expansions and more than $300 million was invested in thirty-eight new industrial plants. Location is also a factor in the area's booming tourism industry, particularly in Sevier County, where more than 11 million people annually visit the Great Smoky Mountains National Park and the many other attractions in Gatlinburg, Pigeon Forge and Sevier-ville.

Knoxville remains an urban center for mining in the Cumberland range. Zinc and coal mining are carried on in the region. Burley tobacco and a variety of food crops are harvested on farms just outside the city, and livestock and dairy products are also important to the local economy.

All major air shipments in Knoxville originate out of McGhee Tyson Airport, located 17 miles south of downtown. It is served by nine national and regional carriers. The city's other major facility is downtown's Island Home Airport, which is a base for smaller general aviation traffic and privately-owned planes. A new cargo facility was constructed in the early 1990s more than doubling the airport's cargo capacity. Main rail service is provided by the Norfolk Southern Railway System and the CSX Transportation system. Knox County, where 172 miles of track cross, is at the junction of major east-west and north-south Southern Railway lines. Direct one-line service is available to most large and small cities in the Southeast, with freight service provided by both railroads' Knoxville freight division offices. In addition, sixty regular-route, common-carrier truck lines have terminals in Knox County. Many irregular routes and special-contract carriers also supply the area with efficient ground freight services.

Because of navigation improvements made by the Tennessee Valley Authority on the Tennessee River system, Knoxville now enjoys barge commerce with twenty-one other states on the Tennessee, Ohio, and Mississippi Rivers. This interconnected inland water system runs from the Gulf of Mexico to the Great Lakes, allowing shipments on water to such distant points as Houston, Tampa, Pittsburgh, Minneapolis, and Little Rock.

Access to the city via car, truck, or bus is made easy by the fact that three of the nation's busiest interstate highways—I-40, I-75, and I-81—intersect in Knoxville. An extension of the Pellissippi Parkway was underway in 1992.

Population (1990)

Total Population and Growth Rate
1990: 604,816
1980: 565,970
1970: 476,538
Growth rate 1970–1990: 27%

Race and Hispanic Origin
White: 92.8%
Black: 6.0%
Asian/Pacific Islander: 0.8%
Native American: 0.2%
Hispanic origin: 0.5%
White not Hispanic: 92.5%

Age
Ages 18 to 20: 5.2%
Ages 21 to 24: 6.2%
Ages 25 to 44: 31.9%
Ages 45 to 54: 11.2%
Ages 55 to 59: 4.7%
Ages 60 to 64: 4.6%
Ages 65 plus: 13.3%

Educational Attainment (1990)
Percent having completed high school: 70.3%
Percent having completed college: 19.2%
Elementary and high school enrollment: 94,053

Federal Funds and Grants Received
Total received in 1989: $3,258,500,000
Funds received per capita: $5,434

Civilian Labor Force
1993 (April): 306,501
1992 average: 306,133
1991 average: 295,399
1990 average: 289,099

Unemployment
1993 (April): 5.5%
1992 average: 5.7%
1991 average: 5.7%
1990 average: 4.9%

Average Annual Pay
1988: $19,035
1987: $18,227
1985: $16,721

Per Capita Personal Income
1991: $16,846
1990: $16,337
1989: $15,414

Business Climate (1987)

Manufacturing
Number of establishments in 1987: 796
Shipments in 1987 ($1,000): $5,336,300
Employees in 1987: 48,800
Change in employment, 1982 to 1987: 0%
Average annual pay for manufacturing work in 1989: $24,044
Average annual pay for production work in 1987: $18,064

Wholesale Trade
Number of establishments in 1987: 1,178
Total sales in 1987 ($1,000): $4,637,600
Change in sales, 1982 to 1987: 14.0%

Retail Trade
Number of establishments in 1987: 4,296
Total sales in 1987 ($1,000): $4,637,600
Retail sales per household in 1987: $18,036
Average annual pay in 1989: $10,805

Service Industry
Selected receipts in 1987 ($1,000): $2,136,400
Average annual pay in 1989: $18,600

Housing
Total number of units in 1990: 260,970
Occupied units in 1990: 237,822
Owner-occupied units in 1990: 68.7%
1993 ACCRA average cost: $98,500
1993 ACCRA average rent for an apartment: $470

Chamber of Commerce
Greater Knoxville Chamber of Commerce, Jack Hammontree, President, 301 E. Church St., PO Box 2688, Knoxville, TN 37901. 615-637-4550

Major Businesses

Company	SIC	Telephone
Albers Inc.	5122	(615) 524-5492
Apac-Tennessee Inc.	1611	(615) 983-3100
Baptist Health System of East Tennessee	8062	(615) 632-5081
Blue Diamond Coal Co.	1222	(615) 588-8511
Chapman Drug Co.	5122	(615) 522-3161
Clayton Homes Inc.	5271	(615) 970-7200
Conagra Fertilizer Co.	5261	(615) 673-5400
East Tennessee Natural Gas Co.	4923	(615) 693-3501
East Tennessee Baptist Hospital	8062	(615) 632-5081
Fort Sanders Alliance	8062	(615) 541-1606
Fort Sanders Regional Medical Center	8062	(615) 546-2811
Goody's Family Clothing Inc.	5137	(615) 966-2000
Hackney, H. T. Co., Inc.	5141	(615) 546-1291
Institutional Jobbers Co.	5141	(615) 970-7800
Knoxville Utilities Board	4931	(615) 524-2911
Lay Packing Co.	2011	(615) 546-2511
Martin Marietta Energy System	2819	(615) 574-3764
Outlet Stores Inc.	5651	(615) 966-2000
Pilot Corp.	5541	(615) 588-7488
Plasti-Line Inc.	3993	(615) 938-1511
Proffitt's Inc.	5311	(615) 983-7000

Major Businesses (Continued)

Company	SIC	Telephone
Ray Industries Inc.	3732	(615) 522-4181
Rentenbach Engineering Co.	1542	(615) 546-2440
Sea Ray Boats (Florida Co.)	3732	(615) 522-4181
Sea Ray Boats (Tennessee)	3732	(615) 522-4181
St. Mary's Health System Inc.	8062	(615) 971-6011
Sun Coal Co.	6719	(615) 558-0300
Tennessee Valley Authority	4911	(615) 632-2101
Watson, IRA Co.	5311	(615) 690-6000

Colleges and Universities

Cooper Institute, Knoxville
Draughons Junior College, Knoxville
Knoxville Business College, Knoxville
Knoxville College, Knoxville
Pellissippi State Technical Community College, Knoxville
Tennessee Institute of Electronics, Knoxville
University of Tennessee, Knoxville, Knoxville

MEMPHIS, TN–AR–MS (MSA)

Geographic Profile

Land Area
2303.0 square miles

Counties and Parishes
Arkansas:
  Crittenden
Mississippi:
  DeSoto
Tennessee:
  Shelby
  Tipton

Additional Cities/Towns within Area
West Memphis, AR

Ranking Highlights

77   *out of 319 in total* land area
185   *out of 319 in* population growth, *1970–1990*
82   *out of 310 in having the lowest* unemployment *rate*
56   *out of 310 in size of* labor force
159   *out of 318 in the percentage of* college graduates
98   *out of 292 in per capita personal* income
59   *out of 319 in number of* manufacturing establishments
54   *out of 318 in* physicians *per 1000 people*
56   *out of 318 in* hospital beds *per 1000 people*
223   *out of 267 in fewest* crimes *per 1000 people*
237   *out of 266 in fewest* violent crimes *per 1000 people*
165   *out of 319 in per capita* federal funds and grants

Quality of Life Indexes (Rate per 1000 population)

Crime rate in 1991:	78.0
Violent crime rate in 1991:	10.4
Physicians rate in 1992:	2.6
Hospital bed rate in 1991:	5.37

ACCRA Cost of Living Indexes

(First quarter 1993, average = 100)

Composite index:	93.8
Utilities index:	87.3
Housing index:	81.3

Overview

At the center of a major distribution network, Memphis works from a broad economic base as it continues to diversify its employment opportunities Historically a trading center for cotton and hardwood, Memphis is the headquarters for major manufacturing, services, and other business concerns.

Services centered in Memphis include a major hotel chain, insurance, banking, and nonprofit organizations. Finance and insurance have grown significantly in importance in recent years, as the movement of several Sedgwick James Insurance divisions added to Memphis's own Crump Companies and National Life to bolster insurance employment. Other major office additions to the Memphis economy are Great Western Finance, the Ducks Unlimited headquarters, and the headquarters of several national fraternities and sororities. The Promus Companies, headquartered in Memphis, operate the Hampton Inns, Homewood Suites, Embassy Suites, and Harrah Casinos hotel and casino chains. International Paper moved its operational headquarters to Memphis in 1987 bringing six hundred workers. Their staff has since grown to 1,500 data processing, telecommunications, operations, and management people.

Other factors in the Memphis-area economy include two military installations. The Memphis Defense Depot stores more than $1 billion worth of military supplies while the Millington Naval Air Station, just north of Memphis, is one of the world's largest inland naval complexes. In addition, Memphis is considered a mid-South retail center and an attractive tourist destination.

Memphis's early and continued role as a major cotton market makes agribusiness an economic mainstay in Memphis. Almost half of the nation's cotton crop is traded in Memphis, home of three of the world's largest cotton dealers: Dunavant Enterprises, Hohenburg Brothers, and the Allenburg Company.

Memphis is important in other areas of agribusiness. The city has long been established as a prime marketing center for hardwood, as well as wood and paper products. Memphis concerns are also major processors of soybeans, meats, and other foods. Enhancing Memphis's position at the center of agribusiness is Agricenter International, a $7.7-million, 140,000-square foot exhibition center for agricultural exhibitions, experimentation, and information exchange. It brings together the most technologically advanced methods of farming and farm equipment available in one location.

Memphis's Uniport combines a Foreign Trade Zone with river, air, rail, and road facilities to make Memphis one of the nation's most important distribution centers.

The Memphis River Port, which connects the city to 25,000 miles of interconnected inland waterways, is one of the largest inland ports on the Mississippi River. There are three still-water harbors which include public terminals, loading facilities, grain elevators, and intermodal connections.

Ninety-six freight trains move in and out of Memphis daily, providing ninety-hour service to and from the West Coast and overnight service to and from Chicago, Illinois. Eight federal highways, three interstate highways, and seven state highways connect the Memphis trucking industry with both the rest of the nation and with other vital forms of transportation.

Federal Express has its headquarters in Memphis, and the city's facility handles more than one million packages per night for overnight delivery. Thanks to this location, local firms have an eight-hour lead over firms located elsewhere.

Located minutes from downtown, Memphis International Airport is served by national, regional, and commuter airlines. Expansion efforts underway in 1988 and valued at $100 million dollars include improvements to the concourse, taxiways, control tower, waiting areas, ticketing operations, parking facilities, and servicing systems, as well as land acquisition for further development. Other airports in the Memphis area include General De Witt Spain Airport, Charles W. Baker Airport, Arlington Municipal Airport, Memphis-Olive Branch Airport, Twinkletown Airport, and West Memphis Municipal Airport. Interstate highway I-40 approaches Memphis from North Carolina to the east and California to the west, while interstate highway I-55 approaches the city from Chicago, Illinois, to the north and New Orleans, Louisiana, to the south. Interstate loop I-240 rings the city. Motor traffic also enters Memphis via U.S. highways 51, 61, 64, 70, 72, 78, and 79.

Population (1990)

Total Population and Growth Rate
1990: 981,747
1980: 913,472
1970: 834,103
Growth rate 1970–1990: 18%

Race and Hispanic Origin
White: 58.1%
Black: 40.6%
Asian/Pacific Islander: 0.8%
Native American: 0.2%
Hispanic origin: 0.8%
White not Hispanic: 57.7%

Age
Ages 18 to 20:   5%
Ages 21 to 24:   6%
Ages 25 to 44: 33.4%
Ages 45 to 54: 9.7%
Ages 55 to 59: 3.9%
Ages 60 to 64: 3.8%
Ages 65 plus: 10.3%

Educational Attainment (1990)
Percent having completed high school: 73.5%
Percent having completed college: 19.0%
Elementary and high school enrollment: 180,877

Federal Funds and Grants Received
Total received in 1989: $2,976,800,000
Funds received per capita: $3,040

Civilian Labor Force
1993 (April):   476,655
1992 average: 473,972
1991 average: 471,556
1990 average: 473,527

Unemployment
1993 (April):   5.9%

1992 average: 5.7%
1991 average: 5.7%
1990 average: 4.6%

Average Annual Pay
1988: $20,371
1987: $19,709
1985: $18,310

Per Capita Personal Income
1991: $18,331
1990: $17,645
1989: $16,601

Business Climate (1987)
Manufacturing
Number of establishments in 1987: 1,178
Shipments in 1987 ($1,000): $9,347,300
Employees in 1987: 60,300
Change in employment, 1982 to 1987: -0.3%
Average annual pay for manufacturing work in 1989: $25,872
Average annual pay for production work in 1987: $18,501

Wholesale Trade
Number of establishments in 1987: 2,241
Total sales in 1987 ($1,000): $22,205,700
Change in sales, 1982 to 1987: 31.5%

Retail Trade
Number of establishments in 1987: 5,404
Total sales in 1987 ($1,000): $22,205,700
Retail sales per household in 1987: $18,010
Average annual pay in 1989: $11,705

Service Industry
Selected receipts in 1987 ($1,000): $2,672,600
Average annual pay in 1989: $18,649

Office Real Estate (1992)
Office space inventory: 18,327,610 square feet
Average class A Central Business District rental range per sq. ft: $13.50

Vacancy Rates
All areas: 18.6%

Vacancy Rates in Central Business District
Class A space: 15.0%
Class B space: 34.8%

Vacancy Rates Outside Central Business District
Class A space: 11.5%
Class B space: 22.8%

Housing
Total number of units in 1990: 385,214
Occupied units in 1990: 356,997
Owner-occupied units in 1990: 61.4%
1993 ACCRA average cost: $91,297
1993 ACCRA average rent for an apartment: $425

Chamber of Commerce
Memphis Area Chamber of Commerce, David W. Cooley, President, 22 N. Front St. #200, PO Box 224, Memphis, TN 38101. 901-575-3500

Major Businesses

Company	SIC	Telephone
ACI America Holdings, Inc.	5039	(901) 767-7111
ACI America Inc.	5039	(901) 767-7111
Autozone, Inc.	5531	(901) 325-4600
Baddour Inc.	5311	(901) 365-8880
Baptist Memorial Hospital	8062	(901) 522-5252
Blazer Financial Services	6141	(901) 757-7500
Crye-Leike Inc.	6531	(901) 756-8900
Dover Elevator International	3534	(901) 342-4300
Federal Express Corp.	4513	(901) 369-3600
Federal Express International	4513	(901) 369-3600
First Tennessee Bank National Association	6021	(901) 523-4444
GKN North America Inc.	3714	(901) 523-7711
GKN Parts Industrial Corp.	5013	(901) 523-7711
Helena Chemical Co.	5191	(901) 761-0050
Holiday Inns Inc.	7999	(901) 762-8600
Holly Farms Corp.	2015	(901) 761-3610
Kraft Food Ingredients Co.	2022	(901) 766-2100
Leader Federal Bank for Savings	6035	(901) 578-2000
Malone & Hyde, Inc.	5141	(901) 325-4200
Maybelline Co.	2844	(901) 320-2011
Memphis Hospital Service Surgical	6324	(901) 529-3092
Methodist Health Systems	8062	(901) 726-2310
Parts Inc.	5013	(901) 523-7711
Plough Inc.	2834	(901) 320-2011
Smith & Nephew Consolidated	3069	(901) 396-2121
TBC Corp.	5014	(901) 363-8030
Union Planters Corp.	6022	(901) 523-6000
Union Planters National Bank	6021	(901) 523-6000
Welcome Wagon International	7319	(901) 523-0350

Colleges and Universities
Christian Brothers University, Memphis
Crichton College, Memphis
Draughons Junior College, Memphis
Lemoyne-Owen College, Memphis
Memphis College of Art, Memphis
Memphis State University, Memphis
Phillips Junior College of Memphis, Memphis
Rhodes College, Memphis
Shelby State Community College, Memphis
State Technical Institute at Memphis, Memphis
University of Tennessee, Memphis, Memphis

NASHVILLE, TN (MSA)

Geographic Profile

Land Area

4073.1 square miles

Counties and Parishes

Cheatham
Davidson
Dickson
Robertson
Rutherford
Sumner
Williamson
Wilson

Additional Cities/Towns within Area

Murfreesboro

Ranking Highlights

25 *out of 319 in total* **land area**

94 *out of 319 in* **population growth,** *1970–1990*

51 *out of 310 in having the lowest* **unemployment** *rate*

47 *out of 310 in size of* **labor force**

110 *out of 318 in the percentage of* **college graduates**

74 *out of 292 in per capita personal* **income**

47 *out of 319 in number of* **manufacturing establishments**

47 *out of 318 in* **physicians** *per 1000 people*

72 *out of 318 in* **hospital beds** *per 1000 people*

153 *out of 267 in fewest* **crimes** *per 1000 people*

232 *out of 266 in fewest* **violent crimes** *per 1000 people*

289 *out of 319 in per capita* **federal funds and grants**

Quality of Life Indexes (Rate per 1000 population)

Crime rate in 1991:	64.3
Violent crime rate in 1991:	10.1
Physicians rate in 1992:	2.75
Hospital bed rate in 1991:	5.11

ACCRA Cost of Living Indexes
(First quarter 1993, average = 100)

Composite index:	91.4
Utilities index:	90.3
Housing index:	85.4

Overview

The area has benefitted from low unemployment, consistent job growth, heavy outside investment and expansion, and a broadening of the labor force. Nashville tends to outperform the state and nation in economic downturns and to recover earlier. Although the city's economy is not reliant on any one area of production, Nashville is a leader in finance and insurance, health care, music and entertainment, transportation technology, higher education, and tourism and conventions. Its shift to a strong service economy is unique because of the high growth in managerial and administrative person-

nel at higher income levels and the consistent growth in manufacturing which many cities lack.

Nashville is the largest publishing center in the Southeast and the sixth largest in the country. Some of the nation's leading printers operate alongside scores of small, family-owned shops. The city is home to Thomas Nelson, the world's foremost publisher of Bibles, and two of the country's largest religious publishing houses.

Of all of the products manufactured in the city, music is what makes Nashville most famous. The local recording industry and its offshoots have not only brought worldwide recognition to what was once a sedate southern city, but they have also pumped millions into the local economy, created a thriving entertainment business scene second only to New York City and Los Angeles, California, and given the city a distinctly cosmopolitan flavor. Nashville music—country, pop, gospel, and rock—generates about a half a billion dollars in record sales each year. As a result, spinoff industries have flourished: booking agencies, music publishing companies, promotional firms, recording studios, trade publications, and performance rights associations such as BMI, Broadcast Music Inc. Most major record labels have offices on Nashville's Music Row, including RCA, Sparrow, MCA, CBS, Warner Brothers, and Polygram.

The Nashville Network, one of the country's largest cable channels, operates eighteen hours a day out of a state-of-the-art complex on the grounds of Opryland USA. The influx of new industry such as this has resulted in hundreds of jobs and on-site training opportunities for local actors, editors, artists, technicians, and other production people. Nashville's entertainment scene brings in more than revenue, however. It draws millions of people to the city each year as well. Tourism is one of Tennessee's biggest businesses, and Nashville is known as the hottest spot in the state.

In November 1991 *Fortune* magazine rated Nashville the fifth best city for business in the country, based on its location, its position to serve markets in the South, East and Midwest, its three intersecting highways, and its American Airlines hub.

Millions of tons of goods are moved through the city each year by truck on any of 135 motor freight lines serving the area. Nashville has become a regional headquarters for the trucking industry primarily because of its tight, efficient network of accessible interstate highways, its conveniently centralized location, and the fact that approximately one hundred local terminals provide easy break-bulk distribution and specialized services for products such as produce (refrigeration), gasoline, and hazardous waste.

The local division of the CSX handles eighty to eighty-five trains per day with either direct rail service or connections to all rail routes, including easy access to foreign markets.

The Cumberland River, an artery of the Ohio River that

weaves in and out of the Nashville Metropolitan area, links the city to points on the Mississippi River and the Gulf of Mexico coast. The stream has eighteen commercial operators, three common carriers, and three public port facilities that service the chemical, agricultural, oil, and mining industries regularly. It is estimated that 15 to 20 percent of shipments originating in Nashville are bound for overseas destinations through Gulf ports, stimulating the city's international trade. The distance to Gulf ports was cut by 563 miles in the mid-1980s when the United States Army Corps of Engineers opened its $1.8 billion Tennessee-Tombigbee Waterway, connecting the Tennessee River in northern Alabama with the Tombigbee River of southern Alabama 234 miles away.

East of the city, the Metropolitan Nashville Airport is approximately a twelve-minute ride from the downtown area and is located just eight miles from the central business district.

Six major highways intersect in the heart of Nashville: Interstate-65 N leads to the industrialized cities of Chicago, Illinois, Indianapolis, Indiana, and Pittsburgh, Pennsylvania; I-40 takes travelers to the cities of Richmond, Virginia, Washington, D.C., and Philadelphia, Pennsylvania, plus the Carolina ports; I-24 E extends to Atlanta, Georgia, and Florida; I-65 S reaches Birmingham, Alabama, New Orleans, Louisiana, and the Gulf; I-40 W leads to Dallas, Texas, Oklahoma, and the West Coast; and I-24 W extends to St. Louis, Missouri, and Kansas City, Missouri, the midwestern heartland.

Population (1990)

Total Population and Growth Rate
1990: 985,026
1980: 850,505
1970: 699,271
Growth rate 1970–1990: 41%

Race and Hispanic Origin
White: 83.1%
Black: 15.5%
Asian/Pacific Islander: 1.0%
Native American: 0.2%
Hispanic origin: 0.8%
White not Hispanic: 82.6%

Age
Ages 18 to 20: 4.8%
Ages 21 to 24: 6.1%
Ages 25 to 44: 34.8%
Ages 45 to 54: 10.5%
Ages 55 to 59: 4.2%
Ages 60 to 64: 3.8%
Ages 65 plus: 10.6%

Educational Attainment (1990)
Percent having completed high school: 74.0%
Percent having completed college: 21.4%

Elementary and high school enrollment: 163,200

Federal Funds and Grants Received
Total received in 1989: $2,134,000,000
Funds received per capita: $2,196

Civilian Labor Force
1993 (April): 544,441
1992 average: 538,905
1991 average: 529,241
1990 average: 531,364

Unemployment
1993 (April): 4.6%
1992 average: 5.0%
1991 average: 5.1%
1990 average: 4.0%

Average Annual Pay
1988: $20,469
1987: $19,737
1985: $17,848

Per Capita Personal Income
1991: $19,089
1990: $18,324
1989: $17,622

Business Climate (1987)

Manufacturing
Number of establishments in 1987: 1,506
Shipments in 1987 ($1,000): $11,727,800
Employees in 1987: 88,600
Change in employment, 1982 to 1987: 12.2%
Average annual pay for manufacturing work in 1989: $25,328
Average annual pay for production work in 1987: $20,399

Wholesale Trade
Number of establishments in 1987: 2,101
Total sales in 1987 ($1,000): $10,742,900
Change in sales, 1982 to 1987: 0%

Retail Trade
Number of establishments in 1987: 5,840
Total sales in 1987 ($1,000): $10,742,900
Retail sales per household in 1987: $19,106
Average annual pay in 1989: $12,799

Service Industry
Selected receipts in 1987 ($1,000): $3,505,800
Average annual pay in 1989: $20,080

Office Real Estate (1992)
Office space inventory: 16,206,636 square feet
Average class A Central Business District rental range per sq. ft: $19.96

Vacancy Rates
All areas: 18.0%

Vacancy Rates in Central Business District

Class A space: 15.9%

Class B space: 23.7%

Vacancy Rates Outside Central Business District

Class A space: 15.9%

Class B space: 19.0%

Housing

Total number of units in 1990: 410,968

Occupied units in 1990: 375,831

Owner-occupied units in 1990: 63.2%

1993 ACCRA average cost: $96,433

1993 ACCRA average rent for an apartment: $452

Chamber of Commerce

Nashville Area Chamber of Commerce, Michael W. Rollins, Exec. Vice President, 161 4th Ave. N., Nashville TN 37219. 615-259-4755

Major Businesses

Company	SIC	Telephone
American General Life Accident Insurance	6311	(615) 749-1000
Bridgestone (U.S.A.), Inc.	3011	(615) 391-0088
Commissary Operations Inc.	4213	(615) 391-5201
Dolgencorp, Inc.	5331	(615) 665-9102
Dollar General Corp.	5399	(615) 665-9102
Electric Power Board	4911	(615) 747-3831
Equicor, Inc.	6321	(615) 320-7608
Equicor Holdings, Inc.	6321	(615) 320-7608
First American Corp.	6021	(615) 748-2000
First American National Bank	6021	(615) 748-2000
Genesco Inc.	3143	(615) 367-7000
Health Services Acquisition	8062	(615) 327-9551
Healthtrust Inc.	8062	(615) 383-4444
Ingram Industries Inc.	4449	(615) 298-8200
Inter-City Products Corp.	3585	(615) 793-0450
Life Casulty Insurance of Tennessee	6311	(615) 749-2000
Murray Ohio Manufacturing	3524	(615) 373-6500
Nissan Motor Manufacturing Corp. USA	3711	(615) 459-1400
Noranda Aluminum Inc.	3334	(615) 377-4300
Noranda Finance Inc.	3334	(615) 377-4300
Norandal USA, Inc.	3353	(615) 371-1250
Northern Telecom Inc.	3661	(615) 734-4000
Opryland USA Inc.	7996	(615) 889-6600
Pen Holdings, Inc.	5052	(615) 371-7300
Shoney's Inc.	5812	(615) 391-5201
Sovran Bank/Central South	6022	(615) 749-3333
Sullivan Graphics, Inc.	2752	(615) 377-0377
Tennessee Farmers Cooperate	5191	(615) 793-8011
Third National Corp.	6021	(615) 748-4000

Colleges and Universities

Aquinas Junior College, Nashville

Belmont College, Nashville

David Lipscomb University, Nashville

Draughons Junior College, Nashville

Fisk University, Nashville

ITT Technical Institute, Nashville

John A. Gupton College, Nashville

Middle Tennessee State University, Murfreesboro

Nashville State Technical Institute, Nashville

Tennessee State University, Nashville

Trevecca Nazarene College, Nashville

Vanderbilt University, Nashville

TEXAS

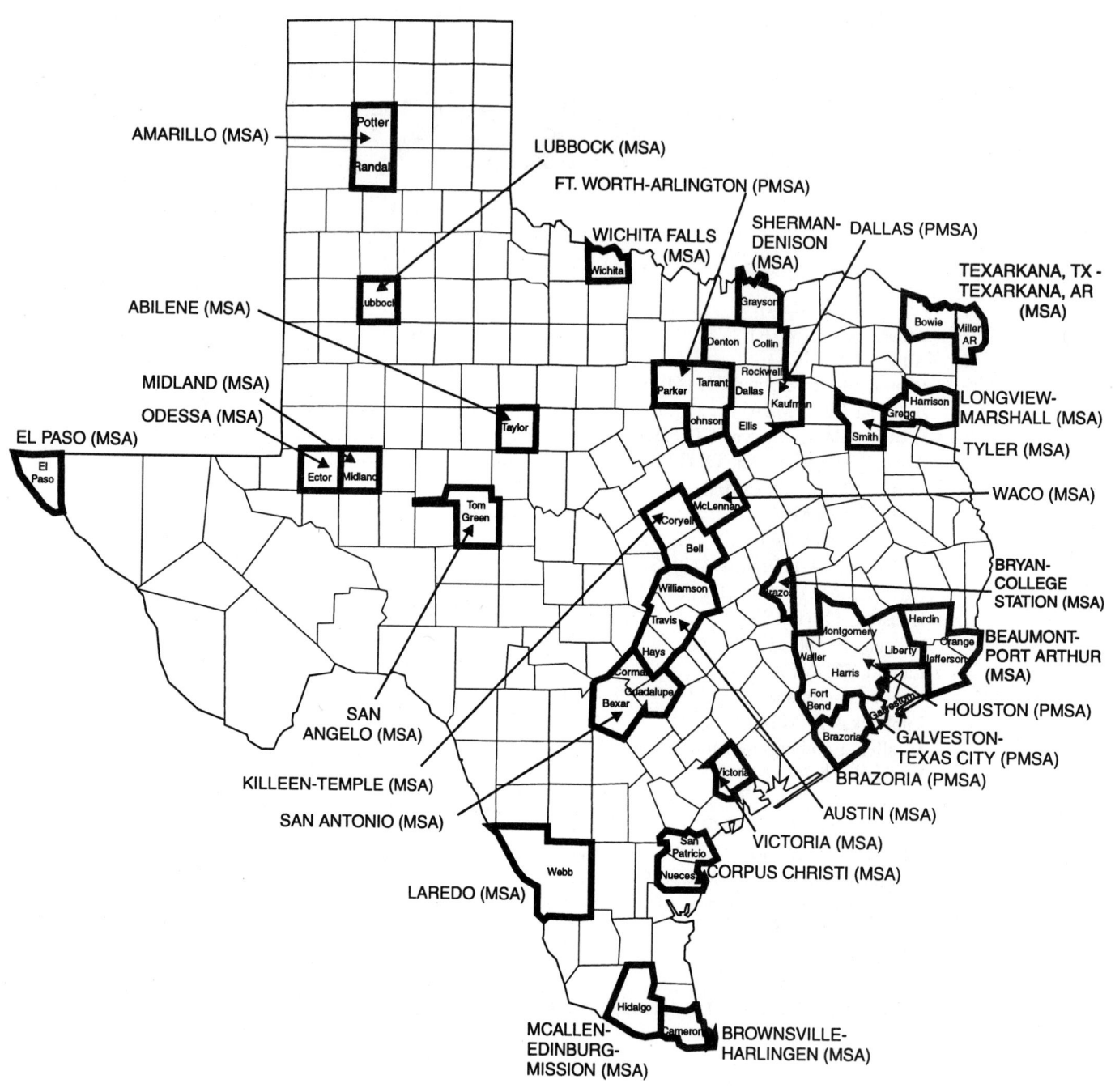

AMARILLO (MSA)

Potter

Randall

LUBBOCK (MSA)

FT. WORTH-ARLINGTON (PMSA)

WICHITA FALLS (MSA)

Wichita

SHERMAN-
DENISON (MSA)

DALLAS (PMSA)

TEXARKANA, TX -
TEXARKANA, AR (MSA)

Bowie

Miller
AR

ABILENE (MSA)

Lubbock

Grayson

Denton

Collin

Rockwall

Parker

Tarrant

Dallas

Kaufman

Harrison

Gregg

LONGVIEW-
MARSHALL (MSA)

MIDLAND (MSA)

ODESSA (MSA)

Taylor

Johnson

Ellis

Smith

TYLER (MSA)

EL PASO (MSA)

El
Paso

Ector

Midland

Tom
Green

McLennan

WACO (MSA)

Coryell

Bell

BRYAN-
COLLEGE
STATION (MSA)

Williamson

Brazos

Hardin

BEAUMONT-
PORT ARTHUR
(MSA)

Travis

Montgomery

Orange

Liberty

Jefferson

SAN
ANGELO (MSA)

Hays

Waller

Harris

HOUSTON (PMSA)

Comal

Fort
Bend

Galveston

GALVESTON-
TEXAS CITY (PMSA)

Guadalupe

Bexar

Brazoria

BRAZORIA (PMSA)

KILLEEN-TEMPLE (MSA)

SAN ANTONIO (MSA)

AUSTIN (MSA)

Victoria

VICTORIA (MSA)

San
Patricio

Webb

Nueces

CORPUS CHRISTI (MSA)

LAREDO (MSA)

Hidalgo

Cameron

BROWNSVILLE-
HARLINGEN (MSA)

MCALLEN-
EDINBURG-
MISSION (MSA)

TEXAS

Population

1990: 16,986,510
1980: 14,229,191

Age

Ages 18 to 20: 836,698
Ages 21 to 24: 1,054,146
Ages 25 to 44: 5,625,196
Ages 45 to 54: 1,628,634
Ages 55 to 59: 661,590
Ages 60 to 64: 627,831
Median age: 30.8

Race and Hispanic Origin

White: 12,774,762
Black: 2,021,632
Asian/Pacific Islander: 319,459
Native American: 65,877
Hispanic origin: 4,339,905

Households

Total: 6,070,937
Persons per household: 2.73

Sex

Male: 8,365,963
Female: 8,620,547

Population Migration

Domestic migration: -899,000
International migration: 474,000

Projection of the Population in 1995

Total: 17,631,000
18 to 64: 10,600,000

Civilian Labor Force

1993: 8,680,100
1992: 8,747,100
1991: 8,526,000
1990: 8,320,600

Manufacturing

1995 Projection: 1,016,900
1992: 970,200
1991: 970,600
1990: 986,400
1989: 969,300

Services

1995 Projection: 2,511,300

1992: 1,844,800
1991: 1,762,800
1990: 1,724,600
1989: 1,640,800

Wholesale and Retail Trade

1995 Projection: 1,996,900
1992: 1,753,400
1991: 1,746,900
1990: 1,733,100
1989: 1,719,900

Unemployment Rate

1993: 8.4%
1992: 8.3%
1991: 6.4%
1990: 5.8%

Employer Unemployment Contributions

Contribution Rate

1992: 1.36%
1991: 1.01%
1990: 1.86%

Average Weekly Benefit

1992: $183.51
1991: $179.12
1990: $162.83

Gross State Product (Million $)

1989: $340,057
1988: $322,125
1987: $302,862
1979: $175,815
Growth rate, 1979 to 1989: 93.4%

Capital Expenditures of Manufacturing Industries

1990: $8,912,700,000
1989: $7,573,300,000
1988: $5,872,400,000
1987: $4,548,000,000

State Tax Rates

Individual income: None.
Corporate income: None.
General property: Local collections. Rates fixed locally, based on true and full value of real and personal property.

General sales: 6.25%
Gasoline: 20¢ per gallon

Income
Median income for a 4 person family: $34,978

Personal per Capita Income
1992: $17,892
1991: $17,248
1990: $16,600

Disposable per Capita Income
1992: $15,965
1991: $15,307
1990: $14,642

Private Employment Weekly Wages

Average
1989: $419
1988: $408
1987: $408

Manufacturing
1989: $394
1988: $511
1987: $489

Services
1989: $384
1988: $371
1987: $361

Wholesale
1989: $548
1988: $531
1987: $503

Retail
1989: $233
1988: $229
1987: $224

Highway Statistics

Total Highway Miles
1990: 305,951
1989: 305,692
1988: 300,444

Federal Highway Aid
1991: $779,920,000
1990: $849,531,000
1989: $943,678,000

Electricity
Average Cost per Kilowatt Hour
1990: 5.77¢
1989: 5.68¢
1988: 5.58¢

Housing (1990)
Owner occupied units: 3,695,115
Median house value: $59,600

Renter occupied units: 2,375,822
Median rent: $328
Total vacant units: 938,062
Homeowner vacancy rate: 3.2%
Rental vacancy rate: 13.0%

State Business Incentives and Assistance

Enterprise Zone Incentives
The local government may: 1) refund the local share of sales and use taxes, 2) reduce or eliminate other fees; 3) provide priority status for local funded projects; 4) amend zoning regulations; 5) waive development fees; 6) reduce municipal utility rates; 7) provide priority status for services; and 8) sales and use taxes refunded for job retention to qualified business.

The State government may: 1) adopt agency rules that encourage development in the zone; 2) waive performance bond for public works less than $200,000; 3) give preference for state loan and grant programs; 4) give refunds of State sales tax of $2,000 per new job created to designated enterprise projects. Maximum refund of state sales tax paid for certain machinery and/or equipment is $1.25 million per state-designated project, 5) franchise tax reduction for state-designated enterprise projects; and 6) sale of publicly owned real property below market value.

Financial and Business Assistance
Industrial Revenue Bonds. Administered by the Department of Commerce, this program issues tax-exempt and taxable bonds to help finance international exporting of Texas products, for new and expanding firms. This program also allows local governments to create nonprofit industrial development corporations through which monies are coordinated and bonds can be issued for manufacturing and industrial development projects.

Small Business Revitalization Program. Administered by the Department of Commerce, this program is designed to promote job creation by making affordable fixed asset financing available to healthy small businesses seeking to expand.

Texas Public Facilities Capital Access Program. Administered by the Business Development Division of the Department of Commerce, this program was established to promote economic development and to assist eligible cities, counties and other subdivisions in financing eligible projects for economic development

Product Commercialization Fund. Administered by the Department of Commerce with an advisory board for the fund, this program is designed to help finance the commercialization of new or improved products in the areas of high technology and agriculture.

Education and Training
Customized Training. Administered by the Work Force Development Division of the Department of Commerce, this program provides customized industrial training for

Major Companies in the State

Company name	Fortune 500 rank	City	Telephone	SIC number
Fortune 500 Companies				
Baker Hughes Inc.	184	Houston	713-439-8600	3533
Baroid Corp.	464	Houston	713-987-4000	2899
Coastal Corp.	046	Houston	713-877-1400	2911
Compaq Computer Corp.	119	Houston	713-370-0670	3571
Cooper Industries Inc.	089	Houston	713-739-5400	3646
Dell Computer Corp.	386	Austin	512-338-4400	3571
Diamond Shamrock Inc.	178	San Antonio	210-641-6800	2911
Dr. Pepper–Seven-Up Companies Inc.	456	Dallas	214-360-7000	2087
Dresser Industries Inc.	116	Dallas	214-740-6000	3563
E Systems Inc.	214	Dallas	214-661-1000	3812
Exxon Corp.	002	Irving	214-444-1000	1311
Fina Inc.	146	Dallas	214-750-2400	2911
Imperial Holly Corp.	446	Sugar Land	713-491-9181	2062
Insilco Corp.	432	Midland	915-684-4411	2731
Kimberly Clark Corp.	075	Dallas	214-830-1200	2676
Lyondell Petrochemical Co.	111	Houston	713-652-7200	2911
Mary Kay Corp.	488	Wilmington	302-998-0592	2844
Maxus Energy Corp.	434	Dallas	214-953-2000	1311
Maxxam Inc.	205	Houston	713-975-7600	3354
Mitchell Energy & Development Corp.	392	Woodlands	713-377-5500	4922
N L Industries Inc.	378	Houston	713-987-5000	2816
NCH Corp.	454	Irving	214-438-0211	2842
Oryx Energy Co.	289	Dallas	214-715-4000	1311
Pennzoil Co.	173	Houston	713-546-4000	2911
Pilgrim's Pride Corp.	403	Pittsburg	903-856-7901	2015
Shell Oil Co.	018	Houston	713-241-6161	2911
Stewart & Stevenson Services Inc.	448	Houston	713-868-7700	3621
Temple Inland Inc.	174	Diboll	409-829-2211	2631
Tenneco Inc.	030	Houston	713-757-2131	3523
Tesoro Petroleum Corp.	369	San Antonio	210-828-8484	2911
Texas Industries Inc.	486	Dallas	214-647-6700	3312
Texas Instruments Inc.	071	Dallas	214-995-2551	3674
Trinity Industries Inc.	312	Dallas	214-689-0592	3743
Union Texas Petroleum Holdings Inc.	442	Houston	713-623-6544	1311
Valero Energy Corp.	309	San Antonio	210-246-2000	2911
Valhi Inc.	402	Dallas	214-233-1700	2063
Other Major Companies in the State				
American Airlines Inc.		Fort Worth	817-963-1234	4512
American General Corp.		Houston	713-522-1111	6311
AMR Corp.		Fort Worth	817-963-1234	4512
Browning Ferris Industries Inc.		Houston	713-870-8100	4953
Burlington Northern Railroad Co.		Fort Worth	817-878-2000	4011
Continental Airlines Holdings Inc.		Houston	713-834-2950	4512
Continental Airlines Inc.		Houston	713-834-5000	4512
Enron Corp.		Houston	713-853-6161	1321
Halliburton Co.		Dallas	214-978-2600	1541
Houston Industries Inc.		Houston	713-629-3000	4911

Major Companies in the State

Company name	Fortune 500 rank	City	Telephone	SIC number
Houston Lighting & Power Co.		Houston	713-228-9211	4911
J C Penney Co. Inc.		Dallas	214-591-1000	5311
Southland Corp.		Dallas	214-828-7011	5411
Sysco Corp.		Houston	713-584-1390	5142
Tandy Corp.		Fort Worth	817-390-3700	5731
Tennessee Gas Pipeline Co.		Houston	713-757-2131	3531
Texas Utilities Co.		Dallas	214-812-4600	4911
Transco Energy Co.		Houston	713-439-2000	4922

new and expanding companies locating in Texas. Start-up training programs may be combined with the Job Training Partnership Act facilities.

Job Training Partnership Act. This program operates with funding from the U.S. Department of Labor. It provides job training and other employment related services.

State Offices

Real estate: Real Estate Commission, Wallace Collins, Administrator, PO Box 12188, Austin, TX 78711-2188. 512-465-3900

Chamber of commerce: Texas State Chamber of Commerce, Larry S. Milner, President, 300 W. 15th St. #875, Austin, TX 78701. 512-472-1594

Economic development: Department of Commerce, Business Development Division, William Taylor, Director, PO Box 12728, 816 South Congress, Austin, TX 78711. 512-472-5059, 512-320-9475

Department of Commerce, Enterprise Zone Program, Camille Berry, Manager, 816 South Congress Street, Suite 1200, Austin, TX 78711. 512-472-5059

Small Business Development Center, Betsy Gatewood, Regional Director, University of Houston, 601 Jefferson, Suite 2330, Houston, TX 77002. 712-752-8444

Small Business Development Center, Robert McKinley, Director, University of Texas at San Antonio, Hemisphere Plaza Building, Suite 448, San Antonio, TX 78205. 512-224-0791

Environmental affairs: Licensing and Regulation Department, Larry E. Kosta, Exec Director, PO Box 12157, Austin, TX 78711. 512-463-3172

Labor: Employment Commission, James J. Kaster, Chairman, 101 East 15th Street, Austin, TX 78778. 512-463-2900

Unemployment: Employment Commission, James J. Kaster, Chairman, 101 East 15th Street, Austin, TX 78778. 512-463-2900

Worker's compensation: Employment Commission, James J. Kaster, Chairman, 101 East 15th Street, Austin, TX 78778. 512-463-2900

Occupational safety and health: Employment Commission, James J. Kaster, Chairman, 101 East 15th Street, Austin, TX 78778. 512-463-2900

Secretary of state: Secretary of State, John Hannah, Secretary of State, PO Box 12887, Austin, TX 78711-2887. 512-463-5701

Taxation and revenue: Comptroller of Public Accounts, Bob Bullock, Comptroller, 111 East 17th Street, Austin, TX 78774. 512-463-4000

Designated Zones for Economic Development

Enterprise Zones

Enacted in: 1988

No. of established zones: 28

Foreign Trade Zones

Zone No. 115, Beaumont, Texas, Grantee: Foreign-Trade Zone of Southeast Texas, Inc., Jefferson County Airport, Bill Kimbrough, 2748 Biterbo Road, Beaumont, TX 77705, 409-835-5367

Foreign Trade Zone No. 62, Brownsville, Texas, Grantee/Operator: Brownsville Navigation District, Port of Brownsville, Judith Adams, PO Box 3070, Brownsville, TX 78523-3070, 512-831-4592

Foreign Trade Zone No. 155, Calhoun/Victoria Counties, Texas, Grantee: Calhoun-Victoria Foreign-Trade Zone, Inc., Doug Lynch, 2206 N. Highway 35 Bypass, Port Lavaca, TX 77979, 512-987-2813

Foreign Trade Zone No. 122, Corpus Christi, Texas, Grantee/Operator: Port of Corpus Christi Authority, Thomas S. Moore, PO Box 1541, Corpus Christi, TX 78403, 512-882-5633

Foreign Trade Zone No. 39, Dallas/Fort Worth, Texas, Grantee/Operator: Dallas/Fort Worth Int'l Airport Board, Dave Rystrom, PO Drawer DFW, DFW Airport, TX 75261, 214-574-3079

Foreign Trade Zone No. 168, Dallas/Fort Worth, Texas, Grantee: Dallas/Fort Worth Maquila Trade Development Corp., Operator: Foreign Trade Zone Company of Texas, Dennis Konopatzke, 1600 Three Lincoln Centre, 5430 LBJ Freeway, Dallas, TX 75240, 214-991-9955

Foreign Trade Zone No. 97, Del Rio, Texas, Grantee/Operator: City of Del Rio, Jeff Pomeranz, City Manager's Office, PO Drawer DD, Del Rio, TX 78840, 512-774-2781

Foreign Trade Zone No. 96, Eagle Pass, Texas, Grantee: City of Eagle Pass, Operator: Maverick Co. Dev Corp, Arthur Pine, PO Box 1188, Eagle Pass, TX 78853, 512-773-6166

Foreign Trade Zone No. 68, El Paso, Texas, Grantee: City of El Paso, Operator: El Paso International Airport, Robert C. Jacob, Jr., El Paso, TX 79925, 915-772-4271

Foreign Trade Zone No. 150, El Paso, Texas, Grantee: Westport Economic Development Corporation, Veronica K. Callaghan, #3 Butterfield Trail Blvd., El Paso, TX 79940, 915-775-1411

Foreign Trade Zone No. 113, Ellis County, Texas, Grantee: Midlothian Trade Zone Corporation, Operator: Trade Zone Operations, Inc., Larry White, PO Box 788, Two Park Avenue, Midlothian, TX 76065, 214-299-5462

Foreign Trade Zone No. 149, Freeport, Texas, Grantee: Port of Freeport, Robert Van Borssum, PO Box 615, Freeport, TX 77541, 409-233-2667

Foreign Trade Zone No. 36, Galveston, Texas, Grantee: City of Galveston, Operator: Port of Galveston, Robert C. Schulz, Galveston Wharves, PO Box 328, Galveston, TX 77553, 409-766-6120

Foreign Trade Zone No. 84, Harris County, Texas, Grantee: Port of Houston Authority, Jack Beasley, PO Box 2562, Houston, TX 77252, 713-739-8522

Foreign Trade Zone No. 94, Laredo, Texas, Grantee: City of Laredo, Operator: Laredo International Airport, Operator of Foreign-Trade Foreign Trade Zone No. 94, Jose L. Flores, 518 Flightline, Building #132, Laredo, TX 78041, 512-722-4933

Foreign Trade Zone No. 12, McAllen, Texas, Grantee/Operator: McAllen Economic Development Corporation, Joyce Dean, 6401 S. 33rd Street, McAllen, TX 78501, 512-682-4306

Foreign Trade Zone No. 171, Liberty County, Texas, Grantee: Liberty County Economic Development Corporation, Ronnie McWaters, PO Box 1733, Cleveland, TX 77327, 713-592-8786 or 713-592-3404/Maureen Hirsch

Foreign Trade Zone No. 165, Midland, Texas, Grantee/Operator: City of Midland, Victor White, Department of Airports, PO Box 60305, Midland, TX 79711, 915-563-1460

Foreign Trade Zone No. 117, Orange, Texas, Grantee: Foreign-Trade Zone of Southeast Texas, Inc., Jefferson County Airport, Bill Kimbrough, 2748 Biterbo Road, Beaumont, TX 77705, 409-835-5367

Foreign Trade Zone No. 116, Port Arthur, Texas, Grantee: Foreign-Trade Zone of Southeast Texas, Inc., Jefferson County Airport, Bill Kimbrough, 2748 Biterbo Road, Beaumont, TX 77705, 409-835-5367

Foreign Trade Zone No. 178, Presidio, Texas, Grantee/Operator: Presidio Economic Development Corporation, Jose Leyva, President, PO Box 1414, Presidio, TX 79845, 915-229-3724

Foreign Trade Zone No. 80, San Antonio, Texas, Grantee: City of San Antonio, Madeleine Hamel, PO Box 839966, San Antonio, TX 78283-3966, 512-554-7107

Foreign Trade Zone No. 95, Starr County, Texas, Grantee/Operator: Starr County Industrial Foundation, Sam Vale, PO Drawer H, Rio Grande City, TX 78582, 512-487-5606

Foreign Trade Zone No. 156, Weslaco, Texas, Grantee: City of Weslaco, Dr. Wai-Lin Lam, 500 South Kansas, Weslaco, TX 78596, 512-968-3181 ext. 224

Labor Unions

Aluminum, Brick and Glass Workers, International Union (AFL-CIO)

Automobile, Aerospace & Agricultural Implement Workers of America, International Union, United, (UAW AFL-CIO)

Carpenters and Joiners of America, United Brotherhood of (AFL-CIO)

Clothing and Textile Workers Union, Amalgamated (AFL-CIO)

Electrical Workers, International Brotherhood of (AFL-CIO)

Food and Commercial Workers International Union, United (AFL-CIO)

Laborers' International Union of North America (AFL-CIO)

Operating Engineers, International Union of (AFL-CIO)

Plumbing and Pipe Fitting Industry of The United States and Canada, United Association of, Journeymen and Apprentices of the (AFL-CIO)

Rubber, Cork, Linoleum and Plastic Workers of America, United (AFL-CIO)

Sheet Metal Workers' International Association (AFL-CIO)

Steelworkers of America, United (AFL-CIO)

Teamsters, Chauffeurs, Warehousemen and Helpers of America, International Brotherhood of, (AFL-CIO)

Universities with Ph.D. Programs

Abilene Christian University, Abilene
Baylor College of Dentistry, Dallas
Baylor University, Waco
Our Lady of The Lake University of San Antonio, San Antonio
Rice University, Houston
St. Mary's University of San Antonio, San Antonio
Sam Houston State University, Huntsville
Southern Methodist University, Dallas
Stephen F. Austin State University, Nacogdoches
Texas A&I University, Kingsville
Texas A&M University, College Station
Texas Chiropractic College, Pasadena
Texas Christian University, Fort Worth
Texas Southern University, Houston

Texas Tech University, Lubbock
Texas Woman's University, Denton
University of Dallas, Irving
University of North Texas, Denton
University of St. Thomas, Houston
University of Texas at Arlington, Arlington
University of Texas at Austin, Austin
University of Texas at Dallas, Richardson
University of Texas at El Paso, El Paso
University of Texas Health Science Center at Houston, Houston
University of Texas Health Science Center at San Antonio, San Antonio
University of Texas Medical Branch at Galveston, Galveston
University of Texas Southwestern Medical Center at Dallas, Dallas

ABILENE, TX (MSA)

Geographic Profile

Land Area
915.7 square miles

Counties and Parishes
Taylor

Ranking Highlights
216 *out of 319 in total* **land area**
287 *out of 319 in* **population growth**, *1970–1990*
139 *out of 310 in having the lowest* **unemployment** *rate*
287 *out of 310 in size of* **labor force**
123 *out of 318 in the percentage of* **college graduates**
197 *out of 292 in per capita personal* **income**
272 *out of 319 in number of* **manufacturing establishments**
178 *out of 318 in* **physicians** *per 1000 people*
155 *out of 318 in* **hospital beds** *per 1000 people*
105 *out of 267 in fewest* **crimes** *per 1000 people*
165 *out of 266 in fewest* **violent crimes** *per 1000 people*
 63 *out of 319 in per capita* **federal funds and grants**

Quality of Life Indexes (Rate per 1000 population)
Crime rate in 1991:	55.5
Violent crime rate in 1991:	7.3
Physicians rate in 1992:	1.74
Hospital bed rate in 1991:	3.9

ACCRA Cost of Living Indexes
(First quarter 1993, average = 100)
Composite index:	93.1
Utilities index:	104.5
Housing index:	83.4

Overview
Abilene ranks among the top twenty cities in the nation according to *Money* magazine. It is a West Central Texas City, located in Taylor County, some 183 miles west of Dallas. The City is the center of a 22-county area called "Big Country". It is the hub of retail trade, manufacturing, farming and ranching, medical care, the petroleum industry and other economic segments in this part of Texas.

Abilene's location on Interstate Highway 20, U.S. highways 80, 83, 84, and 277 and State highways 351 and 36, makes it accessible to all parts of the state as well as the Southwest Region.

The city is home to two major medical centers, three universities, one state junior college and a state vocational/technical school. It is the regional headquarters of numerous county, state and federal agencies, including Dyess Air Force Base. It's airport is served by three major commuter lines with nineteen flights daily.

Population (1990)

Total Population and Growth Rate
1990: 119,655
1980: 110,932
1970: 97,853
Growth rate 1970–1990: 22%

Race and Hispanic Origin
White: 83.8%
Black: 6.3%
Asian/Pacific Islander: 1.2%
Native American: 0.4%
Hispanic origin: 14.6%
White not Hispanic: 77.7%

Age
Ages 18 to 20: 6.2%
Ages 21 to 24: 7.2%
Ages 25 to 44: 30.6%
Ages 45 to 54: 8.8%
Ages 55 to 59: 4.1%
Ages 60 to 64: 3.7%
Ages 65 plus: 12%

Educational Attainment (1990)
Percent having completed high school: 75.4%
Percent having completed college: 20.7%
Elementary and high school enrollment: 21,348

Federal Funds and Grants Received ($1000)
Total received in 1989: 519,000
Funds received per capita: 4,261

Civilian Labor Force
1993 (April):   49,019
1992 average: 51,778
1991 average: 50,384
1990 average: 50,676

Unemployment
1993 (April):   5.6%
1992 average: 6.6%
1991 average: 5.9%
1990 average: 6.1%

Average Annual Pay
1988: $17,697
1987: $17,344
1985: $16,884

Per Capita Personal Income
1991: $16,347
1990: $15,360
1989: $14,876

Business Climate (1987)

Manufacturing
Number of establishments in 1987: 122
Shipments in 1987 ($1,000): $900,600
Employees in 1987: 4,900

Change in employment, 1982 to 1987: -18.3%
Average annual pay for manufacturing work in 1989: $21,651
Average annual pay for production work in 1987: $15,379

Wholesale Trade
Number of establishments in 1987: 296
Total sales in 1987 ($1,000): $1,319,500
Change in sales, 1982 to 1987: -14.0%

Retail Trade
Number of establishments in 1987: 884
Total sales in 1987 ($1,000): $1,319,500
Retail sales per household in 1987: $16,874
Average annual pay in 1989: $11,239

Service Industry
Selected receipts in 1987 ($1,000): $345,400
Average annual pay in 1989: $17,265

Housing
Total number of units in 1990: 49,988
Occupied units in 1990: 43,301
Owner-occupied units in 1990: 62.2%
1993 ACCRA average cost: $95,000
1993 ACCRA average rent for an apartment: $439

Chamber of Commerce
Abilene Chamber of Commerce, Charlie Dromgoole, President, 341 Hickory, PO Box 2281, Abilene, TX 79604. 915-677-7241

Economic Development Office
Abilene Industrial Foundation, Gary Vest, President, 327 Hickory, PO Box 2281, Abilene, TX 79604. 915-673-7349, FAX 915-677-0622

Major Businesses

Company	SIC	Telephone
Arrow Ford Inc.	5511	(915) 692-9500
First Abilene Bankshares	6022	(915) 675-7155
General Beverages of Texas	2086	(915) 673-5243
Hendrick Medical Center	8062	(915) 670-2000
Independent Bankshares Inc.	6022	(915) 677-5550
Independent Grocers Inc.	5141	(915) 692-1440
Merchants, Inc.	4213	(915) 677-1881
Pride SGP Inc.	2911	(915) 677-2223
Sellers, Cecil Cattle Co.	5154	(915) 576-3618
Skinny's Inc.	5411	(915) 672-2882
West Texas Utilities	4911	(915) 674-7000
West Texas Wholesale Supply	5072	(915) 677-2851

Colleges and Universities
Abilene Christian University, Abilene
Hardin-Simmons University, Abilene
Mcmurry University, Abilene

AMARILLO, TX (MSA)

Geographic Profile

Land Area
1823.9 square miles

Counties and Parishes
Potter
Randall

Ranking Highlights

103 *out of 319 in total* land area
129 *out of 319 in* population growth, *1970–1990*
 76 *out of 310 in having the lowest* unemployment *rate*
189 *out of 310 in size of* labor force
165 *out of 318 in the percentage of* college graduates
157 *out of 292 in per capita personal* income
229 *out of 319 in number of* manufacturing establishments
117 *out of 318 in* physicians *per 1000 people*
 68 *out of 318 in* hospital beds *per 1000 people*
195 *out of 267 in fewest* crimes *per 1000 people*
111 *out of 266 in fewest* violent crimes *per 1000 people*
150 *out of 319 in per capita* federal funds and grants

Quality of Life Indexes (Rate per 1000 population)

Crime rate in 1991:	71.1
Violent crime rate in 1991:	5.2
Physicians rate in 1992:	2.04
Hospital bed rate in 1991:	5.17

ACCRA Cost of Living Indexes

(First quarter 1993, average = 100)

Composite index:	89.2
Utilities index:	77.4
Housing index:	80.9

Population (1990)

Total Population and Growth Rate
1990: 187,547
1980: 173,699
1970: 144,396
Growth rate 1970–1990: 30%

Race and Hispanic Origin
White: 84.5%
Black: 5.2%
Asian/Pacific Islander: 1.7%
Native American: 0.7%
Hispanic origin: 13.5%
White not Hispanic: 79.0%

Age
Ages 18 to 20: 4.7%
Ages 21 to 24: 5.7%
Ages 25 to 44: 31.7%
Ages 45 to 54: 9.5%
Ages 55 to 59: 4.4%
Ages 60 to 64: 4.3%
Ages 65 plus: 11.6%

Educational Attainment (1990)

Percent having completed high school: 76.4%
Percent having completed college: 18.7%
Elementary and high school enrollment: 34,660

Federal Funds and Grants Received ($1000)

Total received in 1989: 616,000
Funds received per capita: N/A

Civilian Labor Force

1993 (April):   99,251
1992 average: 98,325
1991 average: 96,783
1990 average: 96,259

Unemployment

1993 (April):   4.6%
1992 average: 5.6%
1991 average: 5.0%
1990 average: 5.1%

Average Annual Pay

1988: $18,328
1987: $19,065
1985: $17,467

Per Capita Personal Income

1991: $17,042
1990: $16,343
1989: $15,741

Business Climate (1987)

Manufacturing
Number of establishments in 1987: 184
Shipments in 1987 ($1,000): $3,122,900
Employees in 1987: 11,000
Change in employment, 1982 to 1987: -12.7%
Average annual pay for manufacturing work in 1989: $20,616
Average annual pay for production work in 1987: $20,086

Wholesale Trade
Number of establishments in 1987: 457
Total sales in 1987 ($1,000): $1,864,600
Change in sales, 1982 to 1987: -16.9%

Retail Trade
Number of establishments in 1987: 1,477
Total sales in 1987 ($1,000): $1,864,600
Retail sales per household in 1987: $20,072
Average annual pay in 1989: $11,675

Service Industry
Selected receipts in 1987 ($1,000): $513,300
Average annual pay in 1989: $18,398

Housing

Total number of units in 1990: 80,734

Occupied units in 1990: 71,897
Owner-occupied units in 1990: 64.2%
1993 ACCRA average cost: $88,833
1993 ACCRA average rent for an apartment: $438

Chamber of Commerce

Amarillo Chamber of Commerce, Tom Patterson, President, 1000 S. Polk St., PO Box 9480, Amarillo, TX 79105. 806-373-7800, FAX 806-373-3909

Economic Development Office

Industrial Development Dept., Santa Fe Railway, R.R. Bagby, 1115 S. Taylor, Amarillo, TX 79101.

Major Businesses

Company	SIC	Telephone
Affiliated Foods Inc.	5141	(806) 372-3851
Amarillo Hospital District	8062	(806) 358-9031
Amarillo National Bank	6021	(806) 378-8000
Attebury Grain Inc.	5153	(806) 335-1639
Cactus Feeders Inc.	5154	(806) 373-2333
Caprock Industries Inc.	0211	(806) 371-3700
Cutberth, Dale	7389	(806) 372-2680
First Amarillo Bancorp	6021	(806) 378-1400
Friona Industries, L. P.	0211	(806) 374-1811
Hastings Books & Records	5735	(806) 376-6251
High Plains Baptist Health System	8062	(806) 358-3151
Kelley, Jack B. Inc.	4213	(806) 353-3553
Maywood Inc.	2431	(806) 374-2835
MESA Limited Partnership	1311	(806) 378-1000
MESA Operating Limited Partner	1382	(806) 378-1000
Nunn Electric Supply Corp.	5063	(806) 376-4581
Southwestern Public Servic Co.	4911	(806) 378-2121
St. Anthonys Health Corp.	8062	(806) 378-6278
St. Anthony's Hospital	8062	(806) 376-4411
Western Merchandisers Inc.	5099	(806) 376-6251

Colleges and Universities

Amarillo College, Amarillo
Texas State Technical Institute-Amarillo Campus, Amarillo

AUSTIN, TX (MSA)

Geographic Profile

Land Area

2791.7 square miles

Counties and Parishes

Hays
Travis
Williamson

Ranking Highlights

54 *out of 319 in total* land area
13 *out of 319 in* population growth, *1970–1990*
51 *out of 310 in having the lowest* unemployment *rate*
58 *out of 310 in size of* labor force
19 *out of 318 in the percentage of* college graduates
109 *out of 292 in per capita personal* income
79 *out of 319 in number of* manufacturing establishments
159 *out of 318 in* physicians *per 1000 people*
296 *out of 318 in* hospital beds *per 1000 people*
247 *out of 267 in fewest* crimes *per 1000 people*
106 *out of 266 in fewest* violent crimes *per 1000 people*
70 *out of 319 in per capita* federal funds and grants

Quality of Life Indexes (Rate per 1000 population)

Crime rate in 1991:	87.3
Violent crime rate in 1991:	5.1
Physicians rate in 1992:	1.8
Hospital bed rate in 1991:	2.13

ACCRA Cost of Living Indexes

(First quarter 1993, average = 100)
Composite index: 97.2
Utilities index: 100.4
Housing index: 88.0

Overview

For decades Austin's economic stability was dependent on two major employers: the University of Texas at Austin and the state government. By the late 1950s, however, the Austin Chamber of Commerce had grown aware of the need for new businesses to stimulate and diversify the economy. Since 1966, when IBM located a major facility in the city, Austin has successfully recruited an ever-increasing number of research and development firms. Ranging in size from international companies such as Motorola, IBM, Lockheed, Texas Instruments, and 3M to small and mid-sized firms, among them Radian, Schlumberger, Unisys, and Intera Technologies, these enterprises have been drawn to Austin by the university, the well-educated labor pool, the quality of life, and the presence of many other research facilities. In 1987, Sematech, a unique public/private sector partnership, chose Austin to begin a research and development facility to improve U.S. competitiveness in the manufacturing of semiconductors. Of Austin's seven hundred manufacturers, two hundred are now high-technology firms which employ 65 percent of the manufacturing workforce.

Robert C. Mueller Municipal Airport, four miles northeast of the city, serves the Austin metropolitan area with nine major carriers that provide direct flights to fifteen American cities and two commuter airlines. In 1992 the city was considering moving the airport to Bergstrom Air Force Base since Bergstrom was scheduled for closure in late 1993. Most visitors have to change planes in Dallas or Houston to reach Austin.

Drivers approach Austin via Interstate Highway 35, which runs north-south through the city and links it with Dallas and San Antonio. Travelers from points east (such as Houston) use U.S. 290.

Population (1990)

Total Population and Growth Rate
1990: 781,572
1980: 536,688
1970: 360,463
Growth rate 1970–1990: 117%

Race and Hispanic Origin
White: 76.8%
Black: 9.2%
Asian/Pacific Islander: 2.4%
Native American: 0.4%
Hispanic origin: 20.5%
White not Hispanic: 67.9%

Age
Ages 18 to 20: 6.7%
Ages 21 to 24: 8.6%
Ages 25 to 44: 37.7%
Ages 45 to 54: 8.6%
Ages 55 to 59: 3.1%
Ages 60 to 64: 2.7%
Ages 65 plus: 7.4%

Educational Attainment (1990)
Percent having completed high school: 82.5%
Percent having completed college: 32.2%
Elementary and high school enrollment: 127,144

Federal Funds and Grants Received
Total received in 1989: $3,041,600,000
Funds received per capita: $4,064

Civilian Labor Force
1993 (April):   481,879
1992 average: 470,310
1991 average: 447,811
1990 average: 434,920

Unemployment
1993 (April):   4.2%
1992 average: 5.0%
1991 average: 4.7%
1990 average: 4.6%

Average Annual Pay
1988: $20,394
1987: $19,701
1985: $18,542

Per Capita Personal Income
1991: $18,081
1990: $17,236
1989: $15,898

Business Climate (1987)

Manufacturing
Number of establishments in 1987: 823
Shipments in 1987 ($1,000): $5,371,600
Employees in 1987: 42,500
Change in employment, 1982 to 1987: 26.1%
Average annual pay for manufacturing work in 1989: $29,619
Average annual pay for production work in 1987: $19,068

Wholesale Trade
Number of establishments in 1987: 1,243
Total sales in 1987 ($1,000): $3,169,800
Change in sales, 1982 to 1987: 49.2%

Retail Trade
Number of establishments in 1987: 4,833
Total sales in 1987 ($1,000): $3,169,800
Retail sales per household in 1987: $17,029
Average annual pay in 1989: $11,244

Service Industry
Selected receipts in 1987 ($1,000): $3,009,600
Average annual pay in 1989: $20,058

Office Real Estate (1992)
Office space inventory: 19,517,404 square feet
Average class A Central Business District rental range per sq. ft: $17.00

Vacancy Rates
All areas: 16.2%

Vacancy Rates in Central Business District
Class A space: 18.9%
Class B space: 24.0%

Vacancy Rates Outside Central Business District
Class A space: 4.3%
Class B space: 18.6%

Housing
Total number of units in 1990: 343,886
Occupied units in 1990: 303,871
Owner-occupied units in 1990: 49.6%
1993 ACCRA average cost: N/A
1993 ACCRA average rent for an apartment: N/A

Chamber of Commerce
Greater Austin Chamber of Commerce, Glenn E. West, President, 111 Congress Ave. #10, PO Box 1967, Austin, TX 78767. 512-478-9383

Major Businesses

Company	SIC	Telephone
Abrams, J. D. Inc.	1611	(512) 322-4000
Abrams International Inc.	1611	(512) 322-4000
Capital Cy Federal Savings Assoc.	6035	(512) 478-1607
CJC Holdings, Inc.	3911	(512) 444-2596
Compuadd Corp.	3571	(512) 250-1489
Dell Computer Corp.	3571	(512) 338-4400
Farm Credit Bank of Texas	6159	(512) 465-0400
Franklin Federal Bancorp	6035	(512) 477-5000
G & S Associates, Inc.	7311	(512) 327-8810
GCR Truck Tire Centers Inc.	5531	(512) 328-3446
Hart Graphics, Inc.	2752	(512) 454-4761
Healthvest	6519	(512) 343-5234
Johnson Leif Ford Inc.	5511	(512) 454-3711
Lower Colorado River Authority	4911	(512) 473-3200
Maund Charles Oldsmbile Cadillac	5511	(512) 458-1111
Mc Coy Corp.	5211	(512) 353-5400
National Western Life Insurance	6311	(512) 836-1010
Radian Corp.	8711	(512) 454-4797
Seton Medical Center	8062	(512) 459-2121
Southern Union Co.	4923	(512) 477-5852
St. David's Hospital	8062	(512) 476-7111
Temple Inland Financial Service	6411	(512) 477-6561
Texas County District Retirement	6733	(512) 476-6651
Texas Commerce Bank-Austin	6021	(512) 479-2444
Texas Medical Liability	6351	(512) 454-6781
Texas Municipal Retirement	6733	(512) 476-7577
Tracor Aerospace Inc.	3489	(512) 926-2800
Tracor Inc.	8711	(512) 926-2800
Westmark Systems, Inc.	8731	(512) 322-0222

Colleges and Universities

Austin Community College, Austin
Concordia Lutheran College, Austin
Huston-Tillotson College, Austin
Institute for Christian Studies, Austin
ITT Technical Institute, Austin
St. Edward's University, Austin
University of Texas at Austin, Austin

BEAUMONT–PORT ARTHUR, TX (MSA)

Geographic Profile

Land Area
2154.4 square miles

Counties and Parishes
Hardin
Jefferson
Orange

Ranking Highlights

81 *out of 319 in total land area*
250 *out of 319 in population growth, 1970–1990*
265 *out of 310 in having the lowest unemployment rate*
126 *out of 310 in size of labor force*
266 *out of 318 in the percentage of college graduates*
147 *out of 292 in per capita personal income*
154 *out of 319 in number of manufacturing establishments*
243 *out of 318 in physicians per 1000 people*
60 *out of 318 in hospital beds per 1000 people*
211 *out of 267 in fewest crimes per 1000 people*
217 *out of 266 in fewest violent crimes per 1000 people*
161 *out of 319 in per capita federal funds and grants*

Quality of Life Indexes (Rate per 1000 population)

Crime rate in 1991:	73.9
Violent crime rate in 1991:	9.6
Physicians rate in 1992:	1.42
Hospital bed rate in 1991:	5.29

ACCRA Cost of Living Indexes

(First quarter 1993, average = 100)
Composite index: 95.4
Utilities index: 102.9
Housing index: 75.9

Population (1990)

Total Population and Growth Rate
1990: 361,226
1980: 373,211
1970: 347,568
Growth rate 1970–1990: 4%

Race and Hispanic Origin
White: 73.2%
Black: 23.4%
Asian/Pacific Islander: 1.6%
Native American: 0.2%
Hispanic origin: 4.2%
White not Hispanic: 70.7%

Age
Ages 18 to 20: 4.3%
Ages 21 to 24: 5.1%
Ages 25 to 44: 30.1%

Ages 45 to 54: 10.2%
Ages 55 to 59: 4.7%
Ages 60 to 64: 4.9%
Ages 65 plus: 13.1%

Educational Attainment (1990)

Percent having completed high school: 73.6%
Percent having completed college: 13.7%
Elementary and high school enrollment: 69,879

Federal Funds and Grants Received

Total received in 1989: $1,115,500,000
Funds received per capita: $3,065

Civilian Labor Force

1993 (April):   177,814
1992 average: 176,578
1991 average: 172,075
1990 average: 164,070

Unemployment

1993 (April):   9.8%
1992 average: 9.1%
1991 average: 7.3%
1990 average: 7.4%

Average Annual Pay

1988: $21,598
1987: $20,864
1985: $20,349

Per Capita Personal Income

1991: $17,361
1990: $16,264
1989: $15,262

Business Climate (1987)

Manufacturing

Number of establishments in 1987: 336
Shipments in 1987 ($1,000): $14,079,200
Employees in 1987: 25,600
Change in employment, 1982 to 1987: -31.4%
Average annual pay for manufacturing work in 1989: $36,654
Average annual pay for production work in 1987: $32,105

Wholesale Trade

Number of establishments in 1987: 571
Total sales in 1987 ($1,000): $1,790,200
Change in sales, 1982 to 1987: -34.9%

Retail Trade

Number of establishments in 1987: 2,251
Total sales in 1987 ($1,000): $1,790,200
Retail sales per household in 1987: $15,875
Average annual pay in 1989: $10,763

Service Industry

Selected receipts in 1987 ($1,000): $878,700
Average annual pay in 1989: $19,048

Housing

Total number of units in 1990: 149,807
Occupied units in 1990: 134,238
Owner-occupied units in 1990: 69.7%
1993 ACCRA average cost: $81,100
1993 ACCRA average rent for an apartment: $466

Chamber of Commerce

Beaumont Chamber of Commerce, James M. Stokes, President, 450 Bowie St., PO Box 3150, Beaumont, TX 77704. 409-838-6581

Economic Development Office

Southeast Texas Inc., James M. Stokes, President, 450 Bowie St., PO Box 3150, Beaumont, TX 77704-3150. 409-838-6800, FAX 409-833-6718

Major Businesses

Company	SIC	Telephone
American Paneling & Plywood	5031	(409) 722-9311
American Valve Hydrant Mfg.	3321	(409) 832-7721
Ami Mid-Jefferson Hospital	8062	(409) 727-2321
Austin Industrial, Inc.	1541	(409) 842-2417
Baptist Hospital of Southeast Texas	8062	(409) 835-3781
Beaumont Motor Co.	5511	(409) 892-5050
Buddy Chevrolet Inc.	5511	(409) 962-8371
Conn Appliances, Inc.	5722	(409) 832-1696
Fair Inc.	5311	(409) 892-6010
First Federal Savings & Loan Association	6035	(409) 838-3901
Gulf States Utilities Commission	4911	(409) 838-6631
International Maintenance	1541	(409) 722-8031
J-K Chevrolet, Inc.	5511	(409) 722-0443
King Savers	5411	(409) 860-4619
Kinsel Motors, Inc.	5511	(409) 838-6611
Kinsel Pontiac Cadillac GMC	5511	(409) 899-4000
M & E Food Mart, Inc.	5411	(409) 727-3104
North Star Steel Texas, Inc.	3312	(409) 768-1211
Ohmstede, Inc.	3443	(409) 833-6375
Polysar Gulf Coast, Inc.	2822	(409) 883-9990
R. Corp.	5511	(409) 892-6696
Raiford Motors Inc.	5511	(409) 962-8383
St. Elizabeth Hospital	8062	(409) 892-7171
Texas Commerce Bank	6021	(409) 838-0234
Thermo Tech Inc.	1799	(409) 883-4344
Tri-Con Inc.	5172	(409) 835-2237
Triangle Engners Construction	1629	(409) 727-5436
US Intec, Inc.	2952	(409) 724-7024

Colleges and Universities

Lamar University, Beaumont
Lamar University-Port Arthur, Port Arthur

BRAZORIA, TX (PMSA)

Geographic Profile

Land Area

1386.9 square miles

Counties and Parishes

Brazoria

Ranking Highlights

146 *out of 319 in total* **land area**

38 *out of 319 in* **population growth,** *1970–1990*

219 *out of 310 in having the lowest* **unemployment** *rate*

196 *out of 310 in size of* **labor force**

233 *out of 318 in the percentage of* **college graduates**

73 *out of 292 in per capita personal* **income**

233 *out of 319 in number of* **manufacturing establishments**

314 *out of 318 in* **physicians** *per 1000 people*

315 *out of 318 in* **hospital beds** *per 1000 people*

56 *out of 267 in fewest* **crimes** *per 1000 people*

80 *out of 266 in fewest* **violent crimes** *per 1000 people*

318 *out of 319 in per capita* **federal funds and grants**

Quality of Life Indexes (Rate per 1000 population)

Crime rate in 1991:	44.4
Violent crime rate in 1991:	4.1
Physicians rate in 1992:	0.89
Hospital bed rate in 1991:	1.66

ACCRA Cost of Living Indexes

(First quarter 1993, average = 100)

Composite index:	N/A
Utilities index:	N/A
Housing index:	N/A

Overview

No central city in this area.

Population (1990)

Total Population and Growth Rate

1990: 191,707

1980: 169,587

1970: 108,312

Growth rate 1970–1990: 77%

Race and Hispanic Origin

White: 80.8%

Black: 8.3%

Asian/Pacific Islander: 1.0%

Native American: 0.4%

Hispanic origin: 17.6%

White not Hispanic: 72.9%

Age

Ages 18 to 20: 4.2%

Ages 21 to 24: 5.3%

Ages 25 to 44: 35.5%

Ages 45 to 54: 10.3%

Ages 55 to 59: 4%

Ages 60 to 64: 3.6%

Ages 65 plus: 7.8%

Educational Attainment (1990)

Percent having completed high school: 75.5%

Percent having completed college: 15.1%

Elementary and high school enrollment: 39,538

Federal Funds and Grants Received

Total received in 1989: $278,700,00

Funds received per capita: $1,510

Civilian Labor Force

1993 (April):	89,951
1992 average:	91,510
1991 average:	93,541
1990 average:	89,083

Unemployment

1993 (April): 7.7%

1992 average: 7.9%

1991 average: 5.6%

1990 average: 5.5%

Average Annual Pay

1988: $25,585

1987: $24,085

1985: $22,569

Per Capita Personal Income

1991: $19,104

1990: $18,378

1989: $17,113

Business Climate (1987)

Manufacturing

Number of establishments in 1987: 171

Shipments in 1987 ($1,000): $7,732,600

Employees in 1987: 14,400

Change in employment, 1982 to 1987: -19.1%

Average annual pay for manufacturing work in 1989: $40,859

Average annual pay for production work in 1987: $36,227

Wholesale Trade

Number of establishments in 1987: 230

Total sales in 1987 ($1,000): $388,000

Change in sales, 1982 to 1987: -3.8%

Retail Trade

Number of establishments in 1987: 953

Total sales in 1987 ($1,000): $388,000

Retail sales per household in 1987: $13,097

Average annual pay in 1989: $11,039

Service Industry

Selected receipts in 1987 ($1,000): $256,700

Average annual pay in 1989: $17,440

Housing

Total number of units in 1990: 74,504
Occupied units in 1990: 64,019
Owner-occupied units in 1990: 69.2%
1993 ACCRA average cost: N/A
1993 ACCRA average rent for an apartment: N/A

Chamber of Commerce

Brazoria Chamber of Commerce, Janet G. Parker, 507 1/2 S. Brooks, PO Box 992, Brazoria, TX 77422. 409-798-6100

BROWNSVILLE– HARLINGEN, TX (MSA)

Geographic Profile

Land Area

905.6 square miles

Counties and Parishes

Cameron

Ranking Highlights

218 *out of 319 in total* **land area**
 30 *out of 319 in* **population growth,** *1970–1990*
300 *out of 310 in having the lowest* **unemployment** *rate*
177 *out of 310 in size of* **labor force**
296 *out of 318 in the percentage of* **college graduates**
292 *out of 292 in per capita personal* **income**
235 *out of 319 in number of* **manufacturing establishments**
310 *out of 318 in* **physicians** *per 1000 people*
222 *out of 318 in* **hospital beds** *per 1000 people*
194 *out of 267 in fewest* **crimes** *per 1000 people*
129 *out of 266 in fewest* **violent crimes** *per 1000 people*
294 *out of 319 in per capita* **federal funds and grants**

Quality of Life Indexes (Rate per 1000 population)

Crime rate in 1991:	70.9
Violent crime rate in 1991:	6.1
Physicians rate in 1992:	0.98
Hospital bed rate in 1991:	3.17

ACCRA Cost of Living Indexes

(First quarter 1993, average = 100)

Composite index:	91.7
Utilities index:	119.3
Housing index:	76.1

Overview

Brownsville, in the Rio Grande Valley (RGV) of Texas, is located in the southern tip of the state and encompasses all of Cameron, Hidalgo, Starr and Willacy counties. It covers an area of 4,244 square miles. It is not really a valley at all, but a fertile plain sloping away in delta fashion from the Rio Grande. It is bounded on the east by the Gulf of Mexico, on the south by the Rio Grande, which forms the international boundary between the United States and Mexico, and on the west and north by Texas ranching counties

Water for the Rio Grande Valley is supplied by Falcon Lake Reservoir and the Amistad Lake Reservoir, both of which lie on the Rio Grande. There is an ample supply of water for individuals and light industry. Water is also furnished on an allocation basis to various water districts for the irrigation of farm land. Raw water is furnished to the various municipalities and then distributed from municipally-owned water plants to industry. The quality of the water is considered good, the prices reasonable.

The Rio Grande Valley economy is based on agriculture, labor intensive industry, and tourism. The major industry in the Valley is comprised of cotton, grain, vegetables, fruit and sugar cane and processing industries connected with their production. Irrigation makes it a lush agriculture area. Labor intensive companies such as cut and sew, electronic assembly, and machine manufacturing are increasing throughout the area because of reasonable wage scales and minimum union involvement. This industry is growing each year. Many "Winter Texans" come to the RGV as early as September and remain until April. The area is considered a gateway to Mexico for Americans traveling south and to the United States for Latinos traveling north. Tourism contributes $500 million per year to the total economy.

The U.S. Customs laws allow a U.S. owned company to assemble products in a foreign country and return the finished product to the United States, paying duty only on the value added (labor, overhead). This program is ideal for manufacturers looking for major cost reduction in a product that is labor intensive; it is especially attractive in Mexico for the low cost (but productive) labor and the lowest possible inventory cost, since the shipping time is substantially less than to any other "offshore" location.

A twin-plant operation is usually a highly automated or technology-oriented U.S. plant and a labor-intensive sister plant on the Mexican side. Components mass-produced in the United States are delivered to the Mexican plant for the time-consuming hand assembly operations.

Population (1990)

Total Population and Growth Rate
1990: 260,120
1980: 209,727
1970: 140,368
Growth rate 1970–1990: 85%

Race and Hispanic Origin
White: 82.4%
Black: .3%
Asian/Pacific Islander: 0.3%
Native American: 0.2%
Hispanic origin: 81.9%
White not Hispanic: 17.4%

Age
Ages 18 to 20: 5.5%
Ages 21 to 24: 5.8%
Ages 25 to 44: 27.4%
Ages 45 to 54: 8.1%
Ages 55 to 59: 3.6%
Ages 60 to 64: 3.8%
Ages 65 plus: 10.6%

Educational Attainment (1990)
Percent having completed high school: 50.0%
Percent having completed college: 12.0%
Elementary and high school enrollment: 70,242

Federal Funds and Grants Received
Total received in 1989: $569,800,000
Funds received per capita: $2,158

Civilian Labor Force
1993 (April):   112,132
1992 average: 112,452
1991 average: 109,146
1990 average: 105,733

Unemployment
1993 (April): 10.2%
1992 average: 12.6%
1991 average: 12.5%
1990 average: 11.6%

Average Annual Pay
1988: $14,589
1987: $14,087
1985: $13,594

Per Capita Personal Income
1991: $9,824
1990: $9,448
1989: $8,709

Business Climate (1987)

Manufacturing
Number of establishments in 1987: 168
Shipments in 1987 ($1,000): $730,500
Employees in 1987: 8,900
Change in employment, 1982 to 1987: -21.9%
Average annual pay for manufacturing work in 1989: $15,317
Average annual pay for production work in 1987: $12,377

Wholesale Trade
Number of establishments in 1987: 393
Total sales in 1987 ($1,000): $838,200
Change in sales, 1982 to 1987: 1.0%

Retail Trade
Number of establishments in 1987: 1,462
Total sales in 1987 ($1,000): $838,200
Retail sales per household in 1987: $14,781
Average annual pay in 1989: $9,961

Service Industry
Selected receipts in 1987 ($1,000): $353,400
Average annual pay in 1989: $13,987

Housing
Total number of units in 1990: 88,759
Occupied units in 1990: 73,278
Owner-occupied units in 1990: 64.4%
1993 ACCRA average cost: N/A
1993 ACCRA average rent for an apartment: N/A

Chamber of Commerce
Brownsville Chamber of Commerce, Edward Weeks, President, 1600 E. Elizabeth St., PO Box 752, Brownsville, TX

78522-0752. 512-542-4341, FAX 512-546-3938

Economic Development Office

Harlingen Area Chamber of Commerce, David E. Allex, President, 311 E. Tyler St., PO Box 189, Harlingen, TX 78551. 800-531-7346, 512-423-5440, FAX 512-425-3870

Economic Development Organizations

Brownsville Economic Development Council, Robert L. Gonzales, President, 1600 E. Elizabeth St., Brownsville, TX 78520. 512-541-1183, FAX 512-546-3938

Major Businesses

Company	SIC	Telephone
Bazaar of Brownsville	5064	(512) 546-6626
Boggus Motor Co. Inc.	5511	(512) 423-2580
Bush Supply Co.	5063	(512) 428-1613
Cardenas Motors, Inc.	5511	(512) 542-3541
De La Garza, E., Inc.	5141	(512) 542-3576
Edelstein's Better Furniture	5712	(512) 542-5605
Gorges Foodservice Inc.	2013	(512) 423-6780
Gulf Packing Co. Inc.	2011	(512) 399-2631
Harlingen National Bancshare	6021	(512) 423-6420
La Casa Del Nylon	5064	(512) 546-4133
Lopez Super Market Inc.	5411	(512) 544-4950
Metex Enterprises Inc.	3442	(512) 423-0912
Pittman & Davis Inc.	5961	(512) 423-2154
Rincon Fabrics Inc.	5949	(512) 546-4430
Rio Grande Oil Mill Ltd.	2074	(512) 423-6540
Rio Grande Valley Suger Growers	2061	(512) 636-1411
Schulgen & Son Inc.	1542	(512) 943-2030
Tex Steel Corp.	3442	(512) 423-0912
Texas Commerce Bank-Brownsville	6022	(512) 546-2461
Tipton Motors, Inc.	5511	(512) 350-5600
Trico Technologies Corp.	3714	(512) 544-2722
Valley Baptist Medical Center	8062	(512) 421-1100
Valley Central Sales, Inc.	5148	(512) 636-1631
Valley Co-Op Oil Mill	2074	(512) 425-4545
Valley Lincoln-Mercury	5511	(512) 423-5130
Valley Nissan, Inc.	5511	(512) 423-6975
Valley Trucking Co. Inc.	4213	(512) 831-4511

Colleges and Universities

Texas Southmost College, Brownsville

Texas State Technical Institute-Harlingen Campus, Harlingen

BRYAN–COLLEGE STATION, TX (MSA)

Geographic Profile

Land Area

585.8 square miles

Counties and Parishes

Brazos

Ranking Highlights

275 *out of 319 in total* **land area**

16 *out of 319 in* **population growth**, *1970–1990*

15 *out of 310 in having the lowest* **unemployment** *rate*

246 *out of 310 in size of* **labor force**

7 *out of 318 in the percentage of* **college graduates**

284 *out of 292 in per capita personal* **income**

303 *out of 319 in number of* **manufacturing establishments**

9 *out of 318 in* **physicians** *per 1000 people*

287 *out of 318 in* **hospital beds** *per 1000 people*

162 *out of 267 in fewest* **crimes** *per 1000 people*

121 *out of 266 in fewest* **violent crimes** *per 1000 people*

298 *out of 319 in per capita* **federal funds and grants**

Quality of Life Indexes (Rate per 1000 population)

Crime rate in 1991:	65.9
Violent crime rate in 1991:	5.6
Physicians rate in 1992:	4.6
Hospital bed rate in 1991:	2.29

ACCRA Cost of Living Indexes

(First quarter 1993, average = 100)

Composite index:	98.6
Utilities index:	99.2
Housing index:	96.9

Overview

Bryan/College Station is home to Texas A&M University, which ranks in the top ten in the nation in funded research. TAMU's presence provides a stable economic base as well as any resources associated with a large university. Bryan/College Station is within a three hour drive of 75% of the state's population. Houston lies 90 miles southeast, Dallas 175 miles north, Austin 100 miles west and San Antonio 150 miles southwest.

Bryan/College Station is the economic hub of the seven-county Brazos Valley region, serving that area with medical services, major retail shopping areas, industrial jobs and cultural and recreational facilities. From mid 1992 to mid 1993 over 3,000 non-agricultural jobs were created in Bryan/College Station.

Population (1990)

Total Population and Growth Rate

1990: 121,862

1980: 93,588

1970: 57,978
Growth rate 1970–1990: 110%

Race and Hispanic Origin
White: 77.8%
Black: 11.2%
Asian/Pacific Islander: 3.5%
Native American: 0.2%
Hispanic origin: 13.7%
White not Hispanic: 71.5%

Age
Ages 18 to 20: 15.2%
Ages 21 to 24: 16.7%
Ages 25 to 44: 28.5%
Ages 45 to 54: 6.7%
Ages 55 to 59: 2.5%
Ages 60 to 64: 2.1%
Ages 65 plus: 6.7%

Educational Attainment (1990)
Percent having completed high school: 79.8%
Percent having completed college: 35.8%
Elementary and high school enrollment: 16,698

Federal Funds and Grants Received
Total received in 1989: $249,900,000
Funds received per capita: $2,144

Civilian Labor Force
1993 (April):   68,386
1992 average: 65,673
1991 average: 63,186
1990 average: 61,784

Unemployment
1993 (April):   3.9%
1992 average: 3.9%
1991 average: 3.6%
1990 average: 3.5%

Average Annual Pay
1988: $16,656
1987: $16,283
1985: $15,658

Per Capita Personal Income
1991: $13,068
1990: $12,430
1989: $11,781

Business Climate (1987)
Manufacturing
Number of establishments in 1987: 87
Shipments in 1987 ($1,000): $283,200
Employees in 1987: 2,400
Change in employment, 1982 to 1987: -25.0%
Average annual pay for manufacturing work in 1989: $20,786
Average annual pay for production work in 1987: $17,813

Wholesale Trade
Number of establishments in 1987: 147
Total sales in 1987 ($1,000): $287,900
Change in sales, 1982 to 1987: 1.5%

Retail Trade
Number of establishments in 1987: 693
Total sales in 1987 ($1,000): $287,900
Retail sales per household in 1987: $14,084
Average annual pay in 1989: $9,125

Service Industry
Selected receipts in 1987 ($1,000): $255,500
Average annual pay in 1989: $16,019

Housing
Total number of units in 1990: 48,799
Occupied units in 1990: 43,725
Owner-occupied units in 1990: 41.9%
1993 ACCRA average cost: $107,120
1993 ACCRA average rent for an apartment: $520

Chamber of Commerce
Bryan-College Station Chamber of Commerce, K. Jack Speer, Exec. Vice President, 401 S. Washington, PO Box 726, Bryan, TX 77806. 409-779-2278

Economic Development Office
Bryan-College Station Economic Development Corp., Robert M. Worley, Exec. Director, 1307 Memorial Dr. Suite 210, Bryan, TX 77802-5205. 409-776-4880, FAX 409-774-0397

Economic Development Organizations
Bryan Development Foundation, Director, PO Box 1000, Bryan, TX 77802. 409-361-3684

Major Businesses

Company	SIC	Telephone
Allen Oldsmobile-Cadillac	5511	(409) 779-3516
Amwest Savings Association	6035	(409) 361-6200
Bossier Chrysler Dodge	5511	(409) 823-8111
Bryan Construction Co.	1629	(409) 776-6000
Bryan Imports, Inc.	5511	(409) 776-7600
Light, Tom Chevrolet Co.	5511	(409) 823-0061
National Feeds Inc.	5153	(409) 776-2700
O. I. Corp.	3826	(409) 690-1711
Producers Coop Association	5999	(409) 778-6000
Readfield Meats & Freezer	5147	(409) 776-4006
Timmons, K. D., Inc.	5171	(409) 822-1394

Colleges and Universities
Texas A & M University, College Station

CORPUS CHRISTI, TX (MSA)

Geographic Profile

Land Area
1527.7 square miles

Counties and Parishes
Nueces
San Patricio

Ranking Highlights

128 *out of 319 in total* **land area**
169 *out of 319 in* **population growth,** *1970–1990*
276 *out of 310 in having the lowest* **unemployment** *rate*
129 *out of 310 in size of* **labor force**
220 *out of 318 in the percentage of* **college graduates**
245 *out of 292 in per capita personal* **income**
183 *out of 319 in number of* **manufacturing establishments**
183 *out of 318 in* **physicians** *per 1000 people*
126 *out of 318 in* **hospital beds** *per 1000 people*
244 *out of 267 in fewest* **crimes** *per 1000 people*
154 *out of 266 in fewest* **violent crimes** *per 1000 people*
152 *out of 319 in per capita* **federal funds and grants**

Quality of Life Indexes (Rate per 1000 population)

Crime rate in 1991:	86.9
Violent crime rate in 1991:	7.0
Physicians rate in 1992:	1.72
Hospital bed rate in 1991:	4.24

ACCRA Cost of Living Indexes

(First quarter 1993, average = 100)
Composite index: 92.3
Utilities index: 109.9
Housing index: 81.1

Population (1990)

Total Population and Growth Rate
1990: 349,894
1980: 326,228
1970: 284,832
Growth rate 1970–1990: 23%

Race and Hispanic Origin
White: 75.7%
Black: 3.9%
Asian/Pacific Islander: 0.8%
Native American: 0.4%
Hispanic origin: 52.0%
White not Hispanic: 43.3%

Age
Ages 18 to 20: 4.6%
Ages 21 to 24: 5.4%
Ages 25 to 44: 31.6%
Ages 45 to 54: 9.4%
Ages 55 to 59: 4.1%
Ages 60 to 64: 4%
Ages 65 plus: 10.2%

Educational Attainment (1990)

Percent having completed high school: 67.6%
Percent having completed college: 16.0%
Elementary and high school enrollment: 77,378

Federal Funds and Grants Received

Total received in 1989: $1,115,000,000
Funds received per capita: $3,114

Civilian Labor Force

1993 (April): 167,927
1992 average: 171,753
1991 average: 165,187
1990 average: 162,370

Unemployment

1993 (April): 7.8%
1992 average: 9.6%
1991 average: 7.9%
1990 average: 6.9%

Average Annual Pay

1988: $19,375
1987: $18,583
1985: $18,387

Per Capita Personal Income

1991: $15,273
1990: $14,521
1989: $13,391

Business Climate (1987)

Manufacturing
Number of establishments in 1987: 258
Shipments in 1987 ($1,000): $6,756,200
Employees in 1987: 11,000
Change in employment, 1982 to 1987: -26.2%
Average annual pay for manufacturing work in 1989: $31,526
Average annual pay for production work in 1987: $24,859

Wholesale Trade
Number of establishments in 1987: 725
Total sales in 1987 ($1,000): $1,832,700
Change in sales, 1982 to 1987: -7.4%

Retail Trade
Number of establishments in 1987: 2,171
Total sales in 1987 ($1,000): $1,832,700
Retail sales per household in 1987: $15,863
Average annual pay in 1989: $10,449

Service Industry
Selected receipts in 1987 ($1,000): $918,200
Average annual pay in 1989: $17,755

Office Real Estate (1992)

Office space inventory: 4,370,000 square feet

Average class A Central Business District rental range per sq. ft: $12.60

Vacancy Rates
All areas: 18.2%

Vacancy Rates in Central Business District
Class A space: 55.1%
Class B space: 16.3%

Vacancy Rates Outside Central Business District
Class A space: 2.0%
Class B space: 62.5%

Housing
Total number of units in 1990: 136,452
Occupied units in 1990: 118,516
Owner-occupied units in 1990: 59.8%
1993 ACCRA average cost: $86,350
1993 ACCRA average rent for an apartment: $473

Chamber of Commerce
Corpus Christi Chamber of Commerce, James D. Bradley, President, 1201 N. Shoreline, PO Box 640, Corpus Christi, TX 78403. 512-882-6161

Economic Development Office
Coastal Bend Council of Governments, John Buckner, Exec. Director, 2910 Leopard, PO Box 9909, Corpurs Christi, TX 78469. 512-883-5743

Economic Development Organizations
Corpus Christi Area Economic Development Corp., Gary Bushell, President, PO Box 640, Corpus Christi, TX 78403. 512-883-5571

Major Businesses

Company	SIC	Telephone
American Chrome & Chemical	2819	(512) 883-6421
Anson Investments, Inc.	6221	(512) 993-9842
Buckner, J. E. Trucks, Inc.	4212	(512) 882-8695
Central Power & Light Co.	4911	(512) 881-5300
Creveling Motor Co.	5511	(512) 992-8000
Driscoll Foundation	8062	(512) 883-5471
Esco Distributors, Inc.	5191	(512) 883-1521
First City Bank of Corpus Christi	6022	(512) 884-3051
Great Western Petro Co.	1311	(512) 880-5935
H & K Construction Co.	1623	(512) 364-3400
Heldenfels Brothers, Inc.	1611	(512) 883-9331
Hicks, Ed Imports	5511	(512) 854-1955
Kane, Sam Beef Processor	2011	(512) 241-5000
Maverick Markets, Inc.	5411	(512) 289-1587
Mbank Corpus Christi	6021	(512) 881-6500
Nueces County Hospital District	8062	(512) 881-4116
Pagan-Lewis Motors Inc.	5511	(512) 855-8400
Port City Pontiac-GMC Trucks	5511	(512) 855-5300
Ryan, Jackson Sears	0212	(512) 882-4301
South Texas Construction Co.	1611	(512) 853-7331

Major Businesses (Continued)

Company	SIC	Telephone
Southwestern Refining Co.	2911	(512) 884-8863
Texline Gas Co.	4922	(512) 882-8407
Thomas Charlie Courtesy	5511	(512) 994-6200
Vista Chevrolet & Isuzu	5511	(512) 855-2100
Whataburger Inc.	5812	(512) 878-0650
York, Paul Toyota BMW	5511	(512) 855-2241

Colleges and Universities
Corpus Christi State University, Corpus Christi
Del Mar College, Corpus Christi

DALLAS, TX (PMSA)

Geographic Profile

Land Area

4471.0 square miles

Counties and Parishes

Collin

Dallas

Denton

Ellis

Kaufman

Rockwall

Additional Cities/Towns within Area

Denton

Irving

Ranking Highlights

19 *out of 319 in total* **land area**

59 *out of 319 in* **population growth**, *1970–1990*

166 *out of 310 in having the lowest* **unemployment** *rate*

10 *out of 310 in size of* **labor force**

34 *out of 318 in the percentage of* **college graduates**

36 *out of 292 in per capita personal* **income**

11 *out of 319 in number of* **manufacturing establishments**

114 *out of 318 in* **physicians** *per 1000 people*

249 *out of 318 in* **hospital beds** *per 1000 people*

261 *out of 267 in fewest* **crimes** *per 1000 people*

257 *out of 266 in fewest* **violent crimes** *per 1000 people*

202 *out of 319 in per capita* **federal funds and grants**

Quality of Life Indexes (Rate per 1000 population)

Crime rate in 1991: 100.4

Violent crime rate in 1991: 13.3

Physicians rate in 1992: 2.05

Hospital bed rate in 1991: 2.92

ACCRA Cost of Living Indexes

(First quarter 1993, average = 100)

Composite index: 102.3

Utilities index: 116.4

Housing index: 95.1

Overview

Despite Texas-sized problems brought on by the national savings and loan crisis, and weaknesses in the oil and defense industries and real estate, Dallas is thriving. In a list of the top two hundred Dallas-area employers, the fields of education, aerospace, defense, manufacturing, transportation, retail trade, and banking are well represented. Dallas remains a center for the graphic arts, publishing, advertising, and printing.

In the last decade Dallas has gained prominence in such diverse areas as high-technology industry, health care, and convention/tourism. Its "Silicon Prairie" development cen-

ters, with more than 165,000 employees, represent the fourth largest center of producers and users of advanced technologies in the nation. In addition, Dallas is second in telecommunications manufacturing employment in the United States. With the proposed construction of the Superconducting Super Collider atom smasher, with its $8.25 billion price tag, Dallas will become a major research and development center.

The hospital complex at the University of Texas Southwestern Medical Center is the cornerstone of the health care industry, which is responsible for 10 percent of the Dallas gross area product. In 1990, the forty major hospitals and clinics in Dallas did about $1.2 billion in referrals, a figure which is expected to reach $4.2 billion by the mid-1990s.

As the nation's second largest host of conventions, Dallas receives tourism revenues of nearly $5 billion. It is consistently ranked among the top three convention cities in America in terms of attendance, facilities, and services.

In addition to its excellent airport services, interstate highways, and railroad connections, Dallas maintains its edge as a leading distribution center of the Southwest with a healthy trucking industry. Approximately one hundred fifty regular-route carriers offer direct service to major points in the United States, and more than two hundred additional motor carriers operate in and around the Dallas area.

Most visitors to Dallas arrive via the Dallas/Fort Worth International Regional (D/FW) Airport, located approximately 17 miles from the downtown areas of both cities. With a U.S. Customs District, a Fish and Wildlife Port of Entry, its own Foreign Trade Zone, and official U.S. Gateway status, the Dallas/Fort Worth Airport is a major U.S. transportation facility. This second busiest airport in the world serviced more than 48 million passengers in 1991.

Prior to construction of D/FW Airport, Dallas's principal airfield was the city-owned Love Field. Today it is both a general aviation and commercial air facility with several local commercial carriers serving other Texas cities and adjacent states. Love Field is conveniently close to Dallas's central business district. Redbird Airport and many smaller municipal airports serve the Metroplex area.

The Dallas area is served by four major highways: I-20 (east-west); I-35 (north-south); I-30 (northeast-west); and I-45 (south). All Dallas highways are connected by a twelve-lane loop—LBJ Freeway (I-635)—that encircles the city.

Population (1990)

Total Population and Growth Rate

1990: 2,553,362

1980: 1,957,430

1970: 1,556,324

Growth rate 1970–1990: 64%

Race and Hispanic Origin

White: 72.6%

Black: 16.1%
Asian/Pacific Islander: 2.6%
Native American: 0.5%
Hispanic origin: 14.4%
White not Hispanic: 66.7%

Age

Ages 18 to 20: 4.5%
Ages 21 to 24: 6.5%
Ages 25 to 44: 37.5%
Ages 45 to 54: 10%
Ages 55 to 59: 3.5%
Ages 60 to 64: 3%
Ages 65 plus: 7.7%

Educational Attainment (1990)

Percent having completed high school: 79.0%
Percent having completed college: 27.6%
Elementary and high school enrollment: 447,551

Federal Funds and Grants Received

Total received in 1989: $6,835,900,000
Funds received per capita: $2,762

Civilian Labor Force

1993 (April): 1,467,297
1992 average: 1,469,067
1991 average: 1,439,893
1990 average: 1,438,554

Unemployment

1993 (April): 5.6%
1992 average: 7.0%
1991 average: 6.0%
1990 average: 5.1%

Average Annual Pay

1988: $24,463
1987: $23,624
1985: $22,069

Per Capita Personal Income

1991: $20,892
1990: $20,291
1989: $19,403

Business Climate (1987)

Manufacturing

Number of establishments in 1987: 4,352
Shipments in 1987 ($1,000): $23,027,900
Employees in 1987: 219,300
Change in employment, 1982 to 1987: 1.1%
Average annual pay for manufacturing work in 1989: $29,791
Average annual pay for production work in 1987: $20,007

Wholesale Trade

Number of establishments in 1987: 7,704
Total sales in 1987 ($1,000): $58,491,400
Change in sales, 1982 to 1987: 25.9%

Retail Trade

Number of establishments in 1987: 15,523
Total sales in 1987 ($1,000): $58,491,400
Retail sales per household in 1987: $20,144
Average annual pay in 1989: $14,573

Service Industry

Selected receipts in 1987 ($1,000): $13,256,200
Average annual pay in 1989: $23,446

Office Real Estate (1992)

Office space inventory: 117,161,000 square feet
Average class A Central Business District rental range per sq. ft: $15.50

Vacancy Rates

All areas: 26.1%

Vacancy Rates in Central Business District

Class A space: 18.6%
Class B space: 37.5%

Vacancy Rates Outside Central Business District

Class A space: 21.8%
Class B space: 28.9%

Housing

Total number of units in 1990: 1,072,830
Occupied units in 1990: 954,728
Owner-occupied units in 1990: 55.1%
1993 ACCRA average cost: $101,204
1993 ACCRA average rent for an apartment: $594

Chamber of Commerce

Greater Dallas Chamber of Commerce, Richard Upton, President, 1201 Elm St. #2000, Dallas, TX 75270. 214-746-6600

Economic Development Office

City of Dallas Economic Development Department, Dennis Martinez, Director, 1500 Marilla Room 4BN, Dallas, TX 75206. 214-670-3052, FAX 214-670-0158

Economic Development Organizations

Greater Dallas Chamber Economic Development Group, Richard W. Douglas, President, 1201 Elm St. Suite 2000, Dallas, TX 75270. 214-746-6600, FAX 214-746-6799

Major Businesses

Company	SIC	Telephone
A & A International Inc.	5065	(817) 390-3150
Aancor Holdings Inc.	3275	(214) 740-4500
American Airlines, Inc.	4512	(817) 963-1234
American Petro Exporting Co.	2911	(214) 750-2400
American Petrofina Inc.	2911	(214) 750-2400
American Petrofina Holding Co.	2911	(214) 750-2400
AMR Corp.	4512	(817) 967-1234
Army and Air Force Exchange	5399	(214) 780-2011
Associates Corp. North America	6141	(214) 541-4000

Major Businesses (Continued)

Company	SIC	Telephone
Associates First Capital	6141	(214) 541-4000
Aviall of Texas Inc.	7699	(214) 956-5000
Beazer West, Inc.	3241	(214) 754-5500
Bell Helicopter Textron Inc.	3721	(817) 280-2011
Burlington Northern Inc.	4011	(817) 878-2000
Caltex Petroleum Corp.	2911	(214) 830-3400
Campbell Taggart Inc.	2051	(214) 358-9211
Centex Corp.	1531	(214) 559-6500
Centex Real Estate Corp.	1521	(214) 559-6500
Central and South West Co.	4911	(214) 754-1000
Commercial Metals Co.	5051	(214) 689-4300
Contran Corp.	2816	(214) 233-1700
Cullum Companies, Inc.	5411	(214) 661-9700
Dresser Industries Inc.	3563	(214) 740-6000
E-Systems, Inc.	3663	(214) 661-1000
Electronic Data Systems	7374	(214) 604-6000
Ensearch Corp.	4923	(214) 651-8700
Federal Home Loan Bank of Dallas	6111	(214) 541-8500
Federal Reserve Bank Dallas	6011	(214) 651-6111
Fina Oil And Chemical Co.	2911	(214) 750-2400
Foxmeyer Corp.	5122	(214) 446-4800
Foxmeyer Drug Co., Inc.	5122	(214) 446-9090
Frito-Lay, Inc.	2096	(214) 351-7000
GLI Bus Operating Holding Co.	4111	(214) 651-7845
Greyhound Lines, Inc.	4111	(214) 744-6500
Halliburton Co.	1389	(214) 978-2600
Harken Energy Corp.	5541	(817) 267-1777
Hoechst Celanese Chemical	2869	(214) 689-4000
Kimberly-Clark Corp.	2621	(214) 830-1200
LTV Aerospace Co.	3761	(214) 979-7711
LTV Corp.	3312	(214) 979-7711
National City Lines Inc.	2063	(214) 233-1700
National Gypsum Co.	3275	(214) 740-4500
NCNB Texas National Bank	6021	(214) 508-6262
Occidental Chemical Corp.	2812	(214) 404-3800
Occidental Chemical Holding	2869	(214) 404-3800
ORYX Energy Co.	1311	(214) 890-6000
Oxy Chemical Corp.	2869	(214) 404-3800
Petrofina Delaware Inc.	2911	(214) 750-2400
Philp Co., Inc.	2911	(214) 871-6500
Sammons Enterprises Inc.	5084	(214) 670-9790
Simmons, Harold C. Family	3533	(214) 233-1700
Southland Corp.	5411	(214) 828-7011
Southwest Airlines Co.	4512	(214) 904-4000
Southwestern Life Insurance Co.	6311	(214) 954-7111
Sun Energy Partners	1382	(214) 890-6207
Sun Operating Ltd. Partner	1311	(214) 890-6000
Tandy Corp.	5731	(817) 390-3700
Texas Instruments Inc.	3674	(214) 995-2011
Texas Oil & Gas Corp.	4922	(214) 954-2000

Major Businesses (Continued)

Company	SIC	Telephone
Texas Utilities Co.	4911	(214) 812-4600
Texas Utilities Electric Co.	4911	(214) 812-8200
Trinity Industries Inc.	3743	(214) 631-4420
Valhi Group Inc.	2816	(214) 386-4110
Zale Holding Corp.	5944	(214) 580-4000

Colleges and Universities

Art Institute of Dallas, Dallas
Baylor College of Dentistry, Dallas
Criswell College, Dallas
Dallas Baptist University, Dallas
Dallas Christian College, Dallas
Devry Institute of Technology, Irving
El Centro College, Dallas
Miss Wade's Fashion Merchandising College, Dallas
Mountain View College, Dallas
North Lake College, Irving
Richland College, Dallas
Southern Methodist University, Dallas
Texas Woman's University, Denton
University of North Texas, Denton
University of Texas Southwestern Medical Center at Dallas, Dallas
University of Dallas, Irving

EL PASO, TX (MSA)

Geographic Profile
Land Area
1013.1 square miles

Counties and Parishes
El Paso

Ranking Highlights
200 *out of 319 in total* **land area**
56 *out of 319 in* **population growth,** *1970–1990*
289 *out of 310 in having the lowest* **unemployment** *rate*
91 *out of 310 in size of* **labor force**
232 *out of 318 in the percentage of* **college graduates**
288 *out of 292 in per capita personal* **income**
106 *out of 319 in number of* **manufacturing establishments**
250 *out of 318 in* **physicians** *per 1000 people*
256 *out of 318 in* **hospital beds** *per 1000 people*
250 *out of 267 in fewest* **crimes** *per 1000 people*
228 *out of 266 in fewest* **violent crimes** *per 1000 people*
110 *out of 319 in per capita* **federal funds and grants**

Quality of Life Indexes (Rate per 1000 population)
Crime rate in 1991:	89.4
Violent crime rate in 1991:	9.9
Physicians rate in 1992:	1.39
Hospital bed rate in 1991:	2.79

ACCRA Cost of Living Indexes
(First quarter 1993, average = 100)
Composite index:	97.1
Utilities index:	90.2
Housing index:	90.7

Population (1990)
Total Population and Growth Rate
1990: 591,610
1980: 479,899
1970: 359,291
Growth rate 1970–1990: 65%

Race and Hispanic Origin
White: 76.5%
Black: 3.7%
Asian/Pacific Islander: 1.1%
Native American: 0.4%
Hispanic origin: 69.6%
White not Hispanic: 25.6%

Age
Ages 18 to 20: 5.7%
Ages 21 to 24: 6.6%
Ages 25 to 44: 30.8%
Ages 45 to 54: 8.7%
Ages 55 to 59: 3.8%
Ages 60 to 64: 3.7%
Ages 65 plus: 8.2%

Educational Attainment (1990)
Percent having completed high school: 63.7%
Percent having completed college: 15.2%
Elementary and high school enrollment: 141,694

Federal Funds and Grants Received
Total received in 1989: $2,031,900,000
Funds received per capita: $3,468

Civilian Labor Force
1993 (April): 261,875
1992 average: 261,704
1991 average: 251,087
1990 average: 250,981

Unemployment
1993 (April): 9.1%
1992 average: 10.8%
1991 average: 10.8%
1990 average: 10.7%

Average Annual Pay
1988: $16,731
1987: $16,142
1985: $15,474

Per Capita Personal Income
1991: $11,764
1990: $11,441
1989: $10,992

Business Climate (1987)
Manufacturing
Number of establishments in 1987: 546
Shipments in 1987 ($1,000): $4,455,400
Employees in 1987: 35,200
Change in employment, 1982 to 1987: -8.1%
Average annual pay for manufacturing work in 1989: $16,364
Average annual pay for production work in 1987: $12,620

Wholesale Trade
Number of establishments in 1987: 909
Total sales in 1987 ($1,000): $2,699,600
Change in sales, 1982 to 1987: -4.6%

Retail Trade
Number of establishments in 1987: 2,813
Total sales in 1987 ($1,000): $2,699,600
Retail sales per household in 1987: $16,659
Average annual pay in 1989: $11,026

Service Industry
Selected receipts in 1987 ($1,000): $1,133,300
Average annual pay in 1989: $16,391

Office Real Estate (1992)
Office space inventory: 3,046,100 square feet

Average class A Central Business District rental range per sq. ft: $15.00

Vacancy Rates
All areas: 7.2%

Vacancy Rates in Central Business District
Class A space: 4.8%
Class B space: 7.8%

Vacancy Rates Outside Central Business District
Class A space: 2.1%
Class B space: 14.2%

Housing
Total number of units in 1990: 187,473
Occupied units in 1990: 178,366
Owner-occupied units in 1990: 58.7%
1993 ACCRA average cost: $98,855
1993 ACCRA average rent for an apartment: $522

Chamber of Commerce
El Paso Chamber of Commerce, Wes Jurey, Exec. Director, 10 Civic Center Plaza, PO Box 9738, El Paso, TX 79987. 915-534-0500

Economic Development Office
El Paso Industrial Development Council, Bert M. Diamond-stein, Vice President, 9 Civic Center Plaza, El Paso, TX 79901. 915-534-0523, FAX 915-534-0516

Major Businesses

Company	SIC	Telephone
Border Steel Rolling Mill	3312	(915) 886-2000
Crinco Investments Inc.	5541	(915) 779-4711
Economy Cash & Carry Inc.	5141	(915) 532-2660
El Paso Electric Co.	4911	(915) 543-5711
El Paso Maquila Sales Ltd.	3679	(915) 775-2581
El Paso Natural Gas Co.	4922	(915) 541-2600
El Paso Refinery	2911	(915) 772-1433
Farah International Inc.	2325	(915) 593-4444
Helen of Troy Corp.	5064	(915) 779-6363
Hunt Building Corp.	1522	(915) 533-1122
Lama, Tony Co. Inc.	3143	(915) 778-8311
Pasotex Corp.	3312	(915) 544-6000
Petro Inc.	5541	(915) 779-4711
Popular Dry Goods Co.	5311	(915) 532-7755
Powell, Edd Inc.	5411	(915) 859-7441
Providence Memorial Hospital	8062	(915) 542-6011
Southwestern Irrigation	5159	(915) 581-5441
Sun Apparel Inc.	2339	(915) 598-1900
Texscan Corp.	3663	(915) 594-3555
Tri State Wholesale Associated	5141	(915) 772-7682

Colleges and Universities
El Paso Community College, El Paso
University of Texas at El Paso, El Paso

FORT WORTH–ARLINGTON, TX (PMSA)

Geographic Profile
Land Area
2496.5 square miles

Counties and Parishes
Johnson
Parker
Tarrant

Ranking Highlights
70 *out of 319 in total* **land area**
50 *out of 319 in* **population growth,** *1970–1990*
157 *out of 310 in having the lowest* **unemployment** *rate*
34 *out of 310 in size of* **labor force**
85 *out of 318 in the percentage of* **college graduates**
86 *out of 292 in per capita personal* **income**
37 *out of 319 in number of* **manufacturing establishments**
253 *out of 318 in* **physicians** *per 1000 people*
70 *out of 318 in* **hospital beds** *per 1000 people*
262 *out of 267 in fewest* **crimes** *per 1000 people*
228 *out of 266 in fewest* **violent crimes** *per 1000 people*
39 *out of 319 in per capita* **federal funds and grants**

Quality of Life Indexes (Rate per 1000 population)
Crime rate in 1991:	101.4
Violent crime rate in 1991:	9.9
Physicians rate in 1992:	1.37
Hospital bed rate in 1991:	5.14

ACCRA Cost of Living Indexes
(First quarter 1993, average = 100)
Composite index: 98.5
Utilities index: 107.1
Housing index: 83.4

Overview
Fort Worth has traditionally been a diverse center of manufacturing and the city demonstrated strong economic growth in the 1980s. Unlike many other parts of the state, the Fort Worth area's economy was not critically affected by the downturn in Texas's oil and banking sectors. Major employers in the area are American Airlines, General Dynamics, Bell Helicopter-Textron, Tandy Corporation, and Delta Airlines. In 1987 the Advanced Robotics Research Institute, a major center for high-technology research, began operations to advance the science of automated manufacturing. In 1991 the U.S. Department of the Treasury started printing 25 percent of the nation's currency at its new Fort Worth facility. As a result printing and publishing, and automation and robotics are projected to emerge as strong sectors of the economy. The city is trying to fight the blow which will result from the closing of Carswell Air Force Base.

The size and proximity of Dallas/Fort Worth International Regional Airport, with its Foreign Trade Zone and U.S. Customs District, make Fort Worth a transportation center and an ideal wholesale and distribution location. Headquarters of approximately forty insurance companies are also located in the area.

The Dallas/Fort Worth International Regional Airport makes the Fort Worth area a major transportation hub. Its Foreign Trade Zone, U.S. Customs Office, and U.S. Port of Entry status afford business and industry easy access to many important services. Nearby Alliance Airport is used solely by distribution and manufacturing firms to reach national and international markets. Commercial motor freight service is provided by several local and long distance carriers. For firms with their own trucks, support services are abundant. A full complement of rail services is available in the city where Burlington Northern, the largest railroad in the nation, is headquartered.

Four interstate highways serve Dallas/Fort Worth: I-20 (east-west), I-35 (north-south), I-30 (northeast-west), and I-45 (south).

Population (1990)

Total Population and Growth Rate
1990: 1,332,053
1980: 973,138
1970: 795,244
Growth rate 1970–1990: 68%

Race and Hispanic Origin
White: 80.3%
Black: 10.8%
Asian/Pacific Islander: 2.3%
Native American: 0.5%
Hispanic origin: 11.3%
White not Hispanic: 75.4%

Age
Ages 18 to 20: 4.5%
Ages 21 to 24: 6.4%
Ages 25 to 44: 36.1%
Ages 45 to 54: 10%
Ages 55 to 59: 3.8%
Ages 60 to 64: 3.3%
Ages 65 plus: 8.6%

Educational Attainment (1990)
Percent having completed high school: 79.1%
Percent having completed college: 22.6%
Elementary and high school enrollment: 234,276

Federal Funds and Grants Received
Total received in 1989: $6,553,200,000
Funds received per capita: $5,076

Civilian Labor Force
1993 (April): 743,292
1992 average: 745,925

1991 average: 737,468
1990 average: 731,726

Unemployment
1993 (April): 5.8%
1992 average: 6.9%
1991 average: 6.5%
1990 average: 5.2%

Average Annual Pay
1988: $21,196
1987: $20,509
1985: $19,147

Per Capita Personal Income
1991: $18,714
1990: $18,153
1989: $17,412

Business Climate (1987)

Manufacturing
Number of establishments in 1987: 2,139
Shipments in 1987 ($1,000): $13,442,600
Employees in 1987: 110,000
Change in employment, 1982 to 1987: 3.7%
Average annual pay for manufacturing work in 1989: $28,255
Average annual pay for production work in 1987: $22,393

Wholesale Trade
Number of establishments in 1987: 2,454
Total sales in 1987 ($1,000): $12,626,900
Change in sales, 1982 to 1987: 22.2%

Retail Trade
Number of establishments in 1987: 7,484
Total sales in 1987 ($1,000): $12,626,900
Retail sales per household in 1987: $18,352
Average annual pay in 1989: $12,548

Service Industry
Selected receipts in 1987 ($1,000): $3,492,500
Average annual pay in 1989: $18,784

Office Real Estate (1992)
Office space inventory: 17,904,748 square feet
Average class A Central Business District rental range per sq. ft: $15.27

Vacancy Rates
All areas: 17.5%

Vacancy Rates in Central Business District
Class A space: 13.5%
Class B space: 23.9%

Vacancy Rates Outside Central Business District
Class A space: 16.4%
Class B space: 21.2%

Housing
Total number of units in 1990: 554,225
Occupied units in 1990: 495,144

Owner-occupied units in 1990: 60.3%
1993 ACCRA average cost: $88,167
1993 ACCRA average rent for an apartment: $528

Chamber of Commerce

Arlington Chamber of Commerce, Ted Willis, President, 316 W. Main, PO Box 607, Arlington, TX 76004-0607. 817-275-2613

Major Businesses

Company	SIC	Telephone
AFG Industries, Inc.	3211	(817) 332-5006
Altai, Inc.	7371	(817) 649-1816
American Excelsior Co.	2499	(817) 640-1555
American Corp.	4512	(817) 967-1234
Arch Petroleum Inc.	1311	(817) 332-9209
Austin Paving Co.	1611	(817) 336-2373
Ben E. Keith Co.	5141	(817) 332-9171
Bizmart, Inc.	5112	(817) 792-5200
Bizmart Inc.	5943	(817) 792-4097
BMS Enterprises, Inc.	1799	(817) 926-5214
Bombay Co., Inc.	5712	(817) 347-8200
Buffton Corp.	3000	(817) 332-4761
Burlington Northern Inc.	4011	(817) 878-2000
Calloway's Nursery, Inc.	5261	(817) 656-1122
Cash America Investments	5932	(817) 335-1100
Ceramic Cooling Tower Co.	3443	(817) 232-4661
Chickasha Cotton Oil Co.	0131	(817) 732-8595
Color Tile, Inc.	5211	(817) 870-9630
Columbia Hospital Corp.	8062	(817) 870-5900
Educators Industries, Inc.	6512	(817) 284-9259
Esco Elevators, Inc.	3534	(817) 478-4251
FFP Partners	5541	(817) 831-0761
First Cash, Inc.	5932	(817) 625-2274
Gainsco, Inc.	6331	(817) 336-2500
Garvey Enterprises Inc.	5153	(817) 335-5881
Howell Instruments, Inc.	3825	(817) 336-7411
Justin Boot Co.	3143	(817) 332-4385
Justin Industries, Inc.	3251	(817) 336-5125
Lomak Petroleum, Inc.	1381	(817) 870-2601
MPI, Inc.	2299	(817) 335-7676
Miller Business Systems	5021	(817) 649-1313
Morrison Supply Co.	5074	(817) 336-0451
NCNB Texas National Bank	6021	(817) 390-6161
Pancho's Mexican Buffet,	5812	(817) 831-0081
Pier 1 Imports, Inc.	5719	(817) 878-8000
Setlowear, Inc.	2326	(817) 332-6492
Shoreline Products Inc.	3799	(817) 465-1351
Six Flags Corp.	7996	(817) 261-5700
Sky Chefs, Inc.	5812	(817) 792-2123
Snyder Oil Corp.	1311	(817) 338-4043
Standard Meat Co.	5147	(817) 831-0981
Sterns Airport Equipment	3535	(817) 294-2020

Major Businesses (Continued)

Company	SIC	Telephone
Stevens Graphics Corp.	3555	(817) 831-3911
Stripling & Cox	5311	(817) 336-4985
Sunbelt Nursery Group, Inc.	5261	(817) 738-8111
Tandy Brands Accessories,	2387	(817) 548-0090
Tandycrafts, Inc.	5948	(817) 551-9600
Technology Development Co.	3825	(817) 640-7274
Tecnol, Inc.	3842	(817) 581-6424
Tecnol Medical Products,	5047	(817) 581-6424
Texas Commerce Bank-Arlington	6022	(817) 469-3100
Texas Refinery Corp.	2952	(817) 332-1161
Texas Steel Co.	3325	(817) 923-4611
TNP Enterprises, Inc.	4911	(817) 731-0099
Transport Life Insurance	6311	(817) 390-8000
Union Pacific Resources Co.	1311	(817) 877-6000
Westbridge Capital Corp.	6321	(817) 878-3300
Williamson-Dickie Mfg. Co.	2326	(817) 336-7201
Wolverine Exploration Co.	1311	(817) 335-4701

Colleges and Universities

Arlington Baptist College, Arlington
Bauder Fashion College, Arlington
ITT Technical Institute, Arlington
Tarrant County Junior College, Fort Worth
Texas Christian University, Fort Worth
Texas Wesleyan University, Fort Worth
University of Texas at Arlington, Arlington

GALVESTON–TEXAS CITY, TX (PMSA)

Geographic Profile

Land Area

398.7 square miles

Counties and Parishes

Galveston

Ranking Highlights

311 *out of 319 in total* **land area**

143 *out of 319 in* **population growth,** *1970–1990*

245 *out of 310 in having the lowest* **unemployment** *rate*

171 *out of 310 in size of* **labor force**

151 *out of 318 in the percentage of* **college graduates**

99 *out of 292 in per capita personal* **income**

262 *out of 319 in number of* **manufacturing establishments**

11 *out of 318 in* **physicians** *per 1000 people*

11 *out of 318 in* **hospital beds** *per 1000 people*

237 *out of 267 in fewest* **crimes** *per 1000 people*

187 *out of 266 in fewest* **violent crimes** *per 1000 people*

239 *out of 319 in per capita* **federal funds and grants**

Quality of Life Indexes (Rate per 1000 population)

Crime rate in 1991:	83.7
Violent crime rate in 1991:	8.2
Physicians rate in 1992:	4.08
Hospital bed rate in 1991:	7.32

ACCRA Cost of Living Indexes

(First quarter 1993, average = 100)

Composite index:	N/A
Utilities index:	N/A
Housing index:	N/A

Population (1990)

Total Population and Growth Rate

1990: 217,399

1980: 195,738

1970: 169,812

Growth rate 1970–1990: 28%

Race and Hispanic Origin

White: 75.5%

Black: 17.6%

Asian/Pacific Islander: 1.6%

Native American: 0.3%

Hispanic origin: 14.2%

White not Hispanic: 66.6%

Age

Ages 18 to 20: 4.1%

Ages 21 to 24: 5.1%

Ages 25 to 44: 33.4%

Ages 45 to 54: 10.5%

Ages 55 to 59: 4.4%

Ages 60 to 64: 4.5%

Ages 65 plus: 10.5%

Educational Attainment (1990)

Percent having completed high school: 75.8%

Percent having completed college: 19.3%

Elementary and high school enrollment: 41,517

Federal Funds and Grants Received

Total received in 1989: $530,200,000

Funds received per capita: $2,525

Civilian Labor Force

1993 (April): 121,162

1992 average: 118,094

1991 average: 112,190

1990 average: 109,833

Unemployment

1993 (April): 7.3%

1992 average: 8.6%

1991 average: 7.0%

1990 average: 7.1%

Average Annual Pay

1988: $20,417

1987: $20,092

1985: $19,321

Per Capita Personal Income

1991: $18,316

1990: $17,549

1989: $16,627

Business Climate (1987)

Manufacturing

Number of establishments in 1987: 138

Shipments in 1987 ($1,000): $7,346,900

Employees in 1987: 8,500

Change in employment, 1982 to 1987: -24.8%

Average annual pay for manufacturing work in 1989: $38,745

Average annual pay for production work in 1987: $33,053

Wholesale Trade

Number of establishments in 1987: 215

Total sales in 1987 ($1,000): $995,700

Change in sales, 1982 to 1987: 121.9%

Retail Trade

Number of establishments in 1987: 1,320

Total sales in 1987 ($1,000): $995,700

Retail sales per household in 1987: $14,966

Average annual pay in 1989: $10,976

Service Industry

Selected receipts in 1987 ($1,000): $341,000

Average annual pay in 1989: $16,495

Housing

Total number of units in 1990: 99,451

Occupied units in 1990: 81,451
Owner-occupied units in 1990: 62.0%
1993 ACCRA average cost: N/A
1993 ACCRA average rent for an apartment: N/A

Chamber of Commerce

Galveston Chamber of Commerce, Jimmy Dike, President, 621 Moody #300, Galveston, TX 77550. 409-763-5326

Major Businesses

Company	SIC	Telephone
American Indemnity Co.	6331	(409) 766-4600
American Indemnity Finance	6331	(409) 766-4600
American National Life Insurance	6311	(409) 763-4661
American Printing Co.	2752	(409) 763-2412
Anrem Corp.	6531	(409) 763-4661
Farmer's Marine Copper	3498	(409) 765-6361
Galveston Newspapers, Inc.	2711	(409) 744-3611
Galveston Wharves	3523	(409) 765-9321
Hornbeck Offshore Service	4499	(409) 762-8228
Seal Fleet, Inc.	4491	(409) 763-8878
Securities Management	6211	(409) 763-2767
Texas City Terminal Co.	4013	(409) 945-4461
U. S. National Bank	6021	(409) 763-1151

Colleges and Universities

College of the Mainland, Texas City
Galveston College, Galveston
Texas A&M University at Galveston, Galveston
University of Texas Medical Branch at Galveston, Galveston

HOUSTON, TX (PMSA)

Geographic Profile

Land Area
5321.8 square miles

Counties and Parishes
Fort Bend
Harris
Liberty
Montgomery
Waller

Additional Cities/Towns within Area
Baytown

Ranking Highlights

  11 *out of 319 in total* **land area**
  41 *out of 319 in* **population growth,** *1970–1990*
181 *out of 310 in having the lowest* **unemployment** *rate*
  8 *out of 310 in size of* **labor force**
 58 *out of 318 in the percentage of* **college graduates**
 48 *out of 292 in per capita personal* **income**
 10 *out of 319 in number of* **manufacturing establishments**
 87 *out of 318 in* **physicians** *per 1000 people*
151 *out of 318 in* **hospital beds** *per 1000 people*
233 *out of 267 in fewest* **crimes** *per 1000 people*
240 *out of 266 in fewest* **violent crimes** *per 1000 people*
282 *out of 319 in per capita* **federal funds and grants**

Quality of Life Indexes (Rate per 1000 population)

Crime rate in 1991:	81.9
Violent crime rate in 1991:	10.8
Physicians rate in 1992:	2.31
Hospital bed rate in 1991:	3.99

ACCRA Cost of Living Indexes
(First quarter 1993, average = 100)

Composite index:	97.8
Utilities index:	101.8
Housing index:	91.7

Overview

Houston, seat of Harris County, Texas, is located on the upper Gulf Coast, 50 miles from the Gulf of Mexico. Annual average nonfarm payroll employment in the Houston PMSA in 1992 declined by .2%. Houston's economy has diversified. Employment in upstream energy sectors declined from 67.4% of the economic base in 1982 to 41.1% in 1992, while jobs in energy-independent sectors rose from 17.1% of the base in 1982 to 40.2% in 1992, according to the University of Houston Center for Public Policy. During 1982-1992, the energy-independent portion of the base grew at a compound annual rate of 7.8%.

Fifteen companies on the 1993 *Fortune 500* list have their corporate headquarters in Houston. Many other *Fortune 500* companies maintain U.S. administrative headquarters in Houston, although their corporate headquarters are elsewhere. Seven of the *Fortune 100 Fastest Growing Companies* are headquartered in Houston. Companies on this list are publicly traded, have at least three years of operating results, were profitable in the last two quarters of 1991 and in 1991 as a whole, and had 1991 sales of at least $82 million. Houston is also a primary location for more than 45 of the world's largest non-U.S. based corporations.

Houston hosts 39 foreign banks representing 12 nations. Fifty-five foreign governments maintain consular offices in the city, ranking Houston's consular corps among the largest in the nation. Twenty-seven foreign governments maintain trade and commercial offices here, and the city has 24 active foreign chambers of commerce and trade associations.

Manufacturing in 1992 accounts for 17.8% of Houston's CMSA Gross Area Produce. Non-durable goods represent 71.7% of the manufacturing total. The Houston-Gulf Coast region has over 45% of the nation's base petrochemical manufacturing capacity. More than 200 chemical companies employing some 40,000 people have manufacturing plants in the Houston area.

Johnson Space Center, a $954-million complex built in 1962, occupies 1,620 acres about 25 miles from downtown Houston.

Among U.S. ports, Houston ranked third in 1990 in total tonnage and first in 1991 in foreign tonnage; world-wide, it ranks eighth. In 1991, 277,764 tons of merchandise valued at $354.7 million entered the Houston Free Trade Zone, and 202,160 tons valued at $275.7 million were shipped from it. Houston is second only to Chicago, Illinois, in the amount of convention space–1.7 million square feet., versus Chicago's 1.8 million.

Population (1990)

Total Population and Growth Rate
1990: 3,301,937
1980: 2,734,617
1970: 1,891,004
Growth rate 1970–1990: 75%

Race and Hispanic Origin
White: 66.3%
Black: 18.5%
Asian/Pacific Islander: 3.8%
Native American: 0.3%
Hispanic origin: 21.4%
White not Hispanic: 56.4%

Age
Ages 18 to 20: 4.5%
Ages 21 to 24: 6.2%
Ages 25 to 44: 36.7%
Ages 45 to 54: 9.9%
Ages 55 to 59: 3.6%
Ages 60 to 64: 3.2%
Ages 65 plus: 7.1%

Educational Attainment (1990)
Percent having completed high school: 75.1%
Percent having completed college: 25.1%
Elementary and high school enrollment: 646,541

Federal Funds and Grants Received
Total received in 1989: $7,219,000,000
Funds received per capita: $2,223

Civilian Labor Force
1993 (April): 1,756,590
1992 average: 1,775,149
1991 average: 1,756,017
1990 average: 1,723,528

Unemployment
1993 (April): 6.7%
1992 average: 7.2%
1991 average: 5.6%
1990 average: 5.2%

Average Annual Pay
1988: $24,410
1987: $23,509
1985: $22,938

Per Capita Personal Income
1991: $20,169
1990: $19,468
1989: $18,020

Business Climate (1987)

Manufacturing
Number of establishments in 1987: 4,468
Shipments in 1987 ($1,000): $37,582,600
Employees in 1987: 160,200
Change in employment, 1982 to 1987: -35.0%
Average annual pay for manufacturing work in 1989: $31,954
Average annual pay for production work in 1987: $23,868

Wholesale Trade
Number of establishments in 1987: 7,813
Total sales in 1987 ($1,000): $71,035,100
Change in sales, 1982 to 1987: -27.7%

Retail Trade
Number of establishments in 1987: 17,374
Total sales in 1987 ($1,000): $71,035,100
Retail sales per household in 1987: $16,944
Average annual pay in 1989: $12,747

Service Industry
Selected receipts in 1987 ($1,000): $15,228,000
Average annual pay in 1989: $23,203

Office Real Estate (1992)
Office space inventory: 135,171,000 square feet

Average class A Central Business District rental range per sq. ft: $16.64

Vacancy Rates

All areas: 21.6%

Vacancy Rates in Central Business District

Class A space: 14.0%

Class B space: 32.6%

Vacancy Rates Outside Central Business District

Class A space: 12.3%

Class B space: 27.8%

Housing

Total number of units in 1990: 1,355,821

Occupied units in 1990: 1,186,375

Owner-occupied units in 1990: 54.9%

1993 ACCRA average cost: $96,900

1993 ACCRA average rent for an apartment: $579

Chamber of Commerce

Greater Houston Chamber of Commerce, Eileen Crowley, President, 1100 Milam Bldg. 25th Fl., Houston, TX 77002. 713-651-1313

Economic Development Office

Greater Houston Partnership, Economic Development Division, Jim Kollaer, CEO, 1100 Milam 25th Fl., Houston, TX 77002. 713-651-1313

Economic Development Organizations

Harris County Commercial Development Agency, Cinda Calderon, Planning Manager, 3100 Timmons Ln. #330, Houston, TX 77023. 713-651-5651

Clear Lake Area Economic Development Foundation, L.H. Pezoldt, President, 2525 Bay Area Blvd. Suite 640, Houston, TX 77058. 713-486-5535

Major Businesses

Company	SIC	Telephone
American General Corp.	6311	(713) 522-1111
Baker Hughes Inc.	3533	(713) 439-8600
BP North America Petroleum	5172	(713) 558-3443
Brown & Root Inc.	8711	(713) 676-3011
Brown & Root USA, Inc.	1629	(713) 676-3011
Browning-Ferris Industries	4953	(713) 870-8100
Coastal Corp.	4922	(713) 877-1400
Coastal Holding Corp.	2911	(713) 877-1400
Coastal Natural Gas Co.	4922	(713) 877-1400
Coastal Refining & Market	5171	(713) 877-1400
Compaq Computer Corp.	3571	(713) 370-0670
Conoco Inc.	2911	(713) 293-1000
Continental Air Holdings	4512	(713) 658-9588
Continental Airlines, Inc.	4512	(713) 834-5000
Cooper Industries Inc.	3469	(713) 739-5400
Cosbel Petroleum Corp.	5171	(713) 877-1400
ELF Trading, Inc.	5172	(713) 953-8000

Major Businesses (Continued)

Company	SIC	Telephone
Enron Corp.	4922	(713) 654-6161
First City BanCorp.	6021	(713) 658-6011
Gotco USA Inc.	5172	(713) 652-5300
Grocers Supply Co. Inc.	5141	(713) 747-5000
Houston Industries Inc.	4911	(713) 629-3000
Houston Lighting & Power Co.	4911	(713) 228-9211
Houston Pipe Line Co.	4922	(713) 853-6161
Kellogg, M. W. Co.	1629	(713) 960-2000
Kern County Land Co.	3531	(713) 757-2131
Kerr-Mcgee Refining Corp.	2911	(713) 831-4700
Lyondell Petrochemical Co.	2869	(713) 652-7200
National Convenience Store	5411	(713) 863-2200
Natural Gas Clearinghouse	5172	(713) 744-1777
Nl Industries Inc.	2816	(713) 987-5000
Panhandle Eastern Corp.	4922	(713) 627-5400
Pennzoil Co.	2911	(713) 546-4000
Permian Partners	5172	(713) 787-2500
Schlumberger Technology Co.	1382	(713) 928-4000
Scurlock Oil Co. Inc.	5172	(713) 739-4100
Shell Oil Co.	2911	(713) 241-6161
Solvay America Inc.	2821	(713) 526-2000
Star Enterprise	2911	(713) 874-7000
Sysco Corp.	5142	(713) 584-1390
Tauber Oil Co.	5171	(713) 869-8700
Tenneco Inc.	3523	(713) 757-2131
Tenneco Interamerica Inc.	3731	(713) 757-2131
Tennessee Gas Pipeline Co.	3523	(713) 757-2131
Texaco Chemical Co.	2911	(713) 961-3711
Texaco Refining and Marke	2911	(713) 650-4000
Texas Commerce Bancshares	6021	(713) 236-4865
Texas Eastern Corp.	4922	(713) 627-5400
Texport Oil Co.	5172	(713) 875-2600
Transco Energy Co.	4922	(713) 439-2000
Transco Gas Co.	4923	(713) 439-2000
Tricentrol Oil Trading, Inc.	5172	(713) 877-8733

Colleges and Universities

Art Institute of Houston, Houston

Houston Baptist University, Houston

Houston Community College System, Houston

ITT Technical Institute, Houston

Lee College, Baytown

National Education Center-Bryman Campus, Houston

North Harris County College District, Houston

Rice University, Houston

San Jacinto College–North Campus, Houston

San Jacinto College–South Campus, Houston

Texas Southern University, Houston

University of Houston, Houston

University of Houston–Clear Lake, Houston

University of Houston–Downtown, Houston

University of St. Thomas, Houston

University of Texas Health Science Center at Houston, Houston

KILLEEN–TEMPLE, TX (MSA)

Geographic Profile

Land Area

2110.8 square miles

Counties and Parishes

Bell

Coryell

Ranking Highlights

85 *out of 319 in total* **land area**

64 *out of 319 in* **population growth,** *1970–1990*

208 *out of 310 in having the lowest* **unemployment** *rate*

184 *out of 310 in size of* **labor force**

226 *out of 318 in the percentage of* **college graduates**

279 *out of 292 in per capita personal* **income**

246 *out of 319 in number of* **manufacturing establishments**

104 *out of 318 in* **physicians** *per 1000 people*

278 *out of 318 in* **hospital beds** *per 1000 people*

74 *out of 267 in fewest* **crimes** *per 1000 people*

113 *out of 266 in fewest* **violent crimes** *per 1000 people*

10 *out of 319 in per capita* **federal funds and grants**

Quality of Life Indexes (Rate per 1000 population)

Crime rate in 1991:	48.4
Violent crime rate in 1991:	5.2
Physicians rate in 1992:	2.12
Hospital bed rate in 1991:	2.43

ACCRA Cost of Living Indexes

(First quarter 1993, average = 100)

Composite index:	91.3
Utilities index:	108.0
Housing index:	82.7

Overview

Several manufacturing and processing plants and wholesale and distribution firms are located in Temple. Their products include plastic laminates, centrifugal and aluminum castings, urethane and polyester fibers, woodworking power tools, hydraulic cylinders, computer-peripheral equipment, cabinets, kiln-dried domestic and hard woods, plastic bags, foam containers, dry pet food, poultry products, food and material handling equipment, corrugated and paper products, auto sunshades, recreational vehicle services, agricultural-farm equipment, adhesives, auto supplies, groceries and retail-wholesale goods, and medical supplies and equipment. One of the largest concentration of school, church, and institutional furniture manufacturers is in Temple.

Ft. Hood, 23 miles from Temple, is one of the three major army facilities in the United States and one of the largest facilities in the world (339 square miles). The base is projected to have a military personnel population of about

45,000 in 1993. Annual financial impact exceeds $1.5 billion.

Rail services are provided by AMTRAK Passenger Service (daily), Union Pacific Railroad, and Santa Fe Railway; bus lines by Greyhound-Trailway Bus Lines, Arrow Bus Lines, and Kerrville Bus Lines; and motor freight by seven major lines, plus moving and storage and truck leasing firms.

Population (1990)

Total Population and Growth Rate
1990: 255,301
1980: 214,587
1970: 159,794
Growth rate 1970–1990: 60%

Race and Hispanic Origin
White: 71.0%
Black: 19.5%
Asian/Pacific Islander: 2.8%
Native American: 0.6%
Hispanic origin: 12.2%
White not Hispanic: 65.6%

Age
Ages 18 to 20: 6.9%
Ages 21 to 24: 10%
Ages 25 to 44: 33.3%
Ages 45 to 54: 7.7%
Ages 55 to 59: 3.1%
Ages 60 to 64: 2.9%
Ages 65 plus: 8%

Educational Attainment (1990)
Percent having completed high school: 79.4%
Percent having completed college: 15.7%
Elementary and high school enrollment: 45,834

Federal Funds and Grants Received
Total received in 1989: $1,908,600,000
Funds received per capita: $7,966

Civilian Labor Force
1993 (April): 105,182
1992 average: 102,423
1991 average: 97,089
1990 average: 96,688

Unemployment
1993 (April): 6.3%
1992 average: 7.7%
1991 average: 7.0%
1990 average: 7.1%

Average Annual Pay
1988: $16,747
1987: $16,043
1985: $15,300

Per Capita Personal Income
1991: $13,742
1990: $13,140
1989: $12,797

Business Climate (1987)

Manufacturing
Number of establishments in 1987: 148
Shipments in 1987 ($1,000): $828,900
Employees in 1987: 7,400
Change in employment, 1982 to 1987: 1.4%
Average annual pay for manufacturing work in 1989: $21,967
Average annual pay for production work in 1987: $16,509

Wholesale Trade
Number of establishments in 1987: 202
Total sales in 1987 ($1,000): $803,100
Change in sales, 1982 to 1987: 37.0%

Retail Trade
Number of establishments in 1987: 1,399
Total sales in 1987 ($1,000): $803,100
Retail sales per household in 1987: $13,705
Average annual pay in 1989: $10,562

Service Industry
Selected receipts in 1987 ($1,000): $375,400
Average annual pay in 1989: $16,403

Housing
Total number of units in 1990: 94,927
Occupied units in 1990: 83,927
Owner-occupied units in 1990: 52.1%
1993 ACCRA average cost: $87,000
1993 ACCRA average rent for an apartment: $522

Chamber of Commerce
Greater Killeen Chamber of Commerce, Rick Murphy, President, 1 Santa Fe Plaza, PO Box 548, Killeen, TX 76540. 814-526-9551

Economic Development Office
Temple Chamber of Commerce, John Mark Bonnet, Exec. Director, 2 N. 5th St., PO Box 158, Temple, TX 76501. 817-773-2105

Economic Development Organizations
Temple Economic Development Corp., Brodie Allen, President, 2 N. 5th St., PO Box 1343, Temple, TX 76503. 817-773-8332, FAX 817-773-0661

Major Businesses

Company	SIC	Telephone
American Desk Manufacturing Co.	2531	(817) 773-1776
Artco-Bell Corp.	2531	(817) 778-1811
BFW Construction Co. Inc.	1542	(817) 778-8941
Bandas Industries Inc.	1611	(817) 773-1535

Major Businesses (Continued)

Company	SIC	Telephone
C & H Die Casting Inc.	3363	(817) 938-2541
Centroplex Ford Inc.	5511	(817) 526-0511
Chafin, Purser Inc.	1794	(817) 634-5567
Delta Centrifugal Corp.	3325	(817) 773-9055
First Federal Savings & Loan Association	6035	(817) 773-5241
First National Bank of Texas	6021	(817) 773-2115
First National Bank of Killean	6021	(817) 634-2161
Fort Hood National Bank	6021	(817) 532-2161
Howe Building Corp.	1542	(817) 773-9966
Howe Equity Corp.	8741	(817) 773-9966
Johnson Brothers Ford Inc.	5511	(817) 773-5257
JSJ Seating Corp.	2522	(817) 939-3517
King's Daughters Hospital Association	8062	(817) 771-8600
Mclane Co. Inc.	5141	(817) 771-7500
Mclane/Pacific Inc.	5141	(817) 778-7500
Mclane/Sunwest, Inc.	5141	(817) 778-7500
Mclane/Western Inc.	5141	(817) 778-7500
Mickey's Enterprises Inc.	5411	(817) 628-0343
Ralph Wilson Plastics Co.	2821	(817) 778-2711
Ringler Don Chevrolet-Sub	5511	(817) 778-4285
SRH Inc.	5511	(817) 526-4191
Scott & White Memorial Hospital	8062	(817) 774-2111
Scott and White Health	6321	(817) 774-3000
Slavonic Benevolent Order	6411	(817) 773-1575
Tranum Buick Inc.	5511	(817) 773-4548
Wendland's Farm Products	2048	(817) 773-5211
Wooley's Inc.	5194	(817) 939-3231

Colleges and Universities
Central Texas College, Killeen
Temple Junior College, Temple
University of Central Texas, Killeen

LAREDO, TX (MSA)

Geographic Profile
Land Area
3357.0 square miles

Counties and Parishes
Webb

Ranking Highlights
  41 *out of 319 in total* **land area**
  33 *out of 319 in* **population growth**, *1970–1990*
269 *out of 310 in having the lowest* **unemployment** *rate*
271 *out of 310 in size of* **labor force**
309 *out of 318 in the percentage of* **college graduates**
290 *out of 292 in per capita personal* **income**
314 *out of 319 in number of* **manufacturing establishments**
315 *out of 318 in* **physicians** *per 1000 people*
352 *out of 318 in* **hospital beds** *per 1000 people*
251 *out of 267 in fewest* **crimes** *per 1000 people*
149 *out of 266 in fewest* **violent crimes** *per 1000 people*
302 *out of 319 in per capita* **federal funds and grants**

Quality of Life Indexes (Rate per 1000 population)
Crime rate in 1991:	89.7
Violent crime rate in 1991:	6.8
Physicians rate in 1992:	0.85
Hospital bed rate in 1991:	2.87

ACCRA Cost of Living Indexes
(First quarter 1993, average = 100)
Composite index:	N/A
Utilities index:	N/A
Housing index:	N/A

Population (1990)
Total Population and Growth Rate
1990: 133,239
1980: 99,258
1970: 72,859
Growth rate 1970–1990: 83%

Race and Hispanic Origin
White: 70.3%
Black: .1%
Asian/Pacific Islander: 0.4%
Native American: 0.2%
Hispanic origin: 93.9%
White not Hispanic: 5.6%

Age
Ages 18 to 20: 5.9%
Ages 21 to 24: 6.6%
Ages 25 to 44: 28.4%
Ages 45 to 54: 8.1%
Ages 55 to 59: 3.3%

Ages 60 to 64: 3.2%
Ages 65 plus: 7.9%

Educational Attainment (1990)
Percent having completed high school: 47.8%
Percent having completed college: 11.1%
Elementary and high school enrollment: 37,107

Federal Funds and Grants Received
Total received in 1989: $256,100,000
Funds received per capita: $1,987

Civilian Labor Force
1993 (April):   58,914
1992 average: 57,967
1991 average: 55,191
1990 average: 53,231

Unemployment
1993 (April):   8.2%
1992 average: 9.4%
1991 average: 9.8%
1990 average: 10.8%

Average Annual Pay
1988: $14,619
1987: $14,093
1985: $13,509

Per Capita Personal Income
1991: $9,529
1990: $8,840
1989: $8,121

Business Climate (1987)
Manufacturing
Number of establishments in 1987: 57
Shipments in 1987 ($1,000): $122,400
Employees in 1987: 1,400
Change in employment, 1982 to 1987: -6.7%
Average annual pay for manufacturing work in 1989: $13,933
Average annual pay for production work in 1987: $1,363

Wholesale Trade
Number of establishments in 1987: 258
Total sales in 1987 ($1,000): $606,600
Change in sales, 1982 to 1987: 52.0%

Retail Trade
Number of establishments in 1987: 791
Total sales in 1987 ($1,000): $606,600
Retail sales per household in 1987: $21,380
Average annual pay in 1989: $10,121

Service Industry
Selected receipts in 1987 ($1,000): $132,400
Average annual pay in 1989: $12,534

Housing
Total number of units in 1990: 37,197

Occupied units in 1990: 34,438
Owner-occupied units in 1990: 60.6%
1993 ACCRA average cost: N/A
1993 ACCRA average rent for an apartment: N/A

Chamber of Commerce
Laredo Chamber of Commerce, Dr. Dianne M. Freeman, Exec. Vice President, 2310 San Bernardo Ave., PO Box 790, Laredo, TX 78042. 512-722-9895

Economic Development Office
Laredo Development Foundation, Frank Leach, Exec. Director, 1 Townlake Plaza Dr., Laredo, TX 78041. 800-533-5736, 512-722-0563

Major Businesses

Company	SIC	Telephone
American Meat Trading Co.	5147	(512) 726-1586
Arguindegui Oil Co.	5171	(512) 722-5251
Brand, Joe Inc.	5611	(512) 722-0771
Casso, Guerra & Co.	5141	(512) 723-4371
Creek Food Products N.V.	5142	(512) 727-0100
International Bancshares	6021	(512) 722-7611
International Bank Commerce	6022	(512) 722-7611
ISE Inc.	5731	(512) 722-4611
Jett Racing and Sales Inc.	5064	(512) 722-3102
Laredo Diesel Inc.	5531	(512) 723-7473
Laredo National Bancshare	6021	(512) 723-1151
Laredo National Bank	6021	(512) 723-1151
Liverpool	5064	(512) 723-2722
Mercy Hospital of Laredo	8062	(512) 727-6222
Powell-Watson Motors Inc.	5511	(512) 722-5182
Sanchez-Obrien Oil & Gas	1382	(512) 722-8092
Tanjore Corp. Ltd.	5051	(512) 722-2942
Texas-Mexican Railway Co.	4011	(512) 722-6411
Union National Bank of Texas	6021	(512) 726-8200
Vilore Foods Co. Inc.	5149	(512) 726-3633

Colleges and Universities
Laredo Junior College, Laredo
Laredo State University, Laredo

LONGVIEW–MARSHALL, TX (MSA)

Geographic Profile

Land Area

1172.9 square miles

Counties and Parishes

Gregg

Harrison

Ranking Highlights

170 *out of 319 in total* **land area**

117 *out of 319 in* **population growth,** *1970–1990*

272 *out of 310 in having the lowest* **unemployment** *rate*

205 *out of 310 in size of* **labor force**

223 *out of 318 in the percentage of* **college graduates**

222 *out of 292 in per capita personal* **income**

174 *out of 319 in number of* **manufacturing establishments**

267 *out of 318 in* **physicians** *per 1000 people*

223 *out of 318 in* **hospital beds** *per 1000 people*

201 *out of 267 in fewest* **crimes** *per 1000 people*

185 *out of 266 in fewest* **violent crimes** *per 1000 people*

214 *out of 319 in per capita* **federal funds and grants**

Quality of Life Indexes (Rate per 1000 population)

Crime rate in 1991:	72.0
Violent crime rate in 1991:	8.0
Physicians rate in 1992:	1.29
Hospital bed rate in 1991:	3.16

ACCRA Cost of Living Indexes

(First quarter 1993, average = 100)

Composite index:	N/A
Utilities index:	N/A
Housing index:	N/A

Population (1990)

Total Population and Growth Rate

1990: 162,431

1980: 151,760

1970: 120,770

Growth rate 1970–1990: 34%

Race and Hispanic Origin

White: 75.3%

Black: 22.1%

Asian/Pacific Islander: 0.4%

Native American: 0.4%

Hispanic origin: 3.1%

White not Hispanic: 74.0%

Age

Ages 18 to 20: 4.8%

Ages 21 to 24: 5%

Ages 25 to 44: 30.2%

Ages 45 to 54: 10%

Ages 55 to 59: 4.4%

Ages 60 to 64: 4.3%

Ages 65 plus: 13.4%

Educational Attainment (1990)

Percent having completed high school: 73.9%

Percent having completed college: 15.9%

Elementary and high school enrollment: 31,389

Federal Funds and Grants Received

Total received in 1989: $443,400,000

Funds received per capita: $2,661

Civilian Labor Force

1993 (April):   79,633

1992 average: 81,656

1991 average: 80,356

1990 average: 79,659

Unemployment

1993 (April): 8.4%

1992 average: 9.5%

1991 average: 8.0%

1990 average: 6.9%

Average Annual Pay

1988: $19,169

1987: $18,640

1985: $18,193

Per Capita Personal Income

1991: $15,839

1990: $15,193

1989: $14,321

Business Climate (1987)

Manufacturing

Number of establishments in 1987: 280

Shipments in 1987 ($1,000): $2,340,500

Employees in 1987: 15,300

Change in employment, 1982 to 1987: -4.4%

Average annual pay for manufacturing work in 1989: $26,976

Average annual pay for production work in 1987: $21,346

Wholesale Trade

Number of establishments in 1987: 424

Total sales in 1987 ($1,000): $1,176,100

Change in sales, 1982 to 1987: 0.6%

Retail Trade

Number of establishments in 1987: 1,421

Total sales in 1987 ($1,000): $1,176,100

Retail sales per household in 1987: $17,972

Average annual pay in 1989: $10,837

Service Industry

Selected receipts in 1987 ($1,000): $313,700

Average annual pay in 1989: $14,804

Housing

Total number of units in 1990: 68,170
Occupied units in 1990: 60,732
Owner-occupied units in 1990: 67.3%
1993 ACCRA average cost: N/A
1993 ACCRA average rent for an apartment: N/A

Chamber of Commerce

Longview Chamber of Commerce, Terry W. Burns, Exec. Vice President, 410 N. Center, PO Box 427, Longview, TX 75606. 214-237-4000

Economic Development Office

Longview Economic Development Foundation, Ronnie Morrison, Director, 410 N. Center St., PO Box 472, Longview, TX 75606. 903-237-4011, FAX 903-237-4049

Economic Development Organizations

Marshall-Harrison County Industry, Mike Strotheide, Exec. Director, 213 W. Austin St., PO Box 520, Marshall, TX 75671. 903-935-9502, FAX 903-935-9982

Major Businesses

Company	SIC	Telephone
Axelson Inc.	3533	(214) 757-6650
Bass Chevrolet Inc.	5511	(214) 757-3720
Carlile & Howell Inc.	1311	(214) 938-6641
Cherco Compressors Inc.	3533	(214) 753-4488
Delta Distributors Inc.	5169	(214) 759-7151
Durham Chevrolet Inc.	5511	(214) 984-2503
East Texas Salt Water Disposal	1389	(214) 984-9216
First Bancshares of Texas	6022	(214) 759-5188
Gibson Management Group Inc.	5912	(214) 297-0766
Good Shepherd Medical Center	8062	(214) 236-2000
Gregg Industrial	1799	(214) 757-5754
Ican Energy Co.	5171	(214) 983-1551
Jones, Cassity Inc.	5211	(214) 759-0736
Lebus Manufacturing Inc.	3462	(214) 759-4424
Lively Olds-Cadillac	5511	(214) 757-6600
Longview Bank & Trust Co.	6022	(214) 237-5500
Longview Regional Hospital	8062	(214) 758-1818
Marathon Le Tourneau Co.	3532	(214) 237-7000
Marshall Exploration Inc.	1311	(214) 938-6641
Martin Gas Corp.	5172	(214) 983-1551
Martin Gas Sales, Inc.	5171	(214) 983-1551
Mid-Valley Pipeline Co.	4612	(214) 757-0251
Motor Supply Warehouse Inc.	5013	(214) 679-3101
Presley, J. F. Oil Co.	5171	(214) 753-7051
Reeves Oil Co. Inc.	5171	(214) 759-0633
Texas Commerce Bank-Longview	6021	(214) 753-5511
Vertex Communications Corp.	3663	(214) 984-0555
Watson, Ralph Oil Co.	5411	(214) 938-0317
West Florida Natural Gas	4924	(214) 983-1551
Westchester Gas Co.	1311	(214) 687-2545

Colleges and Universities

East Texas Baptist University, Marshall
Letourneau University, Longview

LUBBOCK, TX (MSA)

Geographic Profile

Land Area

899.6 square miles

Counties and Parishes

Lubbock

Ranking Highlights

222 *out of 319 in total* **land area**

164 *out of 319 in* **population growth**, *1970–1990*

128 *out of 310 in having the lowest* **unemployment** *rate*

174 *out of 310 in size of* **labor force**

73 *out of 318 in the percentage of* **college graduates**

235 *out of 292 in per capita personal* **income**

179 *out of 319 in number of* **manufacturing establishments**

33 *out of 318 in* **physicians** *per 1000 people*

15 *out of 318 in* **hospital beds** *per 1000 people*

152 *out of 267 in fewest* **crimes** *per 1000 people*

117 *out of 266 in fewest* **violent crimes** *per 1000 people*

233 *out of 319 in per capita* **federal funds and grants**

Quality of Life Indexes (Rate per 1000 population)

Crime rate in 1991:	64.0
Violent crime rate in 1991:	5.4
Physicians rate in 1992:	2.89
Hospital bed rate in 1991:	7.02

ACCRA Cost of Living Indexes

(First quarter 1993, average = 100)

Composite index:	92.0
Utilities index:	83.9
Housing index:	84.3

Population (1990)

Total Population and Growth Rate

1990: 222,636

1980: 211,651

1970: 179,295

Growth rate 1970–1990: 24%

Race and Hispanic Origin

White: 79.1%

Black: 7.7%

Asian/Pacific Islander: 1.2%

Native American: 0.3%

Hispanic origin: 22.9%

White not Hispanic: 68.0%

Age

Ages 18 to 20: 7.3%

Ages 21 to 24: 9.1%

Ages 25 to 44: 31%

Ages 45 to 54: 8.7%

Ages 55 to 59: 3.9%

Ages 60 to 64: 3.6%

Ages 65 plus: 9.9%

Educational Attainment (1990)

Percent having completed high school: 74.2%

Percent having completed college: 23.4%

Elementary and high school enrollment: 40,357

Federal Funds and Grants Received

Total received in 1989: $584,900,000

Funds received per capita: $2,579

Civilian Labor Force

1993 (April):   115,067

1992 average: 116,582

1991 average: 114,515

1990 average: 114,551

Unemployment

1993 (April):   5.0%

1992 average: 6.5%

1991 average: 5.6%

1990 average: 4.8%

Average Annual Pay

1988: $17,564

1987: $17,007

1985: $16,483

Per Capita Personal Income

1991: $15,577

1990: $15,138

1989: $14,301

Business Climate (1987)

Manufacturing

Number of establishments in 1987: 270

Shipments in 1987 ($1,000): $867,400

Employees in 1987: 6,900

Change in employment, 1982 to 1987: -41.0%

Average annual pay for manufacturing work in 1989: $22,747

Average annual pay for production work in 1987: $16,595

Wholesale Trade

Number of establishments in 1987: 598

Total sales in 1987 ($1,000): $2,717,800

Change in sales, 1982 to 1987: 0.1%

Retail Trade

Number of establishments in 1987: 1,487

Total sales in 1987 ($1,000): $2,717,800

Retail sales per household in 1987: $20,090

Average annual pay in 1989: $12,353

Service Industry

Selected receipts in 1987 ($1,000): $597,100

Average annual pay in 1989: $16,803

Housing

Total number of units in 1990: 91,770

Occupied units in 1990: 81,534
Owner-occupied units in 1990: 58.2%
1993 ACCRA average cost: $92,870
1993 ACCRA average rent for an apartment: $443

Chamber of Commerce

Lubbock Chamber of Commerce, John A. Logan, President, 14th & Ave. K, PO Box 561, Lubbock, TX 79408. 806-763-4666

Economic Development Office

Lubbock Board of City Development, Carlton Schwab, Vice President, 2579 S. Loop 289 Suite 200, Lubbock, TX 79423. 806-748-1011

Major Businesses

Company	SIC	Telephone
Alderson Cadillac Co.Inc.	5511	(806) 763-8041
BRG Inc.	5171	(806) 795-8785
BPB Enterprises Inc.	5511	(806) 745-2177
Cafeteria Operators	5812	(806) 792-7151
Carlsbad Auto Co.	5511	(806) 797-3441
Fields & Co. of Lubbock	5074	(806) 762-0241
First Federal Savings Bank	6035	(806) 762-0491
First Lubbock Bancshares	6712	(806) 765-8861
First National Bank at Lubbock	6021	(806) 765-8861
Ford Bank Group Inc.	6712	(806) 763-5993
Furr's Inc.	5411	(806) 763-1931
Furr's/Bishops Cafeterias	5812	(806) 792-7151
Great Plains Pipeline	1623	(806) 747-3132
Griffin Rip Truck Service	5171	(806) 795-8785
K-West Auto Inc.	5511	(806) 763-8585
Lewis, Lee General Contractor	1542	(806) 745-9705
Lubbock American Iron & Metal	5093	(806) 765-8837
Lubbock County Hospital District	8062	(806) 743-3111
Methodist Hospital Lubbock, Texas	8062	(806) 792-1011
Modern Chevrolet Co.	5511	(806) 747-3211
Plains Cooperative Oil	2074	(806) 747-3434
Plains Association	5159	(806) 763-8011
Plains National Bank of Lubbock	6021	(806) 795-7131
Scoggin-Dickey Buick-GMC	5511	(806) 798-4000
South Plains Electric	4911	(806) 762-0406
Supermarket Development Co.	5411	(806) 763-1931
UMS Fulfillment Inc.	8732	(806) 744-6740
United Supermarkets Inc.	5411	(806) 745-4246
Watson Institutional Food	5141	(806) 747-2678
Womble Oldsmobile, Inc.	5511	(806) 796-7777

Colleges and Universities

Lubbock Christian University, Lubbock
Texas Tech University, Lubbock

McALLEN–EDINBURG–MISSION, TX (MSA)

Geographic Profile

Land Area
1569.1 square miles

Counties and Parishes
Hidalgo

Additional Cities/Towns within Area
Pharr

Ranking Highlights

126 *out of 319 in total* land area
  14 *out of 319 in* population growth, *1970–1990*
309 *out of 310 in having the lowest* unemployment *rate*
131 *out of 310 in size of* labor force
305 *out of 318 in the percentage of* college graduates
291 *out of 292 in per capita personal* income
225 *out of 319 in number of* manufacturing establishments
317 *out of 318 in* physicians *per 1000 people*
288 *out of 318 in* hospital beds *per 1000 people*
182 *out of 267 in fewest* crimes *per 1000 people*
104 *out of 266 in fewest* violent crimes *per 1000 people*
303 *out of 319 in per capita* federal funds and grants

Quality of Life Indexes (Rate per 1000 population)

Crime rate in 1991:	68.5
Violent crime rate in 1991:	5.0
Physicians rate in 1992:	0.78
Hospital bed rate in 1991:	2.24

ACCRA Cost of Living Indexes

(First quarter 1993, average = 100)
Composite index: 95.5
Utilities index: 119.8
Housing index: 83.7

Overview

McAllen, in the Rio Grande Valley (RGV) of Texas is located in the southern tip of the state and encompasses all of Cameron, Hidalgo, Starr and Willacy counties. It covers an area of 4,244 square miles. It is not really a valley at all, but a fertile plain sloping away in delta fashion from the Rio Grande. It is bounded on the east by the Gulf of Mexico, on the south by the Rio Grande, which forms the international boundary between the United States and Mexico, and on the west and north by Texas ranching counties.

Water for the Rio Grande Valley is supplied by Falcon Lake Reservoir and the Amistad Lake Reservoir, both of which lie on the Rio Grande. There is an ample supply of water for individuals and light industry. Water is also furnished on an allocation basis to various water districts for the irrigation of farm land. Raw water is furnished to the various municipalities and then distributed from municipally-owned water plants to industry. The quality of the water in the Valley is considered good, the prices reasonable.

The Rio Grande Valley economy is based on agriculture, labor intensive industry, and tourism. The major industry in the Valley is comprised of cotton, grain, vegetables, fruit and sugar cane and processing industries connected with their production. Irrigation makes it a lush agriculture area. Labor intensive companies such as cut and sew, electronic assembly, and machine manufacturing are increasing throughout the area because of reasonable wage scales and minimum union involvement. This industry is growing each year. Many "Winter Texans" come to the RGV as early as September and remain until April. The area is considered a gateway to Mexico for Americans traveling south and to the United States for Latinos traveling north. Tourism contributes $500 million per year to the total economy.

The U.S. Customs laws allow a U.S. owned company to assemble products in a foreign country and return the finished product to the United States, paying duty only on the value added (labor, overhead). This program is ideal for manufacturers looking for major cost reduction in a product that is labor intensive; it is especially attractive in Mexico for the low cost (but productive) labor and the lowest possible inventory cost, since the shipping time is substantially less than to any other "offshore" location.

A twin-plant operation is usually a highly automated or technology-oriented U.S. plant and a labor-intensive sister plant on the Mexican side. Components mass-produced in the United States are delivered to the Mexican plant for the time-consuming hand assembly operations.

Population (1990)

Total Population and Growth Rate
1990: 383,545
1980: 283,323
1970: 181,535
Growth rate 1970–1990: 111%

Race and Hispanic Origin
White: 74.8%
Black: .2%
Asian/Pacific Islander: 0.3%
Native American: 0.2%
Hispanic origin: 85.2%
White not Hispanic: 14.1%

Age
Ages 18 to 20: 5.7%
Ages 21 to 24: 6.1%
Ages 25 to 44: 27.3%
Ages 45 to 54: 7.8%
Ages 55 to 59: 3.2%
Ages 60 to 64: 3.4%
Ages 65 plus: 10%

Educational Attainment (1990)
Percent having completed high school: 46.6%
Percent having completed college: 11.5%
Elementary and high school enrollment: 107,184

Federal Funds and Grants Received
Total received in 1989: $767,300,000
Funds received per capita: $1,978

Civilian Labor Force
1993 (April): 166,060
1992 average: 165,096
1991 average: 163,081
1990 average: 163,342

Unemployment
1993 (April): 13.3%
1992 average: 17.0%
1991 average: 17.6%
1990 average: 19.1%

Average Annual Pay
1988: $13,449
1987: $13,311
1985: $12,979

Per Capita Personal Income
1991: $9,230
1990: $8,807
1989: $8,166

Business Climate (1987)

Manufacturing
Number of establishments in 1987: 190
Shipments in 1987 ($1,000): $734,100
Employees in 1987: 10,400
Change in employment, 1982 to 1987: 46.5%
Average annual pay for manufacturing work in 1989: $13,601
Average annual pay for production work in 1987: $11,171

Wholesale Trade
Number of establishments in 1987: 547
Total sales in 1987 ($1,000): $1,343,900
Change in sales, 1982 to 1987: -1.0%

Retail Trade
Number of establishments in 1987: 1,657
Total sales in 1987 ($1,000): $1,343,900
Retail sales per household in 1987: $14,861
Average annual pay in 1989: $10,544

Service Industry
Selected receipts in 1987 ($1,000): $452,300
Average annual pay in 1989: $14,330

Housing
Total number of units in 1990: 128,241
Occupied units in 1990: 103,479
Owner-occupied units in 1990: 70.3%
1993 ACCRA average cost: N/A

1993 ACCRA average rent for an apartment: N/A

Chamber of Commerce

McAllen Chamber of Commerce, Tommy Joyner, Exec. Director, 10 N. Broadway, PO Box 790, McAllen, TX 78502. 512-682-2871

Economic Development Office

Lower Rio Grande Valley Development Council, Kenneth N. Jones, Exec Director, 4900 N. 23rd St., McAllen, TX 78504. 512-682-3481, FAX 512-631-4670

Economic Development Organizations

Council for South Texas Economic Progress, Director, PO Box 6500, McAllen, TX 78502-6500. 512-682-6371, FAX 512-682-9853

Major Businesses

Company	SIC	Telephone
Azteca Milling Co.	0723	(512) 383-4911
Barbee-Neuhaus Implement	5083	(512) 968-7502
Boggus Motor Sales, Inc.	5511	(512) 686-7411
Cardenas International	5142	(512) 687-7364
Carl's Grocery Co., Inc.	5411	(512) 585-4578
Clark, Charles Chevrolet	5511	(512) 686-5441
Griffin & Brand of Mcallen	0161	(512) 682-6181
H & H Meat Products, Inc.	2011	(512) 565-6366
J & E Oil Inc.	5411	(512) 262-4771
Jones & Jones Inc.	5311	(512) 687-1171
Knapp Medical Center	8062	(512) 968-8567
LFD., Inc.	5712	(512) 686-2271
Liverpool of Mcallen, Inc.	5064	(512) 631-7131
Magic Valley Electric Cooperate	4911	(512) 565-2451
Mc Manus, J. S. Produce Co.	5148	(512) 969-2426
Mission Hospital Inc.	8062	(512) 580-9000
Ogden, Bert Motors Inc.	5511	(512) 381-8131
Payne-Pike Development Co.	5511	(512) 969-2525
Phillips Properties, Inc.	5541	(512) 686-0505
Richann Inc.	5411	(512) 630-2838
San Antonio Federal Savings Bank	6035	(512) 968-5551
Southwest Grain Co., Inc.	5153	(512) 842-3355
Texas Citrus Exchange	2033	(512) 585-8321
Universal Health Services of McAllen	8062	(512) 632-4000
Valley Banana King, Inc.	5148	(512) 843-8456
Valley Shamrock Inc.	5171	(512) 686-0563
Van Burkleo Motors, Inc.	5511	(512) 682-2838
Wilson D. Construction Co.	1542	(512) 686-9573

Colleges and Universities

University of Texas-Pan American, Edinburg, TX

MIDLAND, TX (MSA)

Geographic Profile

Land Area
900.3 square miles

Counties and Parishes
Midland

Ranking Highlights

221 *out of 319 in total* **land area**
 61 *out of 319 in* **population growth,** *1970–1990*
201 *out of 310 in having the lowest* **unemployment** *rate*
289 *out of 310 in size of* **labor force**
 47 *out of 318 in the percentage of* **college graduates**
N/A *out of 292 in per capita personal* **income**
284 *out of 319 in number of* **manufacturing establishments**
283 *out of 318 in* **physicians** *per 1000 people*
228 *out of 318 in* **hospital beds** *per 1000 people*
186 *out of 267 in fewest* **crimes** *per 1000 people*
221 *out of 266 in fewest* **violent crimes** *per 1000 people*
317 *out of 319 in per capita* **federal funds and grants**

Quality of Life Indexes (Rate per 1000 population)

Crime rate in 1991:	69.5
Violent crime rate in 1991:	9.7
Physicians rate in 1992:	1.18
Hospital bed rate in 1991:	3.12

ACCRA Cost of Living Indexes
(First quarter 1993, average = 100)

Composite index:	92.4
Utilities index:	104.9
Housing index:	76.1

Population (1990)

Total Population and Growth Rate
1990: 106,611
1980: 82,636
1970: 65,433
Growth rate 1970–1990: 63%

Race and Hispanic Origin
White: 81.6%
Black: 7.8%
Asian/Pacific Islander: 0.8%
Native American: 0.4%
Hispanic origin: 21.4%
White not Hispanic: 69.9%

Age
Ages 18 to 20: 3.8%
Ages 21 to 24: 4.6%
Ages 25 to 44: 33.7%
Ages 45 to 54: 9.1%
Ages 55 to 59: 4.2%

Ages 60 to 64: 4.3%
Ages 65 plus: 8.9%

Educational Attainment (1990)
Percent having completed high school: 76.8%
Percent having completed college: 26.4%
Elementary and high school enrollment: 21,431

Federal Funds and Grants Received
Total received in 1989: $171,400,000
Funds received per capita: $1,598

Civilian Labor Force
1993 (April): 48,082
1992 average: 49,465
1991 average: 49,020
1990 average: 47,973

Unemployment
1993 (April): 6.5%
1992 average: 7.5%
1991 average: 5.4%
1990 average: 5.4%

Average Annual Pay
1988: $23,728
1987: $22,745
1985: $22,929

Per Capita Personal Income
1991: N/A
1990: N/A
1989: N/A

Business Climate (1987)
Manufacturing
Number of establishments in 1987: 111
Shipments in 1987 ($1,000): $214,800
Employees in 1987: 2,500
Change in employment, 1982 to 1987: -41.9%
Average annual pay for manufacturing work in 1989: $28,710
Average annual pay for production work in 1987: $22,333

Wholesale Trade
Number of establishments in 1987: 289
Total sales in 1987 ($1,000): $1,623,800
Change in sales, 1982 to 1987: -30.4%

Retail Trade
Number of establishments in 1987: 724
Total sales in 1987 ($1,000): $1,623,800
Retail sales per household in 1987: $16,613
Average annual pay in 1989: $11,659

Service Industry
Selected receipts in 1987 ($1,000): $319,900
Average annual pay in 1989: $17,713

Housing
Total number of units in 1990: 45,181

Occupied units in 1990: 38,920
Owner-occupied units in 1990: 65.9%
1993 ACCRA average cost: $85,000
1993 ACCRA average rent for an apartment: $426

Chamber of Commerce
Midland Chamber of Commerce, President, 109 N. Main St., PO Box 1890, Midland, TX 79702. 915-683-3381

Major Businesses

Company	SIC	Telephone
AOI Coal Co.	1221	(915) 684-3773
Adobe Gas Pipeline Co.	5172	(915) 683-4701
Clajon Holdings	4923	(915) 682-1176
Clajon Marketing	4924	(915) 682-1176
Compressor Systems Inc.	7353	(915) 563-1170
Eddins-Walcher Co.	5172	(915) 684-4423
INR Partners	2851	(915) 682-7936
Insilco Corp.	3469	(915) 684-4411
Leonard, Dave Construction	1542	(915) 683-3355
Midland Memorial Hospital District	8062	(915) 685-1111
Parker Parsley Petro Co.	1311	(915) 683-4768
Sherman, Jack Chevrolet Inc.	5511	(915) 694-9601
Union Supply Co.	5084	(915) 684-8841
West Texas Equipment Co.	5082	(915) 563-1863
West Texas Gas Inc.	4923	(915) 682-4349

Colleges and Universities
Midland College, Midland

ODESSA, TX (MSA)

Geographic Profile

Land Area

901.1 square miles

Counties and Parishes

Ector

Ranking Highlights

220 *out of 319 in total* land area

140 *out of 319 in* population growth, *1970–1990*

283 *out of 310 in having the lowest* unemployment *rate*

281 *out of 310 in size of* labor force

307 *out of 318 in the percentage of* college graduates

114 *out of 292 in per capita personal* income

203 *out of 319 in number of* manufacturing establishments

279 *out of 318 in* physicians *per 1000 people*

213 *out of 318 in* hospital beds *per 1000 people*

266 *out of 267 in fewest* crimes *per 1000 people*

172 *out of 266 in fewest* violent crimes *per 1000 people*

319 *out of 319 in per capita* federal funds and grants

Quality of Life Indexes (Rate per 1000 population)

Crime rate in 1991: 120.5

Violent crime rate in 1991: 7.5

Physicians rate in 1992: 1.23

Hospital bed rate in 1991: 3.27

ACCRA Cost of Living Indexes

(First quarter 1993, average = 100)

Composite index: 93.9

Utilities index: 104.9

Housing index: 79.2

Overview

Odessa, the county seat of Ector County, is located approximately mid-way between Dallas/Ft. Worth. The region has one international airport offering service from four airlines and one private airport.

Odessa is the most populous city in the Permian Basin Region and hosts a heavy manufacturing base with oil/gas as its primary industry. Some of the major oil companies represented in the area are Phillips Petroleum, Exxon, Texaco and Shell.

Over the past two years more than 100 new businesses have opened, creating in excess of 2,000 jobs. Other major ventures such as the addition of a Sam's Wholesale Club, Walmart Supercenter, Safe Tire Disposal (tire recycling facility), ABB Randall, and Highland Pump-Rotaflex Division.

Convention facilities include the 8,200 seat Ector County Coliseum. Cultural activities include the Globe Theatre, Presidential Museum, Art Institute of the Permian Basin, and the nearby Petroleum Museum.

Population (1990)

Total Population and Growth Rate

1990: 118,934

1980: 115,374

1970: 92,660

Growth rate 1970–1990: 28%

Race and Hispanic Origin

White: 76.8%

Black: 4.7%

Asian/Pacific Islander: 0.6%

Native American: 0.5%

Hispanic origin: 31.4%

White not Hispanic: 62.9%

Age

Ages 18 to 20: 4.4%

Ages 21 to 24: 5.2%

Ages 25 to 44: 31.7%

Ages 45 to 54: 9.3%

Ages 55 to 59: 4.2%

Ages 60 to 64: 4.2%

Ages 65 plus: 9.3%

Educational Attainment (1990)

Percent having completed high school: 66.9%

Percent having completed college: 11.4%

Elementary and high school enrollment: 25,562

Federal Funds and Grants Received

Total received in 1989: $179,600,000

Funds received per capita: $1,440

Civilian Labor Force

1993 (April): 53,032

1992 average: 54,445

1991 average: 53,214

1990 average: 51,273

Unemployment

1993 (April): 8.9%

1992 average: 10.1%

1991 average: 6.6%

1990 average: 6.0%

Average Annual Pay

1988: $20,278

1987: $21,275

1985: $20,157

Per Capita Personal Income

1991: $17,980

1990: $17,304

1989: $16,271

Business Climate (1987)

Manufacturing

Number of establishments in 1987: 223

Shipments in 1987 ($1,000): $963,000

Employees in 1987: 4,000

Change in employment, 1982 to 1987: -55.6%

Average annual pay for manufacturing work in 1989: $38,037

Average annual pay for production work in 1987: $22,182

Wholesale Trade
Number of establishments in 1987: 473
Total sales in 1987 ($1,000): $1,271,400
Change in sales, 1982 to 1987: -24.3%

Retail Trade
Number of establishments in 1987: 858
Total sales in 1987 ($1,000): $1,271,400
Retail sales per household in 1987: $15,952
Average annual pay in 1989: $11,647

Service Industry
Selected receipts in 1987 ($1,000): $314,300
Average annual pay in 1989: $17,840

Housing
Total number of units in 1990: 48,789
Occupied units in 1990: 42,322
Owner-occupied units in 1990: 65.8%
1993 ACCRA average cost: $91,075
1993 ACCRA average rent for an apartment: $386

Chamber of Commerce
Odessa Chamber of Commerce, Russell S. Autry, CEO, 400 W. 4th St., PO Box 3626, Odessa, TX 79763. 915-332-8180

Economic Development Office
Odessa Economic Development Corp., Neil McDonald,Jr., Director, 400 W. 4th St., Odessa, TX 79760. 915-332-9103

Major Businesses

Company	SIC	Telephone
Arledge Jack Oldsmobile-Cadillac	5511	(915) 332-0441
B-Banc Corp.	6712	(915) 335-7911
Ector County Ind School District	8211	(915) 332-9151
Farmer, E. L. & Co.	4213	(915) 332-1496
Jones Pontiac - GMC Inc.	5511	(915) 332-6422
Permian Tank & Manufacturing	3443	(915) 333-4591
Pinkie's Inc.	5921	(915) 337-6623
Ref-Chem Corp.	1629	(915) 332-8531
Sewell, Buick, Toyota, Inc.	5511	(915) 332-1601
Sivalls Inc.	3443	(915) 337-3571
Southwest Energy Distribution	5172	(915) 332-1301
Standard Sales Co. Inc.	5181	(915) 367-7662
Terk Distributing Co.	5182	(915) 332-9183

Colleges and Universities
Odessa College, Odessa
University of Texas of the Permian Basin, Odessa

SAN ANGELO, TX (MSA)

Geographic Profile
Land Area
1522.2 square miles
Counties and Parishes
Tom Green

Ranking Highlights
129 *out of 319 in total* land area
101 *out of 319 in* population growth, *1970–1990*
 99 *out of 310 in having the lowest* unemployment *rate*
295 *out of 310 in size of* labor force
192 *out of 318 in the percentage of* college graduates
200 *out of 292 in per capita personal* income
294 *out of 319 in number of* manufacturing establishments
168 *out of 318 in* physicians *per 1000 people*
 69 *out of 318 in* hospital beds *per 1000 people*
139 *out of 267 in fewest* crimes *per 1000 people*
130 *out of 266 in fewest* violent crimes *per 1000 people*
115 *out of 319 in per capita* federal funds and grants

Quality of Life Indexes (Rate per 1000 population)
Crime rate in 1991:	61.5
Violent crime rate in 1991:	6.1
Physicians rate in 1992:	1.77
Hospital bed rate in 1991:	5.16

ACCRA Cost of Living Indexes
(First quarter 1993, average = 100)
Composite index: N/A
Utilities index: N/A
Housing index: N/A

Population (1990)
Total Population and Growth Rate
1990: 98,458
1980: 84,784
1970: 71,047
Growth rate 1970–1990: 39%

Race and Hispanic Origin
White: 80.8%
Black: 4.2%
Asian/Pacific Islander: 1.0%
Native American: 0.4%
Hispanic origin: 25.9%
White not Hispanic: 68.7%

Age
Ages 18 to 20: 6.3%
Ages 21 to 24: 6.6%
Ages 25 to 44: 30.2%
Ages 45 to 54: 9%
Ages 55 to 59: 4.1%

Ages 60 to 64: 4%
Ages 65 plus: 12.7%

Educational Attainment (1990)

Percent having completed high school: 71.0%
Percent having completed college: 17.0%
Elementary and high school enrollment: 18,460

Federal Funds and Grants Received

Total received in 1989: $340,100,000
Funds received per capita: $3,426

Civilian Labor Force

1993 (April):   46,019
1992 average: 45,773
1991 average: 44,286
1990 average: 43,588

Unemployment

1993 (April):   5.5%
1992 average: 6.0%
1991 average: 5.3%
1990 average: 5.6%

Average Annual Pay

1988: $16,817
1987: $16,559
1985: $15,982

Per Capita Personal Income

1991: $16,252
1990: $15,334
1989: $14,807

Business Climate (1987)

Manufacturing

Number of establishments in 1987: 102
Shipments in 1987 ($1,000): $478,700
Employees in 1987: 4,100
Change in employment, 1982 to 1987: -19.6%
Average annual pay for manufacturing work in 1989: $19,188
Average annual pay for production work in 1987: $15,172

Wholesale Trade

Number of establishments in 1987: 186
Total sales in 1987 ($1,000): $551,800
Change in sales, 1982 to 1987: -11.2%

Retail Trade

Number of establishments in 1987: 697
Total sales in 1987 ($1,000): $551,800
Retail sales per household in 1987: $16,245
Average annual pay in 1989: $10,564

Service Industry

Selected receipts in 1987 ($1,000): $210,000
Average annual pay in 1989: $16,354

Housing

Total number of units in 1990: 40,135

Occupied units in 1990: 35,408
Owner-occupied units in 1990: 62.3%
1993 ACCRA average cost: N/A
1993 ACCRA average rent for an apartment: N/A

Chamber of Commerce

San Angelo Chamber of Commerce, Doug Kinsinger, Exec. Vice President, 500 Rio Concho Dr., San Angelo, TX 76903. 915-655-4136

Major Businesses

Company	SIC	Telephone
Amalgamated Sugar Co.	2063	(801) 399-3431
American Food & Drug Inc.	5411	(801) 537-3000
American Superstores, Inc.	5411	(801) 539-0112
Associated Food Stores, Inc.	5141	(801) 973-4400
Crossland Savings, Utah	6035	(801) 350-9600
First Security Corp.	6021	(801) 350-6000
Huntsman Chemical Corp.	2821	(801) 532-5200
IHC Hospitals Inc.	8062	(801) 533-8282
Intermountain Power Agency	4911	(801) 262-8807
Jewel Companies, Inc.	5411	(801) 539-0112
Northwest Pipeline Corp.	4922	(801) 583-8800
Price Savers Wholesale, Inc.	5199	(801) 466-7777
Questar Corp.	4924	(801) 534-5600
Smiths Food & Drug Center	5411	(801) 974-1400
Thiokol Corp.	3764	(801) 629-2270
Utah State Retirement Board	6733	(801) 355-3884
Western Dairymen's Cooper	2026	(801) 322-4672

Colleges and Universities

Angelo State University, San Angelo

SAN ANTONIO, TX (MSA)

Geographic Profile

Land Area
2519.6 square miles

Counties and Parishes
Bexar
Comal
Guadalupe

Ranking Highlights

69 *out of 319 in total* **land area**
78 *out of 319 in* **population growth,** *1970–1990*
139 *out of 310 in having the lowest* **unemployment** *rate*
42 *out of 310 in size of* **labor force**
150 *out of 318 in the percentage of* **college graduates**
219 *out of 292 in per capita personal* **income**
58 *out of 319 in number of* **manufacturing establishments**
79 *out of 318 in* **physicians** *per 1000 people*
214 *out of 318 in* **hospital beds** *per 1000 people*
264 *out of 267 in fewest* **crimes** *per 1000 people*
157 *out of 266 in fewest* **violent crimes** *per 1000 people*
66 *out of 319 in per capita* **federal funds and grants**

Quality of Life Indexes (Rate per 1000 population)

Crime rate in 1991:	104.5
Violent crime rate in 1991:	7.1
Physicians rate in 1992:	2.39
Hospital bed rate in 1991:	3.25

ACCRA Cost of Living Indexes

(First quarter 1993, average = 100)

Composite index:	94.5
Utilities index:	79.2
Housing index:	87.1

Overview

The City of San Antonio is located in south central Texas. Northwest of the city, the terrain slopes upward to the Edwards Plateau. To the southeast, it slopes to the Gulf Coastal Plains. Elevations varies from 500-1,500 feet. San Antonio, the tenth largest city in the United States, is projected to grow at an average annual rate of 1.9 to 2.0 percent through the year 2010.

San Antonio's economy is based on services, commercial trade, government employment, tourism, medical facilities and manufacturing. The leading employment sector, with 27.9% and 156,700 jobs, is the service industry. Almost half of these employees work in health (28%) or business services (20%). From December 1985 to December, 1992 this industry has had a consistent increase of jobs, adding 45,700 in a period of seven years. The second leading employment sector is retail and wholesale trade, which, together with services, reflect San Antonio's role as the economic hub of central and south Texas. With 142,600

employed in this sector, San Antonio has become a focal point for the transportation of goods in and out of Mexico. The 10.6 million tourists who visit annually, spending over $2 billion a year, also contribute to the great retail demand. Government is the third leading employer with 22.7%, employing 127,400. This figure includes federal, state and local governments. Manufacturing comprises 8.2% of the work force. Within the San Antonio MSA, manufacturing establishments employ 46,700 workers. Principal products include metal and plastic products, semiconductors, electronic equipment, computer peripheral equipment, air-conditioning equipment, processed meats, beer and clothing.

The San Antonio housing market was ranked the second best in the country by *U.S. News and World Report* and the major companies include Southwestern Bell Corporation, Sony Microelectronics, Bausch and Lomb, World Savings and Loan, Golden Aluminum, and Citicorp. Located in the central time zone and 180 miles from Mexico, the city is very attractive to telecommunications-intensive operations and to companies preparing to benefit from NAFTA. Over 41% of the $58 billion in trade with Mexico travels through San Antonio. San Antonio International Airport makes more than 65 direct flights into Mexico every week.

Health care and biotechnology constitute over a $1.5 billion industry. The Southwest Research Institute is a $231 million research and development contract laboratory, the Southwest Foundation for Biomedical Research conducts ongoing research programs in human and non-human primates, and the Texas Research and Technology Foundation is dedicated to the transfer of technology from the laboratory to the marketplace. The University of Texas Institute of Biotechnology, the Cancer Therapy and Research Center's Institute for Drug Development, and the Southwest Oncology Group headquarters are also located in San Antonio.

The city's cost of living is among the lowest in the nation, with the median price of a home at $78,600. Home to four major museums, symphony, the San Antonio Missions (AA Farm Team of the LA Dodgers), the NBA San Antonio Spurs, Sea World, Fiesta Texas, major golf tournaments and water sports, the list of cultural and recreational activities is endless. A new $180 million Alamodome, a multi-use domed stadium, opened in May of 1993. There are 10 local colleges and universities and less than 7% of the work force is unionized.

Population (1990)

Total Population and Growth Rate
1990: 1,302,099
1980: 1,072,125
1970: 888,179
Growth rate 1970–1990: 47%

Race and Hispanic Origin
White: 75.1%
Black: 6.8%

873

Asian/Pacific Islander: 1.2%
Native American: 0.4%
Hispanic origin: 47.6%
White not Hispanic: 44.3%

Age

Ages 18 to 20: 5.1%
Ages 21 to 24: 6.2%
Ages 25 to 44: 32.3%
Ages 45 to 54: 9.4%
Ages 55 to 59: 4%
Ages 60 to 64: 3.7%
Ages 65 plus: 10.3%

Educational Attainment (1990)

Percent having completed high school: 72.7%
Percent having completed college: 19.4%
Elementary and high school enrollment: 259,974

Federal Funds and Grants Received

Total received in 1989: $5,585,100,000
Funds received per capita: $4,221

Civilian Labor Force

1993 (April): 641,030
1992 average: 629,476
1991 average: 606,655
1990 average: 606,296

Unemployment

1993 (April): 5.5%
1992 average: 6.6%
1991 average: 6.6%
1990 average: 6.9%

Average Annual Pay

1988: $19,325
1987: $18,436
1985: $17,415

Per Capita Personal Income

1991: $15,950
1990: $15,252
1989: $14,855

Business Climate (1987)

Manufacturing

Number of establishments in 1987: 1,193
Shipments in 1987 ($1,000): $4,500,900
Employees in 1987: 44,100
Change in employment, 1982 to 1987: -12.8%
Average annual pay for manufacturing work in 1989: $21,461
Average annual pay for production work in 1987: $15,611

Wholesale Trade

Number of establishments in 1987: 2,111
Total sales in 1987 ($1,000): $9,235,500
Change in sales, 1982 to 1987: 28.0%

Retail Trade

Number of establishments in 1987: 7,292
Total sales in 1987 ($1,000): $9,235,500
Retail sales per household in 1987: $17,049
Average annual pay in 1989: $11,956

Service Industry

Selected receipts in 1987 ($1,000): $3,498,300
Average annual pay in 1989: $17,899

Office Real Estate (1992)

Office space inventory: 17,641,292 square feet
Average class A Central Business District rental range per sq. ft: $13.00

Vacancy Rates

All areas: 23.0%

Vacancy Rates in Central Business District

Class A space: 25.5%
Class B space: 33.9%

Vacancy Rates Outside Central Business District

Class A space: 15.6%
Class B space: 25.2%

Housing

Total number of units in 1990: 504,411
Occupied units in 1990: 451,021
Owner-occupied units in 1990: 59.2%
1993 ACCRA average cost: $97,700
1993 ACCRA average rent for an apartment: $473

Chamber of Commerce

Greater San Antonio Chamber of Commerce, Joseph R. Krier, President, 602 E. Commerce, PO Box 1628, San Antonio, TX 78296. 512-229-2100

Economic Development Office

San Antonio Economic Development Foundation, Mario Hernandez, President, 602 E. Commerce St., PO Box 1628, San Antonio, TX 78296. 512-226-1394

Major Businesses

Company	SIC	Telephone
Associated Milk Producers	5143	(512) 340-9100
Benson, Tom Customer Service	5511	(512) 341-3311
Builders Square Inc.	5211	(512) 731-0500
Butt, H. E. Grocery Co.	5411	(512) 270-8000
Chromalloy Gas Turbine Co.	3724	(512) 333-6010
City Public Service	4931	(512) 227-3211
Datapoint Corp.	3571	(512) 699-7000
Diamond Shamrock Inc.	2911	(512) 641-6800
Frost National Bank	6021	(512) 220-4011
Handy-Andy	5411	(512) 227-8755
Harte-Hanks Communication	2741	(512) 829-9000
HHC Holding Inc.	2711	(512) 829-9000
Kinetic Concepts, Inc.	7352	(512) 225-4092
Leonard & Harral Packing	5147	(512) 924-4403

Major Businesses (Continued)

Company	SIC	Telephone
Luby's Cafeterias, Inc.	5812	(512) 654-9000
Sidermex International, Inc.	5051	(512) 736-4111
Southwest Research Institute	8731	(512) 684-5111
Tesoro Petroleum Corp.	2911	(512) 828-8484
UETA, Inc.	5921	(512) 828-8382
United Services Auto Association	6311	(512) 498-2211
Valero Energy Corp.	2911	(512) 246-2000
Valero Natural Gas Co.	1311	(512) 246-2000
Valero Natural Gas Partner	4922	(512) 246-2000
Valero Refining & Marketing Co.	2911	(512) 246-2000
Winn's Stores Incorporate	5331	(512) 227-4747
Zachry, Inc.	1611	(512) 922-1213

Colleges and Universities

Incarnate Word College, San Antonio
Our Lady of the Lake University of San Antonio, San Antonio
Palo Alto College, San Antonio
St. Mary's University of San Antonio, San Antonio
St. Philip's College, San Antonio
San Antonio Art Institute, San Antonio
San Antonio College, San Antonio
Trinity University, San Antonio
University of Texas at San Antonio, San Antonio
University of Texas Health Science Center at San Antonio, San Antonio

SHERMAN–DENISON, TX (MSA)

Geographic Profile

Land Area
933.7 square miles

Counties and Parishes
Grayson

Ranking Highlights

211 *out of 319 in total* **land area**
205 *out of 319 in* **population growth,** *1970–1990*
201 *out of 310 in having the lowest* **unemployment** *rate*
293 *out of 310 in size of* **labor force**
256 *out of 318 in the percentage of* **college graduates**
192 *out of 292 in per capita personal* **income**
271 *out of 319 in number of* **manufacturing establishments**
200 *out of 318 in* **physicians** *per 1000 people*
46 *out of 318 in* **hospital beds** *per 1000 people*
168 *out of 267 in fewest* **crimes** *per 1000 people*
92 *out of 266 in fewest* **violent crimes** *per 1000 people*
218 *out of 319 in per capita* **federal funds and grants**

Quality of Life Indexes (Rate per 1000 population)

Crime rate in 1991:	66.6
Violent crime rate in 1991:	4.5
Physicians rate in 1992:	1.64
Hospital bed rate in 1991:	5.6

ACCRA Cost of Living Indexes

(First quarter 1993, average = 100)

Composite index:	N/A
Utilities index:	N/A
Housing index:	N/A

Population (1990)

Total Population and Growth Rate
1990: 95,021
1980: 89,796
1970: 83,225
Growth rate 1970–1990: 14%

Race and Hispanic Origin
White: 90.0%
Black: 6.9%
Asian/Pacific Islander: 0.4%
Native American: 1.1%
Hispanic origin: 2.9%
White not Hispanic: 88.7%

Age
Ages 18 to 20: 4.6%
Ages 21 to 24: 5%
Ages 25 to 44: 29%
Ages 45 to 54: 10.3%
Ages 55 to 59: 4.8%

Ages 60 to 64: 4.7%
Ages 65 plus: 16.3%

Educational Attainment (1990)

Percent having completed high school: 72.1%
Percent having completed college: 14.0%
Elementary and high school enrollment: 16,505

Federal Funds and Grants Received

Total received in 1989: $257,000,000
Funds received per capita: $2,624

Civilian Labor Force

1993 (April):   46,024
1992 average: 46,594
1991 average: 46,864
1990 average: 46,899

Unemployment

1993 (April):   6.2%
1992 average: 7.5%
1991 average: 6.6%
1990 average: 5.3%

Average Annual Pay

1988: $19,962
1987: $19,192
1985: $17,902

Per Capita Personal Income

1991: $16,396
1990: $15,833
1989: $15,172

Business Climate (1987)

Manufacturing

Number of establishments in 1987: 127
Shipments in 1987 ($1,000): $1,591,800
Employees in 1987: 10,400
Change in employment, 1982 to 1987: -6.3%
Average annual pay for manufacturing work in 1989: $28,844
Average annual pay for production work in 1987: $21,658

Wholesale Trade

Number of establishments in 1987: 167
Total sales in 1987 ($1,000): $283,400
Change in sales, 1982 to 1987: 3.6%

Retail Trade

Number of establishments in 1987: 700
Total sales in 1987 ($1,000): $283,400
Retail sales per household in 1987: $16,025
Average annual pay in 1989: $10,867

Service Industry

Selected receipts in 1987 ($1,000): $192,800
Average annual pay in 1989: $16,676

Housing

Total number of units in 1990: 44,223

Occupied units in 1990: 36,847
Owner-occupied units in 1990: 69.3%
1993 ACCRA average cost: N/A
1993 ACCRA average rent for an apartment: N/A

Chamber of Commerce

Sherman Area Chamber of Commerce, James E. Heath, President, 1815 S. Sam Rayburn, PO Box 1029, Sherman, TX 75090. 214-893-1184

Major Businesses

Company	SIC	Telephone
Barrett Grocery Co. Inc.	5912	(214) 465-8225
Brooks, Jim Olds Cadillac	5511	(214) 465-3535
Carl's Sausage Co.	2013	(214) 364-2935
Chapman Inc.	5172	(214) 893-8106
Diaper Jeans, Inc.	2361	(214) 465-5795
Grayson Collin Electric Co.	4911	(214) 482-5231
J & W Corp.	5541	(214) 893-8106
Jones Wilson N. Memorial Hospital	8062	(214) 870-4611
Kralis, M. and Co. Inc.	5144	(214) 893-7955
LJH Corp.	7353	(214) 465-6937
Martinek Grain & Bins Inc.	5191	(214) 433-5425
Medical Plaza Hospital	8062	(214) 870-7000
Mit-Con Inc.	1542	(214) 893-6593
Monitor Inc.	3448	(214) 893-6336
Old American Pottery Co.	5999	(214) 532-5547
Perkins, Arnold L.	4493	(214) 465-6330
Plyler, Lloyd Construction	1541	(214) 893-6393
Pogue, Paul Inc.	1542	(214) 892-4696
Red River Chrysler-Plymouth	5511	(214) 892-1578
Sherman Foundry	3321	(214) 893-4307
Smith, W. J. Wood Preserving	2491	(214) 465-6161
Sooner Oil Co.	5172	(214) 893-6576
Taylor Cars Inc.	5511	(214) 893-0144
Thomason Oil Co.	5541	(214) 893-4338
Washington Iron Works Inc.	3599	(214) 892-8145
Young Enterprises Inc.	1731	(214) 892-1508

Colleges and Universities

Austin College, Sherman
Grayson County College, Denison

TEXARKANA, TX – TEXARKANA, AR (MSA)

Geographic Profile

Land Area

1512.0 square miles

Counties and Parishes

Arkansas:

  Miller

Texas:

  Bowie

Ranking Highlights

133 *out of 319 in total* **land area**

186 *out of 319 in* **population growth**, *1970–1990*

230 *out of 310 in having the lowest* **unemployment** *rate*

272 *out of 310 in size of* **labor force**

285 *out of 318 in the percentage of* **college graduates**

261 *out of 292 in per capita personal* **income**

290 *out of 319 in number of* **manufacturing establishments**

193 *out of 318 in* **physicians** *per 1000 people*

 40 *out of 318 in* **hospital beds** *per 1000 people*

195 *out of 267 in fewest* **crimes** *per 1000 people*

170 *out of 266 in fewest* **violent crimes** *per 1000 people*

 48 *out of 319 in per capita* **federal funds and grants**

Quality of Life Indexes (Rate per 1000 population)

Crime rate in 1991:	71.1
Violent crime rate in 1991:	7.4
Physicians rate in 1992:	1.67
Hospital bed rate in 1991:	5.7

ACCRA Cost of Living Indexes

(First quarter 1993, average = 100)

Composite index:	N/A
Utilities index:	N/A
Housing index:	N/A

Population (1990)

Total Population and Growth Rate

1990: 120,132

1980: 113,067

1970: 102,294

Growth rate 1970–1990: 17%

Race and Hispanic Origin

White: 76.9%

Black: 22.0%

Asian/Pacific Islander: 0.3%

Native American: 0.5%

Hispanic origin: 1.4%

White not Hispanic: 75.9%

Age

Ages 18 to 20: 4.2%

Ages 21 to 24: 5%

Ages 25 to 44: 29.9%

Ages 45 to 54: 10.3%

Ages 55 to 59: 4.3%

Ages 60 to 64: 4.5%

Ages 65 plus: 14.3%

Educational Attainment (1990)

Percent having completed high school: 69.6%

Percent having completed college: 12.8%

Elementary and high school enrollment: 23,437

Federal Funds and Grants Received

Total received in 1989: $560,700,000

Funds received per capita: $4,695

Civilian Labor Force

1993 (April):	57,861
1992 average:	57,812
1991 average:	56,850
1990 average:	57,265

Unemployment

1993 (April): 7.0%

1992 average: 8.1%

1991 average: 7.5%

1990 average: 6.4%

Average Annual Pay

1988: $18,111

1987: $17,747

1985: $16,670

Per Capita Personal Income

1991: $15,004

1990: $14,401

1989: $13,506

Business Climate (1987)

Manufacturing

Number of establishments in 1987: 106

Shipments in 1987 ($1,000): $847,200

Employees in 1987: 7,300

Change in employment, 1982 to 1987: 0%

Average annual pay for manufacturing work in 1989: $24,543

Average annual pay for production work in 1987: $21,075

Wholesale Trade

Number of establishments in 1987: 237

Total sales in 1987 ($1,000): $544,900

Change in sales, 1982 to 1987: 15.1%

Retail Trade

Number of establishments in 1987: 771

Total sales in 1987 ($1,000): $544,900

Retail sales per household in 1987: $15,602

Average annual pay in 1989: $11,429

Service Industry

Selected receipts in 1987 ($1,000): $223,700

Average annual pay in 1989: $17,302

Housing

Total number of units in 1990: 50,406
Occupied units in 1990: 44,868
Owner-occupied units in 1990: 70.0%
1993 ACCRA average cost: N/A
1993 ACCRA average rent for an apartment: N/A

Chamber of Commerce

Texarkana Chamber of Commerce, R.E. Lee, President, 819 State Line Ave., PO Box 1468, Texarkana, TX 75504. 214-792-7191

Major Businesses

Company	SIC	Telephone
AP Supply Co.	5085	(501) 773-6586
Arnold, Truman Companies	5172	(214) 794-3835
Buhrman-Pharr Hardware Co.	5072	(501) 773-3122
Coker Buick Inc.	5511	(214) 793-4623
Commercial Box & Lumber Co.	2441	(214) 794-2207
Commercial National Bank of Texas	6021	(501) 773-4561
E Z Mart Stores Inc.	5541	(214) 832-6502
Firstbank	6022	(214) 838-6502
Four Thirteen Inc.	1623	(214) 832-5784
HMB Construction Co.	2951	(214) 838-5541
Humco Laboratory Inc.	5122	(214) 793-3174
J & J Trucking Co.	4213	(214) 792-2002
James, M. L. Construction Co.	1542	(214) 794-2738
Jones, N. E. Oil Co. Inc.	5411	(214) 838-8541
Keaton Truck Lines Inc.	4213	(214) 792-3351
Mankins, Pete Pontiac-Cadillac	5511	(214) 793-5661
Mc Larty Ford Inc.	5511	(214) 792-7121
Miller-Bowie County Farms Assoc.	5191	(214) 794-3631
Miller-Claborn Oil Distributing	5171	(501) 772-8251
Oaklawn Financial Corp.	6022	(214) 838-6502
ORR Inc.	5511	(214) 794-5500
Payne, J-W Construction Co.	1622	(214) 628-6979
Robbins Toyota Inc.	5511	(214) 794-5121
Save-Mart	5411	(214) 667-2624
Smith, Starkey & Stacey	5411	(214) 667-2515
Southwest Ark Electric Coop Co.	4911	(501) 772-2743
Texana Tank Car Manufacturing	7699	(214) 838-5564
Texarkana Memorial Hospital	8062	(214) 793-4511
Texarkana National Bank	6021	(214) 792-7166
Texarkana Water Utilities	4941	(214) 794-3571
Texarkana Wire & Cable Inc.	3357	(501) 772-0100
Walsh-Lumpkin Drug Co.	5122	(214) 794-5141
Wholesale Electric Supply	5063	(214) 794-3404
Wholesale Paneling Inc.	5031	(501) 772-8301

Colleges and Universities

East Texas State University at Texarkana, Texarkana, TX
Texarkana College, Texarkana, TX

TYLER, TX (MSA)

Geographic Profile

Land Area
928.5 square miles

Counties and Parishes
Smith

Ranking Highlights

214 *out of 319 in total* land area
 67 *out of 319 in* population growth, *1970–1990*
184 *out of 310 in having the lowest* unemployment *rate*
218 *out of 310 in size of* labor force
141 *out of 318 in the percentage of* college graduates
105 *out of 292 in per capita personal* income
232 *out of 319 in number of* manufacturing establishments
 91 *out of 318 in* physicians *per 1000 people*
 64 *out of 318 in* hospital beds *per 1000 people*
218 *out of 267 in fewest* crimes *per 1000 people*
132 *out of 266 in fewest* violent crimes *per 1000 people*
278 *out of 319 in per capita* federal funds and grants

Quality of Life Indexes (Rate per 1000 population)

Crime rate in 1991:	75.8
Violent crime rate in 1991:	6.3
Physicians rate in 1992:	2.27
Hospital bed rate in 1991:	5.25

ACCRA Cost of Living Indexes
(First quarter 1993, average = 100)
Composite index: 95.9
Utilities index: 112.7
Housing index: 95.3

Population (1990)

Total Population and Growth Rate
1990: 151,309
1980: 128,366
1970: 97,096
Growth rate 1970–1990: 56%

Race and Hispanic Origin
White: 75.1%
Black: 20.9%
Asian/Pacific Islander: 0.4%
Native American: 0.3%
Hispanic origin: 5.9%
White not Hispanic: 72.6%

Age
Ages 18 to 20: 4.9%
Ages 21 to 24: 5.3%
Ages 25 to 44: 30.4%
Ages 45 to 54: 10%
Ages 55 to 59: 4.4%

Ages 60 to 64: 4.5%
Ages 65 plus: 13.8%

Educational Attainment (1990)
Percent having completed high school: 75.7%
Percent having completed college: 19.8%
Elementary and high school enrollment: 28,005

Federal Funds and Grants Received
Total received in 1989: $344,900,000
Funds received per capita: $2,260

Civilian Labor Force
1993 (April):   76,017
1992 average: 76,579
1991 average: 75,119
1990 average: 74,102

Unemployment
1993 (April):   6.7%
1992 average: 7.3%
1991 average: 6.6%
1990 average: 6.2%

Average Annual Pay
1988: $19,733
1987: $19,416
1985: $18,494

Per Capita Personal Income
1991: $18,159
1990: $17,291
1989: $16,411

Business Climate (1987)
Manufacturing
Number of establishments in 1987: 172
Shipments in 1987 ($1,000): $1,521,000
Employees in 1987: 11,500
Change in employment, 1982 to 1987: -6.5%
Average annual pay for manufacturing work in 1989: $27,066
Average annual pay for production work in 1987: $23,333

Wholesale Trade
Number of establishments in 1987: 372
Total sales in 1987 ($1,000): $953,500
Change in sales, 1982 to 1987: -9.3%

Retail Trade
Number of establishments in 1987: 1,012
Total sales in 1987 ($1,000): $953,500
Retail sales per household in 1987: $17,379
Average annual pay in 1989: $13,006

Service Industry
Selected receipts in 1987 ($1,000): $414,900
Average annual pay in 1989: $18,857

Housing
Total number of units in 1990: 64,369

Occupied units in 1990: 56,800
Owner-occupied units in 1990: 66.5%
1993 ACCRA average cost: $110,050
1993 ACCRA average rent for an apartment: $455

Chamber of Commerce
Tyler Area Chamber of Commerce, James S. Hardy, Exec. Vice President, 407 N. Broadway, PO Box 390, Tyler, TX 75710. 214-592-1661

Major Businesses

Company	SIC	Telephone
Allied Transport Co.	5172	(214) 595-1095
Baker-Lucas Real Estate	6531	(214) 581-4200
Beard, Percy Inc.	5411	(214) 581-7902
Best Equipment Service & Sales	5084	(214) 595-6511
Brookshire Grocery Co.	5411	(214) 534-3000
C. Construction Co. Inc.	1542	(214) 597-1500
Combined Underwriters	6311	(214) 597-3761
East Texas Dodge Inc.	5511	(214) 561-2404
East Texas Hospital Foundation	8062	(214) 597-0351
East Texas Savings and Loan	6035	(214) 534-6400
First City, Texas-Tyler	6021	(214) 595-1941
Hill, Don Construction Co.	1542	(214) 597-8343
Howe-Baker Engineers Inc.	1629	(214) 597-0311
King Chevrolet Co.	5511	(214) 595-4531
Kirby & Kirby Oil Co	5541	(214) 592-3841
Loggins Meat Co. Inc.	5147	(214) 595-1011
Medical Center Hospital	8062	(214) 597-0351
Mediterranean Homes Inc.	6514	(214) 561-6000
Mother Frances Hospital	8062	(214) 531-5000
OGE Oldsmobile Inc.	5511	(214) 581-0600
Petrofac Inc.	1629	(214) 595-5050
Pizza Systems Inc.	5812	(214) 561-8261
Process Systems International	1629	(214) 597-0311
Promoters Supply Inc.	5122	(214) 561-1900
S-3 Inc.	5411	(214) 595-0706
Shtofman Co. Inc.	5139	(214) 592-0861
Sobank Inc.	6021	(214) 531-7111
Southside State Bank	6022	(214) 531-7111
TCA Cable TV Inc.	4841	(214) 595-3701
Teleservice Corp. of America	4841	(214) 595-3701
Tyler Ford Inc.	5511	(214) 597-9331
Tyler Packing Co. Inc.	2011	(214) 593-9592
Tyler Pipe Industries	3321	(214) 882-5511
Wagner Cadillac Co.	5511	(214) 561-1212

Colleges and Universities
Texas College, Tyler
Tyler Junior College, Tyler
University of Texas at Tyler, Tyler

VICTORIA, TX (MSA)

Geographic Profile
Land Area
882.6 square miles

Counties and Parishes
Victoria

Ranking Highlights
224 *out of 319 in total* **land area**
103 *out of 319 in* **population growth,** *1970–1990*
117 *out of 310 in having the lowest* **unemployment** *rate*
305 *out of 310 in size of* **labor force**
253 *out of 318 in the percentage of* **college graduates**
135 *out of 292 in per capita personal* **income**
313 *out of 319 in number of* **manufacturing establishments**
120 *out of 318 in* **physicians** *per 1000 people*
 12 *out of 318 in* **hospital beds** *per 1000 people*
231 *out of 267 in fewest* **crimes** *per 1000 people*
225 *out of 266 in fewest* **violent crimes** *per 1000 people*
307 *out of 319 in per capita* **federal funds and grants**

Quality of Life Indexes (Rate per 1000 population)
Crime rate in 1991:	81.8
Violent crime rate in 1991:	9.9
Physicians rate in 1992:	2.02
Hospital bed rate in 1991:	7.18

ACCRA Cost of Living Indexes
(First quarter 1993, average = 100)
Composite index: N/A
Utilities index: N/A
Housing index: N/A

Population (1990)
Total Population and Growth Rate
1990: 74,361
1980: 68,807
1970: 53,766
Growth rate 1970–1990: 38%

Race and Hispanic Origin
White: 79.7%
Black: 6.6%
Asian/Pacific Islander: 0.3%
Native American: 0.3%
Hispanic origin: 34.1%
White not Hispanic: 58.9%

Age
Ages 18 to 20: 4.3%
Ages 21 to 24: 4.9%
Ages 25 to 44: 31.4%
Ages 45 to 54: 9.8%
Ages 55 to 59: 4.2%
Ages 60 to 64: 4.1%
Ages 65 plus: 10.9%

Educational Attainment (1990)
Percent having completed high school: 70.2%
Percent having completed college: 14.1%
Elementary and high school enrollment: 16,050

Federal Funds and Grants Received
Total received in 1989: $141,600,000
Funds received per capita: $1,907

Civilian Labor Force
1993 (April):   40,125
1992 average: 39,629
1991 average: 37,648
1990 average: 36,055

Unemployment
1993 (April):   5.0%
1992 average: 6.3%
1991 average: 4.9%
1990 average: 5.0%

Average Annual Pay
1988: $18,398
1987: $17,846
1985: $17,804

Per Capita Personal Income
1991: $17,625
1990: $16,677
1989: $15,557

Business Climate (1987)
Manufacturing
Number of establishments in 1987: 58
Shipments in 1987 ($1,000): N/A
Employees in 1987: N/A
Change in employment, 1982 to 1987: N/A
Average annual pay for manufacturing work in 1989: $32,612
Average annual pay for production work in 1987: N/A

Wholesale Trade
Number of establishments in 1987: 186
Total sales in 1987 ($1,000): $594,300
Change in sales, 1982 to 1987: -39.3%

Retail Trade
Number of establishments in 1987: 576
Total sales in 1987 ($1,000): $594,300
Retail sales per household in 1987: $18,315
Average annual pay in 1989: $10,824

Service Industry
Selected receipts in 1987 ($1,000): $209,100
Average annual pay in 1989: $16,815

Housing
Total number of units in 1990: 29,162

Occupied units in 1990: 26,228
Owner-occupied units in 1990: 64.6%
1993 ACCRA average cost: N/A
1993 ACCRA average rent for an apartment: N/A

Chamber of Commerce

Victoria Chamber of Commerce, Robert C. Martin, President, 700 Main Center #101, PO Box 2465, Victoria, TX 77902. 512-573-5277

Major Businesses

Company	SIC	Telephone
Atzenhoffer Chevrolet Inc.	5511	(512) 578-0181
Boyd, Durst & Kuenstler	1381	(512) 573-9121
Brannan Paving Co., Inc.	1611	(512) 573-3130
Central Computers, Inc.	7374	(512) 575-6496
Citizens Medical Center	8062	(512) 573-9181
Detar Hospital, Inc.	8062	(512) 575-7441
Dick's Food Stores	5411	(512) 573-7429
Falstaff Sales Co. of Victoria	5182	(512) 573-5248
First Victoria Corp.	6021	(512) 573-6321
Groce-Wearden Co.	5141	(512) 573-5201
Hogan, Al Builder Inc.	1531	(512) 578-2925
Killibrew Inc.	5511	(512) 575-0483
Kovar, Leonard Ford Co.	5511	(512) 576-1221
New Distributing, Inc.	5171	(512) 575-1981
P W Food Stores, Inc.	5411	(512) 572-8207
South Texas Electric Co-Op	4911	(512) 575-6491
South Texas Savings Bank	6036	(512) 573-5241
Thomas, C. L. Petroleum Inc.	5171	(512) 573-7443
Victoria Advocate Plumbing Co.	2711	(512) 575-1451
Victoria Air Conditioning	1711	(512) 578-5241
Victoria Bank & Trust Co.	6411	(512) 573-5151
Victoria Bankshares Inc.	6022	(512) 573-9432
Victoria County Electric	4911	(512) 573-2428
Zarsky Lumber Co. Inc.	5211	(512) 573-2479

Colleges and Universities

University of Houston-Victoria, Victoria
Victoria College, Victoria

WACO, TX (MSA)

Geographic Profile

Land Area
1041.9 square miles

Counties and Parishes
McLennan

Ranking Highlights

194 *out of 319 in total* land area
141 *out of 319 in* population growth, *1970–1990*
157 *out of 310 in having the lowest* unemployment *rate*
194 *out of 310 in size of* labor force
206 *out of 318 in the percentage of* college graduates
232 *out of 292 in per capita personal* income
189 *out of 319 in number of* manufacturing establishments
226 *out of 318 in* physicians *per 1000 people*
246 *out of 318 in* hospital beds *per 1000 people*
242 *out of 267 in fewest* crimes *per 1000 people*
198 *out of 266 in fewest* violent crimes *per 1000 people*
170 *out of 319 in per capita* federal funds and grants

Quality of Life Indexes (Rate per 1000 population)

Crime rate in 1991: 85.4
Violent crime rate in 1991: 8.8
Physicians rate in 1992: 1.5
Hospital bed rate in 1991: 2.96

ACCRA Cost of Living Indexes

(First quarter 1993, average = 100)
Composite index: 94.3
Utilities index: 111.4
Housing index: 82.7

Population (1990)

Total Population and Growth Rate
1990: 189,123
1980: 170,755
1970: 147,553
Growth rate 1970–1990: 28%

Race and Hispanic Origin
White: 77.3%
Black: 15.6%
Asian/Pacific Islander: 0.7%
Native American: 0.3%
Hispanic origin: 12.5%
White not Hispanic: 71.1%

Age
Ages 18 to 20: 7.2%
Ages 21 to 24: 7.5%
Ages 25 to 44: 28.3%
Ages 45 to 54: 9.1%
Ages 55 to 59: 4.1%

Ages 60 to 64: 4.2%
Ages 65 plus: 13.5%

Educational Attainment (1990)
Percent having completed high school: 71.6%
Percent having completed college: 16.6%
Elementary and high school enrollment: 33,351

Federal Funds and Grants Received
Total received in 1989: $568,300,000
Funds received per capita: $3,022

Civilian Labor Force
1993 (April): 93,217
1992 average: 94,204
1991 average: 92,749
1990 average: 92,091

Unemployment
1993 (April): 5.7%
1992 average: 6.9%
1991 average: 6.4%
1990 average: 5.8%

Average Annual Pay
1988: $17,486
1987: $17,109
1985: $16,371

Per Capita Personal Income
1991: $15,623
1990: $14,771
1989: $14,048

Business Climate (1987)
Manufacturing
Number of establishments in 1987: 249
Shipments in 1987 ($1,000): $1,635,100
Employees in 1987: 13,800
Change in employment, 1982 to 1987: -7.4%
Average annual pay for manufacturing work in 1989: $20,890
Average annual pay for production work in 1987: $16,520

Wholesale Trade
Number of establishments in 1987: 398
Total sales in 1987 ($1,000): $1,061,800
Change in sales, 1982 to 1987: -10.6%

Retail Trade
Number of establishments in 1987: 1,236
Total sales in 1987 ($1,000): $1,061,800
Retail sales per household in 1987: $15,782
Average annual pay in 1989: $10,526

Service Industry
Selected receipts in 1987 ($1,000): $395,200
Average annual pay in 1989: $16,016

Housing
Total number of units in 1990: 78,857

Occupied units in 1990: 70,208
Owner-occupied units in 1990: 58.9%
1993 ACCRA average cost: $89,480
1993 ACCRA average rent for an apartment: $474

Chamber of Commerce
Waco Chamber of Commerce, Curtis Cleveland, President, Civic Center Plaza, PO Box 1220, Waco, TX 76703-1220. 817-752-6551

Major Businesses

Company	SIC	Telephone
Away Marketing Inc.	5171	(817) 772-0590
Beasley-Wilson Inc.	5511	(817) 662-3610
Behrens Inc.	5122	(817) 776-7583
Brazos Electric Power Co.	4911	(817) 750-6500
Brazos Higher Education Authority	6141	(817) 753-0915
Central Freight Lines Inc.	4213	(817) 772-2120
Central Transportation System	4214	(817) 662-2884
Command-Aire Corp.	3585	(817) 840-3244
First Republicbank Waco	6021	(817) 753-6461
First Savings & Loan Association	6035	(817) 753-2411
Hillcrest Baptist Medical Center	8062	(817) 756-8011
K-D Manitou Inc.	3537	(817) 799-0232
Lipsitz, M. & Co., Inc.	5093	(817) 756-6661
Lux Packaging Ltd.	2653	(817) 776-8890
National Group Corp.	6411	(817) 756-5531
PMS Inc.	7389	(817) 776-3260
Phillips, Maynard Toyota	5511	(817) 772-5430
Providence Health Center	8062	(817) 751-4000
Purvis Bearing Service Inc.	5085	(817) 753-6477
Rountree, Gordon Motors	5511	(817) 756-4461
SMI International Inc.	3999	(817) 776-1230
Spenco Medical Corp.	5047	(817) 772-6000
Steakley Brothers Chevrolet	5511	(817) 772-8850
Texas Agriculture Service Co.	5014	(817) 772-3030
Texas Life Insurance Co.	6311	(817) 752-6521
Texas Plantation Foods Co.	0253	(817) 799-6211
Waco Meat Service Inc.	5147	(817) 772-5644
Westpac Industries Inc.	2431	(817) 757-2622
Wolf Manufacturing Co.	2329	(817) 753-7301
Young Brothers Contractor	1611	(817) 754-2324

Colleges and Universities
Baylor University, Waco
Mclennan Community College, Waco
Paul Quinn College, Waco
Texas State Technical Institute-Waco Campus, Waco

WICHITA FALLS, TX (MSA)

Geographic Profile

Land Area

627.7 square miles

Counties and Parishes

Wichita

Ranking Highlights

266 *out of 319 in total* **land area**

265 *out of 319 in* **population growth,** *1970–1990*

184 *out of 310 in having the lowest* **unemployment** *rate*

279 *out of 310 in size of* **labor force**

209 *out of 318 in the percentage of* **college graduates**

146 *out of 292 in per capita personal* **income**

242 *out of 319 in number of* **manufacturing establishments**

113 *out of 318 in* **physicians** *per 1000 people*

169 *out of 318 in* **hospital beds** *per 1000 people*

245 *out of 267 in fewest* **crimes** *per 1000 people*

187 *out of 266 in fewest* **violent crimes** *per 1000 people*

 69 *out of 319 in per capita* **federal funds and grants**

Quality of Life Indexes (Rate per 1000 population)

Crime rate in 1991:	85.8
Violent crime rate in 1991:	8.2
Physicians rate in 1992:	2.06
Hospital bed rate in 1991:	3.73

ACCRA Cost of Living Indexes

(First quarter 1993, average = 100)

Composite index:	89.9
Utilities index:	102.6
Housing index:	78.5

Population (1990)

Total Population and Growth Rate

1990: 122,378

1980: 121,082

1970: 120,563

Growth rate 1970–1990: 2%

Race and Hispanic Origin

White: 83.7%

Black: 9.2%

Asian/Pacific Islander: 1.5%

Native American: 0.7%

Hispanic origin: 8.6%

White not Hispanic: 80.2%

Age

Ages 18 to 20: 6.1%

Ages 21 to 24: 6.1%

Ages 25 to 44: 30.6%

Ages 45 to 54: 9.3%

Ages 55 to 59: 4.6%

Ages 60 to 64: 4.3%

Ages 65 plus: 12.7%

Educational Attainment (1990)

Percent having completed high school: 75.1%

Percent having completed college: 16.5%

Elementary and high school enrollment: 21,081

Federal Funds and Grants Received

Total received in 1989: $507,100,000

Funds received per capita: $4,069

Civilian Labor Force

1993 (April):	50,920
1992 average:	54,544
1991 average:	54,569
1990 average:	54,453

Unemployment

1993 (April): 6.2%

1992 average: 7.3%

1991 average: 6.8%

1990 average: 6.1%

Average Annual Pay

1988: $17,602

1987: $17,261

1985: $16,974

Per Capita Personal Income

1991: $17,363

1990: $16,781

1989: $16,039

Business Climate (1987)

Manufacturing

Number of establishments in 1987: 155

Shipments in 1987 ($1,000): $949,000

Employees in 1987: 7,900

Change in employment, 1982 to 1987: 0%

Average annual pay for manufacturing work in 1989: $25,479

Average annual pay for production work in 1987: $21,121

Wholesale Trade

Number of establishments in 1987: 265

Total sales in 1987 ($1,000): $478,100

Change in sales, 1982 to 1987: -17.1%

Retail Trade

Number of establishments in 1987: 928

Total sales in 1987 ($1,000): $478,100

Retail sales per household in 1987: $17,109

Average annual pay in 1989: $10,440

Service Industry

Selected receipts in 1987 ($1,000): $279,600

Average annual pay in 1989: $15,255

Housing

Total number of units in 1990: 51,413

Occupied units in 1990: 45,271
Owner-occupied units in 1990: 63.4%
1993 ACCRA average cost: $91,075
1993 ACCRA average rent for an apartment: $383

Chamber of Commerce

Wichita Falls Board of Commerce & Industry, Ronald J. Mertens, President, 218 Hamilton Bldg., 8th & Lamar, PO Box 1860, Wichita Falls, TX 76307. 817-723-2741

Economic Development Office

Wichita Falls Board of Commerce & Industry, Ronald Mertens, President, 218 Hamilton Bldg., 900 8th St., PO Box 1860, Wichita Falls, TX 76307. 817-723-2741, FAX 817-723-8773

Major Businesses

Company	SIC	Telephone
Beacon National Insurance Co.	6331	(817) 322-4884
Berend Bros Inc.	5999	(817) 723-2735
Bethania Regional Health Center	8062	(817) 723-4111
Bridwell Oil Co.	1311	(817) 723-4351
Brodie Buick Co.	5511	(817) 766-4191
Burk Royalty Co.	1311	(817) 322-5421
Cantu Services, Inc.	5812	(817) 569-1860
Cavalier Homes Inc.	2451	(817) 485-6073
Davis, George Chevrolet Inc.	5511	(817) 723-6631
Estes Inc.	5191	(817) 766-0163
Eureka Life Insurance Co. of America	6311	(817) 692-5600
First Wichita Bancshares	6021	(817) 322-7861
Grozier & Mann Co.	5172	(817) 767-9415
Herb Easley Motors, Inc.	5511	(817) 767-1445
Mansion Homes Inc.	2451	(817) 723-5523
Mc Alster A. Lander Trucking Co.	4213	(817) 767-9246
Parker Square National Bank	6022	(817) 767-8321
Patterson Oldsmbile-GMC	5511	(817) 766-0293
Pistocco, Joe Pontiac-Cadillac	5511	(817) 322-5451
Preston Dairy, Inc.	2026	(817) 569-1421
Roberts, Ron Ford Inc.	5511	(817) 767-7711
Southwest Buyers Inc.	5722	(817) 691-1112
Star Industries Inc.	2451	(817) 723-5523
Union Square Credit Union	6111	(817) 322-1120
United Texas Financial Corp.	6022	(817) 767-8321
White Fuel Corp.	6512	(817) 322-4884
Wichita General Services	8062	(817) 723-1461

Colleges and Universities

Midwestern State University, Wichita Falls

UTAH

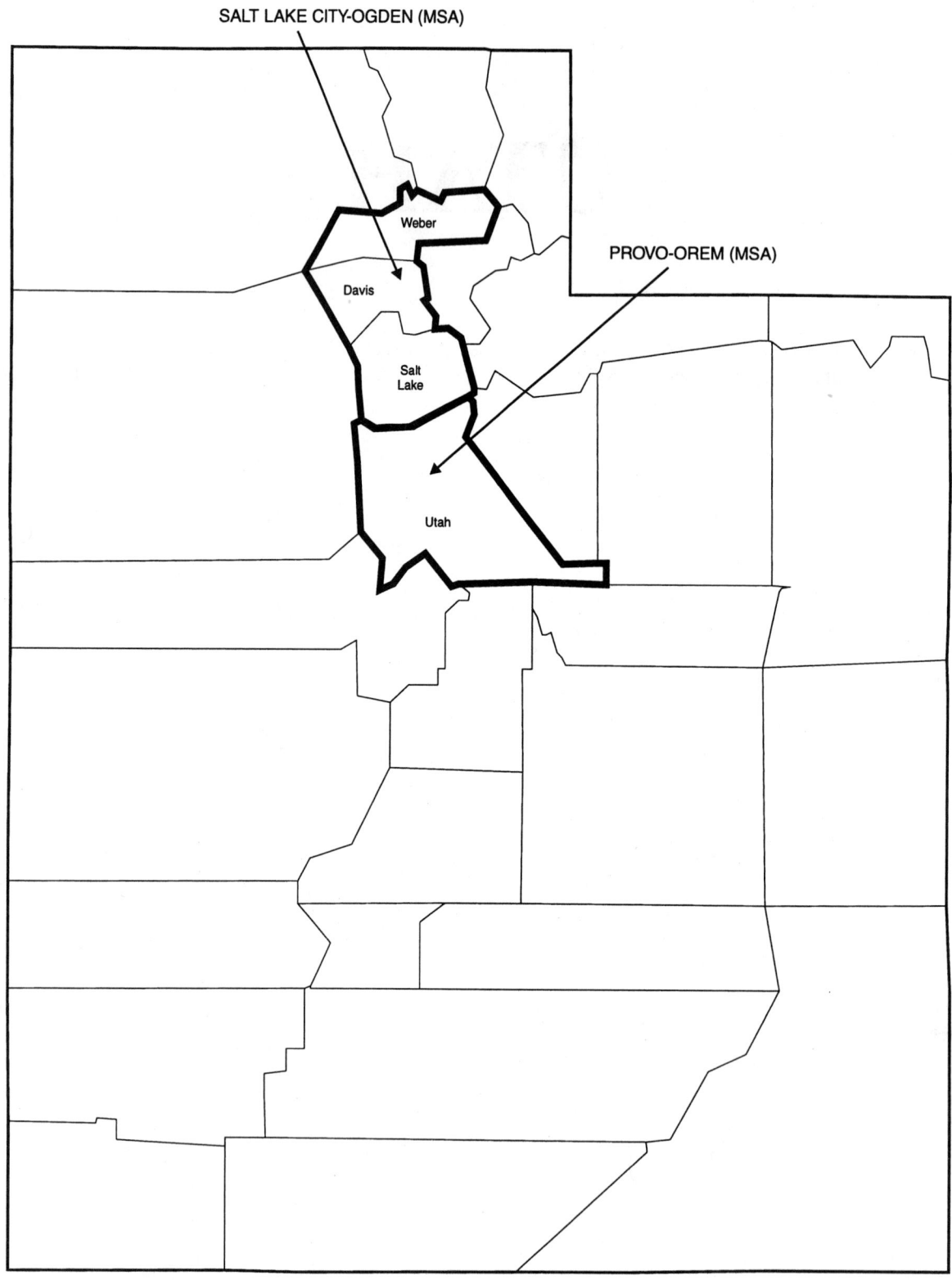

SALT LAKE CITY-OGDEN (MSA)

PROVO-OREM (MSA)

Weber

Davis

Salt
Lake

Utah

UTAH

Population

1990: 1,722,850
1980: 1,461,037

Age

Ages 18 to 20: 90,245
Ages 21 to 24: 109,741
Ages 25 to 44: 499,570
Ages 45 to 54: 138,481
Ages 55 to 59: 54,930
Ages 60 to 64: 52,481
Median age: 26.2

Race and Hispanic Origin

White: 1,615,845
Black: 11,576
Asian/Pacific Islander: 33,371
Native American: 24,283
Hispanic origin: 84,597

Households

Total: 537,273
Persons per household: 3.15

Sex

Male: 855,759
Female: 867,091

Population Migration

Domestic migration: -166,000
International migration: 23,000

Projection of the Population in 1995

Total: 1,841,000
18 to 64: 1,007,000

Civilian Labor Force

1993: 808,900
1992: 812,300
1991: 797,600
1990: 777,000

Manufacturing

1995 Projection: 114,300
1992: 105,800
1991: 106,600
1990: 109,200
1989: 104,000

Services

1995 Projection: 262,700
1992: 196,900
1991: 195,900
1990: 187,600
1989: 172,800

Wholesale and Retail Trade

1995 Projection: 197,700
1992: 184,300
1991: 185,600
1990: 183,700
1989: 176,600

Unemployment Rate

1993: 5.0%
1992: 4.8%
1991: 4.6%
1990: 4.4%

Employer Unemployment Contributions

Contribution Rate

1992: 1.01%
1991: 1.24%
1990: 1.49%

Average Weekly Benefit

1992: $181.91
1991: $177.70
1990: $163.33

Gross State Product (Million $)

1989: $28,135
1988: $26,450
1987: $24,622
1979: $13,493
Growth rate, 1979 to 1989: 108.5%

Capital Expenditures of Manufacturing Industries

1990: $484,600,000
1989: $441,300,000
1988: $428,400,000
1987: $403,500,000

State Tax Rates

Individual income: Range from 2.55% ($1,500 or less) to 7.2% (above $7,500).
Corporate income: 5% of total taxable income.
General property: Sum of state and local rates. Real and tan-

gible personal property based on 100% of reasonable fair cash value.

General sales: 5%

Gasoline: 19¢ per gallon

Income

Median income for a 4 person family: $36,562

Personal per Capita Income

1992: $15,325

1991: $14,628

1990: $14,036

Disposable per Capita Income

1992: $13,355

1991: $12,713

1990: $12,156

Private Employment Weekly Wages

Average

1989: $364

1988: $356

1987: $356

Manufacturing

1989: $343

1988: $454

1987: $438

Services

1989: $334

1988: $325

1987: $316

Wholesale

1989: $465

1988: $451

1987: $425

Retail

1989: $201

1988: $197

1987: $193

Highway Statistics

Total Highway Miles

1990: 43,244

1989: 42,971

1988: 42,935

Federal Highway Aid

1991: $92,541,000

1990: $91,407,000

1989: $95,130,000

Electricity

Average Cost per Kilowatt Hour

1990: 5.49¢

1989: 5.79¢

1988: 6.09¢

Housing (1990)

Owner occupied units: 365,979

Median house value: $68,900

Renter occupied units: 171,294

Median rent: $300

Total vacant units: 61,115

Homeowner vacancy rate: 2.4%

Rental vacancy rate: 8.6%

State Business Incentives and Assistance

Enterprise Zone Incentives

Incentives are available to manufacturing companies which move into, start up or expand within an enterprise zone. However, benefits are not awarded for jobs which are moved into an enterprise zone from elsewhere in Utah. The state will allow credits, to be claimed within five years, against income tax or corporate franchise tax as follows:

1) A tax credit of either $750 or $1,250 for each new full-time position that has been filled for not less than six months during a given tax year.

2) An investment tax credit of 10% of the first $10,000 in investment, 5% of the next $90,000, and 2% of the remaining qualifying investment in plant, equipment or other depreciable property.

Financial and Business Assistance

Industrial Development Bonds. Administered by the Community Development Division of the Community and Economic Development Department, this program authorizes cities, towns, and counties to issue IDBs for private companies. The goal of the program is to stimulate economic growth within the state.

International Business. Administered by the Business and Economic Development Division of the Community & Economic Development Department, this program promotes and stimulates businesses in selling their products and services abroad and helps recruit foreign investment to Utah.

Utah Technology Finance Corporation. Established by the state legislature, the Corporation provides grants and loans for initial stage development for small technology intensive businesses. The Corporation operates four major programs: the Innovation Finance Program, the Venture Capital Program, the Cities & Counties Program, and the Technology Based Business Development Program.

Education and Training

High Technology Training. Administered by the Job Training for Economic Development Office of the Department of Community and Economic Development, this program provides high technology training for any new and existing Utah technology company workers.

Custom Fit Program. Administered by the State Office of Education, this program provides customized training for new or expanding manufacturing, production, assembly, and some service companies.

Major Companies in the State

Company name	Fortune 500 rank	City	Telephone	SIC number
Fortune 500 Companies				
Thiokol Corp.	288	Ogden	801-629-2000	3764
Other Major Companies in the State				
Alta Health Strategies Inc.		Salt Lake City	801-568-5500	6411
American Stores Co.		Salt Lake City	801-539-0112	5411
Bonneville Pacific Corp.		Salt Lake City	801-363-2520	4911
Compania Boliviana De Energia Elect		Salt Lake City	801-521-1024	4911
Evans & Sutherland Computer Corp.		Salt Lake City	801-582-5847	3577
First Security Corp.		Salt Lake City	801-350-5706	6712
Geneva Steel		Vineyard	801-227-9000	3312
Grand Valley Gas Co.		Salt Lake City	801-532-7526	4924
Iomega Corp.		Roy	801-778-1000	3577
JBS Restaurants Inc.		Salt Lake City	801-974-4300	5812
Mountain Fuel Supply Co.		Salt Lake City	801-534-5555	4923
Nature's Sunshine Products Inc.		Spanish Fork	801-798-9861	2833
Northwest Pipeline Corp.		Salt Lake City	801-583-8800	4922
Questar Corp.		Salt Lake City	801-534-5000	4923
Questar Pipeline Co.		Salt Lake City	801-530-2400	4922
Rocky Mountain Helicopters Inc.		Provo	801-375-1124	4522
Skywest Inc.		St George	801-628-2655	4512
Smith's Food & Drug Centers Inc.		Salt Lake City	801-974-1400	5411
Zion's Co. Operative Mercantile Inst		Salt Lake City	801-321-6404	5311
Zions Bancorporation		Salt Lake City	801-524-4787	6712

Job Training Partnership Act. This program operates with funding from the U.S. Department of Labor. It provides job training and other employment related services.

State Offices

Real estate: Commerce Department, Real Estate Division, Elaine E. Twitchell, Director, PO Box 45802, 160 East 300 South, Salt Lake City, UT 84111. 801-530-6762

Chamber of commerce: Utah State Chamber of Commerce Association, Wes Boman, President, 6 N. Main St., PO Box 458, Brigham City, UT 84302. 801-723-3931

Economic development: Community and Economic Development Department, Lynn Blake, Director, 324 South State Street, Suite 200, Salt Lake City, UT 84111. 801-538-UTAH

Community & Economic Development Department, Community Development Division, Director, 324 South State Street, Suite 200, Salt Lake City, UT 84111. 801-538-8700

Community & Economic Development Department, Business & Economic Development Division, Marian Hein, National Business Development Director, 324 South State Street, Suite 200, Salt Lake City, UT 84111. 801-538-8800

Community & Economic Development Department, Business & Economic Development Division, Johnnie Wilkinson, Enterprise Zone Coordinator, 324 South State Street, Suite 230, Salt Lake City, UT 84111. 801-538-8782

Utah Technology Finance Corporation, President, 185 South State Street, Suite 208, Salt Lake City, UT 84111. 801-364-4346

Small Business Development Center, David Nimkin, State Director, University of Utah, 102 West 500 South, Suite 315, Salt Lake City, UT 84102. 801-581-7905

Environmental affairs: Environmental Health Division, Kenneth Alkema, Director, PO Box 16700, Salt Lake City, UT 84116-0700. 801-538-6121

Labor: Industrial Commission, Stephen M. Hadley, Chairman, PO Box 510910, Salt Lake City, UT 84151-0910. 801-530-6880

Unemployment: Employment Security Division, Floyd Astin, Administrator, PO Box 11249, Salt Lake City, UT 84147. 801-533-2400

Worker's compensation: Industrial Commission, Stephen M. Hadley, Chairman, PO Box 510910, Salt Lake City, UT 84151-0910. 801-530-6880

Occupational safety and health: Industrial Commission, Industrial Accidents Division, Joyce Sewell, Director, PO Box 510910, Salt Lake City, UT 84151-0910. 801-530-6817

Secretary of state: Lieutenant Governor Office, W. Val Oveson, Lieutenant Governor, 203 State Capitol, Salt Lake City, UT 84114. 801-538-1040

Taxation and revenue: Tax Commission, R.H. Hansen, Chairman, 160 East 300 South, Salt Lake City, UT 84134. 801-530-6077

Designated Zones for Economic Development
Enterprise Zones
Enacted in: 1988

No. of established zones: 13

Beaver County
Carbon County
Duchesne County
Emery County
Garfield County
Grand County
Iron County
Juab County
Millard County
San Juan County
Sanpete County
Unitah County
Wasatch County
Wayne County

Foreign Trade Zones
Foreign Trade Zone No. 30, Salt Lake City, Utah, Grantee: Redevelopment Agency of Salt Lake City, Richard Turpin, 285 West North Temple, Suite 200, Salt Lake City, UT 84103, 801-328-3211

Labor Unions
Electrical Workers, International Brotherhood of (AFL-CIO)
Jordan Classified Employees Association
National Education Association
Utah Teachers Association
Utah School Employees Association

Universities with Ph.D. Programs
Brigham Young University, Provo
University of Utah, Salt Lake City
Utah State University, Logan

Sources of Additional Information
Utah Facts, 1990-1991. Utah Dept. of Community and Economic Development, n.d. 39p.

Utah, America's Choice: A Business Profile. Utah Dept. of Community and Economic Development, n.d. np.

Utah, America's Choice: Life in the Valley. Utah Dept. of Community and Economic Development, n.d. np.

PROVO–OREM, UT (MSA)

Geographic Profile
Land Area
1998.4 square miles
Counties and Parishes
Utah

Ranking Highlights
93 *out of 319 in total* land area
21 *out of 319 in* population growth, *1970–1990*
24 *out of 310 in having the lowest* unemployment *rate*
167 *out of 310 in size of* labor force
48 *out of 318 in the percentage of* college graduates
286 *out of 292 in per capita personal* income
175 *out of 319 in number of* manufacturing establishments
290 *out of 318 in* physicians *per 1000 people*
303 *out of 318 in* hospital beds *per 1000 people*
34 *out of 267 in fewest* crimes *per 1000 people*
12 *out of 266 in fewest* violent crimes *per 1000 people*
316 *out of 319 in per capita* federal funds and grants

Quality of Life Indexes (Rate per 1000 population)
Crime rate in 1991:	39.5
Violent crime rate in 1991:	1.4
Physicians rate in 1992:	1.13
Hospital bed rate in 1991:	2.06

ACCRA Cost of Living Indexes
(First quarter 1993, average = 100)
Composite index:	95.7
Utilities index:	85.8
Housing index:	97.2

Overview
Provo is the commercial center and county seat of Utah County, and one of the fastest growing areas in the nation. The Provo-Orem area has a diverse economy based on high-technology; electronics; manufacturing; construction; transportation; utilities; finance, insurance, and real estate; government employment; tourism; and the wholesale, retail, and service industries. The area is home to the second largest concentration of software technologies companies in the United States and has the third largest concentration of high-technology companies.

Two of the world's major software companies are located in the area, creating opportunities for more than one hundred fifty small to mid-range high-technology companies. Located in Utah Valley is the WordPerfect Corporation, developer of the country's most popular software programs. Provo is international headquarters to such businesses giants as Novell, Inc., Nu Skin, and Dynix. Other companies with their headquarters in the city are Gazelle Systems, Erying Research, 386 Systems, Folio Corporation, Systems Connection, DHI Commuting Systems, and Jostens/Wicat.

Provo's Aerospace Park is home to Rocky Mountain Helicopters and AVTECH. Only four of the top ten high-technology employers in Utah County have been in existence longer than fifteen years. High-technology companies with divisions in Provo include IBM, Sanyo, R. R. Donnelly, Intel, Smith's Megadiamond, and Ameritech.

Provo is served by the Denver & Rio Grand Western and the Union Pacific railroads, which offer second-morning service to ninety percent of the western markets. The Provo area is served by thirty-two trucking lines, fifteen of which are located in Provo. The local airport can serve and handle most aircraft and is equipped with an instrument-landing system and a weather-reporting capability. The airport is serviced by eight major airlines and three commuter operators. Provo/Orem is intersected by U.S. Highways 50, 89, 91, and 189, as well as by Interstate 15. Provo is located within an hour's drive of Salt Lake City International Airport, which is ranked among the world's busiest.

Population (1990)

Total Population and Growth Rate
1990: 263,590
1980: 218,106
1970: 137,776
Growth rate 1970–1990: 91%

Race and Hispanic Origin
White: 96.2%
Black: .1%
Asian/Pacific Islander: 1.5%
Native American: 0.7%
Hispanic origin: 3.2%
White not Hispanic: 94.5%

Age
Ages 18 to 20: 8.3%
Ages 21 to 24: 10.5%
Ages 25 to 44: 25.2%
Ages 45 to 54: 6.3%
Ages 55 to 59: 2.5%
Ages 60 to 64: 2.4%
Ages 65 plus: 7%

Educational Attainment (1990)
Percent having completed high school: 87.9%
Percent having completed college: 26.2%
Elementary and high school enrollment: 65,181

Federal Funds and Grants Received
Total received in 1989: $398,200,000
Funds received per capita: $1,641

Civilian Labor Force
1993 (April): 122,030
1992 average: 120,199
1991 average: 120,204
1990 average: 115,570

Unemployment
1993 (April): 4.3%
1992 average: 4.3%
1991 average: 4.3%
1990 average: 3.7%

Average Annual Pay
1988: $17,123
1987: $16,260
1985: $15,881

Per Capita Personal Income
1991: $12,467
1990: $11,592
1989: $10,663

Business Climate (1987)

Manufacturing
Number of establishments in 1987: 276
Shipments in 1987 ($1,000): $629,400
Employees in 1987: 9,000
Change in employment, 1982 to 1987: -21.7%
Average annual pay for manufacturing work in 1989: $22,983
Average annual pay for production work in 1987: $16,313

Wholesale Trade
Number of establishments in 1987: 244
Total sales in 1987 ($1,000): $450,300
Change in sales, 1982 to 1987: 58.6%

Retail Trade
Number of establishments in 1987: 1,034
Total sales in 1987 ($1,000): $450,300
Retail sales per household in 1987: $13,971
Average annual pay in 1989: $8,627

Service Industry
Selected receipts in 1987 ($1,000): $510,900
Average annual pay in 1989: $20,347

Housing
Total number of units in 1990: 72,820
Occupied units in 1990: 70,168
Owner-occupied units in 1990: 62.7%
1993 ACCRA average cost: $111,667
1993 ACCRA average rent for an apartment: $480

Chamber of Commerce
Provo-Orem Chamber of Commerce, Steven T. Densley, President, 777 S. State, PO Box 738, Provo, UT 84603. 801-224-3636

Economic Development Office
Provo City Dept. of Economic Development, Gary D. Golightly, Director, 40 South 100 W. St. Suite 100, Provo, UT 84601. 801-379-6160, FAX 801-375-1469

Economic Development Organizations
Comm. for Econ. Dev. in Orem, DeLance W. Squire, Exec. Director, 777 S. State, Orem, UT 84058. 801-226-1521

Major Businesses

Company	SIC	Telephone
Broderick & Howell Construction	1542	(801) 225-9211
Central Bank & Trust	6022	(801) 375-1000
Central Distributing Co., Inc.	5172	(801) 798-9833
Clyde, W.W. & Co.	1611	(801) 489-5616
Crest Distributing Co., Inc.	5171	(801) 373-7970
D H I Computing Service	7374	(801) 373-8518
Dynix Inc.	7373	(801) 375-2770
Dynix Management, Inc.	7372	(801) 375-2770
Eyring, Inc.	7371	(801) 375-2434
Geneva Rock Products Inc.	5032	(801) 225-1012
Geneva Steel	3312	(801) 227-9000
Givan Ford Sales	5511	(801) 373-4060
Harvey, Gene Chevrolet Inc.	5511	(801) 756-3546
Morris Motors Inc.	5511	(801) 373-2114
Mountainland Supply Co.	5074	(801) 224-6050
Natures Sunshine Products	2833	(801) 798-9861
Novell Inc.	7373	(801) 379-5900
P S T Inc.	4213	(801) 785-7525
Professional Lithographer	2752	(801) 373-7335
Rocky Mountain Helicopter	4522	(801) 375-1124
SII Megadiamond	3545	(801) 377-3474
Softcopy Inc.	5045	(801) 224-4000
Valtek Inc.	3494	(801) 489-8611
Warner, Rick Chevrolet-Buick	5511	(801) 373-9500
Western Utility Contractor	1623	(801) 785-3401
Wicat Systems Inc.	7372	(801) 224-6400
Word-Perfect Corp.	7372	(801) 222-4000

Colleges and Universities

Brigham Young University, Provo, UT
Utah Valley Community College, Orem, UT

SALT LAKE CITY–OGDEN, UT (MSA)

Geographic Profile

Land Area

1617.5 square miles

Counties and Parishes

Davis

Salt Lake

Weber

Ranking Highlights

121 *out of 319 in total* land area

65 *out of 319 in* population growth, *1970–1990*

40 *out of 310 in having the lowest* unemployment *rate*

49 *out of 310 in size of* labor force

82 *out of 318 in the percentage of* college graduates

227 *out of 292 in per capita personal* income

49 *out of 319 in number of* manufacturing establishments

90 *out of 318 in* physicians *per 1000 people*

262 *out of 318 in* hospital beds *per 1000 people*

175 *out of 267 in fewest* crimes *per 1000 people*

65 *out of 266 in fewest* violent crimes *per 1000 people*

126 *out of 319 in per capita* federal funds and grants

Quality of Life Indexes (Rate per 1000 population)

Crime rate in 1991:	67.8
Violent crime rate in 1991:	3.7
Physicians rate in 1992:	2.28
Hospital bed rate in 1991:	2.7

ACCRA Cost of Living Indexes

(First quarter 1993, average = 100)

Composite index:	96.8
Utilities index:	89.4
Housing index:	86.0

Overview

Salt Lake City is the state capital and largest city in Utah. The city is the world headquarters of the Church of Jesus Christ of Latter-Day Saints (Mormons). Since its founding, Salt Lake City has been the destination of Mormon converts from all over the world, giving the city an international flavor; it is the commercial and cultural hub for a large area of the western mountain region. The nearby mountains, historical and religious landmarks, and the uniqueness of the Great Salt Lake make the city a prominent tourist attraction.

Salt Lake City was originally a farming community, but it has grown into a diverse economic region. A plentiful supply of ore from the nearby mountains is processed in a number of area plants and mines, including the Bingham Copper Mine, the world's largest open-pit copper mine. The steel industry is also a major contributor to the local economy. Many oil refineries process oil in the Salt Lake City area and ship it to neighboring states through elaborate networks of pipelines. Sugar is also a major industry in the city, with a number of plants refining sugar from locally grown beets.

Agriculture is still a large part of the Salt Lake City economy, with a wide variety of crops grown in the Salt Lake Valley, now a fertile region because of widespread irrigation. The surrounding desert area is deemed ideal for the production and testing of defense equipment such as missiles and rocket engines, and the military presence has attracted a number of high-technology electronics firms.

Salt Lake City is the commercial center for a large portion of the West and a transportation hub for the area between Denver, Colorado, and the West Coast. A number of national financial institutions have established branch offices in the city, making Salt Lake City the center of banking and finance for the region. Salt Lake City is also the largest retail and wholesale market in Utah; the city also supports a thriving tourist industry.

Salt Lake City's status as a Foreign Trade Zone makes it an ideal location for the import and export of goods. The Salt Lake International Airport handles more than one hundred forty million pounds of air cargo and express mail each year. It is the twenty-fifth busiest in the country, handling nearly twelve million passengers each year. Eight major airlines serve the airport, including Delta Airlines, which operates its western hub out of Salt Lake City. Four major railway companies provide convenient rail transportation to major markets in the West, and a number of trucking firms have extensive storage and shipping facilities in the Salt Lake City area. Salt Lake City is at the junction of two major interstate highways, Interstate 15, running north-south, and Interstate 80, running east-west. Interstate 215 forms a commuter loop and by-pass around the inner city.

Population (1990)

Total Population and Growth Rate
1990: 1,072,227
1980: 910,222
1970: 683,913
Growth rate 1970–1990: 57%

Race and Hispanic Origin
White: 93.3%
Black: 1.0%
Asian/Pacific Islander: 2.4%
Native American: 0.8%
Hispanic origin: 5.8%
White not Hispanic: 90.2%

Age
Ages 18 to 20: 4.6%
Ages 21 to 24: 5.8%
Ages 25 to 44: 30.9%
Ages 45 to 54: 8.4%
Ages 55 to 59: 3.3%
Ages 60 to 64: 3%
Ages 65 plus: 8.4%

Educational Attainment (1990)
Percent having completed high school: 85.6%
Percent having completed college: 22.9%
Elementary and high school enrollment: 254,580

Federal Funds and Grants Received
Total received in 1989: $3,545,600,000
Funds received per capita: $3,329

Civilian Labor Force
1993 (April): 541,571
1992 average: 523,317
1991 average: 519,305
1990 average: 513,237

Unemployment
1993 (April): 3.8%
1992 average: 4.7%
1991 average: 4.6%
1990 average: 4.1%

Average Annual Pay
1988: $19,498
1987: $18,856
1985: $17,999

Per Capita Personal Income
1991: $15,687
1990: $15,097
1989: $14,244

Business Climate (1987)

Manufacturing
Number of establishments in 1987: 1,463
Shipments in 1987 ($1,000): $6,985,100
Employees in 1987: 61,000
Change in employment, 1982 to 1987: 7.4%
Average annual pay for manufacturing work in 1989: $24,269
Average annual pay for production work in 1987: $18,019

Wholesale Trade
Number of establishments in 1987: 2,247
Total sales in 1987 ($1,000): $9,684,600
Change in sales, 1982 to 1987: 29.0%

Retail Trade
Number of establishments in 1987: 5,192
Total sales in 1987 ($1,000): $9,684,600
Retail sales per household in 1987: $17,486
Average annual pay in 1989: $11,263

Service Industry
Selected receipts in 1987 ($1,000): $2,861,500
Average annual pay in 1989: $17,695

Office Real Estate (1992)
Office space inventory: 11,029,379 square feet

Average class A Central Business District rental range per sq. ft: $15.81

Vacancy Rates

All areas: 18.0%

Vacancy Rates in Central Business District

Class A space: 19.9%

Class B space: 17.2%

Vacancy Rates Outside Central Business District

Class A space: 23.0%

Class B space: 13.3%

Housing

Total number of units in 1990: 370,967

Occupied units in 1990: 347,531

Owner-occupied units in 1990: 67.4%

1993 ACCRA average cost: $92,281

1993 ACCRA average rent for an apartment: $505

Chamber of Commerce

Salt Lake Area Chamber of Commerce, Fred S. Ball, President, 175 East 400 St., Salt Lake City, UT 84111. 801-364-3631

Economic Development Office

Metro Utah, Inc., E. Joyce Smith, Operations Manager, 6150 State Office Bldg., PO Box 1499, Salt Lake City, UT 84110. 801-538-3055

Major Businesses

Company	SIC	Telephone
Amalgamated Sugar Co.	2063	(801) 399-3431
American Food & Drug Inc.	5411	(801) 537-3000
American Superstores, Inc.	5411	(801) 539-0112
Associated Food Stores, Inc.	5141	(801) 973-4400
Crossland Savings, Utah	6035	(801) 350-9600
First Security Corp.	6021	(801) 350-6000
Huntsman Chemical Corp.	2821	(801) 532-5200
IHC Hospitals Inc.	8062	(801) 533-8282
Intermountain Power Agency	4911	(801) 262-8807
Jewel Companies, Inc.	5411	(801) 539-0112
Northwest Pipeline Corp.	4922	(801) 583-8800
Price Savers Wholesale, Inc.	5199	(801) 466-7777
Questar Corp.	4924	(801) 534-5600
Smiths Food & Drug Center	5411	(801) 974-1400
Thiokol Corp.	3764	(801) 629-2270
Utah State Retirement Board	6733	(801) 355-3884
Western Dairymen's Cooper	2026	(801) 322-4672

Colleges and Universities

Latter-Day Saints Business College, Salt Lake City

Salt Lake Community College, Salt Lake City

Stevens Henager College, Ogden

University of Utah, Salt Lake City

VERMONT

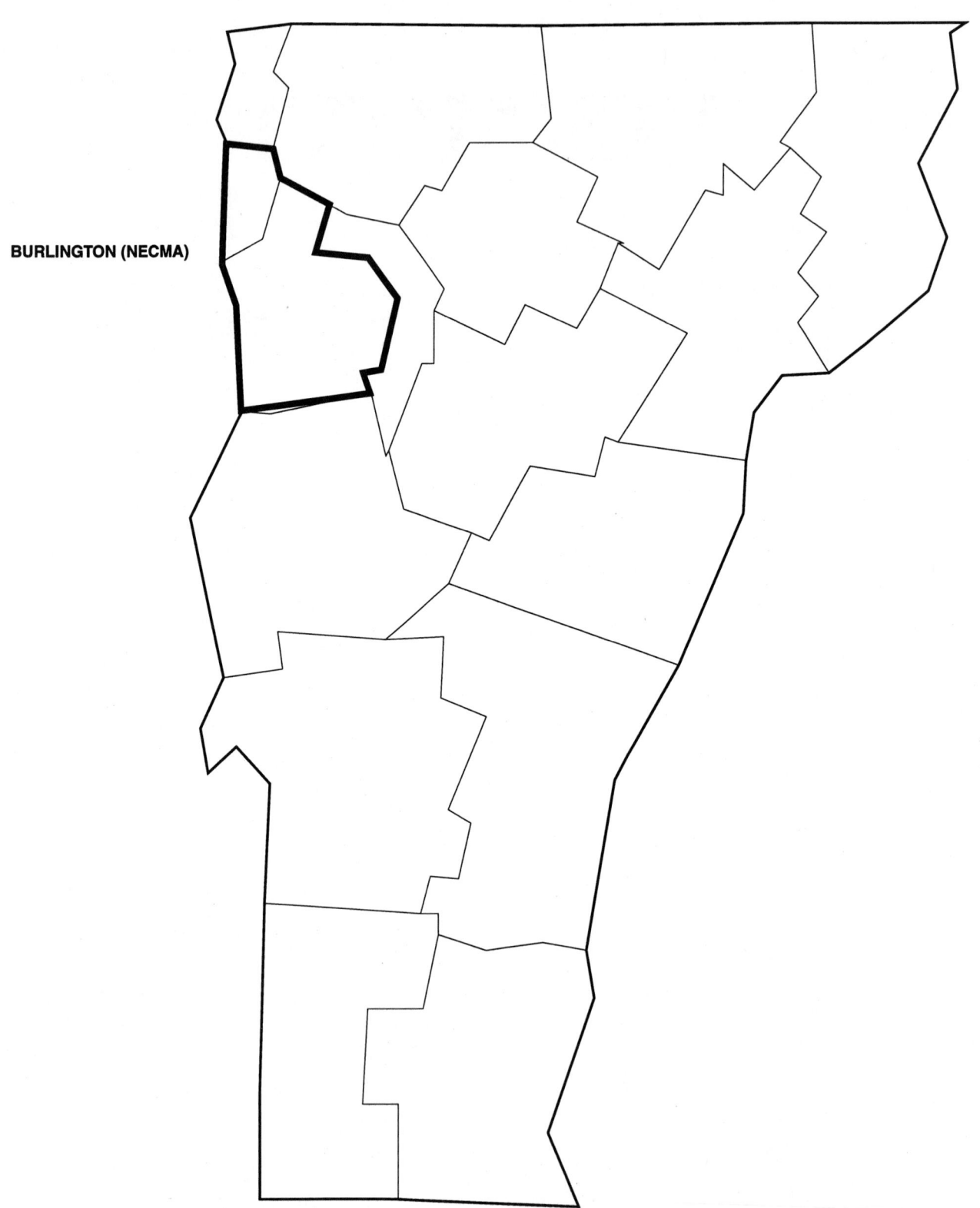

BURLINGTON (NECMA)

VERMONT

Population
1990: 562,758
1980: 511,456

Age
Ages 18 to 20: 29,671
Ages 21 to 24: 33,495
Ages 25 to 44: 187,689
Ages 45 to 54: 57,389
Ages 55 to 59: 22,787
Ages 60 to 64: 22,481
Median age: 33.0

Race and Hispanic Origin
White: 555,088
Black: 1,951
Asian/Pacific Islander: 3,215
Native American: 1,696
Hispanic origin: 3,661

Households
Total: 210,650
Persons per household: 2.57

Sex
Male: 275,492
Female: 287,266

Population Migration
Domestic migration: 15,000
International migration: 1,000

Projection of the Population in 1995
Total: 594,000
18 to 64: 374,000

Civilian Labor Force
1993: 321,100
1992: 309,900
1991: 310,900
1990: 309,700

Manufacturing
1995 Projection: 58,300
1992: 43,700
1991: 43,100
1990: 44,700
1989: 47,000

Services
1995 Projection: 105,600

1992: 69,300
1991: 71,100
1990: 69,500
1989: 68,700

Wholesale and Retail Trade
1995 Projection: 76,300
1992: 58,100
1991: 58,300
1990: 60,700
1989: 63,700

Unemployment Rate
1993: 7.0%
1992: 7.1%
1991: 6.6%
1990: 4.5%

Employer Unemployment Contributions

Contribution Rate
1992: 2.50%
1991: 2.50%
1990: 2.94%

Average Weekly Benefit
1992: $164.22
1991: $158.30
1990: $150.16

Gross State Product (Million $)
1989: $11,502
1988: $10,821
1987: $9,846
1979: $4,498
Growth rate, 1979 to 1989: 155.7%

Capital Expenditures of Manufacturing Industries
1990: $455,600,000
1989: $437,200,000
1988: $380,100,000
1987: $334,400,000

State Tax Rates
Individual income: 28% of taxpayer's Federal tax amount.
Corporate income: Range from 5.5% ($10,000 or less) to 8.25% (above $250,000).

General property: Rates fixed locally. Property is valued at 33.33% to 100%.

General sales: 5%

Gasoline: 15¢ per gallon

Income

Median income for a 4 person family: $40,397

Personal per Capita Income

1992: $18,834

1991: $17,960

1990: $17,630

Disposable per Capita Income

1992: $16,640

1991: $15,802

1990: $15,421

Private Employment Weekly Wages

Average

1989: $370

1988: $354

1987: $354

Manufacturing

1989: $336

1988: $474

1987: $457

Services

1989: $316

1988: $298

1987: $278

Wholesale

1989: $455

1988: $453

1987: $417

Retail

1989: $225

1988: $219

1987: $209

Highway Statistics

Total Highway Miles

1990: 14,121

1989: 14,093

1988: 14,089

Federal Highway Aid

1991: $54,269,000

1990: $53,923,000

1989: $54,350,000

Electricity

Average Cost per Kilowatt Hour

1990: 8.10¢

1989: 7.66¢

1988: 7.62¢

Housing (1990)

Owner occupied units: 145,368

Median house value: $95,500

Renter occupied units: 65,282

Median rent: $378

Total vacant units: 60,564

Homeowner vacancy rate: 2.1%

Rental vacancy rate: 7.5%

State Business Incentives and Assistance

Financial and Business Assistance

The Vermont Industrial Development Authority (VIDA) is set up to promote economic prosperity and increase employment through a variety of financing programs, including direct loans for industrial and agricultural purposes, agricultural operating loans, industrial revenue bonds and mortgage loan insurance. Programs include:

Direct Loan Program. This program is designed to make low-interest loans available to businesses for the purchase of land, the purchase or construction (including renovation) of buildings, and the purchase and installation of machinery and equipment for use in an industrial facility. VIDA may make loans for up to 40% of the cost of a project, not exceeding $500,000, of which no more than $300,000 may be for land and buildings and $200,000 for machinery and equipment. The maximum term for real estate loans is 10 years, amortizable on a 15 year basis. The maximum term for machinery and equipment loans is seven years. A commitment fee of 2% of the loan is payable to VIDA at closing.

Industrial Revenue Bonds. This program is designed to aid businesses through VIDA's issuance of tax-exempt, low-interest bonds to provide funds for acquisition of land, buildings, and/or machinery and equipment for use in a manufacturing facility. Projects smaller than $1.5 million are generally not appropriate for this program. A fee of 5/8 of 1% of the bond amount is payable to VIDA upon final approval of a new bond issue.

Assistance to Local Development Corporation. This program provides loans to nonprofit local development corporations for the purchase of land for industrial parks, industrial park planning and development, and the construction or improvement of speculative buildings or small business incubator facilities. The term of the loan is generally two to five years. Loans for the acquisition and development of land for an industrial park cannot exceed 80% of the developed appraised property value. The local development corporation is expected to provide a minimum of 10% of the project cost. A commitment fee of the loan is payable to VIDA at closing.

Mortgage Insurance Program. This program is designed to aid businesses by VIDA's insurance of mortgage payments required to repay loans from banks. VIDA may insure loans made for the acquisition of land, buildings, machinery and equipment, or working capital for use in an industrial facility. The loan must be secured by fixed assets, appraised for at least 133% of the loan amount if used for working capital. VIDA may insure up to 90% of the principal balance of any mortgage loan, limited to 10 million for any project. VIDA charges an insurance premium of up to five points at closing.

Agricultural Fiance Program. This program is designed to assist family farmers and agricultural facility operators by making available low-interest loans from the Agricultural Development Fund. Loan proceeds may be used to fund real estate and machinery and equipment acquisitions. The maximum loan is $50,000 with special consideration given to projects involving diversified processing of Vermont agricultural products.

Debt Stabilization Program. This program combines Vermont banks' funds with state funds to assist family farms. It is intended to reduce farm operating loan payments by refinancing existing operating loans at lower interest rates, and by making a limited number of new operating loans. The maximum loan available to any applicant is $150,000.

SBA 504 Certified Development Company Program. Administered by the Vermont 503 Corporation, a SBA Certified Development Company, this program may make loans to many types of manufacturing/processing/assembly businesses to fund acquisition, construction or renovation of fixed assets. Businesses with a net worth of less than $6 million and average net income of no more than $3 million for the last two years are eligible to apply. Loans may not exceed $750,000 or 40% of the project cost, whichever is less. Loan terms are either 10 years for machinery and equipment or 20 years for land and building. Interest rates are usually below conventional bank rates. Fees totaling approximately 3% of the loan are payable at closing, plus an annual servicing fee of 1/2% of 1% of the outstanding loan balance.

Vermont Job Start Program. Administered by the Vermont Economic Opportunity Office of the Industrial Development Authority, this program provides financial assistance to Vermont small businesses. It is designed to help Vermont residents with annual gross incomes no more than $14,000 to $24,000 depending on size of household to start, strengthen or expand a small business. Loans are limited to $10,000 per applicant with 8.5% simple interest, four-year maximum term.

Rural Economic Activity Loan Program. Funded with $1 million borrowed from the Farmers Home Administration, this program is intended to assist rural entrepreneurs and former agriculturalists to establish or expand their business. The maximum fixed asset loan is $100,000 or 50% of the project cost, whichever is less. Loans carry a 4% interest rate and terms range from 5-10 years. Working capital loans are limited to $50,000 or 50% of the project amount, with maximum terms of seven years at a fixed

interest rate of 2% below prime rate. A 2% commitment fee is payable at closing.

Education and Training

Job Training Partnership Act. This program operates with funding from the U.S. Department of Labor. It provides job training and other employment related services.

State Offices

Real estate: Real Estate Commission, David Drew, Director, Redstone Bldg., 26 Terrace Street, Montpelier, VT 05602. 802-828-3228

Chamber of commerce: Vermont State Chamber of Commerce, Christopher G. Barbieri, President, PO Box 37, Granger Rd., Montpelier, VT 05601. 802-223-3443, FAX 802-229-4581

Economic development: Agency of Development & Community Affairs, Dept. of Econ. Dev., William Kenerson, Commissioner, 109 State St., Pavilion Bldg., 4th Fl., Montpelier, VT 05602. 802-828-3221, FAX 802-828-3258

Vermont Industrial Development Authority, Robert E. Fletcher, Manager, 58 East State St., Montpelier, VT 05602. 802-223-7226, FAX 802-223-4205

Vermont 503 Corporation, Robert E. Fletcher, Manager, 58 East State St., Montpelier, VT 05602. 802-223-7226

Small Business Development Center, Norris A. Elliott, State Director, Morrill Hall, University of Vermont, Burlington, VT 05405. 802-656-4479

State Economic Opportunity Office, Director, 103 South Main St., Waterbury, VT 05676. 802-241-2450

Development & Community Affairs Agency (Enterprise Zones Office), Curtis Carter, Development Programs Coordinator, 109 State Street, 4th Floor, Montpelier, VT 05609. 802-828-3221

Environmental affairs: Natural Resources Agency, Jan S. Eastman, Secretary, 103 S. Main St., Waterbury, VT 05676. 802-244-8755

Labor: Labor and Industry Department, Dana Cole-Levesaue, Commissioner, 7 Court St., Montpelier, VT 05602. 802-828-2288

Unemployment: Employment and Training Department, Patricia Thomas, Commissioner, PO Box 488, Green Mountain Drive, Montpelier, VT 05601. 802-229-0311

Worker's compensation: Labor and Industry Department, Dana Cole-Levesaue, Commissioner, 5 Court St., Montpelier, VT 05602. 802-828-2286

Occupational safety and health: Labor and Industry Department, Occupational Safety Programs, Robert McLeod Jr., Manager, 7 Court St., Montpelier, VT 05602. 802-828-2765 or 800-622-4124

Secretary of state: Secretary of State, James H. Douglas, Secretary of State, 120 State St., State Office Bldg., Montpelier, VT 05602. 802-828-2386

Taxation and revenue: Taxes Commission, Agency of Administration, Joyce H. Errecart, Commissioner, 109

Major Companies in the State

Company name	Fortune 500 rank	City	Telephone	SIC number
Fortune 500 Companies				
None				
Other Major Companies in the State				
Alcoa International Holdings Co.		Burlington	802-658-2726	2819
Banknorth Group Inc.		Burlington	802-658-9959	6712
Ben & Jerry's Homemade Inc.		North Moretown	802-244-6957	2024
Central Vermont Public Service Corp.		Rutland	802-773-2711	4911
Chittenden Corp.		Burlington	802-658-4000	6712
Community Bancorp		Derby	802-334-7915	6712
Eastern Bancorp Inc.		Williston	802-879-9000	6712
Fund American Companies Inc.		Norwich	802-649-3633	6162
Green Mountain Power Corp.		South Burlington	802-864-5731	4911
Health Insurance of Vermont Inc.		Colchester	802-655-5500	6324
IMTEC Inc.		Bellows Falls	802-463-9502	3579
Independent Bankgroup Inc.		Springfield	802-885-4515	6712
Marble Financial Corp.		Rutland	802-775-0025	6712
Meldon Alumni Inc.		Mendon	802-774-3200	6513
Merchants Bancshares Inc.		Burlington	802-658-3400	6712
NECO Enterprises Inc.		Quechee	802-295-1368	4911
SKI Ltd		Killington	802-422-3333	7011
Vermont Financial Services Corp.		Brattleboro	802-257-7151	6712
Vermont Research Corp.		North Springfield	802-886-2256	3674
Vermont Yankee Nuclear Power Corp.		Brattleboro	802-257-5271	4911

State St., Pavilion Bldg., Montpelier, VT 05602. 802-828-2505.

Designated Zones for Economic Development

Enterprise Zones
Enacted in: 1986
No. of established zones: 3
Poultney
Rockingham
A northeast Vermont consortium of eight towns

Foreign Trade Zones
Foreign Trade Zone No. 55, Burlington, Vermont, Grantee/Operator: Greater Burlington Industrial Corp., C. Harry Behney, PO Box 786, Burlington, VT 05402, 802-862-5726

Foreign Trade Zone No. 91, Newport, Vermont, Grantee/Operator: Northeastern Vermont Dev. Assoc, Henry W. Merrill, Jr., 44 Main Street, St. Johnsbury, VT 05819, 802-748-5181

Labor Unions
Electrical Workers, International Brotherhood of (AFL-CIO)
Food and Commercial Workers International Union, United (AFL-CIO)
National Education Association
Paperworkers International Union, United (AFL-CIO)
Plumbing and Pipe Fitting Industry of The United States and Canada, United Association of, Journeymen and Apprentices of the (AFL-CIO)
State, County and Municipal Employees, American Federation of (AFL-CIO)
Steelworkers of America, United (AFL-CIO)
Teamsters, Chauffeurs, Warehousemen and Helpers of America, International Brotherhood of, (AFL-CIO)
IUE Local 248

Universities with Ph.D. Programs
Middlebury College, Middlebury
University of Vermont, Burlington

Sources of Additional Information
Wage and Fringe Benefit Survey, 1990. Vermont Dept. of Employment and Training, September 1990. 39p.
Summary of Financing Programs. Vermont Industrial Development Authority, October 1989. 8p.
Vermont, A Natural Busienss Environment: Financing Programs. Vermont Dept. of Econ. Development, n.d. 16p.
Starting a Business in Vermont, Sources. Vermont Agency of Development & Community Affairs, Sept. 1990. 8p.

BURLINGTON, VT (NECMA)

Geographic Profile

Land Area

621.6 square miles

Counties and Parishes

Chittenden (part)

Franklin (part)

Grand Isle (part)

Additional Cities/Towns within Area

Chittenden County:

Charlotte

Colchester

Esex

Hinesburg

Jericho

Milton

Richmond

St. George

Shelburne

South Burlington

Williston

Winooski

Franklin County:

Georgia

Grand Isle County:

Grand Isle

South Hero

Ranking Highlights

268 *out of 319 in total* **land area**

118 *out of 319 in* **population growth,** *1970–1990*

29 *out of 310 in having the lowest* **unemployment** *rate*

208 *out of 310 in size of* **labor force**

14 *out of 318 in the percentage of* **college graduates**

66 *out of 292 in per capita personal* **income**

222 *out of 319 in number of* **manufacturing establishments**

8 *out of 318 in* **physicians** *per 1000 people*

131 *out of 318 in* **hospital beds** *per 1000 people*

N/A *out of 267 in fewest* **crimes** *per 1000 people*

N/A *out of 266 in fewest* **violent crimes** *per 1000 people*

105 *out of 319 in per capita* **federal funds and grants**

Quality of Life Indexes (Rate per 1000 population)

Crime rate in 1991:	N/A
Violent crime rate in 1991:	N/A
Physicians rate in 1992:	4.73
Hospital bed rate in 1991:	4.18

ACCRA Cost of Living Indexes

(First quarter 1993, average = 100)

Composite index:	N/A
Utilities index:	N/A
Housing index:	N/A

Overview

This MSA area is situated within partial boundaries of Chittenden, Franklin, and the Grand Isle counties. The Greater Burlington region is Vermont's major economic center and most urban area. It serves as a commercial gateway to the rest of New England for the Montreal, Quebec, Canada, area, only 90 miles north. Montreal can be reached via rail, Interstate 89 and the Burlington International Airport, which also provides direct flights to Boston, Massachusetts, New York City, Newark, New Jersey, Baltimore,Maryland, Washington, D.C., Pittsburgh, Pennsylvania and Chicago, Illinois. Boston is 225 miles to the southeast and New York City 300 miles to the south. There is a market of 75 million people within a 500-mile radius.

Several industrial parks with speculative buildings have been developed in the area by the Greater Burlington Industrial Corporation (GBIC), Winooski Community Development Corporation, and private developers, with industrial sites available from one to 200 acres. GBIC is the Grantee of Foreign-Trade Zone No. 55, located at the Catamount Industrial Park, which includes an industrial facility and available land.

Greater Burlington was recently selected by *Inc. Magazine* and DRI/McGraw-Hill as one of the best places to build and grow a business in the Northeast.

Population (1990)

Total Population and Growth Rate

1990: 137,079

1980: 120,147

1970: 102,705

Growth rate 1970–1990: 33%

Race and Hispanic Origin

White: 97.8%

Black: .6%

Asian/Pacific Islander: 1.1%

Native American: 0.2%

Hispanic origin: 0.9%

White not Hispanic: 97.1%

Age

Ages 18 to 20: 7.6%

Ages 21 to 24: 8.3%

Ages 25 to 44: 33.9%

Ages 45 to 54: 9.4%

Ages 55 to 59: 3.5%

Ages 60 to 64: 3.1%

Ages 65 plus: 7.9%

Educational Attainment (1990)

Percent having completed high school: 86.6%

Percent having completed college: 33.2%

Elementary and high school enrollment: 23,000

Federal Funds and Grants Received

Total received in 1989: $477,900,000

Funds received per capita: $3,551

Civilian Labor Force

1993 (April): 83,245
1992 average: 80,966
1991 average: 82,050
1990 average: 81,550

Unemployment

1993 (April): 4.9%
1992 average: 4.5%
1991 average: 4.5%
1990 average: 3.4%

Average Annual Pay

1988: $21,543
1987: $20,422
1985: $18,621

Per Capita Personal Income

1991: $19,369
1990: $19,030
1989: $18,019

Business Climate (1987)

Manufacturing

Number of establishments in 1987: 197
Shipments in 1987 ($1,000): N/A
Employees in 1987: N/A
Change in employment, 1982 to 1987: N/A
Average annual pay for manufacturing work in 1989: $34,004
Average annual pay for production work in 1987: N/A

Wholesale Trade

Number of establishments in 1987: 269
Total sales in 1987 ($1,000): N/A
Change in sales, 1982 to 1987: N/A

Retail Trade

Number of establishments in 1987: 1,168
Total sales in 1987 ($1,000): N/A
Retail sales per household in 1987: $22,658
Average annual pay in 1989: $11,416

Service Industry

Selected receipts in 1987 ($1,000): $478,900
Average annual pay in 1989: $18,562

Housing

Total number of units in 1990: 52,610
Occupied units in 1990: 48,313
Owner-occupied units in 1990: 64.0%
1993 ACCRA average cost: N/A
1993 ACCRA average rent for an apartment: N/A

Chamber of Commerce

Lake Champlain Regional Chamber of Commerce, A. Wayne Roberts, President, 209 Battery St., PO Box 453, Burlington, VT 05402. 802-863-3489

Economic Development Office

Greater Burlington Industrial Corp., C. Harry Behney, President, PO Box 786, 7 Burlington Square #210, Burlington, VT 05402. 802-862-5726, FAX 802-860-1899

Economic Development Organizations

Colchester Community Development Corp., Roger G. Kilbourn, Exec. Director, 336 Malletts Bay Ave., PO Box 444, Colchester 05446. 802-864-7158, FAX 802-864-7114

Small Business Development Center, Norris A. Elliott, State Coordinator, Morrill Hall, University of Vermont, Burlington, VT 05405. 802-656-4479

Local Incentives for Business

Revolving Loan — Burlington Community Development Dept.

Major Businesses

Company	SIC	Telephone
Bank of Vermont	6022	(802) 658-1810
Banknorth Group, Inc.	6712	(802) 860-5442
BankVermont Corporation	6712	(802) 658-1810
Burlington Free Press	2711	(802) 863-3441
Chittenden Corp.	6712	(802) 658-4000
E. B. & A. C. Whiting Co.	3089	(802) 863-6333
Edlund Co., Inc.	3556	(802) 862-9661
G. S. Blodgett Co., Inc.	3589	(802) 658-6600
George Little Press, Inc.	2752	(802) 658-3300
Howard Bank, N.A.	6021	(802) 658-1010
Independent Food Co.	5141	(802) 862-0800
John Mckenzie Packing Co.	2013	(802) 864-4585
Koffee Kup Bakery, Inc.	2051	(802) 863-2696
Ladd Research Industries	3841	(802) 862-9119
Lane Press, Inc.	2752	(802) 863-5555
Merchants Bancshares, Inc.	6022	(802) 658-3400
Queen City Printers, Inc.	2759	(802) 864-4566
T.A. Haigh Lumber Co., Inc.	5211	(802) 863-3428

Colleges and Universities

Burlington College, Burlington
Champlain College, Burlington
St. Michael's College, Colchester
Trinity College of Vermont, Burlington
University of Vermont, Burlington

VIRGINIA

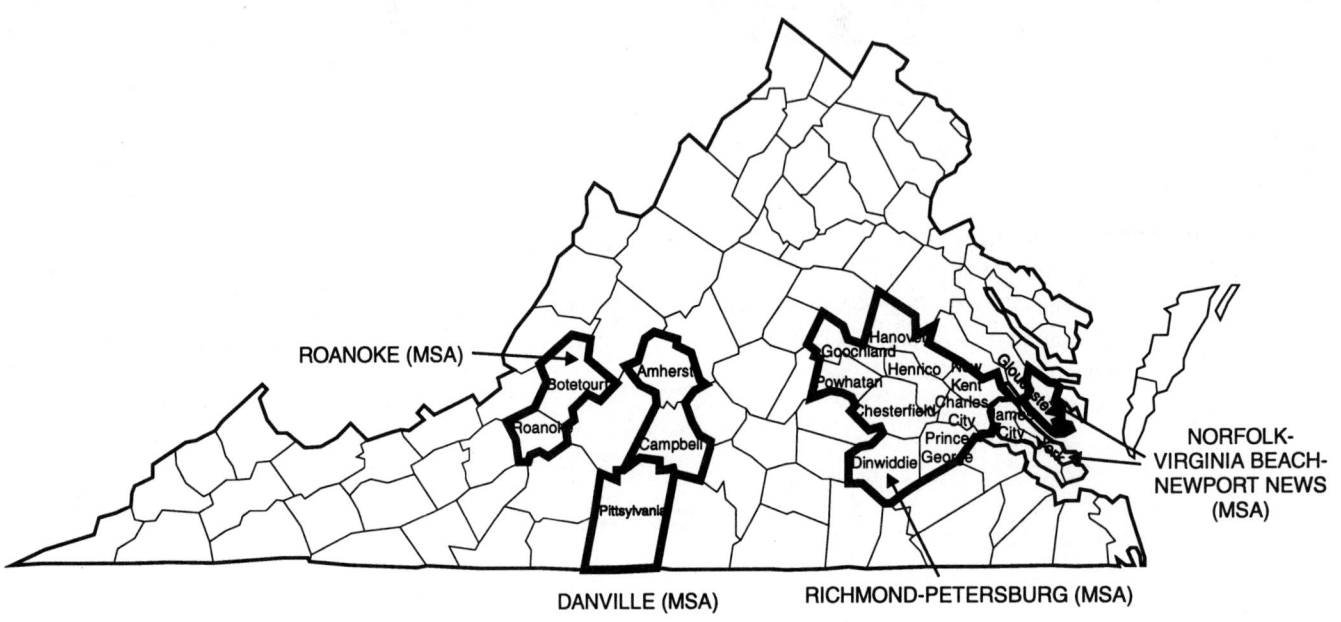

ROANOKE (MSA)

Botetourt

Roanoke

Amherst

Campbell

Pittsylvania

DANVILLE (MSA)

Goochland

Hanover

Henrico

Powhatan

New
Kent

Chesterfield

Charles
City

Prince
George

Dinwiddie

Gloucester

James
City

York

RICHMOND-PETERSBURG (MSA)

NORFOLK-
VIRGINIA BEACH-
NEWPORT NEWS
(MSA)

VIRGINIA

Population
1990: 6,187,358
1980: 5,346,818

Age
Ages 18 to 20: 308,105
Ages 21 to 24: 411,626
Ages 25 to 44: 2,132,444
Ages 45 to 54: 663,332
Ages 55 to 59: 257,207
Ages 60 to 64: 245,436
Median age: 32.6

Race and Hispanic Origin
White: 4,791,739
Black: 1,162,994
Asian/Pacific Islander: 159,053
Native American: 15,282
Hispanic origin: 160,288

Households
Total: 2,291,830
Persons per household: 2.61

Sex
Male: 3,033,974
Female: 3,153,384

Population Migration
Domestic migration: 442,000
International migration: 99,000

Projection of the Population in 1995
Total: 6,544,000
18 to 64: 4,232,000

Civilian Labor Force
1993: 3,315,000
1992: 3,329,800
1991: 3,259,300
1990: 3,132,500

Manufacturing
1995 Projection: 458,300
1992: 407,500
1991: 413,200
1990: 418,300
1989: 428,200

Services
1995 Projection: 1,068,000

1992: 755,600
1991: 749,400
1990: 736,700
1989: 707,100

Wholesale and Retail Trade
1995 Projection: 782,000
1992: 633,000
1991: 658,900
1990: 671,400
1989: 685,200

Unemployment Rate
1993: 6.5%
1992: 7.2%
1991: 5.4%
1990: 4.4%

Employer Unemployment Contributions
Contribution Rate
1992: 0.99%
1991: 0.79%
1990: 0.82%

Average Weekly Benefit
1992: $166.51
1991: $168.61
1990: $146.80

Gross State Product (Million $)
1989: $136,497
1988: $126,668
1987: $115,881
1979: $53,390
Growth rate, 1979 to 1989: 155.7%

Capital Expenditures of Manufacturing Industries
1990: $2,096,200,000
1989: $1,986,700,000
1988: $1,727,000,000
1987: $1,542,700,000

State Tax Rates
Individual income: Range from 2% ($3,000 or less) to 5.75% (above $17,000).
Corporate income: 6% of taxable net income.
General property: Sum of local rates, based on fair market

value of real property and tangible personal property.
General sales: 3.5%
Gasoline: 17.5¢ per gallon

Income
Median income for a 4 person family: $45,090

Personal per Capita Income
1992: $20,629
1991: $20,046
1990: $19,679

Disposable per Capita Income
1992: $18,010
1991: $17,420
1990: $17,039

Private Employment Weekly Wages

Average
1989: $407
1988: $393
1987: $393

Manufacturing
1989: $372
1988: $453
1987: $431

Services
1989: $409
1988: $392
1987: $369

Wholesale
1989: $554
1988: $531
1987: $498

Retail
1989: $235
1988: $228
1987: $219

Highway Statistics

Total Highway Miles
1990: 67,700
1989: 67,282
1988: 66,892

Federal Highway Aid
1991: $269,475,000
1990: $262,499,000
1989: $219,482,000

Electricity
Average Cost per Kilowatt Hour
1990: 6.04¢
1989: 5.90¢
1988: 5.63¢

Housing (1990)
Owner occupied units: 1,519,521

Median house value: $91,000
Renter occupied units: 772,309
Median rent: $411
Total vacant units: 204,504
Homeowner vacancy rate: 2.1%
Rental vacancy rate: 8.1%

State Business Incentives and Assistance

Enterprise Zone Incentives
1) State sales tax exemption for purchases for up to five years.
2) State business income tax credit, starting at 80% during the first year, reducing incrementally to 20% in the fourth and fifth years.
3) Credit against state business income tax based on a portion of the amount of state unemployment taxes, starting at 80% during the first year and declining to 20% during the fourth and fifth years.
4) Additional local incentives.

Financial and Business Assistance
Small Business Financing Authority. Administered by the Small Business and Financial Services Office of the Department of Economic Development, the Authority issues umbrella Industrial Development Bonds, making the funds available to firms which previously were too small to utilize this financial option.

Economic Development Revolving Loan Fund. Administered by the Community Financial Assistance Office of the Department of Housing and Community Development, this program provides loans to industrial development authorities set up in communities qualified for receiving Community Development Block Grants. The loans may be relent to private manufacturing, warehousing, and distribution businesses for the acquisition of land and buildings and renovation of existing plants, machinery and equipment.

Virginia Tech Corporate Research Park. Administered by the Virginia Polytechnic University, the Park is designed to encourage corporate research and development in rural Virginia.

Small Business Incubator. Administered by the Virginia Polytechnic University, this program is designed to encourage start-ups for high-growth technology firms. The incubator facility allows businesses to test and perfect production processes on prototype scale.

Industrial Access Road Program. Administered by the State Secondary Roads Engineer Office of the Department of Transportation, this program constructs roads to provide access to new and expanding industries involved in manufacturing or processing.

Education and Training
Industrial Training. Administered by the Industrial Training Division of the Department of Economic Development, this program provides customized pre-employment, on-

Major Companies in the State

Company name	Fortune 500 rank	City	Telephone	SIC number
Fortune 500 Companies				
E R Carpenter Co.	499	Richmond	804-359-0800	3086
Chesapeake Corp.	388	Richmond	804-697-1000	2621
Dibrell Brothers Inc.	337	Danville	804-792-7511	5193
Ethyl Corp.	161	Richmond	804-788-5000	2824
Gannett Co. Inc.	143	Arlington	703-284-6000	2711
General Dynamics Corp.	58	Falls Church	703-876-3000	3721
James River Corp. of Virginia	113	Richmond	804-644-5411	2676
Lafarge Corp.	271	Reston	703-264-3600	3241
Mobil Corp.	6	Fairfax	703-846-3000	1311
Reynolds Metals Co.	96	Richmond	804-281-2000	3334
Smithfield Foods Inc.	347	Smithfield	804-357-4321	2013
Specialty Coatings International	471	Richmond	804-697-3500	3861
Universal Corp.	160	Richmond	804-359-9311	5159
Other Major Companies in the State				
Appalachian Power Co.		Roanoke	703-985-2300	4911
Best Products Co. Inc.		Richmond	804-261-2000	5311
C&S Sovran Corp.		Norfolk	804-441-4000	6712
Chesapeake & Potomac Telephone Co. of Virginia		Richmond	804-772-2000	4813
Circuit City Stores Inc.		Richmond	804-527-4000	5731
Crestar Financial Corp.		Richmond	804-782-5000	6712
CSX Corp.		Richmond	804-782-1400	4011
Dominion Bankshares Corp.		Roanoke	703-563-7749	6712
Dominion Resources Inc. Virginia		Richmond	804-775-5700	4911
Norfolk & Western Railway Co.		Norfolk	804-629-2682	4011
Norfolk Southern Corp.		Norfolk	804-629-2680	4011
Norfolk Southern Railway Co.		Norfolk	804-629-2682	4011
Owens & Minor Inc.		Glen Allen	804-747-9794	5122
Paramax Inc.		Mclean	703-847-3600	3812
Richfood Holdings Inc.		Richmond	804-746-6000	5141
Signet Banking Corp.		Richmond	804-747-2000	6712
Southern Railway Co.		Norfolk	804-629-2682	4011
USAir Group Inc.		Arlington	703-418-5306	4512
USAir Inc.		Arlington	703-418-7000	4512
Virginia Electric & Power Co.		Richmond	804-771-3520	4911

the-job training to companies with facilities in the state. Additional services provide include recruitment and screening of trainees.

Job Training Partnership Act. This program operates with funding from the U.S. Department of Labor. It provides job training and other employment related services.

State Offices

Real estate: Real Estate Commission, Joan White, Commissioner, 3600 West Broad Street, Richmond, VA 23230. 804-367-8552

Chamber of commerce: Virginia State Chamber of Commerce, Edwin C. Luther III, Exec Vice President, 9 S. 5th St., Richmond, VA 23219. 804-644-1607

Economic development: Department of Economic Development, Hugh D. Keogh, Director, PO Box 798, 1021 East Cary Street, Richmond, VA 23206-0798. 804-371-8100, FAX 804-371-8112

Department of Economic Development, Community and Business Services, Director, PO Box 798, 1021 East Cary Street, Richmond, VA 23206-0798. 804-371-8100

Department of Housing and Community Development, Office of Community Financial Assistance, Associate Director, 205 North Fourth Street, Richmond, VA 23219. 804-786-4474

Department of Housing and Community Development, Enterprise Zones Office, Stanley Kidwell, Associate Director, 205 North Fourth Street, Richmond, VA 23219. 804-786-4966

Department of Economic Development, Small Busienss and Financial Services, Dave O'Donnell, Director, 1021 East Cary Street, Richmond, VA 23219. 804-371-8260

Virginia Small Business Financing Authority, Director, PO Box 798, 1021 East Cary Street, Richmond, VA 23206-0798. 804-371-8100

Virginia Tech Corporate Research Park and Business Incubator, Bill Braun and Charles Forbes, Virginia Polytechnic University, Blacksburg, VA 24061. 703-231-6000

Department of Transportation, State Secondary Roads Engineer Office, Director, 1221 East Broad Street, Richmond, VA 23219. 804-786-2746

Environmental affairs: Council on Environment, Keith J. Buttleman, Administrator, 202 North 9th Street, 9th State Office Bldg., Suite 900, Richmond, VA 23219. 804-786-4500

Labor: Labor and Industry Department, Carol Amato, Commissioner, PO Box 12064, 205 North 4th Street, Richmond, VA 23241. 804-786-2377

Unemployment: Employment Commission, Unemployment Insurance Division, John W. Rusher, Director, 703 East Main Street, Rchmond, VA 23219. 804-786-3004

Worker's compensation: Employment Commission, Ralph G. Cantrell, Commissioner, 703 East Main Street, Rchmond, VA 23219. 804-786-3001

Occupational safety and health: Labor and Industry Department, Occupational Safety & Encorcement Division, William R. Crawfod, Director, PO Box 12064, 205 North 4th Street, Richmond, VA 23241. 804-786-2391

Secretary of state: Secretary of the Commonwealth, Pamela Womack, Secretary of the Commonwealth, 114 9th State Office Bldg., Box 1B, Richmond, VA 23201. 804-786-2441

Taxation and revenue: Taxation Department, W.H. Forst, Commissioner, 2220 West Broad Street, Box 6L, Richmond, VA 23282. 804-367-8005

Designated Zones for Economic Development

Enterprise Zones

Enacted in: 1982

No. of established zones: 18

Foreign Trade Zones

Foreign Trade Zone No. 20, Suffolk, Virginia, Grantee: Virginia Port Authority, Charles Shotton, c/o Atlantic Warehousing, PO Box 466, Suffolk, VA 23434, 804-934-2386

Labor Unions

Air Line Pilots Association, International (AFL-CIO)

Food and Commercial Workers International Union, United (AFL-CIO)

Steelworkers of America, United (AFL-CIO)

Universities with Ph.D. Programs

College of William and Mary, Williamsburg

George Mason University, Fairfax

Old Dominion University, Norfolk

University of Virginia, Charlottesville

Virginia Commonwealth University, Richmond

Virginia Polytechnic Institute and State University, Blacksburg

Washington and Lee University, Lexington

CHARLOTTESVILLE, VA (MSA)

Geographic Profile
Land Area
1177.1 square miles

Counties and Parishes
Albermarle
Fluvanna
Greene

Ranking Highlights
169 *out of 319 in total* **land area**
80 *out of 319 in* **population growth,** *1970–1990*
47 *out of 310 in having the lowest* **unemployment** *rate*
228 *out of 310 in size of* **labor force**
13 *out of 318 in the percentage of* **college graduates**
68 *out of 292 in per capita personal* **income**
250 *out of 319 in number of* **manufacturing establishments**
3 *out of 318 in* **physicians** *per 1000 people*
18 *out of 318 in* **hospital beds** *per 1000 people*
42 *out of 267 in fewest* **crimes** *per 1000 people*
49 *out of 266 in fewest* **violent crimes** *per 1000 people*
184 *out of 319 in per capita* **federal funds and grants**

Quality of Life Indexes (Rate per 1000 population)
Crime rate in 1991:	40.4
Violent crime rate in 1991:	3.0
Physicians rate in 1992:	7.85
Hospital bed rate in 1991:	6.58

ACCRA Cost of Living Indexes
(First quarter 1993, average = 100)
Composite index:	N/A
Utilities index:	N/A
Housing index:	N/A

Population (1990)
Total Population and Growth Rate
1990: 131,107
1980: 113,568
1970: 89,529
Growth rate 1970–1990: 46%

Race and Hispanic Origin
White: 83.2%
Black: 14.4%
Asian/Pacific Islander: 2.0%
Native American: 0.1%
Hispanic origin: 1.1%
White not Hispanic: 82.4%

Age
Ages 18 to 20: 7.7%
Ages 21 to 24: 8.9%
Ages 25 to 44: 33.7%
Ages 45 to 54: 9.4%
Ages 55 to 59: 3.9%
Ages 60 to 64: 3.9%
Ages 65 plus: 10.7%

Educational Attainment (1990)
Percent having completed high school: 76.9%
Percent having completed college: 33.3%
Elementary and high school enrollment: 17,851

Federal Funds and Grants Received
Total received in 1989: $365,100,000
Funds received per capita: $2,949

Civilian Labor Force
1993 (April):	75,472
1992 average:	73,156
1991 average:	72,104
1990 average:	70,998

Unemployment
1993 (April): 3.2%
1992 average: 4.8%
1991 average: 4.5%
1990 average: 3.0%

Average Annual Pay
1988: $19,032
1987: $18,077
1985: $16,600

Per Capita Personal Income
1991: $19,240
1990: $19,081
1989: $18,250

Business Climate (1987)
Manufacturing
Number of establishments in 1987: 146
Shipments in 1987 ($1,000): $848,500
Employees in 1987: 9,600
Change in employment, 1982 to 1987: 26.3%
Average annual pay for manufacturing work in 1989: $22,368
Average annual pay for production work in 1987: $16,656

Wholesale Trade
Number of establishments in 1987: 165
Total sales in 1987 ($1,000): $2,132,500
Change in sales, 1982 to 1987: 0%

Retail Trade
Number of establishments in 1987: 879
Total sales in 1987 ($1,000): $2,132,500
Retail sales per household in 1987: $19,544
Average annual pay in 1989: $11,105

Service Industry
Selected receipts in 1987 ($1,000): $287,400
Average annual pay in 1989: $17,459

Housing

Total number of units in 1990: 51,932
Occupied units in 1990: 48,709
Owner-occupied units in 1990: 59.4%
1993 ACCRA average cost: N/A
1993 ACCRA average rent for an apartment: N/A

Chamber of Commerce

Charlottesville–Albemarle County Chamber of Commerce, Mary Ann Elwood, President, 5th & E. Market Sts., PO Box 1564, Charlottesville, VA 22902. 804-295-3141

Economic Development Office

Greater Charlottesville Area Development Corp., Mary Ann Elwood, President, 5th & Market Sts., PO Box 1293, Charlottesville, VA 22902. 804-295-3144

Major Businesses

Company	SIC	Telephone
Amvest Corp.	1222	(804) 977-3350
Better Living, Inc.	5211	(804) 973-4333
Brady-Bushey Ford Inc.	5511	(804) 977-7960
Central Telephone Co. of Virginia	4813	(804) 399-2500
Comdial Corp.	3661	(804) 978-2500
Faulconer Construction Co.	1629	(804) 973-1568
Haley, Chisholm & Morris	1794	(804) 978-1000
HCM Associates Inc.	5511	(804) 978-3711
Hereford, Frank L.	6798	(804) 974-7377
Jefferson Bankshares Inc.	6021	(804) 972-1100
Lee, R. E. and Son, Inc.	1542	(804) 973-1321
Martha Jefferson Hospital	8062	(804) 293-0111
MBFC Inc.	6162	(804) 979-1191
Mortgage Bankers Financial	6162	(804) 979-1189
Pepsi Cola Bottling Control	2086	(804) 978-2140
Price Chevrolet Co.	5511	(804) 973-1881
Recreational Resorts Ltd.	6552	(804) 973-1250
Sanderson Motors of Charlottesville	5511	(804) 977-3380
Sperry Marine Inc.	3812	(804) 974-2000
Sprigg Lane Investment Co.	3499	(804) 977-1402
University of Virginia Health Service	8721	(804) 295-1000
Wade, R. D. Builder Inc.	1531	(804) 973-7841
Worrell Enterprises	2711	(804) 977-7520

Colleges and Universities

National Business College, Charlottesville
Piedmont Virginia Community College, Charlottesville
University of Virginia, Charlottesville

DANVILLE, VA (MSA)

Geographic Profile

Land Area
1013.9 square miles

Counties and Parishes
Pittsylvania

Ranking Highlights

199 *out of 319 in total* land area
256 *out of 319 in* population growth, *1970–1990*
248 *out of 310 in having the lowest* unemployment *rate*
280 *out of 310 in size of* labor force
316 *out of 318 in the percentage of* college graduates
248 *out of 292 in per capita personal* income
282 *out of 319 in number of* manufacturing establishments
291 *out of 318 in* physicians *per 1000 people*
178 *out of 318 in* hospital beds *per 1000 people*
11 *out of 267 in fewest* crimes *per 1000 people*
27 *out of 266 in fewest* violent crimes *per 1000 people*
258 *out of 319 in per capita* federal funds and grants

Quality of Life Indexes (Rate per 1000 population)

Crime rate in 1991:   32.5
Violent crime rate in 1991:   2.3
Physicians rate in 1992:   1.11
Hospital bed rate in 1991:   3.6

ACCRA Cost of Living Indexes

(First quarter 1993, average = 100)
Composite index: N/A
Utilities index: N/A
Housing index: N/A

Population (1990)

Total Population and Growth Rate
1990: 108,711
1980: 111,789
1970: 105,180
Growth rate 1970–1990: 3%

Race and Hispanic Origin
White: 67.9%
Black: 31.6%
Asian/Pacific Islander: 0.3%
Native American: 0.1%
Hispanic origin: 0.5%
White not Hispanic: 67.7%

Age
Ages 18 to 20: 4.1%
Ages 21 to 24: 5%
Ages 25 to 44: 29.9%
Ages 45 to 54: 11.1%
Ages 55 to 59: 5%

Ages 60 to 64: 5.4%
Ages 65 plus: 16%

Educational Attainment (1990)
Percent having completed high school: 56.8%
Percent having completed college: 9.9%
Elementary and high school enrollment: 17,536

Federal Funds and Grants Received
Total received in 1989: $259,200,000
Funds received per capita: $2,398

Civilian Labor Force
1993 (April): 54,645
1992 average: 54,535
1991 average: 54,473
1990 average: 53,039

Unemployment
1993 (April): 7.0%
1992 average: 8.7%
1991 average: 9.9%
1990 average: 7.6%

Average Annual Pay
1988: $17,376
1987: $16,849
1985: $15,263

Per Capita Personal Income
1991: $15,221
1990: $14,989
1989: $14,175

Business Climate (1987)
Manufacturing
Number of establishments in 1987: 113
Shipments in 1987 ($1,000): $1,790,900
Employees in 1987: 17,100
Change in employment, 1982 to 1987: -9.5%
Average annual pay for manufacturing work in 1989: $21,238
Average annual pay for production work in 1987: $18,288

Wholesale Trade
Number of establishments in 1987: 151
Total sales in 1987 ($1,000): $39,400
Change in sales, 1982 to 1987: -89.4%

Retail Trade
Number of establishments in 1987: 661
Total sales in 1987 ($1,000): $39,400
Retail sales per household in 1987: $14,011
Average annual pay in 1989: $10,358

Service Industry
Selected receipts in 1987 ($1,000): $124,500
Average annual pay in 1989: $16,838

Housing
Total number of units in 1990: 46,158

Occupied units in 1990: 42,325
Owner-occupied units in 1990: 69.3%
1993 ACCRA average cost: N/A
1993 ACCRA average rent for an apartment: N/A

Chamber of Commerce
Danville Area Chamber of Commerce, Allan W. Libby, Exec. Director, 635 Main St., PO Box 1538, Danville, VA 24543. 804-793-5422

Economic Development Office
Danville Development Council, Director, 530 Main St., PO Box 299, Danville, VA 24543. 804-793-1753

Major Businesses

Company	SIC	Telephone
Abercrombie Oil Co. Inc.	5171	(804) 792-8022
American National Bank & Trust Co.	6021	(804) 792-5111
American National Bankshares	6021	(804) 792-5111
Belk-Leggett Co. Inc.	5311	(804) 792-6211
Bivens Winchester Corp.	3589	(804) 797-9241
Blair Construction Inc.	1541	(804) 656-6243
Chatham Oil Co.	5172	(804) 432-0251
Dan River, Inc.	2211	(804) 799-7000
Daniel, John W. & Co.	1542	(804) 792-1111
Dibrell Brothers Inc.	5159	(804) 792-7511
Durham Hosiery Mills	2253	(804) 792-5011
Memorial Hospital of Danville	8062	(804) 799-2100
Southern Processors Inc.	2141	(804) 797-4414
Virginia-Carolina Tools Inc.	5084	(804) 793-0155
Woodall, Robert Chevrolet	5511	(804) 797-1411

Colleges and Universities
Averett College, Danville
Danville Community College, Danville
National Business College, Danville

LYNCHBURG, VA (MSA)

Geographic Profile

Land Area
1029.2 square miles

Counties and Parishes
Amherst
Campbell
Lynchburg

Ranking Highlights

196 *out of 319 in total* land area
202 *out of 319 in* population growth, *1970–1990*
 92 *out of 310 in having the lowest* unemployment *rate*
214 *out of 310 in size of* labor force
213 *out of 318 in the percentage of* college graduates
207 *out of 292 in per capita personal* income
202 *out of 319 in number of* manufacturing establishments
201 *out of 318 in* physicians *per 1000 people*
 67 *out of 318 in* hospital beds *per 1000 people*
 30 *out of 267 in fewest* crimes *per 1000 people*
100 *out of 266 in fewest* violent crimes *per 1000 people*
177 *out of 319 in per capita* federal funds and grants

Quality of Life Indexes (Rate per 1000 population)

Crime rate in 1991:	38.0
Violent crime rate in 1991:	4.9
Physicians rate in 1992:	1.62
Hospital bed rate in 1991:	5.18

ACCRA Cost of Living Indexes
(First quarter 1993, average = 100)
Composite index: 92.2
Utilities index: 85.1
Housing index: 83.4

Population (1990)

Total Population and Growth Rate
1990: 142,199
1980: 141,289
1970: 123,474
Growth rate 1970–1990: 15%

Race and Hispanic Origin
White: 78.0%
Black: 21.2%
Asian/Pacific Islander: 0.5%
Native American: 0.2%
Hispanic origin: 0.6%
White not Hispanic: 77.6%

Age
Ages 18 to 20: 6.5%
Ages 21 to 24: 6.6%
Ages 25 to 44: 29.8%
Ages 45 to 54: 10.7%
Ages 55 to 59: 4.7%
Ages 60 to 64: 4.6%
Ages 65 plus: 14%

Educational Attainment (1990)
Percent having completed high school: 66.1%
Percent having completed college: 16.4%
Elementary and high school enrollment: 22,479

Federal Funds and Grants Received
Total received in 1989: $432,500,000
Funds received per capita: $2,973

Civilian Labor Force
1993 (April): 80,640
1992 average: 78,493
1991 average: 77,468
1990 average: 75,038

Unemployment
1993 (April): 4.6%
1992 average: 5.9%
1991 average: 5.6%
1990 average: 4.8%

Average Annual Pay
1988: $18,910
1987: $18,399
1985: $16,796

Per Capita Personal Income
1991: $16,113
1990: $15,976
1989: $15,259

Business Climate (1987)

Manufacturing
Number of establishments in 1987: 229
Shipments in 1987 ($1,000): $2,380,800
Employees in 1987: 21,000
Change in employment, 1982 to 1987: -8.7%
Average annual pay for manufacturing work in 1989: $25,100
Average annual pay for production work in 1987: $19,575

Wholesale Trade
Number of establishments in 1987: 212
Total sales in 1987 ($1,000): $565,000
Change in sales, 1982 to 1987: 46.7%

Retail Trade
Number of establishments in 1987: 967
Total sales in 1987 ($1,000): $565,000
Retail sales per household in 1987: $17,124
Average annual pay in 1989: $10,836

Service Industry
Selected receipts in 1987 ($1,000): $358,400
Average annual pay in 1989: $16,644

Housing

Total number of units in 1990: 56,839
Occupied units in 1990: 52,922
Owner-occupied units in 1990: 68.5%
1993 ACCRA average cost: $96,833
1993 ACCRA average rent for an apartment: $413

Chamber of Commerce

Greater Lynchburg Chamber of Commerce, C. Parker Hardy, III, Exec. Vice President, PO Box 2027, Lynchburg, VA 24501. 804-845-5966

Economic Development Office

Lynchburg Office of Economic Development, V. Lee Cobb, Director, 900 Church St. 2nd Fl., PO Box 60, Lynchburg, VA 24505. 804-847-1732, FAX 804-845-4304

Major Businesses

Company	SIC	Telephone
Amherst Motors Inc.	5511	(804) 946-7761
Belgium Tool & Die Co.	3565	(804) 239-0358
Consolidated Shoe Co.	5139	(804) 239-0391
Craddock-Terry, Inc.	3143	(804) 847-3500
First Colony Life Insurance	6311	(804) 845-0911
First Federal Savings Bank of Lynchburg	6035	(804) 845-2371
Fleet C. B. Co. Inc.	2844	(804) 528-4000
Flowers Baking Co. of Lynchburg	2051	(804) 528-0441
Frances Denney, Inc.	2844	(804) 845-7073
Frazier Construction Co.	1542	(804) 847-5364
Lane Co. Inc.	2512	(804) 369-5641
Leggett of Virginia, Inc.	5311	(804) 845-6011
Limitorque Corp.	3491	(804) 528-4400
Lynchburg Gas Co.	4924	(804) 847-7721
Lynchburg Steel & Special	3441	(804) 929-0951
Peanut Corp. of America	5159	(804) 525-2618
Progress Printing Co.	2752	(804) 239-9213
Quality Foods Cooperative	5141	(804) 929-6515
Schewel Furniture Co.	5712	(804) 845-2326
Southern Air, Inc.	1711	(804) 385-6200
Watts Petroleum, Inc.	5171	(804) 846-6509

Colleges and Universities

Central Virginia Community College, Lynchburg
Liberty University, Lynchburg
Lynchburg College, Lynchburg
National Business College, Lynchburg
Randolph-Macon Woman's College, Lynchburg

NORFOLK–VIRGINIA BEACH–NEWPORT NEWS, VA (MSA)

Geographic Profile

Land Area
1685.4 square miles

Counties and Parishes
Gloucester
James City
York

Additional Cities/Towns within Area
Chesapeake
Hampton
Poquoson
Portsmouth
Suffolk
Virginia Beach
Williamsburg

Ranking Highlights

115 *out of 319 in total* land area
123 *out of 319 in* population growth, *1970–1990*
157 *out of 310 in having the lowest* unemployment *rate*
40 *out of 310 in size of* labor force
136 *out of 318 in the percentage of* college graduates
160 *out of 292 in per capita personal* income
72 *out of 319 in number of* manufacturing establishments
125 *out of 318 in* physicians *per 1000 people*
243 *out of 318 in* hospital beds *per 1000 people*
170 *out of 267 in fewest* crimes *per 1000 people*
134 *out of 266 in fewest* violent crimes *per 1000 people*
16 *out of 319 in per capita* federal funds and grants

Quality of Life Indexes (Rate per 1000 population)

Crime rate in 1991:   66.9
Violent crime rate in 1991:   6.4
Physicians rate in 1992:   1.98
Hospital bed rate in 1991:   2.99

ACCRA Cost of Living Indexes
(First quarter 1993, average = 100)
Composite index: 97.9
Utilities index: 123.4
Housing index: 90.6

Population (1990)

Total Population and Growth Rate
1990: 1,396,107
1980: 1,160,311
1970: 1,058,764
Growth rate 1970–1990: 32%

Race and Hispanic Origin

White: 67.8%
Black: 28.5%
Asian/Pacific Islander: 2.5%
Native American: 0.3%
Hispanic origin: 2.3%
White not Hispanic: 66.7%

Age

Ages 18 to 20: 5.7%
Ages 21 to 24: 8.1%
Ages 25 to 44: 34.8%
Ages 45 to 54: 8.9%
Ages 55 to 59: 3.6%
Ages 60 to 64: 3.5%
Ages 65 plus: 9%

Educational Attainment (1990)

Percent having completed high school: 79.1%
Percent having completed college: 20.1%
Elementary and high school enrollment: 234,941

Federal Funds and Grants Received

Total received in 1989: $9,559,700,000
Funds received per capita: $6,926

Civilian Labor Force

1993 (April): 676,963
1992 average: 663,556
1991 average: 648,387
1990 average: 626,396

Unemployment

1993 (April): 5.8%
1992 average: 6.9%
1991 average: 6.1%
1990 average: 4.7%

Average Annual Pay

1988: $18,982
1987: $18,268
1985: $16,827

Per Capita Personal Income

1991: $17,030
1990: $16,448
1989: $15,899

Business Climate (1987)

Manufacturing

Number of establishments in 1987: 912
Shipments in 1987 ($1,000): $9,075,100
Employees in 1987: 66,000
Change in employment, 1982 to 1987: 0%
Average annual pay for manufacturing work in 1989: $25,717
Average annual pay for production work in 1987: $21,648

Wholesale Trade

Number of establishments in 1987: 1,681

Total sales in 1987 ($1,000): $7,807,000
Change in sales, 1982 to 1987: 29.4%

Retail Trade

Number of establishments in 1987: 7,604
Total sales in 1987 ($1,000): $7,807,000
Retail sales per household in 1987: $19,023
Average annual pay in 1989: $10,484

Service Industry

Selected receipts in 1987 ($1,000): $3,548,600
Average annual pay in 1989: $17,399

Office Real Estate (1992)

Office space inventory: 15,514,918 square feet
Average class A Central Business District rental range per sq. ft: $16.00

Vacancy Rates

All areas: 12.9%

Vacancy Rates in Central Business District

Class A space: 11.9%
Class B space: 15.4%

Vacancy Rates Outside Central Business District

Class A space: 14.6%
Class B space: 11.9%

Housing

Total number of units in 1990: 537,101
Occupied units in 1990: 493,536
Owner-occupied units in 1990: 58.9%
1993 ACCRA average cost: N/A
1993 ACCRA average rent for an apartment: N/A

Chamber of Commerce

Hampton Roads-Headquarters Chamber of Commerce, John A. Hornbeck, Jr., President, 420 Banks St., PO Box 327, Norfolk, VA 23510. 804-622-2312

Economic Development Office

Forward Hampton Roads, Gregory H. Wingfield, President, 1214 First Virginia Bank Tower, 555 Main St., Norfolk, VA 23510. 804-627-2315, FAX 804-627-3081

Economic Development Organizations

Virginia Beach Department of Economic Development, Director, 770 Lymnhaven Parkway Suite 200, Virginia Beach, VA 23452. 804-498-4567, FAX 804-498-7263

Virginia Peninsula Economic Development Council, J.A. Denton, III, President, 825 Diligence Dr. Suite 114, PO Box 12227, Newport News, VA 23612. 804-873-0000, FAX 804-873-1073

Major Businesses

Company	SIC	Telephone
Birdsong Corp.	5159	(804) 539-3456
Bon Secour-Maryview Health	8062	(804) 398-2200
Bonnie Be-Lo Markets Inc.	5411	(804) 855-1021

Major Businesses (Continued)

Company	SIC	Telephone
Camellia Food Stores, Inc.	5411	(804) 855-3371
Farm Fresh Inc.	5411	(804) 480-6700
Landmark Communications	2711	(804) 446-2010
Marketplace Foods Inc.	5411	(804) 490-0413
Military Distributors	5141	(804) 855-0114
Miller Oil Co. Inc.	5172	(804) 543-5751
Norfolk and Western Railway Co.	4011	(804) 629-2600
Norfolk Shipbuilding Drydock	3731	(804) 494-4000
Norfolk Southern Corp.	4011	(804) 629-2600
Royster Co.	2874	(804) 622-4783
Sentara Health System	8062	(804) 455-7020
Sentara Hospitals	8062	(804) 455-7110
Sovran Financial Corp.	6021	(804) 441-4000
Tarmac Virginia, Inc.	3273	(804) 853-6701
Telecable Corp.	4841	(804) 624-5000
Tidewater Construction Co.	1622	(804) 420-4140
Virginia Natural Gas Inc.	4924	(804) 466-5400

Colleges and Universities

Christopher Newport College, Newport News
Commonwealth College, Norfolk, Norfolk
Commonwealth College, Virginia Beach, Virginia Beach
Commonwealth College, Hampton, Hampton
Hampton University, Hampton
Norfolk State University, Norfolk
Old Dominion University, Norfolk
Thomas Nelson Community College, Hampton
Tidewater Community College, Virginia Beach Campus, Virginia Beach
Tidewater Community College, Chesapeake Campus, Chesapeake
Virginia Wesleyan College, Norfolk

RICHMOND–PETERSBURG, VA (MSA)

Geographic Profile

Land Area
2944.7 square miles

Counties and Parishes
Charles City
Chesterfield
Dinwiddie
Goochland
Hanover
Henrico
New Kent
Powhatan
Prince George

Additional Cities/Towns within Area
Colonial Heights
Hopewell

Ranking Highlights

47 *out of 319 in total* land area
144 *out of 319 in* population growth, *1970–1990*
114 *out of 310 in having the lowest* unemployment *rate*
54 *out of 310 in size of* labor force
71 *out of 318 in the percentage of* college graduates
31 *out of 292 in per capita personal* income
67 *out of 319 in number of* manufacturing establishments
52 *out of 318 in* physicians *per 1000 people*
107 *out of 318 in* hospital beds *per 1000 people*
146 *out of 267 in fewest* crimes *per 1000 people*
125 *out of 266 in fewest* violent crimes *per 1000 people*
122 *out of 319 in per capita* federal funds and grants

Quality of Life Indexes (Rate per 1000 population)

Crime rate in 1991:	62.3
Violent crime rate in 1991:	5.9
Physicians rate in 1992:	2.7
Hospital bed rate in 1991:	4.56

ACCRA Cost of Living Indexes

(First quarter 1993, average = 100)
Composite index: 110.4
Utilities index: 118.3
Housing index: 102.8

Overview

Manufacturing, services, government, and retail trade account for about 20 percent each of all jobs in the Richmond area. Other major blocks of employment are in wholesale trade; in transportation, communications, and public utilities; and in finance, insurance, and real estate. More than one-third of Virginia's primary metal employment is concentrated in the Richmond area, as is 24 percent of the state's printing industry. The chemical industry in Chesterfield County alone accounts for approximately 20 percent of Virginia's chemical employment.

Richmond, as headquarters of the Fifth Federal Reserve District, is a financial nerve center for an industrially strong and diverse region that consists of Maryland, Virginia, West Virginia, North Carolina, South Carolina, and the District of Columbia. Banking has always been a significant employment factor in the Richmond area, and liberalization of banking laws has increased the centralization of headquarters activity in the Richmond area by many of the state's large and regionally oriented banks.

Insurance is also a strong, steady growth industry in the Richmond area. Richmond is headquarters for Life Insurance Company of Virginia, Lawyers Title Insurance Corporation, Fidelity Bankers Life Insurance Company, Home Beneficial Life Insurance Company, Virginia Farm Bureau Mutual Insurance Company, Blue Cross and Blue Shield of Virginia, and Mutual Assurance Company of Virginia.

As for manufacturing concerns, an increasing number of European and Japanese companies like Maruchan, The Wella Corporation, Alfa-Laval Thermal, San-Jirushi Corporation, Wako Chemicals, Hohnore Incorporated, Hauni-Werke, Fiorucci Foods, and G. D. Packaging Machinery, a subsidiary of Degremont, have been attracted to the area in recent years.

Philip Morris, which began in tobacco production, has been a part of Richmond's business community since 1929. Richmond's $200 million Philip Morris Manufacturing Center today is the largest and most modern facility of its kind in the world. Located on a 200-acre site, the 1.6-million-square-foot facility represents the largest single capital investment in Philip Morris history. Richmond has become a major East Coast distribution center and customer service center with the arrival of firms like G.E. Lighting, Mazda Motor of America, J. C. Penney, and Time-Life Books.

Other major companies with substantial capital investment in plants and operations in the Richmond area are DuPont, Allied Corporation, RJR Nabisco, ICI Americas and Bear Island Paper Company, as well as AT&T Technology Systems, with a plant in Henrico County that produces circuit boards. With thirteen *Fortune* 500 headquarters in the city, Richmond is the eighth largest *Fortune* 500 city in the nation. Many of these firms have substantial operations in Richmond. They include Reynolds Metals Company, Ethyl Corporation, C S X Corporation, University Corporation and Dominion Resources. Richmond also is home for firms like Circuit City Stores, Best Products, and Hamilton Beach/Proctor-Silex.

According to the November 4, 1991 *Fortune* magazine review of the best cities for business, "Richmond scores well for its lack of environmental problems and stable fiscal situation."

More than seventy trucking companies, including home-based Overnite, the nation's largest nonunion trucker, serve the Richmond area. Overnight or one-day service is provided within a 500-mile radius to cities such as Atlanta, Georgia, Boston, Massachusetts, New York City, Philadelphia, Pennsylvania, and Washington, D.C. Richmond is also served by thirty courier and business delivery firms.

Three rail lines converge in Richmond: the Richmond, Fredericksburg & Potomac, and the Norfolk CSX Southern. CSX Corporation, the nation's largest railroad, has its corporate headquarters in Richmond.

Richmond is a United Parcel Service (UPS) hub. All major airlines offer air-cargo service and air-freight service is provided by Airborne, Bedmon & Lassitor, Emery, Federal Express, CCX Express, Burlington, DHL, and UPS.

Richmond's deep-water port facilities were rudimentary until recent years. Tobacco constituted the major cargo, and Richmond had the East Coast's only livestock-handling facility (still true today).

Eleven airlines with nonstop and direct flights to more than two hundred cities serve Richmond International Airport, which is located twelve minutes, via Interstate 64, from the center city. General and corporate aviation services are also available at the Chesterfield County Airport.

Crisscrossing the metropolitan area are major north-south and east-west interstates. Interstate 95 provides ready access to markets up and down the East Coast. I-64 is a major corridor from St. Louis, Missouri, to the port of Hampton Roads. I-295 connects with I-95 to the north and south of Richmond.

Population (1990)

Total Population and Growth Rate

1990: 865,640
1980: 761,311
1970: 676,351
Growth rate 1970–1990: 28%

Race and Hispanic Origin

White: 68.8%
Black: 29.2%
Asian/Pacific Islander: 1.4%
Native American: 0.3%
Hispanic origin: 1.1%
White not Hispanic: 68.2%

Age

Ages 18 to 20: 4.6%
Ages 21 to 24: 6%
Ages 25 to 44: 35.1%
Ages 45 to 54: 10.5%
Ages 55 to 59: 4.1%
Ages 60 to 64: 4.1%
Ages 65 plus: 11.3%

Educational Attainment (1990)

Percent having completed high school: 75.8%

Percent having completed college: 23.8%
Elementary and high school enrollment: 139,874

Federal Funds and Grants Received
Total received in 1989: $2,842,300,000
Funds received per capita: $3,367

Civilian Labor Force
1993 (April):   486,954
1992 average: 477,961
1991 average: 473,879
1990 average: 459,350

Unemployment
1993 (April):   4.9%
1992 average: 6.2%
1991 average: 5.4%
1990 average: 3.9%

Average Annual Pay
1988: $21,293
1987: $20,374
1985: $18,566

Per Capita Personal Income
1991: $21,416
1990: $21,310
1989: $20,327

Business Climate (1987)

Manufacturing
Number of establishments in 1987: 1,002
Shipments in 1987 ($1,000): $11,776,100
Employees in 1987: 66,400
Change in employment, 1982 to 1987: 0%
Average annual pay for manufacturing work in 1989: $31,758
Average annual pay for production work in 1987: $24,772

Wholesale Trade
Number of establishments in 1987: 1,753
Total sales in 1987 ($1,000): $11,773,000
Change in sales, 1982 to 1987: 61.2%

Retail Trade
Number of establishments in 1987: 4,959
Total sales in 1987 ($1,000): $11,773,000
Retail sales per household in 1987: $19,832
Average annual pay in 1989: $12,901

Service Industry
Selected receipts in 1987 ($1,000): $2,975,500
Average annual pay in 1989: $18,166

Office Real Estate (1992)
Office space inventory: 17,670,559 square feet
Average class A Central Business District rental range per sq. ft: $21.50

Vacancy Rates
All areas: 18.9%

Vacancy Rates in Central Business District
Class A space: 13.9%
Class B space: 29.6%

Vacancy Rates Outside Central Business District
Class A space: 17.5%
Class B space: N/A

Housing
Total number of units in 1990: 355,467
Occupied units in 1990: 331,824
Owner-occupied units in 1990: 65.0%
1993 ACCRA average cost: $113,406
1993 ACCRA average rent for an apartment: $568

Chamber of Commerce
Metro Richmond Chamber of Commerce, Paul Ellsworth, President, 201 E. Franklin St., PO Box 12324, Richmond, VA 23241-0324. 804-648-1234

Economic Development Office
Industrial Development Authority of the County of Henrico, Frederick Agostino, Exec. Director, 4120 E. Parham Rd., PO Box 27032, Richmond, VA 23288. 804-747-4212, FAX 804-672-0104

Economic Development Organizations
Metro Economic Development Council, A.J. Christopher Wood, Exec Director, 201 East Franklin Street, Richmond, VA 23219. 804-643-3227

City of Richmond, Office of Economic Development, Ronald E. Foster, Acting Director, 900 E. Broad St. Room 305, Richmond, VA 23219. 804-780-5633, FAX 804-780-6793

Major Businesses

Company	SIC	Telephone
American Home Funding, Inc.	6162	(804) 965-6700
Blue Cross Blue Shield	6324	(804) 359-7000
Chesapeake Corp.	2621	(804) 697-1000
Chesapeake Telephone Co. Virginia	4813	(804) 772-2000
Circuit City Stores Inc.	5731	(804) 527-4000
Crestar Bank	6022	(804) 782-5000
Crestar Financial Corp.	6022	(804) 782-5000
CSX Corp.	4011	(804) 782-1400
Dominion Resources Inc.	4911	(804) 775-5700
Ethyl Corp.	2869	(804) 788-5000
Federal Reserve Bank of Richmond	6011	(804) 697-8000
Fidelity Bankers Life Insurance	6311	(804) 323-1011
General Medical Corp.	5047	(804) 264-7500
James River Corp. Virginia	2621	(804) 644-5411
James River Paper Co.	2621	(804) 644-5411
Life Insurance Co. of Virginia	6311	(804) 281-6000
Massey, A. T. Coal Co.,	1221	(804) 788-1800
Media General, Inc.	2711	(804) 649-6000

Major Businesses (Continued)

Company	SIC	Telephone
Overnite Transport Co.	4213	(804) 231-8000
Owens & Minor, Inc.	5047	(804) 747-9794
Reynolds International, Inc.	3334	(804) 281-2000
Reynolds Metals Co.	3411	(804) 281-2000
Richfood, Inc.	5141	(804) 746-6000
Richfood Holdings, Inc.	5141	(804) 746-6000
Signet Banking Corp.	6022	(804) 747-2000
Sovran Bank National Association	6021	(804) 788-2000
Universal Leaf Tobacco Co.	5159	(804) 359-9311
Virginia Electric & Power Co.	4911	(804) 771-3000

Colleges and Universities

Commonwealth College, Richmond, Richmond
J. Sargeant Reynolds Community College, Richmond
Richard Bland College, Petersburg
University of Richmond, Richmond
Virginia Commonwealth University, Richmond
Virginia State University, Petersburg
Virginia Union University, Richmond

ROANOKE, VA (MSA)

Geographic Profile

Land Area
850.8 square miles

Counties and Parishes
Botetourt
Roanoke

Additional Cities/Towns within Area
Salem

Ranking Highlights

227 *out of 319 in total* **land area**
216 *out of 319 in* **population growth,** *1970–1990*
 60 *out of 310 in having the lowest* **unemployment** *rate*
159 *out of 310 in size of* **labor force**
174 *out of 318 in the percentage of* **college graduates**
 63 *out of 292 in per capita personal* **income**
169 *out of 319 in number of* **manufacturing establishments**
 35 *out of 318 in* **physicians** *per 1000 people*
 44 *out of 318 in* **hospital beds** *per 1000 people*
104 *out of 267 in fewest* **crimes** *per 1000 people*
 74 *out of 266 in fewest* **violent crimes** *per 1000 people*
162 *out of 319 in per capita* **federal funds and grants**

Quality of Life Indexes (Rate per 1000 population)

Crime rate in 1991:	55.4
Violent crime rate in 1991:	4.0
Physicians rate in 1992:	2.88
Hospital bed rate in 1991:	5.62

ACCRA Cost of Living Indexes
(First quarter 1993, average = 100)

Composite index:	93.1
Utilities index:	86.1
Housing index:	87.1

Overview

Roanoke is located at the southern end of the Shenandoah Valley, approximately 170 miles west of Richmond and 235 miles southwest of Washington, DC. Two-thirds of the population of the United States is within a 500 mile radius. Lying at the region's crossroads of major rail and highway systems, the city serves as the principal trade, industrial, transportation, medical and cultural center of western Virginia.

In May of 1993, a ground breaking for Transkrit Corporation occurred at the Roanoke Centre for Industry and Technology (RCIT). This manufacturer of business forms will build a 105,000 square foot building, invest $9 million and employ 175, while bringing its headquarters and manufacturing plant to the area. Another company at RCIT, Vitramon, Incorporated, is in the process of expanding. Its 50,000 square foot, $21 million addition was helped by a

$350,000 grant from the Governor's Opportunity Fund and $150,000 from the city for site preparation. Roanoke competed with Mexico and Singapore for this expansion, but won out because of its excellent work force. Vitramon expects to add 200 jobs.

In August, Retired Persons Services (RPS) announced their plans to buy the recently closed Sears Telemarketing Center. The company contracts with AARP to run its mail order pharmacy. Although the total number of jobs was not specified at the announcement, plans are to hire displaced workers from Sears Telecatalog. Employment is expected to be more than 600.

Under construction in the city is the $5 million trash transfer station. This facility will receive trash from members of the new Regional Landfill Resource Authority and load it onto railroad cars for its once daily trip to the Smith Mountain landfill. Plans call for startup of this state-of-the-art plant in October 1993.

Population (1990)

Total Population and Growth Rate
1990: 224,477
1980: 220,393
1970: 199,629
Growth rate 1970–1990: 12%

Race and Hispanic Origin
White: 86.7%
Black: 12.3%
Asian/Pacific Islander: 0.7%
Native American: 0.1%
Hispanic origin: 0.6%
White not Hispanic: 86.3%

Age
Ages 18 to 20: 4.4%
Ages 21 to 24: 5.3%
Ages 25 to 44: 32.2%
Ages 45 to 54: 11%
Ages 55 to 59: 4.8%
Ages 60 to 64: 5.1%
Ages 65 plus: 15.2%

Educational Attainment (1990)
Percent having completed high school: 73.4%
Percent having completed college: 18.1%
Elementary and high school enrollment: 33,492

Federal Funds and Grants Received
Total received in 1989: $676,700,000
Funds received per capita: $3,054

Civilian Labor Force
1993 (April): 133,449
1992 average: 130,225
1991 average: 128,978
1990 average: 123,805

Unemployment
1993 (April): 4.4%
1992 average: 5.2%
1991 average: 4.8%
1990 average: 3.5%

Average Annual Pay
1988: $18,562
1987: $17,654
1985: $16,520

Per Capita Personal Income
1991: $19,417
1990: $19,245
1989: $17,993

Business Climate (1987)

Manufacturing
Number of establishments in 1987: 287
Shipments in 1987 ($1,000): $2,012,200
Employees in 1987: 20,300
Change in employment, 1982 to 1987: 0%
Average annual pay for manufacturing work in 1989: $25,129
Average annual pay for production work in 1987: $18,232

Wholesale Trade
Number of establishments in 1987: 575
Total sales in 1987 ($1,000): $2,527,400
Change in sales, 1982 to 1987: 34.9%

Retail Trade
Number of establishments in 1987: 1,721
Total sales in 1987 ($1,000): $2,527,400
Retail sales per household in 1987: $20,306
Average annual pay in 1989: $11,204

Service Industry
Selected receipts in 1987 ($1,000): $692,200
Average annual pay in 1989: $17,384

Office Real Estate (1992)
Office space inventory: 2,386,442 square feet
Average class A Central Business District rental range per sq. ft: $14.00

Vacancy Rates
All areas: 17.9%

Vacancy Rates in Central Business District
Class A space: 13.0%
Class B space: 62.4%

Vacancy Rates Outside Central Business District
Class A space: 19.5%
Class B space: 12.2%

Housing
Total number of units in 1990: 95,467
Occupied units in 1990: 89,694
Owner-occupied units in 1990: 67.7%
1993 ACCRA average cost: $100,152

1993 ACCRA average rent for an apartment: $430

Chamber of Commerce

Roanoke Regional Chamber of Commerce, C. Thom Robinson, Exec. Vice President, PO Box 0700, Roanoke, VA 24007-0700. 703-983-0700

Economic Development Office

City of Roanoke, Department of Economic Development, Brian Wishneff, Chief, Room 355, Municipal Bldg., 215 Church Ave. S.W., Roanoke, VA 24011. 703-981-2715, FAX 703-981-2773

Economic Development Organizations

Regional Partnership of Roanoke Valley, Mark D. Heath, Exec. Director, 111 Franklin #333, Roanoke, VA 24001. 703-343-1550

Major Businesses

Company	SIC	Telephone
Advance Stores Co. Inc.	5531	(703) 345-4911
Allred Chevrolet Inc.	5511	(703) 562-2001
Appalachian Power Co.	4911	(703) 985-2300
Avis Construction Co, Inc.	1542	(703) 982-3558
Bellsouth Commuter Systems	5065	(703) 983-6000
Blue Ridge Transfer Compay	4213	(703) 342-1835
Brabham Petroleum Co.	5541	(703) 345-6267
Branch Group Inc.	1542	(703) 989-5215
Branch Highways, Inc.	1611	(703) 989-1678
Carilion Health System	8062	(703) 981-7000
Community Hospital of Roanoke Virginia	8062	(703) 985-8000
Dominion Bankshares Corp.	6021	(703) 563-7000
Dominion Bank of Cumberland	6021	(703) 563-7000
Fuel Oil & Equipment Co., Inc.	5032	(703) 345-8866
Grand Piano & Furniture Co.	5712	(703) 343-1701
Halmode Apparel Inc.	2335	(703) 563-2801
Hancock, John W. Jr. Inc.	3441	(703) 389-0211
Hart Motor Co. Inc.	5511	(703) 389-2364
Heironimus S. H. Co., Inc.	5311	(703) 343-6941
Magic City Motor Corp.	5511	(703) 345-0911
Petroleum Marketers Inc.	5983	(703) 362-4900
Roanoke Electric Steel Co.	3312	(703) 342-1831
Roanoke Gas Co.	4924	(703) 344-6651
Roanoke Memorial Hospital	8062	(703) 981-7000
Rowe Furniture Corp. Nevad	2512	(703) 389-8671
Shenandoah Life Insurance Co.	6311	(703) 985-4400
Stop In Food Stores Inc.	5411	(703) 288-4877
Valley Rich Dairy	5143	(703) 344-5143
Valleydale Packers Inc.	2013	(703) 389-5473
Virginia Holding Corp.	6552	(703) 981-4611
Wabash Railroad Co.	6517	(703) 981-4000
Webb's Oil Corp.	5172	(703) 362-3795
Woodson Pontiac Inc.	5511	(703) 366-8888

Colleges and Universities

Community Hospital of Roanoke Valley-College of Health Sciences, Roanoke
Hollins College, Roanoke
National Business College, Roanoke
Roanoke College, Salem
Virginia Institute of Hospitality, Salem
Virginia Western Community College, Roanoke

WASHINGTON

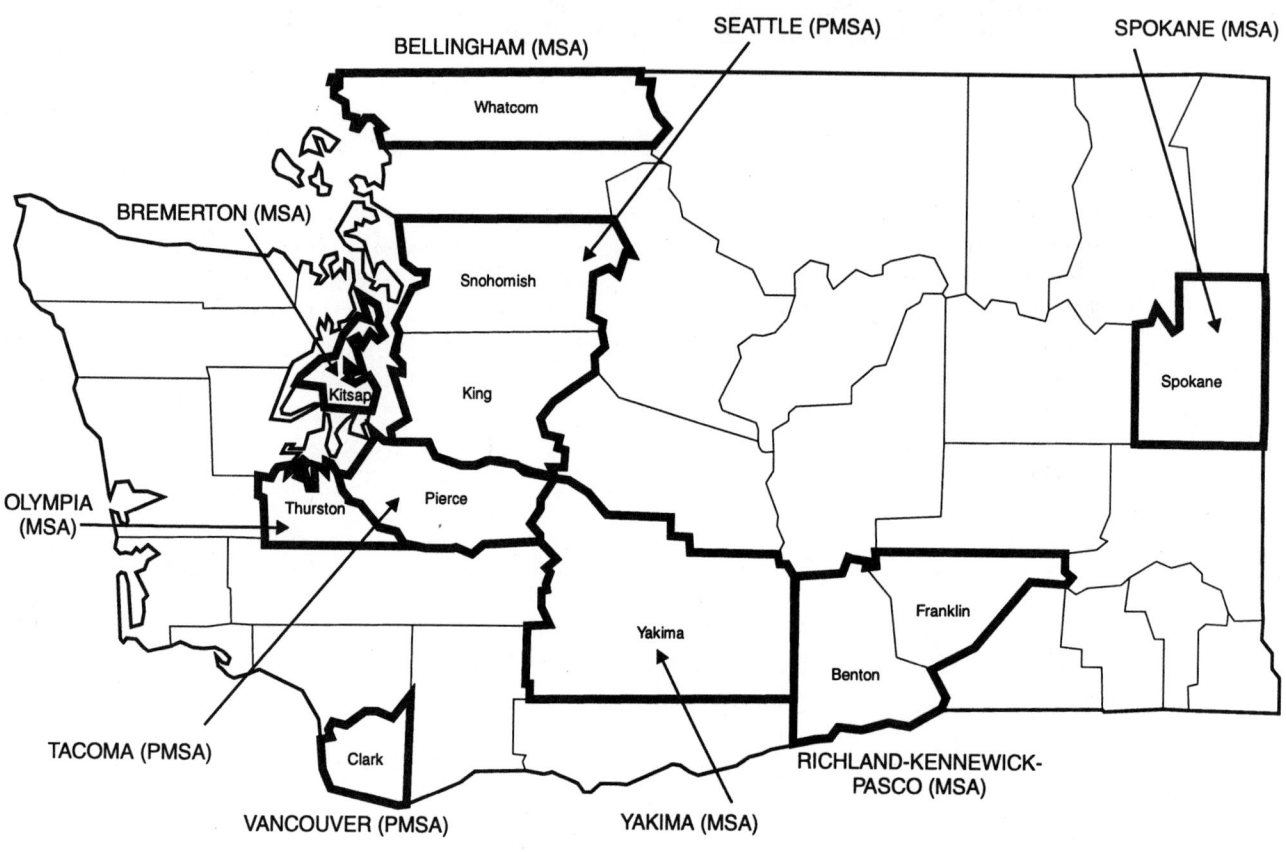

BELLINGHAM (MSA)

SEATTLE (PMSA)

SPOKANE (MSA)

Whatcom

BREMERTON (MSA)

Snohomish

Spokane

Kitsap

King

OLYMPIA
(MSA)

Thurston

Pierce

Franklin

Yakima

Benton

TACOMA (PMSA)

Clark

RICHLAND-KENNEWICK-
PASCO (MSA)

VANCOUVER (PMSA)

YAKIMA (MSA)

WASHINGTON

Population
1990: 4,866,692
1980: 4,132,156

Age
Ages 18 to 20: 210,809
Ages 21 to 24: 277,730
Ages 25 to 44: 1,658,951
Ages 45 to 54: 501,543
Ages 55 to 59: 191,602
Ages 60 to 64: 189,382
Median age: 33.1

Race and Hispanic Origin
White: 4,308,937
Black: 149,801
Asian/Pacific Islander: 210,958
Native American: 81,483
Hispanic origin: 214,570

Households
Total: 1,872,431
Persons per household: 2.53

Sex
Male: 2,413,747
Female: 2,452,945

Population Migration
Domestic migration: 320,000
International migration: 83,000

Projection of the Population in 1995
Total: 5,045,000
18 to 64: 3,142,000

Civilian Labor Force
1993: 2,593,000
1992: 2,534,200
1991: 2,500,300
1990: 2,479,900

Manufacturing
1995 Projection: 377,700
1992: 346,300
1991: 359,000
1990: 365,800
1989: 366,400

Services
1995 Projection: 754,800

1992: 554,100
1991: 530,100
1990: 525,800
1989: 486,900

Wholesale and Retail Trade
1995 Projection: 606,100
1992: 537,900
1991: 522,000
1990: 535,700
1989: 522,600

Unemployment Rate
1993: 9.2%
1992: 8.2%
1991: 5.9%
1990: 6.1%

Employer Unemployment Contributions
Contribution Rate
1992: 2.30%
1991: 2.30%
1990: 2.30%

Average Weekly Benefit
1992: $182.13
1991: $180.36
1990: $170.09

Gross State Product (Million $)
1989: $96,233
1988: $87,864
1987: $81,503
1979: $47,933
Growth rate, 1979 to 1989: 100.8%

Capital Expenditures of Manufacturing Industries
1990: $2,207,800,000
1989: $2,264,600,000
1988: $1,172,900,000
1987: $1,244,800,000

State Tax Rates
Individual income: None.
Corporate income: None.
General property: Sum of state and local rates. Assessed value is 100% of the true and fair cash value of real and

tangible personal property.
General sales: 6.5%
Gasoline: 23¢ per gallon

Income

Median income for a 4 person family: $41,728

Personal per Capita Income

1992: $20,398
1991: $19,521
1990: $18,738

Disposable per Capita Income

1992: $18,038
1991: $17,170
1990: $16,378

Private Employment Weekly Wages

Average

1989: $404
1988: $389
1987: $389

Manufacturing

1989: $376
1988: $557
1987: $543

Services

1989: $337
1988: $321
1987: $311

Wholesale

1989: $494
1988: $477
1987: $457

Retail

1989: $237
1988: $226
1987: $219

Highway Statistics

Total Highway Miles

1990: 81,299
1989: 81,439
1988: 81,546

Federal Highway Aid

1991: $224,603,000
1990: $233,930,000
1989: $278,705,000

Electricity

Average Cost per Kilowatt Hour
1990: 3.48¢
1989: 3.58¢
1988: 3.44¢

Housing (1990)

Owner occupied units: 1,171,580

Median house value: $93,400
Renter occupied units: 700,851
Median rent: $383
Total vacant units: 159,947
Homeowner vacancy rate: 1.3%
Rental vacancy rate: 5.8%

State Business Incentives and Assistance

Financial and Business Assistance

Community Economic Revitalization Board. Administered by the Department of Trade and Economic Development, this Board provides grants and loans to finance local community infrastructure improvements required for private sector development. The funds are awarded as low-cost loans to local governments on an as-needed basis for public works projects.

Development Loan Fund. Administered by the Department of Community Development, this fund is mainly created to provide loans to businesses in distressed areas to assist in reducing unemployment. Loans up to $700,000 may be made.

Job Creation Tax Credit. Growing companies, located in distressed areas and increasing their employment level in a calendar year by 15% over the previous year, may received a tax credit against their state business and occupation tax. For each new full-time position created, the business can take a credit of $1,000.

New Industry Sales Tax Deferral Program. This program is designed to assist the start-up of new businesses and the attraction of new industry to the state.

Distressed Area Sales Tax Deferral Program. Eligible manufacturing, computer service, or research and development investments include expansions or modernizations of existing facilities, as well as start-ups and new locations. The deferral is limited to that portion of the capital investment that creates at least one full-time employees for each $300,000 invested.

Small Business Incubators. Administered by the Department of Community Development, this program program is designed to encourage start-ups for high-growth technology firms. The incubator facility allows businesses to test and perfect production processes on prototype scale.

Education and Training

Job Skills Program. Administered by the State Board for Vocational Education, this program provides grants for customized, quick-start training and retraining projects that have at least 50% matching support from the private sector. The match may include cash, donated or loaned equipment, instructional time contributed by company personnel, use of company facilities, or training materials.

Job Training Partnership Act. This program operates with funding from the U.S. Department of Labor. It provides job training and other employment related services.

Major Companies in the State

Company name	Fortune 500 rank	City	Telephone	SIC number
Fortune 500 Companies				
Boeing Co.	12	Seattle	206-655-2121	3721
Burlington Resources Inc.	251	Seattle	206-467-3838	1311
Longview Fibre Co.	444	Longview	206-425-1550	2653
Paccar Inc.	171	Bellevue	206-455-7400	3537
Weyerhaeuser Co.	51	Tacoma	206-924-2345	2621
Other Major Companies in the State				
Airborne Freight Corp.		Seattle	206-285-4600	4513
Alaska Air Group Inc.		Seattle	206-431-7040	4512
Costco Wholesale Corp.		Kirkland	206-828-8100	5399
Egghead Inc.		Issaquah	206-391-0800	5734
GTE Northwest Inc.		Everett	206-261-5321	4813
Hillhaven Corp.		Tacoma	206-572-4901	8051
Mccaw Cellular Communications Inc.		Kirkland	206-827-4500	4812
Microsoft Corp.		Redmond	206-882-8080	7373
Nordstrom Inc.		Seattle	206-628-2111	5331
Pacific Northwest Bell Telephone Co.		Seattle	303-896-3099	4813
Pacific Telecom Inc.		Vancouver	206-696-0983	4813
Pay N Pak Stores Inc.		Kent	206-854-5450	5211
PNP Prime Corp.		Kent	206-854-5450	5251
Puget Sound Bancorp		Tacoma	206-593-3600	6712
Puget Sound Power & Light Co.		Bellevue	206-454-6363	4911
Safeco Corp.		Seattle	206-545-5000	6331
Seafirst Corp.		Seattle	206-358-3000	6712
Univar Corp.		Kirkland	206-889-3400	5169
Washington Mutual Savings Bank		Seattle	206-464-4400	6035
Washington Water Power Co.		Spokane	509-489-0500	4931

State Offices

Real estate: Real Estate Division, Director, 1100 Olive Way, Suite 1450, Seattle, WA 98105. 206-464-6416

Chamber of commerce: Association of Washington Business, Don Brunell, President, 1414 South Cherry, PO Box 658, Olympia, WA 98507. 206-943-1600, FAX 206-943-5811

Economic development: Department of Trade & Economic Development, Paul Isaki, Acting Director, 101 General Administration Bldg., Olympia, WA 98504. 206-753-5630

Department of Community Development, Director, Ninth and Columbia Building, GH-51, Olympia, WA 98504-4151. 206-586-8976

Business Assistance Center, David Dougherty, Director, 919 Lakeridge Way SW, Olympia, WA 98502. 206-753-5632

Small Business Development Center, Lyle M. Anderson, State Director, Washington State University, College of Business and Economics, Pullman, WA 99164. 509-335-1576

Environmental affairs: Ecology Department, Christine Gre-goire, Director, MS PV-11, Olympia, WA 98504. 206-459-6168

Labor: Labor and Industries Department, Joseph Dear, Director, General Administration Bldg., HC-101, Olympia, WA 98504. 206-753-6307

Unemployment: Employment Security Department, Unemployment Insurance Division, Isreal David Mendoza, Director, 212 Maple Park, Olympia, WA 98504. 206-753-5120

Worker's compensation: Labor and Industries Department, Workers Benefits Section, Ronald Gray, Director, General Administration Bldg., HC-101, Olympia, WA 98504. 206-753-6376

Occupational safety and health: Industrial Safety and Health Division, Alan S. Paja, Assistant Director, PO Box 207, Olympia, WA 98504. 206-753-6500

Secretary of state: Secretary of State, Ralph Munro, Secretary of State, Legislative Bldg., AS-22, Olympia, WA 98504-9000. 206-753-7121

Taxation and revenue: Revenue Department, Dennis I. Okamoto, Director, 415 General Administration Bldg., AX-02, Olympia, WA 98504. 206-753-5574

Designated Zones for Economic Development

Enterprise Zones

No program.

Foreign Trade Zones

Foreign Trade Zone No. 129, Bellingham, Washington, Grantee: Port of Bellingham, Bob Hilpert, PO Box 1737, Bellingham, WA 98227-1737, 206-676-2500

Foreign Trade Zone No. 130, Blaine, Washington, Grantee: Port of Bellingham, Bob Hilpert, PO Box 1737, Bellingham, WA 98227-1737, 206-676-2500

Foreign Trade Zone No. 120, Cowlitz County, Washington, Grantee: Cowlitz Economic Development Council, John C. Thompson, 1338 Commerce, Suite 211, Longview, WA 98632, 206-423-9921

Foreign Trade Zone No. 85, Everett, Washington, Grantee: Puget Sound Foreign-Trade Zone Association, c/o Port of Tacoma, Jerry Ahmann, PO Box 1837, Tacoma, WA 98401-1837, 206-383-5841

Foreign Trade Zone No. 173, Grays Harbor, Washington, Grantee: Port of Grays Harbor, Clifford C. Muller, PO Box 660, Aberdeen, WA 98520-0141, 206-533-9528

Foreign Trade Zone No. 5, Seattle, Washington, Grantee/ Operator: Port of Seattle Commission, Howard Granger, 2700 13th Avenue SW, Seattle, WA 98134, 206-728-3666

Foreign Trade Zone No. 131, Sumas, Washington, Grantee: Port of Bellingham, Bob Hilpert, PO Box 1737, Bellingham, WA 98227-1737, 206-676-2500

Foreign Trade Zone No. 86, Tacoma, Washington, Grantee: Port of Tacoma, Jerry Ahmann, PO Box 1837, Tacoma, WA 98401-1837, 206-383-5841

Foreign Trade Zone No. 128, Whatcom County, Washington, Grantee: Lummi Indian Business Council, Tim Hostetler, 2616 Kwina, Bellingham, WA 98266, 206-734-8180

Labor Unions

Carpenters and Joiners of America, United Brotherhood of (AFL-CIO)

Electrical Workers, International Brotherhood of (AFL-CIO)

Fire Fighters, International Association of (AFL-CIO)

Food and Commercial Workers International Union, United (AFL-CIO)

Hospital and Health Care Employees

Laborers' International Union of North America (AFL-CIO)

National Education Association

Nurses' Association, American

Operating Engineers, International Union of (AFL-CIO)

Professional and Technical Employees

Seattle Police Officers Guild

Tacoma Association of Classroom Teachers

Teachers, American Federation of (AFL-CIO)

Woodworkers of America, International (AFL-CIO)

Universities with Ph.D. Programs

Bastyr College, Seattle

Gonzaga University, Spokane

Seattle University, Seattle

University of Washington, Seattle

BELLINGHAM, WA (MSA)

Geographic Profile
Land Area
2120.1 square miles

Counties and Parishes
Whatcom

Ranking Highlights
  84 *out of 319 in total* **land area**
  66 *out of 319 in* **population growth,** *1970–1990*
191 *out of 310 in having the lowest* **unemployment** *rate*
227 *out of 310 in size of* **labor force**
  97 *out of 318 in the percentage of* **college graduates**
174 *out of 292 in per capita personal* **income**
198 *out of 319 in number of* **manufacturing establishments**
183 *out of 318 in* **physicians** *per 1000 people*
314 *out of 318 in* **hospital beds** *per 1000 people*
102 *out of 267 in fewest* **crimes** *per 1000 people*
  51 *out of 266 in fewest* **violent crimes** *per 1000 people*
  35 *out of 319 in per capita* **federal funds and grants**

Quality of Life Indexes (Rate per 1000 population)
Crime rate in 1991:	55.1
Violent crime rate in 1991:	3.2
Physicians rate in 1992:	1.72
Hospital bed rate in 1991:	1.67

ACCRA Cost of Living Indexes
(First quarter 1993, average = 100)
Composite index:	105.2
Utilities index:	59.7
Housing index:	114.1

Overview
Whatcom County is located in the northwest corner of Washington State. It is bound to the north by British Columbia, Canada, the west by the Puget Sound waterway, the south by Skagit County, and the east by Okanogan County. Major roadways include Interstate 5 and State Routes 9, 539 and 542. Bellingham is the largest city and county seat of Whatcom County, which is 61 miles north of Everett, 89 miles north of Seattle and approximately 60 miles south of Vancouver, Canada. The eastern portion of Whatcom County consists of the Mt. Baker Wilderness area and a part of the North Cascades National Park, all of which are rugged mountainous areas. The terrain of the western portion varies with farmlands in the northern section and rolling hills and mountain foothills in the eastern section, with significant areas of level terrain throughout. Elevation of the county ranges from sea level to a high of 10,778 on Mt. Baker.

The major employer in the area is Western Washington University with 1,475 employees. It is followed by the aluminum producer Intalco with 1,300 employers.

The Bellingham International Airport has a 5,000 ft. asphalt runway and services Horizon, Alaska, and United Express airlines.

The Port of Bellingham has two berths and handles breakbulk and neo-bulk cargo - wood pulp, aluminum, liquid chemicals, fertilizers, containers, logs and lumber, etc. Burlington Northern Railroad Company has 37 active spurs in Whatcom County which includes the areas of Blaine, Bellingham, Ferndale, Lynden and Sumas. Five trucking companies service the area.

Population (1990)
Total Population and Growth Rate
1990: 127,780
1980: 106,701
1970: 81,983
Growth rate 1970–1990: 56%

Race and Hispanic Origin
White: 93.3%
Black: .5%
Asian/Pacific Islander: 1.8%
Native American: 3.1%
Hispanic origin: 2.9%
White not Hispanic: 91.7%

Age
Ages 18 to 20: 5.8%
Ages 21 to 24: 7.3%
Ages 25 to 44: 32.1%
Ages 45 to 54: 9.6%
Ages 55 to 59: 3.7%
Ages 60 to 64: 3.9%
Ages 65 plus: 12.6%

Educational Attainment (1990)
Percent having completed high school: 83.2%
Percent having completed college: 22.0%
Elementary and high school enrollment: 21,174

Federal Funds and Grants Received ($1000)
Total received in 1989: 611,200
Funds received per capita: 5,150

Civilian Labor Force
1993 (April):   72,843
1992 average: 73,321
1991 average: 69,513
1990 average: 68,502

Unemployment
1993 (April):   7.3%
1992 average: 7.4%
1991 average: 6.3%
1990 average: 4.9%

Average Annual Pay
1988: $16,927
1987: $17,093

1985: $16,137

Per Capita Personal Income

1991: $16,754
1990: $16,207
1989: $14,912

Business Climate (1987)

Manufacturing

Number of establishments in 1987: 232

Shipments in 1987 ($1,000): $2,865,400

Employees in 1987: 7,300

Change in employment, 1982 to 1987: 4.3%

Average annual pay for manufacturing work in 1989: $25,761

Average annual pay for production work in 1987: $23,464

Wholesale Trade

Number of establishments in 1987: 239

Total sales in 1987 ($1,000): $511,000

Change in sales, 1982 to 1987: 36.6%

Retail Trade

Number of establishments in 1987: 897

Total sales in 1987 ($1,000): $511,000

Retail sales per household in 1987: $16,543

Average annual pay in 1989: $10,343

Service Industry

Selected receipts in 1987 ($1,000): $225,700

Average annual pay in 1989: $14,021

Housing

Total number of units in 1990: 55,742

Occupied units in 1990: 48,543

Owner-occupied units in 1990: 64.3%

1993 ACCRA average cost: $131,000

1993 ACCRA average rent for an apartment: $575

Chamber of Commerce

Whatcom Chamber of Commerce & Industry, Michael J. Brennan, Exec. Vice President, 1203 Cornwall Ave. #102, Bellingham, WA 98225. 206-734-1330

Economic Development Office

Fourth Corner Economic Development Group, David Bell, Exec. Director, 1203 Cornwall St., #103, PO Box 2803, Bellingham, WA 98227. 206-676-4255, FAX 206-647-9213

Major Businesses

Company	SIC	Telephone
Allsop Inc.	3695	(206) 734-9090
Alpine H & S Inc.	2411	(206) 734-6174
Bellingham Marine Industries	1629	(206) 676-2800
Bellingham National Bank	6021	(206) 676-6300
Bovenkamp Development Inc.	5211	(206) 354-5617
Brown & Cole Inc.	5411	(206) 384-5915

Major Businesses (Continued)

Company	SIC	Telephone
Cedartone Specialties Inc.	2499	(206) 671-1237
Colt Construction Co.	1541	(206) 676-4905
Dealer Info Systems Corp.	7371	(206) 733-7610
Ennen's Food Stores Inc.	5411	(206) 647-2290
Ershig's Inc.	3084	(206) 733-2620
Exports of Washington, Inc.	5399	(206) 332-5961
Farmers Equipment Co.	5083	(206) 354-4451
Ferndale Grain Inc.	5153	(206) 384-1101
Haggen's Inc.	5411	(206) 733-8720
Haskell Corp.	1711	(206) 734-1200
Hawley's Inc.	5551	(206) 734-9660
Hoksbergen Hay Co.	5191	(206) 354-5056
Horizon Bank	6022	(206) 733-3050
Imco General Construction	1622	(206) 671-3936
JIJ Construction Co Inc.	1611	(206) 366-5050
LTI Inc.	4212	(206) 354-2101
Meenderinck Molasses Co., Inc.	2099	(206) 966-5303
Morse Hardware Co.	5072	(206) 734-2400
Mt. Baker Plywood Inc.	2435	(206) 733-3960
Redden Net Co., Inc.	5941	(206) 733-0250
San Juan Seafoods Inc.	5146	(206) 734-8384
Seafood Producers Co.	2092	(206) 733-0120
Technodent Corp.	3843	(206) 988-7911
Trans-Ocean Products Inc.	2091	(206) 671-6886
Video Depot Ltd.	5064	(206) 676-0319
Whatcom Farmer's Co-Op	2875	(206) 354-2108
Wilder Construction Co., Inc.	1611	(206) 733-2060

BREMERTON, WA (MSA)

Geographic Profile

Land Area

396.0 square miles

Counties and Parishes

Kitsap

Ranking Highlights

312 *out of 319 in total* **land area**

27 *out of 319 in* **population growth,** *1970–1990*

117 *out of 310 in having the lowest* **unemployment** *rate*

202 *out of 310 in size of* **labor force**

141 *out of 318 in the percentage of* **college graduates**

140 *out of 292 in per capita personal* **income**

280 *out of 319 in number of* **manufacturing establishments**

250 *out of 318 in* **physicians** *per 1000 people*

316 *out of 318 in* **hospital beds** *per 1000 people*

65 *out of 267 in fewest* **crimes** *per 1000 people*

55 *out of 266 in fewest* **violent crimes** *per 1000 people*

14 *out of 319 in per capita* **federal funds and grants**

Quality of Life Indexes (Rate per 1000 population)

Crime rate in 1991:   46.0

Violent crime rate in 1991:   3.3

Physicians rate in 1992:   1.39

Hospital bed rate in 1991:   1.29

ACCRA Cost of Living Indexes

(First quarter 1993, average = 100)

Composite index: N/A

Utilities index: N/A

Housing index: N/A

Population (1990)

Total Population and Growth Rate

1990: 189,731

1980: 147,152

1970: 101,732

Growth rate 1970–1990: 87%

Race and Hispanic Origin

White: 90.2%

Black: 2.7%

Asian/Pacific Islander: 4.4%

Native American: 1.7%

Hispanic origin: 3.3%

White not Hispanic: 88.5%

Age

Ages 18 to 20: 4.6%

Ages 21 to 24: 6.1%

Ages 25 to 44: 33.6%

Ages 45 to 54: 10.1%

Ages 55 to 59: 3.5%

Ages 60 to 64: 3.5%

Ages 65 plus: 10.7%

Educational Attainment (1990)

Percent having completed high school: 86.6%

Percent having completed college: 19.8%

Elementary and high school enrollment: 33,727

Federal Funds and Grants Received

Total received in 1989: $1,374,700,000

Funds received per capita: $7,601

Civilian Labor Force

1993 (April):   86,650

1992 average: 86,786

1991 average: 83,616

1990 average: 83,198

Unemployment

1993 (April):   6.7%

1992 average: 6.3%

1991 average: 5.2%

1990 average: 4.2%

Average Annual Pay

1988: $19,817

1987: $19,484

1985: $18,772

Per Capita Personal Income

1991: $17,488

1990: $16,859

1989: $16,007

Business Climate (1987)

Manufacturing

Number of establishments in 1987: 114

Shipments in 1987 ($1,000): $133,100

Employees in 1987: 1,500

Change in employment, 1982 to 1987: -6.3%

Average annual pay for manufacturing work in 1989: $24,617

Average annual pay for production work in 1987: $16,800

Wholesale Trade

Number of establishments in 1987: 115

Total sales in 1987 ($1,000): $193,200

Change in sales, 1982 to 1987: 21.8%

Retail Trade

Number of establishments in 1987: 903

Total sales in 1987 ($1,000): $193,200

Retail sales per household in 1987: $12,654

Average annual pay in 1989: $11,011

Service Industry

Selected receipts in 1987 ($1,000): $306,000

Average annual pay in 1989: $16,341

Housing

Total number of units in 1990: 74,038

Occupied units in 1990: 69,267
Owner-occupied units in 1990: 64.3%
1993 ACCRA average cost: N/A
1993 ACCRA average rent for an apartment: N/A

Chamber of Commerce

Bremerton Area Chamber of Commerce, Betti L. Sheldon, Exec. Director, 837 4th St., PO Box 229, Bremerton, WA 98310. 206-479-3579

Economic Development Office

Economic Development Council of Kitsap County, Earle Smith, Jr., President, 4841 Auto Center Way #204, Bremerton, WA 98312. 206-377-9499, FAX 206-479-4653

Major Businesses

Company	SIC	Telephone
Courtesy Ford Inc.	5511	(206) 697-2700
Family Pancake House Management	8741	(206) 479-4137
GNW Financial Corp.	6035	(206) 479-1551
Grey Chevrolet Inc.	5511	(206) 876-8091
Harrison Memorial Hospital	8062	(206) 377-3911
Howe Co. Inc.	5511	(206) 876-4484
Nor Eastern Trawl Systems	2399	(206) 842-5623
Pearce Enterprises Inc.	5511	(206) 479-2100
Stirrett-Johnsen Inc.	1711	(206) 692-6128
Wetzel, Scott Services Inc.	6411	(206) 479-0200
Wilkins Distributing Co., Inc.	5983	(206) 876-4801

Colleges and Universities

Olympic College, Bremerton

OLYMPIA, WA (MSA)

Geographic Profile

Land Area
727.1 square miles

Counties and Parishes
Thurston

Ranking Highlights

248 *out of 319 in total* **land area**
 17 *out of 319 in* **population growth,** *1970–1990*
139 *out of 310 in having the lowest* **unemployment** *rate*
197 *out of 310 in size of* **labor force**
 65 *out of 318 in the percentage of* **college graduates**
115 *out of 292 in per capita personal* **income**
247 *out of 319 in number of* **manufacturing establishments**
147 *out of 318 in* **physicians** *per 1000 people*
230 *out of 318 in* **hospital beds** *per 1000 people*
 75 *out of 267 in fewest* **crimes** *per 1000 people*
 36 *out of 266 in fewest* **violent crimes** *per 1000 people*
 52 *out of 319 in per capita* **federal funds and grants**

Quality of Life Indexes (Rate per 1000 population)

Crime rate in 1991:   48.5
Violent crime rate in 1991:   2.8
Physicians rate in 1992:   1.85
Hospital bed rate in 1991:   3.1

ACCRA Cost of Living Indexes

(First quarter 1993, average = 100)
Composite index: 105.4
Utilities index: 68.1
Housing index: 115.9

Population (1990)

Total Population and Growth Rate
1990: 161,238
1980: 124,264
1970: 76,894
Growth rate 1970–1990: 110%

Race and Hispanic Origin
White: 91.9%
Black: 1.8%
Asian/Pacific Islander: 3.8%
Native American: 1.5%
Hispanic origin: 3.0%
White not Hispanic: 90.2%

Age
Ages 18 to 20: 4.3%
Ages 21 to 24:   5%
Ages 25 to 44: 33.6%
Ages 45 to 54: 10.8%
Ages 55 to 59: 3.9%

Ages 60 to 64: 3.8%
Ages 65 plus: 11.7%

Educational Attainment (1990)
Percent having completed high school: 86.5%
Percent having completed college: 24.7%
Elementary and high school enrollment: 29,105

Federal Funds and Grants Received
Total received in 1989: $718,100,00
Funds received per capita: $4,584

Civilian Labor Force
1993 (April):   88,040
1992 average: 91,199
1991 average: 84,560
1990 average: 83,401

Unemployment
1993 (April):   6.5%
1992 average: 6.6%
1991 average: 5.9%
1990 average: 5.0%

Average Annual Pay
1988: $19,352
1987: $18,763
1985: $17,889

Per Capita Personal Income
1991: $17,966
1990: $17,162
1989: $16,215

Business Climate (1987)
Manufacturing
Number of establishments in 1987: 148
Shipments in 1987 ($1,000): $609,800
Employees in 1987: 3,400
Change in employment, 1982 to 1987: 17.2%
Average annual pay for manufacturing work in 1989: $24,220
Average annual pay for production work in 1987: $22,519

Wholesale Trade
Number of establishments in 1987: 155
Total sales in 1987 ($1,000): $276,600
Change in sales, 1982 to 1987: 43.9%

Retail Trade
Number of establishments in 1987: 879
Total sales in 1987 ($1,000): $276,600
Retail sales per household in 1987: $14,054
Average annual pay in 1989: $11,042

Service Industry
Selected receipts in 1987 ($1,000): $291,200
Average annual pay in 1989: $16,307

Housing
Total number of units in 1990: 66,464

Occupied units in 1990: 62,150
Owner-occupied units in 1990: 64.7%
1993 ACCRA average cost: $139,558
1993 ACCRA average rent for an apartment: $476

Chamber of Commerce
Olympia/Thurston County Chamber of Commerce, Joseph Beaulieu, Exec. Director, 1000 Plum St., PO Box 1427, Olympia, WA 98507. 206-357-3362

Economic Development Office
Thurston County EDC, Kathy Combs, Exec. Director, 721 Columbia S.W., Olympia, WA 98501. 206-754-6320, FAX 206-586-5493

Major Businesses

Company	SIC	Telephone
Capitol Chevrolet Co.	5571	(206) 357-5515
Columbia Beverage Co.	2086	(206) 357-9090
Custom House Inc.	5065	(206) 491-6320
Dapaul Inc.	5099	(206) 943-9844
Harbor Wholesale Grocery	5141	(206) 754-4484
Hardel Mutual Plywood Corp.	2436	(206) 754-6030
L & E Bottling Co. Inc.	2086	(206) 748-0071
Moduline International, Inc.	2451	(206) 491-1130
Olympia Federal Savings & Loan Association	6035	(206) 754-3400
Rotters Automotive Sales	5511	(206) 357-7762
Sunset Life Insurance Co. of America	6311	(206) 943-1400
West Star Corp.	5411	(206) 754-9595

Colleges and Universities
Evergreen State College, Olympia
South Puget Sound Community College, Olympia

RICHLAND–KENNEWICK– PASCO, WA (MSA)

Geographic Profile

Land Area

2945.3 square miles

Counties and Parishes

Benton

Franklin

Ranking Highlights

46 *out of 319 in total* **land area**

63 *out of 319 in* **population growth,** *1970–1990*

245 *out of 310 in having the lowest* **unemployment** *rate*

210 *out of 310 in size of* **labor force**

120 *out of 318 in the percentage of* **college graduates**

144 *out of 292 in per capita personal* **income**

275 *out of 319 in number of* **manufacturing establishments**

273 *out of 318 in* **physicians** *per 1000 people*

269 *out of 318 in* **hospital beds** *per 1000 people*

120 *out of 267 in fewest* **crimes** *per 1000 people*

70 *out of 266 in fewest* **violent crimes** *per 1000 people*

6 *out of 319 in per capita* **federal funds and grants**

Quality of Life Indexes (Rate per 1000 population)

Crime rate in 1991:	58.5
Violent crime rate in 1991:	3.9
Physicians rate in 1992:	1.25
Hospital bed rate in 1991:	2.58

ACCRA Cost of Living Indexes

(First quarter 1993, average = 100)

Composite index: 105.9

Utilities index: 76.3

Housing index: 114.7

Population (1990)

Total Population and Growth Rate

1990: 150,033

1980: 144,469

1970: 93,356

Growth rate 1970–1990: 61%

Race and Hispanic Origin

White: 86.5%

Black: 1.6%

Asian/Pacific Islander: 2.1%

Native American: 0.7%

Hispanic origin: 13.3%

White not Hispanic: 82.4%

Age

Ages 18 to 20: 4.1%

Ages 21 to 24: 4.8%

Ages 25 to 44: 32%

Ages 45 to 54: 10.1%

Ages 55 to 59: 4%

Ages 60 to 64: 3.9%

Ages 65 plus: 10.1%

Educational Attainment (1990)

Percent having completed high school: 80.2%

Percent having completed college: 21.0%

Elementary and high school enrollment: 30,875

Federal Funds and Grants Received

Total received in 1989: $1,237,400,000

Funds received per capita: $8,454

Civilian Labor Force

1993 (April): 83,765

1992 average: 79,880

1991 average: 76,034

1990 average: 74,787

Unemployment

1993 (April): 6.8%

1992 average: 8.6%

1991 average: 8.1%

1990 average: 6.9%

Average Annual Pay

1988: $21,520

1987: $21,266

1985: $20,849

Per Capita Personal Income

1991: $17,398

1990: $16,487

1989: $15,426

Business Climate (1987)

Manufacturing

Number of establishments in 1987: 120

Shipments in 1987 ($1,000): $2,246,400

Employees in 1987: 15,400

Change in employment, 1982 to 1987: 37.5%

Average annual pay for manufacturing work in 1989: $32,527

Average annual pay for production work in 1987: $24,438

Wholesale Trade

Number of establishments in 1987: 236

Total sales in 1987 ($1,000): $597,900

Change in sales, 1982 to 1987: -4.4%

Retail Trade

Number of establishments in 1987: 844

Total sales in 1987 ($1,000): $597,900

Retail sales per household in 1987: $16,051

Average annual pay in 1989: $10,885

Service Industry

Selected receipts in 1987 ($1,000): $810,500

Average annual pay in 1989: $21,675

Housing
Total number of units in 1990: 58,541
Occupied units in 1990: 54,423
Owner-occupied units in 1990: 62.4%
1993 ACCRA average cost: $124,490
1993 ACCRA average rent for an apartment: $647

Chamber of Commerce
Richland Chamber of Commerce, Marv York, Exec. Vice President, 515 Lee Blvd., PO Box 637, Richland, WA 99352. 509-946-1651

Economic Development Office
Kennewick Chamber of Commerce, Ann Philip, Exec. Director, 500 N. Morain Suite 1200, PO Box 6986, Kennewick, WA 99336. 509-736-0510, FAX 509-783-1733

Economic Development Organizations
Greater Pasco Area Chamber of Commerce, Dorothy Schoeppach, Exec. Director, 129 N. 3rd Ave., PO Box 550, Pasco, WA 99301. 509-547-9755

Major Businesses

Company	SIC	Telephone
Balcom & Moe Inc.	0134	(509) 547-3383
C & L Crop Care	5191	(509) 545-9511
Columbia Healthcare System	8062	(509) 946-4611
Columbia Packaging, Inc.	5113	(509) 547-3437
Dean, Russ Ford Inc.	5511	(509) 545-9501
Grant, George A. Inc.	1542	(509) 946-6188
Grigg Enterprises Inc.	5311	(509) 547-0566
Kadlec Medical Center	8062	(509) 946-4611
Kennewick Industrial & Electric	5063	(509) 582-5156
Kennewick Public Hospital District	8062	(509) 586-6111
L & M Feeders Inc.	0211	(509) 547-8864
Lamb-Weston Inc.	2037	(509) 735-4651
Liberty Agriculture Inc.	5083	(509) 547-0541
Morrison Construction Service	1711	(509) 547-9739
NPA, Inc.	4512	(509) 545-6420
Our Lady of Lourdes Hospital	8062	(509) 547-7704
Poland, Ray & Sons Inc.	1623	(509) 586-2158
Prosser Public Hospital District Benton	8062	(509) 786-2222
Public Utility 1 Benton	4911	(509) 582-2175
South Columbia Basin	4971	(509) 547-1735
Westinghouse Hanford Co.	4911	(509) 376-7411
Wondrack Distributing Inc.	5171	(509) 582-5181

Colleges and Universities
Columbia Basin College, Pasco

SEATTLE, WA (PMSA)

Geographic Profile

Land Area
4216.3 square miles

Counties and Parishes
King
Snohomish

Additional Cities/Towns within Area
Auburn
Everett

Ranking Highlights
23 *out of 319 in total* land area
114 *out of 319 in* population growth, *1970–1990*
34 *out of 310 in having the lowest* unemployment *rate*
17 *out of 310 in size of* labor force
27 *out of 318 in the percentage of* college graduates
15 *out of 292 in per capita personal* income
16 *out of 319 in number of* manufacturing establishments
40 *out of 318 in* physicians *per 1000 people*
283 *out of 318 in* hospital beds *per 1000 people*
198 *out of 267 in fewest* crimes *per 1000 people*
126 *out of 266 in fewest* violent crimes *per 1000 people*
82 *out of 319 in per capita* federal funds and grants

Quality of Life Indexes (Rate per 1000 population)
Crime rate in 1991: 71.5
Violent crime rate in 1991: 6.0
Physicians rate in 1992: 2.82
Hospital bed rate in 1991: 2.37

ACCRA Cost of Living Indexes
(First quarter 1993, average = 100)
Composite index: 117.0
Utilities index: 61.8
Housing index: 147.0

Overview
While Seattle has in the past been largely dependent on the aerospace industry, the city's diverse economy is also based on the manufacture of transportation equipment and forest products, as well as food processing and advanced technology. Non-manufacturing activities, however, comprise four-fifths of the Seattle economy; maritime commerce, for instance, is a leading industry. The Port of Seattle, the second largest handler of container cargo in the country, provides a direct connection to the Orient and serves as a major link in trade with markets in Alaska, on the Gulf of Mexico, and on the Atlantic Coast.

With its multifaceted transportation network of freeways, railroads, an airport, a ferry system, and port facilities, Seattle is the principal trade, distribution, financial, and services center for the Northwest. Tourism has become a vital part of the city's economy.

The Seattle Center is the city's major meeting and conference facility. The main arena, with 15,600 square feet of space, provides banquet seating for 1,500 people and theater seating for more than 6,000 persons. The complex also includes eight conference rooms accommodating groups of up to 120 persons, an exhibition hall providing more than forty-three thousand square feet of space, and numerous multi-use rooms.

The Kingdome serves as a site of trade shows; meetings can also be held at the University of Washington's Battelle Conference Center. The Westin Hotel, the Seattle Sheraton, and the Four Seasons Olympic Hotel are among downtown hotels equipped with meeting rooms and exhibition space for both large and small groups. Hotels and motels in the metropolitan area provide a total of 17,500 rooms as well as additional convention and meeting accommodations.

Seattle's economy benefits from Seattle-Tacoma International Airport, which is served by thirteen cargo carriers. The city's most important commercial asset is Elliott Bay, one of the finest deep-water ports in the world. The Port of Seattle can accommodate ships up to fourteen hundred feet in length and provides generous warehouse space. Two transcontinental railroads and more than one hundred seventy motor freight carriers transport goods to and from Seattle.

Air travelers to Seattle are served by the Seattle-Tacoma International Airport (Sea-Tac), one of the country's most modern and efficient air traffic facilities. Thirty airlines, including sixteen international carriers, schedule daily flights to Seattle from points throughout the United States and the world. Two interstate highways serve Seattle: I-5 (north-south) and I-90 (east-west).

Population (1990)

Total Population and Growth Rate
1990: 1,972,961
1980: 1,607,618
1970: 1,424,605
Growth rate 1970–1990: 38%

Race and Hispanic Origin
White: 86.8%
Black: 4.1%
Asian/Pacific Islander: 6.9%
Native American: 1.2%
Hispanic origin: 2.8%
White not Hispanic: 85.3%

Age
Ages 18 to 20: 3.9%
Ages 21 to 24: 5.8%
Ages 25 to 44: 37.6%
Ages 45 to 54: 10.7%
Ages 55 to 59: 3.8%
Ages 60 to 64: 3.6%
Ages 65 plus: 10.7%

Educational Attainment (1990)
Percent having completed high school: 87.7%
Percent having completed college: 29.8%
Elementary and high school enrollment: 293,734

Federal Funds and Grants Received
Total received in 1989: $7,235,300,000
Funds received per capita: $3,886

Civilian Labor Force
1993 (April): 1,162,159
1992 average: 1,148,197
1991 average: 1,112,620
1990 average: 1,123,388

Unemployment
1993 (April):   6.2%
1992 average: 6.2%
1991 average: 4.8%
1990 average: 3.5%

Average Annual Pay
1988: $23,436
1987: $22,543
1985: $20,907

Per Capita Personal Income
1991: $23,329
1990: $22,276
1989: $21,051

Business Climate (1987)

Manufacturing
Number of establishments in 1987: 3,464
Shipments in 1987 ($1,000): $23,363,400
Employees in 1987: 174,500
Change in employment, 1982 to 1987: 4.7%
Average annual pay for manufacturing work in 1989: $32,863
Average annual pay for production work in 1987: $24,341

Wholesale Trade
Number of establishments in 1987: 5,059
Total sales in 1987 ($1,000): $28,184,000
Change in sales, 1982 to 1987: 40.7%

Retail Trade
Number of establishments in 1987: 11,745
Total sales in 1987 ($1,000): $28,184,000
Retail sales per household in 1987: $17,950
Average annual pay in 1989: $13,801

Service Industry
Selected receipts in 1987 ($1,000): $7,531,400
Average annual pay in 1989: $19,645

Office Real Estate (1992)
Office space inventory: 13,536,000 square feet

Average class A Central Business District rental range per sq. ft: $20.16

Vacancy Rates
All areas: 14.4%

Vacancy Rates in Central Business District
Class A space: 14.8%
Class B space: 12.5%

Vacancy Rates Outside Central Business District
Class A space: 15.3%
Class B space: 12.0%

Housing
Total number of units in 1990: 831,285
Occupied units in 1990: 797,505
Owner-occupied units in 1990: 60.4%
1993 ACCRA average cost: $180,228
1993 ACCRA average rent for an apartment: $564

Chamber of Commerce
Greater Seattle Chamber of Commerce, George Duff, President, 600 University St. Suite 1200, Seattle, WA 98101. 206-389-7200, FAX 206-389-7288

Economic Development Office
Auburn Area Chamber of Commerce, Michael P. Morrisette, Exec. Manager, 228 1st St. N.E., Auburn, WA 98002. 206-833-0700

Economic Development Organizations
Everett Chamber of Commerce, Thomas M. Burns, President, 1710 W. Marine View Dr., PO Box 1086, Everett, WA 98201. 206-252-5181, FAX 206-252-3105

Seattle-King County Economic Development Council, Victor Ericson, President, 701 5th Ave. Suite 2510, Seattle, WA 98104. 206-386-5040, FAX 206-386-7821

Economic Development Council of Snohomish County, John E. Thoresen, President, 917 134th St. S.W. Suite 103, Everett, WA 98204. 206-743-4567, FAX 206-745-5563

Major Businesses

Company	SIC	Telephone
Airborne Freight Corp.	4513	(206) 285-4600
Alaska Air Group, Inc.	4512	(206) 431-7040
Alaska Airlines, Inc.	4512	(206) 433-3200
Associated Grocers Inc.	5141	(206) 762-2100
Boeing Co.	3721	(206) 655-2121
Burlington Resources Inc.	4923	(206) 467-3838
Costco Wholesale Corp.	5331	(206) 828-8100
Federal Home Loan Bank of Seattle	6111	(206) 340-2300
Great Northern Insured	6311	(206) 625-1755
Microsoft Corp.	7372	(206) 882-8080
Nordstrom, Inc.	5651	(206) 628-2111
Paccar Inc.	3711	(206) 455-7400
Pacific Bell Telephone Co.	4813	(206) 345-2211

Major Businesses (Continued)

Company	SIC	Telephone
Puget Sound Power Light Co.	4911	(206) 454-6363
Safeco Insurance Co. of America	6331	(206) 545-5000
Safeco Life Insurance Co.	6311	(206) 545-5000
Seafirst Corp.	6021	(206) 358-3000
Seattle First National Bank	6021	(206) 358-3000
Security Pacific Banc	6021	(206) 621-5280
Security Pacific Bank Washington	6021	(206) 621-4111
Services Group of America	5141	(206) 251-9100
Simpson Investment Co.	2621	(206) 224-5000
US West Communications	4813	(206) 345-2211
United Pacific Life Insurance	6311	(206) 952-6770
Univar Corp.	5169	(206) 447-5911
Van Waters & Rogers Inc.	5169	(206) 447-5911
Western Conference Teamsters	6733	(206) 329-4900
Weyerhaeuser Financial Service	6162	(206) 924-2345
Weyerhaeuser Real Estate	6552	(206) 924-2390

Colleges and Universities
Antioch University Seattle, Seattle
Art Institute of Seattle, Seattle
Bastyr College, Seattle
Cornish College of the Arts, Seattle
Everett Community College, Everett
Green River Community College, Auburn
Griffin College, Seattle
ITT Technical Institute, Seattle
North Seattle Community College, Seattle
Seattle Central Community College, Seattle
Seattle Pacific University, Seattle
Seattle University, Seattle
Shoreline Community College, Seattle
South Seattle Community College, Seattle
University of Washington, Seattle

SPOKANE, WA (MSA)

Geographic Profile

Land Area

1763.8 square miles

Counties and Parishes

Spokane

Ranking Highlights

107 *out of 319 in total* **land area**

161 *out of 319 in* **population growth,** *1970–1990*

149 *out of 310 in having the lowest* **unemployment** *rate*

124 *out of 310 in size of* **labor force**

127 *out of 318 in the percentage of* **college graduates**

165 *out of 292 in per capita personal* **income**

114 *out of 319 in number of* **manufacturing establishments**

78 *out of 318 in* **physicians** *per 1000 people*

170 *out of 318 in* **hospital beds** *per 1000 people*

165 *out of 267 in fewest* **crimes** *per 1000 people*

82 *out of 266 in fewest* **violent crimes** *per 1000 people*

141 *out of 319 in per capita* **federal funds and grants**

Quality of Life Indexes (Rate per 1000 population)

Crime rate in 1991:	66.2
Violent crime rate in 1991:	4.2
Physicians rate in 1992:	2.4
Hospital bed rate in 1991:	3.72

ACCRA Cost of Living Indexes

(First quarter 1993, average = 100)

Composite index:	101.3
Utilities index:	56.7
Housing index:	117.5

Overview

Metropolitan Spokane is the economic, financial and service capital of the Inland Northwest, in addition to being a major attraction to parts of southern British Columbia and Alberta, Canada. Spokane is the major trade, medical, financial, cultural, transportation and entertainment center between Seattle, Minneapolis,Minnesota, Salt Lake City, Utah, and Calgary, Alberta, Canada.

The Spokane economy is heavily trade and service oriented, with these industriesaccounting for nearly 60 percent of employment. The manufacturing sector in the Spokane area accounts for thirteen percent of employment. The hospitality industry employs more than 6,000 people and contributes over $250 million annually to the economy.

Because of Spokane's location, it has been the Pacific Northwest's primary inland distribution center and transportation hub since 1881. The Spokane International Airport is the second largest in the state and serves the area with five transcontinental and two regional airlines and 30 airfreight firms. The Union Pacific and Burlington Northern railroads have helped to make Spokane one of the largest rail centers

west of Omaha. Spokane is on the main east-west Amtrak route and is served by several Pacific Northwest and national bus lines. The Spokane Transit Authority provides daily public transportation to Spokane area residents.

Fairchild Air Force Base, located 12 miles southwest of Spokane, is the largest employer in the Spokane MSA with 6,000 military and civilian employees. The total annual payroll of the facility is approximately $240 million.

In 1992 6,069 homes were sold with a record listing volume of $539 million. This valuation represents a 22 percent increase over that of 1991 and is nearly double 1989's volume of $293 million. Total building permit valuation in the county reached a record $428,820,000, and new construction accounted for $345 million. The valuation of new single family housing permits reached a record of $182,745,000.

Nonagricultural wage and salary workers totaled over 164,100 in 1992, an increase of nearly 14% over the 1988 level of 144,300. Total retail sales continue climbing, hitting $4.9 billion for 1992 compared to $4.6 billion one year prior. Taxable retail sales were up 8.22 percent in 1992.

Population (1990)

Total Population and Growth Rate

1990: 361,360

1980: 341,835

1970: 287,487

Growth rate 1970–1990: 26%

Race and Hispanic Origin

White: 94.6%

Black: 1.4%

Asian/Pacific Islander: 1.8%

Native American: 1.5%

Hispanic origin: 1.9%

White not Hispanic: 93.4%

Age

Ages 18 to 20: 4.8%

Ages 21 to 24: 5.8%

Ages 25 to 44: 32%

Ages 45 to 54: 9.8%

Ages 55 to 59: 4%

Ages 60 to 64: 4%

Ages 65 plus: 13.3%

Educational Attainment (1990)

Percent having completed high school: 84.4%

Percent having completed college: 20.6%

Elementary and high school enrollment: 62,839

Federal Funds and Grants Received

Total received in 1989: $1,154,300,000

Funds received per capita: $3,239

Civilian Labor Force

1993 (April): 184,680

1992 average: 181,129

1991 average: 172,641
1990 average: 170,560

Unemployment
1993 (April): 5.9%
1992 average: 6.8%
1991 average: 6.2%
1990 average: 5.4%

Average Annual Pay
1988: $18,009
1987: $17,480
1985: $16,662

Per Capita Personal Income
1991: $16,857
1990: $16,216
1989: $15,290

Business Climate (1987)

Manufacturing
Number of establishments in 1987: 497
Shipments in 1987 ($1,000): $2,359,400
Employees in 1987: 19,600
Change in employment, 1982 to 1987: 22.5%
Average annual pay for manufacturing work in 1989: $24,815
Average annual pay for production work in 1987: $19,683

Wholesale Trade
Number of establishments in 1987: 851
Total sales in 1987 ($1,000): $3,314,700
Change in sales, 1982 to 1987: 16.4%

Retail Trade
Number of establishments in 1987: 2,150
Total sales in 1987 ($1,000): $3,314,700
Retail sales per household in 1987: $16,021
Average annual pay in 1989: $11,347

Service Industry
Selected receipts in 1987 ($1,000): $857,600
Average annual pay in 1989: $15,113

Housing
Total number of units in 1990: 150,105
Occupied units in 1990: 141,619
Owner-occupied units in 1990: 63.7%
1993 ACCRA average cost: $134,768
1993 ACCRA average rent for an apartment: $563

Chamber of Commerce
Spokane Area Chamber of Commerce, George Reitemeier, President, W. 1020 Riverside Ave., PO Box 2147, Spokane, WA 99210. 509-624-1393

Economic Development Office
Spokane Area Economic Development Council, Robert Cooper, President, PO Box 203, Spokane, WA 99210. 509-624-9282

Major Businesses

Company	SIC	Telephone
Acme Concrete Co.	3273	(509) 535-3081
Alloy Trailers Inc.	3715	(509) 455-8650
Camp Chevrolet Inc.	5511	(509) 456-7890
Cominco American Inc.	1031	(509) 747-6111
Consumer's Group Holding	6331	(509) 838-3111
Consumers Group Holding Co.	6311	(509) 838-3111
E-Z Loader Boat Trailers	3799	(509) 489-0181
Empire Health Services Inc.	8062	(509) 458-7960
Interstate Product Credit Association	6159	(509) 838-9300
Itron Inc.	3825	(509) 924-9900
Jensen-Byrd Co. Inc.	5072	(509) 624-1321
Key Tronic Corp.	3575	(509) 928-8000
Medical Service Corp.	6324	(509) 536-4700
Metropolitan Mortgage Security	6211	(509) 838-3111
Montana Tunnels Mining Inc.	1041	(509) 624-4653
Pegasus Gold Corp.	1041	(509) 624-4653
Pentzer Corp.	3825	(509) 459-1350
RSM, Inc.	5411	(509) 326-8900
Rosauers Supermarkets Inc.	5411	(509) 326-8900
Sacred Heart Medical Center	8062	(509) 455-3040
Self-Service Furniture Inc.	5712	(509) 535-7717
System-TWT Transportation	4213	(509) 623-4000
URM Stores Inc.	5141	(509) 467-2620
WTB Financial Corp.	6022	(509) 455-4122
Washington Irrigation Development Co.	1221	(509) 489-0500
Washington Trust Bank	6022	(509) 455-4122
Washington Water Power Co.	4911	(509) 489-0500
Wendle Ford Sales Inc.	5511	(509) 484-4800
Western United Life Assurance	6311	(509) 838-3384
Yokes Foods Inc.	5411	(509) 325-5611
Zortman Mining Inc.	1041	(509) 624-4653

Colleges and Universities
Gonzaga University, Spokane
ITT Technical Institute, Spokane
Phillips Junior College of Spokane, Spokane
Spokane Community College, Spokane
Spokane Falls Community College, Spokane

TACOMA, WA (PMSA)

Geographic Profile

Land Area

1675.6 square miles

Counties and Parishes

Pierce

Ranking Highlights

118 *out of 319 in total* **land area**

88 *out of 319 in* **population growth,** *1970–1990*

219 *out of 310 in having the lowest* **unemployment** *rate*

89 *out of 310 in size of* **labor force**

184 *out of 318 in the percentage of* **college graduates**

151 *out of 292 in per capita personal* **income**

98 *out of 319 in number of* **manufacturing establishments**

188 *out of 318 in* **physicians** *per 1000 people*

301 *out of 318 in* **hospital beds** *per 1000 people*

187 *out of 267 in fewest* **crimes** *per 1000 people*

215 *out of 266 in fewest* **violent crimes** *per 1000 people*

60 *out of 319 in per capita* **federal funds and grants**

Quality of Life Indexes (Rate per 1000 population)

Crime rate in 1991:	69.8
Violent crime rate in 1991:	9.5
Physicians rate in 1992:	1.69
Hospital bed rate in 1991:	2.09

ACCRA Cost of Living Indexes

(First quarter 1993, average = 100)

Composite index: 103.4

Utilities index: 61.8

Housing index: 102.8

Overview

Tacoma-Pierce County is the second most populous metropolitan area in Washington State. *Money* magazine rated Tacoma fourth in the nation as the best place to live in 1990. It is 36 miles from Seattle, 28 miles from Olympia the State Capital, 142 miles from Portland, Oregon, 174 miles from Vancouver, British Columbia, Canada, and 292 miles from Spokane. Located in western Washington on Commencement Bay, west of the Cascade Mountain Range and Mount Rainier, Pierce County covers 1,797 square miles, 118 of which are under water.

There are 10 hospitals, 3,364 hospital beds, and 700 physicians and dentists in Tacoma.

Ft. Lewis Army Post (third largest in nation), McChord Air Force Base, Madigan Army Medical Center, Camp Murray National Guard; 25,757 combined military employment (34,680 total expected by 1995). Civilian employment 8,886 (1992).

The Port of Tacoma is the sixth largest container port in North America and the 20th largest in the world. There has been over 752% growth in containerized shipping through the Port of Tacoma from 1980-1990. The Port of Tacoma airfreight pier pick up includes 20 airfreight forwarders. It is a major port for trade with Pacific Rim countries, up to 2 and 1/2 days closer than other West Coast ports via water. It is the gateway to Alaska, and the Port handles over 80% of waterborne cargo shipped to that state. Over 1,500 ships visit annually, generating over 19,000 jobs and creating up to $1 billion for the local economy. Over 700 acres of land is available for development. Over 900 acres of land and warehouse space is located in Foreign Trade Zone #86.

Seattle-Tacoma International Airport, 20 miles north, serves nearly 800 commercial flights a day and accommodates approximately 20 million passengers a year (1991). Tacoma Narrows Airport, six miles west, serves corporate and business aviation needs. There are three additional general aviation fields, the largest of which is Pierce County Airport (Thun Field), with a runway of 3,300 feet.

Interstate 5 (main north/south route along Pacific Coast), Interstate 90 (main east/west route), several highways and state routes service Tacoma. Pierce Transit operates local bus service, express service to Seattle and Olympia, and door-to-door shuttle service for the disabled. Vanpool, carpool, park and ride, and employer services are offered.

Rail service is provided by two transcontinental systems, Union Pacific and Burlington Northern. Both lines serve two dockside intermodal rail yards at the Port of Tacoma. Trucking service is provided by 30 interstate and 156 intrastate carriers.

Tacoma City Light ranked second lowest in national survey of 106 municipal utilities in industrial electric costs (1991 Annual National Electric Rate Survey/KMPG Pete Marwick). Puget Sound Power and Light, the state's largest investor-owned electric utility, has among the lowest electric rates nationally among investor-owned utilities. (Edison Electric Institute). Washington Natural Gas serves an area of 902 square miles, including Pierce County, with ample supplies of natural gas. Tacoma City Water pumps 72 million gallons per day from the Cascade Mountains via the Green River, supplemented with 58 million gallons of water per day in reserve capacity from 16 area wells.

Population (1990)

Total Population and Growth Rate

1990: 586,203

1980: 485,667

1970: 412,344

Growth rate 1970–1990: 42%

Race and Hispanic Origin

White: 85.1%

Black: 7.2%

Asian/Pacific Islander: 5.0%

Native American: 1.4%

Hispanic origin: 3.5%

White not Hispanic: 83.3%

Age
Ages 18 to 20: 4.8%
Ages 21 to 24: 6.5%
Ages 25 to 44: 33.6%
Ages 45 to 54: 9.7%
Ages 55 to 59: 3.8%
Ages 60 to 64: 3.7%
Ages 65 plus: 10.5%

Educational Attainment (1990)
Percent having completed high school: 83.2%
Percent having completed college: 17.5%
Elementary and high school enrollment: 102,003

Federal Funds and Grants Received
Total received in 1989: $2,461,700,000
Funds received per capita: $4,403

Civilian Labor Force
1993 (April): 264,599
1992 average: 262,238
1991 average: 254,561
1990 average: 255,392

Unemployment
1993 (April): 8.0%
1992 average: 7.9%
1991 average: 6.4%
1990 average: 4.8%

Average Annual Pay
1988: $18,644
1987: $18,091
1985: $17,403

Per Capita Personal Income
1991: $17,184
1990: $16,551
1989: $15,540

Business Climate (1987)
Manufacturing
Number of establishments in 1987: 644
Shipments in 1987 ($1,000): $2,567,900
Employees in 1987: 19,700
Change in employment, 1982 to 1987: -3.4%
Average annual pay for manufacturing work in 1989: $24,738
Average annual pay for production work in 1987: $20,765

Wholesale Trade
Number of establishments in 1987: 686
Total sales in 1987 ($1,000): $3,127,200
Change in sales, 1982 to 1987: 24.5%

Retail Trade
Number of establishments in 1987: 2,805
Total sales in 1987 ($1,000): $3,127,200
Retail sales per household in 1987: $14,547
Average annual pay in 1989: $11,921

Service Industry
Selected receipts in 1987 ($1,000): $1,039,400
Average annual pay in 1989: $15,879

Housing
Total number of units in 1990: 228,842
Occupied units in 1990: 214,652
Owner-occupied units in 1990: 60.3%
1993 ACCRA average cost: $116,000
1993 ACCRA average rent for an apartment: $515

Chamber of Commerce
Tacoma-Pierce County Chamber of Commerce, David W. Graybill, President, 950 Pacific Ave. #300, PO Box 1933, Tacoma, WA 98401. 206-627-2175

Economic Development Office
Economic Development for Tacoma-Pierce County, Erling Mork, President, 950 Pacific Ave. #410, PO Box 1555, Tacoma, WA 98401. 206-383-4726, FAX 206-383-4676

Major Businesses

Company	SIC	Telephone
Absher Construction Co.	1542	(206) 845-9544
Good Samaritan Hospital	8062	(206) 848-6661
Gordco Investment Inc.	5136	(206) 531-9595
Gordon Trucking Inc.	4213	(206) 845-3800
Interstate Distributor Co.	4213	(206) 537-9455
Korum Ford Inc.	5511	(206) 845-6601
Manke Lumber Co. Inc.	2421	(206) 572-6252
Multicare Health System	8062	(206) 594-1253
Multicare Medical Center	8062	(206) 594-1252
Pierce County Medical Bureau	6324	(206) 597-6533
Pierce Transit	4111	(206) 581-8080
Port of Tacoma	4491	(206) 383-5841
Puget Sound Bancorp	6022	(206) 593-3600
Russell, Frank Co.	6411	(206) 572-9500
Simon, Joseph & Sons Inc.	5093	(206) 272-9364
Smith Tractor & Equipment	5082	(206) 922-8718
St. Joseph Hospital & Health Center	8062	(206) 627-4101
Tacoma Boatbuilding Co.	3731	(206) 572-3600
Tacoma Dodge Inc.	5511	(206) 475-7300
US Oil & Refining Co.	2911	(206) 383-1651
Uddenberg, Keith Inc.	5411	(206) 851-6688
Weyerhaeuser Co.	2411	(206) 924-2345
Wilcox Farms Inc.	0252	(206) 458-7774

Colleges and Universities
Pacific Lutheran University, Tacoma
Pierce College, Tacoma
Tacoma Community College, Tacoma
University of Puget Sound, Tacoma

VANCOUVER, WA (PMSA)

Geographic Profile
Land Area
627.9 square miles

Counties and Parishes
Clark

Ranking Highlights
265 *out of 319 in total* **land area**
29 *out of 319 in* **population growth**, *1970–1990*
208 *out of 310 in having the lowest* **unemployment** *rate*
156 *out of 310 in size of* **labor force**
200 *out of 318 in the percentage of* **college graduates**
N/A *out of 292 in per capita personal* **income**
155 *out of 319 in number of* **manufacturing establishments**
292 *out of 318 in* **physicians** *per 1000 people*
317 *out of 318 in* **hospital beds** *per 1000 people*
54 *out of 267 in fewest* **crimes** *per 1000 people*
44 *out of 266 in fewest* **violent crimes** *per 1000 people*
285 *out of 319 in per capita* **federal funds and grants**

Quality of Life Indexes (Rate per 1000 population)
Crime rate in 1991:   43.7
Violent crime rate in 1991:   3.0
Physicians rate in 1992:   1.1
Hospital bed rate in 1991:   1.26

ACCRA Cost of Living Indexes
(First quarter 1993, average = 100)
Composite index: N/A
Utilities index: N/A
Housing index: N/A

Population (1990)
Total Population and Growth Rate
1990: 238,053
1980: 192,227
1970: 128,454
Growth rate 1970–1990: 85%

Race and Hispanic Origin
White: 94.6%
Black: 1.3%
Asian/Pacific Islander: 2.4%
Native American: 1.0%
Hispanic origin: 2.5%
White not Hispanic: 93.1%

Age
Ages 18 to 20:   4%
Ages 21 to 24: 4.8%
Ages 25 to 44: 33.7%
Ages 45 to 54: 10.9%
Ages 55 to 59: 3.8%
Ages 60 to 64: 3.7%
Ages 65 plus: 10.7%

Educational Attainment (1990)
Percent having completed high school: 83.9%
Percent having completed college: 16.8%
Elementary and high school enrollment: 44,440

Federal Funds and Grants Received
Total received in 1989: $499,000,000
Funds received per capita: $2,206

Civilian Labor Force
1993 (April):   135,500
1992 average: 132,368
1991 average: 126,887
1990 average: 127,739

Unemployment
1993 (April):   6.6%
1992 average: 7.7%
1991 average: 6.6%
1990 average: 4.9%

Average Annual Pay
1988: $19,450
1987: $18,710
1985: $18,057

Per Capita Personal Income
1991: N/A
1990: N/A
1989: N/A

Business Climate (1987)
Manufacturing
Number of establishments in 1987: 330
Shipments in 1987 ($1,000): $2,407,200
Employees in 1987: 14,900
Change in employment, 1982 to 1987: 13.7%
Average annual pay for manufacturing work in 1989: $27,692
Average annual pay for production work in 1987: $22,755

Wholesale Trade
Number of establishments in 1987: 284
Total sales in 1987 ($1,000): $585,400
Change in sales, 1982 to 1987: 7.8%

Retail Trade
Number of establishments in 1987: 1,013
Total sales in 1987 ($1,000): $585,400
Retail sales per household in 1987: $11,892
Average annual pay in 1989: $10,933

Service Industry
Selected receipts in 1987 ($1,000): $373,300
Average annual pay in 1989: $14,424

Housing
Total number of units in 1990: 92,849

Occupied units in 1990: 88,440
Owner-occupied units in 1990: 64.3%
1993 ACCRA average cost: N/A
1993 ACCRA average rent for an apartment: N/A

Chamber of Commerce

Greater Vancouver Chamber of Commerce, Donna Canton-wine, President, 404 E. 15th St. Suite 11, Vancouver, WA 98663. 206-693-8279

Economic Development Office

Columbia River Economic Development Council, Robert Levin, President, 100 Columbia Way, Vancouver WA 98661. 206-694-5006

Major Businesses

Company	SIC	Telephone
Cadet Manufacturing Co.	3634	(206) 693-2505
Columbia Machine, Inc.	3559	(206) 694-1501
First Independent Bank	6022	(206) 695-1311
First Independent Investment	6712	(206) 699-4261
Fort Vancouver Plywood Co.	2435	(206) 694-3368
General Brewing Co.	2082	(206) 695-3381
Nerco Exploration Co.	1041	(206) 892-1148
Nerco Minerals Co.	1041	(206) 253-3377
Northwestern Telephone System	4813	(206) 696-0983
Pacific Telecom, Inc.	4813	(206) 696-0983
Portco Corp.	2655	(206) 696-1641
Red Lion Inns Limited Partner	7011	(206) 696-0001
Rovalve Division	3491	(206) 944-1400
U. S. Natural Resources	3531	(206) 892-2650

Colleges and Universities

Clark College, Vancouver

YAKIMA, WA (MSA)

Geographic Profile

Land Area

4296.1 square miles

Counties and Parishes

Yakima

Ranking Highlights

  21 *out of 319 in total* **land area**
128 *out of 319 in* **population growth,** *1970–1990*
298 *out of 310 in having the lowest* **unemployment** *rate*
179 *out of 310 in size of* **labor force**
266 *out of 318 in the percentage of* **college graduates**
204 *out of 292 in per capita personal* **income**
201 *out of 319 in number of* **manufacturing establishments**
268 *out of 318 in* **physicians** *per 1000 people*
258 *out of 318 in* **hospital beds** *per 1000 people*
224 *out of 267 in fewest* **crimes** *per 1000 people*
143 *out of 266 in fewest* **violent crimes** *per 1000 people*
219 *out of 319 in per capita* **federal funds and grants**

Quality of Life Indexes (Rate per 1000 population)

Crime rate in 1991:   78.7
Violent crime rate in 1991:   6.6
Physicians rate in 1992:   1.28
Hospital bed rate in 1991:   2.74

ACCRA Cost of Living Indexes

(First quarter 1993, average = 100)
Composite index: 102.2
Utilities index: 92.4
Housing index: 102.7

Population (1990)

Total Population and Growth Rate

1990: 188,823
1980: 172,508
1970: 145,212
Growth rate 1970–1990: 30%

Race and Hispanic Origin

White: 73.9%
Black: 1.0%
Asian/Pacific Islander: 1.0%
Native American: 4.5%
Hispanic origin: 23.9%
White not Hispanic: 70.0%

Age

Ages 18 to 20: 4.5%
Ages 21 to 24: 5.3%
Ages 25 to 44: 29.4%
Ages 45 to 54: 9.6%
Ages 55 to 59: 3.9%

Ages 60 to 64: 4%
Ages 65 plus: 13%

Educational Attainment (1990)

Percent having completed high school: 66.1%
Percent having completed college: 13.7%
Elementary and high school enrollment: 37,720

Federal Funds and Grants Received

Total received in 1989: $486,100,000
Funds received per capita: $2,620

Civilian Labor Force

1993 (April): 108,954
1992 average: 108,744
1991 average: 100,860
1990 average: 101,971

Unemployment

1993 (April): 12.0%
1992 average: 12.5%
1991 average: 11.6%
1990 average: 9.7%

Average Annual Pay

1988: $14,871
1987: $14,396
1985: $13,992

Per Capita Personal Income

1991: $16,210
1990: $15,306
1989: $14,360

Business Climate (1987)

Manufacturing

Number of establishments in 1987: 231
Shipments in 1987 ($1,000): $1,276,400
Employees in 1987: 8,000
Change in employment, 1982 to 1987: 11.1%
Average annual pay for manufacturing work in 1989: $20,657
Average annual pay for production work in 1987: $18,705

Wholesale Trade

Number of establishments in 1987: 353
Total sales in 1987 ($1,000): $1,381,600
Change in sales, 1982 to 1987: 46.6%

Retail Trade

Number of establishments in 1987: 1,107
Total sales in 1987 ($1,000): $1,381,600
Retail sales per household in 1987: $13,140
Average annual pay in 1989: $10,912

Service Industry

Selected receipts in 1987 ($1,000): $295,600
Average annual pay in 1989: $14,514

Housing

Total number of units in 1990: 70,852

Occupied units in 1990: 65,985
Owner-occupied units in 1990: 63.2%
1993 ACCRA average cost: $114,000
1993 ACCRA average rent for an apartment: $521

Chamber of Commerce

Greater Yakima Chamber of Commerce, Gary W. Webster, General Manager, 10 N. 9th St., PO Box 1490, Yakima, WA 98907-1490. 509-248-2021, FAX 509-248-0601

Economic Development Office

Yakima County Development Association, Timothy P. McGree, Exec. Director, 32 N. Front St., Yakima, WA 98901. 509-575-1140, FAX 509-575-1508

Major Businesses

Company	SIC	Telephone
A & R Supply Co., Inc.	0134	(509) 837-5101
Amikay Development Co.	5541	(509) 248-9640
Blaze Construction Inc.	1521	(509) 248-5880
Bleyhl Farm Service Inc.	5191	(509) 882-1225
Clasen Fruit & Cold Storage	4222	(509) 966-0970
Comet Trailer Corp.	3715	(509) 697-4800
Highland Fruit Growers Inc.	0723	(509) 966-3990
Inland Fruit & Produce Co.	0723	(509) 877-2126
Larson Fruit Co.	0723	(509) 697-7208
MEC Inc.	5082	(509) 248-0862
Mc Guire Lumber Co. Inc.	5031	(509) 575-1600
Michelsen Packaging Co.	5113	(509) 248-6270
Moen, Gilbert H. Co.	1542	(509) 248-0740
Noel Corp.	5141	(509) 248-4545
Roche Fruit Co Inc.	5148	(509) 248-7200
Smith, R. H. Distributing Co.	5171	(509) 882-3377
Snokist Growers	0723	(509) 453-5631
Speck, C. Motors Inc.	5511	(509) 837-5501
Stadelman Fruit Inc.	0723	(509) 452-8571
Sunnyside Community Hospital Association	8062	(509) 837-4070
Tree Top, Inc.	2033	(509) 697-7251
Twin Y Corp.	2431	(509) 248-2601
Van De Graaf Ranches Inc.	0211	(509) 837-3151
Washington Beef Inc.	2011	(509) 248-3350
Western Recreational Vehicle	3792	(509) 457-4133
Yakima Federal Savings & Loan Association	6035	(509) 248-2634
Yakima Hardware Co.	5072	(509) 453-3181
Yakima Valley Grape Products	2033	(509) 882-1223
Yakima Valley Memorial Hospital Association	8062	(509) 575-8000

WEST VIRGINIA

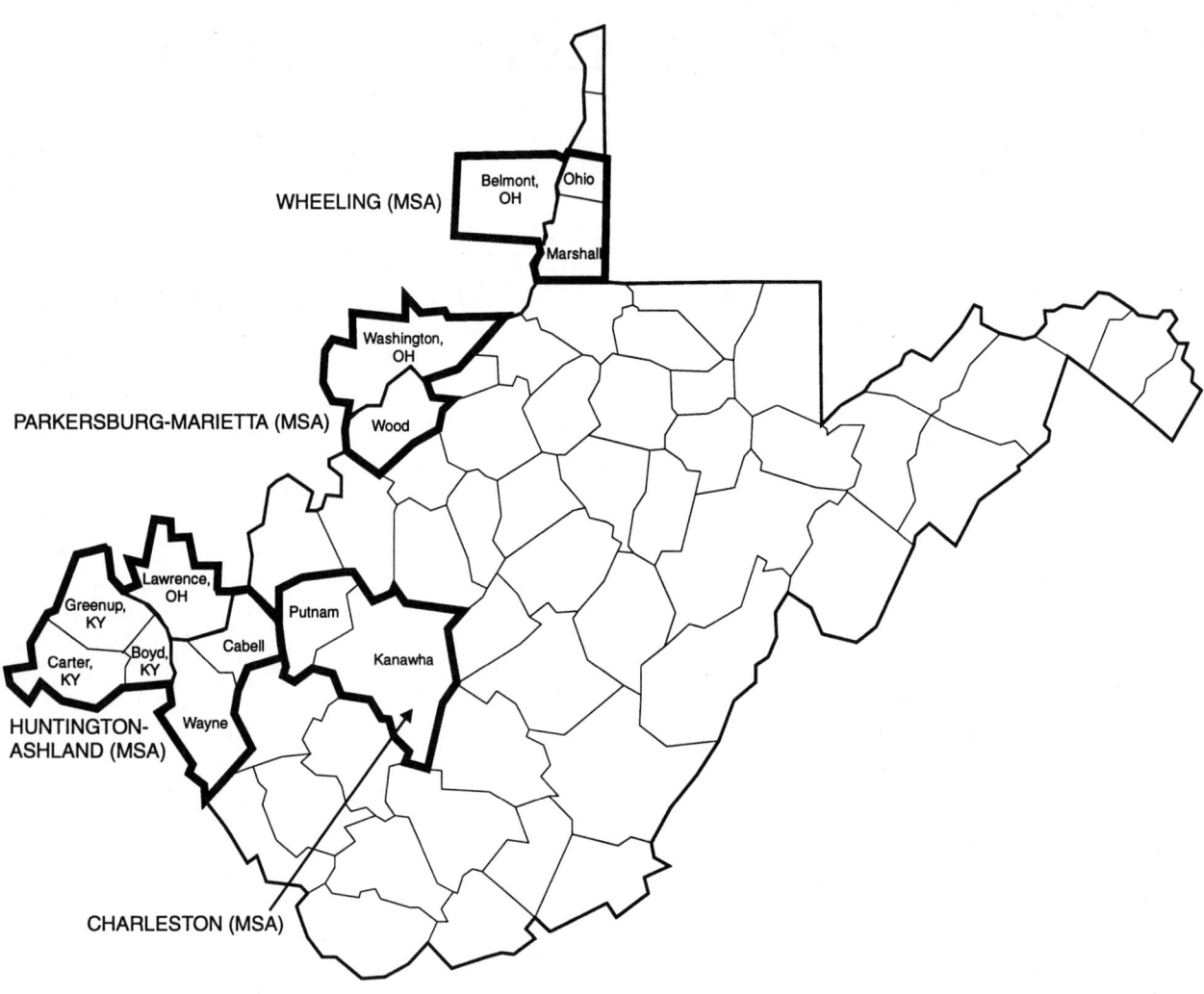

WHEELING (MSA)

Belmont, OH

Ohio

Marshall

PARKERSBURG-MARIETTA (MSA)

Washington, OH

Wood

Lawrence, OH

Greenup, KY

Putnam

Carter, KY

Boyd, KY

Cabell

Kanawha

HUNTINGTON-ASHLAND (MSA)

Wayne

CHARLESTON (MSA)

WEST VIRGINIA

Population
1990: 1,793,477
1980: 1,949,644

Age
Ages 18 to 20: 87,263
Ages 21 to 24: 92,728
Ages 25 to 44: 532,807
Ages 45 to 54: 191,318
Ages 55 to 59: 85,265
Ages 60 to 64: 91,622
Median age: 35.4

Race and Hispanic Origin
White: 1,725,523
Black: 56,295
Asian/Pacific Islander: 7,459
Native American: 2,458
Hispanic origin: 8,489

Households
Total: 688,557
Persons per household: 2.55

Sex
Male: 861,536
Female: 931,941

Population Migration
Domestic migration: -172,000
International migration: 6,000

Projection of the Population in 1995
Total: 1,873,000
18 to 64: 1,118,000

Civilian Labor Force
1993: 765,700
1992: 797,000
1991: 780,500
1990: 768,900

Manufacturing
1995 Projection: 90,100
1992: 82,100
1991: 83,000
1990: 84,400
1989: 87,400

Services
1995 Projection: 191,700
1992: 157,700
1991: 152,900
1990: 149,000
1989: 138,700

Wholesale and Retail Trade
1995 Projection: 172,600
1992: 146,100
1991: 147,800
1990: 148,700
1989: 148,400

Unemployment Rate
1993: 11.8%
1992: 13.9%
1991: 10.0%
1990: 9.2%

Employer Unemployment Contributions
Contribution Rate
1992: 3.00%
1991: 2.90%
1990: 2.10%

Average Weekly Benefit
1992: $165.47
1991: $170.86
1990: $148.14

Gross State Product (Million $)
1989: $27,922
1988: $26,660
1987: $25,025
1979: $17,978
Growth rate, 1979 to 1989: 55.3%

Capital Expenditures of Manufacturing Industries
1990: $753,000,000
1989: $522,400,000
1988: $586,800,000
1987: $434,800,000

State Tax Rates
Individual income: Range from 3% ($10,000 or less) to 6.5% (above $60,000).
Corporate income: 9% of total taxable income.
General property: Property is assessed at 60% of value.

General sales: 6%
Gasoline: 15.5¢ per gallon

Income

Median income for a 4 person family: $31,811

Personal per Capita Income
1992: $15,065
1991: $14,315
1990: $13,722

Disposable per Capita Income
1992: $13,526
1991: $12,795
1990: $12,236

Private Employment Weekly Wages

Average
1989: $384
1988: $376
1987: $376

Manufacturing
1989: $364
1988: $508
1987: $483

Services
1989: $318
1988: $309
1987: $299

Wholesale
1989: $438
1988: $421
1987: $402

Retail
1989: $195
1988: $193
1987: $189

Highway Statistics

Total Highway Miles
1990: 34,592
1989: 34,477
1988: 34,573

Federal Highway Aid
1991: $111,473,000
1990: $110,173,000
1989: $112,037,000

Electricity

Average Cost per Kilowatt Hour
1990: 4.73¢
1989: 4.78¢
1988: 4.80¢

Housing (1990)

Owner occupied units: 510,058
Median house value: $47,900

Renter occupied units: 178,499
Median rent: $221
Total vacant units: 92,738
Homeowner vacancy rate: 2.2%
Rental vacancy rate: 10.1%

State Business Incentives and Assistance

Financial and Business Assistance

The West Virginia Economic Development Authority. WVEDA administers several direct loan programs providing fixed asset financing for new and existing businesses. Uses of loan funds include acquisition, construction and/or renovation of land, buildings and equipment. WVEDA participation levels vary between 30 and 45% of the project's fixed assets and minimum cash equity is required.

West Virginia Certified Development Corporation (SBA 504). This federal program provides long-term, fixed-rate loans for small- and medium-sized firms. Interest rates are tied to U.S. Treasury bond rates of comparable maturity. The maximum loan amount is $750,000.

West Virginia Capital Company Program. The West Virginia Capital Company Act was enacted to stimulate the formation of capital companies to invest in businesses based in West Virginia. Capital companies must have a capital base of at least $1 million but not more than $4 million. Investors in a qualified capital company are entitled to a 50% state tax credit for every dollar invested in a capital company. Unused credit may be carried back three years and carried forward 15 years.

Capital Access Program. CAP is a loan loss reserve fund created to expand the availability of commercial bank loans to businesses in West Virginia.

Community Infrastructure Authority. Administered by the Governor's Office on Community and Industrial Development, the Authority fosters and promotes the provision of adequate capital markets and facilities for borrowing money by counties and municipalities for the financing of public improvements.

Business Investment and Jobs Expansion Tax Credit. Calculation based upon a formula using a qualified investment factor and a job creation factor, this program can allow recovery of up to 90% of a capital investment through state tax credits. The portion of qualified investment allowable as credit is determined by the number of new jobs created that are directly attributable to the taxpayer's qualified investment. This credit can be applied against up to 80% of business and occupation taxes, business franchise taxes, corporation net income taxes, telecommunication taxes and sales or use taxes apportioned to the new investment. This credit also provides for rebate of: 80% of the property taxes attributable to the qualified investment; and 80% of unemployment taxes and 20% of workers' compensation premiums attributable to the new jobs created by the capital investment. Extra rebate amount may

Major Companies in the State

Company name	Fortune 500 rank	City	Telephone	SIC number
Fortune 500 Companies				
Weirton Steel Corp.	338	Weirton	304-797-2000	3312
Other Major Companies in the State				
Allegheny & Western Energy Corp.		Charleston	304-343-4567	4923
American Bancorporation		Wheeling	304-233-5006	6712
Ashland Coal Inc.		Huntington	304-526-3333	5052
CB&T Financial Corp.		Fairmont	304-363-5800	6712
Chesapeake & Potomac Telephone Co. of West Virginia		Charleston	304-343-9911	4813
City Holding Co.		Charleston	304-925-6611	6712
FCFT Inc.		Princeton	304-487-9000	6712
Horizon Bancorp Inc.		Beckley	304-255-7000	6712
Key Centurion Bancshares Inc.		Charleston	304-348-4438	6712
Matewan Bancshares Inc.		Matewan	304-426-8221	6712
Monongahela Power Co.		Fairmont	304-366-3000	4911
Mountaineer Bankshares of West Virginia Inc.		Martinsburg	304-263-1628	6712
National Banc of Commerce Co.		Charleston	304-348-4540	6712
One Valley Bancorp of West Virginia Inc.		Charleston	304-348-7000	6712
Southern Bankshares Inc.		Beckley	304-256-2265	6712
Spectrum Financial Corp.		Wheeling	304-233-0600	6712
Steel of West Virginia Inc.		Huntington	304-696-8200	3312
Twentieth Bancorp Inc.		Huntington	304-526-6200	6712
United Bankshares Inc. West Virginia		Charleston	304-424-8761	6712
Wesbanco Inc.		Wheeling	304-234-9000	6712

be carried forward for a period of up to 12 tax years.

Corporate Headquarters Credit. Additional credit is available to a corporation that relocates its headquarters into West Virginia. If at least 15 new jobs are created the allowable credit is 10% of adjusted qualified investment. For 50 or more new jobs, the allowable credit is 50%. Adjusted qualified investment includes the reasonable and necessary expenses incurred by the corporation to move its corporate headquarters.

Small Business Credit. Tax credits similar to the Business Investment and Jobs Expansion Tax Credit are offered to the small businesses with lower number of created jobs. To qualify, a company must have a annual payroll of at most $1,700,000, annual sales not exceeding $5,500,000, and the median salary of the employees must be at least $12,000 per year. If 10 new jobs are created, the firm is allowed 30% of its qualified investment as credit. An additional 0.5% is allowed for every job created over 10 but not over 50. For 50 or more jobs, the Business Investment and Jobs Expansion Tax Credit benefit will apply.

Warehouse Freeport Tax Exemption. This Exemption allows goods in transit to an out-of-state destination to be exempt from local ad valorem property tax when warehoused in West Virginia.

Other Investment Tax Credits. Credit against Business Franchise taxes for industrial expansion or revitalization is available to manufacturers and persons providing manufacturing services. The credit is 10% of the eligible investment for industrial expansion or revitalization and is applied at the rate of 1/10 per year for 10 years. For more information, please contact the West Virginia State Tax Department.

Education and Training

Job Training Partnership Act. This program operates with funding from the U.S. Department of Labor. It provides job training and other employment related services.

State Offices

Real estate: Real Estate Commission, Donald E. Portis, Exec Secretary, 1033 Quarrier Street, Suite 211, Charleston, WV 25301. 304-348-3555

Chamber of commerce: West Virginia State Chamber of Commerce, John D. Hurd, President, PO Box 2789, 300 Capitol St. #1000, Charleston, WV 25301. 304-342-1115

Economic development: Governor's Office of Community and Industrial Development, Director, 6 Capitol Complex, Rm M-146 Charleston, WV 25305. 304-348-0400, FAX 304-348-0362

Economic Development Authority, Bob Cehi, Exec Director, State Capitol Complex, Bldg. 6, Rm 525, Charleston, WV 25305. 304-348-3650

Business and Industrial Development Division, Director, State Capitol Complex, Bldg. 6, Rm 517, Charleston, WV 25305. 304-348-2234

Governor's Office of Community & Industrial Development (Enterprise Zones Office), Karen Price, Capitol Complex, Room 151, Charleston, WV 25305. 304-348-3255

Small Business Development Center, Eloise Jack, State Director, Governor's Office of Community and Industrial Development, 1115 Virginia Street East, Charleston, WV 25310. 304-348-2960

Environmental affairs: Natural Resources Division, Waste Management Division, Bill Rheinlander, Information Representative, 1356 Hansford St., Charleston, WV 25301. 304-348-5929

Labor: Division of Labor, Bob Miller, Deputy Commissioner, Bldg 3, Rm 319, Capitol Complex, Charleston, WV 25305. 304-348-7890

Unemployment: Employment Security Division, Unemployment Compensation Section, Daniel Light, Supervisor, 112 California Ave., Charleston, WV 25305. 304-348-2624

Worker's compensation: Health and Human Sources Department, Workmen's Compensation Fund, David Caldwell, Director of Employee Relations, 601 Morris St., Charleston, WV 25301. 304-348-0380

Occupational safety and health: Labor Division, Safety & Health Consultation Program, Bob Miller, Deputy Commissioner, Bldg 3, Rm 319, Capitol Complex, Charleston, WV 25305. 304-348-7890

Secretary of state: Secretary of State Office, Bob Wilkinson, Deputy Secretary of State, Bldg 1, Ste. 157-K, Capitol Complex, Charleston, WV 25305. 304-345-4000

Taxation and revenue: Tax and Revenue Department, Mark Muchow, Chief Tax Analyst, Bldg 1, Rm W-300, Capitol Complex, Charleston, WV 25305. 304-348-7890

Designated Zones for Economic Development

Enterprise Zones
Enacted in: 1986
No. of established zones: 0, Program inactive.

Foreign Trade Zones
None

Labor Unions

Aluminum, Brick and Glass Workers, International Union (AFL-CIO)

Boilermakers, Iron Shipbuilders, Blacksmiths, Forgers and Helpers, International Brotherhood of, (AFL-CIO)

Chemical and Atomic Workers

Chemical Workers Union, International (AFL-CIO)

Electrical Workers, International Brotherhood of (AFL-CIO)

Machinists and Aerospace Workers, International Association of (AFL-CIO)

Service Employees' International Union (AFL-CIO)

State, County and Municipal Employees, American Federation of (AFL-CIO)

Steelworkers of America, United (AFL-CIO)

Teamsters, Chauffeurs, Warehousemen and Helpers of America, International Brotherhood of, (AFL-CIO)

Universities with Ph.D. Programs
Marshall University, Huntington
West Virginia University, Morgantown
West Virginia College of Graduate Studies, Charleston

Sources of Additional Information
West Virginia: A Welcome Change. The Governor's Office of Community & Industrial Development, n.d. np.

State of West Virginia Development Assistance Programs. The Governor's Office of Community & Industrial Development, September 1990. np.

Analysis of Receipts and Expenditures. State of West Virginia, State Auditor's Office, Charleston, 1991. 12p.

Vocational Facilities in West Virginia, 1990-91. West Virginia Dept. of Education (304-348-3897), n.d. 8p.

CHARLESTON, WV (MSA)

Geographic Profile

Land Area

1249.4 square miles

Counties and Parishes

Kanawha

Putnam

Ranking Highlights

157 *out of 319 in total* **land area**

282 *out of 319 in* **population growth,** *1970–1990*

252 *out of 310 in having the lowest* **unemployment** *rate*

172 *out of 310 in size of* **labor force**

195 *out of 318 in the percentage of* **college graduates**

148 *out of 292 in per capita personal* **income**

236 *out of 319 in number of* **manufacturing establishments**

82 *out of 318 in* **physicians** *per 1000 people*

48 *out of 318 in* **hospital beds** *per 1000 people*

58 *out of 267 in fewest* **crimes** *per 1000 people*

63 *out of 266 in fewest* **violent crimes** *per 1000 people*

107 *out of 319 in per capita* **federal funds and grants**

Quality of Life Indexes (Rate per 1000 population)

Crime rate in 1991:   44.6

Violent crime rate in 1991:   3.7

Physicians rate in 1992:   2.37

Hospital bed rate in 1991:   5.58

ACCRA Cost of Living Indexes

(First quarter 1993, average = 100)

Composite index: 103.9

Utilities index: 106.2

Housing index: 109.9

Overview

Charleston is the region's hub for transportation, finance, retail, commerce, government, and health care, and acts as a lively center for the arts and recreation while also serving as West Virginia's state capital. The Kanawha Valley owes much of its past and future prosperity to its reputation as a transportation and distribution hub. From river port to interstate hub, the sophisticated transportation routes have lured and kept industry in the region when other parts of West Virginia were troubled with the same economic doldrums that affected much of the nation. Insulated from the boom-or-bust coal industry, the Kanawha Valley has relied on its diversity of natural resources and its importance in the eastern and central states' waterways system, moving goods to the Gulf of Mexico via the Ohio and Mississippi rivers.

Since 1929 the chemical industry has been an economic force in the valley, providing a large, stable employment base for many years. Union Carbide Corporation, Monsanto, E. I. du Pont De Nemours, Rhone-Poulenc, FMC and Olin are among the companies with chemical connected

facilities in the Charleston area. Union Carbide also has its headquarters for research and development in the Tech Center complex in South Charleston. Other Kanawha Valley industries include heavy steel fabricating, glass manufacturing, and energy development; Columbia Gas Transmission Corporation, headquartered in Charleston, employs almost one-third of its workforce in the Charleston headquarters.

Looking at the region as a whole, however, coal and chemicals—the products most often associated with Charleston—actually play a smaller role in the economy than such sectors as government, health services, and wholesale and retail trade. In fact, the city is the retail center of the state. With the 1983 opening of Charleston Town Center—the largest enclosed urban mall east of the Mississippi—retailing got a major boost. The Streetscape project that converted Charleston's traditional downtown into a restored turn-of-the-century village has also helped this district retain its share of the retail market.

The Kanawha Valley's transportation systems may be the region's biggest economic asset, since Charleston is the region's hub for air service, river commerce, and highways. The city has become a distribution center because of its extremely sophisticated transportation routes. Charleston was designated a port of entry by the U.S. Customs Office in 1973, and the business and industrial sectors take advantage of direct shipments from foreign countries. The customs office at Yeager Airport inspects air, barge, rail, and other freight shipments received at locations throughout the region.

Every thirty seconds, a freight car is loaded or unloaded on West Virginia's railways. The cargo can be chemicals, minerals, ores, primary metals, coal, petroleum, stone, or glass. The state has 3,931 miles of track, most of it linking the Atlantic Coast to the Midwest.

The U.S. Army Corps of Engineers maintains a navigation channel three hundred feet wide and a minimum of nine feet deep in the Kanawha River—from the mouth at Point Pleasant on the West Virginia-Ohio border to a point 91 miles east at Deepwater, about 40 miles up river from Charleston. Waterborne commerce has tripled on the Kanawha River since the early 1950s.

Arriving in Charleston by air, travelers land at Yeager Airport—a facility located ten minutes from downtown. First known as the Kanawha Airport, it was built in the late 1940s by shearing off mountaintops and filling in adjacent valleys. Yeager Airport serves ten commercial air carriers and several cargo companies, has private aviation facilities, and is home to the 130th Tactical Airlift Group of the West Virginia Air National Guard.

Arriving by car, visitors approach Charleston via three major interstates, 64, 77, and 79, which intersect near downtown. Charleston is one of thirteen cities in the nation where three interstates merge. I-64 links the Midwest through Charleston to Virginia's eastern seaboard. I-77 links the

Great Lakes area through Charleston to South Carolina and north to Cleveland, Ohio. The West Virginia Turnpike, which originates in Charleston and ends at the Virginia border near Princeton, has been incorporated into the I-77 and I-64 systems. I-79 runs from Erie, Pennsylvania, where it connects with the New York throughways, through Pittsburgh, Pennsylvania, terminating in Charleston.

Population (1990)

Total Population and Growth Rate

1990: 250,454
1980: 269,595
1970: 257,140
Growth rate 1970–1990: -3%

Race and Hispanic Origin

White: 93.6%
Black: 5.6%
Asian/Pacific Islander: 0.6%
Native American: 0.1%
Hispanic origin: 0.4%
White not Hispanic: 93.3%

Age

Ages 18 to 20: 3.8%
Ages 21 to 24: 4.7%
Ages 25 to 44: 31.4%
Ages 45 to 54: 11%
Ages 55 to 59: 5%
Ages 60 to 64: 5.3%
Ages 65 plus: 14.9%

Educational Attainment (1990)

Percent having completed high school: 72.7%
Percent having completed college: 16.9%
Elementary and high school enrollment: 41,913

Federal Funds and Grants Received

Total received in 1989: $908,900,000
Funds received per capita: $3,485

Civilian Labor Force

1993 (April): 119,720
1992 average: 117,960
1991 average: 121,067
1990 average: 118,921

Unemployment

1993 (April): 9.0%
1992 average: 8.8%
1991 average: 7.9%
1990 average: 6.3%

Average Annual Pay

1988: $20,752
1987: $20,352
1985: $19,503

Per Capita Personal Income

1991: $17,343

1990: $16,645
1989: $15,319

Business Climate (1987)

Manufacturing

Number of establishments in 1987: 165
Shipments in 1987 ($1,000): $2,001,100
Employees in 1987: 10,700
Change in employment, 1982 to 1987: -25.7%
Average annual pay for manufacturing work in 1989: $35,857
Average annual pay for production work in 1987: $28,327

Wholesale Trade

Number of establishments in 1987: 558
Total sales in 1987 ($1,000): $1,512,500
Change in sales, 1982 to 1987: -13.3%

Retail Trade

Number of establishments in 1987: 1,531
Total sales in 1987 ($1,000): $1,512,500
Retail sales per household in 1987: $15,882
Average annual pay in 1989: $10,993

Service Industry

Selected receipts in 1987 ($1,000): $642,300
Average annual pay in 1989: $19,115

Housing

Total number of units in 1990: 109,631
Occupied units in 1990: 100,408
Owner-occupied units in 1990: 70.8%
1993 ACCRA average cost: $126,000
1993 ACCRA average rent for an apartment: $551

Chamber of Commerce

Charleston Regional Chamber of Commerce, John A. Chapman, President, 106 Capitol St. #100, Charleston, WV 25301-2610. 304-345-0770

Economic Development Office

Governor's Office of Industrial Development, Ann M. Johnson, Director, State Capitol Complex, Bldg. 6 Room 517, Charleston, WV 25305. 304-348-3810, FAX 304-348-0449

Major Businesses

Company	SIC	Telephone
Allegheny & Wstern Energy	4924	(304) 343-4327
Blue Cross Blue Shield of West Virginia	6324	(304) 347-7600
Camcare Inc.	8062	(304) 348-7696
Cannelton Industries Inc.	1221	(304) 925-1222
Charleston Area Medical	8062	(304) 348-6043
Charleston National Bank	6021	(304) 348-4411
Coal Properties Corp.	1221	(304) 344-0300
Columbia Gas Transmission	4923	(304) 357-2000
Concorp Inc.	1629	(304) 776-6128

Major Businesses (Continued)

Company	SIC	Telephone
Eastern Associated Coal	1221	(304) 340-1700
Hawks Nest Mining Co., Inc.	1221	(304) 343-6550
Holland, Joe Chevrolet Inc.	5511	(304) 744-1561
Imperial-Pacific Investment	5052	(304) 343-6550
Jefferds Corp.	5084	(304) 755-8111
Key Centurion Bancshares	6021	(304) 348-4411
Maple Meadow Mining Co.	1221	(304) 925-1222
Mcjunkin Corp.	5051	(304) 348-5211
Midwest Corp.	3312	(304) 343-8874
Mountaineer Gas Co.	4924	(304) 347-0595
National Banc of Commerce	6712	(304) 348-5000
One Valley Bank of Charleston	6021	(304) 348-7000
St. Francis Hospital of Charleston	8062	(304) 347-6500
Thomas Herb Memorial Hospital Assoociation	8062	(304) 766-3600
Union Boiler Co.	1629	(304) 755-8171
United Bankshares, Inc.	6021	(304) 424-8800
West Virginia Parkways	4785	(304) 925-4906
West Virginia-Merican Water Co.	4941	(304) 345-3474

Colleges and Universities

University of Charleston, Charleston

HUNTINGTON–ASHLAND, WV–KY–OH (MSA)

Geographic Profile

Land Area

2159.9 square miles

Counties and Parishes

Kentucky:
  Boyd
  Carter
  Greenup
Ohio:
  Lawrence
West Virginia:
  Cabell
  Wayne

Ranking Highlights

  80 *out of 319 in total* **land area**

264 *out of 319 in* **population growth,** *1970–1990*

278 *out of 310 in having the lowest* **unemployment** *rate*

158 *out of 310 in size of* **labor force**

290 *out of 318 in the percentage of* **college graduates**

267 *out of 292 in per capita personal* **income**

176 *out of 319 in number of* **manufacturing establishments**

178 *out of 318 in* **physicians** *per 1000 people*

118 *out of 318 in* **hospital beds** *per 1000 people*

  14 *out of 267 in fewest* **crimes** *per 1000 people*

  32 *out of 266 in fewest* **violent crimes** *per 1000 people*

102 *out of 319 in per capita* **federal funds and grants**

Quality of Life Indexes (Rate per 1000 population)

Crime rate in 1991:	33.9
Violent crime rate in 1991:	2.6
Physicians rate in 1992:	1.74
Hospital bed rate in 1991:	4.39

ACCRA Cost of Living Indexes

(First quarter 1993, average = 100)

Composite index:	N/A
Utilities index:	N/A
Housing index:	N/A

Population (1990)

Total Population and Growth Rate

1990: 312,529
1980: 336,410
1970: 306,785
Growth rate 1970–1990: 2%

Race and Hispanic Origin

White: 97.3%
Black: 2.2%
Asian/Pacific Islander: 0.3%
Native American: 0.1%

Hispanic origin: 0.4%
White not Hispanic: 97.0%

Age
Ages 18 to 20: 5.1%
Ages 21 to 24: 5.4%
Ages 25 to 44: 29.2%
Ages 45 to 54: 11.4%
Ages 55 to 59:   5%
Ages 60 to 64: 5.1%
Ages 65 plus: 14.4%

Educational Attainment (1990)
Percent having completed high school: 66.7%
Percent having completed college: 12.6%
Elementary and high school enrollment: 55,182

Federal Funds and Grants Received
Total received in 1989: $1,149,800,000
Funds received per capita: $3,567

Civilian Labor Force
1993 (April):   130,769
1992 average: 131,140
1991 average: 133,236
1990 average: 132,559

Unemployment
1993 (April): 10.2%
1992 average: 9.8%
1991 average: 9.5%
1990 average: 6.9%

Average Annual Pay
1988: $19,506
1987: $18,783
1985: $17,595

Per Capita Personal Income
1991: $14,622
1990: $14,070
1989: $13,164

Business Climate (1987)
Manufacturing
Number of establishments in 1987: 275
Shipments in 1987 ($1,000): $3,754,100
Employees in 1987: 16,600
Change in employment, 1982 to 1987: 0%
Average annual pay for manufacturing work in 1989: $29,972
Average annual pay for production work in 1987: $26,516

Wholesale Trade
Number of establishments in 1987: 458
Total sales in 1987 ($1,000): $1,497,100
Change in sales, 1982 to 1987: 2.2%

Retail Trade
Number of establishments in 1987: 1,833
Total sales in 1987 ($1,000): $1,497,100

Retail sales per household in 1987: $13,170
Average annual pay in 1989: $9,934

Service Industry
Selected receipts in 1987 ($1,000): $433,700
Average annual pay in 1989: $17,842

Housing
Total number of units in 1990: 130,687
Occupied units in 1990: 119,640
Owner-occupied units in 1990: 72.0%
1993 ACCRA average cost: N/A
1993 ACCRA average rent for an apartment: N/A

Chamber of Commerce
Huntington Area Chamber of Commerce, Coleman Trainor, President, 522 9th St., PO Box 1509, Huntington, WV 25716. 304-525-5131

Economic Development Office
Chamber of Commerce of Boyd and Greenup Counties, Raymond B. Graeves, Prsident, 207 15th St. PO Box 830, Ashland, KY 41105-0830. 606-324-5111, FAX 606-325-4607

Economic Development Organizations
City of Ashland Economic Development Department, Jo Ann Bell, Director, PO Box 1839, Ashland, KY 41105. 606-327-2005, FAX 606-327-2055

Economic Development Corp. of Boyd and Greenup Counties, John W. Gatling, President, PO Box 830, Ashland, KY 41105-0830. 606-324-5113, FAX 606-325-4607

Major Businesses

Company	SIC	Telephone
Addington Resources Inc.	1221	(606) 928-3433
Ameriquest Inc.	7699	(606) 325-8845
Arthur's Enterprises Inc.	5063	(304) 523-7491
Ashland Coal Inc.	1221	(304) 526-3333
Ashland Hospital Corp.	8062	(606) 327-4000
Ashland Oil Holdings Inc.	1611	(606) 329-3333
Ashland Oil Inc.	2911	(606) 329-3333
Ashland Pipe Line Co.	4612	(606) 329-5616
Cabell Huntington Hospital	8062	(304) 526-2000
First American Kentucky Bancorp	6036	(606) 329-2222
First Huntington National Bank	6021	(304) 526-4200
Hall, Don Chevrolet Inc.	5511	(606) 329-8777
Inco Alloys International	3356	(304) 526-5100
Jabo Supply Corp.	5051	(304) 736-8333
Kentucky Electric Steel Co.	3312	(606) 928-6441
Kentucky Power Co.	4911	(606) 327-1111
Logan, S. S. Packing Co.	5147	(304) 525-7625
Marathon Acquisition Corp.	3532	(304) 529-4343
Persinger Supply Co.	5064	(304) 486-5401
St. Mary's Hospital Inc.	8062	(304) 526-1234

Major Businesses (Continued)

Company	SIC	Telephone
Service Wire Co.	3643	(304) 522-6053
South Point Ethanol	2869	(614) 377-2765
State Electric Supply Co.	5063	(304) 523-7491
Steel of West Virginia Inc.	3312	(304) 529-7171
Third National Bank of Ashland	6021	(606) 329-2900
Twentieth Street Bank Inc.	6022	(304) 529-2501

Colleges and Universities

Huntington Junior College of Business, Huntington, WV

Marshall University, Huntington, WV

University of Kentucky, Ashland Community College, Ashland, KY

PARKERSBURG–MARIETTA, WV–OH (MSA)

Geographic Profile

Land Area

1002.6 square miles

Counties and Parishes

Ohio:

Washington

West Virginia:

Wood

Ranking Highlights

203 *out of 319 in total* **land area**

253 *out of 319 in* **population growth,** *1970–1990*

259 *out of 310 in having the lowest* **unemployment** *rate*

223 *out of 310 in size of* **labor force**

275 *out of 318 in the percentage of* **college graduates**

229 *out of 292 in per capita personal* **income**

223 *out of 319 in number of* **manufacturing establishments**

286 *out of 318 in* **physicians** *per 1000 people*

46 *out of 318 in* **hospital beds** *per 1000 people*

N/A *out of 267 in fewest* **crimes** *per 1000 people*

N/A *out of 266 in fewest* **violent crimes** *per 1000 people*

131 *out of 319 in per capita* **federal funds and grants**

Quality of Life Indexes (Rate per 1000 population)

Crime rate in 1991: 26.8

Violent crime rate in 1991: N/A

Physicians rate in 1992: 1.17

Hospital bed rate in 1991: 5.6

ACCRA Cost of Living Indexes

(First quarter 1993, average = 100)

Composite index: 94.8

Utilities index: 90.6

Housing index: 94.0

Population (1990)

Total Population and Growth Rate

1990: 149,169

1980: 157,893

1970: 143,978

Growth rate 1970–1990: 4%

Race and Hispanic Origin

White: 98.3%

Black: 1.1%

Asian/Pacific Islander: 0.3%

Native American: 0.2%

Hispanic origin: 0.3%

White not Hispanic: 98.1%

Age

Ages 18 to 20: 4.2%

Ages 21 to 24: 5%

Ages 25 to 44: 30.2%
Ages 45 to 54: 11.6%
Ages 55 to 59: 4.8%
Ages 60 to 64: 4.9%
Ages 65 plus: 14.3%

Educational Attainment (1990)

Percent having completed high school: 75.0%
Percent having completed college: 13.4%
Elementary and high school enrollment: 26,099

Federal Funds and Grants Received

Total received in 1989: $508,400,000
Funds received per capita: $3,293

Civilian Labor Force

1993 (April):   74,178
1992 average: 74,047
1991 average: 73,524
1990 average: 73,090

Unemployment

1993 (April):   8.5%
1992 average: 9.0%
1991 average: 7.9%
1990 average: 6.8%

Average Annual Pay

1988: $19,849
1987: $18,844
1985: $18,044

Per Capita Personal Income

1991: $15,671
1990: $15,080
1989: $14,128

Business Climate (1987)

Manufacturing

Number of establishments in 1987: 195
Shipments in 1987 ($1,000): $2,857,400
Employees in 1987: 14,400
Change in employment, 1982 to 1987: 0%
Average annual pay for manufacturing work in 1989: $30,677
Average annual pay for production work in 1987: $26,129

Wholesale Trade

Number of establishments in 1987: 243
Total sales in 1987 ($1,000): $811,400
Change in sales, 1982 to 1987: 0%

Retail Trade

Number of establishments in 1987: 939
Total sales in 1987 ($1,000): $811,400
Retail sales per household in 1987: $16,038
Average annual pay in 1989: $10,245

Service Industry

Selected receipts in 1987 ($1,000): $332,800
Average annual pay in 1989: $16,112

Housing

Total number of units in 1990: 63,372
Occupied units in 1990: 57,804
Owner-occupied units in 1990: 74.1%
1993 ACCRA average cost: $113,625
1993 ACCRA average rent for an apartment: $377

Chamber of Commerce

Greater Parkersburg Area Chamber of Commerce, George Kellenberger, President, 720 Juliana St., Parkersburg, WV 26101. 304-422-3588

Economic Development Office

Marietta Area Chamber of Commerce, Jack Moberg, President, 316 3rd St. Marietta, OH 45750. 614-373-5176, FAX 614-373-7808

Economic Development Organizations

Buckeye Hills-Hocking Valley Regional Development District, Tom Closser, Exec. Director, Route 1 Box 299D, Marietta, OH 45750. 614-374-9436, FAX 614-374-8038

Major Businesses

Company	SIC	Telephone
American Marietta Corp.	1542	(614) 374-8989
Ames, O. Co.	3423	(304) 424-3000
Benson Truck Bodies Inc.	3713	(304) 489-9020
Blue Cross Blue Shield of West Virginia	6321	(304) 424-7700
Broughton Foods Co.	2026	(614) 373-4121
Camden-Clark Memorial Hospital	8062	(304) 424-2111
Commercial Bancshares Inc.	6712	(304) 424-0300
Commercial Banking & Trust	6022	(304) 424-0300
Connex Pipe Systems Inc.	3498	(614) 373-7541
Dils Motor Co.	5511	(304) 485-6401
Fenton Art Glass Co., Inc	3229	(304) 375-6122
Forma Scientific Inc.	3821	(614) 373-4763
Gatewood Products Inc.	5051	(304) 422-3103
Globe Metallurgical Inc.	3339	(614) 984-2361
Goldsmit-Black Inc.	5194	(304) 295-3341
International Converters	3089	(614) 423-7525
Jim Mc Cutcheon Auction Co.	7389	(304) 485-6561
Kardex Systems Inc.	2542	(614) 374-9300
Kelly, Carl Paving Inc.	1611	(304) 424-7353
Laurel Management Group	1761	(304) 295-3311
Life Sciences International	5049	(614) 373-5763
Marietta Automotive Warehouse	5013	(614) 373-8151
Marietta Memorial Hospital	8062	(614) 374-1400
Marietta Structures Corp.	3272	(614) 373-3211
Mc Clinton Chevrolet Co.	5511	(304) 422-6501
Mountain Co. Inc.	1761	(304) 295-3311
Nelson's Drug Store Inc.	5912	(304) 422-4593
Pizza People Inc.	5812	(614) 373-1102
Ravens Metal Products Inc.	3715	(304) 428-8030

Major Businesses (Continued)

Company	SIC	Telephone
River Gas Co., Inc.	4924	(614) 373-6545
St. Joseph Hospital of Parkersburg	8062	(304) 424-4111
Storck Baking Co., Inc.	2051	(304) 485-5441
United National Bank	6021	(304) 424-8800
Warner, Dick Pontiac Inc.	5511	(304) 422-3503

Colleges and Universities

Marietta College, Marietta, OH
Ohio Valley College, Parkersburg, WV

WHEELING, WV–OH (MSA)

Geographic Profile

Land Area

950.5 square miles

Counties and Parishes

Ohio:
  Belmont
West Virginia:
  Marshall
  Ohio

Ranking Highlights

206 *out of 319 in total* **land area**
317 *out of 319 in* **population growth,** *1970–1990*
265 *out of 310 in having the lowest* **unemployment** *rate*
230 *out of 310 in size of* **labor force**
294 *out of 318 in the percentage of* **college graduates**
239 *out of 292 in per capita personal* **income**
261 *out of 319 in number of* **manufacturing establishments**
117 *out of 318 in* **physicians** *per 1000 people*
 16 *out of 318 in* **hospital beds** *per 1000 people*
N/A *out of 267 in fewest* **crimes** *per 1000 people*
N/A *out of 266 in fewest* **violent crimes** *per 1000 people*
176 *out of 319 in per capita* **federal funds and grants**

Quality of Life Indexes (Rate per 1000 population)

Crime rate in 1991:	N/A
Violent crime rate in 1991:	N/A
Physicians rate in 1992:	2.04
Hospital bed rate in 1991:	6.99

ACCRA Cost of Living Indexes

(First quarter 1993, average = 100)

Composite index:	N/A
Utilities index:	N/A
Housing index:	N/A

Population (1990)

Total Population and Growth Rate

1990: 159,301
1980: 185,566
1970: 181,954
Growth rate 1970–1990: -12%

Race and Hispanic Origin

White: 97.5%
Black: 2.0%
Asian/Pacific Islander: 0.3%
Native American: 0.1%
Hispanic origin: 0.4%
White not Hispanic: 97.2%

Age

Ages 18 to 20: 4.4%
Ages 21 to 24: 4.5%

Ages 25 to 44: 28.7%
Ages 45 to 54: 10.4%
Ages 55 to 59: 4.8%
Ages 60 to 64: 5.8%
Ages 65 plus: 18%

Educational Attainment (1990)
Percent having completed high school: 72.9%
Percent having completed college: 12.2%
Elementary and high school enrollment: 26,327

Federal Funds and Grants Received
Total received in 1989: $510,300,000
Funds received per capita: $2,975

Civilian Labor Force
1993 (April):   71,487
1992 average: 71,417
1991 average: 72,200
1990 average: 72,039

Unemployment
1993 (April):   9.5%
1992 average: 9.1%
1991 average: 7.6%
1990 average: 6.0%

Average Annual Pay
1988: $18,080
1987: $17,501
1985: $16,604

Per Capita Personal Income
1991: $15,396
1990: $14,996
1989: $14,083

Business Climate (1987)
Manufacturing
Number of establishments in 1987: 139
Shipments in 1987 ($1,000): $865,700
Employees in 1987: 5,300
Change in employment, 1982 to 1987: -44.8%
Average annual pay for manufacturing work in 1989: $29,233
Average annual pay for production work in 1987: $19,971

Wholesale Trade
Number of establishments in 1987: 211
Total sales in 1987 ($1,000): $501,800
Change in sales, 1982 to 1987: -0.2%

Retail Trade
Number of establishments in 1987: 1,106
Total sales in 1987 ($1,000): $501,800
Retail sales per household in 1987: $13,478
Average annual pay in 1989: $9,860

Service Industry
Selected receipts in 1987 ($1,000): $256,000
Average annual pay in 1989: $15,304

Housing
Total number of units in 1990: 69,434
Occupied units in 1990: 62,858
Owner-occupied units in 1990: 72.4%
1993 ACCRA average cost: N/A
1993 ACCRA average rent for an apartment: N/A

Chamber of Commerce
Wheeling Area Chamber of Commerce, Richard A. Kennedy, Jr., President, 1000 Boury Center, 1233 Main St., Wheeling, WV 26003. 304-233-2575

Economic Development Office
Ohio Valley Industrial & Business Development Corp., Terry Burkhart, Exec. Director, PO Box 1029, Wheeling, WV 26003. 304-232-7722, FAX 304-232-6022

Major Businesses

Company	SIC	Telephone
Aladdin Food Management Service	5812	(304) 242-6200
American BanCorp.	6021	(304) 233-5006
Bellaire Trucking Co.	4213	(614) 695-5142
Belmont Bancorp	6021	(614) 695-3323
Belmont County National Bank	6021	(614) 695-3323
City Hospital of Bellaire	8062	(614) 671-1200
Cloverland Dairy Inc.	2021	(614) 968-3523
Courtaulds Packaging Inc.	3082	(304) 277-3000
East Ohio Regional Hospital	8062	(614) 633-1100
Federal One Savings Bank	6035	(304) 234-1100
Jarvis, Downing & Emch Inc.	1541	(304) 232-5000
Ohio Valley Medical Center	8062	(304) 234-0123
PAR Enterprises Inc.	5511	(304) 233-2222
Private Brands Ltd.	5014	(304) 547-5921
Reynold's Memorial Hospital	8062	(304) 845-3211
Riesbeck's Food Markets Inc.	5411	(304) 234-6150
Robinson Bob Oldsmobile-Cadillac	5511	(304) 232-1880
Security National Bank & Trust	6021	(304) 233-0600
Sledd, Charles M. Co., Inc.	5194	(304) 243-1820
Spectrum Financial Corp.	6022	(304) 233-0600
Stone & Thomas	5311	(304) 232-3344
United National Bank-North	6021	(304) 233-4500
Valley Welding Supply Co.	5084	(304) 232-1541
Wesbanco, Inc.	6022	(304) 234-9000
Wheeling Hospital Inc.	8062	(304) 243-3000
Wheeling National Bank	6021	(304) 232-0110
Wheeling Power Co.	4911	(304) 234-3000
Wheeling Wholesale Grocer	5141	(304) 845-3807
Wheeling-Pittsburgh Steel	3312	(304) 234-2400
Wilson, W. A. & Sons Inc.	5039	(304) 232-2200

WISCONSIN

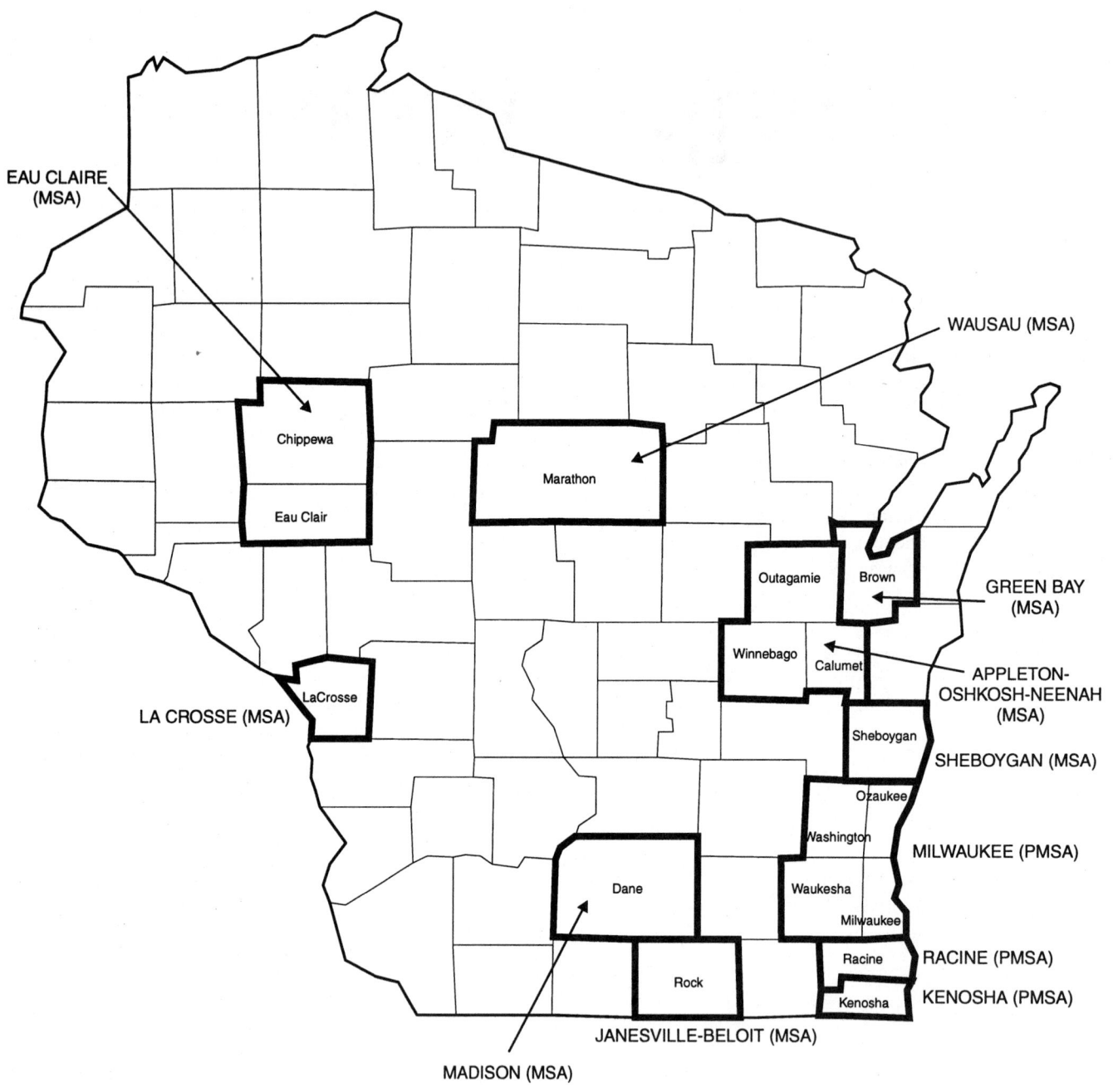

EAU CLAIRE
(MSA)

WAUSAU (MSA)

Chippewa

Eau Clair

Marathon

Outagamie

Brown

GREEN BAY
(MSA)

Winnebago

Calumet

APPLETON-
OSHKOSH-NEENAH
(MSA)

LaCrosse

Sheboygan

SHEBOYGAN (MSA)

LA CROSSE (MSA)

Ozaukee

Washington

MILWAUKEE (PMSA)

Dane

Waukesha

Milwaukee

Rock

Racine

RACINE (PMSA)

Kenosha

KENOSHA (PMSA)

JANESVILLE-BELOIT (MSA)

MADISON (MSA)

WISCONSIN

Population
1990: 4,891,769
1980: 4,705,767

Age
Ages 18 to 20: 225,390
Ages 21 to 24: 286,936
Ages 25 to 44: 1,546,832
Ages 45 to 54: 478,882
Ages 55 to 59: 204,647
Ages 60 to 64: 208,879
Median age: 32.9

Race and Hispanic Origin
White: 4,512,523
Black: 244,539
Asian/Pacific Islander: 53,583
Native American: 39,387
Hispanic origin: 93,194

Households
Total: 1,822,118
Persons per household: 2.61

Sex
Male: 2,392,935
Female: 2,498,834

Population Migration
Domestic migration: -149,000
International migration: 29,000

Projection of the Population in 1995
Total: 5,055,000
18 to 64: 3,082,000

Civilian Labor Force
1993: 2,662,900
1992: 2,594,900
1991: 2,593,900
1990: 2,547,600

Manufacturing
1995 Projection: 583,400
1992: 546,100
1991: 548,400
1990: 553,100
1989: 552,400

Services
1995 Projection: 739,900

1992: 570,500
1991: 554,400
1990: 537,300
1989: 515,800

Wholesale and Retail Trade
1995 Projection: 622,800
1992: 546,400
1991: 545,100
1990: 549,800
1989: 542,600

Unemployment Rate
1993: 5.3%
1992: 5.8%
1991: 4.9%
1990: 5.6%

Employer Unemployment Contributions
Contribution Rate
1992: 2.04%
1991: 2.05%
1990: 2.47%

Average Weekly Benefit
1992: $189.13
1991: $180.71
1990: $172.01

Gross State Product (Million $)
1989: $93,978
1988: $88,559
1987: $81,943
1979: $50,228
Growth rate, 1979 to 1989: 87.1%

Capital Expenditures of Manufacturing Industries
1990: $2,580,400,000
1989: $2,433,500,000
1988: $2,141,000,000
1987: $2,027,400,000

State Tax Rates
Individual income: Range from 4.9% ($10,000 or less) to 6.93% (above $20,001).
Corporate income: 7.9% of total taxable income.
General property: N/A

General sales: 5%
Gasoline: 22.2¢ per gallon

Income

Median income for a 4 person family: $40,557

Personal per Capita Income
1992: $18,727
1991: $17,919
1990: $17,455

Disposable per Capita Income
1992: $16,351
1991: $15,545
1990: $15,110

Private Employment Weekly Wages

Average
1989: $381
1988: $372
1987: $372

Manufacturing
1989: $356
1988: $497
1987: $479

Services
1989: $324
1988: $311
1987: $297

Wholesale
1989: $483
1988: $470
1987: $445

Retail
1989: $193
1988: $186
1987: $178

Highway Statistics

Total Highway Miles
1990: 109,876
1989: 109,813
1988: 109,629

Federal Highway Aid
1991: $213,574,000
1990: $216,076,000
1989: $225,758,000

Electricity

Average Cost per Kilowatt Hour
1990: 5.40¢
1989: 5.44¢
1988: 5.49¢

Housing (1990)

Owner occupied units: 1,215,350
Median house VA lue: $62,500

Renter occupied units: 606,768
Median rent: $331
Total VA cant units: 233,656
Homeowner VA cancy rate: 1.2%
Rental VA cancy rate: 4.7%

State Business Incentives and Assistance

Enterprise Zone Incentives

The Wisconsin Development Zone Program is designed to improve private-sector investment and employment opportunities, particularly for target groups, in the state's economically distressed areas. Businesses locating or expanding operations in development zones can receive tax benefits. These tax credits include:

1) A refundable jobs credit equal to 40% of the first $6,000 in qualified wages for the first and second years of employment. This credit is aVA ilable for hiring members of certain targeted groups.

2) A refundable sales tax credit for the amount of sales tax paid on building materials and equipment used in a trade or business in a development zone.

3) A non-refundable 2.5% location credit for the costs of acquiring, constructing, rehabilitating, remodeling, or repairing real property that is used in a trade or business in a development zone.

4) A non-refundable 2.5% investment credit on depreciable tangible personal property used in a trade or business in a development zone.

5) A non-refundable 5% additional research credit on increased expenditures within a development zone.

Financial and Business Assistance

The Community Based Economic Development Program. Facilitates business development in distressed areas. The program awards up to $30,000 for business and entrepreneurial development and business incubator grants from $25,000.

The Wisconsin Development Fund. Includes approximately $12 million for economic development. It includes the following programs: 1) Major Economic Development Project Program. Supports business-development projects that will have a substantial local, regional, or state-wide impact; 2) Technology Development Fund. Encourages business research leading to a new product or process. Applicant businesses must work with a university on their research. Awards are repaid if the new product or process is successful; 3) Small Business Innovation Research Bridge-Financing Program. Provides bridge or interim financing for companies that have won federal SBIR Phase I awards. They can then continue their research while awaiting federal funding decisions on their Phase II awards and; 4) The Employee Ownership Assistance Loan Program. Can help a group of employees seeking to purchase a business. The business under consideration must have closed or suffered substantial layoffs within one year

Major Companies in the State

Company name	Fortune 500 rank	City	Telephone	SIC number
Fortune 500 Companies				
A. O. Smith Corp.	348	Milwaukee	414-359-4000	3713
Banta Corp.	461	Menasha	414-722-7777	2754
Briggs & Stratton Corp.	351	Wauwatosa	414-259-5333	3519
Consolidated Papers Inc.	382	Wisconsin Rapids	715-422-3111	2672
Fort Howard Corp.	321	Green Bay	414-435-8821	2676
Giddings & Lewis Inc.	480	Fond DuLac	414-921-4100	3541
Harley Davidson Inc.	332	Milwaukee	414-342-4680	3751
Harnischfeger Industries Inc.	282	Brookfield	414-671-4400	3554
Johnson Controls Inc.	105	Milwaukee	414-228-1200	3822
Oshkosh Truck Corp.	468	Oshkosh	414-235-9151	3711
Snap-on Tools Corp.	361	Kenosha	414-656-5200	3423
Terex Corp. Wisconsin	357	Green Bay	414-435-5322	3715
Universal Foods Corp.	389	Milwaukee	414-271-6755	2099
Other Major Companies in the State				
Applied Power Inc.		Butler	414-781-6600	3594
Firstar Corp.		Milwaukee	414-765-4985	6712
Journal Communications Inc.		Milwaukee	414-224-2374	2711
Lands End Inc.		Dodgeville	608-935-9341	5961
Manpower Inc.		Milwaukee	414-961-1000	7363
Marshall & Ilsley Corp.		Milwaukee	414-765-7801	6712
Modine Manufacturing Co.		Racine	414-636-1200	3443
Rex Holdings Inc.		Milwaukee	414-643-3000	3535
Rexnord Corp.		Milwaukee	414-643-3000	3568
Roundy's Inc.		Pewaukee	414-547-7999	5141
Schultz Sav O Stores Inc.		Sheboygan	414-457-4433	5411
Shopko Stores Inc.		Green Bay	414-497-2211	5331
Wicor Inc.		Milwaukee	414-291-7026	4923
Wisconsin Bell Inc.		Milwaukee	414-549-7102	4813
Wisconsin Electric Power Co.		Milwaukee	414-221-2345	4911
Wisconsin Energy Corp.		Milwaukee	414-221-2345	4931
Wisconsin Gas Co.		Milwaukee	414-291-7000	4923
Wisconsin Power & Light Co.		Madison	608-252-3311	4931
Wisconsin Public Service Corp.		Green Bay	414-433-1445	4931
WPL Holdings Inc.		Madison	608-252-3311	4931

prior to the employee-group's application. Maximum award for any business is $35,000.

Wisconsin Innovation Network Foundation. The Foundation receives state funds and donations. It serves as a bridge between entrepreneurs and sources of finance for business.

Tax Incremental Financing. A funding mechanism for financing local economic development projects, created to help cities attract industrial and commercial growth in underdeveloped and blighted areas and to areas in need of rehabilitation. A city designates a specific area and develops a plan to improve property values in the district. The extra taxes generated by the increased property value will be used to pay for land acquisition or public works it must install, such as sewer lines, and street construction.

The Wisconsin Transportation Facilities Economic Assistance and Development Program. Enables the Department of Transportation Secretary to approve transportation facilities improvements when transportation improvement is a part of an economic development project.

The Wisconsin Housing and Economic Development Authority. Offers a linked-deposits program that makes available through Wisconsin lenders short-term, below-market-rate loans to small, minority- or women-owned businesses.

Wisconsin Business Development, Inc. Reviews business financing requests to the federal Small Business Administration and uses SBA loan programs to provide small businesses with fixed rate financing.

The Area Development Manager Program. Assists business expansions, promotes business retention, and helps local development organizations in their respective territories.

Education and Training

Customized Labor Training Fund. Administered by the Department of Development, this program stimulates employment, business expansion of existing businesses, and the attraction and creation of new businesses by helping companies train or retrain workers in specialized skills. The employer needs to provide a 50% cash or in-kind match for the training cost.

Job Training Partnership Act. This program operates with funding from the U.S. Department of Labor. It provides job training and other employment related services.

State Offices

Real estate: Regulation and Licensing Department, Direct Licensing & Real Estate Bureau, Clete Hansen, Director, PO Box 8935, Madison, WI 53708-8935. 608-266-3423

Chamber of commerce: Wisconsin Manufacturers & Commerce, James S. Haney, President, PO Box 352, Madison, 501 E. Washington Ave., WI 53701. 608-258-3400

Economic development: Department of Development, Robert N. Trunzo, Secretary, PO Box 7970, 123 W. Washington Ave., Madison, WI 53707. 800-HELP-BUS or 608-266-1018, FAX 608-267-0436

Department of Development, Katherine Heady, Development Zone Program Manager, PO Box 7970, 123 W. Washington Ave., Madison, WI 53707. 608-267-2045, FAX 608-267-0436

Small Business Development Center, William Pinkovitz, State Director, University of Wisconsin, 432 North Lake Street, Madison, WI 53705-1498. 608-263-7766

Wisconsin Innovation Network Foundation, Diane Curtz, Exec Vice President, PO Box 71, Madison, WI 53701. 608-256-8348

Forward Wisconsin (Wisconsin's Economic Development Marketing Corporation)

Environmental affairs: Dept. of Natural Resources, Carroll D. Besadny, Secretary, PO Box 7921, 101 S. Webster Street, 5th Fl., Madison, WI 53707. 608-266-2121

Labor: Dept. of Industry, Labor, & Human Relations - Job Service, Edith Borden, Division Administrator, PO Box 7903, Rm 201, 201 E. Washington Ave., Madison, WI 53707. 608-266-8561

Unemployment: Dept. of Industry, Labor, & Human Relations - Unemployment Compensation, Bruce Hagen, Division Administrator, PO Box 7905, Rm 371X, 201 E. Washington Ave., Madison, WI 53707. 608-266-7074

Worker's compensation: Dept. of Industry, Labor, & Human

Relations - Worker's Compensation, Greg Frigo, Division Administrator, PO Box 7901, Rm 152, 201 E. Washington Ave., Madison, WI 53707. 608-266-6841

Occupational safety and health: Dept. of Industry, Labor, & Human Relations - Safety & Buildings, Michael Corry, Division Administrator, PO Box 7969, Rm 101, 201 E. Washington Ave., Madison, WI 53707. 608-266-1816

Secretary of state: Secretary of State's Office, Douglas LaFollette, Secretary of State, PO Box 7848, 30 W. Mifflin Street, 9th Fl., Madison, WI 53707. 608-266-5801

Taxation and revenue: Revenue Department, Mark Bugher, Secretary, PO Box 8933, 125 S. Webster Street, Madison, WI 53708. 608-266-6466

Designated Zones for Economic Development

Enterprise Zones

Enacted in: 1988

No. of established zones: 12

Beloit, Steve Lere, Director of Community Development, City of Beloit, 100 State Street, Beloit, WI 53511. 608-364-6700

Fond du Lac, John Angeli, Director of Redevelopment, City of Fond du Lac, PO Box 150, Fond du Lac, WI 54936-0150. 414-929-3311

Green Bay, Gail Niedzwiedz, Economic Development Authority, City of Green Bay, 100 North Jefferson Street, Green Bay, WI 54301. 414-448-3400

Iron County, Clyde W. Eilo, Development Zone Coordinator, PO Box 97, 100 Cary Road, Hurley, WI 54534. 715-561-2922

Lac du Flambeau (Indian ResrVA tion), Emerson Coy, Tribal Planner, Lac du Flambeau Band of Lake Superior Chippewa Indians, PO Box 66, Lac du Flambeau, WI 54538. 715-588-3303

Manitowoc, David Less, City Planner, Manitowoc City Plan Commission, PO Box 1597, 817 Franklin St., Rm. 202, Manitowoc, WI 54221-1597. 414-683-4435

Milwaukee, Michael Brodd, Zone Administrator, Dept. of City Development, PO Box 324, Milwaukee, WI 53201. 414-223-5845

Racine, Thomas N. Wright, Director of City Development, 730 Washington Ave., Racine, WI 53403. 414-636-9151

Richland Center/Town of Richland, Judy Derse Bethke, Exec Director, Richland County Economic Development Corp., PO Box 49, Richland Center, WI 53581. 608-647-4310

Stockbridge-Munsee Community (Indian ReserVA tion), Molly Miller-Gardner, Tribal Planner and Development Zone Administrator, Stockbridge-Munsee Community, Route 1, Bowler, WI 54416. 715-793-4111

Sturgeon Bay, William D. Chaudoir, Exec Director, Door County Economic Development Corp., PO Box 423, Sturgeon Bay, WI 54235. 800-527-3529 or 414-743-3113

Superior, James Kumbera, Community Development Director, City of Superior, 1407 Hammond Ave., Superior, WI 54880. 715-394-0278

Foreign Trade Zones

Foreign Trade Zone No. 167, Brown County, Wisconsin, Grantee: Brown County, Wisconsin, c/o Green Bay Chamber of Commerce, Nevin Limburg, PO Box 969, Green Bay, WI 54305-0969, 414-437-8704

Foreign Trade Zone No. 41, Milwaukee, Wisconsin, Grantee: Foreign Trade Zone of Wisconsin, Ltd., Vincent J. Boever, 2150 E. College Avenue, Cudahy, WI 53110, 414-764-2111

Foreign Trade Zone No. 173, Grays Harbor, Washington, Grantee: Port of Grays Harbor, Clifford C. Muller, PO Box 660, Aberdeen, WA 98520-0141, 206-533-9528

Labor Unions

Automobile, Aerospace & Agricultural Implement Workers of America, International Union, United, (UAW AFL-CIO)

Electrical Workers, International Brotherhood of (AFL-CIO)

Engineers and Architects (Madison)

Fire Fighters, International Association of (AFL-CIO)

Food and Commercial Workers International Union, United (AFL-CIO)

Hotel Employees and Restaurant Employees International Union (AFL-CIO)

Machinists and Aerospace Workers, International Association of (AFL-CIO)

National Education Association

Nurses' Association, American

Operating Engineers, International Union of (AFL-CIO)

Paperworkers International Union, United (AFL-CIO)

State, County and Municipal Employees, American Federation of (AFL-CIO)

Steelworkers of America, United (AFL-CIO)

Teachers, American Federation of (AFL-CIO)

Woodworkers of America, International (AFL-CIO)

Universities with Ph.D. Programs

Marquette University, Milwaukee

University of Wisconsin-Madison, Madison

University of Wisconsin-Milwaukee, Milwaukee

Sources of Additional Information

Wisconsin Economic Profile. Wisconsin Dept. of Development, May 1990. 8p.

Financial Resources Available to Wisconsin Businesses, Quick Reference Guide. Wisconsin Dept. of Development, June 1991. 6p.

APPLETON–OSHKOSH–NEENAH, WI (MSA)

Geographic Profile

Land Area

1398.9 square miles

Counties and Parishes

Calumet

Outagamie

Winnebago

Ranking Highlights

145 *out of 319 in total* **land area**

209 *out of 319 in* **population growth**, *1970–1990*

48 *out of 310 in having the lowest* **unemployment** *rate*

120 *out of 310 in size of* **labor force**

192 *out of 318 in the percentage of* **college graduates**

136 *out of 292 in per capita personal* **income**

105 *out of 319 in number of* **manufacturing establishments**

210 *out of 318 in* **physicians** *per 1000 people*

195 *out of 318 in* **hospital beds** *per 1000 people*

28 *out of 267 in fewest* **crimes** *per 1000 people*

4 *out of 266 in fewest* **violent crimes** *per 1000 people*

156 *out of 319 in per capita* **federal funds and grants**

Quality of Life Indexes (Rate per 1000 population)

Crime rate in 1991:   37.4

Violent crime rate in 1991:   1.1

Physicians rate in 1992:   1.57

Hospital bed rate in 1991:   3.47

ACCRA Cost of Living Indexes

(First quarter 1993, average = 100)

Composite index: 96.8

Utilities index: 90.8

Housing index: 98.6

Population (1990)

Total Population and Growth Rate

1990: 315,121

1980: 291,369

1970: 276,948

Growth rate 1970–1990: 14%

Race and Hispanic Origin

White: 97.4%

Black: .3%

Asian/Pacific Islander: 1.2%

Native American: 0.9%

Hispanic origin: 0.7%

White not Hispanic: 96.9%

Age

Ages 18 to 20: 4.8%

Ages 21 to 24: 6.2%

Ages 25 to 44: 32.7%

Ages 45 to 54: 9.7%
Ages 55 to 59: 4%
Ages 60 to 64: 3.9%
Ages 65 plus: 11.9%

Educational Attainment (1990)
Percent having completed high school: 80.9%
Percent having completed college: 17.0%
Elementary and high school enrollment: 54,611

Federal Funds and Grants Received ($1000)
Total received in 1989: 966,400
Funds received per capita: 3,089

Civilian Labor Force
1993 (April):   184,467
1992 average: 183,701
1991 average: 175,647
1990 average: 183,417

Unemployment
1993 (April):   4.9%
1992 average: 4.9%
1991 average: 5.3%
1990 average: 4.2%

Average Annual Pay
1988: $20,780
1987: $19,965
1985: $18,518

Per Capita Personal Income
1991: $17,618
1990: $17,050
1989: $16,150

Business Climate (1987)
Manufacturing
Number of establishments in 1987: 559
Shipments in 1987 ($1,000): $6,938,700
Employees in 1987: 49,700
Change in employment, 1982 to 1987: 10.4%
Average annual pay for manufacturing work in 1989: $28,093
Average annual pay for production work in 1987: $23,367

Wholesale Trade
Number of establishments in 1987: 548
Total sales in 1987 ($1,000): $2,385,800
Change in sales, 1982 to 1987: 44.3%

Retail Trade
Number of establishments in 1987: 2,005
Total sales in 1987 ($1,000): $2,385,800
Retail sales per household in 1987: $16,663
Average annual pay in 1989: $9,600

Service Industry
Selected receipts in 1987 ($1,000): $606,800
Average annual pay in 1989: $16,191

Housing
Total number of units in 1990: 120,511
Occupied units in 1990: 115,515
Owner-occupied units in 1990: 70.3%
1993 ACCRA average cost: $114,267
1993 ACCRA average rent for an apartment: $451

Chamber of Commerce
Fox Cities Chamber of Commerce, William J. Welch, President, 227 S. Walnut St., PO Box 1855, Appleton, WI 54913-1855. 414-734-7101, FAX 414-734-7161

Economic Development Office
Oshkosh Association of Manufacturing and Commerce, John A. Casper, Exec Vice President, 120 Jackson St., Oshkosh, WI 54901. 414-236-5260, FAX 414-424-0804

Economic Development Organizations
Future Neenah Development Corp., Randy Stadtmueller, Exec. Director, 121 1/2 W. Wisconsin Ave., Neenah, WI 54957. 414-722-1920

Major Businesses

Company	SIC	Telephone
Aid Association for Lutherans	6311	(414) 734-5721
Air Wis Services Inc.	4512	(414) 739-5123
Air Wisconsin Inc.	4512	(414) 739-5123
Appleton Papers, Inc.	2621	(414) 734-9841
Ariens Company	3524	(414) 756-2141
Banta Corp.	2732	(414) 722-7777
Boldt Group Inc.	1541	(414) 739-7800
Curwood Inc.	2671	(414) 236-7300
Fox Valley Corp.	2621	(414) 739-8982
Great Northern Corp.	2653	(414) 739-3671
K-C Aviation Inc.	4581	(414) 747-5723
Menasha Corp.	2631	(414) 751-0200
Miller Electric Manufacturing Co. Inc.	3548	(414) 734-9821
Miller Group Ltd., Inc.	3548	(414) 734-9821
Miron Construction Co., Inc.	1541	(414) 749-3060
Novus Health Group Inc.	8062	(414) 730-0330
Oshkosh B'gosh Inc.	2361	(414) 231-8800
Oshkosh Truck Corp.	3711	(414) 235-9150
Pierce Manufacturing Inc.	3711	(414) 832-3000
Plexus Corp.	3672	(414) 722-3451
Repap USA Inc.	2672	(414) 788-3511
Reynolds Consumer Product	2671	(414) 739-9471
Riverside Paper Corp.	2621	(414) 749-2200
Security Insurance	6331	(414) 739-3161
Shannon, S. C. Co., Inc.	5141	(414) 733-7313
Theda Clark Memorial Hospital	8062	(414) 729-3100
U. S. Oil Co., Inc.	5171	(414) 739-6101
Valley BanCorp.	6022	(414) 738-3830
Voith Inc.	3554	(414) 731-7724
Wisconsin Tissue Mills	2621	(414) 725-7031

Colleges and Universities

Fox Valley Technical College, Appleton
Lawrence University, Appleton
University of Wisconsin-Oshkosh, Oshkosh

EAU CLAIRE, WI (MSA)

Geographic Profile

Land Area

1648.1 square miles

Counties and Parishes

Chippewa
Eau Caire

Ranking Highlights

119 *out of 319 in total* **land area**
178 *out of 319 in* **population growth,** *1970–1990*
60 *out of 310 in having the lowest* **unemployment** *rate*
226 *out of 310 in size of* **labor force**
195 *out of 318 in the percentage of* **college graduates**
228 *out of 292 in per capita personal* **income**
224 *out of 319 in number of* **manufacturing establishments**
147 *out of 318 in* **physicians** *per 1000 people*
20 *out of 318 in* **hospital beds** *per 1000 people*
25 *out of 267 in fewest* **crimes** *per 1000 people*
4 *out of 266 in fewest* **violent crimes** *per 1000 people*
190 *out of 319 in per capita* **federal funds and grants**

Quality of Life Indexes (Rate per 1000 population)

Crime rate in 1991:	37.1
Violent crime rate in 1991:	1.1
Physicians rate in 1992:	1.85
Hospital bed rate in 1991:	6.42

ACCRA Cost of Living Indexes

(First quarter 1993, average = 100)

Composite index:	100.8
Utilities index:	92.2
Housing index:	114.0

Population (1990)

Total Population and Growth Rate

1990: 137,543
1980: 130,932
1970: 114,936
Growth rate 1970–1990: 20%

Race and Hispanic Origin

White: 97.5%
Black: .2%
Asian/Pacific Islander: 1.7%
Native American: 0.4%
Hispanic origin: 0.4%
White not Hispanic: 97.2%

Age

Ages 18 to 20: 6.7%
Ages 21 to 24: 7.2%
Ages 25 to 44: 29.9%
Ages 45 to 54: 9.1%
Ages 55 to 59: 3.8%

Ages 60 to 64: 4%
Ages 65 plus: 13.1%

Educational Attainment (1990)
Percent having completed high school: 79.6%
Percent having completed college: 16.9%
Elementary and high school enrollment: 23,687

Federal Funds and Grants Received
Total received in 1989: $396,500,000
Funds received per capita: $2,864

Civilian Labor Force
1993 (April): 74,270
1992 average: 73,456
1991 average: 71,143
1990 average: 71,984

Unemployment
1993 (April): 6.2%
1992 average: 5.2%
1991 average: 5.5%
1990 average: 4.9%

Average Annual Pay
1988: $17,661
1987: $17,106
1985: $15,886

Per Capita Personal Income
1991: $15,697
1990: $15,261
1989: $14,510

Business Climate (1987)
Manufacturing
Number of establishments in 1987: 192
Shipments in 1987 ($1,000): $1,616,400
Employees in 1987: 10,300
Change in employment, 1982 to 1987: 21.2%
Average annual pay for manufacturing work in 1989: $24,573
Average annual pay for production work in 1987: $20,425

Wholesale Trade
Number of establishments in 1987: 239
Total sales in 1987 ($1,000): $608,000
Change in sales, 1982 to 1987: -18.2%

Retail Trade
Number of establishments in 1987: 972
Total sales in 1987 ($1,000): $608,000
Retail sales per household in 1987: $16,757
Average annual pay in 1989: $9,821

Service Industry
Selected receipts in 1987 ($1,000): $262,100
Average annual pay in 1989: $16,016

Housing
Total number of units in 1990: 53,765

Occupied units in 1990: 50,359
Owner-occupied units in 1990: 68.2%
1993 ACCRA average cost: $130,000
1993 ACCRA average rent for an apartment: $548

Chamber of Commerce
Greater Eau Claire Area Chamber of Commerce, Brenda J. Blanchard, Exec. Vice President, 505 Dewey St. S., Eau Claire, WI 54701. 715-834-1204

Economic Development Office
City of Eau Claire Community Development, Michael Schatz, Economic Development Specialist, 203 S. Farwell St., PO Box 5148, Eau Claire, WI 54702. 715-839-4947

Economic Development Organizations
Eau Claire Area Industrial Development Corp., Craig Carlson, Exec. Director, 505 Dewey St. S. #101, Eau Claire, WI 54701. 715-834-0070, FAX 715-834-1956

Major Businesses

Company	SIC	Telephone
American Materials Corp.	3273	(715) 835-2251
Consumers Cooperative Association	5411	(715) 836-8700
Doro Inc.	5812	(715) 836-6800
First Federal Savings	6035	(715) 834-7741
First Interstate Bank of Wisconsin	6021	(715) 833-2274
First National Bank of Chippewa	6021	(715) 723-5531
First Wisconsin National Bank	6021	(715) 839-6300
Indianhead Food Service	5142	(715) 834-2777
Luther Hospital Inc.	8062	(715) 839-3311
Market & Johnson Inc.	1542	(715) 834-1213
Markquart, Lee Inc.	5511	(715) 833-0444
Mason Shoe Manufacturing	3143	(715) 723-1871
Menard, Inc.	5211	(715) 874-5911
National Presto Industries	3634	(715) 839-2121
North Central Crop Insurance	6331	(715) 834-8155
Northern Cross Arm Co., Inc.	5031	(715) 723-4100
Northern States Power Wisconsin	4911	(715) 839-2424
Owen Ayres and Associates	8711	(715) 834-3161
Phoenix Steel, Inc.	3441	(715) 835-6143
Pope & Talbot Wisconsin, Inc.	2621	(715) 834-3461
River Country Co-Op	5191	(715) 723-2828
Sacred Heart Hospital	8062	(715) 839-4121
Spectrum Industries Inc.	3999	(715) 723-4427
Spickler Enterprises Ltd.	5561	(715) 834-8552
St Josephs Hospital	8062	(715) 723-1811
Video Monitors Inc.	3575	(715) 834-7785

Colleges and Universities
Chippewa Valley Technical College, Eau Claire
University of Wisconsin-Eau Claire, Eau Claire

GREEN BAY, WI (MSA)

Geographic Profile

Land Area
528.7 square miles

Counties and Parishes
Brown

Ranking Highlights

286　*out of 319 in total* **land area**

168　*out of 319 in* **population growth,** *1970–1990*

　29　*out of 310 in having the lowest* **unemployment** *rate*

170　*out of 310 in size of* **labor force**

178　*out of 318 in the percentage of* **college graduates**

　83　*out of 292 in per capita personal* **income**

160　*out of 319 in number of* **manufacturing establishments**

217　*out of 318 in* **physicians** *per 1000 people*

214　*out of 318 in* **hospital beds** *per 1000 people*

　43　*out of 267 in fewest* **crimes** *per 1000 people*

　27　*out of 266 in fewest* **violent crimes** *per 1000 people*

268　*out of 319 in per capita* **federal funds and grants**

Quality of Life Indexes (Rate per 1000 population)

Crime rate in 1991:	41.1
Violent crime rate in 1991:	2.3
Physicians rate in 1992:	1.55
Hospital bed rate in 1991:	3.25

ACCRA Cost of Living Indexes

(First quarter 1993, average = 100)

Composite index:	98.0
Utilities index:	88.7
Housing index:	102.0

Overview

Green Bay area is located 114 miles north of Milwaukee, 204 miles north of Chicago, Illinois and 284 miles east of Minneapolis-St. Paul, Minnesota. The city of Green Bay is in Brown County and is 44 square miles in size. It is part of an 80.7 square miles urban area including Allouez, Ashwaubenon, Bellevue, DePere and Howard. The area is 500 feet above sea level.

The principal industry of Brown County is paper making and allied products, and eleven mills of varying size are located here. About forty percent of local manufacturing is connected with paper making.

Food and kindred products are produced here for national and foreign markets. Cheese is produced in ten plants, meat in four, dairy products (excluding cheese) in seven and vegetables in five. Bakery, pizza and candy producers are also located here.

Brown County is the fourth largest jobbing, wholesale, and distribution point in Wisconsin and is the dominant retail center of northeastern Wisconsin and Upper Michigan. The primary and secondary retail trade areas have a potential of over a half million people, and Brown County is the fourth ranking retail sales county in the state.

The Green Bay area is the transportation hub of northeastern Wisconsin, with one of the only complete beltlines in Wisconsin. U.S. highways 41 and 141 service the area, as do Wisconsin highways 29, 32, 54, and 57. Interstate 43 is a direct route from Green Bay to Milwaukee. Highway 172 links U.S. Highway 41 on the west side of the Fox River and I-43 on the east side.

Forty truck lines offer service to the rest of the country. Cargo service is provided by Green Bay and Western, the Soo Line, Chicago and Northwestern, Escanaba and Lake Superior, and Fox River Valley railroads.

Austin Straubel International Airport is the third largest airport facility in Wisconsin, located just outside of Green Bay's city limits. It is owned and operated by Brown County. The field has over 35 scheduled flights daily by American Eagle, Northwest Airlines, Northwest Airlink, United Express, Skyway/Midwest Express, and Chicago Express.

The Port of Green Bay is an international port for domestic and foreign trade. The 24-foot deep channel serviced 178 commercial ships in 1992, with 14 vessels flying a foreign flag. The 1992 port tonnage was over 1.9 million tons. The navigation season is about April 2 to December 31.

Population (1990)

Total Population and Growth Rate
1990: 194,594
1980: 175,280
1970: 158,244
Growth rate 1970–1990: 23%

Race and Hispanic Origin
White: 95.9%
Black: .5%
Asian/Pacific Islander: 1.3%
Native American: 2.0%
Hispanic origin: 0.8%
White not Hispanic: 95.5%

Age
Ages 18 to 20: 4.8%
Ages 21 to 24: 6.3%
Ages 25 to 44: 34.1%
Ages 45 to 54: 9.6%
Ages 55 to 59: 3.8%
Ages 60 to 64: 3.6%
Ages 65 plus: 10.8%

Educational Attainment (1990)

Percent having completed high school: 82.6%
Percent having completed college: 17.7%
Elementary and high school enrollment: 34,332

Federal Funds and Grants Received

Total received in 1989: $442,800,000

Funds received per capita: $2,315

Civilian Labor Force
1993 (April):   119,888
1992 average: 118,898
1991 average: 113,318
1990 average: 111,083

Unemployment
1993 (April):   4.9%
1992 average: 4.5%
1991 average: 4.6%
1990 average: 3.9%

Average Annual Pay
1988: $20,672
1987: $19,796
1985: $18,755

Per Capita Personal Income
1991: $18,837
1990: $18,230
1989: $17,111

Business Climate (1987)

Manufacturing
Number of establishments in 1987: 315
Shipments in 1987 ($1,000): $4,537,500
Employees in 1987: 23,500
Change in employment, 1982 to 1987: 10.8%
Average annual pay for manufacturing work in 1989: $28,260
Average annual pay for production work in 1987: $23,783

Wholesale Trade
Number of establishments in 1987: 441
Total sales in 1987 ($1,000): $2,086,200
Change in sales, 1982 to 1987: 26.8%

Retail Trade
Number of establishments in 1987: 1,245
Total sales in 1987 ($1,000): $2,086,200
Retail sales per household in 1987: $18,852
Average annual pay in 1989: $11,395

Service Industry
Selected receipts in 1987 ($1,000): $446,800
Average annual pay in 1989: $18,208

Housing
Total number of units in 1990: 74,740
Occupied units in 1990: 72,280
Owner-occupied units in 1990: 65.6%
1993 ACCRA average cost: $114,500
1993 ACCRA average rent for an apartment: $519

Chamber of Commerce
Green Bay Area Chamber of Commerce, Nevin R. Limburg, President, 400 S. Washington St., PO Box 969, Green Bay, WI 54305. 414-437-8704

Economic Development Office
Advance-Green Bay Area Economic Development, Nan Nelson, Exec. Director, 400 S. Washington St., PO Box 1660, Green Bay, WI 54305. 414-437-8704, FAX 414-437-1024

Economic Development Organizations
Green Bay Economic Development Authority, James Schlies, Coordinator, 100 N. Jefferson St. Room 608, City Hall, Green Bay, WI 54301. 414-448-3400, FAX 414-448-3123

Green Bay Economic Development Authority, Development Zone Program, Gail Niedzwiedz, Manager, 100 N. Jefferson St., Green Bay, WI 54301. 414-448-3400

Local Incentives for Business

Financial and Technical Incentives
The state development zone tax credits are among the many financial and technical resources that are available in Green Bay. Others include:

Community Development Revolving Loan Fund.

Tax Incremental Financing.

Industrial Revenue Bonds.

Broadway Historic Economic Development Loan Program.

Brown County Economic Development Loan Program.

Section 108 Loan Guarantee Program.

Community Development Block Grant Float Loan Program.

Brown County Development Corporation-Small Business Administration Loans.

Wisconsin Public Service Corporation Financial Assistance Programs.

Green Bay Economic Development Authority-business assistance and referral assistance.

Small Business Development Center at University of Wisconsin at Green Bay.

Employment Incentives
The development zone jobs tax credits are available, along with the following employment incentive and assistance programs:

Job Opportunities and Basic Skills Program.

Job Service Public Labor Exchange.

On-the-job training supported by the Jobs Training Partnership Act.

Federal Targeted Jobs Tax Credits.

Work Supplementation Wage-Reimbursement for AFDC recipients.

Veterans Training Program.

Wisconsin Division of Vocational Rehabilitation offering job training for disabled persons.

Ex-Offenders Training Programs.

Refugee Assistance Programs.

Customized Vocational Training provided by the Northeast Wisconsin Technical College.—

Major Businesses

Company	SIC	Telephone
Associated Banc-Corp	6021	(414) 433-3166
Employers Health Insurance Co.	6311	(414) 336-1100
Fort Howard Corp.	2656	(414) 435-8821
Frigo Cheese Corp.	2022	(414) 494-2228
Frigo Foods Inc.	2022	(414) 494-2228
Green Bay Packaging Inc.	2631	(414) 433-5311
Krueger International Inc.	2522	(414) 468-8100
Larsen Co.	2033	(414) 435-5301
Miramar Marine Corp.	3732	(414) 822-3214
Northeast Communications of Wisconsin	4813	(414) 822-4000
Packerland Packing Co.	2011	(414) 468-4000
Paper Converting Co.	3554	(414) 494-5601
Schneider National Inc.	4213	(414) 497-2201
Schneider Transport Inc.	4213	(414) 497-2201
Schreiber Foods Inc.	2022	(414) 437-7601
Shopko Stores, Inc.	5331	(414) 497-2211
St. Vincent Hospital	8062	(414) 433-0111
Terex Corp.	3531	(414) 435-5322
Wisconsin Public Service	4939	(414) 433-1598

Colleges and Universities

Bellin College of Nursing, Green Bay
Northeast Wisconsin Technical College, Green Bay
University of Wisconsin-Green Bay, Green Bay

JANESVILLE–BELOIT, WI (MSA)

Geographic Profile

Land Area
720.5 square miles

Counties and Parishes
Rock

Ranking Highlights
250 *out of 319 in total* **land area**
238 *out of 319 in* **population growth**, *1970–1990*
128 *out of 310 in having the lowest* **unemployment** *rate*
221 *out of 310 in size of* **labor force**
277 *out of 318 in the percentage of* **college graduates**
191 *out of 292 in per capita personal* **income**
218 *out of 319 in number of* **manufacturing establishments**
259 *out of 318 in* **physicians** *per 1000 people*
189 *out of 318 in* **hospital beds** *per 1000 people*
 97 *out of 267 in fewest* **crimes** *per 1000 people*
 35 *out of 266 in fewest* **violent crimes** *per 1000 people*
201 *out of 319 in per capita* **federal funds and grants**

Quality of Life Indexes (Rate per 1000 population)
Crime rate in 1991:	54.1
Violent crime rate in 1991:	2.6
Physicians rate in 1992:	1.33
Hospital bed rate in 1991:	3.52

ACCRA Cost of Living Indexes
(First quarter 1993, average = 100)
Composite index:	99.3
Utilities index:	85.7
Housing index:	110.4

Overview
Janesville-Beloit MSA is located in south-central Wisconsin on the Rock River at the Wisconsin-Illinois state line. Major Highways: Interstate 90 and 43, U.S. Highway 51, and Wisconsin highways 81 and 213. Air Service: Commercial air service is available from the Rockford and the Chicago O'Hare Airports in Illinois. The Beloit Development Zone extends northeast from Beloit's downtown and includes residential neighborhood, commercial, and manufacturing areas.

Population (1990)

Total Population and Growth Rate
1990: 139,510
1980: 139,420
1970: 131,970
Growth rate 1970–1990: 6%

Race and Hispanic Origin
White: 93.8%

Black: 4.8%
Asian/Pacific Islander: 0.7%
Native American: 0.3%
Hispanic origin: 1.3%
White not Hispanic: 93.0%

Age
Ages 18 to 20: 4.3%
Ages 21 to 24: 5.5%
Ages 25 to 44: 31%
Ages 45 to 54: 10.6%
Ages 55 to 59: 4.6%
Ages 60 to 64: 4.3%
Ages 65 plus: 12.6%

Educational Attainment (1990)
Percent having completed high school: 78.2%
Percent having completed college: 13.3%
Elementary and high school enrollment: 24,929

Federal Funds and Grants Received
Total received in 1989: $378,000,000
Funds received per capita: $2,773

Civilian Labor Force
1993 (April):   75,034
1992 average: 75,300
1991 average: 73,433
1990 average: 74,426

Unemployment
1993 (April):   6.7%
1992 average: 6.5%
1991 average: 9.7%
1990 average: 5.2%

Average Annual Pay
1988: $20,488
1987: $19,257
1985: $19,172

Per Capita Personal Income
1991: $16,461
1990: $16,454
1989: $15,451

Business Climate (1987)
Manufacturing
Number of establishments in 1987: 200
Shipments in 1987 ($1,000): $4,289,200
Employees in 1987: 17,500
Change in employment, 1982 to 1987: 10.8%
Average annual pay for manufacturing work in 1989: $30,827
Average annual pay for production work in 1987: $25,093

Wholesale Trade
Number of establishments in 1987: 207
Total sales in 1987 ($1,000): $709,600
Change in sales, 1982 to 1987: 69.2%

Retail Trade
Number of establishments in 1987: 911
Total sales in 1987 ($1,000): $709,600
Retail sales per household in 1987: $16,552
Average annual pay in 1989: $10,303

Service Industry
Selected receipts in 1987 ($1,000): $209,300
Average annual pay in 1989: $14,724

Housing
Total number of units in 1990: 54,840
Occupied units in 1990: 52,252
Owner-occupied units in 1990: 68.2%
1993 ACCRA average cost: $128,300
1993 ACCRA average rent for an apartment: $500

Chamber of Commerce
Janesville Area Chamber of Commerce, Jule C. Raith, Exec. Vice President, 60 S. River St., PO Box 998, Janesville, WI 53545. 608-752-7459

Economic Development Office
Janesville Economic Development Agency, Douglas Venable, Director, 18 N. Jackson St., PO Box 5005, Janesville, WI 53545. 608-755-3180, FAX 608-755-3196

Economic Development Organizations
City of Beloit, Dept. of Community Development, Steve Lere, Director, 100 State St., Beloit, WI 53511. 608-364-6700, FAX 608-364-6609

Greater Beloit Economic Development Corp., Bruce Kepner, Exec. Director, 136 W. Grand Suite 100, PO Box 539, Beloit, WI 53511. 608-365-6945

Local Incentives for Business
Financial and Technical Incentives
The state development zone tax credits are available in Beloit. Other incentives include:

Commercial/industrial development revolving loan fund.

Local initiatives to reduce the cost of developable land through municipal purchase, development and resale.

Commercial Facade Revitalization Loan Program.

Tax Increment Financing designation.

Business assistance provided by the University of Wisconsin-Whitewater.

One Stop Permit Program.

Employment Incentives
In addition to the state development zone jobs credits, Beloit offers the following:

Wis JOBS wage subsidy program.

Work Supplementation Wage-Reimbursement program.

Wisconsin Job Service, offering referral and preliminary screening.

Federal Targeted Jobs Tax Credit.

Blackhawk Technical College for basic and customized training.

Opportunities Industrialization Center of Rock County,

offering basic skills training.

Rock County Private Industries Council and Forward Services Corporation, offering programs in basic and occupational skills and vocational training.

On-the-job training supported by the federal Job Training Partnership Act.

Rock County Re-Employment Program for dislocated workers.

Wisconsin Division of Vocational Rehabilitation job training for the disabled.

Major Businesses

Company	SIC	Telephone
Accudyne Corp.	3483	(608) 752-9081
American Builders & Contractors	5031	(608) 362-7777
Baker Manufacturing Co.	5084	(608) 882-5100
Beloit Corp.	3554	(608) 365-3311
Beloit Memorial Hospital	8062	(608) 364-5011
Bryden Motors Inc.	5511	(608) 365-7705
Chambers & Owen Inc.	5194	(608) 752-7865
Cullen, J. P. & Sons Inc.	1542	(608) 754-6601
De Long Co. Inc.	5191	(608) 676-2255
Freeman Shoe Co.	3143	(608) 364-1200
Janesville Auto Transport Co.	4213	(608) 755-4300
Kerry Foods Inc.	2099	(608) 365-5561
Lab Safety Supply Inc.	5099	(608) 754-2345
Lemans Corp.	5013	(608) 884-3461
Mercy Hospital of Janesville Wisconsin	8062	(608) 756-6000
Monterey Mills Inc.	2221	(608) 754-2866
Rollette Oil Co. Inc.	5541	(608) 754-0035
Ryan Inc. Central	1794	(608) 754-2291
SSI Technologies Inc.	3441	(608) 755-1900
Weiser, Bud Motors Inc.	5511	(608) 365-4481

Colleges and Universities

Beloit College, Beloit

Blackhawk Technical College, Janesville

University of Wisconsin Center-Rock County, Janesville

KENOSHA, WI (PMSA)

Geographic Profile

Land Area

272.8 square miles

Counties and Parishes

Kenosha

Ranking Highlights

316 *out of 319 in total* **land area**

227 *out of 319 in* **population growth,** *1970–1990*

 89 *out of 310 in having the lowest* **unemployment** *rate*

273 *out of 310 in size of* **labor force**

288 *out of 318 in the percentage of* **college graduates**

139 *out of 292 in per capita personal* **income**

240 *out of 319 in number of* **manufacturing establishments**

301 *out of 318 in* **physicians** *per 1000 people*

267 *out of 318 in* **hospital beds** *per 1000 people*

 88 *out of 267 in fewest* **crimes** *per 1000 people*

 26 *out of 266 in fewest* **violent crimes** *per 1000 people*

271 *out of 319 in per capita* **federal funds and grants**

Quality of Life Indexes (Rate per 1000 population)

Crime rate in 1991:   51.0

Violent crime rate in 1991:   2.2

Physicians rate in 1992:   1.05

Hospital bed rate in 1991:   2.61

ACCRA Cost of Living Indexes

(First quarter 1993, average = 100)

Composite index: N/A

Utilities index: N/A

Housing index: N/A

Population (1990)

Total Population and Growth Rate

1990: 128,181

1980: 123,137

1970: 117,917

Growth rate 1970–1990: 9%

Race and Hispanic Origin

White: 93.0%

Black: 4.1%

Asian/Pacific Islander: 0.5%

Native American: 0.4%

Hispanic origin: 4.4%

White not Hispanic: 90.7%

Age

Ages 18 to 20: 4.6%

Ages 21 to 24: 5.7%

Ages 25 to 44: 31.8%

Ages 45 to 54: 10.2%

Ages 55 to 59: 4.1%

Ages 60 to 64: 4.1%
Ages 65 plus: 12.6%

Educational Attainment (1990)
Percent having completed high school: 75.1%
Percent having completed college: 12.7%
Elementary and high school enrollment: 22,609

Federal Funds and Grants Received
Total received in 1989: $281,200,000
Funds received per capita: $2,294

Civilian Labor Force
1993 (April):   59,033
1992 average: 57,697
1991 average: 55,250
1990 average: 53,916

Unemployment
1993 (April):   6.4%
1992 average: 5.8%
1991 average: 6.4%
1990 average: 6.3%

Average Annual Pay
1988: $22,362
1987: $20,648
1985: $19,637

Per Capita Personal Income
1991: $17,560
1990: $17,452
1989: $16,771

Business Climate (1987)
Manufacturing
Number of establishments in 1987: 160
Shipments in 1987 ($1,000): $2,360,700
Employees in 1987: 12,600
Change in employment, 1982 to 1987: -11.3%
Average annual pay for manufacturing work in 1989: $30,803
Average annual pay for production work in 1987: $27,588

Wholesale Trade
Number of establishments in 1987: 117
Total sales in 1987 ($1,000): $489,600
Change in sales, 1982 to 1987: 39.2%

Retail Trade
Number of establishments in 1987: 753
Total sales in 1987 ($1,000): $489,600
Retail sales per household in 1987: $13,061
Average annual pay in 1989: $9,407

Service Industry
Selected receipts in 1987 ($1,000): $151,600
Average annual pay in 1989: $15,745

Housing
Total number of units in 1990: 51,262

Occupied units in 1990: 47,029
Owner-occupied units in 1990: 68.8%
1993 ACCRA average cost: N/A
1993 ACCRA average rent for an apartment: N/A

Chamber of Commerce
Kenosha Area Chamber of Commerce, Louis J. Micheln, Exec. Director, 812 56th St., PO Box 518, Kenosha, WI 53141. 414-654-2165

Economic Development Office
Kenosha Area Development Corp., John Bechler, Director, 5455 Sheridan Rd. Suite 101, Kenosha, WI 53140. 414-654-2167, FAX 414-654-1111

Major Businesses

Company	SIC	Telephone
B R Industries Inc.	3325	(414) 633-1844
Badger Cork & Manufacturing Co.	2499	(414) 862-2311
Dallas & Mavis Forwarding	4213	(414) 658-4831
First Financial Associate	6021	(414) 658-2331
First Natopnal Bank of Kenosha	6021	(414) 658-2331
Gander Mountain Inc.	5961	(414) 862-2331
Global Technology Systems	2499	(414) 862-2311
Jockey International Inc.	2254	(414) 658-8111
Jupiter Transport Co.	4213	(414) 658-4831
Kenosha Auto Transport Co.	4213	(414) 658-4831
Kenosha Hospital & Medical	8062	(414) 656-2011
Kenosha Savings & Loan Association	6036	(414) 658-4861
Snap-On Tools Corp.	3423	(414) 656-5200
St. Catherine's Hospital Inc.	8062	(414) 656-3011
Stan's Lumber Inc.	5211	(414) 877-2181

Colleges and Universities
Carthage College, Kenosha
University of Wisconsin-Parkside, Kenosha

LA CROSSE, WI (MSA)

Geographic Profile

Land Area
452.8 square miles

Counties and Parishes
La Crosse

Additional Cities/Towns within Area
None

Ranking Highlights
302 *out of 319 in total* **land area**
171 *out of 319 in* **population growth,** *1970–1990*
34 *out of 310 in having the lowest* **unemployment** *rate*
274 *out of 310 in size of* **labor force**
117 *out of 318 in the percentage of* **college graduates**
149 *out of 292 in per capita personal* **income**
263 *out of 319 in number of* **manufacturing establishments**
18 *out of 318 in* **physicians** *per 1000 people*
23 *out of 318 in* **hospital beds** *per 1000 people*
59 *out of 267 in fewest* **crimes** *per 1000 people*
3 *out of 266 in fewest* **violent crimes** *per 1000 people*
221 *out of 319 in per capita* **federal funds and grants**

Quality of Life Indexes (Rate per 1000 population)
Crime rate in 1991:   44.7
Violent crime rate in 1991:   1.0
Physicians rate in 1992:   3.46
Hospital bed rate in 1991:   6.33

ACCRA Cost of Living Indexes
(First quarter 1993, average = 100)
Composite index: 98.7
Utilities index: 94.9
Housing index: 98.8

Population (1990)

Total Population and Growth Rate
1990: 97,904
1980: 91,056
1970: 80,468
Growth rate 1970–1990: 22%

Race and Hispanic Origin
White: 96.3%
Black: .4%
Asian/Pacific Islander: 2.7%
Native American: 0.3%
Hispanic origin: 0.7%
White not Hispanic: 96.0%

Age
Ages 18 to 20: 7.2%
Ages 21 to 24: 8.3%
Ages 25 to 44: 30.6%
Ages 45 to 54: 8.9%
Ages 55 to 59: 3.9%
Ages 60 to 64: 3.7%
Ages 65 plus: 12.8%

Educational Attainment (1990)
Percent having completed high school: 82.6%
Percent having completed college: 21.1%
Elementary and high school enrollment: 15,848

Federal Funds and Grants Received
Total received in 1989: $249,800,000
Funds received per capita: $2,616

Civilian Labor Force
1993 (April):   58,148
1992 average: 56,865
1991 average: 54,717
1990 average: 54,073

Unemployment
1993 (April):   4.5%
1992 average: 4.6%
1991 average: 4.5%
1990 average: 3.7%

Average Annual Pay
1988: $17,822
1987: $17,178
1985: $16,545

Per Capita Personal Income
1991: $17,253
1990: $16,679
1989: $15,690

Business Climate (1987)

Manufacturing
Number of establishments in 1987: 138
Shipments in 1987 ($1,000): $1,026,800
Employees in 1987: 10,300
Change in employment, 1982 to 1987: 3.0%
Average annual pay for manufacturing work in 1989: $22,977
Average annual pay for production work in 1987: $18,687

Wholesale Trade
Number of establishments in 1987: 186
Total sales in 1987 ($1,000): $1,428,400
Change in sales, 1982 to 1987: 70.7%

Retail Trade
Number of establishments in 1987: 732
Total sales in 1987 ($1,000): $1,428,400
Retail sales per household in 1987: $18,781
Average annual pay in 1989: $9,610

Service Industry
Selected receipts in 1987 ($1,000): $244,900
Average annual pay in 1989: $17,174

Housing
Total number of units in 1990: 38,239
Occupied units in 1990: 36,662
Owner-occupied units in 1990: 62.9%
1993 ACCRA average cost: $115,800
1993 ACCRA average rent for an apartment: $417

Chamber of Commerce
Greater La Crosse Area Chamber of Commerce, William Sorenson, President, 712 Main St., PO Box 219, La Crosse, WI 54602-0219. 608-784-4880

Economic Development Office
La Crosse Area Development Corp., James P. Hill, Exec. Director, 712 Main St., La Crosse, WI 54601. 608-784-5488

Major Businesses

Company	SIC	Telephone
Badger Corrugating Co.	5033	(608) 788-0100
Century Telephone of Wisconsin	4813	(608) 782-9980
Consolidated Midwest Inc.	5172	(608) 781-1010
Dahl Ford-La Crosse, Inc.	5511	(608) 784-9600
Dairyland Power Cooperative	4911	(608) 788-4000
Desmond's Formal Wear, Inc.	7299	(608) 781-7770
Eversole Motors Inc.	5511	(608) 791-3000
First Federal Savngs & Loan Association	6035	(608) 784-8000
Gateway Foods, Inc.	5141	(608) 785-1330
Heileman G. Brewing Co.	2082	(608) 785-1000
Inland Printing Co.	2752	(608) 788-5800
International Footwear Co.	3021	(608) 782-3020
La Crosse Footwear, Inc.	3021	(608) 782-3020
La Crosse Plumbing Supply	5074	(608) 784-3839
La Crosse Truck Center Inc.	5511	(608) 785-0800
Lutheran Hospital-Lacross	8062	(608) 785-0530
Midwest Bottle Gas Co.	5984	(608) 781-1010
Norplex Oak, Inc.	3083	(608) 784-6070
North-West Telecommunication	4813	(608) 784-6920
Randall-Graw Co., Inc.	5084	(608) 784-6228
Reinhart	5141	(608) 782-2660
St. Francis Medical Center	8062	(608) 785-0940
St. Joseph Equipment Inc.	5084	(608) 788-1025
Stansfield, Jim Vending Inc.	5962	(608) 782-7181
White, L.B. Co., Inc	3585	(608) 783-5691

Colleges and Universities
University of Wisconsin-La Crosse, La Crosse
Viterbo College, La Crosse

MADISON, WI (MSA)

Geographic Profile
Land Area
1202.2 square miles
Counties and Parishes
Dane

Ranking Highlights
164 *out of 319 in total* land area
156 *out of 319 in* population growth, *1970–1990*
4 *out of 310 in having the lowest* unemployment *rate*
95 *out of 310 in size of* labor force
11 *out of 318 in the percentage of* college graduates
39 *out of 292 in per capita personal* income
111 *out of 319 in number of* manufacturing establishments
12 *out of 318 in* physicians *per 1000 people*
164 *out of 318 in* hospital beds *per 1000 people*
95 *out of 267 in fewest* crimes *per 1000 people*
58 *out of 266 in fewest* violent crimes *per 1000 people*
87 *out of 319 in per capita* federal funds and grants

Quality of Life Indexes (Rate per 1000 population)
Crime rate in 1991: 53.6
Violent crime rate in 1991: 3.4
Physicians rate in 1992: 3.87
Hospital bed rate in 1991: 3.76

ACCRA Cost of Living Indexes
(First quarter 1993, average = 100)
Composite index: 113.8
Utilities index: 87.9
Housing index: 140.8

Overview
The capital of Wisconsin, Madison is also the seat of Dane County and the focus of a metropolitan statistical area that includes the entire county. Since Madison was founded, the natural beauty of its setting has been enhanced by parks and boulevards with an impressive State Capitol Building and plaza at the center of the city. Madison is the base of the University of Wisconsin, a nationally respected research institution, which is known for a tradition of academic excellence.

The principal economic sectors in Madison are manufacturing, agriculture, services, and government. Meat packing and the production of agriculture and dairy equipment have long been established industries in the city; among other items produced by area manufacturing firms are hospital equipment, advanced instrumentation, storage batteries, and air circulating fixtures. Diversified farming contributes significantly to the Madison economy; nearly one-sixth of all Wisconsin farms are located within the Greater Madison market region. Dane County ranks among the top ten counties in the nation for agricultural production, the primary products being corn, alfalfa, tobacco, oats, eggs, cattle, hogs, and dairy foods.

The home offices of more than thirty insurance companies are located in Madison; included among them are American Family, C U N A Mutual Insurance Group, and General Casualty. The city is also the world headquarters of RAY-OVAC Corporation and Ohmeda and Nicolet Instrument Corporation; Oscar Mayer headquarters are located in Madison as well. Government and education are major economic sectors; about one third of the area work force is employed in federal, state, and local government jobs, and the University of Wisconsin employs more than thirty–six thousand workers. Madison is a banking and finance center, serving the metropolitan region with more than 120 banks, credit unions, and savings and loan institutions. Other service areas important to the local economy are health care and research and development.

Madison is served by the Chicago & Northwestern, Soo/ Milwaukee, and Wisconsin & Calumet Railroads. More than forty motor freight carriers link the city with markets throughout the nation via an extensive interstate highway system. Air cargo is shipped through Dane County Regional Airport by three companies; over eleven million pounds of freight were handled at the airport in 1989 alone. I-90 and I-94, two of Wisconsin's interstate highways, pass through Madison, connecting the city with Chicago, Illinois, Minneapolis, Minnesota, and Milwaukee. The highway system also includes U.S. routes 12, 14, 18, 51, and 151 and state roads 30 and 113. The West Beltline, formed by U.S. 18, 151, 12, and 14, bypasses the city.

Population (1990)

Total Population and Growth Rate
1990: 367,085
1980: 323,545
1970: 290,272
Growth rate 1970–1990: 26%

Race and Hispanic Origin
White: 93.9%
Black: 2.9%
Asian/Pacific Islander: 2.4%
Native American: 0.3%
Hispanic origin: 1.6%
White not Hispanic: 92.9%

Age
Ages 18 to 20: 6.8%
Ages 21 to 24: 8.9%
Ages 25 to 44: 36.5%
Ages 45 to 54: 9.2%
Ages 55 to 59: 3.4%
Ages 60 to 64: 3.2%
Ages 65 plus: 9.3%

Educational Attainment (1990)
Percent having completed high school: 88.9%

Percent having completed college: 34.2%
Elementary and high school enrollment: 51,989

Federal Funds and Grants Received
Total received in 1989: $1,309,500,000
Funds received per capita: $3,711

Civilian Labor Force
1993 (April): 244,456
1992 average: 241,451
1991 average: 229,065
1990 average: 227,000

Unemployment
1993 (April): 2.4%
1992 average: 2.9%
1991 average: 3.1%
1990 average: 2.5%

Average Annual Pay
1988: $20,253
1987: $19,334
1985: $17,728

Per Capita Personal Income
1991: $20,629
1990: $19,950
1989: $18,580

Business Climate (1987)

Manufacturing
Number of establishments in 1987: 517
Shipments in 1987 ($1,000): $2,604,800
Employees in 1987: 22,100
Change in employment, 1982 to 1987: 18.8%
Average annual pay for manufacturing work in 1989: $25,386
Average annual pay for production work in 1987: $19,374

Wholesale Trade
Number of establishments in 1987: 660
Total sales in 1987 ($1,000): $2,394,100
Change in sales, 1982 to 1987: 39.1%

Retail Trade
Number of establishments in 1987: 2,448
Total sales in 1987 ($1,000): $2,394,100
Retail sales per household in 1987: $18,302
Average annual pay in 1989: $10,462

Service Industry
Selected receipts in 1987 ($1,000): $1,133,000
Average annual pay in 1989: $18,738

Housing
Total number of units in 1990: 147,851
Occupied units in 1990: 142,786
Owner-occupied units in 1990: 55.2%
1993 ACCRA average cost: $160,750
1993 ACCRA average rent for an apartment: $663

Chamber of Commerce

Greater Madison Chamber of Commerce, Robert W. Brennan, President, 615 E. Washington Ave., PO Box 71, Madison, WI 53701-0071. 608-256-8348

Major Businesses

Company	SIC	Telephone
Alpha Distributors Ltd.	5141	(608) 241-2107
Am Fam Inc.	6331	(608) 249-2111
American Family Mutual Insurance	6331	(608) 249-2111
American Famly Life Insurance Co.	6311	(608) 249-2111
American TV & Appliance of Madison	5731	(608) 271-1000
Cumis Insurance Society Inc.	6331	(608) 231-7363
Cuna Mutual Insurance Society	6311	(608) 238-5851
Erdman, Marshall & Association	1542	(608) 238-0211
General Casualty of Wisconsin	6331	(608) 837-4440
Greyhund Portfolio Holdings	6351	(608) 257-2527
Madison Gas & Electric Co.	4939	(608) 252-7000
Mayer, Oscar Foods Corp.	2013	(608) 241-3311
Nicolet Instrument Corp.	3826	(608) 271-3333
Rayovac Corp.	3692	(608) 275-3340
SASM of the Midwest Inc.	5411	(608) 246-3670
Viking Insurance Co. of Wisconsin	6331	(608) 836-3000
Wisconsin Housing	6162	(608) 266-7884
Wisconsin Physicians Service	6324	(608) 221-4711
Wisconsin Power and Light	4931	(608) 252-3311
WPL Holdings Inc.	4931	(608) 252-4888

Colleges and Universities

Edgewood College, Madison
Madison Area Technical College, Madison
Madison Business College, Madison
University of Wisconsin-Madison, Madison

MILWAUKEE, WI (PMSA)

Geographic Profile

Land Area
1460.0 square miles

Counties and Parishes
Milwaukee
Ozaukee
Washington
Waukesha

Additional Cities/Towns within Area
Waukesha

Ranking Highlights

138 *out of 319 in total* land area
261 *out of 319 in* population growth, *1970–1990*
 29 *out of 310 in having the lowest* unemployment *rate*
 32 *out of 310 in size of* labor force
112 *out of 318 in the percentage of* college graduates
 45 *out of 292 in per capita personal* income
 23 *out of 319 in number of* manufacturing establishments
 65 *out of 318 in* physicians *per 1000 people*
183 *out of 318 in* hospital beds *per 1000 people*
130 *out of 267 in fewest* crimes *per 1000 people*
111 *out of 266 in fewest* violent crimes *per 1000 people*
197 *out of 319 in per capita* federal funds and grants

Quality of Life Indexes (Rate per 1000 population)

Crime rate in 1991:	60.1
Violent crime rate in 1991:	5.2
Physicians rate in 1992:	2.51
Hospital bed rate in 1991:	3.57

ACCRA Cost of Living Indexes
(First quarter 1993, average = 100)

Composite index: 104.2
Utilities index: 96.3
Housing index: 120.8

Overview

Milwaukee, a commercial and industrial hub for the Great Lakes region, is home to several Fortune 500 industrial companies, banks, and diversified service companies, as well as one of the nation's ten largest insurance firms. The city places among the top manufacturing centers in the United States, although it recently has lost eighty–five thousand manufacturing jobs due to the flight of factories abroad. The economy is dominated by small– to medium–size firms with representatives in nearly every industrial classification.

Metropolitan area firms are engaged primarily in the manufacture of machinery; contrary to Milwaukee's reputation as a brewery capital, less than one percent of the city's industrial output is related to brewing. Major products include industrial controls, X-ray apparatus, steel, mining machinery, hoists, industrial cranes and monorails, speed changers, and drives and gears. Milwaukee companies are also in the forefront of science and technology, producing such items as computers, aircraft components, medical instruments, water desalination systems, electronic circuit boards, and industrial robots.

Milwaukee's foundries rank among the most productive in the nation; they turn out iron, steel, aluminum, brass, and copper castings. Milwaukee is known worldwide for sausage making. Other principal industries include food processing; the manufacture of paper, plastic, rubber, and leather products; and advertising, printing, publishing, and graphic arts. The service sector, which increased substantially in the 1980s, accounts for more than one–fourth of the city's economic base, surpassing manufacturing as the main source of employment. A number of large service firms serving national markets are headquartered in Milwaukee. The service sector, including finance, insurance, real estate, and retail trade, employs more than sixty–one percent of the area's non–farm workforce. Nearly a quarter of the state's high–tech firms, employing over one–third of Wisconsin's technology industry staff, are located in Milwaukee County.

More than 350 multi-service motor freight carriers are engaged in shipping goods from Milwaukee to markets throughout the country. Three railroads provide rail freight service to the metropolitan area. General Mitchell International Airport is the destination for most air traffic into Milwaukee. Situated adjacent to I-94, eight miles south of downtown, Mitchell Airport is served by seventeen commercial airlines. The terminal accommodates more than four million passengers each year and is highly regarded by frequent travelers. Based at General Mitchell International Airport is Midwest Express Airlines, ranked as one of the best airlines in the country, which provides nonstop commuter service to Milwaukee from several major United States cities. The principal general aviation facility for Milwaukee is Timmerman Field.

A 160-mile freeway system permits direct access to central Milwaukee within twenty minutes from points throughout a 10-mile radius, except during the peak rush-hour period.

Population (1990)

Total Population and Growth Rate
1990: 1,432,149
1980: 1,397,020
1970: 1,403,884
Growth rate 1970–1990: 2%

Race and Hispanic Origin
White: 82.6%
Black: 13.8%
Asian/Pacific Islander: 1.3%
Native American: 0.6%

Hispanic origin: 3.6%
White not Hispanic: 80.9%

Age
Ages 18 to 20: 4.2%
Ages 21 to 24: 5.9%
Ages 25 to 44: 32.8%
Ages 45 to 54: 9.8%
Ages 55 to 59: 4.3%
Ages 60 to 64: 4.3%
Ages 65 plus: 12.5%

Educational Attainment (1990)
Percent having completed high school: 79.7%
Percent having completed college: 21.3%
Elementary and high school enrollment: 250,656

Federal Funds and Grants Received
Total received in 1989: $3,938,700,000
Funds received per capita: $2,817

Civilian Labor Force
1993 (April): 780,029
1992 average: 772,180
1991 average: 754,562
1990 average: 759,730

Unemployment
1993 (April): 5.0%
1992 average: 4.5%
1991 average: 4.7%
1990 average: 3.8%

Average Annual Pay
1988: $21,800
1987: $20,838
1985: $19,481

Per Capita Personal Income
1991: $20,325
1990: $19,785
1989: $18,811

Business Climate (1987)

Manufacturing
Number of establishments in 1987: 3,023
Shipments in 1987 ($1,000): $19,104,300
Employees in 1987: 164,000
Change in employment, 1982 to 1987: -9.1%
Average annual pay for manufacturing work in 1989: $28,730
Average annual pay for production work in 1987: $24,210

Wholesale Trade
Number of establishments in 1987: 3,098
Total sales in 1987 ($1,000): $15,624,800
Change in sales, 1982 to 1987: 20.8%

Retail Trade
Number of establishments in 1987: 8,332
Total sales in 1987 ($1,000): $15,624,800

Retail sales per household in 1987: $16,531
Average annual pay in 1989: $10,937

Service Industry

Selected receipts in 1987 ($1,000): $4,228,100
Average annual pay in 1989: $18,713

Office Real Estate (1992)

Office space inventory: 24,145,174 square feet
Average class A Central Business District rental range per sq. ft: $17.80

Vacancy Rates

All areas: 15.3%

Vacancy Rates in Central Business District

Class A space: 12.3%
Class B space: 15.2%

Vacancy Rates Outside Central Business District

Class A space: 13.0%
Class B space: 18.3%

Housing

Total number of units in 1990: 562,031
Occupied units in 1990: 537,722
Owner-occupied units in 1990: 59.4%
1993 ACCRA average cost: $132,680
1993 ACCRA average rent for an apartment: $648

Chamber of Commerce

Metro Milwaukee Association of Commerce, John Duncan, President, 756 N. Milwaukee St., Milwaukee, WI 53202. 414-287-4100, FAX 414-271-7753

Economic Development Office

Waukesha Area Chamber of Commerce, Jean E. Graf, Exec. Director, 223A Wisconsin Ave., Waukesha, WI 53186. 414-542-4249, FAX 414-542-8068

Economic Development Organizations

Milwaukee Dept. of City Development, Michael Brodd, Zone Administrator, PO Box 324, Milwaukee, WI 53201. 414-223-5845

Milwaukee County Economic Development, Timothy M. Casey, Director, 907 N. 10th St. Room 309, Milwaukee, WI 53233. 414-278-4905

Milwaukee Commercial Development Corp., Curtiss E. Harris, Director, 135 W. Wells #428, Milwaukee, WI 53203. 414-272-8300

Waukesha Economic Development Corp., Walt Elish, Exec. Dirctor, N14 W23777 Stone Ridge Dr. Room 170, PO Box 16, Waukesha, WI 53186. 414-523-0330

Local Incentives for Business

Financial and Technical Incentives

The state development zone tax benefits are just one of the incentives available to businesses in Milwaukee. Others include:

Development Zone Loan Program.

Job Opportunity Bond Fund, offering fixed rate tax exempt financing and other bond financing as well.

Second Mortgage Program, offering accessible fixed asset financing for small business.

SBA 504 Debenture Guarantee, offering fixed asset financing for small business.

Women- and Minority-Business Enterprise, offering gap financing for early state enterprises.

High Tech Mortgage Program, providing fixed-asset financing for high-tech firms.

Partnership Loan Program, offering aid to rapidly expanding companies.

Tax Increment Financing.

Permit Information Center.

Land Bank Mortgage Program for Land Bank properties in all three areas.

Three small business incubators.

Technology Development Fund for research.

Employment Incentives

In additional to the state development zone jobs tax credits, the following employment and training incentives are offered:

Wis JOBS wage subsidy program.

Wisconsin Job Service providing referral and preliminary screening.

Federal Targeted Jobs Tax Credits.

The Step-Up Program to assist youth in making a successful transition to the workplace.

Milwaukee County Private Industry Council, offering adult programs in basic and occupational skills and vocational training.

Major Businesses

Company	SIC	Telephone
Beatrice Cheese Inc.	2022	(414) 782-2750
Bergner, P. A. & Co. of Illinois	5311	(414) 347-4141
Bergner, P. A. & Co.	5311	(414) 347-4141
Blue Cross Blue Shield United	6324	(414) 226-5000
Briggs & Stratton Corp.	3519	(414) 259-5333
Diana Corp.	5147	(414) 289-9797
Farm House Foods Corp.	5147	(414) 271-5050
Firstar Corp.	6021	(414) 765-4321
Godfrey Co.	5411	(414) 542-9311
Harley-Davidson Inc.	3751	(414) 342-4680
Harnischfeger Industries	3554	(414) 671-4400
Hoover Universal Inc.	2531	(414) 228-1200
Johnson Controls, Inc.	3822	(414) 228-1200
Journal Communications Inc.	2711	(414) 224-2000
Kohl's Acquisition Inc.	5311	(414) 783-5800
Kohl's Department Stores	5311	(414) 783-5800
Kohl's Food Stores Inc.	5411	(414) 771-8000
Marshall & Ilsley Corp.	6022	(414) 765-7801
Miller Brewing Co.	2082	(414) 931-2000

Major Businesses (Continued)

Company	SIC	Telephone
Northwestern Mutual Life Insurance	6311	(414) 271-1444
Rex-Pt Holdings Inc.	3562	(414) 643-3000
Rexnord Corp.	3562	(414) 643-3000
Roundy's, Inc.	5141	(414) 547-7999
Scot Lad Foods, Inc.	5141	(414) 547-7900
Smith, A. O. Corp.	3714	(414) 359-4000
Time Insurance Co. Inc.	6311	(414) 271-3011
Universal Foods Corp.	2037	(414) 271-6755
Wisconsin Bell Inc.	4813	(414) 549-7102
Wisconsin Electric Power Co.	4911	(414) 221-2345
Wisconsin Energy Corp.	4911	(414) 221-2345

Colleges and Universities

Alverno College, Milwaukee
Cardinal Stritch College, Milwaukee
Carroll College, Waukesha
Columbia College of Nursing, Milwaukee
Marquette University, Milwaukee
Milwaukee Area Technical College, Milwaukee
Milwaukee Institute of Art And Design, Milwaukee
Milwaukee School of Engineering, Milwaukee
Mount Mary College, Milwaukee
Stratton College, Milwaukee
University of Wisconsin-Milwaukee, Milwaukee
University of Wisconsin Center-Waukesha County, Waukesha

RACINE, WI (PMSA)

Geographic Profile

Land Area

333.1 square miles

Counties and Parishes

Racine

Ranking Highlights

315 *out of 319 in total land area*
259 *out of 319 in population growth, 1970–1990*
121 *out of 310 in having the lowest unemployment rate*
200 *out of 310 in size of labor force*
209 *out of 318 in the percentage of college graduates*
 82 *out of 292 in per capita personal income*
140 *out of 319 in number of manufacturing establishments*
259 *out of 318 in physicians per 1000 people*
237 *out of 318 in hospital beds per 1000 people*
147 *out of 267 in fewest crimes per 1000 people*
118 *out of 266 in fewest violent crimes per 1000 people*
295 *out of 319 in per capita federal funds and grants*

Quality of Life Indexes (Rate per 1000 population)

Crime rate in 1991:	62.7
Violent crime rate in 1991:	5.4
Physicians rate in 1992:	1.33
Hospital bed rate in 1991:	3.04

ACCRA Cost of Living Indexes

(First quarter 1993, average = 100)
Composite index: 104.2
Utilities index: 96.3
Housing index: 120.8

Overview

Manufacturing is the largest segment of the economy followed by retail trade and services.

The Wisconsin Electric Power Company provides service to Racine County at various voltages to serve residential, commercial, and industrial uses. Electric rates in the county are among the lowest in the nation. Waste collection is provided by both public and private collection services. Most of the solid waste is landfilled at one large, general-use landfill located within the county and three large landfills located in adjacent counties. Public sanitary sewerage systems serve about 85 percent of the county population. The remainder is served by onsite sewage disposal systems. Most of the communities in Racine County have recently compelted, or are currently undertaking, sewer system and treatment plant rehabilitation and expansion programs. Public water supply is generally available within and adjacent to the urban centers in Racine County, serving approximately 75 percent of the county's population. There are 13 publicly owned water utilities in the county. In addition, there are numerous small, private water utilities serving isolated residential and institutional land uses. The Wisconsin Natural Gas Company and the Wisconsin Southern Gas Company are authorized to operate in Racine County.

I-94 links Racine County with Milwaukee and Chicago, Illinois, while U.S. 45 and state highway's 11, 20, 31, 32, 36, 38, and 83 integrate the county. Statehighway's 75, 142, and 164 connect Racine County with adjacent counties. Rail freight service is provided by the Chicago & North Western Transportation Company, the Wisconsin Central Ltd., and the Soo Line Railroad Company. Rail passenger service is provided by Amtrak. Racine County is located 13 miles from the Port of Milwaukee. Racine County is served by three general aviation airports: John H. Batten Field, Burlington Municipal Airport, and Sylvania Airport, all located within the county. Both John H. Batten Field and Burlington Municipal Airport are capable of handling a wide variety of business aircraft. John H. Batten Field can accommodate aircraft up to and including corporate jets. General Mitchell International Airport, the nearest scheduled air carrier airport, is located seven miles to the north in the City of Milwaukee. Chicago's O'Hare International Airport is located 50 miles to the south. There are 95 widely distributed trucking and warehousing establishments located in Racine County.

Population (1990)

Total Population and Growth Rate
1990: 175,034
1980: 173,132
1970: 170,838
Growth rate 1970–1990: 2%

Race and Hispanic Origin
White: 86.9%
Black: 9.7%
Asian/Pacific Islander: 0.6%
Native American: 0.3%
Hispanic origin: 5.2%
White not Hispanic: 84.4%

Age
Ages 18 to 20: 3.7%
Ages 21 to 24: 5.2%
Ages 25 to 44: 32.1%
Ages 45 to 54: 10.4%
Ages 55 to 59: 4.3%
Ages 60 to 64: 4.3%
Ages 65 plus: 12%

Educational Attainment (1990)
Percent having completed high school: 76.4%
Percent having completed college: 16.5%
Elementary and high school enrollment: 32,162

Federal Funds and Grants Received
Total received in 1989: $374,200,000
Funds received per capita: $2,153

Civilian Labor Force
1993 (April):   89,867
1992 average: 89,791
1991 average: 87,891
1990 average: 89,527

Unemployment
1993 (April):   6.5%
1992 average: 6.4%
1991 average: 6.5%
1990 average: 4.7%

Average Annual Pay
1988: $21,117
1987: $19,978
1985: $18,714

Per Capita Personal Income
1991: $18,894
1990: $18,442
1989: $17,381

Business Climate (1987)

Manufacturing
Number of establishments in 1987: 384
Shipments in 1987 ($1,000): $3,071,700
Employees in 1987: 25,500
Change in employment, 1982 to 1987: 5.8%
Average annual pay for manufacturing work in 1989: $30,590
Average annual pay for production work in 1987: $20,965

Wholesale Trade
Number of establishments in 1987: 234
Total sales in 1987 ($1,000): $732,700
Change in sales, 1982 to 1987: 77.9%

Retail Trade
Number of establishments in 1987: 1,095
Total sales in 1987 ($1,000): $732,700
Retail sales per household in 1987: $16,298
Average annual pay in 1989: $9,641

Service Industry
Selected receipts in 1987 ($1,000): $350,000
Average annual pay in 1989: $16,706

Housing
Total number of units in 1990: 66,945
Occupied units in 1990: 63,736
Owner-occupied units in 1990: 68.3%
1993 ACCRA average cost: N/A
1993 ACCRA average rent for an apartment: N/A

Chamber of Commerce
Racine Area Manufacturing & Commerce, Roger Caron, President, 300 5th RacineSt., Racine, WI 53403. 414-634-1931, FAX 414-634-7422

Economic Development Office
Racine CRacineounty Economic Development Corp., Gor-

don Kacala, Exec. Director, 4701 Washington Ave., Racine, WI 53406. 414-638-0234, FAX 414-638-0250

Economic Development Organizations

Racine City Development, Thomas N. Wright, Director, 730 Washington Ave., Racine, WI 53403. 414-636-9151

Local Incentives for Business

Financial and Technical Incentives

In addition to the state development zone tax benefits, the following programs and agencies are available to provide financial and technical assistance to development zone businesses:

Community Development Block Grant provides funds for business loans, site prepartation, neighborhood infrastructure improvement, and housing rehabilitation.

Small Business Administration 502 and 504 loans. Administered by the Racine County Economic Development Corporation (RCEDC), offering financing of fixed assets for small businesses.

RCEDC assistance in applying for Wisconsin Housing & Economic Development Authority funds for economic development.

Development Zone Tax Increment Financing district in progress.

Low interest loan pool for business expansion and retention.

Technical assistance to development zone business provided by RCEDC.

Employment Incentives

The state development zone jobs tax credit is one of the training and employment incentives available in the zone. Others include:

The Racine County Economic Development Corporation will assist development zone businesses with employee recruitment and training.

Federal Targeted Jobs Tax Credits.

Wisconsin Lakeshore Job Service, offering referral and preliminary screening.

On-the-job training supported by the federal Job Training Partnership Act.

Gateway Technical College, offering standard and customized training.

Economic Dislocation and Worker Adjustment Assistance Program.

Racine Spanish Center, offering job training.

Racine Urban League, offering job training.

Major Businesses

Company	SIC	Telephone
Case Corp.	3523	(414) 636-6011
Case Credit Corp.	6159	(414) 636-6572
First Bank Southeast National Association	6021	(414) 886-3000
Heritage Bank & Trust	6022	(414) 639-6010

Major Businesses (Continued)

Company	SIC	Telephone
Johnson, S. C. & Son, Inc.	2842	(414) 631-2000
Johnson Worldwide Association	3949	(414) 631-2100
Lynch Display Vans Inc.	7532	(414) 763-0147
Modine Manufacturing Co.	3443	(414) 636-1200
Moxness Products Inc.	3069	(414) 554-5050
Open Pantry Food Marts of Wisconsin	5541	(414) 632-3161
Promotions Unlimited Corp.	5199	(414) 554-8484
Reserco Inc.	5541	(414) 632-3161
St. Luke's Memorial Hospital	8062	(414) 636-2011
St. Mary's Medical Center	8062	(414) 636-4011
Twin Disc Inc.	3568	(414) 634-1981
Versa Technologies Inc.	3069	(414) 886-1174
Walker Forge Inc.	3462	(414) 634-7151
Webster Electric Co.	3494	(414) 633-3511
Western Publishing Co.	2731	(414) 633-2431
Wisconsin Natural Gas Co.	4924	(414) 637-7681
Wisconsin Vision Association	5048	(414) 763-7394
Young Radiator Co.	3714	(414) 639-1010

Colleges and Universities

Gateway Technical College, Racine

SHEBOYGAN, WI (MSA)

Geographic Profile

Land Area

513.7 square miles

Counties and Parishes

Sheboygan

Additional Cities/Towns within Area

None

Ranking Highlights

289 *out of 319 in total* **land area**

233 *out of 319 in* **population growth,** *1970–1990*

69 *out of 310 in having the lowest* **unemployment** *rate*

268 *out of 310 in size of* **labor force**

261 *out of 318 in the percentage of* **college graduates**

97 *out of 292 in per capita personal* **income**

194 *out of 319 in number of* **manufacturing establishments**

285 *out of 318 in* **physicians** *per 1000 people*

144 *out of 318 in* **hospital beds** *per 1000 people*

48 *out of 267 in fewest* **crimes** *per 1000 people*

10 *out of 266 in fewest* **violent crimes** *per 1000 people*

299 *out of 319 in per capita* **federal funds and grants**

Quality of Life Indexes (Rate per 1000 population)

Crime rate in 1991:	42.1
Violent crime rate in 1991:	1.3
Physicians rate in 1992:	1.18
Hospital bed rate in 1991:	4.05

ACCRA Cost of Living Indexes

(First quarter 1993, average = 100)

Composite index:	N/A
Utilities index:	N/A
Housing index:	N/A

Overview

Sheboygan is located one hour north of Milwaukee and one hour south of Green Bay. Major state highways form conduits throughout the area. The area is served by more than a dozen common carriers. A municipal airport, with a Fixed Base Operator, is home to 72 corporate aircraft, with a transport airport less than an hour away.

Sheboygan has been recently named one of the Top 10 Livable Cities in the nation by *Money* magazine, based on economic growth, health care, education, tourism and quality of life. The FBI ranks Sheboygan as the third safest city in the nation and the U.S. Census Bureau states that the city has the lowest percentage of people below the poverty level among metropolitan centers studied.

Historic and cultural attractions, road racing, and Lake Michigan sportfishing draw an estimated 750,000 visitors per year and pump nearly $100 million into the county's local economy.

Population (1990)

Total Population and Growth Rate

1990: 103,877

1980: 100,935

1970: 96,660

Growth rate 1970–1990: 7%

Race and Hispanic Origin

White: 96.6%

Black: .4%

Asian/Pacific Islander: 2.0%

Native American: 0.3%

Hispanic origin: 1.6%

White not Hispanic: 95.7%

Age

Ages 18 to 20: 3.7%

Ages 21 to 24: 5.1%

Ages 25 to 44: 31.4%

Ages 45 to 54: 9.9%

Ages 55 to 59: 4.2%

Ages 60 to 64: 4.4%

Ages 65 plus: 14.6%

Educational Attainment (1990)

Percent having completed high school: 77.4%

Percent having completed college: 13.8%

Elementary and high school enrollment: 18,908

Federal Funds and Grants Received

Total received in 1989: $219,500,000

Funds received per capita: $2,131

Civilian Labor Force

1993 (April):	58,013
1992 average:	59,387
1991 average:	58,258
1990 average:	58,130

Unemployment

1993 (April):	3.9%
1992 average:	5.4%
1991 average:	5.6%
1990 average:	4.6%

Average Annual Pay

1988: $19,622

1987: $18,828

1985: $17,354

Per Capita Personal Income

1991: $18,365

1990: $17,896

1989: $17,247

Business Climate (1987)

Manufacturing

Number of establishments in 1987: 236

Shipments in 1987 ($1,000): $2,077,300

Employees in 1987: 18,700

Change in employment, 1982 to 1987: 14.0%

Average annual pay for manufacturing work in 1989: $24,441

Average annual pay for production work in 1987: $21,194

Wholesale Trade

Number of establishments in 1987: 133

Total sales in 1987 ($1,000): $576,300

Change in sales, 1982 to 1987: 44.1%

Retail Trade

Number of establishments in 1987: 594

Total sales in 1987 ($1,000): $576,300

Retail sales per household in 1987: $13,920

Average annual pay in 1989: $10,352

Service Industry

Selected receipts in 1987 ($1,000): $191,700

Average annual pay in 1989: $15,083

Housing

Total number of units in 1990: 40,695

Occupied units in 1990: 38,592

Owner-occupied units in 1990: 70.3%

1993 ACCRA average cost: N/A

1993 ACCRA average rent for an apartment: N/A

Chamber of Commerce

Sheboygan County Chamber of Commerce, Barbara Ebenreiter, Exec. Director, 631 New York Ave., Sheboygan, WI 53081. 414-457-9491, FAX 414-457-6269

Economic Development Office

Sheboygan Development Corp., Martin Crneckiy, President, 631 New York Ave., Sheboygan, WI 53081. 414-457-9491, FAX 414-457-6269

Major Businesses

Company	SIC	Telephone
Brantmeier, Dick Ford Inc.	5511	(414) 458-6111
Donohue & Associates Inc.	8711	(414) 458-8711
Eclipse Manufacturing Co.	3469	(414) 457-2311
First Interstate Bank of Wisconsin	6022	(414) 459-2000
First Wisconsin National	6021	(414) 459-6000
Flagg, Paul Inc.	3111	(414) 278-7946
Gabes Construction Co., Inc.	1623	(414) 459-2600
Heritage Mutual Insurance	6331	(414) 458-9131
Joa, Curt G. Inc.	3554	(414) 467-6136
Kohler Co.	3431	(414) 457-4441
Nemschoff Chairs Inc.	2531	(414) 457-7726
Plyco Corp.	3089	(414) 876-3356
Plymouth Oil Inc.	5171	(414) 893-6851
Prange, H. C. Co.	5311	(414) 459-7144
Quality State Oil Co.,Inc.	5172	(414) 459-5640
Quasius Bros. Inc.	1541	(414) 457-5585
S & R Cheese Corp.	2022	(414) 893-6061
Sargento Cheese Co., Inc.	2022	(414) 893-8484

Major Businesses (Continued)

Company	SIC	Telephone
Sargento Food Service Corp.	5143	(414) 893-8484
Sargento Inc.	2022	(414) 893-8484
Schultz Sav-O Stores, Inc.	5411	(414) 457-4433
Sheboygan Memorial Hospital	8062	(414) 457-5033
St. Nicholas Hospital	8062	(414) 459-8300
Times Printing Co., Inc.	2752	(414) 994-4396
United Savings & Loan Association	6036	(414) 458-3553
Van Horn, Joe Chevrolet Inc.	5511	(414) 893-6361
Vinyl Plastics Inc.	3081	(414) 458-4664
Watry Industries Inc.	3365	(414) 457-4886
Werner, Bob Chevrolet-Cadillac	5511	(414) 459-6840
Willman Industries Inc.	3321	(414) 668-8526
Windway Capital Corp.	3469	(414) 457-8600

Colleges and Universities

Lakeland College, Sheboygan

University of Wisconsin Center-Sheboygan County, Sheboygan

WAUSAU, WI (MSA)

Geographic Profile
Land Area
1545.1 square miles
Counties and Parishes
Marathon

Ranking Highlights
127 *out of 319 in total* **land area**
184 *out of 319 in* **population growth,** *1970–1990*
 92 *out of 310 in having the lowest* **unemployment** *rate*
240 *out of 310 in size of* **labor force**
272 *out of 318 in the percentage of* **college graduates**
187 *out of 292 in per capita personal* **income**
226 *out of 319 in number of* **manufacturing establishments**
208 *out of 318 in* **physicians** *per 1000 people*
291 *out of 318 in* **hospital beds** *per 1000 people*
 10 *out of 267 in fewest* **crimes** *per 1000 people*
  6 *out of 266 in fewest* **violent crimes** *per 1000 people*
265 *out of 319 in per capita* **federal funds and grants**

Quality of Life Indexes (Rate per 1000 population)
Crime rate in 1991:   32.3
Violent crime rate in 1991:   1.2
Physicians rate in 1992:   1.59
Hospital bed rate in 1991:   2.2

ACCRA Cost of Living Indexes
(First quarter 1993, average = 100)
Composite index: 103.2
Utilities index: 100.2
Housing index: 122.9

Population (1990)
Total Population and Growth Rate
1990: 115,400
1980: 111,270
1970: 97,457
Growth rate 1970–1990: 18%
Race and Hispanic Origin
White: 97.2%
Black: .1%
Asian/Pacific Islander: 2.2%
Native American: 0.4%
Hispanic origin: 0.4%
White not Hispanic: 97.0%
Age
Ages 18 to 20: 4.1%
Ages 21 to 24: 5.2%
Ages 25 to 44: 31.6%
Ages 45 to 54: 10.1%
Ages 55 to 59: 4.1%

Ages 60 to 64: 4.2%
Ages 65 plus: 12.7%

Educational Attainment (1990)
Percent having completed high school: 75.9%
Percent having completed college: 13.5%
Elementary and high school enrollment: 21,878

Federal Funds and Grants Received
Total received in 1989: $266,000,000
Funds received per capita: $2,346

Civilian Labor Force
1993 (April):   66,309
1992 average: 66,867
1991 average: 65,118
1990 average: 63,678

Unemployment
1993 (April): 5.5%
1992 average: 5.9%
1991 average: 5.9%
1990 average: 4.5%

Average Annual Pay
1988: $19,024
1987: $18,360
1985: $16,975

Per Capita Personal Income
1991: $16,471
1990: $16,094
1989: $15,098

Business Climate (1987)
Manufacturing
Number of establishments in 1987: 190
Shipments in 1987 ($1,000): $1,843,000
Employees in 1987: 11,200
Change in employment, 1982 to 1987: -7.4%
Average annual pay for manufacturing work in 1989: $24,051
Average annual pay for production work in 1987: $22,256
Wholesale Trade
Number of establishments in 1987: 235
Total sales in 1987 ($1,000): $659,600
Change in sales, 1982 to 1987: 18.0%
Retail Trade
Number of establishments in 1987: 691
Total sales in 1987 ($1,000): $659,600
Retail sales per household in 1987: $15,605
Average annual pay in 1989: $9,514
Service Industry
Selected receipts in 1987 ($1,000): $231,000
Average annual pay in 1989: $17,086

Housing
Total number of units in 1990: 43,774

Occupied units in 1990: 41,547
Owner-occupied units in 1990: 74.7%
1993 ACCRA average cost: $144,625
1993 ACCRA average rent for an apartment: $530

Chamber of Commerce

Wausau Area Chamber of Commerce, Richard A. Olsen, Exec. Vice President, 300 3rd St. Suite 200, PO Box 6190, Wausau, WI 54402-6190. 715-845-6231, FAX 715-845-6235

Economic Development Office

Marathon County Economic Development Council, Roger Allen Luce, Exec. Director, 300 3rd St. Suite 200, PO Box 6190, Wausau, WI 54402-6190. 715-845-6231, FAX 715-845-6235

Major Businesses

Company	SIC	Telephone
29 Super Market Inc.	5411	(715) 848-1316
A & B Process System Corp.	1711	(715) 687-4332
Community Health Care Inc.	8062	(715) 847-2227
Employers Insurance Wausau	6331	(715) 845-5211
Fore Way Express Inc.	4213	(715) 845-1177
Gordon Aluminum Industries	3354	(715) 359-6101
Graebel Companies, Inc.	4213	(715) 848-3399
Graebel Movers Inc.	4213	(715) 848-3399
Graebel Van Lines Inc.	4213	(715) 848-3399
Greenheck Fan Corp.	3444	(715) 359-6171
Hoffers, Inc.	5013	(715) 675-4848
L & S Electric Inc.	5063	(715) 359-3155
Manson, J. N. Agency Inc.	6411	(715) 845-4371
Marathon Cheese Corp.	7389	(715) 443-2211
Marathon Electric Manufacturing	3621	(715) 675-3311
Marmet Corp.	3449	(715) 845-5242
Mid-State Contracting Inc.	1711	(715) 675-2388
Mosinee Paper Corp.	2621	(715) 693-4470
Riiser Oil Co., Inc.	5171	(715) 845-7272
Rosemurgy Motors Inc.	5511	(715) 845-4236
Van Ert Electric Co.	1731	(715) 845-4308
Wausau Coated Products Inc.	2672	(715) 848-2741
Wausau Homes Inc.	2452	(715) 359-7272
Wausau Hospital Inc.	8062	(715) 847-2121
Wausau Metals Corp.	3442	(715) 845-2161
Wausau Paper Mills Co.	2621	(715) 845-5266
Wausau Service Corp.	6311	(715) 845-5211
Wausau Supply Co., Inc.	5033	(715) 842-2181
Wausau Underwriters Insurance	6331	(715) 845-5211
Wergin Co Inc.	1542	(715) 842-2222
Zimpro/Passavant Inc.	1629	(715) 359-7211

Colleges and Universities

Northcentral Technical College, Wausau

University of Wisconsin Center-Marathon County, Wausau

WYOMING

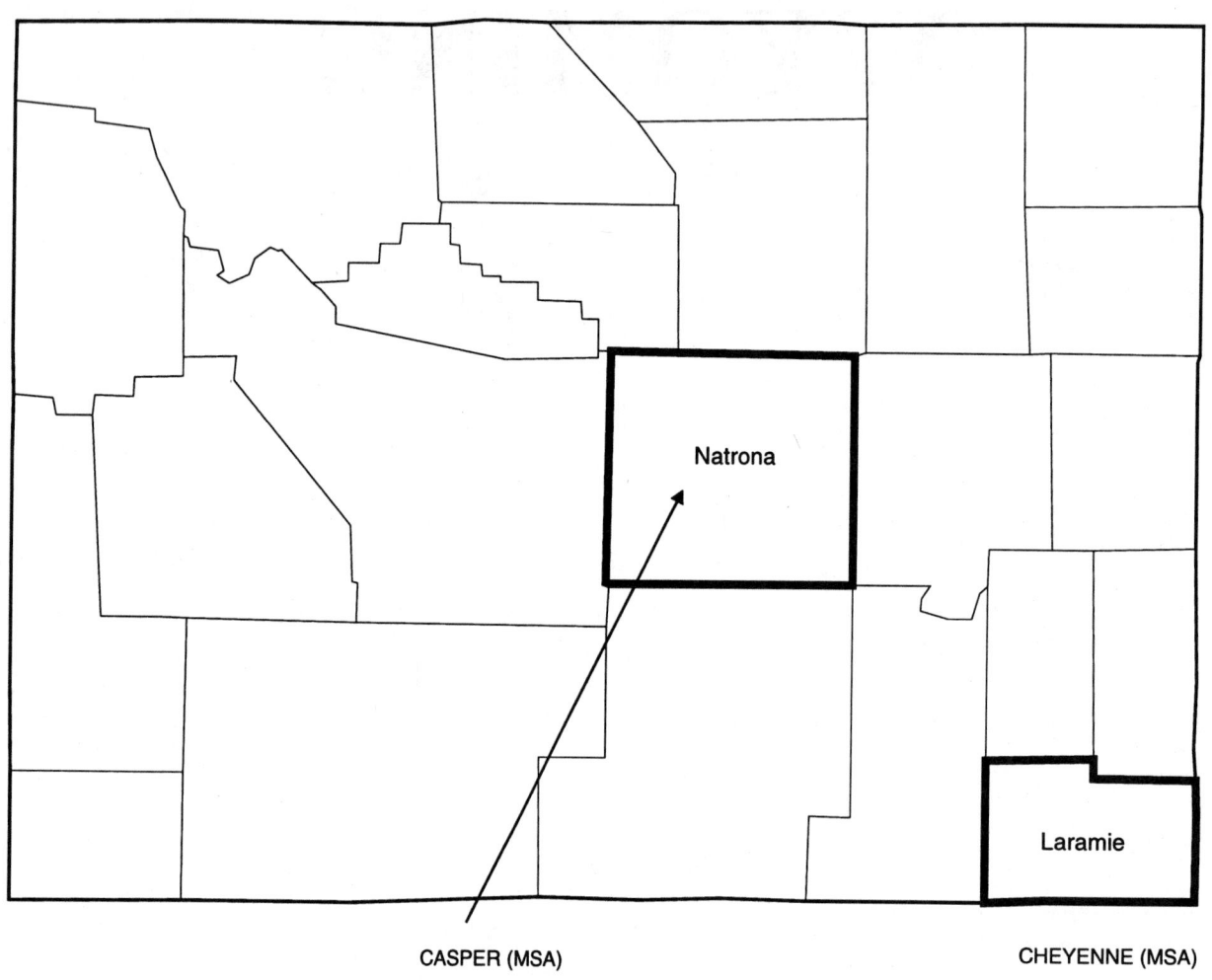

Natrona

Laramie

CASPER (MSA)

CHEYENNE (MSA)

WYOMING

Population

1990: 453,588
1980: 469,557

Age

Ages 18 to 20: 20,025
Ages 21 to 24: 21,361
Ages 25 to 44: 148,495
Ages 45 to 54: 45,497
Ages 55 to 59: 17,893
Ages 60 to 64: 17,597
Median age: 32.0

Race and Hispanic Origin

White: 427,061
Black: 3,606
Asian/Pacific Islander: 2,806
Native American: 9,479
Hispanic origin: 25,751

Households

Total: 168,839
Persons per household: 2.63

Sex

Male: 227,007
Female: 226,581

Population Migration

Domestic migration: -81,000
International migration: 3,000

Projection of the Population in 1995

Total: 474,000
18 to 64: 289,000

Civilian Labor Force

1993: 232,700
1992: 238,900
1991: 242,200
1990: 240,000

Manufacturing

1995 Projection: 11,300
1992: 9,200
1991: 10,000
1990: 9,900
1989: 9,000

Services

1995 Projection: 59,600

1992: 41,700
1991: 36,300
1990: 36,600
1989: 35,300

Wholesale and Retail Trade

1995 Projection: 51,000
1992: 46,600
1991: 45,500
1990: 45,300
1989: 44,600

Unemployment Rate

1993: 6.4%
1992: 7.8%
1991: 5.4%
1990: 6.4%

Employer Unemployment Contributions

Contribution Rate

1992: 2.20%
1991: 2.24%
1990: 3.23%

Average Weekly Benefit

1992: $164.70
1991: $161.47
1990: $158.35

Gross State Product (Million $)

1989: $11,115
1988: $10,782
1987: $10,557
1979: $8,480
Growth rate, 1979 to 1989: 31.1%

Capital Expenditures of Manufacturing Industries

1990: $75,400,000
1989: $68,500,000
1988: $45,400,000
1987: $65,300,000

State Tax Rates

Individual income: None.
Corporate income: None.
General property: Sum of state and local rates. Assessed at 100% of fair market VA lue.

General sales: 3%
Gasoline: 9¢ per gallon

Income

Median income for a 4 person family: $35,620

Personal per Capita Income
1992: $17,423
1991: $16,968
1990: $16,467

Disposable per Capita Income
1992: $15,607
1991: $15,118
1990: $14,667

Private Employment Weekly Wages

Average
1989: $360
1988: $358
1987: $358

Manufacturing
1989: $350
1988: $407
1987: $402

Services
1989: $263
1988: $259
1987: $251

Wholesale
1989: N/A
1988: $432
1987: $427

Retail
1989: $192
1988: $189
1987: $189

Highway Statistics

Total Highway Miles
1990: 39,213
1989: 39,541
1988: 40,502

Federal Highway Aid
1991: $79,650,000
1990: $79,475,000
1989: $81,102,000

Electricity

Average Cost per Kilowatt Hour
1990: 4.22¢
1989: 4.31¢
1988: 4.51¢

Housing (1990)

Owner occupied units: 114,544
Median house value: $61,600

Renter occupied units: 54,295
Median rent: $270
Totalvacant units: 34,572
Homeowner vacancy rate: 3.9%
Rental vacancy rate: 14.4%

State Business Incentives and Assistance

Financial and Business Assistance

Federally Funded Business Loans. This program provides low-interest loans to businesses creating jobs for low-to-moderate-income citizens. Funds can be used to buy or lease land, buildings, machinery and equipment, and for construction and renoVA tion of facilities. The state grants the money to participating cities, towns and counties, which then loan it to businesses at a below market rate based upon need. Loans are limited to 50% of the total project cost. One new job must be created for each $10,000 of loan funds. 51% of the jobs created must be filled by low-to-middle-income citizens.

State Funded Business Loans. This program provides direct loans and loan guarantees for ventures that use state resources, employ state people or otherwise add value to Wyoming goods. The loan cannot exceed 60% of the total project cost. Applicant must contribute at least 20% equity. Funds are loaned at below-market interest rates, and loan terms may not exceed 10 years.

Planning and Marketing Grants. Local governments may apply for grants under this program on behalf of for-profit businesses. Funds may be used to defray the cost of feasibility studies, and for business plan preparation, marketing studies and test marketing. Up to $25,000 is available per applicant, and a 25% match is required.

Main Street Program. Wyoming's Main Street communities have received $800,000 from the Petroleum Violations Fund to implement low-interest, revolving loan programs. These funds must be matched with private funds and may be used for energy conserVA tion related renovation projects in downtown areas.

Science, Technology and Energy Authority. This program is designed to help businesses involved with advanced technology move from research and development to the marketplace. The Authority leverages state funds with private and federal dollars to provide financing.

Wyoming Small Business Act. This program provides fixed-asset financing and fixed-term interest rate subsidies of loans which are to be used for creating jobs. The State Treasurer purchases the guaranteed portions of SBA or Farmers Home Administration loans. All Wyoming residents who own and operate medium-sized industrial or manufacturing firms are eligible. Funds may be used to acquire land and buildings, buy machinery and equipment, and build or renovate facilities.

Link Deposit Program. A fixed-term, fixed-rate interest subsidy is available on loans used for the creation and

Major Companies in the State

Company name	Fortune 500 rank	City	Telephone	SIC number
Fortune 500 Companies				
None				
Other Major Companies in the State				
American Nuclear Corp.		Casper	307-265-7912	1094
Cheyenne Resources Inc.		Cheyenne	307-632-6437	1311
Crested Corp.		Riverton	307-856-9272	6519
Double Eagle Petroleum & Mining Co.		Casper	307-237-9330	1311
EMC Energies Inc.		Casper	307-234-7813	1311
Four Nines Gold Inc.		Riverton	307-856-9271	1623
Hawks Industries Inc.		Casper	307-234-1593	2731
Liberty Media Corp.		Cheyenne	307-638-5835	4841
Metro Cable Corp.		Riverton	307-856-3800	1311
MINEX Resources Inc.		Riverton	307-856-1817	1311
Northwest Gold Inc.		Riverton	307-856-9278	6519
Nugget Exploration Inc.		Casper	307-234-9151	1041
Ruby Mining Co.		Riverton	307-856-9278	1041
S W Financial Corp.		Riverton	307-856-0375	6799
Score Exploration Corp.		Casper	307-265-0382	1311
Star Acquisitions Corp.		Riverton	307-857-3022	6799
Tyrex Oil Co.		Casper	307-234-4260	1311
U S Energy Corp.		Riverton	307-856-9271	6519
Viable Resources Inc.		Casper	307-234-5310	1041
Video Communications & Radio Inc.		Gillette	307-686-9348	7812
Western Standard Corp.		Riverton	307-856-9288	7011
Wyoming National Bancorporation		Casper	307-235-7797	6712
Wyoming Oil & Minerals Inc.		Casper	307-234-9638	1311

retention of jobs. The program allows the State Treasurer to contract with Wyoming financial institutions to supply deposit funds which are then used for below-market interest rates for business loans. The funds may be used to build, remodel, or buy facilities, or to purchase machinery, equipment, land and livestock. Up to $750,000 is available to the borrower, who must certify creation of new jobs.

Wyoming Industrial Development Corporation. This is a private corporation which offers economic development financing and services to Wyoming businesses through several different programs. It also administers a Small Business Administration 504 program statewide.

Office of International Trade. The Office links Wyoming firms with new markets overseas. Wyoming companies are encouraged to export through counseling, educational programs and direct export promotion assistance.

Education and Training

Industrial Training. Administered by the Wyoming Community College Commission, this informal program will assist company to train or retrain workers. The local col-

lege will work with the employers and set up customized training programs.

Job Training Partnership Act. This program operates with funding from the U.S. Department of Labor. It provides job training and other employment related services.

State Offices

Real estate: Real Estate Commission, Connie K. Anderson, Exec Diretor, Herschler Bldg., 4th Fl., 122 West 25th Street, Cheyenne, WY 82002. 307-777-7141

Chamber of commerce: (No State Chamber of Commerce)

Economic development: Economic Development & Stabilization Board of Wyoming, Steve Schmitz, Exec Director, Herschler Bldg., 3rd Fl, East Wing, 122 West 25th Street, Cheyenne, WY 82002. 800-262-3425 or 307-777-7284, FAX 307-777-5840

International Trade Office, J. Vincent Levine, Acting Director, Herschler Bldg., 2nd Fl, West Wing, 122 West 25th Street, Cheyenne, WY 82002. 307-777-6412, FAX 307-777-5840

Division of Corporations, Jeanne Sawyer, Director, Herschler Bldg., Cheyenne, WY 82002. 307-777-5334

Community Development Block Grant Program, Director, Economic Development & Stabilization Board, Herschler Bldg., Cheyenne, WY 82002. 307-777-7284

Science, Technology and Energy Authority, Director, University of Wyoming, PO Box 3985, UW Station, Laramie, WY 83071. 307-766-3842

Wyoming Industrial Development Corporation, Director, PO Box 3599, Casper, WY 82602. 307-234-5351

U.S. Small Business Administration, Business Development Division, Paul Nemetz, District Director, PO Box 2839, Casper, WY 82602. 307-261-5761

Business Assistance Center, University of Wyoming, Director, PO Box 3275, Laramie, WY 82071. 307-766-2363

Community Assessment Program, Economic Development & Stabilization Board, CAP Coordinator, Herschler Bldg., Cheyenne, WY 82002. 307-777-7285 or 800-262-3425

Small Business Development Center, State Director, Casper Community College, 111 West Second Street, Suite 416, Casper, WY 82601. 307-235-4825

Environmental affairs: Environmental Quality Department, Dennis Hemmer, Director, Herschler Bldg., 4th Fl. West, Cheyenne, WY 82002. 307-777-7938

Labor: Labor and Statistics Department, Michael J. Sullivan, Commissioner, Herschler Bldg., 2nd Fl, Cheyenne, WY 82002. 307-777-7261

Unemployment: Employment Security Commission, Unemployment Compensation Division, Elizabeth A. Nelson, Exec Director, PO Box 2760, Casper, WY 82602. 307-235-3254

Worker's compensation: Worker's Compensation, Ann E. Woodward, Director, 122 West 25th Street, Cheyenne, WY 82002-0700. 307-777-7441

Occupational safety and health: Occupational Health and Safety Department, Michael J. Sullivan, Administrator, Herschler Bldg., 2nd Fl. East, Cheyenne, WY 82002. 307-777-7786

Secretary of state: Secretary of State Office, Kathy Karpan, Secretary of State, State Capitol, Cheyenne, WY 82002-0020. 307-777-7378

Taxation and revenue: Revenue and Taxation Department, Nancy Freudenthal, State Tax Commission Chairman, 122 West 25th Street, Herschler Bldg., Cheyenne, WY 82002. 307-777-5285

Designated Zones for Economic Development

Enterprise Zones

No program.

Foreign Trade Zones

Foreign Trade Zone No. 157, Casper, Wyoming, Grantee: Natrona County International Airport, Eddie F. Storer, Zone Administrator, Casper, WY 82604, 307-472-6688, FAX 307-472-1805

Universities with Ph.D. Programs

University of Wyoming, Laramie

Sources of Additional Information

Wyoming, A Business Portfolio. Wyoming International Trade Office and Economic Development and Stabilization Department, n.d. 12p.

Made In Wyoming, Your Kit for Business Development in Wyoming. Division of Economic and Community Development, n.d. 20p.

CASPER, WY (MSA)

Geographic Profile

Land Area

5340.1 square miles

Counties and Parishes

Natrona

Ranking Highlights

9 *out of 319 in total* **land area**

181 *out of 319 in* **population growth**, *1970–1990*

191 *out of 310 in having the lowest* **unemployment** *rate*

309 *out of 310 in size of* **labor force**

130 *out of 318 in the percentage of* **college graduates**

92 *out of 292 in per capita personal* **income**

300 *out of 319 in number of* **manufacturing establishments**

147 *out of 318 in* **physicians** *per 1000 people*

171 *out of 318 in* **hospital beds** *per 1000 people*

159 *out of 267 in fewest* **crimes** *per 1000 people*

107 *out of 266 in fewest* **violent crimes** *per 1000 people*

220 *out of 319 in per capita* **federal funds and grants**

Quality of Life Indexes (Rate per 1000 population)

Crime rate in 1991: 65.4

Violent crime rate in 1991: 5.1

Physicians rate in 1992: 1.85

Hospital bed rate in 1991: 3.67

ACCRA Cost of Living Indexes

(First quarter 1993, average = 100)

Composite index: 99.3

Utilities index: 72.3

Housing index: 102.6

Population (1990)

Total Population and Growth Rate

1990: 61,226

1980: 71,856

1970: 51,264

Growth rate 1970–1990: 19%

Race and Hispanic Origin

White: 96.9%

Black: .7%

Asian/Pacific Islander: 0.5%

Native American: 0.7%

Hispanic origin: 3.7%

White not Hispanic: 94.5%

Age

Ages 18 to 20: 4.1%

Ages 21 to 24: 4.2%

Ages 25 to 44: 33%

Ages 45 to 54: 10%

Ages 55 to 59: 4.2%

Ages 60 to 64: 4.7%

Ages 65 plus: 10.5%

Educational Attainment (1990)

Percent having completed high school: 85.3%

Percent having completed college: 20.4%

Elementary and high school enrollment: 11,769

Federal Funds and Grants Received

Total received in 1989: $169,300,000

Funds received per capita: $2,617

Civilian Labor Force

1993 (April): 29,332

1992 average: 30,354

1991 average: 31,200

1990 average: 32,244

Unemployment

1993 (April): 6.8%

1992 average: 7.4%

1991 average: 5.7%

1990 average: 5.8%

Average Annual Pay

1988: $20,068

1987: $19,632

1985: $19,997

Per Capita Personal Income

1991: $18,461

1990: $18,265

1989: $16,105

Business Climate (1987)

Manufacturing

Number of establishments in 1987: 92

Shipments in 1987 ($1,000): $495,800

Employees in 1987: 1,400

Change in employment, 1982 to 1987: -36.4%

Average annual pay for manufacturing work in 1989: $25,310

Average annual pay for production work in 1987: $24,000

Wholesale Trade

Number of establishments in 1987: 276

Total sales in 1987 ($1,000): $776,600

Change in sales, 1982 to 1987: -48.8%

Retail Trade

Number of establishments in 1987: 492

Total sales in 1987 ($1,000): $776,600

Retail sales per household in 1987: $16,257

Average annual pay in 1989: $11,006

Service Industry

Selected receipts in 1987 ($1,000): $147,500

Average annual pay in 1989: $16,457

Housing

Total number of units in 1990: 29,082

Occupied units in 1990: 23,837
Owner-occupied units in 1990: 68.9%
1993 ACCRA average cost: $130,000
1993 ACCRA average rent for an apartment: $317

Chamber of Commerce

Casper Area Chamber of Commerce, Thomas Lamoureux, Exec. Vice President, 500 N. Center St., PO Box 399, Casper, WY 82602. 307-234-5311, FAX 307-265-2643

Economic Development Office

Casper Area Economic Development Alliance, Carl F. Adrian, President, 111 W. 2nd St. #615, Casper, WY 82601. 307-577-7011, FAX 307-577-7014

Major Businesses

Company	SIC	Telephone
B & B Homes Corp.	3792	(307) 235-1525
Benson Chevrolet, Inc.	5511	(307) 237-2438
Casper Air Service	4522	(307) 472-3400
Coliseum Motor Co.	5511	(307) 237-8491
Crum Electric Supply Co.	5063	(307) 266-1278
Energy Distributing Co.	5171	(307) 237-9363
First Interstate Bank of Casper	6021	(307) 235-4201
Greiner Motor Co Inc.	5511	(307) 266-1680
Kaycee Bentonite Partners	1459	(307) 265-3740
Kloefkorn-Ballard Construction	1542	(307) 265-5950
Northern Gas Co.	4922	(307) 235-1541
Rissler & Mc Murry Co.	1611	(307) 473-9581
SST Energy Corp.	1382	(307) 235-3529
Western Oil Tool & Manufacturing Co.	3441	(307) 235-1591
Wyoming Medical Center	8062	(307) 577-7201
Wyoming National Bancorporation	6021	(307) 235-7797
Wyoming National Bank	6021	(307) 266-1100

Colleges and Universities

Casper College, Casper

CHEYENNE, WY (MSA)

Geographic Profile

Land Area
2686.3 square miles

Counties and Parishes
Laramie

Ranking Highlights

  60 *out of 319 in total* **land area**
132 *out of 319 in* **population growth,** *1970–1990*
  34 *out of 310 in having the lowest* **unemployment** *rate*
307 *out of 310 in size of* **labor force**
123 *out of 318 in the percentage of* **college graduates**
128 *out of 292 in per capita personal* **income**
319 *out of 319 in number of* **manufacturing establishments**
134 *out of 318 in* **physicians** *per 1000 people*
191 *out of 318 in* **hospital beds** *per 1000 people*
  84 *out of 267 in fewest* **crimes** *per 1000 people*
  30 *out of 266 in fewest* **violent crimes** *per 1000 people*
  24 *out of 319 in per capita* **federal funds and grants**

Quality of Life Indexes (Rate per 1000 population)

Crime rate in 1991:	50.5
Violent crime rate in 1991:	2.4
Physicians rate in 1992:	1.91
Hospital bed rate in 1991:	3.51

ACCRA Cost of Living Indexes

(First quarter 1993, average = 100)
Composite index: 98.8
Utilities index: 80.8
Housing index: 103.5

Overview

Cheyenne, the capital of Wyoming, began as a railroad town and, during the height of the colorful cattle days, became the wealthiest city in the world. Cheyenne has retained its Western frontier traditions while keeping pace with the twentieth century. The seat of Laramie County, Cheyenne continues to be a railroad and livestock center; the city is also a primary industrial area in the state as well as the site of a major military base. Cheyenne is known for its quality of life and for high clean air ratings.

Cheyenne's economy is based mainly on light manufacturing, agriculture, the military and government, tourism, services, and transportation. Cattle- and sheep-raising continue to be important in the region, yet the economy of Cheyenne has become diversified with the development of industries such as fertilizer processing plants. Other manufacturing includes electronic products and precision instruments as well as restaurant equipment. F. E. Warren U.S. Air Force Base, site of a major installation of the Strategic Air Command, is the city's largest employer; federal, state, and county government offices are located in Cheyenne. With access to two railroads, interstate freeways, and commercial air service, the city is a vital transportation center for the state of Wyoming.

A major transportation center in the state, Cheyenne routes air cargo service through Cheyenne Municipal Airport. Two railroads provide daily freight transportation, and more than sixteen motor freight carriers move goods through facilities in Cheyenne.

Cheyenne offers four convention facilities accommodating a combined total of 3,110 persons. More than eighteen hundred hotel and motel rooms are located in the Cheyenne area. Several hotels and motels also provide meeting accommodations.

The major routes into Cheyenne are: Interstate 25, which runs north and south contiguous with U.S. 85 and 87; east-west I-80; and U.S. 30, which bisects the city southwest to east.

A charter air carrier and two commercial airlines fly into Cheyenne Municipal Airport, which operates three runways. Rail transportation is provided by Amtrak, and commercial bus service is available from points throughout Wyoming and the nation.

Population (1990)
Total Population and Growth Rate
1990: 73,142
1980: 68,649
1970: 56,360
Growth rate 1970–1990: 30%

Race and Hispanic Origin
White: 90.6%
Black: 3.0%
Asian/Pacific Islander: 1.1%
Native American: 0.7%
Hispanic origin: 10.0%
White not Hispanic: 85.3%

Age
Ages 18 to 20: 4.3%
Ages 21 to 24: 5.7%
Ages 25 to 44: 33.6%
Ages 45 to 54: 10.2%
Ages 55 to 59: 4.1%
Ages 60 to 64: 3.9%
Ages 65 plus: 10.3%

Educational Attainment (1990)
Percent having completed high school: 84.2%
Percent having completed college: 20.7%
Elementary and high school enrollment: 13,271

Federal Funds and Grants Received
Total received in 1989: $450,400,000
Funds received per capita: $5,990

Civilian Labor Force
1993 (April):   35,733

1992 average: 36,541
1991 average: 35,970
1990 average: 37,562

Unemployment
1993 (April): 4.3%
1992 average: 4.6%
1991 average: 4.3%
1990 average: 5.1%

Average Annual Pay
1988: $18,371
1987: $18,103
1985: $17,834

Per Capita Personal Income
1991: $17,664
1990: $17,043
1989: $16,023

Business Climate (1987)
Manufacturing
Number of establishments in 1987: 39
Shipments in 1987 ($1,000): $306,100
Employees in 1987: 1,100
Change in employment, 1982 to 1987: -21.4%
Average annual pay for manufacturing work in 1989: $23,200
Average annual pay for production work in 1987: $24,000

Wholesale Trade
Number of establishments in 1987: 116
Total sales in 1987 ($1,000): $198,200
Change in sales, 1982 to 1987: 0.4%

Retail Trade
Number of establishments in 1987: 464
Total sales in 1987 ($1,000): $198,200
Retail sales per household in 1987: $16,458
Average annual pay in 1989: $10,236

Service Industry
Selected receipts in 1987 ($1,000): $136,800
Average annual pay in 1989: $14,438

Housing
Total number of units in 1990: 30,507
Occupied units in 1990: 28,092
Owner-occupied units in 1990: 65.5%
1993 ACCRA average cost: $108,350
1993 ACCRA average rent for an apartment: $605

Chamber of Commerce
Greater Cheyenne Chamber of Commerce, Larry T. Atwell, Exec. Vice President, 301 W. Lincolnway, PO Box 1147, Cheyenne, WY 82003. 307-638-3388

Economic Development Office
Cheyenne LEADS, Jack Crews, President, 1720 Carey Ave. #401, PO Box 1045, Cheyenne, WY 82003-1045. 307-638-6000

Major Businesses

Company	SIC	Telephone
American National Bank of Wyoming	6021	(307) 634-2121
Cheyenne Outfitters, Inc.	5699	(307) 775-7500
Fleischli Oil Co. Inc.	5172	(307) 634-4466
Key Bancshares of Wyoming	6712	(307) 632-0504
Key Bank of Wyoming	6022	(307) 634-5961
Mecham Inc.	5511	(307) 634-1531
Norwest Bank Cheyenne	6021	(307) 634-3314
Rocky Mountain	6035	(307) 634-2101

Colleges and Universities

Laramie County Community College, Cheyenne

PART II: RANKINGS

RANKINGS

Land Area Rankings—Metropolitan Areas

Land area ranking, largest to smallest, of metropolitan statistical areas. (a)

Metropolitan area	Land area (square miles)	Rank
RIVERSIDE-SAN BERNARDINO, CA (PMSA)	27,269.9	1
PHOENIX, AZ (MSA)	9,204.1	2
TUCSON, AZ (MSA)	9,187.0	3
BAKERSFIELD, CA (MSA)	8,141.6	4
LAS VEGAS, NV (MSA)	7,910.7	5
DULUTH, MN-WI (MSA)	7,534.9	6
RENO, NV (MSA)	6,342.5	7
FRESNO, CA (MSA)	5,963.2	8
CASPER, WY (MSA)	5,340.1	9
SAINT LOUIS, MO-IL (MSA)	5,330.8	10
HOUSTON, TX (PMSA)	5,321.8	11
ATLANTA, GA (MSA)	5,121.5	12
SACRAMENTO, CA (MSA)	5,094.0	13
MINNEAPOLIS-ST PAUL, MN-WI (MSA)	5,051.4	14
TULSA, OK (MSA)	5,014.9	15
KANSAS CITY, MO-KS (MSA)	4,987.9	16
VISALIA-TULARE-PORTERVILLE, CA (MSA)	4,824.3	17
EUGENE-SPRINGFIELD, OR (MSA)	4,554.2	18
DALLAS, TX (PMSA)	4,471.0	19
DETROIT, MI (PMSA)	4,465.6	20
YAKIMA, WA (MSA)	4,296.1	21
OKLAHOMA CITY, OK (MSA)	4,247.4	22
SEATTLE, WA (PMSA)	4,216.3	23
SAN DIEGO, CA (MSA)	4,204.5	24
NASHVILLE, TN (MSA)	4,073.1	25
LOS ANGELES-LONG BEACH, CA (PMSA)	4,060.0	26
GREELEY, CO (MSA)	3,992.8	27
BIRMINGHAM, AL (MSA)	3,981.7	28
WASHINGTON, DC-MD-VA (MSA)	3,966.7	29
LAS CRUCES, NM (MSA)	3,807.4	30
REDDING, CA (MSA)	3,785.7	31
DENVER, CO (PMSA)	3,760.9	32
PORTLAND, OR (PMSA)	3,743.0	33
COLUMBUS, OH (MSA)	3,578.9	34
BISMARCK, ND (MSA)	3,559.6	35
PHILADELPHIA, PA-NJ (PMSA)	3,518.1	36
GREENSBORO--WINSTON-SALEM--HIGH POINT, NC (MSA)	3,452.2	37

(continued)

Land Area Rankings—Metropolitan Areas (Continued)

Land area ranking, largest to smallest, of metropolitan statistical areas. (a)

Metropolitan area	Land area (square miles)	Rank
PITTSBURGH, PA (PMSA)	3,400.0	38
BANGOR, ME (NECMA)	3,396.0	39
CHARLOTTE-GASTONIA-ROCK HILL, NC-SC, (MSA)	3,378.6	40
LAREDO, TX (MSA)	3,357.0	41
SALINAS-SEASIDE-MONTEREY, CA (MSA)	3,321.9	42
ALBANY-SCHENECTADY-TROY, NY (MSA)	3,248.5	43
INDIANAPOLIS, IN (MSA)	3,071.2	44
WICHITA, KS (MSA)	2,967.8	45
RICHLAND-KENNEWICK-PASCO, WA (MSA)	2,945.3	46
RICHMOND-PETERSBURG, VA (MSA)	2,944.7	47
ROCHESTER, NY (MSA)	2,931.5	48
LITTLE ROCK-NORTH LITTLE ROCK, AR (MSA)	2,908.6	49
JOHNSON CITY-KINGSPORT-BRISTOL, TN-VA (MSA)	2,865.6	50
SCRANTON--WILKES-BARRE, PA (MSA)	2,839.9	51
MOBILE, AL (MSA)	2,829.9	52
FARGO-MOORHEAD, ND-MN (MSA)	2,811.0	53
AUSTIN, TX (MSA)	2,791.7	54
MEDFORD, OR (MSA)	2,785.4	55
RAPID CITY, SD (MSA)	2,776.4	56
KNOXVILLE, TN (MSA)	2,774.7	57
SANTA BARBARA-SANTA MARIA-LOMPOC, CA (MSA)	2,738.5	58
GREAT FALLS, MT (MSA)	2,698.0	59
CHEYENNE, WY (MSA)	2,686.3	60
JACKSONVILLE, FL (MSA)	2,635.7	61
BILLINGS, MT (MSA)	2,635.2	62
UTICA-ROME, NY (MSA)	2,624.6	63
BALTIMORE, MD (MSA)	2,609.3	64
FORT COLLINS-LOVELAND, CO (MSA)	2,601.4	65
CHARLESTON, SC (MSA)	2,591.8	66
TAMPA-SAINT PETERSBURG-CLEARWATER, FL (MSA)	2,554.5	67
ORLANDO, FL (MSA)	2,537.9	68
SAN ANTONIO, TX (MSA)	2,519.6	69
FORT WORTH-ARLINGTON, TX (PMSA)	2,496.5	70
BOSTON-LAWRENCE-SALEM-LOWELL-BROCKTON, MA (NECMA)	2,440.3	71
SYRACUSE, NY (MSA)	2,389.5	72
PUEBLO, CO (MSA)	2,388.8	73
JACKSON, MS (MSA)	2,363.0	74
HOUMA-THIBODAUX, LA (MSA)	2,339.9	75
NEW ORLEANS, LA (MSA)	2,308.8	76
MEMPHIS, TN-AR-MS (MSA)	2,303.0	77
LOUISVILLE, KY-IN (MSA)	2,266.1	78
SAINT CLOUD, MN (MSA)	2,189.4	79
HUNTINGTON-ASHLAND, WV-KY-OH (MSA)	2,159.9	80
BEAUMONT-PORT ARTHUR, TX (MSA)	2,154.4	81
COLORADO SPRINGS, CO (MSA)	2,126.7	82
CINCINNATI, OH-KY-IN (PMSA)	2,125.0	83
BELLINGHAM, WA (MSA)	2,120.1	84

(continued)

Land Area Rankings—Metropolitan Areas (Continued)

Land area ranking, largest to smallest, of metropolitan statistical areas. (a)

Metropolitan area	Land area (square miles)	Rank
KILLEEN-TEMPLE, TX (MSA)	2,110.8	85
GREENVILLE-SPARTANBURG, SC (MSA)	2,100.0	86
CHATTANOOGA, TN-GA (MSA)	2,090.6	87
WEST PALM BEACH-BOCA RATON-DELRAY BEACH, FL (MSA)	2,034.3	88
NAPLES, FL (MSA)	2,025.5	89
SANTA FE, NM (MSA)	2,018.7	90
RALEIGH-DURHAM, NC (MSA)	2,015.9	91
MONTGOMERY, AL (MSA)	2,007.5	92
PROVO-OREM, UT (MSA)	1,998.4	93
HARRISBURG-LEBANON-CARLISLE, PA (MSA)	1,990.9	94
AUGUSTA, GA-SC (MSA)	1,947.0	95
MIAMI-HIALEAH, FL (PMSA)	1,944.5	96
MERCED, CA (MSA)	1,928.9	97
SALEM, OR (MSA)	1,926.1	98
OMAHA, NE-IA (MSA)	1,916.5	99
CHICAGO, IL (PMSA)	1,884.3	100
LAKELAND-WINTER HAVEN, FL (MSA)	1,874.9	101
OXNARD-VENTURA, CA (PMSA)	1,846.0	102
AMARILLO, TX (MSA)	1,823.9	103
FORT SMITH, AR-OK (MSA)	1,805.7	104
PEORIA, IL (MSA)	1,796.5	105
SAGINAW-BAY CITY-MIDLAND, MI (MSA)	1,774.5	106
SPOKANE, WA (MSA)	1,763.8	107
JOHNSTOWN, PA (MSA)	1,762.8	108
DES MOINES, IA (MSA)	1,727.7	109
SHREVEPORT, LA (MSA)	1,720.6	110
DAVENPORT-ROCK ISLAND-MOLINE, IA-IL (MSA)	1,708.0	111
LANSING-EAST LANSING, MI (MSA)	1,707.3	112
GLENS FALLS, NY (MSA)	1,705.3	113
ANCHORAGE, AK (MSA)	1,697.7	114
NORFOLK-VIRGINIA BEACH-NEWPORT NEWS, VA (MSA)	1,685.4	115
DAYTON-SPRINGFIELD, OH (MSA)	1,683.7	116
PENSACOLA, FL (MSA)	1,679.5	117
TACOMA, WA (PMSA)	1,675.6	118
EAU CLAIRE, WI (MSA)	1,648.1	119
CHICO, CA (MSA)	1,639.6	120
SALT LAKE CITY-OGDEN, UT (MSA)	1,617.5	121
BATON ROUGE, LA (MSA)	1,586.5	122
VALLEJO-FAIRFIELD-NAPA, CA (PMSA)	1,582.0	123
OCALA, FL (MSA)	1,579.0	124
SANTA ROSA-PETALUMA, CA (PMSA)	1,576.2	125
MCALLEN-EDINBURG-MISSION, TX (MSA)	1,569.1	126
WAUSAU, WI (MSA)	1,545.1	127
CORPUS CHRISTI, TX (MSA)	1,527.7	128
SAN ANGELO, TX (MSA)	1,522.2	129
HARTFORD-NEW BRITAIN-MIDDLETOWN-BRISTOL, CT (NECMA)	1,514.9	130
WORCESTER-FITCHBURG-LEOMINSTER, MA (NECMA)	1,513.2	131

(continued)

Land Area Rankings—Metropolitan Areas (Continued)

Land area ranking, largest to smallest, of metropolitan statistical areas. (a)

Metropolitan area	Land area (square miles)	Rank
CLEVELAND, OH (PMSA)	1,512.2	132
TEXARKANA, TX - TEXARKANA, AR (MSA)	1,512.0	133
MODESTO, CA (MSA)	1,494.6	134
LEXINGTON-FAYETTE, KY (MSA)	1,479.4	135
EVANSVILLE, IN-KY (MSA)	1,467.4	136
ALLENTOWN-BETHLEHEM-EASTON, PA-NJ (MSA)	1,461.0	137
MILWAUKEE, WI (PMSA)	1,460.0	138
OAKLAND, CA (PMSA)	1,457.8	139
COLUMBIA, SC (MSA)	1,457.4	140
GRAND FORKS, ND (MSA)	1,437.9	141
YORK, PA (MSA)	1,424.7	142
GRAND RAPIDS, MI (MSA)	1,422.0	143
STOCKTON, CA (MSA)	1,399.4	144
APPLETON-OSHKOSH-NEENAH, WI (MSA)	1,398.9	145
BRAZORIA, TX (PMSA)	1,386.9	146
TOLEDO, OH (MSA)	1,364.6	147
FORT WAYNE, IN (MSA)	1,355.7	148
TUSCALOOSA, AL (MSA)	1,325.3	149
ALEXANDRIA, LA (MSA)	1,322.7	150
SAN JOSE, CA (PMSA)	1,291.2	151
DECATUR, AL (MSA)	1,275.7	152
JOPLIN, MO (MSA)	1,266.3	153
FLORENCE, AL (MSA)	1,264.1	154
CLARKSVILLE-HOPKINSVILLE, TN-KY (MSA)	1,260.5	155
JOLIET, IL (PMSA)	1,257.4	156
CHARLESTON, WV (MSA)	1,249.4	157
SPRINGFIELD, MO (MSA)	1,238.2	158
WILLIAMSPORT, PA (MSA)	1,234.9	159
YUBA CITY, CA (MSA)	1,233.1	160
BINGHAMTON, NY (MSA)	1,225.6	161
NEWARK, NJ (PMSA)	1,219.9	162
FORT LAUDERDALE-HOLLYWOOD-POMPANO BEACH, FL (PMSA)	1,208.9	163
MADISON, WI (MSA)	1,202.2	164
NASSAU-SUFFOLK, NY (PMSA)	1,198.0	165
BLOOMINGTON-NORMAL, IL (MSA)	1,183.6	166
TALLAHASSEE, FL (MSA)	1,183.0	167
SPRINGFIELD, IL (MSA)	1,182.6	168
CHARLOTTESVILLE, VA (MSA)	1,177.1	169
LONGVIEW-MARSHALL, TX (MSA)	1,172.9	170
MACON-WARNER ROBINS, GA (MSA)	1,171.7	171
GAINESVILLE, FL (MSA)	1,167.5	172
HICKORY-MORGANTON, NC (MSA)	1,167.1	173
ALBUQUERQUE, NM (MSA)	1,166.2	174
NEW YORK, NY (PMSA)	1,147.6	175
SPRINGFIELD, MA (NECMA)	1,147.6	176
DOTHAN, AL (MSA)	1,141.5	177
SIOUX CITY, IA-NE (MSA)	1,136.6	178

(continued)

Land Area Rankings—Metropolitan Areas (Continued)

Land area ranking, largest to smallest, of metropolitan statistical areas. (a)

Metropolitan area	Land area (square miles)	Rank
FORT PIERCE, FL (MSA)	1,128.2	179
WILMINGTON, DE-NJ-MD (PMSA)	1,112.3	180
MONMOUTH-OCEAN, NJ (PMSA)	1,108.2	181
STATE COLLEGE, PA (MSA)	1,107.6	182
COLUMBUS, GA-AL (MSA)	1,106.3	183
DAYTONA BEACH, FL (MSA)	1,105.9	184
LAKE CHARLES, LA (MSA)	1,071.2	185
LAWTON, OK (MSA)	1,069.4	186
PORTSMOUTH-DOVER-ROCHESTER, NH-ME (NECMA)	1,064.1	187
JAMESTOWN-DUNKIRK, NY (MSA)	1,062.1	188
ENID, OK (MSA)	1,058.5	189
BILOXI-GULFPORT, MS (MSA)	1,057.9	190
BOISE CITY, ID (MSA)	1,055.0	191
MIDDLESEX-SOMERSET-HUNTERDON, NJ (PMSA)	1,045.5	192
BUFFALO, NY (PMSA)	1,044.7	193
WACO, TX (MSA)	1,041.9	194
YOUNGSTOWN-WARREN, OH (MSA)	1,031.1	195
LYNCHBURG, VA (MSA)	1,029.2	196
MELBOURNE-TITUSVILLE-PALM BAY, FL (MSA)	1,018.5	197
SAN FRANCISCO, CA (PMSA)	1,015.6	198
DANVILLE, VA (MSA)	1,013.9	199
EL PASO, TX (MSA)	1,013.1	200
LAFAYETTE, LA (MSA)	1,009.8	201
WATERLOO-CEDAR FALLS, IA (MSA)	1,005.3	202
PARKERSBURG-MARIETTA, WV-OH (MSA)	1,002.6	203
CHAMPAIGN-URBANA-RANTOUL, IL (MSA)	997.2	204
CANTON, OH (MSA)	970.9	205
WHEELING, WV-OH (MSA)	950.5	206
FAYETTEVILLE-SPRINGDALE, AR (MSA)	950.2	207
LANCASTER, PA (MSA)	949.1	208
PROVIDENCE-PAWTUCKET-WOONSOCKET, RI (NECMA)	940.9	209
FORT WALTON BEACH, FL (MSA)	935.8	210
SHERMAN-DENISON, TX (MSA)	933.7	211
ATHENS, GA (MSA)	933.4	212
PITTSFIELD, MA (NECMA)	931.4	213
TYLER, TX (MSA)	928.5	214
SAVANNAH, GA (MSA)	919.9	215
ABILENE, TX (MSA)	915.7	216
GARY-HAMMOND, IN (PMSA)	915.2	217
BROWNSVILLE-HARLINGEN, TX (MSA)	905.6	218
AKRON, OH (PMSA)	905.2	219
ODESSA, TX (MSA)	901.1	220
MIDLAND, TX (MSA)	900.3	221
LUBBOCK, TX (MSA)	899.6	222
PINE BLUFF, AR (MSA)	884.8	223
VICTORIA, TX (MSA)	882.6	224
MANCHESTER-NASHUA, NH (NECMA)	876.5	225
READING, PA (MSA)	859.2	226

(continued)

Land Area Rankings—Metropolitan Areas (Continued)

Land area ranking, largest to smallest, of metropolitan statistical areas. (a)

Metropolitan area	Land area (square miles)	Rank
ROANOKE, VA (MSA)	850.8	227
AURORA-ELGIN, IL (PMSA)	841.4	228
LINCOLN, NE (MSA)	838.9	229
PORTLAND, ME (NECMA)	835.6	230
ATLANTIC CITY, NJ (MSA)	816.4	231
ORANGE COUNTY, NY (PMSA)	816.4	232
SIOUX FALLS, SD (MSA)	809.2	233
LIMA, OH (MSA)	805.7	234
HUNTSVILLE, AL (MSA)	805.0	235
FORT MYERS-CAPE CORAL, FL (MSA)	803.6	236
ERIE, PA (MSA)	802.0	237
POUGHKEEPSIE, NY (MSA)	801.7	238
FLORENCE, SC (MSA)	799.2	239
ROCKFORD, IL (MSA)	795.2	240
ANAHEIM-SANTA ANA, CA (PMSA)	789.7	241
JACKSONVILLE, NC (MSA)	766.9	242
PANAMA CITY, FL (MSA)	763.7	243
TERRE HAUTE, IN (MSA)	761.0	244
CUMBERLAND, MD-WV (MSA)	753.1	245
BOULDER-LONGMONT, CO (PMSA)	742.5	246
BRADENTON, FL (MSA)	741.2	247
OLYMPIA, WA (MSA)	727.1	248
PASCAGOULA, MS (MSA)	726.6	249
JANESVILLE-BELOIT, WI (MSA)	720.5	250
ANDERSON, SC (MSA)	718.0	251
CEDAR RAPIDS, IA (MSA)	717.5	252
ANN ARBOR, MI (PMSA)	710.1	253
BATTLE CREEK, MI (MSA)	708.9	254
JACKSON, MI (MSA)	706.7	255
ALBANY, GA (MSA)	685.5	256
COLUMBIA, MO (MSA)	685.4	257
KANKAKEE, IL (MSA)	677.5	258
SHARON, PA (MSA)	671.9	259
NEW LONDON-NORWICH, CT-RI (NECMA)	666.1	260
ASHEVILLE, NC (MSA)	656.3	261
FAYETTEVILLE, NC (MSA)	653.1	262
ROCHESTER, MN (MSA)	653.0	263
FLINT, MI (MSA)	639.7	264
VANCOUVER, WA (PMSA)	627.9	265
WICHITA FALLS, TX (MSA)	627.7	266
BRIDGEPORT-STAMFORD-NORWALK-DANBURY, CT (NECMA)	625.9	267
BURLINGTON, VT (NECMA)	621.6	268
IOWA CITY, IA (MSA)	614.5	269
MONROE, LA (MSA)	611.0	270
ANNISTON, AL (MSA)	608.5	271
DUBUQUE, IA (MSA)	608.2	272
NEW HAVEN-WATERBURY-MERIDEN, CT (NECMA)	605.8	273
HONOLULU, HI (MSA)	600.2	274

(continued)

Land Area Rankings—Metropolitan Areas (Continued)

Land area ranking, largest to smallest, of metropolitan statistical areas. (a)

Metropolitan area	Land area (square miles)	Rank
BRYAN-COLLEGE STATION, TX (MSA)	585.8	275
STEUBENVILLE-WEIRTON, OH-WV (MSA)	581.5	276
DECATUR, IL (MSA)	580.6	277
SARASOTA, FL (MSA)	571.8	278
BENTON HARBOR, MI (MSA)	571.0	279
KALAMAZOO, MI (MSA)	561.9	280
JACKSON, TN (MSA)	557.1	281
NEW BEDFORD-FALL RIVER-ATTLEBORO, MA (NECMA)	556.0	282
KOKOMO, IN (MSA)	553.5	283
TOPEKA, KS (MSA)	549.9	284
GADSDEN, AL (MSA)	534.8	285
GREEN BAY, WI (MSA)	528.7	286
ALTOONA, PA (MSA)	525.9	287
NIAGARA FALLS, NY (PMSA)	523.0	288
SHEBOYGAN, WI (MSA)	513.7	289
MUSKEGON, MI (MSA)	509.2	290
LAFAYETTE-WEST LAFAYETTE, IN (MSA)	499.8	291
MANSFIELD, OH (MSA)	497.0	292
LORAIN-ELYRIA, OH (PMSA)	492.6	293
VINELAND-MILLVILLE-BRIDGETON, NJ (PMSA)	489.3	294
LEWISTON-AUBURN, ME (NECMA)	470.3	295
HAMILTON-MIDDLETOWN, OH (PMSA)	467.3	296
ELKHART-GOSHEN, IN (MSA)	463.8	297
OWENSBORO, KY (MSA)	462.4	298
HAGERSTOWN, MD (MSA)	458.2	299
SOUTH BEND - MISHAWAKA, IN (MSA)	457.3	300
LAWRENCE, KS (MSA)	457.0	301
LA CROSSE, WI (MSA)	452.8	302
ANDERSON, IN (MSA)	452.2	303
LAKE COUNTY, IL (PMSA)	447.8	304
SANTA CRUZ, CA (PMSA)	445.8	305
BEAVER COUNTY, PA (PMSA)	435.3	306
BURLINGTON, NC (MSA)	430.7	307
BERGEN-PASSAIC, NJ (PMSA)	419.3	308
SAINT JOSEPH, MO (MSA)	409.8	309
ELMIRA, NY (MSA)	408.2	310
GALVESTON-TEXAS CITY, TX (PMSA)	398.7	311
BREMERTON, WA (MSA)	396.0	312
BLOOMINGTON, IN (MSA)	394.4	313
MUNCIE, IN (MSA)	393.3	314
RACINE, WI (PMSA)	333.1	315
KENOSHA, WI (PMSA)	272.8	316
TRENTON, NJ (PMSA)	226.0	317
WILMINGTON, NC (MSA)	198.9	318
JERSEY CITY, NJ (PMSA)	46.7	319

(a) Land area data are from the *State and Metropolitan Area Data Book 1991* (a Statistical Abstract supplement), Census Bureau, 755 pages, Washington D.C.: U.S. Government Printing Office, 1991.

Population Growth (1970–1990)—Metropolitan Areas

Ranking of metropolitan statistical areas by population change, with each area placed in descending order, largest to smallest. (a)

Metropolitan area	% Population change	Rank
NAPLES, FL (MSA)	299.84%	1
FORT MYERS-CAPE CORAL, FL (MSA)	218.50%	2
FORT PIERCE, FL (MSA)	218.33%	3
OCALA, FL (MSA)	182.24%	4
LAS VEGAS, NV (MSA)	171.31%	5
WEST PALM BEACH-BOCA RATON-DELRAY BEACH, FL (MSA)	147.43%	6
ORLANDO, FL (MSA)	136.67%	7
SARASOTA, FL (MSA)	130.69%	8
RIVERSIDE-SAN BERNARDINO, CA (PMSA)	127.26%	9
DAYTONA BEACH, FL (MSA)	118.73%	10
PHOENIX, AZ (MSA)	118.50%	11
BRADENTON, FL (MSA)	118.00%	12
AUSTIN, TX (MSA)	116.82%	13
MCALLEN-EDINBURG-MISSION, TX (MSA)	111.28%	14
RENO, NV (MSA)	110.35%	15
BRYAN-COLLEGE STATION, TX (MSA)	110.19%	16
OLYMPIA, WA (MSA)	109.69%	17
FORT COLLINS-LOVELAND, CO (MSA)	107.05%	18
FORT LAUDERDALE-HOLLYWOOD-POMPANO BEACH, FL (PMSA)	102.47%	19
LAS CRUCES, NM (MSA)	94.22%	20
PROVO-OREM, UT (MSA)	91.32%	21
MODESTO, CA (MSA)	90.49%	22
TUCSON, AZ (MSA)	89.63%	23
SANTA ROSA-PETALUMA, CA (PMSA)	89.48%	24
REDDING, CA (MSA)	89.38%	25
TAMPA-SAINT PETERSBURG-CLEARWATER, FL (MSA)	87.05%	26
BREMERTON, WA (MSA)	86.50%	27
SANTA CRUZ, CA (PMSA)	85.58%	28
VANCOUVER, WA (PMSA)	85.32%	29
BROWNSVILLE-HARLINGEN, TX (MSA)	85.31%	30
SAN DIEGO, CA (MSA)	83.97%	31
BOISE CITY, ID (MSA)	83.35%	32
LAREDO, TX (MSA)	82.87%	33
VALLEJO-FAIRFIELD-NAPA, CA (PMSA)	79.66%	34
ANCHORAGE, AK (MSA)	79.09%	35
CHICO, CA (MSA)	78.60%	36
LAKELAND-WINTER HAVEN, FL (MSA)	77.40%	37
BRAZORIA, TX (PMSA)	77.00%	38
OXNARD-VENTURA, CA (PMSA)	76.76%	39
SACRAMENTO, CA (MSA)	74.74%	40
HOUSTON, TX (PMSA)	74.61%	41
MELBOURNE-TITUSVILLE-PALM BAY, FL (MSA)	73.46%	42
GAINESVILLE, FL (MSA)	70.96%	43
BOULDER-LONGMONT, CO (PMSA)	70.86%	44
MERCED, CA (MSA)	70.51%	45
ANAHEIM-SANTA ANA, CA (PMSA)	69.61%	46

(continued)

Population Growth (1970–1990)—Metropolitan Areas (Continued)

Ranking of metropolitan statistical areas by population change, with each area placed in descending order, largest to smallest. (a)

Metropolitan area	% Population change	Rank
PANAMA CITY, FL (MSA)	68.69%	47
COLORADO SPRINGS, CO (MSA)	68.25%	48
ATLANTA, GA (MSA)	68.24%	49
FORT WORTH-ARLINGTON, TX (PMSA)	67.50%	50
SANTA FE, NM (MSA)	67.27%	51
PORTSMOUTH-DOVER-ROCHESTER, NH-ME (NECMA)	67.20%	52
VISALIA-TULARE-PORTERVILLE, CA (MSA)	65.63%	53
STOCKTON, CA (MSA)	65.12%	54
RALEIGH-DURHAM, NC (MSA)	64.88%	55
EL PASO, TX (MSA)	64.66%	56
BAKERSFIELD, CA (MSA)	64.57%	57
TALLAHASSEE, FL (MSA)	64.24%	58
DALLAS, TX (PMSA)	64.06%	59
FORT WALTON BEACH, FL (MSA)	63.04%	60
MIDLAND, TX (MSA)	62.93%	61
FRESNO, CA (MSA)	61.49%	62
RICHLAND-KENNEWICK-PASCO, WA (MSA)	60.71%	63
KILLEEN-TEMPLE, TX (MSA)	59.77%	64
SALT LAKE CITY-OGDEN, UT (MSA)	56.78%	65
BELLINGHAM, WA (MSA)	55.86%	66
TYLER, TX (MSA)	55.83%	67
MEDFORD, OR (MSA)	54.85%	68
MIAMI-HIALEAH, FL (PMSA)	52.79%	69
ALBUQUERQUE, NM (MSA)	52.19%	70
CHARLESTON, SC (MSA)	50.84%	71
MANCHESTER-NASHUA, NH (NECMA)	50.07%	72
SALEM, OR (MSA)	48.95%	73
JACKSONVILLE, FL (MSA)	48.02%	74
GREELEY, CO (MSA)	47.62%	75
MONMOUTH-OCEAN, NJ (PMSA)	47.14%	76
DENVER, CO (PMSA)	46.69%	77
SAN ANTONIO, TX (MSA)	46.60%	78
FAYETTEVILLE-SPRINGDALE, AR (MSA)	46.58%	79
CHARLOTTESVILLE, VA (MSA)	46.44%	80
JACKSONVILLE, NC (MSA)	45.30%	81
ATHENS, GA (MSA)	45.09%	82
WILMINGTON, NC (MSA)	44.93%	83
LAFAYETTE, LA (MSA)	44.86%	84
SALINAS-SEASIDE-MONTEREY, CA (MSA)	43.73%	85
SPRINGFIELD, MO (MSA)	43.16%	86
CLARKSVILLE-HOPKINSVILLE, TN-KY (MSA)	42.45%	87
TACOMA, WA (PMSA)	42.16%	88
JOLIET, IL (PMSA)	42.02%	89
SAINT CLOUD, MN (MSA)	41.86%	90
PENSACOLA, FL (MSA)	41.69%	91
YUBA CITY, CA (MSA)	41.50%	92
LAWRENCE, KS (MSA)	41.20%	93

(continued)

Population Growth (1970–1990)—Metropolitan Areas (Continued)

Ranking of metropolitan statistical areas by population change, with each area placed in descending order, largest to smallest. (a)

Metropolitan area	% Population change	Rank
NASHVILLE, TN (MSA)	40.86%	94
BATON ROUGE, LA (MSA)	40.63%	95
SAN JOSE, CA (PMSA)	40.58%	96
COLUMBIA, SC (MSA)	40.40%	97
SANTA BARBARA-SANTA MARIA-LOMPOC, CA (MSA)	39.83%	98
COLUMBIA, MO (MSA)	38.85%	99
ORANGE COUNTY, NY (PMSA)	38.79%	100
SAN ANGELO, TX (MSA)	38.58%	101
SEATTLE, WA (PMSA)	38.49%	102
VICTORIA, TX (MSA)	38.30%	103
CHARLOTTE-GASTONIA-ROCK HILL, NC-SC, (MSA)	38.29%	104
ANDERSON, SC (MSA)	37.66%	105
BISMARCK, ND (MSA)	37.37%	106
FORT SMITH, AR-OK (MSA)	37.13%	107
RAPID CITY, SD (MSA)	37.06%	108
JACKSON, MS (MSA)	36.98%	109
AUGUSTA, GA-SC (MSA)	36.33%	110
ATLANTIC CITY, NJ (MSA)	36.16%	111
GREENVILLE-SPARTANBURG, SC (MSA)	35.36%	112
LAKE COUNTY, IL (PMSA)	34.96%	113
PORTLAND, OR (PMSA)	34.93%	114
TULSA, OK (MSA)	34.82%	115
LITTLE ROCK-NORTH LITTLE ROCK, AR (MSA)	34.63%	116
LONGVIEW-MARSHALL, TX (MSA)	34.50%	117
BURLINGTON, VT (NECMA)	33.47%	118
OKLAHOMA CITY, OK (MSA)	33.41%	119
IOWA CITY, IA (MSA)	33.26%	120
HONOLULU, HI (MSA)	32.62%	121
LANCASTER, PA (MSA)	32.10%	122
NORFOLK-VIRGINIA BEACH-NEWPORT NEWS, VA (MSA)	31.86%	123
EUGENE-SPRINGFIELD, OR (MSA)	31.34%	124
PASCAGOULA, MS (MSA)	31.00%	125
LEXINGTON-FAYETTE, KY (MSA)	30.64%	126
SIOUX FALLS, SD (MSA)	30.04%	127
YAKIMA, WA (MSA)	30.03%	128
AMARILLO, TX (MSA)	29.88%	129
HICKORY-MORGANTON, NC (MSA)	29.87%	130
BILLINGS, MT (MSA)	29.82%	131
CHEYENNE, WY (MSA)	29.78%	132
TUSCALOOSA, AL (MSA)	29.73%	133
BILOXI-GULFPORT, MS (MSA)	29.71%	134
FAYETTEVILLE, NC (MSA)	29.49%	135
MONTGOMERY, AL (MSA)	29.48%	136
WASHINGTON, DC-MD-VA (MSA)	29.05%	137
HAMILTON-MIDDLETOWN, OH (PMSA)	28.85%	138
AURORA-ELGIN, IL (PMSA)	28.66%	139
ODESSA, TX (MSA)	28.36%	140

(continued)

Population Growth (1970–1990)—Metropolitan Areas (Continued)

Ranking of metropolitan statistical areas by population change, with each area placed in descending order, largest to smallest. (a)

Metropolitan area	% Population change	Rank
WACO, TX (MSA)	28.17%	141
HUNTSVILLE, AL (MSA)	28.08%	142
GALVESTON-TEXAS CITY, TX (PMSA)	28.02%	143
RICHMOND-PETERSBURG, VA (MSA)	27.99%	144
OAKLAND, CA (PMSA)	27.98%	145
BLOOMINGTON, IN (MSA)	27.88%	146
GRAND RAPIDS, MI (MSA)	27.66%	147
FLORENCE, SC (MSA)	27.56%	148
FARGO-MOORHEAD, ND-MN (MSA)	27.47%	149
LINCOLN, NE (MSA)	27.19%	150
KNOXVILLE, TN (MSA)	26.92%	151
GREENSBORO--WINSTON-SALEM--HIGH POINT, NC (MSA)	26.80%	152
YORK, PA (MSA)	26.80%	153
MOBILE, AL (MSA)	26.61%	154
ROCHESTER, MN (MSA)	26.59%	155
MADISON, WI (MSA)	26.46%	156
PORTLAND, ME (NECMA)	26.29%	157
HOUMA-THIBODAUX, LA (MSA)	26.11%	158
LOS ANGELES-LONG BEACH, CA (PMSA)	25.86%	159
DECATUR, AL (MSA)	25.79%	160
SPOKANE, WA (MSA)	25.70%	161
STATE COLLEGE, PA (MSA)	24.70%	162
MINNEAPOLIS-ST PAUL, MN-WI (MSA)	24.33%	163
LUBBOCK, TX (MSA)	24.17%	164
BLOOMINGTON-NORMAL, IL (MSA)	23.75%	165
ELKHART-GOSHEN, IN (MSA)	23.45%	166
MONROE, LA (MSA)	23.23%	167
GREEN BAY, WI (MSA)	22.97%	168
CORPUS CHRISTI, TX (MSA)	22.84%	169
ABILENE, TX (MSA)	22.28%	170
LA CROSSE, WI (MSA)	21.67%	171
ANN ARBOR, MI (PMSA)	20.86%	172
ASHEVILLE, NC (MSA)	20.52%	173
SAVANNAH, GA (MSA)	20.44%	174
MACON-WARNER ROBINS, GA (MSA)	19.85%	175
COLUMBUS, OH (MSA)	19.83%	176
MIDDLESEX-SOMERSET-HUNTERDON, NJ (PMSA)	19.71%	177
EAU CLAIRE, WI (MSA)	19.67%	178
JOPLIN, MO (MSA)	19.57%	179
DOTHAN, AL (MSA)	19.53%	180
CASPER, WY (MSA)	19.43%	181
LAFAYETTE-WEST LAFAYETTE, IN (MSA)	19.40%	182
JACKSON, TN (MSA)	18.56%	183
WAUSAU, WI (MSA)	18.41%	184
MEMPHIS, TN-AR-MS (MSA)	17.70%	185
TEXARKANA, TX - TEXARKANA, AR (MSA)	17.44%	186
HAGERSTOWN, MD (MSA)	16.92%	187

(continued)

Population Growth (1970–1990)—Metropolitan Areas (Continued)

Ranking of metropolitan statistical areas by population change, with each area placed in descending order, largest to smallest. (a)

Metropolitan area	% Population change	Rank
BANGOR, ME (NECMA)	16.91%	188
CHATTANOOGA, TN-GA (MSA)	16.81%	189
POUGHKEEPSIE, NY (MSA)	16.72%	190
JOHNSON CITY-KINGSPORT-BRISTOL, TN-VA (MSA)	16.72%	191
WICHITA, KS (MSA)	16.49%	192
ALBANY, GA (MSA)	16.42%	193
GLENS FALLS, NY (MSA)	16.07%	194
WILMINGTON, DE-NJ-MD (PMSA)	15.83%	195
DES MOINES, IA (MSA)	15.69%	196
GRAND FORKS, ND (MSA)	15.68%	197
LAKE CHARLES, LA (MSA)	15.62%	198
ALLENTOWN-BETHLEHEM-EASTON, PA-NJ (MSA)	15.53%	199
LEWISTON-AUBURN, ME (NECMA)	15.32%	200
HARRISBURG-LEBANON-CARLISLE, PA (MSA)	15.25%	201
LYNCHBURG, VA (MSA)	15.17%	202
LANSING-EAST LANSING, MI (MSA)	14.34%	203
BIRMINGHAM, AL (MSA)	14.32%	204
SHERMAN-DENISON, TX (MSA)	14.17%	205
KANSAS CITY, MO-KS (MSA)	14.07%	206
BALTIMORE, MD (MSA)	14.01%	207
NEW BEDFORD-FALL RIVER-ATTLEBORO, MA (NECMA)	13.96%	208
APPLETON-OSHKOSH-NEENAH, WI (MSA)	13.78%	209
VINELAND-MILLVILLE-BRIDGETON, NJ (PMSA)	13.74%	210
READING, PA (MSA)	13.54%	211
SHREVEPORT, LA (MSA)	12.93%	212
NEW ORLEANS, LA (MSA)	12.64%	213
ANNISTON, AL (MSA)	12.55%	214
INDIANAPOLIS, IN (MSA)	12.46%	215
ROANOKE, VA (MSA)	12.45%	216
BURLINGTON, NC (MSA)	12.14%	217
FLORENCE, AL (MSA)	11.54%	218
ALEXANDRIA, LA (MSA)	11.41%	219
WORCESTER-FITCHBURG-LEOMINSTER, MA (NECMA)	11.41%	220
OMAHA, NE-IA (MSA)	11.21%	221
KALAMAZOO, MI (MSA)	10.85%	222
SPRINGFIELD, IL (MSA)	10.83%	223
NEW LONDON-NORWICH, CT-RI (NECMA)	10.54%	224
OWENSBORO, KY (MSA)	9.69%	225
EVANSVILLE, IN-KY (MSA)	9.62%	226
FORT WAYNE, IN (MSA)	8.70%	228
KENOSHA, WI (PMSA)	8.70%	227
HARTFORD-NEW BRITAIN-MIDDLETOWN-BRISTOL, CT (NECMA)	8.55%	229
SAN FRANCISCO, CA (PMSA)	8.23%	230
NEW HAVEN-WATERBURY-MERIDEN, CT (NECMA)	7.96%	231
ALBANY-SCHENECTADY-TROY, NY (MSA)	7.79%	232
SHEBOYGAN, WI (MSA)	7.47%	233

(continued)

Population Growth (1970–1990)—Metropolitan Areas (Continued)

Ranking of metropolitan statistical areas by population change, with each area placed in descending order, largest to smallest. (a)

Metropolitan area	% Population change	Rank
TRENTON, NJ (PMSA)	7.14%	234
PROVIDENCE-PAWTUCKET-WOONSOCKET, RI (NECMA)	7.10%	235
GADSDEN, AL (MSA)	6.05%	236
CHAMPAIGN-URBANA-RANTOUL, IL (MSA)	5.97%	237
JANESVILLE-BELOIT, WI (MSA)	5.71%	238
LORAIN-ELYRIA, OH (PMSA)	5.56%	239
SCRANTON--WILKES-BARRE, PA (MSA)	5.47%	240
LOUISVILLE, KY-IN (MSA)	5.06%	241
WILLIAMSPORT, PA (MSA)	4.78%	242
CINCINNATI, OH-KY-IN (PMSA)	4.72%	243
JACKSON, MI (MSA)	4.52%	244
ERIE, PA (MSA)	4.52%	245
BRIDGEPORT-STAMFORD-NORWALK-DANBURY, CT (NECMA)	4.39%	246
ROCKFORD, IL (MSA)	4.28%	247
ROCHESTER, NY (MSA)	4.25%	248
PUEBLO, CO (MSA)	4.07%	249
BEAUMONT-PORT ARTHUR, TX (MSA)	3.93%	250
SYRACUSE, NY (MSA)	3.66%	251
TOPEKA, KS (MSA)	3.64%	252
PARKERSBURG-MARIETTA, WV-OH (MSA)	3.61%	253
CEDAR RAPIDS, IA (MSA)	3.40%	255
SPRINGFIELD, MA (NECMA)	3.40%	254
DANVILLE, VA (MSA)	3.36%	256
LAWTON, OK (MSA)	3.09%	257
LIMA, OH (MSA)	3.07%	258
RACINE, WI (PMSA)	2.46%	259
NASSAU-SUFFOLK, NY (PMSA)	2.09%	260
MILWAUKEE, WI (PMSA)	2.01%	261
BOSTON-LAWRENCE-SALEM-LOWELL-BROCKTON, MA (NECMA)	2.00%	262
COLUMBUS, GA-AL (MSA)	1.88%	263
HUNTINGTON-ASHLAND, WV-KY-OH (MSA)	1.87%	264
WICHITA FALLS, TX (MSA)	1.51%	265
TOLEDO, OH (MSA)	1.28%	266
MUSKEGON, MI (MSA)	0.99%	267
SOUTH BEND - MISHAWAKA, IN (MSA)	0.91%	268
ENID, OK (MSA)	0.70%	269
PHILADELPHIA, PA-NJ (PMSA)	0.68%	270
SAINT LOUIS, MO-IL (MSA)	0.61%	271
PINE BLUFF, AR (MSA)	0.19%	272
CANTON, OH (MSA)	0.08%	273
CHICAGO, IL (PMSA)	-0.38%	275
SAGINAW-BAY CITY-MIDLAND, MI (MSA)	-0.38%	274
PEORIA, IL (MSA)	-0.82%	276
SIOUX CITY, IA-NE (MSA)	-1.01%	277
KANKAKEE, IL (MSA)	-1.02%	278
BINGHAMTON, NY (MSA)	-1.43%	279

(continued)

Population Growth (1970–1990)—Metropolitan Areas (Continued)

Ranking of metropolitan statistical areas by population change, with each area placed in descending order, largest to smallest. (a)

Metropolitan area	% Population change	Rank
BENTON HARBOR, MI (MSA)	-1.56%	280
DAYTON-SPRINGFIELD, OH (MSA)	-2.43%	281
CHARLESTON, WV (MSA)	-2.60%	282
KOKOMO, IN (MSA)	-2.91%	283
MANSFIELD, OH (MSA)	-2.97%	284
AKRON, OH (PMSA)	-3.19%	285
DAVENPORT-ROCK ISLAND-MOLINE, IA-IL (MSA)	-3.25%	286
FLINT, MI (MSA)	-3.40%	287
ALTOONA, PA (MSA)	-3.56%	288
JAMESTOWN-DUNKIRK, NY (MSA)	-3.67%	289
DETROIT, MI (PMSA)	-3.78%	290
BATTLE CREEK, MI (MSA)	-4.21%	291
SAINT JOSEPH, MO (MSA)	-4.41%	292
GARY-HAMMOND, IN (PMSA)	-4.55%	293
DUBUQUE, IA (MSA)	-4.64%	294
SHARON, PA (MSA)	-4.89%	295
GREAT FALLS, MT (MSA)	-5.03%	296
CUMBERLAND, MD-WV (MSA)	-5.14%	297
TERRE HAUTE, IN (MSA)	-5.52%	298
ANDERSON, IN (MSA)	-5.67%	299
NEWARK, NJ (PMSA)	-5.80%	300
WATERLOO-CEDAR FALLS, IA (MSA)	-5.81%	301
NEW YORK, NY (PMSA)	-5.84%	302
BERGEN-PASSAIC, NJ (PMSA)	-5.85%	303
DECATUR, IL (MSA)	-6.24%	304
ELMIRA, NY (MSA)	-6.25%	305
NIAGARA FALLS, NY (PMSA)	-6.35%	306
PITTSFIELD, MA (NECMA)	-6.73%	307
UTICA-ROME, NY (MSA)	-7.00%	308
MUNCIE, IN (MSA)	-7.40%	309
JOHNSTOWN, PA (MSA)	-8.21%	310
YOUNGSTOWN-WARREN, OH (MSA)	-8.29%	311
JERSEY CITY, NJ (PMSA)	-9.01%	312
DULUTH, MN-WI (MSA)	-9.56%	313
BEAVER COUNTY, PA (PMSA)	-10.71%	314
CLEVELAND, OH (PMSA)	-11.27%	315
PITTSBURGH, PA (PMSA)	-12.39%	316
WHEELING, WV-OH (MSA)	-12.45%	317
BUFFALO, NY (PMSA)	-13.02%	318
STEUBENVILLE-WEIRTON, OH-WV (MSA)	-14.34%	319

(a) Population change represents the simple percent change between 1970 and 1990. Population growth data is calculated from population numbers from the 1970 and 1990 Census as reported by the Bureau of Economic Analysis.

Unemployment Rate (1992)—Metropolitan Areas

Metropolitan areas ranked by 1992 annual average unemployment rate. (a)

Metropolitan area	Unemployment rate (percent)	Rank
IOWA CITY, IA (MSA)	2.0	1
SIOUX FALLS, SD (MSA)	2.3	2
LINCOLN, NE (MSA)	2.4	3
COLUMBIA, MO (MSA)	2.9	5
MADISON, WI (MSA)	2.9	4
LAWRENCE, KS (MSA)	3.2	6
RAPID CITY, SD (MSA)	3.2	6
ROCHESTER, MN (MSA)	3.3	8
OMAHA, NE-IA (MSA)	3.4	9
HONOLULU, HI (MSA)	3.5	10
FARGO-MOORHEAD, ND-MN (MSA)	3.5	10
FAYETTEVILLE-SPRINGDALE, AR (MSA)	3.6	12
SANTA FE, NM (MSA)	3.6	12
LAFAYETTE-WEST LAFAYETTE, IN (MSA)	3.8	14
DES MOINES, IA (MSA)	3.9	15
RALEIGH-DURHAM, NC (MSA)	3.9	15
GRAND FORKS, ND (MSA)	3.9	15
ENID, OK (MSA)	3.9	15
BRYAN-COLLEGE STATION, TX (MSA)	3.9	15
BOULDER-LONGMONT, CO (PMSA)	4.1	20
SIOUX CITY, IA-NE (MSA)	4.1	20
BOISE CITY, ID (MSA)	4.1	20
TOPEKA, KS (MSA)	4.2	23
LEXINGTON-FAYETTE, KY (MSA)	4.3	24
PROVO-OREM, UT (MSA)	4.3	24
TALLAHASSEE, FL (MSA)	4.4	26
WICHITA, KS (MSA)	4.4	26
BISMARCK, ND (MSA)	4.4	26
FORT COLLINS-LOVELAND, CO (MSA)	4.5	29
MINNEAPOLIS-ST PAUL, MN-WI (MSA)	4.5	29
BURLINGTON, VT (NECMA)	4.5	29
GREEN BAY, WI (MSA)	4.5	29
MILWAUKEE, WI (PMSA)	4.5	29
CEDAR RAPIDS, IA (MSA)	4.6	34
BLOOMINGTON-NORMAL, IL (MSA)	4.6	34
SPRINGFIELD, MO (MSA)	4.6	34
BURLINGTON, NC (MSA)	4.6	34
LA CROSSE, WI (MSA)	4.6	34
CHEYENNE, WY (MSA)	4.6	34
CHAMPAIGN-URBANA-RANTOUL, IL (MSA)	4.7	40
BLOOMINGTON, IN (MSA)	4.7	40
ALBUQUERQUE, NM (MSA)	4.7	40
COLUMBIA, SC (MSA)	4.7	40
SALT LAKE CITY-OGDEN, UT (MSA)	4.7	40
HUNTSVILLE, AL (MSA)	4.8	47
LAKE COUNTY, IL (PMSA)	4.8	47
CHARLOTTESVILLE, VA (MSA)	4.8	47
GAINESVILLE, FL (MSA)	4.9	48

(continued)

Unemployment Rate (1992)—Metropolitan Areas (Continued)

Metropolitan areas ranked by 1992 annual average unemployment rate. (a)

Metropolitan area	Unemployment rate (percent)	Rank
KANSAS CITY, MO-KS (MSA)	4.9	48
APPLETON-OSHKOSH-NEENAH, WI (MSA)	4.9	48
WASHINGTON, DC-MD-VA (MSA)	5.0	51
OKLAHOMA CITY, OK (MSA)	5.0	51
GREENVILLE-SPARTANBURG, SC (MSA)	5.0	51
NASHVILLE, TN (MSA)	5.0	51
AUSTIN, TX (MSA)	5.0	51
INDIANAPOLIS, IN (MSA)	5.1	56
ANN ARBOR, MI (PMSA)	5.1	56
ASHEVILLE, NC (MSA)	5.1	56
GREENSBORO--WINSTON-SALEM--HIGH POINT, NC (MSA)	5.1	56
TUCSON, AZ (MSA)	5.2	60
JOPLIN, MO (MSA)	5.2	60
ROANOKE, VA (MSA)	5.2	60
EAU CLAIRE, WI (MSA)	5.2	60
GREELEY, CO (MSA)	5.3	64
SPRINGFIELD, IL (MSA)	5.3	64
COLUMBUS, OH (MSA)	5.3	64
LAWTON, OK (MSA)	5.3	64
LANCASTER, PA (MSA)	5.3	64
BILLINGS, MT (MSA)	5.4	69
HICKORY-MORGANTON, NC (MSA)	5.4	69
JACKSONVILLE, NC (MSA)	5.4	69
ROCHESTER, NY (MSA)	5.4	69
HARRISBURG-LEBANON-CARLISLE, PA (MSA)	5.4	69
SHEBOYGAN, WI (MSA)	5.4	69
CHARLOTTE-GASTONIA-ROCK HILL, NC-SC, (MSA)	5.5	75
ATHENS, GA (MSA)	5.6	76
DUBUQUE, IA (MSA)	5.6	76
KALAMAZOO, MI (MSA)	5.6	76
SAINT CLOUD, MN (MSA)	5.6	76
CINCINNATI, OH-KY-IN (PMSA)	5.6	76
AMARILLO, TX (MSA)	5.6	76
DENVER, CO (PMSA)	5.7	82
WATERLOO-CEDAR FALLS, IA (MSA)	5.7	82
LOUISVILLE, KY-IN (MSA)	5.7	82
JACKSON, MS (MSA)	5.7	82
CHARLESTON, SC (MSA)	5.7	82
KNOXVILLE, TN (MSA)	5.7	82
MEMPHIS, TN-AR-MS (MSA)	5.7	82
TULSA, OK (MSA)	5.8	89
JOHNSON CITY-KINGSPORT-BRISTOL, TN-VA (MSA)	5.8	89
KENOSHA, WI (PMSA)	5.8	89
TUSCALOOSA, AL (MSA)	5.9	92
SARASOTA, FL (MSA)	5.9	92
LANSING-EAST LANSING, MI (MSA)	5.9	92
ANDERSON, SC (MSA)	5.9	92
JACKSON, TN (MSA)	5.9	92

(continued)

Unemployment Rate (1992)—Metropolitan Areas (Continued)

Metropolitan areas ranked by 1992 annual average unemployment rate. (a)

Metropolitan area	Unemployment rate (percent)	Rank
LYNCHBURG, VA (MSA)	5.9	92
WAUSAU, WI (MSA)	5.9	92
WILMINGTON, DE-NJ-MD (PMSA)	6.0	99
PENSACOLA, FL (MSA)	6.0	99
SAINT LOUIS, MO-IL (MSA)	6.0	99
ALBANY-SCHENECTADY-TROY, NY (MSA)	6.0	99
SAN ANGELO, TX (MSA)	6.0	99
BIRMINGHAM, AL (MSA)	6.1	104
LITTLE ROCK-NORTH LITTLE ROCK, AR (MSA)	6.1	104
ANAHEIM-SANTA ANA, CA (PMSA)	6.1	104
SAN FRANCISCO, CA (PMSA)	6.1	104
ELKHART-GOSHEN, IN (MSA)	6.1	104
FORT WAYNE, IN (MSA)	6.1	104
SAINT JOSEPH, MO (MSA)	6.1	104
GREAT FALLS, MT (MSA)	6.1	104
STATE COLLEGE, PA (MSA)	6.1	104
CHATTANOOGA, TN-GA (MSA)	6.1	104
BRADENTON, FL (MSA)	6.2	114
RICHMOND-PETERSBURG, VA (MSA)	6.2	114
SEATTLE, WA (PMSA)	6.2	114
MACON-WARNER ROBINS, GA (MSA)	6.3	117
RENO, NV (MSA)	6.3	117
VICTORIA, TX (MSA)	6.3	117
BREMERTON, WA (MSA)	6.3	117
MONTGOMERY, AL (MSA)	6.4	121
PHOENIX, AZ (MSA)	6.4	121
AUGUSTA, GA-SC (MSA)	6.4	121
BATON ROUGE, LA (MSA)	6.4	121
PORTLAND, OR (PMSA)	6.4	121
FLORENCE, SC (MSA)	6.4	121
RACINE, WI (PMSA)	6.4	121
OAKLAND, CA (PMSA)	6.5	128
ATLANTA, GA (MSA)	6.5	128
SOUTH BEND - MISHAWAKA, IN (MSA)	6.5	128
TERRE HAUTE, IN (MSA)	6.5	128
EVANSVILLE, IN-KY (MSA)	6.5	128
FAYETTEVILLE, NC (MSA)	6.5	128
TRENTON, NJ (PMSA)	6.5	128
POUGHKEEPSIE, NY (MSA)	6.5	128
DAYTON-SPRINGFIELD, OH (MSA)	6.5	128
LUBBOCK, TX (MSA)	6.5	128
JANESVILLE-BELOIT, WI (MSA)	6.5	128
FORT WALTON BEACH, FL (MSA)	6.6	139
SAVANNAH, GA (MSA)	6.6	139
MUNCIE, IN (MSA)	6.6	139
CLEVELAND, OH (PMSA)	6.6	139
ABILENE, TX (MSA)	6.6	139
SAN ANTONIO, TX (MSA)	6.6	139

(continued)

Unemployment Rate (1992)—Metropolitan Areas (Continued)

Metropolitan areas ranked by 1992 annual average unemployment rate. (a)

Metropolitan area	Unemployment rate (percent)	Rank
OLYMPIA, WA (MSA)	6.6	139
DOTHAN, AL (MSA)	6.7	139
ELMIRA, NY (MSA)	6.7	139
YORK, PA (MSA)	6.7	139
SAN JOSE, CA (PMSA)	6.8	149
BRIDGEPORT-STAMFORD-NORWALK-DANBURY, CT (NECMA)	6.8	149
WILMINGTON, NC (MSA)	6.8	149
MIDDLESEX-SOMERSET-HUNTERDON, NJ (PMSA)	6.8	149
LAS VEGAS, NV (MSA)	6.8	149
BINGHAMTON, NY (MSA)	6.8	149
PITTSBURGH, PA (PMSA)	6.8	149
SPOKANE, WA (MSA)	6.8	149
COLORADO SPRINGS, CO (MSA)	6.9	157
MONROE, LA (MSA)	6.9	157
BILOXI-GULFPORT, MS (MSA)	6.9	157
SYRACUSE, NY (MSA)	6.9	157
AKRON, OH (PMSA)	6.9	157
SALEM, OR (MSA)	6.9	157
FORT WORTH-ARLINGTON, TX (PMSA)	6.9	157
WACO, TX (MSA)	6.9	157
NORFOLK-VIRGINIA BEACH-NEWPORT NEWS, VA (MSA)	6.9	157
NEW LONDON-NORWICH, CT-RI (NECMA)	7.0	166
JACKSONVILLE, FL (MSA)	7.0	166
ORLANDO, FL (MSA)	7.0	166
NEW ORLEANS, LA (MSA)	7.0	166
GRAND RAPIDS, MI (MSA)	7.0	166
DULUTH, MN-WI (MSA)	7.0	166
READING, PA (MSA)	7.0	166
DALLAS, TX (PMSA)	7.0	166
SANTA ROSA-PETALUMA, CA (PMSA)	7.1	174
TAMPA-SAINT PETERSBURG-CLEARWATER, FL (MSA)	7.1	174
OWENSBORO, KY (MSA)	7.1	174
LAFAYETTE, LA (MSA)	7.1	174
PASCAGOULA, MS (MSA)	7.1	174
NASSAU-SUFFOLK, NY (PMSA)	7.1	174
ORANGE COUNTY, NY (PMSA)	7.1	174
DAVENPORT-ROCK ISLAND-MOLINE, IA-IL (MSA)	7.2	181
SHREVEPORT, LA (MSA)	7.2	181
HOUSTON, TX (PMSA)	7.2	181
ANCHORAGE, AK (MSA)	7.3	184
FORT SMITH, AR-OK (MSA)	7.3	184
COLUMBUS, GA-AL (MSA)	7.3	184
ALEXANDRIA, LA (MSA)	7.3	184
BUFFALO, NY (PMSA)	7.3	184
TYLER, TX (MSA)	7.3	184
WICHITA FALLS, TX (MSA)	7.3	184
SAN DIEGO, CA (MSA)	7.4	191
CHICAGO, IL (PMSA)	7.4	191

(continued)

Unemployment Rate (1992)—Metropolitan Areas (Continued)

Metropolitan areas ranked by 1992 annual average unemployment rate. (a)

Metropolitan area	Unemployment rate (percent)	Rank
PEORIA, IL (MSA)	7.4	191
KOKOMO, IN (MSA)	7.4	191
BALTIMORE, MD (MSA)	7.4	191
LAS CRUCES, NM (MSA)	7.4	191
LIMA, OH (MSA)	7.4	191
PHILADELPHIA, PA-NJ (PMSA)	7.4	191
BELLINGHAM, WA (MSA)	7.4	191
CASPER, WY (MSA)	7.4	191
FLORENCE, AL (MSA)	7.5	201
UTICA-ROME, NY (MSA)	7.5	201
EUGENE-SPRINGFIELD, OR (MSA)	7.5	201
MIDLAND, TX (MSA)	7.5	201
SHERMAN-DENISON, TX (MSA)	7.5	201
BATTLE CREEK, MI (MSA)	7.6	206
ERIE, PA (MSA)	7.6	206
FORT MYERS-CAPE CORAL, FL (MSA)	7.7	208
HAMILTON-MIDDLETOWN, OH (PMSA)	7.7	208
KILLEEN-TEMPLE, TX (MSA)	7.7	208
VANCOUVER, WA (PMSA)	7.7	208
SANTA BARBARA-SANTA MARIA-LOMPOC, CA (MSA)	7.8	212
PUEBLO, CO (MSA)	7.8	212
HARTFORD-NEW BRITAIN-MIDDLETOWN-BRISTOL, CT (NECMA)	7.8	212
AURORA-ELGIN, IL (PMSA)	7.8	212
MANCHESTER-NASHUA, NH (NECMA)	7.8	212
CANTON, OH (MSA)	7.8	212
CLARKSVILLE-HOPKINSVILLE, TN-KY (MSA)	7.8	212
MOBILE, AL (MSA)	7.9	219
SACRAMENTO, CA (MSA)	7.9	219
DAYTONA BEACH, FL (MSA)	7.9	219
TOLEDO, OH (MSA)	7.9	219
ALLENTOWN-BETHLEHEM-EASTON, PA-NJ (MSA)	7.9	219
BRAZORIA, TX (PMSA)	7.9	219
TACOMA, WA (PMSA)	7.9	219
VALLEJO-FAIRFIELD-NAPA, CA (PMSA)	8.0	226
JOLIET, IL (PMSA)	8.0	226
BOSTON-LAWRENCE-SALEM-LOWELL-BROCKTON, MA (NECMA)	8.0	226
MONMOUTH-OCEAN, NJ (PMSA)	8.0	226
FORT LAUDERDALE-HOLLYWOOD-POMPANO BEACH, FL (PMSA)	8.1	230
MELBOURNE-TITUSVILLE-PALM BAY, FL (MSA)	8.1	230
WILLIAMSPORT, PA (MSA)	8.1	230
TEXARKANA, TX - TEXARKANA, AR (MSA)	8.1	230
NEW HAVEN-WATERBURY-MERIDEN, CT (NECMA)	8.2	234
GARY-HAMMOND, IN (PMSA)	8.2	234
SAGINAW-BAY CITY-MIDLAND, MI (MSA)	8.2	234
BERGEN-PASSAIC, NJ (PMSA)	8.2	234

(continued)

Unemployment Rate (1992)—Metropolitan Areas (Continued)

Metropolitan areas ranked by 1992 annual average unemployment rate. (a)

Metropolitan area	Unemployment rate (percent)	Rank
ANNISTON, AL (MSA)	8.3	238
DECATUR, AL (MSA)	8.3	238
ANDERSON, IN (MSA)	8.3	238
JAMESTOWN-DUNKIRK, NY (MSA)	8.3	238
OXNARD-VENTURA, CA (PMSA)	8.4	242
MANSFIELD, OH (MSA)	8.4	242
MEDFORD, OR (MSA)	8.4	242
ALBANY, GA (MSA)	8.6	245
GALVESTON-TEXAS CITY, TX (PMSA)	8.6	245
RICHLAND-KENNEWICK-PASCO, WA (MSA)	8.6	245
KANKAKEE, IL (MSA)	8.7	248
NEWARK, NJ (PMSA)	8.7	248
ALTOONA, PA (MSA)	8.7	248
DANVILLE, VA (MSA)	8.7	248
SHARON, PA (MSA)	8.8	252
CHARLESTON, WV (MSA)	8.8	252
GADSDEN, AL (MSA)	8.9	254
PANAMA CITY, FL (MSA)	8.9	254
ROCKFORD, IL (MSA)	8.9	254
HAGERSTOWN, MD (MSA)	8.9	254
DETROIT, MI (PMSA)	8.9	254
OCALA, FL (MSA)	9.0	259
BENTON HARBOR, MI (MSA)	9.0	259
PARKERSBURG-MARIETTA, WV-OH (MSA)	9.0	259
LAKE CHARLES, LA (MSA)	9.1	265
STEUBENVILLE-WEIRTON, OH-WV (MSA)	9.1	265
BEAUMONT-PORT ARTHUR, TX (MSA)	9.1	265
WHEELING, WV-OH (MSA)	9.1	265
SANTA CRUZ, CA (PMSA)	9.2	266
DECATUR, IL (MSA)	9.2	266
NAPLES, FL (MSA)	9.3	268
HOUMA-THIBODAUX, LA (MSA)	9.4	269
YOUNGSTOWN-WARREN, OH (MSA)	9.4	269
LAREDO, TX (MSA)	9.4	269
GLENS FALLS, NY (MSA)	9.5	272
NIAGARA FALLS, NY (PMSA)	9.5	272
SCRANTON--WILKES-BARRE, PA (MSA)	9.5	272
LONGVIEW-MARSHALL, TX (MSA)	9.5	272
LOS ANGELES-LONG BEACH, CA (PMSA)	9.6	276
CORPUS CHRISTI, TX (MSA)	9.6	276
WEST PALM BEACH-BOCA RATON-DELRAY BEACH, FL (MSA)	9.8	278
HUNTINGTON-ASHLAND, WV-KY-OH (MSA)	9.8	278
JACKSON, MI (MSA)	9.9	280
LORAIN-ELYRIA, OH (PMSA)	9.9	280
MIAMI-HIALEAH, FL (PMSA)	10.0	282
NEW YORK, NY (PMSA)	10.1	283
ODESSA, TX (MSA)	10.1	283
ATLANTIC CITY, NJ (MSA)	10.4	285

(continued)

Unemployment Rate (1992)—Metropolitan Areas (Continued)

Metropolitan areas ranked by 1992 annual average unemployment rate. (a)

Metropolitan area	Unemployment rate (percent)	Rank
JOHNSTOWN, PA (MSA)	10.5	286
BEAVER COUNTY, PA (PMSA)	10.6	287
CUMBERLAND, MD-WV (MSA)	10.7	288
EL PASO, TX (MSA)	10.8	289
PINE BLUFF, AR (MSA)	10.9	290
RIVERSIDE-SAN BERNARDINO, CA (PMSA)	11.0	291
LAKELAND-WINTER HAVEN, FL (MSA)	11.3	292
CHICO, CA (MSA)	11.6	293
JERSEY CITY, NJ (PMSA)	11.8	294
MUSKEGON, MI (MSA)	11.9	295
FLINT, MI (MSA)	12.1	296
SALINAS-SEASIDE-MONTEREY, CA (MSA)	12.2	297
REDDING, CA (MSA)	12.5	298
YAKIMA, WA (MSA)	12.5	298
BROWNSVILLE-HARLINGEN, TX (MSA)	12.6	300
VINELAND-MILLVILLE-BRIDGETON, NJ (PMSA)	12.9	301
FORT PIERCE, FL (MSA)	13.9	301
STOCKTON, CA (MSA)	14.3	303
FRESNO, CA (MSA)	14.5	304
BAKERSFIELD, CA (MSA)	15.1	305
VISALIA-TULARE-PORTERVILLE, CA (MSA)	15.3	306
MODESTO, CA (MSA)	16.0	307
MERCED, CA (MSA)	16.5	308
MCALLEN-EDINBURG-MISSION, TX (MSA)	17.0	309
YUBA CITY, CA (MSA)	18.1	310

Metropolitan areas not ranked

BANGOR, ME (NECMA)
LEWISTON-AUBURN, ME (NECMA)
NEW BEDFORD-FALL RIVER-ATTLEBORO, MA (NECMA)
PITTSFIELD, MA (NECMA)
PORTLAND, ME (NECMA)
PORTSMOUTH-DOVER-ROCHESTER, NH-ME (NECMA)
PROVIDENCE-PAWTUCKET-WOONSOCKET, RI (NECMA)
SPRINGFIELD, MA (NECMA)
WORCESTER-FITCHBURG-LEOMINSTER, MA (NECMA)

(a) Data are from an unpublished report dated August 17, 1993, on Local Area Unemployment Statistics from the U.S. Bureau of Labor Statistics, Washington, D.C. The MSA with the lowest unemployment rate in 1992 was ranked number 1.

Labor Force Size (1992)—Metropolitan Areas

Metropolitan areas ranked by 1992 size of the labor force.(a)

Metropolitan area	Labor force (1992)	Rank (1992)
LOS ANGELES-LONG BEACH, CA (PMSA)	4,535,300	1
NEW YORK, NY (PMSA)	3,954,918	2
CHICAGO, IL (PMSA)	3,257,492	3
PHILADELPHIA, PA-NJ (PMSA)	2,435,338	4
WASHINGTON, DC-MD-VA (MSA)	2,262,748	5
DETROIT, MI (PMSA)	2,141,856	6
BOSTON-LAWRENCE-SALEM-LOWELL-BROCKTON, MA (NECMA)	2,126,580	7
HOUSTON, TX (PMSA)	1,775,149	8
ATLANTA, GA (MSA)	1,534,846	9
DALLAS, TX (PMSA)	1,469,067	10
MINNEAPOLIS-ST PAUL, MN-WI (MSA)	1,422,797	11
ANAHEIM-SANTA ANA, CA (PMSA)	1,374,144	12
NASSAU-SUFFOLK, NY (PMSA)	1,343,842	13
SAINT LOUIS, MO-IL (MSA)	1,272,909	14
BALTIMORE, MD (MSA)	1,238,053	15
SAN DIEGO, CA (MSA)	1,195,619	16
SEATTLE, WA (PMSA)	1,148,197	17
RIVERSIDE-SAN BERNARDINO, CA (PMSA)	1,137,617	18
OAKLAND, CA (PMSA)	1,117,769	19
PHOENIX, AZ (MSA)	1,057,209	20
TAMPA-SAINT PETERSBURG-CLEARWATER, FL (MSA)	1,038,694	21
PITTSBURGH, PA (PMSA)	1,032,692	22
MIAMI-HIALEAH, FL (PMSA)	979,613	23
CLEVELAND, OH (PMSA)	951,180	24
NEWARK, NJ (PMSA)	923,578	25
DENVER, CO (PMSA)	890,231	26
SAN FRANCISCO, CA (PMSA)	878,085	27
KANSAS CITY, MO-KS (MSA)	871,186	28
SAN JOSE, CA (PMSA)	821,953	29
CINCINNATI, OH-KY-IN (PMSA)	792,858	30
SACRAMENTO, CA (MSA)	784,443	31
MILWAUKEE, WI (PMSA)	772,180	32
COLUMBUS, OH (MSA)	761,091	33
FORT WORTH-ARLINGTON, TX (PMSA)	745,925	34
PORTLAND, OR (PMSA)	713,670	35
FORT LAUDERDALE-HOLLYWOOD-POMPANO BEACH, FL (PMSA)	688,270	36
INDIANAPOLIS, IN (MSA)	687,552	37
BERGEN-PASSAIC, NJ (PMSA)	677,172	38
ORLANDO, FL (MSA)	665,685	39
NORFOLK-VIRGINIA BEACH-NEWPORT NEWS, VA (MSA)	663,556	40
CHARLOTTE-GASTONIA-ROCK HILL, NC-SC, (MSA)	657,200	41
SAN ANTONIO, TX (MSA)	629,476	42
HARTFORD-NEW BRITAIN-MIDDLETOWN-BRISTOL, CT (NECMA)	594,564	43
MIDDLESEX-SOMERSET-HUNTERDON, NJ (PMSA)	591,085	44
NEW ORLEANS, LA (MSA)	578,455	45

(continued)

Labor Force Size (1992)—Metropolitan Areas (Continued)

Metropolitan areas ranked by 1992 size of the labor force.(a)

Metropolitan area	Labor force (1992)	Rank (1992)
BRIDGEPORT-STAMFORD-NORWALK-DANBURY, CT (NECMA)	543,455	46
NASHVILLE, TN (MSA)	538,905	47
GREENSBORO--WINSTON-SALEM--HIGH POINT, NC (MSA)	533,458	48
SALT LAKE CITY-OGDEN, UT (MSA)	523,317	49
LOUISVILLE, KY-IN (MSA)	514,049	50
ROCHESTER, NY (MSA)	510,471	51
OKLAHOMA CITY, OK (MSA)	492,182	52
MONMOUTH-OCEAN, NJ (PMSA)	486,791	53
RICHMOND-PETERSBURG, VA (MSA)	477,961	54
DAYTON-SPRINGFIELD, OH (MSA)	477,114	55
MEMPHIS, TN-AR-MS (MSA)	473,972	56
JACKSONVILLE, FL (MSA)	470,430	57
AUSTIN, TX (MSA)	470,310	58
BUFFALO, NY (PMSA)	458,160	59
RALEIGH-DURHAM, NC (MSA)	449,405	60
BIRMINGHAM, AL (MSA)	448,689	61
WEST PALM BEACH-BOCA RATON-DELRAY BEACH, FL (MSA)	441,202	62
ALBANY-SCHENECTADY-TROY, NY (MSA)	435,967	63
LAS VEGAS, NV (MSA)	422,716	64
HONOLULU, HI (MSA)	408,196	65
GRAND RAPIDS, MI (MSA)	390,399	66
NEW HAVEN-WATERBURY-MERIDEN, CT (NECMA)	390,296	67
OXNARD-VENTURA, CA (PMSA)	384,528	68
SCRANTON--WILKES-BARRE, PA (MSA)	377,499	69
GREENVILLE-SPARTANBURG, SC (MSA)	349,314	70
OMAHA, NE-IA (MSA)	345,785	71
TULSA, OK (MSA)	344,697	72
ALLENTOWN-BETHLEHEM-EASTON, PA-NJ (MSA)	344,507	73
FRESNO, CA (MSA)	343,006	74
HARRISBURG-LEBANON-CARLISLE, PA (MSA)	342,912	75
AKRON, OH (PMSA)	339,631	76
LAKE COUNTY, IL (PMSA)	332,050	77
TUCSON, AZ (MSA)	321,450	78
SYRACUSE, NY (MSA)	320,650	79
WILMINGTON, DE-NJ-MD (PMSA)	316,071	80
TOLEDO, OH (MSA)	312,910	81
KNOXVILLE, TN (MSA)	306,133	82
BATON ROUGE, LA (MSA)	282,670	83
LITTLE ROCK-NORTH LITTLE ROCK, AR (MSA)	274,133	84
ALBUQUERQUE, NM (MSA)	272,004	85
JERSEY CITY, NJ (PMSA)	267,463	86
WICHITA, KS (MSA)	265,028	87
GARY-HAMMOND, IN (PMSA)	262,395	88
TACOMA, WA (PMSA)	262,238	89
BAKERSFIELD, CA (MSA)	262,147	90
EL PASO, TX (MSA)	261,704	91
COLUMBIA, SC (MSA)	248,551	92
DES MOINES, IA (MSA)	248,449	93

(continued)

Labor Force Size (1992)—Metropolitan Areas (Continued)

Metropolitan areas ranked by 1992 size of the labor force.(a)

Metropolitan area	Labor force (1992)	Rank (1992)
CHARLESTON, SC (MSA)	244,014	94
MADISON, WI (MSA)	241,451	95
LANSING-EAST LANSING, MI (MSA)	240,471	96
LANCASTER, PA (MSA)	235,097	97
JOLIET, IL (PMSA)	233,581	98
YORK, PA (MSA)	232,019	99
JOHNSON CITY-KINGSPORT-BRISTOL, TN-VA (MSA)	227,784	100
YOUNGSTOWN-WARREN, OH (MSA)	226,959	101
MOBILE, AL (MSA)	225,358	102
SANTA ROSA-PETALUMA, CA (PMSA)	219,845	103
CHATTANOOGA, TN-GA (MSA)	213,898	104
VALLEJO-FAIRFIELD-NAPA, CA (PMSA)	213,109	105
STOCKTON, CA (MSA)	212,950	106
MELBOURNE-TITUSVILLE-PALM BAY, FL (MSA)	201,777	107
JACKSON, MS (MSA)	201,336	108
AURORA-ELGIN, IL (PMSA)	200,564	109
AUGUSTA, GA-SC (MSA)	200,513	110
FORT WAYNE, IN (MSA)	199,942	111
CANTON, OH (MSA)	198,178	112
LEXINGTON-FAYETTE, KY (MSA)	195,506	113
COLORADO SPRINGS, CO (MSA)	191,374	114
SAGINAW-BAY CITY-MIDLAND, MI (MSA)	190,148	115
DAVENPORT-ROCK ISLAND-MOLINE, IA-IL (MSA)	188,413	116
MANCHESTER-NASHUA, NH (NECMA)	185,902	117
ATLANTIC CITY, NJ (MSA)	185,470	118
SANTA BARBARA-SANTA MARIA-LOMPOC, CA (MSA)	184,102	119
APPLETON-OSHKOSH-NEENAH, WI (MSA)	183,701	120
FLINT, MI (MSA)	183,637	121
READING, PA (MSA)	181,445	122
LAKELAND-WINTER HAVEN, FL (MSA)	181,416	123
SPOKANE, WA (MSA)	181,129	124
MODESTO, CA (MSA)	180,044	125
BEAUMONT-PORT ARTHUR, TX (MSA)	176,578	126
TRENTON, NJ (PMSA)	175,170	127
PEORIA, IL (MSA)	173,239	128
CORPUS CHRISTI, TX (MSA)	171,753	129
SALINAS-SEASIDE-MONTEREY, CA (MSA)	170,840	130
MCALLEN-EDINBURG-MISSION, TX (MSA)	165,096	131
DAYTONA BEACH, FL (MSA)	164,598	132
ANN ARBOR, MI (PMSA)	163,547	133
ROCKFORD, IL (MSA)	160,953	134
VISALIA-TULARE-PORTERVILLE, CA (MSA)	160,094	135
SHREVEPORT, LA (MSA)	157,887	136
FORT MYERS-CAPE CORAL, FL (MSA)	155,945	137
PENSACOLA, FL (MSA)	154,928	138
EUGENE-SPRINGFIELD, OR (MSA)	148,738	139
SALEM, OR (MSA)	146,081	140
EVANSVILLE, IN-KY (MSA)	144,940	141

(continued)

Labor Force Size (1992)—Metropolitan Areas (Continued)

Metropolitan areas ranked by 1992 size of the labor force.(a)

Metropolitan area	Labor force (1992)	Rank (1992)
SANTA CRUZ, CA (PMSA)	144,502	142
BOULDER-LONGMONT, CO (PMSA)	143,591	143
TALLAHASSEE, FL (MSA)	142,968	144
RENO, NV (MSA)	142,349	145
ERIE, PA (MSA)	141,803	146
MONTGOMERY, AL (MSA)	140,573	147
ORANGE COUNTY, NY (PMSA)	138,757	148
NEW LONDON-NORWICH, CT-RI (NECMA)	138,735	149
SPRINGFIELD, MO (MSA)	137,812	150
HAMILTON-MIDDLETOWN, OH (PMSA)	137,245	151
HUNTSVILLE, AL (MSA)	136,337	152
UTICA-ROME, NY (MSA)	136,235	153
LINCOLN, NE (MSA)	133,518	154
HICKORY-MORGANTON, NC (MSA)	132,633	155
VANCOUVER, WA (PMSA)	132,368	156
MACON-WARNER ROBINS, GA (MSA)	131,850	157
HUNTINGTON-ASHLAND, WV-KY-OH (MSA)	131,140	158
ROANOKE, VA (MSA)	130,225	159
SARASOTA, FL (MSA)	129,412	160
SOUTH BEND - MISHAWAKA, IN (MSA)	128,033	161
BOISE CITY, ID (MSA)	125,929	162
LORAIN-ELYRIA, OH (PMSA)	124,898	163
KALAMAZOO, MI (MSA)	121,300	164
SPRINGFIELD, IL (MSA)	121,010	165
BINGHAMTON, NY (MSA)	120,461	166
PROVO-OREM, UT (MSA)	120,199	167
POUGHKEEPSIE, NY (MSA)	119,184	168
SAVANNAH, GA (MSA)	119,037	169
GREEN BAY, WI (MSA)	118,898	170
GALVESTON-TEXAS CITY, TX (PMSA)	118,094	171
CHARLESTON, WV (MSA)	117,960	172
ANCHORAGE, AK (MSA)	117,700	173
LUBBOCK, TX (MSA)	116,582	174
DULUTH, MN-WI (MSA)	116,436	175
GAINESVILLE, FL (MSA)	113,093	176
BROWNSVILLE-HARLINGEN, TX (MSA)	112,452	177
FORT PIERCE, FL (MSA)	110,202	178
YAKIMA, WA (MSA)	108,744	179
LAFAYETTE, LA (MSA)	108,523	180
BRADENTON, FL (MSA)	107,357	181
SAINT CLOUD, MN (MSA)	107,085	182
FORT COLLINS-LOVELAND, CO (MSA)	104,082	183
KILLEEN-TEMPLE, TX (MSA)	102,423	184
JOHNSTOWN, PA (MSA)	101,987	185
FAYETTEVILLE, NC (MSA)	101,619	186
COLUMBUS, GA-AL (MSA)	100,095	187
CEDAR RAPIDS, IA (MSA)	99,098	188
AMARILLO, TX (MSA)	98,325	189

(continued)

Labor Force Size (1992)—Metropolitan Areas (Continued)

Metropolitan areas ranked by 1992 size of the labor force.(a)

Metropolitan area	Labor force (1992)	Rank (1992)
ASHEVILLE, NC (MSA)	96,632	190
CHAMPAIGN-URBANA-RANTOUL, IL (MSA)	95,560	191
NIAGARA FALLS, NY (PMSA)	94,685	192
TOPEKA, KS (MSA)	94,320	193
WACO, TX (MSA)	94,204	194
FORT SMITH, AR-OK (MSA)	93,184	195
BRAZORIA, TX (PMSA)	91.510	196
OLYMPIA, WA (MSA)	91,199	197
FARGO-MOORHEAD, ND-MN (MSA)	90,462	198
ELKHART-GOSHEN, IN (MSA)	90,418	199
RACINE, WI (PMSA)	89,791	200
BILOXI-GULFPORT, MS (MSA)	89,197	201
BREMERTON, WA (MSA)	86,786	202
OCALA, FL (MSA)	84,136	203
LAKE CHARLES, LA (MSA)	83,767	204
LONGVIEW-MARSHALL, TX (MSA)	81,656	205
CHICO, CA (MSA)	81,419	206
BLOOMINGTON-NORMAL, IL (MSA)	81,203	207
BURLINGTON, VT (NECMA)	80,966	208
MERCED, CA (MSA)	80,386	209
RICHLAND-KENNEWICK-PASCO, WA (MSA)	79,880	210
BENTON HARBOR, MI (MSA)	78,738	211
SIOUX FALLS, SD (MSA)	78,590	212
LIMA, OH (MSA)	78,573	213
LYNCHBURG, VA (MSA)	78,493	214
JOPLIN, MO (MSA)	77,937	215
NAPLES, FL (MSA)	77,219	216
MEDFORD, OR (MSA)	77,014	217
TYLER, TX (MSA)	76,579	218
WATERLOO-CEDAR FALLS, IA (MSA)	76,499	219
ATHENS, GA (MSA)	75,980	220
JANESVILLE-BELOIT, WI (MSA)	75,300	221
SANTA FE, NM (MSA)	74,802	222
PARKERSBURG-MARIETTA, WV-OH (MSA)	74,047	223
COLUMBIA, MO (MSA)	73,883	224
TUSCALOOSA, AL (MSA)	73,496	225
EAU CLAIRE, WI (MSA)	73,456	226
BELLINGHAM, WA (MSA)	73,321	227
CHARLOTTESVILLE, VA (MSA)	73,156	228
ANDERSON, SC (MSA)	72,664	229
WHEELING, WV-OH (MSA)	71,417	230
HOUMA-THIBODAUX, LA (MSA)	70,602	231
MONROE, LA (MSA)	70,471	232
FORT WALTON BEACH, FL (MSA)	69,600	233
STATE COLLEGE, PA (MSA)	69,579	234
GREELEY, CO (MSA)	69,547	235
WILMINGTON, NC (MSA)	68,955	236
LAFAYETTE-WEST LAFAYETTE, IN (MSA)	68,824	237

(continued)

Labor Force Size (1992)—Metropolitan Areas (Continued)

Metropolitan areas ranked by 1992 size of the labor force.(a)

Metropolitan area	Labor force (1992)	Rank (1992)
REDDING, CA (MSA)	68,697	238
MUSKEGON, MI (MSA)	67,322	239
WAUSAU, WI (MSA)	66,867	240
BILLINGS, MT (MSA)	66,711	241
FAYETTEVILLE-SPRINGDALE, AR (MSA)	66,543	242
ROCHESTER, MN (MSA)	66,332	243
PANAMA CITY, FL (MSA)	66,299	244
JACKSON, MI (MSA)	65,791	245
BRYAN-COLLEGE STATION, TX (MSA)	65,673	246
BURLINGTON, NC (MSA)	65,262	247
BATTLE CREEK, MI (MSA)	64,621	248
HAGERSTOWN, MD (MSA)	64,207	249
ALTOONA, PA (MSA)	63,901	250
IOWA CITY, IA (MSA)	63,850	251
SIOUX CITY, IA-NE (MSA)	63,715	252
JAMESTOWN-DUNKIRK, NY (MSA)	63,629	253
DECATUR, IL (MSA)	63,603	254
MANSFIELD, OH (MSA)	63,581	255
BEAVER COUNTY, PA (PMSA)	63,580	256
TERRE HAUTE, IN (MSA)	63,269	257
FLORENCE, AL (MSA)	63,090	258
BLOOMINGTON, IN (MSA)	62,131	259
VINELAND-MILLVILLE-BRIDGETON, NJ (PMSA)	61,840	260
WILLIAMSPORT, PA (MSA)	61,547	261
MUNCIE, IN (MSA)	61,501	262
DECATUR, AL (MSA)	61,406	263
FLORENCE, SC (MSA)	60,614	264
LAS CRUCES, NM (MSA)	60,470	265
DOTHAN, AL (MSA)	59,719	266
PASCAGOULA, MS (MSA)	59,399	267
SHEBOYGAN, WI (MSA)	59,387	268
ALEXANDRIA, LA (MSA)	58,587	269
ANDERSON, IN (MSA)	58,120	270
LAREDO, TX (MSA)	57,967	271
TEXARKANA, TX - TEXARKANA, AR (MSA)	57,812	272
KENOSHA, WI (PMSA)	57,697	273
LA CROSSE, WI (MSA)	56,865	274
STEUBENVILLE-WEIRTON, OH-WV (MSA)	55,914	275
CLARKSVILLE-HOPKINSVILLE, TN-KY (MSA)	54,925	276
SHARON, PA (MSA)	54,841	277
GLENS FALLS, NY (MSA)	54,575	278
WICHITA FALLS, TX (MSA)	54,544	279
DANVILLE, VA (MSA)	54,535	280
ODESSA, TX (MSA)	54,445	281
ALBANY, GA (MSA)	54,419	282
YUBA CITY, CA (MSA)	53,937	283
ANNISTON, AL (MSA)	52,443	284
KANKAKEE, IL (MSA)	51,973	285

(continued)

Labor Force Size (1992)—Metropolitan Areas (Continued)

Metropolitan areas ranked by 1992 size of the labor force.(a)

Metropolitan area	Labor force (1992)	Rank (1992)
PUEBLO, CO (MSA)	51,864	286
ABILENE, TX (MSA)	51,778	287
LAWTON, OK (MSA)	49,629	288
MIDLAND, TX (MSA)	49,465	289
KOKOMO, IN (MSA)	47,593	290
LAWRENCE, KS (MSA)	47,130	291
DUBUQUE, IA (MSA)	46,630	292
SHERMAN-DENISON, TX (MSA)	46,594	293
BISMARCK, ND (MSA)	46,555	294
SAN ANGELO, TX (MSA)	45,773	295
CUMBERLAND, MD-WV (MSA)	45,328	296
OWENSBORO, KY (MSA)	44,716	297
SAINT JOSEPH, MO (MSA)	43,573	298
ELMIRA, NY (MSA)	42,608	299
GADSDEN, AL (MSA)	41,920	300
JACKSON, TN (MSA)	41,891	301
RAPID CITY, SD (MSA)	40,944	302
JACKSONVILLE, NC (MSA)	40,279	303
GREAT FALLS, MT (MSA)	40,085	304
VICTORIA, TX (MSA)	39,629	305
PINE BLUFF, AR (MSA)	37,146	306
CHEYENNE, WY (MSA)	36,541	307
GRAND FORKS, ND (MSA)	34,646	308
CASPER, WY (MSA)	30,354	309
ENID, OK (MSA)	27,405	310

Metropolitan areas not ranked

BANGOR, ME (NECMA)
LEWISTON-AUBURN, ME (NECMA)
NEW BEDFORD-FALL RIVER-ATTLEBORO, MA (NECMA)
PITTSFIELD, MA (NECMA)
PORTLAND, ME (NECMA)
PORTSMOUTH-DOVER-ROCHESTER, NH-ME (NECMA)
PROVIDENCE-PAWTUCKET-WOONSOCKET, RI (NECMA)
SPRINGFIELD, MA (NECMA)
WORCESTER-FITCHBURG-LEOMINSTER, MA (NECMA)

(a) Data are from an unpublished report dated August 17, 1993 on Local Area Unemployment Statistics from the U.S. Bureau of Labor Statistics, Washington, D.C. The MSA with the largest labor force in 1992 was ranked number 1.

Per Capita Personal Income

Metropolitan areas are ranked by per capita personal income, greatest to least, as reported by Wallace K. Bailey, "Comprehensive Revision of Local Area Personal Income Estimates, 1969–1990," *Survey of Current Business,* May 1993, p. 63–68. (a)

Metropolitan area	Per capita personal income (dollars)	Rank
SAN FRANCISCO, CA (PMSA)	30,555	1
WEST PALM BEACH-BOCA RATON-DELRAY BEACH, FL (MSA)	28,097	2
NEW HAVEN-WATERBURY-MERIDEN, CT (NECMA)	28,021	3
TRENTON, NJ (PMSA)	27,263	4
NAPLES, FL (MSA)	26,935	5
SAN JOSE, CA (PMSA)	25,955	6
NEW YORK, NY (PMSA)	25,583	7
WASHINGTON, DC-MD-VA (MSA)	25,338	8
HARTFORD-NEW BRITAIN-MIDDLETOWN-BRISTOL, CT (NECMA)	24,911	9
ATLANTIC CITY, NJ (MSA)	24,856	10
ANCHORAGE, AK (MSA)	24,464	11
OAKLAND, CA (PMSA)	23,545	12
NIAGARA FALLS, NY (PMSA)	23,545	12
BOSTON-LAWRENCE-SALEM-LOWELL-BROCKTON, MA (NECMA)	23,480	14
SEATTLE, WA (PMSA)	23,329	15
BATON ROUGE, LA (MSA)	23,319	16
CHICAGO, IL (PMSA)	22,849	17
WILMINGTON, DE-NJ-MD (PMSA)	22,668	18
FORT LAUDERDALE-HOLLYWOOD-POMPANO BEACH, FL (PMSA)	22,620	19
SANTA BARBARA-SANTA MARIA-LOMPOC, CA (MSA)	22,611	20
SARASOTA, FL (MSA)	22,580	21
RENO, NV (MSA)	22,561	22
SANTA CRUZ, CA (PMSA)	22,554	23
BOULDER-LONGMONT, CO (PMSA)	22,169	24
SANTA ROSA-PETALUMA, CA (PMSA)	22,156	25
HONOLULU, HI (MSA)	22,102	26
PHILADELPHIA, PA-NJ (PMSA)	22,014	27
BALTIMORE, MD (MSA)	21,874	28
MINNEAPOLIS-ST PAUL, MN-WI (MSA)	21,655	29
DENVER, CO (PMSA)	21,441	30
RICHMOND-PETERSBURG, VA (MSA)	21,416	31
ANN ARBOR, MI (PMSA)	21,369	32
ROCHESTER, MN (MSA)	21,354	33
PORTLAND, ME (NECMA)	21,351	34
LOS ANGELES-LONG BEACH, CA (PMSA)	20,967	35
DALLAS, TX (PMSA)	20,892	36
NEW LONDON-NORWICH, CT-RI (NECMA)	20,863	37
ROCHESTER, NY (MSA)	20,784	38
MADISON, WI (MSA)	20,629	39
DETROIT, MI (PMSA)	20,585	40
DES MOINES, IA (MSA)	20,570	41
PITTSFIELD, MA (NECMA)	20,513	42
SAINT LOUIS, MO-IL (MSA)	20,507	43

(continued)

Per Capita Personal Income (Continued)

Metropolitan areas are ranked by per capita personal income, greatest to least, as reported by Wallace K. Bailey, "Comprehensive Revision of Local Area Personal Income Estimates, 1969–1990," *Survey of Current Business,* May 1993, p. 63–68. (a)

Metropolitan area	Per capita personal income (dollars)	Rank
FORT PIERCE, FL (MSA)	20,447	44
MILWAUKEE, WI (PMSA)	20,325	45
ATLANTA, GA (MSA)	20,304	46
RALEIGH-DURHAM, NC (MSA)	20,170	47
HOUSTON, TX (PMSA)	20,169	48
SANTA FE, NM (MSA)	20,154	49
YORK, PA (MSA)	19,998	50
CLEVELAND, OH (PMSA)	19,995	51
KANSAS CITY, MO-KS (MSA)	19,963	52
READING, PA (MSA)	19,868	53
INDIANAPOLIS, IN (MSA)	19,844	54
SPRINGFIELD, IL (MSA)	19,822	55
ORANGE COUNTY, NY (PMSA)	19,802	56
SAN DIEGO, CA (MSA)	19,799	57
ALBANY-SCHENECTADY-TROY, NY (MSA)	19,783	58
PITTSBURGH, PA (PMSA)	19,579	59
SALINAS-SEASIDE-MONTEREY, CA (MSA)	19,572	60
SACRAMENTO, CA (MSA)	19,540	61
TOPEKA, KS (MSA)	19,476	62
ROANOKE, VA (MSA)	19,417	63
BLOOMINGTON-NORMAL, IL (MSA)	19,401	64
FORT MYERS-CAPE CORAL, FL (MSA)	19,392	65
BURLINGTON, VT (NECMA)	19,369	66
CINCINNATI, OH-KY-IN (PMSA)	19,273	67
CHARLOTTESVILLE, VA (MSA)	19,240	68
PORTLAND, OR (PMSA)	19,235	69
WICHITA, KS (MSA)	19,206	70
SPRINGFIELD, MA (NECMA)	19,197	71
ALLENTOWN-BETHLEHEM-EASTON, PA-NJ (MSA)	19,176	72
BRAZORIA, TX (PMSA)	19,104	73
NASHVILLE, TN (MSA)	19,089	74
PROVIDENCE-PAWTUCKET-WOONSOCKET, RI (NECMA)	19,088	75
VALLEJO-FAIRFIELD-NAPA, CA (PMSA)	19,086	76
CEDAR RAPIDS, IA (MSA)	19,079	77
LANCASTER, PA (MSA)	19,071	78
OMAHA, NE-IA (MSA)	19,037	79
GREENSBORO--WINSTON-SALEM--HIGH POINT, NC (MSA)	18,943	80
LOUISVILLE, KY-IN (MSA)	18,912	81
RACINE, WI (PMSA)	18,894	82
GREEN BAY, WI (MSA)	18,837	83
HUNTSVILLE, AL (MSA)	18,763	84
CHARLOTTE-GASTONIA-ROCK HILL, NC-SC, (MSA)	18,757	85
FORT WORTH-ARLINGTON, TX (PMSA)	18,714	86
COLUMBUS, OH (MSA)	18,630	87
SIOUX FALLS, SD (MSA)	18,597	88

(continued)

Per Capita Personal Income (Continued)

Metropolitan areas are ranked by per capita personal income, greatest to least, as reported by Wallace K. Bailey, "Comprehensive Revision of Local Area Personal Income Estimates, 1969–1990," *Survey of Current Business,* May 1993, p. 63–68. (a)

Metropolitan area	Per capita personal income (dollars)	Rank
IOWA CITY, IA (MSA)	18,524	89
LAS VEGAS, NV (MSA)	18,474	90
BUFFALO, NY (PMSA)	18,466	91
CASPER, WY (MSA)	18,461	92
TAMPA-SAINT PETERSBURG-CLEARWATER, FL (MSA)	18,445	93
HARRISBURG-LEBANON-CARLISLE, PA (MSA)	18,430	94
LINCOLN, NE (MSA)	18,429	95
PEORIA, IL (MSA)	18,383	96
SHEBOYGAN, WI (MSA)	18,365	97
MEMPHIS, TN-AR-MS (MSA)	18,331	98
GALVESTON-TEXAS CITY, TX (PMSA)	18,316	99
DAYTON-SPRINGFIELD, OH (MSA)	18,302	100
DECATUR, IL (MSA)	18,258	101
MIAMI-HIALEAH, FL (PMSA)	18,252	102
AKRON, OH (PMSA)	18,234	103
BIRMINGHAM, AL (MSA)	18,210	104
TYLER, TX (MSA)	18,159	105
PHOENIX, AZ (MSA)	18,156	106
LEXINGTON-FAYETTE, KY (MSA)	18,142	107
DAVENPORT-ROCK ISLAND-MOLINE, IA-IL (MSA)	18,092	108
AUSTIN, TX (MSA)	18,081	109
SYRACUSE, NY (MSA)	18,063	110
BINGHAMTON, NY (MSA)	18,048	111
MELBOURNE-TITUSVILLE-PALM BAY, FL (MSA)	18,009	112
GRAND RAPIDS, MI (MSA)	18,008	113
ODESSA, TX (MSA)	17,980	114
OLYMPIA, WA (MSA)	17,966	115
FORT WAYNE, IN (MSA)	17,962	116
JACKSONVILLE, FL (MSA)	17,937	117
ROCKFORD, IL (MSA)	17,936	118
EVANSVILLE, IN-KY (MSA)	17,863	119
WILMINGTON, NC (MSA)	17,840	120
TULSA, OK (MSA)	17,837	121
ORLANDO, FL (MSA)	17,832	122
COLUMBIA, MO (MSA)	17,782	123
LANSING-EAST LANSING, MI (MSA)	17,777	124
KOKOMO, IN (MSA)	17,754	125
TOLEDO, OH (MSA)	17,713	126
COLUMBIA, SC (MSA)	17,708	127
CHEYENNE, WY (MSA)	17,664	128
FORT COLLINS-LOVELAND, CO (MSA)	17,657	129
VINELAND-MILLVILLE-BRIDGETON, NJ (PMSA)	17,654	130
COLORADO SPRINGS, CO (MSA)	17,651	131
SAGINAW-BAY CITY-MIDLAND, MI (MSA)	17,631	132
BOISE CITY, ID (MSA)	17,625	133

(continued)

Per Capita Personal Income (Continued)

Metropolitan areas are ranked by per capita personal income, greatest to least, as reported by Wallace K. Bailey, "Comprehensive Revision of Local Area Personal Income Estimates, 1969–1990," *Survey of Current Business,* May 1993, p. 63–68. (a)

Metropolitan area	Per capita personal income (dollars)	Rank
SOUTH BEND - MISHAWAKA, IN (MSA)	17,625	133
VICTORIA, TX (MSA)	17,625	135
APPLETON-OSHKOSH-NEENAH, WI (MSA)	17,618	136
LITTLE ROCK-NORTH LITTLE ROCK, AR (MSA)	17,610	137
BILLINGS, MT (MSA)	17,608	138
KENOSHA, WI (PMSA)	17,560	139
BREMERTON, WA (MSA)	17,488	140
CHAMPAIGN-URBANA-RANTOUL, IL (MSA)	17,460	141
FLINT, MI (MSA)	17,459	142
ASHEVILLE, NC (MSA)	17,451	143
RICHLAND-KENNEWICK-PASCO, WA (MSA)	17,398	144
KALAMAZOO, MI (MSA)	17,397	145
WICHITA FALLS, TX (MSA)	17,363	146
BEAUMONT-PORT ARTHUR, TX (MSA)	17,361	147
CHARLESTON, WV (MSA)	17,343	148
LA CROSSE, WI (MSA)	17,253	149
HAMILTON-MIDDLETOWN, OH (PMSA)	17,200	150
TACOMA, WA (PMSA)	17,184	151
SAVANNAH, GA (MSA)	17,161	152
MONTGOMERY, AL (MSA)	17,158	153
GREAT FALLS, MT (MSA)	17,104	154
KANKAKEE, IL (MSA)	17,080	155
CHATTANOOGA, TN-GA (MSA)	17,069	156
AMARILLO, TX (MSA)	17,042	157
ALBUQUERQUE, NM (MSA)	17,040	158
BATTLE CREEK, MI (MSA)	17,032	159
NEWARK, NJ (PMSA)	17,030	160
NORFOLK-VIRGINIA BEACH-NEWPORT NEWS, VA (MSA)	17,030	160
NEW ORLEANS, LA (MSA)	16,959	162
SCRANTON--WILKES-BARRE, PA (MSA)	16,912	163
ERIE, PA (MSA)	16,886	164
SIOUX CITY, IA-NE (MSA)	16,857	165
ELKHART-GOSHEN, IN (MSA)	16,857	165
SPOKANE, WA (MSA)	16,857	165
KNOXVILLE, TN (MSA)	16,846	168
HAGERSTOWN, MD (MSA)	16,845	169
GARY-HAMMOND, IN (PMSA)	16,811	170
OKLAHOMA CITY, OK (MSA)	16,799	171
AUGUSTA, GA-SC (MSA)	16,792	172
CANTON, OH (MSA)	16,778	173
BELLINGHAM, WA (MSA)	16,754	174
GAINESVILLE, FL (MSA)	16,743	175
GREENVILLE-SPARTANBURG, SC (MSA)	16,729	176
RIVERSIDE-SAN BERNARDINAO, CA (PMSA)	16,707	177
BISMARCK, ND (MSA)	16,702	178

(continued)

Per Capita Personal Income (Continued)

Metropolitan areas are ranked by per capita personal income, greatest to least, as reported by Wallace K. Bailey, "Comprehensive Revision of Local Area Personal Income Estimates, 1969–1990," *Survey of Current Business,* May 1993, p. 63–68. (a)

Metropolitan area	Per capita personal income (dollars)	Rank
LEWISTON-AUBURN, ME (NECMA)	16,682	179
SPRINGFIELD, MO (MSA)	16,628	180
MACON-WARNER ROBINS, GA (MSA)	16,611	181
REDDING, CA (MSA)	16,579	182
BENTON HARBOR, MI (MSA)	16,576	183
FORT WALTON BEACH, FL (MSA)	16,574	184
ENID, OK (MSA)	16,489	185
ELMIRA, NY (MSA)	16,486	186
SAINT JOSEPH, MO (MSA)	16,471	187
WAUSAU, WI (MSA)	16,471	187
DUBUQUE, IA (MSA)	16,469	189
JANESVILLE-BELOIT, WI (MSA)	16,461	191
TALLAHASSEE, FL (MSA)	16,422	190
SHERMAN-DENISON, TX (MSA)	16,396	192
WATERLOO-CEDAR FALLS, IA (MSA)	16,390	193
OWENSBORO, KY (MSA)	16,387	194
LIMA, OH (MSA)	16,369	195
FARGO-MOORHEAD, ND-MN (MSA)	16,354	196
ABILENE, TX (MSA)	16,347	197
UTICA-ROME, NY (MSA)	16,336	198
SALEM, OR (MSA)	16,255	199
SAN ANGELO, TX (MSA)	16,252	200
HICKORY-MORGANTON, NC (MSA)	16,247	201
STATE COLLEGE, PA (MSA)	16,244	202
WILLIAMSPORT, PA (MSA)	16,234	203
YAKIMA, WA (MSA)	16,210	204
LAFAYETTE-WEST LAFAYETTE, IN (MSA)	16,184	205
EUGENE-SPRINGFIELD, OR (MSA)	16,145	206
LYNCHBURG, VA (MSA)	16,113	207
RAPID CITY, SD (MSA)	16,106	208
TUCSON, AZ (MSA)	16,087	209
MUNCIE, IN (MSA)	16,080	210
GREELEY, CO (MSA)	16,052	211
BANGOR, ME (NECMA)	16,043	212
JACKSON, MI (MSA)	16,039	213
FRESNO, CA (MSA)	15,994	214
JACKSON, MS (MSA)	15,991	215
FAYETTEVILLE-SPRINGDALE, AR (MSA)	15,987	216
DULUTH, MN-WI (MSA)	15,979	217
MEDFORD, OR (MSA)	15,953	218
SAN ANTONIO, TX (MSA)	15,950	219
GLENS FALLS, NY (MSA)	15,933	220
SHREVEPORT, LA (MSA)	15,897	221
LONGVIEW-MARSHALL, TX (MSA)	15,839	222
BAKERSFIELD, CA (MSA)	15,791	223

(continued)

Per Capita Personal Income (Continued)

Metropolitan areas are ranked by per capita personal income, greatest to least, as reported by Wallace K. Bailey, "Comprehensive Revision of Local Area Personal Income Estimates, 1969–1990," *Survey of Current Business,* May 1993, p. 63–68. (a)

Metropolitan area	Per capita personal income (dollars)	Rank
DAYTONA BEACH, FL (MSA)	15,742	224
YOUNGSTOWN-WARREN, OH (MSA)	15,739	225
SHARON, PA (MSA)	15,731	226
EAU CLAIRE, WI (MSA)	15,697	228
SALT LAKE CITY-OGDEN, UT (MSA)	15,687	227
PARKERSBURG-MARIETTA, WV-OH (MSA)	15,671	229
DECATUR, AL (MSA)	15,631	230
JAMESTOWN-DUNKIRK, NY (MSA)	15,628	231
WACO, TX (MSA)	15,623	232
STOCKTON, CA (MSA)	15,582	233
PANAMA CITY, FL (MSA)	15,580	234
LUBBOCK, TX (MSA)	15,577	235
DOTHAN, AL (MSA)	15,564	236
ATHENS, GA (MSA)	15,428	237
COLUMBUS, GA-AL (MSA)	15,401	238
WHEELING, WV-OH (MSA)	15,396	239
FLORENCE, SC (MSA)	15,369	240
LAKE CHARLES, LA (MSA)	15,363	241
MANSFIELD, OH (MSA)	15,348	242
PENSACOLA, FL (MSA)	15,328	243
CORPUS CHRISTI, TX (MSA)	15,273	245
LAKELAND-WINTER HAVEN, FL (MSA)	15,241	244
TUSCALOOSA, AL (MSA)	15,236	246
ALEXANDRIA, LA (MSA)	15,230	247
MODESTO, CA (MSA)	15,221	248
DANVILLE, VA (MSA)	15,221	248
CHARLESTON, SC (MSA)	15,200	250
ALTOONA, PA (MSA)	15,175	251
CHICO, CA (MSA)	15,172	252
MOBILE, AL (MSA)	15,134	253
ALBANY, GA (MSA)	15,133	255
JOHNSON CITY-KINGSPORT-BRISTOL, TN-VA (MSA)	15,121	254
STEUBENVILLE-WEIRTON, OH-WV (MSA)	15,115	256
TERRE HAUTE, IN (MSA)	15,113	257
JOPLIN, MO (MSA)	15,092	258
GRAND FORKS, ND (MSA)	15,020	259
YUBA CITY, CA (MSA)	15,016	260
TEXARKANA, TX - TEXARKANA, AR (MSA)	15,004	261
JOHNSTOWN, PA (MSA)	14,961	262
BLOOMINGTON, IN (MSA)	14,957	263
SAINT CLOUD, MN (MSA)	14,912	264
PUEBLO, CO (MSA)	14,795	265
CUMBERLAND, MD-WV (MSA)	14,768	266
HUNTINGTON-ASHLAND, WV-KY-OH (MSA)	14,622	267
FLORENCE, AL (MSA)	14,600	268

(continued)

Per Capita Personal Income (Continued)

Metropolitan areas are ranked by per capita personal income, greatest to least, as reported by Wallace K. Bailey, "Comprehensive Revision of Local Area Personal Income Estimates, 1969–1990," *Survey of Current Business,* May 1993, p. 63–68. (a)

Metropolitan area	Per capita personal income (dollars)	Rank
LAWRENCE, KS (MSA)	14,590	269
ANNISTON, AL (MSA)	14,434	270
MONROE, LA (MSA)	14,396	271
FORT SMITH, AR-OK (MSA)	14,324	272
VISALIA-TULARE-PORTERVILLE, CA (MSA)	14,248	273
LAFAYETTE, LA (MSA)	14,215	275
OCALA, FL (MSA)	14,158	274
BILOXI-GULFPORT, MS (MSA)	13,930	276
LAWTON, OK (MSA)	13,862	277
PINE BLUFF, AR (MSA)	13,749	278
KILLEEN-TEMPLE, TX (MSA)	13,742	279
GADSDEN, AL (MSA)	13,739	280
FAYETTEVILLE, NC (MSA)	13,582	281
MERCED, CA (MSA)	13,403	282
HOUMA-THIBODAUX, LA (MSA)	13,152	283
BRYAN-COLLEGE STATION, TX (MSA)	13,068	284
CLARKSVILLE-HOPKINSVILLE, TN-KY (MSA)	13,033	285
PROVO-OREM, UT (MSA)	12,467	286
LAS CRUCES, NM (MSA)	11,831	287
EL PASO, TX (MSA)	11,764	288
JACKSONVILLE, NC (MSA)	10,537	289
BROWNSVILLE-HARLINGEN, TX (MSA)	9,824	290
LAREDO, TX (MSA)	9,529	291
MCALLEN-EDINBURG-MISSION, TX (MSA)	9,230	292

Metropolitan areas not ranked

ANAHEIM-SANTA ANA, CA (PMSA)
ANDERSON, IN (MSA)
ANDERSON, SC (MSA)
AURORA-ELGIN, IL (PMSA)
BEAVER COUNTY, PA (PMSA)
BERGEN-PASSAIC, NJ (PMSA)
BRADENTON, FL (MSA)
BRIDGEPORT-STAMFORD-NORWALK-DANBURY, CT (NECMA)
BURLINGTON, NC (MSA)
JACKSON, TN (MSA)
JERSEY CITY, NJ (PMSA)
JOLIET, IL (PMSA)
LAKE COUNTY, IL (PMSA)
LORAIN-ELYRIA, OH (PMSA)
MANCHESTER-NASHUA, NH (NECMA)
MIDDLESEX-SOMERSET-HUNTERDON, NJ (PMSA)
MIDLAND, TX (MSA)
MONMOUTH-OCEAN, NJ (PMSA)

(continued)

Per Capita Personal Income (Continued)

Metropolitan areas are ranked by per capita personal income, greatest to least, as reported by Wallace K. Bailey, "Comprehensive Revision of Local Area Personal Income Estimates, 1969–1990," *Survey of Current Business,* May 1993, p. 63–68. (a)

Metropolitan area	Per capita personal income (dollars)	Rank
MUSKEGON, MI (MSA)		
NASSAU-SUFFOLK, NY (PMSA)		
NEW BEDFORD-FALL RIVER-ATTLEBORO, MA (NECMA)		
OXNARD-VENTURA, CA (PMSA)		
PASCAGOULA, MS (MSA)		
PORTSMOUTH-DOVER-ROCHESTER, NH-ME (NECMA)		
POUGHKEEPSIE, NY (MSA)		
VANCOUVER, WA (PMSA)		
WORCESTER-FITCHBURG-LEOMINSTER, MA (NECMA)		

(a) Per capita personal income was computed using Bureau of the Census midyear population estimates. The 1991 Census county population estimates have been adjusted by the Bureau of Economic Analysis (BEA) to be consistent with 1991 Census State population estimates released in January 1993. The metropolitan area definition used by BEA for its personal income estimates are the county-based definitions issued in December 1992 by the Office of Management and Budget for federal statistical purposes. These areas have been changed to reflect the results of the 1990 Census of Population. For a discussion of the changes in the MSA definitions, please refer to the introduction to this volume.

Manufacturing Establishments—Metropolitan Areas

Metropolitan areas ranked by the number of manufacturing establishments, greatest to fewest. (a)

Metropolitan area	Number of manufacturing establishments	Rank
LOS ANGELES-LONG BEACH, CA (PMSA)	19,753	1
NEW YORK, NY (PMSA)	16,277	2
CHICAGO, IL (PMSA)	11,742	3
DETROIT, MI (PMSA)	8,072	4
PHILADELPHIA, PA-NJ (PMSA)	7,414	5
BOSTON-LAWRENCE-SALEM-LOWELL-BROCKTON, MA (NECMA)	6,796	6
ANAHEIM-SANTA ANA, CA (PMSA)	5,855	7
NASSAU-SUFFOLK, NY (PMSA)	4,948	8
MINNEAPOLIS-ST PAUL, MN-WI (MSA)	4,494	9
HOUSTON, TX (PMSA)	4,468	10
DALLAS, TX (PMSA)	4,352	11
CLEVELAND, OH (PMSA)	4,155	12
NEWARK, NJ (PMSA)	3,887	13
ATLANTA, GA (MSA)	3,878	14
BERGEN-PASSAIC, NJ (PMSA)	3,721	15
SEATTLE, WA (PMSA)	3,464	16
MIAMI-HIALEAH, FL (PMSA)	3,395	17
SAINT LOUIS, MO-IL (MSA)	3,351	18
SAN JOSE, CA (PMSA)	3,298	19
OAKLAND, CA (PMSA)	3,211	20
SAN FRANCISCO, CA (PMSA)	3,153	21
SAN DIEGO, CA (MSA)	3,041	22
MILWAUKEE, WI (PMSA)	3,023	23
PHOENIX, AZ (MSA)	2,803	24
PROVIDENCE-PAWTUCKET-WOONSOCKET, RI (NECMA)	2,791	25
WASHINGTON, DC-MD-VA (MSA)	2,744	26
PORTLAND, OR (PMSA)	2,631	27
TAMPA-SAINT PETERSBURG-CLEARWATER, FL (MSA)	2,546	28
PITTSBURGH, PA (PMSA)	2,518	29
DENVER, CO (PMSA)	2,505	30
RIVERSIDE-SAN BERNARDINAO, CA (PMSA)	2,494	31
BALTIMORE, MD (MSA)	2,311	32
CHARLOTTE-GASTONIA-ROCK HILL, NC-SC, (MSA)	2,276	33
KANSAS CITY, MO-KS (MSA)	2,254	34
CINCINNATI, OH-KY-IN (PMSA)	2,242	35
HARTFORD-NEW BRITAIN-MIDDLETOWN-BRISTOL, CT (NECMA)	2,229	36
FORT WORTH-ARLINGTON, TX (PMSA)	2,139	37
GREENSBORO--WINSTON-SALEM--HIGH POINT, NC (MSA)	1,977	38
INDIANAPOLIS, IN (MSA)	1,813	39
BRIDGEPORT-STAMFORD-NORWALK-DANBURY, CT (NECMA)	1,796	40
NEW HAVEN-WATERBURY-MERIDEN, CT (NECMA)	1,795	41
FORT LAUDERDALE-HOLLYWOOD-POMPANO BEACH, FL (PMSA)	1,790	42
MIDDLESEX-SOMERSET-HUNTERDON, NJ (PMSA)	1,753	43
GRAND RAPIDS, MI (MSA)	1,593	44

(continued)

Manufacturing Establishments—Metropolitan Areas (Continued)
Metropolitan areas ranked by the number of manufacturing establishments, greatest to fewest. (a)

Metropolitan area	Number of manufacturing establishments	Rank
DAYTON-SPRINGFIELD, OH (MSA)	1,588	45
COLUMBUS, OH (MSA)	1,573	46
NASHVILLE, TN (MSA)	1,506	47
WORCESTER-FITCHBURG-LEOMINSTER, MA (NECMA)	1,469	48
SALT LAKE CITY-OGDEN, UT (MSA)	1,463	49
SACRAMENTO, CA (MSA)	1,415	50
ROCHESTER, NY (MSA)	1,391	51
JERSEY CITY, NJ (PMSA)	1,385	52
TULSA, OK (MSA)	1,322	53
BUFFALO, NY (PMSA)	1,310	54
ORLANDO, FL (MSA)	1,249	55
AKRON, OH (PMSA)	1,225	56
LOUISVILLE, KY-IN (MSA)	1,223	57
SAN ANTONIO, TX (MSA)	1,193	58
MEMPHIS, TN-AR-MS (MSA)	1,178	59
GREENVILLE-SPARTANBURG, SC (MSA)	1,172	60
SCRANTON--WILKES-BARRE, PA (MSA)	1,166	61
BIRMINGHAM, AL (MSA)	1,150	62
ALLENTOWN-BETHLEHEM-EASTON, PA-NJ (MSA)	1,091	63
NEW BEDFORD-FALL RIVER-ATTLEBORO, MA (NECMA)	1,072	64
OKLAHOMA CITY, OK (MSA)	1,071	65
SPRINGFIELD, MA (NECMA)	1,066	66
RICHMOND-PETERSBURG, VA (MSA)	1,002	67
MONMOUTH-OCEAN, NJ (PMSA)	996	68
TOLEDO, OH (MSA)	988	69
JACKSONVILLE, FL (MSA)	942	70
NEW ORLEANS, LA (MSA)	937	71
NORFOLK-VIRGINIA BEACH-NEWPORT NEWS, VA (MSA)	912	72
WEST PALM BEACH-BOCA RATON-DELRAY BEACH, FL (MSA)	861	73
ELKHART-GOSHEN, IN (MSA)	855	74
HICKORY-MORGANTON, NC (MSA)	852	75
OXNARD-VENTURA, CA (PMSA)	836	76
RALEIGH-DURHAM, NC (MSA)	834	77
ALBANY-SCHENECTADY-TROY, NY (MSA)	828	78
AUSTIN, TX (MSA)	823	79
LANCASTER, PA (MSA)	821	80
AURORA-ELGIN, IL (PMSA)	800	81
HONOLULU, HI (MSA)	800	82
KNOXVILLE, TN (MSA)	796	83
ROCKFORD, IL (MSA)	772	84
EUGENE-SPRINGFIELD, OR (MSA)	769	85
LAKE COUNTY, IL (PMSA)	760	86
SYRACUSE, NY (MSA)	759	87
YORK, PA (MSA)	759	88
OMAHA, NE-IA (MSA)	702	89
MANCHESTER-NASHUA, NH (NECMA)	697	90
WICHITA, KS (MSA)	697	91

(continued)

Manufacturing Establishments—Metropolitan Areas (Continued)

Metropolitan areas ranked by the number of manufacturing establishments, greatest to fewest. (a)

Metropolitan area	Number of manufacturing establishments	Rank
HARRISBURG-LEBANON-CARLISLE, PA (MSA)	690	92
TUCSON, AZ (MSA)	686	93
FRESNO, CA (MSA)	678	94
FORT WAYNE, IN (MSA)	674	95
SANTA ROSA-PETALUMA, CA (PMSA)	657	96
CHATTANOOGA, TN-GA (MSA)	644	97
TACOMA, WA (PMSA)	644	98
CANTON, OH (MSA)	643	99
YOUNGSTOWN-WARREN, OH (MSA)	637	100
READING, PA (MSA)	624	101
ALBUQUERQUE, NM (MSA)	592	102
LITTLE ROCK-NORTH LITTLE ROCK, AR (MSA)	590	103
PORTSMOUTH-DOVER-ROCHESTER, NH-ME (NECMA)	576	104
APPLETON-OSHKOSH-NEENAH, WI (MSA)	559	105
EL PASO, TX (MSA)	546	106
WILMINGTON, DE-NJ-MD (PMSA)	542	107
ERIE, PA (MSA)	538	108
STOCKTON, CA (MSA)	535	109
SANTA BARBARA-SANTA MARIA-LOMPOC, CA (MSA)	523	110
MADISON, WI (MSA)	517	111
MOBILE, AL (MSA)	517	112
BOULDER-LONGMONT, CO (PMSA)	507	113
SPOKANE, WA (MSA)	497	114
JOHNSON CITY-KINGSPORT-BRISTOL, TN-VA (MSA)	494	115
SOUTH BEND - MISHAWAKA, IN (MSA)	489	116
GARY-HAMMOND, IN (PMSA)	483	117
DES MOINES, IA (MSA)	474	118
LAKELAND-WINTER HAVEN, FL (MSA)	469	119
TRENTON, NJ (PMSA)	468	120
SALEM, OR (MSA)	463	121
BATON ROUGE, LA (MSA)	456	122
DAVENPORT-ROCK ISLAND-MOLINE, IA-IL (MSA)	452	123
COLUMBIA, SC (MSA)	448	124
VALLEJO-FAIRFIELD-NAPA, CA (PMSA)	430	125
ANN ARBOR, MI (PMSA)	428	126
SARASOTA, FL (MSA)	427	127
COLORADO SPRINGS, CO (MSA)	419	128
SAGINAW-BAY CITY-MIDLAND, MI (MSA)	412	129
LAS VEGAS, NV (MSA)	408	130
EVANSVILLE, IN-KY (MSA)	407	131
JOLIET, IL (PMSA)	405	132
LANSING-EAST LANSING, MI (MSA)	399	133
JACKSON, MS (MSA)	394	134
KALAMAZOO, MI (MSA)	393	135
BENTON HARBOR, MI (MSA)	390	136
CHARLESTON, SC (MSA)	389	137
LEXINGTON-FAYETTE, KY (MSA)	388	138

(continued)

Manufacturing Establishments—Metropolitan Areas (Continued)

Metropolitan areas ranked by the number of manufacturing establishments, greatest to fewest. (a)

Metropolitan area	Number of manufacturing establishments	Rank
MELBOURNE-TITUSVILLE-PALM BAY, FL (MSA)	387	139
RACINE, WI (PMSA)	384	140
LORAIN-ELYRIA, OH (PMSA)	382	141
PORTLAND, ME (NECMA)	381	142
MODESTO, CA (MSA)	379	143
SPRINGFIELD, MO (MSA)	378	144
SANTA CRUZ, CA (PMSA)	375	145
UTICA-ROME, NY (MSA)	367	146
ORANGE COUNTY, NY (PMSA)	362	147
DAYTONA BEACH, FL (MSA)	359	148
BAKERSFIELD, CA (MSA)	357	149
RENO, NV (MSA)	357	150
AUGUSTA, GA-SC (MSA)	347	151
SHREVEPORT, LA (MSA)	344	152
MONTGOMERY, AL (MSA)	337	153
BEAUMONT-PORT ARTHUR, TX (MSA)	336	154
VANCOUVER, WA (PMSA)	330	155
MEDFORD, OR (MSA)	326	156
JACKSON, MI (MSA)	324	157
FLINT, MI (MSA)	323	158
PEORIA, IL (MSA)	319	159
GREEN BAY, WI (MSA)	315	160
BINGHAMTON, NY (MSA)	312	161
FORT MYERS-CAPE CORAL, FL (MSA)	305	162
BURLINGTON, NC (MSA)	303	163
VISALIA-TULARE-PORTERVILLE, CA (MSA)	301	164
FORT SMITH, AR-OK (MSA)	298	165
NIAGARA FALLS, NY (PMSA)	294	166
HUNTSVILLE, AL (MSA)	293	167
HAMILTON-MIDDLETOWN, OH (PMSA)	288	168
ROANOKE, VA (MSA)	287	169
ASHEVILLE, NC (MSA)	285	170
DULUTH, MN-WI (MSA)	285	171
BOISE CITY, ID (MSA)	284	172
JOHNSTOWN, PA (MSA)	280	173
LONGVIEW-MARSHALL, TX (MSA)	280	174
PROVO-OREM, UT (MSA)	276	175
HUNTINGTON-ASHLAND, WV-KY-OH (MSA)	275	176
MUSKEGON, MI (MSA)	275	177
FORT COLLINS-LOVELAND, CO (MSA)	274	178
LUBBOCK, TX (MSA)	270	179
JOPLIN, MO (MSA)	265	180
MACON-WARNER ROBINS, GA (MSA)	262	181
PENSACOLA, FL (MSA)	262	182
CORPUS CHRISTI, TX (MSA)	258	183
JAMESTOWN-DUNKIRK, NY (MSA)	255	184
NEW LONDON-NORWICH, CT-RI (NECMA)	255	185

(continued)

Manufacturing Establishments—Metropolitan Areas (Continued)

Metropolitan areas ranked by the number of manufacturing establishments, greatest to fewest. (a)

Metropolitan area	Number of manufacturing establishments	Rank
SALINAS-SEASIDE-MONTEREY, CA (MSA)	252	186
SAINT CLOUD, MN (MSA)	250	187
ATLANTIC CITY, NJ (MSA)	249	188
WACO, TX (MSA)	249	189
LIMA, OH (MSA)	247	190
SAVANNAH, GA (MSA)	244	191
REDDING, CA (MSA)	239	192
LINCOLN, NE (MSA)	237	193
SHEBOYGAN, WI (MSA)	236	194
VINELAND-MILLVILLE-BRIDGETON, NJ (PMSA)	235	195
BANGOR, ME (NECMA)	234	196
CEDAR RAPIDS, IA (MSA)	234	197
BELLINGHAM, WA (MSA)	232	198
FORT PIERCE, FL (MSA)	231	199
WILLIAMSPORT, PA (MSA)	231	200
YAKIMA, WA (MSA)	231	201
LYNCHBURG, VA (MSA)	229	202
ODESSA, TX (MSA)	223	203
CHICO, CA (MSA)	222	204
MANSFIELD, OH (MSA)	219	205
PITTSFIELD, MA (NECMA)	217	206
BRADENTON, FL (MSA)	215	207
FLORENCE, AL (MSA)	214	208
GLENS FALLS, NY (MSA)	213	209
BATTLE CREEK, MI (MSA)	211	210
DECATUR, AL (MSA)	211	211
LAFAYETTE, LA (MSA)	208	212
OCALA, FL (MSA)	208	213
POUGHKEEPSIE, NY (MSA)	207	214
TALLAHASSEE, FL (MSA)	205	215
ANDERSON, SC (MSA)	204	216
COLUMBUS, GA-AL (MSA)	204	217
JANESVILLE-BELOIT, WI (MSA)	200	218
LEWISTON-AUBURN, ME (NECMA)	200	219
GAINESVILLE, FL (MSA)	198	220
ATHENS, GA (MSA)	197	221
BURLINGTON, VT (NECMA)	197	222
PARKERSBURG-MARIETTA, WV-OH (MSA)	195	223
EAU CLAIRE, WI (MSA)	192	224
MCALLEN-EDINBURG-MISSION, TX (MSA)	190	225
WAUSAU, WI (MSA)	190	226
MUNCIE, IN (MSA)	188	227
WATERLOO-CEDAR FALLS, IA (MSA)	188	228
AMARILLO, TX (MSA)	184	229
HOUMA-THIBODAUX, LA (MSA)	178	230
BEAVER COUNTY, PA (PMSA)	172	231
TYLER, TX (MSA)	172	232

(continued)

Manufacturing Establishments—Metropolitan Areas (Continued)

Metropolitan areas ranked by the number of manufacturing establishments, greatest to fewest. (a)

Metropolitan area	Number of manufacturing establishments	Rank
BRAZORIA, TX (PMSA)	171	233
SHARON, PA (MSA)	169	234
BROWNSVILLE-HARLINGEN, TX (MSA)	168	235
CHARLESTON, WV (MSA)	165	236
BILOXI-GULFPORT, MS (MSA)	164	237
MONROE, LA (MSA)	161	238
TERRE HAUTE, IN (MSA)	161	239
KENOSHA, WI (PMSA)	160	240
FARGO-MOORHEAD, ND-MN (MSA)	155	241
WICHITA FALLS, TX (MSA)	155	242
WILMINGTON, NC (MSA)	154	243
TUSCALOOSA, AL (MSA)	152	244
DOTHAN, AL (MSA)	148	245
KILLEEN-TEMPLE, TX (MSA)	148	246
OLYMPIA, WA (MSA)	148	247
BILLINGS, MT (MSA)	147	248
ANCHORAGE, AK (MSA)	146	249
CHARLOTTESVILLE, VA (MSA)	146	250
FAYETTEVILLE, NC (MSA)	146	251
HAGERSTOWN, MD (MSA)	146	252
ALTOONA, PA (MSA)	145	253
ANNISTON, AL (MSA)	143	254
DUBUQUE, IA (MSA)	143	255
FLORENCE, SC (MSA)	143	256
GREELEY, CO (MSA)	142	257
CHAMPAIGN-URBANA-RANTOUL, IL (MSA)	141	258
STATE COLLEGE, PA (MSA)	141	259
FAYETTEVILLE-SPRINGDALE, AR (MSA)	140	260
WHEELING, WV-OH (MSA)	139	261
GALVESTON-TEXAS CITY, TX (PMSA)	138	262
LA CROSSE, WI (MSA)	138	263
SIOUX FALLS, SD (MSA)	138	264
NAPLES, FL (MSA)	136	265
SPRINGFIELD, IL (MSA)	133	266
ANDERSON, IN (MSA)	132	267
SANTA FE, NM (MSA)	130	268
TOPEKA, KS (MSA)	130	269
DECATUR, IL (MSA)	129	270
SHERMAN-DENISON, TX (MSA)	127	271
ABILENE, TX (MSA)	122	272
LAKE CHARLES, LA (MSA)	121	273
MERCED, CA (MSA)	120	274
RICHLAND-KENNEWICK-PASCO, WA (MSA)	120	275
SIOUX CITY, IA-NE (MSA)	119	276
CLARKSVILLE-HOPKINSVILLE, TN-KY (MSA)	117	277
YUBA CITY, CA (MSA)	117	278
FORT WALTON BEACH, FL (MSA)	115	279

(continued)

Manufacturing Establishments—Metropolitan Areas (Continued)

Metropolitan areas ranked by the number of manufacturing establishments, greatest to fewest. (a)

Metropolitan area	Number of manufacturing establishments	Rank
BREMERTON, WA (MSA)	114	280
PANAMA CITY, FL (MSA)	114	281
DANVILLE, VA (MSA)	113	282
KANKAKEE, IL (MSA)	111	283
MIDLAND, TX (MSA)	111	284
GADSDEN, AL (MSA)	110	285
BLOOMINGTON, IN (MSA)	108	286
STEUBENVILLE-WEIRTON, OH-WV (MSA)	107	287
ALEXANDRIA, LA (MSA)	106	288
LAFAYETTE-WEST LAFAYETTE, IN (MSA)	106	289
TEXARKANA, TX - TEXARKANA, AR (MSA)	106	290
ELMIRA, NY (MSA)	102	291
RAPID CITY, SD (MSA)	102	292
SAINT JOSEPH, MO (MSA)	102	293
SAN ANGELO, TX (MSA)	102	294
JACKSON, TN (MSA)	100	295
BLOOMINGTON-NORMAL, IL (MSA)	99	296
ALBANY, GA (MSA)	97	297
OWENSBORO, KY (MSA)	97	298
PUEBLO, CO (MSA)	95	299
CASPER, WY (MSA)	92	300
CUMBERLAND, MD-WV (MSA)	91	301
PASCAGOULA, MS (MSA)	89	302
BRYAN-COLLEGE STATION, TX (MSA)	87	303
COLUMBIA, MO (MSA)	87	304
PINE BLUFF, AR (MSA)	87	305
KOKOMO, IN (MSA)	85	306
BISMARCK, ND (MSA)	83	307
LAWRENCE, KS (MSA)	82	308
IOWA CITY, IA (MSA)	76	309
LAS CRUCES, NM (MSA)	74	310
ROCHESTER, MN (MSA)	66	311
GREAT FALLS, MT (MSA)	60	312
VICTORIA, TX (MSA)	58	313
LAREDO, TX (MSA)	57	314
ENID, OK (MSA)	56	315
LAWTON, OK (MSA)	52	316
GRAND FORKS, ND (MSA)	48	317
JACKSONVILLE, NC (MSA)	48	318
CHEYENNE, WY (MSA)	39	319

(a) Data are from the U.S. Bureau of the Census, *1987 Census of Manufacturers, Geographic Area Series*, (MC87-A-1 through MC87-A-52), as reported in the *State and Metropolitan Area Data Book 1991* (a *Statistical Abstract* supplement), Census Bureau, 755 pages, Washington D.C.: U.S. Government Printing Office, 1991.

Physicians, Rate Per 1,000 People—Metropolitan Areas

Ranking of metropolitan areas by the number of patient care physicians per 1,000 people. (a)

Metropolitan area	Total patient care physicians	Patient care physicians per 1,000 people	Rank
ROCHESTER, MN (MSA)	1,828	17.17	1
IOWA CITY, IA (MSA)	1,019	10.60	2
CHARLOTTESVILLE, VA (MSA)	1,029	7.85	3
ANN ARBOR, MI (PMSA)	1,968	6.96	4
COLUMBIA, MO (MSA)	718	6.39	5
GAINESVILLE, FL (MSA)	1,105	5.41	6
RALEIGH-DURHAM, NC (MSA)	3,544	4.82	7
BURLINGTON, VT (NECMA)	648	4.73	8
BRYAN-COLLEGE STATION, TX (MSA)	560	4.60	9
SAN FRANCISCO, CA (PMSA)	6,759	4.21	10
GALVESTON-TEXAS CITY, TX (PMSA)	888	4.08	11
LEXINGTON-FAYETTE, KY (MSA)	1,350	3.87	12
MADISON, WI (MSA)	1,419	3.87	12
NEW YORK, NY (PMSA)	30,992	3.63	14
BOSTON-LAWRENCE-SALEM-LOWELL-BROCKTON, MA (NECMA)	13,639	3.60	15
NEW HAVEN-WATERBURY-MERIDEN, CT (NECMA)	2,842	3.53	16
NASSAU-SUFFOLK, NY (PMSA)	9,056	3.47	17
LA CROSSE, WI (MSA)	339	3.46	18
SIOUX FALLS, SD (MSA)	408	3.30	19
AUGUSTA, GA-SC (MSA)	1,306	3.29	20
ALBUQUERQUE, NM (MSA)	1,547	3.22	21
BALTIMORE, MD (MSA)	7,634	3.20	22
SPRINGFIELD, IL (MSA)	603	3.18	23
NEW ORLEANS, LA (MSA)	3,933	3.17	24
CLEVELAND, OH (PMSA)	5,811	3.17	24
LITTLE ROCK-NORTH LITTLE ROCK, AR (MSA)	1,613	3.14	26
BERGEN-PASSAIC, NJ (PMSA)	4,012	3.14	26
WASHINGTON, DC-MD-VA (MSA)	12,136	3.09	28
MIAMI-HIALEAH, FL (PMSA)	5,921	3.06	29
PORTLAND, ME (NECMA)	741	3.05	30
JACKSON, MS (MSA)	1,185	3.00	31
PHILADELPHIA, PA-NJ (PMSA)	14,136	2.91	32
PITTSBURGH, PA (PMSA)	5,934	2.89	33
LUBBOCK, TX (MSA)	643	2.89	33
ROANOKE, VA (MSA)	647	2.88	35
BIRMINGHAM, AL (MSA)	2,606	2.87	36
SHREVEPORT, LA (MSA)	960	2.87	36
CHARLESTON, SC (MSA)	1,451	2.86	38
BRIDGEPORT-STAMFORD-NORWALK-DANBURY, CT (NECMA)	2,341	2.83	39
OMAHA, NE-IA (MSA)	1,744	2.82	40
SEATTLE, WA (PMSA)	5,565	2.82	40
HARTFORD-NEW BRITAIN-MIDDLETOWN-BRISTOL, CT (NECMA)	3,149	2.80	42
CHICAGO, IL (PMSA)	16,855	2.78	43

(continued)

Physicians, Rate Per 1,000 People—Metropolitan Areas (Continued)

Ranking of metropolitan areas by the number of patient care physicians per 1,000 people. (a)

Metropolitan area	Total patient care physicians	Patient care physicians per 1,000 people	Rank
WILMINGTON, NC (MSA)	333	2.77	44
NEWARK, NJ (PMSA)	5,052	2.77	44
PORTLAND, OR (PMSA)	3,428	2.76	46
ASHEVILLE, NC (MSA)	481	2.75	47
NASHVILLE, TN (MSA)	2,704	2.75	47
INDIANAPOLIS, IN (MSA)	3,407	2.73	49
TUCSON, AZ (MSA)	1,814	2.72	50
TRENTON, NJ (PMSA)	884	2.71	51
RICHMOND-PETERSBURG, VA (MSA)	2,337	2.70	52
DENVER, CO (PMSA)	4,284	2.64	53
BUFFALO, NY (PMSA)	2,522	2.60	54
MEMPHIS, TN-AR-MS (MSA)	2,548	2.60	54
TOPEKA, KS (MSA)	416	2.58	56
JACKSON, TN (MSA)	201	2.58	56
MIDDLESEX-SOMERSET-HUNTERDON, NJ (PMSA)	2,601	2.55	58
WORCESTER-FITCHBURG-LEOMINSTER, MA (NECMA)	1,803	2.54	59
KALAMAZOO, MI (MSA)	567	2.54	59
SAN JOSE, CA (PMSA)	3,777	2.52	61
WILMINGTON, DE-NJ-MD (PMSA)	1,457	2.52	61
LOUISVILLE, KY-IN (MSA)	2,399	2.52	61
COLUMBIA, SC (MSA)	1,141	2.52	61
MILWAUKEE, WI (PMSA)	3,594	2.51	65
FARGO-MOORHEAD, ND-MN (MSA)	383	2.50	66
ROCHESTER, NY (MSA)	2,507	2.50	66
PROVIDENCE-PAWTUCKET-WOONSOCKET, RI (NECMA)	2,282	2.49	68
HONOLULU, HI (MSA)	2,064	2.47	69
SAINT LOUIS, MO-IL (MSA)	6,033	2.47	69
ANAHEIM-SANTA ANA, CA (PMSA)	5,925	2.46	71
CINCINNATI, OH-KY-IN (PMSA)	3,566	2.45	72
TOLEDO, OH (MSA)	1,497	2.44	73
LOS ANGELES-LONG BEACH, CA (PMSA)	21,556	2.43	74
BILLINGS, MT (MSA)	276	2.43	74
BISMARCK, ND (MSA)	204	2.43	74
PITTSFIELD, MA (NECMA)	336	2.41	77
SPOKANE, WA (MSA)	866	2.40	78
SARASOTA, FL (MSA)	665	2.39	79
SAN ANTONIO, TX (MSA)	3,117	2.39	79
SYRACUSE, NY (MSA)	1,571	2.38	81
CHARLESTON, WV (MSA)	593	2.37	82
MINNEAPOLIS-ST PAUL, MN-WI (MSA)	5,821	2.36	83
SANTA BARBARA-SANTA MARIA-LOMPOC, CA (MSA)	867	2.35	84
GRAND FORKS, ND (MSA)	164	2.32	85
RENO, NV (MSA)	591	2.32	85
SANTA FE, NM (MSA)	270	2.31	87
ALBANY-SCHENECTADY-TROY, NY (MSA)	2,016	2.31	87

(continued)

Physicians, Rate Per 1,000 People—Metropolitan Areas (Continued)

Ranking of metropolitan areas by the number of patient care physicians per 1,000 people. (a)

Metropolitan area	Total patient care physicians	Patient care physicians per 1,000 people	Rank
HOUSTON, TX (PMSA)	7,617	2.31	87
SALT LAKE CITY-OGDEN, UT (MSA)	2,443	2.28	90
SAN DIEGO, CA (MSA)	5,664	2.27	91
TYLER, TX (MSA)	344	2.27	91
HARRISBURG-LEBANON-CARLISLE, PA (MSA)	1,331	2.26	93
OAKLAND, CA (PMSA)	4,682	2.25	94
OKLAHOMA CITY, OK (MSA)	2,157	2.25	94
CHAMPAIGN-URBANA-RANTOUL, IL (MSA)	388	2.24	96
KANSAS CITY, MO-KS (MSA)	3,503	2.24	96
KNOXVILLE, TN (MSA)	1,354	2.24	96
GREENSBORO--WINSTON-SALEM--HIGH POINT, NC (MSA)	2,099	2.23	99
SANTA ROSA-PETALUMA, CA (PMSA)	862	2.22	100
WEST PALM BEACH-BOCA RATON-DELRAY BEACH, FL (MSA)	1,874	2.17	101
SACRAMENTO, CA (MSA)	3,206	2.16	102
COLUMBUS, OH (MSA)	2,944	2.14	103
SPRINGFIELD, MO (MSA)	511	2.12	104
KILLEEN-TEMPLE, TX (MSA)	540	2.12	104
BOULDER-LONGMONT, CO (PMSA)	473	2.10	106
JACKSONVILLE, FL (MSA)	1,891	2.09	107
ATLANTA, GA (MSA)	5,913	2.09	107
PUEBLO, CO (MSA)	255	2.07	109
LAKE COUNTY, IL (PMSA)	1,070	2.07	109
PEORIA, IL (MSA)	701	2.07	109
GREAT FALLS, MT (MSA)	161	2.07	109
WICHITA FALLS, TX (MSA)	252	2.06	113
SAVANNAH, GA (MSA)	497	2.05	114
JOHNSON CITY-KINGSPORT-BRISTOL, TN-VA (MSA)	895	2.05	114
DALLAS, TX (PMSA)	5,224	2.05	114
AMARILLO, TX (MSA)	382	2.04	117
WHEELING, WV-OH (MSA)	325	2.04	117
AKRON, OH (PMSA)	1,337	2.03	119
SPRINGFIELD, MA (NECMA)	1,217	2.02	120
VICTORIA, TX (MSA)	150	2.02	120
PHOENIX, AZ (MSA)	4,242	2.00	122
DETROIT, MI (PMSA)	8,754	2.00	122
ELMIRA, NY (MSA)	190	2.00	122
NORFOLK-VIRGINIA BEACH-NEWPORT NEWS, VA (MSA)	2,767	1.98	125
FORT LAUDERDALE-HOLLYWOOD-POMPANO BEACH, FL (PMSA)	2,478	1.97	126
TAMPA-SAINT PETERSBURG-CLEARWATER, FL (MSA)	4,080	1.97	126
MUNCIE, IN (MSA)	234	1.96	128
POUGHKEEPSIE, NY (MSA)	505	1.95	129
MOBILE, AL (MSA)	923	1.94	130
TALLAHASSEE, FL (MSA)	453	1.94	130

(continued)

Physicians, Rate Per 1,000 People—Metropolitan Areas (Continued)
Ranking of metropolitan areas by the number of patient care physicians per 1,000 people. (a)

Metropolitan area	Total patient care physicians	Patient care physicians per 1,000 people	Rank
RAPID CITY, SD (MSA)	156	1.92	132
CHATTANOOGA, TN-GA (MSA)	831	1.92	132
NAPLES, FL (MSA)	290	1.91	134
MACON-WARNER ROBINS, GA (MSA)	536	1.91	134
FLORENCE, SC (MSA)	218	1.91	134
CHEYENNE, WY (MSA)	140	1.91	134
LINCOLN, NE (MSA)	405	1.90	138
TUSCALOOSA, AL (MSA)	284	1.89	139
MEDFORD, OR (MSA)	277	1.89	139
WICHITA, KS (MSA)	912	1.88	141
BOISE CITY, ID (MSA)	384	1.87	142
MONMOUTH-OCEAN, NJ (PMSA)	1,849	1.87	142
FAYETTEVILLE-SPRINGDALE, AR (MSA)	211	1.86	144
VALLEJO-FAIRFIELD-NAPA, CA (PMSA)	841	1.86	144
EVANSVILLE, IN-KY (MSA)	520	1.86	144
OLYMPIA, WA (MSA)	298	1.85	147
EAU CLAIRE, WI (MSA)	254	1.85	147
CASPER, WY (MSA)	113	1.85	147
WILLIAMSPORT, PA (MSA)	219	1.84	150
ALLENTOWN-BETHLEHEM-EASTON, PA-NJ (MSA)	1,265	1.84	150
JERSEY CITY, NJ (PMSA)	1,013	1.83	152
DAYTON-SPRINGFIELD, OH (MSA)	1,738	1.83	152
REDDING, CA (MSA)	267	1.82	154
NEW LONDON-NORWICH, CT-RI (NECMA)	463	1.82	154
ROCKFORD, IL (MSA)	516	1.82	154
CHICO, CA (MSA)	330	1.81	157
BANGOR, ME (NECMA)	266	1.81	157
DULUTH, MN-WI (MSA)	433	1.80	159
BINGHAMTON, NY (MSA)	477	1.80	159
AUSTIN, TX (MSA)	1,407	1.80	159
ORLANDO, FL (MSA)	1,916	1.79	162
LAFAYETTE-WEST LAFAYETTE, IN (MSA)	234	1.79	162
ALEXANDRIA, LA (MSA)	236	1.79	162
GREENVILLE-SPARTANBURG, SC (MSA)	1,144	1.79	162
HUNTSVILLE, AL (MSA)	425	1.78	166
PENSACOLA, FL (MSA)	614	1.78	166
GRAND RAPIDS, MI (MSA)	1,218	1.77	168
EUGENE-SPRINGFIELD, OR (MSA)	500	1.77	168
SAN ANGELO, TX (MSA)	174	1.77	168
SANTA CRUZ, CA (PMSA)	404	1.76	171
SOUTH BEND - MISHAWAKA, IN (MSA)	435	1.76	171
LEWISTON-AUBURN, ME (NECMA)	185	1.76	171
BILOXI-GULFPORT, MS (MSA)	347	1.76	171
ANCHORAGE, AK (MSA)	396	1.75	175
FRESNO, CA (MSA)	1,167	1.75	175

(continued)

Physicians, Rate Per 1,000 People—Metropolitan Areas (Continued)

Ranking of metropolitan areas by the number of patient care physicians per 1,000 people. (a)

Metropolitan area	Total patient care physicians	Patient care physicians per 1,000 people	Rank
OXNARD-VENTURA, CA (PMSA)	1,168	1.75	175
ABILENE, TX (MSA)	208	1.74	178
HUNTINGTON-ASHLAND, WV-KY-OH (MSA)	544	1.74	178
DOTHAN, AL (MSA)	227	1.73	180
MONROE, LA (MSA)	246	1.73	180
READING, PA (MSA)	582	1.73	180
LAFAYETTE, LA (MSA)	359	1.72	183
CORPUS CHRISTI, TX (MSA)	602	1.72	183
BELLINGHAM, WA (MSA)	220	1.72	183
DUBUQUE, IA (MSA)	147	1.70	186
CUMBERLAND, MD-WV (MSA)	173	1.70	186
YOUNGSTOWN-WARREN, OH (MSA)	831	1.69	188
TACOMA, WA (PMSA)	993	1.69	188
MANCHESTER-NASHUA, NH (NECMA)	564	1.68	190
TULSA, OK (MSA)	1,191	1.68	190
ERIE, PA (MSA)	463	1.68	190
FORT SMITH, AR-OK (MSA)	293	1.67	193
SCRANTON--WILKES-BARRE, PA (MSA)	1,228	1.67	193
TEXARKANA, TX - TEXARKANA, AR (MSA)	201	1.67	193
GADSDEN, AL (MSA)	166	1.66	196
JOHNSTOWN, PA (MSA)	400	1.66	196
FORT WAYNE, IN (MSA)	600	1.65	198
ALTOONA, PA (MSA)	215	1.65	198
SHERMAN-DENISON, TX (MSA)	156	1.64	200
FORT MYERS-CAPE CORAL, FL (MSA)	544	1.62	201
DES MOINES, IA (MSA)	637	1.62	201
LYNCHBURG, VA (MSA)	230	1.62	201
SIOUX CITY, IA-NE (MSA)	185	1.61	204
FLINT, MI (MSA)	691	1.61	204
BATON ROUGE, LA (MSA)	847	1.60	206
ENID, OK (MSA)	91	1.60	206
WAUSAU, WI (MSA)	184	1.59	208
CEDAR RAPIDS, IA (MSA)	266	1.58	209
PASCAGOULA, MS (MSA)	181	1.57	210
APPLETON-OSHKOSH-NEENAH, WI (MSA)	496	1.57	210
MONTGOMERY, AL (MSA)	457	1.56	212
FORT COLLINS-LOVELAND, CO (MSA)	291	1.56	212
ATHENS, GA (MSA)	243	1.56	212
BLOOMINGTON, IN (MSA)	170	1.56	212
GLENS FALLS, NY (MSA)	185	1.56	212
MODESTO, CA (MSA)	574	1.55	217
OWENSBORO, KY (MSA)	135	1.55	217
LANSING-EAST LANSING, MI (MSA)	670	1.55	217
SAINT JOSEPH, MO (MSA)	129	1.55	217
CHARLOTTE-GASTONIA-ROCK HILL, NC-SC, (MSA)	1,796	1.55	217

(continued)

Physicians, Rate Per 1,000 People—Metropolitan Areas (Continued)

Ranking of metropolitan areas by the number of patient care physicians per 1,000 people. (a)

Metropolitan area	Total patient care physicians	Patient care physicians per 1,000 people	Rank
ORANGE COUNTY, NY (PMSA)	478	1.55	217
GREEN BAY, WI (MSA)	301	1.55	217
BRADENTON, FL (MSA)	326	1.54	224
COLUMBUS, GA-AL (MSA)	372	1.53	225
TERRE HAUTE, IN (MSA)	196	1.50	226
CANTON, OH (MSA)	591	1.50	226
WACO, TX (MSA)	283	1.50	226
RIVERSIDE-SAN BERNARDINAO, CA (PMSA)	3,868	1.49	229
WATERLOO-CEDAR FALLS, IA (MSA)	219	1.49	229
SAGINAW-BAY CITY-MIDLAND, MI (MSA)	592	1.48	231
PINE BLUFF, AR (MSA)	126	1.47	232
UTICA-ROME, NY (MSA)	465	1.47	232
COLORADO SPRINGS, CO (MSA)	581	1.46	234
FORT PIERCE, FL (MSA)	366	1.46	234
ALBANY, GA (MSA)	162	1.44	236
ATLANTIC CITY, NJ (MSA)	459	1.44	236
FLORENCE, AL (MSA)	188	1.43	238
SALINAS-SEASIDE-MONTEREY, CA (MSA)	509	1.43	238
MELBOURNE-TITUSVILLE-PALM BAY, FL (MSA)	572	1.43	238
GARY-HAMMOND, IN (PMSA)	862	1.43	238
STATE COLLEGE, PA (MSA)	177	1.43	238
STOCKTON, CA (MSA)	682	1.42	243
LAKE CHARLES, LA (MSA)	238	1.42	243
BEAUMONT-PORT ARTHUR, TX (MSA)	512	1.42	243
GREELEY, CO (MSA)	186	1.41	246
LAS VEGAS, NV (MSA)	1,044	1.41	246
DECATUR, IL (MSA)	164	1.40	248
ANDERSON, SC (MSA)	204	1.40	248
SALEM, OR (MSA)	387	1.39	250
EL PASO, TX (MSA)	825	1.39	250
BREMERTON, WA (MSA)	264	1.39	250
FORT WORTH-ARLINGTON, TX (PMSA)	1,822	1.37	253
DAYTONA BEACH, FL (MSA)	504	1.36	254
AURORA-ELGIN, IL (PMSA)	486	1.36	254
KANKAKEE, IL (MSA)	131	1.36	254
PORTSMOUTH-DOVER-ROCHESTER, NH-ME (NECMA)	472	1.35	257
HICKORY-MORGANTON, NC (MSA)	296	1.34	258
HAGERSTOWN, MD (MSA)	161	1.33	259
JANESVILLE-BELOIT, WI (MSA)	185	1.33	259
RACINE, WI (PMSA)	232	1.33	259
LAKELAND-WINTER HAVEN, FL (MSA)	537	1.32	262
PANAMA CITY, FL (MSA)	167	1.32	262
BLOOMINGTON-NORMAL, IL (MSA)	170	1.32	262
LAWRENCE, KS (MSA)	108	1.32	262
LANCASTER, PA (MSA)	557	1.32	262

(continued)

Physicians, Rate Per 1,000 People—Metropolitan Areas (Continued)

Ranking of metropolitan areas by the number of patient care physicians per 1,000 people. (a)

Metropolitan area	Total patient care physicians	Patient care physicians per 1,000 people	Rank
LONGVIEW-MARSHALL, TX (MSA)	210	1.29	267
FORT WALTON BEACH, FL (MSA)	184	1.28	268
VINELAND-MILLVILLE-BRIDGETON, NJ (PMSA)	177	1.28	268
YAKIMA, WA (MSA)	242	1.28	268
DAVENPORT-ROCK ISLAND-MOLINE, IA-IL (MSA)	446	1.27	271
YORK, PA (MSA)	530	1.27	271
BAKERSFIELD, CA (MSA)	681	1.25	273
BURLINGTON, NC (MSA)	135	1.25	273
LAS CRUCES, NM (MSA)	170	1.25	273
RICHLAND-KENNEWICK-PASCO, WA (MSA)	188	1.25	273
OCALA, FL (MSA)	241	1.24	277
SAINT CLOUD, MN (MSA)	237	1.24	277
LIMA, OH (MSA)	190	1.23	279
ODESSA, TX (MSA)	146	1.23	279
BENTON HARBOR, MI (MSA)	195	1.21	281
SHARON, PA (MSA)	146	1.21	281
BATTLE CREEK, MI (MSA)	161	1.18	283
MIDLAND, TX (MSA)	126	1.18	283
SHEBOYGAN, WI (MSA)	123	1.18	285
LAWTON, OK (MSA)	130	1.17	286
PARKERSBURG-MARIETTA, WV-OH (MSA)	174	1.17	286
MANSFIELD, OH (MSA)	145	1.15	288
JAMESTOWN-DUNKIRK, NY (MSA)	160	1.13	289
PROVO-OREM, UT (MSA)	299	1.13	290
DANVILLE, VA (MSA)	121	1.11	291
NEW BEDFORD-FALL RIVER-ATTLEBORO, MA (NECMA)	556	1.10	292
VANCOUVER, WA (PMSA)	263	1.10	292
ANNISTON, AL (MSA)	127	1.09	294
KOKOMO, IN (MSA)	106	1.09	294
LORAIN-ELYRIA, OH (PMSA)	296	1.09	294
MERCED, CA (MSA)	192	1.08	297
VISALIA-TULARE-PORTERVILLE, CA (MSA)	334	1.07	298
FAYETTEVILLE, NC (MSA)	294	1.07	298
NIAGARA FALLS, NY (PMSA)	236	1.07	298
MUSKEGON, MI (MSA)	167	1.05	301
HAMILTON-MIDDLETOWN, OH (PMSA)	307	1.05	301
CLARKSVILLE-HOPKINSVILLE, TN-KY (MSA)	178	1.05	301
KENOSHA, WI (PMSA)	135	1.05	301
ANDERSON, IN (MSA)	136	1.04	305
JOPLIN, MO (MSA)	138	1.02	306
ELKHART-GOSHEN, IN (MSA)	158	1.01	307
STEUBENVILLE-WEIRTON, OH-WV (MSA)	142	1.00	308
BEAVER COUNTY, PA (PMSA)	185	0.99	309
BROWNSVILLE-HARLINGEN, TX (MSA)	255	0.98	310
HOUMA-THIBODAUX, LA (MSA)	175	0.96	311

(continued)

Physicians, Rate Per 1,000 People—Metropolitan Areas (Continued)

Ranking of metropolitan areas by the number of patient care physicians per 1,000 people. (a)

Metropolitan area	Total patient care physicians	Patient care physicians per 1,000 people	Rank
DECATUR, AL (MSA)	121	0.92	312
JACKSON, MI (MSA)	136	0.91	313
BRAZORIA, TX (PMSA)	171	0.89	314
LAREDO, TX (MSA)	113	0.85	315
JOLIET, IL (PMSA)	320	0.82	316
MCALLEN-EDINBURG-MISSION, TX (MSA)	301	0.78	317
JACKSONVILLE, NC (MSA)	115	0.77	318

Metropolitan areas not ranked

YUBA CITY, CA (MSA)

(a) Data on the number of physicians within a metropolitan area were obtained from *Physician Characteristics and Distribution in the U.S., 1993 Edition,* Chicago: American Medical Association, 1993. Population figures used to calculate the number of physicians per 1,000 people were obtained from the U.S. Census Bureau, *1990 Census of Population,* as reported by the Bureau of Economic Analysis.

Hospital Beds per 1,000 People—Metropolitan Areas

Ranking of metropolitan areas by the number of hospital beds per 1,000 people.

Metropolitan area	Total number of hospital beds	Hospital beds per 1,000 people	Rank
ROCHESTER, MN (MSA)	1,437	13.50	1
IOWA CITY, IA (MSA)	1,108	11.53	2
JACKSON, TN (MSA)	828	10.62	3
COLUMBIA, MO (MSA)	1,023	9.10	4
SPRINGFIELD, IL (MSA)	1,656	8.74	5
BISMARCK, ND (MSA)	655	7.81	6
GREAT FALLS, MT (MSA)	588	7.57	7
SPRINGFIELD, MO (MSA)	1,785	7.42	8
SIOUX FALLS, SD (MSA)	912	7.37	9
MONROE, LA (MSA)	1,043	7.34	10
GALVESTON-TEXAS CITY, TX (PMSA)	1,592	7.32	11
VICTORIA, TX (MSA)	534	7.18	12
SIOUX CITY, IA-NE (MSA)	824	7.16	13
ENID, OK (MSA)	406	7.16	13
LUBBOCK, TX (MSA)	1,562	7.02	15
WHEELING, WV-OH (MSA)	1,113	6.99	16
FLORENCE, AL (MSA)	914	6.96	17
CHARLOTTESVILLE, VA (MSA)	863	6.58	18
GRAND FORKS, ND (MSA)	455	6.44	19
EAU CLAIRE, WI (MSA)	883	6.42	20
SAINT JOSEPH, MO (MSA)	531	6.39	21
FLORENCE, SC (MSA)	731	6.39	21
LA CROSSE, WI (MSA)	620	6.33	23
DUBUQUE, IA (MSA)	541	6.26	24
DECATUR, IL (MSA)	725	6.19	25
LEXINGTON-FAYETTE, KY (MSA)	2,134	6.12	26
ANN ARBOR, MI (PMSA)	1,730	6.11	27
SHREVEPORT, LA (MSA)	2,033	6.08	28
JACKSON, MS (MSA)	2,378	6.01	29
DULUTH, MN-WI (MSA)	1,430	5.96	30
FORT SMITH, AR-OK (MSA)	1,035	5.88	31
OMAHA, NE-IA (MSA)	3,634	5.88	31
LITTLE ROCK-NORTH LITTLE ROCK, AR (MSA)	3,010	5.87	33
ALEXANDRIA, LA (MSA)	768	5.84	34
KANKAKEE, IL (MSA)	558	5.80	35
COLUMBUS, GA-AL (MSA)	1,402	5.77	36
BIRMINGHAM, AL (MSA)	5,227	5.76	37
FAYETTEVILLE-SPRINGDALE, AR (MSA)	651	5.74	38
ELMIRA, NY (MSA)	545	5.73	39
TEXARKANA, TX - TEXARKANA, AR (MSA)	685	5.70	40
OWENSBORO, KY (MSA)	495	5.68	41
ALBANY, GA (MSA)	637	5.66	42
WILLIAMSPORT, PA (MSA)	668	5.63	43

(continued)

Hospital Beds per 1,000 People—Metropolitan Areas (Continued)

Ranking of metropolitan areas by the number of hospital beds per 1,000 people.

Metropolitan area	Total number of hospital beds	Hospital beds per 1,000 people	Rank
ROANOKE, VA (MSA)	1,261	5.62	44
PINE BLUFF, AR (MSA)	480	5.61	45
SHERMAN-DENISON, TX (MSA)	532	5.60	46
PARKERSBURG-MARIETTA, WV-OH (MSA)	835	5.60	46
CHARLESTON, WV (MSA)	1,397	5.58	48
GAINESVILLE, FL (MSA)	1,133	5.55	49
JOPLIN, MO (MSA)	738	5.47	50
ATHENS, GA (MSA)	848	5.43	51
CEDAR RAPIDS, IA (MSA)	914	5.42	52
SHARON, PA (MSA)	653	5.40	53
GADSDEN, AL (MSA)	538	5.39	54
DOTHAN, AL (MSA)	704	5.38	55
MEMPHIS, TN-AR-MS (MSA)	5,271	5.37	56
DES MOINES, IA (MSA)	2,098	5.34	57
EVANSVILLE, IN-KY (MSA)	1,487	5.33	58
CUMBERLAND, MD-WV (MSA)	539	5.30	59
TRENTON, NJ (PMSA)	1,724	5.29	60
BEAUMONT-PORT ARTHUR, TX (MSA)	1,912	5.29	60
PITTSBURGH, PA (PMSA)	10,838	5.27	62
TOLEDO, OH (MSA)	3,231	5.26	63
TYLER, TX (MSA)	795	5.25	64
NEW ORLEANS, LA (MSA)	6,475	5.23	65
PENSACOLA, FL (MSA)	1,794	5.21	66
LYNCHBURG, VA (MSA)	737	5.18	67
AMARILLO, TX (MSA)	969	5.17	68
SAN ANGELO, TX (MSA)	508	5.16	69
ERIE, PA (MSA)	1,417	5.14	70
FORT WORTH-ARLINGTON, TX (PMSA)	6,852	5.14	70
NASHVILLE, TN (MSA)	5,035	5.11	72
AUGUSTA, GA-SC (MSA)	2,020	5.09	73
NEWARK, NJ (PMSA)	9,242	5.07	74
LAKE CHARLES, LA (MSA)	845	5.03	75
LAFAYETTE, LA (MSA)	1,048	5.02	76
ANDERSON, IN (MSA)	655	5.01	77
ALTOONA, PA (MSA)	654	5.01	77
WATERLOO-CEDAR FALLS, IA (MSA)	733	5.00	79
TERRE HAUTE, IN (MSA)	654	5.00	79
SAVANNAH, GA (MSA)	1,209	4.98	81
SARASOTA, FL (MSA)	1,363	4.91	82
MOBILE, AL (MSA)	2,336	4.90	83
BILLINGS, MT (MSA)	554	4.88	84
YOUNGSTOWN-WARREN, OH (MSA)	2,398	4.87	85

(continued)

Hospital Beds per 1,000 People—Metropolitan Areas (Continued)

Ranking of metropolitan areas by the number of hospital beds per 1,000 people.

Metropolitan area	Total number of hospital beds	Hospital beds per 1,000 people	Rank
TUSCALOOSA, AL (MSA)	731	4.86	86
LAFAYETTE-WEST LAFAYETTE, IN (MSA)	635	4.86	86
CLEVELAND, OH (PMSA)	8,873	4.85	88
SAGINAW-BAY CITY-MIDLAND, MI (MSA)	1,915	4.80	89
BUFFALO, NY (PMSA)	4,632	4.78	90
TALLAHASSEE, FL (MSA)	1,113	4.76	91
STEUBENVILLE-WEIRTON, OH-WV (MSA)	678	4.76	91
KNOXVILLE, TN (MSA)	2,868	4.74	93
WICHITA, KS (MSA)	2,296	4.73	94
KOKOMO, IN (MSA)	458	4.72	95
MACON-WARNER ROBINS, GA (MSA)	1,315	4.68	96
GLENS FALLS, NY (MSA)	553	4.67	97
CHAMPAIGN-URBANA-RANTOUL, IL (MSA)	805	4.65	98
GARY-HAMMOND, IN (PMSA)	2,792	4.62	99
WILMINGTON, NC (MSA)	554	4.61	100
CHATTANOOGA, TN-GA (MSA)	1,995	4.61	100
JAMESTOWN-DUNKIRK, NY (MSA)	653	4.60	102
NEW YORK, NY (PMSA)	39,298	4.60	102
RALEIGH-DURHAM, NC (MSA)	3,372	4.58	104
SCRANTON--WILKES-BARRE, PA (MSA)	3,363	4.58	104
JOHNSTOWN, PA (MSA)	1,103	4.57	106
MIAMI-HIALEAH, FL (PMSA)	8,840	4.56	107
RICHMOND-PETERSBURG, VA (MSA)	3,951	4.56	107
BLOOMINGTON-NORMAL, IL (MSA)	588	4.55	109
JOHNSON CITY-KINGSPORT-BRISTOL, TN-VA (MSA)	1,970	4.52	110
PUEBLO, CO (MSA)	555	4.51	111
DAVENPORT-ROCK ISLAND-MOLINE, IA-IL (MSA)	1,576	4.49	112
PEORIA, IL (MSA)	1,516	4.47	113
FORT LAUDERDALE-HOLLYWOOD-POMPANO BEACH, FL (PMSA)	5,543	4.42	114
JERSEY CITY, NJ (PMSA)	2,443	4.42	115
MONTGOMERY, AL (MSA)	1,287	4.40	116
DAYTON-SPRINGFIELD, OH (MSA)	4,184	4.40	116
HUNTINGTON-ASHLAND, WV-KY-OH (MSA)	1,373	4.39	118
LOUISVILLE, KY-IN (MSA)	4,172	4.38	119
INDIANAPOLIS, IN (MSA)	5,444	4.36	120
KANSAS CITY, MO-KS (MSA)	6,783	4.33	121
LEWISTON-AUBURN, ME (NECMA)	453	4.30	122
OKLAHOMA CITY, OK (MSA)	4,112	4.29	123
BENTON HARBOR, MI (MSA)	688	4.26	124
FLINT, MI (MSA)	1,830	4.25	125
CORPUS CHRISTI, TX (MSA)	1,482	4.24	126
LIMA, OH (MSA)	650	4.21	127

(continued)

Hospital Beds per 1,000 People—Metropolitan Areas (Continued)

Ranking of metropolitan areas by the number of hospital beds per 1,000 people.

Metropolitan area	Total number of hospital beds	Hospital beds per 1,000 people	Rank
PHILADELPHIA, PA-NJ (PMSA)	20,392	4.20	128
ANNISTON, AL (MSA)	486	4.19	129
FARGO-MOORHEAD, ND-MN (MSA)	643	4.19	129
BILOXI-GULFPORT, MS (MSA)	824	4.18	131
BURLINGTON, VT (NECMA)	573	4.18	131
BATTLE CREEK, MI (MSA)	566	4.16	133
PORTLAND, ME (NECMA)	1,009	4.15	133
MUSKEGON, MI (MSA)	660	4.15	133
ASHEVILLE, NC (MSA)	725	4.15	133
TULSA, OK (MSA)	2,943	4.15	133
MUNCIE, IN (MSA)	494	4.13	138
ALLENTOWN-BETHLEHEM-EASTON, PA-NJ (MSA)	2,838	4.13	138
TOPEKA, KS (MSA)	661	4.11	140
TAMPA-SAINT PETERSBURG-CLEARWATER, FL (MSA)	8,467	4.09	141
ROCHESTER, NY (MSA)	4,083	4.07	142
CINCINNATI, OH-KY-IN (PMSA)	5,910	4.07	142
NIAGARA FALLS, NY (PMSA)	893	4.05	144
SHEBOYGAN, WI (MSA)	421	4.05	144
DECATUR, AL (MSA)	532	4.04	146
BRADENTON, FL (MSA)	855	4.04	146
BOSTON-LAWRENCE-SALEM-LOWELL-BROCKTON, MA (NECMA)	15,119	4.00	148
SAINT LOUIS, MO-IL (MSA)	9,772	4.00	148
HARRISBURG-LEBANON-CARLISLE, PA (MSA)	2,354	4.00	148
ALBANY-SCHENECTADY-TROY, NY (MSA)	3,486	3.99	151
HOUSTON, TX (PMSA)	13,183	3.99	151
HUNTSVILLE, AL (MSA)	933	3.91	153
CHICAGO, IL (PMSA)	23,763	3.91	153
CANTON, OH (MSA)	1,537	3.90	155
ABILENE, TX (MSA)	467	3.90	155
RENO, NV (MSA)	990	3.89	157
VINELAND-MILLVILLE-BRIDGETON, NJ (PMSA)	534	3.87	158
CHARLESTON, SC (MSA)	1,956	3.86	159
JACKSON, MI (MSA)	573	3.83	160
ATLANTIC CITY, NJ (MSA)	1,221	3.82	161
AKRON, OH (PMSA)	2,511	3.82	161
FORT WAYNE, IN (MSA)	1,380	3.79	163
PANAMA CITY, FL (MSA)	478	3.76	164
MADISON, WI (MSA)	1,382	3.76	164
SOUTH BEND - MISHAWAKA, IN (MSA)	927	3.75	166
RAPID CITY, SD (MSA)	305	3.75	166
BATON ROUGE, LA (MSA)	1,974	3.74	168

(continued)

Hospital Beds per 1,000 People—Metropolitan Areas (Continued)

Ranking of metropolitan areas by the number of hospital beds per 1,000 people.

Metropolitan area	Total number of hospital beds	Hospital beds per 1,000 people	Rank
WICHITA FALLS, TX (MSA)	457	3.73	169
SPOKANE, WA (MSA)	1,346	3.72	170
MANSFIELD, OH (MSA)	463	3.67	171
CASPER, WY (MSA)	225	3.67	171
WEST PALM BEACH-BOCA RATON-DELRAY BEACH, FL (MSA)	3,164	3.66	173
ROCKFORD, IL (MSA)	1,039	3.66	173
DAYTONA BEACH, FL (MSA)	1,349	3.64	175
LINCOLN, NE (MSA)	778	3.64	175
GREENVILLE-SPARTANBURG, SC (MSA)	2,322	3.62	177
SAN FRANCISCO, CA (PMSA)	5,770	3.60	178
DANVILLE, VA (MSA)	391	3.60	178
FORT MYERS-CAPE CORAL, FL (MSA)	1,202	3.59	180
LANSING-EAST LANSING, MI (MSA)	1,555	3.59	180
ALBUQUERQUE, NM (MSA)	1,726	3.59	180
MEDFORD, OR (MSA)	522	3.57	183
MILWAUKEE, WI (PMSA)	5,109	3.57	183
GREENSBORO--WINSTON-SALEM--HIGH POINT, NC (MSA)	3,352	3.56	185
KALAMAZOO, MI (MSA)	793	3.55	186
BRIDGEPORT-STAMFORD-NORWALK-DANBURY, CT (NECMA)	2,928	3.54	187
AURORA-ELGIN, IL (PMSA)	1,263	3.54	187
MODESTO, CA (MSA)	1,306	3.52	189
JANESVILLE-BELOIT, WI (MSA)	491	3.52	189
JACKSONVILLE, FL (MSA)	3,184	3.51	191
HOUMA-THIBODAUX, LA (MSA)	642	3.51	191
CHEYENNE, WY (MSA)	257	3.51	191
NASSAU-SUFFOLK, NY (PMSA)	9,104	3.49	194
ATLANTA, GA (MSA)	9,841	3.47	195
HICKORY-MORGANTON, NC (MSA)	769	3.47	195
LORAIN-ELYRIA, OH (PMSA)	941	3.47	195
APPLETON-OSHKOSH-NEENAH, WI (MSA)	1,092	3.47	195
SAINT CLOUD, MN (MSA)	661	3.46	199
BANGOR, ME (NECMA)	506	3.45	200
CHICO, CA (MSA)	625	3.43	201
MONMOUTH-OCEAN, NJ (PMSA)	3,379	3.43	201
COLUMBUS, OH (MSA)	4,720	3.43	201
BALTIMORE, MD (MSA)	8,125	3.41	204
DETROIT, MI (PMSA)	14,817	3.38	205
SYRACUSE, NY (MSA)	2,230	3.38	205
VALLEJO-FAIRFIELD-NAPA, CA (PMSA)	1,522	3.37	207
FORT WALTON BEACH, FL (MSA)	482	3.35	208
ORLANDO, FL (MSA)	3,572	3.33	209

(continued)

Hospital Beds per 1,000 People—Metropolitan Areas (Continued)

Ranking of metropolitan areas by the number of hospital beds per 1,000 people.

Metropolitan area	Total number of hospital beds	Hospital beds per 1,000 people	Rank
BEAVER COUNTY, PA (PMSA)	616	3.31	210
BERGEN-PASSAIC, NJ (PMSA)	4,191	3.28	211
UTICA-ROME, NY (MSA)	1,039	3.28	211
ODESSA, TX (MSA)	389	3.27	213
SAN ANTONIO, TX (MSA)	4,238	3.25	214
GREEN BAY, WI (MSA)	632	3.25	214
COLUMBIA, SC (MSA)	1,466	3.23	216
WILMINGTON, DE-NJ-MD (PMSA)	1,863	3.22	217
ORANGE COUNTY, NY (PMSA)	986	3.20	218
HARTFORD-NEW BRITAIN-MIDDLETOWN-BRISTOL, CT (NECMA)	3,584	3.19	219
REDDING, CA (MSA)	468	3.18	220
LAKELAND-WINTER HAVEN, FL (MSA)	1,288	3.18	220
BROWNSVILLE-HARLINGEN, TX (MSA)	825	3.17	222
LONGVIEW-MARSHALL, TX (MSA)	513	3.16	223
ANCHORAGE, AK (MSA)	714	3.15	224
BURLINGTON, NC (MSA)	340	3.14	225
ANDERSON, SC (MSA)	456	3.14	225
LOS ANGELES-LONG BEACH, CA (PMSA)	27,700	3.13	227
MIDLAND, TX (MSA)	333	3.12	228
LAWTON, OK (MSA)	347	3.11	229
OLYMPIA, WA (MSA)	500	3.10	230
DENVER, CO (PMSA)	5,010	3.09	231
BINGHAMTON, NY (MSA)	816	3.09	231
READING, PA (MSA)	1,041	3.09	231
PROVIDENCE-PAWTUCKET-WOONSOCKET, RI (NECMA)	2,819	3.08	234
SPRINGFIELD, MA (NECMA)	1,851	3.07	235
ELKHART-GOSHEN, IN (MSA)	478	3.06	236
MINNEAPOLIS-ST PAUL, MN-WI (MSA)	7,501	3.04	237
RACINE, WI (PMSA)	532	3.04	237
TUCSON, AZ (MSA)	2,016	3.02	239
PORTLAND, OR (PMSA)	3,742	3.02	239
HAMILTON-MIDDLETOWN, OH (PMSA)	878	3.01	241
PASCAGOULA, MS (MSA)	346	3.00	242
PITTSFIELD, MA (NECMA)	417	2.99	243
CHARLOTTE-GASTONIA-ROCK HILL, NC-SC, (MSA)	3,470	2.99	243
NORFOLK-VIRGINIA BEACH-NEWPORT NEWS, VA (MSA)	4,179	2.99	243
WACO, TX (MSA)	560	2.96	246
MANCHESTER-NASHUA, NH (NECMA)	990	2.95	247
LANCASTER, PA (MSA)	1,241	2.94	248
DALLAS, TX (PMSA)	7,446	2.92	249
LAKE COUNTY, IL (PMSA)	1,499	2.90	250

(continued)

Hospital Beds per 1,000 People—Metropolitan Areas (Continued)
Ranking of metropolitan areas by the number of hospital beds per 1,000 people.

Metropolitan area	Total number of hospital beds	Hospital beds per 1,000 people	Rank
PHOENIX, AZ (MSA)	6,104	2.88	251
LAREDO, TX (MSA)	382	2.87	252
POUGHKEEPSIE, NY (MSA)	741	2.86	253
NAPLES, FL (MSA)	431	2.83	254
FORT PIERCE, FL (MSA)	702	2.80	255
SANTA BARBARA-SANTA MARIA-LOMPOC, CA (MSA)	1,031	2.79	256
EL PASO, TX (MSA)	1,650	2.79	256
YAKIMA, WA (MSA)	518	2.74	258
MELBOURNE-TITUSVILLE-PALM BAY, FL (MSA)	1,085	2.72	259
BOISE CITY, ID (MSA)	557	2.71	260
LAS VEGAS, NV (MSA)	2,011	2.71	260
SALT LAKE CITY-OGDEN, UT (MSA)	2,897	2.70	262
WASHINGTON, DC-MD-VA (MSA)	10,511	2.68	263
NEW HAVEN-WATERBURY-MERIDEN, CT (NECMA)	2,137	2.66	264
ANAHEIM-SANTA ANA, CA (PMSA)	6,369	2.64	265
BLOOMINGTON, IN (MSA)	285	2.62	266
KENOSHA, WI (PMSA)	334	2.61	267
HONOLULU, HI (MSA)	2,174	2.60	268
COLORADO SPRINGS, CO (MSA)	1,026	2.58	269
GRAND RAPIDS, MI (MSA)	1,773	2.58	269
RICHLAND-KENNEWICK-PASCO, WA (MSA)	387	2.58	269
NEW LONDON-NORWICH, CT-RI (NECMA)	656	2.57	272
HAGERSTOWN, MD (MSA)	312	2.57	272
FRESNO, CA (MSA)	1,681	2.52	274
YORK, PA (MSA)	1,053	2.52	274
SAN DIEGO, CA (MSA)	6,179	2.47	276
WORCESTER-FITCHBURG-LEOMINSTER, MA (NECMA)	1,737	2.45	277
OAKLAND, CA (PMSA)	5,065	2.43	278
KILLEEN-TEMPLE, TX (MSA)	620	2.43	278
LAWRENCE, KS (MSA)	197	2.41	280
MIDDLESEX-SOMERSET-HUNTERDON, NJ (PMSA)	2,436	2.39	281
SANTA FE, NM (MSA)	279	2.38	282
SACRAMENTO, CA (MSA)	3,508	2.37	283
SEATTLE, WA (PMSA)	4,681	2.37	283
OCALA, FL (MSA)	451	2.31	285
EUGENE-SPRINGFIELD, OR (MSA)	654	2.31	285
BRYAN-COLLEGE STATION, TX (MSA)	279	2.29	287
MCALLEN-EDINBURG-MISSION, TX (MSA)	860	2.24	288
RIVERSIDE-SAN BERNARDINO, CA (PMSA)	5,784	2.23	289
SAN JOSE, CA (PMSA)	3,342	2.23	289
BAKERSFIELD, CA (MSA)	1,194	2.20	291
FORT COLLINS-LOVELAND, CO (MSA)	409	2.20	291

(continued)

Hospital Beds per 1,000 People—Metropolitan Areas (Continued)

Ranking of metropolitan areas by the number of hospital beds per 1,000 people.

Metropolitan area	Total number of hospital beds	Hospital beds per 1,000 people	Rank
WAUSAU, WI (MSA)	254	2.20	291
STOCKTON, CA (MSA)	1,051	2.19	294
STATE COLLEGE, PA (MSA)	270	2.18	295
GREELEY, CO (MSA)	281	2.13	296
FAYETTEVILLE, NC (MSA)	586	2.13	296
AUSTIN, TX (MSA)	1,668	2.13	296
JOLIET, IL (PMSA)	828	2.12	299
VISALIA-TULARE-PORTERVILLE, CA (MSA)	656	2.10	300
YUBA CITY, CA (MSA)	256	2.09	301
TACOMA, WA (PMSA)	1,226	2.09	301
SANTA ROSA-PETALUMA, CA (PMSA)	798	2.06	303
PROVO-OREM, UT (MSA)	544	2.06	303
OXNARD-VENTURA, CA (PMSA)	1,372	2.05	305
SALEM, OR (MSA)	542	1.95	306
CLARKSVILLE-HOPKINSVILLE, TN-KY (MSA)	325	1.92	307
MERCED, CA (MSA)	337	1.89	308
PORTSMOUTH-DOVER-ROCHESTER, NH-ME (NECMA)	645	1.84	309
LAS CRUCES, NM (MSA)	240	1.77	310
BOULDER-LONGMONT, CO (PMSA)	387	1.72	311
SANTA CRUZ, CA (PMSA)	390	1.70	312
SALINAS-SEASIDE-MONTEREY, CA (MSA)	602	1.69	313
BELLINGHAM, WA (MSA)	214	1.67	314
BRAZORIA, TX (PMSA)	318	1.66	315
BREMERTON, WA (MSA)	244	1.29	316
VANCOUVER, WA (PMSA)	299	1.26	317
JACKSONVILLE, NC (MSA)	133	0.89	318

Metropolitan area not ranked

NEW BEDFORD-FALL RIVER-ATTLEBORO, MA (NECMA)

Data on the number of hospital beds within a metropolitan area were obtained from *Hospital Statistics, 1992–1993 Edition,* American Hospital Association, Chicago: American Hospital Association, 1992. Population figures used to calculate the number of hospital beds per 1,000 people were obtained from the U.S. Census Bureau, *1990 Census of Population,* as reported by the Bureau of Economic Analysis.

Crime Rate per 1000 Inhabitants—Metropolitan Areas

Metropolitan areas are ranked by the number of crimes committed per 1,000 inhabitants.

Metropolitan area	Crime rate per 1,000 inhabitants	Rank
BEAVER COUNTY, PA (PMSA)	23.2	1
SHARON, PA (MSA)	23.3	2
STEUBENVILLE-WEIRTON, OH-WV (MSA)	24.0	3
ALTOONA, PA (MSA)	24.6	4
CUMBERLAND, MD-WV (MSA)	28.7	5
HAGERSTOWN, MD (MSA)	29.2	6
LANCASTER, PA (MSA)	31.2	7
YORK, PA (MSA)	31.6	8
ALLENTOWN-BETHLEHEM-EASTON, PA-NJ (MSA)	32.0	9
WAUSAU, WI (MSA)	32.3	10
DANVILLE, VA (MSA)	32.5	11
BINGHAMTON, NY (MSA)	32.7	12
SAINT CLOUD, MN (MSA)	33.5	13
HUNTINGTON-ASHLAND, WV-KY-OH (MSA)	33.9	14
BILLINGS, MT (MSA)	34.0	15
UTICA-ROME, NY (MSA)	34.2	16
FLORENCE, AL (MSA)	34.5	17
PITTSFIELD, MA (NECMA)	34.8	18
PITTSBURGH, PA (PMSA)	35.0	19
JOHNSON CITY-KINGSPORT-BRISTOL, TN-VA (MSA)	35.3	20
GLENS FALLS, NY (MSA)	35.5	21
POUGHKEEPSIE, NY (MSA)	35.9	22
ERIE, PA (MSA)	35.9	22
ORANGE COUNTY, NY (PMSA)	36.5	24
EAU CLAIRE, WI (MSA)	37.1	25
NEW LONDON-NORWICH, CT-RI (NECMA)	37.2	26
OWENSBORO, KY (MSA)	37.3	27
APPLETON-OSHKOSH-NEENAH, WI (MSA)	37.4	28
JAMESTOWN-DUNKIRK, NY (MSA)	38.0	29
LEWISTON-AUBURN, ME (NECMA)	38.0	30
LYNCHBURG, VA (MSA)	38.0	30
LORAIN-ELYRIA, OH (PMSA)	38.5	32
READING, PA (MSA)	38.5	32
DECATUR, AL (MSA)	39.5	34
BURLINGTON, NC (MSA)	39.5	34
PROVO-OREM, UT (MSA)	39.5	34
ROCHESTER, MN (MSA)	40.0	37
MIDDLESEX-SOMERSET-HUNTERDON, NJ (PMSA)	40.0	37
MONMOUTH-OCEAN, NJ (PMSA)	40.0	37
KOKOMO, IN (MSA)	40.2	40
ALBANY-SCHENECTADY-TROY, NY (MSA)	40.2	40
CHARLOTTESVILLE, VA (MSA)	40.4	42
GREEN BAY, WI (MSA)	41.1	43
BISMARCK, ND (MSA)	41.2	44

(continued)

Crime Rate per 1000 Inhabitants—Metropolitan Areas (Continued)

Metropolitan areas are ranked by the number of crimes committed per 1,000 inhabitants.

Metropolitan area	Crime rate per 1,000 inhabitants	Rank
FARGO-MOORHEAD, ND-MN (MSA)	41.6	45
ANNISTON, AL (MSA)	41.7	46
NASSAU-SUFFOLK, NY (PMSA)	42.0	47
SHEBOYGAN, WI (MSA)	42.1	48
DULUTH, MN-WI (MSA)	42.3	49
ANDERSON, IN (MSA)	42.5	50
BERGEN-PASSAIC, NJ (PMSA)	42.8	51
BANGOR, ME (NECMA)	43.2	52
SYRACUSE, NY (MSA)	43.3	53
VANCOUVER, WA (PMSA)	43.7	54
OXNARD-VENTURA, CA (PMSA)	44.3	55
HICKORY-MORGANTON, NC (MSA)	44.4	56
BRAZORIA, TX (PMSA)	44.4	56
CHARLESTON, WV (MSA)	44.6	58
LA CROSSE, WI (MSA)	44.7	59
LOUISVILLE, KY-IN (MSA)	44.9	60
SIOUX FALLS, SD (MSA)	45.0	61
GRAND FORKS, ND (MSA)	45.4	62
BOISE CITY, ID (MSA)	45.7	63
BREMERTON, WA (MSA)	46.0	64
CANTON, OH (MSA)	46.3	65
LAFAYETTE-WEST LAFAYETTE, IN (MSA)	46.4	66
OMAHA, NE-IA (MSA)	46.5	67
SANTA ROSA-PETALUMA, CA (PMSA)	46.8	68
MERCED, CA (MSA)	47.2	69
ELKHART-GOSHEN, IN (MSA)	48.0	70
CHICO, CA (MSA)	48.1	71
ELMIRA, NY (MSA)	48.1	71
MEDFORD, OR (MSA)	48.3	73
KILLEEN-TEMPLE, TX (MSA)	48.4	74
SANTA BARBARA-SANTA MARIA-LOMPOC, CA (MSA)	48.5	75
CLEVELAND, OH (PMSA)	48.5	75
PHILADELPHIA, PA-NJ (PMSA)	48.5	75
OLYMPIA, WA (MSA)	48.5	75
REDDING, CA (MSA)	48.9	79
SALINAS-SEASIDE-MONTEREY, CA (MSA)	49.2	80
JACKSONVILLE, NC (MSA)	49.3	81
SAN JOSE, CA (PMSA)	50.4	82
EVANSVILLE, IN-KY (MSA)	50.4	82
CHEYENNE, WY (MSA)	50.5	84
FORT SMITH, AR-OK (MSA)	50.6	85
JOPLIN, MO (MSA)	50.6	85
ANDERSON, SC (MSA)	50.8	87
KENOSHA, WI (PMSA)	51.0	88

(continued)

Crime Rate per 1000 Inhabitants—Metropolitan Areas (Continued)

Metropolitan areas are ranked by the number of crimes committed per 1,000 inhabitants.

Metropolitan area	Crime rate per 1,000 inhabitants	Rank
KNOXVILLE, TN (MSA)	51.9	89
ROCHESTER, NY (MSA)	52.5	90
LAWTON, OK (MSA)	53.2	91
PROVIDENCE-PAWTUCKET-WOONSOCKET, RI (NECMA)	53.2	91
CLARKSVILLE-HOPKINSVILLE, TN-KY (MSA)	53.3	93
LAFAYETTE, LA (MSA)	53.4	94
MADISON, WI (MSA)	53.6	95
FAYETTEVILLE-SPRINGDALE, AR (MSA)	53.9	96
YUBA CITY, CA (MSA)	54.1	97
JANESVILLE-BELOIT, WI (MSA)	54.1	97
ASHEVILLE, NC (MSA)	54.2	99
GRAND RAPIDS, MI (MSA)	54.4	100
BOSTON-LAWRENCE-SALEM-LOWELL-BROCKTON, MA (NECMA)	54.8	101
BELLINGHAM, WA (MSA)	55.1	102
EUGENE-SPRINGFIELD, OR (MSA)	55.3	103
ROANOKE, VA (MSA)	55.4	104
ABILENE, TX (MSA)	55.5	105
MINNEAPOLIS-ST PAUL, MN-WI (MSA)	55.7	106
WILMINGTON, DE-NJ-MD (PMSA)	56.2	107
CINCINNATI, OH-KY-IN (PMSA)	56.7	108
ALEXANDRIA, LA (MSA)	56.8	109
BUFFALO, NY (PMSA)	56.9	110
HARTFORD-NEW BRITAIN-MIDDLETOWN-BRISTOL, CT (NECMA)	57.0	111
PORTLAND, ME (NECMA)	57.0	111
SAINT JOSEPH, MO (MSA)	57.5	113
SPRINGFIELD, MO (MSA)	57.5	113
NEW BEDFORD-FALL RIVER-ATTLEBORO, MA (NECMA)	57.7	115
MANCHESTER-NASHUA, NH (NECMA)	58.1	116
VALLEJO-FAIRFIELD-NAPA, CA (PMSA)	58.2	117
SANTA CRUZ, CA (PMSA)	58.4	118
DAYTON-SPRINGFIELD, OH (MSA)	58.4	118
GREELEY, CO (MSA)	58.5	120
SAGINAW-BAY CITY-MIDLAND, MI (MSA)	58.5	120
RICHLAND-KENNEWICK-PASCO, WA (MSA)	58.5	120
ANAHEIM-SANTA ANA, CA (PMSA)	58.7	123
JACKSON, MI (MSA)	58.7	123
COLUMBUS, GA-AL (MSA)	58.9	125
WASHINGTON, DC-MD-VA (MSA)	59.0	126
LANSING-EAST LANSING, MI (MSA)	59.1	127
HONOLULU, HI (MSA)	59.6	128
GARY-HAMMOND, IN (PMSA)	60.0	129
MILWAUKEE, WI (PMSA)	60.1	130
FORT PIERCE, FL (MSA)	60.2	131

(continued)

Crime Rate per 1000 Inhabitants—Metropolitan Areas (Continued)

Metropolitan areas are ranked by the number of crimes committed per 1,000 inhabitants.

Metropolitan area	Crime rate per 1,000 inhabitants	Rank
DOTHAN, AL (MSA)	60.3	132
NAPLES, FL (MSA)	60.4	133
FORT WAYNE, IN (MSA)	60.5	134
INDIANAPOLIS, IN (MSA)	60.6	135
RAPID CITY, SD (MSA)	60.9	136
VISALIA-TULARE-PORTERVILLE, CA (MSA)	61.2	137
BOULDER-LONGMONT, CO (PMSA)	61.2	137
LEXINGTON-FAYETTE, KY (MSA)	61.5	139
SAN ANGELO, TX (MSA)	61.5	139
TRENTON, NJ (PMSA)	61.6	141
SALEM, OR (MSA)	61.8	142
COLORADO SPRINGS, CO (MSA)	62.0	143
BRIDGEPORT-STAMFORD-NORWALK-DANBURY, CT (NECMA)	62.0	143
MACON-WARNER ROBINS, GA (MSA)	62.2	145
RICHMOND-PETERSBURG, VA (MSA)	62.3	146
RACINE, WI (PMSA)	62.7	147
SAINT LOUIS, MO-IL (MSA)	63.0	148
MANSFIELD, OH (MSA)	63.1	149
GREENVILLE-SPARTANBURG, SC (MSA)	63.1	149
TULSA, OK (MSA)	63.3	151
LUBBOCK, TX (MSA)	64.0	152
NASHVILLE, TN (MSA)	64.3	153
GREENSBORO--WINSTON-SALEM--HIGH POINT, NC (MSA)	64.4	154
CHATTANOOGA, TN-GA (MSA)	64.4	154
SPRINGFIELD, MA (NECMA)	64.6	156
GADSDEN, AL (MSA)	65.0	157
LAS CRUCES, NM (MSA)	65.3	158
CASPER, WY (MSA)	65.4	159
VINELAND-MILLVILLE-BRIDGETON, NJ (PMSA)	65.5	160
BAKERSFIELD, CA (MSA)	65.6	161
BRYAN-COLLEGE STATION, TX (MSA)	65.9	162
RALEIGH-DURHAM, NC (MSA)	66.0	163
ENID, OK (MSA)	66.0	163
DENVER, CO (PMSA)	66.2	165
NEWARK, NJ (PMSA)	66.2	165
SPOKANE, WA (MSA)	66.2	165
BIRMINGHAM, AL (MSA)	66.6	168
SHERMAN-DENISON, TX (MSA)	66.6	168
ANCHORAGE, AK (MSA)	66.9	170
NORFOLK-VIRGINIA BEACH-NEWPORT NEWS, VA (MSA)	66.9	170
MODESTO, CA (MSA)	67.3	172
PANAMA CITY, FL (MSA)	67.4	173
ATHENS, GA (MSA)	67.5	174
PORTLAND, OR (PMSA)	67.8	175

(continued)

Crime Rate per 1000 Inhabitants—Metropolitan Areas (Continued)

Metropolitan areas are ranked by the number of crimes committed per 1,000 inhabitants.

Metropolitan area	Crime rate per 1,000 inhabitants	Rank
SALT LAKE CITY-OGDEN, UT (MSA)	67.8	175
SAN FRANCISCO, CA (PMSA)	67.9	177
ANN ARBOR, MI (PMSA)	67.9	177
NEW HAVEN-WATERBURY-MERIDEN, CT (NECMA)	68.0	179
OCALA, FL (MSA)	68.0	179
SAN DIEGO, CA (MSA)	68.2	181
PUEBLO, CO (MSA)	68.5	182
KALAMAZOO, MI (MSA)	68.5	182
MCALLEN-EDINBURG-MISSION, TX (MSA)	68.5	182
RENO, NV (MSA)	69.2	185
MIDLAND, TX (MSA)	69.5	186
COLUMBUS, OH (MSA)	69.8	187
TACOMA, WA (PMSA)	69.8	187
AUGUSTA, GA-SC (MSA)	70.2	189
LAS VEGAS, NV (MSA)	70.2	189
MELBOURNE-TITUSVILLE-PALM BAY, FL (MSA)	70.4	190
TOLEDO, OH (MSA)	70.4	190
DETROIT, MI (PMSA)	70.6	193
BROWNSVILLE-HARLINGEN, TX (MSA)	70.9	194
AMARILLO, TX (MSA)	71.1	195
TEXARKANA, TX - TEXARKANA, AR (MSA)	71.1	195
MONTGOMERY, AL (MSA)	71.3	197
SEATTLE, WA (PMSA)	71.5	198
SARASOTA, FL (MSA)	71.7	199
BATTLE CREEK, MI (MSA)	71.7	199
LONGVIEW-MARSHALL, TX (MSA)	72.0	201
SACRAMENTO, CA (MSA)	72.1	202
FLORENCE, SC (MSA)	72.1	202
MONROE, LA (MSA)	72.5	204
BALTIMORE, MD (MSA)	72.7	205
PINE BLUFF, AR (MSA)	72.8	206
LAWRENCE, KS (MSA)	72.8	206
JERSEY CITY, NJ (PMSA)	73.1	208
COLUMBIA, SC (MSA)	73.2	209
DAYTONA BEACH, FL (MSA)	73.8	210
BEAUMONT-PORT ARTHUR, TX (MSA)	73.9	211
GREAT FALLS, MT (MSA)	74.5	212
CHARLESTON, SC (MSA)	74.5	212
OAKLAND, CA (PMSA)	74.6	214
KANSAS CITY, MO-KS (MSA)	74.8	215
WICHITA, KS (MSA)	74.9	216
BENTON HARBOR, MI (MSA)	75.2	217
TYLER, TX (MSA)	75.8	218
MUSKEGON, MI (MSA)	76.0	219

(continued)

Crime Rate per 1000 Inhabitants—Metropolitan Areas (Continued)

Metropolitan areas are ranked by the number of crimes committed per 1,000 inhabitants.

Metropolitan area	Crime rate per 1,000 inhabitants	Rank
LINCOLN, NE (MSA)	76.1	220
LOS ANGELES-LONG BEACH, CA (PMSA)	76.2	221
FLINT, MI (MSA)	77.3	222
MEMPHIS, TN-AR-MS (MSA)	78.0	223
YAKIMA, WA (MSA)	78.7	224
BRADENTON, FL (MSA)	79.1	225
SAVANNAH, GA (MSA)	79.5	226
CHARLOTTE-GASTONIA-ROCK HILL, NC-SC, (MSA)	80.4	227
SHREVEPORT, LA (MSA)	79.7	228
OKLAHOMA CITY, OK (MSA)	80.5	229
TUSCALOOSA, AL (MSA)	81.3	230
PHOENIX, AZ (MSA)	81.8	231
VICTORIA, TX (MSA)	81.8	231
HOUSTON, TX (PMSA)	81.9	233
TAMPA-SAINT PETERSBURG-CLEARWATER, FL (MSA)	82.7	234
ATLANTA, GA (MSA)	83.2	235
TUCSON, AZ (MSA)	83.6	236
GALVESTON-TEXAS CITY, TX (PMSA)	83.7	237
STOCKTON, CA (MSA)	83.9	238
JACKSON, MS (MSA)	84.2	239
NEW YORK, NY (PMSA)	84.8	240
FORT LAUDERDALE-HOLLYWOOD-POMPANO BEACH, FL (PMSA)	85.1	241
WACO, TX (MSA)	85.4	242
TOPEKA, KS (MSA)	85.5	243
CORPUS CHRISTI, TX (MSA)	86.9	244
WICHITA FALLS, TX (MSA)	85.8	245
JACKSON, TN (MSA)	87.0	246
AUSTIN, TX (MSA)	87.3	247
BATON ROUGE, LA (MSA)	87.8	248
NEW ORLEANS, LA (MSA)	88.4	249
EL PASO, TX (MSA)	89.4	250
LAREDO, TX (MSA)	89.7	251
ALBUQUERQUE, NM (MSA)	89.8	252
FAYETTEVILLE, NC (MSA)	90.5	253
FRESNO, CA (MSA)	91.0	254
ALBANY, GA (MSA)	90.8	255
JACKSONVILLE, FL (MSA)	92.0	256
LITTLE ROCK-NORTH LITTLE ROCK, AR (MSA)	93.5	257
GAINESVILLE, FL (MSA)	94.6	258
LAKELAND-WINTER HAVEN, FL (MSA)	97.2	259
WILMINGTON, NC (MSA)	97.7	260
DALLAS, TX (PMSA)	100.4	261
FORT WORTH-ARLINGTON, TX (PMSA)	101.4	262

(continued)

Crime Rate per 1000 Inhabitants—Metropolitan Areas (Continued)

Metropolitan areas are ranked by the number of crimes committed per 1,000 inhabitants.

Metropolitan area	Crime rate per 1,000 inhabitants	Rank
ATLANTIC CITY, NJ (MSA)	102.4	263
SAN ANTONIO, TX (MSA)	104.5	264
TALLAHASSEE, FL (MSA)	113.5	265
ODESSA, TX (MSA)	120.5	266
MIAMI-HIALEAH, FL (PMSA)	127.9	267

Metropolitan areas not ranked

AKRON, OH (PMSA)
AURORA-ELGIN, IL (PMSA)
BILOXI-GULFPORT, MS (MSA)
BLOOMINGTON, IN (MSA)
BLOOMINGTON-NORMAL, IL (MSA)
BURLINGTON, VT (NECMA)
CEDAR RAPIDS, IA (MSA)
CHAMPAIGN-URBANA-RANTOUL, IL (MSA)
CHICAGO, IL (PMSA)
COLUMBIA, MO (MSA)
DAVENPORT-ROCK ISLAND-MOLINE, IA-IL (MSA)
DECATUR, IL (MSA)
DES MOINES, IA (MSA)
DUBUQUE, IA (MSA)
FORT COLLINS-LOVELAND, CO (MSA)
FORT MYERS-CAPE CORAL, FL (MSA)
FORT WALTON BEACH, FL (MSA)
HAMILTON-MIDDLETOWN, OH (PMSA)
HARRISBURG-LEBANON-CARLISLE, PA (MSA)
HOUMA-THIBODAUX, LA (MSA)
HUNTSVILLE, AL (MSA)
IOWA CITY, IA (MSA)
JOHNSTOWN, PA (MSA)
JOLIET, IL (PMSA)
KANKAKEE, IL (MSA)
LAKE CHARLES, LA (MSA)
LAKE COUNTY, IL (PMSA)
LIMA, OH (MSA)
MOBILE, AL (MSA)
MUNCIE, IN (MSA)
NIAGARA FALLS, NY (PMSA)
ORLANDO, FL (MSA)
PARKERSBURG-MARIETTA, WV-OH (MSA)
PASCAGOULA, MS (MSA)
PENSACOLA, FL (MSA)
PEORIA, IL (MSA)

(continued)

Crime Rate per 1000 Inhabitants—Metropolitan Areas (Continued)

Metropolitan areas are ranked by the number of crimes committed per 1,000 inhabitants.

Metropolitan area	Crime rate per 1,000 inhabitants	Rank
PORTSMOUTH-DOVER-ROCHESTER, NH-ME (NECMA)		
RIVERSIDE-SAN BERNARDINO, CA (PMSA)		
ROCKFORD, IL (MSA)		
SANTA FE, NM (MSA)		
SCRANTON--WILKES-BARRE, PA (MSA)		
SIOUX CITY, IA-NE (MSA)		
SOUTH BEND - MISHAWAKA, IN (MSA)		
SPRINGFIELD, IL (MSA)		
STATE COLLEGE, PA (MSA)		
TERRE HAUTE, IN (MSA)		
WATERLOO-CEDAR FALLS, IA (MSA)		
WEST PALM BEACH-BOCA RATON-DELRAY BEACH, FL (MSA)		
WHEELING, WV-OH (MSA)		
WILLIAMSPORT, PA (MSA)		
WORCESTER-FITCHBURG-LEOMINSTER, MA (NECMA)		
YOUNGSTOWN-WARREN, OH (MSA)		

Data include crimes of all types, both personal and property. Data are from the Federal Bureau of Investigation, U.S. Department of Justice, *Crime in the United States 1991, Uniform Crime Reports,* Washington, D.C.: U.S. Government Printing Office, 1992.

Violent Crime per 1,000 Inhabitants—Metropolitan Areas

Metropolitan areas are ranked by the number of violent crimes committed per 1,000 inhabitants.

Metropolitan area	Violent crime rate per 1,000 inhabitants	Rank
BISMARCK, ND (MSA)	0.73	1
BILLINGS, MT (MSA)	0.82	2
LA CROSSE, WI (MSA)	1.04	3
APPLETON-OSHKOSH-NEENAH, WI (MSA)	1.09	4
EAU CLAIRE, WI (MSA)	1.09	4
BANGOR, ME (NECMA)	1.18	6
WAUSAU, WI (MSA)	1.18	6
GRAND FORKS, ND (MSA)	1.20	8
SAINT CLOUD, MN (MSA)	1.27	9
SHEBOYGAN, WI (MSA)	1.31	10
ALTOONA, PA (MSA)	1.38	11
PROVO-OREM, UT (MSA)	1.40	12
ROCHESTER, MN (MSA)	1.41	13
JAMESTOWN-DUNKIRK, NY (MSA)	1.42	14
LEWISTON-AUBURN, ME (NECMA)	1.47	15
DULUTH, MN-WI (MSA)	1.81	16
BINGHAMTON, NY (MSA)	1.86	17
LANCASTER, PA (MSA)	1.88	18
MANCHESTER-NASHUA, NH (NECMA)	1.90	19
UTICA-ROME, NY (MSA)	1.94	20
ALLENTOWN-BETHLEHEM-EASTON, PA-NJ (MSA)	1.96	21
YORK, PA (MSA)	2.00	22
JOPLIN, MO (MSA)	2.11	23
GREAT FALLS, MT (MSA)	2.15	24
FAYETTEVILLE-SPRINGDALE, AR (MSA)	2.18	25
KENOSHA, WI (PMSA)	2.22	26
DANVILLE, VA (MSA)	2.26	27
GREEN BAY, WI (MSA)	2.26	27
OWENSBORO, KY (MSA)	2.31	29
CHEYENNE, WY (MSA)	2.37	30
HONOLULU, HI (MSA)	2.40	31
HUNTINGTON-ASHLAND, WV-KY-OH (MSA)	2.55	32
SHARON, PA (MSA)	2.57	33
MIDDLESEX-SOMERSET-HUNTERDON, NJ (PMSA)	2.61	34
JANESVILLE-BELOIT, WI (MSA)	2.63	35
LAFAYETTE-WEST LAFAYETTE, IN (MSA)	2.76	36
PORTLAND, ME (NECMA)	2.76	36
OLYMPIA, WA (MSA)	2.76	36
BOULDER-LONGMONT, CO (PMSA)	2.77	39
MONMOUTH-OCEAN, NJ (PMSA)	2.80	40
JOHNSON CITY-KINGSPORT-BRISTOL, TN-VA (MSA)	2.83	41
HAGERSTOWN, MD (MSA)	2.91	42
NASSAU-SUFFOLK, NY (PMSA)	2.95	43

(continued)

Violent Crime per 1,000 Inhabitants—Metropolitan Areas (Continued)

Metropolitan areas are ranked by the number of violent crimes committed per 1,000 inhabitants.

Metropolitan area	Violent crime rate per 1,000 inhabitants	Rank
VANCOUVER, WA (PMSA)	2.97	44
EUGENE-SPRINGFIELD, OR (MSA)	2.98	45
BOISE CITY, ID (MSA)	3.01	46
SPRINGFIELD, MO (MSA)	3.01	46
BEAVER COUNTY, PA (PMSA)	3.02	48
CHARLOTTESVILLE, VA (MSA)	3.04	49
ELMIRA, NY (MSA)	3.11	50
SIOUX FALLS, SD (MSA)	3.20	51
BELLINGHAM, WA (MSA)	3.20	51
FLORENCE, AL (MSA)	3.21	53
SYRACUSE, NY (MSA)	3.21	53
BREMERTON, WA (MSA)	3.28	55
NEW LONDON-NORWICH, CT-RI (NECMA)	3.30	56
CUMBERLAND, MD-WV (MSA)	3.35	57
MADISON, WI (MSA)	3.40	58
ROCHESTER, NY (MSA)	3.42	59
MEDFORD, OR (MSA)	3.50	60
KOKOMO, IN (MSA)	3.69	61
FORT WAYNE, IN (MSA)	3.71	62
DECATUR, AL (MSA)	3.72	63
CHARLESTON, WV (MSA)	3.72	63
ERIE, PA (MSA)	3.74	65
SALT LAKE CITY-OGDEN, UT (MSA)	3.74	65
POUGHKEEPSIE, NY (MSA)	3.76	67
ANDERSON, IN (MSA)	3.80	68
GREELEY, CO (MSA)	3.83	69
RICHLAND-KENNEWICK-PASCO, WA (MSA)	3.89	70
ASHEVILLE, NC (MSA)	3.91	71
LORAIN-ELYRIA, OH (PMSA)	3.92	72
BERGEN-PASSAIC, NJ (PMSA)	3.94	73
ROANOKE, VA (MSA)	3.98	74
SALEM, OR (MSA)	4.03	75
JACKSONVILLE, NC (MSA)	4.05	76
READING, PA (MSA)	4.07	77
ALBANY-SCHENECTADY-TROY, NY (MSA)	4.11	78
ORANGE COUNTY, NY (PMSA)	4.13	79
BRAZORIA, TX (PMSA)	4.14	80
COLORADO SPRINGS, CO (MSA)	4.22	81
SPOKANE, WA (MSA)	4.24	82
GLENS FALLS, NY (MSA)	4.26	83
PITTSBURGH, PA (PMSA)	4.29	84
REDDING, CA (MSA)	4.36	85
STEUBENVILLE-WEIRTON, OH-WV (MSA)	4.36	85

(continued)

Violent Crime per 1,000 Inhabitants—Metropolitan Areas (Continued)

Metropolitan areas are ranked by the number of violent crimes committed per 1,000 inhabitants.

Metropolitan area	Violent crime rate per 1,000 inhabitants	Rank
FORT SMITH, AR-OK (MSA)	4.41	87
SANTA ROSA-PETALUMA, CA (PMSA)	4.43	88
LAWRENCE, KS (MSA)	4.43	88
HICKORY-MORGANTON, NC (MSA)	4.44	90
BURLINGTON, NC (MSA)	4.51	91
SHERMAN-DENISON, TX (MSA)	4.53	92
CHICO, CA (MSA)	4.58	93
PITTSFIELD, MA (NECMA)	4.62	94
MINNEAPOLIS-ST PAUL, MN-WI (MSA)	4.70	95
SAINT JOSEPH, MO (MSA)	4.72	96
ELKHART-GOSHEN, IN (MSA)	4.75	97
MERCED, CA (MSA)	4.84	98
LOUISVILLE, KY-IN (MSA)	4.87	99
LYNCHBURG, VA (MSA)	4.93	100
RAPID CITY, SD (MSA)	4.94	101
SANTA BARBARA-SANTA MARIA-LOMPOC, CA (MSA)	4.99	102
CANTON, OH (MSA)	4.99	102
MCALLEN-EDINBURG-MISSION, TX (MSA)	5.00	104
ALEXANDRIA, LA (MSA)	5.01	105
AUSTIN, TX (MSA)	5.07	106
PROVIDENCE-PAWTUCKET-WOONSOCKET, RI (NECMA)	5.09	107
CASPER, WY (MSA)	5.09	107
ATHENS, GA (MSA)	5.16	109
LINCOLN, NE (MSA)	5.19	110
AMARILLO, TX (MSA)	5.20	111
MILWAUKEE, WI (PMSA)	5.20	111
SAN JOSE, CA (PMSA)	5.22	113
KILLEEN-TEMPLE, TX (MSA)	5.22	113
OXNARD-VENTURA, CA (PMSA)	5.29	115
SANTA CRUZ, CA (PMSA)	5.34	116
LUBBOCK, TX (MSA)	5.36	117
RACINE, WI (PMSA)	5.39	118
OMAHA, NE-IA (MSA)	5.47	119
LAS CRUCES, NM (MSA)	5.56	120
BRYAN-COLLEGE STATION, TX (MSA)	5.60	121
ANAHEIM-SANTA ANA, CA (PMSA)	5.68	122
MACON-WARNER ROBINS, GA (MSA)	5.75	123
EVANSVILLE, IN-KY (MSA)	5.85	124
RICHMOND-PETERSBURG, VA (MSA)	5.92	125
SEATTLE, WA (PMSA)	5.96	126
SARASOTA, FL (MSA)	6.06	127
LAFAYETTE, LA (MSA)	6.07	128
BROWNSVILLE-HARLINGEN, TX (MSA)	6.08	129

(continued)

Violent Crime per 1,000 Inhabitants—Metropolitan Areas (Continued)

Metropolitan areas are ranked by the number of violent crimes committed per 1,000 inhabitants.

Metropolitan area	Violent crime rate per 1,000 inhabitants	Rank
SAN ANGELO, TX (MSA)	6.12	130
KNOXVILLE, TN (MSA)	6.28	131
SALINAS-SEASIDE-MONTEREY, CA (MSA)	6.34	132
TYLER, TX (MSA)	6.34	132
NORFOLK-VIRGINIA BEACH-NEWPORT NEWS, VA (MSA)	6.36	134
RALEIGH-DURHAM, NC (MSA)	6.39	135
COLUMBUS, GA-AL (MSA)	6.41	136
WILMINGTON, DE-NJ-MD (PMSA)	6.42	137
GRAND RAPIDS, MI (MSA)	6.46	138
CINCINNATI, OH-KY-IN (PMSA)	6.47	139
HARTFORD-NEW BRITAIN-MIDDLETOWN-BRISTOL, CT (NECMA)	6.48	140
WICHITA, KS (MSA)	6.56	141
LANSING-EAST LANSING, MI (MSA)	6.60	142
YAKIMA, WA (MSA)	6.63	143
PANAMA CITY, FL (MSA)	6.69	144
CLEVELAND, OH (PMSA)	6.69	144
FORT PIERCE, FL (MSA)	6.71	146
TOLEDO, OH (MSA)	6.72	147
RENO, NV (MSA)	6.74	148
LAREDO, TX (MSA)	6.76	149
TUCSON, AZ (MSA)	6.89	150
TRENTON, NJ (PMSA)	6.89	150
DAYTON-SPRINGFIELD, OH (MSA)	6.92	152
ANN ARBOR, MI (PMSA)	6.94	153
CORPUS CHRISTI, TX (MSA)	6.97	154
LEXINGTON-FAYETTE, KY (MSA)	7.11	155
ENID, OK (MSA)	7.11	155
ANCHORAGE, AK (MSA)	7.12	157
SAN ANTONIO, TX (MSA)	7.12	157
JACKSON, MS (MSA)	7.16	159
COLUMBUS, OH (MSA)	7.21	160
OKLAHOMA CITY, OK (MSA)	7.24	161
BRIDGEPORT-STAMFORD-NORWALK-DANBURY, CT (NECMA)	7.26	162
ANNISTON, AL (MSA)	7.27	163
YUBA CITY, CA (MSA)	7.28	164
ABILENE, TX (MSA)	7.29	165
DENVER, CO (PMSA)	7.30	166
INDIANAPOLIS, IN (MSA)	7.33	167
GREENSBORO--WINSTON-SALEM--HIGH POINT, NC (MSA)	7.33	167
MELBOURNE-TITUSVILLE-PALM BAY, FL (MSA)	7.34	169
LAWTON, OK (MSA)	7.36	170
TEXARKANA, TX - TEXARKANA, AR (MSA)	7.36	170

(continued)

Violent Crime per 1,000 Inhabitants—Metropolitan Areas (Continued)

Metropolitan areas are ranked by the number of violent crimes committed per 1,000 inhabitants.

Metropolitan area	Violent crime rate per 1,000 inhabitants	Rank
ODESSA, TX (MSA)	7.52	172
VALLEJO-FAIRFIELD-NAPA, CA (PMSA)	7.53	173
AUGUSTA, GA-SC (MSA)	7.53	173
PHILADELPHIA, PA-NJ (PMSA)	7.59	175
ANDERSON, SC (MSA)	7.62	176
PHOENIX, AZ (MSA)	7.71	177
VISALIA-TULARE-PORTERVILLE, CA (MSA)	7.72	178
MUSKEGON, MI (MSA)	7.76	179
NEW HAVEN-WATERBURY-MERIDEN, CT (NECMA)	7.82	180
WASHINGTON, DC-MD-VA (MSA)	7.85	181
LAS VEGAS, NV (MSA)	7.88	182
SACRAMENTO, CA (MSA)	7.94	183
PORTLAND, OR (PMSA)	7.98	184
LONGVIEW-MARSHALL, TX (MSA)	8.00	185
MODESTO, CA (MSA)	8.04	186
GALVESTON-TEXAS CITY, TX (PMSA)	8.24	187
WICHITA FALLS, TX (MSA)	8.24	187
ALBANY, GA (MSA)	8.25	189
WILMINGTON, NC (MSA)	8.27	190
TULSA, OK (MSA)	8.30	191
BOSTON-LAWRENCE-SALEM-LOWELL-BROCKTON, MA (NECMA)	8.32	192
DOTHAN, AL (MSA)	8.35	193
SAVANNAH, GA (MSA)	8.35	193
NAPLES, FL (MSA)	8.49	195
BUFFALO, NY (PMSA)	8.50	196
MONTGOMERY, AL (MSA)	8.54	197
WACO, TX (MSA)	8.76	198
ATLANTIC CITY, NJ (MSA)	8.79	199
SPRINGFIELD, MA (NECMA)	8.84	200
MONROE, LA (MSA)	8.89	201
STOCKTON, CA (MSA)	8.90	202
FORT LAUDERDALE-HOLLYWOOD-POMPANO BEACH, FL (PMSA)	9.08	203
KALAMAZOO, MI (MSA)	9.10	204
DAYTONA BEACH, FL (MSA)	9.12	205
SAGINAW-BAY CITY-MIDLAND, MI (MSA)	9.14	206
BATTLE CREEK, MI (MSA)	9.17	207
BAKERSFIELD, CA (MSA)	9.19	208
SHREVEPORT, LA (MSA)	9.29	209
TOPEKA, KS (MSA)	9.30	210
GARY-HAMMOND, IN (PMSA)	9.33	211
GADSDEN, AL (MSA)	9.38	212
SAINT LOUIS, MO-IL (MSA)	9.38	212

(continued)

Violent Crime per 1,000 Inhabitants—Metropolitan Areas (Continued)

Metropolitan areas are ranked by the number of violent crimes committed per 1,000 inhabitants.

Metropolitan area	Violent crime rate per 1,000 inhabitants	Rank
CHATTANOOGA, TN-GA (MSA)	9.41	214
TACOMA, WA (PMSA)	9.48	215
NEW BEDFORD-FALL RIVER-ATTLEBORO, MA (NECMA)	9.49	216
BEAUMONT-PORT ARTHUR, TX (MSA)	9.62	217
TUSCALOOSA, AL (MSA)	9.65	218
SAN DIEGO, CA (MSA)	9.67	219
FAYETTEVILLE, NC (MSA)	9.67	219
CHARLESTON, SC (MSA)	9.73	221
MIDLAND, TX (MSA)	9.73	221
VINELAND-MILLVILLE-BRIDGETON, NJ (PMSA)	9.79	223
SAN FRANCISCO, CA (PMSA)	9.84	224
VICTORIA, TX (MSA)	9.86	225
LAKELAND-WINTER HAVEN, FL (MSA)	9.88	226
ATLANTA, GA (MSA)	9.88	226
EL PASO, TX (MSA)	9.92	228
FORT WORTH-ARLINGTON, TX (PMSA)	9.92	228
GREENVILLE-SPARTANBURG, SC (MSA)	9.96	230
DETROIT, MI (PMSA)	10.01	231
NASHVILLE, TN (MSA)	10.15	232
OCALA, FL (MSA)	10.17	233
FRESNO, CA (MSA)	10.21	234
NEWARK, NJ (PMSA)	10.29	235
OAKLAND, CA (PMSA)	10.37	236
MEMPHIS, TN-AR-MS (MSA)	10.38	237
BRADENTON, FL (MSA)	10.60	238
MANSFIELD, OH (MSA)	10.62	239
HOUSTON, TX (PMSA)	10.77	240
PINE BLUFF, AR (MSA)	10.86	241
FLINT, MI (MSA)	10.93	242
FLORENCE, SC (MSA)	10.97	243
CLARKSVILLE-HOPKINSVILLE, TN-KY (MSA)	11.07	244
BENTON HARBOR, MI (MSA)	11.17	245
BIRMINGHAM, AL (MSA)	11.28	246
COLUMBIA, SC (MSA)	11.49	247
GAINESVILLE, FL (MSA)	11.52	248
CHARLOTTE-GASTONIA-ROCK HILL, NC-SC, (MSA)	11.59	249
KANSAS CITY, MO-KS (MSA)	11.75	250
JERSEY CITY, NJ (PMSA)	11.91	251
ALBUQUERQUE, NM (MSA)	11.98	252
BALTIMORE, MD (MSA)	12.55	253
TAMPA-SAINT PETERSBURG-CLEARWATER, FL (MSA)	12.65	254
BATON ROUGE, LA (MSA)	12.86	255
JACKSON, MI (MSA)	12.96	256

(continued)

Violent Crime per 1,000 Inhabitants—Metropolitan Areas (Continued)

Metropolitan areas are ranked by the number of violent crimes committed per 1,000 inhabitants.

Metropolitan area	Violent crime rate per 1,000 inhabitants	Rank
DALLAS, TX (PMSA)	13.34	257
PUEBLO, CO (MSA)	13.38	258
JACKSON, TN (MSA)	13.60	259
NEW ORLEANS, LA (MSA)	14.08	260
LITTLE ROCK-NORTH LITTLE ROCK, AR (MSA)	14.09	261
JACKSONVILLE, FL (MSA)	14.47	262
TALLAHASSEE, FL (MSA)	16.71	263
LOS ANGELES-LONG BEACH, CA (PMSA)	17.96	264
NEW YORK, NY (PMSA)	20.44	265
MIAMI-HIALEAH, FL (PMSA)	21.95	266

Metropolitan areas not ranked

AKRON, OH (PMSA)
AURORA-ELGIN, IL (PMSA)
BILOXI-GULFPORT, MS (MSA)
BLOOMINGTON, IN (MSA)
BLOOMINGTON-NORMAL, IL (MSA)
BURLINGTON, VT (NECMA)
CEDAR RAPIDS, IA (MSA)
CHAMPAIGN-URBANA-RANTOUL, IL (MSA)
CHICAGO, IL (PMSA)
COLUMBIA, MO (MSA)
DAVENPORT-ROCK ISLAND-MOLINE, IA-IL (MSA)
DECATUR, IL (MSA)
DES MOINES, IA (MSA)
DUBUQUE, IA (MSA)
FARGO-MOORHEAD, ND-MN (MSA)
FORT COLLINS-LOVELAND, CO (MSA)
FORT MYERS-CAPE CORAL, FL (MSA)
FORT WALTON BEACH, FL (MSA)
HAMILTON-MIDDLETOWN, OH (PMSA)
HARRISBURG-LEBANON-CARLISLE, PA (MSA)
HOUMA-THIBODAUX, LA (MSA)
HUNTSVILLE, AL (MSA)
IOWA CITY, IA (MSA)
JOHNSTOWN, PA (MSA)
JOLIET, IL (PMSA)
KANKAKEE, IL (MSA)
LAKE CHARLES, LA (MSA)
LAKE COUNTY, IL (PMSA)
LIMA, OH (MSA)
MOBILE, AL (MSA)

(continued)

Violent Crime per 1,000 Inhabitants—Metropolitan Areas (Continued)

Metropolitan areas are ranked by the number of violent crimes committed per 1,000 inhabitants.

Metropolitan area	Violent crime rate per 1,000 inhabitants	Rank
MUNCIE, IN (MSA)		
NIAGARA FALLS, NY (PMSA)		
ORLANDO, FL (MSA)		
PARKERSBURG-MARIETTA, WV-OH (MSA)		
PASCAGOULA, MS (MSA)		
PENSACOLA, FL (MSA)		
PEORIA, IL (MSA)		
PORTSMOUTH-DOVER-ROCHESTER, NH-ME (NECMA)		
RIVERSIDE-SAN BERNARDINO, CA (PMSA)		
ROCKFORD, IL (MSA)		
SANTA FE, NM (MSA)		
SCRANTON--WILKES-BARRE, PA (MSA)		
SIOUX CITY, IA-NE (MSA)		
SOUTH BEND - MISHAWAKA, IN (MSA)		
SPRINGFIELD, IL (MSA)		
STATE COLLEGE, PA (MSA)		
TERRE HAUTE, IN (MSA)		
WATERLOO-CEDAR FALLS, IA (MSA)		
WEST PALM BEACH-BOCA RATON-DELRAY BEACH, FL (MSA)		
WHEELING, WV-OH (MSA)		
WILLIAMSPORT, PA (MSA)		
WORCESTER-FITCHBURG-LEOMINSTER, MA (NECMA)		
YOUNGSTOWN-WARREN, OH (MSA)		

Violent crimes are offenses of murder, forcible rape, robbery, and aggravated assault. Data are from the Federal Bureau of Investigation, U.S. Department of Justice, *Crime in the United States 1991, Uniform Crime Reports,* Washington D.C.: US. Government Printing Office, 1992.

Per Capita Federal Funds and Grants—Metropolitan Areas

Metropolitan areas are ranked by the per capita federal funds and grants received. The area receiving the greatest amount of federal funds and grants per capita is ranked number 1.

Metropolitan areas	Total federal funds and grants received ($1,000)	Per capita federal funds and grants received (dollars)	Rank
NEW LONDON-NORWICH, CT-RI (NECMA)	3,613,200	14,591	1
SANTA FE, NM (MSA)	1,389,300	12,353	2
HUNTSVILLE, AL (MSA)	2,711,100	11,453	3
WASHINGTON, DC-MD-VA (MSA)	36,649,900	9,815	4
JACKSONVILLE, NC (MSA)	1,133,900	8,967	5
RICHLAND-KENNEWICK-PASCO, WA (MSA)	1,237,400	8,454	6
MELBOURNE-TITUSVILLE-PALM BAY, FL (MSA)	3,182,700	8,197	7
AUGUSTA, GA-SC (MSA)	3,240,100	8,173	8
LIMA, OH (MSA)	1,279,800	8,165	9
KILLEEN-TEMPLE, TX (MSA)	1,908,600	7,966	10
FAYETTEVILLE, NC (MSA)	1,998,000	7,814	11
FORT WALTON BEACH, FL (MSA)	1,170,400	7,772	12
PASCAGOULA, MS (MSA)	981,200	7,659	13
BREMERTON, WA (MSA)	1,374,700	7,601	14
LAWTON, OK (MSA)	898,400	7,531	15
NORFOLK-VIRGINIA BEACH-NEWPORT NEWS, VA (MSA)	9,559,700	6,926	16
ALBUQUERQUE, NM (MSA)	3,368,200	6,831	17
GREAT FALLS, MT (MSA)	528,400	6,758	18
NEW BEDFORD-FALL RIVER-ATTLEBORO, MA (NECMA)	3,259,600	6,749	19
CLARKSVILLE-HOPKINSVILLE, TN-KY (MSA)	1,052,700	6,627	20
PITTSFIELD, MA (NECMA)	904,900	6,525	21
COLORADO SPRINGS, CO (MSA)	2,445,200	6,208	22
ANNISTON, AL (MSA)	752,600	6,103	23
CHEYENNE, WY (MSA)	450,400	5,990	24
SPRINGFIELD, IL (MSA)	1,106,000	5,769	25
HONOLULU, HI (MSA)	4,784,600	5,706	26
ALBANY-SCHENECTADY-TROY, NY (MSA)	4,791,100	5,631	27
TRENTON, NJ (PMSA)	1,852,200	5,596	28
SACRAMENTO, CA (MSA)	7,746,400	5,592	29
KNOXVILLE, TN (MSA)	3,258,500	5,434	30
COLUMBUS, GA-AL (MSA)	1,306,800	5,293	31
BILOXI-GULFPORT, MS (MSA)	1,081,600	5,277	32
ANCHORAGE, AK (MSA)	1,151,100	5,268	33
SAINT LOUIS, MO-IL (MSA)	12,915,400	5,236	34
BELLINGHAM, WA (MSA)	611,200	5,150	35
SAN JOSE, CA (PMSA)	7,369,200	5,146	36
DOTHAN, AL (MSA)	673,000	5,135	37
TALLAHASSEE, FL (MSA)	1,171,400	5,124	38
FORT WORTH-ARLINGTON, TX (PMSA)	6,553,200	5,076	39
MACON-WARNER ROBINS, GA (MSA)	1,433,000	4,997	40
HARRISBURG-LEBANON-CARLISLE, PA (MSA)	2,918,700	4,938	41

(continued)

Per Capita Federal Funds and Grants—Metropolitan Areas (Continued)

Metropolitan areas are ranked by the per capita federal funds and grants received. The area receiving the greatest amount of federal funds and grants per capita is ranked number 1.

Metropolitan areas	Total federal funds and grants received ($1,000)	Per capita federal funds and grants received (dollars)	Rank
LAS CRUCES, NM (MSA)	649,400	4,919	42
SAN DIEGO, CA (MSA)	11,531,700	4,865	43
TUCSON, AZ (MSA)	3,071,900	4,830	44
CHARLESTON, SC (MSA)	2,456,500	4,809	45
BOSTON-LAWRENCE-SALEM-LOWELL-BROCKTON, MA (NECMA)	17,873,100	4,784	46
DAYTON-SPRINGFIELD, OH (MSA)	4,462,100	4,707	47
TEXARKANA, TX - TEXARKANA, AR (MSA)	560,700	4,695	48
PANAMA CITY, FL (MSA)	584,900	4,661	49
GRAND FORKS, ND (MSA)	325,800	4,624	50
PENSACOLA, FL (MSA)	1,615,200	4,616	51
OLYMPIA, WA (MSA)	718,100	4,584	52
MONTGOMERY, AL (MSA)	1,377,700	4,581	53
BRIDGEPORT-STAMFORD-NORWALK-DANBURY, CT (NECMA)	3,723,800	4,556	54
RAPID CITY, SD (MSA)	372,100	4,537	55
DENVER, CO (PMSA)	7,425,800	4,528	56
TOPEKA, KS (MSA)	740,000	4,490	57
SALINAS-SEASIDE-MONTEREY, CA (MSA)	1,553,200	4,454	58
SANTA BARBARA-SANTA MARIA-LOMPOC, CA (MSA)	1,526,000	4,447	59
TACOMA, WA (PMSA)	2,461,700	4,403	60
BINGHAMTON, NY (MSA)	1,131,300	4,347	61
BALTIMORE, MD (MSA)	10,162,000	4,338	62
ABILENE, TX (MSA)	519,000	4,261	63
SARASOTA, FL (MSA)	1,105,800	4,243	64
VALLEJO-FAIRFIELD-NAPA, CA (PMSA)	1,780,000	4,231	65
SAN ANTONIO, TX (MSA)	5,585,100	4,221	66
HARTFORD-NEW BRITAIN-MIDDLETOWN-BRISTOL, CT (NECMA)	4,569,900	4,123	67
PINE BLUFF, AR (MSA)	370,900	4,085	68
WICHITA FALLS, TX (MSA)	507,100	4,069	69
AUSTIN, TX (MSA)	3,041,600	4,064	70
SAVANNAH, GA (MSA)	992,800	4,063	71
CINCINNATI, OH-KY-IN (PMSA)	5,883,800	4,061	72
DES MOINES, IA (MSA)	1,591,000	4,061	73
LAS VEGAS, NV (MSA)	2,544,600	4,031	74
COLUMBIA, SC (MSA)	1,835,300	4,021	75
WICHITA, KS (MSA)	1,922,900	3,980	76
ORLANDO, FL (MSA)	3,859,600	3,974	77
SCRANTON--WILKES-BARRE, PA (MSA)	2,915,600	3,958	78
BISMARCK, ND (MSA)	339,100	3,954	79
JACKSONVILLE, FL (MSA)	3,528,500	3,929	80

(continued)

Per Capita Federal Funds and Grants—Metropolitan Areas (Continued)

Metropolitan areas are ranked by the per capita federal funds and grants received. The area receiving the greatest amount of federal funds and grants per capita is ranked number 1.

Metropolitan areas	Total federal funds and grants received ($1,000)	Per capita federal funds and grants received (dollars)	Rank
ENID, OK (MSA)	227,100	3,895	81
SEATTLE, WA (PMSA)	7,235,300	3,886	82
UTICA-ROME, NY (MSA)	1,196,600	3,828	83
NASSAU-SUFFOLK, NY (PMSA)	10,087,000	3,822	84
YUBA CITY, CA (MSA)	446,800	3,772	85
WEST PALM BEACH-BOCA RATON-DELRAY BEACH, FL (MSA)	3,040,200	3,715	86
MADISON, WI (MSA)	1,309,500	3,711	87
OKLAHOMA CITY, OK (MSA)	3,574,600	3,709	88
NEW ORLEANS, LA (MSA)	4,824,400	3,691	89
SALEM, OR (MSA)	989,800	3,669	90
SHREVEPORT, LA (MSA)	1,308,900	3,645	91
CEDAR RAPIDS, IA (MSA)	624,900	3,644	92
BAKERSFIELD, CA (MSA)	1,891,300	3,637	93
JOHNSON CITY-KINGSPORT-BRISTOL, TN-VA (MSA)	1,605,400	3,630	94
LANSING-EAST LANSING, MI (MSA)	1,550,600	3,620	95
ALEXANDRIA, LA (MSA)	497,100	3,606	96
OAKLAND, CA (PMSA)	7,222,900	3,600	97
TAMPA-SAINT PETERSBURG-CLEARWATER, FL (MSA)	7,171,800	3,595	98
PITTSBURGH, PA (PMSA)	7,510,300	3,586	99
SAN FRANCISCO, CA (PMSA)	5,676,800	3,570	100
CUMBERLAND, MD-WV (MSA)	365,300	3,568	101
HUNTINGTON-ASHLAND, WV-KY-OH (MSA)	1,149,800	3,567	102
PHILADELPHIA, PA-NJ (PMSA)	17,547,900	3,566	103
SOUTH BEND - MISHAWAKA, IN (MSA)	867,500	3,552	104
BURLINGTON, VT (NECMA)	477,900	3,551	105
LOS ANGELES-LONG BEACH, CA (PMSA)	30,039,300	3,498	106
CHARLESTON, WV (MSA)	908,900	3,485	107
OMAHA, NE-IA (MSA)	2,166,200	3,485	108
CHAMPAIGN-URBANA-RANTOUL, IL (MSA)	597,300	3,471	109
EL PASO, TX (MSA)	2,031,900	3,468	110
DAYTONA BEACH, FL (MSA)	1,206,900	3,464	111
NEW YORK, NY (PMSA)	29,610,700	3,456	112
MONMOUTH-OCEAN, NJ (PMSA)	3,345,900	3,451	113
SYRACUSE, NY (MSA)	2,243,300	3,450	114
SAN ANGELO, TX (MSA)	340,100	3,426	115
KANSAS CITY, MO-KS (MSA)	5,392,500	3,423	116
BATTLE CREEK, MI (MSA)	473,500	3,401	117
RALEIGH-DURHAM, NC (MSA)	2,323,200	3,399	118
BOULDER-LONGMONT, CO (PMSA)	740,500	3,398	119
LITTLE ROCK-NORTH LITTLE ROCK, AR (MSA)	1,741,900	3,395	120
DAVENPORT-ROCK ISLAND-MOLINE, IA-IL (MSA)	1,233,800	3,388	121

(continued)

Per Capita Federal Funds and Grants—Metropolitan Areas (Continued)

Metropolitan areas are ranked by the per capita federal funds and grants received. The area receiving the greatest amount of federal funds and grants per capita is ranked number 1.

Metropolitan areas	Total federal funds and grants received ($1,000)	Per capita federal funds and grants received (dollars)	Rank
RICHMOND-PETERSBURG, VA (MSA)	2,842,300	3,367	122
BENTON HARBOR, MI (MSA)	559,800	3,361	123
BOISE CITY, ID (MSA)	674,600	3,361	124
ANAHEIM-SANTA ANA, CA (PMSA)	7,516,500	3,330	125
SALT LAKE CITY-OGDEN, UT (MSA)	3,545,600	3,329	126
CHATTANOOGA, TN-GA (MSA)	1,455,100	3,321	127
BRADENTON, FL (MSA)	620,200	3,318	128
INDIANAPOLIS, IN (MSA)	4,097,800	3,314	129
JACKSON, MS (MSA)	1,312,700	3,313	130
PARKERSBURG-MARIETTA, WV-OH (MSA)	508,400	3,293	131
MANCHESTER-NASHUA, NH (NECMA)	1,093,000	3,290	132
OXNARD-VENTURA, CA (PMSA)	2,129,300	3,290	133
LINCOLN, NE (MSA)	693,600	3,278	134
ALBANY, GA (MSA)	381,100	3,276	135
PHOENIX, AZ (MSA)	6,642,000	3,273	136
PORTLAND, ME (NECMA)	768,600	3,264	137
FORT WAYNE, IN (MSA)	1,195,000	3,253	138
IOWA CITY, IA (MSA)	281,800	3,250	139
PORTSMOUTH-DOVER-ROCHESTER, NH-ME (NECMA)	1,084,900	3,244	140
SPOKANE, WA (MSA)	1,154,300	3,239	141
DULUTH, MN-WI (MSA)	779,000	3,228	142
BUFFALO, NY (PMSA)	3,091,600	3,225	143
NAPLES, FL (MSA)	443,800	3,203	144
COLUMBUS, OH (MSA)	4,296,200	3,196	145
CLEVELAND, OH (PMSA)	5,879,900	3,187	146
FORT MYERS-CAPE CORAL, FL (MSA)	981,600	3,175	147
HAGERSTOWN, MD (MSA)	370,900	3,149	148
ORANGE COUNTY, NY (PMSA)	921,500	3,139	149
AMARILLO, TX (MSA)	616,000	3,132	150
FARGO-MOORHEAD, ND-MN (MSA)	464,200	3,129	151
CORPUS CHRISTI, TX (MSA)	1,115,000	3,114	152
FORT LAUDERDALE-HOLLYWOOD-POMPANO BEACH, FL (PMSA)	3,690,100	3,109	153
SIOUX FALLS, SD (MSA)	390,000	3,108	154
PUEBLO, CO (MSA)	396,200	3,104	155
APPLETON-OSHKOSH-NEENAH, WI (MSA)	966,400	3,089	156
REDDING, CA (MSA)	431,300	3,086	157
DECATUR, AL (MSA)	408,100	3,077	158
MINNEAPOLIS-ST PAUL, MN-WI (MSA)	7,325,300	3,068	159
TERRE HAUTE, IN (MSA)	406,800	3,067	160
BEAUMONT-PORT ARTHUR, TX (MSA)	1,115,500	3,065	161
ROANOKE, VA (MSA)	676,700	3,054	162

(continued)

Per Capita Federal Funds and Grants—Metropolitan Areas (Continued)

Metropolitan areas are ranked by the per capita federal funds and grants received. The area receiving the greatest amount of federal funds and grants per capita is ranked number 1.

Metropolitan areas	Total federal funds and grants received ($1,000)	Per capita federal funds and grants received (dollars)	Rank
STATE COLLEGE, PA (MSA)	352,700	3,050	163
FLORENCE, AL (MSA)	412,900	3,046	164
MEMPHIS, TN-AR-MS (MSA)	2,976,800	3,040	165
MERCED, CA (MSA)	516,500	3,038	166
FORT PIERCE, FL (MSA)	702,900	3,032	167
JOHNSTOWN, PA (MSA)	759,900	3,032	168
STEUBENVILLE-WEIRTON, OH-WV (MSA)	447,700	3,031	169
WACO, TX (MSA)	568,300	3,022	170
ALTOONA, PA (MSA)	399,100	3,011	171
PROVIDENCE-PAWTUCKET-WOONSOCKET, RI (NECMA)	2,731,900	3,009	172
NEWARK, NJ (PMSA)	5,653,600	2,997	173
ATLANTIC CITY, NJ (MSA)	922,200	2,983	174
WILMINGTON, DE-NJ-MD (PMSA)	1,709,000	2,980	175
WHEELING, WV-OH (MSA)	510,300	2,975	176
LYNCHBURG, VA (MSA)	432,500	2,973	177
OCALA, FL (MSA)	563,700	2,970	178
ELMIRA, NY (MSA)	272,000	2,965	179
MIAMI-HIALEAH, FL (PMSA)	5,376,700	2,965	180
LAKE CHARLES, LA (MSA)	510,900	2,964	181
JAMESTOWN-DUNKIRK, NY (MSA)	418,000	2,957	182
JERSEY CITY, NJ (PMSA)	1,600,800	2,952	183
CHARLOTTESVILLE, VA (MSA)	365,100	2,949	184
SIOUX CITY, IA-NE (MSA)	340,800	2,946	185
SPRINGFIELD, MA (NECMA)	1,731,200	2,923	186
WATERLOO-CEDAR FALLS, IA (MSA)	430,300	2,913	187
NEW HAVEN-WATERBURY-MERIDEN, CT (NECMA)	2,313,700	2,912	188
WILLIAMSPORT, PA (MSA)	339,800	2,873	189
EAU CLAIRE, WI (MSA)	396,500	2,864	190
BANGOR, ME (NECMA)	404,300	2,860	191
LAKE COUNTY, IL (PMSA)	1,413,900	2,854	192
ASHEVILLE, NC (MSA)	491,400	2,839	193
CHICO, CA (MSA)	494,800	2,836	194
ANN ARBOR, MI (PMSA)	758,400	2,832	195
NIAGARA FALLS, NY (PMSA)	612,400	2,823	196
MILWAUKEE, WI (PMSA)	3,938,700	2,817	197
PORTLAND, OR (PMSA)	3,331,700	2,804	198
RIVERSIDE-SAN BERNARDINO, CA (PMSA)	6,372,400	2,798	199
BERGEN-PASSAIC, NJ (PMSA)	3,584,800	2,774	200
JANESVILLE-BELOIT, WI (MSA)	378,000	2,773	201
DALLAS, TX (PMSA)	6,835,900	2,762	202
DUBUQUE, IA (MSA)	251,100	2,762	203
JACKSON, TN (MSA)	215,500	2,754	204

(continued)

Per Capita Federal Funds and Grants—Metropolitan Areas (Continued)

Metropolitan areas are ranked by the per capita federal funds and grants received. The area receiving the greatest amount of federal funds and grants per capita is ranked number 1.

Metropolitan areas	Total federal funds and grants received ($1,000)	Per capita federal funds and grants received (dollars)	Rank
GAINESVILLE, FL (MSA)	568,300	2,737	205
MUSKEGON, MI (MSA)	441,200	2,735	206
KANKAKEE, IL (MSA)	267,000	2,728	207
ATLANTA, GA (MSA)	7,398,300	2,703	208
BIRMINGHAM, AL (MSA)	2,493,900	2,701	209
BATON ROUGE, LA (MSA)	1,448,900	2,700	210
MEDFORD, OR (MSA)	390,700	2,679	211
DETROIT, MI (PMSA)	11,633,500	2,673	212
COLUMBIA, MO (MSA)	282,000	2,666	213
LONGVIEW-MARSHALL, TX (MSA)	443,400	2,661	214
SAINT JOSEPH, MO (MSA)	226,400	2,651	215
WILMINGTON, NC (MSA)	309,400	2,636	216
CHICAGO, IL (PMSA)	16,311,200	2,624	217
SHERMAN-DENISON, TX (MSA)	257,000	2,624	218
YAKIMA, WA (MSA)	486,100	2,620	219
CASPER, WY (MSA)	169,300	2,617	220
LA CROSSE, WI (MSA)	249,800	2,616	221
MOBILE, AL (MSA)	1,269,700	2,615	222
FAYETTEVILLE-SPRINGDALE, AR (MSA)	289,200	2,614	223
BILLINGS, MT (MSA)	303,700	2,608	224
WORCESTER-FITCHBURG-LEOMINSTER, MA (NECMA)	1,754,000	2,597	225
YOUNGSTOWN-WARREN, OH (MSA)	1,302,900	2,597	226
LAWRENCE, KS (MSA)	198,500	2,596	227
GADSDEN, AL (MSA)	266,800	2,594	228
LOUISVILLE, KY-IN (MSA)	2,507,600	2,593	229
ROCHESTER, NY (MSA)	2,541,800	2,593	230
BEAVER COUNTY, PA (PMSA)	491,600	2,590	231
FORT SMITH, AR-OK (MSA)	466,800	2,583	232
LUBBOCK, TX (MSA)	584,900	2,579	233
SHARON, PA (MSA)	315,600	2,579	234
VINELAND-MILLVILLE-BRIDGETON, NJ (PMSA)	354,300	2,559	235
LAKELAND-WINTER HAVEN, FL (MSA)	1,009,800	2,551	236
AKRON, OH (PMSA)	1,664,100	2,547	237
GREENSBORO--WINSTON-SALEM--HIGH POINT, NC (MSA)	2,351,200	2,543	238
GALVESTON-TEXAS CITY, TX (PMSA)	530,200	2,525	239
JOPLIN, MO (MSA)	343,200	2,524	240
TUSCALOOSA, AL (MSA)	366,900	2,524	241
PEORIA, IL (MSA)	857,700	2,520	242
LAFAYETTE-WEST LAFAYETTE, IN (MSA)	314,400	2,508	243
ATHENS, GA (MSA)	362,200	2,503	244
EUGENE-SPRINGFIELD, OR (MSA)	676,100	2,503	245

(continued)

Per Capita Federal Funds and Grants—Metropolitan Areas (Continued)

Metropolitan areas are ranked by the per capita federal funds and grants received. The area receiving the greatest amount of federal funds and grants per capita is ranked number 1.

Metropolitan areas	Total federal funds and grants received ($1,000)	Per capita federal funds and grants received (dollars)	Rank
LEXINGTON-FAYETTE, KY (MSA)	866,700	2,491	246
EVANSVILLE, IN-KY (MSA)	694,600	2,470	247
SPRINGFIELD, MO (MSA)	578,400	2,469	248
ERIE, PA (MSA)	681,600	2,460	249
ANDERSON, IN (MSA)	323,600	2,455	250
AURORA-ELGIN, IL (PMSA)	869,600	2,447	251
STOCKTON, CA (MSA)	1,109,700	2,435	252
BURLINGTON, NC (MSA)	257,700	2,434	253
ALLENTOWN-BETHLEHEM-EASTON, PA-NJ (MSA)	1,642,100	2,425	254
MIDDLESEX-SOMERSET-HUNTERDON, NJ (PMSA)	2,363,700	2,416	255
YORK, PA (MSA)	987,400	2,406	256
SANTA ROSA-PETALUMA, CA (PMSA)	877,900	2,399	257
DANVILLE, VA (MSA)	259,200	2,398	258
CANTON, OH (MSA)	959,900	2,392	259
LEWISTON-AUBURN, ME (NECMA)	247,200	2,392	260
GLENS FALLS, NY (MSA)	276,900	2,384	261
RENO, NV (MSA)	567,200	2,366	262
READING, PA (MSA)	777,800	2,363	263
TOLEDO, OH (MSA)	1,454,100	2,359	264
WAUSAU, WI (MSA)	266,000	2,346	265
FRESNO, CA (MSA)	1,433,300	2,331	266
ROCHESTER, MN (MSA)	235,100	2,329	267
GREEN BAY, WI (MSA)	442,800	2,315	268
DECATUR, IL (MSA)	284,400	2,300	269
JACKSON, MI (MSA)	342,900	2,295	270
KENOSHA, WI (PMSA)	281,200	2,294	271
BLOOMINGTON-NORMAL, IL (MSA)	284,400	2,282	272
FLINT, MI (MSA)	982,800	2,282	273
BLOOMINGTON, IN (MSA)	235,100	2,281	274
SAGINAW-BAY CITY-MIDLAND, MI (MSA)	924,900	2,277	275
VISALIA-TULARE-PORTERVILLE, CA (MSA)	678,400	2,277	276
ROCKFORD, IL (MSA)	638,600	2,263	277
TYLER, TX (MSA)	344,900	2,260	278
TULSA, OK (MSA)	1,633,400	2,245	279
KALAMAZOO, MI (MSA)	487,700	2,238	280
KOKOMO, IN (MSA)	220,700	2,231	281
HOUSTON, TX (PMSA)	7,219,000	2,223	282
MUNCIE, IN (MSA)	265,500	2,211	283
POUGHKEEPSIE, NY (MSA)	578,700	2,207	284
VANCOUVER, WA (PMSA)	499,000	2,206	285
MONROE, LA (MSA)	317,500	2,205	286
OWENSBORO, KY (MSA)	193,200	2,202	287

(continued)

Per Capita Federal Funds and Grants—Metropolitan Areas (Continued)

Metropolitan areas are ranked by the per capita federal funds and grants received. The area receiving the greatest amount of federal funds and grants per capita is ranked number 1.

Metropolitan areas	Total federal funds and grants received ($1,000)	Per capita federal funds and grants received (dollars)	Rank
LORAIN-ELYRIA, OH (PMSA)	594,400	2,198	288
NASHVILLE, TN (MSA)	2,134,000	2,196	289
GRAND RAPIDS, MI (MSA)	1,459,500	2,194	290
MANSFIELD, OH (MSA)	283,100	2,194	291
FLORENCE, SC (MSA)	257,900	2,186	292
GARY-HAMMOND, IN (PMSA)	1,335,100	2,181	293
BROWNSVILLE-HARLINGEN, TX (MSA)	569,800	2,158	294
RACINE, WI (PMSA)	374,200	2,153	295
FORT COLLINS-LOVELAND, CO (MSA)	391,700	2,152	296
MODESTO, CA (MSA)	732,500	2,148	297
BRYAN-COLLEGE STATION, TX (MSA)	249,900	2,144	298
SHEBOYGAN, WI (MSA)	219,500	2,131	299
SAINT CLOUD, MN (MSA)	381,000	2,103	300
ANDERSON, SC (MSA)	294,200	2,056	301
LAREDO, TX (MSA)	256,100	1,987	302
MCALLEN-EDINBURG-MISSION, TX (MSA)	767,300	1,978	303
LANCASTER, PA (MSA)	809,500	1,955	304
CHARLOTTE-GASTONIA-ROCK HILL, NC-SC, (MSA)	2,153,700	1,937	305
GREENVILLE-SPARTANBURG, SC (MSA)	1,186,400	1,909	306
VICTORIA, TX (MSA)	141,600	1,907	307
SANTA CRUZ, CA (PMSA)	431,500	1,903	308
HOUMA-THIBODAUX, LA (MSA)	344,900	1,883	309
HAMILTON-MIDDLETOWN, OH (PMSA)	516,600	1,847	310
GREELEY, CO (MSA)	244,600	1,796	311
LAFAYETTE, LA (MSA)	373,900	1,783	312
HICKORY-MORGANTON, NC (MSA)	385,900	1,737	313
JOLIET, IL (PMSA)	655,000	1,727	314
ELKHART-GOSHEN, IN (MSA)	249,200	1,649	315
PROVO-OREM, UT (MSA)	398,200	1,641	316
MIDLAND, TX (MSA)	171,400	1,598	317
BRAZORIA, TX (PMSA)	278,700	1,510	318
ODESSA, TX (MSA)	179,600	1,440	319

(a) Data are from the *State and Metropolitan Area Data Book 1991* (a *Statistical Abstract* supplement), Census Bureau, 755 pages, Washington D.C.: U.S. Government Printing Office, 1991.

Financial Accountability of 30 Large Cities

1993 rankings of the top U.S. cities in terms of accounting, budgeting, infrastructure controls, and evaluation and measurement. *Source:* "Rating America's Large Cities," by Katherine Barrett and Richard Greene. *Financial World* vol. 162, no. 5 March 2, 1993), pp. 56-60.

Rank	City	Overall	Accounting	Budgeting	Infra-structure con-trol	Evaluation & measurement
1.	Dallas	A	A+	A-	A	A
2.	Phoenix	A-	A	A-	A	A
3.	Portland	A-	A-	A	A	A-
4.	San Jose	A-	A	B+	A+	A-
5.	Milwaukee	B+	A-	A-	B+	A-
6.	Seattle	B+	B+	A-	B+	B+
7.	San Antonia	B+	A	A-	B-	B
8.	Austin	B+	B	A-	B	A-
9.	Indianapolis	B+	A	B+	B	B
10.	Fort Worth	B+	A	A-	C+	B+
11.	Denver	B	A-	B+	B+	B-
12.	Oklahoma City	B	A-	B+	B-	B+
13.	Boston	B	B-	B-	A-	A-
14.	Baltimore	B	B+	A	B	C+_
15.	Memphis	B	A-	B-	B+	C+
16.	El Paso	B	B	B+	B	B-
17.	Cleveland	B	B+	B	B	B-
18.	Los Angeles	B-	B-	B-	A-	B-
19.	San Diego	B-	A-	C-	B+	B
20.	New York	B-	A	C	C+	B+
21.	Columbus	B-	B+	B-	B+	C+
22.	Nashville	B-	B+	B+	B-	C+
23.	Chicago	B-	B-	B-	B-	B+
24.	Jacksonville	B-	B+	B+	B-	C
25.	San Francisco	C+	A	C	B	C-
26.	Houston	C+	B	C+	C	B
27.	Washington DC	C	A	D+	C-	C
28.	New Orleans	C	B-	C	C-	C-
29.	Philadelphia	C-	B+	D+	C-	D
30.	Detroit	D+	C	D-	C-	D+

Accounting—How fairly and thoroughly do the cities present their financial information to experts and to the general public?

Budgeting—Are the cities' budgets in line with fiscal reality? Do they utilize budget tricks? Is there an imbalance between revenutes and expenditures?

Infrastructure Controls—Do the cities effectively monitor the conditions of their infrastructure and act on their findings?

Evaluation & Measurement—How well do the cities evaluate the efficiency and effectiveness with which their dollars have been spent?

Best Cities for Plastics Manufacuters

The study was keyed to a 125-worker injection molding plant occupying 100,000 sq. ft. of space and shipping 20 million lbs. of finished product to markets in North America: *Source:* "New study points processors West," by Jim Callari. *Plastics World* vol. 51, no. 1 (January, 1993, pp. 38-40.

The 10 Least Expensive Cities to Manufacture Plastics

1. Albuquerque, NM
2. Dallas, TX
3. Winnipeg, Manitoba
4. Atlanta, GA
5. Erie, PA
6. Milwaukee, WI
7. Portland, ME
8. Cincinnati, OH
9. Akron, OH
10. Providence, RI

The 10 Most Expensive Cities to Manufacture Plastics:

1. San Jose, CA
2. Vancouver, British Columbia
3. Hartford, CT
4. San Francisco, CA
5. Rochester, NY
6. Stamford, CT
7. Nassau/Suffolk, NY
8. Buffalo, NY
9. Boston, MA
10. Washington, DC

Best Cities for Business

Source: "The Best Cities for Business," by Bill Saporito. *Fortune* vol. 126, no. 10 pp. 40-70.

City	International Present Index	Manufacturing Competitive Index	Pro-Business Attitude Ranking (Total=60)
Top Ten Cities			
1.Seattle	100	114	34
2.Houston	142	110	9
3.San Francisco	133	81	52
4.Atlanta	117	95	7
5.New York	158	81	47
6.Raleigh/Durham	92	138	9
7.Denver	83	105	15
8.Chicago	142	95	31
9.Boston	117	100	48
10.Orlando	75	124	12
Other Major Cities			
Albany	67	81	55
Austin	67	124	44
Baltimore	92	95	42
Birmingham	58	81	34
Buffalo	83	90	45
Charlotte	58	81	1
Cincinnati	83	95	16
Columbus	83	105	6
Dallas	100	110	4
Dayton	58	90	43
Detroit	108	90	53
Fort Lauderdale	67	86	39
Fort Worth	67	114	3
Grand Rapids	58	95	12
Greensboro	67	95	14
Hartford	83	105	56
Honolulu	108	86	60
Indianapolis	75	86	8
Jacksonville	83	105	27
Kansas City, MO	83	86	23
Las Vegas	58	76	20
Los Angeles	142	90	49
Louisville	67	105	26
Memphis	67	100	18
Miami	125	86	24
Milwaukee	75	100	22

(continued)

Best Cities for Business (Continued)

Source: "The Best Cities for Business," by Bill Saporito. *Fortune* vol. 126, no. 10 pp. 40-70.

Minneapolis	92	105	51
Nashville	75	86	2
New Orleans	100	110	54
Norfolk, VA	83	119	11
Oakland	75	114	58
Oklahoma City	67	100	25
Philadelphia	117	90	49
Phoenix	83	124	30
Pittsburgh	83	76	32
Portland, OR	92	100	29
Richmond	75	110	34
Rochester, NY	58	95	40
Sacramento	58	100	59
St. Louis	83	100	17
Salt Lake City	75	110	5
San Antonio	67	86	33
San Diego	92	114	57
San Jose	92	119	46
Scranton	67	95	38
Tampa	92	100	37
Tulsa	67	95	19
Washington, DC	125	90	41
West Palm Beach	75	105	27

Top 10 Cities for International Companies

Top 10 cities for international trade, chosen for their international access, international culture, supporting institutions, education, and the local economy are: *Source:* "Top 10 Cities for International Companies," by Robin Soslow, et al. *World Trade* vol. 5, no. 8 (October 1992), pp. 32–44.

1992

Atlanta, GA
Baltimore, MD
Columbus, OH
Des Moines, IA
Indianapolis, IN
Long Beach, CA
Miani, FL
Pittsburgh, PA
Rochester, NY
Tulsa, OK

1991

Little Rock, AR
Louisville, KY
Memphis, TN
Norfolk, VA
Orlando, FL
Portland, OR
Raleigh, NC
Sacramento, CA
Salt Lake City, UT
San Antonia, TX

Best Places to Live in America

Source: "The Best Places to LIve in America," by Marguerite T. Smith and Debra Englander. *Money* vol. 21, no. 9 (September 1992), pp. 110–124.

Top Ranked 20 Locations

1. Sioux Falls, SD
2. Columbia, MO
3. Austin, TX
4. Minneapolis/St. Paul, MN
5. Fargo, ND
6. San Francisco, CA
7. Honolulu, HI
8. Provo/Orem, UT
9. Gainesville, FL
10. Madison, WI
11. Bremerton, WA
12. Bryan, TX
13. Galveston/Texas Ctiy, TX
14. Duluth, MN
15. Oakland, CA
16. Houston, TX
17. Raleigh/Durham, NC
18. Boston, MA
19. Phoenix, AZ
20. Brownville, TX

Best Places in America to Own a Business

Source: "The 1992 *Inc.* Metro Report: The Best Places in America to Own a Business," by John Case. *Inc.* vol. 14, no. 8 (August 1992), pp. 30–41.

Cities with Most Business Starts, 1989–1991

1. Las Vegas, NV
2. Orlando, FL
3. Phoenix, AZ
4. Atlanta, GA
5. Raleigh-Durham, NC

Cities with Most Young High-Growth Companies, 1989–1991

1. San Jose, CA
2. Las Vegas, NV
3. Anaheim, CA
4. Seattle, WA
5. Houston-Galveston, TX

Manufacturing Climate Evaluation for States

This study evaluates the manufacturing climate in each state by measuring 16 factors. These factors are divided into four categories. *Source: Grant Thornton Manufacturing Climates Study.* Eleventh Annual. Grant Thornton, August 1990. (Publication ceased.)

State and Local Government Fiscal Policites

(Tax effort, 5-year change in tax effort, expenditures vs. personal income growth, and debt vs. personal income growth)

Top 10 Ranking States

1. New Hampshire
2. Nevada
3. Wyoming
4. Vermont
5. West Virginia
6. Massachusetts
7. Maryland
8. Rhode Island
9. Michigan
10. South Dakota

State-Regulated Employment Costs

(Average unemployment compensation benefits, unemployment compensation trust fund net worth, statutory average workers' compensation cost per case, and workers' compensation insurance levels)

Top 10 Ranking States

1. North Carolina
2. Indiana
3. New Jersey
4. Mississippi
5. South Dakota
6. Utah
7. Virginia
8. South Carolina
9. North Dakota
10. Nevada

Labor Costs

(Average hourly wage, 5-year change in hourly wage, percentage of manufacturing workers unionized, and 5-year change in unionization rate)

Top 10 Ranking States

1. New Mexico
2. South Dakota
3. North Dakota

(continued)

1089

4. Arkansas
5. Mississippi
6. Nebraska
7. South CArolina
8. Iowa
9. Idaho
10. Alabama

Productivity of Resources
(Education man hours lost, value added, and energy costs)

Top 10 Ranking States

1. North Dakota
2. Alaska
3. Wyoming
4. Iowa
5. Minnesota
6. Nebraska
7. Delaware
8. New York
9. Louisiana
10. Colorado

Counties Ranked by Growth

Each city or country is graded according to three criteria: 1) the rate of population growth between 1970 and 1990, 2) the rate of increase in per capita income between 1979 and 1987, and 3) the deviation of each county from the median density for all 411 counties. *Source:* "America's Hottest Counties," by G. Scott Thomas. *American Demographics"* vol. 13, no. 9 (September 1991), pp. 34–37.

The Hottest 20 Counties

Rank	
1	Fayette County, GA (Atlanta)
2	Collin County, TX (Dallas-Fort Worth)
3	Gwinnett County, GA (Atlanta)
4	Hernando County, FL (Tampa-St. Petersburg-Clearwater)
5	Denton County, TX (Dallas-Fort Worth)
6	Cherokee County, GA (Atlanta)
7	James City County, VA (Norfolk-Virginia Beach-Newport News)
8	Osceola County, FL (Orlando)
9	Howard County, MD (Baltimore)
10	Loudoun County, VA (Washington, D.C.)
11	Stafford County, VA (Washington, D.C.)
12	Pasco County, FL (Tampa-St. Petersburg-Clearwater)
13	Forsyth County, GA (Atlanta)
14	Paulding County, GA (Atlanta)
15	Douglas County, CO (Dener-Boulder)
16	Henry County, GA (Atlanta)
17	Seminole County, FL (Orlando)
18	Chesterfield County, VA (Richmond-Petersburg)
19	Prince William County, VA (Washington)
20	Palm Beach County, FL (W. Palm Beach-Boca Raton-Delray Beach)

The Coldest 20 Counties:

Rank	
411	Orleans County, LA (New Orleans)
410	Denver County, CO (Denver-Boulder)
409	Cuyahoga County, OH (Cleveland-Lorain)
408	Cook County, IL (Chicago-Gary-Lake County)
407	Wayne County, MI (Detroit-Ann Arbor)
406	Milwaukee County, WI (Milwaukee-Racine)
405	Hopewell County, VA (Richmond-Petersburg)
404	St. Louis County, MO (St. Louis)
403	Washington County, DC (Washington, D.C.)
402	Philadelphia County, PA (Philadelphia-Wilmington-Trenton)
401	Portsmouth County, VA (Norfolk-Virginia Beach-Newport News)
400	Norfolk County, VA (Norfolk-Virginia Beach-Newport News)
399	Osage County, OK (Tulsa)
398	Baltimore County, MD (Baltimore)
397	Hamilton County, OH (Cincinnati-Hamilton)
396	Richmond County, VA (Richmond-Petersburg)
395	Allegheny County, PA (Pittsburgh-Beaver Valley)
394	Queens County, NY (New York-Northern New Jersey-Long Island)
393	Kings County, NY (New York-Northern New Jersey-Long Island)
392	San Francisco County, CA (San Francisco-Oakland-San Jose)

Best Small Cities in America

Summarizing from G. Scott Thomas' book *The Rating Guide to Life in America's Small Cities,* this article provided some information about "Micropolitan Areas." Micropolitan areas are cities of at least 15,000 people in counties of at least 40,000 that are not part of a metropolitan area. *Source:* "The Best Small Cities in America," by Cheryl Russell. *American Demographics* vol. 12, no. 5 (May 19909), pp. 32–34. *=ties

Top 20 Micropolitan Areas

1. San Luis Obispo-Atascadero, CA
2. Corvallis, OR
3. Fredericksburg, VA
*4. Fairbanks, AK
*4. Wenatchee, WA
6. Hattiesburg, MS
*7. Ames, IA
*7. Port angeles, WA
9. Mankato, MN
*10. Aberdeen, WA
*10. Brunswick, GA
12. Vero Beach, FL
13. Longview, WA
14. Marsfield-Wisconsin Rapids, WI
15. Gainesville, GA
16. Rome, GA
17. Cape Giradeau, MO
18. Key West, FL
*19. Carson City, NV
*19. Faribault, MN

Top 10 Northeast Micropolitan Areas

*1. Ithaca, NY
*1. Salisbury, MD
3. Concord, NH
4. Plattsburgh, NY
*5. Batavia, NY
*5. Morgantown, WV
7. Newport, RI
8. Dover, DE
9. Jamestown, NY
10. Kingston, NY

(continued)

Top 10 Midwest Micropolitan Areas

1. Ames, IA
2. Mankato, MN
3. Marshfield-Wisconsin Rapids, WI
4. Cape Girardeau, MO
5. Faribault, MN
6. Findlay, OH
*7. Columbus, IN
*7. Mason City, IA
*7. Salina, KS
*10. Minot, ND
*10. Sandusky, OH

Top 10 South Micropolitan Areas

1. Fredericksburg, VA
2. Hattiesburg, MS
3. Brunswick, GA
4. Vero Beach, FL
5. Gainesville, GA
6. Rome, GA
7. Key West, FL
8. Bartlesville, OK
9. Winchester, VA
10. La Grange, GA

Top 10 West Micropolitan Areas

1. San Luis Obispo-Atascadero, CA
2. Corvallis, OR
*3. Fairbanks, AK
*3. Wenatchee, WA
5. Port Angeles, WA
6. Aberdeen, WA
7. Longview, WA
8. Carson City, NV
9. Pullman, WA
10. Prescott, AZ